Good Beer Guide 2004

Edited by
Roger Protz

Deputy Editor
Jill Adam

Assistant Editor
Kate Green

BOOKS

Campaign for Real Ale
230 Hatfield Road, St Albans,
Hertfordshire AL1 4LW

Sponsored by

Contents

Thanks to the following at CAMRA head office: Cressida Feiler, Publications Co-ordinator, for research and progress chasing for the Breweries section, and her assistant Emma Lloyd. The Campaigns team of Mike Benner, Iain Loe, Louise Ashworth, Tony Jerome, Georgina Haworth, Jonathan Mail and John Cottrell. Ted Bruning and the What's Brewing team. The Administration team: Kirk Winkler, Malcolm Harding, Jean Jones, Gary Fowler, Michael Green, Carwyn Davies, Caroline Clerembeaux and Tatiana Rathore. Special thanks to Peter Feiler for crunching the first draft of the Breweries section.

Beer Index compiled by Jeff Evans.

Cartoons by Mike Flanagan

Thanks to 67,000 CAMRA members who carried out research for the pubs; the Campaign's Regional Directors who co-ordinated the pub entries; CAMRA's Brewery Liaison Officers for their reports on the country's breweries; Paul Moorhouse for assembling the brewery tasting notes; and CAMRA's National Executive for their support and enthusiasm.

The Good Beer Guide production team: Designed by Rob Howells of Howells Design, London W13. Typeset by Ken Millie, T&O Graphics, Bungay, Suffolk. Maps by David and Morag Perrott, PerrotCarto, Machynlleth, Montgomeryshire, Wales. Printed by WS Bookwell Ltd, Finland; British representative David Sowter.

Published by the Campaign for Real Ale Ltd, 230 Hatfield Road, St Albans, Herts, AL1 4LW. Tel 01727 867201. Fax 01727 867670. © Campaign for Real Ale Ltd 2003/2004

E-mail camra@camra.org.uk Web-site www.camra.org.uk ISBN 1-85249-186-8

Beer is back!

Roger Protz hails the real ale revival
as smaller brewers cast off the shackles
of the global giants

A BEER REVOLUTION is underway in Britain. It is ignored by the wine-obsessed media, but as new craft breweries blossom and sales of real ale revive, the country is suddenly awash with fine beer, and choice and diversity have never been greater.

The final decade of the 20th century was a gloomy time for beer lovers. Forty-four breweries closed and sales of cask beer went into serious decline. It seemed that the global brewers and the new breed of pub groups had an armlock on the production and supply of beer, with a growing concentration on expensively advertised ersatz lager and bland nitro-keg.

But many pubgoers have stopped drinking the advertising. There is a growing demand for beer with flavour and character. The demand even has a political dimension: opponents of globalisation and genetically modified food want beer that is natural, unprocessed, and full of goodness rather than chemicals and cheap additives.

The Breweries section of this edition of the Guide lists more than 30 new breweries that have fired their mash tuns and coppers in the past year. A further two dozen are waiting to launch their beers in the next few months. Entry after entry reports that craft breweries are expanding production to keep pace with demand.

The revival is not confined to the minnows of the beer world. First, let us celebrate and shout for joy the fact that McMullen of Hertford has been saved. The future of the brewery had been in doubt for more than a year. Some members of the family that controls the company wanted to sell both brewery and 140 pubs, and retire on the profitable proceeds. But two family directors, David and Fergus McMullen, backed by CAMRA members, the workforce, publicans and customers, were determined to stay in brewing. In the summer of 2003, sufficient non-brewing properties were sold to pay off the rejectionist faction in the family. A year after the closure of Brakspear – the result not of falling beer sales but a venal rush to cash in on the £10 million value of the site in Henley-on-Thames – beer aficionados desperately needed a victory. We salute the determination of all those at McMullen who fought the good beer fight.

Longer hours

A new Licensing Bill became law in July 2003. Among its provisions will be the right for licensees to vary their opening hours to suit local demand. In some urban areas, this could mean that pubs will stay open until later at night; some may even operate on a 24-hour basis. Applications for new licences will be heard between 2004 and 2005. This means that the pub opening times stated in the Guide will hold good for the duration of this edition.

Fergus McMullen (left), a director of McMullen of Hertford, celebrates with his brewing staff winning a gold medal for Castle Pale Ale, shortly after the company was saved.

Further east in Suffolk, Greene King, with 1,600 pubs and some 3,000 free trade accounts, reported in July 2003 an 8 per cent increase in profits to £75 million. Sales of its three main cask beers, Abbot Ale, Old Speckled Hen and IPA, rose respectively by 21, 14 and 6 per cent. Similar stories have flowed from the independent sector, with good sales figures for the likes of Adnams, Batemans, Caledonian, Fuller's, Timothy Taylor, Charles Wells and Young's. Caledonian has seen sales of its Deuchar's IPA rocket as a result of winning CAMRA's Champion Beer of Britain award in 2002, while Tim Taylor has benefited from a surprise accolade from singer Madonna, who said Landlord was her favourite beer. When the 'Material Girl' prefers Landlord to Bud we know the beer world is experiencing a volte-face.

Perhaps the most surprising good news came from Kimberley brewer Hardys & Hansons. This was a brewery earmarked by many for closure following the disappearance of the mining industry in Nottinghamshire. Miners, their clubs and keg beer were the mainstay of the company. But Hardys & Hansons invested in pubs and new cask beers, and has built a dynamic and successful brewing and retailing business. Profits before tax in the first half of 2003 were up 12 per cent, and sales of the brewery's new cask ale, Olde Trip, were said to be encouraging.

In Wiltshire, Wadworth of Devizes is spending £1 million, an astonishing amount for a medium-sized regional brewer, to promote its premium 6X cask beer. In the 1990s, Wadworth leased the brand to

Whitbread to develop national sales. In the clumsy hands of the national group, sales of 6X managed to fall. Wadworth had to buy the brand back at considerable expense and is now investing in it with enormous confidence.

At the global end of the brewing industry, Interbrew is to spend £17 million promoting Draught Bass and Boddingtons, brands it now owns. As the sun set on the old Bass empire, sales of Draught Bass, which once ran into millions of barrels a year, were allowed to slide to 150,000 barrels annually. Predictably, when Whitbread bought Boddingtons, the mass-market philosophy went into overdrive. A nitro-keg version, using the risible slogan 'The Cream of Manchester', was heavily promoted. The cask version of Boddingtons today accounts for only 30 per cent of total sales of the brand. The fact that Interbrew sees a future in cask Draught Bass and Boddingtons shows that redemption is not confined to the road to Damascus.

Cask beer's vigorous revival is due to the persistence, endeavour, determination and even courage of independent brewers, often against overwhelming odds. Interbrew may be spending what seems a vast amount on Draught Bass and Boddingtons, but it's spending money for the global giant, and the main thrust of its activities will go to promoting its premium lager, Stella Artois. Scottish Courage, Britain's biggest brewer, now owns the French lager Kronenbourg, brewed in such famous Gallic centres as Reading-les-Deux-Eglises. There will be little cash to spend on ScotCo's cask brands now that rich pickings can be made from massively-hyped lager.

Coors, American owner of some of the former Bass and Whitbread groups, has shown some slight interest in cask by adding Worthington's 1744 to its portfolio. But in truth 1744, with an identical strength to Draught Bass, is more a spoiler for Interbrew's premium cask ale rather than a serious stab at the real ale market. Carlsberg-Tetley, wholly owned by the Danish group, has Britain's biggest-selling standard ale in its quiver, but – as with ScotCo's John Smith's Bitter – puts most of its muscle behind the nitro-keg version.

Abysmal record

As Martyn Cornell shows in this section, statistics concerning cask beer's share of the total beer market are distorted by the Big Four's abysmal record in the sector. If you strip out sales of the Big Four's real ales, fair and independent statisticians show that cask is doing rather better than the doomsters suggest. Ringwood in the New Forest started life 25 years ago as a tiny micro. Last year it celebrated a quarter century of remarkable growth that has seen Ringwood join the ranks of regional brewers, based in a large, modern site capable of producing 30,000 barrels a year. Titanic of Burslem in the Potteries produced 10 barrels of beer a week when it opened in the 1980s. Last year it moved to a new site with the capacity to grow production to 100 barrels a week. Cottage Brewery in Somerset, which celebrated 10 years of brewing in 2003 and got off to a flying start by winning the Champion of Britain with Norman's Cottage in 1995, has moved from 10 to 30 barrel production.

The national brewers may deride such figures and claim they spill more beer than Cottage or Titanic produce. But the micros have an influence far beyond their size. They have changed the face of brewing. They have broken out of the regionals' straitjacket of Mild, Bitter and a Strong 'Un for Christmas. The micros have been both innovative and fiercely traditional at one and the same time. Golden summer ales that offer an alternative to lager originated with Exmoor and Hop Back. Revivalist porters, stouts and IPAs, wheat beers, spiced and fruit beers, the use of new hop varieties and grains other than barley malt have all been the brainchilds of the micros, who have inspired the regionals to follow suit. Britain is a more exciting country in which to drink – and offers the greatest choice of any nation in the world – as a result of this bibulous revolution from below.

Pubco stranglehold

It would be naive to suggest that all is well in the world of beer and pubs. As Ted Bruning shows in his over-view of the rise of the pub companies, the giant retailers often inflict a stranglehold on choice for both publicans and drinkers. The demands for vast discounts on the wholesale price, often as high as 50%, deter many smaller brewers from selling to the pubcos. As well as discounts, there is the added cost of listing fees: brewers pay the pub companies to place them in promotional material for their pubs. A brewer who sells four beers to a pubco could find himself paying more than £10,000 a year in listing fees. The pub groups have brought to beer retailing the attitudes and ethics of the supermarkets: buy cheap, sell dear, and the devil take the hindmost. While some groups are starting to take more beer from independents, in most cases drinkers are faced by the same boring choice of cheapie national brands.

In 2002 the government said the last rites over the Beer Orders, the early 1990s legislation that permitted the tenants of national brewers' pubs to buy 'guest beers' free of the tie. As the nationals have off-loaded most of their pubs – ScotCo was in the throes of selling its tied estate as the Guide went to press – there are no tenants left to enjoy the guest beer provision. But there is a crying need for tenants to buy guest beers

As a sign of the cask beer upturn, Marston's has launched Old Empire, a true Burton India Pale Ale

John Russell (left) and Bill Bainbridge have reopened the famous Three Tuns brewery attached to a pub in Bishop's Castle, Shropshire.
The All Nations brew-pub in Madeley, Shropshire, has also reopened.

in the vast estates owned by the pub companies. When Patricia Hewitt and Melanie Johnson at the Department of Trade and Industry confidently tell us they are satisfied that 'full and fair competition' exists in brewing and retailing they are either badly advised by their officials or spend too much time being lunched and charmed by the likes of Hugh Osmond of Punch, Ted Tuppen of Enterprise Inns or John Sands of Pubmaster. But guest beer rights in pub companies would be meaningless without a DTI investigation of discounts and listing fees: a level playing field for brewers of all sizes can only operate when these pernicious practices are outlawed.

There is a further, hidden, charge imposed on small brewers by the pubcos. The owner of a micro-brewery in Sheffield has told the Guide that he has stopped supplying beer to one of the national pubcos as, on top of discounts and listing fees, he is expected to deliver on a weekly basis to a depot in Liverpool. It's a long and arduous, cross-Pennine journey. The brewer has a truck, not one of the refrigerated lorries used by bigger brewers. He is concerned that beer that has sloshed around in the back of his truck, then rolled around at the depot, will not reach pubs in the best condition. The absurdity of the situation is that, having arrived in Liverpool, the beer is then trunked all round the country and some finds its way back to Sheffield. It's not only bad for beer, but bad for the environment, too, as expensive diesel and petrol are used to move beer long and often unnecessary journeys. Wherever possible, users of this Guide should drink fresh beer in pubs close to its brewery of origin. Think local...drink local.

Two-edged sword

One reason for the growing strength and presence of the micro-brewery sector was the introduction of Progressive Beer Duty by the government in 2002. Brewers who produce less than 3,000 barrels a year had their duty cut by half, saving around £40 on the cost of each barrel produced. Brewers who make up to 18,000 barrels get a graded discount that could save as much as £120,000 a year in tax. When Chancellor Gordon Brown said PBD would affect 'a majority of brewers in the country' he failed to point out that that majority produces only between one and two per cent of the nation's beer. By setting the ceiling so low, the government cut out all Britain's smaller regional and family-owned breweries. PBD has been a boon for the micros. It has stopped many of

Down in the New Forest something stirred... staff, brewery workers and drivers at Ringwood celebrate 25 years of brewing in 2003, with production close to 30,000 barrels a year.

them going out of business, and has enabled them to invest in new equipment. But the system is not the true sliding scale that brewers have been campaigning for and it unfairly penalises the middle rank. It is nothing short of grotesque that a company such as Ringwood should develop its business from minnow to small regional status and then find itself excluded from the benefits of lower duty rates. CAMRA is lobbying the government to bring in a proper sliding scale of duty by adopting the European Union's ceiling of 200,000 hectolitres or 120,000 barrels a year.

The current levels for PBD act as a disincentive to breweries to develop their businesses. They can even encourage some breweries to scale down production. McMullen, for example, is cutting out all contract brewing at its Hertford brewery and will produce no more than 18,000 barrels a year in order to benefit from PBD. The long-term viability of McMullen, rattling around in a brewery designed to produce 200,000 barrels a year, has to be called into question. The least-worst option may be to move to a new and smaller site. If and when the new Brakspear brewery is built in Oxfordshire it is likely that it, too, will opt for a maximum production level of 18,000 barrels a year. Unless the government overhauls PBD and raises the ceiling it is in effect handing an advantage to the global brewers, who can soak up the beer sales abandoned by downsized regionals.

Green beer

Drinkers can draw comfort from the fact that both brewers and hop growers have moved to meet the demand for beers made without pesticides and fertilisers. The Breweries section lists some two dozen breweries now making organic beers. Britain leads the world in this small but rapidly growing sector of the beer market. At present, most organic hops are

Beer duty review

In July 2003, Customs & Excise announced it would hold a consultation with the brewing industry into the effects of Progressive Beer Duty and to see if it should be extended to medium-sized producers.
It is possible that, as a result of the consultation, the upper limit for PBD could be raised to 122,000 barrels a year.
This would then cover an estimated 27 regional breweries and would give them both a considerable duty relief and enable them to compete more effectively with the giant global breweries.

sourced from New Zealand, where the pests and diseases that attack English hops are unknown. But English farmers, once dab hands at reaching for the spray can, have listened to the advice of the environmental lobby and learnt that it is best to allow nature to deal with such problems as aphid attack. Why kill ladybirds with chemical sprays when the bugs, left to their own devices, will eat aphids and spider mites? Trials of new organic hops are underway and organic versions of new 'hedgerow' hops such as First Gold – which grow to only half the height of conventional varieties – have proved successful. Fullers' Organic Honey Dew has been a runway success and is one of the biggest-selling bottled beers in the country. Greener beer is not only better for consumers, it is also highly beneficial to the environment. These are arguments entirely lost on the global brewers: there is not a single organic beer produced by them.

Good beer in Britain can survive only with constant vigilance on the part of its devotees. CAMRA's continued growth – membership currently stands at 67,000 – is a sure sign that beer lovers recognise the need to lobby government and big brewers, and to support craft breweries and genuine free trade publicans. The fact that beer sales rose in 2003 for the first time in 20 years, and that choice for drinkers today is the best in living memory, are testimony to the impact of the Campaign. Success breeds success. CAMRA needs new members to strengthen its elbow and to encourage new brewers to enter the market. Join us today and, in the words of the prophet, go forth and multiply.

The devil's in the discount

Ted Bruning argues that giant 'pubcos' are squeezing small craft brewers and restricting choice for drinkers

THIS IS AN EVERYDAY story of ruthlessness and greed, and how you and I – as well as brewers and their suppliers, and thousands of publicans – are being screwed by faceless corporations you may never even have heard of.

These corporations, mainly financed by foreign merchant banks, very probably own your local. You may not know who they are, but it's because of them that you have to pay more than you need for your pint. They are the non-brewing pub companies, generally called 'pubcos', a title as unlovely as the entities it denotes; and their avarice and blindness are slowly but surely strangling Britain's breweries and pubs. You are unlikely ever to have seen their names on the signs of your locals, yet they own half of the nation's pubs.

Let me take you back to 1990, and the Beer Orders that followed the Monopolies Commission's enquiry into the brewing industry. This was prompted by the Big Six national brewers' grip on the beer market, and the commission duly declared them to be a complex monopoly operating against the public interest. After much debate a number of correctives were promulgated, chief among them that the Big Six must dispose of some 11,000 of their tied houses, either leasing them free of tie or simply selling them.

The hope was that these 11,000 pubs would be run as free houses, selling the ales their licensees chose. Only it didn't work out that way. Deviously, if not surprisingly, the Big Six found a way of seeming to comply while actually staying in control. Instead of simply freeing selected tenants from the tie, they sold tranches of pubs to newly-created non-brewing companies. In many cases the 'entrepreneurs' behind these new companies were the brewery's own middle managers. Often they were bankrolled by the breweries themselves.

Thus Whitbread disposals formed such chains as CM Group (80 pubs), Discovery Inns (223) and Inn Business (88); 200 ex-Bass pubs were the basis of Centric Inns; and 300 Allied cast-offs reappeared as Sycamore Inns. Consumer benefit was nil, for guess whose beers these pubcos sold? In many cases the brewery signs outside the pubs were never even changed.

How clever the Big Six thought they were! They had done all that was asked of them, yet their power was reduced not a whit. But how wrong they were! For 14 years on, their offspring have grown into psychopathic teenagers who have their parents at their mercy.

Today the country's brewers – national, regional, and micro – own a fraction over 10,000 pubs between them, while the pubcos have more than 30,000. Pubcos dominate just as the Big Six did in 1990. The

biggest of them runs some 8,000 pubs – as many as Bass did in its hey-day. The top three between them own more than 15,000 pubs, with buying power to match. Pub prices may have soared in the last 10 years, but the clout of the pubcos is such that the wholesale price of beer has actually fallen.

As for the Big Six which were household names a decade ago, well, none of them owns pubs any more. Some of them – Courage, Watney's, Bass and Whitbread – have disappeared almost entirely.

Before outlining how this happened, let me dispose of the high-street theme bar chains – the Edwardses, It's A Screams, All Bar Ones and so forth, which have put our high streets out of bounds on a Friday or Saturday night to anyone too old for a crop-top and body piercings. The trade jargon for such bars, YPVs or Young People's Venues, sums them up succinctly enough, and, with the honourable exception of the JD Wetherspoon Organisation's 600-odd pubs, they are entirely innocent of anything anyone of discernment would want to drink. This rash of uncontrolled and uncontrollable binging shops has created a huge social problem, but it is not the subject of this enquiry.

For in terms of numbers, it's the big leased chains that matter – Enterprise, Punch, Pubmaster, and the like. These are the boys who have

---

David and Goliath pub market

Owners of small pub groups have complained bitterly that they are unable to expand because of the 'silly prices' the giant pubcos are prepared to pay for new properties. Chris Holmes, a former chairman of CAMRA who now runs the 24-strong East Midlands-based Tynemill pub group, said in July 2003 that he had not bought a single pub for more than a year. He put the blame for the over-inflated state of the market on the shoulders of the pubcos. Holmes accused one pubco, Punch, of departing from standard valuation guidelines in its rush to snap up new outlets.

'Pubs are going for silly prices,' Holmes said, 'and it's putting the market out of the reach of smaller players. The big pub companies are chasing one another for the sake of growth. Some valuations placed on ordinary pubs in this region are just ridiculous.'

At the same time, London brewer and pub retailer Fuller's also said it was buying fewer new outlets as a result of the inflated prices paid by the national pubcos.

---

bought up Britain's pubs by the thousand, and who now screw the breweries that supply them, the tenants who front for them, and the customers who in the main don't even know they exist. The only people they can't screw are the international bankers who own them.

Breweries axed

Pubcos based on big brewery disposals weren't the only ones to appear in the 1990s. City fad had it that you couldn't be both a brewer and a retailer, and many regionals fell for it – suicidally, as it turned out. Famous names such as Gibbs Mew, Boddingtons, Morrells, and Greenalls axed their breweries, set up as pubcos, and were one by one bought out. (Eldridge Pope and Brakspear currently await the same quietus).

In the mid-90s, with so many pub estates now vulnerable to takeover, a new phenomenon arose: the predatory pubco, heavily backed by foreign banks. For German, American, and Japanese merchant banks were key players in the growth of the giant pubcos. They saw the Great British Pub with its regular flow of rent as a cash-cow, and bought heavily. Nomura at one time owned almost the entire ex-GrandMet empire; Daiwa was the power behind Avebury Taverns; Deutsche Bank part-owns Laurel (the rump of what used to be Whitbread); and an American venture capital house is behind InnSpired, formerly Usher's.

The first of these heavily-backed predators was Enterprise Inns. Founded in 1991 with 372 ex-Bass pubs, its estate had grown to 500 by 1994. Then it hit its stride, snapping up pubco after pubco. John Labbatt Retail, Wirral Inns, Gibbs Mew, Mayfair Taverns, Century Inns fell like ninepins. By 1999 it had 1,500 pubs; and as the Big Six finally shed the last vestiges of their past, it really opened up. In 2001 it bought 900 pubs from Whitbread and Scottish & Newcastle; and in 2002 it did a complicated deal with venture capital partners to snap up the last of the old GrandMet and Whitbread tenanted estates. It now controls more than 8,000 pubs.

Enterprise is the nonpareil of the predatory pubco, but there are others: Punch Taverns, set up in 1998 by Pizza Express bosses Hugh Osmond and Luke Johnson to buy the old Bass leased estate of 1,400 pubs and financed by international bankers, is its nearest rival with around 4,000 pubs.

So have all these corporate shenanigans been of any benefit to the beer drinker? Well, in one way, yes.

In 1991, I was asked to contribute my thoughts on the post-Beer Orders world to the Good Beer Guide. My (fairly obvious) prediction was that as ownership fragmented, so would supply. And so it has.

At first, the pubcos stocked only Big Six beers because they were in the Big Six's pockets. The maelstrom of takeovers since then has snapped the link. The national (or rather multinational) brewers still dominate, partly because they brew all the lager. On the ale front, mass-produced brands such as John Smith's, Tetley, and Boddingtons (all most common in their keg variant) still lead the market; mainly because they're dirt cheap. But many regional brewers have managed to get their flagship ales into the pubcos' estates. Fuller's London Pride, Shepherd Neame Spitfire and Marston's Pedigree are now nationally distributed, while Adnams, Bateman's, Timothy Taylor, and Young's are also well-represented in pubco estates. So in the very narrow sense that pubco tenants can stock a slightly wider range of ales than they could when they were Big Six tied houses, we're better off. But that's where it ends.

For the international banks behind the pubcos are vampires. Where they bite, they feed until their victim is bled white.

So pub tenants have found their rents soaring while the level of service from their landlords has dwindled to nothing; and at the same time they are charged top dollar for their beer. At around £2, you may be paying twice as much for a pint as you did 14 years ago. But don't blame the poor licensee: most pubco tenants are worse off than they were as Big Six tied traders, and a staggering 48 per cent of them, according to a recent survey, loathe their landlords and regret ever having signed their leases.

And don't imagine that the brewers see much of that £2, either. Pubcos typically pay £35-£40 for a 72-pint firkin, and the brewer must pay the duty out of his share. His only chance of profit is to be ruthlessly efficient himself, laying off workers and squeezing his own suppliers, who in turn must do the same. So maltsters pay animal-feed prices for top-quality malting barley, and as that's below the cost of growing it, the farmers depend on subsidies to make a living – subsidies paid by you and me.

Tiny margins

Many regional brewers have disappeared since 1990 either because they couldn't get their cost-base down or because their brands just couldn't cut it. For once a brewer's beer wins a listing with a pubco, he still faces the hugely expensive task of persuading the pubco's tenants to stock it and their customers to ask for it by name. So regional brewers have to invest in marketing on an unprecedented scale to convert the tiny margin the pubcos allow them into a profit worth having – an investment which directly benefits the pubcos.

Wadworth of Devizes found itself in this position last year, when it had to pour £1 million into promoting its famous 6X. As Wadworth only brews 100,000 barrels a year, that's £10 per barrel blown on a single advertising campaign.

Marketing director Fred West says, diplomatically, that Wadworth is 'comfortable' with the prices it gets from its pubco customers.

'Certainly pubcos have some pretty keen buyers,' he says. 'But we can make money out of it by building the brand and public demand for it, so we don't have to be so concerned about the margins the pubco allows us.'

Of course, he adds, it helps to brew 'damned good beer – and that's how the likes of Adnams and Timothy Taylor have flourished despite having few pubs of their own.'

What he doesn't say is that brewers like Wadworth have to make up for the shameful prices paid by pubcos by charging their own tenants more – which, again, means higher prices for you and me.

But if pubcos make life hard for regional brewers, they make it nearly impossible for micros.

Some pubcos have schemes in place which allow tenants to select from a carefully-rationed range of micro-breweries' ales. But the terms they impose and the prices they pay make it hardly worth the micros' while to join such schemes. Especially galling is that suppliers must deliver to a central depot, which might be a hundred miles away – only to see the same cask turn up two weeks later at the pub down the road. Quite apart from the miles added to the beer's journey, and the effect on its condition, there's the question of cask recovery. A firkin costs £80, and the longer each one is out in trade the more the brewery has to have. Twenty years ago a brewer reckoned to need three for each one in trade: now it's more like seven.

Keith Bott runs the Titanic Brewery in Burslem, Staffordshire, and is newly-elected president of the Society of Independent Brewers, which has waged a long campaign for more access to pubco-owned pubs.

'Pubcos own half the pubs in the country and to get our beers to market we have to go through them,' he says. 'But it's a chicken and egg situation. They won't stock our beer until we prove there's a demand for it, and we can't prove there's a demand for it until they start stocking it.

'I'm desperate to get my beer to market. I want to promote quality beer – I'm sure that the reason the beer market is declining is that most of the ales people are faced with are boring, mass-produced national brands. But I can't do it unless the pubcos will deal fairly with me.'

It wouldn't be fair to end this blast at pubcos without mentioning the handful of saints among them. And there are some – but of course, they're tiny.

Companies like Tynemill in the East Midlands, Chapman Inns in Gloucester, Sir John Fitzgerald in Tyneside, Market Town Taverns in West Yorkshire and Burlison Inns in the Home Counties run good locals where tasty craft-brewed real ales are a regular feature.

Gary Burlison, whose mini-empire of eight pubs includes the award-winning Wellington in Bedford and the Sir William Peel brew-pub in Sandy, says that unlike the venture capital-backed giants, his growth has been curbed by unhelpful banks and by the property market distortions created by the reckless acquisitiveness of companies like Punch Taverns.

'It's increasingly difficult to buy single pubs on the open market,' he says. 'If they're any good, someone like Punch will make offers for them which we can't hope to equal. Either that or they're sold in packages too big for us to bid for.'

Gary admits that he doesn't pay his suppliers any too generously. On the other hand, he says, his wholesale profit is his only source of income because he doesn't screw his tenants.

'Micros still like to deal with us because they deal direct so there's no middleman, they know their beer will be served in top condition, and they can get their casks back promptly,' he says. 'And we don't make money out of our rents – we believe that dealing fairly with our tenants is the only way to recruit and keep the best ones, and recruiting and keeping the best tenants is the only way to make the pubs work.'

If only there were more Gary Burlisons around! But he and people like him are a rarity: if small, real ale-friendly chains like his own 100 pubs between them, that's all they own.

Shameless power

So that's pubcos for you: faceless corporations that are abusing you, me, publicans, brewers, maltsters, farmers. They overcharge shamelessly. They underpay equally shamelessly. They have power of life and death over an entire sector of the brewing industry, power which they exercise on behalf of foreign shareholders and investors. They need to be controlled.

So what, you'll want to know, are our protectors, the Office of Fair Trading and the Government, proposing to do to curb the pubcos' market power?

Absolutely nothing, that's what. Last year the OFT turned down a request for an investigation on a technicality. Just before that the Government had revoked the 1990 Beer Orders without proposing to put anything in their place. No one pubco controls enough of the market to trigger a Competition Commission enquiry. So nothing's to be done.

CAMRA and its allies in the brewing industry and licensed trade won't let it rest, though. We'll keep on pressing until the Government acts – or if the Government doesn't, the European Commission does. But we won't rest until our breweries and pubs are safe from the short-termist sharks who are squatting on our culture, our heritage, our way of life.

In the meantime, enjoy your overpriced pint. Or, more likely, stay at home.

Ted Bruning edits *What's Brewing*, CAMRA's national monthly newspaper.

Pass the porter

Fiona Beckett says it's time to put beer on the dining table as the perfect companion for food

I F YOU WERE THROWING a posh dinner party would you put beer or wine on the table? Given you've bought a copy of this Guide, I guess beer might get a look in – but how much thought would you give to whether it went with the food?

Well, Britain's brewers would like you to. Beer and food matching – trying to pair different beers with different dishes – is the new rock 'n' roll, with brewers falling over themselves to prove their beers are food-friendly. Over the past 12 months there has been an avalanche of promotional activity. Greene King, for example, joined forces with celebrity chef Ed Baines to launch a 'Beer to Dine for' campaign, following it up with a bottled beer of the same name. Scottish Courage sponsored a 34-page beer and food supplement in the Observer, Shepherd Neame launched a series of beer dinners, and there was a flurry of beers brewed to go with curry. Not to mention the National Hop Association's annual Beauty of Hops competition, which focused in 2003 on beers to go with cheese.

So why the sudden interest? Don't we all know that beer goes with food? Surely this is a case – if ever there was one – of reinventing the wheel? Beer writer Michael Jackson certainly thinks so. 'I do get quite irritated. I've been telling people all this stuff for 20 years then I have people coming back to me and saying "Did you know you could pair food with beer?" ' Nor is he convinced by the current marketing of beers designed to go with food. 'You can't have one beer that goes with everything. You'd never say that about wine.'

But Britain's brewers have a problem. While wine has become as integral a part of the dinner table as it is for a Frenchman or an Italian, beer is still regarded as the best way to get bladdered on a Saturday night. For many people the term 'lager lout' still represents the typical beer drinker.

'What we're trying to do is reawaken the industry into not focusing on beer as a medium for a male-bonding ritual but more for its product attributes and how you enjoy it,' says Rooney Anand, managing director of Greene King. 'Part of that is how it goes with different types of food. Beer to Dine For at least makes that concrete. It is flexible. It's more floral, paler in colour, slightly less gassy than traditional ales, so it doesn't fill you up. We've tried to make a beer that women will love that isn't lager.'

The fact is that in most pubs there is beer and there is food, with little attempt to link the two. Even the large number of gastropubs that have sprung up seem to be 'gastro' by virtue of having a large wine list rather than being a showcase for the best British beers. When I dined at an award-winning London gastropub there were plenty of people drinking beer on the terrace outside but inside the restaurant there was scarcely a glass to be seen. The admirable White Horse at Parson's Green, Southwest London, remains the only pub I know of that systematically pairs a beer as well as a wine with each course.

Of course you can... a Greene King recipe suggests how to match a delicious dish with Old Speckled Hen

Main Course
Served with OLD SPECKLED HEN
Poached Lamb Fillet wrapped in Parma Ham with Braised Winter Vegetables and Red Pepper Jus

4 Lamb Cannons	12 slices Parma Ham
100gm Butter	Chopped Parsley
Ground Pepper	

Trim any fat off the lamb and leave in the fridge. Soften the butter and fold in the parsley and pepper. Cover each of the fillets with this butter mix, and then, placing cling film on your bench surface, place three slices of Parma ham, overlapping, in the centre of the sheet of cling film. Place the lamb in the centre of the ham and gently wrap the fillet in the ham using the cling film to fold the ham over. Wrap each fillet in an additional piece of cling film and tie the ends tightly. Bring a pot of water to the boil and poach the fillets in this for 12 minutes, then remove from the water.

Braised Vegetables:

1 Celeriac	3 Carrots
4 Potatoes	200gm of the Butter
250ml Chicken Stock	Salt
Thyme	

Peel the vegetables and cut into presentable shapes of about the same size. In a shallow pan, place the butter, thyme, salt and vegetables. Add the chicken stock. Cover with butter paper and boil until the water evaporates, the butter begins to turn golden and the vegetables are cooked to a golden brown colour.

In a typically British way, we tend to look for reasons why serving beer in good restaurants won't work rather than an opportunity to offer the customer something they might enjoy. So far as the trade is concerned, there's the fear that their margins will be eroded. But that's simply not true, says Fiona Smith, Strategic Projects Manager of Interbrew. 'On the contrary, beer is a great revenue generator. Retail outlets can make the same margin per unit of alcohol as they can with other drinks. And it's easier to get people to order one more bottle of beer than another bottle of wine.'

Habit forming

As more people go out to eat on a regular basis, that habit could catch on. 'More people now drink beer with food than without food and we have to recognise that,' adds Fiona Smith. Then there's the question of presentation, the feeling that beer glasses are too big and bottles too small to grace the dinner table.

'People do find the glass size off-putting,' admits Michael Jackson. 'They worry a beer dinner involves having a pint with each course.' But brewers are starting to address that just as they're starting to bottle their beers in wine-sized bottles. 'Big bottles give credence on the table,' says Rooney Anand. 'It makes beer look more like a drink you have

to share with food rather than for the sad dad in his armchair watching football. A smaller bottle says "you". A bigger bottle says "us".

They might also give some thought to names. One of the best beers I've tasted recently, a strong Orkney ale that was brilliant with both blue cheese and chocolate, was called Skullsplitter. That's not going to tempt your average wine-lover to replace his favourite dessert wine or port.

It's not as if the flavours of beer don't work well with food – and I'm not just talking about pies and sandwiches. I would choose a fruit beer over a sweet wine with cheesecake, for example, or a barley wine in preference to red wine with a cheeseboard. I'm more than happy to drink a good lager with a spicy Asian-inspired salad, a wheat beer with grilled fish or a robust ale with a steak.

What we need are more opportunities to try these less conventional combinations. 'We recently held a dinner where we paired a crab and avocado starter with a Chinese-style Sunlik lager, a rich lamb casserole with Bishop's Finger, followed by trifle with a Bellevue Framboise raspberry beer,' says Chris Gregson of Shepherd Neame. 'It really worked. The bitter, astringent flavour of the Bishop's Finger cut through the richness of the lamb perfectly, while the acidity of the framboise was just what you needed to refresh the palate after a mouthful of cheesecake.'

Interbrew, too, had a good response when they hosted a trial beer dinner at the Belper Arms in Newton Burgoland, Leicestershire, despite

the fact that they were charging £25 a head. 'Everyone was really positive – it went really well,' says spokesman Sam Rooke. 'A lot of women said they didn't normally drink beer, and had never tried the ones on the menu, but afterwards they said they would serve them at home. And the landlord said it would be the first of many for him.'

Four ale bar... Rooney Anand of Greene King wants pubgoers to match cask beer and tempting menus

Along with other brewers, they are also planning to introduce linked lunchtime deals where you order a main course and get a glass of an appropriate beer to drink with it for an all-in price. I think all this amounts to what in management jargon they call a 'tipping point' – the moment in time when perceptions change and a previously unusual situation (in this case thinking about matching food with specific beers) becomes the norm.

But it's not just up to the brewers and landlords. It's up to us beer lovers to have the courage of our convictions and share the outstanding beers that this country produces with our wine-drinking friends. Then we will have a beer culture worthy of the name.

Fiona Beckett is a freelance food and drink writer and the author of *How to Match Food and Wine*. She has her own website www.foodandwinematching.co.uk

Image of Beer

BEER IN ITS VARIOUS FORMS – whether it be lager, keg, cask or stout – continues to have an image connected with laddish behaviour, alcoholism, and law and order issues, and has become canon fodder for the lobbying groups who wish to attack our social pastime – our visit to the pub. We need to act, and act now.

Can we look to the continent to learn any lessons? Drinking is more moderate (although regular), and they talk of quality not quantity. It's presented professionally in a branded glass and food is accompanied by beer and regularly drunk at family occasions.

We can also learn from the wine industry which has created an image of vineyards, rolling countryside, the skill and art of wine making, and the enormous range and variety available resulting in consumers having more knowledge of wine than of our own beers. In a recent survey carried out by the National Farmers Union, only 15% of people questioned were aware that the main ingredient in beer was barley.

At long last we are moving towards a more liberalised licensing regime similar to that of our brethren in Europe and no longer will we have to down pints as quickly as possible as the pub will shut at 11 o'clock. This gives us the opportunity once and for all to stop apologising about beer, but instead claim its virtues and prove those doubters wrong and show them that we can be responsible as a nation.

The two component parts of the image of beer are marketing and beer presentation. Marketing has to show leadership and not endorsing current behaviour. Drinks promotions should talk more about the brand values and not the price. Beer is for every occasion, and a great deal of work is now being done by a number of the brewers including Hall & Woodhouse (www.badgerbrewery.com), Greene King with their 'Beer to Dine For' campaign, and Coors with their 'Beer Naturally' initiative.

Beer education has also been championed by Coors

Above: presentation at the Bell at Standerwick, the 200th Hall & Woodhouse licensee to receive Cask Marque accreditation. Pictured (left to right) are Andrew Younger (H&W), Bell licensees Jackie and David Southward, Nick Sellick (H&W) and Paul Nunny of Cask Marque.

(www.beer-naturally.co.uk) and latterly by Refresh UK owners of the Wychwood and Brakspear brands (www.beer-academy.co.uk).

When we talk about beer quality and presentation, this is where Cask Marque can play an important role. Cask Marque, over the past two years, has been setting standards for the industry to enable every pub landlord and his members of staff to serve a 'perfect pint'.

Cellar Manual and Cellar Cards

With the four national brewers, Cask Marque has helped write a cellar handbook to be used to train staff in cellar management – remember the cellar is the engine room of the pub.

Distributor Charter

This lays down best practice for the handling of beer in the supply chain. Beer has never been in better condition when leaving the brewery, but can we guarantee a quality product is delivered to the pub? These guidelines will help in this area.

Glassware

Clean glassware is essential to the appearance and presentation of beer. Any film on the glass will give a dull appearance, but also affect head retention. How often have we been served with a beer that looks dull and unappetising? While this could be due to poor cellar practices, a major contributing factor could be the cleanliness of glassware. To tackle this major issue, Cask Marque has issued a Glasswashing Charter and Troubleshooting Guide.

Bar Staff

The final person in the chain to deliver the 'perfect pint' is the bar person. A survey showed that 67% of staff felt they did not receive sufficient training. To help overcome this problem, Cask Marque has produced a 20-minute video for the bar person and this highlights how to pour the 'perfect pint' and present it to the customer, if possible in a branded glass. We challenge customers to question bar staff if beer is served in the wrong glass as it is very unprofessional. In the last six months over 1,500 copies of the video have been sold and it has also won an award from the British Guild of Beer Writers.

Beer Description

By empowering bar staff with knowledge about beer products, they will impart this information to their customers. Cask Marque are promoting to brewers the concept of a back clip on the cask ale pump which will give details of the ABV, the colour, the description, and the hop variety used.

Cask Marque will continue to play its role in inspecting beer quality in pubs and making awards to licensees who meet the quality standard. Look for the Cask Marque plaque, you are guaranteed better beer quality. This year Cask Marque will carry out over 14,000 visits. When a Cask Marque logo is displayed, do write or e-mail us if beer is not up to standard and do feel free to recommend pubs to be included in our scheme.

For more information, please visit our website on www.cask-marque.co.uk.

The Cask Marque Trust
Seedbed Centre, Severalls Park, Colchester,
Essex CO4 9HT
Fax: 01206 751198
E-mail: info@cask-marque.co.uk

Beer's greasy pole

Martyn Cornell says statistics – and the big brewers – distort real ale's true market share

THERE ARE SEVERAL versions of the famous comment by Andrew Lang, the 19th-century poet and author, about the misuse made of numbers, but this one will do us: 'Statistics play the same role for a policymaker as a lampost does for a drunk – as support, rather than illumination.'

The trouble in the cask ale market is that there are two completely different statistical lamposts available from different research companies. These lend support to wildly opposite conclusions – to the detriment of the drinker.

One firm, AC Nielsen, puts out figures backed by the British Beer and Pub Association (the former Brewers' Society) that claim to show that sales of cask beer are only 8% of the total beer market, at around 2.75 million barrels in 2002, and cask is only 30 per cent of the whole ale market and falling.

The other, a company called CGA, insists that Nielsen and the BBPA have consistently under-reported the true size of the market. Its surveys of more than 5,000 on-trade outlets show that cask ale sales are actually around five million barrels a year, and that cask is in reality more than 20% of total on-trade beer sales, making it the second biggest category after (heavily advertised) standard lager.

Why two teams of researchers are so far apart, with one saying the cask ale market is 45% smaller than the other reckons it is, remains unclear. The two firms cannot even agree on how much market share the national brewers, Coors, Interbrew, Carlsberg-Tetley and Scottish & Newcastle, have between them. Nielsen says the nationals' brands make up 'nearly half' of UK cask ale sales. CGA says the national Big Four sell much less, only 27 per cent of all the cask ale drunk in Britain, with the 40-odd regional brewers taking all of 57 per cent and the country's 450 or so micro-brewers mopping up the final 15 or 16 per cent.

Grip on market

Even if you take the larger estimate for national brewers' cask beer sales, however, that is still a massive under-performance compared with their mail-fisted grip on the rest of the beer market, in a sector that on Nielsen's figures is worth a substantial £1.5 billion a year (CGA says £2.6 billion). Overall, the Big Four make almost four out of five pints of all beer sold in the UK, thanks to their huge and category-dominating lager brands, such as Carlsberg, Carling and Fosters.

Why is their performance in the cask ale market so comparatively bad? Even Nielsen agrees that the nationals are showing the biggest declines in cask ale sales. Is it because they have believed Nielsen's constantly pessimistic figures on the size of the market and cut back on

their efforts on cask ale, while the regional brewers have preferred to rely on the evidence of their ever-growing order books, and have increased their share of the market as a result?

Many would argue that, since the national brewers' power squeezes all choice out of the markets they dominate, their weakness in the cask sector is a huge bonus for those who prefer variety to sameness. In the standard lager sector, nine pints out of ten go to just five national brands. In the cask ale market, the top five brands together make up just one pint in five, and the top 20 brands just two pints in five. There are around 2,500 cask ale brands on sale in the UK, but no more than 40 draught lagers.

All the same, the national brewers' power still means they have the number one and number two cask ale brands, in Tetley Bitter from Carlsberg-Tetley, which sells more than 300,000 barrels a year, and John Smith's, from Scottish & Newcastle, which in its cask form sells 183,000 barrels a year. Whatever the merits of those two beers, they surely ride into many pubs on the coat-tails of those companies' 'must stock' lagers, Carlsberg and Foster's.

Certainly the national brewers like to promote the use of a technique called 'category management', which is used by supermarkets to tell them which brands of, say, baked beans to stock and which ones not to bother with. Surprise, category management allegedly says that, according to Darran Britton, director of ales at Carlsberg-Tetley, pubs should all be stocking a leading national cask ale brand alongside a popular regional brand, and maybe if there's room 'a rotated micro-brewery ale'. Since category management points towards a nightmare where every bar in Britain has only Tetley's and London Pride coming through the handpumps, it is to be hoped pub owners spot the ludicrousness of the idea.

The truth is that what real ale drinkers like most, after consistent quality, is diversity. Big pub companies such as Laurel, Punch, Enterprise and Unique have joined the likes of JD Wetherspoon in stocking a wider range of cask ales to suit local demand, and those retail pub groups that feature cask ale continue to report good sales. So do the regional brewers: Greene King says volume sales of Abbot Ale have risen 20%, with Old Speckled Hen up 13%. Wolverhampton & Dudley confirms 'there is a trend towards more flavoursome beers' and is investing in more production capacity for Marston's Pedigree.

Fuller's announced continued sales growth, with brewing profits up 18% in 2003. Shepherd Neame says sales of Spitfire are up 20%. Jennings and Robinson's report sales up. Hardys & Hansons announced 'a substantial increase in own-brewed brands' for 2003, with seasonal cask ale volumes growing strongly. Sales of Young's Bitter were up 6.6% for 2002/03, while its seasonal dark beer, Winter Warmer, saw sales climb 21%. Adnams' Bitter sales rose 11% while its Broadside increased by 15.5%. And so on.

At the same time, despite gloomy talk about a declining market overall, the number of outlets for cask ale is actually increasing: CGA found that compared to 2001 there were another 1,160 pubs stocking cask ale, a 2.9% increase, which means that 63% of pubs now sell at least one cask ale. As the Punch Pub Company put it, 'cask ale is one of the few defining elements of the British pub'. All the statistics in the world won't alter that.

Martyn Cornell is managing editor of Martin Information, the leading supplier of news and analysis to the leisure and hospitality industry. He worked with CGA to produce the Business Guide to Cask Ale.

Top 10 ale budgets

1 John Smith's: £8.03m*
2 Tetley: £5.16m*
3 Boddingtons: £2.37m*
4 Worthington: £1.32m*
5 Greene King Abbot: £1.13m
6 Shepherd Neame: £1.1m
7 Fuller's: £0.73m
8 Young's: £0.66m
9 Marston's: £0.52m
10 Adnams: £0.38m

*Indicates the beer is available as both cask and nitro-keg: the biggest proportion of these advertising spends is for nitro-keg.

Top 10 lager budgets

1 Budweiser: £13.3m*
2 Carling: £12.9m
3 Stella Artois: £10.22m
4 Carlsberg: £9.52m
5 Foster's: £8.51m
6 Grolsch: £8.01m
7 Kronenbourg: £3.62m
8 Becks: £3.08m
9 Tennents: £1.7m
10 San Miguel: £1.3m

*Denotes the Anheuser-Busch lager, not the Czech Budweiser Budvar.

Figures courtesy Nielsen Media Research

How the Good Beer Guide is compiled for pub lovers

FOR THIRTY-ONE years the Good Beer Guide has been produced with one over-riding belief: that if a pub landlord cares about the quality of the beer in his cellar, then everything else – the welcome, the food, other drinks, accommodation and family facilities, even the state of the toilets – will also be top-notch. Micro-waved food, stale sandwiches and supermarket plonk are usually synonymous with pubs that also sell keg beer and lager.

The Guide is constantly evolving. In its early days, pub descriptions were brief or even non-existent. To recall an old advertising jingle, we were only there for the beer. But society has changed. Pubs face intense competition from other parts of the 'leisure industry' that scarcely existed in the 1970s and '80s. People are no longer satisfied with the spartan world of the four ale bar. The Guide has moved to meet the demand for creature comforts and good food with longer and more useful descriptions that also cover the history and architecture of pubs with advice on other local attractions.

We listen to our readers. This year we include post codes for the first time that will enable Guide users to track down pubs on computerised maps. We have also dropped the 'Inn Brief' sections for each county or region that gave shorter descriptions of selected pubs. Readers (and publicans!) thought the Inn Brief entries meant second-class pubs. That was not the intention, but we have bowed to our readers' wishes and removed Inn Briefs; they have been replaced with additional full entries.

One of the strengths of the Good Beer Guide is that it offers a good choice of pubs in urban as well as rural areas. Some guides give the impression that pubs only exist at the end of country lanes. CAMRA has been at the forefront of the campaign to save threatened rural pubs and they feature in abundance in the following pages. But we do not assume that pubgoers only visit the countryside. They go to such major urban areas as Leeds, Liverpool and Manchester and are well catered for in these pages, whereas the unfortunate users of one pub guide will find one entry in Leeds, two in Liverpool, and three in central Manchester.

As a result of our selection process, there is always a substantial turnover of pubs from one edition to the next. CAMRA has 67,000 members who visit pubs in their localities on a regular basis. We do not rely on single visits or recommendations. Even as we prepare the Guide for press, we delete pubs that CAMRA members feel should be removed as a result of a sudden change of landlord or a decline in beer quality.

Our unique Breweries section is also made possible by the strength of CAMRA, which appoints liaison officers to every brewery in the land. This means we can offer up-to-date information about breweries and their beers, information that spills over into the pubs section as well.

■ You can keep your Guide up to date by visiting the CAMRA website www.camra.org.uk. Click on Good Beer Guide then Updates to the GBG 2004. You will find information on brewery changes; pubs that CAMRA branches consider should be deleted from the Guide as a result of closure or poor beer quality; and pub entries that have experienced changes to opening hours, beer range and facilities.

BEDFORDSHIRE

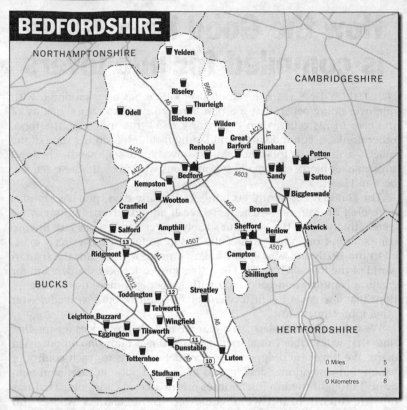

NORTHAMPTONSHIRE

CAMBRIDGESHIRE

Yelden

Riseley

Thurleigh

Odell

Bletsoe

Wilden

Renhold

Great Barford

Blunham

Potton

Bedford

Sandy

Sutton

Kempston

Wootton

Biggleswade

Cranfield

Broom

Salford

Ampthill

Shefford

Henlow

Astwick

Ridgmont

Campton

Shillington

BUCKS

Toddington

Streatley

Tebworth

Leighton Buzzard

Wingfield

Eggington

Tilsworth

HERTFORDSHIRE

Totternhoe

Dunstable

Luton

Studham

0 Miles 5

0 Kilometres 8

AMPTHILL

Engine & Tender ⊘
11 Dunstable Street, MK45 2NJ
🕐 11 (12 Sat)-2.30, 5-11; 11-11 Fri; 12-4, 7-10.30 Sun
☎ (01525) 403319
Greene King IPA, Abbot Ⓗ

Friendly one-bar local on the main road, with a good 'pubby' atmosphere, frequented by the local rugby club. A large patio area to the rear is used for summer drinking. Bar snacks are served weekdays, 12–2. Darts, dominoes and shut the box are played. The landlord possesses an unusual 'snuff engine' – if the pub is not too busy, ask to try it! Ampthill is an attractive Georgian market town, popular for its antique shops. 🏛🏵♣

ASTWICK

Tudor Oaks
Taylors Road, SG5 4AZ (A1)
🕐 11-11; 12-3.30, 7-10.30 Sun
☎ (01462) 834133
website: www.thetudoroakslodge.co.uk
Beer range varies Ⓗ

Oak-beamed pub where seven handpumps serve an ever-changing range of beers, mainly from micro-breweries. Real cider (varies) and perry are served chilled; no nitro-keg beers are sold at all. An extensive bar and restaurant menu offers freshly-cooked food, including Loch Fyne seafood and Aberdeen Angus steaks. The guest accommodation is in 13 rooms set around a central courtyard, some with four-poster beds. 🏛🏵🛏🍴◑🅿♣

BEDFORD

Ship ⊘
St Cuthbert's Street, MK40 3JB
🕐 11-11; 12-10.30 Sun
☎ (01234) 267126
Greene King IPA, Abbot; guest beer Ⓗ

Delightful old coaching inn located close to the town centre by St Cuthbert's Church and the old castle mound. This Greene King house retains three bars, plus front decking and a large rear patio. The two front cabin and public bars bear some genuine beams and both have marvellous wood-burning fires. The back patio, which is heated in winter, is ideal for summer barbecues.
🏛Q🏵◑♣🅿

Wellington Arms ⊘
**40-42 Wellington Street,
MK40 2JA**
(off the Broadway, A6 N of centre)
🕐 12-11; 12-10.30 Sun
☎ (01234) 308033
website: www.wellingtonarms.co.uk
**Adnams Bitter; B&T Two Brewers Bitter,
Shefford Bitter; guest beers** Ⓗ

Award-winning B&T pub in the older part of town. This three-times local CAMRA Pub of the Year attracts customers from miles around; a must to visit when in the area. One of the few pubs in Bedfordshire to stock real mild and real cider (Westons), it also offers a growing selection of Belgian and other assorted imported beers, in bottle and on draught.
🏵♣

BIGGLESWADE

Wheatsheaf ●
5 Lawrence Road, SG18 0LS
⏰ 11-4, 7-11; 11-11 Fri & Sat; 12-10.30 Sun
☎ (01767) 222220
Greene King XX Mild, IPA H
Compact, unpretentious, one-bar local.
Tucked away in a small street, the
Wheatsheaf is an end-of-terrace property
with a small garden to the rear. A loyal
(mostly male) clientele enjoys its no-frills
atmosphere – just good beer and
conversation. It fields active crib and
dominoes teams. The locals' enthusiasm for
football talk is reinforced with live TV
coverage. A weekly meat raffle and frequent
trips to the races are organised. No food is
served, apart from summer barbecues. ❀≈♣

BLETSOE

Falcon ●
Rushden Road, MK44 1QN
⏰ 11-3, 6-11 (11-11 summer Sat); 12-3, 7-10.30
(12-10.30 summer) Sun
☎ (01234) 781222
Wells Eagle, Bombardier; guest beers H
17th-century coaching inn with a large
garden running down to the River Great
Ouse. The splendid oak-panelled restaurant
was once a local courtroom. The excellent
menu is strong on fish and steak, and
includes home-made pastries. The Victorian
traveller and writer Edward Fitzgerald stayed
here while translating the Rubaiyat of Omar
Khayyam. ♨❀◑P⌖

BLUNHAM

Salutation
20 High Street, MK44 3NL
⏰ 12-3, 5.30-11; 12-4, 7-10.30 Sun
☎ (01767) 640620
Greene King IPA, Ruddles County, Abbot H
Fine pub, situated in the centre of the village.
John Donne, poet and one-time Dean of St
Paul's, was rector here in the early 17th
century. The front of the building (including
the leaded windows) dates from this time,
although the rest was added later. There is a
small, comfortable lounge and a large public
bar with pool and table skittles. Behind the
bar is a spacious dining room. ♨❀◑⊟♣P

BROOM

Cock ☆
23 High Street, SG18 9NA
⏰ 12-3 (4 Sat), 6-11; 12-4, 7-10.30 Sun
☎ (01767) 314411
Greene King IPA, Ruddles County, Abbot G
Wonderful old pub with no bar! Beer is
served direct from the cellar. It has featured
in every edition of this Guide and is on
CAMRA's National Inventory. This Grade II
listed building has a number of charming
rooms with flagstone floors and many
fireplaces; a real treasure. Pub games such as
Northants skittles are played, and excellent
food is served. ♨⍝❀◑⊟▲♣P

CAMPTON

White Hart
Mill Lane, SG17 5NX
⏰ 12-3 (not Mon-Thu), 7-11; 12-11 Sat; 12-3, 7-10.30 Sun

☎ (01462) 812567
**Hook Norton Best Bitter; Marston's Pedigree;
Theakston Best Bitter; guest beers** H
This traditional, family-run village free
house has been in this Guide since 1976. A
300-year-old, Grade II listed pub, it features
quarry-tiled floors, two inglenooks and a
wealth of bygones and memorabilia. A large
garden and patio with a petanque piste and
a well-equipped play area complete the
picture. No food is served, but buffets are
available for special occasions.
♨Q❀♣P

CRANFIELD

Carpenters Arms
93 High Street, MK43 0DP
⏰ 12-2.30 (not Mon), 6-11; 12-3, 7-10.30 Sun
☎ (01234) 750232
Wells Eagle, Bombardier; guest beers H
Situated in the centre of Cranfield, the
'Carps' has recently been refurbished in the
character of a traditional pub with wood
floors and cladding, but remains light and
airy. The licensees have over 20 years'
experience as publicans. They offer an
extensive choice of snacks and bar meals
served in a comfortable, no-smoking dining
area. Darts and skittles are played in the bar.
The large car park leads to a patio garden.
♨Q❀⍝◑⊟♣P

DUNSTABLE

Victoria
69 West Street, LU6 1ST
⏰ 11-11; 12-10.30 Sun
☎ (01582) 662682
Beer range varies H
Friendly, town-centre local, strong on pub
games and TV sport. It has just one bar, but
a comfortable function room can be used
when not booked. The house beer, Victoria
Bitter, is brewed by Tring, while four ever-
changing guest beers come from micros and
regional brewers. The paved patio to the
rear hosts summer barbecues. The pub also
stages quarterly beer festivals. Good value
lunches are served at this local CAMRA Pub
of the Year, 1995–2000. ❀◑♣

EGGINGTON

Horseshoes
High Street, LU7 9PD
⏰ 11-2.30 (not Mon), 6-11; 12-10.30 Sun
☎ (01525) 210282
Fuller's London Pride; Wadworth 6X; guest beer H
Picture-postcard pub with four rooms,
consisting of a bar with scrubbed wooden
tables, much used for cards and dominoes, a
snug, a restaurant and an unusual upstairs
room. Originally three farm cottages, it
dates from around 1750. The large garden
has a lawned area that is a real suntrap in
summer. The food (not served Mon) is
superb, and booking is strongly
recommended. ♨Q❀◑♣P

INDEPENDENT BREWERIES

B&T Shefford
Old Stables Sandy
Potton Potton
Wells Bedford

GREAT BARFORD

Anchor Inn ⊘
High Street, MK44 3LF
✪ 12-3, 5.30-11; 12-3, 7-10.30 Sun
☎ (01234) 870364
Wells Eagle, Bombardier; guest beers Ⓗ
Village local overlooking the River Great
Ouse; it is popular with boating people in
summer. The bar food is all home cooked –
specialities include steaks and fresh fish –
and is available every day. The restaurant
opens Sunday lunchtime and
Tuesday–Saturday evenings (booking is
recommended). Three rooms are available
for B&B guests. Two guest beers come from
a varied range. ♨Q⇆◑ ♠P⅊

HENLOW

Engineers Arms ⊘
66 High Street, SG16 6AA
✪ 12-11; 12-10.30 Sun
☎ (01462) 812284 website: www.engineersarms.com
Everards Tiger; Ⓗ **guest beers** Ⓗ/Ⓖ
Bedfordshire CAMRA Pub of the Year 2003 –
a real community pub catering for 18–80
year-olds. It fields several sports teams and
hosts regular blues, comedy and curry
nights. Now sporting nine handpumps, it
offers around 15–20 different beers each
week, mainly from micro-brewers. The
landlord also brews his own at the Bass
Museum Brewery several times a year. This
very friendly pub is enjoyed by villagers and
visitors from far and wide.
♨❀⊡♣

KEMPSTON

Half Moon
108 High Street, MK42 7BN
✪ 12-3 (not Mon), 6 (5 Fri; 7 Sat)-11; 12-3,
7-10.30 Sun
☎ (01234) 852464
Wells Eagle, Bombardier Ⓗ
Conventional, friendly local in the oldest
part of town, it is handy for pleasant walks
by the River Great Ouse. The public bar has
a large games area where skittles and darts
are played. The cheerful landlord will stay
open later at lunchtimes if customers are
still drinking. A large, grassed area has
picnic tables and children's play equipment,
including swings and a rocking horse.
❀⊡♣P

LEIGHTON BUZZARD

Hunt Hotel
19 Church Road, LU7 2LR
✪ 12-2.30 (3 Sat), 5-11; 12-3, 7-10.30 Sun
☎ (01525) 374692
**Fuller's London Pride, ESB; Tetley Bitter; guest
beers** Ⓗ
Built in 1846 and originally named the
Railway Tavern, this family-owned hotel
has a comfortable lounge bar, a restaurant
and a conference room. The food is very
good, but is not served on Sunday. Children
are welcome in the daytime. Live music is
featured on Friday evenings. One of the 12
bedrooms was regularly used in the 1930s
by Edward, Prince of Wales, and Mrs Wallis
Simpson when they visited to hunt with the
Whaddon Chase.
❀⇆◑⇌♣P

Stag ⊘
1 Heath Road, LU7 3AB
✪ 12-2.30, 6-11; 12-3, 7-10.30 Sun
☎ (01525) 372710
**Fuller's Chiswick, London Pride, ESB; seasonal or
guest beer** Ⓗ
This comfortably furnished, wedge-shaped
pub is larger inside than it looks from
outside. Attracting a good cross-section of
local drinkers, it features a long, wood-
panelled bar with a brass footrest. Good
home-cooked food is served, with a no-
smoking area available to diners (no meals
Sun eve). A quiz is held on Tuesday
evening. The car park is unsuited to
limousines, but ample parking is available
nearby. ❀◑♣P

Wheatsheaf
57 North Street, LU7 1EQ
✪ 11-11; 12-10.30 Sun
☎ (01525) 374611 website: www.thewheatie.co.uk
Shepherd Neame Spitfire; guest beer Ⓗ
Small, but lively, two-bar town pub run by
the same licensee for the past 20 years. The
low, beamed front bar is the original part of
the building. The rear bar area is more
recent and features old church pews for
seating and a stage area for live bands
which perform on Fridays, Saturdays and
bank holidays. Local 'star', Paul Young, has
played here three times. The varying guest
beer is invariably rare to the area. Benches
at the front of the pub are for summer
drinking. ❀⊡♣⊟

LUTON

Bricklayers Arms
16-18 Hightown Road, LU2 0DD
✪ 12-2.30, 5-11; 12-11 Fri & Sat; 12-10.30 Sun
☎ (01582) 611017
Everards Beacon, Tiger; guest beers Ⓗ
Friendly, unpretentious town pub, where
three ever-changing guest beers are usually
sourced from micro-breweries. Belgian
bottled beers are also available. Food, served
12–2 weekdays, includes filled rolls, toasted
sandwiches, ploughmans and burgers with
chips. A quiz is held every Monday evening
and Sky TV football is shown. It can get
crowded on Luton Town match days.
❀⇌♣P

Globe
26 Union Street, LU1 3AN
✪ 11-11; 12-10.30 Sun
☎ (01582) 728681
Greene King IPA; guest beers Ⓗ
Popular, street-corner local, just off the
town centre. This one-bar, L-shaped pub
offers two guest ales that change frequently
from micros and regional brewers. It also
stages regular beer festivals. Sport is shown
on TV. Good value food is served at
lunchtime. An enclosed patio area stands to
the rear of the small car park. ❀◑♣P

Two Brewers
43 Dumfries Street, LU1 5BP
✪ 12-11; 12-10.30 Sun
☎ (01582) 616008
Beer range varies Ⓗ
Friendly, street-corner local, now a free
house, stocking up to six guest beers, which
generally include one from Tring Brewery

(the former owners) and a dark ale. An island bar serves two bar areas. Acoustic music sessions are held every Friday, and jazz on alternate Wednesdays. Bottled Belgian beers are available, and an occasional real cider. It hosts beer festivals several times a year. It is popular with both home and away supporters on match days. There is no family room, but children are welcome.

🏚️🏵️🚅♣️🍺

ODELL

Bell
Horsefair Lane, MK43 7AU
🕐 11-3, 6-11; 12-3, 7-10.30 Sun
☎ (01234) 720254
Greene King IPA, Ruddles County, Abbot; guest beers Ⓗ

Handsome, thatched pub at the heart of the village, boasting an aviary of exotic birds and a large garden running almost to the River Great Ouse. This is an excellent stop for walkers, with the Harrold-Odell Country Park just down the lane. Although the cooking deserves its place in CAMRA's Good Pub Food, this is a pub with good food rather than a restaurant with good beer. No evening meals are served Sunday.

🏚️Q🏵️◑P

POTTON

Old Coach House ⊘
12 Market Square, SG19 2NP
🕐 12-2.30, 5.30-11; 12-11 Sat; 12-10.30 Sun
☎ (01767) 260221
website: www.pottoncoachhouse.co.uk
Adnams Bitter; Potton Shannon IPA, Shambles; guest beer Ⓗ

Friendly, family-run inn in the picturesque Georgian market square. It enjoys an excellent reputation for its home-cooked food – try the steak and Potton Ale pie (no food Sun eve). No pub games, TV, or juke box intrude so you can relax in quiet, comfortable surroundings. A separate dining room is available for special occasions. Well-placed for visiting mid-Bedfordshire's attractions, it has 12 centrally-heated, en-suite rooms. The floodlit petanque piste is open to the public.
Q🏵️🛏️◑P✂️

RENHOLD

Polhill Arms
25 Wilden Road, MK41 0JP (Salph End)
🕐 12-2.30 (not Mon; 3 Sat), 6-11 (12-11 summer Sat); 12-10.30 Sun
☎ (01234) 771398 website: www.polhillarms.co.uk
Greene King IPA, Morland Original; guest beer Ⓗ

Traditional village local on a corner towards the Bedford end of the village. The garden has a children's play area. The single bar includes a dining area which is no-smoking. The food is all home cooked and includes take-away fish and chips (Thu–Sat). Pensioners' lunches are available on Tuesday; evening meals are served Wednesday–Saturday. Guest beers include some from outside the standard Greene King range. Occasional themed nights are held.
🏚️🏵️◑♣️P✂️🍴

RIDGMONT

Rose & Crown ⊘
89 High Street, MH43 0TY
🕐 10.30-2.30 (12-3 Sat), 6-11; 12-3.30, 7-10.30 Sun
☎ (01525) 280245
Adnams Broadside; Wells Eagle, Bombardier; seasonal beer or guest beer Ⓗ

Attractive pub, built using local bricks and dating back some 300 years. A multiple award-winner, its latest achievement is Best Real Ale Pub in the entire Wells estate. Highlights are two comfortable bars, good food and a huge garden with approved facilities for camping and caravanning. The use of mobile phones is prohibited in the bars; children are permitted in the dining area. Run by the same licensees for well over 20 years, the pub has been in every edition of this Guide. 🏵️◑Å P

RISELEY

Fox & Hounds ⊘
High Street, MK44 1DT
🕐 11-2.30, 6.30-11; 12-3, 7-10.30 Sun
☎ (01234) 708240
Wells Eagle, Bombardier; guest beers Ⓗ

Extended old village inn with a reputation for good food. It attracts diners from a wide area. Charcoal-grilled steaks, sold by weight, are a speciality (not served Sat lunch). A dining room can be reserved for groups, but no booking is necessary for normal bar meals – meet and drink in the bar while your food is cooked. The large, lawned garden has a covered patio with heaters for inclement weather. Q🏵️◑P

SALFORD

Red Lion Hotel
Wavendon Road, MK17 8AZ (2 miles from M1 jct 13)
🕐 11-2.30, 6-11; 12-2.30, 7-10.30 Sun
☎ (01908) 583117
Wells Eagle, Bombardier; guest beers Ⓗ

Lively, traditional country pub hotel, the Red Lion serves a good selection of real ales. Home-cooked food is available in the bar and no-smoking dining area. At the rear is a large garden with a covered area and children's playground. The bar, warmed by an open real fire in winter offers a selection of board games. Guest rooms are chalet-style with four-poster beds. The Swan in Salford also serves real ales. 🏚️🏵️🛏️◑♣️P

SANDY

Sir William Peel
39 High Street, SG19 1AG
🕐 12 (11 Sat)-11; 12-3, 7-10.30 Sun
☎ (01767) 680607
Everards Beacon; Old Stables Stable Ale; guest beers Ⓗ

Single-bar, traditional pub where a warm welcome is extended to a well-behaved clientele of all ages. The pub is the home of the Old Stables Brewing Co., which offers seasonal beers and the regular brew, Stable Ale. The guest beers are normally supplied by small independent breweries, making for adventurous drinking. Friday night can be hectic. No food is available, but the pub is flanked by a chip shop and Indian restaurant. 🏵️🚅P

SHEFFORD

Brewery Tap
14 North Bridge Street, SG17 5DH
☼ 11.30-11; 12-10.30 Sun
☎ (01462) 628448
B&T Shefford Mild, Shefford Bitter, Dragonslayer, seasonal beers; guest beers Ⓗ
This basic drinkers' pub has a single bar featuring breweriana and bottled beers. There is a family room at the rear and a small patio garden. Over the years the pub has been called the Green Man, Grape Vine and Countryman, but was rescued by B&T Brewery and renamed in 1996. Popular for games, which include table football and skittles, it hosts live music most Friday evenings. Six handpumps serve B&T beers at reasonable prices, plus usually two guests. Food is restricted to hot pies and filled rolls.
ॐ ❀ ♣ P

SHILLINGTON

Musgrave Arms
16 Apsley End Road, SG5 3LX
☼ 12-3, 5-11; 11-11 Sat; 12-4, 7-10.30 Sun
☎ (01462) 711286
Greene King XX Mild, Ⓗ **IPA, Abbot; guest beer** Ⓖ
Cosy, country pub, boasting original Tudor beams. The raised 'public' end, with scrubbed wooden tables, is popular with dominoes players. The no-smoking dining room, where children are welcome, offers excellent food – Tuesday is steak night (no food Mon). The large garden features a patio area, play equipment and two petanque pitches. A Guide regular, the Musgrave was local CAMRA Pub of the Year 2001.
꛰ Q ❀ ◑ ♣ P

STREATLEY

Chequers
171 Sharpenhoe Road, LU3 9PS
☼ 12-11; 12-10.30 Sun
☎ (01582) 882072
Greene King IPA, Ruddles County, Abbot, Old Speckled Hen; guest beers Ⓗ
Busy, friendly pub in a traditional rural setting, next to the village church. The building is Georgian in origin, but has been much extended. The single L-shaped bar offers good food all day and, unusually for the area, oversized glasses are used. The pub is close to the Chiltern Way and is popular with walkers. The garden offers a play area and a patio, and outside jazz sessions are held monthly on Sunday lunchtime. Five guest rooms are available.
꛰ ❀ ⇌ ◑ ♣ P ☗

STUDHAM

Bell
Dunstable Road, LU6 2QG
☼ 11.30-3, 5.30-11; 11.30-11 Sat; 12-10.30 Sun
☎ (01582) 872460
Adnams Bitter; Fuller's London Pride; Greene King IPA, Abbot, Old Speckled Hen Ⓗ
Reputedly haunted 16th-century village pub. The public bar has darts, dominoes and plenty of seating; the saloon bar incorporates a no-smoking dining area. The food is good value, and Sunday lunches are so popular that booking is recommended. The garden offers a panoramic view of the

Chilterns. Whipsnade Zoo is nearby.
❀ ◑ ⇌ ♣ P

SUTTON

John O'Gaunt Inn
30 High Street, SG19 2NG
☼ 12-3, 7-11; 12-3, 7-10.30 Sun
☎ (01767) 260377
Greene King IPA, Old Speckled Hen; guest beer Ⓗ
This traditional pub, comprising two oak-beamed bars, has a timeless feel to it. Very active in all village life, it boasts a floodlit boules pitch and a Northants skittle alley in the public bar. The pub has its own golf society. Social evenings with buffet can be arranged. It hosts occasional folk sessions and morris dancers perform in summer. Admire the village quilt displayed in the lounge bar. A good range of home-cooked food is available every day (not Sun eve).
꛰ Q ❀ ◑ ♣ P ⪥

TEBWORTH

Queen's Head
The Lane, LU7 9QB
☼ 11.30-3, 6.30-11; 12-3, 7-10.30 Sun
☎ (01525) 874101
Adnams Broadside; Ⓖ **Wells Eagle;** Ⓗ **guest beer** Ⓖ
This village local was built in 1926, following the destruction of the former thatched pub by fire – the 'shed' to the side of the car park was the licensee's accommodation, and is a listed building. The current landlord oversees a public bar, with darts and a rickety pool table, and a comfortable lounge bar which hosts a weekly quiz (Thu eve) and live music (Fri eve). In this Guide continuously for over 20 years. ꛰ ❀ ⇌ ♣ P

THURLEIGH

Jackal ⊘
3 High Street, MK44 2DB
☼ 12-3 (2.30 Mon), 6-11; 12-2.30, 7-10.30 Sun
☎ (01234) 771293
website: www.thejackal.fsbusiness.co.uk
Wells Eagle, Bombardier Ⓗ
Attractive, part-thatched pub with an abundance of baskets and pots brimming with flowers all year round. The large, child-friendly garden backs on to rolling fields. The main drinking area is the public bar; the lounge is mostly taken up with the dining area. The high quality bistro-style food is full of innovative dishes using local produce (no food Sun eve or Mon).
꛰ ❀ ◑ ⇌ ♣ P

TILSWORTH

Anchor ⊘
1 Dunstable Road, LU7 9PU
☼ 11-11; 12-10.30 Sun
☎ (01525) 210289
Greene King IPA, Abbot; guest beer Ⓗ
Lively, welcoming village local. The L-shaped bar area has a stone-flagged games area to one end, and has been extended with the addition of a conservatory/restaurant area. Good food from an extensive menu includes many interesting dishes. Families are welcome at all times; the large garden has a patio area and play equipment. ꛰ ❀ ◑ ♣ P

TODDINGTON

Bedford Arms
64 High Street, LU5 6BY
🕐 12-11; 12-10.30 Sun
☎ (01525) 873503
Wells Eagle; seasonal or guest beers Ⓗ
Attractive both inside and out, this
apparently haunted, former farmhouse
offers two heavily-beamed bars to lounge
standard. One bar extends into a no-
smoking conservatory dining area. It has a
large garden and patio area. Antipodean
hosts offer a warm welcome. Good food is
served, but not Sunday evening or Monday.
Tuesday is quiz night. 🏨🌸◑♣P

Oddfellows Arms
2 Conger Lane, LU5 6BP
🕐 12-3 (not Mon-Thu), 5-11; 12-10.30 Sun
☎ (01525) 872021
website: www.theoddfellowsarms.com
Adnams Broadside; Fuller's London Pride; guest beers Ⓗ
This 15th-century pub facing the village
green, comprises a heavily-beamed L-shaped
bar and restaurant. It stocks over 20 Belgian
bottled beers, plus Hoegaarden Wit beer on
draught; all are served in the correct glass. A
sheltered patio area is available for summer
drinking. The extensive menu offers good
value food (not served after 5.30pm Sun)
and several dishes use the Belgian beers.
Beer festivals are held in the spring and
autumn. Local CAMRA Pub of the Year
2002 and 2003. 🏨🌸◑♣

Sow & Pigs ✿
19 Church Square, LU5 6AA
🕐 11-11; 12-10.30 Sun
☎ (01525) 873089 website: www.sowandpigs.co.uk
Greene King IPA, Abbot; seasonal or guest beer Ⓗ
19th-century commercial inn with one long,
narrow, dog-friendly bar, heated by three
real fires, displaying an assortment of pig
and golfing memorabilia and a wide range
of games. Food on offer generally consists of
cold platters and home-made soup. The
upstairs banqueting room can be booked for
parties of 16-24 people, and the spread of
food provided has to be seen to be believed!
Accommodation is in comfortable rooms at
reasonable prices. The Sow has appeared in
every edition of this Guide. 🏨Q🌸⇔♣P

TOTTERNHOE

Old Farm
16 Church Road, LU6 1RE
🕐 12-3, 5.30-11; 12-11 Fri & Sat; 12-10.30 Sun
☎ (01582) 661294 website: www.oldfarminn.co.uk
Fuller's Chiswick, London Pride, ESB Ⓗ
Charming village local in the conservation
area of Totternhoe, nestling under
Dunstable Downs. The public bar has a low,
boarded ceiling and an inglenook, and is
much used for traditional pub games. The
restaurant, which serves commendable,
good value food, is located in the rear bar,
which also boasts an inglenook. Wheelchair
access is via the restaurant. A large, child-
friendly garden is next to the car park.
Q🌸◑⇔♣P

WILDEN

Victoria
23 High Street, MK44 2PB
🕐 12-2.30, 6.30-11; 12-11 Sat; 12-3.30,
7-10.30 Sun
☎ (01234) 772146
Greene King IPA, Abbot; guest beer (occasional) Ⓗ
Friendly village local with one bar and a
restaurant attached. Occasional guest beers
come from the Greene King range. Home-
cooked food includes fish and chips on
Tuesday, special meals for senior citizens on
Wednesday, 'pie and pint' on Thursday and
curry night on Friday. No evening meals are
served Sunday or Monday. Children are
welcome in the restaurant, which has a no-
smoking area. 🏨🐾◑♣P

WINGFIELD

Plough ✿
Tebworth Road, LU7 9QH
🕐 12-3, 5.30-11 (11-11 summer Sat); 12-4, 6-10.30
(closed Sept-Mar eve) Sun
☎ (01525) 873077
Adnams Bitter; Fuller's London Pride, ESB; seasonal or guest beer Ⓗ
Attractive, thatched village inn dating from
the 17th century. Beware the low beams
and entrance. The conservatory at the rear
serves as a restaurant where children are
welcome. The bar is decorated with Royal
Navy memorabilia and rural scenes. The
food is of a high standard (no meals Sun
eve). Tables are set out at the front of the
pub for summer drinking, and the enclosed
prize-winning garden has children's play
equipment. 🏨🌸◑P

WOOTTON

Chequers
47 Hall End, MK43 9HP (from Wootton take
Church Rd and keep going) OS001458
🕐 11.30-2.30, 5.30-11; 12-10.30 Sun
☎ (01234) 768394
Wells Eagle; guest beers Ⓗ
Built as a farm in the 16th century, the
Chequers retains many interesting old
features, not least the heavy beams and low
ceilings that give the lounge bar its intimate
atmosphere. The large, lawned garden, with
seats and tables, is a popular venue in good
weather. The public bar offers the local
version of skittles. A good range of
interesting food varies according to produce
available; all dishes are home made (no
food Sun eve or Mon).
🏨🌸◑⊟♣P

YELDEN

Chequers
High Street, MK44 1AW
🕐 5 (4 Fri; 12 Sat)-11; 12-10.30 Sun
☎ (01933) 356383
Fuller's London Pride; Ⓗ **Greene King Abbot;** Ⓖ
Shepherd Neame Spitfire; Woodforde's Wherry; guest beers Ⓗ
Traditional village pub stocking five real ales
and two ciders. It has a family-cum-skittles
room and a small lounge (no-smoking
except Mon). The large garden houses
children's play equipment and is the venue
for an annual real ale festival over the
spring bank holiday weekend. The main bar
displays rare bottled beers. Yelden is on the
Three Shires Way footpath and boasts the
impressive earthworks of a Norman castle.
🏨🐾🌸▲♣●P⊬

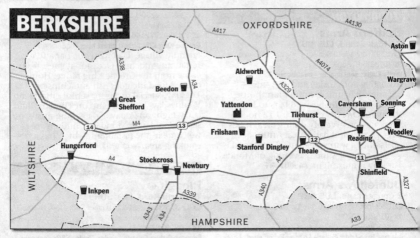

BERKSHIRE

ALDWORTH

Bell ☆
Bell Lane, RG17 9QJ
(follow signs to Aldworth from B4009) OS556797
⏱ 11-3, 6-11; closed Mon; 12-3, 7-10.30 Sun
☎ (01635) 578272
Arkells 3B, Kingsdown; West Berkshire Maggs Magnificent Mild, seasonal beers Ⓗ/Ⓖ
Standing opposite England's deepest well (370ft), the present building dates from the late 15th century, and the same family has played host here since 1830. The main bar is tiny, with painted brick walls and ancient furniture, while the tap room has simple wooden benches and a 300-year-old, one-handed case clock. A cottage garden adjoins the cricket pitch and is popular with hikers from the nearby Ridgeway long-distance footpath. Award-winning filled rolls are irresistible. Old Tyler is West Berkshire's Good Old Boy rebadged. Upton farmhouse cider is stocked. ♨Q❀◑♣♠P

ASCOT

Swinley
29 Brockenhurst Road, South Ascot, SL5 9DJ (on A330)
⏱ 11-11; 12-10.30 Sun
☎ (01344) 621743
Greene King IPA, Ruddles County Ⓗ
Genuine, late-Victorian street-corner local with a comfortable lounge and a truly unspoilt public bar. The landlady, who has run the pub for over 30 years, was given a special Award of Excellence in 2002 by the local CAMRA branch. It was previously called the Railway Arms but was renamed to avoid confusion with the nearby Station Hotel. There is a TV in the lounge. The pub has a cribbage team with darts and shove-ha'penny also played. It can get busy during Royal Ascot week. ♨❀◑Ⓗ&⇌♣P

ASTON

Flower Pot
Ferry Lane, RG9 3DG
⏱ 11-3, 6-11; 12-3.30, 7-10.30 Sun
☎ (01491) 574721
Brakspear Bitter, Special, seasonal beers Ⓗ
Rural, late Victorian hotel, half a mile from Hambleden Lock on the Thames. The

Thames path and the pub's own landing stage are nearby. A bare-boarded public bar adorned with hop bines, complements a smart lounge and dining area. Real fires warm the pub and there are numerous stuffed fish in glass cases. The large garden, with unusual fowl in the adjacent field, offers extensive views of the Chilterns. Good value food is available (not served on Sunday evening), and snacks include jellied eels. ♨❀⇌◑Ⓗ&♣P

BEEDON

Langley Hall Inn
Oxford Road, World's End, RG20 8SA
(1 mile S of village, near A34 intersection with M4, jct 13) OS484761
⏱ 11-11; 12-10.30 Sun
☎ (01635) 248332
West Berkshire Good Old Boy; guest beers Ⓗ
Named after a long-demolished nearby manor, this popular, welcoming local is situated on a quiet road, bypassed by the present A34. A horseshoe-shaped bar dominates, with minimalist decor – no horse brasses here. The adjoining restaurant is a favourite with business people; breakfasts are available before the pub opens. No meals are served on Sunday evening. In fine weather, sit outside on the front patio or in the rear garden. The choice of beers is limited but they are carefully chosen and well kept. Backgammon is played. Piped music can be loud later in the evening. ♨❀⇌◑♣P

BINFIELD

Stag & Hounds
Forest Road, RG42 4HA (on B3034, E of village)
⏱ 11-11; 12-10.30 Sun
☎ (01344) 483553
Courage Best Bitter; guest beer Ⓖ
Very attractive, large country pub, once at the centre of Windsor forest. It is mostly half-timbered with the villagers' bar in an appropriately decorated Georgian addition. The low, beamed main bar has a large inglenook which is a treat on winter days when the beer is served straight from barrels behind the bar. Doorways lead off the main bar to a number of different rooms and seating areas. The large menu includes daily

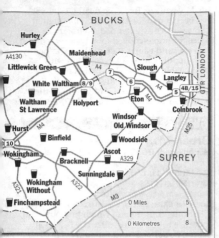

specials. Anyone out walking in the area will find the pub dog-friendly. ♨Q✿❍●⧉P

Victoria Arms ✓
Terrace Road North, RG42 5JA
(N of B3034 at mini-roundabout in village centre)
🕐 11-11; 12-10.30 Sun
☎ (01344) 483856
Fuller's Chiswick, London Pride, ESB, seasonal beers Ⓗ
Friendly and comfortable pub with a single split-level bar, incorporating a central fireplace that divides the room. An extensive collection of old beer bottles adorns the rafters. The absence of gaming machines means the pub is generally quiet enough for conversation, although there is a TV in the lower level of the bar and occasional piped music. A quiz evening is held on Sunday. A wide range of basic pub food is available at reasonable prices, including daily specials. No food is served on Sunday evening. ♨✿❍●P

BRACKNELL

Old Manor ✓
Grenville Place, High Street, RG12 1BP
🕐 11-11; 12-10.30 Sun
☎ (01344) 304490
Courage Directors; Greene King Abbot; Shepherd Neame Spitfire; Theakston Best Bitter; guest beers Ⓗ
Not a typical Wetherspoon's as this is a genuinely historic building that has held a licence for many years. There are two bars, one of which is completely no-smoking and allows children if dining (until 8.30pm). Multi-roomed, the pub features the monk's room, which is characterised by a priest's hole, discovered during renovation. An exceptional range of up to six ever-changing guest beers is available. Berkshire south-east CAMRA Pub of the Year 2002.
Q✿❍&≠♣P⅄

CAVERSHAM

Griffin
10-12 Church Road, RG4 7AD (on A4074)
🕐 11-11; 12-10.30 Sun
☎ (0118) 947 5018
Courage Best Bitter, Directors; Theakston XB; guest beer Ⓗ

Chef & Brewer branded conversion of a 100-year-old pub. Licensed premises have occupied the site for over 300 years. The pub has an olde-worlde feel with fake beams and hop bines around the bar, background jazz music and atmospheric candlelit tables. Restaurant-quality food is served at all times. The guest beer is usually from a regional or small independent brewery. A pleasant, shady patio area is provided for outdoor drinking.
♨✿❍●P

COLNBROOK

Ostrich
42 High Street, SL3 0NZ
🕐 11-11; 12-10.30 Sun
☎ (01753) 682628
Worthington's 1744; guest beers Ⓗ
This old coaching inn is a Grade II listed architectural gem. The third oldest pub in England, most of the building is from the early 1500s, although parts date back to the 12th century. A one-time innkeeper here used to murder rich guests. The large and varied menu includes ostrich steaks. Friendly and attentive staff help maintain a cosy atmosphere. Not a venue for people on tight budgets. Bus route 81 from Slough to Hounslow passes outside. ♨✿❍●P

ETON

Crown & Cushion
84 High Street, SL4 6AF
🕐 11-11; 12-10.30 Sun
☎ (01753) 861531
Brakspear Special; Courage Best Bitter; Greene King Old Speckled Hen; Marston's Pedigree Ⓗ
Friendly local which dates back to 1575 and caters for a true cross-section of the community, from actors who stay during productions at the nearby theatre, to staff from Eton College. A cosy atmosphere pervades, with subdued lighting and glowing embers. Meals are served daily except Friday–Sunday evenings. All pubs in Eton serve real ale.
♨⛾✿⇆❍●≠ (Windsor & Eton Riverside)
♣P⅄

FINCHAMPSTEAD

Queen's Oak
Church Lane, RG11 4LS (off B3016)
🕐 11-3, 5.30-11 (11-11 summer); 12-10.30 Sun
☎ (0118) 973 4855
Brakspear Bitter, Special, seasonal beers Ⓗ
This fine Grade II listed building stands opposite the church and the oak tree that Queen Victoria planted, which inspired the pub's name. The ample garden has a play area, an Aunt Sally and can hold a marquee which is available for private hire. The licensee has once again won a Brakspear award and has introduced a friendly quiz on Wednesday night during winter. Pub meals are served 12–2 and 6.30–9 (no food Sun eve) and there is a no-smoking bar.
♨Q✿❍♣P⅄

INDEPENDENT BREWERIES

Butts Great Shefford
West Berkshire Yattendon

FRILSHAM

Pot Kiln
RG18 0XX (1 mile S of Yattendon
on Bucklebury road) OS552781
☻ 12-2.30 (not Tue), 6.30-11; 12-3, 7-10.30 Sun
☎ (01635) 201366
Arkells 3B; Greene King Morland Original; West Berkshire Brick Kiln Bitter, seasonal beers ⊞
Isolated and hard to find, this determinedly old-fashioned beer house is situated well away from the village among attractive woodland and meadows. Three simply furnished rooms are arranged around a tiny bar, and the entry lobby serves as a tap room, where locals stand and chat, or where summer visitors queue for service. West Berkshire Brewery operates from the outbuildings and brews Brick Kiln Bitter, which is unique to the pub. A daily menu is offered but no food is available on Tuesday and warm filled rolls (only) are served on Sunday.
෴Q❀◑⊟♣P⊁

HOLYPORT

Belgian Arms
Holyport Street, SL6 2JR (E of A330)
☻ 11-3, 5.30-11; 12-3, 7-10.30 Sun
☎ (01628) 634468
Brakspear Bitter, Special ⊞
Traditional, 400-year-old pub originally called the Eagle, its name was changed when German POWs saluted it during WWI. The wisteria-covered frontage faces the village green and a pleasant garden with a pond makes it a particularly attractive spot in summer. The real fire is a cosy prospect in winter. Good value food is served daily except Sunday evening.
෴Q❀◑▷♣P

HUNGERFORD

Hungerford Club ⊘
3 The Croft, RG17 0HY
(off Church St, close to the fire station)
☻ 12-3 (not Mon-Fri), 7-11; 12-3, 7-10.30 Sun
☎ (01488) 682357
Fuller's London Pride, Greene King IPA; guest beers ⊞
This is a welcoming and comfortable club with a saloon bar atmosphere, whose members enjoy lawn tennis and bowls on the well-kept grounds across the village-green-like 'croft'. Two excellent Victorian snooker tables are available, and there is a busy entertainments schedule with live music, quizzes and prize draws. Guest ales are imaginatively chosen, often from micro-breweries, in this former CAMRA Club of the Year runner-up. A copy of this Guide or a CAMRA membership card will gain entry.
❀⇌♣P

HURLEY

Dew Drop Inn
Batts Green, Honey Lane, SL6 6RB
(1 mile S of A4130, off Henley Rd at Hurley Bottom)
OS824815
☻ 12-3, 6-11; 12-3, 7-10.30 Sun
☎ (01628) 824327
Brakspear Bitter, Special, seasonal beer ⊞
Remote, traditional country pub, at the foot of Ashley Hill, that is the only house in Batts Green. Once Queen Anne cottages

used by workers from the nearby estate, it has been a pub for 150 years. The original bar was recently extended, giving more space for home-cooked food (not served Sun eve) and games such as shove-ha'penny and indoor boules. A large garden with picnic tables and gazebos makes it particularly appealing in summer, as confirmed by its local CAMRA Pub of the Season award in 2003. ෴Q❀◑▷♣P

HURST

Green Man
Hinton Road, RG10 0BP (off A321, just before the duckpond)
☻ 11-3, 5.30-11; 12-3, 6-10.30 Sun
☎ (0118) 934 2599
website: www.thegreenman.uk.com
Brakspear Bitter, Special, seasonal beers ⊞
Charming country pub which first obtained a licence to sell ale in 1602. The beams are said to be derived from the timbers of decommissioned ships, returning to their original home in Windsor forest. Although there is a strong emphasis on food, there is a distinct bar area. Decorations include prints and some unusual gadgetry. There is a sizeable rear garden. Meals can be booked via the website. Wheelchair WC.
෴Q❀◑▷P⊁

INKPEN

Swan
Craven Road, Lower Green, RG17 9DX
(on the road from Hungerford Common) OS359643
☻ 11-3, 7-11 (often 11-11 Sat); 12-3,
7-10.30 (often 12-10.30) Sun
☎ (01488) 668326
website: www.theswaninn-organics.co.uk
Butts Bitter; Hook Norton Mild, Best Bitter; guest beer ⊞
This 17th-century, rural pub came perilously close to becoming a private house until a local farmer took up the challenge. Heavy investment has created a friendly, spacious pub with something for everyone, not least a specialism in organic products. They are used in the restaurant and bar meals, and even in the choice of guest ale (when possible). Lambourn Valley cider is sold. It is a good base for walking and cycling (10 new bedrooms). Games are played in the separate flagstoned area and there is a well-stocked farm shop. It is wheelchair-ramped throughout.
෴❀⇐◑▷♣P⊁

LANGLEY

Red Lion ⊘
1 St Marys Road, SL3 7EN
☻ 11-11; 12-10.30 Sun
☎ (01753) 582285
Courage Best Bitter; Greene King IPA, Abbot; guest beer ⊞
Friendly, locals' hostelry that dates back to Tudor times. The fireplace in the saloon bar, although unused, is nonetheless impressive. The 12th-century church opposite is also worth a look. The pub has had a varied history and at one time was a mortuary. The extensive restaurant area has a large menu. The play area out back makes it popular with families in summer.
❀◑▷P

LITTLEWICK GREEN

Cricketers
Coronation Road, SL6 3RA (400 yds S of A4)
🕙 11-3, 5-11; 11-11 Sat; 12-10.30 Sun
☎ (01628) 822888
website: www.thecricketers.demon.co.uk
Badger K&B Sussex, Best; guest beers H

The landlady worked at this former free house (regularly featured in this Guide) and became publican when it was bought by Badger in 2002. The pub overlooks the green and cricket pitch in a pretty village, often seen on TV. Cricketers' pictures adorn the inside walls. One of the three rooms is dominated by an old factory clock above the real log fire. Tables out front and good food make it attractive all year. Accommodation is available.
🏚Q❀🛏◖♣P

MAIDENHEAD

Vine ●
20 Market Street, SL6 8AD
🕙 11-11; 12-10.30 Sun
☎ (01628) 782112
Bateman Mild; Brakspear Bitter, Special H

The oldest building in Market Street, this cosy, town-centre local was once a fire station and was formerly owned by the church. Its welcome tradition of having real mild as a fixture continues. An extensive range of good value food is available Monday–Friday, 11–7, and Sunday lunchtime. The decor features spirit miniatures and two TVs show live sport. Quiz night is Sunday. Public car parks are nearby, and there is roadside seating for summer drinking. ❀◖♣♣

NEWBURY

Hogshead ●
1-3 Wharf Street, RG14 5AN (off market place, towards the wharf)
🕙 12-11; 12-10.30 Sun
☎ (01635) 569895
Bateman XXXB; Greene King Abbot; Taylor Landlord; Wadworth 6X; Young's Special; guest beer H

Located just off the market place, this spacious, open-plan pub is always busy and attracts a wide range of customers. The split-level interior displays posters from the building's former auction-room days. A small terrace overlooks the Kennet & Avon Canal. The weekend choice of 12 different ales is reduced to six during the week. A good selection of continental bottled beers is also available. Meals are served until 8pm.
🏚❀◖&⇌♠

Lock Stock & Barrel ●
104 Northbrook Street, RG14 1AA (next to canal bridge)
🕙 11-11; 12-10.30 Sun
☎ (01635) 42730
Fuller's London Pride, ESB, seasonal beers H

Sizeable one-bar pub that is situated just off the main shopping area adjacent to the canal bridge. Probably the finest positioned pub in Newbury town centre, there is a pleasant patio area beside the Kennet & Avon Canal and a rooftop terrace. Barbecues are held in summer. A no-smoking area is enforced at lunchtime. It is popular with office workers at lunchtime, and drinkers in

the evening. It has convenient wheelchair access, with a WC next to the bar area.
❀◖&⇌

Monument
57 Northbrook Street, RG14 1AN
(near Broadway clock tower)
🕙 11-11; 12-10.30 Sun
☎ (01635) 41964
website: www.themonumentonline.co.uk
Butts Bitter, Barbus Barbus; Gale's HSB; Greene King Old Speckled Hen; guest beers H

Lively, 16th-century high street pub that attracts a wide ranging clientele. The pub is split into three areas, including a snug and an area which boasts computer games, fruit machines, table soccer and a hexagonal rotating pool table. Traditional pub games such as darts and cribbage are also played. Internet access is available. The rear covered courtyard is used as a venue for live music and comedy acts. The CD juke box and TVs are almost constantly in use. Westons Old Rosie cider is sold. ❀◖♣♠

OLD WINDSOR

Jolly Gardeners
92 St Lukes Road, SL4 2QJ
🕙 11-11; 12-10.30 Sun
☎ (01753) 740893
Courage Best Bitter; Wells Bombardier; guest beers H

Genuine, community local where the single horseshoe-shaped bar keeps a public bar/lounge feel. The publicans' stated intent to maintain a traditional pub is as successful as it is laudable, perhaps helped by the fact that the landlord was born next door. Please use your mobile phone outside only. Dogs are welcome until 8pm. ♣♠P

READING

Allied Arms
57 St Mary's Butts, RG1 2LG
🕙 11-11; 12-10.30 Sun
☎ (0118) 959 0865
Courage Best Bitter; Fuller's London Pride; guest beer (occasional) H

Interesting, traditional, town-centre local dating from around 1828. The name commemorates the military campaigns of the 19th century, although inside there is a slight rugby football flavour. Enter from the street into the small Yeoman Lounge, or via the cobbled side passageway into this or the slightly larger Dragoon Bar. The enclosed patio/garden at the rear is a secluded suntrap. One could easily forget that one was drinking in a busy town centre. ❀⇌

Eldon Arms
19 Eldon Terrace, RG1 4DX (off Eldon Rd)
🕙 10.30-3, 5.30-11; 12-3, 7-10.30 Sun
☎ (0118) 957 3857
Wadworth IPA, 6X, seasonal beers; guest beer H

Two-bar, back-street local just 10 minutes' walk from the bustling town centre. The same couple have run the pub for 28 years – the local CAMRA branch presented them with a certificate to celebrate their time at the Eldon Arms. There is a large, busy public bar and a comfortable, cosy lounge. Q◖◖♣

Fisherman's Cottage
224 Kennet Side, RG1 3DW
(on Kennet towpath behind college)

✪ 12-3, 6-11; 11-11 Sat & summer; 12-10.30 Sun
☎ (0118) 957 1553
Fuller's London Pride, ESB, seasonal beers Ⓗ
Pleasant, airy, single-bar canalside pub with a tiny snug/games room. The addition of a glass-roofed conservatory doubled the size of the original building. A delightful suntrap patio garden and towpath seating prove to be a honeypot on sunny summer days. The conservatory side of the bar has a slightly continental café-like feel with murals, hanging baskets and wicker seating. Blake's Lock Museum is on the opposite bank with access over the lock gates. ✿◖▶ ♣

Great Expectations
33 London Street, RG1 4PS
✪ 11-11; 12-10.30 Sun
☎ (0118) 950 3925
Courage Best Bitter; Theakston Best Bitter, Old Peculier; guest beer Ⓗ
A bizarre, if not unique, pub with a strong Dickensian theme – possibly a bit over the top for some, but not tacky. The large bar is divided into many drinking areas with a separate no-smoking room. Although invariably packed (and loud) on Friday and Saturday night, at other times there is usually somewhere to enjoy a relatively peaceful pint. ◖▶ ⊁

Hobgoblin
2 Broad Street, RG1 2BH
✪ 11-11; 12-10.30 Sun
☎ (0118) 950 8119
Wychwood Fiddler's Elbow, Hobgoblin Best Bitter; guest beers Ⓗ
A real ale sweetshop. A back-street boozer in the main thoroughfare, with a front bar leading to cubicles at the rear, allowing respite from the buzz of conversation. Five constantly-changing guest beers, usually from smaller micro-breweries vie with three beers from the Wychwood portfolio, Czech Budvar and the full range of rotating cider and perry from Westons. The wooden floor was recycled from London Zoo Elephant House. The walls and ceiling are covered in pump clips from the 4,000 odd different ales sold in the last 10 years. Pavement tables are provided for summer drinking. ✿ ⇌ ●

Hop Leaf
163-165 Southampton Street, RG1 2QZ
✪ 12 (4 Mon)-11; 12-10.30 Sun
☎ (0118) 931 4700
Hop Back GFB, Best Bitter, Crop Circle, Entire Stout, Thunderstorm, Summer Lightning; guest beer Ⓗ
Former Simonds pub shown by the hop leaf motif on the railings. This pub is halfway up a hill just outside the town centre, close to the historic British School that is currently being renovated. The full range of Hop Back beers is offered, plus others from the Cellarman's Reserve. There is a TV but it is rarely switched on. The emphasis is on beer but food is available, except on Sunday evening and Monday; a no-smoking area is provided for eating. Families are welcome. Ninepin skittles, bar billiards, crib and shove-ha'penny are played. ◖▶ ఉ ♣ ⊁

Retreat
8 St Johns Street, RG1 4EH (E of town centre)
✪ 12-2, 5.30-11; 11-11 Fri & Sat; 12-10.30 Sun
☎ (0118) 957 1593
Beer range varies Ⓗ

Two-bar, back-street, terraced pub with a regularly-changing range of beers, usually including Hook Norton Best Bitter. An Enterprise Inns pub, its licensees make the best possible use of the choice of beers available to them. Local CAMRA Pub of the Year for 2002. The back room has a pool table (and is the home venue for the Hobgoblin pool team). Live music is often featured on a Tuesday or Thursday. ⊠ ⇌

SHINFIELD

Magpie & Parrot
Arborfield Road, RG2 9EA (A327 just S of village)
✪ 12-7; 12-3 Sun
☎ (0118) 988 4130
Fuller's London Pride Ⓗ
Magnificent, refined village pub – despite the fact that the single-bar room barely seats 20 and that the pub closes in the early evening, everyone visiting will be rewarded with a relaxing experience. The decor, furnishings and somewhat bizarre collection of artefacts contribute to the congenial atmosphere. Do not miss the garden in spring and summer – it is an ornithologist's paradise. Bus route 144 Reading to Wokingham stops outside. ⋈Q✿P

SLOUGH

Rose & Crown
312 High Street, SL1 1NB
✪ 11-11; 12-10.30 Sun
☎ (01753) 521114
Beer range varies Ⓗ
Situated at the east end of the High Street, this is a true free house serving an ever-changing range of beers. Real cider is on draught in summer. Small and traditional, this two-bar pub was first licensed in the 1820s. A kitchen extension planned for 2003 will enable food to be served. An excellent range of Rebellion bottled beers is sold. A summer beer festival featuring local brews is popular. There is a roadside patio. ✿ ⇌ ●

Wheatsheaf ⊘
15 Albert Street, SL1 2BE
✪ 11-11; 12-10.30 Sun
☎ (01753) 522019
Fuller's Chiswick, London Pride, ESB, seasonal beers Ⓗ
One of the few traditional pubs left in Slough, this comfortable one-bar establishment has the unusual feature of a working red telephone box. Formerly a bakery, it was first licensed in 1897. The present publicans have run the pub for several years and were the local CAMRA Publicans of the Year 2003. Join the quiz night on Thursday. ✿◖

SONNING

Bull Hotel ⊘
High Street, RG4 6UP (off B481 next to church)
✪ 11-3, 5.30-11; 11-11 Sat; 12-10.30 Sun
☎ (0118) 969 3901
Gale's Butser, GB, HSB, seasonal beers; guest beer (occasional) Ⓗ
Upmarket, oak-beamed, 16th-century inn with hotel facilities, close to the River

Thames. Emphasis is on quality food in the higher price bracket with a range of lighter and more substantial meals served in the main bar and no-smoking dining room. The separate locals' bar, which is reserved for drinkers only, retains a traditional pub atmosphere. The award-winning display of hanging baskets may be admired in summer from the pleasant garden and patio.

🏾Q🌣🚳⬤◗ ⬚且P

STANFORD DINGLEY

Bull
RG7 6LS (150 yds N of only road jct in village)
🕐 12-3, 6-11; 12-3, 7-10.30 Sun
☎ (0118) 974 4409
website: www.thebullatstanforddingley.co.uk
Draught Bass; Brakspear Bitter; West Berkshire Good Old Boy, Dr Hexter's Healer Ⓗ

This small, 15th-century inn, in a pretty Pang valley village, has been recently extended to include guest bedrooms and a new dining room. The original two bars have been enlarged slightly but still retain their traditional cottage character, including a wattle and daub wall, tiled floors and low ceilings. There are folk music sessions on the first Wednesday of the month. The centuries-old game of ring the bull is still played here. No food is served on Sunday evening in winter.

🏾🌣🚳◗⬤ ⬚且🌣♣P

STOCKCROSS

Rising Sun
Ermine Street, RG20 8LG
🕐 12-2.30 (not Mon), 5.30 (7 Sat)-11; 12-3, 7-10.30 Sun
☎ (01488) 608131
Fuller's London Pride; Greene King IPA; guest beers Ⓗ

With its one large remaining bar, this pub was much altered in the 1960s and '70s, but the friendly, unpretentious licensees have ensured a strong and continuing local support while other pubs in the village have closed. Handy for visits to Newbury and nearby Donnington Castle, it is close to the A34/A4 intersection. Live music is performed some weekends. Guest ales may include West Berkshire brews. Take care as the car park exits on to a dangerous bend.

🌣◗⬤🌣♣P⅄

SUNNINGDALE

Nag's Head
28 High Street, SL5 0NG
🕐 11.30-11; 12-10.30 Sun
☎ (01344) 622725
Harveys XX Mild, BB, seasonal beers Ⓗ

A compact entrance leads into the smaller public bar with pool table and darts, and a larger cosy lounge for food and access to the child-friendly garden (with bouncy castle). You will find a warm welcome and excellent Harveys ales, including a regular mild. A side room in the lounge provides a no-smoking and weekday eating area. Comfortable seating, a collection of pewter and the pub cat typify this friendly local that is a short drive from Ascot racecourse.

🌣◗⬚且♣P⅄

THEALE

Fox & Hounds ⊘
Station Road, Hanger Lane, Sunnyside, RG7 4AA (between Theale and Burghfield, 1/2 mile S of canal bridge)
🕐 11 (11.30 Sat)-2.30, 5.30 (6 Sat)-11; 12.30-3, 7-10.30 Sun
☎ (0118) 930 2295
Badger Tanglefoot; Draught Bass; Red Shoot Forest Gold; Wadworth IPA, 6X, JCB Ⓗ

Friendly, one-bar Wadworth house with a separate restaurant area. A large collection of earthenware bottles and paintings decorate the bar. Welcoming locals, bar billiards and comfortable seating add to the atmosphere of the pub. Jazz night is Tuesday and other occasional live music events are staged. The small garden has a play area for children. No food is served on Sunday evening.

🏾🌣◗⬤🌣&♣P

Lamb
22 Church Street, RG7 5BZ
🕐 12-3, 6.30-11; 12-3, 7-10.30 Sun
☎ (0118) 930 2216
Beer range varies Ⓗ

Traditional, late-Victorian village pub, sympathetically modernised and extended in recent years. It features a peaceful, cosy lounge bar and a larger public bar with pool table and TV. It also has a back room and a function room. Normally quiet, but occasionally live music is staged in the public bar. One real ale is stocked (sometimes two), selected from a varied guest list. Lunches are available Monday–Saturday. Do not confuse with the thatched Old Lamb Hotel next door – the two businesses are unrelated.

Q🌣◗⬚且⇌P

TILEHURST

Butcher's Arms
9 Lower Armour Road, RG31 6HH
🕐 11-3 (3.30 Sat), 6-11; 12-3, 7-10.30 Sun
☎ (0118) 942 4313 website: www.butchersarms.org.uk
Flowers IPA; Fuller's London Pride Ⓗ

Pre-dating most of the surrounding suburban housing, this is a welcoming two-bar local. It stands near the top of Armour Hill, on the flanks of which stood the tileworks, reputedly of Roman origin, that gave Tilehurst its name. Popular with darts and cribbage teams, major sporting events are shown on a large-screen TV. A pleasant garden lies to the side of the car park.

🌣⬚且♣P

WALTHAM ST LAWRENCE

Bell ⊘
The Street, RG10 0JJ
🕐 11.30-3, 5-11; 12-10.30 Sun
☎ (0118) 934 1788
Hook Norton Best Bitter; guest beers Ⓗ

Housed in an historic building dating from circa 1400, this large pub has two drinking areas and a separate dining room with a covered well in the floor. Meals are served lunchtime and evening, except on Sunday evening. It is popular with diners. The walls are adorned with numerous pictures of the pub at various stages through its history. Two unique beers are brewed especially for the pub by West Berkshire Brewery but are sold under the name of Waltham St Lawrence Brewing Company. 🏠Q◑▶

Star Inn
Broadmoor Road, RG10 0HY
🕐 11.30-2.30 (3 Sat), 6 (6.30 Sat)-11; 12-3, 7-10.30 Sun
☎ (0118) 934 3486
Wadworth IPA, 6X Ⓗ
The pub has a small restaurant at the back of the bar. This does not seem to detract from the large drinking area. Meals are served 12–2 and 7–9.30, except for Sunday evening. There is a quiz held on Monday night. This pleasant pub is ideal for a quiet pint as it is rarely crowded. The real fire adds to the relaxed atmosphere. 🏠🏵◑▶P

WARGRAVE

Bull ⊘
High Street, RG10 8DE (off A4, on A321 towards Henley)
🕐 11-3, 6-11; 12-4, 7-10.30 Sun
☎ (0118) 940 3120
Brakspear Bitter, Special, seasonal beers Ⓗ
Unspoilt, 17th-century inn on the village-centre crossroads. The emphasis is on food but it caters for drinkers and diners alike. A real log fire is housed in a large, attractive feature fireplace, very welcoming in winter. The pub offers pleasantly furnished, comfortable, character rooms, including an oak-beamed lounge with unusual low-level flint wall. Mobile phones are frowned upon. It provides convenient accommodation for Thames Valley tourist spots but tends to be very busy during Henley Regatta week.
🏠Q🏵🛏◑▶⇌

WHITE WALTHAM

Beehive
Waltham Road, SL6 3SH OS850774
🕐 11-3, 5-11; 12-11 Sat; 12-10.30 Sun
☎ (01628) 822877
Brakspear Bitter; Flowers Original; Fuller's London Pride; guest beer Ⓗ
Traditional pub at the centre of a village with an historic church and private airfield. The Beehive has three areas: public bar; lounge with real fire; and no-smoking conservatory/restaurant, serving home-cooked food. Its front garden overlooks the village cricket pitch. In the large rear garden, bowls, petanque, or (in summer) skittles may be played. Occasionally morris dancers perform. A plaque in the car park records that the pub burned down in May 1861 but was rebuilt by late June.
🏠🏵◑▶🛏&♣P⊁🖥

WINDSOR

Prince Arthur
29 Grove Road, SL4 1JD
🕐 11-3, 5-11; 11-11 Fri & Sat; 12-10.30 Sun
☎ (01753) 832491
Fuller's Chiswick, London Pride, ESB, seasonal beers; guest beers Ⓗ
Welcoming, side-street local which, in summer, is embellished with numerous vivid hanging baskets. Effective lighting is provided by old-style station lamps. It is a popular haunt for antipodeans and can become crowded when big sporting events

are screened. No meals are served on Sunday evening. A courtyard serves as a garden. The splendid tiled exterior is worthy of note. It is quite close to Windsor Arts Centre. 🏵◑▶&♣

Trooper
97 St Leonards Road, SL4 3BZ
🕐 11-11; 12-10.30 Sun
☎ (01753) 670123
Gale's GB, HSB; guest beer Ⓗ
Pleasant, one-bar establishment owned by Gale's Brewery since 2002. It is within walking distance of the town centre and castle. A covered garden room at the rear doubles as a restaurant area. All specials are home made and bar meals are available. Particularly popular with office workers at lunchtime, it tends to get very busy in the evening, especially when there is football on TV. The pub is nearly opposite Windsor Arts Centre.
🏵🛏◑▶⊁

Vansittart Arms ⊘
105 Vansittart Road, SL4 5DD
🕐 12 (11 Sat)-11; 12-10.30 Sun
☎ (01753) 865988 website: www.chipfreezone.co.uk
Fuller's London Pride, ESB, seasonal beers; guest beer Ⓗ
Long-time Guide entry with several recesses, providing a cosy atmosphere. The decor includes rugby memorabilia and a large montage of pub revellers. Live music is staged on Sunday night, when no food is served. The summer beer festival is now well established and takes place on the heated patio. The pub and its menu are chip-free zones – see the website address.
🏠🏵◑▶⇌ (Windsor & Eton Central) ♣

WOKINGHAM

Broad Street Tavern ⊘
29 Broad Street, RG40 1AJ
🕐 11-11; 12-10.30 Sun
☎ (0118) 977 3706
Red Shoot Forest Gold, Tom's Tipple; Wadworth IPA, 6X, JCB Ⓗ
Town-centre pub with one main bar and two small front rooms, one of which is no-smoking. There is a tropical garden but the garden bar does not sell real ale. There are three mini beer festivals each year. Children are not allowed in the pub or in the garden. Beers from Wadworth's micro-brewery, Red Shoot, are regularly available. Lunches are served Monday–Saturday at local CAMRA's Pub of the Year 2003.
🏵◑⇌⊁

Rifle Volunteer ⊘
141 Reading Road, RG41 1HD
(on A329, NW of town centre)
🕐 11-3, 5.30-11; 11-11 Sat; 12-10.30 Sun
☎ (0118) 978 4484
Courage Best Bitter; Fuller's London Pride; guest beer Ⓗ
Popular one-bar local built in 1859. It was initially named the Volunteer, becoming the Rifle Volunteer in 1883. There is a small family room and a large garden with a children's play area. The pub has a team in the local Aunt Sally league. The guest beer changes weekly. Lunches are available Monday–Friday.
♿🏵◑&♣P

Ship ✔
104 Peach Street, RG40 1XH
(on A329)
12-11; 12-10.30 Sun
☎ (0118) 978 0389
Fuller's London Pride, ESB, seasonal beers Ⓗ
Welcoming town local, the listed main building dates from the 1600s and the old stables were incorporated to enlarge the premises about 25 years ago. There are two main bars with a separate bar in the darts area. Gas-effect log fires provide a cosy feeling in winter and the outside patio has high-level heaters and parasols. TVs show major sporting events. Darts and crib are played. Lunchtime snacks and meals are available all week, evening food is served Monday–Thursday. A quiz night is held each Sunday.
❀ⒹⒹ≑♣P

WOKINGHAM WITHOUT

Crooked Billet
Honey Hill, RG40 3BJ
(off Nine Mile Ride) OS826867
11-11; 12-10.30 Sun
☎ (0118) 978 0438
Brakspear Bitter, Special Ⓗ
This weatherboarded country pub is tucked away down a quiet lane on the rural outskirts oF Wokingham, one and a half miles south-east of the town centre. The bar area is surrounded by bench seating, giving a traditional feel with a snug at one end and a welcoming fire in winter. It is a popular choice with walkers and cyclists in summer, as is the peaceful garden. No food is served on Sunday evening. ♔Q❀ⒹⒹ♿♣P⊬

WOODLEY

Inn on the Park
Woodford Park Leisure Centre, Haddon Drive, RG5 4LY (from A4 take Pound Lane towards Woodley, turn right after 1 mile)
11-2.30, 6-11; 11-11 Fri & Sat; 12-10.30 Sun
☎ (0118) 962 8655
website: www.inn-on-the-park.co.uk
Brakspear Bitter, Special; Fuller's London Pride; guest beers Ⓗ
Basic but comfortable bar situated in the local council sports centre. It always has at least one guest ale – often something unusual for the area. It is a good venue for parents with young children in summer as the centre has a patio, play area and paddling pool. No food is available except crisps and nuts as the bar lacks kitchen facilities, but the beer quality compensates for this. ❀♿P

WOODSIDE

Duke of Edinburgh
Woodside Road, SL4 1RZ (off A332)
11-3, 5-11; 11-11 Sat; 12-6 Sun
☎ (01344) 882736
Arkells 2B, 3B, Kingsdown Ⓗ
This eclectic Arkells house has three separate bar areas: one for the sports enthusiasts, with three TV screens, dartboard and memorabilia, a relaxing lounge, with a no-smoking section and finally, the full à la carte restaurant. With comfy sofas and curios, one of the sayings on the wall sums this place up: 'A cloudy day is no match for a sunny disposition'. It is particularly popular with visitors to the nearby Ascot racecourse. The child-friendly and comfortable garden houses a collection of breeding birds. ♔❀ⒹⒹ♣P⊬

Brakspear's coming home

In 2003, the revered brewer of classic pale ales, W H Brakspear of Henley-on-Thames, ceased brewing and became a pub retailer. The brands were sold to Refresh UK, which owns the Wychwood Brewery in Witney, also in Oxfordshire. Refresh said it planned to build a new brewery in the county dedicated to the Brakspear brands. In the meantime, Brakspear Bitter and Special were moved to the Burtonwood Brewery in Cheshire. Refresh earmarked two sites in Oxfordshire for its new brewery, but ran into major planning permission. In July 2003, Refresh announced that it had won planning agreement to extend the Wychwood site. It will build a new brewhouse where it will instal the old Henley equipment, including the famous 'double drop' fermenters. The beers should be available by spring 2004.

Readers should consult the CAMRA website www.camra.org.uk or www.wychwood.co.uk for up-to-date information.

BUCKINGHAMSHIRE

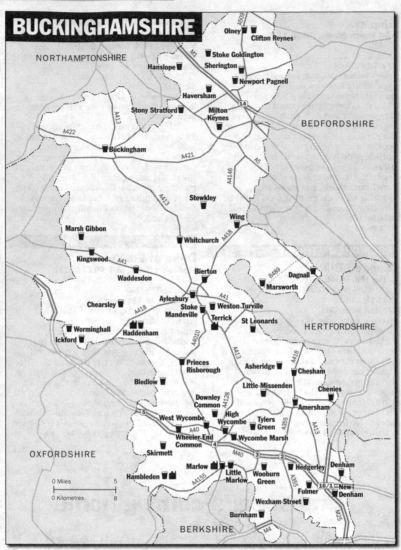

NORTHAMPTONSHIRE

Olney
Clifton Reynes
Stoke Goldington
Hanslope
Sherington
Newport Pagnell
Haversham
Stony Stratford
Milton Keynes
BEDFORDSHIRE
Buckingham
Stewkley
Wing
Marsh Gibbon
Whitchurch
Kingswood
Bierton
Dagnall
Waddesdon
Marsworth
Chearsley
Aylesbury
Stoke Mandeville
Weston Turville
Terrick
St Leonards
Worminghall
Haddenham
HERTFORDSHIRE
Ickford
Princes Risborough
Asheridge
Chesham
Bledlow
Little Missenden
Chenies
Downley Common
Amersham
West Wycombe
High Wycombe
Tylers Green
Wheeler End Common
Wycombe Marsh
OXFORDSHIRE
Skirmett
Hedgerley
Denham
Marlow
Little Marlow
Wooburn Green
Fulmer
New Denham
Hambleden
Wexham Street
Burnham

BERKSHIRE

0 Miles 5
0 Kilometres 8

AMERSHAM

King's Arms
30 High Street, Old Amersham, HP7 0DJ
⊘ 11-11; 12-10.30 Sun
☎ (01494) 726333
website: www.kingsarmsamersham.co.uk
Rebellion IPA; Tetley Burton Ale; ℍ guest beers Ⓖ
Traditional local in the old part of town, attracting a healthy mix of customers. This pub is one of England's oldest and is blessed with a dedicated landlord who is extensively restoring it. Originally two timber-framed houses circa 1450, each side of a covered entrance to the inn yard, the right-hand side is now a restaurant (eve meals Tue–Sat). The bar area has wood floors, an oak-beamed ceiling and sturdy wooden bar, a log-burning stove stands in the grand fireplace. Bar meals are served at lunchtime only.
🏚Q✿⏧♣P⅟

ASHERIDGE

Asheridge Arms
Asheridge Road, HP5 2UX
(2 miles NW from Chesham, through Asheridge Rd Ind Est) OS938046
⊘ 12-2.30, 5.30-11; 12-11 Fri & Sat; 12-10.30 Sun
☎ (01494) 758263 website: www.blueball.org
Fuller's London Pride; Wells Bombardier; guest beer ℍ
Previously known as the Blue Ball, until summer 2003, this is the only pub serving the hamlet. Family-run, it offers a frequently-changing guest ale sourced from a wide variety of breweries. It hosts a general knowledge quiz on Thursday evening and a monthly, challenging musical quiz (Sat). The no-smoking room can be booked for functions. A June beer festival offers 30 micro-brews. Excellent home-made food is supplemented by occasional themed evenings. 🏚✿⏧♣P

AYLESBURY

Queen's Head
1 Temple Square, HP20 2QA
✪ 11.30-11; 12-4, 7-10.30 Sun
☎ (01296) 415484
Adnams Bitter; Courage Directors; Flowers IPA Ⓗ
Very close to the Roald Dahl Museum, this
friendly pub is the closest thing to a village
pub in a town that you can find. Oak beams
throughout set the atmosphere, which is
enhanced by the lack of fruit machines or
juke box. It is especially popular at
lunchtime, when a range of specials
supplement the food menu. The landlord
also runs the nearby King's Head, which is
the oldest courtyard inn in the country.
🏠 Q ✿ 🍴 ⓓ ⇌

BIERTON

Bell
191 Aylesbury Road, HP22 5DS
✪ 11-3, 5-11; 11-11 Sat; 12-10.30 Sun
☎ (01296) 436055
Fuller's Chiswick, London Pride, ESB; guest beer
(occasional) Ⓗ
Small village local, two miles north of
Aylesbury on the Leighton Buzzard road. Its
two bars consist of a small, traditional
public bar and a larger room which acts as
the restaurant. Fuller's ales are occasionally
supplemented by independent guests and
seasonal beers. A good range of food is
always available at very reasonable prices.
This popular pub is now open all day at the
weekend, with food served until 6pm on
Sunday.
ⓓ 🍴 ♣ P

BLEDLOW

Lions of Bledlow
Church End, HP27 9PE (off B4009, between
Chinnor and Princes Risborough) OS776020
✪ 12-3, 6-11; 12-4, 7-10.30 Sun
☎ (01844) 343345
Marston's Pedigree; Wadworth 6X; guest beers Ⓗ
Rambling, unspoilt, 16th-century pub
complete with beams and inglenooks and a
large log fire in winter. It comprises a games
room, restaurant and a large bar where a
wide range of food is listed on blackboard
menus. Originally three shepherd's cottages,
pictures and notes of the pub's earlier days
are displayed. The extensive garden is busy
in summer with walkers and families, while
tables at the front enjoy a picturesque
setting at the junction of footpaths and
bridleways.
🏠 Q ✿ ⓓ P ⼡

BUCKINGHAM

Whale ⊘
14 Market Hill, MK18 1JX
✪ 11-11; 12-10.30 Sun
☎ (01280) 815537
Fuller's Chiswick, London Pride, seasonal beers Ⓗ
Single-bar, town-centre Fuller's house. The
bar is split into three levels, lit by the
original gas mantles. It hosts regular pub
quizzes, and live music. The TV at one end
of the bar does not intrude on drinkers at
the other end. The pub is close to the
historic Town Jail Museum.
✿ 🍴 ⓓ ♿ ♣ P

BURNHAM

George
20 High Street, SL1 7JH
✪ 11-11; 12-10.30 Sun
☎ (01628) 605047
Courage Best Bitter, Directors; Vale Notley Ale Ⓗ
Listed, 16th-century coaching inn named
after George IV. Run by the same licensee
for 36 years it has changed very little in that
time. This local welcomes strangers (and
dogs). Directors is served through a mirror,
or looking-glass, and is known as Alice by
the locals. Pool is popular and dominates
one end of the bar. If the front door is
locked in the afternoon, access is via the
back door from the car park at the rear.
🏠 ♣ P

CHEARSLEY

Bell ⊘
The Green, HP18 0DJ
✪ 12-2.30 (not Mon; 12-3 Sat), 6-11; 12-3,
7-10.30 Sun
☎ (01844) 208077
Fuller's Chiswick, London Pride, ESB, seasonal beers Ⓗ
Traditional, thatched country pub by the
village green, renowned for its excellent
range of food at reasonable prices, from bar
snacks to Sunday lunches, plus vegetarian
and children's options. Evening meals are
served Wednesday–Saturday. Its comfortable
atmosphere is enhanced by open fires. The
large, safe garden has a play area. It was
Aylesbury Vale Council's Best Village Pub
winner in 1998 and 2000. 🏠 Q ✿ ⓓ ♣ P

CHENIES

Red Lion
WD3 6ED
(off A404, between Chorleywood and Little Chalfont)
✪ 11-2, 5.30-11; 12-3, 7-10.30 Sun
☎ (01923) 282722
Vale Best Bitter; Wadworth 6X; guest beers Ⓗ
Popular free house in an attractive village
near the River Chess. A tiny snug can be
found at the back. This is a pub and not a
restaurant, however the superb home-
cooked food is always unusual and
interesting. The guest beers are normally
sourced locally or from micro-breweries.
Local bottled beers are also available. The
house beer, Lion Pride, is brewed by
Rebellion; Vale Best Bitter is known locally
as Ben's. Q ✿ ⓓ ♿ P

CHESHAM

Queen's Head ⊘
120 Church Street, HP5 1JB
✪ 12-11; 12-10.30 Sun
☎ (01494) 778690
Brakspear Bitter; Fuller's London Pride, ESB Ⓗ
Traditonal, old town pub with two bars and
a Thai restaurant upstairs. The public bar is
a classic with old local cricketing photos
and noteworthy fittings. The saloon boasts

INDEPENDENT BREWERIES

Chiltern Terrick
Chiltern Valley Hambleden
Rebellion Marlow Bottom
Vale Haddenham

a large original Fuller's mirror and other pub memorabilia. Thai food is also served in the bars (no food Sun eve). A great drinking and meeting place with olde-worlde-style, where shove-ha'penny can still be played, the Queen's Head has been in this Guide longer than any other pub in Chesham.
🏾 Q ❀ ◑ ➡ ⊖ ♣ P

CLIFTON REYNES

Robin Hood
MK46 5DR
(cul-de-sac village off Emberton-Turvey road)
☺ 12-3, 6.30-11 (closed Mon); 12-4, 7-10.30 Sun
☎ (01234) 711574
Greene King IPA, Abbot Ⓗ
Pleasant pub at the end of a lane into the village off the A509, run by a friendly landlord. Good food is served (not Sun eve) and Northants skittles is played in the public bar. Photographs of sundry portrayals of the outlaw of Sherwood Forest decorate the saloon. A no-smoking conservatory and garden with pet rabbits are added attractions. The fine walk from nearby Olney was immortalised by local poet, William Cowper, although as he observed, it can be muddy!
🏾 Q ❀ ◑ ➡ Å ♣ ✄

DAGNALL

Golden Rule
Main Road South, HP4 1QX (on A4146)
☺ 11.30-3, 5.30-11; 12-3, 7-10.30 Sun
☎ (01442) 843227
Adnams Bitter; Fuller's London Pride, Ⓗ **ESB; Hook Norton Old Hooky; guest beers** Ⓖ
Cosy, rural village free house, newly decorated with an eclectic mix of old wood furniture and beer posters. A warm, friendly welcome is shown to all by the landlord. An ever-changing range of guest beers is stored in a temperature-controlled stillage behind the bar. Four themed beer festivals are held over the year, offering a variety of ales. Food is always available in the form of a Spanish tapas bar menu. A small patio catches the evening sun. 🏾 Q ❀ ◑ ♣ P

DENHAM

Falcon
Village Road, UB9 5BE
(signed from A40 and A412) OS042872
☺ 11-3 (not Fri), 5.30-11; 12-3, 7-10.30 Sun
☎ (01895) 832125
Flowers IPA; Marston's Pedigree; Taylor Landlord; guest beer Ⓗ
Overlooking the green in a delightful olde-worlde village, entry to this 16th-century pub is by well-worn stone steps. It is very popular with diners lunchtime and early evening due to its excellent, mainly seafood, menu. The original small bar area has been retained and is welcoming. Parking can be difficult, but buses stop on the nearby main roads and the station is accessed by a footpath from the opposite side of the green. ➡ ◑ ⇌ ✄

DOWNLEY COMMON

De Spencer Arms
HP13 5YQ (down a track, across the common from village) OS849959

☺ 12-3, 6-11; 12-11 Sat; 12-10.30 Sun
☎ (01494) 535317
Fuller's Chiswick, London Pride, ESB, seasonal beers Ⓗ
This ex-Wethered's brick and flint house, now owned by Fuller's, is remotely situated off Downley Common. A family-oriented local, it is home to Downley Village football and cricket teams. The pub consists of numerous secluded corners, plus a small room off the bar. In summer it hosts barbecues, and two mini beer festivals, set up in a marquee. Pub games include mole in the hole! Bus No. 310 (329 eve) from High Wycombe stops in the village nearby.
🏾 Q ❀ ◑ ♣ P

FULMER

Black Horse ❷
Windmill Road, SL3 6HD
☺ 11-3, 5.30-11; 11-11 Sat; 12-10.30 Sun
☎ (01753) 663183
Greene King IPA, Abbot; guest beer Ⓗ
Friendly pub which the licensees help to make a central part of local life, reflecting its physical position in the village. As well as being accommodating to individuals and families alike, the pub hosts charity events and supports local sports activities. Several cosy rooms are arranged around the bar, itself an object of interest, the front being constructed of timbers salvaged from the local WWII ARP hut. No food is served Sunday evening; half portions are available for children.
🏾 Q ❀ ◑ ♿ P

HADDENHAM

King's Head
52 High Street, HP17 8ET
☺ 12-2.30, 5-11; 12-11 Sat; 12-10.30 Sun
☎ (01844) 291391
Fuller's London Pride; Greene King IPA; Ⓗ
guest beer Ⓗ/Ⓖ
Busy, traditional village pub, in the old part of town, which can be difficult to find despite having two entrances (the other is on Townside). Parts of the pub date back to the 16th century, although it is the recently developed patio drinking area which attracts the customers in summer. There are occasional music evenings and customers can watch Sky Sports. The guest beer alternates on a weekly basis, and is sometimes served by gravity dispense.
🏾 Q ❀ ◑ P

Red Lion
Church End, HP17 8AH
☺ 11.30-3, 5.30-11; 11-11 Sat; 12-10.30 Sun
☎ (01844) 291606
website: www.theredlion.freeserve.co.uk
Adnams Bitter; Ansells Mild; Courage Directors; Young's Bitter Ⓗ
Friendly, two-bar local built in 1939, that still retains the original oak floor and polished tables. It has had only four landlords since it opened, and the present incumbent has been there for over 30 years. It is very active in local leagues, with thriving crib, darts, dominoes and quiz teams. The outdoor drinking area at the front is popular in summer, affording a fantastic view of the village church, green and duckpond. 🏾 Q ❀ ⇌ ◑ ➡ ♣ P

HAMBLEDEN

Stag & Huntsman

RG6 6RP (1 mile N of A4155) OS785866
🕐 11-2.30 (3 Sat), 6-11; 12-3, 7-10.30 Sun
☎ (01491) 571227

Rebellion IPA; Wadworth 6X; guest beer Ⓗ
Unspoilt, characterful local gem, in a
picturesque brick and flint NT village. This
country pub comprises a locals' public bar, a
cosy front bar behind a curtain, and a rear
lounge. An extensive menu is served
throughout the three bars and the dining
room (no food Sun eve). The guest beer
changes weekly and regularly features
Cottage and Eccleshall brews. Thatchers dry
cider is always available on handpump. It is
very popular with hikers and cyclists,
especially on Sunday. Local CAMRA Pub of
the Year 2003. ⚒️❀🛏️🍽️🅳♣ 🍺 P

HANSLOPE

Globe

50 Hartwell Road, Long Street, MK19 7BZ
(between Hanslope and Hartwell on unclassified road)
🕐 12-2.30 (not Tue), 6-11; 12-3, 7-10.30 Sun
☎ (01908) 510336

Banks's Bitter, seasonal beers; guest beers Ⓗ
Former local CAMRA Pub of the Year, this
classic village pub has won awards for its
ales. It has a very community-oriented
public bar in this mixed farming and
commuter village, with a games room off. A
quiet, comfortable lounge leads to the
no-smoking restaurant with cottage-style
decor (drinkers use it outside dining hours).
Booking is advised but food is also served in
the bar. A pleasant garden features an aviary
and well-equipped children's play area. Bus
No. 33 MK–Northampton stops outside (no
evening service). Q❀🍽️🅳♣P

HAVERSHAM

Greyhound

2 High Street, MK19 7DT
(N of MK, go to end of V6 through new part of village,
take right turn. Pub is on corner down hill)
🕐 11-2.30 (3 Sat), 5.30-11; 12-3, 7-10.30 Sun
☎ (01908) 313487
website: www.havershamvillage.co.uk

Greene King IPA, Abbot Ⓗ
There has been a pub on this site since
Domesday times. This is a very pleasant
rural local, which is surprising given its
proximity to Milton Keynes. Very family-
friendly, it has a children's certificate. A
local motorcycle club meets here on
Wednesday evening. It was awarded a Best
Beer Quality certificate by the brewers in
2002. Live music is staged once a month.
The garden has a play area for children.
⚒️Q❀🍽️🅳♣P

HEDGERLEY

White Horse

Village Lane, SL2 3UY OS969874
🕐 11-2.30, 5.30-11; 11-11 Sat; 12-10.30 Sun
☎ (01753) 643225

Greene King IPA; Rebellion IPA; guest beers Ⓖ
Offering up to seven real ales on gravity,
this popular, 15th-century, award-winning
hostelry is highly recommended. The public
bar, patronised mainly by locals, has an
atmosphere you could bottle; the flagstone

floor and inglenook are special features.
Two real ciders and foreign beers add to the
attraction. The beer festival at the end of
May draws customers from far and wide.
You will not find much better than this.
⚒️Q❀🍽️🅳♣ 🍺P

HIGH WYCOMBE

Bell ⊘

Frogmoor, HP13 5DG
🕐 11-11; 12-10.30 Sun
☎ (01494) 521317

Fuller's London Pride, ESB Ⓗ
After a short spell as a night club, the Bell
has now reverted to being a proper pub. The
frontage of the 16th-century building
disguises the fact that it has been extended
to the rear. Despite being in the town centre
it is not part of the 'circuit' and is usually an
oasis of calm. It is opposite the site of one of
Wycombe's three defunct breweries. Note
the fountains. Evening meals are served
Monday–Thursday. ⚒️🛏️🅳 ≢

ICKFORD

Rising Sun

36 Worminghall Road, HP18 9JD
🕐 12-3 (not Mon), 5-11; 12-11 Sat; 12-10.30 Sun
☎ (01844) 339238

**Adnams Bitter; Flowers IPA; Marston's Pedigree;
Young's Bitter** Ⓗ
Popular village local dating back to the 15th
century. Oak beams, a thatched roof and a
welcoming wood-burning stove add to the
traditional feel. Four ales are always on tap,
and food is available most sessions, but is
not obtrusive. The pub is very active in local
games and events, including darts, crib,
pool and quizzes. Aunt Sally is played in the
garden. It is known locally as the
Woodcutters Arms, as the landlord was a
forestry contractor. ⚒️Q❀🅳♣P

KINGSWOOD

Plough & Anchor ⊘

Bicester Road, HP18 0RB
🕐 12-3, 6-11; 12-6 Sun
☎ (01296) 770251

Fuller's London Pride; guest beer Ⓖ
Comfortable, 16th-century, food-oriented
roadside pub, catering mainly for diners,
but drinkers are welcome. The beers are
served on gravity by a custom-built dispense
and cooling system. The guest beer is
sourced from regional and micro-breweries
and is usually under 4% ABV. The open fire
is fuelled by some of the largest logs you
will ever see. A small patio area is available
for outside drinking. ⚒️Q❀🅳P

LITTLE MARLOW

Queen's Head

Pound Lane, Church Road, SL7 3SR
OS873880
🕐 12-3, 6-11; 12-3, 7-10.30 Sun
☎ (01628) 482927

**Adnams Bitter, Broadside; Greene King IPA;
Wells Bombardier** Ⓗ
Quaint, two-bar gem hidden in a cul-de-sac
near a 12th-century church and the local
cricket green. Set in a picturesque village,
just off the main road, the Queen's remains
a true local with an enterprising agenda.

Home-cooked meals are lovingly prepared by the landlady (eve meals Wed–Sat). The pub featured in the final TV episode of Inspector Morse – the great man would have approved of this little treasure. Beer choice may vary. 🏮Q🕭🌑🍴🛏️🦽P

LITTLE MISSENDEN

Crown
HP7 0RD (off A413)
☼ 11-2.30, 6-11; 12-3, 7-10.30 Sun
☎ (01494) 862571
Adnams Bitter; Black Sheep Special; Fuller's London Pride; guest beer Ⓗ

Unchanged, compact, village pub run by the Howe family for over 90 years. Popular with the locals, the very small bar serves two seating areas. Red tiles cover the floor to the left of the bar, with oak parquet flooring on the right. Both areas are edged with built-in wall seats. The lack of music and games machines aids concentration on the fine ales and traditional lunchtime food, served Monday–Saturday. 🏮Q🕭🌑🍀P

MARLOW

Prince of Wales
1 Mill Road, SL7 1PX
☼ 11-11; 12-10.30 Sun
☎ (01628) 482970
Adnams Bitter; Fuller's London Pride; guest beer Ⓗ

Friendly, L-shaped, back-street local with two connecting bars; a comfortable public bar leads into a lounge with a dining area serving excellent Thai cuisine. The landlord puts on occasional dinner theme nights, for example, St George's, Valentine's and Burns' Night. The guest beer is often from the Rebellion portfolio or from independents further afield. It tends to get busy early evening, especially Friday and Saturday. For walkers, it is a short diversion from the Thames path. 🌑🚪🌑🚃P

MARSH GIBBON

Greyhound
West Edge, OX27 0HA
☼ 12-2.30, 6-10 (11 Fri & Sat); closed Mon; 12-4, 7-10.30 Sun
☎ (01869) 277365
Fuller's London Pride; Greene King IPA, Abbot; Ⓗ

Country pub in a quiet Domesday village. A listed building, with some 17th-century brickwork, it was rebuilt after a fire in 1740. Further refurbishment in 1979 is commemorated by a beech tree planted in front of the pub. The oak-beamed interior comprises a restaurant, two drinking areas and an oak-panelled bar. Seating is on comfortable stools and benches; a log fire burns in the main bar. The Greyhound specialises in Thai food, freshly prepared to order (book weekend eves). 🏮Q🕭🌑P🚪

MARSWORTH

Red Lion ⊘
90 Vicarage Road, HP23 4LU
(by canal bridge 130, off B489) OS919147
☼ 11-3, 5-11; 12-3, 7-10.30 Sun
☎ (01296) 668366
Rebellion IPA; Vale Notley Ale; guest beer Ⓗ

This fine old 17th-century free house lies close to the junction of the Aylesbury arm

of the Grand Union Canal. To the left is a split-level, quiet lounge with comfortable sofas and a restaurant, while to the right is a popular public bar with a games room. Here you can play bar billiards, darts, skittles and shove-ha'penny. Children are restricted to the games room. Evening meals are served Tuesday–Saturday. 🏮Q🛏️🌑🍴🛏️🍀P

MILTON KEYNES

Burnt Oak
Egerton Gate, Shenley Brook End, MK5 7HH (off Fulmer S7, V3)
☼ 12-11; 12-10.30 Sun
☎ (01908) 521968
Banks's Bitter; guest beer Ⓗ

Pleasant, spacious, modern estate pub on the western edge of the new city. One large bar is broken up into drinking areas, including one for non-smokers. Enigma code-cracker, Alan Turing lodged in this area during the war, when Shenley was somewhat more rural. Bus Nos. 7 and 9 from Central Milton Keynes station and shopping centre stop outside (journey time 15 minutes). 🏮Q🛏️🌑🍴🦽P🚫

Nag's Head
30 High Street, Great Linford, MK14 5AX (in old village of Great Linford, NE of Milton Keynes)
☼ 12-11; 12-10.30 Sun
☎ (01908) 607449
Draught Bass; Greene King IPA; Tetley Bitter Ⓗ

This 16th-century thatched tavern stands near an 11th-century church and an 18th-century manor house and canal. It just goes to show that there *is* some history in Milton Keynes! Darts and TV in the public bar contrast with the quieter atmosphere in the lounge. A spectacular inglenook fire is featured and oddly touching sepia photographs of village locals, when Linford was a village. It can get crowded, but this Punch Taverns owned, historic pub is a deservedly popular gem. 🏮Q🌑🍴🛏️🍀🚫

Wetherspoon's ⊘
201 Midsummer Boulevard, MK9 1EA (near station)
☼ 10-11; 12-10.30 Sun
☎ (01908) 606074
Courage Directors; Greene King Abbot; Shepherd Neame Spitfire; Theakston Best Bitter; guest beers Ⓗ

One of four JDW outlets in the city, the pub is large and airy. This outlet is based in the business district and should not be confused with those in the theatre district. As in all Wetherspoon's, this one offers good value food and great ales at reasonable prices. There are usually at least two guest beers. It can be busy, especially on Thursday evening when the curry promotion is on. Children are now permitted in the no-smoking area until 6pm. Q🌑🍴🦽🚃🚫

NEW DENHAM

Nine Stiles
52 Newtown Road, UP9 4BD (off A4020)
OS048848
☼ 11-11; 12-10.30 Sun
☎ (01895) 272692
Greene King IPA, Ruddles County, Abbot Ⓗ

Originally two cottages and a barn, then an ale house with a brewery, this pub, right on the edge of Buckinghamshire, was neglected for some time until its recent renovation. The narrow bar area opens out for pool and darts at one end, and dining the other. The front patio is beautifully planted. The home-made food often has a Trinidadian flavour as befits the landlady's origins. An old piano needs a bit of tuning but awaits a player. ✿⌂❍♣P⅍

NEWPORT PAGNELL

Cannon
50 High Street, MK16 8AQ
✿ 11-11; 12-10.30 Sun
☎ (01908) 211495
Banks's Bitter; Marston's Pedigree; guest beers Ⓗ
18th-century listed free house in town centre. The Cannon once had its own brewery and this is reflected in the large number of devotees of good ale that make up the regular drinkers. An ever-changing range of guest ales is offered alongside the regulars from the W&D stable. The single bar features military memorabilia. It can be lively at times. The car park is accessed via Union Street. ⌂♣P

King's Arms ⊘
Tickford Street, MK16 9BY
✿ 12-3, 5-11; 12-11 Sat; 12-4, 7-10.30 Sun
☎ (01908) 610033
Wells Eagle; guest beer Ⓗ
Friendly, old-style roadhouse, though the road concerned is of much lesser status than in the past due to the proximity of Milton Keynes. The pub benefits from ample parking and a large front garden. One guest beer is usually on tap, rising to two in summer. Regular quiz nights are held on Sunday. Near the famous Aston Martin factory, it is only a short walk from the oldest working iron bridge of its type in the UK. Lunches are served Monday–Saturday. ✿❍♣P⅍

OLNEY

Swan Inn & Bistro
12 High Street South, MK46 4AA
✿ 11-11; 12-4 (closed eve) Sun
☎ (01234) 711111
Adnams Bitter; Fuller's London Pride; Hook Norton Best Bitter; Shepherd Neame Best Bitter; guest beer Ⓗ
Bistro-style pub in an attractive market town whose name rhymes with 'pony'. The pub, which dates back to the 17th century, is noted for its great food and romantic candlelit ambience, but also welcomes the drinker, and beer prices are remarkably reasonable for this type of establishment. Watch out for inappropriate sparklers, but bar staff are happy to remove these. Cowper Museum, dedicated to the poet, is nearby and the famous pancake race on Shrove Tuesday runs past here. ⌂Q✿❍P

PRINCES RISBOROUGH

Bird in Hand
47 Station Road, HP27 9DE (off A4010)
✿ 12-3, 5-11; 12-3, 7-10.30 Sun
☎ (01844) 345602
Greene King IPA, Abbot; guest beer Ⓗ
Cosy, terraced boozer, a genuine local, with the accent on games as the trophy cabinet demonstrates. This L-shaped pub was

acquired by Greene King in 1989 and continues to flourish. A short walk from the town centre, it is the nearest pub to the station. A traditional watering-hole for all ages, conversation is top of the agenda. Parking can be difficult, but do not be put off – it is well worth finding. ✿❍≠

ST LEONARDS

White Lion
Jenkins Lane, HP23 6NW (from Chesham, take road to Cholesbury and on to St Leonards) OS918069
✿ 11.30-11; 12-10.30 Sun
☎ (01494) 758387
Greene King IPA; Highgate Dark; guest beers Ⓗ
This former Benskins pub is community- and family-oriented, supporting charity fundraising, hosting summer fêtes (with morris dancers) and fireworks displays. There are also traditional pub games, regular quizzes and other entertainments. The landlord endeavours to obtain beers that are otherwise unavailable locally, particularly from smaller independent breweries. This pub is conveniently situated near the Chiltern Way and Ridgeway walks. The chalkboard menu is not served Sunday evening. The garden has a good-sized play area. ⌂Q✿❍♣P⅍

SHERINGTON

White Hart
1 Gun Lane, MK16 9PE
✿ 12-3, 5-11; 12-3.30, 7-10.30 Sun
☎ (01908) 611953
website: www.whitehartsherington.com
Fuller's London Pride; Young's Bitter; guest beers Ⓗ
Community-centred local, saved from change of use to residential. It offers excellent food (must book), ever-changing guest ales and comfortable accommodation in a former stable. Every May there is a beer and sausage festival in the splendid garden where boules is also played. Live music is staged on alternate Wednesdays (phone for details). This local CAMRA Pub of the Year 2002 and 2003 is hard to find and the car park is on the small side, but it is well worth the effort. No food is served Sunday evening. ⌂Q✿⌂❍♣P⅍

SKIRMETT

Frog ⊘
RG9 6TG (off M40 at jct 5, through Ibstone to Skirmett) OS775903
✿ 11.30-3, 6.30 (6 Fri)-11; 11-3, 6-11 Sat; 12-4 (10.30 summer) Sun
☎ (01491) 638996 website: www.thefrog.tablesir.com
Adnams Bitter; Fuller's London Pride; Hook Norton Best Bitter; guest beers Ⓗ
Affording views across outstanding countryside, this 300-year-old free house is situated in the beautiful Turville valley. The Frog is a family-owned and run concern, exuding warmth and tranquillity. It offers a fine restaurant menu and high quality accommodation. Snacks are available in the bar area where an inviting log fire is always burning in winter. A guest beer is usually available. ⌂Q✿⌂❍♣P⅍

STEWKLEY

Carpenter's Arms ◉
1 Wing Road, LU7 0JB
☼ 12-3 (not Mon), 4.30-11; 12-11 Sat; 12-10.30 Sun
☎ (01525) 240272
website: www.thecarpentersarms.net

Brakspear Bitter; Fuller's London Pride; guest beers ⊞

At the southern end of the long main street, this two-bar pub has gained local acclaim, firstly by being awarded Aylesbury Vale Council's Best Village Pub of the Year 2003 and now recognition in this Guide. Run by a couple who have, amazingly, only been in the pub trade two years, a warm welcome is assured in the small public bar and cosy lounge with dining areas (mostly no-smoking). Food for all tastes includes gluten-free and vegetarian (no food Mon). It hosts occasional comedy and music events.
🅰Q✿◖◗⊟Å♣P

STOKE GOLDINGTON

Lamb
16-20 High Street, MK16 8VR (on B526)
☼ 12-3, 5-11; 12-11 Fri & Sat; 12-10.30 Sun
☎ (01908) 551233

Hook Norton Best Bitter; guest beers ⊞

Free house in a picturesque village, the pub has been extensively, but sypathetically refurbished. The home-cooked food is superb – Sunday lunch is exceptional value. Do not miss the chance to try your hand at Northamptonshire table skittles. The cellar trap door is on the customers' side of the bar – disconcerting when it opens at your feet! Friendly hosts and two scatty dogs make this a relaxing hostelry to linger in, or you may prefer the large, peaceful garden.
🅰Q✿◖◗⊟♣🖐P⊬

STOKE MANDEVILLE

Bull
5 Risborough Road, HP22 5UP
☼ 12-3, 5.30-11; 12-11 Fri & Sat; 12-10.30 Sun
☎ (01296) 613632

Fuller's London Pride; Tetley Bitter; Wells Bombardier ⊞

Small, two-bar local on a main road, well served by public transport. The comfortable lounge bar at the rear tends to be quieter than the public bar at the front, which is very popular with locals interested in watching the football and racing on the TV. An ample garden is at the rear. Lunches are served Monday–Saturday.
Q✿◖◗⊟⇌♣P

STONY STRATFORD

Fox & Hounds
87 High Street, MK11 1AT
☼ 12-11; 12-10.30 Sun
☎ (01908) 563307 website: www.stonystratford.co.uk

Beer range varies ⊞

This two-bar pub offers an ever-changing range of real ales, many from local breweries, and Addlestones cider. Frequent live folk, blues and jazz, plus the odd visitation from morris dancers, puts this pub at the heart of the thriving Stony music scene. It is home to a successful Northamptonshire skittles team. Dick Turpin stabled his horse next door, and the pub is believed to be haunted. Good food is

served Monday–Saturday lunchtime, with a monthly themed evening of something more exotic. Q✿◖◗⊟&♣🖐P⊬

TYLERS GREEN

Horse & Jockey ◉
Church Road, HP10 8EG
☼ 11.30-3, 5-11; 11.30-11 Fri & Sat; 12-10.30 Sun
☎ (01494) 815963

Adnams Broadside; Greene King Abbot; Tetley Bitter; guest beers ⊞

This traditional pub stands near the distinctive church of Tylers Green. The single room is U-shaped with the food servery in the larger left-hand side. Food is available all week from 12–2 and 6–10. The small right-hand side of the room has a more public bar atmosphere with a dartboard. 🅰✿◖◗♣P

WADDESDON

Bell ◉
116 High Street, HP18 0JF
☼ 12-2.30 (3 Sat), 5.30-11; 12-5, 7-10.30 (not winter eve) Sun
☎ (01296) 651320

Adnams Bitter, Broadside ⊞

Spacious, part-thatched pub, set back from the road in front of the church. It stands at the northern end of this historic village, the last medieval remains of which can be found behind the Bell. Two bars; one serves as a restaurant with a deserved reputation for its good food (no meals Sun eve). There is a small outdoor drinking area at the front. It is very handy for Waddesdon Manor, one of the National Trust's top attractions.
🅰Q✿◖◗P

WEST WYCOMBE

George & Dragon
High Street, HP14 3AB (on A40)
☼ 11-2.30 (3 Sat), 5.30-11; 12-3, 7-10.30 Sun
☎ (01494) 464414
website: www.george-and-dragon.co.uk

Adnams Broadside; Courage Best Bitter; Wells Bombardier ⊞

The NT owns this rustic, oak-beamed, 18th-century inn, where the cobbled entrance is through an archway. The food is exemplary. A vintners is also run by the tenants. Two bedrooms have four-poster beds. The garden has children's play equipment. West Wycombe Park and House (NT) stand behind the village; the famous Hellfire Caves, mausoleum and church with golden ball on top can also be visited. Buses run from High Wycombe centre – Nos. 275, 331, 340 and 341. 🅰Q🛏✿🚪◖◗P⊬

WESTON TURVILLE

Chequers
35 Church Lane, HP22 5SJ (parallel to B4544)
☼ 12-3 (not Mon), 6-11; 12-3, 7-10.30 Sun
☎ (01296) 613298

Adnams Bitter; Fuller's London Pride; Greene King IPA; Wadworth 6X ⊞

Unchanging pub and restaurant in the older part of the village. A stone-flagged main bar leads to a small lounge bar and restaurant area in a former barn. The cosy feel is enhanced by a roaring fire and paintings by local artists on the stone walls. It can be busy, so booking is advised for the restaurant (open Tue–Sun lunch and Tue–Sat eve). Arriva bus No. 54 (Aylesbury–Wendover) passes nearby Monday–Saturday daytime. ♨Q❀◑P

WEXHAM STREET

Plough

Wexham Street, SL3 6NJ
✪ 11 (12 Sat)-11; 12-10.30 Sun
☎ (01753) 662613
Courage Best Bitter; Fuller's London Pride; guest beers Ⓗ

Rural gem, in part dating back to the 17th century. Real fires and original low beams create an atmosphere to be savoured. The garden at the back is a good place for children to let off steam. The pub hosts a club night every Wednesday. There are usually five real ales on tap – it is a good choice for a drink after a round of golf at the course opposite. The Sunday roasts are highly recommended. ♨❀◑P

WHEELER END COMMON

Chequers

Bullocks Farm Lane, HP14 3NH (narrow lane off A40 or over M40 from Lane End) OS806926
✪ 11-3, 5.30-11; 11-11 Sat; 12-10.30 Sun
☎ (01494) 883070
Fuller's Chiswick, London Pride, ESB, seasonal beers; guest beers Ⓗ

Picturesque, Fuller's, 17th-century inn with roaring log fires in winter. It stands at the edge of Wheeler End Common (ideal for walking), just across the M40 bridge connection from Lane End. The pub boasts attractive gardens to relax in. The innovative menu, offering home-cooked cuisine, features local estate game, fresh fish from Cornwall and home-smoked duck breasts; Sunday lunches are served 12.30–5. Bus No. 339 from High Wycombe stops at Lane End close by (No. 315 on Sunday and public holidays). ♨Q❀◑♣P

WHITCHURCH

White Swan

10 High Street, HP22 4JT
✪ 11-11; 12-3, 7-10.30 Sun
☎ (01296) 641228
Fuller's Chiswick, London Pride, ESB, seasonal beers Ⓗ

Attractive, part-thatched, 16th-century pub with an intimate atmosphere. It boasts a huge mature garden and distinctive wood panelling in the lounge bar. Good value food is available except Sunday evening, with daily specials (Tue–Sun) and occasional food theme nights. You can eat in either of the bars or the small, no-smoking dining room. The landlord is a Fuller's Master Cellarman and has several appearances in this Guide to his credit. ♨Q❀◑🍴♣P

WING

Cock

26 High Street, LU7 0NR
✪ 11.30-3, 6-11; 12-3, 7-10.30 Sun
☎ (01296) 688214
Courage Directors; Webster's Bitter; guest beers Ⓗ

Former coaching inn that appeals to diners, drinkers and families. Four of its six real ales

come from independent or micro-breweries, often unusual for this area. Cottage, Rebellion and Vale beers are sometimes featured. There are three main drinking areas, one with a dartboard. Food is served both in the bars and the large carvery restaurant which can get busy at weekends. A rather narrow entranceway leads to a large car park. ♨Q❀◑&♣P

WOOBURN GREEN

Queen & Albert

24 The Green, HP10 0EJ
✪ 11-11; 12-10.30 Sun
☎ (01628) 520610
Fuller's London Pride; Greene King IPA; Young's Bitter Ⓗ

Locally known as Steps, this friendly local is popular with all ages due to its pleasant, relaxed, homely atmosphere. The bar is in the main lounge which leads into a lower retreat, with an unobtrusive TV, where children are welcome until 7pm. The front snug is for local debate, along with cards and dominoes, as the regulars put the world to rights. The three ales may change periodically, depending on the locals' palate. The garden has a petanque piste. Q🛏❀◑P

WORMINGHALL

Clifden Arms

75 Clifden Road, HP18 9JR OS640083
✪ 12-3, 7-11; 12-4, 6-11 (12-11 summer) Sat; 12-4, 7.30-10.30 (12-10.30 summer) Sun
☎ (01844) 339273
Adnams Broadside; Brakspear Bitter; Hook Norton Best Bitter; guest beer Ⓗ

Off the beaten track, between Oxford and Thame, this really is a hidden gem. The hub of local activities, its two bar areas feature low beams and local memorabilia. A wide selection of meals, served in the restaurant area, includes vegetarian and children's options: specials include curry nights (Thu) and take-away fish and chips. Aunt Sally is played in the large garden and bar billiards is also available at this local CAMRA Pub of the Year 2001. ♨Q❀◑🍴♣P

WYCOMBE MARSH

General Havelock

114 Kingsmead Road, HP11 1HZ (S of A40)
✪ 12-2.30, 5.30-11; 11-11 Fri & Sat; 12-10.30 Sun
☎ (01494) 520391
Fuller's Chiswick, London Pride, ESB, seasonal beers Ⓗ

Imposing building that used to be a farmhouse, it now finds itself between a ski slope and playing fields. It has had the same licensee since Fuller's acquired it and is a regular in this Guide. It is a locals' type of place and generates a big, happy family atmosphere. Lunches are available all week, plus evening meals on Friday and Saturday. ♨❀◑♣P

> Bread is the staff of life,
> but beer is life itself.
>
> Traditional

CAMBRIDGESHIRE

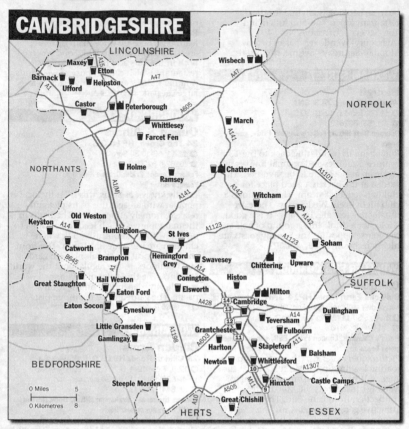

BALSHAM

Black Bull
27 High Street, CB1 6DJ
☼ 11.30-2.30, 6-11; 12-3, 7.30-10.30 Sun
☎ (01223) 893844
Adnams Bitter; Greene King IPA; guest beer Ⓗ
Large, Grade II listed thatched building, dating mostly from the mid-17th century, although now much altered internally. There are several different drinking areas surrounding the island bar plus two dining rooms, one no-smoking. Cerise ceilings, exposed beams and internal timbers emphasise the traditional non-gimmicky feel of the pub. Excellent home-cooked food is available all sessions except Monday (all day) and Sunday evening. Three regularly-changing guest beers are sold. ▲ ❀ ☞ ◑ ▶ P

BARNACK

Millstone
Millstone Lane, PE9 3ET
(down lane off Main Street and 'Hills and Hollows')
☼ 11.30-11; 12-10.30 Sun
☎ (01780) 740296
Adnams Bitter; Everards Tiger, Original; guest beer Ⓗ
The Millstone is now even more popular with drinkers as the old cellar has been converted to a traditional bar with pub games. It has won numerous awards for beer quality and excellent food. Enjoy the sun in the large, walled patio and conservatory. An ancient quarry, known as

the 'Hills and Hollows', is part of the village. Stone was extracted from here to build Peterborough Cathedral. The site is now a pleasant nature reserve. Q ❀ ◑ ◑ 吕 ♣ P ⊁

BRAMPTON

Grange Hotel
115 High Street, PE28 4RA
(jct of Grove Rd and High St)
☼ 11-11; 12-2.30, 6-10.30 Sun
☎ (01480) 459516
website: www.grangehotelbrampton.co.uk
Greene King IPA; guest beers Ⓗ
This pleasant Georgian building has been used for various purposes in the past: it has been a private girls' school, a residence, and then, during WWII, it became the headquarters of the American Eighth Air Force and subsequently that of the RAF Air Training Corps. Since 1981, it has been a private hotel and now boasts interesting food (not served Sun) and an ever-changing selection of real ales, one always from a local brewery. The decor is subdued with photographs of its military past.
Q ❀ ☞ ◑ ◑ 占 P

CAMBRIDGE

Cambridge Blue ⊘
85-87 Gwydir Street, CB1 2LG (off Mill Rd)
☼ 12-2.30 (3 Sat), 5.30-11; 12-3, 6-10.30 Sun
☎ (01223) 361382
Beer range varies Ⓗ

Fine beer, wine and food in quiet surroundings. Inside is no-smoking and mobile phone-free and there is a large garden. Well-behaved children and dogs are welcome. Rowing features strongly – the pub has its own club. Beers are mainly from East Anglia, with a regular set including Adnams Broadside, Iceni Fine Soft Day and Elgood's Black Dog Mild. The local Cassels cider is served in summer. ≜Q☜☺◑♣♠⌇

Castle Inn
38 Castle Street, CB3 0AJ
☼ 11.30-3, 5 (6 Sat)-11; 12-3, 7-10.30 Sun
☎ (01223) 353194
Adnams Bitter, Broadside, seasonal beers; Fuller's London Pride, ESB; Wells Bombardier; guest beers Ⓗ
Adnams' western flagship is a textbook example of sensitive pub renovation. The ground floor offers five separate drinking areas and there are three more upstairs. The suntrap patio garden is bordered by the mound of the long-gone Cambridge Castle. Nine real ales are usually on tap with beers from regional brewers complementing Adnams' own products. First-class food is served at every session. ≜☺◑⌇

Champion of the Thames
68 King Street, CB1 1LN
☼ 11-11; 12-10.30 Sun
☎ (01223) 352043
Greene King IPA, Abbot; guest beers Ⓗ/Ⓖ
One of the few remaining traditional pubs in the city centre. The two cosy bars both have wood panelling, leather upholstered benches and stout wooden tables. There are many interesting nooks and crannies. The pub's name commemorates a famous oarsman, depicted in action on fine etched windows. Inside, the rowing theme continues with prints of boat races along with scenes of Cambridge life. Students and locals enjoy the convivial atmosphere here. ≜Q◑♣

Elm Tree
Orchard Street, CB1 1JS
(behind Parkside School)
☼ 12-2.30, 4-11; 12-11 Sat; 12-10.30 Sun
☎ (01223) 363005
website: www.homepage.ntlworld.com/theelmtree
Adnams Broadside; Wells Eagle, Bombardier; guest beers Ⓗ
This relaxing back-street pub has a huge range of board games available, with the mood set by the large fish tank and background jazz music. Guest beers include JW Lees, Caledonian, Badger (Tanglefoot), plus Wells' seasonals. There is live jazz on Monday, Thursday and Sunday nights. Major sports events are shown on TV. Tables and chairs are set out on the pavement in summer. ☺♣

Empress
72 Thoday Street, CB1 3AX
☼ 11-2.30, 6.30-11; 12-2.30, 7-10.30 Sun
☎ (01223) 247236
Castle Eden Ale; Marston's Pedigree; Taylor Landlord; guest beers Ⓗ
The pubs in this part of town are by and large an unprepossessing bunch, but this terrific back-street local is very much the exception. It also proves that if you get the essentials spot on – ace beer in a welcoming atmosphere – then you do not need to offer

food to attract the crowds. Westons Old Rosie cider is sold. The interior has been extended over the years, but the original public bar and lounge are still identifiable within the open-plan layout. ☺♣♠

Free Press ✿
Prospect Row, CB1 1DU
☼ 12-2.30 (3 Sat), 6-11; 12-3, 7-10.30 Sun
☎ (01223) 368337
Greene King XX Mild, IPA, Abbot; guest beers Ⓗ
This is one of the two no-smoking and no-mobile-phone pubs in Cambridge. It looks old inside but was in fact restored after being saved from redevelopment in the 1970s. The snug bar is a popular feature. Guest beers from the Greene King range and draught Budweiser Budvar are served. 'Upmarket' food is available at each session. A great pub for conversation. ≜Q☺◑♣⌇🖳

Kingston Arms
33 Kingston Street, CB1 2NU (off Mill Rd)
☼ 12-2.30 (not Mon); 5-11; 12-11 Sat; 12-10.30 Sun
☎ (01223) 319414
Lidstones Rowley Mild, Session Bitter, Lucky Punter, Oat Stout, Bookies Revenge, Rawalpindi IPA Ⓗ
Under its previous ownership this was arguably the worst pub in Cambridge; many would now say it is the best. The impressive array of 10 handpumps dispense not only Lidstones own beers but an ever-changing selection of beers from other micro-breweries. The freshly-cooked food has acquired an excellent reputation and advance booking is wise. The enclosed garden is a pleasant spot in summer; the pub itself is a wonderful place to be at anytime. ≜Q☺◑⇌

Live & Let Live
40 Mawson Road, CB1 2EA
(200 yds off Mill Road)
☼ 11.30-2.30; 5.30 (6 Sat)-11; 12-2, 7-10.30 Sun
☎ (01223) 460261
Adnams Bitter; Everards Tiger; Nethergate Umbel Ale; guest beers Ⓗ
Friendly back-street local dating from the 19th century. It takes its name from an early landlord's protest against the Beer Act. Modern wood panelling, bare floorboards, and a large collection of pump clips, all contribute to the homely feel. The extensive range of ales includes guests from around Britain. There is also a respectable selection of bottled Belgian beers and single malt whiskies. Cider is from Cassels. Good, home-cooked food is available except on Sunday evening, when the pub hosts live acoustic music. Q◑⇌♣♠⌇

Portland Arms
129 Chesterton Road, CB4 3BA
☼ 11-11; 12-10.30 Sun
☎ (01223) 357268 website: www.come.to/theportland
Greene King XX Mild, IPA, Ruddles Best, Abbot; guest beers Ⓗ

INDEPENDENT BREWERIES
City of Cambridge Chittering
Elgood's Wisbech
Fenland Chatteris
Milton Milton
Oakham Peterborough

Largely unaltered example of a Greene King 1930s 'improved public house' in neo-Georgian style. The lounge is opulently panelled and the public also retains many original fittings (but it now operates as a 'net bar', offering Internet access and good coffee). The large back room plays host to live music most nights. The extensive menu includes Mexican and Indian dishes, no meals are served on Sunday or Monday evenings. The lounge may close in the afternoon. ♨◑▶ ⊟♣

St Radegund
129 King Street, CB1 1LD
🕒 5 (12 Sat)-11; 12-2, 6.30-10.30 Sun
☎ (01223) 311794
Fuller's London Pride; Shepherd Neame Spitfire Ⓗ
True free house where much is packed into a small space. It is named after a 5th-century Frankish queen and nun, founder of a priory on the site of nearby Jesus College. An array of reference books and a collection of ties are notable behind the bar. The ceiling has smoked etchings of college society names. Elsewhere are invitations to join Friday's Vera Lynn club, Wednesday's Cuban cocktail night or participate in the 'King Street Run'. Background jazz does not intrude and neither should your mobile phone. Habit is brewed by local Milton Brewery especially for the pub.

CASTLE CAMPS

Cock Inn
High Street, CB1 6SN
🕒 7 (12 Sat)-11; 12-3, 7-10.30 Sun
☎ (01799) 584207
Greene King IPA, Abbot; guest beer Ⓗ
Cosy, two-bar village inn off the beaten track in one of the county's southernmost outposts. A recent face-lift includes chalet accommodation at very reasonable rates. The main bar houses a plate collection in an unusual roof arrangement as well as a very large cockerel on the wall. The unobtrusive TV in the small front bar is mainly for sport. This bar also houses the traditional sing-around-the-room folk club every second Monday of the month. Home-cooked food is served evenings (Thu–Sun) and Sunday lunch as bar meals or in the dining room, or dine outside in the summer. The secluded patio and garden are beyond the new extension. ♨❀▭◑▶P

CASTOR

Prince of Wales Feathers
38 Peterborough Road, PE5 7AL
🕒 12-3 (not Thu), 6-11; 12-3, 7-10.30 Sun
☎ (01733) 380936
Adnams Bitter; Greene King Ruddles County; John Smith's Bitter; guest beers Ⓗ/Ⓖ
This welcoming pub, in a charming village, has recently been attractively refurbished. Five real ales are on offer and freshly-made sandwiches are sold Tuesday–Saturday lunchtimes. A lively pub that caters for all ages, it hosts a Sunday quiz, live music monthly, and fields teams in crib, dominoes and pool. ♨❀点♣

Royal Oak Inn
24 Peterborough Road, PE5 7AX (off A47)
🕒 12-2.30 (not Mon), 5-11; 11-11 Sat; 12-10.30 Sun

☎ (01733) 380217
Tetley Bitter, Burton Ale; guest beers Ⓗ
17th-century, stone built, thatched pub with three bars, a long-standing entry in this Guide. The outside patio is somewhat quieter now that the main A47 has bypassed the village and is consequently used much more. Good lunchtime meals are served (Mon–Sat). The pub is popular with ramblers and locals. Boules and ring the bull are played.
♨Q❀◑♣▶⊬⊟

CATWORTH

Fox
Fox Road, PE28 0PW (off A14)
🕒 11-11; 12-10.30 Sun
☎ (01832) 710363
Greene King IPA; guest beers Ⓗ
The Fox sits perched above the A14 and is reached via a slip road to the B606. The car park leads to a patio and garden with a children's play area. Entering the pub, there is one open-plan area, with a bar in the centre. Paintings associated with nearby WWII airfields adorn the walls. A wide range of real ales is on offer, many from micro-breweries, along with an extensive blackboard menu – the pub opens for breakfast at 9am on Saturday. An annual beer festival is held in June to July. ♨❀◑▶P

CHATTERIS

Walk the Dog
34 Bridge Street, PE16 6RN
(on main road into town, from Ramsey End)
🕒 12-2.30, 6.30-11; 12-2.30, 7-11 Sun
☎ (01354) 693695
Adnams Bitter; Fuller's London Pride; guest beers Ⓗ
Traditional, family-owned community pub, this free house often has one of the local Fenland Brewery beers on offer. Bottle-conditioned beers are also available. A variety of pub games can be enjoyed including Scrabble, chess, darts, dominoes and petanque. New for locals is a sailing club to blend with the pub golfing society. Theme nights are often held and Sunday is quiz night. Charity fundraising is very important in this pub. A couple of benches in front of the pub act as a suntrap in summer. Lunchtime food is offered Monday–Saturday. ♨Q❀◑♣P

CONINGTON

White Swan ⊘
Elsworth Road, CB3 8LN (½ mile off A14)
🕒 12-3, 6-11; 12-3, 7-10.30 Sun
☎ (01954) 267251
Greene King IPA, Abbot; guest beer Ⓗ
1760s' country pub of Tudoresque appearance with red brickwork, hooded windows and diamond-shaped window panes. A thriving six o'clock club collects in the main bar area which leads to the brick-floored games/family room with bar billiards and dominoes. Quiz night is Sunday. The dining room extends to a dining patio in summer. Home-made pies top the popularity list of the reasonably-priced dishes which include four vegetarian options and a children's menu (no food on Sun eve). A large front patio and grass surrounds make up a vast outdoor drinking

area which includes a secure children's play section and a footbridge over a stream.
🏠⚲◐♣P

DULLINGHAM

Boot
18 Brinkley Road, CB8 9UW
⊙ 11-2, 5-11; 11-11 Sat; 12-2.30, 7-10.30 Sun
☎ (01638) 507327
Adnams Bitter, Broadside; guest beer Ⓗ
Very much a local success story. Back in 2001, Greene King closed this pub, and were intending to convert it into a private house. Fortunately for the villagers though, one resident (the current landlord) came to the rescue and took the pub over, turning it into a friendly village local with a single, uncluttered, L-shaped bar. Excellent Adnams beers are on tap all the time, supplemented by an ever-changing guest beer, usually from an East Anglian brewery. Evening meals are available until 8pm.
🏠⚲◐≉♣P

EATON FORD

Barley Mow ⊘
27 Crosshall Road, PE19 3AB
⊙ 11.30-3, 5-11; 11-11 Fri & Sat; 12-10.30 Sun
☎ (01480) 474435
Greene King IPA, Ruddles County Ⓗ
The Barley Mow is a simple one-bar pub. What makes it special, other than the excellent beer, is the customers – it is a true community pub, with a wide variety of activities focused on the 'regulars'. A long bar dominates the drinking area with its decor a mix of plaster, brick and wood panelling. The highlights of past pub social events are featured in a display of photographs, some date back to the early 1900s. Petanque is played and a covered patio tempts outdoor drinkers. ⚲◐♣P

EATON SOCON

Rivermill Tavern
School Lane, PE19 8GW
⊙ 12-11; 12-10.30 Sun
☎ (01480) 219612
Greene King IPA, Abbot; guest beers Ⓗ
Popular riverside pub converted from a flour mill at Eaton Socon lock on the River Ouse. Its facilities include a galleried area above the main bar, housing an à la carte restaurant. Extensive bar snacks feature a Mexican selection. Children are well catered for in a family room that offers a host of activities. Live music is popular with two sessions per week (Wed and Fri eves). A quiz is held on Sunday evening. In summer the patio area is busy and offers splendid views of the river and marina. Moorings on the river are available close by. Up to three guest beers from independent breweries are on tap.
≥⚲◐♿P⌿

ELSWORTH

Poacher
1 Brockley Road, CB3 8JS (take Elsworth turn at New Cambourne roundabout off A428)
⊙ 12-2.30, 6 (6.30 Mon-Wed)-11; 12-2.30, 7-10.30 Sun
☎ (01954) 267219

Greene King IPA, Abbot, Old Speckled Hen; Potton Shambles; guest beers Ⓗ
This small, thatched pub (circa 1650) has a warm and cosy interior with a log fire in winter. The small servery boasts a fine range of ales with Greene King IPA as a constant, and guests which include beers from Adnams, Elgood's and Nethergate. The bric-à-brac reflects the family history of the licensee; model trains, cars and interesting pictures are on show. A good snack lunchtime menu is served with a more substantial emphasis in the evening; home-made steak and kidney and chilli are highly recommended. The garden is superb with ample seating.
🏠Q⚲◐P⌿

ELY

Fountain
1 Silver Street, CB7 4JF
⊙ 5-11; 12-2, 6-11 Sat; 12-2, 7-10.30 Sun
☎ (01353) 663122
Adnams Bitter, Broadside (winter), **Regatta** (summer); **Fuller's London Pride; guest beers** Ⓗ
A short walk from the station, city centre and very close to the cathedral, this intriguing pub with wood floor and real fire is not to be missed. Pictures of militaria and classes from the local King's School compete with the stuffed animals, antler rack and buffalo horns. Children are welcome, however the pub gets very busy after 7pm, particularly Friday and Saturday. Cider is occasionally stocked. There are rings on the outside wall of the pub to secure your bike.
🏠Q≥≉⚭

Prince Albert
62 Silver Street, CB7 4JL
(across street from Barton Road car park)
⊙ 11-3 (not Tue; 3.30 Thu-Sat), 6.30-11; 12-3.30, 7-10.30 Sun
☎ (01353) 663494
Greene King XX Mild, IPA, Abbot; guest beers Ⓗ
Traditional, English pub within easy reach of city-centre attractions, only 10 minutes' walk from the station. Recently redecorated inside and out, it has a splendid, cosy interior and a prize-winning garden. Generous portions of home-cooked lunchtime food are served Monday–Saturday (no meals winter Tue). There is an ever-changing choice of two guest ales.
Q⚲◐≉♣⌿

ETTON

Golden Pheasant
1 Main Road, PE6 7DA
(400 yds N of B1443 Glinton-Helpston road)
⊙ 11-11; 12-10.30 Sun
☎ (01773) 252387
website: www.thegoldenpheasant.co.uk
Adnams Broadside; Fuller's London Pride; Rooster's Yankee; guest beers Ⓗ
Former Georgian rectory/manor house set in grounds of more than an acre. The à la carte restaurant provides lunches and dinner. Outdoor facilities include a children's play area, plenty of garden tables and a petanque court. The Golden Pheasant holds two annual beer festivals with up to 24 different cask ales and ciders.
🏠Q≥⚲◐♿⚭P

EYNESBURY

Chequers
St Mary's Street, PE19 2TA
✪ 10.30-2.30, 7-11; 12-2 (closed eve) Sun
☎ (01480) 472116 website: www.chequers.cambs.com
Beer range varies Ⓗ
This 16th-century inn may be the oldest house in Eynesbury. It has seen many additions and much restoration over the years to extend and enlarge it. Manor courts were held here in the 18th century and a wealth of beams and wood panelling give it olde-worlde charm. There is a comfortable lounge bar with areas set aside for dining; the food is excellent. ♨✿◖P

FARCET FEN

Plough
Milk and Water Drove, Ramsey Road, PE7 3DR (on B1095, 2 miles S of A605 jct)
✪ 12-3 (not Mon-Fri), 5.30 (6 Sat)-11; 12-10.30 Sun
☎ (01733) 844307
website: www.members.tripod.co.uk/ploughfarcet
Elgood's Black Dog Mild; Oakham JHB; John Smith's Bitter; guest beers Ⓗ
Situated on an open fen road between Peterborough and Ramsey, this white-painted pub stands out in the sparsely populated landscape. It is renowned for its quality, reasonably-priced food and choice of real ales. The local farming community ensures a steady turnover of cask ales. An extensive garden and play area welcome families in the summer months. Grand uninterrupted views of the open fens, and wonderful sunsets enhance this rural gem. ♨Q✿◖⊟☖▲♣♠P☂

FULBOURN

Six Bells
9 High Street, CB1 5DH
✪ 11.30-2.30, 6-11; 12-11 Sat; 12-10.30 Sun
☎ (01223) 880244
Adnams Bitter; Flowers IPA; Tetley Burton Ale; guest beer Ⓗ
Some intriguing 15th-century parts were discovered here during repairs following a fire in 1999. A traditional, friendly village local with cosy corners, it offers a good, varied menu of home-cooked food served in the restaurant (not Sun or Mon eves). Live jazz is hosted twice monthly. The warm, comfortable atmosphere is enhanced by open fires and a wide selection of real ales in the three bars. One of the bars focuses on pub games. A large garden and patio prove popular in summer. ♨Q⦿✿◖⊟☖P

GAMLINGAY

Cock
25 Church Street, SG19 3JH
✪ 11.30-3, 5.30-11; 11.30-11 Sat; 12-4, 7-10.30 Sun
☎ (01767) 650255
Greene King IPA, Abbot; guest beers Ⓗ
This 400-year-old pub is the only survivor of the great fire of Gamlingay, which destroyed most of the village in 1660. The pub boasts many wooden beams and features a large inglenook. Excellent, good value meals are available and a separate restaurant is accessed through the lounge bar (no food on Sun or Mon eves). The

public bar caters for sports fans, but you should look around and observe the collection of cocks. A well-stocked patio area leads to the garden and petanque pitch, which caters well for young children with play equipment and a menagerie. ♨⦿✿◖⊟♣P

GRANTCHESTER

Blue Ball Inn
57 Broadway, CB3 9NQ
✪ 11.30-3, 6-11; 12-3, 7-10.30 Sun
☎ (01223) 840679
Adnams Bitter; guest beer Ⓗ
There has been a Blue Ball in Grantchester since the mid-18th century but the present building dates from Victorian times. It comprises just two small rooms and only five tables. Photographs of the pub and village are displayed along with a list of all landlords since 1767. Food is available but meals must be booked in advance. Local CAMRA Pub of the Year 2002, ring the bull, shove-ha'penny and cards are popular here. ♨Q✿☖◖♣

GREAT CHISHILL

Pheasant
24 Heydon Road, SG8 8SR
✪ 12-3, 6-11; 12-11 Sat; 12-10.30 Sun
☎ (01763) 838535
Greene King IPA; guest beers Ⓗ
Peaceful, cheery free house with an outstanding garden (steps up). The single, L-shaped bar is replete with beams and brass, plus an inglenook. Bar snacks and restaurant standard food provided at all sessions, represent excellent value for money. ♨Q✿◖♣P

GREAT STAUGHTON

White Hart
56 The Highway, PE19 5DA (on B645)
✪ 12-2, 5-11; 12-3, 7-11 Sat; 12-3, 7-10.30 Sun
☎ (01480) 860345
Bateman XB, XXXB, seasonal beers Ⓗ
Fine example of a 16th-century coaching inn, and driving through the narrow coachway entrance transports you back to the days of horse-drawn coaches. The pub itself has been extended and altered since Cromwell's days, but still warrants a Grade II listing; unusually, an interior staircase is Grade I listed. The main bar was once several rooms. There is a small dining room at the front of the pub. A separate games area offers darts, pool and table skittles. This, reputedly haunted, pub is an excellent outlet for Bateman beers. ♨Q✿◖♣P✄

HAIL WESTON

Royal Oak ⊘
79 High Street, PE19 5JW (off B645)
✪ 12-11; 12-10.30 Sun
☎ (01480) 472527
Adnams Broadside; Marston's Pedigree; Wells Eagle Ⓗ
The Royal Oak is a traditional village pub; the heart, soul and social centre of Hail Weston. The building dates from the 16th century. The main bar is dominated by a vast open fire, with many exposed beams and horse brasses. Adjoining the bar is an

intimate restaurant, and a varied blackboard menu is offered. At the rear of the pub, leading to the extensive garden, is a family room, with children's games. Petanque is also played. Off the family room is a community Internet access room, used as part of a council-sponsored education venture. ♨Q♿☢♣♠P

HARLTON

Hare & Hounds
60 High Street, CB3 7ES
✪ 12-3 (not Mon), 5-11; 12-3, 7-10.30 Sun
☎ (01223) 262672
Wells Eagle, Bombardier; guest beer Ⓗ

Welcoming village free house set in typical Cambridgeshire countryside. A community meeting place, well supported by local clubs and typified by the Friday meat raffle. The single bar is big enough comfortably to accommodate the normal passing trade, including diners for the home-cooked bar meals such as stew and dumplings (eve meals Tue–Sat). The large garden features a petanque pitch and hosts the occasional traction engine rally. ♨Q☢♣♠P

HELPSTON

Blue Bell
10 Woodgate, PE6 7ED
✪ 5.30-11; 12-3, 6-11 Sat; 12-3, 7-10.30 Sun
☎ (01733) 252394
Bateman XB; John Smith's Bitter; guest beers Ⓗ

Traditional village local with a wood-panelled lounge, comfortable bar and plenty of rural charm. A barn at the rear is used for a June beer festival. The 'peasant poet', John Clare, was born in the village in 1793 and was said to have stayed in the pub in later years. An annual festival is held in his honour in the village when the pub hosts poetry readings, folk singing and morris dancing. ♨Q☢♣♠P

HEMINGFORD GREY

Cock
47 High Street, PE28 9BJ
✪ 11.30-3, 6-11; 12-4, 6.30-10.30 Sun
☎ (01480) 463609
Adnams Bitter; Elgood's Black Dog Mild; Oakham JHB; Woodforde's Wherry Ⓗ

Superbly revamped local in a stylish village. The small bar features simple furnishings, a solid fuel stove and a relaxing food-free atmosphere. The selection of local ales is unprecedented in the area. Excellent food is served in the large restaurant (closed Sun eve). Speciality sausages are a popular feature and there are usually several fresh fish and game dishes. Booking is advisable at all times. No food is served in the bar. ♨Q☢♣P

HINXTON

Red Lion
32 High Street, CB10 1QY (near jct 9 M11/A11)
✪ 11-2.30, 6-11; 12-2.30, 7-10.30 Sun
☎ (01799) 530601
Adnams Bitter; Greene King IPA; Woodforde's Wherry; guest beer Ⓗ

16th-century coaching inn with a compartmented L-shaped bar and busy, award-winning dining-room extension. It

blends sympathetically with the original brickwork, which is punctuated throughout by fine old clocks, horse brasses and stuffed animals. Note the unusual polished copper doorsteps. The pub fields a cricket team and cribbage is popular (Wed). Morris men visit each June as do passing participants in the annual London–Cambridge cycle ride. Lunches are available Monday–Saturday. ♨Q☢♣P

HISTON

Red Lion
27 High Street, CB4 4JD
✪ 11-3, 5 (4 Fri)-11; 11-11 Sat; 12-6, 7-10.30 Sun
☎ (01223) 564437
Everards Beacon, Tiger; Milton Minotaur; guest beers Ⓗ

Two-bar free house, comprising a quiet(ish) lounge where food is served and a more boisterous public bar with a fine collection of bottled beers on display. There is a wide range of breweriana throughout, including old pub signs and water jugs, plus old photographs. Two beer festivals are staged annually: an Easter 'apéritif' and the main event in early September with a marquee in the garden and live entertainment each evening. A range of Belgian bottled beers complements the ever-changing selection of guest ales. An anti-mobile phone policy is upheld rigorously. ♨Q☢♣P

HOLME

Admiral Wells
41 Station Road, PE7 3PH
✪ 12-2.30, 5-11; 12-11 Sat; 12-10.30 Sun
☎ (01487) 831214
Everards Tiger; Woodforde's Wherry; guest beers Ⓗ

This Victorian, yellow-brick pub is situated next to the main east coast railway line. Named after one of Nelson's pall bearers at his funeral, the pub is in the 'sinking fens' area. Nearby the Holme posts show how much the land has sunk over the years. Up to five beers are on offer, with a choice of three drinking areas. A large, shaded garden is at the side of the pub with a separate dining room. It is popular with ramblers and cyclists. ♨Q♿☢♣♠P

HUNTINGDON

Old Bridge Hotel ✔
1 High Street, PE29 3TQ (on ring road, by river)
✪ 11-11; 12-10.30 Sun
☎ (01480) 424300
Adnams Bitter; guest beers Ⓗ

This relaxing hotel bar provides splendid surroundings for local real ale drinkers, residents and diners. The handsome, ivy-clad 18th-century building was a former private bank and stands next to the River Great Ouse in the birthplace of Oliver Cromwell. A local brewery often supplies one of the two guest beers. The imaginative, quality food and fine wines are stylishly served in the informal atmosphere of the mural-adorned 'terrace', or the intimate, but more formal, dining room. ♨Q☢♣P

Samuel Pepys ✔
146 High Street, PE29 3TF
✪ 11-11; 12-10.30 Sun
☎ (01480) 437877 website: www.thesamuelpepys.com

Courage Best Bitter; Ⓗ **guest beers** Ⓗ/Ⓖ
Previously an Irish-theme bar, now a large single-bar pub providing an eclectic mix of drinking choices and a welcome addition to Huntingdon's pub scene. Popular at lunchtime catering for town office workers and shoppers, food is available until 6pm and in the evening it becomes a lively circuit venue. East Anglian independent brewers and micro-breweries usually feature among the constantly changing range of cask beers. Oldershaw beers are often stocked. ⊛◁≢

KEYSTON

Pheasant
Village Loop, PE18 0RE (off A14)
✪ 12-3, 6-11; 12-3, 7-10.30 Sun
☎ (01832) 710241 website: www.huntsbridge.co.uk
Adnams Bitter; Potton Village Bike; guest beer Ⓗ
The Pheasant is a converted from a series of thatched cottages and has an idyllic setting. Inside, the pub has a number of open-plan rooms with oak beams and farm implements hanging from the ceiling. The main bar is a lounge drinking area with an imposing fireplace. There are three dining areas, two no-smoking, all comfortable with simple wooden furniture. A constantly-changing range of real ales is drawn from local micro-breweries and independents. Belgian beers are also on offer. The food is modern in style with a Mediterranean emphasis.
🌜Q⏴⊛◁P⚲

LITTLE GRANSDEN

Chequers
71 Main Road, SG19 3DW
✪ 12-2.30, 5-11; 11-11 Sat; 12-3, 7-10.30 Sun
☎ (01767) 677348
Adnams Bitter; guest beers Ⓗ
Run by the same family for the last 50 years, its history has been well researched and documented by the landlord, and provides interesting reading. While retaining an excellent basic public bar, a comfortable lounge has been added. The landlord has devised a secret weapon in winter to stop people hanging around in front of the bar; you will soon find out if you linger too long. There is always an unusual guest beer.
🌜⏴⊛⏴♣P

MARCH

Rose & Crown
41 St Peter's Road, PE15 9NA
(B1099 off High St, old A141)
✪ 12-2.30 (not Wed; 3 Sat), 7-11; 12-3, 7-10.30 Sun
☎ (01354) 652879
Archers Village; guest beers Ⓗ
Family-owned, traditional free house just south of the town centre. A comfortable bar plus a popular, no-smoking lounge cater for a broad range of locals and visitors. The seven handpumps normally include a mild and over 2,000 different beers have been served. Two ciders plus a perry are on gravity from the ultra-modern cellar. Over 100 whiskies fight for space on the well-stocked back bar in this CAMRA multi-award winning pub. Bar snacks are available (Thu–Sat) in a welcoming atmosphere with no disturbance from TV, juke box or video

games. A small floral patio area at the rear is pleasant for those better days.
Q⊛⏴⊛♣♠P⚲

MAXEY

Blue Bell
37-39 High Street, PE6 9EE (on A15)
✪ 5.30-11; 12-4, 7-11 Sat; 12-4, 7-10.30 Sun
☎ (01778) 348182
Fuller's London Pride; guest beers Ⓗ
The front bar has been extensively modernised in keeping with the traditional surroundings and features a Yorkshire range fireplace. Built in 1645 using local limestone, it became a free house in 1997 saving it from the fate of Maxey's other pubs. Much improved in recent years, it now figures at the centre of village life. The front bar is a no-smoking zone and is available for meetings. The pleasant garden has tranquil views of the surrounding countryside. 🌜Q⊛⏴♣P⚲🖳

MILTON

Waggon & Horses
39 High Street, CB4 6DF
✪ 12-2.30 (3 Sat), 5 (6 Sat)-11; 12-3, 7-10.30 Sun
☎ (01223) 860313
Elgood's Black Dog Mild, Cambridge, Pageant Ale, seasonal beers; guest beers Ⓗ
Elgood's most southerly house, this imposing mock-Tudor one-roomed pub boasts a large collection of hats. The sizeable garden is safe for children and offers a slide, swings, and a petanque terrain. Games include bar billiards and shove-ha'penny. A popular quiz is held on Wednesday and baltis are the speciality on Thursday evening. All meals represent good choice and value. The real cider is from local producer, Cassels. 🌜⊛◁▸♣♠P🖳

NEWTON

Queen's Head
Fowlmere Road, CB2 5PG (off A10)
✪ 11.30-2.30, 6-11; 12-2.30, 7-10.30 Sun
☎ (01223) 870436
Adnams Bitter, Broadside, seasonal beers Ⓖ
Classic, timeless village pub, which has had only 18 licensees since 1729. The achingly traditional public bar has wooden benches, a high-backed settle, tiled floor and the comforting tick of a large old clock. In the tiny games annexe you can play devil among the tailors or shove-ha'penny. The cosy lounge features a roaring fire and built-in seating. Simple, satisfying food is freshly cooked to order. Cassels cider is sold. The head on the sign is that of Anne of Cleeves. George V and the Kaiser had a drink here before WWI. This gem has appeared in every edition of this Guide.
🌜Q⊛◁▸⏴♣♠P⚲

OLD WESTON

Swan
Main Street, PE17 5LL (B660, off A14)
✪ 6.30-11; 12-2.30, 7-11 Sat; 12-3.30, 7-10.30 Sun
☎ (01832) 293400
Adnams Bitter, Broadside; Greene King Abbot; guest beers Ⓗ
16th-century, oak-beamed village pub, with a central bar area, a dining area and a games

section offering hooded skittles, darts and pool. The central bar has a large inglenook. The pub started life as two private houses that have since been merged, and the building has evolved and grown over the years. At the turn of the century the pub had its own brewery. The Swan offers a varied menu of home-cooked traditional pub food including home-made puddings (Sat and Sun only, lunch and evening).
ᐁQ⌖❀❀◗♣P

PETERBOROUGH

Brewery Tap
80 Westgate, PE1 2AA
⏱ 12-11 (2am Fri & Sat); 12-10.30 Sun
☎ (01733) 358500
Oakham JHB, Bishops Farewell; guest beers Ⓗ
Converted from an employment exchange, it incorporates bits of old brewery kit to create a large, airy pub. A glass panel shows views of the Oakham Ales Brewery. The walls display more than 70 of the brewery's awards. The simple tables and chairs have now been complemented by leather armchairs and low tables which together with bamboo and more muted colours, help create a softer, more relaxing atmosphere. Excellent Thai food is served. A door charge operates after 11pm on Friday and Saturday, when there is usually a disco and occasionally live music. An annual beer festival is held in March. Belgian bottled beers are sold and a mild is always available. The dress code is casual but smart for weekend evenings. Still under threat of demolition to make way for shops. ◗❀≈⊬

Charters
Town Bridge, PE1 1DG
⏱ 12-11 (1.30am Fri & Sat); 12-10.30 Sun
☎ (01733) 315700 website: www.charters-bar.co.uk
Draught Bass; Hop Back Summer Lightning; Oakham JHB; Taylor Landlord; Ⓗ **guest beers** Ⓗ/Ⓖ
Large, converted Dutch barge moored at Town Bridge, always 12 beers available, plus Dutch Korenwolf and Belgian bottled beers. The wide range of customers ensures that the pub has the feel of a local. Live blues is performed (Fri and Sat) so there is usually an entry charge after 9.30pm. The large garden provides a refuge from the traffic above. The upper deck houses a fine oriental restaurant, East, and oriental food and snacks are available in the bar. It is popular with local football supporters on match days when entry restrictions may apply. A footpath from the garden leads to Nene Valley Railway, Railworld and the shops. Local CAMRA Pub of the Year 2002.
❀◗❀≈⊬

Coalheavers Arms
5 Park Street, Fletton, PE2 9BH (on A15 S of city, down side street off London Rd)
⏱ 12-2.30, 5.30-11; 12-11 Fri & Sat; 12-3, 7-10.30 Sun
☎ (01733) 565664
Milton Minotaur, Jupiter, Pegasus; guest beers Ⓗ
A new addition to the city's south side selection of fine pubs. This small, back-street gem was revived in August 2002 by a consortium of business partners, one of which is Milton Brewery of Cambridge. Hence the regular selection of Milton beers, which are complemented by an ever-

changing range of guest ales from micro-brewers. The one-roomed bar has been sympathetically refurbished with wood furnishings and a flagstone floor. It is run by a couple with high standards. Bottled continental beers are also available.
Q❀≈●▯

Goodbarns Yard ✓
64 St John's Street, PE1 5DD
(edge of city centre, 500 yds from market)
⏱ 11 (12 Sat)-11; 12-10.30 Sun
☎ (01733) 551830
website: www.mysite.freeserve.com/GoodBarnsYard
Adnams Broadside; Black Sheep Best Bitter; guest beers Ⓖ
Goodbarns Yard was voted local CAMRA 2001 Pub of the Year. Situated on the edge of the city centre, this modern pub's exterior hides a deceptively warm and friendly interior. Sample the excellent ales, served on gravity. Food is available and children are welcome. This community pub is a treat. ❀❀◗⬧≈♣P⊬

Hand & Heart ☆
12 Highbury Street, PE1 3BE
(off Lincoln Rd in Millfield area)
⏱ 11-11; 12-10.30 Sun
☎ (01733) 564653
Draught Bass; John Smith's Bitter; guest beers Ⓗ
Splendid, friendly, two-roomed community local with a characterful interior. Leatherette bench seating features in both rooms, and the Smoke Room has a serving-hatch. The lovely black and white tiled drinking corridor with a glass serving hatchery, adds to the charm. 'Warwick's' windows reflect an earlier owner. Darts, crib and dominoes teams are supported and the local CAMRA cricket team is sponsored. A recently improved garden adds another dimension for warmer times. Children are welcome in the back room. ᐁQ❀❀♣

New England Club and Institute
Occupation Road, New England, PE1 2LJ
(between present A15 and old A15)
⏱ 11-3 (5 Sat), 6.30-11; 12-3, 7-10.30 Sun
☎ (01733) 564021
Draught Bass; Camerons Strongarm; Tetley Bitter; Worthington's Bitter; guest beers Ⓗ
This late Victorian establishment opened in 1901 as a social club and bath house. Upstairs became a family lounge and large snooker room in 1990, and in 1993 a concert room was built for weekend entertainment, special functions and big-screen sports (this has wheelchair access). Cecil the ghost is said to haunt upstairs and the ornate staircase. Regular teams compete at snooker, darts, pool, crib and dominoes. The original public bar is lively. Regular pensioners' events take place. A former winner of the champion CAMRA Club of East Anglia, it is the best example of a multi-roomed club in the area.
Q❀❀⬧≈♣P

Palmerston Arms
82 Oundle Road, PE2 9PA
⏱ 12-11; 12-10.30 Sun
☎ (01733) 565865
Beer range varies Ⓖ
This stone-built, corner pub is one of the oldest buildings in Peterborough, dating back to 1600. Popular with the locals, the

pub is devoid of all electrical inventions except lighting, meaning good conversation can be enjoyed along with one of up to 14 ales, poured direct from the cask. Real cider and/or perry, as well as country wines and continental bottled beers are also available. Old artefacts and breweriana fill every nook and cranny, and an extensive list of malt whiskies is offered. A small courtyard serves as a garden. Beware, this pub operates a highly restrictive entry policy, which may be activated by the licensee at any time!
Q❀✿♣☙

RAMSEY

Jolly Sailor ✿
43 Great Whyte, PE26 1HH (on B1040)
✪ 11-3, 5.30 (6 Sat)-11; 12-3, 7-10.30 Sun
☎ (01487) 813388
Adnams Bitter, Broadside; Tetley Bitter; Wells Bombardier; guest beers Ⓗ

The half-dozen handpumps on the central bar serve three rooms of differing character in this Grade II listed real ale mecca, which has been a pub for 400 years. No food, no music and a mature clientele make it a great place for conversation. Toilets and the rear lounge are easily accessed by wheelchairs from the car park (entry via Newtown Road). Daytime buses connect Ramsey with Peterborough, Whittlesey, St Ives and Huntingdon, but evening/Sunday services are sparse. Council boat moorings are a five-minute walk away. The weekly Saturday market is held in front of the pub. A secluded courtyard is available for alfresco drinking. ♒Q❀ఉ♣P

ST IVES

Floods Tavern
27 The Broadway, PE27 5BX
✪ 11.30-11; 12-10.30 Sun
☎ (01480) 467773
Elgood's Cambridge, Greyhound Strong, seasonal beer Ⓗ

Lively and friendly, single-bar town pub providing a welcome outpost for the Fenland brewers, Elgood's. The rear riverside garden is an idyllic refuge with superb views across the River Great Ouse and its water meadows. Enlarged photographs of historic local flood scenes adorn the walls in the bar. Steak night (Wed) is the only evening for food. Karaoke is staged on Thursday night, live music on Saturday evening and jam sessions on Tuesday. ❀◑

SOHAM

Carpenters Arms
76 Brook Street, CB7 5AE
✪ 12-11; 12-10.30 Sun
☎ (01353) 722026
Greene King IPA; guest beers Ⓗ

On first appearances the outside of the pub looks deceptively small, but on entering it opens up to a large bar area, leading to a quiet drinking corner and games room with pool table. This is very much a drinkers' pub with no food served, only crisps and bar snacks. The sizeable garden hosts an annual beer festival in the late summer. This pub is well worth finding for the traditional drinker as you will be guaranteed a warm welcome. ❀ఉ♣

STAPLEFORD

Longbow
2 Church Street, CB2 5DS
✪ 11-3, 6 (5 summer)-11; 11-11 Fri; 12-3, 7-10.30 Sun
☎ (01223) 566855
Adnams Bitter, Broadside; guest beers Ⓗ

The somewhat unprepossessing interior, is more than compensated for by a genuinely welcoming atmosphere and a superb selection of ever-changing guest beers. The Longbow attracts a wide cross-section of the local community. The games room provides a pool table and bar billiards. An extensive range of food is advertised on blackboards, all excellent value (eve meals Mon-Sat). ⊱❀◑≢(Shelford)♣P⌿

STEEPLE MORDEN

Waggon & Horses
19 Church Street, SG8 0NJ
✪ 12-3, 6-11; 12-11 Sat; 12-10.30 Sun
☎ (01763) 852829
Greene King XX Mild, IPA; guest beers (summer) Ⓗ

Deep in the heart of South Cambridgeshire's countryside, this 300-year-old pub provides a welcoming retreat. Your thirst can be slaked with an excellent pint of the rare Greene King XX Dark Mild. The tile-floored public bar, with pool table, leads to a cosy lounge boasting a large inglenook (children welcome). There is a CC-registered site at the rear of the pub (must be booked). Petanque is played. Look out for the former WWII American Air Force base memorial, which is close by. ♒⊱❀✿⚑▲♣P

SWAVESEY

White Horse
1 Market Street, CB4 5QG
✪ 12-2.30, 6-11; 11.30-11 Sat; 12-10.30 Sun
☎ (01945) 232470
Adnams Bitter; guest beers Ⓗ

Large, well-run pub in the village centre. It has a comfortable, food-oriented lounge and a characterful public bar with tiled floor and roaring fire in winter, plus a pool/family room at the back. The spacious garden hosts barbecues and has a children's play area. Food is served all sessions except Sunday evening; Sunday lunchtime roasts are renowned. A beer festival is held on May bank holiday weekend. ♒⊱❀◑⚑♣⌿

TEVERSHAM

Rose & Crown
1 High Street, CB1 5AF
✪ 11.30-2.30, 6 (5 Fri)-11; 12-11 Sat; 12-3, 7-10.30 Sun
☎ (01223) 292245
Ansells Mild; Greene King IPA; guest beer Ⓗ

Friendly village pub with plenty to offer. The extended garden includes a children's play area. The bar area is Z-shaped and usually has adequate seating. Well-behaved children are welcome. A pool table is at one end and local radio is sometimes played without being intrusive. The beer is always of a high standard with a regular mild and a frequently-changing guest. Pub games, including darts, are available on request. ♒Q❀◑ఉ♣P

UFFORD

White Hart

Main Street, PE9 2PA

⏲ 12-11; 12-10.30 Sun

☎ (01780) 740250

Adnams Bitter; Oakham JHB, White Dwarf Wheat Beer; guest beer Ⓗ

This 17th-century former farmhouse is a traditional two-bar pub. Both bars are small with open fires. The public bar has a large, tiled fireplace, bench seats and a collection of old railway lamps and signs. Games nights are held on a regular basis and small groups of different associations meet here. It is a centre for village activity, but the piano has been replaced by a TV. The garden is safe for children and pleasant for summer drinking. ♨Q⚲✿⊟♿P

UPWARE

Five Miles from Anywhere, No Hurry

Old School Lane, CB7 5ZR (2 miles off A1123, between Wicken and Stretham)

⏲ closed Mon; 11-3, 7-11 (12.30am Wed; 2am Fri; 11-2am summer Sat); 12-10.30 Sun

☎ (01353) 721654 website: www.fivemiles.co.uk

City of Cambridge Hobson's Choice; guest beers Ⓗ

Unusual pub that successfully caters for many different types of customer, including walkers, boaters and families with children. Outside, almost four acres of grounds include a fully-equipped children's play area, extensive moorings and a heated terrace for dining. Children love the bouncy castle in summer. Live entertainment is hosted (Fri and Sat eves) and monthly jazz (on third Sun lunchtime). The lounge bar stocks a choice of three real ales, the public has a large-screen TV. The pub holds a children's certificate. ✿◐◑⊟P

WHITTLESEY

Bricklayers Arms

9 Station Road, PE7 1UA

⏲ 11-4, 7-11; 12-4, 7-10.30 Sun

☎ (01733) 202593

John Smith's Bitter; guest beers Ⓗ

Two-roomed local with a long, plainly furnished public bar and a smaller, cosy, no-smoking lounge. It holds a well-deserved CAMRA gold award for serving a large range of real ales, one of which is always a mild. Strong language is not tolerated and the clientele spans all ages. Situated close to the council boat moorings, it is handy for the station and near the bus route to Peterborough (limited evening service). The pub has a large garden and is HQ for the famous Whittlesey Straw Bear Festival. Wheelchair access is via the garden door from the car park. ✿⊟♿⇌♣P⊁⊓

Hero of Aliwal

75 Church Street, PE7 1DG (on B1040, 1/4 mile S of A605 jct)

⏲ 11-3 (not Mon or Tue), 7-11; 12-3, 7-10.30 Sun

☎ (01733) 203736

Adnams Bitter; Ⓗ **guest beers** Ⓗ/Ⓖ

Family-owned, fenland free house with a large public bar and a lounge containing a 65-seater restaurant. Wheelchair access is to public bar WCs only. Usually two guest ales are on offer, sometimes more and occasionally on gravity dispense. Rudgate and Oakham Breweries are frequently featured. The pub is on a riverside site, handy for boat moorings, and has a patio with a grassed children's play area, plus a floodlit petanque terrain. Darts, dominoes and pool complete the games scene. Folk music nights and visits from local dance teams are popular. The pub is just five minutes' walk from the main bus stops (limited evening services). Q✿⛟◐◑⊟♿♣P⊓

WHITTLESFORD

Bees in the Wall

36 North Road, CB2 4NZ

⏲ 12-3, 6-11; 12-11 Sat; 12-10.30 Sun

☎ (01223) 834289

Badger IPA; Taylor Landlord; guest beers Ⓗ

Two-bar pub on the village's northern frontier, which actually does have bees in the wall. The public bar oozes atmosphere, especially when the fire is blazing. The long, split-level lounge opens on to the huge, well-tabled paddock-style gardens. It is a focal point for village activities, and convenient for visitors to the magnificent Imperial War Museum at Duxford (two miles away). The two guest beers change every week. Inexpensive food is served 12–2, Monday–Saturday, and evening meals feature chilli and pasta on Wednesday, and fish and chips on Thursday. ♨Q✿◐◑⊟♣P

WISBECH

Rose Tavern

53 North Brink, PE13 1JX (follow the river upstream from the town centre)

⏲ 12-3, 6-11; 12-3, 7-10.30 Sun

☎ (01945) 588335

Adnams Broadside; Fuller's London Pride; Shepherd Neame Spitfire; Woodforde's Wherry; guest beers Ⓗ

A traditional pub on the north bank of the River Nene in Wisbech; a charming market town. The characterful interior has oak beams on the walls and ceiling and an imposing open fireplace. Nine handpumps are used during busy periods. Pub games are played including 'spoof'. The lunchtime menu has recently been praised by press critics – no food is available at weekends. Children are welcome during the day. A beer festival takes place every summer with 40 ales.

♨Q✿◐♣

WITCHAM

White Horse

7 Silver Street, CB6 2LF (off A142)

⏲ 12-3 (not Mon & Tue), 6.30-11; 12-3, 7-10.30 Sun

☎ (01353) 778298

Adnams Bitter; guest beers Ⓗ

Now the only pub in Witcham village, this tucked-away local is well worth finding. It serves an ever-changing range of guest ales and a real cider in summer. Freshly-cooked meals are available with a carvery on Sunday lunchtime and a senior citizens' carvery on Wednesday lunchtime (no food on Sun or Mon eves). This family-run open-plan pub has three distinctive areas: a restaurant (booking advised), a lounge bar, and a carvery.

✿◐◑♣🍎P

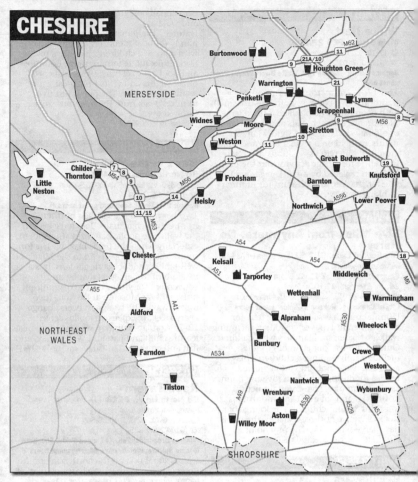

CHESHIRE

ALDFORD

Grosvenor Arms
Chester Road, CH3 6HJ
☼ 11.30-11; 12-10.30 Sun
☎ (01244) 620228
Flowers IPA; guest beers Ⓗ
Lying close to the Duke of Westminster's country estate, this classy, substantial Victorian free house oozes both quality and efficiency. Solidly furnished and decorated throughout with wood floors, quirky prints and bric-à-brac, rooms include a large, panelled library and a quieter snug with a fireplace. An airy, terracotta-tiled conservatory, complete with verdant low-hanging baskets looks out on a suntrap terrace and sizeable lawned beer garden. A fine beer range complements the appetising, highly popular, home-made fare featured on the blackboard menu.
♙Q❀◑க்P

ALPRAHAM

Travellers Rest ☆
Chester Road, CW6 9JA (on A51)
☼ 6.30-11; 12-4.30, 6.30-11 Sat; 12-3, 7-10.30 Sun
☎ (01829) 260523
Marston's Pedigree; Tetley Dark Mild, Bitter Ⓗ

Close to the canal (Bunbury Lock), this family-owned rural local is in a 1950/60s time warp; twice winner of CAMRA's South Cheshire Pub of the Year. A wall divides the bar into two separate rooms; one ❀ is a hub of conversation, where locals and strangers are made very welcome. The darts/dominoes room is notable for the unusual 1950s furniture. The toilets, like the bowling green, are to the rear. **Q❀♣P**

ALSAGER

Mere
58 Crewe Road, ST7 2HA (on B4077)
☼ 11-11; 12-10.30 Sun
☎ (01270) 882019
Flowers IPA; guest beers Ⓗ
Situated close to the attractive mere, this award-winning pub draws a wide range of customers. Five handpumps dispense an excellent range of guest beers, rotating weekly. A description of the monthly beer list is displayed and the week's guests are highlighted on a blackboard. The pub has a large-screen satellite TV in the bar and a separate games room with TV, pool and bar football. Live music is featured on Tuesday night. Hot snacks are served all day.
❀⇌♣P

and memorabilia of local village life and Bhurtpore fortress in India make fascinating viewing. Eleven beers are normally available (including mild), plus real cider, draught Belgian, German and Czech beers, with extensive ranges of malt whiskies and Belgian bottled beers. Excellent food, including home-made curries, is served in both the bar and the smoke-free restaurant. The July beer festival should not be missed.
Ⓠ✿🛏🌙❶🍴🅐🚭🅰⇄ (Wrenbury) ♣ ☞ P ✕

BARNTON

Barnton Cricket Club
Broomsedge, Townfield Lane, CW8 4PP (400 yds from A533 via Stoneheyes Lane, Broomfield Lane)
☼ 6.30 (5 Sat)-11; 12-3, 6.30-10.30 Sun
☎ (01606) 77702
Boddingtons Bitter; Hydes Dark, Bitter; guest beer Ⓗ
Family club for the local community that welcomes visitors. The main function room with TV, darts and pool table may host events such as live entertainment at weekends. The quieter lounge offers an alternative, for conversation, playing cards or dominoes. For a panoramic view of the cricket field, opt for the front patio. Hydes Traditional Mild appears as Barnton Classic Ale. An annual beer festival is held in November. Bar meals are available Thursday–Saturday (7–11) and Sunday (12–3). Please show this Guide or CAMRA membership card on arrival. Local CAMRA Club of the Year 2003. ✿❶♣P

BOLLINGTON

Poachers Inn
95 Ingersley Road, SK10 5RE
(edge of village on road to Rainow)
☼ 12-2 (not Mon), 5.30 (7 Sat)-11; 12-2.30, 7-10.30 Sun
☎ (01625) 572086
website: www.thepoachersinnbollington.co.uk
Boddingtons Bitter; Taylor Landlord; guest beers Ⓗ
Genuine free house offering a warm atmosphere with two or three regularly changing guest beers, often from local breweries such as Storm Brewing. Converted from five stone-built terraced cottages, it now comprises a single room pub, plus a no-smoking restaurant, serving good value, home-prepared food. Close to the Peak District National Park, Gritstone Trail and ideally placed for many other attractive walks, popular special events taking place include quizzes and food theme nights.
✿❶P

Queen's Arms
40 High Street, SK10 5PH (off Palmerston St, B5090)
☼ 2 (12 Fri & Sat)-11; 12-10.30 Sun
☎ (01625) 573068
Robinson's Hatters, Best Bitter Ⓗ

ASTBURY

Egerton Arms
Audley Road, CW12 4RQ (signed on the A34)
☼ 11.30-11; 12-3, 7-10.30 Sun
☎ (01260) 273946 website: www.egertonarms.com
Robinson's Best Bitter, Ⓟ **Frederics** Ⓗ
16th-century country village inn, across the road from a stunning 12th-century parish church. The interior of the pub is spacious and so relaxed, you wonder why you do not visit more often. An extensive, imaginative bar menu offers unusual specials. There are eight guest rooms (with special weekend rates) and a restaurant. The garden is a haven for families, being well equipped, well maintained and fenced off.
Ⓠℤ✿🛏❶P✕🅱

ASTON

Bhurtpore Inn
Wrenbury Road, CW5 8DQ (off A530)
☼ 12-2.30 (3 Sat), 6.30-11; 12-10.30 Sun
☎ (01270) 780917
Hanby Drawwell; guest beers Ⓗ
Now celebrating its eleventh appearance in this Guide, this wonderful free house returned to the same family ownership in 1991 after 90 years. Historical photographs

INDEPENDENT BREWERIES

Beartown Congleton
Burtonwood Burtonwood
Coach House Warrington
Khean Congleton
Paradise Wrenbury
Storm Macclesfield
Weetwood Tarporley

Solidly-built stone pub, typical of many Robinson's houses in the area. Modernised in the early 1980s, it still maintains a traditional ambience with a friendly welcome. Situated in the centre of a small mill town, it is close to the old market place, near Macclesfield Canal and footpaths to White Nancy. Popular for TV sporting events; favourite pub games include women's netball, pool, darts, league dominoes and crib. A quiz night is held every other Sunday. A pleasant garden and occasional barbecues add to summer drinking pleasure. ✿♣

BUNBURY

Dysart Arms
Bowesgate Road, CW6 9PH
☼ 11.30-11; 12-10.30 Sun
☎ (01829) 260183
website: www.dysartarms-bunbury.co.uk
Taylor Landlord; Thwaites Bitter; guest beers Ⓗ
Recently extended old village pub with stone-flagged floors, lying opposite the church, with a pleasant lawned garden to the side. Although popular for meals, it is still widely used by villagers as a regular pub. A beer festival is held every April, featuring about 50 beers from local micro-breweries. ♨Q✿◑♿▲♣P⚥

BURTONWOOD

Bridge Inn
Phipps Lane, WA5 4HD
☼ 11.30-11; 12-10.30 Sun
☎ (01925) 225709
Burtonwood Bitter Ⓗ
Four-roomed community pub with an island bar to serve a room which houses a dartboard, the licensee's rugby-playing mementos and a wide-screen TV; and a lounge with pictures of old Burtonwood. A singer performs live on Saturday evening. The pool room has old Burtonwood Brewery memorabilia including bottles embedded in the wall. Families are welcome in the conservatory and pool room. A small drinking area lies outside at the front, and a bowling green at the rear. Many local sports teams are based here, such as a ladies' rounders team. The pub is served by buses from Warrington (weekdays daytime) and St Helens. Lunches are offered weekdays. ♿✿◑🍴♣P

CHESTER

Albion
Park Street, CH1 1RN (close to the river)
☼ 11-3.30, 5 (6 Sat)-11; 12-2.30, 7-10.30 Sun
☎ (01244) 340345
website: www.albioninnchester.co.uk
Banks's Bitter; Taylor Landlord; guest beer Ⓗ
Classic Victorian street-corner pub situated just off the Roman walls, a short walk from the city centre. The interior, however, is pure Edwardian with flowered wallpaper, period furnishing and a piano. The landlord is an avid collector of WWI memorabilia, with artefacts and period prints on every wall, while Kitchener gazes at you from all corners. Outstanding home-cooked bar food is on offer; this pub is a regular winner of local CAMRA awards including Pub of the Year in 2001 and 2002. ♨Q◑🍴

Duttons
10-12 Godstall Lane, CH1 1LN
(access from St Werburgh St or Eastgate Row)
☼ 11-11; 12-10.30 (5.30 winter) Sun
☎ (01244) 403018
Lees Bitter; seasonal beers Ⓗ
A pleasing blend of old and modern, this city-centre venue combines traditional wooden furnishings, luxuriant armchairs and a stainless steel bar top. The emphasis, especially at lunchtime, is on food, and diners can take advantage of a varied menu that offers everything from snacks to steaks (served until 9pm). Tables and chairs are available immediately outside the bar which is situated along a quaint alley that runs from opposite the cathedral towards the main shopping area. Doormen may enforce a dress code on weekend evenings. Q◑♿⚥

Mill Hotel
Milton Street, CH1 3NF
(adjacent to the canal just off the ring road)
☼ 11-11; 12-10.30 Sun
☎ (01244) 350035 website: www.millhotel.com
Cains Bitter; Theakston Cool Cask; Weetwood Best Bitter; guest beers Ⓗ
The choice of up to 15 ales, mostly brewed by independents and always including a mild, is probably unsurpassed in the county. Mill Premium is a house beer brewed by Coach House. While its interior resembles a hotel lounge bar, the atmosphere is invariably one of a busy local with an even mix of regulars and overnight guests. Sky Sports is usually on in the background, except on Monday when it is jazz night. This popular canalside hotel is located just outside the city centre. Good value food is served all day until 10pm. Q✿🛏◑♿⚭P⚥

Ship Victory
47 George Street, CH1 3EQ (opp. fire station)
☼ 12 (11 Sat)-11; 12-10.30 Sun
☎ (01244) 376453
Tetley Bitter; guest beer Ⓗ
Compact and welcoming oasis in the middle of a city-centre car park. The pub has built up a deserved reputation as a friendly community venue. Evenings are never dull and live music, karaoke, darts and quiz nights are regular features. The landlord often organises charity events which are enthusiastically supported by the local clientele. The guest beer is usually an interesting choice from one of the smaller independents. Take a moment to stand outside and look at the pub building – does the shape remind you of anything? ♿⚭♣

Telford's Warehouse
Tower Wharf, CH1 4EZ
(turn left at top end of Northgate St, down Canal St)
☼ 11-1am (12.30am Thu; 1.30am Fri & Sat);
12-midnight Sun
☎ (01244) 390090
website: www.telfordswarehouse.com
Taylor Landlord; Theakston Best Bitter; Weetwood Eastgate Ale; guest beer Ⓗ
In a superb location on Chester's canal basin, this spacious pub bears some original features from its role as warehouse for the barges on the Shropshire Union. A large open bar with high ceiling and stone walls houses some industrial artefacts while the

glass frontage provides a tranquil scene overlooking the water. Upstairs has large comfy sofas while the lower area is reserved for the popular music nights the pub offers. A fine balance of customers exists, all attracted by Telford's bohemian image. Excellent food is on offer. There may be an admission charge on music evenings. Table football, and canalside tables complete the picture. ⌘◑♣P

Union Vaults
44 Egerton Street, CH1 3ND
(adjacent to canal, just off St Oswalds Way)
✪ 11-11; 12-10.30 Sun
☎ (01244) 322170
Greenalls Bitter; guest beer Ⓗ
Welcoming street-corner local comprising a simple main bar, offering satellite TV and bagatelle, and a quieter, more comfortable drinking area on an upper tier. Occasional impromptu folk sessions and a regular and often high-spirited clientele help make for one of the best traditional pub atmospheres in the city. It is situated around the corner from the Mill Hotel and the Shropshire Union Canal. Q➤♣

CHILDER THORNTON

White Lion
New Road, CH66 5PU (off A41)
✪ 11.30-11; 12-10.30 Sun
☎ (0151) 339 3402
Thwaites Mild, Bitter, Lancaster Bomber Ⓗ
Small, friendly country pub on the outskirts of Ellesmere Port, this former regional CAMRA Pub of the Year is popular with all sections of the community. The bar has a recently revealed original brick fireplace and the two compact lounges are popular with families at lunchtime, who spill outside into the garden in summer. It is convenient for the Boat Museum and Cheshire Oaks, the largest designer outlet in Europe. Reasonably-priced meals and bar snacks are available at lunchtime (not Sun) – try the home-made chicken tikka. ▲Q⌘◑P

CONGLETON

Beartown Tap
18 Willow Street, CW12 1RL (A54 Buxton Road)
✪ 12-2, 4-11; 12-11 Fri & Sat; 12-10.30 Sun
☎ (01260) 270990
website: www.beartownbrewery.co.uk
Beartown Bear Ass, Kodiak Gold, Bearskinful, Polar Eclipse; guest beer Ⓗ
Five or six ales are usually on offer at the very first pub owned by Beartown Brewery. Efforts are made to have guests, usually from another micro. Non-regular beers vary according to the time of year. Black Bear (ABV 5%) is available in the winter months and lower strength Ambeardextrous is sold in summer. A good selection of Belgian bottled beers is stocked. Frequently changing real cider is usually available. No games machines or music spoil the atmosphere. Street parking can be found nearby. Local CAMRA Pub of the Year 2002. ▲Q➤♣♠⌁

Congleton Leisure Centre
Worral Street, CW12 1DT (by Congleton Park)
✪ 10-1 (not Mon), 7-11 (9.30 Sat); 8-10.30 Sun
☎ (01260) 271552

Beer range varies Ⓗ
Unusually, a municipal leisure centre that sells an ever-changing choice of three real ales. Efforts have been made to create a pub environment in the bar; the walls are adorned with brewery posters and beermats, and it has a snug feel. By contrast, the no-smoking family room is a little bland. The bar is open to all; no need to use the sporting facilities and no entrance fee is payable. Q➤♿❄P⌁

Queen's Head
Park Lane, CW12 3DE
(opp. station, at bridge 75 of Macclesfield Canal))
✪ 11-11; 12-10.30 Sun
☎ (01260) 272546
Ansells Mild; Greene King Abbot; Marston's Pedigree; Tetley Bitter; guest beers Ⓗ
Canalside pub with its own moorings, popular with locals and canal users. The huge garden has a children's play area and stages occasional outdoor events in summer. Originally built for the railway trade, the pub has enjoyed something of a revival in recent years under the current landlord. One room has a pool table, while food is served in a separate area at the back; it is mostly home-cooked, and there is a changing specials boards. Guest beers are frequently from local breweries. ⌘◁◑➤♣P⌁

Wharf
121 Canal Road, CW12 3AP
(near Dog Lane aqueduct)
✪ 11-11; 12-10.30 Sun
☎ (01260) 272809
Greenalls Mild, Bitter; guest beer Ⓗ
Smart, friendly pub on the outskirts of town, offering fresh home-cooked food from a very varied menu. The large garden has a children's play area. The guest ale is constantly changing. This pub is popular with canal users as it stands only 50 yards from the Cheshire Ring Canal. ➤⌘◑➤♣P

CREWE

Borough Arms
33 Earle Street, CW1 2BG
(on Earle St railway bridge in town centre)
✪ 7 (3 Fri)-11; 12-4, 7-11 Sat; 12-3, 7-10.30 Sun
☎ (01270) 254999
Titanic Iceberg; guest beers Ⓗ
Good conversation is forthcoming in this welcoming haven for real ale drinkers. Eight handpumps (plus one for real cider) all change regularly, sourced from small breweries and micros. Six Belgian beers are on tap, five are ever-changing. Over 100 bottled beers are stocked from six countries – mainly Belgian. The pub has a split-level interior, with access from Thomas Street, up some steps. The walls are adorned with breweriana. ➤♠

Crown
25 Earle Street, CW1 2BH
✪ 11-11; 12-10.30 Sun
☎ (01270) 257295
Robinson's Hatters, Best Bitter, Old Tom (winter), **seasonal beers** Ⓗ
Friendly, family-run pub in the town centre. This is a three-storey Victorian building next to Crewe's municipal buildings, which

it pre-dates. Carefully refurbished, it is now an open-plan pub with a central bar. The walls display interesting Victorian prints. This is a rare outlet for Old Tom on handpump in winter. ♣♣

Rising Sun
Middlewich Road, Wistaston Green, CW2 8SB (on A530, between Crewe and Nantwich)
☼ 11-11; 12-10.30 Sun
☎ (01270) 213782
Courage Directors; Theakston Best Bitter; Titanic Premium Bitter, White Star; guest beers ⊞
Traditional country pub offering a large range of beers, especially for a Chef & Brewer. The food is excellent value, and there is a very good vegetarian choice. Nine ales are usually on tap, and in summer cider is stocked. Two beer festivals are held a year. Background music is played, mainly jazz or classical. ✿◑●P¼

FARNDON

Farndon Arms
High Street, CH3 6PU (on B5130)
☼ 11-3, 5-11; 12-3, 7-10.30 Sun
☎ (01829) 270570
Worthington's Bitter; guest beers ⊞
This locals' pub near the English/Welsh border is a traditional former coaching house with a fittingly decorated and furnished interior. A good range of beers is on offer with guest beers from small breweries. The lounge area contains a real fire at one end and a restaurant at the other. Brasses and plates are displayed on the walls, and TV and a pool table are provided. A range of guides by the door will help visitors enjoy the local attractions.
▨✿⇔◑♣P

Greyhound
High Street, CH3 6PU (on B5130)
☼ 5 (12 Sat)-11; 12-10.30 Sun
☎ (01829) 270244
Greenalls Bitter; Tetley Mild; guest beers ⊞
Friendly local which shows its commitment to real ale with an impressive display of pump clips behind the bar. Located in the village of Farndon by the River Dee, its two regular beers are supported by guest ales. Two seating areas can be found with easy access to the bar, the TV does not interfere with the enjoyment of customers who prefer a quiet drink. The restaurant area has pasta, pizza and a Thursday curry night.
▨⛵✿⇔◑♣P

FRODSHAM

Helter Skelter
31 Church Street, WA6 6PN
☼ 11-11; 12-10.30 Sun
☎ (01928) 733361
Weetwood Best Bitter; guest beers ⊞
Originally two cottages, now named after a past local attraction. Four rotating guests and 'one of the month' are supported by a locally-brewed house bitter; all are reasonably priced. A range of imported bottled beers is stocked. A long side bar is surrounded by a choice of seating with a raised deck in the far corner. It may be crowded on Friday and Saturday evening when village nightlife is in full swing! An interesting choice of freshly-prepared and

highly commended food is available 12–2.30 (4 Sun) and 5.30–8 Monday–Saturday.
◑⇌●⊟

GAWSWORTH

Harrington Arms ☆
Church Lane, SK11 0PH
(just off A536, 500 yds from church)
☼ 12-3, 6-11; 12-3, 7-10.30 Sun
☎ (01260) 223224
Robinson's Hatters, Best Bitter ⊞
This delightful 17th-century coaching inn, part of a working farm, is situated just off the Macclesfield to Congleton road. An unspoilt atmosphere pervades the several small rooms furnished with wood settles and scrubbed tables. No TV or piped music is played. No official menu exists, sandwiches or pies are made from whatever ingredients happen to be available on the day. A folk club meets here on Friday evening. Limited parking in front of the pub or in the lane, the pub is convenient for Gawsworth Hall.
▨Q✿P

GRAPPENHALL

Grappenhall Community Centre
Bellhouse Farm, Bellhouse Lane, WA4 2SG
(off A50)
☼ 7.30 (2 Sat)-11; 2-10.30 Sun
☎ (01925) 268633 website: www.grappenhall.com
Greene King Ruddles Best; guest beers ⊞
This large private club and social centre supports a wide range of groups and activities. Converted from an old farmhouse and barn, a central bar serves the different areas. The games room, where pool and darts are played, doubles as a family room and is the venue for the Wednesday quiz. The comfortably furnished lounge has a no-smoking area, while the old barn houses the function room, the venue for the spring beer festival. CAMRA National Club of the Year finalist 2002, production of a CAMRA membership card gains admission.
✿♿♣P¼

GREAT BUDWORTH

George & Dragon
High Street, CW9 6HF (off A559)
☼ 11.30-11; 12-10.30 Sun
☎ (01606) 891317
Tetley Bitter; guest beers ⊞
The George & Dragon is an essential ingredient of this well cared-for historic village; search out the stocks, well, and fascinating lime tree avenue. It is a fine centre for short drives to the country hall, parkland, museums, and refurbished Anderton boat lift. The rural surroundings suit walkers and cyclists. The good value varied meals appeal to all ages, children to pensioners. Upstairs is a restaurant and a useful 40-seater function room. The large, lively public bar and cosy front lounge prove popular. Changing guest beers are prominently displayed on the blackboard by a family proud of their long-standing hospitality.
Q⛵✿◑⊟♣P¼

HELSBY

New Helsby Arms

Chester Road, WA6 0JE (1/2 mile from M56 jct 14)

🕐 12-11; 12-10.30 Sun

☎ (01928) 724618

Black Sheep Best Bitter; guest beer Ⓗ

Open-plan interior with separate areas for drinking and dining (no-smoking), where a large real open fire welcomes you on cold evenings. Three ever-changing guest beers are always available in a relaxed drinking area. Full bar lunches are provided six days a week as well as a restaurant service (12–3 and 6–9 Mon–Sat, and 12–8 Sun) offering a wide range of New World cuisine with an extensive wine list and imported bottled beers. Background music is played throughout the pub and there is a pleasant outdoor patio for summer drinking. Disabled parking is provided. 🏛️❀◑&P✗

HENBURY

Cock Inn

Chelford Road, SK10 3LH

🕐 11-3, 4.30-11; 11-11 Fri & Sat; 12-10.30 Sun

☎ (01625) 425659

Robinson's Hatters, Hartleys XB, Snowdon, seasonal beers Ⓗ

Village pub on the main road, two miles west of Macclesfield. The lounge and restaurant can be busy with diners at weekends enjoying the wholesome food. There is a children's room off the lounge with a playground at the rear – a welcome alternative to the more commercial children's pubs. This is a genuine village public bar with dartboard and team. There is a ramp and level access to the pub (and toilets) but there are no special disabled facilities. Robinson's seasonal beers are stocked, including Old Tom in winter. 👫❀◑⊟♣P

HIGHER SUTTON

Hanging Gate ⊘

Meg Lane, SK11 0NG

(follow Ridge Hill Road from village centre for 1 1/2 miles)

🕐 12-3, 7 (5.30 Fri)-11; 12-11 Sat; 12-10.30 Sun

☎ (01260) 252238

Hydes Bitter, Jekyll's Gold, seasonal beers Ⓗ

An unusual building, dating from 1621, built on a hillside with small rooms on three levels; the lowest affords a wonderful panorama of the hills and Cheshire Plain, stretching to the Welsh mountains. Despite the exposed setting, inside is cosy and welcoming with blazing fires in winter. Family-run, the pub is popular with walkers and diners, with a reputation for good home-cooked food. Local CAMRA Pub of the Year 2000, it is a rare outlet for Hydes in the area. 🏛️👫❀◑P✗

HOUGHTON GREEN

Millhouse

Ballater Drive, WA2 0LX

🕐 12-11; 12-10.30 Sun

☎ (01925) 811405

Holt Mild, Bitter Ⓗ

Large 1980s pub built on the edge of an extensive residential area. A spacious bar, with pool and darts is offered and a comfortable lounge to the side. Food is served weekday lunchtime only. No excuse for not knowing the time for last orders, as there are five clocks above the fire! This is a rare outlet for Holt beers outside the Manchester area. ◑⊟P

KELSALL

Olive Tree

Chester Road, CW6 0RS

(from A54 follow signs for Kelsall village)

🕐 11.30-11; 12-10.30 Sun

☎ (01829) 751291

Weetwood Best Bitter, Ambush Ale; guest beers Ⓗ

Formerly known as the Morris Dancer, this village-centre pub is a favourite with both drinkers and diners. High quality meals are available in the bar and the separate restaurant. The Chester folk festival takes place next to the pub at the end of May each year. Various social events are hosted, such as race nights, throughout the year and there are regular quizzes. Beers from the nearby Weetwood Brewery are featured regularly. 🏛️❀◑⊟&AP

KETTLESHULME

Bull's Head

Macclesfield Road, SK23 7QU (on B5470)

🕐 3 (5 Mon)-11; 12-11 Fri & Sat; 12-10.30 Sun

☎ (01663) 733225

Boddingtons Bitter; guest beer Ⓗ

Stone, end-of-terrace pub in the centre of the village, with two comfortable rooms. The smaller is cottage-style with pine seating, the larger has a farmhouse feel and has a natural stone floor, open fire, and darts area. Blues-based background music is often playing and live bands perform about once a month. Food is not normally available but groups (such as hikers) can book food in advance. One regularly changing guest beer is always available. The pub is surrounded by good walking country. 🏛️❀&♣P

Swan

Macclesfield Road, SK23 7QU (on B5470)

🕐 12-3 (not Mon), 5.30-11; 12-11 Sat; 12-10.30 Sun

☎ (01663) 732943

Thwaites Bitter; guest beers Ⓗ

15th-century, whitewashed pub in a hollow alongside the B5470. The classic interior of this small rural inn features original timber beams, stone fireplaces and log fires (in winter). Three ever-changing guest beers are always available, one often from the Khean Brewery in Congleton. Families and hikers are welcome. Lunches are served Tuesday–Sunday. This picturesque Peak District National Park village is surrounded by excellent walking country. 🏛️❀◑♣P

KNUTSFORD

Cross Keys

52 King Street, WA16 6DT

🕐 11.30-3, 5.30 (7 Sat)-11; 12-3, 7-10.30 Sun

☎ (01565) 750404

Boddingtons Bitter; Taylor Landlord; Tetley Bitter; guest beers Ⓗ

Set on an attractive shopping street, this 18th-century coaching inn was largely rebuilt in 1909. A glass and timber screen separates the lounge from the vault with its pool table and TV. Bar meals are sold at lunchtime, while the restaurant, reached by a barrel-vaulted tunnel, opens Tuesday–Saturday evening. The fine choice of cask ales sets the Cross Keys apart: a gleaming bank of polished brass handpumps features three constantly-changing guest beers. Real cider is often available.

🛏️◀️◑🍴🍸☕P⅟

LITTLE NESTON

Harp Inn
19 Quayside, CH64 0TB (from Burton Road down Marshlands Road to bottom, turn left)
✪ 11-11; 12-10.30 Sun
☎ (0151) 336 6980
Holt Bitter; Taylor Landlord; guest beers Ⓗ
Delightful, two-roomed pub served by a single bar. Converted from two cottages, it subsequently became a miners' pub and obtained a full licence in 1960. The superb public bar has a roaring fire and low beams. Enjoy the wonderful views across the Dee, but beware high tides. This pub may be difficult to find, but it is well worth the effort: a little gem.
🏚️Q❀◑P

LOWER PEOVER

Crown
Crown Lane, WA16 8QB (on B5081, off the A50 S of Knutsford))
✪ 11.30-3, 5.30-11; 12-10.30 Sun
☎ (01565) 722074
Boddingtons Bitter; Flowers IPA; Greene King Old Speckled Hen; Taylor Landlord; Tetley Dark Mild; guest beer Ⓗ
The cobbled frontage tempts the passer-by into this homely 17th-century country inn with low ceilings and beams enhancing the cosy atmosphere. The stone-flagged bar has a well-used dartboard, while the smart front room is used mainly by diners enjoying the home-cooked meals. Thursday is quiz night and a gooseberry competition is held in July. Pleasingly, cask mild is usually available, and the guest beer is generally from one of Cheshire's independent brewers, typically Weetwood.
🏚️🛏️❀◑🍸♣P

LYMM

Barn Owl ⊘
Agden Wharf, Warrington Lane, WA13 0SW (off A56 Lymm-Altrincham road)
✪ 11-11; 12-10.30 Sun
☎ (01925) 752020 website: www.thebarnowlinn.co.uk
Marston's Bitter, Pedigree; guest beers Ⓗ
Open-plan pub in a converted boatyard building on the banks of the Bridgewater Canal. It enjoys a thriving local trade, despite the rural location. Popular with canal tourists and local cruising clubs, walkers on the opposite towpath can summon the pub's own ferry by ringing the bell. It hosts live music on Saturday and a quiz on Thursday. Home-cooked food and a children's certificate make it popular with diners. The no-smoking conservatory is a pleasant spot for a peaceful drink.
❀◑🖨♣P⅟

MACCLESFIELD

British Flag
42 Coare Street, SK10 1DW
✪ 7 (4 Sat)-11; 12-3, 7.30-10.30 Sun
☎ (01625) 425500
Robinson's Hatters, Best Bitter, Ⓗ **Old Tom** (winter), Ⓖ **seasonal beers** Ⓗ
This is an old-fashioned and friendly town local, where four rooms surround a central bar. Pub games are popular, with table skittles played and one room dedicated to pool. The tap room, apart from darts and cards, is home to the landlord's local trophy cabinet of Macclesfield Town FC memorabilia. There is also a large-screen TV for sport. In the 1860s the pub was a ginger beer brewery. It has a reputation as the local of the neighbouring King's School, being frequented by many of its staff. ⇌♣

Dolphin
76 Windmill Street, SK11 4HS
✪ 12-2.30, 5.30-11; 12-11 Sat; 12-10.30 Sun
☎ (01625) 616179
Robinson's Hatters, Best Bitter, Ⓗ **Old Tom** (winter), Ⓖ **seasonal beers** Ⓗ
Friendly, traditional street-corner local, opposite playing fields, with two distinct drinking areas served by the central bar and a separate room to the left. This is a true community local, with darts, dominoes and crib teams, and is popular with several generations of local families. Robinson's seasonal beers are always stocked, as well as the award-winning Old Tom strong ale in the winter months. Home-cooked lunches are available, but not on Sunday. Local CAMRA Pub of the Season, winter 2002.
🏚️🛏️◑🍸♣

Prince of Wales (Porters)
33 Roe Street, SK11 6UT
✪ 11.30-11; 12-10.30 Sun
☎ (01625) 424796
website: www.portersprinceofwales.co.uk
Banks's Original; Draught Bass; Theakston Best Bitter; guest beers Ⓗ
Comfortable and friendly town-centre pub, opposite the heritage centre, and refurbished in 'Porters' style. The one large room has quiet corners away from the bar, a real fire and hops dangling from the ceiling. The pub has close links with Macclesfield Rugby Club and fields its own quiz, pool and crib teams; backgammon and dominoes are also played. The two frequently-changing guest beers are usually from independent breweries. A few seats are provided in the small back yard during summer. 🏚️❀⇌♣

Railway View
Byrons Lane, SK11 7JW (off London Rd, off A523, at lights on Langley-Wincle road)
✪ 4 (12 Fri; 11 Sat)-11; 12-10.30 Sun
☎ (01625) 423657
Beer range varies Ⓗ
Very pleasant pub, 100 yards from the main London road. The beer range includes Dr Duncans from Cains and seven changing guest beers from around the country, often from small micros. This is a pub that is well worth visiting. On Monday and Wednesday evenings beer is offered at reduced price. The pub is half a mile from Macclesfield football ground. Free sandwiches are

provided on Friday and Saturday evenings from 10pm onwards. During the rest of the week tasty home-made pies and sandwiches are sold. 🏚🏯🐾👌♣♣

Waters Green Tavern
98 Waters Green, SK11 6LH
✪ 11.30 (11 Sat)-3, 5.30 (7 Sat)-11; 12-3, 7-10.30 Sun
☎ (01625) 422653
Taylor Landlord; guest beers Ⓗ
Close to the bus and train stations, this is a popular town pub, where beer quality is a priority. Traditional home-cooked food is served. The interior has been slightly opened out to create three areas with a pool room to the rear. The long bar to the left stocks seasonal and more unusual beers, often including some from north of the border. This local CAMRA Pub of the Year 1999 fields thriving darts, pool and quiz teams. 🏚Q◖≈♣♣

MIDDLEWICH

Royal British Legion Club ⊘
100 Lewin Street, CW10 9AS
✪ 12-3, 7-11; 12-11 Sat; 12-3, 7-11 Sun
☎ (01606) 833286
Hydes Bitter; guest beers Ⓗ
This club, in a large, imposing building, is very sports-oriented. Three large snooker tables dominate one bar, while the back bar commonly features sport on TV; a bowling green completes the facilities. The two function rooms host many events, these are the only occasions when children are admitted. A beer festival in November showcases local beers. Entry can be gained on production of a valid CAMRA membership card or a copy of this Guide. Q🏯🗄👌♣P

MOBBERLEY

Bull's Head
Mill Lane, WA16 7HX (off Town Lane, signed from B5085)
✪ 11.30-11; 12-10.30 Sun
☎ (01565) 873134
Boddingtons Bitter; Taylor Landlord; Tetley Bitter; guest beers Ⓗ
This traditional country local is an integral part of its community, with all manner of social and charitable events, and a good reputation for its food. It hosts quiz nights, occasional beer festivals, traction engine rallies and music. Down a quiet lane, the pub has an attractive cobbled frontage and a bowling green to the rear. Dominoes, darts, cards and pool are played in addition to the bowls. Formerly three cottages, now an unusual fireplace divides the main room. The licensee has installed three guest beers, and custom is building up well. 🏚🛲🏯◖🗄♣P

Roebuck
Mill Lane, WA16 7HX (off Town Lane, signed from B5085)
✪ 12-3, 5-11; 12-11 Sat; 12-10.30 Sun
☎ (01565) 873322
Taylor Landlord; Tetley Bitter; guest beers Ⓗ
This fashionable restaurant was converted from a traditional pub, with a partly open three-room layout. The floor is timber and tiled; the tables scrubbed wood. A log fire warms the room to the right. The decor is stylish, with a wine bar atmosphere. The adventurous menu features excellent home-cooked food, with prices not unreasonable for the location. Although dining is important to the trade, the beer quality is consistently good. Four gleaming handpumps offer two regularly changing guest beers. 🏚🏯◖P¥

MOORE

Red Lion
Runcorn Road, WA4 6UD
(off A56 between Warrington and Daresbury)
✪ 12-11; 12-10.30 Sun
☎ (01925) 740205
Greenalls Bitter; guest beers Ⓗ
This traditional pub, dating from the 17th century, has a separate bar and larger comfortable lounge area. Attractively presented with interesting bric-à-brac, the pub has a rotating choice of three guest beers, and is convenient for the Bridgewater Canal and local footpaths. It is due to be extended, to enlarge the tap room and kitchen areas. A wide selection of food is served. Please check for times. ◖🗄P

NANTWICH

Black Lion
29 Welsh Row, CW5 5ED
(just outside town centre over river bridge)
✪ 4 (1 Fri & Sat)-11; 1-10.30 Sun
☎ (01270) 628711
Titanic White Star; Weetwood Best Bitter, Old Dog, Oasthouse Gold Ⓗ
Fairly small, old black and white, half-timbered pub between River Weaver and Shropshire Union Canal. The three cosy downstairs rooms have two serving areas and candle-lit tables. Chess is played most evenings, although there is also the buzz of lively conversation. Upstairs there is a comfortable meeting room with TV. The outside drinking area is covered and heated during winter months. Entertainment includes a quiz on Wednesday night and live music on Friday and Saturday evening. 🏚Q🏯≈♣♣

Vine ⊘
42 Hospital Street, CW5 5RP
✪ 11-11; 12-10.30 Sun
☎ (01270) 624172
Hydes Bitter, Jekyll's Gold, seasonal beer; guest beer Ⓗ
This old pub has characterful low windows and doors, and an entrance way that slopes down to the main room below street level. Standing on one of Nantwich's shopping streets, it is well used at lunchtime, and bustles with activity in the evening. A dining room lies to the rear of the pub. The guest is usually one of the Hydes seasonal beers. ◖≈

NORTHWICH

Penny Black ⊘
110 Witton Street, CW9 5AB
✪ 10-11; 12-10.30 Sun
☎ (01606) 42029
Boddingtons Bitter; Cains Mild; Greene King Abbot; Shepherd Neame Spitfire; Tetley Bitter; guest beer Ⓗ
A typical Wetherspoon's conversion from

the old post office buildings, situated towards the top of the main street. From the front door you walk past distinct areas to left and right, the right being the family area, to a large, airy bar area with natural light. The long, straight bar is dominated by an orange ventilating duct which runs the entire bar length. Disabled access is to the side of the pub.
Q ⅏ ⊛ ◑ ⅍ ≠ P ⅍

PENKETH

Ferry Tavern
Station Road, WA5 2UJ
(off Tannery Lane, off A562)
☼ 12-3, 5.30-11; 12-11 Sat; 12-10.30 Sun
☎ (01925) 791117 website: www.ferrytavern.com
Boddingtons Bitter; Courage Directors; Greene King Old Speckled Hen; guest beers ⒣
Worth seeking out, the pub is located between the River Mersey and the Sankey Canal, and is situated on the Trans-Pennine trail, so it is popular with walkers in the summer months. Access to the pub from the car park is by crossing a railway line and the canal. Six handpumps in the bar are complemented by real cider and over 300 whiskies, including one of the largest collections of Irish whiskies outside Ireland. Food is limited to pies and sandwiches. Local CAMRA branch Pub of the Year 2002.
⚶ ⊛ ♣ P

PEOVER HEATH

Dog
Wellbank Lane, WA16 8UP
(off A50 at the Whipping Stocks pub)
☼ 11.30-3, 5-11; 12-10.30 Sun
☎ (01625) 861421
Hydes Bitter; Moorhouses Black Cat; Weetwood Best Bitter, Old Dog ⒣
Set on a quiet lane and converted from a row of 18th-century cottages, this local CAMRA Pub of the Season, summer 2002, features in CAMRA's Good Pub Food (booking is advisable). The tap room offers pool and darts, an open fire warms the lounge, and the restaurant boasts local produce. Beams, dried flowers and photos of old village life add interest, and regular quiz nights feature. Flower tubs and hanging baskets grace the patio.
⚶ Q ⊛ ⇔ ◑ ⊟ ⅍ ♣ P ⅍

PRESTBURY

Admiral Rodney
New Road, SK10 4HT
(200 yds downhill from train station)
☼ 11-3, 5.30-11; 11-11 Fri & Sat; 12-3, 7-10.30 Sun
☎ (01625) 829484
Robinson's Hatters, Best Bitter ⒣
Situated at the village centre, less than five minutes' walk from the station, this Grade II listed building dates from 1730. The interior is most attractive, with small rooms, low ceilings and exposed beams. The furnishings are also appealing, with some of the tables being constructed from old barrels. Named after a famous British naval officer in the Napoleonic Wars, the pub benefits from a total absence of juke box, pool table or other annoying machines.
Q ⊛ ◑ ≠ P

RAINOW

Rising Sun
Hawkins Lane, SK10 5TL (2 miles out of Macclesfield, on the B5470 Whaley Bridge road)
☼ 12-3 (not Mon), 6-11; 12-10.30 Sun
☎ (01625) 424235
Marston's Bitter, Pedigree; guest beers ⒣
Traditional stone-built pub on the road through Rainow, alongside Kerridge Ridge. There are impressive views of the ridge and White Nancy from the two-level garden, which backs on to open fields. The interior is divided by a central bar, with a small separate dining/function room. The pub is popular with locals and passing trade alike, especially on Monday night when the landlord's free dish of the day is featured. The regular beers are supplemented by a great variety of guest ales. ⅏ ⊛ ◑ P

STRETTON

Cat & Lion
Tarporley Road, WA4 4NB (on A49)
☼ 11-11; 12-10.30 Sun
☎ (01925) 730451
Courage Directors; Greenalls Bitter; guest beer ⒣
Attractive sandstone-faced building on a busy junction just north of M56, junction 10. Built around 1700, it was once owned by the Lyons family who incorporated a Cheshire cat into their coat of arms. The interesting pub sign states 'the lion is strong and the cat is vicious, my ale is strong and so are my liquors'. The large interior is broken up into various areas – one with TV, a small no-smoking alcove, and a conservatory-style eating area to the rear. The interior is finished in rustic bare brick and exposed beams but a long-due refurbishment is planned. A Millers Kitchen food operation supports the Premier Lodge accommodation. A small patio is provided at the rear, and additional tables to the front. ⊛ ⇔ ◑ ⅍ P ⅍

Ring O' Bells
Northwich Road, Lower Stretton, WA4 4NZ
(on A559, just off M6 jct 10)
☼ 12-3 (3.30 Sat), 5.30 (7 Sat)-11; 12-3, 7-10.30 Sun
☎ (01925) 730556
Tetley Dark Mild, Bitter; guest beer ⒣
Traditional pub in an area dominated by family eating houses – a real gem. What was once a row of cottages is now a small, cosy, friendly local. No fruit machines or music, so conversation tends to be lively. The main room has an inviting real fire and tables made from old sewing machines. The two smaller side rooms are quieter and there is a compact outside drinking area to the rear. Soup and sandwiches are sold at lunchtimes. The guest beer is from the Pubmaster list. The pub is on Warrington Borough Transport bus routes 45 and 46.
⚶ Q ⊛ ◑ P

TILSTON

Carden Arms Hotel
SY14 7HH (off A41 Whitchurch Road)
☼ 12-2.30 (not Mon or Tue), 5-11; 11-11 Fri & Sat; 12-10.30 Sun
☎ (01829) 250214
Greenalls Bitter; guest beers ⒣

Ancient inn at the centre of the village with a cobbled area outside the front door, and a warm and relaxing atmosphere inside. There are real fires and the walls are decorated with old photographs and prints. This pub acts as a focus for local interests such as horse-riding and a pub ghost adds to the atmosphere. ♨✿◑◐ ▲♣ P

WARMINGHAM

Bear's Paw Hotel ✇
School Lane, CW11 3QN
✪ 5 (12 Sat)-11; 12-10.30 Sun
☎ (01270) 526317 website: www.thebearspaw.co.uk
Boddingtons Bitter; guest beers Ⓗ

A traditional country house hotel and restaurant at the picturesque heart of a small village. Excellent food, reasonably priced and freshly prepared, is available in the restaurant, leaving the large bar area free for drinkers. A no-smoking section and separate games room complete the layout. Children are welcome throughout. Guest beers are mainly from local breweries. ♨◑ P

WARRINGTON

Bull's Head
33 Church Street, WA1 2SX
✪ 12-11; 12-10.30 Sun
☎ (01925) 635680
Cains Bitter; Greenalls Bitter; Tetley Mild; Wells Bombardier; guest beer Ⓗ

Just off the town centre, this attractive pub dates back to the 17th century. The single bar serves a front lounge and a bar with a pool table. Behind are two smaller rooms, a larger sports/function bar (with large-screen TV and displays of rugby memorabilia) and a bowling green. Lunches are sold Monday–Friday. The pub is home to many sports teams and offers a welcoming, unspoilt drinking experience. ✿◑⊟≠ (Central) ♣

Lower Angel
27 Buttermarket Street, WA1 2LY
✪ 11-11; 12-4 Sun
☎ (01925) 633299
Tetley Mild, Bitter, Burton Ale; guest beer Ⓗ

Traditional town-centre pub (a rarity in Warrington) with a public bar and a more comfortable lounge. Windows still display the name of the pub's former owners (Walkers). Satellite TV is provided in the bar area and proves popular on football or rugby nights. The guest beer is from the Punch range. ⊟≠ (Central)

Wilkies Tavern
25 Church Street, WA1 2SS
(on A49, 500 yds from centre)
✪ 2 (12 Fri & Sat)-11; 12-10.30 Sun
☎ (01925) 416564
Beer range varies Ⓗ

Warrington's only true free house, where the single bar features a continually changing range of six beers, with an emphasis on smaller breweries and micros. The rear courtyard hosts popular beer festivals at Easter and early December, which attract drinkers from near and far. An Irish theme is reflected in the expanding range of Irish whiskies. The bar can be busy at weekends with rugby league or football on the big-screen TV. ✿≠ (Central) ♣ ●

WESTON

Prospect
70 Weston Road, WA7 4LD
✪ 11-11; 12-10.30 Sun
☎ (01928) 561280
Boddingtons Bitter; Cains Mild, Bitter; Courage Directors; Tetley Bitter; guest beer Ⓗ

Set on the side of Weston Point, this traditional-style pub sets the standard, offering a warm and friendly atmosphere. A hub of the local village, it comprises a lively bar and relaxing lounge area. There is a wide range of food available and a busy quiz night on Tuesday. The car park to the rear has panoramic views of the Mersey and local chemical industry. ♨Q◑◐ ⊟P

WETTENHALL

Little Man
Winsford Road, CW7 4DL OS628601
✪ 12-3 (not Tue), 7-11; 12-3, 7-10.30 Sun
☎ (01270) 528203
Beer range varies Ⓗ

A truly rural pub with a friendly atmosphere serving the local farming and equestrian communities. One side of the pub has a public bar feel, with televised sport featured; the other opens out into a comfortable dining area with a welcoming fire in winter. Children and dogs are welcome. A new wheelchair access ramp has been added. There are normally three beers, often from small breweries, and this, combined with the good food, makes the pub worth seeking out. ♨✿◑◐ ♿P╤

WHEELOCK

Commercial Hotel ☆
2 Game Street, CW11 3RR
(off Crewe Road, on the square by the canal bridge)
✪ 12-11; 12-10.30 Sun
☎ (01270) 760122
Boddingtons Bitter; Thwaites Bitter; guest beers Ⓗ

This building has been a pub since 1742 and became a hotel early last century. The bar offers four handpumps serving two regular beers and two guests. An interesting collection of older bottled beers is displayed above the bar with the latest bottled beers for sale behind. The pub comprises four large rooms: bar, lounge, no-smoking family room and a games room with snooker, table, dartboard and TV. Dominoes and skittles are also played. Baps are sold at lunchtime, and Westons Old Rosie cider is available in the summer. Behind the pub is a large enclosed beer garden and orchard. ♨⌕✿♣●✕

WIDNES

Four Topped Oak
2 Hough Green Road, Hough Green, WA8 4PE (at the jct of Chapel Lane and Hough Green Road midway between Cronton and Ditton)
✪ 12-11; 12-10.30 Sun
☎ (0151) 257 8031
Tetley Bitter; guest beers Ⓗ

Fully refurbished in 2002 with a stylish, modern decor, the Four Topped Oak has separate rooms and alcoves with comfortable seating and leather armchairs. This is a friendly and inviting pub with no juke box, real fires in winter and an outside area for summer drinking. There is no loud music and children under 14 are not allowed inside at any time. There are no-smoking areas available, including the bar. Tetley Bitter is a regular with two changing guest beers. ♨Q☮◑&P✗

Horse & Jockey
18 Birchfield Road, WA8 7SU
(300 yds S of station)
✪ 11-11; 12-10.30 Sun
☎ (0151) 420 2966
Greenalls Bitter; Tetley Bitter; guest beer Ⓗ
Friendly, one-roomed pub, close to the town centre and train and bus services. Frequently busy, the pub hosts dominoes and quiz evenings and is alive with conversation and banter. Over a century old, it backs on to a park and has a fully enclosed garden suitable for children. It is much favoured by the local community and has no juke box. The guest beer changes weekly. ☮≈P

WILLEY MOOR

Willey Moor Lock Tavern
Tarporley Road, SY13 4HF (300 yds off A49)
OS534452
✪ 12-2.30 (3 summer), 6-11; 12-2.30, 7 (6 summer)-10.30 Sun
☎ (01948) 663274
Theakston Best Bitter; guest beers Ⓗ
Accessed by footbridge over the Llangollen Canal with its rushing bywash, this attractive former lock-keeper's cottage is one of those rare breeds – a genuine free house. Popular with narrowboat enthusiasts and walkers on the adjacent sandstone trail, it features several carpeted rooms, comfortably furnished with padded wall-seats, chairs, stools and dimpled copper tables as well as longcase clocks, local watercolour paintings and an eye-catching collection of teapots. For warmer months there is an outside terrace plus a safety-fenced beer garden. ♨☮◑P

WILMSLOW

Coach & Four ✔
69-71 Alderley Road, SK9 1PA
(on the main road just S of town centre)
✪ 11.30-11 (12 Thu-Sat); 12-10.30 Sun
☎ (01625) 525046

Hydes Light, Bitter, Jekyll's Gold, seasonal beers Ⓗ
This large, rambling former coaching inn on the road to Alderley Edge (owned by one of Manchester's excellent traditional brewers) features cask mild and a seasonal speciality. The attractive, beamed interior was well refurbished recently, the semi open-plan layout retains many discrete areas for the diners who form an important part of the trade. The clientele is mixed, and sport on TV can be watched at the bar. Light and bitter are reduced during the evening happy hour. ☎☮◑&≈P

King William
35 Manchester Road, SK9 1BQ
(just N of town centre, on a roundabout)
✪ 11.30-2.30, 5-11; 12-2, 6.30-11 Sat; 12-3.30, 7-10.30 Sun
☎ (01625) 524022 website: www.kingwilliam.20m.com
Robinson's Hatters, Best Bitter Ⓗ
An oasis of consistency in the Wilmslow maelstrom of change. Retaining much of its traditional atmosphere, this pub is run by serial winners of the brewery's Best-Kept Cellar award. An old coaching inn, it still has rooms for B&B and offers an unfussy lunchtime menu, Monday–Friday. Beams, settles, old prints and traditional tables lend a solid feeling of permanence. The main bar is complemented by a snug at the front and a two-part lounge up steps to the left. A courtyard is available for summer drinking. ☮⌂◑≈P

WYBUNBURY

Swan
2 Main Road, CW5 7NA (next to church tower)
✪ 12 (5 Mon)-11; 12-10.30 Sun
☎ (01270) 841280
Greene King Abbot; Jennings Bitter, Cumberland Ale, Cocker Hoop, Sneck Lifter; guest beers Ⓗ
In an attractive village setting, this large white inn stands next to a tower, all that remains of the original parish church. There are spacious bars with two inviting log fires. Excellent food is served including snacks and main meals (not Mon). There is a bar for games and the pub has a thriving darts team. A rare Jennings house in this area, the pub holds a beer festival in May/June when 15 additional ales are available. ♨Q☮⌂◑♣P✗

Learned drinker

He was a learned man, of immense reading, but is much blamed for his unfaithful quotations. His manner of Studie was thus, he wore a long quilt cap, which came two or rather three inches at least over his eies, which served him as an Umbrella to defend his Eies from the light. About every three houres his man was to bring him a roll and a pot of Ale to refocillate (refresh) his wasted spirits so he studied, and dranke, and munched some bread and this maintained him till night, and then he made a good supper.

An Oxford man, William Prynne (1600-69), as described by **John Aubrey** (1626-97) in *Brief Lives,* ed. John Buchanan-Brown, 2000

CAMRA's Beers of the Year

The beers listed below are CAMRA's Beers of the Year. They were short-listed for the Champion Beer of Britain competition in August 2003, and the Champion Winter Beer of Britain competition in January 2003. The August competition judged Dark and Light Milds; Bitters; Best Bitters; Strong Bitters; Speciality Beers; and Bottle-conditioned Beers, while the winter competition judged Old Ales and Strong Milds; Porters and Stouts; and Barley Wines. Each beer was found by panels of trained CAMRA judges to be consistently outstanding in its category, and they all receive a 'full tankard' ⬤ symbol in the Breweries section.

DARK AND LIGHT MILDS
Batemans Dark Mild
Bazens Black Pig
Brains Dark
Harvey's Dark Mild
Lidstone's Rowley Mild
Taylor's Golden Best
Titanic Mild

BITTERS
Bullmastiff Gold
Caledonian Deuchars IPA
Daleside Bitter
Dark Star Hop Head
Glastonbury Mystery Tor
Goose Eye Barmpot
Harviestoun Bitter & Twisted
Holden's Black Country Bitter
Mighty Oak IPA
Milton Pegasus
Oakham JHB
Triple fff Alton Pride
Woodforde's Wherry
Yates Feverpitch

BEST BITTERS
Bath Barnstormer
Batham Best Bitter
Crouch Vale Brewers Gold
Eccleshall Slater's Supreme
Fuller's London Pride
Harvey's Sussex Best Bitter
Hobson's Town Crier
Orkney Red MacGregor
Phoenix Arizona
Rooster's Hooligan
Taylor's Landlord
Triple fff Moondance
West Berkshire Full Circle
Winter's Golden

STRONG BITTERS
Adnams Broadside
B&T S.O.S
Fuller's ESB
Hop Back Summer Lightning
Oakham Bishop's Farewell
RCH East Street Cream
St Austell HSD

OLD ALES AND STRONG MILDS
Gale's Festival Mild
Harvey's Old
Sarah Hughes Dark Ruby Mild
Orkney Dark Island
Rudgate Ruby Mild
Theakston Old Peculier
Woodforde's Norfolk Nog

PORTERS AND STOUTS
Burton Bridge Top Dog Stout
Hop Back Entire Stout
Nethergate Old Growler
O'Hanlon's Port Stout
Oldershaw Grantham Stout
RCH Old Slug Porter
Wentworth Oatmeal Stout

BARLEY WINES
Adnams Tally Ho
Harvey's Christmas Ale
Lees Moonraker
Museum No 1 Barley Wine
Orkney Skullsplitter
Robinson's Old Tom
Woodforde's Headcracker

SPECIALITY BEERS
Cheriton Village Elder
Fraoch Heather Ale
Daleside Morocco
Harviestoun Schiehallion
Hebridean Isle of Skye Gold
Oakham White Dwarf
Titanic Iceberg

BOTTLE-CONDITIONED BEERS
Burton Bridge Porter
Fuller's 1845
Hop Back Summer Lightning
O'Hanlon's Port Stout
RCH Old Slug Porter
Worthington's White Shield
Young's Special London Ale

CHAMPION WINTER BEER OF BRITAIN
Nethergate Old Growler

CHAMPION BEER OF BRITAIN
Harviestoun Bitter and Twisted

CORNWALL

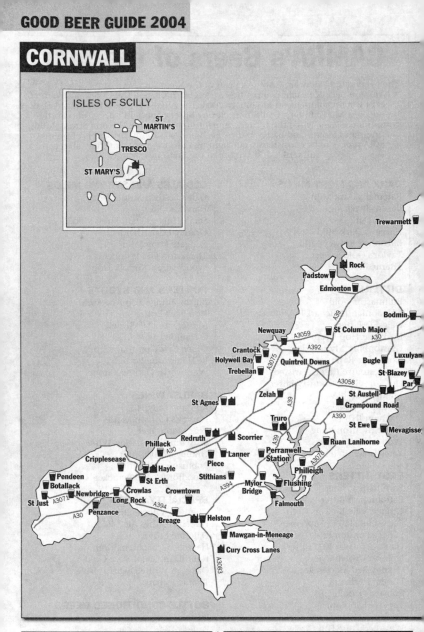

ISLES OF SCILLY

ST MARTIN'S

TRESCO

ST MARY'S

Trewarmett

Rock

Padstow

Edmonton

Bodmin

Newquay — A3059 — St Columb Major

Crantock — A392

Holywell Bay — Quintrell Downs

Trebellan

Bugle — Luxulyan

St Blazey — Par

Zelah — A3058

St Austell

St Agnes — Grampound Road

Truro

St Ewe — Mevagissey

Redruth — Scorrier

Phillack — Ruan Lanihorne

Piece — Lanner — Perranwell Station

Cripplesease — Hayle — Philleigh

St Erth — Stithians — Flushing

Pendeen — Mylor Bridge

Botallack — Crowlas — Crowntown — Falmouth

St Just — Newbridge — Long Rock

Penzance

Breage — Helston

Mawgan-in-Meneage

Cury Cross Lanes

ALBASTON

Queen's Head
PL18 9AJ (S of A390, SW of Gunnislake)
☼ 11.30-3, 6-11; 12-3, 7-10.30 Sun
☎ (01822) 832482
Draught Bass; Courage Best Bitter; Fuller's London Pride; guest beer Ⓗ
Welcoming and pleasant two-bar local, run by the same family for two generations. Interesting local memorabilia; photographs are displayed plus a small mineral collection and tinplate railway items. Up to two guest beers are served, and there is occasionally live music. The nearby branch line runs trains to Plymouth until late evening. The pub is on the Tamar Valley rail ale trail.
⚫Q⚫⚫⚫≢ (Gunnislake) P

ALTARNUN

Rising Sun
PL15 7SN
(1 mile N of village on Camelford road)
☼ 11-3, 6-11; 11-11 Sat & summer; 12-10.30 Sun
☎ (01566) 86332
Greene King IPA; Sharp's Doom Bar; guest beers Ⓗ
Originally a 16th-century farmhouse, this pub retains many original features. There are normally four ever-changing real ales, increasing to five at weekends plus six in summer. Camping is allowed in the pub grounds – caravans are welcome. The pub offers an excellent value food menu. It is near the Inny Valley recreational walk and is dog-friendly. Pool is played.
⚫Q⚫⚫⚫⚫ AP

George & Dragon
St Nicholas Street, PL31 1AB
(40 yds from Shire House on Lostwithiel road)
☀ 11-11; 12-10.30 Sun
☎ (01208) 72514
St Austell Black Prince, Tinners, HSD Ⓗ
Small, single-bar local with a warm atmosphere. Pub games are played, and teams compete in local leagues for darts, pool and euchre. Bar snacks are available at reasonable prices. The pub's location on the edge of the town centre, means that local attractions are all within a few hundred yards and the bus network is just 20 yards away. B&B is offered at reasonable rates.
Q ➳ 🕮 🛏 ◑ ♣

Mason's Arms
5-9 Higher Bore Street, PL31 2JS
(near town wall, on Lanivet road)
☀ 11-11; 12-10.30 Sun
☎ (01208) 72607
Sharp's Cornish Coaster; Marston's Pedigree; guest beers Ⓗ
This pre-Napoleonic pub claims to be the oldest in town. The lively public bar with slate-flagged floor provides games, music and occasional live entertainment. The lounge is quieter and preferred by locals wanting a more relaxed pint and general chat. Autumn sees the annual conker contest and beer festival, champion beers and boyish fun. On the edge of town, the Mason's has a good local trade but visitors are always welcome.
🏚 Q 🕮 ◑ 🜨 🜊 ♣ P

Queen's Arms
TR19 7QG (off B3306)
☀ 6.30 (11 summer)-11; 12-11 Sat; 12-10.30 Sun
☎ (01736) 788318
Beer range varies Ⓗ
Friendly, traditional, granite-built village local, not far from Land's End. There are always one or two ever-changing local Cornish ales, while a house beer from Skinner's is called Tallack Tipple. Although converted to a single bar, there are distinct drinking areas, a separate family room, and a spacious beer garden. Mining pictures reflect the once-dominant local industry. Opening times may vary according to demand – if in doubt, phone before visiting.

0 Miles 10
0 Kilometres 16

Blisland Inn
The Green, PL30 4JF (signed from A30, N of Bodmin)
☀ 11.30-11; 12-10.30 Sun
☎ (01208) 850739
Beer range varies Ⓗ/Ⓖ
Friendly, rural community pub by the only village green in Cornwall; CAMRA's Pub of the Year in 2000 is a strong supporter of real ale from small breweries. There are around six ever-varying guest beers, at least two of them from Cornwall, while the cider also constantly changes. With two separate bars and a collection of barometers and toby jugs, it serves excellent food made from local produce. In the family room, an iguana keeps a watchful eye on proceedings. 🏚 Q ➳ 🕮 ◑ 🜨 ♣ ☗

Ales of Scilly St Mary's
Blackawton Saltash
Blue Anchor Helston
Doghouse Scorrier
Driftwood St Agnes
Keltek Lostwithiel
Organic Cury Cross Lanes
Redruth Redruth
Ring O' Bells Launceston
St Austell St Austell
Sharp's Rock
Skinner's Truro
Wheal Ale Hayle
Wooden Hand Grampound Road

The pub is known for imaginative and good quality food, served every evening and weekend lunchtimes. ⚲Q♿☺⊕P

BREAGE

Queen's Arms
TR13 9PD (off A394)
🕐 11.30-2.30, 6.30-11; 12-10.30 Sun
☎ (01326) 573485
website: www.thequeensarmsinn.co.uk
Draught Bass; Greene King Abbot; Sharp's Doom Bar; guest beers Ⓗ

Lively village inn with enthusiastic landlord and efficient staff. Open fires blaze at both ends of the long bar, and there is a games area around the corner. The no-smoking dining room serves food until 9pm. Children and dogs are welcome. There is plenty of space outside with more tables across the lane in a walled play area. Seven handpumps are usually in action, including one for Bulmers West Country cider. Former runner-up in Cornwall CAMRA's Pub of the Year; swingtime jazz is hosted on Thursday evening. ⚲☺⊕♣☙P

BUDE

Bencoolen Inn
Bencoolen Road, EX23 8PJ
🕐 12-11 (11-11 summer); 12-10.30 Sun
☎ (01288) 354694
Ring O' Bells Dreckly; Sharp's Doom Bar, Own; guest beer (summer) Ⓗ

The Bencoolen is named after a merchantman that foundered off the coast here in 1862 en route from Liverpool to Bombay, loaded with iron. The story is told on the wall of the pub in the words of the official report and even more graphically shown in a large mural. The regular Cornish beers are supplemented by a guest ale in summer, and indexed by several during Bude jazz festival week, when the pub is a hive of activity. Accommodation is available in summer. ☺⇔⊕▲♣P

BUGLE

Bugle Inn ⊘
57 Fore Street, PL26 8PB
🕐 11-11; 12-10.30 Sun
☎ (01726) 850307 website: www.bugleinn.co.uk
St Austell IPA, Tinners, Tribute, seasonal beer Ⓗ

This friendly, locals' pub has been refurbished to a comfortable standard and caters for all age groups. It is situated in the Cornish china clay district, not far from the Eden Project, which has added to its popularity. It is supposedly named after the sound of the horn as the stagecoach passed through. Food is available all day, breakfast starting at 8am for residents and visitors. A no-smoking conservatory has recently been added at the back. The five bedrooms are all en-suite. ⚲☺⇔⊕⇌♣P⅄

CRANTOCK

Old Albion
Langurroc Road, TR8 5RB
🕐 12-11; 12-10.30 Sun
☎ (01637) 830243
Courage Best Bitter; Skinner's Betty Stogs Bitter; guest beers Ⓗ

Picture-postcard pub by the church lych

gate, this partly-thatched village inn has a long history of smuggling activity with secret tunnels to the caves on the beach and the nearby church. It attracts a good mix of locals and visitors who usually enjoy the choice of meals available in the summer. The safe, sandy beach is within easy walking distance, as are many camping/caravan sites. Car parking may appear limited but can be shared with the pub opposite (Cornishman). Outdoor seating is available in the garden. ⚲☜☺⊕▲P

CRIPPLESEASE

Engine Inn
TR20 8NF (on B3311)
🕐 11-2.30, 6-11 (11-11 summer); 12-10.30 Sun
☎ (01736) 740204
Greene King Old Speckled Hen; Marston's Pedigree; Sharp's Doom Bar Ⓗ

This 17th-century inn, high on the edge of the wild Penwith moorland, was once the counthouse for nearby Giew mine, whose engine house still stands. Families and dogs are welcome. Food is available whenever the pub is open, and Sunday roast lunches are served. Live entertainment is hosted occasionally in the evening, otherwise the pub is 'quiet'. The patio affords great views across the moors and amusements for the children include a family of guinea pigs. ⚲Q♿☺⊕▲♣P

CROWLAS

Star Inn
TR20 8DX (on A30)
🕐 11-11; 12-10.30 Sun
☎ (01736) 740375
Beer range varies Ⓗ

This striking and friendly old pub on the A30 could be easily missed on the drive west, which would be a pity as it is a local mecca for real ale. The single long bar sports several handpumps dispensing ever-changing ales from many sources. This is a beer-drinkers' local where conversation rules – there is no food. Good value B&B offers an excellent base for local pub crawling. A regular bus service (including coaches to London) serves the pub. Q⇔▲♣P

CROWNTOWN

Crown Inn
TR13 0AD (on B3303, Camborne-Helston road)
🕐 12-2.30 (not Mon-Thu in winter), 6 (5.30 winter)-11; 12-3, 7-10.30 Sun
☎ (01326) 565638
Ring O' Bells Bodmin Boar, Dreckly; Skinner's Cornish Knocker; guest beer Ⓖ

Large, friendly, old free house that offers a single bar with ample seating, a separate room for the pool table and a walled beer garden, it also houses the village post office. This is a community pub where conversation dominates, although there may be occasional live entertainment and a quiz night. The guest beers are varied frequently, and favour Cornish breweries. The ales are dispensed by gravity, straight from the cellar, despite the array of four handpumps (complete with clips) on the bar. Q☺⇔⊕P

EDMONTON

Quarryman Inn ✪
PL27 7JA (just off A39, near Wadebridge)
☼ 12-11; 12-10.30 Sun
☎ (01208) 816444
Sharp's Eden Ale; Skinner's Coast Liner; guest beer
(summer) Ⓗ

Close to the Camel Trail and county showground, this popular, family-friendly free house exudes character and bonhomie, attracting both town and country tipplers. The homely single-bar interior accommodates public and lounge bars plus dining. With an emphasis on local produce, the varying beer menu is complemented by high quality meals. Concentrating on sport and field pursuits, the decor is eclectic throughout. It was originally part of a 19th-century, purpose-built housing complex for local quarrymen. Adjoining workers' cottages, now holiday lets, provide an unusual quadrangular background for the beer garden. ⚒Q❀◗▲P

FALMOUTH

Mason's Arms ✪
31 Killigrew Street, TR11 3PW
☼ 11-11; 12-10.30 Sun
☎ (01326) 311061
St Austell Tribute, HSD Ⓗ

Cosy little town-centre pub favoured by locals, which is keen to emphasise its traditional values ('no discos, no karaoke'), although there is a juke box. Good value real ale is dispensed without sparklers. The tiny bar serves a small single room, which nonetheless has room for a spot of private drinking. Pub games are available over the bar on request. No meals, but the pub advertises nearby takeaways with an invitation to bring in your own food. ⚒≠

Seven Stars ☆
The Moor, TR11 3QA
(town centre, by bus terminus)
☼ 11-3 (3.30 Sat), 6-11; 12-3, 7-10.30 Sun
☎ (01326) 312111
Draught Bass; Sharp's Special; Skinner's Cornish Knocker Ⓖ

A priest runs this unspoilt old pub, which has a lively, if narrow, tap room and a quiet snug at the back. The planked bar ceiling is festooned with an impressive collection of key fobs, while the ancient, unpolished bar-top shows distinct signs of warping, and is often covered in an eclectic selection of bar towels. An old clock proclaims the time as permanently GMT; mobile phones are banned. The pub is on the CAMRA National Inventory of historic pub interiors. The paved frontage serves as an area for outdoor drinking. Q❀⊟≠ (Penmere)

FLUSHING

Royal Standard
St Peters Hill, TR11 5TP (off A393 at Penryn)
☼ 11-2.30 (3 Fri & Sat), 6.30-11 (varies winter); 12-3, 7-10.30 (varies winter) Sun
☎ (01326) 374250
Draught Bass; Sharp's Cornish Coaster, Doom Bar Ⓗ

Friendly local, run by the present landlord for over 30 years. Home-made pasties and apple pies are specialities on the menu. Fine views of Falmouth and the Penryn River can be enjoyed from the front patio. Drivers – beware of swans in the road nearby. The pub is accessible from Falmouth by foot ferry across the river. ⚒❀◗♣

FOWEY

Galleon
12 Fore Street, PL13 1AQ
☼ 11-11; 12-10.30 Sun
☎ (01726) 833014
Draught Bass; Sharp's Cornish Coaster, Doom Bar; guest beer Ⓗ

This 400-year-old pub has been comprehensively refurbished and provides congenial drinking areas, including a patio beside the town quay, overlooking the river. This view can also be enjoyed from the lounge and some of the bedrooms. The traditional feel of the public bar is provided by imaginative use of timber beams and solid wood furniture. Children are welcome and nappy-changing facilities are provided. Accommodation includes two family rooms with air conditioning. Live music is performed on Sunday lunchtime. Guest beer is only available on seasonal occasions, and Addlestones cider is served in summer. Q⏱❀⊭◗⊟&▲◆

HAYLE

Cornish Arms ✪
86 Commercial Road, TR27 4DJ (on B3301, between Copperhouse and Hayle)
☼ 11.30-2.30, 6-11 (11-11 Sat & summer); 12-10.30 Sun
☎ (01736) 753237
St Austell IPA, Black Prince, Tinners, Dartmoor Best, HSD Ⓗ

Roomy, convivial two-bar locals' pub, set back from the main road. Lunchtime clientele tend to be older, with a broader cross-section in the evening. The 'public' doubles as a pool room, although the spacious lounge hosts the dartboard; a lounge extension serves as a restaurant area as required. One of the few pubs to feature most, if not all, of St Austell's real ales, as the array of handpumps will testify – check both bars to see the full range available. ⚒❀◗⊟▲≠♣P

HELSTON

Blue Anchor
50 Coinagehall Street, TR13 8EU
☼ 10.30-11; 12-10.30 Sun
☎ (01326) 562821
Blue Anchor Spingo Jubilee, Middle, Bragget (summer)**, Special, seasonal beers** Ⓗ/Ⓖ

Thatched, 15th-century brew-pub in the heart of town. There are two main bars with low, beamed ceilings and flagstone floors. The small back bar has an inglenook. A compact family room is on the left. A garden and sitting-out area are to the rear, past the brewery and cellar. The skittle alley also has its own bar, open for special functions and entertainments. It is convenient for buses to and from Redruth, Camborne, Truro and Penzance. Accommodation is available at the pub's own B&B next door. ⚒Q⏱❀⊭◗⊟♣

HOLYWELL BAY

St Piran's Inn
TR8 5PP
✪ 11 (7 winter)-11; 12-10.30 (varies winter) Sun
☎ (01637) 830205
St Austell Tribute, HSD; guest beers Ⓗ

Level walking to a golden sandy beach makes this friendly free house a good location for a refreshing drink or a meal. Up to four guest ales, many from local micros, may be renamed by the landlord with his own pump clips (St Austell HSD is Diesel). There may be a refundable car parking charge in summer. It is convenient for the many caravan/camping sites that boost summer trade. The beach featured in the opening sequence of the Bond film, Die Another Day. ♨ Q ⦵ ❀ ⑪ ♿ ♣ A P

KINGSAND

Rising Sun
The Green, PL10 1NH
✪ 12-11 (not winter Mon); 12-10.30 Sun
☎ (01752) 822840
Courage Best Bitter; Skinner's Cornish Knocker; guest beer Ⓗ

Cosy and welcoming village inn which is at once both popular and quiet. The pub was the former Customs and Excise house in this village of narrow streets, close to the coastal footpath and off the beaten track. Parking is limited to only four cars. The excellent locally-produced food may include crab dishes and the famous half-yard of sausage. It hosts occasional live entertainment, especially on Friday; food is served all day on Saturday and Sunday. ♨ Q ❀ ⑪ P

LANNER

Lanner Inn
The Square, TR16 6EH
(on A393 Redruth-Falmouth road)
✪ 12-3 (not Mon), 4.30-11 (may vary); 12-11 Fri & Sat; 12-3, 7-10.30 Sun
☎ (01209) 216668
Sharp's Cornish Coaster, Doom Bar; guest beer Ⓗ

Busy and convivial community pub, whose keen landlord varies the guest beer as advised by his locals. This is not a food-oriented pub; the emphasis is on real ale, conversation, and games such as darts, euchre, pool, dominoes and quizzes, while good value B&B accommodation (four rooms) is especially welcoming for real ale enthusiasts on holiday. A delightful orchard doubles as the beer garden and children's play area in summer. Frequent buses run to local towns, including weekday evenings. ♨ Q ❀ ⇔ ⊞ ♣ P

LONG ROCK

Mexico Inn
Gladstone Terrace, TR20 8JB
(off A30, near Penzance)
✪ 11-2.30, 5-11; 12-3, 7 (5 summer)-10.30 Sun
☎ (01736) 710625
Sharp's Eden Ale; Skinner's Cornish Knocker; guest beer Ⓗ

Once part of a tin mine, this popular free house has the bare granite walls characteristic of the area. The single L-shaped beamed bar has a dining

extension. The ales are usually local, with a house beer from Skinner's Brewery. The pub is especially popular in summer, being close to the beach. Good bus services pass the door; car parking is very limited. Good quality food is available either as bar meals, or in the no-smoking restaurant in the evening. ♨ Q ❀ ⑪ ♣ A P

LOSTWITHIEL

Royal Oak
Duke Street, PL22 0AG (close to A390)
✪ 11-11; 12-10.30 Sun
☎ (01208) 872552
website: www.angelfire.com/ky/royaloak
Fuller's London Pride; Marston's Pedigree; guest beers Ⓗ

Lostwithiel was the old capital of Cornwall and the Royal Oak (just off the main road) is a 13th-century inn known for its excellent ales and delicious food (often prepared with local produce). Keltek Royal Oak Special is the house beer, a selection of bottle-conditioned ales come from small local Cornish breweries. Restormel Castle was reputed to have a bolt hole from its dungeons to the inn's cellar.
Q ❀ ⇔ ⑪ ⊞ ♿ ♣ A ≈ ♣ P

LUXULYAN

King's Arms ❷
Bridges, PL30 5EF
✪ 12-11; 12-10.30 Sun
☎ (01726) 850202
St Austell Tinners, Tribute, HSD Ⓗ

This village pub, known locally as Bridges, has been carefully refurbished and has one bar that is still partially divided into lounge and bar sections. The latter area houses a pool table. There is no family room but children are welcome. Home-cooked food is served daily (except for Mon eve). The pub can be reached via the beautiful Luxulyan Valley, which still shows many remnants of the area's industrial past. The famous Eden Project is less than two miles away and the Par to Newquay railway line passes close by – the station is a request stop.
❀ ⑪ ♿ A ≈ ♣ P ✂

MAWGAN-IN-MENEAGE

Old Court House
TR12 6AD (off Helston-St Keverne road, B3293)
✪ 11-11; 12-10.30 Sun
☎ (01326) 221240
Beer range varies Ⓗ

Although tucked away down a leafy lane, this friendly village pub is the centre for local life. Up to four real ales, mostly from Cornish micros can accompany home-cooked food. A talkative parrot (Nibbles), black dog and black cat will also entertain you with their antics. Well-behaved children are welcome. ♨ Q ❀ ⑪ A P

MEVAGISSEY

Fountain Inn
3 Cliff Street, PL26 6QH
✪ 11.30-11; 12-10.30 Sun
☎ (01726) 842320
St Austell Tinners, HSD Ⓗ

The inn's slate floors and low, beamed ceiling declare its 15th-century origins. The

two bars have a cosy feel and abound in interesting features. Just off the end of Fore Street, close to the harbour, the pub is within easy motoring distance of the famous Lost Gardens of Heligan. The friendly landlord, once a fisherman, keeps the ale in tip-top condition. There are three guest rooms; evening meals are served in summer. Regular buses run to St Austell.
♨Q⇌◑◐⊟⛺

MYLOR BRIDGE

Lemon Arms ✔
Lemon Hill, TR11 5NA (off A393 at Penryn)
⊛ 11-3, 6-11; 12-3, 7-10.30 Sun
☎ (01326) 373666
St Austell Tinners, Tribute, HSD Ⓗ
Friendly, one-bar, village-centre pub frequented by local sports teams. Good home-cooked food is available, and families with children are made welcome. The real ales from the St Austell Brewery may vary from time to time. There is a patio for summer drinking. Hourly buses from Falmouth serve the pub on weekday lunchtimes.
♨❀◑◐♣P

NEWBRIDGE

Fountain Inn ✔
TR20 8QH (on A3071 Penzance-St Just road)
⊛ 12-2 (not winter Mon), 6-11; 12-11 Fri, Sat & summer; 12-10.30 Sun
☎ (01736) 364075
St Austell IPA, Tinners, Tribute, HSD Ⓗ
This charming Grade II listed Cornish inn, set in a quiet hamlet on the Penzance–St Just road, was voted Cornwall CAMRA Pub of the Year 2002. It has solid stone walls, flagstone floors, and a carpeted dining area with real fire in an enormous granite fireplace. Some tables are made from old wooden casks and disused dartboards. Cornish language lessons are held here weekly. Popular for good quality meals, the pub welcomes families. A good bus service passes the door. Camping is available (for tents only) behind the pub in summer.
♨Q❀◑◐⛺♣P

NEWQUAY

Skinner's Ale House
58 East Street, TR7 1BE
⊛ 12-11; 12-10.30 Sun
☎ (01637) 876391 website: www.skinnersbrewery.com
Skinner's Betty Stogs Bitter, Cornish Knocker, Cornish Blonde Wheat Beer, seasonal beers; Ⓗ **guest beers** (occasional) Ⓖ
A real ale haven among various theme bars, this is the brewery's flagship pub. Expect to find the latest brews from the Truro-based brewery alongside more regular offerings, including Goofy Ale, which is a house beer. Free monkey nuts provide the 'sawdust' on the bare wooden floor, but good value, more substantial meals can be enjoyed, too. Live music is popular most weekend evenings, while the pub supports several sports teams in winter. If the brewer and family are in, expect surfing discussion. Two beer festivals are generally held each year in spring and autumn. Pavement tables are available for summer drinking.
❀◑◐⇌

PADSTOW

Golden Lion Inn
Lanadwell Street, PL28 8AN (off market square)
⊛ 11-11; 12-10.30 Sun
☎ (01841) 532797
Draught Bass; Sharp's Cornish Coaster, Doom Bar Ⓗ
Padstow's oldest pub, well over 400 years old and unspoilt. It is used as the stable for the Red 'Oss which makes its appearance on May Day during the famous 'Obby 'Oss celebrations. The low beamed and slate-flagged public bar is normally busy, while the quieter lounge is spacious and comfortable. Favoured by the locals, it is situated away from the busy harbour area but can still become crowded in the summer season. ♨❀⇌◑◐⊟

PAR

Royal Inn
66 Eastcliffe Road, PL24 2AJ
⊛ 11.30-11; 12-10.30 Sun
☎ (01726) 815601
Greene King Abbot; Sharp's Doom Bar, Will's Resolve; Skinner's Cornish Knocker; Tetley Burton Ale Ⓗ
Large family pub close to the railway station, popular for eating out; there is a separate dining room. The beer range (six handpumps) is varied, but normally includes ales from Sharp's as well as another local brewery. The house beer, called Royal Cornish, is also from Sharp's. Known to older hands as the Par Royal, the pub is part of a small local group, Ladybird Inns, which also owns the Galleon, Fowey. Background music provided, with live performances hosted on Friday night. ❀◑◐⛺⇌P

PENDEEN

North Inn ✔
TR19 7DN (on B3306, St Just-St Ives road)
⊛ 12-11; 12-10.30 Sun
☎ (01736) 788417
St Austell IPA, Tinners, Tribute, HSD Ⓗ
Welcoming locals' pub in a famous tin mining district. The bar room is decorated with artefacts from nearby Geevor, the last local working mine to be closed and now a museum. Voted CAMRA Cornwall Pub of the Year, the inn is in an area of outstanding natural beauty, with nearby cliffs and good walking; a small upstairs restaurant affords outstanding views over the sea. Two double rooms are available for B&B, as well as a campsite round the back. A regular bus service passes the door.
♨Q❀⇌◑◐⛺♣P

PENZANCE

Alexandra Inn
Alexandra Road, TR18 4LY (off the promenade)
⊛ 11.30-2.30, 5-11; 11.30-11 Sat & summer; 12-3.30, 6-10.30 (12-10.30 summer) Sun
☎ (01736) 365165
Organic Lizard Point; Sharp's Eden Ale; guest beers Ⓗ
Near the seafront and rugby ground, and about 20 minutes' walk from the railway station, this pleasant town pub has been attractively modernised, with bar carpeting and woodwork much in evidence. Up to six real ales are usually on offer, with the emphasis on Cornish brews. The keen and friendly landlord holds a beer festival in

March to celebrate the feast of St Piran, Cornwall's patron saint. The house beer is Skinner's Pirates Pride. Home-cooked food is of a good 'pub-grub' variety with a vegetarian option available. Q ❁ ◑ ♣ ♠

PERRANWELL STATION

Royal Oak
TR3 7PX
⊛ 11-3, 6-11 (may vary summer); 12-3, 7-10.30 (may vary summer) Sun
☎ (01872) 863175
Draught Bass; Flowers IPA; Sharp's Special Ⓗ
Small, friendly, cottage pub dating from the 18th century, now a free house with a deserved reputation for good food, and tapas at the bar (bookings for tables advisable). It has a cosy drinking area at the bar, where a guest beer may be available. A bus service stops outside, connecting with Truro and both Cornish coasts. Q ❁ ◑ ⇌ P

PHILLACK

Bucket of Blood ⊘
14 Churchtown Road, TR27 5AE
⊛ 11 (12 winter Mon)-2.30 (3 Sat). 6-11; 12-4, 7-10.30 Sun
☎ (01736) 752378
St Austell IPA, Dartmoor Best, HSD Ⓗ
Friendly old pub near the dunes of Hayle Towans, whose name is linked to a gory legend. The notice 'Familiarity breeds contempt' attached to one of the very low beams serves as a warning rather than a proverb. Sensitively refurbished to render the structure safe, the single-bar room houses the pool table at one end, and a cosy drinking/eating area at the other, with settles and a recently-exposed old fireplace. No food is served on winter lunchtime, or on Sunday or Monday. ⚊ ⏆ ❁ ◑ ⏏ P

PHILLEIGH

Roseland Inn
TR2 5NB (King Harry ferry from Truro or via Tregony)
⊛ 11-3, 6-11; 12-3, 6-10.30 Sun
☎ (01872) 580254
Marston's Pedigree; Ringwood Best Bitter; Sharp's Doom Bar Ⓗ
Picturesque, 16th-century village inn on the Roseland Peninsula, with slate floors, exposed beams, real fires, a lounge bar and a snug. The bars are both made of single pieces of oak. The interesting and varied menu has quality-sourced food, that has won many awards. Pig roasts and barbecues feature in summer. The pub is accessible from Truro via the King Harry ferry or land route via Tregony. Situated on the new national cycle trail, it is bicycle-, child- and dog-friendly. ⚊ Q ❁ ◑ ⏏ P

PIECE

Countryman Inn
TR16 6SG (on Pool-Four Lanes road)
⊛ 11-11; 12-10.30 Sun
☎ (01209) 215960
Courage Best Bitter; Greene King Old Speckled Hen; Sharp's Own; Skinner's Cornish Blonde Wheat Beer; Theakston Old Peculier; guest beers Ⓗ
This lively country pub, set high among the old copper mines near the prominent landmark of Carn Brea, was once a miners'

grocery shop. There are two bars, the larger hosting some form of entertainment every night, plus Sunday lunchtime (which includes a raffle for local charities). A range of up to 10 ales is offered, several from local brewers. A house beer from Sharp's Brewery is called No-Name, as it was never given one! Food is available all day.
⚊ ⏆ ❁ ◑ ⏏ P

POLPERRO

Blue Peter
Quay Road, PL13 2QZ
⊛ 11-11; 12-10.30 Sun
☎ (01503) 272743
St Austell HSD; Sharp's Doom Bar, Own, Special; guest beer Ⓗ
Named after a naval flag, this friendly, split-level pub on the coastal path is reached by steps at the end of the quay. It has wooden floors and interesting hidden corners, while it boasts the only sea view from a pub in town – if you can find the right window! Guest ale may appear in summer, usually from a local brewery. No food, but you may take in your own sandwiches. Haye Farm cider is stocked. Live music is performed on Saturday evening and Sunday lunchtime.
⚊ Q ⏆ ❁ ▲ ♠

QUINTRELL DOWNS

Two Clomes
East Road, TR8 4PD (on A392)
⊛ 12-3, 7-11 (12-11 summer); 12-3, 7-10.30 (12-10.30 summer) Sun
☎ (01637) 871163
Sharp's Doom Bar; guest beers Ⓗ
Conveniently situated on the outskirts of Newquay, the pub is named after the fireside ovens. The emphasis here is on food, but a mix of locals make sure the real ale choice is good and varied regularly. It is advisable to book a table for the large no-smoking restaurant, even in winter. Popular and convenient for local camping/caravan sites. ⚊ Q ❁ ◑ ▲ ⇌ P

REDRUTH

Tricky Dickie's
Tolgus Mount, TR15 2AP
(NE off old Redruth bypass A3047) OS686427
⊛ 11-3, 6-11; 11-11 Fri & Sat; 12-10.30 Sun
☎ (01209) 219292
Sharp's Own; guest beers Ⓗ
Imaginatively converted former tin mine smithy, with several corners in which to hide, including a small no-smoking room. The pub is decorated with 'before' and 'after' pictures. A wide range of reasonably-priced food is served until 10pm and a good selection of wines. A covered outside barbecue is available for hire. On site are squash courts and a fitness centre with a separate accommodation block including conference facilities. Live jazz is performed on Tuesday evening, other music on Thursday (late licence). Families are welcome. Tricky Dickie's is well worth finding. ❁ ⇌ ◑ ⏚ ▲ P ⊬

RILLA MILL

Manor House Inn
PL17 7NT (on B3254, NE of Liskeard)

☼ 11-3, 6-11; 12-3, 7-10.30 Sun
☎ (01579) 362354
Draught Bass; Ring O' Bells Dreckly; guest beers
(summer) ᴴ
Traditional, 17th-century inn and
restaurant in the Lynher Valley. Guest beers
and cider are available in summer. Food is
served 11.30–2.30 and 6.30–9. The pub is
close to Sterts Open Air Theatre and Lynher
Dairy, home of Yarg cheese.
Q ⟡ ⬤ ⟠ ⦅◗

RUAN LANIHORNE

King's Head Inn
TR2 5NX
☼ 12-2.30, 6.30-11 (not winter Mon); 12-2.30,
7-10.30 Sun
☎ (01872) 501263
Beer range varies ᴴ
One of the many fine pubs situated on the
Roseland Peninsula, this free house
overlooks the upper reaches of the Fal
estuary. The village can be reached from the
A3078 at Tregony. Alternatively, the King
Harry ferry route can be used when
approaching from the west. The sunken
garden is a popular suntrap in the summer.
Two house beers are always on, King's Ruan
from Skinner's and Which King's Best from
Sharp's. Good home-cooked meals are
served; the Sunday lunches are a favourite.
Note that the pub is closed on Monday in
winter. ⬤Q ⟡ ⬤⦅◗ ⬤ ⬤⬤ ⬤ ⬤P⌿

ST AGNES

Driftwood Spars
Quay Road, Trevaunance Cove, TR5 0RT
☼ 11-11 (midnight Fri-Sat); 12-10.30 Sun
☎ (01872) 552428 website: www.driftwoodspars.com
**Draught Bass; Driftwood Cuckoo Ale; St Austell HSD;
Sharp's Own; Tetley Bitter; guest beers** ᴴ
Former mine workhouse and sail loft, now a
vibrant family-run hotel with micro-
brewery. It is built from granite, slate and
enormous ships' spars. Beamed ceilings,
leaded light windows, granite fireplaces plus
a 'wreckers' tunnel form a cosy,
atmospheric three-bar interior. The nautical
decor includes a fine collection of ships'
clocks. Popular with locals and tourists, it
enjoys easy access for surfing and cliff
walks. An extensive menu offers excellent
meals, and entertainment includes a
monthly theme night, live theatre and
music at the weekend.
⬤Q ⟡ ⬤⟠ ⦅◗ ⬤P

ST AUSTELL

Stag Inn
5 Victoria Place, PL25 5PE (near church)
☼ 10.30-11; 12-10.30 Sun
☎ (01726) 67148
**Draught Bass; Greene King Old Speckled Hen; Sharp's
Doom Bar; guest beer** ᴴ
Built in the 1700s, this inn was the second
to be established in the then village of St
Austell. It is now a small, friendly, town-
centre house currently owned by
Pubmaster, who provide an excellent
selection of ales (six are always available).
Bulmers medium traditional cider is
served. A traditional drinkers' pub with
bare floorboards where conversation
remains all-important, meals are served

daily except Sunday. Live entertainment is
usually staged on Friday evening. The
Eden Project and bus and railway stations
are close by. Q ⟠ ⦅◗ ⬤ ⬤ ⬤ ⬤

ST BLAZEY

Packhorse Inn
Fore Street, PL24 2NH (on A390)
☼ 11-2.30, 5-11; 12-3, 5-10.30 Sun
☎ (01726) 813970
Skinner's Coast Liner; Taylor Landlord; guest beer ᴴ
This pub was once a part of the Devenish
estate but is now a free house. It stands on
raised ground next to the main road (A390)
in the centre of the village. Reputedly it is
located on the site of an old battleground.
Originally a tax office, then a coaching inn,
it is now a friendly locals' pub. The original
licensee can be traced back to the 1800s
when the pub was under its present name.
The Eden Project is within a couple of miles.
⬤⬤⟠ ⦅◗ ⬤ ⬤ (Par) ⬤P

ST COLUMB MAJOR

Ring o' Bells
3 Bank Street, TR9 6AT
☼ 12-2 (not Mon), 5-11; 12-3, 7-10.30 Sun
☎ (01637) 880259
Sharp's Doom Bar, Eden Ale; ᴴ **guest beers** ᴳ
This charming, 15th-century free house was
established to commemorate the parish
church tower. Attracting rural and town
custom, it was a former brew-pub and is the
oldest in town. The narrow frontage
disguises the capacious, beamed slate-
floored, three-bar interior. Each bar has a
different feel and draws a different crowd:
youngsters tend to choose the front bar,
while mature drinkers opt for the middle
and back. Wood-burning stoves and
assorted wood furnishings, including settles,
provide a welcoming, rustic ambience
throughout. The adjoining former brewery,
now a comfortable restaurant, provides an
extensive and varied menu. ⬤Q ⟡ ⬤⦅◗ ⬤⬤

ST ERTH

Star Inn
1 Church Street, TR27 6HP
(off A30 near Hayle Causeway)
☼ 11-11; 12-10.30 Sun
☎ (01736) 752068
Draught Bass; guest beer ᴴ
Traditional, 17th-century, award-winning
village pub with a rather rambling interior,
decorated with antiques and bric-à-brac. Up
to four real ales may appear at busy times,
and these are frequently rotated. Families
and dogs are welcome; the pub supports
euchre and pool teams and holds a whist
drive on the third Monday in the month.
Live entertainment is held most Saturday
nights (there may be a small fee at the
door). Buses linking with Penzance run
nearby until late evening.
⬤⬤⟠ ⦅◗ ⬤ ⬤ ⬤P

ST EWE

Crown Inn ⬤
PL26 6EY (2 miles W of Mevagissey)
☼ 12-3, 5-11 (11-11 summer); 12-3, 6-10.30
(12-10.30 summer) Sun
☎ (01726) 843322

St Austell Tinners, Tribute, HSD, seasonal beer (summer) ⓗ

This cosy, 16th-century inn set in an unspoilt and remote village, has a low, beamed ceiling and slate-flagged floor in the bar. There is a restaurant in an upper level extension. The open fire in the bar features a working spit. A marquee is erected in summer in the garden for children and families to use. The landlord – John Green – was a co-founder of the famous Lost Gardens of Heligan, which are just over a mile away.

🏚Q❀⇔❶❻ⒼⓐP

ST JUST

Star Inn
1 Fore Street, TR19 7LL
✪ 11-11; 12-10.30 Sun
☎ (01736) 788767
St Austell Black Prince, Tinners, Dartmoor, HSD, ⓗ seasonal beers Ⓖ

Popular, 18th-century granite inn, St Just's oldest. The atmospheric single bar is full of interest, recalling a long association with tin mining. A slate floor, assorted wood furnishings and an open fire create a cosy ambience. The adjoining 'snuggery' provides a comfy family room. With beer the priority, food is limited to substantial bar snacks. A real drinkers' pub, locals enjoy a humorous yarn or two. The centre of the local folk scene, singalongs are guaranteed most evenings, but particularly on Monday; traditional pub games also thrive.

🏚Q⛵❀⇔❶Ⓖⓐ🅰❤❺

SALTASH

Union Inn
Tamar Street, PL12 4EL
✪ 11-11; 12-10.30 Sun
☎ (01752) 848952
Draught Bass; Ⓖ Courage Best Bitter; Flowers IPA; Fuller's London Pride; ⓗ Greene King Abbot; Ⓖ guest beer ⓗ

Basic riverside local below the Tamar bridges, with a frontage painted as a union flag. The single bar offers a selection of regular and ever-changing guest ales, some on gravity in the cellar – see the blackboard above the bar for the complete list. Food is confined to filled bread rolls at lunchtime. Regular live music evenings are held – jazz on Tuesday, other performances on Wednesday and Saturday. Real cider is Inch's Stonehouse on handpump, driven by a jetflow system.

≈❤P

STITHIANS

Seven Stars
Church Road, TR3 7DH
✪ 12-2.30, 7 (6 Fri)-11; 11-11 Sat; 12-3, 7-10.30 Sun
☎ (01209) 860003
Beer range varies ⓗ

Lively 100-year-old village free house used by a good cross-section of the community, where euchre is enthusiastically played. The pub was a farmhouse extension, purpose-built to serve the drinking needs of tin miners. Up to four ever-changing ales are stocked, usually including two Cornish brews. The original bar and lounge have been opened out to form one drinking area,

while a more modern extension houses the pool table. Good quality, reasonably-priced meals are available except Monday evening and Tuesday. There is a front patio and rear area for summer drinking.

🏚❀❶❺❖

STRATTON

King's Arms
EX23 9BX
✪ 12-2.30, 6.30-11; 12-11 Fri & Sat; 12-10.30 Sun
☎ (01288) 352396
Exmoor Ale; Sharp's Doom Bar, Own; guest beer ⓗ

Just off the A39, close to Bude, the King's Arms is a warm, friendly local at the heart of the village. The pub dates from the 17th century and has many original features including a fine floor of delabole slate in the bar and a small bread oven, discovered while renovating the large open fireplace in the lounge. The regular local beers are supplemented by one guest beer, rising to two in summer. Cider is stocked in summer.

🏚❀⇔❶🅰❖❤P

TREBELLAN

Smugglers' Den Inn
TR8 5PY (off A3075 towards Cubert then signed)
✪ 11.30-2.30 (not winter Mon-Wed), 6-11 (11-11 summer); 12-2.30, 6-10.30 (12-10.30 summer) Sun
☎ (01637) 830209
website: www.thesmugglersden.co.uk
Beer range varies ⓗ

Tucked down a narrow lane, this 400-year-old thatched inn boasts an Elizabethan courtyard, as well as a garden. The popular no-smoking restaurant serves a wide variety of daily specials. The large fireplace is a focal point in winter. The friendly owners offer a varying range of ales, with mainstays from St Austell, Skinner's and Sharp's; Addlestones cider is available in summer. An ale and pie festival is held annually (the last weekend in April). A good bus service stops 10 minutes' walk from the pub.

🏚⛵❀❶🅰❤P

TREWARMETT

Trewarmett Inn
PL34 6ET (opp. garden centre)
✪ 12-2.30 (not Mon), 7-11; 12-2.30, 7-10.30 Sun
☎ (01840) 770460
Ring O' Bells Dreckly; Sharp's Doom Bar; guest beers ⓗ

Welcoming village pub, parts of which date back 300 years. A traditional Cornish local, it features low beams, slate floors and stone walls in its two drinking rooms and dining area where good food is served. Popular folk music sessions attract locals and visitors on Wednesday and Saturday evening. Look out for the varied collection of instruments.

🏚Q❀⇔❶P

TRURO

City Inn
Pydar Street, TR1 3SP
(B3284, beside railway bridge)
✪ 11-11; 12-10.30 Sun
☎ (01872) 272623
Courage Best Bitter; Sharp's Doom Bar; Skinner's Betty Stogs Bitter; guest beer ⓗ

Busy community pub off the shopping

centre, popular with local residents. The Skinner's beers are regularly varied, as is the guest ale; real Cornish cider from Haye Farm is also usually on offer on gravity, fetched from the cellar. The lounge has several drinking corners and boasts an impressive collection of water jugs, while the public bar is more spartan and sports-oriented. The large beer garden is a summer suntrap, with a new covered drinking area providing shelter when needed.
✿🚲🍴🍺🖾🌳♣🚶

Old Ale House
11 Quay Street, TR1 2HD
✿ 11-11; 12-10.30 Sun
☎ (01872) 271122 website: www.oldalehouse.co.uk
Draught Bass; Courage Directors; Sharp's Doom Bar; Ⓗ guest beers Ⓖ
This busy ale house in the city centre was once a department store. It benefits from a superb, central location and is less than one minute's walk from the bus station. The guest beers, including some excellent local ales, are fed on gravity; Skinner's Kiddleywink is a house beer, and is named after an 18th-century unlicensed beer shop. Regular live music is staged.
Q🍴♿

Wig & Pen ⊘
Frances Street, TR1 3DP
✿ 11-11; 12-8 (10.30 summer) Sun
☎ (01872) 273028
St Austell IPA, Black Prince, Dartmoor Best Ⓗ
Pleasant, town-centre pub with a quiet, friendly atmosphere. The single-bar carpeted interior is comfortable with wood furnishings throughout. A screen separates the dining area from the bar. Once called the Star, the pub was renamed on the relocation of the nearby county court. A judicial theme is reflected in the decor. Corner sited, the patio provides a relaxing area for tipplers, weather permitting. Quality beer is served and can be enjoyed

with the excellent meals available from the ever-changing menu. The pub is within walking distance of the rail station.
Q✿🍴

WIDEMOUTH BAY

Bay View Inn
EX23 0AW
✿ 11-3, 6-11 (11-11 summer); 12-3, 6-10.30 (12-10.30 summer) Sun
☎ (01288) 361273 website: www.bayviewinn.co.uk
Sharp's Doom Bar, Own Ⓗ
This small, welcoming inn has magnificent views over the broad expanse of Widemouth Bay, and is popular with surfers and families. The house beer, Kitch's Klassic, is brewed to the landlord's own recipe by Skinner's and in fact is now the same recipe used for their regular Coast Liner, though it is further dry hopped before being served here. There is always one guest ale, rising to two in summer.
🛏🚲🚗🍴🏕♣🚶P

ZELAH

Hawkins Arms
High Road, TR4 9HU (off A30)
✿ 11-3, 6-11; 12-3, 7-10.30 Sun
☎ (01872) 540339
Doghouse Wet Nose, Retriever, Biter, Loyal Corgi, Bow Wow, Dingo Lager; Tetley Bitter Ⓗ
Although alphabetically the last recommendation in the county, this unspoilt village pub should be one of the first on your list. Recently acquired by the local Doghouse Brewery, it usually boasts the full Doghouse range of ales on handpump. The pub offers five fully refurbished en-suite rooms for B&B. An extensive à la carte menu is offered, together with a children's menu. This is an ideal stop, with easy access, just off the A30. Lined glasses are available on request.
🛏Q✿🚲🍴♿♣🚶P🍽

Ruby the barmaid

Most barmaids are called Ruby, and they usually come from Portsmouth. It is hard to say why (our local Ruby could possibly furnish an explanation if you asked her, but this is something I do not advise, for it would mean violating a certain rule of etiquette generally observed in conversations between barmaid and customer). You can talk to a barmaid on any subject in the world – oh, yes, she's very broad-minded – except on the subject of barmaids: To acknowledge the existence of such a breed in her presence would be an impropriety of the most boorish kind. For although there is nothing discreditable in her calling, the word 'barmaid' has an unfortunate ring about it which suggests otherwise. It is a survival of the days when a pub was either a fine, flaring gin-palace or a seamy, sinful beer shop; and from the higher-minded of his ancestors the average man has inherited an ability to say 'barmaid' without sounding a faint note of contumely.

T.E.B. Clarke, *What's Yours?* 1938

CUMBRIA

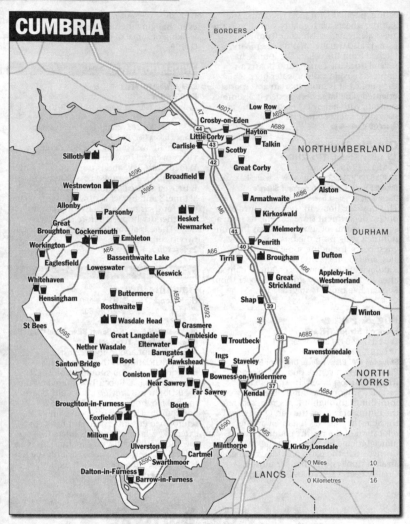

Ship Hotel
Main Road, CA15 6QF
(on B5300 N from Maryport)
☼ 12-3 (not winter Mon), 7-11; 12-3, 7-10.30 Sun
☎ (01900) 881017
Yates Bitter, Premium; seasonal beers Ⓗ
Overlooking the Solway Firth with its
glorious sunsets, this 17th-century coaching
inn offers the rare opportunity to sample
three Yates beers. The focal point of this
peaceful village, fielding darts, pool and
quiz teams, it is also the HQ of the village
cricket eleven. Good local support ensures
success for charity events which often raise
funds for the extensive children's
playground, located alongside the beach.
There is ample parking and the pub offers
attractive accommodation in oak beamed
rooms. ♨♿⚑◑▲♣P

ALSTON

Angel Inn
Front Street, CA9 3HU

☼ 11-4, 7-11 (not Tue); 12-3, 7-10.30 Sun
☎ (01434) 381363
Flowers IPA; Greene King Old Speckled Hen Ⓗ
Alston's town hall until the late 1800s when
a new building was opened, it was soon
converted into a pub serving miners and
large numbers of people visiting this, the
highest market town in England. Well
modernised, to retain a pub feel, a large
open fire is lit on cool summer days if
needed. The six guest rooms are an
excellent base for visiting the narrow gauge
railway, mines, Pennines and other local
attractions. ♨♿⚑◑⇌♣P

AMBLESIDE

Golden Rule
Smithy Brow, LA22 9AS
(100 yds off A591, towards Kirkstone)
☼ 11-11; 12-10.30 Sun
☎ (015394) 32257
**Robinson's Old Stockport, Hartleys XB, Cumbria Way,
Best Bitter, Frederics** Ⓗ
Long-standing Guide entry which has held
steadfast in offering no keg ales, hot meals,

pool, juke box or piped noise. Enjoyed instead for sticking to what it does best – being a traditional pub where (almost) the entire range of Robinson's beers and good conversation are the order of the day. Good walking, boating and fishing can be had nearby. A suntrap, sheltered patio is great for sunny days, while a real fire is lit in cooler weather. ᴀᴀQ❀♣✲

Queen's Hotel ⊘
Market Place, LA22 9BU
✪ 10-11; 12-10.30 Sun
☎ (015394) 32206
Jennings Bitter; Tetley Bitter; guest beers Ⓗ
Although primarily a hotel, the quality and variety of the beers on offer here have, deservedly, gained an enthusiastic following from locals and visitors. The guest beers are sourced from regional and local micro-breweries. Meals, of hefty proportions, are served all day in the bar and the (no-smoking) dining room. The cellar bar opens at weekends and for big matches on Sky TV.
ᴀᴀ⇌◑

APPLEBY-IN-WESTMORLAND

Golden Ball
4 High Wiend, CA16 6RD
✪ 12-11; 12-10.30 Sun
☎ (017683) 51493
Jennings Bitter, Cumberland Ale Ⓗ
Rare example of a basic pub that works and therefore does not need any fixing. The bar to the right has a (quiet) juke box and dartboard; the lounge to the left has sundry seating and a gas fire in winter. It now offers meals but they do not detract from its reputation as an unaltered gem. There is a sheltered outdoor area to the rear.
❀⇌◑⇌⇌♣

ARMATHWAITE

Fox & Pheasant ⊘
CA4 9PY
(2 miles E of A6, between Carlisle and Penrith)
✪ 12-3, 6-11; 12-11 Sat; 12-11 Sun
☎ (016974) 72400
Jennings Bitter, Sneck Lifter; guest beers Ⓗ
With a warm welcome, beamed ceilings, partially flagged floor, open fire, a fine selection of real ales and superb food from an extensive menu – this pub deserves its excellent reputation. A former coaching inn, it lies in the lovely village of Armathwaite, straddling the River Eden and on the Carlisle–Settle railway. Meals in the large stable bar are on a first come, first served basis, but early booking is advisable for the three other dining areas.
ᴀᴀQ❀◑ ⇌⇌P

BARROW IN FURNESS

Ambrose Hotel
237 Duke Street, LA14 1XT (off A590)
✪ 12-11; 12-10.30 Sun
☎ (01229) 830990 website: www.ambrosehotel.co.uk
Beer range varies Ⓗ
Once a neglected hotel on the northern edge of the town centre, this is a perfect example of the transformation that care and dedication can bring about. Now with 17 guest rooms, and excellent value meals, it stocks a constantly-changing selection of

cask beers. The main area is semi-divided by a partition wall housing a coal fire. To the rear, a room given over to pool and TV has another area off to one side; both rooms are served from a central bar.
ᴀᴀ⇌⇌◑⇌♣ ●P✲

Dominics ⊘
32 Rawlinson Street, LA14 2DS
✪ 12-11; 12-10.30 Sun
☎ (01229) 824788
Robinson's Hatters, Old Stockport, Best Bitter, Frederics Ⓗ
Recently renovated, this friendly Robinson's house has lost none of its northern England, street-corner-local character. It is a rare outlet in the area for Frederics which is always available. The pub and its staff are an excellent source of local history – just ask!
Q⇌♣

BASSENTHWAITE LAKE

Pheasant ⊘
CA13 9YE
(S off A66, midway between Keswick and Cockermouth)
✪ 11-2.30; 5.30-10.30 (11 Sat); 12-2.30, 6-10.30 Sun
☎ (017687) 76234 website: www.the-pheasant.co.uk
Draught Bass; Jennings Cumberland Ale; Theakston Best Bitter Ⓗ
Quintessential example of an unspoilt English coaching inn. The Pheasant is steeped in 500 years of history and has a public bar that has the feel of a bygone age and where the preferred tipple of the locals is Draught Bass. The bar has mellow polished walls and oak settles; in summer the garden is a delight. The hotel accommodation has been seriously upgraded in recent years and the restaurant is now one of the best in Lakeland. Nearby an osprey's nest sits atop a tall leafless tree.
ᴀᴀQ❀⇌◑ ⇌⇌P

BOOT

Brook House Inn
CA19 1TG
(E from Ambleside via Wrynose and Hardnott Passes)
✪ 11-11; 12-10.30 Sun
☎ (019467) 23288 website: www.brookhouseinn.co.uk
Taylor Landlord; Theakston Best Bitter; guest beers Ⓗ
A short walk from Dalegarth Station in Eskdale, at the end of the famous La'al Ratty railway, this superbly positioned inn offers a well presented range of beers; of the four guests usually one is Cumbrian. For walkers, it is surrounded by some of the highest fells

INDEPENDENT BREWERIES

Barngates Barngates
Beckstones Millom
Bitter End Cockermouth
Coniston Coniston
Dent Dent
Derwent Silloth
Foxfield Foxfield
Great Gable Wasdale Head
Hawkshead Hawkshead
Hesket Newmarket Hesket Newmarket
Jennings Cockermouth
Tirril Brougham
Yates Westnewton

in Lakeland and some magnificent scenery; close by are the remains of the Roman Fort at Hardnott. The inn comprises a very comfortable bar and a no-smoking room which has a children's certificate. The food and accommodation are excellent.
🏠Q🛏⚘◑Ⅾ Å⇌♣P⅄

BOUTH

White Hart
LA12 8JB (off A590, 6 miles NE of Ulverston)
☾ 12-2, 6-11; 12-11 Sat; 12-10.30 Sun
☎ (01229) 861229 website: www.whitehartbouth.co.uk
Black Sheep Best Bitter; Jennings Cumberland Ale; Tetley Bitter; guest beers Ⓗ
Beamed country village inn on the edge of the Lake District, five miles from the Grizedale Forest, offering good walking routes. Bouth often wins Best Kept Village awards and boasts a good play area on the green. The pub has a games room, an upstairs dining room and a patio that gets busy in summer with diners, drinkers and families. The varied menu represents good value. A mild or dark beer often features in the excellent guest beer range. 🏠⚘P

BOWNESS-ON-WINDERMERE

Village Inn
Lake Road, LA23 3DE
☾ 11-11; 12-10.30 Sun
☎ (015394) 43731
Black Sheep Best Bitter; Boddingtons Bitter; Castle Eden Ale; Jennings Cumberland Ale; guest beers Ⓗ
Multi-roomed, centrally located inn in a popular Lakeland tourist resort. The guest beer range, mainly from local micro-breweries, increases through summer. Meals are served in the bar area all day until 8.30pm (until 10pm in the adjoining restaurant). The split-level front patio offers a good vantage point from which to view passers-by and the fine parish church opposite. Lake steamer trips and boat hire are available from the nearby piers. ⚘◑Ⅾ &P

BROADFIELD

Crown Inn
Southwaite, CA4 0PT
(4 miles S of Carlisle racecourse)
☾ 12-3 (not Tue), 6.30-11; 12-3, 7-11 Sun
☎ (016974) 73467
Greene King Ruddles Best; guest beer Ⓗ
Isolated at a crossroads, this superb free house is popular with locals and visitors alike. It has a small bar, but food is served in a separate area. It also has a good restaurant where booking is essential. A patio provides space for outdoor drinking. 🏠Q⚘◑Ⅾ & Å P

BROUGHTON-IN-FURNESS

Manor Arms
The Square, LA20 6HY
☾ 12 (may be later in winter)-11; 12-10.30 Sun
☎ (01229) 716286
Coniston Bluebird; Taylor Best Bitter; Yates Bitter; guest beers Ⓗ
This popular pub, overlooking the imposing Georgian village square, offers a beer festival in miniature. Invariably there are six beers on handpump (no keg or smooth beer here) and Liefmans Kriek on draught, plus an occasional cider. The pub regularly receives

awards for the quality of its ale and its hospitality. In winter the 18th-century fire basket (one of only 10 made) is put to good use, warming the hop-strewn bar.
🏠Q⚘🛏◑Ⅾ ♣♠🖵

BUTTERMERE

Bridge Hotel
CA13 9UZ
(on B5289 from Keswick, via Honister Pass)
☾ 10.30-11; 12-10.30 Sun
☎ (017687) 70252 website: www.bridge-hotel.com
Black Sheep Best Bitter; Theakston Old Peculier; Tirril Old Faithful Ⓗ
This 18th-century hotel nestles between Crummock Water and Buttermere and is an ideal spot for those seeking to explore the Buttermere and Lorton valleys, with their walking and climbing opportunities. The views from the bar extend to the fells surrounding the lakes. The two comfortable bars serve good value meals throughout the day. There is also a restaurant and the hotel offers a range of accommodation, it can be very busy in summer. Q⚘🛏◑Ⅾ ÅP

CARLISLE

Carlisle Rugby Club
Warwick Road, CA1 1CW
(off A69, next to Carlisle Utd FC)
☾ 7 (5.30 Fri; 6 Sat)-11 (1-11 Sat in rugby season); 12-3, 7-10.30 Sun
☎ (01228) 521300
Tetley Bitter; Yates Bitter; guest beer (occasional) Ⓗ
Friendly club, with a cosy lounge and recently refurbished bar, it is often crowded when neighbouring Carlisle United play at home. Show this Guide or CAMRA membership to be signed in at this regular winner of Cumbria CAMRA's Club of the Year award. Guest beers are stocked during the rugby season. 🏠⚘P

Cumberland Inn ☆
22 Botchergate, CA1 1QS (near station)
☾ 11-11; 12-10.30 Sun
☎ (01228) 536900
Black Sheep Best Bitter; guest beer (occasional) Ⓗ
The best preserved ex-State Management scheme pub in Carlisle, dating from 1929, it is included in CAMRA's National Inventory. Redfern-designed, with wood panelling throughout, it has featured on BBC TV. The pub's games room displays much railway memorabilia, reflecting its proximity to the station; however, this is no museum-piece, but a popular town-centre pub, now run by a landlord keen to promote real ale. A guest beer is usually available at weekends.
🏠⚘⇌♣

Gosling Bridge
Kingstown Road, CA3 0AT
(on A7, 1½ miles N of centre)
☾ 11-11; 12-10.30 Sun
☎ (01228) 515294
Marston's Pedigree; Theakston Best Bitter; guest beer Ⓗ
Former local CAMRA Pub of the Season, the 'Goz' is a large, 1980s hotel, named after a nearby stream. Traditionally furnished, it is divided into light and airy 'rooms' and a bar area. Very family-friendly, meals are served here all day. Bus No. 63 from the city centre will take you there. ⚘🛏◑Ⅾ &P⅄

Howard Arms
107 Lowther Street, CA3 8ED
(next to the Lanes shopping centre)
✪ 11-11; 12-3, 7-10.30 Sun
☎ (01228) 532926
Derwent Carlisle State Bitter; Theakston Best Bitter Ⓗ
Popular pub, boasting a superb tiled exterior, with several small rooms – a regular Guide entry. Like all Carlisle's pubs over 30 years old, the Howard Arms is an ex-State Management scheme pub, and has changed little since those days. The city's late-lamented theatre stood opposite the pub, which numbered Charlie Chaplin, Laurel and Hardy and other music hall legends among its customers. Old photos and posters are a reminder of its theatrical links. No food is served Sunday. ⊛Ⓒ≢

King's Head
Fisher Street, CA3 8RF
✪ 11-11; 12-10.30 Sun
☎ (01228) 533797
Yates Bitter, seasonal beers; guest beer Ⓗ
Situated in the middle of the city, this pub has become very popular since it reopened in January 2002, when real ale was put back on the bar. Carlisle Cathedral, Tullie House Museum and Carlisle Castle are all within a short walk. The pub became the first in the city centre to sell Yates' beers regularly. Food is served in the upstairs dining room, 12-3 Monday–Saturday; drinks can be ordered from the main bar. Ⓒ≢⅄

Maltsters Arms
John Street, CA2 5TR (opp. old State Brewery)
✪ 5.30 (12 Sat)-11; 12-3, 7-10.30 Sun
☎ (01228) 520499
Jennings Cumberland Ale; guest beers Ⓗ
Traditional local where you are assured of a friendly welcome. The single room has areas for darts and pool. It was voted Solway CAMRA Pub of the Season in spring 2002. In the Caldergate area of Carlisle, the Jovial Sailor in Port Road also sells real ale. ♣

King's Arms
The Square, LA11 6QB
✪ 11-11; 12-10.30 Sun
☎ (015395) 36200
Beer range varies Ⓗ
On the bank of the river, overlooking the 12th-century priory, this fine country inn is set back from the square in a small cobbled courtyard for outside drinking. The central bar serves a large lounge, semi-divided to create distinctive areas. There is also a pool room and snug, plus a spacious riverside dining room (no smoking) and patio. Meals are served all day Saturday and Sunday. The inn bears black beams throughout and gleams with polished brass. ⅍⊛Ⓒ▲♣⅄

Bitter End ⊘
15 Kirkgate, CA13 9PJ (off market place)
✪ 12-2.30 (3 summer), 6-11 (11.30-11 summer Sat); 12-3, 7-10.30 Sun
☎ (01900) 828993 website: www.bitterend.co.uk
Bitter End Farmers Ale, Cuddy Lugs; Jennings Bitter, Cumberland Ale, seasonal beers; guest beers Ⓗ

This popular brew-pub won local CAMRA Pub of the Year awards for four consecutive years from 1999. Its fine choice of beers includes two from its own brewery (visible from the back bar), a selection from other Cumbrian breweries, plus two from further afield. A range of foreign bottled beers is stocked. This comfortable hostelry won a civic award for its renovation; the bars are adorned with old pictures of Cockermouth. The pub raises funds for local charities and offers a good range of bar food. ⋈Ⓒ▷▲●

Bush Hotel ⊘
Main Street, CA13 9JS
✪ 11-11; 12-10.30 Sun
☎ (01900) 822064
Jennings Bitter, Cumberland Ale, Cocker Hoop, Sneck Lifter; guest beers Ⓗ
Comfortable, 18th-century pub in the heart of the town. A warm, old-fashioned atmosphere prevails with plenty of conversation. You can sample the fullest range of Jennings beers in the town here. A large public car park is located less than 100 yards away and buses stop outside the door. Home-cooked food is served daily at lunchtime, with soup and sandwiches available to walkers through the afternoon. The licensee is a keen supporter of local charities, particularly Cockermouth's mountain rescue team. ⋈Ⓒ▲

Black Bull
Yewdale Road, LA21 8DN
✪ 11-11; 12-10.30 Sun
☎ (015394) 41668
Coniston Bluebird, Bluebird XB, Old Man Ale; guest beers Ⓗ
Large, but friendly pub situated at the centre of Coniston village. The pub is home to Coniston Brewery and serves the full range of their own beers. An old inn, built during Drake's time, it still offers accommodation, with one room featuring a four-poster bed. In winter, phone to book a room rather than arriving 'on spec'. The bar is warm and welcoming; in summer outside seating is available. ⋈Q⅍⊛≢Ⓒ●P

Sun Inn
LA21 8HQ (up hill from bridge)
✪ 11-11; 12-10.30 Sun
☎ (015394) 41248
website: www.thesun@hotelconiston.com
Moorhouses Black Cat; Coniston Bluebird; guest beers Ⓗ
This 400-year-old inn reveals many original features, including flagged floors, a beamed ceiling and a beautiful old range in the fireplace. A single bar serves three drinking areas. The east-facing restaurant affords views over the village to Coniston Water. Donald Campbell stayed here during his later attempts at the water speed record. The Sun is an ideal halt for walkers, being at the junction of three footpaths.
Q⅍⊛≢Ⓒ▲♣P⅄

Stag Inn
CA6 4QN (on loop road off A689, E of Carlisle)
✪ 12-2.30, 6-11 (12-11 summer); 12-3, 6-10.30 Sun
☎ (01228) 573210

Jennings Bitter, Cumberland Ale, Sneck Lifter Ⓗ
Sympathetically extended some years ago, this pub stands at the centre of a peaceful village. It serves a range of Jennings beers and enjoys a reputation for good food. It has four inter-connected rooms on the ground floor (one no-smoking), where partially flagged floors, exposed stone and brick walls, low ceilings and open fires make for an intimate atmosphere. Upstairs, a large restaurant offers an extensive menu which is also available downstairs.
ᐃQ❀◑⊟⏣P⅊

DALTON-IN-FURNESS

Black Dog Inn
Holmes Green, Broughton Road, LA15 8JP
(1/2 mile from wildlife park on Ireleth road) OS233761
🕓 5 (12 Sat & summer)-11; 12-10.30 Sun
☎ (01229) 462561
Beer range varies Ⓗ
Serving up to six ever-changing guest ales (many rare for the area) and three or four ciders and perries, this pub is a frequent winner of local CAMRA awards. Two open fires, exposed beams and tiled floors provide a warm atmosphere in which to enjoy the good value meals, served daily until 8pm. The menu includes a selection of vegetarian and children's options. Outside, a benched terrace by the stream offers an additional drinking area. Dogs are welcome.
ᐃQ🐾❀☖◑❀P⊟

Brown Cow
10 Goose Green, LA15 8LP
(on old main road, S of town)
🕓 11-11; 12-10.30 Sun
☎ (01229) 462553
Beer range varies Ⓗ
Possibly 900 years old, this family-run pub and restaurant provides a cosy spot for sampling good food and drink. The small, beamed bar, warmed by a coal fire, stocks a very varied range of constantly-changing guest beers. It can be busy with diners in transit to and from the large upstairs dining room. Nestling below the tower of St Mary's Church, the warmer, lighter days can be spent relaxing in the garden or on the patio at the front. ᐃQ🐾❀☖◑⅚≢P⅊

DENT

Sun Inn
Main Street, LA10 5QL
🕓 11-2.30, 6-11 (11-11 Sat & school holidays); 12-10.30 Sun
☎ (015396) 25208
Dent Bitter, Aviator, Kamikaze, T'owd Tup, seasonal beers Ⓗ
Traditional pub, set on the cobbled main street of this popular Dales village. The L-shaped bar area includes a no-smoking annexe and a games room with a juke box. The full range of Dent beers, brewed a couple of miles away, is complemented by good value meals. The George & Dragon, also Dent Brewery-owned, and almost next door, is usually open if the Sun is closed.
ᐃQ❀☖◑Å❀P⅊

DUFTON

Stag Inn
CA16 6DB

🕓 12-3 (not winter Mon), 6-11; 12-11 Sat & summer; 12-10.30 Sun
☎ (017683) 51608
Black Sheep Best Bitter; Flowers IPA; guest beers Ⓗ
Go down a few steps (or ramp) from the village green, across the patio to the entrance of the Stag, which opens into a front bar with flagged floor and a kitchen range, and the dining area. The rear lounge leads to the garden. Guest beers, which may be limited in winter, are usually sourced from local micro-breweries. On the Coast-to-Coast walk, the Stag makes a good touring base.
ᐃQ❀☖◑Å❀P

EAGLESFIELD

Black Cock
CA13 0SD (S from A66 at Cockermouth)
🕓 8 (5 Sat)-11; 12-10.30 Sun
☎ (01900) 822989
Jennings Bitter Ⓗ
Rare example of an unchanged village pub which has retained its character over a great many years. Winner of a local CAMRA Pub of the Season award, the wood panelling, beams and open fire give the bar a truly homely feel. The considerable amount of gleaming brassware that adorns the walls add to the warmth. Only Jennings Bitter is served, but it is a superb pint. Affectionately known locally as 'Annie's' (after the long-serving landlady), this is a pub well worth seeking out. Parking is limited.
ᐃQ❀P

ELTERWATER

Britannia Inn
LA22 9HP
🕓 11-11; 12-10.30 Sun
☎ (015394) 37210 website: www.britinn.co.uk
Coniston Bluebird; Dent Aviator; Jennings Bitter; guest beers Ⓗ
Busy pub in this popular Lakeland village, offering a variety of beers from near and far. The slate flagged bar area is to the right, ahead is a hallway and rear room, to the left is a no-smoking dining room. The village green is used as an overflow from the patio. The inn is free from juke box, pool, TV and machines. Evening booking is advised for the dining room.
ᐃQ❀☖◑Å❀P

EMBLETON

Wheatsheaf Inn
CA14 9XP
🕓 12-3 (not Mon-Fri), 6-11 (12-11 Mon-Sat summer); 12-3, 6-10.30 (12-10.30 summer) Sun
☎ (017687) 76408
Jennings Bitter, Cumberland Ale, seasonal beers Ⓗ
Comfortable pub in a small village to the east of Cockermouth on what used to be the main road, prior to the construction of the present A66. The single bar benefits from well-spaced tables and a no-smoking area. Live jazz and folk music are performed on alternate Thursday evenings. A good selection of bar meals is served in the evenings and on summer Saturday lunchtime. The family room is also equipped with some games; there is a garden.
ᐃQ🐾❀❀P⅊

FAR SAWREY

Claife Cryer Bar
LA22 0LQ
(1 mile from ferry on W side of Windermere, B5285)
☼ 11-11; 12-10.30 Sun
☎ (015394) 43425 website: www.sawreyhotel.co.uk
Black Sheep Best Bitter; Hawkshead Bitter; Jennings Cumberland Ale; Theakston Best Bitter, Old Peculier Ⓗ
Formerly an old stable block, this is now part of a popular hotel near the Windermere ferry. With only 10 landlords in 144 years, this small but cosy bar offers a fine selection of real ales. The bar is named after the ghost of Claife Heights (a local hill). It retains several original features, such as mangers and water troughs.
🏨🛏☕🍴◖🚲♣♿

FOXFIELD

Prince of Wales
LA20 6BX (off A595, opp. station)
☼ 5 (12 Fri & Sat)-11; closed Mon & Tue; 12-10.30 Sun
☎ (01229) 716238
website: www.princeofwalesfoxfield.co.uk
Beer range varies Ⓗ
Friendly pub, ideally situated for buses and the station (no trains Sun). Darts, board games and bar billiards are available. The ever-changing beers always include a mild, and usually a beer from the licensee's own Tigertops or Foxfield breweries. Specialities include draught foreign wheat and fruit beers, plus a good selection of bottled continental beers; the cider varies. Themed mini beer festivals are a regular feature, but the hospitality is permanent.
🏨Q☕🚋♣♣🅿🍺

GRASMERE

Traveller's Rest
LA22 9RR (on A591, ½ mile N of village)
☼ 11-11; 12-10.30 Sun
☎ (015394) 35604 website: www.lakelandinns.com
Jennings Bitter, Cumberland Ale, Sneck Lifter; guest beer Ⓗ
Popular roadside pub near the Coast-to-Coast walk, affording excellent fell views. The cosy bar area leads to a raised family/games room and two dining areas (the no-smoking one is down a couple of steps). Good food is served all day in summer. Try walking over Helvellyn to the King's Head at Thirlspot (same ownership) or take the bus between the two pubs (stops outside both). 🏨Q🛏☕🍴◖♣🅿

GREAT BROUGHTON

Punchbowl
19 Main Street, CA13 0YJ (off A66)
☼ 11 (7 Mon)-11; 12-10.30 Sun
☎ (01900) 824708
Coniston Bluebird; Jennings Bitter Ⓗ
Welcoming, traditional village pub that has featured in this Guide many times over the past 27 years. The building dates back to the early 17th century and was a coaching inn; Lord Leconfield used to hold his annual court there. The walls are adorned with Rugby League memorabilia, and a collection of water jugs hangs from the low, beamed ceiling. The pub is the HQ of the West Cumbrian Woodcarvers and the licensees are active fundraisers for a number of charities. 🏨♣

GREAT CORBY

Corby Bridge Inn
CA4 8LL (¾ mile S of A69)
☼ 12-11; 12-10.30 Sun
☎ (01228) 560221
Thwaites Mild, Bitter; guest beer Ⓗ
Grade II listed building of architectural and historical significance, situated alongside the Carlisle–Newcastle railway line, a short, but stunning walk across the viaduct from Wetheral Station. The pub offers a friendly welcome in its three open-plan rooms and holds special gourmet food nights (no food Mon). It was Solway CAMRA Pub of the Year in 2002 and 2003.
🏨Q☕🍴🚄🅿

GREAT LANGDALE

Old Dungeon Ghyll
LA22 9JY
☼ 11-11; 12-10.30 Sun
☎ (015394) 37272 website: www.odg.co.uk
Black Sheep Special; Jennings Cumberland Ale; Theakston Cool Cask, Old Peculier; guest beers Ⓗ
Basic walkers' and climbers' bar adjacent to the hotel, characterised by its hard floor and benches and kitchen range. Solid pub grub makes this an ideal pit-stop for wet and weary visitors. A good choice of guest beers and spectacular fell views from the patio make this a regular Guide entry. A bus service runs from Ambleside. Non-residents can book dinner (served at 7.30pm) in the hotel which has its own bar.
🏨Q☕🍴◖Å♣🅿🍺

GREAT STRICKLAND

Strickland Arms
CA10 3DF
☼ 12-3 (not Wed), 6-11; 12-10.30 Sun
☎ (01931) 712238
Black Sheep Best Bitter; Jennings Cumberland Ale; Tetley Bitter, Burton Ale; guest beer Ⓗ
Village-centre local with a low ceilinged front bar, where quiet classical music plays, and a games area. A comfortable rear lounge boasts a fine sandstone fireplace. There is a safe back garden. A rare regular outlet for Burton Ale, it is well worth a detour from the M6 (junction 39 or 40). It also makes a good base from which to explore Lakeland to the west and the Hugills/Pennines to the east. 🏨☕📷◖Å♣🅿

HAWKSHEAD

King's Arms Hotel
The Square, LA22 0NZ
☼ 11-11; 12-10.30 Sun
☎ (015394) 36372
Black Sheep Best Bitter; Coniston Bluebird; Hawkshead Bitter; Tetley Bitter Ⓗ
Pleasant pub, situated on the north side of the village square. The Hawkshead Bitter is brewed just down the road. Among the bar's many original features is an unusual roof support – an Acrow prop, now disguised as a sculpture by local artist, Jim Whitworth. The pub's accommodation, which includes two self-contained cottages,

makes a useful base for Lakes visitors. A cider is stocked in summer. 🏠Q🛏️🏮🍴◐● ♿✂

HAYTON

Stone Inn
Bracken How, CA8 9HR (½ mile S of A69)
⊕ 11-3, 5.30-11; 11-11 Sat; 12-3, 7-10.30 Sun
☎ (01228) 670498
Thwaites Mild, Bitter; guest beer (occasional) Ⓗ
At the centre of a pleasant village, the Stone really is at the heart of its local community. The walls are decorated with naval and agricultural artefacts and prints, worthy of a second look. The clientele is 95% local but a warm and welcoming atmosphere awaits allcomers. Upstairs a private function room is equally well adorned with interesting antiquities. Toasties are available at this local CAMRA Pub of the Season for winter 2002. 🏠Q♣P

HENSINGHAM (WHITEHAVEN)

Lowther Arms
18 Ribton Moorside, CA28 8PU
(off B5295, ½ mile SE of centre of Whitehaven)
⊕ 12.30-3 (not Mon), 6.30-11; 12.30-3, 7-10.30 Sun
☎ (01946) 695852
Robinson's Hartleys XB, Best Bitter, seasonal beers Ⓗ
Robinson's pub stocking seasonal beers in a cellar that has recently been re-equipped and uprated. There is a restaurant called Kit Horns after a former landlord of the pub. The main bar, filled with nostalgic sporting photographs, has a warm and comfortable ambience; it is supplemented by a quiet lounge area. 🏠Q🛏️🏮◐● 🍴&Å≉♣P✂

HESKET NEWMARKET

Old Crown Inn
CA7 8JG
⊕ 12-3 (not Mon), 5.30-11; 12-11 Sat; 12-3, 7-10.30 Sun
☎ (016974) 78288
Hesket Newmarket Great Cockup Porter, Blencathra Bitter, Skiddaw Special, Hellvelyn Gold, Doris's 90th Birthday Ale, Old Carrock Strong Ale Ⓗ
CAMRA Pub of the Year 2001 for Cumbria, Solway and North Pennines indicates how highly this pub is regarded by real ale aficionados. On the edge of the Caldback Fells, it is the start (and finish) point for many walkers. It serves as the tap for the village brewery, situated in a converted barn to the rear. The rooms may be small, but the welcome is large in what is one of the few pubs in the country owned by a local co-operative. 🏠Q🏮◐● Å♣●

INGS

Watermill Inn ●
LA8 9PY (just off A591)
⊕ 12-11; 12-10.30 Sun
☎ (01539) 821309 website: www.watermillinn.co.uk
Black Sheep Best Bitter; Coniston Bluebird; Jennings Cumberland Ale; Lees Moonraker; Theakston Old Peculier; guest beers Ⓗ
Full marks here if you can spot the odd area of wall not covered by an award certificate! Family run, it went from guest house to an instant success as a pub in 1990. The unbeatable range of beers can be enjoyed in an atmosphere created by the absence of TV, pool, juke box or piped sound. Good

quality meals, a beckside patio and real fires complete the picture.
🏠Q🛏️🏮◐● &♣●P✂

KENDAL

Burgundy's Wine Bar
19 Lowther Street, LA9 4DH
⊕ 11.30-3.30 (not Mon-Wed), 6.30-11 (not Mon); 7-10.30 Sun
☎ (01539) 733803
website: www.burgundyswinebar.com
Beer range varies Ⓗ
Multi-level, town-centre bar with a difference – no juke box, armchairs or chrome fittings. Under the tile-roofed bar will be found an ever-changing variety of beers – usually including one from Dent, Derwent, or other local micro. It also offers a good range of draught and bottled European beers and hosts a spring beer festival, plus parties on St Patrick's and St George's day. Evening meals are available by arrangement. It is served by good bus connections. ◐≉●

Castle Inn
13 Castle Street, LA9 7AA
⊕ 11-11; 12-10.30 Sun
☎ (01539) 729983
Jennings Cumberland Ale; Tetley Bitter; guest beers Ⓗ
Bustling pub at the edge of the town centre. The lounge houses a well-stocked fish tank, while the bar has TV, an original Duttons Brewery window and a games area (up a step). It serves good value lunches, including a Sunday roast. Of an evening darts, pool and quizzes make for a true community local. Families with children are welcome until 6pm, and a couple of pavement benches are put out in summer. Usually a Dent beer and/or one from Black Sheep is stocked. ◐≉♣

KESWICK

Dog & Gun
2 Lake Road, CA12 5BT
⊕ 12-11; 12-10.30 Sun
☎ (017687) 73463
Theakston Best Bitter, Old Peculier; Yates Bitter; guest beers Ⓗ
Probably the busiest pub in Keswick, and deservedly so, as it has a reputation for good, inexpensive food and a fine pint of ale. At time of writing it is the only Keswick pub selling Yates Bitter. The pub is stone flagged and oak beamed, warmed by a roaring fire in winter. The nearby market place has been pedestrianised (only essential traffic permitted); the historic Moot Hall is its centrepiece. Close by, the Theatre by the Lake is gaining international acclaim for its brilliant productions. 🏠◐● Å

KIRBY LONGDALE

Snooty Fox Tavern
Main Street, LA6 2AH
⊕ 11-11; 12-10.30 Sun
☎ (015242) 71308
Black Sheep Best Bitter; Taylor Landlord; Theakston Best Bitter Ⓗ
A pub 'in the round': to the left is a lounge bar with marble topped tables and high-backed settles; beyond are several dining areas, then we are in the back bar with slate

floor, juke box and TV. A courtyard to the rear has parking and benches in summer. Renowned for its beer, meals and accommodation, nearby is Devil's Bridge, popular with bikers and daring jumpers into the River Eden below. 🏠Q✿⛽✉◑🌙⊟🅰P

KIRKOSWALD

Crown Inn ✓
CA10 1DQ (on B6413, 6½ miles NE of Penrith)
✿ 12-3.30 (not Wed), 6-11 (12-11 summer Sat); 12-10.30 Sun
☎ (01768) 898435
Jennings Cumberland Ale; guest beer (winter) Ⓗ
Built in 1750, this former coaching inn stands next to the cobbled market square in this historic, attractive village overlooking the Eden Valley – read the potted history of the area on the wall. Cheerful staff greet you as you enter directly at the bar. Low ceilings and an open fire contribute to the cosy atmosphere – but beware of the resident ghost! Upstairs, a pool room in the old hayloft features bare stone walls and exposed beams. Evening meals at the weekend require reservations. 🏠Q✿✉◑🌿

LITTLE CORBY

Haywain
CA4 8QQ (500 yds from Corby Hill crossroads on A69)
✿ 12-2 (not Mon-Fri), 7 (6 Fri & Sat)-11; 12-10.30 Sun
☎ (01228) 560598
Robinsons Best Bitter, Cumbria Way, seasonal beers Ⓗ
Known as the Plough until 1957, this was the nearest free house to Carlisle during the many years of state control in the area. Extensively altered four years ago, one end of the single long room is a bar area popular with locals playing darts and dominoes or watching TV, while the other end consists of a comfortable lounge with subdued lighting. Food is served Friday–Sunday evenings and Saturday and Sunday lunchtimes. Solway CAMRA Pub of the Season summer 2002. 🌿◑👌🌿P

LOWESWATER

Kirkstile Inn
CA13 0RU (off B5292/B5289)
✿ 11-11; 12-10.30 Sun
☎ (01900) 85219 website: www.kirkstile.com
Coniston Bluebird; Jennings Bitter; Tirril Old Faithful; Yates Bitter Ⓗ
Classic Lakeland inn, replete with original beams and stone walls. Between Loweswater and Crummock Water it enjoys a fantastic setting, dominated by Melbreak Fell. Good food is served in the two rooms that comprise the bar. It also has a restaurant and good value accommodation. The beers are well chosen from Cumbrian breweries. The inn has won many awards, including a local CAMRA Pub of the Season and a newspaper Best Country Pub award. Its own micro-brewery should be operational late in 2003. 🏠Q✿✉◑👌P

LOW ROW

Railway Inn
CA8 2LE (3 miles E of Brampton, N of A69)
✿ 12-3, 5.30-11; 12-3, 6.30-10.30 Sun
☎ (016977) 46222

Thwaites Bitter; guest beers Ⓗ
Built as a byre (cowshed) and converted into an inn around 1850, it is tucked away in its own grounds, just off the main road through the village. It takes its name from the Carlisle–Newcastle railway line; the footrest is an old section of railway track. On a clear day the views across the Pennines are superb. Q✿◑🅰P

MELMERBY

Shepherds' Inn
CA10 1HF
✿ 11-3, 6-11; 12-3, 7-10.30 Sun
☎ (0870745) 3383
Dent T'Owd Tup; Jennings Cumberland Ale; guest beers Ⓗ
Built in 1789, this fine pub stands at the centre of the village. An attached barn has been converted into a bar area, creating two split-level rooms, one with a raised pool table. The good beer is complemented by highly recommended food, earning it the Cheeseboard Pub of the Year award. 🏠Q✿◑🅰🌿🐾P⊟

MILNTHORPE

Cross Keys Hotel
1 Park Road, LA7 7AD
✿ 12-11; 12-10.30 Sun
☎ (015395) 62115
Robinson's Hartleys XB, Best Bitter, seasonal beers Ⓗ
Spacious former coaching inn at the centre of a market town. Recent modernisation and major refurbishment have been carried out with care. The limed oak panelling in the ground-floor bar area and restaurant has been retained. There is a large function room upstairs. The pub is several times winner of the annual Hartley's Best Kept Cellar competition. The free car park to the rear is barrier-operated. 🏠✿✉◑👌🌿P

NEAR SAWREY

Tower Bank Arms
LA22 0LF
(6 miles S of Ambleside on B5285) OS371956
✿ 11-3, 6 (5.30 summer)-11; 12-3, 6-10.30 (12-10.30 summer) Sun
☎ (015394) 36334
website: www.sales@towerbankarms.fsnet.co.uk
Theakston Best Bitter, Old Peculier; Wells Bombardier; guest beers Ⓗ
Popular, small, country inn that featured in Beatrix Potter's Jemima Puddleduck and stands next door to Hill Top, the author's former home. The bar has a stone-flagged floor, comfortable chairs and photographs of celebrities who have stayed there, but no juke box, pool or machines. The guest beers are often from local breweries of which there are a growing number. Ideally situated for walking and sailing, this typical Lakeland pub has a licence for fishing. 🏠Q✿✿✉◑P

NETHER WASDALE

Screes Inn
CA20 1ET
(E off A595 at Gosforth, follow signs for 4 miles)
✿ 11-11; 12-10.30 Sun
☎ (019467) 26262
website: www.thescreesinnwasdale.com

Black Sheep Best Bitter; Worthington's Bitter; Yates Bitter; guest beers 🅗

The Screes is one of two first-class sources of real ale in this tiny hamlet, hidden deep in the heart of the Lake District. Close by are Great Gable, Scawfell Pike and brooding Wastwater. Loyal patrons support jazz and folk nights and the annual Wasdale real ale festival hosted by the two pubs. A homely, friendly pub, the bar is on two levels where oddly-shaped beams support an ancient structure. Walkers and family groups are welcome. 🏚Q☕🛏🕩🍴🅑♿🅰♣P⌗

PARSONBY

Horse & Jockey
CA7 2DD (on B5301, S from Aspatria)
🕐 11-11; 10.30-10.30 Sun
☎ (016973) 20482
website: www.horseandjockeypub.co.uk
Jennings Mild, Bitter 🅗

Situated between Aspatria and Cockermouth, this friendly roadside pub is one of the few regular local outlets for Jennings Mild – the landlord's own preferred tipple. The open fireplace, flagged floor and oak beams add to the atmosphere, as do the fascinating collection of artefacts on a porcine theme, the wall mirrors and the aquarium. An unusual gallery of pictures drawn by customers' children is a feature which visitors are invited to add to. The food is largely home-made.
🏚☕🕩🅰♣P

PENRITH

Gloucester Arms
Great Dockray, CA11 7DE
🕐 11-11; 12-10.30 Sun
☎ (01768) 863745
Beer range varies 🅗

16th-century listed building, boasting several original features. King Richard III is known to have stayed here during his incursions into Cumbria. Nowadays a lively town-centre pub, with a wood-panelled main bar, a pool room at the rear, and rooms available for functions or meetings, it usually has at least two real ales on tap. For further variety, call at the Miners Arms, a free house on Southend Road.
🏚☕🕩⇌♣P

Lowther Arms
3 Queen Street, CA11 7XD
🕐 11-3, 6-11; 11.30-2.30, 6-10.30 Sun
☎ (01768) 862792
Courage Directors; Fuller's London Pride; Theakston Best Bitter; guest beers 🅗

Built in 1662 as a coaching inn and recently sympathetically extended, the interior has a split-level lounge and drinking area with wood and stone floors. The decor, along with the open fire, gives a cosy olde-worlde feel. An ever-changing range of guest beers and excellent food are on offer here. The pub is a past winner of the Penrith in Bloom competition for their floral hanging baskets, and CAMRA Pub of the Season, summer 2003. 🏚🕩

RAVENSTONEDALE

King's Head Hotel ✓
CA17 4NH (signed from A685)

🕐 11-11; 12-10.30 Sun
☎ (015396) 23284
Black Sheep Best Bitter; guest beers 🅗

Originally four cottages, this long, 16th-century inn once housed the local court. There is a snug and a dining room to the left (both no-smoking); the bar area to the right has a games/family room down a small step. Up to four guest beers are usually sourced from micro-breweries. Note the vast collection of over 200 water jugs, arranged on shelves and hanging from the beams. Reputedly haunted, it is worth the short detour from the A685. 🏚☕🛏🕩🅰♣●P⌗

ROSTHWAITE

Scafell Hotel
CA12 5XB (S on B5289 from Keswick)
🕐 11-11; 12-10.30 Sun
☎ (017687) 77208 website: www.scafell.co.uk
Theakston Best Bitter, XB, Old Peculier 🅗

Situated in the jaws of Borrowdale, this hotel has been in the same capable hands for many years. Even the barman has been there longer than most people can recall! There is a balcony where drinkers can sit, near an icy stream of rushing crystal-clear water. This is the very heart of the Lake District, and the rainfall levels from Keswick to Borrowdale increase dramatically up the valley, to Seathwaite – the wettest place in England. A great place for walking, climbing or just taking photographs.
🏚⇥☕🛏🕩🅑♿🅰♣P

ST BEES

Queen's Hotel
Main Street, CA27 0DE
🕐 12-3, 5.30-11; 12-3, 7-10.30 Sun
☎ (01946) 822287
website: www.queenshotel-stbees.com
Jennings Bitter, Cumberland Ale; Yates Bitter 🅗

17th-century pub and hotel in the middle of the village. An extensive menu of mainly traditional fare includes Cumberland sausage and Waberthwaite ham. The guest beer is likely to be from the Jennings range. The village, home to a medieval priory and a 400-year-old public school, is close to the western fells and stands at the start of the Coast-to-Coast walk (St Bees to Robin Hood's Bay). Parking is limited.
🏚Q☕🛏🕩🅑♿🅰⇌P⌗

SANTON BRIDGE

Bridge Inn ✓
CA19 1UX
(from A595, turn E at Holmbrook, follow signs)
🕐 11-11; 11-10.30 Sun
☎ (019467) 26221
Jennings Bitter, Cumberland Ale, Cocker Hoop, Sneck Lifter; guest beer 🅗

The Bridge Inn was once a modest coach halt, but is now a well-situated inn, offering good food and accommodation. It is the home of 'the biggest liar' competition, held each November. The bar has a yesteryear feel with oak beams and comfortable seating in alcoves. Surrounded by excellent walking and climbing areas, the ascent to Scafell Pike is within easy reach. Licensed for civil marriage ceremonies, it also caters for private functions.
🏚Q☕🛏🕩🅰P

SCOTBY

Royal Oak
47 Scotby Village, CA4 8EP
(1 mile S of A69, 3 miles E of Carlisle)
☼ 11-3, 5-11; 12-10.30 Sun
☎ (01228) 513463
Theakston Best Bitter, Hesket Newmarket Skiddaw Special Bitter Ⓗ
One and a half miles from the M6 (junction 43) and three miles from the city centre, this is the nearest real ale village pub to Carlisle. With a partially flagged floor and exposed stone chimney breasts, a convivial atmosphere is enhanced by the layout: two cosy seating areas either side of the entrance. It is well supported by locals, but also has a healthy dining custom, attracted by the quality of the food. ⊛◑ᗺ♣

SHAP

Greyhound Hotel
Main Street, CA10 3PW
☼ 11-11; 12-10.30 Sun
☎ (01931) 716474
Greene King Old Speckled Hen; Jennings Bitter, Cumberland Ale; Young's Special; guest beer Ⓗ
Large, former coaching inn, built in 1684. A rare example of a working revolving door leads into a spacious bar area with a games section. There are separate dining and function rooms. Bunk house accommodation is available – handy for those following the Coast-to-Coast walk on a budget. The hotel is a good base for the far eastern Lakeland Fells and the Eden Valley.
♨⊛⇆◑♣P

SILLOTH

Golf Hotel
Criffel Street, CA7 4AB (opp. green)
☼ 11-11; 12-10.30 Sun
☎ (016973) 31438 website: www.golfhotelsilloth.co.uk
Derwent Carlisle State Bitter; guest beers
(summer) Ⓗ
Opened in 1865, this family-run hotel overlooks a green and the Solway Firth. The comfortable, spacious lounge has a small bar in one corner. The rooms display pictures of old Silloth, and are mobile phone-free zones. The hotel is used by various groups as a meeting place. Occasional guest beers, in the summer, are from the local Derwent Brewery.
Q⇆◑Å♣

STAVELEY

Eagle & Child
Kendal Road, LA8 9LP
☼ 11-11; 12-10.30 Sun
☎ (01539) 821320 website: www.eaglechildinn.co.uk
Black Sheep Best Bitter; Coniston Bluebird; guest beers Ⓗ
The bar counter is at one end of the U-shaped ground floor. This memorabilia-filled pub always stocks a beer from Yates and supports other local micro-breweries. The function room upstairs is decorated as a medieval banqueting hall. There is a garden to the rear and another by the river, across the road. A regular bus service between Kendal and Keswick stops outside the door.
♨⊛⇆◑Å⇌♣P

SWARTHMOOR

Miners Arms
1 Fox Street, LA12 0HY
(on A590, near Ulverston)
☼ 12-3.30, 7-11; 12-3.30, 7-10.30 Sun
☎ (01229) 583941
Barngates Cracker Ale; Thwaites Lancaster Bomber; guest beer Ⓗ
On the main A590, Ulverston–Barrow road. This small building houses a single bar room, large enough to hold a pool table and TV. The walls display newspaper reports charting the highlights of the pub's history, including the day when the men of Barrow walked the eight miles to get here after their home town ran out of beer! Although the garden has only a few tables, it does have a large grassed area. ⊛♣

TALKIN

Blacksmith's Arms
CA8 1LE (3 miles S of Brampton)
☼ 12-3, 6-11; 12-3, 6-10.30 Sun
☎ (016977) 3452
website: www.blacksmithsarmstalkin.co.uk
Black Sheep Best Bitter; Jennings Cumberland Ale; Tetley Bitter Ⓗ
This popular free house attracts locals and many visitors drawn to the area by the natural beauty of the northern Pennines. Nearby are Talkin Tarn Country Park and Brampton Golf Course. Originally a 17th-century smithy, it now has a warm, welcoming atmosphere and a reputation for excellent meals. It comprises a dining room, lounge, bar and garden room – a second (no-smoking) eating area leading to a neat and colourful garden. It was local CAMRA Pub of the Season for spring 2003.
♨Q⊛⇆◑ÅP⊁

TIRRIL

Queen's Head
CA10 2JF
☼ 12-3, 6-11; 12-11 Fri & Sat ; 12-10.30 Sun
☎ (01768) 863219 website: www.queensheadinn.co.uk
Tirril John Bewsher's Best Bitter, Brougham Ale, Old Faithful, 1823, Academy Ale; guest beers Ⓗ
Multi-level, two bar inn which housed the Tirril Brewery – now relocated to nearby Brougham (pronounced Broom) Hall. The house beer names have a local connection. The front bar has a part-flag, part-wood floor and an award-winning fireplace. The back bar houses a juke box and pool table. Good quality meals are served in the no-smoking dining room and in the bars. While in the area, pay a visit to the Jennings pub, the Sun at Pooley Bridge.
♨⊛⇆◑⇌♣P

TROUTBECK

Queen's Head
LA23 1PW (on A592)
☼ 11-11; 12-10.30 Sun
☎ (015394) 32174
website: www.queensheadhotel.com
Boddingtons Bitter; Coniston Bluebird; guest beers Ⓗ
Well-appointed, 17th-century former coaching inn on the old Windermere–Penrith packhorse route. The bar incorporates a four-poster bed frame from Appleby Castle. The guest beers

include one from the Jennings range and usually one from another Cumbrian micro. Noted for its high quality meals served in the bar area or the several dining rooms (some no-smoking), evening booking is recommended – essential in summer. Admire the fine fell and valley views from the patio.
🏨⌾🍴◧◖⟐♿♠P✠

ULVERSTON

Farmer's Arms
Market Place, LA12 7BA
✪ 11-11; 11-10.30 Sun
☎ (01229) 584469
website: www.farmersrestaurant-thelakes.co.uk
Theakston Best Bitter; guest beers Ⓗ
Popular town-centre pub overlooking the market (Thu & Sat) with an extensive dining area at the rear serving good quality, popular meals. The original imposing fireplace in the bar area adds character. Breakfast is available from 10.30am; daily newspapers are provided. Busy at weekends, especially evenings, the guest beers change often, with the emphasis on local brews. Children are welcome until 9pm (if not too busy). A pleasant area at the front allows you to sit outside and watch the world go by.
⌾◖Å≉

Stan Laurel Inn
31 The Ellers, LA12 0AB (off A590)
✪ 7-11; 7-10.30 Sun
☎ (01229) 582814
Tetley Dark Mild, Bitter; guest beers Ⓗ
Situated close to the centre of Ulverston (Stan Laurel's birthplace), the Stan is sufficiently away from the boisterous weekend pub circuit, to allow a conversational environment. Serving two guest beers, the main beamed bar area is decorated with an unobtrusive display of Laurel and Hardy memorabilia. Pool, darts, TV and a juke box are in an adjacent room, popular with darts and quiz teams, while a third room can accommodate groups for meetings.
◧≉♣P

WASDALE HEAD

Wasdale Head Inn
CA20 1EX (E off A595 at Gosforth, follow signs for approx 9 miles) OS187087
✪ 11-11; 12-10.30 Sun
☎ (019467) 26229 website: www.wasdale.com
Great Gable Great Gable, Wasd'ale, Scawfell, Yewbarrow, seasonal beers; guest beers Ⓗ
Situated nine miles from Gosforth, off the A595, this world-famous inn is surrounded by England's tallest mountains. The area was the birthplace of climbing, but walkers enjoy it, too. A good choice of ales is supplied by the Great Gable Brewery which is located next to the inn. Excellent home-cooking uses produce from local farms. A variety of accommodation is available, from camping to en-suite rooms. The pub is also famous for 'the World's Biggest Liar' – former landlord, Will Ritson, huntsman and raconteur.
Q🛏⌾◧◖⟐Å♣P✠⎕

WESTNEWTON

Swan Inn
CA7 3PQ (N on B5301 from Aspatria)
✪ 12-3 Sat (and summer Tue-Fri), 6-11; 12-3, 7-10.30 Sun
☎ (016793) 20627
website: www.theswaninncumbria.co.uk
Jennings Cumberland Ale; Yates Fever Pitch Ⓗ
Friendly, traditional village pub that is at the thriving heart of the community. Westnewton is a charming village between the northern fells and the Solway. It is also the home of Yates Brewery. Guest accommodation is available – the bedrooms are in the process of being refurbished as we go to press. Food is served in the bar or restaurant, which has a no-smoking section. A fun quiz is held every Sunday evening.
🏨Q⌾🍴◧◖♣

WHITEHAVEN

Welsh Arms
Tangier Street, CA28 7UZ
✪ 11-11 (1am Fri & Sat); 12-10.30 Sun
☎ (01946) 66288
Robinson's Old Stockport, Hartleys XB, seasonal beer Ⓗ
A friendly town-centre pub, its single room was created from original premises and the next door building. Look out for the ring in the beam over the original cellar drop. The pub is a popular venue for watching football and rugby league matches on satellite TV. A fourth beer is stocked (on a rotating basis).
♿≉

WINTON

Bay Horse
CA17 4HS (signed off A685)
✪ 12-4 Sat & summer, 6.30-11; 12-4, 6.30-10.30 Sun
☎ (017683) 71451
Black Sheep Best Bitter; Theakston Cool Cask; guest beer Ⓗ
Unpretentious local by the village green. The flagged bar area has a dining section beyond and a games room up a step to the rear. Opening hours and guest beer availability may be restricted in winter, but a warm welcome is always assured. It is well worth the minor detour off the A685 and is handily placed 'twixt the Lake District and the Pennines. 🏨Q⌾🍴◧◖⟐♣P

WORKINGTON

George IV (Minnie's)
Stanley Street, CA14 2JD
✪ 11-3, 7-11; 12-3, 7-10.30 Sun
☎ (01900) 602266
Jennings Bitter Ⓗ
Affectionately known locally as 'Minnie's' after the landlady, who is reputed to be England's oldest and longest serving, this very homely end of terrace pub is located in one of the oldest parts of Workington. It is a gem, hidden away from the town centre, but well worth a visit. A short walk from the railway station, it is also close to the port of Workington and the town's rugby league, football and speedway stadia. 🏨≉

Support our historic pubs

This new pamphlet is vital for all beer drinkers who cherish
Britain's unique treasure-trove of historic pubs.
The pamphlet gives far more detail, including brief
descriptions and addresses, than is possible in the
Good Beer Guide, and is illustrated throughout, plus maps.
Edited by David Gamston, it costs £3.50 including postage.

The pamphlet is available from CAMRA, 230 Hatfield Road,
St Albans, Herts, AL1 4LW; cheques or postal orders made out to 'CAMRA'.
To order by Access or Visa, phone 01727 867201 between 9am and 5pm,
Monday to Friday (answerphone outside office hours).
Allow 28 days for delivery.

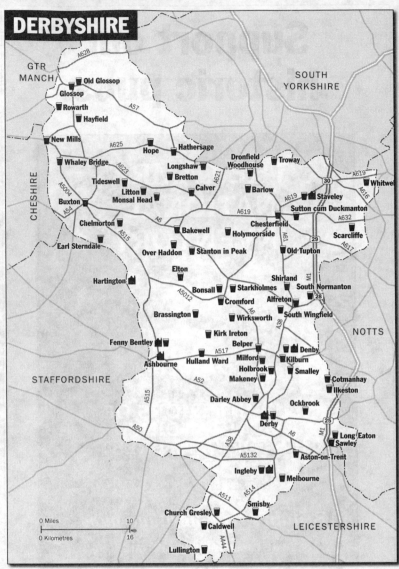

DERBYSHIRE

ALFRETON

Victoria Inn
80 Nottingham Road, DE55 7EL
(on B600)
⊕ 1 (12 Sat)-11; 12-10.30 Sun
☎ (01773) 520156
Taylor Landlord; guest beers Ⓗ
Extensively refurbished, busy but friendly
two-roomed local served by a central bar.
The lounge features an illuminated
aquarium, while pump clips of previously
featured beers are displayed on beams in
the public bar, which has a pool table
and Sky TV. Guest beers change regularly
and showcase local micro-breweries; a
summer beer festival is held. The outdoor
terrace houses long alley skittles. A
limited snack menu is available. Parking
is difficult; the town centre is nearby.
⊛Ⓠⓐ≒♠

ASTON-ON-TRENT

Malt Shovel
16 The Green, DE72 2AA (off Derby Rd)
⊕ 11.30-11; 12-10.30 Sun
☎ (01332) 792256
**Draught Bass; Fuller's London Pride; Marston's
Pedigree; Wells Bombardier; guest beers** Ⓗ
The brewer's Tudor exterior marks this as a
latecomer among the hand-made bricks of
surrounding buildings. It has two rooms,
plus a restaurant – an extension of the
original lounge. The bar retains its unspoilt
inter-war oak-panelled decor, while the
quieter lounge is decked out with copper,
brass and horse tack. A reference library
provides reading matter. Guest beers vary
between regionals and micro-breweries'
products, with a house beer brewed by
Wyre Piddle. Regular buses run from Derby
(No. 73). ▲ⓆⓈⓄⓓⓆⓖⓐ♠P

DERBYSHIRE

BAKEWELL

Peacock Hotel
Bridge Street, DE45 1DS
✪ 11-11; 12-10.30 Sun
☎ (01629) 812994
Tetley Bitter; guest beers Ⓗ

Cosy, stone inn dating back to 1819, situated in this busy Peak District market town. The pub, which can be very busy on market day (Mon), has five en-suite bedrooms in what were originally the inn's stables. The Peacock hosts occasional live music on Saturday and Sunday evenings. If visiting Bakewell, remember to try the famous Bakewell pudding, 'invented' by complete accident at the nearby Rutland Hotel. ❀⇆◑▶ P

BARLOW

Hare & Hounds Inn
32 Commonside Road, S18 7SJ (off B6051)
✪ 11-11; 12-10.30 Sun
☎ (0114) 289 0464
Draught Bass; Stones Bitter Ⓗ

Standing proud, and affording superb views across the picturesque Cordwell Valley, this much-expanded pub remains at the heart of the local rural community. Fine ales and the hearty banter of conversation are the key elements here. The pub resists the temptation to serve cooked food – why bother when fresh local produce is available in such quantities? Cheese, eggs, gammon, vegetables and pickles are all available to take home. ⋈Q⏂❀♣ P

BELPER

Cross Keys ✆
Market Place, DE56 1FZ
✪ 12-11; 12-10.30 Sun
☎ (01773) 599191
Draught Bass; Bateman Mild, XB, XXXB; guest beer Ⓗ

This early 19th-century pub was formerly used as accommodation for visiting theatre troupes, and as a meeting place for Druids and Oddfellows; it has also witnessed at least one murder! Two-roomed, with a central bar, the pub has enjoyed a renaissance since being bought by Bateman's, all of whose beers have proved popular locally; a summer beer festival is held. A real fire warms the lounge. Lunchtime and evening snacks are available; bar billiards and shove-ha'penny are played. ⋈Q❀⏚♣♣

Queen's Head
29 Chesterfield Road, DE56 1FF (on Ripley bus route)
✪ 4 (12 Fri & Sat)-11; 12-10.30 Sun
☎ (01773) 825525 website: www.thequeenshead.net
Caledonian Deuchars IPA; Tetley Bitter, Burton Ale; guest beers Ⓗ

Built during the Victorian era, this popular roadside inn comprises three rooms with a central bar, an upstairs function room, and a pleasant patio area, providing panoramic views over the town and countryside. The public bar has a real fire and old photographs of Belper. Reputedly haunted, the pub hosts regular themed beer festivals, quizzes and entertainment, usually blues or folk, at the weekends. It is a short walk uphill from the market place. ⋈Q❀⏚≈♣♠

Thorn Tree Inn
21 Chesterfield Road, DE56 1FF
(on Ripley bus route)
✪ 5 (4 Fri & Sat)-11; 12-10.30 Sun
☎ (01773) 823360
Draught Bass; guest beers Ⓗ

Roadside inn, situated at the junction of two roads, just below the Queen's Head, a 10-minute walk uphill from the market place. This split-level pub has two distinct drinking areas, with separate entrances, based around a central bar. After being closed and boarded up, this former keg pub was reopened and rescued from neglect in the summer of 2000, and is now a thriving local, showcasing interesting guest beers. Q⏚

BONSALL

Barley Mow
The Dale, DE4 2AY (off the Via Gellia, A5012)
✪ 6 (12 Sat)-11; 12-10.30 Sun
☎ (01629) 825685
website: www.barleymowbonsall.co.uk
Greene King Abbot; Whim Hartington Bitter; guest beer (summer) Ⓗ /Ⓖ

Situated on the ancient route to Winster, the pub is best approached by turning left at the gothic fountain before you enter the village centre. This friendly local makes incredible use of limited space, pushed as it is into the rocks from which the cellar was hewn in the 17th century. Good food is served evenings and weekends. The pub is renowned for guided UFO-spotters' walks (leaflets available), regular live music and the world championship hen races in August. ⋈❀◑▶♣ P

BRASSINGTON

Olde Gate Inne ☆
Well Street, DE4 4HJ (off A5023)
✪ 12-2.30, 6-11; 12-3, 7-10.30 Sun
☎ (01629) 540448
Marston's Pedigree, seasonal beers Ⓗ

Family-run, ivy-clad gem, built in 1616, now Grade II listed and reputedly haunted. Oak beams feature throughout, with gleaming copper utensils hanging around three open fireplaces. The main bar boasts pewter jugs and a black-leaded range, while a pipe rack in the snug dates from the 17th century. An extensive menu includes home-cooked dishes and game in season (no food Mon eve). No children under 10 are admitted. Boules is played here. The tourist attraction of Carsington Water is nearby. ⋈Q❀◑♿Ⓐ♣ P✗

BRETTON

Barrel Inn
S32 5QD OS201779

INDEPENDENT BREWERIES

Brunswick Derby
Haywood Ashbourne
Leadmill Denby
Leatherbritches Fenny Bentley
John Thompson Ingleby
Townes Staveley
Whim Hartington

93

☼ 11-3, 6-11; 11-11 Sat; 12-10.30 Sun
☎ (01433) 630856
Greene King Abbot; Marston's Pedigree; Tetley Bitter; guest beer Ⓗ

This inn takes pride in its origins in 1597 but has seen a lot of changes since then, most recently an accommodation block. The bar now serves one large L-shaped room which is decorated with local paintings and photographs. Bretton Edge is narrow at this point and there are extensive views both north and south on a clear day. The main road network does not reach here, but the pub is popular with motorists and as a starting point for various walks.
🏛🐾⊛🚐◖⎒⌖&▲P

Baker's Arms
26 West Road, SK17 6HF
☼ 12-2, 6 (4 Fri; 7 Sat)-11; 12-3, 7-10.30 Sun
☎ (01298) 24404
Greene King Abbot; Tetley Bitter; guest beers Ⓗ

You enter the pub through a porch into a small, two-roomed, friendly local, where an L-shaped bar has only enough room for two staff. With bench seating and small tables in both rooms, there is just enough room to play darts at the rear of the larger room. This very popular local maintains good connections with sporting clubs; note the many trophies on display. It stocks an ever-changing selection of guest beers and bottled foreign beers. ⊛▲⇌P

George
The Square, SK17 6AZ
☼ 11-11; 12-10.30 Sun
☎ (01298) 24711
Beer range varies Ⓗ

This large, busy pub in the centre of Buxton is the latest to start serving real ale and has gone from strength to strength. It now has a range of up to six ever-changing beers on at a time. The pub gets very lively in the evening, with varied live music, so a visit simply to sample the beer range is best done in the afternoon or early evening. Good quality, home-cooked food is served all day and well worth trying. There is a small patio at the front of the pub. 🏛⊛◖▲⇌♣

Ramsey's Bar
1 Burlington Road, SK17 9AS
☼ 12-2, 6-11; 12-3, 6-10.30 Sun
☎ (01298) 70481
website: www.buckinghamhotel.co.uk
Taylor Landlord; Wells Bombardier; guest beers Ⓗ

This large public bar and restaurant form part of the Buckingham Hotel. The name originates from the fact that No. 1 Burlington Road was the home and studio of local artist, George Ramsey in the early part of the last century; his engraved signature is still to be found on one of the windows. With up to six beers regularly on tap, this bar is becoming very popular. A wide choice of food ranges from simple bar meals to a full-blown carvery. ⊛🚐◖▲⇌P

Royal Oak
Main Street, DE12 6RR
☼ 11-11; 12-10.30 Sun
☎ (01283) 761486

Marston's Pedigree; guest beer Ⓗ

18th-century, beamed free house and genuine community pub, attracting clientele from beyond the small village. Cyclists and ramblers are welcome. A small, narrow public bar has stairs leading up to a smart, split-level lounge with log fire at the rear. Part of the building used to be a bakery, and the garden was once a burial ground for plague victims! Limited parking at the side is supplemented by a field beyond in dry weather. Local CAMRA Country Pub of the Year 2002. 🏛⊛⎒▲P

Bridge Inn
S32 3XA (on A623)
☼ 11.30-3 (3.30 Sat), 5.30-11; 12-3.30, 7-10.30 Sun
☎ (01433) 630415
Hardys & Hansons Bitter, seasonal beers Ⓗ

This sturdy stone inn has a strong local trade but also welcomes visitors. It has two lounge bars; one, retaining the atmosphere of a public bar, sports a collection of local guide books. The other has a display of antique fire-fighting equipment. The garden fronts on to the River Derwent and faces the impressive Calver Mill, recently converted into apartments. The pub has been 11 consecutive years in this Guide. No evening meals are served Monday or winter Sunday.
🏛Q⊛◖&▲P⌿⎕

Church Inn
Main Street, SK17 9SL
☼ 12-3.30, 7-11 (12-11 summer Sat); 12-3.30, 7-10.30 (12-10.30 summer) Sun
☎ (01298) 85319
Adnams Bitter; Marston's Bitter, Pedigree; guest beer (summer) Ⓗ

Set in beautiful surroundings, opposite the local church, this traditional village pub caters for both locals and walkers alike. Even though the main room is laid out with dining tables and good home-cooked food is on offer, a cosy atmosphere is still maintained with a low ceiling and real fire, and the pub is run primarily as a local serving good quality beer. A quiz is held on Monday evening. Parking is available on the dead-end road outside the pub. 🏛Q⊛◖♣

Derby Tup
387 Sheffield Road, Whittington Moor, S41 8LS
☼ 11.30-3, 5-11; 11.30-11 Wed-Sat; 12-4, 7-10.30 Sun
☎ (01246) 454316
Greene King Abbot; Kelham Island Easy Rider; Theakston Old Peculier; Whim Hartington Bitter; guest beer Ⓗ

The Tup was already a well-established mecca for real ale drinkers before it was purchased in 1990 by Tynemill. A selection of bottled continental beers and malt whiskies supplement the choice of four regular beers and six guest ales. Home-made food, prepared from local produce is available at lunchtime; a set menu is served weekday evenings. A Sunday quiz and occasional live music complete the welcome at this hostelry. Q◖♣⚫⌿

Peacock

412 Chatsworth Road, Brampton, S40 3BQ

☼ 12-3.30, 5.30-11; 12-4, 7-10.30 Sun

☎ (01246) 275115

Black Sheep Best Bitter; Caledonian Deuchars IPA; Stones Bitter; Tetley Bitter; Wells Bombardier; guest beers ⒣

Friendly, two-roomed pub with exposed beams and real fires. A central bar offers a good selection of real ales and ever-changing guest beers. To the rear is a large garden and seating area, ideal for families in summer. Entertainment includes darts and a quiz night. The pub is part of the 'Brampton Mile' – a renowned crawl of a dozen or so pubs on the outskirts of Chesterfield. Discerning drinkers will include the Peacock as part of the mile.
㎃Q⊛⛾♣

Royal Oak

43 Chatsworth Road, Brampton, S40 2AH

☼ 11.30-11; 12-10.30 Sun

☎ (01246) 277854

Theakston Best Bitter, XB; Whim Arbor Light, Hartington Bitter; guest beers ⒣

Busy, street-corner local, situated at the start (or end) of the 'Brampton Mile'. Sport, pool and horse racing are all popular here. It can get very busy, particularly on live music nights, when many customers come for the entertainment. Try it at midday when it attracts a quieter, more discerning clientele. It hosts the popular Oakstock on bank holidays, featuring local bands.
㎃Q⛞P

Rutland

23 Stephensons Place, S40 1XL

☼ 11-11; 12-10.30 Sun

☎ (01246) 205857

Boddingtons Bitter; ⒣ **Caledonian Deuchars IPA;** ⒢/⒣ **Castle Eden Ale; Greene King Abbot; Taylor Landlord;** ⒣ **guest beers** ⒣/⒢

Next to the famous crooked spire, part of this pub was the former vicarage to St Mary's and All Saints Church. A wide range of guest beers can be enjoyed in this wood-panelled beer emporium. Watch out for regular mini beer festivals. The friendly atmosphere is completed by the provision of real fires in winter and a no-smoking area all year round. Good value food is served all day. ㎃⊛◖▷≠♣●⤨

Victoria

21-23 Victoria Street West, Brampton, S40 3QY (off A619 near Safeway roundabout)

☼ 12-4, 7-11; 12-4, 7-10.30 Sun

☎ (01246) 273832

Adnams Bitter; Caledonian Deuchars IPA; Stones Bitter; Tetley Mild, Bitter; guest beers ⒣

Tucked away, off the main Chatsworth road, this traditional, two-roomed back-street pub is well worth seeking out. Favoured by many locals this community pub has plenty of charm and character. It usually stocks two guest beers. A selection of local produce – eggs, cheese and pickled onions, etc – is usually for sale here.
Q⊛⛾♣P

Winsick Arms

Mansfield Road, Hasland, S41 0JH

☼ 12-11; 12-10.30 Sun

☎ (01246) 206847

John Smith's Bitter; Tetley Bitter; Theakston Best Bitter; guest beers ⒣

This impressive white-walled hostelry resembles an alpine hotel with its decorative shutters. A cosy atmosphere is created by the stone archways and wooden beams and rafters. An excellent range of five guest ales complements the great value, home-cooked meals made from local produce. A conservatory leads into the large beer garden with its child-friendly, well-equipped play area. Children can mingle with free-ranging pets, such as chickens, rabbits and quails. Musical events are arranged outdoors.
⊛◖▷⛾P⤨

Rising Sun

77 Church Street, DE11 9NR

☼ 11.30 (12 Fri & Sat)-11; 12-10.30 Sun

☎ (01283) 217274

Draught Bass; Marston's Pedigree ⒣

Late 19th-century free house, close to non-league Gresley Rovers football ground. In the L-shaped drinking area, an arch links the busy public bar with the marginally quieter lounge and another small lounge beyond. Special features include an unusual porch, bar tops inlaid with over 6,000 old pennies, and an old red telephone box (with working telephone) in a corner of the public bar. A large meeting/function room upstairs boasts impressive carved oak beams. Limited parking is possible on the forecourt.
㎃⊛⛾♣

Bridge Inn

15 Bridge Street, DE7 8RD

☼ 11-11; 12-10.30 Sun

☎ (0115) 932 2589

Hardys & Hansons Mild, Bitter ⒫

This friendly, traditional, two-roomed pub is well worth seeking out. It stands by the Erewash Canal and is frequented by anglers, boaters and walkers. The bar is popular with locals for pub games. There is also a large, comfortable lounge. The garden has a drinking area right on the canal bank. Occasional live music is staged. Dogs are welcome.
Q⊛⛾♣P⛗

Boat Inn

Scarthin, DE4 3QF (off market place)

☼ 12-3, 6-11; 12-11 Sat; 12-10.30 Sun

☎ (01629) 823282

Marston's Pedigree; guest beers ⒣

Popular free house, originally built to slake the thirsts of Arkwright's millworkers. A cosy atmosphere is created by low, beamed ceilings, bare stone walls, open fires and barrel tables. It hosts regular live music (folk nights Tue) and quizzes, as well as beer festivals in the cellar bar and summer barbecues. A Springhead beer is often stocked and the guests are usually sourced locally (Burton Bridge, Leatherbritches, etc.); all are available in bargain four-pint pitchers. Cider is sold in summer.
㎃⊛◖▷♿▲≠♣●

DARLEY ABBEY

Abbey Inn
Darley Street, DE22 1DX (on riverside)
✪ 11.30-2.30, 6-11; 12-11 Sat; 12-10.30 Sun
☎ (01332) 558297
Samuel Smith OBB Ⓗ
This erstwhile, 15th-century guesthouse is all that remains of the Augustinian Abbey of St Mary De Pratis, the most powerful abbey in Middle England before the Dissolution. Rescued from long neglect in 1978, it won a national award for conversion to its present use. A lower-level bar, with stone-flagged floor and roaring fire, is complemented by an upper level, longer bar, with original church pews, reached by an impressive stone spiral staircase. Darley Park is nearby.
⚲Q✿❀◖⊟♣P

DENBY

Leadmill Old Stables Bar
Park Hall, Park Hall Road, DE5 0PS
(off B6179)
✪ 5 (12 Sat)-11; closed Mon-Thu; 12-10.30 Sun
☎ (01332) 883577
Leadmill Marehay Mild, Saigon, IPA, Curly Blonde, Red River, Derby Festival Stout, Sidewinder, B52, Park Hall Porter; guest beers Ⓗ
Set in the grounds of the imposing Park Hall, this converted stable building now acts as the tap for the Leadmill Brewery, directly opposite. With proper stable door, sawdust-covered floor, low lighting and much brewery memorabilia, the place has real atmosphere. An impressive range of 11 handpumps dispenses all the company's beers, plus a selection of guests. Brewery tours are given by prior arrangement. Easily reached by the No. 92 bus from Derby, the pub opens at the weekend. Q✿♣P

DERBY

Alexandra Hotel
203 Siddals Road, DE1 2QE (near station)
✪ 11-11; 12-3, 7-10.30 Sun
☎ (01332) 293993
Barnsley Bitter; Draught Bass; Castle Rock Nottingham Gold; York Yorkshire Terrier; guest beers Ⓗ
Named after the Danish princess who married the Prince of Wales (later Edward VII) in 1863, the Alex was originally the Midland Coffee House. The end wall once advertised Zacharia Smith's Shardlow Ales, but both sign and brewer have slipped into history. Long a Shipstone's house, it subsequently went to Bateman's and latterly to Tynemill, since when it has been a strong champion of small breweries. Two-roomed, with a central bar, the pub was the birthplace of Derby CAMRA in 1974.
Q✿⚲◖⊟⊞⇋♣●P↯

Babington Arms ◉
11-13 Babington Lane, DE1 1TA
(off St Peter's St)
✪ 11-11; 12-10.30 Sun
☎ (01332) 383647
Courage Directors; Greene King Abbot; Shepherd Neame Spitfire; Theakston Best Bitter; Wyre Piddle seasonal beer; guest beers Ⓗ
The second Wetherspoon's pub in Derby stands in what used to be the grounds of

Babington House, former home of Anthony Babington, who plotted to assassinate Elizabeth I and replace her with Mary, Queen of Scots, which cost him his head. Fronted with a verandah for fairweather drinking, the ample interior extends far back, with a dining area to the rear. It was in the neighbouring Grand Theatre that the first performance of Bram Stoker's Dracula was given in 1924. Q✿❀◖⊟↯

Bishop Blaise
114 Friar Gate, DE1 1EX
✪ 11-midnight; 12-midnight Sun
☎ (01332) 297065
Draught Bass; Burton Bridge Bridge Bitter; Oakham JHB; Taylor Landlord; Whim Hartington IPA; guest beers Ⓗ
Near the town centre on one of Derby's older streets, now a café bar quarter and refurbished in similar ilk, the former Friargate pub still offers a range of real ales. The modern, trendy setting offers an outdoor drinking area and piped music to boot. This Victorian tavern replaced the Sun, a much older timber-framed inn and lies almost opposite the now-defunct church where Dr Samuel Johnson married Tetty Porter in 1735. Car park to rear.
❀◖⊟P

Brunswick Inn
1 Railway Terrace, DE1 2RU
✪ 11-11; 12-10.30 Sun
☎ (01332) 290677
Draught Bass; Brunswick Mild, Triple Hop, Second, Railway Porter, Triple Gold; Everards Tiger; Ⓗ **guest beers** Ⓗ/Ⓖ
Built by the Midland Railway as the centrepiece of the railway village that is now a conservation area, it was closed in 1974 and fell into disrepair. Rescued and restored by the Derbyshire Historic Buildings Trust, it opened as Derby's first multiple real ale house some 14 years later. A purpose-built brewery was added and it rapidly became one of the best known free houses in the country. It was sold to Everards in 2002; thankfully both pub and brewery remain unchanged.
Q➰✿◖⊟⇋●↯

Crompton Tavern
45 Crompton Street, DE1 1NX
✪ 11-11; 12-10.30 Sun
☎ (01332) 733629
Banks's Original; Marston's Pedigree; Taylor Landlord; guest beers Ⓗ
Tucked away in a cul-de-sac off Green Lane and picked out at night by a fringe of fairy lights, the former Queen's Hotel was originally a guest house for visiting thespians at the nearby Grand Theatre. Two front doors open on to different sides of the same U-shaped room, with lower level wings on each side of a central bar, whose walls frequently double as a free gallery for local artists. A pleasant rear garden provides a welcome haven. ⚲❀♣

Falstaff
74 Silver Hill Road, Normanton, DE23 6UJ
✪ 12-11; 12-10.30 Sun
☎ (01332) 342902
Greene King Abbot; Leatherbritches Hairy Helmet; Marston's Pedigree; guest beers Ⓗ
Known locally as The Folly, the Falstaff was

built as a latter-day coaching inn for Pountain, Girardot & Forman before the surrounding area was built up, closing it in. Formerly owned by Allied, it is now free of tie and the best real ale house in Normanton. The curved bar is flanked on one side by a small lounge, with a real fire in winter, and on the other by a games room with occasional entertainment. Not posh, but a real local. There are plans to reopen the brewery. 🏚Q🌳🍴♣

Flowerpot
23-25 King Street, DE1 3DZ
🕐 11-11; 12-10.30 Sun
☎ (01332) 204955
Draught Bass; Ⓖ **Marston's Pedigree; Whim Arbor Light;** Ⓗ **guest beers** Ⓗ/Ⓖ

Just up from the cathedral and round Clockhouse Corner, this is one of the pubs that spearheaded Derby's free trade expansion in the 1990s to become a virtual showcase for small breweries. Much expanded from its original premises, it reaches far back from the small, roadside frontage and divides into several interlinking rooms, the furthest provides the stage for a lively ongoing gig scene and another houses a glass cellar wall, revealing row upon row of stillaged firkins.
Q🌳🍴🔥🚻⌖♣

Furnace Inn
9 Duke Street, DE1 3BX
(upriver from market place)
🕐 11-11; 12-3, 6.30-10.30 Sun
☎ (01332) 331563
Hardys & Hansons Mild, Bitter, Olde Trip, seasonal beers Ⓗ

Just off St Mary's Bridge with its 15th-century chapel, the pub stands on the west bank of the Derwent at the edge of Darley Park. The name preserves its close connection with Handyside's Britannia foundry of which it was once part. Although opened out, it retains distinct drinking areas around a central bar. Scenes of bygone Derby adorn the walls and bartop. A bustling community local, it provides a handy watering-hole for riverside cyclists and walkers. 🌳♿♣P

Olde Dolphin Inne ☆
5a Queen Street, DE1 3DL
🕐 10.30-11; 12-10.30 Sun
☎ (01332) 267711
Adnams Bitter; Draught Bass; Black Sheep Best Bitter; Cains Mild; Caledonian Deuchars IPA; Greene King Abbot; Marston's Pedigree; guest beers Ⓗ

Standing below the great gothic tower of the cathedral, the timber-framed Dolphin is Derby's oldest surviving pub, although much restored. The beamed interior divides into bar, upper and lower lounges, snug and an upstairs steak bar, each with its own character. Reputedly haunted, regular themed evenings are supplemented by an annual beer festival in July, which spreads out on to a splendid, raised patio. Local CAMRA's City Pub of the Year in 2002, it is a gem, not to be missed. 🏚Q🌳🍴🚻⌖P

Old Silk Mill
19 Full Street, DE1 3AF (near cathedral)
🕐 10.30-11; 12-10.30 Sun
☎ (01332) 369748
Draught Bass; Caledonian Deuchars IPA; Fuller's

London Pride; guest beers Ⓗ

The Old Silk Mill selling Nottingham Rock Ales was demolished in 1924, its namesake being built four years later. Distinguished by an elegant stone front and unique mural depicting the historic silk trades lock-out of 1833, the present pub attracts custom as much for its food as for its beer. The Silk Mill itself, housing the industrial museum, is close by, while on the green opposite stands an equestrian statue of Bonnie Prince Charlie, where his incursion into England ended. 🌳🍴♿

Rowditch Inn
246 Uttoxeter New Road, DE22 3LL
(1 mile from centre)
🕐 12-2 (not Mon-Thu), 7-11; 12-2, 7-10.30 Sun
☎ (01332) 343123
Hardys & Hansons Bitter, Olde Trip, seasonal beers; Marston's Pedigree; guest beers Ⓗ

The pub stands on the borough's ancient boundary, once marked by a defensive dyke or rough ditch (whence Rowditch). A plain-fronted, but warmly welcoming roadside pub, its unexpectedly deep interior divides into two drinking areas and a small snug. A downstairs cellar bar opens occasionally, and the long rear garden is a positive haven in warmer weather. Regular beer festivals supplement an ever-changing range of guest ales, as is borne out by a large collection of pump clips around the bar area. 🏚🌳♣✂

Smithfield
Meadow Road, DE1 2BH
(downriver from market place)
🕐 11-11; 12-10.30 Sun
☎ (01332) 370429
Draught Bass; Oakham JHB, Bishops Farewell; Phoenix Arizona; Whim Hartington IPA; guest beers Ⓗ

Bow-fronted riverside pub built to serve the cattle market, which has since moved to a new site, leaving the Smithy in a bit of a backwater. A long, basic bar is flanked on one side by a games/TV room that admits children until 9pm, and on the other by a cosy lounge with stone fireplace and old settles, overlooking a pleasant riverside patio. Exceptional beer has helped earn the pub local CAMRA's Pub of the Year award for 2003. 🏚🛏🌳🍴🚻♣P

Station Inn
12 Midland Road, DE1 2SN
🕐 11.30-2.30, 5 (7 Sat)-11; 11.30-11 Fri; 12-3, 7-10.30 Sun
☎ (01332) 608014
Draught Bass; Ⓖ **Worthington's 1744** Ⓗ

This modest pub, but for its elaborate frontage and stained glass, was named after the Midland Railway's classical station nearby, needlessly swept away in 1983 to be replaced by the present uninspiring edifice. A traditional bar, with panelled counter, cast iron footrail and quarry-tiled floor, is flanked by a games area to the right and a large lounge to the rear that acts as dining area and function room. Many cellar awards attest to the skills of the licensee.
🍴🚻♿🚃♣🍽

Jolly Farmer
Pentland Road, S18 8ZQ
🕐 12-11; 12-10.30 Sun

☎ (01246) 418018

Black Sheep Best Bitter; Greene King Ruddles County; Tetley Bitter; guest beers Ⓗ

This pub was built in 1976 as part of a large private housing development. The original owners, former Nottingham brewers, Shipstone's, were taken over by Greenalls who turned it into an ale house with real ale to the fore, notably with casks on stillage behind a glass panel. Despite many changes of ownership since then, the pub's character remains much the same and it attracts a mixed clientele, mostly from the immediate area. Quizzes and games take place regularly. No evening meals Sunday.
❀◑&♣

EARL STERNDALE

Quiet Woman
SK17 0BU (off B5053)
⊕ 12-3.30, 7-11; 12-3.30, 7-10.30 Sun
☎ (01298) 83211
Mansfield Dark Mild; Marston's Bitter, Pedigree; guest beers Ⓗ

This unspoilt local, at the heart of the Peak District National Park, stands opposite the village church and green. The cosy, beamed room has a real fire and a small bar; one of the beams displays a collection of original Marston's pump clips of long-lost beers. Pub games are played, with dominoes tables in the main bar and a games room. Local cheeses, fresh eggs and traditional pork pies can be purchased from the bar. Walkers are welcome. Live folk music is performed every Sunday. ♒Q❦❀◑A♣P

ELTON

Duke of York ☆
Main Street, DE4 2BW
⊕ 8.30-11; 12-3, 8.30-10.30 Sun
☎ (01629) 650367
Adnams Bitter; Mansfield Cask Ale Ⓗ

In the same hands for the past 36 years, this is a basic, unspoilt village local, worthy of its place in CAMRA's National Inventory. Real fires blaze in all three rooms which, with their original decor, make this a pub of great character. No food, no frills – just good beer and company. Note the limited opening hours.
♒Q⊟P⊟

FENNY BENTLEY

Bentley Brook Inn
DE6 1LF (on A515)
⊕ 11-11; 12-10.30 Sun
☎ (01335) 350278
website: www.bentleybrookinn.co.uk
Leatherbritches Goldings, Ashbourne Ale, Hairy Helmet, Bespoke; Marston's Pedigree; guest beers Ⓗ

Just inside the National Park and set back off the main road, this imposing country house hotel is home to Leatherbritches Brewery, an award-winning restaurant, a smokehouse, a baker's and sausage shop, a restored Victorian kitchen garden and a skittle alley. Extensive grounds, with camping facilities, host the annual spring bank holiday beer and music festival in a large marquee, featuring over 100 beers. With fine views and superb facilities it is the ideal base for Derbyshire's major tourist attractions. ♒❦❀☒◑&A♣●P⊬

GLOSSOP

Friendship
3 Arundel Street, SK13 7AB
⊕ 4 (3 Fri; 12 Sat)-11; 12-3, 7-10.30 Sun
☎ (01457) 855277 website: www.thefriendship.co.uk
Robinson's Hatter, Best Bitter, seasonal beers Ⓗ

Street-corner local, run by a committed licensee whose sympathetic refurbishments have kept the pub's character. A semi-circular bar and wood-panelled interior are features of the open-plan lounge. The back tap room is served by a hatch. It is used by fans of the nearby Glossop cricket and football clubs. Over 30 malt whiskies are sold. Children are welcome until 8pm. Note the impressive lamp over the front door, circa 1900. The secluded garden is reached via the pub. ♒❦❀♣♠

Old Gloveworks
Riverside Mill, George Street, SK13 8AY
⊕ 12-11 (may close early Mon-Wed); 12-10.30 Sun
☎ (01457) 858432
website: www.theglovewordsglossop.com
Beer range varies Ⓗ

This converted mill, previously a wine bar, offering six varying guest beers, is completely free of tie. It boasts a roof terrace and riverside patio, affording views over Glossop brook. A licence extension until midnight applies on Friday and Saturday (admittance before 10.45pm). A discretionary age limit (over 25) is imposed by the landlord. Entertainment includes local bands (Thu), discos (Fri and Sat) and cabaret (from 4pm Sun). Weekday lunches are served. ❀◑⇌P

HATHERSAGE

Little John Hotel
Station Road, S32 1DD
⊕ 12-11; 12-10.30 Sun
☎ (01433) 650225
Beer range varies Ⓗ

Popular free house serving four regularly-changing guest beers in four seating areas: a lounge, a bar with bar billiards and pool, a spacious family area and a function room, all recently refurbished. Generous portions of home-cooked food are prepared using fresh produce; meals are served all day Saturday and Sunday. Visitors to the Peak District National Park are accommodated in the hotel rooms and holiday cottages. Baby changing facilities are available and dogs are welcome. A real cider is sold March–December.
❦❀☒◑⊟&A⇌♣●P⊬

HAYFIELD

Kinder Lodge
10 New Mills Road, High Peak, SK22 2JG
⊕ 12-11; 12-10.30 Sun
☎ (01663) 743613
Banks's Bitter; Black Sheep Best Bitter; Taylor Best Bitter; guest beers Ⓗ

Stone pub, entirely in keeping with its surrounding environment, it stands close to the village centre, near the bypass. Formerly known as the Railway, its open-plan interior allows for a separate games area. Popular, and well used by locals and visitors alike, it is an example of a good village local doing what it should do well. ❀☒◑♣

Royal Hotel
Market Street, SK22 2EP

✪ 11-3, 6-11; 11-11 Sat; 12-10.30 Sun

☎ (01663) 742721

website: www.royalhotel.hayfield@virgin.net

Marston's Pedigree; Tetley Bitter; guest beers Ⓗ

This imposing stone pub blends well into its surroundings – an attractive Peak District village. This former vicarage stands near the church and cricket ground. The River Sett in front of the pub flows down from Kinder Scout. The traditional interior boasts original oak panels and pews which, aided by real fires, give a pleasant, relaxing atmosphere. A restaurant and a function room complete the facilities.
₩Q☎❀⇔⏻⚅ΔP⅊

HOLBROOK

Wheel Inn
14 Chapel Street, DE56 0TQ

✪ 12-2.30 (Thu & Fri), 6 (5 Fri)-11; 11-11 Sat; 12-10.30 Sun

☎ (01332) 880006

Archers Golden; Ⓖ Courage Directors; Kelham Island Pale Rider; Leatherbritches Hairy Helmet; Marston's Pedigree; Whim Hartington Bitter; guest beers Ⓗ

Warm, 18th-century pub with a brewer's Tudor frontage, but much altered inside. Several interconnected rooms include a restaurant area to the rear, offering a good range of reasonably-priced, home-cooked food (not Sun eve or Mon). The patio and award-winning garden are a joy to behold in summer and form a useful overspill for the regular beer festival held in an outbuilding. A good range of malt whiskies is stocked. Regular buses run from Derby (No. R71). ₩❀⏻

HOLYMOORSIDE

Lamb Inn
16 Loads Road, S42 7EU

✪ 12-3 (not Mon-Fri), 7-11; 12-3, 6-10.30 Sun

☎ (01246) 566167

Everards Home Bitter; guest beers Ⓗ

Cosy and immaculate local in a village close to the Peak District National Park on the edge of Chesterfield. Warmed by a roaring real fire in the bar, this proud holder of numerous local CAMRA awards boasts up to six ever-changing guest ales, showing what can be achieved in a modest-sized pub given the desire and application. A pleasant outdoor drinking area is ideal for summer evenings. This pub opens at lunchtime on bank holiday Mondays. ₩Q❀♣P

HOPE

Cheshire Cheese
Edale Road, S33 6ZF

✪ 12-3, 6-11; 12-11 Sat; 12-4, 6-10.30 Sun

☎ (01433) 620381 website: www.cheshire-cheese.net

Barnsley Bitter; Black Sheep Best Bitter; Whim Hartington Bitter; guest beers Ⓗ

Visitors to the Peak District can try the guest ales supplied by Cottage, Eccleshall and Kelham Island within this 16th-century free house are three seating areas furnished with upholstered chairs and benches; the lower section becomes a restaurant when the excellent meals are being served. A range of wines and malt whiskies are

stocked. Children are welcome, except in the immediate vicinity of the bar. Take care outside; the car park is small and the road narrow. ₩Q❀⇔⏻ΔP⅊

HULLAND WARD

Black Horse Inn ⊘
DE6 3EE (on A517)

✪ 12-2.30, 6-11; 12-3, 7-10.30 Sun

☎ (01335) 370206

Harviestoun Bitter & Twisted; guest beers Ⓗ

This traditional, 300-year-old country inn stands in an elevated village, in some of the most picturesque country outside the Peak, close to Carsington Water. Its split-level, multi-roomed drinking area, with low, beamed ceilings and quarry-tiled floors, is served by a central bar, offering rotating guest ales. An extensive bar menu is complemented by a popular Sunday carvery in the restaurant. Some guest rooms boast four-poster beds. ❀⇔⏻♣P⅊

ILKESTON

Dewdrop Inn
24 Station Street, Ilkeston Junction, DE7 5TE

✪ 12-2.30 (4 Sat), 7-11; 12-5, 7-10.30 Sun

☎ (0115) 932 9684 website: www.eggpie.com

Draught Bass; Taylor Best Bitter; guest beers Ⓗ

Previous CAMRA East Midlands Pub of the Year (1997) and a winner of several local awards, visitors to this three-roomed local may enjoy up to five real ales and a real cider. The pub is now open on a Saturday lunchtime and accommodation is available to CAMRA members. It is run by a former Oakham Brewery employee (ask him who named the White Dwarf beer); the pub was formerly known as the Middleton.
₩Q☎❀⏻⚅⚅♣●⅊

Spanish Bar
76 South Street, DE7 5AJ

(100 yds from A609/A6007 jct)

✪ 11-11; 12-10.30 Sun

☎ (0115) 930 8666

Mallard Best Bitter; guest beers Ⓗ

Small, bustling, European café-style bar that was converted from a shop three years ago. The bright and cheerful decoration is based on a Spanish theme. A varied, friendly clientele enjoys guest beers from local micro-breweries. This pub is something out of the ordinary from other entries in this area and well worth a visit. ₩

White Cow
Nottingham Road, DE7 5NX (on A6007)

✪ 11-11; 11-10.30 Sun

☎ (0115) 930 4825

Draught Bass; Greene King IPA; Mallard Duckling; Marston's Pedigree; guest beers Ⓗ

Believed to be the only White Cow in England, this traditional two-roomed pub is about a mile from the town centre. Recently extended and refurbished, it now offers two en-suite rooms and five single rooms, plus an enlarged restaurant. This is the landlord's first venture into running a pub and he has been awarded local CAMRA's Pub of the Year 2003. Wednesday is folk night, and a quiz is held on Thursday evening. Locals and visitors alike receive a warm welcome here. ₩❀⇔⏻⚅⚅♣P

INGLEBY

John Thompson Inn
Ingleby Lane, DE73 1HW
✪ 10.30-2.30, 7-11; 12-2, 7-10.30 Sun
☎ (01332) 862469
John Thompson JTS XXX Bitter, JTS Rich Porter, JTS Summer Gold; Tetley Burton Ale Ⓗ

John Thompson is the former fruit grower who revived Derbyshire's brewing industry in 1977, having made his family home into a highly individual pub eight years earlier. Comprising a large, comfortable lounge with smaller rooms opening off, the pub is rich in local interest, displaying many prints and watercolours. Close to the banks of the River Trent, in open country just outside the village, it also has a spacious patio and large garden with the brewery housed in outbuildings. ➘❀◑⅁♣P✚

KILBURN

Traveller's Rest
114 Chapel Street, DE56 0NT
(1 mile off B6179)
✪ 12-4 (not Mon-Thu), 5.30-11; 12-4, 7-10.30 Sun
☎ (01332) 880108
Greene King Abbot; Tetley Bitter, Burton Ale; guest beer Ⓗ

Traditional, friendly two-roomed village local, in a former mining area, dating back to the 1850s. Known locally as Mamma's after a former landlady, it enjoys a good standing in several pub games leagues. Look for the photograph of the old Kilburn railway station which stood nearby. A small back garden houses an open skittle alley. The guest beer is usually from Leadmill's range. A mile from Denby Pottery, a good bus service runs from Derby (Nos. 91 and 125). ▦❀⅁♣P

KIRK IRETON

Barley Mow ☆
Main Street, DE6 3JP (off B5023)
✪ 12-2, 7-11; 12-2, 7-10.30 Sun
☎ (01335) 370306
Hook Norton Old Hooky; Marston's Pedigree; Whim Hartington IPA; guest beers Ⓖ

Set in an olde-worlde village overlooking the Ecclesbourne Valley, this exceptionally characterful gabled Jacobean building was originally a farmhouse. Several interconnecting rooms of different size and character have low, beamed ceilings, mullioned windows, slate-topped tables, well-worn woodwork and open fires set in stone fireplaces. A small serving-hatch reveals a stillage with beer dispensed straight from the cask. There are not many pubs left like this rural gem. ▦Q❀⇔Å♣●P✚

LITTON

Red Lion
Main Street, SK17 8QU
✪ 12-3, 6-11; 12-11 Fri & Sat; 12-10.30 Sun
☎ (01298) 871458
Jennings Cumberland Ale; Oakwell Barnsley Bitter; Shepherd Neame Spitfire; guest beer Ⓗ

The only pub in the village and one of which residents of many surrounding villages must feel jealous. It acts as the hub of its community in the traditional way.

Attractively situated, facing a green complete with stocks, it is cosy inside with three small rooms and a huge open fireplace. It houses a collection of books of local interest. Quizzes and other events take place on Monday evenings. The accommodation is a new addition for 2004. No evening meals are served Sunday. ▦Q❀⇔◑Å♣P✚

LONG EATON

Hole in Wall
6 Regent Street, NG10 1JX
✪ 10.30-4, 6-11; 10.30-11 Fri & Sat; 12-10.30 Sun
☎ (0115) 973 4920
website: www.hiw.pub@ntlworld.com
Draught Bass; guest beers Ⓗ

Over 100 years old, this back-street local is a big supporter of micro-breweries' products, with those from Nottingham Brewery frequently on tap. A previous winner of local CAMRA's Pub of the Season awards, it has two distinct drinking areas; the lively bar with pool table is supplemented by a quieter elevated lounge. The pub also boasts a small serving-hatch. Lunchtime snacks are available. Close to the Erewash Canal and town centre, nearby is a large public car park and bus stops. ❀⅁P

LONGSHAW

Grouse Inn
S11 7TZ (on A625) OS258779
✪ 12-3, 6-11; 12-11 Sat; 12-10.30 Sun
☎ (01433) 630423
Banks's Bitter; Marston's Pedigree; guest beers Ⓗ

In an area of bleak moorland, but on a popular main road out of Sheffield, the pub is well known by Peak District visitors and has built up a strong following. There is a cosy front lounge, a bar doubling as a function room and a conservatory. On display is a collection of bank notes, both exotic and familiar, and some fine colour photographs of local gritstone edges and other features. Lunches are served Tuesday–Sunday. ▦Q➘❀◑⅁♣P⍿

LULLINGTON

Colvile Arms
Main Street, DE12 8EG
✪ 12-2 (not Mon-Fri), 7-11; 12-3, 7-10.30 Sun
☎ (01827) 373212
Draught Bass; Marston's Pedigree; guest beer Ⓗ

Popular, 18th-century free house, leased from the Lullington Estate, at the heart of an attractive hamlet at the southern tip of the county. The snug, featuring high-backed settles and wood panelling, together with a comfortable lounge, are served from a central bar. A second lounge/function room overlooks the garden with its own bowling green. Three quiz teams and the local cricket team meet here, provoking some lively conversation at local CAMRA's Country Pub of the Year 2001. ❀⅁♣P

MAKENEY

Holly Bush Inn
Holly Bush Lane, DE56 0RX OS352447
✪ 12-3, 5-11; 12-11 Fri & Sat; 12-10.30 Sun
☎ (01332) 841729

Brains Dark; Ⓗ Greene King Ruddles County;
Marston's Pedigree; Ⓖ guest beers Ⓗ
Grade II listed, and once a farmhouse with a
brewery on the Strutt Estate, this late 17th-
century, former Offilers' house positively
oozes character. It stood on the Derby
turnpike before the Strutts opened the
valley route in 1818; Dick Turpin is known
to have drunk here. The enclosed wooden
snug is sandwiched between two bars. Up to
five guest beers are offered, supplemented
by regular beer festivals.
ₘₐQ ⏃ ❀ ⌂P

MELBOURNE

Blue Bell
53 Church Street, DE73 1EJ
✪ 11-11; 12-10.30 Sun
☎ (01332) 865764
**Shardlow Best Bitter, Reverend Eaton's Ale; guest
beer** (occasional) Ⓗ
In the traditional prime spot close to the
hall and Norman church, in a well-pubbed
locality, the Blue Bell stands out as the
Shardlow Brewery tap, although it is several
miles from the brewery itself. The bar of this
old country pub bears a sporting emphasis,
while the lounge opens on to a patio with
barbecue. Run on traditional lines with
seasonal beers and a house mild, it offers
occasional guests, too. The regular
Derby–Swadlincote bus No. 69/69A stops
nearby. ❀⌂◑ ⌂Ⓛ♣

MILFORD

King William
The Bridge, Derby Road, DE56 0RR (on A6)
✪ 12-3, 5.30-11; 12-11 Sat; 12-10.30 Sun
☎ (01332) 840842
**Draught Bass; Marston's Pedigree; Taylor Landlord;
Wells Bombardier; guest beers** Ⓖ
Long, single-roomed, stone roadhouse at
the foot of a sandstone cliff, it is a
contemporary of the elegant stone bridge
that straddles the adjacent River Derwent. A
warm welcome is assured from the landlady
who has restored the interior to its former
glory, retaining softwood beams, the
original tiled floor and open fire. The
Derwent Valley, whose mills and factories
were seminal in the Industrial Revolution, is
now a World Heritage site. Regular buses
run from Derby (Nos. R61–R64).
ₘₐ⌂◑ ♿

MONSAL HEAD

Monsal Head Hotel
DE45 1NL (on B6465)
✪ 11-11; 12-10.30 Sun
☎ (01629) 640250 website: www.monsalhead.com
**Courage Directors; Taylor Landlord; Theakston Best
Bitter, Old Peculier; Whim Hartington Bitter; guest
beers** Ⓗ
The early 19th-century inn here was
demolished to make way for a hotel when
the railway was built to pass through a
tunnel underneath. The stable bar was part
of the original inn and is where most of the
real ale is stocked. The Monsal Head is
situated at a popular beauty spot
overlooking a sharp bend in the limestone
gorge of Monsal Dale, complete with its
now-disused railway viaduct.
ₘₐQ ❀⌂◑ Ⓛ♣P

NEW MILLS

Pack Horse
Mellor Road, SK22 4QQ
(1 mile from town centre on Marple Bridge road)
✪ 12-3, 5-11; 12-11 Sat; 12-10.30 Sun
☎ (01663) 742365
Tetley Bitter; guest beers Ⓗ
Stone pub, in keeping with the farmhouses
dotted around the surrounding countryside,
it nestles in the fold of the back road from
New Mills to Mellor and Marple Bridge.
There are good views up the valley to
Hayfield and beyond and south over
Ollersett Moor. A comfortable, well-
appointed single room serves good quality
food until late. Catering for all tastes, this is
a friendly, relaxing place to drink and dine.
ₘₐQ ❀⌂◑P

OCKBROOK

Royal Oak
55 Green Lane, DE72 3SE
(off A52, follow Ilkeston signs)
✪ 11.30-2.30 (3 Sat), 6-11; 12-3, 7-10.30 Sun
☎ (01332) 662378
Draught Bass; guest beers Ⓗ
Set back from the road across a cobbled
courtyard, this fine pub, local CAMRA's
Country Pub of the Year 2003, was the
regional award winner in 2000. In the same
family since coronation year and little
changed, each of the five rooms has its own
distinctive character and clientele. Three
ever-changing guest beers are supplemented
by an annual beer festival in October.
Excellent home-cooked food is served
(evening meals on weekdays). Separate
gardens cater for adults and families.
Q❀◑Ⓛ♣P✗

OLD GLOSSOP

Queens
1 Shepley Street, SK13 7RZ
✪ 11-11; 12-10.30 Sun
☎ (01457) 862451
**Black Sheep Best Bitter; Jennings Cumberland Ale;
Marston's Pedigree; Worthington's Bitter;
guest beers** Ⓗ
A pleasant 10-minute walk through
Glossop's Manor Park brings you to the
Queens, in a quaint old area of the town.
Comfortably furnished, it is open plan with
a partially flagstoned floor. Popular locally
for good bar food, a new à la carte
restaurant has opened on the second floor
(Thu–Sat), doubling as a function room.
Another room houses a large-screen TV,
popular for football. Completely refurbished
late 2002, after severe flash flooding; the
pub attracts walkers, being at the foot of
Bleaklow. Q❀◑Ⓛ♣✗

OLD TUPTON

Royal Oak
Derby Road, S42 6LA
(3 miles S of Chesterfield on A61)
✪ 12-11; 12-10.30 Sun
☎ (01246) 862180
**Daleside Bitter; John Smith's Bitter, Magnet; Wells
Bombardier; Whim Hartington IPA; guest beers** Ⓗ
A friendly welcome awaits in this 100-
year-old, red brick free house. The Oak is
at the centre of its village community and

holds bank holiday rambles that draw dozens of local revellers. The games room sports a giant Jenga and skittles is played outside next to the garden and wooden play area. The tap room, snug and best room complete the choice of accommodation for enjoying the excellent range of ales on offer from the pub's Master Cellarman.
🏨❀◑ 🛏🛆♣P🖵

OVER HADDON

Lathkil Hotel
DE45 1JE
(off B5055, Bakewell-Monyash road) OS206665
☼ 11.30-3, 7-11; 11.30-11 Sat & summer; 12-10.30 Sun
☎ (01629) 812501 website: www.lathkil.co.uk
Wells Bombardier; Whim Hartington Bitter; guest beers Ⓗ
One of the gems of the Peak for the discerning drinker, this popular free house stands in an idyllic setting, affording spectacular views across the Lathkill Dale, beloved by visiting walkers, who enjoy the important nature reserve. The bar features oak panelling and stocks up to five ales. Superior accommodation and quality meals are available – look out for the specials board. The family room is open at lunchtime at this regular local CAMRA award-winner.
🏨Q🍴❀🛏◑♣P🖵

ROWARTH

Little Mill Inn
SK22 1EB
(signed off Shiloh road, 1/2 mile E of Mellor)
☼ 11-11; 12-10.30 Sun
☎ (01663) 743178
Banks's Bitter; Camerons Strongarm; Marston's Pedigree; guest beer Ⓗ
Originally a candlewick mill, this pub features a fully working waterwheel. To the front is a large open area bordering a stream, which incorporates a children's adventure playground. A huge log fire dominates the lounge and home-cooked food is served all day. To reach the pub from New Mills or Mellor, use the unclassified road and take the Shiloh road at the five road junction.
🏨Q🍴❀🛏◑🛏🛆♣P🖵

SAWLEY

Harrington Arms ✱
392 Tamworth Road, NG10 3AU (on B6540)
☼ 11-11; 12-10.30 Sun
☎ (0115) 973 2614
website: www.harringtonarms.co.uk
Hardys & Hansons Bitter, Olde Trip, seasonal beers Ⓗ
This former coaching inn stands close to the River Trent and the Trent and Mersey Canal. It features traditional decor of panelled walls and low, beamed ceilings in a spacious, open-plan area. An open fire and wood-burning stove add to its charm. The extended patio and garden, warmed by large outdoor heaters, hosts the annual beer festival in August. Freshly-cooked food, with international dishes, is served in the restaurant area, but the bar menu is just as good.
🏨❀◑≈P✂

Nag's Head
1 Wilne Road, NG10 3AL
☼ 11-11; 12-10.30 Sun
☎ (0115) 973 2983
Mansfield Cask Ale; Marston's Pedigree; guest beers Ⓗ
Early 19th-century, two-roomed local close to the River Trent and Sawley Marina, it has only had four landlords since WWII; the present incumbent has been here for 12 years. The lounge has a homely feel and a wood-burning stove warms the bar during colder months. Traditional pub games are played, including long alley skittles. Guest beers, selected from Wolverhampton & Dudley's portfolio, change monthly. This pub is the company's fourth largest seller of Pedigree. 🏨Q❀🛏♣P

SCARCLIFFE

Horse & Groom
Rotherham Road, S44 6SU (on B6417)
☼ 12-4, 6-11; 12-3, 7-10.30 Sun
☎ (01246) 823152
Draught Bass; Greene King Abbot; Stones Bitter; Tetley Bitter; guest beers Ⓗ
This free house is what village pubs should be like – a rural gem. Offering a warm welcome, with friendly customers and no electronic slot machines or meals, it is a proper pub where good conversation is the norm. The lounge bar features dark wood panelling, a copper-topped bar, pictures, plates and ornaments of hunting scenes. The traditional tap room is used for games. A covered verandah at the rear, complete with a barrel water feature, can accommodate children. 🏨Q❀🛏♣P

SHIRLAND

Hay
135 Main Road, DE55 6BA
(on A61 between Chesterfield and Alfreton)
☼ 3 (6 Mon)-11; 12-3, 6-11 Sat; 12-10.30 Sun
☎ (01773) 835383
Caledonian Deuchars IPA; guest beers Ⓗ
Traditional one-roomed local, offering a refreshing selection of real ales in a mainly keg area. Situated on the main A61, this previously keg-only pub was bought in 2002 by long-standing, award-winning CAMRA members. Their beer policy is to offer three ever-changing guests, one of which is always a mild, and to include beers not normally seen in the area. Belgian bottled beers and English country wines may also be enjoyed at this pub which is well worth seeking out. 🛆♣P

SMALLEY

Bell Inn ✱
35 Main Road, DE7 6EF (on A608)
☼ 11.30-3, 5-11; 11-11 Sat; 12-10.30 Sun
☎ (01332) 880635
Adnams Broadside; Mallard Duckling; Oakham JHB; Whim Hartington Bitter, Hartington IPA; guest beers Ⓗ
This mid 19th-century inn has three rooms and a large, attractive, child-friendly garden. Accommodation is offered in three flats in a converted stable adjoining the pub. Brewing and other memorabilia adorn the walls. Top quality beer and food helped earn the Bell

the local CAMRA Pub of the Year award in 2002. Situated on the main Derby–Heanor road, near Shipley Country Park, it can be reached via the H1 bus service (every 20 minutes from Derby bus station).
🏠Q❄️🛏️📶🍴&P

SMISBY

Smisby Arms
Main Street, LE65 2UA
☼ 12-3, 6 (5.30 Fri & Sat)-11; 12-3, 7-10.30 Sun
☎ (01530) 412677
Marston's Pedigree; guest beers Ⓗ
Popular village free house. While parts of the building are thought to be about 350 years old, the pub originates from the 19th century and, despite extension and renovation in recent decades, it retains much of its original character. From the spacious upper lounge, with brick pillars and beamed ceiling, steps lead down to the snug with bench seats and open fire, then more steps down to the rear entrance and conservatory. Enjoying a good reputation for food, no meals are served Sunday evening. 🏠Q❄️🍴♣P

SOUTH NORMANTON

Clock Inn ⊘
107 Market Street, DE55 2AA
(off B6019, 1½ miles from M1 jct 28)
☼ 11-11; 12-10.30 Sun
☎ (01773) 811396 website: www.theclockinn.co.uk
Greene King Abbot; Marston's Bitter; Shepherd Neame Spitfire, Original Porter; guest beers Ⓗ
This free house has picked up two Pub of the Season awards from local CAMRA in the last two years, alongside a Cask Marque accreditation. Attractions include an ever-changing range of guest beers and meals cooked to order in generous helpings. The house jazz band plays on the first Monday evening of each month. Look out for the twice-yearly beer festivals (May and Oct), each offering around 20 real ales and ciders.
Q🍴❄️🍴🍴&P✄

SOUTH WINGFIELD

Old Yew Tree
51 Manor Road, DE55 7NH
☼ 5-11; 12-3, 6.30-11 Sat; 12-4, 7-10.30 Sun
☎ (01773) 833763
Cottage seasonal beers; Marston's Pedigree; guest beers Ⓗ
A regular Guide entry, this very busy, family-run free house is situated near the magnificent remains of the 15th-century Wingfield Manor, destroyed by Cromwell during the Civil War. Guest beers regularly showcase local micro-breweries. Good home-cooked food includes excellent Sunday lunches (no food Sun eve). The award-winning landlord was runner-up Ind Coope Master Cellarman and the pub has won the Amber Valley Clean Air award. There is limited parking space.
🏠❄️🍴&AP✄

STANTON IN PEAK

Flying Childers Inn
Main Road, DE4 2LW (off B5056 between Bakewell and Ashbourne)
☼ 12-2 (not Mon; 12-3 Sat); 7-11; 12-3, 7-10.30 Sun

☎ (01629) 636333
Beer range varies Ⓗ
Created from four cottages in the 18th century, this free house has been in the same hands for 20 years. The changing guests come from a range including Shepherd Neame, Townes, Fuller's and Charles Wells. The cosy, timeless bar is enhanced by a real fire, settles and exposed beams; the lounge has a gas fire and leather seating – both rooms are adorned with copious brass. Cobs and sandwiches are available every lunchtime. The pub is handy for walkers exploring the magical Stanton Moor.
🏠Q❄️🍴A♣P

STARKHOLMES

White Lion Inn
195 Starkholmes Road, DE4 5JA
(signed from Matlock Green)
☼ 12-3, 5-11; 11-11 Sat; 12-10.30 Sun
☎ (01629) 582511
Burtonwood Bitter; Marston's Pedigree; guest beer Ⓗ
Comfortable village local on the old coach road, overlooking Matlock Bath and the Derwent Valley. Low ceilings, open fires and an interesting array of fire insurance plaques feature. A small no-smoking area is provided beyond the central bar. Starkholmes is served by the No. 158 bus, which runs hourly until 6pm (last bus 8pm), no Sunday service. The pub sign features Edward IV, whose insignia bore a white lion.
🏠Q🛏️🍴AP✄

STAVELEY

Speedwell Inn
Lowgates, S43 3TT
☼ 6-11; 6-10.30 Sun
☎ (01246) 472252
Townes Golden Bud, Speedwell Bitter, IPA; Pynot Porter; Staveleyan; guest beer Ⓗ
Home of the Townes Brewery since 1998, this unassuming pub won the local CAMRA Pub of the Year awards in 2000 and 2003. Simple and comfortable surroundings provide real ale lovers with a desirable venue. Townes' regular special brews and bottle-conditioned beers always feature at the bar. Regular bus services 70, 74 (eves only) and 77 from Chesterfield stop near the pub.
Q♣✄

SUTTON CUM DUCKMANTON

Arkwright Arms
Chesterfield Road, S44 5JG (on A632)
☼ 11-11; 12-10.30 Sun
☎ (01246) 232053
Marston's Pedigree; guest beers Ⓗ
This mock-Tudor fronted boozer consists of a bar and lounge separated by a shared bar, with a restaurant at the rear. The three guest ales are normally from local micro-breweries and the Easter beer festival is a real treat. The fresh home-cooked food is great value. Open fires add to the warm welcome in this friendly free house. Conveniently situated on the A632 between Chesterfield and Bolsover Castle, this is a real gem.
🏠❄️🍴🍴♣♣P🍴

TIDESWELL

Star
High Street, SK17 8LD
☼ 5 (12 Sat)-11; 12-10.30 Sun
☎ (01298) 872397
Tetley Bitter; guest beers Ⓗ
This pub, despite the address, is tucked away from the main road through the village. It has become the social centre of the village, drawing a strong local trade. It consists of several small rooms surrounding a central bar, plainly and sensibly decorated. There are usually two guest beers from a wide-ranging selection. A pizza oven has recently been acquired; meals are served right through the afternoon on Sunday. Bar billiards is played here. ✿⊯◑ᗒ▲♣⅄♬

TROWAY

Black-a-Moor
Snowdon Lane, S21 5RU (on B6056)
☼ 12-3, 6-11; 12-10.30 Sun
☎ (01246) 413180
website: www.blackamoor.fsbusiness.co.uk
Beer range varies Ⓗ
This 1930s mock-Tudor comfortable roadside pub places an emphasis on food, but has a strong commitment to real ale and always stocks two or three constantly-changing guest ales, often from micro-breweries. The conservatory and terrace garden provide panoramic views over the Moss Valley. Two beer festivals are held each year in the summer months.
❀◑ᗒ♣P⅄♬

Gate Inn
Main Road, S21 5RU (from B6056, Snowdon Lane, turn at Black-a-Moor pub)
☼ 12-3, 7-11; 12-3, 7-10.30 Sun
☎ (01246) 413280
Burtonwood Bitter, Top Hat; guest beer Ⓗ
Relax and soak up the charm of this small, friendly pub in good walking country on the south side of the Moss Valley. Usually a dog or two is sprawled in front of the fire in the bar, where TV sport is kept on in the background. The cosy lounge and peaceful little garden are equally attractive havens for the drinker. Monthly guest beers add variety. ✿Q❀⊟♣P♬

WHALEY BRIDGE

Shepherd's Arms
7 Old Road, SK23 7HR
☼ 2 (4 Mon)-11; 12-11 Sat; 12-10.30 Sun
☎ (01663) 732840
Banks's Original; Marston's Bitter, Pedigree; guest beer Ⓗ
Attractive, whitewashed stone pub, formerly a farmhouse, this is an ageless local of the type that is sadly becoming rare. It has an interesting layout with a comfortable lounge, but the pub's pride and joy is its traditional tap room where an open fire, stone flags and scrubbed tables make it one of the best examples for miles around. An attractive garden is an asset to a pub that should not be missed.
✿Q❀⊟⇌♣P

WHITWELL

Mallet & Chisel
Hillside, S80 4PF
(off Bakestone Moor at the Spar shop)
☼ 12-3, 5.30-11; 12-11 Sat; 12-10.30 Sun
☎ (01909) 720343
Mansfield Dark Mild; guest beers Ⓗ
Hidden away in a picturesque village, this local is well worth seeking out. A beer house until 1967, it serves a mild (the landlord's tipple) and three guests, usually from Black Sheep, Charles Wells, Fuller's, Shepherd Neame or a micro. The lounge and public bar are warmed by real fires. Good value, home-cooked food is served (eve meals 5.30–7.30). The pub is depicted on the bar front by local artist, Shirley Mottershead. Chesterfield–Worksop bus No. 77 stops nearby.
✿Q❀◑⊟⇌♣P

WIRKSWORTH

Royal Oak
North End, DE4 4FG (off B5035)
☼ 8-11; 12-3, 7.30-10.30 Sun
☎ (01629) 823000
Draught Bass; Taylor Landlord; Whim Hartington IPA; guest beers Ⓗ
Excellent, small, ultra-traditional local in a stone terrace near the market place. The bar features some good breweriana. Genuinely free of tie, the Oak combines a long-standing reputation for Bass with a choice of guests. Reached by No. R61 bus from Derby, Wirksworth (or Wuzzer, as it's affectionately known), should become even more accessible with the planned opening of the Ecclesbourne Valley railway from Duffield during 2003.
Q♣

George and the Dragon

Belated traveller arrives at an inn, the George and Dragon. He bangs on the door for a long time. Eventually an upstairs window opens and a furious female head is thrust out. 'What the hell d'you want at this time o' night?' 'Can I speak to George, please?'

Yorkshire story

Beers with bottle

The new, fourth edition of CAMRA's Good Bottled Beer Guide, written by Jeff Evans and sponsored by Safeway, is fully revised, updated and greatly expanded. The Good Beer Guide's little brother is now not so little and features more than 500 bottled real ales – a massive 40% increase on the last edition – from around 120 British breweries. Included is information on how to buy, keep and serve bottled real ale and how to stage a tasting for friends, plus features on foreign bottled beers, organic bottles, beer and food matching, and more. An expanded Beer Shops section, now with web sites, helps you track down the bottled real ales covered in the book. A must for all armchair beer fans. £10.99 including postage.

DEVON

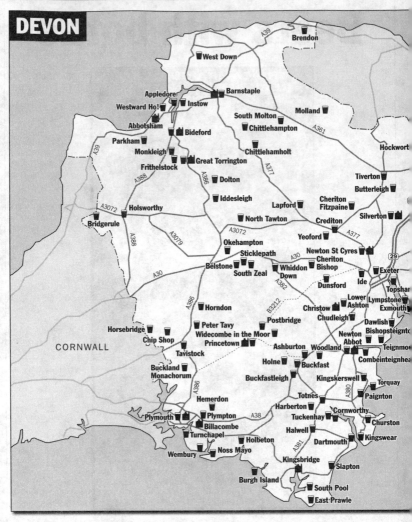

APPLEDORE

Beaver Inn
Irsha Street, EX39 1RY
(take A386 N from Bideford)
☼ 11-3.30, 6-11; 12-11 Sat; 12-10.30 Sun
☎ (01237) 474822
Draught Bass; guest beers Ⓗ
Fantastic vistas over the estuary can be
enjoyed by visitors to this pub. Meals are
served on a raised area, ensuring that diners
get a good view. The pub name dates back
to the old fur trading days, but there are no
recorded links. A games room is used for
pool and darts and copious amounts of
reading matter are provided. If you can not
drink any more of the local guest ales, there
is a tremendous selection of whiskies from
which to choose a night cap. The cider is
supplied by Ostler's. ⌂❀❍▲♣✿

ASHBURTON

Exeter Inn
26 West Street, TQ13 7DU
☼ 11-2.30, 5-11; 12-3, 7-10.30 Sun
☎ (01364) 652013
Badger Best; Greene King IPA Ⓗ
The oldest pub in Ashburton, it was built in
1131 (with 17th-century additions) to
house the men building the church. The
inn was frequented by Sir Francis Drake on
his many journeys from Plymouth to
London. The main bar has a rustic, dark
wood-panelled, L-shaped bar and canopy
with two drinking areas. The drink
dispensing area is incorporated into a
disused fireplace edged by two old
millstones. A serving-hatch at the rear of
the bar serves the lounge of this friendly
local. ⌂Q❀❍▲♣

AXMINSTER

Red Lion
Lyme Street, EX13 5AY
☼ 12 (11 Thu)-2.30, 7 (5 Thu)-11; 12-2.30,
7-10.30 Sun
☎ (01297) 32016
Beer range varies Ⓗ
Town pub converted from three old
buildings. TV is usually on in the

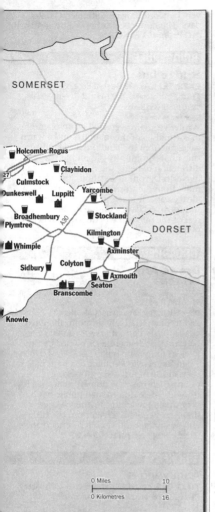

background, often with news or sport (especially cricket); Saturdays are always busy for a big match. There is a quiet dining area off the main bar, and the good value menu includes an interesting specials board. Children are welcome. The large car park opposite can get full on Thursday (market day). There are always four real ales on tap, including varying brews from Branscombe Vale and Cotleigh. ◖▶≉●P

AXMOUTH

Ship Inn
Church Street, EX12 4AF
☼ 11-2.30, 6-11; 12-10.30 Sun
☎ (01297) 21838 website: www.axmouth.com
Draught Bass; Otter Bitter; Young's Special Ⓗ
This creeper-clad village pub was rebuilt in 1880 after the original 10th-century building was destroyed by fire. Note the collections of Guinness memorabilia and costumed dolls from around the world. The decked garden provides a home for convalescing owls, while the skittle alley doubles as a children's room. Live music is

performed on Sunday afternoon. The Ship has been in every edition of this Guide, run by the same family, for all that time.
Q☂❀◖▶ 뮤&ȦP

BARNSTAPLE

Marshals
95 Boutport Street, EX31 1SX
☼ 11-11; 12-10.30 Sun
☎ (01271) 376633
Draught Bass; Ⓗ **guest beers** Ⓗ/Ⓖ
A typical town pub, it is situated on one of Barnstaple's main shopping streets near the Queen's Theatre. A true local, stocking ever-changing guest beers, the single bar is very popular for lunchtime food. All meals are home-cooked using local ingredients. Much is done in support of various charities – beware the fines for using a mobile phone.
◖≉♣

Reform Inn
Reform Street, Pilton, EX31 1PD
☼ 11.30-11; 12-10.30 Sun
☎ (01271) 323164
Beer range varies Ⓗ
Well established at the heart of the Pilton community; its skittle alley is the place to be for the annual beer festival during the Green Man celebrations in July. Pool and music are played in the larger bar on the left, while the bar on the right is quieter. The pub frequently hosts live music, and annual events, such as a conker competition. The beers are from the Barum Brewery behind the pub; plastic containers are available for takeaways. Q❀≉●

BELSTONE

Tors
EX20 1QZ OS619935
☼ 11-3, 6-11 (11-11 summer); 12.3.30, 7-10.30 (12-10.30 summer) Sun
☎ (01837) 840689
Sharp's Doom Bar; guest beers Ⓗ
The Tors is a large granite building next to the church in an unspoilt village near Okehampton. The long, single bar acts as a friendly local for the many walkers who come to enjoy the open moorland or river valleys leading to the moor. The Tarka Trail passes through the village and pony

INDEPENDENT BREWERIES

Barum Barnstaple
Beer Engine Newton St Cyres
Blackdown Dunkeswell
Blewitts Kingsbridge
Branscombe Vale Branscombe
Clearwater Great Torrington
Country Life Abbotsham
Exe Valley Silverton
Jollyboat Bideford
O'Hanlon's Whimple
Otter Luppitt
Points West Plymouth
Princetown Princetown
Scattor Rock Christow
Summerskills Billacombe
Sutton Plymouth
Teignworthy Newton Abbot

trekking is available nearby. Although the beer range varies regularly, the accent is on West Country products; this goes for the food, too. Gray's cider is sold in summer. 🏚🏵🚾🕻🍴♣♠

BIDEFORD

Appledore Inn
18 Chingswell Street, EX39 2NF
🕛 11-11; 12-10.30 Sun
☎ (0137) 472496
Country Life Old Appledore; Jollyboat Mainbrace Ⓗ
This Grade II listed inn is now open plan. The nearest inn to Bideford FC ground, it is popular with sports-minded locals; the licensee is a former sports editor with a national newspaper. The building was used, in the days when the water was closer than now, to sort mail prior to loading on to a boat for Appledore, hence the inn's name. The pub has a piano and stages live music on Sunday. Three guest rooms opened in 2003. 🏚🏵🚾🕻♣

BISHOPSTEIGNTON

Bishop John de Grandisson
Clanage Street, TQ14 9QS
🕛 11-2.30, 5-11; 11-11 Sat; 12-10.30 Sun
☎ (01626) 775285
Draught Bass; Greene King Old Speckled Hen; guest beers Ⓗ
Friendly, old village pub where an L-shaped bar leads to a cosy, split-level dining room, serving home-cooked food. Well supported by the community, it fields games teams and stages regular events. Most locals live within walking distance. The outside seating area overlooks the village. 🏚🏵♿♣♠P

BRANSCOMBE

Fountain Head
Strete, EX12 3BG
🕛 11.30 (11 Sat)-2.30, 6.30 (6 Sat)-11; 12-2.30, 6.30-10.30 Sun
☎ (01297) 680359
Branscombe Vale Branoc, Draymans, seasonal beers Ⓗ
This traditional pub, over 500 years old, was previously a forge and cider house. It has retained its original wood-panelled walls and flagstone floor. Every June a beer festival is held, with live music, on the nearest weekend to the longest day. Branscombe Vale brew the house beer, Jolly Jeff and other seasonal offerings; Green Valley cider is stocked. Good value pub food is served; accommodation is in two self-catering cottages. It is popular with walkers, but children are not encouraged. 🏚Q🌣🏵🚾🕻🍴♣♠P✗

BRENDON

Rockford Inn
EX35 6PT OS756478
🕛 12-3, 6.30 (7 winter)-10.30; 12-3, 7-10.30 Sun
☎ (01598) 741214 website: www.therockfordinn.com
Cotleigh Barn Owl Ⓗ/Ⓖ
An absolutely delightful pub, set in the most idyllic surrounding scenery to be found in North Devon. Not the easiest pub to find, but a treat when you do! The patio provides the best outdoor drinking for many miles. The two open fires make for

very cosy drinking conditions on cooler days. The house beer is brewed by St Austell. 🏚Q🌣🏵🚾🕻🍴▲♣♠P✗

BRIDGERULE

Bridge Inn
EX22 7EJ (take A39 Bideford-Bude, then B3254)
🕛 12-2 (not Mon-Fri), 6.30-11; 12-3, 7-10.30 Sun
☎ (01288) 381316
Beer range varies Ⓗ
Winter visitors are greeted by an open fire in the middle of the main bar and a warm welcome from the landlord and landlady. A true rural community pub, it has the distinction of being the most westerly pub in North Devon. Its location, just a few miles from the Cornish coast, makes it an ideal escape. It may open lunchtimes on summer weekdays – phone to check. At the rear of the pub you will discover an aviary. 🏚Q♿▲

BROADHEMBURY

Drewe Arms
EX14 3NF
🕛 11-3, 6-11; 12-3, 7-10.30 (closed winter eve) Sun
☎ (01404) 841267
Otter Bitter, Bright (summer), **Ale, Head** Ⓖ
Picturesque, relatively unspoilt, thatched Grade II listed inn. It is set in a village of cob and thatched cottages owned by the Drewe family who built Castle Drogo in the Teign Valley. Predominantly a food pub, specialising in fish dishes (booking essential), it has won numerous awards for its food. The old-fashioned public bar is very small; the lounge features a large fireplace. Beers are served from the casks, enclosed in a wooden chill cabinet; Lane's cider is stocked. 🏚Q🏵🕻♣♠P

BUCKFAST

Abbey Inn ⊘
TQ11 0EA (just off A38 on route to Buckfast Abbey)
🕛 11-2.30, 6-11; 11-11 Sat & summer);
12-10.30 Sun
☎ (01364) 642343
St Austell IPA, Tribute, HSD Ⓗ
Large inn situated inside the Dartmoor National Park, close to the famous Buckfast Abbey. The large oak-panelled bar is traditionally furnished to create a warm, welcoming interior. A spacious dining room serves an excellent range of food. In an idyllic setting, its terrace overlooks the unspoilt River Dart. There are many visitor attractions in the vicinity. 🏚Q🏵🚾🕻♿▲P

BUCKFASTLEIGH

White Hart
2 Plymouth Road, TQ11 0DA
🕛 12-3 (not Mon), 6-11; 12-11 Sat (Tue-Sat summer);
12-3.30, 7-10.30 Sun
☎ (01364) 642337 website: www.stayanight.com
Greene King Abbot; Teignworthy Beachcomber; guest beer Ⓗ
Pleasant pub, with a single, open-plan bar area, plus a dining area. There is also a restaurant room at the rear of the pub that is not open all year round. Outside, a courtyard provides additional seating and hosts barbecues in summer. A good range of fresh, home-cooked food is available at

reasonable prices. The house beer is brewed by Teignworthy, while the varied guest beers are sourced from all over the country, with one always on tap.

BUCKLAND MONACHORUM

Drake Manor Inn
PL20 7NA
🕑 11.30-2.30 (3 Sat), 6.30-11; 12-3, 7-10.30 Sun
☎ (01822) 853892
Courage Best Bitter; Greene King Abbot; Sharp's Doom Bar Ⓗ

Cosy, 16th-century pub with a public bar, relaxed lounge/snug and a restaurant that enjoys a good reputation. Local produce is used as much as possible in the 'specials'. The small cellar room behind the bar admits children. A stream runs through the peaceful garden. Admire the impressive floral displays around the pub in summer. Shove-ha'penny and darts are played. The pub's car park has limited space. A daytime Citybus No. 55 from Yelverton serves the village. 🏚Q🍺❀🕭🍴🛗✄

BURGH ISLAND

Pilchard
Burgh Island, TQ7 4BG (stop at Bigbury-on-Sea car park; cross the beach, or take the sea tractor)
🕑 11-11; 12-10.30 Sun
☎ (01548) 810514
Draught Bass; guest beers Ⓗ

Located on an island, the Pilchard is cut off by the tide twice a day, when only the sea tractor can get you back. Dating from 1336, with slate floors, exposed beams and stone walls, smuggler Tom Crocker was shot outside and reputedly haunts the place. The pub has featured in episodes of Poirot and Lovejoy. It is lit by ship's lanterns. Look out for the stuffed parrot in the glass case. Children are welcome until 9pm. Evening meals are served Thursday–Saturday; cider is stocked in summer. 🏚🍺❀🕭🍴🛗✄

BUTTERLEIGH

Butterleigh Inn
EX15 1PN
🕑 12-2.30, 6 (5 Fri)-11; 12-3, 7-10.30 Sun
☎ (01884) 855407
website: www.thebutterleighinn.co.uk
Cotleigh Tawny, Barn Owl; guest beers Ⓗ

This is just what a country pub should be; in a charming spot, this splendid 400-year-old Devon cob building is full of character. The main bar area is supplemented by a snug and a no-smoking dining area/lounge. The open fire in the bar and wood-burner in the lounge make this a warm, welcoming place on cold winter evenings. In summer, enjoy the views of the surrounding rolling hills from the attractive secluded garden. 🏚Q❀🕭🛗♣P

CHERITON BISHOP

Old Thatch Inn
EX16 6JH
(1 mile from A30, Exeter-Okehampton road)
🕑 11.30-3, 6-11; 12-3, 7-10.30 Sun
☎ (01647) 24204
Branscombe Vale Branoc; Otter Ale; guest beer Ⓗ

Traditional, 16th-century thatched country free house on the north-eastern edge of Dartmoor, boasting exposed beams and a magnificent open stone fireplace. The pub comprises a small bar, a larger restaurant area and a no-smoking room. The three ales come from independent breweries, and at least two are sourced locally. The bar snack and restaurant menus offer a varied selection of good food. En-suite accommodation is available. 🏚❀🛗🕭 ⚓P

CHERITON FITZPAINE

Ring of Bells
EX17 4JG
🕑 12-2.30 (not Mon-Fri), 6.30-11; 12-4.30, 7-10.30 Sun
☎ (01363) 866374
Beer range varies Ⓗ

This charming, 14th-century inn is situated in beautiful countryside. Notable for its thatched roof, open fires and exposed beams, the central bar serves both the pub and the dining area. It is the hub of the Crediton folk festival, held annually in the village in April. Boules and skittles are played. Excellent bar/restaurant menus are prepared by a progressive chef – look out for theme nights. Three beers are available in winter and up to six in the summer. 🏚❀🕭♣P

CHIP SHOP

Chip Shop Inn
PL19 8NT (off A384, 13 miles W of Tavistock)
OS437751
🕑 12-2.30, 5-11; 11-11 Sat; 12-10.30 Sun
☎ (01822) 832322
Sharp's Doom Bar; Worthington's 1744; guest beers Ⓗ

This remote pub is well worth finding – it is a gem. The area had numerous lead and tin mines and the pub's name comes from the mine company's habit of paying its employees partly in chips, exchangeable at the company shop (nothing to do with fish). The pub is renowned for its collection of mirrors. The skittle alley is very popular and the garden is child-friendly, with a playhouse. Being a country pub it welcomes well-behaved dogs, whether pets or working animals. 🏚Q❀🕭 ⚓P

CHITTLEHAMHOLT

Exeter Inn
EX37 9NS (off A3227, South Molton-Great Torrington road)
🕑 11.30-2.30, 7-11 (11.30-11 summer); 12-3, 7-10.30 Sun
Greene King Abbot; St Austell Dartmoor Best Ⓗ

This pub is another fine example of a traditional village local. The thatched roof and original exposed beams make this pub the sort that every visitor expects to see in this part of the country. Fine ales are accompanied by good food and a warm welcome. Accommodation is available in self-catering cottages. If staying in the area, the Old George Inn at High Bickington keeps a range of guest beers. ❀🕭P

CHITTLEHAMPTON

Bell Inn
The Square, EX37 9QL (off B3227, South Molton-Great Torrington road)

✪ 11-3, 7-11; 11-11 Sat; 12-3, 7-10.30 Sun
☎ (01769) 540368
Draught Bass; Fuller's London Pride; Ⓗ
guest beers Ⓗ/Ⓖ
Situated at the village centre, opposite the
church, this pub is truly the focus for the
community. The village football and cricket
teams are based here – why they ever get on
the field is a mystery – as are other local
groups. Ales are sold on gravity as well as on
handpump, so always ask what is available
from the list. Families with children are
welcome.
✿◑☕P

CHUDLEIGH

Bishop Lacy
Fore Street, TA13 0HY (signed off A38)
✪ 11-11; 12-10.30 Sun
☎ (01626) 854585 website: www.bishoplacy.com
O'Hanlon's Fire Fly; Ⓗ **Princetown Jail Ale;** Ⓖ
**Shepherd Neame Spitfire; Skinner's Cornish
Knocker;** Ⓗ **guest beers** Ⓖ
Grade II listed, this 14th-century church
house is now a bustling local. It has built up
a reputation for serving a good selection of
real ales, mostly on gravity. The pub has
two bars, both warmed by open fires.
Home-cooked food is served in a no-
smoking restaurant area. Beer festivals are a
regular event at this local CAMRA Pub of
the Year 2000 (and regional winner in
1998). Children (and dogs) are welcome.
🏨Q✿◑⊕▲♣P

CHURSTON

Weary Ploughman
Brixham Road, TQ5 0LL (on A3022, between
Brixham and Paignton)
✪ 11-11; 12-10.30 Sun
☎ (01803) 844702
Sharp's Doom Bar; John Smith's Bitter; guest beers Ⓗ
Built as the Railway Hotel, this large
roadside pub has served a variety of uses,
although it has always been a pub or hotel.
It was once known as the Churston Links,
when HQ of Churston Golf Club. The bar
and eating area is mainly open plan, but
there is a no-smoking section, and a child-
friendly area. Top of the range pub food is
served at reasonable prices. Two or three
guest beers are available. Visit the steam
railway station next door.
🏃🏨◑P

CLAYHIDON

Half Moon Inn
EX15 3TJ
✪ 12-2.30, 7-11 (closed Mon); 12-3 (closed eve) Sun
☎ (01823) 680291
Cotleigh Tawny, Old Buzzard; guest beers Ⓗ
Set in the Blackdown Hills, near the
Somerset border, the inn benefits from
outstanding views over the Culm Valley. It
is very popular, both with locals and
visitors. A traditional country inn, it is
noted locally for its varied range of
reasonably-priced meals, served in the bar
and restaurant area. The Half Moon is
believed to have been built by stone masons
for their accommodation while building the
church; in the 18th century it was known as
the Church House.
🏨✿◑▲♣P✕

COLYTON

Gerrard Arms
Rosemary Lane, EX24 6LN
✪ 11-3, 6 (4.30 winter Sat)-11; 12-3, 7-10.30 Sun
☎ (01297) 552588
Draught Bass; Ⓗ **Branscombe Vale Branoc;** Ⓖ
guest beer Ⓗ
Busy, one-bar pub next to the church in this
delightful little town, full of lovely old
cottages and a tangle of narrow streets and
alleyways. Very popular with locals, the pub
has a well-used skittle alley at the rear and a
garden for families. The home-made food is
good value and a traditional roast is served
on Sunday. Seaton tramway runs in
summer, and it is an easy walk, or you can
ride in a horse-drawn wagon, from Colyton
Station.
✿◑▲⊖⊖

COMBEINTEIGNHEAD

Wild Goose
TQ12 4RA (between Newton Abbot and Shaldon,
S of Teign estuary)
✪ 11.30-2.30, 6.30-11; 12-2.30, 7-10.30 Sun
☎ (01626) 872241
Beer range varies Ⓗ
This 17th-century free house stands at the
heart of the village. A long, single bar
features large, open fireplaces and seating
areas at each end. There are normally six
constantly-changing ales on tap, many of
them local. On the other side of the pub is a
recently revamped dining area, affording
rural views across the River Teign. All food
is home cooked, with fresh fish and
vegetarian options always available. The
house beer (Goose Bitter) is brewed by St
Austell. 🏨Q✿◑⅛&♣P

CORNWORTHY

Hunter's Lodge Inn
TQ9 7ES
✪ 11.30-2.30, 6.30-11; 12-3, 7-10.30 Sun
☎ (01803) 732204 website: www.hunterslodgeinn.com
Teignworthy Reel Ale; guest beers Ⓗ
An archetypal country inn in a delightful,
hilly Devon village with low, beamed
ceilings and a log fire. Opening in 1804 as
the New Inn, it became the Globe in 1880,
before settling as the Hunter's Lodge.
Providing good quality beers and wines, and
home-cooked food, the menu specialises in
fish dishes and buys local produce wherever
possible. Children are welcome in the
dining area. Two or three guest beers are
kept. South Devon CAMRA Pub of the Year
2003. 🏨Q✿◑♣&♣P✕

CREDITON

Crediton Inn
28A Mill Street, EX17 1EZ (opp. Somerfield)
✪ 11-11; 12-2, 7-10.30 Sun
☎ (01363) 772882 website: www.crediton-inn.co.uk
Sharp's Doom Bar; guest beers Ⓗ
Located just off the town centre, this well-
established, friendly free house is a regular
entry in this Guide. Four ales are always
available, with the guest beers often coming
from regional independent breweries. The
pub runs its own angling club and fields a
pool team. The skittle alley doubles as a
function room. A modest menu of cooked

meals is available and occasional quiz/theme nights are held. This is a real gem. ◑☞♨♣P

Culm Valley Inn
EX15 3JJ
✪ 12-3, 6-11 (12-11 summer Sat); 12-10.30 Sun
☎ (01884) 840354
Beer range varies Ⓖ

This 300-year-old village inn sits by the River Culm where it emerges from the Blackdown Hills. The car park was formerly the railway sidings of the Tiverton light railway and the pub was previously called the Railway Inn. Local produce, often free range and organic, is sourced for the pub's menu. Recent improvements have included a new kitchen, toilets and, most importantly, a new cellar where all the beer is stillaged on automatic tilters and dispensed by gravity. ♨Q☞❀✿◑♣●

Cherub Inn
13 Higher Street, TQ6 9RB
✪ 11-2.30, 5.30-11 (11-11 summer); 12-10.30 Sun
☎ (01803) 832571 website: www.the-cherub.co.uk
Beer range varies Ⓗ

This Grade II listed building, originally the home of a wool merchant, is the oldest house in Dartmouth, only becoming a pub in 1972. It has a small, cosy, beamed bar, warmed by an open fire in winter. It is popular with locals and visitors alike. A steep spiral staircase leads to the restaurant which has earned a good reputation for local fish and seafood. Three beers (two in winter), mainly from south-western breweries, complement the house beer from Summerskills. ♨Q◑

Windjammer Inn
23 Victoria Road, TQ6 9RT (opp. old market hall)
✪ 11-3, 5.15-11; 12-3, 6-10.30 Sun
☎ (01803) 832228
Draught Bass; Princetown Dartmoor IPA; guest beer Ⓗ

A typical town pub exterior conceals a large, single bar, furnished in light coloured woods. The pub bears a nautical theme, providing yachting information on a blackboard. It has a good reputation for home-cooked, reasonably-priced food. It is free from gaming machines and piped music. The guest beer changes constantly. ♨Q◑

Smugglers Inn
27 Teignmouth Road, EX7 0LA
(on A379 coastal road to Teignmouth)
✪ 11-11; 12-10.30 Sun
☎ (01626) 862301
Draught Bass; Scattor Rock Devonian; Teignworthy Reel Ale; guest beer Ⓗ

This large roadhouse, half a mile from Dawlish Station (two miles from Teignmouth Station) boasts a massive car park and stunning coastal views. New owners in 2001 have revitalised the attraction of cask ales, to the extent of having occasional mini-festivals, with half a dozen extra ales on gravity. Families with

children are made welcome and a most attractive no-smoking restaurant serves a daily carvery. The disabled facilities are exemplary. ♨☞❀◑♿⚲♨P

Union Inn
EX19 8QH
✪ 12-2.30, 6-11; 12-2.30, 7-10.30 Sun
☎ (01805) 804633
Clearwater Cavalier; St Austell Tribute Ⓗ

16th-century cob long house, comprising two bars, a restaurant and a function room. A log fire helps create a warm, friendly atmosphere in the bars with their unspoilt interiors. Excellent food is sourced locally. Note the interesting snuff box on the bar. It once had an orchard in the garden growing Pig's Nose cider apples. The pub offers special rates for three-day breaks in its three en-suite guest rooms. ♨Q❀✿◑⚏⚲♣P

Royal Oak
EX6 7DA (follow B3212 from Exeter) OS284084
✪ 12-2.30, 6.30 (7 Mon; 6 Fri)-11; 12-2.30, 7-10.30 Sun
☎ (01647) 252256
Greene King Abbot; Princetown Jail Ale; Sharp's Cornish Coaster; Doom Bar Ⓗ

Popular local, set in a small village on the edge of the Dartmoor National Park. A pleasant and convenient stopping-place when visiting the moor, the accommodation is in converted barns. It stages a quiz every Thursday evening and 'mystery ales' are offered at a lower price on Friday evening. Children are welcome and catered for on the wide-ranging menu. The pub has a small garden. No piped music or games machines disturb the atmosphere. ♨Q❀✿◑⚲P⚏

Pig's Nose Inn
TQ7 2BY
✪ 12-2.30, 7 (6.30 Sat)-11; 12-3, 7-10.30 Sun
☎ (01548) 511209 website: www.pigsnoseinn.co.uk
Fuller's London Pride; Sutton Eddystone; guest beers (summer) Ⓖ

Old, three-roomed smugglers' inn, set on the village green. Children (and dogs) are welcome; adults are asked to behave themselves. The beer is stored in a specially-made rack behind the bar. It is a haven for birdwatchers and coastal walkers alike. Home-made meals are produced using local ingredients. Occasional live music, performed at weekends in a hall adjoining the pub, helps to make this a popular venue. ♨Q☞❀✿◑♿⚲♣

Brook Green
31 Well Street, EX4 6QL
(near St James Park Station)
✪ 12-2.30 (not Mon or Tue), 5-11; 11-3, 6-11 Sat; 12-3, 7-10.30 Sun
☎ (01392) 495699
Butcombe Bitter; Fuller's London Pride; guest beers Ⓗ

Welcoming, traditional pub serving the local community. The friendly landlady always offers six beers at reasonable prices. Close to Exeter City football ground, it is student-friendly. It fields two league darts teams and hosts regular meetings of the Victorians cricket team. It has a small car park, and parking locally is difficult, however, it is a mere 100 yards from St James Park Station on the Exmouth line from St Davids or Central stations. Q ⑤ ⇌ (St James Pk) ♣ P

Double Locks Hotel

EX2 6LT (road access is from Marsh Barton trading estate) OS933901
🌣 11-11; 12-10.30 Sun
☎ (01392) 256947
Adnams Broadside; Branscombe Vale Branoc; Everards Original; Young's Bitter, Special; guest beers H /G

This famous pub is best approached on foot or cycle from Exeter's historic quayside via the Riverside Country Park, but road access and parking are good. Popular with walkers, cyclists, families and dog-owners, it sits in extensive grounds beside the ancient canal. It serves home-cooked food all day and has a seasonal barbecue bar. It normally stocks a dozen cask ales, with Young's predominating, plus local Gray's Farm cider. Live music is performed Thursday, Friday and Saturday. ⋈ ⊛ ⓞ ⚫ P

Great Western Hotel

Station Approach, St David's, EX4 4NU
🌣 11-11; 12-10.30 Sun
☎ (01392) 274039
Adnams Broadside; Draught Bass; Fuller's London Pride; Taylor Landlord; guest beers H

Bustling, friendly railway hotel/pub. Cheerful, knowledgeable staff greet you when you enter this oasis of real ales. More than four regular ales are accompanied by up to 14 guest ales. Probably the best ale pub in the city, it is a mecca for locals and the travelling public alike. Great value, unusual food is served in the bar and restaurant. Q ⋈ ⓞ ⊟⇌ (St David's) P

Hour Glass

Melbourne Street, EX2 4AU (off Topsham Rd/Holloway St)
🌣 12-2.30, 5.30-11; 12-2.30, 7-10.30 Sun
☎ (01392) 258722
Greene King Abbot; Otter Ale; guest beers H

Delightful, 19th-century back-street pub, just outside the city centre. It retains a City Brewery etched window, but has been sympathetically restored and opened out, using old timbers and oak panelling. Over the last three years the range of ales has been improved, along with its reputation for food. Seafood and vegetarian options are specialities here. Most diners choose to eat in the cellar restaurant. Q ⓞ

Royal Oak

Fore Street, Heavitree, EX1 2RN
🌣 11-3, 6-10.30 (5-11 Fri); 11-11 Sat; 12-10.30 Sun
☎ (01392) 254121
Fuller's London Pride; Otter Ale; guest beer H

This multi-roomed, 17th-century pub used to be the manor house for the old hamlet of Heavitree. It is full of bric-à-brac, including a cell door from Dartmoor Prison. Good value home-cooked lunches are served. Home to a clay pigeon syndicate and euchre teams, it also hosts a general knowledge

quiz every Wednesday. It is the only pub in Exeter to have retained a thatched roof. Q ⊛ ◁ ♣

Well House

Cathedral Yard, EX1 1HD
🌣 11-11; 12-10.30 Sun
☎ (01392) 223611
O'Hanlons Port Stout; Otter Ale; Skinner's Spriggan Ale; guest beers H

Not a conventional appearance – a plate glass shop-front window looks out on to the lovely Cathedral Green in the historic heart of the city – but this is an ale drinker's haven. The six handpumps always serve two beers from Otter's range, one each from O'Hanlon's and Skinner's plus two guests (and three ciders on gravity). Three week-long beer festivals each year see another six ales on gravity. Its strong regular following is rewarded, by a dedicated management, with well-supported brewery trips and outings. ◁⇌ (Central) ⚫

EXMOUTH

Powder Monkey ⊘

2-2A The Parade, EX8 1RG
🌣 10-11; 12-10.30 Sun
☎ (01395) 280090
Courage Directors; Greene King Abbot; Shepherd Neame Spitfire; Theakston Best Bitter; guest beers H

In the middle of a lovely seaside resort, this Wetherspoon's is smaller than their average outlet, but has a good, friendly atmosphere. The family area is nicely separated but not isolated, while the toilets and disabled facilities are to the usual high standard for this company. Popular all year round with all ages during the day, it is a major venue for the under 30s in the evenings. Up to three guest ales are usually available, a couple from West Country brewers.
Q ⑤ ⊛ ⓞ ⑤ ⇌ ⚏

FRITHELSTOCK

Clinton Arms

EX38 8JH
(off A386, between Torrington and Bideford)
🌣 11-3, 6-11; 12-3, 6 (7 summer)-10.30 Sun
☎ (01805) 623279
Clearwater Cavalier, seasonal beers H

This quiet village inn enjoys a tranquil setting, opposite ancient abbey ruins. Its large walled garden and lawns are a great venue for functions in summer, and include a play area for children. The pub grows its own vegetables and herbs for the kitchen and is currently trialling its own cider. Skittles and pool can be played here. Disabled facilities should be in place by 2004. Accommodation is in four en-suite rooms; special fishing breaks can be arranged. ⋈ Q ⑤ ⊛ ⋈ ⓞ ⑤ ♣ ⚫ P

GREAT TORRINGTON

Black Horse

High Street, EX38 8HN
🌣 11-3, 6-11; 11-11 Sat; 12-4, 7-10.30 Sun
☎ (01805) 622121
Courage Best Bitter, Directors; guest beer H

Famous for its use as an office during the Civil War by both sides, Sealed Knot members now use it when in town for commemorative gatherings. Modernised in places, but still mostly 16th-century, a regularly-changing guest ale makes this a popular meeting place for other local groups. Pump clips on the ceiling show some of the 1,000-plus ales that have been served in the 15 years under the present landlord, who has just celebrated 10 years in this Guide. 🏠Q🍴◑🌳

HALWELL

Old Inn
TQ9 7JA (on A381, Totnes-Kingsbridge road)
🕙 11-3, 6-11; 12-3, 6-10.30 Sun
☎ (01803) 712329
website: www.the-old-inn.freeserve.co.uk
RCH PG Steam, East Street Cream Ⓗ
Friendly, family-run, roadside pub, with a warm village atmosphere. Situated next to the beautiful Norman church, the present inn was built in 1874; the original Old Inn had been destroyed by fire in the 17th century. The single bar has seating and dining tables in the bar area, but there is also a no-smoking dining room. Excellent food at reasonable prices features oriental dishes as a speciality. En-suite accommodation and cider in summer are added attractions. 🏠Q🕭❀🍴◑🌳🚶P✄

HARBERTON

Church House Inn
TQ9 5SF (off A381, Totnes-Kingsbridge road)
🕙 12-3, 6-11; 12-3, 7-10.30 Sun
☎ (01803) 863707
Beer range varies Ⓗ
This friendly, 12th-century pub was built to house the masons working on the church. It then became a chantry house for monks. In 1327 the Abbot handed the property to the poor and in 1950 it passed out of the church's hands. A Tudor window frame and latticed window containing panes of 13th-century hand-made glass can still be seen. Heavy beams and a stone floor characterise the bar and dining area where an extensive range of excellent food is available. Beer can be expensive. 🏠Q🕭❀🍴◑🌳🚶P✄

HEMERDON

Miner's Arms
PL7 5BU (between Plympton and Sparkwell)
🕙 11-2.30l 5.30-11; 12-3, 7-10.30 Sun
☎ (01752) 336040
Draught Bass; Ⓗ/Ⓖ **Sutton XSB; guest beer** Ⓗ
Unspoilt, friendly village pub that has been run by the same family since 1870. The large public bar boasts original beams and a massive stone fireplace, complete with baker's oven; it was used as a regular, cosy backdrop in a TV series about local pubs. The name reflects the days when tin, arsenic and wolfram were mined in the locality. The garden houses a small children's playground and affords views towards the outskirts of Plymouth. 🏠Q❀🕭🚶P

HOCKWORTHY

Staple Cross Inn
TA21 0HN
🕙 11-11; 12-10.30 Sun
☎ (01398) 361374
Cotleigh Tawny; Exmoor Ale Ⓗ

Unspoilt, 400-year-old local, recently reopened following active village and CAMRA action against a planning application to change to residential use. This quiet country pub on the Somerset border comprises two bars, one with a quarry-tiled floor, the other a carpeted lounge area. It offers a friendly welcome and good food, served in the bar or dining area. 🏠Q❀◑🕭🚶⚓♣P

HOLBETON

Mildmay Colours Inn
Fore Street, PL8 1NA
🕙 11-3, 6-11; 12-3, 7-10.30 Sun
☎ (01752) 830248
website: www.mildmay-colours.co.uk
Beer range varies Ⓗ
Built in the reign of King James I, in 1617 the pub was renamed in the honour of the late Anthony Mildmay. This popular village local sells a house beer brewed by Skinner's and regular local guest beers. The bar menu specialises in locally-sourced home-cooked food and a carvery is served in the upstairs restaurant on Sunday. The family room provides entertainment for children. A beer festival is held on August bank holiday, with live entertainment. The cider is from local producer, Symons. 🏠Q🕭❀🍴◑🚶P✄

HOLCOMBE ROGUS

Prince of Wales
TA21 0PN
🕙 12-3 (not winter Mon-Thu), 6.30-11; 12-3, 7-10.30 Sun
☎ (01823) 672070
Otter Bitter; guest beers Ⓗ
Pleasant, 17th-century country pub, not far from the Grand Western Canal, which is popular with cyclists and walkers. Note the unusual cash register handpumps that have been lovingly restored. A large restaurant area offers home-cooked food, including vegetarian options, or you can just relax in the lounge by the log-burning stove. A skittle alley, pool and darts areas are well used. An attractive walled garden completes the facilities here. 🏠Q❀◑🚶🚶P

HOLNE

Church House Inn
TQ13 7SJ 0S706696
🕙 12-2.30 (12-3 Sat), 7 (6.30 Sat)-11; 12-3, 7-10.30 Sun
☎ (01364) 631208
website: www.churchhouse-holne.co.uk
Butcombe Bitter; Palmer IPA Ⓗ
Grade II listed 14th-century inn in Dartmoor National Park. The pub has two bars, one leading to the dining area and the other basically for drinkers. Excellent fresh food is cooked to order from local ingredients. Families with children, dogs and walkers are all most welcome. Two house beers brewed by Summerskills and Ring o' Bells are served. 🏠Q🕭🍴◑⚓🚶

HOLSWORTHY

King's Arms Hotel ☆
The Square, EX22 6DL
🕙 11-11; 12-3.30, 7-10.30 Sun
☎ (01409) 253517

113

Draught Bass; Sharp's Doom Bar H

This 17th-century inn comprises three bars with entrances on two streets, which results in two post codes! Whichever way you enter you are certain of a warm welcome and fine ale. The snug and public bars are separated by a fine snob screen – an original feature. The display of pub and beer memorabilia is noteworthy, particularly the pictures.

ᴹᴬQ☺⊞♣↯

HORNDON

Elephant's Nest Inn

PL19 9NQ (1½ miles E of Mary Tavy on A386, follow signs) OS517800

☼ 12-3, 6.30-11 (closed Mon, Jan-Easter); 12-3, 6.30-10.30 (closed winter eve) Sun

☎ (01822) 810273

Palmer Copper Ale, IPA; St Austell HSD; guest beers H

Many years ago this was the New Inn, but this picturesque 16th-century pub, prompted by a former landlord, had an unusual name change. The large garden offers superb views of Dartmoor and has its own cricket pitch. The traditional bar features many elephantine items, including a mural, figures, curios and 'elephant' spelt in many languages on the ceiling beams. The bar is supplemented by two rooms suitable for children. It supports local cricket, rugby, darts and pony clubs.

ᴹᴬQ☎☺◑♣☻P↯

HORSEBRIDGE

Royal Inn

PL19 8PJ (signed off A388)

☼ 11.30-3, 7-11; 12-3, 6.30-10.30 Sun

☎ (01822) 870214 website: www.royalinn.co.uk

Draught Bass; Sharp's Doom Bar; guest beers H

The inn stands on an historic little bridge over the River Tamar joining Devon and Cornwall. Monks built both the bridge and the pub, which was originally a nunnery. It retains features to illustrate its earlier use. The main bar is half-panelled, while the lounge bears hops and horse brasses. A third, small room is no-smoking. Up to six real ales are available in summer. The pub is isolated, but well worth finding. The food is excellent, but pricey.

ᴹᴬQ☺◑♣↯

IDDESLEIGH

Duke of York

EX19 8BG (on B3217)

☼ 11-11; 12-10.30 Sun

☎ (01837) 810253

Adnams Broadside; Cotleigh Tawny; guest beers G

This 14th-century inn is situated in a quiet village. Its welcoming, friendly atmosphere is enhanced by a huge log fire, with a rocking chair. It was originally built as four cottages to house craftsmen building the church next door. The food is mostly supplied from the landlord's own farm and market garden and is served in farmer's-sized portions. The bar gets quite busy, despite its remote location. Be prepared for occasional outbursts of song from the locals.

ᴹᴬQ☺☎◑♣☻

IDE

Poacher's Inn

High Street, EX2 9RW

☼ 12-3 (not Mon), 6-11; 12-3, 6-10.30 Sun

☎ (01392) 273847

Draught Bass; Otter Ale; guest beer H

This traditional village pub has a welcoming, cosy atmosphere created by an attractive variety of comfy seating and cottage-style furniture. It places a major emphasis on good quality food, including fish and seafood, for which it has an excellent reputation (no meals Sun eve). In summer, the large garden, overlooking rolling hills and valleys, is rightly popular. It is sometimes possible that no more than two of the four handpumps will be in service. ᴹᴬ☺☛◑P

INSTOW

Quay Inn

Marine Parade, EX39 4HX (off A39, between Barnstaple and Bideford)

☼ 11-11; 12-10.30 Sun

☎ (01271) 860624

Beer range varies H

Set on the estuary, this interesting little pub is full of character. A welcome stop for walkers on the Tarka Trail, it attracts a mixed clientele; all ages, both locals and visitors ensure an interesting time when sampling the ales. Most beers are locally brewed and products from a new brewery may appear soon. If visiting the area, the New Inn at nearby Fremington also sells real ale. ◑

KILMINGTON

New Inn

The Hill, EY13 7SF (100 yds S of A35)

☼ 11-2.30, 6-11; 12-3, 7-10.30 Sun

☎ (01297) 33376

Palmer Bridport Bitter, IPA H

Village pub, overlooking the Axe Valley; its safe garden houses aviaries and boasts impressive summer flower displays. This chocolate-box thatched Devon long house dates from the 14th century, becoming a pub around 1800. In every edition of this Guide, it is well supported by local teams most nights in winter, and has a good skittle alley. Snacks are sold at lunchtime, with a fuller evening menu, and Sunday roasts. Children are welcome in the small no-smoking dining room or family room. ᴹᴬQ☺☎◑♠♣P⊟

Old Inn

EX13 7RD (on A35, 1 mile W of Axminster)

☼ 12-2.30 (11-3 summer), 6-11; 12-2.30, 7-10.30 Sun

☎ (01297) 32096

Branscombe Vale Branoc H

This thatched pub, Branscombe Vale's first, is run by one of the brewery's partners and his wife. They have a policy of sourcing produce as far as they can from the south-west. A second Branscombe ale is stocked alongside the Branoc. The small bar, popular with locals, displays cricketing memorabilia, while a larger lounge features an inglenook and a restaurant; evening meals in winter are served Wednesday–Saturday. Outside is a fenced

patio and lawn with an adjoining skittle alley and boules pitch.
⛰Q✿◐⊟▲●P

KINGSKERSWELL

Bickley Mill Inn

Stoneycombe, TQ12 5LN (midway between Ipplepen and Kingskerswell, nr quarry) OS864665
☉ 12-3, 6.30-11; 12-3.30, 7-10.30 Sun
☎ (01803) 873201 website: www.bickleymill.co.uk
Greene King IPA; Teignworthy Springtide, seasonal beer; guest beers Ⓗ
Delightful 13th-century free house, originally a mill, in a beautiful valley. Beamed bars each feature a log fire and comfortable seating while the attractive gardens have shady seating. Centrally located, within 10 minutes of Torbay, Totnes and Newton Abbot, it offers a varied home-cooked menu of local produce with a daily specials board; local beers are used in the cooking. Pleasant bed and breakfast accommodation, a comfortable family room and good disabled facilities make this a splendid choice for all visitors.
⛰Q⛟✿⛽◐♿▲P☐

KINGSWEAR

Ship Inn

Higher Street, TQ6 0AG (just up from steam railway station)
☉ 12-3, 6-11; 7-10.30 Sun
☎ (01803) 752348
Draught Bass; Flowers IPA; Otter Ale Ⓗ
Tucked away behind the church and village hall, this 15th-century, three-roomed pub is worth seeking out. A small, comfortable lounge with oak panelling and roughcast walls leads to a spacious dining room. Views from the window, or the front terrace are spectacular, taking in the steam railway station, marina, Dartmouth and on up the River Dart towards Dittisham. The accommodation is completed by an unpretentious public bar. Q◐⊟

KNOWLE

Dog & Donkey

24 Knowle Village, EX9 6AL
☉ 11-2.30, 6-11; 12-3, 7-10.30 Sun
☎ (01395) 442021
Draught Bass; guest beer Ⓖ
Lively, friendly, village pub retaining many original features, where old photos tell the pub's story. It is a haven for walkers, cyclists and Caravan Club members, free from electronic music. Regular music evenings, including singalongs and live bands, are staged. The guest ales change weekly. Local produce features on an interesting, great value menu. Skittles, euchre and pool teams play here regularly. The pub has received an Award of Excellence from the local environmental health department.
⛰Q⛟✿⛽◐⊟♿▲♣●P⚟☐

LAPFORD

Old Malt Scoop Inn

EX17 6PZ (1/2 mile from A377)
☉ 12-3, 6-11; 11-11 Fri & Sat; 12-4, 7-10.30 Sun
☎ (01363) 83330
Badger Best; Marston's Pedigree; Sharp's Doom Bar, Ⓗ **Special; guest beers** Ⓖ
Popular village local with a friendly welcome on both sides of the bar. Just half a mile from Lapford Station, it supports skittles, darts, pool and soccer teams and hosts folk music sessions. Dating from the 16th century, the pub comprises small, cosy rooms and a no-smoking restaurant. The excellent food is also served in the bar (no meals Mon). In an attractive village setting amid rolling countryside – this is everything a village pub should be, lucky folks of Lapford. ⛰Q✿◐≋♣●P

LOWER ASHTON

Manor Inn

EX6 7QL
(off B3193, between Dunsford and Chudleigh)
☉ 12-2 (2.30 Sat), 6.30-11; closed Mon; 12-2.30, 7-10.30 Sun
☎ (01647) 252304
Princetown Jail Ale; RCH Pitchfork; Teignworthy Reel Ale; guest beers Ⓗ
This small country pub is well known for the high standards of its ale and food. In a delightful setting at the heart of the Teign Valley, it attracts visitors and cyclists, and is easily accessible from Exeter and Torbay. Wood fires in the winter add to the cosy atmosphere of this unaltered pub, while the small garden is popular in summer. There are no fruit machines or piped music in either of the two rooms. ⛰Q✿◐⊟▲●P

LYMPSTONE

Redwing Inn

Church Road, EX8 5JT (off A376, between Exeter and Exmouth)
☉ 11.30-4, 6-11; 11.30-11 Sat; 12-10.30 Sun
☎ (01395) 222156
Greene King Abbot; Otter Bitter; Palmer IPA; guest beer Ⓗ
This friendly pub, that has survived closure in the past, continues to thrive as a village local. Four beers and Thatchers cider are complemented by excellent food – seafood is a speciality. Live jazz on Tuesday and other music on Friday, quiz nights and local sports teams combine to make this a seriously good village pub. ✿◐⊟≋●P

MOLLAND

London Inn

EX36 3NG (2 miles N of B3227)
☉ 12-2.30, 6-11; 12-2.30, 7-10.30 Sun
☎ (01769) 550269
Cotleigh Tawny; Exmoor Ale Ⓖ
Delightful old village pub set on the edge of Exmoor, popular both with locals and visitors to the area. Comprising several small rooms and a restaurant, it can be quite busy during the shooting season – the pub is full of displays connected with shooting and hunting. Molland has a second real ale pub worth a visit, the Black Cock, which is a free house. ⛰Q⛟✿◐

MONKLEIGH

Bell

EX39 5JS (off A386, Bideford-Great Torrington road)
☉ 12-11; 12-10.30 Sun
☎ (01805) 622338
Beer range varies Ⓗ
The focal point of the village, with the

community's shop in the grounds, the pub has a partially thatched roof and is based around a 15th-century building. The garden affords good views. Excellent home-cooked food is served, with some interesting dishes on the menu; a no-smoking area is available for diners. Pool is played here. 🏵🌘🔥♣P

NEWTON ABBOT

Dartmouth Inn
63 East Street, TQ12 2JP (opp. hospital)
🕐 12-3, 4.30-11; 11-11 Sat; 12-10.30 Sun
☎ (01626) 353451
Princetown Dartmoor IPA; H guest beers H /G
This 17th-century free house has been locally described as the village pub within the town. The warm, friendly three-roomed pub, with open fires and a cosy atmosphere, boasts a good selection of guest ales from local micro-breweries, as well as those from further afield. At weekends guest beers are sometimes available on gravity. The cider comes from Devon producer, Winkleigh. This 2002 local CAMRA Pub of the Year has two en-suite guest rooms. 🏠🐕🏵🛏♣🍺

Wolborough Inn
55 Wolborough Street, TQ12 1JQ
🕐 5 (12 Thu)-11; 11-11 Sat; 12-3, 7-10.30 Sun
☎ (01626) 361667
Beer range varies H
Also known locally as the First & Last and the Little House, on account of being the smallest pub in Newton Abbot, the Wolborough is cosy and friendly. It is a basic, town-centre, terraced pub on the main Newton Abbot to Totnes road. Recently refurbished, it has a single room with a bare wood floor, the bar area is to one side, and a small seating area to the other. The old Starkey, Knight and Ford Brewery etched windows have been retained. ♣

NEWTON ST CYRES

Beer Engine
EX5 5AX (1 mile off A377, by station)
🕐 11-11; 12-10.30 Sun
☎ (01392) 851282
Beer Engine Rail Ale, Piston Bitter, Sleeper Heavy, seasonal beers H
Built as a railway hotel in 1850, the pub is home to Devon's oldest brewery (opened in 1983). The pub is a single room, with a dining area, plus a restaurant (children encouraged). The kitchen has recently been refurbished and enlarged; try the locally-made sausages. The bar is decorated with hops, artworks and many photographs of the village. The brewery can be viewed downstairs through glass. Note: all ales are served with sparklers (brewer's policy, but removed on request). 🏠Q🏵🌘🔥🅰🚆♣P🍺

NORTH TAWTON

Railway
Whiddon Down Road, EX20 2BE
(1 mile S of North Tawton) OS666001
🕐 12-2 (not Mon, Wed or Thu), 6-11; 12-3, 7-10.30 Sun
☎ (01837) 82789
Teignworthy Reel Ale; guest beers H
Set in a rural location, the Railway is a friendly, single bar local that is part of a working farm. It stands next to the former North Tawton Station (closed in 1971), which it predates, and the bar decor includes railway memorabilia and old station photos. The beer range, although changing regularly, is generally West Country based, as is the cider stocked in summer. The dining room is popular in the evening (no food Thu eve); just light meals are served at lunchtime. 🛏🌘♣P

NOSS MAYO

Ship Inn
PL8 1EW
🕐 11-11; 12-10.30 Sun
☎ (01752) 872387 website: www.nossmayo.com
Exmoor Gold; Princetown Dartmoor IPA; Shepherd Neame Spitfire; Summerskills Tamar; guest beers H
The recent refurbishment of this pub ensured that its original character has been kept. Situated alongside the River Yealm, it has its own moorings (contact the pub to ascertain the tides). Comfortable seating, inside and out, enables you to enjoy the river views or to peruse the papers and magazines provided. The pub is an ardent supporter of craft ales and local food producers. It is handy for walkers on the South Devon Coastal Path. Children are welcome until 7pm.
🏠Q🏵🌘🔥♣🍺P🚫

OKEHAMPTON

Plymouth Inn
26 West Street, EX20 1HH
🕐 12-11; 12-10.30 Sun
☎ (01837) 53633
Beer range varies G
This 16th-century former coaching inn, stands near the bridge over the West Okement River, at the western end of town. A friendly pub, it brings the welcome and atmosphere of a village local to an old market town. Walking and cycling groups are informally organised in summer, and two beer festivals are held (normally May and Nov). The constantly-changing beer range places the accent on West Country breweries. Occasional live music is performed at this local CAMRA Pub of the Year 2002.
🐕🏵🌘♣🍺

PAIGNTON

Isaac Merritt ⊘
54-58 Torquay Road, TQ3 3AA
🕐 10-11; 12-10.30 Sun
☎ (01803) 556066
Courage Directors; Greene King Abbot; Shepherd Neame Spitfire; Theakston Best Bitter; guest beers H
Busy, town-centre ale house, popular with all ages. Its comfortable, friendly atmosphere is enhanced by cosy seated alcoves and it is accessible to wheelchair-users, with a designated ground floor WC. This superb Wetherspoon's has a deserved reputation for its excellent ever-changing guest beers from all over the country. The house beer, Isaac's Tipple, is brewed by Blackawton. Good value meals are available all day. Fully air-conditioned, it was local CAMRA Pub of the Year 2001.
Q🐕🌘🔥🚆♣🍺🚫

PARKHAM

Bell
EX39 5PL (off A39, between Bideford and Bude)
🕐 12-3, 6-11; 12-3, 7-10.30 Sun
☎ (01237) 451201
Draught Bass; Exmoor Stag; Greene King IPA; Fuller's London Pride Ⓗ

Popular village pub under a thatched roof. One part of the building was recently converted into the local shop, thus cementing its place as the focal point of the community. Visitors to the area might like to try the various real ales that are on offer at another local pub, the Hoops Inn at Horns Cross. ⚫Q🍴🛏◖P

PETER TAVY

Peter Tavy Inn
PL19 9NN
🕐 12-2.30 (3 Sat), 6.30 (6 Fri & Sat)-11; 12-3, 6-10.30 Sun
☎ (01822) 810348
Fuller's London Pride; Princetown Jail Ale; Summerskills Tamar; guest beers Ⓗ

In a quiet village on the edge of Dartmoor, a good range of local beers can be found in the small, central bar of this 15th-century inn. Two larger rooms complement this, one of which is the no-smoking-cum-family room. There is also a patio and hidden garden. The pub is renowned for its food, but drinkers are also welcome. It is situated near a caravan and camping site and is on the No. 27 cycle route. ⚫Q🍴🅿🛏◖ ▲P✂

PLYMOUTH

Blue Peter
68 Pomphlett Road, PL9 7BN
(off A379, follow signs for Turnchapel)
🕐 11-11; 12-10.30 Sun
☎ (01752) 402255
Beer range varies Ⓗ

Once a real ale desert, this area of Plymouth is now blessed with an oasis in the shape of this pub. Two or three constantly-changing guest beers bring relief to local real ale lovers. Home-cooked food and a friendly welcome await visitors to the pub. The large public bar houses a TV and has a games area; background music is played in the lounge.
⚫🅿◖♣P

Britannia Inn ⊘
1 Wolseley Road, Milehouse, PL2 3AE
🕐 10-11; 12-10.30 Sun
☎ (01752) 607596
Courage Directors; Greene King Abbot; Shepherd Neame Spitfire; Theakston Best Bitter, Old Peculier; guest beers Ⓗ

Typical Wetherspoon's conversion from a run-down Edwardian pub into a fine, busy local that truly serves its community, attracting mostly regular locals. It stands by a busy road junction, near the Mayflower Sports Centre in Plymouth's largest public park. The friendly staff serve good quality food. The pub sponsors a player from nearby Plymouth Argyll and admits football supporters on match days, when the atmosphere always remains good-humoured. They stock, on average, four guest beers plus an occasional cider.
Q🅿◖♿≠✂

Commercial Inn
75 Lambhay Hill, The Barbican, PL1 2NR
🕐 11-3, 7-11 (11-11 summer Sat) summer weekdays vary); 12-5 Sun
☎ (01752) 268329
Flowers Original Ⓖ

Beyond and above the hustle of the Barbican and the Mayflower Steps Monument, this single-bar pub sits mid-terrace, and affords a fantastic view across the water to Mount Batten. A strong naval theme is followed with photographs and over 100 ships' plaques. Popular with locals and visitors, only one regular cask feature in winter but there may be guests in summer. Cold snacks are available at lunchtime. It is definitely worth the climb up the steps from Madeira Road.

Dolphin
14 The Barbican, PL1 2LS
(opp. Dartington Glass)
🕐 10-11; 12-10.30 Sun
☎ (01752) 660876
Draught Bass Ⓖ

A must; the only unspoilt pub in Plymouth's historic centre. Opposite the old fish market, it is convenient for the National Aquarium and Mayflower Steps. Paintings of the landlord by a celebrated local artist decorate the walls. The pub windows depict the original Octagon Brewery, which was sold to Plymouth Breweries; the pub is now owned by Punch Taverns. The Tolpuddle Martyrs stayed here on their return to England. The facilities are basic. ⚫Q

Fawn Private Members' Club
39 Prospect Street, North Hill, PL4 8NY
🕐 12 (11 Sat)-11; 12-10.30 Sun
☎ (01752) 660540
Courage Best Bitter; guest beers Ⓗ

Named after HMS Fawn. Formerly a pub, this is now a private members' club; CAMRA members are welcome on production of a current membership card. This no-frills establishment draws from a mainly local clientele. A large-screen TV, dartboard and pool table in the single room ensure a sporting following. Euchre, dominoes and cricket fans are also catered for. Sharp's beers are regularly on tap here. 🅿♿≠♣

Fishermans Arms ⊘
Lambhay Hill, Barbican, PL1 2NN
🕐 11-11; 12-10.30 Sun
☎ (01752) 661457
St Austell Tribute, HSD Ⓗ

Hidden away behind the famous Barbican, and because of its location, used mostly by locals, this pub has two bars. The public bar is lively and the place to go if you want to talk to a local – the lounge bar is comfortable, with a raised area used for diners. This is a welcoming pub in a tourist area, that is worth finding. The view from the front over the Queen Anne Battery is worth the walk. It is one of the few St Austell brewery pubs in Plymouth. ◖🍺♣

Fortescue ⊘
37 Mutley Plain, PL4 6JQ
🕐 11-11; 12-10.30 Sun
☎ (01752) 660673

Draught Bass; Greene King Abbot; guest beers ⒣
This local is situated in a student area, but frequented by a cross-section of the community. It has been described as bohemian. Live sport is not shown in the main bar so as not to spoil the conversational atmosphere, but the cellar bar houses a large-screen TV for major events, and is a venue for musical evenings. The patio garden at the rear is popular in summer. Two or three changing guest beers include some exotic and unusual brews.
⊛◖≠ (North Rd)

Hill Park Inn
32 Hill Park Crescent, Greenbank, PL4 8JP
✪ 11-11; 12-10.30 Sun
☎ (01752) 212177
Draught Bass; Courage Best Bitter; Sharp's Doom Bar ⒣
Recently refurbished two-room pub where the bar is dominated by a large-screen TV and pool table. The quieter lounge has a dartboard and is popular with students. Opposite the fire station, this is one of the closest pubs to Lipson, Plymouth's 'dry' area, ensuring a healthy supply of thirsty regulars. ⇔⊛◖⅋≠♣

Minerva
31 Looe Street, Bretonside, PL4 0EA
(near bus station)
✪ 12-11; 12-10.30 Sun
☎ (01752) 223047
Courage Best Bitter; Greene King Abbot; Sharp's Doom Bar; Wadworth 6X ⒣
Built before the Spanish Armada in 1588, it is not known exactly when the Minerva became an inn. However, it is recognised as the oldest pub in Plymouth. It boasts a fine leaded window and picturesque lantern outside and contains a curious wooden spiral staircase, made from the mast of a captured Spanish galleon. It stages a varied repertoire of live music on four evenings a week. There is a small, sheltered patio for use in summer. ⇔⊛♣♠

Prince Maurice
3 Church Hill, Eggbuckland, PL6 5RJ
✪ 11-3, 7-11; 11-11 Fri & Sat; 12-4, 7-10.30 Sun
☎ (01752) 771515
Adnams Broadside; Badger Tanglefoot; Draught Bass; Courage Best Bitter; Summerskills Best Bitter; guest beers ⒣
Cosy, friendly, two-bar pub close to the church and dating from the 16th century. It is situated in an area that still has a village atmosphere, despite now being surrounded by residential development. Prince Maurice was the nephew of Charles I, who stayed nearby during the Civil War while leading the Royalist offensive against the local Parliamentarian stronghold. The pub is a frequent winner of Plymouth CAMRA's Pub of the Year award. ⇔⊛♣♠P

Royal Albert Bridge Inn
930 Wolseley Road, Saltash Passage, PL5 1LB
✪ 11-11, 12-10.30 Sun
☎ (01752) 361108
Draught Bass; Courage Best Bitter; guest beer ⒣
Small pub enjoyed by locals and visitors alike. Standing in the shadow of Brunel's famous railway bridge, it affords views across the River Tamar to Cornwall, and

features much maritime memorabilia. Good, freshly-cooked food, includes very popular Sunday roasts, and a tempting range of desserts. An Italian Motorcycle Club meets here every month. Note the memorial to the US troops who left from here on D-Day, just outside the pub.
Q⊛◖⅋≠ (Ferry Rd/St Budeaux) ♣⊁

Thistle Park Brewhouse
32 Commercial Road, Coxside, PL4 0LE
(between Aquarium and Warner village)
✪ 11-2am; 12-12.30am Sun
☎ (01752) 204890
Sutton Plymouth Pride, XSB, Comfort, Eddystone, seasonal beers; guest beer (occasional) ⒣
This friendly, basic pub can be reached by foot via a swing bridge from the historic Barbican. It has bare floorboards and an air of a village pub within the city. The beers come from the adjacent Sutton Brewery, plus an occasional guest. Those with strong jaws should try the biltong, a delicacy from the landlord's native South Africa. 'Lunches' are served until 5pm. Pavement tables are set out in fine weather. Live music is staged regularly; note the late licence. ⊛◖♣

London Inn
Church Road, PL7 1NH
✪ 11-11; 12-10.30 Sun
☎ (01752) 337025
Courage Best Bitter; Greene King Ruddles County; guest beers ⒣
Two-bar, 17th-century former coaching inn, situated just off Fore Street in a conservation area. The walls of the lounge are adorned with ship's crests and other naval memorabilia. An upstairs function room is available, and regular food theme nights featuring ethnic cuisines are held. The garden lies across the road and off a passageway, near the church.
⇔Q⊛◖⅋♣P

Blacksmith's Arms
EX15 2JU
✪ 12-2.30 (not Mon), 6-11; 12-3, 7-10.30 Sun
☎ (01884) 277474
Banks's Hanson's Mild; O'Hanlons Fire Fly; Otter Ale; guest beers ⒣
This 18th-century popular village pub enjoys a reputation for good food, that is usually sourced locally; a children's menu is available. Occasional live music and quiz nights are staged; skittles and boules are played. From easy chairs around the log-burner admire the oak-beamed interior, decorated with blacksmith's tools, diving memborabilia and a collection of deer antlers. In summer this friendly local holds barbecues and plays host to local and touring cricket sides. ⇔Q⊛◖♣P

Warren House Inn
PL20 6TA (on B3212, Mortonhampstead road)
✪ 11-3, 6-11; 11-11 Fri, Sat & summer; 12-10.30 Sun
☎ (01822) 880208
Butcombe Gold; Moor Old Freddy Walker; Sharp's Doom Bar; guest beer ⒣
The third highest inn in England, this

isolated hostelry is a welcome sight on wild Dartmoor. A great place to seek shelter and refreshment when crossing the moor by whatever means, it is well worth a visit. The new dining area opens during summer for groups and is no-smoking, unlike the fire that has burnt continuously since 1845. A good range of home-cooked food is served – light lunches and a fuller evening menu. Countryman cider is stocked in summer.
🏨Q🍴🛏️🛉⏰♿🅿️✂️

PRINCETOWN

Plume of Feathers
The Square, PL20 6QQ
⏰ 11-11; 12-10.30 Sun
☎ (01822) 890240
website: www.plumeoffeathers-dartmoor.co.uk
Draught Bass; Princetown Dartmoor IPA; Jail Ale Ⓗ
Princetown's oldest building (1785) features copper-topped bars, a slate floor and granite walls. Attracting locals, visitors, walkers, runners and all, the range of different rooms includes a family room with its own bar. Outside, the accommodation offered includes a campsite, bunkhouses and three guest rooms, with good facilities for all. The cider is from Countryman. A wide range of food, including a good children's menu, is served all day. A ghost (Moaning Myrtle?) reputedly haunts the ladies' loo.
🏨Q🍴🛏️🛉⏰♿🅿️🔌♿♣🅿️

Prince of Wales
Tavistock Road, PL20 6QF
⏰ 11-11; 12-10.30 Sun
☎ (01822) 890219
Draught Bass; Princetown Dartmoor IPA, Jail Ale; guest beers Ⓗ
Just down the road from the main square, this is the tap for the Princetown Brewery, at the rear. The main bar leads to a small pool room and the restaurant, which doubles as a no-smoking area for drinkers. The pub holds a children's certificate and stages occasional live music, including informal folk evenings, on the last Thursday of the month. The Yelverton–Princetown cycle route ends conveniently behind the pub. Home-cooked dishes include Jail Ale pie. 🏨🛏️⏰♿♣🅿️✂️

Railway Inn
Two Bridges Road, PL20 6QT
⏰ 11-11; 12-10.30 Sun
☎ (01822) 890232
Sutton Dartmoor Pride; Teignworthy Old Moggie; Wadworth 6X Ⓗ
Although Princetown's railway closed in 1956, the walls of this cosy pub are hung with its memorabilia. The numerous rooms offer a homely alternative to its famous neighbour (the prison) and include a family room and skittle alley. Appealing to locals and visitors alike, meals from the menu and specials board are served all day. The Luscombe organic cider is worth a try (even though kept in a keg). The pub fields darts and skittles teams. 🏨Q🛏️🛉🛏️⏰♿♣🅿️

SIDBURY

Red Lion
Fore Street, EX10 0SD
⏰ 12-2.30 (not Tue), 6-11; 12-3, 7-10.30 Sun
☎ (01395) 597313

Adnams Broadside; guest beers Ⓗ
Step inside this popular 400-year-old coaching inn, replete with beams, original floorboards, hops and brass, to take in the atmosphere of a real village pub/post office. Cheerful, helpful staff greet you in the pleasant bar and dining area. It holds a beer festival every Easter and stages live bands. It is home to Sidbury cricket club. The skittle alley doubles as a function room. Suggestions to the landlord for guest ales are always appreciated.
Q🛉🛏️⏰🔌♿♿♣

SILVERTON

Lamb Inn
Fore Street, EX5 4HZ
⏰ 11-2.30, 6-11; 11-11 Sat; 12-10.30 Sun
website: www.thelamb-inn.com
Draught Bass; Ⓗ **Exe Valley Dob's Best Bitter; guest beers** Ⓖ
Family-run village pub: all stone floors, stripped timber and old pine furniture. Most ales are served from a temperature-controlled stillage behind the bar. A multi-purpose function room houses a skittle alley and bar. Good value, home-cooked food includes a specials board which always features a vegetarian option; monthly steak nights are held with low prices. Village organisations, such as bell ringers and short mat bowlers use the pub as a meeting place.
🏨⏰♿♣✂️

SLAPTON

Queen's Arms
TQ7 2PN (signed off A379)
⏰ 12-3, 6-11; 12-3, 7-10.30 Sun
☎ (01548) 580800
website: www.slapton.org/queensarms
Princetown Dartmoor IPA; Teignworthy Reel Ale; guest beers Ⓗ
South Devon free house; this single bar, with a traditional atmosphere and large open fire, stocks one or two guest ales depending on the time of year. A full menu is served, with the chef's home-made pies a speciality (takeaways available). See the many old photos of the area, including those of wartime evacuation. Peaceful, secluded walled gardens and a patio add to its appeal. Children and dogs are welcome.
🏨Q🛉🔌⏰♣🅿️

SOUTH MOLTON

King's Arms
4 King Street, EX36 3BL
⏰ 10.30-11; 12-10.30 Sun
☎ (01769) 572679
Draught Bass; Cotleigh Tawny; guest beer Ⓗ
No-nonsense local, attracting a varied clientele, depending on the time of day. It can be noisy, but the games machines, pool table and TV are at one end of the long bar; a quieter area, with ample seating, overlooks the town square. You will find a warm welcome and plenty of conversation – everyone seems to know each other. No food is advertised, but basic snacks are available on request. The guest beer is supplied by Cotleigh.
♣🍺

SOUTH POOL

Millbrook Inn
TQ7 2RW (off A379 at Chillington, E of Kingsbridge)
OS776402
🕐 12-2.30, 6-11 (10.30 winter); 12-3, 7-10.30 Sun
☎ (01548) 531581 website: www.millbrookinn.co.uk
Draught Bass; G Fuller's London Pride; guest beers Ⓗ
The Millbrook is situated at the head of the Salcombe estuary. The main section of the pub dates back to the early 17th century, with the top bar (where children are welcome) added later. The pub is busy in summer, with most of its trade coming from boaters and walkers. Famed for its crab sandwiches; no Sunday evening meals are served January–March. Note: no debit or credit cards are accepted. Dogs are welcome.
🏚Q🏶◑Ⓖ♣

SOUTH ZEAL

King's Arms
EX20 2JP
🕐 12-2.30, 5.30-11; 12-10.30 Sun
☎ (01837) 840300
Adnams Bitter; Greene King Abbot; Otter Ale; Young's Special Ⓗ
Thatched, 14th-century ale house (or more accurately a former cider house), which is still a popular meeting place. It stands towards the top of the hill at the western end of the village. The landlord is active in the local folk music scene, so live music is not an uncommon occurrence in one of the two bars; this is usually acoustic, but sometimes jazz, and sometimes impromptu.
🏚🏶◑♿Å♣P

STICKLEPATH

Devonshire Inn
EX20 2NW
🕐 11-3, 5-11 (11-11 school holidays); 12-3, 7-10.30 Sun
☎ (01837) 840626
Draught Bass; St Austell Tinners, HSD Ⓖ
At the end of what was a terrace of Elizabethan cottages in this North Dartmoor village, the Devonshire is an unspoilt thatched local, with low ceilings and a large open fire. A leat, running past the back wall of the pub, helps to cool the stillage for the beers, as well as powering the waterwheels of the Finch Foundry Museum (NT) next door. The Exeter–Okehampton bus service stops outside, and a number of footpaths access the Dartmoor countryside.
🏚Q🏶Å♣P

Taw River Inn
EX20 2NB
🕐 12-3, 5-11, 11-11 Thu-Sat; 12-10.30 Sun
☎ (01837) 840377
Greene King Abbot; Sharp's Doom Bar; guest beer Ⓗ
The Taw River is an active village local on the old A30. The large, single bar is usually lively; numerous sports and pub games are followed by the regulars. The Exeter–Okehampton bus service stops nearby and the area is popular for walking in the summer. The Finch Foundry Museum is just across the road. There is a camping barn behind (but not owned by) the pub.
🏚🏶◑Å♣P

STOCKLAND

King's Arms Inn
EX14 9BS
🕐 12-3, 6.30-11; 12-3, 6.30-10.30 Sun
☎ (01404) 881361 website: www.kingsarms.net
Exmoor Ale; Otter Bitter, Ale; guest beers Ⓗ
This 16th-century former coaching inn is set on the eastern edge of the picturesque Blackdown Hills. Its large public bar is very popular, especially for live music on Saturday and Sunday evenings. There is also a smaller lounge and a well-used skittle alley. The no-smoking restaurant is renowned for good quality food; bar meals are also available at lunchtime. Two ever-changing guest beers always include an O'Hanlon's beer; Inch's and Jack Rat cider are sold in summer. 🏚Q🏶🛏◑Ⓖ♣♣P🛈

TAVISTOCK

Trout & Tipple
Parkwood Road, PL19 0JS
🕐 12-2.30 (not Tue), 6-11; 12-3, 6 (7 winter)-10.30 Sun
☎ (01822) 618886 website: www.troutandtipple.co.uk
Princetown Jail Ale; Blackawton seasonal beers; guest beers Ⓗ
Situated just a mile north of Tavistock, this hostelry features a traditionally-appointed bar, with a large, no-smoking conservatory and dining area. A games room and a small patio complete the picture. Nearby is a trout fishery from which its name derives, so not surprisingly trout appears on the menu; alongside good value alternatives. The pub holds a children's certificate (children welcome until 9pm). The car park is across the road. 🏚Q⛵🏶◑Å♣P⌀

TEIGNMOUTH

Blue Anchor Inn
Teign Street, TQ14 8EG (close to docks)
🕐 11-11; 12-10.30 Sun
☎ (01626) 772741
Beer range varies Ⓗ
Small locals' pub, close to the docks, regularly serving up to six real ales. A single bar, warmed by stoves at each end, contains a juke box, pool table and dartboard. The small garden hosts summer barbecues. Full of local character and charm, it nonetheless has a cosmopolitan atmosphere. The car park is small. 🏶🚉♣P

Golden Lion
85 Bitton Park Road, TQ4 5NG (on A379)
🕐 12-4, 6-11; 12-4, 7.30-10.30 Sun
☎ (01626) 776442
Beer range varies Ⓗ
Friendly and welcoming, this typical two-bar pub, overlooks the docks. There is a cosy, L-shaped lounge bar with beamed ceilings and a larger public bar housing an L-shaped bar and a pool table. Three ever-changing real ales are served on handpump at very reasonable prices. This darts-oriented pub boasts no less than three dartboards. Parking outside is limited. Ⓖ🚉♣P

TIVERTON

White Ball Inn 🏅
Bridge Street, EX16 5LY
🕐 10-11; 12-10.30 Sun

☎ (01884) 251525
Blackdown Premium; Courage Directors; Exmoor Stag;
Shepherd Neame Spitfire; Theakston Best Bitter;
guest beers Ⓗ
This spacious, multi-roomed pub close to
the River Exe, offers an extensive outdoor
area, overlooking the river. An old well can
be observed in the bar area, through a
reinforced glass panel in the floor – quite
disconcerting. Handy for the town centre,
many regulars enjoy Wetherspoon's
inexpensive ale and food at this friendly
pub. ⚌Q⚏❀◑▣♿

TOPSHAM

Bridge Inn ☆
Bridge Hill, EX3 0QQ (by River Clyst on Exmouth
road)
✪ 12-2, 6-10.30 (11 Fri & Sat); 12-2, 7-10.30 Sun
☎ (01392) 873862 website: www.cheffers.co.uk
Adnams Broadside; Branscombe Vale Branoc,
seasonal beers; guest beers Ⓖ
Grade II listed inn overlooking the River
Clyst, with no juke boxes, no fruit machines
and no lager other than occasional
Schiehallion. Regular beers generally
include Branscombe Vale and other local
and regional beers. Simple fare includes
home-made soup and ploughmans. The
Queen has visited this pub, which has been
run by the same family for over 100 years.
For lovers of real ale, it is a pub not to be
missed. ⚌Q❀❅⇌P

Lighter Inn ⊘
The Quay, Fore Street, EX3 0HZ
✪ 11-11; 12-10.30 Sun
☎ (01392) 875439
Badger Best, Tanglefoot, seasonal beers Ⓗ
Formerly a customs house, this attractive,
spacious pub is situated on Topsham's old
quay, benefiting from splendid views across
the river. The most westerly of Hall &
Woodhouse's pubs, it attracts a good mix of
tourists and locals. A maritime theme is
carried throughout; of the two no-smoking
areas, one is for family use. Food is
prominent with lots of fresh fish, plus
vegetarian options. Extensive
refurbishment, scheduled for November
2003, will involve temporary closure for up
to four months. ⚌⚏❀◑⇌✂

TORQUAY

Crown & Sceptre
2 Petitor Road, St Marychurch, TQ1 4QA
✪ 11-3 (12-4 Fri), 5.30-11; 11-4, 6.30-11 Sat;
12-4, 7.30-10.30 Sun
☎ (01803) 328290
Draught Bass; Courage Best Bitter, Directors; Fuller's
London Pride; Greene King Old Speckled Hen; Young's
Special; guest beers Ⓗ
200-year-old, characterful coaching house,
featuring exposed stone walls in the
lounge where a collection of chamber pots
hangs. A constant entry in this Guide for
27 years, with a friendly, outgoing
atmosphere, it has a wide following of
devotees. Jazz is staged on Sunday and
Tuesday evenings; other live music on
Saturday and folk on the second Thursday
in the month. It has two enclosed
gardens; children are welcome at this dog-
friendly pub. No food is served Sunday.
⚌Q❀◑▣♣P

Hole in the Wall
6 Park Lane, The Strand, TQ1 5AU
✪ 11-11; 12-10.30 Sun
☎ (01803) 298020
Draught Bass; Courage Best Bitter; Wells Bombardier;
guest beers Ⓗ
Tucked away in the centre of Torquay, only
a few yards from the harbour, is Torquay's
oldest inn (circa 1540). For hundreds of
years smugglers, men of the sea, business
types, locals and visitors alike have enjoyed
drinking in this authentic, comfortable
establishment with its listed cobbled floors,
beamed ceilings and warm atmosphere.
Dogs on leads are welcome. Food is served
all day in summer. ⚏❀◑▣

TOTNES

Rumours Wine Bar
30 High Street, TQ9 5RY
✪ 10-11; 6-10.30 Sun
☎ (01803) 864682
Beer range varies Ⓗ
Typical, town-centre wine bar that serves
three real ales, plus farm cider and a wide
range of continental bottled beers and
lagers; Black Pearl Stout and draught
Erdinger wheat beer are also stocked. This
14th-century town house has an open-plan
bar that is extremely popular with locals, as
much for the good food and extensive wine
list as for the range of beers. The talented
young chef does a good line in home-
cooked takeaway pizzas. ⚌◑⇌♠

TUCKENHAY

Maltster's Arms
Bow Creek, TQ9 7EQ
(signed from A381, Totnes-Kingsbridge road)
✪ 11-11; 12-10.30 Sun
☎ (01803) 732350 website: www.tuckenhay.com
Princetown Dartmoor IPA; guest beers Ⓗ
Marvellous pub overlooking the peaceful,
wooded Bow Creek. Tables by the water and
boat moorings are available. The pub's
narrow main bar links two other cosy
rooms, the snug and another with red-
painted seats and kitchen chairs on a wood
floor. The restaurant serves excellent food,
while barbecues and live music are held in
summer at the creek's edge.
Accommodation is available (10% discount
for card-carrying CAMRA members); the
beer is expensive. Heron Valley cider is
stocked in summer.
⚌Q⚏❀⊠◑♣♠P

TURNCHAPEL

New Inn
1 Boringdon Road, PL9 9TB
(on A379, follow signs to Mountbatten and Turnchapel)
✪ 12-3 (not Mon-Thu), 6-11; 12-11 Sat; 12-10.30 Sun
☎ (01752) 402675
Draught Bass; Princetown Jail Ale; Sharp's Doom Bar;
Taylor Landlord; guest beers Ⓗ
This village pub was originally three
buildings: a bakery, a butcher's and a
tavern. On the outskirts of Plymouth, the
new inn stands at the waterside, looking out
across the Cattewater to Plymouth Hoe.
Enjoying an excellent reputation for both
beer and food, the pub is accessible from
Plymouth city centre by bus or water taxi

from the Barbican. Some of the inn's five quiet, en-suite guest rooms benefit from sea views. ⚄Q⊯⊲◑♣P

WEMBURY

Odd Wheel
Knighton Road, PL9 0JD
☼ 12-3, 6.30-11; 12-11 Sat; 12-4, 7-10.30 Sun
☎ (01752) 862287
Courage Best Bitter; Princetown Jail Ale; Skinner's Coast Liner; Sutton XSB; guest beers Ⓖ
Friendly pub in the South Hams, on a regular bus route from Plymouth. It comprises a large lounge with dining tables and comfortable seating, plus a lively public bar. The pub runs its own golfing society and is the meeting place for a sailing club, darts and football teams. The garden affords views of the rolling countryside. Close to Wembury Bay and the Mewstone, it makes a good start, or finishing point, for a coastal walk. Home-cooked food includes dishes with a Mediterranean flavour.
⚄Q❀◑⊲P

WEST DOWN

Crown Inn
The Square, EX34 8NV (1 mile off A3123)
☼ 12-3; 7 (6 summer)-11; 12-10.30 Sun
☎ (01271) 862790
Barum Original; Draught Bass; guest beer Ⓗ
Archetypal village inn, set on the square of this quiet rural village. Dating from the 17th century, but sympathetically refurbished, the small bar on the right houses a TV and pool table, while the long bar to the left leads around to the dining area. The wonderful country garden is a pleasure on a nice summer's evening. Thatcher's cider appears on the bar in summer. CAMRA members receive discounts on accommodation.
⚄Q❀⊯◑⊲⚓▲♣P⊁

WESTWARD HO!

Nelson
5 Nelson Road, EX39 1LP
☼ 11-11; 12-10.30 Sun
☎ (01237) 474745
Fuller's London Pride; guest beer Ⓗ
This pub was originally built for residential purposes. There is a separate dining area and large-screen TV in the bar for major sporting events. A second guest beer is stocked in summer. You are always assured of a warm welcome here, despite the tourist location.
❀⊯◑⊲▲♣P

WHIDDON DOWN

Post Inn
Exeter Road, EX20 2QT
☼ 11-11; closed Tue; 12-10.30 Sun
☎ (01647) 231242
Beer range varies Ⓗ
Built in the 16th century as the post office on the old coaching road to the west, the Post is a pleasantly refurbished country pub, handy for the A30 and keen to cater for modern travellers (meals are available 11–11). The central bar serves three rooms; the two side rooms, although generally laid out for diners, are available for no-smoking

drinkers. The ales follow a West Country theme, and the cider is local. Occasional beer festivals are held. ⚄Q◑⊲▲♣P⊓

WHIMPLE

New Fountain Inn
Church Road, EX5 2TA (leave A30 at Daisymount, follow signs)
☼ 12-3, 6.30-11; 12-3, 7-10.30 Sun
☎ (01404) 822350
Branscombe Vale Branoc; Teignworthy Reel Ale; O'Hanlon's Fire Fly, Yellowhammer Ⓖ
Friendly, two-bar, village pub, serving an excellent menu at superb value prices. Well-behaved children are welcome. Special events here include wassailing in January (the village was the original home of Whiteways Cider), occasional charity quiz nights and live music. Visit the Heritage Centre, situated in a building in the car park. ⚄Q❀◑⊲⚓⇌♣P

WIDECOMBE IN THE MOOR

Rugglestone Inn
TQ13 7TF (¼ mile S of village centre) OS721766
☼ 11-3, 7-11 (11-11 summer); 12-3, 7-10.30 (12-10.30 summer) Sun
☎ (01364) 621327 website: www.rugglestone.f9.co.uk
Butcombe Bitter; St Austell Dartmoor Best Ⓖ
Unspoilt cosy pub in a splendid Dartmoor setting. The small bar area has some seating and a stone floor; beer is also available through a small serving-hatch in the passageway. The lounge is warmed by an open fire. The pub is named after a local 'Logan' stone. Children under 14 are not allowed inside, but across the stream is a large grassed seating area with a shelter for use in bad weather. The car park is just down the lane. ⚄Q❀◑▲♣P

WOODLAND

Rising Sun
TQ13 7JT (signed on A38 to Plymouth) OS790697
☼ 11.45-3 (not Mon), 6-11 (not winter Mon); 12-3, 7-10.30 Sun
☎ (01364) 652544
website: www.risingsunwoodland.co.uk
Princetown Jail Ale; guest beers Ⓗ
Lovely, spacious, free house in beautiful countryside between Torbay and Dartmoor. The long, single bar has large open-plan drinking and dining areas, with small screens offering some privacy. An additional children's area lies off the main bar. Note the collection of keys hanging from the ceiling. Extensive grounds have seating and a children's play area. Excellent food – try the home-made pies. Accommodation is available and the pub is suitable for parties and functions. ⚄Q⛄⊯◑AP⊁

YARCOMBE

Yarcombe Angel
EX14 9BD (on A30)
☼ 12-3, 6.30-11; 12-3, 7.30-10.30 Sun
☎ (01404) 861676
Draught Bass; Black Sheep Best Bitter; Greene King Abbot; Taylor Landlord; guest beers Ⓖ
The 14th-century building was part of the estate given to Francis Drake by Elizabeth I. The landlord is enthusiastic about beer, and is often 'helped' in the bar by his friendly

'Dulux' dog. The interior has been refashioned to give a long room, with the bar at one end and a fire at the other. There is also a back room with a pool table, and a skittle alley upstairs. Occasional mini-fests and music nights are staged.
🅰Q🍴◖❚P

YEOFORD

Mare & Foal
The Village, EX17 5JD
🕐 12-2.30, 6-11; 12-2.30, 7-10.30 Sun

☎ (01363) 84348
Beer range varies Ⓗ/Ⓖ
Although built in the 1830s to serve the expanding railway, its appearance is that of a pub rather than a railway hotel. An open fire, interconnecting rooms, a skittle alley and a dining room characterise this pub. The house food speciality is steaks. Traditional beer is to the fore, with usually one from Sharp's and one from Otter, but do not be disappointed if the gravity beer is off – the locals cannot get enough of it!
🅰Q📶🐕◖❧♣◖P✂

Hold the front page...

Members of CAMRA receive a free monthly newspaper, What's Brewing. It is packed with up-to date information about beer, brewing and pubs, and will keep you informed about all the latest developments in the beer world. What's Brewing also lists CAMRA beer festivals throughout the country, along with CAMRA branch and regional activities.

What's Brewing has the best and most authoritative writers. It is edited by Ted Bruning, and regular columnists include Jeff Evans, Good Beer Guide editor Roger Protz, and Arthur Taylor. John Reynolds surveys the City scene while laughter is provided by veteran cartoonist Bill Tidy with his Kegbuster strip.

What's Brewing is worth the price of CAMRA membership alone. To receive your monthly copy, sign up for membership by using the form at the back of the Guide.

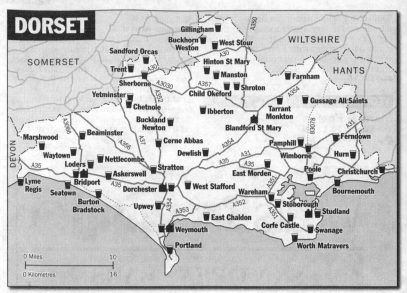

DORSET

ASKERSWELL

Spyway
DT2 9EP (signed off A35 E of Bridport) OS529933
☼ 11.30-2.30, 6-11; closed Mon; 12-3, 7-10.30 Sun
☎ (01308) 485250
Greene King Abbot; Goldfinch Tom Brown; Palmer IPA (summer)**; Quay Best Bitter, JD 1742** Ⓖ
Situated above the village on an old road called Spyway, this smugglers' inn dates from 1600. The south-facing garden provides stunning views of the surrounding walking country. Inside is a comfortable lounge, dining room and cosy, beamed bar with open fire, settles and horse brasses. The ample food menu uses local farm produce. The local theme continues with beers from Dorset breweries at Bridport, Dorchester and Weymouth, all served direct from the cask.
🏨Q❀🚐🌢P

BEAMINSTER

Greyhound Inn
The Square, DT8 3AW
☼ 11-2.30, 6.30-11; 12-3, 7-10.30 Sun
☎ (01308) 862496 website: www.grey-hound-inn.co.uk
Palmer Bridport Bitter, Copper Ale, IPA, 200, Tally Ho! Ⓗ
Attractive, rendered pub with lichen-spotted roof and slatted window shutters that belie the even more attractive 18th-century character interior. A spacious flagstoned bar, with a stone fireplace opens into a comfortable dining area. A shadowy passage, hung with local photos and Guinness cartoons leads to an intimate family/function room. The pub caters for local and visiting trade, with a varied menu including local fish, steaks, pasta and vegetarian dishes. Dogs are welcome.
🏨Q🌢🌢♣👤

BOURNEMOUTH

Goat & Tricycle ⊘
27-29 West Hill Road, BH2 5PP
☼ 12-3, 6-11; 12-3, 7-10.30 Sun
☎ (01202) 314220
Red Shoot Tom's Tipple; Wadworth IPA, 6X, JCB, seasonal beers; guest beers Ⓗ
Split-level pub with a central bar, this was formerly two neighbouring pubs that have been cleverly knocked together. It keeps the full range of Wadworth beers plus seasonal brews and guest ales. A courtyard, which is covered, is a riot of colour in the summer, with well-planted hanging baskets and tubs; just watch out for the gnomes. Good food is served lunchtime and early evening.
🏨Q🌢❀🌢

Porterhouse ⊘
113 Poole Road, Westbourne, BH4 8BY
☼ 11-11; 12-10.30 Sun
☎ (01202) 768586
Ringwood Best Bitter, Fortyniner, Old Thumper, seasonal beers; guest beers Ⓗ
This small but busy pub sells the whole range of Ringwood beers plus guest ales and a traditional cider. Wood floors, panelling and settles give the pub a cosy atmosphere. This Ringwood house has won local CAMRA's Pub of the Year award six times in nine years. Lunches are served Monday–Saturday.
Q🌢⇌(Branksome)♣👤

Shoulder of Mutton
1010 Ringwood Road, BH11 9LA
☼ 12-2.30, 6-11; 12-4.30, 7-11 Sat; 12-3.30, 7-10.30 Sun
☎ (01202) 573124
Flowers Original; guest beers Ⓗ
Bournemouth's third oldest pub and one of the few still with a separate public bar. The large car park adjoins the children's play area. The pub stands alongside the original Ringwood road, now overshadowed by the dual carriageway. The pub has been extended at both ends of the building, but has retained its heart, where the flagstoned floor was laid over 200 years ago. Ask to play on the century-old shove-ha'penny slate in the public bar.
❀🌢🌢♣P

BRIDPORT

Hope & Anchor
13 St Michaels Lane, DT6 3RA
✿ 11-11; 12-10.30 Sun
☎ (01308) 422160
Beer range varies Ⓗ
Unspoilt, back-street local presided over by a welcoming landlady. It hosts live music, mainly blues, on Sunday lunchtime and most Friday and Saturday evenings. An ever-changing selection of three real ales from West Country brewers is supplemented by occasional beer festivals in summer. Three ciders are also served: Taunton, Burrow Hill and Cheddar Valley. The pub has no parking space but both the bus station and a municipal car park are next door. ♨✿♣👜

BUCKHORN WESTON

Stapleton Arms
Church Hill, SP8 5HS (signed from A30)
✿ 11-3, 6-11; 12-3, 6-10.30 Sun
☎ (01963) 370396
website: www.thestapletonarms.co.uk
Butcombe Bitter; Ringwood Best Bitter; guest beers Ⓗ
This outstanding village pub, now into its third year under the present ownership, continues to thrive as a true hub for its community. This is largely due to the popularity, locally and further afield, of its beer and its food, and also to its welcome to both visitors and to regulars. The children's play area next to the attractive garden has been further developed. The cider is Westons Old Rosie. ♨✿🛏◑♣👜P

BUCKLAND NEWTON

Gaggle of Geese
DT2 7BS (E of village, 600 yds from B3143)
✿ 12-2.30, 6.30-11; 12-3, 7-10.30 Sun
☎ (01300) 345249 website: www.gaggleofgeese.co.uk
Badger Best; Butcombe Bitter; Ringwood Best Bitter, Fortyniner; guest beers Ⓗ
Excellent village pub at the head of the Piddle Valley. A genuine free house, it provides the village with an Internet connection, as well as goose auctions, combined with car boot sales. The bars are different levels and a large garden is an added attraction. The menu is extensive, offering many home-made dishes. Popular with walkers and cyclists alike, the adjacent Caravan Club members site is run from the pub. ♨Q♿◑♿♣P👜

BURTON BRADSTOCK

Three Horseshoes
DT6 4QZ
✿ 11-11; 12-10.30 Sun
☎ (01308) 897259
Palmer Copper Ale, IPA, Dorset Gold, 200, Tally Ho! Ⓗ
Attractive, thatched building in a pretty village close to Chesil Beach. Extensive restaurant and bar menus specialise in local fish and game and it is one of the few pubs in the area to sell Tally Ho! There are two outdoor areas: a secluded garden and a series of south-facing benches. Inside, the low beams and open fire make this a popular pub in winter, too. Good quality live music is regularly performed. ♨✿◑🅿P

CERNE ABBAS

Royal Oak
23 Long Street, DT2 7JG
✿ 11.30 (11 Sat)-3, 6-11; 12-3, 7-10.30 Sun
☎ (01300) 341797
Butcombe Bitter; Greene King Old Speckled Hen; Quay Best Bitter; Wadworth IPA, 6X Ⓗ
Picturesque, thatched, stone pub, easily noticed by the creeper hanging all down the front. Built in 1540, it has three bars with stone flags and much timber. The decor features wooden settles, armchairs and a huge collection of horse brasses. The pub is well known for its good food. Walking from the pub, past the handsome church and remains of Cistercian abbey, a footpath leads towards the hill sporting the famous priapic giant. ♨Q✿◑♣

CHETNOLE

Chetnole Inn
DT9 6NU
✿ 11-2.30, 6-11; 12-3, 7-10.30 Sun
☎ (01935) 872337
Branscombe Vale Branoc; Butcombe Bitter; Palmer IPA; guest beers Ⓗ
This popular village pub, opposite the church, is a 15-minute walk from the tiny halt on the Weymouth–Bristol line. It is surrounded by unspoilt countryside, criss-crossed by footpaths. The inn has two bars; the lounge has a cosy eating area. Tables outside catch all the sun and there is also a garden and skittle alley. Each bank holiday there are several extra beers available. No food is served Sunday evening, or Wednesday. ♨Q🛏◑🚆♿🅰♣P👜

CHILD OKEFORD

Saxon Inn
Gold Hill, DT11 8HD OS829135
✿ 11-2.30 (not Tue; 3 Sat), 7-11; 12-3, 7-10.30 Sun
☎ (01258) 860310
Butcombe Bitter; guest beers Ⓗ
This welcoming pub stands at the north end of the village, nestling against the foot of Hambledon Iron Age hill fort which offers spectacular views across the River Stour and Vale of Blackmoor. The pub was converted from three cottages in 1949, but looks older, with a low, beamed ceiling and settles. Two rooms are served from one small bar. Excellent food is cooked to order (no eve meals Tue or Sun). It also has a large garden. ♨Q✿◑♿🅰♣P

CHRISTCHURCH

Olde George Inn
2A Castle Street, BH23 1DT
✿ 11-11; 12-10.30 Sun
☎ (01202) 479383
Flowers Original; Hampshire Strong's Best Bitter; Ringwood Fortyniner; guest beers Ⓗ
Former Tudor coaching inn, with two low-

INDEPENDENT BREWERIES

Badger Blandford St Mary
Goldfinch Dorchester
Isle of Purbeck Studland
Palmer Bridport
Quay Weymouth

ceilinged rooms, one set aside for diners. A covered courtyard, where children are permitted, is heated in winter. This leads to a barn bar which hosts jazz on Thursday evening and folk bands on Friday; admission is free to these very popular events. Two ciders are normally on tap along with a dark mild (usually Brains Dark). ⚞⊛◑◔

CORFE CASTLE

Greyhound Inn
The Square, BH20 5EZ
🕓 11-3, 6-11; 11-11 Sat; 12-10.30 Sun
☎ (01929) 480205
Beer range varies Ⓗ
This perfectly situated pub nestles at the foot of the castle, and its garden affords a splendid view of the ruins. The main bar area serves the long, curved front bar and some smaller sections at the back of the pub. An extensive food menu complements the ever-changing guest ales. A beer festival is held in the spring.
🏚Q⚞⊛◑Ⓐ♣

DEWLISH

Oak at Dewlish
DT2 7ND OS775981
🕓 11.30-3, 6.30-11; 12-3, 7-10.30 Sun
☎ (01258) 837352
Ringwood Best Bitter; Ⓖ **guest beer** Ⓗ
Welcome return for this small country pub, which was closed for some time and its future looked bleak. The village boasts a Stuart house, and a park; the remains of a medieval village can be detected opposite the pub. The interior consists of an L-shaped bar decorated in stripped pine; one area is set aside for diners enjoying the interesting menu. One beer is served from a wooden stillage behind the bar. A cider is sometimes stocked in summer.
🏚Q⚞◑♿♣P

DORCHESTER

Colliton Club
Colliton House, Colliton Park, DT1 1XJ
(opp. County Hall)
🕓 12-2.30 (3 Fri & Sat), 7-11; closed Sun
☎ (01305) 224503
Badger Best; Greene King IPA, Abbot; Palmer IPA; Ringwood Best Bitter; guest beer Ⓗ
Local government club located in the grounds of Dorset County Council offices. It will admit CAMRA members and anyone carrying a current edition of this Guide. It always has a choice of six very reasonably-priced real ales. Pub games include skittles, darts, pool and snooker; this Wessex region CAMRA Club of the Year 2002 is busy most evenings, as it is home to many games teams. Snacks are available at lunchtime.
⊛≉♣

Tom Brown's
47 High East Street, DT1 1HU
🕓 11-11; 11-3, 5.30-11 Tue & Wed; 12-4, 7-10.30 Sun
☎ (01305) 264020
Goldfinch Tom Brown, Flashman's Clout, Midnight Blinder Ⓗ
The tap of the Goldfinch Brewery takes the form of an old public bar, with bare

floorboards and plain wooden tables and chairs. Conversation rules in this friendly pub, only occasionally disturbed by the ancient, outstandingly good value, juke box. The brewery is situated to the rear of the building in what used to be a night club, and is partially visible from the corridor. Three Goldfinch beers are always available at this local CAMRA Pub of the Year 2002. 🛏◑≉♣

EAST CHALDON

Sailors Return
DT2 8DN (1 mile S of A352) OS791834
🕓 11-2.30, 6-11 (11-11 Easter-autumn); 12-3, 7-10.30 Sun
☎ (01305) 853847
Hampshire Strong's Best Bitter; Ringwood Best Bitter; guest beer Ⓗ
This thatched inn is situated on the fringe of a small hamlet. It provides a welcome refreshment stop for ramblers on the nearby Dorset Coastal Path and can get extremely busy on summer weekends. Excellent food in generous portions dominates in the numerous flagstoned rooms while the main bar retains the air of a local. Up to seven beers are served in high season, five normally. A tented beer festival is held in late spring. Westons traditional cider is sold.
Q⊛◑♣🍺P

EAST MORDEN

Cock & Bottle
BH20 7DL (on B3075, off A35 near Wareham)
🕓 11-3, 6-11; 12-3, 7-10.30 Sun
☎ (01929) 459238
Badger K&B Sussex, Best, Tanglefoot Ⓗ
Lovely village pub, unspoilt by development. An open fire is the main feature in the warm public bar. Well-used by locals, it attracts a lot of custom for its meals, served in the cosy dining area. Bar snacks are also available, all at reasonable prices. The garden is well situated to enjoy a summer pint as the village is not on a main road. Wheelchair access is excellent and there are designated disabled facilities.
🏚Q◑🍺♿♣P

FARNHAM

Museum Inn
DT11 8DE (between A354 and B3081)
🕓 12-3, 6-11; 12-3, 7-10.30 Sun
☎ (01725) 516261 website: www.museuminn.co.uk
Ringwood Best Bitter; Taylor Landlord; guest beer Ⓗ
Originally built for visitors to a local museum, from which it took its name, this 17th-century, part-thatched country inn retains flagstone floors and a large inglenook, despite a recent extensive refurbishment. With a varied food and wine menu, ever-changing guest beer and accommodation, this inn is well worth a visit. It is handy for nearby Larmer Tree Gardens and Cranborne Chase in excellent walking country. 🏚Q⚞⊛🛏◑♿P

FERNDOWN

Nightjar ⊘
94 Victoria Road, BH22 9JA
🕓 10-11; 12-10.30 Sun
☎ (01202) 855572

Boddingtons Bitter; Courage Directors; Theakston Best Bitter; guest beers Ⓗ

Split-level pub in the middle of Ferndown. As with all Wetherspoon's pubs the beer and varied food menu are reasonably priced. This former supermarket is now put to much better use as a comfortable drinking haven. Popular with all ages, it gets very busy on Friday and Saturday evenings. A small car park is at the rear of the pub. Q⬢🕪&P⚲

GILLINGHAM

Buffalo
Lydfords Lane, Wyke, SP8 4NS
(100 yds from B3081, Wincanton road)
🕒 12-2.30, 5.30 (6 Sat)-11; 12-3, 7-10.30 Sun
☎ (01747) 823759
Badger K&B Sussex or IPA, Best, seasonal beers Ⓗ

The pub's name comes from the symbol of the former Matthews Brewery, whose converted buildings still stand opposite the entrance to Lydfords Lane. Two linked bars feature partial stone flooring and exposed beams; in one bar the Drum and Monkey sign is believed to show the pub's original name. The Buffalo used to be the hub of Wyke as a separate community, now merged into Gillingham; nevertheless the pub retains a rural feel. No evening meals are served Sunday. 🏚Q🏵🕪♣P

Phoenix Inn ✓
The Square, SP8 4AY
🕒 10-2.30 (3 Sat), 7-11; 12-3, 7-10.30 Sun
☎ (01747) 823277
Badger K&B Sussex, Best, seasonal beers Ⓗ

The Phoenix was built in the 15th century and developed in the 17th, complete with its own brewery. During WWII it was famous (or infamous) for risqué parties, attended by celebrities such as Laurence Olivier, David Niven, Robert Newton and (perhaps surprisingly) General Eisenhower. This thriving pub has now expanded with a separate dining area, leaving the bar for drinkers. The main entrance is in the High Street, with the outside patio drinking area overlooking the quiet town square. 🏚🏵🕪⇌♣

GUSSAGE ALL SAINTS

Drovers Inn
BH21 5ET (between A354 and B3078) OS003106
🕒 11.45-3, 6-11; 12-3, 7-10.30 Sun
☎ (01258) 840084
Ringwood Best Bitter, Fortyniner, Old Thumper, seasonal beers Ⓗ

This part-thatched, 17th-century village inn became Ringwood Brewery's fourth tied house, saving it from permanent closure. Formerly the Earl Haig, its two bar areas, featuring beams, flagstone floors and an old bread oven, are warmed and divided by a large inglenook. An extensive front garden affords good views over the surrounding countryside. Excellent, home-cooked food is popular with both locals and visitors; no meals served Monday evening. 🏚Q🏵🕪♣P

HINTON ST MARY

White Horse
DT10 1NA (100 yds from B3092) OS787162
🕒 11.30-3, 6.30-11; 12-3, 7-10.30 Sun

☎ (01258) 472723 website: www.avoncauseway.co.uk
Young's Bitter; guest beers Ⓗ

Splendid village pub – the hub of its community – centred on the flagstoned public bar. The dining room is more sedate. The small garden adjoins Charlie Dimmock's showpiece. The licensees, now in their third year, maintain the pub's previous standards and selection of guest beers (one below and one above 4% ABV) and the same high quality food. They have also continued the Friday night tradition of £1 per pint off a selected guest ale – lucky Hinton St Mary! 🏚Q🏵🕪🔲♣🍴P

HURN

Avon Causeway Hotel ✓
BH23 6AS (off B3073, behind road bridge)
🕒 11-11; 12-10.30 Sun
☎ (01202) 482714 website: www.avoncauseway.co.uk
Red Shoot Forest Gold; Ringwood Best Bitter, Old Thumper; Wadworth IPA, 6X, JCB Ⓗ

This pub was the Hurn railway station until 1935. The old platform is complete and houses a carriage, used as a restaurant and a venue for Murder Mystery evenings. The public bar, which welcomes walkers with dogs bears a railway theme with many old artefacts. The lounge bar leads to the family area and garden, where a children's play section has swings and a slide, as well as an aviary. The hotel has 14 rooms – one a bridal suite. 🛏🏵🛌🕪&AP⚲

IBBERTON

Crown Inn
Church Lane, DT11 0EN
(4 miles off A357) OS788077
🕒 11-2.30 (not Mon), 7-11; 11-11 summer; 12-3, 7-10 (12-10.30 summer) Sun
☎ (01258) 817448
Ringwood Best Bitter; guest beers Ⓗ

Idyllic country pub nestling below Bulbarrow Hill, its 15th/16th century origins can be seen in the huge oak door leading to the bar which boasts an original flagstone floor and inglenook. A small brook runs alongside the attractive garden. Off the beaten track, this Guide regular is well worth the effort of tracking down. The guest beer is usually from Cottage Brewery and the cider is from Burrow Hill. 🏚Q🛏🏵🕪&♣🍴P

LODERS

Loders Inn
DT6 3SA
🕒 11.30-3, 6-11; 12-3, 6-10.30 Sun
☎ (01308) 422431
Palmer Bridport Bitter, IPA, 200 Ⓗ

The inn stands in a pretty village on the River Asker valley, surrounded by steep hills, etched with ancient field terraces. There is a stone-flagged, long, thin bar area with hops decorating the bar itself. The menu is varied and represents good value. Children (and dogs) are welcome here. Camping is permitted beyond the car park. Games include chess and Connect Four. 🏚Q🏵🛌🕪A♣🍴P

LYME REGIS

Nag's Head
32 Silver Street, DT7 3HS
⊕ 11-2, 5-11; 11-11 Sat; 12-10.30 Sun
☎ (01297) 442312
Beer range varies Ⓗ
Friendly local, benefiting from a fine view of the town across to the bay. Good food is served in the bar and dining room. Live music is performed most Saturdays – otherwise background music is classic rock kept at a reasonable level, so conversations can and do develop. The house beer is from Quay Brewery while a beer from Otter is usually available. Children are allowed in the lower level area off the main bar.
🏚❀⌂❀◑❀♣

Volunteer Inn
31 Broad Street, DT7 3QE
⊕ 11-11; 12-10.30 Sun
☎ (01297) 442214
Draught Bass; Fuller's London Pride; guest beers Ⓗ
Cosy, old bar with low beams, gas log-effect fire and an excellent bar atmosphere. The four beers are well kept; Otter and Adnams appear regularly while the house beer, named Donegal Ale to reflect the landlord's roots, is brewed by Branscombe Vale and served from a stillage behind the bar. Meals are served in the bar and the family/dining room (no food Mon). Background music is kept low and there are no electronic games machines.
🕭◑❀♣

MANSTON

Plough
Shaftesbury Road, DT10 1HR (on B3091, 2½ miles NE of Sturminster Newton)
⊕ 11.30-2.30, 6.30-11.30; closed Mon; 12-3, 7-10.30 Sun
☎ (01258) 472484
Palmer IPA; Sharp's Cornish Coaster; Ⓗ **guest beers** Ⓗ/Ⓖ
The Plough stands on a sharp bend on the B3091, just east of the village. One large bar caters both for drinkers and for diners; the latter have to sit closer to the mysterious plasterwork fertility symbols on the far wall. The garden offers petanque and sometimes skittles, on a pitch opposite the marquee used mainly for the popular beer festival (usually held in July).
🏚❀◑♣P

MARSHWOOD

Bottle Inn
DT6 5QJ (on B3165)
⊕ 12-3, 6.30-11; (closed winter Mon); 12-3, 7-10.30 Sun
☎ (01297) 678254 website: www.thebottleinn.co.uk
Greene King Old Speckled Hen; Otter Bitter; guest beers Ⓗ
Thatched inn on the B3165, almost in Devon. A single bar serves two small rooms, and there is a large garden overlooking Marshwood Vale. The interesting menu includes vegetarian and vegan dishes, as well as local organic meat. The pub hosts a nettle-eating competition in June (organic of course). Children are not forgotten; organic cola and crisps are available.
🏚Q🕭❀◑ÅP

NETTLECOMBE

Marquis of Lorne
DT6 3SY (easiest approach is from A3066)
OS517956
⊕ 12-2.30, 7-11; 12-3, 7-10.30 Sun
☎ (01308) 485236 website: www.marquisoflorne.com
Palmer Copper Ale, IPA, 200 Ⓗ
Old stone pub overlooking a pretty valley, at the foot of Eggardon Hill in beautiful countryside. The main bar has a homely, cosy look with wood panelling, armchairs by the fireplace, books and a piano. There is plenty of accommodation for those wanting a peaceful break. The menu is interesting, if a little pricey.
🏚Q🕭❀⌂◑♣P⅄

PAMPHILL

Vine ☆
Vine Hill, BH21 4EE (off B3082)
⊕ 11-2.30, 7-11; 12-3, 7-10.30 Sun
☎ (01202) 882259
Fuller's London Pride; Ⓗ **guest beers** Ⓖ
Pretty pub, built as a bakehouse over 200 years ago, it is close to Kingston Lacey House and Badbury Rings (both NT). Run by the same family for three generations, it has two small bars and an upstairs games room. The large garden, with ample seating, is very popular with walkers and cyclists. Sandwiches and ploughmans are served at lunchtime. A true free house, this 2003 local CAMRA Rural Pub of the Year serves real ales from many small breweries.
Q❀❀♣❀P╤

POOLE

Angel
28 Market Street, BH15 1NR
⊕ 11-11; 12-10.30 Sun
☎ (01202) 666431
Ringwood Best Bitter, Fortyniner, Old Thumper, seasonal beers Ⓗ
This is the fifth Ringwood pub to be added to their estate. There has been an inn on this site since 1789; it was rebuilt in 1890 and has seen many alterations since then. It was opened in September 2002 by Ringwood after a refurbishment that gave a reassuringly traditional feel to the pub, with wood furniture and fittings predominating. A real log fire makes it welcoming on a cold winter's day. Meals are served 12–7 (12–2 Sun).
🏚❀◑❀≠♣

Bermuda Triangle
10 Parr Street, Lower Parkstone, BH14 0JY
⊕ 12-2.30, 5.30 (6 Fri)-11; 12-11 Sat; 12-10.30 Sun
☎ (01202) 748087
Beer range varies Ⓗ
Refurbished as a free house in 1990, it soon established a reputation for well-kept, varied real ales and its popularity and standards remain undiminished to this day. The small bar boasts four constantly-changing guests. Seating is spread across three distinctive sections, all featuring Bermuda Triangle Mystery-related items; note the section of an aircraft wing suspended from the ceiling. Winner of many local CAMRA awards, it is a must for visitors to the area.
❀◑≠ (Parkstone)

Blue Boar
29 Market Close, BH15 1NE
☼ 11-3, 5 (6 Sat)-11; 12-3, 7-10.30 Sun
☎ (01202) 682247
Cottage Southern Bitter; Courage Best Bitter, Directors; guest beers Ⓗ
Former merchant's house, circa 1750, this popular free house is located in old Poole, near the High Street. The lounge bar is comfortable and stylish, while the atmospheric cellar bar stages live music Wednesday (folk club), Friday and Sunday. Both bars are bedecked with nautical artefacts, many from the landlord's diving days. The outdoor drinking area is used by morris dancers on May Day. A magnificent function/conference room is available at this former local CAMRA Pub of the Year.
Q ✿ ◖ ≠ ♣

Branksome Railway Hotel
420 Poole Road, BH12 1DQ
☼ 11-11; 12-10.30 Sun
☎ (01202) 769555
Fuller's London Pride; Hampshire Strong's Best Bitter; guest beers Ⓗ
Built in 1864, this Victorian coaching inn is situated halfway between Bournemouth and Poole town centres, on the main road opposite Branksome Station. Two bars are connected by an arch: the public bar has a pool table and dartboard, while the lounge bar has plenty of comfortable seating. Live music is performed, particularly on a Sunday afternoon; theme nights are staged during the week. The food and accommodation are both excellent (discount for CAMRA members on the latter).
⇌ ◖ ≠ (Branksome) ♣ P

Brewhouse
68 High Street, BH15 1DA
☼ 11-11; 12-10.30 Sun
☎ (01202) 685288
Milk Street Gulp, seasonal beers Ⓗ
This pub was formerly the home of Poole Brewery. The brewery has now closed and the pub has been sold to Milk Street Brewery. Apart from being redecorated the pub has not changed; its single bar serves a split-level room. At the front a seating area overlooks the pedestrian precinct, to the rear two pool tables are in constant use. This busy town pub sells the Milk Street range, plus the seasonal brews at reasonable prices.
≠ ♣

Bricklayers Arms
41-45 Parr Street, Parkstone, BH14 0JX
☼ 12-2.30, 5-11; 12-11 Sat; 12-10.30 Sun
☎ (01202) 740304
Greene King Abbot; Hop Back Summer Lightning; Ringwood Best Bitter, Fortyniner Ⓗ
Upmarket, single-roomed free house; on entering you will encounter an L-shaped layout with handpumps immediately opposite. To the right is a real fire and comfortable armchairs, to the left a sofa and more seating at the rear. Greenery punctuates the tasteful furnishings, while outside to the front is a small seating area complemented by a secluded rear garden.
⇌ ✿ ◖ ≠ (Parkstone)

Oakdale
Kingsmill Road, BH17 8RQ
☼ 11-11; 12-10.30 Sun
☎ (01202) 672055
Ringwood Best Bitter; guest beers Ⓗ
This pub is set off the main dual carriageway, and is accessed from Canford Heath Road. The public and lounge bars have separate entrances from the car park. Inside they are joined by an internal door. The bar runs the length of both rooms. The public bar is basic, with a hard floor, pool table and a dartboard. The lounge bar is more plush with carpets and Tudor-style decor; a door leads to a large, enclosed garden.
⇌ ✿ ◖ ≠ ⇦ P

Royal Oak & Gas Tavern
25 Skinner Street, BH15 1RQ
☼ 11-11; 12-10.30 Sun
☎ (01202) 672022
Hampshire Strong's Best Bitter, Ironside Ⓗ
Traditional, truly local back-street pub, dating back to 1798. Many of the original features remain – note the windows and wood-panelled walls. An enclosed garden is used in summer as an extra function room; the pleasant indoor function room has space for up to 100 people. Close to Poole Quay, the pub is off the beaten track so in the busy summer holidays it is a haven of peace. ✿ ≠ ♣

PORTLAND

George Inn
133 Reforne, Easton, DT5 2AP
☼ 11-11; 12-10.30 Sun
☎ (01305) 820011
Greene King Abbot; Ringwood Best Bitter; guest beer Ⓗ
This 17th-century pub stands across the road from the cricket ground, a location that is appreciated by locals on summer evenings. The original bar is partly built with beams from long-gone sailing ships, and is a place for conversation. By contrast, the larger Quarr Bar, a recent addition, hosts live bands at the weekend. The food is wholesome and reasonably priced. The guest beer is from Pubmaster's monthly list.
Q ✿ ◖ ≠ ♣

SANDFORD ORCAS

Mitre
DT9 4RU (N of Sherborne, signed from B3148)
OS626205
☼ 11.30-2.30, 7-11; 12-3, 7-10.30 Sun
☎ (01963) 220271
Adnams Bitter; Greene King Abbot; guest beers Ⓗ
Visiting the Mitre (mind your head) is an experience of true rural pub life. The welcome is warm, the home-cooked food excellent, the seating comfortable (armchairs in the bar) and beers in top condition. Flagged floors extend from the bar area to the dining room; well-behaved children are welcome. Outside is an elevated garden where one can just enjoy the peace of rural England. No food is served Monday. Beers are selected from the Punch Tavern guest beer list.
⇌ Q ✿ ◖ & ♣ P

SEATOWN

Anchor
DT6 6JU

✪ 12-3, 6-11; (12-11 summer); 12-3, 7-10.30 Sun
☎ (01297) 489215

Palmer Bridport Bitter (summer)**, Dorset Gold, IPA, 200** ⊞

Accessed by a single track road from Chideock or by foot along the Dorset Coastal Path, this comfortable inn is situated nearly on the beach. Run by a friendly landlord, it is popular with tourists and local walkers alike. Public parking space is available opposite. Occasionally, live jazz groups perform at weekends. Opening times may vary, depending on sea conditions and the season – phone beforehand if travelling far. ♨Q✿⇌◑ Å♣

SHERBORNE

Digby Tap
Cooks Lane, DT9 3NS

✪ 11-2.30, 5.30-11; 12-3, 7-10.30 Sun
☎ (01935) 813148

Ringwood Best Bitter; guest beers ⊞

Lively, long-established free house close to the Abbey, station and all town-centre amenities. Four discrete drinking areas, all have flagged floors and cosy corners. It enjoys a strong regular trade, but is nonetheless very welcoming. A favourite haunt of rugby and hockey players, it fields cricket and pool teams. Brewery visits are arranged, and occasional live music. It has a no mobile phones policy. Three or four ever-changing beers, mostly come from independent brewers. Good, unpretentious food is served. ♨Q◑⇌♣

SHROTON (IWERNE COURTNEY)

Cricketers
Main Street, DT11 8QD (off A350)

✪ 11.30-3, 6.30-11; 12-3, 7-10.30 Sun
☎ (01202) 860421

Butcombe Bitter; guest beers ⊞

Large, airy bar with a sports bar area on the left and a cosy snug opposite the main bar. A large corridor leads to the restaurant which has won various awards and featured in the Country Life magazine. A true free house, its ever-changing guest beers are served on cricket bat-style handpumps. It is heavily involved with the local cricket team – the pitch is opposite. The accommodation is highly recommended.
Q✿⇌◑♣♣P⊁

STOBOROUGH

King's Arms
3 Corfe Road, BH20 5AB (adjacent to B3075)

✪ 11-11; 12-10.30 Sun
☎ (01929) 552705

Greene King Abbot; Ringwood Best Bitter; Taylor Landlord; guest beers ⊞

Affording views of nearby River Frome, this 17th-century pub has a small, intimate bar area. The restaurant, in an extension of the building, sells excellent food; summer meals are also served in a large outdoor drinking area. Children are welcome provided they are well behaved. A beer festival is held in summer in a field behind the pub.
✿◑♣ÅP

STRATTON

Saxon Arms
Dorchester Road, DT2 9WG

✪ 11-3, 6-11; 12-3, 7-10.30 Sun
☎ (01305) 260020

Fuller's London Pride; Greene King Abbot; Palmer IPA ⊞

Stratton is bypassed by the A37 north of Dorchester. Newly built in 2001, this thatched country pub is now well established as the centre of village life. It features flagged floors, an open fire and really good food. Located next to the village church, it is frequented by villagers and tourists alike. The experienced landlord ensures that the beer is of the highest quality. Two Palmer's beers are always available, one being the house beer.
♨✿◑♣P

STUDLAND

Bankes Arms Hotel
Manor Road, BH19 3AU (signed from village)

✪ 11-11; 12-10.30 Sun
☎ (01929) 450225

Beer range varies ⊞

This picturesque National Trust-owned Purbeck stone pub has a large garden that enjoys spectacular sea views. Nearby is the start of the beautiful coastal path and the pub is popular with walkers and cyclists. Dogs are welcome. Eight ever-changing beers are available, and the pub now has its own brewery. There is an annual summer beer festival. In winter the large open fires are especially welcome.
♨✿⇌◑ Å♠

SWANAGE

Black Swan Inn
159 High Street, BH19 2NE

✪ 12-2, 6.30-11; 12-2, 7-10.30 Sun
☎ (01929) 422761

Beer range varies ⊞

Lovely, comfortable pub, the building is 400 years old and has been a pub for 200 years. The lounge is L-shaped, decorated with many pictures, mainly of Swanage. The pub has a good, varied menu including vegetarian specials. A patio serves as a small outside drinking area. Bed and breakfast is also available. Dogs are welcome on a lead. Archaeologists should ask to view the 140,000,000-year-old fossil (footprint).
✿⇌◑⇌P

TARRANT MONKTON

Langton Arms
DT11 8RX (off B3082 from Wimborne, or off A354 from Blandford) OS944088

✪ 11.30-11; 12-10.30 Sun
☎ (01258) 830225
website: www.thelangtonarms.co.uk

Beer range varies ⊞

This multi-award winning, 17th-century gem is centrally situated in a picturesque hamlet that nestles in the Tarrant Valley. The rustic public bar houses a pool table and dartboard. The beamed lounge bar boasts an array of handpumps (over 30 guests each month). The restaurant-cum-function room serves excellent food, while the accommodation is of superior quality. A beer festival is held annually.

🏚Q🐾🌳🚪⟨◗🍺🕭♣P✂

TRENT

Rose & Crown
DT9 4SL
🕰 12-3, 7-11; closed Mon; 12-2.15 (closed eve) Sun
☎ (01935) 850776
Butcombe Bitter; Sharp's Doom Bar; guest beers Ⓗ

Charming stone pub near the church, but on the edge of the village overlooking fields. It is a genuine free house, although it is leased from the trust that owns the village. The stone floor in the main bar probably remains from the original farmhouse that once sold beer. The conservatory benefits from a view over the countryside. The menu offers an interesting mix of main meals, bar meals and salads.

🏚Q🐾🌳🌸⟨◗🕭♣P✂

UPWEY

Royal Standard
700 Dorchester Road, DT3 5LA
🕰 11-3, 6-11; 12-10.30 Sun
☎ (01305) 812558
Butcombe Bitter; Greene King IPA; guest beers Ⓗ

Genuine two-bar pub on the main approach road to Weymouth. The lounge reflects the landlord's interest in railways, with pictures and models. Outside at the rear an aviary contains a magnificent eagle owl, which could be said to be the licensee's pride and joy were it not for his equal passion for vintage motor cycles. More modern interests are not forgotten – there is Internet access but beware the fine should your mobile ring in the public bar.

🏚Q🌸🚪♣P

WAREHAM

Duke of Wellington
East Street, BH20 4NN
🕰 11-11; 12-10.30 Sun
☎ (01929) 553015
Beer range varies Ⓗ

Cosy pub in the middle of Wareham. The main bar leads to a small restaurant and to an attractive courtyard with access to a public car park. Guest ales vary but there is a high percentage of beers from Palmer's Brewery. A good range of food suits all tastes.

🏚Q🐾🌸⟨◗🅰♣

WAYTOWN

Hare & Hounds
DT6 5LQ
🕰 11.30-3, 6.30-11; 12-3, 7-10.30 Sun
☎ (01308) 488203
Palmer Dorset Gold, IPA Ⓖ

Tucked away in a small hamlet (best reached from the Netherbury end), this unspoilt country pub offers Palmer's ales on gravity dispense. A single counter serves two drinking areas. The garden offers superb views and it makes an excellent stopping-place for the many walks that you can take in one of the prettiest parts of West Dorset. No food is served Sunday evening or Monday in winter. Taunton cider is stocked.

🏚Q🌸⟨◗🅰♣P

WEST STAFFORD

Wise Man
DT2 8AG
🕰 11-3, 6-11; 12-4.30 (closed eve) Sun
☎ (01305) 263694
Ringwood Best Bitter; guest beers Ⓗ

This 400-year-old, thatched, ivy-strewn pub in a quiet village has retained the public bar but the lounge is now almost exclusively used as a restaurant, serving a wide food selection. Appropriate guest beers, linked with suitable guest beers, are served on special occasions, eg Burns Night and St Patrick's Day. The guest beers are chosen from the Pubmaster list and occasional beer festivals are planned. 🏚Q🌸⟨◗🚪♣P

WEST STOUR

Ship Inn
SP8 5RP (on A30)
🕰 12-3, 6-11; 12-3.30, 7-10.30 Sun
☎ (01747) 838640 website: www.shipinn-dorset.com
Ringwood Best Bitter; Palmer 200; guest beer Ⓗ

This coaching inn, severely damaged by fire soon after its construction in the 1740s, was rebuilt with ships' timbers, hence its name. Sited on the A30, enjoying scenic views of the Blackmore Vale, the inn (with CAMRA's help) was saved from conversion to four terraced houses. Two stone-walled bars lead to a popular restaurant. The resident ghost is said to do little, apart from bang doors. One regular beer is from Palmer's, rare in this corner of Dorset. 🏚Q🌸🚪⟨◗♣P

WEYMOUTH

Boot Inn
High West Street, DT4 8QT (behind fire station)
🕰 11-11; 12-10.30 Sun
☎ (01305) 770327
Ringwood Best Bitter, Fortyniner, Old Thumper, seasonal beers; guest beers Ⓗ

Weymouth's oldest pub can be difficult to find, hidden as it is behind the fire station. The single bare-boarded bar area leads to comfortable rooms at each end. The full Ringwood beer range is supplemented with the landlord's choice of guests and Cheddar Valley cider. The pub's popularity leads to a spillage of customers on to the pavement (seating provided) in clement weather. A true pub where conversation rules, occasionally bar snacks are available – really excellent pork pies! 🏚Q🌸≈♣🍺

Dolphin Hotel
67 Park Street, DT4 7DE (100 yds from station)
🕰 11-11; 12-10.30 Sun
☎ (01305) 786751
Hop Back GFB, Best Bitter, Crop Circle, Entire Stout, Summer Lightning, seasonal beers Ⓗ

A recent addition to the Hop Back estate, it is conveniently situated for the station. A full range of Hop Back beers is available, together with a selection of Belgian bottled beers and a good choice of wines. There is no regular food served . Quiz night is Wednesday. The skittle alley is off the main bar and available for functions. Bar prices are very reasonable for the area. 🕭≈♣

Old Rooms Inn
Hope Square, DT4 8TT
🕰 11-11; 12-10.30 Sun

☎ (01305) 771130

Courage Best Bitter; Quay Harbour Master, Steam Beer Ⓗ

Commodious corner pub on the quayside, close to the former Devenish Brewery. In recent years the pub has greatly extended into the ex-brewery offices and, although predominantly food-driven, the entrance area retains the air of a public bar. Food is served all day and the pub is extremely busy in summer when visitors sit outside and take in the scenery. Usually two Quay beers are available; sparklers are used but will be removed on request. ⚲ ❀ ◖ ᗡ ⇌

Red Lion
Hope Square, DT4 8TR
✪ 11-11; 12-10.30 Sun
☎ (01305) 786940

Courage Best Bitter, Directors; guest beers Ⓗ

Situated opposite the former Devenish Brewery, now the home of Quay Brewery who supply three of its beers, the pub is regarded as the brewery tap. It is a single-bar, bare-boarded pub decorated with boating, and particularly RNLI, artefacts. In summer and on sunny winter weekends it is extremely popular as there is a lot of outdoor seating in the square. Breakfast is served all day at these times. Beware when crowded – the toilet facilities are limited! ⚲ ❀ ◖ ⇌ ♣

WIMBORNE

Crown & Anchor ⊘
6 Wimborne Road, Walford Bridge, BH21 1NN
✪ 11-2.30, 6-11; 12-3, 7-10.30 Sun
☎ (01202) 841405

Badger K&B Sussex, Best Ⓗ

A pub since 1823 and refurbished in 2000, this friendly local is one of the finest outlets for Badger beers in East Dorset, hence its long-standing inclusion in this Guide. It also offers splendid lunches. A small garden beside the River Allen, overlooks Walford Craft Mill. Conversation rules, except for Thursday evening when it plays host to the local folk club. A short walk along a pretty stretch of the river leads to the centre of the ancient town of Wimborne. Q ❀ ◖ ♣ P

Horns Inn
Butts Hill, Deansgrove, Colehill, BH21 7AA
✪ 11-2.30 (4 Fri & Sat), 6-11; 12-4, 7-10.30 Sun

☎ (01202) 883557

Badger K&B Sussex, Best Ⓗ

Totally rebuilt after burning to the ground in the 1930s, this rural gem also survived the threat of closure early in 2001, thanks in part to a vigorous local campaign. Bouncing back under new tenants, the Horns offers good food and a large garden with views over rising green fields. In summer its exterior is a riot of hanging baskets. The interior is decorated in classic Hall & Woodhouse style – well worth a visit. ⚲ ❀ ◖ ▲ ♣ P

WORTH MATRAVERS

Square & Compass ☆
BH19 3LF (off B3069) OS974777
✪ 12-3, 6-11; 12-11 Sat; 12-3, 7-10.30 (closed winter eve) Sun
☎ (01929) 439229

Badger Tanglefoot; Ringwood Best Bitter; guest beers Ⓖ

Run by the Newman family since 1907 and listed in every edition of this Guide, this rural classic features real ale from the cask (no bar), a rare drinking corridor and flagstone floors. Its own museum displays the largest public fossil collection from the Purbeck coastline. Views across field systems and the sea make this a highly popular stop for walkers. A beer festival is held in October, a cider festival in November, plus frequent live music. Timeless – an experience not to be missed. ⚲ Q ❀ ▲ ♣

YETMINSTER

White Hart Inn
High Street, DT9 6LF
✪ 12-2.30, 7-11; 12-3, 7-10.30 Sun
☎ (01935) 872338

Greene King IPA; guest beers Ⓗ

This 400-year-old, thatched inn is located at the village centre, a pleasant stroll from the railway halt. The convivial public bar is basically furnished and caters for pub games. An imaginative menu, including vegetarian dishes is served in the more comfortable lounge area. The pub provides accommodation in an adjoining converted barn. The skittle alley at the rear features its own bar, while the garden has a play area for children.
Q ⋈ ◖ ⊟ ᗡ ⇌ ♣ P

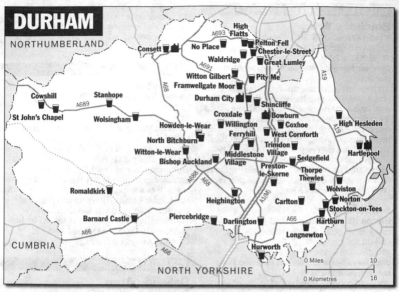

DURHAM

NORTHUMBERLAND

Co Durham incorporates part of the former county of Cleveland

BARNARD CASTLE

Coach & Horses
22 Galgate, DL12 8BH
☼ 11-11; 12-10.30 Sun
☎ (01833) 638369
Jennings Mild, Bitter, Cumberland Ale Ⓗ

Charming, 18th-century inn situated in the centre of this historic market town, gateway to the reaches of upper Teesdale, it has the 12th-century castle close by. With its friendly atmosphere, it is popular with locals, visitors and walkers. Two camping and caravan sites are not far away. Many local buses stop outside the door. One of the few Jennings outlets to be found in this area despite the close proximity of Cumbria.
🛏 ❀ 🛏 Å ♣

BISHOP AUCKLAND

Newton Cap
Newton Cap Bank, DL14 7PX (from market place head for viaduct, off roundabout)
☼ 12-4 (not Tue), 7-11; 12-4, 7-10.30 Sun
☎ (01388) 605445
Camerons Bitter, Strongarm Ⓗ

An old style, small pub just off the town centre, enjoyed by locals and visitors alike, comprising a compact bar area with seating and two separate rooms to the rear, one housing a pool table, the other seating and tables – perfect for meetings or a quiet drink. Darts, dominoes and cards are all available in the main bar as is a game called the bull ring – you had better ask the landlady about that one!
🛏 ♣

Station Hotel
201 Newgate Street, DL14 7EJ (on main shopping street, close to railway station)
☼ 11-11; 11-10.30 Sun
☎ (01388) 605780
John Smith's Magnet; guest beer Ⓗ

Bustling, town-centre pub recently redecorated and renovated. It has one large bar and seating area with a split-level area housing a pool table. Darts, dominoes and cards are all available. The pub enters teams in the local darts, dominoes and football leagues. Thursday is quiz night. It is only about three minutes' walk from the train station and eight minutes from the bus station. Lunchtime food is served 12–2, Monday–Friday.
◁≈ ♣

CARLTON

Smith's Arms
TS21 1EA
☼ 12-2 (not Mon or Tue), 5-11; 11-11 Fri & Sat; 12-10.30 Sun
☎ (01740) 630471
Beer range varies Ⓗ

Fine end-of-terrace, Victorian red-brick pub in the heart of the village, where cheery staff provide a warm welcome for all. The bustling public bar tends to be full on big match occasions. The quieter, cosy lounge has comfortable settees on which it is all too easy to nod off after a few pints. The restaurant is in the old stables. The meals, which include vegetarian options, represent excellent value for money. There is even a children's tuck shop. The pub has something to suit all tastes, and combined with the landlord's commitment to supply a constantly-changing range of Britain's finest ales, it is definitely worth a visit. No food is served on Sunday evening.
Q ❀ ◁▷ 🛏 ♣ P 🖰

INDEPENDENT BREWERIES

Camerons Hartlepool
Derwent Rose Consett
Durham Bowburn
Hill Island Durham City

CHESTER-LE-STREET

Butcher's Arms
Middle Chare, DH3 3QD (just off Front St)
✪ 11-4, 6.30-11; 12-4, 7-10.30 Sun
☎ (0191) 388 3605
Camerons Strongarm; Marston's Pedigree; guest beer Ⓗ
An ideal place for the discerning drinker and diner. This pub has a good local reputation for home-cooked food, pies are a speciality made on the premises and the fish is freshly delivered. Comfortable bedrooms are available for weary travellers. The landlord is very proud of the quality and availability of his cask beers. Tea and coffee are also on offer. Small meetings can be accommodated. A fine array of porcelain is displayed. Q ⊛ 🛏 ◖ ◕ ≠

Smith's Arms
Brecon Hill, Castledene, DH3 4HE (uphill from county cricket ground, left after roundabout 400 yds)
✪ 4 (12 Sat)-11; 12-5, 7-10.30 Sun
☎ (0191) 385 6915
Black Sheep Best Bitter; Courage Directors; Taylor Landlord; guest beer Ⓗ
Popular, country pub tucked away near Brecon Woods. It has a cosy, traditional bar with a Yorkshire range which enhances the friendly atmosphere. Opt for the comfortable lounge or games room which has a pool table. Upstairs, is a much-visited, high quality restaurant. The floors of both rooms slope – this effect increases with ale.
🏚 Q ◖ ⊟ ♣ P 🍴

CONSETT

Grey Horse
115 Sherburn Terrace, DH8 6NE
(off A692, between town centre and Leadgate)
✪ 12-11; 12-10.30 Sun
☎ (01207) 502585 website: www.thegreyhorse.co.uk
Beer range varies Ⓗ
This former coaching inn has its own brewery (Derwent Rose) and boasts a varied selection of real ales as well as over 100 malt whiskies. The quaint decor, open coal fires and total absence of any loud, piped music invest this grand old family-run pub with a traditional atmosphere all of its own. It has always been one of the leading contenders for Durham CAMRA Pub of the Year since it gained this honour in 2000. It is handy for the Coast-to-Coast cycle route. A forecourt with tables and chairs serves as a garden.
🏚 Q ⅓ ⊛ ◖ ⊟ ♣ P

COWSHILL

Cowshill Hotel
DL13 1JQ
✪ 12-2, 7-11; 12-2, 7-10.30 Sun
☎ (01388) 537236
Tetley Bitter Ⓗ
Imposing, three-storey establishment that has been in the same family since the 1960s. It is in the centre of the village in this rural upland area. Only a couple of miles from the Kilhope Leadmining Centre, it is a popular watering-hole for tourists, cyclists and walkers. Those venturing out on the Pennine Fells must respect the weather at this high altitude; if in doubt, stick to the beer! Take bus No. 101 from Stanhope, but check the return times

especially on Sundays and bank holidays – it's a long walk to civilisation! Sunday lunch, and evening meals on Friday and Saturday are served, it is essential to book.
🏚 ◖ ◕ ♣ P

COXHOE

Cricketers
Victoria Terrace, DH6 4EA (off A177)
✪ 7-11; 12-3, 7-10.30 Sun
☎ (0191) 377 0510
Camerons Strongarm; Marston's Pedigree; guest beer Ⓗ
Another remnant of the defunct Vaux empire, this pub is now run by Pubmaster. Open plan, it has one large, L-shaped bar/lounge. Named after the Coxhoe cricket team, it is a popular haunt for cricketers and the football team. This pub has retained the qualities that ensure it is a thriving community local. Coxhoe is served by bus services 20, 56, 57, 235/6, 13 and XI. Contact Arriva for further details. ⊛ ♣

CROXDALE

Daleside Arms
Front Street, DH6 5HY
(on B6288, 3 miles S of Durham, off A167)
✪ 12-2.30 (3 Sat; not Mon-Thu), 7-11; 12-3, 7-10.30 Sun
☎ (01388) 814165
Beer range varies Ⓗ
Fine ale, great food, a local pub with a big heart. The beers continue to flow from all over Britain. Local brews also figure and include a house special from Hill Island. A warm welcome and a good atmosphere abound in a bar decorated with sporting memorabilia and pump clips of previous beers. See which ones you have missed. Mike and Sandra continue to run this gem in the usual winning way. Booking advised for the unbeatable waist-expanding food – available 5–9, Wednesday–Saturday and Sunday lunchtime. Bus route 724 serves the pub. Q ⅓ ⊛ 🛏 ◖ ⊟ ₺ P 🍴

DARLINGTON

Binns Department Store (off-licence)
1-7 High Row, DL3 7HH
✪ 9-5.30 (6 Sat); 11-5 Sun
☎ (01325) 462606
House of Fraser department store with a fabulously-stocked bottled beer section in the basement. Highly commended in British Guild of Beer Writers Take Home Beer Awards. Over 400 quality beers are available, including dozens of British and Belgian bottle-conditioned ales, plus an array of matching glasses. If they do not have what you want, the manager John, will try to get it. The own-label Binns' beer comes from Springhead. Frequent Saturday tasting session are often hosted by brewers. ≠

Britannia
Archer Street, DL3 6LR
✪ 11.30-3, 5.30-11; 11-11 Fri & Sat; 12-3, 7-10.30 Sun
☎ (01325) 463787
Camerons Strongarm; John Smith's Bitter; guest beers Ⓗ

Friendly, much-loved local just across the ring road from the town centre but well-removed from the frenetic circuit. A bastion of cask beer for 140 years, it is a frequent entry in this Guide. The pub retains much of the appearance and layout of the private house it originally was: a modestly-enlarged bar and domestic-proportioned parlour (used for meetings) sit either side of a central corridor. Listed for historical associations, it was the birthplace of teetotal, 19th-century publisher JM Dent. Up to three guest beers are available. ≉♣P🖰

Darlington Cricket Club
South Terrace, DL1 5JD
(S of town centre, off Feethams South)
✪ 7.30 (4 Sat)-11; 12-10.30 Sun
☎ (01325) 250044
Mansfield Cask Ale; guest beer 🅷
Traditional-style pavilion in the last shared English venue for County cricket and League football. The comfortable lounge is decorated with local cricket memorabilia. There is TV for sport and a separate snooker room. The function room overlooks the cricket field. The bar opens earlier for certain sports fixtures. The members select the guest ale each month. Show this Guide or CAMRA membership for entry.
🏵&≉♣P

Number Twenty-2 ◉
22 Coniscliffe Road, DL3 7RG
✪ 11-11 (closed some bank holidays); closed Sun
☎ (01325) 354590
Village White Boar, Bull, Old Ruby; guest beers 🅷
Popular, classy bar on the edge of the town centre, with surely the biggest sale of cask ale for miles. Winner of numerous CAMRA awards since opening in 1995, large, curved windows and a high ceiling give an airy character even when packed, which is often the case. In all, 13 handpumps serve nine beers, mainly from small micros. This is the home of Village Brewer beers, commissioned from Hambleton by the licensee. Nightmare Stout is sold here as Yorkshire Stout, and imported Erdinger Weissbier and Liefmans Frambozen are also on tap. No spirits or alcopops available. Lunches are prepared Monday–Saturday, prepared with the freshest seasonal produce.
Q🆑&≉🖰

Old Yard Tapas Bar
98 Bondgate, DL3 7JY
✪ 11-11; 12-10.30 Sun
☎ (01325) 467385 website: www.tapasbar.co.uk
John Smith's Magnet; Theakston Cool Cask, Old Peculier; guest beers 🅷
Interesting mixture of small town-centre bar and Mediterranean-style taverna, with a range of five real ales sold alongside the sangria, ouzo, tapas and mezes. It is perfectly acceptable to simply pop in for a pint. It is licensed for pavement drinking in summer, when tables are set out. Public car parks are within 50 yards. The TV shows the football only. Two guest beers are on tap.
🏵🆑≉

Quaker Coffee House
2 Mechanics Yard, DL3 7QF
(yard off High Row next to Binns store)
✪ 11-11; 12-10.30 Sun
☎ (07818) 848213

website: www.darkangel-rock.co.uk/quaker
Beer range varies 🅷
Unusual bar in one of Darlington's oldest buildings, tucked away in one of the hidden town-centre historic yards. The upstairs café is open 7.30–4 (12–4 Sun) and acts as a function room in the evening. It is a popular venue for visiting football fans and has live music on Wednesday. It was voted local CAMRA Pub of the Year 2003 and on two other occasions. Quaker Ghost is the house beer, brewed by Darwin in memory of Ethel, the resident ghost. Up to five guest ales are available. 🆑&≉♣🖰

Tanners Hall ◉
63-64 Skinnergate, DL3 7LL
✪ 10-11; 12-10.30 Sun
☎ (01325) 369939
Courage Directors; Shepherd Neame Spitfire; Theakston Best Bitter; guest beers 🅷
Typical town-centre Wetherspoon's pub, it is spacious with a no-smoking area, and plenty of old pictures of Darlington and its railway history are displayed. A single, long bar serves drink and food. A wide range of drinks at highly competitive prices draws the crowds, particularly at weekends, when the pub tends to be very busy. Good value meals are served all day. A patio area is available for outdoor drinking. A public car park is adjacent. Families are welcome.
🏵Q🏵🆑&≉⌽

Bridge
40 North Road, DH1 4SE
✪ 11-11; 12-10.30 Sun
☎ (0191) 386 8090
Theakston Best Bitter; guest beers 🅷
The run down, smallish pub that was the Bridge has become a comfortable, larger, airy cask ale venue. Attractively furnished, the interior provides an ideal setting to enjoy home-cooked food and good ale. Just sit back and watch the busy world go by. It will appeal to the rail fan as it sits below the famous viaduct. Guests from the Scotco guest programme usually include Speckled Hen or Wells Bombardier on rotation. 🆑≉

Colpitts
Colpitts Terrace, DH1 4EG
✪ 12-11; 12-10.30 Sun
☎ (0191) 386 9913
Samuel Smith OBB 🅷
Basic, friendly, street-corner local, serving the cheapest cask ale in the city. Unspoilt, it continues to be an anachronism in the modern age. The pub is made up of a small lounge, public bar and pool room, check out the off-sales hatch; a rare sight. What a contrast to the mundane plastic pubs forced on us these days. It is less than 10 minutes' walk from both rail and bus stations.
🏵Q🆑≉♣

Court Inn
Court Lane, DH1 3AW
✪ 11-11; 12-10.30 Sun
☎ (0191) 384 7350
Draught Bass; guest beers 🅷
The name of this pub is derived from its location next door to the county court rooms and city prison. It is one of the few venues in the city to provide a

comprehensive menu of 'real food' throughout the day; it is popular with warders, students and locals, especially at lunchtime. The large area at the rear is no-smoking. The absence of games machines adds to the relaxing atmosphere. Two guest beers are usually on offer. ⛬✿◖&✁

Dun Cow
37 Old Elvet, DH1 3HN
✪ 11-11; 12-4, 7-10.30 Sun
☎ (0191) 386 9219
Boddingtons Bitter; Castle Eden Ale Ⓗ
Ever-popular with a wide variety of clientele, this traditional pub dates from the 16th century. The intimate, beamed snug (entered by a passageway) has remained unchanged in living memory. Continue further down the passageway to reach the more spacious lounge. Opposite this entrance, a plaque tells of the legend of the Dun Cow. Good value snacks are available with a specials board on Friday. A rare outlet for Hill Island in the city; the house beer is Hill Island Dun Cow bitter.
Q⛬◖🍴&♣

Elm Tree
12 Crossgate, DH1 4PS
✪ 12-3, 6-11; 11-11 Sat; 12-10.30 Sun
☎ (0191) 386 4621
Adnams Bitter; Draught Bass; Camerons Strongarm; Tetley Bitter Ⓗ
Former Vaux city flagship pub and old coaching inn whose interior has suffered neglect since Pubmaster took over. It has a split bar area with separate lounge and small rear patio, with a very restricted car park. Folk music is staged on Tuesday evening and a popular quiz on Wednesday evening. Students flock to the pub at weekends, so it tends to be busy. Limited accommodation available. Q✿🛏🍴≈P

Half Moon
New Elvet, DH1 3AQ (end of Elvet Bridge)
✪ 11-11; 12-10.30 Sun
☎ (0191) 383 6981
Draught Bass; Worthington's Bitter; guest beer Ⓗ
Yet another historic city-centre pub, the Victorian interior and back bar are listed. Very popular with visitors and locals alike, the pub is one of the few in the city to be able to offer guest beers from the Durham Brewery on a regular basis. A big screen and a TV show all the major sporting events. Newspapers are provided during the daytime as are a selection of sandwiches and toasties. ✿♣

Hogshead ⊘
58 Saddler Street, DH1 3NU
(between market place and cathedral)
✪ 11-11; 12-10.30 Sun
☎ (0191) 386 9550
Black Sheep Best Bitter; Caledonian Deuchars IPA; Castle Eden Ale; guest beers Ⓗ
This typical Hogshead pub (owned by Laurel) still tries to offer a good range of beers. Like many Pubcos, the choice is restricted but Beer Seller's guest list is put to good use. The beers are pricey but in excellent condition and it is an ideal venue for young and old to try cask ales. It tends to be very busy at weekends. Refurbishment of the wooden interior has given an airy, bright feel. ◖&≈

Queen's Head Hotel
2 Sherburn Road, Gilesgate, DH1 2JR
✪ 12-11; 12-4, 7-10.30 Sun
☎ (0191) 386 5649
Greene King Old Speckled Hen; Marston's Pedigree; guest beer Ⓗ
The ubiquitous Pedigree and Speckled Hen somehow seem to taste better than usual at this well-managed hotel. This leads to speculation that the Queen's would be a true real ale paradise if only its licensee's masters allowed her a wider choice of guest beers. However, it is still worth the short bus ride from the city centre to enjoy the friendly welcome awaiting all customers. The meal choice is varied and reasonably priced – the broth starter is a must.
✿🛏◖🍴♣P

Victoria ☆
86 Hallgarth Street, DH1 3AS
✪ 11-3, 6-11; 12-2, 6-10.30 Sun
☎ (0191) 386 5269
Daleside Greengrass; Marston's Pedigree; McEwan 80/-; Theakston Best Bitter; guest beer Ⓗ
On CAMRA's National Inventory with a listed interior, this remains one of the best adverts anywhere for a friendly, unspoilt thriving cask pub. A welcome is assured from the locals and staff alike. Great pride is taken in the congenial atmosphere and cracking ale. Two open fires and a rear snug create a cosy atmosphere – incentive to go out on a winter's night. Darwin Ghost is sold regularly and many good guest ales feature. Local and Scottish brews are popular; just brilliant.
🏚Q🛏🍴≈♣

Woodman Inn
23 Gilesgate, DH1 1QW
(10 minutes' walk past Gala Theatre via Claypath)
✪ 12-11; 12-10.30 Sun
☎ (0191) 386 7500
Greene King Ruddles County; guest beers Ⓗ
The Woodman picked up Durham CAMRA's Pub of the Year in 2002, shortly followed by a change of hosts. A new tenancy agreement with Scotco cut the guests available but four are still sold at a time. Regular beer festivals featuring rare or local beers are the main pull, hopefully their success will spur Scotco to allow the pub more freedom. Still very much worth a visit, a comfortable pub for all. Arriva services 63 and 64 run from the city. ≈

FERRYHILL

Manor House
Market Street, DL17 8JH
(100 yds E of the market place)
✪ 11-11; 12-10.30 Sun
☎ (01740) 654322
Beer range varies Ⓗ
Reputedly haunted, this is one of Ferryhill's oldest buildings, dating in part from the 1640s. It was converted from a private house in 1990, and boasts exposed beams and bare stone walls and floors. A priest's hole can still be found in the panel room. A large, sheltered garden is a pleasant place to enjoy a pint – choose from the ever-changing guest beers, many from local independents.
✿🛏◖&P

FRAMWELLGATE MOOR

Tap & Spile
Front Street, DH1 5EE (off A167 bypass, 1½ miles N of Durham centre)
☼ 11.30-3 , 6 (5 Fri)-11; 12-3, 7-10.30 Sun
☎ (0191) 386 5451
Black Sheep Best Bitter; Jennings Cumberland Ale; guest beers Ⓗ
This Enterprise house offers a restricted range of ales but the choice has improved. The basic interior decor of wood is in need of refurbishment to complement the external face-lift. A mild strong ale, stout or porter is regularly on offer, not available in many pubs. A greater freedom of ale choice and investment would benefit this potential cask ale gold mine. Stotties and real cider, usually Westons Old Rosie, are available. Buses 723, 724, 54, 754 and XI pass the door. A bar billiards table is housed in the family room. Q🕏🕯️🍴♣🖐

GREAT LUMLEY

Old England
Front Street, DH3 4JB
☼ 11-11; 12-10.30 Sun
☎ (0191) 388 5257
Beer range varies Ⓗ
Large, friendly village pub with spacious public and lounge bars. A pool table, dartboard, satellite and big-screen TV are on offer in the popular public bar; the peaceful, comfortable lounge is divided into distinct areas and has a no-smoking eating section. Lunches are served Friday–Sunday, and evening meals from Monday–Saturday. Regular entertainment includes a quiz held twice a week, on Tuesday and Thursday. Three local guest ales are available.
Q🕯️🍴🖐♣P

HARTBURN

Masham Hotel
87 Hartburn Village, TS18 5DR
☼ 11-11; 12-3, 7-10.30 Sun
☎ (01642) 580414 website: www.themasham.co.uk
Black Sheep Special; Draught Bass; guest beer Ⓗ
Walk into this fine local and its origins as a public 'house' are immediately apparent. A bustling public bar is supplemented by three other rooms. Extensive gardens to the rear play host to regular barbecues in the summer months. Regular live music events, often with an Irish theme, are a feature of the pub, with the licensee often jamming along. The guest beer is from Punch Taverns' finest cask range. Meals are served Monday–Saturday, 12–2.30 and 5.30–7.30.
Q🕏🕯️🍴🖐♣P🖐

HARTLEPOOL

Causeway
Vicarage Gardens, Stranton, TS24 7QT (beside Stranton Church)
☼ 11-11; 12-10.30 Sun
☎ (01429) 273954
Banks's Original, Bitter; Camerons Strongarm; guest beers Ⓗ
Nestling beside Camerons Brewery is this Victorian red-brick gem, widely regarded as the brewery tap, but not owned by them. A lively public bar lies to one side of the entrance, with two small snugs, one no-

smoking, to the other. The pub is deservedly popular with both Camerons and Pubmaster staff from adjacent premises. The licensee is a keen musician, so regular acoustic music evenings are held – phone for details. Lunches are served Monday–Saturday, 12–2. Q🕯️🍴♣🖐🖐

Jackson's Wharf
The Highlights, Hartlepool Marina, TS24 0XN
☼ 11-11; 12-10.30 Sun
☎ (01429) 862963
Camerons Bitter, Strongarm; guest beers (summer) Ⓗ
Superbly located on the recently revitalised marina, next to the historic quay, where HMS Trincomalee (built in 1817 and the oldest ship afloat in Britain) and preserved paddle steamer PSS Wingfield Castle are both berthed. This nautically-themed pub is deceptively large with many distinct drinking areas, including a large no-smoking section. There are separate games and big-screen TV areas. Camerons' ales are still sold under a supply deal with W&D following the recent sale of the town brewery by W&D to Castle Eden. Guest ales are served during summer as holiday trade picks up. Good quality, reasonably-priced food is served all day. A pub with something for everybody, enjoyed by locals and visitors, a marine-side terrace serves as a garden. Q🕯️🍴🖐≢🖐🖐

White House
Wooler Road, TS26 0DR
☼ 11-11; 12-10.30 Sun
☎ (01429) 224392
Draught Bass; Tetley Bitter; Worthington's 1744; guest beers Ⓗ
Aptly-named, truly stunning conversion of a Victorian mansion set in its own grounds, in an affluent part of the town. It has reputedly seen service as a wartime convalescent home and as St Francis RC Grammar School. The gentlemen's club style interior has leather furniture and a home-from-home feeling. The licensee serves three rotating guest ales. A springtime 'champions' beer festival includes a fun contest to see who can serve a full pint with the largest head, and known locally as a banker. A south-facing terrace, value-for-money food served all day, and first-class staff all enhance the experience.
🛏Q🕯️🍴🖐≢P🖐

HEIGHINGTON

George & Dragon
4 East Green, DL5 6PP
☼ 12-3, 5-11; 11-11 Sat; 12-10.30 Sun
☎ (01325) 313152
Black Sheep Best Bitter; John Smith's Magnet; Wells Bombardier; Worthington's Bitter; guest beers Ⓗ
Friendly village pub where locals warmly welcome visitors. An old coaching inn complete with stables, it has been refurbished in a more modern style with a spacious lounge and a separate bar. Bar meals are served in the lounge and a conservatory-style restaurant offers outstanding home-cooked food, which has an excellent reputation. Regular live music and quiz nights are held.
🕯️🍴🖐♣P

HIGH FLATTS

Plough Inn
DH2 1BL OSNZ2652
☼ 2-11 (flexible hours); 12-10.30 Sun
☎ (0191) 388 2068
Wadworth 6X; guest beer Ⓗ
Traditional, country ale house but very close to the town centre. A regular bus service passes seven days a week. Quizzes are held three times a week, attracting contestants from all over the area. The landlord has boosted the cask ale sales. The walls are adorned with many brass and copper implements, together with photographs of a bygone era. The panoramic views include glimpses of the Angel of the North and Pensaw Monument. There is a private airstrip to the rear, and an adjacent caravan site. Quoits, darts and dominoes are played. ❀⊟♿Å♣P

HIGH HESLEDEN

Ship Inn
TS27 4QD (½ mile off B1281, Blackhall Colliery)
☼ 12-3, 6-11; 12-3, 7-10.30 Sun
☎ (01429) 836453
Beer range varies Ⓗ
Described as 'an oasis in the desert', this friendly, welcoming pub is continuing to thrive. The landlord is a real ale enthusiast, most of the beers are from the area. Westons Old Rosie cider is sold. Displaying a nautical theme, the spacious bar offers excellent meals, it is advisable to book for the separate restaurant. Theme nights are organised throughout the year, as well as an August beer festival. Well worth a visit.
🏛Q⛄❀🍴◑⊟♿Å♣P⤶🗓

HOWDEN-LE-WEAR

Plantation
40 High Street, DL15 8EZ
☼ 6 (7 Tue & Thu)-11; 12-3, 7-10.30 Sun
☎ (01388) 766450
Courage Directors; John Smith's Bitter; guest beers Ⓗ
Recently returned to a cask ale house by new owners, this pub has been transformed into a proactive cask outlet with a high turnover of guest ales. Formerly called the Garden House, the Plantation has rapidly built up a clientele from the surrounding area. Quiz and bingo are held on Thursday night. Bus routes Arriva 1 and Weardale 101 to Howden-le-Wear serve the pub, bus stops are close by. Evening meals are served on Monday, Wednesday, Friday and Saturday, 6–9 and lunch on Sunday only.
❀◑♣P

HURWORTH

Bay Horse
45 The Green, DL2 2AA
☼ 11-3, 5 (4.30 Fri)-11; 11-11 Sat; 12-10.30 Sun
☎ (01325) 720663
Courage Directors; John Smith's Magnet; guest beers Ⓗ
Attractive inn, situated in an equally charming village by the River Tees, home of the famous mathematician, William Emerson. It consists of a cosy, two-part lounge, bustling bar and a conservatory/dining room at the rear. Two guest beers are available, from which a weekly guest

is selected from the SIBA list. A carriage arch leads to a small car park and garden at the rear. There is a quiz every Tuesday.
🏛Q❀◑▯⊟Å♣P🗓

LONGNEWTON

Vane Arms ◕
Darlington Road, TS21 1DB
☼ 11.30-3, 5.30-11; 11.30-11 Fri & Sat;
12-10.30 Sun
☎ (01642) 580401
Draught Bass; John Smith's Magnet; guest beers Ⓗ
Cosy, two-roomed pub, in what was originally a Hammond's house. Plenty of memorabilia includes a 1935 bottle of Vaux Maxim and a six-pack of bottled Bass, brewed to celebrate the brewery's 200th anniversary. Besides the two regular beers, two guest ales, selected from the Enterprise stable, are also available. The large, south-facing beer garden is ideal in summer, while open fires feature in winter. A quiz night is held on the last Sunday of the month. Good value home-cooked food, fine ales and a warm welcome are assured from this family-run pub. Lunches are available daily and evening meals on Thursday–Saturday.
🏛Q❀◑⊟P

MIDDLESTONE VILLAGE

Ship
Low Road, DL14 8AB
☼ 4 (12 Fri & Sat)-11; 12-10.30 Sun
☎ (01388) 810904
Beer range varies Ⓗ
This pub was saved by a local CAMRA campaign after it was closed by Vaux Brewery as unviable. Since then it has gone from strength to strength. It now has six cask ales from local and regional independent breweries, usually including Durham and Daleside with another four from across the country. It was awarded local CAMRA Pub of the Year 2001 and 2002 and north-east Pub of the Year 2002. A quiz night is hosted on Thursday and beer festivals are held in May and November. A rooftop patio offers an unusual place to enjoy a pint on summer evenings with superb views of the Cleveland Hills. The local bus service stops outside the door. 🏛❀♣P🗓

NO PLACE

Beamish Mary Inn ◕
Front Street, DH9 0QH
(600 yds off A693, 1 mile from Beamish museum)
☼ 12-11; 12-10.30 Sun
☎ (0191) 370 0237
Black Sheep Special; Courage Directors; Jennings Cumberland Ale; Theakston Old Peculier; guest beers Ⓗ
This pub remains one of the stars of Durham County. Beers are brewed exclusively for the Beamish Mary, including a house beer, No Place Bitter. A separate hall acts as a venue for live music, and an annual beer festival takes place. This is an excellent, sociable pub – well loved by locals. 🏛Q❀🛏◑▯⊟

NORTH BITCHBURN

Red Lion
North Bitchburn Terrace, DL15 8AL

(on A689, 3 miles NW of Bishop Auckland)
☼ 12-3, 7-11; 12-3, 7-10.30 Sun
☎ (01388) 763561

Black Sheep Special; Greene King Abbot; Marston's Pedigree; John Smith's Bitter; guest beer Ⓗ

This friendly, old, roadside free house has been in the same hands for over 16 years. The pub oozes character and offers high quality food and real ale, with locals happily mixing with people from further afield; look for the caricature of the landlord in the pub sign. Guest beers change regularly and are from all over Britian, pump clips cover the walls, giving testament to the variety of guests. Bulmers Traditional cider is sold. Bus route 1B Darlington–Tow Law, stops by the door.
Ⓜ Q ⚘ ◑ ♣ ♠ P ⏸

NORTON

Unicorn

147 High Street, TS20 1AA
☼ 12-3.30, 5.30-11; 11-11 Fri & Sat; 12-4, 7-10.30 Sun
☎ (01642) 643364

John Smith's Magnet Ⓗ

Superb, old village gem in the High Street conservation area. It has a fascinating layout with several small rooms off a central corridor. Local pride is all – any changes to this historic building would be met with stiff resistance! An unsympathetic owner tried to box in a girder bearing the local maker's name, Dorman Long; the result was almost civil war. Unlike most pubs in this Guide with their bewildering choice of real ales, this pub serves only one – supremely well. Q ⏦ ⚘ ◑ ⊟ ♣ ♠

PELTON FELL

Moorings

Front Street, DH2 3JU (into Chester-le-Street under viaduct, 2 miles signed on left)
☼ 11.45-11; 11.45-10.30 Sun
☎ (0191) 370 1597

Black Sheep Special; Theakston Cool Cask; guest beer Ⓗ

Well turned out country pub with a nautical theme. The pub is on a hill, so the facilities are on two levels. The landlord is a Master Cellarman and prides himself on the quality of the beer and the food. Meals include high quality fish dishes in the restaurant. Q ⚘ ◑ P

PIERCEBRIDGE

Carlbury Arms

DL2 3SJ (just off A67)
☼ 11-11; 12-10.30 Sun
☎ (01325) 374286

Beer range varies Ⓗ

Traditional inn set in this picturesque village which dates back to Roman times, when it was a fort and settlement known as 'Magis'. Formerly known as the Wheatsheaf, it is run by the area's youngest licensee and consists of two rooms along with a restaurant. The choice of up to three guest beers available, and the food on offer, give something to suit everyone. The beer garden consists of a picnic area with rustic water features. There is a quiz on alternate Mondays.
Ⓜ Q ⚘ ◑ ♣ P

PITY ME

Lambton Hounds

62 Front Street, DH1 5DE (off A167 roundabout, 2 miles from Durham City)
☼ 11-11; 12-10.30 Sun
☎ (0191) 386 4742

Black Sheep Best Bitter; Caledonian Deuchars IPA Ⓗ

This popular, ex-coaching inn provides good ale, tasty food (booking advised), accommodation and a warm welcome. The three-roomed pub includes bar fittings from the Olympic, the Titanic's stablemate. The staff are ready to share a laugh with locals and strangers alike and make this a pub you will want to revisit. Locally referred to as 'Pops' for over 50 years, it is on the same bus route as the Tap & Spile.
Q ⏦ ⚘ ◑ ⊟ ♣ ⅁

PRESTON-LE-SKERNE

Blacksmith's Arms

Ricknall Lane, DL5 6JH
(off A167, at Gretna Green)
☼ 5.30-11; closed Mon; 12-3, 7-10.30 Sun
☎ (01325) 314873
website: www.blacksmithsarms.co.uk

Beer range varies Ⓗ

Long, narrow, family-run free house standing by itself. A lengthy corridor separates the bar and lounge, while the beamed lounge is set in a farmhouse style, complete with Welsh dresser. Up to four guest ales are available, the special cask ale night on Sunday offers good value for money. Excellent home-cooked food is served. Hens, peacocks and guinea fowl roam free in the garden, and there is even a helicopter landing pad. Former local CAMRA Rural Pub of the Year. ⚘ ◑ ⊟ P

ROMALDKIRK

Kirk Inn

The Green, DL12 9ED
☼ 12-3 (not Tue), 6-11; 12-3, 7-10.30 Sun
☎ (01833) 650260

Black Sheep Best Bitter; Jennings Cumberland Ale; Taylor Landlord; Village White Boar Ⓗ

Overlooking the large, attractive green, this one-roomed pub doubles as a village post office until lunchtime (weekdays, not Tue), but it is impossible to detect at other times. Evening meals are served daily, except on Tuesday and Sunday. Background classical music creates a restful atmosphere. The pub is popular with walkers. Ⓜ Q ⚘ ◑ ⅁ ♣ P

ST JOHN'S CHAPEL

Blue Bell

12 Hood Street, DL13 1QJ (W end of village)
☼ 5 (11 Sat)-11; 12-3, 7-10.30 Sun
☎ (01388) 537256

Tetley Bitter Ⓗ

A new landlord runs this pub but the high standards have been maintained and it is still one of the few outlets in the region for cask cider (Addlestones). This fine, old, traditional pub is very popular with the local community and is located in excellent hill walking and cycling country, in an area known as 'England's last wilderness'. However, the weather can be very unpredictable in winter and spring. The pub is served by Weardale bus 101 from

Stanhope – please check return times before travelling, especially on Sundays and bank holidays. ✿ Å ♣ ♠

SEDGEFIELD

Ceddesfield Hall
Sedgefield Community Association, Rectory Row, TS21 2AE (behind church in centre)
✿ 7.30-10.30; 8-11 Sat; 8-11 Sun
☎ (01740) 620341
Beer range varies Ⓗ
This club is unusual in the north east as it sells an ever-changing range of cask ales and holds an annual beer festival on the first weekend of July. Voted CAMRA Club of the Year, again, in 2002, it has a resident ghost – 'the pickled parson' may no doubt have sampled the odd guest (beer!). Friendly, reasonably-priced and accessible to CAMRA members, the club is a credit to the volunteers of Sedgefield Community Association. Q ✿ ⊟ & P ▯

Dun Cow Inn
23 Front Street, TS21 3AT
✿ 11-3, 6.30-11; 11.30-3, 7-10.30 Sun
☎ (01740) 620894
Theakston Best Bitter; guest beers Ⓗ
This small but characterful hotel has built up an excellent reputation for both its food and excellent cask ales. The pub is popular with drinkers of all ages. Food can be taken in the main lounge/bar area or simply sample an ale in the snug or olde-worlde back bar. The pub stocks many beers rare to the area and is a definite change from the mundane. Check out the exterior in summer – a floral delight. Q ⇔ ◑ ⊟ P

Nag's Head
8 West End, TS21 2BS
✿ 12 (5 Mon)-11; 12-10.30 Sun
☎ (01740) 620234
Taylor Landlord; Theakston Cool Cask; guest beers Ⓗ
The Nag's Head is conveniently situated in the village close to Sedgefield racecourse. It is a free house, run as an old-fashioned local to attract all age groups; families with well-behaved children are most welcome. There is a compact, comfortable bar and a smaller quaint lounge. A separate restaurant uses fresh local ingredients – no food is served on Sunday evening. The three guest beers are usually mid-strength (4–5%). There are traditional pub games available, such as shove-ha'penny. The landlord and landlady both come from the village. ✿ ◑ ⊟ & P ⊬

SHINCLIFFE

Seven Stars
High Street North, DH1 2NU (on A177, 1¾ miles S of Durham)
✿ 12-11; 12-10.30 Sun
☎ (0191) 384 8454 website: www.sevenstarsinn.co.uk
Black Sheep Best Bitter; Castle Eden Ale; Courage Directors; Theakston Best Bitter Ⓗ
Situated at the end of a quaint pretty village, this old coaching inn is popular with both regulars and visitors. The customer can enjoy conversation in a pleasant atmosphere, undisturbed by any loud, piped music. The food menu is imaginative, if perhaps a little upmarket, and has many devotees. The forecourt, with tables and chairs, serves as a garden. The

pub is a good centre for many fine country walks and the attractions of Durham City are close to hand.
Q ✿ ⇔ ◑ ⊟ ⊞

STANHOPE

Grey Bull
17 West Terrace, DL13 2PB
✿ 2 (12 Sat)-11; 12-10.30 Sun
☎ (01388) 528177
Jennings Cumberland Ale; guest beer (occasional) Ⓗ
This fine house, with a long-held reputation for good ale, has recently become a Jennings pub. Ideally situated at the edge of town near the ford, open-air swimming pool and playgrounds, from here roads head north and south over high wilderness moors that are a match for the best mountain bikers. This popular pub can be busy during darts and pool nights but the casual visitor can be assured of a warm welcome and good pint. Bus No. 101 runs from Crook and Bishop Auckland to the market place – check if going to Horn Hall or 'up-dale', otherwise five minutes' walk. ▥ ⍾ Å

STOCKTON-ON-TEES

Fitzgeralds
9-10 High Street, TS18 1UB
✿ 11.30-3 (3.30 Fri; 4 Sat), 6.30-11; 7-10.30 Sun
☎ (01642) 678220
Taylor Landlord; guest beers Ⓗ
Imposing, stone-built edifice with shap granite pillars built originally as a gentleman's club with an upstairs billiards room. Converted to a pub many years ago, and modernised in the 1970s – all formica and plastic – then-owners, Sir John Fitzgerald, carried out a much more sympathetic restoration, with wood, cut glass and snob screens to create the fine pub that exists today. The licensee stocks guest ales from breweries rarely seen in this area. It is not open Sunday lunchtime. ◑ ⇌ ♣

THORPE THEWLES

Hamilton Russell Arms
Bank Terrace, TS21 3JW
✿ 12-11; 12-10.30 Sun;
☎ (01740) 630757
Courage Directors; John Smith's Magnet; Wells Bombardier Ⓗ
Historic pub overlooking the picturesque village green. Originally part of the estate of the Marchioness of Londonderry, it was named following the 1828 marriage of Gustavson Hamilton and Emma Maria Russell. Recently extended and refurbished, the pub retains its snug and games room, together with a large no-smoking area. There is an extensive south-facing garden, while open fires feature in winter. Fine dining at pub prices, from an extensive menu, with fish and vegetarian options, is available all day. Cheery, dedicated staff ensure that the 'Hammy' continues to be a pub to suit all tastes. ▥ Q ✿ ◑ ⊟ & P ⊬

TRIMDON VILLAGE

Bird in Hand
Salters Lane, TS29 6JQ (on B1278)

⊛ 11-11; 12-3, 7-11 Mon; 12-10.30 Sun
☎ (01429) 880391
Black Sheep Best Bitter; guest beers Ⓗ
Large, friendly, 1950s, locals' pub on the
edge of the village, overlooking open
country. It has a central serving area, a bar
at one side and a spacious lounge/restaurant
at the other. The landlord is a real ale
enthusiast and stages six themed beer
weekends a year. There are old-fashioned
games nights; games played include devil
among the skittles. August bank holiday is
the 'Battle of the Bands' (rock and blues);
regular live entertainment is staged.
Trimdon folk club meets on the first Friday
of the month. Look for mementos of the
landlord's time in Star City as a trainee
cosmonaut. ☎✿◖◗❶♣P

WALDRIDGE

Waldridge Tavern
DH2 3RY OSNZ2550
⊛ 11.30-11; 11.30-10.30 Sun
☎ (0191) 389 0439
Tetley Bitter; guest beers Ⓗ
Well-appointed pub with a cosy,
comfortable ambience. The restaurant
serves international and vegetarian dishes,
and a good selection of wines. A children's
menu is available with novelties. Speciality
coffees and cocktails can be sampled. The
function room (free) caters for party nights,
meetings and the like. The adjacent fell is
popular with walkers. Enjoy a drink on the
roof terrace which offers splendid views
across the valley. ☎✿◖◗❶&P⌿

WEST CORNFORTH

Square & Compass
7 The Green, DL17 9JQ
⊛ 12-5, 7-11; 12-11 Sat; 12-10.30 Sun
☎ (01740) 654030
Beer range varies Ⓗ
A locals' pub, ideally situated at the top of
the green which is the oldest part of the
village. Accommodation comprises a large,
open-plan bar/lounge and a small games
room. This is a free house, one of the ales is
usually from the nearby Durham Brewery.
Entertainment includes a popular quiz on
Thursday, and live music hosted on
Saturday. ♨&♣P

WILLINGTON

Black Horse Inn
42 Low Willington, DL15 0BD (on A690,
Durham road)
⊛ 7 (12 Sat)-11; 12-10.30 Sun
☎ (01388) 746340
Beer range varies Ⓗ
Popular pub on the edge of town and one of
only a few in the area to sell cask ale. Two
beers are always available from both
regional and local breweries. Situated in an
area rich in Roman roads and
encampments, the Black Horse Inn is
reputed to have a Roman ghost who
rearranges beermats and table decorations.
A quiz night is held on Sunday. It is on the
X46 bus route from Durham to Crook and
route 108 from Bishop Auckland stops by
the front door. Local CAMRA Pub of the
Year 2000.
Q✿❶♣P⏚

WITTON GILBERT

Glendenning Arms
Front Street, DH7 6SY (off A691, Consett Road
bypass, 2 miles from Durham)
⊛ 4 (11 Sat)-11; 12-10.30 Sun
☎ (0191) 371 0316
Draught Bass; Boddingtons Bitter; Tetley Bitter Ⓗ
Contemporary village pub that is popular
with locals. Warm and friendly, it offers a
bar with the original 1970 Vaux handpulls,
and seat dividers that were installed three
years ago. There is also a comfortable
lounge, both rooms have real fires. In
summer, seats are installed in the car park,
which then serves as a garden. The
Glendenning Arms has appeared in this
Guide for 19 years. ♨Q✿◖❶♣P

Travellers Rest
Front Street, DH7 6TQ (off A691, Consett Road
bypass, 2 miles from Durham)
⊛ 11.30-3, 5.30-11; 11-11 Sat; 12-10.30 Sun
☎ (0191) 371 0458
Theakston Best Bitter; guest beers Ⓗ
Smart, country-style pub with a diverse
cultural food menu. Meals are served in
three of the four distinct pub areas. The
conservatory doubles as the family room
(no-smoking) with high chairs available on
request. The large car park has an area for
outdoor drinking. An eat in or takeaway
pizza service is available. One of the guest
beers is usually from Durham Brewery.
♨Q☎✿◖◗P⌿

White Tun
Sacriston Lane, DH7 6QU
⊛ 12-3, 6-11; 12-11 Fri & Sat; 12-10.30 Sun
☎ (0191) 371 0734
Camerons Nimmos XXXX; guest beers Ⓗ
Neat, estate pub with spacious bar and
smaller lounge. One of the three beers is
often discounted and from Durham
Brewery. Traditional food is served during
opening hours except on Sunday evening. It
usually sells Camerons' range of beers with
a guest ale. The White Tun has a friendly
atmosphere; the bar has a large-screen TV
for football. Part of the car park serves as an
area for outdoor drinking. Q✿◖◗❶♣P

WITTON-LE-WEAR

Dun Cow
19 High Street, DL14 0AY
⊛ 6 (12.30 Fri & Sat)-11; 12-10.30 Sun
☎ (01388) 488294
John Smith's Bitter; Wells Bombardier; guest beer Ⓗ
Traditional village pub dating from 1799,
overlooking the village green. Popular with
locals and users of the Wear Valley Way
long-distance footpath and the nearby Low
Barns nature reserve, a thriving leek club
holds its annual show in September. The
soon-to-be-preserved Weardale railway
station, is close by, as is the local bus stop. It
is a quiet pub with no juke box, pool table
or piped music, but is reported to have a
ghost who has been spotted in the passage
at night. ♨✿▲P

WOLSINGHAM

Black Bull
27 Market Place, DL13
⊛ 12-11; 12-10.30 Sun

☎ (01388) 527332
Ansells Best Bitter; guest beer Ⓗ
Former coaching house in the village market place. The historic buildings in Wolsingham cover many architectural periods and the nearby back roads and lanes are perfect for an afternoon stroll before retiring to the Bull for an evening's refreshment. The landlord is a chef of high repute and the restaurant can be busy; best to book in advance. Sunday evening meals are only available in summer. The bar is popular on darts nights, although the lounge bar is usually a place for peaceful contemplation. Bus route 101 from Crook and Bishop Auckland stops in the market place, and there are public car parks opposite. ⚲☞❀☎◑⊟▲♣

WOLVISTON

Ship Inn
50 High Street, TS22 5JX
🕑 12-2.30, 5-11; 12-3.30, 7-10.30 Sun
☎ (01740) 644420
Black Sheep Best Bitter; guest beer Ⓗ
Former coaching inn with stables still standing to the rear, the current 1900s pub occupies a much earlier site. A no-smoking

area and efficient ventilation system ensure comfort for all. The Ship has an enviable reputation for food, all of which is prepared and cooked on the premises from fresh ingredients – no portion control or microwave 'ping' in these kitchens. Meals are served 12–2.45 (3 on Sunday) and 5–8.45. Selected by local CAMRA as Pub of the Season in 2000, it is still as good today. ❀◑⊅♣P⌇

Wellington
31-33 High Street, TS22 5JY
🕑 11-11; 12-5, 7-10.30 Sun
☎ (01740) 646901
Draught Bass Ⓗ
Old, whitewashed pub with pantiled roof, guarding a crossroads on what was once the main road north. The interesting façade advertises Bass Burton ales. The pub has a large function room used regularly for live music events and a comfortable lounge area leading into the busy public bar. The two pubs in the village, both featured in this Guide, have a long and unswerving commitment to real ale. Lunches are served daily and evening meals from 5.30–8.30 Monday–Friday.
❀◑♣P

Dowie's ale

Johnnie Dowie was the sleekest and kindest of landlords. Nothing could equal the benignity of his smile when he brought in a bottle of 'the ale' to a company of well-known and friendly customers. It was a perfect treat to see his formality in drawing the cork, his precision in filling the glasses, his regularity in drinking the healths of all present in the first glass (which he always did, and at every successive bottle), and then his douce civility in withdrawing. Johnnie lived till within the last few years (he died in 1817), and, with laudable attachment to the old costume, always wore a cocked hat, and buckles at the knees and shoes, as well as a cane with a cross top, somewhat like an implement called by Scottish gardeners 'a dibble'.

William Hone, *The Year Book*, 1839

Dowie's Tavern in Edinburgh was famously frequented by Robert Burns. Other habitués included Henry Raeburn, Adam Smith and the ballad collector, David Herd. The ale served was invariably Younger's, whose reputation the inn helped to make. After Dowie's death it became Burns Tavern but was demolished in 1831.

Leave the car at home

Public transport to pubs

BUSES

Bus Traveline
Most bus timetable enquiries are now dealt with through the National Traveline which is operated under a standard call number by local authorities across the UK for countrywide information
Telephone: (0870) 608 2608
Textphone: (0870) 241 2216

Information & Journey Planner Websites - some may cover other transport modes.
www.internet.xephos.com
www.pti.org.uk www.traveline.org.uk

Other sources of information can be found through your local County, District or Unitary Council or Passenger Transport Executive (see PTE Websites below) to ascertain correct contact details. Details of these together with train operating company telephone numbers appear in full in the National Rail Timetable (from main stations and W H Smith shops), or others in the www.ukbus.co.uk website.

www.ukbus.co.uk Station Master Bus & Train Information & Journey Planners with telephone numbers

www.arriva.co.uk Arriva Buses, Trams & Trains

www.firstgroup.com First Group Buses, Trams & Trains

www.stagecoachplc.com Stagecoach Buses, Trams & Trains

www.go-ahead.com Go Ahead Group

www.londontransport.co.uk for all London.

www.lothianbuses.co.uk for Edinburgh & Lothian area.

Other large Bus Groups include Blazefield Holdings, East Yorkshire Motor Services, Wellglade (Trent) and Yorkshire Traction, often with websites for their local operating companies.

Other Information Websites
Other important local authority public transport websites often give information - the main ones in metropolitan areas are as follows:

www.gmpte.gov.uk Greater Manchester
www.merseytravel.gov.uk Merseyside

www.nexus.org.uk Tyne & Wear
www.centro.org.uk West Midlands
www.southyorks.org.uk South Yorkshire
www.wymetro.com West Yorkshire
www.spt.co.uk Glasgow & Strathclyde
www.edinburgh.gov.uk Edinburgh & Lothian
www.cardiff.gov.uk Cardiff area

Many of the other Shire Counties & UAs have a website, often www. ending in .gov.uk

COACHES

National Express Scottish City Link

For longer distance coach service timetables & planners contact National Express - their line number is:

National Express (08705) 808080
www.gobycoach.com
www.nationalexpress.co.uk

Scottish Citylink (08705) 505050
www.citylink.co.uk

TRAINS

National Train Information Line

The national hotline for all train information is:
(08457) 484950
Minicom: (0845) 60 50 600

Other Rail Timetable & Fare Information + Journey Planning Websites

Enquiries:
www.nationaltrainenquiries.co.uk
www.railtrack.co.uk

Planning:
www.travelinfosystems.com

Current state of rail services:
www.nationalrail.co.uk

Booking services:
www.thetrainline.com

London:
www.londontransport.co.uk
(This covers Buses, Trams, Underground, River, Docklands Rail and Victoria Coach Station)

Many of the above websites often refer to a further local site for additional detailed information, and most of the train operating companies also have websites.

Important Note
Don't rely on information from websites being 100% accurate and up-to-date – contact the appropriate telephone service to check before travelling.

The lists shown are not exhaustive due to space limitations but many smaller operators have websites too.

For other information about transport websites and other contacts, but not timetable or service enquiries, please contact the CAMRA Public Transport Task Group by email MikePCAMRA@aol.com or by post or email via CAMRA Headquarters.

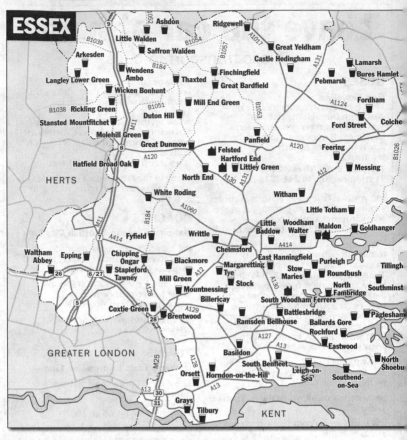

ESSEX

(Map of Essex showing towns including:)
Ashdon, Ridgewell, Little Walden, Saffron Walden, Great Yeldham, Castle Hedingham, Lamarsh, Arkesden, Wendens Ambo, Finchingfield, Bures Hamlet, Langley Lower Green, Thaxted, Great Bardfield, Pebmarsh, Wicken Bonhunt, Great Dunmow, Mill End Green, Fordham, Rickling Green, Duton Hill, Ford Street, Colche, Stansted Mountfitchet, Molehill Green, Panfield, Feering, Hatfield Broad Oak, Felsted, Hartford End, Littley Green, Messing, HERTS, North End, Witham, White Roding, Little Totham, Fyfield, Writtle, Chelmsford, Little Baddow, Woodham Walter, Maldon, Goldhanger, Waltham Abbey, Epping, Chipping Ongar, Stapleford Tawney, Blackmore, Margaretting Tye, East Hanningfield, Purleigh, Tillingh, Mill Green, Stock, Stow Maries, Roundbush, North Fambridge, Southminst, Mountnessing, South Woodham Ferrers, Coxtie Green, Billericay, Battlesbridge, Paglesham, Brentwood, Ramsden Bellhouse, Ballards Gore, Rochford, GREATER LONDON, Basildon, Eastwood, North Shoebu, Orsett, Horndon-on-the-Hill, South Benfleet, Leigh-on-Sea, Southend-on-Sea, Grays, Tilbury, KENT

AINGERS GREEN

Royal Fusilier
Aingers Green Road, CO7 8NH
☼ 11-2.30 (3.30 Sat), 5.30-11; 12-4, 7-10.30 Sun
☎ (01206) 250001
Beer range varies Ⓗ
This large, two-bar pub at the edge of the village, started life as a beer house well over 50 years ago. The present landlord and landlady are approaching their half century working here – an amazing achievement. The bars are traditional in appearance, with brickwork and timbers from a previous era. The two pleasures in visiting this pub are to discover which beers are available and what tales the landlord has to tell. Great Bentley railway station is one mile away. ♨🚲🕷❀♣P

ARKESDEN

Axe & Compasses ✓
CB11 4EX (2 miles N of B1038) OS483344
☼ 11-2.30, 6-11; 12-3, 7-10.30 Sun
☎ (01799) 550272
Greene King IPA, Abbot, Old Speckled Hen Ⓗ
Partly-thatched, 17th-century village inn with a public bar and restaurant that has won awards for good, if slightly pricey, food. A community pub with a very friendly atmosphere, it is the centre for much of village life, and locals actually talk to strangers here. It is frequented by walkers using the extensive local network of

footpaths in this beautiful locality. The peace is sometimes interrupted by a 1971 Wurlitzer juke box in the public bar.
♨Q❀◑⊟♣P

ASHDON

Rose & Crown
Crown Hill, CB10 2HB
(NE of Saffron Walden) OS587422
☼ 12-2, 6-11; 12-4, 7-10.30 Sun
☎ (01799) 584337
Adnams Bitter, Broadside; Greene King IPA, Abbot Ⓗ
Ashdon was the scene of an agricultural workers' strike in 1912 which led to farming reform. This 16th-century three-roomed pub retains much character from the past; reputedly haunted, it has a room known as the Cromwell Room still with its 'original' decoration. The pub is undergoing renovation in consultation with the local planning authority. Access at the front is via steps as the pub is above the road. Evening meals are served Tuesday–Sunday.
♨Q🚲❀◑P

BALLARDS GORE

Shepherd & Dog
Gore Road, SS4 2DA
(2½ miles from Rochford through Stambridge)
☼ 12-3, 6-11; 12-4, 6.30-10.30 Sun
☎ (01702) 258279 website: www.shepndog.com
Beer range varies Ⓗ

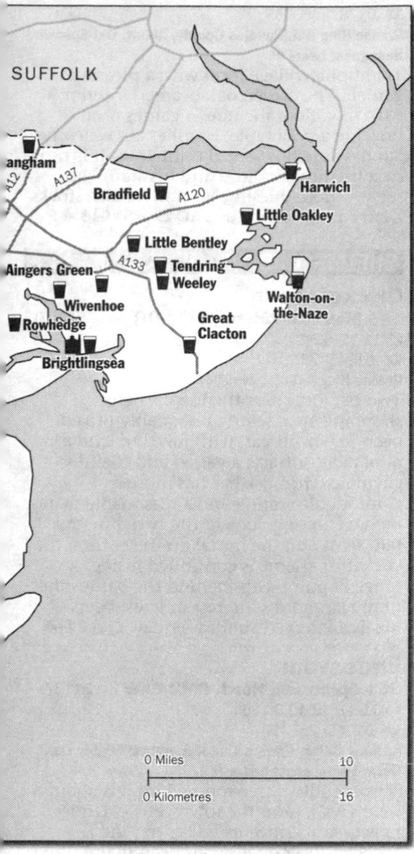
SUFFOLK
angham
A137
A12
Bradfield
A120
Harwich
Little Oakley
Little Bentley
A133
Aingers Green
Tendring
Weeley
Wivenhoe
Walton-on-the-Naze
Rowhedge
Great Clacton
Brightlingsea
0 Miles
10
0 Kilometres
16

Family-run country pub where timber features highly – in beams, bar panels and the floor. A frequently-changing range of ales comes from small and independent breweries; a variety of real ciders is stocked in summer. Highly commended food is served at all sessions. Popular with walkers and cyclists, the garden is safe for children (under 12s not allowed in the pub) and overlooks the adjacent golf course and lakes. A classic motorcycle club meets frequently at local CAMRA's Rural Pub of the Year 2002. ❀◐◑♣●P

BASILDON

Moon on the Square ✔

1-11 Market Square, SS14 1DF
⊙ 10-11; 12-10.30 Sun
☎ (01268) 520360
Courage Best Bitter, Directors; Shepherd Neame Spitfire; Theakston Best Bitter; guest beers Ⓗ
Typical Wetherspoon's outlet situated at the heart of this new town next to the market and frequented by an often lively crowd. It stocks a better than average range of ales from the frequently-changing list of this chain that is well known for its bargain prices. Other promotions are commonplace, such as beer festivals, food specials and the regular curry nights. It is well served by public transport with both bus and rail stations nearby.
◐◑♿⇌⊁

BATTLESBRIDGE

Barge

Hawk Hill, SS11 7RE
(off A130, follow signs for antiques centre) OS781947
⊙ 11-11; 12-10.30 Sun
☎ (01268) 732622
Adnams Bitter; guest beers Ⓗ
Traditional Essex weatherboarded Grade II listed historic pub on the north bank of the River Crouch. An antiques and craft centre now occupies the adjacent former mill and surrounding buildings. It can be reached from the small village station, with an hourly London service. A beer festival is held each April over the week covering St George's Day. A cash machine, unusual guest beers and a wheelchair WC complete the amenities, and ensure that the pub is often crowded, especially on a Sunday.
⛬❀◐◑♿⇌♣P⊁

BILLERICAY

Coach & Horses

36 Chapel Street, CM12 9LU
(by Waitrose, near B1007)
⊙ 10-11; 12-10.30 Sun
☎ (01277) 622873
Adnams Bitter; Greene King IPA, Abbot; guest beer Ⓗ
Comfortable town-centre pub, just off the High Street. This Gray & Sons house is popular with locals. Note the excellent collection of jugs and tankards. Good home-made food is served at lunchtime and evenings, with roast available all day on Sunday; home-made pies are a speciality. A 'DES' (DESignated driver) scheme operates for drivers to help combat the problem of drink-driving. ⛬❀◐◑⇌♣P

BLACKMORE

Leather Bottle

Horsefayre Green, CM4 0RL OS603009
⊙ 11-11; 12-10.30 Sun
☎ (01277) 821891
Adnams Bitter; Ridleys IPA; guest beers Ⓗ
Spacious pub in a well-appointed village. The bar has a flagstone floor and comfortable seating; the pool table, fruit machine and dartboard are separated from the general drinking area. A reasonably-priced guest beer is generally available (for about £1.50 a pint). Food is only available in the restaurant; run by an outside franchise, the excellent home-made meals are competitively priced and highly recommended. The cider is Westons Old Rosie. ⛬❀◐◑⊟♣●P

BRADFIELD

Village Maid

Heath Road, CO11 2UZ OS142302
⊙ 11.30-3, 6-11; 12-10.30 Sun
☎ (01255) 870329

INDEPENDENT BREWERIES

Crouch Vale South Woodham Ferrers
Felstar Felsted
Maldon Maldon
Mighty Oak Maldon
Railway Tavern Brightlingsea
Ridleys Hartford End

Greene King IPA, Abbot; guest beer Ⓗ

Popular, one-bar village local with a restaurant. Surprisingly these days, the village is served by a frequent bus service (every 30 minutes at peak times). The numerous beams in the bar and restaurant were taken from a dismantled barn during a previous renovation. There are separate bar and restaurant menus, and take-away fish and chips are available every day.
Q❄◐▣&P

BRENTWOOD

Swan ⊘
123 High Street, CM14 4RX (on A1023)
🕐 11-11; 12-10.30 Sun
☎ (01277) 211848
Draught Bass; Boddingtons Bitter; Brakspear Bitter; Greene King IPA; Wadworth 6X; Young's Special; Ⓗ **guest beers** Ⓗ/Ⓖ

Despite refurbishment, this 15th-century pub still retains much of its wood panelling and some interesting photographs of old Brentwood are displayed. There is a small patio to the rear. A varied range of guest beers is available – some on gravity stillage. The pub has limited parking which may not be available at lunchtime. ⋒❄◐▶≈

BRIGHTLINGSEA

Railway Tavern
58 Station Road, CO7 0DT (on B1029)
🕐 5 (3 Fri; 12 Sat)-11; 12-10.30 Sun
☎ (01206) 302581
Crouch Vale Crouch Best; Railway Tavern Crab & Winkle Mild, seasonal beers; guest beers Ⓗ

The Railway is a basic boozer – no frills, no music, no TV. You may hear the folk singers practising occasionally in the back bar, but you will see the front bar full of regulars drinking the house mild, Crab & Winkle, and the seasonal Old, Bladderwrack or Porter. All are products of the back room brewery. A sense of humour is desirable here. An important celebration is the May cider festival. This pub, with its varied activities, was local CAMRA Pub of the Year 2002. ⋒Q❄❦♣●

BURES HAMLET

Swan
1 Station Hill, CO8 5DD
(near B1508, 200 yds from station)
🕐 11.30-11; 12-10.30 Sun
☎ (01787) 228121
Greene King IPA, Abbot Ⓗ

Delightful, two-bar pub on the Suffolk border. The unspoilt public bar features wall benches, a terracotta tiled floor and an open fire. It contrasts nicely with the plush lounge and restaurant area. Throughout the pub there is a wealth of exposed beams that add to its character. Easily accessible by train, it also attracts its fair share of walkers and cyclists in addition to the strong support it receives from the friendly locals. Evening meals are served Monday–Saturday. ⋒❄◐▶▣≈♣P

CASTLE HEDINGHAM

Wheatsheaf ⊘
High Street, CO9 3EX
🕐 12-2.30, 5-11; 12-11 Sat; 12-10.30 Sun

☎ (01787) 460555
Greene King IPA, Ruddles County, Abbot, Old Speckled Hen; guest beers Ⓗ

Traditional village local with a pleasant garden. The carved oak-beamed interior with tiled floor includes a games room, housing a pool table. Families are welcome. Sunday lunch is served until 4pm. It is run by a friendly landlord and his staff who serve various guest beers, and he also stocks a large range of wines. ⋒Q➻❄◐▶▣&♣P

CHELMSFORD

Cricketers
143 Moulsham Street, CM2 0JT (near B1007)
🕐 11-11; 12-10.30 Sun
☎ (01245) 261157
Greene King Abbot; guest beers Ⓗ

Two-bar local near the town's main shopping area, selling reasonably-priced beer. The front bar, with juke box and a pool table, attracts a varied and friendly clientele. The back bar has more comfortable seating and a reasonable piano. Before entering, look at the two different pub signs and the mural on the corner; the cricketing theme is continued inside. A range of pump clips behind the bar testifies to the landlord's interest in guest beers. Meals are served Sunday–Friday. Q❄◐▣♣

Endeavour
351 Springfield Road, CM2 6AW (on B1137)
🕐 11-11; 12-10.30 Sun
☎ (01245) 257717
Adnams Bitter; Greene King IPA, Abbot; Mighty Oak Oscar Wilde; guest beers Ⓗ

This friendly, three-roomed local is about a mile's walk from the town centre. Under new tenants since its last entry, the excellent beer quality has been maintained by the landlord. Two or three guest beers are usually available but the mild may not be on sale during the hottest summer months. Good food includes fresh Lowestoft fish on Friday and Saturday, and Saturday steak nights. On Sunday a meat raffle takes place. Low-level background music does not intrude.
⋒◐▶♣⑂

Original Plough
28 Duke Street, CM1 1HY (by station, near A138)
🕐 12-11; 12-10.30 Sun
☎ (01245) 250145
Draught Bass; Greene King IPA; guest beers Ⓗ

Large, open-plan pub offering up to five guest beers, mainly from family breweries and larger micros. Popular with local office workers and commuters, it also attracts a younger crowd at weekends – Friday and Saturday evenings can be noisy. Major sporting events are shown on TV and it hosts occasional live music, mainly rock and soul bands. A mild is often on sale. A no-smoking area is available at lunchtime. Evening meals are served Monday–Thursday until 8pm.
❄◐▶≈♣P⑂

Queen's Head
30 Lower Anchor Street, CM2 0AS (near cricket ground and B1007)
🕐 12 (11 Sat)-11; 12-10.30 Sun
☎ (01245) 265181
website: www.queensheadchelmsford.co.uk

Crouch Vale Crouch Best, Brewers Gold; guest beers H
Hugely popular back-street local, owned by Crouch Vale Brewery, but selling up to six interesting guest beers from small breweries. A mild and a second dark beer are always available. The pub is decorated with brewing and cricketing memorabilia. Home-made food is served Monday–Saturday at reasonable prices. Live jazz is performed on the last Sunday lunchtime of every month, and an annual beer festival is staged on the last weekend of September.
🏛Q✿◖⑂⬥♣P

White Horse
25 Townfield Street, CM1 1QJ
(behind station, near A138)
✿ 11-11; 12-10.30 Sun
☎ (01245) 269556
Adnams Bitter, Broadside; Ansells Mild; Fuller's London Pride; Young's Bitter; guest beers H
Back-street local, selling eight or nine real ales, mainly from family breweries. Lunchtime trade consists mainly of workers from nearby offices; local residents and commuters being more in evidence in the evening. Major sporting events are shown on TV, in both the bar and the lounge end. The pub has a dartboard and one of the area's few bar billiards tables. Smoking is permitted throughout. A mild is always available at this local CAMRA Pub of the Year 2003. Weekday lunches are served.
✿◖⪦♣

CHIPPING ONGAR

Cock Tavern
218 High Street, CM5 9AB (on A128)
✿ 11-3, 5.30-11; 11-11 Fri & Sat; 12-10.30 Sun
☎ (01277) 362615
website: www.pickapub.co.uk/thecocktavern.htm
Greene King IPA; guest beers H
400-year-old pub where recent alterations have improved the standing area by changing the bar layout; seating areas are spaced around, with the old saloon retaining its cosy intimacy. It normally stocks three guest beers. Occasional live music is staged at weekends; the function room, with its own bar, is available by arrangement. Part of the Gray's pub group, it is in the town centre, next to a public car park. 🏛◖▶♣

COLCHESTER

Bricklayers
27 Bergholt Road, CO4 5AA (near station, between A134 and B1508)
✿ 11-3, 5.30-11; 11-11 Fri & Sat; 12-3, 7-10.30 Sun
☎ (01206) 852008
Adnams Bitter, Fisherman, Broadside, seasonal beers; guest beers H
Flagship Adnams town pub, with a public bar, a spacious, split-level lounge bar and a sun lounge (no-smoking at lunchtime). Up to three guest beers are supplemented by Adnams seasonal ales. A favourite with local CAMRA members, it has won numerous local awards. A high quality, good value menu includes a vegetarian option, as well as the extremely popular Sunday roasts, for which it is best to arrive early. Served by frequent buses from the town centre, it is handy for rail travellers, too.
✿◖⪦(North) ♣⬥P

Dragoon
82 Butt Road, CO3 3DA
(B1026, near police station)
✿ 11-11; 12-10.30 Sun
☎ (01206) 573464
Adnams Bitter, seasonal beers; Everards Tiger H
Welcoming local, just a short walk from the town centre, the Dragoon has a seated area and a games area with pool, darts and a large-screen TV for live sports. The pub is a favourite with Colchester United fans on match days, when an infamous chilli is served (not for the faint-hearted). Fish and chips are available on Fridays, and a popular Sunday roast is served (1–4pm).
✿◖⪦(Town) ♣

Foundry Arms
83 Artillery Street, CO1 2JQ (off A134)
✿ 11-11; 12-10.30 Sun
☎ (01206) 505159
Beer range varies H
This back-street free house in the new town district of Colchester is worth seeking out for its good selection of real ales. They mainly come from Shepherd Neame but can vary. Live music is staged on Sunday evening. The landlord has introduced bar snacks, and Sunday lunches are available. The pub is best reached by foot or cycle as parking in the area is very restricted. The pub keeps a range of bottle-conditioned beers. ✿♣⬥

Fox & Fiddler
1 St John Street, CO2 7AA
✿ 11-11; 12-10.30 Sun
☎ (01206) 560520
Greene King IPA, Old Speckled Hen; guest beer H
This town-centre pub has its origins in the 15th century. The single front bar opens off the street, but there are two other drinking areas in the pub's rambling interior. As you might expect it is allegedly haunted. It has had a few name changes over the years. The landlord, although new to the trade, has rapidly established a reputation for the quality of his beer and the warmth of his welcome. ✿◖⪦(Town)

Hospital Arms
123-125 Crouch Street, CO3 3HA
(opp. Essex County Hospital, near A1124)
✿ 11-11; 12-10.30 Sun
☎ (01206) 573572
Adnams Bitter, Fisherman, Broadside; Fuller's London Pride H
This friendly local on the edge of the town centre eschews music and pool, but concentrates on its ale. You will quite often find local thespians here in the evenings, as the establishment attracts actors and actresses from the nearby Mercury Theatre; if humorous banter is your cup of tea, this is the place for you. Split in half by the bar, the rear of the pub is quiet and full of intimate recesses, leading to a small courtyard. Colchester's oldest Indian restaurant is next door. Q✿◖🍴

Odd One Out
28 Mersea Road, CO2 7ET
(on B1025, 300 yds from Town Station)
✿ 4.30 (12 Fri; 11 Sat)-11; 12.30-10.30 Sun
☎ (01206) 578140
Archers Best Bitter; Ridleys Prospect; guest beers H

Basic, comfortable, free house attracting a wide-ranging clientele interested in decent beer and conversation. Up to five guest beers, including a dark and a strong beer, are offered, plus at least three ciders (often Crone's or Biddenden) and a selection of Scotch and Irish malt whiskies, all at sensible prices. Food is limited to cheese rolls. Local CAMRA's Pub of the Year 2003 is within walking distance of the town's rail and bus stations. ⚄✿≠(Town) ♣ ♠ ¾

Prettygate
102 The Commons, CO3 4NW (near B1022)
✿ 11-11; 12-10.30 Sun
☎ (01206) 563501
Courage Best Bitter; guest beers ⊞
Refurbished estate pub, a short bus ride (No. 1) from the town centre, it is well worth a visit. Ever-changing guest beers are stocked, mainly from the smaller breweries. The pub has recently been converted to one bar but still retains its separate games area. It also now offers a no-smoking area at the front. Despite being a comparative newcomer to this Guide, it has already achieved Town Pub of the Year status for 2003 from local CAMRA. ⓘ♭♿P¾

Spinnaker
Hythe Quay, CO2 8JB (on A134)
✿ 11-11; 11-3, 7.30-11 Sat; 12-3, 7.30-10.30 Sun
☎ (01206) 793176
Shepherd Neame Spitfire; Wells Bombardier; guest beers (occasional) ⊞
This traditional, friendly local has doggedly remained open despite the closure of the port and nearby factories. The Spinnaker is now deservedly starting to benefit from local regeneration, and plans are afoot to extend the bar and eating areas. Already a real ale oasis in an area otherwise bereft of a decent pint, this augurs well for the future. Weekday lunches are available.
ⓘ≠(Hythe) ♣

Stockwell Arms
18 West Stockwell Street, CO1 1HN (off High Street)
✿ 11-11; 11-5, 6.30-11 Sat; 12-4, 7-10.30 Sun
☎ (01206) 575560
Brakspear Special; Caledonian Deuchars IPA; Fuller's London Pride; Nethergate Suffolk County; Shepherd Neame Spitfire; guest beers ⊞
In Colchester's historic Dutch quarter, the Stockwell is best described as a village local in the middle of town. Dating from the 14th century, oak-beamed inside and out, it is reputed to have been the home of author, Daniel Defoe. The long-serving landlord has been awarded for charity work, including many fundraising walks across Scotland. Walkers and cyclists are particularly welcome, with regular monthly country walks organised (last Saturday). Booking is recommended for Sunday lunch.
✿ⓘ♣

COXTIE GREEN

White Horse
173 Coxtie Green Road, CM14 5PX
(1 mile W of A128)
✿ 11.30-11; 12-10.30 Sun
☎ (01277) 372410
Adnams Bitter; Fuller's London Pride; Ridleys Rumpus; guest beers ⊞

This splendid, two-bar local goes from strength to strength. It has been recently refurbished and redecorated throughout (including new toilets). Three guest beers are sourced from anywhere and everywhere, and a cider is usually available on draught. Each July a very popular beer festival is held in the extensive garden, normally with 30 or 40 beers on tap. The pub has its own golf society and occasional quizzes are held. Very good value lunches are served daily, except Sunday.
✿ⓘ♿♣♠P

DUTON HILL

Three Horseshoes
CM6 2DX (1/2 mile W of B184, Dunmow-Thaxted road) OS606268
✿ 12-2.30 (not Mon-Wed), 6-11; 12-3, 6-11 Sat; 12-3, 7-10.30 Sun
☎ (01371) 870681
Archers Village; Ridleys IPA; guest beers ⊞
Cosy village local, with a large garden overlooking the Chelmer Valley and open farmland. It hosts an open-air theatre one weekend in July. The wildlife pond is home to frogs and newts. A millennium beacon in the garden, breweriana and a remarkable collection of Butlins memorabilia are interesting features of this unpretentious pub. Food is served Thursday–Monday (not Mon lunch), but this is definitely a village pub not a restaurant. A beer festival is held on the late spring bank holiday. Local CAMRA Pub of the Year 2003.
⚄✿ⓘ♣P☐

EAST HANNINGFIELD

Windmill Tavern
The Tye, CM3 8AA (signed from old A130)
✿ 11-11; 12-10.30 Sun
☎ (01245) 400315
Beer range varies ⊞
Friendly village pub and restaurant selling good, home-made food seven days a week, including a full Sunday roast. It offers lower food prices for the over 55s Wednesday and Thursday lunchtimes. Children are welcome if well-behaved, otherwise there is a garden! A quiz is held on Wednesday evening. The pub has ample parking – you are welcome to leave your car here while exploring the village.
⚄✿ⓘ♣P

EASTWOOD

Oakwood
564 Rayleigh Road, SS9 5HX (on A1015)
✿ 11-11; 12-10.30 Sun
☎ (01702) 429000 website: www.theoakwood.co.uk
Draught Bass; Fuller's London Pride ⊞
Cheery pub with two rooms and a garden. One area houses darts and pool tables and shows live sport on TV. The smaller bar is quieter, with comfortable seating and a piano. Observe the original stained glass windows (preserved in the ceiling by the stage). It hosts live entertainment on Saturday evening. This local CAMRA Town Pub of the Year 2002 is served by bus routes Arriva 9 and First 20 from Southend or Rayleigh. No food is served Sunday evening.
✿ⓘ♿P

EPPING

Forest Gate
111 Bell Common, CM16 4DZ
(off B1393, Ivy Chimneys road) OS451011
⚙ 10-3, 5.30-11; 12-3 (4 summer), 7-10.30 Sun
☎ (01992) 572312
Adnams Bitter, Broadside, Ⓗ **Tally Ho;** Ⓖ
Ridleys IPA, Ⓗ **Woodforde's Wherry** Ⓖ
Timeless, 17th-century country free house, owned and run by the same family for many years. Situated on the edge of Epping Forest, it is popular with walkers. It specialises in real ale; the juke box, music and fruit machines are remarkable for their absence. Snacks are usually available and a renowned turkey broth is served in winter. A large, lawned area at the front of the pub is used for summer drinking. Dogs are welcome. ⚌Q✿◑♣P

FEERING

Sun Inn
3 Feering Hill, CO5 9NH (on B1024)
⚙ 11-3, 6-11; 12-3, 6-10.30 Sun
☎ (01376) 570442
Beer range varies Ⓗ
A true free house featuring carved beams, this pub stocks an ever-changing range of six real ales, mainly from small breweries, plus a cider or perry. A wide-ranging food menu is available every day. The food is wholesome and the portions large, but try to save room for a dessert. Two log fires provide an additional welcome in winter, while in summer you can relax in the shady garden. ⚌Q✿◑⇌(Kelvedon)♣♣P

FINCHINGFIELD

Red Lion
6 Church Hill, CM7 4NN (on B1053)
⚙ 11.30-11; 12-10.30 Sun
☎ (01371) 810400
website: www.red-lion-finchingfield.com
Ridleys IPA, Prospect, Old Bob Ⓗ
In one of the most picturesque villages in Essex, the Red Lion stands on a hill opposite the church and Guildhall. Set on several levels, access is difficult for the less mobile. Cosy, and heavily beamed, with a log fire in the main bar, it is popular for food. You can dine in the restaurant, but home-cooked food is served throughout this 500-year-old pub. ⚌✿⇌◑♣P

FORD STREET (ALDHAM)

Coopers Arms
CO6 3PH (on A1124, 4 miles W of Colchester)
⚙ 12-3, 5-11; 12-4, 7-11 Sat; 12-3, 7-10.30 Sun
☎ (01206) 241177
Greene King IPA, Abbot; Woodforde's Wherry; guest beers Ⓗ /Ⓖ
One glimpse of the comfy, leather sofas shows you are in a place that cares; a glance at the ample beerboard followed by a visit to the bar will bring a smile to your face. The wide range of ales makes this village local a must, but it also boasts 'real grub' – and it certainly is. Do not worry about a starter – the main course will sink you (no food Sun lunch). The atmosphere is subdued; the ideal pub for a beer or two, followed by a gourmet evening. ✿◑♣P

FORDHAM

Three Horseshoes
74 Church Road, CO6 3NJ
(off A1124, 4 miles W of Colchester)
⚙ 11-11; 12-10.30 Sun
☎ (01206) 240195
website: www.thethreehorseshoes.freeserve.com
Ridleys IPA; guest beers Ⓗ
Although this village local is off the beaten track, it is well worth seeking out. An L-shaped bar is split in two: the upper level has pool and darts, while the lower area boasts a fireplace big enough to walk inside. Mind your head on the beams – people were obviously shorter when the pub was built 400 years ago. Any beer could be on tap when you visit, as the range changes all the time. The dining room is open 2–9 Wednesday–Friday (7–9 Sat; 12–2 Sun). ⚌✿◑⇌♣P

FYFIELD

Queen's Head
Queen Street, CM5 0RY (by B184)
⚙ 11-3.30 (11-4 Sat), 6-11; 12-4, 7-10.30 Sun
☎ (01277) 899231
Adnams Bitter, Broadside; guest beers Ⓗ
Busy country pub in the middle of the village. It retains a cosy feel, with a long bar, some partitions, a beamed ceiling and wood flooring around the bar. Popular for food, it can get very busy at lunchtimes; evening meals are served Monday–Saturday. The garden overlooks the Roding River. The guest beers – normally four – are usually from small micro-breweries, sometimes one guest is replaced by a real cider. ⚌Q✿◑♣P

GOLDHANGER

Chequers Inn
The Square, CM9 8AS
(off B1026, past Agricultural Museum)
⚙ 11-11; 12-10.30 Sun
☎ (01621) 788203
website: www.thechequersgoldhanger.com
Greene King IPA, Old Speckled Hen; Ridleys Tolly Original, Old Bob; guest beers Ⓗ
Built in 1410 and gradually extended, this glorious village local recently changed hands, but is the new owner's third successive Guide pub. Committed to good ales and fine food, it hosts an annual beer festival in March. An extensive menu at reasonable prices, includes a monthly curry night (third Sunday); otherwise no meals are served Sunday evening. The decor varies in the many bars and games rooms, including farming and fishing memorabilia. Games include bar billiards and shove-ha'penny. Sea fishing packages with accommodation are available. ⚌Q⛴✿⇌◑⇌Å♣P⌷

GRAYS

Grays Athletic Football Club
Bridge Road, RM17 6BZ (end of club ground)
⚙ 5 (12 Fri & Sat)-11; 12-10.30 Sun
☎ (01375) 377753
Beer range varies Ⓗ
The social club of Grays Athletic Football Club admits card-carrying CAMRA members, or bearers of this Guide. It usually keeps three guest beers, often including a

mild, and hosts a beer festival (normally January). The bar overlooks an indoor five-a-side football pitch and the main ground. A large-screen TV shows sport in the bar. Parking is limited at the club, but ample space is available in the public car park opposite. Local CAMRA's Club of the Year 2003. & ♣ P

Theobald Arms
King's Walk, RM17 6HR
🕐 10.30-3, 5-11; 10.30-11 Fri & Sat; 12-4, 7-10.30 Sun
☎ (01375) 372253
Courage Best Bitter; guest beers Ⓗ
Family-run local in the recently rejuvenated riverside area of Grays, opposite the refurbished Grays town wharf and near Thurrock Yacht Club. Three constantly-changing guest beers are listed on chalkboards in both bars. The public bar features an unusual revolving round pool table. An annual beer festival is held in June, when one of the former stables at the rear is converted into a bar. Both bars have outdoor drinking areas; the public bar one is more secluded. Excellent value food is served weekday lunchtimes. ❀◖🖰 & ⇌ ♣ P

GREAT BARDFIELD

Bell
Dunmow Road, CM7 4SA (on B1057)
🕐 11-11; 12-10.30 Sun
☎ (01371) 811097
Adnams Bitter; Greene King IPA; guest beers Ⓗ
This cosy, friendly, two-bar local in the village centre is popular with locals. The 500-year-old structure means the lively public bar is at a higher level than the saloon bar, which houses a large brick open fireplace and an inlaid game table. The pub is said to be haunted by two ghosts. If you fancy a pint of Ridleys for a change, try the Vine, also in Dunmow Road. ⚏◖♣ P

GREAT CLACTON

Plough
1 North Road, CO15 4DA (near B1032)
🕐 11-11; 12-10.30 Sun
☎ (01255) 429998
Flowers Original; Greene King IPA; Tetley Bitter; guest beers Ⓗ
Great Clacton possibly contains most of the historic buildings in the area. The 12th-century church is now back in use after renovation and the 200-year-old Plough has never been out of use. Its snug bar hosts a myriad of conversations in its timeless atmosphere, while the L-shaped public bar is the perfect setting for the lively chatter and games of the younger element; both bars have an upright piano. A regular bus service runs from Clacton Station. ⚏❀♣

GREAT DUNMOW

Boar's Head
37 High Street, CM6 1AB (on B184)
🕐 11-11; 12-10.30 Sun
☎ (01371) 873630
Adnams Bitter; Young's Bitter; guest beers Ⓗ
Town-centre pub by the main public car park. Around 400 years old, low ceilings, beams, pictures of old Dunmow and a tropical fish tank are notable features here.

This timber-framed, lathe and plaster building 'bends' when delivery lorries 'bump' it while negotiating the tight bend. Quiet at lunchtimes, it gets lively in the evenings and weekends but is mainly frequented by locals. The little pub with a big atmosphere is run by a former thatcher. ❀P

GREAT YELDHAM

Waggon & Horses
High Street, CO9 4EX (on A1017)
🕐 11-11; 12-10.30 Sun
☎ (01787) 237936
website: www.waggonandhorses.net
Greene King IPA, Abbot, guest beers Ⓗ
16th-century inn at the village centre, where ales, including the guests come from various Anglian brewers. This popular local serves traditional pub food (all day at weekends). Games vary from pool to shove-ha'penny. Reasonably-priced B&B is provided in the main pub and a recently-built annexe. It is handy for visiting nearby Hedingham Castle and the Steam Railway Museum. The pub attracts all ages, and a friendly welcome from the landlord is assured. ❀🛏◖🖰 & ♣ P

White Hart
Poole Street, CO9 4HJ (on A1017)
🕐 11-11; 12-10.30 Sun
☎ (01787) 237250
website: www.whitehartyeldham.co.uk
Adnams Bitter; guest beers Ⓗ
This imposing, timber-framed inn, at the edge of the village, was built in 1505. Original beams, a Norfolk pammet floor in the bar and octagonal chimneys are features of this Grade I* listed building, which boasts extensive riverside gardens. Guest ales from local brewers, such as Adnams and Mighty Oak, change weekly and Belgian bottled beers are stocked. High quality, freshly-prepared food is served in both the bar and restaurant; an excellent wine list is a bonus. ⚏Q❀◖🖰 & P

HARWICH

Hanover Inn
65 Church Street, CO12 3DR
🕐 10.30-2.30, 6.30-11; 12-4, 7-10.30 Sun
☎ (01255) 502927
website: www.hanover-inn-harwich.co.uk
Greene King IPA; guest beers Ⓗ
Right at the heart of historic old Harwich, the Hanover is one of only a handful of survivors from a time when the old seaport had the highest density of pubs in the land. Situated next to the church, this free house offers lively conversation, good beer and a cosy, nautical charm. Accommodation makes this pub perfect for an overnight stop for the ferry, or a base from which to explore the area. ⚏🛏⇌ (Town) ♣

HATFIELD BROAD OAK

Cock
High Street, CM22 7HF (on B183)
🕐 12-2.30, 6-11; 12-4, 7-10.30 Sun
☎ (01279) 718306
website: www.pickapub.co.uk/thecockinnhbo.htm
Adnams Bitter; Fuller's London Pride; guest beer
(occasional) Ⓗ

Traditional 16th-century pub in the middle of a pretty Essex village, attracting a good mix of regulars and visitors. An extensive menu is served daily at lunchtime (when it is popular with walkers and cyclists) and Monday–Saturday evenings. A small room is set aside for non-smokers. 🏚Q◑&P⚥

HORNDON-ON-THE-HILL

Swan
121 High Road, SS17 8LD
(near B1007, off A13/A1014)
☼ 11-3 (not Mon), 6-11; 12-4.30, 6-10.30 Sun
☎ (01375) 640617
Adnams Bitter; guest beers Ⓗ
Welcoming, 400-year-old, two-bar village pub. Hops hang from exposed beams and the bar top is covered with pre-decimal coinage. There is a designated no-smoking area. A lively folk group plays every Sunday evening – everyone is welcome to join in. This local CAMRA Pub of the Year 2003, usually offers a guest ale from a micro-brewery. 🏚Q❀◑⊟&ᴧ♣P⚥

LAMARSH

Lamarsh Lion
CO8 5EP (1mile from B1508)
☼ 12 (11 Sat)-3.30, 6-11; 12-3, 7-10.30 Sun
☎ (01787) 227918 website: www.lamarshlion.com
Marston's Pedigree; Nethergate IPA, Augustinian Ale; guest beer (occasional) Ⓗ
It is well worth seeking out, this isolated rural pub set on the surprisingly steep side of the Stour Valley, affording fine views towards Sudbury. There is no public transport, but Bures Station is only 30 minutes' walk away. This 14th-century coaching inn has beams throughout, and a spacious dining area. An excellent menu features both local and international cuisine, and three guest rooms are available. 🏚Q❀❀≋◑ᴧ♣P

LANGHAM

Shepherd & Dog
Moor Road, CO4 5NR
(4 miles N of Colchester, off A12)
☼ 11-3, 5.30-11; 11-11 Sat; 12-10.30 Sun
☎ (01206) 272711
website: www.shepherdanddog.fsnet.co.uk
Greene King IPA, Ruddles County, Abbot; guest beer Ⓗ
This restaurant-cum-pub has such a good reputation that it was bought by Julian Dicks, the ex-West Ham United star. The three regular beers are supported by a changing guest ale. The pub has no less than three dining areas, offering an extensive range of first-class meals (try the mango sorbet). It is fair to say that this village local is not an ale drinker's paradise, but its mix of good beer, excellent cuisine and friendly atmosphere make it a must. 🏚Q❀◑P

LANGLEY LOWER GREEN

Bull
CB11 4SB (turn N off B1083 at Clavering)
OS436345
☼ 12-2.30, 6-11; 12-3, 7-10.30 Sun
☎ (01279) 777307
Adnams Bitter; Greene King IPA Ⓗ

Classic Victorian village local, with original cast iron lattice windows and fireplaces. In a tiny isolated hamlet, less than a mile from the Hertfordshire border, it has a devoted band of regulars and is used by local groups, including football and cricket teams. This friendly pub, in beautiful rolling countryside, is worth a visit. A pitch-penny game (penny in the hole) is concealed beneath a bench in the saloon bar. Meals can be arranged with advance notice. 🏚❀⊟♣P

LEIGH-ON-SEA

Broker
213-217 Leigh Road, SS9 1JA
☼ 11-3, 6-11; 11-11 Thu-Sat; 12-10.30 Sun
☎ (01702) 471932
website: www.brokerfreehouse.co.uk
Everards Tiger; Fuller's London Pride; Ridleys IPA; Shepherd Neame Spitfire; guest beer Ⓗ
Run by three generations of the same family, the Broker is a regular Guide entry. Children are permitted in one area of the pub until early evening. This sporty pub hosts quizzes and boasts an original Pacman machine and a plasma TV. Other attractions include a selection of wines and whiskies, and food specials including a curry night on Thursday. Evening meals are served Thursday–Saturday. ☎❀◑≋(Chalkwell) ♣

LITTLE BADDOW

Rodney
North Hill, CM3 4TQ OS778080
☼ 11.30-2.30 (3 Sat), 6-11; 12-10.30 Sun
☎ (01245) 222385
Greene King IPA, Old Speckled Hen; guest beer Ⓗ
A pub since the early 1800s, when it sold beer from the Chelmsford Brewery, the Rodney started out as a farmhouse around 1650, and has also served as a grocer's and a bakery. This comfortable, friendly, two-roomed beamed pub, has a public bar with a pool table and a small snug and a compact drinking/dining area. The decor includes brasses, posters, seafaring prints and pump clips. The pub is renowned for its food, all home made. Q❀◑⊟♣P

LITTLE BENTLEY

Bricklayer's Arms
Rectory Road, CO7 8SL (off A120 and A133)
☼ 12-3, 6.30-11; 12-4, 7-10.30 Sun
☎ (01206) 250405
Greene King IPA, Ruddles County Ⓗ
This delightful village pub forms the hypotenuse of a small, tree-lined green. There is, about the two-bar interior, a clear hint of the theatre, with the larger bar set inside a proscenium arch. Here witty banter is regularly exchanged between the locals and the landlady, who is never lost for the appropriate riposte. The food is 'real' and the beers always first class, as is the welcome. Q❀◑P

LITTLE OAKLEY

Olde Cherry Tree
Clacton Road, CO12 5JH (by B1414)
☼ 11-2.30, 5-11; 12-3, 7-10.30 Sun
☎ (01255) 880333 website: www.cherrytreepub.com
Adnams Bitter, Broadside; Fuller's London Pride; guest beers Ⓗ

This historic village local is close to Harwich and yet is in a truly rural setting with views of the North Sea. Five handpumps dominate the bar, two serving constantly-changing guest ales. Superb home-cooked food and a large open fire complete the award-winning formula that attracts regulars from all walks of life. The pub features a good-sized garden which is the venue for the beer festival and hog roast every June. ⚆Q🕮◑♣♠P🗇

LITTLE TOTHAM

Swan
School Road, CM9 8JJ (2 miles SE of B1022, between Tiptree and Great Totham) OS889117
⊙ 11-11; 12-10.30 Sun
☎ (01621) 892689
website: www.theswanpublichouse.co.uk
Adnams Bitter; Crouch Vale Brewers Gold; Fuller's London Pride; Mighty Oak Oscar Wilde, Maldon Gold; guest beers Ⓖ
CAMRA's national Pub of the Year 2002 and Essex Pub of the Year 2003 is a gem. This archetypal village pub has low, beamed ceilings, a friendly atmosphere and service; everything you could expect from a 400-year-old beer house. The recently-added dining room serves excellent food and complements the cosy lounge. A large, enclosed garden is a regular haunt of morris sides. The public bar is the hub of the village community, supporting many local activities. A beer festival is held each June. The pub stocks four guests.
⚆Q🕮◑♨🕮♿Å♣P🗇

LITTLE WALDEN

Crown
High Street, CB10 1XA
(on B1052, 2 miles NE of Saffron Walden)
⊙ 11.30-2.30, 6-11; 12-10.30 Sun
☎ (01799) 522475
Adnams Broadside; City of Cambridge Boathouse Bitter; Greene King Abbot; guest beers Ⓖ
Charming, 18th-century, beamed country pub, featuring a large inglenook. It offers an extensive menu with evening meals available Tuesday–Saturday. Racked cask stillage is used for dispensing an excellent selection of real ales. This recently extended pub in a quiet country hamlet attracts many locals and business folk from Saffron Walden. It is used for local club meetings and hosts trad jazz on Wednesday evening.
⚆Q🛏🕮◑♿♣P

LITTLEY GREEN

Compasses
CM3 1BU
(turn off B1417 at Ridleys Brewery) OS699172
⊙ 12-3, 6 (7 Sat)-11; 12-3, 7-10.30 Sun
☎ (01245) 362308
Ridleys IPA, Rumpus, Old Bob Ⓖ
Ridley's Brewery tap is tucked away in a quiet hamlet about a mile from the brewery. The interior is simply fitted-out with benches and rustic furniture. Beer is drawn direct from the cask and carried up from a half-cellar. There are no electronic games and the only music is at the monthly folk evening (third Mon). The large garden has picnic tables. Substantial bar snacks (lunch and evening) are mainly jacket potatoes and huffers (a local large triangular breadcake) with a wide variety of fillings.
⚆Q🛏🕮♣P🍴

MALDON

Queen's Head
The Hythe, CM9 5HN
⊙ 10.30-11; 12-10.30 Sun
☎ (01621) 854112
Greene King IPA, Abbot, Old Speckled Hen; Mighty Oak Maldon Gold, Burntwood; guest beers Ⓗ
Pleasant pub, some 600 years old, on the quay overlooking the River Blackwater with its sailing barges. Ale can be supped around a log fire, with friendly conversation from the landlord and staff. The rear bars afford river views and are decorated with old photos of sailing craft. The third bar gives access to the restaurant. Bench tables line the quay for outdoor drinkers. Bar food includes soup and Essex 'huffers'; Sunday meals are served 12–6. Parking is limited.
⚆Q🕮◑🕮♿♣P

Swan Hotel ⊘
73 High Street, CM9 5EP
⊙ 11-11; 12-10.30 Sun
☎ (01621) 853170
website: www.swanhotel-maldon.co.uk
Greene King IPA, Ruddles County, Abbot; Mighty Oak IPA Ⓗ
Grade II listed building dating from the late 15th century, it became a hotel 200 years ago. Now this single-bar Gray & Sons house, with a games room, provides ale, food, lodging and more. The varied food menu features daily specials using local produce. The Bewick function suite hosts not only the weekly music club and the monthly farmers' market but also many other local events. 🛏◑🕮♿♣●P

MARGARETTING TYE

White Hart
Swan Lane, CM4 9JX OS684011
⊙ 11.30-3, 6-11; 12-10.30 Sun
☎ (01277) 840478 website: www.thewhitehart.uk.com
Adnams Bitter, Broadside; Mighty Oak IPA; Ⓗ **guest beers** Ⓗ/Ⓖ
This single, beamed bar is set amid farmland, close to Chelmsford. It is sometimes referred to as Tigers Island, due to the 19th-century railway workers' bare-knuckle fights that took place there. A genuine free house, it pursues a vigorous guest beer policy. The restaurant in the conservatory serves home-made daily specials. The large garden has a children's play area and a pets' corner. It stages two beer festivals – in June and October. Darts and cribbage teams play here regularly. ⚆🛏🕮◑♿Å♣P🍴

MESSING

Old Crown Inn
Lodge Road, CO5 9TU
(1 mile N of B1022) OS898190
⊙ 12-2.30, 6-11; 12-4, 7-10.30 Sun
☎ (01621) 815575
Ridleys IPA, Prospect; guest beers Ⓗ
Comfortable, pleasant, old timbered inn at centre of the village with an open main bar area and a restaurant. Recommended for its good food, it can get busy at weekends. A small display area commemorates the visit

of George Bush (senior), ex-President of the USA. The front of the building was rebuilt in 1885 after an earthquake destroyed it and is possibly the reason for its resident ghost. ⚌Q☺◖P

MILL END GREEN

Green Man
CM6 2DN
(1 mile E of B184, Dunmow-Thaxted road) OS619260
✪ 12-3, 7-11; 12-5, 7-10.30 Sun
☎ (01371) 870286
Adnams Bitter; Greene King IPA; Ridleys IPA Ⓗ
15th-century pub on a quiet road in open countryside. Oak studwork and very low beams characterise the cosy bar, with padded settles. The adjacent dining area has seating for 30-plus. The central open fireplace is controlled by an adjustable hood. The landlord is also the chef, offering a varied menu of home-prepared fresh dishes. The excellent garden has a mesh-covered pond and a tennis court available for hire, as well as the more usual patio and barbecue area. ⚌Q☺✍◖P

MILL GREEN

Viper
Mill Green Road, CM4 0PT OS641018
✪ 12-3, 6-11; 12-3, 7-10.30 Sun
☎ (01277) 352010
Mighty Oak Oscar Wilde; Ⓗ **Ridleys IPA; guest beers** Ⓗ/Ⓖ
Lovely, unspoilt country pub, comprising a wood-panelled public bar and snug and a comfortable lounge. Usually two or three guest beers are available and the Oscar Wilde may occasionally be replaced by a different mild. The landlord, the third generation of his family to run the pub, is a bit of a 'chilli-head'; he makes his own chilli-pickled eggs and usually has some other chilli-based snacks on sale. Lunchtime food includes real ale sausages and ploughmans. ⚌Q☺◖♣♠P

MOLEHILL GREEN

Three Horseshoes
CM22 6PQ (1 mile from Stansted on Takeley-Elsenham road) OS563247
✪ 11-11; 12-10.30 Sun
☎ (01279) 870313
website: www.thethreehorseshoes.info
Greene King IPA, Abbot Ⓗ
Historic, thatched, ex-drovers' pub that still has a grazing meadow. Low beams and an inglenook with a real fire provide a pleasant, welcoming atmosphere. Aviation plates and other curios adorn the walls. The large garden is ideal for summer plane-spotting. The pub makes a good start or finish point for local walks. Attracting a good mix of locals and visitors, it has become a focal centre of the community, and is at the forefront of the Stop Stansted Expansion campaign. ⚌☺◖♿P

MOUNTNESSING

Prince of Wales
199 Roman Road, CM15 0UG (on B1002)
OS632979
✪ 12-3, 5-11; 12-3, 7-10.30 Sun
☎ (01277) 353445

Ridleys IPA, Prospect, Rumpus, Old Bob Ⓗ
This Ridleys' tied house stands opposite a windmill and a large cricket field. The timbered interior divides into two distinct drinking areas, one of which has a no-smoking section with individual partitioned tables. Evening meals are served Tuesday–Saturday. ⚌◖ ⊟P✍

NORTH END

Butcher's Arms
Dunmow Road, CM6 3PJ
(on A130, between Chelmsford and Dunmow)
✪ 12-3, 6-11; 12-11 Sat; 12-10.30 Sun
☎ (01245) 237481
Ridleys IPA, Prospect, Old Bob Ⓗ
Attractive, welcoming, 16th-century roadside pub bearing many original features – note the beams and fireplace. Up to five Ridleys' beers are always available. Very good home-cooked food, including locally-renowned fish and chips, is served in the bar and the no-smoking dining area. Booking is advised; evening meals are served Tuesday–Saturday. An award-winning garden makes this a pleasant place for families in summer. ⚌Q☺◖♣P

NORTH FAMBRIDGE

Ferry Boat Inn
Ferry Road, CM3 6LR
(signed from B1012, follow sign to river) OS853968
✪ 11.30-3, 6.30-11; 12-4, 6.30-10.30 Sun
☎ (01621) 740208 website: www.ferryboat.net
Shepherd Neame Best Bitter, Spitfire, Bishops Finger; guest beers (occasional) Ⓗ
The Ferry Boat is a cosy, unspoilt 500-year-old inn on the bank of the River Crouch. In its maritime setting, low beams and a log fire create a real olde-worlde feel. Families are welcome in two areas; the conservatory gives a good view of the garden where children can play. The six guest rooms are separate from the pub; one room has been designed to cater for disabled visitors. Good home-cooked food is served. Games include bar skittles. The publican has served here for 22 years. ⚌Q☞☺✍◖♿♣P

NORTH SHOEBURY

Angel
Parsons Corner, SS3 8UD (at A13/B1017 jct)
✪ 11-3.30, 5.30-11; 12-3.30, 7-10.30 Sun
☎ (01702) 589600
Greene King IPA, Abbot; guest beers Ⓗ
An attractive collection of cottages has been sympathetically restored as the Angel. On the edge of a large housing estate, it is more like a traditional country pub. The soft background music allows easy conversation in this deservedly popular local. The no-smoking restaurant, with children's licence, serves high quality food at reasonable prices. The four guest beers per week feature local micro-brews, with a Whitsun beer festival. It is handy for the Asda store. ⚌☞☺◖P✍

ORSETT

Foxhound
18 High Road, RM16 3ER (on B188)
✪ 11-3.30, 6-11; 11-11 Sat; 12-3.30, 7-10.30 Sun
☎ (01375) 891295

153

Courage Best Bitter; Crouch Vale Essex Boys Bitter;
guest beers H

A pub that has retained its traditions and originality: the saloon bar bears many hunting artefacts, including a striking carpet featuring foxhound heads; the public bar is basic but full of character. The Fox's Den dining room provides excellent meals at lunchtimes and Wednesday–Saturday evenings. Lively monthly quizzes are held, and, several times a year even livelier auctions that raise funds for guide dogs.
🏚Q❀◑〇🍽৬♣P

PAGLESHAM

Punchbowl

Church End, SS42 2DP (off A127, to Rochford, then follow signs Canewdon and Paglesham)
☼ 11.30-3, 6.30-11; 12-2.30, 6.30-10.30 Sun
☎ (01702) 258376

Adnams Bitter; Ridleys Old Bob; guest beers H

Three-storey, 16th-century free house, formerly a sailmakers, in a quiet, one-street village. Its single, low-beamed bar is decorated with brassware and pictures, while a small restaurant to one side affords pleasant views across open countryside. Dining tables outside in front of the pub, face south. Two guest beers are always available, changing regularly. An extensive menu includes vegetarian options and a pensioner's deal. There is a children's play area at the rear. Q❀◑P

PANFIELD

Bell

37 Kynaston Road, CM7 5AQ (off B1053, between Braintree and Saffron Walden) OS735252
☼ 11-11; 12-10.30 Sun
☎ (01376) 324641

Ridleys IPA, Old Bob H

This 16th-century, timber-framed pub is roofed with locally-made red clay tiles. Its two bars are connected by a long corridor. This sporting pub fields two football teams and boasts its own pitch; darts, dominoes and crib are also played. The pub even has its own racehorse, a two-year-old filly called Panfield Belle, owned and trained by the landlord and regulars. Good value meals and a large garden with a play area for children complete the facilities.
🏚❀◑〇🍽৬A♣P

PEBMARSH

King's Head

The Street, CO9 2NH (1½ miles E of A131)
OS851335
☼ 12-3, 6-11 (closed Mon); 12-6 (closed eve) Sun
☎ (01787) 269306

Greene King IPA; guest beers H

This old drovers' inn, dating from 1450, has been bought by the bar manager, ensuring that standards have been maintained. Popular with villagers, walkers and tourists, the oak-beamed interior and a large open fire ensure a warm welcome whatever the weather. The garden and patio are a summer attraction, with a bouncy castle for children; pub games and guest beers from small breweries guarantee entertainment for the adults. Regular events include curry nights, Greek meals and race nights.
🏚Q❀◑🍽♣P

PURLEIGH

Bell

The Street, CM3 6QJ (off B1010, next to church)
☼ 11-3, 6-11; 12-3, 7-10.30 Sun
☎ (01621) 828348

Adnams Bitter; Ridleys IPA; guest beer H

Attractive old pub, extensively refurbished in the 16th century. It is situated in a conservation area, near the church and other original buildings, on top of a hill. The pub affords fine views over the Blackwater Estuary. Popular with walkers using St Peter's Way and other footpaths, well-behaved dogs are welcome. Good food is available at this friendly, traditional hostelry. 🏚Q❀◑〇🍽♣P

RAMSDEN BELLHOUSE

Fox & Hounds

Church Road, CM11 1PW OS718948
☼ 11-11; 12-10.30 Sun
☎ (01268) 710286
website: www.pickapub.co.uk/fox&hounds.htm

Greene King IPA; guest beers H

Popular village pub, where a family-friendly beer festival is held on the last weekend in July. On the bar, interesting guest ales appear alongside the two regulars. Menus range from an à la carte/Sunday roast served in the no-smoking restaurant, to snacks and light meals served in the bar. Children are welcome – a play area and extensive garden will keep them amused. ❀◑🍽♣P

RICKLING GREEN

Cricketers Arms

CB11 3YG (½ mile W of B1383, near Quendon)
OS511298
☼ 12-11; 12-10.30 Sun
☎ (01799) 543210
website: www.cricketers.demon.co.uk

Flowers IPA; Fuller's ESB; Wadworth 6X; guest beers G

This cricket-themed pub stands next to the green where, in 1882, the highest score – 920 runs – ever scored in a single innings on a single day was achieved. A famous one day pro-am tournament is held annually. The pub has an outdoor boules pitch and a giant Jenga game indoors. Dating from the 17th century, it has been extended to provide accommodation for tourists and Stansted Airport, which is conveniently near but not obtrusive.
🏚⛺❀❀◑〇🍽♣P

RIDGEWELL

White Horse

Mill Road, CO9 4SG (on A1017)
☼ 11-3 (not Tue), 6-11; closed Mon; 12-3, 7-10.30 Sun
☎ (01440) 785532

Beer range varies H

Popular local, serving ever-changing guest beers, whose landlord is always happy to stock customers' requests. Note the old pennies that make up the bar counter. A wide-ranging menu is available in the restaurant, as well as bar snacks. Occasional live music is staged. A recent refurbishment has restored the pub to its former glory.
❀◑৬♣P

ROCHFORD

Golden Lion
35 North Street, SS4 1AB
✪ 12-11; 12-10.30 Sun
☎ (01702) 545487
Greene King Abbot; Taylor Landlord; guest beers Ⓗ
Classic, 16th-century pub, complete with
traditional Essex weatherboard and stained
glass windows. It is a regular local CAMRA
Pub of the Year winner, including 2003.
Muddy boots and dogs are welcome, but
not children. The juke box, which caters for
all tastes, is often loud, particularly on
Friday evening, but can be avoided in
quieter areas of the pub. Occasional live
music is staged. An unobtrusive TV shows
sport (by request). There is always a dark
beer stocked, and often some interesting
guests. ≠ ♣ ● ▯

Milestone
Union Lane, SS4 1AP
✪ 10-11; 12-10.30 Sun
☎ (01702) 544229
Greene King IPA, Abbot; guest beer Ⓖ
Tucked away in a courtyard over the road
from the station, this is Rochford's newest
pub and its best-kept secret. Open all
permitted hours, strangers soon become
part of the crowd in its cosy bar. The
landlord has had 30 years' experience in
various local pubs. His collection of soda
syphons is worth a look. The Thai
restaurant upstairs has a take-away service.
The TV is tuned to sport.
✿ ▶ ⅄ ≠

ROUNDBUSH (PURLEIGH)

Roundbush
Fambridge Road, CM9 6NN (on B1010)
✪ 11-2.30 (4 Sat), 6 (5 Fri)-11; 12-10.30 Sun
☎ (01621) 828354
Greene King IPA; guest beers Ⓖ
Traditional Gray's house with a cosy saloon
and simply furnished public bar which is
served via a hatch from the bar. It is a
favourite with the inhabitants of several
surrounding villages, who make less
frequent visitors welcome. Beers are served
from a stillage behind the bar. An excellent
menu is available in the dining room; the
pub also owns the café next door (open
8.30–2).
≞ Q ✿ ▯ ♣ P

ROWHEDGE

Walnut Tree
Fingringhoe Road, CO5 7JH (1 mile E of B1025)
OS021216
✪ 7.30 (7 Sat)-11; closed Mon & Wed; 12-3,
7.30-10.30 Sun
☎ (01206) 728149
Beer range varies Ⓗ
Cosy, lively one-bar pub on the outskirts of
the village. Popular for its mostly local,
independent beers on five handpumps, it
stocks no draught lager or keg beer. A vinyl
juke box, pinball machine and pool table
add to the atmosphere. Long-standing
owners welcome friendly dogs, while Nutty,
the goat, munches on in the large garden
unperturbed. Local CAMRA's rural Pub of
the Year 2002 offers good value food.
≞ ✿ ▶ ♣ P

SAFFRON WALDEN

King's Arms
8 Market Hill, CB10 1HQ
✪ 11-11; 12-10.30 Sun
☎ (01799) 522768
Draught Bass; Greene King IPA Ⓗ
Unusual, and architecturally-interesting,
pub just off the town's market square. A
welcoming log fire surrounded by sofas
and armchairs gives the bar a 'clubby' feel
on winter evenings. Its meeting room is
used by many clubs and societies. Jazz is
staged once a month on a Sunday
lunchtime. Note the display of caricatures
on the walls. Backgammon is played in
the bar and Rugby Union internationals
shown on TV.
≞ Q ✿ ▯ P

Old English Gentleman
11 Gold Street, CB10 1ES (near B184/B1052)
✪ 11-11; 12-10.30 Sun
☎ (01799) 523595
Adnams Bitter; Greene King IPA; guest beers Ⓗ
18th-century, town-centre pub with log
fires and a welcoming atmosphere, serving a
selection of regularly-changing guest beers.
An extensive lunchtime menu includes
special dishes that change daily. Meals can
be taken in the bar or the no-smoking
dining area, where artworks are displayed.
Saffron Walden is busy on market days,
Tuesday and Saturday. The pub has a
pleasant patio at the rear.
≞ ✿ ▯

Temeraire ✪
55 High Street, CB10 1AA
✪ 10-11; 12-10.30 Sun
☎ (01799) 516975
**Courage Directors; Greene King IPA; Shepherd Neame
Spitfire; Theakston Best Bitter; guest beers** Ⓗ
Spacious Wetherspoon's house in a former
working men's club on the main
thoroughfare of this attractive market town.
It is named after a battleship featured in a
famous painting by Turner and its tenuous
local connection is explained in displays
around the pub. Beer festivals are staged
three times a year; the well-trained staff
assiduously apply a 'try before you buy'
policy. A pleasant, secluded outside
drinking area at the rear is a bonus. It is
popular with younger people at weekends.
Q ✿ ▯ ⅄ P ⅍

SOUTH BENFLEET

Hoy & Helmet
24-32 High Street, SS7 1NA (on B1014)
✪ 11-11; 12-10.30 Sun
☎ (01268) 792307
**Adnams Bitter, Broadside; Courage Directors; guest
beers** Ⓗ
Situated in a conservation area, this
historic, 500-year-old Grade II listed pub
has many rooms, including a pool room.
With low beams and open fireplace, it
attracts a very mixed clientele. A large
garden at the rear contains a play area
with a bouncy castle. An extensive menu
is served until 9.30pm; local seafood is
available nearby at times. A surprisingly
varied range of rotating guest beers is
stocked at this Scotco outlet.
≞ Q ⌂ ✿ ▯ ≠ ♣ P

SOUTHEND-ON-SEA

Cork & Cheese
10 Talza Way, Victoria Plaza, SS2 5BG
(lower ground floor of shopping centre)
☼ 11-11; closed Sun
☎ (01702) 616914 website: www.corkandcheese.co.uk
Nethergate IPA; guest beers Ⓗ

Central Southend's only real pub, where shoppers, bankers and punks happily mix among the plastic beams and breweriana. Three TVs show sport (only by request). Micro-brews rule with over 2,000 different beers offered over 10 years at reasonable prices. Bring dark glasses for a trip to the loo. Local CAMRA Pub of the Year six times in 11 years, you will find it on the ground floor beneath the car park and shopping centre. Some tables are put outside in summer. ✿◖≉(Victoria/Central) ♣ ✿

SOUTHMINSTER

Station Arms
39 Station Road, CM0 7EW
(near B1020/B1021 jct)
☼ 12-2.30, 6-11; 12-11 Sat; 12-4, 7-10.30 Sun
☎ (01621) 772225
Adnams Bitter; Crouch Vale Brewers Gold; Ridleys IPA; guest beers Ⓗ

This delightful, weatherboarded pub is a former CAMRA East Anglian Pub of the Year, and is a must for beer lovers. Frequently-changing beers showcase micro-breweries. Simple furnished on a railway theme, a warm welcome and friendly atmosphere are assured here. Beer festivals, utilising the restored barn and outbuildings, are held in late January, the late May bank holiday and August bank holidays. Live blues evenings are staged monthly. Meals are served Thursday–Saturday evenings in the restaurant – booking advisable.
♨Q✿◖≉♣✿

STANSTED MOUNTFITCHET

Rose & Crown
31 Bentfield Green, CM24 8HX
(½ mile W of B1383) OS507255
☼ 11.30-3.30, 6-11.30; 12-3.30, 7-10.30 Sun
☎ (01279) 812107
Adnams Bitter; Fuller's London Pride Ⓗ

Typical Victorian pub near a duckpond on the edge of a small hamlet, now part of Stansted Mountfichet village. This free house has been modernised to provide one large bar but keeps the friendly, caring atmosphere of a village local. Note the outstanding floral display at the front. The landlady, who seems to know every customer's name, makes everyone welcome and the pub is well used by locals. Food is simple but reliably excellent and good value (no eve meals Sun). ✿◖♣P

STAPLEFORD TAWNEY

Moletrap
Tawney Common, CM16 7PU (3 miles E of Epping, 1½ miles from Toot Hill. Left turn on Epping road after Toot Hill to Tawney Common) OS501014
☼ 12-3, 6.30 (6 summer)-11; 12-4, 7-10.30 Sun
☎ (01992) 522394
Fuller's London Pride; guest beers Ⓗ

Truly great country pub, enjoying good views and a fine reputation for real ale and food. The three ever-changing guest beers are mostly from small micros. A lovely selection of home-made dishes are all at good value prices (no food Sun eve). Always a contender for local CAMRA's Pub of the Year, it is easy to see why – warm and inviting in winter, in summer everyone sits outside while goats, geese and chickens wander around. Why the name Moletrap? Ask at the pub. ♨Q✿◖P

STOCK

Hoop
21 High Street, CM4 9BD (on B1007)
☼ 11-11; 12-10.30 Sun
☎ (01277) 841137
Adnams Bitter, Broadside; Crouch Vale Brewers Gold; Ⓗ **guest beers** Ⓗ/Ⓖ

Small pub in an upmarket village. Up to four ever-changing guest beers are mostly on gravity dispense; the cider varies. The cosy, beamed bar houses a dartboard, and the pub sponsors Stock United football club. The food (available all day in summer) is prepared on the premises. Behind the pub are some friendly dogs, outside toilets, and a large, well-tended garden crammed with tables, which are cleared for the legendary late May bank holiday beer festival. Regular buses run from Billericay and Chelmsford.
Q✿◖♣✿

STOW MARIES

Prince of Wales
Woodham Road, CM3 6SA (near B1012)
OS830993
☼ 11-11; 12-10.30 Sun
☎ (01621) 828971
Beer range varies Ⓗ/Ⓖ

With its friendly atmosphere, this is a popular village pub in a 17th-century building. The 19th-century bread oven is used for regular home-made pizza nights. Other food theme evenings include fish and barbecues. An excellent range of beer, includes Belgian brews. Live music and beer festivals are staged several times a year.
♨Q✿≈✿◖✿P

TENDRING

Cherry Tree Inn
Crow Lane, CO16 9AP (on B1035)
☼ 11-3, 6-11; 12-7 Sun
☎ (01255) 830340
Adnams Bitter; Greene King IPA, Abbot; guest beers Ⓗ

A regular Guide entry for the past decade, this country pub is busy even on the most wintry of evenings. The ideal combination of real ale and real food ensures its continued survival in an area where other pubs have foundered. Conversation and good humour flourish in the quiet atmosphere. The Cherry Tree is worth a detour from the A133 for the quality of the real ale and the imaginative menu.
♨✿◖P

THAXTED

Star
Mill End, CM6 2LT (on B184)
☼ 11-11; 12-10.30 Sun
☎ (01371) 830368

Adnams Bitter, Broadside; Fuller's London Pride; guest beers Ⓗ

The Star is popular with locals and visitors alike. It is now open plan, but exposed beams and a large open fireplace have been retained. Thaxted is an architectural gem – do not miss its steep High Street, Guildhall, windmill, almshouses and, towering above all, its parish church of cathedral proportions. The latter hosts a month-long annual music festival and the town also stages an annual gathering of morris dancers when visiting teams from all over the country dance in the streets and at local pubs. ⚒ ❀ ◑ ♣ P

TILBURY

Anchor ✅
Civic Square, RM18 8AD (near A126)
🕐 10-11; 12-10.30 Sun
☎ (01375) 850560
Courage Directors; Hop Back Summer Lightning; Shepherd Neame Best Bitter; Theakston Best Bitter; guest beers Ⓗ

Sympathetic conversion of an old Charrington's pub by JD Wetherspoon has brought excellent value and interesting guest beers to a predominantly keg town. Locals favour the front of the pub, while the no-smoking area to the rear is used mainly by diners and families with children, and can therefore be rather noisy. Scenes of Tilbury Docks, together with profiles of local characters feature in the decor. The pub is often very busy.
🛏 ❀ ◑ & ♣ P ✂

TILLINGHAM

Cap & Feathers
8 South Street, CM0 7TH (on B1021)
🕐 12-3, 5.30-11; 11-11 Sat; 12-10.30 Sun
☎ (01621) 779212
Crouch Vale Essex Boys Bitter, Crouch Best, Brewers Gold; guest beers Ⓗ

Welcoming, 15th-century, Grade II listed weatherboarded pub in a picturesque village. The single bar is divided into three areas, each with its own character. The menu offers a good range of home-cooked food. A family room and comfortable bed and breakfast accommodation are additional amenities.
⚒ Q 🛏 ❀ ⇔ ◑ ♣ ❁ P

WALTHAM ABBEY

White Lion
11 Sun Street, EN9 1ER (near B194)
🕐 11-11; 12-10.30 Sun
☎ (01992) 718673
McMullen AK Ⓗ

Small, single-bar pub in a pedestrianised shopping area. It is popular with local darts players – league matches are played here on Monday, Tuesday and Wednesday. It hosts live music on some Saturday evenings. This is a very friendly, wood-panelled pub, where the landlady does not use cask breathers. ♣

WALTON-ON-THE-NAZE

Walton Tavern
30-31 The Parade, CO14 8AP (near B1034)
🕐 11-11; 12-10.30 Sun
☎ (01255) 676000

Adnams Bitter; Ridleys IPA, Rumpus; guest beers Ⓗ

This pub has been renamed many times. It boasts an enviable view of the pier and the North Sea from the bay windows. This family-run pub has undergone considerable refurbishment in recent years. Its large bar area is frequented by the sporting fraternity. Numerous photographs of Walton's past are displayed. The large dining area ably caters for the visitors in the summer season and some roadside tables are set out in fine weather.
❀ ⇔ ◑ ⇌ ♣

WEELEY

White Hart
Clacton Road, Weeley Heath, CO16 9ED (on B1441)
🕐 12-2.30, 4.30-11; 12-11 Fri; 11-11 Sat; 12-10.30 Sun
☎ (01255) 830384
Beer range varies Ⓗ /Ⓖ

Lively roadside pub whose regulars compete in local darts and pool leagues. It runs a beer club which organises visits to Guide-listed pubs and CAMRA beer festivals near and far. Its popularity is based on real ale from a variety of breweries. The publican has introduced a policy of regular beer weeks dedicated to beers from specific breweries, sometimes served by gravity dispense. A warm welcome is guaranteed at this pub on the village link bus route.
❀ ♣ P 🍺

WENDENS AMBO

Bell
Royston Road, CB11 4JY (on B1039, W of village) OS511363
🕐 11.30-2.30, 6-11; 11.30-11 Sat; 12-10.30 Sun
☎ (01799) 540383
Adnams Bitter, Broadside; Ansells Mild; guest beer Ⓗ

Beamed country pub at the centre of a picturesque village. The large rear garden houses a crazy golf course and hosts occasional bank holiday beer festivals. The two goats in the field belong to the pub. The Bell was local CAMRA's Pub of the Year 2002. There is easy access from Audley End Station (Liverpool Street–Cambridge line) and buses from Saffron Walden will bring you to this welcoming hostelry. No food is served Monday evening.
⚒ Q ❀ ◑ ⇌ (Audley End) P

WHITE RODING

Black Horse
Chelmsford Road, CM6 1RF (on A1060, opp. Abbess Roding jct)
🕐 11.30-3 (not Mon), 5.30 (6 Sat)-11; 12-3, 7-10.30 Sun
☎ (01279) 876322 website: www.theblackhorse.org.uk
Ridleys IPA, Old Bob Ⓗ

Traditional pub where the public bar dates back to the 17th century. Several additions have been made over the years, including a saloon bar which is mainly used for dining. Good quality food is available, except Sunday evening and Monday lunchtime; fish is a speciality Thursday–Saturday evenings. Legend has it that the pub has its own ghost called George, who can be heard playing the piano.
Q ❀ ◑ ⊟ ♣ P ✂

157

WICKEN BONHUNT

Coach & Horses
Wicken Road, CB11 3UG (on B1038)
OS498332
✪ 12-11; 12-10.30 Sun
☎ (01799) 540516
website: www.wickenbonhunt.com
Greene King IPA, Old Speckled Hen; guest beer H
Thatched pub at the centre of the village.
Some shoes discovered in one of the
chimneys are now on display; these were
thought to ward off evil spirits. Popular
with walkers, the pub lies close to
footpaths connecting to the Harcamlow
Way. A friendly pub, hosting jazz once a
month, on Sundays, it has a very small car
park.
🏚Q⊛◑⋑⊟♣P

WITHAM

Woolpack
7 Church Street, Chipping Hill, CM8 2JP
(near B1018)
✪ 11.30-11; 12-10.30 Sun
☎ (01376) 511195
Beer range varies G
Small, friendly local, dating from the
14th/15th century, where interesting
features include a built-in hide in the attic,
and a table converted from a large
cartwheel. Also look out for the collection
of bottles and soda fountains, many of
which bear the stamps of defunct breweries.
The house beer is Badger IPA.
🏚⊟≈♣

WIVENHOE

Horse & Groom ✪
55 The Cross, CO7 9QL (on B1028)
✪ 10.30-3, 5.30 (6 Sat)-11; 12-3.30, 7-10.30 Sun
☎ (01206) 824928
Adnams Bitter, seasonal beers; guest beers H
The Horse & Groom lies on the outskirts of
this delightful riverside town. The landlord
is proud to have been in this Guide for the
past 20 years. It is very much a local,
catering for both young and old. The public
bar is a hotbed of enthusiasm for pub
games. The lounge bar is quieter and ideal
for conversation. Although this is an
Adnams house, guest beers are often
available. There is a regular bus service to
Colchester.
⊛◑⊟♣P

WOODHAM WALTER

Bell
The Street, CM9 6RF (off A414, near Danbury)
✪ 12-3, 7-11; 12-3, 7-10.30 (not winter eve) Sun
☎ (01245) 223437
Adnams Broadside; Greene King IPA; guest beer H
This picturesque, 16th-century coaching
house is timber-framed with exposed
beams. Central to the village, the traditional
pub is popular with ramblers and is close to
the Chelmer Navigation and areas of
common land. Friendly and relaxing, it
offers good home-produced food, including
daily specials, grills, fish and vegetarian
dishes, plus eight varieties of ploughmans.
A room is available for parties. Evening
meals are served Tuesday–Saturday.
🏚Q⥁⊛◑♣P✠

WRITTLE

Inn on the Green
57 The Green, CM1 3DT
✪ 11-3, 6-11; 11-11 Wed-Sat; 12-10.30 Sun
☎ (01245) 420266
**Brakspear Bitter; Mighty Oak IPA, English Oak; Taylor
Landlord;** H **guest beers** H/G
This popular free house has one long, single
bar divided into two distinct drinking areas
and a raised dining area. Two or three guest
beers are generally sourced from
independents, with one occasionally on
gravity dispense. A real cider is sometimes
stocked. Good home-cooked food includes
daily specials; upstairs is a function
room/restaurant. An Easter beer festival,
held in a marquee, features over 40 beers.
The pub is listed in a book of Essex walks.
🏚⊛◑♣🌶P

Wheatsheaf
70 The Green, CM1 3DU (³/₄ mile S of A1060)
✪ 11-3, 5.30-11; 11-11 Sat; 12-10.30 Sun
☎ (01245) 420695
website: www.wheatsheafph-writtle.co.uk
Greene King IPA, Abbot; guest beers H
Small, friendly, traditional village local
converted from a pair of cottages, which has
been selling beer since 1851. A small public
bar with wooden benches is connected to a
more comfortable, but even smaller, lounge.
The two guest beers come from the Gray's
list and usually feature a Mighty Oak brew.
Note the Gray & Sons sign in the public bar,
rescued from the brewery which was closed
in 1974. Q⊛⊟♣P

Recipe for Buttered Beer

Take a quart or more of Double Beere and put to it a good piece
of fresh butter, sugar candie an ounce, or liquerise in powder,
or ginger grated, of each a dramme, and if you would have it
strong, put in as much long pepper and Greynes, let it boyle in
the quart in the maner as you burne wine, and who so will
drink it, let him drinke it as hot as he may suffer. Some put in
the yolke of an egge or two towards the latter end, and so they
make it more strength-full.

Thomas Cogan, *The Haven of Health*, 1584

Family-friendly pubs

Campaign for Real Ale — CAMRA

Pubs
for families

Adrian Tierney-Jones

Adrian Tierney-Jones starts his guide with a plea to publicans to 'make kid-friendly pubs'. He argues that taking children into pubs at an early age is the best way for them to become sensible and moderate drinkers later in life – as well as preferring cask beer! The guide lists pubs throughout the country that offer family and child facilities, and also lists other attractions close to the pubs. With maps and illustrations, it's an essential companion for those who travel with children and who like to enjoy a quiet beer while the youngsters play happily and safely. £10.99 including postage.

Available from all good bookshops or from CAMRA, 230 Hatfield Road, St Albans, Herts, AL1 4LW; cheques or postal orders made out to 'CAMRA'. To order by Access or Visa, phone 01727 867201 betwen 9am and 5pm, Monday to Friday (answerphone outside office hours). Allow 28 days for delivery.

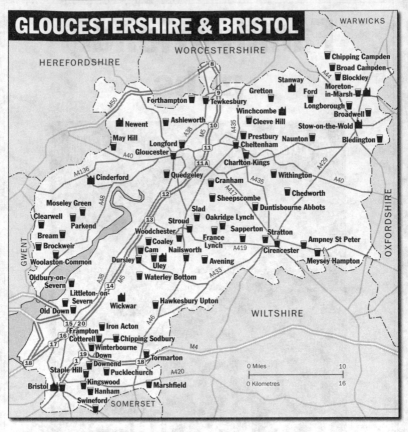

GLOUCESTERSHIRE & BRISTOL

WARWICKS

WORCESTERSHIRE

HEREFORDSHIRE

Chipping Campden
Broad Campden
Blockley
Moreton-in-Marsh
Stanway
Gretton
Ford
Longborough
Broadwell
Winchcombe
Cleeve Hill
Stow-on-the-Wold
Forthampton
Tewkesbury
Newent
Ashleworth
Prestbury
Cheltenham
Naunton
Bledington
May Hill
Longford
Gloucester
Charlton Kings
Withington
Cinderford
Quedgeley
Cranham
Chedworth
Sheepscombe
Duntisbourne Abbots
Moseley Green
Slad
Oakridge Lynch
Clearwell
Parkend
Stroud
Sapperton
Stratton
Bream
Woodchester
France Lynch
Ampney St Peter
Brockweir
Coaley
Nailsworth
Cirencester
Woolaston Common
Cam
Avening
Meysey Hampton
Dursley
Uley
Oldbury-on-Severn
Waterley Bottom
Littleton-on-Severn
Wickwar
Hawkesbury Upton
Old Down
WILTSHIRE
Iron Acton
Frampton Cotterell
Chipping Sodbury
Winterbourne Down
Tormarton
Staple Hill
Downend
Pucklechurch
Bristol
Kingswood
Hanham
Marshfield
Swineford
SOMERSET

OXFORDSHIRE
GWENT

0 Miles — 10
0 Kilometres — 16

AMPNEY ST PETER

Red Lion ☆

GL7 5SL (on A417)
⊙ 6-10.30; 12-2.30, 6-10.30 Sat; 12-2.30,
7-10.30 Sun
☎ (01285) 851596
Hook Norton Best Bitter; Taylor Landlord or Flowers IPA Ⓗ

Superb, 400-year-old pub, caught in a time warp. The two tiny flagstoned rooms are superbly preserved and little appears to have changed since the jovial veteran landlord was a babe in arms. Without a bar counter, service is from the corner of one room. An open fire in each room completes the welcoming appeal of this gem. Two pub signs grace the outside, one in the distinctive oval frame of the defunct Stroud Brewery. No food at all, but the beer is keenly priced. Open bank holiday lunchtimes. ⋈Q❀⊟P

ASHLEWORTH

Boat Inn

The Quay, GL19 4HZ OS819251
⊙ 11-2.30 (not winter Wed), 6 (7 winter)-11; closed all day Mon Oct-Apr; 12-3, 7-10.30 Sun
☎ (01452) 700272
Beer range varies Ⓖ

This pub is an absolute gem – an unspoilt, tranquil haven on the banks of the River Severn. Owned by the same family for 400 years, it serves beers direct from the cask;

---

the ever-changing range mainly comes from smaller local breweries. Rolls and ploughmans are available at lunchtime. Several small rooms are furnished with antiques. Outside is a courtyard, with some tables under cover. A frequent CAMRA award-winner, the Boat holds an annual autumn beer festival.
Q❀⊞♣P

AVENING

Bell

29 High Street, GL8 8NF
⊙ 12-2.30, 5.30-11; 11-11 Fri, Sat & summer;
12-2.30, 5.30-10.30 Sun
☎ (01453) 836422
Wickwar BOB; guest beers Ⓗ

Pleasantly refurbished old stone inn located at the centre of the village. Efficiently run and comfortable, the exposed stone walls, adorned with horse brasses and tankards, lend a traditional, rustic appearance to the interior. Two regularly-changing guest beers are supplied by independent local breweries. Good typical pub fare is served seven days a week; the menu includes weekday 'specials'.
⋈Q❀⊞◁▯♿&♣P⚲▯

BLEDINGTON

King's Head

The Green, OX7 6XQ OS243228
⊙ 11-3, 6-11; 12-3, 6.30-10.30 Sun
☎ (01608) 658365 website: www.kingsheadinn.net

Hook Norton Best Bitter; Wadworth 6X;
guest beers Ⓗ

Delightful 16th-century honey-coloured
stone inn overlooking the village green with
its brook and ducks. The original old beams,
inglenook with kettle and military brasses,
flagstone floors and high-backed settles and
pews create a convivial atmosphere. High
quality food is served in the restaurant
(reservations recommended); 12 rooms offer
charming accommodation, where
supposedly Prince Rupert of the Rhine
lodged prior to the Battle of Stow in 1614.
Bledington is a regular winner of the
Bledisloe Cup (Best Kept Village award).
🏚Q🐾⛲🐕🍴♿⚓🅰🚃(Kingham) ♣P

BLOCKLEY

Great Western Arms
Station Road, GL56 9DT
(on B4479 towards Paxford)
🕐 11.30-2.30 (11-3 Sat), 6-11; 12-3, 7-10.30 Sun
☎ (01386) 700362
Hook Norton Best Bitter, Old Hooky, seasonal beers;
guest beer Ⓗ

This pub offers a friendly welcome,
interesting history and a range of Hook
Norton ales. It was originally built for
navvies constructing the nearby railway
from which the name derives. Various
railway artefacts are displayed, together
with old village photographs, both in the
modern style lounge and in the public bar,
which also houses a pool table. Home-
cooked food can be taken on the patio area
while enjoying beautiful views over the
valley in which this picturesque, sprawling
Cotswold village lies.
Q🐾🍴🅰🚃🅿P

BREAM

Rising Sun
High Street, GL15 6JF (opp. war memorial)
🕐 12-2.30, 6.30-11; 12-11 Sat; 12-10.30 Sun
☎ (01594) 564555 website: www.therisingsun.uk.com
Goff's Jouster; guest beers Ⓗ

This spacious 300-year-old stone pub
benefits from spectacular views over the
Forest of Dean. It houses a friendly main
bar, with overspill into two adjoining
rooms, a restaurant and a function room. It
offers five constantly-changing real ales,
Belgian and Czech beers, plus a small range
of Belgian bottled beers; the cider varies.
Local CAMRA's Pub of the Year 2003 holds
an annual beer festival. Superb beer and
food (booking advised) make the trip to
Bream worthwhile.
🏚Q🐾🍴👥♣🍴P✗

BRISTOL

Bag O'Nails
141 St George's Road, Hotwells, BS1 5UW
🕐 12-2.15, 5.30-11; 12-11 Fri & Sat; 12-10.30 Sun
☎ (0117) 940 6776 website: www.bagonails.org.uk
Beer range varies Ⓗ

Gaslit, with wood panelling and
floorboards, this small, friendly pub is just a
few minutes' walk from the city centre. It
usually features at least six ales, sometimes
more, mostly from small breweries. Neither
fruit machines nor bar meals dominate this
pub – the Bag is a beer drinker's delight; you
will also find an extensive range of quality

bottled beers here. An annual mini beer
festival is staged in November. Sandwiches
are usually available at lunchtime.

Brewery Tap
6-10 Colston Street, BS1 5BD
🕐 11-11; 12-6 Sun
☎ (0117) 921 3668 website: www.smiles.co.uk
Smiles Original, Best, IPA, Heritage, seasonal beers Ⓗ

The only Smiles-owned pub left in Bristol. A
friendly, traditional pub of two rooms, the
D-shaped bar is in the smoking room.
Checked floor tiling, wooden seats and
hops adorning the ceiling are its main
features. Steep stairs between the bars lead
to the toilets. A newspaper rack is provided
and special food nights are a weekly event.
The brewery next door offers tours and the
shop sells their merchandise. An historic,
15th-century almshouse just down the hill
is worth a look, too. Q🍴✗

Bridge Inn
16 Passage Street, BS2 0JF (past fire station
and across bridge)
🕐 11-11; 12-10.30 Sun
☎ (0117) 949 9967
Bath SPA, Gem, Barnstormer Ⓗ

The split-door, single entrance leads straight
into this cosy and intimate one-roomed
pub. This is one of the smallest pubs in
Bristol and it does not take many customers
to create a busy atmosphere. Old movie
posters decorate the walls; a TV and fruit
machine provide amusement. Lunchtime
food is served every day except Sunday.
🍴🚃(Temple Meads)

Bunch of Grapes
Denmark Street, BS1 5DG
🕐 11.30-2.30, 5-11; 11.30-11 Fri & Sat; 6-10.30 Sun
☎ (0117) 987 0500 website: www.bunchofgrapes.net
Wickwar Cotswold Way; guest beers Ⓗ

Popular, back-street pub near the Bristol
Hippodrome, displaying posters of
entertainers who have performed there. The
single bar normally keeps five guest ales,
mainly from micro-breweries. Lively and
enterprising, it hosts regular live music:
Tuesday blues, Thursday jazz and usually
rock on Friday; stand-up comedy is staged
on Sunday evening. It can get very busy,
particularly at weekends. The rock juke box
is superb. The amiable landlord allows food
from the chip shop next door to be brought
in.

Coronation
18 Dean Lane, Southville, BS3 1DD
🕐 12-11; 12-10.30 Sun
☎ (0117) 940 9044

INDEPENDENT BREWERIES

Bath Ales Bristol
Donnington Stow-on-the-Wold
Freeminer Cinderford
Goff's Winchcombe
Home County Wickwar
North Cotswold Moreton-in-Marsh
Smiles Bristol
Stanway Stanway
Uley Uley
Whittington's Newent
Wickwar Wickwar

Hop Back GFB, Best Bitter, Crop Circle, Summer Lightning; guest beers [H]

Popular Hop Back Brewery pub, offering a warm welcome to both locals and visitors. It comprises a main bar and a secluded area to the left. On Saturday there is a 'happy hour' special when all Hop Back beers are £1.50 a pint until 6pm. It is a rare outlet for award-winning Westcroft cider; excellent pizzas are available every evening. Quiz night is Monday. A must when visiting Bristol, it is well worth the short walk from the city centre.
⇌ (Temple Meads/Bedminster) ♣●

Hare on the Hill
41 Thomas Street North, Kingsdown, BS2 8LX
⚙ 12-2.30, 5-11; 12-11 Fri & Sat; 12-10.30 Sun
☎ (0117) 908 1982 website: www.bathales.co.uk
Bath SPA, Gem, Barnstormer, seasonal beer or guest beer [H]

Set on a steep hill overlooking the Stokes Croft area, this busy local sells paintings by local artists. The imaginative menu features daily specials at competitive prices. It stocks a good range of British and Continental bottled beers. Bath Ales' first pub won the local CAMRA Pub of the Year award in 1998. L-shaped, with a dartboard and TV (for Sky Sports), it normally keeps a guest beer from an independent brewery, occasionally replaced by a seasonal brew.
◑◗♣

Highbury Vaults
164 St Michael's Hill, Kingsdown, BS2 8DE
⚙ 12-11; 12-10.30 Sun
☎ (0117) 973 3203
Brains SA; Smiles Best, Heritage; Young's Bitter, Special [H]

Dark and atmospheric pub with a tiny front snug, and a larger rear bar. The walled patio area can be used year-round as it is warmed by several gas heaters. Good value food is served daily at lunchtime and Monday–Friday evenings. The pub is close to the university and can be very busy with students taking time off from their gruelling academic workloads. Bar billiards is played here. ❀◑◗♣

King's Head ☆
60 Victoria Street, BS1 6DE
⚙ 11-3, 5-11; 11-11 Wed-Fri; 7.30-11 Sat; 12-3, 7-10.30 Sun
☎ (0117) 927 7860
Draught Bass; Courage Best Bitter; Smiles Original [H]

This pub, with Victorian decor, dates back to the 1660s and retains much charm and character. The single, narrow bar leads to a cosy snug; photographs of old Bristol and beer memorabilia adorn the walls. Within walking distance of the station, shops and offices, it enjoys a lively lunchtime trade; good food is served weekdays. The mostly business clientele at lunchtime is replaced by locals in the evening. Three pavement tables cater for outdoor drinkers.
Q❀◑⇌ (Temple Meads) ♣

Lamplighters
Station Road, Shirehampton, BS11 9XA
(250 yds off the Portway)
⚙ 11-3, 6-11; 12-10.30 Sun
☎ (0117) 982 3549
website: www.the-lamplighters.co.uk
Butcombe Bitter; Bath Gem; Fuller's London Pride; guest beers [H]

Riverside pub dating from the 18th century, overlooking Pill on the other side of the River Avon. Comprising a neat, tidy single lounge bar with a function room upstairs and a children's room, it is situated in a private housing estate. Popular with locals, it is also used by anglers and members of the yacht club nearby. The large garden stages an annual beer festival in September. No food is served Sunday evening.
⛰❀◑◗⇌ (Shirehampton) ♣P

Magic Box ✔
135-137 Cheltenham Road, BS6 5RR
(N of Broadmead shopping centre on A38)
⚙ 10-11; 12-10.30 Sun
☎ (0117) 970 5140
Draught Bass; Courage Directors; Greene King Abbot; Theakston Best Bitter; guest beers [H]

This building was once a cinema, hence the name, and a Christadelphian meeting hall. It opened as a Wetherspoon's in October 2000 catering for a diverse range of customers. It offers highly competitive deals on beers and food. There is a curry club twice a week (Tue and Thu) and two to three beers available from an extensive guest list. It actively supports the April, October and Christmas beer festivals. The patio adjoins the A38 and is entertainingly level with passengers – the double-decker buses stop outside. Q❀◑◗♿⇌●⚟

Merchants Arms
5 Merchants Road, Hotwells, BS8 4PZ
⚙ 12-2.30, 5-11; 12-11 Fri & Sat; 12-10.30 Sun
☎ (0117) 904 0037
Bath SPA, Gem, Barnstormer; guest beer [H]

Situated close to the Cumberland basin/floating harbour area is Bath Ales' third pub. A guest beer from an independent brewery is joined by a second at busy times. Bottle-conditioned beer, carry-outs and commemorative gift packs are available from this small, simply furnished pub. A lower, rear area is set aside for non-smokers. Filled rolls and toasties are served but no meals. On alternate Mondays a fiendish quiz is staged. A great pub for conversation, not to be missed; it has limited parking. ⚟

Old Fox Inn
60 Fox Road, Eastville, BS5 0YB
⚙ 7.30-11 (closed July-August and Christmas/New Year); 7.30-10.30 Sun
☎ (0117) 952 2674
RCH Pitchfork; Taylor Landlord; guest beers [H]

This 300-year-old, back-street local has a panelled interior displaying old photographs of the locality and its mines. Local hero, WG Grace, is said to have drunk in this inn, which was restored in the 1970s when owned by CAMRA Investments; it is now a free house in private hands. Six real ales from independent breweries are normally available, including a low ABV session beer and a stout/porter, together with a good range of bottled beers.
Q⇌ (Stapleton Rd) ♣⚟

Penny Farthing ✔
115 Whiteladies Road, Clifton, BS8 2PB
⚙ 11-11; 12-10.30 Sun
☎ (0117) 973 3539

Badger Tanglefoot; Draught Bass; Butcombe Bitter; Ⓟ Wadworth IPA, 6X, JCB; Ⓗ guest beers Ⓟ
Converted from a bank in the 1990s, this wood-panelled pub gives the impression of much greater maturity than its years. With up to 11 real ales, it is a breath of fresh air in an area renowned for themed pubs and café-bars. The walls are adorned with collages of photos and artefacts, including an ancient penny farthing bicycle. Over the road from Clifton Down shopping centre and station, outside pavement drinking is possible. ❀◖≉(Clifton Down)

Port of Call
3 York Street, Clifton, BS8 2YE
(near top of Blackboy Hill)
✪ 12-2.30, 5.30-11; 12-11 Sat; 12-5 Sun
☎ (0117) 973 3600
Draught Bass; Fuller's London Pride; Shepherd Neame Spitfire; Smiles Best; Theakston Old Peculier; Young's Special; guest beers Ⓗ
Dating back to at least 1776, this pub consists of an L-shaped bar; pictures of harbours and ships decorate the walls. Up to 12 ales are on offer, two of which are ever-changing guests, often from micro-breweries. Pump clips on beams and behind the bar record past beers. A varied menu includes fish dishes (booking advised at weekends for meals served 12–6). This comfortable, cosy pub is ideally situated for The Downs; the garden is great in summer (no children admitted). ❀◖

Post Office Tavern
17 Westbury Hill, Westbury on Trym, BS9 3AG
✪ 11-11; 12-3, 7-10.30 Sun
☎ (0117) 940 1233
Draught Bass; Ⓖ Bath SPA; Butcombe Bitter; Courage Best Bitter; Otter Bitter; guest beer Ⓗ
This popular pub, at the top of Westbury Hill, operates a dress code. Once the old village post office, it still displays plenty of memorabilia, including a red telephone box in the bar. This free house keeps six real ales and a guest beer; Otter Bitter is rarely seen in Bristol. There is a no-smoking bar. Evening food is restricted to excellent pizzas, available Monday–Saturday. Q◖⌇

Prince of Wales
84 Stoke Lane, Westbury on Trym, BS9 3SP
✪ 11-3, 5.30 (5 Fri)-11; 11-11 Sat; 12-4, 7-10.30 Sun
☎ (0117) 962 3715
Draught Bass; Bath SPA; Butcombe Bitter; Courage Best Bitter; Fuller's London Pride; guest beers Ⓗ
This popular pub, only a five-minute walk from the village centre, boasts an attractive garden, and is one of just a few free houses left in Bristol. Memorabilia and unusual sporting prints decorate the various comfortable seating areas. The menu is imaginative, with daily specials, and competitively priced. It sponsors badminton, football, rugby and cricket teams and can get busy when the large foldaway TV screen is lowered for rugby. A no-smoking area is available at lunchtime. Q❀◖⌇

Red Lion
26 Worrall Road, Clifton, BS8 2UE (off Blackboy Hill)
✪ 12-3, 5-11; 12-11 Fri & Sat; 12-4, 7-10.30 Sun
☎ (0117) 903 0989

Draught Bass; Bath SPA; Courage Best Bitter Ⓗ
A 1937 newspaper article, celebrating a local's 100th birthday, called the Red Lion 'a comfortable house whose customers meet night after night in friendly intercourse and in which exists a spirit of friendship and goodfeeling, the beer is always in first-rate condition'. Little has changed. The pub remains a genuine two-bar local, close to The Downs end of Whiteladies Road. The spacious, flagstoned bar and a snug, wood-panelled lounge offer an extensive wine list and local Thatchers cider.
Q◖⊟≉(Clifton Down) ♣♠

Sugar Loaf
51 St Mark's Road, Easton, BS5 6HX
✪ 11-11; 12-10.30 Sun
☎ (0117) 939 4498
Greene King IPA, Abbot; Marston's Pedigree Ⓗ
This popular community pub is situated next to Stapleton Road Station and possibly the best spice shops in Bristol, as is reflected in the menu (evening meals are served 5.30–7.30). The pub has two bar areas, one of which houses a CD juke box that satisfies most musical tastes. The other is quieter and leads to a pool room with three tables. The house beer, Easton Bitter, is brewed by Moles; Thatchers cider is stocked.
❀◖≉(Stapleton Rd) ♣♠

Victoria ◉
20 Chock Lane, Westbury on Trym, BS9 3EX
✪ 12-2.30, 5-11; 12-3, 5.30-10.30 Sun
☎ (0117) 950 0441
Draught Bass; Wadworth IPA, 6X, seasonal beers Ⓗ
Hidden away behind the imposing parish church, the Victoria is a welcoming local. Its elevated garden catches the evening sun. The substantial 18th-century building served as a village court house. The comfortable bar has a no-smoking area. The pub is known for excellent food, served lunchtime and until 8pm; home-cooked pizzas are available until 10pm. See the many photographs and prints of Westbury on Trym, when it was a village, quite separate from Bristol.
Q❀◖♣⌇

Wellington Hotel
Horfield, BS7 8UR (on A38, near Horfield Common, opp. stadium)
✪ 12-2.30 (3 Sat), 5 (6 Sat)-11; 11 Fri & summer Sat; 12-10.30 Sun
☎ (0117) 951 3022
Bath SPA, Gem, Barnstormer, seasonal beers; guest beers Ⓗ
The Wellington has been the subject of a refurbishment in Bath Ales' own inimitable style, to create the atmosphere of an old drinking house. A rolling guest beer complements Bath Ales' own range. A good selection of Belgian and German bottled beers, German and Czech lagers on draught and organic bottled cider are also stocked. The closest pub to the Memorial Stadium, it welcomes football and rugby supporters, providing special match day menus (no food Sun eve). ❀⊟◖P⌇

White House
24 High Street, Westbury on Trym, BS9 3DZ
✪ 11-11; 12-10.30 Sun
☎ (0117) 950 7622

Sharp's Cornish Coaster; Worthington's 1744; guest beer (occasional) G

Known locally as the Hole in the Wall, as one bar is served via a window of the original building into the Georgian extension. The multiple rooms cover six centuries of development. The main bar has a flagstoned floor. Beers are served straight from the barrels kept cool in a 14th-century vault. Seating ranges from modern tables and chairs to ancient carved wooden settles. Children are welcome in rooms without a bar until 7pm. The pub can be busy on weekend evenings, and is sometimes smoky. Q ❀ ◑ ♣ ●

BROAD CAMPDEN

Bakers Arms
GL55 6UR (signed from B4081)
✪ 11.30-2.30, 4.45-11; 11.30-11 Fri, Sat & summer; 12-10.30 Sun
☎ (01386) 840515
Donnington BB or SBA; Hook Norton Best Bitter; Stanway Stanney Bitter; Wells Bombardier; guest beer H

Dating from 1724, this fine old country pub is free from music and machines. A 1905 photograph shows it as a bakery and grain store. It is characterised by Cotswold stone walls, exposed beams, an inglenook and an attractive oak bar counter where the local Stanney Bitter can be tried. A framed handwoven rug, depicting the inn, took 1,000 hours to make in 1969. Home-cooked meals are available in the newly-opened, no-smoking dining room extension. Local CAMRA Pub of the Year 2003.
🏨 Q ❀ ◑ Å ♣ ● P ✗

BROADWELL

Fox Inn
The Green, GL56 0UF (off A429 in village centre)
✪ 11-2.30, 6-11; 12-2.30, 7-10.30 Sun
☎ (01451) 870909
Donnington BB, SBA H

Traditional, attractive, one-bar stone pub, overlooking the village green. Original flagstone flooring is retained in the main bar area, where jugs hang from beams. Good pub food is served in a no-smoking dining area; special dietary requirements are catered for with prior notice (no meals Sun eve). Tables are set on gravel in the rear garden, where Aunt Sally is sometimes played. A caravan site is in the field behind. Visit the National Trust-owned Chastleton House nearby.
🏨 Q ❀ ◑ Å ♣ ● P

BROCKWEIR

Brockweir Country Inn
NP16 7NG (off A466, Monmouth-Chepstow road)
✪ 12-3, 6.30-11; 12-3, 7-10.30 (12-10.30 summer) Sun
☎ (01291) 689548
Adnams Broadside; Badger Tanglefoot; Butcombe Bitter; Hook Norton Best Bitter H

This cosy, beamed, two-roomed pub, close to the River Wye is popular with walkers. Tintern Abbey and Offa's Dyke are nearby. The home-made food represents good value and a warm welcome is assured here. The building contains beams from a ship built in the village. Reasonably-priced

accommodation completes the facilities on offer at the inn.
🏨 Q ⇔ ◑ ◑ ⊞ ♣ ● P

CAM

Berkeley Arms
High Street, GL11 5LA
✪ 11-2.30 (not Mon), 5 (7 Mon)-11; 12-11 Sat; 12-10.30 Sun
☎ (01453) 542424
Fuller's London Pride; Wickwar BOB H

Friendly single bar locals' pub, built in 1890, with a skittle/function room. The imposing Stroud Brewery tiled frontage includes an impressive gilded Berkeley family crest. The pub has quiz, skittles and dart teams. Live music is usually staged on Friday and Saturday. The enthusiastic landlord runs a beer festival over the early May bank holiday. The pleasant, secluded walled garden is a bonus. ❀ ≉ ♣

CHARLTON KINGS

Merryfellow Inn
2 School Road, GL53 8AU
✪ 11-11; 12-10.30 Sun
☎ (01242) 525883 website: www.merryfellowinn.co.uk
Black Sheep Best Bitter; Greene King IPA; Wadworth 6X; guest beers H

This busy, modernised, but comfortable pub at the village centre retains its original Stroud Brewery window. An extensive outdoor area houses an aviary and provides a safe area for supervised children. The front part of the pub is a no-smoking area. Different lunch and evening (6–9) menus are provided. Darts and quoits are played; the skittle alley doubles as a function room. See the Jack Russell print of the England and Australian cricket teams, signed by the players. Stagecoach service B runs from Cheltenham. ❀ ◑ ♣ P ✗

CHEDWORTH

Seven Tuns
Queen Street, GL54 4AE
(NE of village, near church) OS053121
✪ 11-3, 6-11 (11-11 summer); 12-3, 7.30-10.30 Sun
☎ (01285) 720242
Young's Bitter, Special, seasonal beer; guest beer H

Unspoilt, but spacious Young's pub, with an attractive garden, in one of England's longest villages. The various rooms and dining areas are pleasantly furnished, displaying local rural artefacts and old photographs. The food menu is extensive with exotic dishes such as zebra and regular specials; there is a comprehensive wine list. The pub supports village sporting activities and a skittle alley is available for hire.
🏨 Q ❀ ◑ ♣ P ✗

CHELTENHAM

Adam & Eve
8 Townsend Street, GL51 9HD
✪ 10.30-3, 5-11; 10.30-11 Sat; 12-3, 7-10.30 Sun
☎ (01242) 690030
Arkells 2B, JRA, 3B H

This unpretentious, friendly, terraced local was Cheltenham CAMRA's Pub of the Year 2002. Some 15 minutes' walk from the centre, it is readily accessible by public transport (Stagecoach C and No. 41). The public bar and small, comfortable lounge have a strong community focus; the pub is home to many skittles teams and local quiz league teams. The friendly landlady has run the pub for 25 years. Arkells JRA is a favourite with regulars, but may be replaced by other seasonal offerings. Q ⇘ ♣

Mitre's

23 Sandford Street, GL53 7EW
✪ 12-3, 5-11; 12-11 Fri & Sat; 12-10.30 Sun
☎ (01242) 516655
Greene King IPA; guest beers Ⓗ

This modernised community pub was Cheltenham CAMRA's Pub of the Year 2003. Despite its wine bar appearance, this free house remains very much a popular back-street pub. Up to three beers, mainly from local brewers, are always available in the single bar, which also serves the cellar and conservatory. Live music sessions and fun nights are regular events. Centrally located, close to the hospital, Playhouse Theatre and town hall, it offers reasonably-priced accommodation. ⇘◁▷

Portland Bar

22 St Margarets Road, GL50 4DZ (on inner ring road)
✪ 11-3, 6-11; closed Mon; 12-4 Sun
☎ (01242) 231600
Goff's Jouster; guest beer Ⓗ

Formerly the Portland Club, it has been a bar since December 2001, when refurbishment was completed. The name derives from a Cheltenham MP of the Victorian era. The bar bears a racing theme and sports collections of blow torches and tankards. The function room is used for a men's business club and for weddings.
Q ◁▷ &

Volunteer Inn

Lower High Street, GL55 6DY (W end of village)
✪ 11.30-3, 5 (6 Sat)-11; 12-3, 7-10.30 Sun
☎ (01386) 840688
Hook Norton Best Bitter; North Cotswold Genesis; Stanway Stanney Bitter; guest beers Ⓗ

300-year-old stone inn, run by the same family for 18 years, named after the volunteer army of the 1840s. Local brewers are well represented here. The front bar features a huge stone fireplace and cushioned seats in the bay windows; the walls and beams are adorned with old village photos, army paintings, helmets, bugles and hops. There is a pretty garden and courtyard decked with hanging baskets. The Cotswold Way starts close to this local CAMRA Pub of the Year 2002.
≝Q ❀⇘◁▷♣ ♠

Squire Inn

67 Broad Street, BS37 6AD
✪ 11-3, 5-11; 11-11 Fri & Sat; 12-10.30 Sun
☎ (01454) 312121
Draught Bass; Wadworth 6X; Wickwar BOB; guest beer Ⓗ

Situated in the main town square, restoration work in 1986 revealed an open fireplace in the lounge bar. This spacious, 18th-century coaching inn has low ceilings and flagged floors. The restaurant serves

good value, no-nonsense food – the meat is locally sourced. The three rooms are supplemented by a skittle alley and garden. Friendly and welcoming, it gets very busy at weekends. The guest beer is normally from Marston's, Charles Wells or Fuller's.
≝❀◁▷♣

Twelve Bells

Lewis Lane, GL7 1EA
✪ 11-11; 12-10.30 Sun
☎ (01285) 644549
Beer range varies Ⓗ

A beer drinker's haven and Gloucestershire CAMRA Pub of the Year 2003; recently spruced up, this old, panelled pub, with open fires in all three rooms, is now even better. The landlord, who possesses a wry sense of humour, holds court in the lively front bar, while the back rooms are quieter. Five constantly-changing beers are complemented by excellent, varied meals, freshly prepared using food from local suppliers. Portions are substantial – abandon all diets, ye who enter here!
≝⇗❀◁▷&♠P

Lamb

The Cross, Newland Road, GL16 8JU
✪ 12-3 (not Mon-Thu), 6-11 (not Mon or Tue); 12-3, 7-10.30 Sun
☎ (01594) 835441
Beer range varies Ⓖ

Comfortable, country pub, comprising two rooms with log fires: a delightful snug has old settles, the other room is divided into cosy seating areas and is used for pub games. Up to three real ales are served directly from the cask in the cellar. Clearwell is en route to the Wye Valley and Clearwell Caves are nearby. ≝Q❀⇘&♠P

High Roost

GL52 3PP (on B4632, top of Cleeve Hill)
✪ 11.30-3, 7-11; 12-4.30 (closed eve) Sun
☎ (01242) 672010
Hook Norton Best Bitter; Goff's Jouster or guest beer Ⓗ

This imposing Victorian villa is reached by a flight of steps. A family-run free house, perched on the highest point of the Cotswolds, it affords spectacular views over the Severn basin to the Black Mountains in Wales. The pub is open plan, with a dartboard and TV discreetly tucked away; bar skittles is played. A terrace provides outdoor drinking space. Good value food (at least 20 choices) includes Welsh sirloin steaks; an evening menu is served Thursday–Saturday. ❀◁▷♣P

Fox & Hounds

The Street, GL11 5EG
✪ 12-3 (not Mon), 7-11; 12-3, 7-10.30 Sun
☎ (01453) 890366
Black Sheep Best Bitter; Uley Bitter; guest beers Ⓗ

This 300-year-old traditional Cotswold stone free house has one cosy bar, warmed by a wood-burning stove. The function room houses a skittle alley and the restaurant serves an extensive home-cooked menu at reasonable prices. The south-facing garden affords a fine view to Coaley Peak. Famous for its acoustic jazz, Irish and Cajun music on Saturday (and occasionally Fri), this community pub extends a warm welcome to visitors. ⚶Q✿◑▲P

CRANHAM

Black Horse
GL4 8HP (off A46)
☼ 11.45-3, 6.30-11; 12-3, 7 (8 winter)-10.30 Sun
☎ (01452) 812217
Hancock's HB; Hook Norton Best Bitter; Jennings Cumberland Ale; Wickwar BOB; Worthington's 1744 Ⓗ

Unspoilt, stone, 17th-century free house, tucked away off the narrow road that winds through Cranham village. A large open log fire, red tiled floor and red leather upholstery contribute warmth in the main bar. A second bar and rooms upstairs contain extra seating. Extensive woods that crowd the nearby Cotswold escarpment attract walkers whose appetites can do justice to the pub's country-sized meals; even its sandwiches have substantial fillings (no food Sun eve). ⚶Q✿◑▲P

DOWNEND

Downend Tavern
125 Downend Road, BS16 5BE
☼ 11-11; 12-10.30 Sun
☎ (0117) 987 3413
Draught Bass; Butcombe Bitter; Courage Best Bitter; Worthington's Bitter; guest beers (occasional) Ⓗ

Traditional, street-corner local in a residential suburb of Bristol, that hosts popular live music evenings on Thursday, Friday and Saturday. On display in the bar is probably the most extensive array of photographs of old Bristol to be found anywhere in the city. The pub has a skittle alley, and stages bingo or a quiz every Sunday evening. No food is served Sunday. ✿◑&♣

DUNTISBOURNE ABBOTS

Five Mile House ☆
Old Gloucester Road, GL7 7JR
(on old A417; follow services sign)
☼ 12-3, 6-11; 12-3, 6-10.30 Sun
☎ (01285) 821432
Beer range varies Ⓗ

Refurbishments of unspoilt pubs with Grade II listed interiors are rarely as successful as this. The tiny bar, virtually unchanged and food-free, leads to a smart, no-smoking dining room; the food is deservedly popular. To the left of the entrance is a small tap room created by two venerable curving settles around a wood-burning stove; steps lead down to a snug and the old cellar. The main road has been moved a few yards, leaving the old Ermin Street empty, if not exactly quiet. ⚶Q✿◑▲P

DURSLEY

Old Spot Inn
Hill Road, GL11 5JQ (next to bus station)
☼ 11-3, 5-11; 11-11 Fri & Sat; 12-10.30 Sun
☎ (01453) 542870

Otter Bitter; Uley Old Ric; guest beers Ⓗ

Award-winning free house named after the Gloucestershire breed of pig. Sympathetically restored by the owner, this pub of 100 years has an intimate atmosphere, with bar billiards table, log fires and brewery memorabilia in the four drinking areas. It offers an extensive, healthy lunch menu (strictly chip-free). A convivial local on the Cotswold Way, the secluded garden has a boules piste. ⚶✿(♣✕

FORD

Plough Inn
GL54 5RU
(on B4077, 5 miles W of Stow-on-the-Wold
☼ 11-11, 12-10.30 Sun
☎ (01386) 584215
Donnington BB, SBA Ⓗ

This characterful, 16th-century stone inn with its low, beamed ceilings, flagstone floors and inglenooks, is ideally situated for Cotswold attractions. A former courthouse, the cellars acted as cells to hold sheep stealers. The remains of indoor stocks are visible. Shove-ha'penny is still played here. Famous for its asparagus suppers, all the food is home cooked. Across the road is Jackdaw's Castle, the racing gallops of trainer Jonjo O'Neill. The connection is evident around the pub, especially after a big win! ⚶✿⇌◑&♣♠P

FORTHAMPTON

Lower Lode Inn
GL19 4RE OS878317
☼ 12-3 (not winter Mon or Tue), 6-11; 12-11 Sat; 12-10.30 Sun
☎ (01684) 293224
Donnington BB; guest beers Ⓗ

15th-century brick pub, standing in three acres of lawned River Severn frontage, looking across to Tewkesbury Abbey. The bar has parquet and flagstone flooring, and an exposed brick wall; at the rear is a games room. Two cask ales are always available (four in summer). There are public mooring facilities and a private slipway. A licensed Camping and Caravan Club site is adjacent and day fishing tickets are available. Approach roads are liable to flooding in winter. ⚶Q✿⇌◑&♠♣P

FRAMPTON COTTERELL

Rising Sun
43 Ryecroft Road, BS36 2HN
☼ 11.30-3, 5.30-11; 11.30-11 Fri & Sat; 12-3, 6-10.30 Sun
☎ (01454) 772330
Draught Bass; Butcombe Bitter; Wadworth 6X; Wickwar Coopers WPA, BOB; guest beer Ⓗ

Classic, real ale oasis where top quality beer is the trade mark. Up to six beers are on offer, including a changing guest. The bar sports period prints and a flagstoned floor. The rear upper level is a smoking area, while the hop-strewn conservatory is for non-smokers, where children are also welcome. A wide range of food includes Sunday lunches. The adjacent skittle alley doubles as a function room. The front patio is a sunny drinking area. ✿◑♣P✕

FRANCE LYNCH

King's Head
GL6 8LT OS903035
☼ 12-2.30, 6-11; 12-4, 7-10.30 Sun
☎ (01453) 882225
Archers Best Bitter; Hook Norton Best Bitter; guest beers Ⓗ
Friendly, single-bar pub, hidden away at the heart of a village of winding streets; well worth finding. The village name implies Huguenot connections; French and Flemish weavers came to this wool-rich area in search of work, when their native industries foundered. The superb reclaimed garden has a safe children's play area and a creche is provided on Friday evening (7–9). Live jazz, blues or folk is performed on Monday evening. Evening meals are served Monday–Saturday. ﷽Q♥☼♣Ⓓ▲♣P

GLOUCESTER

Black Swan Inn
68-70 Southgate Street, GL1 2DR
(200 yds S of the Cross)
☼ 11-11; 12-3, 7-10.30 Sun
☎ (01452) 523642
website: www.pubs2000.com/blackswan
Wickwar Cotswold Way; guest beers Ⓗ
As this Guide went to press, this mid 19th-century listed free house was about to be restored to the size it had been before Whitbread demolished half of it. The expansion will give extra guest accommodation and a restaurant, but the bar will be largely unchanged. Five ever-changing guest beers come from craft brewers around the British Isles. Excellent home-cooked food is served Monday–Saturday. Live music is performed Tuesday and Sunday evenings. Wheelchair WC. ☼♪Ⓓ♣P

England's Glory ⊘
66-68 London Road, GL1 3PB
☼ 11.30-2.30, 5-11; 12-11 Sat; 12-10.30 Sun
☎ (01452) 302948
Wadworth IPA, 6X, JCB, seasonal beer; guest beer Ⓗ
Although rebuilt internally in 1992, the lounge bar of this popular community pub has an older feel, thanks to its fine log fire, high-backed chairs, pews, old tables and old photographs. The public bar houses a large-screen TV for sporting events and there is a double skittle alley. A large blackboard lists a wide selection of home-cooked food at reasonable prices. Regular quizzes and folk evenings are staged. Wheelchair WC. ﷽Q☼Ⓓ♣♣≈♣P✗

Fountain Inn
53 Westgate Street, GL1 2NW
☼ 10.30-11; 12-10.30 Sun
☎ (01452) 522562 website: www.fountainglos.co.uk
Black Sheep Best Bitter; Fuller's London Pride; Greene King Abbot; Taylor Landlord; Wickwar BOB Ⓗ
Approached through a passage from Westgate Street, this ever-popular, 17th-century inn occupies the site of a former 13th-century ale house. A wall plaque overlooking the flower bedecked courtyard records William of Orange's ascent on horseback up outside stairs to show contempt for Jacobites who met in an upper room. Orange Room is the name recently bestowed on the sympathetically

refurbished subsidiary bar and dining room (no eve meals Sun–Tue). Live entertainment is staged Tuesday evening. Wheelchair WC. ﷽Q☼♣Ⓓ♣♣

Linden Tree ⊘
73-75 Bristol Road, GL1 5SN
(on A430, S of docks)
☼ 11.30-2.30, 6-11; 11.30-11 Sat; 12-10.30 Sun
☎ (01452) 527869
Red Shoot Tom's Tipple; Wadworth IPA, 6X, JCB, seasonal beers; Ⓗ **guest beers** Ⓖ
This end property of a Grade II listed Georgian terrace is a popular community pub, attracting a mature local clientele. Its modest entrance masks an interior not untypical of a Cotswold pub. An open fire, warm colour scheme and slightly eccentric decorative features contribute to a homely atmosphere. A popular skittle alley is opened up to create extra space when required. Guest ales are from mainly southern family brewers. Substantial home-made meals (not served Sun eve) and bargain accommodation are a bonus. ﷽Q☼♣Ⓓ♣

New Inn Hotel
16 Northgate Street, GL1 1SF
☼ 11-11 (1.30am Thu-Sat); 12-12.30am Sun
☎ (01452) 522177 website: www.newinnglos.com
Beer range varies Ⓗ
This 15th-century Grade I listed building, regarded as the finest medieval galleried inn in Britain, is a major social centre in the city, as reflected in its late weekend opening hours. The ale bar usually keeps a minimum of six ever-changing beers from small breweries, plus Black Rat cider from Moles. The inn has its own coffee shop, restaurant, two other bars and a function room. Fine accommodation is offered at Gloucester CAMRA's Pub of the Year 2003. ☼♣Ⓓ≈♣♠

GRETTON

Royal Oak
GL54 5EP (1½ miles from Winchcombe)
☼ 12-3, 6-11; 12-4, 7-10.30 Sun
☎ (01242) 604999
website: www.royal-oak-at-gretton.co.uk
Goff's Jouster, White Knight, seasonal beers; guest beer Ⓗ
This pub with olde-worlde charm has been newly refurbished by Goff's Brewery as their tap, serving the full range of their excellent beers. A mix of wood and flagstone floors and chamber pots hanging from exposed beams add character. The no-smoking conservatory, affording outstanding views, serves traditional food with a twist (no meals Sun eve). Close to Sudeley Castle and Toddington Steam Railway, the pub holds a beer festival every June. A tennis court is an unusual facility here. ﷽☼Ⓓ♣▲♣♠P

HANHAM

Queen's Head
29 Lower Hanham Road, BS15 8QP
(on main Kingswood-Hanham road)
☼ 11.30-2.30, 6.30-11; 12-3, 7-10.30 Sun
☎ (0117) 967 4995
Wadworth IPA, 6X, JCB, seasonal beers Ⓗ
The single open-plan lounge has a wood-panelled bar frontage and central stone

167

fireplace. Taken over by Wadworth in 2002, it is a welcome addition to the area for ale drinkers. One side of the bar is for non-smokers, while the no-smoking conservatory caters for diners, who come for the popular, freshly-cooked meals – the specials are changed daily. It is within walking distance of the centre of Hanham, although uphill. Q❀◑●P✂

HAWKESBURY UPTON

Beaufort Arms
High Street, GL9 1AU
✪ 12-11; 12-10.30 Sun
☎ (01454) 238217
Wickwar BOB; guest beers 田
Traditional Cotswold stone pub, popular with locals and passing trade in its public and lounge bars. Note the period dentist's chairs and collection of brewery and local memorabilia. The no-smoking dining area offers good value food. Added attractions include a pleasant garden and a skittle alley/function room with a well. A third guest beer is put on at the weekend. This pub deserves its local CAMRA Pub of the Year awards for 2002 and 2003 and is well worth a visit. ♨Q❀❀◑❑♿♣●P

IRON ACTON

Rose & Crown
High Street, BS37 9UG (off B4058)
✪ 5 (6 Sat)-11; 12-3, 7-10.30 Sun
☎ (01454) 228423
Draught Bass; Flowers IPA; Marston's Pedigree; Uley Old Spot, Pig's Ear 田
Excellent community local, dating from the 17th century. In this Guide for the last 10 years and in the same hands for much longer, the owners have always preferred to concentrate on drink, so no food is sold. There are two distinct bars, both warmed by log fires. A strong supporter of local brewers, it is a rare outlet for Uley beers. A full-sized football pitch to the rear is owned by the pub. ♨Q❀❑❑♣

KINGSWOOD

Colliers ✔
94-96 Regent Street, BS15 8HP
✪ 10.30-11; 12-10.30 Sun
☎ (0117) 967 2247
Draught Bass; Butcombe Gold; Greene King Abbot; Theakston Best Bitter; guest beers 田
This purpose-built Wetherspoon's bar is built on the site of a former market. Pictures of the old Kingswood coal mines adorn the walls and give the pub its name. The garden is large and full of interesting plants. Up to nine beers, including three guests are regularly served. Food is available all day; curry night is Thursday. There is a large no-smoking area at the rear. Access to the wheelchair WC is difficult. No children's area at time of survey. Q❀◑✂

LITTLETON-ON-SEVERN

White Hart
BS35 1NR
✪ 12-3, 6-11; 12-4, 7-10.30 Sun
☎ (01454) 412275
Smiles Best; Young's Bitter, Special, Waggle Dance or Winter Warmer 田

Lovely, homely, country pub dating back to 1680. Originally a farmhouse, many features survive including two inglenooks. The interior has six distinct areas, all with flagstone floors and beamed ceilings. The food is high quality and reasonable in price, however no bookings are taken. The front garden affords views over the River Severn and the rear patio has heaters. Waggle Dance replaces the Winter Warmer in summer. ♨Q❀❀❀❑◑♣P✂

LONGBOROUGH

Coach & Horses
GL56 0QU (off A424)
✪ 11-2 (3 summer), 7-11; 12-2 (3 summer), 7-10.30 Sun
☎ (01451) 830325
Donnington BB 田
Only one mile from the renowned Donnington Brewery, this unspoilt one-bar pub is the only regular outlet for their XXX Mild. In a quiet village with morris dancing connections, the friendly landlady has been in charge here for 34 years. Firefighting memorabilia reflects the proximity of Moreton Fire Services College. No food is served but customers may bring in sandwiches. Parking can be difficult in summer; it is ideally situated for a visit to the historic House of Sezincote. ♨Q❀♣

LONGFORD

Queen's Head
84 Tewkesbury Road, GL2 9EJ
(on A38 N of A40 jct)
✪ 11-3 (2.30 Mon & Tue), 5.30 (6 Sat)-11; 12-3, 7-10.30 Sun
☎ (01452) 301882
Draught Bass; Boddingtons Bitter; Fuller's London Pride; Goff's Jouster; Greene King Old Speckled Hen; Ringwood Best Bitter 田
This partly timber-framed building dates from the 1730s, but has been a pub for just 100 years. It is extremely popular, both as a warm, welcoming community pub and a quality eating house. The public bar area boasts a stone-flagged floor and open fire. The lounge contains two dining areas, set back to the side and rear, where sensibly priced, award-winning food makes booking always advisable. Fine flower basket displays brighten the pub in summer.
♨Q◑❑P

MARSHFIELD

Catherine Wheel
High Street, SN14 8LR
✪ 11-3 (not Mon), 6-11; 12-3, 7-10.30 Sun
☎ (01225) 892220
Abbey Bellringer; Draught Bass; Brains Buckley's Best Bitter; Courage Best Bitter 田
This is a beautifully restored Georgian pub. On entering, have a look at the very pretty dining-room to the left. The extensive main bar leads down from the original wood-panelled area, via stone-walled rooms to the cosy patio garden at the rear. In winter there is usually a superb open fire. The food, served in the bar and garden, is imaginative and well presented; evening meals are served Monday–Saturday (no lunchtime food Mon). ♨Q❀❑◑P

MAY HILL

Glasshouse Inn

Glasshouse Hill, GL17 0NN

(off A40, W of Huntley) OS710213

✪ 11.30-3, 6.30-11; 12-3, 7-10.30 Sun

☎ (01452) 830529

Draught Bass; Butcombe Bitter; guest beers Ⓖ

Charming old building, recently extended, using reclaimed timbers and flagstones to retain its character. Divided into three rooms, one houses an old, black-leaded range, another a roaring open fire. The addition of a new kitchen means the owners can provide good home-cooked food six days a week. Three real ales are always available, one a changing guest. The fenced garden, with an historic yew hedge, is ideal for families. ▲Q✿◑🅟 🖳🕭♣P

MEYSEY HAMPTON

Mason's Arms

28 High Street, GL7 5JT

✪ 11.30-2.45, 6-11; 12-4, 7-10.30 (not winter eve) Sun

☎ (01285) 850164

website: www.smoothhound.co.uk/hotels/mason

Hook Norton Best Bitter; guest beers Ⓗ

This Grade II listed, 17th-century inn enjoys a picturesque setting on the village green. A large inglenook at one end of the knocked-through bar area and a wood-burning stove at the other combine with the exposed stone walls, parquet floors, hops and farm implements to provide a warm, rustic ambience. The three constantly-changing guest beers are usually from micro-breweries. A centre for the village community, it also appeals to visitors for its accommodation and reasonably-priced restaurant. Lunchtime food is served Monday–Thursday (no food Sun). ▲✿🖳◑

MORETON-IN-MARSH

Inn on the Marsh

Stow Road, GL56 0DW (on A429, S end of village)

✪ 12-2.30, 7-11; 11-3, 6-11 Fri, Sat & summer; 12-3, 7-10.30 Sun

☎ (01608) 650709

Banks's Original; Marston's Bitter, Pedigree; guest beer Ⓗ

This former bakery has a bar which is reminiscent of an Amsterdam 'brown café' where the Dutch game of schoolen can be played. Baskets hanging from the rafters are a reminder of Moreton's basket weaving past, while the main area has comfortable armchairs, old photographs and hanging hops. Food in the conservatory bears a Dutch East Indies influence from the landlady/chef (no food Mon eve). A former coach wash in the garden is now a duckpond. Q✿◑🖳⅄≈♣P⅃

MOSELEY GREEN

Rising Sun

GL15 4HN OS632087

✪ 11-3, 6.30-11 (11-11 summer Sat); 12-3, 7-10.30 (12-10.30 summer) Sun

☎ (01594) 562008

Freeminer Speculation; Greene King Abbot; guest beers Ⓗ

Built in the early 1800s to serve the coal mining community, it was renovated and extended in 1982, adding a skittle alley-cum-function room and a balcony. A patio area, seating 50, was created in 1989 to commemorate 50 years of service at the inn by the same family. A children's play area and barbecue have been added since; the latter is used when local brass bands play on summer Sunday evenings. Family meals are always available. Enjoy the panoramic forest views.
Q✿❀◑♣🖳P⅃🛏

NAILSWORTH

George Inn

Newmarket, GL6 0RF

(¹/₂ mile uphill from bus station)

✪ 11-3, 6-11; 12-3, 7-10.30 Sun

☎ (01453) 833228

Draught Bass; Moles Tap Bitter; Taylor Landlord; Uley Old Spot Ⓗ

Traditional village local looking south over the valley above Nailsworth. The George is a 15-minute walk from the Forest Green Rovers ground. Three chimneys confirm that the inn was originally three cottages, becoming a pub in 1820 and renamed in 1910 to honour the incoming King, George V – the George features in CAMRA's Good Pub Food and the award-winning chef uses only fresh ingredients; the imaginative, keenly-priced menu is served in the small restaurant (booking essential) or the bar. Q✿◑P

NAUNTON

Black Horse

GL54 3AD (off B4068) OS119234

✪ 11.30-3, 6-11; 12-3, 7-10.30 Sun

☎ (01451) 850565

website: www.blackhorse-naunton.co.uk

Donnington BB, SBA Ⓗ

Traditional Cotswold stone village inn, offering a friendly welcome. The interior features black beams, stripped stonework, flagstone floors, wood settles and cast iron-framed tables. Home-cooked food is served in the no-smoking area of the old snug. Unspoilt Naunton boasts a magnificent dovecot (circa 1600) and an old mill. Ask at the pub for a leaflet on the Black Horse walk, a full day's ramble that is popular with walkers and the horse racing fraternity alike.
Q✿❀◑🖳🕭♣P

OAKRIDGE LYNCH

Butcher's Arms

GL6 7NZ (at N end of village) OS915038

✪ 11-3, 6-11; 12-4, 7-10.30 Sun

☎ (01285) 760371

Archers Best Bitter; Greene King Abbot; Tetley Bitter; Wickwar BOB Ⓗ

Popular, two-bar stone local, serving four regular ales. The restaurant opens Wednesday–Saturday and Sunday lunchtime; food is also available in the bars (not Sun eve or Mon). There is a skittle alley and the pub runs a team in the local league. It also fields its own cricket eleven which plays friendly matches against neighbouring pubs. Noted for both its beer and excellent food, the pub boasts a fine garden.
Q✿◑🖳🕭♣P

OLDBURY-ON-SEVERN

Anchor Inn
BS35 1QA

✪ 11.30-2.30, 6.30-11; 11.30-11 Sat; 12-10.30 Sun
☎ (01454) 413331

Draught Bass; Ⓖ Butcombe Bitter; Theakston Old Peculier; Wickwar BOB Ⓗ

This 17th-century two-bar pub has a restaurant at the rear where children are welcome. In the main bar, the accent can be on food, sourced locally and of exceptionally good quality (no lunches Sat). The public bar is smaller and popular with locals. The pub enjoys the benefit of a large garden which, although next to a river, is safety fenced, and has a petanque pitch. This well-run pub has been in this Guide for many years.
🏨Q🏠🕪🍴🌳♣P

OLD DOWN

Old Fox
The Inner Down, BS32 4PR (1½ miles from A38)

✪ 12-3 (2.30 Sat), 6-11; 12-10.30 Sun
☎ (01454) 412507

Draught Bass; Flowers IPA; Moles Best Bitter; guest beer Ⓗ

Friendly, free house where the ambience is enhanced by the low ceiling and exposed beams. The stone bar serves an L-shaped drinking area. A small, no-smoking children's room leads to a patio and garden with a play area. A popular menu now includes Sunday lunch (no food Sun eve). Live entertainment features on Saturday evening, otherwise the pub is music free. Look out for the home-made pub sign. Black Rat cider is served. Guest beers are often from Bath Ales.
🏨Q🐕🏠🕪♣🍴P✕

PARKEND

Fountain Inn and Lodge
GL15 4JD (4 miles N of Lydney, A48) OS616078

✪ 12-2.30, 6-11; 12-11 Sat; 12-2.30, 7-10.30 Sun
☎ (01594) 562189
website: www.thefountaininnandlodge.com

Draught Bass; Freeminer Bitter; guest beer Ⓗ

Traditional village inn, centrally situated in the Forest of Dean, popular with locals. An open fire and exposed stone walls provide a cosy atmosphere; the beams throughout are adorned with old tools and knick-knacks. An extensive menu offers a good choice, including curries, light snacks, main meals, vegetarian dishes and an award-winning children's menu. A bunkhouse, sleeping 32, caters for ramblers, in addition to the eight en-suite guest rooms. Quoits is played here.
🏨🏠🛏🕪🍴🏃P

PRESTBURY

Royal Oak
The Burgage, GL52 3DL

✪ 11.30-2.30, 5.30-11 (11.30-11 summer Sat); 12-3.30, 7-10.30 (12-10.30 summer) Sun
☎ (01242) 522344

Archers Village or Best Bitter; Greene King IPA; guest beer Ⓗ

Small, popular local in what is reputedly Britain's most haunted village. The public bar features exposed beams and low ceilings, while the lounge serves as a restaurant until 9pm. All food is home made and features cheeses from a local producer, while meat is mainly sourced directly from Smithfield. A large garden at the rear leads to a skittle alley-cum-function room. Parking is possible opposite the pub.
🏨Q🏠🕪

PUCKLECHURCH

Rose & Crown
68 Parkfield Road, BS16 9PS

✪ 11.30-3, 6-11; 12-4, 7-10.30 Sun
☎ (0117) 937 2351

Draught Bass; Wadworth IPA, 6X, JCB Ⓗ

Close to the Bristol–Bath cycle path, this large, traditionally-styled, popular country pub comprises a lounge bar, side rooms, a public bar and a restaurant. It enjoys a reputation for good food, served in the restaurant (booking advised), lounge bar and small adjoining rooms. Evening meals are served Tuesday–Saturday; pensioners' specials offer good value. Children are welcome in the restaurant and side rooms. The pub provides a warm, comfortable welcome to all.
🏨🏠🕪♣P

Star Inn
37 Castle Road, BS16 9RF

✪ 11-11; 12-10.30 Sun
☎ (0117) 937 2391

Draught Bass; Ⓖ Wadworth 6X Ⓗ

Large pub, opposite the playing fields that are central to village activities. The Bass is brought up from the cellar by the jug; three real ciders are also available, usually Cheddar Valley Red, Taunton Traditional and Thatchers Dry. An annual beer festival is held on the third weekend in June. The Star is popular for its good value food (not served Sun eve), so booking is advised at the weekend. The No. 689 bus from central Bristol stops outside.
🏠🕪♣P

QUEDGELEY

Little Thatch Hotel
141 Bristol Road, GL2 4PQ (on B4008)

✪ 12-2.30, 6.30-11; 12-3, 7-10.30 Sun
☎ (01452) 720687

Otter Bitter; guest beers Ⓗ

Magnificently preserved building of 1351 that was known as Queen Anne's Farm before being licensed in the 1950s. Legend has it that in 1535 Anne Boleyn stayed here while Henry VIII faced the mostly Catholic population of Gloucester, who refused to recognise his divorce from Catherine of Aragon. Today, the original building contains two bar areas and a very pleasant dining room, while a modern extension provides hotel accommodation. Two guest beers come from craft breweries. It stages occasional Murder Mystery evenings.
Q🏠🛏🕪P

SAPPERTON

Daneway Inn
Daneway, GL7 6LN

✪ 11-2.30 (3 Sat), 6.30-11; 12-3, 7-10.30 Sun
☎ (01285) 760297

Wadworth IPA, 6X, JCB, seasonal beers Ⓗ

Old characterful pub, built in 1784 as three cottages for canal workers near one end of the now-disused Sapperton Tunnel. It was later used as lodging for bargees and tunnel leggers until licensed premises gradually took over all the cottages. The comfortable lounge is dominated by a magnificent carved fireplace. Popular with walkers, the large garden has a children's area and there is a no-smoking room for families. Simple but wholesome food is served daily, except Monday evening.

🏚Q🌣⛱◑◗ ⊟P⅄

SHEEPSCOMBE

Butcher's Arms
GL6 7RH (signed from A46 and B4070) OS892104
✪ 12-3, 6.30 (6 Fri & Sat)-11; 12-3.30, 7-10.30 Sun
☎ (01452) 812113 website: www.cotswoldinns.co.uk
Hook Norton Best Bitter; Uley Old Spot; guest beer Ⓗ

Cosy, 17th-century village pub and restaurant cooking fresh produce. It is part of Blenheim Inns, a privately-owned company which breathes life into tired pubs. Quoits is played. Its sign, with a butcher supping a pint of ale with a pig tied to his leg, is probably the most photographed in the country. It is thought that butchering went on here when Henry VIII hunted deer in Sheepscombe Valley.

Definitions

bivvy – beer

bumclink – inferior beer

bunker – beer

cooper – half stout, half porter

gatters – beer

shant of gatter – glass of beer

half and half – mixture of ale and porter, much favoured by medical students

humming – strong (as applied to drink)

ponge or pongelow – beer, half and half

purl – mixture of hot ale and sugar, with wormwood infused

rot-gut – bad

small beer shandy – gaffs ale and gingerbeer

shant – pot or quart (shant of bivvy – quart of beer)

swipes – sour or small beer

wobble-shop – shop where beer sold without a licence

J.C. Hotten,
The Slang Dictionary, 1887

Enjoy the staggering views from the tables behind the pub.

🏚Q🌣⛱◑◗♣ P⅄⊟

SLAD

Woolpack
GL6 7QA (on B4070)
✪ 12-3, 6-11; 11.30-11 Sat; 12-10.30 Sun
☎ (01452) 813429
Uley Bitter, Laurie Lee's Bitter, Old Spot, Pig's Ear; guest beer Ⓗ

Popular, 16th-century inn, affording superb views of the Slad Valley. It achieved fame through the late Laurie Lee, author of Cider With Rosie, who was a regular. It has been thoughtfully restored, with the addition of wooden settles in the end bar. Well-behaved children are welcome in the end room. The award-winning Uley beers, are served to three separate rooms from the bar; draught cider and perry are available in summer. Lunches are served daily and evening meals Tuesday–Saturday.

🏚Q🌣⛱◑◗ ⊟♣ ♠P⅄

STAPLE HILL

Humpers Off-Licence
26 Soundwell Road, BS16 4QW (on A4017)
✪ 12-2, 5-10.30 (12-10.30 summer Sat); 12-2, 5-10.30 (12-10.30 summer) Sun
☎ (0117) 956 5525
Draught Bass; Butcombe Bitter, Gold; Hop Back Summer Lightning; Smiles Best; Ⓗ **guest beers** Ⓖ

Bristol's only real ale off-licence has been in this Guide for 12 years. Five beers are kept on handpump, with up to three guests on gravity. Thatchers and Westons organic real ciders are served at prices well below pub prices; bring your own container or buy one here. Up to 40 bottled beers are available, most of them bottle-conditioned. Guest ales can be specially ordered. Opening hours may vary. ♣

STRATTON

Drillman's Arms
34 Gloucester Road, GL7 2JY
✪ 11-2.30, 5.30-11; 11-11 Sat; 12-4, 7-10.30 Sun
☎ (01285) 653892
Archer's Best Bitter; Draught Bass; Moles Best Bitter; guest beer Ⓗ

Do not be put off by the two looming fruit machines in the lounge – the low, beamed ceilings, open fire, horse brasses, brewery pictures and excellent beer more than compensate. A pool table is available in the rear bar while the function room houses a skittle alley. The immaculate loos are brightened by fresh flowers. Very reasonably-priced, standard pub fare is served. A summer beer festival is held each year. Outside seating is in the small car park at the front.

🏚⛱◑◗♣P

STROUD

Queen Victoria
5 Gloucester Street, GL5 1QG
(close to Merrywalks shopping centre)
✪ 10-11; 12-10.30 Sun
☎ (01453) 762396
website: www.thequeenvicstroud.co.uk
Smiles Best; guest beers Ⓗ

This imposing building formerly housed the Gloucester Street forge. Records show that it was owned by the Nailsworth Brewery in 1891. The large, single bar always keeps three guest beers, sourced from small, independent micro-breweries. The spacious function room hosts beer festivals in March and September. This community pub fields quiz, darts and pool teams in local leagues and stages live music (Thu, Fri and Sat eves).
🏚️❀⇌♣🕭

SWINEFORD

Swan
Bath Road, BS30 6LN
(1 mile SE of Bitton, on A431)
✪ 11-3, 5-11; 12-3, 7-10.30 Sun
☎ (0117) 932 3101
Draught Bass; Ⓖ Butcombe Bitter; Ⓗ Courage Best Bitter; Ⓖ Worthington's Bitter Ⓗ
Free house in a tiny hamlet between Bristol and Bath, the pub is popular with locals, walkers and residents of nearby villages. It provides home-prepared pub meals; booking is advisable for Sunday lunch. A no-smoking room, between the main bar and the restaurant, is used by drinkers and those enjoying bar meals. Children are welcome in the pub. In winter the open log fire provides a pleasant focal point.
🏚️❀◑Ⓟ⌇

TEWKESBURY

Berkeley Arms ✅
8 Church Street, GL20 5PA (on A38)
✪ 11.30-3, 5-11; 11.30-11 Fri & Sat; 12-4, 7-10.30 Sun
☎ (01684) 293034
Wadworth IPA, 6X, JCB; guest beer Ⓗ
Superb, 16th-century, half-timbered Grade II listed building. The public bar entrance is on the street, while the lounge is accessed by one of Tewkesbury's many alleyways. At the rear a barn, believed to be the oldest non-ecclesiastical building in this historic town, is used for dining in summer; good value food is served. Live music is performed on Saturday evening.
Q◑⇌♣

White Bear
Bredon Road, GL20 5BU
✪ 11-11; 12-10.30 Sun
☎ (01684) 296614
Wye Valley Bitter; guest beers Ⓗ
Lively local on the edge of the town centre. It has a single L-shaped bar, with one end dominated by a pool table, the other has a dartboard. This good value, family-run pub stocks an ever-changing range of beers, often from smaller breweries. Close to Tewkesbury Marina, it is popular with river users. It fields crib, darts and pool teams and its skittle alley is the venue for Tewkesbury CAMRA's winter ale festival, held each February. ❀♣🕭Ⓟ🍴

TORMARTON

Portcullis
High Street, GL9 1HZ (near M4 jct 18)
✪ 12-3, 6-11; 12-3, 7-10.30 Sun
☎ (01454) 218263
Draught Bass; Butcombe Bitter, Otter Bitter; Wadworth 6X; guest beers Ⓗ

The focal point of the ancient village of Tormarton was built in the 1700s. Its modest virginia creeper-covered stone frontage belies its spacious, unassuming main bar. The oak-panelled, no-smoking restaurant provides freshly-cooked, generous meals at modest prices. The friendly landlord/owner takes pride in his fine selection of beers, sourced mainly from local breweries.
🏚️Q❀⇌◑Å♣Ⓟ

ULEY

Old Crown
The Green, GL11 5SN
✪ 11.30-2.30 (3 Sat), 7-11; 12-3, 7-10.30 Sun
☎ (01453) 860502
Uley Bitter, Pig's Ear; guest beers Ⓗ
Welcoming, attractive, whitewashed, 17th-century free house set in the picturesque Uley Valley, within its own pleasant walled garden. The main bar has a low, timbered ceiling. Close to the Uley Brewery and the Cotswold Way, it is popular with walkers. Live music can be enjoyed on Tuesday and Friday. The pub was local CAMRA's Pub of the Year 2001. The landlady serves over 150 guest beers a year, mainly from micro-breweries and serves home-cooked meals at reasonable prices.
🏚️Q❀⇌◑♣Ⓟ

WATERLEY BOTTOM

New Inn
GL11 6EF
(signed from North Nibley) OS758964
✪ 12-2.30 (not Mon), 6 (7 Mon)-11; 12-11 Sat; 12-10.30 Sun
☎ (01453) 543659
Bath SPA, Gem; Cotleigh Tawny; Greene King Abbot; guest beer Ⓗ
Lovely free house, situated in a small hamlet surrounded by steep hills. During the 19th century it was a cider house, frequented by mill workers on their daily journey to Dursley. A beer festival is held over the last weekend of June. On the following Wednesday, a traditional ball throwing event takes place. The pub has two bars, and the attractive garden houses a boules piste. No food is served Monday. Children are welcome. Thatchers cider is served straight from the cask.
🏚️Q❀◑⇌♣🕭Ⓟ

WINTERBOURNE DOWN

Cross Hands Inn
85 Down Road, BS36 1BZ
✪ 12 (11 Sat)-11; 12-10.30 Sun
☎ (01454) 850077
Draught Bass; Courage Best Bitter; Greene King Old Speckled Hen; Moles Tap Bitter; guest beer Ⓗ
Popular free house that is a proper pub. It hosts live music every Friday, with free entry. No meals are served, but hot snacks are available all day and DIY barbecues are popular in summer in the pub's large, attractive garden. In winter you can enjoy a glass of hot mulled wine while playing devil among the tailors (table skittles). Thatchers and Rich's ciders are always available; the latter is rarely found in the area on draught.
❀♣🕭

WITHINGTON

King's Head
King's Head Lane, GL54 4BD
(off Yanworth road) OS036153
✪ 11-2.30, 6-11; 12-2.30, 7-10.30 Sun
☎ (01242) 890216

Hook Norton Best Bitter; Wickwar Cotswold Way Ⓗ

Quiet and unspoilt community-centred local that has been in the same family for over 90 years. The welcome is always friendly from the landlady who keeps this pleasant, comfortable pub. There is a pool table plus other traditional pub games, with live music evenings around the piano in the lounge. Food is not normally available, except sandwiches if requested. Children are allowed in the lounge anteroom. Chedworth Roman Villa is nearby.
🏚Q✿❄♣●P

WOODCHESTER

Ram Inn
Station Road, South Woodchester,
GL5 5EQ (signed from A46)
✪ 11-11; 12-10.30 Sun
☎ (01453) 873329

John Smith's Bitter; Uley Old Spot; Wickwar BOB; guest beers Ⓗ

The Ram is more than 400 years old and is situated in superb walking country, near Woodchester Mansion. A planned extension will add a no-smoking area, disabled access and a new toilet block to the inn. Three guest ales from all parts of the country are stocked. An Irish beer festival coincides with the Cheltenham Gold Cup in March, while an anti-Beaujolais celebration in November promotes English beer and food. The pub has a restaurant area. 🏚Q✿◑♿▲●P⌀

Royal Oak Inn
Church Road, North Woodchester,
GL5 5PQ (signed from A46)
✪ 12 (5 Mon)-11; 12-11 Sun
☎ (01453) 872735

Archers Best Bitter; Bath SPA; Wickwar BOB; guest beer Ⓗ

Pretty, whitewashed, late 16th-century cottage inn with two elegant bars. This lively, friendly local attracts customers from miles around to sample its ales and imaginative, freshly-cooked meals at reasonable prices. The dining area boasts a magnificent open fireplace with a log fire. The pub's patio garden affords stunning views over a typical Cotswold valley. A monthly live music night features folk, jazz or blues.
🏚Q✿◑♣●P

WOOLASTON COMMON

Rising Sun
GL15 6NU
(1 mile from A48 at Woolaston) OS590009
✪ 12-2.30 (not Wed), 6.30-11; 12-3, 7-10.30 Sun
☎ (01594) 529282

Fuller's London Pride; Wye Valley Bitter; guest beers Ⓗ

This 350-year-old country pub, benefiting from fine views, is on the route of the circular pub walk of the Forest of Dean. It is popular with both ramblers and cyclists. The landlord and the locals make this a welcoming refuge. The pub has undergone many sympathetic improvements over the years and now features a large bar and small, intimate snug. The meals represent good value.
🏚Q✿◑♣P

Fizz warning

Some national breweries produce both cask-conditioned and 'nitro-keg' versions of their beers. Boddingtons Bitter, John Smith's Bitter, Tetley's Bitter and Worthington fall into this category. Nitro-keg beers, often promoted as 'smooth' or 'cream-flow' products, are filtered and pasteurised in the brewery, and served in pubs by a mix of applied carbon dioxide and nitrogen gases. They are bland, served extremely cold, and any hop character is lost by the use of applied gas. To add insult to injury, the keg founts that serve such beers are often topped by small dummy handpumps. As a result of lobbying by CAMRA, some producers of cask and nitro versions of the same beer now include the word 'cask' on pump clips for the genuine article. For example, both John Smith's Bitter and Tetley's Bitter now carry the word 'cask' on pump clips for the real thing. For the sake of brevity, and as the Good Beer Guide lists only cask-conditioned beers, we refer simply to John Smith's Bitter and Tetley Bitter. The Interbrew brand, Worthington, is labelled Worthington Bitter in cask form, and – bizarrely – Worthington Best Bitter in the nitro-keg version. Always choose the living rather than the dead.

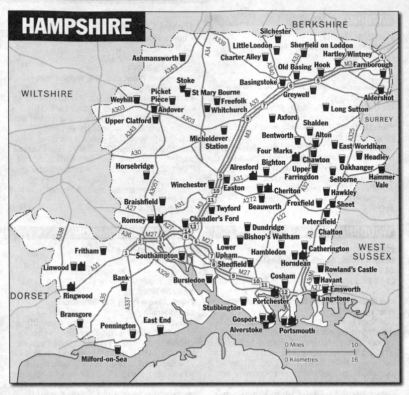

HAMPSHIRE

ALDERSHOT

Red Lion
Ash Road, GU12 4EZ
☉ 5 (12 Thu-Sat)-11; 12-4, 7-10.30 Sun
☎ (01252) 686700

Courage Best Bitter; guest beers Ⓗ
This imposing roadside pub was rebuilt
in 1926 after it burnt down. There are
three drinking areas, each boasting its
own log fire. Oak doors, various ceramic
collections and barley twist footrails
enhance the quiet air of this comfortable
pub, away from the excesses of the town
centre. A genuine free house, an
interesting selection of five guest beers
from local and not-so-local micro-
breweries changes each week (over 2,000
different real ales under the current
landlord).
▲Q❀≠P

Royal Staff ✓
37A Mount Pleasant Road, GU12 4NW
☉ 12-3, 5-11; 12-11 Sat; 12-10.30 Sun
☎ (01252) 408012

Fuller's Chiswick, London Pride, seasonal beers Ⓗ
At the high end of Waterloo Road, this
well illuminated pub is handy for
Aldershot Town football ground. Inside
there is Sky TV for football or golf. The
pub has its own golf society, plus ladies',
and gents' darts teams. Doors to the left
of the bar lead to a child-friendly garden,
featuring a fully carpeted Wendy house,
and less obviously, hops growing among
the hedges. It hosts a quiz on Sunday
evening with a meat raffle.
❀

ALTON

Crown Hotel
High Street, GU34 1BN
☉ 11.30-11; 12-10.30 Sun
☎ (01420) 84567

Shepherd Neame Spitfire; Wells Bombardier; guest beers Ⓗ
Formerly a 16th-century coaching inn, it
now has a single bar, with exposed beams
and brickwork, arranged as a series of bays,
with comfortable seating. Good, honest pub
food is offered at reasonable prices (there is
a no-smoking restaurant). The beer range
varies on an irregular basis, usually
featuring regional breweries. The decked
drinking area on this corner site contributed
to this pub winning the Alton in Bloom
competition. No meals served Sunday
evening. ▲❀✦◁◑≠P

Eight Bells
33 Church Street, GU34 2DA
☉ 11-11; 12-10.30 Sun
☎ (01420) 82417

Hogs Back TEA; guest beers Ⓗ
Excellent free house just outside the town
centre on the old Alton–Odiham turnpike.
The building dates from 1640 and is
steeped in history. Opposite stands the
ancient St Lawrence Church, around
which the Civil War Battle of Alton was
fought. The pub has one small, oak-
beamed bar with an extra drinking area to
the rear, and a bijou garden with a well.
The house ale, Leaping Trout, is brewed
by Hogs Back and may be accompanied
by hearty filled rolls.
▲Q❀♣♠

French Horn
The Butts, GU34 1RT (near A31 western jct)
☼ 11-3, 5.30 (6 Sat)-11; 12-4, 7-10.30 (12-10.30 summer) Sun
☎ (01420) 83269
Draught Bass; Courage Best Bitter; Gale's HSB; Young's Bitter; guest beers Ⓗ
Consistently popular, historic pub renowned for its food. It overlooks the medieval archery butts, now a public open space. A warming fire in winter lights up a tankard collection gracing the beams. Several grassed drinking areas afford good views of the Watercress Line trains on the nearby embankment. The regulars' corner near the fire is a welcoming spot. A skittle alley is available. No children under 14 are allowed in the main building. ⚫Q❀☙◑ⓅP

Market Hotel
3 Market Square, GU34 1HD
☼ 11-11; 12-10.30 Sun
☎ (01420) 82350
Courage Best Bitter; guest beers Ⓗ
Situated in the pedestrianised ancient market square, this pub has two high-ceilinged bars: the larger one offers modern pub games and is popular with younger drinkers; the bare-boarded public bar is quieter and boasts a striking mural commemorating Alton's extinct livestock market. Both bars have juke boxes and TVs. Food is sensibly priced, with usually a choice of home-made soups. This pub normally has one guest at a time to ensure rapid turnover. Evening meals are served Sunday–Thursday. ⚫Q❀☙◑Ⓠ⇌♣

Railway Arms
26 Anstey Road, GU34 2RB
(opp. end of Station Rd)
☼ 11-11; 12-10.30 Sun
☎ (01420) 88218
Triple fff Alton's Pride, Pressed Rat & Warthog, Moondance; guest beers Ⓗ
Close to the Watercress Line and main line station, the U-shaped bar has one side divided into cosy areas. During the day, quiet background music is played, but at other times it is busy and can be noisy. Leased by the owner of Triple fff Brewery, his beers are by no means the only ones on offer; seven handpumps display a frequently-changing range from a host of micros. There are tables outside, under a striking sculpture of a steam locomotive. ❀◑⇌♣◑

ALVERSTOKE

Alverbank
Stokes Bay Road, PO12 2QT
☼ 11-11 (may close early winter midweek); 12-10.30 Sun
☎ (023) 9251 0005
website: www.alverbank.clara.co.uk
Beer range varies Ⓗ
Victorian country house hotel bar in an attractive setting overlooking Stokes Bay and once frequented by Lillie Langtry. Up to five real ales from independent and micro-breweries are supplied by East-West Ales. The house ale is Ringwood Best Bitter rebadged. The restaurant is open daily, except Sunday evenings, and barbecues are held on summer Sunday lunchtimes. A

newly-built function room with a wheelchair WC caters for weddings and there is occasional live music. ⚫❀☙◑ⒶP

ANDOVER

John Russell Fox ✓
10 High Street, SP10 1NY
☼ 10-11; 12-10.30 Sun
☎ (01264) 320920
Courage Directors; Hop Back Summer Lightning; Shepherd Neame Spitfire; Theakston Best Bitter; guest beers Ⓗ
This recent addition to the Wetherspoon's estate is located in the former printing shop of the Andover Advertiser, and named after the newspaper's founder. The pub has an L-shaped layout on three levels; the lower level forms the main drinking area. The bar is on the middle level while the upper level is used principally for eating (children welcome here until 6pm if dining). Printing memorabilia is much in evidence, including an old typesetting machine. Lifts are provided. Q◑&

Lamb Inn
21 Winchester Street, SP10 2EA (opp. police station)
☼ 11-3, 6 (5 Fri; 7 Sat)-11; 12-2.30, 7-10.30 Sun
☎ (01264) 323961
Wadworth IPA, 6X; guest beers Ⓗ
One of Andover's last remaining traditional pubs, it had a long history under the now-defunct Heath and Crowley breweries, before becoming Wadworth's first Andover pub in 1954. The licensee is the brewery's longest-serving landlady. It is not unusual to find board games being played in the homely lounge around the log fire. A Thai restaurant is in the old public bar, and traditional pub fare is also available. The Lamb refers to Knights Templar' heraldry. ⚫Q❀☙Ⓠ♣

ASHMANSWORTH

Plough Inn
RG20 9SL
(1 mile off A343, S of Highclere village) OS415575
☼ 12-2.30 (not Tue), 6-11; closed Mon; 12-3, 7.30-10.30 Sun
☎ (01635) 253047
Archers Village, Best Bitter, Golden; guest beer Ⓖ
This superb local is the village's last remaining pub; the shop and post office have already closed. The Plough is popular with walkers and cyclists exploring Hampshire's highest village and the Wayfarer's Walk. All beers are gravity-drawn from stillage behind the single bar. A small selection of lunchtime snacks is normally

INDEPENDENT BREWERIES

Cheriton Cheriton
Gale's Horndean
Hampshire Romsey
Itchen Valley Alresford
Oakleaf Gosport
Packhorse Portsmouth
Portchester Portchester
Red Shoot Linwood
Ringwood Ringwood
Triple fff Four Marks

available. The risk of closure is always present, so support for this former local CAMRA Pub of the Year is encouraged. Parking is limited. ♨Q❀♣P

AXFORD

Crown Inn
RG25 2DZ (on B3046 S of Basingstoke)
✪ 12-3, 6-11; 12-3, 7.30-10.30 Sun
☎ (01256) 389492
Fuller's London Pride; guest beers Ⓗ
Set at the entrance to a small village, on a hill providing a split-level garden above the pub and a large patio, this is a good watering-hole in picturesque rolling countryside, featuring places such as Gobley Hole and Flockmoor Cott. There are two bars and a restaurant area overlooking the patio; food is available throughout the pub. Comfortably furnished, its pleasant decor enhances the friendly, relaxing atmosphere.
♨❀◑▸P

BANK (LYNDHURST)

Oak
Pinkney Lane, SO43 7FE (1¼ miles W of Lyndhurst) OS286072
✪ 11.30-3, 6-11 (11.30-11 Sat & Easter-autumn); 12-10.30 Sun
☎ (023) 8028 2350
Holden's Special; Ringwood Best Bitter; guest beers Ⓟ
This welcoming pub stands in a New Forest hamlet, frequented by walkers and cyclists. The low-ceilinged, beamed bar is adorned with unusual ornaments and graced by a fireplace surround once owned by the Rev. Charles L. Dodgson (Lewis Carroll). The varied menu uses fresh ingredients; Sunday meals are served 12-7. An annual beer festival is held in July. Daytime bus services, X34 and X35 (Southampton–Ringwood–Bournemouth) stop nearby at Bank turn. Mobile phone use is frowned upon.
♨❀◑▸♣P

BASINGSTOKE

Basingstoke & North Hants Cricket Club ⊘
Mays Bounty, Fairfield Road, RG21 3DR
(5 minutes' walk S of old town centre)
✪ 12-2.30, 5-11; 12-11 Fri & Sat; 12-10.30 Sun
☎ (01256) 473646 website: www.bnhcc.freewire.co.uk
Adnams Bitter; Fuller's London Pride; Greene King IPA; guest beers Ⓗ
Founded by the owner of May's Brewery, which ceased brewing in the 1940s, this is a members-only club; visitors are welcome on production of a valid CAMRA membership card. The club fields cricket, football, squash, snooker and darts teams. The beer range changes often, with small breweries well represented; it arguably has the best range in town. The atmosphere is often described as more pub than club. A good selection of food is served. Local CAMRA Club of the Year 2003.
❀◑▸♣P⪥❒

Bounty Inn
81 Bounty Road, RG21 3BZ (follow signs for Fairfields Arts Centre)
✪ 11-2.30, 5.30-11; 11-11 Sat; 12-10.30 Sun
☎ (01256) 320071 website: www.bountyinn.co.uk

Courage Best Bitter; Greene King Abbot; Oakleaf Hole Hearted; guest beers Ⓗ
Formerly known as the Cattle Market, the pub's name was changed in the mid-20th century to reflect its location next to May's Bounty cricket ground – a gift to the people of Basingstoke a century ago by Lt Col. John May, the town's great benefactor and brewer. Gentlemen of a cold-blooded disposition may not appreciate the outside WC. The no-smoking family room doubles as a function room. No food is served on Monday evening. Parking is limited.
♨❀◑▤♣P⪥

Soldiers Return
80 Upper Sherborne Road, RG21 5RP
✪ 11-2.30, 5.30-11; 11-11 Fri & Sat; 12-10.30 Sun
☎ (01256) 322449
website: www.mysite.freeserve.com/Soldiers_Return
Courage Best Bitter; guest beers Ⓗ
Originally a privately-owned beer house built in the 1860s for soldiers returning from the Crimean war. It was extended by Farnham United Breweries in 1927 becoming a public house. In the 1960s, under Courage, further extension resulted in a lounge, public bar, children's room and inside toilets. The Soldiers is now a lively free house offering four real ales mainly sourced from small breweries. It has its own football and pool teams and is home to the Basingstoke Motorcycle Action Group
☕❀◑▤P

BEAUWORTH

Milbury's
SO24 0PB (S of A272, 1 mile beyond Beauworth hamlet) OS570246
✪ 12-11; 12-10.30 Sun
☎ (01962) 771248
Hop Back Best Bitter; Theakston Old Peculier; guest beers Ⓗ
18th-century, hilltop free house, worth finding; its classic interior boasts a wealth of oak beams, flagstone and quarry-tiled floors and bare brick walls – ancient settles and gnarled, uneven tables add to its charm. One room features a 300ft hand-dug well, with a gigantic treadmill to raise the bucket. A skittle alley is available. The wide-ranging menu offers many home-made dishes; portions are generous. The house beer is from the local Triple fff Brewery; guest beers are usually from small breweries.
♨Q☕❀◑▲♣P⪥

BENTWORTH

Sun Inn
GU34 5JT (off A339) OS671403
✪ 12-3, 6-11; 12-10.30 Sun
☎ (01420) 562338
Cheriton Pots Ale; Ringwood Best Bitter; Stonehenge Pigswill; guest beers Ⓗ
This 17th-century inn has three connected rooms, each with a log fire. The central bar has a low ceiling with oak beams and an inglenook. Families with children can use the side room, which is also used by diners. Scrubbed wood tables, old brass and farm implements complete the rural picture. Beers from local micro-breweries are always available and the house beer is from Hampshire Brewery. The inn is well known for its quality home-made food. ♨Q☕❀◑▸P

BIGHTON

Three Horseshoes

Bighton Road, SO24 9RE (2 miles NE of Alresford, off B3046) OS614344

☼ 12-2.30 (not Mon), 6 (6.30 Sat)-11; 12-2.30, 7-10.30 Sun

☎ (01962) 732859

Gale's Butser, HSB; Otter Bright; guest beer (summer) Ⓗ

Tiny, remote inn, a pub for 400 years with two contrasting bars. The public has ancient woodblock floors, settles, beams, an inglenook and a display of old tools from country crafts. The no-smoking, carpeted lounge is like a private room, displaying a large collection of Matchbox vehicles. The lunch menu offers simple, sustaining fare but the evening choice is more extensive (no food Sun eve). The large garden has a pets' corner. ♨Q◖◑⊟⅄♣P⅄

BISHOP'S WALTHAM

Bunch of Grapes

St Peter's Street, SO32 1AD (off High St)

☼ 10-2, 6-11; 12-2, 7-10.30 Sun

☎ (01489) 892935

Courage Best Bitter Ⓖ

Ancient pub in a narrow, medieval street leading to the parish church, run by one family since 1913. The door opens into the tiny, single bar where you can expect to be drawn into topical conversations (although the decor suggests that topical could involve 'digging for victory'). Many regulars belong to the flourishing golf society. Just one ale cask sits on the table; no food but truly a must visit pub. ❀♣

BRAISHFIELD

Newport Inn

Newport Lane, SO51 0PL (lane opp. phone box) OS372249

☼ 11-3, 6-11; 12-2.30, 7-10.30 Sun

☎ (01794) 368225

Gale's Butser, Winter Brew, HSB, Festival Mild (summer) Ⓗ

Trapped in a time warp, only the prices have changed since the 1960s. No food symbols are shown, yet customers come from all over the county to eat here! The choice is ham or cheese in either a ploughman's or a sandwich; however the portions, quality and value are unsurpassed. At weekends be prepared to join in a singsong around the ancient piano. An extraordinarily mixed clientele are loyal to this 'pub in aspic'. There is a large, unrestrained garden. ♨Q❀⅄♣P

Wheatsheaf

Braishfield Road, SO51 0QE OS375246

☼ 11-11; 12-10.30 Sun

☎ (01794) 368372

Hook Norton Old Hooky; Ringwood Best Bitter; Taylor Landlord; Wadworth 6X Ⓗ

The large garden of this pub, a woodland walk away from the Hillier Arboretum, affords views of rolling fields and wooded hills. The interior comprises several discrete, handsomely furnished areas in which to enjoy the excellent, home-prepared, award-winning food (weekend diners are advised to book). Wines are of good quality and clay pipes are on sale. There is one bus per weekday from Romsey, three miles away, but walkers have many riparian and bosky options. ♨❀◑⅄♣P⅄

BRANSGORE

Three Tuns ✓

Ringwood Road, BH23 8JH (A35 from Christchurch to Lyndhurst, right at Hinton)

☼ 11.30-2.30, 6-11; 12-3, 7-10.30 Sun

☎ (01425) 672232 website: www.3tuns.com

Greene King IPA; Ringwood Fortyniner; Taylor Landlord Ⓗ

Built in 1640, this beautiful, two-roomed, thatched pub sits on the edge of the New Forest. The snug is in fact an extension, but looks very old, it has a wood-burning stove with coopers' tools over the fireplace. The pub is renowned for its excellent food and much of the main bar is taken up by tables for eating, but the comfortable surroundings, friendly staff and locals make visitors welcome. A beer festival is hosted in the summer. ♨Q❀◑⅄⅄

BURSLEDON

Jolly Sailor ✓

Lands End Road, Old Bursledon, SO31 8DN (park at Bursledon Station; follow signed footpath)

☼ 11-11; 12-10.30 Sun

☎ (023) 8040 5557

Badger K&B Sussex, Best, Tanglefoot, seasonal beers Ⓗ

Cosy, multi-roomed, waterside two-bar pub, full of historic maritime artefacts. All are welcomed, from both land and water. Enjoy the splendid views across the River Hamble to a busy marina from the waterside bar, patio and covered jetty. The open log fire completes the cosy rear bar area. Superb food, from a comprehensive menu, including fresh seafood, suits all tastes. The pub is due a major refurbishment involving closure during the life of this Guide. ♨Q❀◑⊟≈⅄

CATHERINGTON

Farmer

300 Catherington Lane, PO8 0TD

☼ 12-2.30, 5-11; 12-11 Sat; 12-10.30 Sun

☎ (023) 9259 2402

Gale's GB, HSB Ⓗ

Village pub, constructed in typical Gale's pre-war style, close to the ancient Catherington down and church. Although it has two bars, the lounge doubles as a Thai restaurant on Thursday–Saturday evenings; daily lunches, including Sunday roasts, are English. The comfortable public bar has an unusual wooden fenced darts stage. Occasional barbecues and spit roasts are held in the large, secure fenced garden, which has a children's play area and an adjacent donkey paddock. ♨Q❀◑⊟P⅄

CHALTON

Red Lion ✓

PO8 0BG OS231160

☼ 11-3, 6-11; 12-3, 7-10.30 Sun

☎ (023) 9259 2246

Gale's Butser, GB, HSB, seasonal beers; guest beers Ⓗ

Built in 1167 to accommodate workmen building the church opposite, it became a pub in 1503 – reputedly the oldest in the county. The thatched building nestles cosily in the South Downs near the old London–Portsmouth coaching route. Despite its remoteness and lack of public transport, its popularity with visitors as well as locals prompted an extension to the car park. The traditional public bar boasts a splendid inglenook. No meals are served Sunday evening. ♛❀◐⊟P⚡

CHANDLER'S FORD

Cleveland Bay

Pilgrim Close, Valley Park, SO53 4ST

⏲ 11-11; 12-10.30 Sun

☎ (023) 8026 9814

Wadworth IPA, 6X, JCB, seasonal beers; guest beers Ⓗ

Spacious, 1980s pub, well hidden in the middle of Valley Park housing development. A central, semi-island bar is surrounded by a large drinking space with a number of gazebo-like seating areas. These, and masses of light wood and high ceilings with exposed roof trusses, give a light, airy atmosphere. The menu includes daily specials; no food is served Sunday evening (quiz night). Guest beers are from Wadworth's list. It fields a flourishing golf society and darts is played.

♛❀◐♿♣P⚡

CHARTER ALLEY

White Hart

White Hart Lane, RG26 5QA

(1 mile W of A340, 1 mile E of A339)

⏲ 12-2.30 (3 Sat), 7-11; 12-3, 7-10.30 Sun

☎ (01256) 850048

website: www.whitehartcharteralley.com

Oakleaf Bitter; Otter Ale; Taylor Landlord; guest beers Ⓗ

The oldest building in the village, built next to the forge in 1819, it was the meeting point for folks to stop and natter, hence Chatter Alley (later becoming Charter Alley). A delightful rural ambience is enhanced by exposed beams, a skittle alley, and fires in winter. In summer, still cider is stocked. The menu offers vegetarian meals, children's portions, a variety of steaks and the speciality – home-made pies (made with real ale). No meals are served Sunday or Monday evening. ♛Q❀◐⊟♣●⚡

CHAWTON

Greyfriar

Winchester Road, GU34 1SB (opp. Jane Austen's cottage)

⏲ 12-11; 12-10.30 Sun

☎ (01420) 83841

Fuller's Chiswick, London Pride, ESB, seasonal beers or guest beer Ⓗ

Originally three cottages, standing opposite Jane Austen's house, the single, L-shaped bar has ancient exposed beams. An irregular plan generates a series of separate areas, one of which is the no-smoking restaurant area where excellent food is served; no meals Sunday evening. A tied pub, it is a local exemplar of what Fuller's beers should taste like. A Saturday treat is London Pride served by gravity dispense from a cask on the bar – delicious. Q❀◐P

CHERITON

Flower Pots Inn

SO24 0QQ

(1/2 mile N of A272 between Winchester and Petersfield)

⏲ 12-2.30, 6-11; 12-3, 7-10.30 Sun

☎ (01962) 771318

Cheriton Pots Ale, Village Elder, Best Bitter, Diggers Gold Ⓖ

Home of the Cheriton Brewhouse, this fine two-bar, red-brick pub was built in the 1800s. A log fire and a 30ft well in the public bar add to the character and charm of this country gem, which is situated on the edge of a pretty village, close to the source of the River Itchen. Popular with walkers, good food is served every day except Sunday evening. A beer festival is held in August. Camping is usually available, May–September (phone ahead).

♛Q❀◐⊟♿⛺P

COSHAM

First Post ✔

42A High Street, PO6 3AG

⏲ 10-11; 12-10.30 Sun

☎ (023) 9221 0331

Courage Directors; Greene King Abbot; Oakleaf Blake's Gosport Bitter; Shepherd Neame Spitfire; Theakston Best Bitter Ⓗ

This is one of the smaller Wetherspoon's at only 2,400 square feet. But this belies the size of the genuine welcome that awaits, especially for families with children, who are admitted for meals from 10am until 8pm every day. Originally a John Menzies shop, it was converted in a modern style. Its most noticeable feature is the macabre painting on the theme of waiting for service, which you never do here, due to the efficiency of the staff. Q❀◐♿⇌⚡

DUNDRIDGE

Hampshire Bowman

Dundridge Lane, SO32 1GD

(1 1/2 miles E of B3035) OS578184

⏲ 12-3, 6-11; 12-11 Fri & Sat; 12-10.30 Sun

☎ (01489) 892940

website: www.hantsbowman.f9.co.uk

Ringwood Fortyniner; guest beers Ⓖ

Headquarters of the Portuguese Racing Sardine Club, the Bowman is off the beaten track but well worth finding. This former Gale's pub, built in 1865, is almost unchanged, with brick floors, old furniture and a wood-burning stove. Real ales are served from a stillage behind the bar. It is popular with walkers (and their dogs). An archery club meets in the field next door. Quiz night is Monday. Good pub grub is served, except Sunday evening.

♛Q❀◐⛺♣P

EAST END (LYMINGTON)

East End Arms

Lymington Road, SO41 5SY

(3 miles E of Lymington) OS362968

⏲ 11.30-3, 6-11 (not Mon eve); 12-9 Sun

☎ (01590) 626223

Ringwood Best Bitter, Fortyniner; guest beer Ⓖ

This unpretentious country pub has two bars with distinctly different characters: the stone-floored public bar, preferred by the locals; and a larger, carpeted lounge, providing a more comfortable environment to indulge in the excellent food (not served Mon). The pub has a children's certificate until 8pm. It is well worth a detour, especially from the Solent Way or the Lymington ferry. ♨Q❀✪❍⊕♣P

EASTON

Cricketers Inn ✿
Church Lane, SO21 1EJ (½ mile S of B3047)
☼ 12-3.30, 6-11; 12-3.30, 7-10.30 Sun
☎ (01962) 779353
Fuller's London Pride; Ringwood Best Bitter; Taylor Landlord; guest beers Ⓗ
Rural free house in the Itchen Valley, described as an architect's 'googly', built in 1906. It has a no-smoking dining room (as well as serving meals in the main bar) but it is a true village pub, supporting the local cricket team and offering entertainment and special events. The decor owes much to cricket and a wide range of reference books can be consulted. The menu is interesting and meals excellent. Guest beers come from small regional and craft brewers.
♨❀⊯❍Ⓐ♣P

EAST WORLDHAM

Three Horseshoes ✿
Cakers Lane, GU34 3AE (on B3004)
☼ 12-3, 6-11; 12-3, 7-10.30 Sun
☎ (01420) 83211
Gale's Butser, GB, HSB, seasonal beers or guest beer Ⓗ
The Worldhams were once the centre of an extensive hop-growing district; the pub you now see, reputedly haunted, is an 1884 replacement for an older building, both serving the itinerant workers. A single bar is comfortably broken up into informal areas; a no-smoking section for drinkers leads to a small, but attractive restaurant, serving good food. ♨Q❀⊯❍♣P

EMSWORTH

Coal Exchange ✿
21 South Street, PO10 7EG
☼ 10.30-3, 5.30-11; 10.30-11 Sat; 12-10.30 Sun
☎ (01243) 375866
Gale's Butser, GB, HSB, seasonal beers; guest beers Ⓗ
As the name suggests, this 17th-century building was used by local farmers to trade their produce with merchants delivering coal by sea to the local harbour. No longer commercial, the harbour is now popular with yachtsmen. The pub bears an unusual green-tiled frontage and the single L-shaped bar houses a dartboard. The curry nights (Tue) and international nights (Thu) attract many customers, so an early arrival is advised. ♨❀❍≉♣

Lord Raglan
35 Queen Street, PO10 7BJ
☼ 11-3, 6-11; 12-10.30 Sun
☎ (01243) 372587 website: www.thelordraglan.com
Gale's Butser, HSB, seasonal beers; guest beers Ⓗ
Popular flint-faced pub on the eastern edge of town, by the Sussex border. The extensive garden affords views of the harbour and the River Ems estuary, which has in the past flooded the pub. A good range of home-cooked meals (especially fish

dishes) is served every session. The pub can be busy and noisy on Sunday evening when local bands perform in the single remaining bar (the other bar has been converted to a small, comfortable restaurant). ♨Q❀✪❍Ⓐ≉

FARNBOROUGH

Prince of Wales ✿
184 Rectory Road, GU14 7EW (near Farnborough North Station)
☼ 11.30-2.30, 5.30-11; 12-10.30 Sun
☎ (01252) 545578
Badger Tanglefoot; Fuller's London Pride; Hogs Back TEA; Ringwood Fortyniner; Young's Bitter; guest beers Ⓗ
This local CAMRA Pub of the Year 2003 offers a very wide range of beers. The regular beers greet you by the front door, but do not miss up to five guests in the snug bar. These include ales from Hampshire and Berkshire breweries, as well as a monthly changing session beer. A convivial and traditional pub, where lunches are served Monday–Saturday and a beer festival is held in October, it is one mile east of the town centre. ❀❍≉ (North) P

Swan
91 Farnborough Road, GU14 6TL
(on A325, S of centre)
☼ 11-11; 12-10.30 Sun
☎ (01252) 554654
Courage Best Bitter; guest beers Ⓗ
Basic, Victorian pub named after the first landlord. Situated near the end of the runway, the walls are adorned with pictures from the biennial Farnborough Airshow. The single bar serves two rooms: a public bar where pool and darts can be played, and a large, simply furnished lounge, incorporating a raised dining/no-smoking area. Up to six beers are served, from a mix of national, regional and micro-breweries. Sky TV is available. ⊯❍⊕♣P⊬

Thatched Cottage
122 Prospect Road, GU14 9NU
☼ 11.30-11; 12-10.30 Sun
☎ (01252) 543118
Courage Best Bitter, Directors; guest beers Ⓗ
Aptly-named, friendly pub, about 10 minutes' walk from the main shopping centre. It has the feel of a country pub, reflected in its mostly local trade, and is handy for Farnborough Town Football Club. Either side of the TV bar there are areas with tables, sometimes used for dining. Games are chosen from the toy box on Monday evening. Due to the age of the Cottage, you may find that height restrictions apply. ❀❍≉P

FREEFOLK

Watership Down
Freefolk Priors, RG28 7NJ (off B3400)
☼ 11.30-3, 6-11; 12-3, 7-10.30 Sun
☎ (01256) 892254
Young's Bitter; guest beers Ⓗ
Welcoming free house, named after the famous book by local author, Richard Adams. The story of the rabbits is set in the downland to the north of the pub. Five handpumps serve a changing range of small brewers' beers, always including a real mild

179

– rare in this area. Two rooms house displays of pump clips, awards and an impressive array of penny arcade machines. Buses stop near this local CAMRA Pub of the Year 2002, which is popular with walkers and cyclists.
🏮🌓🚶♣P⅊🕆

FRITHAM

Royal Oak ⊘
SO43 7HJ (1 mile S of B3078) OS232141
🕙 11.30-2.30 (11-3 summer), 6-11; 11-11 Sat ; 12-10.30 Sun
☎ (023) 8081 2606
Hop Back Summer Lightning; Ringwood Best Bitter, Fortyniner; guest beers Ⓖ
Small, thatched pub at the end of a New Forest track, many times local CAMRA's Pub of the Year. One main bar, with several levels of interconnected rooms feature black beams and bare floors. Lunchtime food is typically ploughmans, soup or quiche. A Supper Club operates Monday and occasionally other evenings (check in advance). In summer the vast garden hosts barbecues, hog roasts and a mid-September beer festival. It is perfect for walkers, cyclists or equestrians (facilities provided); dogs abound.
🏮Q🌓🅰♣

FROXFIELD

Trooper Inn
Alton Road, GU32 1BD
(3 miles from Petersfield) OS727273
🕙 12-3, 6-11; 12-3, 7-10.30 Sun
☎ (01730) 827293 website: www.trooperinn.com
Cheriton Pots Ale; Ringwood Best Bitter; guest beers Ⓗ
Remote but friendly free house that serves four beers from independent breweries. Set high up in Hampshire's rolling countryside, it draws a mixed clientele, but is popular with the country set. The atmosphere is enhanced by the candlelit bar and tables. Worth seeking out for the food alone, the extensive menu varies on a monthly basis. The restaurant is open from 8am for breakfast, although booking is essential. Walls are adorned with paintings from local artists, some for sale.
🏮🌓🚲🅐P

GOSPORT

Clarence Tavern
1 Clarence Road, PO12 1BB
🕙 11-11; 12-10.30 Sun
☎ (023) 9252 9726
Oakleaf Bitter, Hole Hearted, Blake's Gosport Bitter Ⓗ
Brewery tap for the Oakleaf Brewery across the road, with some brewing capacity on the premises, this pub won its first local CAMRA award in 2002. It comprises a main bar area, a restaurant and function room. At busy times, there are additional guest beers from Oakleaf and other breweries; beer festivals are held over the Easter and August bank holidays. A folk group meets on Wednesday evening. No food is served Sunday evening; occasional special events, such as 'medieval' banquets, are staged.
🏮Q🌓🅐⅄♣P⅊

Queen's Hotel
143 Queen's Road, PO12 1LG
🕙 11.30-2.30, 7-11; 11.30-11 Sat; 12-3, 7-10.30 Sun
☎ (023) 9258 2645
Badger Tanglefoot; Rooster's Yankee; Young's Bitter; guest beers Ⓗ
Popular, back-street local enjoying a national reputation; this genuine free house has won many CAMRA awards. The licensee has been here since 1983 and in this Guide since 1986. The bar is divided into three drinking areas, but the focal point is an old open fire with an elegant, carved wood surround. Two guest beers are normally available from the Beer Seller's list, while a sixth handpump dispenses real cider in summer and a dark beer in winter.
🏮♣

GREYWELL

Fox & Goose
The Street, RG29 1BY
🕙 11-11; 12-10.30 Sun
☎ (01256) 702062
Courage Best Bitter; Gale's HSB; Oakleaf Bitter Ⓗ
Popular, 16th-century pub set in an attractive village, a short distance from Basingstoke Canal; an ideal stop in a good walking area. Very child-friendly, customers with well-behaved dogs are also welcome in the pub and garden. A large field behind the pub is used for various village events. A variety of traditional pub games is available, along with a selection of local newspapers.
🏮Q🌓🅐🅰♣P🕆

HAMBLEDON

Bat & Ball ⊘
Hyden Farm Lane, Clanfield, PO8 0UB (2½ miles from village on Clanfield road)) OS677167
🕙 11.30-3 (12-3 Sat), 6-11; 12-4, 7-10.30 Sun
☎ (023) 9263 2692
Gale's Butser, GB, HSB Ⓗ
Remote pub, high on Broadhalfpenny Down, opposite the famous ground known as the cradle of cricket. The pub is now a museum for the great game, displaying memorabilia from both local and national teams. One wall commemorates the monument erected next to the ground and another has the lyrics of a song by Richard Stillgoe marking the visit of the late Brian Johnson to the ground and pub.
🏮🌓🅐♣P

Vine
West Street, PO7 4RW
🕙 11.30-3.30, 6-11; 12-4.30, 7-10.30 Sun
☎ (023) 9263 2419
Gale's Butser; Ringwood Best Bitter; Taylor Landlord; Wells Bombardier; guest beer Ⓗ
Village pub built in the 16th century, it now has a single bar serving several distinct drinking areas. This beamed pub boasts old fireplaces and a glass-covered well within the bar area. The walls and ceiling are covered in bric-à-brac, mainly relating to country life. It has a relaxed, friendly atmosphere with clientele being mainly local. A shove-ha'penny board is fixed to one wall. No meals are served Sunday evening.
🏮Q🌓🅐♣⅄

HAMMER VALE

Prince of Wales
Hammer Lane, GU27 1QH (1 mile S of A3, ½ mile from B3121) OS868326
✪ 12-3, 6-11; 12-11 Sat; 12-10.30 Sun
☎ (01428) 652600
Gale's Butser, HSB, seasonal beers; guest beers G

Set in a wooded valley near Haslemere, the present building was designed by the daughter of George Gale and was built in 1927. Inside, the long bar runs from the public bar, with its refectory type tables and wood-burning stove, to the compact restaurant area. Interesting food is well priced, and always served with fresh vegetables (evening meals Tue–Sat). The large children's play area and patio seating are ideal for families; ramblers are welcome. ♨Q✿◗◱&▲♣P

HARTLEY WINTNEY

Waggon & Horses
High Street, RG27 8NY
✪ 11-11; 12-10.30 Sun
☎ (01252) 842119
Courage Best Bitter; Gale's HSB; guest beers H

Village pub where a lively public bar contrasts well with the smaller, quieter lounge. A winner of many local CAMRA awards, the landlady serves good value food at lunchtime. Although prone to being absolutely packed on weekend evenings, it is still a great place for refreshment after browsing through the many antique shops that crowd the village. At the rear of the pub is a pleasant courtyard garden. ♨Q✿◗◱♣🍴

HAVANT

Old House at Home ✓
2 South Street, PO9 1DA
✪ 11-11; 12-10.30 Sun
☎ (023) 9248 3464
Gale's Butser, GB, HSB, seasonal beers; guest beers H

Despite the date carved in the outside wall, this brick and timber building behind the church dates from the 16th century. Originally five cottages, it was a bakery, then finally a two-bar pub. The public bar has some interesting antiques and the post to which the last dancing bear in England was reputedly tethered. The larger lounge boasts a splendid open fireplace. The pub can be particularly busy on Saturday evening when live music is performed. No meals Sunday evening. ♨✿◗◱♣🍴

Robin Hood
6 Homewell, PO9 1EE
✪ 11-11; 12-10.30 Sun
☎ (023) 9248 2779
Gale's Butser, HSB, Festival Mild, seasonal beers, G **guest beers** H

Surprisingly large, single-bar pub at the centre of town, opposite the church. Unusually for this area, all the regular beers are served direct from their casks mounted on individual trollies behind the bar. A solitary handpump is used for the guest beers. The pub is a rare but regular outlet for Festival Mild. Water from the nearby underground stream was reputedly used for making the parchment for the Magna Carta and the Treaty of Versailles. ♨✿◗≈

HAWKLEY

Hawkley Inn
Pococks Lane, GU33 6NE OS747291
✪ 12-2.30 (3 Sat), 6-11; 12-3, 7-10.30 Sun
☎ (01730) 827205
Beer range varies H

Considering its rural location, this pub is surprisingly busy. Maybe the six regularly rotating beers (all from small breweries) and the landlord's own cider, Swamp Donkey, account for its popularity. A single bar serves two small but distinct areas (one no-smoking). One of the two fireplaces has a moose's head above it, complete with hat and cigarette! Live music is played most Saturday evenings in winter; a beer festival is held in June. Lunches are served daily, evening meals Monday–Saturday. Portsmouth & South-East Hampshire CAMRA Pub of the Year 2003. ♨Q✿◗◍🍴

HEADLEY

Hollybush
High Street, GU35 8PP (on B3002, W of Borden)
✪ 11-3, 5-11; 11-11 Sat; 12-4, 7-10.30 Sun
☎ (01428) 712211
Courage Best Bitter; Gale's HSB; Greene King IPA; guest beer H

This Victorian pub has a central bar, with a single, airy drinking area, and a no-smoking restaurant. Families are welcome and are drawn to the large garden in summer. The guest beer changes monthly and good food is served 12–2 and 6.30–9, except Sunday evening. A bus service runs from Farnham and Haslemere – even on Sunday. Difficult to spot if motoring; the pub is on a tight bend. ♨✿🛏◗&♣P

HOOK

Crooked Billet ✓
London Road, RG27 9EH
(on A30, approx. 1 mile E of Hook)
✪ 11.30-3, 6-11; 12-3, 7-10.30 Sun
☎ (01256) 762118
Courage Best Bitter, Directors; guest beers H

Spacious, roadside pub, built on the site of an older property that used to house the navvies working on the nearby Basingstoke Canal. A large lounge is complemented by a smaller dining area to one side. Guest beers are usually from Lake District micro-breweries. On the August bank holiday weekend, a plastic duck race is held on the River Whitewater that runs alongside the pleasant garden. ♨Q✿◗♣P

HORNDEAN

Brewers Arms
1 Five Heads Road, PO8 9NW
✪ 12-2 (not Mon; 12-4 Sat); 5 (6 Sat)-11; 12-3, 7-10.30 Sun
☎ (023) 9259 1325
Draught Bass; Courage Directors; Fuller's London Pride; Ringwood Best Bitter; guest beers H

Pre-war, half-brick tiled pub, set back off the main Portsmouth Road; it is referred to by regulars as 'a proper pub' – a genuine local where people come to drink and talk. See plans in the lounge of the previous 1929 layout, prior to internal alterations carried out by previous owners, Gale's, in the early 1970s. Four regular beers are stocked, plus two guest ales which go on each Friday night, generally from small breweries. Q❀♿⊟♣P

Ship & Bell ⊘
6 London Road, PO8 0BZ
✪ 11-11; 12-10.30 Sun
☎ (023) 9259 2107
Gale's Butser, GB, HSB, seasonal beers; guest beers Ⓗ
Gale's Brewery tap. This former 17th-century coaching inn is the site of the original Gale's Brewery. The current Victorian brewery is right next door. There are two bars; off the lounge bar is a restaurant, which is also the breakfast room for the pub's 15 en-suite rooms. The larger public bar has a large-screen TV for sporting occasions, and can be quite lively with the younger set weekend evenings. No meals are served Sunday evening. Q⇔◖⊟P✂

HORSEBRIDGE

John O' Gaunt
SO20 6PU (½ mile W of A3057) OS346304
✪ 11-2.30 (3 Fri & Sat), 6-11; 12-3, 7-10.30 Sun
☎ (01794) 388394
Palmer IPA; Ringwood Best Bitter, Fortyniner Ⓗ
Victorian building, opened just before completion of the railway – the long-lamented LSWR Andover to Southampton line. Definitely a pub, not a restaurant, but it offers an extensive, frequently-changing and popular menu. To guarantee 'pubiness', tables cannot be booked and credit cards are eschewed. The food is mostly home-cooked local produce, frequently featuring game. Set in the idyllic Test Valley, the pub is often busy with practitioners of country pursuits – the bar even supplies trout flies! ⛺Q◖P

LANGSTONE

Ship Inn ⊘
Langstone Road, PO9 1RD
✪ 11-11; 12-10.30 Sun
☎ (023) 9247 1719
Gale's Butser, GB, HSB, seasonal beers; guest beers Ⓗ
This large single-bar pub overlooks Langstone Harbour, a popular yachting venue. The much-missed Hayling Island branch line and the old Roman Wade Way crossed the water to Hayling Island nearby. Until 1963 you could view the diminutive train carrying holidaymakers over the swing bridge and the pub's first patrons could have watched wagons being loaded on to the Isle of Wight train ferry (ceased in 1888). Nowadays, the pub is a watering-hole for the many attractive local walks, including the old railway line. ⛺❀◖♿ΔP✂

LINWOOD

Red Shoot ⊘
Toms Lane, BH24 3QT (3 miles E of A338, Ellingham Cross) OS187094
✪ 11-3, 6-11; 11-11 Sat & summer; 12-10.30 Sun
☎ (01425) 475792 website: www.redshootinn.co.uk

Red Shoot Forest Gold, Tom's Tipple; Wadworth IPA, 6X, seasonal beers Ⓗ
Spacious pub, where the multi-level, L-shaped bar is divided into distinct areas. The tiny brewery plant, visible from the bar, is used to produce two regular beers, as well as special brews for the beer festivals held in April and October. Other events include a music quiz (Thu) and live music on Sunday. Excellent value food is served daily. ⛺Q☜❀◖ΔP

LITTLE LONDON

Plough Inn
Silchester Road, RG26 5EP
(1 mile off A340, S of Tadley)
✪ 12-2.30, 6-11; 12-3, 7-10.30 Sun
☎ (01256) 850628
Ringwood Best Bitter, XXXX Porter, Fortyniner; Ⓗ **guest beers** Ⓖ
Village pub where you will find no loud music or other distractions, just an informal atmosphere in a sympathetically restored cottage. In winter porter is served. A good range of baguettes is available lunchtime and evenings (except Sun eve) and jacket potatoes are served on quiz night (third Mon of month). Musicians perform popular songs every second Monday of the month. It is ideally located for ramblers visiting the Roman ruins at Silchester or Pamber Wood. ⛺Q☜❀♿♣P

LONG SUTTON

Four Horseshoes
The Street, RG29 1TA
(1 mile E of village) OS748471
✪ 12-2.30, 6.30-11; 12-3, 7-10.30 Sun
☎ (01256) 862488 website: www.fourhorseshoes.com
Fuller's London Pride; Gale's Butser, HSB; guest beers Ⓗ
East of Long Sutton village, this hostelry is everything a rural pub should be. The single bar and separate family area welcome everyone. Good food (not served Sun eve) complements three regular and two guest beers that invariably include a mild. A regular meeting point for the local car club, the large garden offers good views and a petanque terrain. Its appearance in many CAMRA guides underlines its wide appeal and ensures people keep coming back. ⛺Q☜❀⇔Δ♣P

LOWER UPHAM

Woodman
Winchester Road, SO32 1HA OS524194
✪ 12-2.30 (5.30 Sat), 7-11; 12-5.30, 7.15-10.30 Sun
☎ (01489) 860270
Greene King IPA; guest beers Ⓗ
The public and lounge bars, equally welcoming, are in contrasting styles: one plain and a haven for conversation, the other cottagey and more intimate. In summer fine floral displays bring a blaze of colour to the front of the pub. More than 200 malt whiskies are on offer. A quiz is staged every Tuesday evening, and live blues on the first Wednesday of the month. Stagecoach bus No. 69 (Winchester to Bishop's Waltham, Fareham and Southsea) stops within 100 yards. ⛺❀⊟♣P♟

MICHELDEVER STATION

Dove Inn

Andover Road, SO21 3AU (signed off A303)
🕐 11.30-3 (not Mon; 11.30-4 Sat), 6-11;
12-3, 7-10.30 Sun
☎ (01962) 774288

Fuller's London Pride; Ringwood Best Bitter; guest beer Ⓗ

Situated next to the main Winchester–Waterloo railway line, the bare-boarded bar is spacious and features a comfortable corner, complete with three-piece suite. The bar is separated from the adjacent games room by a large open fire that warms both areas. Traditional English food is served in the bar, while a Thai themed restaurant is also attached (serving meals eves only, not Sun). ♨⊛🛏◑≠P

MILFORD-ON-SEA

Red Lion ⊘

32 High Street, SO41 0QD
🕐 11.30-2.30, 7-11; 12-3, 7-10.30 Sun
☎ (01590) 642236 website: www.redlionmilford.co.uk

Cheriton Best Bitter; Fuller's London Pride; Ringwood seasonal beers Ⓗ

Friendly, comfortable village-centre pub. The large main bar provides a number of discrete areas, without losing a sense of space. The no-smoking dining area is available for drinkers after food service is finished. A central ramp facilitates wheelchair access. The games room, converted from the old stable block, is well integrated into the main bar. The large garden at the rear is isolated from passing traffic, peaceful and colourful.
♨Q⊛🛏◑&♣P

OAKHANGER

Red Lion

GU35 9JQ (2 miles W of A325) OS770360
🕐 11-3, 6-11; 12-3, (closed eve) Sun
☎ (01420) 472232

Courage Best Bitter, Directors; guest beer Ⓗ

Very traditional, rural hostelry boasting an increasingly rare feature – a true public bar. Wood-panelled, adorned by hop bines and with a log fire in the winter – you will not want to leave. An open fire is also a feature of the more refined and food-oriented lounge bar, which, like the rest of the pub, has a relaxed atmosphere. Children are not allowed in the bar but can enjoy the garden and play area. ♨Q⊛◑⊖♣P

OLD BASING

Bolton Arms

91 The Street, RG24 7DA
🕐 11.30-2.30, 5.30 (6 Sat)-11; 12-3 (closed eve) Sun
☎ (01256) 322085 website: www.boltonarms.com

Courage Best Bitter; guest beers Ⓗ

Olde-worlde inn, with a traditional black and white frontage. Parts of the 16th-century pub were built using bricks from the nearby Old Basing House, besieged by Oliver Cromwell. The two beamed bars have low level lighting and copper-topped tables. A secluded garden is at the rear. A barn has been well converted to provide a no-smoking restaurant and a skittle alley. This popular village pub provides guest beers from local micro-breweries. ⊛◑&P

PENNINGTON (LYMINGTON)

Musketeer

26 North Street, SO41 8FZ
(off A337, at White Hart roundabout)
🕐 11.30-3, 5.30-11; 12-3, 7-10.30 Sun
☎ (01590) 676527

Ringwood Best Bitter, Fortyniner; Young's Bitter; guest beer Ⓗ

This imposing brick and tile detached building is an example of that increasingly rare breed, a genuine free house, run by the same family for all of its 24 appearances in this Guide. The home-cooked food, served Monday–Saturday, is excellent and very good value. The log fire is cosy in winter; the small patio is warmed by the sun. The family room houses the dartboard. ♨◑♣P

PETERSFIELD

Good Intent ⊘

40-46 College Street, GU31 4AF
🕐 11-3, 5.30-11; 12-3, 7-10.30 Sun
☎ (01730) 263838 website: www.thegoodintent.com

Gale's Butser, GB, HSB, seasonal beers; guest beers Ⓗ

Just off the town centre, this 16th-century, oak-beamed pub is known as the country pub in the town. The single bar serves a split-level room with candlelit tables. Hop bines hang from the beams and two log fires set the scene. Further rooms leading off the main room, include the restaurant. The pub has won awards for its food, including fresh fish (weekends), and is well known for its sausages. Live music is performed Sunday evening. ♨⊛🛏◑≠P⅙

PICKET PIECE (ANDOVER)

Wyke Down Country Pub & Restaurant ⊘

SP11 7QL (follow signs for Wyke Down from A303)
🕐 11-2.30, 6-11 (may vary); 12-3, 6-10.30 Sun
☎ (01264) 352048 website: www.wykedown.co.uk

Exmoor Ale; guest beers Ⓗ

The main part of the pub is housed in a converted 19th-century barn, to which has been added a modern, well-appointed restaurant; excellent food is served throughout. A large, comfortable, conservatory and adjacent games rooms complete the indoor facilities. Outside is a children's play area and a golf driving range. A large year-round camping site, complete with enclosed outdoor swimming pool, also forms part of the complex. Some hard-standing pitches are available for caravans. ♨⛺⊛◑♠&♣P

PORTSMOUTH

Druids Arms

11-15 Binsteed Road, PO2 7PH
🕐 12-11; 12-10.30 Sun
☎ (023) 9266 5936

Gale's GB, HSB, Festival Mild Ⓗ

Lively, street-corner local in a mainly residential part of town. The surprisingly large public bar has darts and pool. It hosts regular live music evenings and a Friday evening disco with records from the 1950s to the present day. The smaller lounge is comfortable. The patio is used for barbecues and similar functions, thanks to its purpose-built kitchen. Winner of local CAMRA's

Most Improved Pub award 2002, it is a rare outlet for Festival Mild in the city. ✿♣♠

Fifth Hampshire Volunteer Arms
74 Albert Road, Southsea, PO5 2SL
🕐 12-11; 12-10.30 Sun
☎ (023) 9282 7161
Gale's GB, Winter Brew, HSB; guest beer Ⓗ
Popular pub in an area of Southsea, blessed with several good pubs and a variety of restaurants. The public bar features TV sport, darts, a rock juke box and an eclectic collection of tin hats. By contrast, the lounge bar is decorated with naval and military memorabilia and their collection of certificates presented by the local CAMRA branch (founded here in 1974). Guest beers are supplied through Gale's with Festival Mild making an occasional appearance.
Q❧🕩♠

Florence Arms
18-20 Florence Road, Southsea, PO5 2NE
🕐 11-11; 12-10.30 Sun
☎ (023) 9287 5700
Adnams Broadside; Ringwood Fortyniner; Young's Bitter, Special; guest beers Ⓗ
Although basically a street-corner pub, situated near the shops, seafront and the Southsea Gardens, this pub is more than 'traditional'. Maroon glazed tiles and etched windows characterise the exterior; inside are three quite distinct bars. One bar houses a pool table and a ceiling-mounted TV; another serves as a comfortable, quiet lounge, while the third, the largest, doubles as a restaurant and function room. Beers unusual to the area are featured. Evening meals are served weekdays.
◑◐❧♣

Florist
324 Fratton Road, Fratton, PO1 5JX
(opp. Lake Rd jct)
🕐 11-2, 5-11; 11-4, 4.30-11 Sat; 12-10.30 Sun
☎ (023) 9282 0289
Wadworth IPA, 6X, seasonal beers Ⓗ
Welcoming corner local, identifiable by its glazed brick exterior and witch's hat tower. The comfortable lounge bar has been recently refurbished and provides an area of calm away from the often bustling public bar with its thriving darts teams, juke box and pool table. Old photographs of the pub and local area adorn the walls, alongside certificates detailing funds raised for the local church at the annual May Fayre.
Q❧≠(Fratton)♣

Hole in the Wall
36 Great Southsea Street, Southsea, PO5 3BY
🕐 6 (5 Fri & Sat)-11; 6-10.30 Sun
☎ (023) 9229 8085
Oakleaf Nuptu'ale, Squirrel's Delight, Hole Hearted, seasonal beers Ⓗ
Converted restaurant, once called the Beeton Track, this small, back-street pub has attractive Victorian decor and candlelit tables. Next door is the student-dominated India Arms. It is a welcoming pub for those wanting a quiet pint. Reduced price four-pint jugs are available before 9pm and

Belgian beers are stocked. A popular quiz is held on Thursday evening; well worth a visit. ≠(Portsmouth & Southsea)●⊁♉

Isambard Kingdom Brunel ⊘
2 Guildhall Walk, Southsea, PO1 2DD
🕐 10-11; 12-10.30 Sun
☎ (023) 9229 5112
Courage Directors; Hampshire seasonal beers; Hop Back Summer Lightning; Oakleaf Blake's Gosport Bitter; Theakston Best Bitter Ⓗ
This Wetherspoon's has graced the Portsmouth pub scene since 1996. Its appeal lies not just in the war memorials in the entrance, nor its Victorian architecture, but also in the friendliness and efficiency of the staff, plus the beer range sourced, unusually, from local breweries. The sympathetically refurbished bar has a raised no-smoking seating area. Extremely popular, it can be crowded in the evenings during university term time. It has appeared in each edition of this Guide since 1996.
Q❧◑◐♿≠(Portsmouth & Southsea)●⊁

Old Oyster House
291 Locksway Road, Milton, Southsea, PO4 8LH (off A288, near university's Langstone site)
🕐 12-11; 12-10.30 Sun
☎ (023) 9282 7456
Beer range varies Ⓗ
Traditional drinkers' pub, where four real ales and a scrumpy (Thatchers) are always available. Beers are supplied by small and national breweries. The pub sits by the only remaining section of Portsea Canal, and takes its name from the oyster beds in Langstone Harbour. The pub was built in 1930 next to the original oyster house, and bears a nautical theme; worth seeking out.
🚗✿♣●

Red, White & Blue
150 Fawcett Road, Southsea, PO4 0DW
🕐 11-11; 12-10.30 Sun
☎ (023) 9278 0013
Gale's Butser, GB, Winter Brew, HSB Ⓗ
Small, street-corner local where the single bar is decorated with bank notes, military badges and equine artefacts. Football fans are welcome whatever their allegiance. Food is only served on Saturday lunchtime and on Canada Day in July when breakfast is served, washed down with moose's milk. A wide variety of board games is played, including uckers – a form of killer ludo played to naval rules. Live jazz is played each Wednesday evening.
Q≠(Fratton)♣

Winchester Arms
99 Winchester Road, Buckland, PO2 7PS
🕐 12 (4 Mon)-11; 12-10.30 Sun
☎ (023) 9266 2443
Oakleaf Nuptu'ale, Hole Hearted, Blake's Gosport Bitter, seasonal beers Ⓗ
Friendly, back-street local, refurbished as part of the Winchester Ale Houses chain in 1999. Former home of the defunct Buckland Brewery, now owned by Innspired, it has one large main bar with a cosy snug and a patio. The pub serves up to five of the regular Oakleaf Brewery beers, along with seasonal offerings.

Sunday lunches need to be booked by the previous Friday.
🏠Q☸◑♣✄

ROMSEY

Abbey Hotel
11 Church Street, SO51 7DE
☺ 11-3, 6-11; 12-3, 7-10.30 Sun
☎ (01794) 513360
website: www.abbeyhotelromsey.co.uk
Courage Best Bitter, Directors H

This 19th-century pub stands opposite Romsey Abbey, close to the tourist information office and King John's house. The Victorian-style interior is split into two areas, one for drinkers and one aimed at diners; in both sections conversation rules except during the Sunday evening quiz, when no food is served. Hampshire Brewery's bottled Pride of Romsey augments the choice of real ales. Services of varying frequency depart from the nearby bus station to Southampton, Winchester, Salisbury and the New Forest.
🏠Q☸≠◑⇌P

Star
13 Horsefair, SO51 8EZ
☺ 11.30-3, 5.30-11; 12-10.30 Sun
☎ (01794) 516353
Wadworth IPA, 6X, JCB, seasonal beers H

The Star stands near the former entrance to the once great, but long-defunct, Strong's Brewery, where just the tower, maltings and offices remain. The 17th-century pub has a single bar, one end of which contains an inglenook, sofa and armchair. It attracts an eclectic crowd and the occasional (non-malevolent) spirit. Live folk music is staged on alternate Saturday evenings, and a quiz on Sunday evening. Photographs of old Romsey abound. A Sunday roast lunch is served. 🏠☸≠⇌♣

Tudor Rose
3 Cornmarket, SO51 8GB
☺ 10 (11 Tue-Thu)-11; 12-4, 7-10.30 Sun
☎ (01794) 512126
website: www.tudorroseromsey.co.uk
Courage Best Bitter; guest beer H

Modest, town-centre, single-bar pub with a varied history: previously a guildhall, brothel and workhouse. The impressive bar, with original, 15th-century oak beams and handsome fireplace, attracts a wide range of customers, especially on Friday when the weekly guest ale appears. A folk group performs on the first Sunday of the month. Reasonably-priced food is served at lunchtime Monday–Saturday, and on summer evenings. It has appeared in this Guide 29 times in 31 years. 🏠☸◑

William IV
45 Latimer Street, SO51 8DF
☺ 11-11; 12-5, 6-10.30 Sun
☎ (01794) 521831
Fuller's London Pride; Hampshire Strong's Best Bitter H

First time in this Guide for a basic town pub, situated between the twon centre and railway station. Run by a friendly Scot with a most un-Hampshire accent, the pub is set back to provide a small car park. Inside, a large split-level room is enhanced by an unusual angled fireplace behind the front

door, creating a cosy corner at the end of the bar. The upper level has a pool table, juke box and large-screen TV.
🏠≈♣P

ROWLAND'S CASTLE

Castle ✓
1 Finchdean Road, PO9 6DA
☺ 11-3, 5-11; 11-11 Fri & Sat; 12-10.30 Sun
☎ (023) 9241 2494
Gale's Butser, GB, HSB; guest beers H

Typical village pub, tucked behind the railway bridge, by the entrance to Stansted House. It has two bars, both with open fires and bare boards or flagstones. The public bar is traditional, while the second bar is split into two, separated by a central open fireplace. This room doubles as a pleasant restaurant, serving daily lunches and evening meals, Tuesday–Saturday. The large, fenced garden, is safe for small children. Wheelchair access is via the rear entrance. 🏠Q☸◑♿≈♣P

ST MARY BOURNE

Coronation Arms ✓
SP11 6AR (on B3048, on NW side of village)
☺ 11-3, 6.30-11 (11-11 summer Sat); 12-3, 7-10.30 (12-10.30 summer) Sun
☎ (01264) 738432
Draught Bass; Ringwood Best Bitter, Fortyniner; guest beer H

In one of Hampshire's prettiest villages, this genuine free house is a popular meeting place for locals and visitors alike. The spacious bar, with its log fire, is the main drinking area. Two further rooms serve as dining areas. A large, well-kept garden with a play area is a bonus. Good home-cooked food is served at all sessions, except Sunday evening. The pub name commemorates the coronation of Edward VII in 1901, the year the pub was rebuilt after a fire. 🏠☸≠◑♣P

SELBORNE

Selborne Arms
High Street, GU34 3JR
☺ 11-3, 6 (5.30 Fri)-11 (11-11 summer Sat); 12-10.30 Sun
☎ (01420) 511247 website: www.selbornearms.co.uk
Cheriton Pots Ale; Courage Best Bitter; Ringwood Fortyniner; guest beers H

Ancient building situated at the foot of Selborne Hanger and near the Wakes Museum, home of Gilbert White, and the mouth and foot painting artists' gallery. The guest beers in this free of tie house, feature local micro-breweries' beer and the food is widely known for its quality. The extensive grassed drinking areas and a children's play space can become very busy in summer.
🏠Q☸◑⊟P

SHALDEN

Golden Pot
Odiham Road, GU34 4DJ (on B3349)
☺ 12-11; 12-10.30 Sun
☎ (01420) 80655
Greene King IPA, Ruddles Best, Abbot, Old Speckled Hen; guest beer H

A Greene King acquisition, this pub demonstrates what their beer should taste like. The pub is an 1860s rebuild, after a fire, on a slightly different site. The name is derived frm the local area, whose origin is the subject of whimsical theories. In the light, airy L-shaped bar the exposed beams are entirely cosmetic. The pub has a growing reputation for its food at competitive prices (not served Sun eve). The large garden houses children's play equipment. ▲⊛◖P

SHEDFIELD

Wheatsheaf Inn
Botley Road, SO32 2JG (on A334)
☼ 12-11; 12-10.30 Sun
☎ (01329) 833024
Cheriton Pots Ale, Village Elder, Diggers Gold; guest beers Ⓖ

Lively and friendly pub with a comfortable public bar and a small lounge. Beer is served straight from the casks which are mounted on an impressive tiered stillage behind the bar. The real cider varies. Dogs on leads are allowed in the garden and public bar; children may be permitted in the lounge. The car park is opposite. Take care of the dangerous main road when entering or leaving. Q⊛◖♣●P

SHEET

Queen's Head
Sheet Green, GU32 2AH
☼ 12-2.30, 5.30 (6 Sat)-11; 12-3, 7-10.30 Sun
☎ (01730) 264204
Fuller's London Pride; Hampshire Strong's Best Bitter, Ironside; guest beer Ⓗ

Typical local, in a pleasant setting, next to the village green. The public bar is 400 years old with a stone floor, exposed beams and a log fire. The lounge was added later (the front part was once the village butcher's). The restaurant, open Tuesday–Saturday evenings, has an Italian chef who serves up traditional dishes from his country. The pub has been run by the same family since 1959. ▲Q⊛◖⌂♣P

SHERFIELD ON LODDON

White Hart
Old Reading Road, RG27 0BT (100 yds off A33)
☼ 11-2.30, 6-11; 12-10.30 Sun
☎ (01256) 882280
Courage Best Bitter; guest beers Ⓗ

Traditional country pub dating from the 18th century, on an old coaching route. The open-plan main bar is dominated by a large fireplace. There are also two dining areas, one is no-smoking and admits children. The kitchen specialises in home-made food with lots of daily specials. This free house offers two guest beers, normally from the smaller breweries, changing regularly. At the rear is a large garden. ▲Q⊛◖♿P

SILCHESTER

Calleva Arms
Little London Road, RG7 2PH
☼ 11-3, 5.30-11; 11-11 Sat; 12-10.30 Sun
☎ (0118) 970 0305
Gale's Butser, GB, HSB, seasonal beers; guest beers Ⓗ

Standing by a well-used village green, the pub is popular with cyclists and walkers. It is also an attraction for visitors to the

186

remains of the Roman town of Calleva Atrebatum, which boasts some fine examples of town walls around the settlement that can be walked; do not miss the amphitheatre. Parts of the pub date back to the 18th century. A pleasant conservatory has been added for non-smokers wanting a quiet drink (no music here), and there is a large garden. ▲Q☽◖♿♣P✍

SOUTHAMPTON

Bitter Virtue (off licence)
70 Cambridge Road, Portswood, SO14 6US
☼ 10.30-8.30; closed Mon; 10.30-2 Sun
☎ (023) 8055 4881 website: www.bittervirtue.co.uk
Beer range varies Ⓖ

Independent beer shop with up to 300 bottled beers available, together with glasses, T-shirts and some books. The cider range is limited but of good quality. Bottles from Belgium, Britain and Germany dominate the shelves, specialising in micro-breweries – especially local ones. A selection of gueuze is always available. At least one draught beer is always on tap, with well over 100 beers served to date.

Crown Inn
9 Highcrown Street, Highfield, SO17 1DE
☼ 11-11; 12-10.30 Sun
☎ (023) 8031 5033
Draught Bass; Boddingtons Bitter; Flowers Original; Fuller's London Pride; Hampshire Strong's Best Bitter; Ringwood Best Bitter Ⓗ

Large brick pub, close to the university and common, tucked away down an alley. The single bar has a country feel but avoids being like a large barn. It draws a mix of locals and academics, whether eating out, watching the pub TV or just meeting for a drink and chat. The covered patio has canvas sides and gas heating for winter use. Children under 14 are not admitted. ⊛◖P

Dolphin ⊘
30 Osborne Road South, St Denys, SO17 2EZ (by footbridge from St Denys Station)
☼ 12-11; 12-10.30 Sun
☎ (023) 8039 9369
Adnams Bitter; Gale's HSB; Taylor Landlord; guest beers Ⓗ

Single bar, but with several distinctive, comfortable corners. Live music is provided at least twice a week, mainly by local groups and musicians, to appeal to a wide range of tastes. Customers range from mature locals to students. The landlord offers an ever-changing range of guest ales and always has a Wychwood beer on tap. The delicious food is all cooked by the landlady. The large garden provides a pleasant summer drinking environment. ▲⊛◖≠(St Denys) P✍

Endeavour
7 Simnel Street, SO14 2BE
☼ 11-2.30, 6-11; 12-2.30, 6-10.30 Sun
☎ (023) 8021 1879
Greene King XX Mild, IPA, seasonal beers Ⓗ

Named after the losing 1934 America's Cup challenger, this recently refurbished and redecorated pub offers a welcome beer oasis within a short walk of the West Quay shopping centre. The home-made food is excellent value, with vegetarian options always available; on Sunday a roast lunch is served. Strong Suffolk Ale is available in bottles – and on draught when possible. The bar billiards table is an unusual sight in a city pub. Q ⌂ ◖◗

Guide Dog ⊘
38 Earl's Road, SO14 6SF
🕑 11-11; 12-10.30 Sun
☎ (023) 8022 5642
Beer range varies 🅷

Recently established free house, having been sold by Wadworth. This small, back-street local offers an ever-changing range of guest beers, with a bias towards local breweries, such as Itchen Valley and Cheriton. Darts teams, meat draws and raffles are well supported by locals. About 10 minutes from the St Mary's Stadium, food is available only on match days. A basic, but comfortable pub, only quiet background music and conversation distract from the quality of the beer. ♣

Humble Plumb ⊘
Commercial Street, Bitterne, SO18 6LY
🕑 11-3, 5-11; 11.30-11 Fri & Sat; 12-10.30 Sun
☎ (023) 8043 7577
Wadworth IPA, 🅷 **6X;** 🅖 **guest beers** 🅷

Formerly known as the Commercial, it was closed during most of the 1970s until a local builder added it to his small chain of pubs, and fitted it out with a split-level bar and a tiled roof over the serving counter. It was taken over by Wadworth a few years ago. Up to five guest beers from Wadworth and other regional brewers are available. The pub is frequented by locals and users of the nearby Bitterne Leisure Centre.
❀ ◖◗ P

Platform Tavern
Town Quay, SO14 2NY
🕑 12-11; 12-10.30 Sun
☎ (023) 8033 7232 website: www.platformtavern.com
Fuller's London Pride; Itchen Valley Godfathers; guest beers 🅷

This pub incorporates part of the original south walls of the city. 'Eclectic' describes almost every aspect of the pub, from its stunning African ornaments, leather lounge seating, wood-floored bar area, bewildering musical variety, both live and recorded, international cuisine and, most importantly, the range of guest beers from far and near. Live music is featured on Tuesday, Thursday and Sunday when a small surcharge is applied to drinks prices during the performance. Sunday meals are served 12–5. ◖◗

Richmond Inn ⊘
108 Portswood Road, Portswood, SO17 2FW
🕑 11-11; 12-10.30 Sun
☎ (023) 8055 4523
Greene King XX Mild, IPA, Abbot; guest beers 🅷

Two-bar, traditional town pub: a busy, boisterous public bar featuring darts, a juke box and TV; and a quieter, more comfortable lounge. The walls carry many pictures of ocean liners associated with Southampton, and other maritime art. Note the wonderful antique brass till shared between the two bars. To the rear, a pleasant secluded garden houses a function room. The long-established staff cheerfully

remove sparklers upon request.
❀ ⇌ (St Denys) ♣

South Western Arms
38-40 Adelaide Road, St Denys, SO17 2HW
(by St Denys Station)
🕑 4 (1.30 Fri; 12 Sat)-11; 12-10.30 Sun
☎ (023) 8032 4542
Badger Tanglefoot; Fuller's London Pride; Ringwood Best Bitter; Wadworth 6X; 🅷 **guest beers** 🅷/🅖

Large, two-storey pub where many corners provide a surprisingly intimate atmosphere. The landlord takes great pride in his constantly-changing range of beers, regularly stocking 10 or more. The pub won the local and regional CAMRA Pub of the Year award in 2002. Live music is featured at least once a month, and the juke box has a superb selection to suit all tastes. The patio garden provides a pleasant summer drinking venue.
❀ ⇌ (St Denys) P

Waterloo Arms
101 Waterloo Road, Freemantle, SO15 3BS
🕑 12-11; 12-10.30 Sun
☎ (023) 8022 0022
Hop Back GFB, Best Bitter, Crop Circle, Entire Stout, Summer Lightning; guest beers 🅷

Former Strong's pub and the first to join Salisbury's Wyndham Arms in Hop Back Brewery's small estate, this mock-Tudor building is just over half a mile from Central Station, although poorly served Millbrook is closer. The single L-shaped bar has light wood panelling and hosts a quiz night (Tue). Although gas, the coal-effect fires are convincing. Spring and autumn each year see a beer festival in the enclosed patio and garden to the rear.
❀ ◖◗ ⇌ (Millbrook) ♣

Wellington Arms
56 Park Road, Freemantle, SO15 3DF
🕑 12-11; 12-10.30 Sun
☎ (023) 8022 7356
Fuller's London Pride; Ringwood Best Bitter, Old Thumper; guest beers 🅷

Back-street, two-bar pub dating from the 1860s where a dimly lit, intimate atmosphere prevails; a shrine to the Iron Duke. Four guest beers and a good malt whisky selection are attractions. Customers can choose the wines stocked at tastings held every two months. Food is served in the bars or the no-smoking restaurant. Evening meals are served Thursday–Saturday. The landlord is a qualified signer for the deaf.
❀ ◖◗ ⇌ (Central/Millbrook)

STOKE

White Hart
SP11 0NP (off B3048)
🕑 12-2.30 (not Mon or Tue winter), 6-11 (may vary winter); 12-3, 7-10.30 Sun
☎ (01264) 738830
Cheriton Pots Ale; Worthington's 1744; guest beers 🅷

Spacious pub with a large garden set in the rural Bourne Valley. Following a closure in the late 1990s and a refusal for change of use to residential, the new owner has extensively refurbished the pub, however the bar area remains unaltered. There is a large dining area

and function room. Rural pubs in small villages like Stoke will disappear without support; this pub is well worth seeking out, but check opening times first, particularly in winter.
🏚Q❀◑♣P🖫

STUBBINGTON

Golden Bowler
122 Stubbington Lane, PO14 2NQ
✪ 11-11; 12-10.30 Sun
☎ (01329) 662845
Draught Bass; guest beers Ⓗ
Modern free house, originally a Victorian country house, attached to a nursery, which became a licensed premises in the 1960s. The present owners have been here for over 20 years. Normally three guest ales are available, including beers from local micro-breweries, such as Oakleaf and Portchester, and occasional dark beers in winter. The large main bar is supplemented by a restaurant and TV/function room. Children are welcome in some areas until 8pm. No evening meals are served Monday. ❀◑P⅄

TWYFORD

Phoenix
High Street, SO21 1RF
(on B3335, 1 mile S of M3 jct 11)
✪ 11.30-2.30 (3 Fri & Sat), 6-11; 12-3, 7-10.30 Sun
☎ (01962) 713322
Greene King IPA, Abbot; guest beer Ⓗ
The hub of village life; once a many-roomed wayside inn, it is now a single, comfortably-furnished room, entered from the car park. The dining area is no-smoking; one step down is the long bar space with stools for drinkers. The guest beer is from Greene King's limited selection. A good range of home-cooked food is available, including Sunday roasts. Accommodation can be arranged in nearby cottages – ask for introductions. Functions can be booked in the skittle alley. 🏚Q❀◑♣P⅄

UPPER CLATFORD

Crook & Shears
SP11 7QL (off A343, S of Andover)
✪ 12-3 (not Tue), 6-11; 12-3, 7-10.30 Sun
☎ (01264) 361543
Fuller's London Pride; Ringwood Fortyniner; Taylor Landlord; guest beer Ⓗ
Attractive, thatched 17th-century free house at the heart of a typical Hampshire village on the outskirts of Andover. The smaller of the two low-ceilinged bar rooms leads to a tiny dining area. The larger, bare-boarded bar is popular with locals, walkers and cyclists. Good quality food is served. A skittle alley, with its own bar, is available for functions when not being used by the pub's eight-team skittle league. Parking can be difficult. 🏚Q❀◑♣

UPPER FARRINGDON

Rose & Crown Inn
Crows Lane, GU34 3ED (off A32) OS715350
✪ 12-3, 6-11; 12-11 Sat; 12-10.30 Sun
☎ (01420) 588231
Adnams Bitter; Courage Best Bitter; Greene King IPA; Triple fff Stairway to Heaven; Worthington's 1744 Ⓗ
The village is off the beaten track and this

friendly pub is pretty well its only remaining amenity. The L-shaped bar progresses from a comfy seating area with magazines near the fire, through formal tables to a modern restaurant (no food Mon eve). Families are encouraged, with a large garden and a selection of boxed games in the bar. Food is a feature; an imaginative chalkboard restaurant selection is supplemented by lunchtime bar snacks. Dogs and walkers are welcomed. 🏚Q❀◑P

WEYHILL

Weyhill Fair ⊘
SP11 0PP (on A342, 3 miles W of Andover)
✪ 11.15-3, 6 (5 Fri)-11; 12-3, 7-10.30 Sun
☎ (01264) 773631 website: www.weyhillfair.co.uk
Fuller's Chiswick, London Pride, seasonal beers; guest beers Ⓗ
Popular free house serving an ever-changing range of guest beers. Once a private house, it was extended to provide accommodation for livestock drovers who attended the now-defunct fair. A field at the back provides space for camping (well used during the pub's annual beer festival in July). Families are welcome in the no-smoking dining area. Local CAMRA Pub of the Year 2003 and Regional Pub of the Year 2001. Buses stop outside; a cycle route runs from Andover to the pub. 🏚Q❀◑&Å♣P⅄🖫

WHITCHURCH

Prince Regent
104 London Road, RG28 7LT
✪ 11-11; 12-10.30 Sun
☎ (01256) 892179
Hop Back GFB, Summer Lightning; Otter Ale; guest beer Ⓗ
Unspoilt, traditional town pub where a warm welcome is assured. The single-bar pub stands above one of England's smallest towns and is well worth the walk up from The Square. The friendly landlord is always ready for a lively chat and takes great personal pride in the quality of the ale. The pub fields strong pool and quiz teams. Buses stop outside, serving the nearby towns of Basingstoke, Winchester and Andover. Parking is limited. Lunchtime snacks are available. ➤♣🕭P

Red House
21 London Street, RG28 7LH
✪ 11.30-3, 6-11; 12-3, 7-10.30 Sun
☎ (01256) 895558
Cheriton Pots Ale; guest beers Ⓗ
Unpretentious, 16th-century coaching inn that caters for all tastes. The flagstoned public bar, with its log fire and benches, contrasts with the pleasant, light and open lounge. Beers are always from local micro-breweries, and the pub is renowned for its high quality, home-cooked food at reasonable prices. The large garden has an area for young children. If visiting Whitchurch with its silk mill, fine walks and seven other pubs, the Red House should not be missed. 🏚Q❀◑🖭➤♣P

WINCHESTER

Bell ⊘
83 St Cross Road, St Cross, SO23 9RE
(on B3335)

✪ 11-3, 5-11 (11-11 Fri, Sat & summer); 12-4, 7-10.30 Sun
☎ (01962) 865284
Greene King IPA, Abbot; guest beer Ⓗ
Widely contrasting bars allow a choice of drinking area in this comfortable, traditional pub. A quiet, carpeted, conversational lounge complements a busy, cosmopolitan, flagstoned public. A large, safe garden with children's play equipment is reached via the public bar patio doors. The Bell adjoins the Hospital of St Cross, England's oldest (1132) almshouse. It is a tranquil mile's stroll from the city through water meadows that inspired Keats' To Autumn. Good food includes Sunday roasts (no meals Wed eve). ⌂Q✿ⓘ⊟♣P

Black Boy
1 Wharf Hill, SO23 9NQ (off B3330, Chesil St, near M3 jct 10)
✪ 11-3, 5-11; 12-3, 7-10.30 Sun
☎ (01962) 861754
Cheriton Pots Ale; Hop Back Summer Lightning; Ringwood Best Bitter; guest beers Ⓗ
Free house across the River Itchen from Wolvesey Palace. Centuries old, its L-shaped bar is divided by a central fireplace. An adjoining converted old barn is more spacious and has plenty of comfortable seating. An attractive patio garden is a bonus. The idiosyncratic decor displays old signs and engineering pieces, with ceilings covered in collections of spectacles, pocket watches and keys. Numerous table games can be played. Guest beers come from Hampshire breweries. No food Monday; evening meals are served Tuesday–Thursday. ⌂✿ⓘ♣

Fulflood Arms
28 Cheriton Road, SO22 5EF
✪ 12-2 (3 Sat), 5-11; 12-3, 6-10.30 Sun
☎ (01962) 622006 website: www.fulfloodarms.co.uk
Greene King IPA, Abbot; guest beer Ⓗ
This 19th-century pub, standing proudly on a street corner in a residential area, has a strong loyal local following. The attractive exterior, with much glazed brickwork, bears clear evidence of the pub's association with the long-departed Winchester Brewery. The single bar hosts a quiz every Wednesday evening. Live music of various styles is staged on the last Sunday in the month. ✿≢♣✂

Hyde Tavern
57 Hyde Street, SO23 7DY (on B3047)

✪ 12-2 (3 Sat), 5 (6 Sat)-11; 12-10.30 Sun
☎ (01962) 862592
Greene King IPA; guest beer Ⓗ
Small, 15th-century, timber-framed building, dominated by twin dormer windows. In a street where ale has been sold for over 700 years, this unspoilt, two-roomed pub is below street level – beware low beams and ceilings, undulating floors and walls. A place for drinking and conversation (expect to be drawn in), it upholds old-fashioned values. Hyde Abbey's ruins and King Alfred's grave lie close by. The Tavern's ghost's footsteps are reputedly heard in the bar after hours.
Q✿≢⊟♣

St James Tavern ✅
3 Romsey Road, SO22 5BE
(B3040, near county hospital)
✪ 11.30-2.30, 5.30-11; 11.30-11 Sat; 12-3, 6.30-10.30 Sun
☎ (01962) 861288
Butcombe Bitter; Wadworth IPA, 6X, seasonal beers Ⓗ
Close to the 13th-century Westgate, on an acute terrace corner, this pub has wood floors, light wood panelling and lofty ceilings. A raised no-smoking extension houses a coal-effect gas fire, while at the far end of the single, L-shaped bar is one of Winchester's last two bar billiards tables, and a TV for sports events. Fun quiz nights are held on Monday and many games are available. Popular with students and hospital staff, it serves a wide selection of good value food.
✿ⓘ≢♣✂

Wykeham Arms ✅
71 Kingsgate Street, SO23 9PE
✪ 11-11; 12-10.30 Sun
☎ (01962) 853834
Draught Bass; Gale's Butser, GB, HSB; guest beer Ⓗ
Rambling, many-roomed, Georgian pub, yards from the gates of Winchester College and the Cathedral Close. The bric-à-brac and antiquities could furnish every pub in the city – 2,000 (allegedly) tankards adorn the walls; canes cover a ceiling; Nelsoniana abounds; old school desks make compact tables. The menu rates a Michelin award, evening booking is advisable (no meals Sun eve). Trollope called it a 'third-rate hostelry', now rooms are certainly first-rate and priced accordingly. Dogs are welcome. Busy, but always civilised.
⌂Q⇔ⓘP

Burton beer

In 1925 Matilda, daughter of Nicholas de Shobenhale, released to the Abbott and Convent of Burton-on-Trent certain tenements and interests within and without the town: for which release they granted her daily for life two white loaves from the Monastery, two gallons of the Convent beer, and one penny, besides seven gallons of beer for the men and other considerations.

Frank A. King, *Beer has a History,* 1947

Beer Festival Calendar 2004

The Campaign for Real Ale's beer festivals are magnificent shop windows for cask ale and they give drinkers the opportunity to sample beers from independent brewers rare to particular localities. Beer festivals are enormous fun: many offer good food and live entertainment, and – where possible – facilities for families. Some seasonal festivals specialise in spring, autumn and winter ales. Festivals range in size from small local events to large regional ones. The Campaign holds two national festivals, for winter beers in January, and the Great British in August; the latter features around 500 beers. The festivals listed are those planned for 2004. For up-to-date information, contact the CAMRA website: www.camra.org.uk and click on 'CAMRA Near You'.

By joining CAMRA – there's a form at the back of the Guide – you will receive 12 editions of the Campaign's newspaper What's Brewing, which lists every festival on a month-by-month basis. Dates listed are liable to change: check with the website or What's Brewing

JANUARY
Great British Winter Beer Festival, Burton-on-Trent 23-25 Jan
Atherton Bent Bongs Beer Bash
Burton winter festival
Cambridge winter festival
Chelmsford winter festival
Exeter winter festival
Hitchin winter festival
St Neots winter festival

FEBRUARY
Ashfield winter festival
Battersea
Bishops Auckland
Bodmin
Bradford
Bristol
Chesterfield
Derby winter festival
Dorchester
Dover winter festival (no beers under 5%)
Fleetwood
Gosport
Hucknall
Liverpool
Northampton
Plymouth
Richmond & Hounslow
Rotherham
Salisbury
Sussex/Brighton
Tewkesbury
Wear Valley

MARCH
Banbury
Darlington spring festival
Ely
Hitchin
Leeds
Leicester
Loughborough
London Drinker
Oldham
South Devon
Wigan
York

APRIL
Bury St Edmunds
Chippenham
Coventry
Dunstable
Farnham
Gainsborough
Maldon
Mansfield
Newcastle upon Tyne
Paisley
Walsall

MAY
Alloa
Cambridge
Chester
Colchester
Doncaster
Fife (Glenrothes)
Hitchin
Macclesfield
Newark
Ongar
Reading (May Day Bank Holiday weekend)
Rugby
St Ives, Cornwall
Stockport
Stourbridge
Wolverhampton
Yapton

JUNE
Accrington
Catford
Colchester
Doncaster
Exeter
Kingston (Surrey)
Northampton
Salisbury
Scottish Traditional Beer Festival, Edinburgh
Stalybridge
Southampton
South Downs (Sussex)
Thurrock
Woodchurch, near Ashford, Kent: Rare Breeds (first weekend of month)

JULY
Ardingly
Boston
Canterbury: all Kent branches
Chelmsford
Cotswolds
Derby
Devizes
Fenland
Louth
Woodcote Steam Rally

The dog's driving ... a family enjoys a summer beer fest

AUGUST
Great British Beer Festival, London, 6-10
Barnsley
Clacton
Heart of Warwickshire
Harbury
Larling (Norfolk)
Moorgreen
Peterborough (CAMRA's second biggest
festival after GBBF, held in marquees
between the river and the cathedral)
Mumbles, Swansea
Worcester

SEPTEMBER
Ayrshire
Birmingham
Cleethorpes
Burton-on-Trent
Chappel (Essex)
Darlington
Falmouth
Grimsby
Hull
Ipswich
Keighley
Letchworth
Lincoln
Maidstone
Norths Notts
Northwich
Portsmouth
St Albans
St Ives, Cambs
Scunthorpe
Sheffield
Shrewsbury
Somerset
Southport
South Devon
Tamworth
Troon
Ulverston
Quorn

OCTOBER
Alloa
Bath
Bedford
Belfast
Birkenhead/Wirral
Carmarthen
Cardiff Great Welsh & Cider Festival
Croydon
Gravesend
Harlow
Huddersfield
Jersey
Loughborough
Middlesbrough
Norwich
Nottingham
Overton
Oxford
Poole
Solihull
Stoke-on-Trent
Twickenham
Wakefield
Westmorland/Kendall
Worthing

NOVEMBER
Aberdeen
Barnsley winter festival
Chatham/Medway festival
Dudley winter festival
Eastleigh (Hants)
Erewash
Hull
Loughborough
Luton
Medway
Rochford
Swindon
Watford
Woking
Wolverton, near Milton Keynes

DECEMBER
Cockermouth
Pig's Ear (East London)
Harwich
Ipswich winter festival

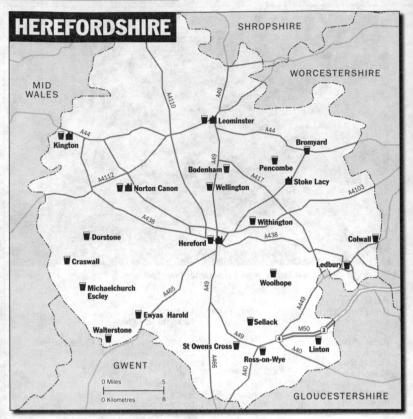

HEREFORDSHIRE

SHROPSHIRE

WORCESTERSHIRE

MID WALES

Kington

Leominster

Bromyard

Bodenham

Pencombe

Norton Canon

Wellington

Stoke Lacy

Withington

Dorstone

Colwall

Hereford

Craswall

Ledbury

Michaelchurch Escley

Woolhope

Ewyas Harold

Sellack

Walterstone

St Owens Cross

Linton

Ross-on-Wye

GWENT

0 Miles 5

0 Kilometres 8

GLOUCESTERSHIRE

BODENHAM

England's Gate Inn
HR1 3HE (just off A417)
☼ 11-11; 12-10.30 Sun
☎ (01568) 797286
Marston's Pedigree; Wye Valley Bitter, Butty Bach; guest beer Ⓗ
This 17th-century, black and white inn has been opened out internally and extensively modernised. It retains fine, original timbers and a flagstone floor. The single, large bar contrasts with a number of more intimate nooks and crannies. The guest beer is usually from a local brewery. This pub has a strong following for its excellent and affordable pub food served weekdays, with traditional lunch on Sundays; no meals on Sunday evening.
ⓌⓈ◑⊁P

BROMYARD

Bay Horse
21 High Street, HR7 4AA
☼ 11-3, 5.30-11; 12-3, 7-10.30 Sun
☎ (01885) 482600
Hobsons Best Bitter; Marston's Pedigree; guest beers Ⓗ
Attractive, well-run, black and white timbered pub in the town centre. Having recovered completely from a ruthless 1980s refurbishment, this pub now has great character. Original wood panelling, cosy seating and cushioned benches, make for comfort and encourage conversation. There

is a pleasant patio and garden to the rear.
Ⓢ◑P

Rose & Lion
5 New Road, HR7 4DE
☼ 11-3, 6-11; 11-11 Fri & Sat; 12-10.30 Sun
☎ (01885) 482381
Wye Valley Bitter, Butty Bach, Dorothy Goodbody's Wholesome Stout; guest beer Ⓗ
Herefordshire CAMRA Pub of the Year 2001, this is the least spoilt and most interesting pub in Bromyard. Run by a dynamic young landlady, it sets the standard for the town's pubs. Careful renovation has brought out the architectural merits of this traditional building. It has a very loyal local following and welcomes visitors. QⓈⒹ♣P

COLWALL

Chase
Chase Road, Upper Colwall, WR13 6DJ
(off B4218, signed British Camp) OS766431
☼ 12-2.30 (not Tue), 6-11; 12-2.30, 7-10.30 Sun
☎ (01684) 540276
Donnington SBA; Hobsons Best Bitter; Wye Valley HPA, seasonal beer Ⓗ
Two-bar free house located in a wooded backwater on the western slopes of the Malvern Hills, comprising a quiet lounge and a comfortable bar, with a pool table. The garden offers superb views across Herefordshire and the Welsh Marches. The only Donnington outlet in the county, it is well worth the 25-minute uphill walk from Colwall railway station. There is a limited

but very wholesome lunch menu – the home-cooked ham is a speciality; no food on Sunday. Q❀◑P

CRASWALL

Bull's Head

HR2 0PN (on Longtown to Hay road) OS278360
🕑 11-11 (closed winter Mon); 11-4 (closed eve) Sun
☎ (01981) 510616
Wye Valley Butty Bach; guest beer (summer) Ⓖ

Unique and utterly unspoilt, this old drovers' inn had been in the Lewis family for over 125 years, before it changed hands in 1998. The isolated pub's subsequent transformation has been remarkable. It now offers real ale and an exciting range of food that has established a national reputation (booking advisable at weekends). Westons GWR and Old Rosie cider are served on gravity. Ideally located for walking the nearby Hay Bluff and Offa's Dyke Path, the pub offers hostel-type B&B and camping in nearby fields. ▲Q☎❀⇔◑Ⅎ♣●

DORSTONE

Pandy Inn

HR3 6AN (by the village green, signed off B4348)
OS313416
🕑 12-3, 6-11; 12-11 Sat; 12-3, 6-10.30 Sun
☎ (01981) 550273 website: www.pandyinn.co.uk
Wye Valley Bitter, Butty Bach or seasonal beer Ⓗ

The original inn here is claimed to have been built in 1185 by one of the knights who killed Thomas à Becket. The interior has been knocked through but retains discrete areas; one of these is a restaurant, while the other two invite drinkers. The welcoming feel is enhanced by the timber framing, exposed stone walls and a huge fireplace. Good food features strongly, including a selection of vegetarian meals and a few South African dishes. Bottled local cider is available. ▲❀◑♣P⊁

EWYAS HAROLD

Temple Bar

HR2 0EU (just off B4347)
🕑 11-3, 6-11; 11-11 Sat; 12-10.30 Sun
☎ (01981) 240423 website: www.templebarinn.com
Hobsons Best Bitter; Worthington's Bitter; guest beers Ⓗ

Large 200-year-old, stone-built, village-centre pub whose name derives from its role as a courthouse in the 18/19th century. The small lounge and two restaurants are in the oldest part of the building. The Victorian stables have been converted to provide the large main bar. Children are welcome in this very popular pub, which holds a beer festival every spring bank holiday. Food ranges from bar snacks to full à la carte, there is also a children's menu.
▲Q❀◑⇔♣P

HEREFORD

Barrels

69 St Owen Street, HR1 2JQ
🕑 11-11; 12-10.30 Sun
☎ (01432) 274968
Wye Valley Bitter, HPA, Butty Bach, Dorothy Goodbody's Wholesome Stout, seasonal beers; guest beer (occasional) Ⓗ

Enjoying a cult status among city drinkers and discerning visitors alike, it was the base of the Wye Valley Brewery from 1987 until 2002 and is still the flagship, stocking most of the beer range. Bulmers Traditional cider is stocked. With its four separate rooms ranging in style from spartan to cosy and in ambience from boisterous to quiet, the Barrels caters for all tastes and age groups. A pool table occupies one bar and another has a large-screen TV for major sporting events. A charity music and beer festival is held on August bank holiday. ❀⇔♣♠●

Kings Fee

49-53 Commercial Road, HR1 2BJ
🕑 10-11; 12-10.30 Sun
☎ (01432) 373240
Greene King Abbot; Shepherd Neame Spitfire; Spinning Dog Chase Your Tail; Theakston Best Bitter; guest beers Ⓗ

It will surprise visitors that this building was a single floor Kwik Save supermarket before its conversion by J D Wetherspoon. The large main bar leads to an elevated family section and an outdoor drinking area. Decor and furnishings are modern in style. Local history panels are displayed alongside a local artist's contemporary woodcuts. This pub has brought a welcome choice of guest ales to Hereford and excellent food is served all day. Full disabled facilities are provided.
Q⇔❀◑&≠⊁

Victory ⊘

88 St Owen Street, HR1 2QD
🕑 11-11; 12-10.30 Sun
☎ (01432) 274998
Spinning Dog Mutleys Dark, Chase Your Tail, Top Dog. Mutley's Revenge, seasonal beers; guest beer Ⓗ

Home of the Spinning Dog Brewery, the Victory also offers the city's best range of real ciders (Bulmers Traditional, Thatchers, Cheddar Valley and Westons Old Rosie) and a guest beer often from local breweries. The bar is in the shape of a galleon and the nautical theme runs through to the large bar/function room at the rear. Herefordshire CAMRA Pub of the Year 2000, it is a venue for local bands and holds fairly frequent beer festivals. The pub dog may be seen demonstrating the behaviour that earned the brewery its name. The generous portions of home-cooked food are recommended. ▲❀◑⇔&≠♣●P

KINGTON

Olde Tavern

22 Victoria Road, HR5 3BX
🕑 5.30-11; 12-3, 6-11 Sat; 12-3, 6-10.30 Sun
☎ (01544) 231384
Dunn Plowman Brewhouse Bitter, Winners; guest beer Ⓗ

The Olde Tavern proves that refurbishment is not always bad news – the pub has reopened to near universal acclaim, and was voted CAMRA runner-up Pub of the Year for

INDEPENDENT BREWERIES

Bridge Street Kington
Dunn Plowman Kington
Marches Leominster
Shoes Norton Canon
Spinning Dog Hereford
Wye Valley Stoke Lacy

Herefordshire in 2002. The side room has been opened up, with a serving-hatch to the bar. Retaining its great character, this pub is taking a more significant role in the local community. It is now the tap for the nearby Dunn Plowman Brewery. Q ♣

Swan Hotel
Church Street, HR5 3AZ
🕑 12-2.30, 6-11; 12-2.30, 7-10.30 Sun
☎ (01544) 230510
website: www.swanhotelkington.co.uk
Draught Bass; Worthington's Bitter; guest beer H
This fine 17th-century hotel has recently been refurbished. A chimney breast divides the one-room bar into two areas; one has chairs for bar meals, the other has comfortable settees. There is also a separate restaurant area with an à la carte menu. It used to be known as the Upper Swan to distinguish it from another (Lower) Swan in the High Street. ⊛⇦⪅ⓘⓓP⅏

LEDBURY

Olde Talbot Hotel
14 New Street, HR8 2DT
🕑 11.30-3, 5-11; 11-11 Sat; 12-4; 7-10.30 Sun
☎ (01531) 632963 website: www.talbotledbury.co.uk
Wadworth IPA, 6X; Wye Valley Butty Bach; guest beer H
This superb, black and white hotel, dating back to 1596, never disappoints. The plush, but lively bar boasts an impressive fireplace and an extra drinking area to the rear, while the beautiful oak-panelled dining room with its fine carved overmantle was once the scene of fighting between Cavaliers and Roundheads. Traditional English food features on the menu. An ideal place to spend a short break, it is convenient for local shops. ⇦ⓘⓓ≈♣P

LEOMINSTER

Black Horse
74 South Street, HR6 8JF
🕑 11-2.30, 6-11; 11-11 Sat; 12-3, 7-10.30 Sun
☎ (01568) 611946
Dunn Plowman Brewhouse Bitter; Hobsons Town Crier; guest beers H
An old coaching inn to the south of the town centre, the Black Horse has a public bar, a long, narrow lounge and a dining area to the rear. Comfortable and friendly, the range and quality of the beers amply compensate for the tired decor of the lounge. It was a former home to the Dunn Plowman Brewery. Home-cooked bar snacks and meals are served, with Sunday lunches a speciality; no food on Sunday evening. Games include petanque and quoits. Access to the car park is through the narrow courtyard entrance. ⪅⊛ⓘⓓ♣P

Grape Vaults
2 Broad Street, HR6 8BS
🕑 11-11; 12-10.30 Sun
☎ (01568) 611404
Banks's Original, Bitter; Marston's Pedigree; guest beers H
An unpretentious exterior fails to prepare the visitor for the delightful wood-panelled interior of this wonderfully unspoilt pub. Once a 'hard-core' cider house, this central pub has much to commend it. The discrete nooks offer the drinker a cosy retreat; the

snug bar is a marvel. A pub to enjoy at one's leisure. ⪅Qⓘⓓ

LINTON

Alma
HR9 7RY (off B4221, W of M50 jct 3) OS659255
🕑 12-2.30 (not Mon-Fri), 6.30 (6 Fri & Sat)-11; 12-2.30, 7-10.30 Sun
☎ (01989) 720355
Butcombe Bitter; RCH Pitchfork; Smiles Best; Malvern Hills Red Earl or guest beer H
Herefordshire CAMRA Pub of the Year for 2002, it usually serves four beers, all from independents. The Alma demonstrates that rural pubs can survive if they prove to be friendly, comfortable places to drink good ale – rather than being turned into restaurants. The large, welcoming lounge contrasts with the games area at the rear and another small bar. The extensive gardens are the venue for an ambitious annual music and beer festival that attracts people from afar. ⪅Q⊛⇦♣P⅏

MICHAELCHURCH ESCLEY

Bridge Inn
HR2 0JW OS318341
🕑 11-2.30 (not winter Mon), 6-11 (11-11 summer); 12-10.30 Sun
☎ (01981) 510646
Wye Valley Butty Bach, HPA or seasonal beer H
Charming, 16th-century house with a rare Welsh stone roof, beautifully set by Escley brook – an ideal venue for a summer's evening. The interior is impressive, with a beamed ceiling and an inglenook separating the family room from the main bar. Try the Gwatkins cider. The pub serves locally sourced, home-cooked food in the bars and in the restaurant. The short menu changes often and always includes steaks. ⪅Q⪚⊛ⓘ⚓♣P

NORTON CANON

Three Horseshoes
HR4 7BH (on A480)
🕑 12-3 (Wed & Sat only), 6-11; 12-3, 7-10.30 Sun
☎ (01544) 318375
Shoes Norton Ale, Canon Bitter, Farriers Beer H
This unpretentious roadside inn, home of the Shoes Brewery, was local CAMRA Pub of the Year 1999. It comprises two contrasting bars: to the left as you enter is a small lounge furnished with comfortable old sofas and a piano; the main community bar, to the right, leads to a large pool room. Farriers Beer is now available on draught as well as bottled, served by gravity despite the handpump. ⪅Q⊛⚓⚓♣P

PENCOMBE

Wheelwrights Arms
HR7 4RN OS598528
🕑 12-2.30 (not Mon or Tue), 6-11; 12-2.30, 7-10.30 Sun
☎ (01885) 400358
Adnams Broadside; Black Sheep Best Bitter; Greene King Abbot; Taylor Landlord; guest beer H
Is this the ultimate all-round village inn? It sits physically and metaphorically at the heart of its community; well supported by the friendly locals. Wholesome, excellent value food is provided, prepared from local

ingredients; no lunches are served on Monday or Wednesday. The Wheelwrights Arms is the focus for many community events including a folk jam session on the first Tuesday of the month.
♨⊛🛏◑♣

ROSS-ON-WYE

Riverside
20 Wye Street, HR9 7BT
✪ 11-11; 12-10.30 Sun
☎ (01989) 564688
Goff's Jouster; Teme Valley That; Wye Valley Butty Bach Ⓗ
Occupying a delightful position on the banks of the River Wye, this pub was recently converted from a café/restaurant. Not relying on a fickle tourist trade, this is a real pub run with imagination and vigour. The single, L-shaped bar has views of the river, a pool table in an alcove, and a separate dining room. The dynamic young landlord supports local breweries in a town that offers little to the drinker. Traditional home-cooked bar food is served.
♨⊛🛏◑♣

ST OWENS CROSS

New Inn
HR2 8LQ (at A4137/B4521 jct)
✪ 12-2.30 (3 Sat), 6-11; 12-3, 7-10 Sun
☎ (01989) 730274
Draught Bass; Tetley Bitter; Wadworth 6X; guest beers Ⓗ
Excellent, black and white, 16th-century pub, the split-level main bar has several cosy nooks and crannies. All the beers are served through a six-gang pewter beer engine rescued from a long-closed pub in Ross-on-Wye. The pub serves traditional English home-cooked snacks and meals in the main bar and in the dining room. The garden, with views of the Black Mountains, features hanging baskets in summer.
♨⊛🛏◑♣P

SELLACK

Loughpool
HR9 6LX (1 mile NW of A49 at Peterstow)
OS558268
✪ 11.30-2.30, 6.30-11; 12-2.30, 6.30-10.30 Sun
☎ (01989) 730236
John Smith's Bitter; Wye Valley Bitter, Butty Bach; guest beer Ⓗ
This 16th-century black and white pub is superb. The long, low bar has two small alcoves and an open fire at one end, and there is a no-smoking restaurant. The accent is on original food, which is of a very high standard, using local produce where possible. This is not, however, to the exclusion of drinkers. The guest beer is usually local and bottled local ciders and perries are available. From the large grassed area outside, there are excellent views of the delightful surrounding countryside.
♨Q⊛◑P

WALTERSTONE

Carpenters Arms
HR2 0DX
✪ 12-11; 12-10.30 Sun

☎ (01873) 890353
Wadworth 6X or seasonal beers Ⓖ
Sitting close by the church in a scattered hamlet with views of the Skirrid Mountain, this lovely old pub, known locally as the Gluepot, is a favourite of ramblers. Hidden behind the tiny bar is a cask from which the beer is drawn directly into the glass. The unobtrusive restaurant to the rear does not detract from the unspoilt atmosphere of the pub; a splendid hearth graces one of the two drinking areas. No lunchtime food is served in winter. Early Hancock's posters and signage decorate the pub. ♨Q⊛◑P

WELLINGTON

Wellington Inn
HR4 8AT (½ mile W of A49)
✪ 12-3 (not Mon), 6-11; 12-3, 7-10.30 Sun
☎ (01432) 830367
Hancock's HB; Hobsons Best Bitter; Wye Valley Butty Bach Ⓗ
The single bar in this traditional village pub has wooden benches, contrasting neatly with opulent leather sofas, plus a rustic barn conversion-style restaurant. Beers from regional breweries and local micros alternate as guest beers. Food is a real speciality with bar snacks and a full menu. A carvery is offered on Sunday and special bangers and mash on Monday. The cider is Westons. Family board games can be played.
♨⊛◑♣♠P

WITHINGTON

Cross Keys
HR1 3NN (on A465 in Withington Marsh)
✪ 5 (12 Sat)-11; 12-4.30, 7-10.30 Sun
☎ (01432) 820616
Greene King Abbot or Speckled Hen; Wye Valley Butty Bach; guest beer Ⓗ
This local has been run by the same landlord for over 30 years. It is a family pub where conversation rules. A single bar serves two drinking areas, each with original stone walls, woodwork, a real fire and basic bench seating. A folk jam session is held on the last Thursday in the month. The pub is on the Hereford to Bromyard bus route (418/419/420); camping can be arranged nearby. On Saturday, filled rolls are available.
♨⊛▲♣P

WOOLHOPE

Crown
HR1 4QP OS611357
✪ 12-2.30, 6.30 -11; 12-11 Sat; 12-3, 6.30-10.30 Sun
☎ (01432) 860468
Smiles Best; Wye Valley Bitter; guest beer Ⓗ
A food-oriented pub next to the church, it is deservedly popular with out-of-town diners, but drinkers are also welcome and now have a new area in a small conservatory by the front door. Meals are served in the restaurant, and, more informally, in the large bar. The food is all home prepared and the extensive, appetising menu includes a large choice of vegetarian dishes. Food gift vouchers are on sale. Booking for weekend meals is advised.
⊛◑P

Upstairs, downstairs
How beer reaches your glass

Real ale is known to brewers as cask-conditioned beer: unlike keg beers and lagers, it is neither filtered nor pasteurised in the brewery. It leaves the brewery in an unfinished state and reaches maturity in its cask in the pub cellar as a result of a secondary fermentation, when yeast turns remaining malt sugars into alcohol and carbon dioxide gas.

As it leaves the brewery, additional hops may be added – known as 'dry hopping' – to give the beer extra aroma and flavour. Finings (isinglass) is added to clear the beer during second fermentation. In the pub cellar, the cask lies on a cradle or stillage. A tap is knocked into the bung hole at the flat end of the cask, while a porous wooden peg, a spile, is knocked through the shive hole on top. The peg allows some

of the carbon dioxide to escape, but sufficient must be retained to give the beer a natural sparkle or condition. After a day, the soft spile is replaced by a hard one that retains the remaining gas inside the cask. The temperature in the cellar is maintained at 12 to 13 degrees C (52 to 55 F), though some strong beers such as winter warmers can benefit from a slightly higher temperature. Cask beer has to be monitored with care: the cellarman will check the condition of the beer on a regular basis. When he is satisfied that secondary fermentation is over and the beer has 'dropped bright' (yeast and protein have settled at the foot of the cask) then the beer is ready to be served. A cask must be emptied within a few days, otherwise the beer will become oxidised and take on cardboard or vinegary flavours.

Methods of dispense

Air pressure
This is used only in Scotland. Originally air pressure was produced by water engines – lavatory cisterns in reverse – but they have been replaced by 'English' handpumps. A few outlets use electric compressors that drive the beer to tall founts on the bar.

Gravity
This is the oldest and simplest method of serving beer. A tap is inserted into the cask and the beer flows naturally into the glass. The cask is often kept on the bar or close to the bar area: the only problem is keeping the beer at a cool temperature. Some pubs serve beer by gravity from casks kept in the cellar or a ground-floor room kept at a suitable temperature.

Handpump
Most real ale is served by a beer engine connected to the familiar handpump or handpull on the bar top. The engine is a simple suction pump that raises the beer from cask to bar. In a growing number

of pubs, the beer 'lines' are encased in thicker tubes known as pythons that contain cold water and keep the beer cool on its journey. Beer engines are often encased in cooling jackets as well. When a pub cellar is exceptionally deep or some distance from the bar, the beer engine may need assistance: this may come in the form of an electric pump placed in the line between cellar and bar, or by a pump powered by cellar gasses, carbon dioxide or nitrogen. Although powered by gas, it does not come into contact with the beer.

Electric pump
This type of pump does the work without the manual effort. Electric pumps are rarely seen these day, and they can be confused with gas-powered keg pumps. If in doubt, ask.

Bottle-conditioned beer
'Real ale in a bottle' contains live yeast and some malt sugars to allow fermentation and maturation to take place.

Methods not approved by CAMRA

Blanket and top pressure
A cylinder of gas – usually carbon dioxide or sometimes a mix of carbon dioxide and nitrogen – is connected to the cask via the spile hole to prevent air entering the cask as beer is pulled off. This can stop the beer reaching maturity and tasting 'green'. Blanket pressure is the term used when only a light pressure of gas is used. Top pressure involves a higher level of pressure that forces the beer from cask to bar.

Cask breather
A refinement of the blanket pressure method, the breather is a demand valve that admits a volume of gas (carbon dioxide and/or nitrogen) to replace beer as it is drawn off. It prevents oxidation and, arguably, some beers reaching full maturity. It does little to prevent beer losing condition and becoming flat. Publicans who rotate stock and use the right size of cask to meet demand should not need pressurised methods of dispense.

HERTFORDSHIRE

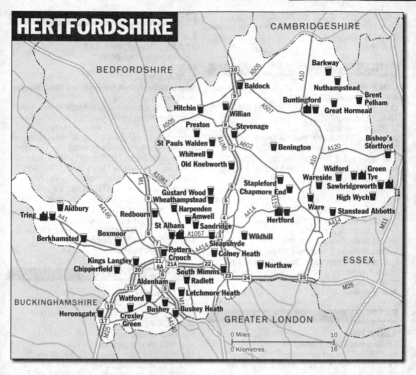

ALDBURY

Greyhound
Stocks Road, HP23 5RT (2 miles E of Tring)
✪ 11-11; 12-10.30 Sun
☎ (01442) 851228
website: www.greyhound.aldbury.wi@freshnet
Badger IPA, Best, Tanglefoot; guest beer Ⓗ
Welcoming pub with a relaxed atmosphere.
Situated in a photogenic village in front of a
pond, it has a traditional feel. This is the
furthest outpost of the Hall & Woodhouse
empire. Bar snacks an and extensive menu
are served all day. Dogs are made welcome.
Functions can be catered for in the spacious
conservatory which offers ample seating.
🏾❀❶❸P

Valiant Trooper ✪
Trooper Road, HP23 5RW (2 miles E of Tring)
✪ 11.30-11; 12-10.30 Sun
☎ (01442) 851203
Fuller's London Pride; guest beers Ⓗ
Busy pub situated in a much-filmed village, it
serves up to five very well-kept beers from
a central bar area. It has been a pub since
1752, and superb food is available in the
restaurant at one end, with bar snacks and
specials offered throughout the two main
drinking areas. The atmosphere is warm and
relaxed, and the seating interesting in this
superb, welcoming pub. 🏾Q❀❶♣P

ALDENHAM

Roundbush
Roundbush Lane, WD25 8BG (just off B462)
✪ 12-11; 12-10.30 Sun
☎ (01923) 855532
**Greene King IPA, Abbot; Marston's Pedigree; Tetley
Bitter** Ⓗ

Genuine 17th-century country pub,
originally a cottage, where an extension has
been sympathetically added. There are two
distinct drinking areas: one has a benched
and tiled floor and offers darts, cards and
TV; the other is a carpeted, beamed eating
and drinking area. The pub caters for all
ages and has a secluded garden with
children's play equipment and well-used
bird boxes. ❀❶♣P

AMWELL

Elephant & Castle ✪
Amwell Lane, AL4 8EA (left fork at top of
Brewhouse Hill, Wheathampstead) OS167133
✪ 12-2.30, 5.30-11; 12-11 Sat; 12-10.30 Sun
☎ (01582) 832175
**Greene King IPA, Morland Original, Abbot;
guest beer** Ⓗ
Friendly, deservedly popular 18th-century
pub (formerly three cottages) in a peaceful
setting and beautifully situated. See the 200-
foot well in the bar. The floors in the front
bars are laid with attractive terracotta tiles.
With the added asset of two large gardens
(one is for adults only), this highly
successful country pub has gone from
strength to strength. The landlord is of the
old school, rating good beer and customer

INDEPENDENT BREWERIES

Buntingford Buntingford
Garden Barber Hertford
Green Tye Green Tye
McMullen Hertford
Sawbridgeworth Sawbridgeworth
Tring Tring
Verulam St Albans

satisfaction high on his list of priorities. Lunches are served daily and evening meals Tuesday–Saturday.
🏚 ❀ ◖ ♣ P

BALDOCK

Cock ✔
43 High Street, SG7 6BG
🕓 12-2 (Wed), 5-11 (Mon-Fri); 12-3, 5-11 Sat; 12-4, 7-10.30 Sun
☎ (01462) 892366
Greene King XX Mild, IPA, Ruddles County, Abbot, Old Speckled Hen; guest beers Ⓗ

The Cock is a 17th-century inn with a beamed interior and open log fire. The split-level drinking area enhances the pub's character. An enclosed patio is available in suitable weather. The pub is highly popular and won the local CAMRA Pub of the Season award in autumn 2002. Baldock is an ancient market town on the old Great North Road coaching route. Market day is Wednesday and visitors should note that the pub does not open at lunchtime on other weekdays. Food is available by prior arrangement only.
🏚 ❀ ♿ ≠ ♣

BARKWAY

Tally Ho
London Road, SG8 8EX
(on B1368 at S end of village)
🕓 11.30 (12 Sat)-3, 5.30 (6 Sat)-11; 12-later Sun
☎ (01763) 848389
Nethergate Suffolk County; guest beers Ⓖ

This friendly, rural free house provides a regular outlet for local independent brewers, and some from further afield. There are often dark beers, milds and porters available. Awarded local CAMRA Most Improved Pub 2000, it has a welcoming atmosphere for stimulating conversation in the bar, where snacks are available on request. Alternatively, order fresh home-cooked food in the separate restaurant. With open log fires, a beer garden, and regularly-changing beers, the pub offers something all year round. Sunday closing is variable – the pub usually shuts when there are no customers left.
🏚 ❀ ◖ P

BENINGTON

Lordship Arms
42 Whempstead Road, SE2 7LL
(3 miles E of Stevenage via B1037) OS308227
🕓 12-3, 6-11, 7-10.30 Sun
☎ (01438) 869665
Fuller's London Pride, ESB; Young's Special; guest beers Ⓗ

Originally named the Cricketers, this excellent one-bar pub is one of the best free houses in Herts. It was voted local CAMRA Pub of the Year in 1997, '99 and 2002. Its regular range of ales is complemented by an ever-changing selection of beers from small breweries, together with draught cider and various fruit wines. The pub features telephone memorabilia, even the handpumps are modelled on different styles of phone. Curry nights are a popular Wednesday evening institution.
🏚 ◖ ♣ P ⛾

BERKHAMSTED

Lamb
277 High Street, HP4 1AJ
(Northchurch end of High St)
🕓 11-11; 12-10.30 Sun
☎ (01442) 862615
Adnams Bitter; Fuller's London Pride; Tring Ridgeway; guest beer Ⓗ

Located at the end of the High Street, two front doors lead into the two bars that are joined inside by an open doorway. Welcoming and friendly, it is very much of the old school with the public bar devoted to the dartboard. High streets were once filled with pubs like this – a real drinkers' pub. Delicious home-cooked food of magnificent proportions is served on weekday lunchtimes only. There is a small patio at the rear. The Lamb retains most of its original features; the only modern concessions are the juke box and games machine. It is a regular outlet for Tring Brewery. ❀ ◖ ⊟ ≠ ♣

BISHOP'S STORTFORD

Half Moon
31 North Street, CM23 2LD
🕓 11-11; 12-10.30 Sun
☎ (01279) 834500
Beer range varies Ⓗ

The Half Moon has been a pub since 1751. The two main bars are at different levels, with a no-smoking snug to one side. The large function room is a regular venue for music of all types. Up to seven guest beers are offered and include a large number of seasonal and special brews. One of the choices is normally a mild, stout or porter. Westons Old Rosie cider is stocked. Dutch graffiti can be seen in the top bar, drawn by WWII US aircrew based in local aerodrome – now known as Stansted Airport.
❀ ◖ ≠ ● P ⅍

BOXMOOR

Steam Coach
86 St Johns Road, HP1 1NP
(1/2 mile from A4146, Station Road)
🕓 12-11; 12-10.30 Sun
☎ (01442) 244480
Greene King IPA, Abbot; guest beers Ⓗ

Sensitively refurbished one-bar pub in a village location, opposite the local cricket pitch. The part-timber, part-rendered walls and central brick pier add to the appeal of the open-plan layout in this charming, edge-of-town pub. The split-level interior has a mix of fully upholstered furniture and sturdy tables and chairs. To the rear of the pub is a large room for diners and drinkers alike, and this can be used for functions. The patio is to the right of the main entrance. Evening meals are served Wednesday–Friday until 8pm.
❀ ◖ ≠ (Hemel Hempstead) P

BRENT PELHAM

Black Horse
SG9 0AP
(150 yds from church, off B1038) OS433311
🕓 12-2.30, 5-11; 12-11 Fri & Sat; 12-10.30 Sun
☎ (01279) 777305
Greene King IPA, Abbot; guest beer Ⓗ

This 400-year-old building was once a dairy and lies next to the church of St Mary the Virgin. A tomb in the church wall is said to hold the remains of the 23-foot giant, Piers Shonks, who slayed a dragon and cheated the devil. The long building is split into three areas: a games room, the general bar and a no-smoking settle room. A friendly welcome, wood fires and home cooking (curries a speciality) make you feel right at home. Food is always available. ▲ 🌑 🕭 ◑ P

BUNTINGFORD

Crown Inn
17 High Street, SG9 9AB
🕛 12-3, 6-11; 12-3, 7-10.30 Sun
☎ (01763) 271422
Archers Best Bitter; Ridleys IPA; guest beer Ⓗ
Popular town-centre pub with a large front bar and cosy back bar. This is a real locals' local. The long-standing landlord is justly proud of running a pub which serves food and not a restaurant which serves beers. Children are welcome in the covered patio and lovely, secluded garden. Theme nights, offering speciality food, are regularly held. A large function room is available for meetings and social events. A Guide entry for 14 consecutive years, it was local CAMRA Best Community Pub 2000 and 2003. 🖢 🌑 ◑

BUSHEY

Swan
25 Park Road, WD23 1EE (off A411)
🕛 11-11; 12-10.30 Sun
☎ (020) 8950 2256
Adnams Bitter; Ansells Mild; Young's Bitter, Special Ⓗ
This small, back-street pub is making its 29th appearance in this Guide. The walls are adorned with old photographs of Bushey, four local CAMRA Pub of the Year awards and various curios. Pub games, a piano and real fires (in winter) add to the character and atmosphere of the Swan. The ladies' loos are in the small back garden. Located close to Bushey Museum, bus routes 142 and 258 stop close by in the High Street. ▲ 🌑 ♣

BUSHEY HEATH

Black Boy
19 Windmill Street, WD23 1MB
🕛 12-11; 12-4, 7-10.30 Sun
☎ (020) 8950 2230
Adnams Bitter; Greene King Abbot; guest beers Ⓗ
One-bar, back-street pub which continues to serve five handpulled beers at most times. It is a five-minute walk from the A4140 (buses 142/258 from Bushey or Watford Stations). Food is served until 10pm. Three times winner of local CAMRA Pub of the Year, it is now in its eighth consecutive year in this Guide. Guest ales tend to be from regional brewers. 🌑 ◑ P

CHAPMORE END

Woodman
30 Chapmore End, SG12 0HF (off B158, ¼ mile SW of A602) OS328164
🕛 12-3, 6 (5.30 Fri)-11; 12-11 Sat; 12-10.30 Sun
☎ (01920) 463143 website: www.woodmanpub.com

Greene King IPA, Morland Original, Abbot, seasonal beers; guest beers Ⓖ
This gem is located in a quiet hamlet, complete with duckpond. The cosy two-bar pub serves cooled ale in splendid condition straight from the cask in the cellar (a step down behind the public bar). Lunches are served every day and a special evening meal every Thursday. There are large gardens at the rear with a children's play area. Petanque and other games are played. Enjoy the carol singing and other entertainment in season. ▲ Q 🌑 ◑ 🕭 ♣ P

CHIPPERFIELD

Royal Oak
1 The Street, WD4 9BH
(on crossroads at Bovingdon end of village)
🕛 12-3, 6-11; 12-3, 7-10.30 Sun
☎ (01923) 266537
Adnams Broadside; Draught Bass; Young's Bitter, Special; guest beer Ⓗ
This street-corner drinkers' pub has featured in all but one edition of this Guide. The public and saloon bars are served by a central two-sided bar. The public is dressed with local photos, historic car pictures and has a growing collection of book matches. Much of the seating is upholstered beer casks. The saloon is slightly more open but is still furnished with dark wood and brasses. Home-made lunches are served (evening meals are offered by prior arrangement).
▲ Q 🌑 ◑ ♣ P

COLNEY HEATH

Crooked Billet
88 High Street, AL4 0NP (signed from A414)
🕛 11-2.30, 5.30-11; 11-11 Sat; 12-2.30, 7-10.30 Sun
☎ (01727) 822128
Greene King IPA; guest beers Ⓗ
Popular and friendly cottage-style village pub dating back over 200 years. Greene King IPA is sold plus at least two guests usually from micro-breweries. A wide range of good value food is available. The large garden has children's play equipment. The pub is an ideal stop-off point for walks on many local footpaths.
▲ 🌑 ◑ 🕭 ♣ P

CROXLEY GREEN

Sportsman
2 Scots Hill, WD3 3AD
(on A412 at jct with the green)
🕛 12-11; 12-10.30 Sun
☎ (01923) 443360
Draught Bass; Tring Side Pocket for a Toad; guest beers Ⓗ
Single bar with large collection of unusual sporting equipment and 'The Simpsons' cartoon murals adorning the walls. Guests change weekly and include local micros and regional beers. Live music (mainly blues), every Saturday, reflects the strong music following, supplemented by folk and blues jams each month which are increasingly popular with musicians. Decking supplements the sheltered rear patio, and 'the shed' provides a separate room with its own bar where occasional beer festivals are held. 🌑 ◑ ♣ P

GREAT HORMEAD

Three Tuns
SG9 0NT (on B1038) OS402300
☼ 12-2.30, 6-11; closed Mon; 12-6 Sun
☎ (01763) 289409
Greene King IPA, Old Speckled Hen Ⓗ
This attractive, 18th-century, thatched pub lies in a village that once featured in a paint advert. The pub was carefully restored in 1992 by Greene King, following an electrical fault which set fire to the thatch. A restaurant annexe was added in the rebuild. On entering the oak-beamed pub, you will be warmly welcomed by the landlord, the pub dog and a lovely fire. Many of the customers are there for the excellent cuisine. Booking is essential at the weekend, especially for Sunday lunch. 🏨❀◖P

GREEN TYE

Prince of Wales
SG10 6JP (off B1004) OS443184
☼ 12-2.30 (not Mon), 5.30-11; 12-11 Sat; 12-10.30 Sun
☎ (01279) 842517
Greene Tye Union Jack; McMullen AK; guest beers Ⓗ
Small village community pub that is a popular stop-off point for cyclists and walkers. The Green Tye Brewery (adjacent to the pub) normally provides one or two regular beers plus Union Jack. Other guests are from micros. This former local CAMRA Pub of the Year is open all day on bank holidays. There is occasional live music at weekends – check the pub notice board for details. Darts matches on Wednesdays mean the pub can be very busy for home fixtures. For special events a marquee is set up in the garden. A regular May Day weekend beer festival is held; an old English event with live music and traditional games. 🏨❀◖♣P

GUSTARD WOOD

Cross Keys
Bullslough Hill, AL4 8LA (off B651, 1 mile N of Wheathampstead)
☼ 11-3, 5.30-11; 12-5, 7-10.30 Sun
☎ (01582) 832165
Fuller's London Pride; Greene King IPA; guest beers Ⓗ
Charming, 17th-century pub serving reasonably-priced, home-cooked food; ideal for ramblers. The pub boasts a large inglenook and a multitude of clocks – only one showing the correct time. The family room is not always open. 🏨Q♿❀♣◖P⊬

HARPENDEN

Carpenters Arms
14 Cravells Road, AL5 1BD (off A1081)
☼ 11-3, 5.30-11; 12-3, 7-10.30 Sun
☎ (01582) 460311
Adnams Bitter; Courage Best Bitter; Greene King Abbot; guest beer Ⓗ
What more can one say about this perennial Guide entry? It is Harpenden's smallest pub, winner of local CAMRA awards for Pub of the Year 2001 and for long-term services to the real ale cause, as well as council awards in the Hertfordshire in Bloom competition and an award for services to the community. The landlord is a classic car and Harley fanatic and a fervent supporter of guest ales from micro-breweries, particularly mild. Simple, good value food (not served Sun) and a warm welcome await you. 🏨Q❀◖P

HERONSGATE

Land of Liberty, Peace & Plenty
Long Lane, WD3 5BS
(½ mile from M25 jct 17) OS023949
☼ 11.30-11; 12-10.30 Sun
☎ (01923) 282226 website: www.landofliberty.co.uk
Courage Best Bitter; Fuller's London Pride; guest beers Ⓗ
A welcome return to this Guide for this true free house. The new owners are locals who have rejuvenated the pub. Five handpulled beers are usually available, although a greater emphasis on food (not served Sun eve) means drinkers may be short of space on Friday and Saturday evenings. Guest beers often include Tring seasonal ales. Live music has also been introduced – mainly jazz. 🏨❀⊨◖P

HERTFORD

Old Cross Tavern
8 St Andrew Street, SG14 1JA
☼ 11.30-11; 12-10.30 Sun
☎ (01992) 583133
Fuller's London Pride; Mighty Oak IPA; Oakham JHB; guest beers Ⓗ
Splendid, welcoming recreation of a town pub of yesteryear. This single bar has historic memorabilia on display. At least seven beers are available, always in superb condition. They include guests from craft/micro-brewers from near and far, usually featuring a dark beer of character. A real cider and reasonable, sound house wines are offered. Lunches are served Monday–Saturday, try Bev's famous fish pie and the daily specials. Q◖≢ (North/East) ♦

White Horse
33 Castle Street, SG14 1HH
☼ 12-2.30, 5.30-11; 12-11 Fri & Sat; 12-10.30 Sun
☎ (01992) 501950
Adnams Bitter; Fuller's Chiswick, London Pride, ESB, seasonal beers; guest beers Ⓗ
Attractive, old timber-framed building near the castle with two downstairs bars and upstairs no-smoking rooms (open to children until 9pm). There is a bar billiards room for over 18s. A log fire downstairs warms the pub in winter. Alongside Fuller's beers, are guest beers of character from craft brewers, all invariably in excellent order. Beer festivals with 50 ales are staged in May and late autumn. Excellent, reasonably-priced lunches are served every day, together with a good choice of coffees and country wines. 🏨Q♿◖⊨≢ (North/East) ♣⊬

HIGH WYCH

Rising Sun
CM21 0HZ
(1 mile W of Sawbridgeworth, on B1184) OS464143
☼ 12-2.30, 5.30-11; 5-11 Fri; 12-3, 7-11 Sat; 12-3, 7-10.30 Sun
☎ (01279) 724099
Courage Directors; guest beers Ⓖ
There is not much that can be said about this gem of a pub that has not been said in

this Guide previously. It has never used handpumps, never sold keg beer or lager, and is proud to be a pub rather than a restaurant. The only food available is pickled eggs and crisps. All beer is served direct from the cask behind the bar. Guest ales are from small independent breweries. Fines are imposed for the use of mobile phones, and the money is added to the charity box. This classic pub is known locally as 'Sid's'. ⚘Q⚘🍺🔥♿P

HITCHIN

Coopers Arms ⊘
81 Tilehouse Street, SG5 2DY
🕐 11-11; 12-10.30 Sun
☎ (01462) 459497
McMullen AK, Country; guest beer ⊞
This old coaching inn, once on the main A505, now thankfully stands in a quiet backwater close to the market square. Although the pub dates back to 1860, it is housed in a much older building. Look out for the old ecclesiastical windows. It has been systematically refurbished to produce an open-plan drinking area with two bars. The high roof provides an airy feel. Meals are served in a smoke-free environment and include 'over 55s' specials. Sky TV is available. ⚘⚘◑P

Victoria
1 Ickleford Road, SG5 1TJ
🕐 12-3, 5-11; 12-11 Sat; 12-4, 7-10.30 Sun
☎ (01462) 432682
Greene King IPA, Ruddles County, Abbot ⊞
Friendly pub on the main road from the station to the market square, it has regular passing trade but not the weekend circuit crawlers. Much-refurbished, this wedge-shaped pub was built in 1865. It has a split-level drinking area with plenty of seating. It is a true local that caters for all age groups, and has successful games and quiz teams. ⚘◑≉♣P

KINGS LANGLEY

Saracen's Head
47 High Street, WD4 9HU
🕐 11-2.30 (3 Sat), 5 (6 Sat)-11; 12-3, 7-10.30 Sun
☎ (01923) 400144
Fuller's London Pride, ESB; Tring Ridgeway; guest beer ⊞
This building has been a pub since at least 1619. The single bar greets you with a comfortable atmosphere with beams, a collection of old bottles and in winter a real fire. At the rear of the bar, close to a bench-lined area, an interesting record of the licensees (dating back to 1826) can be found. During the summer, award-winning hanging baskets complete a pleasant streetside table area. The pub has its own golf society. No food is served on Sunday. No children are admitted. ⚘◑P

LETCHMORE HEATH

Three Horseshoes
The Green, WD25 8ER
🕐 11-3, 5.30-11; 11-11 Fri & Sat; 12-10.30 Sun
☎ (01923) 856084
Adnams Broadside; Draught Bass; Tetley Bitter; guest beers ⊞
A beer house since the 18th century, the

building was recorded in 1586 with a smithy adjoining. The earliest part is the timber hall circa 16th century, with a 17th-century frontage. Substantial reconstruction took place in 1803. The pub has featured in films since the 1920s, in addition to numerous TV appearances. There are two separate bars, a flagstoned public and genuine oak-beamed lounge. An extensive menu is available. Q◑🍺P

NORTHAW

Two Brewers
1 Northaw Road, EN6 4NW
🕐 11.30-11; 12-10.30 Sun
☎ (01707) 655557
Adnams Bitter; Greene King IPA; Tetley Burton Ale ⊞
One-bar village pub situated next to a picturesque 19th-century church. Formerly owned by Allied-Domecq, this Punch Taverns house is divided into several drinking areas which helps to maintain an intimate atmosphere. The exterior is particularly attractive in summer when the window boxes are a blaze of colour. There is a garden to the rear and a patio to the front, plus a barbecue. Recent new management has revitalised the place and the future looks secure for this establishment. ⚘⚘◑♣P✂

NUTHAMPSTEAD

Woodman Inn
SG8 8NB (signed off A10) OS413346
🕐 11-3.30, 5.30-11; 11-11 Sat; 12-4, 7-10.30 Sun
☎ (01763) 848328
website: www.thewoodman-inn.co.uk
Adnams Bitter; Fuller's London Pride; guest beer ⊞
This 17th-century free house features an L-shaped bar and wonderful open fires. The restaurant offers à la carte meals as well as house specials and snacks (no food Sun eve). Accommodation is available, making this an excellent base for visiting local attractions, such as Duxford Imperial War Museum. During WWII the USAF 398th bomber group was based locally. The B-17 Flying Fortresses flew many missions over Europe and the pub displays original photographs and memorabilia. A memorial is located outside. The pub has been a regular winner of the local CAMRA Pub of the Season. ⚘Q⚘🛏◑P🍺

OLD KNEBWORTH

Lytton Arms
Park Lane, SG3 6QB OS229202
🕐 11-11; 12-10.30 Sun
☎ (01438) 812312 website: www.thelytton-arms.co.uk
Adnams Bitter, Broadside; Fuller's London Pride; Woodforde's Wherry; guest beers ⊞
Popular, large Lutyens inn adjoining the Knebworth estate. Built in the 19th century, it features fascinating photos of Knebworth House and its pop festivals, and of the locals, past and present. The pub has featured for over a decade in this Guide and thousands of different ales have been served. A range of Belgian beers (bottled and draught) is available. Recently refurbished, it also offers an extensive selection of food and draught cider. The pub has won numerous CAMRA awards and hosts regular beer festivals. ⚘⚘◑♿♣👜P✂

POTTERS CROUCH

Hollybush ⊘
Bedmond Lane, AL3 4AL (off A4147) OS116053
✪ 11.30 (12 Sat)-2.30, 6 (7 Sat)-11; 12-2.30,
7-10.30 Sun
☎ (01727) 851792
Fuller's Chiswick, London Pride, ESB; seasonal beers (occasional) ⊞

Attractive, early 18th-century, oak-beamed pub in rural surroundings. It is well furnished throughout with large oak tables and period chairs. The landlord is a top Fuller's Master Cellarman and a winner of many brewery awards. The huge array of award certificates displayed in the bar confirms that this is one of the best quality Fuller's outlets in the area. Good lunchtime snacks are served (not Sun). The pleasant large garden is ideal in summer. ⚲Q P

PRESTON

Red Lion
The Green, SG4 7UD (signed from B651)
✪ 12-2.30, 5.30-11 (hours vary Sat); 12-3,
7-10.30 Sun
☎ (01462) 459585
Greene King IPA; guest beers ⊞

Attractive Georgian-style free house on the village green. It was Britain's first community-owned pub in the 1980s. It features guest beers from many micro-breweries. The freshly home-cooked food is second to none, with many local sources of supply. No evening meals are served on Tuesday. It has many cricket teams and is involved in fundraising events. It was the local CAMRA Pub of the Year 2001, and Hertfordshire CAMRA Pub of the Year 2001. In the Morning Advertiser Pub Industry Awards, the Red Lion won the silver medal in 2003. ⚲Q❀《❶ ⊞♣ P

RADLETT

Red Lion
78-80 Watling Street, WD7 7NP (on A5183)
✪ 11-11; 12-10.30 Sun
☎ (01923) 855341
Young's Bitter, Special, seasonal beers ⊞

This Victorian hotel, opposite Radlett railway station, was originally a Temperance establishment. Things have now changed and Young's bought the freehold in 2000. The bar area has been extended, and the 60-seat restaurant refurbished. There are 14 guest rooms and a function room. Meals are served 12–3 and 6–10. There is a flower-bedecked patio at the front of the building overlooking the street. ❀⚄《❶ & ⇌P

Cat & Fiddle
14 Cobden Hill, Watling Street, WD7 7JR (on A5183)
✪ 11-11; 12-10.30 Sun
☎ (01923) 469523
Greene King IPA; Shepherd Neame Spitfire; Young's Bitter ⊞

Mostly 18th-century, the pub has three oak-panelled bars on different levels (some parts of the building are older). Games and quizzes are popular in the public bar and the pub fields a football team. There is a cosy snug and a comfortable lounge with carved furniture. Admire the fantastic collection of china cats and two fiddles. An

---

attractive patio and large car park are to the rear. Q❀《⇌♣P

REDBOURN

Chequers
1 St Albans Road, AL3 7AD
✪ 11-11; 12-10.30 Sun
☎ (01582) 782359
Courage Best Bitter; guest beers ⊞

Originally a 14th-century coaching station, the building was first shown on the map in 1760. More recently its owners, Chef & Brewer, refurbished it in 2000, but the thatched roof and the original timber frames in the dining area have been retained. The landlord has been here for three years and has access to an extensive range of guest ales. Beer drinkers are welcome to drink anywhere in the dining area (the landlord stresses the Chequers is not a restaurant per se). ⚲Q❀《❶ ⊞&P⊁

Hollybush
Church End, AL3 7DU (in cul-de-sac by St Mary's Church, off the common)
✪ 11-2.30 (3 Sat), 5.30 (7 Sat)-11; 12-3,
7-10.30 Sun
☎ (01582) 782423
Adnams Bitter; Tetley Bitter; guest beers ⊞

Charming two-bar pub set in picturesque Church End, just off Chequer Lane and opposite almshouses. The building is 16th-century, the first official records state it was a pub in 1595. This is Redbourn's true free house, serving three ever-changing guest beers from a variety of independent brewers. These include Archers, Cottage, Church End, Mauldons, Nethergate, Rebellion, Vale and Wolf. There is a folk music evening every Thursday. Lunches are served Monday–Saturday. ⚲Q❀《❶⊞P

ST ALBANS

Farmer's Boy
134 London Road, AL1 1PQ
✪ 11-11; 12-10.30 Sun
☎ (01727) 766702
Verulam Best Bitter, Special, IPA, Farmers Joy, seasonal beers ⊞

Cosy, cottage-style pub, now the home of the Verulam Brewery, which moved here from Harpenden in 1996. All the beers are brewed on site, including good value Best Bitter and monthly seasonal beers. An assortment of German and Belgian bottled beers is also available. All the food is home made and served from 11.30–9.30 every day, with roasts on Sundays and barbecues on the patio in summer. Satellite TV is provided. Look out for the unusual ashtrays on the bar. ⚲❀《❶⇌ (City) ♣

King Harry
2 King Harry Lane, AL3 4BL
✪ 12-11; 12-10.30 Sun
☎ (01727) 846904
Beer range varies ⊞

Vastly improved M&B pub (dating from mid-18th century) situated at the southern entrance to the city. An interesting selection of up to six beers is available at premium prices. Belgian bottled beers are also stocked as well as an extensive wine list. A wide range of home-cooked food is served daily. The beer garden has halogen-heated lamps.

Quiz night is Monday. Live musical duos perform every six weeks. Pub games on offer include draughts, chess and Jenga.
❀◑≠(Abbey) P✕

Lower Red Lion
34-36 Fishpool Street, AL3 4RX
✪ 12-2.30, 5.30-11; 12-11 Sat; 12-3, 7-10.30 Sun
☎ (01727) 855669
Fuller's London Pride; Oakham JHB; guest beers Ⓗ
17th-century, two bar coaching inn located near the cathedral and Roman Verulamium. This genuine free house stocks seven changing guest beers from micro-breweries, Dutch, Czech and Belgian beers on draught, Belgian bottled beers and malt whiskies. Regular beer festivals, including May Day and August bank holiday weekends, feature up to 50 unusual beers. It offers comfortable B&B with full English breakfast. Lunch is served every day, including Sunday roasts with up to 10 vegetables. Quiz night is Wednesday. ⚑Q❀⇚◑♣P

Mermaid
98 Hatfield Road, AL1 3RL
✪ 12-11 (midnight Wed & Fri); 11.30-midnight Sat; 12-10.30 Sun
☎ (01727) 837758
Adnams Bitter; Everards Tiger; guest beers Ⓗ
A beer house until 1950, this ex-Everards pub dates back to 1830. The L-shaped bar boasts beers from smaller brewers such as Nethergate and B&T. The Mermaid is now owned by English Inns, the small enterprising pub chain. Wednesday evenings feature an 'open mike' night for musicians to perform. Live bands play occasionally on Saturdays. A cashpoint machine is available. ❀◑≠(City) ♣P

White Hart Tap
4 Keyfield Terrace, AL1 1QJ
✪ 12-11; 12-10.30 Sun
☎ (01727) 860974 website: www.whiteharttap.co.uk
Adnams Broadside; Caledonian Deuchars IPA; Fuller's London Pride; guest beer Ⓗ
Much-improved one-bar, back-street local, featuring two guest beers per week. Parking is possible nearby. Daily lunchtime meals are offered including Sunday roasts. Barbecues are held in the spacious garden in summer. Occasional food nights are hosted, live music can be heard with local bands performing on Saturday nights. The pub is twinned with the 'Bar No Limit' in Belgrade and a visit there was featured on Carlton Television. ⚑❀◑♣

ST PAULS WALDEN

Strathmore Arms
London Road, SG4 8BT (on B656)
✪ Closed Mon, Tue & Wed; 12-2.30 Thu; 12-11 Fri & Sat; 12-10.30 Sun
☎ (01438) 871654
Fuller's Chiswick, London Pride; guest beers Ⓗ
This is a refurbished pub on the Bowes-Lyon estate. The landlord has run an independent pub before, at Hitchin. He has changed this pub completely, and offers a fine selection of beers, including many from micro-breweries. A selection of real ciders will be introduced soon. The pub is close to the church and proves popular with the local bellringers.
Q⚘❀◑▲♣P

SANDRIDGE

Green Man
High Street, AL4 9VD
✪ 11-3, 5.30-11; 11-11 Fri & Sat; 11-10.30 Sun
☎ (01727) 854845
website: www.thegreenman@sandridge.co.uk
Adnams Broadside; Ⓖ **Draught Bass;** Ⓗ **Bateman XXXB;** Ⓖ **Greene King IPA,** Ⓗ **Abbot** Ⓖ
Comfortable one-bar pub located in the middle of the High Street. The landlord has resided here for 16 years – the longest-serving in Sandridge. It is very much a locals' pub but all discerning beer drinkers are most welcome. Evening meals are served on Friday and Saturday. A local cycling club meets every Thursday. There are usually three beers served straight from the cask, these come from a separate cellar and are located nearby at floor level. ⚑Q⚘❀◑♣P

SAWBRIDGEWORTH

Gate
81 London Road, CM21 9JJ
✪ 11.30-2.30; 11.30-11 Fri & Sat; 12-10.30 Sun
☎ (01279) 722313
Greene King Abbot; Taylor Landlord; Ⓗ **guest beers** Ⓗ/Ⓖ
Small pub that caters for the local community. Host to the Sawbridgeworth Brewery (in the car park), the pub aims to keep nine real ales at all times and a real cider is sold in summer. The front bar has over 2,000 pump clips from the ales they have served. The rear bar is home to the pub's sports teams and a younger clientele. There are small patio areas at the front and side for summer drinking. The very small car park will tax any driver's three-point-turn ability. ❀◑&≠♣●P

SLEAPSHYDE

Plough
Sleapshyde Lane, AL4 0SB (off A414 towards Hatfield via Small ford Rd and Sleapshyde lane)
✪ 11.30-2.30, 5.30-11; 11-3, 6-11 Sat; 12-3, 7-10.30 Sun
☎ (01727) 823730
Fuller's London Pride; Greene King Abbot; Tetley Bitter Ⓗ
Popular, friendly pub located in the centre of a small hamlet, parts of it date back to the 14th century. The original building has a wealth of exposed beams and an inglenook, with the more recent addition of a larger bar and restaurant area behind. The menu is good value, and offers some unusual dishes. ⚑⚘❀◑♣P

SOUTH MIMMS

Black Horse
65 Blackhorse Lane, EN6 3PS
(off B556 near A1/M25 jct)
✪ 11-3, 5.30-11; 11-11 Fri & Sat; 12-10.30 Sun
☎ (01707) 642174
Greene King IPA, Abbot, seasonal beers Ⓗ
It may not seem possible that the narrow, winding Blackhorse Lane was once the main road linking the north-west of England to London. This is, of course, why the pub is on the site. This busy two-bar local also caters for passing trade. The lively public bar has a thriving darts team. The cosy lounge has a horsy theme, an open

fire, interesting furniture and bric-à-brac. The secluded garden overlooks farm buildings. The Black Horse has a reputation for good food. ✿✿⊄⊞♣P

STANSTEAD ABBOTTS

Lord Louis
36 High Street, SG12 8AG
✪ 11-11; 12-10.30 Sun
☎ (01920) 870121
Fuller's Chiswick, London Pride, ESB Ⓗ
Large town-style pub that stands in a small village. This was once a multi-roomed house as is evident by the different floorings (wood, tile and stone) as you walk through. Many of the chairs have previously been used in a church. The pub now attracts fewer youngsters than in the past. The car park is very small. ⊄▶⇌ (St Margarets) P

STAPLEFORD

Papillon (at the Woodhall Arms)
17 High Road, SG14 3NW
✪ 11-3, 5-midnight; 12-3, 6.30-10.30 Sun
☎ (01992) 535123
Adnams Bitter or Greene King IPA; guest beers Ⓗ
Spacious pub-restaurant that retains a pub atmosphere in its main entrance bar. The restaurant areas have a reasonably priced, wide choice of superb food and bar meals and children's menus are also offered. There are four beers on handpump, guests are from noted craft/micro-brewers and always in excellent order. B&B accommodation is available. There is a disabled WC and wheelchair access, but there is a step to each separate dining area. ✿≠⊄⊞⚲P

STEVENAGE

Our Mutual Friend
Broadwater Crescent, SG2 8EH (1 mile off A1(M) jct 7, off A602, roundabout at Esso garage)
✪ 12-11; 12-10.30 Sun
☎ (01438) 312282
Black Sheep Best Bitter; Caledonian Deuchars IPA; Tetley Dark Mild; guest beers Ⓗ
Boasting a name derived from a Dickens's novel, this lively two-bar estate pub has been brought back to 'real ale' life by four CAMRA members. Close to Stevenage football ground, three permanent beers (one always a dark mild) and rotating guests have drawn drinkers back to their local. Watch live sports, play pool and darts in the public bar, or enjoy peace and quiet, and read a novel by Dickens in the lounge bar. Beer festivals and live music sessions are held regularly. Local CAMRA Pub of the Season and Most Improved Pub 2002. Good pub grub is served Monday–Saturday (12–3.30) and Sunday roasts (12.30–2.30). Q✿⊄⊞♣♠P

Squirrel Tavern
Chells Way, SG2 0LA (off Sixhills Way)
✪ 12-11; 12-10.30 Sun
☎ (01438) 312037
Greene King IPA; Potton Shannon IPA; guest beers Ⓗ
Large, light, airy community pub with a central bar area, ample seating and air conditioning. There are plenty of sports channels, a pool table and dartboard. The pub runs its own successful football team and holds regular pub quiz nights. There

is a large patio garden to the front of the pub with wooden benches and hanging baskets. Entertainment nights are held every two weeks. Lunches are served Monday–Friday (12–5) and Saturday and Sunday (12–4).
✿⊄⊞P

TRING

King's Arms
King Street, HP23 6BE
(Aylesbury end of town, B4635)
✪ 12-2.30 (3 Fri), 7-11; 11.30-3, 7-11 Sat; 12-4, 7-10.30 Sun
☎ (01442) 823318
Wadworth 6X; guest beers Ⓗ
This back-street 1830s town pub exudes a welcoming country feel. Its grand pillared entrance contrasts with the subdued green, half-panelled interior that boasts real fires, brewing mirrors and plaques. The ever-changing range of guest beers never disappoints. Bottled Belgian beers are also available, as is a take-away service. There is a seasonally-changing menu, with an international flavour. Dishes made to home-cooked original recipes use locally supplied bread, meat and vegetables. This local and regional CAMRA Pub of the Year 2002, has a no-smoking area at lunchtime. The canopied patio is heated in spring and autumn.
♨Q✿⊄▶⚲

Robin Hood ✔
1 Brook Street, HP23 5ED
(on roundabout at B4635/B486 jct)
✪ 11-2.30 (3 Sat), 5.30 (6.30 Sat)-11; 12-3, 7-10.30 Sun
☎ (01442) 824912
Fuller's Chiswick, London Pride, ESB, seasonal beer Ⓗ
Brilliant white with distinctive Fuller's logo, this pub nestles down to the side of the main road at the lower end of the High Street. The beers are in superb condition; the landlord has twice been awarded Fuller's Master Cellarman of the Year. The pristine interior has a single bar and gleaming handpumps. The inset marine montage in one corner suggests the food speciality. The cosy layout has a mixture of booths, chairs and stools, the latter clustered around a wood-burning stove. There is a no-smoking seating area to the rear.
♨Q✿⊄▶⚲

WARE

Crooked Billet
140 Musley Hill, SG12 7NL
(via New Rd from Ware High St)
✪ 12-2.30 (not Mon, Wed or Thu), 5.30-11; 12-11 Sat; 12-10.30 Sun
☎ (01920) 462516
Greene King XX Mild, IPA, Morland Original, seasonal beers Ⓗ
Justifiably popular local, some 20 minutes' walk from the station and well worth tracking down. There are two main bar areas, one relaxed and cosy, the other more animated, with a pool table and Sky Sports. Carlisle United fans are always welcome. The beers normally include the hard-to-find Greene King's XX dark mild. Bar snacks are available. ♨✿♣

WARESIDE

Chequers Inn
SG12 7QY
(on B1004, in centre of village) OS395156
✪ 12-2.30, 6-11; 12-11 Sat; 12-10.30 Sun
☎ (01920) 467010
Adnams Bitter, Broadside; guest beers Ⓗ
Once a traditional 17th-century coaching inn, this characterful, cosy pub has a most interesting interior with low, beamed ceilings. It offers three distinct drinking areas and a restaurant converted from the old stables. All the food is freshly cooked; local game is a speciality and there is a good range of vegetarian dishes. Small independent breweries predominate among the guest beers. There is a patio at the front of the pub facing the road. Live jazz is played on Sunday evening. ▲Q❀◒◑❶P

WATFORD

Estcourt Arms
2 St Johns Road, WD1 1PT (¼ mile SE of Watford Junction Station)
✪ 11-11; 12-10.30 Sun
☎ (01923) 220754
Adnams Bitter; Fuller's London Pride; Tetley Bitter; guest beer (occasional) Ⓗ
This is a smallish, street-corner town pub with a strong Irish influence. The main bar is complemented by a small snug, the door to which is not always opened at the first attempt! Live Irish music is played late Sunday afternoon/early evening. The pub is known locally as 'Lynch's' after the landlord. Lunches are served Monday–Friday. ❀◒≠ (Junction)

WHEATHAMPSTEAD

Swan
56 High Street, AL4 8AR
✪ 12-11; 12-10.30 Sun
☎ (01582) 833110
Adnams Broadside; Draught Bass; Shepherd Neame Spitfire; Ⓖ **Tetley Burton Ale** Ⓗ
Cheerful, welcoming, one-bar pub, just off the mini roundabout in the High Street. First officially recorded as a pub in 1756, the building is evidently older, as is suggested by the low, timber frames and inglenook (now housing a gas fire). It is reputed to be the first watering-hole between London and the North – stables once existed where the bottle stall now sits. Brocket Hall and the NT's Shaw's Corner (formerly home of George Bernard Shaw) are local attractions. ❀◒P

WHITWELL

Maiden's Head
67 High Street, SG4 8AH (signed from B656)
✪ 11.30-3 (4 Sat), 5 (6 Sat)-11; 12-3, 7-10.30 Sun
☎ (01438) 871392
Draught Bass; McMullen AK, Country; guest beers Ⓗ
One of the flagship McMullen's pubs, this is a popular two-bar local. The landlord celebrated 20 years in residence in October 2002. He has won numerous McMullen's Cellarman of the Year awards, and he won the Ted and Josie Arnold award a few years ago for the Best Community Pub. A collection of Dinky toys is on display in the public bar while photographs and awards

decorate the wall, showing the true village pub. Lunchtime food is served Monday–Saturday, and evening meals Tuesday–Sunday. ▲❀◒◑❶♣P

WIDFORD

Green Man
High Street, SG12 8GR (on B1004) OS420159
✪ 12-3, 5.30-11; 12-11 Sat; 12-10.30 Sun
☎ (01279) 842846
Adnams Bitter; McMullen AK; guest beer Ⓗ
This pub is popular with village locals and is also a welcome stop-off point for walkers and cyclists. The B&B is often oversubscribed, so book in advance. New accommodation in the adjacent barn should solve the problem – due for completion in 2004. Guest beers (at least one, but more at weekends) are from independent breweries. Being a true free house, guest ales are selected by quality not by price. No food is served on Monday lunchtime, evening food should be available sometime in 2004. ❀◒◑♿P

WILDHILL

Woodman
45 Wildhill Road, AL9 6EA (between A1000 and B158) OS265068
✪ 11.30-2.30, 5.30-11; 12-2.30, 7-10.30 Sun
☎ (01707) 642618
Greene King IPA, Abbot; McMullen AK; guest beers Ⓗ
An absolute gem, a small, friendly village pub specialising in beers from micro-breweries. Popular with office workers at lunchtime, it is also busy on Sunday lunchtimes although no food is served that day. Bus service 201 stops outside the pub on Tuesday and Thursday. The Woodman is close to the estate of the late Dame Barbara Cartland. It is a popular watering-hole for Saracens rugby fans (the landlord is a keen supporter). The pub is the cheapest genuine free house in Herts and a winner of many local CAMRA awards, including Pub of the Year 2002. It is well worth a visit. Q❀◒♣P

WILLIAN

Three Horseshoes
Baldock Lane, SG6 2AE (tiny lane opp. the church, 1 mile from jct 9 A1(M))
✪ 11-11; 12-10.30 Sun
☎ (01462) 685713
Greene King IPA, Morland Original, Ruddles County, Abbot, Old Speckled Hen Ⓗ
This pub was originally two 18th-century cottages. The 'Shoes' remained a two-roomed tavern for over two centuries until 1975 when it was converted into the cosy single bar of today. Popular with locals, it is very much a community pub with darts, cribbage and quiz teams. Weekly raffles raise funds for charity. A marquee provides a venue for up to 20 people. It is a former winner of the local CAMRA Community Pub of the Year. ▲❀◒♣P

> Keep your Good Beer Guide up to date by visiting the CAMRA website www.camra.org.uk, then Good Beer Guide, then Updates to GBG.

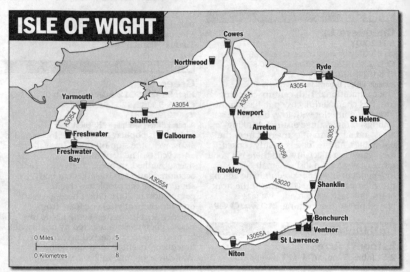

ISLE OF WIGHT

Cowes
Northwood
Ryde
A3054
Yarmouth
A3054
Newport
St Helens
Shalfleet
Calbourne
Arreton
A3055
Freshwater
A3056
Freshwater
Bay
Rookley
A3055A
A3020
Shanklin
A3055A
Bonchurch
Ventnor
St Lawrence
Niton

0 Miles 5
0 Kilometres 8

BONCHURCH

Bonchurch Inn
The Chute, PO38 1NU (off Shanklin road)
☼ 11-3, 6.30-11; 12-3, 7-10.30 Sun
☎ (01983) 852611 website: www.bonchurch-inn.co.uk
Courage Best Bitter, Directors Ⓖ
Superbly preserved stone pub, tucked away
in a Dickensian courtyard and former
stables of the adjacent Manor House. Little
has changed since first gaining its licence in
the 1840s, making this one of the most
unspoilt pubs on the island. As well as
featuring in an episode of TV's The
Detectives, there are mementos and
keepsakes from many of the stars who have
popped in when visiting the island. There is
an Italian restaurant across the courtyard.
Q ☼ ⚘ ⏩ ◑ ☖ ♣ P ⊁

CALBOURNE

Sun
Sun Hill, PO30 4JA
☼ 11-3, 5-11; 12-3, 6-10.30 Sun
☎ (01983) 531231 website: www.sun-calbourne.co.uk
**Adnams Bitter; Black Sheep Best Bitter; Greene King
IPA, Abbot; Ringwood Fortyniner; Taylor Landlord** Ⓗ
Family-friendly village pub, overlooking
Westover cricket ground, with a traditional
public bar. Splendid views can be had of
Westover and Brighstone Forest and of
Freshwater Cliffs in the distance. It benefits
from a garden and patio and a very large car
park. Good home-made food includes a
daily roast. It stocks an excellent selection
of ales and an ever-changing range of guest
beers. Winkle Street is but a short stagger
away. ☼ ⚘ ◑ ☖ ♣ P

COWES

Kingston Arms
176 Newport Road, PO31 7PS
☼ 11-2.30, 6-11; 11-11 Fri & Sat; 12-4, 7-10.30 Sun
☎ (01983) 293393
Gale's HSB; guest beers Ⓗ
On the main road out of Cowes towards
Newport, you cannot miss the Kingston
Arms. This friendly, family and locals' pub

near the yachting centre, provides good
value bed and breakfast accommodation. A
lively public bar offers darts, pool, petanque
and any other variety of game that takes
your fancy. Beer is always in good order and
an interesting variety of guest ales adds to
the pub's appeal. ⚌ ⚘ ⏩ ◑ ☖ ♣ P

Union Inn
Watch House Lane, PO31 7QH
(just off the Parade)
☼ 10.30-3, 6-11 (10.30-11 summer); 12-10.30 Sun
☎ (01983) 293163
Gale's GB, HSB; guest beer (summer) Ⓗ
One three-sided bar serves the lounge, a
snug, a dining area and the airy
conservatory that had originally been the
yard. The beer range is limited but always in
tiptop condition, with a guest ale from the
Gale's portfolio during the summer months.
A roaring fire in winter adds to the overall
cosy atmosphere. The long-standing
landlord has built up the trade for good
value accommodation in both the winter
and summer months. ⚌ Q ☼ ⚘ ◑ ☖ ⊁

FRESHWATER

Prince of Wales
Princes Road, PO40 9ED
☼ 11-11; 12-10.30 Sun
☎ (01983) 753535
**Boddingtons Bitter; Greene King Abbot; Tetley Mild;
Wadworth 6X** Ⓗ
Fine, unspoilt town pub run by possibly the
longest-serving landlord on the island. A
strong games section adds to the lively
atmosphere. Situated just off the main
Freshwater shopping centre, there is a large
garden to relax in and a pleasant snug bar
to sample the ales. A barrel of cider is now
kept out the back. Should you have one too
many of an evening, no need to phone for a
taxi – the landlord has one.
⚘ ◑ ☖ ⅙ ▲ ♣ ♦ P ⎚

FRESHWATER BAY

Fat Cat Bar
Sandpipers, Coastguard Lane, PO40 9QX

☼ 11-3, 6-11; 12-3, 6-10.30 Sun
☎ (01983) 758500 website: www.fatcattrading.co.uk
Beer range varies Ⓗ

A real gem, tucked away within the Sandpipers Hotel, situated between Freshwater Bay and the Afton Nature Reserve. An ever-changing range of ales (usually four on tap), mainly from smaller breweries, is served in convivial surroundings. Well frequented by young and old alike; for children, there is an adventure playground, and for adults, a choice of patio or garden area for outside drinking. The traditional public bar has been replaced by a games area with pool table, darts and the like, popular with locals.
ᴁQ ▓ ⊛ ⇆ ◑ ⅃PⰔ

NEWPORT

Bargeman's Rest
Little London Quay, PO30 5BS
(signed from dual carriageway)
☼ 10.30-11; 12-10.30 Sun
☎ (01983) 525828 website: www.bargemansrest.co.uk
Badger IPA, Best, Tanglefoot; guest beers Ⓗ

This locally-owned, massive pub development is located in what has been an animal feed store, a sail loft and a rigging loft for servicing the commercial barge fleet. The outdoor drinking area is only a few feet from the bustling River Medina. The food is consistently good and is available all day. Entertainment is staged most of the week and beer festivals are held in conjunction with the other three pubs in the group.
Q ▓ ⊛ ◑ PⰔ

Prince of Wales
36 South Street, PO30 1JE (opp. bus station)
☼ 10.30-11; 12-4, 7-10.30 Sun
☎ (01983) 525026
Goddards Special Bitter; Oakleaf Hole Hearted; Usher's Best Bitter; guest beers Ⓗ

Formerly the tap for the adjacent (now demolished) Green Dragon, this excellent mock-Tudor single-bar, street-corner local has built up a fine reputation for its ale and tasty food. Although in the centre of town, opposite Safeway supermarket, this is very much a locals' pub that has resisted the temptation to be 'tarted up', and retains its public bar atmosphere. ᴁQ ◑ ♣ ⊟

Railway Medina
1 Sea Street, PO30 5BU
☼ 11-11; 12-10.30 Sun
☎ (01983) 528303
Gale's HSB; Webster's Green Label; guest beers Ⓗ

Excellent, popular and comfortable, unspoilt street-corner local. Enjoy the pleasant, cosy atmosphere at this regular Guide entry. Its name comes from being the closest to the now-demolished Newport railway station and the pub contains many old IW railway photographs and artefacts. It was purchased from Gale's without tie by the incumbent landlord.
ᴁ ⊛ ◑ ⊟ ♣

NITON

Buddle Inn
St Catherine's Road, PO38 2NE (follow signs to St Catherine's lighthouse)
☼ 11-11; 12-10.30 Sun
☎ (01983) 730243

Adnams Bitter; Flowers Original; Greene King Abbot; guest beers Ⓗ

16th-century farmhouse that reputedly became a smugglers' inn during the 18th century. Extensively refurbished in recent years, it retains its ancient flagstones, beams and inglenook. The adjoining smugglers' barn was a cattle shed until 1934 when it was transformed into a dance hall. Very popular with the seasonal trade, with an ample area outside to take advantage of the south-facing views, it has an excellent reputation for good quality food. At least six ales are stocked, chosen to suit the landlord's taste. ᴁ ▓ ⊛ ◑ ♣ PⰔ

NORTHWOOD

Travellers Joy
85 Pallance Road, PO31 8LS
(on A3020, Yarmouth road)
☼ 11-2.30, 5-11; 11-11 Fri & Sat; 12-3, 7-10.30 Sun
☎ (01983) 298024 website: www.tjoy.com
Goddards Special Bitter; guest beers Ⓗ

Offering one of the best choices of cask ales on the Isle of Wight, this well-renovated and extended old country inn, was the island's first beer exhibition house. The island's beer drinkers owe much to the Travellers Joy, and it has deservedly won local CAMRA's Pub of the Year award on no less than five occasions. Always at least eight beers are on offer from national, local and micro-breweries. A good range of home-cooked food is served.
ᴁ ▓ ⊛ ◑ Å ♣ PⰔ ⊟

ROOKLEY

Chequers Inn
Niton Road, PO38 3NZ (off A3020)
☼ 11-11; 12-10.30 Sun
☎ (01983) 840314
website: www.chequers-inn.demon.co.uk
Courage Best Bitter, Directors; Gale's HSB; Greene King Old Speckled Hen; John Smith's Bitter Ⓗ

This country pub at the heart of the island benefits from beautiful views. Considering its present popularity after an extensive rebuild, it is astonishing that Whitbread closed the pub and sold it. Dating from the mid-1800s it was once a customs and excise house. It is heavily food- and family-oriented, but retains a flagstone public bar and a fine pint of beer. Very good children's facilities include a large outdoor play area and changing room. Food is served all day.
ᴁ ▓ ⊛ ◑ ⊟ Å ♣ PⰔ

Rookley Inn
Main Road, PO38 3NG
☼ 2-11 (11-12.30am summer); 12-10.30 (11-12.30am summer) Sun
☎ (01983) 721800
Fuller's London Pride; Greene King Abbot; guest beers Ⓗ

Over the years, this amenity built to enhance the enjoyment of the Country Park has become a fine pub, offering an excellent

INDEPENDENT BREWERIES

Goddards Ryde
Scarecrow Arreton
Ventnor Ventnor
Yates St Lawrence

selection of up to six real ales. It enjoys a following from across the island. Outside is a good children's playground, arcade and pitch and putt. Nightly entertainment (March–Nov) includes a Kids Club. Set in 22 acres, Rookley Country Park, and adjacent lake, is the ideal centre for a holiday. Evening meals are served in summer. The late licence also applies on Friday and Saturday in winter. ⌂❀☙❮❙&❀P

RYDE

Railway
68 St John's Road, PO33 2RT
(by St John's Station)
☼ 11-11; 12-10.30 Sun
☎ (01983) 615405
Beer range varies Ⓗ
Refurbished to a standard that enhances the drinking experience, and re-named back to the original Railway, its paint job in yellow and green sounds bizarre but looks very good. This pub has a following for its range of at least six beers, two of which are local. Having once been a very ordinary town pub it is now a major venue under the guidance of its latest tenants. ⌂⌂❀☙❮≢(St John's)

Simeon Arms
21 Simeon Street, PO33 1JG
(opp. swimming pool and canoe lake)
☼ 11-3, 6-11; 11-11 Fri & Sat; 12-10.30 Sun
☎ (01983) 614954
Courage Directors; Goddards Special Bitter; guest beers Ⓗ
Thriving, yet unlikely gem, tucked away in Ryde's back streets, with a Tardis-like interior and separate function hall. The pub is immensely popular with the local community who participate in all the various indoor leagues, such as darts, crib and pool, plus petanque on the enormous floodlit pitch during the summer. With such a throughput of customers, the beer is always in pristine condition. Evening meals are served Friday and Saturday.
⌂❀☙❮≢(Esplanade) ❀

Solent Inn
7 Monkton Street, PO33 1JW
(by parade of shops)
☼ 11-11; 12-10.30 Sun
☎ (01983) 563546
Greene King IPA; guest beers Ⓗ
Excellent, street-corner local, that has improved considerably under its present landlord. The range of real ales has increased to four (five in summer), due to demand by the regulars, and varies frequently. Parts of the pub are very ancient, and the public bar slopes downhill alarmingly. Friday is music night, when the landlord and many local musicians jam together on a variety of instruments, including flutes and (astonishingly) a concert harp. ❀❮❙≢(Esplanade) ❀

ST HELENS

Vine Inn
Upper Green Road, PO33 1UJ
☼ 11-11; 12-10.30 Sun
☎ (01983) 872337
Fuller's London Pride; Greene King IPA, Abbot, Old Speckled Hen; guest beers Ⓗ
Friendly, two-bar pub overlooking the

208

village green. An interesting selection of guest beers includes some unlikely to be found anywhere else on the island. A restaurant is at the rear, adjoining the garden. Adequate public parking space can be found behind the children's playground on the green opposite. ⌂❀☙❮▲❀

SHALFLEET

New Inn
Main Road, PO30 4NS
☼ 12-3, 6-11 (12-11 summer); 12-3, 6-10.30 Sun
☎ (01983) 531314 website: www.thenew-inn.co.uk
Badger Best; Draught Bass; Ventnor Golden; guest beers Ⓗ
The New Inn has stood at the entrance to Mill Road for 300 years. An ancient, and largely unspoilt, country local with flagstoned floor and huge log fire, the good beer and food, especially fish and seafood for which the pub is noted, continue to entice locals from inland and seafarers up the lane from Shalfleet creek. The roaring log fire is a delight and, in summer, there are rustic chairs and tables outside and an ample back garden to enjoy.
⌂⌂❀☙❮▲❀P✂

SHANKLIN

King Harry's Bar
Glenbrooke Hotel, Old Village, PO37 6NU
☼ 11-11; 12-10.30 Sun
☎ (01983) 863119
Fuller's London Pride; guest beers Ⓗ
Charming, 19th-century thatched property with parking at the front and rear. The amenities here include two established Tudor bars inside, and decking, gardens and a chine walk outside. The long-established Henry VIII Kitchen specialises in steaks and grills. It is well worth a visit for an ever-changing range of beer and an interesting menu. It stages entertainment and other functions can be catered for.
❀☙❮❙&❙≢❀P

VENTNOR

Spyglass Inn
Esplanade, PO38 1JX
☼ 10.30-11; 12-10.30 Sun
☎ (01983) 855338
Badger Best, Tanglefoot; Ventnor Golden; guest beers Ⓗ
The inn has considerable character and boasts a large collection of seafaring memorabilia. Wisely, the temptation was avoided to knock all the rooms into one; instead they have been skilfully incorporated into the overall layout. Local seafood is a speciality (meals are served all day at weekends and in summer). A small beer festival is held every year. Regular entertainment is provided most evenings and on Sunday lunchtime. The outdoor drinking area is huge. ⌂❀☙❮❙P

Volunteer
30 Victoria Street, PO38 1ES
(near bus terminus)
☼ 11-11; 12-10.30 Sun
☎ (01983) 852537
website: www.thevolunteer.demon.co.uk
Badger Best; Greene King Abbot; Ventnor Golden; guest beers Ⓗ

Built in 1866, the Volunteer is probably the smallest pub on the Isle of Wight. It operated as a beer house between 1869 and 1871 and retains many original features. It is well known for the quality of its beer which has been recognised by the many awards in CAMRA's local Pub of the Year competition. No chips, no children, no fruit machines, no video games, just a pure adult drinking house, this is one of the few places where you can still play rings. ♨ Q ♣

YARMOUTH

Wheatsheaf Inn
Bridge Road, PO41 0PH

☼ 11-11; 12-10.30 Sun
☎ (01983) 760456
Brakspear Special; Ⓗ **Goddards Fuggle-Dee-Dum;** Ⓖ **Greene King Old Speckled Hen; Wadworth 6X** Ⓗ
Old coaching house, now with additional rooms. Spacious and comfortable, it has a large conservatory to the rear for families and pleasant summer evenings. The large public bar receives its fair share of visiting yachtsmen, tracing the few yards from the harbour. The beer complements the interesting, good value, freshly-cooked food. The Wheatsheaf is ideal for summer days and snug for winter evenings.
Q ☎ ❀ ◑ ⌂ ≠ (Wightlink Ferry) ♣

Food for thought

Ale is an enemy to idlenesse, it will worke and bee working in the braine as well as in the Barrel; if it be abused by any man, it will trip up his heeles, and give him either a faire or fowle fall, if hee bee the strongest, stowtest, and skilfullest Wrastler either in Cornwall or Christendome. But if Ale bee moderately, mildly, and friendly dealt withall it will appease, qualifie, mitigate, and quench all striffe and contention, it wil lay anger asleepe, and give a furious man or woman a gentle Nap, and therefore it was rightly called Nappy ALE, by our Learned and Reverend Fore-fathers.

Besides it is very medicinable, (as the best Physitians doe affirme) for Beere is seldom used or applyed to any inward or outward maladies, except sometimes it bee warmed with a little Butter to wash the galled feete, or toes of a weary Traveller; but you shall never knowe or heare of a usuall drinker of ALE, to bee troubled with the Hippocondra, with Hiopocondragacall obstructions or convulsions, nor are they vexed (as others are) with severall paines of sundry sorts of Gowts, such as are the Gonogra, Podegra, Chirocgra, and the lame Hop-halting Sciatica, or with the intollerable griefe of the Stone in the Reines, Kidneys, or Bladder.

Beere is a Dutch Boorish Liquor, a thing not knowne in England, till of late dayes an Alien to our Nation, till such time as Hops and Heresies came amongst us, it is a fawcy intruder into this Land, and it's sold by usurpation; for the houses that doe sell Beere onely, are nickname Ale-houses; marke beloved, an Ale-house is never called a Beere-house, but a Beere-house would have but small custom, if it did not falsely carry the name of an Ale-house; also it is common to say a Stand of Ale, it is not onely a Stand, but it will make a man understand, or stand under; but Beere is often called a Hogshead, which all rational men doe knowe is but a swinish expression.

John Taylor (1580-1653), Ale ale-vated into the Ale-titude, 1651

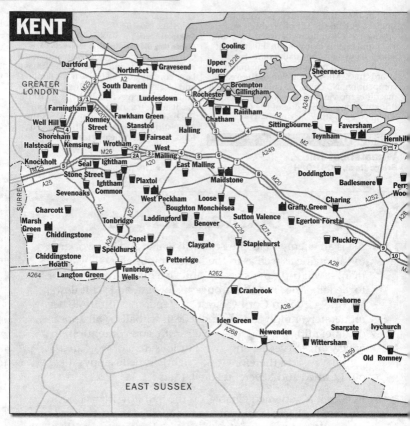

KENT

ASHLEY

Butcher's Arms
Chapel Lane, CT15 5HX
🕐 12-2 (3 Sat), 7-11; 12-5 Sun
☎ (01304) 825925
Shepherd Neame Master Brew Bitter; guest beer Ⓗ
Set in the village of Ashley (Studdal) the Butcher's is a classic village pub. Just off the North Downs Way, it is popular with walkers and cyclists. The patio and garden are open in warmer weather. No meals are served but bar snacks include pickled eggs and cockles. There is a cosy public bar and bar billiards in the games room. Ales vary, with one from a regional and some micro-brewery products usually available.
🍴Q✿⊞♣P

BADLESMERE

Red Lion
Ashford Road, ME13 0NX
🕐 12-3, 6-11; 12-11 Fri & Sat; 12-10.30 Sun
☎ (01233) 740320
Fuller's London Pride; Greene King Abbot; Shepherd Neame Master Brew Bitter; guest beers Ⓗ
Situated on the busy A251, five miles south of Faversham, this free house is noted for its food, prepared using local produce, some from the landlady's father's farm; no food is served Sunday evening. The pub dates from 1546 and its naturally cool cellar was once a morgue. Beer festivals are held over Easter and August bank holidays. Live bands perform on Friday evening. A mild is

usually offered, as is Johnson's cider from Sheppey (known locally as Marsh Monkey).
🍴✿🕓 Å♣ ♠P

BARFRESTONE

Yew Tree Inn
CT15 7JH
🕐 12-3 (not Mon), 6 (7 Mon)-11; 12-11 Fri & Sat;
12-7 (10.30 summer) Sun
☎ (01304) 831619 website: www.barfrestone.co.uk
Beer range varies Ⓗ
The Yew Tree, which has a long colourful history, specialises in Kentish ales sourced from most of the county's independent brewers, particularly Hopdaemon and Whitstable. A mild is always available and Biddenden cider is served from a cask. The food is restaurant quality and very popular, however the drinker always comes first at this delightful country pub. Evening meals are served Monday-Saturday.
🍴Q🕓✿🕓♠P

BENOVER

Woolpack Inn
Benover Road, ME18 6AS (on B2162, between Yalding and Collier Street) OS705482
🕐 12-3, 6-11, 7-10.30 Sun
☎ (01892) 730356
Shepherd Neame Master Brew Bitter Ⓗ
A warm welcome is always assured at this 15th-century country inn, where antique farm tools decorate the walls. Look for the skeleton in the cupboard and the brick floor

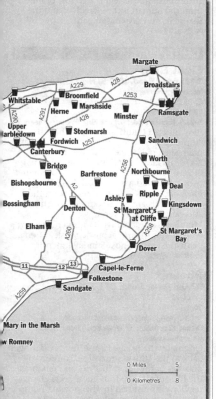

play area. Home-made food is served in both the bar and the attractive modern conservatory, which is a good place to organise celebratory meals. Barbecues are planned for the summer. A good pub for walkers and cyclists, it is surrounded by rolling fields, woodland and heath.
🏚Q🌣🍽🌑◐♣P✂

BOUGHTON MONCHELSEA

Cock Inn
Heath Road, ME17 4JD (off A229, S of Maidstone) OS776508
🕛 11-11; 12-10.30 Sun
☎ (01622) 743166
website: www.cockinn@youngs.co.uk
Young's Bitter, Special, Waggle Dance (summer), Winter Warmer Ⓗ

This 16th-century, Grade I listed coaching inn has been owned by Young's since 1999 and managed by real ale enthusiasts who previously ran a Guide-listed pub in Derbyshire. The kitchen produces good quality, home-cooked food, featuring local ingredients as much as possible, and everything is cooked to order. Fish and shellfish dishes are a speciality. Backgammon and other board games are played here. 🏚Q🌑◐💺♣P

BRIDGE

Plough & Harrow
86 High Street, CT4 5LA
🕛 11-3, 5-11; 11-11 Sat; 12-3, 7-10.30 Sun
☎ (01227) 830455
Shepherd Neame Master Brew Bitter Ⓗ

This 300-year-old former maltings has no garden or food or music, but takes pride in being a traditional village pub. It is home to over 30 clubs and teams; bar billiards and shut the box are played. The vicar works behind the bar once a month. There is a strong emphasis on conversation and visitors are welcomed. The back bar has been renovated recently. An easy detour from the A2, it is served by buses from Canterbury; limited parking. 🏚Q♣P

BROADSTAIRS

Brown Jug
204 Ramsgate Road, CT10 2EW
🕛 12-3, 6-11; 12-11 Sat; 12-10.30 Sun
☎ (01843) 862788
Greene King IPA; guest beers Ⓗ

This delightful pub, between Broadstairs and Ramsgate, exudes olde-worlde charm, with its shuttered, leaded windows and flint façade; outside toilets and public and saloon bars are in keeping. It was reputed to have been used as an officers' billet during the

in the public bar. A regular Guide entry, this pub serves excellent food. Other Shepherd Neame ales (dispensed using pressure but still excellent) are available. There is a real fire in winter and a large garden for the summer. Bus No. 23 (not Sun) from Maidstone stops outside. 🏚🌑◐🍴P

BISHOPSBOURNE

Mermaid
The Street, CT4 5HX (off A2 at B2065 jct)
🕛 12-3 (3.30 Sat), 6.10-11; 12-3, 7-10.30 Sun
☎ (01227) 830581
Shepherd Neame Master Brew Bitter, seasonal beers Ⓗ

Well worth the short detour from the A2, this attractive community pub is in its 23rd year in this Guide. One of the three small bars has a basket grate, secondhand books and darts. The pub is just off the North Downs Way; dogs are welcome with well-behaved owners. It is a pleasant half-hour walk from here to the Plough & Harrow at Bridge (see below), passing the former home of author, Joseph Conrad. 🏚Q🌑◐🍴♣

BOSSINGHAM

Hop Pocket
The Street, CT4 6DY
🕛 12-3, 7-11; 12-3, 7-10.30 Sun
☎ (01227) 709866
Beer range varies Ⓗ

Warm, friendly country pub hung with hops. The large garden contains a children's

INDEPENDENT BREWERIES

Flagship Chatham
Goacher's Maidstone
Hopdaemon Canterbury
Larkins Chiddingstone
Millis South Darenth
Ramsgate Ramsgate
Shepherd Neame Faversham
Swan West Peckham
Whitstable Grafty Green

Napoleonic Wars. Note the large brown jug over the public bar entrance. The pub supports flourishing petanque and quiz teams and keeps a selection of board games to play. Lunchtime opening times can be erratic. ⚔Q🏃❀🍴₤≑(Dumpton Pk) ♣P

Lord Nelson
11 Nelson Place, CT10 1HQ
✪ 11-11; 12-10.30 Sun
☎ (01843) 861210
Greene King IPA, Abbot; Morland Original; guest beer Ⓗ

Welcoming local, a short walk from the town's harbour and the main beach. Built in 1805 on what used to be a tea garden, as a tailor and draper's, it opened as a pub 10 years later. Named in honour of Lord Nelson, the admiral's body was on the Victory when it laid anchor in Viking Bay on its way home from the Battle of Trafalgar. The guest beer is one of Greene King's brews. ⚔❀≑♣P

Neptune's Hall ☆
1-3 Harbour Street, CT10 1ET
✪ 11-11; 12-10.30 Sun
☎ (01843) 861400
Shepherd Neame Master Brew Bitter, Spitfire, seasonal beers Ⓗ

Lively old fishermen's pub, close to the town's harbour, it is popular with locals and visitors alike. Built in 1815 on the site of some old fishermen's cottages, it was used in the 1920s as an hotel. One of its patrons at the time was the celebrated JH Somerton, better known as 'Uncle Mac', who performed on the pier. The pub's interior was listed in 1999. It hosts regular jam sessions, especially during the town's annual Folk Week in August. ❀🍴≑♣♠

BROMPTON

King George V
1 Prospect Row, ME7 5AL
✪ 11.45-11; 12-10.30 Sun
☎ (01634) 842418
Beer range varies Ⓗ

This single-bar town house boasts four ever-changing beers. The pub is close to the historic Chatham Dockyard, now a visitor attraction, and displays much naval memorabilia. A whisky club meets in the pub once a month; wines by the glass are also available. The pub offers an enterprising menu (no meals Sun, or Mon eve). See the old photographs of this quiet pub when it was called the King of Prussia. 🏠🍴♣

BROOMFIELD

Huntsman & Horn
Margate Road, CT6 7AF (signed from A299)
✪ 11.30-11; 12-10.30 Sun
☎ (01227) 365995
Ansells Best Bitter; Young's Bitter Ⓗ

This attractive listed building houses a welcoming pub with cosy decor and large open fire. There are two bar areas and a restaurant with children's certificate. Sunday lunches and weekday senior citizens' lunch specials (two courses for £4.95) are very popular (no food Sun eve or Mon). The large garden features a bat and trap pitch. The friendly landlord is a real ale

enthusiast. Broomfield is a couple of miles from the Roman fort of Reculver and the Saxon Shore Way coastal path. ⚔🏃❀🍴♣P

CANTERBURY

Eight Bells
34 London Road, CT2 8LN (off A2050 roundabout on ring road)
✪ 3 (12 Fri & Sat)-11; 12-10.30 Sun
☎ (01227) 454794
Fuller's London Pride; Greene King IPA; guest beers Ⓗ

Very much a traditional local, where the emphasis is on conversation, the Eight Bells has been a pub since 1702. It was rebuilt 200 years later but retained many original beams. The small, L-shaped bar is decorated with curios and a dark red ceiling. Home-made meat pies and stews feature on the menu; meals are served Sunday lunchtime and early summer evenings, Monday–Saturday. Live bands perform twice a month, and acoustic music (often a pianist) is staged most Sunday lunchtimes. ❀🍴≑(West) ♣

Phoenix
67 Old Dover Road, CT1 3DB
✪ 11-11; 12-4, 7-10.30 Sun
☎ (01227) 464220
website: www.thephoenix-canterbury.co.uk
Greene King Abbot; Ⓖ **Wells Bombardier; Young's Bitter; guest beers** Ⓗ

Originally the Bridge House Tavern, dating back to the 18th century, this comfortable pub was burnt down in 1962 and renamed the Phoenix. Up to four guest beers change regularly, as testified by the growing pump clip collection; a popular beer festival is held in December. Close to the county ground, it displays a collection of cricketing memorabilia. Regular fun quiz nights are held. Senior citizens qualify for meal discounts; meals, including all-day breakfasts, are served 11–9.30. ❀🏠🍴≑(East) ♣P

Thomas Ingoldsby ❷
5-9 Burgate, CT1 2HG
✪ 10-11; 12-10.30 Sun
☎ (01227) 463339
Courage Directors; Shepherd Neame Spitfire; Theakston Best Bitter; guest beers Ⓗ

Formerly a furniture shop, this busy Wetherspoon's outlet is close to Canterbury's jewel, the medieval cathedral. The pub is also ideally situated for the shops and bus station. The walls are adorned with historic prints of Canterbury, and two local authors, Joseph Conrad and the creator of the Ingoldsby Legends. Another literary work, the Canterbury Tales, is celebrated in a visitor attraction in the city. Q❀🍴&≑(West/East) ✂

Unicorn
61 St Dunstans' Street, CT2 8BS (by level crossing)
✪ 11-11; 12-10.30 Sun
☎ (01227) 463187
Shepherd Neame Master Brew Bitter; guest beers Ⓗ

Celebrating its 400th birthday this year, this comfortable pub stands near the ancient Westgate. The Unicorn boasts an attractive suntrap garden. An unobtrusive satellite TV in the back bar shows sporting events; bar

billiards is played here and a quiz is held weekly on Sunday. The menu is extensive but unpretentious, featuring a daily special (no food Sun eve). At least one guest beer is usually from a local brewery.
⌂❀◑◗≹(West) ♣

CAPEL

Dovecote Inn ✔

Alders Road, TN11 6SU (2 miles W of A228, between Colts Hill and Tudeley) OS643441
12-3 (or later), 6-11; 12-3 (or 4), 7-10.30 Sun
☎ (01892) 835966
Adnams Broadside; Badger K&B Sussex; Harveys BB; Larkins Chiddingstone; guest beer Ⓖ
The Dovecote stands in an idyllic rural location near hopfields in the middle of a row of cottages. Enjoy the warm, welcoming atmosphere in its bare brick interior. Four ales are served direct from the cask by a knowledgeable landlord with Cask Marque accreditation. The good value food is particularly popular on Thursday (curry night) when booking is recommended. Chiddingstone real cider is stocked. The attractive garden houses a dovecot and a large children's climbing frame.
⌂Q❀◑◗⅄●P

CAPEL-LE-FERNE

Royal Oak

New Dover Road, CT18 7HY (on B2011, E of village) OS263387
11.30-4, 7-11; 12-4, 7.30-10.30 Sun
☎ (01303) 244787
Shepherd Neame Master Brew Bitter; guest beers Ⓗ
Originally a farmhouse and long barn, the pub is not far from the cliff edge, affording outstanding views of the Channel and (occasionally) the French coast. The main bar acts as a tacking shop and sometime cribbage school; the barn is used for other games. Food is cooked to order. Guest ales come from regional and micro-breweries. The handy Folkestone–Dover bus stops outside. ⌂❀◑◗⅄♣P

CHARCOTT

Greyhound

TN11 8LZ (1/2 mile N of B2027 and Chiddingstone Causeway) OS522472
12-3 (not Tue), 6-11; 12-3, 7-10.30 Sun
☎ (01892) 870275
Adnams Bitter; Badger K&B Sussex; Flowers Original; Harveys BB Ⓗ
Small, brick and tiled free house which provides a focal point for the locals living in the hamlet and nearby villages. A small extension to the rear forms the dining area where good quality food is served (no meals Tue). The interior is decorated with assorted pictures and has a real fire in winter. Penshurst Station is a short walk along a footpath. The flat land to the south was once an airfield. Boules is played in the garden in summer. ⌂❀◑◗≹(Penshurst) ♣P

CHARING

Bowl Inn

Egg Hill Road, TN27 0HG (at jct of five lanes, including Bowl Road) OS950514
5 (12 Fri & Sat)-11; 12-10.30 Sun
☎ (01233) 712256 website: www.bowl-inn.co.uk
Fuller's London Pride; guest beers Ⓗ
A remote pub, it sits on the top of the Downs overlooking the Weald of Kent. The large garden has amenities for camping (book). For the colder months there is a magnificent open fire. It has been a regular CAMRA award-winner since 1994 and hosts a beer festival every July when over 20 real ales are offered. There are always three guest beers on tap in this free house; food is restricted to bar snacks. ⌂❀⅄♣P⅓

CHATHAM

Ropemakers Arms

70 New Road, ME4 4QR (on A2)
12-3 (not Sat), 7-11; 12-3, 7-10.30 Sun
☎ (01634) 402121
Goacher's Light; Greene King Abbot; guest beers Ⓗ
Although situated on the main road, there is car parking behind and adjacent to the pub. The L-shaped bar bears four handpumps. A monthly quiz night is always well attended (first Wed). In the back room, pool and darts can be played; the pub also has a bar billiards table. Close to the station and High Street, the pub is worth seeking out. No food is served Sunday. A mural of a dockyard shed was painted by local artist, Jamie Montgomery. ◑≹♣

CHIDDINGSTONE HOATH

Rock

Hoath Corner, TN8 7BS (1½ miles S of Chiddingstone, via Wellers Town) OS497431
11.30-3, 6-11; closed Mon; 12-3, 7-10.30 Sun
☎ (01892) 870296
Larkins Traditional, Best, Porter Ⓗ
Located in the Kentish Weald, the Rock, owned by the local Larkins Brewery, is a fine country pub with a brick floor, brick-built bar, and hop-strewn beams. Outside seating is provided at the front of the pub as well as in the garden to the rear, while inside a wood-burning stove provides winter comfort. No meals are available on Sunday evening. Ring the bull is played here. ⌂Q❀◑◗⊟♣P

CLAYGATE

White Hart

TN12 9PL (approx 4 miles S of Yalding on B2162)
11-11; 12-10.30 Sun
☎ (01892) 730313 website: www.thewhitehart.biz
Adnams Bitter; Fuller's London Pride; Goacher's Light; guest beers Ⓗ
Large two-bar country pub, half of which is given over to a no-smoking restaurant seating up to 60 and serving large portions of home-cooked food at reasonable prices. The one-acre garden provides a pleasant retreat. The pub is a new venture for the successful landlord and landlady who were formerly tenants of the Bull at East Farleigh and previous winners of local CAMRA's Pub of the Year award. This genuine free house has a children's certificate and wheelchair WC. ⌂Q❀◑◗♿⅄P

COOLING

Horseshoe & Castle

The Street, ME3 8DJ
11-3, 7-11; 12-4, 7-10.30 Sun
☎ (01634) 221691

website: www.horseshoeandcastle.co.uk
Adnams Bitter; Draught Bass; guest beers ⊞
In the middle of a peaceful village, this pub
is close to an RSPB bird and nature reserve.
The pub specialises in seafood on an
interesting menu; evening meals are served
Tuesday–Saturday. The nearby ruined castle
was once owned by Sir John Oldcastle, on
whom Shakespeare's Falstaff was modelled,
while the local graveyard boasts the
tombstones that were used in Charles
Dickens' Great Expectations, where young
Pip was surprised by Magwitch. The pub is
in danger of demolition if the Cliffe Airport
is built. ⚄Q☸≠◑ ⬤

CRANBROOK

George Hotel ⊘
Stone Street, TN17 3HE
✪ 10.30-11; 12-10.30 Sun
☎ (01580) 713348 website: www.georgehoteluk.co.uk
Harveys BB; guest beers ⊞
Historic hotel, in a tranquil Weald town,
dating back to 1300, although much of the
interior is 15th century. The restaurant
boasts connections with Elizabeth I, who
visited the town in 1573. Three guest beers
are usually available, with occasionally a
mild on tap. The high-ceilinged main
lounge bar is uncluttered, with comfy sofas
and armchairs blending with simple tables
and chairs. A smaller bar has TV and music,
while the restaurant features an impressive
fireplace. ⚄Q☸≠◑P

DARTFORD

Malt Shovel
3 Darenth Road, DA1 1LP (on A226)
✪ 11-2.30, 5-11; 11-11 Fri & Sat; 12-3, 7-10.30 Sun
☎ (01322) 224381
Young's Bitter, Special, seasonal beers ⊞
Traditional town pub with a country
atmosphere. Dating from the late 17th
century, it retains an olde-worlde charm
with low ceilings and time-worn woodwork,
particularly in the small public bar. Bric-à-
brac hangs from the ceilings and an
authentic Dartford Brewery mirror is
displayed in the conservatory which
doubles as the family room. The garden,
overlooking the town centre, is pleasant in
good weather. Good value food includes a
specials board; evening meals are served
Tuesday–Saturday.
⚄ⓢ☸◑ ⊟≠P

DEAL

Admiral Penn
79 Beach Street, CT14 6JA
✪ 6-11; closed Sun
☎ (01304) 374279 website: www.admiralpenn.com
**Draught Bass; Fuller's London Pride;
Wells Bombardier** ⊞
Smart bar in a prime seafront location,
offering panoramic views of passing
shipping. The nautical theme, combined
with a Dutch flavour, works well. A range
of continental spirits and liqueurs is
stocked, including such specialities as
Dutch Kopstoot and Jagermeister, cold
from the fridge. In spite of, or maybe
because of, limited opening hours, the
pub is invariably well patronised and
lively. ⚄≠

Saracen's Head
1 Alfred Square, CT14 6LS (N end of High St)
✪ 11-11; 12-10.30 Sun
☎ (01304) 381650
**Shepherd Neame Master Brew Bitter, Spitfire,
seasonal beers** ⊞
Shepherd Neame tied house serving the
north end of town. It overlooks the
distinctive Alfred Square, Deal's only square.
This cheerful street-corner local is home to
several darts and pool teams. The games
area on the left, and the area of seating by
the bar blend well together, making for a
good atmosphere that attracts a wide range
of customers. Lunches are served
Monday–Saturday. ☸◑♣

Ship
141 Middle Street, CT14 6JZ
✪ 11-11; 12-10.30 Sun
☎ (01304) 372222
**Draught Bass; Hook Norton Best Bitter; Shepherd
Neame Master Brew Bitter; guest beers** ⊞
Cosy, traditional pub with two drinking
areas – one is a secluded back room. This
historic tavern in the heart of Deal's
conservation area is surely light years away
from the haunt of blackguards and ruffians
who must have frequented these mean
streets in days gone by. The pub's walls
display, naturally, a nautical theme. Freshly-
made rolls and coffee are available at the
bar. Beware historical re-enactment events
in season!
⚄☸≠

DENTON

Jackdaw
The Street, CT4 6QZ (on A260)
✪ 11-11; 12-10.30 Sun
☎ (01303) 844663
Shepherd Neame Spitfire; guest beers ⊞
Tucked away in a deep valley on the busy
A260 in a tiny hamlet, this distinctive pub
successfully combines food and drink
operations. Originally it was the Red Lion, a
name revived for the 1960s Battle of Britain
film when it was used for the public bar
shots. Lydden motor racing circuit is a
couple of miles away through narrow lanes.
Beers come mainly from regional breweries,
but Spitfire seems most appropriate here.
Buses from Folkestone stop outside.
☸◑P

DODDINGTON

Chequers Inn
The Street, ME9 0BG
✪ 11-3, 7 (6 Fri)-11; 11-11 Sat; 12-3, 7-10.30 Sun
**Shepherd Neame Master Brew Bitter,
seasonal beers** ⊞
Classic, timeless pub nestling in a fold of
the North Downs. Two bars: the public
has a pool table and the saloon is entered
via an old stable-type door. In winter a
cosy fire burns in the large fireplace.
Popular with cyclists and walkers, it is also
home to the Norton Motorcycle Owners
Club. Locally-made cheese and sausages
are on the menu, among other delights.
Folk music is performed now and then.
Outside seating is provided for the warmer
nights.
⚄ⓢ☸◑ ⊟♣P

DOVER

Eagle Inn
324 London Road, CT17 0SX
✪ 11-11; 12-10.30 Sun
☎ (01304) 212929
**Hopdaemon Golden Braid, Incubus;
Old Kent Opener** Ⓗ
Imposing former hotel which looks down
the High Street towards the town hall
(Maison Dieu). A gilded eagle stares from
the rooftop at the shoppers below.
Successfully rebuilt after a failed attempt at
a mock-Irish bar, it is now a modern version
of the traditional 'stand-up' public bar, with
a back room for sports TV and pool.
Hopdaemon beers are a permanent feature,
including the bottle conditioned
Greendaemon lager.
⌨≈ (Priory)

Golden Lion
11 Priory Street, CT17 9AA (at A256/B2011 jct)
✪ 10-11; 12-10.30 Sun
☎ (01304) 202919
Adnams Bitter; Marston's Pedigree; guest beer Ⓗ
Just off the High Street, this one-bar, street-
corner local enjoys a significant regular
following, as well as making visitors feel
very welcome. It provides a sanctuary from
the surrounding busy streets. The Golden
Lion serves its community well, with its
Winkle Club raising a lot of money for local
schools and charities – see the photos of
some of the work that has been done and
regular customers. Inexpensive filled rolls
are available. ≈ (Priory)

Mogul
5 Chapel Place, CT17 9AS (near A256/A20 jct at
York St roundabout)
✪ 11-11; 12-10.30 Sun
☎ (01304) 205072
Beer range varies Ⓖ
Former Kent CAMRA Pub of the Year, the
Mogul places an emphasis on ales from
micro-breweries; the range changes daily,
with popular brews returning regularly. The
garden affords views of the castle and
harbour. Music plays gently in the
background, allowing lively banter at the
bar. Pictures of old Dover and Imperial
India feature alongside brewery posters and
chalk caricatures by local artist, Chris
Baxter. Easier to find on foot than by car, it
is well worth seeking out. The landlady
signs for the hearing-impaired.
ﷺQ❀≈ (Priory) ♣🍴✧

EAST MALLING

King & Queen
1 New Road, ME19 6DD
✪ 11.30-2.30, 6-11; 12-3.30 (closed eve) Sun
☎ (01732) 842752
Beer range varies Ⓗ
This 16th-century, central village pub goes
from strength to strength. With a large,
comfortable saloon bar, a public bar and a
no-smoking room for diners, there is no
shortage of seating space, including an
attractive garden. Four handpumps serve a
range of guest beers of consistently high
quality and good, freshly-cooked food is
always available. With a friendly landlord
and staff, this pub is well worth a visit.
Q❀⌨▻⌨≈P

Rising Sun
125 Mill Street, ME19 6BX
✪ 12-11; 12-10.30 Sun
☎ (01732) 843284
**Goacher's Light; Shepherd Neame Master Brew Bitter;
guest beer** Ⓗ
Family-run free house noted for its keen
pricing policy. The guest beer is usually
from a micro-brewery. The pub supports
several darts teams – the rear of the pub
is the games area, while the front part
offers comfortable seating. This true local
makes visitors feel very welcome.
Weekday lunches are served. East Malling
had five pubs four years ago – now it has
just two.
❀⌨≈♣

EGERTON FORSTAL

Queen's Arms
Forstal Road, TN27 9EH OS893464
✪ 11.30-2, 6.30-11 (11-11 summer); 12-10.30 Sun
☎ (01233) 756386
**Goacher's Mild; Shepherd Neame Master Brew Bitter;
guest beers** Ⓗ
Village local, with beamed ceilings and a
restaurant area. It is hard to find, but well
worth the effort; certainly many do make it
here as it can be busy. Up to six changing
guest beers are stocked, showcasing Kent
breweries as well as micros from further
afield.
ﷺ❀⌨♣P

ELHAM

Rose & Crown
High Street, CT4 6TD
✪ 11-3, 6-11; 12-3, 7-10.30 Sun
☎ (01303) 840141 website: www.roseandcrown.co.uk
**Hopdaemon Golden Braid; Greene King Ruddles Best;
guest beer** Ⓗ
Handsome, mainly 18th-century building
with a heavily beamed bar area leading to
a no-smoking dining room. Comfortable
and cosy, with settees in front of the fire,
it is populated by sleeping cats and dogs.
A comprehensive menu is offered, with
fresh fish a speciality. Up to four beers are
available, with a preference for local
brews such as Hopdaemon.
Accommodation is available in the old
coaching stables, now converted to six
en-suite guest rooms.
ﷺQ❀►⌨P

FAIRSEAT

Vigo
Gravesend Road, TN15 7JL
(on A227, 1 mile N of A20)
✪ 12-3.30 (not Mon-Fri), 6-11; 12-3.30, 7-10.30 Sun
☎ (01732) 822547
Harveys BB, Old; Young's Bitter, Special; guest beers
(summer) Ⓗ
Unspoilt and unchanging former drovers'
inn on the main road at the top of a steep
hill on the North Downs. Named in honour
of a local resident distinguished in the
famous Crimean battle, the pub has been
run by the same family since 1930 and has
withstood the test of time. Enjoy the quiet
atmosphere, except when dadlums (Kentish
skittles) is being played.
ﷺQ⌨Å♣P✧🍴

FARNINGHAM

Chequers ◉
87 High Street, DA4 0DT
(250 yds from A20, off M25 jct 3)
☼ 11 (12 Sat)-11; 12-10.30 Sun
☎ (01322) 865222
Fuller's London Pride, ESB; Oakham JHB; Taylor Landlord; guest beers Ⓗ

Excellent, one-bar, corner local in a charming riverside village, which still has a family butcher, grocer, post office and curry house. Near the Darenth Valley footpath and river and easily accessible by major roads, the pub attracts a wide-ranging clientele. Up to eight beers include a rotating range of guests, especially from micro-breweries. Nearby cottages display outstanding floral arrangements in spring and summer. This regular CAMRA haunt is well worth visiting. Lunches are served Monday–Saturday. ⌖◗♣

FAVERSHAM

Anchor
52 Abbey Street, ME13 7BP
☼ 12-11; 12-3, 6-11 Mon; 12-10.30 Sun
☎ (01795) 536471 website: www.upanchor.co.uk
Shepherd Neame Master Brew Bitter, Best Bitter, Spitfire, seasonal beers Ⓗ

Dating from the 17th century, the pub is one of the three original Shepherd Neame pubs. It straddles the end of historic Abbey Street, near Standard Quay where many types of sailing vessels are berthed. The pub's main beams are old ships' timbers. It enjoys a well-deserved reputation for its food, on a varied menu (no meals Sun eve). Live music is performed every week. Well-behaved children are welcome; the large garden overlooking the creek is popular in summer. ⌂Q⌖◗⌸♣

Bear
3 Market Place, ME13 7AG
☼ 10.30-3, 5.30-11; 10.30-11 Sat; 12-10.30 Sun
☎ (01795) 532668
Shepherd Neame Master Brew Bitter, Spitfire, seasonal beers Ⓗ

This classic market town pub retains its early 19th-century layout of three distinct bars off a long side corridor. It stands opposite the ancient Guildhall where tables for outside drinking are set out in summer. Notable features include a carved wooden bear and a clock with figures replaced by the letters of the pub's name. Excellent home-cooked food includes toad in the hole with Spitfire Ale sausages. Popular with local folk musicians, the pub recreates times past in terms of atmosphere and friendliness. Q⌖◗⌸≢

Chimney Boy
59 Preston Street, ME13 8PG
☼ 11-4, 5.30 (6 Sat)-11; 12-4, 7-10.30 Sun
☎ (01795) 532007
Shepherd Neame Master Brew Bitter, seasonal beers Ⓗ

Close by the station, this pub, formerly a convent and later an hotel, is home to a wide selection of clubs and societies, including the very popular Faversham Folk Club that meets every Wednesday evening in the upstairs function room. This pub was renamed in the 1970s after steps were found

in an old chimney. The pub is noted for its restaurant (no meals Sun eve) and it has a room for pool. ⌖◗≢♣P

Crown & Anchor
41 The Mall, ME13 8JN
☼ 10.30-3, 5.30-11; 10.30-4, 6-11 Sat; 12-3.30, 7-10.30 Sun
☎ (01795) 532812
Shepherd Neame Master Brew Bitter Ⓗ

Conveniently located less than five minutes from the station, on the opposite side to the town centre, this single-roomed pub is a true local with no juke box or TV to disturb conversation. There is a separate area for pool and darts. The landlord is a keen horticulturist, his speciality being orchids, and these beautiful plants decorate the bar. A regular Guide entry for over 10 years, it serves weekday lunches. ◗♣

Elephant
31 The Mall, ME13 8JN
☼ 12-11; 12-10.30 Sun
☎ (01795) 590157
Beer range varies Ⓗ

Community pub, handy for buses and trains, with a loyal following. An ever-changing range of beers includes two from owner, Flagship Brewery, and an occasional mild. The house beer, Elephant's Trunk, is Flagship's Admiral Bitter rebadged. It stocks a good choice of draught and bottled Belgian beers and local bottled cider. Frequent beer festivals, quiz nights and other events are staged. It boasts the best juke box in town. The walled garden is popular with families. ⌖◗≢♣

Shipwright's Arms
Hollowshore, off Ham Road, ME13 7TU
(from Davington School, go along Ham Rd, left at end, first right) OS017636
☼ 11-3 (4 Sat), 6-11 (closed winter Mon); 12-4, 6-10.30 Sun
☎ (01795) 590088
Goacher's Mild, Gold Star Ale; Hopdaemon Skrimshander IPA; guest beer (summer) Ⓖ

Remote, historic pub set in the marshes at the confluence of Faversham and Oare creeks. It has a special atmosphere and stocks beers from Kentish breweries only, plus a cider in summer. Shipwrecked is a house beer brewed by Goacher's. CAMRA regional Pub of the Year 2001 and Kent award-winner 2002, it is best to book for meals, served Wednesday–Saturday and Sunday lunch. Children (and dogs) are welcome. Real fires, real food and real character! ⌂Q⌖◗♣●P⋇

Sun Inn
10 West Street, ME13 7JE
☼ 11-11; 12-10.30 Sun
☎ (01795) 535098
Shepherd Neame Master Brew Bitter, Spitfire, seasonal beers Ⓗ

Ancient pub, among the old buildings of West Street, a stone's throw from the historic Guildhall in the market place. It has well-preserved wood panelling and a beautiful fireplace, used throughout the colder months. In summer outside drinking is possible on the rear patio or at tables on the pedestrianised street at the front. In summer 2003 the pub was extended into the adjacent town house to provide guest accommodation and a new restaurant (no eve meals Sun). ⚑✿☎◑⊙≢

Three Tuns
16 Tanners Street, ME13 7JP
✪ 11-3, 7-11; 12-3, 7-10.30 Sun
☎ (01795) 532663
Shepherd Neame Master Brew Bitter Ⓗ
Genuine local, hosting many social activities. Very old, it is one of the three original Shepherd Neame pubs. It has been suggested that the pub is where Horatio Nelson, then a mere captain, paid off his Faversham crew members. On a split level, a comfortable upper bar is complemented by a lower bar where darts and pool are played. A pretty walled garden houses petanque and bat and trap pitches. The landlord's home-cooked lunches, served Tuesday–Saturday, are very good value. ✿◑≢♣

FAWKHAM GREEN

Rising Sun
Valley Road, DA3 8NL
✪ 11.30-11; 12-10.30 Sun
☎ (01474) 872291
Courage Best Bitter, Directors; guest beers Ⓗ
Enterprising rural pub, pleasantly located on the village green, about one mile north of Brands Hatch racing circuit and within earshot of the M20. Three changing beers come from independent suppliers, including local breweries; the cider comes from Biddenden. It has earned a good reputation for food in the adjoining restaurant and its comfortable accommodation is recommended; some rooms have four-poster beds. Well worth seeking out. ⚑✿☎◑ ⊡♣☙P

FOLKESTONE

British Lion
10 The Bayle, CT20 1SQ
✪ 11-4 (5 Sat), 7-11; 12-5, 7-10.30 Sun
☎ (01303) 251478
Greene King IPA, Abbot, Old Speckled Hen; guest beer Ⓗ
An ale house was first recorded on this site in 1460. It is situated close to the town centre but has a comfortable back-street atmosphere and is decorated with various local prints. The pub fields a team in the local quiz league and both crib and chess are played regularly. The food is notable for the generous portions; the restaurant is a no-smoking area. ✿◑♣

Clifton Hotel
The Leas, CT20 2EB
✪ 11-3, 6-11; 12-3.30, 6.30-10.30 Sun
☎ (01303) 223949 website: www.thecliftonhotel.com
Draught Bass Ⓗ
Hotel bar close to the Leas Cliff Hall entertainment centre. The central bar has stools and comfortable armchair seating around the room. Only one beer is stocked, but it is always in excellent condition. The Clifton is Folkestone's premier three-star hotel, affording spectacular views of the English Channel. Q✿☎◑≢(Central)

Guildhall
42 The Bayle, CT20 1SQ
✪ 12-11; 12-10.30 Sun
☎ (01303) 251393

Draught Bass; Greene King IPA; guest beers Ⓗ
This traditional family-run pub has a single bar which splits neatly into a pool and darts area at one end and tables around the fire at the other. Usually two guest beers complement the regular brews. Excellent pub food is available; the tempting puddings are hard to resist. The pub is on the Bayle, off the pedestrianised precinct, near the top of the old High Street. ✿◑≢(Central)♣

Happy Frenchman
Christchurch Road, CT20 2SX
(by clock tower at west end of town)
✪ 11-11; 12-10.30 Sun
☎ (01303) 259815
Draught Bass; Shepherd Neame Spitfire; Wells Bombardier; guest beers Ⓗ
Spacious, one-bar pub, with a large area for pool and darts. Live music performed on Friday and Saturday evenings varies (phone for details). A big-screen TV is used for Sky Sports. Biker-friendly, the pub's decor is spartan with post-revolutionary French influences (no guillotine involved). It is close to the town centre and Leas Cliff Hall. The spectacular annual Shepway Air Show on the Leas promenade is normally held at the beginning of September and well worth a visit. ≢(Central)♣

FORDWICH

Fordwich Arms
King Street, CT2 0DB
(400 yds from A28 at Sturry)
✪ 11-11; 12-3, 7.30-10.30 Sun
☎ (01227) 710444
Flowers Original; Shepherd Neame Master Brew Bitter; Wadworth 6X; guest beers Ⓗ
This classic, friendly 1930s pub has a large bar, with a splendid fireplace, and a restaurant. The garden and terrace overlook the River Stour, on which summer Sunday boat trips can be booked (in advance). Folk, country music or blues is played most Sunday evenings and an annual music festival is staged at local CAMRA's Pub of the Year 2003. Fordwich claims to be England's smallest town; the ancient, tiny town hall stands opposite the pub. No evening meals are served on Sunday.
⚑Q✿◑≢P

GILLINGHAM

Barge
63 Layfield Road, ME7 2QY
✪ 12-3 (not Tue or Fri), 7-11; 4-11 Fri; 12-11 Sat; 12-10.30 Sun
☎ (01634) 850485
website: www.myofficesecretary.com/thebarge
Beer range varies Ⓗ
A pub worth seeking out, located at the end of a no-through road towards the Strand end of Gillingham. The decking in the rear garden affords views of the River Medway. Monday evening is free folk music night. The pub is totally candlelit in the evenings. Named after the landlord's son, Joshua Ale is the house ale brewed by Chatham's Brewery, Flagship. Local artist Jamie Montgomery painted the walls of the pub, depicting life below decks on a sailing ship.
✿≢♣

217

Dog & Bone
21 Jeffrey Street, ME7 1DE (off High St)
✪ 11-11; 12-10.30 Sun
☎ (01634) 576829
Beer range varies Ⓗ
The pub has undergone a few changes since its last inclusion in this Guide. A flagstone floor has been laid in the larger of the two bars and the conservatory now houses the restaurant. Four handpumps offer the real ale drinker a good, varying choice. The smaller bar caters for the younger element with fruit machines, juke box, pool table and a large-screen TV. Away football supporters visiting Gillingham FC are welcome. ♨✿◖♣♠

Frog & Toad ✿
38 Burnt Oak Terrace, ME7 1DR
✪ 11-11; 12-10.30 Sun
☎ (01634) 852231 website: www.thefrogandtoad.com
Beer range varies Ⓗ
Medway CAMRA Pub of the Year for three years running, this busy single bar townhouse was redecorated during 2003 (note the carpet design). The pub holds two beer festivals a year in its garden, over the late May and August bank holidays. The pub stocks 30-plus Belgian bottled beers, each served in its own branded glass. Barbecues are staged in summer; live entertainment and meat raffles at other times. Q✿☀≈♣♠

Scruffy Duck
97 Skinner Street, ME7 1LD
✪ 11-11; 12-10.30 Sun
☎ (01634) 851210
Greene King IPA, Abbot; guest beers Ⓗ
Street-corner local, just off the High Street. The single bar, with wood floor and ceiling beams, has an olde-worlde feel, where the themed courtyard gives a more Mediterranean ambience. Home-cooked food represents good value. It hosts regular quiz nights and a weekly fun darts knockout competition. A friendly atmosphere and a warm welcome are assured in a pub previously called Jolly Jake and before that the Victory. No food is served Sunday evening. ♨✿◖➤≈

Upper Gillingham Conservative Club
541 Canterbury Street, ME7 5LF
(top of Canterbury St, near A2)
✪ 11-2.30, 7-11; 11-3, 6.30-11 Sat; 12-2.30, 7-10.30 Sun
☎ (01634) 851403
Shepherd Neame Master Brew Bitter; guest beers Ⓗ
Medway CAMRA's Club of the Year for the fourth consecutive year, it was a runner-up nationally in 2001. You are assured of a friendly welcome here but will need to show a current CAMRA membership card or copy of this Guide in order to be signed in. The club has a TV room and snooker room. It was a military store until 1922. A U-shaped bar serves two distinct drinking areas. ♣

Will Adams
73 Saxton Street, ME7 5EG
(off lower end of Canterbury St)
✪ 12-3 (not Mon-Fri), 7-11; 12-4, 8-10.30 Sun
☎ (01634) 575902

Hop Back Summer Lightning; guest beers Ⓗ
This friendly one-bar, back-street local enjoys a well-deserved reputation for its beer. Up to three guest beers are supplemented by a real cider (Westons Old Rosie or Moles Black Rat) plus 25 malt whiskies. The pub fields darts and pool teams and can get very busy when Gillingham FC are playing at home. Lunches are served on match days and the hours are extended. The name honours the navigator/adventurer whose exploits are depicted on a mural inside. ≈♣●✄

GRAVESEND

British Tar
15 Milton Road, DA12 2RF (opp. clock tower)
✪ 11-2.30, 7-11; 12-3, 7-10.30 Sun
☎ (01474) 533891
Everards Tiger; Fuller's London Pride; Young's Bitter Ⓗ
Old, timber-framed building with a Dutch-style pointed roof, which pre-dates the adjoining Georgian colonnade. The licensee is the longest-serving landlord in Gravesend and little has changed here since the 1960s. This basic two-bar former waterman's hostelry is a quiet refuge from the modern revamped town-centre theme bars. ◖◻≈♣

Crown & Thistle
44 The Terrace, DA12 2BJ (off inner ring road, near river)
✪ 11-11; 12-10.30 Sun
☎ (01474) 326049
website: www.crownandthistle.org.uk
Daleside Shrimpers; guest beers Ⓗ
This small Georgian pub has no TV, fruit machines or children; a relaxing atmosphere allows drinkers to enjoy up to five ales from micro-breweries around the country. Indian and Chinese meals can be ordered at the bar (eves) to be eaten on or off premises. It stages occasional live music and raises funds for the RNLI. Note the Russells of Gravesend brewery pictures and the hundreds of pump clips (all beers sold within the last two years) at local CAMRA Pub of the Year 2003. ✿≈●✄

Windmill Tavern
45 Shrubbery Road, DA12 1JW
✪ 11-11; 12-10.30 Sun
☎ (01474) 352242
Fuller's London Pride; Greene King IPA; Harveys BB; Shepherd Neame Master Brew Bitter, Spitfire; guest beer Ⓗ
Three-bar pub near the middle of town, with a country pub feel. It runs an active bowls and tennis club in the adjoining park. The pub's attractive, award-winning garden is pleasant in summer. A popular locals' 'public bar', a snug/private bar and a comfortable saloon bar complete this village local in the town. Notable visitors in the past are believed to include Charles Dickens and Lord Nelson. ✿◖◻≈♣

HALLING

Homeward Bound
72 High Street, ME2 1BY
✪ 12-3, 5 (7 Sat)-11; 12-3, 7-10.30 Sun
☎ (01634) 240743
Shepherd Neame Master Brew Bitter Ⓗ
Formerly a Mason's of Maidstone house,

this friendly village local forms part of a Victorian terrace. Various old photographs of the village adorn the walls. Every Tuesday the car park is full of assorted motorcycles of all ages as the Medway Triumph Club holds its meetings here. A traditional Kent dartboard (no trebles) is used by the darts team on Thursday evenings. The pub has appeared in 26 editions of this Guide.
Q❀≠♣P

HALSTEAD

Rose & Crown
Otford Lane, TN14 7EA OS489611
☼ 12-11; 12-10.30 Sun
☎ (01959) 533120
Courage Best Bitter; Harveys BB; Larkins Traditional; guest beers H
Two-bar free house in a flint-faced listed building of the 1860s. Originally named the Crown, it was part of Fox and Son's brewery estate and then a Stile and Winch house. Pictures show the pub in earlier times. Lunches are served weekdays. Bat and trap is played in the garden where children are welcome; they may also use the games room. Three guest beers change regularly – a tribute to the knowledgeable landlady. Ask her about Humphrey the benign ghost.
Q❅❀❨❞♣P

HERNE

Smuggler's Inn
1 School Lane, CT6 7AN
☼ 11-11; 12-10.30 Sun
☎ (01227) 741395
Shepherd Neame Master Brew Bitter, seasonal beers H
The attic of this well-kept pub was used by smugglers as a lookout, while a tunnel linked the cellars to the church. The recently refurbished games bar is fitted with a binnacle and the prow of a whaler. The beamed saloon bar features hops and brass. A regular bus service runs from Canterbury and Herne Bay. Just across the road is the recommended Herne florist and real ale off-licence. Meals are served Monday–Saturday.
Q❅❀❨❞♣

HERNHILL

Three Horseshoes
46 Staple Street, ME13 9UA (follow Bull Lane from Boughton-under-Blean, then right) OS080601
☼ 12-3, 5-11; 12-11 Fri & Sat; 12-3, 7-10.30 Sun
☎ (01227) 750842
Shepherd Neame Master Brew Bitter, Spitfire, seasonal beers G
Traditional country pub, dating from 1690, in a small hamlet among fruit orchards and hop gardens, close to Mount Ephraim Gardens and Farming World. The beers are served direct from casks behind the bar. A warm welcome is extended to all who visit this friendly village local. Home-made food is served Tuesday–Sunday. Live music (jazz or blues) is performed on the last Saturday of each month and regular quiz nights are staged. Local Crippledick cider is offered in bottles (to take away only).
Q❀❨▲♣P

IDEN GREEN (BENENDEN)

Woodcock Inn
Woodcock Lane, TN17 4HT (off Benenden-Sandhurst road towards Standen Street) OS807313
☼ 11-11; 12-10.30 Sun
☎ (01580) 240009
Greene King IPA, Morland Original, Ruddles County; Rother Valley Level Best H
It is unlikely that you will come across this popular rural pub by chance as it is extremely well hidden. The interior is dominated by low, exposed timbers and brickwork; an inglenook opposite the bar forms a centrepiece. The dining area offers a diverse menu of home-cooked food, with something to satisfy most tastes. Behind is a large garden, with a window to allow customers to order drinks directly from the bar. Q❀❨❞P

IGHTHAM

Chequers
The Street, TN15 9HH
☼ 11-3, 6-11; 12-3, 7-10.30 Sun
☎ (01732) 882396
Greene King IPA, Abbot, seasonal beer; guest beer H
Pleasant, traditional, welcoming one-bar village local with a large open stone fireplace at one side and a no-smoking section for diners at the other end of the mock Tudor-style bar. However, diners are welcome to eat in all areas and booking is advisable as the pub has a strong reputation for good food, available during all sessions. The Chequers supports local charities including the Kent Air Ambulance.
Q❀❨P⚓

IGHTHAM COMMON

Old House ☆
Redwell Lane, TN15 9EE (½ mile SW of Ightham Village, between A25 and A227) OS590559
☼ 12-3 (not Mon-Fri), 7-11 (9 Tue); 12-3, 7-10.30 Sun
☎ (01732) 882383
Daleside Shrimpers; G **Flowers IPA;** H **Oakham JHB; Otter Bitter; guest beers** G
Converted from a row of red brick cottages, on a steep hill in a narrow lane, with a small forecourt for parking, the pub is difficult to find as it has no sign. However, it has a strong local following and the atmosphere buzzes with convivial conversation. Four beers are kept on stillage in a room behind the bar. The main room boasts a large open fireplace and exposed beams (partly 16th century); the quiet parlour features an old cash register, retired after 28 years' service. Q❨▲P

IVYCHURCH

Bell Inn
Ashford Road, TN29 0AL (off A2070/A259 jct)
☼ 12-2 (3 summer), 6-11; 12-4, 7-10.30 Sun
☎ (01797) 344355
Greene King IPA; Harveys BB; guest beers H
A 'church house' pub once situated on glebe land, the Bell is known locally for its stained glass windows. Two regular ales and one or two guests are served to wash down the simple, local food. Frequented by walkers and cyclists, banger racing is held in an adjacent field three or four times a year. These days a warm welcome is assured here,

but in the past, strangers were treated with hostility as both the pub and church were used by 'owlers' as contraband warehouses.
🏚⚘◐↧P

KEMSING

Rising Sun
Cotmans Ash Lane, TN15 6XD OS563599
✪ 11-3, 6-11; 12-3, 7-10.30 Sun
☎ (01959) 522683
Beer range varies Ⓗ
This isolated, hilltop pub stands in scenic countryside near the North Downs Way and several local footpaths. Visitors are advised to phone for directions. The main bar area is a converted hunting lodge, displaying old agricultural implements; an ageing African Grey parrot resides by the large open fireplace. Five handpumps dispense an ever-changing selection of beers from small independent and micro-breweries; a cider is stocked in summer. A popular venue for diners, excellent home-cooked English food comes in generous portions. 🏚Q☆☺◐Ⅰ♣P▯

KINGSDOWN

King's Head
Upper Street, CT14 8BJ (1 mile E of A258)
✪ 12-3 (not Mon-Thu), 5-11; 12-10.30 Sun
☎ (01304) 373915
Draught Bass; Greene King IPA; guest beer Ⓗ
Halfway down the main village street, towards the sea, this convivial, split-level pub appeals to locals and visitors alike. Divided into several bars, its oldest part dates back to the turn of the 18th/19th centuries. The lower bar sports a collection of old firearms and a frosted glass door bearing the name of the long-defunct local brewery, Thompson of Walmer. The secluded garden has a skittle alley. The guest ale selection concentrates on local brews. 🏚⚘◐Ⅰ♣

KNOCKHOLT

Three Horseshoes
The Pound, TN14 7JD
✪ 11.30-3, 6-11; 12-3, 7-10.30 Sun
☎ (01959) 532102 website: www.t3hsk.co.uk
Courage Best Bitter; Fuller's London Pride; Greene King IPA; Harveys BB Ⓗ
Imposing building at the village centre. The roomy saloon bar is decorated with pictures of cars and trains, while the panelled snug displays pictures of military occasions – the landlord is a former band sergeant major of the Irish Guards. There are four handpumps in the saloon and two in the snug. The North Downs Way passes about 600 yards to the south of the pub. No meals are served Sunday evening. Wheelchair access is at the rear. The pub hosts vintage car rallies.
Q⚘◐Ⅰ♣P

LADDINGFORD

Chequers Inn ✔
The Street, ME18 6BP
✪ 12-3, 5-11; 12-11 Sat; 12-10.30 Sun
☎ (01622) 871266
Adnams Bitter; Fuller's London Pride; Young's Bitter; guest beers Ⓗ
A warm welcome awaits at this lovely

15th-century weatherboarded inn at the heart of the village, and not just in winter with the central open fire. An enthusiastic supporter of local charities, the pub holds a number of fundraising events. Each April, a popular weekend-long beer festival is staged. One wall of the pub is covered with certificates, including many for the floral displays that cover the front of the pub in summer.
🏚⚘↧◐ⅠP

LANGTON GREEN

Hare
Langton Green, TN3 0JA
✪ 11-11; 12-10.30 Sun
☎ (01892) 862419
website: www.brunningandprice.co.uk
Everards Tiger; Greene King IPA, Ruddles County, Abbot Ⓗ
Large, comfortable Victorian Greene King pub, on the edge of the village green. Recently refurbished, it features wood floors and open fireplaces, with three eating areas and a bar. Four real ales are always available, while good food on a daily changing menu keeps six chefs busy. No TV, fruit machines or play area for children, make this predominantly an adults' pub, although children are welcome in the eating areas.
🏚Q⚘◐Ⅰ♿♣

LOOSE

Walnut Tree
657 Loose Road, ME15 9UX (on A229)
✪ 11-3 (4 Fri), 6-11; 12-3, 7-10.30 Sun
☎ (01622) 743493
Shepherd Neame Master Brew Bitter, Spitfire, seasonal beers Ⓗ
Popular local, consisting of two bars in an L-shape with a log-effect fire between them. The main area is decorated with horse brasses, WWII prints, caricatures and an unusual collection of chamberpots, while the other bar has water jugs and a dartboard. The landlord has been here for 18 years. Reasonably-priced bar snacks and hot meals, available every day except Sunday, include vegetarian dishes. Petanque can be played in the garden.
Q⚘◐Ⅰ♣P

LUDDESDOWN

Cock Inn ✔
Henley Street, DA13 0XB OS664672
✪ 12-11; 12-10.30 Sun
☎ (01474) 814208
Adnams Bitter, Broadside; Goacher's Mild; Shepherd Neame Master Brew Bitter; guest beers Ⓗ
Excellent, independently-owned free house offering at least six real ales, three ciders and the occasional perry. The welcoming landlord devises and hosts a popular free quiz on Tuesday evening, and the extended conservatory is used for various functions. The saloon bar features WWII memorabilia, while the public bar has a classic car theme and offers a choice of dartboards including quads, Kentish and London fives. Petanque is played regularly. No food is served Saturday evening or Sunday.
🏚Q⚘◐Ⅰ♿♣P

MAIDSTONE

Druid's Arms
24 Earl Street, ME14 1PP (near Hazlitt Theatre)
◑ 11-11; 12-10.30 Sun
☎ (01622) 758516
Draught Bass; Fuller's London Pride; Greene King Abbot; guest beers Ⓗ

Busy, lively, town-centre pub within easy walking distance of both rail and bus stations as well as other Guide-listed pubs. The outdoor drinking area is popular in summer with younger customers. Modestly priced food is available seven days a week. Why not combine a visit to the county town of Kent and its shopping centre with lunch at the Druid's Arms?
✿◑➤ (East/West)

Pilot ⊘
23-25 Upper Stone Street, ME15 6EU
(on A229)
◑ 12-3 (4 Sat), 6 (7 Sat)-11; 12-5, 7-10.30 Sun
☎ (01622) 691162
Harveys XX Mild, BB, Armada, seasonal beers Ⓗ

Friendly pub with an open fire and terraced garden, just to the south of the town centre. It hosts live music most Sundays and fields petanque and quiz teams. Home-cooked meals and bar snacks are served. It is within walking distance of buses and trains and other Guide-listed pubs. ⌂Q♿✿◑

Rifle Volunteers
28 Wyatt Street, ME14 1EU
◑ 11-3 (may vary), 6 (7 Sat)-11; 12-3 (may vary), 7-10.30 Sun
☎ (01622) 758891
Goacher's Mild, Light, Crown Imperial Stout Ⓗ

This quiet, street-corner, single bar is one of the two tied houses owned by the local Goacher's Brewery. Its three beers include the rarely seen Crown Imperial Stout, available here all year round. Excellent value, no-nonsense lunches are produced mainly for the regular clients from the nearby old people's home; evening meals can be arranged. The pub runs two quiz league teams. Toy soldiers are given as beer tokens for customers not yet ready for a refill. Q✿◑➤ (East) ♣

Swan Inn
2 County Road, ME14 1UY
◑ 11-11; 12-10.30 Sun
☎ (01622) 751264
website: www.swan-inn-maidstone.com
Shepherd Neame Master Brew Bitter, Bishops Finger, seasonal beers Ⓗ

Fine, community-based Shepherd Neame pub whose landlord has won many Cellarmanship awards. Delicious authentic Indian meals are available. It is home to the Maidstone quiz and bar billiards leagues. Note the collection of porcelain swans, all gifts from regulars. The pub is actively engaged in raising money for local charities. It always carries the full range of Shep's seasonal ales and award-winning Kent honey is sold. ✿◑➤ (East) ♣⎕

MARGATE

Orb
243 Ramsgate Road, CT9 4EU
◑ 11-11; 12-10.30 Sun
☎ (01843) 220663

Shepherd Neame Master Brew Bitter Ⓗ

Superb pub, close to the area's main hospital. It started out as a small farm cottage and stable on the Chappel Hill estate; the change to a pub was brought about by its excellent position on the Margate–Ramsgate road that made it a good stop-off point for horse-drawn traffic. The pub today, with extensions to incorporate a dining area and games room, is a lively local. A second Shepherd Neame beer changes regularly. Lunches are served weekdays.
⌂✿◑

Spread Eagle ⊘
25 Victoria Road, CT9 1LW
◑ 11-3, 5-11; 11-11 Sat; 12-10.30 Sun
☎ (01843) 293396
Fuller's London Pride; Greene King IPA; guest beer Ⓗ

This back-street local was built in 1762 as a boarding academy, although this never materialised; the change to a beer house in 1830, it became fully licensed in 1838. A Victorian frontage was added to the Georgian façade and two adjoining cottages have been incorporated over the years. It supports award-winning quiz and darts teams. Food is served every day except Sunday. It is one of only two local outlets to have achieved Cask Marque accreditation.
✿◑♣

MARSH GREEN

Wheatsheaf Inn
TN8 5QL
◑ 11-11; 12-10.30 Sun
☎ (01732) 864091
Harveys BB; guest beers Ⓗ

Friendly country pub, the focal point for the village community. At least six to eight real ales, including a mild, are always available and change regularly. Biddenden cider is also stocked. An annual beer festival is held in early summer, to coincide with the village fête, offering over 30 ales on gravity. The pub has several rooms, including a conservatory, and serves a wide range of home-cooked food, with vegetarian options. Darts, cribbage and shove-ha'penny are played.
⌂Q♿✿◑♿♣♠P½

MARSHSIDE

Gate Inn
Boyden Gate, CT3 4EB
(take Chislet turning off A28 at Upstreet)
◑ 11-2.30, 6-11; 12-4, 7-10.30 Sun
☎ (01227) 860498
Shepherd Neame Master Brew Bitter, Spitfire, seasonal beers Ⓖ

In this Guide under the same landlord since 1975, this unspoilt pub has a tiled floor and is hung with hops. Set in marshland, the garden has a duckpond, stream and apple trees. There is a strong emphasis on the local community, staging charity events such as mummers' plays, hoodeners and morris dancing. The excellent value menu is based on fresh local ingredients; in winter evening meals are served Wednesday–Saturday. It is a worthwhile detour from the A28 or Thanet Way.
⌂Q♿✿◑▲♣P½

MINSTER (THANET)

New Inn
2 Tothill Street, CT12 4AG
✪ 11.30-3, 6 (5 Tue)-11; 11.30-11 Wed-Sat; 12-10.30 Sun
☎ (01843) 821294
Greene King IPA, Abbot; guest beer H

This delightful local, with a warm, friendly atmosphere, was built in 1837 as a replacement for the original hostelry in William Buddell's pleasure gardens complex, when the gardens were extended. Today the pub's garden is all that remains of the ample pleasure gardens and houses an aviary, rabbit warren and a climbing frame. An extension has provided a better dining area and venue for live music. Note the Cobb's windows. No food is served Monday or Sunday evening. ✿◑▣≈♣P

NEW ROMNEY

Prince of Wales
Fairfield Road, TN28 8HW
✪ 12-3, 6 (5 Thu)-11; 12-11 Fri & Sat; 12-10.30 Sun
☎ (01797) 362012
Shepherd Neame Master Brew Bitter; Tetley Burton Ale; guest beer H

Friendly local, a short walk from the RH & D light railway station, it is a rare outlet for Burton Ale. Games played here include crib, pool and darts. The pub has two bars with low ceilings. Fairfield Road is inland from, and parallel to, the A259, near the superstore. ▨✿▣A♣

NEWENDEN

White Hart
Rye Road, TN18 5PN (on A28)
✪ 11-11; 12-10.30 Sun
☎ (01797) 252166
Fuller's London Pride; Harveys BB; Rother Valley Level Best; guest beer H

Typical inn, offering a wide range of home-cooked food in pleasant surroundings. Petanque is played in the garden in summer. Boat and steam railway trips are available to Bodiam Castle; it is a short stroll from the Kent & East Sussex steam railway. Rother Valley Brewery is only a few hundred yards away, across the river in Sussex. Six newly refurbished en-suite bedrooms are available. ▨Q☜✿▣◑♿♣P

NORTHBOURNE

Hare & Hounds
The Street, CT14 0LG
✪ 11-3 (3.30 Sat, 6-11); 12-3, 7-10.30 Sun
☎ (01304) 365429
Draught Bass; Greene King Abbot; Harveys BB; Shepherd Neame Master Brew Bitter H

This 300-year-old village local stands on the ancient route between Canterbury and Sandwich, close to the site of St Augustine's Abbey. Originally three rooms, it was converted into one space in the 1970s, but has managed to retain its original character. A full menu of home-cooked food attracts diners, but it still finds time and space to ensure drinkers are welcome, with beers from Kent and further afield. The garden has a children's play area. Occasional quiz nights are staged. ▨Q✿◑♣P

NORTHFLEET

Campbell Arms
1 Campbell Road, DA11 0JZ
✪ 12-11; 12-10.30 Sun
☎ (01474) 320488
Courage Best Bitter; guest beers H

Popular, one-bar, back-street, corner pub in an old residential area on the Gravesend border. It gets especially busy early weekday evenings. The pub runs both darts and football teams and features a pool table. There is a Courage Best mirror in the bar and an old Mann, Crossman & Paulin one behind the bar. Up to three guest beers are available, regularly including a mild, a rarity for the area. This basic, but good value, local is a welcome recent convert to real ale. ✿♣

OLD ROMNEY

Rose & Crown
Swamp Road, TN29 9SQ (off A259)
✪ 11.30-11; 12-10.30 Sun
☎ (01797) 367500
website: www.roseandcrown-oldromney.co.uk
Fuller's London Pride; Greene King XX Mild, IPA, Abbot; Young's Bitter H

Pretty country inn, built in 1689, it became a pub in 1806. Under the wide skies and surrounded by the sometimes bleak landscape of Romney Marsh, it is easily accessible, just off the A259. The large garden, offering many facilities for families, is complemented by the no-smoking area in the conservatory. Biddenden cider is served straight from the cask. No food is served on Sunday evenings in winter. Well worth seeking out; there is a games room and petanque is also played. ▨✿▣◑A♣♿P⊁

PERRY WOOD

Rose & Crown
ME13 9RY (1 mile S of Selling village) OS042552
✪ 11-3, 6.30-11; 12-3, 7-10.30 Sun
☎ (01227) 752214
Adnams Bitter; Goacher's Mild; Harveys BB; guest beer H

Located in the midst of Perry Wood, next to East Kent's highest point, this pub is well known locally for the quality of its beers and food. Its garden, which has won several national awards, houses a bat and trap pitch and a children's play area. Inside, it is very comfortable and displays a Pub Coal Fire award; it has also been a previous winner of Swale CAMRA's Pub of the Year. Evening meals are served Tuesday–Saturday. ▨Q✿◑♣P

PETTERIDGE

Hop Bine
Petteridge Lane, TN12 7NE
(1 mile SW of Brenchley) OS668413
✪ 12 (11 Sat)-2.30, 6-11; 12-3, 7-10.30 Sun
☎ (01892) 722561
Badger Best, seasonal beers H

Traditional, unspoilt, brick and white weatherboarded pub, off the beaten track; it is well worth seeking out. The L-shaped bar is warmed by an open fire. A former King & Barnes house, taken over by the distant Badger Brewery, it has been in this Guide for 15 years. The menu, supplemented by a daily specials board, represents excellent value; no food is served on Wednesday.

🏚 Q ⏣ ◐ ⅃ ♣ ♠ P

PLAXTOL

Golding Hop
Sheet Hill, TN15 0PT
(E off A227 into Bewley Lane, first right down Sheet Hill)
☼ 11-3, 6 (5.30 Fri)-11; 11-11 Sat; 12-3.30
(4 summer), 7-10.30 Sun
☎ (01732) 882150
Adnams Bitter; Young's Special, seasonal beers; guest beers Ⓖ

Particularly attractive, ancient country pub in an idyllic setting, notable for its range of ciders, one of which is made on the premises. The homely interior is on three levels with whitewashed walls, original dark wood beams and log-burning stoves. Good bar food is available (except Mon/Tue eves). Outside is a flower-filled terraced garden and a tranquil seating area with a stream; petanque is played. Eggs are often available from resident ducks, geese and chickens.
🏚 ⏣ ◐ ♣ ♠ P

PLUCKLEY

Dering Arms
Station Road, TN27 0RR
☼ 12-2, 6-11; 12-2, 7-10.30 Sun
☎ (01233) 840371
Dering Ale Ⓗ

Built as a hunting lodge for the Dering estate, with stone flagged bars, the pub serves a house beer, Dering Ale (brewed by Goacher's) and excellent food. This absolute gem is situated a little way from the village, but right outside Pluckley Station, so it is very convenient for the trains.
🏚 Q 🛏 ◐ ⇌

RAINHAM

Mackland Arms
213 Station Road, ME8 7PS
☼ 10-11; 12-10.30 Sun
☎ (01634) 232178
Shepherd Neame Master Brew Bitter, Best Bitter, Spitfire, Bishops Finger, seasonal beers Ⓗ

A real local; this small L-shaped bar offers all you can want in a pub: good beer, good conversation and good humour. The last unchanged pub in the area, run by a long-standing landlord, it is popular with a wide range of drinkers. ⇌ ♣

RAMSGATE

Artillery Arms
36 Westcliffe Road, CT11 9JS
☼ 12-11; 12-10.30 Sun
☎ (01843) 853282
Beer range varies Ⓗ

Superb, unpretentious, little pub with attractive leaded bow windows that depict soliders and guns from the Napleonic Wars. Allegedly built in 1812, it was used as an officers' billet and a brothel before becoming a beer house and, in 1869, a fully licensed pub. The 'Arty' was refurbished and the interior rebuilt in 1992. Since then, although it has seen several landlords, the emphasis has always been on real ale, with an ever-changing roster of beers. Å ♠

Brewhouse & Bakers
98 Harbour Street, CT11 8LP
☼ 10am-midnight (1am Fri & Sat); 12-10.30 Sun
☎ (01843) 594758
website: www.ramsgatebrewhouse.com
Ramsgate Gadds No. 7, Gadds No. 5, Gadds No. 3 Ⓗ

Two beer enthusiasts opened this lively café-bar, whose full title is the Ramsgate Royal Harbour Brewhouse and Bakers, in 2002 after a painstaking refurbishment of a former restaurant. As its name suggests, it houses a brewery (the brewing equipment can be seen at the rear) and a bakery which produces much of the bar's bread and pastries. As well as the brewery's beers, the bar serves over 70 draught and bottled Dutch and Belgian beers. 🏚 ◐ Å ♠ ▯

Churchill Tavern
18-20 The Paragon, CT11 9JX
☼ 11-11 (midnight Fri & Sat); 12-10.30 Sun
☎ (01843) 587862
Courage Best Bitter, Directors; Fuller's London Pride; Ringwood Old Thumper; Taylor Landlord; guest beers Ⓖ

This large pub, with views across the Channel, is popular with locals, visitors and students from nearby language schools. It evolved out of the bars and lounges of the Paragon Hotel, when it lost its hotel function, and was rebuilt in the late 1980s to resemble a country pub, using old beams and church pews and given its present name. All the real ales are served direct from the cask. 🏚 ◐ Å ♣

Montefiore Arms
1 Trinity Place, CT11 7HJ
☼ 12-2.30, 7-11; closed Wed; 12-3, 7-10.30 Sun
☎ (01843) 593296
Ridleys Tolly Original; guest beer Ⓗ

This busy, friendly local, serving the Hereson Road district of town, started life as two cottages. Its unique name honours the legendary centenarian and philanthropist, Sir Moses Montefiore, a campaigner for Jewish rights, who is remembered locally as a benefactor to the town's poor. He lived in the town much of his life and is buried in a mausoleum nearby. The Monty holds regular theme nights throughout the year.
Q 🛏 ⇌ (Dumpton Pk) ♣

St Lawrence Tavern
High Street, St Lawrence, CT11 0QH
☼ 11-11; 12-10.30 Sun
☎ (01843) 592337
Beer range varies Ⓗ

This lively pub and restaurant was formerly known as the White Horse and is now part of the successful local Thorley Tavern chain. The original Cobb's Brewery pub was built in the 18th century, some 300 yards away. Demolished in 1851, it reappeared on the present pub's car park, before finally settling on its present site in 1969. Football matches are regularly shown here on a large-screen TV.
🏚 ⏣ ◐ Å ⇌ ♣ P

RIPPLE

Plough Inn
Church Street, CT14 8JH
☼ 11-4, 6-11; 11-11 Sat; 12-10.30 Sun
☎ (01304) 360209

Fuller's ESB; Shepherd Neame Master Brew Bitter,
Spitfire, seasonal beers Ⓗ

Popular, single-bar, village local enjoying
a good trade for its wide range of home-
cooked meals. The heavily-beamed
interior is decorated with old farm
implements, horse brasses, pump clips
and a wagon wheel. Note the unusual
chain mail fire curtain and the fine two-
pump beer engine by the main entrance
(unfortunately no longer used). A wide
selection of country wines is stocked.
Children are welcome in the small seating
area by the main entrance.
🏚🏵🚄⓵🍴♣P

ROCHESTER

Britannia Café Bar
376 High Street, ME1 1DJ
✪ 11-11; 12-10.30 Sun
☎ (01634) 815204
website: www.britannia-bar-cafe.co.uk
Beer range varies Ⓗ

Busy at lunchtimes with a mainly business
clientele, it serves an extensive and popular
menu daily, plus traditional Sunday lunches
(breakfast is also served 10am–noon). A very
friendly and cosy atmosphere extends into
the evening. A stylish bar leads out into a
small walled garden that is a suntrap in
summer. Live music is performed every
Monday evening and occasionally on
Friday. A monthly quiz and occasional
theme and dinner nights are also held.
Q🏵⓵⇌

Cooper's Arms
10 St Margarets Street, ME1 1TL
(near castle and cathedral)
✪ 11-3, 5.30-11; 11-11 Fri & Sat; 12-10.30 Sun
☎ (01634) 404298
Courage Best Bitter, Directors; guest beers Ⓗ

This ancient and attractive inn is said to be
the oldest in Kent and is mentioned in
the Domesday Book. It features an
overhanging upper storey and
weatherboarded sides. Two comfortable
bars contain some interesting items of
historic interest. The food (not served
Sun) is good value and includes a daily
home-cooked special. Summer barbecues
(Fri eve) are held in the prize-winning
garden. Apart from the castle and
cathedral there are many other
interesting buildings and the River
Medway nearby.
🏚Q🏵⓵⇌

Man of Kent
6-8 John Street, ME1 1YN
✪ 12-11; 12-10.30 Sun
☎ (01634) 818771
Beer range varies Ⓗ

Small, back-street ale house with a single
L-shaped bar. Its rare, original tiled
exterior is badged Style & Winch, a
Maidstone Brewery taken over and closed
by Courage. Specialising in beers from
Kent micro-breweries, normally five
handpumps are in operation. Two
draught ciders, again sourced in Kent, are
usually on tap; a selection of Kent wines
and German beers are also stocked. The
small rear garden is used occasionally for
summer barbecues.
🏚Q🏵⇌🍴

ROMNEY STREET

Fox & Hounds
Romney Street, TN15 6XR
(2 miles up hill from Eynsford war memorial) OS550614
✪ 12-3 (not Mon), 6-11; 12-11 Sat; 12-10.30 Sun
☎ (01959) 525428
Beer range varies Ⓗ

Remote hilltop country pub in the hamlet
of Romney Street; a friendly stopping place
for hikers, it also enjoys a loyal, regular
trade. Traditional games such as shove-
ha'penny and shut the box are available.
Good traditional food is served every
lunchtime and early evening (Thu–Sat)
providing welcome sustenance for ramblers.
Four rotating guest beers include at least
one from a micro-brewery. The large,
attractive garden is the venue for an annual
beer festival in June. A wheelchair ramp and
camping facilities are available on request.
🏚🏵⓵♿▲♣P⅄

ST MARGARET'S AT CLIFFE

Smugglers
High Street, CT15 6AU (on B2058)
✪ 12-3, 5-11; 12-11 Sat; 12-4, 7-10.30 Sun
☎ (01304) 853404
Fuller's London Pride; Greene King IPA; guest beers Ⓗ

St Margaret's at Cliffe supports four pubs
within 200 yards of each other. The smallest
is the Smugglers, comprising a long, single
bar with an unusual semi-circular servery.
Low-ceilinged, with much dark wood and
subdued lighting, it combines a popular
local and good restaurant (Mexican dishes a
speciality). Bus services to Dover and Deal
operate until early evening. The guest ale
appears only at the weekend in winter. A
late drinking extension is available to
diners. 🏵⓵

ST MARGARET'S BAY

Coastguard
The Beach, CT15 6DY
✪ 11-11; 12-10.30 Sun
☎ (01304) 853176 website: www.thecoastguard.co.uk
Adnams Bitter; guest beer Ⓗ

Formerly the Green Man, the pub was
shelled during WWII and rebuilt. It lies just
above the high water mark, north of Dover
Harbour in the classic village of St
Margaret's Bay. The village boasts
associations with Ian Fleming, Noel Coward
and Lord Byron. The pub showcases Kent's
independent brewers and stocks European
bottled beers. It is an ideal venue for
watching the maritime traffic in the Dover
straits.
Q🛏🏵⓵▲P

ST MARY IN THE MARSH

Star
TN29 0BX OS064279
✪ 11-3, 7-11; 12-3, 7-10.30 Sun
☎ (01797) 362139
**Shepherd Neame Master Brew Bitter, Spitfire,
seasonal beers** Ⓗ

Friendly local, with a stone-flagged floor, in
a village on the Romney Marsh. This is an
unspoilt part of the county, three miles
north of New Romney (home of the
Romney, Hythe and Dymchurch Light
Railway). The landscape can be a bit bleak

and windswept in winter, making this pub a welcome sight.
🏠🏵️⛴️◑♣P

SANDGATE

Clarendon Inn
Brewers Hill, CT20 3DH
(take stepped passageway up hill by phone box, next to Sandgate Hotel)
🕑 12-3, 6-11; 12-5 Sun
☎ (01303) 248684
Shepherd Neame Master Brew Bitter, Best Bitter, Spitfire, Bishops Finger, seasonal beers Ⓗ
To reach this historic pub you must climb 80 yards from Sandgate Esplanade (A259). Well worth the climb – stepping inside the hop-bedecked interior you will see a classic Victorian back bar laden with at least 16 single malts and fruit gins made on the premises. Home-cooked food is prepared from the finest local ingredients. An interesting assortment of memorabilia lines the walls of this local CAMRA Pub of the Year 2002. Ring for details of live music performances. 🏠Q🏵️⛴️◑🏠♣✠🗄️

SANDWICH

Fleur-de-Lis
6 Delf Street, CT13 9BZ
🕑 11-11; 12-10.30 Sun
☎ (01304) 611311
Fuller's London Pride; Greene King IPA; guest beers Ⓗ
This old coaching inn was considerably altered during the 1990s, providing three distinct areas for dining, drinking, TV and pool. The guest ale changes weekly and is often from a micro-brewery, for example, Sharp's or Oakham. Its central location means that all of the charms of this original Cinque Port are within five minutes' walk.
⛴️◑≷

SEAL

Five Bells
25 Church Street, TN15 0AU
(100 yds N of High St, A25)
🕑 11.30-11; 12-10.30 Sun
☎ (01732) 761503
Harveys BB; guest beer Ⓗ
This friendly local was converted from three 18th-century cottages. Nicely decorated, it features wood panelling, old local photos and a working upright piano for impromptu entertainment – there is no juke box. Four ales are stocked, with guests sourced from small breweries; a mild is often available. A lunchtime bar snack menu is offered on weekdays. There are benches outside for summer drinking. **Q**

SEVENOAKS

Anchor
32 London Road, TN13 1AS
🕑 11-3 (10.30-4 Fri & Sat), 6 (7 Sat)-11; 12-3, 7-10.30 Sun
☎ (01732) 454898
Harveys BB; guest beers Ⓗ
Pleasant pub where guest beers are often sourced from small breweries and good value food is served. Monthly live jazz is staged (first Wed eve). The licensee, the longest-serving in Sevenoaks, is chairman of the Licensed Victuallers Association. Note

the unusual curved entrance doors – the inner and outer doors form an almost completely circular lobby. Look out for beer festivals in future. ◑♣

Chequers
71 High Street, TN13 1LD
🕑 11-11; 12-10.30 Sun
☎ (01732) 454377
Draught Bass; Tetley Bitter; guest beers Ⓗ
An old timber-framed building that has survived in the town centre. The guest beers number between six and nine, depending on the time of the year, frequently featuring ales from small breweries. This pub usually offers the best choice of quality real ale in the town, and is an ideal place to eat. Good food is served from a varied menu – Sunday lunches, served 2–5, are especially recommended. Food is served all day on Saturday until 9pm.
🏵️◑♣✠

SHEERNESS

Red Lion
61 High Street, Bluetown, ME12 1RW
🕑 11-11; 12-10.30 Sun
☎ (01795) 663163
Beer range varies Ⓗ
In the historic Bluetown area of the town, the pub faces the old dockyard wall. Behind it is the country's largest concrete garden gnome factory and it is adjacent to O'Hagans sausage shop. The interior displays a host of maritime memorabilia, including old photographs of naval ships associated with the town. Three or four real ales are normally available and it is a rare outlet for Johnson's cider, made on the Isle of Sheppey. The upstairs restaurant opens on summer evenings.
🏠🏵️◑≷●

SHOREHAM

Olde George Inne
Church Street, TN14 7SB
🕑 11-11; 12-10.30 Sun
☎ (01959) 522017
Harveys BB; Worthington's 1744; guest beer Ⓗ
Friendly, 15th-century free house on the edge of the village and close to the picturesque Darenth Valley. The pub is divided into three bars, with oak beamed ceilings, and is home to three darts teams. Two of the four handpumps dispense beers not normally seen in the area. Good value food is served 12–3 and 7–9. Roadside tables are put out for summer drinking.
🏠🏵️◑≷♣P

SITTINGBOURNE

Old Oak
68 East Street, ME10 4RT
🕑 10.30-2.30, 7-11; 12-2.30, 7-10.30 Sun
☎ (01795) 472685
Beer range varies Ⓗ
This 150-year-old pub is situated among the various small shops and takeaways in East Street. Inside, the wood-panelled pub has changed little over the last 50 years, giving it a settled and comfortable feel. Run by Sittingbourne's longest-serving landlord, it was joint winner of Swale CAMRA Pub of the Year in 1998. Extremely good value

food is offered and there are always two beers from micro- and regional brewers.
❀◖≈♣⊁

Red Lion
58 High Street, ME10 4PB
✪ 11-3, 6-11; 12-3, 7-10.30 Sun
☎ (01795) 472706
Fuller's London Pride; guest beers Ⓗ
This historic town-centre pub, part of which dates back to the 15th century, is a former coaching inn. The outdoor drinking area is the former stable yard. In 1835 the pub was divided into private dwellings, with only the eastern end remaining as a public house. It was completely rebuilt in 1896, the western end becoming Martins Bank (now housing Woolwich Building Society). There is a quiz every Sunday evening. Normally five guest beer are stocked from regional breweries. ❀◖≈

SNARGATE

Red Lion ☆
TN29 9UQ (on B2080, 1 mile from Appledore Station)
✪ 12-3, 7-11; 12-3, 7-10.30 Sun
☎ (01797) 344648
Goacher's Light; guest beers Ⓖ
Locally known as Doris's, this pub, dating from 1540, has been in the same family since 1911, run with love and devotion. Three or four beers from independents, particularly local breweries, usually include a mild. The pub is a legend and this is its 20th consecutive entry in this Guide. In 1999 the pub was CAMRA's regional Pub of the Year, and was runner-up for the national award. A beer festival is held annually in June, on the weekend of the longest day. Double Vision cider is sold.
▨Q❀♣⊌P

SPELDHURST

George & Dragon
Speldhurst Hill, TN3 0NN (3 miles W of Tunbridge Wells)
✪ 11-11; 12-10.30 Sun
☎ (01892) 863125
website: www.george-and-dragon-speldhurst.co.uk
Harveys Pale Ale, BB; Larkins Traditional; guest beers Ⓗ
This 13th-century, timber-framed building is warmed by large open fires in both bars. The Village Bar has a flagstone floor and dark wood panelling while the Buttery is an informal dining room, with a daily blackboard menu (eve meals Tue–Sat). The Oak Room restaurant upstairs, with its magnificent beam spanning the entire room, provides a sumptuous setting in which to appreciate fine food and drink. A garden to the front is complemented by a newly-decked area at the rear for outdoor drinking. ▨❀◖⊟⅋♣P

STANSTED

Black Horse
Tumblefield Road, TN15 7PR (1 mile N of A20) OS606621
✪ 11-11; 12-10.30 Sun
☎ (01732) 822355
Larkins Traditional; guest beers Ⓗ
In a secluded downland village near Brands

226

Hatch, this somewhat austere Victorian building is a second home for the local community and welcomes walkers and other visitors. A large natural garden includes a safe children's play area. The pub hosts a Kent Week in July, when all the real ales, ciders and wines come from local producers; Biddenden cider is always available. Thai cuisine (Tue–Sat eves) and excellent Sunday lunches are served. The bed & breakfast accommodation is recommended.
▨▱❀⅋⊨◖⚲♣P⊁

STAPLEHURST

Lord Raglan
Chart Hill Road, TN12 0DE (left off A229 from Maidstone at Cross At Hand) OS786472
✪ 12-3, 6-11; closed Sun
☎ (01622) 843747
Goacher's Light; Harveys BB; guest beer Ⓗ
This popular, unspoilt pub has no music or other distractions, so conversation reigns supreme. A real gem of a country pub, it is run with devotion. Two log fires keep you warm in winter and hops hang all around the bar. Lunchtime and evening meals are served from an excellent menu. Three real ales are stocked – the guest beer is always changing; a cider is available in summer.
▨Q❀◖⅋♣P

STODMARSH

Red Lion
Stodmarsh Road, CT3 4BA
(3½ miles from A257)
✪ 11-11; 12-10.30 Sun
☎ (01227) 721339
Greene King IPA; guest beer (occasional) Ⓖ
Lively, slightly eccentric pub with lots of character. Hanging hops, fresh flowers, low ceilings, curios and intimate areas for eating and drinking are attractive features. A strong emphasis is placed on good food, with a changing menu (no food Sun eve). Bat and trap is played in the attractive garden. Curry and jazz nights take place on the first Wednesday of the month; music workshops and jam sessions are generally held on the first Sunday. The River Stour, lakes and a nature reserve are nearby.
▨Q❀⊨◖⚲♣P

STONE STREET

Padwell Arms
Stone Street Road, TN15 0LQ OS569551
✪ 12-3, 6-11; 12-3, 7-10.30 Sun
☎ (01732) 761532
Badger Best, Tanglefoot; Harveys BB; Hook Norton Old Hooky; guest beers Ⓗ
Attractive old rural pub in a leafy lane on the edge of the village. The inviting interior features beams, wood panelling, polished old copper measures and log fires, while the spacious, south-facing terrace overlooks orchards. Four reliable regular beers are joined by a good variety of guests. Generous portions of well-presented food from the varied menu are served every lunchtime and Tuesday–Saturday evenings. Walkers and cyclists are welcome.
▨❀◖♣P⊁

SUTTON VALENCE

Swan
Broad Street, ME17 3AJ (off A274)
❁ 11.30-3 (not Tue), 6-11; 11.30-11 Fri & Sat;
12-10.30 Sun
☎ (01622) 843212
website: www.gswanningaround@aol.com
Adnams Bitter; Fuller's London Pride; Harveys BB Ⓖ
This unspoilt 15th-century inn is one of the
oldest in Kent. It overlooks the picturesque
village of Sutton Valence at the front and
has a small farm at the rear, with goats and
geese. The interior reflects a traditional
village pub with a hop-strewn bar, timbered
ceilings and a log fire in winter. A wide
choice of food is available. The pub is a
regular outlet for mild and occasionally
stocks real cider. ⚠Q❁❍P

TEYNHAM

Dover Castle
London Road, ME9 9QS
❁ 11-11; 12-10.30 Sun
☎ (01795) 521214
**Shepherd Neame Master Brew Bitter, Spitfire,
seasonal beers** Ⓗ
This is a pub that has successfully combined
a popular restaurant trade with a warm
welcome for drinkers. Situated on the A2,
London–Dover road, this old coaching inn
dates back to the 16th century. The pub's
garden, which is home to one of the few bat
and trap pitches in the area, backs on to an
attractive old orchard. The pub fields two
darts teams and also holds a regular quiz on
Mondays. ⚠❁❍➺♣P⚹

TONBRIDGE

Ivy House
199 High Street, TN9 1BW
❁ 11-11; 12-10.30 Sun
☎ (01732) 352382
Adnams Bitter; Harveys BB; Wadworth 6X Ⓗ
A friendly welcome awaits in this popular
two-roomed pub, one of the oldest
buildings in Tonbridge. The restaurant area
serves meals Tuesday–Saturday. Full of
character, with a good vibrant atmosphere,
the pub hosts regular quizzes and other
themed events which are detailed on a
display board outside the pub. There is
plenty of outside seating for use in good
weather. ⚠Q❁❍➺♣P

TUNBRIDGE WELLS

Cross Keys ⊘
236 St Johns Road, TN4 9XD
(on A26 towards Southborough)
❁ 11-11; 12-10.30 Sun
☎ (01892) 536761
Harveys BB; guest beers Ⓗ
This old-fashioned roadhouse has been
serving the local community for over 100
years. It has a long L-shaped bar, plus a
room for dining; carpeted throughout, it
has dark wood furniture and subdued wall
lighting. A large external patio is
supplemented by an extensive garden to the
rear, away from the road, that hosts music
and barbecues on sunny Sunday afternoons.
The pub shows most major sporting events
on TV.
❁❍➺ (High Brooms) ♣🐾P⚹

Grove Tavern
19 Berkley Road, TN1 1YR
❁ 12-11; 12-10.30 Sun
☎ (01892) 526549
Harveys BB; guest beers Ⓗ
Small, back-street pub close to the historic
sights of Tunbridge Wells, in the old part of
town. Active in pool, darts and crib leagues,
the landlord encourages a good local
atmosphere. The menu is limited, but food
is always home-cooked. Grove Park nearby
offers pleasant green surroundings and a
children's play area. Anyone wishing to
enjoy an unpretentious pub in pure English
style would enjoy this.
⚠❍➺♣

Rose & Crown
47 Grosvenor Road, TN1 2AY
❁ 10.30-2.30, 5-11; 10.30-11 Fri & Sat; 12-3,
7-10.30 Sun
☎ (01892) 522427
**Brains Dark; Greene King IPA; Wadworth 6X; guest
beers** Ⓗ
Victorian town-centre pub, where a
partition is used in the evenings to form
public and saloon bars. The landlord prides
himself on running a traditional town pub;
he always has a mild on tap and guest beers
favour small local breweries. A good range
of lunchtime food makes it popular with
office workers; the evening trade is mainly
local residents. A weekly raffle and a
monthly quiz are held. Bar billiards is
played.
⚠Q❍➺♣

UPPER HARBLEDOWN

Plough Inn
London Road, CT2 9AW (near A2/A2050 jct)
❁ 12-11; 12-10.30 Sun
☎ (01227) 463131
Shepherd Neame Master Brew Bitter; guest beers Ⓗ
Just off the A2, the Plough stands on a quiet
street that used to be the main road. The
pub is attractive and comfortable, with a
stripped wood floor and tables, and a sofa
by the fireplace. The restaurant offers
authentic Thai food, including a special
lunch menu; meals are available
Tuesday–Sunday. The guest beer is usually
from a local brewery. Games played here
include crib and backgammon.
⚠❁❍♣P

UPPER UPNOR

Tudor Rose
29 High Street, ME2 4XG
❁ 11-11; 12-4, 7-10.30 Sun
☎ (01634) 715305
**Wells Bombardier; Young's Bitter, Special; guest
beers** Ⓗ
At the foot of the cobbled High Street,
next to Upnor Castle, this multi-roomed
pub boasts old cooking ranges in two of
its rooms. An annual beer festival takes
place every May Day bank holiday. The
garden is partly surrounded by a 17th-
century wall and is child-friendly. No food
is served Sunday evening or Monday. It
stocks three ever-changing guest beers.
Use the public car park at the top of the
village.
⚠🚲❁❍♣

WAREHORNE

World's Wonder
TN26 2LU (on B2067, between Ham Street and Woodchurch)
✪ 11.30-3, 6-11; 12-3, 6.30-10.30 Sun
☎ (01233) 732431
Bateman XXXB; guest beer Ⓗ
This isolated country pub attracts custom from a wide area – a friendly welcome awaits all who find it. Originally two cottages, it became a pub in the early 1930s, before this beer was sold from the garden shed. The licensees are collectors; note the clocks in the restaurant, the 200-plus bottles of beer in the lounge bar and over 30 whiskies behind the bar. The house beer is brewed by Goacher's. The pub is not far from the Woodchurch Rare Breeds Centre, where the local CAMRA annual beer festival takes place. ✪◑ ⊟♣P

WELL HILL

Kent Hounds
Pump Lane, BR6 7PL (off A224) OS497643
✪ 10-2.30, 5.30 (6 Sat)-11; 12-3, 7-10.30 Sun
☎ (01959) 534288
Courage Best Bitter; Harveys BB; Shepherd Neame Master Brew Bitter; Wells Bombardier Ⓗ
Delightfully located, high up on the border of Kent and Greater London, but well hidden from the access lane (Well Hill), it is marked by a prominent pub sign. Pump Lane is now an unmade bridleway. Note the large collection of key fobs, miscellaneous china items and the doodlebug shell. The large garden contains an aviary. Ramblers are welcome, but large groups should give prior notice. 🚃✪◑♣P

WEST MALLING

Joiners Arms
64 High Street, ME19 6LU
✪ 11-3; 5-11; 12-10.30 Sun
☎ (01732) 840723
Shepherd Neame Master Brew Bitter, Spitfire, seasonal beers Ⓗ
Welcome back to this Guide for a friendly, two-bar local at the centre of West Malling. Owned by Shepherd Neame and recently refurbished (including an extension to the rear bar area), there are usually two regular beers on offer, plus the current seasonal brew. Occasionally live music is performed. Bar snacks and hot meals are available at lunchtime. Bus No. 70 from Maidstone and No. 151 from Tunbridge Wells and Medway stop nearby. 🚃✪◐≢♣

Scared Crow
79 Offham Road, ME19 6RV
(off High St, via West St)
✪ 11-3, 5-11; 12-10.30 Sun
☎ (01732) 840408
Adnams Bitter Ⓗ
This is a rarity – a bistro/wine bar serving excellent beer. The ceiling has festoons of hops entwined with fairy lights, and candles are placed on the tables. The mainly Tex-Mex menu is displayed on blackboards, around the walls, interspersed by varied collections of artefacts. The wine list is supplemented by a selection of fruit wines. A bookcase holds a quantity of volumes concerning the Royal Family. An enclosed outside area provides extra seating for fair weather. ✪◑▶

WEST PECKHAM

Swan on the Green
The Green, ME18 5JW
(1 mile W of B2016) OS644525
✪ 11-3 (4 Sat), 6-11 (earlier winter Mon eve); 12-5 Sun
☎ (01622) 812271
website: www.swan-on-the-green.co.uk
Swan Whooper Pale, Ginger Swan, Trumpeter Best Ⓗ
An out-of-the-way village pub, but one that rewards a beer-lover's visit, the Swan has been a licensed inn for over 300 years; now its own micro-brewery supplies a full range of cask-conditioned beers to keep six handpumps well occupied. Delightfully situated by the cricket green, its constantly varying menus offer good food in a bistro-style setting. The landlord's commitment to brewing excellence and his cellar expertise are obvious. Check the website for local events and more. 🚃Q✪◑P

WHITSTABLE

New Inn
30 Woodlawn Street, CT5 1HQ
✪ 11-11; 12-4, 7-10.30 Sun
☎ (01227) 264746
Shepherd Neame Master Brew Bitter Ⓗ
Built in 1844 as the Bricklayer's Arms, this back-street pub is a survivor from the days when Whitstable had a pub or general store on every corner. Etched glass windows show the original tiny drinking areas, which are remembered by many long-standing customers. Darts, pool and quiz nights are well supported and the Jubilee street party was a great success; a true community pub, welcoming all-comers. Whitstable's timeless charm can be experienced here. ど≢

Prince Albert
Sea Street, CT5 1AN
✪ 11.30-11; 12-10.30 Sun
☎ (01227) 273400
Fuller's London Pride; Greene King IPA; Worthington's 1744; guest beer (occasional) Ⓗ
Just a few yards from the beach, yet within the town centre, the Albert is a small, friendly one-bar pub opposite the new Horsebridge development. Note the original Tomson and Wootton windows and a line showing the level reached in a 1953 flood. The small, secluded garden is a real suntrap. An excellent range of good value, home-cooked food includes fisherman's pie and steak and oyster pie. ✪◑≢

Ship Centurion ✪
111 High Street, CT5 1AY
(opp. Whitstable Playhouse)
✪ 11-11; 12-7 Sun
☎ (01227) 264740
Adnams Bitter; Elgood's Black Dog Mild; guest beers Ⓗ
The only pub in town always to offer mild, this busy central inn is festooned with colourful hanging baskets in summer. Fascinating old photographs of Whitstable hang in the public bar. Entertainment includes Sky TV and live music on Thursday evening. Guest beers change frequently. Home-cooked bar snacks often feature authentic German produce; the only food

available on Saturday is German schnitzels; a free seafood selection is put on the bar on Sunday. A public car park is in Middle Wall nearby. ⚅◖◗⇲🖃

WITTERSHAM

Swan
1 Swan Street, TN30 7PH (on B2082, between Tenterden and Rye)
✪ 11-11; 12-10.30 Sun
☎ (01797) 270913
website: www.swan-wittersham.co.uk
Goacher's Mild, Light; Harveys BB; guest beers Ⓗ
Friendly local dating from the 17th century, at the centre of village life. Twice-yearly beer festivals are held (visit the website for details); live music is performed occasionally and a conker championship is staged. Two bars offer up to six ales, often including a mild, plus Biddenden and Double Vision cider. The No. 12 bus stops outside. It was voted local CAMRA Pub of the Year in 2001 and again in 2003.
🏨⚅◖◗⊟👗♣🐾P

WORTH

Blue Pigeons
The Street, CT14 0DE (off A258)

✪ 11-11; 12-10.30 Sun
☎ (01304) 613245
Ansells Best Bitter; Draught Bass; Young's Bitter; guest beers Ⓗ
Revitalised village local with a restaurant attached. Although tucked away in a quiet village, it is within walking distance of Sandwich railway station. It stands opposite the church, near the pond and memorial. It is served by buses from Deal and Canterbury. ⚅◖◗⊟♣P

WROTHAM

Rose & Crown
High Street, TN15 7AE
✪ 12-3, 5.30 (6 Sat)-11; 12-4, 7-10.30 Sun
☎ (01732) 882409
Shepherd Neame Master Brew Bitter, Spitfire, Bishops Finger, seasonal beers Ⓗ
Popular local at the village centre that has been pleasantly altered and modernised without destroying its traditional character. The dining area serves a good range of food at lunchtime, plus evening meals Friday and Saturday. Home to long-established morris dancers, it hosts various social and sporting activities, with weekly quiz nights. It has been a local CAMRA favourite since the early 1970s. 🏨⚅◖◗♣P

Nottingham Ale

Ye Bishops and Curates, Priest, Deacons, and Vicars,
When once you have tasted, you'll own it is true,
That Nottingham ale is the best of all liquors,
And none understand what is good like to you.
It dispels ev'ry vapour, saves pen, ink, and paper,
For, when you've a mind in the pulpit to rail,
'Twill open your throats, you may preach without notes,
When inspir'd with a bumper of Nottingham ale.

Ye Doctors, who more executions have done,
With powder and potion, and bolus and pill,
Than hangman with halter, or soldier with gun,
Or miser with famine, or lawyer with quill;
To despatch us the quicker, you forbid us malt liquor,
Till our bodies consume, and our faces grow pale;
Let him mind you who pleases – what cures all diseases is
A comforting glass of good Nottingham ale.

This song, to the tune of *'Lillibulero'*, was reputedly written in the second half of the eighteenth century by a naval officer called Gunthorpe, in return for the gift of a cask of ale from his brother, a Nottingham brewer. By a simple substitution of name it was also claimed for Newcastle.

LANCASHIRE

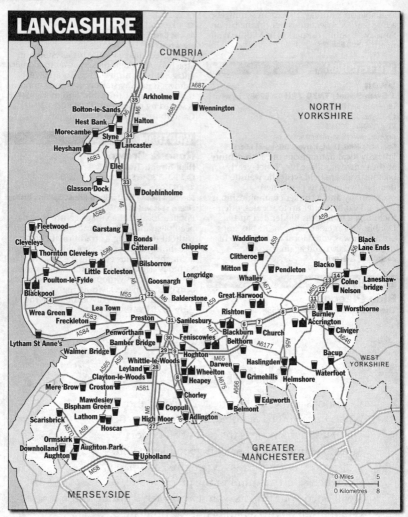

Red Lion
6 Moorgate, Green Haworth, BB5 3SJ
(off Blackburn Road, 1½ miles up Willows Lane)
☻ 12-3, 7-11; 12-11 Fri & Sat; 12-10.30 Sun
☎ (01254) 233194
**Picks Moorgate Mild, Bedlam Bitter, Porter,
Lions Pride** Ⓗ

This long-established pub is the tap for
Picks Brewery. The plant has been relocated
to a more spacious industrial unit – much
less cramped than the pub's cellar! During
the day the pub can be reached by bus, but
healthy thirsts can be stimulated by a two-
mile walk from Accrington centre. Bar food
is on offer at lunchtime. At the weekend a
fifth Picks beer (Lions Main or Pale Ale) is
on tap. All beer is sold in oversized lined
glasses. ⊛◖♣PⓊ

Sydney Street Working Men's
Club
Sydney Street, BB5 6EG (off A679)
4.30 (7 Wed)-11; 11.30-11 Fri & Sat; 12-10.30 Sun
01254) 233868

John Smith's Bitter, Magnet; guest beers Ⓗ
The open-plan layout is typical of working
men's clubs in the area. Amenities include a
full-length snooker table, other games and a
large-screen TV. The lounge is separated
from the games area by a screen. The guest
beer changes regularly, with occasionally
two on tap at once. The club is located on
the site of the long-gone Sidney Street
Brewery (note different spelling) and uses
part of the old building. ♣

Victoria
161 Manchester Road, BB5 2NY (on A680)
☻ 3-11, 1-11 Fri & Sat; 1-10.30 Sun
☎ (01254) 237727
Thwaites Mild, Bitter Ⓗ

Large, open-plan pub located on the main
road to Manchester, a short distance out of
the town centre. The single, large, U-
shaped room has a central bar area with
seating on either side. A small games area
with a pool table is to the left. This is a
popular pub with both the local
community and passers-by and is primarily
frequented by drinkers. ⊛♣

ADLINGTON

Spinners Arms
23 Church Street, PR7 4EY (on A6)
✪ 12-2, 5-11; 12-11 Fri & Sat; 12-10.30 Sun
☎ (01257) 483331
Coniston Bluebird; Taylor Landlord; guest beers Ⓗ
Large pub, built in 1838, on the main A6,
well placed for rail and bus services. There is
a sizeable bar area with alcoves, plus a
dining room serving an extensive menu;
steaks are a speciality. At the front of the
pub is an attractive drinking area with
pleasant views. Next door, a former church
is now an Indian restaurant. Guest beers are
mainly sourced from micro-breweries. It is
known locally as the Bottom Spinners to
distinguish it from the other Spinners Arms
at the top end of the town. ⚏◑➔P✂

White Bear
5A Market Street, PR7 4HE (on A6)
✪ 12 (11 Fri & Sat)-11; 12-10.30 Sun
☎ (01257) 482357
Holt Bitter; Theakston Best Bitter; guest beers Ⓗ
Large stone pub on the A6; its attractive
exterior is enhanced by canopies and
window boxes. The spacious front bar has
separate dining and drinking areas, plus a
rear bar and a games area; a large-screen TV
shows sporting events. The rear garden and
benches to the front of the pub are ideal for
summer drinking. Good value, home-
cooked meals are offered; Sunday lunches
are popular. It is handy for bus and rail
services. ⚏♨⚲⚱◑➔P✂

ARKHOLME

Bay Horse
LA6 1AS (on B6254)
✪ 11.30-3 (not Mon), 6-11; 12-3, 6-10.30 Sun
☎ (015242) 21425
**Black Sheep Best Bitter; Boddingtons Bitter; guest
beer** Ⓗ
This old village inn retains a homely, rustic
feel. The three-roomed pub boasts a
bowling green and an outdoor drinking area
with seats to the front. Most of the pub's
customers now arrive in cars for meals, but
you can get here using buses 286, 443, 445
or L2. Q⚏◑P✂

Redwell
Kirkby Lonsdale Road, LA6 1BQ (on B6254)
✪ 11-11; 12-10.30 Sun
☎ (015242) 21240 website: www.redwellinn.co.uk
Beer range varies Ⓗ
Although the postal address is Arkholme,
this pub is closer to Gressingham and Over
Kellet. The 17th-century building now has a
single large bar, a function room and a pool
room. Good food is served; Monday is steak
night and Friday is fish night. The two beers
are usually from micros in the surrounding
region. Good views can be enjoyed from the
garden. Served by an infrequent bus service
(445), the 'Carnforth Connect' L2 bus will
call here if booked. ⚏⚏◑♣P

AUGHTON

Derby Arms ✓
Prescot Road, L39 6TA (off B5197)
✪ 11.30-11; 12-10.30 Sun
☎ (01695) 422237
Beer range varies Ⓗ
Traditional country pub practically in the
middle of nowhere. Full of nooks and
crannies, it is quite unspoilt. The roaring
real fires, the warm welcome given to
visitors, and the array of interesting
artefacts around the walls combine to create
a relaxing environment. Local and small
breweries are supported and there is always
something out of the ordinary in the beer
range. It is worth organising a walk (or a
drive) for a visit. ⚏⚏◑♣P✂

Stanley Arms
24 St Michael Road, L39 6SA (just off A59)
✪ 11.30-3, 5-11; 11.30-10.30 Sun
☎ (01695) 423241
Marston's Pedigree; Tetley Dark Mild, Bitter Ⓗ
The Stanley Arms is an attractive pub
almost opposite the village church – body
and soul properly catered for in one spot.
Inside, the pub has been sympathetically
modernised to retain many of its original
features. The bar serves several, largely
separate, drinking areas which are decorated
with brasses and other relics of a bygone
era. On music nights, when live bands play,
there is an electric atmosphere, with
standing-room only. Q⚏◑➔ (Town Green) P

AUGHTON PARK

Dog & Gun
233 Long Lane, L39 5BU (off B5197)
✪ 5-11; 12-3, 6-11 Sat; 12-2, 7-10.30 Sun
☎ (01695) 423303
Burtonwood Bitter, Top Hat Ⓗ
This Edwardian treasure is well worth a
major detour. A traditional, friendly inn, it
has been run by the same landlady for over
30 years. It remains firmly rooted in the
1950s, a time when pubs catered for the
surrounding community. It has a central
room and two unspoilt snugs, all with the
unfussy (but well-kept) decor of half a
century ago. Outside is an excellent bowling
green. ⚏Q⚏➔♣P

BACUP

Crown
Greave Road, OL13 9HQ
(50 yds off Todmorden Road, ³/₄ mile from town centre)
✪ 7 (5 Fri; 1 Sat)-11; 12-10.30 Sun
☎ (01706) 873982 website: www.barearts.com
Pictish Bare Arts, IBA; guest beer Ⓗ
Hidden under a bank, just off Todmorden
Road, this gem has only just been
discovered by the local CAMRA branch.
Already it has won their Pub of the Season
award (winter 2002). The pub has a long,
flag-floored lounge with a prominent bar

stretching most of its length. It is a mecca for lovers of the arts; upstairs is a studio for painting and sculpting. The house beer, Bare Arts, reflects this passion. Occasional impromptu acoustic sessions are the only sounds to break the conversation. The guest beer is also often supplied by Pictish. ♨Q❀P

BALDERSTONE

Myerscough
Whalley Road, BB2 7LE (on A59)
🕒 12-2.30, 5-11; 12-10.30 Sun
☎ (01254) 812222
Robinson's Hatters, Best Bitter, seasonal beers Ⓗ
Homely, country inn close to Samlesbury Aerodrome. It comprises a wood-panelled lounge with bay windows and authentic beams and a small no-smoking room with a real fire. Pictures of aeroplanes adorn the walls. The pub is a base for 10 clubs, including car enthusiasts, anglers and motorcyclists. There is a large garden to the rear. Comfortable accommodation is provided in three en-suite rooms. Genuine home-cooked food includes Lancashire dishes; Sunday meals are served 12–7. Quiz night is Wednesday. ♨Q❀☎◑♣P⌿

BAMBER BRIDGE

Olde Original Withy Trees
157 Station Road, PR5 6LA (on B6258)
🕒 11-11; 12-10.30 Sun
☎ (01772) 330396
Burtonwood Bitter; guest beer Ⓗ
Originally a 17th-century farm, this popular local has a higher level vault at the rear, a side lounge and a front drinking area surrounding a central bar. A large TV is popular for watching football. The pub is now the only Withy Trees as the other one over the road has changed its name. A convenient bus stop outside is served by regular buses from Preston, Chorley, Bolton and Manchester. ❀☎⇌♣P

BELMONT

Black Dog Hotel
Church Street, BL7 8AB (on A675)
🕒 12-11; 12-10.30 Sun
☎ (01204) 811218
Holt Mild, Bitter, seasonal beers Ⓗ
Rare outlet for Holt beers in East Lancs, and so it probably offers the lowest-priced pint in the area. Originally a farmhouse dating from the 1750s, it became a pub in 1825. During the 19th century the small area in front of the bar served as the village court. This comfortable pub has separate rooms for non-smokers and for pool. Buses run from Bolton and Blackburn. ❀☎◑P⌿

BELTHORN

Grey Mare
Elton Road, BB3 2PG (on A6177, 1½ miles S of M65 jct 5)
🕒 12-2.30, 6-11; 12-11 Fri & Sat; 12-10.30 Sun
☎ (01254) 53308
Thwaites Mild, Bitter, Lancaster Bomber, seasonal beers Ⓗ
On its own, 1163ft above sea level, on a clear day this roadside inn offers moor views as far as Blackpool Tower and the

Ribble estuary. Well known for its excellent food (booking advisable), the Grey Mare also keeps up to four Thwaites beers on tap. Demand for food is such that the seating areas are for diners, but drinkers are made welcome at the small bar. ♨❀♣P

BILSBORROW

'Owd Nell's Canalside Tavern ✿
Guy's Thatched Hamlet, Canalside, PR3 0RS
(50 yds down St Michaels Road, off A6 at Bilsborrow)
🕒 11-11 (including Sun)
☎ (01995) 640010
website: www.guysthatchedhamlet.com
Boddingtons Bitter; guest beers Ⓗ
'Owd Nell's is the public bar of Guy's Thatched Hamlet, a popular 'eatin', drinkin', stayin' and playin'' place. This free house offers a splendid choice of real ales, often from local breweries at most reasonable prices, including a daily 99p special. The house beer 'Owd Nells is brewed by Moorhouses. A guest cider is stocked in summer. Good value food includes a Bush Tucker menu of Australian dishes. It stages an autumn stout and oyster festival, and regular cricket matches on its own ground. This reputedly haunted canalside pub has everything, including a children's play pavilion.
♨Q❀☎◑🖂🅰️♣P⌿

BISPHAM GREEN

Eagle & Child
Malt Kiln Lane, L40 3SG (off B5246)
🕒 12-3, 5.30-11; 12-10.30 Sun
☎ (01257) 462297
Moorhouses Black Cat; Thwaites Bitter; guest beers Ⓗ
Outstanding 16th-century local boasting antique furniture and stone-flagged floors. Renowned for its food, a popular feature is the monthly curry club (usually the first Mon – booking advisable). An annual beer festival is held over the May bank holiday in a marquee behind the pub. Tables around the well-kept bowling green offer wonderful views of the surrounding countryside, while the front of the pub overlooks the village green.
♨Q⛄❀◑♣P⌿

BLACKBURN

Fox & Grapes Hotel
3 Limefield, Preston New Road, BB2 6BT (on A677, 1 mile W of centre)
🕒 12-3.30, 5.30-11; 12-11 Fri & Sat; 12-10.30 Sun
☎ (01254) 53902
Thwaites Mild, Bitter, Lancaster Bomber, seasonal beers Ⓗ
The comfortably furnished lounge has plenty of bar space, while a further large room to the rear houses a snooker table and is used for meetings. An unchanged snug behind the bar can be used as a family room. Sales of handpulled mild are greater than those of bitter. It stands on the X63 bus route from Preston to Burnley. 🖂♣P

Navigation Inn
2 Canal Street, Mill Hill, BB2 4DL (off A6062 near Ewood, by bridge No. 96A on Leeds/Liverpool canal)
🕒 10.30-11; 12-10.30 Sun
☎ (01254) 53230

Thwaites Mild, Bitter H

Popular, unpretentious local run by one of the town's longest-serving landladies; a warm welcome is assured as is some good conversation. The pub has retained its character through sympathetic refurbishment. It is within walking distance of Ewood Park, home of Blackburn Rovers. A cobbled parking area slopes down to the pub and there are a couple of benches for watching canal craft pass by. There are moorings for barges on the pub side and plenty of shops nearby. Buses 21 and 22 run from the town centre. ⬤⧫ (Mill Hill) ♣

St Mark's Conservative Club
Preston Old Road, Witton, BB2 2SS (on A674, 1 mile W of centre))
✪ 6-11; 11.30-2.30, 6.30-11 Sat; 12-3, 7-10.30 Sun
☎ (01254) 52962

Thwaites Mild, Bitter; guest beer H

Near Witton Country Park, this comfortable club comprises two lounges, a games room and a concert room extension at the back. Entertainment is provided on Saturday evening, while Sunday is given over to dancing or karaoke. In addition, charity fundraising nights are held. The guest beer is usually a session bitter from a well-known independent brewer. Show this Guide or CAMRA membership card to gain admittance. Catch buses 123, 124 and 152 from the town centre. Q⧫ (Mill Hill) ♣P

Hare & Hounds ⊘
Skipton Old Road, BB8 7EP (between Skipton and Colne on unclassified road) OS929432
✪ 12-midnight; 12-10.30 Sun
☎ (01282) 863070

Black Sheep Best Bitter; Taylor Golden Best, Landlord; Tetley Bitter; guest beer H

An exceptional range of beer is kept in this very pleasant pub on the Yorkshire border. In a rural setting, it is welcoming to walkers, with boot washing facilities. The guest beer sometimes comes from Riverhead Brewery. Log fires at each end warm the pub. Enjoy great views over the moors in the garden area that hosts summer barbecues; the food is always popular here. Famous for no football on TV, the only dogs allowed are guide dogs. ⌂❀◑P✁

Cross Gaites Inn
Beverley Road, BB9 6RF (off A682, Gisburn road) OS867416
✪ 12-2, 6-11; 12-11 Sat; 12-10.30 Sun
☎ (01282) 616312

Burtonwood Bitter; guest beer H

16th-century inn in a rural setting, this semi-open plan pub has a separate small room. Both rooms have real fires. A good range of food is on offer at reasonable prices and the pub is popular with families at mealtimes. The Nelson–Blacko bus stops at the pub. ⌂❀P

Bispham Hotel
Red Bank Road, Bispham, FY2 9HY
✪ 11-11; 12-10.30 Sun
☎ (01253) 351752

Samuel Smith OBB H

Although mainly used by locals, the Bispham Hotel also attracts tourists, particularly in the season. A vault houses a pool table, dartboard and TV so the lounge area is relatively quiet, apart from the piped music. Buses No. 3 and 4 stop outside and the tram stop on the promenade is nearby. Lunches are served weekdays – everything is reasonably priced. The car park is small. ◑⬤⊖♣P

Dunes
561 Lytham Road, FY4 1RD (500 yds from airport)
✪ 11-11; 12-10.30 Sun
☎ (01253) 403854

Boddingtons Bitter; guest beers H

A real local community pub with a separate public bar. The pub keeps up to three guest beers, usually from micro-breweries, with one normally from the local Hart Brewery. The guest beers tend to be available mainly at weekends. The pub holds a quiz every Sunday evening. It is on the No. 11 bus route from the town centre. ❀◑⬤⬥ ⧫ (Squires Gate) ⊖ (Harrowside Tram) ♣P

Number 4 & Freemasons
Layton Road, FY3 8ER (B5266/Newton Drive jct)
✪ 12-11; 12-10.30 Sun
☎ (01253) 302877

Thwaites Bitter H

The first meeting of Blackpool's Freemasons is said to have taken place in this smart, friendly pub which is a short walk from Stanley Park. It has a large lounge and a bar with pool and darts. Meals are served until 7pm, after which music and younger drinkers tend to dominate. The small forecourt has picnic benches. The car park is shared with the adjoining fitness centre, while bus No. 2 from the town centre stops outside. ❀◑⬤♣P

Shovels
260 Commonedge Road, Marton, FY4 5DH (on B5261, 1/2 mile from A5230 jct)
✪ 11.30-11; 12-10.30 Sun
☎ (01253) 762702

Beer range varies H

This large, award-winning pub offers five ever-changing guest beers, usually from micros and brew-pubs. Local CAMRA's Pub of the Year 2003, The Shovels holds a week-long beer festival in October. The pub is home to many sports teams and has a large-screen TV; quiz night is Thursday. It stands on the No. 14 bus route from the town centre. The landlord writes a regular column for the local CAMRA magazine. ⌂❀◑⬥♣P✁

Wheatsheaf
194 Talbot Road, FY1 3AZ (100 yds from train and bus stations)
✪ 10.30-11; 12-10.30 Sun
☎ (01253) 625062

Theakston Mild, Best Bitter, Old Peculier; guest beers H

Lively, down-to-earth, characterful drinking house with just a touch of sophistication (a chandelier in the lounge). This gem has collections of flags, giant fish, mannequins and wartime posters. The atmosphere is enhanced by a real fire and a pianist (Tue eve). A small patio is available for barbecues and a full menu is served from midday until 8pm. ⚜Q✿❁⊄ᴑ➥(North) ⊖♣P

BOLTON-LE-SANDS

Blue Anchor
68 Main Road, LA5 8DN (on A6)
✪ 11-11; 12-10.30 Sun
☎ (01524) 843241
Boddingtons Bitter; Tetley Bitter; guest beers Ⓗ
Bolton-le-Sands is mostly a large dormitory settlement, but the old village, where this pub stands, remains quite attractive and rural. A 17th-century building, attracting a mainly local crowd, its single bar is made up of two rooms knocked together. A small games room is at the rear. A large-screen TV shows sporting events. Buses 55 and 55A pass here. ⚜✿⇔▲♣↙

BONDS

Church
33 Bonds Lane, PR3 1ZB (on B6430)
✪ 11-3, 6-11; 12-3, 6-10.30 Sun
☎ (01995) 602387
Theakston Best Bitter; guest beer Ⓗ
Within easy reach of Garstang town centre, but retaining a rural feel, the Church benefits from a good bus service – Nos. 40, 41 and 42 stop right outside and run until late. Despite the twin entrances, there is now only one bar but with distinct games and dining areas. The guest beer is often from a remote brewery. If you are hungry, the home-made specials are worth investigating.
Q✿⊄ᴑ♣P

BURNLEY

Coal Clough
41 Coal Clough Lane, BB11 4PG (200 yds E of M65 jct 10)
✪ 11-11; 12-10.30 Sun
☎ (01282) 423226 website: www.coalcloughpub.co.uk
Adnams Broadside; Cains Bitter; Museum Massey's Bitter; Worthington's Bitter; guest beer Ⓗ
This end-of-terrace community local is always busy and friendly; the games room is popular. The Massey's Bitter is specially brewed by Bass Museum to an old local brewery recipe. It hosts a folk club (Tue), quiz night (Wed), and live music on Thursday. The pub was East Lancs CAMRA Pub of the Year 2002. Check the website for beer festivals based on Bass Museum special brews.
➥(Barracks) ♣

Garden Bar
131-137 Church Street, BB11 1PG (off Centenary Way/Church St roundabout)
✪ 11-11; 12-10.30 Sun
☎ (01282) 414895
Lees Bitter Ⓗ
Situated just off the town centre, this friendly, popular pub is the only Lees outlet in East Lancs. A varied clientele is welcomed at different times of the day and week. The lunchtime trade is supported by shoppers and office workers wanting a decent bar snack, while weekday evenings and Sundays attract the local gay community. Friday and Saturday are disco nights for the young and young at heart. Truly, a pub for everyone.
⊄&➥(Central)

Ministry of Ales
9 Trafalgar Street, BB11 1TQ (off A682 Manchester Rd/Centenary Way roundabout)
✪ 5 (12 Thu & Fri; 11.30 Sat)-11; 12-10.30 Sun
☎ (01282) 830409
Moonstone Black Star; guest beers Ⓗ
The pub is situated 100 yards below Manchester Road Station. It houses the Moonstone micro-brewery which can be viewed in the room on the right. It features regular art exhibitions displaying local talent. Guest beers are sourced from a wide variety of micro-brewers, sometimes complemented by special in-house brews. A friendly welcome and good conversation is the norm here. ➥(Manchester Rd)

CATTERALL

Pickerings
Garstang Road, PR3 0HD (on B6430)
✪ 11-11; 12-10.30 Sun
☎ (01995) 600999
Theakston Best Bitter; guest beers Ⓗ
16th-century residence in its own extensive grounds, much extended and altered and now a hotel with all the facilities you would expect, but with a surprising selection of beer in the small bay-windowed bar. Four guest beers are stocked, they could be drawn from anywhere, but small Lancashire breweries tend to be favoured. The attractive garden has a play area and view of the fells. Bus Nos. 40, 41 and 42 stop close by.
✿⇔ᴑP

CHIPPING

Sun Inn
Windy Street, PR3 2GD
✪ 12-3, 5.30-11; 12-11 Fri & Sat; 12-10.30 Sun
☎ (01995) 61206
Black Sheep Best Bitter; Boddingtons Bitter; Flowers IPA; Theakston Mild Ⓗ
Reputedly haunted pub in a prize-winning village, it is used by locals and visitors to the Trough of Bowland. The front entrance is up some steep steps, but it can be entered from a rear courtyard with outside seating and an aviary housing birds of prey. The central bar has three rooms off: a lounge with real fire; a large games room and a smaller room where ring the bull is played. Upstairs is a snooker room. Traditional Lancashire dishes are a speciality – try the delicious pies with mushy peas and the local Chipping cheese.
⚜Q✿⊄▲♣

CHORLEY

Albion
29 Bolton Street, PR7 3AA (on A6, S of centre)
✪ 11-11; 12-10.30 Sun
☎ (01257) 416957
Tetley Dark Mild, Bitter Ⓗ
Traditional local, just south of the town centre, its unspoilt wood-panelled interior comprises a cosy lounge and a public bar/games room. The cask mild is of particularly good quality and is a popular choice with the locals. The pub stands near Chorley's Big Lamp landmark in the centre of the nearby roundabout.
Q⇔⊞➥❏

Malt & Hops
Friday Street, PR6 0AH (behind station)
☻ 12-11; 12-10.30 Sun
☎ (01257) 260967
Taylor Landlord; guest beers Ⓗ
Resembling a long-standing street-corner local, this has only been a pub for about 14 years, having been converted from a shop. The Victorian-style decor gives an ale house atmosphere and emphasises that this is a pub for drinkers – no food is served. There is a quiz on Wednesday evening at this dog-friendly pub. Being privately-owned there is no tie and usually eight ales are on tap. At Chorley Station use the platform 2 exit to get to the pub. ⇌

Potters Arms
42 Brooke Street, PR7 3BY
(on A6 ring road, next to Morrison's)
☻ 12 (7 Wed)-11; 12-3.30, 7-11 Sat; 12-5, 7-10.30 Sun
☎ (01257) 267954
Marston's Pedigree; Moorhouses Premier; Tetley Bitter; guest beers (occasional) Ⓗ
Small, friendly-run free house named after its owners, situated at the bottom of Brooke Street, alongside the railway line. The central bar serves the games area, while the two comfortable lounges are popular with locals. The Potters displays a fine collection of photographs from the entertainment world as well as beer bottles from long-closed breweries. Occasional guest beers come from independent breweries such as Greene King, Jennings and Adnams. ⇌ ♣ P

Prince of Wales ⊘
9-11 Cowling Brow, PR6 0QE (off B6228)
☻ 11-11; 12-10.30 Sun
☎ (01257) 413239
Jennings Mild, Bitter, Cumberland Ale, seasonal beers; guest beers Ⓗ
This stone terraced pub lies in the south-eastern part of town near the Leeds–Liverpool Canal. Its unspoilt interior incorporates a traditional tap room, a games area, a large lounge and a comfortable snug, complete with a real fire. The pub is noted for its love of jazz and stages live music for all tastes at weekends. Note the collections of brewing artefacts and saucy seaside postcards. Guest ales are from a range of regional breweries. This was the first pub in Chorley to be awarded Cask Marque accreditation. ♨ ❀ ⊟ ♣ ✂

Stag Inn
1 Bank Street, BB5 4HH (off A679, Henry St)
☻ 12-11; 12-10.30 Sun
☎ (01254) 399906
Holt Bitter; Moorhouses Black Cat; guest beer (occasional) Ⓗ
Typical, two-roomed local whose regulars are heavily into games such as dominoes and darts. The area has several residential homes for older people and the pub organises many events to involve them. This is a perfect example of a successful community pub. It sold only keg beers for many years, then was boarded up for another year or two until the present landlord purchased the lease. Now real ale sells well. ⊟⇌ (Church & Oswaldtwistle) ♣

Halfway House
470 Preston Road, PR5 7JB (on A6)
☻ 12-11; 12-10.30 Sun
☎ (01772) 394477
Lees GB Mild, Bitter, Moonraker, seasonal beers Ⓗ
This large, roadside inn has been recently refurbished in the traditional style, including a tap room with games area, a large lounge, dining room and a no-smoking area. Recently acquired by Lees Brewery, the pub is situated on the main A6 road between Preston and Chorley and gets its name from being reputedly exactly halfway between London and Glasgow. It is noted for good value meals.
♨ ⏚ ❀ ◑ ⊟ & ♣ P ✂

Victoria
183 Victoria Road West, FY5 3PZ
☻ 11-11; 12-10.30 Sun
☎ (01253) 853306
Samuel Smith OBB Ⓗ
Imposing 1930s building on a corner site on the main road, in a residential area close to the town centre. Conveniently located on bus routes, it is a short walk to the Blackpool–Fleetwood tramway. Half a mile from the seafront, this outstanding, popular local has a spacious, well-appointed main lounge and a dining area, warmed by two real fires. The pub serves one of the lowest-priced regular cask beers in Lancashire. A no-smoking meeting room is available.
♨ Q ◑ ⊟ & ⊖ ♣ P ✂

New Inn
Parsons Lane, BB7 2ZT
(from interchange, head west towards castle)
☻ 11 (10.30 Sat)-11; 12-10.30 Sun
☎ (01200) 423312
Caledonian Deuchars IPA; Coach House ESB; Gunpowder Mild; Taylor Landlord; guest beer Ⓗ
Listed in this Guide for the last 11 years, this superb ale house nestles below the ruins of Clitheroe Castle. A central bar area connects four rooms, of which two are warmed by real fires. This busy pub is frequented by people from all walks of life, who enjoy the quiet atmosphere, free from juke box or piped music. The inn stands next to the open market, with parking nearby. ♨ Q ❀ ♣ ♣

Queen
412 Burnley Road BB10 4SU (on A646)
☻ 1-11; 12-10.30 Sun
☎ (01282) 436712
John Smith's Bitter; guest beers Ⓗ
Small, friendly, roadside local with two rooms, both with coal fires in winter. Conversation and good beer are the order of the day here, with no music or machines to get on your nerves. Situated amid the spectacular scenery of the Cliviger Gorge, the pub keeps up to four guest beers, usually from micro-breweries. A collection of old and new photos may give you an excuse to get into conversation. ♨ Q ♣

COLNE

Admiral Lord Rodney
Waterside Road, Mill Green, BB8 0TA (off A56 at Colne Station)
☼ 11-11; 12-10.30 Sun
☎ (01282) 866565
Old Bear Original; guest beers ⒣
Excellent local in the Waterside part of town. The industrial history of this area is displayed on the walls of an inner room; note, too, the ornate tiling. A house beer is usually available from Goose Eye Brewery. Excellent value meals are served (not Sun eve or Mon) and it is popular on quiz night. You can enjoy a pleasant walk here from the station (ask for directions). ♨⒤▸≉♣

COPPULL

Red Herring
Mill Lane, PR6 5AN (off B5251)
☼ 12-11; 12-10.30 Sun
☎ (01257) 470130
Lees Bitter; guest beers ⒣
Classic red-brick pub: a cask oasis in a village dominated by keg outlets. The building itself was the former offices of the imposing mill next door. Converted to a pub some years ago, the bar serves a large single room that has recently been extended. TV sports addicts are catered for, along with the fishing fraternity who use the millpond to the front of the pub. Regular music nights and free barbecues are a feature at this former local CAMRA award-winning pub. ♨❀⒤◖▲♣P⊁

CROSTON

Grapes
67 Town Road, PR26 9RA (on A581)
☼ 12-3 (not Mon or Tue), 6 (7.30 Mon)-11; 12-10.30 Sun
☎ (01772) 600225
Boddingtons Bitter; Taylor Landlord; guest beers ⒣
Old whitewashed pub at the historic heart of Croston, set opposite the ancient parish church and the cross which gives the village its name. Records show that the Grapes has been an inn since at least 1799 and it once served as a custom house and a magistrates' court. Three rooms are complemented by a restaurant, although meals are served in all parts of the pub. There are usually two changing guest beers on tap. Bus Nos. 106, 107 and C7 run from Chorley, No. 103 and 112 from Preston. ⎈❀⒤▸≉P

DARWEN

Black Horse
72 Redearth Road, BB3 2AF (off A666)
☼ 12-11; 12-10.30 Sun
☎ (01254) 873040
Bank Top Flat Cap; guest beers ⒣
This friendly, welcoming community local has four handpumps delivering rare ales and a real cider. The annual rare beers festival, showcasing over 40 ales on the late May bank holiday weekend draws visitors from far and wide. The pool and darts teams are well supported. Special Sunday afternoon meal deals and Tuesday evening cheese nights are a feature here. A large enclosed area to the rear has picnic tables. ❀⒤≉♣▵

Britannia
104 Bolton Road, BB3 1BZ (on A666)
☼ 11-11; 12-10.30 Sun
☎ (01254) 701326
Thwaites Mild, Bitter ⒣
This unchanged pub boasts its original, fully-lined entrance, with more tiling inside. The front window suggests the pub used to sell H. Shaw & Co.'s noted ales. From the steps up to the front door you can look across to the 200ft India Mills chimney; the mill also houses a preserved mill engine and print machine. The Britannia is the only Thwaites Mild outlet in the town. A small tap room is complemented by popular games rooms. Outside is an enclosed rear children's play area and picnic area which get very busy in summer. ❀♣

DOLPHINHOLME

Fleece
Bay Horse, LA2 9AQ (on Galgate-Oakenclough road, ½ mile W of village) OS509532
☼ 12-11; 12-10.30 Sun
☎ (01524) 791233 website: www.thefleece.org.uk
Black Sheep Best Bitter; Boddingtons Bitter; Flowers Original; guest beers ⒣
At first sight, this former farmhouse is in the middle of nowhere, but as the nearby village and the country beyond have no pubs, it is the local for quite a large community. The main entrance opens on to an old-fashioned hall with a long-case clock. The main bar is oak-beamed, with an oak settle and (usually) a roaring fire. The back room doubles as a family room. Up to three guest beers are stocked, depending on the season. The restaurant is closed on Monday. ♨❀⒤▸♣P

DOWNHOLLAND

Scarisbrick Arms ⊘
2 Black-a-Moor Lane, L39 7HX (just off A5147)
☼ 12-2.30, 5-11; 12-10.30 Sun
☎ (0151) 526 1120
Cains Bitter; Greene King Old Speckled Hen; Tetley Bitter; guest beer ⒣
Between Maghull and Southport and right by the Leeds–Liverpool Canal, the Scarisbrick Arms is a natural oasis for travellers (and worth getting lost for). Its substantial restaurant enjoys a reputation for good food. The smallish bar area offers a range of four cask ales. The attractive garden affords views of the canal. ♨❀⒤▸P

EDGWORTH

Black Bull
167 Bolton Road, BL7 0AF (off High St, B6391)
☼ 11.30-11; 12-10.30 Sun
☎ (01204) 852811
Lees Bitter; Tetley Bitter; guest beers ⒣
Traditional rural country pub, formerly two cottages. Until 1955 only the two front rooms were licensed (no spirits) and women were restricted to the 'back nanny pen' (kitchen), now the lounge. In these more enlightened times the bar unites the lounge (two handpumps for regular ales) and the front tap room (pumps for two guests) – beers change so often that the staff cannot keep up with the names, so pump clips are reversed. A rustic-style extension houses an

award-winning Mediterranean restaurant.
🏚️❀◑🗄️♣P

ELLEL

Graduate College Bar
Lancaster University Complex, Barker House Village, Green Lane, LA2 0PF (off A6)
✪ 12-2.30 (not Sat), 7 (6 Thu & Fri)-11; 7-11 Sun
☎ (01524) 65201 ext. 92824
website: www.gradbar.co.uk
Beer range varies 🅷

Modern student bar, more like a pub than most, and with a better beer range. As the name suggests, it is aimed at a slightly higher age range, but undergraduates drink here, too. Only university members, staff, guests and people carrying a Good Beer Guide are served. It stocks at least two beers, maybe many more, with a bias towards nearby breweries, especially Bryson's; Phoenix beers are always on tap. The university is served by several buses. From the stop, walk south to Grizedale College, across the perimeter road and Green Lane and along the covered walkway. ❀♣P

FENISCOWLES

Feildens Arms
673 Preston Old Road, BB2 5ER
(A674/A6062 jct)
✪ 12-11; 12-10.30 Sun
☎ (01254) 200988
Boddingtons Bitter; Flowers IPA; Tetley Dark Mild; guest beers 🅷

Welcoming, stone pub at a busy road junction. The licensee worked at the Matthew Brown Brewery in Blackburn (demolished by S&N after they had said it was 'sacrosanct'). The guest beers come from small breweries. Some lively evenings, such as Lancashire folk night and a soul night have been successful. Live football is shown regularly. It is served by bus routes 123, 124 and 152 from Blackburn town centre. 🏚️❀◑≢(Pleasington) ♣P

FLEETWOOD

North Euston Hotel ❷
The Esplanade, FY7 6BN
✪ 11-11; 12-10.30 Sun
☎ (01253) 876525
Moorhouses Black Cat; Webster's Bitter; guest beers 🅷

Historic building boasting a spectacular semi-circular frontage, the work of Decimus Burton, who designed the new town of Fleetwood in the 1840s. A focal point of the old town, and its main hotel, its location is full of interest, with superb views across the Wyre Estuary and Morecambe Bay. The terminus of the Blackpool–Fleetwood tram line and two Burton-designed lighthouses are nearby. A trad jazz band, Wyre Levee Stompers, plays monthly (first Sun afternoon). The regularly-changing guest beers usually include a bitter from Moorhouses. A no-smoking area is available until 8pm. ⛌🏚️◑♿⊖(Ferry) P⌿

Queen's Hotel
Beach Road, FY7 6DT (Poulton Rd jct)
✪ 12-11; 12-10.30 Sun
☎ (01253) 876740
Thwaites Bitter 🅷

Suburban local, serving a large residential area; this traditional community pub has a pronounced bias towards sport. It fields thriving football, cricket, golf, angling and gun clubs and major televised sporting events are shown. A quiz, often with a theme, is held on Thursday evening and a sports quiz on Sunday afternoon. Meals are not normally served, but food can be provided for functions.
Blackpool–Fleetwood bus No. 14 stops outside. ❀♿♣P

Steamer
1 Queens Terrace, FY7 6BT
✪ 11-11 (midnight Fri & Sat); 12-10.30 Sun
☎ (01253) 771756
John Smith's Bitter; Wells Bombardier; guest beers 🅷

Old Dockside local dating back to 1842, it was the only Fleetwood outlet of former Blackburn Brewery, Matthew Brown. Convenient for the market and the ferry/bus/tram terminal, children are welcome. Basic but excellent bar food is available at lunchtime; Fleetwood fish is a speciality. The restaurant is open 12–8. Market days are especially busy. Snooker and darts are played. ◑⊖(Ferry/Victoria St) ♣

Thomas Drummond ❷
London Street, FY7 6JY (between Lord St and Dock St)
✪ 11-11; 12-10.30 Sun
☎ (01253) 876740
Boddingtons Bitter; Shepherd Neame Spitfire; Theakston Mild, Best Bitter; guest beers 🅷

Thomas Atkinson Drummond was one of the first building contractors to be involved in the construction of the new town of Fleetwood, arriving in 1837. He built most of Fleetwood's churches and cottages. The pub is adorned with pictures of Fleetwood's founding fathers, including Sir Peter Hesketh Fleetwood, the town's original sponsor and Decimus Burton, its architect. An excellent range of bargain meals includes the popular Thursday curry club. This is one of the best Wetherspoon's houses. Q❀◑♿⊖(Preston St) ⌿

Wyre Lounge Bar ❷
Marine Hall, The Esplanade, FY7 6HF
✪ 11-4, 7-11; 12-4, 7-10.30 Sun
☎ (01253) 771141
Courage Directors; Moorhouses Pendle Witches Brew; Phoenix Navvy; guest beers 🅷

Council-owned lounge bar known locally as the Municipal Arms, it is part of the Marine Hall entertainment complex, the home of Fleetwood's beer festival. Enjoy the spectacular views across Morecambe Bay to the mountains of the Lake District; the Isle of Man can often be seen on clear summer evenings. It is convenient for outdoor activities at the Marine Gardens where crown green bowling, crazy golf and pitch and putt are played. A particularly enterprising guest beer policy is in operation. ⛌❀♿⊖(Ferry) P

FRECKLETON

Coach & Horses
6 Preston Old Road, PR4 1PD (off A584)
✪ 11-11; 12-10.30 Sun
☎ (01772) 632284
Boddingtons Bitter; guest beer 🅷

Welcoming, community-minded pub, known locally as Ponkey's, in the centre of a large village. Of the three beamed rooms, one is a quiet, comfortable lounge, another has a real fire with a Ponkey's inscription. Ponkey was the school playground nickname of a previous landlord, hence the house beer, Ponkey's Ale (brewed by Titanic). The pub fields darts teams and a golf society, but has no juke box or pool table. It is easily reached by bus from Preston or Blackpool.
⛼Q❀◖♣P

GARSTANG

Royal Oak
Market Place, PR3 1ZA
⏲ 11-3 (4 Thu), 6-11; 11-11 Fri & Sat; 12-10.30 Sun
☎ (01995) 603318
Robinson's Hatters, Hartleys XB, Best Bitter Ⓗ
This 17th-century coaching inn has been sympathetically renovated. It retains four small rooms alongside the main bar and restaurant. The pub has seats outside on the old market square – markets now take place elsewhere. Buses 40, 41 and 42 (southbound) stop nearby on Bridge Street; the northbound stop is on Park Hill Road.
⛼Q❀◖◗⅄♣P

GLASSON DOCK

Dalton Arms
Ten Row, West Quay, LA2 0BZ (approached from S side of dock)
⏲ 12-2 (4 Sat), 7-11; 12-10.30 Sun
☎ (01524) 751213
Thwaites Bitter, Lancaster Bomber Ⓗ
The four cottages that became this pub were built in 1780, 34 years after the dock. The dock still does a brisk trade, especially considering its small size, with both commercial and pleasure traffic. Crews of many nations often end up in this pub, where an unofficial currency exchange operates. Glasson is picturesque enough to attract day-trippers – it stands at the end of a cycleway from Lancaster. Locals complete the varied clientele. Quiz nights are held (Wed) and occasional indoor putting. Buses Nos. 88 and 89 stop nearby. Evening meals are served at weekends.
⛼◖◗♣P

GOOSNARGH

Grapes
Church Lane, PR3 2BH (off B5269)
⏲ 12-3, 5.30 (7 Mon)-11; 12-11 Thu-Sat; 12-10.30 Sun
☎ (01772) 865234
Boddingtons Bitter; Jennings Bitter; guest beers Ⓗ
Attractive free house, close to the village green. Enjoy the wonderful real fire on cold nights; other amenities include a pool room and bowling green, cobbled drinking area at the front and a rear garden. It stands near the supposedly haunted Chingle Hall. The landlord sources most of the four guest beers himself rather than relying on beer agencies, concentrating on small breweries in North Yorkshire and the Lake District. An occasional cider is stocked in summer. No food is served Monday evening. ⛼❀◖◗♣P⚡

GREAT HARWOOD

Victoria Hotel ☆
St Johns Street, BB6 7EP (off Blackburn road, B6535)
⏲ 3 (12 Sat)-11; 12-10.30 Sun
☎ (01254) 885210
John Smith's Bitter; Lees seasonal beers; guest beers Ⓗ
Multi-roomed local, built in 1905 by Alfred Nuttall. Little-altered, the pub is Grade II listed. The main room has full height cream and green Art Nouveau glazed tiling; four other rooms lead off this room. An alternative name for the pub is Butcher Brig, after a now-defunct slaughterhouse that stood alongside. The bowling green at the rear benefits from spectacular views. ⛼❀P

GRIMEHILLS

Crown & Thistle
Roman Road, BB3 3PN (the old Darwen-Edgworth road)
⏲ 12-2.30 (not Mon), 6-11; 12-11 Fri & Sat; 12-10.30 Sun
☎ (01254) 702624
Everards Tiger; Thwaites Bitter; guest beers Ⓗ
Traditional, country roadside inn, replete with beams and decorative brasses. It has a wonderful homely atmosphere enhanced by a piano, open fire, wooden tables, chairs and pews, and displays of breweriana, whisky jars and dolls. The bar has four handpumps to quench your thirst after a walk on the moors. Food is the main theme here – its award-winning restaurant serves an international menu including vegetarian options and Sunday lunches, complemented by a fine wine list. ⛼❀◖◗P

HALTON

White Lion
Church Brow, LA2 6LR (W of village, near River Lune)
⏲ 12-3 (not Mon), 6-11; closed Tue; 12-10.30 Sun
☎ (01524) 811210
Everards Beacon; Jennings Cumberland Ale; guest beers Ⓗ
In the lowest, oldest part of the village (low enough to be flooded occasionally) this pub backs on to an historic churchyard. A cosy, traditional village local with a single bar, it has a room available for functions and customers avoiding tobacco smoke. Food (which never dominates the atmosphere) includes tapas. The locals like strong pale ales, so often one is available, along with a second guest beer. Buses 49 and 490 pass here. ❀◖◗♣P

HASLINGDEN

Griffin Inn
86 Hudrake, BB4 5AF (near A680/A677 jct)
⏲ 12-11; 12-10.30 Sun
☎ (01706) 214021
Porter Dark Mild, Bitter, Rossendale Ale, Porter, Sunshine, seasonal beer Ⓗ
Home of the Porter Brewery, this is a fine community pub. Its fairly open-plan layout has areas for pub games. The lounge features a picture window overlooking the northern side of town, while the window by the bar overlooks the shortest and steepest approach to the pub. The most outstanding

aspect here is the ale. With the brewery located in the cellar, owner Dave Porter keeps a constant check on what flows through the wickets. The guest cider varies. 🏚♣👍

HEAPEY

Top Lock
Copthurst Lane, PR6 8LS (alongside canal at Johnsons Hillock)
☼ 11-11; 12-10.30 Sun
☎ (01257) 263376
Black Sheep Best Bitter; Coniston Bluebird; guest beers ⊞
An annual beer festival is held in October at the picturesque Top Lock which sits beside the Leeds–Liverpool Canal at the series of locks known as Johnsons Hillock. A fine example of a country pub, it comprises a single bar downstairs and an upstairs dining area. An authentic Indian menu is served alongside more traditional pub fare. Popular with walkers and narrow boat owners, at least five guests are usually on sale, including a dark mild. ❀◖▮P

HELMSHORE

Robin Hood
280 Holcombe Road, BB4 4NP (follow brown signs to Helmshore Textile Museum)
☼ 4 (1 Sat)-11; 1-10.30 Sun
☎ (01706) 213180
Tetley Bitter; guest beer ⊞
Small pub divided in several areas with a minute bar by the entrance. Cigarette card collections and ornamental ducks adorn every wall and cranny. Look out for the etched window of the Glen Top Brewery of Waterfoot. A terraced garden to the side and rear of the pub overlooks an old mill lodge, now part of the Helmshore Textile Museum. The guest beer is usually from the Phoenix Brewery. 🏚❀♣

HEST BANK

Hest Bank
2 Hest Bank Lane, LA2 6DN (near canal bridge No. 116)
☼ 11.30-11; 12-10.30 Sun
☎ (01524) 824339
Boddingtons Bitter; Cains Bitter; Robinson's Best Bitter; Taylor Landlord; guest beers ⊞
Over a pint you can read about the history of this pub, as the last stop for travellers beginning the perilous crossing of the sands. Transport developments and suburban sprawl have cut it off from the sea, but left it with a pleasant canalside garden. To the left as you enter from the front is the locals' bar in the older part of the pub, with the oldest room behind; to the right a number of linked spaces on different levels are used mainly by diners. It is served by bus No. 55A, or No. 5 that runs along the A5109 over the canal.
🏚Q❀◖▲♣P⊬

HIGH MOOR

Rigbye Arms
2 Whittle Lane, WN6 9QB (off B5246)
☼ 12-3, 5.30-11; 12-11 Sat; 12-10.30 Sun
☎ (01257) 462354

Greene King Old Speckled Hen; Marston's Pedigree; Tetley Mild, Bitter ⊞
Although only three miles from the M6 (junction 27), this pub nestles at the heart of rural Lancashire. Always a hostelry, it was built in the 17th century and retains the character and distinct flavour of those bygone days. A Lancashire Life award-winner for its food, the public bar is popular with ramblers who warm up by its log-burning stove. The main lounge bar includes a snug where children are welcome. A well-kept bowling green sits to the rear of the car park. 🏚Q❀◖⊟P

HOGHTON

Royal Oak
Blackburn Old Road, Riley Green, PR5 0SL (A675/A674 jct)
☼ 11.30-3, 5.30-11; 12-10.30 Sun
☎ (01254) 201445
Thwaites Mild, Bitter, Lancaster Bomber, seasonal beers ⊞
Traditional stone pub on the old road between Preston and Blackburn. Close to the Riley Green basin on the Leeds–Liverpool Canal, the Royal Oak is popular with diners and drinkers alike. Rooms and alcoves radiate from the central bar, and there is a dining room. The pub has low, beamed ceilings and numerous brasses adorn the walls. This Thwaites tied house is a regular outlet for the brewery's seasonal beers. Visitors may want to visit the local attraction, Hoghton Tower, which is steeped in history. 🏚Q❀◖P⊬

HOSCAR

Railway Tavern
Hoscar Moss Road, L40 4BQ (by station)
☼ 12-11; 12-10.30 Sun
☎ (01704) 892369
Jennings Bitter; Tetley Mild, Bitter; guest beers ⊞
The Railway Tavern is a superb, unspoilt, rural local, popular with cyclists and those out on a country drive. It stands next to Hoscar Station, which is itself in the middle of nowhere. We can only assume they built the station for the benefit of discerning beer drinkers! The pub's three rooms are served by a central bar; two coal fires create a welcoming atmosphere. Railway memorabilia and pictures of military aircraft adorn the walls. 🏚Q☕❀◖⊟♿⧓♣P

LANCASTER

John O'Gaunt
53 Market Street, LA1 1JG (near City Museum)
☼ 11-3 (5 Sat), 6 (7 Sat)-11; 12-4, 7-10.30 Sun
☎ (01524) 65356
Boddingtons Bitter; Jennings Bitter; Tetley Bitter, Burton Ale; guest beers ⊞
Hidden behind its handsome, original frontage, this narrow, single bar is not big enough for the trade it attracts. The walls are crammed with objects collected by the licensee: beer mats, jazz posters, photos of musicians and an array of awards. At lunchtime, most of the customers come from nearby banks and offices; in the evening, it is mostly regulars – come before 9pm if you want a seat. Varied live music is performed (Mon-Thu eves) and jazz Sunday

lunchtime. Hot pies are available at most times (no food Sun). ♿◗≢

Water Witch
Tow Path, Aldcliffe Road, LA1 1SU (on Lancaster Canal, stone ramp off A6)
🕐 11-11; 12-10.30 Sun
☎ (01524) 63828
Beer range varies Ⓗ
This former canal company stable block assumed its present name and function in 1978 – the first true canalside pub on this canal. Wedged between the towpath and a retaining wall, it is very long and narrow. The decor is spartan; bare stonework is only relieved by some mirrors. A mezzanine floor is mainly used for dining – there is a talented chef here. Popular with students, beers from Lancashire, especially Hart, Thwaites and Bryson's, feature strongly. It is most easily found via the towpath from the Infirmary bus stop. ♿◗

Yorkshire House
2 Parliament Street, LA1 1PB (near bus station)
🕐 7-11; 7-10.30 Sun
☎ (01524) 64679
website: www.yorkshirehouse.enta.net
Everards Beacon, Tiger; guest beer Ⓗ
On the fringe of the town centre, the pub sports an austere bare-boarded style, although there is a cosy corner around the fire. Pictures of old rock stars, film posters and table football complete the picture. Upstairs, a spacious room is used for live music (Fri and Sat) and a jazz club (Thu). The patio opens for summer drinking. ♨♿

LANESHAWBRIDGE

Hargreaves Arms
Keighley Road, BB8 7EJ (on A6068, 3 miles N of Colne)
🕐 12-2, 6-11; 12-11 Sat; 12-10.30 Sun
☎ (01282) 863470
Moorhouses Black Cat; John Smith's Bitter; Taylor Golden Best, Landlord Ⓗ
Standing back from the main road, this pub is sometimes called the Monkroyd; its atmosphere is pleasant and cosy. The emphasis is on superb quality food from an extensive menu which is always available. The restaurant is open Wednesday–Saturday lunch and evening, plus Sunday 12–5.30. Situated in beautiful countryside, it makes an ideal base for exploring the adjacent Wycollar Countryside Park.
♨Q✍◗P

LATHOM

Briars Hall Hotel
Briars Lane, L40 5TH (on A5209 E of Burscough)
🕐 11.30-11; 12-10.30 Sun
☎ (01704) 892368 website: www.briarshallhotel.co.uk
Tetley Dark Mild, Bitter; Thwaites Bitter; guest beers Ⓗ
The hotel is an imposing building set in its own landscaped grounds. It was built in the 19th century as a private residence for a wealthy local corn-milling family. Some original features have been retained and the stable block is particularly impressive. The style is that of a residential hotel and restaurant, nevertheless, the areas set aside for drinkers are comfortable.
Q♿✍◗♿Å≢ (Burscough Jct) P⤸

Ship
4 Wheat Lane, L40 4BX (off A5209 by canal)
🕐 11.30-11; 12-10.30 Sun
☎ (01704) 893117
Moorhouses Black Cat, Pendle Witches Brew; John Smith's Bitter; Theakston Best Bitter, Old Peculier; guest beers Ⓗ
Situated at the junction of the Rufford branch canal and the Leeds–Liverpool Canal, the Ship is at the heart of a conservation area with early boatmen's cottages, locks and a dry dock all within a few yards. 200 years old, this multi-roomed, oak-beamed pub today offers an adventurous beer range, a varying real cider and home-cooked food in pleasant surroundings. It is known locally as the Blood Tub for reasons obscurely connected with the making of black puddings.
♿♿◗♿♣♠P⤸

LEA TOWN

Smiths Arms (Slip Inn)
Lea Lane, PR4 0RP (opp. BNFL east gate)
OS476312
🕐 12-2, 4.30-11; 12-10.30 Sun
☎ (01772) 726906
Thwaites Mild, Bitter Ⓗ
Cosy, family-run, country pub, known locally as the Slip Inn from the time when farmers would walk cattle from the Fylde to Preston market and would slip in for a drink. Food is served 12–2 and at teatime Friday–Sunday – a really ruthless chilli is a speciality. A lunchtime food take-away service is popular with workers at the nearby factory. Handy for the canal and the new Ribble link, camping facilities are available in an adjacent field. ♨♿◗Å♣P

LEYLAND

Eagle & Child
Church Road, PR25 3AA (on B5248)
🕐 11.45-11; 12-10.30 Sun
☎ (01772) 433531
Burtonwood Bitter; guest beers Ⓗ
Ancient inn, nestling snugly behind the 1,000-year-old parish church, to which it is said to be connected by a secret tunnel. Next door, the old grammar school serves as South Ribble's museum. The pub's original separate rooms have been opened out and the bar has been sympathetically restored. Unlike some nearby pubs, all ages are catered for here. The pub's crown bowling green is across the road. Two guest beers are usually available. Weekday lunches are served. Bus No. 111, Preston–Leyland, runs every 10 minutes (half-hourly eves and Sun). ♿◗♣P

LITTLE ECCLESTON

Cartford Hotel
Cartford Lane, PR3 0YP (1/2 mile off A586, by toll bridge)
🕐 12 (11.30 Sat)-3; 6.30-11; 12-10.30 Sun
☎ (01995) 670166 website: www.cartfordinn.co.uk
Fuller's London Pride; Hart Dishy Debbie; Phoenix Arizona; Rooster's Yankee; guest beers Ⓗ
Converted 17th-century farmhouse set on the banks of the River Wyre. A genuine free house, with a range of ever-changing guests, it usually stocks beer from Hart brewed

behind the hotel, plus a cider in summer. It is popular with walkers, cyclists and caravanners in summer, and is a frequent winner of local CAMRA's Pub of the Year award. A comprehensive menu features curries, vegetarian dishes and children's meals. A play area for small children is provided. The guest rooms have en-suite facilities. ♨☺☎⊯◑♣●P✗

LONGRIDGE

Old Oak
111 Preston Road, PR3 3BA
(B6243/B6244 jct)
☼ 12-11; 12-10.30 Sun
☎ (01772) 783648
Theakston Mild, Bitter; Wells Bombardier; guest beers Ⓗ
Welcoming, community local with wood settles and a real fire in the comfortable lounge. The large games room has big-screen TV for sport. The two guest beers change regularly. A large array of pump clips and stuffed cartoon characters are displayed around the pub. It has its own beer appreciation society and runs competitions such as big onion, pie-making and alcoholic jelly contests. There is a no-smoking area at lunchtime where meals are served (12–4). This characterful pub has an award-winning rear patio.
♨☺◑♣P

LYTHAM ST ANNE'S

Taps ⊘
12 Henry Street, FY8 5LR (behind Clifton Arms Hotel)
☼ 11-11; 12-10.30 Sun
☎ (01253) 736226 website: www.thetaps.com
Beer range varies Ⓗ
Busy, basic but excellent, cosy ale house offering a changing range of nine guest beers, which always includes a mild. The house beer is brewed by Titanic. A regular CAMRA prize-winner, it was West Pennines Pub of the Year 2002, and only just failed to reach the top four pubs for the national award. The rear patio is heated. No food is served Sunday. Bus Nos. 7, 11 and 167/8/9 from Blackpool stop in the square.
♨☺◑&≢●

MAWDESLEY

Black Bull
Hall Lane, L40 2QY (off B5246)
☼ 12-11; 12-10.30 Sun
☎ (01704) 822202
Tetley Dark Mild, Greenalls Bitter; Taylor Landlord; Theakston Best Bitter; guest beer Ⓗ
This stone inn, dating from 1580, has been a pub since 1610. The low-ceilinged building boasts some magnificent oak beams. Older residents of the village know the pub as 'Ell 'Ob – a reference to a coal-fired cooking range. There is a games room upstairs and a boules pitch outside. Many certificates in the bar record the pub's success in the Lancashire Best-Kept Village competition. In summer the hanging baskets are splendid. No food is served Monday evening. Bus No. 347, Chorley–Southport, passes (four times a day, not Sun).
♨☺◑&♣P✗

Robin Hood Inn
Bluestone Lane, L40 2RG
(off B5250) OS506163
☼ 11.30 (11 Sat)-11; 12-10.30 Sun
☎ (01704) 822275 website: www.robinhood-inn.com
Boddingtons Bitter; Taylor Landlord; guest beers Ⓗ
Charming white-painted inn at the crossroads between the three old villages of Mawdesley, Croston and Eccleston. The 15th-century building was substantially altered in the 19th century. The pub has been in the same family for over 30 years. It enjoys a reputation for good food, but still finds room for the drinker, with four guest ales on tap. Bar food is served all day at the weekend; Wilson's Restaurant, upstairs, is open Tuesday–Sunday evenings. Bus No. 347, Chorley–Southport, serves the pub.
☎☺◑P

MERE BROW

Legh Arms ⊘
82 The Gravel, PR4 6JX (off A565 at B5246 jct)
☼ 11-11; 12-10.30 Sun
☎ (01772) 812359
Courage Directors; Taylor Landlord; Tetley Bitter; guest beer Ⓗ
This former Higson's house is situated close to the Tarleton leisure lakes compex. The Legh Arms is a friendly local in a peaceful village, just off the Preston–Southport bypass. It has a quiet, pleasant lounge with French windows looking out on to the garden and a popular public bar where games are played. There is a small snug at the rear. Coal fires help create a welcoming atmosphere throughout. ♨Q☺◑⊟♣P

MITTON

Aspinall Arms
Mitton Road, BB7 9PQ (B6245)
☼ 12-3, 6-11; 12-11 Sat; 12-10.30 Sun
☎ (01254) 826223 website: www.aspinallarms.co.uk
Greene King IPA; Shepherd Neame Spitfire; Taylor Landlord; guest beers Ⓗ
At the heart of this Ribble Valley, the Aspinall is a typical country pub. The emphasis is on good beer, good food and good service. The pub is semi-open plan with one or two nooks and crannies. The restaurant is open during pub hours, with last food orders taken half an hour before closing time. An extensive garden overlooks the River Ribble. The Aspinall is well used by locals, tourists and walkers, being located next to the Ribble Way.
♨☺◑P

MORECAMBE

Smugglers' Den
56 Poulton Road, LA4 5HB
(off B5274, near police station)
☼ 11-3, 7-11; 12-10.30 Sun
☎ (01524) 421684
Boddingtons Bitter; Tetley Bitter; guest beers Ⓗ
The pub's current name and decor – dark, with low beams, stone-flagged floors and tables shaped like casks – date from 1960. Since then there has been a single change of licensee, from father to son. The pair have accumulated a vast collection of mainly nautical artefacts; note also the impressive stained glass windows. The garden houses

caged birds. The pub lies at the centre of the old fishing village of Poulton. **P**

NELSON

Station ⊘
13 Hibson Road, BB9 9SB (opp. station)
✪ 11-11, 12-10.30 Sun
☎ (01282) 877910
Moorhouses Black Cat; guest beers Ⓗ
This Wetherspoon's pub just outside the station is a veritable oasis in the beer desert that is Nelson town centre. An imposing building, the interior does full justice to the exterior. The first thing you notice is the beautifully-restored horseshoe bar: wood, glass and slate in perfect harmony. The rest of the pub is kitted out in the same fashion; warm and comfortably furnished with areas to suit everyone. Q❀◑➅✹≠

ORMSKIRK

Eureka
78 Halsall Lane, L39 3AX (off A59)
✪ 12-11, 12-10.30 Sun
☎ (01695) 572585
Taylor Landlord; Tetley Mild, Bitter Ⓗ
Its name might conjure up an image of a trendy high street wine bar, but the Eureka is in fact a traditional back-street local, offering well-kept beer in an unpretentious but pleasant setting. It is on a residential road and caters for the local community, while being entirely welcoming to visitors. It is worth wandering off the main road to find this pub. No meals are served on Monday. Q◑➅♣P✹

Greyhound
100 Aughton Street, L39 3BS (on B5319)
✪ 11.30-11, 12-10.30 Sun
☎ (01695) 576701
Tetley Dark Mild, Bitter Ⓗ
A genuine local, the Greyhound is a turn of the century pub (the century in question being the 19th), with its original multi-room design still intact. Despite its traditional character, the pub has modern furnishings, apart from the small vault which has a timeless atmosphere. Visitors are assured of a friendly welcome. It is easy to reach from the town centre. ➅≠♣P

Hayfield
22 County Road, L39 1NN (on A59)
✪ 12-11, 12-10.30 Sun
☎ (01695) 571157
Beer range varies Ⓗ
The Hayfield is a popular, modern pub where the spacious, comfortable interior is served by a long L-shaped bar. Although it is open plan, a platform area, rails and screens give the illusion of separate rooms. The pub prides itself on its adventurous range of beers, which are often drawn from smaller breweries; a real cider is often available too. The winner of a number of local CAMRA awards, it has a strong following among younger people and buzzes at the weekend. Q❀◑➅♣P⊟

Yew Tree
Grimshaw Lane, L39 1PD (off A59)
✪ 11.30-3; 6-11; 12-11 Sat; 12-4, 7-10.30 Sun
Cains Mild, Bitter; Robinson's Best Bitter; guest beers Ⓗ

A delightful, time-warp, 1950s-style pub on a pleasant estate, the Yew Tree is a haven for beer drinkers. An excellent choice is always available – proof that a local does not have to be unambitious in its range of beers. The pub boasts a perfectly preserved post-war lounge and a traditional tap room. A small, but charming, walled garden is an added attraction. Q❀◑➅♣P

PENDLETON

Swan with Two Necks
BB7 1PT (off A59) OS755396
✪ 12-2 (not Mon or Tue), 7 (6 Sat)-11; 12-10.30 Sun
☎ (01200) 423112
Moorhouses Premier; Phoenix Arizona; guest beer Ⓗ
This superb, traditional local doubles as the village post office. The long main room has two warming coal fires in winter. A small back room and an upstairs restaurant, offering an extensive, good value menu, enhance this attractive pub. At the rear is a pleasant, safe garden, while at the front a river splits the main street (mind the ducks). It makes an excellent starting and finishing point for walks around the delightful Pendle Hill. ⌂Q❀◑P

PENWORTHAM

Fleece
39 Liverpool Road, PR1 9XD (on A59)
✪ 11-11; 12-10.30 Sun
☎ (01772) 745561
Boddingtons Bitter; Wells Bombardier; guest beers Ⓗ
Old coaching inn situated next to a former water tower – Penwortham's most prominent feature. At the front a cosy, village inn appearance is maintained, although the pub has seen several refurbishments in recent years. It holds a beer festival each February when some 35 beers are available over a 10-day period. A former bowling green has been converted to an outdoor drinking area and children's playground. Two guest beers are usually on tap. ❀◑♣P✹

POULTON-LE-FYLDE

Thatched House
12 Ball Street, FY6 7BG
✪ 11-11; 12-10.30 Sun
Boddingtons Bitter; Theakston Cool Cask; guest beers Ⓗ
This picturesque town-centre pub is a local institution. Standing in the graveyard of the parish church, it is an unspoilt gem, where any restoration has served only to enhance its character. The landlord has been allowed by Scottish Courage to source one of his guest beers locally. He has chosen the award-winning Hart Brewery and presents their immaculate beer well. A busy pub, attracting a mature clientele (no food, children, alcopops or music), it comes close to perfection. ⌂Q➅➅A≠

PRESTON

Ashton Institute
10-12 Wellington Road, PR2 1BU (off A5072)
✪ 7 (4 Fri)-11; 1-10.30 Sun
☎ (01772) 726582
Thwaites Bitter; Worthington's Bitter; guest beers Ⓗ
Small club, situated among rows of terraced

housing; it is hard to find but well worth the effort. Free of tie for cask ales, the guest beers can be interesting. Of the two rooms, one is used for functions, the other has pool and snooker tables. It is the oldest club in Preston, situated in its original premises (opened on 4.4.1944). An annual beer festival is held on the last weekend in October each year. Show a CAMRA card or copy of this Guide for entry. ♣

Black Horse ☆
166 Friargate, PR1 2EJ (near market)
🕐 10.30am-11pm (may close early Mon, Tue & Wed); 12-3.30 (closed eve) Sun
☎ (01772) 204855
Robinson's Hatters, Best Bitter, Frederics, seasonal beers Ⓗ
Classic, Grade II listed pub in the main shopping area close to the historic open market. With its exquisite tiled bar and walls and superb mosaic floor, it is an English Heritage/CAMRA award-winner. There are two front rooms displaying photos of old Preston, and the famed 'hall of mirrors' seating area to the rear. Memorabilia collected by a previous landlord is displayed in a glass partition. The modern upstairs bar (no real ale) is usually open at weekends. ≢

Hogshead
99 Fylde Road, PR1 2XQ (on A583)
🕐 11-3, 6-11; 12-10.30 Sun
☎ (01772) 252870 website: www.hogshead.co.uk
Caledonian Deuchars IPA; Taylor Landlord; Worthington's Bitter; guest beers Ⓗ
Now in its tenth year, this spacious pub is as popular as ever. A pool table and bar football are recent additions. Plenty of fun nights are held to keep the students from the nearby university amused. The pub is a former doctor's surgery and has listed status. The cellar is visible from the drinking area. Multi-channel sports are available and the garden is popular when the sun comes out. ❄ⓓ▷♿♣P✂

Limekiln
288 Aqueduct Street, PR1 7JP
(off Fylde Road, A583)
🕐 11-11; 12-10.30 Sun
☎ (01772) 493247
Banks's Original, Bitter, seasonal beers Ⓗ
This tile-fronted local welcomes visitors as well as regulars. The aqueduct which carried the Lancaster Canal into Preston centre was removed in the 1960s and canal terminus is now only 200 yards from the pub. A central bar serves four drinking areas, including pool and darts rooms. Entertainment includes karaoke night (Sat) and an organ singalong (Sun). In summer tables are set up outside the pub. ⓓ♣P

Market Tavern
33-35 Market Street, PR1 2ES
🕐 10.30-11; closed Sun
☎ (01772) 254425 website: www.market-tavern.com
Beer range varies Ⓗ
Overlooking Preston's impressive Victorian market, this small pub was totally rebuilt internally and now consists of a range of seating areas around the bar, including some intimate booths. Fascinating prints of old Preston adorn the walls. There is a jam night every Monday and live bands perform

monthly (last Thu). Of the three ever-changing guest beers, one is usually from the Pictish Brewery. It is becoming well known for its selection of German and Belgian bottled beers. The second largest bus station in Europe is nearby. ≢

New Britannia Inn
6 Heatley Street, PR1 2XB (off Friargate)
🕐 11-3, 6-11; 11-11 Sat; 7-10.30 Sun
☎ (01772) 253424
Boddingtons Bitter; Castle Eden Ale; Marston's Pedigree; Goose Eye Brontë; guest beers Ⓗ
This CAMRA multi-award-winning single-bar, town-centre pub attracts real ale enthusiasts from far and wide. It enjoys an excellent reputation for its beers which are lovingly cared for by the landlady and her dedicated staff. The pub is very comfortable inside, and attractive outside with floral decorations in winter and summer. Note the splendid Britannia windows. The excellent home-made food represents good value. ❄ⓓ♿≢●

Old Blue Bell
114 Church Street, PR1 3BS (near bus station)
🕐 11-11; 12-10.30 Sun
☎ (01772) 251280
Samuel Smith OBB Ⓗ
Small, white-fronted pub, just off the main shopping areas. There is a small lounge off the main room and a snug at the rear. An extensive array of prints covers the walls. The pub, which dates from 1722, has the remains of a passageway to the nearby minster in the cellar. It offers the cheapest beer in a brewery-owned pub in the city. With its real fire, it is peaceful (no juke box) and an excellent place for conversation. Good value, home-cooked lunches are served. ᛘQ ⓓ

Olde Dog & Partridge
44 Friargate, PR1 2AT (NW of Ringway)
🕐 11-2, 6-11; 12-3, 7-10.30 Sun
☎ (01772) 252217
Fuller's London Pride; Highgate Dark; Marston's Pedigree; guest beers Ⓗ
This well established rock pub attracts a diverse clientele. Both the DJ (Thu and Sun) and landlord have been at the pub well over 20 years. It is the only Preston pub to sell both real mild and cider (Addlestones). During the summer an impressive array of motorbikes often assembles in front of the pub. Weekends can be busy. Cheap, basic food is served lunchtimes (not Sun) and the area has many fast food outlets. Guest beers come from the Punch list. ⓓ≢♣●

Stanley Arms
24 Lancaster Road, PR1 1DD (next to Guild Hall)
🕐 12-11; 12-10.30 Sun
☎ (01772) 254004
Courage Directors; Theakston Mild, Best Bitter; guest beers Ⓗ
This local is close to, but not part of the 'circuit'. A rare outlet for mild in the town centre, three guest beers are also regularly available; one, a 'landlord's choice' may come from anywhere in the country. The single lounge bar tends to be busy. Bar meals are served 12–5.30 daily. An impressive, ornate listed building, the pub's name refers to the Earls of Derby, once the landowners in the area. ⓓ≢♣

RISHTON

Rishton Arms
Station Road, BB1 4HF
☼ 7 (12 Sat)-11; 12-10.30 Sun
☎ (01254) 886396
Thwaites Mild, Bitter, seasonal beer Ⓗ
Large, comfortable local next to the station, comprising a spacious lounge and a smaller tap room, with darts, pool and a large-screen TV. One of the best Thwaites outlets that you will find, it has deservedly been in this Guide for 11 years.
❀⏚⇌♣P

SAMLESBURY

New Hall Tavern
Cuerdale Lane, PR1 4TA (on B6230)
☼ 11.30-11; 12-10.30 Sun
☎ (01772) 877217
website: www.btinternet.com/-newhall
Boddingtons Bitter; guest beers Ⓗ
Welcoming country pub on a rural crossroads. This ex-Matthew Brown pub was acquired by Whitbread when its large brewery was built nearby. A spacious, central, single bar area is comfortably furnished with side areas for diners. Traditional home-cooked food is popular and reasonably priced (served all day Sun). The varied beer range is favoured by locals and visitors; usually a locally-brewed beer is available. Live music is performed Thursday evening. The No. 217 Preston–Mellor bus passes (infrequent service).
🚋🛏❀⏃&Å♣P⌇

SCARISBRICK

Heatons Bridge Inn
2 Heatons Bridge Road, L40 9QE (by Leeds-Liverpool Canal bridge No. 28, on B5242)
☼ 11-11; 12-10.30 Sun
☎ (01704) 840549
Tetley Mild, Bitter; guest beer Ⓗ
The Heatons Bridge is a traditional pub, still divided into dark little rooms full of atmosphere and character, the way country pubs used to be. A perfect place to meet and talk, or just to read – newspapers are supplied for solitary drinkers. In good weather you can sit outside and watch the canal boats – a great place to end up after a country walk. Good food is served.
Q❀⏃P

SLYNE

Slyne Lodge ✔
92 Main Road, LA2 6AZ (on A6)
☼ 11-11; 12-10.30 Sun
☎ (01524) 825035 website: www.slynelodge.co.uk
Jennings Mild, Bitter, Cumberland Ale Ⓗ
Elegant Georgian house with a terraced garden. It was a country club until 1981 but once it gained a full licence it slowly changed, through a succession of owners, into an eating-house. Jennings have made it more of a pub again. A large central servery, dark wood panelling, soft lights and a log fire characterise this place. There is a rustic galleried restaurant on one side (closed weekday lunchtimes) and a modern conservatory on the other. Buses 55, 555 and 556 pass here.
🚋🛏🛌⏃♣P

THORNTON CLEVELEYS

Bay Horse
Station Road, FY5 5HY (by level crossing)
☼ 11-11; 12-10.30 Sun
☎ (01253) 852324
Greene King Abbot; Tetley Bitter Ⓗ
Cosy local with a great community spirit. Inside is a snug area with a fire, a restaurant and a traditional vault with darts and dominoes. Outside a barbecue area and south-facing garden with play space add to its appeal. Food is served all day, every day. The pub is 460 years old; originally a stable and inn for travellers on their way to Wardleys Creek, it later became a house of ill-repute and a Masonic meeting place.
❀⏃⏚&♣⌇

UPHOLLAND

Old Dog
6 Alma Hill, WN8 0NW (off A577)
☼ 5 (3 Sat)-11; 12-10.30 Sun
☎ (01695) 623487
Boddingtons Bitter; guest beers Ⓗ
Halfway along the steep Alma Hill, this small, stone pub is worth the short climb from the village. It retains an original Greenall Whitley (St Helens) etched window and one showing the pub name. Its three small, heavily beamed rooms are all on different levels, with a small bar area. In the lower lounge, an extensive collection of decorative plates is displayed. The rear rooms benefit from wonderful views across Wigan to the Pennine Hills.
Q♣

White Lion
10 Church Street, WN8 0ND (off A577)
☼ 5 (12 Sat)-11; 12-10.30 Sun
☎ (01695) 622727
Thwaites Bitter Ⓗ
This multi-level pub is built into the hillside facing Upholland church. Inside are four rooms: two lounges, a games room to the rear and a small snug at the front. Photographs of old Upholland line the walls of the front lounge, which also houses the TV. High on the outside front wall the pub name can be seen alongside the date 1921, although the building appears to be much older. The graveyard opposite is the burial place of local highwayman, George Lyon.
♣P

WADDINGTON

Lower Buck
Edisford Road, BB7 3HU (behind the church)
☼ 12-11; 12-10.30 Sun
☎ (01200) 423342
Black Sheep Best Bitter; Moorhouses Premier, seasonal beer; Taylor Landlord Ⓗ
Splendid example of a village local in a picturesque setting; a genuine free house run by a landlord with a passion for real ale. Each room has its own fire; there is a room for the pool table which also contains the TV. The pub is a short walk from the village centre and is ideally placed for walkers. Moorhouses seasonal beers are available during winter months.
🚋Q❀⏃⌇

WALMER BRIDGE

Longton Arms

2 Liverpool Old Road, PR4 5HA (off A59)
✪ 12.30 (1 Sat; 2 Mon & Tue; 3 Thu)-11;
12-10.30 Sun
☎ (01772) 612335
Cains Mild; Greenalls Bitter Ⓗ
End-of-terrace village pub, a fine
community local. Hanging baskets and
window boxes add to its charm. The pub
offers a splendid small front snug, side bar
and rear lounge with serving hatch and a
big-screen TV. Note the duck frieze over the
bar in the snug – a haunt of wildfowlers
from nearby Longton Marsh. The pub is
also home to a golf society, football team
and the Longton picnic club which raises
money for charity by organising days out.
Stagecoach buses regularly pass the pub.
🏠❀Ⓓ♣P

WATERFOOT

Jolly Sailor

Booth Place, BB4 9BD (off B6238)
✪ 5-11; 12-11 Fri & Sat; 12-10.30 Sun
☎ (01706) 226340
**Adnams Broadside; Jennings Cumberland Ale; Taylor
Landlord; guest beer** Ⓗ
Built in 1825, the pub's name may
commemorate the first landlord's seafaring
life. Rebuilt once, and extended, the Jolly
Sailor is now a friendly, mainly open-plan
pub. The separate games room has hatch
access to the bar. A slightly raised wooden
stage area is used for live music (folk,
occasionally Sun) and monthly karaoke
(Sat). Freshly-prepared hot and cold snacks
and main meals are available, with a roast
lunch on Sunday. 🏠❀Ⓓ♣

WENNINGTON

Bridge

LA2 8NL (on B6480, S of station)
✪ 12-3, 6-11; 11-11 Fri & Sat; 12-10.30 Sun
☎ (015242) 21236
**Black Sheep Best Bitter; Boddingtons Bitter; guest
beer** Ⓗ
The bar is small, low-beamed and cosy and
it is hard not to get drawn into the
conversation. There are also two dining
rooms where children are admitted. Located
in a pretty isolated spot, but with a
surprisingly large number of regular
customers, the pub features in a Turner
painting. 🏠Q❀🚲Ⓓ♿Å≠♣P

WHALLEY

Dog Inn

35 King Street, BB7 9SP (on B6246)
✪ 11-11; 12-10.30 Sun
☎ (01254) 823009
Theakston Best Bitter; guest beers Ⓗ
At the village centre, and originally a
stables, in 1877 the Dog was first licensed as
a one-room ale house. It has since been
extended to become a multi-area pub. The
rear of the building is considerably lower
than the front, requiring a step in the
L-shaped bar. The guest beers tend to be
from one brewery's range, that brewery
changing monthly; there can be up to six
real ales at a time. The pub gets very lively
on weekend evenings. ❀Ⓓ♣♣

WHEELTON

Dressers Arms

Briers Brow, PR6 8HD (near A674)
✪ 11-11; 12-10.30 Sun
☎ (01254) 830041
website: www.dressers.arms@virgin-net
**Boddingtons Bitter; Taylor Landlord; Tetley Bitter;
Worthington's Bitter; guest beers** Ⓗ
Home to Old Wheelton Brewery, one of
whose beers is always on sale, this pub has
been converted over the years from a
number of terraced cottages into a spacious,
multi-roomed establishment. The bar is
complemented by a lounge, games room
and a snug. The no-smoking room looks on
to the brewery. Good food is served
downstairs (all day Sat and Sun) and an
authentic Chinese restaurant upstairs is an
added attraction. 🏠⇆❀Ⓓ♣P✂

WHITTLE-LE-WOODS

Royal Oak

216 Chorley Old Road, PR6 7NA (off A6)
✪ 2.30-11; 12-10.30 Sun
☎ (01257) 276485
**Boddingtons Bitter; Jennings Cumberland Ale; Wells
Bombardier** Ⓗ
This small, single-bar, terraced village local
was built in 1820 to serve the adjacent
branch of the Leeds–Liverpool Canal (now
filled in). This local CAMRA award-winning
pub has been in this Guide for 28 years
consecutively. Long and narrow, with a
small bar and separate games room, it is
very much a community pub and haunt of
mature motorcycle enthusiasts. Wheelchair
access is at the rear. 🏠❀♣♣

WORSTHORNE

Crooked Billet Inn

1 Smith Street, BB10 3NQ
✪ 5 (3 Fri; 12 Sat)-11; 12-10.30 Sun
☎ (01282) 429040
**Taylor Landlord; Tetley Dark Mild, Bitter; Theakston
Best Bitter; guest beers** Ⓗ
Fine local situated just off the main square
of the village, which is on the outskirts of
Burnley. It is handy for moorland walks.
The pub retains its wood panelling and has
a fine bar. The rooms have been opened out
somewhat but the pub still has distinct
drinking areas. Meals are served at the
weekend, 12–6.
🏠❀Ⓓ♣P✂

WREA GREEN

Villa ⊘

Moss Side Lane, PR4 2PE
(on B5259 towards Lytham)
✪ 11-11; 12-10.30 Sun
☎ (01772) 684317 website: www.the-villahotel.com
Jennings Bitter, Cumberland Ale Ⓗ
Originally a 19th-century gentlemen's
country residence, the Villa received a
multi-million pound facelift from Jennings
Brewery, before being sold on. This hotel is
a jewel in a spectacular setting. Although
primarily an upmarket hotel and restaurant,
the bar is very much treated by locals as the
village pub and no pressure is put on
drinkers to buy food. It is extremely
comfortable and intimate.
🏠Q❀🚲Ⓓ♿Å≠(Moss Side) P✂

Farmers back small brewers

A growing number of farmers' markets, which sell produce direct to consumers free from middle-men and supermarkets, include stalls run by micro-brewers. As small brewers find it difficult to sell their beers to pub groups that demand enormous discounts, and with the number of genuine free trade pubs in decline, farmers' markets offer valuable outlets. CAMRA and the National Association of Farmers' Markets (01225 787914) now have links on their web sites. Readers are encouraged to support micro-brewers by buying their products at farmers' markets. Usually only bottled beers are available but some brewers sell draught beer in polypins or other take-home containers. If bottled beers are filtered rather than bottle-conditioned, farmers' markets are ideal venues for face-to-face discussions about going the extra mile to bottle-conditioning and using organic ingredients as well.

Web sites: **www.farmersmarkets.net**
email: **nafm@farmersmarkets.net**
www.camra.org
email: **camra@camra.org**

BERKSHIRE
Chiltern Brewery sells beer at **Reading Farmers' Market** on the first and third Saturdays in every month.
Contact Mark Hillyer, market co-ordinator
☎ (0118) 933 1924.

Berkshire Farmers' Market meets the first Thursday of every month in Wokingham (Market Place), with beers supplied by Glebe Wine Company (see National Farmers' Market web site).

CUMBRIA
The following farmers' markets sell bottled beers from Dent Brewery, including T'Owd Tup, Ramsbottom and Kamikaze:

Brampton: fourth Saturday of every month

Carlisle: first Friday of every month

Egremont: third Friday of every month

Kendal: last Friday of every month

Orton: second Saturday of every month (www.ortonfarmers.co.uk)

Ulverston: third Saturday of every month

Whitehaven: first Saturday of every month

Plus

Holker Hall: end of May, beginning of June every year

Lowther Horse Driving Trials: August every year

Westmorland Show: September every year

Ulverston Dickensian show: 22-23 November 2003.

Consult www.madeincumbria.co.uk

HERTFORDSHIRE

Chiltern Brewery has a stall at **Hatfield Farmers' Market**, White Lion Square, first Saturday of every month. Contact **m.donovan@welhat.gov.uk**

NORFOLK

Iceni Brewery, which has been the pace-setter among small breweries of selling at farmers' markets, regularly has its beers at the **Sunday Norwich Farmers' Market**, which meets on the fourth Sunday of every month. The market takes place at the Norfolk Showground, just off the Norwich southern by-pass; access from A47, Norwich southern by-pass at the A1074 junction (Longwater Interchange).

Iceni sells beer at the annual **Royal Norfolk Show** in June and the brewery's beers are also on sale in authorised shops in Thetford Forest.

For information about **Norfolk Farmers' Market** contact the organiser Rick Holland:

rickholland@btopenworld.com
Iceni Brewery: **icenibrewe@aol.com**
☎ (01842) 878922; fax (01842) 879216. Also contact Iceni for information about a small brewers' co-operative that has been set up in East Anglia.

SOMERSET

Hecks Cider from Street is sold at the **Farmers' Market in Weston-super-Mare** (Town Square) on the second Saturday of every month, 9.30am-2pm. Contact **graham.quick@n-somerset.gov.uk**
www.n-somerset.govuk/econ-dev

SUFFOLK

Old Chimneys Brewery beers are sold at **Needham Market Farmers' Market** at Alder Carr Farm, Creeting St Mary, Ipswich, on the third Saturday of every month.
☎ (01449) 720820.

YORKSHIRE

Organic beers from North Yorkshire Brewery are sold at **Pinchinthorpe Hall Farmers' Market** on the first Sunday of every month, 10am-2pm. The brewery is based at the hall and is open to visitors. Contact **anneblueprintpublicity@ntworld.com** or **www.pinchinthorpehall.co.uk**

SCOTLAND

Bottle-conditioned and organic beers from Black Isle Brewery are sold at the following Scottish Farmers' Markets:

Aberdeen: on fourth Saturday of every month. Contact: **john@apardion.co.uk**

Edinburgh: on the first and third Saturdays of every month at Castle Terrace. Contact:
www.edinburghcc.com

Glasgow: on second and fourth Saturdays of every month. Contact:
safm@fentonevents.com

Haddington: on fourth Saturday of every month. Contact as for Glasgow.

Inverness: on first Saturday of every month. Contact as for Glasgow.

Perth: first Saturday of every month. Contact as for Glasgow.

Black Isle Brewery
www.blackislebrewery.com
greatbeers@blackislebrewery.com
☎ (01463) 811871.
Scottish Association of Farmers Markets
www.scottish farmers.com

Brendan Moore (right) of Iceni Brewery in Norfolk, launching his bottle-conditioned Hogs Wash now on sale at farmers' markets

■ The Good Beer Guide would like to hear of other farmers' markets that sell beer. Information to:
roger.protz@camra.org.uk

LEICESTERSHIRE & RUTLAND

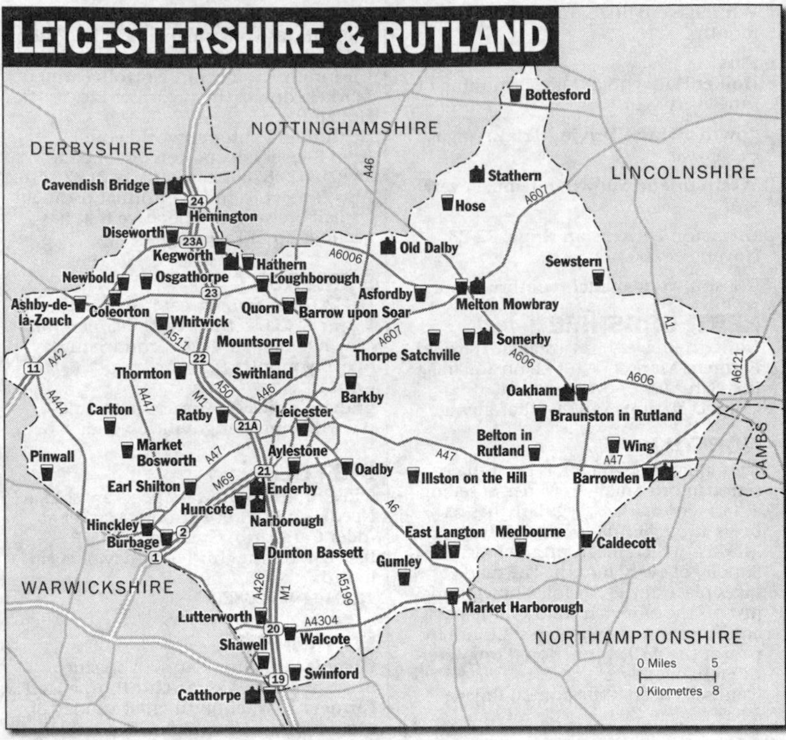

ASFORDBY

Crown Inn

106 Main Street, LE14 3SA

✪ 6.30 (4 Fri; 12 Sat)-11; 12-10.30 Sun

☎ (01664) 812175

Beer range varies Ⓗ

This 18th-century, friendly local has low, beamed ceilings, and nooks to sit in. Local stone has been used for the bar, but beware of its sloping top. The pub was saved from becoming a private residence by the locals. Renovation work carried out a few years ago, has added to the pub's character. The Crown is a free house and the beer range is constantly changing, often one of the local micro-breweries is featured. Lunches are offered on Sunday, and evening meals on Friday and Saturday. Daytime buses from Loughborough, Grantham and Leicester serve the pub, with an evening bus only from Leicester and Melton.

♔Q❀◐♿♣P

ASHBY-DE-LA-ZOUCH

Plough ✔

The Green, North Street, LE65 1JU

✪ 11-11; 12-10.30 Sun

☎ (01530) 412817

website: www.theploughashby.co.uk

Draught Bass; Marston's Pedigree; guest beers Ⓗ

Parts of this pub date back to the 1580s and, although modernised into a single bar, it has been split into various cosy areas. A friendly local, it fields darts, dominoes and cribbage teams; major rugby matches are screened. It has a rural feel, despite being in the centre of a small historic town. The guest beers are constantly changing and a guest cider is sometimes available. Home-cooked food represents excellent quality and value. An annual beer festival is held here during the August bank holiday with a minimum of 30 guest ales, plus live music.

♔Q❀◐♣P

AYLESTONE

Black Horse

65 Narrow Lane, LE2 8NA (off Sanvey Lane)

✪ 11-3, 5-11; 11-11 Fri & Sat; 12-4, 7-10.30 Sun

☎ (0116) 283 2811

Everards Beacon, Tiger, seasonal beers; guest beers Ⓗ

Cracking, three-bar community local dating from late Victorian times. It offers a very comfortable lounge and smoke-free snug. All bars have open log fires in winter. There is a function room upstairs and a large garden at the rear with children's play area and aviary. A long alley skittles room is available for hire. A short step from the Grand Union Canal and the Great Central Way, it is popular with boaters and walkers.

♔Q❀♣

BARKBY

Brookside

35 Brookside, LE7 3QO (off Barkby Holt Lane)

✪ 12-3 (not Tue), 6-11; 12-4, 7-10.30 Sun

☎ (0116) 260 0092

Burtonwood Bitter, Top Hat; guest beer Ⓗ

Cheery and welcoming pub with the air of a country local. It is two-roomed, with a traditional bar and a cosy lounge with a log fire for those cold winter nights. There is a separate no-smoking restaurant leading from the lounge. Meals are not available on

Sunday evening or on Tuesday. Darts and petanque are popular. The pub has a scenic setting with a brook at the front with plenty of ducks, and a pleasant garden.
⛏❀◑ ⊟♿♣P

Malt Shovel
27 Main Street, LE7 3QG
11-11; 12-4, 6.30-10.30 Sun
☎ (0116) 269 2558
Banks's Bitter; Marston's Pedigree; guest beers Ⓗ
The large, U-shaped bar dominates at this pub. Five real ales are on tap, three of them are rotating guests. The mantelpiece over the fireplace is filled with unopened bottles of British and European beers. Pictures of the local cricket club, and other memorabilia decorate the interior. Access to the pub is via the car park, under cover of a stable block roof. ❀◑♣P

BARROW UPON SOAR

Navigation
87 Mill Lane, LE12 8LQ
11-3, 5.30-11; 11-11 Sat; 12-3, 7-10.30 Sun
☎ (01509) 412842 website:
www.countryfocus.co.uk/barrowuponsoar/navigation
Adnams Bitter; Belvoir Star Bitter; Grainstore Triple B; Greene King Abbot; Marston's Pedigree; guest beer Ⓗ
Thriving free house by the side of the Grand Union Canal and built at the same time – in the 1760s. This waterside pub is popular with the locals and passing summer boat trade (moorings are available nearby). The main bar boasts a bar top inlaid with old pennies, plus much brass and bric-à-brac. The cosy snug has its own bar. The outdoor seating area affords a rural view across the canal. There are regular bus and train services from Leicester and Loughborough during the daytime, but during the evening public transport is limited. The bus stop and station are just a short walk away.
⛏Q❀◑≠♣

BOTTESFORD

Rutland Arms
2 High Street, NG13 0AA
11-11; 12-10.30 Sun
☎ (01949) 843031
Draught Bass; Greenalls Bitter; Tetley Mild; guest beer Ⓗ
One of three excellent pubs in a delightful village that is accessible by public transport. The Rutland Arms has two rooms, plus a restaurant. Mild is always available. The beamed bar is equipped with a pool table, dominoes and darts; the lounge is carpeted and comfortable. Horseshoes and plates decorate the panelled restaurant. Good value English food is served, with inexpensive curries on Tuesday, and steaks on Friday. Not food is available Sunday evening. ⛏❀◑ ⊟♿≠♣P

BURBAGE

Sycamores Inn
60 Windsor Street, LE10 2EF
11-11; 12-10.30 Sun
☎ (01455) 239268
Marston's Bitter, Pedigree Ⓗ
Named after the two trees that stood on this site until the pub was built in 1925, the Sycamores has two rooms; a basic tile-floored bar, and a lounge where children are admitted. The landlord here founded the successful campaign to save Marston's Bitter in 1998. Marston's Bitter outsells Pedigree in this area, strange as it may seem. Note the Banks's beers here are nitro-keg. ❀♣P

CARLTON

Gate Hangs Well
Barton Road, CV13 0DB
12-3 (4 Sat), 6-11; 12-4, 7-10.30 Sun
☎ (01455) 291845
Draught Bass; Greene King Abbot; Marston's Bitter, Pedigree Ⓗ
Comfortable, cosy country inn where singers perform twice a week, on Wednesday and Saturday evening. A conservatory is available for families with children to use until mid-evening, and there is a garden. This local is in Leicestershire, but is virtually on the Warwickshire border.
Q❀♣P

CATTHORPE

Cherry Tree
Main Street, LE17 6DB
5 (12 Sat)-11; 12-10.30 Sun
☎ (01788) 860430
Ansells Best Bitter; Draught Bass; Hook Norton Best Bitter; guest beers Ⓗ
Popular, small, cheery free house that is very much a locals' pub but attracts customers from a wide area. It has a compact, comfortable bar with a wood-burning stove, and a smaller lounge/games room with table skittles. Outside, above the front door, the old Phipp's of Northampton brewery sign can just be seen. Catthorpe is the home of the Dow Bridge Brewery.
⛏Q❀♣P

CAVENDISH BRIDGE

Old Crown
DE74 2HL (400 yds off A6 at Trent Bridge)
11.30-3, 5-11; 12-5, 7-10.30 Sun
☎ (01332) 792392
website: www.oldcrownpub@yahoo.com
Draught Bass; Marston's Pedigree; guest beers Ⓗ
Once a 17th-century coaching inn, now a cosy, atmospheric village pub on the southern bank of the River Trent. Several hundred water jugs hang from the lounge ceiling, while the walls are crammed full of brewery and railway memorabilia; the display even extends into the lavatories. Up to four guest beers are on tap, often featuring beers from the Shardlow Brewery,

INDEPENDENT BREWERIES

Belvoir Old Dalby
Blencowe Barrowden
Brewster's Stathern
Dow Bridge Catthorpe
Everards Narborough
Featherstone Enderby
Grainstore Oakham
John O'Gaunt Melton Mowbray
Langton East Langton
Parish Somerby
Shardlow Cavendish Bridge
Wicked Hathern Hathern

just across the river. Lunches are home cooked. There is a limited daytime bus service from Loughborough and Derby.
♨Q❀☎◗▣℥♿Å P

COLEORTON

King's Arms
187 The Moor, LE67 8GD
🕓 11-3 (not Mon), 5.30-11; 12-10.30 Sun
☎ (01530) 815 4355
Hook Norton Old Hooky; Marston's Pedigree; guest beer Ⓗ
Small village pub originally attached to a miners' hostel, when part of the miners' wages would be paid in beer. It has been extended into a neighbouring cottage and comprises a separate bar and lounge/dining area. Lunches and evening meals are offered. The extensive grounds are being transformed into a garden for all ages.
♨Q❀◗▣❑➕♣P

DISEWORTH

Bull & Swan
Grimesgate, DE74 2QD
🕓 11.30-2.30, 5.30 (5 Fri; 7 Sat)-11; 12-10.30 Sun
☎ (01332) 853960
Draught Bass; Marston's Pedigree; Theakston Best Bitter; guest beers Ⓗ
This building was originally two pubs – the Bull's Head and the Swan. It has a number of rooms on different levels and plenty of cosy corners. Watch your head on the low beams and doorways. There is an upstairs function room and a pool room. Copper and brass bric-à-brac decorate most rooms. A fenced, child-friendly patio that overlooks the parish church is a recent addition. Although close to East Midlands Airport and popular with its staff, the tranquility of this pub is not disturbed by aircraft noise. A warm and friendly welcome is guaranteed at this old village local. There are regular daytime bus services from Loughborough.
♨Q❀◗▣♣P

DUNTON BASSETT

Merrie Monk
38 Station Road, LE17 5LQ (50 yds from A426)
🕓 11-11; 12-10.30 Sun
☎ (01455) 209117
Draught Bass; Greene King IPA; Marston's Pedigree Ⓗ
This U-shaped pub always offers a cheery welcome. It is located on the opposite side of the A426 to the main village, almost in Ashby Magna. Formerly called the Station until the nearby Great Central Line closed, it is now probably named after the Marston's strong mild, Merrie Monk, whose pub it was until three years ago. Sport events are usually shown on TV, but they do not disrupt the whole pub. Private parties are catered for by arrangement. A guest beer is sometimes offered at weekends.
♨❀♣P

EARL SHILTON

Dog & Gun
72 Keats Lane, LE9 7DR (100 yds from A47)
🕓 12-2.30 (not Mon-Thu), 5.30-11; 11.30-3.30, 5.30-11 Sat; 12-3, 7-10.30 Sun
☎ (01445) 842338
Banks's Original; Marston's Bitter, Pedigree Ⓗ

250

Just a short distance from the A47, the pub is set back from the rest of the buildings on the street, as it was built behind the original village pub (which was demolished in 1932). It has three rooms, including a snug. The bar has a tiled floor and a large log fire. With a number of walking routes in this area, the pub runs its own rambling club and participates in many local charity events. The attractive garden is a regular award-winner. ♨❀◗▣♣P

EAST LANGTON

Bell Inn
Main Street, LE16 7TW
🕓 11.30-2.30, 7 (6 Fri & Sat)-11; 12-4, 7-10.30 Sun
☎ (01858) 545278
Greene King IPA, Abbot; Langton Caudle Bitter, Bowler Strong Ale; seasonal beers guest beers Ⓖ
This 17th-century listed building is at the heart of Leicestershire's hunting country. A pretty walled garden, very low beams and an open log fire all add to its appeal. Quality food, produced from local ingredients, is freshly prepared each session, offering anything from a light bite to a banquet. Should you wish to extend your stay, B&B accommodation is provided in en-suite bedrooms. Langton Brewery, which started up in 1999, is situated in buildings behind the inn. ♨Q❀☎◗P

GUMLEY

Bell Inn
2 Main Street, LE16 7RU
🕓 12-3, 6-11; 12-3, (closed eve) Sun
☎ (0116) 279 2476
Bateman XB; Everards Tiger; Greene King IPA; guest beers Ⓗ
Early 19th-century free house, popular with local rural and commuting urban clientele. Cricketing artefacts decorate the entrance hall, while pictures of fox hunting scenes hang in the bar and restaurant. The beamed interior comprises an L-shaped bar and a no-smoking restaurant, serving an extensive menu. Behind the pub lies a large patio garden, but please note this is not for the use of children or dogs. ♨Q❀◗♣P

HATHERN

Dew Drop
49 Loughborough Road, LE12 5HY
🕓 12-2, 6-11; 12-3, 7-11 Sat; 12-3, 7-10.30 Sun
☎ (01509) 842438
Hardys & Hansons Mild, Bitter, seasonal beers Ⓗ
Long-established, traditional two-roomed pub on the main A6 through Hathern. A friendly local, it stocks a good selection of malt whiskies. It fields dominoes and darts teams. Regular bus services run from Loughborough. ♨Q❀▣♣P

HEMINGTON

Jolly Sailor
21 Main Street, DE74 2RB
🕓 11.30-2.30, 4.30-11; 11-11 Sat; 12-10.30 Sun
website: www.midlandspubs.co.uk/leicestershire/jollysailor
Draught Bass; Everards Beacon; Greene King Abbot; Marston's Pedigree; M&B Mild; guest beers Ⓗ
Small, friendly, village pub that started life as a farmhouse, before being converted some time around the mid-19th century.

Both of the heavily-timbered rooms are warmed by real fires in winter, the exposed beams are festooned with a collection of brass blow lamps. As well as two changing guest beers, Stowford Press cider is available with other real ciders making guest appearances in summer. There is also an extensive range of malt whiskies. A restaurant has been created from a former sitting room and is open Friday and Saturday evening; lunches are served Tuesday–Saturday. ♨Q❀◑▷ ⅏ ♣ ⬤P

HINCKLEY

Railway Hotel
Station Road, LE10 1AP
✪ 12-11; 11-3.30, 7-11 Sat; 12-3.30, 7-10.30 Sun
☎ (01455) 615285
Banks's Original; Marston's Bitter, Pedigree Ⓗ
Opposite the station, this is a spacious, two-roomed, basic local, the bar is adorned with railway pictures. The comfortable lounge regularly hosts live music, while a conservatory houses a pool table and acts as the family area. A function room can be booked. Bed and breakfast is also available.
Q☎❀🛏◀⇆♣P

HOSE

Black Horse
21 Bolton Lane, LE14 4JE OS734294
✪ 12-2 (not Mon & Tue), 6-11; 12-4, 7-10.30 Sun
☎ (01949) 860336
Draught Bass; Castle Rock Farriers Gold; Everards Home Bitter; guest beers Ⓗ
Traditional pub where the carpeted lounge features beams and a brass ornamental brick fireplace. Pictures and blackboard menus surround a wooden corner bar. The unspoilt public bar has a tiled floor, wooden furniture, mirrors and a brick fireplace. Current ales are shown on a blackboard. A wood-panelled restaurant, with an embellished fireplace and rustic artefacts, serves a menu based on local produce.
♨Q❀◑▷⅏⬤Å♣P⅊

Rose & Crown
43 Bolton Lane, LE14 4JE OS734295
✪ 12-2.30 (not Mon-Wed), 7 (5 Fri; 6.30 Sat)-11; 12-3, 7.30-10.30 Sun
☎ (01949) 860424
Greene King IPA, Abbot; guest beers Ⓗ
The stone bar divides the area into two distinct sections, each features beams and a stone fireplace. The comfortable lounge leads to a separate restaurant area, the bar has a dartboard and a pool table. A patio and large, attractive garden are popular in summer. Up to five ales are served, always including a mild. Note the low prices.
♨❀◑▷⅏Å♣P

HUNCOTE

Red Lion
Main Street, LE9 3AU
✪ 12-2.30 (not Mon-Tue), 5-11; 12-11 Sat; 12-10.30 Sun
☎ (0116) 286 2233 website: www.red-lion.biz
Everards Beacon, Tiger; guest beer Ⓗ
Built in 1892, the Red Lion is a friendly locals' pub with beamed ceilings throughout. It has a cosy lounge with a wooden fireplace and a traditional log fire.

There is a bar area with adjoining dining room and a separate pool room. The sizeable garden has picnic tables and a children's play section. The pub serves good value home-cooked lunches – meals are not offered on Saturday or Monday. Long alley skittles can be played by prior arrangement.
♨❀◑⊟♣P⅊

ILLSTON ON THE HILL

Fox & Goose
Main Street, LE7 9EG (off B6047, near Billesdon)
✪ 12-2.30 (not Mon or Tue), 5.30 (7-Mon)-11; 12-2.30, 7-10.30 Sun
☎ (0116) 259 6340
Everards Beacon, Tiger, Original; guest beer Ⓗ
A gem: a cosy village pub with a timeless feel, displaying a fascinating collection of local mementoes and hunting memorabilia. In 1997, when structural work was needed, every item on the walls was photographed and later returned to its exact place. That's how unchanged it is! Popular annual events include a conker championship, onion-growing competition and fundraising auction for local charities. The pub is tucked away, but well worth seeking out.
♨Q❀♣♠

KEGWORTH

Red Lion
24 High Street, DE74 2DA
✪ 11-11; 12-10.30 Sun
☎ (01509) 672466
Adnams Bitter; Banks's Original; Courage Directors; Greene King Abbot; guest beers Ⓗ
Partly dating from the 15th century, this central pub has three bars and a no-smoking family room. A special feature at the bar is a range of Polish and Ukrainian vodkas, as well as a good selection of malt whiskies and up to four guest beers. Petanque is a popular game, with five courts available; the pub also boasts a skittle alley and two darts rooms. The large garden, with a children's play area, makes a good vantage point for viewing aircraft approaching East Midlands Airport. Evening meals are served weekdays, 5.30–8; no food is available on Sunday. ♨Q❀◑▷♣⬤P

LEICESTER

Ale Wagon
27 Rutland Street, LE1 1RE
✪ 11-11; 12-3, 7-10.30 Sun
☎ (0116) 262 3330 website: www.alewagon.co.uk
Beer range varies Ⓗ
A real local atmosphere pervades the 1930s interior of this pub run by the Hoskins family. It boasts an original oak staircase, and tiled and parquet floors in its two rooms, with a central bar. It is popular with rugby fans and ale drinkers visiting Leicester. ♨⊟⇆♣⅊

Criterion
44 Millstone Lane, LE1 5JN
✪ 12-3, 5.30-11; 12-11 Fri & Sat; 12-10.30 Sun
☎ (0116) 262 5410
website: www.swanandrushes.co.uk
Hardy & Hansons Bitter; Oakham JHB; guest beers Ⓗ
Friendly, modern, city-centre pub designed for comfort and to store, display and serve a wide range of the world's finest beers. The

front bar features darts and bar billiards, while the lounge is dominated by a long, dark, gleaming bar where you are encouraged to linger and gaze at the six fridges packed with continental special beers. The changing range of six beers expands to 12 on festival weekends. Home-baked, Italian-style pizzas are a house speciality. ◐❶🏠♣P🚲🚬

Globe

43 Silver Street, LE1 5EU
(300 yds from clock tower)
☼ 11-11; 12-10.30 Sun
☎ (0116) 262 9819

Everards Beacon, Tiger, Original; guest beers Ⓗ

City-centre pub, that earned the local CAMRA Pub of the Year title in 1977 for being Everards' first pub to return to a full real ale range, after seven years as keg only. Major renovations were carried out in 2000, moving the bar to the centre of the pub and creating four drinking areas. The yard was incorporated into the pub and the snug and gas lighting retained. A room is available for meetings – used for Leicester CAMRA's first-ever meeting in 1974, their 25th anniversary in 1999 and for regular branch meetings. Guest beers come from Everards Old English Ale Club. Meals are served from 12–7. ◐🏠&

Hat & Beaver

60 Highcross Street, LE1 4NN
☼ 12-11; 12-10.30 Sun
☎ (0116) 262 2157

Hardys & Hansons Mild, Bitter, Ye Olde Trip Ale Ⓗ

Basic, two-roomed local with a relaxed atmosphere, one of Leicester's few remaining traditional pubs. It has a TV in the bar and on certain evenings, a table skittles game in the lounge. Well-filled, good value cobs are usually available at lunchtime and early evening. It is handy for the Shires shopping centre nearby. ♣

Leicester Gateway

52 Gateway Street, LE2 7DP (near Leicester Royal Infirmary and De Montfort University)
☼ 11-11; 12-10.30 Sun
☎ (0116) 255 7319

Beer range varies Ⓗ

Friendly, air-conditioned local, a converted hosiery factory, frequented by nearby infirmary and university staff and students. Close to both Leicester City football and rugby grounds, it supports sporting fixtures. Owned by Tynemill, it stocks usually up to six real ales from Castle Rock, and guests, plus a range of British and continental bottled beers and an occasional summer cider. Home-cooked food, on a varied menu, including vegetarian choices is available 12–9 on weekdays and 12–6 on Saturday and Sunday; a Sunday carvery is offered. ◐&♣🚲

Old Horse

198 London Road, LE2 1ND (opp. Victoria Park)
☼ 11-11; 12-10.30 Sun
☎ (0116) 254 8384

Everards Beacon, Tiger, Original Ⓗ

Large, open-plan pub with two smaller adjoining rooms to main area, one with a log fire. A 10-minute uphill walk along London Road from the station, it stands opposite Leicester's major open space,

Victoria Park. A courtyard to the rear houses an aviary with four owls and leads to a substantial garden. The impressive flower baskets and herb garden won the pub the Everards Spencer Memorial 2002 award for the class. A large dining area and conservatory complete the facilities here. Meals are served Monday–Saturday 12–9, and 12–4 on Sunday. 🛏🚂◐&🚲♣P🚬

Swan & Rushes

19 Infirmary Square, LE2 5WR (on Oxford St)
☼ 12-11; 12-10.30 Sun
☎ (0116) 233 9167
website: www.swanandrushes.co.uk

Hardys & Hansons Bitter; Oakham JHB; guest beers Ⓗ

Triangular, comfortable, two-bar 1930s boozer, now a shrine to great beer from Britain and beyond. Between five and seven real ales usually feature, including a mild. Four imported draughts and over 100 top-rated bottled beers, mainly from Belgium and Germany, are also available. Occasional beer festivals and interesting breweriana add to the appeal. Cheddar Valley cider is stocked. Close to Leicester's rugby and football grounds, it can be busy before major games. 🚂◐🏠🚲♣🍴🚬

Vaults

1 Wellington Street, LE1 6HH
☼ 5 (12 Fri & Sat)-11 (10.30 Mon); 12-3, 7-10.30 Sun
☎ (0116) 255 5506 website: www.the-vaults.co.uk

Brewster's Hophead; guest beers Ⓗ

Small cellar bar with cheery atmosphere, a genuine free house only selling beers from micro-breweries, with seven constantly changing ales. The pub has now sold over 3,000 different beers since opening in 1997. Awarded Leicester CAMRA Pub of the Year 2002, it is a rare town outlet for real cider, three are usually available. Live music on Saturday afternoon means it can get quite busy. An entry charge is sometimes imposed on Sunday evening for live bands. 🚲♣🍴🚬

LOUGHBOROUGH

Albion

Canal Bank, LE11 1QA
☼ 11-3 (4 Sat), 6-11; 12-3, 7-10.30 Sun
☎ (01509) 213952

Brains Dark; Robinson's Best Bitter; guest beers Ⓗ

Tranquil canalside pub, with a bar, darts room and a quiet lounge. There are moorings outside the pub for boats. The canal bank or patio, which houses an aviary, are ideal for summer drinking. The lounge is designated a no-smoking area until 8pm. Home-cooked food is served lunchtime and early evening. Car parking is available, but take care when driving along the wide towpath to the pub. The wicked Hathern Albion Special is a house beer. 🛏Q🚂◐&🚲♣P🚬

Swan in the Rushes

21 The Rushes, LE11 5BE
☼ 11-11; 12-10.30 Sun
☎ (01509) 217014

Archers Golden; Castle Rock Rushes Gold; Tetley Bitter; guest beers Ⓗ

This traditional pub (owned by Tynemill) has three rooms (one no-smoking) and is popular with the locals for its constantly changing range of six guest beers which always includes a mild. You can be entertained by musicians in the function room most weeks. Two beer festivals are staged each year, one during the spring and the other during the autumn, when 30-plus beers are available. A limited range of continental beers is stocked, both draught and bottled, plus a good selection of malt whiskies. All food is freshly cooked; evening meals are served Monday–Friday.

🏠Q♿🛏️🏮🌳◖❶🚲🍴♣♠Ｐ✠

Tap & Mallet
36 Nottingham Road, LE11 1EU
✪ 12-2.30, 5-11; 11.30-11 Sat; 12-10.30 Sun
☎ (01509) 210028
Church End Gravediggers; Courage Best Bitter; Marston's Pedigree; guest beers Ⓗ

Genuine free house, located between the town centre and the mainline railway station. Up to five guest beers are usually available, most of them from micro-breweries, often local. Church End's Gravediggers Mild may sometimes be replaced by a mild from another micro-brewery. Erdinger Wiessbier is available on draught. There is only one bar/lounge, however the lounge can be partitioned off for private functions. The pub fields several darts teams, and there is a pool table in the bar area. At the rear is a pleasant walled garden with an extensive lawn, plus a children's play section and a pets' corner.

🏠Q🏮♣♠❶

LUTTERWORTH

Unicorn Inn
29 Church Street, LE17 4AE
(off A426 on one-way system near church and library)
✪ 10.30-3, 5-11; 10.30-11 Fri & Sat; 12-10.30 Sun
☎ (01455) 552486
Draught Bass; Greene King IPA; M&B Brew XI; Robinson's Best Bitter Ⓗ

Corner pub near the church, with a black and white frontage and award-winning window boxes. The entrance lobby still has the old off-sales hatch. The busy bar, with darts and skittles, has wall benches and plenty of tables and a well-stocked trophy cabinet near the fire. The small, comfortable lounge with old local photographs is separated from the no-smoking dining area by a central fireplace. The good value lunchtime meals, including daily specials, are also available in the bar. 🏠🏮🌳◖❶◖❶♣Ｐ

MARKET BOSWORTH

Olde Red Lion Hotel
1 Park Street, CV13 0LL
✪ 11-2.30, 5.30-11; 10-3, 5.30-11 Wed; 11-11 Fri; 10-11 Sat; 11-10.30 Sun
☎ (01455) 291713
website: www.theredlion.dabsol.co.uk
Banks's Original, Bitter; Camerons Bitter; Greene King Abbot; Marston's Pedigree; Theakston Old Peculier; guest beers Ⓗ

Popular, friendly pub, near the old market square, with a large, beamed bar and dining area. There is an open fire in winter. The range of beers, including guests, is extensive. A varied choice of food is offered, daily from 12–2 and from 6–8.30 Tuesday–Saturday. The accommodation here is reasonably priced, with characterful bedrooms, two with four-poster beds. It is an ideal base for exploring. Visit the site of

the Battle of Bosworth, where Richard III was killed in 1485, Bosworth Water Park and Mallory Park motorsport circuit.
🏠🏮🛏️◖❶♣Ｐ✠

MKT HARBOROUGH (Little Bowden)

Cherry Tree
Church Walk, Kettering Road, LE16 8AE
✪ 12-2.30, 5-11; 12-11 Fri & Sat; 12-10.30 Sun
☎ (01858) 463525
Everards Beacon, Tiger, Original Ⓗ

This spacious pub is characterised by low beams and a thatched roof. Drinkers and diners can choose from many small alcoves and seating areas. The pub is actually situated in Little Bowden, but is very much part of the Market Harborough community. A beer festival is held outside over August bank holiday weekend. Meals are served at lunchtime (daily) and from 7–9, Tuesday–Saturday. 🏮◖❶🚲♣✠

MEDBOURNE

Nevill Arms
12 Waterfall Way, LE16 8EE
✪ 12-2.30, 6-11; 12-3, 7-10.30 Sun
☎ (01858) 565288
Adnams Bitter; Fuller's London Pride; Greene King Abbot; guest beers Ⓗ

The initials MGN over the door are those of Captain Nevill, who was heir to the nearby Holt estate when this former coaching inn was rebuilt in 1863, after the original building was destroyed by fire in 1856. Folklore suggests that a spark caused the fire after the village blacksmith wagered he could support an anvil on his chest while a horseshoe was forged upon it. A warm welcome awaits in the heavily-beamed bar with its large inglenook. 🏠🏮🛏️◖❶♣Ｐ

MELTON MOWBRAY

Boat
57 Burton Street, LE13 1AF
✪ 5 (12 Sat)-11; 12-10.30 Sun
☎ (01664) 560518
Burtonwood Bitter, Top Hat; guest beer (occasional) Ⓗ

Dating from around the 17th century, the pub's name was originally the Fox & Hounds, however, when the Melton & Oakham navigation canal was built during the mid-1700s the name was changed to the Boat. The basin where the barges unloaded, which was next to the pub, disappeared in 1893 when the railway came to Melton. The walls are oak-panelled throughout and have remained unchanged since 1958. Photographs and prints of Melton with canal memorabilia adorn the walls, while various water jugs hang from the beamed ceiling. A quiet, very traditional, friendly local with a great atmosphere; petanque is played here.
🏠Q🏮🐾♣

Crown Inn
10 Burton Street, LE13 1AE
✪ 11-3, 7-11; 11-11 Sat; 12-4, 7-10.30 Sun
☎ (01664) 564682
Everards Beacon, Tiger, Original; guest beer Ⓗ

Sociable, two-roomed town pub, run by a long-serving landlord. The lounge is designated a no-smoking area when lunches

are being served. Popular with office workers and shoppers at lunchtime, it attracts all ages in the evening. Note the old photographs of Melton Mowbray around the walls. Close to the station and town centre, regular bus services run from Leicester, Loughborough, Grantham, Nottingham and Stamford.
🏚Q🛏🌝🌓◖❶◗🫱♣♠

Mash Tub
58 Nottingham Street, LE13 1NW
🕐 11-11; 12-10.30 Sun
☎ (01664) 410051
Banks's Mansfield Dark Mild, Bitter; guest beers Ⓗ
The pub has a single multi-level room, with several well-defined seating areas. It has a local custom during the week, but attracts younger folk at weekends. It fields two well-established darts teams. The guest beer changes monthly; the cider is the award-winning Westons Old Rosie. ◖♣♠

MOUNTSORREL

Swan
10 Loughborough Road, LE12 7AT
🕐 12-11; 12-10.30 Sun
☎ (0116) 230 2340 website: www.jvf.co.uk/swan
Greene King Ruddles County; Theakston Best Bitter, XB, Old Peculier; guest beer Ⓗ
On the old A6, this pub dates back to the 1700s. It has a split-level bar with a stone floor, while the dining area has a polished wood floor. The secluded gardens reach down to the River Soar; no moorings are available here, but moorings for narrow boats are not far away. Low ceilings make it very cosy. The restaurant serves top quality home-cooked food to order; the menu changes each week. Booking is advised, particularly at weekends. 🏚Q🌝◖P

NEWBOLD

Cross Keys
9 Worthington Lane, LE67 8PJ
🕐 5.30 (5 Mon; 11 Sat)-11; 12-10.30 Sun
☎ (01530) 224799
Greene King Old Speckled Hen; Marston's Pedigree; Wells Bombardier Ⓗ
Traditional village local built around 1900, it has two rooms, one a bar with dartboard and pool table, the other is a lounge. There is a small restaurant area attached. The pub fields two pool teams. There is also an outdoor seating area. This pub is an ideal base for walkers and cyclists. A limited daytime bus service runs to Loughborough, Ashby and Coalville. 🏚Q🌝🫱◖❶♣♠P

OADBY

Cow & Plough
Stoughton Farm Park, Gartree Road, LE2 2FB (close to BUPA Hospital)
🕐 5-7 (12-10 Sat) winter; 12-3, 5-10 (12-10 Sat) summer; 12-4, 7-10.30 (all year) Sun
☎ (0116) 272 0852 website: www.steamin-billy.co.uk
Fuller's London Pride; Greene King Abbot; Steamin' Billy Scrum Down Mild, Bitter, Skydiver Ⓗ
Housed in a converted barn with a no-smoking conservatory, this pub is decked out with breweriana, pub mirrors and signs. Pictures of many of Leicester's historic pubs hang on the walls. Twice East Midlands CAMRA Pub of the Year, it regularly holds

beer festivals in the conservatory and function rooms. It is home to Steamin' Billy beers, named after the owner's Jack Russell, who features in the logo. Steamin' Billy ales are brewed under licence by Grainstore. Guest beers change daily and Westons cider is sold. Q🛏🌝◖❶❹♣♠P🫱

OSGATHORPE

Storey Arms
41 Main Street, LE12 9TA
🕐 12-3, 7.30-11; 12-3, 7.30-10.30 Sun
☎ (01530) 224166
Marston's Pedigree; guest beer Ⓗ
Traditional country pub built on the site of a former inn which local knowledge remembers as being the Cock & Mitten. It has a 1960s style bar and lounge. The pub fields both men's and ladies' darts teams and holds popular quiz nights. Barbecues are hosted in summer and a beer festival features in mid-September. Occasionally on Saturday evening live music is staged for the entertainment of regulars. There is a very limited daytime bus service here. 🏚🌝♣♠P

PINWALL

Red Lion
Main Road, CV9 3NB (on B4116, 1 mile from A5)
🕐 11-11; 12-10.30 Sun
☎ (01827) 712223
Draught Bass; Marston's Pedigree; Taylor Landlord; guest beers Ⓗ
Very rural, cosy locals' pub on the B4116 about a mile from the A5. It is one of only five or six buildings that make Pinwall. The village is not actually shown on most maps. The Red Lion incorporates a restaurant and nine-room hotel, these do not spoil the character of this pub. Room prices may be negotiated at weekends. Usually two guest beers are on tap. No evening meals are served on Sunday. 🏚Q🌝🫱◖P

QUORN

White Hart ⊘
32 High Street, LE12 8DT
🕐 12-2, 5-11; 12-11 Fri & Sat; 12-10.30 Sun
☎ (01509) 412704
Caledonian Deuchars IPA; Greene King IPA; Taylor Landlord; Tetley Burton Ale; guest beers Ⓗ
This pub dates from 1690 and is the oldest in Quorn. However, over the years it has been modernised and little evidence remains to show its true age. Although open plan, there are three distinct areas, all with open wood-burning fires; one section doubles as a dining area. Apart from the usual pub food, an extensive vegetarian menu is available and all food is freshly prepared on the premises. Lunches are served 12–1.30, Monday–Saturday and 12–3.30 on Sunday. There is an illuminated outdoor seating area and additional seating near the petanque courts, where you can watch or play this game. A regular bus service runs to Loughborough and Leicester. 🏚Q🌝◖♣♠P

RATBY

Plough Inn
6 Burrough Road, LE6 0XZ
🕐 11.30-3, 6-11; 11.30-11 Sat; 12-10.30 Sun

☎ (0116) 239 2103
Banks's Original, Bitter; Marston's Bitter, Pedigree; guest beer Ⓗ

Tucked away off a quiet side road, in the centre of the village, this 600-year-old pub comprises a cosy, low, beamed snug which leads into a large bar and dining area. There is a spacious restaurant/function room off the bar. The sizeable garden and smaller terraced drinking area are pleasant in summer. While very much a locals' pub, it is also popular with diners. The pub won Leicester CAMRA's first ever Pub of the Month award in 1978. ▲Q❀◑♣P

SEWSTERN

Blue Dog Inn
46 Main Street, NG33 5RQ
◑ 6-11; 12-3, 6-11 Sat; 12-10.30 Sun
☎ (01476) 860097
Boddingtons Bitter; Fuller's London Pride; guest beer Ⓗ

Quiet, friendly country pub set in the centre of an unspoilt village on the Viking Way. Cyclists, walkers and dogs are welcome. This listed, stone building dates from the 1650s. The comfortable, quiet snug bar has a real fire, old village photographs and a reading corner. The large main public bar has pool, darts and another real fire. Other games include shove-ha'penny, carom, and devil among the tailors. There is a small rear garden behind the petanque piste, and a sunny patio to the front. An annual beer festival is held on May Day bank holiday. Camping is possible, by arrangement. ▲Q❀◑⊟♣P

SHAWELL

White Swan Inn
Main Street, LE17 6AG (signed off jct A5/A426)
◑ 7-11; closed Mon; 12-2.30, (closed eve) Sun
☎ (01788) 860357
Greene King IPA, Ruddles County, Abbot Ⓗ

Classic, welcoming village pub with an unusual layout. Parts of the building date back to the 17th century. The wood-panelled bar has several plush seating areas, complete with real fires. An excellent restaurant serves à la carte meals and Sunday roasts. The bar area can get busy and noisy in the evening when the local skittles teams are playing. Benches are provided in front of the pub for summer drinking. Accommodation comprises 24 guest rooms. ▲Q❀⊭♣P

SOMERBY

Old Brewery Inn
39 High Street, LE14 2PZ
◑ 12-2.30, 6.30-11; 12-10.30 Sun
☎ (01664) 454777
Draught Bass; Bateman XXXB; Parish Special, Baz's Bonce Blower Ⓗ

Formerly the Three Crowns, this 15th-century pub was given by Sir Richard Sutton to Brasenose College, Oxford in 1508. At that time the pub was thatched, with stabling for hunting horses, a coach house and adjoining walled gardens. The pub has changed much, but remains a cosy place. The outbuildings have been in use by the Parish brewery since 1991. This brewery brewed the strongest beer in the world (23%

ABV). The strongest beer at the bar is Baz's Bonce Blower at 11% ABV, but you can obtain it bottled to take home. Note the unusual glass-topped well next to the bar. Live music is performed every Saturday. No food is served on Sunday evening. ▲Q❀◑♣P

Stilton Cheese
High Street, LE14 2QB
◑ 12-3, 6-11; 12-3, 7-10.30 Sun
☎ (01664) 454394
Marston's Pedigree; Tetley Bitter; guest beers Ⓗ

Late 16th-century pub that is built from the local ironstone as are most of the older buildings in this village. Beware of the low, beamed ceiling and door. Note the wide range of pump labels fixed to the beams. There are two rooms, one is no-smoking. Real cider is always available; customers are looking forward to when a Somerby-produced cider will be available. This is a popular place for meals and it is advisable to book, particularly at weekends. There is a function room upstairs. ▲Q❀◑♣♣P⊬

SWINFORD

Chequers
High Street, LE17 6BL (by church)
◑ 12-2.30, 6 (7 Mon)-11; 12-3, 6-11 Sat; 12-3, 7-10.30 Sun
☎ (01788) 860318
Ansells Mild; Greene King IPA; guest beer Ⓗ

Within easy reach of the M1 and its interchange with the M6 and the A14, this traditional pub has a warm welcome and is family-friendly. Inside, is a pleasant wood floored bar area with a skittle table. Meals can be enjoyed in the dining section. The spacious garden with extensive play area is popular in summer. In July, the car park is given over to a large marquee and a small beer festival takes place. Close to the village is the 16th-century Stanford Hall. ❀◑♣P

SWITHLAND

Griffin Inn
174 Main Street, LE12 8TJ
◑ 11-2.30, 5.30-11; 11-11 Sat; 12-10.30 Sun
☎ (01509) 890535
Adnams Bitter; Everards Beacon, Tiger, Original; guest beer Ⓗ

Friendly local comprising three comfortable rooms and a small games/family area with long alley skittles. The pub has a regular Wednesday night quiz and murder mystery evenings. Set in the heart of Charnwood Forest, there are many cycling and walking routes nearby. Guest beers are from Everards Old English Ale Club. Meals are served from 12–2.30 and 6–10 on weekdays, and all day on Saturday and Sunday. ▲Q❀◑♣♣P

THORNTON

Bricklayer's Arms
213 Main Street, LE67 1AH
◑ 12-3 (not Mon), 6 (6.30 Mon)-11; 12-11 Sat; 12-10.30 Sun
☎ (01530) 230808
Everards Tiger; guest beer Ⓗ

Village pub partly built in the 16th century, and refurbished in early 2003. It has, in its time, served as a surgery, baby clinic, coroner's court and mortuary. There is a

255

cosy, beamed bar, a larger dining room-cum-lounge, and small lounge with TV and darts. The pleasant garden has furniture, a children's play area, ducks, rabbits and a view over Thornton Reservoir. No food is served in the larger dining room after 9pm when it becomes a lounge area; no meals are offered on Monday or Sunday evenings. A chilled version of Everards Tiger is also available. 🏠🌣◑♿♣P

THORPE SATCHVILLE

Fox
13 Main Street, LE14 2DQ
✪ 6.30-11 Mon; 12-11 Tue-Sat; 12-10.30 Sun
☎ (01664) 840257
John O'Gaunt Robin a Tiptoe, Duke of Lancaster; Mansfield Cask Ale; guest beer Ⓗ
This pub is essentially the tap for the John O'Gaunt Brewery, and is surprisingly modern, given its rural location. It was built in the 1930s and has a lounge, bar and dining area. It fields cribbage, darts, petanque, pool and skittles teams. A friendly village local, it caters for all ages. It is popular with walkers and cyclists. The village has a limited daytime bus service from Melton Mowbray. 🏠🌣◑♿♣♦P

WALCOTE

Black Horse
25 Lutterworth Road, LE17 4JU (on A4304, 1 mile from M1 jct 20)
✪ 12-2 (not Mon-Thu or Sat), 6.30 (5.30 Fri)-11; 12-3, 6.30-10.30 Sun
☎ (01455) 552684
Greene King Abbot; Oakham JHB; Taylor Landlord; guest beers Ⓗ
Single-bar free house, well worth the one mile detour from the M1 motorway (junction 20), but note it is closed most lunchtimes. As well as the regular beers, two guests are sourced from independent breweries. Home-cooked Thai food is a speciality here. Lunches are served Friday and Sunday. 🏠🌣◑P

WHITWICK

Forest Rock ⊘
Leicester Road, LE67 5GQ
✪ 12-4 (not Mon-Fri), 6-11; 12-4, 7-10.30 Sun
☎ (01530) 831495
Marston's Pedigree; Wells Bombardier; guest beers Ⓗ
Formerly an hotel dating from the 17th century, and built from the locally quarried pink granite, it hides its age well. It became solely a pub in 1830. The original three rooms have been opened out in to a single room with three distinct areas, one of which has been designated no-smoking. Brass and copperware adorn the walls along with old pictures. The pub holds a regular quiz on Sunday. It is an uphill walk from the nearest bus stop about 1,200 yards away, where you can catch buses to Leicester or Coalville. 🏠Q🌣❀✄

Three Horshoes ☆
11 Leicester Road, LE67 5GN
✪ 11-3, 6.30-11; 12-2, 7-10.30 Sun
☎ (01530) 837311
Draught Bass; M&B Mild Ⓗ
This unspoilt, traditional ale house, known locally as Polly's, is listed on CAMRA's

National Pub Inventory. Its basic bar is popular with locals, while the tiny smoke room is furnished with pews and decorated with commemorative plates which record this area's involvement with the coal mining industry, now sadly defunct. There are regular bus services from Coalville, Leicester and Loughborough. 🏠Q🖼♣⊘

Rutland

BARROWDEN

Exeter Arms
28 Main Street, LE15 8EQ
✪ 12-2, 6-11; 12-3, 7-10.30 Sun
☎ (01572) 747247
Blencowe Beach Boys, seasonal beers; guest beers Ⓗ
In an idyllic setting, the pub looks down over the village green and duckpond, with southerly views across the Welland Valley to the good walking area of Wakerley Woods. Blencowe Brewery is situated in a barn at the end of the garden. The pub has a fine stone exterior, under Collyweston roof tiles. Inside, there is one long room with a dining area at one end and the bar and drinking area at the other. Live music is performed regularly. The use of mobile phones is prohibited inside. Cider is available at the spring bank holiday festival. Meals are available Tuesday–Saturday, plus Sunday lunch. Petanque is played. 🏠🌣✍◑♣P

BELTON IN RUTLAND

Sun Inn
24a Main Street, LE15 9LB (½ mile from A47)
✪ 12-2 (3 Sat), 6-11; 12-10.30 Sun
☎ (01572) 717227
Banks's Bitter; Marston's Pedigree Ⓗ
This compact, cosy pub is tucked away in a small, quiet village and is well worth the detour from the nearby A47, to visit. Originally a Phipp's pub, until swallowed up by Watneys in the early 1970s, it is on three levels, one of which is the games room. One or two minor changes have been made since the 1960s, it remains a typical country local, unspoilt by progress. Belton in Rutland is the village name to distinguish it from the Belton some 20 miles away in Leicestershire.
🏠Q♣♣

BRAUNSTON IN RUTLAND

Old Plough Inn
2 Church Street, LE15 8QY
✪ 11.30-3, 6 (5 Fri)-11; 11.30-11 Sat; 12-10.30 Sun
☎ (01572) 722714
Draught Bass; Greene King IPA; guest beers Ⓗ
Country pub with a public bar, a cosy, low, beamed lounge, conservatory restaurant and a patio garden. Guest beers are usually chosen after recommendation by regular customers. Not all the pub's spirits are bottled; footsteps and slamming doors have been heard long after closing time. Regular jazz evenings are held. The village name is Braunston in Rutland to distinguish it from the large housing estate in Leicester. Usually, two guest beers are on tap. Meals are served Monday–Saturday 12–2.30, 6.30–9 and 12–9 on Sunday.
🏠Q🌣✍◑♿P

CALDECOTT

Castle Inn

Main Street, LE16 8RT (on B6003 to
Rockingham) OS867934
☼ 12-3, 6-11; 12-3, (closed eve) Sun
☎ (01536) 770641
Grainstore Triple B; Taylor Landlord; guest beers Ⓗ
This free house takes its name from
Rockingham Castle which nestles on the
opposite side of the Welland Valley. The
pub offers accommodation at the Castle
Sleeper, situated across the road on the site
of the former Rockingham railway station
on the LNWR line from Rugby to Stamford
(opened 1850, closed 1966). The pub's
ambience and character have been created
by local craftsmen during refurbishment in
1998. ⚏Q❀⌂⍋◑☕P⌫

OAKHAM

Grainstore

Station Approach, LE15 6RE
☼ 11-2.30, 5-11; 11-11 Fri & Sat; 12-10.30 Sun
☎ (01572) 770065
**Grainstore Rutland Panther, Cooking, Triple B,
Steamin Billy Bitter, Ten Fifty, seasonal beers** Ⓗ
This pub is on the ground floor of a former
Victorian railway grainstore, the tap for the
Grainstore Brewery on the upper floor. The
large bar area features five large cast-iron
columns supporting the floor above. Two
sets of handpumps are in use, one set with
swan necks, the other without. Third-pint
sampling glasses are available. The station,
on the Peterborough–Leicester line is next
door. There is a good selection of Belgian
bottled beer. Filled baguettes are usually
sold Monday–Saturday lunchtime. Live
music is staged twice monthly.
Q❀❧☕☕♣P⌷

White Lion

30 Melton Road, LE15 6AY
☼ 11.30-3 (not Mon), 6-11; 12-3, 7-10.30 Sun
☎ (01572) 724844
Draught Bass; Worthington's Bitter; guest beers Ⓗ
This 18th-century former coaching inn is
situated near the level crossing gates not far
from the station. Coaches once passed into
the back yard and this makes an impressive
entrance to the pub. The interior consists of
one large room at two different levels; the
higher level close to the entrance being a
drinking and dining area, the lower level
down a few steps containing the bar and
being primarily a drinking area. There is one
guest beer in winter and two guests are
available in summer. Meals are served daily
except Monday lunch and Sunday evening.
⚏Q❀⌂◑☕♣P

WING

Cuckoo

3 Top Street, LE15 8SE
☼ 11.30-2.30 (not Tue), 6.30-11; 12-4, 7-10.30
(12-10.30 summer) Sun
☎ (01572) 737340
Beer range varies Ⓗ
Unspoilt, 17th-century free house in a
village of limestone buildings. The interior
is beamed and has two distinct drinking
areas, one in which food is served, the other
a games area. In common with many other
pubs in Rutland, there is a petanque piste
with a team in one of the thriving league
divisions. There are four guest beers always
on offer, all bitters and mostly from micro-
breweries. Nearby is a rare turf maze used by
kneeling penitents in medieval times. No
food is available on Tuesday.
⚏Q❀◑Å♣P

257

LINCOLNSHIRE

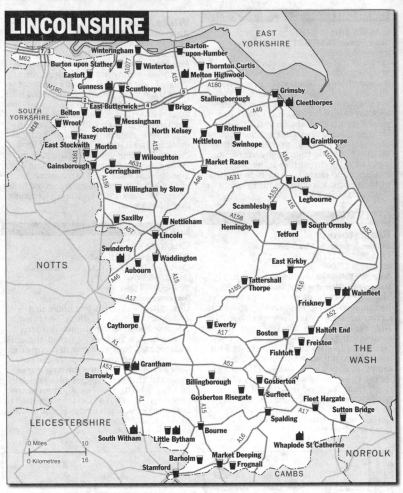

AUBOURN

Royal Oak
Royal Oak Lane, LN1 3PS (2 miles S of A46)
🕐 12-3, 7-11; 12-3, 7-10.30 Sun
☎ (01522) 788291
Bateman XB; Greene King Abbot; Tetley Bitter; guest beers Ⓗ
Delightful country local in a pleasing village, popular with both locals and people from far and wide who come to try the excellent ales. The guest beers usually include one from a local micro-brewery. Fine food is served at lunchtime and in the evening. The large garden is used for a wide range of functions. Be sure to go the right way around the one-way system.
🏚🏃😋🕪🍴♣P

BARHOLM

Five Horseshoes
Main Street, PE9 4RA (end of short lane, off sharp bend in main street)
🕐 5 (12.30 Sat)-11; 12-10.30 Sun
☎ (01778) 560238
Adnams Bitter; Oakham JHB; guest beers Ⓗ
This 18th-century, three-roomed pub, constructed of locally-quarried Barnack stone, can be difficult to find. Situated in a very quiet hamlet, open fires greet visitors on chilly nights. Outside is a creeper-covered patio and large, attractive gardens with a bouncy castle for children in summer and a petanque terrain. It concentrates on selling beer, with four guests always on offer, frequently strong beers, and normally sourced from micro-breweries. An occasional house beer is brewed by Rooster's. 🏚Q🏃😋Å♣P

BARROWBY

White Swan ✓
High Road, NG32 1BH (½ mile from A1 and A52)
🕐 11.30-11; 12-10.30 Sun
☎ (01476) 562375
Adnams Bitter, Broadside; guest beers Ⓗ
On the main road, this pleasant village local is the only pub in Barrowby. It always keeps four real ales, usually two from Adnams. The pub appeals to all tastes, having two distinctly different bars; the comfortable lounge is quiet, but in the larger public bar there is music and a pool table, plus games (darts, cribbage and dominoes). The pleasant old garden has apple trees, a swing and bench seating. Q😋🕪♣P

BARTON-UPON-HUMBER

Wheatsheaf Hotel
3 Holydyke, DN18 5PS (opp. market place)
☼ 11-3.30, 6-11; 11-11 Fri & Sat; 12-10.30 Sun
☎ (01652) 633175
John Smith's Bitter; Stones Bitter; Theakston Mild, Best Bitter; guest beers Ⓗ
Popular pub in the centre of Barton. One central bar serves a large lounge and bar area and a cosy snug; wood panels and beams feature throughout. The lounge is dominated by diners at lunchtime, but there is plenty of room for beer drinkers by the bar and in the snug. There are two regular guest beers, one rotated weekly and the other on a monthly basis. The pub has designated no-smoking areas in the lounge.
❀◖P✗

BELTON

Crown
Church Lane, Churchtown, DN9 1PA (off A161, behind church)
☼ 4 (12 Sat)-11; 12-10.30 Sun
☎ (01427) 872834
Glentworth seasonal beers; Marston's Pedigree; John Smith's Bitter; Theakston Best Bitter; guest beer (occasional) Ⓗ
Welcoming local, tucked away behind All Saints Church. A friendly welcome is guaranteed in this proper drinkers' pub. No food is served here, and no smooth beers. Glentworth beers have become a permanent fixture after they found favour with local drinkers of all ages. This local CAMRA Pub of the Season summer 2002 is worth seeking out. ♨❀♣P♖

BILLINGBOROUGH

Fortescue Arms
27 High Street, NG34 0QB
☼ 12-2.30, 6-11; 12-3, 7-10.30 Sun
☎ (01529) 240229
Bateman XB; Greene King IPA; Tetley Burton Ale Ⓗ
Fine, comfortable, country inn with olde-worlde charm, set in a village with spring wells and grand old buildings. Two restaurants serve excellent home-made food (booking advisable). Hanging baskets and tubs of shrubs and plants brighten three sides of the pub. Nearby is the site of Sempringham Abbey with a monument to Gwenllian, daughter of the Prince of Wales who was confined to the priory in the 12th century. Stone from the abbey was used to build parts of the inn. ♨Q❀◖⊟♣P

BOSTON

Ball House ✪
Wainfleet Road, PE21 9RL (on A52, 2 miles from centre)
☼ 11.30-3, 6.30-11; 12-3, 7-10.30 Sun
☎ (01205) 364478 website: www.the ballhouse.co.uk
Draught Bass; Bateman XB, XXXB; guest beer Ⓗ
Friendly pub, dating from the early 13th century, it is the oldest public house still to hold a justice licence within the Borough of Boston. The supposed site of a cannonball store for nearby Rochford Tower gives the pub its name. Award-winning floral displays feature in summer, when an enclosed play area is available. A wide-ranging menu offers meat, fish, poultry and locally-grown

vegetables; small adult portions can be ordered. ♨Q❀◖P

Coach & Horses ✪
86 Main Ridge, PE21 6SY
(100 yds E of John Adams Way)
☼ 5 (6 Fri)-11; 11-3, 7-11 Sat; 12-3, 7-10.30 Sun
☎ (01205) 362301
Bateman XB, XXXB Ⓗ
A friendly landlord and regulars, assure a warm welcome at this pub. This one-roomed hostelry fields thriving dominoes, pool and darts leagues. Handy for Boston United home fixtures, you need to get in early on match days. This pub is well worth the short walk from the centre to seek out the XXXB. ♨❀♣⊟

Cowbridge
Horncastle Road, PE22 7AX
(on B1183, N of town)
☼ 11-3, 6-11; 12-4, 7-10.30 Sun
☎ (01205) 362597
Everards Home Bitter; Greene King Old Speckled Hen; Theakston Mild; guest beers Ⓗ
This out-of-town pub is popular with drinkers and diners. Of its three bars, one has a no-nonsense drinking and darts environment, displaying a large collection of football scarves. The smaller lounge is very cosy with an open fire; this opens out into a restaurant which serves excellent freshly-cooked food. The pub is handy for Boston Golf Club. ♨❀◖⊟♿♣P

Eagle
West Street, PE21 8RE (near station)
☼ 11-11; 12-10.30 Sun
☎ (01205) 361116
Adnams Broadside; Banks's Bitter; Castle Rock Gold; Taylor Landlord; guest beers Ⓗ
Part of the Tynemill chain, this two-roomed pub has a friendly atmosphere. The small, comfortable lounge has an open fire in winter. The L-shaped bar houses a pool table and a large-screen for live sports events. On Thursday a free quiz is staged. Good value hot snacks are sold Monday–Saturday, 12–2. The pub stocks an ever-changing range of guest beers, with at least two on sale at all times and the regular Castle Rock Gold is rebadged as Golden Nugget; the cider comes from Biddenden or Stowford Press. ♨Q❀⊟≋♣●

Mill Inn
148 Spilsby Road, PE21 9QN (on A16)
☼ 11-11; 11.30-3, 5.30-11 Mon; 12-3.30, 5.30-10.30 Sun
☎ (01205) 352874
Bateman XB, XXXB; guest beers Ⓗ

INDEPENDENT BREWERIES

Bateman Wainfleet
Blue Bell Whaplode St Catherine
Blue Cow South Witham
DarkTribe Gunness
Donoghue Grainthorpe
Highwood Melton Highwood
Newby Wyke Little Bytham
Oldershaw Grantham
Poachers Swinderby
Riverside Wainfleet
Willy's Cleethorpes

Situated a short distance to the north of the town centre on the A16, this popular, welcoming public house is well worth seeking out. One unusual feature is the bar counter that is covered in old penny coins. The main bar leads to two dining areas where high quality, home-cooked food, using mainly local produce, is served.
🏠Q🌳🅒🕭 ⊟P

Ship Tavern
Custom House Lane, PE21 6HH
(off South Square, opp. quayside)
🕑 11-11; 12-10.30 Sun
☎ (01205) 358156
Bateman Mild, XB; Greene King IPA; guest beer 🅗
This town-centre pub has a traditional feel, comprising one large L-shaped room with an area for darts and pool. Seating is a mix of wooden pews, farmhouse tables and benches and upholstered seats. Breweriana abounds in this cosy pub. There is a small patio to the rear. No hot food is served, but pre-packed sandwiches are available.
🏠🌳🦶♣

BOURNE

Smith's
25 North Street, PE10 9AE
🕑 11-11; 12-10.30 Sun
☎ (01778) 426819 website: www.smithsofbourne.co.uk
Fuller's London Pride; Oakham JHB; guest beers 🅗
Opened in 2002, it was the Smith family grocery store for the previous 150 years, but had been a pub prior to that. The front of this three-storey Georgian building is listed and the fine Victorian shop sign is still in place. A front bar and a back bar are on the ground floor, while attractive rooms on ground and first floors stretch back some distance. Much thought and expense has been given to the refurbishment. 🏠🌳🦶🕭🅒

BRIGG

Black Bull
3 Wrawby Street, DN20 8JH
🕑 11-3 (4 Thu), 7-11; 11-11 Sat; 12-3, 7-10.30 Sun
☎ (01652) 652153
Highwood Tom Wood's Harvest Bitter; John Smith's Bitter; guest beers 🅗
Popular, town-centre pub with a homely feel, busy on market days (Thu and Sat). It usually stocks a regular beer from Highwood and an additional guest that constantly changes. The garden and car park are behind the pub, which is centrally situated for shoppers. Brigg is on the No. 909 bus route that serves Doncaster, Sheffield, Grimsby and Hull; the train service only operates on Saturday. 🌳🕭🚲♣P

BURTON UPON STATHER

Ferry House
Stather Road, DN15 9DJ (follow campsite signs)
🕑 7-11; 12-5, 7 (6 summer)-11 Sat; 12-10.30 Sun
☎ (01724) 721783
Beer range varies 🅗
Homely village pub, overlooking the River Trent; a large, single room with discrete drinking areas. Normally two guest beers are available, often from the local Highwood Brewery. Outdoor live music is staged during the summer months. Camping and caravanning facilities are available nearby.

Additional space has been created by a new lounge extension opening on to the river bank; perfect for watching the ships go by.
🌳🦶🅐♣P

CAYTHORPE

Red Lion
62 High Street, NG32 3DN (off A607)
🕑 12-3, 6-11; 11-11 Fri & Sat; 12-10.30 Sun
☎ (01400) 272632
Draught Bass; Fuller's London Pride; guest beers 🅗
The present landlord of this 400-year-old free house started refurbishment in 2001. The pub now boasts a large bar area, a 60-seater restaurant and an annexe for watching Sky Sports on a large-screen TV. It hosts a quiz every Wednesday evening and live music on the last Saturday of the month. One guest beer is usually from a local micro-brewery. The pub is situated on a regular bus route from Lincoln and Grantham. 🏠🌳🕭🅒 ⊟♣P

CLEETHORPES

Crow's Nest
Balmoral Road, DN35 9ND
🕑 11-3, 7-11; 12-4, 7-10.30 Sun
☎ (01472) 698867
Samuel Smith OBB 🅗
Classic, two-roomed estate pub, that has remained basically unaltered since being built in the 1950s. It keeps only one real ale, proving that quality outweighs quantity. This pub is the only recipient of multiple merit awards from the local CAMRA branch. Quizzes are staged on Monday and Thursday. Slightly off the beaten track, it is well worth the effort to find. The No. 4 bus service from Grimsby and Cleethorpes passes the end of the road. Q🌳🚲🕭 ⊟♣P✂

No. 1 Refreshment Rooms
1 Station Approach, DN35 8AX
🕑 11-11; 12-10.30 Sun
☎ (01472) 691707
Beer range varies 🅗
The former offices of the railway station now serve as a comfy retreat at the busy end of this resort. Recently acquired by Highwood Brewery, whose beers are normally on offer, up to five real ales can usually be tried here. The handpumps are located in the lounge, so if you are in the bar just ask for the choice. It is well worth the effort of seeking out. 🏠🕭🅒⊟♣♣

Smugglers
High Cliff Road, DN35 8RQ
🕑 12-11; 12-10.30 Sun
☎ (01472) 200866
Banks's Original, Bitter; Marston's Pedigree; guest beers 🅗
The Smugglers was converted from the cellars of a former hotel, situated at the quieter end of the resort. Good quality, home-cooked meals are available daily at lunchtime and early evening, Monday–Thursday. Pub games may be played here and there is an outdoor drinking area. 🌳🕭🚲♣P✂

Willy's Pub and Brewery
17 High Cliff Road, DN35 8RQ
🕑 11-11; 12-10.30 Sun
☎ (01472) 602145

Bateman XB; Willy's Original Bitter; guest beers Ⓗ
This pub is a must for real ale drinking visitors and locals alike. The home of Grimsby and Cleethorpes' only brewery, which can be viewed from the bar, the pub is run by beer enthusiasts for beer enthusiasts. An active policy of seeking out unusual and new beers ensures an ever-changing range. Excellent home-made food is served at lunchtime; a supper club operates on Monday and Tuesday, while Thursday is curry night. ❀◑≢

CORRINGHAM

Beckett Arms
25 High Street, DN21 5QP (off A631)
✪ 12-2, 5.30-11; 11-11 Sat; 12-10.30 Sun
☎ (01427) 838201
Barnsley Bitter; guest beers (occasional) Ⓗ
This converted farmhouse has been a pub for the last 100 years. It has split-level rooms, with a bar area serving the pool room and lounge areas, there are two other rooms on the upper level and a lounge bar and restaurant on the lower level offering vegetarian and children's meals. Guest accommodation in four rooms includes a family room. ⛺Q❀≅◑❅♣P

EAST BUTTERWICK

Dog & Gun
High Street, DN17 3AJ (off A18, at Keadby Bridge)
✪ 6 (5 Thu & Fri; 12 Sat)-11; 12-10.30 Sun
☎ (01724) 783419
John Smith's Bitter; guest beer Ⓗ
Old-fashioned village local, nestling on the bank of the River Trent. Basic, but welcoming, the central bar serves three distinct drinking areas, one with a pool table. Renowned for its real fire in winter, it has long been an outlet for local micro-brewery DarkTribe. These beers are now rotated with Daleside beers as available. The hub of village life, visitors are always welcome. ⛺♣P

EAST KIRKBY

Red Lion
Main Road, PE23 4BZ
✪ 12-2.30, 7-11; 12-3, 7-10.30 Sun
☎ (01790) 763406
Draught Bass; Broadstone Best Bitter; guest beers Ⓗ
Friendly village pub, well frequented by locals and visitors alike. It is close to a former WWII airfield, once fully operational, and now a museum. This three-roomed inn is full of old clocks, tools, breweriana and antiques. The Red Lion offers a warm welcome and good home-cooked food. ⛺Q❀◑▲♣P

EAST STOCKWITH

Ferry House
27 Front Street, DN21 3DJ
✪ 11.30-3, 6.30-11; closed Mon; 12-10.30 Sun
☎ (01427) 615276
John Smith's Bitter; Webster's Bitter; guest beers Ⓗ
Free house on the bank of the River Trent which caters for a wide range of clientele. Excellent value food is all cooked on the premises. The large bar has facilities for pool, darts and dominoes. There is a dining room and a large room for functions. Three

guest rooms, with Trent views offer well-priced bed and breakfast. Two guest beers come from independent brewers. A quiz is held on alternate Wednesdays.
⛺❀≅◑♣P

EASTOFT

River Don Tavern
Sampson Street, DN17 4PQ (on A161)
✪ 12-2, 5 (7 winter) -11; 12-11 Sat; 12-10.30 Sun
☎ (01724) 798040
DarkTribe seasonal beers; Highwood seasonal beers; John Smith's Bitter; guest beers Ⓗ
Local CAMRA award-winning village pub, decorated with dark wood beams and agricultural implements. The bar serves one large room divided into discrete drinking/eating areas, plus a restaurant. Excellent home-cooked food (served Wed–Sun) includes popular hot skillet meals. Five or six real ales are normally available, with guest beers from the likes of Hambleton and Moorhouses. It hosts an annual beer festival in June, regular party theme nights and ferret racing in season (Oct–Feb). ⛺❀◑❅♣P

EWERBY

Finch Hatton Arms
Main Street, NG34 9PH
✪ 12-3, 6-11; 12-3, 6-10.30 Sun
☎ (01529) 460363
Black Sheep Best Bitter; Everards Tiger; guest beer Ⓗ
Built in the early 1870s as the Angel Inn, it was bought by Lord Winchelsea in 1875 and given his family name until the mid-1960s. The old Finch Hatton family motto is shown on the pub sign. From a traditional, brewery-owned village pub, it then started the transition into the free house it is today. Now a fully-equipped small hotel, it retains the charm of its past. The extensive menu is varied in both taste and price. ⛺Q❀≅◑P

FISHTOFT

Red Cow Inn
Gaysfield Road, PE21 0SF
✪ 5.30-11; 11-11 Sat; 12-10.30 Sun
☎ (01205) 367552
Bateman Mild, XB Ⓗ
Long-serving Bateman's tenants have established a thriving, atmospheric village pub. It fields plenty of pub teams, including pool, and hosts occasional entertainment evenings – karaoke, local bands, quizzes and race nights. It is close to the Pilgrim Fathers Memorial Park and the many angling and birdwatching sites on the Wash. A warm welcome is assured here. ⛺❀▲♣P▯

FLEET HARGATE

Bull
Old Main Road, PE12 8LH (off A17/A151 jct)
✪ 12-11; 12-10.30 Sun
☎ (01406) 426866
Bateman XB; guest beer Ⓗ
Although ideally situated for passing trade, just off the A17, the Bull manages to retain a village local feel. Pump clips adorn the walls, testifying to the variety of guest ales, many from micro-brewers, including a fair number of dark ales. Pub games feature

strongly in the evenings, with several teams being fielded in local leagues. Beer prices are reduced Tuesday–Thursday; evening meals are served Thursday–Saturday. There is a camping/caravan site in the village.
🏕🚪◑◖⬦Å♣P

FREISTON

King's Head ✅
Church Road, PE22 0NT
☼ 11-2.30, 6.30-11; 11.30-11 Sat; 12-10.30 Sun
☎ (01205) 760368
Bateman Mild, XB Ⓗ
This welcoming village local is a regular finalist in Bateman's floral display competition – it looks a treat in summer. Good home-cooked food includes Friday fish nights which are excellent value. Pub games are played and local league teams in darts and dominoes are supported. Local amenities include the Wash banks for angling and birdwatching. ⩗Q🏕◑◖Å♣P⊟

FRISKNEY

Barley Mow
Sea Lane, PE22 8SD (on A52, between Boston and Skegness)
☼ 12-2.30 (3 Sat; not Mon-Thu); 6.30 (6 Sat; 7 Wed)-11; closed Mon & Tue; 12-10.30 Sun
☎ (01745) 820883
Bateman XB; guest beers Ⓗ
Situated on the busy Boston–Skegness road, this 300-year-old hostelry is known locally as the Barley Mow (pronounced cow). Frequented by locals and visitors alike, it is especially popular during the summer months. A wide selection of home-cooked meals features on their imaginative, very reasonably-priced menu. A conservatory is to be added soon. ⩗Q🏕◑◖⬦♣P

FROGNALL

Goat
155 Spalding Road, PE6 8SA
(on B1525, E of Deeping St James)
☼ 11.30-2.30, 6-11; 12-3, 6-10.30 Sun
☎ (01778) 347629
website: www.goat.frognall@virgin.net
Beer range varies Ⓗ
This award-winning pub consists of one bar and two dining areas (one a separate room). It dates from 1647 and the low-ceilinged bar houses several beer engines; there are always five cask ales on offer, sourced from small regional or micro-breweries. Since 1994 over 2,000 beers have been offered from 430 breweries. Delicious food is cooked to order. Families are made welcome – the spacious garden has a children's play area; under fives are catered for with a variety of toys. ⩗Q🏕◑ÅP⊟

GAINSBOROUGH

Eight Jolly Brewers
Ship Court, Silver Street, DN21 2DW
(behind market place)
☼ 11-11; 12-10.30 Sun
☎ (01427) 677128
Broadstone Best Bitter; Glentworth Lightyear; Highwood Tom Wood's Best Bitter; Taylor Landlord; guest beers Ⓗ
In addition to the regular beers, an ever-changing selection of up to five others from small brewers increases the appeal of this small, town-centre pub. Real cider and Belgian Leffe beer are also on draught, and one or two beers are always heavily discounted. A wide selection of foreign bottled beers is stocked. A lively downstairs bar is always well patronised, while upstairs is a more quiet drinking area, except when the folk club meets on alternate Fridays.
Q🏕♣●P⥥⊟

GOSBERTON

Bell Inn
High Street, PE11 4NJ
☼ 11.30-3, 6-11; 11.30-11 Sat; 12-3, 7-10.30 Sun
☎ (01775) 840186
Beer range varies Ⓗ
Family-run pub at the centre of the village. It has no regular real ale but offers a changing selection of two or three ales, mainly from micro-breweries. This pub is popular with locals and fields darts and quiz teams. There are occasional Sunday evening jazz sessions which the landlord plans to make a regular event. A small patio caters for outside drinkers. ⩗🏕◑♣P

GOSBERTON RISEGATE

Duke of York
105 Risegate Road, PE11 4EY
☼ 12-2.30, 6-11; 12-11 Fri & Sat; 12-2.30, 7-10.30 Sun
☎ (01775) 840193
Bateman XB; Black Sheep Best Bitter; guest beers Ⓗ
Lively, village pub at the centre of community life, supporting local charities and running a number of sports and social teams. It enjoys a justified reputation for good quality beers and food at sensible prices. It has a no-smoking dining room and a games room. The guest beer list is always changing, giving the opportunity to sample a wide range. A large garden with a play area, goats and other animals, provides an added attraction. ⩗🏕◑⬦Å♣P⊟

GRANTHAM

Beehive
10-11 Castlegate, NG31 6SE
☼ 12-11; 12-10.30 Sun
☎ (01476) 404554
Newby Wyke Bear Island, White Squall, seasonal beers; guest beer Ⓗ
This busy, town-centre local, hosts a regular quiz on Monday evening. It boasts a very large, enclosed beer drinking area at the rear, while the interior consists of two rooms. The bar is L-shaped with pool and darts and the lounge is a quiet area with comfortable seating. Peruse the fascinating collection of old photos of the pub's famous living sign, but beware of the bees. Evening meals are available on Friday; the home-made curries and chilli are recommended.
🏕◑⬦&

Blue Pig
9 Vine Street, NG31 6RQ
☼ 11 (10.30 Sat)-11; 12-10.30 Sun
☎ (01476) 5653704 website: www.bluepiginn.com
Draught Bass; Flowers Original; Taylor Landlord; York Yorkshire Terrier; guest beer Ⓗ
This traditional 17th-century pub is a fine example of a Tudor-style building with a

wealth of history within. Offering fine ales and great food, it is no wonder that it won Grantham CAMRA's Pub of the Year in 2003. The beer range varies, and what could be better than to sit among the brewery memorabilia, soaking up the atmosphere? The varied menu includes home-made dishes in generous portions (served all day Sat and Sun). The Blue Pig should not be missed. ⚠️◑⊟✂

Chequers
25 Market Place, NG31 6LR
☀ 12-11; 12-10.30 Sun
☎ (01476) 401633
Beer range varies Ⓗ
Victorian building retaining its charm inside. It attracts a cosmopolitan clientele, with rock discos being held on Friday evening and occasional live music on Saturday. Up to four cask ales are usually available and the landlord discovers rare beers – mainly from Scotland and Ireland. It can be noisy on Saturday nights, but a warm welcome is assured.
≢♣

Hunting Tower Arms
93 Harlaxton Road, NG31 6AJ
☀ 11.30-3, 6.30-11; 11-11 Sat; 12-10.30 Sun
☎ (01476) 563814
Newby Wyke White Squall, seasonal beers; guest beers Ⓗ
Busy pub just outside the town centre and 10 minutes from the station. Various rooms were converted from a small pub about five years ago. Well known for its high standard of real ale, and live music, its pub quiz also attracts a large audience. A long bar greets the visitor with delightful touches in the decor. This friendly boozer makes you want to keep coming back.
⚠️🍴◑≢♣

Lord Harrowby
65 Dudley Road, NG31 6AC
☀ 4 (12 Sat)-11; 12-10.30 Sun
☎ (01476) 402121
Draught Bass; Worthington's Bitter; guest beer Ⓗ
Small, friendly, back-street local situated among chimney pots. The pub boasts two darts teams, pool and cribbage teams. Probably the cheapest pub in the area, it bears a 1930s-style decor and retains a lounge and separate bar area. The lounge is dedicated to aviation with many pictures capturing the spirit of Grantham's links with the RAF. The Dambusters made their plans at nearby St Vincents.
⚠️Q☸⊟♣

Nobody Inn
9 North Street, NG31 6NU (opp. Asda)
☀ 12-11; 12-10.30 Sun
☎ (01476) 565288 website: www.nobodyinn.com
Oakham JHB; Samuel Smith OBB; guest beers Ⓗ
One of the last independently-owned public houses in Grantham town, its six handpulls on the bar are all aimed at supporting the micro-brewers in the Grantham area, such as Oldershaw and Oakham. The Grantham Gold is brewed especially for the pub by Newby Wyke. Warm, welcoming and atmospheric, the pub's clientele ranges from 18 to 80. It is one of the few pubs which has not lost its traditional British character.
≢♣

Royal Oak
190 Victoria Street, DN31 1NX
☀ 11.30-11; 12-10.30 Sun
☎ (01472) 354562
Draught Bass; Theakston Mild; guest beer Ⓗ
The attractive Tudor-style front and leaded lights suggest a traditional interior. Despite some changes over the years, it still has two distinct rooms. A pleasant lounge complements the bar, with its working man's feel, demonstrated by the clatter of dominoes and the thud of darts, where you may view the tropical fish and have a chat without having to shout. The Oak is 300 yards from the town-centre bus station and seven minutes' walk from the railway station. ☸⊟≢(Town) ♣

Rutland Arms
26-30 Rutland Street, DN31 3AF
(1/2 mile off A180)
☀ 11-11; 12-10.30 Sun
☎ (01472) 268732
Old Mill Mild, Bitter Ⓗ
One-roomed drinkers' pub in an area of town not served too well by other hostelries. It is a handy port of call for visitors to Grimsby Town football matches. Converted from a derelict social club in 1988, the Rutland is a regular in this Guide, and was a former local CAMRA Pub of the Year. ≢(New Clee) ♣

Swigs
21 Osborne Street, DN31 1EY
☀ 11-11; 12-10.30 Sun
☎ (01472) 354773
Taylor Landlord; Willy's Original Bitter; guest beers Ⓗ
The second outlet for Willy's Brewery of Cleethorpes, Swigs has a continental café feel and offers excellent home-made food. Ever-present in this Guide since opening 12 years ago, it can be busy with shoppers and office workers at lunchtime. In the evenings students often add to a boisterous atmosphere. ◑≢(Town)

Tivoli Tavern
Old Market Place, DN31 1DT
☀ 11-11; 12-10.30 Sun
☎ (01472) 347563
Draught Bass; M&B Mild; Worthington's Bitter Ⓗ
Intimate, one-roomed pub in the town centre, a perfect stop during a busy day's shopping in the nearby Freshney Place centre. It serves no food, just great beer and is full of local character. ≢(Town)

Castle Inn
Wainfleet Road, PE22 0PF
(on A52, 4 miles N of Boston)
☀ 11.30-11; 12-10.30 Sun
☎ (01205) 760393
Bateman Mild, XB, XXXB; Greene King Abbot Ⓗ
The spacious bar area and large garden are well looked after here. The Castle stages regular, lively entertainment evenings and fields many teams in local pub game leagues. Good home-cooked food from a wide menu includes children's meals. One of a small number of Boston area pubs serving XXXB, it is worth a visit en-route to or from bracing Skegness. ⚠️☸◑♣P

HAXEY

Loco
31-33 Church Street, DN9 2HY
(from A161, follow B1396 into village)
☼ 2 (12 Sat)-11; 12-10.30 Sun
☎ (01427) 752879
John Smith's Bitter; guest beer Ⓗ
Unusual pub, converted from the village Co-op and chip shop about 20 years ago. A must for railway enthusiasts, an engine smokebox protrudes from one wall. Guest beers (usually two) are mostly sourced from local breweries, such as Highwood and Broadstone, with occasional beers from smaller breweries elsewhere. Pictures of the Haxey Hood (a game played on 6th Jan each year) and Indian cuisine add interest. ◖◗

HEMINGBY

Coach & Horses
Church Lane, LN9 5QF (1 mile from A158)
☼ 12-2 (not Mon or Tue), 7 (6 Wed-Fri)-11; 12-3, 7-10.30 Sun
☎ (01507) 578280
website: www.coach-horses.sagenet.co.uk
Bateman Mild, XB; guest beer Ⓗ
The only pub in a quiet village on the edge of the Lincolnshire Wolds. This proper country pub has all the essential features – low, beamed ceilings, open fire, brasses and plates for decoration and settles. The garden has plenty of seating, plus play equipment for children. A range of home-cooked food is available at sensible prices (not served Sun eve). At least one guest beer is always available, changing once or twice a week.
🏚Q⛱◖◗Å♣P

LEGBOURNE

Queen's Head
Station Road, LN11 8LL
☼ 12-2.30 (not Mon), 7 (5 Fri)-11; 12-11 Sat; 12-10.30 Sun
☎ (01507) 603839
Draught Bass; Bateman XB; guest beers Ⓗ
Friendly village pub, frequented by young and old alike. The single bar is horseshoe-shaped, giving two drinking areas. A quiz night is held every Thursday and regular themed food nights on alternate Fridays. Well-behaved dogs are allowed in, when food is not being served. The garden incorporates a children's adventure play area; the village cricket team meets here.
🏚⛱◖◗Å♣P

LINCOLN

Golden Eagle
21 High Street, LN5 8BD
☼ 11-11; 12-10.30 Sun
☎ (01522) 521058
Bateman XB; Everards Beacon, Tiger; guest beers Ⓗ
This friendly, basic but developing, two-bar pub stands near to the City football ground. In the lounge football memorabilia and historic City pictures are displayed. The bar at the back is a much livelier area with a TV; pub games are played and league teams encouraged. Unusually, a petanque piste is available in summer. Beer festivals are held as well as charity events. Good, honest pub food is served all day to complement the many guest beers. ⛱◖◗♣🍴P

264

Lord Tennyson
72 Rasen Lane, LN1 3HD
(200 yds from Museum of Lincolnshire Life)
☼ 11-3, 5.30-11; 12-3, 7-10.30 Sun
☎ (01522) 889262
Draught Bass; Greene King IPA; Tetley Bitter; guest beer Ⓗ
Former Ward's house, the Tennyson is a white-fronted traditional town pub appealing to locals and visitors alike. Named after the county's famous Poet Laureate, the Victorian double bay-fronted building has a later rear extension. One bar serves two drinking areas and a dining area. Photos of bygone Lincoln add interest. Pool and darts are played at the rear. Good value meals, mostly home-cooked, are served. The piped music is unobtrusive. ⛱◖◗♣P

Morning Star
11 Greetwell Gate, LN2 4AW
☼ 11-11; 12-10.30 Sun
☎ (01522) 527079
Draught Bass; Greene King Ruddles Best, Abbot; Tetley Bitter; Wells Bombardier; guest beer Ⓗ
This is a very traditional pub, situated five minutes' walk east from the cathedral. Apart from an obvious extension to the bar at one end and inside toilets, it has not changed in living memory. The atmosphere is always warm and welcoming. On Saturday evening the piano is played; it is believed to be the only pub in the city where this still happens. Games include shut the box and table skittles, but not darts. Lunches are served Monday–Saturday. 🏚Q⛲⛱◖◗♣P

Peacock Inn
23 Wragby Road, LN2 5SH
☼ 11.30-11; 12-10.30 Sun
☎ (01522) 524703
Hardys & Hansons Mild, Bitter, Classic; guest beer Ⓗ
This old coaching inn is in the picturesque uphill area of Lincoln between the cathedral, the hospital and the prison. Recently the dining room was much extended; the food is good and very popular, so booking is advisable (meals served 12–9). The bar, with open fire, TV and dartboard, is a warm, friendly and busy place and usually has the complete Hardys & Hansons' range of beers on tap. ⛱◖◗♣P

Portland
50 Portland Street, LN5 7JX (off High St)
☼ 11-11; 12-10.30 Sun
☎ (01522) 560564 website: www.will.lisa@virgin.net
Bateman XB; John Smith's Bitter; guest beers Ⓗ
A recent refurbishment has given a more homely feel to the Portland. Between the bar and an area where the pool table is located, there is a small no-smoking area; children are admitted during meal times – evening meals finish at 7.30pm. Two regular beers and five guest ales, including a mild, are on offer at all times. Quiz night is Thursday and football fans will find the ground within easy walking distance.
⛱◖◗🍴≉♣P✄

Lincoln Post Office Sports & Social Club
Maitland Block, Dunkirk Road, LN1 3UJ
(off Burton Rd)
☼ 11-3 (not Tue-Thu; 11-4 Sat), 6.30-11; 12-10.30 Sun

☎ (01522) 524050

Marston's Pedigree; John Smith's Bitter; guest beer Ⓗ
No-frills club serving beers at club prices. It is home to an enthusiastic horse racing club. Currently housed in former army barracks, the club is due to move into a new purpose-built building just across the road. Show a CAMRA membership card or this Guide to gain entry. ♣P

Reindeer Hotel
8 High Street, LN5 8BG
❀ 12-11; 12-4, 7-10.30 Sun
☎ (01522) 520024
John Smith's Bitter; Tetley Dark Mild; guest beers Ⓗ
Late 18th-century brick and stone former coaching inn (note the thick walls), close to what was the old southern city gate. The front door opens into a panelled lounge with comfortable bench seating. Behind is the livelier public bar with juke box, TV, unplayed piano, and an adjoining pool room. Both bars are packed for the popular Sunday quiz night. The friendly landlord has been here for 16 years, through several changes of ownership; it is now an Enterprise Inn. Q↺⌂⊟♣P

Sippers
26 Melville Street, LN5 7HW
(near railway and bus stations)
❀ 11-2, 5 (7 Sat)-11; 11-11 Fri; 7-10.30 (closed lunch) Sun
☎ (01522) 527612
Courage Directors; Greene King Old Speckled Hen; Marston's Pedigree; John Smith's Bitter; guest beers Ⓗ
Once the Crown & Cushion, this has been Sippers for nearly 20 years; the current licensee has been here for over 15. It is a consistent Guide entry. The building, a survivor of road schemes and demolitions, is unspectacular outside but comfortable within, with plenty of seating areas tucked away. Close to the city centre, this is useful for meals both lunchtime and evening (until 8pm Mon–Sat). ◖▮≉♣

Strugglers Inn
83 Westgate, LN1 3BG
❀ 11.30-11; 12-10.30 Sun
☎ (01522) 535023
Draught Bass; Black Sheep Best Bitter; Fuller's London Pride; Greene King Abbot; guest beer Ⓗ
Two-roomed pub set beneath the castle walls, isolated between coach and car parks. The pub was originally registered in 1863 as the Struggler in the Globe; the public gallows stood nearby. The bustling bar contrasts well with the smaller, cosy snug. The sheltered patio is popular with families in the summer and has barbecue facilities. Q❀⊟

Tap & Spile
21 Hungate, LN1 1ES
❀ 11.30-11; 12-10.30 Sun
☎ (01522) 534015
Beer range varies Ⓗ
City-centre oasis for real ale, tucked away from the disco bars on the High Street. A friendly welcome awaits in this open-plan, stone-flagged Tap & Spile. The pub is divided into three areas: bar, lounge and no-smoking section. It stages live music on Friday evening, a general knowledge quiz (Sun) and music quiz (Wed); look out for

the occasional comedy nights. It is home to a 'round' chess table club. ❀≉♣⅄

Victoria
6 Union Road, LN1 3BJ (next to castle)
❀ 11-11; 12-10.30 Sun
☎ (01522) 536048
Bateman XB; Taylor Landlord; guest beers Ⓗ
Fine free house next to the castle, opposite the Lawn visitor centre. Up to eight beers are available at a time, including a guest mild and a beer from Castle Rock. Westons or Biddenden cider is stocked. Two beer festivals are held annually (June and Christmas), offering a large range of beers. Food, served every lunchtime, includes an enormous late breakfast on Saturday. This member of the Tynemill chain is well worth visiting. Q❀◖⊟⅊♣♨

Willoughby Arms ✪
Station Road, NG33 4RA
❀ 12-2.30, 5-11; 12-11 Sat; 12-10.30 Sun
☎ (01780) 410276
Newby Wyke Sidewinder, Lord Lancaster; guest beers Ⓗ
Traditional pub surrounded by open countryside where a large garden provides the setting for two beer festivals each year. Regular mini-fests are staged as well. The award-winning Newby Wyke Brewery is at the rear. A cellar bar hosts regular live music. Meals may be taken in the main bar area in front of an open fire, or in the no-smoking dining room. Curries and game dishes are specialities; fish and chips nights are Monday and Wednesday. Guest accommodation is in well-appointed rooms.
⇞❀↺◖▮⊟♣⅊P⅁

Boar's Head
12 Newmarket, LN11 9HH
❀ 11-2 (not Mon-Wed; 9.30-2 Thu), 5.30-11; 12-10.30 Sun
☎ (01507) 603561 website: www.whoresbed.co.uk
Bateman XB; Highwood Tom Wood's Best Bitter; guest beers Ⓗ
Located five minutes' walk from the bustling town centre, this pub opens early on Thursday to cater for visitors to the nearby cattle market. Inviting open fires burn in winter; one has a boar's head hanging above. Pool, darts and shove-ha'penny can be played. Currently run by local Highwood Brewery, it stocks seasonal guest beers. It attracts all ages and hosts occasional live entertainment. Outside drinking space is at two tables. A free council car park provides ample space next to the pub. ⇞❀↺♣⅊

Masons Arms Hotel
Cornmarket, LN11 9PY
❀ 11-11; 11-3, 7-10.30 Sun
☎ (01507) 609525 website: www.themasons.co.uk
Bateman XB, XXXB; Marston's Pedigree; Samuel Smith OBB; Taylor Landlord; guest beers Ⓗ
Early 18th-century posting inn on the market square, formerly a meeting place for the Louth Masonic Lodge, it is now Grade II listed. Recognisable Masonic symbols can be seen on fireplaces, doors and windows. The friendly, family-run hotel bar offers

excellent home-made fare (children are welcome while food is being served); the upstairs restaurant is open Friday and Saturday evenings and Sunday lunchtime. Q♿◐🕒&

Newmarket Inn
133 Newmarket, LN11 9EG
✪ 7-11; 12-3, 7-10.30 Sun
Adnams Bitter; Robinson's Hartleys XB; guest beer Ⓗ
Formerly known as the Brown Cow, this pub was renamed in 1972 by the present owner's family. This pleasantly decorated, two-roomed pub in a rural location, is popular with all ages. A guest beer is available at weekends, generally from Black Sheep Brewery. A free quiz is held every Sunday evening. It is worth checking if Hurdles Bistro is open before visiting as seasonal variations are possible, and booking is recommended. Sunday lunches are available. Parking is limited. ♨Q❀▶P

Olde Whyte Swanne
45 Eastgate, LN11 9NP
✪ 10-11; 10-10.30 Sun
☎ (01507) 601312
website: www.louth.org/swan/swan.html
Black Sheep Best Bitter; Caledonian Deuchars IPA; Greene King Old Speckled Hen; Theakston Old Peculier; guest beers Ⓗ
16th-century coaching inn at the centre of a busy market town, offering a friendly welcome. The bar and dining room are both warmed by log fires. It serves a wide range of food, based on local produce, throughout the day. The small bar is very cosy, and several blackboards give the daily menus. It cannot have changed much for many years.
♨Q🍴♿◐🕒&P

Wheatsheaf ⊘
62 Westgate, LN11 9YD
✪ 11-3, 5-11; 12-4, 7-10.30 Sun
☎ (01507) 606262
Boddingtons Bitter; Flowers Original; guest beers Ⓗ
Tucked away in the conservation area of a thriving market town, this 17th-century inn has three bars, all with coal fires and low, beamed ceilings. A beer and bangers festival held in May/June is a popular annual event. The magnificent St James Church spire is a wonderful sight from the garden, as are the pub's large hanging baskets. The house beer, Tipsy Toad, comes from an undisclosed source. Lunches are served Monday–Saturday. ♨Q❀◐&P

Woolpack Inn
Riverhead Road, LN11 0DA
✪ 11-3 (not Mon), 5 (7 Mon)-11; 12-4, 7-10.30 Sun
☎ (01507) 606568
Bateman Mild, XB, XXXB, seasonal beers; Greene King Abbot; guest beers Ⓗ
Built in the early 1770s to serve the trade from the newly-constructed Louth Canal, this Grade II listed building has been an inn ever since. Situated one mile east of the town centre at the head of the canal, the inn is a recommended starting point for the 'round Louth walk'. The inn comprises two L-shaped bars, both with open fires, and separate dining areas. This long-standing Guide entry has only missed one edition due to a management change. No food is served Monday. ♨Q❀◐♿&♣P✂

Vine ⊘
19 Church Street, PE6 8AN
✪ 11.30-2, 5.30-11; 11.30-3, 6.30-11 Sat; 12-3, 7-10.30 Sun
☎ (01778) 342387
Wells Eagle, Bombardier; guest beer Ⓗ
Friendly local, close to the centre of Market Deeping. This attractive building of local limestone was originally a Victorian prep school. Inside, is a low-ceilinged front bar with a cosy snug at the back. The landlord is a keen thespian who regularly takes roles in the summer productions of the Stamford Shakespeare Company. Two beer festivals a year are held in the outdoor drinking area at the back of the pub. The car park is small.
Q❀▲♣P

Red Lion
45 King Street, LN8 3BB
✪ 11.30-2, 7-11; 11-3, 7-11 Sat; 12-3, 7-10.30 Sun
☎ (01673) 842424
Draught Bass; Tetley Bitter; guest beer Ⓗ
On entering this traditional free house you are quickly given a friendly reception. The oldest pub in town, it retains lounge and public bars. It is well supported by a wide range of customers who enjoy their darts, dominoes and pool, as well as the juke box and honest pub grub. There is a small garden. The third handpump offers beers from the more established breweries.
♨❀◐♿&➭♣P

Horn Inn
61 High Street, DN17 3NU
✪ 11-11; 12-10.30 Sun
☎ (01724) 762426
John Smith's Bitter; guest beers Ⓗ
Hospitable roadside local in a village on the Scunthorpe, Gainsborough and Lincoln bus routes (services 351 and 353). Essentially a one-roomed pub, its three discrete, comfortably-furnished drinking areas are served by a central bar. Coal fires, rural artefacts and friendly banter create a convivial TV-free atmosphere. Two guest beers are always available and good home-cooked food is served (booking is recommended Sunday). Busy for live music on Wednesday evening and occasional Saturdays, the Monday quiz is also popular. Wheelchair WC.
♨❀◐&♣P

Crooked Billet
1 Crooked Billet Street, DN21 3AG
✪ 12-11; 12-10.30 Sun
☎ (01427) 612584
Beer range varies Ⓗ
Lively Victorian village pub, comprising several large rooms. The pub hosts numerous activities, such as table football, pinball, bingo and quizzes; there is Sky TV and occasional live music. Local sports teams meet here. There is a quiet room for those seeking an opportunity just to chat. Two guest beers change on a regular basis.
♨Q♿♣🍴

NETTLEHAM

Black Horse

Chapel Lane, LN2 2NX

☼ 11.30-3, 6-11; 11.30-11 Fri & Sat; 12-10.30 Sun

☎ (01522) 750702

Bateman XB; Brains Dark; John Smith's Bitter;
Highwood Tom Wood's Best Bitter; guest beers Ⓗ

This consistent Guide entry in recent years
operates a committed guest beer policy,
including bottled beers. This popular stone
pub, reputedly haunted, encompasses the
former village workhouse, which inspired
the name of the Workhouse Folk and Blues
Club where top name artists regularly
appear. Good quality, home-cooked meals
are served (eves until 8pm); booking for
Sunday lunch is advised. A no-smoking
policy applies in the dining area. ᛘ◑⬭⬛&♣

Plough

1 The Green, LN2 2NR

☼ 12-11; 12-10.30 Sun

☎ (01522) 750275

Draught Bass; Bateman Mild, XB, XXXB Ⓗ

Pleasant community village local serving a
Lincoln suburb. People come from far and
wide to try the fine beers and excellent food
served both in the bar and attic dining
room (open evenings and Sunday lunch).
The pub is adorned with brasses and bric-à-
brac which add to the rural atmosphere. It
hosts a quiz on Wednesday evening and a
variety of games teams are supported.
❀◑♣⬛

NETTLETON

Salutation Inn

Church Street, LN7 6NP

☼ 12-3, 6-11; 12-3, 7-10.30 Sun

☎ (01472) 851228

Draught Bass; Highwood Tom Wood's Best Bitter;
Taylor Landlord; Wadworth 6X Ⓗ

This relaxed, friendly and quiet pub on the
A46, serves good food in the bar and the
adjoining no-smoking dining room.
Children are catered for in the family room
and enjoy the garden, which houses a
collection of farm animals. On the edge of
the Wolds, it is a good stop for walkers.
ᛘQ⬗❀◑&▲♣P

NORTH KELSEY

Butchers Arms

Middle Street, LN7 6EH

☼ 4 (12 Sat)-11; 12-10.30 Sun

☎ (01652) 678002

Highwood Tom Wood's Best Bitter, Tom Wood's
Harvest Bitter; guest beers Ⓗ

Owned by Highwood Brewery, this is a
traditional village pub, hidden away down a
side street. The single U-shaped room is
decorated in farmhouse style, with two bay
windows; a real fire gives it a cosy
atmosphere. Children (and dogs) are made
welcome. The outdoor drinking area is
alongside the car park, but is divided by a
row of mature trees. ᛘ❀&P

Royal Oak

High Street, LN7 6EA

(on B1434, off A1084 to Caistor)

☼ 7-11 (may vary summer); 12-3, 7-10.30 Sun

☎ (01652) 678544 website: www.pubs247.com

Barnsley Bitter; Taylor Landlord Ⓗ

Well-furnished pub in a quiet village. The
lounge is the biggest of three rooms,
warmed by a wood-burning stove; a snug-
cum-bar houses a dartboard. It boasts a
good-sized garden and a large car park. New
licensees have plans for further
development of the amenities; at the
moment Sunday lunch is the only meal
offered. Families are welcome.
⬗❀⬛♣P⌿⬛

ROTHWELL

Blacksmith's Arms

Hill Rise, LN7 6AZ

☼ 11.30-3, 5-11; 11.30-11 Sat; 12-10.30 Sun

☎ (01472) 371300

Courage Directors; Marston's Pedigree; Theakston
Best Bitter; guest beer Ⓗ

Nestling at the heart of the Lincolnshire
Wolds, this pub oozes rural charm. With its
low, beamed ceilings and real fires it is an
archetypal English pub – the kind of place
you would love to introduce to foreign
visitors. Mainly open plan, with a small bar
to one side and a large function room to the
rear, as soon as you sit down with a pint,
you feel immediately comfortable, and
dream about persuading someone else to
drive home. ᛘ❀◑♣P

SAXILBY

Anglers

65 High Street, LN1 2HA

☼ 11.30-2.30 (3 Sat), 6 (5 Fri; 7 Sat)-11; 12-3,
7-10.30 Sun

☎ (01522) 702200

Everards Home Bitter; Theakston Best Bitter;
guest beer Ⓗ

This busy, friendly local fields darts, crib,
dominoes and pool teams. Match nights
can be hectic, but lunchtimes are quieter
and table skittles are played then. The
lounge, displaying photos of the village, is
regularly used by local clubs and societies
for meetings. The pub was built in 1850 as
the Railway but changed to its present
name in 1900 when large numbers of
fishermen came by train to fish in the
nearby Foss Dyke. ❀⬛⇌♣P

SCAMBLESBY

Green Man

Old Main Road, LN11 9XG (off A153)

☼ 12-11; 12-10.30 Sun

☎ (01507) 343282

Black Sheep Best Bitter; guest beer Ⓗ

Motorbike and ale-loving licensees run this
200-year-old free house in a village off the
A153. Viking Way walkers and
motorcyclists visiting nearby Cadwell Park
Circuit are welcomed. The bar features a
games area, a log fire and Harry, the pub
dog, while the small, beamed lounge has
rocking chairs and, possibly, a ghost. A
second guest beer is usually available on
bank holidays. Good value food is served
daily, 12–9. ᛘQ⬗❀⬔◑⬛▲♣P

SCOTTER

White Swan

9 The Green, DN21 3UD

☼ 11.30-3, 6.30-11; 11.30-11 Fri & Sat;
12-10.30 Sun

☎ (01724) 762342
John Smith's Bitter; Webster's Bitter; guest beers Ⓗ
Smart, well-appointed village local, tucked away off the main road, comprising a refurbished bar area and a large restaurant, extended to overlook the garden and the tiny River Eau. It places a strong emphasis on food, but still offers an interesting range of beers, usually with three guests. Good quality accommodation is available in 15 rooms; a relaxing place to eat, drink or stay. ❀🛏◑P

SCUNTHORPE

Blue Bell ✓
1-7 Oswald Road, DN15 7PU
✪ 10-11; 12-10.30 Sun
☎ (01724) 863921
Courage Directors; Greene King Abbot; Shepherd Neame Spitfire; Theakston Best Bitter; guest beers Ⓗ
Wetherspoon's town-centre pub keeps two or three guest ales and serves food until 10pm Monday–Saturday (9.30pm Sun). Children's meals are available until 7pm Sunday–Thursday and 5pm Friday and Saturday. It gets busy Friday and Saturday evenings. Beer festivals are held twice a year. The patio area is used by both drinkers and diners in summer. Q❀◑ㅤ🖘P⅄

Honest Lawyer
70 Oswald Road, DN15 7PG (near station)
✪ 11-11; 12-10.30 Sun
☎ (01724) 849906
Daleside Bitter; guest beers Ⓗ
The pub's long, narrow bar area is fitted out in old-style dark wood, bearing a legal theme. An upstairs drinking area houses a large-screen TV and the downstairs 'snug' also has a small TV, both of which are popular with sports fans. Newspapers are provided daily by the genial licensee, and the pub is a favourite among real ale drinkers. An outdoor drinking area is set up in front of the pub during summer. ❀◑🖘●

Malt Shovel
219 Ashby High Street, DN16 2JP
✪ 11-11; 12-10.30 Sun
☎ (01724) 843318
Courage Directors; John Smith's Bitter; Tetley Bitter; Theakston Old Peculier; guest beers Ⓗ
Use the right-hand side entrance for the large, comfortable bar where rustic beams, leaded windows and a brick fireplace give the impression of a more rural location than a main shopping street. Popular lunchtime and early evening for good value meals, at other times, quieter surroundings allow you to savour four regular and two changing guest beers – Glentworth and Abbeydale are particular favourites. Membership is available for the licensed snooker facilities in left-hand bar (real ale also served). Q❀◑

Queen Bess
Derwent Road, Ashby, DN16 2PE
✪ 11.30-3.30 (4 Sat), 6-11; 12-3.30, 7-10.30 Sun
☎ (01724) 840827
Samuel Smith OBB Ⓗ
This estate pub was named after a local iron-making furnace. A central bar serves a tidy lounge and a public bar. The large function room is used by local societies, for special celebrations and for live music. The pub

holds a children's certificate. Snacks are available. This regular Guide entry serves the best Sam Smith's in town and is a holder of several local CAMRA awards. ᴍ❀🍽♣P

SOUTH ORMSBY

Massingberd Arms
Brinkhill Road, LN11 8QS
(1½ miles from A16 turn at Swaby)
✪ 12-3 (not winter Mon), 5.30-11; 12-5, 7-10.30 Sun
☎ (01507) 480492
Beer range varies Ⓗ
Dating back to the 19th century, and set in the beautiful Lincolnshire Wolds, this was a favourite haunt for aircrew from local bomber stations during the war. It is now a quiet, village pub serving two real ales on handpump (three in summer) and home-cooked food which includes game, such as venison, rabbit and pheasant. The bar features a collection of woodworking tools, made by the landlord's father; note the pump clips, depicting regulars, painted by a local artist. ᴍ❀◑♣P⅄

SPALDING

Lincoln Arms
4 Bridge Street, PE11 1XA (off market place)
✪ 11-3 (3.30 Sat), 7-11; 12-4, 7.30-10.30 Sun
☎ (01775) 722691
Banks's Mansfield Dark Mild, Original, Riding Bitter, Cask Ale; guest beers Ⓗ
Traditional, 18th-century local, overlooking the River Welland by the Town Bridge. The interior is comfortably furnished, providing a welcoming atmosphere. The pub is home to the Spalding Folk Club which holds monthly gigs (first Wed). The landlord's pursuit of quality and perfection means that the pub has appeared in this Guide for 10 consecutive years. 🛏🖘

Red Lion Hotel
Market Place, PE11 1SU
✪ 11-11; 12-10.30 Sun
☎ (01775) 722869
website: www.redlionhotel-spalding.co.uk
Draught Bass; Fuller's London Pride; Greene King Abbot; Marston's Pedigree Ⓗ
Attractive hotel bar on the corner of the market place, looking a little like a French villa. It has been richly refurbished to provide a warm, welcoming atmosphere, but it can get a bit smoky at times. Tremendously popular with locals and visitors to the fens, it is home to the Spalding Blues Club which presents fortnightly bands in the Blues Café to the rear of the main bar. No food is served on Sunday evening. ᴍQ❀🛏◑🖘

STALLINGBOROUGH

Stallingborough Grange
Riby Road, DN41 8BU
(on A1173, outskirts of village)
✪ 11-11; 12-10.30 Sun
☎ (01469) 561302
website: www.stallingborough-grange.com
Tetley Bitter; Burton Ale; guest beers Ⓗ
Dating back to the 18th century, this picturesque, thatched country house is steeped in local history. Set in beautiful and tranquil gardens, it has now been converted into a privately-owned hotel. The

comfortable, modern public lounge provides a friendly atmosphere where a good choice of bar meals is available. There is also a restaurant and a large function room. The regular guest beers are changed every two or three months. ✿✍◑&♣P

Crown Hotel
6 All Saints Place, PE9 2AG
✿ 11-11; 12-10.30 Sun
☎ (01780) 763136
website: www.crownhotelstamford.co.uk
Adnams Bitter; Draught Bass; Taylor Landlord; guest beers Ⓗ
This impressive, multi-roomed hotel is overlooked by All Saints Church. The abundance of flowers and plants in the mosaic-tiled lobby give an expectation of what to find within. Mobile phones are prohibited in public areas, as is smoking, except from the bar area where meals and snacks may be enjoyed informally, although there are two designated dining areas. The decor celebrates local rural pursuits. Good selections of fine wines and malt whiskies are stocked. Q✿✍◑⬚≉P✗

Green Man
29 Scotgate, PE9 2YQ
✿ 11-11; 12-10.30 Sun
☎ (01780) 753598
Theakston Best Bitter; guest beers Ⓗ
A real gem for drinkers of all ages and preference. A stone-built former coaching inn dating back to 1796, it has a split-level L-shaped bar, and secluded patio garden where bi-annual beer festivals are held, Easter and mid-September. Six regularly-changing guests from micro-breweries, include beers from Newby Wyke and Rooster's, brewed especially for the pub. A good range of European and American bottled beers (15–20) plus at least half a dozen ciders or perries are stocked. Many artefacts of the brewing industry are displayed. The juke box is on free vend during happy hour. ▲✿✍◑≉♣●🍴

Periwig
7 All Saints Place, PE9 2AG
✿ 11-11; 12-10.30 Sun
☎ (01780) 762169
Adnams Bitter; Fuller's London Pride; Hop Back Summer Lightning; Oakham JHB; guest beers Ⓗ
Multi-level pub, especially popular with the younger element at weekends. It offers regular promotions and 'happy hour' lasts from 11–2 and 5–7. Guest beers are usually from micro-breweries. It is handy for both bus and rail stations. Redecoration at Easter 2003 included new lighting and soft leather furnishings in the upstairs area. It serves good value food and can get busy at lunchtimes (no meals Sun). ◑≉

Mermaid
2 Gosberton Road, PE11 4AB (on B1356)
✿ 11-11; 12-10.30 Sun
☎ (01775) 680275
Adnams Broadside; guest beers Ⓗ
Once the site of a brewery, this good-sized pub stands on the bank of the River Glen. Its large garden features tropical-style

thatched parasols and an outdoor bar in summer (weather permitting); there is a good play area for children. Excellent value meals make this a popular eating place, and much of the bar area is often occupied by diners, which can be a problem for drinkers, especially at weekends. A varied selection of guest ales is offered. ▲Q✿✍◑P

Anchor
280 Bridge Road, PE12 9SH
(1 mile W of bridge)
✿ 11-4, 7-11; 12-3, 7-10.30 Sun
☎ (01406) 350302
Blue Bell Olde Honesty; Greene King IPA; guest beer Ⓗ
A long bar serves three adjoining areas, each with its own identity, although a comfortable relaxed feel is a common factor throughout. The simple bar and pool table area caters for the pub's many games teams, while the cosy lounge displays an interesting collection of model sailing boats. Good, homely food is served in the lounge or the dining room. ▲✍◑⬚♣P✗

Click'em Inn
LN8 6BS (2 miles N of Binbrook on B1203)
✿ 12-3 (not Mon), 7-11; 11.30-11 Sat; 12-3, 7-10.30 Sun
☎ (01472) 398253
Theakston XB; guest beers Ⓗ
Welcoming country pub in the Lincolnshire Wolds. It is popular with both locals and diners due to the good quality meals served in the bar and conservatory. The house beer, Click'em Bitter, comes from an undisclosed source. ✿◑♣P

Bluebell Inn
Thorpe Road, LN4 4PE
✿ 12-2.30, 7-11; 12-2.30, 7-10.30 Sun
☎ (01526) 342206
Everards Tiger; Highwood Tom Wood's Bomber County; Poachers Bluebell Pathfinders Ale; guest beers Ⓗ
One of Lincolnshire's oldest inns, dating back to the 13th century, it bears a wealth of beamed ceilings and historical charm. This pub was the watering-hole of the famous Dambusters 617 RAF Squadron during WWII. Numerous photographs hang on the walls, and the low ceilings have been signed by many service personnel. ▲Q✿◑⬚P

White Hart Inn
East Road, LN9 6QQ OS333747
✿ 12-4, 7-11; 12-5, 7-10.30 Sun
☎ (01507) 533255
Adnams Bitter; Fuller's London Pride; Greene King Abbot; guest beer (summer) Ⓗ
At the heart of the village, the pub comprises several bars of varying shapes and sizes. The 'public' bar has a fire that burns from the hearth and an old, bowed settle that is quite unique. The sign on entry, 'please take off your muddy boots' indicates that walkers from the Viking Way are

frequent visitors; in the past it applied to farm labourers, no doubt. The pub is on the Meridian Line, so calling time is no problem! ♨Q♿☎🖰🆑◐🖰♿♣▲♣♠P✄

THORNTON CURTIS

Thornton Hunt Inn
Main Street, DN39 6XW
(on A1077, between Wooton and Barton)
🕑 12-3, 6-11; 12-3, 7-10.30 Sun
☎ (01469) 531252
Highwood Tom Wood's Bomber County; Taylor Landlord; Tetley Bitter Ⓗ

Cosy, well-appointed village local decorated in rural fashion with beams, brasses and hunting pictures. Popular for bar meals, the pub also has its own bistro. Two regular real ales are supplemented by a different Highwood beer each season. The garden features a fun trail play area for children. The pub lies close to the ruins of Thornton Abbey. ❀🖰🆑♿P

WADDINGTON

Three Horseshoes
High Street, LN5 9RF
🕑 12-4, 7-11; 11-11 Fri & Sat; 12-10.30 Sun
☎ (01522) 720448
John Smith's Bitter; Wells Bombardier; guest beers Ⓗ

This 220-year-old, red brick, back-street local is a free house that always has two guests on tap; at Christmas polypins of seasonal beers can sometimes be found on the bar. The local fishing, cricket and football clubs meet here and adult education classes are held at the pub. The name commemorates horse racing that used to happen locally – the stables stood nearby, but the church bells gave the pub its nickname of the Clangers. ♨☎❀♣P

WAINFLEET

Jolly Sailor
19 St John Street, PE24 4DL (off main square)
🕑 12-2, 4-11; 11-3, 7-11 Sat; 12-3, 7-10.30 Sun
☎ (01754) 880275
Bateman XB, seasonal beers Ⓗ

Typical, back-street boozer, and the nearest Bateman's house to the brewery, where a warm, friendly atmosphere prevails. It enjoys an excellent reputation with the locals for the quality of its beer. It boasts a coal fire and has a large function room (for auctions and bingo). It fields a darts team and runs brewery trips. If you are extremely lucky you may be entertained by the local town crier. ♨Q☎🖰⊟≈♣P

WILLINGHAM BY STOW

Half Moon
23 High Street, DN21 5JZ
🕑 12-2 (not Mon), 5 (7 Mon)-11; 12-11 Sat; 12-10.30 Sun
☎ (01427) 788340
Wells Bombardier; guest beers Ⓗ

This two-roomed local, just off the main road through the village, serves three real ales, two of which are regularly-changing guests. Its home-cooked food is recommended, especially the fish and chip suppers. A quiz is held every Thursday evening; bar skittles and shove-ha'penny are played and it fields darts, dominoes and

football teams. A converted agricultural labourer's cottage, it has beamed ceilings. A beer festival usually takes place in the summer, offering 12–15 beers. ♨Q❀🆑⊟♣

WILLOUGHTON

Stirrup Inn
Templefield Road, DN21 5RZ (off B1398)
🕑 7.30 (12 Sat)-11; 12-10.30 Sun
☎ (01427) 668270 website: www.pubs247.com
Eccleshall Slaters Top Totty; John Smith's Bitter Ⓗ

Family-run free house for the past 13 years, it won local CAMRA's Pub of the Season award for winter 2001. The guest beer changes on a weekly basis. Home to the local football teams, dominoes and darts are played here. A single bar serves an L-shaped room, split into bar and lounge areas by a central fireplace. Unusually for a village pub, it does not have to provide meals to attract visiting trade. ♨Q❀⊟♣P

WINTERINGHAM

Bay Horse Inn
2-6 West End, DN15 9NS
🕑 12 (4 Mon)-11; 12-10.30 Sun
☎ (01724) 732865
Tetley Bitter; guest beers Ⓗ

Popular local, where Dick Turpin reputedly slept. Hops and brasses cover exposed beams. Two guest beers are available and an annual beer festival is held in summer. Home-cooked food is served at lunchtime Friday–Sunday, and Tuesday–Sunday evenings 7–9pm, from an extensive menu. A quiz is held (Sun eve). The function room houses the pool table. Four en-suite guest rooms, and a wheelchair WC complete the facilities here. ♨❀🖰🆑♿♣P

WINTERTON

Lion's Head
55 Park Street, DN15 9UP
🕑 5 (11.30 Fri & Sat)-11.30; 12-10.30 Sun
☎ (01724) 733343
Black Sheep Best Bitter; guest beer Ⓗ

Friendly village local, with brass bedecked beams, it has an L-shaped lounge bar with an area for darts, plus a warm, welcoming snug. The guest beer changes fortnightly; a quiz is run weekly. Weekend entertainment is provided on a regular basis. The pub fields its own cricket and football teams and a vintage motorcycle club holds its meetings here. A walled garden area and patio are added attractions. ♨Q❀⊟♣P

WROOT

Cross Keys
High Street, DN9 2BT
(signed off B1396) OS714034
🕑 4 (2 Sat)-11; 12-3, 5.30-10.30 Sun
☎ (01302) 770231
Glentworth seasonal beer; Theakston Best Bitter Ⓗ

Isolated inn in Lincolnshire's most westerly village, which was an island until drained in the 17th century. Popular with locals, the present landlord has introduced beers from the local Glentworth Brewery, occasionally displaced by a beer from another brewer. Local teams are prevalent here, as are letters from charities and local causes that the pub has supported. Well worth finding. ♨❀♣P

CAMRA's National Inventory
of Pub Interiors of Outstanding Historic Interest

The pubs listed here have interiors that are of national historic significance. The listing details pubs whose internal arrangements have remained more or less intact since World War Two. They are a diverse group ranging from basic street-corner locals to some of the most ornate pubs in the land. Further details about National Inventory pubs may be found on the CAMRA website – www.camra.org.uk – and in a booklet advertised in this edition of the Guide. Most, but by no means all, the pubs sell real ale.

ENGLAND

Bedfordshire
Broom: Cock
Luton: Painter's Arms

Berkshire
Aldworth: Bell

Buckinghamshire
West Wycombe: Swan

Cambridgeshire
Peterborough: Hand & Heart

Cheshire
Alpraham: Travellers Rest
Barthomley: White Lion
Bollington: Holly Bush
Gawsworth: Harrington Arms
Macclesfield: Castle
Wheelock: Commercial

Cornwall
Falmouth: Seven Stars

Cumbria
Broughton Mills: Blacksmiths Arms
Carlisle: Cumberland Inn

Derbyshire
Brassington: Gate Inn
Derby: Old Dolphin
Elton: Duke of York
Kirk Ireton: Barley Mow
Wardlow Mires: Three Stags' Heads

Devon
Drewsteignton: Drewe Arms
Holsworthy: King's Arms
Luppitt: Luppitt Inn
Topsham: Bridge Inn

Dorset
Pamphill: Vine
Worth Matravers: Square & Compass

County Durham
Durham City: Shakespeare
Durham City: Victoria

Gloucestershire & Bristol
Ampney St Peter: Red Lion
Bristol: King's Head
Duntisbourne Abbots:

Five Mile House
Purton: Berkeley Arms
Willsbridge: Queen's Head

Hampshire
Steep: Harrow

Herefordshire
Leintwardine: Sun Inn
Leysters: Duke of York

Kent
Broadstairs: Neptune's Hall
Ightham Common: Old House
Snargate: Red Lion

Lancashire
Great Harwood: Victoria
Preston: Black Horse

Leicestershire
Hinckley: Holly Bush
Whitwick: Three Horseshoes

Greater London
Central: EC1, Hatton Garden: Olde Mitre
EC4, Blackfriars: Black Friar
WC1, Holborn: Cittie of Yorke; Princess Louise
WC2, Covent Garden: Salisbury
East: Ilford: Dr Johnson
North N4: Finsbury Park: Salisbury
North-West: NW6 Kilburn: Black Lion
Harrow: Castle
South Kenton: Windermere
South-West: SW1, St James's: Red Lion
SW10, West Brompton: Fox & Pheasant
West: W1, Soho: Argyll Arms
W8, Kensington: Windsor Castle
W9, Maida Vale: Warrington Hotel

Greater Manchester
Altrincham: Railway
Eccles: Lamb; Royal Oak; Stanley Arms
Farnworth: Shakespeare
Gorton: Plough
Heaton Norris: Nursery Inn
Manchester: Briton's Protection; Circus Tavern; Hare & Hounds; Mr Thomas's; Peveril of the Peak

Mum's the word ... enjoying a pint in the Old Swan (Ma Pardoe's) in Netherton

Rochdale: Cemetery Hotel
Salford: Coach & Horses
Stalybridge: Grosvenor
Stockport: Alexandra; Arden Arms; Bishop Blaize; Swan with Two Necks
Westhoughton: White Lion

Merseyside
Birkenhead: Stork Hotel
Liverpool: Belvedere; Lion; Peter Kavanagh's; Philharmonic; Vines
Walton: Prince Arthur
Lydiate: Scotch Piper

Norfolk
Warham: Three Horseshoes

Northumberland
Berwick upon Tweed: Free Trade
Netherton: Star Inn

Nottinghamshire
Nottingham: Old Trip to Jerusalem
Sherwood: Five Ways

Oxfordshire
Bix: Fox
Steventon: North Star
Stoke Lyne: Peyton Arms
Stoke Talmage: Red Lion

Shropshire
Edgerley: Royal Hill

Halfway House: Seven Stars
Selattyn: Cross Keys
Shrewsbury: Loggerheads

Somerset
Appley: Globe
Bath: Old Green Tree; Star
Crowcombe: Carew Arms
Faulkland: Tucker's Grave Inn
Midsomer Norton: White Hart
Witham Friary: Seymour Arms

Staffordshire
Rugeley: Red Lion
Tunstall: Vine

Suffolk
Brent Eleigh: Cock
Bury St Edmunds: Nutshell
Ipswich: Margaret Catchpole
Laxfield: King's Head ('Low House')
Pin Mill: Butt & Oyster

East Sussex
Firle: Ram
Hadlow Down: New Inn

West Sussex
The Haven: Blue Ship

Tyne & Wear
Newcastle upon Tyne: Crown Posada

Warwickshire
Five Ways: Case is Altered

West Midlands
Birmingham: Anchor; Bartons Arms; Bellefield; Britannia; British Oak; Market Tavern; Marlborough; Red Lion; Samson & Lion; Villa Tavern; White Swan; Woodman
Bloxwich: Romping Cat; Turf Tavern
Dudley: Shakespeare
Netherton: Old Swan ('Ma Pardoe's')
Oldbury: Waggon & Horses
Rushall: Manor Arms
Sedgley: Beacon Hotel
Smethwick: Waterloo Hotel
Wednesfield: Vine

Wiltshire
Easton Royal: Bruce Arms
Salisbury: Haunch of Venison

Worcestershire
Bretforton: Fleece
Clent: Bell & Cross
Defford: Cider House ('Monkey House')
Hanley Castle: Three Kings
Worcester: Paul Pry Inn

Yorkshire: East Yorks
Beverley: White Horse Inn ('Nellie's')
Hull: Olde Black Boy; Olde White Harte
Skerne: Eagle Inn

North Yorks
Beck Hole: Birch Hall Inn
Harrogate: Gardeners Arms
York: Blue Bell; Golden Ball; Swan

South Yorks
Barnburgh: Coach & Horses
Sheffield: Bath Hotel

West Yorks
Bradford: Cock & Bottle; New Beehive
Leeds: Adelphi; Whitelock's; Cardigan Arms; Rising Sun; Garden Gate; Beech

WALES

Mid Wales
Hay-on-Wye: Three Tuns
Llanfihangel-yng-Ngwynfa: Goat
Welshpool: Grapes

North-east Wales
Ysceifiog: Fox

North-west Wales
Bethesda: Douglas Arms
Conwy: Albion Hotel

West Wales
LLandovery: Red Lion
Pontfaen: Dyffryn Arms

SCOTLAND

Dumfries & Galloway
Stranraer: Grapes

Fife
Kincardine: Railway Tavern
Kirkcaldy: Feuars Arms
Leslie: Auld Hoose

Grampian
Aberdeen: Grill

The Lothians
Edinburgh: Abbotsford; Bennet's Bar; Café Royal; Oxford Bar; Leslie's Bar
Leith: Central Bar

Strathclyde
Auldhouse: Auldhouse Arms
Glasgow: Horseshoe Bar; Old Toll Bar; Steps Bar; Portland Arms
Larkhall: Village Tavern
Lochgilphead: Commercial ('The Comm')
Paisley: Bull
Renton: Central Bar
Shotts: Old Wine Store

Tayside
Dundee: Clep; Speedwell; Tay Bridge

NORTHERN IRELAND

County Antrim
Ahoghill: Gillistown House
Ballycastle: House of McDonnell
Ballyeaston: Carmichael's
Bushmills: Bush House

County Armagh
Portadown: Mandeville Arms (McConville's)

Belfast
Belfast: Crown; Fort Bar (Gilmartin's)

County Fermanagh
Enniskillen: Blake's Bar
Irvinestown: Central Bar

More information about National Inventory pubs and the National Inventory itself can be found in a booklet pice £2.50 from CAMRA, 230 Hatfield Road, St Albans AL1 4LW, and by visiting the CAMRA website www.camra.org.uk

Compiled by Geoff Brandwood, Dave Gamston and Mick Slaughter

GREATER LONDON

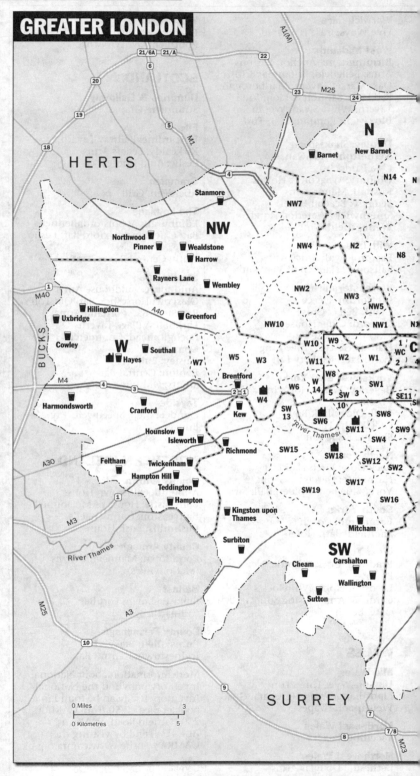

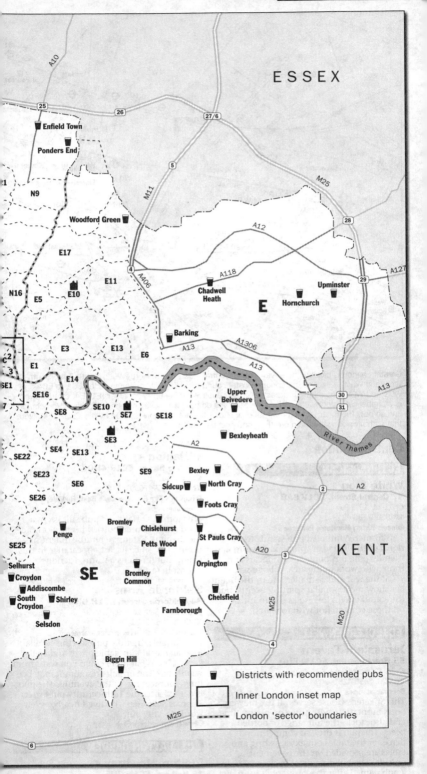

ESSEX

Enfield Town
Ponders End

N9

Woodford Green

E17

N16

E5   E10   E11

E3   E13   E6

E1

E14

SE16

SE8   SE10   SE18

SE7

SE3

SE4   SE13

SE22

SE23   SE6

SE26

Penge   Bromley

SE25

Selhurst

Croydon

Addiscombe

South   Shirley
Croydon

Selsdon

SE

Chadwell
Heath

E

Hornchurch

Upminster

Barking

Upper
Belvedere

Bexleyheath

Bexley

Sidcup   North Cray

Foots Cray

Chislehurst

Petts Wood

St Pauls Cray

Orpington

Bromley
Common

Chelsfield

Farnborough

KENT

Biggin Hill

River Thames

Districts with recommended pubs

Inner London inset map

London 'sector' boundaries

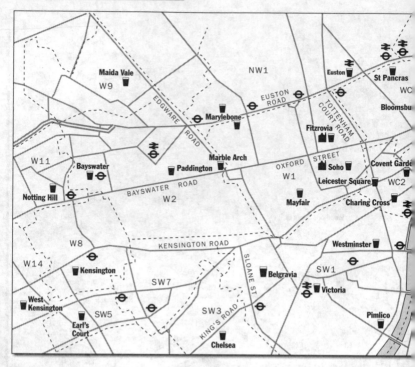

Greater London is divided into seven areas: Central, East, North, North-West, South-East, South-West and West, reflecting the London postal boundaries. Central London includes EC1 to EC4 and WC1 and WC2. The other six areas have their pubs listed in numerical order (E1, E4, etc) followed in alphabetical order by the outlying areas which do not have postal numbers (Barking, Hornchurch, and so on). The Inner London map, above, shows the area roughly covered by the Circle Line. Note that some regions straddle more than one postal district.

Central London

EC1: BARBICAN

White Lion
37 Central Street, EC1V 8AB
🕓 11-11; 12-6 Sun
☎ (020) 7689 4313
Adnams Bitter; Marston's Pedigree Ⓗ
This former Whitbread pub stands to the north of the Barbican complex. A warm and friendly pub, it is popular with locals and those who work in the area. A large-screen TV at the rear and a smaller one in the main bar show most popular sporting events, but the sound is kept low, so as not to intrude on those who do not wish to watch. ≠ ⊖

EC1: CLERKENWELL

Jerusalem Tavern
55 Britton Street, EC1M 5UQ
🕓 11-11; closed Sat & Sun
☎ (020) 7450 4281
Beer range varies Ⓐ
This St Peter's House serves all the brewery's beers in rotation, with three on at any time, and also stocks the full range of bottled beers. The pub is tiny, so competition is fierce for the tables but extra seating and tables are provided on the pavement outside. The building dates back to 1720 but a pub named after the Priory of St John of Jerusalem has been in the area since the 14th century. 🏚 Q ✿ ◖ ≠ (Farringdon) ⊖

O'Hanlon's
8 Tysoe Street, EC1R 4RQ
🕓 11-11; 12-10.30 Sun
☎ (020) 7278 7630
O'Hanlon's Fire Fly, Blakeley's Best, Red Ale; guest beers Ⓗ
This former O'Hanlon's pub still keeps a good range of their bottled beers, alongside the draught. Extensive refurbishment has taken place since its last appearance in this Guide, but it retains a warm, friendly atmosphere. ◖

Sekforde Arms
34 Sekforde Street, EC1R 0HA
🕓 11-11 (6 Sat); 11-4 Sun
☎ (020) 7253 3251
Young's Bitter, Special, Winter Warmer Ⓗ
Comfortable, friendly pub serving excellent food all day at affordable prices and well-kept beers. What more could you want from your local? The upstairs restaurant may be hired for meetings in the evening. The pub is named after the 16th-century publisher, Thomas Sekforde, who lived nearby. Well worth seeking out.
◖ ≠ (Farringdon) ⊖ ♣

EC1: HATTON GARDEN

Melton Mowbray ⊘
18 Holborn, EC1N 2LE
🕓 11-11; closed Sat & Sun
☎ (020) 7405 7077

Areas with recommended pubs
Brewery
Circle Line station
Rail connections
---- Postal District

is a short walk from the Old Bailey. On two levels, the first floor is accessed by a spiral staircase from the bar. The upstairs room is often let out for private functions in the evening. The pub is decorated with pictures and other memorabilia of the various trades of the area, including, of course, the famous Smithfield meat market which is just over the road.

◑ & ≹ (City Thameslink) ⊖ (Barbican)

EC3: CITY

Counting House ⊘
50 Cornhill, EC3V 3PD
🕙 11-11; closed Sat & Sun
☎ (020) 7283 7123
Fuller's Chiswick, London Pride, ESB, seasonal beers; guest beer (occasional) Ⓗ
This pub has been well converted from a bank to retain a period feel and much of the original decor. Many historical prints of London are displayed on the marble-tiled walls. There is plenty of extra space on the balcony and in the bank's former offices at the rear of the pub. Guest beers are stocked occasionally. Q ◑ & ≹ (Liverpool St) ⊖ (Bank)

Crosse Keys ⊘
7-12 Gracechurch Street, EC3Y 0DR
🕙 10-11 (7 Sat); closed Sun
☎ (020) 7623 4824
Fuller's London Pride; Shepherd Neame Spitfire; guest beers Ⓗ
This is not the biggest Wetherspoon's, but it is among the most impressive and the beer range is simply marvellous. At the heart of the city, this is probably the chain's flagship, offering a regularly-changing selection of up to 12 guest beers – often rare brews from micros across the country. The main bar, boasting marble pillars and an ornate ceiling with glass domes contrasts with the comfortable, smaller rooms at the rear. At busy times, the attendant in the toilet will offer perfumes and sweets to help you freshen up. Q ⟱ ◑ ≹ (Fenchurch St/ Liverpool St) ⊖ (Monument) ⠽

Elephant
119 Fenchurch Street, EC3M 5BA
🕙 11-9; closed Sat & Sun
☎ (020) 7623 8970
Young's Bitter, Special, seasonal beers Ⓗ
Old pub, now incorporated into a modern office block. To find the front entrance look for the unusual pub sign. A back stairway, from the adjacent alleyway down to the cellar bar, is even more difficult to locate. The ground-floor bar serves as a basic public

Fuller's Chiswick, London Pride, ESB, seasonal beers Ⓗ
This Fuller's Ale & Pie house is situated between London's famous legal and jewellery areas. The pub stands opposite the magnificent Prudential building and in good weather you can sit at the pavement tables to admire it. Although a small building, the pub makes good use of space, providing ample seating both on and under a mezzanine floor at the rear of the bar.
Q ⊛ ◑ & ⊖ (Chancery Lane)

Old Mitre ☆
1 Ely Court, Ely Place, EC1N 6SJ
🕙 11-11; closed Sat & Sun
☎ (020) 7405 4751
Adnams Bitter; Draught Bass; Tetley Bitter, Burton Ale Ⓗ
Unless you know of this pub you are unlikely to spot it – Ely Court is a path between Ely Place and Hatton Garden, near Holborn Circus. The pub is definitely worth finding though. The Elizabethan building retains many original features, while the seating in the lounge bar dates from the 18th century. Bar snacks, including its famous toasties, are available all day until 9.30pm. ⌚Q ⊛⟱≹ (City Thameslink/ Farringdon) ⊖ (Chancery Lane)

EC1: SMITHFIELD

Butcher's Hook & Cleaver ⊘
61 West Smithfield, EC1A 9DY
🕙 11-11; closed Sat & Sun
☎ (020) 7600 9181
website: www.butchers.hook@fullers.co.uk
Fuller's Chiswick, London Pride, ESB, seasonal beers Ⓗ
This Fuller's pub is situated between Smithfield market and St Bart's Hospital and

INDEPENDENT BREWERIES

Battersea SW11
Freedom W1 and WC2
Fuller's W4
Grand Union Hayes
Haggards SW6
Mash W1
Meantime SE7
Pacific Oriental EC2
Pitfield N1
Sweet William E10
Young's SW18
Zerodegrees SE3

bar for stand-up drinking while the cellar bar provides comfortable seating. Excellent food is served. The TV screens downstairs usually show Sky news or sports events, but neither these, nor the sound from fruit machines is obtrusive. The pub may close early evening if quiet.
◖≢ (Fenchurch St) ⊖ (Aldgate/Tower Hill)

Lamb Tavern
10-12 Leadenhall Market, EC3V 1LR
◷ 11-9; closed Sat & Sun
☎ (020) 7626 2454

Young's Bitter, Special; seasonal beers Ⓗ
Splendid, Grade II listed pub in the famous Leadenhall market. The impressively tiled basement bar is only open during the day. The main bar stays open into the evening, often with drinkers standing in the market itself, where some extra seating is available. There is another bar on the first floor. The pub has been in this Guide every year except 1985, when Young's first took over.
Q ❀◖≢ (Liverpool St/Fenchurch St)
⊖ (Monument) ⚬

Swan ⊘
Ship Tavern Passage, 78 Gracechurch Street, EC3V 1LY
◷ 11-9; closed Sat & Sun
☎ (020) 7283 7712

Fuller's Chiswick, London Pride, seasonal beers Ⓗ
Look for the covered passage next to Marks and Spencer for this small, but popular, pub. The stone-flagged, ground-floor bar is often difficult to get into and drinkers spill out into the passage for more space. The upstairs bar is a little more spacious but also fills up quickly at lunchtime and early evening. The pub occasionally stays open later if trade demands.
Q ❀◖≢ (Fenchurch St) ⊖ (Monument)

Three Lords
27 Minories, EC3N 1DD
◷ 11-11; closed Sat & Sun
☎ (020) 7481 4249

Young's Bitter, Special, Winter Warmer Ⓗ
Despite its external Victorian appearance, this is a 1985 copy of its predecessor, and the third pub of this name on the site since 1799. Inside is a light, airy bar and a downstairs function room which serves as a restaurant at lunchtime. The Three Lords were supporters of Bonnie Prince Charlie and were executed on nearby Tower Hill for their part in the 1745 Jacobite Rebellion.
◖≢ (Fenchurch St) ⊖ (Tower Hill DLR/Tower Gateway)

EC4: BLACKFRIARS

Cockpit
7 St Andrews Hill, EC4V 5BY
◷ 11-11 (9 Sat); 12-4, 7-10.30 Sun
☎ (020) 7248 7315

Courage Best Bitter, Directors; Marston's Pedigree Ⓗ
Halfway up St Andrews Hill, this wedge-shaped building dates from 1843 although there has been a pub on this site since the 16th century. The name derives from its origin as a cockfighting venue, although this stopped soon after opening in 1846. The decoration dates from the 1960s when the gallery around the top of the pub was put in to emulate the original layout. Note the fold-down shove-ha'penny board set

against the wall. This pub has had only three landlords since the 1930s. The trade comes mostly from locals, workers and members of St Paul's Cathedral choir.
Q ◖≢ (Blackfriars) ⊖ ♣

EC4: CITY

Bell
29 Bush Lane, EC4R 0AN
◷ 11-10; closed Sat & Sun
☎ (020) 7626 7560

Courage Best Bitter, Directors; Shepherd Neame Spitfire Ⓗ
Originally on a steep lane leading down to the riverside, this Grade II listed pub is now surrounded by offices. Its proximity to the river may have helped save it from the Great Fire of 1666. Its friendly atmosphere is enjoyed by local shop and office workers. This quiet pub (no music, TV or games machines) is decorated with pictures and artefacts collected during the licensee's family's many years in the trade; this is the current landlady's 43rd year here.
Q ≢ (Cannon St) ⊖

EC4: FLEET STREET

Harrow ⊘
32 Whitefriars Street, EC4Y 8JJ
◷ 11-11; closed Sat & Sun
☎ (020) 7427 0911

Fuller's London Pride Ⓗ
This long-established pub, just off Fleet Street, is busy with city workers at lunchtime and early evening. A pub of two halves, the main split-level bar and the small back bar (only accessible from Primrose Street) are dedicated to the memory of Daily Mail columnist, Vincent Mulchrone, who habitually drank here. The story goes he was there when the news broke of Kennedy's assassination. The no-smoking oak-panelled dining area is open lunchtime. Tables are put outside in good weather.
❀◖≢ (Blackfriars/Cannon St) ⊖ (Temple)

Old Bank of England ⊘
194 Fleet Street, EC4A 2LT
◷ 11-11; closed Sat & Sun
☎ (020) 7430 2255

Fuller's Chiswick, London Pride, ESB, seasonal beers Ⓗ
Large Fuller's pub in what was (until 1975) the law courts branch of the Bank of England. The interior is centred on an imposing oval bar, overlooked by a quieter balcony, and there are several adjoining side rooms. The present building was built on the site of Sweeney Todd's barber shop and adjacent pie shop. Coincidentally the pub is a branded Ale & Pie house, where food is served all day until 9pm. Q ◖▷ ⊖ (Temple)

WC1: BLOOMSBURY

Calthorpe Arms
252 Gray's Inn Road, WC1X 8JR
◷ 11-11; 12-10.30 Sun
☎ (020) 7278 4732

Young's Bitter, Special, seasonal beers Ⓗ
On the corner of Wren Street, this comfortable, friendly single-bar pub is popular with locals and office staff alike. It was once used as a temporary magistrates'

court after the first recorded murder of an on-duty policeman in 1830. The upstairs dining room is open at lunchtime; evening meals are also available 6–9.30 Monday–Friday. The upstairs room can also be hired for functions. There is no music to spoil the enjoyable atmosphere of this pub. Outside drinking is on a paved patio area.
❀◖❍ ⇌ (King's Cross) ⊖ (Russell Sq)

King's Arms
11a Northington Street, WC1N 2JF
✪ 11-11; closed Sat & Sun
☎ (020) 7405 9107
Draught Bass; Greene King IPA; guest beer Ⓗ
This is a relaxing and friendly single-bar pub, just off Gray's Inn Road, that retains a number of the better features from its days under Charringtons. There has been a pub on this site from at least 1756, originally backing on to the stables of a local brewery. Adnams Broadside is a regular guest beer. Upstairs there are two meeting rooms; the larger holds up to 50, the smaller is no-smoking and holds about 20. Meals are available at lunchtime. There is a small pavement patio area outside where seating is provided in summer.
Q ❀◖⊖ (Russell Sq) ♣ ✁

Lamb
94 Lamb's Conduit Street, WC1N 3LZ
✪ 11-11; 12-4, 7-10.30 Sun
☎ (020) 7405 0713
Young's Bitter, Special, seasonal beers Ⓗ
Named after William Lambe (1495–1580), a philanthropist who brought water to the area in 1577, this is an attractive, Grade II listed building, decorated with green upholstery, and original Victorian snob screens. The island bar has a small snug towards the rear on one side, and a sunken lounge area on the other, which leads to the outside courtyard. The pub also boasts a working music hall polyphon, a Victorian forerunner of the record player, which may be played in aid of charity. There is an upstairs dining room, open for meals except Saturday and Sunday evening.
❀◖❍ ⊖ (Russell Sq) ♣ ✁

Pakenham Arms ⊘
1 Pakenham Street, WC1X 0LA
✪ 9am-1.30am; 9am-10.30pm Sun
☎ (020) 7837 6933
Adnams Bitter; Fuller's London Pride; Harveys BB; guest beers Ⓗ
Spacious pub with a central bar, that is popular with locals, office staff and postal workers from nearby Mount Pleasant sorting office. Up to five beers are available, with Adnams, Fuller's and Harveys regularly on tap. Food is served every day – breakfasts from 9–12 and a full menu from 12–3 and 6–10. Popular for watching sports events, with a number of large-screen TVs and projection screens, it can get crowded, especially at weekends. There is some seating on a pavement patio area for when the weather is fine.
❀◖❍ ⇌ (King's Cross) ⊖ (Russell Sq) ♣

WC1: CLERKENWELL

Apple Tree
45 Mount Pleasant, WC1X 0AE
✪ 11-1am; closed Sat & Sun

☎ (020) 7837 2365
Greene King IPA, Abbot; guest beer Ⓗ
Recently refurbished, this large pub is popular with staff from the nearby Mount Pleasant sorting office, and increasingly with office staff from Gray's Inn Road. The pub windows are decorated with small apple tree motifs. A large-screen TV is generally switched on for football matches. In addition, there are pool tables and a dartboard in the large upstairs room. Meals are available from noon–10pm weekdays. Outside seating is available on a reasonably-sized pavement patio area.
❀◖❍ ⇌ (Farringdon) ⊖ ♣

WC1: HOLBORN

Cittie of Yorke ☆
22 High Holborn, WC1V 6BS
✪ 11.30-11; 12-11 Sat; closed Sun
☎ (020) 7242 7670
Samuel Smith OBB Ⓗ
Situated next to the gatehouse to Gray's Inn, a pub has stood on this site since 1430. In 1685 it was rebuilt, well back from the road with a garden in front (only benches in summer now) and was called the Gray's Inn Coffee House. The cellar bar (open from 6pm) is the old cellar of the original coffee house. The front bar (on the left as you enter) is wood panelled, with plenty of seating. The real splendour lies in the rear bar, with its vaulted ceiling, long bar, handsome screenwork, compartments for private drinking (although most customers prefer to stand) and massive mounted vats.
Q ❀◖❍ ⊖ (Chancery Lane)

Dolphin Tavern
44 Red Lion Street, WC1R 4PF
✪ 11-11; 12-11 (5 winter) Sat; 12-3, 7-10.30 Sun
☎ (020) 7831 6298
Brakspear Bitter; Fuller's London Pride; Shepherd Neame Spitfire Ⓗ
This small, one-bar house has been a pub since the 18th century. However, it had to be rebuilt in 1915 when a German Zeppelin dropped a bomb on it, killing three men. By the bar is a clock that stopped at 10.40, when the bomb hit. It is a cosy but busy place with copper and pottery artefacts giving it a cottagey feel. Food is served weekday lunchtime; for a quick evening meal, try the Fryer's Delight on Theobalds Road. Outside benches are put out when the weather is warmer. Phone to check weekend hours. ❀◖⊖

Penderel's Oak ⊘
283-288 High Holborn, WC1V 7HJ
✪ 10-11; 12-10.30 Sun
☎ (020) 7242 5669
Courage Directors; Fuller's London Pride; Greene King Abbot; Shepherd Neame Spitfire; guest beers Ⓗ
Legend has it that a man with local associations, Richard Penderel, sheltered King Charles I in his oak tree during his flight from Parliamentary forces. A huge Wetherspoon's conversion, unusually the downstairs bar features several large-screen TVs for sport and music, so it can be noisy; however, the noise in the upstairs bar comes from contented drinkers. It is as well designed as can be from the former premises of the meteorological office, providing clearly defined and some semi-

private drinking areas. At the rear is an area where supervised children can eat – last food orders for them is at 5pm. Four or more guest beers are stocked. Q ⏃◗ ⅙ ⊖⅄

WC1: ST PANCRAS

Mabel's Tavern
9 Mabledon Place, WC1H 9AZ
✪ 11-11; 12-10.30 Sun
☎ (020) 7387 7739
Shepherd Neame Master Brew Bitter, Best Bitter, Spitfire, Bishops Finger, seasonal beers ⊞
Comfortable, traditionally decorated street-corner pub, where bright carpets and upholstery are complemented by cream and plum paintwork. The body of the single room is flanked by two raised areas, one of them no-smoking. The full range of Shepherd Neame brews is served here and the bar is gratifyingly free of nitro-keg ale. It lies equidistant from Euston and King's Cross. ⌘◗⇌ (Euston) ⊖⅄

Skinners Arms
114 Judd Street, WC1H 9NT
✪ 12-11; closed Sat & Sun
☎ (020) 7837 6521
Greene King IPA, Abbot; guest beer ⊞
Friendly, one-bar pub, which was refurbished in the 1990s, moving the island bar to flank one wall. It has a raised seating area, wood panelling and a Skinners Arms clock. The rear area is for non-smokers. Run by Greene King until 2002, it is now independently owned, but you would have trouble noticing the difference. Popular with local office workers, it is close enough to St Pancras and King's Cross stations for a visit before you begin your travels.
⌘◗⇌ (King's Cross) ⊖⅄

WC2: CHARING CROSS

Ship & Shovell ✓
1-3 Craven Passage, WC2N 5PH
✪ 11 (12 Sat)-11; closed Sun
☎ (020) 7839 1311
Badger K&B Sussex, IPA, Best, Tanglefoot, seasonal beers ⊞
This Hall & Woodhouse pub straddles Craven Passage in two halves. The main bar is fully carpeted with mirrored walls and old prints showing naval battles of the 17th century. The smaller bar, across the passage, has snugs and an upstairs function room; this bar opens 12–3 and 5–11. The name of the pub is a reference to the times when the River Thames was a hive of activity and commemorates the dockers who serviced the ships. ◗⇌⊖

WC2: COVENT GARDEN

Hogshead
23 Wellington Street, WC2E 7DA
✪ 11-11; 12-10.30 Sun
☎ (020) 7836 6930
Adnams Bitter; Boddingtons Bitter; Fuller's London Pride; Hook Norton Old Hooky; guest beers ⊞
Formerly called the Gilbert & Sullivan, this small pub stands next to the Lyceum Theatre and can get very busy before a performance begins. The main bar area has clear windows and stools by the windows so you can watch people walking by and enjoying the next door restaurant. There is

an upstairs bar known as the upper circle which can take the overflow, but real ale must be purchased in the main downstairs bar. Guest beers are mainly from regional breweries. Food is available all day. ◗◗ ⊖

WC2: LEICESTER SQUARE

Bear & Staff
11 Bear Street, WC2H 7AS
✪ 11-11; 12-10.30 Sun
☎ (020) 7930 5260
Beer range varies ⊞
Dating from 1878, this Mitchell & Butlers pub operates an adventurous guest beer policy, with a selection mainly from larger micros and regional breweries. The pub draws a mainly tourist clientele, enjoying the food that is available all day. The music can be loud at times, but there is an upstairs area with its own bar where a pint can be supped in peace. ◗◗⇌ (Charing Cross) ⊖

WC2: SOHO

Moon Under Water ✓
105-107 Charing Cross Road, WC2H 0BP
✪ 10-11; 12-10.30 Sun
☎ (020) 7287 6039
Courage Directors; Greene King Abbot; Shepherd Neame Spitfire; Theakston Bitter; guest beers ⊞
Wetherspoon's conversion of the famous Marquee Club which hosted fledgling bands such as the Rolling Stones and the Who. This spacious pub stretches between Charing Cross Road and Greek Street. The Greek Street entrance has a smaller bar with no real ale and a no-smoking area overlooking the main bar. The main bar area is situated on the lower level, with alcove seating alongside the wall and tables and easy chairs in one corner. A smaller upstairs balcony with tables and chairs serves as a second no-smoking area. Even though this is a large pub, owing to its location this venue can get packed during the evening.
Q ◗◗ ⅙ ⊖ (Leicester Sq/Tottenham Ct Rd)⅄

East London

E1: SPITALFIELDS

Pride of Spitalfields
3 Heneage Street, E1 5LJ
✪ 11-11; 12-10.30 Sun
☎ (020) 7247 8933
Fuller's London Pride, ESB; guest beers ⊞
This small pub is just off Brick Lane which boasts many superb curry houses. The pub is always packed and customers tend to spill out onto the street in good weather. The pub is decorated with prints of historical East End life, especially on the canals. Old jugs and bottles jostle for space with the many pump clips from previous guest beers. The guests always include one Crouch Vale beer and usually one other. This is a really friendly East End local.
◗⇌ (Liverpool St) ⊖ (Aldgate East)

E1: WHITECHAPEL

Black Bull
199 Whitechapel Road, E1 1DE
✪ 11-11; 12-10.30 Sun
☎ (020) 7247 6707

Nethergate Suffolk County, Old Growler; guest beers Ⓗ

This large pub is close to the London Hospital and is well used by staff and patients alike, as well as the local market traders. The mock-Tudor exterior leads into a large single room, which is dominated by a big-screen TV in the corner. The atmosphere is always friendly. ◖⊖

E3: BOW

Coburn Arms
8 Coburn Road, E3 2DA
☼ 11-11; 12-10.30 Sun
☎ (020) 8980 3793

Young's Bitter, Special, seasonal beers Ⓗ

Situated in the middle of an elegant Georgian terrace, this single-bar pub is just a short distance off the busy Mile End Road. Cleverly divided by the horseshoe-shaped bar, it is a real local, with a friendly and welcoming atmosphere. Additional seating is provided in a large side room that also houses one of the pub's two dartboards.
⊛◖◗♿⊖(Mile End/Bow Rd) ♣

E5: CLAPTON

Anchor & Hope
15 High Hill Ferry, E5 9HG (10 mins N from Lea Bridge Road along towpath)
☼ 11-3, 5.30-11; 11-11 Sat; 12-10.30 Sun
☎ (020) 8806 1730

Fuller's London Pride, ESB Ⓗ

Small, one-bar drinkers' pub on the banks of the River Lea. The landlord, Leslie Heath OBE, celebrated his golden jubilee here in July. Little has changed since he took over in 1953; note the large Fuller's mirror over the brick fireplace. Check for the mistakes on the painting of the pub hanging in the small back room. The TV is switched on for sport, competing with the background music and darts in back. Drink your pint outside by the river and watch the world go by. ⊛⇌

Princess of Wales
146 Lea Bridge Road, E5 9QB
☼ 11-11; 12-10.30 Sun
☎ (020) 8533 3463

Young's Bitter, Special, seasonal beers Ⓗ

Attractive, wood-panelled pub by the Lea bridge. It has a traditional public bar and comfortable saloon bar with picture windows facing the river. A popular watering-hole for passing walkers, the pictures on the wall show that this pub was originally known as the Prince of Wales, but was renamed in 1998. A large patio and picnic area make for a pleasant summer's drink by the river; it is handy, too, for the Lea Valley ice rink. It stocks a range of Young's bottled beers. Q⊛◖◗⊟⇌♣

E6: EAST HAM

Millers Well ⊘
419-423 Barking Road, E6 2JX
☼ 10-11; 12-10.30 Sun
☎ (020) 8471 8404

Courage Directors; Greene King Abbot; Hop Back Summer Lightning; Shepherd Neame Spitfire; Theakston Best Bitter; guest beers Ⓗ

Opposite Newham town hall on the busy Barking road, this Wetherspoon's is decorated in the usual fashion with wood panelling and information boards showing local history and photos. Originally shop premises, the pub was doubled in size in 1987, allowing for the addition of a garden area and a rear skylit 'conservatory'. Very busy at evenings and weekends (especially if nearby West Ham United are at home), the customers are mostly locals and office workers popping in at the end of the day. Q⊛◖◗⊖⊬

E10: LEYTON

Drum ⊘
557-559 Lea Bridge Road, E10 7EQ
☼ 10-11; 12-10.30 Sun
☎ (020) 8539 6577

Courage Directors; Greene King Abbot; Hop Back Summer Lightning; Shepherd Neame Spitfire; Theakston Best Bitter; guest beers Ⓗ

This corner pub was recently refurbished after a fire. Close to the Baker Arms junction, it is not typical of Wetherspoon's style. The pub is split into areas with a raised bar at the back, while the conservatory admits children until 7.30. The patio area has gas heaters for chilly evenings. The friendly staff and locals add to the enjoyment. Up to five guest ales are chosen from a list of 100.
♨Q⌂⊛◖◗⇌(Midland Rd) ⊬

E11: LEYTONSTONE

Birkbeck Tavern
45 Langthorne Road, E11 4HL
☼ 11-11; 12-10.30 Sun
☎ (020) 8539 2584

Beer range varies Ⓗ

Several times winner of local CAMRA's Pub of the Year award, this large, two-bar corner pub offers an exceptionally warm welcome. Two guest beers – normally from micro-breweries – are usually available, in addition to a house beer, Rita's Special. Raising the standard still higher are the regular beer festivals. The pub maintains strong ties to the local community, hosting darts matches several nights a week. Supporters of local team, Leyton Orient, can be found drowning their sorrows here on match days.
⊛⊟⊖(Leyton) ♣

North Star
24 Browning Road, E11 3AR
☼ 12-11; 12-10.30 Sun
☎ (020) 8989 5777

Adnams Broadside; Draught Bass; Fuller's London Pride Ⓗ

There is much local debate over the name of this pub – one faction claims that it was named after a train (hence the photos around the walls) while the other holds that a ship was the inspiration. Whichever is correct, the fact that the pub was created from two cottages knocked together in the 19th century is undisputed. Part of the Voyager estate, quality is a byword in this wonderful pub, where a friendly atmosphere and a strong sporting interest prevail. ⊛◖◗⊟⊖♣

E11: WANSTEAD

Duke of Edinburgh
79 Nightingale Lane, E11 2EY

✪ 11-11; 12-10.30 Sun
☎ (020) 8989 0014
website: www.intheteam.com/dukes
Adnams Broadside; Draught Bass; Young's Bitter Ⓗ
The brick and mock-Tudor frontage and
wood panelling inside make this pub appear
older than it really is. Although it only has
one bar, there are several distinct areas
within it – a games area for darts, pool and
watching the big-screen TV; a central area
with tables for drinking; and finally at the
end a small dining area (meals served
12–6.30; not Sun). Beware the kink in
Nightingale Road – keep walking and you
will find the pub eventually. If you fancy a
game of shove-ha'penny, look for the board
fixed to the wall. ⚘◖⊖ (Snaresbrook) ♣P

George ⊘
159 High Street, E11 29GL
✪ 10-11; 12-10.30 Sun
☎ (020) 8989 2921
**Courage Directors; Greene King Abbot; Hop Back
Summer Lightning; Ridleys Rumpus; Shepherd Neame
Spitfire; guest beers** Ⓗ
This grandiose corner pub, directly opposite
Wanstead tube station, does not have the
normal Wetherspoon's feel about it. With a
marble porch and partly frosted windows
there are distinct drinking areas, and a
balcony bar (open Fri and Sat eves). Pictures
of old Wanstead in its heyday and also
famous Georges abound, but Saint George is
not forgotten, with a dragon's chair and a
dragon bursting through the ceiling of the
downstairs bar.
♨Q⌇⚘◖⊟⚘⊖

E13: PLAISTOW

Black Lion
59-61 High Street, E13 0AD
✪ 11-3.30, 5-11; 11-11 Thu-Sat; 12-10.30 Sun
☎ (020) 8472 2351
Courage Best Bitter, Directors; guest beers Ⓗ
This former coaching inn dates back 450
years, although the frontage was rebuilt in
1875. Its many rooms are on different levels
– the split-level front bar is bare-boarded
with half-panelled walls and carved wooden
seating. To the left is a comfortable lounge
(Grade II listed). The old stables are now
used by the West Ham Boys and Amateur
Boxing Club – George Walker and Michael
Watson are just two successes to have
trained here. Evening meals are served
5–7.30. Q⚘◖⊟⊖

E14: LIMEHOUSE

Grapes
76 Narrow Street, E14 8BP
✪ 12-3.30, 5.30-11; 12-11 Sat; 12-10.30 Sun
☎ (020) 7987 4396
Adnams Bitter; Draught Bass; Tetley Burton Ale Ⓗ
In all respects, this is a very traditional pub,
from the etched glass frontage to the range
of superbly-kept beers available at the bar.
Upstairs you will find a renowned, award-
winning seafood restaurant, while those
craving fresh air should head straight for the
river front deck overlooking the Thames
at the rear of the main bar. Bar meals are
available daily, including an excellent roast
on Sunday lunchtime; evening meals are
served weekdays.
Q⚘◖⇌(Limehouse) ⊖(DLR Westferry) ♣

E17: WALTHAMSTOW

Coppermill
205 Coppermill Lane, E17 7HP
✪ 11-11; 12-10.30 Sun
☎ (020) 8520 3709
Courage Best Bitter; Fuller's London Pride, ESB Ⓗ
This small, busy, corner pub has a strong
community focus – as is evident from the
constant hum of conversation. There is also
a definite sporting interest, with notice
boards providing information on
everything from football to sub-aqua. Take
the time to look at the various artefacts
decorating the pub – hanging from the
ceiling, around the walls, and on every
available surface; especially notable are the
display cases housing miniature
handpumps. ⚘⇌(St James St) ♣

Flower Pot
128 Wood Street, E17 3HX
✪ 11-11; 12-10.30 Sun
☎ (020) 8520 3600
Draught Bass; guest beers Ⓗ
This large, one-bar community pub is in
Walthamstow's Wood Street shopping area.
The beer range has recently been expanded
and now two guests are regularly on tap,
often from Young's and Charles Wells. The
pub has a strong commitment to real ale,
and displays several brewery mirrors,
including one from the now-defunct
Wenlock Brewery. Football matches are
shown on a big-screen TV and live music is
occasionally performed. ⚘⇌(Wood St) ♣

Village
31 Orford Road, E17 9NL
✪ 11-11; 12-10.30 Sun
☎ (020) 8521 9982
Fuller's London Pride; guest beers Ⓗ
A favourite local in this area, especially for
those going on to clubs. It can get noisy at
times, not just with the music, but also
because of the crowds. It does stay quieter
in the snug at the rear and also in the large
yard behind the pub which has plenty of
seating. There are usually three or four
guests from all over the country.
⚘◖⇌(Central) ⊖

BARKING

Britannia
1 Church Road, IG11 8PR (near A123)
✪ 11-3, 5-11; 12-11 Sat; 12-10.30 Sun
☎ (020) 8594 1305
**Young's Bitter, Special, Winter Warmer, seasonal
beers** (occasional) Ⓗ
Young's only tied house in the area, it is a
long-standing entry in this Guide and has
been local CAMRA's Pub of the Year several
times, including 2003. A roomy,
comfortable, saloon bar contrasts with a
more basic public bar where games are
played. The caryatids on the pub's frontage
are a rare (and possibly the only remaining)
example in East London. Food is available
at lunchtime and early evening.
⚘◖⊟⇌⊖♣P

CHADWELL HEATH

Eva Hart ⊘
1128 High Road, RM6 4AH (on A118)
✪ 10-11; 12-10.30 Sun

☎ (020) 8597 1069
Courage Best Bitter, Directors; Ridleys Prospect, Old Bob; Shepherd Neame Spitfire, Bishops Finger; guest beers Ⓗ

This large, comfortable Wetherspoon's was converted from a former police station, on the site of the old village stocks. Eva Hart, who was the longest-lived survivor of the Titanic disaster, was a well-known singer and music teacher and there is plenty of memorabilia commemorating her life. The pub operates an excellent guest beer policy, stocking three or more beers and often Westons Old Rosie cider. A children's licence is in force for the no-smoking gallery until 7pm. Good value food is available all day. Q ☼ ☜ ⊛ ◖◗ & ≢ ● P ✁

HORNCHURCH

Chequers
North Street, RM11 1ST (near A124)
✪ 11-11; 12-10.30 Sun
☎ (01708) 442094
Ansells Best Bitter; Draught Bass; Greene King Abbot Ⓗ

This small local has somehow managed to retain its character despite recent refurbishment. Situated on a traffic island, it sells good value beers and is definitely a drinker's pub. A very busy local, especially early evening, it enjoys a keen darts following and fields several teams. There is an unobtrusive TV in one corner for sports fans, away from the main seating area. It was deservedly local CAMRA's Pub of the Year 1997–1999, and 2001–2002. Lunches are served Wednesday–Friday.
◖◗ ≢ (Emerson Pk) ♣ P

UPMINSTER

Crumpled Horn ⬤
33-37 Corbets Tey Road, RM14 2AJ (on B1421)
✪ 11-11; 12-10.30 Sun
☎ (01708) 226698
Gale's GB; Wells Bombardier; guest beers Ⓗ

Opened in September 2000, this Wizard Inn is an attractive conversion of three shop units in the centre of Upminster. The four real ales usually available are supplemented by occasional beer festivals. The pub provides a welcome boost to the limited local real ale scene. Food is available for most of the day. A quiz is held on Tuesday evening. The pub's name was chosen in a competition and was taken from a nearby (now defunct) dairy. ◖◗ & ≢ ⊖ ✁

WOODFORD GREEN

Cricketers ⬤
299-301 High Road, IG8 9HQ (on A1199)
✪ 11-11; 12-10.30 Sun
☎ (020) 8504 2734
McMullen AK, Country, seasonal beers; guest beer Ⓗ

Comfortable, friendly pub, almost opposite the famous statue of Sir Winston Churchill on the green. The cosy, peaceful saloon bar displays wooden plaques of various county cricket clubs. The more basic public bar features a dartboard. Regular monthly quiz nights are held. Excellent weekday lunches are served, including very good value pensioners' specials. This attractive pub last year won the Silver Rose in the McMullen

in Bloom competition. There is a small patio at the front.
⊛ ◖ ⊟ & ♣ P

Traveller's Friend
496-498 High Road, IG8 0PN (on A104)
✪ 11-11; 12-4, 7-10.30 Sun
☎ (020) 8504 2435
Courage Best Bitter, Directors; Greene King Abbot; Ridleys IPA; guest beer Ⓗ

Small, but characterful single-bar pub on an access road, just off the busy High Road. As far as is known no keg bitter has ever been sold here; during the dark days of ubiquitous keg, Draught Bass was the mainstay here. The walls of the horseshoe-shaped bar are panelled with oak; on one side the original snob screens are still in place. The sociable couple who have run the pub for many years organise a beer festival annually in April. This splendid local is well worth a visit, if only to view the collection of pub brewery memorabilia. Limited parking. Q ⊛ ◖◗ & P

North London

N1: HOXTON

Beershop
14B Pitfield Street, N1 6EY
✪ 11-7 (not Mon); 10-4 Sat; closed Sun
☎ (020) 7739 3701
website: www.pitfieldbeershop.co.uk
Beer range varies Ⓗ

This modestly proportioned off-licence is crammed with many delights. Organic wines, craft-made cider, home brewing supplies, breweriana, books and glasses jostle for space with a huge number of British bottled ales, including those of the neighbouring Pitfield Brewery. According to author Tim Webb it stocks the best range of Belgian beer in London. German and American beers are also well represented.
≢ (Old St) ⊖

Prince Arthur
49 Brunswick Place, N1 6EB
✪ 11-11; 12-6 Sun
☎ (020) 7253 3187
Shepherd Neame Master Brew Bitter, Best Bitter, Spitfire Ⓗ

Situated between City Road and Pitfield Street (close to the Pitfield Beer Shop), this small, pleasant single-bar, back-street local attracts drinkers from nearby offices. There is a dartboard in a sunken area towards the rear, and the pub fields both ladies' and men's dart teams. The pub has been redecorated recently. Outside seating is available for fine summer weather. ⊛ ≢ (Old St) ⊖ ♣

Wenlock Arms ⬤
26 Wenlock Road, N1 7TA
✪ 12-11; 12-10.30 Sun
☎ (020) 7608 3406 website: www.wenlock-arms.co.uk
Adnams Bitter; Crouch Vale Brewers Gold; guest beers Ⓗ

Established in 1835, and formerly the Wenlock brewery tap, this lively street-corner pub near Regent's Canal was rescued from oblivion in 1994. Since then the Wenlock has been North London CAMRA's Pub of the Year three times. An island bar with alcove seating, this pub attracts locals

and visitors from afar, who come to sample the ever-changing range of beers. Up to five guests, including a mild are stocked, plus a draught cider or perry. It stages occasional music nights in addition to regular Sunday lunchtime jazz. Bar food includes their famous salt beef 'sandwedges'.
♨ ⇌ ⊖ (Old St) ♣ ♠

N1: ISLINGTON

Compton Arms
4 Compton Avenue, N1 2XD
✪ 12-11; 12-10.30 Sun
☎ (020) 7359 6883
Greene King IPA; Ruddles County, Abbot; guest beer Ⓗ
Small, attractive, cottage-style building, in a narrow side street opposite some modern flats. Inside, with its compact dimensions and wooden beams, you get even more of a country pub atmosphere. The main part of the pub is a narrow bare-boarded area. Towards the rear is a smaller dining area that features old local prints on the walls. There is also a lower lounge area that leads out to the patio courtyard. Food is served 12–2.30 and 6–8.30 weekdays (except Tue), and 12–4 at the weekend. It gets crowded before kick-off when Arsenal play at home.
❀◐⇌ (Highbury & Islington) ⊖

Duke of Cambridge
30 St Peter's Street, N1 8JT
✪ 12-11; 12-10.30 Sun
☎ (020) 7359 3066
Pitfield Singhbolton, Shoreditch Stout, Eco Warrier; St Peter's Organic Best Bitter Ⓗ
This large, open-plan pub was transformed into a gastro-pub after being closed for two years, squatted and vandalised. What makes this different, even for the Islington area, is that almost all the food and drink is based on organic ingredients. The pub itself is furnished with large wooden tables, while outbuildings have been turned into a waiter-service restaurant (you can also eat in the main bar). It can get very busy in the evenings with food dominating, but you still feel comfortable, just having a beer. Expensive, even for this area.
Q ❀◐ ⊖ (Angel) ✂

Prince of Wales
1A Sudeley Street, N1 8HP
✪ 11-11; 12-10.30 Sun
☎ (020) 7837 6173
Adnams Bitter; Young's Special Ⓗ
Knocked through, L-shaped, wood-panelled, street corner local, retaining some original features. Situated by the Regents Canal, the Prince of Wales is a welcome retreat from the hubbub of Upper Street. A couple of tables for outside drinking are provided in summer. Home-made oriental cooking is a speciality and the menu also features pinoy jerk chicken, curry and lasagne. Meals are served weekdays 12–3 and 6–8pm.
◐ ⊖ (Angel) ♣

N2: EAST FINCHLEY

Madden's
130 High Road, N2 9ED
✪ 11-11; 12-10.30 Sun
☎ (020) 8444 7444

Fuller's London Pride; Greene King Abbot; guest beers Ⓗ
Authentic Irish-run pub, where it is tricky to find the entrance due to abundant foliage. Recent refurbishment shows off the wood panelling and stone floor. Note the eclectic collection of artefacts, including jazz figurines, Charlie Chaplin memorabilia and the 1999 Grand National winning jockey's shirt. A big-screen TV is switched on for sports in the back area which has cosy leather sofas. A smaller TV is above the door in the front area. Unusually, food is brought in from the recommended Chinese restaurant next door. The house beers are brewed by Cottage. It hosts occasional live music. ⅚ ♣ ♠

N8: CROUCH END

Harringay Arms
153 Crouch Hill, N8 9QH
✪ 12-11; 12-10.30 Sun
☎ (020) 8340 4243
Courage Best Bitter, Directors Ⓗ
This welcoming, single-bar local at the heart of Crouch End is frequented by a devoted clientele. The wood-panelled interior displays many old pictures of the area and copies of documents showing the history of this old pub. A TV often is quietly on at the back, but conversation rules. Behind the pub is a walled courtyard with seating. Filled rolls are available at lunchtime. Quiz night is Tuesday. ❀⇌ (Crouch Hill) ♣

N8: HORNSEY

Tollgate ⊘
26-30 Turnpike Lane, N8 0PS
✪ 10-11; 12-10.30 Sun
☎ (020) 8889 9085
Courage Directors; Greene King Abbot; Shepherd Neame Spitfire; Theakston Best Bitter; guest beers Ⓗ
Recently refurbished Wetherspoon's pub that has kept its character as a community local and as the area's best ale house. In addition to the regular beers, five guest beers are served, usually from the company's seasonal list. Good value food is served until an hour before closing. It can be very noisy on weekend evenings.
Q ❀◐⇌ ⊖ (Turnpike Lane) ✂

N9: LOWER EDMONTON

Beehive
24 Little Bury Street, N9 9JZ
✪ 11-11; 12-10.30 Sun
☎ (020) 8360 4358
Adnams Bitter; Draught Bass; Marston's Pedigree; Tetley Bitter Ⓗ
1930s suburban estate pub serving a mainly local clientele. Once two bars, it has been knocked through with a central bar. One end has a pool table with a distinctive purple cloth. Also noteworthy is an unusual coat and umbrella stand. Evening meals are available on weekdays. The TV is switched on for sports events. Small garden. ❀◐ ♣ P

N14: SOUTHGATE

New Crown ⊘
80-84 Chase Side, N14 5PH
✪ 10-11; 12-10.30 Sun
☎ (020) 8882 8758

Courage Best Bitter, Directors; Greene King Abbot;
Hop Back Summer Lightning; Shepherd Neame
Spitfire; guest beers Ⓗ
Large Wetherspoon's conversion of a former
supermarket, frequented by local office and
business workers. In the evening and at
weekends it is mainly taken over by the
younger generation. Three or four guest
beers usually come from smaller breweries.
It stages two beer festivals a year. A good
value menu is served all day (it opens at
10am for breakfast); curry night is
Thursday. Pictures of old Southgate, its
history and local luminaries decorate the
walls. Cider is kept in summer. Q ◐ ⊖ ⚫ ⅍

Woolpack
52 High Street, N14 6EB
✪ 11-11; 12-10.30 Sun
☎ (020) 8886 5051
**Courage Best Bitter or Directors; Greene King Old
Speckled Hen; guest beer Ⓗ**
Victorian pub that has retained its
character. Split levels open out into various
drinking areas, part bare-boarded and part
carpeted, and furnished in country style. It
is located midway between the village green
and shopping centre. A very playful
Rottweiler sometimes appears during
opening hours. The Woolpack is popular
with students at the local college. The meals
are home cooked. Pool and darts are played.
❀ ◐ ⊖ ♣

N16: STOKE NEWINGTON

Rochester Castle ✅
145 Stoke Newington High Street, N16 0NY
✪ 10-11; 12-10.30 Sun
☎ (020) 7249 6016
**Courage Best Bitter, Directors; Fuller's London Pride;
Greene King Abbot; Hop Back Summer Lightning;
Shepherd Neame Spitfire; guest beers Ⓗ**
Refurbished in spring 2003, this is a busy
and popular Wetherspoon's, drawing
customers from all walks of life. A welcome
relief from the hustle and bustle of the
thriving cosmopolitan thoroughfare, this is
a quiet pub where conversation is very
much alive. It keeps regular guest beers. The
no-smoking conservatory leads out to the
garden. Chess is played. Q ⇆ ❀ ◐ ⇌ ♣ ⅍

N21: WINCHMORE HILL

Orange Tree
18 Highfield Road, N21 3HA
✪ 11-11; 12-10.30 Sun
☎ (020) 8360 4853
Greene King IPA; guest beers Ⓗ
Traditional, back-street local with a friendly,
welcoming atmosphere, signposted off
Green Lanes. There is one large bar with a
dartboard and a large-screen TV for sporting
events, as well as a semi-separate room with
a pool table. The large garden at the rear has
a barbecue and children's play area. The
local CAMRA branch voted this Pub of the
Year in 1999, 2000 and 2002. ❀ ◑ ⇌ ♣ ♣

BARNET

Albion
74 Union Street, EN5 4HZ
✪ 12 (11 Sat)-11; 12-10.30 Sun
☎ (020) 8441 2841
Greene King IPA, Abbot; Tetley Burton Ale Ⓗ

Archetypal, popular and friendly back-street
boozer. Tucked away behind the High
Street, it still has an outside gents loo. One
bar serves two distinct areas; the smaller
public side has a dartboard and games set
into table tops, while the lounge area has a
TV for loyal sports fans (mostly rugby). It
boasts a fascinating collection of WWI
memorabilia. A surprisingly large garden
has a children's play area. The pub is a rare
outlet for draught cider (Addlestones).
❀ ⊖ (High Barnet) ⚫

Lord Nelson
14 West End Lane, EN5 2SA (off Wood St)
✪ 11-2.30, 5-11; 11-3, 6-11 Sat; 12-4, 7-10.30 Sun
☎ (020) 8449 7249
**Adnams Bitter; Fuller's London Pride; Greene King
IPA, Abbot; Jennings Cumberland Ale Ⓗ**
Friendly, back-street free house. Smartly
refurbished, with patio tables at the front,
the interior bears a nautical theme,
displaying model ships in the front bay and
above the bar. A framed poem on the wall
by Richard Burton, is a reminder that he
and Liz Taylor frequented this pub when
filming at Elstree in the 1960s. Meals
include a fish and chips evening (Mon) and
steak evening (Wed); no other evening
meals are served and there is no food
Sunday. Ask for games (for example,
cribbage) if you wish to play. ❀ ◐ ♣

Mitre Inn
58 High Street, EN5 5SJ
✪ 12-11; 12-10.30 Sun
☎ (020) 8449 6582
**Adnams Bitter; Ansells Mild; Tetley Bitter; guest
beers Ⓗ**
Once a famous coaching inn for sometimes
dangerous journeys into Hertfordshire or
London, the pub's character has changed
little. Having seen celebrated visitors such as
General Monk and Dr Johnson, it is worth
noting the wonderful inscriptions on the
walls. Lively in the evenings, particularly if
sport is on TV, it is quieter in the afternoon.
The high side of the bar is a no-smoking
area. With regularly-changing guest ales and
good value food (served 12–8; 12–6
weekends), this is a deservedly popular pub.
Limited parking. ❀ ◐ ⊖ (High Barnet) ♣ P ⅍

Monken Holt
193 High Street, EN5 5SU
✪ 11-11; 12-10.30 Sun
☎ (020) 8449 4280
**Adnams Bitter; Greene King IPA; Taylor Landlord;
guest beers Ⓗ**
Privately-owned town pub, representing
good value for both beer and food (served
all day). An amusing menu gives the A–Z of
ordering at the bar. The name derives from
General Monk, who camped in Barnet on
his way to restore Charles II to the throne. A
conservatory (with five unobtrusive TVs)
leads to a suntrap garden. Note the two
CAMRA mirrors and a sign on the fireplace
stating that foul language is not tolerated.
The pub fields a crib team and hosts a
Thursday quiz. ❀ ♣

Sebright Arms
9 Alston Road, EN5 4ET
✪ 12 (5 Mon)-11; 12-10.30 Sun
☎ (020) 8449 6869
McMullen AK, Country, seasonal or guest beer Ⓗ

Friendly, community pub where the enterprising tenants decline to use the cask breather. The lively public bar has a TV for sport and a photographic display dedicated to Barnet FC. A hand-painted sporting mural decorates one wall. The quieter lounge has a real fire. Bus No. 384 passes the door. ♨ ⊞ ♣

ENFIELD TOWN

Old Wheatsheaf
3 Windmill Hill, EN2 6SE
✪ 11-11; 12-10.30 Sun
☎ (020) 8363 0516
Adnams Bitter; Greene King IPA; Tetley Bitter; guest beers ⊞
This pub is well known for its outside floral displays for which many prize certificates hang in the public bar. This comfortable bar has a fruit machine and a TV for sporting events. The quieter saloon bar to the side of the pub displays pictures of the old Enfield. There are tables outside for use in summer. The quiz nights are popular with locals. Lunches are served weekdays.
◑ ⊞ ≓ (Enfield Chase)

NEW BARNET

Railway Bell ✔
13 East Barnet Road, EN4 8RR
✪ 10-11; 12-10.30 Sun
☎ (020) 8449 1369
Courage Best Bitter, Directors; Greene King Abbot; Shepherd Neame Spitfire; guest beers ⊞
Unlike many Wetherspoon's establishments there has always been a pub on this site. There are usually three or four guest beers on tap. Admire the railway memorabilia on the walls and, as it is situated by the railway, it is possible to sit in the garden and watch the trains go by. The conservatory at the back includes the no-smoking area. It attracts a good mix of patrons and is justifiably popular with locals. Q ❀ ◑ ≓ P ⅟

PONDERS END

Picture Palace ✔
Howard's Hall, Lincoln Road, EN3 4AQ
✪ 10-11; 12-10.30 Sun
☎ (020) 8344 9690
Courage Directors; Greene King Abbot; Shepherd Neame Spitfire; Theakston Best Bitter; guest beers ⊞
Excellent Wetherspoon's conversion of a derelict council community hall and former cinema. The main bar area is rather attractive and includes some comfortable leather sofas among the more conventional tables and chairs. Murals high on the walls depict early cinema stars to remind customers of the building's history. Facilities for the disabled, including two low sections of bar, and two family areas, help to make this a popular pub, and a welcome addition to the area.
Q ⌂ ❀ ◑ ⅓ ≓ (Southbury) ♣ P ⅟

North-West London

NW1: CAMDEN TOWN

Spread Eagle
141 Albert Street, NW1 7NB
✪ 11-11; 12-10.30 Sun

☎ (020) 7267 1410
Young's Bitter, Special, seasonal beers ⊞
This elegant pub is divided into two rooms, featuring old framed prints and extensive dark wood panelling. The elongated bar is carpeted and furnished with benches and stools. The other room boasts picture windows. Food is served lunchtime and early evening (pizzas). There is an outside drinking area with benches and tables along the quieter side road. ❀ ◑ ⊖ ♣

NW1: EUSTON

Head of Steam
1 Eversholt Street, NW1 1DN
✪ 11-11; 12-10.30 Sun
☎ (020) 7383 3359
Holt Bitter; Hop Back Summer Lightning; guest beers ⊞
Close enough to offer a handy waiting place for trains, there is a good beer range here, including a mild. The pub, which is full of railway memorabilia, is reached by a flight of stairs. The bar area has a TV and bar billiards. A raised no-smoking area allows bus travellers to keep an eye out for the right bus. Evening meals are served 5–8 weekdays; no food Sunday. Ask for the code to use the toilets. ◑ ≓ ⊖ ♣ ♠ ⅟

NW1: MARYLEBONE

Perseverance
11 Shroton Street, NW1 6UG
✪ 11-11; 12-10.30 Sun
☎ (020) 7723 7469
Draught Bass; Greene King IPA ⊞
Friendly pub used by both locals and workers. Originally an inn catering for stagecoaches, it had two bars which were knocked through into one in the early 1990s. Later in that decade it suffered two major floods when a mains pipe in nearby Lisson Grove burst, completely flooding the cellar and rising up into the bar itself. A genuine local in central London.
❀ ◑ ≓ ⊖ (Baker St)

NW2: CRICKLEWOOD

Beaten Docket ✔
50-56 Cricklewood Broadway, NW2 3DT
✪ 10-11; 12-10.30 Sun
☎ (020) 8450 2972
Courage Directors; Greene King Abbot; Shepherd Neame Spitfire ⊞
A beacon of real ale in an area said by humorist Alan Coren to be unpossessed of either wood or crickle. This is a fairly typical Wetherspoon's conversion of a former retail premises. With the passage of time it has become very comfortably worn in, with a series of well-defined drinking areas disguising the vastness of the place. The pub's name refers to a losing betting slip; plenty of prints and paraphernalia reinforce the theme. There is a good choice of excellent value restaurants nearby (try the Khana). Benches are outside all year long for the hardy. A local CAMRA Pub of the Season winner. Q ❀ ◑ ⅓ ≓ ⅟

NW3: HAMPSTEAD

Duke of Hamilton
23 New End, NW3 1JD

✪ 12-11; 12-10.30 Sun
☎ (020) 7794 0258

Fuller's London Pride, ESB; guest beers Ⓗ

A consecutive entry in this Guide for 12
years, and local CAMRA Pub of the Year
2002 and 2003, this good value
community local is an oasis in a
wilderness of gastro-pubs and coffee bars.
Named after a Civil War Royalist, this
200-year-old pub has a single bar and a
large front terrace. The bar displays an
extensive collection of brewing, rugby and
cricketing memorabilia, and old local
photographs. Draught Czech lager is also
available, along with a selection of more
than 15 malt whiskies.
Q ❀ ◖≉ (Hampstead Heath) ⊖ ♦

Holly Bush ⊘
22 Holly Mount, NW3 6SG (up Heath St to Holly
Steps)
✪ 12-11; 12-10.30 Sun
☎ (020) 7435 2892

**Adnams Bitter, Broadside; Fuller's London Pride;
Harveys BB; Hook Norton Double Stout** Ⓗ

A true gem, nestling in the quiet streets of
Hampstead. Grade II listed status applies as
the pub is unspoilt and retains many
original features. Built from stables in the
early 19th century, the single-bar pub has
many side rooms. Features include a real
coal fire, a large Benskins enamel sign, and
original wood fittings. A resident ghost
enhances the period atmosphere. Food is
cooked on the premises. The pub has
several famous customers.
🏠Q ❀ ◖≉ (Hampstead Heath) ⊖ ♣

NW4: HENDON
Greyhound
52 Church End, NW4 4JT
✪ 11-11; 12-10.30 Sun
☎ (020) 8457 9730

Young's Bitter, Special, seasonal beer or guest beer Ⓗ

First mentioned as an inn in 1655, the
Greyhound is idyllically located between a
picturesque 18th-century church and the
Charles II period Church Farmhouse
Museum. This large, busy pub is decorated
with photos of old Hendon and is handy for
the town hall and Middlesex University. A
large-screen TV is switched on for sporting
events. The guest beer is usually from
Smiles. ◖

NW5: TUFNELL PARK
Dartmouth Arms
35 York Rise, NW5 1SP
✪ 11 (10 Sat)-11; 10-10.30 Sun
☎ (020) 7485 3267

Adnams Bitter; guest beers Ⓗ

Relaxed, community pub that combines a
traditional two-room layout with
contemporary decor. Good food is available
until 10pm every day, and ranges from a
breakfast menu to a selection of daily
specials. A different well-priced set menu is
served each Thursday. One of the two guest
beers often comes from a micro-brewery
such as Boggart Hole Clough or Cottage. It
hosts frequent wine tastings; a cider is
stocked in summer. There is a cigar
humidor next to the pub's own bookshop.
Quiz night is Tuesday.
🏠 ❀ ◖ ⊖ ♣ ♦

NW7: MILL HILL
Rising Sun
137 Marsh Lane, Highwood Hill, NW7 4EY
(³/₄ mile from A41/A1 jct)
✪ 12-11; 12-10.30 Sun
☎ (020) 8959 1357

Adnams Bitter; Greene King Abbot; Young's Bitter Ⓗ

Intimate, 17th-century country pub on the
edge of London, set at the top of a hill. Its
long history includes ghost stories and
ownership by Stamford Raffles, founder of
London Zoo. An unspoilt interior features a
small bar, a quaint, raised snug room, a
lounge bar and a restaurant converted from
a barn. Good quality meals are served in
generous portions, from 12–9.30 (8.30 Sun).
❀ ◖ ♣ P

NW10: HARLESDEN
Grand Junction Arms
Acton Lane, NW10 7AD
✪ 11-11; (1am Fri; midnight Sat); 12-10.30 Sun
☎ (020) 8965 5670

Young's Bitter, Special, seasonal beers Ⓗ

Imposing pub, alongside the Grand Union
Canal (moorings available), comprising
three contrasting bars, together with
extensive gardens, a patio and children's
amusements. The front bar has pool tables
and a large-screen TV for sport. The middle
bar is more intimate and regularly features
sport on a smaller TV. The beamed back bar
opens on to the canal and has a children's
certificate until 7pm at weekends. Good
food is served all day until 9pm (cold snacks
3–6). Cooked on the premises, many dishes
include beer.
❀ ◖ 🍽 ≉ ⊖ ♣ P

HARROW
Moon on the Hill ⊘
373-375 Station Road, HA1 2AW
✪ 10-11; 12-10.30 Sun
☎ (020) 8863 3670

**Courage Directors; Theakston Best Bitter;
guest beers** Ⓗ

A relatively small and cosy Wetherspoon's
pub, it is always well patronised. The
clientele consists of office workers, shoppers
and local Harrovians. The pub keeps five
real ales, including unusual guests and takes
part in twice-yearly beer festivals. It opens
for breakfast at 10am and serves good value
meals until late evening. The pub is on two
levels; the lower level, which has several
booths, is the designated no-smoking
section.
Q ◖ ✂

NORTHWOOD
Sylvan Moon ⊘
27 Green Lane, HA6 2PX
✪ 10-11; 12-10.30 Sun
☎ (01923) 820760

**Courage Best Bitter, Directors; Fuller's London Pride;
Hop Back Summer Lightning; Shepherd Neame
Spitfire; guest beers** Ⓗ

The frontage of this corner Wetherspoon's
house, is festooned with attractive hanging
baskets in summer. Framed photos of old
Northwood village decorate the walls inside.
A good mix of all ages frequents this busy
local, especially Thursday and Friday

evenings, when students from the nearby college join the throng. At least two guest beers are on tap at any one time.
Q ◑ ♿ ⊖ ✗

PINNER

Oddfellows
2 Waxwell Lane, HA5 3EN
⊛ 11-3, 5.30 (6 Sat)-11; 12-3, 7-10.30 Sun
☎ (020) 8866 7372
Fuller's London Pride; Greene King IPA; Young's Special Ⓗ
This Grade II listed building was named in recognition of Thomas Ellement, who founded the Pinner branch of the Oddfellows Society in 1848. A very comfortable 'village' local at the end of the High Street, a recent redecoration has resulted in the loss of the old prints and memorabilia. Large garden.
⊛ ◑ ⊖

Queen's Head
31 High Street, HA5 5PJ
⊛ 11-11; 12-10.30 Sun
☎ (020) 8868 9844
Adnams Bitter; Ansells Best Bitter; Draught Bass; Greene King Abbot; Tetley Bitter; Young's Special Ⓗ
This Grade II listed building is the oldest pub in Pinner, partly dating back to 1540, although an ale house is believed to have been on this site since the first Pinner Fair in 1336. The attractive decor includes exposed beams and plenty of stained wood panelling. An open fire and lack of music give this a true pub feel. A no-smoking area is available at lunchtime. ⚑ Q ⊛ ◑ ⊖ P ✗

RAYNERS LANE

Village Inn ⊘
402-408 Rayners Lane, HA5 5DY (lower end of one-way system)
⊛ 10-11; 12-10.30 Sun
☎ (020) 8868 8551
Courage Directors; Greene King Abbot; Hop Back Summer Lightning; Shepherd Neame Spitfire; Theakston Best Bitter; guest beers Ⓗ
Typical Wetherspoon's shop conversion at the junction of Village Way and Rayners Lane. It stocks at least two guest beers, more during the beer festivals held twice a year. Parking at the rear is difficult – the Pay and Display opposite is easier. A mix of booths and stools and a display of local photographs complete the picture.
Q ⊛ ◑ ♿ ⊖ P ✗

STANMORE

Man in the Moon ⊘
1 Buckingham Parade, The Broadway, HA7 4EB (on A410 at the foot of Stanmore Hill, A4140)
⊛ 10-11; 12-10.30 Sun
☎ (020) 8954 6119
Courage Best Bitter, Directors; Greene King Abbot; Shepherd Neame Spitfire; guest beers Ⓗ
Large, busy, town-centre Wetherspoon's displaying plenty of photos and history of old Stanmore. With the food and children's dining area tucked away at the back of the pub, there is a pleasant smoke-free atmosphere for dining. As well as the regular beers, there are two or three ever-changing guest ales usually available.
Q ◑ ♿ ⊖ ✗

WEALDSTONE

Royal Oak
60 Peel Road, HA3 7QU
⊛ 11-11; 12-10.30 Sun
☎ (020) 8426 0981
Adnams Bitter; Tetley Bitter; guest beers Ⓗ
Although rather hard to find (the route along Peel Road from the High Street having been severed by a multi-storey car park and a bypass), once negotiated, the best beer for miles around can be sampled. A former Burton Ale Master Cellarman, the landlord recently received local CAMRA's 10-year award for continuous entries in this Guide. Good food can be enjoyed (not Sat or Sun eve) in one of several distinctive areas in this 1930s-built establishment, including a newish conservatory, built at the expense of the public bar. ⊛ ◑ ⇌ ⊖ P

WEMBLEY

JJ Moons ⊘
397 High Road, HA9 6AA
⊛ 10-11; 12-10.30 Sun
Courage Directors; Greene King Abbot; Shepherd Neame Spitfire; guest beers Ⓗ
Long-standing Wetherspoon's pub near the Wembley complex. Five beers are usually available, including two guests from smaller breweries, all sold at very competitive prices. The pub opens at 10am to serve breakfast and continues to supply good food throughout the day. The combination of good quality and value attracts a varied clientele that reflects the diversity of the local community. ⚑ Q ⊛ ◑ ♿ ⊖ ✗

South-East London

SE1: BANKSIDE

Founders Arms
52 Hopton Street, SE1 9JH (riverside)
⊛ 11-11; 12-10.30 Sun
☎ (020) 7928 1899
Young's Bitter, Special, seasonal beers Ⓗ
This 1970s Young's pub, part of the first regeneration of the area, has now been joined by Tate Modern in the adjacent former bankside power station. The Millennium Footbridge and Globe Theatre are also nearby. The pub has recently been extended and revamped, large windows giving impressive views across the Thames to St Paul's. Outside seating is on the riverside. It offers an extensive wine list, and has separate coffee and food counters (open at 9am) and summer evenings. Busy weekends and summer evenings.
⊛ ◑ ♿ ⇌ (Blackfriars) ⊖ (Southwark) ✗

SE1: BOROUGH

George Inn
77 Borough High Street, SE1 1NH
⊛ 11-11; 12-10.30 Sun
☎ (020) 7407 2056
website: www.georgeinn-southwark.co.uk
Flowers Original; Fuller's London Pride; Greene King Abbot; guest beers Ⓗ
Until the latter end of the 19th century, London had a number of galleried coaching inns in the Borough. Most were demolished for road or rail schemes. The NT-owned George, the only survivor, had two of its

three wings destroyed by the Great Northern Railway. First mentioned in Stow's Survey of London 1598, the building dates from 1677 (the original inn was destroyed in the Southwark fire of 1676). The first room is the most original of the five on the ground floor. House beer is brewed by Adnams. No meals Sunday evening.
Q ❀ ◖❙ ≈ (London Bridge) ⊖ ⊬

Lord Clyde
27 Clennam Street, SE1 1ER
✪ 11-11; 12-4, 8-11 Sat; 12-4, 8-10.30 Sun
☎ (020) 7407 3397
Courage Best Bitter; Fuller's London Pride; Shepherd Neame Spitfire; Young's Bitter Ⓗ
Interesting, back-street local, in the same family since 1956. This 300-year-old pub was rebuilt in 1913 with tiles covering the exterior. The interior is divided into two rooms: larger main bar, and a smaller, quiet room with a serving-hatch and dartboard. A short walk up Southwark Bridge Road leads to the Globe Theatre and Tate Modern.
Q ◖❙ ≈ (London Bridge) ⊖ ♣

Market Porter
9 Stoney Street, SE1 9AA
✪ 11-11; 12-10.30 Sun
☎ (020) 7407 2495
Beer range varies Ⓗ
Busy pub, where no less than eight handpumps offer a large selection of ales from around the country. At least 1,000 different beers have been sold here over the past few years. Across the street from Borough market, it is popular with a wide section of the community. The area is a perfect location for many period dramas.
≈ (London Bridge) ⊖ ♣

Royal Oak ⊘
44 Tabard Street, SE1 4JU
✪ 11-11; closed Sat & Sun
☎ (020) 7357 7173
Harveys XX Mild, Pale Ale, BB, seasonal beers Ⓗ
Harvey's only tied house in London. Although well hidden, the pub is in fact quite close to the tube station. The original Tabard Inn was destroyed by fire in 1676, rebuilt, renamed the Talbot and eventually demolished in 1873. A tabard was a sleeveless coat worn by knights and heralds and gave its name to the inn from which pilgrims started their journey in Chaucer's Canterbury Tales. Today's pilgrims, in search of Harveys' full range of beers, enjoy a ready welcome in the Royal Oak's two rooms. Q ◖❙ ≈ (London Bridge) ⊖

Shipwright's Arms
88 Tooley Street, SE1 2TF
✪ 11-11; 12-10.30 Sun
☎ (020) 7378 1486
Beer range varies Ⓗ
Spacious, one-room pub with an island bar. The pub features a large tilework picture of the Pool of London. It always has three ales on handpump. Convenient for the many tourist attractions on the South Bank, including Tower Bridge and the London Dungeon. The new Mayor of London's office is also close by. ◖≈ (London Bridge) ⊖

Wheatsheaf
6 Stoney Street, SE1 9AA
✪ 11-11; 12-8 Sat; closed Sun

☎ (020) 7407 7242
Smiles IPA; Young's Bitter, Special, seasonal beers Ⓗ
Recently acquired by Young's, the brewery has redecorated the Wheatsheaf sympathetically, retaining the original layout. Candles, fairy lights and spotlights provide a glowing atmosphere here, enhanced by a real fire. The full range of Young's bottled beers is stocked. Attracting a mixed clientele, it is handy for the Borough food market, where ingredients for the home-cooked food are sourced.
🚭 ❀ ◖❙ ≈ (London Bridge)

SE1: TOWER BRIDGE

Bridge House ⊘
218 Tower Bridge Road, SE1 2UP
✪ 11-11; 12-10.30 Sun
☎ (020) 7407 5818
Adnams Bitter, Broadside, seasonal beers Ⓗ
The only Adnams-owned pub in London, it is very different from the traditional pubs in Adnams home area. The unashamedly modern bar is decorated in a light, modern style, with an upmarket menu to match. Although Adnams' beers are not hard to find in London, this pub is the only one that regularly offers four of their brews, including seasonal specials. Prominently situated on Tower Bridge Road, it is the closest pub to Tower Bridge itself.
◖❙ ≈ (London Bridge)

Pommelers Rest ⊘
196-198 Tower Bridge Road, SE1 2UN
✪ 10-11; 12-10.30 Sun
☎ (020) 7378 1399
Courage Directors; Fuller's London Pride; Greene King Abbot; guest beers Ⓗ
Typical Wetherspoon's experience, this family-friendly pub is convenient for Tower Bridge and the Thames Path, which meanders past the tourist attractions of the South Bank. This pub stands right at the edge of the congestion charging zone, near the old Courage Anchor Brewery that has now been converted into luxury flats. Meals are served all day.
Q ◖❙ ≈ (London Bridge) ⊖ (Tower Hill)

SE4: BROCKLEY

Brockley Barge ⊘
184 Brockley Road, SE4 2RR
✪ 10-11; 12-10.30 Sun
☎ (020) 8694 7690
Courage Best Bitter, Directors; Greene King Abbot; Hop Back Summer Lightning; Shepherd Neame Spitfire; guest beers Ⓗ
Wetherspoon's undertook a major refit of the Breakspeare Arms, that had been closed for many years, and reopened in 2000. The new name recalls the old Croydon canal that was filled in during 1830 to form the bed of the railway from New Cross Gate to West Croydon. This pub group's usual range of inexpensive food and drink attracts a very cosmopolitan crowd and the bar can get boisterous at times, but it is a useful oasis in an area where real ale is rare.
Q ❀ ◖❙ ♿ ≈ ⊬

SE6: CATFORD

Catford Ram
9 Winslade Way, SE6 4JU

✪ 11-11; 12-10.30 Sun
☎ (020) 8690 6206
Young's Bitter, Special, Winter Warmer Ⓗ
Located at the Broadway entrance to the
Catford shopping centre and near the street
market, this large pub is popular with
shoppers. There is a large raised seating area
and plenty of standing space. Despite
having no windows it has a light and airy
feel created by the comfortable
spaciousness, light decor and air-
conditioning. Sporting events are shown on
the big-screen TV. It is handy for the
Broadway Theatre where the Catford Real
Ale festival is held every June. Lunches are
served Monday–Saturday. ◖◗&≷

London & Rye ✪
109 Rushey Green, SE6 4AF
✪ 10-11; 12-10.30 Sun
☎ (020) 8697 5028
**Courage Best Bitter, Directors; Greene King Abbot;
Shepherd Neame Spitfire; guest beers** Ⓗ
With a more modern touch to the design
than is usual, this Wetherspoon's pub is
tucked away in a busy parade of shops. It
caters for a wide variety of customers. All
the usual Wetherspoon features are
available: curry club, affordable prices,
engaging bar staff. It opens for breakfast at
10am. Q◖◗&≷⊱

SE8: DEPTFORD

Dog & Bell ✪
116 Prince Street, SE8 3JD
✪ 12-11; 12.30-3.30, 7.30-10.30 Sun
☎ (020) 8692 5664
Fuller's London Pride, ESB; guest beers Ⓗ
Take a walk down the Thames Path and you
happen across this two-times CAMRA
national Pub of the Year. A little way off the
beaten track, this excellent, genuine free
house is well worth a detour. Guest beers
change constantly and 20 malt whiskies are
stocked. Quiz night is Sunday; bar billiards
and shove-ha'penny are played. There is
storage space for bicycles and a secluded
garden. Go on, treat yourself. Buses 47 and
199 stop nearby. ⋈Q✿◖◗♣♠

SE9: ELTHAM

Howerd Club
447 Rochester Way, SE9 6PH
✪ 12-3 (not Mon-Fri), 7.30-11; 12-2.30,
7.30-10.30 Sun
☎ (020) 8856 7212
**Fuller's London Pride; Shepherd Neame Master Brew
Bitter** Ⓗ
Small, but comfortable, friendly and
homely, this club is like a large family –
everyone knows everyone else. Many
generations of the same family come to the
club; grandparents, parents and children.
Popular among the local community, a lot
of the members live just a couple of streets
away. ≷

SE10: GREENWICH

Admiral Hardy
7 College Approach, SE10 9HY
✪ 12-11; 12-10.30 Sun
☎ (020) 8858 6452
**Flagship Admiral's; Greene King Ruddles Best;
Shepherd Neame Spitfire; guest beers** Ⓗ

Open, traditional bar with wood and
upholstered seating, this pub dates from
1830. It was named after the famous
admiral of Nelson's Victory, who was
Governor of the Royal Naval Hospital at the
time the pub was built. It is a step away
from the lively Greenwich market, where
you can enjoy a leisurely drink in a covered
area. It is convenient, too, for both the
Cutty Sark and the National Maritime
Museum. ✿≷⊖(DLR Cutty Sark)

Greenwich Union
56 Royal Hill, SE10 8RT
✪ 11-11; 12-10.30 Sun
☎ (020) 8692 6258
Meantime Blonde Ⓗ
A real ale haven for many years, this pub
has seen a few changes since being taken
over by the local Meantime Brewery.
Formerly known as both the Fox & Hounds
and McGowans, it has been completely
revamped in a pleasing, bright, modern
style. Most beers are dispensed under
pressure, but the cask Blonde is brewed by
Rooster's as a house beer. A good
contemporary menu, friendly service and
live music add to its appeal.
✿◖◗≷⊖(DLR) ⊟

Plume of Feathers
19 Park Vista, SE10 9LZ
✪ 11-11; 12-10.30 Sun
☎ (020) 8858 0533
**Adnams Bitter; Fuller's London Pride, ESB; Young's
Special; guest beer** (occasional) Ⓗ
Welcoming pub, dating from 1691, on the
edge of Greenwich Park and close to the
National Maritime Museum. It caters for all
ages. A choice of regional beers is
supplemented by the occasional guest.
There is also a good menu with a vegetarian
option; the dining area is to the rear of the
pub. Major sports events are shown on TV.
⋈✿≷(Maze Hill) ⊖(DLR Cutty Sark)

Richard I (Tolly's)
52-54 Royal Hill, SE10 8RT
✪ 11-11; 12-10.30 Sun
☎ (020) 8692 2996
**Young's Bitter, Special, Winter Warmer,
seasonal beers** Ⓗ
Also known as Tolly's through its past
association with the now-defunct Tolly
Cobbold Brewery of Ipswich, this 18th-
century former cottage now serves a fine
range of Young's beers in its two bars. There
is a large rear garden, extremely popular in
summer, where barbecues are held; large gas
heaters help keep you warm on the cooler
evenings. ✿◖◗&≷⊖(DLR Cutty Sark) ♣

Spanish Galleon
48 Greenwich Church Street, SE10 9BL
✪ 11-11; 12-10.30 Sun
☎ (020) 8293 0949
**Shepherd Neame Master Brew Best Bitter, Spitfire,
Bishops Finger** Ⓗ
Traditional, Shepherd Neame pub with a
relaxed atmosphere in easy reach of the
Cutty Sark, the Maritime Museum and
Greenwich Park and Observatory. An
unpretentious haven in the centre of the
tourist trail, its two bars are joined by a food
counter, serving a range of meals and
snacks. Furnishings are simple, with wood
chairs and benches on bare boards. The

nautical decor is in keeping with its location. The tiled conservatory is for non-smokers. ⛵◗Ⓓ♿♨⊖ (DLR Cutty Sark) ✂

SE11: KENNINGTON

Prince of Wales
48 Cleaver Square, SE11 4EA
🕐 12-11; 12-10.30 Sun
☎ (020) 7735 9916
Shepherd Neame Master Brew Best Bitter, Spitfire, seasonal beers Ⓗ
Small, attractive pub tucked away in the corner of a quiet, tree-lined Georgian square. Popular with MPs and media folk (Parliament is a short walk away), it is close to Lambeth county court. It is rumoured that Charlie Chaplin once danced outside. Regulars occasionally organise boules tournaments in the square. Food is mostly home made.
🏨🐕◗Ⓓ⊖ (Oval) ♣

SE13: LEWISHAM

Dacre Arms
11 Kingswood Place, SE13 5BV
🕐 12-11; 12-10.30 Sun
☎ (020) 8852 6719
Courage Best Bitter; Greene King IPA; guest beers Ⓗ
There is a relaxed, genteel atmosphere in this affable jewel of a local in a salubrious residential back-street on the Lewisham/Blackheath border. The cosy wood-panelled bar has an eclectic mix of comfortable soft furnishings, brass knick-knacks, china and pictures. It offers a regularly-changing mix of guest ales. Founded by local landowners, Lord and Lady Dacre in around 1720, the present building dates from the 1900s.
🐕≢ (Blackheath)

Watch House ⊘
198-204 Lewisham High Street, SE13 6JP
🕐 10-11; 12-10.30 Sun
☎ (020) 8318 3136
Courage Directors; Greene King Abbot; Hop Back Summer Lightning; Ridleys Rumpus; Shepherd Neame Spitfire; guest beers Ⓗ
Busy, town-centre pub in the original Wetherspoon's style. It has the typical atmosphere and range of beers and food associated with the chain. Notices giving details of local history and celebrities who once frequented the area complement the wood-panelled alcoves, shelves lined with passed-over books and floral carpet. It was named after the original village green – now the pedestrianised shopping area.
🐕◗Ⓓ♿≢⊖✂

SE16: ROTHERHITHE

Ship & Whale
2 Gulliver Street, SE16 7LT
🕐 12-3, 6-11; 11-11 Sat; 12-10.30 Sun
☎ (020) 7237 7072
Shepherd Neame Master Brew Bitter, Spitfire Ⓗ
Sofas, chairs and pews provide comfortable seating in this old Docklands pub that has been refurbished to a high standard. Newspapers and board games are provided for entertainment, as well as occasional live music. Children are welcome and can choose from their own menu.
🐕◗Ⓓ⊖ (Surrey Quays/Canada Water) ♣

SE17: WALWORTH

Beehive
60-62 Carter Street, SE17 3EW
🕐 11-11; 12-10.30 Sun
☎ (020) 7703 4992
Courage Directors; Fuller's London Pride; Greene King Old Speckled Hen; Wadworth 6X Ⓗ
Approached down Penrose Street (opposite East Street market), this back-street local is very upmarket for the area. The bar staff are smartly attired in white aprons and black bow ties. There is an extensive wine list and the food is top quality, ranging from snacks to unusual full meals. The plain furnishings create a homely atmosphere, while the walls are packed with political memorabilia that maintains a careful balance between the parties. The TV is used for sport.
♿◗Ⓓ⊖ (Kennington)

SE18: WOOLWICH

Prince Albert (Rose's)
49 Hare Street, SE18 6NE
🕐 11-11; 12-3 (closed eve) Sun
☎ (020) 8854 1538
Beer range varies Ⓗ
Do not ask where the Prince Albert is! Until 1985 this genuine free house, near Woolwich Ferry roundabout, was owned by EJ Rose & Co (their sign is still displayed), hence the nickname by which this cracking pub is ubiquitously known. At least three constantly-changing ales are always on tap, as is real cider on Friday and Saturday. This is a 100% town-centre boozer. Generously-filled rolls and hot snacks are available at most times. Good value accommodation.
Q🛏≢ (Woolwich Arsenal) ♣🚶

SE20: PENGE

Moon & Stars ⊘
164-166 High Street, SE20 7QS
🕐 10-11; 12-10.30 Sun
☎ (020) 8776 5680
Courage Directors; Greene King Abbot; Hop Back Summer Lightning; Theakston Best Bitter; guest beers Ⓗ
Deservedly the most popular Wetherspoon's in South-East London. Built in 1994, this spacious pub was originally intended to be a cinema conversion but the building proved unsafe and was demolished. As a result this is one of the best designed new pubs in the estate. It has a number of partitioned alcoves around a large bar area, thus avoiding the barn-like feel of many modern drinking establishments. Note the superb woodwork throughout.
Q🐕◗Ⓓ♿≢⊖ (Beckenham Rd Tramlink) P✂

SE22: EAST DULWICH

Herne Tavern
2 Forest Hill Road, SE22 0RR
🕐 11-11; 12-10.30 Sun
☎ (020) 8299 9521
Courage Best Bitter, Directors Ⓗ
Facing Peckham Rye Park, this pub boasts an imposing Victorian exterior – its fine leaded-light windows are Grade II listed. Inside, this spacious three-roomed community local is equally impressive with wood-panelled walls throughout. A

conservatory at the rear leads to a large garden and children's play area; it hosts occasional barbecues. No lunches are served on Saturday. Shut the box is played. Buses 12, 63 and 312 stop close by. Q❀◐♣

SE23: CATFORD

Blythe Hill Tavern

319 Stanstead Road, SE23 1JB

11-11; 12-10.30 Sun

☎ (020) 8690 5176

Courage Best Bitter; Fuller's London Pride H

Between Forest Hill and Catford on the South Circular road, this three-roomed, two-bar pub is larger than the exterior suggests. The front room is dedicated to golf, with some very old items on display; the room to the rear is devoted to horse racing while the third contains old brewery items and Temperance Movement posters. It is definitely a pub for browsers. The garden has a children's play area; small car park. Q❀≷♣P

SE26: SYDENHAM

Dulwich Wood House

39 Sydenham Hill, SE26 6RS

11-11; 12-10.30 Sun

☎ (020) 8693 5666

Young's Bitter, Special, seasonal beers H

Designed as a private residence by Sir Joseph Paxton (architect of the Crystal Palace) in 1857, this deservedly popular hostelry has recently been sympathetically extended to provide a large no-smoking bar. The spacious garden has many seats and can be accessed through both the old and new bars and directly from the road. Near the Dulwich & Sydenham Hill Golf Club, the pub has its own long-standing golf society. Buses 63 and 202 stop nearby. No evening meals are served Sunday.

Q❀◐▶ ≷ (Sydenham Hill) ♣P

ADDISCOMBE

Claret Free House

5a Bingham Corner, Lower Addiscombe Road, CR0 7AA (on A222, near tram stop)

11.30 (11 Sat)-11; 12-10.30 Sun

☎ (020) 8656 7452

Palmer IPA; Shepherd Neame Spitfire; guest beers H

Excellent, small ale house in an attractive parade of shops. Four constantly-changing guest beers come from small breweries – see the beer menu with its interchangeable hook-on descriptions. Real cider is brought from the cellar. Fake beams reflect the mock-Tudor exterior, while brewery mirrors and old photographs complete the decor. Two TV sets mean it is busy during big matches. No food is served, except rolls on Saturday lunchtime. Trams and buses 289, 312, 494 stop nearby. ⊖ (Tramlink) ♣

BEXLEY

Black Horse

63 Albert Road, DA5 1NJ (200 yds along road behind library)

11.30-11; 12-4, 7-10.30 Sun

☎ (01322) 523371

Courage Best Bitter; guest beers H

Friendly, back-street local offering good value lunches in comfortable, uncrowded surroundings. The open-plan bar is split into two areas, the front and left providing an open area with a dartboard, the right-hand side offering a small, more intimate area and a bar leading to the garden. The pub supports a golf society. Beers vary – the publican aims to ensure a different guest beer every time a barrel runs out – a noble ambition. ❀◐≷♣

King's Head

65 Bexley High Street, DA5 1AA

11-11; 11-4, 6-11 Sat; 2-4, 7-10.30 Sun

☎ (01322) 526112

Courage Best Bitter; Greene King IPA, Abbot H

Popular pub, busy at lunchtime and early evening with commuters. Dating from the 16th century, this is one of the oldest buildings in historic Bexley village; it has been a pub for around 300 years. Its weatherboarded exterior makes it a local landmark. The interior boasts many original oak beams (and a few replacements following Victorian alterations). The function room stages live jazz (Mon eve) and doubles as a restaurant for Sunday lunch. ❀◐≷

BEXLEYHEATH

Robin Hood & Little John

78 Lion Road, DA6 8PF

11-3, 5.30 (7 Sat)-11; 12-4, 7-10.30 Sun

☎ (020) 8303 1128

Brains Rev James; Brakspear Bitter; Flagship Futtock, seasonal beers; Fuller's London Pride; Harveys BB; guest beers H

With its bizarre pub sign, this back-street local of 1854 retains its country origins. The wood-panelled walls and old Singer sewing machine tables provide the perfect setting for enjoying excellent lunches (not served Sun), supplemented by several daily themed specials which feature pasta dishes. However, the real ale is the biggest draw, combined with friendly, efficient service. CAMRA Greater London Pub of the Year winner 2000 and 2001 and local branch winner for the last four years, it admits over 21s only. ❀◐

Rose

179 Broadway, DA6 7ES

11-11; 12-10.30 Sun

☎ (020) 8303 3846

Greene King IPA; Tetley Bitter; guest beers H

Situated opposite Christ Church, this double bay-windowed building of 1834 was destroyed by a bomb in 1941 and rebuilt in 1955. The inside is quite small and basically U-shaped; outside there is a small drinking area at the front, with a patio at the rear. Home-cooked food, including daily specials, is served 12–2 (not Sun). Football matches are shown live (although without sound). It stocks a limited range of guest ales from independent breweries. Over 21s only are admitted. ❀◐

Royal Oak (Polly Clean Stairs)

Mount Road, DA6 8JS

11-3, 6-11; 11-11 Sat; 12-3, 7-10.30 Sun

☎ (020) 8303 4454

Courage Best Bitter; guest beers H

Highly attractive, weatherboarded pub (circa 1863) that retains its rural charm despite being overtaken by 1930s housing.

The nickname refers to a houseproud landlady who washed the front steps every day. The inside is best described as cosy, with lots of different comfortable seating areas. Plates adorn the walls and tankards hang from the ceiling; horse brasses add the final country feel. Children are allowed in the garden. Lunchtime rolls and sandwiches are available (not Sun). Q❀P

BIGGIN HILL

Old Jail
Jail Lane, TN16 8AX (1 mile from A233)
OS435594
✪ 11.30-3, 6-11; 12-11 Sat; 12-10.30 Sun
☎ (01959) 572979
Greene King IPA; Harveys BB; Shepherd Neame Spitfire; guest beers Ⓗ
Popular pub, between Biggin Hill and Cudham. Perhaps never a prison, but it certainly has strong links with the nearby WWII airfield, now a civil airport. Numerous wartime photographs are displayed around the walls. The pub hosts meetings of the Spitfire and Hurricane associations. The large garden has a well-equipped children's play area; bat and trap is played. No food is served on Sunday evening. ❀◖▶♣P

BROMLEY

Bitter End (off-licence)
139 Masons Hill, BR2 9HY
✪ 12-3 (not Mon), 5-10 (9 Mon); 11-10 Sat; 12-2, 7-9 Sun
☎ (020) 8466 6083 website: www.thebitterend.biz
Beer range varies Ⓖ
Just the job for those occasions when you do not want to go to the pub. Whether you just fancy a couple of pints at home or are planning a party, this off-licence has a good range of beers and ciders on hand and, given a little notice, polypins and firkins can be obtained from a range of over 500 beers. It also stocks an interesting range of British and imported bottled beers (some bottle-conditioned). Glasses and equipment can be hired or borrowed. ⇌(South)

Bromley Labour Club
HG Wells Centre, St Marks Road, BR2 9HA
✪ 11-11; 12-10.30 Sun
☎ (020) 8460 7409
Shepherd Neame Master Brew Bitter; guest beers Ⓗ
Friendly, popular club, convenient for Bromley town-centre shops and High Street. The club has a spacious bar with comfortable padded seats, plus a pool table in a separate area and a patio. A nicely decorated, large hall is available for functions. CAMRA members are welcome to visit the club if they have their membership cards. ❀⇌(South)♣P

Red Lion
10 North Road, BR1 3LG
✪ 11-11; 12-10.30 Sun
☎ (020) 8460 2691
Greene King IPA, Abbot; Harveys BB; guest beers Ⓗ
Former winner of South-East London CAMRA Pub of the Year, this is a popular friendly pub in a quiet back street. It still has some of the original tiling. The large collection of pump clips around the bar indicates the range of guest beers that have

featured (there are normally two guests on tap). The TV is used with discretion for major sporting events. Evening meals finish at 7pm. Q❀◖▶⇌(North)♣

Tom Foolery ⊘
204-206 High Street, BR1 1HB
✪ 11-11; 12-10.30 Sun
☎ (020) 8290 2039
Fuller's Chiswick, London Pride, ESB, seasonal beers Ⓗ
More like an upmarket wine bar, this modern pub in the town centre is decorated in a mix of pastels and vibrant colours. Popular with groups of women and office parties, it offers the full range of Fuller's beers and an extensive wine list. The bar, with comfortable seating in the form of upholstered armchairs and sofas, has a restful atmosphere. ◖▶ ⓵⇌(North/South)✠

BROMLEY COMMON

Bird in Hand
62 Gravel Road, BR2 8PF (car access from Oakley Rd and Cross St)
✪ 11-11; 12-10.30 Sun
☎ (020) 8462 1083
Courage Best Bitter; Fuller's London Pride; Greene King IPA; Theakston Old Peculier; Wells Bombardier; Young's Special Ⓗ
Friendly, comfortable pub, featuring traditional wood panelling. Very much a family pub, it has a pleasant atmosphere and a large garden. A private room (for hire) has a separate bar. It is popular with locals watching horse racing and football on Saturday afternoon. The conservatory/function room, where children are welcome, is delightful. An English menu is served at lunchtime. ⏁◖♣

Two Doves
37 Oakley Road, BR2 8HD
✪ 12-3, 5.30 (5 Mon & Fri; 6 Sat)-11; 12-3, 7-10 Sun
☎ (020) 8462 1627
Beer range varies Ⓗ
Quiet, homely free house only 15 minutes away by bus from the bustle of Bromley High Street. The choice of three real ales usually on offer from independent breweries changes regularly. A passageway from the bar leads to the attractive, no-smoking conservatory and the immaculate garden. Occasional specialist barbecues are held in summer (booking essential). Saucy seaside postcards are displayed in the spotless loos. No. 320 Biggin Hill–Bromley North bus stops outside every half-hour until 11.30pm. Q❀✠

CHELSFIELD

Five Bells
Church Road, BR6 7RE
✪ 11-11; 12-10.30 Sun
☎ (01689) 821044
Courage Best Bitter; Greene King IPA; Old Speckled Hen; guest beer Ⓗ
Friendly, unspoilt village pub, handy for the public golf course at Chelsfield Lakes and close to the historic St Martin of Tours parish church. Both bars display old photographs of the pub and village, some dating back to the 19th century. Shove-ha'penny and shut the box are played. Evening meals are served

Wednesday–Saturday. The R3 bus via Orpington stops outside. If walking from Chelsfield Station (one mile) follow the footpath behind the hedgerow and spot the London Eye. ✿✸▢❦P

CHISLEHURST

Bull's Head
Royal Parade, BR7 6NR (near war memorial, A222/A208)
✿ 11-11; 12-10.30 Sun
☎ (020) 8467 1727
Young's Bitter, Special, Winter Warmer Ⓗ
Large, traditional pub and hotel. Smart and comfortable, the lounge bar has the atmosphere of a gentleman's club, with wing chairs and chesterfield sofas. Bare brick walls and dark wood panelling give a restful feel. The pub, a former Kent newspaper Town Pub of the Year, is very popular at weekends. Q➥✿☎◀▢❧⇌P

CROYDON

Dog & Bull
24 Surrey Street, CRO 1RG (just off High St, A235)
✿ 11-11; 12-10.30 Sun
☎ (020) 8667 9718
Young's Bitter, Special, seasonal beers Ⓗ
Grade II listed building in the street market. An island bar serves the main drinking area and other areas to the rear and side (the latter is designated no-smoking at lunchtime). Like the market outside, the pub is busy by day, but quieter in the evening. Tuesday is quiz night. At the back is a well-equipped courtyard (no dogs or children admitted), with a food and drink servery. On fine summer days barbecues may be held. Q✿☎◀⇌(East/West) ⊖(Church St/George St Tramlink) ♣

Fishermans Arms
78 Windmill Road, CRO 2XP (on A213)
✿ 12 (11 Sat)-11; 12-10.30 Sun
☎ (020) 8689 7887
Fuller's London Pride, ESB Ⓗ
The single bar is on two levels: the lower, older, side offers pool and darts, while the other level is decorated with items relating to fishing. The garden has been commended by Fuller's in their competition; it has facilities for both petanque and croquet. Occasional guest and seasonal beers are available, to supplement the regular brews. Bus No. 450 from West Croydon passes the door. ✿◀♣

Princess Royal
22 Longley Road, CRO 3LH (off A235, London Rd)
✿ 12-3, 5.30 (6 Sat)-11; 12-11 Fri; 12-3, 8-10.30 Sun
☎ (020) 8240 0046
Banks's Original; Greene King IPA, Abbot; guest beers Ⓗ
Small, friendly, back-street pub, also known as the Gluepot. A rare outlet for mild, this pub is an oasis in a beer desert. There are usually three guest beers available, alongside good quality food at all times, including good value Sunday roasts. Live acoustic music is performed occasionally on Saturday evening. Well-behaved dogs are welcome (but not children). The secluded outdoor drinking area has a large fishpond.

Croydon CAMRA Pub of the Year 2003.
Q✿◀⇌(West) ⊖(Tramlink) ♣

Royal Standard ✿
1 Sheldon Street, CRO 1SS (off A235, near flyover)
✿ 12-11; 12-10.30 Sun
☎ (020) 8688 9749
Fuller's Chiswick, London Pride, ESB, seasonal beers Ⓗ
Small, intimate local in the shadow of Croydon's flyover. Its very traditional interior was recently repainted. From the pleasant garden opposite, you can sit and watch the traffic jams build up. This Fuller's house is a regular in this Guide and it is easy to see why. Good food is available at most times. A very friendly place, it gets busy at weekends and is a welcome retreat after shopping in the town centre. Quiz night is Tuesday; it fields a keen darts team.
Q✿◀⇌(East/West) ⊖(Church St/George St Tramlink) ♣

Ship of Fools ✿
9-11 London Road, CRO 2RE (opp. W. Croydon Station)
✿ 10-11; 12-10.30 Sun
☎ (020) 8681 2835
Courage Directors; Greene King Abbot; Hop Back Summer Lightning; Shepherd Neame Spitfire; Theakston Best Bitter; guest beers Ⓗ
This Wetherspoon's pub can be found at the north end of the High Street. Opposite West Croydon Station and near a tram stop, it is handy for shoppers and commuters. This pub offers an ever-changing choice of guest ales and hosts the occasional beer festival. Scenes of local history are displayed on the walls.
Q◀⇌(West) ⊖(Tramlink) ✂

Tamworth Arms
62 Tamworth Road, CRO 1XW (near Reeves Corner)
✿ 11-11; 12-10.30 Sun
☎ (020) 8681 1328
Young's Bitter, Special Ⓗ
This detached, 19th-century building boasts an attractive tiled exterior and stepped doorways. The pub was closed for many months during the construction of Croydon's tram system. The worst was feared, but Young's did reopen it. Now this single-bar pub is back in business with an enterprising licensee who hopes the new shopping centre nearby will bring more life back to the area; also perhaps a tram stop nearby? ⚌✿◀⇌(West) ⊖(Church St/Reeves Corner Tramlink) ♣P

FARNBOROUGH

Woodman
50 High Street, BR6 7BA
✿ 12-11; 12-10.30 Sun
☎ (01689) 852663
Shepherd Neame Master Brew Bitter, Spitfire, seasonal beers Ⓗ
Comfortable, welcoming village local, catering for all ages. A good selection of food, includes decent vegetarian options. Evening meals are served Wednesday–Saturday; no lunches are available on Saturday. Various board games can be played and books can be borrowed. A no-smoking area is at one end of the bar

area. The Woodman is served by the 358 bus route (Crystal Palace–Orpington Station). ⚄✿◑♪✉

FOOTS CRAY

Seven Stars
Foots Cray High Street, DA14 5HJ
✪ 11.30-11; 12-6 Sun
☎ (020) 8300 2057
Draught Bass; Greene King IPA Ⓗ
16th-century local in what was once a quaint village, now rather over-developed. It comprises three main drinking areas and a dining area. The decor combines a mix of old and new, where many original features contrast with gaming machines. Live music is staged Friday and Saturday evenings, but check schedules. ✿◑P

NORTH CRAY

White Cross
146 North Cray Road, DA14 5EL
✪ 11-11; 12-10.30 Sun
☎ (020) 8300 2590
Courage Best Bitter, Directors; guest beers Ⓗ
A survivor of the dual carriageway development of the 1960s, the pub was known as the Red Cross from 1730 until 1935. The front bar displays an impressive array of copper and brass utensils; this is where the locals drink. The pub is popular for meals, particularly at lunchtime; food is served all day on Saturday and Sunday. Vehicle access is from the northbound carriageway. It is on the No. 492 bus route. ✿◑P

ORPINGTON

Cricketers
93 Chislehurst Road, BR6 0DQ
✪ 12-3, 5-11; 12-11 Sat; 12-10.30 Sun
☎ (01689) 812648
Adnams Bitter, Broadside; guest beer Ⓗ
Popular back-street pub, a few minutes' walk from the High Street and overlooking Broomhill Common. A single bar with traditional decor plus a family/no-smoking room, the Cricketers and Rose Cottage were purchased in 1867 by local brewery, Fox & Sons of Green Street Green. Acquired by Courage in 1905, it has been run by the same family for many years. Framed cigarette cards of cricketers and boxing champions are displayed. This pub is very dog-friendly – dog biscuits are provided on request. Q↻✿✉

PETTS WOOD

Sovereign of the Seas ◉
109-111 Queensway, BR5 1DG
✪ 10-11; 12-10.30 Sun
☎ (01689) 891606
Courage Directors; Greene King Abbot; Shepherd Neame Spitfire; Theakston Best Bitter; guest beers Ⓗ
The pub takes its name from a Navy warship, built in 1638 by local shipbuilder, Peter Pett. The area also derives its name from the Pett family. Wetherspoon's converted this pub from a former furniture shop in 1995. Photos around the walls depict local history. This pub makes an effort for special events like Hallowe'en, Burns Night, etc and stages regular beer

festivals. Bus routes 208, R3 and N47 pass outside. Children are welcome in the no-smoking area until 9pm. Q↻✿◑♿≈✉

ST PAULS CRAY

Bull Inn
Main Road, BR5 3HS (near Homebase on Sevenoaks Way)
✪ 11-11; 12-10.30 Sun
☎ (01689) 821642
Boddingtons Bitter; Flowers Original; Greene King Old Speckled Hen Ⓗ
Popular, 16th-century pub, decorated in traditional style where four distinct drinking areas surround a central bar. A double-sided fireplace is the main feature between two areas, and the smell of burning logs is welcome on cold winter nights. A lively pub quiz is held every Tuesday at 9pm. The freshly-cooked food is popular, so booking is advised. ⚄Q✿◑

SELHURST

Two Brewers
221 Gloucester Road, CR0 2DW (off A213)
✪ 11-11; 12-10.30 Sun
☎ (020) 8684 3544
Shepherd Neame Master Brew Bitter, Best Bitter, Spitfire, Bishops Finger, Porter Ⓗ
This compact, Shepherd Neame house has maintained its local country atmosphere with a flower-bedecked exterior and compact, well-laid-out interior. The bar staff are welcoming and the local clientele add to the friendly atmosphere. Situated off the main roads, there is not much passing trade, but this does help to give a family feel. Sunday is quiz night. ⚄✿◑≈♣

SELSDON

Sir Julian Huxley ◉
152-154 Addington Road, CR2 8LB (on A2022)
✪ 10-11; 12-10.30 Sun
☎ (020) 8657 9457
Shepherd Neame Spitfire; Theakston Best Bitter; guest beers Ⓗ
Former shop premises converted by Wetherspoon's into a split-level café-bar. The bar is on the lower level, with a further drinking area and the non-smoking/eating area on the upper level. There is a conservatory at the back and stairs lead down to the garden. Three or four guest ales are usually available at this highly successful oasis in a former real ale desert. Q✿◑♿✉

SHIRLEY

Orchard
116 Orchard Way, CR0 7NN (between A232 and A214, on corner of Radnor Walk)
✪ 12-11; 12-10.30 Sun
☎ (020) 8777 9011
Harveys BB; Shepherd Neame Master Brew Bitter; guest beer Ⓗ
Modern pub at the end of a suburban shopping parade. Despite the pub's name the two large trees outside at the front are evergreens. Front and side doors lead into two adjoining bars. The front bar is open plan, but the side bar has a number of alcoves, each with a table and facing bench seats. Very much a local at the heart of a

residential area, the guest beer is aimed at the weekend trade and may not be available midweek. The TV is used for sports events. Bus No. 367 runs nearby. ◗♣P

SIDCUP

Alma
10 Alma Road, DA14 4EA
✪ 11-2.30, 5.30-11; 11-11 Fri; 11-3, 6-11 Sat; 12-3, 7-10.30 Sun
☎ (020) 8300 3208
Courage Best Bitter; Fuller's London Pride; Shepherd Neame Spitfire ⊞
Back-street local near Sidcup Station, popular with commuters recovering from their train journey home. The building dates from 1868, when it began life as the Railway Tavern. It was extended in 1897 by the addition of a large billiards room, now used for functions. The pub was extended again in 1934 but still has a reasonable-sized garden which is popular in summer. The interior retains some of its Victorian character. Lunches are served on weekdays. The car park is tiny. Q✪◗♣P

SOUTH CROYDON

Rail View
188 Selsdon Road, CR2 6PL (off A235)
✪ 11-11; 12-10.30 Sun
☎ (020) 8688 2315
Adnams Bitter; Fuller's London Pride; Hancock's HB ⊞
Quiet, good old-fashioned local, compriing two bars. The saloon is furnished in deep-blue upholstery (old first-class railway colours) and the walls are decorated with pictures of steam locomotives from a bygone age. The public bar, furnished with tables and chairs, has a dartboard as well as traditional board games. A quiz is hosted on Sunday evening. Note the original stained glass fanlight windows at the front of the pub. ✪◗♿≢♣P

UPPER BELVEDERE

Fox
79 Nuxley Road, DA17 5JU
✪ 11-11; 12-10.30 Sun
☎ (01322) 435557
Courage Best Bitter; Sharp's Special ⊞
The building which dates from 1853 was refronted in 1921 to give an attractive, bold appearance. The interior is L-shaped, comfortable and functional. Meals are served every day between 11–5, including inexpensive Sunday roasts; fresh seafood is also often available. Family events, sometimes for charity, take place on summer weekends and bank holidays. There is a children's playground in the garden. Live music is performed some Saturday evenings. ✪◗

South-West London

SW1: BELGRAVIA

Duke of Wellington
63 Eaton Terrace, SW1W 8TR
✪ 11-11; 12-10.30 Sun
☎ (020) 7730 1782
Shepherd Neame Master Brew Bitter, Spitfire, Bishops Finger ⊞
Excellent pub with loads of character, now

owned by Shepherd Neame. Built in 1826, and named after the first Duke of Wellington (1769–1852), this late Georgian building is very well furnished, with oil paintings adding a touch of class. It can get very busy in the evening, but earlier in the day it can be quiet. There is a cigarette machine (under the menu board) where, it is claimed, Arthur Wellesley (the first duke) used to buy his Woodbines. No food is served Sunday.
◗▣≢(Victoria) ⊖(Sloane Sq)

Horse & Groom
7 Groom Place, SW1X 7BA
✪ 11-11; closed Sat & Sun
☎ (020) 7235 6980
Shepherd Neame Master Brew Bitter, Spitfire ⊞
Owned by Greene King until 1996, then acquired by Shepherd Neame, this fine pub is wood panelled throughout, and furnished to the same standards as its two nearby sisters, the Cask & Glass in Palace Street and the Duke of Wellington (qv). The pub serves good food during the day and a dartboard is available upstairs. Usually quiet during the day, it can get busy in the evening. It is handy for the Caledonian Club nearby.
Q◗⊖(Hyde Pk Cnr) ♣

Nag's Head
53 Kinnerton Street, SW1X 8ED
✪ 11-11; 12-10.30 Sun
☎ (020) 7235 1135
Adnams Bitter, Broadside, seasonal beers ⊞
Still more or less unspoilt, there are bars on two levels here; the front one boasts possibly the lowest bar counter in London. Built circa 1833, it was first licensed as a beer house around 1870. Benskins acquired the pub later that century. Now free of tie, it stocks the full range from Adnams. There are photographs galore, etched glass, mirrors and assorted bric-à-brac. Pencil drawings of actors, Nigel Davenport and James Mason grace the bar. Food is served all day until 9.30pm.
♨Q✪◗▣⊖(Hyde Pk Cnr)

Star Tavern ✪
6 Belgrave Mews West, SW1X 8HT
✪ 11-11; 12-10.30 Sun
☎ (020) 7235 3019
Fuller's Chiswick, London Pride, ESB, seasonal beers ⊞
The Star is reputedly where the Great Train Robbers used to meet. Here Biggs and Co. planned their heist with the help of a train of ashtrays, a bridge of beermats, a fleet of quick get-away glasses and a box of matchstick men. Its other claim to fame is to have had an entry in every edition of this Guide. West London CAMRA Pub of the Year 2001.
♨Q◗▣⊖(Hyde Pk Cnr/Knightsbridge)

SW1: PIMLICO

Morpeth Arms
58 Millbank, SW1P 4RW
✪ 11-11; 12-10.30 Sun
☎ (020) 7834 6442
Young's Bitter, Special, seasonal beers ⊞
The Morpeth used to be a part of the Millbank Penitentiary, one of whose inmates attempted to escape when he heard he was to be deported to Australia. He died

in the labyrinthine interconnecting tunnels. Even today he can still send a shiver around the bar when the word Australia is mentioned – or is it the Australian cricket team that does that? Alongside Tate Britain, the Morpeth is handy for a post-gallery visit. Q ❀⊄◑ ⇌ (Vauxhall) ⊖

SW1: VICTORIA

Cask & Glass
39 Palace Street, SW1E 5HN
✪ 11-11; 12-8 Sat; closed Sun
☎ (020) 7834 7630
Shepherd Neame Master Brew Bitter, Best Bitter, Spitfire Ⓗ
Best visited during spring or summer when its floral displays, which have won several awards, are in full bloom. Take a measuring tape along with you if you wish to confirm its claim to be the second smallest pub in London. What it lacks in space is compensated for with fine hospitality. Punch cartoons, prints, caricatures, and a squadron of model aeroplanes decorate the walls.
Q ⇌ ⊖

Jugged Hare ⊘
172 Vauxhall Bridge Road, SW1V 1DX
✪ 11-11; 12-10.30 Sun
☎ (020) 7828 1543
Fuller's Chiswick, London Pride, ESB, seasonal beers Ⓗ
Once a branch of the National Westminster Bank, the pub is well worth seeking out. Very much in the 'Ale & Pie' style, it resembles the Jack Horner, another of this company's establishments in Tottenham Court Road. Food is served all day. The weekends can be quiet since the clientele are mainly business folk. Locals come from the Warwick Way and Tachbrook Street market. MPs visit sometimes. The upstairs balcony doubles as a function room and is very different in style.
⊄◑ ⇌ ⊖ ⅄

SW1: WESTMINSTER

Buckingham Arms
62 Petty France, SW1H 9EU
✪ 11-11; 11-5.30 Sat; 12-5.30 Sun
☎ (020) 7222 3386
Young's Bitter, Special, seasonal beers Ⓗ
The pub is named after George Villiers, who was Gentleman of the Bedchamber to James I. On your way to the toilet, look in on the odd corridor bar at the back where customers sup their beer in single file. This is the place to be when you do not want to be seen.
⊄◑ ⇌ (Victoria) ⊖ (St James's Pk)

Lord Moon of the Mall ⊘
16-18 Whitehall, SW1A 2DY
✪ 10-11; 12-10.30 Sun
☎ (020) 7809 7701
Courage Directors; Fuller's London Pride; guest beers Ⓗ
Once a bank, this Wetherspoon's pub retains a cash dispenser from that time. There are lots of prints on the walls, depicting local scenes and posters of theatre land. The no-smoking area towards the rear of the main floor includes a family area (children welcome until 5pm). Trafalgar

Square is just up the road, as is the National Gallery. The Whitehall Theatre is next door. Meals are served until 9pm.
Q ⛬ ⊄◑ ♿ ⇌ (Charing Cross) ⊖ ⅄

Royal Oak
2 Regency Street, SW1P 4BZ
✪ 11-11; closed Sat; 12-4 Sun
☎ (020) 7834 7046
Young's Bitter, Special, seasonal beers Ⓗ
Corner pub, close enough to Victoria to be handy for the shops and the theatre, but far enough away to retain a local atmosphere. A clear glass frontage allows you to see if you fancy going in without having to poke your head around the door. Bare floorboards, with most of the seating around the walls, give the Royal Oak a light, airy feel. ◑⇌ (Victoria) ⊖ (St James's Pk)

Sanctuary House Hotel ⊘
33 Tothill Street, SW1H 9LA
✪ 11-11; 12-10.30 Sun
☎ (020) 7794 4044
website: www.sanctuaryhousehotel.com
Fuller's Chiswick, London Pride, ESB, seasonal beers Ⓗ
An Ale & Pie house furnished in very much traditional style, there is a split-level seating area at one end of the pub which has polished wood floors, benches and bar stools. Handy base for sightseeing in central London, the hotel has 34 rooms, all en-suite and immaculately furnished. Two rooms can accommodate families. The hotel has no restaurant, but pub meals are available 12–9 daily. The pub has a children's certificate.
⛬ ⇨ ⊄◑ ⇌ (Victoria) ⊖ (St James's Pk)

SW2: STREATHAM HILL

Crown & Sceptre ⊘
2A Streatham Hill, SW2 4AH
✪ 10-11; 12-10.30 Sun
☎ (020) 8671 0843
Courage Best Bitter, Directors; Hop Back Summer Lightning; Shepherd Neame Spitfire; guest beers Ⓗ
This large, busy pub is the foremost Wetherspoon's in south-west London. A former notorious music pub, this was the company's earliest conversion in the area. Its fascia, proclaiming Trumans Ale of London and Burton was restored at the request of the Streatham Society. Different levels and distinct areas give the pub its character. Draught beer sales are very high here and there are rarely less than six guest beers on tap. Q ⛬ ❀ ⊄◑ ⇌ (Hill) P ⅄

SW3: CHELSEA

Crown (at Chelsea)
153 Dovehouse Street, SW3 6LB
✪ 11-11; 12-10.30 Sun
☎ (020) 7352 9505
Adnams Bitter; Fuller's London Pride Ⓗ
Just what the doctor ordered! In the midst of the Royal Marsden and Royal Brompton Hospital complex lies a quiet refuge and place of convalescence for stressed London dwellers. This long, narrow pub with a soothing colour scheme in pale green and cream, fits a quart into a pint pot. The small bar area, with bare floor and stools at the front, is a cosy meeting-place for regulars, a few out-patients and doctors in the evening.

The rear section is mainly for diners (eve meals Tue–Thu); the TV caters for sports fans. ◑▶ ⊖ (S Kensington)

Surprise (in Chelsea) ⊘
6 Christchurch Terrace, SW3 4AJ
✪ 12–11; 12-10.30 Sun
☎ (020) 7349 1821
Adnams Bitter; Fuller's London Pride Ⓗ
A surprise indeed – especially if you can even find it… in a back street in leafy Chelsea. Most notable is its country pub feel: tranquil most of the day, attracting a faithful local following; evenings are more boisterous, but always civilised. A good conversation pub despite background music. Dating from 1853, its fine bar counter, topped by a painted frieze, is worth a closer look, and the large leaded windows are a special feature. Three interconnected rooms, include one with a TV and bar billiards, and a rear snug.
❀◑▶ ⊖ (Sloane Sq) ♣

SW4: CLAPHAM

Manor Arms
128 Clapham Manor Street, SW4 6ED
✪ 11–11; 12-10.30 Sun
☎ (020) 7622 2894
Adnams Bitter; Black Sheep Best Bitter; Fuller's London Pride; Taylor Landlord; guest beer Ⓗ
Just a few yards off bustling Clapham High Street, the Manor is an oasis of peace and quiet. The narrow bar area is enough to escape from the TV which shows sporting events. There is a marquee at the rear (where children are welcome) and a space out front with heaters. Draught beer is an important consideration for the enlightened management team here. Clapham Manor baths stand opposite.
⌘◑▶⇌ (High St) ⊖ (North/Common)

Rose & Crown
2 The Polygon, SW4 0JG
✪ 12–11; 12-10.30 Sun
☎ (020) 7720 8265
Greene King IPA, Abbot; guest beers Ⓗ
Near the other Polygon pubs, this one stands out for several reasons. With its fascia for Simonds Noted Ales to attract the curious, this is still a beer house. It draws in a regular crowd for its traditional ales, and the 'circuit' crowd in the guest beers and food. The pub's one bar is split into different areas by pillars and wooden partitions. ❀◑⊖ (Common) ♣

SW5: EARL'S COURT

Blackbird ⊘
209 Earl's Court Road, SW5 9AR
✪ 11–11; 12-10.30 Sun
☎ (020) 7835 1855
Fuller's Chiswick, London Pride, ESB Ⓗ
Located at the heart of busy Earl's Court, this pub is a welcome haven. The extensive wood panelling is a reminder that the pub was converted from a bank in 1993. The furnishings and fittings seem to create a certain 'gin palace' ambience. Although not spacious, the limited bare-boarded area at the front and the carpeted area at the rear create an impression of greater space and diversity. This Fuller's Ale & Pie house serves food every day. ◑▶ ⊖

SW6: PARSONS GREEN

Duke of Cumberland
235 New King's Road, SW6 4X6
✪ 11–11; 12-10.30 Sun
☎ (020) 7736 2777
Young's Bitter, Special, seasonal beers Ⓗ
This large, late Victorian pub stands proud on the green. The exterior is grand, while internally there is much to admire, despite many alterations. The main bar boasts a marvellous tiled wall (once part of a side corridor), and a panel describing the life of the Duke. The rear bar, added in the 1980s, has been refurbished and is now more in sympathy with the rest. It attracts a younger clientele who enjoy loud music and sport on plasma screens, as well as table football.
♨❀◑▶⌖⊖♣

White Horse ⊘
1-3 Parsons Green, SW6 4UL
✪ 11–11; 12-10.30 Sun
☎ (020) 7736 2115 website: www.whitehorsesw6.com
Adnams Broadside; Draught Bass; Harveys BB; Oakham JHB; Rooster's Yankee Ⓗ
Originally two properties, this upmarket pub is situated in an attractive location, directly beside Parsons Green. Well known for the variety of real ales on offer, food is also a major feature at this popular pub. The staff take pride in the quality of cellar management and breweriana is on display. Regular beer festivals are held during the year and barbecues are also organised. This local CAMRA Pub of the Year 2001 holds a children's certificate.
❀◑▶ ⊖

SW8: SOUTH LAMBETH

Mawbey Arms
7 Mawbey Street, SW8 2TT
✪ 11–11; 12-10.30 Sun
☎ (020) 7622 1936
Shepherd Neame Master Brew Bitter; Young's Bitter; guest beers Ⓗ
Friendly south London local whose customers are known for their impromptu singalongs. Four darts teams meet at the pub and cribbage is available. It gets busy at weekends, especially during televised sports. Bar food can be arranged in advance for the evening, otherwise meals are only served at lunchtime.
Q❀◑⇌ (Vauxhall) ⊖ (Stockwell) P

Priory Arms ⊘
83 Lansdowne Way, SW8 2PB
✪ 11–11; 12-10.30 Sun
☎ (020) 7622 1884
Adnams Bitter; Harveys BB; Hop Back Summer Lightning; guest beers Ⓗ
A true free house where the two guest beers from micro-breweries are constantly changing. It stocks a good selection of foreign bottled beers and a German beer festival is staged in October. Special celebrations are organised for Saints' Days (St George's Day, etc), Hallowe'en, Burns' Night and Pancake Day. The friendly landlady, landlord and their staff are committed to serving a wide range of interesting beers at this six times winner of South-West London CAMRA Pub of the Year.
◑⊖ (Stockwell) ♣ ♠

SW9: BRIXTON

Trinity Arms
45 Trinity Gardens, SW9 8DR
🕐 11-11; 12-10.30 Sun
☎ (020) 7274 4544
Young's Bitter, Special, Winter Warmer, seasonal beers Ⓗ

Single-bar pub, a few yards from Brixton town centre. Customers include local regulars and casual visitors who come for the well-kept beers. The pub stands in Trinity Gardens which is a quiet area; the name derives from Trinity Asylum which stood in nearby Acre Lane, founded in 1824. A good variety of lunches is served on weekdays and Sunday; on Saturday food is available 1–6.
Q❀❀⊁⊖

SW9: CLAPHAM

Landor
70 Landor Road, SW9 9PH
🕐 12-11; 12-10.30 Sun
☎ (020) 7274 4386 website: www.landor.com
Greene King IPA; Shepherd Neame Spitfire; guest beers Ⓗ

Vibrant pub, decorated with various artefacts. It gets very busy when the upstairs, highly regarded theatre is open (Tue–Sat). The staff give first-class service and are always pleasant and helpful. The home-cooked food is excellent and represents good value; coffee is a speciality (no food Sun eve or Mon). The pub boasts three pool tables which are always in use; a large-screen TV shows sports events on request.
◑⊁ (High St) ⊖ (North) ♣

SW10: WEST BROMPTON

Chelsea Ram
32 Burnaby Street, SW10 0PL
🕐 11-11; 12-10.30 Sun
☎ (020) 7351 4008
Young's Bitter, Special, seasonal beers Ⓗ

The regenerated, affluent area off Lots Road, near the King's Road and Chelsea Harbour benefits from this fine Young's pub, catering to the needs of the many younger locals. The old pub was given a stylish make-over in the form of scrubbed oak tables, padded benches and artwork. The rear section, lit by a skylight, is quiet and mainly for diners. Emphasis on quality pub fare and a decent wine list does not, however, detract from its genuine, friendly pub atmosphere. Q◑

SW11: BATTERSEA

Castle
115 Battersea High Street, SW11 3JR
🕐 12-11; 12-10.30 Sun
☎ (020) 7228 8181
Young's Bitter, Special, seasonal beers Ⓗ

This pleasant 1960s pub, built in typical Young's post-war style, has established a firm reputation for high quality food at reasonable prices for the area. It can therefore be rather busy at peak dining times, but the beer is excellent. The pub's attractions include a conservatory and secluded patio area at the rear, as well as a recently redecorated back bar with leather sofas. Note the rare carved wooden pub sign at the gable end of the building.
❀◑⊁ (Clapham Jct) P

Grove ✅
279 Battersea Park Road, SW11 4NE
🕐 11-11; 12-10.30 Sun
☎ (020) 7220 5198
Adnams Broadside; Boddingtons Bitter; Fuller's London Pride Ⓗ

Clean and spacious community local, something of an oasis for real ale in an area where many pubs are no longer serving it. The Grove attracts a wide cross-section of locals. Do not be put off by the rather forbidding architecture of this post-war estate pub – a warm welcome awaits within. It serves excellent value Sunday lunches and fresh fish from Billingsgate on Friday lunchtime (booking advised).
❀◑⊁ (Battersea Pk) ⊁

SW12: BALHAM

Nightingale
97 Nightingale Lane, SW12 8NX
🕐 11-11; 12-10.30 Sun
☎ (020) 8673 1637
Young's Bitter, Special, seasonal beers Ⓗ

Brick-built Victorian pub, on the affluent northern fringes of Balham. It has won numerous awards over the years, and is well-known for its annual charity walk. A small conservatory at the rear acts as a no-smoking-cum-family room. This leads through to an attractive patio and garden, which can be a real suntrap in the summer. Evening meals are available Monday–Friday.
Q❀❀◑⊁ (Wandsworth Common) ♣⊁

SW13: BARNES

Coach & Horses
27 Barnes High Street, SW13 9LW
🕐 11-3, 5.30-11; 11-11 Fri, Sat & summer; 12-10.30 Sun
☎ (020) 8876 2695
Young's Bitter, Special, seasonal beers Ⓗ

Former coaching inn, first leased by Young's in 1831. It has a distinct village-pub feel, as befits its location in one of London's so-called villages. Its single bar is quite small, but the sizeable garden (large enough for a boules pitch) is popular with families, especially for summer weekend barbecues. Excellent lunches are served daily, and sandwiches until 9pm Monday–Saturday. A large function room is available.
Q❀◑⊁ (Barnes Bridge) ♣

SW15: PUTNEY

Green Man
Putney Heath, SW15 3NG (off A219)
🕐 11-11; 12-10.30 Sun
☎ (020) 8788 8096
Young's Bitter, Special, seasonal beers Ⓗ

One of the first pubs bought by Young's Brewery (1831), this two-roomed country inn-style pub was built on the site of Thomas Cromwell's (Earl of Sussex) birthplace. Routemaster buses begin their journey into central London opposite. On warm days, drinkers can imbibe on the concreted areas surrounding the pub or in the rear garden. Food is served 12–2 weekdays (12–4 Sat and Sun). Barbecues are

held on warm weekends in the garden. Ring the bull is played here.
Q❀◖❶♣

SW15: ROEHAMPTON

Angel
11 Roehampton High Street, SW15 4HL
🕓 11-11; 12-10.30 Sun
☎ (020) 8788 1997
Young's Bitter, Special Ⓗ
Charming, two-bar Young's house, tucked away in what seems to be a back street off Roehampton Lane. This locals' favourite is welcoming to passers-by. Sport is a popular conversation topic and the public bar has a large-screen TV on which major events are shown. A quieter pint can be enjoyed in the saloon bar. ◖❶◿

SW16: STREATHAM

Hogshead
68-70 Streatham High Road, SW16 1DA
🕓 11-11; 12-10.30 Sun
☎ (020) 8696 7587
Draught Bass; Fuller's London Pride; Gale's HSB; Ⓗ **Harveys BB;** Ⓖ **Young's Bitter** Ⓗ**; guest beers** Ⓗ/Ⓖ
An enthusiastic management team ensures this pub is a real gem, avoiding interference from the pub company hierarchy. It is laid out on several levels displaying many old prints of local historical interest. One beer is always sold cheaply and a small range of Belgian bottled beers is stocked. Music is kept to a reasonable level and various board games are available; Wednesday is quiz night. Food is served 12–9 weekdays (7 Sat; 8 Sun); there are special deals on meals at certain times.
◖❶⇌ (Hill) ♣✄

Pied Bull
498 Streatham High Road, SW16 3BQ
🕓 11-11; 12-10.30 Sun
☎ (020) 8764 4003
Young's Bitter, Special, Winter Warmer Ⓗ
Near the common, this brightly-lit pub features a large-screen TV for sports and subdued music. An island bar serves three distinct areas, attracting a mixed crowd. There are comfortable sofas and upholstered chairs; pictures and prints adorn every wall. The pub dates from around 1768 and was a stopping-place along the road from London for coaches. The garden is popular with families.
❀◖❶⇌P

SW17: TOOTING

JJ Moons ✓
56A Tooting High Street, SW17 0RN
🕓 10-11; 12-10.30 Sun
☎ (020) 8672 4726
Courage Directors; Greene King Abbot; Shepherd Neame Spitfire; Theakston Best Bitter; guest beers Ⓗ
One of South London's early Wetherspoon's shop conversions; a long, narrow pub with a quieter no-smoking area at the rear, but bustling at the front. Very close to Tooting Broadway, the pub's clientele reflects the area's rich ethnic mix. Note the photographs of Edwardian Tooting along the walls. One or two guest beers are normally on offer.
Q⛭◖❶⊖ (Broadway) P✄

SW18: SOUTHFIELDS

Gardeners Arms
266-268 Merton Road, SW18 5JL
🕓 11-11; 12-10.30 Sun
☎ (020) 8874 7624
Young's Bitter, Special, seasonal beers Ⓗ
Clean, commodious corner pub with a friendly atmosphere. The large island bar with its cast iron gantry is the focal point of the interior, while a side room, formerly a shop, increases the seating capacity. An unpretentious local in an otherwise unremarkable stretch of Merton Road, running between Wandsworth and Wimbledon, it is easily accessible by bus. The present building dates from 1931 and retains its exterior tiling. ❀◖❶⊖

Grid Inn ✓
22 Replingham Road, SW18 5LS
🕓 10-11; 12-10.30 Sun
☎ (020) 8874 8460
Courage Best Bitter, Directors; Greene King Abbot; Shepherd Neame Spitfire; guest beers Ⓗ
Wetherspoon's free house whose small size and cosily partitioned interior are not typical of the chain. Otherwise, standard JDW comforts and beer policies are in evidence. The pub takes its name from the somewhat unimaginative pattern of streets between Southfields and Wimbledon Park. The sparse decoration centres on the history of the area, with early photographs of the nearby station.
Q◖❶♿⊖✄

SW18: WANDSWORTH

Cat's Back
86-88 Point Pleasant, SW18 1NN
🕓 11-11; 12-10.30 Sun
☎ (020) 8877 0818
Eccleshall Slaters Supreme; O'Hanlon's Blakeley's Best, Yellowhammer; Ringwood Old Thumper Ⓗ
The only true free house in Wandsworth borough and the first O'Hanlon's outlet after O'Hanlon's original pub. Now usually serving the rotating O'Hanlon's beers, one Slaters, often Ringwood Old Thumper and occasionally a Young's beer, it keeps up to four real ales at any time. Homely furniture, old photographs, original paintings, a stained glass window behind the bar, bizarre artefacts and dim lighting, all contribute to a great atmosphere. Superb lunches; breakfast is served weekdays, 10–4.
🏠◖⇌ (Town) ⊖ (E Putney)

SW19: MERTON

Princess of Wales
98 Morden Road, SW19 3BP
🕓 11-3, 5-11; 11-11 Fri & Sat; 12-10.30 Sun
☎ (020) 8542 0573
Young's Bitter, Special, seasonal beers Ⓗ
Cosy one-bar Young's house; the main bar leads to a lounge area which is usually quiet, while to one side is the former public bar with darts. The pub dates from around the mid-19th century and has evolved over the years, but retains its Victorian frontage. The pub is twinned with the Horse Brass Pub in Portland, Oregon. It is home to the Young's Brewery cricket team who play on the nearby Abbey recreation ground. Good value,

home-cooked food is served lunchtime and weekday evenings (6–8.30).
🏚Q🌢◑⊖(Morden Rd/S Wimbledon) ♣P

SW19: SOUTH WIMBLEDON

Sultan
78 Norman Road, SW19 1BT
⊘ 12-11; 12-10.30 Sun
☎ (020) 8542 4532
Hop Back GFB, Summer Lightning, seasonal beers 🅗
Hop Back's sole London pub is situated on a quiet residential street. This two-bar pub has a quiet side for darts and cards, which is usually only open in the evening. This is a beer pub which hosts an annual beer festival (Sept) and a beer club (Wed 6–9) with discounted real ale. A walled patio is used for outside drinking and barbecues. Note: Hop Back Entire Stout is served with a cask breather. CAMRA 2002 London Pub of the Year. 🌢🖴🕭🌢♣P

SW19: WIMBLEDON

Brewery Tap ⊘
68-69 High Street, SW19 5EE
⊘ 11-11; 12-10.30 Sun
☎ (020) 8947 9331
Adnams Bitter; Fuller's London Pride; guest beers 🅗
Open-plan, modernised pub, which maintains a lively atmosphere and appeals to a broad mix of customers. The Wimbledon Brewery stood next door but was destroyed by fire in 1889. The three guest beers often include a choice of a mild, a dark beer and a micro-brewery beer. The TV shows major sporting events. Lunch and breakfast are served every day (Sun from 11am) and on Wednesday evening, tapas. Fish and chips are available on big match football nights (except tapas night). ◑≑⊖

Crooked Billet
15 Crooked Billet, SW19 4RQ
⊘ 11-11; 12-10.30 Sun
☎ (020) 8946 4942
Young's Bitter, Special, seasonal beers 🅗
Dating in part from the 18th century, this pub has been selling Young's beers since the 1880s and the brewery has owned it since 1928. There is a large restaurant area at the rear and a small courtyard at the side. However many customers prefer to drink on the green opposite in summer. The pub televises many sporting events and will even provide breakfast during rugby internationals. Seasonal beers include Winter Warmer and Waggle Dance.
🖴🌢◑🗲

Hand in Hand
6 Crooked Billet, SW19 4RQ
⊘ 11-11; 12-10.30 Sun
☎ (020) 8946 5720
Young's Bitter, Special, seasonal beers 🅗
Originally a bakery, beer has been sold here since the 1860s when the pub was rented from the Watney family. The pub was bought by Young's in 1974 when a full licence was obtained. It was refurbished in the '80s and consists of a horseshoe-shaped bar surrounded by several drinking areas. The shady courtyard is popular in summer, as is the green opposite. Seasonal beers include Winter Warmer and Waggle Dance. 🖴🌢◑🗲

Rose & Crown
55 High Street, SW19 5BA
⊘ 11-11; 12-10.30 Sun
☎ (020) 8947 4713
Young's Bitter, Special, seasonal beers; guest beer (occasional) 🅗
Welcoming, 17th-century coaching inn at the top of Wimbledon Village, just off the common. A popular, very spacious pub with a central bar, it was impressively extended in 2002 to provide a large family conservatory, 13 luxurious hotel bedrooms and a deep cellar. Fine traditional English food is served (not winter Sun eve). It stocks an occasional guest beer from Smiles. An attractive patio is at the rear. Live rugby and cricket are shown on the TVs; Sunday quiz.
🏚Q🖴🌢🛏◑🕭🗲

CARSHALTON

Greyhound Hotel
2 High Street, SM5 3PE (on A232)
⊘ 11-11; 12-10.30 Sun
☎ (020) 8647 1511
Young's Bitter, Special, seasonal beers 🅗
Grade II listed building in a picturesque setting opposite Carshalton ponds. Close by are the ancient parish church and the Sutton Heritage Centre. The original building dates from about 1706, while the brick and stone western end was added in the 1830s. The Swan Bar boasts a real fire, grandfather clock and antique artefacts; the main bar is U-shaped. An extension houses a 21-bedroom hotel, that offers reduced weekend rates. A traditional and contemporary menu is served all day (12–7 Sun). Sutton CAMRA Pub of the Year 2003.
🏚Q🌢🛏◑≑♣P

Railway Tavern ⊘
47 North Street, SM5 2HG
⊘ 12-2.30, 5-11; 11-11 Sat; 12-10.30 Sun
☎ (020) 8669 8016
Fuller's London Pride, ESB 🅗
Traditional, friendly, one-bar pub where the walls are adorned with railway memorabilia. On a pillar opposite the main door into the pub is a certificate showing the landlord's Fuller's Master Cellarman award (2002). Also on show are many prizes for the pub's hanging baskets which are a blaze of colour in the summer. Disabled customers may enter the pub via the garden entrance. Lunchtime snacks are available. 🌢≑♣

Windsor Castle
378 Carshalton Road, SM5 3PT
(at A232/B278 jct)
⊘ 11-11; 12-10.30 Sun
☎ (020) 8669 1191
Fuller's London Pride; Hancock's HB; guest beers 🅗
Detached building combining an L-shaped bar and drinking area with a restaurant end. A courtyard leads to a small garden and detached function room. Six handpumps dispense the regular and guest ales; pump clips on the ceiling beams show the range of guests sold over the years. It hosts live music on Saturday evening and first Monday evening in the month, plus a weekly quiz. An annual beer festival is held on spring bank holiday weekend. Evening meals are served Tuesday–Saturday.
🌢◑≑(Beeches) ♣P

CHEAM

Claret Wine Bar
33 The Broadway, SM3 8BL (off A232)
☼ 11-11; 12-10.30 Sun
☎ (020) 8715 9002
Shepherd Neame Master Brew Bitter; guest beers Ⓗ
Converted retail premises in a parade of shops: a narrow bar and drinking area at the front opens out at the back. Light-coloured wood used for furniture, floors and panelling gives a spacious impression. Due to become a Claret Free House, discounts are given on four-pint jugs of ale. Quiz night is Monday and curry night, Thursday. The iron spiral staircase at the front leads up to the restaurant (open Wed–Sat evenings and for Sunday lunch). Q ◑ ▶ �

Prince of Wales
28 Malden Road, SM3 8QF (off A232)
☼ 11-11; 12-10.30 Sun
☎ (020) 8641 8106
Adnams Bitter; Fuller's London Pride; Young's Bitter; guest beer Ⓗ
Pleasant, traditional local; note the collection of pewter tankards and interesting clock near the dartboards. It has a restaurant and children's area; dogs are also welcome. Interesting historic buildings in the area include Henry VIII's Nonsuch Palace and Whitehill, a weatherboarded house. Real ale is a big seller here. The locals are very friendly; a TV is available for major sporting occasions. Special events, such as Valentine's Day and Mother's Day are celebrated with gusto. Q ⌂ ⊛ ◑ ≈ ♣ ● ⚞

KEW

Coach & Horses Hotel
8 Kew Green, TW9 3BH
☼ 11-11; 12-10.30 Sun
☎ (020) 8940 1208
Young's Bitter, Special, seasonal beers Ⓗ
A Young's house since 1831, the Coach & Horses now has a modern hotel, complete with underground car park, at the rear. Its reopening in 2001 also saw a refurbishment of the bar area, creating more space and allowing a side no-smoking room to be used mainly for dining. It enjoys a justifiably excellent reputation for its home-cooked food, which includes fish specialities – best to book for Sunday lunch. Close to Kew Gardens, it is on bus route 65.
♨ Q ⊛ ⋈ ◑ ≈ (Bridge) ⊖ (Gardens) P ⚞

KINGSTON UPON THAMES

Canbury Arms
49 Canbury Park Road, KT2 6LQ
☼ 11-11; 12-10.30 Sun
☎ (020) 8288 1882
Courage Best Bitter; guest beers Ⓗ
Victorian drinkers' pub close to central Kingston, offering a good range of up to five guest beers, usually on the stronger side. The interior features mock beams and a small raised seating area; there is a pool table and other pub games are played. It hosts live music Friday and Saturday evening and a quiz on Sunday. The children's area is a small back room away from the TV where most live sports are shown. This is a former local CAMRA Pub of the Year. ⌂ ⊛ ≈ ♣ ● P ⊟

Park Tavern
19 New Road, KT2 6AP (off B351)
☼ 11-11; 12-10.30 Sun
Fuller's London Pride; Young's Bitter; guest beers Ⓗ
Excellent pub, tucked away down a small side road, not far from Richmond Park's Kingston gate. The single bar is decorated with old pictures, clocks and a display of the many pump clips used over the years. There is a patio at the front of the pub and a garden which is used for the annual November fireworks. Three or four guest beers are available, from a variety of brewers, small and large. Filled rolls are available at lunchtime. ♨ ⊛

Richmond Park
178 Kings Road, KT2 5HJ (off A307)
☼ 11 (12 Sat)-11; 12-3, 7-10.30 Sun
☎ (020) 8296 0894
Fuller's London Pride Ⓗ
Large pub on a corner site. The lounge is dominated by a central fireplace and is decorated with pictures of Richmond Park down the side. It has a raised seating area in one corner and a large collection of old bottles on high level shelving. The plainer public bar is sports-oriented with a large-screen TV. A DJ is employed on Saturday evening; a quiz is held on Wednesday. No meals are served at weekends. Q ⊛ ◑ ⊟ ♣ P

Willoughby Arms ⊘
47 Willoughby Road, KT2 6LN
☼ 10.30-11; 12-10.30 Sun
☎ (020) 8546 4236
Caledonian Deuchars IPA; Fuller's London Pride; Marston's Pedigree; Taylor Landlord; guest beer Ⓗ
Two beer festivals are held each year here, on St George's Day and Hallowe'en. This two-bar local attracts a friendly clientele. A cat, three dogs, games (including three dartboards and pool) and local papers add interest. The walls of the front bar are covered with stories of the pub featured in the press. The pub has received its third Cask Marque accreditation. Cheddar Valley cider is stocked. ⊛ ☺ ♣ ●

Wych Elm ⊘
93 Elm Road, KT2 6HT
☼ 11-3, 5-11; 11-11 Sat; 12-10.30 Sun
☎ (020) 8546 3271
Fuller's Chiswick, London Pride, ESB, seasonal beers Ⓗ
Very traditional, two-bar pub: a basic public bar, with lino floor and dartboard contrasts with the more comfortable and decorative lounge. It has been run for more than 20 years by a charismatic landlord from Spain, who looks after his pub and his beers superbly. There is a pleasant garden at the rear. The pub has won several awards for its floral displays and Christmas decorations. Home-cooked food is served Monday–Saturday. ⊛ ◑ ⊟ ≈

MITCHAM

King's Arms
260 London Road, CR4 3HG
☼ 11-11; 12-5.30, 8-10.30 Sun
☎ (020) 8648 0896
Young's Bitter, Special, seasonal beers Ⓗ
Situated in the pedestrianised area of the town centre, an island bar commands the

room. Various old prints adorn the walls and resident cats, Doris and Mr Brown prowl or commandeer chairs by the fire. There is an outside drinking area and a function room on the first floor. Main meals are available weekday lunchtimes. Quizzes are held on Thursday and Sunday evening. Sound is kept at a reasonable level on the TV and games machine. ♨✿◖

RICHMOND

Marlborough ◉
46 Friars Stile Road, TW10 6NQ
✪ 12-11; 12-10.30 Sun
☎ (020) 8940 0572
Fuller's London Pride; guest beer Ⓗ
Recently refurbished in a modern style, this former hotel has retained some stained glass panels and two real fires. The clientele is mixed but it appeals to younger people. Sofas, armchairs and benches are spread throughout two drinking and dining areas. Mediterranean-influenced food is served all hours, plus summer barbecues. It has the largest pub garden in Richmond, with a bandstand that hosts summer jazz concerts. ♨✿◖

Red Cow
59 Sheen Road, TW9 1YJ
✪ 11-11; 12-10.30 Sun
☎ (020) 8940 2511
website: www.redcowpub.activehotels.com
Young's Bitter, Special, seasonal beers Ⓗ
Popular local, a few minutes' walk from Richmond's shops and station. There are three distinct drinking areas, where rugs on bare floorboards and period furniture create a traditional atmosphere. The first floor has four en-suite bedrooms. Good lunches are served daily, and evening meals until 8.30pm on weekdays. Tuesday is quiz night, and live music is performed on Thursday evening. ♨✿⌂◖≈♣♠

Triple Crown
15 Kew Foot Road, TW9 2SS
✪ 11-11; 12-10.30 Sun
☎ (020) 8940 3805
Beer range varies Ⓗ
True free house serving four regularly changed ales. It stands by Richmond Athletic Ground, close to Old Deer Park and Kew Gardens, and is convenient for the station. A fairly small and narrow pub, it is popular for the Tuesday evening quiz and Sunday afternoon jazz. There are a couple of tables on the front pavement, and an upstairs function room has its own bar (with handpumps) and a small balcony. Lunches are served Monday–Saturday. ✿◖≈⊖

White Cross
Riverside, Water Lane, TW9 1TJ
✪ 11-11; 12-10.30 Sun
☎ (020) 8940 6844
Young's Bitter, Special, seasonal beers Ⓗ
A prominent feature on Richmond's waterfront, the pub dates from 1835, but a stained glass panel is a reminder that it stands on the site of a former convent of the Observant Friars, whose insignia was a white cross. It is reached by steps for good reason – the river often floods here. An island bar serves two side rooms (one a

mezzanine). An unusual feature is a working fireplace beneath a window. A ground-level patio bar opens at busy times (plastic glasses are used for outside drinking). ♨Q✿◖≈⊖

SURBITON

Cap in Hand ◉
174 Hook Rise North, KT6 5DE
✪ 10-11; 12-10.30 Sun
☎ (020) 8397 3790
Courage Best Bitter; Fuller's London Pride; Greene King Abbot; Hop Back Summer Lightning; Shepherd Neame Spitfire; guest beers Ⓗ
Large Wetherspoon's roadhouse, formerly known as the Southborough Arms. Regular guest beers alternate every month or so. Plenty of local memorabilia is displayed; singer, Petula Clark was born and raised in nearby Chessington. Friendly and very family-oriented, children are allowed in the conservatory. The outdoor seating area overlooks the busy Ace of Spades junction of the A3. The cider is Westons Old Rosie. ♨Q⛄✿◖&♣P⅙

Coronation Hall ◉
St Marks Hill, KT6 4TB (on B3370)
✪ 10-11; 12-10.30 Sun
☎ (020) 8390 6164
Courage Best Bitter, Directors; Greene King Abbot; Shepherd Neame Spitfire; guest beers Ⓗ
Opened in 1997, a splendid conversion from an old music hall (latterly the Ritz bingo hall and once a nudist health club). Decorated on a film theme, pictures of film stars and articles of old cinema equipment abound. The entrance has mixed seating (for families) where one can watch passers-by. Going in up the steps is the long bar and a more enclosed seating area; an upstairs balcony at the end provides a view of the bar. Food is served all day, from 10am. Q⛄◖&≈⅙

Lamb
73 Brighton Road, KT6 5NF (on A243)
✪ 11-11; 12-10.30 Sun
☎ (020) 8390 9229
Greene King IPA; guest beers Ⓗ
Small, one-bar local with a welcome for all. The beer range features a constantly-changing guest as well as a beer of the month. There always seems to be something happening here, with a Tuesday quiz, karaoke on the first Saturday of the month, and charity events, including the annual pub olympics. Football matches and rugby internationals are shown on a large-screen TV. A good range of pub grub, includes real chips; no food Sunday. ✿◖≈♣

New Prince ◉
117 Ewell Road, KT6 6AL (on A240)
✪ 11-11; 12-10.30 Sun
☎ (020) 8296 0265
Gale's Butser, GB, HSB Ⓗ
Locals' pub catering for all ages. The beamed interior features advertising for Gale's beers. The main room houses the bar counter and the no-smoking area (at lunchtime) leads off from this. The pub fields a team in the local darts league and hosts a monthly quiz in winter (Tue). Sports matches are shown on TV. A duo occasionally performs live music. ✿◖≈♣⅙

303

Waggon & Horses
1 Surbiton Hill Road, KT6 4TW (on A240)
🕐 11-11; 12-10.30 Sun
☎ (020) 8390 0211
Young's Bitter, Special, Winter Warmer Ⓗ
Good, traditional Young's pub at the bottom of Surbiton Hill. The name is due to the pub supplying horses to assist heavy loads up the hill. Of its two bars, one is a more open public bar at the front, with a lounge to the side which is ideal for eating your Thai meal in. At the rear is the wood-panelled, carpeted lounge bar with a raised seating area that leads out to the garden.
Q 🍴 🕯️◗ ≠ ♣ ✁

SUTTON

Little Windsor ✓
13 Greyhound Road, SM1 4BY
🕐 11.30-11; 12-10.30 Sun
☎ (020) 8643 2574
Fuller's Chiswick, London Pride, ESB, seasonal beers; guest beer Ⓗ
Friendly little local which was Sutton CAMRA Pub of the Year 2002 – look for the certificate under the most unusual light! Recently extended to accommodate, among other things, a big-screen TV, it sells beer in four-pint jugs at a discount. A quiz night is held most Tuesdays. It screens all major televised sport, but occasionally the constant TV in the corner can be distracting. There is a garden and deck out the back, and a small roadside seating area at the front. 🕯️◗ ≠

Lord Nelson
32 Lower Road, SM1 4QP
🕐 12-11; 12-4, 7-10.30 Sun
☎ (020) 8642 4120
Young's Bitter, Special, seasonal beers Ⓗ
Young's pub, traditionally decorated with a lot of green paint and external tiles. It has lost one of its original three bars, but retains two. The main bar is surprisingly long; the smaller bar has a darts area; note the etched windows. This friendly pub hosts occasional barbecues in the garden. 🕯️◗ ≠

New Town
7 Lind Road, SM1 4BX
🕐 12-3, 5-11; 12-11 Fri & Sat; 12-10.30 Sun
☎ (020) 8770 2072
Young's Bitter, Special, seasonal beers Ⓗ
A couple of hundred yards from the A232, this former hotel has an interesting lounge bar on three levels as well as a public bar. The lounge bar features several old wooden barrels, while the public bar has a pool table (an unusual asset in this area). It carries the usual range of Young's beers. Food is available lunchtime and evening. 🕯️◗ 🍴≠

Robin Hood
52 West Street, SM1 1SH (behind UCI cinema)
🕐 11-11; 12-10.30 Sun
☎ (020) 8643 7584
Young's Bitter, Special; guest beer (occasional) Ⓗ
Recently refurbished, this spacious and comfortable, 19th-century, one-bar pub is located just behind the cinema. It benefits from a strong local trade; regulars have raised over £9,000 for charity over the past four years. A real fire burns in winter and a small courtyard and pavement seating are

used in summer. The full range of Young's bottled beers is available. Meals are served Monday–Saturday. Shove-ha'penny and cribbage can be played here. 🏠Q🕯️◗ ≠ ♣

WALLINGTON

Duke's Head Hotel
6 Manor Road, SM6 0AA (A237/A232 jct)
🕐 11-11; 12-10.30 Sun
☎ (020) 8647 1595
Young's Bitter, Special, seasonal beers Ⓗ
A listed building in the oldest part of Wallington, it was originally called Bowling Green House; records go back to 1726. The present building is Victorian, in an attractive setting on the village green, it was recently expanded with hotel accommodation, a new restaurant and no-smoking area. All the work has been sympathetic to the building's character. The public bar has a TV, juke box and darts; the saloon bar and lounge offer a quiet, more mature atmosphere.
🏠Q🕯️🛏️◗ 🍴♿≠♣P✁

West London

W1: FITZROVIA

Hope
15 Tottenham Street, W1T 2AJ
🕐 11-11; 12-6 Sun
☎ (020) 7637 0896
Adnams Bitter; Fuller's London Pride; Taylor Landlord; guest beers Ⓗ
Lovely pub, famed for its food; the specials change daily and a fixed menu is served 12–4. A good range of Thai dishes is also available. An upstairs room can be booked for private functions. Board games played here include Scrabble, Monopoly and chess. Its two rooms have been knocked through to a single bar where lots of colour photographs and prints decorate the walls, together with a wonderful old Buchanan's black and white mirror. ◗➡(Goodge St) ♣

One Tun
58 Goodge Street, W1T 4ND
🕐 11.30-11; 12-10.30 Sun
☎ (020) 7209 4105
Young's Bitter, Special, seasonal beers Ⓗ
Formerly a Finches house, now a deservedly popular Young's pub near Tottenham Court Road, Bass mirrors grace the walls and darts is played towards the rear. The pub, served by an island bar, is fully carpeted, keeping the noise of music down to an acceptable level and helping you to enjoy the pub and its beers in peace. During the summer the front patio doors can be opened and it is possible to sit at the front of the pub and watch the world go by. Tuesday is quiz night. ◗➡(Goodge St)

W1: MARYLEBONE

Beehive
7 Homer Street, W1H 4NU
🕐 11-11; 12-10.30 Sun
☎ (020) 7262 6581
Fuller's London Pride; Young's Bitter Ⓗ
Small, friendly, one-bar pub with frosted windows, carpeted floors and prints of London street life. On the wall is a mechanism for weighing sacks of grain.

This pub has a very loyal local following which reflects that London is made up of several villages. Strangers are also made to feel welcome and it is popular with actors from a famous soap opera. This is what a pub should be like and is a haven from nearby Edgware Road, famous for its many ethnic restaurants and coffee houses.
🏨 ◖≉♿ (Edgware Rd)

Carpenters Arms ✔
12 Seymour Place, W1H 7NE
🕐 11-11; 12-10.30 Sun
☎ (020) 7723 1050
Fuller's London Pride; guest beers Ⓗ
Sister pub to the Market Porter near London Bridge, this pub is smaller and mainly attracts a clientele who appreciate Sky Sports. It is a mecca for beers from micros and regional breweries, not normally found in London. This pub had an unsavoury past in medieval London in that a tunnel, now blocked off, connected to the Masons Arms (Hall & Woodhouse pub) where prisoners were kept shackled before being hanged at nearby Tyburn Gate. The main entrance to the pub has an original tiled wall. The back part can be reserved for parties and hosts darts on Tuesday evening. ◖♿ (Marble Arch)

Golden Eagle
59 Marylebone Lane, W1V 2NY
🕐 11-11; 12-10.30 Sun
☎ (020) 7935 3228
Brakspear Bitter; Fuller's London Pride; guest beer Ⓗ
Small, back-street local, not far from bustling Oxford Street. During the day it can be very quiet, with a small contingent of regulars catching up on the local gossip. The clientele changes during the evenings with workers coming in for a drink. On Thursday and Friday a pianist plays popular tunes; this may be extended to other evenings. At lunchtime it sells baguettes stuffed with Biggles sausages from the award-winning shop also located in Marylebone Lane where CAMRA members can get a discount. ♿ (Bond St)

Wargrave Arms
40 Brendon Street, W1H 5HE
🕐 11-11; 12-10.30 Sun
☎ (020) 7723 0559
Young's Bitter, Special, seasonal beers Ⓗ
Former Finches pub acquired by Young's in the 1980s. It is open plan, but a carpeted floor helps to keep noise levels down. The pub reflects 1950s style; leather chairs with small tables run along the wall close to the bar. One area is used for dining. It attracts an eclectic clientele, either deep in conversation or playing chess on certain nights. Evenings can be busy with local couples and business people relishing the end of the day. ❀◖≉ (Edgware Rd) ♿♣

W1: MAYFAIR

Guinea
30 Bruton Place, W1J 6NL
🕐 11-11; 11-6.30 Sat; closed Sun
☎ (020) 7409 1728
Young's Bitter, Special, seasonal beers Ⓗ
Upmarket Mayfair local which is also a grill and restaurant that has won many awards for its food. There has been a pub on this site since 1423 and this building dates back to 1675. The pub consists of a small front bar with a dividing screen and door separating the corridor leading to the restaurant at the back of the pub. Prints of Mayfair gentlemen during the time of Dickens are displayed. Clientele is mainly local business people. Q ♿ (Bond St)

W1: SOHO

Coach & Horses
29 Greek Street, W1D 5DH
🕐 11-11; 12-10.30 Sun
☎ (020) 7437 5920
Fuller's London Pride; Marston's Pedigree; Tetley Burton Ale Ⓗ
Famous Soho institution run by Norman Balon since the 1960s. The pub is fully carpeted with 1960s bench seating and tables. The walls are veneered in wood, bearing cartoons of the landlord and also of Jeffrey Bernard feeling unwell, with an ambulance waiting outside the pub. With the Cambridge Theatre next door, the pub can get packed in the evening with theatre-goers. Sunday–Friday 11–4 is happy 'hour'. Sandwiches are available all day.
♿ (Leicester Sq/Piccadilly Circus)

Ship ✔
116 Wardour Street, W1F 0TT
🕐 11-11; closed Sun
☎ (020) 7437 8446
Fuller's London Pride, ESB, seasonal beers Ⓗ
Only Fuller's outlet in the West End, this small pub is situated close to Chinatown and the former red light area. During WWII a gas explosion destroyed the pub. It was rebuilt, preserving the etched glass windows and etched mirror behind the bar. The clientele is fairly mixed, attracting media students and Soho types and is handy for Berwick Street market. Being in the heart of Soho, the pub can be packed in the evenings and the music can be loud. ◖♿

W2: BAYSWATER

Prince Edward ✔
73 Princes Square, W2 4NY
🕐 11-11; 12-10.30 Sun
☎ (020) 7727 2221
Badger K&B Sussex, Best, Tanglefoot Ⓗ
The pub's attractive interior features etched glass, pictures, mirrors, plates and assorted bric-à-brac. The function room doubles as a small dining area. It hosts gigs on Saturday evening, but the pub is usually quiet early in the day. Sunday lunches are served from 12–3. ❀◖♿ (Queensway) ♣

W2: MARBLE ARCH

Tyburn ✔
18-20 Edgware Road, W2 2EN
🕐 10-11; 12-10.30 Sun
☎ (020) 7723 4731
Fuller's London Pride; Greene King Abbot; Shepherd Neame Spitfire; guest beers Ⓗ
Café-style Wetherspoon's pub with stone flooring and raised seating in the no-smoking area. The pub has been converted from a Whistlestop supermarket and the name refers to the notorious Tyburn Gate where public hangings took place. With the spartan furnishing the pub can get noisy with the chat in several different languages

from tourists and the local population. This pub hosts several beer festivals and weekly promotions. ◖▣⊖⅄

W2: PADDINGTON

Archery Tavern ⊘
4 Bathurst Street, W2 2SD
✪ 11-11; 12-10.30 Sun
☎ (020) 7402 4916
Badger K&B Sussex, Best, Tanglefoot, seasonal beers 🅷
This Badger outlet is just one of 11 pubs that Hall & Woodhouse have in the capital. It dates from 1840 and is located next to a mews and old stables. Well furnished and comfortable throughout, it is a handy stop en-route to the West End for the many tourists who pass through its doors. Some pub games are available, plus a dartboard at the rear of the pub. The food on offer is quite varied and wholesome and is served all day Sunday (12–9).
❀◖▣⇌ (Lancaster Gate) ⊖♣

Mad Bishop & Bear ⊘
First Floor, The Lawn, Paddington Station, W2 1HB
✪ 7.30am-11pm; 8.30am-10.30pm Sun
☎ (020) 7402 2441
Fuller's Chiswick, London Pride, seasonal beers; guest beers 🅷
Breakfast is served from 7.30am weekdays and 8.30am on Sunday. The pub is entered by ascending the escalators by the check-in desks. Ample seating is provided within and without. There is a regular turnaround on the guest beers and the food menu changes regularly, with dishes to suit all palates. Similar to the Wetherspoon's at Victoria Station, with the trains only minutes away, this is very much a pub to enjoy.
⅊❀◖▣⇌⊖⅄

Royal Exchange
26 Sale Place, W2 1PU
✪ 11-11; 12-10.30 Sun
☎ (020) 7723 3781
Boddingtons Bitter; Brakspear Bitter 🅷
A good, traditional local. Among the many monochrome prints on the walls, appears a front page from the Daily Express during WWII. The landlord is a keen fan of the turf, as is quite evident from framed cigarette cards and the fine portrait of a racehorse which hangs alongside some country scenes. The food menu is good and changes daily, including a Friday 'special' (no food Sun eve). The licence dates back to 1841 and the name refers to letters being exchanged between horse-drawn Royal Mail coaches. Q◖▣⇌⊖

Victoria ⊘
10A Strathearn Place, W2 2NH
✪ 11-11; 12-10.30 Sun
☎ (020) 7724 1191
Fuller's Chiswick, London Pride, ESB, seasonal beers 🅷
This is a very attractive pub boasting old prints and etched mirrors throughout. There is a TV to one side for Sky fans. Benches outside, together with some plants, afford a barrier to the traffic noise. An upstairs bar and a smaller room, the library, can be hired for functions. Queen Victoria is said to have been a visitor here on her way

to open Paddington Station. The beers complement an excellent, varied menu, served all day. ❀◖▣⇌⊖ (Lancaster Gate)

W3: ACTON

Duke of York
86 Steyne Road, W3 9YU
(off Horn Lane near Safeway)
✪ 11-11; 12-10.30 Sun
☎ (020) 8992 0463
Courage Best Bitter; Fuller's London Pride 🅷
Friendly free house, comprising a single dog-leg bar, pool room, a dining room (serves food 12–4, 6–9 Mon–Sat, 12–6 Sun) and a function room upstairs for hire. Its regular clientele is occasionally augmented by local celebrities. The garden has heaters to extend its use. Traditional games available here include draughts and cribbage. ❀◖▣⊖♣

King's Head
214 High Street, W3 9NX
✪ 11-11; 12-10.30 Sun
☎ (020) 8992 0282
Fuller's Chiswick, London Pride, ESB 🅷
This spacious, comfortable single bar offers distinct areas for drinking, dining, playing pool and watching TV. The pub occupies a prominent position towards the western end of central Acton, near Safeway supermarket. A paved frontage provides space for benches for outdoor drinking. Meals are served Monday–Saturday, 12–3 and 6–8.30. ❀◖▣⇌ (Central)

W4: CHISWICK

Bell & Crown
11-13 Thames Road, Strand-on-the-Green, W4 3PL (E of Kew Bridge, on N bank of Thames)
✪ 11-11; 12-10.30 Sun
☎ (020) 8994 4164
Fuller's Chiswick, London Pride, ESB, seasonal beers 🅷
The Bell & Crown has two conservatories overlooking the river. One forms an entrance and part of the main bar, the other (without an exit) is a no-smoking area which both drinkers and diners can use. The riverside patio can be quite crowded in comparison to the rest of the pub in summer, when many walkers pop in to quench their thirst. ♨❀◖▣⇌ (Kew Bridge)

George & Devonshire ⊘
8 Burlington Lane, W4 2QE (southside of Hogarth roundabout, A4/A316)
✪ 11-11; 12-10.30 Sun
☎ (020) 8994 1859
Fuller's Chiswick, London Pride, ESB, seasonal beers 🅷
Rare in an area where many pubs have been converted into single bars, the George & Devonshire has a more traditional feel with its saloon bar and bare-boarded public bar. There is some seating at the rear of the pub by the car park, or the more adventurous can sit out the front and watch the endless stream of traffic on Hogarth roundabout. ♨❀◖▣⊖⅊

Old Pack Horse ⊘
434 Chiswick High Road, W4 5TA
✪ 11-11; 12-10.30 Sun

☎ (020) 8994 2872
Adnams Bitter; Fuller's London Pride, ESB, seasonal beers 🄷
Large Fuller's pub, which has its own Thai restaurant to the side of the main bar. The main bar area displays an extensive array of theatre memorabilia. Towards the rear there is a little snug area, warmed by a real fire. Behind the pub is a small paved area, separated from the pavement, with seating for the odd sunny day. No meals are served on Sunday evening.
♨✿◐◑ ⇌ (Gunnersbury) ⊖ (Chiswick Pk)

Tabard
2 Bath Road, W4 1LN
🕓 11-11; 12-10.30 Sun
☎ (020) 8994 3492
Adnams Broadside; Draught Bass; Greene King IPA; Marston's Pedigree; Tetley Bitter 🄷
Built as part of the Bedford Park estate, the Tabard is ideally situated between the local underground and the housing estate. It was refurbished two years ago as the first pub of the Oak Inns brand. Apart from cleaning up the interior, it remains unchanged. The main bar and seating area is supplemented by a superb snug that doubles as the no-smoking area, and a large side room that can also be used for functions.
✿◐◑ ⊖ (Turnham Green)

W5: EALING

Castle ✔
36 St Mary's Road, W5 5EU (on B455)
🕓 11-11; 12-10.30 Sun
☎ (020) 8567 3285
Fuller's Chiswick, London Pride, ESB 🄷
The striking exterior is the first thing you notice about this traditional local, opposite Thames Valley University. Mainly open plan, a small snug bar has been retained. The main bar has a genuine stone-flagged floor. The menu offers mainly Thai dishes. Meals are served practically all day until 9.30pm (no service between 3pm and 4pm).
✿◐◑ ♿ ⊖ (South)

Fox & Goose ✔
Hanger Lane, W5 1DP (NW of gyratory system)
🕓 11-11; 12-10.30 Sun
☎ (020) 8998 5864
Fuller's Chiswick, London Pride, ESB, seasonal beers 🄷
Part of Fuller's English Inns chain, with a 73-bed hotel and restaurant attached. Popular with nearby office workers, it is generally quiet in the evenings, but is always a haven for those seeking respite from the nearby gyratory system. Refurbished when the hotel was added in the 1990s, the pub retains several distinct drinking areas, ranging from the old public bar, which regularly presents live TV sports coverage, through to the quieter back room overlooking the garden. The no-smoking area is available until 3pm.
✿🛏◐◑ ♿ ⊖ (Hanger Lane) P

Questors Grapevine Club ✔
12 Mattock Lane, W5 5BQ
🕓 7-11; 12-2.30, 7-10.30 Sun
☎ (020) 8567 0011
website: www.questors.org.uk/grapevine
Fuller's London Pride, seasonal beers; guest beers 🄷
Set opposite Walpole Park, this friendly club bar lies away from the busy town centre. It serves members of the Questor's Theatre and their guests; non-members are obliged to sign the visitors' book. The club is managed and staffed entirely by volunteers. Regularly awarded Cask Marque accreditation, it holds a beer festival every autumn. Q ⇌ (Broadway) ⊖P

Red Lion ✔
13 St Mary's Road, W5 5RA
🕓 11-11; 12-10.30 Sun
☎ (020) 8567 2541
Fuller's Chiswick, London Pride, ESB, seasonal beers; guest beers 🄷
A major refurbishment in 2002 doubled the size of this single-bar institution. However, the essential character of the original section at the front has, thankfully, been retained. The extension has allowed a greater emphasis to be placed on food. Also known as Stage 6, derived from nearby Ealing Film Studios, this link is reinforced by the numerous photographs and other memorabilia that line the walls. West Middlesex CAMRA's Pub of the Year 2002.
✿◐◑ ⇌ (Broadway) ⊖ (South)

TJ Duffy's ✔
282 Northfield Avenue, W5 4UB
🕓 11-11; 12-10.30 Sun
☎ (020) 8932 1711 website: www.tjduffy.co.uk
Fuller's London Pride; Greene King Abbot; guest beer 🄷
Warm, friendly pub converted from a wine bar some years ago. High quality, hands-on management is the key here; the proprietor used to run the similarly-named Duffy's elsewhere in Ealing. The beer policy is always to include a guest ale from a small independent brewery. Meals are available daily, served right through the day, Saturday. The food is good and reasonably priced; booking is recommended for Sunday lunch. ◐◑ ⊖ (Northfields)

Wheatsheaf ✔
41 Haven Lane, W5 2HZ
🕓 11-11; 12-10.30 Sun
☎ (020) 8997 5240
Fuller's Chiswick, London Pride, ESB 🄷
The Wheatsheaf is tucked away up a side street just north of the town centre. Inside, it is deceptively large and seems to have been constructed almost entirely of wood. There is a small public bar at the front, connecting with a comfortable saloon. This in turn leads on to an open-plan area at the rear. TVs show sport, but do not generally dominate. It enjoys a good reputation locally for food. ◐◑ ⇌ (Broadway) ⊖

W6: HAMMERSMITH

Andover Arms ✔
57 Aldensley Road, W6 0DL
🕓 11-11; 12-3.30, 7-10.30 Sun
☎ (020) 8741 9794
Fuller's Chiswick, London Pride, ESB, seasonal beers 🄷
Situated in an area that estate agents call Brackenbury Village, this traditional local stands in peaceful surroundings. It is a cosy pub with padded seats; the bar has a few snob screens. It hosts a quiz on Sunday night. An English menu is served at lunchtime and Thai food in the evening.

Lunches are served weekdays; no evening meals on Sunday.
Q ◑▸ ⊖

Brook Green Hotel
170 Shepherd's Bush Road, W6 7NB
✪ 11-11; 12-10.30 Sun
☎ (020) 7603 2516
Young's Bitter, Special, seasonal beers Ⓗ
Modernised 'gin palace', retaining many original features, this is a spacious pub with a high ceiling. It has a hard floor but comfort is provided with padded seats and armchairs, and a few sofas. There is a large-screen TV for sport, but this remains a basically quiet pub. It is very handy for the supermarket. The basement houses a comedy club. Q ✿⇔◑▸ ⊖

Cross Keys ⊘
57 Black Lion Lane, W6 9BG
✪ 11-11; 12-10.30 Sun
☎ (020) 8748 3541
Fuller's London Pride, ESB Ⓗ
The Cross Keys lies in the middle of a quiet residential street. The floor is wood at the front, giving way to tiles at the rear. The spacious, high-ceilinged interior has padded settles and stools; the oak panelling is striking. There is a large patio at the rear. Quiet background music is often played.
✿◑▸ ⊖ (Stamford Brook)

Dove ⊘
19 Upper Mall, W6 9TA
✪ 11-11; 12-10.30 Sun
☎ (020) 8748 5405
Fuller's Chiswick, London Pride, ESB, seasonal beers Ⓗ
Picturesque pub by the river: four distinct drinking areas inside and a terrace overlooking the water. It boasts what is reputedly the smallest bar in England. There are low beams and old photographs of the area. It is a five-minute walk from Hammersmith Bridge, in a very peaceful location. Q ✿◑▸ ⊖ (Ravenscourt Pk)

Plough & Harrow ⊘
120-124 King Street, W6 0QU
✪ 11-11; 12-10.30 Sun
☎ (020) 8735 6020
Courage Best Bitter; Greene King Abbot; Shepherd Neame Spitfire; guest beers Ⓗ
Rare example of the reopening of a pub after over 40 years as a car showroom. It was a Fuller's pub until 1960, rebuilt in 1903 as a 'modern drinking palace' replacing a coaching inn reputedly dating from 1419. It features large black-edged windows on the frontage and two sets of double doors lead through into a long bar in modern style with stone-flagged flooring, maroon and white decor, light pine furniture, a black 'starlight' ceiling and metallic bar top. An Holiday Inn Express Hotel occupies the upper storeys. Q ➥◑▸ ♿⊖↯

Salutation ⊘
154 King Street, W6 0QU
✪ 11-11; 12-10.30 Sun
☎ (020) 8748 3668
Fuller's Chiswick, London Pride, ESB Ⓗ
A striking tiled exterior opens into a bright, spacious pub. Background music is played and there is a TV for sport. A superb skylight is a notable feature and at the rear

there is a large garden. The seating is comfortable, including some sofas. The pub is on the north side of King Street, five minutes from the tube station, near the town hall. ✿◑▸ ⊖

W7: HANWELL

Fox
Green Lane, W7 2PJ
✪ 11-11; 12-10.30 Sun
☎ (020) 8567 3912
Brakspear Bitter; Fuller's London Pride; Taylor Landlord; guest beers Ⓗ
Standing 100 yards from the Grand Union Canal and the River Brent, this early 19th-century, family-centred free house is firmly established in the area. Beer festivals are extremely busy and guest beers are always available. Home-cooked Sunday lunches are popular and barbecues are held during the summer. In keeping with its community spirit, accompanied children (and dogs) are always welcome. ✿◑P

W8: KENSINGTON

Britannia
1 Allen Street, W8 6UX
✪ 11-11; 12-10.30 Sun
☎ (020) 7937 6905
Young's Bitter, Special, seasonal beers; guest beer Ⓗ
Former tap of the William Wells Britannia Brewery the pub became tied to Young's in 1824. Recent work has resulted in the loss of the public bar but it retained the conservatory towards the rear where families are made welcome. A separate bar is also opened when trade demands. The pub is well furnished with a maroon carpet, tables and chairs and pew bench seating along one wall. The pub still enjoys a regular following among locals and workers from the busy Kensington High Street.
Q ➥◑▸ ⊖ (High St)

Churchill Arms ⊘
119 Kensington Church Street, W8 7LN
✪ 11-11; 12-10.30 Sun
☎ (020) 7727 4242
Fuller's Chiswick, London Pride, ESB, seasonal beers Ⓗ
CAMRA's West London Pub of the Year 2002 stands halfway between Kensington High Street and Notting Hill Gate. It has leaded windows and an enormous collection of bric-à-brac. The highly-regarded landlord has won numerous awards which are prominently displayed. Pictures of Winston Churchill and wartime newspapers abound. Two TVs relay major sporting events, but this remains a traditional pub. No food is served Sunday evening. Q ◑▸ ⊖ (Notting Hill Gate)

Uxbridge Arms
13 Uxbridge Street, W8 7TQ
✪ 12-11; 12-10.30 Sun
☎ (020) 7727 7326
Brakspear Bitter; Fuller's London Pride; guest beers Ⓗ
Tucked away behind the main shopping area and quite difficult to find, this is very much a local, carpeted and wood-panelled throughout, with various photographs and pictures on the walls; the pub boasts a fine collection of plates. A selection of dimple

jugs hang from a bar that sports three old sherry pins. The TV is used occasionally. ♨Q❀⊖ (Notting Hill Gate) ♣

W9: MAIDA VALE

Warrington Hotel ☆
93 Warrington Crescent, W9 1EH
☼ 11-11; 12-10.30 Sun
☎ (020) 7286 2929
Fuller's London Pride, ESB; Young's Special; guest beers Ⓗ

Grade II listed Victorian pub dating to 1859, with decorated marble pillars, ornate gas light standards and a mosaic floor by the front entrance. The saloon bar has a semi-circular marble-topped bar with ornate glass shelves and a dome with scantily clad nubile girls, reflecting the days when this was a whore house. An etched glass screen separates the public and the saloon bars; note too, the old Bass Pale Ale mirror. Upstairs a Thai restaurant serves food lunchtime and evening. ♨Q❀🍴⊖

Warwick Castle
6 Warwick Place, W9 2PX
☼ 12-11; 12-10.30 Sun
☎ (020) 7432 1331
Draught Bass; Fuller's London Pride Ⓗ

Small, back-street Victorian local near Little Venice on the Grand Union Canal. The outside wall bears a horseshoe-shaped ornate lamp standard. The interior has been sympathetically refurbished, preserving the smaller side room and rear room with fire, etched windows and original prints, especially William Firth's print of Paddington Station of 1861. This pub is popular with locals and visitors calling in for refreshments after watching the narrow boats. ♨Q❀🍴⊖

W10: KENSAL GREEN

Paradise (By Way of Kensal Green)
19 Kilburn Lane, W10 4AE
☼ 11-11; 12-10.30 Sun
☎ (020) 8969 0098
Shepherd Neame Spitfire Ⓗ

Large three-roomed pub situated just off Harrow Road. The main bar has a blue/grey decor with bare floorboards and a mix of secondhand tables, chairs and settles. The corner has a bust of an angel overlooking the customers. At the back of the pub is the dining area with table service. A smaller area at the front features a fire and a collection of books. There are several upstairs rooms that host music functions and can be hired. 🍴

W11: NOTTING HILL

Cock & Bottle
17 Needham Road, W11 2RP
☼ 12-11; 12-10.30 Sun
☎ (020) 7229 1550
Fuller's London Pride; Greene King IPA Ⓗ

Formerly called the Swan, this three-roomed corner local dates back to 1851. The main bar area is quite small with ornate pillars alongside the bar and lead glass panels above the windows depicting a Swan enjoying a swim. The lounge area is accessible through Venetian swing doors,

where a real log fire can be enjoyed on a cold winter's night. To the left of the bar is a smaller room which has a dartboard where play can be enjoyed without disturbing other customers. A quiz is held on Tuesday after 9pm. ♨🍴⊖ (Notting Hill Gate)

W14: WEST KENSINGTON

Radnor Arms
247 Warwick Road, W14 8PX
☼ 11-11; 12-10.30 Sun
☎ (020) 7602 7708
Everards Tiger; guest beer Ⓗ

Formerly an Everards house, now owned by Oak Taverns, this is still a regular outlet for Everards beers. The pub was once part of a terrace and now stands alone on the busy Warwick road next to some 1930s apartments. The premises has a small bar, surrounded by tables and chairs, and a raised area towards the rear with Sky TV and a dartboard. This pub has been known to offer the full range of Everards beers during the week of the Great British Beer Festival in nearby Olympia. ≉ (Olympia) ⊖

BRENTFORD

Brewery Tap
47 Catherine Wheel Road, TW8 8BD
☼ 11-11; 12-10.30 Sun
☎ (020) 8560 5200
Fuller's Chiswick, London Pride, ESB, seasonal beers Ⓗ

Originally the tap of the William Gomm Brewery which was acquired by Fuller's in 1908 (but subsequently closed). Of Victorian origin, the pub is reached by steps from road level as the river used to flood here. A recent development, following vigorous campaigning against demolition, is access from the rear to a small patio. Well-known for its jazz (Tue and Thu eves) it now has a Monday quiz and other music at weekends. Lunches are popular (book Sun). ❀🍴≉♣

Express Tavern
56 Kew Bridge Road, TW8 0EW
☼ 11.30-3, 5.30 (6.30 Sat)-11; 12-10.30 Sun
☎ (020) 8560 8484
Draught Bass; Young's Bitter, Special; guest beer Ⓗ

Over 200 years old, the Express has too much history to detail, but if you are interested in the origins of Brentford FC, the former Brentford market, the 'Buffalos' and indeed CAMRA, then you have to come here. Locally renowned for its Bass, supplemented by the Young's and now a guest beer, it is a haven from the busy roads outside. Little has changed over the years in its two bar areas and quiet rear lounge. Ring the bell on the side gate for wheelchair access. Q❀🍴&≉ (Kew Bridge)

Magpie & Crown
128 High Street, TW8 8EW
☼ 11-11; 12-10.30 Sun
☎ (020) 8560 5658
Beer range varies Ⓗ

Mock-Tudor pub opposite the magistrates' court, set back from the road, so providing an outside drinking area. Four regularly-changing ales (over 1,000 in six years) have made it a magnet for real ale lovers. A varying cider (occasionally perry) is available, plus draught Budvar and Hoegaarden and a range of continental bottled beers. Major sports events are shown on TV; Friday is karaoke night. Local CAMRA Pub of the Year 1999 and 2000. ✿≋♣◑

COWLEY

Paddington Packet Boat
High Road, UB8 2HT
✿ 12-11; 12-10.30 Sun
☎ (01895) 442392
Fuller's London Pride, ESB Ⓗ
Spacious 200-year-old pub which, despite having been completely modernised, retains some old fittings and mirrors, and displays memorabilia relating to the old packet boat service to Paddington. It draws a good passing trade, although most of its customers are local, and include workers from the almost adjacent Grand Union Canal. It hosts live music on Friday and Saturday evenings and a weekly quiz on Tuesday. No food is served Sunday evening. ✿≋◑&♣P

CRANFORD

Jolly Gardeners
144 High Street, TW5 9PD
✿ 11-11; 12-10.30 Sun
☎ (020) 8897 6996
Tetley Bitter; guest beers Ⓗ
Small, community-oriented pub whose hub is a vibrant public bar, separated only by a doorless arch from the cosy, but less busy, saloon. Try the good value, plentiful, lunches which offer the best in hearty British cuisine (not served Sat). Weekday accommodation is available in two reasonably-priced twin bedrooms which make a rustic alternative to the many clinical, anonymous hotels in the area. Look out for the Vortons, a '60s revival band, when they land! ⚏✿≋◑♣P

Queen's Head
123 High Street, TW5 9PB
✿ 11-11; 12-10.30 Sun
☎ (020) 8897 0722
Fuller's Chiswick, London Pride, ESB Ⓗ
Large roadhouse, rebuilt in 1931 in an attractive Tudor style, complete with a manorial banqueting hall (where the food servery is located). It was the first pub in the country to be granted a full liquor licence. The two halves of the building operate much in the way of two separate bars, although there is no physical distinction between them. A welcome return as a full entry for this perennial of the Guide's first 20 years. ⚏Q✿◑♣P

FELTHAM

Moon on the Square ✅
30 The Centre, High Street, TW13 4AU
✿ 11-11; 12-10.30 Sun
☎ (020) 8893 1293
Courage Directors; Greene King Abbot; Shepherd Neame Spitfire; Theakston Best Bitter; guest beers Ⓗ
Flourishing real ale oasis, stocking up to eight different beers at one time, often with a Scottish slant – a far cry from the former Cricketers which it replaced.

Pictures and history panels on the walls depict the changing Feltham landscape over 90 years. Families with children are welcome in the no-smoking area until 6pm. Q◑&≋✔

GREENFORD

Bridge Hotel
Western Avenue, UB6 8ST (NE side of flyover, A40)
✿ 11-11; 12-10.30 Sun
☎ (020) 8566 6246
Young's Bitter, Special, seasonal beers Ⓗ
Old Young's house that grew into an hotel but managed to keep its own identity. The expansion in 1989 added 68 bedrooms, conference facilities and an excellent restaurant. Hotel guests mingle happily with locals in the three bar areas: a comfortable lounge, the more secluded back room and, between them, the curving main bar which features several drinking booths. The Bridge offers the full Young's wine list, by bottle or glass. ✿≋◑&≋⊖P

HAMPTON

Jolly Coopers
16 High Street, TW12 2SJ
✿ 11-3, 5-11; 11-11 Sat; 12-10.30 Sun
☎ (020) 8979 3384
Brakspear Bitter; Courage Best Bitter; Hop Back Summer Lightning; Marston's Pedigree Ⓗ
Popular pub, dating back to the early 1700s. The restricted space on entering opens up on both sides of the U-shaped bar. The left-hand side leads to the restaurant (Squiffy's) and the rear patio from where there is wheelchair access. The bar area is adorned with numerous beer, whisky and water jugs and bottled beers. The restaurant is open weekdays and Sunday lunchtime, plus Tuesday–Saturday evenings; bar food is available weekday lunchtimes. ✿◑&≋

HAMPTON HILL

Roebuck
72 Hampton Road, TW12 1JN
✿ 11-11; 12-10.30 Sun
☎ (020) 8255 8133
Badger K&B Sussex, Best, Tanglefoot; guest beers Ⓗ
Popularity is bringing an extra handpump each year (now five) to this friendly, welcoming pub. It is festooned with bric-à-brac and transport-related memorabilia – ships, trains, buses, and working traffic lights that change for last orders and closing time. Guest beers change monthly and lunches are served weekdays. Four bedrooms are available. Bus Nos. 285 and R68 pass by. Past readers note: it is in Hampton Hill after all – not Teddington! ⚏✿≋◑≋ (Fulwell)

HARMONDSWORTH

Five Bells
High Street, UB7 0AQ
✿ 11-11; 12-10.30 Sun
☎ (020) 8579 4713
Adnams Bitter, Broadside; Fuller's London Pride; guest beers Ⓗ
Despite handpumps being only located in the saloon, the (rare for the area) public bar is still worth a look. Under threat from the

government's third runway proposals, along with the village itself, the pub has wholeheartedly embraced the campaign against further Heathrow Airport growth. It is a regular outlet for a special beer produced by nearby Grand Union Brewery (5p from each pint donated to the protest group). This vibrant community pub hosts a popular quiz on Saturday. Evening meals are served weekdays. Q❀◖▣⌂♣

HAYES

Botwell Inn ❷
25-29 Coldharbour Lane, UB3 3EB
🕓 10-11; 12-10.30 Sun
☎ (020) 8848 3112
Courage Best Bitter, Directors; Greene King Abbot; Hop Back Summer Lightning; Shepherd Neame Spitfire; guest beers Ⓗ
Large, light and airy Wetherspoon's conversion. Two areas are designed for non-smokers, diners and families. A small patio at the rear is supplemented by tables on the front pavement. Smoking is not permitted at the marble-topped bar. It offers the usual Wetherspoon's all-day catering – order and pay for food (not forgetting your table number) and allow 15–20 minutes (rarely more) for it to arrive. Wetherspoon's free magazine provides a good read – now 60-plus pages. Q❀◖▣⬆⇌⥼

HILLINGDON

Master Brewer Hotel
Freezeland Way, UB10 9NX
🕓 11.30-11; 12-3, 6-10.30 Sun
☎ (01895) 251199
Fuller's London Pride, ESB Ⓗ
Following extensive road changes, the hotel is now situated off the main A40 dual carriageway. Its proximity to Hillingdon underground station gives easy access into central London. The bar is well lit with comfortable seating. It stocks an excellent selection of bottle-conditioned beers. The 105-room hotel has two large function rooms available for hire. Q⛌◖⬆⊖P

Oak Tree
132 Ryefield Avenue, UB10 9DA
🕓 11-11; 12-10.30 Sun
☎ (01895) 238085
Fuller's London Pride, ESB Ⓗ
Built in 1953, to serve a 1920s housing estate, this traditional, back-street local is tucked away. Everyone is on first-name terms here and the pub fields darts and pool teams. To the left of the foyer is a large bar, divided by movable screens into a lounge and a public bar. To the right is an unusually small private bar which is available for functions. Children are welcome at the manager's discretion. ⬗Q❀P

HOUNSLOW

Cross Lances ❷
236 Hanworth Road, TW3 3TU (on A314)
🕓 11-11; 12-10.30 Sun
☎ (020) 8570 4174
Fuller's London Pride, ESB, seasonal beers Ⓗ
Dark-red tiled Victorian local, now with an extended saloon giving wheelchair access from the award-winning garden. Excellent

beers are complemented by the huge lunches (including Sunday roasts – best to book), with a senior citizens' discount on Tuesday, and evening food. Fielding football, pool and darts teams, it also hosts crib, quiz and music evenings, plus jazz and barbecues in the garden on Sunday afternoons of bank holiday weekends. It is a dog-friendly pub. ❀◖▣⬆⇌♣

Moon under Water ❷
84-88 Staines Road, TW3 3LF (W end of High St, just past Safeway)
🕓 11-11; 12-10.30 Sun
☎ (020) 8572 7506
Courage Best Bitter, Directors; Greene King Abbot; Hop Back Summer Lightning; guest beers Ⓗ
Local history panels feature in this early Wetherspoon's outlet, since enlarged. Very popular, it has many regular customers, some of whom travel from some distance away. Its beer range is more extensive than most, with up to three guests usually available. At festival times all 12 handpumps may have different beers. The large no-smoking area now accommodates families. Q❀◖⬆⇌⊖ (Central) ⥼

ISLEWORTH

Coach & Horses
183 London Road, TW7 5BQ (on A315)
🕓 11-midnight (11 Wed); 12-10.30 Sun
☎ (020) 8560 1447
Smiles IPA; Young's Bitter, Special, seasonal beers Ⓗ
First leased by Young's in 1831, this is one of the few remaining coaching houses that were once abundant on this road. There have been a few changes since it was mentioned by Dickens in Oliver Twist, but it is still a pub of great character. Music evenings, with a midnight extension, are regular – usually jazz Monday, folk or blues Tuesday, and various bands Thursday–Saturday; Wednesday is quiz night. Meals are served (not Sun eve) either in the bar or the Thai-based restaurant. ⬗❀◖⇌ (Syon Lane) ♣P

Red Lion
92-94 Linkfield Road, TW7 6QJ
🕓 11-11; 12-10.30 Sun
☎ (020) 8560 1457 website: www.red-lion.info
Young's Bitter; guest beers Ⓗ
Spacious two-bar free house with a very strong community focus. There is often something going on here – it might be a pantomime, or a summer production in the garden, by their own theatre group, or live music (Sat and Sun eves), a quiz (Thu), or themed 'retro' nights, darts and pool competitions. It also hosts summer barbecues and twice-yearly beer festivals, featuring champion beers. Normally there are up to six beers complementing the Young's, always with tasting notes provided. Lunches are served weekdays. ❀◖▣⇌♣

Royal Oak
128 Worton Road, TW7 6EP
🕓 12-11; 12-10.30 Sun
☎ (020) 8560 2906
Fuller's Chiswick, London Pride, ESB; guest beer Ⓗ
Built in 1843, the Royal Oak is in an entirely residential area, served by bus route H20, by the Duke of Northumberland's

River. It is totally traditional, featuring dark wood partitions, etched glass, upholstered seating and bric-à-brac. Old photos of local interest adorn the walls and ceiling, alongside the long-serving landlord's many awards and cellarmanship certificates. With a riverside patio, TV at the back for sports, and food from a comprehensive menu served all day, it is the perfect local. ❀◐◑

SOUTHALL

Southall Conservative & Unionist Club

Fairlawn, High Street, UB1 3HB

✪ 11.30-2.30 (not Mon), 7 (6 Mon, Fri & Sat)-11; 12-3, 7-10.30 Sun

☎ (020) 8574 0261

Rebellion IPA, seasonal beers Ⓗ

Difficult to find (behind the old fire station), the club is now one of only two such establishments in the town. Only those with a current CAMRA card or this Guide can gain entry but, once inside, enjoy the Rebellion on offer. Other facilities include darts, snooker and wholesome weekday lunches. Try pitting your wits against such luminaries as the Buccaneers, Nifties and Pops on Monday quiz nights; on Saturday evening, live music is often performed. The patio overlooks a bowling green. ❀◐≥♣P

TEDDINGTON

Lion ✔

27 Wick Road, TW11 9DN

✪ 12-11; 12-10.30 Sun

☎ (020) 8977 6631 website: www.thelionpub.co.uk

Fuller's London Pride; Greene King Abbot; Young's Bitter; guest beer Ⓗ

Victorian single-bar pub that has been transformed by CAMRA award-winning tenants, establishing an excellent reputation for both beer and food, that attracts customers from far afield. The food is from a modern menu (not served Sun eve) but does not overlook the traditional. An attractive garden hosts summer barbecues. Live music Saturday evening, and an annual beer festival all add to its appeal. It is a short walk from Hampton Wick Station.
⚔❀◐◑≥(Hampton Wick)♣

Queen Dowager

49 North Lane, TW11 0HU

✪ 11-11; 12-10.30 Sun

☎ (020) 8943 3474

Young's Bitter, Special, seasonal beers Ⓗ

Tucked away off Broad Street, near Tesco's car park, this family pub was refurbished and extended in 2003. The former public bar has been opened up to the main area and designated a dining and no-smoking area. Sunday lunches are now offered and a bar billiards table has appeared. A pub site since 1747, the present building dates from 1906 and commemorates Queen Adelaide, widow of William IV and Ranger of Bushy Park, who lived in nearby Bushy House.
❀◐≥♣⚡

TWICKENHAM

Eel Pie ✔

9-11 Church Street, TW1 3NJ

✪ 11-11; 12-10.30 Sun

☎ (020) 8891 1717

Badger K&B Sussex, IPA, Best, Tanglefoot, seasonal beers; Gribble Inn Fursty Ferret Ⓗ

Perhaps suprisingly, the Eel Pie has only been a pub for 20 years – it was previously a wine bar. It has all the feel of a traditional pub, with a choice of drinking areas, a distinctly 'historic' look, and much rugby-oriented paraphernalia. All the food is home made, with lunches daily – Sunday roasts are popular – and lighter evening meals (not served Sun). A bar billiards table is available. ◐◑≥

Moon Under Water ✔

53-57 London Road, TW1 3SZ

✪ 10-11; 12-10.30 Sun

☎ (020) 8744 0080

Courage Best Bitter, Directors; Greene King Abbot; Hop Back Summer Lightning; Shepherd Neame Spitfire; guest beers Ⓗ

An early, now extended, Wetherspoon's pub, serving two changing guest ales (one often from Ridleys) and Westons Old Rosie cider. Wood-panelled and carpeted, it is attractive and comfortable, with quiet areas. It has the usual JDW food and special offers. Close to the station and shops, in common with other central Twickenham pubs, it uses plastic glasses on international rugby days.
Q◐◑♿≥●⚡

UXBRIDGE

Load of Hay

33 Villier Street, UB8 2DU (near Brunel University)

✪ 11-3, 5.30-11; 12-3, 7-10.30 Sun

☎ (01895) 234676

website: www.loadofhay-uxbridge.co.uk

Beer range varies Ⓗ

This popular free house is a frequent local CAMRA Pub of the Year winner. Originally the officers' mess of the Elthorne Light Militia, it became a pub in the 1870s. It used to be linked to the pub opposite, long since closed, but a tunnel still connects the cellars. The main part of the pub is an old stable block conversion with a small, quiet front bar. The beers are mainly from micros, with normally three available. No evening meals served Sunday. Q♨❀◐◑♣P

> Here old John Randal lies,
> Who counting from this tale,
> Lived three score years and ten,
> Such vertue was in ale.
> Ale was his meat,
> Ale his drink,
> Ale did his heart revive,
> And if he could have drunk his ale,
> He still had been alive.
>
> Epitaph of 1699, formerly at Great Wolford, Warwickshire

Perfect Pints and Pillows

Tim Hampson has scoured the country to find the best pubs for accommodation – and beer. Broken down into regions, it gives full details of accommodation and other facilities, with directions on how to find pubs, essential price details, and other handy advice such as proximity to sports grounds, theatres, and places of historic interest. It's an essential guide for those who travel and prefer traditional pubs to plastic motels. £10.99 including postage.

GREATER MANCHESTER

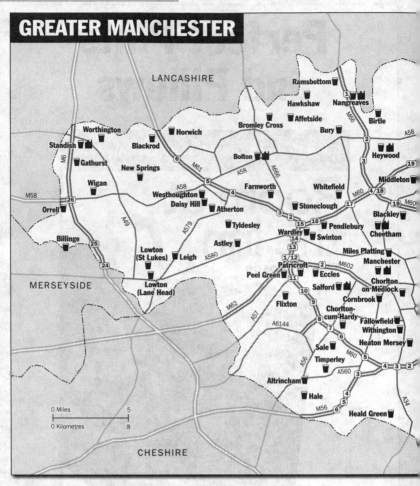

AFFETSIDE

Pack Horse
52 Watling Street, BL5 3QW
(approx 2 miles NW of Walshaw) OS755136
☼ 12-3, 5-11; 12-11 Sat; 12-10.30 Sun
☎ (01204) 883802
Hydes Light, Bitter, Jekyll's Gold (occasional),
seasonal beers Ⓗ
This country pub benefits from panoramic
views, thanks to its situation, high up on a
Roman road. The bar area and cosy lounge
(with real fire), are the original parts of the
pub, dating from the 15th century. It has a
function and pool room, while the Hightop
Bar is used as a family room. Many stories
are told relating to the ghost of the local
man whose skull is on view behind the bar.
Excellent food is served (all day Sat and
Sun). ⚌Q❀❀ⓓ▲P

ALTRINCHAM

Old Market Tavern
Old Market Place, WA14 7RT
☼ 12-3, 5-11; 12-11 Fri & Sat; 12-10.30 Sun
☎ (0161) 927 7062
Beer range varies Ⓗ
Old coaching inn, the present building
dates from the mid-19th century and was

extended towards the end of the century to
serve as the town hall. Opened out inside in
the early 1990s, in a bare-boarded beer
house-style it serves an ever-changing range
of up to 10 beers and good, basic pub
lunches (weekdays). ⚌❀❀ⓓ⇌⊖⅍

Orange Tree
15 Old Market Place, WA14 4DE
☼ 12-11; 12-10.30 Sun
☎ (0161) 928 2935
Tetley Bitter; guest beers Ⓗ
Friendly local on the old market square.
Note the old photos around the bar which
show neighbouring pubs, now gone. There
is an upstairs function room for hire where
an occasional mini beer festival is held.
Home-cooked meals are served at lunchtime
(until 5.30pm on Sunday). A patio area
provides space for outside drinking.
❀ⓓ⇌⊖⅍

ASHTON-UNDER-LYNE

Caledonia Hotel
13 Warrington Street, OL6 6AS
☼ 11.30-11 (9.30 Mon & Wed); 12-4, 7-10.30 Sun
☎ (0161) 339 7117
Robinson's Hatters, Best Bitter, Frederics Ⓗ
Three-storey pub situated in the town-

centre pedestrian zone. Comprising three distinct drinking areas and a raised dining area, dark stained wood and fabrics lend a warm feel to a friendly, sociable atmosphere. The pub serves good value food, winning awards from its owner's, Robinson's and national awards for its pies. An ideal place for B&B, evening meals are served 5–7 (not Sun or Mon and 5–8 Fri and Sat).
❀⇄❶⇥P

Dog & Pheasant
528 Oldham Road, Waterloo, OL7 6PQ
☼ 12-11; 12-10.30 Sun
☎ (0161) 330 4894
Banks's Original; Marston's Bitter, Pedigree; guest beers Ⓗ
Known locally as the Top Dog, this popular, friendly local stands near the Medlock Valley Country Park. A large bar serves three areas, plus another room at the front. Good value food is available (not Sun eve); the extensive menu includes vegetarian options. Twice weekly (Tue and Thu eves), music is performed and the regular quizzes are well attended. Monthly entertainment is also staged on Sunday teatime.
♨❀❶P

Junction Inn
Mossley Road, Hazlehurst, OL6 9BX
☼ 12-11; 12-10.30 Sun
☎ (0161) 343 1611
Robinson's Hatters, Best Bitter, Frederics Ⓗ
Small stone pub of great character, which remains little altered close to open country and Ashton golf course. Like so many of the borough's pubs, it was built in the 19th century and was intended to last. The small cosy rooms make it very welcoming and the unpretentious tap room is traditional in every aspect. If you are hungry, try the home-made rag pudding – well worth it. Weekday lunches are served, plus an evening meal on Friday (5–7.30).
Q❀❶⇥♣P

Oddfellows Arms
1-7 Alderley Street, Hurst, OL6 9EE
☼ 11-11; 12-10.30 Sun
☎ (0161) 330 6356 website: www.theoddies.com
Robinson's Hatters, Best Bitter, seasonal beers Ⓗ
This street-corner, terraced local, run by the same family since 1914, is an established Guide entry. A small hatch and screen leads to the fine polished bar with its stained glass and nooks and crannies; on the left the small tap room has been opened out, leaving the tiny 'vestry' untouched. Adjoining the comfortable lounge is the no-smoking Tom's Room, named after the late landlord. The walled patio is used for barbecues and contains a Koi carp pool.
Q❀♿⇥✂

ASTLEY

Cart & Horses
221 Manchester Road, M29 7SD
☼ 12-11; 12-10.30 Sun
☎ (01942) 870751
Holt Mild, Bitter Ⓗ
You may like to bring a camera on a visit to the Cart, to record its cobbled frontage, large etched windows and roof sign proclaiming the pub as a Holt's house. This popular roadside local is home to Astley Golf Society. Inside, the large lounge is composed of three rooms; part of the original hall tilework has remained. There is

INDEPENDENT BREWERIES

Bank Top Bolton
Bazens Salford
Boggart Hole Clough Moston
Facers Salford
Greenfield Greenfield
Holt Cheetham
Hydes Manchester
Lees Middleton Junction
Leyden Nangreaves
Lowes Arms Denton
McGuinness Rochdale
Marble Manchester
Mayflower Standish (moving to Wigan)
Phoenix Heywood
Pictish Rochdale
Ramsbottom Nangreaves
Robinson's Stockport
Saddleworth Uppermill
Shaws Dukinfield

also a raised no-smoking lounge and a vibrant traditional vault. ❀◖◗ ⌑♣P⤶

ATHERTON

Atherton Arms
6 Tyldesley Road, M46 9DD
✪ 12-11; 12-10.30 Sun
☎ (01942) 882885
Holt Mild, Bitter Ⓗ

This spacious, former Labour Club has now lost its club-style, but the games room retains both snooker and pool tables, with ample seating to watch sporting events on TV. The lounge holds popular karaoke at weekends. If you require a quiet area, the hall, with its own serving hatch, is a haven on busy nights. The concert room at the rear is available for hire. ⌑≹♣P

Pendle Witch
2-4 Warburton Place, M46 0EQ
✪ 4 (may be earlier summer)-11; 12-11 Sat;
12-10.30 Sun
☎ (01942) 884537
Moorhouses Black Cat, Premier, Pendle Witches Brew, seasonal beers Ⓗ

Access to the Witch is via an alley off Market Street. This small, popular local manages to fit in a raised seating area, cosy bench seat, tables, a pool table and a bar. It hosts occasional rock discos and beer festivals in summer. The garden is a good distraction from shopping. ❀

BILLINGE

Jarvis Bar
191 Main Street, WN5 7PB (on A581)
✪ 12-11; 12-10.30 Sun
Beer range varies Ⓗ

Large, one-roomed pub, back from 20 years in the keg wilderness. With a good social mix, it is popular for big matches on TV, especially Rugby League, when its neutral location attracts both Wigan and St Helens supporters. It stocks an excellent range of bottled beers. It has its own bowling green. ❀◖◗P

BIRTLE

Pack Horse Inn
Elbut Lane, BL9 7TU (approx 800 yds N of B6222 near Jericho) OS836125
✪ 11.30-11; 12-10.30 Sun
☎ (0161) 764 3620
Lees GB Mild, Bitter, seasonal beers Ⓗ

Cosy, rural stone pub dating from the 18th century, replete with horse brasses, grandfather clocks and copper kettles. The impressive firegrate was made at the Yewtree Ironworks in Hollinwood. A derelict barn has been converted into a restaurant, decorated with a large tableau featuring a farm cart, milk churns and hop sacks. A more modern conservatory allows drinkers and diners to enjoy views over adjoining fields. Two small snugs provide quiet areas for conversation. ⋈❀◖◗ &P

BLACKLEY

Golden Lion
47 Old Market Street, M9 8DX (off Rochdale Rd, by hospital)
✪ 11-11; 12-10.30 Sun

☎ (0161) 794 1944
Holt Mild, Bitter, seasonal beers Ⓗ

Impressive Edwardian pub opposite the church, where it is said that clergy escaped persecution via a tunnel leading to the cellar of the former pub on the same site. The lounge has been opened out, with doors leading to a patio with seating and a bowling green. By the central bar is an imposing staircase, lit by an attractive stained glass window on the landing. Artistes perform live at weekends. ❀⌑♣

BLACKROD

Thatch & Thistle
Chorley Road, BL6 5LA
(on A6 1 mile from M61 jct 6)
✪ 12-11; 12-10.30 Sun
☎ (01257) 474044 website: www.thatchandthistle.com
Beer range varies Ⓗ

Welcoming thatched pub, on the busy main road out of Blackrod. It comprises a stone-flagged bar and four main eating/drinking areas. The pub has gained a reputation for serving good food and, with three changing guest beers (one usually from the Banktop Brewery), it is deservedly very busy at weekends. There is a patio area at the front and children's play area and garden at the rear. Jazz night is Tuesday and quiz night, Wednesday. ⋈Q❀❀◖◗ &P⤶

BOLTON

Ainsworth Arms ⊘
606 Halliwell Road, BL1 8BY (at A58/A6099 jct)
✪ 11.30-2 (not Tue-Thu), 5-11; 11.30-11 Sat;
12-10.30 Sun
☎ (01204) 840671
Taylor Landlord; Tetley Mild, Bitter; guest beers Ⓗ

Close to Smithills Hall, a Grade I listed building, this is a friendly local. The bar serves three areas: one is raised with alcoves, another is a tap room, complete with bell pushes, last used in 1981. It has a long association with football and is the meeting place for many local sports teams; TV sport is also available, although the juke box will only be switched on by request. Lunches are served Friday–Sunday. Q❀◖♣

Bob's Smithy
1448 Chorley Old Road, BL1 7PX (on B6226, 1/2 mile uphill from A58 ring road)
✪ 12-3 (not Mon), 4.30-11; 12-11 Sat; 12-10.30 Sun
☎ (01204) 842622
Draught Bass; Boddingtons Bitter; Taylor Best Bitter; Tetley Dark Mild, Bitter; guest beers Ⓗ

Cosy, stone hostelry on the edge of the moors, handy for walkers and visitors to the Reebok Stadium. A genuine free house, run by friendly, enterprising owners, the pub has been in existence for around 200 years and is named after a regular, Bob the blacksmith, who used to work across the road. The guest beers are usually from small independent breweries. ⋈❀P

Dog & Partridge
22 Manor Street, BL1 1TU
✪ 7 (12 Sat)-11; 7-10.30 Sun
☎ (01204) 388596
website: www.dogandpartridgepub.com
Thwaites Bitter, seasonal beers Ⓗ

Unspoilt, three-roomed local situated on the edge of the town centre. The pub dates from the 18th century and features a traditional vault with a curved bar. The small games room at the back has an acid-etched Cornbrook Ales window; the larger side room houses a pool table and hosts weekend discos/acoustic sessions. Use public car parks nearby. ⊕≠(Bolton) ♣

Hope & Anchor
747 Chorley Old Road, BL1 5QH
(on B6226, 400 yds from A58 ring road)
☼ 3 (12 Sat)-11; 12-10.30 Sun
☎ (01204) 842650
Lees Bitter; Taylor Landlord; Tetley Mild, Bitter Ⓗ
Compact local where a central bar serves two distinct snugs, used for different functions, including quizzes, darts, dominoes and family gatherings. It is known by the locals as the Little Cocker, due to the proximity of Doffcocker Lodge, a nature reserve. Less than two miles from the town centre, take bus No. 519 from the bus/rail interchange, or Nos. 125 or 126 from Moor Lane bus station. The outdoor drinking area adjoins the car park. ☎❀♣P

Howcroft
36 Pool Street, BL1 2JU (300 yds from Topp Way, A673)
☼ 12-11; 12-10.30 Sun
☎ (01204) 526814
Bank Top seasonal beers; Taylor Landlord; Tetley Mild, Bitter; guest beers Ⓗ
Exceptional, multi-roomed local, one of a dying breed. A 1980s refurbishment won CAMRA's Joe Goodwin award for Best Pub Conservation. It stages regular folk/acoustic nights and a well-kept bowling green is available for hire; the crown green is covered by a marquee for the October Bolton beer festival. The lunchtime menu is very good value, especially on Sunday. Take bus No. 501 from the Crown Court to Vernon Street. ♨Q◑♣P

King's Head
52-54 Junction Road, Deane, BL3 4NA
(off A676, Wigan road)
☼ 12 (3.30 winter)-11; 12-10.30 Sun
☎ (01204) 62609
Taylor Landlord; Tetley Mild, Bitter; guest beers Ⓗ
This 300-year-old Grade II listed pub stands next to the Deane Clough Nature Trail. It was refurbished in 1991 to provide three distinct drinking areas; the largest has stone flooring and an authentic-looking range. Piped music and TV underlie the buzz of conversation. A well-used bowling green is available for hire, and a small children's play area to its side has seating and tables. Bank Top Executioner is the house bitter. Meals are served 5–7 Thursday–Saturday and 2–7 Sunday. ❀➊♣P

Olde Man & Scythe
6-8 Churchgate, BL1 1HL
☼ 11-11; 12-10.30 Sun
☎ (01204) 527267 website: www.manandscythe.co.uk
Boddingtons Bitter; Caledonian Deuchars IPA; Flowers Original; Greene King Old Speckled Hen; Holt Bitter; Tetley Bitter Ⓗ
One of the oldest pubs in Britain, its barrel-vaulted cellar was probably built before 1200. The first record of the pub's existence was 1251, but the present building dates from 1636. In 1651 the seventh Earl of Derby spent his last hours here before his

execution outside for his part in the 1644 Bolton Massacre. A stone-flagged floor is flanked by two rooms. It hosts many events and entertainment. Inexpensive snacks, a cash machine and Internet complete the facilities. ☎❀◑≠♣●

Traveller's Call
402 Stockport Road West, SK6 2DT
☼ 12-11; 12-10.30 Sun
☎ (0161) 430 2511
Lees Bitter, seasonal beers Ⓗ
Solidly traditional, commercial inn whose continued presence today results from a road-widening scheme being shelved. With the threat of demolition now lifted, the pub was given a very sympathetic and high quality refit that retained the multiplicity of drinking, dining and games areas. Another beneficiary was the kitchen, and a range of well-priced pub meals makes the pub popular throughout the week. It is a rare outlet for Lees seasonal beers in the area. ❀◑≠P⊬

Flag Inn ⊘
50 Hardmans Lane, BL7 9HX
(off B6472, Darwen Road)
☼ 12-11; 12-10.30 Sun
☎ (01204) 598267
Boddingtons Bitter; guest beers Ⓗ
Enterprising management and constantly-changing guest beers, sourced from small independent breweries, make this popular beer drinkers' mecca well worth seeking out. Although not immediately apparent, the building's history has been traced back over 300 years. The old brick arched cellars were originally stables. In a spacious open-plan interior, TV screens attract sports enthusiasts, but do not dominate, or impede conversation. It gets very busy at weekends. ♨❀≠

Arthur Inn
97 Bolton Road, BL8 2AH
☼ 12-11; 12-10.30 Sun
☎ (0161) 797 3860
Porter Dark Mild, Floral Dance, Bitter, Rossendale Ale, Porter, Sunshine; guest beer Ⓗ
Community local on the main road between Bolton and Bury. When purchased by the Porter Brewing Company, it was in need of considerable refurbishment. Since then it has been transformed into a comfortable, friendly outlet for their excellent beers. The main lounge is complemented by a small games room and a no-smoking side room. A guest beer, usually from a micro, has joined the guest real cider on the bar. The frequent No. 471 Bury–Bolton bus will drop you practically at the front door. ⊖●⊬

Dusty Miller
87 Crostons Road, BL8 1AL (at B621/B6214 jct)
☼ 2 (12 Fri & Sat)-11; 12-10.30 Sun
☎ (0161) 764 1124
Moorhouses Black Cat, Premier, Pendle Witches Brew Ⓗ

This is a proudly traditional local that caters for a mixed clientele. Its position at a busy road junction makes parking difficult, but it is well worth making the effort to visit. Divided into two rooms served by a central bar, there is also a covered courtyard and outdoor seating for summer drinking. It is one of only a small number of tied Moorhouses' pubs. ⌂⊖

Trackside
East Lancs Railway, Bolton Street, BL9 0EY
✪ 12 (11 Sat)-11; 12-10.30 Sun
☎ (0161) 764 6461
Beer range varies Ⓗ
Genuine free house situated on a platform of the East Lancs Steam Railway. Nine handpumps offer an impressive choice of micro-brewed beers from near and far; an interesting range of foreign bottled beer is also stocked. A useful coding scheme aids you in your choice of beer. Large windows give this rectangular room plenty of light and afford a good view of the railway platform. Good value food is available daily. Q◖&⇌(E Lancs Bolton St) ⊖

Wyldes
4 Market Street, BL9 0LH
✪ 12-11; 12-10.30 Sun
☎ (0161) 797 2000
Holt Mild, Bitter, seasonal beers Ⓗ
Large, modern two-storey pub, right at the centre of town. Once a bank, it has been impressively converted by Manchester brewer, Joseph Holt. There is a long bar on the ground floor and a smaller one upstairs. Seating is a mix of chairs and comfortable sofas. A no-smoking mezzanine area is the perfect place to dine. Food is served until 7pm weekdays and 4pm on Sunday. Although it gets very busy at times, its size means it rarely appears overcrowded. ◖&⊖⌿

CHEADLE HULME

Church
90 Ravenoak Road, SK8 7EG (on A5149)
✪ 11-11; 12-10.30 Sun
☎ (0161) 485 1897
Robinson's Hatters, Old Stockport, Best Bitter, seasonal beers Ⓗ
A Robinson's house since 1880, the licence has been held by the Bromley family for many years. A warm traditional atmosphere, with a strong local following, awaits behind the attractive cottage-style exterior. One of its two comfortable lounges, warmed by open fires, is used for dining. Service is always efficient, even during busy periods; the excellent food is not available on Sunday evening. This compact pub also has a small vault. Seasonal beers replace Old Stockport on the bar as available. ⌂Q⌂◖⌂♣P

CHEETHAM

Queen's Arms
6 Honey Street, M8 8RG (200 yds from A665)
✪ 12-11; 12-10.30 Sun
☎ (0161) 834 4239
website: www.queensarmsmanchester.co.uk
Phoenix Bantam; Taylor Landlord; guest beers Ⓗ
Overlooking the industrialised Irk Valley, just outside Manchester city centre, this tile-

fronted free house offers a range of up to six guests, plus a wide range of bottled Belgian beers; the real cider is from Biddenden. Excellent food is available daily (until 8pm) which in good weather can be enjoyed in the back garden, where supervised children are welcome. Bikers are catered for in 'Harley Corner' and a quiz is held on Tuesday. ⌂Q⌂◖⇌(Victoria) ⊖♠

CHORLTON-CUM-HARDY

Bar
533 Wilbraham Road, M21 0UE
✪ 12-11; 12-10.30 Sun
☎ (0161) 861 7576 website: www.marblebeers.co.uk
Beer range varies Ⓗ
Continental-style café bar with pavement seating, offering a selection of Marble organic beers brewed in Manchester, alongside a range of continental and Belgian beers. The bar section opens into a slightly raised larger seating area with wood floors throughout. The menu, including daily specials, is served until 8pm; meals may be eaten in the back room which is smoke-free during dining hours. A quiz is held on Monday evening. ⌂◖

Beech Inn
72 Beech Road, M21 9EZ
✪ 11-11; 12-10.30 Sun
☎ (0161) 881 1180
Flowers Original; Hydes Trophy Bitter; Marston's Pedigree; Taylor Best Bitter, Landlord Ⓗ
This busy three-roomed pub is popular with serious drinkers. Situated close to the village green it has a garden at the rear and a pavement seating area. No music is played but a large-screen TV, mainly used for sporting events, is installed in the back room. Monday evening is musicians' night, when all are welcome; a quiz is held on Thursday evening. ⌂⌂♣

Marble Beer House
57 Manchester Road, M21 0PW
✪ 12-11; 12-10.30 Sun
☎ (0161) 881 9206 website: www.marblebeers.co.uk
Marble Chorlton-cum-Hazy, Cloudy Marble, Manchester Bitter, Ginger Marble; guest beers Ⓗ
Converted from a shop into a continental-style bar, owned by the Marble Beer House, it offers a range of their organic beers, as well as a good range of Belgian and continental beers. Snacks, supplied by the local health food shop, are available all day at the bar. A new extraction system has been fitted to reduce smokers' fumes. A quiz is held monthly (first Tue). Q⌂

CHORLTON ON MEDLOCK

Kro Bar
325 Oxford Road, M13 9PG
(on B5117 at Dover St Jct)
✪ 11-11; 12-10.30 Sun
☎ (0161) 274 3100 website: www.kro.co.uk
John Smith's Magnet; Theakston Cool Cask; Taylor Landlord; guest beers Ⓗ
Former premises of the Manchester Temperance society, the stylish interior and rear conservatory extension were designed by local architects, Stephenson Bell, successfully incorporating a modern bar into a listed Georgian building. Rooms upstairs have a more traditional feel and

display old Temperance memorabilia found during the building's restoration. The bar is lively, as you would expect, given its location opposite the university students' union. Food, served 12–9.30, is good and often has a Scandinavian accent – Kro is Danish for country pub.
❀◐◗♿

Mawson ✔
74-80 Frances Street, M13 9SQ
(off Brunswick St)
✪ 11-11; 12-10.30 Sun
☎ (0161) 273 2157
Coach House Dick Turpin; Tetley Mild, Bitter Ⓗ
Traditional, multi-roomed pub, retaining many original features including extensive wood panelling. It caters for a diverse range of customers and offers a warm welcome to all. This is a remarkable survivor, as a busy, thriving local in an area where all too many pubs have closed. Weekday lunches are served. ◐♣

COMPSTALL

Andrew Arms
George Street, SK6 5JD
✪ 11.30-11; 12-10.30 Sun
☎ (0161) 427 2281
Robinson's Hatters, Best Bitter Ⓗ
Detached stone pub in a quiet village off the main road close to Etherow Country Park, with its wildlife and river valley walks. This pub has been a continuous entry in this Guide since the mid-1970s and deservedly so. With a small, traditional tap room and a comfortable lounge, it is a true local catering for all tastes.
❀◐♣P

CORNBROOK

Hope Inn
297 Chester Road, M15 4EY
✪ 11-4, 7.30-11; 12-5, 7.30-10.30 Sun
☎ (0161) 848 0038
Hydes Light, Bitter Ⓟ
Traditional, street-corner local on the main road to Old Trafford cricket and football grounds, comprising two small rooms where TV and chat predominate. It is visible, but sadly inaccessible from Cornbrook tram station which is only open for interchange between routes.
⇌ (Deansgate) ⊖ (G-Mex) ♣

DAISY HILL

Rose Hill Tavern
321 Leigh Road, Westhoughton, BL5 2JQ
(on B5235)
✪ 12-11; 12-10.30 Sun
☎ (01942) 815776
Holt Mild, Bitter Ⓗ
Large, welcoming, open-plan pub that retains the outline of its old room plan, with two of the rooms taken up by games of all sorts. It is often referred to by locals as the Bug since a workhouse (the bug house) was demolished to make way for the pub. It was built in 1889, the year after the railway came to the village. It was formerly an Oldfield Brewery (of Poolstock) house – their crest can be seen over the door.
❀⇌♣P

DELPH

Royal Oak (Th' Heights)
Broad Lane, Heights, OL3 5TX
(1 mile above Denshaw Rd) OS982090
✪ 7-11; 12-4, 7-10.30 Sun
☎ (01457) 874460
Boddingtons Bitter; Moorhouses Black Cat; Phoenix Arizona; guest beers Ⓗ
Isolated, 250-year-old stone pub on a packhorse route, overlooking the Thame valley. Set in a popular walking area, it offers outstanding views. The pub comprises a cosy bar and three rooms, each with an open fire. The refurbished side room has a hand-carved stone fireplace, while the comfortable snug has exposed beams and old photos of the pub. Good home-cooked food (Fri–Sun eves) often features game and home-bred pork and beef. The house beer is brewed by Moorhouses. Q❀◗P⊁

DENTON

Lowes Arms
301 Hyde Road, M34 3FF
✪ 12-3, 5-11; 12-11 Sat; 12-10.30 Sun
☎ (0161) 336 3064
Boddingtons Bitter; Lowes Arms seasonal beers Ⓗ
Imposing pub in a river valley by the main A57 road. Rescued from obscurity by an enterprising management, it is now well known for both beer and food. The beers are mostly supplied by the on-site LAB (Lowes Arms Brewery), named in keeping with the local area. Generally two or three are available and the choice changes frequently. The food ranges from simple bar meals to a very well-regarded and popular menu in the cosy restaurant area. ❀◐◗♣P

DIGGLE

Diggle Hotel
Station Houses, OL3 5JZ
(1/2 mile off A670) OS011081
✪ 12-3, 5-11; 12-11 Sat; 12-10.30 Sun
☎ (01457) 872741
Black Sheep Special; Boddingtons Bitter; Taylor Landlord; guest beer Ⓗ
Stone pub in a pleasant hamlet close to the recently reopened Standedge canal tunnel under the Pennines. Built as a merchant's house in 1789, it became an ale house and general store on the construction of the nearby railway tunnel in 1834. Affording fine views of the Saddleworth countryside, this makes a convenient base in a popular walking area. With a bar area and two rooms, the accent is on home-cooked food (served all day Sat and Sun). Brass bands play on bank holidays. ❀◐◗♣P

DOBCROSS

Swan Inn (Top House)
The Square, OL3 5AA
✪ 12-3, 5.30-11; 12-3, 7.30-10.30 Sun
☎ (01457) 873451
Jennings Mild, Bitter, 1828, Cumberland Ale, Cocker Hoop, Sneck Lifter; guest beers Ⓗ
This village local, circa 1765, was built for the Wrigley family of chewing gum fame, but part of the building was later used as a police court and cells. Overlooking the attractive village square, the pub has been well renovated, with flagged floors and

three distinct drinking areas. It gets busy
during events, such as the Whit Friday brass
band contest and the August Rushcart
Festival. Good value home-cooked food
includes Indian dishes (no food Sun eve).
🏠Q🅿🌳◗🍴

ECCLES

Albert Edward
142 Church Street, M30 0LS (on A57)
◷ 12-11; 12-10.30 Sun
☎ (0161) 707 1045
Samuel Smith OBB Ⓗ

Renovations early in 2003 restored this
small, low-ceilinged old pub to its original
layout. Old photographs indicated a single,
central door as opposed to two side doors.
Reinstating this door meant moving the bar
towards the back of the pub and creating
four distinct rooms. Named after the Prince
of Wales, later King Edward VII, the pub has
a cosy, lived-in feeling and provides a
welcome change from Eccles' many Holt's
houses. 🏠Q🅿🛏♿🌳⊖ (Eccles Cross) ♣🍴

Lamb Hotel ✩
33 Regent Street, M30 0BP
(opp. tram terminus)
◷ 11.30-11; 12-10.30 Sun
☎ (0161) 789 3882
Holt Mild, Bitter, seasonal beers Ⓗ

Rebuilt in 1906, with a lofty red-brick
façade and a spiked cupola atop the roof,
the Edwardian interior is superbly
preserved with its rich mahogany, curved
etched glass and tiling. Of the three Eccles
area pubs with a billiards room, it is the
only one to retain a full-sized table.
Handy for the metro tram terminus and
bus station as well as the new West One
retail park.
Q🛏🌳⊖♣P

FALLOWFIELD

Friendship
353 Wilmslow Road, M14 6XS (on B5093)
◷ 11.30-11; 12-10.30 Sun
☎ (0161) 224 5758
Hydes Bitter, Jekyll's Gold, seasonal beers Ⓗ

This busy local is situated in the student
heartland of Manchester. A large central bar
serves all areas, while to the rear can be
found a snug, decorated with old sporting
prints. Outside is a raised patio area where
you can watch the world go by. 🅿◗P

FARNWORTH

Britannia
34 King Street, BL4 7AF
(opp. bus station, off A6053)
◷ 11-11; 12-10.30 Sun
☎ (01204) 571629
Moorhouses Premier Ⓗ

Typical, lively, town-centre pub that has a
small, recently refurbished lounge and a
larger basic vault; the central bar serves
both areas. The pub hosts two popular
mini beer festivals (May and August bank
holidays), with around six beers served at a
time from a specially-built (covered)
outside bar. The lunches are wholesome
and well-priced – worth trying. A free car
park lies behind the pub.
🅿◗🛏🌳♣

FLIXTON

Church Inn
34 Church Road, M41 6HS
◷ 11-11; 12-10.30 Sun
☎ (0161) 748 2158
**Greenalls Bitter; Holt Mild; Robinson's Best Bitter;
Taylor Landlord** Ⓗ

Comfortable village-style pub in the old
part of Flixton, divided into distinct seating
areas. One draught mild is always available.
It is a five-minute walk from Flixton Station
on the Manchester–Warrington main line.
Meals are served at lunchtime, but on
Thursday–Saturday service is extended until
6.30pm (5pm Sun). 🅿◗🌳♣P

GATHURST

Navigation Inn
162 Gathurst Lane, WN6 8HZ
(on B5206 between Shevington and Orrell)
◷ 12-11; 12-10.30 Sun
☎ (01257) 252866 website: www.thenavigationinn.com
Taylor Landlord; Tetley Bitter; guest beers Ⓗ

The pub was named after the Douglas
Navigation Company, who kept the
adjacent River Douglas navigable in the
19th century. The transfer point for barges
to move between river and canal is still
visible alongside the nearby locks. The pub
is popular with all Leeds–Liverpool Canal
users, including walkers and cyclists. It is
situated next to Bridge 46. Boules is played
here. Bulmers cider is sold in summer.
🏠🅿◗🌳♣P🍴

GORTON

Plough ✩
927 Hyde Road, M18 7FB (on A57)
◷ 11-11; 12-10.30 Sun
☎ (0161) 223 4310
Robinson's Hatters, Best Bitter, Ⓗ **Old Tom** (winter) Ⓖ

Large, multi-roomed building, first licensed
around 1800 and little changed since the
1890s; note the Victorian tiling in the
lobby. In the public bar, check out the
parquet floor, carved bar frontage and fitted
wooden seating. Upstairs, etched windows
announce commercial rooms, which were
used to collect union subs. The Plough is
still at the heart of the community. Families
are made welcome in daytime. Darts and
cribbage teams compete on a rare
Manchester log end board.
Q🅿🛏🌳 (Ryder Brow) ♣P

GREENFIELD

King William IV
134 Chew Valley Road, DL3 7DD (on A669)
◷ 11.30-11; 12-10.30 Sun
☎ (01457) 873933
**Draught Bass; Lees Bitter; Tetley Mild, Bitter; guest
beers** Ⓗ

Detached stone pub on the main road in
the village centre. Its cosy, friendly
interior is where the locals meet to discuss
village life, uninterrupted by a juke box.
Food is served until 7pm each day. On
Monday evening it hosts a popular quiz.
Handy for walks over the nearby
Saddleworth Hills, the Nos. 180 and 183
bus services from Oldham and
Manchester pass the pub.
🅿◗🌳♣P

Railway

11 Shaw Hall Bank Road, OL3 7JZ (opp. station)

☺ 5 (12 summer Fri)-11; 12-11 Sat; 12-10.30 Sun

☎ (01457) 878323

John Smith's Bitter; Taylor Landlord; Wells Bombardier; guest beers Ⓗ

Friendly, no-frills village local in a stone terrace, with a central bar and games area. The public bar displays a collection of old Saddleworth photos. In a picturesque area, close to the recently reopened Huddersfield Narrow Canal, it provides a good base for walking, rock climbing and other outdoor pursuits. Regular live music, including cajun, R&B and jazz is performed. Accommodation is in reasonably-priced rooms, two afford good views over Chew Valley.

🏨🍴⊕Å≈♣P

GUIDE BRIDGE

Boundary

2 Audenshaw Road, M34 5HD

☺ 11-11; 12-10.30 Sun

☎ (0161) 330 1677

Beer range varies Ⓗ

Friendly, busy pub on a major road junction by Guide Bridge railway station and the Ashton Canal. Good value meals are a feature at the pub which usually hosts a beer festival in June. All in all, it is an excellent pub, doing a very good job.

◐⊕⊟≈♣P

HALE

Railway

128-130 Ashley Road, WA14 2UN

☺ 11-11; 12-10.30 Sun

☎ (0161) 330 1677 website: www.railwayhale.co.uk

Robinson's Hatters, Old Stockport, Best Bitter, seasonal beers Ⓗ

Friendly local with a substantial, loyal following. A relaxed atmosphere is enhanced by wood panelling and newspapers to read. Its busy main bar contrasts with the quiet, no-smoking room, while the traditional tap room has TV and darts. It reputedly sells more beer than any other Robinson's pub in Greater Manchester, and is an important part of the Hale village scene. Next to Hale Station, it is within walking distance of Atrincham Metrolink. A good range of home-cooked food is served.

Q ✿❀◐⊕⊟≈♣⌶

HAWKSHAW

Red Lion ⊘

81 Ramsbottom Road, BL8 4JS (on A676)

☺ 12-3, 6-11; 12-10.30 Sun

☎ (01204) 856600

Jennings Bitter, Cumberland Ale; guest beers Ⓗ

Attractive stone pub, nestling in a picturesque village. Inside you will find a single large room, friendly locals and an excellent menu. Popular with diners, you can choose to eat either in the pub or in the adjacent restaurant, which offers an extensive range of freshly prepared delights (meals all day Sun). The pub is on the outskirts of Bury but is popular with both locals and those from further afield. 🍴◐

HEALD GREEN

Griffin

124 Wilmslow Road, SK8 3BE (on B5358)

☺ 12-11; 12-10.30 Sun

☎ (0161) 437 1596

Holt Mild, Bitter, seasonal beer Ⓗ

There has been a pub on this site for some 120 years, the current building since the 1960s. This large, three-roomed house, boasts a quiet snug and a lounge, both decorated with original Victorian and Edwardian photographs, while the vault displays a fine collection of 1930s postcard-type pictures, mainly of sporting events. This thriving, often bustling, pub stages live entertainment on Thursday. Weekday lunches are served. ✿◐⊕♣P

HEATON MERSEY

Griffin

552 Didsbury Road, SK4 3AJ (on A5145)

☺ 12-11; 12-10.30 Sun

☎ (0161) 443 2077

Holt Mild, Bitter Ⓗ

Former local CAMRA Pub of the Year, this busy, multi-roomed local is dominated by a superb mahogany and etched glass bar area. The pub has acquired a reputation for good quality lunchtime food. A very pleasant garden, complete with aviary and water feature, is a bonus. Good quality local beers at reasonable prices make this pub well worth a visit. ✿◐P⌶

HEATON NORRIS

Navigation

11 Manchester Road, SK4 1TY (top of Lancashire Hill, A626)

☺ 12-11; 12-10.30 Sun

☎ (0161) 480 6626

Beartown Ambeardextrous, Kodiak Gold, Bearskinful, Polar Eclipse, Wheat Beer; guest beers Ⓗ

In little over 12 months this ex-Wilson's keg pub has become Beartown's premier cask ale outlet, serving seven beers and up to five traditional ciders. The ciders are served direct from the cellar – see the blackboard in the lounge. Overshadowed by a large flour mill, this outwardly plain pub has won many hearts with its keen prices and charming staff. The range of Belgian and German beers at this local CAMRA Pub of the Year 2003 seems to be continuously increasing. ✿⊕♿♣♦P

Nursery ☆

258 Green Lane, SK4 2NA (off A6, Wellington Road North by Dunham Jaguar)

☺ 11.30-3, 5.30-11; 11.30-11 Sat; 12-10.30 Sun

☎ (0161) 432 2044

Hydes Mild, Bitter, Ⓟ Jekyll's Gold, seasonal beers Ⓗ

CAMRA's national Pub of the Year 2001, and a Guide regular, the Nursery is a classic, unspoilt 1930s pub, well hidden away in a pleasant suburban area. The multi-roomed interior includes a traditional vault, with its own entrance and a spacious wood-panelled lounge, used as a dining room at lunchtimes. The home-made food draws customers from many miles around, particularly for Sunday lunch; children are welcome if dining. The pub's immaculate bowling green is well used by local league teams. ✿◐⊕♣P⌶

HEYWOOD

Edwin Waugh ✓
10 Market Street, OL10 4LY
🕐 10-11; 12-10.30 Sun
☎ (01706) 621480
Courage Directors; Hop Back Summer Lightning; Shepherd Neame Spitfire; guest beers Ⓗ

The Edwin Waugh was named after a local dialect poet known as the 'Burns of Lancashire'. Look out for excerpts of his poems etched into the glass over the bench seating. Previously the town's Woolworth's, now converted into a Wetherspoon's house, it is always busy and often noisy. This vibrant, popular venue attracts all sections of the community, young and old. Inexpensive food, served until 10pm, includes a good range of vegetarian options with breakfast available from 10am (except Sun). Up to five guest beers change weekly.
Q❀◑♿✦

Wishing Well
89 York Street (on A58)
🕐 12-11; 12-10.30 Sun
☎ (01706) 620923
Tetley Bitter; guest beers Ⓗ

Popular free house in the centre of Heywood that attracts real ale drinkers from near and far. There are several comfortable drinking areas to choose from as you ponder the extensive beer list. Unsurprisingly, local brewery, Phoenix, often features alongside other micro-brewers. The long-standing landlord has received many awards over the years and his efforts are reflected in the quality of the beer. The frequent No. 471 Bury–Rochdale bus stops outside. ◑P

HIGH LANE

Royal Oak
Buxton Road, SK6 8AY
🕐 12-3, 6-11; 12-10.30 Sun
☎ (01663) 762380
Burtonwood Bitter; guest beer Ⓗ

Well-appointed pub, with a pleasing external appearance, on a busy main road. Although open plan, there are three distinct drinking areas, one of which is used for games. Live entertainment is staged most Friday evenings. An innovative menu is served at all sessions. Burtonwood beers make a welcome addition to the usual range in the area. The pub has a garden and play area for children. Q➳❀◑⊟♿♣P☐

HORWICH

Crown
1 Chorley New Road, BL6 7QJ
(at A673/B6226 jct)
🕐 11-11; 12-10.30 Sun
☎ (01204) 690926
Holt Mild, Bitter, seasonal beers Ⓗ

Large pub on the edge of town, not too far from the Reebok Stadium for a drink before the game. Mainly open plan, it comprises a well furnished drinking area, a vault and a games room at the rear. This friendly pub serves good value food. Wednesday is quiz night. It is well worth a visit to take in the views of Rivington Pike. Sunday evening is busy when locals take part in free and easy singalongs. ♨❀◑⊟♿♣P

HYDE

Sportsman Inn
57 Mottram Road, SK14 2NN
🕐 11-11; 12-10.30 Sun
☎ (0161) 368 5000
Phoenix Bantam; Plassey Bitter; Moorhouses Black Cat; Taylor Landlord; Whim Hartington Bitter; guest beers Ⓗ

Outstanding example of a true free house with a mouth-watering selection of micro and regional brewery beers, including rotating guests, plus an occasional cider. Rescued from the Whitbread stable and now very much at the heart of the local community, it fields many sports teams and provides a venue for clubs and charitable associations. Simply decorated, it has two main rooms, plus a meeting room upstairs, housing a well-used, full-sized snooker table. ♨❀Ⓔ⇌ (Newton/Central) ♣♦P☐

LEIGH

Bowling Green
Manchester Road, WN7 2LD
🕐 12-midnight; 12-10.30 Sun
☎ (01942) 673964
Holt Bitter; guest beers Ⓗ

Although open plan in style, the lounge bar retains several discrete seating areas, so there is plenty of room for the pub's share club and golf society to meet. The tap room fields darts, pool and football teams and hosts live music on Saturday evening. The family room is spacious. Evening meals are served early (4.30–7); on Saturday and Sunday food is available all day until 7pm. The pub is situated close to Butts Bridge (No. 64) and Butts Basin on the Leigh branch of the Bridgewater Canal. ➳❀◑P

Nevison
96B Plank Lane, WN7 4QE
🕐 12-2 (not Mon or Tue), 5 (6.30 Mon)-11; 12-11 Wed; 11-11 Sat; 12-10.30 Sun
☎ (01942) 671394
Beer range varies Ⓗ

Situated on the outskirts of the town, the Nevison stands close to Plank Lane swing bridge on the Leigh branch of the Leeds–Liverpool Canal. This local is named after the highwayman William Nevison. Its cosy front parlour and bar contain a vast array of plates and brassware. A later addition to the pub is the long games room. The large rear garden has a playground; children are welcome until 9pm. ❀◑♣P

LITTLEBOROUGH

Moorcock Inn
Halifax Road, OL15 0LD (on A58)
🕐 11.30-11; 12-10.30 Sun
☎ (01706) 378156 website: www.themoorcockinn.com
Marston's Bitter; Taylor Landlord; guest beers Ⓗ

Built as a farmhouse in 1641 and first licensed in 1840, this gem, nestling in the Pennine foothills is worth a visit for the view alone. Although boasting a fine 80-seat restaurant, the pub section is kept apart by clever use of floor space, so two guest beers (usually from local brewers) are served in amenable surroundings. Being near the Pennine Way, ramblers and equestrians (tethers provided for horses) join the varied clientele. ♨➳❀⌂◑♿▲P✦

LOWTON (LANE HEAD)

Red Lion
324 Newton Road, WA3 1HE
🕿 12-11; 12-10.30 Sun
☎ (01942) 671429
Greenalls Bitter;Tetley Dark Mild; guest beers Ⓗ

Commodious, friendly local, with three lounge areas and a pool room where a big-screen TV shows various sporting events. It is one of the few pubs in the area to boast a bowling green. The pub is a good starting point for visiting the local attractions, Pennington Park and Haydock Park race course. A friendly quiz is staged on Tuesday evening. Children are welcome until 9pm.
🕸🍴◑●♣P

LOWTON (ST LUKES)

Hare & Hounds
1 Golborne Road, WA3 2DP
🕿 11-11; 12-10.30 Sun
☎ (01942) 728387
Tetley Bitter; guest beers Ⓗ

Situated at St Lukes crossroads which now boasts an Indian restaurant, road improvements have given the pub more prominence. The Hare attracts customers of all ages. Due to many alterations, the pub has distinctive drinking areas, from the sunken dining area to the low-ceilinged tap room. For children there is a small play barn and a safe playground outside; for adults there are two paved areas. 🕸◑●♣P⅄

LYDGATE

White Hart
51 Stockport Road, OL4 4JJ (at A669/A6050 jct)
🕿 12-11; 12-10.30 Sun
☎ (01457) 872566 website: www.thewhitehart.co.uk
Draught Bass; Boddingtons Bitter; Lees Bitter; Moorhouses Pendle Witches Brew; Taylor Landlord; guest beers Ⓗ

Stone hostelry commanding impressive views over the hills above Oldham. Adjoining the local school and parish church, the pub has four rooms, each with an open fire; two are used for dining. A small snug has its own bar servery and features Victorian gothic backpanels and high-backed wooden seats. The popular bar area boasts eight handpumps, while a new extension, with bar, provides a brasserie-style restaurant used for gourmet meals and weddings. A good base for visiting the Saddleworth moors with en-suite accommodation. Q🕸🍴◑●&P

MANCHESTER CITY CENTRE

Bar Fringe
8 Swan Street, M4 5JN (30 yds from A665/A62 jct)
🕿 12-11; 12-10.30 Sun
☎ (0161) 835 3815 website: www.barfringe.co.uk
Beer range varies Ⓗ

Four handpumps always serve beers from small brewers, such as Bank Top and Boggart Hole Clough. The Belgian-style bar also has continental beers on draught and in bottle; real cider is from the barrel. The 'Fringe Twins' delight in giving customers the Bar Fringe experience – friendly, humorous and robust. The decor includes changing wall posters and

ornaments. A secluded outside seating area in a back alley is festooned with red lights. Hot and cold food is served 12–6 Monday–Thursday.
🕸◑●≋(Victoria) ⊖(Market St) 🍎

Britons Protection ☆
50 Great Bridgewater Street, M1 5LE
🕿 11-11; 12-10.30 Sun
☎ (0161) 236 5895
Jennings Bitter; Robinson's Best Bitter; Tetley Bitter; guest beer Ⓗ

Friendly, city pub with a long, narrow bar leading to two more cosy rooms at the rear. Deserving of its listing on CAMRA's National Inventory, it boasts beautiful preserved tiling both inside and out. The food is venison and game pie, plus specials. Situated opposite the Bridgewater Concert Hall, it is also handy for the G-Mex exhibition centre.
🏚Q🕸◑≋(Deansgate) ⊖(G-Mex)

Café Bar Centro
74 Tib Street, M4 1LG (off A665)
🕿 12-midnight (1am Thu-Sat); closed Sun
☎ (0161) 835 2863 website: www.centrobar.co.uk
Beer range varies Ⓗ

Up to three handpumps supply beers from Bazens, Boggart Hole Clough, Pictish and Spinning Jenny. The café bar has atmosphere without attitude – customers can unwind and/or celebrate. The bar does a lot to attract women to real ale, as well as stocking a permanent (rotating) cider on handpump and a good selection of continental beers, draught and bottled. A large upstairs room with retro bar is the hub, with seating and a small dance floor downstairs. Interesting food is always available.
◑≋(Victoria) ⊖(Market St) 🍎

Castle
66 Oldham Street, M4 1LE (near A62/A665 jct)
🕿 12-11; 12-10.30 Sun
☎ (0161) 236 2945
Robinson's Hatters, Old Stockport, Hartleys XB, Cumbria Way, Best Bitter, Frederics, seasonal beers Ⓗ

The only pub in the city to sell the complete range of Robinson's ales is situated close to the infamous Northern Quarter, and is a mecca for local real ale worshippers. The 18th-century Grade II listed building has a bustling front parlour, and a small snug with a piano. The passage leads to a larger, basic back room housing a pool table. Q≋(Piccadilly/Victoria) ⊖(Piccadilly Gdns/Market St)

Circus Tavern ☆
86 Portland Street, M1 4GX (50 yds N of Princess St)
🕿 11-11; 12-10.30 Sun
☎ (0161) 236 5818
Tetley Bitter Ⓗ

This utterly unspoilt pub is a tremendous survivor in bustling central Manchester. This early 19th-century stuccoed building, has a matchboard panelled drinking corridor on the left, leading to two simply-fitted public rooms, one behind the other, on the right. The servery is under the stairs and is only large enough for one person to perform the noble act of serving beer.
Q≋(Piccadilly/Oxford Rd) ⊖(St Peters Sq)

City Arms
48 Kennedy Street, M2 4BQ
🕓 11.30-11; closed Sun
☎ (0161) 236 4610
Tetley Bitter; guest beers Ⓗ
Listed, two roomed, city pub, notable for its attractive tiled exterior. An ever-changing range of up to six guest beers comes from a variety of breweries. Popular with office workers, it can be crowded at lunchtime but generally less hectic in the evenings and on Saturday. There is no room to expand though – the City Arms is wedged between two other pubs (the Vine and the Waterhouse). ◖≠(Oxford Rd) ⊖(St Peters Sq)

Hare & Hounds ☆
46 Shudehill, M4 4AA (near tram station)
🕓 11-11; 12-10.30 Sun
☎ (0161) 832 4737
Holt Bitter; Tetley Bitter Ⓗ
The Hare & Hounds has a second entrance at the back on Salmon Street, now a quiet cul-de-sac adjacent to new developments within the preserved shell of the old Smithfield wholesale market. However, this popular pub is much the same as it was when the market flourished. Most of the original tiling, mahogany and leaded glass remains intact in this Grade II listed building. It retains the atmosphere of a small town local, despite its proximity to the city centre. ❀≠(Shudehill) ♣♣

Jolly Angler
47 Ducie Street, M1 2JW
🕓 12-3, 5.30-11; 12-11 Sat; 12-5, 8-10.30 Sun
☎ (0161) 236 5307
Hydes Bitter, seasonal beers Ⓗ
The pub has been with the same family for over 17 years. While Irish theme bars have largely been and gone, the much-loved Jolly Angler remains authentically Irish. A basic two-roomed pub that has been opened out, its corner bar is the source of lively banter, warmed by a coal (and at times, peat) fire. Folk singers have a session on Sunday evening, with Irish music on Thursday and Saturday evenings. ♨≠(Piccadilly) ⊖♣

Knott
374 Deansgate, M3 4LY (under railway viaduct)
🕓 12-11; 12-10.30 Sun
☎ (0161) 839 9229
Marble Manchester Bitter, Ginger Marble, Lagonda IPA; guest beers Ⓗ
This popular, modern bar features an eclectic array of furniture and background music. Beer, wine and food are all of interest; a varied menu is available until 8pm. The location (near Deansgate Locks) is handy for the tourist sights of Castlefield. Stone blocks support the railway above, but only long freight trains are loud enough to be heard. The continental ambience is helped by a wide selection of Belgian and German beers, bottled and on draught; guest beers come from local micros. ❀◖≠(Deansgate) ⊖(G-Mex) ●

Marble Arch
73 Rochdale Road, M4 4HY
🕓 11.30-11; 12-10.30 Sun
☎ (0161) 832 5914
Marble Cloudy Marble, Manchester Bitter, Ginger Marble, Lagonda IPA, seasonal beers; guest beers Ⓗ
Busy free house, home to the Marble Brewery, whose beers are entirely organic. The brewery can be viewed from the rear lounge. The mosaic floor notoriously slopes from the front entrance to the corner bar. Below the tiled ceiling is an impressive frieze showing names of various drinks. A large McKenna's Brewery mirror and a range of seating enhance the period feel. Up to five Marble beers are supplemented by guests from micro-breweries around the country, usually including a mild. ◖≠(Victoria) ⊖

Peveril of the Peak ☆
127 Great Bridgewater Street, M1 5JQ
🕓 11.30-3 (not Sat), 5 (7 Sat)-11; 7-10.30 Sun
☎ (0161) 236 6364
Boddingtons Bitter; Marston's Pedigree; Wells Bombardier; guest beer Ⓗ
This almost triangular, three-roomed Grade II listed building is well worth a visit to see the superb exterior tiling and stained glass in the bar. A TV and football table are in the bar, but the large lounge and small triangular snug are quiet, except on Tuesday evening when Irish folk musicians gather to entertain. There is some pavement seating. It opens Saturday afternoons when Manchester United play at home (2.30–11); food is then served, in addition to weekday lunches. ❀◖⊟≠(Oxford Rd) ⊖(St Peters Sq)

Pot of Beer
36 New Mount Street, M4 4DE
🕓 12-11; closed Sun
☎ (0161) 834 8579
Robinson's Dark Mild; guest beers Ⓗ
Small back-street, free house, hidden away off Rochdale Road. Formerly a Marston's house, it became free of tie in 1996. Two bare-boarded drinking areas are divided by a low partition. A fine collection of mirrors adorns the walls. Usually three guest beers are sourced from micro-breweries, plus Moles Black Rat cider. Good value food is served daily (times vary). ❀◖≠(Victoria) ⊖●

Rain Bar
80 Great Bridgewater Street, M1 5JG
🕓 11-11 (midnight Fri & Sat); 12-10.30 Sun
☎ (0161) 235 6500
Lees GB Mild, Bitter, Moonraker, seasonal beers Ⓗ
Former Manchester CAMRA Pub of the Year, conveniently located for concert-goers near the Bridgewater Hall. The name derives from its former existence as an umbrella factory, converted into a pub. The patio overlooks the Rochdale Canal, and is overlooked itself by an increasing number of modern apartments. Take the rare opportunity to sample all Lees beers on the ground floor (the first floor is more café-bar style). An interesting menu and wide range of quality wines by the glass are served. ❀◖ₒ≠(Oxford Rd) ⊖(St Peters Sq)

Smithfield Hotel & Bar
37 Swan Street, M4 5JZ
🕓 12-11; 12-10.30 Sun
☎ (0161) 839 4424
Greene King XX Mild; guest beers Ⓗ
Popular hotel bar, very much an integral part of the Northern Quarter circuit. A single, narrow room, with pool table at the

front, opens out to the rear with more seating and a large TV, often on for football. Six of the eight handpumps dispense micro and regional brews. The house bitter is from Phoenix. Jugs from the cellar supplement the handpumps at occasional beer festivals, which attract drinkers from far and wide. Good value accommodation is an added attraction. ⌂≠(Victoria) ⊖(Shudehill) ♣

White House
122 Great Ancoats Street, M4 6DE (opp. Central Retail Park)
⊙ 12-4 (4.30 Fri & Sat), 8-11 (not Tue eve); 12-4.30, 8-10.30 Sun
☎ (0161) 228 3231
Holt Bitter; guest beer ℍ
Quality real ale is the byword for a pub, which has had the same tenant for over 18 years. Guests include beers from Barnsley, Jennings and Phoenix breweries. The large lounge is adorned with pictures of Hollywood movie greats, while the small vault – dominated by a pool table – has glass cabinets on each wall displaying trophies of both the men's and women's pool and darts teams. ❀⌂≠(Piccadilly) ⊖♣

Railway
223 Stockport Road, SK6 6EN
⊙ 11.45-11; 12-10.30 Sun
☎ (0161) 427 2146
Robinson's Hatters, Best Bitter ℍ
This impressive pub opened in 1878 alongside Rose Hill Station, whose commuters still number among its customers. Replacing a former pub called the Gun Inn, the pub was opened by Bell's Brewery of Hempshaw Brook, Stockport and is little changed externally. Handy for walkers and cyclists on the nearby Middlewood Way, its two pleasant rooms, in open-plan style, have an airy, relaxing atmosphere. Children are welcome until 3pm. ❀◑≠(Rose Hill) P

Ring O' Bells ✆
130 Church Lane, SK6 7AY
⊙ 11.30-3, 5.30-11; 11.30-11 Sat; 12-10.30 Sun
☎ (0161) 427 2300
Robinson's Hatters, Best Bitter, seasonal beers ℍ
The pub is situated alongside the Macclesfield Canal near the top lock at Marple. Comfortable, it is semi open-plan, with two small additional rooms, offering a welcome for all. Externally, the years have brought little change and the pub still serves as a community focal point. ❀◑P

Lane Ends
Glossop Road, SK6 5DD
⊙ 4-11 (12 Fri & Sat); 12-10.30 Sun
☎ (0161) 427 5226
Adnams Broadside; Tetley Bitter ℍ
Stone-built hostelry on the edge of Marple Bridge village, bordering open countryside. It offers a warm welcome to the whole family. Outdoor drinking and play areas afford rural views, while a cosy open-plan interior on two levels is fully carpeted with an open fire. The Glossop and Hazel Grove bus, No. 394, passes the door. Ample parking is available. ⌂❀◑P

Oddfellows Arms ✆
73 Moor End Lane, SK6 5PT
(2 miles from Marple Bridge)
⊙ 11-3 (not Mon), 5.30-11; 12-3, 7-10.30 Sun
☎ (0161) 449 7826
Adnams Bitter; Flowers IPA; Marston's Pedigree; guest beer
The Oddfellows is an elegant three-storey pub, totally in keeping with its picture-postcard setting. Internally restored many years ago, a good social atmosphere prevails in its comfortable bar and lounge. The pub maintains a reputation for high quality food served in the no-smoking restaurant upstairs and also in the pub. ⌂Q❀◑&P⊟

Old Boar's Head
111 Long Street, M24 6UE
⊙ 11-11; 12-10.30 Sun
☎ (0161) 643 3520
Lees GB Mild, Bitter ℍ
This old, multi-roomed, flagstone-floored, half-timbered building dates back to at least 1632, the date being engraved into a cellar lintel. It has had many uses over the years, including a stopping-point for stage coaches and a spell as a magistrates' court. The pub was completely and stunningly restored by Lees in 1986. An excellent range of meals is supplied and the pub exudes a warm, inviting atmosphere with its many rooms providing something for everyone. ⌂❀◑P

Tandle Hill Tavern
Thornham Fold, Thornham Lane, M24 2HB
(1 mile off A664 or A627, along unmetalled road)
OS898091
⊙ 7 (12 Sat)-11; 12-10.30 Sun
☎ (01706) 345297
Lees GB Mild, Bitter ℍ
True hidden gem on a hilltop near Tandle Hill Country Park, this two-roomed pub is hard to find the first time, but well worth the effort. First licensed in 1850 as a beer house, it was purchased by Lees in 1932. In a small farming community, it draws its custom from far and wide, including farmers and walkers. Simple soup and sandwich lunches are available at weekends. Phone to check opening times if planning a midweek visit. ⌂❀

Ace of Diamonds
241 Oldham Road, M40 7UR
⊙ 12-11; 12-10.30 Sun
☎ (07811) 332421
Beer range varies ℍ
This is a real ale fairy story come true. The owner of a nearby demolition firm bought the pub to knock down for expansion, until a friend in the pub trade suggested otherwise. The former neglected keg house is now a pleasant and welcoming one-roomed pub serving real ale from Holts, Saddleworth and Thwaites, among others. There is a long bar, plus a snug and a vault area. Frequented by mature regulars, the Ace is an oasis in a beer desert. ❀♣

MOSSLEY

Britannia Inn
217 Manchester Road, OL5 9AJ
☼ 11-11; 12.30-10.30 Sun
☎ (01457) 832799
Marston's Bitter; guest beers Ⓗ

Like all the local 19th-century buildings, this pub is built of millstone grit. Standing three storeys high, it faces the Manchester–Huddersfield railway line and Mossley Station. Recently refurbished, this former Marston's house is enjoying a new lease of life under the Pyramid Pub Co, who have created an open-plan interior, complete with pool table, darts and Sky TV. The two guest beers are from the company's list. Meals are served 12–7 (5 Sun).
❀◖≄♣♠

Church Inn
82 Stockport Road, OL5 0RF
☼ 11-11; 12-10.30 Sun
☎ (01457) 832021
John Smith's Bitter; Theakston Cool Cask; guest beers Ⓗ

The exterior of this inn is typical of many northern town pubs – built at the end of a long, stone terrace of houses, and giving an impression of permanence. A traditional local, catering for all ages, it has a tap room, served from a through bar. The two guest beer pumps offer a good choice of ales, including those from local micros, Shaws and Greenfield. The pub is home to the Mossley morris men.
❀◖≄♣P

Rising Sun
235 Stockport Road, OL5 0RQ
☼ 4 (12 Sat)-11; 12-10.30 Sun
☎ (01457) 834436
Black Sheep Best Bitter; Taylor Landlord; Tetley Bitter; guest beers Ⓗ

The Rising Sun, now a well established free trade outlet, appears to be squeezed into the hillside which rises to 956 feet behind. This perhaps explains why, on entering, the interior seems larger than expected. A small games room allows the darts and crib team to compete in the local league and hosts a folk music session (Tue), notwithstanding the bridge veterans. Three of the six cask ales are guests, frequently from local micro-breweries, Shaws and Greenfield. Q♣P

MOTTRAM

White Hart
91 Market Street, SK14 6JQ
☼ 11-11; 12-10.30 Sun
☎ (01457) 766953
Lees Bitter; Moorhouses Black Cat; Phoenix Bantam; Plassey Bitter; Taylor Landlord; guest beers Ⓗ

Village-centre local in a conservation area, opposite the old courthouse. Its comfortable lounge, tap room and bare-boarded floors around the bar, are complemented by a Cuban, Caribbean and Tapas restaurant upstairs (open Thu–Sat, 6–10), offering a wide vegetarian choice. Formerly a keg-only pub, it is now by far the most popular pub locally. The cider changes constantly. Regular bus services run from Glossop and Hyde. The community spirit is enhanced by three pool and two darts teams.
♨Q◖♿♣♠⚘

NANGREAVES

Lord Raglan
Mount Pleasant, BL9 6SP
☼ 12-2.30, 7-11; 12-10.30 Sun
☎ (0161) 764 6680
Beer range varies Ⓗ

This inn is the home of the Leyden Brewery and several of their beers feature on the bar. The Leyden family have run this charming country local for half a century. It is decorated throughout with many items of interest, including antique glassware and pottery. There are also old photographs and pictures on the walls. The pub is renowned for its good food and the chef is also the head brewer. Food is served all day Sunday until 9pm. ❀◖▮P

NEW SPRINGS

Colliers Arms
192 Wigan Road, WN1 1DU
(on B5238 between Wigan and Aspull)
☼ 1.30-5.30 (not Wed or Thu), 7.30-11; 1.30-11 Sat; 1-5.30, 7.30-10.30 Sun
☎ (01942) 831171
Burtonwood Bitter Ⓗ

Known locally as the Stone, this popular two-roomed inn is making its 20th consecutive appearance in this Guide, a feat unrivalled by any other pub in the area. A striking mock-Tudor building dating from 1700, it displays much memorabilia from former local collieries, including a pit helmet (used to illuminate the lounge fireplace). Many bottles are displayed around the bar, alongside books on walking and rambling. It is handy for the nearby attractions of Haigh Hall and the Leeds–Liverpool Canal. ♨Q❀P

OLDHAM

Bridgewater Hotel
197 Manchester Road, Hollinwood, OL8 4PS (on A62)
☼ 11.30-11; 12-10.30 Sun
☎ (0161) 628 8464
Holt Mild, Bitter Ⓗ

Built on the site of the old Bridgewater Hotel, this modern, low-level, two-roomed Holt's outlet, has a vibrant, noisy vault that contrasts with an open-plan lounge, with lots of mahogany fittings. Large windows in the vault allow a view of televised sport from the lounge area. Live music and singsongs, mostly for retired folk, take place on Thursday afternoon. Note the large glass case housing pool trophies in the vault.
◖♣P

Gardener's Arms
Dunham Street (Millbottom), Lees, OL4 3NH
☼ 12-11; 12-10.30 Sun
☎ (0161) 624 0242
Robinson's Hatters, Best Bitter Ⓗ

Less than two miles out of Oldham town centre, on the outskirts of Lees, this pub nestles in a dip on the old road to Yorkshire, next to the River Medlock. It retains many original features from when it was rebuilt in the 1930s, with its layout of separate rooms boasting plenty of woodwork, tilework and fireplaces. Brassware around the bar adds to the atmosphere. Live groups perform occasionally on Saturday evening. Weekday lunches are served. ❀◖♣P

Royal Oak
176 Manchester Road, Werneth, OL9 7BN
(on A62 opp. Werneth Park)
✪ 2-11; 12-5, 8-11 Sat; 12-10.30 Sun
☎ (0161) 624 5795
Robinson's Hatters, Best Bitter Ⓗ
Traditional Robinson's pub, where four drinking areas are served from a central bar. This community local features wood panelling, old-fashioned cast iron radiators and an old Gledhill cash register. A rare Robinson's Old Tom mirror hangs in the games room alongside old black and white photographs. It is handy for the local station at Werneth. Q ⇌ ♣

ORRELL

Robin Hood
117 Sandy Lane, WN5 7AZ
✪ 12-11; 12-10.30 Sun
☎ (01695) 627479
Beer range varies Ⓗ
Small, unspoilt, sandstone, family-run pub where the two rooms are themed on the well-known freedom fighter from Sherwood Forest. Pictures of Robin Hood abound and the fairer sex can freshen up in the 'damsels'. It looks like the sort of place that ought to sell real ale and now does, after many years in the keg wilderness (the Greenalls is still keg, though).
Q ◖ ᗕ⇌♣P

PATRICROFT

Stanley Arms
295 Liverpool Road, M30 0QN (on A57, near Bridgewater Canal)
✪ 12-11; 12-10.30 Sun
☎ (0161) 788 8801
Holt Mild, Bitter Ⓗ
The large corner door of this small 19th-century pub is permanently closed, so use the side door on Eliza Ann Street. The Stanley is one of only six Holt's tenancies, and everything oozes quality. The front vault is always busy and drinkers often huddle in the tiny lobby with its single table. There is a smart 'best room' and at the end of the corridor a door marked 'Private' leads to a public room with a restored cast iron range, used mostly at weekends.
ᗰ⇌♣

PEEL GREEN

Grapes Hotel
439 Liverpool Road, M30 7HD (on A57)
✪ 11-11; 12-10.30 Sun
☎ (0161) 789 6971
Holt Mild, Bitter, seasonal beers Ⓗ
The Grapes celebrated its centenary in 2003, when the exterior was given a sympathetic makeover. Inside this large, listed pub many original features remain: the mahogany bar, etched glass, wall tiling and mosaic floor. It is one of three pubs in the Eccles area to boast a billiards room (which only houses a pool table at present). With five distinct areas, including an airy and lively vault, the Grapes has been used occasionally as a film set for TV dramas.
Q ᗕ⇌ (Patricroft) ♣P

PENDLEBURY

Newmarket
621 Bolton Road, M27 5EJ (on A666)
✪ 11-11; 12-10.30 Sun
☎ (0161) 794 3650
Holt Mild, Bitter Ⓗ
The Newmarket was built in 1896 on the site of a pub called the Volunteer, to coincide with the opening of the new market across the road. Sadly, this once thriving market no longer exists, the pub though, still retains something of the atmosphere of a Victorian beer house. As you enter, on the right is a small vault, the bar, and a small opened-out back room. The central corridor opens to the main lounge on the left. ❀⇌ (Swinton) ♣P

RAMSBOTTOM

Hare & Hounds
400 Bolton Road West, Holcombe Brook, BL0 9RY
✪ 12-11; 12-10.30 Sun
☎ (01706) 822107
Beer range varies Ⓗ
This is a very large, one-roomed pub, split into distinct drinking areas, including a raised no-smoking area. Eight handpumps dispense a variety of beers, often from local breweries. Beer festivals are held twice yearly. The abundance of TVs testifies to the locals' interest in sport and it gets very busy at weekends and on match days. In an area not renowned for choice, customers are attracted by the good service and excellent beer quality. Food is served daily until 9.30pm. ᗰQ◖ ᗙ&P⅃

ROCHDALE

Albion
600 Whitworth Road, OL12 0SW
✪ 12-2.30, 5-11; 12-11 Sun
☎ (01706) 648540
Boddingtons Bitter; Lees Bitter; Phoenix Monkeytown Mild; Taylor Best Bitter, Landlord; guest beers Ⓗ
A true free house, this is a neat, multi-roomed local with a bistro attached. The pub is built into the side of a hill, to such an extent that the garden is almost on the roof. It is popular with locals and visitors alike, who come for the excellent beer and the superb home-cooked food, which features many African specialities. It usually stocks two guest beers, and a well chosen range of wines is always available.
ᗰQ❀◖

Cask & Feather
1 Oldham Road, OL16 1UA
✪ 11-11; 12-10.30 Sun
☎ (01706) 711476
website: www.mcguinnessbrewery.com
McGuinness Feather Pluckers Mild, Best Bitter, Junction Bitter, Tommy Todd's Porter Ⓗ
Halfway between the town centre and the station, on the main route to Oldham, the pub provides a welcome break at the top of a long climb. An old stone building with one L-shaped room and a long bar, the McGuinness Brewery is situated at the rear, and this pub is its only tied outlet. Most of the beers are usually on tap and occasionally seasonal beers make an appearance. Pay and display parking is

available nearby and many bus routes pass by. ◖⇌

Cemetery Hotel ☆
470 Bury Road, OL11 5EU
✪ 12-11; 12-10.30 Sun
☎ (01706) 645635
Black Sheep Best Bitter; Jennings Cumberland Ale; John Smith's Bitter; Taylor Landlord; guest beers Ⅱ
At a road junction, about a couple of miles out from the town centre, this pub has been a popular venue for many years, particularly with fans from the not-too-distant Rochdale Football Club at Spotland. It retains many features, such as etched windows, tiling, woodwork, and the original room layout, from the days of its ownership by Crown Brewery of Bury. ♣

Healey Hotel
172 Shawclough Road, OL12 6LW (on B6377)
✪ 12 (3 Tue & Wed)-11; 12-10.30 Sun
☎ (01706) 645453
Robinson's Best Bitter, Cumbria Way, Old Tom, seasonal beers Ⅱ
This terraced stone pub, at the entrance to Healey Dell Nature Reserve, is a gem. Many original features remain, including a splendid bar, tiles and oak doors. The traditional layout consists of a quiet, no-smoking front parlour, a rear gentlemen's room with a sporting motif and a bar/lounge displaying film star portraits. The extensive gardens boast a well-used petanque piste. ⚲Q✿▲♣⅌

Merry Monk
234 College Road, OL12 6AF (near A6060/B6222 jct)
✪ 12-11; 12-5, 7-10.30 Sun
☎ (01706) 646919
Hydes Dark, Bitter, Jekyll's Gold; guest beers Ⅱ
Victorian, detached brick local, first licensed in 1850. A glimpse of its history can be seen in the fine pair of Phoenix of Heywood tile sets in the entrance. The pub passed to Bass via Cornbrook and was purchased as a free house in 1984. There are always one or two guest beers available. The open-plan layout is home to strong darts and quiz teams; ring the bull and other games are also played, while outside are two international petanque pistes. ✿♣P

Puckersley Inn
22 Narrowgate Brow, Fir Lane, OL2 6YD (off A671, via Dogford Road)
✪ 11-11; 12-10.30 Sun
☎ (0161) 624 4973
Lees GB Mild, Bitter Ⅱ
Popular, detached stone-fronted pub on the edge of the green belt, with panoramic views over Royton and Oldham from the car park and garden. Recently extended to provide a restaurant area, the lounge bar and snug room both enable customers to enjoy a conversation in comfortable surroundings. The lively vault has no juke box, pool table or other distractions. The No. 408 bus passes the pub. Q✿◖⇌♣P

Railway Hotel
2 Oldham Road, OL2 6DN
✪ 11-11; 12-10.30 Sun
☎ (0161) 624 2793

Lees GB Mild, Bitter Ⅱ
This is a very popular, traditional local that attracts a wide mix of customers. A large pub, dominating the main town-centre junction, it comprises three distinct drinking areas. The busy vault is nicely complemented by a spacious central lounge and a cosy snug. Table football is one of the games favoured by the locals. ◖⇲♣

King's Ransom ⊘
Britannia Road, M33 2AA
✪ 11.30-11; 12-10.30 Sun
☎ (0161) 969 6006
Boddingtons Bitter; Hardys & Hansons Bitter, seasonal beers Ⅱ
A rare Hardy & Hanson's outlet in Greater Manchester, the pub is situated beside the Bridgewater Canal and features a moored floating pontoon as an outdoor drinking area. The pub was built six years ago, but the exterior looks much older. The site required extensive preparatory work, including dredging of the canal. During this work the price of the derelict site increased, causing the developer to remark that it was costing a king's ransom – hence the pub's name. ✿◖&⊖P⅌

Albert Vaults
169 Chapel Street, M3 6AD
(on A6, near Central Station)
✪ 11-11; 12-10.30 Sun
☎ (0161) 819 1368
Phoenix Arizona; guest beer Ⅱ
Very much a local, it caters for the mature drinker. The central entrance leads into the main bar area; note the unusual round coloured glass feature above the bar. The room to the left has a small stage area for occasional live acts, while the back vault acts as the games room. The guest beer comes from a local micro-brewery. The pub was previously a Tetley's 'free' house, then leased to Burtonwood. Weekday lunches are served. ◖⇲⇌ (Central) ♣

Crescent
18-21 The Crescent, M5 4PF (100 yds from A6/A5066 jct)
✪ 11.30-11; 12-10.30 Sun
☎ (0161) 736 5600
Hydes Bitter; Rooster's Special; guest beers Ⅱ
A long-standing Guide entry, this terraced, bare-boarded free house offers up to eight guest beers, including a mild. Its central bar serves three very different rooms. Regular beer festivals are held in the side games room which is also used for meetings. An extensive range of draught and bottled foreign beers come served in their traditional glasses. The excellent value food is recommended, particularly on Wednesday evening, which is curry night (eve meals Tue–Fri). ⚲✿◖⇌ (Crescent) ♣✿P☐

Eagle Inn (Lamp Oil)
19 Collier Street, Greengate, M3 7DW (250 yds from A6041/A6042 jct)
✪ 11-11; 12-10.30 Sun
☎ (0161) 832 4919
Holt Mild, Bitter Ⅱ

Delightful example of a Holt's basic, back-street boozer. The double bow-fronted windows at the front lead to three small rooms; a tap, games room and a snug. Look for the sign in the tap room, 'nutters corner – no vacancies'; Pre-Raphaelite prints decorate the snug. Affectionately known as the Lamp Oil – the outside light shows the historical connection – it caters mainly for locals, but for the visitor, once found (can be tricky), its welcoming atmosphere is never forgotten. ⬤≠(Central) ⊖(Victoria) ♣

King's Arms
11 Bloom Street, M3 6AN
(200 yds from Central Station)
🕒 12-11; 12-7 Sun
☎ (0161) 839 7722
Bazens Pacific; Caledonian Deuchars IPA; guest beers Ⓗ
Unusually-shaped free house, just off the main A6, now surrounded by newly-built luxury apartments. A corridor leads past a small side room to the curved main room and bar area, where a blackboard lists the drinks available. Guest beers are often from local micro-breweries. The main room can get smoky. Live music is a regular feature. Food is served 12–3 daily. ◖≠(Central)

Star Inn
2 Bk Hope Street, Higher Broughton, M7 2FR
🕒 1.30-4.30 (5.30 Sat), 8-11; 1.30-11 Fri; 1.30-5.30, 8-10.30 Sun
☎ (0161) 792 4184
Robinson's Hatters, Best Bitter, seasonal beer Ⓗ
Hidden away, and surrounded by cobbled streets in a conservation area known as 'Cliffside', the pub is an attractive white pebble dashed cottage. Through the porch, a half-opening hinged door opens on to a tiny original vault and bar – the hub of the Star, where the locals gather. There is also a long saloon, largely unspoilt, and a games room, housing a Manchester log end dartboard. The most unusual feature is outside in the yard – the ladies' loo. ❀⬤♣

Pineapple Inn
18 Kenworthy Street, SK15 2DX
🕒 4 (12 Fri & Sat)-11; 12-10.30 Sun
☎ (0161) 338 2542
Robinson's Hatters, Best Bitter, seasonal beers Ⓗ
Biker-friendly community pub, just off the redeveloped town centre, far enough away to avoid the worst of the weekend revellers doing the 'Stalyvegas' circuit. An open-plan interior is split into three distinct areas, including one dedicated to pub games. Frequent live music events add to the pub's popularity. The function room upstairs boasts full-sized snooker and billiards tables. The large garden is a rarity in the area. ❀≠♣P

Station Buffet Bar
Platform 1, Stalybridge Station, Rassbottom Street, SK15 1RF
🕒 11-11; 12-10.30 Sun
☎ (0161) 303 0007 website: www.buffetbar.co.uk
Draught Bass; Boddingtons Bitter; Flowers IPA; guest beers Ⓗ
This licensed buffet was so authentically restored that you find yourself glancing

around for Trevor Howard and Celia Johnson. Four distinct rooms all have their own cosy atmosphere, but it is around the marble-topped bar, close by the impressive fireplace that its heart lies. Some come in to wait for a train, some for food (including the famous black peas), but many come for the five guest beers from independent breweries, or the traditional cider. Unmissable. ♨Q❀◖≠♣P

Boar's Head
Wigan Road, WN6 0AD
(on A49, halfway between Wigan and Standish)
🕒 11.30-3, 5.30-11; 11.30-11 Sat; 12-3, 7-10.30 Sun
☎ (01942) 749747
Burtonwood Bitter; guest beer Ⓗ
Built in 1271 as a coaching inn, it is thought to be the second oldest pub in England. It divides into several distinct areas, plus a small conservatory-style function room. The open log fire complements the oak beams and array of whisky jugs; motorcycle pictures adorn the walls. Outside is a lovely private garden with a patio and a well-kept bowling green. ♨⯅❀◖♣P

Dog & Partridge
33 School Lane, WN6 0TG
🕒 1-11; 12-10.30 Sun
☎ (01257) 401218
Tetley Mild, Bitter; guest beers Ⓗ
Popular drinkers' pub offering several guest beers, mostly from micro-breweries. One central bar serves both sides of the pub; one side is popular for football and rugby matches on TV, while the other is quieter. Definitely the best pub in Standish for a good selection of interesting beers, it hosts an annual charity beer festival. ♣P

Horseshoe Inn
1 Wigan Road, WN6 0BG
🕒 12-11; 12-10.30 Sun
☎ (01257) 400716
Burtonwood Bitter; guest beer Ⓗ
Recently renovated and now open plan, it has definitely benefited from its facelift. TVs and snob screens are much in evidence, with darts and pool available at either end of the pub. Popular with diners, it can get busy at weekends; the home-cooked food represents good value. Children are welcome until 9pm. ❀◖P

Arden Arms ☆
23 Millgate, SK1 2LX (behind Asda)
🕒 12-11; 12-10.30 Sun
☎ (0161) 480 2185 website: www.ardenarms.com
Robinson's Hatters, Best Bitter, Ⓗ
Old Tom (winter), Ⓖ **seasonal beers** Ⓗ
Grade II listed, this pub warrants a visit for the building alone: note the fine bar, tiled lobby, grandfather clocks, two real fires and the splendid snug (only accessible through the serving area). The food is of a very high standard (the licensees formerly ran a restaurant) – the four or five specials always include a vegetarian option. The cobbled courtyard testifies to the Arden's past as a coaching inn; there are mortuary slabs in

the cellar for those whose journey finished earlier than expected. 🏚️🍴◑P

Armoury
31 Shaw Heath, SK3 8BD
❂ 11-11; 12-10.30 Sun
☎ (0161) 477 3711
Robinson's Hatters, Best Bitter, Ⓗ Old Tom Ⓖ
Of the three rooms, the best room, the lounge, is fitted out in a muted rustic decor, with much 1930s light oak, especially the understated bar. Photos of old Stockport and a beaten copper fireplace provide interest. The other two rooms are more simply decorated as befits their status – a vault, with darts and Old Tom on bar stillage and a fairly spartan snug. The glass in the doors features the room name and a pair of bells, from former owners' Bells Brewery's time.
🏚️◑🖢♣♠

Blossoms
2 Buxton Road, Heaviley, SK2 6NU (at A6/Bramhall Lane jct)
❂ 12-3, 5-11; 12-11 Sat; 12-10.30 Sun
☎ (0161) 477 2397
Robinson's Hatters, Best Bitter, Ⓗ Old Tom Ⓖ
Cosy, multi-roomed Victorian pub, comprising a drinking lobby and three rooms: one given over to pool; a tap room with ornate coloured glass windows and a pleasant rear smoke room featuring a carved wooden fireplace. Together, they create a relaxing atmosphere. The lunchtime food, served Monday–Saturday, may include home-made pies. Blossoms was local CAMRA's Pub of the Year in 1998.
Q◑♣P

Boars Head
2 Vernon Street, SK1 1TY
❂ 11-11; 12-10.30 Sun
☎ (0161) 480 3918
Samuel Smith OBB Ⓗ
Victorian pub in Stockport's historic market square. Four rooms lead off from a central bar area and outside there are five tables. The pub can be very busy on market days (Tue, Fri and Sat). A recent high quality refurbishment has, remarkably, resulted in the reinstatement of some internal walls. Very keen beer prices and a normally bustling, vibrant atmosphere add to its appeal. No food is served on Monday.
🏚️🖢◑🖢♿≠

Crown ✅
154 Heaton Lane, SK4 1AR (just off Mersey Square)
❂ 12-3 (not Mon-Wed), 6-11; 12-11 Fri & Sat; 7-10.30 Sun
☎ (0161) 429 0549
Jennings Bitter; guest beers Ⓗ
Still Stockport's number one pub for choice and quality; nine handpumps dispense an array of guest beers, with one each reserved for the products of Bank Top, Whim, Pictish and Phoenix breweries, and another dedicated to a guest mild. A changing guest cider is sold on gravity. This attractive pub retains much of its Victorian layout and fittings, and is undergoing loving restoration by the licensees. It is becoming well established on the local music scene, hosting a range of styles.
🖢◑◑🖢≠♠⚥✁

Little Jack Horner's
28 Lord Street, SK1 3NA (off A6)
❂ 11.30-11 (11-4, 7-11 Sat); 12-3, 7-10.30 Sun
☎ (0161) 477 3086
Camerons Strongarm; Marston's Pedigree; Tetley Bitter; Worthington's Bitter Ⓗ
Historic building set among 1960s and '70s office development. The three rooms are on separate levels: the bar and snug are on the middle tier; a large upper section is more modern and rustic, while the bottom part is a couples' meeting area before moving on. Many rare prints of old Stockport hang on the walls. One of the town's more haunted pubs, the ghosts of a number of former licensees reputedly make appearances. Popular with local office staff at lunchtimes, weekday meals are served. ◑≠

Olde Vic
1 Chatham Street, Edgeley, SK3 9HE
❂ 5 (7 Sat)-11; 7-10.30 Sun
☎ (0161) 480 2410
Beer range varies Ⓗ
Small, one-roomed pub run with irrepressible style. A tightly-run ship (strictly no swearing) underpins the easy-going atmosphere where no-one is a stranger for long. Four changing guest beers are always stocked and the impressive pump clip-bedecked ceilings testify to the choice available. Westons Special Vintage cider completes the handpump range. The enclosed patio, a suntrap in summer, is almost as big as the pub and is a welcome venue in the warmer months. Beware of the cat! 🏚️🖢≠♠

Olde Woolpack
70 Brinksway, SK3 0BY (on A560)
❂ 11.30-3, 5-11; 11.30-11 Fri; 11.30-4.30, 7.30-11 Sat; 12-10.30 Sun
☎ (0161) 476 0688
Theakston Best Bitter, Cool Cask; guest beers Ⓗ
Rescued from dereliction in the late 1980s, its fortunes started to turn under the present licensee. It has gone from strength to strength, majoring on quality cask ales and good home-cooked food – both much appreciated by the occupants of Stockport's landmark blue pyramid that dwarfs the pub. The Woolpack retains much of its original layout of front and rear lounges, drinking lobby and well-used vault. It has won a clutch of CAMRA awards, both local and regional. Q🖢◑♣P

Pineapple
159 Heaton Lane, SK4 1AQ (100 yds from A6 at Debenhams)
❂ 11.30-11; 12-10.30 Sun
☎ (0161) 480 3221
Robinson's Hatters, Best Bitter, Ⓟ seasonal beers Ⓗ
Originally a coaching house dating from 1822, the building later became HQ for the Stockport Botanical Society. Bells Brewery turned it into a pub in 1901. When you walk to the bar you may feel that you have already had one too many, but it is only the undulating floor. There is a choice of three rooms; the front lounge displays innumerable commemorative plates. Even many Stopfordians have yet to discover the 'Chunky' and it is time they did. No food is served on Sunday. ◑≠♣

Railway

1 Avenue Street, SK1 2BZ (off A560)
🕐 12-11; 12-10.30 Sun
☎ (0161) 429 6062
Porter Dark Mild, Floral Dance, Bitter, Railway Sleeper, seasonal beers; guest beers Ⓗ

There is something for everyone in this friendly one-roomed pub. Porter's wide range of distinctive, reasonably-priced beers is complemented by guests from micro-breweries, an extensive choice of foreign bottled beers, and a varying chilled cider. A hard-working licensee and friendly staff have won the pub numerous awards, including regional CAMRA Pub of the Year and national runner-up in 2002. It draws a good mix of customers. Appetising home-cooked food is served Monday–Saturday.
🏠🌑♣🕯

Red Bull

14 Middle Hillgate, SK1 3AY
🕐 11.30-11; 12-3, 7-10.30 Sun
☎ (0161) 480 2087
Robinson's Hatters, Best Bitter Ⓗ

The entrance to this whitewashed building is up some well-worn steps. A breathtaking interior, featuring dark wood, is served by a large three-sided bar, and has the look and feel of a country pub. Various areas include a traditional stone-flagged snug with pew seating and a plusher lounge snug with an open fire and its own bar for busy times. Mirrors, brass ornaments and drawings of old Stockport abound. The pub is popular with Robinson's directors, especially at lunchtime for the weekday meals.
🏚Q🌑◑⇋P

Tiviot

8 Tiviot Dale, SK1 1TA
🕐 11-11; 12-4 Sun
☎ (0161) 480 4109
Robinson's Hatters, Best Bitter, Ⓟ Old Tom Ⓖ

Town-centre pub run by one of the area's longest-serving licensees, with a homely, down-to-earth ambience. The lounge bears photos recording Tiviot Dale over the years since the war. The games room sports an aged table football game, while the corridor joining the bar with the dining room features line drawings of some of the gems of the local pub scene. The pub is busiest at lunchtime when good value food is served in the dining room (no meals Sun).
◑🏠♣P🍴

STONECLOUGH

Market Street Tavern

131 Market Street, Radcliffe, M26 1HF
(on A667)
🕐 12-11; 12-10.30 Sun
☎ (01204) 572985
Tetley Bitter; guest beer Ⓗ

Busy main road pub with a lounge and vault. The landlord works hard to keep a tidy pub, with well-kept beers; Flat Cap from Bank Top Brewery is a regular guest. Both beers are very keenly priced. There is a drinking area at the front and parking at the rear. A free juke box all day, a wide-screen TV and a Monday evening quiz add to its appeal; well worth a visit.
🏠⇋(Kearsley) ♣P

SWINTON

Football

33 Swinton Hall Road, M27 4BL
🕐 11-11; 12-10.30 Sun
☎ (0161) 950 8178
Boddingtons Bitter; Tetley Dark Mild, Bitter Ⓗ

This Victorian red-brick pub is named after the game of rugby league football – Swinton Lions' ground once stood nearby. The two front rooms are more or less original, but the back was partially opened out some years ago. Extremely good value lunches attract a loyal brand of older customers and the pub is busy in the evenings, too, drawing a mixed clientele. Q🏠◑🕀⇋♣

White Lion

242 Manchester Road, M27 4TS
(at A6/A572 jct)
🕐 12-11; 12-10.30 Sun
☎ (0161) 288 0434
Robinson's Dark Mild, Best Bitter, Snowdon, seasonal beers Ⓗ

At the back of this late 18th-century pub is an annexe featuring photographs and other memorabilia of Swinton Lions RL team. The link goes back to when the ground was just across the road (it has since moved three times). Swinton Folk Club also meets in this room on Monday. Recently extended into an old cottage site next door, the rest of the pub consists of a lounge, vault and new snug, together with a modern kitchen. Children are welcome until 6.30pm.
Q🛏🏠🕀♣P

White Swan

186 Worsley Road, M27 5SN
🕐 12-11; 12-10.30 Sun
☎ (0161) 794 1504
Holt Mild, Bitter, seasonal beers Ⓗ

This 1920s building reflects much of the earlier style of Holt's pubs of the 1900s, but with wood panelling replacing the ceramic tiling. In the 1990s the entrance was altered and two rooms were partially combined. The three remaining rooms – a vault, a lounge and a large function room at the back – remain unaltered. The mild handpump is in the vault, so be sure to ask for traditional at the other two bars. The family room is open on Sunday until 5pm.
Q🛏🏠🕀♣P

TIMPERLEY

Quarry Bank Inn

Bloomsbury Lane, WA15 6TU
🕐 11.30-11; 12-10.30 Sun
☎ (0161) 903 9483
Hydes Mild, Bitter, seasonal beers Ⓗ

Thriving, popular, suburban pub on the edge of the old village centre. A well-used vault contrasts with a quieter lounge and restaurant area. It boasts a floodlit crown bowling green, an unusual asset in an area where almost all pubs once had one. It is reputed to have the highest beer sales of any Hydes' pubs. Q🏠◑🕀♣P

TYLDESLEY

Half Moon

115-117 Elliot Street, M29 8FL
🕐 11-11; 12-10.30 Sun
☎ (01942) 873206

Holt Bitter; guest beers Ⓗ
Local bar run by a local landlord, who welcomes visitors. This long-established Holt's outlet also stocks guest beers. The bar has various seating areas, with a quiet lounge to the side and a pleasant garden to the rear. Well worth a visit. ⊛

Mort Arms
235-237 Elliot Street, M29 8DG
🕔 12-11; 12-10.30 Sun
☎ (01942) 883481
Holt Mild, Bitter Ⓗ
Popular, edge-of-town local. Rebuilt in the late 1930s, the front entrance leads to a traditional vault and the lounge, complete with bowed bar, polished oak panels and etched glass. Comfortable seating around the lounge accommodates participants for the regular quiz nights; old pictures of Tyldesley adorn the walls. ⊟♣

UPPERMILL

Cross Keys
OL3 6LW (off A670)
🕔 11-11; 12-10.30 Sun
☎ (01457) 874626
Lees GB Mild, Bitter, Moonraker, seasonal beers Ⓗ
This attractive 18th-century stone building with exposed beams throughout, overlooks Saddleworth church. The bar boasts a stone-flagged floor and a Yorkshire range. The centre for many activities, including mountain rescue, a clay pigeon club, Saddleworth Runners and the Garland Girls, it is busy during annual events, such as the charity beer walk (June) and the Saddleworth Rushcart Festival (Aug). It hosts folk nights (Wed and Sun) in the barn. Good value, home-cooked food is served until 7pm. Children's certificate.
🏛Q⌘⊛◖⊟♣P

Waggon Inn
34 High Street, OL3 6HR
🕔 11.30-11; 12-10.30 Sun
☎ (01457) 872376
Robinson's Cumbria Way, Best Bitter, seasonal beers Ⓗ
Mid-19th-century stone pub in a picturesque village, opposite Saddleworth Museum and the Huddersfield Narrow Canal. With a central bar, three rooms and a restaurant, it now offers high quality en-suite B&B. The venue for many local events, including the Whit Friday brass band contest, the July Saddleworth Folk Festival, and in August, the 'Yanks' weekend, live music is performed regularly on Friday evening. Good value, home-cooked food includes 'early bird' specials.
Q⊛🚪◖⊟Å⇌♣P

WARDLEY

Morning Star
520 Manchester Road, M27 9QW (on A6)
🕔 12-11; 12-10.30 Sun
☎ (0161) 794 4927
Holt Mild, Bitter Ⓗ
This Edwardian building, situated between Swinton and Walkden, is a popular community pub. To the right of the central bar is a small lounge which leads through to the large main lounge. To the left is a traditional vault which is the hub of the

social activities, including men's and ladies' darts teams and a dominoes team. There is usually live entertainment on Saturday evening and excellent value home-made lunches are available Monday–Friday.
⊛◖⊟⇌(Moorside) ♣P

WESTHOUGHTON

Robert Shaw ⊘
34-40 Market Street, BL5 3AN (near town hall)
🕔 10-11; 12-10.30 Sun
☎ (01942) 844110
Cains Mild; Courage Directors; Greene King Abbot; Shepherd Neame Spitfire Ⓗ
Former supermarket, dramatically converted into a modern, large open-plan ground-floor pub with a small drinking area (and toilets) upstairs. Despite many objections (mainly from other publicans), this Wetherspoon's pub has hit this small, historic town by storm since its recent opening. Always busy, it offers many special promotions on both food and drink.
Q⌘◖⅊⇌(Daisy Hill/Westhoughton) P✗

WHITEFIELD

Coach & Horses
71 Bury Old Road, M45 6TB (on A665)
🕔 12-11; 12-10.30 Sun
☎ (0161) 798 8897
Holt Mild, Bitter Ⓗ
Traditional multi-roomed local that still bears many of its original characteristics. Built in 1830, it derives its name from its use as a stopping-place on the Burnley–Manchester mail run. It also served as a stop on the daily omnibus service between Manchester and Bury. There is much local debate as to whether it belongs to Whitefield or Prestwich, as it stands on the boundary. It comprises a tap room, snug and lounge.
Q⊛⊖(Besses o' th' Barn) ♣P

Eagle & Child
Higher Lane, M45 7EY (at A665/A56 jct)
🕔 12-11; 12-10.30 Sun
☎ (0161) 766 3024
Holt Mild, Bitter Ⓗ
Large black and white pub set back from the road. It has an L-shaped main bar and a cosy side room. The well-kept bowling green at the rear is popular in summer. The building dates from 1936, replacing the original Eagle & Child, built in 1802, which was the first hostelry on Higher Lane. The other five pubs that served this lane are long gone. Once a Whitefield Brewery pub, it has been a Holt's house since 1907.
⊛⊖(Besses o' th' Barn) P

WIGAN

Anvil ⊘
Dorning Street, WN1 1ND (by bus station)
🕔 11-11; 12-10.30 Sun
☎ (01942) 239444
Caledonian Deuchars IPA; Hydes Mild, Bitter; guest beers Ⓗ
There is a very modern feel to this town-centre pub that lies between the town's bus and railway stations, and in the shadow of the parish church. Local CAMRA Pub of the Year 2003, its varied guest beers supplement the regular Hydes' range. A wide-screen TV

caters for sports aficionados in their own room. ⊛◖≼ (North Western/Wallgate)

Black Bull
140 Hardybutts, WN1 1NE
🕐 12.30-3, 7-11; 12.30-11 Fri & Sat; 12-10.30 Sun
☎ (01942) 243452
Tetley Bitter Ⓗ
Small, friendly local, tucked away from the main road, but only 10 minutes' walk from the town centre. Televised sport is always available; the games area is covered in local sporting colours. An open-plan conversion allows everyone to enjoy the Saturday evening live music. Children welcome. ♣

Brocket Arms ⊘
Mesnes Road, WN1 2DD
🕐 11-11; 12-10.30 Sun
☎ (01942) 820372
Courage Directors; Shepherd Neame Spitfire; Theakston Best Bitter; guest beers Ⓗ
This former small hotel has been restored to its original use and now also offers function rooms. The 1950s exterior opens into a light, airy, open-plan room decorated in a contemporary style. It is carefully divided to offer an almost separate no-smoking and family room (until 7pm). Intimate booths with fixed benches, together with flexible seating, accommodate various party sizes. An outdoor terrace is open in good weather. ⊱⊨◖▯P⅄

Moon under Water ⊘
5-7a Market Place, WN1 1PE
🕐 11-11; 12-10.30 Sun
☎ (01942) 323437
Courage Directors; Shepherd Neame Spitfire; Theakston Best Bitter Ⓗ
Wigan's first and best Wetherspoon's is situated at the very centre of town. A former Halifax Building Society office, a tailor's shop and photography store were all knocked into one large pub. Fully opening, full-length windows create an alfresco atmosphere in sunny weather. Very busy at weekends, a side entrance opens on to the no-smoking area, via the Wiend (Wigan's historic shopping street).
Q◖▯℥≼ (North Western/Wallgate) ⅄

Orwell
Wigan Pier, Wallgate, WN3 4EU
🕐 11.30-3, 5-11; 11.30-11 Fri & Sat; 12-10.30 Sun
☎ (01942) 323034 website: www.wiganpier.co.uk
Beer range varies Ⓗ
Converted Victorian cotton warehouse, on the Leeds–Liverpool Canal, approximately 10 minutes' walk from the JJB Stadium (home of Wigan Athletic and the Warriors). The menu includes a large selection of home-made soups and hot or cold snacks; there is a no-smoking dining area. This true free house is a former local CAMRA Pub of the Year and offers the widest range of beers from micro-breweries in the area. A cobbled area by the canal is used by drinkers in summer. ⊛◖℥≼ (North Western/Wallgate) ♣P

Silverwell
117 Darlington Street East, WN1 3BS
🕐 12-11; 12-10.30 Sun
☎ (01942) 243648
Holt Mild, Bitter Ⓗ
Roomy pub that has been tastefully returned to its 'boozer' status. 10 minutes'

walk from town centre, pictures of old Wigan adorn the walls. Sport is shown regularly on TV; live music is performed on Saturday evening. A small central bar serves all areas of the pub. ⊛◖▯♣P

Swan & Railway
80 Wallgate, WN1 1BA
🕐 12 (11 Sat)-11; 12-10.30 Sun
☎ (01942) 495032
Banks's Original, Bitter; Mansfield Dark Mild; guest beers Ⓗ
Classic, largely unspoilt boozer, saved from unsympathetic treatment by the successful campaign of the local CAMRA branch. The mosaic porch and the tiled bar are particular highlights here, but also of interest are the attractive stained glass inserts in the vault, commemorating local locomotives, and the numerous Victorian still life prints. A pool table now occupies the front snug.
⊨◖≼ (North Western/Wallgate) ♣

Victoria ⊘
438 Wilmslow Road, M20 3BW (on B5093)
🕐 11.30-11; 12-10.30 Sun
☎ (0161) 448 1083
Hydes Mild, Bitter, Jekyll's Gold, Ⓗ **seasonal beers** Ⓖ
With its well-lit brick and stone exterior and etched windows, the Victoria provides a welcome sight. The slightly different floor levels inside are evidence that it was originally two shops in the 19th century. Each area has its own character: the front lounge displaying old photos of Hydes Brewery; the rear lounge with plush leather seating. Lunches are served Saturday and Sunday. ⊛◖♣

Davenport Arms (Thief's Neck)
550 Chester Road, SK7 1PS (on A5102)
🕐 11-3.30, 5.15-11; 11-11 Sat; 12-3, 7-10.30 Sun
☎ (0161) 439 2435
Robinson's Hatters, Best Bitter, Old Tom (winter), **seasonal beers** Ⓗ
A real pub among many identikit dining venues, run by the same family for over 70 years. Its mellow red-brick exterior features impressive floral displays, while inside a variety of cosy rooms includes a traditional tap and a no-smoking snug (children welcome at lunchtime). The excellent food is mostly home made, with some adventurous specials. There is an attractive garden. ⋈Q℥⊛◖▯♣P⅄

White Crow
Chorley Road, WN1 2XL
🕐 12-2.30, 5.30-11; 11-11 Fri & Sat; 12-10.30 Sun
☎ (01257) 474344
Boddingtons Bitter; Theakston Cool Cask; guest beers Ⓗ
Commodious pub, refurbished in olde-worlde style, with a games area and large-screen TV at one end, a no-smoking dining area and children's room at the other. It serves an extensive menu and has earned a deserved reputation for its food. Close to Worthington Lakes, the pub has a large car park and children's play area next to the stables at the rear. ⋈℥⊛◖▯℥P⅄

MERSEYSIDE

BARNSTON

Fox & Hounds
107 Barnston Road, CH61 1BW
🕐 11-11; 12-10.30 Sun
☎ (0151) 648 7685
Theakston Best Bitter; Old Peculier; Webster's Bitter; guest beers Ⓗ
Built in 1911 on the site of an 18th-century pub, the Fox & Hounds has a lounge, a snug, and a traditional tiled bar. Plenty of memorabilia, old photos and brasses add to the country atmosphere. Guest beers give good support to micro-brewers, and home-cooked pub food is served. The flowery courtyard makes a welcome resting point during the local CAMRA summer pubs walk. ♨Q♿⚅♫◖⊟♣P

BEBINGTON

Traveller's Rest
169 Mount Road, CH63 8PJ
🕐 12-11; 12-10.30 Sun
☎ (0151) 608 2988
Boddingtons Bitter; Cains Bitter; Flowers IPA; Greene King Abbot; Taylor Landlord; guest beers Ⓗ
Reputedly over 300 years old, this cosy pub is decorated throughout with brasses and bric-à-brac. All beers are served from a central bar feeding two other rooms (one no-smoking), the beer list regularly features micro-brewery beers. A winner of many local CAMRA awards, its licensee was the 2003 Wirral Publican of the Year and regularly supports local charities. Popular
334

for its award-winning lunches (not served Sun), the Monday night quiz is well attended. Q◖⚅♿✄

BIRKENHEAD

Crown Ale House ⊘
128 Conway Street, CH41 6JE
(opp. main bus terminus)
🕐 11-11; 12-10.30 Sun
☎ (0151) 647 0589
Cains Bitter; Greenalls Mild; John Smith's Bitter; guest beers Ⓗ
Large, listed building on the fringe of the shopping centre, a local CAMRA award-winning pub which over the last decade has become the town's best-known real ale outlet. After a degree of neglect, the present licensee has revitalised the pub and made the most of its fine fixtures and fittings. A bar, lounge and rear lounge are all served by a central area. An extensive menu is served from noon to 6pm daily. There is a large enclosed garden and usually four guest ales are available. ♿◖⊟⇌ (Conway Pk) ⊖♣P

Old Colonial ⊘
167 Bridge Street, CH41 1AY
🕐 12-11; 12-10.30 Sun
☎ (0151) 650 1110
Cains Mild, Bitter, FA; guest beers Ⓗ
Refurbished Cains pub adjacent to the Tram Museum garage: trams run from Woodside bus and ferry terminus on bank holidays and weekends and stop near the pub. Live jazz bands play every Thursday. A pool table

and dartboard are provided. Set meals and specials are available every lunchtime (including Sun), and 5–7 Monday–Friday. There is a raised decking area for outdoor drinking. ❀◖≉(Hamilton Sq) P

Stork Hotel ☆
41-43 Price Street, CH41 6JN
🕐 11.30-11; 12-10.30 Sun
☎ (0151) 647 7506
Beer range varies Ⓗ

Wirral CAMRA Pub of the Year 2002 and 2003, a superb example of extravagant but practical architecture, it rightly features in the CAMRA National Inventory of Pub Interiors. Built in 1840, it has many original fittings, including an ornate circular bar with leaded stained glass and lighting. This street-corner pub has a colourful ceramic exterior and wonderful mosaic floor. The 'newsroom' with its original bell pushes, etched door and windows is a no-smoking area. This is a must for traditional pub lovers. Four ever-changing guests are available. Food is served Monday–Friday (12–2 and 4.30–6.30). Children are welcome until 9pm.
❀◖ ◲⊖(Hamilton Sq/Conway Pk) ♣⊬

CROSBY

Crow's Nest
63 Victoria Road, L23 7XY
🕐 11.30-11; 12-10.30 Sun
☎ (0151) 924 6953
Cains Bitter; guest beers Ⓗ

Charming, small pub which is a Grade II listed building; a popular local with a cosy bar, tiny snug and comfortable lounge. The interior has several interesting features, including a tiled floor on entry and original etched windows. Friendly staff ensure a warm welcome for locals and visitors alike. Tables are placed outside the pub for summer drinking. A list of forthcoming beers is displayed; you are sure to want to return to this suburban gem.
Q❀◲≉(Blundellsands/Crosby) P

Stamps Wine Bar/Bistro
4 Crown Buildings, L23 5SR
🕐 10.30-11; 12-10.30 Sun
☎ (0151) 286 2662 website: www.stampsbistro.co.uk
Beer range varies Ⓗ

This small bar has a community atmosphere. It has built a reputation for good beer and has increased its range to four ales. There are two levels. The upstairs lounge holds poetry evenings on Monday. A successful mini beer festival is held annually. This is a lively place which also has Internet access. Last year, Stamps was runner-up for a national music award for the variety and quality of the live performances it provides.
◖ ⅋≉(Blundellsands/Crosby)

EASTHAM

Tap
1A Ferry Road, CH62 0AU
🕐 12 (11.30 Sat)-11; 12-10.30 Sun
☎ (0151) 327 6089
Burtonwood Bitter; guest beers Ⓗ

Formerly known as the Pier bar, and not to be confused with the neighbouring Ferry Hotel, the Tap is situated below Eastham Country Park by the old pier. Enjoy the superb views across the Mersey from Liverpool centre to the airport. Ships using the Manchester Ship Canal pass within a few yards of the front door. This small, friendly pub attracts a wide range of customers including walkers, families visiting the country park, and bikers (particularly Sun eve). ⚏❀♣P

EGREMONT

Brighton
133 Brighton Street, CH44 8DT
(opp. Wallasey town hall)
🕐 11.30-11; 12-10.30 Sun
☎ (0151) 638 1163
Cains Bitter Ⓗ

This very impressive listed sandstone building is over 120 years old and stands on the main route from Birkenhead to New Brighton. It offers two lounges and a public bar, all served from a central bar. There is a separate TV room. At the entrance to the middle lounge there are two attractive, coloured leaded glass panels which are thought to be original. The pub boasts successful darts and pool teams, plus a Crown Green bowls team. ◲⅃♣

FORMBY

Freshfield Hotel
1A Massams Lane, L37 7BD
🕐 12-11; 12-10.30 Sun
☎ (01704) 874871 website: www.blemon.demon.co.uk
Boddingtons Bitter; Castle Eden Bitter; Flowers IPA; Moorhouses Black Cat; Taylor Landlord; guest beers Ⓗ

The Freshfield is 15 minutes' walk from the National Trust area of Formby Point, one of the last strongholds of the red squirrel in the UK. It always has 12 real ales available and has won many local CAMRA awards for the quality and variety of its beers. Smaller brewers are favoured for guest beers. The lounge area is open-plan, with a public bar at the side. Wood floors and a real fire add character. Lunches are served Monday–Friday. ⚏Q◖◲≉(Freshfield) ♣P

GREASBY

Irby Mill ✔
Mill Lane, CH49 3NT
🕐 12-11; 12-10.30 Sun
☎ (0151) 678 2565
Cains Bitter, FA; Taylor Landlord; Theakston Best Bitter; Wells Bombardier; guest beers Ⓗ

Traditional country pub built on the site of an ancient mill, a favourite haunt of bikers and hikers in the 1920s. Two rooms are linked by a narrow bar full of regulars and friendly banter. A real haven with 13 handpumps, it now hosts regular beer festivals. It was awarded Birkenhead's Pub of the Festival 2000 and the industry's Cask Pub of the Year 2001. Popular with country

INDEPENDENT BREWERIES

Beecham's St Helens
Cains Liverpool
Cambrinus Knowsley
Liverpool Liverpool
Wapping Liverpool

walkers, close to Royden Park, this superb pub, with no slot machines or music, promises a warm welcome. Q✿◑P

HESWALL

Dee View
Dee View Road, CH60 0DH
✪ 12-11; 12-10.30 Sun
☎ (0151) 342 2320
Boddingtons Bitter; Cains Bitter; Taylor Best Bitter; guest beers Ⓗ
Traditional, homely pub built in the 1800s. The single bar offers a friendly atmosphere and lively weekly quiz night. Good home-cooked food is served along with six handpumped ales. A changing guest beer ensures micro-brewers are well supported. It sits on a hairpin bend opposite the war memorial and features on the local CAMRA summer pubs walk. ✿◑♣P

Johnny Pye
Pye Road, CH60 0DB (opp. bus station)
✪ 11-11; 12-10.30 Sun
☎ (0151) 342 8215
Banks's Original, Bitter; Camerons Bitter Ⓗ
Lively, modern Banks's pub, named after a local 1920s entrepreneur, John Pye, who operated a local omnibus company. The bright, open-plan interior with polished wood floor, features a selection of pictures of historic Heswall. The raised lounge seating area is L-shaped with a similar separate section set aside for non-smokers. It provides large-screen TV for sports and can be busy during the more popular football matches. A pub quiz is held on Thursday evening. No food is served on Sunday. ✿◑♿♣P⌿

HIGHTOWN

Hightown Hotel ✪
Lower Alt Road, L38 0BA
✪ 11-11; 12-10.30 Sun
☎ (0151) 929 2650
Cains Bitter; Fuller's London Pride; Greene King Old Speckled Hen; Shepherd Neame Spitfire; Worthington's Bitter Ⓗ
The Hightown Hotel is a real ale oasis in this growing village that has developed by the mouth of the River Alt among the dunes of the north-west coast. A large, lively pub, it is perfectly placed for walkers coming up the coast from Crosby. For the lazier drinker, it is immediately adjacent to Hightown railway station. ⛟◑♿⇌P

KINGS MOSS

Collier's Arms
37 Pimbo Road, WA11 8RD
(off B5205, Rainford Road, near Billinge)
✪ 12-11; 12-10.30 Sun
☎ (01744) 892894
Beer range varies Ⓗ
Built in 1850, this traditional pub is situated in the tiny hamlet of Kings Moss, near Billinge. The atmosphere is warm and friendly; there are comfortable dining/lounge areas and a separate public bar with an open fire. The pub usually offers three guest beers and good home-cooked food is available lunchtime and evening and all day on Sunday. The pub's name originates from the time when local miners

collected their wages here during bad winter weather. ♨✿◑Ⓓ♿♣P⌿

LISCARD

Saddle
30 Withens Lane, Wallasey, CH44 1DE
✪ 11-11; 12-10.30 Sun
☎ (0151) 639 2534
Greene King IPA; John Smith's Bitter; guest beers Ⓗ
Small, welcoming pub close to the local shopping area (Liscard) and even closer to the local police station! The licensee thinks that the pub was once originally two cottages and could be over 150 years old. The guest beers rotate weekly and are usually from micros. The new conservatory, built at the side of the pub, caters for the increasing number of diners the pub attracts.
✿◑Ⓓ♿♣P

Stanley's
83 Seaview Road, CH45 4LE
(between Liscard shops and Asda superstore)
✪ 11-11; 12-10.30 Sun
☎ (0151) 639 9736
McEwan 80/-; Theakston Cool Cask; guest beers Ⓗ
A mixture of church pews, bare brick walls and farmhouse kitchen tables give this pub, built eight years ago, a characterful yet homely feel. One of the area's best real ale outlets, with appeal across all age groups, it can get very busy especially at weekends. Four changing guests, mainly from micros, an always interesting range of daily specials from around the world (kangaroo sausages anyone?) and a popular Monday evening quiz, ensure there is something for everybody.
✿◑Ⓓ♿P

LIVERPOOL: ALLERTON

Inn in the Park (Allerton Hall)
Clarke Gardens, Springwood Avenue, L25 7UN
✪ 11.30-11; 12-10.30 Sun
☎ (0151) 494 2664
Cains Bitter; Marston's Pedigree; guest beers Ⓗ
This is an excellent family pub. An enjoyable walk around Clarke Gardens, where animals are kept, will build up your thirst. The pub is part of the Premier Lodge chain, but does not yet offer accommodation. Millers Kitchen meals are available. There are up to four ever-changing guest beers, usually from independent breweries.
⛟✿◑♿⇌ (Allerton) P

Storrsdale
43-47 Storrsdale Road, L18 7JY (250 yds from jct of B5180 Mather Ave and Storrsdale Rd)
✪ 3 (12 Sat)-11; 12-10.30 Sun
☎ (0151) 724 3464
Taylor Landlord Ⓗ
Friendly local pub with a separate large wood-panelled lounge and public bar. There is a quiz on Wednesday and a live artist performance on Saturday evening. The pub has a dartboard in the bar and a juke box. Original leaded windows are typical of the 1930s construction. The pub attracts a mix of locals and thirsty sportsmen from the nearby playing fields drawn by the relaxed atmosphere and good beer. There is a small

yard with tables and benches to the side of the pub for outdoor drinking.
❄☕≉(Mossley Hill) ♣

ANFIELD

Strawberry Tavern
Breckfield Road South, L6 5DR
✪ 12-11; 12-10.30 Sun
☎ (0151) 260 6158
Oakwell Barnsley Bitter, Old Tom Ⓗ
Welcoming suburban pub with a good atmosphere, which has reopened after a lengthy closure. The pub provides a rare local outlet for Barnsley's Oakwell Brewery. Formerly open-plan, the pub has been partitioned to form a lounge and separate bar area, which has a well-used dartboard. Situated off West Derby Road the pub provides a handy stop-off point if travelling to Liverpool Football Club. ❄☕☕&♣P

CHILDWALL

Childwall Abbey
Score Lane, L16 5EY (corner Childwall Abbey Rd)
✪ 11-11; 12-10.30 Sun
☎ (0151) 722 5293
Burtonwood Bitter, Top Hat; guest beer Ⓗ
This 17th-century Grade I listed building was never an abbey and looks more like a castle. Unlike other Burtonwood pubs in the area, this one remains committed to real ale. The guest beer changes monthly. There are some great weekday food offers. Meals are served from 12–2 and 5–8.15 and up to 6.45 on Sunday. Sky Sports can be watched in the bar. The pub has seven guest rooms.
⌂❄☕☕♣P⊟

CITY CENTRE

Augustus John
Peach Street, L3 5TX
✪ 11.30-11; closed Sat & Sun
☎ (0151) 794 5507
Cains Bitter; guest beer Ⓗ
Large, modern open-plan pub located in the heart of Liverpool University campus next to Blackwells bookshop. Popular with students and university staff, it can get busy at times. Cains Bitter, Tetley Bitter and a constantly rotating guest beer are offered and lunchtime sandwiches and light snacks are available. A pool table and bar football table provide the usual student distractions, together with the music which can get loud at times. Karaoke night is held on Wednesday. ❄≉(Lime St) ⊖(Central) ♣

Baltic Fleet
33 Wapping, L1 8DQ
✪ 12 (11.30 Fri & Sat)-11; 12-10.30 Sun
☎ (0151) 709 3116
Cains Mild, Bitter; Wapping Bitter, Baltic Extra, seasonal beers; guest beers Ⓗ
A Grade II listed building, located close to the Albert Dock. This 'flat-iron' pub not only physically resembles a ship but the interior is adorned with nautical memorabilia. The excellent range of innovative house beers from the Wapping Brewery has enhanced the reputation of the pub, it sustains an enviable combination of top quality ales and delicious food. The Sunday roasts are first-rate and the Saturday brunches are rapidly achieving a legendary

status. The CAMRA Pub of the Year award in 2000 was well deserved.
⌂☕◑⊖(James St) ●P⚲

Cambridge
51-53 Mulberry Street, L7 7EE
✪ 11.30-11; closed weekends out of summer term; 12-10.30 Sun
☎ (0151) 708 7150
Burtonwood Bitter, Top Hat; guest beer Ⓗ
Small pub within the precincts of Liverpool University. An attractive Burtonwood tied house, popular with students and university staff, the pub has a cosmopolitan and friendly atmosphere, and tends to be bustling during term time. In addition to one rotating guest beer, good value basic bar meals are available at lunchtime. However, the pub's speciality is Sunday breakfast. A popular quiz is held on Sunday evening.
❄☕≉(Lime St) ⊖(Central) ♣

Carnarvon Castle
5 Tarleton Street, L1 1DS
✪ 11-11 (8 Mon & Tue); 12-6 Sun
☎ (0151) 708 0516
Cains Mild, Bitter; guest beer Ⓗ
City-centre pub close to Central Station, just off Church Street, in the main shopping area. It has a small snug area to the rear and a long, narrow front bar. The many display cases contain collections of bric-à-brac, particularly model cars. Although rather crowded during the day with shoppers and regular customers, the welcome is very warm and friendly. Bar snacks are available, so enjoy a lunchtime 'toastie' or one of the freshly-made sandwiches sold all day.
⌂Q☕≉(Lime St) ⊖(Central)

Cornmarket
Old Ropery, L2 7NT (off Fenwick St)
✪ 11.30 (7.30 Sat)-11; closed Sun
☎ (0151) 236 2131
Wells Bombardier; guest beer Ⓗ
Surprisingly large pub, comprising a long bar and additional separate bar in the lower section which concentrates on lunchtime food, for city business workers. It takes its name from the time when traders would have met here or in the corn exchange to trade cargoes of corn. The guest beer is from the Enterprise Inns range. Enjoy the good value food which is served until 6pm. The lower dining section is closed in the evening, including the entrance; try the other end. ◑

Crown ⊘
43 Lime Street, L1 1JQ
(50 yds from Lime St Station)
✪ 11-11; 12-10.30 Sun
☎ (0151) 707 6027
Fuller's London Pride; guest beers Ⓗ
An impressive Art Nouveau-style pub just a few seconds' walk from Lime Street Station. This is one of Liverpool's architectural gems. With a small, but excellently-kept, range of beers, it caters for a wide range of patrons and provides reasonably-priced food until early evening, served by friendly and efficient staff. To the delight of customers, the original interior decoration has been retained in the two downstairs rooms and the upstairs function area.
Q◑≉(Lime St) ⊖(Central)

Dispensary ✪
87 Renshaw Street, L1 2SP
(10-minute walk from Lime St Station)
✪ 11.30-11; 12-10.30 Sun
☎ (0151) 709 2160
Cains Mild, Bitter, seasonal beers; guest beers Ⓗ
Busy, Victorian-style corner pub, which was
an original Robert Cain pub; a winner of
numerous awards from the local CAMRA
branch, including Pub of Excellence,
together with the CAMRA/English Heritage
Pub Refurbishment award. The Cains'
products are superb and a regular supply of
equally good guest ales make this pub
popular with a large regular clientele and
groups of visitors. Customers will have the
opportunity to sample quality beer in fine
company. ≠ (Lime St) ⊖ (Central)

Doctor Duncan's ✪
St John's House, St John's Lane, L1 1HF
✪ 11.30-11; 12-10.30 Sun
☎ (0151) 709 5100
**Cains Mild, Dr Duncans IPA, Bitter, FA, seasonal
beers; guest beers** Ⓗ
Cains' flagship tied house with usually four
guest beers complementing the full Cains'
range. CAMRA regional Pub of the Year
2000, the Victorian tiled room, which was
originally the entrance to the Pearl
Assurance, dates back to when Doctor
Duncan became the first officer to
implement a public health policy. An
imaginative menu of quality food is served
daily, including curry night on Tuesday. A
friendly, lively atmosphere is created by an
enthusiastic licensee, it can be busy at
weekends.
⊛◑▶≠ (Lime St) ⊖

Everyman Bistro
5-9 Hope Street, L1 9BH
✪ 12-midnight (1am Thu, 2am Fri & Sat); closed Sun
☎ (0151) 708 9545
Beer range varies Ⓗ
Popular bistro and bar beneath the
Everyman Theatre and close to the
Philharmonic Hall, Liverpool University
and the Catholic cathedral. Well used,
especially by students and theatregoers, it
has three, large 'basement' rooms, which
have an interesting display of advertising
memorabilia. One of the rooms is the bar,
the second has a food servery, offering
choices from an extremely interesting,
varied menu, with a good selection of
vegetarian dishes, while the third room is a
quieter restaurant-style area. No meals are
served on Sunday. Q ◑▶

Excelsior
121 Dale Street, L2 2JH
✪ 11-11; 7.30-10.30 Sun
☎ (0151) 236 6486 website: www.excelsiorpub.co.uk
**Cains Bitter; Greene King Old Speckled Hen;
guest beer** Ⓗ
This pub, popular with students, offers an
extensive programme of social events. These
include quizzes, forfeits nights and disco
theme nights, as well as two evenings of live
music a week. The double bar dominates
the main room, while a back room provides
additional seating. Food is served all
afternoon and consists of standard pub fare.
Winner of local CAMRA Pub of Merit 2002.
◑≠ (Lime St) ⊖ (Moorfields)

Flying Picket
24 Hardman Street, L1 9AX
✪ 12 (7 Sat)-11; closed Sun
☎ (0151) 709 3995
**Cains Bitter; Coach House Coachman's Best Bitter,
Gunpowder Mild; Marston's Pedigree** Ⓗ
Part of the Trade Union Resource Centre,
the Flying Picket is a small, recently
refurbished, comfortable bar and popular
music venue, tucked away behind gates and
across an enclosed courtyard. The bar
displays its music heritage in a collection of
framed record covers. The Coach House
mild is excellent value at £1.10 a pint.
Visitors please note the restricted weekend
opening hours ⊛♿♣

Globe
17 Cases Street, L1 1HW
✪ 11-11; 12-10.30 Sun
☎ (0151) 707 0067
Cains Bitter, Bitter, FA; guest beers Ⓗ
Popular, two-roomed Victorian pub in the
city centre, close to Central Station and
Clayton Square shopping area. This friendly
little pub is frequented by regulars and
thirsty shoppers and can get very busy.
However, it is worth a visit, especially as it is
more than 115 years old and has had an
interesting history. In the quiet back room
there is a plaque commemorating the
inaugural meeting of the Merseyside branch
of CAMRA in January 1974.
Q≠ (Lime St) ⊖ (Central)

Lion Tavern ☆
67 Moorfields, L2 2BP
✪ 11-11; 12-10.30 Sun
☎ (0151) 236 1734
Lees Bitter; Taylor Landlord; guest beers Ⓗ
Victorian splendour lives on in this Grade II
listed, traditional street-corner pub. Some of
the architectural highlights include a glass
cupola in a rear room, panelled wood
pilasters and etched glass panels behind the
windows. The front bar serves the no-frills
public bar, while there are two comfortable
lounges in the back. The pub offers two
guests and is a rare outlet for Lees Bitter in
the city. Food is served daily, and includes
an excellent cheese board.
◑≠ (Lime St) ⊖ (Moorfields)

Ma Boyle's
Tower Buildings, Tower Gardens, L3 1AB
(off Water St)
✪ 11-11; 12-8 Sat; closed Sun
☎ (0151) 236 1717
Hydes Bitter; guest beer Ⓗ
Traditional haunt where business deals are
struck over a pint and a plate of Galway Bay
oysters. Well worth seeking out, not just for
the beer but also for the great food served
until 9pm weekdays and all day on
Saturday. If you tire of beer, prawns can be
bought by the pint instead. A friendly
welcome is guaranteed in either the upstairs
or quieter downstairs bars, which may be
hired for private parties. Jazz night is held
on Wednesday. Q ◑▶ ⊖ (Moorfields/James St)

Peter Kavanagh's ☆
2-6 Egerton Street, L8 7LY
✪ 12-11; 12-10.30 Sun
☎ (0151) 709 3443
Cains Bitter; Greene King Abbot; guest beers Ⓗ

The original terraced structure of this wonderful back-street pub is over 150 years old, with stained glass windows and wooden shutters. The interior is fascinating, with a quiet snug at each end of the bar, each of which boasts period wall paintings and wooden benches with carved arms. There are many small, interestingly-shaped rooms, with plenty of bric-à-brac. The staff are happy to give visitors a potted history of the pub and point out various unusual features. Q ❀ ♣ ✲

Philharmonic ☆
36 Hope Street, L1 9BX
✪ 12-11; 12-10.30 Sun
☎ (0151) 707 2837
Cains Bitter; guest beers Ⓗ
Described as the most ornate pub in England, the Grade II* listed 'Phil' was designed by Walter Thomas for Robert Cain. The entrance through the magnificent wrought iron and copper gate leads to a bar with adjoining front bar, smoke rooms – known as Brahms and Liszt – and a former billiards room, the grand lounge, which has copper panels and a plaster frieze. It was designed as a gentlemen's club with renowned marble toilets, mosaic floors and a riot of Victorian flamboyance and mahogany joinery. It stocks two or three guest beers and wholesome food, catering for theatregoers, students and tourists.
🛏 ◁≉ (Central) ⊖ (Lime St)

Pig & Whistle
12 Covent Garden, L2 8UA (off Chapel St)
✪ 11-11; closed Sun
☎ (0151) 236 4760
Cains Bitter; Taylor Landlord; guest beer Ⓗ
Located in the city business area close to the pier head, this cosy pub has two split-level rooms, plus an upstairs bar open at lunchtime and for private functions. Maritime pictures and charts add a sense of history, while bench seating, wood finishes and period lighting create a mellow atmosphere. It is popular for good value lunchtime food served Monday–Saturday (11.30–3), the menu includes daily specials.
♨ ◁ ⊖ (Moorfields)

Poste House
23 Cumberland Street, L1 6BU
✪ 11-11; 12-10.30 Sun
☎ (0151) 236 4130
Cains Mild, Bitter; guest beers Ⓗ
Small, busy Victorian pub tucked away, just off Dale Street, with two cosy rooms and a very welcoming, friendly environment. Recently rescued from demolition by a spirited campaign led by regular customers, local newspapers and CAMRA members, this hospitable little pub will now be integrated into the redevelopment scheme that was meant to replace it. One of Liverpool's oldest pubs, it has been visited by a number of famous people over the years. ≉ (Lime St) ⊖ (Moorfields)

Roscoe Head
26 Roscoe Street, L1 2SX
✪ 11-11; 12-10.30 Sun
☎ (0151) 709 4365
Jennings Bitter, Cumberland Ale; guest beer Ⓗ
The only Merseyside pub to have featured

in every edition of this Guide. This unspoilt back-street local has a congenial atmosphere and has been run by the same family for almost 20 years. A small bar leads into a front snug; a rear lounge/snug and tiny front bar complete the picture. Entertainment includes a popular quiz night on Tuesday, and cribbage night on Wednesday. The home-cooked lunches can be ordered by phone.
◁≉ (Lime St) ⊖ (Central)

Ship & Mitre ✔
133 Dale Street, L2 2JH
✪ 12-11; 12-10.30 Sun
☎ (0151) 236 0859 website: www.shipandmitre.co.uk
Beer range varies Ⓗ
The Ship & Mitre has built its reputation on the number (up to 12), range and quality of its beers, which are complemented by two ciders and an ever-changing selection of continental beers. Quarterly beer festivals are held. The atmosphere is warm and welcoming and reasonably-priced lunches are available on weekdays. Thursday is quiz night. Look out for Wurzel Gummidge in the rear lounge. Awarded local CAMRA Pub of the Year for 2001 and 2002, together with Pub of Excellence for the past four years. ◁≉ (Lime St) ⊖ (Moorfields) ♣ ☙ ☷

Swan Inn
86 Wood Street, L1 4DQ
✪ 12-11; 12-10.30 Sun
☎ (0151) 709 5281
Cains Bitter; Hydes Bitter; Jekyll's Gold; Phoenix Wobbly Bob; Taylor Landlord; guest beers Ⓗ
After closure for refurbishment, the Swan has returned and retains its distinctive atmosphere. The popular rock juke box still dominates the downstairs bar. Customers can enjoy an increased range of ales; five regular and three constantly-changing and interesting guest beers. The plush upstairs bar features live sport on the big screen, both during the week and at weekends. Enjoy a drink in the new third-level bar which attracts good crowds on Friday and Saturday. ◁♿≉ (Lime St) ⊖ (Central) ☙

Vernon Arms
69 Dale Street, L2 2HJ
✪ 11.45-11; closed Sun
☎ (0151) 236 4525
Coach House Gunpowder Mild; guest beers Ⓗ
This friendly pub is located near the business district, and serves six constantly-changing guest beers along with a regular mild. One of the guests is usually supplied by the owners, the Liverpool Brewing Company. The pub is divided into three main areas: a main bar, a small snug to the front, and a back room. The sloping floor has been known to catch out the unwary. The food is excellent quality and the day's specials are displayed on a chalkboard near the bar. The home-made chips are always a popular choice with meals. Winner of a local CAMRA Pub of Excellence award for the past three years.
◁▷≉ (Lime St) ⊖ (Moorfields)

Welkin ✔
7 Whitechapel, L1 6DS
✪ 8-11; 10-10.30 Sun
☎ (0151) 243 1080
Beer range varies Ⓗ

One of Wetherspoon's five pubs in Liverpool, located in the centre of the shopping area. There is a large L-shaped room on the lower floor and a smaller room with dining area and second bar upstairs. The Welkin offers an ever-changing choice of beers, including seasonal promotions. Do not be afraid to ask for a 'top up' or a sample taste, as this is acceptable. Reasonably-priced food is available all week, with a very popular curry club night on Thursday. Breakfast is served between 8–12 Monday–Saturday and 10–12 Sunday.
◑▷&⇌(Lime St) ⊖(Central)

White Star (Quinn's)
2-4 Rainford Gardens, L2 6PT
✪ 11.30-11; 12-10.30 Sun
☎ (0151) 231 6861
Beer range varies Ⓗ
Situated in Liverpool's famous Cavern Quarter, the pub is a real ale oasis, offering five cask beers. Friendly staff offer a warm welcome to all. The front bar has pictures of local boxing legends, together with prints of various White Star liners. The rear lounge has a corner dedicated to the Beatles, but is dominated by a huge Bass mirror. The pub is twinned with pubs in Norway and the Czech Republic. Big-screen satellite TV features all the major sporting events.
🜋⇌(Lime St) ⊖(Moorfields/Central)

KNOTTY ASH

Wheatsheaf
186 East Prescot Road, L14 5NG
✪ 12-11; 12-10.30 Sun
☎ (0151) 228 5080
Cains Bitter Ⓗ
Many original features are retained in this Victorian pub, including the etched windows of Joseph Jones Brewery, which was situated nearby. The pub has three rooms: a spacious public bar, lounge area and a snug. Both the lounge and snug offer waiter service. Standing on a main road this pub is served by a frequent bus service. A quiz night is held on Monday. Q 🜋P

NETHERLEY

Falcon
Caldway Drive, L27 0YB
✪ 12-11; 12-10.30 Sun
☎ (0151) 487 9994
Oakwell Barnsley Bitter, Old Tom Ⓗ
Two-roomed modern pub on the edge of Netherley housing estate. It reopened in mid-2001 after a long closure. The rear public bar has a pool table and there is an outside drinking area with tables. The beers are very competitively priced. The pub is an Oakwell Brewery tied house. It is a rare real ale gem in an area that is predominantly smoothflow-only. ❀🜋♣P

TOXTETH

Brewery Tap
35 Grafton Street, L8 5XJ (adjoins Cains Brewery – on busy bus route to Speke)
✪ 11-11; 12-10.30 Sun
☎ (0151) 709 2129
Cains Mild, Dr Duncans IPA, Bitter, FA, seasonal beers; guest beers Ⓗ
Set within the walls of the Robert Cain

Brewery, the Tap was magnificently restored from the Grapes, whose name is still in the Victorian terracotta façade. The full range of Cains' beers is served alongside usually three guest beers. Host to the Cains' brewery tours, the single bar can be very busy. An interesting collection of breweriana, especially beer labels from former Merseyside brewers, adorns the walls. The pub is 15 minutes' walk from the centre, past the Anglican cathedral. Lunches are served on weekdays. Use the brewery car park; a street-side area is available for summer drinking. ❀◑♣P

WAVERTREE

Edinburgh
4 Sandown Lane, L15 8HY
✪ 12-11; 12-10.30 Sun
☎ (0151) 475 2648
Cains Mild, Bitter, FA, seasonal beers; guest beers Ⓗ
Small, street-corner local just off the bustling Wavertree High Street. A frequent Guide entry when it was a Peter Walker tied house, it was rescued by the local Cains Brewery in the late 1990s from the fate of smoothflow conversion, which has befallen most of its neighbours. This little gem of a pub consists simply of a small lounge area and an even smaller bar, but while compact in size, it is always big on welcome and is well worth seeking out.
🜋⇌(Wavertree Technology Pk)

Willowbank
329 Smithdown Road, L15 3JA
(20 yds from A562 jct)
✪ 12-11; 12-10.30 Sun
☎ (0151) 733 5782
Beer range varies Ⓗ
Friendly pub which is popular with students and cask ale drinkers alike. It has a large lounge area and a small enclosed public bar. The patio, with tables and benches to the front of the pub, is popular in the summer months. The pub publishes its own newsletter. An ever-changing range of up to 11 beers plus regular beer festivals, make this a pub not to be missed. Good value meals are served daily (12–2 and 5–8). Join the excellent quiz night on Wednesday.
❀◑🜋♣P

WOOLTON

Gardeners Arms
101 Vale Road, L25 7RW
✪ 4 (12 Sat)-11; 12-10.30 Sun
☎ (0151) 428 1443
Cains Mild, Bitter Ⓗ
Traditional suburban local with the feel of a country pub. The large central bar serves two very comfortable lounge areas, one of which is principally for non-smokers. A warm and friendly welcome is assured, as well as a fine pint of Cains Bitter or Mild. The pub is home to a number of sports teams and has its own golf society. Sky TV shows sporting events and a popular quiz is run on Tuesday evening. &🍴

White Horse
2 Acrefield Road, L25 5JL
✪ 12-11; 12-10.30 Sun
☎ (0151) 428 1862
Black Sheep Best Bitter; Cains Bitter Ⓗ

Attractive white-painted pub close to the centre of Woolton village. Three drinking areas and a central bar create a warm atmosphere, with wood panelling, brasswork, local maps and pictures of old Woolton adorning the walls. Waiter service brass buttons remain in situ but are not in use. This cosy village local serves good value lunches and a daily special Monday–Saturday (12–3) and Sunday roasts (12–5). ✿◑

LYDIATE

Scotch Piper ☆
Southport Road, L31 4HD
✪ 12-3, 5.30-11; 12-11 Sat; 12-10.30 Sun
☎ (0151) 526 0503
Burtonwood Bitter, Top Hat Ⓗ
Fine pub situated on the Southport Road (A5147) on the outskirts of Lydiate, easily reached on the No. 300 bus route from Liverpool and Southport. The pub claims to be the oldest in the county with a date of 1320 over the door. A small, cosy three-roomed pub, each area has its own real fire. The main bar is where most people congregate. The pub is warm and welcoming and is popular with locals, visitors and bikers. ⚌Q✿◐✣P

NEW BRIGHTON

Clarence Hotel
89 Albion Street, CH45 9JQ
✪ 11-11; 12-10.30 Sun
☎ (0151) 639 3860
Cains Bitter; Caledonian Deuchars IPA; Fuller's London Pride; Greene King Abbot; guest beers Ⓗ
A 10-minute walk from the resort of New Brighton, this pub has been recently refurbished and extended. It has a split-level lounge (children are restricted to the lower level) and a function room. Pub games, including darts, are played. A varied range of up to five real ales is available. Tasty home-cooked food is offered from Wednesday–Sunday. There is a patio for summer drinking. ⌣✿◑◱≢✣✍

Commercial Hotel ⦿
19 Hope Street, CH45 2LN
✪ 11-11; 12-10.30 Sun
☎ (0151) 639 2105
Cains Mild, Bitter, seasonal beers; guest beers Ⓗ
Traditional, street-corner local, refurbished by Robert Cain. The bar, with upright piano, is devoted to TV sports, with football and horse racing to the fore. The bar serves the comfortable lounge through a hatch and the pub is one of the few on the Wirral to retain a table waiting service. Plenty of old photographs of New Brighton add to the interest of this splendid pub that has regained the high standards that earned it local CAMRA awards when it was a Walkers house. Q◱≢✣

PRESCOT

Clock Face
54 Derby Street, L34 3LL
(take M57 jct 2 then A57 to Prescot)
✪ 11-3, 7-11 Sat; 11-3, 7-10.30 Sun
☎ (0151) 292 4121
Thwaites Bitter Ⓗ
Attractively decorated and comfortably

furnished, this multi-roomed pub offers a sumptuous setting. Converted from a Georgian mansion, it retains much of its former glory. Lofty windows offer superb views; the pub benefits from an open aspect which makes sitting at the benches and tables outside particularly enjoyable in summer. Quiz night is Monday. You may spot a ghost or two. It is a rare outlet for Thwaites beers on Merseyside. ✿◑≢✣P

Old Mill
8 Mill Street, L34 6MA (just off A57)
✪ 12-11; 12-10.30 Sun
☎ (0151) 430 6826
Hydes Bitter, Jekyll's Gold, seasonal beers Ⓗ
Extensively and sympathetically refurbished by Hydes Brewery, this is their only tied house in Merseyside to date. The pub consists of a single bar serving the main lounge, sunken games area and the restaurant section. Real fires add to the congenial atmosphere, which is generated by the clientele and the efficient bar staff. The well-laid out garden to the rear is very pleasant in good weather. ⚌✿◑

RABY

Wheatsheaf Inn
Raby Mere Road, CH63 4JH
(from M53 jct 4 take B5151 second right to Raby village)
✪ 11.30-11; 12-10.30 Sun
☎ (0151) 336 3416
Cains Bitter; Greene King Old Speckled Hen; Theakston Best Bitter, Old Peculier; Wells Bombardier; guest beer Ⓗ
This quaint pub, sitting in the hamlet of Raby, is probably the oldest on the Wirral. It specialises in handpulled cask ales of which there are always at least nine on the bar. It is a pub for all seasons, whether enjoying a pint in front of the coal fire in winter, or lazing in the garden, which is a suntrap in summer. No evening meals are served on Sunday or Monday. Children are admitted at lunchtime only.
⚌Q⌣✿◑◱♿P

RAINHILL

Commercial
12 Station Road, L35 0LL (off A57)
✪ 11-11; 12-10.30 Sun
☎ (0151) 430 8473
Cains Bitter Ⓗ
Overlooking Rainhill Station, this section of the line is a significant location in railway history for the trials in 1829 in which Stephenson's Rocket emerged victorious. The event is depicted pictorially inside the pub, alongside scenes of old Rainhill and Prescot. The pub is always busy. The TV racing channel is popular during the afternoon. It is well worth breaking your journey here if travelling between Manchester Victoria and Liverpool. ◱✣≢P

ST HELENS

Beecham's Bar & Brewery
Water Street, WA10 1PR (A58, off Westfield Street)
✪ 12-11; closed Sun
☎ (01744) 623420
Beecham's Crystal Wheat Beer, seasonal beers; Greene King Abbot; guest beers Ⓗ

This one-roomed bar is part of the former Beecham's Powders building, which has a distinctive bell tower. It is now part of the local college and students can gain brewing and management skills at the in-house micro-brewery. There is a discount for NUS and CAMRA members. This is a safe haven for the real ale enthusiast amid a plethora of trendy bars on Westfield Street. Try the in-house brews with crystal wheat and one or two current extras and guests, served in oversized glasses.
⅋≠ (Central) ⌷

Hope & Anchor
174 City Road, WA10 2UD
🕐 12-11; 12-10.30 Sun
☎ (01744) 24199
Beer range varies Ⓗ
Heralding a much-deserved return to the Guide, with three rotating guest beers, this community local is situated at the junction of City Road and Bishop Road, at the edge of Victoria Park (close to the A580). It is a former Tetley house and displays distinctive etched windows. Located next to Cowley Hall glass works, a large mirror with the works' logo and Pilkington name, takes pride of place in the lounge. Pool, darts and dominoes teams are supported and a large-screen TV shows sporting events. A good juke box is provided in the comfortable lounge.
⅋♣

Sutton Oak ✓
73 Bold Road, WA9 4JG
(B5204, Bold Road, near jct with Helena Road)
🕐 12-11; 12-10.30 Sun
☎ (01744) 813442 website: www.thesuttonoak.co.uk
Black Sheep Best Bitter; guest beers Ⓗ
Small, friendly community pub built in 1870, offering traditional pub games including dominoes, darts, pool and cribbage. It is located close to a nature trail through a wildlife conservation area. The pub has its own angling club which meets regularly, and also holds karaoke and quiz nights. A large-screen TV features sport. The garden area is fenced off and safe for children. Barbecues are organised occasionally in the summer.
⛱◖⅋≠ (Jct) ♣P

Baron's Bar, Scarisbrick Hotel ✓
293 Lord Street, PR8 1NZ (entrance off the pedestrianised thoroughfare, next to the hotel, or through the hotel reception area)
🕐 11-11; 12-10.30 Sun
☎ (01704) 543000 website: www.scarisbrickhotel.com
Taylor Landlord; Tetley Bitter; guest beers Ⓗ
Baron's Bar is furnished in the style of a medieval baronial hall with weaponry and heraldry decorating the walls. Despite this, the bar is comfortable rather than grand, and a popular spot for holidaymakers coming off the beach. The Flag & Turret is the bar's own beer, and is very cheaply priced. Baron's Bar holds an annual beer festival during the first week of May, commencing on May Day at 6am! There are tables on the pedestrianised street for outdoor drinking.
Q⛱⋈⅋≠

Berkeley Arms Hotel
19 Queens Road, PR9 9HN
🕐 4 (12 Sat)-11; 12-10.30 Sun
☎ (01704) 500811
Adnams Bitter; Camerons Strongarm; Moorhouses Black Cat, Pride of Pendle, Pendle Witches Brew; guest beers Ⓗ
Popular locals' bar with an excellent reputation for its home-made pizza, as well as for its range of beers. Although it looks like an imposing B&B, it is roomy inside, with the drinking area divided into a small, cosy bar with a golfing theme (it used to be pigs!) and a larger bar, part of which is no-smoking. A regular in this Guide, it has changed name twice in the past four years. Tables are provided at the front for summer drinking. Q⛵⛱⋈◖P⅋

Cheshire Lines
81 King Street, PR8 1LQ
🕐 11-11; 12-10.30 Sun
☎ (01704) 532178
Tetley Dark Mild, Bitter Ⓗ
This small, half-timbered property with attractive hanging baskets is situated in a quiet back street surrounded by small hotels and B&Bs. Inside, it contains many railway prints plus an old stone hearth from the original Cheshire Lines railway, whose terminus used to be on nearby Lord Street. Although largely opened up, it retains a small snug with newspapers for the solitary visitor. Music nights are held Thursday–Saturday. Q⛱◖≠♣

Falstaff
68 King Street, PR8 1LG
🕐 11.30-11; 12-10.30 Sun
☎ (01704) 501116
Courage Directors; Theakston Mild, Best Bitter; Wells Bombardier; guest beers Ⓗ
Half of this building was once a bicycle shop, and the other half is rumoured to have once had striptease; even worse, it once sold only keg. However, the Falstaff is now highly respectable and an essential stop in any exploration of real ale in Southport. With a wide range of beers on offer, it has pleasant open-plan seating with traditional furnishing and decoration. Popular with senior citizens because of the good value food on offer, it was local CAMRA Pub of the Year 2001. Outdoor tables to the front are provided for summer drinking. Q⛱◖⅋≠♣

Guest House
16 Union Street, PR9 0QE
🕐 11-11; 12-10.30 Sun
☎ (01704) 537660
Boddingtons Bitter; Cains Bitter; Courage Directors; Wells Bombardier; guest beers Ⓗ
This unspoilt Edwardian gem is situated just off the northern end of historic Lord Street. The double-fronted, elegantly styled exterior, hung with flowering baskets, is complemented by a traditional interior with wood-panelled walls and glazed panelling over the bar. The decoratively tiled entrance hall leads to two comfortably furnished rooms. A further, equally comfortable, drinking area can be found to the left of the bar. All the rooms have traditional fireplaces.
Q⛱♣

London
14 Windsor Road, PR9 0SQ
⊙ 12-11; 12-10.30 Sun
☎ (01704) 542885
Oakwell Barnsley Bitter, Old Tom Ⓗ
This community pub is the only outlet in Southport for the famous Barnsley Bitter brewed by Oakwell, in South Yorkshire. The London is a large, relaxing pub, attractively furnished and decorated to a high standard. The main drinking area is spacious and divided into distinct sections. The pub boasts a tap room as well as a separate family room. The walls are decorated with the trophies of a number of successful local sports teams, most notably in connection with bowling; it has its own bowling green.
Q ⅋ ❀ ⊈ ♣ P

Wetherspoon's ✪
93-97 Lord Street, PR8 1RH
⊙ 10-11; 12-10.30 Sun
☎ (01704) 530217
Cains Mild; Courage Directors; Shepherd Neame Spitfire; Theakston Best Bitter; guest beers Ⓗ
Typical Wetherspoon's pub on the ground floor of what was once a 19th-century department store. Before going in, it is worth looking at the building for a moment, as it is a good example of the fine Victorian architecture to be found down Lord Street. This branch of Wetherspoon's is of relatively recent origin but is now established as a key provider of cask ales at some of the lowest prices in Southport.
Q ⊄ ⅋ ≢ ✁

WALLASEY

Farmer's Arms
225 Wallasey Village, CH45 3LG
(near Grove Rd Station)
⊙ 11.30-11; 12-10.30 Sun
☎ (0151) 638 2110
Cains Mild, Bitter; Tetley Bitter; Theakston Best Bitter; guest beer Ⓗ
A former local CAMRA Pub of the Month,

Pub of the Year and regional winner, the much-respected and long-standing licensee has ensured entries in each of the last 10 editions of this Guide. A front bar, side snug and back lounge cater for all ages and tastes. Weekday lunches are offered, with stir fries a speciality. Quiz nights are run on Tuesday. The guest beer pump is in the bar.
⊄ ⊈ ≢ (Grove Rd)

WATERLOO

Brooke Hotel
51 Brooke Road East, L22 2BE
⊙ 12-11; 12-10.30 Sun
☎ (0151) 924 7304
Greene King Old Speckled Hen; Taylor Landlord Ⓗ
The Brooke is a friendly, busy and welcoming pub. Its newly designed, open-plan layout helps to combine a feeling of space, yet has cosy, intimate areas. A pleasant, attractive garden at the rear creates a desire for warm summer evenings where you can sit and relax after a hard day at work. Weekends are lively with music or discos on Friday and Saturday night. Themed events are also popular, and recent highlights have included Caribbean, Medieval, Hallowe'en and Elvis nights.
❀ ⊄ ≢ (Blundellsands/Waterloo) P

Volunteer Canteen ✪
45 East Street, L22 8QR
⊙ 12-11; 12-10.30 Sun
☎ (0151) 928 6594
Cains Bitter; guest beer Ⓗ
Cosy, traditional local with a central bar serving both the public bar and rear lounge, where table service is still available. The comfortable lounge area boasts wood panelling, etched windows and an interesting display of local photographs. Guest beers for the coming month are displayed in both bars. The pub has a relaxed atmosphere, where the sound of conversation and the rustle of newspapers take the place of the juke box – heaven.
Q ⊄ ≢ ♣

NORFOLK

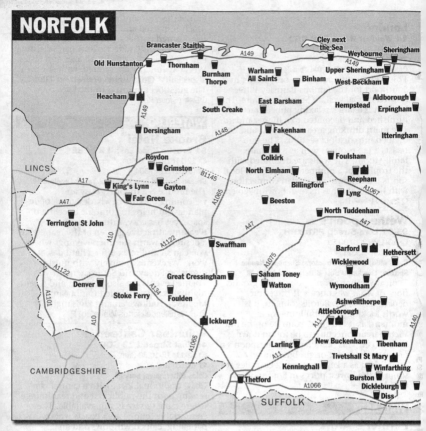

ALDBOROUGH

Old Red Lion
The Green, NR11 7AA
(2 miles W of Aylsham-Cromer road)
🕏 12-11; 12-10.30 Sun
☎ (01263) 761451
Taylor Landlord; Winter's Golden; Wolf Golden Jackal; guest beers Ⓗ

This 17th-century pub, open all day, seven days a week, is situated in a quaint setting offering delightful views of the large village green. The main bar is fairly small but well furnished with cream-painted walls and wooden beams. The dining area is large and contains some comfortable chairs. An extensive food menu is available both lunchtime (but book in advance) and evening. On summer afternoons the dining room becomes a tea room offering a cream tea menu until 6pm. Buses to North Walsham and Aylsham run daily through the village. ♨🚫🏡⌖🍺🔑♿🍴⌀

ALPINGTON

Wheel of Fortune
Wheel Road, NR14 7NL
(turn left 1 mile S of Poringland, B1332)
🕏 12-3, 5.30-11; 12-11 Sat; 12-10.30 Sun
☎ (01508) 492712
Adnams Bitter; Greene King IPA; Tetley Imperial; guest beer Ⓗ

Classic village pub that stands on the boundary with Yelverton (near the

school); difficult to find but it is marked on OS maps. The pub dates from the 17th century, is thatched, with brick and flint walls and inside there are real beams and low ceilings. It retains a two-bar layout, with a central chimney-stack with real fires. The lounge is traditional and comfortable, with some fine woodwork – a room to relax in. The public bar is a community centre, busy and boisterous, but retains a friendly welcome for visitors. The bar backs with Watney signage are a rare survival of a 1960s refurbishment. The beer garden includes a petanque court. There are plenty of good country walks to enjoy in the area.
♨🚫🕏🍺🔑P

ASHWELLTHORPE

White Horse
49-55 The Street, NR16 1AA
🕏 12-2.30 (not Mon or Tue), 5.30-11; 7-10.30 Sun
☎ (01508) 489721
Adnams Bitter; Fuller's London Pride; guest beers Ⓗ

Village local featuring original beams and an inglenook plus brasses and other artefacts in the bar. There is an attractive, extensive garden at the rear and tables at the front. The pub has a large car park. A wide-ranging food menu is available during the evening and at lunchtime. There is a separate dining room.
♨🚫🕏🍺P

to the building. The menu comprises a changing range of home-cooked fare made with local produce. No food is offered on Sunday evening. ❁🏠🌓🍴🚲🐾P

BARFORD

Cock Inn
Watton Road, NR9 4AS (on Norwich-Watton road)
🕐 12-3, 6-11; 12-3, 7-10.30 Sun
☎ (01603) 757646
Blue Moon Easy Life, Sea of Tranquillity, Moon Dance, Dark Side, Hingham High 🅷

A former coaching inn, this fine old pub is now the home of two breweries, Blue Moon and Spectrum. There are two bars, a small one with a wooden floor and welcoming real fire, the other, a large, long bar which is carpeted. In addition, an eating area comprises a small restaurant and two smaller alcoves, which are private from the main restaurant. There is a bowling green and camping area outside. A regular bus service runs past the pub between Dereham and Norwich, Monday–Saturday. ♨❁🌓🏕🐾P

BEESTON

Ploughshare
The Street, PE32 2NF
🕐 12-2.30, 5.30-11; 11-11 Sat; 12-10.30 Sun
☎ (01328) 701845 website: www.theploughshare.co.uk
Greene King IPA; Woodforde's Wherry 🅷

Friendly village pub in middle Norfolk, complete with beams, inglenook and a crisp-loving terrier. The home-cooked food, from mostly local produce, is served throughout the day on Sunday. Pictures of Beeston-born prize fighter, Gem Mace, are displayed in the main bar along with others of Wendling Airfield during the war. The smaller bar has a no-smoking area. The guest beers come from independent breweries, often local. There is a large garden and children (and dogs) are welcome, but not in the main bar. B&B accommodation is a new addition to the facilities. ♨Q❁🏠🌓🐾P✗

BERNEY ARMS

Berney Arms
NR30 1SB OS467052
🕐 11-11 (phone ahead early/late season); closed end Oct-Mar; 12-10.30 Sun

ATTLEBOROUGH

Bear
Exchange Street, NR17 2AG
🕐 11-3, 5.30-11; 12-3, 7-10.30 Sun
☎ (01953) 454421
Wolf Bitter; guest beers 🅷

An old, but recently refurbished free house with low ceilings, beams, bare boards, pamments and an inglenook in the main bar. There is also a second bar, a cosy, peaceful snug and a covered south-facing courtyard outside. The guest beers come from a wide variety of brewers. There is a dining area and the home-cooked food is good value. Live music features on Thursday.
♨Q❁🏠🌓🚲🐾

Griffin Hotel
Church Street, NR17 2AH
🕐 10.30-3, 5.30-11; 10.30-11 Fri & Sat; 12-4, 7-10.30 Sun
☎ (01953) 452149
Greene King Abbot; Wolf Bitter; Worthington's 1744; guest beers 🅷

A Guide regular, the wainscotted bar of this 16th-century former coaching inn features mellow brickwork and many exposed beams. The much more recently built bar was constructed with reclaimed materials, and includes the oldest timber in the premises. There is also a smaller public bar, a function room, and a dining area which occupies part of the 17th-century extension

INDEPENDENT BREWERIES

Alewife Starston
Blanchfields Colkirk
Blue Moon Barford
Buffy's Tivetshall St Mary
Captain Grumpy Stoke Ferry
Chalk Hill Norwich
Fox Heacham
Humpty Dumpty Reedham
Iceni Ickburgh
Reepham Reepham
Spectrum Barford
Tindall Seething
Uncle Stuarts Lingwood
Winter's Norwich
Wolf Attleborough
Woodforde's Woodbastwick

☎ (01493) 700303
Greene King IPA; Woodforde's Wherry; guest beers Ⓗ
Isolated and remote, this 200-year-old free house is accessible by train, boat or, for the determined, via the Weavers Way footpath. It is popular with Broads boaters in the summer and birdwatchers in the autumn. The Berney Arms offers a glimpse of what a Norfolk pub was like in years gone by, while providing modern facilities. Reasonably-priced food is available. 🅰Q🌣🏠⊛◑❦♣

BILLINGFORD

Forge
Bintree Road, NR20 4RE
✪ 11-2.30, 7-11; 12-3, 7-10.30 Sun
☎ (01362) 668720
Adnams Bitter, Broadside; Greene King Abbot; guest beer Ⓗ
The Forge was indeed a forge until about 1980 when it was converted into a pub, the village having been publess for the previous 10 years. The multi-level bar area is long, beamed and characterful. To the rear is a large garden adjoining the village playing field and cricket pitch. There is also a dining area where you can order home-cooked food. ⊛◑♣P🗒

BINHAM

Chequers
Front Street, NR21 0AL
✪ 11.30-3, 5.30-11; 12-3, 7-10.30 Sun
☎ (01328) 830297
Adnams Bitter; Greene King IPA, Abbot; Woodforde's Wherry Ⓗ
Attractive local set in the centre of this charming North Norfolk village. One end of the long, narrow bar area is no-smoking, the other end has the original bar, with impressive fireplace and beams. This welcoming pub is owned by the village charity. Good quality bar meals are available at reasonable prices. Nearby is the medieval Binham Priory, now owned by English Heritage, which is well worth a visit. 🅰🚌◑♣⊛🚲

BRANCASTER STAITHE

Jolly Sailors
Main Road, PE31 8BJ (on A149 coast road)
✪ 11-11; 12-10.30 Sun
☎ (01485) 210314 website: www.jollysailors.co.uk
Adnams Bitter; Woodforde's Wherry; guest beers Ⓗ
Fine free house in an increasingly popular tourist location. Situated just across from the staithe (local name for a harbour), the pub has developed an excellent reputation for quality real ale as well as good food (meals available 12-9). Cider is sold in summer. There is an extensive outdoor garden/drinking area with ample seating as well as a cool conservatory if the weather warms up. A general knowledge quiz is held each Tuesday night. 🅰Q🌣⊛◑🏠Å♣⊛P🚲🗒

White Horse
Main Road, PE31 8BY (on A149 coast road)
✪ 11-11; 12-10.30 Sun
☎ (01485) 210262
website: www.whitehorsebrancaster.co.uk
Adnams Bitter, Fisherman; Greene King IPA; guest beer Ⓗ

A much improved drinking establishment in a thriving tourist area. The award-winning White Horse has a large restaurant attached and has been expanded to include eight more en-suite bedrooms. The front bar very much retains a genuine 'pub' feel and includes a bar billiards table. Many local photographs adorn the walls. From the outside decking, there are outstanding sea views across the salt marshes and beyond to Scolt Head island. 🅰🌣⊛🚌◑🏠Å⊛♣P🚲🗒

BURNHAM THORPE

Lord Nelson
Walsingham Road, PE31 8HL
✪ 11-2.30 (3 Sat), 6-11; closed Mon in winter; 12-3, 7-10.30 (closed winter eve) Sun
☎ (01328) 738241 website: www.nelsonslocal.com
Greene King IPA, Abbot Ⓖ
Close to Nelson's birthplace, this pub features many original paintings and prints celebrating his life. Beer is brought to your table, direct from the casks in the cellar room. The bar dates back over 300 years and still has the original settles and stone-flagged floor. More recent additions include a dining room, a large wooden play area for children and, for those drinking in the garden, a serving-hatch. 🅰Q🌣⊛◑🏠♣P🚲

BURSTON

Crown Inn
Crown Green, IP22 3TW
✪ 12-2 (Wed-Fri), 6.30-10.30 (11 Fri & Sat); closed Mon & Tue; 12-6 Sun
☎ (01379) 741257
Beer range varies Ⓖ
Dating from 1580, this free house offers good beer and imaginative food in pleasant surroundings. Both bars are beamed and comfortable, the one with the inglenook near the dining area is no-smoking. Vegetarian, vegan and children's dishes are made to order. The accommodation (from late 2003) is self-catering, or camping is available in front of the pub. The house beer is by Old Chimneys, and the toilets are notably decorated. The famous Strike School is nearby, and there are weekday buses from Norwich and Diss. 🅰Q⊛🚌◑Å♣P🚲

CLAXTON

Beauchamp Arms
Buckingham Ferry, NR14 6DH (down long drive from Loddon Road)
✪ 11-3, 6-11; 11-11 Sat; 12-10.30 Sun
☎ (01508) 480247
Adnams Bitter; Woodforde's Wherry; guest beer Ⓗ
Large, multi-roomed rural pub situated on the River Yare with free mooring facilities for the many holidaymakers using this peaceful area. There are two games rooms with pool and darts and a dining room serving food all day with vegetarian options. The large outdoor area has tables and a children's play section. Accommodation is available; single, double or family rooms. ⊛🚌◑🏠🚲♣P

CLEY NEXT THE SEA

Three Swallows
Newgate Green, NR25 7TT

(1/2 mile S of main A149, coast road)
☼ 11-11; 12-10.30 Sun
☎ (01263) 740526
Adnams Bitter; Greene King IPA; guest beer
(summer) Ⓗ
With the parish church behind it and the
village green in front, this old pub certainly
looks the part. The very cosy interior
consists of three bars. On the side of the
main bar there are some intriguing
woodcarvings. The walls are covered with
many fascinating old photographs of local
scenes featuring the village's maritime past.
There are roaring log fires at each end of the
pub. Food is available throughout the day at
weekends. Children are allowed in the
dining area. On warm summer days, one
can sit outside and look across the green
with a fine view of the river, once the site of
a bustling port. Daily bus services pass
through the village centre along the North
Norfolk coast road between Sheringham
and King's Lynn.
⚏Q❀🛏◑⤸

COLKIRK

Crown
Crown Road, NR21 7AA
☼ 11-2.30, 6-11; 12-3, 7-10.30 Sun
☎ (01328) 862172
Greene King XX Mild, IPA, Abbot; guest beer Ⓗ
Large, three-roomed pub with two bars, one
laid out with traditional bar stools and
tables, and the other with a log fire and
church-style pews. The third room is a
dining room with a large glass door leading
on to a patio. An extensive menu is
available including full restaurant meals or
bar snacks. The pub is possibly unique in
the area in having a dark mild as a
permanent fixture. A large car park and
pleasant garden lie to the rear of the pub.
⚏❀◑⚑&▲P

CROMER

Red Lion Hotel
Brooke Street, NR27 9EX
☼ 10-11; 12-10.30 Sun
☎ (01263) 512834
Adnams Bitter; Draught Bass; guest beers Ⓗ
Victorian hotel situated in the town centre
at the top of the cliff with a commanding
view of the North Sea. There are two bars,
one an Edwardian-style bar complete with
ornate mahogany partitions between the
seats, the other bar is flint-walled with
many photographs of Cromer lifeboats
and lifeboat crewmen. An extensive food
menu is available. 🛏◑P⤸

DENVER

Bell
2 Ely Road, PE38 0DW (opp. church)
☼ 12-2.30 (not Mon), 6-11; 12-11 Sat; 12-10.30 Sun
☎ (01366) 382173
Greene King IPA; guest beers Ⓗ
Friendly village pub with three guest
pumps. The spacious front bar has a TV and
there is a restaurant downstairs. The large
garden offers a children's play area. The
front bar hosts a Christmas carol service.
The Bell is close to Denver's working
windmill (fresh bread) and the 'Denver
complex' of recreational facilities. The pub

was third in the 2002 Village Pub of the
Year awards, organised by the Morning
Advertiser. ⚏❀◑♣P

DERSINGHAM

Feathers
Manor Road, PE31 6LN
☼ 11-2.30, 4.30-11 (11-11 summer); 12-10.30 Sun
☎ (01485) 540207
website: www.thefeathershotel.co.uk
Adnams Bitter; guest beers Ⓗ
Close to the Sandringham estate, the
Feathers offers a couple of wood-panelled
bars for drinkers, a restaurant for those who
want more than bar snacks, and a large
garden with a selection of toys for the
children. In addition, there is a stable bar
with loud music, discos and live bands, far
enough away not to intrude on those who
want a quiet pint. Add to this, good value
meals, accommodation, and events such as
quiz nights and you find it offers something
for everyone. ❀🛏◑P

DICKLEBURGH

Crown
The Street, IP21 4NQ
☼ 12-3, 7 (5 Fri)-11; 12-11 Sat; 12-10.30 Sun
☎ (01379) 741475
website: www.dickleburghcrown.co.uk
Greene King IPA; guest beers Ⓗ
This 16th-century hostelry is situated on the
former Norwich to Ipswich turnpike. The
single bar is long and heavily beamed, and
effectively comprises three separate areas,
with pool tables at the top end and back-to-
back fireplaces and the chimney breast
neatly partitioning off the front part of the
pub. The atmosphere is relaxing with comfy
armchairs. The guest beers are often from
local breweries. The well-priced food is not
available on Wednesday. ⚏❀🛏◑♣P

DISS

Cock Inn
**63 Lower Denmark Street, Fair Green,
IP22 4BE** (SW of town centre)
☼ 11.30-3, 5-11; 11.30-11 Fri & Sat; 12-10.30 Sun
☎ (01379) 643633
Adnams Bitter; guest beers Ⓗ
Situated opposite Fair Green, this is a
sublimely comfortable, 17th-century town
pub which provides a relaxed, friendly and
atmospheric refuge for those wishing to
avoid 'restaurant pubs'. The beamed bar
areas both have an inglenook (one fire, one
woodburner) and comfy leather armchairs.
In addition to the tables in front of the pub,
the green opposite is a pleasant place to sit
with a beer in summer. ⚏❀♣P

EARSHAM

Queen's Head
Station Road, NR35 2TS
☼ 12-3, 6-11; 12-3, 7-10.30 Sun
☎ (01986) 892623
Beer range varies Ⓗ
Parts of this pub date from 1684, it is the
only remaining village pub, and doubles as
the local post office. The welcoming main
bar has a clay and tiled floor, plenty of
beams and a real fire. The side room houses
the pool table and there is a separate dining

room (evening meals by arrangement). The micro-brewery at this pub should be operational by autumn 2003. There are three ever-changing, well-kept real ales, making this a popular pub with locals and visitors. It is convenient for Earsham Otter Trust. ₳Q❀◑▲♣P⏚

EAST BARSHAM

White Horse Inn
Fakenham Road, NR21 0LH
(2 miles N of Fakenham)
⊕ 11.30 (12 Sat)-3, 6.30-11 (1.30am Sat);
12-3, 6.30-10.30 Sun
☎ (01328) 820645
Adnams Bitter, Broadside; Wells Eagle; guest beer (summer) ⊞
Fine old Grade II listed building situated on a bend on the main Fakenham to Walsingham road, which is on the main pilgrimage route to Walsingham Shrine. King Henry VIII once stayed at the ornate red-brick Tudor Barsham Hall (just down the road) while making a pilgrimage to the shrine. The interior of this open-plan pub is large and welcoming, with a huge, roaring inglenook fire at one end. There is a restaurant on an upper level at one end, but bar meals are also served in the main pub. Accommodation is offered both at the pub and an adjoining cottage. ₳Q❧❀≈◑P⅄

ERPINGHAM

Spread Eagle
Eagle Lane, NR11 7QA
⊕ 11-3, 6.30-11; 12-3, 7-10.30 Sun
☎ (01263) 761571
Adnams Bitter; Woodforde's Wherry; guest beers ⊞
This 16th-century inn is situated opposite the old Woodforde's brewery. It was the former brewery tap. The long, open-plan pub is well furnished and includes a traditional games room with a pool table, a lounge area and a separate dining section. This traditional, family-run pub with a friendly local atmosphere offers excellent home cooking along with a choice of cask ales. There is occasional live music at weekends. Children and pets are welcome. Buses run through the village to and from Aylsham on a daily basis. ₳❀◑♣P

FAIR GREEN

Gate Inn
PE32 1RW
⊕ 12-2.30, 7-11; 12-3, 7-10.30 Sun
☎ (01553) 840518
Greene King IPA; guest beer ⊞
Pleasant village local, situated just north of the A47 near Middleton, which attracts a wide range of customers. There is not the range of beer seen in some pubs, but the comfortable bar, a games room and a small dining area make it a worthwhile place to visit. No meals are served on Monday evening. In summer, the garden is an excellent place to drink, and the award-winning hanging baskets add to the appeal. ₳❀◑♣P

FAKENHAM

Star
44 Oak Street, NR21 9DY

⊕ 11-2.30, 7-11; 12-3, 7-10.30 Sun
☎ (01328) 862895
Ridleys Tolly Original; guest beer ⊞
Comfortable, friendly local close to the centre of Fakenham, a busy north-west Norfolk market town. The pub dates from the 16th century and its interior contains some unusual decorative features such as pink pastel-coloured plastered walls with black columns, rounded wooden coving and white wooden boarded ceiling planks. There is a pool room, and a very large, secure garden with children's playing area at the rear of the building. Lunch is offered on market days only. Fakenham is well served by public transport, with regular bus services to Norwich, Swaffham, King's Lynn and various resorts on the North Norfolk coast. ❀♣P

FOULDEN

White Hart
White Hart Street, IP26 5AN
⊕ 11-11; 12-10.30 Sun
☎ (01366) 328638
Elgood's Black Dog Mild; Greene King IPA, Abbot; guest beers ⊞
You will receive a warm welcome at this superb, family-run village local. A varied menu of excellent value home-cooked food is on offer – Sunday lunchtime roast only; no food Tuesday lunchtime. Children are allowed in the conservatory. Local CAMRA Pub of the Year 2003, it pub is a gem. ₳❀≈◑♿♣P⅄

FOULSHAM

Queen's Head ●
2 High Street, NR20 5AD
⊕ 12-2.30 (not Mon), 6-11 (not Jan-Feb Mon);
11-11 summer; 1-3, 7-10.30 (not Jan-Feb,
12-10.30 summer) Sun
☎ (01362) 683339
website: www.queens-head-foulsham.co.uk
Adnams Bitter; ⊞ **guest beers** ⊞/⑤
Off the beaten track, this 16th-century village free house is, however, on route 1 of the national cycle network. The beamed and comfortable main bar is warmed by two fires, and the no-smoking ex-snug is now a 'magic bar' for families/children (the landlord is a member of the Magic Circle). Camping (including caravans) is possible in the garden, as are croquet, bowls and boules. No food offered on Sunday. Broadoak cider is sold. ₳❧❀◑▲♣●P⅄

GAYTON

Crown ●
Lynn Road, PE32 1PA
⊕ 11.30-2.30 (3 Sat), 6 (5.30 Fri)-11; 12-3,
7-10.30 Sun
☎ (01553) 636252
Greene King XX Mild, IPA, Abbot, Old Speckled Hen; guest beer ⊞
Delicious food is a feature of this village local, but it does not dominate. The bars and snug provide plenty of room for drinkers, and there is also a games room and garden. Regular guest ales supplement the Greene King beers, and there are often events such as live music taking place. A roaring log fire helps to make this a wonderful place on a cold winter's evening. ₳❧❀◑♣P

GORLESTON-ON-SEA

Dock Tavern
Dock Tavern Lane, NR31 6PY
✪ 12-11; 12-10.30 Sun
☎ (01493) 442255
Draught Bass; Elgood's Black Dog Mild; Greene King IPA; guest beers ℍ
Close to the river, this pub has been subject to flooding over the years as can be seen by the flood levels at the front door. An upturned fishing boat is an unusual feature over the bar. Occasional entertainment takes place at weekends. Situated just off the High Street, it is served by several bus routes. Try the varied selection of guest beers. ✿

Lord Nelson
33 Trafalgar Road West, NR31 8BS
✪ 11-11; 12-10.30 Sun
☎ (01493) 301084
Adnams Bitter, Broadside; guest beers ℍ
Not easy to find, but worth seeking out, this cosy, two-bar pub has a wealth of Nelson memorabilia plus a collection of over 4,000 cigarette lighters. The function room that doubles as a family area. The lounge has a real fire and attractive Nelson windows. A take-away pizza service is available. ⌂Q☕✿

New Entertainer
30 Pier Plain, NR31 6PG
✪ 11-11; 12-10.30 Sun
☎ (01493) 441643
Greene King IPA; guest beers ℍ
This former Lacons pub still has the original window in the unusual rounded end. The single bar serves three separate areas, including the comfortable lounge. Unusually, the pub is completely surrounded by highway, without any pavement, as it stands between two roads. Six guest beers are on tap, one is usually from Timothy Taylor. Q♣

GREAT CRESSINGHAM

Windmill Inn
Water End, IP25 6NN
✪ 11-3, 6-11; 12-3, 6.30-10.30 Sun
☎ (01760) 756232
Adnams Bitter, Broadside; Greene King IPA; guest beers ℍ
Ever-popular, multi-roomed country pub with two large car parks and an enclosed garden with sandpit and children's activities. It has been run by the same friendly family for over 45 years. The pub is renowned for its extensive menu and good quality value meals at all times. The house beer is brewed by Bass. Music is staged each Tuesday and Thursday in one room only. Memorabilia and paraphernalia dominate throughout. All in all, something for everyone here; it can get very busy at weekends. Camping is possible in the pub grounds and you can play Aunt Sally. ⌂Q☕✿◑&Å♣P

GREAT YARMOUTH

St John's Head
58 North Quay, NR30 1JE
✪ 11-11; 12-10.30 Sun
☎ (01493) 843443
Elgood's Cambridge; guest beers ℍ

Single-bar drinking pub with a large-screen TV for sporting events. Located between the river and the town centre, it is handy for the railway station. One beer is always offered at 'sale' price, and Addlestones cider is stocked. ✿◑Å≈ (Vauxhall) ♦

Talbot ✓
4 Howard Street North, NR30 1PQ
✪ 11-11; 12-10.30 Sun
☎ (01493) 843175
Greene King Abbot; guest beers ℍ
The interior of this single-bar pub with a wooden floor and wood panelling has an old-fashioned appeal. Seating is comfortable and there is an island drinking area. The juke box has an excellent choice of classic hits ranging from the 1960s to the '80s. The interesting, varied selection of guest ales and relaxed atmosphere make this a pub well worth visiting. ≈ (Vauxhall)

GRIMSTON

Bell
1 Gayton Road, PE32 1BG
✪ 11.30 (5 Mon)-11; 12-10.30 Sun
☎ (01485) 601156
Beer range varies ℍ
This village pub has changed a great deal over the past few years. Much of the original pub is now used for guest accommodation. A total refurbishment retained the small public bar to the rear, and created a tea room. Do not be deterred by the café-style appearance, two or three ales are available. Winter opening hours may vary. ✿⌂◑P

HAPPISBURGH

Hill House
NR12 0PN
✪ 12-2.30, 7-11; 12-11 Thu-Sat; 12-10.30 Sun
☎ (01692) 650004
Shepherd Neame Spitfire; guest beer ℍ
Charming, 16th-century beamed pub of character, with a log fire. The two bars serve three ales; the house beer is called Elementary after Sherlock Holmes, whose author, Sir Arthur Conan Doyle, stayed here in 1903. A well-laid-out dining room provides good meals and special theme nights. An old signal box features as one of the three guest houses. A five-day Solstice beer festival is held every year with up to 40 real ales available. ⌂Q☕✿⌂◑Å♣P

HEACHAM

Fox & Hounds
22 Station Road, PE31 7EX
✪ 12-11; 12-10.30 Sun
☎ (01485) 570345
Draught Bass; Fox Heacham Gold; guest beers ℍ
The home of Fox Brewery, this is a thriving one-roomed locals' bar with five handpumps. The guest beers served here are generally from this brewery. There is a popular beer festival held annually in mid-July, featuring a superb range of beers not seen often locally. ✿◑P

HEDENHAM

Mermaid
Norwich Road, NR35 2LB (on B1332)

✪ 12-3, 7 (5 Fri)-11; 12-4, 7-10.30 Sun
☎ (01508) 482480
Greene King IPA; Tindall Best Bitter; guest beer Ⓗ
Just when you thought that every roadside free house had been modernised out of recognition, you come across a charming pub like this, with original oak beams, brick floors, open fires and atmosphere by the bucketful. Over 300 years old, this former coaching inn stands by the main road, with a regular bus service. It offers a separate restaurant – no food served on Sunday evening – and an outdoor play area for children.
ⒶⓆ❀◖ Ａ♣ P

HEMPSTEAD

Hare & Hounds
Baconsthorpe Road, NR35 6LD
(2 miles SE of Holt)
✪ 11-3, 6.30-11; 12-10.30 Sun
☎ (01263) 712329
Adnams Bitter; Woodforde's Wherry Ⓗ
Situated on the parish boundary on a side road between Hempstead and Baconsthorpe and north of the main village, this pub has only recently reopened. It has been extensively refurbished after being closed for the last two years. Three cask ales are served in the bar. It has a well-appointed dining area with a comprehensive menu serving reasonably-priced food in generous portions. There is a large children's play area in the gardens. Infrequent bus services to Holt and Sheringham pass through Hempstead and Baconsthorpe villages.
Ⓐ⊨◖ Ａ

HETHERSETT

King's Head
36 Old Norwich Road, NR9 3DD
✪ 11-2.30, 5.30-11; 12-3, 7-10.30 Sun
☎ (01603) 810206
Adnams Bitter; Fuller's London Pride (summer);
Greene King IPA; Theakston Old Peculier (winter) Ⓗ
The public bar of this 17th-century former coaching inn is relaxed and characterful. It has exposed beams, a pamment floor, and an unusual inglenook. This is in contrast to the separate lounge bar which is larger and more comfortable. There is also a no-smoking dining room. All the food is home cooked, but there are no meals on Sunday evening. A shove-ha'penny board is available, and there is a play area in the garden. ⒶⓆ❀◖ ⊟♣ P

HORSEY

Nelson's Head
Beach Road, NR27 3LT (300 yds off B1159)
✪ 11-3, 6-11 (10 winter); 12-3, 7-10.30 Sun
☎ (01493) 393378
Woodforde's Wherry, Nelson's Revenge Ⓗ
Close to the coast road on Horsey Marsh, the location attracts a mix of locals, naturalists and Broads holidaymakers in the summer. In the winter, the pub takes on a mellower character with its large log fire and subdued lighting. A separate dining room displays paintings that are available for purchase – they are by local artists.
Ⓐ❀◖ ♣ P

ITTERINGHAM

Walpole Arms
The Common, NR11 7AR
(NW of Aylsham, just off B1354)
✪ 12-3, 6-11; 12-11 Sat; 12-10.30 Sun
☎ (01263) 587258
website: www.thewalpolearms.co.uk
Adnams Bitter, Broadside; guest beer Ⓗ
Large, upmarket, food-oriented pub that welcomes families. The pub consists of two large rooms, one a traditional bar with old exposed beams, and a roaring log fire at one end, the other a large, well-appointed dining room. Although there is an emphasis on food, this very friendly establishment caters for the casual drinker. There is a drinking-only area near the long bar with three large tables set aside. Guest beers from local breweries are served here, along with an extensive list of bottle-conditioned Belgian beers and French cider. Walpole Arms Bitter is a house beer (brewed by Woodforde's).
ⒶⓆ❀◖ ♣ P

KENNINGHALL

Red Lion ⊘
East Church Street, NR16 2GP
✪ 12-3, 6.30-11; 12-11 Fri & Sat; 12-10.30 Sun
☎ (01953) 887849
Greene King IPA, Ⓗ **Abbot;** Ⓖ **Woodforde's Mardler's, Wherry; guest beer** Ⓗ
Situated opposite the parish church, this fine old inn has pink walls and grey tiles. The multi-roomed interior comprises a main bar with wooden floorboards and intriguing old photographs, a compact wood-panelled snug and a huge open-plan restaurant. It was awarded local CAMRA Pub of the Year, 2000. Accommodation is in converted outhouses at the rear and an additional attraction is the bowling green.
ⒶⓆ❀⊨◖ ♿ ＡP

KING'S LYNN

Fenman
Blackfriars Road, PE30 1NT
✪ 11-11; 12-3, 7-10.30 Sun
☎ (01553) 761889
Greene King IPA, Abbot; guest beer Ⓗ
This busy one-roomed locals' bar can be found opposite the railway station. The guest beer may or may not be from the Greene King stable. A pool table can be found in the bar area. The regulars often meet here to watch football.
❀≑♣

Live & Let Live ⊘
18 Windsor Road, PE30 5PL
✪ 12 (11 Sat)-11; 12-10.30 Sun
☎ (01553) 764990
Beer range varies Ⓗ
Traditional, back-street locals' pub with two bars: a cosy lounge and a larger public bar. It can be found just off London Road, opposite the Catholic church. It has changed very little since the middle of the last century. Three beers are on offer, typically including a mild or stout. There is a small public car park nearby which can be reached by turning off London Road at Guanock Terrace, near the Southgates.
⊟≑♣ ⊓

Ouse Amateur Sailing Club
Ferry Lane, PE30 1NN
(off King St near Arts Centre)
✪ 12-4, 7-11; 12-11 Fri & Sat; 12.30-4, 8-10.30 Sun
☎ (01553) 772239
Beer range varies Ⓗ
Located at the end of Ferry Lane, this popular, cosy, one-roomed bar has a wooden verandah overlooking the river. Seven beers and a cider are normally available, including an ordinary bitter, a premium bitter, a strong beer and a dark beer. It was awarded CAMRA national Club of the Year in 1998 and runner-up in 2001. Lunch is served daily except Sunday. Show this Guide or a CAMRA membership card to gain entry. ⊛Ⓒ♣

Stuart House Hotel
35 Goodwins Road, PE30 5QX
✪ 7-11; 12-3, 7-10.30 Sun
☎ (01553) 772169
website: www.stuart-house-hotel.co.uk
Beer range varies Ⓗ
Situated at the end of a gravel drive, off Goodwins Road, close to the park, this independent hotel has a comfortable bar, open to non-residents. Many locals are attracted by the relaxed atmosphere and the special events such as Friday night blues and Sunday lunchtime jazz. There is also a beer festival towards the end of July. Note that the bar is normally closed at lunchtime, except on Sunday. ⇴⊛⊯◗P

Tudor Rose
St Nicholas Street, PE30 1LR
(near Tuesday market)
✪ 11-11; 12-10.30 Sun
☎ (01553) 762824 website: www.tudorrose-hotel.co.uk
Fuller's London Pride; guest beers Ⓗ
This attractive hotel, which dates from circa 1500, offers two bars: a quiet lounge at the front, in the older part of the building, with no music, and a livelier public bar at the rear with a juke box. There are four beers on tap, three of them are changing guests.
Q⊛⊯◗◖⊟≠

White Horse
9 Wootton Road, PE30 4EZ
✪ 11-3, 5.30-11; 11-11 Fri & Sat; 12-10.30 Sun
☎ (01553) 763258
Greene King IPA; Shepherd Neame Spitfire; guest beer Ⓗ
Popular, bustling local, with two separate bars, located near the Gaywood clock. Over the years customers have enjoyed an interesting range of guest ales, some rare to the district. This is a traditional drinkers' pub where games are keenly played. Regulars also often gather here to watch the football. ⊟♣P

LARLING

Angel Inn
NR16 2QU
(just off A11, 1 mile S of Snetterton market/track)
✪ 10.30-11; 12-10.30 Sun
☎ (01953) 717963
Adnams Bitter; guest beers Ⓗ
It may now be bypassed by the A11, but do not pass by without sampling quality ale and food in one of Norfolk's landmark pubs. Enthusiastic locals are the backbone of the public bar, where the turnover of ale through five handpumps ensures variety. Mild is a staple here (unusual outside Norwich), it is much in demand by the farming and football fraternities. A popular watering-hole for discussing Norwich City FC, away fans are welcome. Book early for accommodation, especially at beer festival time. A campsite is also now up and running. Good quality home-cooked food is always available – booking is advised. ⇴⊛⊯◗◖⊟Å≠ (Harling Rd – limited service) ♣P⊟

LYNG

Fox & Hounds
The Street, NR9 5AL
✪ 12-3, 5-11; 12-11 Sat; 12-4, 7-10.30 Sun
☎ (01603) 872316
Adnams Bitter; Greene King IPA, Abbot; Woodforde's Wherry Ⓗ
Charming, old village pub, the main bar has a low, beamed ceiling, inglenook, fairy lights and old photographs of the building. The separate dining area is no-smoking and there is a games room which can also be used for functions. Mrs Bailey, a former landlady, is now the resident ghost with a penchant for changing keys in locks. Folk music is staged on the first Wednesday of the month. A sociable, community pub, there is a garden to the rear and tables set out to the front. ⇴⊛◗◖♣P

NEATISHEAD

White Horse Inn
The Street, NR12 8AD
(in centre of village E of A1151, NE of Wroxham)
✪ 11-3, 7-11; 11-11 Fri, Sat & summer; 12-3, 7-10.30 (12-10.30 summer) Sun
☎ (01692) 630828 website: www.thewhitehorse.net
Adnams Bitter, Broadside; Greene King IPA, Abbot; guest beers Ⓗ
Situated between Wroxham and Stalham, a short walk from the moorings off Barton Broad and close to the RAF museum, this traditional village local was reputedly built in 1815. There is a friendly atmosphere, and you can enjoy real fires in winter and a courtyard in summer. A good range of home-cooked food (using local produce) is available (no fast food) – booking is advised in summer. A variety of musical and other events are held – often in support of Caister lifeboat. Note the interesting photograph gallery of local sailing craft in the back bar. Children are allowed in the no-smoking café bar area. ⇴Q⊛◗◖⊟♣P⊬

NEW BUCKENHAM

King's Head
Market Place, NR16 2AN
✪ 12-3, 7-11; 12-3, 7-10.30 Sun
☎ (01953) 860487
Adnams Bitter; guest beers Ⓗ
Friendly, rural local, centrally situated in this old South Norfolk village on the green and opposite the 17th-century market-house. The interior of the pub consists of two bars with stone floors and the original old wooden panels and beams. The bars are furnished with an eclectic mix of tables and chairs. Children are allowed into the public bars. The pub is well situated for visiting the

nearby 12th-century Norman castle. Plenty of parking is available around the village green. 🏨 🕽 ♣

NORTH ELMHAM

Railway
Station Road, NR20 5HH
(on B1145, E of main village)
🕓 11-11; 12-10.30 Sun
☎ (01362) 668300
Beer range varies Ⓗ
Set back from the road, this brick and flint building, formerly the Railway Hotel, is now a relaxed and comfortable village local. It offers beers from Elgood's and assorted micro-breweries. The no-smoking area provides comfy armchairs around the fire. Just off the bar is the small dining area where the home-cooked food is served. Camping is possible in the garden, and a real cider is sometimes available in summer. There are occasional beer festivals.
Q ✿ 🕽 ▲ ♣ P ⌀

NORTH TUDDENHAM

Lodge
Main Road, NR20 8DJ
🕓 11-11; 12-10.30 Sun
☎ (01362) 637257
Reepham Rapier; guest beers Ⓗ
Well worth a stop, this 18th-century former coaching inn is now a friendly village local, and a rare regular outlet for Reepham Brewery. Many of the guests are also from Reepham. The wainscotted and beamed bar is relaxed and homely, and there is also a dining area on the other side of the building. The home-cooked food is good value, available all day, and features a wide range of dishes. Music is performed each Thursday. 🏨 ✿ 🕽 ♣ P

NORWICH

Alexandra Tavern
16 Stafford Street, NR2 3HH
(just off the Dereham road)
🕓 10.30-11; 12-10.30 Sun
☎ (01603) 627772
Chalk Hill Tap, CHB, Flintknapper's Mild; guest beers Ⓗ
If there ever was a pub that fits the cliché, 'friendly corner local', this does, but appearances are not everything. The landlord and landlady are well known in the Norwich area for their battle with Courage and their leasing terms, which gained them a considerable amount of publicity. Now completely free of tie, the pub has been transformed. It offers something for everyone and a warm welcome. The two-bar layout has been retained, and there are two real fires, a wealth of interesting memorabilia, plenty of games (darts, cards, bridge among others), bar snacks from 12.30–7, a patio area to the front and Banham cider (in season).
🏨 ♣ ♣ 🍺

Angel Gardens
96 Angel Road, NR3 3HT
🕓 11-3, 5.30-11; 11-11 Fri & Sat; 12-10.30 Sun
☎ (01603) 427490 website: www.norwichinns.com
Adnams Bitter, Broadside; Buffy's Bitter; guest beers Ⓗ
Set back from the road in Victorian suburbs just north of the old city, this pub keeps an interesting selection of beers, mainly from the smaller breweries, with the added attraction of home-cooked lunches and evening meals. Norfolk Farm cider is sold. With a main bar, sports area and function room, complete with its own bar, plus a pleasant garden to the rear, this welcoming local is convenient for the newly renovated Waterloo Park. The pub holds a children's certificate. City service bus stops are nearby.
♿ ✿ 🕽 ♣ 🍺 P

Billy Bluelight
27 Hall Road, NR1 3HQ (top end of Hall Rd, about 10 minutes' walk from main shopping area)
🕓 11-11; 12-10.30 Sun
☎ (01603) 623768
Woodforde's Great Eastern, Ⓖ **Mardler's, Wherry,** Ⓗ **Nelson's Revenge, Norfolk Nog,** Ⓖ **Admiral's Reserve, seasonal beers; guest beer** Ⓗ
This Woodforde's flagship house has the entire range of beers available, either from handpump or gravity served from a tap room situated alongside the bar. A monthly special from the Woodforde's portfolio is Beer of the Month. The pub is named after a popular Norwich character of the late 19th century. In summer, barbecues are held in the patio area. On Sunday, lunch is served until 4pm, no evening meals. The Norwich Poetry Society meets here every month. Games include crib, dominoes and skittles and a bar billiards table is provided in the main bar. Come and listen to the live music (acoustic) performed once a month.
🏨 ✿ 🕽 ♣

Champion ✿
101 Chapelfield Road, NR2 1SE
🕓 11-11; 12-10.30 Sun
☎ (01603) 765611
Buffy's Bitter; Elgood's Black Dog Mild; Greene King IPA, Morland Original; guest beers Ⓗ
Offering a number of separate bars, this is very much a friendly, traditional and genuine house, run by owners Don and Pat. The excellent selection of beers includes a number from local Norfolk breweries including Buffy's. Lunchtime snacks are served 11–3. The Champion is a former winner of the local paper's Pub of the Year award. It is located just across the road (underpass) from the shopping and bus stops of St Stephen's Street, and close to the bus station Q 🕽 ♣

Coachmakers Arms
9 St Stephen's Road, NR1 3SP
🕓 11-11; 12-10.30 Sun
☎ (01603) 662080
Greene King IPA, Abbot; Wolf Golden Jackal; Woodforde's Wherry Ⓖ
This pub is unusual in that it serves all its real ales from gravity dispense behind the bar. It is popular with all walks of life, from office workers to students. A former coaching inn, it now has a covered courtyard converted to a pleasant drinking area, and a patio. The pub is situated only a few yards from the main shopping area in St Stephens. Wooden beams predominate in the bar. Wolf mild is sold in bottles (cask conditioned). A monthly film quiz is held on the second Sunday in the month, on a big screen in the courtyard. The

Coachmakers dates from the 17th century, it is possibly even older, and is built on the foundations of an asylum – it is supposedly haunted by a 'friendly' ghost. ⚏ ❀ ◖◗ ♣

Coach & Horses
82 Thorpe Road, NR1 1BA
(500 yds from rail station)
☼ 11-11; 11-10.30 Sun
☎ (01603) 477077
Chalk Hill Tap, CHB, Dreadnought, Flinknapper's Mild, Old Tackle; guest beer Ⓗ
Situated just up the road from the railway station, this is the brewery tap for Chalk Hill Brewery (visible at the rear of the building). The pub attracts a mixture of customers from local office workers to football supporters – it is popular on match days. It serves generous portions of good food (from 12–9) from a varied menu that changes daily – the emphasis is on fish of the exotic variety. On Sunday the pub opens at 11am and serves coffee and breakfast until noon. Popular as a first port of call from the railway, it is very much a local pub. Shut the box, cards, draughts and chess are played. Banham cider is sold.
⚏ ❀ ◖◗ ⇌ (Thorpe) ♣ ● P

Duke of Wellington
91-93 Waterloo Road, NR3 1EG
(10 minutes' walk from Anglia Square)
☼ 12-11; 12-10 Sun
☎ (01603) 441182
Elgood's Black Dog Mild; Fuller's London Pride; Wolf Golden Jackal; Ⓗ **guest beers** Ⓗ/Ⓖ
Lying to the north of the city centre, this pub serves a wide variety of cask conditioned ales from the smaller breweries around the country. The house beer, Welly Boot, is brewed by Wolf. Up to 12 ales are available on gravity from the tap room just behind the bar. These always include Greene King Abbot and Hop Back Summer Lightning. Kingfisher cider is sold. Carefully renovated, the pub features mainly small areas for quiet drinking. Food consists of lunchtime rolls. An unusual selection of foreign beer is stocked, including German bottled beers, Bavarian lager and Belgian beers. To the rear of the pub is a bomb shelter which can be viewed through a glass panel in the floor. Beer festivals take place twice a year (March and Sept). ❀ ♣ ● P

Fat Cat
49 West End Street, NR2 4NA
☼ 12-11; 12-10.30 Sun
☎ (01603) 624364 website: www.fatcatpub.co.uk
Adnams Bitter; Greene King Abbot; Hop Back Summer Lightning; Kelham Island Pale Rider; Oakham Bishop's Farewell; Ⓖ **Woodforde's Wherry; guest beers** Ⓗ
Award-winning, real ale house that serves an ever-changing choice of 19 ales from around the country. The guests include at least one mild and a dark ale (stout/porter). Special themed weeks are held throughout the year. It was CAMRA national Pub of the Year in 1998. The only food sold consists of rolls. Situated just off the Dereham road, (EC routes 19, 20, 21, 22), this very friendly pub caters for a wide range of customers, from students to local business people. Many ales are dispensed from a tap room to the rear of the bar. The pub also sells up to 30 Belgian bottled beers and up to six on draught. Famed for its quality of service, visitors to Norwich should not miss out on this ale drinkers' paradise. ❀ ◖ ● ▯

Ketts Tavern
29 Ketts Hill, NR1 4EX (¾ mile from station)
☼ 11-11; 12-10.30 Sun
☎ (01603) 628520
Buffy's Bitter; guest beers Ⓗ
Welcoming free house, situated only a short distance from the railway station, it is a friendly local with a wide range of up to 10 real ales from regional and micro-breweries. The warm, cosy and inviting interior has seating in several nooks and crannies. The conservatory leads to a small garden area, where a marquee is erected for the beer festivals held throughout the year (winter, spring, summer and autumn). It was local CAMRA Pub of the Year 2001. A varied menu of pub fare, including curries, is offered; there is a no-smoking area at lunchtime only. ❀ ◖◗ ⇌ ♣ ● P ⊁

King's Arms
22 Hall Road, NR1 3HQ
☼ 11-11; 12-10.30 Sun
☎ (01603) 766361
Adnams Bitter; Greene King Abbot; Wolf Coyote; guest beers Ⓗ
Award-winning real ale house with a regularly-changing range of beers from around the country; it specialises in East Anglian micro-breweries. Up to 10 guests are on tap, and a mild and dark ale (stout/porter) are always stocked. The pub, unusually, allows customers to bring in their own food from nearby outlets. Otherwise, snack lunches are served (not Mon). The new garden and conservatory area to the rear enhances the already excellent reputation of this premium drinking establishment. It was CAMRA regional Pub of the Year 1999. Every three months, a themed week of ales takes place with the range of beers having a common denominator. Staff and regulars always offer a friendly welcome. Chess, bridge, crib and backgammon are played. The pub can be busy on football match days, when Norwich are at home. ❀ ♣ ▯

Nelson
122 Nelson Street, NR2 4DR (just off the Dereham road, about 100 yards from Fat Cat pub)
☼ 11-11; 12-10.30 Sun
☎ (01603) 626362 website: www.nelsonpub.co.uk
Adnams Broadside; Woodforde's Wherry; guest beers Ⓗ
Spacious pub dating from the middle of the 19th century, it offers up to two guests from a wide selection of micro-breweries. Regular folk music is hosted on Tuesday night and a quiz is held on Sunday. There are two separate drinking areas with live sports events being shown in the larger room. A distinct Nelson theme runs through the decor with appropriate memorabilia. A number of speciality rums and gins are available. Bar snacks are served. There is plenty of space for outdoor drinking, with a patio and a large garden area, barbecues are planned for the summer. ❀ ♣ P

Rosary Tavern
95 Rosary Road, Thorpe Hamlet, NR1 4BX
☼ 11.30-11; 12-10.30 Sun

☎ (01603) 666287 website: www.rosarytavern.cwc.net
Adnams Bitter; Black Sheep Best Bitter; Ⓗ **Fuller's London Pride;** Ⓖ **guest beers** Ⓗ

Friendly, community-oriented local that is a few minutes' walk from Norwich railway station. The Rosary stocks an ever-changing range of guests from around the country and Kingfisher cider. It has a back room which is available for meetings and socials, indeed, the pub plays host to quiz teams, darts and football. The small garden can be used for summer barbecues. Plenty of pub games are played, including bar billiards, crib, darts, shove-ha'penny and shut the box. The pub offers a varied menu and an unusual feature is the pasta evening on Wednesday. ⅓ ⊛ ◑ ⇌ (Thorpe) ♣ ● P

Trafford Arms ●
61 Grove Road, NR1 3RL
✪ 11-11; 12-10.30 Sun
☎ (01603) 628466 website: www.traffordarms.co.uk
Adnams Bitter; Tetley Bitter; guest beers Ⓗ

Welcoming, well-run local with a mixture of customers from students to local business people. It is situated only a short walk from the city centre, just behind Sainsbury's supermarket. Ales on offer include Barley Boy, brewed for the pub by local brewers, Woodforde's and up to seven guests. A popular Valentine's beer festival is now in its tenth year. Kingfisher and Addlestones cider are available. Major sporting events are shown, and quiz nights and low-key music sessions (mainly folk) take place. The pub has a quiet ambience and is a real ale haven. Outside, fixed to the wall, is a cycle rack, a fitting memorial to a former CAMRA colleague and campaigner, Terry Storer.
⊛ ◑ ● P

Wig & Pen
6 St Martins at Palace Plain, NR3 1RN
(close to cathedral and law courts)
✪ 11-11; 12-5 Sun
☎ (01603) 625891 website: www.thewigandpen.com
Adnams Bitter; Buffy's Bitter; guest beers Ⓗ

Formerly the White Lion, the pub changed its name when the new law courts opened nearby. A true locals' pub in one of the quieter parts of the city, it is popular with office workers and tourists. Delicious food is served lunchtime and evening – watch out for the landlord's choice and soup of the day. It is an ideal place to watch the annual lord mayor's street procession (July) when the pub puts on an excellent barbecue. The house beer, when available, is Courage Best.
♨ ⊛ ◑ ⅄

OLD HUNSTANTON

Ancient Mariner
Golf Course Road, PE36 6JJ
✪ 11-11; 12-10.30 Sun
☎ (01485) 534411 website: www.lestrangearms.co.uk
Adnams Bitter, Broadside; Draught Bass; guest beers Ⓗ

Attached to the Le Strange Arms Hotel, the pub was converted from old barns and retains a comfortable, timbered feel. It occupies a quiet spot away from the main resort of Hunstanton. The Mariner is family-friendly with two family rooms, the one in the attic has superb sea views. The garden has extensive seating, a pond and a children's play area and leads directly to the beach. Unusually for the east coast, you can watch the sun set over the sea with a beer in hand. ♨ ⅓ ⊛ ⊠ ◑ ♣

ORMESBY ST MARGARET

Grange Hotel
Yarmouth Road, NR29 3QG
✪ 11-11; 12-10.30 Sun
☎ (01493) 731877
Beer range varies Ⓗ

This hotel stands in extensive grounds on the main coast road. There are two bars, both very comfortable. A pool room adjoins the main bar and sports fans are well catered for in the smaller bar. Beers come from far and wide with a strong emphasis on Welsh ales. Accommodation is available both in the hotel and in self-catering cottages. The garden has a children's corner.
⅓ ⊛ ⊠ ◑ ▲ ♣ P

PORINGLAND

Royal Oak
The Street, NR14 7JT (on B1332)
✪ 12-3, 5-11; 12-3, 7-10.30 Sun
☎ (01508) 493734
Adnams Bitter; Mauldons Moletrap; guest beers Ⓗ

This large village local (built in 1845) has developed into a semi open-plan layout, with plenty of separate drinking areas; some comfortably furnished, but most for drinkers. This is primarily an ale house, with a wide and varying selection of interesting beers always available. The house beer is Delia's Delight. The absence of food means the ales can be enjoyed without the pervading smell of garlic or chips. The Royal Oak holds spring and autumn beer festivals, as well as special party nights to celebrate St George's Day and Trafalgar Day. Adjacent is a handy fish and chip shop. Carry-outs are available. Regular quiz nights take place. ⊛ ♣ ● P

PULHAM ST. MARY

King's Head
The Street, IP21 4RD
✪ 11.30-3, 5.30-11; 11.30-11 Sat & summer; 12-10.30 Sun
☎ (01379) 676318
Adnams Bitter; guest beers Ⓗ

Friendly, 17th-century local situated in the village centre. It serves quality cask ales, the house beer is Hancock's HB. Welcoming B&B is offered for those wishing to explore the many local walks. The garden is a big attraction for children, with a bouncy castle in the summer and a tree house. A bowling green will please those preferring a more gentle activity with their pint. Good value meals are served all day Saturday and Sunday. A champagne quiz is held on alternate Thursdays. ♨ ⊛ ⊠ ◑ ♣ P

REEPHAM

King's Arms
Market Place, NR10 4JT
✪ 11.30-3, 5.30-11; (11.30-11 summer Sat); 12-3, 7-10.30 Sun
☎ (01603) 870345
Adnams Bitter; Courage Best Bitter, Directors; Greene King Abbot; guest beer Ⓗ

Fine old listed building (circa 1725) situated

in one corner of the market place of this historic mid-Norfolk market town. Internally, it is a large, rambling, half-timbered, open-plan pub with two serving areas and plenty of seating space. There is a large conservatory and if you walk to the back of the pub you can look down an old glass-topped well. Meals include traditional Sunday lunches when you can dine to the sound of live jazz music. Ample parking is available in the market square outside. ⌂➤❀◑♣✂

ROYDON

Blacksmiths Arms
30 Station Road, PE32 1AW
🕑 12 (4.30 Tue & Wed)-11; 12-10.30 Sun
☎ (01485) 601347
Greene King IPA; Ⓗ **guest beers** Ⓖ
This is a very busy locals' bar with a welcoming real fire. Traditional games are popular and the pub is involved in a number of local leagues. Unlike many country inns, this is a drinkers' pub that does not serve meals. It also sells Westons Old Rosie cider, which is not very common in this part of the country. There are generally three beers on tap, two of them being varied guest beers. ⌂❀♣◐P

RUSHALL

Half Moon
The Street, IP21 4QD (near Diss)
🕑 12-3, 6 (5 Sat)-11; 12-10.30 Sun
☎ (01379) 740793
website: www.rushallhalfmoon.co.uk
Adnams Bitter; Woodforde's Wherry Ⓗ
This charming, food-oriented pub was once a 16th-century coaching inn. The public bar has a large inglenook. The Half Moon has an excellent reputation for fine meals. The no-smoking conservatory dining area seats up to 40. Gifts are for sale. There are 10 guest rooms available. Waveney Valley is within easy reach. ⌂❀✿◑ ♣P☐

SAHAM TONEY

Old Bell
1 Bell Lane, IP25 7HD
🕑 11-3, 5-11; 11-11 Sat; 12-10.30 Sun
☎ (01953) 884934
Adnams Bitter; guest beers Ⓗ
Traditional village pub overlooking the oldest mere in the country. This fine family-run free house offers a choice of ever-changing guest ales. The selection includes Frog Island Shoemaker, Kelham Island Easy Rider and Old Chimneys Polecat Porter. A wide range of home-made food (using local produce) is provided; the meat is from an award-winning butcher. The chef's own desserts include home-made ice cream. A children's menu is also available. It is advisable to book at weekends. ⌂Q❀◑ ⊟♣P

SHERINGHAM

Lobster
13 High Street, NR26 8JB
🕑 11.30-11; 12-10.30 Sun
☎ (01263) 822716 website: www.the-lobster.com
Adnams Bitter, Broadside; Greene King Abbot; Marston's Pedigree; guest beers Ⓗ

This traditional family pub is located at the seaward end of the High Street and has retained a two bar layout while acquiring additional facilities, including a function room and 80-cover restaurant to the rear. The food style is modern/trad English, sourced locally by its French-trained chef/owner. Close ties are maintained with the town's lifeboat and the local fishermen; a football team is sponsored, skittles and boules are played, and the pub is the spiritual home of the Lobster Potties morris side. ⌂➤❀◑♿⇌♣P✂

SHOTESHAM

Globe
The Common, NR15 1YC
(on unclassified road, 1 mile SE of Stoke Holy Cross)
🕑 12-11; 12-10.30 Sun
☎ (01508) 550475
Adnams Bitter; Greene King IPA Ⓖ
Traditional pub, situated on the road running through this pleasant linear village. It overlooks the picturesque river valley and the whole area is ideal walking country. Beers are served by gravity because that's how the regulars prefer it. One is instantly made welcome, and you soon feel at home in this pub. Morning teas and coffee are offered. The intimate, small dining room has an interesting traditional menu. It is popular for Sunday lunches. Enquire about weekday lunches as they are available with notice. Children will enjoy the swings and other play equipment. Handy for the nearby nudist camp. ❀◑♿P✂

SMALLBURGH

Crown Inn
NR12 9AD
(on A149 between North Walsham and Stalham)
🕑 12-3 (not Mon), 5.30-11; 7-11 Sat;
12-3 (closed eve) Sun
☎ (01692) 536314
Adnams Bitter, Broadside; Greene King IPA, Abbot; guest beer Ⓗ
Welcoming, friendly and full of character, this comfortable, thatched, village local was once a 15th-century coaching inn and retains some original timbers. The log fire in winter enhances the already cosy atmosphere. A good selection of home-cooked meals, using local produce when available, is served in the bar or dining room. There is a tranquil tree-lined garden at the rear. This locally renowned pub is situated close to the North Norfolk coast and Norfolk Broads. A gem. ⌂Q❀✿◑⊟♣P

SOUTH CREAKE

Ostrich Inn
1 Fakenham Road, NR21 9PB (on B1355, Fakenham-Burnham Market road)
🕑 12-3 (not Tue), 7-11; 12-3, 7-10.30 Sun
☎ (01328) 823320 website: www.ostrichinn.co.uk
Greene King IPA, Abbot; Woodforde's Nelson's Revenge; guest beer Ⓗ
This free house, a 17th-century, Grade II listed inn, is centrally located in a long, straggling village. Its long, single bar is divided into different areas: a comfortable bar area, restaurant, and cosy armchairs round a wood-burning stove, plus a separate

section with a pool table. Wheelchair WC and baby changing facilities are available. A superb menu includes vegetarian and ostrich dishes. The accommodation, which includes one unit to disability standards, is handy for the North Norfolk coast. Limited bus services run between Fakenham and Burnham Market. The Ostrich is the crest of the Coke family of the nearby Holkham estate. ♨☸♿⏱◑ఉ♠P

STRUMPSHAW

Shoulder of Mutton
Norwich Road, NR13 4NT
☼ 11-11; 12-10.30 Sun
☎ (01603) 712274
Adnams Bitter, Broadside; guest beers Ⓗ
Welcoming pub-restaurant that is set back from the main road; it offers a wide range of ales with an Adnams emphasis. Booking is advisable for the restaurant – no meals on Sunday evening. Unusually for this area, the pub has several petanque courts at the rear, and an extensive garden can make summer visits a relaxing experience. ☸♣P

SWAFFHAM

George Hotel
Station Street, PE37
☼ 11-2.30, 6.30-11; 12-2, 7-10.30 Sun
☎ (01760) 721238
Greene King IPA, Abbot Ⓗ
Town-centre hotel with a public bar, built in the 18th century, with a modern extension. The George is a stone's throw from Swaffham's beautiful medieval church and historic market place. The food is highly original with constantly-changing specials. The bar has a relaxed, olde-worlde feel. ⏱◑P⌿

Lydney House Hotel
Norwich Road, PE37 7QS
(note blue signs in town centre)
☼ 11-11; closed Sun
☎ (01760) 723355
website: www.lydney-house.demon.co.uk
Woodforde's Wherry; guest beers Ⓗ
The excellent beers kept at this small hotel mean Swaffham has come up in the real ale world. The guest beers are from local sources such as Iceni. The bar has an extensive collection of pub games – including traditional pinball and bar skittles. Bar meals are available Monday–Saturday, as well as a full restaurant menu. The hotel is on the other side of the church from the George, allowing a visit to both venues in one day. ☸⏱◑♣P

TERRINGTON ST JOHN

Woolpack
Main Road, PE14 7RR
☼ 11-2.30, 6-11; 12-3, 7-10.30 Sun
☎ (01945) 881097
Greene King IPA; Wells Eagle; guest beer Ⓗ
Rarely has a pub become so popular in such a short space of time. The Australian couple that took over an empty shell have introduced excellent beer, great food and a wonderful atmosphere. The addition of a dining room has allowed more space for those who just wish to drink, but it can still become very crowded. The landlady is an

extremely talented artist, and has also done a fine job in selecting the pictures, which decorate the bars. ☸☀◑P

THETFORD

Albion ⊘
93-95 Castle Street, IP24 2DN
(opp. Castle Hill park/ancient monument)
☼ 11-2.30 (3 Fri & Sat), 6 (5 Fri)-11; 12-3, 7-10.30 Sun
☎ (01842) 752796
Greene King IPA, Abbot; guest beer (occasional) Ⓗ
Pleasantly situated among a row of cottages, this well-established and popular local looks out across Castle Park towards Castle Hill, the town's highest point. This small, two-roomed pub is basic but friendly and comfortable. The main bar offers conversation; the lower area caters for pool and darts fans. Add an intimate enclosed patio for relaxed summer drinking and it is easy to see why this pub retains its traditional reputation. Simple food is on offer – sandwiches and jacket potatoes from Monday–Saturday. ♨Q☸P

THORNHAM

Lifeboat Inn
Ship Lane, PE36 6LT
☼ 11-11; 12-10.30 Sun
☎ (01485) 512236 website: www.lifeboatinn.co.uk
Adnams Bitter; Greene King IPA, Abbot; Woodforde's Wherry; guest beer Ⓗ
Things have changed a lot since the 16th century, when this was a smugglers' ale house. Today, the North Norfolk coast is fashionable and busy all year round. The Lifeboat has responded by expanding its food and accommodation side but has managed to retain the character of the pub. It is still dark and cosy in the main bar with log fires, panelling and paraffin lamps. A bright, airy conservatory, clothed in summer by a huge, beer-fed vine provides a modern touch. Westons Old Rosie cider is stocked. ♨Q☸⏱◑♣●P⌿🍴

TIBENHAM

Greyhound
The Street, NR16 1PZ
☼ 6.30-11 (not Tue); 12-3, 6.30-11 Fri; 12-11 Sat; 12-10.30 Sun
☎ (01379) 677676
Adnams Bitter; Greene King IPA; guest beers Ⓗ
Cosy, old, two-roomed pub whose low, beamed interior consists of a carpeted lounge with old real fire and a bar with stone floors and a dartboard. Memorabilia of WWII USA Liberator bombers adorn the walls, reminding us that a wartime US air base was once situated nearby. Guest ales on sale here usually include a Shepherd Neame beer. There is a separate pool room in a barn outside. A large car park and camping facilities can be found to the rear. ♨Q☸◑Å♣P

TRUNCH

Crown ⊘
Front Street, NR28 0AH
☼ 12-2.30, 5.30-11; 12-2.30, 5.30-10.30 Sun
☎ (01263) 722341
website: www.thecrowninntrunch.co.uk

Adnams Bitter, Broadside; Greene King IPA; guest beers H

Once part of the old brewery, this well-run, attractive village pub is exceptionally bright and friendly with a blazing log fire to welcome customers. This free house has a single bar with frequently-changing real ales from all parts of the country. It is well furnished with a local 'old gits corner'. A small, cosy restaurant leads from the bar.
🏚Q✿①⊟♣P

UPPER SHERINGHAM

Red Lion
The Street, NR26 8AD
(on B1157, 1 mile from Sheringham)
☼ 11.30 (12 winter)-3, 6.30-11; 12-4, 6.30-10.30 (closed winter eve) Sun
☎ (01263) 825408
Greene King IPA; Woodforde's Wherry; guest beer (occasional) H

One mile inland from the coastal town, on the Cromer Ridge, this pub has survived big brewery neglect and closure to become a popular destination. With its flint-clad exterior, fine coastal views, tiled floor interior and woodburners, bar dining, and a separate no-smoking room, the emphasis is on food without compromising the welcome of a traditional pub. Accommodation is provided in three cottage-style bedrooms while the pub is convenient for visitors to the nearby NT Sheringham Hall. 🏚🛏✿🚪①▲♣P✂

UPTON

White Horse
17 Chapel Road, NR13 6BP
☼ 11-11; 12-10.30 Sun
☎ (01493) 750696
Adnams Bitter, Broadside; Mauldons Bitter; guest beers H

Old established free house close to the staithe and handy for the Norfolk Broads. A traditional pub with a homely atmosphere, it attracts locals and tourists. Reasonably-priced meals are served in the restaurant. The take-away fish and chips are a local legend. Addlestones cider is available.
🏚Q✿①▲♣♠P

WALCOTT

Lighthouse Inn ⊘
Coast Road, NR12 0PE (main coast road, close to church)
☼ 11-11; 12-10.30 Sun
☎ (01692) 650371 website: www.lighthouseinn.co.uk
Adnams Bitter; Greene King Abbot; Woodforde's Wherry; guest beers H

This village pub is not only popular with locals, many holidaymakers flock to the Lighthouse. Four real ales are offered and there is a no-smoking dining room serving food all day. Many events are organised throughout the year and the pub has its own pool and darts teams. There is ample space outside, barbecues are held and there is a play area, making it popular with families. 🏚Q🛏✿①▲♣P

WARHAM ALL SAINTS

Three Horseshoes ☆
Bridge Street, NR23 1NL

☼ 11.30-2.30, 6-11; 12-2.30, 6-10.30 Sun
☎ (01328) 710547
Greene King IPA; H **Woodforde's Wherry;** G **guest beer** H

Access is only from the rear of the pub. The main bar is genuine 1920s and the serving area is via a hatch at one end. Some of the cask beers are served by gravity. The rest of the pub has been extended in recent years and is modern but still retains the old atmosphere of the original bar. Parking at the pub is restricted but there is a large overspill car park in a field opposite. The modern toilets have full disabled access.
🏚Q✿🚪①♿♣P

WATTON

Breckland Wines
80 High Street, IP25 6AH
☼ 9-9 Mon-Sun
☎ (01953) 881592
Beer range varies G

Traditional off-licence catering to the beer enthusiast. Delights include a draught beer from the Iceni range – available to take away. It offers the most extensive range of bottled beers from Norfolk brewers found anywhere. It is the only outlet for Old Chimneys and Woodforde's bottled beers in south-west Norfolk. There are plans to produce a house beer.

WEST BECKHAM

Wheatsheaf
Church Road, NR25 6NX (1 mile S of A148)
☼ 12-3, 6.30-11 (may close earlier winter Mon-Fri); 12-3, 7-10.30 Sun
☎ (01263) 822110 website: www.wheatsheaf.org.uk
Woodforde's Wherry, Nelson's Revenge, H **Norfolk Nog,** G **Admiral's Reserve,** H **Headcracker;** G **guest beers** H

Popular with locals and tourists, the Wheatsheaf is family- and dog-friendly. Two frequently-changing guest beers include one usually sold at a special low price. Bar snacks and an extensive menu offer value and variety; no meals on Sunday evening. A games room and a large beer garden are provided. On display, is a child's latchet tie shoe, a 1770s relic found in a chimney breast during renovation from farmhouse to pub in 1984. The Woodforde's Norfolk Nog poster is less venerable, but still the last of its type on display, according to the brewery. Self-catering accommodation is available on site. Bus X98, King's Lynn to Cromer, passes through the village daily. 🏚Q🛏✿🚪①♣P

WEYBOURNE

Ship
The Street, NR25 7SZ (on A149 coast road)
☼ 12-3, 6 (7 winter)-11; 11-11 Sat; 12-4, 7-10.30 Sun (phone to confirm)
☎ (01263) 588721 website: www.norwichinns.com
Beer range varies H

Located opposite the church on a sharp bend, this is a stylish, 19th-century brick and flint building, retaining a verandah and Steward & Patteson Brewery windows. The public bar has wooden floors, open fires and an attached pool room while a lounge/dining room enjoys a good reputation for its locally-based menu.

Popular with visitors to the Muckleburgh military collection, the North Norfolk Railway, and walkers, the pub also supports a beer festival. Banham cider is available in summer. The Coastliner bus stops outside.
🏧❀🅲🅳🖴🅰♣🍺P

WICKLEWOOD

Cherry Tree
116 High Street, NR18 9QA
🕒 12-3, 7-11; 12-3, 7-10.30 Sun
☎ (01953) 606962
Buffy's Norwich Terrier, Bitter, Polly's Folly, Hopleaf; guest beer Ⓗ/Ⓖ

This old inn, parts of which date back to the 17th century, has plenty of character. There is a large car park and beer garden with many tables outside. The pleasant interior is L-shaped with stone floors and low ceilings. There is a separate carpeted dining area at one end where home-cooked food is available. Smoking is not allowed in parts of the bar or the dining area. The pub is leased by Buffy's and cask ales, all of which are from the Buffy's range (usually about seven at any one time), are served by either handpump or gravity direct from the cellar. The bar area now boasts a grand piano and occasional live music and quiz nights have become regular features. Q❀🅲🅳🅰♣P✂

WINFARTHING

Fighting Cocks
The Street, IP22 2ED
🕒 11-2.30 (not Mon), 5.30-midnight; 12-4, 7-10.30 Sun
☎ (01379) 643283
Adnams Bitter; Ⓖ **guest beers** Ⓗ

Independent, 16th-century free house, a thriving, friendly village local that boasts darts and pool teams. The large opened-up bar area has many beams and an inglenook. There is also a games room. Rallies and gatherings are hosted here, and there is plentiful free camping (including caravans) behind the pub. Guest beers come from a variety of small brewers. A weekday bus service runs from Diss. The home-made food is reasonably priced.
🏧❀🅲🅳🅰♣P

WINTERTON-ON-SEA

Fisherman's Return
The Lane, NR29 4BN (off B1159)
🕒 11-2.30, 6.15-11; 11-11 Sat; 12-10.30 Sun
☎ (01493) 393305
Adnams Bitter; Woodforde's Wherry; guest beers Ⓗ

Traditional, flint-faced, 300-year-old inn with an attractive wood-panelled public bar. It is run by a long-standing landlord and landlady who were championing real ale in their pub when Norfolk was a 'Watneys desert'. Guest ales come from local East Anglian breweries, and real cider drinkers are well catered for with Westons Old Rosie on handpump. Old photographs of former local pubs are mute witness to the pub closure programme carried out following the takeover of Norfolk's breweries in the 1960s and '70s. The village stands on the site of the original village of Bulmer, Winterton having long since disappeared under the sea.
🏧🛏❀🚳🅲🅳🖴🅰♣🍺P✂

WOODBASTWICK

Fur & Feather
Slad Lane, NR13 6HR
🕒 11-2.30, 6-11 (11-11 summer); 12-10.30 Sun
☎ (01603) 720003
Woodforde's Mardler's, Wherry, Great Eastern, Nelson's Revenge, Norfolk Nog Ⓖ

Rural restaurant set in an award-winning village. Converted from three cottages, it sits by the brewery, which offers its own shop and visitors centre. Originally a pub which was intended to be the brewery tap, a full range of beers is available, including a house ale, Fur & Feather. In summer, drinkers can enjoy a pint in the garden. One of the few places where Woodforde's entire range is available.
❀🅲🅳♿P

WYMONDHAM

Feathers
13 Town Green, NR18 0PN
(¼ mile NW of town centre)
🕒 11-2.30, 7 (6 Fri)-11; 12-2, 7-10.30 Sun
☎ (01953) 605675
Adnams Bitter; Greene King Abbot; Marston's Pedigree; guest beers Ⓗ

Cosy, beamed, one-bar town local, the walls of which are adorned with an absolute plethora of rustic implements and assorted memorabilia. The drinking area is sub-divided into small sections as it rambles towards the courtyard and garden at the rear of the building. The menu is straightforward and good value. The house beer is by Mauldons, and the guests come from a wide variety of breweries.
🏧❀🅲🅳♣

Green Dragon
6 Church Street, NR18 0PH
🕒 11-3, 6-11; 12-3, 7-10.30 Sun
☎ (01953) 607907
Adnams Bitter, Broadside; Greene King IPA; guest beer (summer) Ⓗ

Historic, 14th-century town pub which also offers accommodation. The scorch marks on the front of the building date from a great fire of 1615. The single-room bar has a dining area and the decor, as you might expect, features many old beams and much wood panelling, as well as a large Tudor fireplace in the bar. A splendid place for a quiet pint if it is not too busy; no food is served on Sunday evening. A small, sheltered courtyard offers an alternative on a summer's day.
🏧Q❀🛏🅲🅳⇌♣P

> Charles Collins liveth here,
> Sells rum, brandy, gin and beer;
> I make this board a little wider
> To let you know I sell
> good cyder.
>
> Seventeenth-century notice at the Arrow, Knockholt, Kent

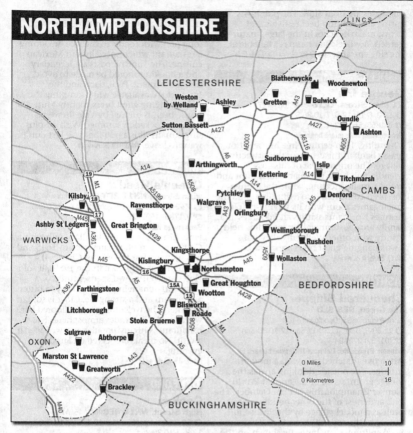

NORTHAMPTONSHIRE

ABTHORPE

New Inn
Silver Street, NN12 8QR (off A43/B4525 main st)
☼ 12-3, 6-11; 12-10.30 Sun
☎ (01327) 857306
Hook Norton Best Bitter, seasonal beers; guest beers Ⓗ

A welcome return to this Guide, after many years' absence for a quiet country pub hidden in a cul-de-sac off the corner of the village green. Built from mellow sandstone, the New Inn was once a thatched farmhouse, although it is now tiled and provides the villagers with a more popular amenity. The appealing interior has an inglenook, a long games bar, and a restaurant on a lower level in the Elton John snug. A beer festival is held over August bank holiday weekend. Aunt Sally is played here. ♨Q❀◗◑ ⊟Å♣P⅄

ARTHINGWORTH

Bull's Head
Kelmarsh Road, LE16 8JZ (off A508)
☼ 12-3, 6-11 (12-11 summer); 12-10.30 Sun
☎ (01858) 525637
website: www.thebullshead@btconnect.com
Adnams Bitter; Everards Tiger; Wells Eagle; guest beers Ⓗ

Large, thriving 19th-century brick-built pub, converted from a former farmhouse. The spacious oak-beamed bar is L-shaped with log fires. Olde-worlde barn conversions provide overnight accommodation, which, as with the main building, retain the original charm and character. Fresh home-cooked meals prepared by a fully qualified chef are available and may either be eaten in the restaurant or on the heated patio. Up to three guest beers supplement the regular range. ♨Q❀➤◗◑ ⊟♣P⅄

ASHBY ST LEDGERS

Olde Coach House
Main Street, CV23 8UN
☼ 12-3, 5-11; 12-11 Sat and summer; 12-10.30 Sun
☎ (01788) 890349
website: www.traditional-freehouses.com
Everards Original; Flowers Original; Frog Island Best Bitter; Taylor Landlord; guest beers Ⓗ

This former 19th-century farmhouse is a popular village inn and regular Guide entry. Built of local golden ironstone, like the rest of the picturesque village, it consists of a bar with Sky TV, and a series of interconnected rooms leading to the award-winning restaurant. Beams, wood panelling and high-backed benches complement the walk-in fireplace. Children are welcome throughout and the pool room is set aside for families. The

INDEPENDENT BREWERIES

Frog Island Northampton
Hoggleys Kislingbury
Rockingham Blatherwycke

359

guest ales are from SIBA. The pub hosts spring and autumn beer festivals and occasional barbecues in the large, mature garden. A wheelchair ramp is available at the side entrance. ♨Q❄☺☏◑▣♣P⏣

ASHLEY

George Inn
21 Main Street, LE16 8HF (off A427)
✪ 12-2, 6-11; 12-3, 7-10.30 Sun
☎ (01858) 565642
Greene King IPA; guest beers Ⓗ
Charming, 18th-century free house set on a grassy bank in the centre of this attractive village. The original bar of this cosy, friendly pub has a red quarry-tiled floor and wood-panelled seating, while the lounge has been converted into a dining room. The small games room with its serving-hatch features Northants skittles and doubles as a family area. A summer beer festival is held jointly with other Welland Valley pubs. Two changing guest beers are on tap.
♨Q❄☺◑☖♣P

ASHTON

Chequered Skipper
The Green, PE8 5LD
(1 mile from A605, Oundle jct)
✪ 11.30-3, 6-11; 11.30-11 Sat; 12-10.30 Sun
☎ (01832) 273494
Adnams Broadside; Oakham JHB; guest beers Ⓗ
Attractive thatched pub with a modern interior. The outside drinking area is the village green, scene of the annual World Conker Championship held in October. The pub and most of the other buildings were built as a model village by the Rothschild family in the early 20th century. The name is taken from a rare butterfly shown on the unusual pub sign and displayed as one of the butterfly exhibits in the pub. Two guest beers are normally sold and the pub is popular with drinkers and diners. The food is recommended and booking is advised at weekends. Q❄◑☖P

BLISWORTH

Royal Oak
1 Chapel Lane, NN7 3BU (on old A43)
✪ 12-2.30, 6-11; 12-11 Fri & Sat; 12-10.30 Sun
☎ (01604) 858372
Hook Norton Best Bitter; Marston's Pedigree; guest beers Ⓗ
Traditional, 300-year-old village pub on the main road, where the single main bar area boasts an inglenook and old oak beams characterise the snug area. The no-smoking dining room offers home-cooked food all year round. An extensive garden includes a children's play area, while the large games/function room has facilities for Northants skittles, darts and pool. Popular with users of the canal, 200 yards away, the pub stocks four guest ales. ♨Q❄☺◑♣P

BRACKLEY

Greyhound
101 High Street, NN13 7BW
✪ 12-3 (summer only), 7-11; 12-4, 6-midnight Sat; 12-4, 7-10.30 Sun
☎ (01280) 703331 website: www.pubssearch.com
Beer range varies Ⓗ

A warm welcome is guaranteed in this traditional pub to the north of the town. Built as a coaching inn in 1760, it is now a long pub with rooms to the side, including a restaurant which specialises in Mexican cuisine. The Sunday roasts are legendary and a booking should be made to avoid disappointment. Pool, darts and the Internet are available while sampling the ever-changing guest beers. Skinny Mutt, the house beer, is brewed by Vale Brewery. Cider is stocked in summer. With 40-plus single malts, it is a pub that you just don't want to leave. ♨❄◑☖♠♣☝

BULWICK

Queen's Head
Main Street, NN17 3DY (500 yds from A43)
✪ 12-2.30, 6-11; closed Mon; 12-3, 7-10.30 Sun
☎ (01780) 450272
Beer range varies Ⓗ
Fine, historic, stone-built village pub with a Collyweston roof. It dates back to 1645 and was named after the wife of Charles II – Catherine of Braganza. In the 1950s, it sold Holes ales but now dispenses three constantly-changing beers – always a bitter, a premium and a strong ale. Cider is sold in summer. The welcoming stone-floored bar, with a real fire, exudes atmosphere. The restaurant is highly popular and well worth a visit. No meals are served on Sunday evening.
♨❄◑☖♣P

DENFORD

Cock ⊘
High Street, NN14 4EC (off A45/A14)
✪ 12-3 (not Mon), 5.30-11; 12-4, 6.30-11 Sat; 12-3, 7-10.30 Sun
☎ (01832) 732565 website: www.cock-inn.co.uk
Draught Bass; Flowers Original; guest beers Ⓗ
Picturesque Nene Valley pub only 200 yards from the river on the old Northampton to Peterborough mail-coach run. Once a saddler's, bootmaker's and blacksmith's, the Cock now has an L-shaped bar with a low, beamed ceiling, bare floorboards, small leaded windows and a roaring open fire. Games include Northants skittles and shut the box. The landlady is a qualified chef and serves home-cooked food in the restaurant, renowned for its curries. The enterprising landlord now serves three changing guests beers. To the rear is an enclosed garden for the children, while benches are laid out to the front of the small village green for fair weather days.
♨Q❄◑☖♣

FARTHINGSTONE

King's Arms
Main Street, NN12 8EZ
✪ 12-3 (not Mon-Fri), 7-11 (not Mon or Wed); 12-3, 9-10.30 Sun
☎ (01327) 361604
Hook Norton Best Bitter; guest beers Ⓗ
Idyllic, 18th-century pub in an attractive location opposite the church. The L-shaped bar, which includes a comfortable armchair lounge area, is decorated with interesting ornaments. In a warm, friendly atmosphere, home-cooked food is served at weekends (booking advised); traditional British

cheeses are a speciality. Full of shrubs and herbs, the beautiful garden is a very restful place to enjoy a beer. A side room is used for Northants skittles. Up to three guest beers are offered. ♨☆◑Å♣P

GREAT BRINGTON

Fox & Hounds
Main Street, NN7 4EW (2 miles from A428)
☼ 11-11; 12-10.30 Sun
☎ (01604) 770651
website: www.althorpe-coaching-inn.co.uk
Fuller's London Pride; Greene King IPA, Abbot, Old Speckled Hen; guest beers Ⓗ

A handy refreshment stop on the Diana Spencer memorial trail, this friendly village local offers up to six guests alongside its regular beers. Much of the pub is given over to diners in the busy lunchtime and early evening but reverts to lively banter later, with live music on Tuesday evening. The atmosphere is enhanced by the flagstoned floor, idiosyncratic nouveau-rustic wooden beams and the real fire in the enormous inglenook. The courtyard becomes a pleasant outdoor drinking area in summer. A collection of china bedpans graces the ladies' toilets. A 'happy hour' is featured 5–7 on weekdays. ♨☆◑●P

GREAT HOUGHTON

White Hart
39 High Street, NN4 7AF (off A428)
☼ 12-3, 5.30 (6 Sat)-11; 12-3, 7-10.30 Sun
☎ (01604) 762940
Greene King IPA; Hook Norton Best Bitter; guest beers Ⓗ

Popular, traditional, thatched village pub on the outskirts of Northampton. The main bar is divided into three individual eating/drinking areas with reasonably priced home-cooked food and regularly changing guests. It has a large, well-maintained beer garden. Quiz nights are held every Thursday evening and several local clubs (including Alfa Romeo) meet monthly at the pub. A free taxi service is offered for diners within a five-mile radius. Q☆◑P

GREATWORTH

Inn
Chapel Road, OX17 2DT
☼ 12-2 (not Mon or Tue), 6.30-11; 12-3, 6.30-10.30 Sun
☎ (01295) 710976
Hook Norton Best Bitter, Old Hooky, seasonal beers; guest beer Ⓗ

Warm and cosy, 16th-century, classic village pub with the plainest of names. Inside are three interconnected rooms that are heavily decorated with brass, photographs, plates and aircraft prints. The small bar is an integral part of the middle room where the locals enjoy the roaring winter fire in the inglenook. Aunt Sally is played in the garden at the rear. ♨Q☆◑●♣P

GRETTON

Blue Bell Inn
90 High Street, NN17 3DF (off A6003)
☼ 12-2.30, 5-11; 12-11 Sat; closed Mon; 12-10.30 Sun
☎ (01536) 770404
Greene King IPA, Abbot; guest beers Ⓗ

This 15th-century pub is located in the middle of a row of mellow yellow limestone houses, on a hill that overlooks the Welland Valley. It is close to the Welland Viaduct, the longest viaduct across a valley on the national rail network. Inside this former bakehouse are two rooms and a restaurant where three guest ales are regularly served. The Blue Bell is one of the pubs that forms the Welland Valley beer festival in the summer. ♨☆◑● ●♣⌖

ISHAM

Lilacs ✓
39 Church Street, NN14 1HD
☼ 12-3, 5.30-11; 12-11 Fri; 11-11 Sat; 12-4, 7-10.30 Sun
☎ (01536) 723948
Greene King IPA, Ruddles Best Bitter; guest beers Ⓗ

Traditional village pub with three drinking areas: the bay-fronted lounge has a log fire; there is a snug and a large games room where Northants skittles can be played. This pub is community-focused and supports various charities. Several clubs hold regular meetings here, such as the Jaguar and Reliant enthusiasts, and the singles club. Frequent theme nights are organised, and a classic car show takes place in summer. ♨☞☆●●♣P

ISLIP

Rose & Crown
1 High Street, NN14 3JS (off A14/A6116)
☼ 12-2.30, 4.30-11; 12-11 Sat; 12-5, 7-10.30 Sun
☎ (01832) 733118
Oakham Bishops Farewell; RCH East Street Cream; guest beers Ⓗ

A former Mansfield-badged pub built from local ironstone and featuring a Collyweston tiled roof. Dating from 1691, the interior consists of two rooms with low, beamed ceilings and a warm, welcoming fire for cold winter days. A small patio and long garden lead down to the River Nene. In fact, the Nene Valley Way actually runs through the garden. The pub is considered a drinkers' local, and for this reason food is only served at lunchtime. Children's play equipment is provided outside. ♨Q☞☆●P

KETTERING

Alexandra Arms
39 Victoria Street, NN16 0BU
(400 yds from bus station)
☼ 2 (12 Sat)-11; 12-10.30 Sun
☎ (01536) 522730
Frog Island Best Bitter; Greene King IPA; guest beers Ⓗ

As you walk into the lounge through the main entrance, note the brewery memorabilia. The lounge separates into two sections, one half has comfortable sofas. Through the door to the left of the bar, a long corridor leads to the games room on the right and unlabelled toilets to the left. The games room has traditional Northants skittles and a dartboard. Six guests are usually available in this new entrant to this Guide. ⌖●≈♣

Piper ⊘
Windmill Avenue, NN15 6PS
(off A6003, by Wicksteed Park)
🕓 11-3 (4 Sat), 5 (6 Sat)-11; 12-10.30 Sun
☎ (01536) 513870
Hook Norton Best Bitter; Theakston Old Peculier; guest beers ⒣

Popular, 1950s, two-roomed estate pub, close to Wicksteed Park. It was voted local CAMRA Pub of the Year in 2001. The landlord supplies a particularly varied beer range with five guests. The lively bar/games room is frequented by younger drinkers. The pub sign depicts two different pipers. If only all estate pubs could be like this.
✿◑🕮♣P

KILSBY

George Hotel ⊘
Watling Street, CV23 8YE (at A361/A5 jct)
🕓 11.30-3, 5.30 (6 Sat)-11; 12-10.30 Sun
☎ (01788) 822229
Adnams Bitter; Draught Bass; Greene King IPA, Abbot; guest beers ⒣

This superb village local is situated just off the A5 and close to junction 18 of the M1. Under impressive management, the pub has gained a reputation for the consistency of its ales and its commitment to fine home-cooked meals, much of which is made from local produce; no meals on Sunday evening. The bar hosts live music on the first and third Saturday of each month and is a venue to watch the home rugby internationals. Q✿🚄◑🕮♣P

KINGSTHORPE

Queen Adelaide
50 Manor Road, NN2 6QJ
🕓 11.30-3, 5.30-11; 11.30-11 Fri & Sat; 12-3, 7-10.30 Sun
☎ (01604) 714524
Adnams Bitter, Broadside; Greene King IPA; Tetley Bitter; Webster's Bitter; guest beer ⒣

With a distinctive white-painted frontage this attractive, listed, stone-built pub has much to offer. The split-level front bar has a Northants skittles table in the lower room and the upper area retains the original dark wood with a snug and homely appeal. The lounge/eating area has many pictures and posters and leads on to a large suntrap garden with a number of benches. There is also outdoor seating to the front of the pub.
Q✿◑♣P

LITCHBOROUGH

Old Red Lion
4 Banbury Road, NN12 8JF
🕓 11-3, 6.30-11; 12-3, 6.30-10.30 Sun
☎ (01327) 830250
Marston's Pedigree; guest beer ⒣

Cosy, compact and homely, this stone village pub boasting flagstones, beams and a huge inglenook, is a very pleasant place to visit. One room offers pool, while another contains darts and Northants skittles. The pub fields a number of games teams. No food or bar snacks are served, however, the pub is the only village amenity and is popular with locals, walkers and cyclists. Fruit wines are available.
🚄Q✿♣P📖

MARSTON ST LAWRENCE

Marston Inn
OX17 2DB (off A43/A422)
🕓 12-2.30, 7-11; 12-3, 7-10.30 Sun
☎ (01295) 711906
Hook Norton Mild, Best Bitter, seasonal beers ⒣

Traditional stone pub on the end of a terrace of identical cottages. It comprises three small interconnected rooms, with one acting as the restaurant. There is a large garden to the rear and an Aunt Sally pitch to the front. Despite the size of the village, the Marston Inn is well supported with darts and dominoes teams. A rare outlet for mild in the county, no food is served on Tuesday evening. 🚄Q✿◑🕮♣△♣P📖

NORTHAMPTON

Fish Inn
11 Fish Street, NN1 2AA (pedestrianised area)
🕓 11-11; 7-10.30 Sun
☎ (01604) 234040
Courage Directors; Marston's Pedigree; Theakston Best Bitter; guest beers ⒣

From the outside, the Fish looks like a Victorian gin palace, cloaked in red. However, what you are actually seeing is a pub style that survives an 1896 rebuilding. The interior is fairly plush, with wood floors in both bars, plus a dining room. Despite its central location, it is not on the local circuit and appeals to a wide range of customers, mostly over-25s. A T&J Bernard-owned pub, it offers a regularly-changing choice of beers. Food is served 11–9.30, Monday–Saturday. 🚄◑⇌♣

Malt Shovel Tavern
121 Bridge Street, NN1 1PF
(facing Carlsberg Brewery)
🕓 11.30-3, 5-11; 12-3, 7-10.30 Sun
☎ (01604) 234212
Banks's Bitter; Frog Island Natterjack; Fuller's London Pride, Tetley Bitter; guest beers ⒣

Much lauded, East Midland CAMRA Pub of the Year 2001. This pub is full of memorabilia from Watney's forerunners, Phipp's and NBC Breweries, which both brewed on the Carlsberg site opposite (falling to Watney's in 1974). Up to nine guest beers are available, including a dark mild. The many bottled Belgian beers (plus a draught) and gins, supplemented by English country wines and up to 50 single malt whiskies, make this a discerning drinkers' paradise, free from sparklers and gaming machines. Tasty home-cooked food is sold (not Sun) and it is a top live blues venue on Wednesday evening.
Q✿◑♿⇌♣●

Racehorse
15 Abington Square, NN1 4AE
🕓 11-11; 12-10.30 Sun
☎ (01604) 631997
Beer range varies ⒣

A diverse range of customers is found at this town-centre pub; including punks, pensioners, building workers, social workers, music lovers and beer lovers. The manager and the bar staff are friendly. The large main room with a central bar hosts bands and DJs and there is a quiz on Monday. The spacious back room holds live gigs and jam sessions. Six or seven handpumps are in action at all times with a wide range of beer featuring Oakham, Nethergate, Bateman, Sharp's, Barnsley and Harviestoun. The pub benefits from a very large garden which is busy in summer. ⊛P

Romany
Trinity Avenue, NN2 6JN
(between A508 and A43)
☼ 11.30-11; 12-10.30 Sun
☎ (01604) 714647
Cains Dr Duncans IPA; Fuller's London Pride; guest beers Ⓗ
Imposing, 1930s two-roomed community pub standing in the fork of a junction, one and a half miles from the town centre. This is very much a sport/games-oriented pub with a large TV, Northants skittles, pool and darts. Live music, usually by rock bands, is performed every Thursday, Saturday and Sunday evening. The landlord always has six guest ales on tap and over 400 beers have been stocked in the past two years. Draught cider is sold. Card-carrying CAMRA members receive a 10% discount on ales on Tuesday and Wednesday evening. Take bus route 8 or 25 from the town centre. It was voted local CAMRA Pub of the Year in 2002. ⊛ⒸⒹ♣♠P

ORLINGBURY

Queen's Arms
11 Isham Road, NN14 1JD (off A509/A43)
☼ 12-2, 6-11; 12-11 Sat; 12-10.30 Sun
☎ (01933) 678258
Taylor Landlord; Tetley Bitter; guest beers Ⓗ
Comfortable, carpeted village pub with a central lounge divided into three distinct areas. There is a no-smoking dining section to the right of the entrance and a snug to the left. The sizeable garden has trestle tables and children's play equipment. A beer festival is hosted in a marquee in early summer. The pub is leased from Inn Partnership and has up to six guest ales. ⊛ⒸⒹ♣P

OUNDLE

Ship Inn
18 West Street, PE8 4EF
☼ 11-11; 12-10.30 Sun
☎ (01832) 273918
website: www.theshipinn-oundle.co.uk
Draught Bass; Hop Back Summer Lightning; Oakham JHB; guest beers Ⓗ
Grade II listed building in the main street, 100 yards from the town centre, this Collyweston-slated pub is reputedly haunted by a previous landlord who flung himself from an upstairs window. A more regal pub ghost, Mary, Queen of Scots, can be found at the Talbot Hotel just around the corner. The Ship is divided into several drinking areas which makes for a homely and cosy atmosphere. It hosts a live jazz night on the last Sunday of each month. ⋈Q⊛⇔ⒸⒹP⅃

PYTCHLEY

Overstone Arms
The Stringers Hill, NN14 1ES
☼ 12-2.30, 7 (6.30 Sat)-11; 12-2.30, 7-10.30 Sun
☎ (01536) 790215
Adnams Bitter; Marston's Pedigree; guest beers Ⓗ

Large, attractive, stone-built village pub with a small single bar and a separate no-smoking restaurant. The excellent food is very popular (booking is advised), meals are also served in the bar area. Two ever-changing guest ales are always available. This pub has come a long way since its previous life under a former landlord. ⋈Q⊛ⒸⒹP

RAVENSTHORPE

Chequers
Church Hill, NN6 8EP (off A428)
☼ 12-3, 6-11; 12-11 Sat; 12-3, 7-10.30 Sun
☎ (01604) 770379
Fuller's London Pride; Greene King IPA; Tetley Bitter; Thwaites Bitter; guest beer Ⓗ
Opposite the Church of Dionysius and its 13th-century tower, this Grade II listed building was a farmhouse until 1900, when it became a pub. It features an L-shaped bar and stone fireplace which makes a welcoming sight on a cold winter's evening. To the rear is a small, intimate restaurant which serves excellent home-cooked fresh food. A games room, housing Northants skittles and pool, can be found across the courtyard. The northern beers that often appear here are keenly priced. ⋈⛢⊛ⒸⒹP

ROADE

Cock at Roade
1 High Street, NN7 2NW
(A508 to Roade, follow Hartwell sign to village)
☼ 12-11; 12-10.30 Sun
☎ (01604) 862544
Greene King IPA; Hook Norton Best Bitter; Shepherd Neame Spitfire; Taylor Landlord Ⓗ
Warm, welcoming pub on the village green with an L-shaped bar decorated with rustic chicken pictures and old adverts. The beer range has stabilised to the four listed, after demand from locals to keep on the Taylor Landlord. Quality control is a priority for the landlord, Max, who is also proud of the standard of food in the no-smoking restaurant. A quiz night is held on Tuesday if the numbers warrant. The large garden has a marquee in summer. It is worth making a short detour from the M1, junction 15. ⋈Q⊛ⒸⒹPⓉ

RUSHDEN

Rushden Historical Transport Society
The Station, Station Approach, NN10 0AW
(N end of A6 one-way system)
☼ 12-3 (not Mon-Fri), 7.30-11; 12-3, 7.30-10.30 Sun
☎ (01933) 318988 website: www.rhts.co.uk.
Fuller's London Pride; guest beers Ⓗ
Railways and great beer come together at this wonderful preserved station that was the CAMRA joint winner of Club of the Year 2000 and East Midlands winner 2002. The main bar is gaslit and contains many railway artefacts, while the museum is further down the platform. The Society operates live steam five times a year, when a jazz band plays alongside the barbecue on the platform. At other times Doctor Busker entertains with his squeezebox. Six changing guest ales are stocked, 300-plus a year. The local CAMRA branch hold their meetings aboard the Gresley buffet coach.

Not to be missed – day membership is 50p.
The station platform serves as a garden.
🏮Q🏮P🏮

STOKE BRUERNE

Boat Inn
Bridge Road, NN12 7SB
(off A508, opp. Canal Museum)
🕛 9am-3, 6-11 (9am-11pm summer); 12-10.30 Sun
☎ (01604) 862428 website: www.boatinn.co.uk
Adnams Bitter; Banks's Bitter; Frog Island Best Bitter; Marston's Bitter, Pedigree; guest beer Ⓗ
Popular canalside pub with a multitude of
customers ranging from Canal Museum
visitors to morris dancers who perform
regularly. Dating from 1877, the thatched
bars occupy the oldest part of the building
and retain stone-flagged floors. A small
games room provides Northants skittles.
The lounge offers bar snacks, and the bistro
serves breakfasts and main meals. The main
restaurant (upstairs) overlooks the canal
lock. Boat trips to the historic Blisworth
Tunnel are available aboard the Indian
Chief narrowboat. 🏮🏮🏮🏮🏮🏮🏮P

SUDBOROUGH

Vane Arms
Main Street, NN14 3BX (off A6116)
🕛 12-3 (not Mon), 5.30-11; 12-11 Sat; 12-5,
7-10.30 Sun
☎ (01832) 733223
Beer range varies Ⓗ
Situated in a quiet, picturesque village, this
16th-century stone-built thatched pub
features a low, beamed ceiling and an open
fire creating a cosy atmosphere. A lounge,
separate bar to the rear and upstairs
restaurant complete the pub. No food is
served on Monday evening. Games include
Northants skittles, pool and darts. Draught
Belgian Kriek beers and real cider
complement the ever-changing six guests.
Three guest rooms with en-suite facilities
are in a separate converted annexe.
🏮Q🏮🏮🏮🏮🏮🏮P🏮

SULGRAVE

Star Inn
Manor Road, OX17 2SA
(off A43, follow brown tourist signs for Sulgrave Manor)
🕛 11-3, 6-11; 12-5 Sun
☎ (01295) 760389
Hook Norton Best Bitter, Old Hooky, seasonal beers; guest beer Ⓗ
Beautiful ivy-clad, stone pub set in an idyllic
village. The 300-year-old Star Inn is
festooned with hanging baskets during the
summer months. The front bar is relatively
unchanged with its stone-flagged floor,
beamed ceilings, wooden settles, glass
partitions and an inglenook. To the rear, is
a restaurant where the home-cooked food is
prepared by the resident chefs; no lunch is
served on Monday. The pub is almost
opposite Sulgrave Manor, the ancestral
home of George Washington's family. A
skittle alley is available on request.
🏮Q🏮🏮🏮🏮🏮P

SUTTON BASSETT

Queen's Head
Main Street, LE16 8HP (on B664)

🕛 12-3, 5-11; 12-11 Sat & summer; 6-10.30 Sun
☎ (01858) 463530
Adnams Bitter; Taylor Landlord Ⓗ
Turn of the century, brick-built, rural pub
overlooking the Welland Valley. There are
two rooms, front and rear with a central bar
serving both areas, connected by a corridor.
Low, beamed ceilings, and subdued wall
lights create an intimate atmosphere. Spot
the piano in the back room which also
houses two upholstered settles. Food is
served and the pub is open all day in
summer. Q🏮🏮🏮🏮P🏮

TITCHMARSH

Dog & Partridge
6 High Street, NN14 3DF (1/2 mile off A605)
🕛 12-4 (not Mon-Fri), 6 (6.30 Sat)-11; 12-4.30,
7-10.30 Sun
☎ (01832) 732546
Wells Eagle, seasonal beers; guest beer Ⓗ
Centrally situated in the village, the pub
offers a warm welcome from the landlord
who has now been in residence for 25 years.
The interior consists of one long room with
a raised games area at one end. Northants
skittles and table football are played.
Outside there is a pleasant patio area. This
regular Guide entry is well worth a visit.
🏮Q🏮🏮P

WALGRAVE

Royal Oak
Zion Hill, NN6 9PN (off A43)
🕛 12-3, 6-11; 12-10.30 Sun
☎ (01604) 781248
Adnams Bitter; guest beers Ⓗ
Comfortable, stone-built village local,
popular for food as well as for a changing
range of up to four guest beers. The front
bar is partitioned into three areas, with
dining at the side and a central smoking
and drinking area. A small back bar serves a
cosy lounge and a separate dining room.
Northants skittles is played in a room across
the car park. Barbecues are held in the
garden on Sunday evenings in summer.
🏮Q🏮🏮🏮P

WELLINGBOROUGH

Old Grammarians Association
46 Oxford Street, NN8 4JH (off one-way system)
🕛 12-2.30, 7-11; 12-11 Fri & Sat; 12-10.30 Sun
☎ (01933) 226188
Greene King IPA; Hook Norton Best Bitter, Old Hooky; guest beers Ⓗ
This sports and social club fields teams for
most outdoor activities, including a
successful rugby team. It is a friendly, town-
centre club, with a small TV lounge, long
bar and function/games room. Access is
from the rear car park – press the voicecom
button; a stair lift is provided for
wheelchairs. Open to all, regular visitors
will be asked to join. There are always three
guest beers on tap at this former CAMRA
East Midlands Club of the Year. 🏮🏮🏮P

WESTON BY WELLAND

Wheel & Compass
Valley Road, LE16 8HZ (off B664)
🕛 12-3, 6-11; 12-3, 6-10.30 Sun
☎ (01858) 565864

Banks's Bitter; Greene King Abbot; Marston's Bitter, Pedigree; guest beers Ⓗ
Popular local, situated on the edge of the village, with an L-shaped bar and side restaurant with excellent food. The Poachers Bar to the front is on a lower level and provides a more intimate place to drink. The rear garden includes benches and seats, and provides an ideal overspill where children can be supervised on the slides and swings. Guest beers are on the side bar. This is the closest pub to the river for those taking part in the summer Welland Valley beer festival. ♨Q❀◖♿P

WOLLASTON

Crispin Arms
14 Hinwick Road, NN29 7QT (E of A509)
🕧 12-11; 12-10.30 Sun
☎ (01933) 664303
Caledonian Deuchars IPA; Fuller's London Pride; Shepherd Neame Spitfire; Theakston Best Bitter; guest beer Ⓗ
Small, two-roomed pub which is very popular with the locals, some of whom can be found playing cards, dominoes, darts or cribbage. It is very cosy and welcoming, especially in winter, with its real fire. A good range of regular beers and two guests are usually available. A paved area in the rear car park is used by drinkers in summer. ♨❀⌖♣P

WOODNEWTON

White Swan
22 Main Street, PE8 5EB

🕧 12-2, 7 (6 Fri)-11; closed Mon; 12-2.30 (closed eve) Sun
☎ (01780) 470381
Adnams Bitter; Camerons Bitter; Marston's Pedigree; Otter Bright Ⓗ
Located in the centre of the village, this pub consists of one long room with a wooden partition separating the bar and drinking area by the entrance, and the popular restaurant at the far end. The food is good quality and cooked to order. Coco the Clown used to frequent the pub, and he is buried in the local churchyard. The garden boasts a petanque pitch. Addlestones cider is sold. Q❀◖♿♣♠P

WOOTTON

Wootton Working Men's Club
23 High Street, NN4 6LP
(off A508, close to M1 jct 15)
🕧 12-2 (2.30 Sat; not Thu), 7-11; 12-5, 7-10.30 Sun
☎ (01604) 761863
Greene King IPA; guest beers Ⓗ
This club enjoys an excellent reputation, having been voted the regional CAMRA Club of the Year in 1994, 1997 and 1998. With air-conditioning throughout, the Club was once a pub, and now comprises a bar, lounge, concert room and games room where Northants skittles, pool and darts are often played. With a beer festival in September, and live entertainment on Saturday evening, this club is well supported by the local CAMRA members. The ever-changing five guest beers are sourced from micro-breweries around Britain. Q☺♿♣P

The sign of the Bell

Mr Jones and Partridge travelled on to Gloucester. Being arrived here, they chose for their house of entertainment the sign of the Bell; an excellent house, and which I do most seriously recommend to every reader who shall visit this ancient city. The master of it is brother to the great preacher, Whitfield, but is absolutely untainted with the pernicious principles of Methodism, or of any other heretical sect. He is indeed a very honest, plain man, and in my opinion not likely to create any disturbance either in Church or State. His wife hath, I believe, had much pretension to beauty, and is still a very fine woman. Her person and deportment might have made a shining figure in the politest assemblies; but though she must be conscious of this and many other perfections, she seems perfectly contented with, and resigned to the state of life to which she is called – To be concise, she is a very friendly, good-natured woman; and so industrious to oblige that the guests must be of a very morose disposition who are not extremely well satisfied in her house.

Henry Fielding (1707-54), *The History of Tom Jones*, 1749

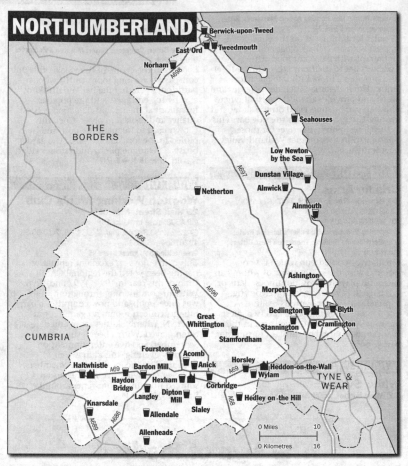

NORTHUMBERLAND

Berwick-upon-Tweed
East Ord • Tweedmouth
Norham

THE BORDERS

Seahouses

Low Newton by the Sea
Dunstan Village
Alnwick

Netherton

Alnmouth

Ashington
Morpeth

Bedlington • Blyth
Stannington • Cramlington

CUMBRIA

Great Whittington
Stamfordham
Fourstones
Acomb
Haltwhistle
Bardon Mill
Anick
Horsley
Heddon-on-the-Wall
Wylam
TYNE & WEAR
Haydon Bridge
Hexham
Corbridge
Langley
Dipton Mill
Knarsdale
Slaley
Hedley on the Hill
Allendale
Allenheads

0 Miles 10
0 Kilometres 16

ACOMB

Miners Arms
Main Street, NE46 4PW
☼ 5-11; 12-11 Sat (& school holidays); 12-10.30 Sun
☎ (01434) 603909
Yates Bitter; guest beers Ⓗ

The pub name is the only reminder of the once prominent mining activity that took place in Acomb. Situated at the top of the hill that is the main street, the Miners offers excellent refreshment. Usually four ales are available with at least one from each of Durham and Mordue breweries. An unusual central staircase effectively splits the pub into two drinking areas: a small, cosy bar and a comfortable lounge with a real fire. A dining room is to the rear. Tyne Valley buses 880/882 link Hexham to Acomb but most of them omit Main Street which means a half mile walk up the hill!
🅼❀◑♣⛫

ALLENDALE

King's Head
Market Place, NE47 9BD
☼ 12-11; 12-10.30 Sun
☎ (01434) 683681
Jennings Mild, Bitter, Cumberland Ale, Cocker Hoop, Sneck Lifter, seasonal beers; guest beers Ⓗ

The public bar of a former coaching inn,
built in the early 18th century. It claims to be the oldest premises continuously used as a pub in the area. Its customers are a good mix of locals, cyclists, ramblers and other tourists attracted by the town's location within an area of outstanding natural beauty. The function room hosts live music nights. The No. 688 Hexham–Allenheads bus passes about every two hours, less frequently Sunday. 🅼🚌◑Å

ALLENHEADS

Allenheads Inn
NE47 9HJ
☼ 12-4, 7-11; 12-11 Fri & Sat; 12-10.30 Sun
☎ (01434) 685200
website: www.theallenheadsinn.co.uk
Greene King IPA, Abbot; guest beers Ⓗ

Built in the 18th century as the family home of Sir Thomas Wentworth, it is now the social heart of a village claiming to be the highest in England. It features an extensive eclectic assembly of memorabilia, antiques and equipment throughout its many rooms: public bar, lounge, games and dining rooms. A good selection of guest beers attracts hikers and walkers, the Coast-to-Coast cycle route and a ski slope are also nearby. The No. 688 Hexham–Allenheads bus passes about every two hours, less frequently Sunday. 🅼❀🚌◑♣⚹

ALNMOUTH

Red Lion Inn
22 Northumberland Street, NE66 2RT
✪ 11-11 (closed winter Mon); 12-10.30 Sun
☎ (01665) 830584
Beer range varies Ⓗ

Over 350 years old, this half-timbered former coaching inn has a welcoming public bar to the rear and a dining room. Atmospheric, with beams and a real fire, its wood panelling is believed to come from the Carpathia, the first vessel to reach survivors of the Titanic. Another unusual feature in a guest bedroom is an 18th-century excisemen lookout window. Note the unusual mural in the gents. Pleasant sandy beaches and a golf course are very close by. The No. 518 Newcastle–Alnwick bus passes hourly. 🏰❀🛏️❶▶♣P⚲

ALNWICK

John Bull Inn
12 Howick Street, NE66 1UY
✪ 12-3 (not Wed; 11-2 Sat), 7-11; 12-3, 7-10.30 Sun
☎ (01665) 602055
Tetley Bitter; guest beers Ⓗ

Small, cosy local set within a row of terraced houses. Recent alterations have increased the drinking area in this bar that offers regularly-changing guest beers and one of the largest selections of malt whiskies in Northumberland. The Bier Shoppe offers every known Belgian bottle-conditioned beer, including Trappist brews and Duvel. Triominoes (three-sided dominoes) is played. The sheltered beer garden is a bonus.
Q❀♣

ANICK

Rat Inn
NE46 4LN
✪ 11-3, 6-11; 12-3 Sun
☎ (01434) 602814
Greene King Ruddles Best, Old Speckled Hen; John Smith's Bitter; guest beers Ⓗ

Classic country pub; an old stone building in a tiny hamlet, two miles from Hexham. Its charming interior features a black-leaded range with a roaring fire. Collections of chamber pots, jugs and drinking mugs hang from the ceiling. It has a conservatory and dining area with great views down the Tyne Valley. Regular guest beers come from local micros, including Mordue. Excellent food is served.
🏰☕❀❶♣P

ASHINGTON

Bubbles Wine Bar
58A Station Road, NE63 9UJ
✪ 11-11 (2am Fri & Sat); 12-10.30 Sun
☎ (01670) 850800 website: www.bubblesbar.co.uk
Beer range varies Ⓗ

Finding a pub as good as Bubbles in this former mining town dominated by CIU clubs is a treat. Handily located near the pedestrianised town centre, it offers a welcoming spot to try a good selection of beers. There is something happening almost every evening here, with full details on their lively website. During the day it is very relaxing, but the pub becomes more active

when popular bands play live. If you leave by the back door you will find their companion pub, the Black Diamond. ❀❶

BARDON MILL

Bowes Hotel
NE47 7HU
✪ 12-2.30 (not Mon), 4.30-11; 12-11 Sat & summer; 12-10.30 Sun
☎ (01434) 344237
Black Sheep Best Bitter; guest beers Ⓗ

Prominent village-centre hotel opposite the village green. The etched glazing in doors and screens give clues as to its former interior layout; one marked Bottle & Jug opens into the dining room (home to the famous 'Bowes leek pudding'). Drinkers are well catered for in the cosy public bar and games room. Local attractions include a pottery and glassworks. The village is also popular with visitors to Hadrian's Wall and the National Trust woodland at Allen Banks. Bus No. 685 Newcastle–Carlisle stops at the door. 🏰Q❀🛏️❶▶♣⚲

BEDLINGTON

Northumberland Arms
112 Front Street East, NE22 5AA
✪ 11-3 (not Mon or Tue), 7-11; 11-11 Thu-Sat; 12-10.30 Sun
☎ (01670) 822754
Beer range varies Ⓗ

Three handpumps provide a regularly-changing selection of real ales. A pleasant atmosphere prevails in the comfortable bar/lounge. The pub is well supported by the many fans who attend matches on the nearby Bedlington Terriers FC ground. A popular feature is the weekly quiz held on Monday evening. The pub has a pool room and an upstairs function room. Lunches are served Wednesday–Saturday. ❶♣

Wharton Arms
Burdon Terrace, NE22 6DA
✪ 11-11; 12-10.30 Sun
☎ (01670) 822214
Greene King Abbot; Tetley Bitter Ⓗ

This pub enjoys regular and loyal support from its local clientele and visitors are welcomed. A lively atmosphere prevails in this terraced town-centre pub with a bar and lounge featuring wood panelling. Darts and pool are played here. ▶♣

BERWICK-UPON-TWEED

Barrels
Bridge Street, TD15 1ES
✪ 11.30 (4 Tue-Thu, Jan-March)-11; 12-10.30 Sun
☎ (01289) 308013
Boddingtons Bitter; Fuller's London Pride; Taylor Landlord; guest beers Ⓗ

Two ground-floor rooms present various styles of decor and furnishings; note, for example, the space invaders machine, various types of chair including the 'throne'

INDEPENDENT BREWERIES

Black Bull Haltwhistle
Hexhamshire Hexham
Northumberland Bedlington
Wylam Heddon-on-the-Wall

in the side room and torches outside. The basement is popular as a live music and entertainment venue. The pub's unthemed nature is reflected in its wide range of customers. Bottled Belgian beers are available. The River Tweed and its famous swans, the old Berwick road bridge and Elizabethan town walls are all close by. Meals are served in summer. ◁≈

Foxtons ✪
Hide Hill, TD15 1AB
✪ 11-11; closed Sun
☎ (01289) 303939
Caledonian Deuchars IPA; guest beers Ⓗ

A wine bar-cum-bistro is an unusual outlet for real ale and very different from the traditional British pub. However, do not be put off by appearances, for good quality real ale thrives here in this busy environment alongside the excellent food, coffee, cakes and draught Italian beer which is rare for north Northumberland. The bar is handy for the Elizabethan town walls and River Tweed. ❀◁▷≈

BLYTH

Oliver's Bar
60 Bridge Street, NE24 2AP
✪ 11 (1 Sat)-11; 12.30-10.30 Sun
☎ (01670) 540356
Greene King Old Speckled Hen; Taylor Landlord; Wells Eagle; guest beers Ⓗ

Located approximately five minutes' walk from Blyth bus station, this pub is a welcome oasis in a town that is a real ale desert. Good ales are available in the one room of what used to be a newsagent's shop, now converted to provide a comfortable and welcoming atmosphere. No main meals served but sandwiches are sold at lunchtime. Q

CORBRIDGE

Angel of Corbridge
Main Street, NE45 5LA
✪ 11-11; 12-10.30 Sun
☎ (01434) 632119
Black Sheep Best Bitter; guest beers Ⓗ

A former Georgian coaching inn, the Angel offers hotel accommodation, a restaurant and public bar. Real ale (including guests from local micros) is served in the bright, contemporary bar, used by locals and visitors alike. The adjacent lounge, by contrast, is panelled in dark wood, with sofas and a piano. In the evenings it is reserved for restaurant diners (no eve meals at weekends). Corbridge is the ideal base for visitors to the Tyne Valley and Hadrian's Wall. Bus No. 685 Newcastle–Carlisle passes every hour. Q❀≈◁▷≈P⚲

Dyvels
Station Road, NE45 5AY
✪ 12-11; 12-10.30 Sun
☎ (01434) 633633
Draught Bass; Black Sheep Best Bitter; guest beers Ⓗ

Small, welcoming public bar in a family-owned country hotel offering good food (Tue–Sun). Situated on the south side of the River Tyne, away from the main part of the village, it has the advantage of being right next to the railway station. Recent refurbishment has seen improved access

from the bar to the garden and heated terrace area. Bus No. 602 Newcastle–Hexham passes every half hour during the day. ≈Q❀≈◁▷≈♣P

CRAMLINGTON

Plough
Middle Farm Buildings, NE23 9DN
✪ 11-11; 12-10.30 Sun
☎ (01670) 737633
Theakston XB; guest beers Ⓗ

In the former village centre of an expanding new town, this fine pub faces the parish church. Once a farm, the old buildings were sympathetically converted into the present establishment some years ago. The bar is small and busy with a door to the outside seating area. The lounge is larger and comfortable with a round 'gin gan' acting as an extra sitting room. Guest beers are often from local micro-breweries. ❀◁▷≈&≈P

DIPTON MILL

Dipton Mill Inn
Dipton Mill Road, NE46 1YA
(2 miles from Hexham on the Whitley Chapel road)
✪ 12-2.30, 6-11; 12-4, 7-10.30 Sun
☎ (01434) 606577
Hexhamshire Devil's Elbow, Shire Bitter, Devil's Water, Whapweasel, Old Humbug; guest beers Ⓗ

The tap for Hexhamshire Brewery, this small, low-ceilinged pub boasts a large garden. The landlord brews excellent beers which are always available. Great home-cooked meals complement the beers. The cosy atmosphere and the warm welcome help visitors to understand why the pub has won several CAMRA awards in recent years; well worth seeking out. The garden has a stream running through it and there is plenty of countryside to explore.
≈Q❀◁▷P

DUNSTAN VILLAGE

Cottage Inn
NE66 3SZ
✪ 12-11; 12-10.30 Sun
☎ (01665) 576658
Wylam Bitter Ⓗ

Less than a mile from possibly the best part of the Northumbrian coastline, this inn has something for everyone. It is surprisingly spacious with a bar, restaurant, conservatory and covered and open patios. Half a mile from Craster village, famed for its kippers, the inn is ideally located for birdwatchers, walkers, golfers and tourists. Good food is served. ≈Q⚳❀≈◁▷≈&P

EAST ORD

Salmon Inn
TD15 2NS
✪ 11-3, 5-11; 11-11 Fri & Sat; 12-10.30 Sun
☎ (01289) 305227
Caledonian Deuchars IPA, 80/-; guest beer Ⓗ

On the main street, the inn has been modernised in the ale house bare boards style, but remains very much a village local, attracting a wide range of customers of all ages, both English and Scots. The menu offers locally-produced food prepared in-house. The L-shaped bar has a welcoming real fire at its heart, a pool table and TV.

Convenient for the Tweed Cycleway and handy for angling on the River Tweed, the No. 23 Berwick–Kelso bus passes about every 90 minutes during the day. 🚶🌳◗

FOURSTONES

Railway Inn
NE47 5DG (off B6319, 3 miles NW of Hexham)
☼ 12 (11 summer)-11; 12-10.30 Sun
☎ (01434) 674711
Jennings Cumberland Ale; seasonal beers ⊞

Stone pub with a warm welcome, situated next to a long-closed station on the still active Newcastle–Carlisle railway line. Fourstones lies on Stane-gate, an old Roman road that pre-dates nearby Hadrian's Wall. The inn is the focal point of the village and is also popular with walkers exploring the River South Tyne and the nearby Roman forts. At the time of survey building work had commenced to extend the pub by adding a restaurant and installing disabled access. On Tyne Valley bus route 881 from Hexham. No evening meals are served Sunday or Tuesday. 🚶Q🌳◗ ⊟♣P

GREAT WHITTINGTON

Queen's Head Inn
NE19 2HP
☼ 12-2.30, 6-11; closed Mon; 12-3, 7-10.30 Sun
☎ (01434) 672267
Hambleton Bitter; guest beers ⊞

This inn, dating from the 15th century, is reputedly the oldest in the county. The house beer, Queen's Head Bitter, is brewed by Hambleton. At the heart of Hadrian's Wall country the pub makes an ideal watering-hole for visitors. The food is excellent – made with local produce wherever possible; the extensive menu has dishes to suit all tastes. There is a small friendly bar, warmed by a roaring fire, in which to enjoy the ales on offer. 🚶Q◗P

HALTWHISTLE

Black Bull
Market Square, NR49 0RL
☼ 12-3 (not Mon-Thu; 12-4 Sat), 7-11; 12-3, 7-10.30 Sun
☎ (01434) 320463
Jennings Cumberland Ale; guest beers ⊞

At the centre of the town that lays claim to be at the geographic centre of Britain, lies this superb pub. A small, low-ceilinged bar is warmed in winter by an open fire and all year round by a warm, friendly welcome. The bar counter proudly boasts six handpumps dispensing a wide range of northern micros' beers. In addition, the former pool room houses the Black Bull Brewery whose products also grace the bar. Bus No. 685 Newcastle–Carlisle stops feet away from the pub. 🚶Q⊟≠♣

HAYDON BRIDGE

General Havelock
9 Ratcliff Road, NE47 6ER
☼ 12-2.30, 7-11; closed Mon; 12-2.30, 7-10.30 Sun
☎ (01434) 684376
Beer range varies ⊞

Warm, friendly pub and restaurant in a small village. The owner likes to support local businesses, so the ales are from north-eastern micros and the food from local producers. The outdoor area stretches down to the River Tyne. General Havelock's mother lived three miles away, hence the name. Bus No. 685 Newcastle–Carlisle passes the door. Hadrian's Wall and wonderful countryside are within easy reach. 🚶Q🌳◗≠♣

HEDLEY ON THE HILL

Feathers
NE43 7SW
☼ 12-3 (not Mon-Fri), 6-11; 12-3, 7-10.30 Sun
☎ (01661) 843607
Boddingtons Bitter; Mordue Workie Ticket; guest beers ⊞

Wonderful, friendly old pub in a hillside village, professionally run with no airs and graces. It serves high quality food and four real ales in two bars, both with open fires. The pub hosts a mini beer festival every Easter and on Easter Monday there is a barrel race among local drinkers – the contestants have to roll a barrel uphill to the pub! The winners are well rewarded (with beer obviously). 🚶🌳🍴◗P

HEXHAM

Tap & Spile
Battle Hill, NE46 1BA
☼ 11-11; 12-3, 7-10.30 Sun
☎ (01661) 602039
Black Sheep Best Bitter; Theakston Best Bitter; guest beers ⊞

Always bustling and busy, this town-centre, street-corner local is popular with shoppers, locals and tourists. It upholds the Tap & Spile concept of a constantly-changing selection of guest ales, providing the drinker with the best range of beers available locally. The pub is split into bar and lounge, served from a central bar with a hatch to the lounge. Regular music sessions include Northumbrian folk, R&B and rock. It makes an ideal watering-hole after a visit to the abbey. No food is served on Sunday. Q◗⊟≠

HORSLEY

Lion & Lamb
NE15 0NS
☼ 12-3, 6-11; 12-11 Fri & Sat; 12-10.30 Sun
☎ (01661) 852952
Caledonian Deuchars IPA; Castle Eden Ale; Marston's Pedigree; guest beers ⊞

This well-appointed, roadside pub is very popular with diners. Parts of the building date from 1718 with low, beamed ceilings; the inscriptions to 'mind ya heed' are not there for decorative purposes! Despite an emphasis on food (no meals Sun eve), six handpumps dispense a wide range of real ales in a bar area furnished with scrubbed-top tables. Guest beers are usually sourced from local micros. On bus route 685 Newcastle–Carlisle. 🚶🌳◗⊟P

KNARSDALE

Kirkstyle Inn
CA8 7PB (off A689, approx. 3 miles S of Lambley)
☼ 12-3 (not winter Mon-Wed, or summer Tue), 6-11; 12-3, 7-10.30 Sun
☎ (01434) 381559

Yates Bitter; guest beer Ⓗ

Both the Pennine Way and the South Tyne Trail pass nearby, bringing walkers and cyclists to Knarsdale. The River South Tyne, within view of the bar, is popular with anglers. The front bar features drawings of regulars and the pub in days gone by. There is a games room to the rear and a small dining room. Self-catering accommodation is available in an adjacent cottage. The once-a-day post bus is the only public transport link during opening hours.
⋈Q❀☼⌂◁◑ ⅄♣P

LANGLEY

Carts Bog Inn
NE47 5NW (3 miles off A69 on A686 to Alston)
✪ 12-3, 7-11; 12-3, 7-10.30 Sun
☎ (01434) 684338
Jennings Cumberland Ale; Yates Bitter; guest beers Ⓗ
An unspoilt country pub; the current building dates from 1730 and is built on the site of an ancient brewery (circa 1521). The new owners are enthusiastic about real ale and buy their guests from local micro-breweries. An unusual fire divides the two rooms and heats both. The pub name is derived from a steeply-banked corner on the old road, where on wet days, the horse-drawn carts were invariably bogged down. Excellent home-cooked food is available, making this a popular venue, especially for Sunday lunch. ⋈Q⏃❀◁◑ ⅃♣P

LOW NEWTON BY THE SEA

Ship Inn
Newton Square, NE66 3EL
✪ 11-4, 8-11; 11-11 Sat & summer; 12-10.30 Sun
☎ (01665) 576262
Black Sheep Best Bitter; guest beers Ⓗ
Enjoying an unrivalled position, literally within yards of the beach, the pub stands in a courtyard of cottages, all arranged in an open-ended square around a small green. All the buildings are of stone and date back to the late 18th century, when they were originally built as fishermen's cottages. A traditional, cosy atmosphere, fine ale and food make this a good resting point when exploring the beautiful Northumberland coastline. ⋈⏃❀⌂◁◑

MORPETH

Joiners Arms
3 Wansbeck Street, NE61 1XZ
✪ 12 (11 Wed, Fri & Sat)-11; 12-10.30 Sun
☎ (01670) 513540
Draught Bass; Caledonian Deuchars IPA; Fullers London Pride; Tetley Bitter; guest beers Ⓗ
This Fitzgerald's pub is a friendly place to enjoy a good pint of real ale. It often showcases local micro-breweries as guests. Here you will discover the real character of Morpeth; you will also find an extraordinary collection of stuffed animals in glass cases ranged around the bar. The lounge has a pleasant view of the River Wansbeck. Tuesday is quiz night. Q⇪

Tap & Spile
23 Manchester Street, NE61 1BH
✪ 12-2.30, 4.30-11; 12-11 Fri & Sat; 12-10.30 Sun
☎ (01670) 513894
Beer range varies Ⓗ

True to the original Tap & Spile concept, this pub is popular with locals and visitors and boasts eight handpumps, serving a varied range of real ales and Westons Old Rosie cider. The bar can get crowded, while the comfortable, quiet lounge, where children are welcome, hosts Northumbrian pipers on Sunday lunchtime. Well worth a visit and easy to get to, it is only three minutes' walk from Morpeth bus station. Q♣☙

NETHERTON

Star Inn ☆
NE65 7HD (off B634 from Rothbury)
✪ 7-10.30 (11 Fri & Sat); winter hours may vary; 12-1.30, 7-10.30 Sun
☎ (01669) 630238
Castle Eden Ale Ⓖ
This unspoilt gem has remained unchanged for the last 80 years. The pub is privately owned and as you go in you feel as though you are entering someone's living room. The beer is served from the cellar at a hatch in the panelled entrance hall. The bar area is basic with benches round the wall. It is the only pub in Northumberland to appear in every edition of this Guide. Opening hours may vary, especially in winter, so please ring. Children are not allowed in the bar. Q P

NORHAM

Masons Arms
16 West Street, TD15 2LB
✪ 12-3, 7-11; 12-3, 7-10.30 Sun
☎ (01289) 382326
Camerons Strongarm, seasonal beers; guest beers (summer) Ⓗ
Attractive, wood-panelled bar with a welcoming fire bearing a Wm Younger mirror above it. Collections of angling equipment, carpentry tools, water jugs and photographs of the River Tweed in flood and bygone Norham add to the atmosphere. Shooting, fishing and golfing enthusiasts are well catered for, with plenty of facilities on hand (packages available). Regular folk music nights feature both the Northumbrian and Scottish traditions. The Tweed Cycleway and a 12th-century castle are both nearby. The No. 23 Berwick–Kelso bus passes about every 90 minutes in daytime. ⋈Q⌂◁◑

SEAHOUSES

Olde Ship Hotel
7-9 Main Street, NE68 7RD
✪ 11-4, 6-11; 11-11 Fri & Sat; 12-10.30 Sun
☎ (01665) 720200 website: www.seahouses.co.uk
Beer range varies Ⓗ
Dating back to the 18th century and licensed for nearly 200 years, the hotel has been in the proprietor's family since 1910. The saloon bar, with ship's decking wooden floor and stained glass windows, is virtually a nautical museum, displaying figureheads, fish baskets, oars, model boats and diving helmets. A real fire adds to the atmosphere. The other bar, a beamed snug, is quieter, smaller, and no-smoking. Convenient for boat trips to the Farne Islands, it is served by infrequent bus services from Newcastle, Alnwick and Berwick. ⋈Q⌂◁ ⅄♣P

SLALEY

Travellers' Rest
NE46 1TT (on B6306, 1 mile N of village,
4 miles S of Hexham)
🕓 12-11; 12-10.30 Sun
☎ (01661) 673231

Black Sheep Best Bitter; guest beers Ⓗ

Licensed for over 100 years, this welcoming
inn started life in the 16th century as a
farmhouse. Living up to its name, it offers
the traveller an excellent choice of guest
beers, wonderful food and accommodation.
The bar has several distinct, cosy areas and a
large open fire. Stone walls, flag floors and
comfortable furniture add to its appeal.
There is a restaurant, but meals are also
served in the bar; the extensive menu is
creative and uses local produce (no eve
meals Sun). Children are welcome; there is a
safe play area beside the pub. ⚲Q❀✿ⓓP

STAMFORDHAM

Bay Horse Inn
NE18 0PB (on B6309)
🕓 11.30-3, 6.30-11; 12-3, 7-10.30 Sun
☎ (01661) 886244

Castle Eden Ale; Marston's Pedigree; guest beers Ⓗ

Overlooking the village green, next to an
11th-century church, this splendid pub
dates back to around 1590 and was
originally a fortified farm before becoming a
coaching inn. En-suite bedrooms have
replaced the old hayloft and a relaxing
lounge/bar is in the original farmhouse.
Situated in an area steeped in the history of
the Romans and the border reivers, the bar
is popular with both visitors and locals.
⚲❀✿ⓓP

STANNINGTON

Ridley Arms
NE61 6EL
🕓 11.30-11; 12-10.30 Sun
☎ (01670) 789216

**Black Sheep Best Bitter; Taylor Landlord;
guest beers** Ⓗ

A Fitzgerald's house, the Ridley Arms is a
many-roomed pub that caters for all tastes.
Wide doors and ramps ensure easy access
for disabled visitors. Children are welcome.
Two guest ales are always available. Quiz
night is Tuesday. Good food and good beer
make this pub well worth a visit.
⚲Q❀ⓓ♿P

TWEEDMOUTH

Angel
Brewery Bank, TD15 2AQ
🕓 11-11; 12-10.30 Sun
☎ (01289) 303030

Hadrian & Border Rampart; guest beers Ⓗ

Once the brewery tap for Border Brewery,
the Angel has two rooms, one with a pool
table. The interior displays the handiwork
of the nearby Crawfords joinery whose
wooden fittings were installed by a former
director of Border Brewery. The house beer
is brewed by Hadrian & Border. The pub is
handy for football and speedway up the
road at Shielfield Park.
🍺≠P

WYLAM

Boathouse
Station Road, NE41 8HR
🕓 11-11; 12-10.30 Sun
☎ (01661) 853431

Beer range varies Ⓗ

Excellent, two-roomed pub, right next to
the railway station, in the historic village
where George Stephenson was born. The
large bar features nine handpumps serving
an ever-changing range of north-eastern
micros' beers, with a particular emphasis on
those from the local Wylam Brewery, based
at nearby Heddon-on-the-Wall. The
Boathouse acts as the brewery tap and
stocks all the brews as available. Well worth
a visit; a warm welcome is guaranteed at all
times at CAMRA's Northumberland Pub of
the Year 2003. Meals are served at the
weekend.
⚲Q❀ⓓ🍺≠♣P

THIS BEER IS TOTALLY PALE AND TASTELESS!!

YOUR GLASS IS EMPTY, YOU NEED A REFILL!

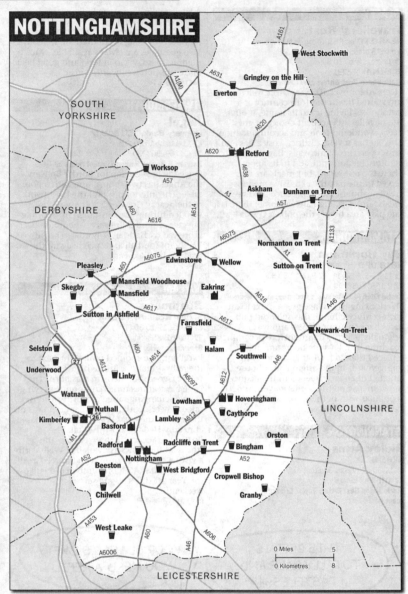

NOTTINGHAMSHIRE

SOUTH YORKSHIRE

DERBYSHIRE

LINCOLNSHIRE

LEICESTERSHIRE

West Stockwith
Gringley on the Hill
Everton
Retford
Worksop
Askham
Dunham on Trent
Normanton on Trent
Edwinstowe
Wellow
Sutton on Trent
Pleasley
Mansfield Woodhouse
Eakring
Skegby
Mansfield
Sutton in Ashfield
Farnsfield
Newark-on-Trent
Selston
Halam
Southwell
Underwood
Linby
Watnall
Lowdham
Hoveringham
Nuthall
Lambley
Caythorpe
Kimberley
Basford
Orston
Radford
Radcliffe on Trent
Bingham
Beeston
Nottingham
West Bridgford
Cropwell Bishop
Chilwell
Granby
West Leake

0 Miles 5
0 Kilometres 8

ASKHAM

Duke William
Town Street, NG22 0RS
(4 miles from Retford)
☼ 12-11; 12-10.30 Sun
☎ (01777) 838564
Broadstone Best Bitter; Taylor Landlord; guest beers H

A warm welcome is assured to all visitors at this small, cosy pub, situated in the centre of the village. There is a small quarry-tiled bar at the front, with a pool table. The rear lounge has its own bar. Food is served daily and the pub was extended in the summer of 2003 with the opening of a restaurant.
🏠 Q ❀ ◑ ♣ P 🖵

BEESTON

Victoria Hotel
Dovecote Lane, NG9 1JG
☼ 11-11; 12-10.30 Sun
☎ (0115) 925 4049
Bateman XB; Caledonian Deuchars IPA; Castle Rock Rylands Gold, Hemlock; Everards Tiger; guest beers H

There are several rooms in this busy free house, including a no-smoking dining area, a drinkers' bar and a covered outside courtyard. A wide choice of constantly-changing beers always includes a mild. It also stocks two ciders, continental beers, good wines and one of the largest selections of malts in the area. The excellent varying menu includes good vegetarian options. Other attractions are live music every Sunday and Monday, a

summer beer festival and themed evenings.
⛫Q❀◑ ⊟♿≠●P

BINGHAM

Horse & Plough ✔
25 Long Acre, NG13 8AS
⏲ 11-11; 12-10.30 Sun
☎ (01949) 839313
Caledonian Deuchars IPA; Wells Bombardier; guest beers 🄷
This award-winning free house is a warm, friendly one-roomed pub with an olde-worlde cottage-style interior with a flagstoned floor. The four guest ales on the bar change regularly and the pub has a 'try before you buy' policy. Before being converted into a pub, this former Methodist chapel housed a bookie's and a butcher's shop. The 42-seater restaurant on the first floor is popular with diners from miles around (open 7–9.30 Tue–Sat, 12–2.30 Sun).
◑♿≠

CAYTHORPE

Black Horse
Main Street, NG14 7ED (near station)
⏲ 11.45-3 (not Mon), 5 (6 Sat)-11; 12-4, 7-10.30 Sun
☎ (0115) 966 3520
Adnams Bitter; Caythorpe Dover Beck Bitter; guest beers 🄷
Fine example of what a village pub should be – dating back some 300 years, it was said to be the haunt of highwayman, Dick Turpin. Magnificent home cooking is a speciality, using seasonal ingredients – try the fish. Your meal can be savoured with a pint of Caythorpe beer, brewed on the premises. Guest beers often include a second Caythorpe brew. Booking for evening meals (not served Sun) is essential. The pub maintains a friendship with a darts team from Bavaria. ⛫Q♘⊟♿⛺P

CHILWELL

Cadland
342 High Road, NG9 5EG
⏲ 11.30-11; 12-10.30 Sun
☎ (0115) 951 8911
Draught Bass; M&B Mild; Worthington's 1744; guest beers 🄷
Since its refurbishment in 2001, the pub has enjoyed a new lease of life. Although now just a single bar, the layout provides discrete areas, separated by fireplaces, walls and glass shelved ornament displays. The relaxed, welcoming atmosphere is enhanced by the friendly staff and comfortable seating. A genuine pub atmosphere pervades even though food is provided. It hosts weekly quiz nights and a beer festival in March.
⛫❀◑♿P⊁

CROPWELL BISHOP

Wheatsheaf
11 Nottingham Road, NG12 3BP
⏲ 12 (4 Tue & Thu)-11; 12-10.30 Sun
☎ (0115) 989 2247
Banks's Riding Bitter, Mansfield Cask Ale; Marston's Pedigree 🄷
Beamed former coaching inn, thought to be at least 400 years old and a reputed haunt of Dick Turpin. The carpeted, split-level lounge has pictures and brasses on the walls; the public bar is tiled. A raised rear area contains a pool table and TV. Upholstered seats surround wooden tables throughout. Superb authentic Chinese banquets can be booked for parties of eight or more in an upstairs room. ❀⊟♣P

DUNHAM ON TRENT

Bridge Inn
Main Street, NG11 6QT (on A57)
⏲ 12-3, 5-11; 12-11 Sat; 12-10.30 Sun
☎ (01777) 228385
Beer range varies 🄷
Situated beside the A57, just before the toll bridge on the Lincolnshire border, this welcoming village local has a large bar area which is full of interesting rural and brewing memorabilia. There is also a dining room. Changing guest ales are served, along with the pub's house beer, Stumbling Bitter, produced by local Broadstone Brewery. This beer is always keenly priced.
⛫Q❀⛟◑♿⛺♣P

EDWINSTOWE

Forest Lodge Hotel
4 Church Street, NG21 9QA
(at A6075/B6034 jct)
⏲ 11.30-2.30, 5.30-11; 12-3, 6.30-10.30 Sun
☎ (01623) 824443 website: www.forestlodge.co.uk
Wells Bombardier; guest beers 🄷
This 17th-century coaching inn, with its regular local trade, still exudes a warm welcome to visitors to Sherwood Forest, a stone's throw away and offers accommodation at reasonable prices. It comprises a cosy lounge bar, with a real fire, a restaurant, smoking and no-smoking areas for both diners and drinkers, plus a family room. Traditional pub games are played; this is a pub not to miss. The house beer is from Kelham Island Brewery.
⛫Q♘⛟◑♿♣P⊁

EVERTON

Blacksmith's Arms
Church Street, DN10 5BQ
⏲ 12-2, 5-11; 12-10.30 Sun
☎ (01777) 817281
Barnsley Bitter; John Smith's Bitter; Theakston Old Peculier; guest beers 🄷
Local CAMRA's autumn Pub of the Season 2002, this genuine 18th-century free house stands at the heart of the village. Drinking areas include the locals' bar with its original tiled floor; duck under the old beams and you enter the games room (formerly the smithy). The comfortable lounge area leads

INDEPENDENT BREWERIES

Alcazar Basford
Broadstone Retford
Castle Rock Nottingham
Caythorpe Hoveringham
Hardys & Hansons Kimberley
Holland Kimberley
Mallard Nottingham
Maypole Eakring
Nottingham Radford
Springhead Sutton on Trent

to a large restaurant, where the emphasis is on fresh home-cooked food (booking advisable). Outside is a Mediterranean-style garden. En-suite accommodation is available in the converted stables.
🏨 Q ⛲ ❀ 🍴 ◑ 🍺 ᴦ ♣ P

FARNSFIELD

Red Lion
Main Street, NG22 8EY
✪ 11-3, 5.30-11; 12-3, 7-10.30 Sun
☎ (01623) 882304
Banks's Riding Bitter, Mansfield Cask Ale; Marston's Pedigree; guest beers Ⓗ
Friendly, family-run pub in a picturesque village, in Robin Hood country. It is very popular for meals, both in the bar and adjoining spacious restaurant area. An 'early bird' menu (5.30–7pm) offers 'lite bites'; a specials boards and menus for older people are also featured. This beamed pub has a dark wood-panelled bar, displaying a fine collection of toby jugs. This is a somewhat rare outlet for the Riding Bitter. 🏨 Q ❀ ◑ ᴦ P

GRANBY

Marquis of Granby
Dragon Street, NG13 9PN
✪ 12-2.30, 5.30-11; 12-11 Sat; 12-10.30 Sun
☎ (01949) 850461
Draught Bass; Ⓖ **Brewster's Marquis; guest beers** Ⓗ
Believed to be the original Marquis of Granby, dating back to 1760 or earlier, this is a small, two-roomed pub, which has risen rapidly from near extinction to become the local CAMRA Pub of the Year. Over 300 different ales have been served in the last year. York stone floors throughout complement naturally-shaped yew bar tops in beamed rooms. The wide range of beers usually includes a guest mild.
🏨 Q ❀ ◑ 🍺 ᴦ ♣ P

GRINGLEY ON THE HILL

Blue Bell
High Street, DN10 4RF
✪ 6 (12 Sat)-11; 12-10.30 Sun
☎ (01777) 817406 website: www.seatlestyle.com
Courage Directors; Fuller's London Pride; John Smith's Bitter; Taylor Landlord; guest beers Ⓗ
At the heart of the village you will be welcomed by an open fire in the winter. One small bar serves all the rooms, including a lounge with a large oak table and easy chairs. An unusual feature is the basement pool room. This busy village pub prides itself on its food, which is served daily, except Monday. Tuesday is pub quiz night. 🏨 Q ◑ ♣

HALAM

Waggon & Horses
The Turnpike, Mansfield Road, NG22 8AE (off B6386)
✪ 11.30-3, 5.30-11; 11.30-11 Sat; 12-10.30 Sun
☎ (01636) 813109
Thwaites Bitter, Thoroughbred, Lancaster Bomber; guest beers Ⓗ
Popular pub, in a quiet village centre, that has been carefully modernised. The open-plan bars all have beamed ceilings and comfortable benches or chairs in country style. The no-smoking dining room is

separated from the main area by brick arches and an interesting wrought iron screen. Traditional pub games are played in one area. A summer beer festival and occasional live music add to the appeal of this rural pub. Q ❀ ♣ P

HOVERINGHAM

Reindeer
Main Street, NG14 7JR (1 mile from A612)
✪ 12-2, 6-11; 12-10.30 Sun
☎ (0115) 966 3629
Marston's Bitter, Pedigree; guest beers Ⓗ
Cottage-style pub, split between a bar and restaurant. A Victorian cricket hatch serves directly on to the village cricket pitch, believed to be the only one in the county. Open log fires and beamed ceilings are features of both bar and restaurant; this cosy, welcoming pub is lit by candles most of the year. It stocks a fast-changing range of good beers. The Marquis of Granby across the road is also worth a visit.
🏨 Q ❀ ◑ 🍺 ⇌ (Thurgarton) P

KIMBERLEY

Nelson & Railway ✪
12 Station Road, NG16 2NR (opp. brewery)
✪ 11.30-11; 12-10.30 Sun
☎ (0115) 938 2177
website: www.nelsonandrailway.fsnet.co.uk
Hardys & Hansons Bitter, Olde Trip, seasonal beers Ⓗ
Fine local, less than 150 yards from Hardys & Hansons Brewery. A traditional, friendly bar complements the beamed lounge with adjoining dining area. The front garden is popular in summer and the pub is renowned for its good value food and accommodation; Sunday meals are served 12–6. The pub has been kept by the same family for over 30 years. ❀ 🍴 ◑ 🍺 ♣ P

Stag Inn
67 Nottingham Road, NG16 2NB
✪ 5 (4.30 Fri; 1.30 Sat)-11; 12-10.30 Sun
☎ (0115) 938 3151
Boddingtons Bitter; Greenalls Bitter; Marston's Pedigree; Tetley Mild; guest beer Ⓗ
Characterful, beamed pub dating from 1537. Old-fashioned slot machines, in full working order, are found in both rooms; traditional games are also played. Although situated on the busy Nottingham Road, the pub attracts mainly a local clientele. The regular R1 bus service from Nottingham stops outside. The garden, at the rear of the building, is the venue for occasional beer festivals.
Q ❀ 🍺 ♣ P

LAMBLEY

Robin Hood & Little John
82 Main Street, NG4 4PP
✪ 12-4 (11 Fri & Sat); 12-4, 7-10.30 Sun
☎ (0115) 931 2531
Mansfield Dark Mild, Banks's Bitter, Mansfield Cask Ale; Marston's Pedigree Ⓗ
Friendly, popular pub, said to be the oldest in the village, comprising a lounge, bar, function room and skittle alley. Lunchtime and evening meals are served. 1970s and '80s music is played in the background. The pub fields a darts team.
🏨 Q ⛲ ❀ ◑ 🍺 P ⊬

LINBY

Horse & Groom
Main Street, NG15 8AE
☼ 12-11; 12-10.30 Sun
☎ (0115) 963 2219
Everards Home Bitter; Theakston Mild; guest beers Ⓗ
Multi-roomed gem of a pub, set in a picturesque, award-winning village, north of Nottingham. The public bar, snug and green room all have open fires, the one in the public bar is an inglenook. Four cask ales are stocked, often coming from small local breweries. This pub has a deserved reputation for excellent quality meals which are served in all areas, in addition to the restaurant. Regular music nights, hosted by a pianist, are staged (Tue) and quiz nights (Thu). 🏚Q🏃⊕🕮♣P⊁

LOWDHAM

Old Ship Inn
Main Street, NG14 7BE
☼ 11.30-2.30, 5.30-11; 12-10.30 Sun
☎ (0115) 966 3049 website: www.oldshipinn.co.uk
Courage Directors; John Smith's Bitter; guest beers Ⓗ
Large village pub, popular with locals for the beers but also for the very good menu in the much extended restaurant. Open fires warm both bars, enhancing the friendly atmosphere. An ever-changing variety of guest ales adds interest. A large, open garden and lawns host barbecues in summer. The accommodation is in comfortable rooms.
🏚Q🏠🛏⊕🕮♣P

World's End Inn
Plough Lane, NG14 7AT
(500 yds from A612/A6097 roundabout)
☼ 12-3, 5.30-11; 12-4, 7-10.30 Sun
☎ (0115) 966 3857
Banks's Bitter, Mansfield Cask Ale; Marston's Bitter, Pedigree Ⓗ
Lovely village pub, circa 1744, brightened by a nice floral display during the summer. There is a flagpole, easily seen from the road, that was purchased from Notts Forest FC; evidently the pole contains some very old coins. The pub interior features exposed beams and a collection of jugs and various items of brass. Good food is served.
🏚Q🏠⊕🕮P

MANSFIELD

Bold Forester ✅
Botany Avenue, NG18 5NF
(½ mile from bus station, along A38)
☼ 11-11; 12-10.30 Sun
☎ (01623) 623970
Draught Bass; Black Sheep Best Bitter; Boddingtons Bitter; Castle Eden Ale; Greene King Abbot; guest beers Ⓗ
Large pub on the outskirts of the town centre, offering a warm, friendly welcome. A range of six guest beers from regional and micro-brewers change constantly. Popular quiz nights are staged three times a week and live bands play every Sunday evening. Good value meals are served lunchtime and early evening in a no-smoking restaurant area, but food does not dominate here. An established annual beer festival around St George's Day offers over 30 beers.
🏠⊕🕮♿🚆●P⊁

Nell Gwyn
117 Sutton Road, NG18 5EX
(50 yds from A38/B6014 jct)
☼ 12-4, 7-11; 12-3, 7-10.30 Sun
☎ (01623) 659850
Beer range varies Ⓗ
Nell Gwyn (formerly Bleak House) is a free house offering two guest beers that change regularly. A homely atmosphere is due to both the landlord and regulars. This small establishment has a lounge and a games room, served from a central bar area. Traditional pub games are encouraged along with TV for special sporting events in the games room. Background music is kept to a minimum allowing for the traditional art of conversation.
🏚Q♿♣

Railway Inn
9 Station Street, NG18 1EF
☼ 11-11; 12-10.30 Sun
☎ (01623) 623086
Bateman XB; guest beers Ⓗ
A long-serving licensee runs this pub, stocking one guest ale, at the best price in the area. The home-cooked food is reasonably priced too, but sells out very quickly due to high demand. The choice of bottled beer has to be seen, and the large choice of spirits starts at £1.50 for a double! The Railway often features on TV and in the local press. Very old-fashioned, with a number of small rooms, it is ideal for meetings of small groups.
Q🏠⊕🕮🚆(Robin Hood Line)⊁

Widow Frost ✅
Leeming Street, NG18 1NB
☼ 10-11; 12-10.30 Sun
☎ (01623) 666790
Courage Directors; Marston's Pedigree; Shepherd Neame Spitfire; guest beers Ⓗ
Spacious, single room Wetherspoon's conversion, executed to a high standard of fitting, with a large no-smoking area for families that can be used by all drinkers. Local beers are available at the manager's discretion. There are the usual old pictures of the town and its history, together with a full story of the pub's name on display. The menu is standard Wetherspoon's, but the Sunday lunch is well worth a try, washed down with the first-class choice of local guest beers.
Q⊕♿🚆⊁

MANSFIELD WOODHOUSE

Greyhound Inn
82 High Street, NG19 8BD
☼ 12-11; 12-3, 7-10.30 Sun
☎ (01623) 464403
Courage Directors; Everards Home Bitter; Mansfield Cask Ale; Theakston Mild; guest beer Ⓗ
Friendly, popular local of stone construction, reputedly 17th century, situated in the village near the old market square. It consists of two rooms; a quiet, comfortable lounge and a lively tap room with pool table, dartboard and traditional games. The pub fields both ladies' and gents' teams and hosts a quiz on Monday and Wednesday evenings. It has been 10 consecutive years in this Guide.
Q🏠🕮🚆♣P🎵

NEWARK-ON-TRENT

Castle & Falcon
10 London Road, NG24 1TW
(50 yards from Beaumont Cross)
☼ 12-3 (not Tue-Thu; 11-3 Fri), 7-11; 12-3,
7-10.30 Sun
☎ (01636) 703513
John Smith's Bitter; guest beers Ⓗ
Dating back to the early 1800s, this former coachhouse on the main London–York run, stands in the shadow of the now converted James Hole's Castle Brewery. This town-centre pub, catering mainly for regulars, is split into three distinct areas: bar, lounge and conservatory. The guest beers change on a regular basis and tasters are offered to help you decide. The pub is very sporting, fielding darts, pool, dominoes and skittles teams; there is something happening most evenings. ❀♫≠(Castle) ♣

Fox & Crown
4-6 Appletongate, NG24 1JY
(near market square)
☼ 11-11; 12-10.30 Sun
☎ (01636) 605820
Caledonian Deuchars IPA; Castle Rock Nottingham Gold, Hemlock; Everards Tiger; Hook Norton Best Bitter; guest beers Ⓗ
Opened by Tynemill in 1997, following closure by Courage in 1974, this popular town pub has an open aspect, but with distinct drinking areas. An excellent range of up to five guest beers is complemented by bottled beers from Belgium and across Europe, plus over 60 malts. Good value food is freshly prepared using local produce. Freshly ground coffee is supplied by the local roasting house. A typical Tynemill no-nonsense drinking establishment, it hosts monthly brewery nights and occasional live music. Q◑&≠(Castle/Northgate) ♣⌇

Mail Coach
13 London Road, NG24 1TN
☼ 11.30-3, 5.30-11; 11.30-11 Sat; 12-3,
7-10.30 Sun
☎ (01636) 605164
Flowers IPA, Original; guest beers Ⓗ
This is a friendly and popular free house dating back to 1778, which offers home-cooked food Tuesday–Sunday, and usually a minimum of two guest beers. The pub is divided into three different drinking areas and there are two real fires to keep customers warm in winter. Outside is a patio garden. Live music is played most Thursdays (jazz or blues).
♫❀≠◑≠(Castle) P

Old Malt Shovel
25 North Gate, NE24 1HD
☼ 11.30-11 (11.30-3, 5.30-11 winter Mon & Tue);
12-10.30 Sun
☎ (01636) 702036
website: www.theoldmaltshovel.co.uk
Adnams Broadside; Caledonian Deuchars IPA; Taylor Landlord; Wells Bombardier; Worthington's 1744; guest beers Ⓗ
On the site of a 16th-century bakery, this comfortable single-roomed pub offers a wide range of beers, usually including a mild. It runs its own real ale tasting society (RATS). Outside is a patio/garden area and a covered skittle alley. The restaurant is open every day, and bar snacks are also available.

The pub is a member of the Campaign for Real Food and specialises in European dishes. ♫Q⌣❀◑&≠(Castle) ♣⌇

NORMANTON ON TRENT

Square & Compass
Eastgate, NG23 6RN (10 miles N of Newark via A1)
☼ 12-11; 12-10.30 Sun
☎ (01636) 821439
website: www.squareandcompass.co.uk
Maypole Lion's Pride; guest beers Ⓗ
Friendly, one-roomed village free house, parts of which are 500 years old and atmospheric with log fire and exposed beams. A curry and quiz night is staged on Wednesday. The dining area is entirely no-smoking. A safe, imaginatively laid-out adventure play area is a bonus for families with children. Wheelchair-users have good access throughout the pub, the WC and one chalet (the accommodation is recommended). This is the Maypole Brewery tap and always features their beer plus two guests.
♫Q❀≠◑&▲♣P

NOTTINGHAM: *CENTRAL*

Bell Inn ✿
18 Angel Row, Old Market Square, NG1 6HL
☼ 11-11; 12-10.30 Sun
☎ (0115) 947 5241 website: www.thebell-inn.com
Hardys & Hansons Mild, Bitter, Olde Trip, seasonal beers; Nottingham Legend Ⓗ
Built on a labyrinth of sandstone caves, this Georgian-fronted, Grade II listed inn is one of the oldest in Nottingham. The Tardis-like quality of this 15th-century pub reveals several bar areas, recently restored to their full. Live music (including jazz) is performed Sunday–Wednesday in the Tudor Bar, where good food is also served. More substantial meals are available in the upstairs Belfrey Restaurant. Pavement tables with waitress service are set outside in the summer. William Clarke Strong Ale is brewed by Hardys & Hansons for the Bell and another Nottingham pub, Ye Olde Trip to Jerusalem. Q❀◑⌇

Fellows, Morton & Clayton
54 Canal Street, NG1 7EH
☼ 11-11 (midnight Fri & Sat); 12-10.30 Sun
☎ (0115) 950 6795
website: www.fellowsmortonandclayton.co.uk
Boddingtons Bitter; Castle Eden Ale; Fellows Bitter, Post Haste; Fuller's London Pride; guest beers Ⓗ
One-roomed pub with split-level areas, converted from a warehouse in the late 1970s; a boat building firm provided the name. Adjacent to the canalside development, it is extremely popular with a diverse clientele. Home of the city centre's first brew-pub (note that malt extract is used), it is a regular outlet for local Mallard beers. An excellent, good value restaurant is situated at the rear of the pub; meals are served all day (until 6pm Sun). Big-screen TV sports are shown.
❀◑≠⊖

Lincolnshire Poacher
161 Mansfield Road, NG1 3FW
(300 yds from Victoria Centre)
☼ 11-11; 12-10.30 Sun
☎ (0115) 941 1584

Bateman XB, XXXB; Castle Rock Poacher's Gold; Oakham JHB; guest beers Ⓗ

Two-roomed traditional pub with wood floors; the smaller room is for non-smokers. There is a garden and large conservatory at the rear. Very popular at lunchtime with ale fans doing the Mansfield Road crawl, it offers an ever-changing variety of beers with many brewery nights showcasing micro-breweries. Occasional live music includes morris dancers performing in the garden. A varied and tasty menu is served.
Q ⌂ ⊛ ◑ ⅃ ♣ ♠ ⅄

Lloyds No. 1 Bar ⊘
1 Carlton Street, Hockley, NG1 1NL
☼ 11-midnight; 12-midnight Sun
☎ (0115) 988 1660
Beer range varies Ⓗ

No loud music is played during the day, so it is ideal for a chat. It serves competitively priced beer and food all day. The bar gets very lively at night, as music is turned up loud to appeal to the younger generation. It was converted from a bank and features unusual high ceilings and a polished wood floor. Families with children are welcome until 9pm. ◑ ◐ ⅃ ⅄

Newshouse
123 Canal Street, NG1 7HB
☼ 11-11; 12-10.30 Sun
☎ (0115) 950 2419
Castle Rock The Daily Gold; Everards Tiger; guest beers Ⓗ

Recently refurbished by new owners Tynemill, who have retained the original two-room layout, tiles feature in the decor – blue on the outside and white, depicting brewery names, on the inside. Historic events are remembered with pages from the local paper displayed on the walls. Accompanying the changing selection of ales are continental beers, both on draught and bottled, a wide choice of malts, Westons Old Rosie cider and speciality teas and coffees. Q ◑ ♣ ⇌ ⊖ ♣ ♠

Olde Trip to Jerusalem ☆
1 Brewhouse Yard, NG1 6AD (below castle)
☼ 11-11; 12-10.30 Sun
☎ (0115) 947 3171 website: www.triptojerusalem.com
Hardys & Hansons Mild, Bitter, Olde Trip, seasonal beers Ⓗ

The world famous Ye Olde Trip to Jerusalem, with 1189 AD painted on the wall, has a number of rooms downstairs, some cut out of the castle rock. Upstairs, the Rock Lounge is home to a haunted galleon and a modern tapestry depicting Nottingham's history. Meals are served until 6pm. The top bar can be reserved for private functions. A must for visitors to Nottingham; William Clarke Strong Ale, brewed by Hardys & Hansons, is only available here and at the Bell in Nottingham, as mentioned. Q ⊛ ◑ ⇌ ⊖ ♣ ⅄

Rose of England
36-38 Mansfield Road, NG1 3JA
☼ 11-11 (midnight Thu-Sat); 12-10.30 Sun
☎ (0115) 947 2739
Adnams Broadside; Greene King Abbot; Tetley Mild; Wells Bombardier; guest beers Ⓗ

Probably Nottingham's finest example of a Victorian pub. This architectural gem was designed by local architect Fothergill

Watson in 1898, sporting a charming and unusual exterior that must be seen. Recently refurbished and reverted to its original name, the pub houses a long bar with 10 handpumps, with three more in the upstairs function room. Guest ales change on a regular basis. Hot food is served 11.30–4 Monday–Saturday. ◑ ⅄

Vat & Fiddle
12-14 Queen's Bridge Road, NG2 1NB
(near station)
☼ 11-11; 12-10.30 Sun
☎ (0115) 985 0611
Castle Rock Meadows Gold, Hemlock; guest beers Ⓗ

Well-regarded, down-to-earth, local at the edge of the city centre. Between the station and the football grounds, it stands next to Tynemill's Castle Rock Brewery. This single-roomed pub displays photos of long-demolished pubs in the nearby Meadows area. Ten handpulls serve up to four beers from Castle Rock (at least one mild); German and Belgian beers and up to 70 malt whiskies are also stocked. It hosts occasional beer festivals. No meals are served Sunday evening. Q ⊛ ◑ ⇌ ⊖ ♠

NOTTINGHAM: *EAST*

Lord Nelson ⊘
11 Thurgarton Street, Sneinton, NG2 4AJ
(near Green's windmill)
☼ 11-3, 5-11; 11-4, 5.30-11 Sat; 12-4, 7-10.30 Sun
☎ (0115) 911 0069
Hardys & Hansons Mild, Bitter, Olde Trip, seasonal beers Ⓗ

Originally two country cottages, this unusual pub has the appearance of a traditional rural inn, albeit in the city. The 400-year-old former coaching inn now consists of four rooms where generally the emphasis is on convivial conversation. Again, unusual for a town pub, it has a fine sheltered garden which helps make it a popular summer venue. Smoking restrictions apply at lunchtime. It hosts a weekly quiz. Only 300 yards away is a working windmill. ⚲ Q ⊛ ◑ ♣ ♠

Magpies
Meadow Lane, Daleside Road, Sneinton, NG2 3GG
☼ 11-3, 5-11; 11-11 Fri & Sat; 12-3, 7-10.30 Sun
☎ (0115) 911 8877
Adnams Broadside; Brewster's Meek & Mild; guest beers Ⓗ

Friendly local offering good value, home-cooked food (eve meals Mon–Fri). It comprises a traditional bar area, complete with pool table and Sky TV, plus a comfortable lounge. Built in the 1950s, the pub displays a wonderful selection of old Nottingham photos and sketches in both rooms. It attracts sports fans due to its proximity to Notts County and Forest, Colwick Racecourse, Trent Bridge cricket and the National Ice Arena. The house beer, Magpie Bitter is from Brewster's.
⊛ ◑ ♣ ▲ ⇌ ♣ P ⊟

NOTTINGHAM: *NORTH*

Gladstone
45 Loscoe Road, Carrington, NG5 2AW
☼ 5 (12 Sat)-11; 12-10.30 Sun
☎ (0115) 912 9994

Fuller's London Pride; Greene King IPA; Old Speckled Hen; Shepherd Neame Spitfire; guest beer Ⓗ
Friendly, two-roomed traditional local, built around 1880, just off Mansfield Road in Carrington. The public bar displays various sporting memorabilia and screens TV sporting events, while the lounge features many books, available for customers to read. Five beers are stocked. A quiz takes place every Thursday and the upstairs function room hosts the local folk club on Wednesday evening. ⚽🍴♣♠

Fox & Crown
33 Church Street, Old Basford, NG6 0GA
❊ 12-11; 12-10.30 Sun
☎ (0115) 942 2002
website: www.alcazarbrewingco.com
Alcazar Ale, Nottingham Nog, New Dawn, Brush Bitter, Vixen's Vice Ⓗ
This pleasant, welcoming pub is the Alcazar Brewery tap. The central circular bar boasts 12 handpumps serving the brewery beers and at least one ever-changing guest. Beer festivals are also held through the year. The brewery can be viewed through the glass wall and is accessible from the garden. The pub stocks a large selection of bottled continental and fruit beers. Pizzas are available in the early evening. 🛏️⚽♿⊖P

Horse & Groom ⊘
462 Radford Road, Basford, NG7 7EA
❊ 11-11; 12-10.30 Sun
☎ (0115) 970 3777
Belvoir Star Bitter; Courage Directors; Wells Bombardier; guest beers Ⓗ
Genuine free house in the shadow of the former Shipstone's Brewery, the pub's original owner. The outside retains the old Shipstone's sign while the inside contains various memorabilia. Eight beers are always on tap, many from micro-breweries. There is a snug and a large function room at the rear where an 'open mike' evening is hosted every Tuesday and bands perform occasionally. 🛏️◖⊖

Lion Inn ⊘
44 Mosley Street, New Basford, NG7 7FQ
(off Radford Road)
❊ 11-11; 12-10.30 Sun
☎ (0115) 970 3506 website: www.overall-online.co.uk
Draught Bass; Bateman XB, seasonal beers; guest beers Ⓗ
Busy, back-street pub, just off the main road, catering for both the local community and lovers of rock/blues, jazz and tribute bands who come from far and wide. One large room with a central bar gives a feeling of separate areas. Micro-breweries, especially local ones, are well represented in the guest portfolio. Although owned by Bateman, the guest range is that of a good free house. 🛏️⚽◖♿⊖♣♠P

NOTTINGHAM: SOUTH

Globe
152 London Road, NG2 3BQ (near Trent Bridge)
❊ 11-11; 12-10.30 Sun
☎ (0115) 986 6881
Belvoir Star Bitter; Broadstone Best Bitter; guest beers Ⓗ
Light, airy, popular pub located near Nottingham's cricket and football grounds. The function room caters for up to 100

people and occasionally shows matches on a big screen. The varied menu is competitively priced; meals are served 12–8 (5 Sun). Recently refurbished, up to six handpumps serve ales from mainly local breweries. Seating ranges from bar stools to settles in a cosy alcove, with a fire in winter. Ask about the CAMRA discount. Frequent buses run from the city centre. ◖⇌P

NOTTINGHAM: WEST

Plough
17 St Peters Street, Radford, NG7 3EN
❊ 12-2.30, 5-11; 12-11 Thu-Sat; 12-10.30 Sun
☎ (0115) 942 2649
Nottingham Rock Ale Mild, Rock Ale Bitter, Legend, Extra Pale Ale, Bullion; guest beers Ⓗ
A real pub for real people. This 1840s local is the tap for the Nottingham Brewery (in buildings at the rear). Live Irish music is performed on Thursday evening, with free chilli. Curry is only £1.50 on Tuesday evening and live music accompanies the popular lunches some Sundays. Regional CAMRA Pub of the Year runner-up 2002, it won a Pub of Excellence award in January 2002 from Nottingham CAMRA. The place to enjoy Nottingham's ales – 'beers to be proud of', the cider comes from Mahoralls Farm. 🛏️Q⚽◖♿♣🐕P

Red Lion
21 Alfreton Road, Canning Circus, NG7 3JE
(at Canning Circus)
❊ 11-11; 12-10.30 Sun
☎ (0115) 952 0309
Boddingtons Bitter; Marston's Pedigree; guest beers Ⓗ
Up to eight different real ales are available in this one-roomed, split-level pub, situated on the western edge of the city centre. Sporting events can be viewed on an unobtrusive TV at the back of the pub. An unusual outside drinking terrace is accessed up a flight of stairs. Good value food is served at lunchtime (limited choice Sat); try the Tuesday evening special – buy a pint and get a meal of bangers and mash for 95p extra. The pub opens at 11 o'clock on Sunday for brunch. ⚽◖

NUTHALL

Three Ponds ⊘
Nottingham Road, NG16 1DP (off M1 jct 26)
❊ 11-11; 12-10.30 Sun
☎ (0115) 938 3170
Hardys & Hansons Bitter, Olde Trip, seasonal beers Ⓗ
Comfortable, popular pub with an established food trade as one of the brewery's 'Value for Money' pubs. The front bar area has retained its pub feel, while the rear caters more for diners. Meals are served 11–9 (12–8 Sun). At the rear is a patio and a spacious children's play area; the pub has a children's certificate. A fine display of old photos of the area features throughout the pub. ⚽◖♿P

ORSTON

Durham Ox
Church Street, NG13 9NS
❊ 12-3, 6-11; 11.30-11 Sat; 12-10.30 Sun
☎ (01949) 850059
website: www.orston.pub@virgin.net

Everards Home Bitter; Marston's Pedigree; Theakston Best Bitter; guest beers Ⓗ
Delightful village pub for locals and visitors alike, with a garden and pavement café tables in summer and a roaring fire in winter. There is ample parking and hitching rails for horses. The divided room stocks an interesting whisky collection in one half and aviation pictures and memorabilia elsewhere. No hot food is served but filled rolls are made to order. Popular pub games are played. ⚲Q☎⚑&♣P✗⌂

PLEASLEY

Olde Plough
Chesterfield Road North, NG19 7SP
(3 miles NW of Mansfield on A617 to Chesterfield)
✪ 11.30-3, 5.30-11; 11-11 Sat; 12-3, 7-10.30 Sun
☎ (01623) 810386
Marston's Bitter, Pedigree; guest beers Ⓗ
Busy and deservedly popular open-plan pub, but quite cosy as well, providing a comfortable setting in which to enjoy an excellent pint. The extensive menu of home-cooked food includes daily specials and a 'lite bites' section. Food is available all week, except Sunday evening. Quiz nights are a regular feature on Tuesday and Sunday. Q☎◑P✗

RADCLIFFE ON TRENT

Black Lion
Main Road, NG12 2FD
✪ 12 (11 Sat)-11; 12-10.30 Sun
☎ (0115) 933 2138
Courage Directors; Everards Home Bitter; guest beers Ⓗ
Spacious, comfortable pub at the village centre, serving three ever-changing guest beers. Separate from the smart lounge is an extended public bar, housing a large-screen TV for sport. Regular live music is performed upstairs. Food is served 12–8.45, with an emphasis on home-cooked dishes and an extensive specials board. The enclosed garden, with children's play area, is popular with families. Black Rat cider is sold in summer. ⚲☎◑⊟&≒♣●P

RETFORD

Joiner's Inn
London Road, DN22 6AZ
(next to GK Ford Garage)
✪ 11-11; 12-10.30 Sun
☎ (01777) 704492
Barnsley Bitter; John Smith's Bitter Ⓗ
Single-storey building on the edge of the town centre. It comprises a large public bar area, with a pool table and dartboard and a lounge bar. While only serving two real ales they are always on good form, with the Barnsley Bitter keenly priced. You would most certainly call this establishment a drinking person's pub. Q⊟≒♣P

Market Hotel
West Carr Road, DN22 7SN
✪ 11-3, 6-11; 11-11 Sat; 12-4.30, 7-10.30 Sun
☎ (01777) 703278
Adnams Bitter; Fuller's London Pride; Young's Bitter; guest beers Ⓗ
This pub has been run by the same family for over 40 years. The comfortable, deservedly popular single bar serves up to

10 real ales (three or four as guests). On the outskirts of town, it is just a few minutes' walk from the railway station. Well known locally for its quality food, particularly the Sunday carvery, children are welcome early evening. There is a restaurant and a large banqueting suite. Q☎◑●≒P

Rum Runner
Wharf Road, DN22 6EN (near fire station)
✪ 11.30-11; 12-10.30 Sun
☎ (01777) 860788
Broadstone Two Water Grog; Taylor Landlord; guest beers Ⓗ
This popular pub is presently north Nottinghamshire's only brew-pub and was local CAMRA Pub of the Year in 2002. Broadstone beers are produced in the converted stables; Two Water Grog is brewed solely for the pub. It always has three guest beers on tap, together with a wide selection of bottled beers. A full range of hot drinks is also available. The no-smoking lounge has large comfortable sofas and can get very busy at the weekends. ⚲☎◑≒♣✗⌂

Turk's Head
Grove Street, DN22 6LA (near market square)
✪ 11-3, 7-11; 11-11 Sat; 12-3, 7-10.30 Sun
☎ (01777) 702742
Adnams Bitter; Courage Directors; Theakston Best Bitter; guest beers Ⓗ
Attractive, oak-panelled pub off the town centre. A warm welcome is assured at this real ale supporter. Food is served daily and the pub is noted for the quality of its Sunday roasts. While there is a pool table, there are plenty of quiet little corners where you can sit and enjoy a conversation over a good pint of beer. ⚲Q◑♣

SELSTON

Horse & Jockey
Church Lane, NG16 6FB
(½ mile off B6018) OS464539
✪ 12-2.30, 5-11; 12-3, 7.30-10.30 Sun
☎ (01773) 781012
Draught Bass; Ⓗ **Greene King Abbot;** Ⓖ **Taylor Landlord; guest beers** Ⓗ/Ⓖ
Family-run village local, dating back to 1664 and reputedly haunted. Allegedly only 12 pubs in England are older than this former local CAMRA Pub of the Year. Low, beamed ceilings and flagstoned floors feature in all rooms – the main bar, snug, a lounge with a working cast iron range and a games room (pool and darts). Wednesday is folk night when all are very welcome – bring your own instrument. Good food is served weekdays, with freshly carved roast meats most days. ⚲Q☎⚑◑&♣●P

SKEGBY

Fox & Crown
116 Dalestorth Road, NG17 3AA
(at A6075/B6014 jct, ¼ mile off A38)
✪ 11-11; 12-10.30 Sun
☎ (01623) 552436
Mansfield Cask Ale; Theakston Mild, XB; guest beer Ⓗ
This very popular Steak & Ale pub is spacious and open plan, with a no-smoking area and restaurant. Dark wood panelling features extensively and pictures of the surrounding area adorn the walls. A regular

lunch stop for the working community, the pub also acts as a traditional local with large-screen TV sports shown regularly. Food is served daily, 11–9.30 (12–8 Sun); quizzes are held on Tuesday and Sunday. The pub has an outdoor children's play area. ⊛◑♣P✖

SOUTHWELL

Old Coach House
69 Easthorpe, NG25 0HY
(on A612, near racecourse)
✪ 5 (4 Fri; 12 Sat)-11; 12-10.30 Sun
☎ (01636) 813289
Draught Bass; guest beers Ⓗ

This friendly, welcoming, 17th-century free house offers an average of 20 different beers each week; six at any one time – shot glasses are used for sampling. On cold days three open fires make it easy to feel at home. Many games are available, including cribbage, rare for the area. Southwell racecourse and minster are close by and the pub lies conveniently on the Newark–Nottingham bus route. Cider is stocked in summer. ⚔⊛⊕♣●

SUTTON IN ASHFIELD

King & Miller ◉
King's Mill Road East, NG17 4JP
(on A38 near King's Mill hospital & reservoir)
✪ 11-11; 12-10.30 Sun
☎ (01623) 553312
Hardys & Hansons Bitter, Olde Trip, seasonal beers Ⓗ

This spacious Cask Marque-accredited pub has an open-plan design; half of the pub is devoted to family dining, with an adjoining indoor children's play area. The public bar hosts regular quiz nights and various special promotions. The patio area adjoins a second children's play area outside which is very popular in summer. ⊛◑♣P✖

Picture House ◉
Forest Street, NG17 1DA (near bus station)
✪ 10-11; 12-10.30 Sun
☎ (01623) 554627
Greene King Abbot; Mansfield Dark Mild; Shepherd Neame Spitfire; Theakston Best Bitter Ⓗ

Converted from a cinema, this is the largest real ale pub in the town centre. Busy at weekends it still maintains a sociable atmosphere. Open-plan and carpeted throughout, its high ceiling helps create a buzzing atmosphere when busy. The decor mixes different styles: wood panels on the upper level, Art Deco behind the bar, gothic light fittings and an eye-catching fibre-optic feature above the front door. Daily papers are provided, along with Wetherspoon's house magazine. Meals are served all day. Q◑♿✖

UNDERWOOD

Red Lion
134 Church Lane, NG16 5HD (off B600)
✪ 12-3, 5.30-11; 12-11 Sat; 12-10.30 Sun
☎ (01773) 810482
Greene King IPA; Marston's Pedigree; guest beers Ⓗ

300-year-old beamed village pub, run by a friendly landlord and his staff. The bar area has a quarry-tiled floor with a step up to a raised carpeted dining area (children are welcome in the latter). A good variety of

excellent meals and snacks is supplemented by barbecues in summer. The large garden has a paved patio, a lawn and a children's play area. On Monday evenings a general knowledge quiz is held. The pub has won a number of local CAMRA awards. ⊛◑P

WATNALL

Queen's Head
40 Main Street, NG16 1HU
✪ 12-3, 5.30-11; 12-11 Fri, Sat & summer;
12-10.30 Sun
☎ (0115) 938 3148
Everards Home Bitter; Greene King Ruddles Best; guest beers Ⓗ

Traditional 300-year-old country pub with a friendly welcome for all. An unusual snug is hidden behind the serving area, while the main bar boasts a grandfather clock and a specially-built table. The famous Moorgreen Show takes place to the rear of the pub. An extensive garden and children's play area are a bonus. The Queen's Larder is famous for its fish and chips and general good value selection; meals are served all day in summer (12–8). Hikers and bikers are welcome. ⚔⊛◑⊟P

WELLOW

Red Lion
Eakring Road, NG22 0EG (off A616)
✪ 11.30-3.30, 6-11; 11-11 Sat; 12-10.30 Sun
☎ (01623) 861000
Black Sheep Best Bitter; Castle Eden Ale; Wells Bombardier Ⓗ

Local CAMRA Pub of the Season, summer 2002, this 400-year-old pub with exposed beams stands opposite the village maypole. The walls of the bar are covered with old photographs and drawings which depict the history of both the pub and the village. There is also a small lounge bar and a dining area. Good quality, home-cooked food is available daily. It is close to both Clumber and Rufford Country Parks and Center Parks holiday village.
Q⊛◑⊟⚔♣P✖

WEST BRIDGFORD

Meadow Covert ◉
Alford Road, Edwalton, NG12 4AT
✪ 11-11; 12-10.30 Sun
☎ (0115) 923 2074
Hardys & Hansons Mild, Bitter, Olde Trip, seasonal beers Ⓗ

To the north of Edwalton, this two-roomed community pub has a games-oriented public bar, housing two pool tables and a large-screen TV. The comfortable L-shaped lounge is commodious, offering plenty of room both for drinkers and diners. Meals are served all day until 7.30 (6pm weekends). The outdoor skittle alley is new, while the pub's garden has a children's play area and hosts summer barbecues. It runs occasional beer festivals. Q◑⊟♿♣P

Southbank Bar
1 Bridgford House, Trent Bridge, NG2 6GJ
✪ 10-midnight; 10-10.30 Sun
☎ (0115) 945 5541 website: www.southbank-bar.co.uk
Fuller's London Pride; Mallard Duck & Dive; Taylor Landlord; guest beers (occasional) Ⓗ

Popular, lively bar on Trent Bridge, which is

handy for both football grounds and the cricket. Sport is featured on several TVs and games are shown on a large screen. Food is served all day until 9pm daily and the menu offers an interesting mix of hot and cold dishes. Monday night is curry night. The spacious beer garden overlooks the river; it is the sister pub to the Globe, just over the bridge. ⊛⊕⊅&

Stratford Haven
2 Stratford Road, NG2 6BA
✪ 10.30-11; 12-10.30 Sun
☎ (0115) 982 5981
Bateman XB; Caledonian Deuchars IPA; Castle Rock Gold, Hemlock; Hook Norton Old Hooky; guest beers Ⓗ

Busy, no-gimmicks Tynemill pub, tucked away next to the Co-op supermarket, between the town centre and Trent Bridge cricket ground. Named as a result of a competition in the local press, the winning entry is on display. The beer range includes at least one mild and a Castle Rock house beer. Monthly brewery nights feature all the selected brewery's beers and usually have live music. A good menu served 12–8 (6 Sun), includes a vegetarian choice (no chips). ⊛⊕&⊌✕

Test Match ❷
Gordon Square, NG2 5LP
✪ 11-11; 12-10.30 Sun
☎ (0115) 981 1481 website: www.thetestmatch.co.uk
Hardys & Hansons Mild, Bitter, Olde Trip, seasonal beers Ⓗ

This Art Deco masterpiece has been restored to its original glory. The main lounge area has been extended to fully show the pub's architectural features; large and comfortable, it boasts a 16-foot mural depicting George Parr and William Clarke, famous cricketers from the 1800s. The traditional bar area has been impressively restored and even the toilets contain many original features. The upstairs cocktail lounge is available for private parties. ⊛⊕&♣P

WEST LEAKE

Star
Melton Lane, LE12 5RQ
✪ 11-2.30, 6-11; 12-3.30, 7-10.30 Sun
☎ (01509) 852233
Draught Bass; guest beers Ⓗ

On the village outskirts, the Star is known locally as the Pit House after two nearby and long-disused clay pits. The attractive, white-painted exterior conceals a quintessentially English country bar, complete with beamed ceiling, quarry-tiled floor, open fire and high-backed settles. Leading off is the no-smoking family room, not so long ago part of an adjoining cottage, while the comfortable, wood-panelled lounge features a central open hearth; a haven of tranquillity. Evening meals are served Tuesday–Saturday. ♨Q➥⊛⊠⊕&P✕

WEST STOCKWITH

White Hart
Main Street, DN10 4ET
✪ 11.30-11; 12-10.30 Sun
☎ (01427) 890176
Taylor Landlord Ⓗ

Small country pub with a small garden, overlooking the River Trent, Chesterfield Canal and West Stockwith Marina. One bar serves the through bar and lounge and the dining area. Daleside Brewery beers are stocked to accompany the freshly-cooked food. The area is especially busy during the summer, due to the volume of river traffic; West Stockwith is where the Chesterfield Canal ends and enters the River Trent. ⊛⊕&▲♣P

WORKSOP

Mallard
Station Approach, Carlton Road, S81 7AG
✪ 5 (2 Fri; 12 Sat)-11; 12-4 Sun
☎ (01909) 530757
Beer range varies Ⓗ

Formerly the Worksop station buffet, this pub offers a warm, friendly welcome in one small, cosy, comfortable bar. The building is within the old station, overlooking the railway line. Two guest beers are constantly changing and there is also a fine selection of Belgian beers and country wines. A further room is available downstairs for special occasions. This local CAMRA Pub of the Season, spring 2002 stages regular beer festivals. Q▲⇌♣P

Newcastle Arms
Carlton Road, S80 1PS (near station)
✪ 11-11; 12-10.30 Sun
☎ (01909) 485384
Greene King IPA; guest beers Ⓗ

This small pub dates from 1910, but became a pool and snooker hall during the early 1980s. It reopened in the mid-1980s to offer a warm, friendly environment. The pub is less than a minute's walk from Worksop's main railway station and just over five minutes' walk from the town centre. A long bar dispenses three real ales; a further room houses a pool table. ⊛⊕&⇌Ⓣ

Shireoaks Inn
West Gate, S80 1LT (near market place)
✪ 11.30-4, 6-11; 11.30-11 Sat; 12-4.30, 7-10.30 Sun
☎ (01909) 472118
Barnsley Bitter; guest beers Ⓗ

Warm, friendly pub that was converted from cottages. The public bar has both a pool table and large-screen TV. There is a comfortable lounge bar and a dining area where good value, home-cooked food is served daily. A small outside area has tables for summer drinking. Q⊛⊕⊠▲⇌♣P✕

> Twas as she tript from cask
>   to cask
> In a bung hole quickly fell
> Suffocation was her task
> She had not time to say
>   farewell
>
> Epitaph at King's Stanley,
> Gloucestershire, to Ann Collins,
> a barmaid who died in 1800,
> aged 49

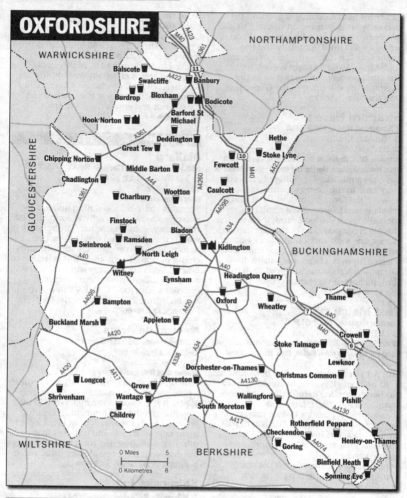

OXFORDSHIRE

APPLETON

Plough
Eaton Road, OX13 5JR
🕐 12-3, 7-11; 12-4, 7-10.30 Sun
☎ (01865) 862441
Greene King XX Mild, IPA, Morland Original Ⓗ
This picturesque, 17th-century, stone
building is still badged as a Morland house
but is now one of the better Greene King
pubs in the area. It consists of three small
connected rooms served from a single bar.
There are no meals except occasional
sandwiches at the bar. The menu is beer
and conversation and the landlord looks
after both. All are welcome at this village
local. ⋈Q✿🐕🛋🍺♣P

BALSCOTE

Butcher's Arms
Shutford Road, OX15 6JQ
(1/2 mile S of main A422 Banbury-Stratford road)
🕐 12-2 (not Mon or Tue), 6.30-11; 12-3.30, 6.30-11
Sat; 12-3.30, 7-10.30 Sun
☎ (01295) 730750 website:
www.hooknorton.tablesir.com/thebutchersarms-balscote
Hook Norton Best Bitter, seasonal beers;
guest beers Ⓖ

Built of local honey-coloured stone and
overlooking the village church, this is a
friendly pub with a homely atmosphere.
The open-plan bar has a real fire at one end
and a pool table at the other. Beers are
served straight from casks visible behind the
bar. Darts, Aunt Sally and dominoes are
played and, on alternate Tuesdays, informal
folk sessions are held. In summer, the
gardens (with resident goat) are a fine place
in which to relax. ⋈✿🐕🍺♣P

BAMPTON

Morris Clown
High Street, OX18 2JW
🕐 5 (12-Sat)-11; 12-10.30 Sun
☎ (01993) 850217
Courage Best Bitter; Vale Notley Ale; guest beers Ⓗ
Former Courage-owned local, with a single,
L-shaped bar, it was saved from closure
many years ago by the present landlord and
his father. There is a huge log fire at one
end of the bar. Aunt Sally and darts are
played in local leagues, although the village
is best known for its morris dancing
connections. The local morris men frequent
this pub, which was awarded Oxford City
CAMRA Pub of the Year 2003. ⋈Q✿🐕♣P

BANBURY

Bell ✓
12 Middleton Road, OX16 4QJ (near station)
☼ 12-3, 7-11; 12-11 Sat; 12-5, 8-10.30 Sun
☎ (01295) 253169
Hancock's HB; Highgate Dark; guest beers Ⓗ

A regular entry in the Guide, this is the archetypal friendly local serving the community. There are two distinct drinking rooms, a bar with a pool table and a lounge for conversation. Run by David and Shirley for 19 years, the pub is a haven for sports teams of all types, including the local Aunt Sally. Sandwiches are available at lunchtime. The pub is very handy for the railway and bus stations, and the canal is close by. ♨❀Ⓓ🚆🚭♣P

BARFORD ST MICHAEL

George Inn
Lower Street, OX15 0RH
(½ mile off B4031, 6 miles S of Banbury)
☼ 12-3 (not Mon-Fri), 7-11;
12-4, 7-10 (not winter eve) Sun
☎ (01869) 338226
Greene King IPA; Hook Norton Best Bitter; guest beers Ⓗ

The George is a thatched pub with mullioned windows and, as stated in Pevsner's Buildings of England, dates from 1672. It was refurbished about 1998 in keeping with the character of this village local. It has regular, well-attended quiz nights, live bands playing anything from pop to folk music and themed food nights with freshly-prepared dishes. Weddings and special functions can be catered for in the marquee in the large gardens. The setting offers scenic views, and a game of Aunt Sally can be played. ♨❀&♣P

BINFIELD HEATH

Bottle & Glass
Harpsden Road, RG9 4JT (N off A4155)
☼ 11-3.30, 6-11; 12-3.30, 7-10.30 Sun
☎ (01491) 575755
website: www.thebottleandglass.co.uk
Brakspear Bitter, Special Ⓗ

Attractive country pub, parts of which date from the 14th century. The thatched roof, genuine beams and flagstones in the main bar add to the ambience. A no-smoking area is available in the smaller bar on the right-hand side. The food is home cooked and good value with a variety of dishes including vegetarian options – no meals served on Sunday evening. The large, attractive garden is ideal for summer drinking and includes several interesting features to explore. Q❀Ⓓ♣P⧗

BLADON

White House
1 Grove Road, OX20 1RQ
☼ 11.30-11; 12-10.30 Sun
☎ (01993) 811582
website: www.whitehousebladon.com
Greene King IPA, Ruddles County, Abbot, Old Speckled Hen; guest beer Ⓗ

A much extended village pub comprising one long, open-plan room with the bar and real fire at one end, and tables throughout. Excellent food is served. A portrait of Sir

Winston Churchill hangs on the wall, appropriate as the pub is very close to Churchill's grave and Blenheim Palace. ♨❀Ⓓ♠♣P

BLOXHAM

Elephant & Castle
Humber Street, OX15 4LZ
(off A361, 4 miles W of Banbury)
☼ 11-3, 5-11; 11-11 Sat; 12-10.30 Sun
☎ (01295) 720383
website: www.elephantandcastle.tablesir.com
Hook Norton Best Bitter, seasonal beers; guest beers Ⓗ

This 16th-century coaching inn once straddled the old Banbury to Chipping Norton turnpike. It has a wide carriage entrance to the garden and car park. The original bread oven stands behind the Aga in the restaurant. The pub has been run by the same landlord for over 30 years. It is warm in winter, with open fires and reasonably-priced, home-cooked meals and snacks at lunchtime, Monday–Saturday. There is a pleasant terrace for sunny days. Aunt Sally is played, and Bulmers Traditional cider is on offer. ♨Q❀Ⓓ🍴&♣🐕P

BODICOTE

Plough Inn
9 High Street, OX15 4BZ
(off A4260, 2 miles S of Banbury)
☼ 11-3, 6-11; 12-3, 7-10.30 Sun
☎ (01295) 262327
website: www.banbury-cross.co.uk/bodicotebrewery
Bodicote Bitter, No. 9, Life Sentence, seasonal beers Ⓗ

Charming, beamed, friendly village pub, parts of which are believed to date from the 13th century. After 45 years running the pub, Jim and Doreen Blencowe retired and now it is run by their son, Jimmy and his wife Denise. Food is cooked to order and five beers (plus seasonal beers) are brewed, as for the past 21 years, by Jimmy. There is a winter beer weekend with guest ales and a popular summer beer festival. ♨QⒹ🍴&♣

BUCKLAND MARSH

Trout at Tadpole Bridge
Tadpole Bridge, SN7 8RF
(off A420, towards Bampton) OS335004
☼ 11.30-3, 6-11; 12-3, (7-10.30 May-Sept) Sun
☎ (01367) 870382 website: www.trout-inn.co.uk
Archers Village; Young's Bitter; guest beer Ⓗ

This Grade II listed building was built in the 17th century from local stone. It has been a pub for over 100 years. The garden runs down to the River Thames and the pub is ideally situated for walks on the Thames path. Children are welcome throughout the pub, which offers excellent cuisine and wines. Six-room accommodation is built on to the pub and includes en-suite amenities and one room with disabled facilities; this

INDEPENDENT BREWERIES

Bodicote Bodicote
Hook Norton Hook Norton
Oxford Kidlington
Wychwood Witney

extension matches the pub building closely. River moorings are available.

🏛🕭🖛🕽🕭🗟🟤🐾P✂

BURDROP, SIBFORD GOWER

Bishop Blaize Inn

OX15 5RQ (½ mile W of B4035, between Sibford Gower and Sibford Ferris) OS359379

🕒 12-2.30, 6-11; 12-3, 7-10.30 Sun

☎ (01295) 780323 website: www.bishopblaize.co.uk

Vale Best Bitter; guest beers Ⓗ

Friendly, family-run village pub with a large, landscaped garden and superb views towards the Sib Valley. Sympathetically extended and refurbished, this 17th-century inn retains many original features. The main bar area boasts an oak-beamed ceiling and a huge inglenook housing a wood-burning stove. An extensive home-cooked menu is available in the dining area which has french doors out to the patio and garden. A separate games room offers a dartboard and quiz machine. 🏛Q🕭🕽🕭🟤P

CAULCOTT

Horse & Groom

Lower Heyford Road, OX25 4ND (on B4030 midway between Middleton Stoney and Lower Hexford)

🕒 11-3, 6-11; 12-3, 7-10.30 Sun

☎ (01869) 343257

Hook Norton Best Bitter; guest beers Ⓗ

Rural, small but pleasant thatched inn with a pleasant roadside garden; this pub is a real ale rural gem. Step inside and you will find excellent food on offer. Three constantly changing ales ensure a wonderful variation of tastes. Lunchtime and evening meals complement the beers, especially after a tour of the nearby Cherwell Valley where there is plenty of good walking, through meadows and alongside river and canal. It was local CAMRA Pub of the Year winner, and deservedly so, in 2000 and 2001. 🏛Q🕭🕽🗟🟤

CHADLINGTON

Tite Inn

Mill End, OX7 3NY (off A361, 2 miles S of Chipping Norton)

🕒 12-2.30, 6.30-11; closed Mon; 12-3, 7-10.30 Sun

☎ (01608) 676475 website: www.titeinn.com

Beer range varies Ⓗ

Family-run Cotswold stone free house, that has had the same owners for 16 years. The attractive garden offers fine views; colourful shrubs line the path from the car park. Two comfortably furnished connecting bars and a restaurant are supplemented by the garden room in the summer. Excellent, freshly-prepared food is offered. It is a focus for village activities, including an annual pantomime, cricket team, Easter egg rolling and an investors' club. 🏛Q🕭🕽🗟🟤🐾P

CHARLBURY

Rose & Crown

Market Street, OX7 3PL

🕒 12 (11 Sat)-11; 12-10.30 Sun

☎ (01608) 810103 website: www.topbeerpub.co.uk

Young's Bitter; guest beers Ⓗ

Popular, traditional town-centre free house, 18 years in this Guide. It has a simply furnished split-level bar and games room.

The patio courtyard features a small pond. On the Oxfordshire Way long distance path, it does not serve meals but walkers are welcome to eat their own food; a pub for the discerning drinker who enjoys a good pint without cooking smells. With five guests, it offers one of the best selections of real ale in the area, and focuses on micro-breweries. CAMRA North Oxfordshire Pub of the Year 2002 and 2003. 🕭🟤🕭🐾

CHECKENDON

Black Horse

Burncote Lane, RG8 0TE

(E off A4074) OS667841

🕒 12-2 (2.30 Sat), 7-11; 12-3.30, 7-10.30 Sun

☎ (01491) 680418

Beer range varies Ⓖ

Hidden up a narrow lane outside the village, this ex-coaching inn has three distinct drinking areas and a small bar where the beer is served on gravity. Run by the same family for a century, this delightful pub has real charm and a homely feel about it. Snacks are available most lunchtimes. The beer range varies, but usually includes ales from West Berkshire Brewery. Hard to find, but worth the effort. 🏛Q🕭🟤P

CHILDREY

Hatchet (Free House)

High Street, OX12 9UF

(off the B4507, Wantage-Ashbury road)

🕒 12-2.30 (3.30 Sat), 7-11; 12-3.30, 7-10.30 Sun

☎ (01235) 751213

Greene King Morland Original; guest beers Ⓗ

Friendly local in a picturesque downland village setting. White-painted externally, it has changed little in over 100 years, its interior featuring beams adorned with horse brasses, beer taps and brass hatchets. It stocks a good range of ever-changing guest beers of varying strengths. A single bar, it has areas for dining and a quiet pint; at one end there is a pool table and a TV at the other. In addition to pool, a number of games are played – Aunt Sally, darts, dominoes and crib. Nestling at the foot of the Ridgeway gives easy access to walkers and the landlord is sympathetic to passing campers. A bus stops close by, providing access to the market town of Wantage. 🕭🕽🐾🟤P

CHIPPING NORTON

Chequers ✅

Goddards Lane, OX7 5NP (next to theatre)

🕒 11-11, 12-10.30 Sun

☎ (01608) 644717 website: www.chequers-pub.co.uk

Fuller's Chiswick, London Pride, ESB, seasonal beers Ⓗ

Cheery, comfortable, 17th-century, town-centre pub with four seating areas and a covered courtyard restaurant, it is designed for conversation and warmth. Josh, the landlord for 12 years, has a well-deserved Cask Marque accreditation. It is particularly handy for the small but popular theatre next door. It has received two awards for Fuller's Pub of the Year and it was local CAMRA Pub of the Year in 1999. The food is very popular; it is not served on Sunday evening. 🏛Q🕽

Stones
1A Middle Row, OX7 5NH
☼ 10-11; 11-10.30 Sun
☎ (01608) 644466
Greene King IPA; guest beers Ⓗ
Popular, town-centre, modern bar with a
decor emphasising brass and pine, it was
completely opened out during a recent
refurbishment. There are ever-changing
guest beers, many from local micro-
breweries, and several Belgian bottled beers
to try. It boasts a busy, separate restaurant
area which specialises in cooking fresh food
to order – no meals on Sunday evening in
winter. A heated patio hosts occasional beer
festivals. The pub is named after Edward
Stone, a local vicar, who discovered the
healing effects of willow bark. ⏣◑▶

CHRISTMAS COMMON

Fox & Hounds
OX49 5HL (off B480/B481 and B4009) OS715932
☼ 11.30-3 (3.30 Sat), 6-11; 12-10.30 Sun
☎ (01491) 612599
Brakspear Bitter, Special, seasonal beers Ⓗ/Ⓖ
The Fox & Hounds retains much charm and
character despite a major make-over, which
added a barn-like restaurant and an
upgrading of other facilities. The original
pub area is comfortable with an authentic
feel. The service is efficient and friendly,
still finding plenty of space for drinkers,
despite an emphasis on food. Organic food
is a speciality and booking is essential at
busy times – no meals are served on Sunday
evening. ♨Q⏣◑▶ ⊟⅄▲♣P

CROWELL

Shepherd's Crook
The Green, OX39 4RR (off B4009 between
Chinnor and M40 jct 6) OS744997
☼ 11.30-3, 5-11; 11-11 Sat; 12-10.30 Sun
☎ (01844) 351431
**Batham Best Bitter; Hook Norton Best Bitter; Taylor
Landlord; guest beers** Ⓗ
In the foothills of the Chilterns, this
comfortable inn was known as the
Catherine Wheel until 1991. The current
landlord, who took over in 1996, is a real
ale fanatic and this is one of the few pubs to
sell Batham's Bitter locally. A former fish
merchant, the landlord obtains supplies
directly from the West Country and
shellfish from the Norfolk coast, while
excellent steak and kidney pies and steaks
come from a local butcher.
♨Q⏣◑▶♣P

DEDDINGTON

Crown & Tuns
New Street, OX15 0SP (on A4260)
☼ 12-3 (may vary afternoons), 6-11;
12-3, 7-10.30 Sun
☎ (01869) 337371
**Hook Norton Mild, Best Bitter, seasonal beers; guest
beers** (occasional) Ⓗ
This 16th-century, traditional, two-bar
pub was originally a coaching inn on the
main Oxford to Banbury road and has two
bay windows which overlook this road. It
is one of only 17 pubs to have appeared in
every edition of this Guide. It has a
homely atmosphere with a real fire and

caters for all ages. Aunt Sally is played in
the garden during the summer months.
B&B is available. ♨⏣⊨♣

Deddington Arms Hotel
Horsefair, OX15 0SH
(off A4260 towards market square)
☼ 10-11; 10-10.30 Sun
☎ (01869) 338364
website: www.deddington-arms-hotel.co.uk
Greene King IPA; Tetley Bitter; guest beers Ⓗ
Formerly the King's Arms, this 16th- to
17th-century gabled and stuccoed building
has been completely refurbished in keeping
with its age. It has sunny window seats
overlooking the market square and old
wooden flooring and a real fire in the bar.
Two of the bedrooms have four-poster beds.
There are also two function rooms. Tables
on the pavement to the front of the pub
serve as an area for summer drinking.
♨Q⏣⊨◑▶⊟⅄P

DORCHESTER-ON-THAMES

Chequers
20 Bridge End, OX10 7JP (sharp turn at bridge)
☼ 12-2 (not Mon or Wed; 2.30 Fri; 3 Sat), 7-11; 12-3,
7-10.30 Sun
☎ (01865) 340015
**Courage Best Bitter; Hook Norton Best Bitter;
Wadworth IPA** Ⓖ
Friendly and relaxed, privately-owned free
house, hidden away near Dorchester bridge.
A large fireplace, which had been boarded
up in the 1960s, was rediscovered and adds
an interesting touch, together with the
flagstoned and tiled floors. Bar billiards is
popular, and Aunt Sally and darts are also
played. It provides a good base for exploring
the surrounding countryside or the old
Roman town. The beer range is selected by
the locals. ♨Q⏚⏣♣P⅄

EYNSHAM

Queen's Head
17 Queen Street, OX29 4HH
☼ 12-2.30, 6-11; 12-11 Fri & Sat; 12-3, 7-10.30 Sun
☎ (01865) 881229
Greene King IPA; guest beers Ⓗ
This 18th-century village inn offers two
bars; one room is peaceful, while the other
has a more vibrant atmosphere with a pool
table and televised sport. Railway pictures
and memorabilia decorate both bars. The
guest beer is selected from the Greene King
list – it is worth asking what is available.
The pub has a large, pleasant garden.
♨⏣⊨◑▶⅄♣

FEWCOTT

White Lion
Fritwell Road, OX27 7NZ (off B430)
☼ 7 (12 Sat)-11; 12-5, 7-10.30 Sun
☎ (01869) 346639
Beer range varies Ⓗ
Lively, 18th-century, stone village pub with
a spacious, but cosy, open bar. It offers a
constantly-changing range of four guest
ales, with support for a porter or mild.
These typically are from outside the region
and include rarely seen micros, so there is
usually something new and interesting to
try. The pub has a keen emphasis on games,
darts and pool in a separate room, and Aunt

Sally is played in the large, quiet garden. The pub is also the base for the local football team. 🏃❀◑&♣P

FINSTOCK

Plough Inn
The Bottom, OX7 3BY (off B4022, N of Witney)
✪ 12-2.30 (3 Sat), 6-11; 12-3.30, 7-10.30 Sun
☎ (01993) 868333
Beer range varies Ⓗ
Thatched pub in an attractive setting: two comfortable beamed bars, plus a snug. Interesting features include an inglenook, old clocks, a lending library, old photographs of village life and a piano. Two acres of well-kept gardens attract customers in summer. Walkers, children and dogs are welcome at this sociable pub that enjoys a reputation for fine real ale, wine and food, much of which is free range and organically produced. Cider is available in summer and autumn. 🏃Q❀◒◑⊟♣❀P

GORING

Catherine Wheel
Station Road, RG8 9HB
✪ 11.30 (12 Sat)-3, 6-11; 12-3, 7-10.30 Sun
☎ (01491) 872379
Bateman Mild; Brakspear Bitter, Special, seasonal beers Ⓗ
Delightful, smart village pub with a long L-shaped bar. Children are welcome in the restaurant area, which is decorated with rowing artefacts and used to be a blacksmith's shop. The 'pit' at the other end of the pub has a large inglenook fire for cosy winter drinking. Good value home-cooked food is available, except on Sunday evening. An ideal refreshment spot when exploring the village or travelling the nearby Ridgeway or Thames footpath.
🏃Q❀◒◑⊜♣

GREAT TEW

Falkland Arms ⊘
OX7 4DB (off A361 and B4022)
✪ 11.30-2.30 (3 Sat), 6-11 (11.30-11 summer Sat); 12-3, 7-10.30 (12-10.30 summer) Sun
☎ (01608) 683653 website: www.falklandarms.org.uk
Wadworth IPA, 6X; guest beers Ⓗ
In an idyllic thatched village, this award-winning pub is a haven for drinkers who enjoy an unspoilt, relaxed atmosphere without the intrusion of modern life. Mobile phones are banned. Simple wooden furniture, oak settles, flagstoned and bare-boarded floors, an inglenook and gentle lighting create a wonderful ambience, complemented by four guest beers, a range of malt whiskies, country wines, real cider, snuffs and clay pipes. This rural gem offers high quality food (not served Sun eve) and accommodation (advisable to book).
🏃Q❀◒◑♣❀

GROVE

Volunteer
Station Road, OX12 0DM
(on A338, 2 miles N of Wantage)
✪ 11-11; 12-10.30 Sun
☎ (01235) 769557
Hook Norton Best Bitter, Old Hooky; guest beer Ⓗ
Large, open-plan pub situated on the A338,

just past the Williams Formula One factory outside Wantage. It is the only Hook Norton pub in the Vale region and serves the changing seasonal Hook Norton beer as a third real ale. Cider is sold in summer. Food is served at lunchtime. There is a large garden and car park and it is also on the bus route from Wantage to the Hanneys.
❀◑♣❀P⊟

HEADINGTON QUARRY

Mason's Arms
3A Quarry School Place, OX3 3LH
✪ 5 (7 Mon; 12 Sat)-11; 12-4, 7-10.30 Sun
☎ (01865) 764579
Black Sheep Best Bitter; Shepherd Neame Spitfire; guest beer Ⓗ
This family-run free house, licensed since 1871, is hidden away in Headington Quarry, but well worth tracking down. The single bar is spacious and there is a heated outdoor decking area and garden, where Aunt Sally is played. The pub is home to the Headington Quarry morris men and the annual Headington Beer Festival. There are popular Saturday quiz nights and monthly comedy nights. Guest ales change weekly. The function room doubles as a family room. ⊱❀&♣P

HENLEY-ON-THAMES

Bird in Hand
61 Greys Road, RG9 1SB
✪ 11.30-2.30, 5-11; 11.30-11 Sat; 12-10.30 Sun
☎ (01491) 575775
Beer range varies Ⓗ
Superb free house, only a few minutes' walk from the town centre, popular with locals and other enthusiasts of quality beer. Good, friendly service is assured from a landlord who knows his ales. The attractive garden has enough to keep the children entertained. The pub fields darts teams and has a regular quiz night. Good value weekday lunches are served. The beer range varies but usually includes a mild and beers from micros. It is a pleasant contrast to the Wetherspoon's which now dominates the centre of Henley. Q⊱❀◑▲♣❀

HETHE

Whitmore Arms
Main Street, OX27 8ES (off A421)
✪ 12-2.30 (not Mon-Fri), 7 (6 Fri)-11; 12-2.30, 7-10.30 Sun
☎ (01869) 277654
Brakspear Bitter; Hook Norton Best Bitter, Ⓗ **seasonal beer;** Ⓖ **guest beer** (occasional) Ⓗ
This 18th-century, stone-built pub is set in a typical north Oxfordshire village. It was originally called the Maltsters Arms and apparently gained its present name in 1810 when the landlord left it to his friend, Thomas Whitmore. A large inglenook with welcoming open fire and flagstone floor occupy one end of the open bar area with a collection of old implements adorning the walls. Good value meals are on offer Tuesday–Saturday evening, 7–9.30, in a quiet atmosphere. At weekends lunches are available. The peaceful garden has a barbecue area. This locality offers plenty of easy walks in scenic surroundings.
🏃Q❀◑▲♣P

HOOK NORTON

Pear Tree Inn
Scotland End, OX15 5NU (near brewery)
⊙ 11.30-2.30, 6-11; 11.30-11 Sat; 12-4,
7-10.30 Sun
☎ (01608) 737482
website: www.peartree.freeserve.co.uk
**Hook Norton Mild, Best Bitter, Generation, Old Hooky,
seasonal beers** Ⓗ
Small, 18th-century brick pub close to Hook
Norton Brewery and its visitor centre. The
oak beams in the single bar are often
festooned with dried hops. There is a cosy
log fire and walking sticks are for sale.
Tables are set out to the front of the pub
and the large rear garden has a children's
area. There is reasonably-priced home-
cooked bar food – not served on Sunday
evening. Three guest rooms are available for
bed and breakfast. Indoor and outdoor
chess, board games, dominoes and cards are
played. This is a traditional country inn in
an ideal location. ♨Q✿⋈◑▯♣P✲

KIDLINGTON

King's Arms
4 The Moors, OX5 2AJ
⊙ 11-2.30, 6-11; 11-11 Sat; 12-10.30 Sun
☎ (01865) 373004
Draught Bass; Greene King IPA; guest beer Ⓗ
Popular village local that was built in 1890.
Two small bars and a covered patio provide
a varied drinking atmosphere where locals
and visitors enjoy cheap lunchtime meals. A
recent hard battle by the landlord with
Punch has resulted in a future guest beer
policy. The pub usually wins the local best
flower arrangement competition.
☙✿◑▯♣P

LEWKNOR

Olde Leatherne Bottel
1 High Street, OX49 5TW (near M40 jct 6)
⊙ 11-2.30, 6-11; 12-3, 7-10.30 Sun
☎ (01844) 351482
Brakspear Bitter, Special Ⓗ
Deservedly popular, 17th-century country
inn; two good-sized bars with authentic
beams and fireplaces add to the
atmosphere. It is popular at lunchtime and
evening with diners but still has plenty of
room for drinkers. The food is varied and
good value. It is very close to the M40, but
you would hardly notice. There is a no-
smoking family room and the pleasant
garden has a children's play area.
♨☙✿◑P✲

LONGCOT

King & Queen
Shrivenham Road, SN7 7TL
⊙ 12-3, 6-11; 7-10.30 Sun
☎ (01793) 783611
Adnams Bitter; Taylor Landlord; guest beer Ⓗ
Located just off the A420 between
Watchfield and Faringdon, this
quintessential, welcoming village pub has
an open-plan bar and a restaurant to one
side. The bar serves a single guest beer, often
Marston's Pedigree. Traditional pub games
are played, including darts and Aunt Sally.
Six guest rooms are available for those
wishing to stay overnight. ♨☙✿⋈◑♣P✲

MIDDLE BARTON

Carpenter's Arms
122 North Street, OX7 7DA
⊙ 12-3, 6-11; 12-11 Fri & summer Sat; 12-10.30 Sun
☎ (01869) 340378
**Greene King IPA, Abbot; Marston's Pedigree;
Theakston Best Bitter; guest beer** Ⓗ
This popular village local has a lively public
bar with an inglenook displaying
woodworker's tools (including an array of
wooden planes). A separate entrance leads
to a quieter, beamed bar and dining room
featuring extensive collections of glass and
earthenware bottles, brass objects and
decorated chamber pots. Home to
dominoes and Aunt Sally teams, a number
of trophies are on show in the public bar.
Guest beers are chosen from the Pubmaster
approved list. A wide choice of food is
served. The patio and garden include a
children's play section and a pets' corner.
Q✿◑▯♣P

NORTH LEIGH

Woodman ✔
New Yatt Road, OX29 6TT
(off A4095, Woodstock-Witney road)
⊙ 12-2.30, 6-11; 12-10.30 Sun
☎ (01993) 881790
Greene King IPA; Wadworth 6X; guest beers Ⓗ
Well-used, comfortable, community pub
that is home to local societies and clubs. A
well-kept garden with Aunt Sally is a bonus
in the summer. Long-established beer
festivals (now in their thirteenth year) are
held at Easter and August bank holidays. A
spacious bar, with simple wooden furniture,
offers plenty of space for drinkers and
diners; fresh flowers on the tables add a nice
touch. There is an impressive 30ft deep
illuminated well in the bar. ♨☙✿⋈◑♣P

OXFORD

Butcher's Arms ✔
5 Wilberforce Street, Headington, OX3 7AN
(first left, then first right after the 'Shark')
⊙ 12-2.30, 5-11; 12-11 Fri & Sat; 12-10.30 Sun
☎ (01865) 761252
**Fuller's Chiswick, London Pride, ESB, seasonal
beers** Ⓗ
You will find a warm welcome and
attractive well-lit interior in this cheery,
Victorian local, which has good wheelchair
access. The extended single bar has plenty
of wooden seating and tables for drinkers
and those wishing to take advantage of the
food on offer, now available every
lunchtime. There is also a heated patio area
that can be booked for barbecues. Major
sporting events are shown on TV and there
are popular weekly quiz nights and meat
raffles. ♨☙✿&♣

Far from the Madding Crowd
10-12 Friar's Entry, OX1 2BY
(between Gloucester Green and Magdalen St)
⊙ 11-11; 12-10.30 Sun
☎ (01865) 240900
**Black Sheep Best Bitter; Taylor Landlord; guest
beers** Ⓗ
New city-centre pub striving to become a
haven for real ale drinkers. No alcopops or
drinks served in bottles are sold. It enjoys an
extremely central location but is still off the

beaten track. Four regular annual beer festivals are held and contemporary art exhibitions are displayed and change regularly. It is rapidly becoming Oxford's theatre pub with play previews, poetry readings and book launches. Live acoustic music is performed on Sunday evening. A wide range of constantly-changing guest beers is available. Access ramps and wheelchair WC are provided. ◑ ⅃ ♣ ⌿

Harcourt Arms
1-2 Cranham Terrace, OX2 6DG
(near Phoenix cinema)
☼ 12-2.30, 5.30-11; 12-2.30, 7-10.30 Sun
☎ (01865) 310630
Fuller's Chiswick, London Pride, ESB Ⓗ
Convivial and characterful, wood-panelled local with two real fires. The pub has a 1950s feel, board games are available and jazz background music plays. Bar snacks include sandwiches, soup and jacket potatoes. Prawn and cheese toasties are a must. The congenial landlord takes pride in his bar. There is an unusual collection of banknotes behind the bar. Beer jugs are available, and wine is served in small pail, pail and bucket. Watch out for ESB! Located in the Jericho area, near Walton Street, this is a good pub for conversation.
♨ ❀ ◑ ♿ ⇌ ♣

Hobgoblin
108 St Aldates, OX1 1BU (opp. town hall)
☼ 11-11; 12-10.30 Sun
☎ (01865) 250201
Wychwood Shires; guest beers Ⓗ
Formerly the Bulldog, the Hobgoblin has been a real ale haven since it was refurbished in 1998. Six beers are usually available – one or two from Wychwood and the remainder are guests from all over the UK. In excess of 1,500 different beers have been served since 1998, testified by the wealth of pump clips on the ceiling. Local CAMRA Pub of the Year in 2000, it serves lunch daily, 12–3. ◑ ⇌

Jude the Obscure
54 Walton Street, OX2 6AE
☼ 12-11; 12-10.30 Sun
☎ (01865) 557309
Greene King IPA, Abbot; guest beers Ⓗ
Sociable, open-plan ex-Morrells house featuring three changing guest ales. Note the huge brewery mirror to the right of the bar. The pub is rarely quiet: the raised seating area to the rear is used for live performances, and there is a regular, well-attended quiz night. The garden is a great place to relax on a sunny day. It is handy for the Phoenix cinema and Jericho's varied and vibrant restaurant scene. ❀ ◑

Lamb & Flag
12 St Giles, OX1 1JU
☼ 11-11; 12-10.30 Sun
☎ (01865) 515787
Fuller's London Pride; Palmer IPA, seasonal beer; Skinner's Betty Stogs Bitter; Theakston Old Peculier; guest beer Ⓗ
Rambling, 15th-century coaching inn, now part of St John's College, accessed from a passageway off St Giles; the local CAMRA branch won its first victory preventing the college from closing this interesting building. Rare Palmer's and Skinner's beers

are now a regular choice. This multi-roomed hostelry boasts connections with Tolkien and CS Lewis, with Inspector Morse a more recent visitor. Q ⅃ ⇌

Next Door
38 Holywell Street, OX1 3SW
☼ 11-11; 12-10.30 Sun
☎ (01865) 793316 website: www.nextdoor.tablesir.com
Young's Bitter, Special, seasonal beer Ⓗ
This pub was opened in 2002, having been converted from Blackwell's music shop. The glass floor outside provides a view of the cellar. Some original features are retained, not least the glass atrium containing a pomegranate tree which is the centrepiece of the bar. There are three separate levels: comfortable sofas and dining tables on the ground level lead down to the bar and lower seating area, all wheelchair-friendly. The food features local produce and includes many share options. Low-key jazz and subtle lighting create a relaxing atmosphere. ◑ ⅃ ⌿

Rose & Crown
14 North Parade Avenue, OX2 6LX
☼ 11-3, 5 (6 Sat)-11; 12-4, 7-10.30 Sun
☎ (01865) 510551
Adnams Bitter; Marston's Pedigree Ⓗ
Superb, mid-Victorian north Oxford local where two small rooms and a corridor are served by a single bar and a hatch. The large, covered garden is heated in winter. This is a pub for conversation, free from intrusive machines and music, and has been run for 20 years by the current licensees. Chess is played weekly, and souvenirs adorn the back room, provided by regulars who pursue more active pastimes – ice hockey and formula one motor racing. Q ❀ ◑

Turf Tavern
4 Bath Place, OX1 3SU
☼ 11-11; 12-10.30 Sun
☎ (01865) 243235
website: www.turftavern.oxford@laurelpubco.com
Archers Golden; guest beers Ⓗ
Classic, 18th-century tavern, popular with all those who find it. Tucked between two alleyways – Bath Place off Holywell Street and St Helen's Passage in New College Lane – it lies just past the Bridge of Sighs. Inside, two low-ceilinged bars offer an ever-changing range of up to 10 guests. Food is available from 12–7.30 daily in all bars and in the smoke-free zone at the rear of pub. Outside, three distinct flagstoned patios provide respite from the crowded bar, and are heated and covered in winter. Westons Old Rosie cider is sold. Q ❀ ◑ ♣ ⌿

Wharf House
14 Butterwyke Place, OX1 1TT
(corner of Speedwell St and Thames St)
☼ 11-3, 6-11; 11-11 Sat; 12-4, 7-10.30 Sun
☎ (01865) 246752
Hook Norton Best Bitter; RCH Pitchfork; Ⓗ
guest beers Ⓗ/Ⓖ
Built as offices for the adjacent wharf, it became a pub in 1851 and is one of only two original buildings in the ancient St Ebbes parish. Real ales and cider are served from all over, plus authentic foreign kegs and a range of Belgian beers. The plain and simple character of the pub, without fruit machines and bright lights, attracts a wide

range of customers. A warm welcome awaits the stranger; be sure to make friends with the dog. Vinyl records are played. Q❀≈♠P

White Horse
52 Broad Street, OX1 3BB
✪ 11-11; 12-10.30 Sun
☎ (01865) 728318
Fuller's London Pride; Taylor Landlord; Tetley Burton Ale Ⓗ
This small, 16th-century, classic, city-centre pub is sandwiched between the entrances of Blackwell's main bookshop. The single, long, narrow and usually crowded bar has brown wood-panelling and the walls are adorned with photographs of Oxford sporting clubs. There is a tiny snug at the rear for those who require more seclusion. One of Inspector Morse's favourite watering-holes, six beers are on dispense (three guests). Lunches are served between 12 and 4. Q◐⊖

Crown
RG9 6HH (on B480)
✪ 11.30-2.30, 6-11; 12-3, 7-10.30 Sun
☎ (01491) 638364 website: www.crownpishill.co.uk
Hook Norton Best Bitter; guest beer Ⓗ
Delightful, 15th-century coaching inn, complete with leaded-light windows and adorned with wisteria. The small front bar with flagstones and old pictures leads to a comfortable lounge. Children are welcome in the large, splendid restaurant – no food is served on Sunday evening. Although highly regarded for its meals, this is still very much a pub to stop off and enjoy a drink when exploring the glorious countryside nearby. High quality accommodation is provided in a one-bedroomed cottage, and the grounds also house a 400-year-old thatched barn which has been converted into a function room. The inn is about a mile from Stonor House and its magnificent parkland. ♨Q❀⇄◐⊑P

Royal Oak
High Street, OX7 3AU
✪ 11-3, 6.30-11; 12-3, 7-10.30 Sun
☎ (01993) 868213
Adnams Broadside; Hook Norton Best Bitter; guest beer Ⓗ
This popular, 17th-century free house has an excellent reputation for imaginative food and a choice of real ales. Comfortably furnished in traditional style, the main bar has an attractive inglenook and at the rear is a small snug bar. A spacious restaurant opens on to a courtyard for summer drinking. No music, TV, fruit machines or games, this is a pub for conversation. Children, dogs and walkers are welcome. Comfortable, en-suite accommodation is available in the former coach house and stable block. ♨Q❀⇄◐♿P♒

Red Lion
Peppard Common, RG9 5LB
✪ 12-11; 12-10.30 Sun
☎ (01491) 628329
Brakspear Bitter, Special Ⓗ

Set back from the road, overlooking the common, this village local can trace its origins to the 17th century. Comfortable and smart, with two small bars and a separate dining area, it offers good, reasonably-priced food. It is liberally decorated with sporting and military memorabilia. The pleasant garden is a venue for barbecues in summer and is child-friendly. ♨❀◐♣P

Prince of Wales
14 High Street, SN6 8AF
✪ 12-3, 6-11; 12-3 (closed eve) Sun
☎ (01793) 782268
website: www.shrivenham.org/powerpage.htm
Wadworth IPA, 6X, JCB, seasonal beers; guest beers Ⓖ
Grade II listed, 17th-century pub with original beams. Handpumps are not used and all beers are dispensed by gravity. All guest ales are from independent and family breweries. The pub provides board games, daily newspapers and four-pint carry containers, and hosts a Tuesday quiz night. Look out for the 'on this day' history board, researched by the landlord. A good range of home-cooked meals includes vegetarian options. Children are welcome in the separate dining area; there is a no-smoking area during mealtimes. Barbecues are hosted on bank holiday Mondays. ♨❀◐♣P

Flowing Spring
Henley Road, RG4 9RB
✪ 11.30-11; 12-10.30 Sun
☎ (0118) 969 3207
website: www.theflowingspring.com
Fuller's Chiswick, London Pride, ESB, seasonal beers Ⓗ
This pub makes an interesting stop on the Reading to Henley road. The island bar is on the upper level reached by steps from the car park via a large verandah providing a good viewing point over the surrounding countryside. The pub boasts a large garden suitable for children but is open to the car park. Evening meals are served Wednesday–Saturday with extra evenings in summer. The car park can occasionally flood during wet winter periods as may be witnessed by the pictures on display in the bar. ♨☎❀◐▲♣P♒

Crown
High Street, OX11 9AG (off A4130)
✪ 11-3, 5.30-11; 12-3, 7-10.30 Sun
☎ (01235) 812262
Wadworth IPA, 6X; guest beers Ⓗ
Genuine community local, with friendly service, which attracts a varied mix of clientele. The large bar area, furnished in rustic style, caters for drinkers and diners alike, while the smaller public bar style area has a popular bar billiards table. The food is good value with booking advisable at busy times. An ever-changing range of up to two guest beers is usually from regional or micro-breweries. ☎❀◐♣P

STEVENTON

Cherry Tree ●
33 High Street, OX13 6RZ
(off A4130 at bottom of Steventon Hill)
☼ 11-2.30, 5-11; 12-11 Fri & Sat; 12-10.30 Sun
☎ (01235) 831222
Red Shoot Tom's Tipple; Wadworth IPA, 6X; guest beers ⒣
Popular village pub managed by a very welcoming publican and his staff. It has exposed beams throughout its two main bar areas and there is a no-smoking dining area to the rear. Two guest beers are always available as well as the three regulars. Mini beer festivals are held approximately twice a year with a selection of ales from all parts. Folk music is staged every third Sunday of the month. A variety of good home-made food is served throughout the week.
♨Q❀⒟P⅟

STOKE LYNE

Peyton Arms ☆
Main Street, OX27 8SD
(½ mile off B4100, near M40 jct 10)
☼ 12-2.30 (not Mon or Tue), 6.30 (6 Fri)-11; 12-11 Sat; 12-5.30, 6.30-10.30 Sun
☎ (01869) 345285
Hook Norton Mild, Best Bitter, Old Hooky, Haymaker, seasonal beers ⒢
Step into this small, quiet village hideaway and you are into an era of simple, basic, rural pubs. The Peyton Arms offers a refuge from the distractions of fast, modern life. The beers are dispensed from wooden casks reserved especially for the pub by Hook Norton Brewery. Recent improvements have made the pub cosier and now food is available in the evening. Listed on CAMRA's National Inventory, this is a 'must visit' real ale pub. Nearby, Stoke Wood can be seen, for its spring display of bluebells.
♨Q❀⒟⒢⅟

STOKE TALMAGE

Red Lion ☆
OX9 7ES (1¼ miles S of A40 at Tetsworth)
OS681994
☼ 12-2 (not Mon-Thu; 2.30 Sat), 6-11 (not Mon); 12-3.30, 7-10.30 Sun
☎ (01844) 281651
Beer range varies ⒣
Do not be put off by the restricted opening times of this pub. Step back in time to a friendly, relaxed atmosphere and enjoy this basic, unspoilt treasure. Saved from closure in the 1960s by the landlord and run by his family for over 60 years, mementos in the bar provide a reminder of its previous ownership by Morland Brewery. Beers from local micros are strongly represented. Bar billiards and hook the fish are played. The pleasant garden has a children's play area and Aunt Sally pitch. ♨Q▷❀⒢♣ Å♣♠P

SWALCLIFFE

Stag's Head
The Green, OX15 5EJ
(6 miles W of Banbury on B4035)
☼ 11.30-2.30 (3 Sat), 6.30-11; closed Mon; 12-3, 7-10.30 Sun
☎ (01295) 780232
website: www.stagsheadswalcliffe@dial.pipex.com

Black Sheep Best Bitter; Brakspear Bitter; guest beer ⒣
Traditional, thatched inn dating from the 15th century in the heart of an historic and picturesque village on the edge of the Cotswolds. The cosy main bar has scrubbed pine tables, wooden pews, a heavily beamed ceiling and a large inglenook. A no-smoking dining area off the main bar is decorated with old photographs of local scenes and serves an excellent menu and extensive wine choice. A patio and terraced garden with ample shade affords delightful views over a small stream. ♨Q❀⇔⒟♣P⅟

SWINBROOK

Swan Inn
OX18 4DY (off A40)
☼ 11.30-3, 6.30-11; 12-3, 7-10.30 Sun
☎ (01993) 822165
Archers Village; Greene King IPA, Old Speckled Hen; Wadworth 6X ⒣
Wisteria-clad, unspoilt, 16th-century country inn by the River Windrush. The comfortable tap room has a flagstone floor, old settles, corner cupboard and log-burning stove in an inglenook. The main bar features hops, a charming mirror and an impressive beam supported by ancient oak pillars in front of the bar. An open fire warms the cosy dining room with its settle and unusual alcove seats. The pub has a superb reputation for food and real ale. There is ample space for outdoor drinking with a large garden plus seating to the front. A pub for conversation and relaxation.
♨Q❀⒟♣♠P

THAME

Swan Hotel
9 Upper High Street, OX9 3ER
☼ 11-11; 12-10.30 Sun
☎ (01844) 261211
Brakspear Bitter; Hook Norton Best Bitter; guest beers ⒣
Nothing much changes (thankfully) at this market town hotel of 16th-century origin. The beer, including two changing guests, is excellent, as is the food – in the bar or in the upstairs restaurant (note the Tudor painted ceiling). The bar areas have been repainted; the interesting furniture and fittings remain. An ideal place for a quiet drink or meeting friends, in winter there is a real fire, in warmer months, outside seating is set in the small shopping alley. Accommodation includes some four-poster beds. ♨❀⇔⒟

WALLINGFORD

Cross Keys
48 High Street, OX10 0DB
☼ 12-3, 5-11; 12-11 Fri & Sat; 12-10.30 Sun
☎ (01491) 826377
Brakspear Bitter, Special, seasonal beers ⒣
Unspoilt, street-corner local, over 300 years old, pleasantly situated opposite the recreation ground. The small public bar leads to the games room, while the lounge gives access to the dining area, which doubles as the family room. Pub games include crib, darts and dominoes, and there is an Aunt Sally pitch next to the car park. The good-sized outside drinking area is

suitable for children. The town's museum is nearby and what remains of the Wallingford Brewery is across the street. Occasional live music is performed. ✿◖▲P

WANTAGE

Royal Oak Inn
Newbury Street, OX12 8DF
🕐 5.30-11; 12-2.30, 7-11 Sat; 7-10.30 Sun
☎ (01235) 763129
Wadworth 6X, JCB; West Berkshire Maggs Magnificent Mild, Dr Hexter's Wedding Ale, Dr Hexter's Healer; Ⓗ/Ⓖ **guest beers** Ⓗ

Three handpumps serve regular beers but these and all guest beers can be served by gravity on request. Wadworth 6X and JCB are served from wooden casks. There are usually between six and 10 beers available. Two of West Berkshire Brewery's beers are named after the longstanding landlord, Paul Hexter. The pub is named after a succession of Royal Navy ships. There are pictures and photographs in the bar. The local branch of the Royal Naval Association meets here.
🛏️◄🏠♣🍺

Shoulder of Mutton
38 Wallingford Street, OX12 8AX
🕐 11-11; 12-10.30 Sun
☎ (01235) 762835
website: www.shoulderofmuttonwantage.com
Greene King Morland Original, Abbot; guest beer Ⓗ

A short distance from the market place, the Shoulder of Mutton is a delightful, unspoilt locals' pub with a choice of four drinking areas. Sup your pint in the public bar to the left, the larger, more spacious bar to the right, the tiny, quiet no-smoking snug or even in the 'layby' in the corridor. In summer, you may also use the small courtyard at the back. Although it has not changed much in the past 100 years, this must be the first ever cyber-pub in Wantage. The landlord is an avid real ale enthusiast who is always willing to discuss his beers with the cognoscenti.
🏛️Q✿◄♣✂

WHEATLEY

Railway
24 Station Road, OX33 1ST
🕐 12 (4 Mon)-11; 12-10.30 Sun
☎ (01865) 874810 website: www.railwaywheatley.co.uk
Fuller's London Pride, ESB, seasonal beer Ⓗ

Trains no longer serve Wheatley, but this Victorian pub is packed with railway memorabilia from the former branch line. The spacious central bar attracts customers of all ages; families are welcome and there is a large, safe garden. Excellent value food is served, except on Monday. The function room has a late licence and is available for hire. Entertainment includes live music weekends, regular jazz and curry nights and a popular Thursday night quiz. The owners are now in their eleventh year at the helm and have recently won the prestigious titles of Fuller's Most Outstanding Pub and Best Country Pub of 2002. 🏛️✿❀♣✂

WOOTTON, WOODSTOCK

Killingworth Castle Inn ✔
Glympton Road, OX20 1EJ (on B4027)
🕐 12-2.30, 6.30-11; 12-2.30, 7-10.30 Sun
☎ (01993) 811401
website: www.killingworthcastle.tablesir.com
Greene King IPA, Morland Original, Ruddles County; guest beer Ⓗ

This 17th-century Cotswold coaching inn comprises a long, beamed bar with a log-burning stove, and a small back bar with games, including bar billiards. Flagstone and timber floors, simple pine furniture, bookcases and original country artefacts make this cheerful pub a popular gathering place for locals, walkers and tourists. An established venue for folk music – every Friday for 30 years – it also hosts modern jazz. A large, well-kept garden is available and there is comfortable, en-suite accommodation in a modern barn conversion. Stylish pub fare is served all week from an extensive menu.
🏛️Q➰✿🛏️◖♣P

SHROPSHIRE

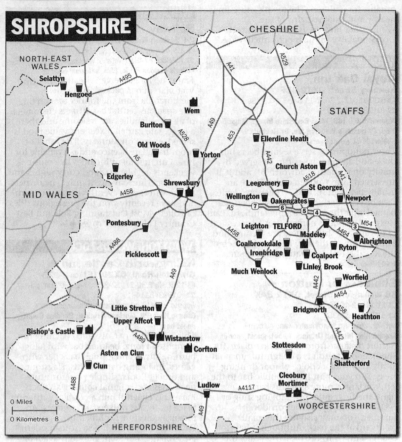

ALBRIGHTON

Harp Hotel
40 High Street, WU7 3JF
⏰ 12-11; 12-10.30 Sun
☎ (01902) 374381

Beer range varies Ⓗ

Basic, two-roomed locals' pub which gets busy on music nights. It is an internationally-known jazz venue. Many pictures of artists who have played at the Harp are displayed in the lounge. Terry, the landlord, has been proprietor for 20 years and has recently started mini beer festivals (four to date). Beers come from local Shropshire breweries and some from further afield. Bulmers Traditional cider is stocked. Summer drinking is pleasant on the green to the front of the pub. ✿⏏Å⇌♣♠P

ASTON ON CLUN

Kangaroo
Clun Road, SY7 8EW (on B4368, between Craven Arms and Clun) OS503981
⏰ 12-3 (not Mon or Tue), 6 (7 Mon & Tue)-11; 12-11 Fri & Sat; 12-10.30 Sun
☎ (01588) 660263 website: www.kangarooinn.co.uk

Six Bells Roo Brew; Wells Bombardier; guest beers Ⓗ

The unusual name dates from the 19th century. This cosy, friendly village local offers a public bar, games room and a large garden. Home-cooked food features (not served Sun–Tue eves); try the 'theme'

evenings. Summer barbecues and the annual beer festival are well supported by locals and visitors. Roo Brew is the 'house' beer. The pub is half a mile from Broome Station. ⚌✿⏏Å⇌(Broome) ♣P⅟

BISHOP'S CASTLE

Castle Hotel
Market Square, SY9 5BH
⏰ 12-2.30, 6.30-11; 12-2.30, 7-10.30 Sun
☎ (01588) 638403

Hobsons Best Bitter; Six Bells Big Nev's; Worthington's 1744; guest beers Ⓗ

Fine, period hotel comprising a dining room, public bar, lounge and small snug bars with much original woodwork. Excellent fresh food and two Shropshire beers are served at their best. The landlord supplies an interesting range for the town's annual beer festival (July). The large water garden provides an ideal spot for families. Situated at the high point of the town, visitors are impressed by the quality of beer, food and the overall ambience. The owners have lovingly cared for all aspects over the past 14 years. ⚌Q✿⏏⏏♣P

Six Bells
Church Street, SY9 5AA
⏰ 12-2.30 (not Mon), 5-11; 12-11 Sat; 12-10.30 Sun
☎ (01588) 630144

Six Bells Big Nev's, Marathon Ale, Cloud Nine, Duck & Dive, seasonal beers Ⓗ

This 17th-century, two-bar coaching inn is the tap of Six Bells Brewery. It is a former local CAMRA award-winner with a reputation for participating in village events, such as the beer festival (July) and Michaelmas fair. The small bar has exposed beams, stonework and a wood-burning stove. The larger bar has seating and tables together with a chalkboard menu; it offers freshly-prepared rolls and excellent meals (except Mon) all day and Sunday evening. The superb house ales are rightly enjoyed by all comers. Sunday buses from Shrewsbury pass every two hours. ₳Q❀◑ ⊕♣

Three Tuns
Salop Street, SY9 5BW
🕐 12-3, 5-11; 12-11 Fri & Sat; 12-10.30 Sun
☎ (01588) 638797
website: www.thethreetunsinn.co.uk
Beer range varies Ⓗ
Pending refurbishment of the pub's own brewery, local breweries (such as Hobsons and Salopian) have stepped in to supply house beers. The hotel is a popular venue for music events, with a good reputation for its cuisine (no meals served Mon lunchtime). There are three distinct bars: public, lounge and conservatory and an area for outside drinking. Food is served in the lounge and the bar features settles and a stove. There are plans to stock beer from the re-established on-site brewery which started production in September 2003. Self-catering accommodation is available. ₳Q❀⊨◑ ⊕P

BRIDGNORTH

Bell & Talbot
Salop Street, High Town, WV16 4QU
🕐 5 (2 Fri; 12 Sat)-11; hours can vary – phone ahead; 12-10.30 Sun
☎ (01746) 763233
Batham Best Bitter; Holden's Mild, Bitter; guest beers Ⓗ
This 250-year-old coaching inn retains many original features and has three attractive bars, two with open log fires. The Severn Valley Railway is within a short walk. Live music is staged Friday, Saturday and sometimes Sunday. A good selection of changing guest beers can be expected. Evening meals are served Wednesday-Sunday until 9pm. ₳⊨◑ ⊕Å≷ (SVR) ♣

Black Horse
4 Bridge Street, Low Town, WV15 6AF
🕐 5.30 (12 Sat)-11; 12-10.30 Sun
☎ (01746) 762415
Banks's Original, Bitter; Batham Best Bitter; Enville Ale; Hobsons Town Crier; guest beers Ⓗ
Classic, mid-1700s English ale house that offers a small front bar (with an antique back bar fitting) and a wood-panelled main bar, typical of the period, with a low ceiling. The courtyard is pleasant for outdoor drinking and has marvellous floral displays in summer. A popular venue for fishermen after a hard day on the nearby River Severn, food is only available during the summer months. ❀⊨◑ ⊕≷ (SVR) ♣P ☖

Railwayman's Arms
Platform One, Severn Valley Railway Station, Hollybush Road, WV16 5DT
🕐 12 (11 summer)-4, 6-11; 11-11 Sat; 12-10.30 Sun
☎ (01746) 764361 website: www.svr.co.uk

Batham Mild, Best Bitter; Hobsons Best Bitter; guest beers Ⓗ
A Guide regular, this characterful, charismatic drinking spot is a must for beer drinkers and steam railway enthusiasts. Sit out on the platform with your drinks and savour the atmosphere of the steam era, or opt for the bar, part of which is the original licensed refreshment room. Note the superb Cheshire's Brewery (Smethwick) mirror above the welcoming coal fireplace. The three guest beers tend to be from smaller brewers, frequently local to the area. Bulmers Traditonal cider is now available all year. ₳Q❀≷ (SVR) ♠P

BURLTON

Burlton Inn
SY4 5TB (on A528, near B4397 jct)
🕐 11-3, 6-11; 12-2, 7-10.30 Sun
☎ (01939) 270284
Banks's Bitter; guest beers Ⓗ
This attractive, free of tie, country pub is situated near the North Shropshire lakes between Shrewsbury and Ellesmere. It offers three constantly-changing guest beers and award-winning, home-cooked food based on local produce (not served Sun eve). Largely geared to eating, drinkers are nonetheless welcome and a new quiet drinking area is provided. Tucked away behind the inn, are new cottages offering six individually designed en-suite bedrooms. ₳Q❀⊨◑ ⅄P

CHURCH ASTON

Last Inn
Wellington Road, TF10 9EJ
(approx 1½ miles from Newport on A518)
🕐 12-11; 12-10.30 Sun
☎ (01952) 820469
Banks's Original, Bitter; Everards Tiger; Hobsons Best Bitter; guest beers Ⓗ
The Last Inn attracts a cosmopolitan clientele. Originally a two-roomed 19th-century pub, it has been extended to provide a spacious dining area and a sizeable garden with a water feature. Ever-changing guest beers in addition to regular beers make this a must for ale enthusiasts. Local CAMRA Pub of the Season, winter 2001–02, it is popular for its food – you can enjoy a good meal with a fine pint. Q❀◑P

CLEOBURY MORTIMER

Stables Tavern
1 Talbot Square, DY14 8BQ
(in alleyway next to Talbot Hotel)

INDEPENDENT BREWERIES

All Nations Madeley
Corvedale Corfton
Dolphin Shrewsbury
Hanby Wem
Hobsons Cleobury Mortimer
John Roberts Bishop's Castle
Salopian Shrewsbury
Six Bells Bishop's Castle
Three Tuns Bishop's Castle
Wood Wistanstow
Worfield Madeley

✪ 12-11; 12-10.30 Sun
☎ (01229) 270382
Banks's Original, Bitter; guest beers Ⓗ
Multi-roomed pub on various levels with a pool room at the back, enabling the pub to cater for all types of customer. The three guest beers change on a regular basis with at least one of them being from a local brewery; the cider is Thatchers. A good range of food is on offer here. The Talbot Square public car park serves as the pub car park. The Old Lion on Lower Street is a free house that also sells real ale. ◖◗ ♣ ♠

CLUN

White Horse Inn ✓
The Square, SY7 8JA
✪ 12-11; 12-10.30 Sun
☎ (01588) 640305
Salopian Shropshire Gold; Worthington's Bitter; Wye Valley Butty Bach, seasonal beers; guest beers Ⓗ
Comfortable, 18th-century coaching inn and post house that stands in the old market square at the centre of a wonderfully timeless village, two minutes from the castle. This friendly local has an L-shaped bar with low beams. A range of board games can be borrowed and the excellent, reasonably-priced food is home made. Westons First Quality cider is stocked. Relax over a quiet pint in the secluded garden at the rear. Accommodation is available.
🏠 Q ✿ ⛺ ◖◗ ♣ ♠

EDGERLEY

Royal Hill ☆
SY10 8ES (between Pentre and Melverley, off A5 to Oswestry) OSSJ3517
✪ 12-2, 6.30-11; 12-2, 7-10.30 Sun
☎ (01743) 741242
Salopian Shropshire Gold, Golden Thread, seasonal beers Ⓗ
This pub is an absolute gem, set on a quiet road, it offers spectacular views of the River Severn. The 18th-century building, recently added to CAMRA's National Inventory, has two cosy rooms and a tiny bar. Canoeists, anglers and campers are always given a genuine welcome by the locals. The garden, across the road on the river bank, is somewhere to tuck into fish and chips on a summer evening, available from a visiting van on Thursday evening. 🏠 Q ☕ ⛺ ⛺ ⛴ Å ♣

ELLERDINE HEATH

Royal Oak
TF6 6RL (midway between A53 and A442) OS603226
✪ 12 (11 Sat)-11; 12-10.30 Sun
☎ (01939) 250300
Hobsons Best Bitter; Salopian Shropshire Gold; Shepherd Neame Master Brew Bitter; Wye Valley HPA; guest beer Ⓗ
Known locally as the Tiddlywink, this small, friendly, country pub should have had an extension and disabled facilities completed by the time this Guide is produced. Very busy for such a rural location, it draws both young and old customers into the cosy central bar with its coal fire and lively conversation. There is a games room and outside play area for children and a very reasonably-priced menu for all. The annual July cider festival, like the regular beer

selection, covers the whole of Great Britain as well as locally produced beverages. Westons cider is normaly stocked. No food is served on Tuesday. 🏠 Q ✿ ◖◗ ♿ Å ♣ ♠ P

HEATHTON

Old Gate
WV5 7EB (between B4176 and A458 near Halfpenny Green) OS814923
✪ 12-2.30, 6.30-11; closed Mon; 12-3, 7-10.30 Sun
☎ (01746) 710431 website: www.oldgateinn.co.uk
Enville Ale; Greene King Abbot; Wells Bombardier Ⓗ
Busy pub in a rural part of the county serving food of restaurant quality (no meals Sun eve). The extensive menu is fairly priced and caters for all tastes. The two bars are decorated as you would expect a typical 16th-century inn to be, with welcoming log fires and a cosy atmosphere. Music is played at low volume, so conversation is still possible. Addlestones cider is sold. Children are welcome and the large garden has a safe play area. Well worth a visit. 🏠 ✿ ◖◗ ♠ P ⛔

HENGOED

Last Inn
SY10 7EU (off B4579, 3 miles N of Oswestry) OS680979
✪ 7-11; 12-3, 7-10.30 Sun
☎ (01691) 659747
Beer range varies Ⓗ
A 1960s-style, one-bar pub, embracing an older structure but with a traditional welcome, in the Welsh Border area that is popular with tourists. Hengoed is Welsh for old wood; the pub derives it name from its days as a cobbler's. In this Guide for 22 years continuously, and in all editions of CAMRA's Good Pub Food, the five ever-changing guest beers are predominantly from regional and micro-breweries. A fine collection of vintage photographs (connected to the pub) and a large collection of brewery trays are displayed. Evening meals are offered (except Tue) and Sunday lunch. 🏠 Q ⛴ ◗ ♣ P

LEIGHTON

Kynnersley Arms
SY5 6RN (off B4380) OS610055
✪ 12-2 Thu (& Tue, Wed summer), 5-11 Mon-Thu;
12-11 Fri & Sat; 12-10.30 Sun
☎ (01952) 510258
Banks's Original; Draught Bass; Tetley Bitter; guest beer Ⓗ
Unique building in small village that has been a flour mill, furnace and forge. Channel 4's Time Team dug on the site and their work can be seen. The pub has its own Heritage Trust fund to continue renovation and investigation. The mill is in the Domesday Book (c1086) and was still grinding corn until around 1936, it can be viewed through a glass floor panel in the pub. Organic produce from local suppliers is used whenever possible in the varied menu and crêpes are one of the French cook's specialities. 🏠 Q ⛴ ✿ ◖◗ Å ♣ P ⛔

LINLEY BROOK

Pheasant Inn
Britons Lane, WV16 4TA
(off B4373, Bridgnorth-Broseley road) OS680979

✪ 12-2, 7 (6.30 summer)-11;
12-3, 7 (6.30 summer)-10.30 Sun
☎ (01746) 762260
Beer range varies Ⓗ
Set in idyllic countryside halfway between
Bridgnorth and Broseley, this picturesque,
low, beamed inn has had a long
commitment to real ale. Run by the same
licensee for 20 years, every year it has
appeared in this Guide. Visiting this
unspoilt, rural gem is like entering a time
warp, the only sound to be heard is polite
conversation and the crackle of the roaring
fire. This is the kind of inn that makes city
dwellers want to settle in the countryside.
⌂Q✿◑●♣P⊟

LITTLE STRETTON

Ragleth Inn
Ludlow Road, All Stretton, SY6 6RB
(just off A49, S of Church Stretton)
✪ 12-3, 6-11; 12-11 Sat; 12-10.30 Sun
☎ (01694) 722711 website: www.theraglethinn.co.uk
Hobsons Best Bitter; guest beers Ⓗ
In good walking country, close to the Long
Mynd and other vast tracts of National
Trust-owned land, the Ragleth is named
after a local hill across the valley. Dated
1650, this warm, quiet inn has an
inglenook, oak beams, antiques and a brick
and tiled floor. It is a true community pub
used by many local social groups. The
attractive garden has climbing frames, a
children's trampoline and a rare tulip tree.
There is always a Shropshire beer or two on
tap and a selection of over 80 malt whiskies.
Traditional games played in the bar include
shove-ha'penny and skittles.
⌂Q✿◑●A♣P✿

LUDLOW

Charlton Arms
Ludford Bridge, SY8 1PJ
✪ 12-11; 12-10.30 Sun
☎ (01584) 872813
Hobsons Best Bitter; guest beers Ⓗ
This pub has a superb location on the
River Teme by Ludford Bridge, on the
outskirts of Ludlow. Five guest ales are
supplied from local breweries, and real
perry and cider are sometimes available.
An extensive menu offers good value,
home-cooked food. This old coaching inn
offers accommodation with a full
Shropshire breakfast. Regular folk nights
are a feature.
⌂✿◑●A♣P⊟

Church Inn
Buttercross, SY8 1AW
✪ 11-11; 12-10.30 Sun
☎ (01584) 872174 website: www.thechurchinn.com
**Brains Bitter; Hobsons Town Crier; Hook Norton Old
Hooky; Weetwood Eastgate Ale; Wye Valley Bitter;
guest beers** Ⓗ
The Church Inn is the oldest pub in
Ludlow and the only free house within
the town walls. A new lounge bar is now
open upstairs. German and Belgian
bottled beers are stocked and good food is
served to complement them. The landlord
is a former mayor of Ludlow and a
CAMRA member. Situated close to the
market square and castle, this is a must. If
you would like to stay longer,

accommodation is available.
⌂Q✿◑●A≈✿⊟

Nelson Inn
Rocks Green, SY8 2DS
(A4117, Kidderminster road)
✪ 12-2.30, 6 (7 Tue)-11; 12-11 Fri & Sat;
12-10.30 Sun
☎ (01584) 872908
website: www.thenelson.fsbusiness.co.uk
**Banks's Original; Worthington's Bitter, 1744; guest
beers** Ⓗ
Wonderful, 300-year-old rural pub on the
outskirts of Ludlow, comprising two rooms.
The lounge bar is decked out with musical
instruments and a collection of mugs. One
of the regular guest beers is Black Beard
Stairway to Heaven, brewed for the pub by
Nottingham. Two beer festivals are held
each year at Easter and in September. Live
music nights are regularly staged.
⌂Q✿◑●⊞♣●P

MUCH WENLOCK

George & Dragon
2 High Street, TF13 6AA (by town square)
✪ 12-3, 6-11; 12-11 Fri, Sat & summer;
12-10.30 Sun
☎ (01952) 727312
Adnams Bitter; Hobsons Town Crier; guest beers Ⓗ
Intimate and popular market town local,
with roots as far back as 1714, providing a
friendly atmosphere for visitors and
regulars. The pub is a focal point of the
town, with quiz nights, day trips and
involvement in many of the town's
festivals. It is conveniently positioned for
walkers enjoying Wenlock Edge. Behind the
busy, but welcoming, bar is a roomy, 40-
seater restaurant, with tables set into cosy
alcoves, and a regularly changing menu of
local fare. Booking is advisable; no food is
served on Sunday evening or Wednesday.
Everyone is always welcome, but due to the
age of the building, wheelchair access is
restricted. Q≈◑●

NEWPORT

New Inn
2 Stafford Road, TF10 7LX
(50 yds from town centre car park)
✪ 12 (11.30 Sat)-11; 12-10.30 Sun
☎ (01952) 814729
Bank's Original; Ⓟ **Draught Bass; guest beers** Ⓗ
Typical, old-style pub with quarry tiles and
latch locks, the type of place that is sadly
disappearing. Frequented by a friendly
clientele, it is one of only two pubs not on
the High Street. The public car park is only
50 yards away, next to a fish and chip shop.
There is an attractive garden in which to
enjoy a break. A must for those wishing to
visit an old heritage pub. ⌂✿♣

OLD WOODS

Romping Cat
SY4 3AX (near Bomere Heath)
✪ 1-3 (not Wed or Fri), 7-11; 12.30-3.30, 7-11 Sat;
12-2.30, 7-10.30 Sun
☎ (01939) 290273
**Boddingtons Bitter; Fuller's London Pride; Oakham
JHB; Taylor Landlord; Weetwood Eastgate Ale** Ⓗ
Nestling in the Shropshire countryside, this
pub is a haven of peace and quiet, popular

with discerning drinkers. In summer, the seating outside provides a pleasant diversion, away from the hustle and bustle of nearby Shrewsbury; security for cycles is thoughtfully provided. Originally called the Railway, a Southam's (Shrewsbury) pub, it has always been known by locals as the Cat, for reasons lost in the mists of time. It underwent a name change in the 1980s.
🏚Q❀♣P🍴

PICKLESCOTT

Bottle & Glass
SY6 6NR (off A49, at Dorrington)
🕏 7-11 (12-2.30, 7-11 Tue-Thu summer); 11-11 Sat; 12-3, 7-10.30 Sun
☎ (01694) 751345
M&B Mild; Salopian Shropshire Gold; Wood Parish, Shropshire Lad; guest beers H
Charming, 17th-century, stone-built, cottage-style inn, situated in a tucked away, picturesque village on the northern end of the Long Mynd. The pub's interior is comfortable, with the ambience of a friendly country local. The public bar, with its low beams, exposed walls and large open fire, is particularly attractive. There is a cosy lounge and a separate restaurant. Lunches are served on Saturday and Sunday; no evening meals Sunday. Westons and Bulmers cider are sold. You may encounter two landlords – one is a ghost.
🏚Q❀🛏🍴❶🏚🛆♣P🍴

PONTESBURY

Horseshoes
Minsterley Road, SY5 0QJ
🕏 12-4 (not Mon-Fri), 6-11; 12-4, 7-10.30 Sun
☎ (01743) 790278
Castle Eden Ale; Salopian Shropshire Gold (summer); **guest beers** H
Busy, friendly local on the edge of a large village and convenient for walking in the South Shropshire hills. Very active in the local games league, including pool, darts and dominoes, the pub hosts a Thursday quiz night. Regular guest beers are from local brewers and from Wye Valley, Cottage and through the Beer Seller. Two B&B rooms are available. Evening meals and weekend lunches are available; Sunday lunch is particularly popular. ❀🛏❶🍴

RYTON

Fox
Great Ryton, SY5 7LS (5½ miles S of Shrewsbury, 1 mile E of A49) OSSJ4903
🕏 12-2.30 (3 Sat; not Mon), 7-11; 12-4, 7-10.30 Sun
☎ (01743) 718499
Brains Rev James; Hobsons Mild, Best Bitter; guest beers H
A warm welcome is assured in this quiet country pub overlooking the Stretton Hills. Entry is from the ample car park via a patio with tables and umbrellas in summer. The Fox is at the heart of the local community and popular with residents from neighbouring villages. There is an ongoing programme of musical, quiz and special cuisine nights. An extensive and interesting menu is available in the evening, plus a bar menu at lunchtime. Shropshire beers are always stocked. Assistance in mounting steps is

offered to wheelchair users.
🏚Q❀❶🏚🛆P

SELATTYN

Cross Keys ☆
Glyn Road, SY10 7DN (on B4579 between Oswestry & Glyn Ceiriog)
🕏 7-11; 12-4, 7-10.30 Sun
☎ (01691) 650247
Banks's Original; guest beers H
A mile from Offa's Dyke, this 17th-century gem of a village local is now a free house. A CAMRA National Inventory pub, it offers a cosy atmosphere. There is a bar with quarry-tiled floor, a snug where music sessions and meetings are held, a games room and a larger function room. The safe garden is ideal for children and has splendid views over the Shropshire plain. It is an ideal resting place for pony trekkers and walkers in this attractive border country as by phoning ahead, or even knocking, groups can be catered for outside the stated opening hours. Accommodation is self-catering. 🏚Q🛏❀🏚🛆♣P

SHATTERFORD

Red Lion
Bridgnorth Road, DY12 1SU
🕏 11-2.30, 6.30-11; 12-3, 7-10.30 Sun
☎ (01299) 861221
website: www.redlionshatterford.co.uk
Banks's Original, Bitter; Ⓟ **Batham Best Bitter; guest beers** H
Home of the hottest little coal fire in Shropshire, this popular pub was built in 1834 after the Duke of Wellington's beer house reform. The pub lies on the Worcestershire border, a mile outside the village. The restaurant and one bar are no-smoking. Ramps and extra-wide doors have been fitted as well as a wheelchair WC and dedicated parking. Local seasonal produce is used (vegetables, game and meat) and the pub enjoys a good reputation for its fish dishes. Outside is a boules piste and the pub hosts a successful team. 🏚Q❀❶🛆ⱯP🍴🍴

SHIFNAL

White Hart ⊘
High Street, TF11 8BB
🕏 12-3, 5.30-11; 12-11 Fri & Sat; 12-10.30 Sun
☎ (01952) 461161
Enville Ale; Holden's Mild, Bitter; Wye Valley Butty Bach; guest beers H
Well-deserved winner of 2002 local CAMRA Pub of the Year award. It is an outstanding example of a traditional British pub, a 400-year-old classic, half-timbered building with two bars. Seven handpumped ales are always on offer, four local and three guests – two premium plus one session beer. Friendly patrons and staff ensure a warm welcome to all. Excellent home-cooked food is served at lunchtime, except Sunday, including the range of famed burgers. Children are welcome until 7pm. ❀❶🏚♣P

SHREWSBURY

Armoury
Victoria Quay, Victoria Avenue, SY1 1HH
🕏 12-11; 12-10.30 Sun
☎ (01743) 340525

website: www.armoury-shrewsbury.co.uk
Boddingtons Bitter; Wadworth 6X; Wood Shropshire Lad; guest beers Ⓗ

Three regular and five constantly-changing guest beers aim to suit a wide range of tastes. The tasting notes are provided on blackboards above the bar as well as a 'coming soon' list. Some 70 malt whiskies and 20 bourbons are also kept. An excellent range of food on an original menu is served in the bar or no-smoking dining area. Children are welcome until 9pm. Once an armoury, it was renovated and appropriately renamed in 1995. A spacious room, it is furnished with a large table and chairs; books and memorabilia adorn the walls. Board games are available on request. Quiet during the day, it turns into a busy evening pub.
🏚Q◖▣ঌ➾♣½

Coach & Horses
Swan Hill, SY1 1NP (to rear of Music Hall)
✪ 11-11; 12-10.30 Sun
☎ (01743) 365661
Draught Bass; guest beers Ⓗ

Set on a corner in quiet street just off the main shopping area, the Coach & Horses can provide a quiet haven. In summer it has a magnificent floral display (see the certificates). Victorian in style, the pub has a wood-panelled bar, a small side snug area and a large lounge which is the lunchtime restaurant, occasionally used in the evening by booked parties. Lighter dishes (available until 4pm) complement the full lunchtime menu. Phoenix Arizona and a Salopian beer often appear as guest beers.
Q◖▣

Dolphin
48 St Michael's Street, SY1 2EZ
✪ 5-11; 12-3, 7-10.30 Sun
☎ (01743) 350419
website: www.thedolphinbrewery.co.uk
Dolphin Best Bitter; guest beers Ⓗ

Popular ale house, within easy walking distance of Shrewsbury railway station. It is gaslit, and symmetrical in style, with one side being the bar, the other the lounge. The Dolphin Brewery has been brewing since December 2000 at the rear of the pub, and at least two house beers are usually on tap here. Up to five real ales are available altogether, plus an occasional cider (Westons) in summer. Q▣➾♦

Loggerheads ☆
1 Church Street, SY1 1UG
(just off St Mary's Street)
✪ 11-11; 12-3, 8-10.30 Sun
☎ (01743) 355457
Banks's Original, Bitter; Draught Bass; Marston's Pedigree; guest beer Ⓗ

One of the few pubs that Banks's has not been able to spoil by progress! It is run by different generations of the same family. Situated in the heart of town, this classic Grade II listed boozer retains its original layout of four distinctive cosy bars. Three of these, including the lounge, are served from hatchways – two via a stone-flagged corridor. One, the former gentlemen-only bar, has traditional settles and scrubbed-topped tables. The other, the poet's room, is wood panelled. The guest beers change regularly and a policy of no

music is pursued. No food is offered on Sunday.
Q◖▣➾♣♠

Three Fishes ⊘
Fish Street, SY1 1UR
✪ 11.30-3, 5-11; 11.30-11 Fri & Sat; 12-10.30 Sun
☎ (01743) 344793
Adnams Bitter; Fuller's London Pride; Taylor Landlord; guest beers Ⓗ

A friendly atmosphere awaits in this award-winning pub, that is family-run, and proudly defends a no-smoking policy throughout. It has a range of up to six beers including one local brew. The 15th-century building stands in the shadow of two churches, St Alkmond's and St Julian's, within the maze of streets and passageways in the medieval quarter of the town. Freshly-prepared food is available lunchtime and early evening (except Sun eve). ◖▣➾½

STOTTESDON

Fighting Cocks
1 High Street, DY14 8TZ
✪ 6 (5 Fri; 12 Sat)-11; 12-10.30 Sun
☎ (01746) 718270
Hobsons Best Bitter, Town Crier; guest beers Ⓗ

This black and white split-level, unspoilt building has a comfortable bar, a no-smoking dining room and a family dining room. It began its days as a pub in 1830, when the village blacksmith became the first landlord. It was also once a slaughterhouse – a giant pulley (used as a carcass hoist) still remains. As the name suggests, it was a centre for cockfighting. The menu of home-cooked food places a strong emphasis on traditional country meals, including Sunday roasts, using produce from local farms. Award-winning pies are not to be missed. Meals are served Wednesday–Sunday, 12–3 and 7–9 from May until September (just Sat and Sun Oct–April). 🏚Q🏠☺◖▣♣P

TELFORD: COALBROOKDALE

Coalbrookdale Inn
12 Wellington Road, TF8 7DX
✪ 12-3, 6-11; 12-3, 7-10.30 Sun
☎ (01952) 433953
website: www.coalbrookdale-inn.co.uk
Adnams Broadside; Fuller's London Pride; guest beers Ⓗ

Lively pub that is full of beer and brewing artefacts, plus other amusing items. In this former National CAMRA Pub of the Year, the customer is presented with an outstanding choice, not only of real ales, but food, too (not served Sun). The toilets are of note – and the landlord will happily invite customers to view them. A good venue to return to after going around the new 'Enginuity' display in the Museum of Iron, opposite. 🏚Q☺◖♦P

COALPORT

Shakespeare Inn
High Street, TF8 7HT
(from M54 jct 5, follow signs to Blists Hill museum)
✪ 5 (12 Sat)-11; closed Mon; 12-10.30 Sun
☎ (01952) 580675
Enville Ale; Everards Tiger; guest beers Ⓗ

Situated in the heart of the Ironbridge

Gorge, a World Heritage Site, the Shakespeare Inn is over 200 years old. It is within easy walking distance of the Coalport China Museum, the Blists Hill Museum, the Maws Craft Centre and the famous Ironbridge itself. The Silkin Way runs alongside, offering ideal walks around the gorge. This friendly, family-run pub has recently been refurbished and offers English, Mediterranean and European dishes. Weekend lunches are served 12–3, including traditional Sunday lunch with an extensive wine list. Evening meals are offered 6–8.30. Booking is highly recommended. Views from the tiered garden are panoramic. Q☼❄⌀◖❯P⚥

IRONBRIDGE

Golden Ball
Newbridge Road, TF8 7BA
(near jct of Madeley Rd and Wesley Rd)
☼ 12-3, 5-11; 12-11 Sat; 12-10.30 Sun
☎ (01952) 432179 website: www.goldenballinn.com
Everards Tiger; Taylor Landlord; guest beers Ⓗ
This interesting inn has been licensed since 1728. It is off the beaten track but well worth finding. It is close to the Ironbridge Gorge and museums. The inn has a warm and friendly atmosphere (even warmer fire) and varied seating spaces on different levels. Superb home-cooked food is available in the bar and separate restaurant, but booking is advisable at weekends. The two regular beers plus guest ales usually include local products. The inn also sells an impressive range of Belgian bottled beers.
🏨☼❄⌀◖❯P⚥🚭

Robin Hood
33 Waterloo Street, TF8 7HQ (on B4373)
☼ 11-11; 12-10.30 Sun
☎ (01952) 433100
website: www.yeolderobinhoodinn.co.uk
Banks's Original; Salopian Golden Thread; guest beers Ⓗ
Overlooking the River Severn and the modern Jackfield Free Bridge, the customer has a choice of enjoying the views from the patio or the cosiness of this convivial watering-hole (licensed since 1828). Good food is served lunchtime and evening in intimate surroundings. Children are catered for with an adventure playground but must vacate the pub by 9pm. There is an interesting range of guest beers and the pub has received the local CAMRA Pub of the Season award. Live music features on Thursday evening. ❄⌀◖❯🌽P⚥

LEEGOMERY

Malt Shovel
Hadley Park Road, TF1 6QG
(off A442 Leegomery roundabout)
☼ 12-2.30 (3 Sat), 5-11; 12-3, 7-10.30 Sun
☎ (01952) 242963
Banks's Original; Marston's Pedigree; Tetley Burton Ale; guest beers Ⓗ
Traditional, two-roomed pub with open fires in the bar and lounge. There is a fine collection of brasses in the lounge and rugby memorabilia around the bar. A wide range of reasonably-priced meals is served Monday–Friday, with a varied selection of rolls at other times. A busy pub, catering for the locals' interests in sport, Sunday

afternoon hours are flexible depending on sporting fixtures and TV schedules.
🏨Q❄◖⌀❯P🚭

OAKENGATES

Crown Inn ✓
Market Street, TF2 6DU
(rear door adjacent to bus station)
☼ 12.30-3, 7-11; 12-11 Thu-Sat; 12.30-10.30 Sun
☎ (01952) 610888
website: www.crown.oakengates.com
Hobsons Best Bitter; guest beers Ⓗ
This friendly pub (built in 1835) has three rooms, adorned with beer-transport paraphernalia. It hosts the world's largest pub-based handpulled beer festivals (Thu–Mon, on the first weekend in May and Oct) with 29 cooled handpulls. The pub uses 13 throughout the year for beers from the independents. Telford Acoustic Club plays on Wednesday evening (not in August), recorded classical music features on Saturday and Sunday afternoons and a range of events, such as baking competitions and beer themed days are regularly held. Wheelchair access is via the rear door. Board games are available. Weekday home-made lunches are offered. The pub has a no-smoking area at certain times of the week. 🏨❄◖⌀🚹⬆≈🌽❯P⚥🚭

Station Hotel
42 Market Street, TF2 6DU
☼ 11-11; 12-2.30, 7-10.30 Sun
☎ (01952) 612949
website: www.stationhotel.oakengates.com
Fuller's London Pride; Salopian Shropshire Gold; Worthington's 1744; guest beers Ⓗ
Popular, town-centre pub near both bus and train stations. Originally called the Talbot, it offers a traditional bar with a quarry-tiled floor, a lounge, pool room and a separate no-smoking dining room. A wide range of reasonably-priced meals is served on Monday and Wednesday–Friday, 12–2.30 (including vegetarian options). Saturday live rock and blues music events are held once a month. ◖⌀≈🌽🍴

ST GEORGES

St Georges Sports & Social Club
Church Road, TF2 9LU
☼ 7 (12 Sat)-11; 12-5, 7-10.30 Sun
☎ (01952) 612911
Banks's Original, Bitter; guest beers Ⓗ
This club, catering to all sections of the local community, has a dedication to real ale that has won it various CAMRA awards. It supports local breweries from Shropshire and the Black Country. The club acts as the base for numerous sports teams, and many trophies are displayed. It overlooks one of Shropshire's County Cricket grounds. The verandah makes a pleasant outdoor drinking area in the summer with views of the idyllic surroundings. 🛋❄🌽P

WELLINGTON

Cock Hotel
148 Holyhead Road, TF1 2DL
☼ 4 (12 Thu-Sat)-11; 12-4, 7-10.30 Sun
☎ (01952) 244954
Hobsons Best Bitter; guest beers Ⓗ

Originally an 18th-century coaching inn, the old stable courtyard is now an outdoor drinking area. It has been local CAMRA Pub of the Year for five out of the last six years, also winning county and regional awards. The six guest beers always include a mild and stout, the eighth handpump permanently dispenses cider, normally Westons, but it can change occasionally. Two out of the three rooms are no-smoking. This lively, popular pub attracts a good mix of customers.
Q ⊛ ⊨ 🛏 ≠ ♣ ♠ P ⅍ 🖫

UPPER AFFCOT (CHURCH STRETTON)

Travellers Rest Inn
SY6 6RL
(on A49, between Church Stretton and Craven Arms)
🕐 11-11; 12-10.30 Sun
☎ (01694) 781275
website: www.travellersrestinn.co.uk
Draught Bass; Boddingtons Bitter; Hobsons Mild, Best Bitter; Wood Shropshire Lad; guest beers Ⓗ
Spacious roadside pub, a welcome stop for travellers as food is served all day. Accommodation consists of 12 en-suite rooms, two are suitable for wheelchair users. Camping is available in the pub's own grounds. Despite its name, the pub attracts locals and has thriving darts and dominoes teams. While the drinking area is one extended room, there are many different sections including a quieter one and space for games, plus a no-smoking conservatory. Cider is available all year. The pub has a children's certificate.
Q ⊛ ⊨ ◑ Ⓓ Ⓖ & ▲ ♣ ♠ P ⅍

WISTANSTOW

Plough Inn
SY7 8DG (take A489 off A49)
🕐 11-2.30, 6.30-11; closed Mon; 12-2.30, 7-10.30 Sun
☎ (01588) 673251
Wood Parish, Special, Shropshire Lad, seasonal beers; guest beers Ⓗ
This pub is the Wood Brewery tap. The building dates from 1782. There are two main bars; the public bar, a few steps down from the entrance, is in two main sections. A games area is separated by a real fire from the drinking space. The lounge is large and serves as a restaurant. Food is served except

Monday and Sunday evening; meals are home made using as much Shropshire produce as possible. Presentation packs of Wood's beer are on sale. Note the large collection of royal wedding beers. A visit to the nearby Discovery Centre is very rewarding. ⊯ Q ⊛ ◑ Ⓓ Ⓖ & ♣ ♠ P

WORFIELD

Dog Inn (Davenport Arms)
Main Street, WV15 5LF
(off A454, 3 miles E of Bridgnorth)
🕐 12-2.30, 7 (6) Sat-11; 12-3, 7-10.30 Sun
☎ (01746) 716020
Courage Best Bitter; Highgate Dark; Wadworth 6X; Wells Bombardier; guest beers Ⓗ
A friendly welcome awaits at this two-bar locals' pub. The well-kept beer and home-cooked food attract a wide clientele. The pub has a separate no-smoking restaurant area. The bar and lounge have been recently modernised and redecorated, creating a pleasant drinking atmosphere. The pub is situated in a no-through road in the charming village of Worfield. Dominoes are played on Monday in the bar. The pub has a children's certificate. ⊯ ⊛ ◑ Ⓓ Ⓖ & ♣ P

YORTON

Railway Inn
SY4 3EP
(200 yds from Yorton railway station) OS SJ2450
🕐 12-3.30, 6.30-11; 12-3.30, 7-10.30 Sun
☎ (01939) 220240
Salopian Golden Thread; Wadworth 6X; Wood Special, Shropshire Lad; guest beers Ⓗ
Located near the picturesque village of Clive, this small, friendly country pub has been run by the same family for 66 years. The simple bar with settle seating, quarry-tiled floor, dartboard and dominoes tables is favoured by the locals. The well-appointed lounge area, popular in summer, displays a fine collection of trophies, including 'Pinkie', a large carp caught at a local pool many years ago. This room is a regular venue for social events and meetings. Due to its close proximity to the station, the pub is very popular with rail travellers. It is a former regional CAMRA Pub of the Year winner. There is a small area for outdoor drinking. Bar food is available on request.
⊯ Q ⊛ ◑ Ⓓ Ⓖ ≠ ♣ P 🖫

Beer, not brandy

Before brandy, which has now become common and sold in every little alehouse, came to England in such quantities as it now doth, we drank good strong beer and ale, and all laborious people (which are the greater part of the kingdom), their bodies requiring after hard labour some strong drink to refresh them, did therefore every morning and evening used to drink a pot of ale or a flagon of strong beer, which greatly helped the promotion of our grains and did them no great prejudice; it hindereth not their work, neither did it take away their senses nor cost them much money, whereas the prohibition of brandy would prevent the destruction of his majesty's subjects, many of whom have been killed by drinking thereof, it not agreeing with their constitution.

Petition to the House of Commons, 1673

SOMERSET

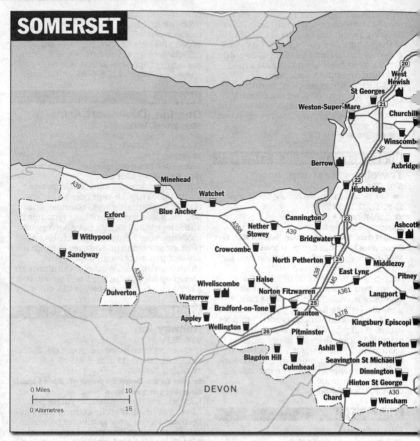

0 Miles 10
0 Kilometres 16

DEVON

APPLEY

Globe Inn ☆
TA21 0HJ
(2½ miles N of A38 at White Ball Hill) OS071215
🕒 11-3, 6.30-11; closed Mon; 12-3, 7-10.30 Sun
☎ (01823) 672327

Cotleigh Tawny; Palmer IPA; guest beer Ⓗ

Rural gem near the Devon border. A serving-hatch opens on to a brick-floored corridor leading to several rooms displaying curios and collectables. One is for dining and another is no-smoking. Well-behaved children are tolerated, but have more scope in the garden, which has some play equipment. The Globe serves excellent food and booking is recommended (essential at weekends). A new toilet block and extension to the skittle alley have been built. Definitely worth the journey.
🏚 Q ✿ ◑ 🍽 Å ♣ P ✕

ASHCOTT

Ring O' Bells
High Street, TA7 9PZ (off A39)
🕒 12-2.30, 7-11; 12-2.30, 7-10.30 Sun
☎ (01458) 210232 website: www.ringobells.com
Beer range varies Ⓗ

Traditional multi-level inn near the village hall and church. It has cosy bar areas, a restaurant, a new function room with a skittle alley, and an attractive garden. One beer from Ashcott's Moor Beer Company is

usually featured, plus two guests from a wide and varying range; Wilkins' cider is stocked. The pub has won several awards for its home-cooked food (same menu in bars and restaurant). Families are welcome at Somerset CAMRA's Pub of the Year 1998.
🏚 ✿ ◑ ⅃ & ♣ ● P

ASHILL

Square & Compass
Windmill Hill, TA19 9NX (off A358) OS310166
🕒 12-2.30 (not Tue-Thu), 6.30-11; 12-3, 7-10.30 Sun
☎ (01823) 480467

Exmoor Ale; guest beers Ⓗ

Inviting, friendly country pub situated off the A358 near Ashill. The pub's extensive menu offers a wide choice of home-made food, prepared by their own chef. Superb views over the Blackdown Hills are a bonus. The large, pleasant garden has a children's area. Exmoor Ales are the beers of choice, with guest beers always available. Some good walks can be enjoyed in the area.
🏚 Q ✿ ◑ P

AXBRIDGE

Crown Inn
St Mary's Street, BS26 2BN (off village square)
🕒 12-3, 7-11; 12-4, 6-11 Fri & Sat;
12-4.30, 7-10.30 Sun
☎ (01934) 732518

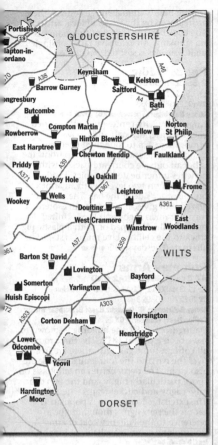

BARTON ST DAVID

Barton Inn
TA11 6BZ (turn off at W end of Keinton Mandeville)
🕑 12.30-2, 4-11; 12-11 Sat; 12-10.30 Sun
☎ (01458) 850451
Beer range varies H

This red-brick, 1930s pub retains most of its original features. Local ciders are sold from a barrel behind the bar throughout the summer months. The beer range features ales from many West Country breweries such as Archers, Glastonbury and Teignworthy, as well as others from further afield. An interesting menu, including organic and vegetarian choices, uses local produce, and also offers excellent curries and steaks. 🏚🛏🕙🍴♿🅰♣🐾👜P🍴🏕

BATH

Bell
103 Walcot Street, BA1 5BW
🕑 11.30-11; 12-10.30 Sun
☎ (01225) 460426 website: www.walcotstreet.com
Abbey Bellringer; Bath Gem; Smiles Best; RCH Pitchfork; Stonehenge Danish Dynamite; H **guest beers** H/G

Popular, city-centre pub where an excellent range of ales is supplemented by five or six guests. The Bell stages live bands on the small central stage on Monday and Wednesday evenings and Sunday lunchtime. There is a long main bar and a collection of smaller rooms at the rear. At the back of the pub is an unexpectedly large terraced garden with plenty of seating. Much of the wall space is taken up with posters for local gigs and other forthcoming events in the Walcot area, which is well known for its bohemian atmosphere.
🕙≍♣🐾

Coeur de Lion
17 Northumberland Passage, BA1 5AR
🕑 11-11; 12-8 Sun
Ridleys Tolly Original; Wells Bombardier; guest beers H

Situated in a narrow passageway opposite the Guildhall in the centre of Bath, this pub claims to be the city's smallest. As it contains only four tables in the single small bar, this may well be true. There is an intimate, bohemian atmosphere, enhanced by fresh flowers and candles. In warm weather, the seating capacity is increased by tables and chairs outside the pub. The stained glass window at the front of the pub is a good example of its

Cotleigh Tawny; guest beer H
Friendly, two-bar free house, which was once a coaching inn, believed to be several hundred years old. There is a busy back bar with a juke box and a quieter front bar. Local Thatchers cider is sold. The Crown is popular for pub games which include skittles, darts, pool, shove-ha'penny and table skittles (two teams). The guest beer normally features one of the Cottage Brewery's range or another local micro.
🏚🕙🛏♣🐾

BARROW GURNEY

Prince's Motto
Barrow Street, BS48 3RU (off A370)
🕑 10.30-11; 12-10.30 Sun
☎ (01275) 472282
Draught Bass; Butcombe Bitter; Wadworth IPA, 6X P
Friendly and comfortable, this three-roomed village inn is decorated in traditional fashion. The jovial landlord has been associated with the pub for a long time and arranges regular outings for the locals. Sport is popular here, too – the pub fields a cricket team and darts is enjoyed by many. Situated conveniently between Bristol and Weston-Super-Mare, many visit for the excellent home-cooked weekday lunches.
🏚🕙🍴♣🐾🍴

INDEPENDENT BREWERIES

Abbey Ales Bath
Berrow Berrow
Blindmans Leighton
Butcombe Butcombe
Cotleigh Wiveliscombe
Cottage Lovington
Exmoor Wiveliscombe
Glastonbury Somerton
Milk Street Frome
Moor Ashcott
Oakhill Oakhill
Odcombe Lower Odcombe
RCH West Hewish

kind. Note the early closing on Sunday evening.
◁≉♣

Hop Pole
Albion Buildings, Upper Bristol Road, BA1 3AR (opp. Victoria Park)
✪ 12-3, 5-11; 12-11 Fri & Sat; 12-10.30 Sun
☎ (01225) 446327
Bath SPA, Gem, Barnstormer; Butcombe Gold; guest beers Ⓗ
Bath Ales' first pub in the city, the Hop Pole is a friendly place, lying between Victoria Park and the River Avon. Its mixed clientele ranges from students to lawyers and resting hacks from the local paper. Normally, two guest ales, a range of bottled foreign beers and an organic cider are stocked. High quality food is served; Sunday lunches are popular. Near the Bath–Bristol cycle path, cycle racks are provided in the spacious garden. Casks and micro-casks of Bath's products can be ordered for parties, etc.
❀◁♣✄

Lambretta's
8-10 North Parade, BA2 4AL
✪ 11-11; 12-10.30 Sun
☎ (01225) 463384 website: www.paradepark.co.uk
Abbey Bellringer; Banks's Bitter; Fuller's London Pride; guest beers Ⓗ
The large bar has been created by revitalising a previously derelict part of the Parade Park Hotel. Continued association with the hotel provides the extensive accommodation facilities. The bar retains the oak panelling which was originally in the room, together with the wooden shutters on the windows. There is a pervading sense of nostalgia for the eponymous scooter and the bar contains many posters and other memorabilia, together with a well-preserved example of the real thing. ❀⌂◁♣♣

Old Farmhouse
25 Belvedere, 1 Lansdown, BA1 5EE
✪ 12-11; 12-10.30 Sun
☎ (01225) 316162
Abbey Bellringer; Butcombe Bitter; Wadworth IPA, 6X Ⓗ
Rebuilt in 1892 on the site of a farmhouse dating from 1600, the pub is instantly recognisable by its mock-Tudor style, which stands out from its Georgian surroundings. Inside is a large bar, divided into two areas. Live jazz is performed in the rear bar most nights, as reflected in the decor which includes many photographs and posters of jazz groups. The pub fields a football team and there is a keen following for shove-ha'penny. The pub sign is a caricature of the landlord. ❀♣P

Old Green Tree ☆
12 Green Street, BA1 2JZ
✪ 11-11; 12-10.30 Sun
Otter Ale; RCH Pitchfork; Wickwar BOB; Mr Perretts Traditional Stout; guest beers Ⓗ
This is a classic example of the traditional, unspoilt pub. Situated in a 300-year-old building in a narrow street near the city centre, its atmosphere of dim cosiness pervades all three of the small, oak-panelled rooms. The comfortable lounge bar at the front is decorated with the owner's collection of pictures of WWII aircraft.

During Bath's annual Fringe Festival, these are replaced by the works of local artists. The back bar, the largest of the rooms, is no-smoking. An extensive range of single malt whiskies is stocked. ♨Q◁≉♣✄

Pig & Fiddle
2 Saracen Street, BA1 5PL
✪ 11-11; 12-10.30 Sun
☎ (01225) 460868
Abbey Bellringer; Theakston XB; guest beers Ⓗ
Large, busy, city-centre pub with a varied clientele, friendly staff and a relaxed atmosphere. Up to four guest beers are available. One end is an old shop front, the other an outside courtyard packed with benches under heated canopies. Inside is a long room on two levels, with an annexe on the other side of the bar. The partially glazed roof gives an airy feel. An esoteric mix of framed rugby and Leeds United memorabilia is topped off with a plastic pig stuck to the ceiling. Live music is staged alternate Tuesdays. ❀◁≉♣●

Pulteney Arms
37 Daniel Street, BA2 6ND
✪ 11-3, 5.30-11; 11-11 Sat; 12-10.30 Sun
☎ (01225) 463923
Abbey Bellringer; Ⓖ **Draught Bass; Brakspear Bitter; Smiles Best; Wadworth 6X** Ⓗ
Dating from 1759, the building is known to have been a pub in 1812. The three rooms all contain some gaslights, there are five over the bar and the four lamps outside are also gaslit. The decor carries an emphasis on sport, particularly rugby, and the pub can raise rugby and cricket teams when invited. The extensive food menu is popular. The cat on the pub sign is thought to be a reference to the Pulteney coat of arms. A no-smoking room is available at lunchtime.
⌇◁●≉♣✄

Rummer
5 Newmarket Row, Grand Parade, BA1 4AW
✪ 11-11; 12-10.30 Sun
☎ (01225) 339345
Bath Gem, Barnstormer; Hop Back Crop Circle Ⓗ
A fine blend of traditional and modern in a recently refurbished pub near Bath's famous Pultney Bridge. The main nicotine-coloured street-level bar is supplemented by two small first-floor rooms, one overlooking the River Avon and the weir. The bar's cosy atmosphere is enhanced with gas fires and wooden panelling. Next to the pub is the old east gate of the city, in a sunken passageway that leads to the river. Evening meals finish at 8pm.
◁●≉

Salamander
3 John Street, BA1 2JL
✪ 12-11; 12-10.30 Sun
☎ (01225) 428889
Bath SPA, Gem, Barnstormer; guest beers Ⓗ
This former 18th-century coffee house has undergone many changes over the years, the most recent in 2001, from 'youf' bar to Bath Ales pub is a definite improvement. Refurbished in their now familiar house style, with bare floorboards, wood panelling and hanging hops, it is subtly divided downstairs, with a restaurant upstairs. It offers relaxed late Sunday lunches and a

Sunday brunch. A selection of bottled Belgian beers is stocked. Bath Ales' merchandise and beers to take home can also be purchased. ◑⇌⅄

Star Inn ☆ ◉
23 The Vineyards, BA1 5NA
❂ 12-2.30, 5.30-11; 12-11 Sat; 12-10.30 Sun
☎ (01225) 425072 website: www.star-inn-bath.co.uk
Abbey Bellringer; Ⓗ Draught Bass; Ⓖ guest beers Ⓗ
The pub, a listed building, is one of the oldest in Bath – first licensed in 1760. A recent refurbishment, by local brewer Abbey Ales, has enhanced the superb interior. The many small rooms feature oak panelling and 19th-century bar fittings. Barrels of Bass are brought up by a special lift through a trap door behind the bar. It is then served, as it has been for many years, from jugs. The smallest bar, used by the older regulars, contains a long wooden bench known as 'death row'. ⚄Q➹⇌♣

BAYFORD

Unicorn Inn
BA9 9NL (on old A303)
❂ 12-2 (not Mon), 7-11; 12-2, 7-10.30 Sun
☎ (01963) 32324
Draught Bass; Butcombe Bitter; Fuller's London Pride; guest beer Ⓗ
This 270-year-old coaching inn serves excellent food; fresh fish is a speciality and the menu includes vegetarian options. Four real ales are usually kept, including an ever-changing guest, that tends to be a session beer. Accommodation is in four en-suite rooms, one of which boasts a four-poster bed. The owners have successfully developed the Unicorn's role as the hub of Bayford. ⚄Q❀⇌◑▯P

BLAGDON HILL

White Lion
TA3 7SG (4 miles S of Taunton) OS211185
❂ 12-3 (not Mon), 7-11; 12-3, 7-10.30 Sun
☎ (01823) 421296
Exmoor Ale, Hart, Stag Ⓗ/Ⓖ
This 17th-century coaching inn is an unspoilt, friendly village pub. It serves local beers and is a popular eating place, offering a typical pub menu of freshly-cooked, locally supplied produce. The bar area features a beamed ceiling and a cosy inglenook. There is a garden for summer use. Skittles, darts, cards and pool are all played here. Cider is stocked in summer.The Exmoor Hart and Stag alternate.
⚄Q➹❀◑▯♣P⅄

BLUE ANCHOR

Blue Anchor Hotel
TA24 6JP (at Watchet end of seafront)
❂ 11.30-3, 6-11; 12-3, 6-10.30 Sun
☎ (01984) 640239
Courage Directors; guest beers Ⓗ
This commodious seafront pub offers a multi-level drinking/eating area with a pleasant atmosphere. The garden and some seats inside afford splendid views over the sea towards Minehead. A varied menu aims to suit all tastes (including children) at reasonable prices. Outside, a large children's play area helps make this a very suitable pub for families. Beers are often from West

Country micros; the guest beer changes weekly, and a second guest is added in summer. ❀⇌◑▯Ａ⇌(W Somerset Rlwy) P

BRADFORD-ON-TONE

White Horse Inn
Regent Street, TA4 1HF
(off A38, Taunton-Wellington road)
❂ 11.30-3, 5.30-11; 12-3, 7-10-30 Sun
☎ (01823) 461239
Butcombe Bitter; Cotleigh Tawny; Fuller's London Pride Ⓗ
This pub, at the heart of the village, is very much a community affair, housing a post office and stores in the outbuildings and hosting many local activities. Visitors receive a warm welcome. The main bar offers bar billiards and a TV, while the restaurant provides excellent home-cooked food. Bar snacks are also available. There are real fires in both bars. The skittle alley has its own bar and doubles as a function room. The beautiful, large garden hosts summer barbecues. ⚄❀◑♣P⅄

BRIDGWATER

Fountain Inn ◉
1 West Quay, TA6 3HL (near town bridge)
❂ 11.30 (11 Fri & Sat)-3, 6.30-11; 12-3, 7-10.30 Sun
☎ (01278) 424115
Butcombe Bitter; Wadworth IPA, 6X; guest beers Ⓗ
This historic, one-roomed, riverside pub by the impressive town bridge has a warm and friendly atmosphere, making it a favourite meeting place for locals. The art of conversation is actively encouraged here. Many old artefacts, including pictures of old Bridgwater are on display. Up to four beer festivals are held annually, each showcasing an average of 12 real ales. Live music, usually blues, is performed on the last Saturday of the month. Evening meals are available in summer. Q◑⅃⇌♣

CANNINGTON

Malt Shovel Inn
Blackmore Lane, TA5 2NE
(off A39, E of Cannington)
❂ 11.30-3, 6.30 (7 winter)-11; 12-3, 6.30-10.30 (not winter eve) Sun
☎ (01278) 653432 website: www.cannington.org.uk
Butcombe Bitter; Exmoor Fox; guest beers Ⓗ
In this Guide since 1985, this 300-year-old free house lies to the north of the Quantock Hills near the coast and attracts walkers and cyclists. Two guest ales are stocked. The bar area has an inglenook with woodburner; there is also a snug, a dining room, a family room (high chairs provided), a function room and a large garden. Good value, home-cooked food is served.
⚄Q➹❀◑♣♣P

Rose & Crown
30 High Street, TA5 2HF
❂ 12-11; 12-10.30 Sun
☎ (01278) 653190
Caledonian Deuchars IPA; Greene King IPA, Abbot, Old Speckled Hen; Ⓗ guest beers Ⓖ
Single bar with a tiled floor, warmed by a roaring fire in winter. This old-fashioned village pub dates from the 17th century. The original oak beams are covered by an interesting array of objects. The bar houses

table skittles, a pool table and numerous clocks. The garden won a Pub in Bloom award in 2002. No food is served. Two guest rooms are available. ᴹ🌼♿♣P

CHARD

Bell & Crown
Coombe Street, Crimchard, TA20 1JP
(towards Combe St Nicholas from town centre)
☼ 12-2.30 (not Mon; 12-3 Sat), 7-11; 12-3, 7-10.30 Sun
☎ (01460) 62470
Otter Bitter; guest beers Ⓗ
Converted from cottages, this pub has retained gaslighting around the bar. The beer range comes mainly from West Country brewers, but some are from further afield. During the winter months (Sept–May), a monthly beer festival of local ales, (generally held the first weekend), adds variety to the usual choice. The cider is Westons scrumpy. The food represents good value. 🌼◖♣♣P

CHEWTON MENDIP

Waldegrave Arms
High Street, BA3 4LL (on A39)
☼ 11.30-2.30, 6-11; 12-10.30 Sun
☎ (01761) 241384
website: www.waldegravearms.co.uk
Butcombe Bitter; Courage Best Bitter; guest beers Ⓗ
This excellent free house stands on the edge of the Mendips. Until 100 years ago it was part of the Waldegrave estate, as was most of the area. It is very strong on darts (five teams and many cups) and quiz teams. The lounge has a no-smoking area (priority is given to diners); a wide range of food is served (supper licence to midnight for diners). Two local guest beers and an award-winning garden add to its appeal. Try the informative website. Q🌼♿◖🖵♣P✂

CHURCHILL

Crown Inn
The Batch, Skinners Lane, BS25 5PP
(S of A38/A369 jct)
☼ 11.30-11; 12-10.30 Sun
☎ (01934) 852995
Draught Bass; Bath SPA; Hop Back GFB; Palmer IPA; RCH PG Steam; guest beers Ⓖ
This multi-roomed, stone-floored building can be mistaken for a cottage. Two log fires heat both halves of the pub, which was local CAMRA's Pub of the Year in 1999. At least two guest beers and Rich's cider are available in this free house. Local produce is used where possible for the home-cooked lunches. Popular with walkers visiting the nearby Dolebury Warren, part of the Mendips, it is also handy for the Avon Ski Centre (dry ski slope). ᴹQ🌼◖Å♣P

CLAPTON-IN-GORDANO

Black Horse
Clevedon Lane, BS20 7RH
(5 mins from M5 jct 19) OS472739
☼ 11-2.30, 5-11; 11-11 Fri & Sat; 12-4, 7-10.30 Sun
☎ (01275) 842105
Draught Bass; Ⓗ **Courage Best Bitter; Smiles Best;** Ⓖ **Webster's Green Label;** Ⓗ **guest beer** Ⓖ
Fine traditional village local, a real community pub. This 14th-century inn

features flagstones, exposed beams and wooden settles. Look out, too, for the collections of firearms and mugs and old photos of local scenes. A single bar serves an L-shaped drinking area. The garden is suitable for children. Thatchers cider is stocked and bar snacks are available Monday–Saturday lunchtime. Difficult to find – ring for directions if required. ᴹQ🌼♿P

COMPTON MARTIN

Ring O' Bells
Bath Road, BS40 6JE
☼ 11.30-3, 6.30-11; 12-3, 7-10.30 Sun
☎ (01761) 221284
Butcombe Bitter, Gold; Wadworth 6X; guest beer Ⓗ
Owned by Butcombe Brewery, this is very much a pub for everyone. It has an excellent family room, a lovely garden – ideal for balmy summer days – and a varied menu to suit all tastes at reasonable prices. One room houses traditional games, including the popular table skittles. A former local CAMRA Pub of the Year, this has been a Guide regular for many years. With very pleasant countryside close by, it is always worth a visit. ᴹQ👶🌼◖Å♣P✂

CONGRESBURY

Plough
High Street, BS49 5JA (off A370)
☼ 11-3, 4.30-11; 11-11 Sat; 12-10.30 Sun
☎ (01934) 832475 website: www.plough-inn.co.uk
Draught Bass; Ⓟ **Butcombe Bitter;** Ⓗ **Worthington's Bitter; guest beers** Ⓟ
Friendly pub, well-used by local clubs and organisations, it is the HQ of the Mendip morris men. Sunday is quiz night and there is a boules court in the garden for summer use. Local Thatchers cider is available. No meals are served other than rolls and sandwiches at lunchtime, with the result that the pub is very dog-friendly and the landlord concentrates on providing quality cask beers for his discerning customers. Buses serve Congresbury from Bristol and Weston-Super-Mare. ᴹ🌼Å♣P

CORTON DENHAM

Queen's Arms
DT9 4LR (3 miles from A303, S of Sparkford)
☼ 12-2.30, 7-11; 12-3 Sun
☎ (01963) 220317
Cheriton Best Bitter; Cotleigh Tawny; guest beers Ⓗ
Beers from all over the country are offered at this pub that boasts one of the best selections of real ale in the area. The blackboard lists the forthcoming guests. There is also an excellent range of home-cooked meals to choose from (no food Mon). The pub is situated in ideal walking country and makes a superb base for outings as bed and breakfast accommodation is available. ᴹQ🌼🛏◖🖵♣P

CROWCOMBE

Carew Arms ☆
TA4 4AD
(signed from A358, between Taunton and Williton)
☼ 12-3, 6-11; 12-3, 7-10.30 Sun
☎ (01984) 618631 website: www.carewarms.co.uk

Exmoor Ale; guest beers Ⓗ

Unspoilt village pub, forgotten by time. The public bar retains all its olde-worlde charm in its original features. The rear bar is equipped with comfortable seating. Well-cooked, wholesome meals are offered at reasonable prices. A good centre for exploring the Quantock Hills, the West Somerset Railway is nearby. On CAMRA's National Inventory of pubs with interiors of outstanding interest, the Carew is well worth a visit.
🏚Q❀◑ ⊖P

CULMHEAD

Holman Clavel

TA3 7EA (5 miles S of Taunton)
🕑 12-3, 5-11; 12-11 Tue, Thu & Sat; 12-3, 7-10.30 Sun
☎ (01823) 421432

Butcombe Bitter, Gold; guest beers Ⓗ

This country inn, dating from the 14th century, is the only pub with this unusual name in England. The name refers to a 'clavel', which is the lintel or beam above the fireplace, made of holm oak. The pub is reputedly haunted by the ghost of a defrocked monk. Home-cooked meals specialise in local fish and game. Guest beers are often from Hop Back and Church End. 🏚Q❀◑ Å♣P

DINNINGTON

Dinnington Docks

TA17 8SX (approx. 3 miles E of Ilminster, off Crewkerne road) OS404132
🕑 11.30-3.30, 6-11; 12-4, 7-10.30 Sun
☎ (01460) 52397

Butcombe Bitter; Wadworth 6X; guest beers Ⓗ

An official name change occurred in 2002, from the Rose & Crown to Dinnington Docks. This old pub is popular with the friendly locals, who support regular charity functions. The bar area is decorated with old transport pictures and signs. The varied menu offers a curry night (Tue), a steak night (Wed) and a roast lunch every day. Outside, the large garden has a children's play area; families, dogs – all are welcome. Burrow Hill cider is stocked.
🏚Q⌂❀◑ ♣●P

DOULTING

Abbey Barn Inn

BA4 4QD
🕑 12-2.30, 6-11; 12-2.30, 7-10.30 Sun
☎ (01749) 880321

Draught Bass; Oakhill Best Bitter; guest beers Ⓗ

Having separate public and lounge bars, together with a skittle alley allows the pub to cater for a mixed trade. Traditional cider is sold, along with regular guest beers. Ask at the bar about the selection of snuffs to try out. The pub is thought to have been rebuilt in 1725; the name, and the medieval tithe barn opposite may point to a link with Glastonbury Abbey. Food is always available. The guest rooms are individually decorated. 🏚❀⇌◑ ⊖&♣●

DULVERTON

Rock House Inn

1 Jury Road, TA22 9DU

🕑 11-3, 6-11 (11-11 Fri & Sat in summer); 12-10.30 Sun
☎ (01398) 323131 website: www.rockhouseinn.co.uk

Draught Bass; Cotleigh Golden Eagle; guest beers Ⓗ

Once owned by Hancock's of Wiveliscombe, this lively, friendly free house stands at the top of this bustling Exmoor town. Built on the side of a rockface, it was first licensed in 1837. The locals tend to congregate in the single bar, which adjoins the lounge area and no-smoking family room. The guest beer is always reasonably priced and often comes from Butcombe Brewery; the cider is Rich's. Look out for the cabinet of curios as you enter. 🏚⌂⇌◑ Å♣●⅄

EAST HARPTREE

Castle of Comfort

BA40 6DD
(on B3134, between Wells and Burrington)
🕑 12-3, 6-11; 12-10.30 Sun
☎ (01761) 221321

Draught Bass; Butcombe Bitter; guest beers Ⓗ

At the top of the Mendip Hills, the pub is just five minutes' drive from the famous Cheddar Gorge and Chew Valley Lake. Dating from the 17th-century, it used to provide refreshments to prisoners on their way to being hanged nearby, in Judge Jeffreys' time. Excellent food is served in generous portions, and a real cider (Thatchers) is available. Children welcome; a big fenced-in field, behind, has a play area. Up to three guest beers are usually on tap. 🏚❀◑ ♣●P

EAST LYNG

Rose & Crown

TA3 5AU (on A361, 6 miles E of Taunton)
🕑 11-2.30, 6.30-11; 12-3, 7-10.30 Sun
☎ (01823) 698235

Butcombe Bitter, Gold; Palmer 200 Ⓗ

The timeless quality of this 13th-century coaching inn is enhanced by comfortable antique furniture and a large stone fireplace where a log fire burns in winter. The no-smoking dining room features old oak beams and an inglenook. Meals are also served in the large bar area; a varied menu includes vegetarian dishes and other home-cooked meals (booking recommended at weekends). The attractive garden is a pleasant spot to enjoy the local ales.
🏚❀⇌◑ &♣P

EAST WOODLANDS

Horse & Groom

BA11 5LY (1 mile S of A361/B3092 jct)
🕑 11.30-2.30 (not Mon), 6.30-11; 12-3, 7-10.30 Sun
☎ (01373) 462802

Branscombe Vale Branoc; Butcombe Bitter; Wadworth 6X; guest beer Ⓖ

Attractive pub and pleasant garden tucked away down a narrow country lane on the edge of Longleat estate. An open fire, flagstone floor and comfortable settles characterise the public bar where games are played. The ale range seldom varies as 'our regulars like them' but Czech Budvar on draught gives variety. The lounge bar, conservatory and restaurant cater for diners (no meals Sun eve). An imaginative menu uses, where possible, local ingredients, with food freshly cooked to order. All bread is made on the premises. ⚲Q✿⚓◑⌂♣P

EXFORD

White Horse Inn
TA24 7PY (by bridge over River Exe)
✪ 11-11; 12-10.30 Sun
☎ (01643) 831229
Exmoor Ale, Gold; Marston's Pedigree (summer); **guest beers** Ⓗ
Ivy-clad hotel at the heart of Exmoor, popular with both locals and visitors. The Dalesman Bar is cosy and compact, while the Tap Bar is larger with rustic settles, benches and tables for dining. See the collection of photographs of Exmoor, which were mostly taken by the landlord. An excellent Sunday carvery includes local venison in season. In the summer, enjoy a pint outside by the River Exe. ⚲✿⚓◑Ä P

FAULKLAND

Tucker's Grave ☆
BA3 5XF (on A366, 1 mile E of village)
✪ 11-3, 6-11; 12-3, 7-10.30 Sun
☎ (01373) 834230
Draught Bass; Butcombe Bitter Ⓗ
This is a real classic and was voted local CAMRA Pub of the Year 2002; a genuine country local that has not changed in many years (apart from new loos). The regulars are a friendly lot who enjoy the local cider. The beers are kept in barrels in the bay window in the tiny middle room, from where the landlady will serve you. You can then take it to the comfortable parlour or the settle-lined snug across the hall. Out the back is a pretty garden where you can admire the amazing roofline of this ancient pub. Tucker, by the way, hanged himself nearby. ⚲Q✿♣P

FROME

Griffin Inn
Milk Street, BA11 3DB
✪ 5-11; 5-10.30 Sun
☎ (01373) 467766
website: www.milkstreetbrewery.co.uk
Milk Street Gulp, Nick's, seasonal beers Ⓗ
The Griffin, situated in the older part of Frome, has been sympathetically renovated by the present owners, Milk Street Brewery. A small brewhouse was constructed in the former function room to produce a wide range of good quality ales. The beers on sale in The Griffin, depend on what has been brewed recently. The single bar has retained many original features, open fires, etched glass windows and wood floors, giving a basic but very popular pub. Unusually, African food is available on Wednesday. Note, the pub is open evenings only. ⚲Q✿◑⇌♣PⓊ

HALSE

New Inn
TA4 3AF (off B3227, signed from A358) OS142280
✪ 12-2.30, 6-11; 12-2.30, 7-10.30 Sun
☎ (01823) 432352 website: www.newinnhalse.co.uk
Bishops Somerset Ale; guest beers Ⓗ
This free house is a typical village inn, dating from the 17th century. There is a

woodburner and old oak beams feature in the quiet, cosy bar. Three or four ales are served, coming from local and other micro-breweries. The no-smoking candlelit dining room has high chairs available and serves delicious, home-cooked food. The large skittle alley doubles as a function room. The inn is popular with visitors to the West Somerset Railway, 1^1/$_2$ miles away. Bottled beers and carry-outs are available. A micro-brewery is planned. ⚲Q⚘✿⚓◑♣P

HARDINGTON MOOR

Royal Oak (Sonny's)
Moor Lane, BA22 9NW
(take Hardington Mandeville road from A30)
✪ 12-2.30 (not Mon), 7 (6 Fri & Sat)-11; 12-2.30, 7-10.30 Sun
☎ (01935) 862354 website: www.sonnysroyaloak.co.uk
Branscombe Vale Branoc; Butcombe Bitter; guest beers Ⓗ
The pub's nickname comes from a previous landlord. Situated some four miles west of Yeovil, this former farmhouse is notable for its hanging baskets. Inside, the open-plan bar offers a friendly welcome and a good range of food (not served Mon). The present landlord is a keen biker and welcomes motorcyclists. An annual beer festival is held in May. Two parrots preside over proceedings here. ⚲Q✿◑♣♠P

HENSTRIDGE

Bird in Hand
2 Ash Walk, BA8 0RA (100 yds off A30/A357)
✪ 11-2.30, 5.30-11; 11-11 Sat; 12-3, 7-10.30 Sun
☎ (01963) 362255
Draught Bass; guest beers Ⓗ
An old stone-walled pub, it is cosy in winter with fires in the bar, and cool in summer. It caters for all, with its skittle alley/function room and games room which are separate from the main bar. Bass is the favoured real ale, but landlords, Tony and Mark, continually rotate guest ales, bringing back old favourites from time to time. This is not a restaurant but do try one of the excellent bar snacks. ⚲Q✿◑♿♣♠P

HIGHBRIDGE

Cooper's Arms
Market Street, TA9 3BD (by station)
✪ 11-3.30, 5-11; 11-11 Fri & Sat; 12-4, 7.30-10.30 Sun
☎ (01278) 783562
Fuller's London Pride; RCH East Street Cream, Double Header, seasonal beers; guest beers Ⓗ
This large pub is unusual in having a skittle alley within the bar area, which makes it popular for fundraising events and league games. Most guest beers are 5% ABV or over, due to demand. One lounge area is quiet, while another houses a large-screen TV for sporting events. A cosy atmosphere is enhanced by subtle lighting and exposed beams. Occasionally, RCH brews ales exclusively for this pub, so keep an eye on the blackboards. Q✿⊟Ä⇌♣P

HINTON BLEWITT

Ring o' Bells
BS18 5AN (between A37 and A368 on hill above Bishop Sutton) OS594570

✪ 11-3.30, 5 (6 Sat)-11; 12-3.30, 7-10.30 Sun
☎ (01761) 452239 website: www.ringobells.net
Wadworth 6X; guest beers Ⓗ
Located in a maze of minor roads between
Bishop Sutton and Temple Cloud, this
hilltop village inn benefits from views of
Chew Valley. A small, friendly local, it is set
back from the village green; the entrance is
through a yard with outside tables.
Enjoying a good reputation for its food, it is
popular in summer with ramblers and
cyclists. Children (and dogs) are welcome.
This regular Guide entry supports many
sports teams.
🏚Q❀◑Å♣🛏P

HINTON ST GEORGE

Lord Poulett Arms
High Street, TA17 8SE
✪ 12-2.30 (not Mon; 12-3 Sat); 6.30 (7 Mon)-11;
12-3, 7-10.30 Sun
☎ (01460) 73149 website: www.lordpoulettarms.co.uk
Butcombe Bitter; Ⓗ **guest beers** Ⓖ
This hamstone inn is set in a picturesque
conservation village. The real ale stillage is
behind an L-shaped bar, serving both the
lounge and public bars. A range of bottle-
conditioned beers is stocked. Food, from bar
snacks to full meals, is prepared by a
professional chef (eve meals Tue–Sat). Bed
and breakfast accommodation is in four
double bedrooms, all en-suite. The secluded
garden contains the remains of a pelota wall
built during the Napoleonic Wars, which is
now a listed monument.
🏚Q❀🛏◑🍽♣🛏P⨰

HORSINGTON

Half Moon
BA8 0EF (200 yds off A357, between Wincanton
and Templecombe)
✪ 12-2.30 (3 Sat), 6-11; 12-3, 7-10.30 Sun
☎ (01963) 370140
Beer range varies Ⓗ
Old stone pub, gently slumbering in
pleasant Blackmore Vale countryside. Over
the years, the present owners have gradually
increased the range of ales until now there
are up to six on tap at any one time. These
range from local products such as Hobden's,
Milk Street and Hop Back, to the more
distant, for example Wadworth, RCH, Quay
and Church End. A beer festival held in
May each year offers a choice of 20 or so
ales. 🏚Q⛄❀🛏◑🍽♣🛏P

HUISH EPISCOPI

Rose & Crown (Eli's)
Wincanton Road, TA10 9QT
(on A372, 1 mile E of Langport)
✪ 11.30-2.30, 5.30-11; 11.30-11 Fri & Sat;
12-10.30 Sun
☎ (01458) 250494
Teignworthy Beachcomber; guest beers Ⓗ
This 17th-century thatched inn (locally
known as Eli's) has been in the same
family for several generations, preserving
its original and unusual character. The
drinks are served from a flagstoned tap
room. Farmhouse cider is drawn from
wooden barrels. Good home-cooked food
is available at lunchtime and early
evening. Unlike many pubs with one large
bar, this one has several small, cosy rooms

where locals and visitors can drink and
chat. Skittles, darts and pool are played
here. Q⛄❀◑🍽🛏♣🛏P

KELSTON

Old Crown
Bath Road, BA1 9AQ (on A431, 3 miles from Bath)
✪ 11.30-2.30, 5-11; 11.30-11 Sat; 12-10.30 Sun
☎ (01225) 423032
**Draught Bass; Bath Gem; Butcombe Bitter; Gold;
Wadworth 6X** Ⓗ
Superb, low-ceilinged, 18th-century
coaching inn. Owned by Butcombe
Brewery, it features a flagstone floor and
church pew seats; note the old beer engine
in the main bar. A friendly atmosphere and
competitively-priced, home-cooked food
make this a busy, popular pub with a small
restaurant (eve meals Tue–Sat). No children
under 14 are admitted. There is a large,
attractive garden at the rear, and a roadside
drinking area; the car park lies across a busy
road. 🏚Q❀🛏◑P

KEYNSHAM

Lock Keeper
Keynsham Road, BS31 2DD
(opp. Cadbury's factory)
✪ 11-11; 12-10.30 Sun
☎ (0117) 986 2383
**Smiles Best; Young's Bitter, Special,
seasonal beers** Ⓗ
This 350-year-old former lock-keeper's
house stands on its own island between the
river and the Kennet and Avon Canal. A
refurbishment in 2003 has extended the
dining facilities, but the pub's original
drinking areas remain unchanged. Within
five minutes of the Bristol–Bath cycle path,
it caters for both locals and passing trade.
An extensive menu includes changing daily
specials; meals are served all day until
9.30pm, at the weekend. The garden houses
a petanque pitch. ❀◑≈♣P

KINGSBURY EPISCOPI

Wyndham Arms
TA12 6AT
✪ 12-3, 6.30-11; 12-3, 7-10.30 Sun
☎ (01935) 823239 website: www.wyndhamarms.com
**Fuller's London Pride; Worthington's Bitter;
guest beers** Ⓗ
Pleasing old hamstone inn, with open fire,
flagstone floor and original beams. It has
remained unaltered for many a year. The
friendly ambience is enhanced by a good
mix of customers, often including visiting
walkers and cyclists. A good range of food is
available at all sessions. The two guest beers
are likely to be from Glastonbury, Otter or
Teignworthy; local Burrow Hill cider is
stocked. The thriving Wyndham Blues &
Roots Club is based in a large upstairs room.
🏚❀◑♣🛏P

LANGPORT

Old Custom House
Bow Street, TA10 9PQ
✪ 12-2.30 (not Mon), 4.30-11 (12-11 summer
Fri & Sat); 12-3.30, 7-10.30 Sun
☎ (01458) 250332
Beer range varies Ⓗ
Two-bar town pub, offering three real ales,

mostly from West Country breweries and always one from Teignworthy; usually an average and a higher ABV beer are stocked. The menu features a hot daily special and other freshly-cooked local produce (eve meals Tue–Sat). A secluded garden, with a barbecue area, leads to a free car park. Cycle hire, with access to the River Parrett Trail, is available nearby. An August beer festival is usually held over the bank holiday weekend. Q ✿ ◑ ⊟ ♣ P

LOWER ODCOMBE

Masons Arms
41 Lower Odcombe, BA22 8TX
(off old Yeovil-Montacute road)
✪ 12.30-3 (not Mon or Tue), 7-11; 12-11 Sat; 12-3, 7-10.30 Sun
☎ (01935) 862591
Butcombe Bitter; Odcombe Lower, Higher, seasonal beers; guest beer Ⓗ
Unpretentious village local – the only outlet for Odcombe Ales. The brewery is within this pleasing old hamstone and thatch inn and the landlord will usually host impromptu brewery tours on request. Food, which is only served on Thursday and Friday evenings and Sunday lunchtime, includes an authentic curry on Thursday, fish and chips on Friday and roast lunches on Sunday, often using home-grown produce. Free range eggs are for sale here. A festival of interesting beers is held in September. Taunton traditional cider is on handpump.
✿ ⊨ ◑ Å ♣ ♠ P

MIDDLEZOY

George Inn
42 Main Road, TA7 0NN
(1 mile from A372/A361 jct) OS378327
✪ 12-2.30 (not Mon), 7-11; 12-3, 7-11 Sat; 12-3, 7-10.30 Sun
☎ (01823) 698215
Butcombe Bitter; guest beers Ⓗ
17th-century village pub, replete with oak beams, stone flags and a log fire, located on the Somerset Levels. Home-cooked food is served (eve meals Tue–Sat) and there is always an excellent selection of cask ales, with regular appearances by favourites such as Hop Back, Otter, Eccleshall, Church End and Moor. Over 500 different ales have been offered in the last five years – a beer festival 365 days a year. The George was Somerset CAMRA's Pub of the Year 2000.
♨ Q ✿ ⊨ ◑ ♣ P ⌿

MINEHEAD

Old Ship Aground
Quay Street, TA24 5UL (next to harbour)
✪ 11-11; 12-10.30 Sun
☎ (01643) 702087
Courage Best Bitter; Greene King Ruddles County; St Austell Dartmoor Best, Tribute Ⓗ
Victorian-era pub in the old part of Minehead. The public bar, overlooking the harbour, is full of character and has a real fire. This is where you will find the locals and the pool table. Next door is a large dining/drinking area. The exposed beams bear dozens of travellers' chalked messages. Maritime photos and a collection of old Somerset beer labels are also on display.

Folk nights are staged once a month. Parking can be difficult.
♨ ⌂ ✿ ⊨ ◑ ♠ Å ⇌ (W Somerset Rlwy) ♣ P

Queen's Head Inn
Holloway Street, TA24 5NR (off the parade)
✪ 12-3, 6.30-11; 12-3, 6.30-10.30 Sun
☎ (01643) 702940
Draught Bass; Exmoor Gold, Hart; Greene King IPA; guest beer (summer) Ⓗ
Comfortable, popular town pub in a small side street off the main thoroughfare. Inside, there is a large, single bar with plenty of room, while a raised area doubles as a dining and family space. An area for games is to the rear. Pine furniture and old photos of Minehead feature in the decor. Beers are kept in a traditional brick-floored cellar and served at the optimum temperature. ◑ Å ⇌ (W Somerset Rlwy) ♣ ⌿

NETHER STOWEY

Rose & Crown
St Mary's Street, TA5 1LJ
✪ 12-11; 12-5, 7-10.30 Sun
☎ (01278) 732265
Beer range varies Ⓗ
This 16th-century coaching inn lies at the centre of this lovely village at the foot of the Quantock Hills. An ideal base for walkers, the pub enjoys a strong local following which ensures a good turnover of beers, many of which are from local breweries. The restaurant, open Wednesday–Saturday, serves home-cooked meals using home-grown produce. Coleridge Cottage can be found nearby, together with other local places of interest. Q ✿ ⊨ ◑ ⊟ ♣ ♠

NORTH PETHERTON

Globe Inn
High Street, TA6 6NQ
(100 yds W of A38 in old part of village)
✪ 12 (11 Mon & Fri)-11; 12-10.30 Sun
☎ (01278) 662999
Butcombe Bitter; Fuller's London Pride; Ⓗ
guest beers Ⓖ
A warm welcome awaits the visitor to this recently refurbished traditional pub situated among some of the oldest buildings in the village. Photographs of bygone days, often referred to by the friendly locals, hang on the bar room walls. Outside are a patio and children's play area. Euchre and skittles are played here and a selection of real cider completes the scene in this genuine Somerset local, the like of which is now only rarely found. Q ✿ ♣ ♠ P

NORTON FITZWARREN

Cross Keys
Minehead Road, TA2 6NR
(at A358/B3227 jct, W of Taunton)
✪ 11-11; 12-10.30 Sun
☎ (01823) 333062
Courage Best Bitter, Directors; guest beers Ⓗ
Large Chef & Brewer pub where the guest beer changes at least twice a week. The wide-ranging menu is complemented by specials created by the pub's talented chefs. An extensive wine list is also available. The pub dates from 1860 and a large garden at the side and rear offers a very pleasant drinking area. The pub seats over 120, and

extends a warm, friendly welcome to all. A good bus service runs from Taunton seven days a week; the stop is outside the pub. ♨✿◑P

NORTON ST PHILIP

Fleur de Lys
BA2 7LG
🕐 11-3, 5-11; 11-11 Sat; 12-3, 7-10.30 Sun
☎ (01373) 834333
Butcombe Bitter; Wadworth IPA, 6X Ⓗ
This ancient stone building has been extensively but sympathetically refurbished. The repositioned bar is on the site of the old passageway, through which the pub ghost reputedly passes on his way to the gallows in the rear garden! Licensed since 1584, the inn has welcomed Queen Anne, wife of James I, and Samuel Pepys. Very good value, tasty food is served. Opposite is the medieval George Inn, an ale house since 1323. ♨Q☎◑♣P

PITMINSTER

Queen's Arms
TA3 7AZ (between Corfe and Blagdon Hill)
🕐 11-11; 12-10.30 Sun
☎ (01823) 421529
Butcombe Bitter, Gold; Cotleigh Tawny; Otter Bitter Ⓗ
Friendly village local boasting stone walls, genuine oak beams and a wood-burning stove. Parts of the building date from 1036 when it was the earliest recorded watermill in the area – at one time the miller doubled as the publican. The small, cosy bar usually stocks three local ales, plus an occasional guest. The restaurant areas offer a wide range of home-cooked food, specialising in seafood. ♨Q☎✿◑🍴♣P✕

PITNEY

Halfway House
Pitney Hill, TA10 9AB (on B3153)
🕐 11.30-3, 5.30-11; 12-3.30, 7-10.30 Sun
☎ (01458) 252513
Branscombe Vale BVB; Butcombe Bitter; Hop Back Crop Circle, Summer Lightning; Teignworthy Reel Ale; guest beers Ⓖ
Village pub serving a wide variety of local ales, Hecks cider and an expanding international bottled beer selection. No juke box or games machines detract from the buzz of conversation. Flagstone floors make it ideal for walkers' boots. An excellent choice of home-cooked curries is served in the evening, other food at lunchtimes (no food Sun). Somerset CAMRA's Pub of the Year 1995, 1997, 2001, 2003 and national CAMRA Pub of the Year 1996, it is a real gem. Bus No. 54, Taunton–Yeovil, stops outside. Children are welcome here. ♨Q✿◑🍴♣P

PORTISHEAD

Windmill Inn
58 Nore Road, BS20 6JZ
🕐 11-11; 12-10.30 Sun
☎ (01275) 843677
Draught Bass; Butcombe Gold; Courage Best Bitter; RCH Pitchfork; guest beer Ⓗ
This free house on the coast road affords lovely views over the Severn estuary to Wales, and the second Severn crossing. The

pub is on three levels; the lower one is a no-smoking family room. A heavy emphasis on food has led to a reputation for quality and value. Meals are served 12–9 (9.30 Fri and Sat). A strong supporter of local award-winning RCH Brewery, the pub also sells Thatchers cider. It is a good venue for walkers, families and just about anyone! Q☎✿◑&♣P

PRIDDY

Hunter's Lodge Inn
BA5 3AR OSST5250
🕐 11.30-2.30, 6.30-11; 12-2, 7-10.30 Sun
☎ (01749) 672275
Butcombe Bitter, Gold; Exmoor Ale Ⓖ
Isolated on a crossroads about a mile from Priddy village, the inn is often frequented by cavers, potholers and walkers. A real 'time warp' of three rooms, it features an old oven in the main bar and barrels of beer lining the wall behind the bar. The current landlord has been at the helm for 33 years, while the pub itself dates from the end of the 18th century. The food is basic, but excellent and remarkable value. Two gardens at the back have picnic tables. ♨Q✿◑🍴♣P

ROWBERROW

Swan Inn
nr Winscombe, BS25 1QL
(off A38, ¾ mile S of A368)
🕐 12-3, 6-11; 12-3, 7-10.30 Sun
☎ (01934) 852371
Draught Bass; Butcombe Bitter, Gold; guest beer Ⓗ
Originally a farmhouse, this Butcombe pub now consists of two large, but cosy, bars warmed by open fires in winter. It is located near Black Down, the highest point on the Mendips, and is an ideal base for hillwalking, in an area of outstanding beauty. A varied menu of good quality, home-cooked dishes makes the Swan a popular destination for diners. A large, well-landscaped garden opposite offers fine views of Dolebury Hill Fort to the north. ♨Q✿◑P

ST GEORGES

Woolpack
Shepherds Way, BS22 7XE
(near M5 jct 21, off A370 to Weston-Super-Mare)
🕐 12-3, 6-11; 12-3, 7-10.30 Sun
☎ (01934) 521670
Beer range varies Ⓗ
Welcoming, 17th-century former coaching house and woolpacking station, it now comprises two bar areas and a dining area, plus a large function room with a skittle alley. Four real ales are always on offer. Somerset breweries such as RCH and Cottage are regularly featured, as well as award-winning beers from around the UK. The pub enjoys a good reputation for its interesting, varied menu. ♨✿◑⇌ (Worle) ♣P

SALTFORD

Bird in Hand
58 High Street, BS31 3EJ
🕐 11-3 (3.30 Sat), 6-11; 12-4, 6-10.30 Sun

☎ (01225) 873335
Abbey Bellringer; Draught Bass; Courage Best Bitter; Moles Tap Bitter Ⓗ
Fine country pub in a very pleasant setting near the River Avon in the older part of Saltford. The Bristol–Bath cycle track runs adjacent to the car park and is also good for walks. Home-cooked food is served at reasonable prices in the no-smoking conservatory dining section. Children are welcome in the small family area. The garden has a small pond and a petanque pitch. Thatchers cider is stocked.
❀◖ὀ♣♣P✗

SANDYWAY

Sportsman's Inn
EX36 3LU (on road between Withypool and North Molton) OS793332
✪ 12-3 (not Mon), 6.30-11; 12-3, 7-10.30 Sun
☎ (01643) 831109 website: www.sportsmans.co.uk
Exmoor Ale, Fox; Ⓗ **guest beers** Ⓗ /Ⓖ
High up on Exmoor, the Sportsman's Inn lies in a small hamlet on the road between Withypool and North Molton. Converted from two cottages in the mid-1800s, it affords superb views of the moors. Inside, it features heavy wood beams, two inglenooks at either side of the roomy bar and dining area, and an old well in the bar. Beers tend to come from Exmoor Brewery and food is supplied by local producers. Hancock's cider is served.
⚔Q❀🛏◖♣P

SEAVINGTON ST MICHAEL

Volunteer Inn
TA19 0QE (3 miles E of Ilminster)
✪ 12-2.30, 6.30-11; 12-2.30, 7-10.30 Sun
☎ (01460) 240126
Beer range varies Ⓗ
Traditional, two-bar, village pub with low beams. It has been recently refurbished but retains all its character. A warm welcome is guaranteed to all. St Austell beers are regularly served as part of the varying guest list. Good value meals, to suit all pockets, are offered at all sessions. A selection of malt whiskies is stocked.
⚔Q❀🛏◖♣♣P✗

SOUTH PETHERTON

Brewer's Arms ⊘
18 St James Street, TA13 5BV
(½ mile off A303)
✪ 11.30-2.30, 6-11; 12-10.30 Sun
☎ (01460) 241887
Otter Bitter; Worthington's Bitter; guest beers Ⓗ
Just off the A303, this 17th-century coaching inn is at the centre of a beautiful hamstone village. Guest beers change regularly and real cider is served. A beer festival is staged on the late May bank holiday weekend, while August bank holiday sees a Somerset beer and cider festival. The restaurant boasts an 18th-century bread oven. A courtyard and new garden are ideal for fine weather drinking. A free public car park is 100 yards away. Somerset CAMRA Pub of the Year 1999.
⚔🍂❀🛏◖Å♣♣

TAUNTON

Hankridge Arms ⊘
Hankridge Way, Riverside, TA1 2LR
(in retail park, off M5, jct 25)
✪ 11-11; 12-10.30 Sun
☎ (01823) 444405
Badger Best, Tanglefoot, seasonal beers or guest beers Ⓗ
This Grade I listed former farmhouse, with carefully renovated original features, such as inglenooks, flagstones, exposed timbers and a priest's hole, dates from the 16th century. The single bar provides ample seating for both drinking and eating, and there is a separate restaurant. Good value meals are all home cooked using fresh ingredients. Guest beers are from Hall & Woodhouse's King & Barnes range, or the Gribble Brewery.
⚔❀◖ὀÅP

Harpoon Louies
75 Station Road, TA1 1PB (near station)
✪ 6-11 (11.30 diners); 7-10.30 Sun
☎ (01823) 324404
Otter Ale; guest beers Ⓗ
Friendly bar/restaurant where up to four real ales are sourced from micro-breweries, both local and from further afield. The subtly-lit restaurant is on split levels, with wood floors and stone walls; as well as the restaurant menu, a good range of bar meals is served at reasonable prices. Close to the cricket ground, it is a favourite haunt of fans. There is always lively conversation at the bar, where a variety of games are available. ◖⇌♣

Masons Arms
Magdelene Street, TA1 1SG
(by St Mary's Church)
✪ 10.30-3, 5-11; 10.30-11 Sat; 12-4,
(closed eve) Sun
☎ (01823) 288916
website: www.masonsarms.freeuk.com
Otter Bitter; guest beers Ⓗ
Traditional, town-centre free house with a convivial atmosphere. This pub dates back to 1809 and has an interesting history, which Taunton's longest-serving licensee will be happy to relate. The three or four beers on tap are kept in excellent condition, partly due to the cellar within the stone foundations, directly below the bar. An interesting menu, including grillstone steaks, is complemented by a good wine list. Somerset CAMRA's Pub of the Year 2002.
Q❀🛏◖♣P

Wyvern Club
Mountfields Road, TA1 3BJ
(off B3170 towards Corfe)
✪ 7-11; 12-2.30, 7-10.30 Sun
☎ (01823) 284591
Exmoor Ale; guest beers Ⓗ
This busy sports and social club serves evening meals, bar snacks and Sunday lunches. Guest beers are often from local micro-breweries or further afield. Refurbished early in 2003, the club has a warm and friendly atmosphere. The bar also opens when cricket, football or rugby is played at home. The spacious function room and skittle alley are for hire. Show this Guide or CAMRA membership card for entry to the region's Club of the Year 2002.
🛏❀◖ὀ♣P

WANSTROW

Pub
Station Road, BA4 4SZ
✪ 12-2.30 (not Mon; 12-3 Fri & Sat), 6-11;
12-3, 7-10.30 Sun
☎ (01749) 850455
**Blindmans Mine Beer; Greene King IPA; Hop Back
Entire Stout; Ⓗ guest beers Ⓖ**
A gem; friendly village local where the cosy
lounge bar with open fire and flagstone
floors leads to a small restaurant. The public
bar, also having an open fire, offers three
guest beers on gravity, while the three
regulars are kept on handpump, along with
two farmhouse ciders. The guest beers
change on a regular basis. A skittle alley
leads off the public bar. A small but very
imaginative menu is offered, all food is
home made. Well worth a visit.
🚶Q🅰🅳🅳🅳♣🍽P

WATCHET

Star Inn
Mill Lane, TA23 0BZ
(200 yds from harbour, on Blue Anchor road)
✪ 12-3.30, 7-11; 12-3.30, 7-10.30 Sun
☎ (01984) 631367
Beer range varies Ⓗ
Converted from three cottages built in
1680, a warm, welcoming atmosphere is
enhanced by the low ceilings. Good food is
served in the bar or dining room, where
children are welcome. Close to the sea,
there is public parking within 100 yards;
West Somerset Railway is five minutes'
walk. A recent addition is the attached
cottage providing accommodation. An
extensive garden lies behind the pub. Guest
ales, changed regularly, place an emphasis
on local beers.
🚶Q🅱🅰🅳🅳🅳⇌ (W Somerset Rlwy)

WATERROW

Rock Inn
TA4 2AX
(on B3227, between Wiveliscombe and Bampton)
✪ 11-2.30, 6-11; 12-3, 7-10.30 Sun
☎ (01984) 623293
Cotleigh Tawny, Barn Owl; Exmoor Fox Ⓗ
The inn is set against a rock face that forms
the rear wall of part of the bar area. It has a
public-style bar at one end, the lounge and
restaurant at the other. Home-cooked food
is based on local produce, and draught local
cider (Sheppys) is sold in summer. The
games room offers darts and pool. The pub
benefits from a beautiful location in a
valley, with the river running below.
🚶Q🅰🅳🅳🅳♣🍽P✆

WELLINGTON

Cottage Inn
31 Champford Lane, TA21 8BH
✪ 11-3, 6-11; 12-4, 7-10.30 Sun
☎ (01823) 664650
**Bishops Somerset Ale; Fuller's London Pride; Otter
Bitter; guest beer Ⓗ**
Friendly local, with limited parking, just off
the main street, near the Wellesley Cinema
and Theatre. The bar is divided by a large
chimney breast into a public-style area, with
pool table and darts, and a lounge bar area.
The lounge features brass knick-knacks,

black beams, pictures and old maps. Home
to darts and skittles and a carnival club, there is
usually someone to chat with. 🅰🅳🅳🅳🅰♣P

WELLOW

Fox & Badger
Railway Lane, BA2 8QG
✪ 11.30-3.30, 6-11; 11.30-11 Fri & Sat;
12-10.30 Sun
☎ (01225) 832293 website: www.foxandbadger.co.uk
**Badger K&B Sussex Best; Draught Bass; Butcombe
Bitter Ⓗ**
Cosy, two-bar, 16th-century pub at the
village centre. Unusually, the public bar has
wood floors, while the lounge has
flagstones. There is a skittle alley at the rear.
A long-term guest beer is usually on for
some months. An extensive and good value
menu of traditional and more unusual
dishes is served; the landlord specialises in
top-notch ploughmans lunches. Parking
can be difficult. 🚶🅱🅰🅳🅳🅳♣🍽

WELLS

City Arms
69 High Street, BA5 2AG
✪ 10-11; 12-10.30 Sun
☎ (01749) 673916
Butcombe Bitter, Gold; Palmer IPA; guest beers Ⓗ
In a cobbled courtyard, part of this splendid
old city-centre pub used to be the city jail.
One of the few bastions of real ale left in
Wells where alcopops seem to rule, the
landlord maintains an old-style hostelry,
with the emphasis on good beer and food.
The regular beers include a dark offering in
winter, and are supported by a wide range
of guests. There is a good choice of British
bottled beers too. Food, freshly cooked, uses
local ingredients where possible. 🅱🅰🅳🅳♣🍽

WEST CRANMORE

Strode Arms
BA4 4QJ (S of A361, E of Shepton Mallet)
✪ 11.30-2.30, 6.30-11; 12-3, 7-10.30 Sun
☎ (01749) 880450
**Castle Rock Nottingham Gold; Wadworth IPA, 6X, JCB;
guest beer Ⓗ**
In an idyllic setting, in a pretty village
overlooking the duckpond, the pub stands
next to the East Somerset steam railway.
Originally a 15th-century farmhouse, a
roaring log fire, complete with railway line
fender, greets you in winter. Outside is a
comfortable terrace area. No-smoking bar
and restaurant areas are available. A varied
menu is offered, with all food made on the
premises using fresh ingredients.
🚶Q🅰🅳🅳P✆

WESTON-SUPER-MARE

Dragon Inn ⊘
15 Meadow Street, BS23 1QG
✪ 10-11; 12-10.30 Sun
☎ (01934) 621304
**Courage Directors; Shepherd Neame Spitfire;
Theakston Best Bitter; guest beers Ⓗ**
Large Wetherspoon's outlet in the usual
company format, displaying old
photographs and snippets of interest about
the town. A wide range of guest beers is
always on offer. These can come from
anywhere in the UK but the pub is a

particularly strong supporter of Somerset breweries, with Cottage, RCH, Butcombe and Exmoor beers regularly featured. A popular pub, it is invariably busy and service is occasionally slow. Westons Old Rosie cider is served straight from the cask.
Q ✿ ⟐ ⬥ Ⓐ ⚌ ❀ ✗

Off the Rails
Station Approach, Station Road, BS23 1XY
✪ 10-11; 12-10.30 Sun
☎ (01934) 415109
Beer range varies ℍ
Located on the station platform, this venue comprises one large room, divided into a bar area and a station buffet. The bar usually has at least two ales available, mostly from West Country breweries. Branscombe Vale, Sharp's and the local RCH breweries are particular favourites of the landlord, who is happy to source beers requested by customers. Children are welcome in the buffet area of this small, friendly hostelry. Ⓐ ⚌

WINSCOMBE

Winscombe Club
Sandford Road, BS25 1HD
✪ 11-2.30, 6.30-11; 12-3, 7-10.30 Sun
☎ (01934) 842624
Theakston XB; Wickwar BOB; guest beer ℍ
This village social club was awarded the local CAMRA Club of the Year award in 2002. Various activities take place, including skittles, darts, pool, quiz nights and fortnightly live music. The beers are reasonably priced and local Thatchers cider is sold. CAMRA members are welcome on production of a membership card. An upstairs function room is available for hire. There is a free car park across the road. A small patio has tables for summer drinking.
✿ ♣ ❀

WINSHAM

Bell Inn
11 Church Street, TA20 4HU
✪ 12-2.30 (3 Sat; not winter Mon), 7-11; 12-3.30, 7-10.30 Sun
☎ (01460) 30677
Branscombe Vale Branoc; guest beer ℍ
Popular, two-roomed pub at the centre of the village. It comprises a large, open-plan bar and a function room where darts and skittles are played. In summer, the patio hosts many village activities. Children are welcome here. The house beer, called Newcomer, is brewed by Branscombe Vale. Good value food is served; the home-made pies are a speciality.
⌂ Q ✿ ⟐ ♣ ❀ P

WITHYPOOL

Royal Oak Inn
TA24 7QP (few yards uphill from Barle River bridge)
✪ 11-3, 6-11; 12-3, 7-10.30 Sun
☎ (01643) 831506
website: www.royaloakwithypool.co.uk
Exmoor Ale, Stag ℍ
Two-bar inn, displaying hunting and shooting memorabilia, including some amazing antlers. At the heart of Exmoor National Park, it is an ideal base for walking, riding and fishing. An excellent menu

makes use of local game and produce. Families use the top bar; Jake's Bar (named after the helpful barman) down below, is where locals gather and visitors are encouraged. Note the letter written by Eisenhower in 1944 when he stayed in the pub prior to D-Day. Bottled White Shield is available.
⌂ Q ⛺ ✿ ⟐ ⟐ ⊟ Ⓐ P

WIVELISCOMBE

Bear Inn
10 North Street, TA4 2JY (off main square)
✪ 11-11; 12-10.30 Sun
☎ (01984) 623537
Cotleigh Tawny, seasonal beers; Otter Bitter; guest beers ℍ
Friendly, former coaching inn at the town centre. This recently extended pub has a comfortable bar area with a new pool room alongside. Children are welcome in the bar area and restaurant, where good home-made food is served. Outside the large garden has an enclosed play area. The old market town of Wiveliscombe is on the old Taunton–Barnstaple road and is ideally placed for forays into Exmoor and the nearby Brendon Hills.
⌂ ⛺ ✿ ⟐ ⟐ ⬥ ♣ P

WOOKEY

Burcott Inn
Wookey Road, BA5 1NJ
(on B3139, 2 miles W of Wells)
✪ 11-2.30, 6-11; 12-3, 7-10.30 Sun
☎ (01749) 673874
Beer range varies ℍ
Deservedly popular country pub where at least two different ales are served across the copper-topped, L-shaped bar. Old pine tables, settles and a real fire help create a welcoming atmosphere. There is something for everyone here: a games room for darts, shove-ha'penny and cribbage competitions (every Thu); an excellent menu, including daily specials (no eve meals Sun or winter Mon); and the extensive garden boasts the remains of a cider press and splendid views of the Mendips.
⌂ Q ⛺ ✿ ⟐ Ⓐ ♣ P

WOOKEY HOLE

Wookey Hole Inn
BA5 1BP (opp. caves)
✪ 12-3, 6-11; 12-4 (closed eve) Sun
☎ (01749) 676677 website: www.wookeyholeinn.com
Beer range varies ℍ
This is a wonderful example of how daring to be different can pay off. Three constantly-changing guest ales, plus Wook Ale (Milk Street's Mermaid in disguise) are joined by seven draught Belgian beers. Add this to the best pub food known to this reviewer and a friendly, if slightly odd interior and you have a great package. A bright pink side room is a no-smoking refuge. The huge landscaped garden seats 100. The five bedrooms have to be seen (ask if it is quiet). Live jazz is staged Sunday; other music Friday evening.
⌂ ✿ ⟐ ⟐ Ⓐ ❀ P

YARLINGTON

Stag's Head
Pounds Head, BA9 8DG
✪ 12-2.30, 6-11; closed Mon; 12-3 (closed eve) Sun
☎ (01963) 440393
Draught Bass; Greene King IPA; guest beer Ⓗ

Traditional country pub, free from piped music, fruit machines and pool. A screened area at the centre of the bar creates a third drinking area. Of the two other rooms, one has an open fire and candlelit tables, the other has a wood-burning stove. The restaurant menu features fresh meat, game and fish. The guest beer changes regularly; a real cider is stocked in summer.
♨Q❀◖♦P

YEOVIL

Armoury
1 The Park, BA20 1D (next to Job Centre)
✪ 11.30-3, 6-11; 11-11 Fri & Sat; 12-10.30 Sun
☎ (01935) 471047
Butcombe Bitter; Wadworth IPA, 6X, JCB, seasonal beers; guest beers Ⓗ

Lively town pub, formerly an armoury, where bar meals are available. Traditional pub games are played by several home teams; the refurbished skittle alley can be viewed on closed circuit TV in the adjoining bar. The pub has limited parking, but there is a free car park opposite (waiting is limited to one hour).
❀◖⅊♣P

Of Ale

Ale is made of malte and water, and they the which do put any other thynge to ale than is rehersed, except yest, barme or godisgood (other forms of yeast) do sofysticat (adulterate) theyr ale. Ale for an englysshe man is a natural drynke. Ale must have these propertyes, it must be freshe and cleare, it must not be ropy (cloudy) or smoky, nor it must have no welt nor tayle (sediment or dregs). Ale should not be dronke under V days olde. Newe ale is unholsome for all men. And soure ale and deade ale the which doth stande a tylt is good for no man. Barly malte maketh better ale then oten malte or any other corne doth, it doth engendre grosse humoures, but yette it maketh a man stronge.

Of Bere

Bere is made of malte, of hoppes, and water, it is a natural drinke for a dutche man. And nowe of late dayes it is moche used in Englande to the detryment of many englysshe men, specyally it kylleth them the which be troubled with the colycke and the stone & strangulion (quinsy), for the drynke is a colde drynke: yet it doth make a man fat and doth inflate the bely, as it doth appere by the dutche mens faces & belyes. If the beer be well served and be fyned & not newe, it doth qualify ye heat of the lyver.

Andrew Boorde (c.1490-1549), *A Compendyous Regyment or a Dyetary of Helth*, 1542

STAFFORDSHIRE

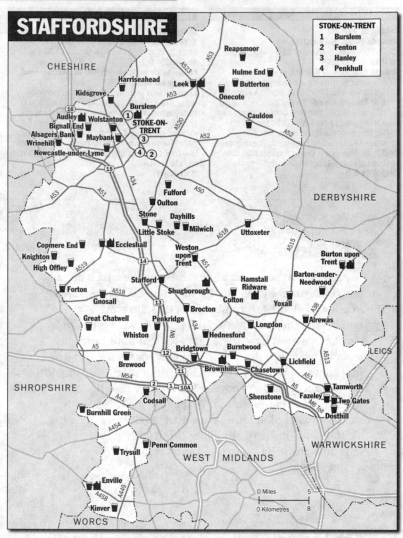

STOKE-ON-TRENT
1 Burslem
2 Fenton
3 Hanley
4 Penkhull

CHESHIRE

Reapsmoor

Harriseahead
Kidsgrove
Leek
Hulme End
Butterton
Onecote

Burslem
STOKE-ON-TRENT
Cauldon

Audley
Wolstanton
Bignall End
Alsagers Bank
Maybank
Wrinehill
Newcastle-under-Lyme

DERBYSHIRE

Fulford
Oulton
Stone
Dayhills
Little Stoke
Milwich
Uttoxeter

Copmere End
Eccleshall
Weston upon Trent
Knighton
High Offley
Burton upon Trent
Barton-under-Needwood
Forton
Stafford
Hamstall Ridware
Gnosall
Shugborough
Colton
Yoxall
Great Chatwell
Penkridge
Brocton
Alrewas
Whiston
Hednesford
Longdon
Bridgtown
Burntwood
Brewood
Brownhills
Chasetown
Lichfield
Codsall
Shenstone
Fazeley
Tamworth
Two Gates
Burnhill Green
Dosthill

SHROPSHIRE

Penn Common
WEST MIDLANDS
Trysull
WARWICKSHIRE

Enville
Kinver

WORCS

LEICS

0 Miles 5
0 Kilometres 8

ALREWAS

Crown Inn
7 Post Office Road, DE13 7BS
🕐 11-2.30, 5-11; 11-11 Sat; 12-10.30 Sun
☎ (01283) 790328
Draught Bass; Greene King Abbot; Marston's Pedigree; guest beer Ⓗ
Traditional 500-year-old village local, once the village post office and some 300 yards from the Trent & Mersey Canal. It features a cosy public bar and a lounge with an adjacent snug. It is apparently haunted by a ghost called Mary! Enjoy the good value home-cooked food with regular specials nights (fish on Thursday) and barbecues in summer. Families are well catered for in terms of food and facilities. It received the Midlands Pub in Bloom award.
🏚Q⛵☺◑🍴&♣P⏘🚲

ALSAGERS BANK

Gresley Arms
High Street, ST7 8BQ (on B5367)

🕐 12-3, 6-11; 12-11 Sat; 12-10.30 Sun
☎ (01782) 720297
Beer range varies Ⓗ
Busy, family-run village pub benefiting from superb views at the rear over Cheshire plain and beyond. Multi-roomed, the pub has a traditional bar, popular lounge, games-cum-children's room, restaurant, beer garden and play area. It caters for locals, families and walkers. Choose from six ever-changing ales from micros and smaller independent brewers. A rotating real cider is stocked, and good value food and bar snacks are always available.
⛵☺◑🍴&♣P

BARTON-UNDER-NEEDWOOD

Royal Oak
74 The Green, DE13 8JD
🕐 11.30-11; 12-10.30 Sun
☎ (01283) 713852
website: www.burtonpubsports.co.uk/pubs/royaloak_bart
Marston's Pedigree; guest beer Ⓗ/Ⓖ
Community local on the southern edge of

the village. While parts of the building date back to the 16th century, the pub has only existed since the late 1800s. The basic public bar has a red tiled floor and is linked to two lounge areas. All sections are served from a single bar where beer is poured direct from the cask on request. It is noted for its pub games teams, over-40s football team, summer beer festival, and annual bonfire night celebration. A conservatory to the side of the pub, opening on to the enclosed garden, serves as the family room but is open in summer only. ⌂❀♠P

Shoulder of Mutton
16 Main Street, DE13 8AA
🕐 12-3, 5-11; 12-11 Fri & Sat; 12-10.30 Sun
☎ (01283) 712568 website:
www.shoulderofmutton.com
Draught Bass; Marston's Pedigree; guest beers Ⓗ
This 17th-century former coaching inn, with some 19th-century additions, is located at the centre of the village, opposite the church. The low beamed ceiling, wood panelling and inglenook in the lounge give way to a plainer, more modern decor in the public bar. Guest beers are regularly available. Food is home-cooked, with specials and themed food nights – no meals are served on Sunday evening. The landscaped garden incorporates a picturesque patio and children's play area.
♨❀◑ ⊟P⌿

Plough
2 Ravens Lane, ST7 8PS
(B5500, ½ mile E of Audley)
🕐 12-3, 7-11; 12-11 Fri & Sat; 12-10.30 Sun
☎ (01782) 720469
Banks's Bitter; guest beers Ⓗ
CAMRA Potteries Pub of the Year 1995 and 2002, this friendly roadside inn has been family-run since 1991. The constantly-changing guest beers come mainly from small independents and micro-breweries: Holden's, Oakham, Titanic, Townhouse (brewed one mile away) and Whim, to name just a few. A range of continental bottled beers completes the diverse choice. The layout of the pub comprises a traditional bar and split-level lounge with a dining area serving excellent value meals – no food on Sunday evening.
❀◑ ⊟♠♠P

Swan Hotel
15 Market Place, ST19 9BS
🕐 12-2.30 (4 Sat), 7-11 (may open all day Sat);
12-10.30 Sun
☎ (01902) 850330
Courage Directors; Theakston XB; guest beers Ⓗ
Comfortable, former coaching inn, with low, beamed ceilings and pictures of old Brewood displayed. There are two cosy snugs, and a skittle alley upstairs. Normally two guest beers are available, chosen with flair. The house beer is Courage Best rebadged. A regular CAMRA award-winner at local level, and once regional Pub of the Year, the Swan is not far from the Shropshire Union Canal. A bus from Wolverhampton stops right outside. No food is served on Sunday lunchtime. ◑♠P

Stumble Inn
264 Walsall Road, WS11 3JL
(200 yds from A34 and A5 jct, by railway bridge)
🕐 11-3, 6 (5 Fri)-11 (7-midnight Sat); 12-10.30 Sun
☎ (01543) 502077
Banks's Original; guest beers Ⓗ
Well-decorated, one-roomed pub with a split-level interior, a pool area and separate small function room. Each Saturday live rock music is performed. Popular within the local community, the pub hosts regular charity nights. Weekday lunches are served from 12–3 (no food at weekends). ❀◑♠♠P

Chetwynd Arms
Cannock Road, ST17 0ST (on A34)
🕐 11-11; 12-10.30 Sun
☎ (01785) 661089
Banks's Original, Bitter; Marston's Pedigree; guest beer Ⓗ
The bustling public bar, with traditional pub games, is a haven for drinkers, while the comfortable lounge accommodates both drinkers and diners, with meals served all day until 9.30pm. The garden includes a children's play area. Brocton is an ideal base for exploring Cannock Chase, an area of natural beauty. The pub is involved in local charities, the highlight event being the annual harvest festival. ❀◑ ⊟♠♠P

Dartmouth Arms
Snowdon Road, WV6 7HU OS787006
🕐 12-3, 6-11 Tue-Sat (may open Mon in summer);
12-3, 6-10.30 Sun
☎ (01746) 783268
Hobsons Best Bitter, Town Crier Ⓗ
This is the estate pub for the Earl of Dartmouth's Patshull Park country estate. It has continued to thrive despite the demise of the stately home it used to serve. It retains its rural feel with two low, oak-beamed rooms filled with hops, horse brasses and memorabilia. Excellent home-cooked food is served in a no-smoking area and is accompanied by real ale from Hobsons and perry from Westons. Q❀◑♠P

Drill Inn
Springle Styche Lane, WS7 9HD OSSK0610
🕐 12-11; 12-10.30 Sun
☎ (01543) 674092

INDEPENDENT BREWERIES

Beowulf Brownhills
Blythe Hamstall Ridware
Burton Bridge Burton upon Trent
Eccleshall Eccleshall
Enville Enville
Leek Leek
Marston's Burton upon Trent
Old Cottage Burton upon Trent
Shugborough Shugborough
Titanic Burslem
Tower Burton upon Trent
Townhouse Audley

Marston's Pedigree; Tetley Bitter; **guest beer** H
Comfortable inn situated in farmland north of Burntwood and within easy reach of Cannock Chase. The spacious beamed main room has a separate area for diners and serves food on weekdays from 12–3 and 5–9. ⑃ ⊛ ◖ P

BURTON UPON TRENT

Museum of Brewing (Burton Bar) ⊘
Horninglow Street, DE14 1YQ (on A511)
☼ 11-7 (5 Sat); 12-5 Sun
☎ (01283) 513513 website: www.bass-museum.com
Draught Bass; Museum Worthington E; Worthington's 1744; guest beers H
Large, comfortable, single-roomed bar inside the museum, now owned by Coors Brewers. It has a conservatory and picnic tables in the garden, and the Wheelwrights Restaurant is adjacent. There is a constantly-changing range of cask beers, many brewed on site by the Museum Brewing Company. This local CAMRA Pub of the Year 2001 is the home of the famous Worthington's White Shield. Free admission is given to current card-carrying CAMRA members, and includes entry to the museum itself.
Q ⑃ ⊛ ◖ ≠ ♣ P

Burton Bridge Inn
24 Bridge Street, DE14 1SY
(on A511 at western end of Trent Bridge)
☼ 11.30-2.15, 5.30-11; 12-2, 7-10.30 Sun
☎ (01283) 536596
Burton Bridge Golden Delicious, Bridge Bitter, Porter, Festival, seasonal beers; guest beer H
This 17th-century pub is the Burton Bridge Brewery tap and fronts the brewery itself. It was joint winner of the Pub Design Award for Refurbishment in 2002 following sensitive renovation. The small front room has wooden pews, and walls covered with awards and brewery memorabilia. The oak-beamed and panelled back room is no-smoking, with oak tables and chairs. Both rooms are served from a central bar. Sample the good range of malt whiskies and fruit wines. A function room and skittle alley are upstairs. Local CAMRA Pub of the Year 2002, where lunches are offered Monday–Saturday. Q ⊛ ♣ ⊁

Derby Inn
17 Derby Road, DE14 1RU (on A5121)
☼ 11-3, 5.30-11; 11-11 Fri & Sat; 12-3, 7-10.30 Sun
☎ (01283) 543674
website: www.tv13.freeserve.co.uk/derbyinn/
Marston's Pedigree H
Friendly, traditional brick-built local situated towards the northern edge of the town, less than a mile from the railway station. The bar features railway pictures and related memorabilia, whereas in the small, wood-panelled lounge the theme is one of racehorses. Very much a community pub, locally-produced fruit, vegetables, eggs and cheese are sold in the bar, mainly at weekends. Take a step back in time to a slower, more relaxed, pace of life. Q ⊟ ≠ ♣ P

Elms Inn
36 Stapenhill Road, DE15 9AE
☼ 12-11; 12-10.30 Sun
☎ (01283) 535505
Draught Bass; Worthington's 1744 H

Free house on the east side of the Trent, overlooking the river. Built as a private house in the late 19th century and converted into a pub soon afterwards, this is one of Burton's original 'parlour pubs'. Recently renovated internally in a Victorian style, with two small rooms at the front and a larger one to the rear, the intimate and friendly atmosphere has been retained. It is rapidly establishing a local reputation for excellent food. A Tower beer is available alongside the regulars – the choice varies.
🛏 Q ⊛ ◖ ⊟ ♣

Lord Burton ⊘
154 High Street, DE14 1JE
☼ 10-11; 12-10.30 Sun
☎ (01283) 517587
Greene King Abbot; Marston's Pedigree; Old Cottage Stout, Halcyon Daze; Shepherd Neame Spitfire; guest beers H
Large, busy, single-roomed, typical Wetherspoon's pub, formerly a branch of Woolworths, close to the town centre and main shopping area. Old photographs of Burton adorn the walls. A wide choice of real ales is available, including a selection from nearby small breweries at locally low prices, together with good value food from the standard Wetherspoon's menu. It has an attractive, enclosed grassed and paved patio area at the rear, with access to the Memorial Gardens overlooking the Trent.
Q ⊛ ◖ ⅏ ⊁

Oak & Ivy
119-122 Wellington Street, DE14 2DP
☼ 10.30-11; 12-10.30 Sun
☎ (01283) 532508
Marston's Pedigree; guest beers H
Popular, lively, end-of-terrace local on the western side of town, a short walk from the railway station. The comfortably furnished public bar and lounge are both served from a central bar. Brewery memorabilia is displayed on shelving around the walls. Bar snacks are enhanced on Sunday lunchtime by a speciality cheese board. There is an enclosed beer garden. ⊛ ⊠ ≠ ♣

Old Cottage Tavern
36 Byrkley Street, DE14 2EG
(off Derby St, A5121)
☼ 12-11; 12-10.30 Sun
☎ (01283) 511615
Old Cottage Oak Ale, Stout, Halycon Daze, seasonal beer; guest beer H
Formerly the British Oak, this cheery and welcoming back-street local is now the Old Cottage Brewery tap. The main lounge at the front and pool room at the rear are served from a central bar. There is a cosy no-smoking snug on one side of the lounge, a small restaurant beyond the pool room, plus a function room, with its own bar, upstairs. Rapidly gaining a reputation for quality home-cooked pub food; no meals are served on Sunday evening or Monday.
🛏 Q ⑃ ⊛ ◖ ⅏ ♣ ⊁

Thomas Sykes
Anglesey Road, DE14 3PF
(off A5189, 1/2 mile S of railway station)
☼ 11-2.30, 5 (7 Sat)-11; 11.30-11 Fri; 12-2.30, 7-10.30 Sun
☎ (01283) 510246
Draught Bass; Marston's Pedigree, guest beers H

Classic ale house in the former stables and wagon sheds of the old Thomas Sykes Brewery, and now a listed building. The high ceiling, cobblestoned floor and breweriana of the main bar create an unspoilt, traditional atmosphere. The separate, small snug is served through a hatch, and skittles can be played in the large function room. Note the unusual anvil table. Two guest beers are normally available. Children are admitted until 8.30pm. The old brewery yard serves as a garden. Q ☽ ⊛ ⊕ ≄ ♣ P

BUTTERTON

Black Lion

ST13 7SP (village signed from B5053)
🕒 12-2 (not Mon), 7-11; 12-2, 7-10.30 Sun
☎ (01538) 304232
Draught Bass; Everards Tiger; Taylor Landlord; Theakston Best Bitter; guest beers Ⓗ

Friendly, 18th-century, stone-built inn, not far from the Manifold Valley. Set across from the church, in a conservation village, the inn is included in many local walks. The outside terrace is wonderful in summer as it looks over the surrounding hills. The cosy interior offers four rooms, one has an old black leaded range and a fire (one of three). Watch out for the low beams. A pool table is provided in the games room; note the large clothes peg outside. Well-kept ales and tasty food are guaranteed at this gem of a pub. ⚌ Q ☽ ⊛ ⊯ ⊕ ⊕ ⏦ ♣ P ⊬

CAULDON

Yew Tree Inn

ST10 3EJ (off A52/A523) OS077493
🕒 11-3, 6-11; 12-3, 7-10.30 Sun
☎ (01538) 308348
Draught Bass; Burton Bridge Bridge Bitter Ⓗ

Nationally-known, stone country hostelry, in the same family for over 40 years and now a Guide regular. The collection of antiques, including working polyphons and pianola, a penny farthing, and a selection of bottled King ale, must be seen. A true country local, that attracts customers from far and wide, value for money bar snacks are sold – try the pork pies and pickled eggs. Camping is possible in the pub grounds, and games such as darts and table skittles are played. ⚌ Q ☽ ⊛ ⊕ ⏦ ♣ P

CHASETOWN

Uxbridge Arms

2 Church Street, WS7 8QL
🕒 12-3, 5.30-11; 12-11 Fri & Sat; 12-10.30 Sun
☎ (01543) 674853
Draught Bass; Worthington's 1744; guest beers Ⓗ

Welcoming, popular local close to Chasewater Country Park. There is a large public bar with an extended comfortable lounge to accommodate diners. It was awarded local CAMRA Pub of the Year in 2001. The three guest beers are always available, and usually come from small breweries. The pub offers a full range of fruit and country wines, plus an extensive food menu – not served on Sunday evening. There is a round pool table and the forecourt is used for summer drinking. ⊛ ⊕ ⊕ ♣ P

CODSALL

Codsall Station

Chapel Lane, WV8 2EH
🕒 11.30-2.30, 5-11; 11-11 Sat; 12-10.30 Sun
☎ (01902) 847061
Holden's Bitter, Golden Glow, Special, seasonal beers; guest beer Ⓗ

Staffordshire CAMRA Pub of the Year 2003, this sensitively restored building is a working main line station, and hosts an annual September beer festival. The comfortable interior, displaying worldwide railway memorabilia, comprises a snug, conservatory, bar and lounge. A chalkboard announces forthcoming guest ales and food specials – no meals on Sunday evening. Outside is a floodlit boules pitch and a raised terrace, where you can sit in peace and watch the trains go by. ⚌ Q ⊛ ⊕ ⏦ ≄ ♣ P

COLTON

Greyhound

Bellamour Way, WS15 3LN
🕒 5.30 (12 Sat)-11; 12-10.30 Sun
☎ (01889) 586769
Banks's Original; Fuller's London Pride; Greene King Abbot; Wadworth 6X; guest beer Ⓗ

Classic, unspoilt, village pub, dating back to the early 1800s, and refurbished in the mid-1980s. The attractive bar incorporates a brick-lined fireplace, stone floor and authentic wooden beams. The lounge has a similar homely feel and doubles as a dining room. Meals are available Thursday–Saturday evening and Sunday lunchtime. The pub lies a mile north of Rugeley Trent Valley railway station and two miles south of Blithfield Reservoir. ⚌ Q ⊛ ⊕ ⊕ ♣ P

COPMERE END

Star

ST21 6EW (1½ miles W of Eccleshall) OS803294
🕒 12-3 (not Mon), 6-11; 12-4 Sun
☎ (01785) 850279
Draught Bass; Mansfield Cask Ale; Worthington's 1744 Ⓗ

Off the beaten track, this cosy establishment is popular with walkers, cyclists and anglers, as well as locals. Parts of the building are thought to be around 200 years old. The Star angling club makes good use of Cop Mere, a 42-acre lake situated opposite. The garden is set out with tables and has a large lawned area with trees and children's swings. Delicious home-cooked meals are served – not Monday evening. ⚌ Q ⊛ ⊕ ⊕ P

DAYHILLS

Red Lion

ST15 8RU (on B5027, 1 mile W of Milwich)
🕒 6.30-11; 12-3, 6-10.30 Sun
☎ (01889) 505474
Draught Bass; Ⓗ/Ⓖ Worthington's Bitter; guest beer Ⓗ

Situated in the tiny hamlet of Dayhills, this is one of the most traditional pubs in Staffordshire. The pub and the adjoining farm have been in the same family for nearly a century. It is affectionately known as the Romping Cat. The regulars always

417

make visitors feel welcome. Basically a one-roomed pub, but when busy a second room is commissioned. It plays host to darts, dominoes and crib teams. The Bass is gravity served in winter. ⚲Q♣P

DOSTHILL

Fox
105 High Street, B77 1LQ
✿ 12-3, 6-11; 12-3, 6-10.30 Sun
☎ (01827) 280847
Ansells Mild; Draught Bass; Greene King Abbot; Tetley Bitter; guest beers Ⓗ
Welcoming local on the southern edge of the Tamworth area, about three miles south of the town centre on the A51. There is a traditional bar, comfortable lounge, restaurant (booking is advisable) and a garden. In addition to the normal offerings, two guest beers are often available and regularly feature the output of Church End. Best to phone to check availability of meals on Sunday evening. Q✿◑⫐♣P

ECCLESHALL

George Inn
Castle Street, ST21 6DF
✿ 11-11; 12-10.30 Sun
☎ (01785) 850300
website: www.thegeorgeinn.freeserve.co.uk
Eccleshall Slaters Bitter, Original, Premium, Shining Knight, Supreme Ⓗ
As the home of the Eccleshall Brewery, the George Inn is best known for stocking nearly the full range of Slaters award-winning, hoppy ales. Since being bought by the Slater family 12 years ago, the neglected 17th-century coaching inn has been thoughtfully renovated. It now has attractive bar and lounge areas, excellent meals, which can be taken in the pub's own café bar, and 10 luxurious guest rooms. Deservedly popular, the George is situated at Eccleshall's main crossroads. ⚲⇔◑P

ENVILLE

Cat
Bridgnorth Road, DY7 5HA (on A458)
✿ 12-3 (2.30 Mon & Tue), 7-11; closed Sun
☎ (01384) 872209
Enville Ale; Tetley Bitter; guest beers Ⓗ
The nearest outlet to Enville Brewery, this 16th-century inn boasts four rooms containing many original features. The pub is popular with locals and visitors. Bar snacks are served in the pub and more elaborate meals in the highly recommended restaurant. Liquid refreshment comes in the form of four guest beers and a selection of fruit wines. Unusually, the pub only has a six-day licence and does not open on Sunday. This may change in the future. ⚲Q✿◑♣P

FAZELEY

Longwood
Deer Park Road, B78 3QP (halfway between centre of Fazeley and Mile Oak on B5404)
✿ 12-11; 12-10.30 Sun
☎ (01827) 284965
Banks's Bitter; Marston's Pedigree; guest beer Ⓗ
Recent refurbishment has seen this pub converted to a single room. Divided into a

number of distinct areas, some allow emphasis to be given to dining, others to drinking. Typically one guest ale joins the two regulars. Although there is no separate family room, children are admitted until 9pm. A quiz takes place twice a week on Thursday and Sunday, and there is occasional live entertainment. ✿◑੬P⚲

FORTON

Swan
Shay Lane, TF10 8BY
(on A519, 1/2 mile from jct with A41)
✿ 12-3, 5-11; 12-10.30 Sun
☎ (01952) 812169
website: www.traditionalfreehouses.com
Beer range varies Ⓗ
Family-run and family-friendly, 18th-century coaching inn, that serves good food in the bar and conservatory restaurant (with a carvery at weekends). Five ever-changing guest beers are on tap. Nine-room accommodation is available in the converted barn. Parties can be catered for in a separate function room, and the pub has a small beer garden. ✿⇔◑▲P

FULFORD

Shoulder of Mutton
Meadow Lane, ST11 9QS OS953380
✿ 12-3, 7-11; 12-10.30 Sun
☎ (01782) 388960
Greene King IPA, Abbot; Marston's Pedigree; guest beers Ⓗ
Formerly a 17th-century farm with ale house, the pub still uses the natural cellar that is carved out of solid rock. The ghost of Mrs Kent, a former landlady, is occasionally seen standing by the fireplace. Ken Brayford, the present landlord, has kept three pubs that have featured in this Guide since 1980. Beer festivals are sometimes hosted. ⚲✿◑▲♣P

GNOSALL

Horns ✿
21 High Street, ST20 0EX (off A518)
✿ 12-11; 12-10.30 Sun
☎ (01785) 822441
website: www.thehorns.rout56.co.uk
Draught Bass; Fuller's London Pride; Tetley Bitter; guest beer Ⓗ
Friendly and lively community local with a bar that is sports-mad. Declare your team and suffer the banter. If you prefer a quieter time then try the carefully refurbished lounge. This is one of the oldest buildings in the village, parts of the pub date back to the 17th century. There is a frequently changing guest beer and the landlord is open to suggestions for future ales. Fortnightly folk nights and local fundraising events are held. The vegetarian restaurant opens Thursday–Saturday evening and for Sunday lunch. ⚲੬♣P

GREAT CHATWELL

Red Lion
TF10 9BJ (2 miles E of A41, near Newport)
✿ 5 (12 Sat)-11; 12-10.30 Sun
☎ (01952) 691366
Everards Beacon, Tiger; Flowers IPA; guest beers Ⓗ
Family-run country pub in a small village,

comprising two bars, a restaurant and a large games room. Part of the building dates from the 18th century. This family-friendly pub boasts a spacious garden, well-maintained play area and an aviary. A popular local venue in summer, its good value food is available at all times.
🏚 🖙 🏵 ◑ 🍺 🛦 ♣ P

HARRISEAHEAD

Royal Oak
42 High Street, ST7 4JT
🕑 12.30-3 (not Mon-Fri), 7-11; 12-3, 7-10.30 Sun
☎ (01782) 513362
Courage Directors; John Smith's Bitter; guest beers H
Two-roomed, 19th-century free house that is deservedly popular with locals and is always welcoming. Three guest beers are on tap from small brewers and micro-breweries. An upstairs function room is available, which adds to the range during pub beer festivals. Choose from a varied selection of interesting continental bottled beers. Monthly quizzes in aid of local charities are held. The route to the car park at the rear can appear to be an adventure – through the door marked 'ladies'. 🍺 ♣ P 🕳

HEDNESFORD

Bell & Bottle
42 Mount Street, WS12 4DE
(10-minute walk from station via Station Rd)
🕑 12-3 (3.30 Fri & Sat), 7 (6.30 Fri & Sat)-11; 12-3.30, 7-10.30 Sun
☎ (01543) 422839
Draught Bass; M&B Brew XI; guest beers H
Built in the 1870s, this pub now boasts two large and comfortable lounge bars. Good beer and tasty food can be enjoyed in pleasant, relaxing surroundings. Lunches are served daily, 12–2 and evening meals 7–9, Monday–Saturday. A quiz night takes place each Tuesday. Q ◑ 🍺 🖙 ♣ P ⌿

Queen's Arms
37 Hill Street, WS12 5DJ (off A460 between town centre and Hednesford Town FC)
🕑 12-3, 6.30 (7 Sat)-11; 12-3, 7-10.30 Sun
☎ (01543) 878437
Draught Bass; Highgate Dark; Worthington's Bitter P
Popular, pleasant, two-roomed local, situated on the Cannock to Rugeley road. There has been a pub on this site since 1866. The bar is decorated with many fine horse brasses. Regular quiz nights are held in this traditional boozer. Home-made lunches are offered 12–2, Monday–Saturday. Q 🏵 ◑ 🍺 🖙 ♣ P

HIGH OFFLEY

Anchor
Peggs Lane, Old Lea, ST20 0NG
(by bridge 42 of Shropshire Union Canal) OS775256
🕑 12-3 (not Mon-Fri winter), 7 (7.30 winter Fri & Sat only)-11; 12-3, 7.30-10.30 (not winter eve) Sun
☎ (01785) 284569
Marston's Pedigree (summer)**; Wadworth 6X** G
On the Shropshire Union Canal, this Victorian two-bar inn is a rare example of an unspoilt, country pub. Cask ales are dispensed by jug from the cellar. This free house has been run by the same family since 1870, when it was called the Sebastopol. Busy in the summer with canal

traffic, it has a canalware gift shop at the rear. This local CAMRA Pub of the Year 2000 is not easily found by road, but is well worth the trip. 🏚 Q 🏵 🛦 A P

HULME END

Manifold Inn
SK17 0EX (on B5054, 2 miles W of Hartington)
🕑 12-2.30, 7-11; 12-2.30, 7-10.30 Sun
☎ (01298) 84537
Whim Hartington Bitter; Worthington's Bitter; guest beer H
Impressive stone hotel, set in picturesque countryside by the banks of the Manifold river, formerly known as the Light Railway, due to its proximity to the terminus of the Manifold Light Railway, now converted to a popular path for walkers and cyclists. Right in the heart of the Peak District, rooms are available with prices ranging from £40–£80 per night. Alternatively, there is a campsite opposite the pub. 🏚 Q 🏵 🛏 ◑ 🛦 ♣ P

KIDSGROVE

Blue Bell
25 Hardingswood, ST7 1EG
(off A50, by canalside near Tesco)
🕑 7.30-11; 1-4, 7-11 Sat; closed Mon; 12-4, 7-10.30 Sun
☎ (01782) 774052
Beer range varies H
CAMRA Staffordshire Pub of the Year 2000–02 and Potteries Pub of the Year 1999–2001. Six ever-changing cask beers are on offer from a wide variety of breweries. This genuine free house has stocked over 1,300 different beers since reopening five years ago. Real cider and/or perry, German and Czech draught lagers, around 30 Belgian and German bottled beers, plus a selection of genevers provide real choice. No juke box, TV or bandits disturb the peace, and there is a no-smoking room. On Sunday evening folk musicians perform. Q 🏵 🖙 ♣ P ⌿

KINVER

Plough & Harrow
82 High Street, DY7 6HD
🕑 5 (12 Sat)-11; 12-10.30 Sun
☎ (01384) 872659
Batham Mild, Best Bitter H
Lively, two-roomed pub known locally as the Steps as its various areas are on ascending levels the further back you go. At the front and bottom is the no-frills public bar, behind and above that is a split-level lounge which hosts live music on Sunday and Thursday. The pub is about half a mile from the Staffs & Worcs Canal. Food is served all day at weekends but not at all in the week. Traditional cider is sometimes available in summer. 🏵 ◑ 🍺 ♣ P

Whittington Inn
Whittington, DY4 6NY (on A449 S of A458 jct)
🕑 11.30-11; 12-10.30 Sun
☎ (01384) 872110
Banks's Original; Marston's Pedigree, seasonal beers; guest beers H
This historic 14th-century inn was originally the manor house of the de Whittingtons. Richard, a grandson of the first owner, became Lord Mayor of London

419

on four occasions. Visited by Charles II after the Battle of Worcester, it boasts panelled walls and moulded ceilings together with a priest's hole and the remains of a Tudor walled garden. It is near Bridge 28 on the Staffs & Worcs Canal. Food is served all day. ⋈Q✿◗P⋊⊟

KNIGHTON

Haberdasher's Arms
ST20 0QH
(between Adbaston and Knighton) OS753275
✪ 12.30 (5 Wed)-11; 12-10.30 Sun
☎ (01785) 280650
Banks's Original, Bitter; guest beer Ⓗ
Built about 1840, the Dashers is a fine example of a traditional community local. A small bar counter serves the three original rooms and a fourth built at the entrance. The large garden is used for local events including the annual potato club show. It was threatened with closure several years ago, with planning permission granted for conversion to a private house. The former local CAMRA Pub of the Year was saved after a vigorous campaign by regulars and CAMRA. ⋈Q⋎✿⊟Ⓐ♣P

LEEK

Bull's Head
35 St Edward Street, ST13 5DN
✪ 5 (12 Wed, Fri & Sat)-11; 12-10.30 Sun
☎ (01538) 370269
Leek Staffordshire Gold, Staffordshire Bitter, St Edwards Ale; guest beers Ⓗ
A Tardis pub on one of the best streets for a real ale crawl. It is more spacious than it looks from the exterior. A narrow, long drinking area extends back, rising up several levels, and has a serving area in the middle. The rock-oriented juke box will not be to everyone's taste, but has an excellent selection. The ale attracts a wide variety of customers, and the choice now includes the recently formed Leek Brewing Company range. Westons Old Rosie cider is sold. ♣◗

Den Engel
Bodkin House, Stanley Street, ST13 5HG
✪ 5 (7 Mon)-11; 12-midnight Fri & Sat; 12-3, 7-10.30 Sun
☎ (01538) 373751
Beer range varies Ⓗ
Genuine, Belgian-style bar in a prominent brick building, it complements the other worthy establishments within walking distance. Internally, a high-ceilinged bar area serves up to four ever-changing cask ales, on top of a selection of 100 plus Belgian bottled beers, all served in the correct glass by waiters. A small, cosy Flemish restaurant on the first floor offers beer-based cuisine including Stoverij (beef in Belgian beer). Lunches are served on Friday and Saturday, evening meals Wednesday–Saturday. Q◗◗◗

Wilkes' Head
16 St Edward Street, ST13 5DS
✪ 11-11; 12-10.30 Sun
☎ (01538) 383616
Whim Arbor Light, Hartington Bitter, Hartington IPA, Black Christmas; guest beers Ⓗ
Leek's second oldest pub, a former coaching inn circa 1800. Enter via the narrow swing

doors, the small bar is on the right and on the left is the music/family room. A range of locally brewed Whim ales, plus occasional guests satisfy the thirst. On Monday night acoustic musicians play – and all are welcome. On summer Sundays, regular music days are hosted in the garden. ⋎✿♣P

LICHFIELD

Acorn Inn ⊘
12 Tamworth Street, WS13 6JH
✪ 11-11; 12-10.30 Sun
☎ (01543) 263400
Courage Directors; Greene King Abbot; Shepherd Neame Spitfire; Theakston Best Bitter; guest beers Ⓗ
Large Wetherspoon's pub in a popular drinking area of the city centre. It offers a very good choice of real ales at competitive prices, with the addition of seasonal mini festivals. The vast emporium caters for the Friday and Saturday night crowds, of all ages. Beer is delivered to the stillage via a purpose-built bridge over the drinking area. Acorn is the original name of a neighbouring pub.
Q◗◗&⪰(City)⋊

Earl of Lichfield Arms
10 Conduit Street, WS13 6JR
✪ 11-11; 12-10.30 Sun
☎ (01543) 251020
Marston's Bitter, Pedigree; guest beer Ⓗ
The only remaining market square pub, this popular split-level, wooden floored house is known locally as the Drum; the name dates from the 1800s when the army drummed up recruits. The old brick and timber construction can be seen through the arched entrance. Photographs are displayed showing how the pub used to look before its current interior. Lunches are served Monday–Saturday, and an extensive coffee menu is available. ✿◗⪰(City)

George & Dragon
28 Beacon Street, WS13 7AJ
✪ 3 (1 Fri; 12 Sat)-11; 12-4.30, 8-10.30 Sun
☎ (01543) 253667
Banks's Original, Bitter; Ⓟ **Marston's Pedigree** Ⓗ
Welcoming, two-roomed drinkers' pub with a basic public bar to the right and an exceptionally cosy lounge to the left. This pub is a fine example, retaining the old social traditions where conversation, pub games, and sport take priority. It is well worth the 10-minute walk from the market place to its location just beyond the cathedral. Look for the St George's flag flying from the pole over the front door. ✿⊟⪰(City)♣P

Queen's Head
Queen Street, WS13 6QD
✪ 12-11; 12-3, 7-10.30 Sun
☎ (01543) 410932
Adnams Bitter; Marston's Pedigree; Taylor Landlord; guest beers Ⓗ
As the most regular Guide entry for Lichfield, this single-roomed pub is always a favourite haunt of real ale lovers, from near and far. The wooden floored interior narrows by the entrance lobby, marking the original divide between the former lounge and bar. Good value home-cooked food is available at lunchtime, Monday–Saturday, it

is always possible to purchase bread, cheese and paté from the specialist counter beside the bar. Q ◐ ⇌ (City) ♣

LITTLE STOKE

Little Stoke Cricket Club

The Sid Jenkins Cricket Ground, Uttoxeter Road, ST15 8RA
(on B5027, 500 yds from level crossing)
✪ 5 (12 Sat)-11; 12-10.30 Sun
☎ (01785) 812558 website: www.littlestoke.com
Tetley Bitter, Imperial; Wells Bombardier; guest beer Ⓗ

Little Stoke Cricket Club's motto – 'non progredi est regredi' – not to advance is to go back, can certainly be applied to the cask ales here. Four handpumps dispense a good range of ales mainly from the Carlsberg–Tetley portfolio. It is like a pub within a club, and boasts dominoes, crib and darts teams as well as cricket. The public are always made welcome by the members. ❀ ♿ ♣ P

LONGDON

Swan with Two Necks

40 Brook End, WS15 4PN (off A51)
✪ 12-2.30 (3 Sat), 7-11; 12-3, 7-10.30 Sun
☎ (01543) 490251
Ansells Best Bitter; Marston's Pedigree; Tetley Burton Ale; guest beers Ⓗ

A Guide regular for 25 years, this pub is an excellent example of a friendly village local. It has a central role in the community, and is welcoming, with real fires in winter. It is run by a French landlord and his English wife, and they continue to maintain high standards, both in the range and quality of regular and guest beers and the excellent food. A separate restaurant is open on Friday and Saturday evening, 7–9 and the Sunday hours are 12–1.45 and 7–8.30. This pub is a must for real ale lovers. Children under 14 are not admitted. ⋒ Q ❀ ◐ ◑ P

MAYBANK

Cricketers Arms

Alexandra Road, ST5 9PL
✪ 3 (12 Fri & Sat)-11; 12-10.30 Sun
☎ (01782) 619169
Draught Bass; Courage Directors; John Smith's Bitter; guest beers Ⓗ

There has been a pub on this site since the 1830s and the present building was completed during the 1930s. What the building lacks from the exterior, the interior more than compensates for, with three separate rooms and a corridor. The smoke room is a must for visitors, with its atmospheric 1930s marine ply panelling and dim lighting, the room has the feel of a bygone era. The pub serves four real ales, one of which is a varying guest. It tends to be busy at weekends. ⋒ Q ❀ ⊟ ♣ P

MILWICH

Green Man

ST18 0EG (on B5027)
✪ 12-2.30 (not Mon-Wed), 5-11; 12-11 Sat; 12-10.30 Sun
☎ (01889) 505310
Draught Bass; Marston's Pedigree; Worthington's Bitter; guest beer Ⓗ

Superb village local that dates from the 15th century; a list of landlords since 1792 is displayed in the bar. The pub is popular with cyclists, hikers and locals alike. Guest ales move quickly and range from well-known brands to obscure micros. The pub has a large grass plot with benches. Lunches are available Thursday–Sunday. ⋒ ❀ ◐ ♣ P

NEWCASTLE-UNDER-LYME

Albert Inn

1 Brindley Street, ST5 2DA
(off A34/A53 ring road)
✪ 11-3 (not Tue-Thu), 5-11; 12-11 Fri; 11-4, 7-11 Sat; 12-3.30, 7-10.30 Sun
☎ (01782) 615125
Burtonwood Bitter, Top Hat Ⓗ

Victorian, street-corner local distinguished by its tiled mural on the exterior. Named after Queen Victoria's consort, its licensees have been traced back to 1861, the year of Albert's death. Popular with all ages, the single drinking area is comfortably furnished with bench seats down both sides. The walls display photographs of old Newcastle and a collection of clay pipes hangs over the entrance. ♣

Museum

29 George Street, ST5 1JU (on A52)
✪ 12-11; 12-10.30 Sun
☎ (01782) 623866
Draught Bass; Worthington's Bitter; guest beers Ⓗ

Two-roomed, friendly, corner local that offers a traditional, cosy bar where pub games, conversation and televised sports are enjoyed. Next door there is a quiet lounge – note the fake window on the back wall. The pub was originally called the Farmer's Arms, the present name comes from a 'museum of curiosities' that was once located here. Check out the full history posted in the bar. Three rotating guest beers are normally available. A welcoming local not to be missed. ❀ ⊟ ♣

Old Brown Jug

Bridge Street, ST5 2RY (off A52/A34 ring road)
✪ 6-11 (midnight Wed); 4.30-midnight Fri; 12-midnight Sat; 7-10.30 Sun
☎ (01782) 711393
Banks's Riding Bitter; Marston's Pedigree; guest beers Ⓗ

A welcome break from the bright lights and noises that make up most of Newcastle's drinking scene. A dividing wall splits the one opened-up room into areas for drinking and conversation. Popular, regular jazz nights are held on Wednesday, mixed music nights take place on Sunday. Two ever-changing guests are available. A late licence has been granted for music nights. This is a rare Staffordshire outlet for real ciders with normally two stocked. ❀ ♣ 🍎 P

ONECOTE

Jervis Arms

ST13 7RU (on B5053, off A523)
✪ 12-3, 7 (6 Sat)-11; 12-10.30 Sun
☎ (01538) 304206
Draught Bass; guest beers Ⓗ

Popular, family-oriented country inn with a large garden running down to the banks of the River Hamps, which is ideal in summer. It is famous for its excellent food (available at all sessions), but this does not detract from the pub's character. A small bar serves the main bar and two family rooms dispensing a range of guest beers, mainly from micro-breweries. Admiral Jervis was an aide to Nelson. Q ⌂ ⊛ ◖ ₠ P ⊱

OULTON

Brushmaker's Arms
8 Kibblestone Road, ST15 8UW
☼ 12-3, 6.30-11; 12-10.30 Sun
☎ (01785) 812062
Draught Bass; Worthington's Bitter; guest beer Ⓗ
Situated one mile north-east of Stone, this timeless pub has an ambience and charm all of its very own. The bar is basic and unspoilt with black and white photographs and postcards decorating the walls. The lounge is small and very comfortable. The guest ales are varied and dispensed through one handpump. The bar plays host to darts and dominoes teams. The pub has won floral awards for its small rear patio, which is ideal for summer lunchtimes. ⌘ Q ⊛ ₠ ♣ P

PENKRIDGE

Railway ⊘
Clay Street, ST19 5AF (on A449)
☼ 12-2.30, 5-11; 12-11 Fri & Sat; 12-10.30 Sun
☎ (01785) 712685
Banks's Original, Bitter; Ⓟ guest beer Ⓗ
Converted in the 1830s from cottages to a pub for railway construction workers who were barred from the village's other pubs, the Railway is much quieter and more welcoming now. The extended original building houses the lounge and small restaurant. The bar has been a garage, mortuary and auctioneers' office in its time. The licensee worked at Banks's Brewery for many years, and sells far more of their beer than any other Pubmaster house in the area. The quality meals are excellent value; no food served on Sunday evening.
⌘ ⊛ ◖ ₠ ⇌ ♣ P

PENN COMMON

Barley Mow
Pennwood Lane, WV4 5JN
(follow signs for Penn Golf Club from A449) OS949902
☼ 12-2.30, 6-11; 12-11 Sat; 12-10.30 Sun
☎ (01902) 333510
Banks's Original; Greene King Abbot; Tetley Burton Ale; guest beers Ⓗ
Small pub dating from the 1630s, on the outskirts of Wolverhampton. A small extension was added in 1999. Next to Penn Common and the golf club, it has a growing reputation for its excellent food, with the meat supplied from the landlord's own butcher's shop. The garden and children's play area are very popular in good weather. The Barley Mow stands at the end of Seven Cornfields path, which is well worn by Wolverhampton beer drinkers. If over 5'5", remember to duck or grouse on entering the pub. ⊛ ◖ P

REAPSMOOR

Butcher's Arms
SK17 0LL
☼ 7-11; lunchtime hours vary phone ahead;
12-3, 7-10.30 Sun

☎ (01298) 84477
Beer range varies Ⓗ
Isolated, rural gem that is difficult to find, but well worth the effort. A former farm-pub that is stone-built and located in open moorland, it comprises several small rooms that have been opened out yet retain their character. A good choice of two real ales is guaranteed. Food is available Sunday lunchtime and in the evenings, at other times it is on request. Excellent walking can be enjoyed in the Peak District National Park. Free camping is available to pub customers. ⌘ Q ⌂ ◖ ₠ Ⓐ ♣ P

SHENSTONE

Fox & Hounds
42 Main Street, WS14 0NB
☼ 12-2.30, 5-11; 12-11 Sat; 12-10.30 Sun
☎ (01543) 480257
Ansells Best Bitter; Jennings Cumberland Ale; Marston's Pedigree; Taylor Landlord Ⓗ
Popular village local consisting of a lounge and separate split-level bar. Diners take priority for seating in the lounge, while the bar is for drinkers only. The quality of the cask beer is equalled by the friendly welcome, efficient service, and good value home-cooked food. The fixed menu is complemented by an extensive blackboard of specials. No meals are served on Sunday evening. The patio is a welcome retreat during the summer months. Q ⊛ ◖ ⇌ P

STAFFORD

Lamb ⊘
Broadeye, ST16 2QB
(on inner ring road, opp. Sainsburys)
☼ 11-11; 12-10.30 Sun
☎ (07946) 403433
Banks's Original; Everards Tiger; Marston's Pedigree; guest beer (occasional) Ⓗ
Following the redevelopment of Stafford town centre, this corner local now finds itself on the inner ring road, surrounded by shops, car parks and Stafford College. Acquired by Punch Taverns in 1999 and extensively refurbished, the Lamb is now a bright, airy hostelry with good value food and a friendly atmosphere. Evening meals are served Monday–Thursday, until 8pm.
◖ ⇌ ♣

Railway
23 Castle Street, ST16 2EB
☼ 12-11; 12-10.30 Sun
☎ (01785) 605085
Draught Bass; Greene King Abbot; Tetley Bitter; guest beer Ⓗ
Like the surrounding terraced housing of Castletown, the inn was built shortly after the Grand Junction Railway reached Stafford, soon after Queen Victoria's coronation in 1837. It remains Stafford's best example of a Victorian back-street local. Parking is sometimes difficult, but it is just a five-minute walk from both the station and the town centre. ⌘ ⊛ ₠ ⇌ ♣

Spittal Brook
106 Lichfield Road, ST17 4LP (on A34, close to railway bridge, 1 mile SE of town centre)
☼ 12-3, 5-11; 12-11 Sat; 12-4, 7-10.30 Sun
☎ (01785) 245268
Marston's Pedigree; Tetley Bitter; guest beer Ⓗ

Originally a beer house, the Spittal Brook was renamed the Crown Inn to commemorate the coronation of Queen Victoria. It reverted to its former name in 1998. This thriving, traditional two-roomed pub adjacent to the west coast main line has been much improved in recent years. The refurbished lounge boasts a lending library and a selection of board games. Accommodation comprises four twin-bedded rooms. No food is served on Sunday evening. Addlestones Cloudy cask cider is sold. Entertainment includes a folk night each Tuesday, and a quiz on Wednesday evening.
🛏🏶🚄❶🖃🔔♣♠P

Stafford Arms
43 Railway Street, ST16 2DS
🕐 12-11; 12-4, 7-10.30 Sun
☎ (01785) 253313
Titanic Best Bitter, White Star; guest beers Ⓗ
Close to the station, the Stafford Arms has long been a convenient stopping-off point for beer-loving rail travellers. The pub offers a range of at least five ales, mostly from small breweries. At least two Titanic beers are regularly available, reflecting former ownership by Titanic Brewery before being bought by Punch Taverns in 1999. The Arms is well known for its support for Tigercare and a variety of local and national charities. Welcoming to discerning drinkers, the pub also offers accommodation. Addlestones Cloudy cask cider is sold.
Q🏶🚄❶➤♣♠P

Tap & Spile
59 Peel Terrace, ST16 3HE (off B5066)
🕐 4.30 (2 Fri; 12 Sat)-11; 12-10.30 Sun
☎ (01785) 223563
Beer range varies Ⓗ
Thriving beer house, selling an incredible volume and variety of cask ales. The local CAMRA Pub of the Year award for 2002 was well deserved. Built early last century, the name change, from Cottage by the Brook, 10 years ago, coincided with a sensitive refurbishment, four distinct drinking areas being retained. The first pub locally with a proper no-smoking area, the Tap & Spile also has a free bar billiards table, several sports teams and Saturday evening music.
🛏🏶♣✂

STOKE-ON-TRENT: *BURSLEM*

Bull's Head
14 St John's Square, ST6 3AJ
🕐 5-11; 12-11 Fri & Sat; 12-10.30 Sun
☎ (01782) 834153
Titanic Best Bitter, Iceberg, Premium, White Star; guest beer Ⓗ
Titanic's brewery tap in the Potteries' 'mother town'. It always keeps at least two guest or seasonal beers from Titanic and other independent brewers. Beer festivals are held in May and September. The traditional bar contains table skittles, bar billiards and a vintage juke box. The lounge is quieter and more comfortable. The pub has a nautical theme as the captain of the ill-fated Titanic (after which the brewery is named) was originally from Stoke-on-Trent. Westons cider is stocked occasionally. Wheelchair access is at the rear.
🛏Q🏶❶&♣♠

FENTON

Malt 'n' Hops
295 King Street, ST4 3EJ
🕐 12-4, 7-11; 12-3.30, 7-10.30 Sun
☎ (01782) 313406
Courage Directors; Tower Tower of Strength; guest beers Ⓗ
Busy, genuine free house, extended over the years to cope with its popularity. The split-level layout gives the impression of two rooms: a traditional bar through the main entrance leading to a comfortable lounge. At least four ever-changing guest beers, including a mild, come from micro-breweries, and the house beer, Bursley Bitter, is from Tower Brewery of Burton. Draught and bottled Belgian ales are stocked. It is very much a beer-oriented pub. Good value snacks and sandwiches are available at lunchtime. ⇌(Longton) ⊖

Potter
432 King Street, ST4 3DB
🕐 12 (11 Sat)-11; 12-10.30 Sun
☎ (01782) 311968
Draught Bass; Coach House Dick Turpin; M&B Brew XI; guest beers Ⓗ
An established drinking venue on the Fenton scene, this multi-roomed pub appeals to customers of all ages. Three excellent guest beers are backed up by three regulars. One of the rooms is set aside for pool and darts. A minor refurbishment has not changed the original feel of the pub. Very busy during live televised sporting events, a warm welcome awaits visitors.
🛏🏶⇌(Longton) ♣

HANLEY

Unicorn
40 Piccadilly, ST1 1EG (opp. Regent Theatre)
🕐 12-11; 12-3, 7-10.30 Sun
☎ (01782) 281809
Draught Bass; Fuller's London Pride; guest beers Ⓗ
Friendly lounge bar in the cultural quarter of the city centre. Comfortable and welcoming, shoppers and office workers mingle during the day, while the evening attracts theatregoers mixing with locals and clubbers in a convivial atmosphere. It is busy at weekends. Interval drinks can be ordered by those attending the Regent Theatre opposite. The pavement serves as a summer drinking area. 🏶

PENKHULL

Beehive
103 Honeywall, ST4 7HU (off A52)
🕐 12-11; 2.30-11 Sat (12-11 Sat when Stoke City at home); 12-4, 7-10.30 Sun
☎ (01782) 846947 website:
www.thebeehivestoke.co.uk
Marston's Pedigree; guest beer Ⓗ
A warm welcome awaits the traveller halfway up Honeywall hill at the Beehive. This single L-shaped room is bedecked with clocks, ornaments, pictures and prints. The real fire adds to the ambience during the winter months. Traditional pub games are played (crib and dominoes). Freshly-cooked food is available daily, except on Sunday evening. It can get very busy on Tuesday quiz nights and when Stoke City are playing at home. Well worth a visit. 🛏🏶❶⇌♣P

Greyhound
6 Manor Court Street, ST4 5DW
✪ 11-3, 5.30-11; 11-11 Fri & Sat; 12-10.30 Sun
☎ (01782) 848978
Greene King Old Speckled Hen; Marston's Pedigree; Wadworth 6X; guest beer Ⓗ
This local retains a village atmosphere despite the city having expanded around it. Parts of the building date from 1540 and were used as the manor court for 250 years before it became a pub. A former local CAMRA Community Pub of the Year, it runs evening quizzes and darts matches, plus curry night (Tue). It is HQ of the Penkhull Institute of Sunday Tipplers. The landlord is Australian, so expect no sympathy during test matches. The bar has a TV, opt for the lounge for a more peaceful drink. There is a patio area and outside benches to the front. No meals are served on Monday or Sunday evening.
♨Q❀◑ Ⓓ♣P

Marquis of Granby
51 St Thomas's Place, ST4 7LA
(55 yds from B5041, London road)
✪ 12-11; 12-10.30 Sun
☎ (01782) 847025
Banks's Original; Marston's Bitter, Pedigree; guest beer Ⓗ
Imposing local in the centre of the village, a pub and brewhouse have been on this site since the 16th century. The current building dates from the 19th century. Note the original etched windows and tiled entrance. In the bar you can watch sports TV or play traditional pub games. There is also a comfortable lounge split into distinct areas. Keenly-priced meals are available at lunchtime, and on Thursday–Saturday evening. The sizeable beer garden attracts customers in summer. ❀◑Ⓓ♣P

STONE

Langtrys
1 Oulton Road, ST15 8EB
(off A520, on way out of town centre towards Leek)
✪ 12-3, 5-11; 12-11 Sat; 12-10.30 Sun
☎ (01785) 818724
Boddingtons Bitter; Castle Eden Ale; Flowers Original; Marston's Pedigree; guest beer Ⓗ
This pub was once called the Bridge Inn and was built in 1852. It has an excellent mix of customers. The comfortable lounge is adorned with pictures of Lillie Langtry. The bar has two separate areas. Football is popular even with the Evertonian licensee, who is a former mayor of the town. The pub has crib and dominoes teams, based in the bar. ♨Ⓓ⇌♣P

Red Lion
25 High Street, ST15 8AJ
✪ 10-11; 12-10.30 Sun
☎ (01785) 814500
Everards Tiger; guest beers Ⓗ
Reputedly Stone's third oldest pub, the earliest licensee recorded was 1793. It has a quiet lounge which overlooks the pedestrianised High Street. The bar is spacious and lively. Jazz nights are held every Monday, pool and darts are available at the rear of the bar. Good value food is served Monday–Saturday. The guest ales are from the Punch Taverns portfolio. ◑Ⓓ⇌

Swan Inn
18 Stafford Street, ST15 8QW
(on A520 by Trent & Mersey Canal)
✪ 10-11; 12-10.30 Sun
☎ (01785) 815570
Coach House Gunpowder Mild, John Joule Old Knotty, Old Priory, Victory; guest beers Ⓗ
This 18th-century, Grade II listed building was carefully renovated in 1999. The John Joule beers (brewed at Coach House) are complemented by the numerous guest ales, many from obscure micros. The pub hosts a beer festival every July. Tuesday is quiz night, and live music is performed up to three nights a week. A free buffet is served every Sunday lunchtime at 12.30. Excellent lunchtime snacks are offered (Mon-Sat) and it opens at 10am for breakfast, an excellent starter before selecting from the nine handpumps. ♨❀◑⇌♦

TAMWORTH

Albert
32 Albert Road, B79 7JS (near railway station)
✪ 12-3, 5-11; 12-11 Sat; 12-10.30 Sun
☎ (01827) 64694
Banks's Original, Bitter; Marston's Pedigree; guest beer (occasional) Ⓗ
A warm welcome is guaranteed at this popular local that is handy for the railway station. This previous local CAMRA Pub of the Year has roadside seating for outdoor drinking during the summer months. The guest beer is available weekends only and is from the W&D portfolio. Sunday lunches are served until 5pm. Bus route 776 to Polesworth/Atherstone and Nuneaton stops directly outside the front door.
❀⋈◑Ⓓよ⇌♣P

Moat House
Lichfield Street, B79 7QQ
✪ 12-11; 12-10.30 Sun
☎ (01827) 311972
Banks's Bitter; guest beers Ⓗ
This popular family pub and restaurant, housed in a 15th-century building, attracts drinkers and diners alike. Since becoming a free house in 2002, up to three guest beers are available, from regional and micro-breweries. The large garden at the rear is ideal during the summer. The current licensees are committed to offering choice for the drinker, making the Moat House one of the best real ale outlets in the Tamworth area. ❀◑よ⇌P⅄

White Lion
Aldergate, B79 7JJ (next to council offices)
✪ 11-11; 12-10.30 Sun
☎ (01827) 64630
Banks's Original, Bitter; Marston's Pedigree; guest beer Ⓗ
Lively, two-roomed town-centre pub, popular with all ages; it can get busy at weekends. The guest beer is ever-changing and can be unusual for the area. It is a mere two-minute walk from the annual Tamworth beer festival, held in September. よ⇌P

TRYSULL

Bell
Bell Road, WV5 7JB

◎ 11.30-3, 5-11; 11-11 Sat; 12-10.30 Sun
☎ (01902) 892871
Batham Best Bitter; Holden's Bitter, Golden Glow, Special; guest beer Ⓗ
A warm welcome awaits at this three-roomed village hostelry. The interior is attractively decorated. Food is available at all times, except Sunday evening and all day Monday. Set in lovely countryside, the pub can get very busy in summer and at weekends. It is popular with locals and visitors alike. Can you spot the pheasant in one of the rooms? ◑ ☖ੳ ♣ P ▯

TWO GATES

Bull's Head
Watling Street, B77 1HW (at A51/B5404 jct)
◎ 12-2.30 (3 Sat), 6.30 (7 Sat)-11; 12-2.30, 7-10.30 Sun
☎ (01827) 287820
Banks's Original; Marston's Pedigree Ⓗ
Friendly, community local which, although in the middle of a housing/industrial area, has the appearance of a Victorian farmhouse. This theme is also apparent in the comfortable, split-level lounge. There is a traditional style bar and a patio area. It has a keen sporting following including a golf society. Good value meals are served Monday–Saturday lunchtime, while on Sunday evening there is a quiz to which all are welcome. Q ✿ ◑ ☖ ⇌ (Wilnecote) P

UTTOXETER

Vaults
Market Place, ST14 8HP
◎ 11-3 (4 Wed, Fri & Sat), 5.30 (5 Fri; 7 Sat)-11; 12-3, 7-10.30 Sun
☎ (01889) 562997
Draught Bass; Marston's Pedigree; Worthington's Bitter Ⓗ
One of the town's oldest pubs where wine used to be made on the premises, the Vaults is a sound ale house which has remained virtually unchanged for decades. Lined up behind the narrow, terraced frontage are three rooms, each having an emphasis on games; darts is keenly played in the front and back rooms while table skittles can be enjoyed in the middle. Acoustic instrumental jam sessions take place on the last Sunday of each month. ☖ Å ⇌ ♣

WESTON UPON TRENT

Woolpack
The Green, ST18 0JH
◎ 11-11; 12-10.30 Sun
☎ (01889) 270238
Banks's Original, Bitter Ⓗ
Locally known as the Inn on the Green, the Woolpack is a welcoming village local with an extensive dining area. Four bays inside the pub are evidence that the building was originally a row of cottages, and it is recorded as being owned by the Bagot family in the 1730s. Over the years the pub has been thoughtfully extended, and is an imposing sight. ⚏ ✿ ◑ ☖ ♣ P

WHISTON

Swan
ST19 5QH (2 miles W of Penkridge) OS895144
◎ 6 (12 Sat)-11; 12-10.30 Sun

☎ (01785) 716200
Banks's Original; Holden's Bitter; guest beer Ⓗ
With an emphasis on excellent beer and superb food, new owners have transformed the Swan from an unviable pub into a thriving one. It has recently been extended. Midlands micro-brewers supply most of the guest beers. As much local produce as possible is used for the wide range of meals. Built in 1593, the oldest part of the pub is the small bar that caters well for the local farming community. The six acres of grounds include a children's obstacle course. ⚏ ✿ ◑ ☖ Å ♣ P

WOLSTANTON

New Smithy Inn (aka Archer)
21 Church Lane, ST5 0EH
◎ 11-11; 12-10.30 Sun
☎ (01782) 740467
Draught Bass; Everards Beacon, Tiger; guest beers Ⓗ
This pub was saved from the bulldozers by a local residents' campaign. It is particularly popular at weekends. In the summer the outside drinking area is often busier than inside. This is a one-roomed, split-level pub, thoughtfully renovated throughout by the current lessee. There are up to five real ales available, two of which vary.
✿ ♣ P ▯

WRINEHILL

Crown Inn
Den Lane, CW3 9BT
(just off A531 between Newcastle and Crewe)
◎ 12-3 (not Mon), 6-11; 12-4, 6-10.30 Sun
☎ (01270) 820472
Adnams Bitter; Banks's Original; Marston's Bitter, Pedigree; guest beer Ⓗ
Welcoming village pub, formerly a coaching inn on the London to Chester road. A genuine free house for 26 years, the owners have a strong commitment to real ale. Five cask beers are always stocked, and the guest changes frequently. It won the 'Taste of Staffordshire good food awards – real ale award' (Oct 2002). The pub has one comfortable, U-shaped lounge bar with no-smoking area, inglenook and open fire. No TV, juke box, bandits or pool spoil the peace. The food menu changes monthly: steaks, fresh fish, vegetarian options and fresh vegetables.
⚏ Q ✿ ◑ P ⤢

YOXALL

Golden Cup
Main Street, DE13 8NQ (on A515)
◎ 12-3, 5-11; 12-11 Sat; 12-10.30 Sun
☎ (01543) 472295 website: www.thegoldencup.com
Marston's Pedigree; guest beers Ⓗ
Impressive 300-year-old inn at the centre of the village, opposite St Peter's Church. The smart lounge caters for diners, with an extensive menu on offer. Crib, darts, dominoes and pool are played in the public bar. The pub has award-winning gardens that stretch down to the River Swarbourn and the grounds include a camping area. Attractive hanging baskets are displayed throughout the spring and summer. Yoxall is accessible on the 812 bus service from Burton and Lichfield.
⚏ ✿ ⌂ ◑ ☖ੳ Å ♣ P

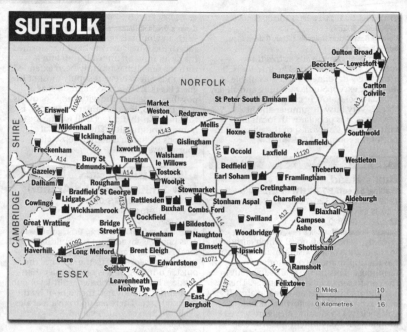

SUFFOLK

Mill Inn
Market Cross Place, IP15 5BJ
☼ 11-3, 6-11; 11-11 Fri & Sat; 12-10.30 Sun
☎ (01728) 452563 website: www.themillinn.com
Adnams Bitter, Broadside, seasonal beers Ⓗ
Almost on the beach, opposite the historic
Moot Hall, this timbered inn, with its
leaded windows, is a second home to many
a fisherman; buy the freshest of fish from
their huts across the road. This dog-friendly
pub is very comfortable both in the front
bars and the dining room at the rear. Many
local RNLI photographs are displayed, as the
landlord is a crew member of the Aldeburgh
lifeboat the Freddie Cooper. 🛏◗

White Hart
222 High Street, IP15 5AJ
☼ 11-11; 12-10.30 Sun
☎ (01728) 453205
Adnams Bitter, Broadside, seasonal beers Ⓗ
At the end of the High Street, next to
Aldeburgh's chip shop, this small single-
room pub was once the town reading room
and is still a great place to read the paper
while enjoying a pint. Always busy with
locals and tourists to this popular seaside
town, no-frills seating and scrubbed tables
give a real drinkers' pub atmosphere. Tables
outside at the rear and benches to the front
are provided for sunny days. This pub never
changes – why would it? 🏠❀🛏♣

BECCLES

Bear & Bells
Old Market, NR34 9AP (next to bus station)
☼ 11.30-3, 5.30-11; 12-3, 7-10.30 Sun
☎ (01502) 712291
Adnams Bitter; Greene King IPA; guest beers Ⓗ
Large, Victorian, town-centre pub by the
bus station and close to the River Waveney,
so it is handy for visitors to the Broads. At

least three guest beers are available in
winter, one is often a dark ale. Wholesome
food is available, except Monday. Live folk
music is played on Sunday evening. A
spacious function room is for hire, where
skittles can be played by prior arrangement.
Please note that mobile phones must be
switched off. Q❀◗●♣♠P

BEDFIELD

Crown
Church Lane, IP13 7JJ (head N from Earl Soham)
☼ 11.30-3 (not Tue; may vary), 6-11;
12-4, 7-10.30 Sun
☎ (01728) 628431
Greene King IPA; guest beer Ⓗ
Thatched, 15th-century, rural pub with low
beams and tiled floor – well worth seeking
out. Disparate wall displays include a
Luftwaffe photograph of the area,
instructions for constructing this timber-
framed building and the largest wooden
spoon ever seen. All the traditional pub
games are played, plus bar billiards, shut the
box, and the extremely rare caves. It hosts a
quiz (Sun), plus monthly karaoke and
country and western. Internet facilities are
available. Meals are served in summer.
🏠❀◗●Å♣P⌿

BILDESTON

King's Head
132 High Street, IP7 7ED
☼ 12-3, 5-11; closed winter Mon; 12-10.30 Sun
☎ (01449) 741434
website: www.bildestonkingshead.co.uk
Beer range varies Ⓗ
Home of the King's Head Brewery since
1996 with three beers usually on tap. If
plans approved by the local council go
ahead, the bar area will be reduced by
conversion of part of this historic village-
centre inn to residential use. Always a

lively venue, it hosts live music on Saturday evening. High, heavily moulded beamed ceilings and large brick inglenooks give the bar great character. Accommodation is in two en-suite rooms or a self-catering flat. Meals are served all day Sunday.
🏠❀⛵◑P

BLAXHALL

Ship Inn
IP12 2DY (on A1152 from Woodbridge)
🕓 7-11 (not Mon or Tue); 12-2.30, 7-11 Sat; 12-2.30 Sun
☎ (01728) 688316 website: www.shipinnblaxhall.co.uk
Adnams Bitter; Woodforde's Wherry, Nelson's Revenge (summer); guest beers Ⓗ
Traditional, low-beamed, 18th-century village inn with a rich history of smuggling and poaching. Traditional music nights are staged. Accommodation is offered in a converted stable block close to the pub; all rooms have en-suite facilities. Home-cooked food includes locally-caught fish (lunches at weekends). A large sandstone block, weighing about five tons, at nearby Stone Farm is thought to have been deposited during the Ice Age. However, locals have other stories, and some claim it is growing in size!
🏠Q❀⛵◑♣P✂

BRADFIELD ST GEORGE

Fox & Hounds
Felsham Road, IP30 0AB
🕓 11.30-3, 5.30-11; closed Mon; 12-3, 7-10.30 Sun
☎ (01284) 386379
website: www.maypolegreenbarns.co.uk
Earl Soham Victoria; Nethergate Suffolk County; guest beer Ⓗ
On the village outskirts, close to the historic coppiced woodland of the Suffolk Wildlife Trust, this free house and country restaurant is a beautifully restored Victorian inn. Refurbished to provide a combination of a real ale pub with a full menu and B&B accommodation, it offers excellent service. The comfortable, attractive interior has two wood-fronted bar areas, one of which has a woodblock floor, pine seating and a wood-burning stove.
🏠Q❀⛵◑P

BRAMFIELD

Queen's Head
The Street, IP19 9HT
🕓 11-3, 6-11; 12-2.30, 7-10.30 Sun
☎ (01986) 784214
Adnams Bitter, Broadside, seasonal beers Ⓗ
16th-century pub by the side of the thatched church that has an unusual round detached tower. The main room boasts an impressive inglenook; just the place to be on a winter's night. A few steps lead to a lower level where children are admitted. Farming implements abound – guess the use of some! Through the passageway is a smaller room, mostly for diners. The food has won many awards and is noted for being based on organic produce from local suppliers.
🏠Q❀◑P

BRENT ELEIGH

Cock ☆
Lavenham Road, CO10 9PB OS941478
🕓 12-3, 6-11; 12-3, 7-10.30 Sun
☎ (01787) 247371
Adnams Bitter; Greene King IPA, Abbot Ⓗ
Absolute gem! This pub manages to transport you back to a time most pubs have long forgotten. In winter both the tiny bars are snug and warm, in summer, with the door open, the bar is at one with its surroundings. Good conversation is guaranteed – sit and listen and you will be involved. Close to Lavenham and the beautiful Brett Valley, the comfortable accommodation is recommended. The pub is CAMROT (Campaign for Real Outside Toilets) approved. Do not miss it.
🏠Q❀⛵⛁♣●P

BRIDGE STREET

Rose & Crown
CO10 9BQ
🕓 11.30-3, 6-11; 12-3, 7-10.30 Sun
☎ (01787) 247022
Greene King IPA; guest beer Ⓖ
Conveniently located between Bury St Edmunds and Sudbury, this pub prides itself on offering a varied and freshly-cooked menu and excellent beer straight from the cask (the guest beer is supplied by Greene King). Feature menus are offered for special occasions and Friday is the popular 'fish day' when a selection of freshly-caught fish is offered. This is a friendly place for the local community and visitors to the tourist destinations of Long Melford and Lavenham. 🏠Q❀◑P

BUNGAY

Fleece
St Mary's Street, NR35 1AX
🕓 11-11; 12-10.30 Sun
☎ (01986) 892192
Adnams Bitter; Fuller's London Pride; guest beer Ⓗ
Spacious, 16th-century pub tied to Adnams, formerly called the Cross Keys, situated opposite the Buttercross Market and close to the castle. The main bar has an olde-worlde feel with a large open fire and beams. Drinking/eating areas include a snug and no-smoking area. There is a pool table and large-screen TV for sporting events in the

INDEPENDENT BREWERIES

Adnams Southwold
Bartrams Rougham
Bury Street Stowmarket
Cox & Holbrook Buxhall
Earl Soham Earl Soham
Green Dragon Bungay
Greene King Bury St Edmunds
Kings Head Bildeston
Lidstones Wickhambrook
Mauldons Sudbury
Nethergate Clare
Old Cannon Bury St Edmunds
Old Chimneys Market Weston
Oulton Oulton Broad
St Peter's St Peter South Elmham

room which was previously the next door property.

🏠🛏️🕮🍴🛋️🅿️✕

Green Dragon
29 Broad Street, NR35 1EE
✪ 11-3, 4.30-11; 11-11 Fri & Sat; 12-3, 7-10.30 Sun
☎ (01986) 892681
Green Dragon Chaucer Ale, Bridge Street Bitter, Ⓗ **seasonal beers** Ⓖ/Ⓗ

The Green Dragon beers and bottle-conditioned seasonal ales are brewed in outbuildings next to the car park at the rear of this property (brewery tours by appointment only). This town pub consists of a public bar, a lounge and a dining area that doubles as a family room and leads through to the secluded garden. Flexible hours depend on demand; in summer the pub is open all day Sunday if busy.

🏠🛏️🕮🍴🛋️♿🅿️

BURY ST EDMUNDS

King's Arms
23 Brentgovel Street, IP33 1EB
✪ 11-11; closed Sun
☎ (01284) 761874
Greene King IPA, Abbot, Old Speckled Hen; guest beers Ⓗ

Just outside the main town square, this one-bar pub is popular with customers of all ages. A fascinating photo collection and interesting artefacts are displayed. The 'happy hour' ales are served in large pint-and-a-half glasses. It is one of very few pubs in the town centre offering an outside drinking area, which not surprisingly is well used in summer. The unusually named meals are excellent value and served promptly.

🏠🕮🍴

Old Cannon
86 Cannon Street, IP33 1JR
✪ 12-3 (not Mon), 5-11; 12-3, 7-10.30 Sun
☎ (01284) 768769 website: www.oldcannon.co.uk
Old Cannon Best Bitter, Gunner's Daughter, seasonal beers; guest beers Ⓗ

Formerly the St Edmund's Head, this pub/brewery is on the same site as the original Cannon Brewery (established in 1847). It reopened in December 1999 and has rapidly become known as the place in town for real ale fans. The Old Cannon beers are brewed on site, with the brewing vessels on view in the bar. At least two guest beers from around the country are sold. A high quality menu and accommodation are available (booking is essential). Pub games include lie dice.

🏠Q🕮🛏️🍴♣🅿️🍴

Rose & Crown
48 Whiting Street, IP33 1NP
✪ 11.30-11; 11.30-3, 7-11 Sat; 12-2.30, 7-10.30 Sun
☎ (01284) 755934
Greene King XX Mild, IPA, Abbot; guest beer Ⓗ

Highly recommended and still very much a town local, this listed red-brick and tile-faced street-corner pub has been run by the same family for 28 years. Retaining two bars plus a rare off-sales counter, both bars bear a subtle porcine theme. Within sight of Greene King's Westgate Brewery, it is frequented by all ranks of staff, and is well-

known for the mild which nearly outsells the IPA. Good value lunches are served Monday–Saturday. Ⓗ♣

BUXHALL

Buxhall Crown
Mill Road, IP14 3DW
(signed off B1115, W of Stowmarket)
✪ 12-3, 6.30-11; 12-3 (closed eve) Sun
☎ (01449) 736521
Beer range varies Ⓗ

Benefiting from fine views over open countryside, beside an old windmill, the Crown is an imposing building of two halves. The public bar on the right is of Victorian white brick, decorated with hops and local memorabilia, and sits higher than the older restaurant, which is very cosy, with low ceilings and a log fire. The beers (usually three on tap) change weekly and showcase local breweries. An interesting menu is complemented by over 30 wines and champagnes sold by the glass.

🏠🕮🍴🛋️🅿️

CAMPSEA ASHE

Dog & Duck
Station Road, IP13 0PT (1½ miles from A12)
✪ 11-2.30 (not Wed), 7-11; 12-2.30, 7-10.30 Sun
☎ (01728) 748439
Adnams Bitter, Oyster Stout (winter), **Woodforde's Mardler's, Wherry** Ⓗ

Friendly, local, one-bar country inn opposite Wickham Market Station. Accommodation is available in five en-suite rooms, two of which are family rooms and one is adapted for disabled guests. Ideal for touring the Suffolk countryside, good, home-cooked food is served. A spacious garden has ample seating for summer.

🏠🕮🛏️♿🚲(Wickham Market) ♣🅿️

CARLTON COLVILLE

Bell Inn
The Street, NR33 8JR (off B1384)
✪ 11-3, 7-11; 11-11 Fri & Sat; 12-10.30 Sun
☎ (01502) 582873
Oulton Bitter, Nutford Mild, Nautilus, Gone Fishing, seasonal beers; guest beer Ⓖ

Recently extended inn owned by Oulton Ales with car parking at the front and a garden at the rear. This open-plan pub has a central fireplace separating the drinking area from the restaurant with its original flagstone floor. Beers are now served by gravity dispense from a new temperature-controlled room, but handpumps are occasionally used. Good quality food is served throughout the inn (booking for the restaurant advisable). The no-smoking area doubles as a family room.

🏠Q🛏️🕮🍴♿🅿️✕

CHARSFIELD

Three Horseshoes
The Street, IP13 7PY (off B1078) OS5257564
✪ 12-3, 6-11; 12-10.30 Sun
☎ (01473) 737330
Adnams Bitter, Broadside; Earl Soham Victoria (summer)**; Fuller's London Pride** Ⓗ

Homely village pub noted for its good food in generous portions, based on local produce and well-kept ales. The landlord's

extensive collection of Laurel and Hardy memorabilia is on show in the bar. Ronald Blythe's book, Akenfield, Portrait of an English Village is based on Charsfield.
ᴁ Q ⊛ ◑ ♣ P

COCKFIELD

Three Horseshoes
Stows Hill, IP30 0JB (on A1141)
✪ 11-3 (not Tue), 6-11; 12-3, 7-10.30 Sun
☎ (01284) 828177
website: www.threehorseshoespub.co.uk
Greene King IPA; guest beers Ⓗ
Part-thatched, 14th-century inn where the restaurant boasts one of the oldest king post roofs in Suffolk and serves home-cooked meals and specials. Pub games such as ring the bull are played. The cosy, beamed bar has three handpumps, one dispenses a house beer brewed by Mauldons. The garden affords rural views; camping and caravanning facilities are available on site.
ᴁ ⊛ ◑ ⌺ ♿ ♠ ♣ P

COMBS FORD

Gladstone Arms
2 Combs Ford, IP14 2AP
(on Needham road, 1 mile from Stowmarket)
✪ 11-3, 5 (6 Sat)-11; 12-3, 7-10.30 Sun
☎ (01449) 612339
Adnams Bitter, Broadside Ⓗ
Adnams' tied house in a hamlet on the southern outskirts of the market town of Stowmarket. The large bar is divided into several distinct drinking areas, with an eating area at one end. A garden can be found beyond the car park, beside a small stream. Lunches are served 12–2 daily and evening meals, 7–9 (not Sun). Just a mile away, the Museum of East Anglian Life, is well worth a visit (open Easter-autumn).
⊛ ◑ ♣ P

COWLINGE

Three Tuns
Queen's Street, CB8 9QD
(1½ miles N of A143 Haverhill-Bury St Edmunds road)
✪ 12-2 (not Mon), 5.30 (6 Mon; 5 Fri)-11; 12-11 Sat;
12-10.30 Sun
☎ (01440) 821847
Adnams Bitter, Broadside; guest beer Ⓗ
This gem of a village local was revived in 2001 after many doldrum years with periods of inactivity; vigorous local and CAMRA protests thwarted permanent closure. The superb beamed bar is estimated to be 16th century and the name Three Tuns indicates an ancient pub. A new dining area has been opened in former living accommodation (eve meals Tue–Sun). Cowlinge is a dispersed village with no real centre, so do not despair if the pub is not apparent immediately. ᴁ Q ⊛ ◑ ♣ P

CRETINGHAM

Bell
The Street, IP13 7BJ OS228603
✪ 11-2.30, 6-11; 12-10.30 Sun
☎ (01728) 685419
Adnams Bitter; Earl Soham Victoria; Mauldons Suffolk Pride; guest beer (summer) Ⓗ
Situated in a pretty village in the upper reaches of Deben Valley, nearby Monewden

has two plant-rich meadows managed by the Suffolk Wildlife Trust. The pub, formerly four cottages, provides a superb combination of good food and good beer in a pleasant atmosphere. The ales come from four local breweries, while the menu is extremely varied to suit all tastes. Shove-ha'penny can be played here.
ᴁ Q ⊛ ⋈ ◑ ♣ P⌿

DALHAM

Affleck Arms
Brookside, CB8 8TG (on B1085)
✪ 5 (6 Sat)-11; 12-10.30 Sun
☎ (01638) 500306
Adnams Bitter; Greene King IPA; guest beers Ⓗ
Pretty, Elizabethan, thatched inn on the bank of the River Kennett, amid picturesque countryside. Keen pricing by the enterprising family owners has made this inn well used by passing trade. No food, just good ales, usually four on tap, featuring Nethergate and Woodforde's among the guests. Self-contained accommodation is available in an annexe. ᴁ ⋈ P

EARL SOHAM

Victoria
The Street, IP13 7RL
(on A1120 at west end of village)
✪ 11.30-3, 6-11; 12-3, 7-10.30 Sun
☎ (01728) 685758
Earl Soham Gannet Mild, Victoria, Sir Roger's Porter, Albert Ale, Jolabrugg Ⓗ
No airs and graces in this popular village pub. An interesting and radical menu uses fresh, and where possible, local produce. Tons of friendly atmosphere go well with the excellent range of beers brewed just across the road. The neighbouring Victoria Terrace was formerly a barley maltings. Outside drinking takes place on the green in front of the pub. ᴁ Q ⊛ ◑ ♣ P

EAST BERGHOLT

Hare & Hounds
Heath Road, CO7 6RL
✪ 12-2.30, 5-11; 12-2.30, 6-10.30 Sun
☎ (01206) 298438
Adnams Bitter, Broadside; Ⓗ **guest beers** Ⓖ
Friendly, traditional village pub with a relaxed, cosy atmosphere where the long-standing landlord and landlady have celebrated over 25 years service. Built in the 15th century, it retains a pargetted ceiling (deep plaster relief), circa 1590, in the lounge. Guest beers are mainly from local breweries. No food is served Tuesday. This fine pub offers something for everyone, including a family room and a pleasant garden. Q ⌂ ⊛ ◑ ⌺ ♿ ♣ P

EDWARDSTONE

White Horse
Mill Green, CO10 5PX OS951429
✪ 12-2 (not Mon, Tue or Thu), 6.30-11; 12-3,
7-10.30 Sun
☎ (01787) 211211
website: www.the-white-horse-inn.co.uk
Greene King IPA; guest beers Ⓗ
Off the beaten track, an OS map will help to find this two-bar free house. It boasts a collection of enamel signs in both bars, and

a wide choice of pub games in the public includes ring the bull. Note the Oliver's Brewery lettering outside, taken over by Greene King in 1919. One of the guests is usually a dark beer. Accommodation is in holiday chalets in the pub grounds. In early summer listen for nightingales calling from the nearby woods. ♨Q⊛✿🛏◑⊕A♣P

ELMSETT

Rose & Crown
The Street, IP7 6PA
✪ 12-3 (not Mon, Tue or Thu), 7-11; 12-3, 7-10.30 Sun
☎ (01473) 658482
Woodforde's Wherry, Nelson's Revenge, Norfolk Nog Ⓗ

Genuine, community pub set in a small, dispersed village which has been fortunate to retain its post office, shop, village hall and church. Recently refurbished, it has an L-shaped main bar, plus a pool area. The landlord endeavours to cater for a wide variety of local drinkers and diners and also organises social trips, both within UK and further afield. It is especially busy at weekends.
♨⊛◑♣P🖩

ERISWELL

Chequers
The Street, IP27 9BH
✪ 11-3, 5.30-11; 12-4, 7-10.30 Sun
☎ (01638) 532478
Greene King IPA, Abbot Ⓗ

In a village within the Elveden estate, now owned by the Guinness family, this tidy 150-year-old pub offers fine facilities for visitors to the area, including good food and a new no-smoking conservatory. The village was built to serve an estate much older than the current one; ask the landlord about the small NEC plaques on the attractive flint-faced houses. Thetford Forest nearby offers fine walks for nature lovers; call at the visitor centre near Brandon for information.
Q⊛◑♣P⍀

FELIXSTOWE (WALTON)

Half Moon
303 Walton High Street, IP11 9QL
✪ 12-2.30, 5-11; 12-11 Sat; 12-3, 7-10.30 Sun
☎ (01394) 216009
website: www.halfmoonfelixstowe.com
Adnams Bitter, Broadside; guest beer Ⓗ

Traditional community pub – no fruit machines, recorded music or food, just good beer and conversation. Note the stained glass screens above the bar. Darts, dominoes, cribbage and backgammon can all be played. The lounge has a small area partitioned off for non-smokers. Plenty of reading matter is provided, but do not fret if you have forgotten your specs – a pair may be borrowed! Ask the landlord about the 'word of the week'. Euros are accepted.
♨Q⊛⊕♣P⍀

FRAMLINGHAM

Station Hotel
Station Road, IP13 9EE (on B1116)
✪ 12-2.30, 5-11; 12-2.30, 7-10.30 Sun
☎ (01728) 723455

Earl Soham Gannet Mild, Victoria, Sir Roger's Porter, Albert Ale, Jolabrugg Ⓗ

Spacious bar with a rare five-handpull font. An excellent menu is supplemented by speciality soups that are out of this world. Railway-themed memorabilia reflect the link with Framlingham's history and old station. The pub is a short walk from this delightful old town's market square and castle, where Mary Tudor was proclaimed Queen. ♨Q🛏⊛◑♣P

FRECKENHAM

Golden Boar Inn
The Street, IP28 8HZ
(2½ miles from A11 on B1102 from Mildenhall)
✪ 12-11; 12-4.30 Sun
☎ (01638) 723000
Adnams Bitter; Courage Directors; Fuller's London Pride; guest beer Ⓗ

16th-century former coaching inn, where many old features were exposed during building work; most impressive is the fireplace in the lounge. Recent additions are four new guest rooms on the premises, to supplement the two self-contained chalets. The dining room extension used reclaimed materials, while the kitchen and cellar were enlarged to cope with demand from the acclaimed restaurant. Meals are prepared using the freshest ingredients. ⊛🛏◑&P

GAZELEY

Chequers Inn
The Green, CB8 8RF
✪ 12-3.30 (not Mon; 12-4 Sat), 6-11; 12-11 Fri; 12-4, 7-10.30 Sun
☎ (01638) 750050
Greene King IPA, Abbot; guest beer Ⓗ

Village-centre local just off the through road. The building is around 400 years old and, although not a classic coaching inn, it may have been intended to serve travellers on the ancient 'Bury road' that passes nearby, crossing the superb packhorse bridge in Moulton and passing on to Bury via Higham. The large rear garden houses a petanque terrain. ♨Q◑⊕♣P

GISLINGHAM

Six Bells
High Street, IP23 8JD
✪ 12-3, 7 (6 Fri)-11; 12-3, 7-10.30 Sun
☎ (01379) 783349
Beer range varies Ⓗ

Spacious village-centre pub. It supports micro-breweries and a fine display of pump clips decorates the walls. Good home-made food is served in the bar or in the no-smoking Columbine restaurant (no food Mon). Note the well which is illuminated to show the drop to the water. The Columbine has connections with the local church where it is believed that the 15th-century stained glass window featuring these flowers is one of the earliest pictorial records of them in the country. Q🐕⊛◑⊕♣P

GREAT WRATTING

Red Lion
School Road, CB9 7HA
✪ 11-2.30, 5-11; 11-11 Sat; 12-3, 7-10.30 Sun
☎ (01440) 783237

Adnams Bitter, Broadside; guest beer (summer) Ⓗ
One of the prettiest and most instantly recognisable pub exteriors in the county, notable for its distinctive whalebone arch over the doorway. This family-run Adnams' tied house comprises a restaurant and a cosy public bar. Functions are catered for in the summer months in a permanent marquee erected to the rear of the pub overlooking the gardens and meadows. ♨Q❀◑ ⊟P

HAVERHILL

Queen's Head
Queen Street, CB9 9DZ
◷ 11-11; 12-10.30 Sun
☎ (01440) 702026
Courage Best Bitter; Greene King Old Speckled Hen; Nethergate Suffolk County, Augustinian Ale; guest beers Ⓗ
Handsome Grade II listed building, dating from 1470, quite possibly the oldest property in town. Etched glass in the ground-floor windows gives character to a popular pub in the main shopping area (pedestrianised during the day). Inside, a cosy atmosphere is created by three bars; one has games, such as pool, while the two smaller rooms are gems and just invite settling down for a pint. Straightforward pub food is available Monday–Saturday.
◑⊟♣P

HOXNE

Swan ❷
Low Street, IP21 5AS (follow signs from Eye)
◷ 11-3, 6-11; 12-10.30 Sun
☎ (01379) 668275
Adnams Bitter, Broadside; Ⓖ guest beers Ⓗ
Impressive pub next to the river, built in 1480 by the Bishop of Norwich as a centre for rest and relaxation. This vibrant village pub features a number of impressive timber-framed rooms which still offer 'R and R' for any weary traveller. Children are welcome until 9.30pm in the family room. Look out for the beer festivals in May and November when a good selection of beers from various local and not-so-local micro-breweries can be tried. ♨Q❦❀◑♣P

ICKLINGHAM

Plough
62 The Street, IP28 6PL
◷ 11.30-3, 6.30-11 (closed winter Mon); 12-3, 7-10.30 Sun
☎ (01638) 711770
Greene King IPA; Woodforde's Wherry; guest beer Ⓗ
Attractive village local, now reviving under the stewardship of an experienced landlord. The building, once two or even three workers' dwellings, retains a fine flint cottage appearance, but is much more spacious than it appears from outside. The River Lark runs by to the rear and is possibly the key to the origins of the pub as it used to be navigable up to Bury St Edmunds. Visit West Stow Country Park close by, with its replica Saxon village.
♨Q❀◑♣P⏚

IPSWICH

Fat Cat
288 Spring Road, IP4 5NL

◷ 12 (11 Sat)-11; 12-10.30 Sun
☎ (01473) 726524 website: www.fatcatipswich.co.uk
Adnams Bitter; Ⓗ Fuller's London Pride; Hop Back Summer Lightning; Oakham JHB; Woodforde's Wherry; guest beers Ⓖ
Award-winning pub, this classic Victorian boozer is full of original enamel advertising signs and brewery posters. Simply decorated, with bench seating and bare floorboards, you can sit in the conservatory or garden, shaded by the hop bines. The hops have been used by Old Chimneys to produce special ales. Many of the 15 or so beers from the tap room, visible from the bar, are supplied by local micro-breweries. Belgian bottled beers, and Leffe Blond on draught, plus Broadland fruit wines from Norfolk are also stocked.
Q❀≈(Derby Rd)♣P

Greyhound
9 Henley Road, IP1 3SE
◷ 11-2.30, 5-11; 11-11 Sat; 12-10.30 Sun
☎ (01473) 252862
Adnams Bitter, Broadside, seasonal beers; Fuller's London Pride; guest beers Ⓗ
Pleasant, two-roomed pub within easy walking distance of the town centre, close to Christchurch Park with its splendid mansion. The relaxed, friendly atmosphere is enhanced by welcoming staff. Well used by locals, the Greyhound is also a popular meeting place for town-centre workers. The food is of high quality, prepared on the premises, with an interesting menu that changes regularly.
❀◑⊟♣P

Lord Nelson ❷
81 Fore Street, IP4 1JZ
(opp. Wherry Lane from the marina)
◷ 11-2.30 (not Sat unless Ipswich match on), 5 (6 Sat)-11; 12-4 Sun
☎ (01473) 254072
website: www.ipswichlordnelson.com
Adnams Bitter, Broadside, seasonal beers Ⓖ
Grade II listed building, originally two cottages. Its earliest reference was in the reign of Charles II when it was a billet for soldiers. Between 1790 and 1805, it was known as the Noah's Ark. Adorned with Nelson and nautical memorabilia, in the no-smoking area a display cabinet of 18th-century artefacts includes mummified rats. Mostly open plan, with low, exposed beams, an open fire and high-backed settle add character. Handy for rapidly developing wet dock area; no food is served Sunday evening. ❀◑♣⏚

Mannings ❷
8 Cornhill, IP1 1DF
◷ 11-11; 12-5 Sun
☎ (01473) 254170
Adnams Bitter, Broadside; guest beers Ⓗ
Tucked away on Cornhill (which is reputedly the oldest public square in Britain), Mannings combines the attributes of an English pub with those of a continental bar where you can sit for hours 'people watching' through the large front windows. Outside, the pub looks tiny, but it stretches back much further than the frontage suggests. Perfect for a break from shopping, it is also popular with people working in the town centre. This little gem is worth popping into. ❀◑&

Milestone Beer House
5 Woodbridge Road, IP4 2EA (opp. Odeon)
✪ 12-3, 5-11; 12-11 Fri & Sat; 12-10.30 Sun
☎ (01473) 252425
website: www.milestonebeerhouse.co.uk
Adnams Bitter, Ⓗ **Broadside;** Ⓖ **Greene King IPA, Abbot, Old Speckled Hen;** Ⓗ **guest beers** Ⓗ /Ⓖ
Impressive mock-Tudor pub near the town centre, where the range rarely drops below 15 real ales, plus two ciders.. You are guaranteed a beer to suit most dishes on the good value menu. As well as a place of pilgrimage for real ale drinkers, the Milestone is a mecca for live music fans, offering excellent entertainment. Shows at the Regent Theatre opposite, often finish in time for a final pint here. Excellent beer festivals are held in May and November.
🏨☸◑&♠♣P🖫

IXWORTH

Greyhound
49 High Street, IP31 2HJ
✪ 11-3, 6-11; 12-3, 7-10.30 Sun
☎ (01359) 230887
Greene King XX Mild, IPA, Abbot; guest beers Ⓗ
This traditional three-bar pub retains a marvellously intimate snug. An inn has stood on this site since Tudor times. Pub games are keenly promoted here: dominoes, crib, darts and pool are played; games evenings are held to raise funds for local charities. Bar meals are served daily (11–2 and 6–8). The pub takes party bookings with a choice of catering for 8-20 people.
☸◑🖛Ⓐ♣P

LAVENHAM

Angel
Market Place, CO10 9QZ
✪ 11-11; 12-10.30 Sun
☎ (01787) 247388
website: www.lavenham.co.uk/angel
Adnams Bitter, Broadside; Greene King IPA; Nethergate Suffolk County Ⓗ
The Angel is a 15th-century, family-run inn at the heart of England's finest medieval village. Great food, atmosphere and a warm welcome awaits you. All eight bedrooms are comfortable and well equipped with sparkling new bathrooms. It offers good value midweek breaks and a relaxing place to stay for exploring Constable country and the Suffolk coast. Local real ales are complemented by a good value wine list. Well-behaved children are welcome.
🏨Q☸🛏◑&P

LAXFIELD

King's Head (Low House) ☆
Gorams Mill Lane, IP13 8DW
✪ 12-3, 6-11; 12-3, 7-10.30 Sun
☎ (01986) 798395
Adnams Bitter, Broadside, seasonal beers; Fuller's London Pride Ⓖ
Not to be missed, this former CAMRA East Anglian Pub of the Year has no bar – in the finest tradition of the beer house, all ales are dispensed by gravity from the tap room. Multi-roomed, high-backed settles, quarry-tiled floors and low ceilings give it character, while the absence of fruit machines and electronic music enhances

the atmosphere. Tuesday afternoon sees informal traditional music sessions. The pub is best approached on foot via the nearby churchyard. Evening meals in winter are served Tuesday–Saturday. 🏨Q☸◑♣P

LEAVENHEATH HONEY TYE

Lion ⊘
Honey Tye, CO6 4NX (on A134)
✪ 11-3, 5.45-11; 12-10.30 Sun
☎ (01206) 263434 website:
www.thelionleavenheath.co.uk
Adnams Bitter; Greene King IPA Ⓗ
Large free house on the main Sudbury–Colchester road near Leavenheath. The single bar leads to an informal drinking/dining area, then on to a separate restaurant. The emphasis here is on food, but drinkers are welcome; it enjoys a regular trade. The food is varied and freshly prepared and has achieved a high local standing. Wheelchair access is via the restaurant. 🏨Q☸◑♣P

LIDGATE

Star Inn
CB8 9PP (on B1063)
✪ 12-3, 5 (6 Sat)-11; 12-4, 7-10.30 Sun
☎ (01638) 500275
Greene King IPA, Abbot, Old Speckled Hen Ⓗ
A taste of the Mediterranean in rural Suffolk; proof that with an enterprising partnership both good food and ale can result. This 16th-century beamed inn serves freshly-prepared Spanish fare, while boards display dishes to suit all tastes. No meals are served Sunday evening. Unusual under-bar beer engines serve Greene King ales. Bar billiards can be played here. 🏨🛏☸◑♣P

LONG MELFORD

Swan ⊘
Hall Street, CO10 9JQ
✪ 11.30-2.30, 5-11; 12-3, 7-10.30 Sun
☎ (01787) 378740
Greene King IPA, Abbot, guest beer (summer) Ⓗ
Opened in 1767 as a brew-pub, part of the two-storey brewhouse remains as a garage. Very much a village pub, many teams are fielded, including Suffolk's only bobsleigh team which raises money for local charities. A display of local history in the lounge has been collected by the landlord. Part of the rear bar, designated 'Tudor Corner', is used by the participants in Kentwell Hall's Tudor recreations – just one of Melford's attractions. No food is served Monday evening. 🏨Q☸◑♣

LOWESTOFT

Oak Tavern
Crown Street West, NR32 1SQ (off B1074)
✪ 10.30-11; 12-10.30 Sun
☎ (01502) 537246
Adnams Bitter; Greene King Abbot; guest beers Ⓗ
Large pub, situated on the northern side of town. Four real ales are always available, with dark beers often served during the winter. An extensive range of Belgian bottled beers, served in the appropriate glasses, is supplemented by De Koninck and Leffe on tap. The open-plan bar divides into two areas, one is festooned with Belgian

brewery memorabilia, the other, used for pool and darts, has a large-screen TV for sporting events. ❀≉♣P

Triangle Tavern
29 St Peter's Street, NR32 1QA
✪ 11-11; 12-10.30 Sun
☎ (01502) 582711
Beer range varies Ⓗ
Lively town pub stocking ales sourced from all over the country, including bottle-conditioned beers from home and Europe. Known locally as Lowestoft's permanent real ale festival, a new brewery under construction here will brew all Green Jack beers – at present Green Jack's Canary sold here is brewed elsewhere. Live music is staged twice weekly in the cosy front bar. Customers are welcome to bring their own food from nearby takeaways. Overall a fantastic pub. ⚄Φ≉♣♠

MARKET WESTON

Mill Inn
Bury Road, IP22 2PD
(between Stanton and Garboldisham)
✪ 12-3, 7-11; closed Mon; 12-3, 7-10.30 Sun
☎ (01359) 221018
Old Chimneys Military Mild; Greene King IPA; guest beer Ⓗ
Tall, white, brick and flint building, set on a crossroads on the B1111. The welcome and facilities inside belie the slightly austere frontage of this historic roadside inn. It is the closest outlet for Old Chimneys Brewery on the other side of the village. Free of tie, an interesting range of beers complements the superb fresh food. QΦ♣P

MELLIS

Railway Tavern
The Common, Yaxley, IP23 8DU
(next to railway, 1 mile W off A140)
✪ 12 (3.30 Mon & Tue)-11; 12-10.30 Sun
☎ (01379) 783416 website: www.mellistavern.co.uk
Adnams Bitter, Broadside, seasonal beers; Greene King IPA; Woodforde's Wherry; guest beers Ⓗ
Situated by the largest common in Suffolk, a nature conservation area, it is only a short drive from Thornham Walks nature trails. Near a disused station, the pub has pictures of steam trains in the L-shaped bar. It supports a wide range of activities, including sports teams, quizzes and folk music. Pool, darts, dominoes, cards and piano may all be played. Lunchtime food is available daily; evening meals in summer and occasionally at other times. ⚄➤ΦÅ♣P

MILDENHALL

Queen's Arms
42 Queensway, IP28 7JW
(follow signs to West Row)
✪ 12-2.30, 4.30-11; 12-11 Fri & Sat; 12-10.30 Sun
☎ (01638) 713657
Greene King XX Mild, IPA, Abbot; guest beer Ⓗ
Comfortable local, well attended by many regulars. Visitors are welcome, and it is favoured by the annual cycle rally. A community centre in every respect, it fields darts teams and many pub games are played; monthly quiz nights are well supported. Excellent home-cooked food is available at lunchtime and most evenings

(phone first); Sunday lunches are superb value. A good-sized garden is a bonus. ❀➤ΦÅ♣P

NAUGHTON

Wheelhouse
Whatfield Road, IP7 7BS (400 yds from B1078)
✪ 5 (12 Fri & Sat)-11; 12-10.30 Sun
☎ (01449) 740496
Adnams Bitter; Greene King IPA; Nethergate Suffolk County; guest beers Ⓗ
Parts of this thatched and pantiled Grade II listed building date back to around 1200. This remote pub is one of the few genuine free houses in Suffolk. Low beams abound so mind your head. Both smoking and no-smoking bars adjoin a no-smoking dining area. Walkers with or without dogs are welcome here, and in winter can warm themselves by a wood stove set in an old inglenook. A real rural gem. Evening meals are served Friday and Saturday (other times by arrangement). ⚄Q❀Φ♣♠P⌿

OCCOLD

Beaconsfield Arms
Mill Road, IP23 7PU
✪ 12-3, 6-11; 12-4, 6.30-10.30 Sun
☎ (01379) 678033
Adnams Bitter; Greene King IPA, Ⓗ **Abbot;** Ⓖ **guest beers** (summer) Ⓗ
This 300-year-old, village-centre local lies close to the pleasant little town of Eye. The main bar area has a low, beamed ceiling, flagstone floor and a large open fireplace. The traditional country pub ambience is completed by a lively and varied clientele. The food is excellent. Dominoes, pool and cribbage may be played. Extensive, safe children's play facilities are outside. Enjoy a rare opportunity to drink Abbot, served straight from the cask. ⚄Q❀Φ♣P

RAMSHOLT

Ramsholt Arms Hotel
Dock Road, Ramsholt Quay, IP12 3AB
(off B1083) OS307415
✪ 11.30-11; 12-10.30 Sun
☎ (01394) 411229 website: www.ramsholtarms.co.uk
Adnams Bitter, Broadside; Mauldons Suffolk Pride (summer)**; Woodforde's Norfolk Nog** (summer) Ⓗ
Former shooting lodge in a delightfully remote riverside location; take in the beautiful views from the bar. Popular with walkers and the sailing fraternity, the tiny hamlet on the bank of the River Deben consists of only the pub, half a dozen houses, a jetty and a Norman church, half a mile to the north. ⚄Q❀➤Φ♣P

RATTLESDEN

Five Bells
High Street, IP30 0RA
✪ 12-11; 12-10.30 Sun
☎ (01449) 737373
Adnams Bitter; guest beers Ⓗ
Lively community pub, with always something going on. Originally owned by Colchester Brewery, this busy free house reopened in 1991 after several years' closure. Deceptively spacious, with three bar areas, it fields football, pool and cribbage games. The outside drinking area opens on

433

to the pub's meadow which hosts village fêtes and other events. Toasted sandwiches are the only food available, but visitors may bring picnics. 🏚❀♣👄

REDGRAVE

Cross Keys
The Street, IP22 1RW (off B1113)
🕐 11.30-11 (not Mon lunch); 12-10.30 Sun
☎ (01379) 898510
Adnams Bitter; Bateman XB; Greene King IPA; guest beers Ⓗ
Built some 450 years ago for pilgrims along the route from London to Walsingham, it has been a pub for 250 years. Ideally situated by the village green and pond, it is well supported by local trade and walkers visiting the nearby ancient fens of Redgrave and Lopham. A varied menu includes home-made pies and daily specials. It stages folk music on Thursday evening, and an Easter sausage and beer fest (15 beers), with mini beer fests every bank holiday. The bar holds a children's certificate; no-smoking restaurant. 🏚Q❀◑🍴♣P

SHOTTISHAM

Sorrel Horse
Hollesley Road, IP12 3HD
🕐 12-3, 7-11; closed Mon; 12-3, 7-10.30 Sun
☎ (01394) 411617
Adnams Bitter or Greene King IPA; guest beers (summer) Ⓖ
Attractive, thatched village pub retaining two distinct bars; one is very basic, with a tiled floor and is dominated by games; the other is mainly used as a restaurant. Food is freshly prepared daily (booking advisable); discounts for pensioners apply some lunchtimes. It offers plenty of vegetarian options and Sunday roasts, too; evening meals served Wednesday–Sunday. It is popular with local campers and weekend visitors. 🏚Q☎❀◑🍴👍Å♣P⌿

SOUTHWOLD

Harbour Inn
Blackshore, IP18 6TA
🕐 11-11; 12-10.30 Sun
☎ (01502) 722381
Adnams Bitter, Broadside, seasonal beers Ⓗ
This pub is a walk of about one mile from the town centre, it stands on the riverside harbour, where there is always something to see. The lower bar has a quarry-tiled floor and a warming stove in winter. Children are welcome in here until 9pm. The upper bar though small is very welcoming. An extension into a former grain store provides extra dining space. Outside, there is a paved section to the front and to the rear the grassed area offers views over the marshes to Southwold town. 🏚❀◑ÅP

Lord Nelson
42 East Street, IP18 6EJ
🕐 10.30-11; 12-10.30 Sun
☎ (01502) 722079
Adnams Bitter, Broadside, seasonal beers Ⓗ
Popular pub, close to the beach and next to the former town reading room, now a museum. It offers three drinking areas; children are allowed in the side bar. There is also a shady patio to the rear. As expected,

there is a wealth of Nelson memorabilia, but a large collection of soda siphons provides a contrast. Expect a warm, friendly welcome from the longest-serving landlord in town at this dog-friendly pub. 🏚❀◑Å

STONHAM ASPAL

Ten Bells
The Street, IP14 6AF (on A1120)
🕐 11.30-3, 5-11; 12-3, 7-10.30 Sun
☎ (01449) 711601 website: www.tenbells.co.uk
Adnams Bitter; Greene King IPA; Ridleys Tolly Mild; guest beer Ⓗ
This thriving, traditional 16th-century pub is at the heart of the community in a picturesque village. The three rooms each have a distinctive atmosphere. This relaxed pub is a rare outlet for Tolly Mild (now brewed by Ridleys) and is noted for its excellent value, traditional food, which always includes vegetarian options. There is a no-smoking dining room, but food can be enjoyed anywhere in the pub. Amusements here include shove-ha'penny.
🏚Q❀◑👍♣P

STRADBROKE

Queen's Head
Queen's Street, IP21 5HG
🕐 11.30-3, 6-11; 12-3, 7-10.30 Sun
☎ (01379) 384384
Adnams Bitter; Greene King IPA, Abbot; Woodforde's Wherry; guest beer Ⓗ
One of three pubs in the village, the Queen's Head has a real community feel. You can challenge the young villagers to a game of pool or just sit and admire the impressive collection of naval artefacts that adorn part of the main drinking area. The beer range is mainly sourced from East Anglian brewers. During the annual beer and jazz festival in spring camping is available (by prior arrangement) in a nearby field. 🏚❀◑👍♣P⌿

SUDBURY

Waggon & Horses
Acton Square, CO10 1HJ
🕐 11-3, 6.30 (5 Fri)-11; 12-3, 7.30-10.30 Sun
☎ (01787) 312147
Greene King IPA; guest beers Ⓗ
Local in the back streets of Sudbury, its single bar has several drinking areas, with games, such as pool, at the far end. There is a small dining area (booking is advised) where the food is home cooked. The landlord is a local councillor and is active within the Sudbury in Bloom organisation. Guest beers tend to come from the Greene King list. 🏚Q☎❀🍴◑≈♣

SWILLAND

Moon & Mushroom
High Road, IP6 9LR
🕐 12-2.30 (not Mon), 6-11; 12-2.30, 7-10.30 Sun
☎ (01473) 785320
Buffy's Norwich Terrier, Hopleaf; Nethergate Umbel Ale; Wolf Coyote; Woodforde's Wherry, Norfolk Nog Ⓖ
Popular pub, about five miles from Ipswich run by a welcoming landlord and landlady. Oak beams, low ceilings, tiled floors, an open fire and a broad cross-section of customers all help to create an authentic,

traditional atmosphere. An unusual range of real ales comes from local micros, all served by gravity from cooled casks. Excellent home-cooked meals include a vegetarian choice. Dominoes, shove-ha'penny, backgammon and cards are available at this award-winning pub. ♨Q⊛◑♣P✂

THEBERTON

Lion
The Street, IB16 4RU
✪ 11-2.30, 6-11; 12.30-2.30, 7-10.30
☎ (01728) 830185 website: www.thelioninn.co.uk
Adnams Bitter; Woodforde's Wherry; guest beers Ⓗ
An easy-to-find red-brick free house on the main road through the village, just opposite the small, but very fine, thatched church. The guest beers change very quickly; hurry or you will miss one. The Lion is popular with locals and visitors to the bird reserve just down the road. At the rear is a patio leading through to the camping and caravan area. Live jazz is staged on the first Sunday of the month. ♨⊛◑ÅP

THURSTON

Fox & Hounds
Barton Road, IP31 3QT
✪ 12-2.30, 5-11; 12-11 Sat; 12-3, 7-10.30 Sun
☎ (01359) 232228
Adnams Bitter; Greene King IPA, Old Speckled Hen; guest beer Ⓗ
Friendly village pub, a listed building from the 1800s. At the heart of the village, it stands opposite the station on the Bury St Edmunds–Ipswich line. A fine selection of real ales is supplemented by weekly guests and home-cooked food. Evening meals are served Tuesday–Saturday. ⊛◑⊟Å⇌P

TOSTOCK

Gardener's Arms ⊘
Church Road, IP30 9PA
✪ 11.30-2.30, 7-11; 12-3, 7-10.30 Sun
☎ (01359) 270460
Greene King IPA, Abbot, seasonal beers Ⓗ
Close to the village green, this splendid old building retains many original low beams. The lively public bar has a stone floor and offers darts, pool and crib. The lounge bar boasts a large open fireplace and carver chairs. There is a no-smoking dining area serving reasonably-priced home-made food; tasty snacks are also available (no food Sun or Mon eve). This popular pub has an extensive garden and patio that are wonderful in summer. ♨⊛◑⊟Å♣P

WALSHAM LE WILLOWS

Six Bells ⊘
Summer Road, IP31 3AH
✪ 11.30-2.30, 5.30 (6.30 Sat)-11; 12-2, 7-10.30 Sun
☎ (01359) 259726
Greene King XX Mild, IPA, Ruddles Best, Abbot Ⓗ
Former wool merchant's house at the centre of a pretty village. This substantial, thatched, 16th-century building features heavily carved timbers in the bar. The six individual rooms and two bars offer a great variety. Use of open studs allow some rooms to be light and airy, while huge fireplaces and dark timbers create a cosy atmosphere. The licensees concentrate on

beer sales so only sandwiches are served (no food Sun). ♨Q⊛⊟♣P

WESTLETON

White Horse
Darsham Road, IP17 3AH
✪ 12-3 (4 Sat), 7-11; 12-4, 7-10.30 Sun
☎ (01728) 648222
Adnams Bitter, Broadside, seasonal beers Ⓗ
Adnams' tied house, attractively situated by the village green and duckpond. A brick-built local with distinctive Dutch-style gables, the main bar divides into two distinct areas, with a dining room down a few stairs. This is a good stopping-off point for walkers on the Heritage Coast; en-suite accommodation is offered. Close to the RSPB Reserve at Minsmere, it is an ideal birdwatchers' retreat. ♨⊛⇔◑♣P

WOODBRIDGE

Cherry Tree ⊘
73 Cumberland Street, IP12 4QG
✪ 11-3, 5-11; 11-11 Sat; 12-10.30 Sun
☎ (01394) 384627
Adnams Bitter, Broadside, seasonal beers; guest beers Ⓗ
Originally a row of cottages on the main road to Ipswich, the Cherry Tree is a cosy, single-bar pub, popular with drinkers of all ages. Despite being an Adnams' tied house, it offers a good range of guest beers from outside Suffolk. The varied menu should have a dish to suit most tastes. A cosy fire makes for a pleasant winter's night drinking with a pint of Adnams Tally Ho! Well worth a visit. ♨⊛◑⇌♣P✂

Thomas Seckford
Seckford Street, IP12 4LZ
✪ 12-3, 5 (6 Sat)-11; 12-4, 7-10.30 Sun
☎ (01394) 384446
Beer range varies Ⓗ
Just off the town centre, near Fen Meadow (common land) this early Victorian free house offers an excellent menu of home-cooked food, Tuesday–Saturday, and an interesting selection of six local real ales. The comfortable decor features many unusual pieces of furniture and antiques. The public area is larger than at first appears, since the bar helps to divide the narrow building and initially hides the drinking and eating areas to the rear. Beware of the heated footrail around the bar servery (it's hot!). Q⊛◑⊟♣⊓

WOOLPIT

Bull Inn
The Street, IP30 9SA
✪ 11 (11.30 Sat)-3, 6-11; 12-3.30, 7-10.30 Sun
☎ (01359) 240393 website: www.bullinnwoolpit.co.uk
Adnams Bitter; guest beers Ⓗ
A true community pub supporting numerous local charities and sports teams. This family-run business offers good home-cooked food throughout the week, except Sunday evening. A large car park by the garden leads off the former main Cambridge–Ipswich road. This small, but ancient, village once had 10 pubs and two annual fairs; it is interesting to walk around and St Mary's Church is a must to visit. ⇖⊛⇔◑⊟♣P

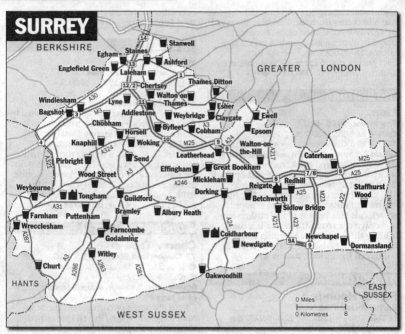

SURREY

BERKSHIRE

Stanwell
Egham
Staines
Ashford
Englefield Green
Laleham
GREATER LONDON
Chertsey
Thames Ditton
Windlesham
Lyne
Walton on Thames
Esher
Bagshot
Addlestone
Weybridge
Claygate
Ewell
Chobham
Byfleet
Epsom
Horsell
Cobham
Knaphill
Woking
Walton-on-the-Hill
Caterham
Pirbright
Send
Leatherhead
Wood Street
Effingham
Great Bookham
Weybourne
Mickleham
Redhill
Staffhurst Wood
Tongham
Guildford
Dorking
Reigate
Farnham
Puttenham
Bramley
Betchworth
Wrecclesham
Albury Heath
Sidlow Bridge
Farncombe
Coldharbour
Newchapel
Godalming
Newdigate
Dormansland
Witley
Churt
Oakwoodhill
HANTS
WEST SUSSEX
EAST SUSSEX
KENT

0 Miles 5
0 Kilometres 8

ADDLESTONE

Queen's Arms
107 Church Road, KT15 1SF (on B3121)
🕒 11-3, 5.30-11; 11-11 Sat; 12-3, 7-10.30 Sun
☎ (01932) 847845
Courage Best Bitter; Young's Bitter, Special Ⓗ
Small pub on the outskirts of the town centre. It is quiet and cosy except when football is on the TV. A former Ashby's pub which originally opened in the 1850s, it once boasted three bars and a skittle alley but now just has a single bar. The exterior has changed little in the intervening years. The pub is 20 minutes' walk from Addlestone Station and on the No. 461 bus route. ❀♣P

ALBURY HEATH

William IV
Little London, GU5 9DG (S of Shere) OS066467
🕒 11-3, 5.30-11; 12-3, 7-10.30 Sun
☎ (01483) 202685
Flowers IPA; Greene King Abbot; Hogs Back TEA, Hop Garden Gold Ⓗ
Traditional, 16th-century country pub, popular with walkers. The lower part of the bar is divided into two areas and boasts flagstones, beams and a large inglenook. A third, carpeted area at the back, up a few steps, is mainly used by diners; evening meals are served Tuesday–Saturday.
ᛗQ❀◑♣P

ASHFORD

King's Head ⊘
4 Feltham Road, TW15 2ER (on B377)
🕒 11-11; 12-10.30 Sun
☎ (01784) 244631
Adnams Broadside; Courage Best Bitter; Worthington's Bitter, 1744 Ⓗ
Local pub with a dedicated restaurant and large bar area with plenty of comfortable seating. Bar snacks (baguettes, sandwiches and jacket potatoes) are available for those not using the restaurant; food is served all day. Pub golf society meetings are held here.
Q❀◑▷P

BAGSHOT

Foresters Arms
173 London Road, GU19 5DH (on A30)
🕒 12-2.30, 5.30-11; 12-3, 7-10.30 Sun
☎ (01276) 472038
Cains Dr Duncans IPA; Courage Best Bitter; Fuller's London Pride; Hogs Back TEA; Taylor Dark Mild; guest beers Ⓗ
This is a modest but comfortable little pub, just outside Bagshot village centre. Landlord, Peter Savage can be rightly proud of the reputation of his beers, which now include a regular mild due to local demand, after trial as a guest. Wife, Gill, meanwhile, caters for a busy lunchtime trade with good pub grub ranging from sandwiches to roasts. The pub competes in local darts leagues, runs a golf society, and also has a skittle alley that is available for private hire, with its own bar. ❀◑♣P

BETCHWORTH

Dolphin Inn
The Street, RH3 7DW (off A25)
🕒 11-3, 5.30-11; 11-11 Sat; 12-10.30 Sun
☎ (01737) 842288
Young's Bitter, Special, Waggle Dance (summer), **Winter Warmer** (winter) Ⓗ
This managed house is noted for serving some of the best pints of Young's around. The building dates from the 16th century and features a flagstone floor with two wood-burning inglenooks. In the summer, drinkers take advantage of the many seats outside the pub and in the garden. This

busy local is also popular with visitors. A good selection of food is served in the three bars, with specials always available. A range of fine wines is kept. ⚌Q🌣⊄♣P

BRAMLEY

Jolly Farmer
High Street, GU5 0HB (on A281)
⌚ 11-3, 6-11; 12-2, 7-10.30 Sun
☎ (01483) 893355 website: www.jollyfarmer.co.uk
Badger Best; Hogs Back TEA; Taylor Landlord; guest beers Ⓗ
Wonderfully rambling free house with a commitment to an excellent range of real ales. There is always a strong food trade, but it never becomes a restaurant, with the beer remaining paramount. The L-shaped bar effectively gives the impression of different drinking areas. The walls and ceilings are richly decorated by an amazing range of esoteric items. Expect to find stuffed animals, old bank notes, beermats from defunct breweries, a 1960s one-armed bandit and much more. Just what a real free house should be like. 🌣⊨⊄♦♣P

BYFLEET

Plough ⊘
104 High Road, KT14 7QT (off A245)
⌚ 11-3, 5-11; 12-3, 7-10.30 Sun
☎ (01932) 353257
Courage Best Bitter; Fuller's London Pride; guest beers Ⓗ
Superb free house whose popularity among the real ale fraternity remains undiminished with seven handpumps dispensing a constantly-changing range of highly varied ales. There are effectively three drinking areas, including a no-smoking conservatory that welcomes children. Elsewhere, enjoy the two magnificent fireplaces in winter, solid furniture and a highly convivial atmosphere conducive to contented drinking. Do not attempt to disturb this ambience by using your mobile phone – they are banned. All in all, this is a must for any discerning drinker when in the area. ⚌Q🌣🌣⊄♣P

CATERHAM

King & Queen ⊘
34 High Street, CR3 5UA (on B2030)
⌚ 11-11; 12-10.30 Sun
☎ (01883) 345438
Fuller's Chiswick, London Pride, ESB Ⓗ
A pub since the 1840s, it was converted from 400-year-old cottages. The three distinct drinking areas comprise a front bar, a middle room with a high ceiling, large inglenook and a small space reserved for diners, and another room with darts – the pub fields three teams. The freshly-cooked food, served Monday–Saturday, includes authentic oriental dishes. There is a small, fenced patio garden at the rear for the summer. It is a regulars' pub which welcomes passers-by. ⚌🌣⊄♣P

CHERTSEY

Coach & Horses ⊘
14 St Anns Road, KT16 9DG (on B375)
⌚ 12-11; 12-3, 7-10.30 Sun
☎ (01932) 563085

Fuller's Chiswick, London Pride, ESB, seasonal beers Ⓗ
Consistently good beers, served by friendly and helpful staff are the hallmarks of this busy Fuller's pub. Situated near the main High Street, the Coach & Horses welcomes locals and visitors in search of a good pint. There is a TV at one end of the bar, those preferring a quiet drink will find a more peaceful area at the other. The pub is ideal for a pint while watching cricket played at weekends on nearby Abbey Fields. 🌣⊨⊄♣P

CHOBHAM

Castle Grove
Scotts Grove Road, GU24 8EE OS970611
⌚ 11-2.30 (3 Fri; 3.30 Sat), 5.30 (6 Sat)-11; 12-3, 7-10.30 Sun
☎ (01276) 858196
Adnams Bitter; Greene King IPA; Young's Bitter; guest beer Ⓗ
Deservedly popular village local, the large public bar displays a selection of photographs of old Chobham. The paintings hanging in the saloon are for sale, and there is a swapping library, full of books. The same landlord has run the pub for 20 years. Originally the building was going to be a station for a railway line that was never built. This theme is echoed in the garden with a large bouncy castle in the shape of a train. Evening meals are served Thursday–Saturday only. 🌣⊄⊟♣P

CHURT

Crossways Inn
Churt Road, GU10 2JE (on A287)
⌚ 11-3.30, 5-11; 11-11 Fri & Sat; 12-4, 7-10.30 Sun
☎ (01428) 714323
Cheriton Best Bitter; Courage Best Bitter; Ringwood Fortyniner; Ⓗ **guest beers** Ⓖ
This popular and well-run pub lies on the A287, Farnham to Haslemere road. The interior comprises a functional public bar served by a hatchway and a comfortable L-shaped saloon which caters for drinkers and diners alike. There is always an interesting selection of five or six guest ales from small breweries, kept on stillage in the cellar. Lunchtime food is good homely fare at reasonable prices. Biddenden cider is stocked. Q🌣⊄⊟♣▲♣P

CLAYGATE

Foley Arms
Foley Road, KT10 0LZ OS153636
⌚ 11-11; 12-10.30 Sun
☎ (01372) 463431
Young's Bitter, Special, seasonal beers Ⓗ
This imposing Victorian hostelry stands midway between the station and the church. It offers much in addition to beer. The old stables near the traditional public bar are the gymnasium and ring of the Foley Amateur Boxing Club. Alongside the quieter lounge bar, is a hall used by the

INDEPENDENT BREWERIES

Hogs Back Tongham
Leith Hill Coldharbour
Pilgrim Reigate

Thames Valley morris dancers and a folk club, while a bridge club also meets at the pub. Traditional English food is provided at lunchtime and there is a well-equipped children's play area in the large garden.
🏚Q🏵◐🖳≈♣P

Griffin
58 Common Road, KT10 0HW OS160635
🌠 11-11; 12-10.30 Sun
☎ (01372) 463799
Fuller's London Pride; Oakham JHB; guest beers ⊞
A two-bar pub on a back road, the Griffin is worth tracking down (and is on the K3 bus route). The landlord augments the regular beers with micro-brewery guests. Home-cooked food is served at lunchtime and on Friday and Saturday evenings. The public bar features a large-screen TV and the saloon boasts fine Mann, Crossman and Paulin windows. 🏚Q🏵◐🖳♣P

COBHAM

Little White Lion ✿
17 Portsmouth Road, KT11 1JF (on A245)
🌠 11-11; 12-10.30 Sun
☎ (01932) 862409
Fuller's London Pride, ESB; guest beer ⊞
Large roadside pub, which has reverted to its original name after a period as the Snail. It has a traditional bar area and a large additional room which, contrary to first impressions, is not a restaurant and caters for both drinkers and diners. Outside seating is available by the roadside. The house beer, Flying Pig (the landlord's nickname) is Fuller's Chiswick. Food ranges from sandwiches and simple bar meals to restaurant-style main courses; fresh fish is served daily. No meals are provided on Sunday evening. 🏵◐🖳♣P⌿

COLDHARBOUR

Plough Inn
Coldharbour Lane, RH5 6HD
(on Leith Hill to Dorking road) OS152441
🌠 11.30-3, 6-11; 11.30-11 Sat; 12-10.30 Sun
☎ (01306) 711793 website: www.ploughinn.com
Leith Hill Crooked Furrow, Tallywhacker; Ringwood Old Thumper; Shepherd Neame Spitfire; Taylor Landlord; guest beers ⊞
Nestling among the Surrey hills, with the St George's Cross flying outside, this is a gem of a rural brew-pub. The cosy bar features eight handpumps, one being devoted to Biddenden cider. Excellent home-made meals are served at all sessions, both in the dining room and, in summer, in the large rear garden. A converted barn serves as the family room. The two-barrel Leith Hill Brewery is located on site. En-suite guest accommodation is available.
🏚Q➳🏵⇔◐♣P

DORKING

Bull's Head ✿
11 South Street, RH4 2DY (on A25, one-way system, westbound)
🌠 11-11; 12-10.30 Sun
☎ (01306) 885720
Draught Bass; Gale's Butser, GB, HSB, seasonal beers ⊞
Boisterous (especially when Chelsea FC are on TV) town-centre pub with one L-shaped

bar. It is situated next to Pump Corner with its 19th-century pump, and just over the road from the site of the old King's Head, which was probably Dickens's Marquis of Granby. When Gale's are between production of seasonal beers, a guest beer may make an appearance. Lunches are on offer Monday–Saturday. ◐♣

Cricketers ✿
81 South Street, RH4 2JU
(on A25, one-way system, westbound)
🌠 12-11; 12-10.30 Sun
☎ (01306) 889938
Fuller's Chiswick, London Pride, ESB, seasonal beer ⊞
This Fuller's pub features one central L-shaped bar, with chairs and tables around it. Bare brick walls are decorated with old photographs and mirrors; the TV is used to show major sporting events. The brick-lined cellars are in ancient sandstone caves which allegedly once concealed smuggled liquor, and now keep the beer in prime condition. Behind the pub is a Georgian walled garden. 🏵◐

King's Arms
45 West Street, RH4 1BU
(on A25, one-way system, eastbound)
🌠 11-11; 12-3, 7-10.30 Sun
☎ (01306) 883361
Fuller's London Pride; Greene King IPA, Old Speckled Hen; Marston's Pedigree; guest beers ⊞
Attractive, beamed pub in a street that is famous for its antique shops. The large interior is cosily divided into areas of differing character. This busy pub has regular Sunday evening music and a monthly quiz. Good food is served in the bars and restaurant or on the covered patio area. The pub is a perfect stopping-off point during a shopping trip. The guest beers change frequently and are usually from micro-breweries. 🏵◐≈(West) P

Old House at Home
24 West Street, RH4 1BY
(on A25, one-way system, eastbound)
🌠 12-3, 5.30-11; 12-11 Wed-Sat; 12-10.30 Sun
☎ (01306) 889664
Young's Bitter, Special, seasonal beer ⊞
One-bar, town-centre pub in a street crowded with antique shops. It is a good pub for conversation as the TV is rarely on, only for occasional football matches. The quiz attracts customers on Thursday evening; the prize is beer. Traditional pub fare is served at lunchtime. Cheerful and welcoming, the Old House at Home has won awards for its floral displays.
🏚🏵◐≈(West) ♣

Pilgrim
Station Road, RH4 1HF
🌠 11-3, 5-11; 11-11 Fri & Sat; 12-10.30 Sun
☎ (01306) 889951
Adnams Bitter; Fuller's London Pride; Ringwood Old Thumper; guest beer (occasional) ⊞
Locals' pub next to Dorking West Station (slightly restricted service) and a few minutes' walk from the town centre. The restaurant area is to the left as you enter, with the pool table and dartboard down a couple of steps to the right. There is also a large garden. The occasional guest beer will probably be from one of the larger independent breweries. 🏵⇔◐≈(West) ♣P

Queen's Head ✔

Horsham Road, RH4 2JS (on A25, one-way system, westbound)
11-11; 12-10.30 Sun
☎ (01306) 883041
Fuller's Chiswick, London Pride, ESB H

Lively, family-run pub, mainly frequented by locals, with an attractive exterior featuring a distinctive mansard roof. The L-shaped bar has two TVs, mainly used for football and rugby, two dartboards and a pool table. There is also a surprisingly large, fenced garden, ideal for children in the summer. Lunches are served Monday–Friday. ❀☾♣P

DORMANSLAND

Old House at Home

63 West Street, RH7 6QP
11-3, 6-11; 12-3, 7-10.30 Sun
☎ (01342) 832117
Shepherd Neame Master Brew Bitter, Best Bitter, G **Spitfire, Bishops Finger, seasonal beer** H

This charming, 16th-century inn is found away from the village centre and is well known for the quality of its food. All meals are home made – there is a larger choice available from Wednesday–Saturday, but no meals on Sunday evening. The bar front has a number of barrels and the bar is decorated with hops. The walls are covered with well-polished brasses. A small room to the side houses a dartboard. ⛫Q❀☾☽⊟♣P

EFFINGHAM

Plough

Orestan Lane, KT24 5SW OS118538
11-3, 5.30-11; 12-3, 7-10.30 Sun
☎ (01372) 458121
Young's Bitter, Special, seasonal beers H

Delightful rural retreat, that gives the impression of being deeper in the countryside than it actually is, given the close proximity to the busy A246. A rare Young's outlet for this part of Surrey. The country inn image is reinforced by the attractive exterior and entrance porch leading to one bar and two drinking areas. The meals are high quality and varied with frequent specials, but this can make it very crowded, especially in the early evening and at weekends. At other times the pub is quieter with more discerning drinkers. A long way from Wandsworth in both the geographical and sociological senses. Q❀☾☽P

EGHAM

Crown

38 High Street, TW20 9DP (on B388)
11-11; 12-10.30 Sun
☎ (01784) 432608
Adnams Bitter, Broadside; Brakspear Special; Fuller's London Pride; Greene King Abbot, seasonal beers H

Cosy, old-style pub with exposed beams and wood floors. The central bar, run by friendly staff, splits the pool and TV area from the quieter side. It is popular with students, locals and shoppers. Children are welcome and there is a garden and conservatory at the rear. The full food menu includes home-made specials. Beer and cider festivals are held in May and August. ❀☾☽⇌♣P

ENGLEFIELD GREEN

Happy Man

12 Harvest Road, TW20 0QS
(off A30, at Egham Hill)
11-11; 12-10.30 Sun
☎ (01784) 433265
Courage Best Bitter; Taylor Landlord; guest beers H

This pub maintains a local feel, it has four, small, distinct rooms served centrally. It attracts students from the local Holloway College. Situated in a back street off the busy A30, it offers two regular beers and two guests. The landlord is a keen chef and provides an extensive range of home-cooked food. It is 15 minutes' walk from Egham railway station.
❀☾☽♣

EPSOM

Barley Mow ✔

12 Pikes Hill, KT17 4EA (off A2022)
11-11; 12-10.30 Sun
☎ (01372) 721044
Fuller's Chiswick, London Pride, ESB H

Back-street pub that was converted from three cottages. Several distinct seating areas surround a central bar. The smaller, more cosy areas are to the left, and the more open area on the right leads to a conservatory, which is due to be extended, and a large garden which can get busy in summer. Park your car in the top left-hand corner of the Upper High Street public car park – a short alleyway then leads to the pub. Food is available at all sessions except Friday, Saturday or Sunday evenings.
⛫Q❀☾☽♿⇌♣

ESHER

Bear

71 High Street, KT10 9RQ (on A307)
11-11; 12-10.30 Sun
☎ (01372) 469786
Young's Bitter, Special, seasonal beers H

Nelson and assorted royals have stayed at this handsome 18th-century coaching inn. There are seven en-suite rooms and food is offered at all sessions. The full-size bears which look down from the roof are linked to the crest of the Earl of Warwick, the former local landowner. A long, single bar links several drinking areas (one no-smoking). The pub is convenient for those attending Sandown Races.
⛫🛏☾☽P⚟

EWELL

Eight Bells ✔

78 Kingston Road, KT17 2DU (off A240/B2200)
12-11; 12-10.30 Sun
☎ (020) 8393 9973
Greene King IPA, Abbot; guest beers H

Large, Edwardian pub (dating from 1905), which caters for locals and visitors alike. It provides an ever-changing range of guest beers. Previous incumbents can be seen on the bar walls (a myriad of pump clips). Live music is performed on Saturday evening, otherwise the background music is at a reasonable level. Bridge is played. The garden includes a children's play area.
❀☾☽♿⇌(West) P⚟

FARNCOMBE

Cricketers ✪
37 Nightingale Road, GU7 2HU
⏰ 12-3, 5.30-11; 12-11 Sat; 12-10.30 Sun
☎ (01483) 420273
Fuller's Chiswick, London Pride, ESB, seasonal beers ⊞
First-rate, suburban, back-street local situated in a residential area on the other side of the level crossing from the town centre. Effectively a corner pub, approached by steep steps, it provides a small outside drinking area. A strong food trade exists, but the beer is never allowed to play second fiddle. Now 15 consecutive years in this Guide, the landlord proudly shows all previous stickers in a special display area. As the name suggests, there is a strong cricketing theme, continued with the new Long Room dining area. The pleasant rear garden is elevated above the general level of the pub. ⊛◑➡

FARNHAM

Lamb
43 Abbey Street, GU9 7RJ (off A287)
⏰ 11-2.30, 5-11; 11-11 Fri & Sat; 12-10.30 Sun
☎ (01252) 714133
Shepherd Neame Best Bitter, ⊞ **Spitfire, seasonal beers** Ⓖ
Friendly and welcoming, back-street local between the town centre and the railway station; handy for that last pint before the train home. A rare outlet for Shepherd Neame beers in this part of Surrey, it is even more unusual to find some of the beers on gravity. Enduringly popular among all age groups, the pub provides live music on Friday, a small games area, and tasty food; meals are not available on Tuesday or Sunday evenings. Do not miss the superb rooftop terraced garden that becomes a suntrap in summer months. ⋒⊛◑➡

Shepherd & Flock ✪
22 Moor Park Lane, GU9 9JB (on A31/A325 jct)
⏰ 11-3, 5.30-11; 11-11 Fri & Sat; 12-10.30 Sun
☎ (01252) 716675
Courage Best Bitter; Hogs Back TEA; Ringwood Old Thumper; guest beers ⊞
Located at the eastern end of town, just off the Farnham bypass, this pub stands on an enormous roundabout that requires local knowledge for access. For safety, pedestrians should use the subway on the town side. A genuine free house, eight handpumps, with five interesting ever-changing beers are displayed along a narrow bar area just inside the 'front' door. The car park door opens into a dining section which is also used for quizzes. Two outside drinking areas include a pleasant back garden as well as seating at the front, where you can watch the 'near misses' among the passing traffic. ⋒⊛◑P

GODALMING

Red Lion
1 Mill Lane, GU7 1HF
⏰ 11-11; 12-10.30 Sun
☎ (01483) 415207
Harveys BB; guest beers ⊞
One of the best free houses imaginable, with an enterprising landlord who has steadily built up a deserved reputation for

range and quality. An historic building, dating from 1696, it is now an oasis in marked contrast to more recent developments in the town centre. The public bar has an airy, high ceiling and a gallery. This complements a smaller and more intimate front saloon. Regular beer festivals and special events are held. Evening meals are offered Tuesday–Saturday. Not surprisingly, it was voted local CAMRA Pub of the Year in 2002. Q⊛◑⊟&♣♠

GREAT BOOKHAM

Anchor
161 Lower Road, KT23 4AH
(off A246, via Eastwick Rd)
⏰ 11-3 (3.30 Sat), 5.30-11; 12-3, 7-10.30 Sun
☎ (01372) 452429
Courage Best Bitter, Directors; guest beer ⊞
A Guide regular, this is a characterful, 16th-century Grade II listed establishment. Deservedly popular, the inglenook, beams, wood floor and single bar structure combine to create an authentic olde-worlde air. The fine ale is also complemented by quality food from Monday–Saturday. Proof, if ever the public need reminding, that 'genuine' old pubs are a cut above the 'pretend' old created by certain pub companies. The pretty front garden includes a pond and a set of stocks. ⋒⊛◑♣P

GUILDFORD

Plough
16 Park Street, GU1 4XB
(on central one-way system)
⏰ 11-11; 12-10.30 Sun
☎ (01483) 570167
Fuller's London Pride; guest beers ⊞
This easy-going locals' pub is less than two minutes' walk from Guildford train station. Pewter tankards hang from the low, beamed ceiling, while photographs of local scenes from the past and old-fashioned foot rails at the bar, all add to the cosy atmosphere and genuine down-to-earth character. Always friendly, it is often lively with sports TV. Unusually, the cellar is upstairs and there is a dry bar, built by one of the regulars. ◑➡

Robin Hood
Sydenham Road, GU1 5RH
⏰ 11-3, 5-11; 11-11 Fri & Sat; 12-5 Sun
☎ (01483) 888307
Draught Bass; Young's Bitter ⊞
Just a short walk up from Guildford Castle, this is a traditional pub with a friendly atmosphere. The pub is renowed for its quality ales and its home-made lunches, making it especially handy for the shopping facilities nearby. One end of the bar leads to a raised seating area by a coffin-shaped phone booth. Live bands play at the other end at weekends, when it can get very busy. The pub has its own cricket club. Occasional big-screen TV sports are shown. ◑P

Varsity Bar
Egerton Road, GU2 5XV
(off A3 at university exit, near hospital)
⏰ 12-11; 12-10.30 Sun
☎ (01483) 306224 website: www.unisport.co.uk
Beer range varies ⊞
Surely one of the best university sports bars

in the country, with three ever-changing beers from independent brewers. Off campus, it is open to the public with access via the shop at the lower level. Excellent beer festivals are held twice a year in the spring and autumn, but throughout the rest of the year there is an enthusiastic commitment to real ale. Capable of being very quiet, or the epitome of all that is boisterous on Wednesday and Saturday match days. Good value deals can be had on four-pint jugs. Lunches are on offer Monday–Saturday. A must if in the Guildford area, it is easily reached by bus from the town centre. If only all student bars were like this. ⓓP

HORSELL

Crown
104 High Street, GU21 4ST
⊙ 11-11; 12-10.30 Sun
☎ (01483) 771719
Adnams Bitter; Fuller's London Pride; guest beers Ⓗ
Revitalised, village-centre pub located opposite the war memorial. Note the enterprising management and the arrival of interesting guest beers, including Beckett's and Sharp's. It is very much a locals' pub, especially the bustling village bar where live music is staged on alternate Saturdays. The lounge is quieter, more relaxing and reflective. The large rear garden is ideal for children and has a petanque terraine. Beer festivals have been held in an outside marquee. Bus No. 28, Woking to Guildford, stops outside. ⊛ⓓP

KNAPHILL

Knap
134 High Street, GU21 2QH
⊙ 12-11; 12-10.30 Sun
☎ (01483) 473174
Young's Bitter; guest beers Ⓗ
This pub is set on a crossroads on the edge of the village and used to be called the Garibaldi. An excellent addition to the real ale scene, having started cautiously with one handpump, it is now approaching its 150th beer. The pub has dark wooden flooring and a cosy, intimate atmosphere with a no-smoking rear drinking area. The strong community focus is demonstrated by the production of a pub newsletter, charity quiz nights held on Sunday, as well as a number of special events. A 'booze and blues' beer festival takes place during the summer in the excellent, safe garden (with children's Wendy house). Q⊛ⓓP⊁

LALEHAM

Feathers
The Broadway, TW18 1RZ (on B377)
⊙ 11-11; 12-10.30 Sun
☎ (01784) 453561
Courage Best Bitter; Fuller's London Pride; guest beers Ⓗ
Fake beams feature in this friendly village local but the ale is real enough! A pub for over 180 years, now extended to provide two linked drinking areas, the main bar at the front has a dartboard, the rear part is shared with diners. For outdoor drinking opt for the shady patio garden at the rear, or the benches at the front. The Thames is a

short walk away. There is a good beer range with three changing guests and occasional beers festivals are held. Entertainment involves a quiz night on Monday and a noisier music quiz on Friday. Tasty, good quality food is on offer, but not on Sunday evening.
𝔐⊛ⓓ Å♣P

LEATHERHEAD

Running Horse ⊘
38 Bridge Street, KT22 8BZ (off B2122)
⊙ 11-11; 12-10.30 Sun
☎ (01372) 372081
Courage Directors; Fuller's London Pride; Greene King IPA, Old Speckled Hen; Tetley Burton Ale; Young's Bitter Ⓗ
This charming, Grade II* listed pub, with origins dating back to the 15th century, is conveniently situated for the town centre and the nearby River Mole. However, it feels more like a country pub. Apparently Elizabeth I spent the night here. The large main bar has various seating areas extending into a rear room and there is a smaller public bar. A courtyard garden is available for summer drinking. An enterprising menu offers reasonably-priced food, though not on Sunday evening.
Q⊛ⓓ ⊟よ⇌P

LYNE

Royal Marine
Lyne Lane, KT16 0AN OS012663
⊙ 11-2.30, 5.30-11; 12-3 (closed eve) Sun
☎ (01932) 873900
website: www.downourlocal.com/royalmarine
Courage Best Bitter; Hogs Back TEA; guest beers Ⓗ
After an absence of 14 years, it is a welcome return to the Guide for this quiet, friendly country free house that dates from 1847. A change of landlord in 2001 has seen beers from small independent breweries introduced, particularly Hogs Back. The pub contains Royal Marines memorabilia and there is a visitors' book for marines, past and present. The peaceful garden backs on to the village green where cricket matches can be enjoyed in summer. Note the pub is closed on Sunday evening.
𝔐Q⊛ⓓ♣

MICKLEHAM

King William IV
Byttom Hill, RH5 6EL
(off A24, southbound, behind Frascati restaurant)
⊙ 11-3, 6-11; 12-3, 7-10.30 Sun
☎ (01372) 372590 website: www.king-williamiv.com
Adnams Bitter; Badger Best; Hogs Back TEA; guest beer Ⓗ
Characterful, 18/19th-century rural pub situated on the fringe of the North Downs. Its renowned, pretty garden is very busy in summer and autumn, affording fine views across Norbury Park. Two-bar in layout, the main bar houses an open fire and has a strong food accent. The smaller (tiny) bar adds to the pub's rustic charm. The establishment has a deserved local reputation for fine home-made cuisine (no food Sun eve). The pub shares a car park with the restaurant at the bottom of the hill.
𝔐Q⊛ⓓP

NEWCHAPEL

Blacksmith's Head ⊘
Newchapel Road, RH7 6LE (on B2028, off A22)
☼ 11 (12 Sat)-3, 5.30 (6 Sat)-11; 12-10.30 Sun
☎ (01342) 833697
**Fuller's Chiswick, London Pride; Harveys BB;
guest beer** Ⓗ

Single-bar pub with a no-smoking
restaurant to one side. The plant-lover's
garden bears testament to the owners'
previous occupation as landscape gardeners.
Varied menus offer freshly-prepared food
for all tastes and there is an extensive wine
list. The guest beer is usually from one of
the small independents. Quiz nights feature
and the pub has two darts teams.
🏚Q✿⌘⒪Å♣P

NEWDIGATE

Surrey Oaks
Parkgate Road, Parkgate, RH5 5DZ
(between Newdigate and Leigh) OS205436
☼ 11.30-2.30 (3 Sat), 5.30 (6 Sat)-11; 12-3,
7-10.30 Sun
☎ (01306) 631200 website www.surreyoaks.co.uk
Adnams Bitter; Harveys BB; guest beers Ⓗ
Regular CAMRA award-winner (current East
& Mid Surrey Pub of the Year), the 'Soaks'
has done more to promote micro-breweries
than any pub for miles. Two guest beers are
always available – these change with every
cask. Dark beers are popular in winter, with
wheat beers often on sale in summer. This
attractive, 16th-century pub has stone-
flagged floors, a large inglenook, and a
choice of drinking areas, each with its own
set of regulars. Good quality food is also on
offer, both in the bar and in the separate
restaurant, except on Sunday and Monday
evenings. Outside is a large pleasant garden.
A beer festival is run over the August bank
holiday. 🏚Q✿⒪♣●P

OAKWOODHILL

Punchbowl ⊘
Oakwoodhill Lane, RH5 5PU (off A29)
☼ 11-11; 12-10.30 Sun
☎ (01306) 627249
Badger Best, Tanglefoot; Gribble Fursty Ferret Ⓗ
Delightful pub, opposite the village cricket
green. Originally two cottages dating from
the 15th century, it became a tavern in the
1800s and remains popular with walkers,
anglers and the local hunt. Its proximity to
Stane Street, the London–Chichester Roman
road, adds to the air of antiquity. The
building is tile-hung and incorporates a
large inglenook and huge local flagstones.
Even the pigsty (in the car park) is a listed
building. Excellent home-cooked food is
supplemented by a magnificent barbecue
area outside in summer. The pub is used
regularly by several vintage motorcycle
clubs. 🏚Q✿⒪⌷♣P✲

PIRBRIGHT

Royal Oak ⊘
Aldershot Road, GU24 0DQ (on A324)
OS945544
☼ 11-11; 12-10.30 Sun
☎ (01483) 232466
**Draught Bass; Flowers IPA, Original; Hogs Back TEA;
guest beers** Ⓗ

Definitely all a country pub should be, the
attractive picture-book exterior is adorned
with colourful plants and flowers. The inn
lies beside a stream, and has a massive
garden to challenge even the most energetic
of children. Approached via a porch
entrance, it opens up to reveal low beams
and a variety of cosy drinking areas.
Although there is a strong food emphasis,
beer still plays a key role with a range of
interesting guests. If you do not wish to take
the car, then the No. 28 bus from Woking
to Guildford stops 100 yards away.
🏚Q✿⒪⌷⅊P✲

PUTTENHAM

Good Intent
62 The Street, GU3 1AR (off B3000)
☼ 11-2.30, 6-11; 11-11 Sat; 12-10.30 Sun
☎ (01483) 810387
**Courage Best Bitter; Theakston Old Peculier;
Young's Bitter; guest beers** Ⓗ
Wonderful, relaxing retreat, off the beaten
track in an attractive, unspoilt village.
Dating from the 16th-century, the pub does
not quite seem to have caught up with the
21st! It is, however, easily accessible from
the nearby, busy A31. There is something
for everyone here, customers are a happy
mix of locals and walkers (with their canine
friends) from the nearby North Downs
Way, and diners. Fish and chips in
newspaper is a popular Wednesday night
treat, and children are welcome in the
designated dining area. Evening meals are
served Tuesday–Saturday. The pub is
dominated by a magnificent fireplace and
hops adorn both the bar and the low
beams. Cheddar Valley cider is available.
🏚Q✿⒪Å♣●P

REDHILL

Garland ⊘
5 Brighton Road, RH1 6PP
(on A23, S of town centre)
☼ 11-11; 12-3, 7-10.30 Sun
☎ (01737) 760377
**Harveys XX Mild, Pale Ale, BB, Armada,
seasonal beers** Ⓗ
If Harveys brew it, then the Garland sells it!
This excellent town local dates from 1865,
and is decorated in traditional style. The
landlord is proud to be a Harveys' tenant,
and lovingly looks after all their beers.
Including seasonal ales, up to seven beers
may be available – when all six handpumps
are busy, others will be sold direct from the
cellar. Bottled beers are not overlooked –
they even have their own menu. Darts is
popular, but does not intrude, and the pub
has a collection of over 2,000 clowns. Good
value food is available at lunchtime on
weekdays. CAMRA Surrey & Sussex regional
Pub of the Year 2002. ✿⒪⇌♣P

Hatch
**44 Hatchlands Road, Shaws Corner,
RH1 6AT** (on A25, towards Reigate)
☼ 12-2.30 (3 Sat), 5.30-11; 12-3, 7-10.30 Sun
☎ (01737) 764593
**Shepherd Neame Master Brew Bitter, Best Bitter,
Spitfire, Bishop's Finger, seasonal beer** Ⓗ
Friendly, one-bar local with an adjoining
function room. Prints of Edwardian music
hall stars adorn the walls and there is an

impressive mirrored fireplace. The Grade II listed building was a former 17th-century forge; a quiet snug area with open fire is to the rear. Live music is played every other Saturday and Monday is quiz night. The horseshoe-shaped bar offers plenty of alcove areas that contribute to the cosy atmosphere. Pool and darts are played. Sunday roasts and other tasty lunchtime food is available. ✹♣♣

Home Cottage
3 Redstone Hill, RH1 4AW
(on A25 behind railway station)
✪ 10.30-11; 12-10.30 Sun
☎ (01737) 762771
Young's Bitter, Special, seasonal beers Ⓗ
This large, busy community pub offers three distinct drinking areas. The front section tends to be fairly sedate and houses a real fire. The back bar is the livelier public bar area where big-screen football and rugby matches are shown. The final drinking area is a large conservatory, where children are admitted. Note the unusual, fine bank of handpumps in the front bar.
🏚🌳✹❶➤♣Ｐ✓

SEND

New Inn
Send Road, GU23 7EN (on A247)
✪ 12-2.30, 5.30-11; 12-2.30, 7-10.30 Sun
☎ (01483) 724940
Adnams Bitter; Fuller's London Pride; Marston's Pedigree; guest beers Ⓗ
The original inn stood across the road, but moved to its present site into a building that was once a mortuary. It adjoins the historic Wey Navigation (built in the 1660s to move flour, ground in Guildford, to the London market). Now immensely popular with modern-day boaters, walkers, diners and anybody else leaving the concrete jungle of Woking for a retreat and a relaxing experience, the pub has three drinking sections (watch the step into the far bar) and a pleasant outdoor area. It tends to be crowded in summer. Q✹❶Ｐ

SIDLOW BRIDGE

Three Horseshoes ●
Ironsbottom, RH2 8PT
(off A217 by the Peugeot garage) OS252461
✪ 12-2.30, 5.30-11 (8.30 Mon); 12-3, 7-10.30 Sun
☎ (01293) 862315 website: www.sidlow.com
Fuller's London Pride, ESB, seasonal beer; Harveys BB, Old Ale (winter); **Young's Bitter** Ⓗ
Good country local that is convenient for Gatwick Airport. Recent improvements have seen the introduction of accommodation and a meeting room. The lunchtime food is particularly good value and quality. Well-known for the quality of its real ale, huge amounts are sold; the London Pride is regarded as a local legend.
Q✹🛏❶Ｐ✓

STAFFHURST WOOD

Royal Oak
Caterfield Lane, RH8 0RR
✪ 11-3, 5-11; 11-11 Sat; 12-10.30 Sun
☎ (01883) 722207
Adnams Bitter; Draught Bass; Larkins Traditional; guest beer Ⓗ

Fine, rural pub with a reputation for excellent meals, especially fish. Happy hour food is sold at reduced prices from Monday–Friday, 6–7. No meals are prepared on Sunday evening. In splendid walking country, the pub caters for hikers, locals and visiting diners in equal measure. Although open plan and on three different levels, the pub has distinct public bar, lounge and restaurant areas and two real fires. Biddenden cider is sold on gravity. This pub is well worth seeking out. 🏚✹❶➤♣♣Ｐ

STAINES

Beehive
35 Edgell Road, TW18 2ET
(approx ½ mile S of town centre, off B376)
✪ 11-11; 12-10.30 Sun
☎ (01784) 452663
Courage Best Bitter; Fuller's London Pride Ⓗ
Three-roomed pub, tucked away from the hustle and bustle of central Staines. The public bar has a bank of four handpumps. A real fire warms the lounge, especially pleasant on a cold winter's evening. This wood-panelled room sports an extensive collection of stone bottles. There are a few ceramic beehives dotted here and there. Nostalgic (!) gents' loos are outside.
🏚✹🛏❶➤♣

Bells
124 Church Street, TW18 4ZB
(W of town centre, off B376)
✪ 11.30-3, 5-11; 11.30-11 Fri; 11-11 Sat; 12-10.30 Sun
☎ (01784) 454240
Young's Bitter, Special, seasonal beers Ⓗ
Cheerful, comfortable Young's pub on the quieter western side of Staines with excellent disabled access and helpful staff. Seasonal beers from Young's appear throughout the year and a good selection of their bottled beer is always available. Serving the local community and businesses, the Bells is within easy reach of the town centre and River Thames. It was awarded local CAMRA Pub of the Year for the second year running in 2002. No food is prepared on Sunday or Monday evenings.
✹❶♿

George ●
2-8 High Street, TW18 2EE (on A308)
✪ 11-11; 12-10.30 Sun
☎ (01784) 462181
Courage Best Bitter, Directors; Greene King Abbot; Shepherd Neame Spitfire; guest beers Ⓗ
Typical, well-upholstered, town-centre Wetherspoon's on the site of an early 1800s pub of the same name, and more recently a department store. A wide range of rapidly-changing guest beers, with smaller regionals and micros well-represented, augment the JDW staples. There are 11 handpumps on the ground floor and more pumps on the quieter upper level. Thursday is curry night. There is good wheelchair access to the ground-floor bar and a wheelchair WC.
Q❶♿➤✓

STANWELL

Rising Sun
110 Oaks Road, TW19 7LA
✪ 11-11; 12-10.30 Sun

☎ (01784) 244080
Greene King Abbot; Tetley Burton Ale Ⓗ
This one-bar pub is adjacent to the
Longford and Duke of Northumberland
Rivers footbridge to Heathrow Airport cargo
area. Although off the beaten track, the pub
is well supported by staff from the airport
and is one of the best bets for a good pint in
the village. Two TVs cover sporting events
and model aircraft and football scarves
adorn the bar. An ATM cash facility is
available inside the bar. ❀◑▶♣Ⓒ

THAMES DITTON

Ferry Tavern
Portsmouth Road, KT7 0XY (on A307)
❀ 11-11; 12-10.30 Sun
☎ (020) 8398 1749
**Greene King IPA; Marston's Pedigree; Young's Bitter;
guest beers** Ⓗ
Traditional-style local with seating arranged
around a single bar. Sports events are
shown, but the TV is unobtrusive, and there
is a fortnightly quiz held on Tuesday in
winter. The pictures and prints on the walls
are for sale. No food is served Sunday
evening or Monday. Good value pub grub is
available, though it is advisable to book.
There is limited parking at the front in
winter (in summer replaced by seats) but
there is a large car park behind the pub
opposite. ❀◑▶P

TONGHAM

Hogs Back Brewery Shop
Manor Farm, The Street, GU10 1DE (off A31)
❀ 10-6 (8.30 Wed-Fri); 9-6 Sat; 10-4.30 Sun
☎ (01252) 784495 website: www.hogsback.co.uk
Beer range varies Ⓗ
Wonderful off-licence attached to an award-
winning brewery. Only Hogs Back beers are
available on draught, but up to 200 bottled
beers from all over the world are stocked.
Clothing and gifts are also sold. Westons
and Great Western Revival cider can be
bought. Admire this impressive old building
with views of the brewery; a discount on
draught beer is given to card-carrying
CAMRA members. ♣P

WALTON ON THAMES

Regent ⊘
19 Church Street, KT12 2QP (on A3050)
❀ 10-11; 12-10.30 Sun
☎ (01932) 243980
**Courage Best Bitter; Fuller's London Pride; Greene
King Abbot, Old Speckled Hen; Shepherd Neame
Spitfire; guest beers** Ⓗ
Wetherspoon's pub in the town centre,
converted from a former cinema. Up to five
guest ales are usually available, including
one from Itchen Valley Brewery. The decor
reflects local associations with the film
industry. Addlestones cider is sold. Q◑▶♣¾

WALTON-ON-THE-HILL

Chequers
Chequers Lane, KT20 7SF (on B2220)
❀ 11-11; 12-10.30 Sun
☎ (01737) 812364
**Young's Bitter, Special, Waggle Dance,
Winter Warmer** Ⓗ
Large, 19th-century pub comprising a

number of rooms served from a single bar.
The back bar is the largest, with several
others to the front, it leads to a patio and
garden where summer barbecues are held.
Good quality food is sold throughout the
pub, with fish a speciality. A splendid range
of wine is available. Food is served all day
Saturday and until 8pm on Sunday. A large
number of societies meet in this hospitable
pub which is situated in a horse-training
area. Boules is played. ♨❀◑▶♣P

WEYBOURNE

Running Stream ⊘
66 Weybourne Road, GU9 9HE (on B3007)
❀ 11-3, 5-11; 11-11 Fri & Sat; 12-3, 7-10.30 Sun
☎ (01252) 323750
**Greene King IPA, Ruddles Best, Morland Original,
Abbot; guest beer** Ⓗ
The pub is named after the old method of
using a stream to control the cellar
temperature. The single horseshoe bar has
distinct drinking areas with individual
character, provided by thoughtful
decoration. One end of the bar has darts,
the other features ornamental fruits in
display cases. Another area pays testament
to the pub's understated, but enthusiastic
charity work. Numerous pub-keeping and
beer quality certificates are displayed.
Novelty clocks above the bar provide a
continual theme of horological confusion.
The garden has a slide and Wendy house to
entertain the children. ❀◑▶P

WEYBRIDGE

Jolly Farmer
41 Princes Road, KT13 9BN (off A317)
❀ 11-3, 5-11; 12-3, 7-10.30 Sun
☎ (01932) 856873 website: www.hopback.co.uk
**Hop Back Best Bitter, Crop Circle, Summer Lightning,
seasonal beers** Ⓗ
This Hop Back house is convenient for both
Weybridge cricket club and the Queen's
Road shopping parade. The large garden is
popular during the summer months. A
lunchtime menu is available. The L-shaped
country-style single bar is surrounded by
upholstered bench seats and has a low,
beamed ceiling. Photographs of old
Weybridge are displayed on the walls. ❀◑

Prince of Wales ⊘
Anderson Road, Oatlands, KT13 9NX
(off A3050)
❀ 10.30-11; 12-10.30 Sun
☎ (01932) 852082
Adnams Bitter; Fuller's London Pride, ESB Ⓗ
This spacious local is tucked behind the
shopping parade, in a suburb of Weybridge.
A separate restaurant area serves home-
cooked food, except on Sunday or Monday
evenings. The house beer is Old Tosser,
actually Fuller's Chiswick Bitter. There are
two main bar areas with a large open fire at
one end. The pub exterior has a vivid floral
display. ♨◑

WINDLESHAM

Bee
School Road, GU20 6PD
(40 yds from A30, on B386)
❀ 11-11; 12-10.30 Sun
☎ (01276) 479244

Brakspear Bitter; Courage Best Bitter; Hop Back
Summer Lightning; Shepherd Neame Spitfire;
guest beer Ⓗ

Unspoilt rural pub with five beers and good
food ranging from sandwiches to curries
(not Mon). It has been an inn since around
1865 and is well supported by the local
community, having not only a darts team
but also a golf society and two clay-pigeon
shooting teams. Live jazz/blues bands play
on some Thursday or Saturday evenings.
Weather permitting, garden barbecues take
place on Sunday lunchtime during summer
months, often with live trad jazz and/or
morris dancers. The garden has a children's
play area. The pub is 20 minutes' walk from
Bagshot Station. ✿◖ ♣P

WITLEY

Star
Petworth Road, GU8 5LU (on A283)
✪ 11-2.30, 4.30-11; 11-11 Fri Sat; 12-3, 7-10.30 Sun
☎ (01428) 684656
Adnams Broadside; Greene King IPA; Jennings
Cumberland Ale; guest beers Ⓗ

Grade II listed building on the corner of a
'T' junction and facing in two directions. It
has an industrial heritage, having been a
woollen mill in the 17th century and was
then converted into a pub in the mid-19th
century. An excellent and traditional public
bar boasts low, oak beams supported by
original cast-iron pillars. The rear saloon is
more modern, airier, quieter and more
food-oriented with a dominating fireplace.
No meals are served on Sunday evening. A
safe, enclosed garden is ideal for children.
Q ⇆ ✿◖ 丫 ♣P

WOKING

Wetherspoon's ✪
51-59 Chertsey Road, GU21 5AJ
✪ 10-11; 12-10.30 Sun
☎ (01483) 722818
Courage Directors; Hogs Back TEA; Shepherd Neame
Spitfire; Theakston Best Bitter; guest beers Ⓗ

An oasis of real ale choice, quality, value
and discernment in an area dominated by
trendy bars and clubs. The pub serves up to
four guest beers that come and go very
quickly given the popularity of the pub. Old
photographs of Woking's previous existence
adorn the walls and there is much tribute to
HG Wells, who lived locally. A metal
sculpture of an invisible man stares down
implacably, while a push-button time
machine dominates the ceiling. The
impression of separate drinking areas is
cleverly created by screens and booths.
Overall, a metamorphosis from a
Woolworths store to an integral part of
Woking's social scene. Q ◖ ⅙ ⇌ ● ⅓

WOOD STREET

Royal Oak
89 Oak Hill, GU3 3DA
✪ 11-3 (3.30 Sat), 5-11; 12-2.30, 7-10.30 Sun
☎ (01483) 235137
Courage Best Bitter; Hogs Back TEA; guest beers Ⓗ

Traditional pub, full of conversation, run by
a friendly landlord carefully supervised by
his pet cat, Oliver. The range of six real ales
is well managed, and always includes a
mild. A few pump clip collections are

displayed behind the bar, including beers
brewed specially for the pub. Look up for
advance notice of ales coming soon.
Thatchers dry cider is sold. Wholesome
home-cooked lunches are served
Monday–Saturday to the three seating areas
and big back garden which has swings and a
windmill for the children. CAMRA Surrey
Pub of the Year 2003. ✿◖ ● P

WRECCLESHAM

Bat & Ball
15 Bat & Ball Lane, Boundstone, GU10 4RA
(follow the Bourne stream, off Upper Bourne Lane)
OS834444
✪ 12-3, 5.30-11; 12-11 Fri & Sat; 12-10.30 Sun
☎ (01252) 794564
website: www.batandball.fsnet.co.uk
Archers Village; Fuller's London Pride; Young's Bitter;
guest beers Ⓗ

Excellent free house, sporting seven
handpumps, relatively isolated, despite
being close to housing. Access is either via a
private road or take the public footpath off
Sandrock Hill. The pub is popular with
drinkers and diners and is famous for its
curries. No food is served on Sunday
evening. Children are well catered for with
an adventure playground in the ample
garden and they are allowed in the
conservatory, which also sports a bar
billiards table. ⋈ Q ⇆ ✿ ⋈ ◖ ♿ ♣ ● P

Sandrock
Sandrock Hill, Upper Bourne, GU10 4NS
(off B3384) OS830444
✪ 11-11; 12-10.30 Sun
☎ (01252) 715865
Batham Best Bitter; Enville Ale; Cheriton Pots Ale;
guest beers Ⓗ

Real ale mecca, recently under a change of
management. However, the beer quality is
still excellent and the food selection has
been increased to attract more people to its
rural location. The pub is small and
atmospheric, with old wooden benches and
tables and real fires. A bar billiards table is
provided. ⋈ Q ✿◖ ♣

Noted ales

At one time or another nearly
every county town in England of
any size has been noted for its
beers or ales. Yorkshire claims not
only stingo but also Hull and
North Allerton ales whilst
Nottingham, Lichfield, Derby,
Oxford and Burton have almost
branded their ales. During the
eighteenth century the fame of
Dorchester beer almost equalled
the popularity of London porter.

Frank A. King,
Beer has a History, 1947

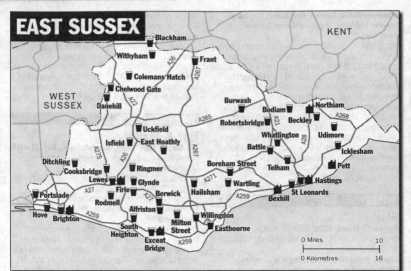

EAST SUSSEX

ALFRISTON

Smugglers Inn
Waterloo Square, BN26 5UE
🕐 11-3, 6.30-11; 12-3, 7-10.30 Sun
☎ (01323) 870241
Harveys BB, seasonal beers; Sussex Pett Progress Ⓗ
Pub with two names – it is also known locally as the Market Cross. It retains much character in the main bar and has a rambling set of other small, low-ceilinged rooms, replete with exposed beams. Reputedly haunted by two ghosts, it is frequented by walkers on the South Downs Way. The pub gets very busy with diners in good weather.
Q❄️◑

BATTLE

Chequers Inn
Lower Lake, TN33 0AT (at A2100/Marley Lane jct)
🕐 11-11; 12-10.30 Sun
☎ (01424) 772088
Fuller's London Pride; Harveys BB; guest beers Ⓗ
Busy, 15th-century inn, a haven for real ale drinkers and lovers of fine food. The pub, to the south of the High Street, has a long rectangular bar, exposed beams, two open fires and a no-smoking dining room, featuring a large inglenook and an original outside wall (now internal). The garden overlooks the site of the Battle of Hastings. Very much part of the community, concerts are often given by local musicians on the terrace on summer evenings.
🏠🛏️❄️◑🍴➡️♣P

BECKLEY

Rose & Crown
Northiam Road, TN31 6SE (at B2188/B2165 jct)
🕐 11-3, 5.30-11; 11-11 Fri & Sat; 12-10.30 Sun
☎ (01797) 252161
Fuller's ESB; Harveys BB; Hook Norton Best Bitter; guest beers Ⓗ
First-class free house serving a great range of beers at their very best; many of them come from distant breweries. This

spacious, family pub has separate areas for drinkers and diners. The long bar is noted for its wood floor and decorative hops. Locals and visitors are made most welcome to this country pub which offers an excellent menu and fine views from the garden.
🏠Q❄️♣P

BERWICK

Cricketers Arms ⊘
BN26 6SP (S of A27 just W of Drusilla's roundabout)
🕐 11-3, 6-11; (11-11 summer); 12-10.30 Sun
☎ (01323) 870469
website: www.cricketersberwick.co.uk
Harveys BB, seasonal beers Ⓖ
After sympathetic updating, this pub remains a gem, with a quarry-tiled floor in the main bar and dining area. All the beers are served straight from casks, kept in a room behind the bar, so do not look for handpumps. Once three cottages, it became a pub in the 18th century. Excellent gardens front and rear, are ideal for summer evenings. Being near Alfriston, it gets busy in summer – and it is not a big place. Toad in the hole is played here.
🏠Q❄️◑♣P

BLACKHAM

Sussex Oak
TN3 9UA (on A264) OS487392
🕐 11-3, 6-11; 12-3, 6.30-10.30 Sun
☎ (01892) 740273 website: www.sussex-oak.co.uk
Shepherd Neame Master Brew Bitter, Best Bitter, Spitfire Ⓗ
Large country pub situated on the A264 between East Grinstead and Tunbridge Wells (served by No. 238 bus). The pub has a traditionally-themed bar where you can choose from a wide range of Shepherd Neame beers. The restaurant serves a varied menu with influences from India and Ireland; occasional food theme nights are held and takeaways are available.
🏠🛏️❄️◑♿➡️ (Ashurst) ♣P⅟

BODIAM

Castle

TN32 5UB (opp. entrance to castle)

✪ 11-3, 6-11; (11-11 summer Sat); 12-10.30 Sun

☎ (01580) 830330

Shepherd Neame Master Brew Bitter, Spitfire, seasonal beers Ⓗ

Rural Shepherd Neame pub in the scenic Rother Valley on the Kent border. Bodiam Castle, the impressive National Trust property, stands opposite, and it is well worth making a visit to both Castles. An extensive menu, featuring local produce, is displayed in the main bar above the imposing fireplace. This pleasant, quiet pub is ideal for a peaceful pint.

🅰Q❀◑➤ (Kent & East Sussex Rlwy) P

BOREHAM STREET (nr Herstmonceux)

Bull's Head ❷

BN27 4SG

✪ 12-3, 6-11; 12-4, 7-10.30 Sun

☎ (01323) 831981

Harveys BB, seasonal beers Ⓗ

This welcoming village inn has been a Harvey's pub since the early 19th century. Recently sympathetically renovated to retain many original features, a log-burning stove in the dining area creates a cosy atmosphere, where excellent meals are cooked to order. The menu is based largely on local produce. In the spacious bar, the decor is modern with a wood floor and two fireplaces. It stages frequent live music evenings and fields darts and shove-ha'penny teams.

🅰❀◑P

BRIGHTON

Basketmakers Arms ❷

12 Gloucester Road, BN1 4AD

✪ 11-11; 12-10.30 Sun

☎ (01273) 689006

Gale's Butser, GB, Winter Brew, HSB, Festival Mild Ⓗ

Traditional, street-corner pub situated in the bohemian North Laine area, worth the short walk from the town centre or Theatre Royal. This Gale's tied house attracts a diverse clientele and is deservedly popular for its beers, food and the range of whiskies on offer. The walls are covered with old signs and food containers, some of which have been known to contain obscure messages. Evening meals are served weekdays 5.30–8.30.

Q◑➤

Battle of Trafalgar

34 Guildford Road, BN1 3LW

✪ 11-11; 12-10.30 Sun

☎ (01273) 327997

Fuller's London Pride; Harveys BB; guest beers Ⓗ

Popular pub a short walk up a steep hill from the station where five handpumps serve guest ales. The small frontage is deceptive, with a designated dining area. The decor features pictures of old sea battles and other nautical memorabilia; note the collection of bottles above the bar. In winter, live music is sometimes staged (Sun eve); background music (jazz or blues) is kept at a sensible level. It would be easy to miss your train here.

❀◑➤

Bedford Tavern

30 Western Street, BN1 2PG (just off seafront)

✪ 11-11; 12-10.30 Sun

☎ (01273) 739495 website: www.bedfordtavern.com

Butcombe Gold; Harveys BB; guest beers Ⓗ

This neat two-bar corner pub is on the Hove boundary between the seafront peace statue and the Western Road shops. Fireplaces in each bar and leaded glass windows in the front make this a cosy hostelry, especially in winter. Two ever-changing guest ales provide a good beer choice. Food is served lunchtimes, except Monday, and consists of a substantial cold platter or steak, and a roast on Sunday. ❀◑

Dover Castle

43 Southover Street, BN2 2UE

✪ 12-11; 12-10.30 Sun

☎ (01273) 688276 website: www.dovercastle.uk

Shepherd Neame Master Brew Bitter, Spitfire, seasonal beers Ⓗ

Corner pub with something going on most nights: Sunday is 'reggae roast', Tuesday evening is 'open mike' and Friday is curry night. A DJ plays on Friday and Saturday when it can be a little noisy. If you wish to escape all this, there is a covered garden that is heated in winter; children are welcome in the conservatory. Euro/Asian food is usually available. 🅰⛄❀◑♣

Evening Star

55-56 Surrey Street, BN1 3PB

(bear right out of station)

✪ 12 (11.30 Sat)-11; 12-10.30 Sun

☎ (01273) 328931

website: www.eveningstarbrighton.co.uk

Dark Star Hophead, Sunburst, seasonal beers; guest beers Ⓗ

Tap of the Dark Star Brewery; this friendly pub stocks an ever-changing selection of house and guest beers, as well as two ciders and a good range of Belgian beer. Live music is regularly performed, with an 'open mike' session on Monday. Occasional beer festivals are also held. Food is available most lunchtimes and some evenings.

◑➤♠

Hand in Hand

33 Upper St James's Street, BN2 1JN

✪ 3 (12 Sat)-11; 12-10.30 Sun

☎ (01273) 699595

website: www.kemptownbrewery.com

Kemptown Brighton Bitter, Kemptown, Old Trout Ale, Dragons Blood; guest beers Ⓗ

Reputed to be the smallest pub in Britain with its own tower brewery. Resembling a large front room with a bar, and wallpapered with old newspapers, the collection of ties, fairy lights and earthenware pots decorating the ceiling provide a comfortable atmosphere. Note the original stone wall. Kemptown ales, brewed

INDEPENDENT BREWERIES

Cuckmere Haven Exceat Bridge

First Inn Last Out Hastings

Harveys Lewes

Kemptown Brighton

Rother Valley Northiam

Sussex Pett

White Bexhill

on the premises, are supplemented by a range of imported draught and bottled beers. Q

Lord Nelson Inn ✅
36 Trafalgar Street, BN1 4ED (downhill E of station)
☼ 11-11; 12-10.30 Sun
☎ (01273) 695872
website: www.thelordnelsoninn.co.uk
Harveys XX Mild, Pale Ale, BB, Armada, seasonal beers Ⓗ

A pub like pubs ought to be! This traditional tied house serves a full range of Harveys beers, including seasonal ales, and provides excellent lunches. Two cosy front bars are complemented by a small back room with bench seating. There is also a spacious gallery room, which houses exhibitions by local artists and is available for meetings. Newspapers are provided, and the walls are covered with sporting prints and pictures.
♨Q◖≩♠

Prestonville ✅
64 Hamilton Road, BN1 5DN
☼ 5 (12 Fri & Sat)-11; 12-10.30 Sun
☎ (01273) 701007
Gale's Butser, GB, HSB, seasonal beers; guest beer (occasional) Ⓗ

Good, single-bar, street-corner pub, a little out of the way but well worth a visit. No pool tables or electronic games here, but live music and quizzes are staged. The beers from Gale's are supplemented by occasional guests, plus a wide range of malt whiskies. A good menu is served lunchtime and evening, including daily specials. ❀◖◗

Regency Tavern
32-34 Russell Square, BN1 2EF
☼ 11-3, 6 (6.30 Sat)-11; 12-3, 7-10.30 Sun
☎ (01273) 325652
Draught Bass; Fuller's London Pride; Greene King Abbot; Harveys BB; Tetley Bitter; guest beer Ⓗ

This is pure, instant Brighton: a classy bar converted from three town houses on the footpath link between Russell Square and Regency Square. Plush green and gilt decor does not overshadow the six ales, which include a varying house beer from a local micro-brewery. With its dramatic lighting, this could be a theatre bar, yet few have such showy toilets. Allegedly haunted by three ghosts; the Prince Regent would have loved it! Q◖≩

Royal Sovereign
66 Preston Street, BN1 2HE
☼ 10.30-11; 12-10.30 Sun
☎ (01273) 323829
Greene King Old Speckled Hen; Harveys BB, seasonal beers Ⓗ

Town-centre pub with a traditional top bar displaying pictures of old Brighton. The bottom bar is a cocktail/sports bar. Lunchtime food is served all week, with roasts on Sunday; a carvery is planned for the near future. The pub is situated in Preston Street, famous for its many restaurants and is very close to the infamous West Pier. ❀◖

Sir Charles Napier ✅
50 Southover Street, BN2 2UE
☼ 5 (12 Fri & Sat)-11; 12-10.30 Sun
☎ (01273) 601413

Gale's Butser, GB, HSB, seasonal beers; guest beers Ⓗ

Surprisingly roomy corner pub, with a small walled garden at the rear. The interior is decorated with all manner of (mostly local) memorabilia, including old maps that show many more pubs in the area than exist nowadays. Among the items is a letter written by 'Black Charlie' Napier, a former naval Commander-in-Chief in the Crimean War, two years before his death. The guest beers come from the Independent Family Brewers of Britain range. ❀◖♣

BURWASH

Rose & Crown ✅
Ham Lane, TN19 7ER (off A265)
☼ 12-11; 12-10.30 Sun
☎ (01435) 882600
website: www.roseandcrownburwash.co.uk
Harveys Pale Ale, BB, seasonal beers Ⓗ

Traditional, 16th-century country inn at the centre of the village, boasting a large inglenook. It was always a fine pub, but a change of landlord some time ago has extended the beer range. The food is served, to suit all tastes, in a well-appointed restaurant area. The Sunday carvery is popular; no food Monday.
♨Q❀⌂◖♣P

CHELWOOD GATE

Red Lion
Lewes Road, RH17 7DE
☼ 12-11; 12-10.30 Sun
☎ (01825) 740265
Shepherd Neame Master Brew Bitter, Spitfire, Bishops Finger, seasonal beers Ⓗ

Dating from 1867, this is one of Shepherd Neame's Mullberry Inns, but still run as a country pub. An extensive range of meals (not served Sun eve) complements the beers. Former prime minister Harold Macmillan lived nearby and once called in for a drink with American President John F. Kennedy, shortly before the latter's assassination. The pub, pleasantly situated in Ashdown Forest, also featured in the first episode of the cult TV series, The Hitch-Hikers Guide to the Galaxy.
≩❀◖♿♇✂

COLEMANS HATCH

Hatch Inn
TN7 4EJ (400 yds S of B2110) OS452335
☼ 11.30-3, 5.30-11 (11-11 summer Sat); 12-10.30 Sun
☎ (01342) 822362 website: www.hatchinn.co.uk
Harveys BB; Larkins Traditional; guest beers Ⓗ

On the northern edge of Ashdown Forest, this popular pub, originally cottages dating back to 1430, displays a wealth of timber beams – beware, some are very low. It enjoys support for local ales and offers a good range of food, with a small no-smoking dining area available. Evening meals are served Tuesday–Saturday. Daily newspapers are provided for customers. Parking can be difficult, even during weekdays. Bus service No. 291 stops a short walk away.
♨❀◖P✂

COOKSBRIDGE

Pump House
Main Road, BN8 4SW
🕐 11-3, 6-11; 11-11 Sat; 12-10.30 Sun
☎ (01273) 400528
Harveys BB; guest beers Ⓗ
This local, standing next to the station, usually has guest beers from micro-breweries on tap. Noted for friendly conversation at the bar, there are comfortable, quiet sections to sit in as well. Live music is often staged on Friday evening. Bar snacks are available, and excellent food is served in the restaurant. There is a pleasant garden, and the pub is child-friendly. ﾒ🏠🕐🐕👦A🚲♣P

DANEHILL

Coach & Horses
School Lane, RH17 7JF (1 mile E of crossroads in village, from A275) OS412288
🕐 11.30-3 (12-4 Sat), 6-11; 12-4, 6-10.30 Sun
☎ (01825) 740369
Harveys BB; guest beers Ⓗ
A portrait of Queen Victoria greets you as you enter this country pub, dating from 1840. Set in rolling farmland, the views may be enjoyed from the large surrounding garden. A small bare-boarded, basic bar is to the right; the main bar to the left leads down steps to a restaurant area, where roof trusses are decorated with hops. No evening meals are served on Sunday. ﾒQ🏠🕐🐕♣P

DITCHLING

White Horse ⊘
16 West Street, BN6 8TS (opp. church)
🕐 11-11 (midnight Fri & Sat); 12-10.30 Sun
☎ (01273) 842006
Harveys BB; guest beers Ⓗ
1998 Local CAMRA Pub of the Year and a runner-up for years since, the pub faces the village church and a house once owned by Anne of Cleves is next door. The pub is a short walk from the foot of the highest point in South Downs – Ditchling Beacon. The pub serves great food (vegetarian and meat dishes). A dedicated games area is at the rear. The cellar is reputedly haunted. ﾒ🏠🕐♣P

EASTBOURNE

Arlington Arms ⊘
360 Seaside, BN22 7RY
(on main road to Hastings)
🕐 11-11; 12-10.30 Sun
☎ (01323) 724365
Harveys XX Mild, Pale Ale, BB, Old, Armada, seasonal beers Ⓗ
A two-bar pub, very much a local. The side bar houses the darts and pool table. The dining room is off the saloon bar where there is also a door to the garden. It gets very busy at weekends. 🏠🕐♣P

Buccaneer
10 Compton Street, BN21 4BW (next to Devonshire Theatre)
🕐 11-11; 12-10.30 Sun
☎ (01323) 732829
Marston's Pedigree; Tetley Bitter, Burton Ale; guest beers Ⓗ
Large, one-bar pub at the heart of Eastbourne's theatreland. Pictures of old Eastbourne are displayed alongside autographed theatre posters. A raised no-smoking area at the rear of the pub overlooks the Devonshire Park tennis courts. On one side of the bar is a partitioned sitting area. Guest beers change quickly here. Q🏠🕐🚲

Hurst Arms ⊘
76 Willingdon Road, BN21 1TW
(on A2270, 1½ miles N of centre)
🕐 11-11; 12-10.30 Sun
☎ (01323) 721762
Harveys Pale Ale, BB, Old, Armada, seasonal beers Ⓗ
A welcome return for this lively local – an imposing Victorian, street-corner pub. The public bar can get boisterous, with its pool and bar billiards tables, fruit machine, juke box and satellite TV. The saloon bar is much quieter with plenty of seating. A west-facing garden to the front of the pub overlooks the main road. This is very much a no-nonsense working men's pub serving excellent beer. 🏠🍺

Terminus ⊘
153 Terminus Road, BN21 3NU
(½ mile from station)
🕐 11-11; 12-10.30 Sun
☎ (01323) 733964
Harveys BB, seasonal beers Ⓗ
Old-fashioned pub in a busy town centre, used by shoppers and students. The Terminus has a large function room upstairs and a restaurant downstairs. Although it has no garden, there is a large pavement drinking area and good seating in the olde-worlde bar. It stages entertainment every Tuesday from April until September, hosting bands, soloists and duos. Q🏠🕐🚲♣

EAST HOATHLY

King's Head
1-3 High Street, BN8 6DR (½ mile off A22)
🕐 11-4, 6-11; 12-4, 7-10.30 Sun
☎ (01825) 840238
Fuller's London Pride; Harveys BB; guest beers Ⓗ
Spacious village-centre pub, much used by locals and visitors. Over the year unusual competitions are organised to raise money for charity. The restaurant serves food of the highest quality (booking advisable) while bar food includes fresh fish cooked in beer batter to eat in or take away. Tables and chairs are provided on the forecourt. There are many interesting places to visit nearby, including a vineyard. Parking is limited. 🏠🕐P

EXCEAT BRIDGE

Golden Galleon
BN25 4AB (on A529, E of Seaford)
🕐 11-11; 12-4 (10.30 summer) Sun
☎ (01323) 892247 website: www.goldengalleon.co.uk
Cuckmere Haven Downland Bitter, Guvnor, Golden Peace, seasonal beers; guest beers Ⓗ/Ⓖ
Situated beside the Seven Sisters Country Park, this is a popular stop for walkers from the nearby South Downs Way. The pub's extensive gardens offer magnificent views down the river estuary to the English Channel. The Cuckmere Haven Brewery can be seen, situated in a conservatory next to the main entrance at the top of the steps. A

small bar is supplemented by spacious dining areas, where an extensive menu of first-class food is served. ⚏❀◑⌖🅰🅿

FIRLE

Ram Inn ☆
The Street, BN8 6NS (½ mile off A27)
⊕ 11.30-11; 12-10.30 Sun
☎ (01273) 858222
Harveys BB; guest beers Ⓗ

Village local with a main bar, a family room and a no-smoking bar. The inn was used by local magistrates to hold court until 1880. The South Downs Way runs nearby. A good range of food, including a children's menu, is available at all times. There is a children's play area and, unusually, baby changing facilities in both toilets. Local societies regularly meet to make use of the bars and play local music and games.
⚏Q╲❀◑♣🅿⌿🍺

FRANT

Abergavenny Arms
High Street, TN3 9DB (on A267)
⊕ 12-3, 6-11; 12-3, 7-10.30 Sun
☎ (01892) 750233
Fuller's London Pride; Harveys BB; Rother Valley Level Best; Taylor Landlord; guest beer Ⓗ

Spacious, roadside country pub, close to Tunbridge Wells. The pub is on two levels and generally has five or six beers on tap. Dating back to the 15th century, what is now the lounge bar was at one time used as a courtroom, while the cellar served as cells.
⚏Q◑♣🅿

GLYNDE

Trevor Arms ⊘
The Street, BN8 6SS
(½ mile off A27, near station)
⊕ 11-11; 12-10.30 Sun
☎ (01273) 858208
Harveys Pale Ale, BB, seasonal beers Ⓗ

Multi-roomed country pub characterised by open fires, bare floorboards and old furniture. It comprises a public bar, snug and restaurant, although food may also be eaten in the public bar. It caters for a variety of customers, including visitors and musicians from the world-famous Glyndebourne Opera House, which is only a short walk away. The large garden is very popular with families. ⚏◑⇌♣🅿⌿

HAILSHAM

Grenadier Hotel
67 High Street, BN27 1AS
⊕ 10.30-11; 12-10.30 Sun
☎ (01323) 842152 website: www.grenadier2000.com
Harveys XX Mild, BB, Armada, seasonal beers; guest beers Ⓗ

Bustling, town-centre pub, one of Harvey's oldest. Two distinct bars, plus a small hatch, indicate that this once had a public saloon and jug and bottle bar. Its Milk and Ale Club has raised over £100,000 for Guide Dogs for the Blind. When licensing hours were relaxed there was no change at this market licensed pub. The garden has a play area and the pub holds a children's certificate. Close to the Cuckoo Trail, it is easily reached by walkers. Q❀⊟♣🅿

HASTINGS

First In Last Out
14 High Street, Old Town, TN34 3EY
⊕ 11-11; 12-10.30 Sun
☎ (01424) 425079
Filo Crofters, Cardinal; guest beers Ⓗ

The refurbished Filo Brewery is now fully working and can be viewed through the large internal window to the rear of the pub. This pub stands near the top of the High Street in the picturesque Old Town. Featuring alcove seating and a central fireplace, it is very cosy throughout the year. Especially busy at weekends, it hosts mini beer festivals in the garden on most bank holidays. In summer Filo Gold is generally available. ⚏Q❀◑♣🅰🅿

HOVE

Cliftonville Inn ⊘
98-101 George Street, BN3 3YE
⊕ 10-11; 12-10.30 Sun
☎ (01273) 726969
Courage Directors; Greene King Abbot; Shepherd Neame Spitfire; Theakston Best Bitter; guest beers Ⓗ

Formerly a DIY shop, this large, open-plan Wetherspoon's pub in the centre of Hove is convenient for the main shopping area and events at Hove Town Hall – a good range of beers is normally on offer at prices that are attractive, compared to other pubs in the area. A strong emphasis on food at lunchtimes tends to attract an older clientele. Q◑♣⇌⌿

Eclipse ⊘
33 Montgomery Street, BN2 5BF
(S of railway, between Hove and Aldrington)
⊕ 11-11; 12-10.30 Sun
☎ (01273) 272212
Harveys Pale Ale, BB, Armada, seasonal beers Ⓗ

Comfortable, two-bar corner pub, with an upstairs function room. The larger public bar is dominated by pool and TV, whereas the sedate, wood-panelled saloon provides comfort and conversation. Two racehorses, Eclipse and Diamond, are to be found, both as external reflief panels and on the pub sign. Q◑⊟⇌ (Aldrington/Hove)♣

Sussex Cricketer
Eaton Road, BN3 3AF
⊕ 12-11; 12-10.30 Sun
☎ (01273) 771645
Draught Bass; Harveys BB; Shepherd Neame Spitfire Ⓗ

A cricketing theme has been abandoned, and clean, modern lines are now the keynotes in the decor of this large pub, next to the Maurice Tate gates of the Sussex County Cricket Club ground. Good food is a feature of this contemporary, adult drinking pub – a Mitchells & Butlers Ember Inn. ⚏❀◑♣

ICKLESHAM

Queen's Head
Parsonage Lane, TN36 4BL
(off A259, opp. football pitches)
⊕ 11-11; 12-10.30 Sun
☎ (01424) 814552
Courage Directors; guest beers Ⓗ

This timeless country inn usually stocks five beers. The interior boasts no less than three log fires in winter, giving this pub a rather cosy feel. Food is available all day with many choices. It can get busy as it is universally popular; a must if you are in the area. It stages live music on Tuesday evening. ᴹQ⊛◁▷♣♠P⅄⏃

ISFIELD

Laughing Fish
Station Road, TN22 5XB (W off A26, 2 miles S of Uckfield)
☼ 12-3, 4.30-11 (12-11 Sat & summer); 12-10.30 Sun
☎ (01825) 750349
Greene King XX Mild (summer), **IPA, Morland Original; guest beers** Ⓗ

Victorian village local, next to the Lavender Line preserved railway. An underground stream helps to maintain the cellar temperature. The pub has been sympathetically refurbished, retaining its character, but with the addition of a children's play area and a delightful garden graced by a pergola. Home-prepared food is served every lunchtime, plus Friday and Saturday evenings (every evening in summer). ᴹ⅋⊛◁▷Å♣P

LEWES

Brewers Arms
91 High Street, BN7 1XN
☼ 10.30-11; 12-10.30 Sun
☎ (01273) 479475
Harveys BB; guest beers Ⓗ

Comfortable, plush, friendly local comprising two bars: a smart lounge at the front and a busy, boisterous games bar at the rear. Situated in the historic High Street near Bull House, there has been a pub on this site since 1540. Look out for the vintage architect's drawing, and the Page & Overton ceramic plaques outside. Biddenden cider is on handpump; the guest beers from small independent breweries. Q◁▷⊟≠♠

Gardener's Arms
46 Cliffe High Street, BN7 2AN
☼ 11-11; 12-10.30 Sun
☎ (01273) 474808
Harveys BB; guest beers Ⓗ

The pub is near Harveys Brewery and the River Ouse; too near in fact, as in October 2000 the cellar became part of the river. Extensive refurbishment has restored the bar with no sign of modernisation. The landlord is a football fan, supporting local teams, but his heart is with Swindon Town, as borne out by the memorabilia from Arkells and Archers breweries. One of their products usually features among the five beers on tap, plus Biddenden cider. ≠♠

Lewes Arms
1 Mount Place, BN7 1TH
☼ 11-11; 12-10.30 Sun
☎ (01273) 473152
Greene King IPA, Abbot; Harveys BB, Old Ⓗ

Built into the castle ramparts, this comfortable pub hosts many charity events, such as the world pea throwing championships. The upper level terrace is accessible via the stairs, as is the function room, home to a folk club and local dramatic productions. Well-behaved children may use the games room until

8pm, where the traditional game of toad in the hole is played. Lunchtime food is available, plus a more limited evening menu (7–9, Mon–Thu). Mobile phones are used at your peril. ᴹQ⊛◁▷⊟≠♠

Snowdrop Inn
119 South Street, BN7 2BU
☼ 11-11; 12-10.30 Sun
☎ (01273) 471018 website: www.snowdrop.co.uk
Harveys BB; Hop Back Summer Lightning; guest beers Ⓗ

This friendly, back-street local on two levels boasts an unusual horseshoe-shaped bar. A free house, serving a range of organic, vegetarian and seafood dishes, it is both child- and dog-friendly (until 9pm for children). It hosts live jazz every Monday and live music most Saturdays. The pub is not named after the flower, but commemorates an avalanche that destroyed a row of cottages nearby in 1836 (a tablet in South Malling Church remembers those who died). ⊛◁▷⅄

White Star
36 Lansdown Place, BN7 2JU
☼ 11-2.30, 5-11; 11-11 Fri & Sat; 12-2.30, 7-10.30 Sun
☎ (01273) 480623
Black Sheep Best Bitter; Harveys BB; Taylor Landlord; guest beers Ⓗ

Quality beer to match the good conversation, is the motto of this comfortable, air-conditioned pub close to the station. Blissfully free from music, pool and darts, it is a perfect haven for commuters and visitors. Decorated with pictures of the liners from which the pub takes its name, it has become an established part of the local CAMRA ale trail. Can you spot the TV? This is only used to show F1 racing, of which the landlord is an aficionado. Q≈

MILTON STREET

Sussex Ox
BN26 5RL (signed off A27) OS534041
☼ 11-3, 6-11 (12-10.30 summer); 12-10.30) Sun
☎ (01323) 870840
Harveys BB, seasonal beers; Hop Back Summer Lightning; guest beers Ⓗ

Spacious country pub situated in the Cuckmere Valley, commanding outstanding views of the surrounding landscape. The pub comprises a traditional bar area with seating, a family room and a restaurant (booking advisable). Four beers are always available with a range of strengths and styles to suit everyone. Reasonably-priced, fresh food is served in all areas. A small campsite (access by prior permission) is well placed for the South Downs. Q⅗⊛◁▷ÅP⅄

PORTSLADE

Stanley Arms
47 Wolseley Road, BN41 1SS
☼ 1 (12 Fri & Sat)-11; 12-10.30 Sun
☎ (01273) 430234 website: www.thestanley.com
Beer range varies Ⓗ

A local CAMRA regular Pub of the Year award-winner. A corner local among Victorian terraced houses, the Stanley has pulling power well beyond its local area, especially for its beer festival (August). The

decorated, oversized glasses have been acquired from various beer festivals. Stained glass panels over the bar, a piano, varnished wood and a collection of Reader's Digest condensed books complete the homely atmosphere. It hosts live music some weekends; children's certificate held. Organic bottled cider is stocked.
🏚Q❀⊟≷ (Fishersgate) ♣ ☐

RINGMER

Cock Inn
Uckfield Road, BN8 5RX (off A26)
❂ 11-3, 6-11; 11-11 Fri & Sat; 12-3, 7-10.30 Sun
☎ (01273) 812040 website: www.cockpub.co.uk
Fuller's London Pride; Harveys BB, Old; guest beers Ⓗ
Dating from the 16th century, in a cul-de-sac off the A26 near the Ringmer turn, the Cock places a great emphasis on food, so the bar area can be very crowded at peak meal times. Children are most welcome in the dining areas. The stone steps to the main door double as an outside drinking area. The bar boasts a great inglenook. The pub lies on a bus route from Lewes to Uckfield. 🏚▷❀◑P

ROBERTSBRIDGE

Ostrich
Station Road, TN32 5DG (opp. station)
❂ 11-11; 12-10.30 Sun
☎ (01580) 881737
Adnams Bitter; Harveys BB; guest beer Ⓗ
Spacious, open-plan pub that was once the Station Hotel. Many interesting pictures adorn the interior and its superb Italian-style garden, with many tropical plants, should not be missed. Basic bar snacks are available at lunchtime. Very much part of the community, the pub has a games room.
🏚❀⊭≷P

RODMELL

Abergavenny Arms
Newhaven Road, BN7 3EZ
❂ 11-3.30, 5.30-11; 11-11 Sat & summer;
12-10.30 Sun
☎ (01273) 472416
Dark Star Hophead; Harveys BB; guest beers Ⓗ
Strategically located close to the South Downs Way and Virginia Woolf's former home, this is a favourite of walkers. Situated within an attractive flint-built village, part of the building was mentioned in the Domesday Book and some of its timbers came from wrecks of the Spanish Armada. The pub also boasts an indoor well. The annual beer festival is held in November. Bus service 123 from Lewes to Newhaven passes the door. No meals are served Sunday evening or Monday. 🏚❀◑P

ST LEONARDS

Bull
530 Bexhill Road, TN38 8AY
❂ 12-3, 6-11; 12-4, 7-10.30 Sun
☎ (01424) 424984
Shepherd Neame Master Brew Bitter, Best Bitter, Spitfire or seasonal beer Ⓗ
Welcoming roadside pub, noted for its range of Shepherd Neame beers served at their very best. This local also offers an excellent menu (book at weekends; no food

Sun eve). There is a dining room, a bar billiards table in one corner and a large car park at the rear, which offers much more space than appears at first. At the western end of St Leonards, it is convenient for the Glynde Gap shops. 🏚Q◑▷♣P

Dripping Spring
34 Tower Road, TN37 6JE (off A2100)
❂ 12-3, 5-11; 11-11 Fri & Sat; 12-3, 7-10.30 Sun
☎ (01424) 434055
website: www.thedrippingspring.fsnet.co.uk
Goacher's Light; Taylor Best Bitter; Young's Bitter; guest beers Ⓗ
The Drip, as it is known to its ever-increasing circle of devotees, has simply the best range of guest beers for miles. Winner of Sussex CAMRA's Pub of the Year award three years running, and a total of over 2,000 different ales to date, make this a must. It stages a beer festival in September and occasional themed weekends as well as a Sunday night quiz, so this is a busy pub at times. ❀≷ (Warrior Sq) ♣ ● ☐

Duke
48 Duke Road, Silverhill, TN37 7DN
(between A21 and B2159)
❂ 11-11; 12-10.30 Sun
☎ (01424) 436241
Greene King IPA; Old Speckled Hen; guest beers Ⓗ
Busy, two-bar pub in the central Silverhill part of town, situated on a street corner. Usually five beers are on tap from the Greene King range – mainly on the strong side. An excellent beer festival is held in May in the garden. Q❀⊟♣

Horse & Groom
Mercatoria, TN38 0EB
❂ 11-11; 12-10.30 Sun
☎ (01424) 420612
Adnams Broadside; Greene King IPA; Harveys BB; guest beers Ⓗ
At the heart of old St Leonards, this first-class free house serves a good range of beers at their very best. The 1829 listed building has an unusual horseshoe bar, dividing two separate bars; one leads to a further quieter room at the rear of the pub. Good bar food is served Monday–Saturday lunchtimes; the adjoining restaurant is open Tuesday–Saturday and for Sunday lunch. Warrior Square Station is nearby, and it is only a short walk to the sea.
🏚Q❀◑≷ (Warrior Sq)

SOUTH HEIGHTON

Hampden Arms
Heighton Road, BN9 0JJ (off B2109)
❂ 12-11; 12-10.30 Sun
☎ (01273) 514529
Greene King Old Speckled Hen; Harveys BB; guest beers Ⓗ
Thankfully unspoilt, this pub, tucked away on the South Downs, is a pleasant local with a tiled frontage and strong community spirit. Pub games are important here, a point emphasised by the three separate areas for darts, toad-in-the-hole and pool, and underlined by the impressive display of trophies above the bar. The landlord and landlady ensure that charities are not forgotten by staging many fundraising events.
🏚❀⊟♣P

TELHAM

Black Horse
Hastings Road, TN33 0SH (on A2100, between Battle and Hastings)
🕐 11-3, 6-11; 12-3, 7-10.30 Sun
☎ (01424) 773109
Shepherd Neame Master Brew Bitter, Spitfire, seasonal beers Ⓗ

Splendid pub on the outskirts of Battle. It has a skittle alley in the attic and two boules pistes in the garden. The annual music festival, held in a marquee every spring bank holiday, is going from strength to strength, and is often referred to as the 'biggest little festival' in Britain. Monthly jazz is performed in the bar every fourth Wednesday; occasional folk music sessions are held as well. Good food is served from an extensive menu, with many home-cooked specials. ▲Q❄◑♣P

UCKFIELD

Alma ⊘
Framfield Road, TN22 5AJ
(on B2102, E of centre)
🕐 11-2.30, 6-11; 12-2, 7-10.30 Sun
☎ (01825) 762232
Harveys XX Mild, Pale Ale, BB, Old, Armada, seasonal beers Ⓗ

The only pub for miles around to serve a full range of beers from Harveys. The saloon bar-cum-no-smoking room is large, bright and very comfortable (no dogs allowed in here). The public bar has all the same great features but smoking and dogs are permitted. The same family has run this local for generations, winning several awards. The small garden is beside the car park. No food is served on Sunday.
Q▷❄◑🖳&≠P⊬🍴

UDIMORE

King's Head
Rye Road, TN31 6BG (B2089, W of village)
🕐 11-4 (not winter Mon), 5.30-11; 12-4, 7-10.30 (not winter eve) Sun
☎ (01424) 882349
Harveys BB; guest beers Ⓗ

Built in 1535 and extended in the 17th century, this traditional village ale house boasts exposed beams, two open fires, wood floors and a very long oak bar, which was installed in the 1930s and has to be seen (and leant on) to be believed. The pub serves excellent home-cooked food and has a no-smoking dining room. Situated in an area of outstanding natural beauty, there are many scenic walks nearby.
▲Q▷❄◑&♣P

WARTLING

Lamb Inn
BN27 1RY (on road between Pevensey and Windmill Hill)
🕐 11-2.30 (3 summer), 6-11 (11-11 summer Sat; closed winter Mon); 12-6 (10 summer) Sun
☎ (01323) 832116
Cuckmere Haven Guvnor; King Red River Ale; Rother Valley Level Best Ⓗ

Grade II listed, 17th-century country inn close to the Herstmonceux Greenwich Observatory. The bar area, with adequate seating, serves a good range of beverages, including three local beers. The adjoining lounge is a good place to relax. The restaurant (booking advisable) serves a range of local produce, freshly prepared and cooked on premises, but food is served in all areas (no meals Sun eve). Wartling has many interesting historical sites nearby and is handy for river and lake fishing, and good walking and cycling routes. ▲Q❄◑●P⊬

WHATLINGTON

Royal Oak
Woodmans Green, TN33 0NJ
(on A21, between Robertsbridge and Sedlescome)
🕐 11-3, 5.30-11; 12-4, 7-10.30 Sun
☎ (01424) 870492
Harveys BB; guest beers Ⓗ

Fine old inn, five miles from Hastings in the small hamlet of Whatlington. With a split-level interior, one of the two upper levels is a no-smoking area. A deep well inside the pub near the bar is an unusual feature, and a splendid large inglenook holds a roaring log fire in winter. An extensive menu is served. ▲Q❄◑⊬

WILLINGDON

Red Lion ⊘
99 Wish Hill, BN20 9HQ (off A2270)
🕐 11-3, 5-11; 11-11 Sat; 12-10.30 Sun
☎ (01323) 502062
Badger K&B Sussex, Best, Tanglefoot; Gribble K&B Mild, Fursty Ferret Ⓗ

Friendly, Victorian village local that serves food only at lunchtime, although a curry night (on the first Thu of the month), is an exception. All curries are home-cooked, including an excellent king prawn. The pub comprises a large bar, a no-smoking lounge and a banked garden. Bar billiards has a big following here, as is borne out by a well-stocked trophy cabinet. The pub is handy for the local beauty spot of Butts Brow on the South Downs. ❄◑P⊬

WITHYHAM

Dorset Arms ⊘
TN7 4BD
(on B2110, between Hartfield and Groombridge)
🕐 11.30-3, 6-11; 12-3, 7-10.30 Sun
☎ (01892) 770278 website: www.dorsetarms.co.uk
Harveys Pale Ale, BB, seasonal beers Ⓗ

Picturesque old pub, built in 1556 in what once was the industrial heartland of England. Its unspoilt, low-ceilinged bar bears a floor of unvarnished local oak. The restaurant serves good food (eve meals Tue–Sat). The large grassed area in front of the pub gets busy with drinkers on warm days. Ashdown Forest, not far away, is worth visiting. The No. 291 bus runs regularly from East Grinstead and Tunbridge Wells, Monday–Saturday during the day. ▲Q❄◑🖳♣P

> Mary Uff
> She sells good stuff
> And that's enough.
>
> Notice formerly at the Crooked Billet,
> Wotton, Buckinghamshire

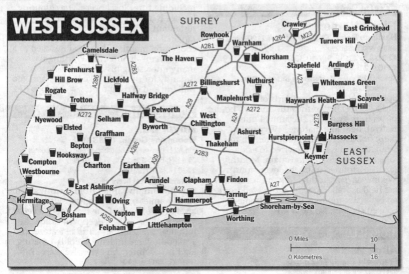

WEST SUSSEX

ARDINGLY

Oak Inn
Street Lane, RH17 6UA (200 yds from B2028)
☼ 11.30-2.30, 5-11; 11.30-11 Thu-Sat; 12-10.30 Sun
☎ (01444) 892244 website: www.theoakardingly.co.uk
Harveys BB; guest beers Ⓗ
Originally three labourers' cottages dating from the 14th century, this friendly pub features an inglenook and oak beams (crash helmets may be required in some places), the ghost of the 'grey lady' sometimes sits in the bar. The restaurant serves excellent food, plus take-away fish and chips (Fri eve); no food Sunday evening. Guest beers change frequently and usually come from local independent breweries. Walkers are welcome; daytime bus Nos. 81, 82 and 88 run to Haywards Heath and Crawley.
🏚Q🐕🏵◑⊟🔥♣P✖

ARUNDEL

King's Arms
36 Tarrant Street, BN18 9DN
☼ 11-3, 5.30-11; 11-11 Sat; 12-10.30 Sun
☎ (01903) 882312
Fuller's London Pride; Young's Special; guest beers Ⓗ
This traditional, unspoilt, two-bar local offers an oasis for beer drinkers among Arundel's tea rooms and antique shops. Recent research has shown that the King's Arms has been a pub for 500 years. Situated on a corner, downhill from the cathedral, it offers a friendly welcome and attracts a cosmopolitan clientele. A genuine free house, it is always worth a detour to check out the guest beers. 🏵◑⊟🅰≠♣

ASHURST

Fountain Inn
Horsham Road, BN44 3AP
(on B2135, 2 miles N of A283)
☼ 12-2.30, 5.30-11; 12-3, 7-10.30 Sun
☎ (01403) 710219
Adnams Bitter; Harveys BB; Shepherd Neame Master Brew Bitter; King Horsham Best Bitter; Ⓗ
guest beers Ⓖ
This wonderful, historic rural pub was local
454

CAMRA's Pub of the Year 2001, and is still a firm favourite. Two main bars and a dining area, with low exposed beams, flagstone floors and open fires, lead off the narrow entrance. The large garden features a restored cider press, while the renovated barn doubles as a skittle alley and function room. Good fresh food is served – snacks only on Sunday and Monday – making the pub popular with drinkers and diners.
🏚Q🏵◑P

BEPTON

Country Inn
Severals Road, GU29 0LR
(1 mile SW of Midhurst) OS870206
☼ 11-3, 5-11 (11-11 Fri, Sat & summer);
12-10.30 Sun
☎ (01730) 813466
Draught Bass; Ballard's Midhurst Mild; Taylor Landlord; Young's Bitter; guest beer Ⓗ
Situated a mile from the A286, this single-bar village local enjoys a busy weekend food trade; no food is available on winter Sunday evenings, but book for Sunday lunch and monthly special food nights. It also hosts occasional live entertainment. At the rear is a large garden. A guest beer from an independent brewer is always on tap. Games include shove-ha'penny and table skittles. 🏚🏵◑♣P

BILLINGSHURST

Railway Inn
40 Station Road, RH14 9SE
☼ 11-11; 12-10.30 Sun
☎ (01403) 782928
Adnams Bitter; Badger Tanglefoot; Flowers IPA; Gale's HSB; Greene King IPA Ⓗ
Spacious Victorian pub with the same licensee since 1984. A large horseshoe-shaped bar, serves an extensive menu, including Sunday lunch with four choices. Opposite Billingshurst Station level crossing, the pub benefits from a good rail service and is also served by Compass bus Nos. 75 and 76 (two-hourly service Mon–Sat). Occasional live music is performed. ◑&≠P

BOSHAM

White Swan
Station Road, PO18 8NG (on A259)
☼ 12-3, 5-11; 12-4.30, 6-11 Sat; 12-4.30,
7-10.30 Sun
☎ (01243) 576086
**Courage Best Bitter; Hop Back Crop Circle, Summer
Lightning; Young's Bitter; guest beer** Ⓗ

An inn for 300 years, this roadside local is
commodious but cosy, with beams, bare
bricks and a log fire. Easily reached by road
or rail, it now has a larger car park, and
improvements to the patio garden make it
more family-friendly without detracting
from its traditional pub atmosphere. The
skittle alley doubles as a family room. The
excellent restaurant offers locally-caught
fish as a speciality. Highly recommended.
🏠Q🕸🅾🕭🍴♿️🏧🚆♣P🍴

BURGESS HILL

Watermill
1 Leylands Road, World's End, RH15 0QF
(E of Wivelsfield Station)
☼ 11-11; 12-10.30 Sun
☎ (01444) 235517
**Fuller's London Pride; Greene King Old Speckled Hen;
Young's Bitter; guest beers** Ⓗ

Friendly, community local situated in the
World's End area of Burgess Hill. The beer
range includes a guest from a SIBA (Society
of Independent Brewers) brewer every
weekend. The enclosed garden provides a
safe area for families and a venue for
barbecues. The TV is turned on for major
sporting events. The pub is a regular on the
local CAMRA trail. Evening meals are served
Friday and Saturday. 🕸🅾🚆 (Wivelsfield) ♣P

BYWORTH

Black Horse Inn
GU28 0HL (off A283, 1 mile from Petworth)
☼ 11-11; 12-10.30 Sun
☎ (01798) 342424
Cheriton Pots Ale; guest beers Ⓗ

Popular pub in the hamlet of Byworth. This
former tannery dates back to 1564 and has
been extended over the centuries, adding
character. Full of nooks and crannies, it
boasts original floorboards and exposed
beams; the bar has an old wooden trap door
with a traditional beer cellar below. It hosts
an all-year-round calendar of events. Try the
Elizabethan dining room upstairs (must
book) and enjoy wonderful views of
Petworth and the Downs from the garden.
🏠Q🕸🅾P

CAMELSDALE

Mill Tavern
Liphook Road, Shottermill, GU27 3QE
(on B2131)
☼ 11-3, 6-11; 12-4, 7-10.30 (12-10.30 summer) Sun
☎ (01428) 643183
**Fuller's London Pride; Greene King IPA; Shepherd
Neame Spitfire; guest beers** Ⓗ

This 15th-century mill now makes a
wonderful country pub, full of character
and serving excellent beers. The main bar
with heavy wood beams, a log fire and
charming decor is supplemented by two
dining rooms, offering a varied and
extensive menu. All food is prepared on the

premises and largely home made. A must
for serious beer drinkers, it also caters very
well for families with babies and young
children who enjoy the spacious family
room. 🏠🛏🕸🅾🍴♿️P

CHARLTON

Fox Goes Free
PO18 0HU (1 mile E of A286 at Singleton)
☼ 11-3, 5.30-11 (11-11 Sat and summer Fri);
12-10.30 Sun
☎ (01243) 811461
**Ballard's Best Bitter; Fuller's London Pride;
Ringwood Fortyniner** Ⓗ

This fine Sussex flint pub lies at the heart of
a sleepy little downland village. With red
brick floors, three inglenooks and many
original features retained from its 400-year
history, it just oozes character. Deservedly
popular for its food; former stables and the
village bakery now form part of the
restaurant. Family-run, a recent addition is
the en-suite accommodation – handy for all
the nearby attractions at Goodwood. Enjoy
fine views from the large garden. Try the
house beer. 🏠Q🕸🛏🅾🍴♿️🏧♣🖤P

CLAPHAM

Coach & Horses
Arundel Road, BN13 3UA
(on A27 just outside Worthing)
☼ 11-3, 5.15-11; 12-4, 7-10.30 Sun
☎ (01903) 264665
**Fuller's London Pride; Greene King Abbot; Harveys BB;
guest beer** Ⓗ

A warm welcome awaits in this former
coaching inn. Built in 1741 as the Rose &
Crown, its name was changed in 1763. The
walls are hung with old pictures of
Worthing and the pub itself. The dining
area offers an imaginative menu; the chef
once cooked for the Queen. Children (and
dogs) are welcome in the rear bar. This
community pub is often involved in charity
events. It hosts monthly jazz/blues nights
and a weekly quiz (Tue). Listen for the ghost
in the cellar. 🏠🛏🕸🅾🍴♣P

COMPTON

Coach & Horses
The Square, PO18 9HA (on B2146)
☼ 11.30-2.30, 6-11; 12-3, 7-10.30 Sun
☎ (02392) 631228
Fuller's ESB; guest beers Ⓗ

16th-century pub in a remote, charming
downland village. The front bar features
two open fires, a bar billiards table, sliding
wooden shutters and pine panelling from
its Henty & Constable days. There is a small
rear bar and a restaurant in the oldest part
of the building. A blackboard menu offers
home-cooked fish dishes and local game.
With up to five interesting guest beers on

INDEPENDENT BREWERIES

Arundel Ford
Ballard's Nyewood
Dark Star Haywards Heath
Gribble Inn Oving
Hepworth Weltons Horsham
King Horsham
Rectory Hassocks

tap, this local CAMRA Pub of the Year 2001 is well worth seeking out. ᴍ☼◖♣

CRAWLEY

Swan ✓
1 Horsham Road, West Green, RH11 7LY
◷ 11-11; 12-10.30 Sun
☎ (01293) 527447
Flowers Original; Fuller's London Pride; Young's Special; Ⓗ **guest beers** Ⓗ/Ⓖ
The Swan has been in this Guide many times over the years. The pub dates back to the coming of the railway in 1848. The present tenants employ a lively guest ale policy which has seen over 200 different ales pass through the pub. The active public bar hosts live music on Friday evening, while the saloon bar is much quieter. Cider is available seasonally. Evening meals are served 5–7pm. This pub is well worth a visit.
☼◗≉♣

White Hart ✓
65 High Street, RH10 1BQ
◷ 10-11; 12-10.30 Sun
☎ (01293) 520033
Harveys Pale Ale, BB, seasonal beers Ⓗ
Popular, busy pub that has a happy hour, Monday–Wednesday, 5–6pm and hosts live music on Sunday evening. Good bar food and a no-smoking restaurant make this a very attractive venue. One of the oldest buildings in the town centre, this Harveys tied house enjoys a loyal following.
☼◖≉♣P

EARTHAM

George Inn
Brittens Lane, PO18 0LT OS938094
◷ 11-11; 12-10.30 Sun
☎ (01243) 814340
Arundel seasonal beers; Greene King Abbot; Palmer IPA; guest beers Ⓗ
At the centre of a village in good walking country, midway between the A27 and A285, the George has a lounge, a locals' bar with stone-flagged floor and a restaurant. The food ranges from bar snacks to a full, quality menu, featuring local produce and game. Outside is a large, south-facing garden. It is on the Chichester–Petworth No. 99 bus route. ᴍ☼◖♿♣P

EAST ASHLING

Horse & Groom
PO18 9AX (on B2178, 2½ miles NW of Chichester)
◷ 12-3, 6-11; 12-6 (closed eve) Sun
☎ (01243) 575339 website:
www.horseandgroom.sageweb.co.uk
Draught Bass; Harveys BB; Hop Back Summer Lightning; Young's Bitter Ⓗ
Originally a forge, this 17th-century inn retains much character, with its flagstone floor, old settles and half-panelled walls in the bar, heated by a fine old commercial range. Sympathetically extended, with much use of knapped Sussex flints, the comfortable dining area offers a diverse menu of home-made dishes, to a high standard (no food Sun eve). An integral 17th-century flint barn, sensitively converted, now offers accommodation in oak-beamed, en-suite rooms.
ᴍQ☼⌂◖Å♣♠P

EAST GRINSTEAD

Ship Inn
RH19 4EG
◷ 11-11; 12-10.30 Sun
☎ (01342) 312089
Young's Bitter, Special, seasonal beers Ⓗ
Recently extensively refurbished, this is now a nicely decorated single-bar pub, which is quite spacious and very friendly. There is plenty of room for both drinkers and diners, with an extensive choice of food for the latter. Located just off the historic High Street, it is an ideal location for a few days' break.
ᴍ☼⌂◖♿≉♣P⌖

ELSTED

Three Horseshoes
GU29 0JY (between Midhurst and Harting)
◷ 11-2.30, 6-11; 12-3, 7-10.30 Sun
☎ (01730) 825746
Ballard's Best Bitter; Cheriton Pots Ale; Fuller's London Pride; Taylor Landlord Ⓖ
Traditional village pub built originally as a drovers' inn, it was later extended into the shop next door. The four small rooms with open fires, panelled walls and beamed ceilings make a wonderful setting for a drink or a meal from the quality menu. The pub's downland setting means views from the huge garden are splendid.
ᴍQ☼◖P

FELPHAM

Old Barn
42 Felpham Road, PO22 7PL
◷ 11-11; 12-10.30 Sun
☎ (01243) 821564
Ringwood Best Bitter; Gale's GB; Hop Back Summer Lightning; guest beers Ⓗ
Old flint building, once part of Felpham Farm. During the last century it was a private residence, a guest house, a rest home, then a club; for the last 30 years it has been a free house. Divided into three distinct areas: at the front is a cosy locals' bar; in the middle is the boisterous section where two of the TVs are switched on for sport; at the far end is the games area, housing pool, darts, pinball and a trivia machine. ☼◖P

FERNHURST

King's Arms
Midhurst Road, GU27 3HA
(on A286, 3/4 mile S of village)
◷ 11.30-3, 5.30 (6.30 Sat)-11; 12-3, 6.30-10.30 (not winter eves) Sun
☎ (01428) 652005
Hogs Back TEA; Ringwood Best Bitter; guest beers Ⓗ
Sussex sandstone free house, set below Henley Hill. A pub since the 17th century, the wood-panelled interior is divided into a bar and restaurant, plus a private dining room. The monthly changing seasonal menu regularly features local fish and game. Outside is an enclosed garden and a Sussex barn that hosts an excellent beer festival in August. An interesting guest beer is always stocked; the house beer is brewed by Ventnor. It is served by the Haslemere–Midhurst No. 70 bus route.
ᴍQ☼◖Å♣P

Red Lion
The Green, GU27 3HY
(¼ mile E of A286 crossroads)
✪ 12-3, 5-11; 12-11 Thu, Fri & Sat; 12-10.30 Sun
☎ (01428) 653304
Fuller's Chiswick, London Pride, ESB, seasonal beers Ⓗ

Nestling by the village green, the Red Lion has been providing hospitality to all since the first licensee was recorded in the parish in 1592. Now a Fuller's tied house, their full range is on offer, including the elusive Chiswick and seasonal brews. Just off the Midhurst–Haslemere road, it is definitely in Sussex despite the Surrey postal address. No meals are served Monday evening.
🛏Q✿🍴◑P⅄

FINDON

Findon Manor Hotel
High Street, BN14 0TA
✪ 12-2.30, 6-11; 12-10.30 Sun
☎ (01903) 872733 website: www.findonmanor.com
Black Sheep Best Bitter; Greene King Abbot; Fuller's London Pride; Harveys BB Ⓗ

The Snooty Fox bar in this attractive, 16th-century country house hotel, serves real ale. The building was originally the village rectory. It was also Montgomery's billet during WWII, but as a teetotaller, the range of real ales would have been wasted on him! A quiet bar for relaxing in, with a log fire in winter, it attracts a mixture of locals and diners. 🛏Q✿🛌◑♿P

GRAFFHAM

Foresters Arms
GU28 0AQ (3 miles W of A285) OS931177
✪ 11-2.30, 6-11;
12-3, 6.30-10.30 (not winter eve) Sun
☎ (01798) 867202
Cheriton Pots Ale; Taylor Landlord; guest beers Ⓗ

Fine, traditional country pub, built in 1609 and extended in Victorian times. Formerly run by Chichester brewers, Henty & Constable, the name comes from its use as a meeting place for the Free Foresters. An attractive garden and an impressive inglenook with blazing logs in winter make this a popular venue, as does its proximity to the South Downs Way and other fine walking country. Four en-suite guest rooms were added in 2003.
🛏Q✿🛌◑P

HALFWAY BRIDGE

Halfway Bridge Inn
GU28 9BP
(on A272, halfway between Midhurst and Petworth)
✪ 11-3, 6-11; 12-3, 7-10.30 Sun
☎ (01798) 861281 website: www.thesussexpub.co.uk
Cheriton Pots Ale; Fuller's London Pride; Gale's HSB; guest beers Ⓗ

Multi-roomed country inn with an emphasis on good quality food, but which still finds room and a welcome for drinkers in the rear bar. The pub boasts no less than five open fires and a wealth of exposed beams and panelling. Built as an inn in 1710, it has recently added eight rooms for guests. Biddenden cider is served. The patio area is secluded for a quiet drink.
🛏Q✿🛌◑♣P

HAMMERPOT

Woodman's Arms ✓
BN16 4EV (just off A27 at Angmering)
✪ 11-3, 6-11; 12-3, 7-10.30 Sun
☎ (01903) 871240
website: www.thewoodmansarms.co.uk
Gale's GB, HSB; guest beers Ⓗ

This 16th-century pub is characterised by stone floors, an inglenook and low beams. The spacious central bar, mainly for drinkers, is complemented by a more food-oriented bar to the right and a cosy bar to the left. Due to the construction of the Angmering bypass, the large car park can only be accessed from a westerly direction. Well worth a visit. 🛏⛵✿🍴◑♣P⅄

THE HAVEN

Blue Ship ☆
RH14 9BS (1 mile S of A281 at Bucks Green)
OS084306
✪ 11-3, 6-11; 12-3.30, 7-10.30 Sun
☎ (01403) 822709
Badger K&B Sussex, Tanglefoot Ⓖ

Wonderful, atmospheric, old country pub in the truest sense. Time seems to have stood still here over the last 100 years. Beer is served straight from the barrel through two serving-hatches. Sit in the cosy main bar, or one of several areas for drinkers in the adjoining rooms. The pub is noted for its dog breeding awards. A real haven for beer drinkers where you will find an honest welcome; evening meals are served Tuesday–Saturday. 🛏Q⛵✿🍴◑🍽♣P⅄

HERMITAGE

Sussex Brewery
36 Main Road, PO18 8AU
(on A259, ½ mile E of Emsworth)
✪ 11-11; 12-10.30 Sun
☎ (01243) 371533
Smiles IPA; Young's Bitter, Special, seasonal beers Ⓗ

Situated at the edge of the fishing village of Emsworth, this cosy, bare-boarded local, with its roaring open fire in winter, is still a traditional pub in the best sense of the word, but also now offers a quality fish menu and an unusual speciality sausage menu. The lovely walled garden is an added attraction. The house beer is brewed by Young's. 🛏Q✿◑🐕🚂(Emsworth) P

HILL BROW

Jolly Drover
GU33 7QL (at B2070/B3006 jct)
✪ 11-2.30, 6-11; 12-3 (closed eve) Sun
☎ (01730) 893137
Draught Bass; Black Sheep Best Bitter; Taylor Landlord; Young's Bitter; guest beer Ⓗ

Built in 1820 by a drover, this watering-hole lies midway between Petersfield and Liphook on the old A3, just outside Liss. Family-run country local, the atmosphere is enhanced by original beams, an extremely large log fire and two chesterfields. Varied bric-à-brac includes a bar price list from the 1950s. The well-proportioned bar and dining area offer over 20 home-made daily specials. The five cask ales include an independent changing guest; Swamp Donkey real cider is sold.
🛏Q✿◑🐕P

HOOKSWAY

Royal Oak
PO18 9JZ
(¼ mile off B2141, near North Marden) OS815162
☼ 11.30 (12 winter)-2.30, 6 (7 winter)-11; closed Mon;
12-3, 6-10.30 (not winter eve) Sun
☎ (01243) 535257
**Exmoor seasonal beers; Gale's HSB; Taylor Landlord;
guest beer** ⊞

Tucked away in a valley close to the South
Downs Way, this rural gem was built as a
lunch stop for the 'guns' on West Dean
Estate shoots. King Edward VII was a
frequent patron, but now walkers and
cyclists enjoy its peaceful setting.
Reasonably-priced, home-cooked food
complements the four ales which include
Hooksway Bitter from Hampshire Brewery,
and often a strong dark beer. A brass shell
case is struck to call 'time'.
♨Q☜❀◑▲♣P✄

Olde King's Head
Carfax, RH12 1EG
☼ 11-11; 12-3 (closed eve) Sun
☎ (01403) 253126
**King Horsham Best Bitter, Red River Ale, seasonal
beers** ⊞

Town-centre hotel, with a large,
comfortable bar. The building dates from
1401 and once served as the local tax office.
Inland Revenue Office is still clearly visible
on the exterior, but do not let that put you
off as excellent beer is served, without a
taxman in sight (except the duty on the
beer). Three handpumps serve WJ King's
ales and seasonal brews.
Q⇔◑&≈P✄

HORSHAM

Malt Shovel
Springfield Road, RH12 2PG
☼ 11-11; 12-10.30 Sun
☎ (01444) 254543 website: www.maltshovel.com
Adnams Bitter; Draught Bass; Taylor Landlord; ⊞
guest beers ⑤

Olde-worlde type of pub, well known for its
Mild in May events. If you like rugby then
this is the place for you. A beer festival is
usually held in February and March with
100-plus beers sold over at least six weeks; a
passport and prizes add to the fun. Three
beers are regularly served on gravity;
Biddenden cider is always available.
Excellent home-cooked food is served until
5pm daily.
♨❀◑≈♣P

HURSTPIERPOINT

White Horse
Albourne Road, BN6 9SP
☼ 11-11; 12-10.30 Sun
☎ (01273) 834717
Harveys BB; guest beers ⊞

This 15th-century listed building stands at
the western edge of the village. Its many
rooms include a large public bar and a
restaurant that can be accessed via the
small, quiet, cosy saloon bar. Meals may
also be eaten in the bars. Old photographs
displayed in the saloon bar include one of a
Hurst Brewery dray. The guest beer range
varies.
♨Q❀◑♣

458

KEYMER

Greyhound
Keymer Road, BN6 8QT
☼ 11-3, 6-11; 11-11 Sat; 12-10.30 Sun
☎ (01273) 842645
Courage Best Bitter; Harveys BB; Young's Special ⊞

Over 450 years old, this pub, opposite the
local church, boasts many old beams and
artefacts of breweries long-gone. Some time
ago an extension was added to make a
dining area and it blends in very well; no
food is served on Sunday evening or
Monday. The public bar houses a bar
billiards table and dartboard, but no pool
table. A piano player entertains on Sunday
lunchtime. ♨Q❀◑⊟&♣P

LICKFOLD

Lickfold Inn
GU28 9EY (4 miles NE of Midhurst) OS926263
☼ 11-3, 5.30-11; 11.30-3, 6-11 (12-11 summer) Sat;
12-3, 7-10.30 Sun
☎ (01798) 861285
**Ballard's Best Bitter; Hop Back Crop Circle, seasonal
beers; King seasonal beers; Young's Bitter; guest
beers** ⊞

Smart, Grade II listed, 15th-century pub
with an accent on high quality meals in the
upstairs restaurant, most evenings or bar
food, downstairs. The wood-panelled family
room opens out on to a terraced garden.
This delightful country pub may prove hard
to find, but is worth the effort. Usually four
guest beers from small, local, independent
brewers are stocked. ♨Q❀◑&♣P

LITTLEHAMPTON

Dew Drop Inn
96 Wick Street, BN17 7JS
☼ 11-3, 5.30-11; 11-11 Sat; 12-10.30 Sun
☎ (01903) 716459
Gales's Butser, HSB; Ringwood Porter; guest beers ⊞

Small, friendly local in the suburbs of
Littlehampton. The long and narrow public
bar is devoted to traditional pub games;
somewhat spartan, it is nonetheless
welcoming. The saloon bar is reminiscent of
a lounge in a private house. A small patio
completes the picture. Q❀⊟♣

MAPLEHURST

White Horse
Park Lane, RH13 6LL
(2 miles S of Mannings Heath) OS190246
☼ 12 -2.30 (11.30-3 Sat), 6-11; 12-3, 7-10.30 Sun
☎ (01403) 891208
Harveys BB; Weltons Pride & Joy; guest beers ⊞

Wonderful country pub where a warm
welcome is assured. The large bar has
several areas rambling off it. The
conservatory doubles as a family room.
Although the pub provides a good range of
food, the emphasis is still very much on
good beer and conversation. The pub has
been local CAMRA Pub of the Year two
years running, and under the guidance of
the same licensees for over 20 years. Local
cider is always available. ♨Q☜❀◑♣●P

NUTHURST

Black Horse ⊘
Nuthurst Street, RH13 6LH

🕒 12-3, 6 (5 Fri)-11; 12-11 Sat; 12-10.30 Sun
☎ (01403) 891272 website: www.theblackhorseinn.info
Fuller's London Pride; Harveys BB; King Horsham Best Bitter, Red River Ale; guest beers Ⓗ

Large, 17th-century village pub where climbing plants cover half the frontage. A small river runs through the garden. Interesting features include an inglenook and an exposed section of wattle and daub wall – beer festivals are held every bank holiday. Food is served all day Saturday and Sunday. A quiz is held Thursday evening. The No. 108 post bus runs from Horsham. 🏚🕸🕩🍴🎁P✂

OVING

Gribble Inn ⊘
Gribble Lane, PO20 6BP
🕒 11-3, 5.30-11; 12-4, 7-10.30 Sun
☎ (01243) 786893
Badger Best; Gribble Fursty Ferret, Ale, Reg's Tipple, Pig's Ear, seasonal beers Ⓗ

Originally two agricultural workers' cottages, it is hard to believe the Gribble has not always been a pub. With its oak beams, thatched roof, open fires and cottage garden, it is the quintessential English country inn. Add the micro-brewery and skittle alley and you can see why it is a popular venue for all ages. Drinkers and diners mix in all the bars. 🏚Q🐾🕸🕩🚶♣🎁P✂

PETWORTH

Star Inn
Market Square, GU28 0AH (on A272)
🕒 11-11; 12-10.30 Sun
☎ (01798) 342569
Fuller's Chiswick, London Pride, ESB, seasonal beer or guest beer Ⓗ

There has been a pub on this site since 1591. Formerly known as the Black Bull, the bar has been given a modern make over. Pleasant meals can be enjoyed from a regularly changed menu; evening meals are served Tuesday–Saturday. A decked patio lets you sit in the sun and sample the Fuller's ales. 🕩✂

ROGATE

White Horse Inn
East Street, GU31 5EA (on A272)
🕒 12-3, 6-11; 12-11 Sat; 12-10.30 Sun
☎ (01730) 821333
Ballard's Best Bitter, Wassail; Cheriton Pots Ale; Hop Back Summer Lightning; Ringwood Fortyniner; guest beers Ⓗ

A coaching inn since 1598, now a popular village pub, with oak beams, a flagstone floor and a huge log fire in its large bar. It usually stocks six real ales, plus an occasional cider. The car park at the rear backs on to the village sports field. The pub supports its own cricket, rugby, and darts teams. An excellent restaurant serves home-made meals; bar snacks are also available. 🏚Q🕸🛏🕩♣♠🎁P

ROWHOOK

Chequers
RH12 3PY OS125343
🕒 11.30-3, 6-11; 12-3, 7-10.30 Sun
☎ (01403) 790480

Fuller's London Pride; Harveys BB; Young's Bitter; guest beers Ⓗ

The Chequers is a rural pub situated on the Roman road of Stane Street. Plenty of low beams and an inglenook give the place a rustic feel. Run by a master-chef and his wife, they enjoy a well-deserved reputation for both the bar and restaurant food. It can be challenging to find, but very rewarding once you arrive. 🏚Q🕸🕩✂

SCAYNE'S HILL

Sloop
Freshfield Lock, Sloop Lane, RH17 7NP
OS385244
🕒 12-3, 6-11; 12-10.30 Sun
☎ (01444) 831219
Greene King XX Mild, IPA, Ruddles County, Abbot; seasonal beers; guest beers Ⓗ

The Sloop stands by the River Ouse, near the Bluebell Railway preserved line. The pub has been carefully refurbished to retain its character, especially in the public bar area which is decorated with railway memorabilia. The oldest part of the pub has been a watering-hole since 1815 and was originally a pair of lock-keepers' cottages. Good food is served throughout the pub and extensive garden. It hosts occasional live music and the Sloop Festival in July. 🏚🕸🕩🚶♣P

SELHAM

Three Moles
GU28 0PN (1 mile S of A272, midway between Midhurst and Petworth) OS935206
🕒 12-2, 5.30-11; 11.30-11 Sat; 12-10.30 Sun
☎ (01798) 861303 website: www.thethreemoles.co.uk
Ballard's Midhurst Mild; King Horsham Best Bitter; Skinner's Betty Stogs Bitter; guest beers Ⓗ

Traditional, small country pub, well off the beaten track in the Rother Valley. Opened in 1872 to serve Selham Station, it has long outlived the railway line. This welcoming free house of great character offers up to three guest beers, mainly from southern micros, and hosts a garden beer festival in June. The unusual name comes from the coat of arms of the owners, the Mitford family. CAMRA Sussex Pub of the Year 2002, it was the local branch winner in 2003. 🏚Q🕸♠🎁P

SHOREHAM-BY-SEA

Buckingham Arms
35-39 Brunswick Road, BN43 5WA
🕒 11-11; 12-10.30 Sun
☎ (01273) 453660
Badger Best; Greene King Abbot; Harveys BB; Hop Back Summer Lightning; Taylor Landlord; guest beers Ⓗ

Flint-faced free house, just south of the level crossing at Shoreham Station, its front garden has been turned into a small car park. A brilliant range of beers includes three guests; a regular clientele keeps the turnover high. Tiffin comes out at six. The toilets are not well signed, and ignore the historic cabin clock (right twice a day!), especially if catching a train. Two popular beer festivals are held on August bank holiday and at the end of February. 🕸🕩⇌♣P

Red Lion
Old Shoreham Road, BN43 3TE
(opp. old toll bridge)
✪ 11-3, 5.30-11; 11.30-11 Sat; 12-10.30 Sun
☎ (01273) 453171
Beer range varies Ⓗ

This cosy, comfortable free house dating back to the 16th century, has a rich history; Tennyson's poem, Rizpah, was based on an event in the pub in 1792. The main bar has a low, beamed ceiling and an open fire; it was here a local blacksmith would lift the heavy oak tables – one in each hand. Added attractions are the six changing guest beers, good food and the annual Adur beer festival at Easter (plus a smaller one in September).
🏚Q✿◖◗⊟P✄

Royal Sovereign
6 Middle Street, BN43 5DP
(by Marlipins Museum)
✪ 11-11; 12-10.30 Sun
☎ (01273) 453518
Badger K&B Sussex; Castle Eden Ale; Flowers Original; Taylor Landlord; Young's Bitter Ⓗ

Classic, side-street pub featuring a green tiled frontage, with original leaded windows of the Portsmouth United period. It is noted for its good food and friendly ambience. Car parking is available next door; the Marlipins Museum is nearby. 🏚Q◖≠

STAPLEFIELD

Jolly Tanners
Handcross Road, RH17 6EF
✪ 11-3, 5.30-11; 11-11 Sat; 12-10.30 Sun
☎ (01444) 400335
Fuller's Chiswick, London Pride; Harveys BB; guest beer Ⓗ

Popular free house, circa 1600, on the north corner of the village green. A comfortable pub, with two bars at different levels, the upper one has an open fire. A smaller bar is used when the main bars are busy, and for meetings. A good selection of home-cooked food is served. Often used as a stopping-off point on various London–Brighton events, this regular Guide entry was local CAMRA's Pub of the Year 2002. A mild ale (varies) is always available. 🏚Q✿◖◗♣P

TARRING

George & Dragon
1 High Street, BN14 7NN
✪ 11-3, 5.30-11; 11-11 Sat; 12-10.30 Sun
☎ (01903) 202497
Courage Directors; John Smith's Bitter; Hop Back Summer Lightning; Wells Bombardier; Young's Bitter; guest beers Ⓗ

This superb pub enjoys a sizeable local following, and rightly so. An excellent selection of six real ales, including a guest, are served by the friendly staff, from a bar dominated by a large illuminated Watneys display. The split-level interior houses a number of rooms; one acts as a no-smoking dining area for the good value food (no meals Sun). There is a small, secluded garden to the rear. Q✿◖≠ (West) P✄

Vine ✓
27-29 High Street, BN14 7NN
✪ 12-3, 5.30-11; 12-11 Fri & Sat; 12-10.30 Sun
☎ (01903) 202891

Badger Best, Tanglefoot; Gribble K&B Mild, Fursty Ferret; Wadworth 6X Ⓗ

In a well-preserved street, the Vine attracts a wide cross-section of customers. It stages live music Monday evening and a quiz on Thursday. Although good beer and conversation are the main criteria, it also offers good value food, with children's meals on request. Parsons Brewery operated at the Vine; see the brewery memorabilia and old Tarring photographs. The large garden appeals to families in summer; on 5th January, morris dancers perform the custom of wassailing around the apple tree.
◖◗P

THAKEHAM

White Lion
The Street, RH20 3LP (300 yds from B2139)
✪ 11-3.30, 5.30-11; 12-4, 6.30-10.30 Sun
☎ (01798) 813141
Greene King IPA, Abbot, Old Speckled Hen; Fuller's London Pride; guest beers Ⓗ

A warm welcome from the landlord and locals alike is just one of the many attractions of this unspoilt, 16th-century, village pub situated in a picturesque village street, just off the B2139. The pub is filled with local colour and the historic interior features an unusual fireplace. There are two main rooms to the bar and a third snug where children are welcome. Excellent food and an enclosed patio and garden complete the amenities on offer.
🏚Q✿◖◗Å♣P

TROTTON

Keeper's Arms
GU31 5ER
(250 yds E of Trotton Bridge traffic lights on A272)
✪ 12-2.30, 5.30-11; 12-11 Fri & Sat; closed Mon; 12-10.30 Sun
☎ (01730) 813724
Ballard's Best Bitter; Cheriton Pots Ale; Hop Back Summer Lightning; guest beer Ⓗ

Delightful country pub, close to the church. An oak-panelled bar, wood floor, beams and homely soft furnishings around a log fire provide total relaxation. Note the private collection of intriguing ornaments and furniture. Reservations are recommended for the excellent restaurant (closed Sun eve); bar food is available 12–2. The patio is very popular in summer. The beer range includes seasonal brews; the cider varies.
🏚Q✿◖◗P

TURNERS HILL

Red Lion ✓
Red Lion Lane, RH10 4NU
✪ 11-3, 5.30-11; 12-10.30 Sun
☎ (01342) 715416
Harveys XX Mild, BB, seasonal beers Ⓗ

Excellent, traditional village pub with an upstairs restaurant (also available for functions). The Sunday lunch roast is highly recommended; evening meals are served Friday and Saturday evenings. This Harveys house is popular and always welcoming. Pub games include marbles. Metro bus Nos. 82, 84 and 85 will take you there from Crawley or East Grinstead.
🏚Q✿◖◗♣P

WARNHAM

Sussex Oak ✪
Church Street, RH12 3QW
✪ 11-11; 12-10.30 Sun
☎ (01403) 265028
Adnams Bitter; Fuller's London Pride; Taylor Landlord; Young's Bitter; guest beer Ⓗ
Spacious village pub dating from the 16th century. The attractive beamed interior includes an inglenook which is appreciated on winter days. For summer outdoor drinking there is a large garden. Diners enjoy the good quality meals in the no-smoking restaurant area (evening meals Tue–Sat). The pub still has a strong community feel and many local charities are supported. The best bet for a good pint in the area, and bar billiards can be played, too. ﹏Q✿✪◗&♣P

WESTBOURNE

Cricketers Inn
Commonside, PO10 8TA OS757083
✪ 12-3, 5-11; 12-11 Fri & Sat; 12-10.30 Sun
☎ (01243) 372647
Ballard's Best Bitter; Hop Back Summer Lightning; Ringwood Fortyniner; guest beer Ⓗ
This 300-year-old pub stands on the northern outskirts of the village. The spacious L-shaped, wood-panelled pub is popular with locals. It hosts a weekly quiz (Thu) and occasional live music. A new kitchen will open before going to press, so food will be available, but phone first. The guest beers usually come from small independent brewers in Sussex and Hampshire. ﹏✿◗♣P

WEST CHILTINGTON

Five Bells
Smock Alley, RH20 2QX (signed on Storrington-West Chiltington road)
✪ 12-3, 6-11; 12-4.30, 7-10.30 Sun
☎ (01798) 812143
Badger K&B Sussex; guest beers Ⓗ
The genial landlord of this regular Guide entry offers an ever-changing range of ales (always including a mild) as well as Biddenden cider served straight from the barrel. The pleasant open-plan bar is supplemented by a conservatory restaurant overlooking a peaceful garden (no food Sun or Mon eves). Recent sympathetic structural alterations have now made it possible to offer accommodation to those travellers unable to tear themselves away from this delightful rural gem. ﹏Q✿🛏◗♣♣P

WHITEMANS GREEN

Ship Inn
RH17 5BY (N of Cuckfield on B2115/B2114 jct)
✪ 12-2.30, 5.30-11; 12-11 Sat; 12-3, 7-10.30 Sun
☎ (01444) 413219
Fuller's London Pride; Harveys BB; guest beers Ⓖ
Located on a bend next to a petrol station, this village local serves real ales by gravity from the barrel. Good food is available at lunchtime and evening, with a no-smoking area for diners. The bar area is large, but cosy, with an open fire for cold weather. Books and newspapers are available to read on the comfy sofas. There is a games room, with a pool table. ﹏Q✿🛏◗▲♣P

WORTHING

Castle Tavern
1 Newland Road, BN11 1JX
(400 yds from station)
✪ 11-2.30, 5-11; 11-11 Fri & Sat; 12-10.30 Sun
☎ (01903) 601000
Greene King Abbot; Harveys BB; Shepherd Neame Spitfire; guest beers Ⓗ
Friendly little pub, long ago knocked into one U-shaped bar, with views from the front bay windows over a busy roundabout. Note the unusual cast iron tractor seat bar stools and the decorative collection of musical instruments and brewery bric-à-brac. Monday folk nights create a great atmosphere, and other live music is staged on Wednesday and Saturday. An annual April beer festival is very popular. Evening meals are available Friday and Saturday; limited parking. ✿◗≠(Central)♣P

Selden Arms ✪
41 Lyndhurst Road, BN11 2DB (near hospital)
✪ 11 (12 Sat)-11; 12-10.30 Sun
Harveys BB; Ringwood Fortyniner; guest beers Ⓗ
Small, friendly local, formerly a Whitbread house sold into the free trade, acquired in 1998 by the present licensees who transformed it into local CAMRA Pub of the Year 2000 and 2002. An ale lover's paradise with six handpumps, four constantly-changing guest ales from independent breweries include a dark beer; it also stocks bottled Belgian beers. The menu changes often, providing liberal portions at very reasonable prices; an evening meal is available on Friday. ﹏Q◗≠(Central)♣🍴

Swan
79 High Street, BN11 1DN (opp. Safeway)
✪ 11-2.30, 6 (5.30 Fri)-11; 11-11 Sat; 12-10.30 Sun
☎ (01903) 232923
Greene King Abbot; Harveys BB; Shepherd Neame Spitfire; guest beer Ⓗ
Comfortable old pub with log fires; note the two attractive Kemptown Brewery windows in the back bar and the plethora of brass articles (227 at the last count). Bar billiards is played in the main bar area, where dogs are allowed at quiet times. It hosts a quiz night (Wed) and weekly food themed evenings; folk sessions are held monthly and discos at the weekend. Guest beers are from Punch Taverns Finest Cask range. ﹏✿◗≠♣

YAPTON

Maypole Inn
Maypole Lane, BN18 0DP
(off B2132, ½ mile N of village) OS978041
✪ 11.30-3, 6-11; 11-11 Fri & Sat; 12-10.30 Sun
☎ (01243) 551417
Ringwood Best Bitter; guest beers Ⓗ
Small, flint-built pub, tucked down a lane away from the village centre. The lane was cut off by the railway in 1846 and the Maypole has enjoyed its quiet isolation ever since. The cosy lounge boasts an imposing log fire. An imposing row of seven handpumps dispenses a range of beers from local and West Country independents, including a mild. The large public bar has darts and pool, and a skittle alley is available (book). ﹏Q✿◗🍺♣P

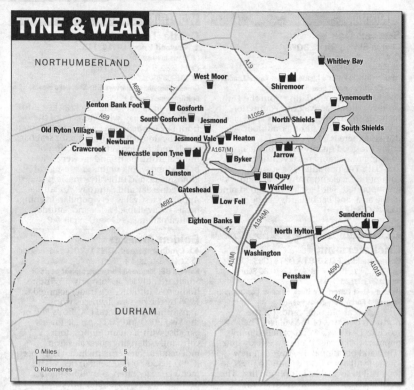

TYNE & WEAR

NORTHUMBERLAND

Whitley Bay

West Moor

Shiremoor

Tynemouth

Kenton Bank Foot

Gosforth

South Gosforth

Jesmond

North Shields

South Shields

Old Ryton Village

Newburn

Jesmond Vale

Heaton

Crawcrook

Newcastle upon Tyne

Byker

Jarrow

Dunston

Bill Quay

Wardley

Gateshead

Low Fell

Eighton Banks

Sunderland

North Hylton

Washington

Penshaw

DURHAM

0 Miles 5
0 Kilometres 8

BILL QUAY

Albion

Reay Street, NE10 0TY (foot of hill on river bank)
⏱ 4 (12 Sat)-11; 12-10.30 Sun
☎ (0191) 469 2418
Jarrow Bitter, Joblings Swinging Gibbet, Old Cornelius; guest beers ⓗ

Overlooking a wide bend in the river, this square-shaped, comfortable lounge bar benefits from excellent views across heavily industrialised Tyneside. Its committed owners run the Jarrow Brewery and support real ales produced by micro-breweries in the north-east. Unusually for the area they also sell a real cider (Westons Old Rosie). Regular quiz nights and live music sessions are added attractions, while the conservatory houses a pool table.
🏚 ❍ (Pelaw) ♣ P

BYKER

Cumberland Arms

Byker Buildings, NE6 1LD
(below E end of Byker Bridge)
⏱ 5 (4.30 Fri)-11; 6-10.30 Sun
☎ (0191) 265 6151
Beer range varies ⓗ/ⓖ

Standing alone, looking down the Lower Ouseburn Valley, this was once one of the very few outlets for real ale in Newcastle. It is now returning to past glories under the careful control of a new owner. The pub hosts a number of traditional activities including Northumbrian music, rapper dancing and poetry readings. The beers are generally local and the drinker can choose to have them served by handpump or

gravity. The pub has bare boards, but a warm welcome.
🏚Q❀⌂❍P

Free Trade

St Lawrence Road, NE6 1AP
⏱ 11-11; 12-10.30 Sun
☎ (0191) 265 5764
Hadrian & Border Gladiator; Mordue Workie Ticket; guest beers ⓗ

This traditional pub looks upstream to the Newcastle bridges and skyline. There can be few better ways of spending an evening than drinking beer and watching the dramatic sunsets over the city from within this fine, deliberately basic, pub. The high standard of graffiti in the gents is often remarked upon. The free juke box is crammed with golden classics from the '50s to the '90s and there's a free quiz on Wednesday evening. 🏚❀

Tyne

1 Maling Street, NE6 1LP
⏱ 12-11; 12-10.30 Sun
☎ (0191) 265 2550 website: www.thetyne.com
Black Sheep Best Bitter; Durham Magus, seasonal beers; Mordue Five Bridge Bitter, Workie Ticket, seasonal beers ⓗ

This fine, comfortable, single-roomed pub sits almost underneath Glasshouse Bridge, which gives a clue to one of the traditional local industries now swept away. The bridge provides an unusual beer garden under one of its arches, while more conventional outdoor seating is available alongside the Ouseburn as it joins the River Tyne. There are frequent live music sessions, with Sunday lunchtime generally offering more gentle and mellow tunes. At other times customers can make use of an interesting, free juke box. ✿

CRAWCROOK

Rising Sun
Bank Top, NE40 4EE
(½ mile S of main crossroads)
❋ 12-11; 12-10.30 Sun
☎ (0191) 413 3316
Boddingtons Bitter; Castle Eden Ale; Mordue Workie Ticket; guest beers Ⓗ

Well situated on most of the Tyne Valley routes between Blaydon and Hexham, this lively, thriving local offers something for everyone. The spacious interior affords numerous different drinking areas and a balance between good value meals and a haven for the discerning drinker. There are always two guest ales on tap, often from local micros. ✿◖▶P

EIGHTON BANKS

Lambton Arms ✓
Rockcliffe Way, NE9 7XR
❋ 11-11; 12-10.30 Sun
☎ (0191) 487 8137
Flowers Original; Greene King Abbot, Old Speckled Hen; Taylor Landlord Ⓗ

A good range of quality real ales is served here in pleasant surroundings. Food is available every day from noon until 9.15pm. There is a warm atmosphere and children are welcome, except in the area near the bar. The pub overlooks the Team Valley and the surrounding countryside; admire the views from the benches outside the pub. ✿◖▶P⊁

GATESHEAD

Borough Arms
80-82 Bensham Road, NE8 1PS
(250 yds from metro station via subway)
❋ 12-3, 6-11; 11-11 Fri & Sat; 12-10.30 Sun
☎ (0191) 478 1323
Draught Bass; Black Sheep Best Bitter; Wells Bombardier; guest beers Ⓗ

One-roomed local in a residential area, close to the bus and metro interchange. It offers the only real ale in the district (including the town centre). The pub is lively, with hands-on management, but without juke box or pool table. Note the pub's sign; it depicts Gateshead borough's former coat of arms which shows the origin of the town's name – a goat's head. Handy for Windmill Hills Park, it stands on the area's historic trail. It hosts a weekly pop quiz and live music. Children are not welcome. ♨✿⊖♣P

GOSFORTH

County
70 High Street, NE3 1HB
❋ 12 (11 Fri & Sat)-11; 12-10.30 Sun
☎ (0191) 285 6919
Courage Directors; Greene King Old Speckled Hen; Marston's Pedigree; Theakston Best Bitter; Wells Bombardier; guest beers Ⓗ

Unspoilt and impressive ale house at the southern end of Gosforth's High Street. The Victorian building is listed and retains many original features. Part of the T&J

Bernard chain, the imposing L-shaped bar offers six regular beers and two ever-changing guests. A mixed clientele means it can get very busy at weekends, but a small, quiet, back room offers some respite. This room is also available for hire. Read about the pub's history on the plaques outside. Meals are served 12–9 (5 Fri and Sat, no food Sun). ♨Q◖▶⊖(Regent Centre) P

Gosforth Hotel
Salters Road, NE3 1HQ
❋ 12-11; 12-10.30 Sun
☎ (0191) 285 6617
Draught Bass; Black Sheep Best Bitter; Taylor Landlord; Tetley Bitter; Wells Bombardier; guest beers Ⓗ

Popular local at the northern end of the High Street at a busy road junction. Although no longer offering accommodation, the pub has been recently refurbished to give it a more café-bar feel which attracts a wide clientele, from students to office workers at the nearby business park. A separate quiet bar at the back is open evenings only, occasionally offering exclusive guest beers not available in the main bar. Meals are served weekdays. Q◖⊖(Regent Centre)

HEATON

Chillingham
Chillingham Road, NE6 5XN
❋ 11-11; 12-10.30 Sun
☎ (0191) 265 5915
Black Sheep Best Bitter; Mordue Workie Ticket; Theakston Best Bitter; guest beers Ⓗ

Two-roomed, roadside pub with separate entrances leading to two different drinking areas. The bar has a pool table, quiz machine and large TV; it can get quite noisy in the evening. The lounge is open plan, with a small snug to the left of the entrance. It boasts an impressive fireplace which unfortunately is not used. Note the small wooden casks on the back bar fitting. Wednesday is quiz night. Evening meals are served Monday–Thursday, 5.30–8.30. ◖▶⊖(Chillingham Rd)

JARROW

Ben Lomond ✓
Grange Road West, NE32 3JY
❋ 10-11; 12-10.30 Sun
☎ (0191) 483 3839
Courage Directors; Shepherd Neame Spitfire; Theakston Best Bitter; Wadworth 6X; guest beers Ⓗ

Spacious, two-storey Wetherspoon's pub near the Viking shopping centre. The ground-floor bar is a large room with a no-smoking area. The walls are decorated with scenes from old Jarrow. There is additional seating on the first floor. In common with all Wetherspoon's pubs, it offers good value ales and food. Q◖▶&⊖⊁

INDEPENDENT BREWERIES

Big Lamp Newburn
Darwin Sunderland
Federation Dunston
Hadrian & Border Newcastle upon Tyne
Jarrow Jarrow
Mordue Shiremoor

Robin Hood
Primrose Hill, NE32 5UB (off A194)
✪ 12-11; 12-10.30 Sun
☎ (0191) 428 5454
Jarrow Bitter, Joblings Swinging Gibbet, Riley's Army, Old Cornelius; guest beers ⒣
This well refurbished pub is home to the Jarrow Brewing Company. The brewery is located at the rear of the pub through impressive doors. The pub has a bar, brewery bar, lounge and a recommended conservatory restaurant (no food Sun eve or Mon). The outdoor drinking area is on the banks of the River Don. It stages live acoustic music (Sun) and a monthly jazz night; Wednesday is quiz night. Three guest beers and Westons Old Rosie cider supplement the brewery's beers.
✤⊕◗ ⊖ (Fellgate) ⬤P

JESMOND

Punch Bowl
125 Jesmond Road, NE2 1JY
✪ 11-11; 12-10.30 Sun
☎ (0191) 281 2552
Courage Directors; Marston's Pedigree; Theakstons Cool Cask, XB ⒣
A pub for around 130 years, it offers modern features such as TV and juke box but at the same time maintains the tradition of a separate bar along with a comfortable lounge. No main meals are served, but toasties and pizzas are available any time. A popular quiz takes place every Monday. ⊟⊖P

JESMOND VALE

Blue Bell
Spring Bank Road, NE2 1PH
(lower side of Heaton Park, off Goldspink Lane)
✪ 12-11; 12-10.30 Sun
☎ (0191) 232 1774
website: www.bongosbluebell.co.uk
Beer range varies ⒣
The Blue Bell is a small and friendly S&N pub on the border between Sandyford and Heaton. It has just one handpump, often serving a beer from the local Mordue Brewery. The pub is split into a lounge and a bar – the latter is frequently used as a venue for live music. Children are welcome until 7pm, dogs welcome anytime! The pub's website lists upcoming events.
✤⊟P

KENTON BANK FOOT

Twin Farms
22 Main Road, NE13 8AB
✪ 11-11; 12-10.30 Sun
☎ (0191) 286 1263
Mordue Workie Ticket; Taylor Landlord; guest beers ⒣
Newly built on the site of an old farm in a traditional style, the pub has a spacious open-plan room with an additional area on the left-hand side. The use of alcoves creates a feeling of several small rooms. Two real fireplaces at either end, plus a huge kitchen range add character. There are several no-smoking areas and the whole place is air-conditioned. The guest beers change weekly and food is available all day. Occasional beer festivals are held.
♨Q✤◗⬤ ⊖ (Bank Foot) P⅊

LOW FELL

Aletaster
706 Durham Road, NE9 6JA
(Chowdene Bank jct)
✪ 12 (11 Sat)-11; 12-10.30 Sun
☎ (0191) 487 0770
Black Sheep Best Bitter; Everards Tiger; Jennings Cumberland Ale; Marston's Pedigree; Taylor Landlord; guest beers ⒣
This former coaching inn is a local newspaper award-winner. Designed in ale house style, bare boards and nicotine-coloured walls in the bar contrast well with a cosy, carpeted, quieter snug. Justifiably proud of its range and quality of real ales, 11 handpulls offer four guest beers, plus a real cider – a local rarity. It boasts some attractive leaded glass and the pub's allegiance to Newcastle United is tastefully displayed. A quiz is held weekly, plus occasional live music and beer festivals.
✤⊟♣⬤P

NEWBURN

Keelman
Grange Road, NE15 8NL
✪ 12-11; 12-10.30 Sun
☎ (0191) 267 0772 website: www.biglampbrewery.com
Big Lamp Bitter, Summerhill Stout, Prince Bishop Ale, Premium, seasonal beers ⒣
A converted Grade II listed building now houses the Keelman and Big Lamp Brewery. The pub is the brewery tap offering the full range of Big Lamp beers. Since its careful restoration in 1997 it has built up a strong following for the beers. Reasonably-priced food is always available and a dining area is set aside from the drinking area. The Keelman's Lodge offers quality accommodation so guests may sleep, eat and drink in very pleasant surroundings. The keelmen, who carried coal on the River Tyne, are commemorated in old photographs. ✤⊯◗&P

NEWCASTLE UPON TYNE

Bodega
125 Westgate Road, NE1 4AG
✪ 11-11; 12-10.30 Sun
☎ (0191) 221 1552
Big Lamp Prince Bishop Ale; Durham Magus; Mordue Workie Ticket; guest beers ⒣
The highlight of every visit to this pub, apart from the good beer selection, is a study of the two original glass ceiling domes. The pub is popular with both football fans and music fans as it stands next to the Tyne Theatre and Opera House. All customers mix together, giving an excellent atmosphere. The single bar room offers various standing and seating spots, including snug cubicles. The house beer (Number 9) is brewed by the local Mordue Brewery and reflects the footballing interests, being the shirt number worn by generations of famous centre forwards for the Magpies. No food Sunday. ◗⇌ (Central)⊖

Bridge Hotel
Castle Square, NE1 1RQ
✪ 11.30-11; 12-10.30 Sun
☎ (0191) 232 6400
Black Sheep Best Bitter; Caledonian Deuchars IPA; Mordue Workie Ticket; guest beers ⒣

Standing next to the high level bridge, the pub has a single, spacious public bar divided into a number of seating and standing areas. Prints of old Newcastle and railway memorabilia adorn the walls. The upstairs function room hosts what is reputed to be one of the oldest folk clubs in the country. The patio garden at the side of the high level bridge overlooks the Tyne.
❀◑≉ (Central) ⊖

Crown Posada ☆
33 The Side, NE1 3JE
🕑 11 (12 Sat)-11; 7-10.30 (closed lunch) Sun
☎ (0191) 232 1269
Draught Bass; Jennings Bitter; guest beers 🅷
Tiny but always welcoming, this pub is architecturally possibly the finest in Newcastle. Beautiful stained glass windows, unusual ceilings and wood-clad walls all add to its appeal. Long and narrow (known locally as the Coffin), it has comfortable seating at one end and a tiny snug at the other. It can get busy as it is now on the circuit following the regeneration of the quayside. However, if you are visiting Newcastle and only have time to visit one pub, make it this one.
Q≉ (Central) ⊖ (Monument)

Hotspur
103 Percy Street, NE1 7RY
🕑 11-11; 12-10.30 Sun
☎ (0191) 232 4352
Courage Directors; McEwan 80/-; Theakston Old Peculier; guest beers 🅷
This popular, single-roomed, city-centre pub is run by a manager who endeavours to keep four guest beers available at all times, alongside his regular products. It draws an interesting mixture of visitors due to its position near the heart of the city's major shopping area, a hospital and university and a bus station which serves eastern Northumberland. The large front windows make the place feel light and open, and allow the drinker to watch for the bus. The pub can be very busy on match days or if Newcastle United are on TV.
❀◑ ⊖ (Haymarket)

New Bridge
2 Argyle Street, NE1 6PE
🕑 11-11; 12-10.30 Sun
☎ (0191) 232 1020
Beer range varies 🅷
The single room is split by partitions featuring photographs of the building of the Tyne Bridge and some old mirrors. The Millennium Bridge can be seen from the side door. The customers consist of regulars, students and people visiting the multi-screen cinema opposite. The changing guests are mainly from local micro-breweries. Food is served at lunchtime – Sunday lunches are popular. Wednesday is quiz night. ◑ (Manors)

Newcastle Arms
57 St Andrews Street, NE1 5SE
🕑 11-11; 12-10.30 Sun
☎ (0191) 221 2519
Black Sheep Best Bitter; Fuller's London Pride; guest beers 🅷
Near St James' Park football ground, this one-roomed pub can get very busy on match days. There is a seating area but also some tables for standing drinkers and stools in the bay window. Food is available at lunchtime (Mon–Sat). Pictures of old Newcastle adorn the walls of this friendly pub which has a large-screen TV for sporting events. ◑⊖ (St James)

Shipwright's Hotel
Ferryboat Lane, SR5 3HW
(off A1231, ½ mile from A19)
🕑 11-4, 7-11.30; 12-3, 7-10.30 Sun
☎ (0191) 549 5139
Brains SA; Greene King Abbot; Jennings Cumberland Ale; Marston's Pedigree 🅷
Situated on the banks of the River Wear, close to the A19 at Hylton Bridge, this 350-year-old former ship chandler's and post office is celebrating 25 consecutive years in this Guide. It has a small bar/lounge area with two adjacent rooms replete with beams and brasses. Its popular food menu includes unusual dishes, such as kangaroo and crocodile. ⊯◑P

Three Horseshoes
Washington Road, SR5 3HZ
(opp. Nissan factory entrance)
🕑 11-11; 12-10.30 Sun
Caledonian Deuchars IPA; Camerons Strongarm; Greene King Ruddles Best, Old Speckled Hen 🅷
Spacious former Vaux pub adjacent to the North-East Aircraft Museum and the Nissan car factory, comprising a bar and lounge. The large lounge is popular with families enjoying meals; the long, narrow bar has a games area at one end. An outside drinking area stands across from the car park. Tuesday is quiz night; no evening meals are served on Sunday. Q❀⊯◑ ⊟P

Magnesia Bank
Camden Street, NE30 1NH
🕑 11-11 (midnight Fri & Sat); 12-10.30 Sun
☎ (0191) 257 4831 website: www.magnesiabank.co.uk
Black Sheep Best Bitter; Durham Magus; Jarrow Bitter; Mordue Workie Ticket; guest beers 🅷
Excellent, town-centre pub, a past winner of local CAMRA's Pub of the Year, it has also received awards for its food, music and beer. Comedy nights are held fortnightly; new country music is performed on the first Wednesday of each month and themed international food nights on the second Tuesday. A no-smoking restaurant has been added and is proving popular.
⊯◑ ⊖

Porthole
11 New Quay, NE29 6LQ
🕑 11-11; 12-10.30 Sun
☎ (0191) 257 6645
Courage Directors; Durham Magus; guest beers 🅷
Dating from 1834 and rebuilt around 1900, the Porthole is close to North Shields ferry landing. The two bar areas are separated by the nautically-themed food serving area. The management is keen to encourage real ale drinkers, hence two regular real ales and a guest are usually available. A lunchtime jazz club is held on Wednesday and entertainment on Sunday and Friday; Monday is quiz night.
◑⊖P

Prince of Wales
2 Liddell Street, NE30 1HE
(follow signs for Fish Quay)
✪ 12-3 (not Tue), 7-11; 12-11 Fri & Sat; 12-10.30 Sun
☎ (0191) 296 2816
Samuel Smith OBB Ⓗ

This pub was first recorded in 1627, but the current building dates from 1927 and is faced with green glazed brick. The premises were empty for some years before being restored by Sam Smith's in a traditional style, featuring French embossed windows. The bar and pool room are served from the central bar, the sitting room from the hatch in the corridor. Pool, darts and dominoes are played. Situated on the fish quay, crab sandwiches are a speciality. ▲Q ⬓ ◖Ⓔ ♣ ♠

Tap & Spile ⊘
184 Tynemouth Road, NE30 1EG
✪ 12-11; 12-10.30 Sun
☎ (0191) 257 2523
Caledonian Deuchars IPA; Everards Tiger; Greene King Ruddles County; guest beers Ⓗ

A Tap & Spile true to the tradition, where the landlord makes the most of his Pubco beer list to offer as interesting and varied a selection as possible. This is enhanced by regular themed beer festivals. Live music is staged in the small public bar. There is a designated no-smoking area in the larger lounge. The landlord is a big speedway fan, hence the regular meetings involving the Newcastle Diamonds (both team and supporters) and the models on display. This local CAMRA Pub of the Year 2003, stocks Westons Old Rosie cider. ◖Ⓔ⊖♣ ♠P⅓

Old Cross
NE40 3QP (from B6317 follow signs for village)
✪ 11 (4 winter)-11; 12-11 Sat; 12-10.30 Sun
☎ (0191) 413 4689
John Smith's Magnet; Wells Bombardier; guest beers Ⓗ

Originally a coaching house serving the Gateshead–Hexham route, the present building dates from 1909 and is situated close to the village cross, hence the name. It has a large one-roomed bar with a raised area to the rear; doors open on to a patio area. The clientele is mainly local and very friendly. The upper floor houses an authentic Italian restaurant serving excellent food, with interesting decor and unusual furnishings. Evening meals are served at weekends. ❀◖◗

Grey Horse
Old Penshaw, DH4 7ER
✪ 12 (4 Mon)-11; 12-10.30 Sun
☎ (0191) 512 6080
Black Sheep Best Bitter; Tetley Bitter; Wells Bombardier Ⓗ

This village local lies near Herrington Country Park and the folly, Penshaw Monument. The pub has recently been refurbished and is now open plan, with an area set aside for diners. A pool table occupies the other end of the bar. The number of regular real ales on offer has been increased to three. Evening meals are served Tuesday–Friday. ❀◖◗P

Shiremoor Farm
Middle Engine Lane, NE29 8DZ
✪ 11-11; 12-10.30 Sun
☎ (0191) 257 6302 website: www.sjf.co.uk
Mordue Workie Ticket; Taylor Landlord; guest beers Ⓗ

An award-winning conversion of derelict stone farm buildings, this Fitzgerald pub retains many original features, such as the conical raftered 'gin gan' which is now the highly recommended restaurant. No-smoking areas and air-conditioning ensure comfort. Children are welcome in the granary areas. This superb pub is well worth seeking out. Q ⬓ ❀◖◗P⅓

Victory
Killingworth Road, NE3 1SY
✪ 12-11; 12-10.30 Sun
☎ (0191) 285 6617
Courage Directors; Taylor Landlord; Theakston Best Bitter; guest beers Ⓗ

Small, friendly local, set away from the A189 spine road, it opened in the late 19th century to quench the thirst of mine-workers from the local collieries. The pub has survived the downturn of that and other industries but retains its original character with many old photographs and mining memorabilia. Popular with students and locals, the bar is divided into small but cosy drinking areas. Benches outside during summer also attract the crowds. Live music is staged Thursday. Snacks are available. ▲Q⊖

Alum House
Ferry Street, HE33 1JR (by ferry landing)
✪ 11-11; 12-10.30 Sun
☎ (0191) 427 7245
Banks's Bitter; Marston's Pedigree; guest beers Ⓗ

Old-fashioned pub at the heart of the regenerated market docks area, the site was once a chemical factory, hence the name. Reputedly haunted by six ghosts; one, named Giggling Nellie, has often been heard. The regular beers are well supplemented by an ever-changing range of guests. Quizzes are held on Sunday, while Thursday is buskers' night. ⊖⛨

Bamburgh ⊘
175 Bamburgh Avenue, NE34 6SS
(coast road to Marsden)
✪ 11-11; 12-10.30 Sun
☎ (0191) 427 5523
Caledonian Deuchars IPA; Flowers Original; Harviestoun Schiehallion; Orkney Red MacGregor Ⓗ

Affording spectacular views over the coast and the finishing line of the Great North Run, the Bamburgh is popular with visitors during the summer. The spacious open-plan pub, with a split-level seating area, offers good value food. There is a family room, separate from the main bar, and an outside seating area in front of the pub. ⬓ ❀◖◗ ▲P

Beacon
Greens Place, NE33 2AQ (Lawe Rd jct)
✪ 11-11; 12-10.30 Sun
☎ (0191) 456 2876
Adnams Broadside; Marston's Pedigree; guest beer Ⓗ

An open-plan pub on three levels, it boasts spectacular views over the mouth of the Tyne. The decor is on a nautical theme and photographs of old South Shields and paintings of Tyneside by local artists are displayed. There is a TV in the bar, but the volume tends to be low. Good value meals are served. Visitors are made welcome; it is convenient for the nearby Roman fort and museum. ◑ ⊖

Dolly Peel

137 Commercial Road, NE33 1SQ

11-11; 12-10.30 Sun

☎ (0191) 427 1441

Courage Directors; Taylor Landlord; guest beers H

Small, quiet, two-roomed pub close to the banks of the Tyne. There is no music or TV and the pub attracts a mostly mature clientele. Up to three guest beers are available and occasional beer festivals are held. The pub takes its name from an 18th-century fishwife and smuggler.

Q ⊖ (Chichester)

Riverside

3 Mill Dam, NE33 1EQ (near ferry landing)

12-11; 12-3, 7-10.30 Sun

☎ (0191) 455 2328

Black Sheep Best Bitter; Courage Directors; Taylor Landlord; Theakston Cool Cask; guest beers H

Popular pub, just offset from the town centre, it comes to life at the weekend when the older generation make for this real ale haven. It stocks three regular and three guest ales, plus a cider is usually available. A single large room on two levels, it features conservative, but tasteful, decor. Background music allows conversation, but the toilets situated on the first floor restrict wheelchair-users. Tuesday is quiz night.

⊖

Stag's Head

45 Fowler Street, NE33 1NS

11-11; 12-10.30 Sun

☎ (0191) 456 9174

Draught Bass; Stones Bitter; Theakston Cool Cask; Worthington's Bitter H

Dating back to 1897, the Stag's Head claims to be the oldest bar in South Shields still serving real ale. The very busy, small bar (handy for shoppers, the metro and bus station), is decorated with old photos of South Shields. It hosts popular theme nights ('60s, '70s and '80s) during the week. An upstairs room is opened to relieve the crowded bar at weekends.

⊖

Steamboat

51 Mill Dam, NE33 1EQ

(near Customs House Theatre)

12-11; 12-10.30 Sun

☎ (0191) 454 0134

Wells Bombardier; guest beers H

One of the oldest pubs in South Shields, it stands on Mill Dam near the River Tyne. Full of maritime memorabilia, including steering wheels, ships' lamps and flags, it also displays many local photographs of times gone by. The bar can get busy at weekends, but there is a quieter lounge area for those who prefer a more sedate atmosphere. The pub offers a range of guest ales.

⊖

Waterfront

9 Mill Dam, NE33 1AZ

11-11 (midnight Fri & Sat); 12-10.30 Sun

☎ (0191) 455 7658

Bateman XXXB; Courage Directors; Fuller's London Pride; Mordue Workie Ticket; Wells Bombardier H

One of three pubs on Mill Dam selling real ale, it was called the Railway until refurbishment. The large ground-floor room is served by a central bar with a games area at the back. There is a function room/restaurant on the first floor. It is handy for the Customs House Theatre. ◑ ⊖

Wouldhave ✓

16 Mile End Road, NE33 1TA

10-11; 12-10.30 Sun

☎ (0191) 427 6014

Courage Directors; Shepherd Neame Spitfire; guest beers H

Convenient for the town centre, in typical Wetherspoon's style, the pub comprises one large room with a slightly raised area. The beers include two regular and four guest ales and all are priced in line with Wetherspoon's policy. Although there is no TV or music, conversation can be difficult when the pub is busy, particularly at weekends. A reasonable food menu represents value for money. Q ◑ ⊖

SUNDERLAND

Fitzgerald's

10-12 Green Terrace, SR1 3PZ

11-11; 12-10.30 Sun

☎ (0191) 567 0852

Beer range varies H

The local CAMRA Pub of the Year for 2002 is a real ale oasis in an area teeming with café-bars. The large main bar features much brass and stained glass, while the smaller chart room bears a maritime theme and a large TV for live football. The pub offers 10 cask beers, and is a keen supporter of local micro-breweries; a beer from Darwin is always available. Tuesday is quiz night in the chart room. ⇌ ⊖ (Park Lane/University)

Harbour View

Benedict Road, Roker, SR6 0NL

11-11; 12-10.30 Sun

☎ (0191) 567 1402

Beer range varies H

Single-roomed lounge bar with a raised bare-boarded seating area and a carpeted bar/lounge area. Its brick walls are broken up with pictures and pub mirrors. Wood-panelled ceilings, from which three TVs are suspended, complete the decor. It serves four constantly-changing beers, often from local breweries. Popular with all age groups, it can get busy at weekends.

⊖ (Stadium of Light)

Ivy House

Worcester Terrace, SR2 7AW (off Stockton Rd)

11-11; 12-10.30 Sun

☎ (0191) 567 3399

Beer range varies H

Single-roomed pub with a long central bar, situated near Park Lane interchange. Popular with students as it is close to the university, it also attracts a wide range of other customers. Several TV screens throughout the bar feature sports; on home match days the pub is very busy. A quiz is held on Wednesday evening and on Thursday there is live music featuring a number of bands. Up to six beers are on tap, with Caledonian beers regularly available. Weekday lunches are served.

🏚◐≢⊖ (Park Lane/University)

King's Arms
Beach Street, SR4 6BU (behind B&Q)
🕓 4.30 (12 Sat)-11; 12-10.30 Sun
☎ (0191) 567 9804
Taylor Landlord; guest beers Ⓗ
Traditional, single-roomed pub situated away from the main road but well worth finding. A framed account of the pub's history is displayed on a wall by one of two open fires. Live music is performed at weekends. The management provides a shuttle bus between the King's Arms, Ropery and Saltgrass at weekends. Local micro-breweries are well represented among the guest ales.
🏚❀⊖ (University/Millfield)

New Derby ◉
Roker Baths Road, SR6 9TA
🕓 11-11; 12-10.30 Sun
☎ (0191) 548 6263
Draught Bass; guest beers Ⓗ
Large, open-plan local, next to Roker Park. The rear of the pub houses a games area, which, along with various raised seating areas, is served from a single bar. Four handpumps offer a range of real ales, mostly from independent brewers. There is some form of entertainment most evenings, with a quiz on Tuesday. Although Roker Park football ground has gone, the pub remains a popular pre-match venue.
◐⊖ (Stadium of Light) ♣

Ropery
Webster's Bank, Deptford, SR4 6BU
🕓 12-3, 5-11 (midnight Fri & Sat); 12-10.30 Sun
☎ (0191) 514 7171
Beer range varies Ⓗ
Multi-roomed pub in a converted 18th-century ropeworks on the banks of the River Wear; it lies in the shadow of the Queen Alexandra Bridge. There are two bars, a function room and a restaurant. Live music is staged at weekends and occasionally midweek. Three cask ales are available. A free minibus links the pub with the Saltgrass and King's Arms on Friday and Saturday.
❀◐⊖ (Pallion) ♣P

Saltgrass
36 Ayres Quay, Deptford, SR4 6BY
🕓 11-2.30, 4.30-11; 11-11 Fri & Sat; 12-10.30 Sun
☎ (0191) 565 7229
Draught Bass; Jennings Cumberland Ale; Marston's Pedigree; guest beers Ⓗ
Nestled at the foot of a steep hill, next to the old shipyards, the pub consists of a small public bar, decorated in a nautical style, complete with a real fire, and a lounge area. Interesting artefacts scattered around include a collection of pewter mugs hanging from the bar ceiling. A quiz is held on Tuesday evening and a free mini bus runs to the Ropery and King's Arms at weekends.
🏚◐⊞⊖ (University/Millfield)

TYNEMOUTH

Tynemouth Lodge Hotel
Tynemouth Road, NE30 4AA
🕓 11-11; 12-10.30 Sun
☎ (0191) 257 7565
Draught Bass; Belhaven 80/-; Caledonian Deuchars IPA; guest beer Ⓗ
This attractive, tiled free house was built in 1799 and has been in this Guide consecutively from 1984 to the current edition following its purchase by its CAMRA member owner. This comfortable, single-room lounge bar is noted in the area for featuring Scottish real ales and reputedly selling the highest volumes of Draught Bass on Tyneside. It stands next to Northumberland Park and is handy for the Coast-to-Coast cycle route.
🏚Q❀⊖P

WARDLEY

Green
White Mare Pool, NE10 8YB (at A184/B1288 jct)
🕓 11.30-11; 12-10.30 Sun
☎ (0191) 495 0171
Courage Directors; Fuller's London Pride; Taylor Landlord; guest beers Ⓗ
Commanding a position near a major road/motorway intersection means that this large pub is popular with drivers. Part of the real ale-oriented Sir John Fitzgerald pub company, it offers an upmarket, comfortable public bar (open evenings) with a large-screen TV, separate restaurant and glass-walled lounge. Inspired by the design of golfer Gary Player's South African home, appropriately it stands next to a golf course. Weekly general knowledge and sports quizzes are held, plus occasional beer festivals. A cash machine is a useful addition. ❀◐⊞♿P

WASHINGTON

Steps
47-49a Spout Lane, The Village, NE38 7HP
🕓 11-11; 12-10.30 Sun
☎ (0191) 416 7396
Beer range varies Ⓗ
Part of the Sir John Fitzgerald chain, this small lounge bar stands near Washington Old Hall and is the only pub in the village centre selling real ale. There is a large TV in the main bar, while the smaller room is decorated with scenes from Old Washington. The three real ales frequently come from local micro-breweries; one beer is sold at a special price on Tuesday. ◐

WEST MOOR

George Stephenson ◉
Great Lime Road, NE12 0NJ
🕓 12-11; 12-10.30 Sun
☎ (0191) 268 0173
McEwan 80/-; John Smith's Magnet; guest beers Ⓗ
Much altered over its 100 years, the pub has recently been extended, retaining two separate areas which, when required, can become a single room by opening the dividing doors. A well-established music venue, it hosts live bands on Wednesday, Thursday and Saturday, a Monday quiz and other events. The frequently-changing guest beers often feature smaller breweries,

including those in the local area. A repeat winner of North Tyneside in Bloom for outstanding external displays, the patio borders the main rail line. ❀P⏚

WHITLEY BAY

Briar Dene
71 The Links, NE26 1UE
⊘ 11-11 (public bar may close afternoons); 12-10.30 Sun
☎ (0191) 252 0926
Beer range varies Ⓗ
This former toll house enjoys a well-earned reputation for good quality beer and food. The manager hosts a continuous beer festival with seven handpumps dispensing constantly-changing beers from all over the country, many not normally available in the area. The well-lit lounge has coloured leaded glass above the bar and overlooks the links, St Mary's lighthouse and the sea. An indoor children's play area leads off this large lounge. The smaller rear bar features TV, pool and darts. ⏚❀◑⚲♿ᚹ♣P⋌

Fat Ox
278 Whitley Road, NE26 2TG
⊘ 12 (11 Sat)-11; 12-10.30 Sun

☎ (0191) 251 3852 website: www.fatox.20m.com
Caledonian Deuchars IPA; John Smith's Bitter; guest beers Ⓗ
A warm welcome awaits in this lively, large traditional one-roomed pub. Situated on a corner site, the pub offers various areas for enjoying a pint in relaxing surroundings. Live music is staged on Friday and Saturday, plus a quiz on Tuesday. Curry nights are a regular feature. Pool is played here and the guest ales change frequently; Westons Old Rosie cider is also stocked. ⊖♣♠

Rockcliffe Arms
Algernon Place, NE26 2DT
⊘ 11-11; 12-10.30 Sun
☎ (0191) 253 1299
Beer range varies Ⓗ
Compact, Sir John Fitzgerald's one-roomed community pub, it offers old-style drinking in pleasant surroundings. Enter by the snug or the lounge doors, attractively decorated with stained glass. The single bar is partitioned to serve two distinct drinking areas. Regular darts and dominoes nights are held and also a quiz night. ❀⊖♠

Warwickshire Beer

At Ilmington four kinds were brewed: Black Strap, Ruffle-me-Cap, Fine and Clear, and Table Beer. At Alderminster Mrs Keyte made Double Ale, Single Ale, Very Good, Twine in the Belly, Twice as Many, Tip Tap, Wuss than That, and Pin. She gave a labourer some Tip Tap to drink and asked him why he laughed afterwards: 'Oi was wondering as 'ow you could brew two worse nor that.' Bad beer was said to be 'sour as varges' (crab apples), and there was a children's beer called Tilly Willy.

At Pillerton a quarter of malt brewed 100 gallons, 20 each of Strong ale, Table beer, Tit-me-Tat and Worse than That. Brewing was done mainly in March, with the last barley of one harvest, and October, with the first of the next. After brewing, a household would invite the neighbours who would come in with crusts of bread to dip in the new beer. This was called 'taking the shot'. Till recent times Lord Willoughby de Broke preserved the old custom of keeping a large leathern jack filled twice a day with his October brew. It stood on the sideboard and callers could help themselves. Winter favourites were mulled ale, cider, or elder wine. These were spiced and heated in a cone-shaped muller or hooter, as it was called in Stratford. Each beverage was drunk in the proper vessel beer, in a pewter tankard; stout, in a china mug; and cider, in a horn cup.

Roy Palmer, *The Folklore of Warwickshire*, 1976

WARWICKSHIRE

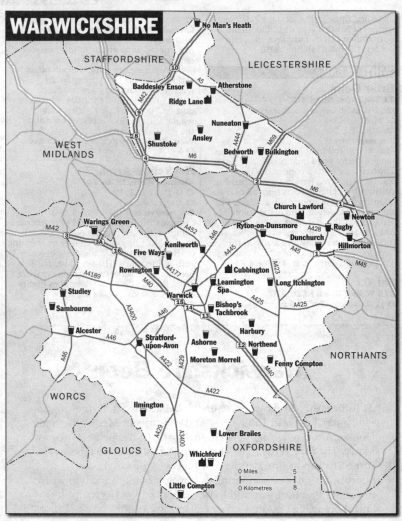

ALCESTER

Holly Bush
Henley Street, B49 5QX (behind church)
🕐 11-11; 12-10.30 Sun
☎ (01789) 762482
Banks's Bitter; Black Sheep Best Bitter; Cannon Royall Fruiterer's Mild; Uley Bitter; guest beers Ⓗ
This former hotel is hidden behind the church and town hall in this delightful market town. It boasts five separate rooms (one no-smoking) as well as a function room and walled garden with a barbecue. Oak and pine panelling abound, while floors are flagged or bare wood. Normally seven or eight real ales are available, and festivals are held in October and June, the latter as part of the Alcester and Arden Folk Festival. The regular folk sessions, 'singarounds' and informal music-making are popular. Westons and Biddenden cider available. ♨ Q ⊛ ◑ ▯ ♣ ● ✠

Three Tuns
High Street, B49 5AB (next to post office)
🕐 12-11; 12-10.30 Sun

☎ (01789) 762626
Goff's Jouster; Hobsons Best Bitter; guest beers Ⓗ
The small, clear bull's-eye windows make this single-bar pub look more like an antique shop. Inside, there are original low beams, flagstone floors and a glass panel in one wall where the wattle and daub construction is exposed. No piped music, no pool table, no food – it is just how real pubs always used to be. An ever-changing range of eight beers is on tap, from micros and independents, plus a selection of fruit wines. Q ♣

ANSLEY

Lord Nelson Inn
Birmingham Road, CV10 9PG
🕐 12-2, 6-11; 12-11 Sat; 12-10.30 Sun
☎ (024) 7639 2305
Draught Bass; M&B Brew XI; Taylor Landlord; guest beers Ⓗ
Large, roadside, family-run free house, with two restaurants. The larger 90-seater Victory offers excellent cuisine, Tuesday is fresh Grimsby fish night. In the Mary Rose, good

value tasty bar meals are available (see the specials board). The bar has a superb range of guest beers, some from local breweries. For public transport users, the No. 17 bus stop is adjacent (no Sunday service).
♨☆◑ ⊟♣P

ASHORNE

Cottage Tavern

CV35 9DR (off B4001) OS303577
✪ 12.30-3 (not Mon or Tue), 5-11 (8 Mon); 12-3, 5-11 Sat; 12-4 (3 winter) Sun
☎ (01926) 651410
Adnams Bitter; John Smith's Bitter; guest beers Ⓗ
Attractive, friendly, village pub with a warm, welcoming atmosphere. A traditional drinking area around the bar, with a cosy log fire during winter, is complemented by a dining section at the other end. The pub is well supported by the local community including the village cricket club in summer. Guest beers are often from the many micro-breweries around the area. Good value evening meals are served Thursday–Saturday, and lunches Wednesday–Sunday. Darts, dominoes and crib are played. A genuine free house.
♨☆☎◑♣👐

ATHERSTONE

Market Tavern

Market Street, CV9 1ET
✪ 12-11; 12-10.30 Sun
Warwickshire Best Bitter, Lady Godiva, Golden Bear, King Maker, seasonal beers Ⓗ
Busy, town-centre pub offering beers to suit all tastes from the Warwickshire Brewery. Definitely worth a visit, it was awarded local CAMRA Pub of the Year in 2002. A discount is given to card-carrying CAMRA members. The pub has two rooms, a congenial atmosphere and a welcoming real fire in the bar. ♨⊟≢

BADDESLEY ENSOR

Red Lion

The Common, CV9 2BT
(off A5 at Grendon, up Boot Hill)
✪ 7-11; 12-3, 7-11 Sat; 12-3, 7-10.30 Sun
☎ (01827) 713009
Banks's Original; Marston's Pedigree; guest beers Ⓗ
Candles and flowers on the tables feature in this one-roomed village pub. A roaring fire in winter months and a wealth of brasses enhance the cosy atmosphere. Up to three guest beers are on tap from independent breweries. A no-smoking area has been recently introduced. Well worth a visit, but note the restricted weekday opening hours. Parking is available opposite. ♨Q✔

BEDWORTH

Travellers Rest

Bulkington Road, CV12 9DG
✪ 12-11; 12-10.30 Sun
☎ (024) 7631 3687
Beer range varies Ⓗ
Originally built in 1871, the old surroundings have now been demolished and replaced with new housing, but this small corner pub is still the heart of the community. The larger bar is games-oriented, with darts, dominoes, crib teams and no less than four football teams. The smaller, quieter lounge can be entered by the side door, making it feel more like a snug. ⊟≢♣P

White Swan

All Saints Square, CV12 8NL
✪ 11-11; 12-10.30 Sun
☎ (0204) 7631 2164
Wells Eagle, Bombardier Ⓗ
Ideally situated in the town centre, near all local bus stops, this large corner pub has a bar with a games area to one end. The spacious lounge is the venue for discos at the weekends and can get busy. Folk clubs meet here (second Wednesday each month) and at the end of November the National Folk Festival is held in Bedworth. The bar and lounge then bustle with folk musicians attracted from around the country. Lunchtime food is served Monday–Saturday. ☆◑⊟≢♣

BISHOP'S TACHBROOK

Leopard

Oakley Wood Road, CV33 9RN
✪ 12-3, 6-11; 12-11 Sat; 12-10.30 Sun
☎ (01926) 426466
Flowers IPA; Greene King Abbot; Hook Norton Old Hooky; Taylor Landlord; guest beers Ⓗ
This Grade II listed pub has been much improved by its present owners. An L-shaped bar serves stand-up drinkers at one end, near the large open fire, which hides resident 'horror' Doris, who has been up there for many years. The long side of the bar serves a seating/eating area and a small lobby. A cosy lounge has a second open fire, plush leather sofas and a secluded dining room. A new informal function/dining room caters for up to 45.
♨☆◑⊟P✔

BULKINGTON

Olde Chequers Inn

Chequers Street, CV12 9NH
✪ 12-3.30 (3 Thu), 7-11; 12-11 Fri, Sat & summer Thu; 12-10.30 Sun
☎ (024) 7631 2182
website: www.oldechequersinn.co.uk
Draught Bass; M&B Brew XI; guest beers Ⓗ
Excellent, well-known village free house; the popular bar has regular guest ales, some from micro-breweries. At the rear is the restaurant giving diners a good choice of meals (opening times vary summer/winter, see website). Lunches are served on Sunday (advisable to book), evening meals on Friday and Saturday all year, and Thursday in summer. The pub has two football teams in local leagues, darts and dominoes are also played here in the separate games area. There is a small patio area and across the car park, the well-kept beer garden. No bus service runs in the evening, on Sunday or bank holidays.
♨☆◑♣P

INDEPENDENT BREWERIES

Church End Ridge Lane
Frankton Bagby Church Lawford
Warwickshire Cubbington
Wizard Whichford

Weavers Arms
12 Long Street, Ryton, CV12 9JZ (off Wolvey Rd)

☼ 12-3.30, 5-11; 12-11 Wed, Fri & Sat; times may vary; 12-3.30, 7-10.30 Sun

☎ (024) 7631 4415

Draught Bass; M&B Brew XI; guest beers ⊞

A regular in this Guide, secluded, but worth finding. A two-roomed free house with a popular stone-floored bar, it is cosy in the winter next to the open log fire. Leading off the bar is a small wood-panelled games room with a bar billards table. The pub is well supported in all its activities, fundraising for charities, a float in the local carnival, darts and dominoes teams, and the pork pie club (Thursday night). Barbecues are held in the beer garden. Public transport is limited in the Nuneaton area; no service is available in the evening, on Sunday or bank holidays. Lunches are offered Wednesday–Saturday. ♨Q🕸◑🍴♣

DUNCHURCH

Dun Cow
The Green, CV22 6NJ

☼ 11-11; 12-10.30 Sun

☎ (01788) 810305

Draught Bass; Tetley Bitter ⊞

Large, village-centre pub which is very popular with diners and locals. The Dun Cow dates back many hundreds of years, it was shut and looked lost a decade ago. It has been rejuvenated, following extensive refurbishment and has gone from strength to strength. Today the pub is split into four separate rooms (one of which is no-smoking). Each room has an open fire, creating a cosy ambience in winter. The shaded courtyard is a superb place to while away warm sunny days with a pint of their excellent Bass. If you are hungry, try the quality food which is tasty and good value for money. ♨Q🕸🛏◑🛌♣P½

FENNY COMPTON

Wharf Inn ✅
Wharf Road, CV47 2FE (on A423 Banbury-Southam road, near Fenny Compton village)

☼ 11-11.20; 12-10.30 Sun; Breakfast from 8am all week

☎ (01295) 770332

Adnams Broadside; Fuller's London Pride; Hook Norton Best Bitter; guest beer ⊞

Popular, comfortable, canalside pub that has been recently refurbished. The bar and restaurant are separate in one long room. This friendly, welcoming inn offers a canalboat shop, fitness studio, and good food. Watch out for special events; entertainment includes a Guy Fawkes firework display, August bank holiday and May Day events and New Year's Eve fireworks. The adjacent campsite admits caravans.

♨Q🕸◑🛌▲P

FIVE WAYS

Case is Altered ☆
Case Lane, CV35 7JD (off Five Ways road at A4141/A4177 jct) OS225701

☼ 12 (11.30 Sat)-2.30, 6-11; 12-2, 7-10.30 Sun

☎ (01926) 484206

472

Greene King IPA; Hook Norton Old Hooky; Ⓖ
Jennings Mild; ⊞ **guest beers** ⊞/Ⓖ

Traditional, 350-year-old country pub unspoilt by a sympathetic refurbishment that has provided disabled access and WCs. Gravity beers are dispensed from a stillage behind the bar using unique antique cask pumps. A separate room is adjacent to the main bar and the lounge bar is open Friday and Saturday evening and Sunday lunchtime. No children, dogs, music, games machines or mobile phones are permitted – just enjoy the excellent ales and good-humoured conversation. There are usually two guest beers, often including at least one from an independent brewery.
Warwickshire CAMRA Pub of the Year 1996 and 2001. ♨Q🕸&♣P

HARBURY

Gamecock
Chapel Street, CV33 9HT

☼ 1 (12 Fri & Sat)-11; 12-10.30 Sun

☎ (01926) 613255

Banks's Bitter; Greene King Abbot ⊞

Situated at the heart of the village, this traditional local has retained its character despite some modernisation. Customers have remained loyal, with many village societies meeting at the pub. It was originally called the New Inn but confusion with another village pub, The Old New Inn led to the name change. The Gamecock welcomes strangers to this drinkers' pub, and they will soon be introduced to some of the locals. On Sunday night the pub hosts a particularly challenging quiz. ♨Q🕸◑♣

HILLMORTON

Stag & Pheasant
School Street, CV21 4BW

☼ 12-11; 12-10.30 Sun

☎ (01788) 844855

Ansells Mild, Best Bitter; Marston's Pedigree; guest beer ⊞

Old village local with a traditional bar and a comfortable, L-shaped lounge. This busy pub has a frequently-changing guest beer and a loyal base of customers. The rear patio is pleasant for summer drinking. Q🕸◑🛏P

ILMINGTON

Howard Arms
Lower Green, CV36 4LT

☼ 11-2.30, 6-11; 12-3, 6-10.30 Sun

☎ (01608) 682226 website: www.howardarms.com

Everards Tiger; North Cotswold Genesis; guest beers ⊞

Rambling, multi-level, stone-built inn on the green in a pretty village on the edge of the Cotswolds. Flagstone floors and a log-burning fire in an inglenook, enhance the olde-worlde atmosphere. The pub is rapidly gaining a reputation for fine food and service. This is an ideal base for a walking and sightseeing holiday. Both regular beers are relatively uncommon in the area.
♨Q🕸🛏◑▲♣P½

KENILWORTH

Albion Tavern
81 Albion Street, CV8 2FY

☼ 12 (11 Sat)-11; 12-10.30 Sun

☎ (01926) 852793
M&B Brew XI; Tetley Bitter Ⓗ
Unspoilt, Victorian local with a friendly atmosphere. The car park is enormous for the size of the pub and the area. Traditional games such as darts and dominoes thrive here, and live music is staged on the last Saturday of the month. The separate bar and lounge have been preserved, and have not been dominated by food service. In fact the only food available is filled rolls at lunchtime. ᕦ♣P

Clarendon Arms
44 Castle Hill, CV8 1NB
✪ 12-3, 5.30-11; 11-11 Sat; 12-10.30 Sun
☎ (01926) 852017
M&B Brew XI; Worthington's 1744; guest beers Ⓗ
Large, busy but friendly, five-roomed pub near Kenilworth Castle with an emphasis on food. A front snug and side bar accommodate drinkers. To the rear there are two dining rooms, one of which is no-smoking. A small patio serves as a beer garden. Upstairs there is a large function/overflow room. The extensive, variable menu ranges from snacks to full meals and is available lunchtime and evening. ❀◑P

Earl Clarendon
127 Warwick Road, CV8 1HY (on A452)
✪ 12-2, 5-11; 12-11 Sat; 12-10.30 Sun
☎ (01926) 854643
Marston's Bitter, Pedigree Ⓗ
Traditonal local on the main road that is otherwise dominated by theme bars. Known locally as Bottom Clad, this welcoming pub has two distinct drinking areas, a comfortable public bar to the front and a quieter lounge to the rear, both served from a central bar. The back garden provides respite from the busy road. The doorstep sandwiches served at lunchtime are renowned; no food available on Sunday or Monday. ❀◑

Old Bakery Hotel
12 High Street, CV8 1LZ (near A429/A452 jct)
✪ 12-2 (not Mon-Fri), 5-11; 12-2, 6.30-10.30 Sun
☎ (01926) 864111
website: www.theoldbakeryhotel.co.uk
Black Sheep Best Bitter; Hook Norton Best Bitter; Taylor Landlord Ⓗ
This small, family-run hotel, a short distance from the imposing castle ruins, is in the oldest and most picturesque area of Kenilworth. Parts of it date from the 17th century, it has been carefully restored and extended, and warmly welcomes residents and visitors. The two-roomed drinking area with single bar is free from music, TV or games machines. Local CAMRA award-winner in 2001 and Warwickshire CAMRA Pub of the Year in 2002; it is well worth a visit. Wheelchair access is at the rear. Outside, a small patio area has a few seats around the covered 17th-century well.
Q❀⚓&P

LEAMINGTON SPA

Hogshead
43-45 Warwick Street, CV32 5JX
(off The Parade)
✪ 11-11; 12-10.30 Sun
☎ (01926) 339885 website: www.hogshead.com

Boddingtons Bitter; Brakspear Bitter; Caledonian Deuchars IPA; Greene King Abbot, Old Speckled Hen; Wadworth 6X Ⓗ
Large, airy, open-plan, town-centre Hogshead that caters for a mix of shoppers, regulars and diners. A raised no-smoking area is not partitioned off. There is a variety of seating with comfortable leather chairs and sofas at the rear of the pub. It has both piped music and a TV. Bottled Belgian beers are available. A mobile ramp allows disabled access. ◑&✘

LITTLE COMPTON

Red Lion
GL56 0RT (signed from A44)
✪ 12-2.30, 6-11; 12-2.30, 6-10.30 Sun
☎ (01608) 674397 website: www.red-lion-inn.com
Donnington BB, SBA Ⓗ
Warwickshire's only Donnington tied house is in the county's southernmost village, a couple of miles from the megalithic Rollright Stones. Built of local stone, it serves good food and is renowned for its steaks and fresh fish, while retaining a strong involvement with the local community, evidenced by a real public bar and an Aunt Sally pitch. It makes an ideal base for a touring holiday or for visiting the Cheltenham races. A portable ramp ensures disabled access to the restaurant.
▥Q❀⚓◑ ᕦ&♣P

LONG ITCHINGTON

Harvester Inn
6 Church Road, CV47 9PG
✪ 11-3, 6-11; 12-10.30 Sun
☎ (01926) 812698
Hook Norton Best Bitter, Old Hooky; guest beers Ⓗ
Family-run free house since 1976, the Harvester is quite unpretentious. It has a long association with Hook Norton beers, and this Guide. The pub is a conversion from two houses built around 1800. To one side of the main room is a small bar with pool table; to the other, a restaurant seating 30. Camping facilities are in the grounds of another pub nearby; there are moorings on the Grand Union Canal – about five minutes' walk.
Q◑ ⚓P

LOWER BRAILES

George Hotel
High Street, OX15 5HN (on B4035)
✪ 11-11; 12-10.30 Sun
☎ (01608) 685223
Hook Norton Mild, Best Bitter, Generation, Old Hooky; seasonal beers Ⓗ
This sympathetically restored, Grade II coaching inn incorporates elements from the 16th to 18th centuries. The extensive garden includes a loggia and an Aunt Sally pitch. Live jazz and blues nights are staged each week, plus more informal sessions. There is a coin-operated Internet terminal on the upstairs landing. Frequent theme evenings and costume dinners are held in the restaurant, plus take-away curry on Monday, and fish and chips on Wednesday. Morris men and mummers gather here to celebrate St George's Day (23 April).
▥Q❀⚓◑ ᕦ&⚓♣P✘

MORETON MORRELL

Black Horse
CV35 9AR
✪ 11.30-3, 7-11; 12-3, 7-10.30 Sun
☎ (01926) 651231
Hook Norton Best Bitter; guest beer Ⓗ
Rural pub in the centre of the village that has a cosy, compact bar with wooden settles ranged around the walls. As well as regulars, it is popular with students from the local agricultural college and with walkers. A relaxing atmosphere prevails. The guest beer is usually from a small independent brewery. The tasty baps are good value. Enjoy a relaxing drink in the peaceful garden. The pub is handy for M40 junction 12. ✿⚶

NEWTON

Stag & Pheasant
Main Street, CV23 0DY
✪ 12-3, 6-11; 12-4, 7-10.30 Sun
☎ (01788) 860326
Banks's Original, Bitter; guest beers Ⓗ
Excellent village pub that boasts a thatched roof and is reputed to be the oldest A-frame building in Warwickshire. Good value meals are served at lunchtime and in the evening until 9pm. This community local hosts fêtes and charity events in the large car park in summer, and has various pub teams. The cellar supposedly houses a ghost. A small garden with play area is available. ✿⑩♣P⛛

NO MAN'S HEATH

Four Counties Inn
Ashby Road, B79 0PB
(on B5493, 1 mile from M42/A42 jct 11)
✪ 11.30-3, 6.30-11; 12-3, 7-10.30 Sun
☎ (01827) 830243
Banks's Original; Everards Original; Marston's Pedigree; guest beer Ⓗ
Former coaching inn on the border of four counties, that legend suggests was once the haunt of highwaymen. The guest beer is more often than not from one of the smaller breweries (with a strength of over 4% ABV). Pub games such as darts, crib and dominoes are played, and there are quiz nights. Children are welcome before 9pm. The pub has many regulars and attracts passing trade, the charming landlady welcomes all visitors. Enjoy good quality pub food and excellent quality ale in pleasant, convivial surroundings. ⚶Q✿⑩♿♣P⛛

NORTHEND

Red Lion
Bottom Street, CV47 2TJ
(signed off B4001, opp. army camp)
✪ 11.30-2.30, 6-11; 12-3, 6-11 Sat; closed Mon; 12-3, 7-10.30 Sun
☎ (01295) 770308
Taylor Landlord; guest beers Ⓗ
Situated at the foot of the Burton Dassett hills, this idyllic country pub offers a warm welcome and is very popular with locals, ramblers and cyclists. The garden, with a marvellous panoramic view, is ideal in warmer weather. A genuine free house, it serves Taylor Landlord as standard and an ever-changing guest beer. The separate no-

smoking restaurant has a comprehensive menu of excellent, freshly-prepared food. Booking is advisable for Sunday lunch. Bar snacks are also available. ⚶Q✿⑩♣P

NUNEATON

Fox Inn
The Square, Attleborough, CV11 9AR
✪ 11-11; 12-10.30 Sun
☎ (024) 7638 3290
Mansfield Cask Ale; Marston's Pedigree Ⓗ
Well-used, traditional, two-roomed local, the bar has a carpeted games area to one end, with a pool table. Darts and dominoes are also played. Lunches are served Monday–Saturday. The well-appointed lounge is comfortable. In summer, the exterior is picturesque with colourful hanging baskets at the front and a patio garden at the rear. For public transport users, note there are no buses in the evening, on Sunday or bank holidays. ✿⑩♿♣

Lloyds
10 Bond Street, CV11 4BX
✪ 11-11 (midnight Fri & Sat); 12-10.30 Sun
☎ (024) 7637 3343
Greene King Abbot, Old Speckled Hen; guest beers Ⓗ
Many real ale drinkers will remember this pub as a non-brewing Firkin, it still retains much of the original layout. The large, split-level bar with a games area to one side is really popular with the young and old. The beer range is from independent breweries, local beers from Church End and Warwickshire feature here regularly. No food is served on Sunday. Situated midway between the rail and bus stations, the pub is very accessible by public transport. ✿⑩▬≠♣

ROWINGTON

Cock Horse
Old Warwick Road, CV35 7AA (on B4439)
✪ 12-11; 12-10.30 Sun
☎ (01926) 842183
Adnams Broadside; Ansells Best Bitter; Flowers Original; Fuller's London Pride Ⓗ
Located just outside the village, this popular, traditional, oak-beamed pub offers an extensive beer and food menu for its size. It has a small lounge/bar and a separate restaurant. The pub has a beer festival on August bank holiday when more than 20 ales are on offer. Live music is performed on some weekdays at this community pub which welcomes everyone. ⚶✿⑩♦P

RUGBY

Alexandra Arms
72-73 James Street, CV21 2SL
(next to multi-storey car park)
✪ 11.30-3, 5-11; 11.30-11 Fri & Sat; 12-10.30 Sun
☎ (01788) 578660
website: www.rugbycamra.org.uk/alexandraarms
Ansells Best Bitter; Fuller's London Pride; Greene King Abbot; guest beers Ⓗ
The only pub to be awarded Rugby CAMRA Pub of the Year four years running. The L-shaped lounge is comfortable, and lively debate among the locals is guaranteed. The games room is popular with rock fans attracted by the well-stocked juke box. The

ex-bowling green serves a more useful purpose as a venue for summer beer festivals. Guest ales, including milds, stouts and porters, come from independent breweries. The draught beers are complemented by a range of bottled Belgian beers. Skittles and bar billards are played, and there is a garden plus a covered seating area. Q ⊛ ◖◗ ≈ ♣ ♠

Merchant Inn
5 Little Church Street, CV21 3AW
✪ 11.30-2.30, 5-11 (1am Fri & Sat); 12-10.30 Sun
☎ (01788) 571119
B&T Shefford Bitter; Everards Tiger; guest beers Ⓗ
Rugby CAMRA Pub of the Year 2002, the Merchant has seen several identities although it has only been a pub for a relatively short time. For many years this fine old building belonged to a local wine merchants. It now boasts a flagstone floor, plenty of wooden seating, comfortable sofas and an abundance of brewery memorabilia. The pub has a late licence on Friday and Saturday. It stocks two regular beers, six guest ales, and a superb selection of Belgian beers, and occasionally hosts beer festivals. ⚌ ◖◗ & ♣

Raglan Arms
30 Dunchurch Road, CV22 6AD
✪ 12-2.30 (not Mon & Tue), 5-11; 11.30-11 Sat; 12-3.30, 7-10.30 Sun
☎ (01788) 544441
Ansells Mild, Best Bitter; Fuller's London Pride; Greene King Abbot; Marston's Pedigree; guest beer Ⓗ
Small, traditional, friendly pub, close to the town centre. The Rugby Football Museum is close by and Rugby School is just over the road. There is a traditional bar to the rear, and a cosy lounge to the front. There is also a separate small function room. The pub has been a regular meeting place for Rugby CAMRA for many years. The landlord is an ex-professional rugby player and the pub has strong sporting associations with no less than two football teams. There are also darts, dominoes and crib teams. With five regular beers alongside a guest, this is still one of the best pubs in town for both range and quality of real ale. Q P

Seven Stars ⊘
Albert Square, CV21 2SH
✪ 10.30-2.30, 7-11; 12-11 Sat; 12-10.30 Sun
☎ (01788) 544789
Wells Eagle, Bombardier; guest beers Ⓗ
Tucked away, the Seven Stars is easily missed, which would be a shame. The pub is undergoing refurbishment to provide a more traditional public bar area, an extended lounge, and a games room/conservatory for darts, skittles, pool, dominoes and crib. There is live music regularly on Friday (blues) and Sunday (jazz). Up to two guest beers are on tap from a wide range of breweries, with some of the less obvious choices. It is one of the few pubs in Rugby with Cask Marque accreditation ⌂ ≈ ♣

Victoria
1 Lower Hillmorton Road, CV21 3ST
✪ 12-2.30, 6 (5.30 Fri)-11; 12-11 Sat; 12-2.30, 7-10.30 Sun
☎ (01788) 544374
Beer range varies Ⓗ

Triangular-shaped local just on the edge of town, it is well worth a visit. Pool and darts are played in the public bar. The lounge, decorated in a Victorian style, provides a good environment to enjoy a pint. There is a varied selection of up to three guest ales. Lunches are served Monday–Saturday. Q ◖◗ ⊞ ≈ ♣

RYTON-ON-DUNSMORE

Old Bull & Butcher
Oxford Road, CV8 3EP
(on A423, 1½ miles SE of Peugeot factory)
✪ 12-2.30, 5-11; 12-10.30 Sun
☎ (024) 7630 1400
Courage Directors; Highgate Dark; guest beers Ⓗ
Large, two-roomed, country free house with a conservatory and children's outdoor play area. The pub has recently been refurbished and has attractive decor. Guest beers often come from local micro-breweries. The conservatory is a no-smoking area. ⚌ ⊛ ◖◗ ⊞ & P ⊁

SAMBOURNE

Green Dragon
The Village Green, B96 6NU
(between A435 and A441)
✪ 11.30-3, 6-11; 12-3, 7-10.30 Sun
☎ (01527) 892465
Draught Bass; Hobsons Best Bitter; M&B Brew XI Ⓗ
The half-timbered, rambling buildings of this pub overlook the picturesque village green in true picture-postcard style. No wonder then that the Green Dragon is a favourite with ramblers and tourists. The central bar serves five rooms (without walls) giving the pub an intimate atmosphere yet still offering plenty of space. There is a no-smoking restaurant if you require a formal meal. The six double rooms make this an ideal base to enjoy the surrounding delights. ⚌ ⊛ ⌂ ◖◗ P

SHUSTOKE

Griffin Inn
Church Road, B46 2LB
(on B4116 on sharp bend)
✪ 12-2.30, 7-11; 12-2.30, 7-10.30 Sun
☎ (01675) 481205
Banks's Original; Marston's Pedigree; Theakston Old Peculier; Wells Bombardier; guest beers Ⓗ
Choose from nine beers, five change often to surprise you on every visit. Local CAMRA Pub of the Year 1998, 2000 and 2001, this is one of the few real English pubs left unspoilt to be enjoyed by clientele from near and far. Set in the Warwickshire countryside, it has fine views from the garden, a large car park, and a conservatory for rainy days. A jewel not to be missed. ⚌ Q ⊃ ⊛ ◖◗ & ⚲ P

STRATFORD-UPON-AVON

West End
Bull Street, CV37 6DT
(in centre of 'old town', SW of town centre)
✪ 11-11; 12-10.30 Sun
☎ (01789) 268832
Black Sheep Best Bitter; Hook Norton Old Hooky; Taylor Landlord; Uley Old Spot, Pig's Ear Ⓗ
The West End in its present form has been

open since 2001, previously it was known as the Sportsman. New management and a substantial refit have created a pub which treads a fine line between bar and wine bar. Though the original two rooms have been knocked into one continuous L-shaped bar, the streetside part is no-smoking and is largely occupied by those eating, whereas the back room is 'smoking' and slightly less formal. Customers are a curious mix of regular, beer-drinking locals and wine-drinking diners. There is also a small 'snug' off to the right of the main bar. This pub is off the beaten track, but well worth the walk from the centre of town.
🏮◑⌁

Little Lark
108 Alcester Road, B80 7NP
(on A435/Tom's Town Lane jct)
🕒 12-3, 6-11; 12-11 Sat; 12-3, 6.30-10.30 Sun
☎ (01527) 853105
Ansells Mild; Usher's Best Bitter; Wadworth 6X Ⓗ
An unusual pub that caters equally for locals and visitors, many visiting for the first time when the pub was on 'Mad O'Rourke's' passport-linked drinking trail. The Lark is loosely based on a newspaper theme and in the past printed its own amusing news-sheet. Nowadays, it is a comfortable street-corner pub and restaurant and the licensee, who is also the chef, offers a varied range of dishes, some quite exotic, including vegetarian options.
🏮◑♣

Cape of Good Hope
66 Lower Cape, CV34 5DP
🕒 12-11; 12-10.30 Sun
☎ (01926) 498138
website: www.capeofgoodhope.co.uk
Boddingtons Bitter; Greene King Abbot; Tetley Bitter; guest beers Ⓗ
Welcoming pub alongside Warwick top lock on the Grand Union Canal. Built around 1800 just after the canal was opened, it has given its name to the lock and surrounding area. There is a traditional public bar to the front with TV, dartboard and games. The quieter lounge bar is to the rear. Good value food is offered. The house beer, called Lock, Stock and (served) Straight from the Barrel, is from Weatheroak. Small car park available, but plenty of room for narrow boats. It tends to be busy with canal traffic in summer. Watch the action from the canalside patio.
Q🏮◑⌂♣P

Globe Hotel
10 Theatre Street, CV34 4DP
🕒 11-11; 12-10.30 Sun
☎ (01926) 492044
website: www.thaielephant-warwick.co.uk
M&B Brew XI; guest beers Ⓗ
Opened in 1788 as the Globe Inn Commercial and Posting House, the varied exterior elevations reveal the many alterations and extensions over the years. Situated just off the market place, until the 1960s it could be approached by an iron bridge over the ravine-like street of the Hollway. Do not be put off by the elephants guarding the entrance and the signs for the Thai Elephant restaurant. Patrons just requiring drinks are most welcome in the comfortable bar. The restaurant is popular, booking is advised (no lunches Sat). 🛏◑ ▲P

Old Fourpenny Shop Hotel
27-29 Crompton Street, CV34 6HJ
(near racecourse within 1/2 mile of town centre)
🕒 12-2.30 (3 Sat), 5.30-11; 12-11 Fri; 12-3, 6-10.30 Sun
☎ (01926) 491360
Greene King Ruddles Best; RCH Pitchfork; guest beers Ⓗ
This is the 13th consecutive Guide entry for the Fourpenny Shop. Four guest beers are always available. There has been a pub on this site since 1780. The current Grade II listed Georgian building is circa 1800. At that time navvies building the canals could buy a tot of rum and a coffee for 4d – hence the name. The warm colours of the single bar reflect the welcome and atmosphere – no music or TV permitted. The quality food is freshly cooked (not served Sun eve). There are 11 en-suite bedrooms.
Q🛏◑

Blue Bell
Warings Green Road, B94 6BP
(S of Cheswick Green off Ilshaw Heath road) OS129742
🕒 11-11; 12-10.30 Sun
☎ (01564) 702328
Beer range varies Ⓗ
Traditional country pub situated on the Stratford Canal, with a friendly, welcoming atmosphere. It has a separate bar with a dartboard, real fire and TV. The large lounge, also with a real fire, consists of a number of the original rooms knocked into one. There is a separate conservatory area for families. The three guests are from local micros and nationals, and change on a daily basis. Popular canal festivals and pig roasts are held throughout the summer.
🏮🛌🏮◑⌂♣🐾P⌁

Norman Knight
CV36 5PE
🕒 12-2.30, 7-11; 12-2.30, 7-10.30 Sun
☎ (01608) 684621
website: www.thenormanknight.co.uk
Hook Norton Best Bitter; Wizard Whichford Bitter; guest beers Ⓗ
Traditional village pub, with a stone-flagged floor and exposed beams, in an idyllic setting facing the extensive village green. Its name commemorates Sir John de Mohun, a garter knight who is buried in the nearby parish church. The Wizard Brewery commenced brewing here in February 2003. Guest beers show an adventurous variety, and come from micros and small independents. The pub has its own caravan site and two holiday cottages. No food is offered on Tuesday, and evening meals are served on Friday and Saturday only. Aunt Sally and shove-ha'penny are played.
🏮🏮◑⌂▲♣P

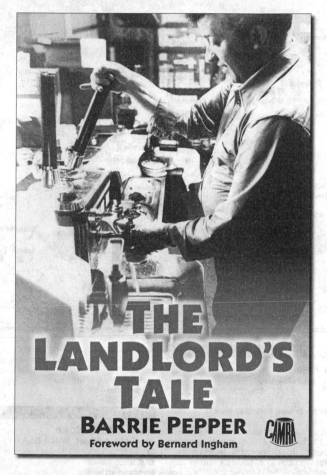

WEST MIDLANDS

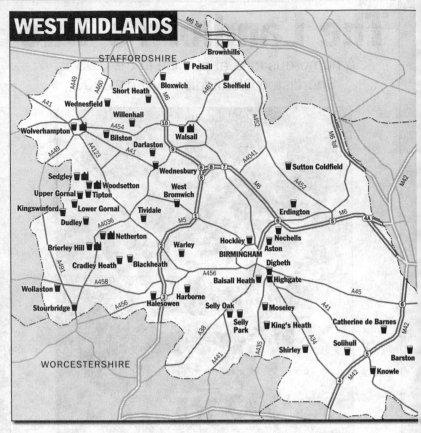

BARSTON

Bull's Head
Barston Lane, B92 0JU
⊕ 11-2.30, 5.30-11; 11-11 Sat; 12-10.30 Sun
☎ (01675) 442830
**Adnams Bitter; Draught Bass; M&B Brew XI;
guest beer** Ⓗ
Beamed, genuine village local, parts of
which date back to 1490. Always welcoming
and friendly, this supporter of independent
breweries won the local CAMRA Pub of the
Year award in 1998, 2000 and 2002, and has
been listed in this Guide for 11 consecutive
years. The pub has two bars, each with a log
fire and horse-racing memorabilia, plus a
restaurant in the oldest part of the building.
It offers superb home-cooked food
Monday–Saturday. ₳Q❀◖◗P

BALSALL COMMON

Railway
547 Station Road, CV7 7EF
⊕ 12-11; 12-3, 7-10.30 Sun
☎ (01676) 533284
**Adnams Broadside; Draught Bass; M&B Brew XI;
Taylor Landlord** Ⓗ
Right next to Berkswell Station, this small,
one-roomed pub was formerly part of
railway workers' cottages, dating from 1846.
Divided into two sections, it resembles a
station buffet bar. At one side of the bar is a
drinking area with a TV, the other side
houses a pool table and dartboard. Popular

with young people, this pub hosts regular
karaoke nights and occasional live music.
Lunchtime bar food is available. Car
parking space is limited.
❀◖≉ (Berkswell) ♣P

BILSTON

Olde White Rose
20 Lichfield Street, WV14 0AG
⊕ 12-11; 12-3.30, 7-10.30 Sun
☎ (01902) 498339
Beer range varies Ⓗ
A Grade II listed frontage leads into a
narrow interior. Wolverhampton's CAMRA
Pub of the Year 2002 stocks 12 beers, many
unusual for the area. Recent improvements
include a garden, Bierkeller, conservatory
and conference room. There is a no-
smoking eating area where food is served
12–9 at reasonable prices; the Sunday lunch
is highly recommended (booking advised).
Children are welcome until 9pm.
Convenient for bus and metro stations
linking Wolverhampton and Birmingham, a
discount is given to card-carrying CAMRA
members. ❀◖◗ ⊖ (Bilston Central) ♣⊬◫

Trumpet
58 High Street, WV14 0EP
⊕ 11-3, 7.30-11; 12-3, 7-10.30 Sun
☎ (01902) 493723 website: www.trumpetjazz.org
Holden's Mild, Bitter, Golden Glow; guest beer Ⓗ
This well-known pub started life as the
Royal Exchange. Its name was changed to

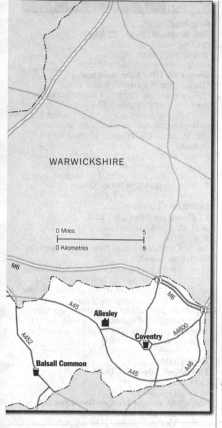

☎ (0121) 440 1954

Ansells Best Bitter; Enville Ale; Greene King Abbot; guest beer Ⓗ

The Old Mo is situated at the end of a terrace in an open space, affording a city-centre view that at night has been compared to more exotic locations. There are three rooms: a public bar, a lounge and a pool room upstairs. It is 10 minutes' walk from Edgbaston Cricket Ground and Birmingham's 'Balti belt'. The bar walls are hung with framed articles about the exploits of regulars and publicity for the pub cricket team. Meals are restricted to Tuesday and Thursday – curry nights. ❀▷⏴

CITY CENTRE

Bull
1 Price Street, B4 6JU
🕐 11-11; closed Sun
☎ (0121) 333 6757
Adnams Broadside; Marston's Pedigree; guest beer Ⓗ
Friendly, two-bar, ex-Heritage Inn on the edge of the city centre, in the Gun Quarter. Dating from the 18th century, the pub has seen little alteration and retains an etched Ansells window. The two rooms are quiet and comfortable; the decor includes a collection of jugs and decorated tableware. A varied menu of good value hot and cold food is served until 10pm. Q⏢⏴▷

Darwins
57 Grosvenor Street West, B16 8AJ
🕐 12-11; 12-10.30 Sun
☎ (0121) 643 6064 website: www.darwinspub.co.uk
Adnams Bitter; Ansells Mild; Greene King Abbot Ⓗ
Traditional back-street pub behind bustling Broad Street, comprising a traditional public bar with pool table, and a lounge/restaurant where a mixture of lounge and dining furniture includes some easy chairs. The pub is cheap for the area, and is a rare outlet for Ansells Mild. The lounge bar windows and toilet doors feature drawings to illustrate Darwin's Theory of Evolution. New 'yuppie' apartments have been built nearby.
Q⏴▷⏢⇄ (Five Ways/Snow Hill) ⊖ (Snow Hill)

Figure of Eight ⊘
236 Broad Street, B1 2HQ
🕐 10-11; 12-10.30 Sun
☎ (0121) 633 0917
Boddingtons Bitter; Courage Directors; Hop Back Summer Lightning; Shepherd Neame Spitfire; Theakston XB; guest beers Ⓗ
Spacious Wetherspoon's outlet at the heart of the city centre, usually serving several guest ales as well as the regular range. See the large collection of old books and pictures of bygone Birmingham. Popular with local office workers, and as a meeting place for a night on the town, it is usually

the Trumpet due to its popularity as a jazz venue. A different style of jazz is showcased here every evening and Sunday lunchtime. Entry is free, but a collection plate is passed around. The walls and ceiling are covered in jazz memorabilia: instruments, music, scores, photographs and posters. Both the bus and metro station are only a couple of minutes' walk away. ⊖ (Bilston Central) ⏇

BIRMINGHAM: ASTON

Bartons Arms ☆
144 High Street, B6 4UP
🕐 12 (11 Sat)-11; 12-10.30 Sun
☎ (0121) 333 5988 website: www.bartons-arms.co.uk
Oakham JHB, White Dwarf, Bishops Farewell, seasonal beers; guest beers Ⓗ
A welcome entry back in this Guide for this splendid Victorian pub. Built in 1901, it is renowned for its magnificent tiled decoration and snob screens and features on CAMRA's National Inventory. Restored by Oakham Ales to full glory, it is popular with locals and visitors. The Thai food served (not Mon) complements the beers; a wide range is available, including Belgian beers. It is a seven-minute bus ride from the city, on services 33, 34, 51 and 52. ♨Q⏴▷P

BALSALL HEATH

Old Moseley Arms
Tindal Street, B12 9QU
🕐 12-11; 12-10.30 Sun

INDEPENDENT BREWERIES

Banks's Wolverhampton
Batham Brierley Hill
Goldthorn Wolverhampton
Highgate Walsall
Holden's Woodsetton
Sarah Hughes Sedgley
Olde Swan Netherton
Rainbow Allesley

crowded and the prices are a welcome antidote to the expensive bars nearby. A sizeable garden at the back is a bonus.
⚬◖▮ & ⇌ (Five Ways/Snow Hill) ⊖ (Snow Hill)✂

Old Fox
54 Hurst Street, B5 4TD (opp. Birmingham Hippodrome)
⚬ 12-midnight (2am Fri & Sat); 12-10.30 Sun
☎ (0121) 622 5080
Greene King Old Speckled Hen; Marston's Pedigree; Tetley Bitter; guest beers Ⓗ
The pub stands opposite the Birmingham Hippodrome and is convenient for the Chinese Quarter. It is reported that Charlie Chaplin and other stars used the pub when they were appearing at the theatre. Its theatrical links are illustrated by memorabilia around the pub. There is usually a choice of four or five real ales served in the two rooms from an island bar. Tables and chairs are set out on the pavement in fine weather. Meals are served Tuesday–Saturday, until 7.30pm.
⚬◖▮ & ⇌ (New St)

Old Royal
53 Church Street, B3 2DP
(turning off Colmore Row)
⚬ 12-11; 12-10.30 Sun
☎ (0121) 200 3841
Fuller's London Pride; Greene King IPA Ⓗ
This listed building is over 100 years old and retains its original stained glass windows. Popular with office workers at lunchtime and early evening, it can become very busy. The single-room bar has recently been refurbished and now features a large-screen TV. There is a large function room upstairs. Food served 12–8, Monday–Friday.
◖▮ ⇌ (New St/Snow Hill)

Prince of Wales
84 Cambridge Street, B1 2NN
(next to National Indoor Arena)
⚬ 12-11; 12-10.30 Sun
☎ (0121) 643 9460
Adnams Broadside; Ansells Mild, Best Bitter; Brains SA; Greene King Abbot; Marston's Pedigree Ⓗ
The 150-year-old building was refurbished in 1998, when the original two bars were knocked into one. It provides a welcome relief from most of the pubs in the nearby Broad Street area, with a choice of eight real ales. It attracts workers and visitors from the National Indoor Arena and the International Convention Centre and also users of the local canal network. Good value food is the norm here. ◖▮ &

Wetherspoon's
Unit 31, Paradise Place, B3 3HJ
⚬ 10-11; 12-10.30 Sun
☎ (0121) 214 8970
Courage Directors; Greene King Abbot; Shepherd Neame Spitfire; guest beers Ⓗ
Bright, airy, single-bar pub, converted from a former café-bar. It is convenient for the central library, museum and art gallery; also the repertory theatre and International Convention Centre. Three regular real ales are supplemented by two guests which are changed on a regular basis. No-smoking and family areas are provided within the one-level bar.
Q & ⇌ (New St/Snow Hill) ⊖ (Snow Hill) ✂

DIGBETH

Anchor ☆
308 Bradford Street, B5 6ET
⚬ 11-midnight; 12-10.30 Sun
☎ (0121) 622 4516
website: www.the-anchor-inn.fsnet.co.uk
Ansells Mild; Tetley Bitter; guest beers Ⓗ
The Anchor is a large Grade II listed building next to Digbeth Coach Station on the corner of Rea Street. The public bar is on the Bradford Street side, a large lounge lies to the rear, and a nominally no-smoking bar on the Rea Street side. Known for its range of cask ales, regular beer festivals and foreign bottled beers, a Belgian beer and two German beers are normally also on draught. The cider varies, but is mostly Thatchers. ⚬◖▮ ⊞⇌ (Moor St/New St) ◗

Horans Tavern
92 Floodgate Street, B5 5SR
⚬ 11-11; 12-3 (closed eve) Sun
☎ (0121) 643 3851
Ansells Mild; Fuller's London Pride; Greene King Abbot; guest beers Ⓗ
Quiet, basic, back-street boozer in the Irish quarter of the city, with two rooms and a small dining area next to the kitchen. There is no music or gaming machines. The pub is popular with workers from the many small businesses in the surrounding area. Food is served at lunchtime, bar snacks in the evening. Q ◖

Woodman ☆
106 Albert Street, B5 9LS
⚬ 11-11; 12-6 Sun
☎ (0121) 643 1959
Ansells Mild; Courage Directors; Greene King Old Speckled Hen; guest beer Ⓗ
Classic Victorian Grade II listed pub, opposite The Thinktank at Millennium Point, and next to the preserved Curzon Street Station. The pub has a tiled, L-shaped bar with etched windows and a cosy snug. A sympathetic renovation of the interior has recently been completed. Note the unusual collection of artefacts. ◖⊞

ERDINGTON

Charlie Hall ⊘
49 Barnabas Road, B23 6SH (opp. Little Market)
⚬ 10-11; 12-10.30 Sun
☎ (0121) 384 2716
Boddingtons Bitter; Hop Back Summer Lightning; Marston's Pedigree; Shepherd Neame Spitfire; Theakston Best Bitter; guest beers Ⓗ
This large Wetherspoon's house, which is named after a locally born actor who appeared in some 30 Laurel & Hardy films, was formerly a bingo hall. Many photographs of the comic duo are displayed on the walls. The pub has been well refurbished and consists of one long room with two ceiling heights. Wood panelling has been used throughout and there are a number of alcoves for privacy. The rear patio is a bonus when the weather is clement. Q ⚬◖▮ & ⇌ ✂

Lad in the Lane
28 Bromford Lane, B24 8BJ (400 yds N of A38)
⚬ 11-11; 12-10.30 Sun
☎ (0121) 377 7471
Ansells Mild; Marston's Pedigree; Tetley Bitter Ⓗ

The oldest pub in Birmingham, it was originally constructed in 1306 and has been magnificently renovated. The view from the outside is of a timber-framed building with leaded windows. Inside, black exposed joints and rafters make an immediate impact. The lounge is in three different sections on two levels. Decorative touches include a Welsh dresser and a wooden bicycle. The large garden is popular with regulars and visitors in summer. Lunches are served Monday–Saturday. ❀◖♣P

HARBORNE

Bell Inn
11 Old Church Road, B17 0BB
(700 yds from A4040 by St Peter's Church)
✪ 12-11; 12-10.30 Sun
☎ (0121) 427 0931
Fuller's London Pride; guest beer Ⓗ
Overlooked by St Peter's Church in the leafy suburb of Harborne, the Bell has the ambience of a village pub even though it is only a short distance from the city centre. Previously the parish clerk's house, it has been an inn for 300 years. The large lounge has oak-beamed walls, and there is an unusual corridor bar. A rear snug, served by a hatch to the bar, often hosts bowling club meetings; the outdoor seating area is by the well-kept bowling green. ❀◖P

White Horse
2 York Street, B15 2ES
✪ 11-11; 12-10.30 Sun
☎ (0121) 427 2063
Adnams Broadside; Marston's Pedigree; Tetley Bitter, Burton Ale; Wadworth 6X; Wells Bombardier Ⓗ
Much-changed Tetley Festival Ale House, now serving a range of ales from nationals and larger regional breweries. An island bar dominates this lively pub, popular with locals, students and local business folk. Pictures of old Harborne adorn the walls of this busy, side-street local. Various events take place – from jam sessions and Sky TV matches to local outings. Food is served 12–7, Monday–Saturday. An occasional cider is stocked. ◖⊟♣⬥

HIGHGATE

Lamp Tavern
257 Barford Street, B5 6AH (off A441)
✪ 12-11; 7-10.30 Sun
☎ (0121) 622 2599
Church End Gravediggers; Everards Tiger; Marston's Pedigree; Stanway Stanney Bitter; guest beers Ⓗ
This small, cosy, back-street local attracts a varied clientele, many of whom travel some distance to drink here. It is still the only regular outlet for Stanway beers in Birmingham. The small front bar is popular at lunchtimes and in the early evening, while the rear function room hosts live music and is a meeting place for many local societies and clubs. Regular guest beers are available at weekends. ◖�≠(New St/Moor St)

HOCKLEY

Black Eagle
16 Factory Road, B18 5JU
(near Soho House Museum)
✪ 11.30-3, 5.30-11; 11.30-11 Fri; 12-3, 7-11 Sat; 12-3 (closed eve) Sun

☎ (0121) 523 4008
Ansells Mild, Best Bitter; Marston's Pedigree; Taylor Landlord; guest beers Ⓗ
Very friendly pub, four times winner of Birmingham CAMRA's Pub of the Year award. Rebuilt in 1895, it retains most of the original features, including Minton tiles. It is Birmingham's sole entry in CAMRA's Good Pub Food. Close to the Soho House Museum, and the famous Jewellery Quarter, it is an ideal destination for the ale connoisseur and sightseer. It hosts an annual beer festival in July.
❀◖⊟Ө(Benson/Soho Rd)

Church Inn
22 Great Hampton Street, B18 6AQ
(take A41 from city centre)
✪ 11.45-11; 12-3, 6-11 Sat; closed Sun
☎ (0121) 515 1851
Batham Best Bitter; guest beer Ⓗ
This excellent, old-fashioned pub is a previous Birmingham CAMRA Pub of the Year. Over 160 years old, it has a warranted reputation for the quality of its food – an extensive menu specialises in steaks, grills and roasts – and the portions are huge. Choose from over 80 whiskies, mostly single malts. The bar is divided into two and shares one serving bar; many old photographs adorn the walls. Another small bar, with a collection of film star photographs, is opened on request.
◖⊟≠(Jewellery Qtr/Snow Hill) Ө(St Paul's)

White House
99 New John Street West, B19 3TZ
✪ 11-11; 12-10.30 Sun
☎ (0121) 523 0782
Holden's Mild, Bitter, Golden Glow, seasonal beers Ⓗ
Imposing, two-roomed corner pub, the only outlet for Holden's beers within the city boundary. The pub has a basic bar and a roomy lounge, with an alcove for diners, where the walls display the landlord's collection of photographs of old Birmingham scenes. A strong community ethos attracts local workers and residents from the surrounding estates. No food is served at weekends. Q◖⊟

KING'S HEATH

Pavilions
229 Alcester Road South, B14 6EB
✪ 12-11; 12-10.30 Sun
☎ (0121) 441 3286
Banks's Original, Bitter; Marston's Pedigree Ⓗ
This 1860s building has been transformed into a modern, welcoming local, situated on the busy No. 50 bus route. This two-roomed pub has a very stylish interior, displaying old photos of King's Heath. A good menu complements the three beers. A quiz is held on Monday and Wednesday evenings.
◖P⊟

MOSELEY

Highbury
Dads Lane, B13 8PQ (500 yds from A441)
✪ 12 (11 Sat)-11; 12-10.30 Sun
☎ (0121) 414 1529
Banks's Original; M&B Brew XI; guest beer Ⓗ
Spacious pub, comprising front and side lounges, a pool room and a family room to the rear (not always open). The large garden

481

has a children's play area. A big-screen TV in the front room shows music videos, live premiership games and other events. Irish-themed music is played, with a juke box for variety. Owned by the Punch Group, guest ales are limited to their list, but often include smaller brewers as well as more recognised names such as Adnams. It is close to the River Rea cycle route.
♨❀♿P⚟▯

Prince of Wales
118 Alcester Road, B13 8EE
12-10.45; 12-10.30 Sun
☎ (0121) 449 4198
Ansells Mild; Greene King Abbot; Tetley Burton Ale; Wells Bombardier Ⓗ
The Prince of Wales has only had one change of landlord in the last 10 years, and the current incumbent was reputedly selected by the previous landlords on their retirement. As a consequence, the character of the pub has changed little in this time. A relaxed pub on weekdays and a lively social venue at weekends, the pub has a public bar and two back rooms. A large outside drinking area lies to the rear of the pub. ❀⊟

NECHELLS

Villa Tavern ☆
307 Nechells Park Road, B7 5PD
11.30-2.30, 5-11; 11.30-11 Fri & Sat; 12-4, 7-10.30 Sun
☎ (0121) 326 7466
Ansells Mild, Best Bitter; Marston's Pedigree Ⓗ
A sign on the outside of this Victorian-style building indicates that it was built in 1897, whereas it actually dates from 1925. It has a splendid interior – note the stained glass bow window in the lounge. The three rooms (bar, lounge and function room) are served by a single bar. This is very much a community pub which supports two dominoes teams and a pool team. Lunches are served on weekdays. Q◖⊟⇌(Aston) ♣P

SELLY OAK

Country Girl
1 Raddlebarn Road, B29 6HJ
(by hospital, 1/2 mile from station)
12-11; 12-10.30 Sun
☎ (0121) 414 9921
Draught Bass; M&B Brew XI; guest beer Ⓗ
Extensive renovation has resulted in a large one-roomed pub with generous seating and an understated but comfortable look, displaying local photos and modern art prints on the walls. Unobtrusive chart music is played. Disabled parking spaces are marked at the front of the building. Customers tend to be groups of locals and students from the nearby university. Close to Selly Oak Hospital, Bournville and Cadbury World, it is the best bet for a decent meal in the area. ❀◖◗⇌P⚟

SELLY PARK

Selly Park Tavern
592 Pershore Road, B29 7HQ
(500 yds from A4029/A441 jct)
12-11; 12-10.30 Sun
☎ (0121) 414 9941
Draught Bass; Fuller's London Pride; M&B Brew XI Ⓗ
Typical example of the Ember Inns chain, with bright, modern decor and open gas fires; old photographs of the locality adorn the walls. Situated close to the BBC studios at Pebble Mill, Cannon Hill Park and the Birmingham Nature Centre, it serves food seven days a week; a comfortable no-smoking area is a bonus, as is the excellent service from the staff. Chart music is played; a quiz is held Monday and Wednesday evenings. Q❀◖◗P⚟

BLACKHEATH

Bell & Bear Inn
71 Gorsty Hill Road, Rowley Regis, B65 0HA (on A4099 halfway down the hill)
11.30-11; 12-4, 7-10.30 Sun
☎ (0121) 561 2196
Adnams Broadside; Taylor Landlord; Tetley Bitter; guest beers Ⓗ
This 400-year-old listed pub is popular with diners for its excellent home-cooked food and with drinkers for the guest beers on tap (up to four). The single large, but cosy, room has a small area set aside for non-smokers. The large garden and patio afford fine views across the Black Country. Barbecues and children's fun days are held in summer; Monday is curry night and Thursday is quiz night. Meals are served 12–9 (12–3 Sun). ♛❀◖◗⇌(Old Hill) P⚟

Lighthouse ✔
153 Coombes Road, B62 8AF
(on A4099, 1/2 mile from A459 jct)
12-11; 12-10.30 Sun
☎ (0121) 602 1620
Enville Ale; Holden's Bitter; guest beers Ⓗ
As its name suggests, the Lighthouse bears a strong nautical theme. Not only is the interior decked out with shipping bric-à-brac, but one external wall is given over to an unusual lighthouse mural. The interior comprises an L-shaped bar, together with several smaller lounge areas and an upstairs function room. Sky Sports are often shown, while Wednesday generally sees live music performances. ❀◖◗♿●P

Waterfall ✔
132 Waterfall Lane, B64 6RE (near A4100 Blackheath-Cradley Heath road)
12-3, 5-11; 12-11 Fri & Sat; 12-10.30 Sun
☎ (0121) 561 3499 website: www.midlandspubs.co.uk
Batham Best Bitter; Enville Ale; Holden's Bitter; Hook Norton Old Hooky; Marston's Pedigree; guest beers Ⓗ
A short walk from Blackheath town centre or up the steep hill from Old Hill Station, this real ale haven remains a firm favourite with locals and visitors alike. In addition to the five regular beers it also keeps five guests and the unusual Enville Ginger Beer is often available along with a variety of real cider. Food is served in the front lounge, while darts can be played in the quiet, comfortable rear bar.
❀◖◗⊟⇌(Old Hill) ●P⚟

BLOXWICH

Lamp Tavern
34 High Street, WS3 2DA (on B4210)
12-11; 12-10.30 Sun
☎ (01922) 479681
Holden's Mild, Bitter, seasonal beers Ⓗ
This cosy, gleaming, one-roomed pub, just south of Bloxwich town centre, was created

out of former farm buildings and stables. It retains much olde-worlde charm. Community-centred, it fields darts, dominoes and crib teams. The restaurant serves balti meals. ⚒Q☺⚒♣P

Stag
Field Road, WS3 3JB (off A34)
✪ 11-11; 12-10.30 Sun
☎ (01922) 405775 website: www.stagbloxwich.co.uk
Adnams Bitter; Banks's Original; Oakham JHB; guest beers Ⓗ
1930s Art Deco pub that has been refurbished in splendid form. An impressive building from the outside, inside one large bar serves three distinct areas. Action by the local community and CAMRA has saved the pub from demolition and redevelopment and it is now very successful. Up to eight guest beers change frequently and often include micro-brewery products. It also stocks Belgian beer on draught and in bottles. Sunday meals are served 12–4.
⚒Q☺⚒◑⚑♣P

Turf Tavern ☆
13 Wolverhampton Road, WS3 2EZ
(off A34, by park)
✪ 12-3, 7-11; 12-3, 7-10.30 Sun
☎ (01922) 407745
RCH Pitchfork; guest beers Ⓗ
Walsall CAMRA's Pub of the Year for the last three years, this Grade II listed building lies within a conservation area. An unspoilt gem, known locally as Tinky's, it has been run by the same family for over 130 years. The tiled floor in the bar adds to the pub's character, while the other two rooms are steeped in nostalgia. A respite from noisy pubs, normally the only sound is the buzz of conversation. Q☺⚑⇌

Rose & Crown
161 Bank Street, DY5 3DD (off High St)
✪ 12-3, 6-11; 12-3, 7-10.30 Sun
☎ (01384) 77825
Holden's Mild, Bitter, Ⓟ **Special** Ⓗ
Situated on the edge of Brierley Hill town centre, this pleasant pub retains its cosiness following a recent refurbishment which saw the bar extended into a new conservatory-like addition. Holden's ales are served in oversized lined glasses. The bar is adorned with a large display of foreign bank notes. Handy for the Civic Hall and police station, it serves a good choice of reasonably-priced meals. ☺◑⚑☺♣PⒽ

Vine (Bull & Bladder)
10 Delph Road, DY5 2TN
(near Merry Hill shopping centre)
✪ 12-11; 12-10.30 Sun
☎ (01384) 78293
Batham Mild, Best Bitter, XXX Ⓗ
Batham's Brewery tap has a number of rooms, including a small, but lively front bar, a long back room and an award-winning lounge which was created by knocking a small snug through into the adjacent former butcher's shop from which the pub gets its nickname. The Shakespearean quotation on the front of the pub could not be more apt. Hearty lunchtime snacks include proper pork pies.
⚒☻☺⚑♣P

Waterfront ⊘
6-7 Level Street, DY5 1XE
(next to Merry Hill shopping centre)
✪ 10-11; 12-10.30 Sun
☎ (01384) 262096
Banks's Original, Bitter; Courage Directors; Shepherd Neame Spitfire; Theakston Best Bitter Ⓗ
Situated on the bank of the Dudley No. 1 Canal, this welcoming Wetherspoon's is right at the heart of the Waterfront complex. It is popular with office workers weekday lunchtimes and as a pre-club gathering point in the evening, when it can get very busy. The standard Wetherspoon's food is always available and can be ordered by fax (01384 263488). The famous Delph Locks are just a short stroll away. Q◑☺⚑

Pear Tree Cottage
Pear Tree Lane, WS8 7NF
✪ 12-11; 12-10.30 Sun
☎ (01543) 454786
Greene King Old Speckled Hen; guest beers Ⓗ
Recently taken over by David and Mary Grieve, the Pear Tree has been refurbished to provide a welcoming, modern but well decorated pub, boasting a good collection of old local photographs and original leaded windows. A comfortable through room provides a pool table and a dartboard in regular use, with local league matches most Monday evenings. A quiz on Tuesday evening completes the fun. No meals are served Wednesday evening or Sunday.
☺◑♣P

Royal Oak ⊘
68 Chester Road, WS8 6DU (on A452)
✪ 12-3 (3.30 Sat), 6-11; 12-3.30, 7-10.30 Sun
☎ (01543) 452089
Ansells Mild, Best Bitter; Greene King Abbot; Tetley Bitter, Burton Ale; guest beer Ⓗ
This large, roadside pub built in 1937 and decorated in an Art Deco style, is known locally as the Middle Oak. The pub has a pleasant, friendly bar and a comfortable, well decorated lounge, alongside a no-smoking dining room, renowned for its good quality and reasonably-priced food. Regular quiz nights are held on Wednesday. Guest beers are normally sourced from local breweries. No evening meals are served Sunday.
Q☺◑⚑☺♣P

Boat Inn
222 Hampton Lane, B91 2TJ
✪ 11.30-11; 12-10.30 Sun
☎ (0121) 704 0474
Courage Directors; Tetley Bitter; guest beers Ⓗ
Traditional, popular local, a Miller's Kitchen pub with individual character, which is an enthusiastic supporter of real ale. The single large wood-panelled lounge is divided into discrete sections; the large family dining area caters well for children. Local CAMRA Pub of the Year 2001 and joint winner 2002, it is situated close to the Grand Union Canal and is ideal for boaters. An annual beer festival is held in early summer; regular theme nights and special promotions are an added attraction. ☺◑☺♣P

COVENTRY

Caludon Inn
St Austell Road, Wyken, CV2 5AF
(½ mile from A4600, Ansty road)
☼ 12-3, 6-11; 12-3, 7-10.30 Sun
☎ (024) 7645 3669
Ansells Best Bitter; guest beers ℍ
This friendly estate pub comprises two rooms and fields darts and dominoes teams. Home-made steak pies are a speciality here; no meals are served on Sunday evening. Quizzes are staged on Wednesday and Sunday evenings. Q❀◑ ⊟♣P

Craven Arms
58 Craven Street, Chapelfields, CV5 8DW
(1 mile W of city centre, off B4106)
☼ 11 (4 Tue)-11; 12-4, 7-10.30 Sun
☎ (024) 7671 5308
Flowers Original; Hook Norton Best Bitter; Taylor Landlord ℍ
Popular community pub run by friendly bar staff in the old watch-making district of the city where some of the buildings retain their original 'top shops'. The area was featured in a Time Team TV programme. Live entertainment is provided on Sunday evening. There is a welcoming fire in winter and barbecues are held on the patio in summer. Pool and darts are played in the games area. ♨❀◑♣

Farmhouse ⊘
215 Earlsdon Avenue, CV5 6HB
(300 yds from Canley Station level crossing)
☼ 11-11; 12-10.30 Sun
☎ (024) 7671 4332
Hardys & Hansons Bitter, seasonal beers ℍ
Coventry's only Hardys & Hansons' house, this is a large open-plan pub providing a restaurant area on one side and a drinking area with comfortable seating, pool table, games machines and TV on the other. A monthly changing beer from the brewery at Kimberley is always available. Food is served from opening until 9pm (10pm Fri and Sat). A children's play area is in the garden. It can be busy when the funfair or circus sets up on the adjacent Hearsall Common.
❀◑&≠(Canley) P

Gatehouse Tavern
46 Hill Street, CV1 4AN (near Belgrade Theatre)
☼ 11-3; 11-11 Thu-Sat; 12-10.30 Sun
☎ (024) 7663 0140
Draught Bass; Fuller's London Pride; guest beer ℍ
A Guide regular since it was rebuilt by the landlord from being a semi-derelict former mill gatehouse. The building now features stained glass windows depicting six nations rugby, giving a clue to the landlord's passion. A large garden has been created, which is unusual in the city centre. Guest beers are normally from the local Church End Brewery. Meals are served Monday–Saturday. ❀◑

Malt Shovel
93-95 Spon End, CV1 3HF
(on B4101, off inner ring road at jct 7)
☼ 12 (4 Mon & Tue)-11; 12-10.30 Sun
☎ (024) 7622 0204
Donnington SBA; Tetley Bitter; guest beers ℍ
One of the oldest pubs in Coventry, dating from 1620, a single bar serves three drinking areas, combining both traditional and

cosmopolitan elements; the paintings are the landlord's own work. Outside is a pleasant patio for summer drinking. A large tent, with its own bar, accessed through the pub, hosts live music every Friday and Saturday evening. Filling Sunday lunches are served but no other meals. Up to three guest beers, often from Church End, are usually available. ♨❀P

Nursery Tavern
38-39 Lord Street, Chapelfields, CV5 8DA
(1 mile W of centre, off Allesley Old Road)
☼ 11-11; 12-10.30 Sun
☎ (024) 7667 4530
Banks's Original; Courage Best Bitter; John Smith's Bitter; guest beers ℍ
Set in an historic watch-making quarter, this is a thriving community local where the hosts have recently celebrated 10 years in charge. Of the three rooms, two are served by a central bar; the third room at the rear is quieter, welcomes families and is used for traditional games. The pub organises regular social events and runs enthusiastic Rugby Union and Formula One supporters' clubs. Beer festivals are held in June and December. Biddenden cider is stocked. Q❧❀◑♣●

Old Windmill
22-23 Spon Street, CV1 3BA
☼ 11-11; 12-3, 7-10.30 Sun
☎ (024) 7625 2183
Banks's Bitter; Courage Directors; Greene King Old Speckled Hen; Theakston Old Peculier; Wychwood Hobgoblin; guest beers ℍ
Welcoming, medieval, multi-roomed pub at the entertainment end of the town centre, with a flagged floor and a large fireplace. The back room, formerly the brewery, retains its old brewing vessel. It offers a home-cooked lunchtime menu with options suitable for vegetarians and vegans. Popular with the local folk scene, regular music evenings are a feature. ♨❧◑≠♣¼

Rose & Woodbine
40 North Street, CV2 3FW (near football ground)
☼ 12-4, 7-11; 12-11 Fri & Sat; 12-5, 7-10.30 Sun
☎ (024) 7645 1480
Ansells Mild; Draught Bass; M&B Brew XI; Tetley Bitter ℍ
Friendly, unpretentious Victorian local on a residential street corner about one and a half miles north-east of the city centre. Inside is a large L-shaped lounge, and a bar/games room with pool tables. The pub fields darts, pool and dominoes teams, while the local homing pigeon society's hut stands next to the garden. Near Coventry City Football Club, the pub is popular on match days. It is one of Coventry's few regular outlets for real mild. ❀◑♣

Royal Oak
22 Earlsdon Street, Earlsdon, CV5 6EJ
☼ 5-11; 12-3, 7-10.30 Sun
☎ (024) 7667 4140
Ansells Mild; Draught Bass; Tetley Bitter; guest beers ℍ
Busy pub, run by the same licensee for 10 years, which attracts a mixed clientele. The front rooms have a convivial atmosphere and boast a bar top and large clock fashioned from slate. Table service, a rare feature in the area, is available during busy

WEST MIDLANDS

periods. The patio, which leads to the rear bar, has magnificent hanging baskets and provides a pleasant outdoor drinking area in warm weather. ⚄Q☸

Town Wall Tavern
Bond Street, CV1 4AH (behind Belgrade Theatre)
☕ 11-11; 12-10.30 Sun
☎ (024) 7622 0963
Adnams Bitter, Broadside; Draught Bass; M&B Brew XI; guest beer Ⓗ
Pleasant city-centre pub, conveniently located for thirsty theatregoers and handy for the main shopping area. Its three rooms include a snug which is probably the smallest in the city and is known to all as the 'Donkey Box'. The owner is a baker by profession and supplies a variety of fresh rolls to the pub on a daily basis. Note the front gable that carries the crest of the long-defunct Atkinson's Brewery.
⚄Q☎◑🍴♠

Whitefriars Olde Ale House
114-115 Gosford Street, CV1 5GN
☕ 11-11; 12-10.30 Sun
☎ (024) 7625 1655
Tetley Bitter; guest beers Ⓗ
Historic building (circa 1335), sympathetically renovated and transformed into a true free house. With two (and a bit) rooms downstairs and a labyrinth of smaller rooms upstairs, each floor boasts a roaring fire. Exposed brickwork, beams, flagstone and wood floors, murals and subtle lighting all add to the ambience; daily newspapers are provided. Occasional garden beer festivals and impromptu music sessions add interest. Lunches are served Monday–Saturday. ⚄Q☸◑&

CRADLEY HEATH

Moon Under Water ⊘
164-166 High Street, B64 5HJ
☕ 10-11; 12-10.30 Sun
☎ (01384) 565419
Banks's Original; Courage Directors; Hop Back Summer Lightning; Shepherd Neame Spitfire; Theakston Best Bitter; guest beers Ⓗ
Wetherspoon's shop conversion at the heart of this famous old Black Country town. One large room is decorated in ersatz Victorian/Edwardian style. The familiar JDW range of comestibles is served until 10pm. Several local bus services stop nearby and the railway station is within easy walking distance.
Q☸◑&≠⌕

DARLASTON

Boat
20 Bentley Road South, WS10 8LW
☕ 12-2.30 (3 Sat), 6 (5 Fri; 7 Sat)-11; 12-3, 7-10.30 Sun
☎ (0121) 526 5104
Banks's Original, Bitter; Greene King IPA; guest beers Ⓗ
Very friendly, two-roomed pub next to Bentley Bridge and the Walsall Canal. Increasingly popular, the Boat now sells seven real ales (four guests), and has won the Avebury Taverns award for cask excellence for three successive years. The bar has a TV (not Sky) for sport only. Occasional barbecues are held in the garden. Lunches are served Tuesday–Friday and hot pork sandwiches on Thursday evening and Friday lunchtime. ⚄☸◑♣P

Fallings Heath Tavern
248 Walsall Road, WS10 9SN (on A4038)
☕ 12-3, 7.15-11; 12-2.30 Sun
☎ (0121) 526 3403
Ansells Mild, Best Bitter; guest beers Ⓗ
Three-roomed roadside pub built in 1937 between Walsall and Darlaston; the bar is noted for its pig memorabilia. Popular pub games are played here. A family room adjoins the garden. The seats in the lounge still have service buttons on the back but are no longer in operation – this room is quiet and comfortable. At weekends an additional guest ale is stocked. An off-licence is at the front of the building.
Q☎☸🍴♣P🍴

DUDLEY

Lamp Tavern
116 High Street, DY1 1QP
☕ 12-11; 12-10.30 Sun
☎ (01384) 254129
Batham Mild, Best Bitter, XXX Ⓗ
Do not be fooled by the address of this Black Country boozer. It is situated at the top of Blower's Green Road. It has two contrasting rooms: a no-frills front bar and a quiet, comfy rear lounge. The former Queen's Cross Brewery behind the pub is now used for live music and other functions. Buses bound for Halesowen and Stourbridge stop near the pub or at the top of the road.
☸⇆◑&♣P⌕

HALESOWEN

Hawne Tavern
76 Attwood Street, B63 3UG
☕ 4.30 (12 Sat)-11; 12-10.30 Sun
☎ (0121) 602 2601
Banks's Original, Bitter; Batham Best Bitter; guest beers Ⓗ
A free house since 1991, the inn was taken over by the present owners who attract a real ale following by offering three popular local beers and five ever-changing guests. The landlord also puts on three mini beer festivals every year. This old tavern was once a tiny pub which has absorbed neighbouring cottages to create a sizeable bar, with seating alcoves, TV area, pool table and darts corner, plus a quiet lounge. Lunches are served on Saturday.
⚄☸◑&♣🍴

Somer's Sports & Social Club
The Grange, Grange Hill, B62 0JH
(at A456/B4551 jct)
☕ 12-2.30, 6-11; 12-2, 7-10.30 Sun
☎ (0121) 550 1645
Banks's Original, Bitter; Batham Mild, Bitter; Olde Swan Original; guest beers Ⓗ
A long bar, with an impressive row of handpumps, serves a comfortable drinking area, extending to a large alcove overlooking a bowling green. Up to six guest beers are on tap, and a house beer, Percy's Bostin' Bitter. The club has won CAMRA's national and regional Club of the Year awards. Non-members can gain admission by showing either a CAMRA

485

membership card or this Guide to the steward or his staff; groups of five or more should phone ahead to check for admittance. ☎❀P

Waggon & Horses
21 Stourbridge Road, B63 3TU
(on A458, ¼ mile from bus station)
✪ 12-11; 12-10.30 Sun
☎ (0121) 550 4989
Batham Best Bitter; Enville Ale; Nottingham Extra Pale Ale; guest beers Ⓗ

A long-standing Guide regular, the focus at the Waggon & Horses is firmly on conversation and real ale, with up to 15 beers available at any one time. Do not be surprised to find beers from micro-breweries as far flung as Cornwall or Scotland on sale, alongside some of the more familiar names in the real ale world. Handily situated on the No. 9 bus route, this is a must on any Black Country pub crawl.
Ⓠ♣☺

KINGSWINFORD

Park Tavern
182 Cot Lane, DY6 5QZ (off A4101)
✪ 12-11; 12-3, 7-10.30 Sun
☎ (01384) 287178
Ansells Best Bitter; Draught Bass; Batham Best Bitter; guest beer Ⓗ

This top-notch suburban local is convenient for the Broadfield House Glass Museum. Enjoy the jovial banter in the sporty bar or sup a more peaceful pint in the comfortable lounge or on the terrace. Several buses stop near the pub on their way to Dudley, Stourbridge or Wolverhampton.
❀Ⓠ♣P

KNOWLE

Vaults
St John's Close, B93 0JU
✪ 12-2.30, 5-11; 11-11 Sat; 12-10.30 Sun
☎ (01564) 773656
Ansells Mild; Greene King IPA; Tetley Bitter, Burton Ale; guest beers Ⓗ

This traditional pub, just off the picturesque High Street, was relocated early in 2002 into adjacent premises. It has retained its olde-worlde decor, while benefiting from unobtrusive air conditioning and smoke extraction. One of the few pubs in the area offering a real cider (usually Westons), the guest beer choice is adventurous, often showcasing micro-breweries rarely seen in the area. The pub holds occasional beer festivals and an annual pickled onion competition!
❀Ⓠ&♣☺

LOWER GORNAL

Black Bear
86 Deepdale Lane, DY3 2AE (off A459)
✪ 5-11; 12-4, 7-11 Sat; 12-3.30, 7-10.30 Sun
☎ (01384) 253333
Shepherd Neame Master Brew Bitter; guest beers Ⓗ

Originally an 18th-century farmhouse, this hillside local now finds itself surrounded by a brand spanking new housing estate. Its decor has the individual character that comes from gradual evolution rather than total refurbishment. Usually three guests join the one regular beer on tap. The

10-minute ascent from Lower Gornal bus station can be broken by calling in at the Fountain and the Old Bull's Head (see below). ⚶♣♣

Five Ways
Himley Road, DY3 2PZ (at A4175/B4176 jct)
✪ 12-11; 12-10.30 Sun
☎ (01384) 252968
Batham Best Bitter; Highgate Dark; Holden's Bitter; guest beer Ⓗ

Welcoming roadside hostelry on the outskirts of Dudley offering good ale and wholesome home-cooked weekday lunches. The plush interior has the appearance of two rooms knocked into one J-shaped area. Major sporting events can be viewed on a large-screen TV. It is an easy walk from Lower Gornal bus station.
❀Ⓠ♣P

Fountain
8 Temple Street, DY3 2PE (off A459)
✪ 12-11; 12-10.30 Sun
☎ (01384) 242777
Enville Ale; Everards Tiger; Holden's Golden Glow, Special; Hook Norton Old Hooky; guest beers Ⓗ

Vibrant free house just 'up the bonk' from Gornal Wood bus station and round the corner from the Old Bull's Head (see below). Up to half a dozen guest beers, two traditional ciders, Czech Budweiser and Hoegaarden Cloudy Wheat Beer complete a formidable draught range. A small selection of Belgian bottled ales is also stocked. A recent extension has added a new dining room and kitchen, attracting increasing numbers of diners to local CAMRA's Pub of the Year 2002 and 2003; no evening meals are served Sunday.
❀Ⓠ▷♣☺✖

Old Bull's Head
1 Redhall Road, DY3 2NU (off B4175)
✪ 4 (12 Sat)-11; 12-10.30 Sun
☎ (01384) 231616 website: www.oldbullshead.co.uk
Banks's Original, Bitter; guest beers Ⓗ

Imposing Victorian pub, two minutes' climb from Lower Gornal bus station. A spacious front bar has been extended to the left, forming a raised area for non-smokers, when not being used as a stage on music nights. There is a games-oriented room at the rear to the right. The former Bradley's Tower Brewery, with some old equipment still intact, rises behind the pub. The No. 541 Dudley–Wolverhampton bus stops right outside.
⚶❀Ⓠ♣P✖

Miners Arms
Ruiton Street, DY3 2EG (off B4175)
✪ 4 (12 Fri & Sat)-11; 12-10.30 Sun
☎ (01902) 882238
Holden's Mild, Ⓟ Bitter, Special, seasonal beers; guest beers Ⓗ

Friendly, back-street watering-hole at the bottom of the steep hill between Upper and Lower Gornal. It has one L-shaped room. Alongside an extensive selection from Holden's own range, there is a guest beer or two and Knights traditional cider. Food is not generally available, but snacks, such as hot pork sandwiches appear occasionally. The pub is served by the Nos. 257 and 541 bus routes.
❀♣☺

NETHERTON

Old Swan ☆
89 Halesowen Road, DY2 9PY (on A459)
🕐 11-11; 12-4, 7-10.30 Sun
☎ (01384) 253075
Olde Swan Original, Dark Swan, Entire, Bumblehole, seasonal beers Ⓗ

Characterful brewery tap on the main road between Dudley and Old Hill. The bar retains its unspoilt atmosphere and the cosy snug, with its real fire, is enlivened by the quick-witted banter of the regulars. The outstanding restaurant offers Black Country delicacies and a wider-ranging à la carte choice (under-14s are not admitted; booking is advisable particularly at weekends). The upstairs function room is used extensively, particularly at Christmas, when the seasonal fare is excellent.
🏚Q❀⊕Ⓓ➡☕P

PELSALL

Old Bush
Walsall Road, WS3 4BP (opp. Pelsall Common)
🕐 12-11; 12-10.30 Sun
☎ (01922) 423690
Wells Bombardier; guest beer Ⓗ

This lively pub benefits from pleasant views over Pelsall Common. The base for many activities including a golf society, two football teams and folk music, the interior consists of a split-level lounge and a bar area. Food is available throughout the day. A small patio at the rear of the pub can be used by drinkers in summer. ❀⊕ⒹP

SEDGLEY

Beacon Hotel ☆
129 Bilston Street, DY3 1JE (on A463)
🕐 12-2.30, 5.30-10.45 (11 Fri); 12-3, 6-11 Sat; 12-3, 7-10.30 Sun
☎ (01902) 883380
Sarah Hughes Pale Amber, Sedgley Surprise, Dark Ruby, Snow Flake; guest beers Ⓗ

Authentically restored Victorian brewery tap, comprising four varied rooms. Families with children are well catered for in their own room and an outdoor play area. A snob-screened island bar dispenses one or two guest beers as well as the full Sarah Hughes range. The No. 545 bus from Dudley to Wolverhampton stops right outside, while the more frequent No. 558 stops in the town centre, just a short walk away. Q➢❀♣P

SHELFIELD

Four Crosses
11 Green Lane, WS4 1RN (off A461)
🕐 12-11; 12-3, 7-10.30 Sun
☎ (01922) 682518
Banks's Original, Bitter; Ⓟ **guest beers** Ⓗ

Imposing, detached pub over 200 years old; part of the building was once a blacksmith's. On entering, note the mosaic flooring and stained glass, remnants of a bygone age. The traditional saloon bar is warmed by a coal fire. The guest beers are dispensed in the quieter, comfortable lounge. It is the nearest thing to a good old basic boozer in the area. Children, accompanied by adults, may use the passageway. 🏚Q➢❀Ⓓ♣P

SHIRLEY

Bernie's Real Ale Off-Licence
266 Cranmore Boulevard, B90 4PX
🕐 12-2 (not Mon), 5.30-10 (9.30 Fri); 11-3, 5-9.30 Sat; 12-2, 7-9.30 Sun
☎ (0121) 744 2827
Beer range varies Ⓗ/Ⓟ

Bernie's is almost an institution in the eyes of Solihull's real ale drinkers, 20 years in this Guide. It is the place to go to try beers from micro-breweries, always served on top form. A 'try before you buy' system operates and the welcome is as high in quality as the beer. If you are looking for a real ale pub in Shirley, try the Red Lion in Stratford Road.

SHORT HEATH

Duke of Cambridge
82 Coltham Road, WV12 5QD
🕐 12-3.30, 7-11; 12-3.30, 7-10.30 Sun
☎ (01922) 408895
Draught Bass; Greene King Old Speckled Hen; Ⓗ **Highgate Dark;** Ⓟ **Taylor Landlord; guest beers** Ⓗ

Family-run free house, originally a 17th-century farm cottage, it has been a pub since the 1820s. The public bar is warmed by a wood-burning stove and displays model commercial vehicles. The lounge is split into two, with an aquarium in the dividing wall and original beams exposed in the front hall. Both bar and lounge have electronic air cleaners. The large family room houses pool and bar football tables. Filled rolls are sold at lunchtime.
🏚Q➢Ⓓ♣P

SOLIHULL

Saddlers Arms ✓
Warwick Road, B91 3DX
🕐 11-11.30 (12.30am Thu-Sat); 12-10.30 Sun
☎ (0121) 711 8001
Adnams Broadside; Young's Bitter; guest beer Ⓗ

Lively, L-shaped town-centre pub, popular for TV sport. On the site of the oldest pub in Solihull (circa 1860), it was substantially rebuilt in the 1920s. Recently sympathetically refurbished in traditional style, it bears wood panelling throughout. It has plenty of comfortable seating and a no-smoking area at the far end of the bar (note, the no-smoking rule is not strictly adhered to on weekend evenings). A patio area by the front doors overlooks Warwick Road.
❀⊕Ⓓ🚻➡☕

STOURBRIDGE

Hogshead ✓
21-26 Foster Street, DY8 1EL
(off ring road, near bus and rail stations)
🕐 12-11; 12-10.30 Sun
☎ (01384) 370140
Boddingtons Bitter; Caledonian Deuchars IPA; Enville White; Hook Norton Old Hooky; guest beers Ⓗ

Formerly a newspaper office, this spacious, single room has a long bar, where various seating areas on two levels add character. Televised sporting events are shown on a large screen. Weekly quizzes carry a cash prize. The cider range varies, with usually a choice of two available. A well-priced menu includes adventurous specials as well as standard Hogshead fare. The outside tables and seating are in a pedestrianised area, by

the ring road, with subway access to the rail and bus stations.
♿◑▶ &≒(Town) ●⚬

Plough & Harrow
107 Worcester Street, DY8 1AX
(at Heath Lane jct of B4186)
✪ 12-2.30, 6-11; 12-11 Sat; 12-3.30, 7-10.30 Sun
☎ (01384) 397218
Enville White; Greene King IPA; Marston's Pedigree; guest beers Ⓗ
This friendly pub was given local CAMRA's Pub of the Year award in 2002. It always has a guest ale on tap. The single room is served from a U-shaped bar. Meals are available Wednesday–Saturday and Sunday lunchtime (booking is advisable at weekends). The pub is situated opposite the popular Mary Stevens Park, but be warned, the park's car park is locked in the evenings. The well-kept garden is accessed through the pub.
♨Q☸◑▶

Royal Exchange
75 Enville Street, DY8 1XW (on A458)
✪ 1 (12 Sat & summer)-11; 12-10.30 Sun
☎ (01384) 396726
Batham Mild, Best Bitter, seasonal beers Ⓗ
Popular pub in the Batham's estate, with a lively bar and a small lounge, plus a large paved patio area, all accessed from a narrow passageway. The upstairs room is not normally open, but is available for private hire. This terraced pub does not have its own car park but there is a public car park opposite. Snacks are usually available.
Q☸⊞♣

Shrubbery Cottage
28 Heath Lane, Oldswinford, DY8 1RQ
(on B4186, ¼ mile W of A491)
✪ 2 (12 Fri & Sat)-11; 12-3, 7-10.30
(12-10.30 summer) Sun
☎ (01384) 377598
Holden's Mild, Bitter, Special, seasonal beers Ⓗ
This regular Guide entry remains dedicated to good ale and conversation; low level background music replaced a juke box many years ago. There is no dartboard to detract from the friendly atmosphere, although Sky TV is switched on for major sporting events, particularly golf tournaments, as the landlord is a fanatic (note the memorabilia). Quizzes are held on a regular basis, usually on a Sunday evening.
Q☸≒ (Junction) P

Bishop Vesey ✔
63 Boldmere Road, Boldmere, B73 5UY
(in central shopping area)
✪ 10-11; 12-10.30 Sun
☎ (0121) 355 5077
Courage Directors; Greene King Abbot; Shepherd Neame Spitfire; Theakston Best Bitter; guest beers Ⓗ
Named after Sutton Coldfield's benefactor, Bishop Vesey (hence the pulpit feature in the bar area), this Wetherspoon's, previously a camping and outdoor shop, offers friendly and efficient service. The usual open-plan layout and upstairs seating are supplemented by a cosy, book-lined conservatory at the far end of the bar, leading to a patio area with seating.

Children are allowed in the no-smoking area from 10–5. A good, changing selection of guest beers is stocked.
Q☸◑▶ &≒(Wylde Green) ⚬

Duke Inn
Duke Street, Maney, B72 1RJ
✪ 11-11.30; 12-10.30 Sun
☎ (0121) 355 1767
Ansells Mild, Best Bitter; Draught Bass; Tetley Bitter, Burton Ale Ⓗ
Traditional, friendly and very well-run local, tucked away off the busy Birmingham Road. In addition to a large following of regulars, it attracts a number of visitors. The bar has Sky TV and a darts area; a back room is served from a hatch in the passage at the side of the bar. Regular quizzes are held. The garden is popular in summer. Filled baguettes are served at lunchtime in this refuge from the many modern and themed pubs in the area. **Q☸⊞≒♣P**

Laurel Wines
63 Westwood Road, B73 6UP
✪ 3 (12 Sat)-10.30; 12-2, 7-10 Sun
☎ (0121) 353 0399
Beer range varies Ⓖ
This well-frequented real ale off-licence offers a constantly-changing range of beers. Sample tasting of cask beers is encouraged. With an extensive range of British and continental bottled beer, wines and spirits, it offers something for everyone.

Port 'n' Ale
178 Horseley Heath, DY4 7DS (on A461)
✪ 12-3, 5-11; 12-11 Fri & Sat; 12-4.30, 7-10.30 Sun
Hop Back Summer Lightning; RCH Pitchfork; guest beers Ⓗ
Genuine free house on the main West Bromwich–Dudley road, halfway between Great Bridge bus station and Dudley Port railway station. Up to six real ales are generally available, as well as two traditional ciders. The pub has two rooms, the larger of which is divided by a glass screen. The No. 74 bus from Birmingham or Dudley stops nearby.
☸⊞≒ (Dudley Port) ●P

Rising Sun
116 Horseley Road, DY4 7NH (off A461)
✪ 12-3, 5-11; 12-3, 7-10.30 Sun
☎ (0121) 530 2308
Banks's Original; Oakham JHB; guest beers Ⓗ
Imposing Victorian hostelry, comprising two high-ceilinged rooms. The bar, on the right, is full of pictures of local sporting heroes, while the comfortable lounge boasts two open fires. The rear courtyard has become an annual venue for the Mikron Theatre Company, and charitable events take place throughout the year. It keeps four guest ales, often from micros, and two draught ciders. Great Bridge bus station is a 10-minute walk and Dudley Port Station is a mile away. **♨☸◑⊞♣●⊟**

Waggon & Horses
131 Toll End Road, DY4 0ET (on A461)
✪ 5 (12 Fri & Sat)-11; 12-3.30, 7-10.30 Sun
☎ (0121) 502 6453
Banks's Hanson's Mild; Olde Swan Entire; Worthington's Bitter; guest beers Ⓗ

Thriving mock-Tudor house, encompassing a spacious public bar to the left of the front door and a comfortable lounge to the right. An attractively landscaped back garden is used for summer barbecues; no food is available at other times. The regular beers are joined by up to five guest ales, often from micro-breweries. The pub is served by Nos. 311, 312 and 313 buses and is less than a mile from Wednesbury Parkway metro stop. Cider is stocked in summer. ⌂🏠♣♦

TIVIDALE

Barley Mow
City Road, B69 1QS (off A4123)
🕐 4 (12 Fri & Sat)-11; 12-3, 7-10.30 Sun
☎ (01384) 254623
Ansells Mild; Tetley Bitter; guest beers Ⓗ
Friendly, three-roomed pub, comprising a bar, cosy lounge and restaurant. The latter is designated no-smoking and is open 6–9 Tuesday–Thursday and from 7pm Friday–Sunday. Children under 12 are not normally admitted to the restaurant, but a Sunday lunchtime carvery is open to all the family. In addition to the regular beers, two guest beers and Rich's medium cider are served. ⌂🏠♣♦P

UPPER GORNAL

Britannia Inn
109 Kent Street, DY3 1UX (on A459)
🕐 12-3 (4 Fri), 7-11; 12-11 Sat; 12-4, 7-10.30 Sun
☎ (01902) 883253
Batham Mild, Best Bitter, XXX Ⓗ
Characterful local on the high road from Dudley to Wolverhampton. Entering through the front door, one passes the recently refitted main lounge via a tile-floored corridor. Off to the right is a brand new TV room, on the left the unspoilt 19th-century tap room, which is now for non-smokers. Straight ahead, the picturesque back yard is a riot of flowers in summer. The No. 558 bus stops close by. ⌂🏠✄

Jolly Crispin
Clarence Street, DY3 1UL (on A459)
🕐 11-11; 12-10.30 Sun
☎ (01902) 672220 website: www.jollycrispin.co.uk
Wells Bombardier; guest beers Ⓗ
Originally a cobbler's shop in the 1700s, this genuine free house, on the No. 558 bus route, lies at the Sedgley end of Upper Gornal. Up to nine guest ales grace the bars, along with 15 fruit wines. The pub held its first beer festival in January 2003, which will become a regular event. The lunchtime food trade (Mon–Sat) is being developed, along with a range of light snacks on Sunday evening. Sadly, the welcoming coal fires have recently been snuffed out. 🏠♣♦P

WALSALL

Tap & Spile
5 John Street, WS2 8AF
(near magistrates' court, off B4210)
🕐 12-3, 5.30-11; 11-11 Fri & Sat; 12-3, 7-10.30 Sun
☎ (01922) 627660
Wells Eagle; guest beers Ⓗ
Welcoming, Victorian, two-roomed local, known as the Pretty Bricks, due to the tiled frontage. Meals of good value and quality

are served daily at lunchtime and Tuesday–Saturday evenings. Usually seven guest beers are on offer. A quiz is held on Wednesday evening; the pub also hosts curry nights. An upstairs function room is available for hire. ⌂Q🏠♣♦

Victoria
23 Lower Rushall Street, WS1 2AA
(off A34, by Safeway)
🕐 12-11; 12-3, 7.30-10.30 Sun
☎ (01922) 725848
Brains SA; Everards Tiger; Greene King IPA, Old Speckled Hen; Taylor Dark Mild; guest beer Ⓗ
This comfortable, two-roomed traditional ale house originally dates from 1800 but was rebuilt in 1901, when the Tower Brewery was added (now a private residence). Up to 10 cask beers on tap include a mild. Known locally as Katz, it is used regularly by the friendly locals. There is a small function room upstairs. ⌂🏠♣♦

Walsall Arms
17 Bank Street, WS1 2EP (behind Royal Hotel)
🕐 12-3, 6-11; 12-5, 7-10.30 Sun
☎ (01922) 626660
Mansfield Dark Mild, Cask Ale; Marston's Bitter, Pedigree; guest beers Ⓗ
Friendly, traditional drinkers' pub without the distraction of music in the background. It has an attractive saloon bar with tiled floor and a smaller, more intimate public bar. A particular feature in this local is the excellent and popular skittle alley. Although it is a little way from the shopping area, it is easily accessible from the Birmingham to Walsall main bus route. Q♣♦

Walsall Cricket Club
Gorway Road, WS1 3BE
(off A34, by college campus)
🕐 7.30 (12 Sat)-11; 12-11 (closed winter afternoon) Sun
☎ (01922) 622094
website: www.walsallcricketclub.com
Adnams Bitter; Banks's Original; Marston's Bitter; guest beers Ⓗ
Established in 1830, Walsall Cricket Club has occupied this site since 1907. It is affiliated with Walsall Hockey and Bowls Clubs. The comfortable lounge has a friendly, sporting atmosphere. Most of the week the bar is manned by members themselves. Five cricket teams, plus juniors, are supported, and for match days in good weather the lounge is opened on to a patio area, affording a view right across the green. Emphasis is placed on family socials. Admission is by CAMRA membership card. 🏠♣P

White Lion ⊘
150 Sandwell Street, WS1 3EQ
🕐 12-3, 6-11; 12-11 Sat; 12-4.30, 7-10.30 Sun
☎ (01922) 628542
Adnams Bitter; Ansells Mild, Best Bitter; Fuller's London Pride; Tetley Burton Ale; guest beer Ⓗ
Imposing Victorian back-street local, the classic and lively L-shaped bar is probably the best in town. A plush, comfortable lounge caters for the drinker who likes to languish, while the pool room has two tables. It hosts occasional live music and, during summer months, garden barbecues. Caught at the right moment, this pub is an instant party. 🏠♣♦

WARLEY

Plough
George Road, Oldbury, B68 9LN (off A4123)
☼ 12-3.30, 5.30-11; 12-11 Fri & Sat; 12-10.30 Sun
☎ (0121) 552 3822
Adnams Bitter; Banks's Original; M&B Mild; guest beer Ⓗ

This community pub, originally an 18th-century farmhouse, is committed to real ale. Its lively bar focuses on pub games and widescreen TV sport. The lounge divides into four distinct cosy drinking areas on different levels. The No. 128 Birmingham–Blackheath bus stops outside and the more frequent No. 126 Birmingham–Wolverhampton service stops nearby on the main road (A4123). ⍝P

WEDNESBURY

Bellweather
3-4 Walsall Street, WS10 9BZ
☼ 10-11; 12-10.30 Sun
☎ (0121) 502 6404
Banks's Bitter; Greene King Abbot; Hop Back Summer Lightning; Shepherd Neame Spitfire; guest beers Ⓗ

Typical, purpose-built Wetherspoon's town pub. Around the walls are various framed prints depicting the local history of Wednesbury, including past dignitaries and local heroes from Saxon times, through the English Civil War and American Civil War up until recent times. The guest beers always include at least two from Walsall's Highgate Brewery. There is a no-smoking family area where children, accompanied by an adult, can eat until 5pm.
⍟◑ ⊖ (Great Western) ⌿

Old Blue Ball
19 Hall End Road, WS10 9ED
☼ 12-3, 5-11; 12-11 Fri; 11.15-5, 7-11 Sat; 7-10.30 Sun
☎ (0121) 556 0197
Draught Bass; Everards Original; Ⓗ **Highgate Dark;** Ⓟ **guest beers** Ⓗ

Three rooms are joined by a central corridor: first on the right is the small front bar where a row of four handpumps is immediately visible. From the ceiling hang mugs, toby jugs and chamber pots. Brewery mirrors adorn one wall and drinks miniatures feature behind the bar. A serving-hatch opens into the corridor, where you can find a short history of Everards Brewery. On the left is the large family room and on the right, the cosy snug with just three tables. Q⍥⍟⍝♣⎗

WEDNESFIELD

Pyle Cock
Rookery Street, WV11 1UN
(on old Wolverhampton-Wednesfield road)
☼ 10.30-11; 12-10.30 Sun
☎ (01902) 732125
Banks's Original, Bitter; guest beer Ⓗ

A splendid rare survivor, this circa 1867 unspoilt pub has been given local listed status. Its three rooms are reached via the entrance corridor; the traditional public bar boasts wooden settle backs. The small smoke room and rear lounge are served by a hatchway in the corridor. A guest beer is now stocked and you can expect to be drawn into conversation. On a showcase

bus route from the city, frequent services make it easy to visit by public transport.
⍟⍝P

Vine ☆
35 Lichfield Road, WV11 1TN
(over canal bridge at end of High St)
☼ 11-3, 7-11; 12-3 (closed eve) Sun
☎ (01902) 733529
Flowers IPA; guest beers Ⓗ

Built in 1938, the Vine is a rare example of its type that has seen very little alteration. This has been recognised by its recent Grade II listing and inclusion in CAMRA's National Inventory. Its three rooms, each with a coal fire, are a delight to sit in and enjoy an excellent pint in this friendly local. The showcase bus route from the city stops frequently outside, making it easy to visit without a car. The real cider is Westons. ⍫Q⍟⍝♣P

WEST BROMWICH

Old Crown
56 Sandwell Street, B70 8TJ
(near A41/A4031 jct)
☼ 12-3.30, 5-11; 12-11 Sat; 12-3.30, 7-10.30 Sun
☎ (0121) 525 4600
Beer range varies Ⓗ

Cosy free house about 10 minutes' walk from the town centre, dispensing guest ales and home-made baltis to an enthusiastic audience. Popular with workers at lunchtime, it is also busy in the evening. No food is served Saturday or Sunday. Bus No. 74 Birmingham–Dudley and No. 79 to Wolverhampton, among others, stop on the nearby High Street.
◑ ⊖ (Dartmouth St)

Wheatsheaf
379 High Street, B70 9QW
☼ 11-11; 12-10.30 Sun
☎ (0121) 553 4221
Holden's Mild, Ⓟ **Bitter;** Ⓟ/Ⓗ **Golden Glow, Special;** Ⓟ **seasonal beers; guest beers** Ⓗ

Superb Black Country local at the heart of the Carter's Green concentration of pubs, restaurants, fast food outlets and, lately, even a casino. The pub has a bustling front bar and a more sedate extended lounge at the back. Two guests compete with the excellent range of Holden's beers for pump space. Lunchtime food, including local speciality, grey peas and bacon, is served daily. See the Old Crown for bus services.
⍟◑⍝⊖ (Dartmouth St/Dudley St) ♣⎗

WILLENHALL

Falcon
77 Gomer Street West, WV13 2NR
(off B4464, behind flats)
☼ 12-11; 12-10.30 Sun
☎ (01902) 633378
Greene King Abbot; Olde Swan Dark Swan; RCH PG Steam, Pitchfork; guest beers Ⓗ

Spacious, two-roomed 1930s pub situated just off Willenhall town centre. This popular pub can get very busy, which is not surprising considering it has up to 10 cask ales on at any time. The beers are listed on a blackboard in the lounge. This friendly, welcoming hostelry is well used by the local community.
Q⍟⍝♣⌿⎗

Robin Hood
54 The Crescent, WV13 2QR
(off B4464, near McDonald's)
🕐 12-3; 5 (7 Sat)-11; 12-3, 7-10.30 Sun
☎ (01902) 608006
Tetley Bitter, Burton Ale; guest beers Ⓗ
Next to the railway line, the Robin Hood has a single, comfortable, U-shaped room. Regulars support the many charity nights and events that take place during the year. A local archery club meets Saturday and Sunday mornings after practising in the adjacent field. Usually two guest beers are available. A quiz is held every other Monday evening. Currently, drinking is possible in a paved area by the car park, but a garden is due to open soon. ✿♣P

WOLLASTON

Foresters Arms
Bridgnorth Road, DY8 3PL
(on A458 towards Bridgnorth)
🕐 12-3, 6-11; 12-11 Sat; 12-3, 7-10.30 Sun
☎ (01384) 394476
Draught Bass; Enville Ale; guest beers Ⓗ
This friendly local is well known for its good value food. The T-shaped room conveniently provides a no-smoking area for diners (no meals Sun eve). As well as being home to the Foresters Golf Society, the pub holds regular quizzes, usually on the first Sunday of the month. Situated at the edge of the village, on the road towards Bridgnorth, it is convenient for Stourbridge Rugby Club. ♨✿ⓓP

Unicorn
145 Bridgnorth Road, DY8 3NX (on A458)
🕐 12-11; 12-4, 7-10.30 Sun
☎ (01384) 394823
Batham Mild, Best Bitter, seasonal beers Ⓗ
This former brewhouse was purchased by Batham's some 10 years ago and has earned a reputation for serving one of the best pints in the estate. The old brewhouse remains at the side of the pub but, sadly, will never brew again as costs are prohibitive. The pub itself is a basic two-roomed traditional drinkers' house, popular with all ages. A sandwich may be ordered at most times. The Unicorn is genuinely 'unspoilt by progress'. Q✿ⱿP

WOLVERHAMPTON

Chindit ⊘
113 Merridale Road, WV3 9SE
🕐 12 (later in winter)-11; 12-10.30 Sun
☎ (01902) 425582
Beer range varies Ⓗ
This popular two-roomed local was built after WWII, and named in honour of the soldiers of the South Staffordshire Regiment who served in Burma. The history of the Chindits is displayed on the lounge wall. The pub serves three guest beers, usually from small brewers. Acoustic music nights are staged every Friday and an annual beer festival is held over the first bank holiday in May. Bus Nos. 513 and 543 from the city centre stop outside. ✿Ⱡ♣P

Clarendon Hotel
38 Chapel Ash, WV3 0TN
🕐 11-11; 12-10.30 Sun
☎ (01902) 420587
Banks's Original, Bitter; Marston's Pedigree; guest beers Ⓗ
Prominent Victorian street-corner brewery tap. The unspoilt frontage is matched internally with the smoke room which alone retains its olde-worlde atmosphere. The pub serves a busy office trade, providing breakfast from 8am, lunches and takeaways. A large-screen TV shows major football games. ⏰ⓓⱾ

Combermere Arms
90 Chapel Ash, WV3 0TY (at A41/A454 jct)
🕐 11-3, 5.30-11; 12-11 Fri & Sat; 12-10.30 Sun
☎ (01902) 421880
Banks's Hanson's Mild, Bitter, Mansfield Cask Ale; guest beer Ⓗ
A vibrant pub in a terrace dating from the late 19th century, the Combermere maintains its appeal with events such as weekly quizzes, occasional music nights and participation in charity events. Seating is shared between three smallish rooms and a covered patio. There is also a small garden. It was named after Viscount Combermere, second in command to Wellington during the 1810 Peninsular War. It is famous for the tree growing in the gents. ♨✿ⓓP

Great Western
Sun Street, WV10 0DJ (off A4124)
🕐 11-11; 12-3, 7-10.30 Sun
☎ (01902) 351090
Batham Bitter; Holden's Mild, Bitter, Golden Glow, Special; guest beer Ⓗ
Built in 1869 on the corner of two terraced streets, opposite the now disused low level railway station, it is the only building from these streets to survive. The original pub has been extended, but in accordance with its listed status. With its speedy service of excellent home-cooked food and quality beers, it attracts a wide range of customers and gets very busy on Wolves match days. Note the railway and football memorabilia. ✿ⓓ≠P

Hogshead ⊘
186 Stafford Street, WV1 1NA
🕐 11-11; 12-10.30 Sun
☎ (01902) 717955
Boddingtons Bitter; Brakspear Bitter; guest beers Ⓗ
City-centre ale house, serving up to 10 cask ales, plus a selection of Belgian beers. Popular with all ages; on Friday and Saturday 18–25s dominate. The pub has two no-smoking areas either side of the entrance. Originally called the Vine, it was built to serve soldiers of the South Staffordshire Regiment, whose drill hall stood behind the pub. After a period as offices, it was reborn as the Hogshead in the mid-1990s. Beers from local Enville and Goldthorn micro-breweries are usually available. ✿ⓓ≠⊖ (St George's) ♠Ⱦ

Homestead
Lodge Road, Oxley, WV10 6TQ
(off A449 at Goodyear island)
🕐 12-2.30 (3 Sat), 6-11; 12-3, 7-10.30 Sun
☎ (01902) 787357
Tetley Bitter; guest beers Ⓗ
Converted from an old farmhouse, this large estate pub has been a consistent Guide entry for over two decades. Throughout this period is has been run by the same family.

The pub consists of a sizeable bar, popular with darts players, and a spacious comfortable lounge. Excellent home-cooked food and two guest beers are added attractions. Bus Nos. 503, 504 and 506 stop on the main Stafford road (ask for the stop after Goodyear island). ❀⇔◑ 🍴♣P

Newhampton
Riches Street, WV6 0DW (off A41)
✪ 11-11; 12-10.30 Sun
☎ (01902) 745773
Courage Best Bitter, Directors; Fuller's London Pride; Marston's Pedigree; Wells Bombardier; guest beer Ⓗ
Outwardly a street-corner local, the pub is Tardis-like inside, with four bars and a function room. The three main bars cater for all sections of the community. The garden boasts a large crown bowling green and a children's play area. Quality home-made food is available; the smoke room becomes non-smoking when meals are served. At busy times the pub can get through three or four guest beers in a session.
♨Q❀◑♣👹

Queen's Arms
Graiseley Row, WV2 4HJ (off A449)
✪ 12-11; 12-10.30 Sun
☎ (01902) 425233
Burtonwood Bitter, Top Hat; guest beer Ⓗ
Small, back-street local in an industrial area. Still known as the Home Brew from when it brewed its own beer (up until the 1960s), it is a rare outlet for Burtonwood beers. It normally stocks two guest ales. Entertainment ranges from darts to karaoke. Despite being knocked into a single room it retains a cosy atmosphere. It is easily reached from the No. 256 bus route along the Penn road (A449). Good value food is served; evening meals finish at 7pm.
❀◑♣P

Royal Oak
7 School Road, Tettenhall Wood, WV6 8EJ
✪ 12-11; 12-10.30 Sun
☎ (01902) 754396
Banks's Original, Bitter Ⓟ
Attractive Grade II listed building in a conservation area, this small pub is over 200 years old. It was runner-up in the national hanging baskets competition 2002. The bar has cable TV for sport, and fields a local league dominoes team. The cosy lounge seats just 12. A large, fenced garden contains a function room, a volleyball/five-a-side pitch and a children's play area; it

hosts summer pig roasts and barbecues. Meals are served 12–2 (all day in summer).
❀◑ 🍴♣👹

Swan (at Compton)
Bridgnorth Road, Compton, WV6 8AE
(on A454)
✪ 11-11; 12-10.30 Sun
☎ (01902) 754736
Banks's Original, Bitter Ⓗ
Grade II listed building dating from 1777, a basic, unspoilt gem in the Compton area of the city. Its traditional bar, with wooden settles and exposed beams, and the L-shaped snug are served by a central servery. The lounge doubles as a games room, with a bar billiards table. Together, they offer a friendly and convivial atmosphere in which to drink excellent beer, now delivered by newly-installed handpulls. Buses stop nearby.
Q❀🍴♣P

Tap & Spile
35 Princess Street, WV1 1HD
✪ 11-11; 12-10.30 Sun
☎ (01902) 713319
Banks's Original, Bitter; guest beers Ⓗ
City-centre pub, comprising three rooms: a narrow bar and two snugs. The bar is dominated by a large-screen TV, and another three TVs around the pub are used to show sports events or music programmes. Very popular with Wolves fans on match days, it also attracts weekend clubbers due to its central location. Food is served weekday lunchtimes and occasionally on Saturday. An enterprising choice of beers is stocked at reasonable prices. It is handy for buses and the metro.
◑♿➔⊖ (St George's) ♣👹

WOODSETTON

Park Inn
George Street, DY1 4LW (off A457)
✪ 12-11; 12-10.30 Sun
☎ (01902) 661279
Holden's Mild, Bitter, Golden Glow, Special, seasonal beers Ⓗ
Lively, family-oriented brewery tap, just off the main Tipton–Sedgley road. Its interior is dominated by a spacious U-shaped bar decorated in a modern style with bare floorboards. Seasonal events have proved popular and the conservatory at the back is available for meetings and functions. There is live entertainment at weekends. The No. 545 bus route passes the pub. ♨❀◑♣P

Fat ale

A judicious labourer would probably always have some ale in his house, and have small beer for the general drink. There is no reason why he should not keep Christmas as well as the farmer; and when he is mowing, reaping, or is at any other hard work, a quart, or three pints, of really good fat ale-a-day is by no means too much.

William Cobbett (1763-1835), *Cottage Economy*, 1822

Low Down on the Low Countries

In the new edition of this popular guide, Tim Webb has travelled through Belgium, the Netherlands and Luxembourg to trackdown all the renowned beers from Trappist, abbey, lambic, ale and wheat beer producers, along with a sidewise look at the behaviour of the big producers. With details on how to get to the countries, where to eat and drink when you've arrived, plus maps and drawings of cafes, this is an indispensible guide for lovers of traditional European beer. £12.99 including postage.

WILTSHIRE

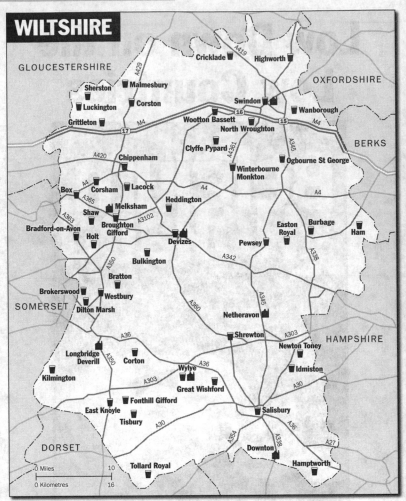

BOX

Quarryman's Arms
Box Hill, SN13 8HN
(in a maze of lanes, ring for directions)
✪ 11-3, 6-11; 11-11 Fri & Sat; 12-10.30 Sun
☎ (01225) 743569
website: www.thequarrymans-arms.co.uk

Butcombe Bitter; Moles Best Bitter; Wadworth 6X; guest beer Ⓗ

Many people get lost trying to find this pub, as it is hidden away in a maze of lanes, but the effort is well worthwhile. The landlord will be happy to give you directions if you ring. The main bar is decorated with maps of the old stone mines that riddle the hill underneath the village. Enjoy the superb views over the Box Valley from the windows of the dining area while you tuck into the excellent food. ♨ ➲ ✿ ⇄ ◑ ▲ ♣ P

BRADFORD-ON-AVON

Beehive
263 Trowbridge Road, BA15 1UA
(next to canal)
✪ 12-2.30, 7-11; 12-3, 7-10.30 Sun
☎ (01225) 863620

Butcombe Bitter; Ⓗ **guest beers** Ⓗ /Ⓖ

Situated close to the Kennet and Avon Canal, this former brothel, now a first class pub, was built in the early 19th century to provide refreshment for the canal trade. The large garden to the rear houses a children's play area and chickens. Five guest beers are served on gravity or from genuine Victorian handpumps. The old Watney's Red Barrel pump on the bar is a talking point. No lunches are served Tuesday or evening meals Sunday. ♨ Q ✿ ◑ ♣ P

Bunch of Grapes
14 Silver Street, BA15 1JY
✪ 12-11; 12-10.30 Sun
☎ (01225) 863877

Smiles Best, IPA; Young's Bitter, Special Ⓗ

This town-centre pub, near the antique shops, is easily recognised by the grapevine growing over the front and the newly-painted pink exterior. A welcoming pub, with wood floors and panelled walls, drinking areas are spread over three levels. Booking is advised for the upstairs restaurant. It can get very busy at times and, as it is not big, it can appear crowded. A rare Young's pub in this area. ✿ ◑ ⇌

BRATTON

Duke
BA13 4RW
🌞 11.30-3, 7-11; 12-3, 7-10.30 Sun
☎ (01380) 830242
Moles Best Bitter; guest beers Ⓗ
Situated in a village at the base of Westbury White Horse, the Duke has won many accolades, including Sunday Roast Pub of the Year and Best Pub Loos. Formerly an Usher's house, it is now affiliated to Moles. Together, the cosy lounge bar/restaurant (possibly becoming totally no-smoking) and a friendly public bar, frequented by locals, cater for two very different types of clientele. The landlord is an excellent chef, producing a varied menu (no food Sun eve).
🏚🚱◑➡🚻♣♠P½

BROKERSWOOD

Kicking Donkey
BA13 4EG (between A36 and A350, near Westbury)
🌞 11.30-2.30 (3 Fri & Sat), 6 (6.30 Fri & Sat)-11 (11.30-11 summer); 12-10.30 Sun
☎ (01373) 823250
Butcombe Bitter; Fuller's London Pride; Wadworth 6X; guest beers Ⓗ
Handsome, but well hidden, 17th-century inn, formerly known as the Yew Tree, replete with exposed beams, brasses and stone flags. The interior is divided into three drinking areas, plus a restaurant serving exceptionally good food. The popular garden caters well, with seating for 200, a children's play area and, in the summer, a bouncy castle. An easy-walking mile away is the Brokerswood Country Park, a family-oriented nature reserve, with camping and caravan sites.
🏚Q🐕🚱◑♠P

BROUGHTON GIFFORD

Bell on the Common
SN12 8LX (2 miles W of Melksham, off B3107)
🌞 11-11; 12-10.30 Sun
☎ (01225) 782309
Wadworth IPA, 6X, seasonal beers Ⓗ
Fine old pub on the edge of the extensive village green. Inside are two contrasting bars: a smart bar, with a copper top, attached to the restaurant; and the public bar, very much a locals' hangout, complete with wooden settles and old tables. A games-cum-family room is next to the public bar. The garden is large and safe for families; in summer boules is played and barbecues are held. The food in both the restaurant and the bars is highly rated.
🏚🐕🚱◑➡♣P

BULKINGTON

Tipsy Toad
High Street, SN10 1SJ OS942583
🌞 12-3, 6-11; 12-3, 7-10.30 Sun
☎ (01380) 828741 website: www.tipsytoad.co.uk
Beer range varies Ⓗ
Village pub, rebuilt after WWI, and more recently refurbished, popular with the small community it serves. A new conservatory, with underfloor heating provides a pleasant dining area (no-smoking), overlooking a small garden. A new skittle alley is now available. This unpretentious, friendly local is keeping pace with the times. As a free house, it has a changing range of three real ales and Black Rat cider. No evening meals are served Sunday.
🚱◑♣♠P

BURBAGE

Three Horseshoes ⊘
Stibb Green, SN8 3AE (off A346 bypass)
🌞 12-2 (not Mon), 6-11; 12-2, 7-10.30 Sun
☎ (01672) 810324
Wadworth IPA, 6X; guest beer Ⓗ
This small, cosy, thatched pub stands on the edge of Savernake Forest. Numerous railway artefacts and pictures decorating the walls add to its traditional character. Good food is served, except on Sunday evening and Monday – try the pies, some of which have unusual fillings.
🏚Q🚱◑➡♣P½

CHIPPENHAM

Old Road Tavern
Old Road, SN15 1JA (near station)
🌞 11-4, 5.45-11; 11-11 Fri & Sat; 12-10.30 Sun
☎ (01249) 652094
Courage Best Bitter; Fuller's London Pride; Greene King Old Speckled Hen; guest beer Ⓗ
Old Road was the original road from Chippenham to Malmesbury; the pub also has a gate on to New Road, leading to an unexpected garden for summer drinking. The Tavern is a true beer drinkers' pub, also offering good value food. A centre for folk and blues music, the Chippenham morris dancers meet here. Regular folk sessions are held on Sunday and gigs are sometimes arranged for Saturday night, but it is not unusual to find impromptu jam sessions almost any time.
🚱◑➡≠♣

CLYFFE PYPARD

Goddard Arms
SN4 7PY OS074769
🌞 12-2.30, 7-11; 11-11 Sat; 12-10.30 Sun
☎ (01793) 731386
Wadworth 6X; guest beers Ⓗ
Possibly one of the oldest pubs in Wiltshire – a Cleeve Inn is listed in the Domesday Book. The village of Cleeve is known nowadays as Clyffe Pypard and the pub, the Goddard Arms. A focus for many local activities, including dog shows and vintage car rallies; the skittle alley often hosts exhibitions from local artists. The two guest beers change frequently and normally come from smaller breweries. The pub offers a varied menu to suit all tastes and en-suite accommodation in two guest rooms.
🏚🚱◑➡♣P

INDEPENDENT BREWERIES

Archers Swindon
Arkells Swindon
Hidden Wylye
Hobden's Longbridge Deverill
Hop Back Downton
Moles Melksham
Stonehenge Netheravon
Wadworth Devizes

CORSHAM

Great Western
21 Pound Pill, SN13 9JA
☼ 11-3 (not Mon), 5.30-11; 12-11 Sat; 12-4,
7-10.30 Sun
☎ (01249) 713838
**Abbey Bellringer; Fuller's London Pride; Wadworth 6X;
Young's Bitter; guest beers** (occasional) ℍ
A typical railway inn, dating from the late
19th century, this popular free house stands
about one mile from Brunel's famous box
tunnel. The two-bar local draws a good mix
of customers of all ages. Tea and coffee are
available in the bar, along with a good
range of food. Corsham is not well known,
but boasts many fine old buildings of local
stone in the mostly pedestrianised High
Street. ♨Q❀◖🍴🍺♣P

Two Pigs
38 Pickwick, SN13 9BU
☼ 7-11; 12-2.30, 7-10.30 Sun
☎ (01249) 712515
Stonehenge Pigswill, Danish Dynamite; guest beers ℍ
On entering this pub you are greeted by a
sign saying that lager drinkers are tolerated,
but not catered for. Essentially one long
room, it does have a very smoky
atmosphere. The pig theme runs
throughout. Background music is played –
blues or jazz – but there is no juke box or
gaming machines. A live band (usually
blues), plays Monday evening. On the old
London–Bath coach road (Pickwick) took the
name of the pub's road (Pickwick) for one of
his best-loved characters. ❀

CORSTON

Radnor Arms
SN16 0HD
☼ 12-3 (not Tue), 5.30-11; 12-11 Sat; 12-10.30 Sun
☎ (01666) 823389
Hook Norton Best Bitter; guest beers ℍ
19th-century village pub between
Malmesbury and the M4. Guest beers
change regularly and usually showcase local
breweries. Black Rat cider is stocked in
summer. An extensive menu includes a hog
roast on bank holiday Mondays. The
Radnor fields a darts team and hosts a quiz
on Mondays; a pool table is available in the
barn in summer. Corston has only a
handful of houses, with the pub as the focal
point; all the buildings tend to be stone, like
the Cotswolds, further north.
♨❀◖🍴♣🍺P

CORTON

Dove
BA12 0SZ
☼ 12-3, 6.30-11; 12-4, 7-10.30 Sun
☎ (01985) 850109 website: www.thedove.co.uk
Butcombe Bitter; Hop Back GFB; guest beer ℍ
Welcoming village pub in the heart of the
Wylye Valley. Facilities include a candlelit
conservatory and a restaurant, where
children are served. The large bar area has a
polished wood floor and an open fire. The
food is excellent, with a varied lunchtime
menu and a more sophisticated evening
choice, using local ingredients where
possible, including game and fish. There is a
large, pleasant garden. Corton is situated on
the Wiltshire Cycleway. ♨Q❀🛏◖🍴P

CRICKLADE

Red Lion
74 High Street, SN6 6DD
☼ 12-11; 12-10.30 Sun
☎ (01793) 750776
Beer range varies ℍ
Friendly, 16th-century ale house, looking to
serve their 1,000th different ale this year.
The pub champions real ale and the
brewer's craft, with up to eight changing
guests from local and micro-brewers. This is
a pub surviving on real ale, with no food
apart from snacks. At the time of survey
there was a competition going on over the
accolade of who is the most miserable
landlord! Local CAMRA Pub of the Year
2003. ♨❀🛏&♣P⅍

DEVIZES

British Lion
9 Estcourt Street, SN10 1SQ
☼ 11-11; 12-10.30 Sun
☎ (01380) 720665
Beer range varies ℍ
Free house on the outskirts of town, that
has been sympathetically refurbished with
wooden floors and seating. The landlord is
committed to real ale, stocking a wide range
of up to eight different beers weekly, from
all over the country, and rarely seen in
Wiltshire. The bar, housing a popular pool
table, is run by friendly staff and attracts
interesting customers. A good selection of
snacks is served. A real gem, it supports the
annual CAMRA beer festival held on the
first Saturday in July. ❀♣🍺P🍽

Hare & Hounds ⊘
Hare & Hounds Street, SN10 1LZ
☼ 11-3, 7-11; 12-3, 7-10.30 Sun
☎ (01380) 723231
Wadworth IPA, 6X, JCB ℍ
For the full flavour of this friendly, back-
street local, see any one of the last umpteen
editions of this Guide. The horseshoe-
shaped bar creates the feel of a two-bar pub.
It is deceptively old – old enough to have
the street named after it. If you want to
know what Wadworth's beers should taste
like, then this is the pub to visit. ♨Q❀◖♣P

DILTON MARSH

Prince of Wales
94 High Street, BA13 4DZ
☼ 12-3 (not Mon or Tue), 7-11; 12-3, 7-10.30 Sun
☎ (01373) 865487
Wadworth 6X; Young's Bitter; guest beers ℍ
Village local where a single bar serves two
drinking areas, plus a small pool table
annexe and a large skittle alley. The pub
participates in local skittles, crib and pool
leagues. In addition, there is a Sunday
evening quiz every week. The factually
incorrect pub sign has featured in a
Japanese pub sign guide! Can you spot the
error? ❀◖≋♣P

EAST KNOYLE

Fox & Hounds
The Green, SP3 6AU (signed from B3089,
1½ miles from A303 jct) OS871313
☼ 11.45-3.30, 6-11; 12-3.30, 7-10.30 Sun
☎ (01747) 830573

Young's Bitter, Special, seasonal beers Ⓗ
Free house leased to Young's, well worth seeking out for the stunning views across the countryside towards Shaftesbury and Gillingham. Popular with walkers and cyclists, in better weather you can sit on the green opposite the pub; in winter enjoy a real fire in the large inglenook. The pub has a good reputation for its varied food menu. Bar billiards can be played here. The cider is supplied by Inch's or Cheddar Valley.
ⓂQ☵❀◑🖰♣♠P✁

EASTON ROYAL

Bruce Arms ☆
Easton Road, Pewsey, SN9 5LR
(on B3087 towards Pewsey)
☀ 12-2.30 (3 Sat), 6-11; 12-3, 7-10.30 Sun
☎ (01672) 810216
Wadworth IPA, 6X; guest beer Ⓗ
This traditional pub, established in the 1840s warrants a listing in CAMRA's National Inventory. Although a fair distance outside the village, it still manages to attract 'locals'. It boasts its own cricket pitch on the opposite side of the road. The large back room features a skittle alley and pool tables, while the front room is more akin to a private living room. The tables and benches are believed to be more than 150 years old.
ⓂQ☵❀♣♠P

FONTHILL GIFFORD

Beckford Arms
SP3 6PX
(midway between Tisbury and Hindon) OS931312
☀ 12-11; 12-10.30 Sun
☎ (01747) 870385
Greene King Abbot; Taylor Landlord; guest beers Ⓗ
Look for the Beckford at a crossroads, deep in this extraordinarily scenic, but little-known, corner of Wiltshire. This fine, 17th-century inn has spacious bars; behind the lounge lie cosy dining areas, leading to the garden room and beyond to quiet tree-shaded lawns. The guest beers are usually sourced from smaller regional breweries. If you plan to eat, it is best to book.
ⓂQ🖰◑🖰♣P

GREAT WISHFORD

Royal Oak
Langford Road, SP2 0PD
(½ mile off A36 at Stoford)
☀ 12-2.30, 6-11 (12-11 summer Sat); 12-10.30 Sun
☎ (01722) 790079
Hop Back GFB; guest beers Ⓗ
Traditional village pub run by Frenchman, Nick Deschamps and his family. Situated in the pleasant Wylye Valley, walks, cycling and fishing can all be enjoyed nearby. Generally, six ales are available, five of which as guests that any festival would be proud of. Alongside the ales are fine wines and excellent food. Each year a small beer festival is staged to coincide with the village celebrations of Oak Apple Day on May 29th. ⓂQ❀🖰◑A♣P✁

GRITTLETON

Neeld Arms
The Street, SN14 6AP
☀ 12-3, 5.30-11; 12-3, 6-10.30 Sun

☎ (01249) 782470 website: www.neeldarms.uk
Brains Buckley's Best Bitter; Brakspear Special; Wadwich 6X; Wychwood Fiddler's Elbow; guest beer (occasional)
17th-century inn set in a beautiful South Cotswold village, popular with locals and visitors, as it is within easy reach of many tourist locations, such as Castle Combe, Lacock and Bath. A good selection of home-made food is offered. The range of real ales is interesting, as most are not usually available in this area. The cosy, single bar is warmed by a welcoming log fire in winter.
ⓂQ❀🖰◑♣P

HAM

Crown & Anchor
SN8 3RB OS331629
☀ 11.30-3 (not Mon), 5-11; 11-11 Sat; 12-10.30 Sun
☎ (01488) 668242
Archers Best Bitter; Wadworth 6X; guest beer Ⓗ
Only just in Wiltshire, this pub is beside the village green. There is a single bar, with a log fire, and a restaurant. It makes a handy stop for walkers on the Wayfarer's path, overnight accommodation is available in three rooms. Evening meals are served Tuesday–Saturday. Ⓜ❀🖰◑♣P

HAMPTWORTH

Cuckoo
SP5 2DU (1 mile from A36, Landford jct)
☀ 11.30-2.30, 6-11; 11.30-11 Sat; 12-10.30 Sun
☎ (01794) 390302
Badger Tanglefoot; Cheriton Pots Ale; Hop Back GFB, Summer Lightning; Wadworth 6X; guest beers Ⓖ
On the edge of the New Forest, this rustic, thatched pub has a genuine and friendly atmosphere. The beers are served on gravity from the ground-floor cellar. Four small bars cater for all and beer, conversation and traditional pub games are the priorities here. The cider is supplied by Thatchers. The large garden has petanque terrains, an area for children and a peaceful section for adults. ⓂQ❀♣♠P✁

HEDDINGTON

Ivy
Stockley Road, SN11 0PL
(2 miles off A4 from Calne)
☀ 12-3, 6.30-11; 12-4, 7-10.30 Sun
☎ (01380) 850276
Wadworth IPA, 6X Ⓖ
Originally three 15th-century cottages, this outstanding thatched village local has evolved to cater for its present customers. On the one hand, it remains a focal point for the village, with the harvest auction and a visit from the Mummers being annual fixtures. On the other hand, its food enjoys an enviable reputation locally (eve meals Thu–Sat). Within a mile of the site of the Battle of Roundway Down (1643) on the North Wessex downs, it is a favourite with hikers. Ⓜ❀◑♣P

HIGHWORTH

Wine Cellar
10 High Street, SN6 7AG
☀ 7 (5.30 Wed & Thu; 1 Fri; 12 Sat)-11; 12-5, 7-10.30 Sun
☎ (01793) 763828

Archers Village, Best Bitter; guest beer Ⓖ
It is well worth visiting this unusual little
pub; follow the steps behind the door next
to the takeaway on the south side of the
market square. The cellar used to be the
kitchen of a house, and extends under the
road. There is a large choice of wine, and 50
or so malt whiskies, plus Black Rat cider, as
well as the beer. A discount is offered to
CAMRA members on production of a valid
membership card.
♣⌫

HOLT

Tollgate Inn
Ham Green, BA14 6PX
(on B3105 between Bradford-on-Avon and Melksham)
✪ 11.30-2.30, 6.30-11; 12-2.30 (closed eve) Sun
☎ (01225) 782326 website: www.tollgateholt.co.uk
Beer range varies Ⓗ
This old village pub is a gem. The range of
four or five ales, which changes every week,
is very imaginative, with a good selection of
local beers and many from smaller brewers
from further afield. The food in both the
upstairs restaurant and the bar is excellent.
The garden overlooks a pretty valley
(although rather spoiled by the Nestlé
factory!). The pub has an upmarket
atmosphere with comfortable sofas in the
bar, but drinkers are very welcome.
🏠❀⌂⌐Ⓓ P

IDMISTON

Earl of Normanton
Tidworth Road, SP4 0AG
✪ 11-3, 6-11; 12-3, 7-10.30 Sun
☎ (01980) 610251
Cheriton Pots Ale, Best Bitter; guest beers Ⓗ
Voted Salisbury CAMRA Pub of the Year
2002, this popular roadside pub boasts an
enviable selection of real ales. Four
handpumps always provide at least one
Cheriton ale as the Earl has strong ties
with the brewery. Triple fff and Hop Back
provide some of the varied guest beers.
The single bar focuses on food, which is
both appetising and good value. There is
a small, pleasant garden, albeit a bit
steep!
🏠Q❀Ⓓ P

KILMINGTON

Red Lion Inn ⊘
BA12 6RP
(on B3092, 2½ miles N of A303 at Mere)
✪ 11.30-2.30, 6.30-11; 12-3, 7-10.30 Sun
☎ (01985) 844263
Butcombe Bitter; Butts Jester; guest beer Ⓗ
The National Trust owns the Red Lion,
originally a 16th-century farmworker's
cottage. It lies on an isolated stretch of
the B3092, near Stourhead Gardens (also
NT). The bar covers the width of the
building, with a flagstone floor and fires
at both ends; a no-smoking area is
designated for customers having lunch.
The attractive gardens afford fine views
of the Wiltshire Downs. The licensee,
who celebrated his 25th anniversary here
in 2003, welcomes all visitors – but
challenge him at shove-ha'penny at your
peril!
🏠Q❀Ⓓ♣P⌫

LACOCK

Bell Inn
The Wharf, SN15 2PQ
✪ 11.30-2.30 (not Mon), 6-11; 11.30-11 Sat;
12-10.30 Sun
☎ (01249) 730308
Wadworth 6X; Wickwar Coopers WPA; guest beers Ⓗ
Free house in a converted 140-year-old
cottage, on the former Wilts & Berks
canal. The line of the long-closed canal is
difficult to trace, but a new Sustrans
cycleway, following the route, is shortly to
open. The pub is in the attractive hamlet of
Bowden Hill, between the National Trust
village of Lacock and a highly thatched
village, Sandy Lane. Renowned for its meals,
the Bell is equally welcoming to drinkers.
❀Ⓓ♿⌐AP⌫

Rising Sun
32 Bowden Hill, SN15 2PP (1 mile E of Lacock)
✪ 12-3, 6-11; 12-5, 7-10.30 Sun
☎ (01249) 730363
**Moles Tap Bitter, Best Bitter, Molennium,
Molecatcher, seasonal beers** Ⓗ
Built in the 17th century, this pub was an
ale house until the early 1980s when a spirit
licence was obtained. It now serves as the
brewery tap for Moles, based in nearby
Melksham. The garden affords spectacular
views across the Avon Valley to the
Salisbury Plain, some 10 miles away. A
comprehensive range of food is listed on
the menu board; evening meals are served
Wednesday–Saturday. Live music is
performed every Wednesday evening.
🏠Q❀Ⓓ▲♣P

LUCKINGTON

Old Royal Ship
SN14 6PA (on B4040 Malmesbury-Bristol road)
✪ 11.30-2.30, 6-11; 11.30-11 Sat; 12-4,
7-10.30 Sun
☎ (01666) 840222
**Archers Village; Draught Bass; Wadworth 6X; guest
beer** Ⓗ
Sitting on the edge of the village green, this
friendly pub, recently extended to provide a
skittle alley, acts as a focal point for the
village. The guest beer is sourced from a
local brewery. An extensive menu is
available throughout the week. It is a
suitable stop for walkers and cyclists alike,
not to mention horse riders – Badminton is
just up the road and Gatcombe Park close
by. Q❀Ⓓ♿♣P

MALMESBURY

Whole Hog
8 Market Cross, SN16 9AS
✪ 11-11; 12-10.30 Sun
☎ (01666) 825845
**Archers Best Bitter; Wadworth 6X; Young's Bitter;
guest beers** Ⓗ
This unusual pub, situated next to the
superb, 15th-century market cross, has in
the past served as a cottage hospital and a
café/restaurant. It is now a popular, town-
centre watering-hole, with a restaurant area
(meals may also be taken in the bar; no
food Sun eve). Read the newspapers
provided while enjoying one of the
regularly changed guest ales. Behind the
pub, Malmesbury Abbey, partly ruined, now

serves as the parish church; see the campanile in the churchyard.
Q ◖❶❷

NEWTON TONEY

Malet Arms
SP4 0HF (1 mile off A338)
✪ 11-3, 6-11; 12-3, 7-10.30 Sun
☎ (01980) 629279
Butts Barbus Barbus; Stonehenge Heel Stone; Wadworth 6X; guest beer Ⓗ
Classic country village pub named after a local family, which is well represented in the nearby churchyard. Comprising two comfortable bars, plus a restaurant, the larger bar boasts a huge fireplace and a window reputed to come from an old galleon. In summer, boules is played in the normally dry river bed in front of the pub. Wadworth 6X is always served from the wood; the guest beer changes regularly.
❧Q✿◖❶✲❖P

NORTH WROUGHTON

Check Inn
79 Woodland View, SN4 9AA
✪ 11.30-3.30, 6.30-11; 11.30-11 Fri & Sat; 12-10.30 Sun
☎ (01793) 845584
Beer range varies Ⓗ
Genuine free house serving eight real ales, plus imported lagers and bottled beers. The guest beers change frequently and are usually from local and independent brewers. This roadside stop has been cut off by the M4 and isolated in a cul-de-sac. It has a terraced drinking area outside and boules can be played in the back garden. Good home-cooked food is available at a reasonable price; hot pot night (Tue) offers a bargain at 95p. ❧Q✿✱◖❖P✂❶

OGBOURNE ST GEORGE

Old Crown
Marlborough Road, SN8 1SQ (off A346)
✪ 12-3 (not Mon), 6-11; 12-3 (closed eve) Sun
☎ (01672) 841445
website: www.theinnwiththewell.com
Wadworth 6X; guest beer Ⓖ
There is something of interest for both diners and drinkers in this cosy pub, which is over 300 years old. A 90ft deep well is a feature of the restaurant, while every pint of beer is drawn by hand straight from the barrel in the cellar. An accommodation block makes this pub a good base for walking the Ridgeway Path and Og Valley; there is also a campsite within 500 yards.
❧Q✿✱◖Å❖P✂

PEWSEY

Coopers Arms
37-39 Ball Road, SN9 5BL (off B3087)
OS170595
✪ 12-2, 6-11; 12-11 Sat; 12-10.30 Sun
☎ (01672) 562495
Butts Barbus Barbus; Fuller's London Pride; Wadworth 6X; guest beer Ⓗ
This back-street pub takes some finding, but is worth the effort. The thatched building exudes character, both inside and out, but, unusually, it upholds a well-publicised pro-smoking policy. Live music, comedy and quiz nights are hosted regularly; pool is played in a separate room. Sunday lunches are served and a real cider is stocked in summer. ❧✿✱Å≈ (Pewsey Vale) ❖P

SALISBURY

Deacons
118 Fisherton Street, SP2 7QT
✪ 5 (4 Fri; 12 Sat)-11; 12-10.30 Sun
☎ (01722) 504723
Draught Bass; Cheriton Village Elder; Hop Back GFB; Summer Lightning; guest beer (occasional) Ⓗ
This split-level pub is convenient for the city centre and the station. Bare floorboards characterise the front bar area; the back bar has table football and a TV for sporting events. Popular with locals, this pub also attracts a lot of passing trade. It always uses lined glasses and usually stocks a beer from the Triple fff brewery. ❧✿◗≈❖❶

Red Lion Hotel
Milford Street, SP1 2AN
✪ 11-2.30 (3 Tue), 6-11; 11-11 Sat; 12-3, 6-10.30 Sun
☎ (01722) 323334
Draught Bass; Ringwood Best Bitter; guest beer Ⓗ
Situated at the centre of Salisbury, this is a fine example of an ancient coaching inn. The oldest part of the hotel dates back to the 13th century and originally served as accommodation for draughtsmen working on the nearby cathedral. The comfortable, beamed bar is entered via a cobbled courtyard which serves as a pleasant outdoor drinking area. With only gentle background music, this is a good place for a quiet pint or conversation. ✿◗◖P✂

Royal George
17 Bedwin Street, SP1 3UT
✪ 11-11; 12-10.30 Sun
☎ (01722) 327782
Adnams Bitter; Hop Back GFB; Ringwood Best Bitter; guest beer Ⓗ
An inn since the 15th century, this Grade II listed pub is named after the sister ship of the HMS Victory. Genuinely welcoming, this city pub has a country feel, and is popular with locals. The pub has a serious involvement in crib, darts, football and pool leagues. Good value lunches are well received on weekday lunchtimes. ✿◗❖P

Tom Brown's
225 Wilton Road, SP2 7JY
✪ 6-11; 12-3, 7-10.30 Sun
☎ (01722) 335918
Goldfinch Tom Browns, Flashman's Clout, Midnight Blinder Ⓗ
This Goldfinch Brewery house has a strong community spirit; it is popular with locals and enters teams in pool and darts leagues. A TV shows sport, such as rugby and Formula One Grand Prix races; at other times there is background music and the buzz of conversation. A Goldfinch seasonal beer occasionally replaces one of the regulars. ❖

Village Free House
33 Wilton Road, SP2 7EF
(on A36, near St Paul's roundabout)
✪ 12 (4 Mon)-11; 12-10.30 Sun
☎ (01722) 329707
Abbey Bellringer; Taylor Landlord; guest beers Ⓗ

At this city local the three ever-changing guest beers are chosen by customers. It specialises in beers unusual in the area, normally including a mild or a stout – the only regular outlet for such beer in the city. Close to the station, it is popular with visitors arriving by rail and many railway artefacts are displayed. Teams are entered in crib and quiz leagues and an annual charity bike ride is organised by this local CAMRA Pub of the Year 2001. ≈ ♣

Winchester Gate
113 Rampart Road, SP1 1JA
✪ 3 (12 Fri & Sat)-11; 1-10.30 Sun
☎ (01722) 322834 website: www.milkstreetbrewery.co.uk
Milk Street Gulp, seasonal beer or guest beer Ⓗ
Welcoming pub run by the Milk Street Brewery in Frome. A former coaching inn on the site of the city's eastern toll gate, it is now separated from the city centre by the ring road. Live music is played on Friday and Saturday evenings; monthly folk and jam sessions are also staged. A hop festival is held in October and in summer, live music events and barbecues are held in the large garden. ♨ ❀ ❑ ♣ P

Wyndham Arms
27 Estcourt Road, SP1 3AS
✪ 12-2.30 (not Mon), 4.30-11; 12-11 Sat; 12-10.30 Sun
☎ (01722) 331026
Hop Back GFB, Best Bitter, Crop Circle, Entire Stout, Summer Lightning, seasonal beers Ⓗ
Still regarded as the home of Hop Back Brewery, although brewing has long since moved to Downton, this is the brewery tap. The head of Bacchus above the front door greets you as you enter this haven of real ale. A single, long, narrow bar has two small rooms adjacent, one of which is no-smoking and welcomes families. A true local, the Wyndham Arms attracts customers, young and old, from all walks of life. A must if visiting Salisbury. ☙ ✂

SHAW

Golden Fleece
Folly Lane, SN12 8HB
✪ 11-2.30 (3 Sat), 6-11; 12-3, 7-10.30 Sun
☎ (01225) 702050
Butcombe Bitter, Gold; Marston's Pedigree; Wickwar BOB Ⓗ
This old coaching inn on the main road from Bath comprises a comfortable bar and a restaurant in a pleasant extension. Outside, the large, pretty garden overlooks the village cricket pitch. At the front of the pub is the skittle alley. Beers include Wickwar's Brand Oak Bitter, more popularly known as BOB and quite rare in this area. The bar food is simple and filling, while the restaurant offers normal pub fare. ❀ ◑ ♣ P

SHERSTON

Rattlebone
Church Street, SN16 0LR
✪ 12-11; 12-10.30 Sun
☎ (01666) 840871
website: www.therattleboneinn.co.uk
Smiles Best, IPA; Young's Bitter, Special, Winter Warmer Ⓗ
Lively, friendly pub at the centre of a

bustling village where a warm welcome is guaranteed, enhanced by log fires in winter. The several rooms include a public bar, lounge and restaurant areas. This is one of just a few Young's pubs in the area. It has its own boules piste and the village holds an annual boules tournament in July. Sherston is one of those villages that is almost a small town with a wide main street.
♨ ☙ ❀ ◑ ❑ ♿ ♣

SHREWTON

George Inn
London Road, SP3 4DH (½ mile off the A360)
✪ 11.30-2.30, 6-11; 11.30-11 Sat; 12-3, 7-10.30 Sun
☎ (01980) 620341
Courage Best Bitter; Wadworth 6X; guest beers Ⓗ
This friendly local benefits from a good passing trade. The large, unspoilt bar offers a relaxing atmosphere, where the two guests are often the less readily available beers from local micro-breweries. A beer festival is staged on August bank holiday weekend and traditional music is performed outdoors most summer weekends. The George has a thriving food trade, with meals served in a no-smoking dining room. A skittle alley completes the amenities here. ♨ ❀ ◑ ♣ ♦ P

SWINDON

Beehive
Prospect Hill, SN1 3JS (behind college)
✪ 12-11; 12-10.30 Sun
☎ (01793) 523187 website: www.bee-hive.co.uk
Greene King IPA, Ruddles County, Old Speckled Hen; guest beer Ⓗ
The multi-levelled, bare-boarded bar is divided into four areas, populated mainly by students as the college is nearby. Live music is performed every Sunday and recorded music is played at most other times. Rolls are available at lunchtime. Quite often art exhibitions feature on the walls. Drinks can be expensive. ♨ ♣

Duke of Wellington
27 Eastcott Hill, SN1 3JG
✪ 12-2, 6.30-11; 12-11 Sat; 12-3, 7-10.30 Sun
☎ (01793) 534180
website: www.swindonweb.com/arkells/dukeofwellington
Arkells 3B, seasonal beer Ⓖ
The pub is named after the duke as a tribute to his 1830 Beer House Act allowing private houses to sell beer. Arkells bought two houses and converted them into this unspoilt pub which opened in March 1869 just before the law was repealed in October that year. It is the only pub in Swindon to serve Arkells on gravity. This is a typical back-street local, consisting of a bar and snug, where crib and darts are played. ♨ ❀ ≈ ♣

Glue Pot
5 Emlyn Square, SN1 5BP (5 mins from station)
✪ 11-11; 12-10.30 Sun
☎ (01793) 523935
Moles Best Bitter; guest beers Ⓗ
Formerly the Archers Brewery tap, now a free house set at the heart of Swindon's historic Railway Village, the Glue Pot offers a range of seven constantly-changing guest beers. This is a real locals' pub, while still offering a welcome to visitors. Lunchtime

food (served weekdays) ranges from an all-day breakfast to the landlord's special, Rourke's Drift (springbok stew). 🏠🍽️≋♣

Steam Railway
14 Newport Street, SN1 3DX
(old town, opp. the Co-op)
🕐 12-11; 12-10.30 Sun
☎ (01793) 538048
Wadworth 6X; Wells Bombardier; guest beers H

Large pub, that was expanded years ago and can be quite noisy at weekends. The traditional real ale bar is on the right, it has a low ceiling and wood panelling. Nine handpumps offer a regularly-changing selection of guest beers, including some lesser known brews. The bar gets busy when major sporting events are on TV, but at other times it is possible to have a quiet drink. Meals are served 12–6, including a roast on Sunday. 🏚🚲🏠🍽️&P

Boot Inn
High Street, SP3 6PS
🕐 11-2.30, 7-11; 12-3, 7-10.30 Sun
☎ (01747) 870363
Flowers Original; guest beers G

Built of Chilmark stone in the 17th century, this fine village pub has been licensed since 1768. Ron Turner has been landlord here since 1976 and maintains a friendly, relaxed atmosphere which appeals to locals and visitors alike. The beers are stillaged behind the bar with two guests normally on offer. Good food is served and the large, uncluttered garden is ideal for summer evenings. 🏚🍽️🅰≋♣P

South Western Hotel
Station Road, SP3 6JT
🕐 12-3.30, 6-11; 11-11 Fri & Sat; 12-3.30, 7-10.30 Sun
☎ (01747) 870160
Fuller's London Pride; Young's Bitter; guest beer (occasional) H

Opposite the station, this Victorian railway inn offers a warm, vibrant welcome to regulars and visitors. There are several drinking areas, so a quiet corner can be found or you can just join in the conversation at the bar. Although handpumps are in place, beer is often served direct from the cask in the ground-floor cellar. Items of local and railway interest decorate the walls. Food is served daily, except Thursday. 🏠🏚🍽️🅰≋♣P

King John
SP5 5PS (on B3081, between Shaftesbury and Sixpenny Handley)
🕐 11-3, 6-11; 12-10.30 Sun
☎ (01725) 516207
Ringwood Best Bitter; Wadworth 6X; guest beers H

Situated in splendid walking and riding country, the King John, built of old mellow brick, nestles in the tiny hamlet of Tollard Royal. Reputed to be the site of King John's hunting lodge, the pub caters for all with its local ales and good food. The large, square bar, boasting beams and a log fire is a comfortable, relaxed haven. Madonna's local when she is at home, this pub is well worth a visit. 🏚Q🚲🏠🏚🍽️&♣P

Harrow
High Street, Lower Wanborough, SN4 0AE
🕐 12-2.30 (3 Sat), 6-11; 12-3, 7-10.30 Sun
☎ (01793) 790622
website: www.theharrowinnwanborough.com
Adnams Bitter; Wadworth 6X; guest beers H

By far the oldest pub in Wanborough, the Harrow & King's Head, as it was then known, was old in 1747, when the earliest dated deed changed hands. At some time in the 19th century it was a brew-pub, but the equipment was removed when the Wanborough Brewery opened next door. This popular two-bar pub serves a wide range of food (no meals Sun eve). The two inglenooks burn some of the largest logs you will ever see. 🏚Q🏠🍽️⊟P

Plough
High Street, Lower Wanborough, SN4 0AE
🕐 12-2.30 (3 Sat), 5-11; 12-11 Fri; 12-3, 7-10.30 Sun
☎ (01793) 790523
Draught Bass; Fuller's London Pride; Moles Tap Bitter; Wadworth 6X; guest beer H

The only Wanborough pub always to have sold real ale, this attractive, thatched Grade II listed building opened as a beer house after 1830. In 1854 the local constable commented that it was the most disorderly house in the village. The present licensee's father gutted the bland 1950s interior himself, exposing the beams, bare walls and open fireplaces. It is now a cosy, characterful pub. Look out for the skull behind the bar. Meals are served Monday–Friday, plus Saturday evening. 🏚Q🏠🍽️♣P

Horse & Groom
Alfred Street, BA13 3DY
🕐 12-3, 7-11; 12-11 Sat; 12-10.30 Sun
☎ (01373) 822854
Beer range varies H

Much welcomed resurrection of a former Guide pub. Over the last 18 months the new landlord has introduced a continually-changing selection of at least four ales, with the emphasis on smaller breweries. This is a true local, offering crib and quiz nights as well as skittles. The food is simple, honest pub grub and the welcome is genuine. A good place to refresh yourself after a hike up to the Westbury White Horse! 🏚Q🏠🍽️≋♣P⅙

New Inn
SN4 9NW (follow signs off A4361, N of Avebury)
🕐 11-3 (not winter Mon), 6-11; 12-3, 6-10.30 Sun
☎ (01672) 539240
Greene King IPA; Wadworth 6X; guest beers H

Friendly local, just off the Swindon–Devizes road, north of Avebury, with a cosy bar warmed by a real fire, plus a restaurant area. The bar is decorated with replica swords and other weapons that have been collected by the landlord over many years. The two guest beers often come from smaller breweries; the real cider varies. The food here is recommended and children's portions are available. The five guest rooms all have en-suite facilities. 🏚🏠🏚🍽️🅰♣🔌P

WOOTTON BASSETT

Five Bells
Wood Street, SN4 7BD (off High St)
☼ 12-2.30, 5-11; 12-11 Sat; 12-10.30 Sun
☎ (01793) 849422
Fuller's London Pride; Hancock's HB; Young's Bitter; guest beers Ⓗ

Cosy, little, thatched local with a black and white façade. Despite the low, beamed ceiling and open fire, on entering one's gaze is drawn towards the bar with its six handpumps and the blackboards, showing a good selection of home-made dishes. There is a front bar and a back room where wood panelling, bric-à-brac and local pictures combine with ample seating and tables, to create a pleasant, homely environment. Evening meals are available on Wednesday, 6–8.30. ♨Q♣ⓓ❀♣♠🍴

WYLYE

Bell Inn
High Street, BA12 0QP
☼ 11.30-2.30, 6-11; 12-3, 7-10.30 Sun
☎ (01985) 248338 website: www.thebellatwylye.co.uk
Beer range varies Ⓗ

As far as it is known, the Bell was built in 1373 as a coaching inn and, with the exception of 'mod cons' such as electricity, the interior is authentic – and very comfortable. A large inglenook houses a huge log fire in winter. The food is adventurous and appetising, but is not typical pub grub. There are usually four real ales available, generally from local breweries, with one pump set aside for something a little different.
♨Q❀🛏ⓓP✄

Directions to the butler

If any one desires a Glass of Bottled Ale, first shake the Bottle, to see whether any thing be in it, then taste it to see what Liquor it is, that you may not be mistaken; and lastly, wipe the Mouth of the Bottle with the Palm of your hand, to shew you Cleanliness.

Take special Care that your Bottles be not musty before you fill them, in order to which, blow strongly into the Mouth of every Bottle, and then if you smell nothing but your own Breath, immediately fill it. If you are curious to taste some of your master's choicest Ale, empty as many of the Bottles just below the Neck as will make the quantity you want; but then take care to fill them up again with clean Water, that you may not lessen your Master's Liquor. Because Butlers are apt to forget to bring up their Ale and Beer time enough, be sure to remember to have yours two Hours before Dinner; and place them in the sunny Part of the Room, to let People see that you have not been negligent. If a gentleman dines often with your Master, and gives you nothing when he goes away you may use several Methods to show him some Marks of your Displeasure, and quicken his Memory: If he calls for Bread or Drink, you may pretend not to hear, or send it to another who called after him: If he asks for Wine, let him stay a while, and send him Small-beer.

Jonathan Swift (1667-1745), *Directions to Servants,* 1745

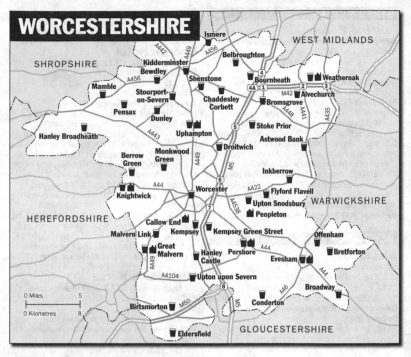

WORCESTERSHIRE

ALVECHURCH

Weatheroak Ales
25 Withybed Lane, Withybed Green, B48 7NX (behind the Red Lion pub)
⏱ 5.30-8.30 Tue-Thu; 5-9 Fri & Sat; closed Sun & Mon
☎ (0121) 445 4411
Weatheroak Light Oak, Ale, Redwood, Triple Tee; guest beer Ⓗ
The owner of Weatheroak Brewery runs this real ale off-licence, located in a residential area. The full range of Weatheroak beers may not be available – phone first to check. Bottled real ale, draught and bottled cider (including Biddenden) and bottled perry are usually stocked. ♠

Weighbridge
Scarfield House, Scarfield Hill, B48 7SQ
(follow signs to marina from village centre)
⏱ 12-3, 7-11 (closed Tue & Wed); 12-3, 7-10.30 Sun
☎ (0121) 445 5111
website: www.the-weighbridge.co.uk
Beer range varies Ⓗ
This friendly pub is part of Alvechurch marina on the Worcester & Birmingham Canal; it comprises three cosy rooms for eating and drinking. Note the unusual collections of 'old luggage' and canal-related memorabilia. Good value bar meals feature popular lunchtime specials, booking is recommended. A classic reminder of how pubs used to be. ♨Q◑≠P✂

ASTWOOD BANK

Oddfellows Arms
24 Foregate Street, B96 6BW (A441 Evesham Rd to lights, Feckenham road 20 yds right)
⏱ 12-11; 12-10.30 Sun
☎ (01527) 892806
M&B Brew XI; guest beer Ⓗ
Small, two-roomed, back-street pub with a friendly local atmosphere. Various games and events take place every week. The bar is to the front, lounge at the rear, and the Outside Inn restaurant doubles as a function room. The restaurant offers home-cooked meals, Tuesday–Friday and Sunday 12–2, and Wednesday, Friday and Saturday, 6.30–9. Booking is essential; Thursday is curry/balti night. Beer festivals are held occasionally. There is a patio garden and children's play area.
♨❀◑⬚♣

BELBROUGHTON

Queens
Queens Hill, DY9 0DU (on B4188)
⏱ 11.30-3, 5.30 (6 Sat)-11; 12-4, 7-10.30 Sun
☎ (01562) 730276
Marston's Bitter, Pedigree; guest beers Ⓗ
Standing next to a brook in a pretty commuter village, this smart, popular inn has prices to match. Three lounge areas are served by one bar. A comprehensive menu of excellent, high quality food is available. The pub is often very crowded at weekends (all tables tend to be reserved) and booking is advisable if you intend to eat. The village hosts a Scarecrow weekend in the autumn. Two guest beers are on tap.
♨❀◑⬚P

INDEPENDENT BREWERIES

Brandy Cask Pershore
Cannon Royall Uphampton
Evesham Evesham
Malvern Hills Great Malvern
St George's Callow End
Teme Valley Knightwick
Weatheroak Weatheroak
Wyre Piddle Peopleton

BERROW GREEN

Admiral Rodney
Berrow Green, near Martley, WR6 6PL
(on B4197) OS748583
✪ 11-3 (not Mon), 5-11; 11-11 Sat; 12-10.30 Sun
☎ (01886) 821375
Greene King IPA; Wye Valley Bitter; guest beers H
Named after Admiral George Brydges
Rodney (1718-92), this large pub lies in the
heart of the countryside on the
Worcestershire Way footpath.
Sympathetically refurbished in 2001, it now
has two bars (one no-smoking), an area
with comfortable settees and a split-level
50-cover barn restaurant, all with
characterful beams. Lunches are served 12–2
and evening meals 6.30–9. A skittle alley is
an added bonus. With the emphasis on real
ales, one guest often comes from a local
brewery. ⛪Q⚪❄⛵◖Ⅱ&♣♠P⅄

BEWDLEY

Black Boy
50 Wyre Hill, DY12 6GT
(follow Sandy Bank from B4194 at Welch Gate)
✪ 12-3, 7-11; 12-3, 7-10.30 Sun
☎ (01299) 403523
**Banks's Original, Bitter, seasonal beers; Marston's
Pedigree** H
Take the steep, but rewarding, climb from
Bewdley town centre to reach this
comfortable local. The pub has separate
rooms, including a small games area that
may be used by families at the landlord's
discretion. Numerous cellar awards are
proudly displayed, and the pub has featured
in this Guide for many years. Its history,
along with other buildings in the
immediate area, dates back several hundred
years. ⛪Q❄⚪❄♣

Black Boy Hotel
Kidderminster Road, DY12 1AG (on B4190)
✪ 11-11; 12-10.30 Sun
☎ (01299) 402199 website: www.blackboyhotel.co.uk
Enville Ale; Greene King Abbot; guest beer H
Close to the River Severn, this former
coaching inn comes complete with a barn
in the car park. A single bar serves the two
main drinking areas and there is a small,
homely alcove. The main room has exposed
beams, a real fire and old settles, it leads to
the no-smoking dining room and the
second drinking area which has a real fire
and a number of tables and chairs. The pub
offers a warm welcome and a wide choice of
menus in the bar and restaurant.
⛪❄⛵◖Ⅱ⇌(SVR) ♣P

Cock & Magpie
1 Severnside North, DY12 2EE
(riverfront, upstream of Bewdley Bridge)
✪ 11-11; 12-10.30 Sun
☎ (01299) 403748
Banks's Original, Bitter P
Friendly, and often busy local situated on
the riverfront adjacent to Telford's bridge.
There are two rooms, and tables are often
provided in summer on the restored
quayside to the front of the pub. The public
bar features pictures of the many floods that
have limited access to all but a hardy few, at
intervals over the years – now hopefully a
thing of the past with the advent of the
Bewdley flood barrier. This pub is a regular

Guide entry, and welcomes locals and
visitors. It may close during the afternoon
on quiet winter days. Q⚪⇌(SVR) ♣Ⅱ

George Hotel
64 Load Street, DY12 2AW
✪ 11-11; 12-10.30 Sun
☎ (01299) 402117
website: www.georgehotelbewdley.co.uk
Tetley Bitter, Burton Ale; guest beer H
A centrepiece in the Georgian town of
Bewdley, this former coaching inn dates
from 1608. The small, cosy bar is known
locally as the Smoke Room, and families are
welcome in the lounge to the front of the
hotel. Note that dogs are discouraged in the
George. As well as bar meals, breakfast is
available from 10–12 and hot and cold
snacks from 2.30–5.30. There is a separate
restaurant and a large function room
upstairs; (lunches only in the restaurant on
Sunday). A covered passageway serves as a
garden. This Grade II listed hotel is said to
be haunted by the Grey Lady who walks in
the ballroom at night. ⛪Q❄⛵◖Ⅱ⇌(SVR) P

Little Pack Horse
31 High Street, DY12 2DH (near Lax Lane)
✪ 12-3, 6-11; 12-11 Sat; 12-10.30 Sun
☎ (01299) 403762
website: www.bewdley.actinet.net/packhorse
**Tetley Burton Ale; Usher's Best Bitter, seasonal
beer** H
An unusual entrance, with a mosaic wall
decoration, leads to this popular pub with
cosy interconnecting rooms. A central bar
serves three drinking areas, each is
decorated with an array of unusual
memorabilia. Hop garlands adorn the walls
and beams, and there are humorous
touches dotted around. There is a variety of
seating and a real fire adds to the relaxed
atmosphere. The food is excellent and
reservations are recommended.
⛪Q⛄◖Ⅱ⇌(SVR)

BIRTSMORTON

Farmer's Arms
Birts Street, WR13 6AP (off B4208) OS790363
✪ 11-4, 6-11; 12-4, 7-10.30 Sun
☎ (01684) 833308
Hook Norton Best Bitter, Old Hooky; guest beer H
Classic black and white village pub, tucked
away down a quiet country lane. The large
bar area with a splendid inglenook is
complemented by a cosy lounge with very
low beams (mind your head). Good value,
home-made, traditional food is on offer,
including classic desserts such as Spotted
Dick. Lunches are served until 2pm and
evening meals until 9.30pm. The guest beer
usually comes from a local independent
small brewery. The spacious, safe garden
with swings provides fine, distant views of
the Malvern Hills. ⛪Q❄◖Ⅱ P

BOURNHEATH

Nailer's Arms
62 Doctors Hill, B61 9JE
✪ 12-11; 12-10.30 Sun
☎ (01527) 873045 website: www.thenailersarms.com
**Enville White; Greene King Old Speckled Hen; guest
beers** H
Originally a 1780s nail maker's workshop-
cum-brewery, this whitewashed, three-

gabled building has a traditional quarry-tiled bar with a real fire. The lounge/restaurant is accessible via a corridor, or a separate entrance. The decor, with comfortable seating and sofas, creates a distinctively modern, Mediterranean feel. Two guest ales and a real cider are usually available. No meals are served on Monday. Awarded local CAMRA Pub of the Season, spring 2002. ▲⚙◑ ⊟& ♣ ⊜P✗

BRETFORTON

Fleece ☆
The Cross, WR11 7JE (near the church)
🕔 11-3, 6-11; 11-11 Sat & summer; 12-10.30 Sun
☎ (01386) 831173 website: www.thefleeceinn.co.uk
Ansells Best Bitter; Hook Norton Best Bitter; Uley Pig's Ear; guest beers Ⓗ

Famous old National Trust pub where the interior is untouched by the passage of time: several small rooms, inglenooks, three open fires, antique furniture and a world-famous collection of 17th-century pewterware are its hallmarks. One of the stars of CAMRA's National Inventory, it was left to the NT by former licensee, Lola Tamplin. There is a large garden with a play area and orchard, ideal for families. The pub holds a famous asparagus auction in the (very short) season. Another unusual offering is the fortnightly informal folk music gathering in the Pewter Room. Fruit wines and Westons Old Rosie cider are available. ▲Q⚙◑ ⊟♣ ● ✗

BROADWAY

Crown & Trumpet
Church Street, WR12 7AE
(on the road to Snowshill)
🕔 11-2.30 (3 summer Mon-Thu), 5-11 (11-11 summer Fri & Sat); 12-10.30 Sun
☎ (01386) 853202
website: www.cotswoldholidays.co.uk
Flowers Original; Greene King Old Speckled Hen; Hook Norton Old Hooky; Stanway Stanney Bitter, seasonal beers Ⓗ

Fine 17th-century Cotswold stone inn on the road to Snowshill, complete with oak beams and log fires in a comfortable interior. Plenty of Flowers Brewery memorabilia can be seen, including an (almost) complete set of beermats. Deservedly popular with locals, tourists and walkers, it offers an unusual range of pub games including devil among the tailors, shut the box, Evesham quoits, shove-ha'penny and ring the bull. Live music is performed on Saturday evening. The menu features specials using locally-grown fruit and vegetables (no meals Sun). Stanway Cotteswold Gold is brewed exclusively for this pub. One of the bedrooms features a Breton wedding bed (not a four-poster). ▲⚙⇌◑ ♣P

BROMSGROVE

Ladybird
2 Finstall Road, Aston Fields, B60 2DZ
(on A448, adjacent to the railway station)
🕔 11-11; 12-10.30 Sun
☎ (01527) 878014 website: www.ladybirdinns.co.uk
Batham Best Bitter; Hobsons Best Bitter; guest beer Ⓗ

Formerly the Dragoon, this pub has been transformed since it was saved from closure in 1997. The use of pine gives a light, airy feel to the bar and lounge. The dining area remains no-smoking even when the good value food is not being served. There are three function rooms, the largest is on the ground floor, and the other two are upstairs and can cater for up to 120 people. Located on the outskirts of town, within a residential community, the pub is well served by public transport. Hobsons Town Crier is usually available as a third cask ale. ⚙⇌◑ ⊟&⇌P✗

Red Lion ⊘
73 High Street, B61 8AQ
🕔 11-11; 12-3, 7-10.30 Sun
☎ (01527) 835387
Banks's Hanson's Mild, Original, Bitter; guest beers Ⓗ

Good, honest town pub with a convenient location in the main shopping area, the bus station is nearby. The single, bright room has a music theme and is attractively decorated. The enthusiastic licensee is justifiably proud of the range and quality of ales on offer. The pub gets very busy at lunchtime when hot and cold bar snacks are sold. There is a small outside drinking area to the rear beside the car park. A mini beer festival is held in July, and Wednesday is quiz night. Three guest beers are from the Banks's portfolio. It was local CAMRA"s Pub of the Season for spring 2003. ⚙♣P

CHADDESLEY CORBETT

Fox Inn
Bromsgrove Road, DY10 4ON
(on A448 past village)
🕔 11-2.30, 5-11; 12-10.30 Sun
☎ (01562) 777247
Enville Ale; Theakston Best Bitter; guest beer Ⓗ

The Fox Inn stands on the roadside on the edge of this attractive village. It is a comfortable pub with a friendly atmosphere and offers several areas for eating and drinking. Families with well-behaved children are welcome at local CAMRA's Pub of the Season for summer 2003. Thatchers cider is sold. Good value food is available; bar meals or a restaurant menu. ▲⚙◑ ● ●

CONDERTON

Yew Tree Inn
GL20 7PP
🕔 12-3, 5.30-11; 12-4, 7-10.30 Sun
☎ (01386) 725364
Wadworth 6X, seasonal beers; guest beer Ⓗ

This charming, roadside pub is built of Cotswold stone, and stands in the middle of the village on the edge of Bredon Hill. Composed of several rooms, it has traditional wooden seating and beams, a no-smoking dining area, and a large garden. The pub serves lunchtime and evening food from a changing menu. ▲⚙◑ ⊟

DROITWICH

Old Cock
77 Friar Street, WR9 8EQ
(near Norbury Theatre, close to town centre)
🕔 11.30-3, 5.30-11; 12-3.30 (closed eve) Sun
☎ (01905) 774233
Banks's Original, Mansfield Cask Ale; Marston's Bitter, Pedigree Ⓗ

Droitwich's oldest licensed premises, a 17th-century inn in the old part of the town. The central bar serves four open-plan rooms decorated with interesting old artefacts and local photographs. There is a function room and a patio garden. The five real ales are complemented by the excellent food. The small, intimate restaurant is delightful with set meal and à la carte menus. Guest beers are from the Banks's portfolio. ⊛◑≠

DUNLEY

Dog Inn
Stourport Road, DY13 0UE
(on A451, Stourport-Great Witley road)
⏰ 11.30-2.30, 5-11; 11.30-11 Fri & Sat;
12-10.30 Sun
☎ (01299) 822833
Banks's Original; Hobsons Best Bitter; guest beers Ⓗ
This wisteria-clad pub has a bar, lounge and small snug. The L-shaped lounge has a no-smoking dining section and a real fire. The menu offers a variety of meals including venison and ostrich at times. A function room for 20–30 people is available and there are three en-suite rooms (one double and two twin). The garden offers a well-equipped, enclosed play area for children and there is a bowling green for hire.
ᨕQ⊛⋈◑⊞♣P

ELDERSFIELD

Greyhound
Lime Street, GL19 4NX
(N of B4211/B4213 jct) OS814305
⏰ 11.30-2.30 (3 Sat), 6 (7 Mon)-11; 12-3,
7-10.30 Sun
☎ (01452) 840381 website: www.greyhoundinn.co.uk
Draught Bass; Butcombe Bitter; guest beer Ⓖ
You will need a good map to find your way to this classic hostelry but the effort is well worthwhile. This friendly, mellow brick, country pub has bentwood seating and a wood-burning stove in the bar. Pub games such as quoits and skittles are played. Excluding Monday and Sunday evening, food is served in the comfortable, no-smoking lounge (with roast lunches on Sunday). A large, safe garden provides plenty of space for children. Two beer festivals are held each year, in June and October. Accommodation comprises a one-bedroom self-catering cottage.
ᨕQ⊛⋈◑♣P⅊

EVESHAM

Old Swanne Inne ⊘
66 High Street, WR11 4HG
⏰ 11-11; 12-10.30 Sun
☎ (01386) 442650
Greene King Abbot; Shepherd Neame Spitfire; Theakston Best Bitter; guest beers Ⓗ
The Swanne has been an inn since 1586, so has experienced many changes. It opened as a Wetherspoon's in late 1998. Evesham Civic Society commended the refurbishment, which 'transformed a scruffy and derelict building into one which is an asset to the town'. Many photographs of old Evesham decorate the walls, together with paintings from earlier times and explanatory texts. Eight handpumps serve three regular and two or three guest beers, regular mini festivals are hosted throughout

the year. Situated on the High Street by what passes for a bus station in Evesham, it is an ideal place to pop into after an afternoon's shopping. A children's area is now provided up to 6pm (last food orders 5pm). Disabled toilets and braille menus are available.
Q⅊⊛◑⅄≠⅊

FLYFORD FLAVELL

Boot Inn
Radford Road, WR7 4BS
⏰ 12-2.30, 5-11; 11-3, 5-11 Sat; 12-3, 7-10.30 Sun
☎ (01905) 820462
Draught Bass; Fuller's London Pride; Greene King Old Speckled Hen; guest beers Ⓗ
This busy local pub enjoys a flourishing trade in food and drink. It was once a farmhouse, and dates back to the 1800s. The restaurant to the rear is housed in an even older 14th-century, timber-framed building (originally the dairy), with a modern conservatory attached. On Saturday evening, the restaurant is run on a strictly walk-in basis. There is a large car park to the front. Five en-suite bedrooms are available.
ᨕ⊛⋈◑⊞P

GREAT MALVERN

Great Malvern Hotel
Graham Road, WR14 2HN
(by crossroads with Church St)
⏰ 10-11; 11-10.30 Sun
☎ (01684) 563411
website: www.great-malvern-hotel.co.uk
Flowers IPA; Fuller's London Pride; guest beers Ⓗ
Victorian hotel bar in the town centre, its proximity to the theatre complex makes it ideal for pre- or post-performance refreshment. Two guest beers are often from the Wood or Hobsons breweries. The comprehensive food menu features local produce, including award-winning sausages from the butcher in the next street. Meals can be enjoyed in the bar or no-smoking brasserie area. No food is served on Sunday. Limited parking. The newly opened 50s themed 'Great Shakes' bar downstairs is keg-only.
⅊⋈◑≠♣P⅄

Malvern Hills Hotel
Wynds Point, WR13 6DW
(A449/B4232 jct, by British Camp hill fort)
⏰ 10-11; 12-10.30 Sun
☎ (01684) 540690
website: www.malvernhillshotel.co.uk
Black Sheep Best Bitter; Greene King Old Speckled Hen; Hobsons Best Bitter; Wye Valley Butty Bach; guest beer Ⓗ
The large, oak-panelled bar and heated patio are the main areas for drinking and bar meals. A separate restaurant serves à la carte dishes while 'Trappers' downstairs provides the home for pool and darts. Walkers spending time in the Malverns and on the nearby Worcestershire Way are warmly welcomed. The landlord has a share in a racehorse (see photo in bar) but the main horsy 'craic' occurs in March when the hotel teems with residents attending the Cheltenham Festival. Come and listen to the live music on Tuesday and Friday evening.
ᨕ⊛⋈◑♣P⅄

HANLEY BROADHEATH

Fox Inn
WR15 8QS (on B4204)
⏰ 5-11; 12-11 Fri & Sat; 12-10.30 Sun
☎ (01886) 853189
Batham Mild, Best Bitter; Hobsons Best Bitter; guest beer ⊞

Imposing, black and white timber building with beamed lounge bar, another bar is predominantly for pool and darts, and a small snug doubles as a family room. The menu, available Thursday–Saturday evening and Sunday lunch only, is purely Thai as influenced by the landlord's Thai mother, but more traditional pub fare can be cooked if ordered in advance. The Batham ales are collected and delivered personally by a local. The guest beer is usually Hobsons Town Crier but it does vary. Cider is served in summer. ♨Q♿☼◑ ⊞♣ ♠P

HANLEY CASTLE

Three Kings Inn ☆
Church End, WR8 0BL (off B4211) OS838420
⏰ 12-3 (may vary), 7-11; 12-3, 7-10.30 Sun
☎ (01684) 592686
Butcombe Bitter; Thwaites Bitter; guest beers ⊞

This 15th-century country inn of great character is a real gem, not to be missed. Awarded local CAMRA Pub of the Year in 2002, it has twice reigned as national champion. The same family has held the licence for over 90 years. An impressive inglenook dominates the tiny quarry-tiled snug with its settle wall and serving hatch. Nell's bar next door is more spacious and features another fire, hops and beams. An annual beer festival is held in November. Organised music is staged on Sunday and occasionally on Saturday; informal jam sessions take place anytime. Westons Old Rosie cider is stocked. No evening meals are served on Sunday. ♨Q♿☼⊞◑♣♠

INKBERROW

Old Bull Inn
The Green, WR7 4DZ (on A422)
⏰ 12-11; 12-10.30 Sun
☎ (01386) 792428
Courage Directors; Flowers Original; Tetley Bitter ⊞

This attractive 'picture-postcard', black and white village local is well-known for its 'Archers' connection. The Bull in Ambridge is modelled on this Bull. Framed photographs of the cast grace the lounge, and there is an exposed inglenook. Evening meals are on offer in the summer only. ♨♿◑♣P

ISMERE

Waggon & Horses
Stourbridge Road, DY10 1RS (on A451)
⏰ 11.30-3.30, 6-11; 12-3, 7-10.30 Sun
☎ (01562) 700298
Banks's Original, Bitter; Ⓟ **Marston's Pedigree; guest beer** ⊞

This country pub has a very quiet front bar with a quarry-tiled floor, etched windows and panelled bar front. The L-shaped side lounge is busier and incorporates the dining section adjacent to the main seating area. The beamed lounge has two open fireplaces and a display of whisky containers. There is

a good, varied menu including children's meals. Thai food is served on Sunday. The guest beer is from the Banks's range. ♨Q☼◑⊟♣P♿

KEMPSEY

Walter de Cantelupe
34 Main Road, WR5 3NA (on A38)
⏰ 12-2, 6-11 (closed Mon); 12-2, 7-10.30 Sun
☎ (01905) 820572
website: www.walterdecantelupeinn.com
Cannon Royall King's Shilling; Everards Beacon; Taylor Landlord; guest beer ⊞

An interesting free house, it is 10 minutes' walk from the River Severn and convenient for the M5 (junction 7). A large inglenook dominates the bar, there is an eating area for the thriving food trade and also an attractive, walled garden (dogs are welcome). The high quality food menu complements a wide selection of beers and wine; ploughmans and sandwiches made with local bread and cheeses are specialities. No food is offered on Sunday evening. Regular special events are staged throughout the year, such as an outdoor paella party in July. Three en-suite rooms are available. ♨Q☼⊭◑P♿

KEMPSEY GREEN STREET

Hunstman Inn
Green Street, WR5 3QB
(from A38 at Kempsey, via Post Office Lane, 2 miles)
⏰ 12-2 (not Mon), 5.30-11; 12-3, 5.30-11 Sat; 12-3.30, 6.30-10.30 Sun
☎ (01905) 820336
Batham Best Bitter; Everards Beacon, Tiger ⊞

Comfortable and welcoming free house of several rooms. The owners undertake a 100-mile round trip to collect the Batham Best Bitter, while (unusually) the Everards is delivered direct from the brewery. Exposed beams and open fires throughout the bar and restaurant area make it a deservedly popular venue, attracting locals and visitors. The impressive skittle alley has its own bar. A huge car park is available. ♨Q♿☼◑⊟P

KIDDERMINSTER

Boar's Head
39 Worcester Street, DY10 1EW
(opp. Safeway)
⏰ 11.30-11, 7-10.30 Sun
☎ (01562) 68776
Banks's Original, Bitter; Camerons Strongarm; Marston's Pedigree; guest beers ⊞

CAMRA-friendly, town-centre Victorian pub. Both the bar and cosy, wood-panelled lounge have solid fuel-burning stoves and there is a covered courtyard complete with working red telephone box, bar for bottled beers and cocktails at busy times. Indeed there is something for everybody here, from good value lunchtime food, a free mineral water dispenser for drivers and Simpsonesque-type murals in the gents' loos. Local talent is encouraged with both live music nights and occasional art exhibitions. ♨Q☼◑≠♠

King & Castle
SVR Station, Comberton Hill, DY10 1QX (next to mainline station)
⏰ 11-3; 11-11 Sat; 12-10.30 Sun

☎ (01562) 747505

Batham Best Bitter; Highgate Dark; Wyre Piddle Royal Piddle; guest beers Ⓗ

A Guide regular, this comfortable pub is a 1980s recreation of a GWR refreshment room of the 1930s at the Kidderminster end of the Severn Valley Railway. The single, long room has ample seating; railway memorabilia and fittings are in character, including an original-pattern carpet complete with GWR logo. A wheelchair WC, on the platform, is open when the trains are running. The Royal Piddle is exceptional value and brewed especially for the pub. ♨Q✿◑≉

KNIGHTWICK

Talbot

WR6 5PH (on B4197, 400 yds from A44 jct) OS572560

✪ 11-11; 12-10.30 Sun

☎ (01886) 821235 website: www.temevalley.co.uk

Hobsons Best Bitter; Teme Valley This, That, seasonal beer Ⓗ

Family-owned hotel, partly 14th-century, in an idyllic setting next to the old coach bridge over the Teme. The Teme Valley Brewery, also owned by the family, is to the rear. Imaginative, good quality food, made wherever possible from local (even home-grown) produce can be enjoyed in the bar or the oak-panelled dining room. A take-away menu is also available. A monthly farmers' market is held outside the hotel (second Sunday). ♨Q✿⊭◑⏛♣P

MALVERN LINK

Nag's Head

Bank Street, WR14 2JG

✪ 11-11; 12-10.30 Sun

☎ (01684) 574373

website: www.thenagsheadmalvern.com

Banks's Bitter; Batham Best Bitter; Greene King IPA; Marston's Pedigree; Taylor Landlord; Wood Shropshire Lad; guest beers Ⓗ

Full of interesting nooks and crannies, and converted from three 18th-century cottages, this is a popular local. There are 15 pumps in the pub, with an average of four regularly-changing guest beers, in addition to those listed above. Food is served between 6:30–8:30 in the evening, after which the restaurant reverts to a bar. Look out for the glass window, set in the floor, with a view into the cellar. ♨✿◑≉P

MAMBLE

Sun & Slipper

DY14 9JL (signed from A456, approx ¼ mile)

✪ 12-3, 6.30-11 (closed Mon); 12-3, 7-10.30 Sun

☎ (01299) 832018

Banks's Original, Bitter; Hobson's Best Bitter; guest beer Ⓗ

Set on the village green, close to Mamble Craft Centre, this country pub comprises a bar, with a pool table, and dining room. The bar often has a blazing fire in the grate and, with its collection of brasses, hops hanging from the beams and coat hooks on the bar, it has a cosy, welcoming feel. The pub has a reputation for fine food and does a good value, set three-course lunch as well as evening meals.

♨✿◑♣P⏢

MONKWOOD GREEN

Fox

WR2 6NX (follow signs to Wichenford, off A443 at Hallow) OS803601

✪ 12.30-2.30 (not Mon-Thu), 6.30-11.30; 12-5, 7-11 Sat; 12-5, 7-10.30 Sun

☎ (01886) 889123 website: www.4avisit.com/sw3

Cannon Royall Arrowhead, Muzzle Loader; guest beer Ⓗ

Bordering common land, this single-bar country pub comprises two drinking areas, one with an inglenook and beamed ceiling. It is a rare outlet for Barker's farmhouse cider and perry. Popular with walkers and cyclists as it is close to Monkwood Nature Reserve, bar snacks made from local produce are served at lunchtime. Evening cooked meals can be prepared for parties by arrangement. Many games are on offer, both traditional (darts, skittles) and unusual (devil among the tailors, petanque). Some opening hours are flexible – phone beforehand if travelling far. ♨Q✿◑Å♣♠P

OFFENHAM

Bridge Inn

Boat Lane, WR11 8QZ

(follow signs to the ferry; although there is no ferry!)

✪ 11-11; 12-10.30 Sun

☎ (01386) 446565

Caledonian Deuchars IPA; Donnington BB; guest beers Ⓗ

This ancient riverside inn has its own moorings and a garden leading down to the Avon. It is known locally as the 'Boat' since the bridge was washed away in the 17th century and was replaced by a ferry. Devastated by the 1998 floods, the pub has been completely refurbished. It retains a vibrant public bar, which serves as unofficial HQ to several local clubs and sports teams. Westons cider is served in summer. ♨Q✿◑⏛Å♣♠P

PENSAX

Bell

WR6 6AE (on B4202, Clows Top-Great Witley Rd)

✪ 12-2.30 (not Mon), 5-11; 12-10.30 Sun

☎ (01299) 896677

Hobsons Best Bitter; Taylor Best Bitter; guest beers Ⓗ

2002 CAMRA County Pub of the Year, this country pub has an L-shaped bar, a snug and a separate no-smoking dining room. The bar features pew-style seating, wood panelling and a wood-burning stove. Above the bar there is an array of interesting old beermats. Opposite the entrance is a small serving-hatch, which is handy for the snug (where children are welcome) and dining room. Guest beers usually come from local independents, and two beers are usually under 4% ABV; the cider is from Westons. ♨Q⏚✿◑Å♠P

PERSHORE

Brandy Cask

25 Bridge Street, WR10 1AJ

✪ 11.30-2.30 (3 Sat), 7-11; 12-3, 7-10.30 Sun

☎ (01386) 552602

Brandy Cask Whistling Joe, Brandysnapper, John Baker's Original; Greene King Ruddles Best, Old Speckled Hen; guest beers Ⓗ

Busy, town-centre free house, home of the Brandy Cask Brewery. The large, landscaped garden running down to the River Avon is popular in the summer, particularly during the annual pub beer festival (August bank holiday). Occasionally Ale Mary joins the regular Brandy Cask brews, but there are usually two further guests. Enjoyable bar food and a good restaurant complete the package. In winter, no meals are served on Tuesday. ♨Q❀☕◐▷⅏

SHENSTONE

Plough

DY10 4DL (off A450/A448) OS865735
☼ 12-3, 6-11; 12-3, 7-10.30 Sun
☎ (01562) 777340

Batham Mild, Best Bitter, XXX (winter) Ⓗ

Tucked away just off the main road, this Batham's beer house (bar snacks only), with past Led Zeppelin links, is a traditional pub with a real fire and well worth seeking out. One bar serves a cheery public bar and walk-through lounge, which is divided into two sections, one of which displays Falkland War pictures. Children are not allowed in the bar or lounge but are permitted in the spacious, enclosed, covered courtyard. Definitely worth a visit to sample the excellently priced ale.
♨Q☜❀☕▲⇌⅏▽

STOKE PRIOR

Navigation Inn

Hanbury Road, Stoke Wharf, B60 4LB
(on B4091)
☼ 11-11; 12-10.30 Sun
☎ (01527) 870194

Fuller's London Pride; John Smith's Bitter; guest beers Ⓗ

Traditional local near the Worcester & Birmingham Canal; the spacious public bar (with pool table) and comfortable lounge with separate dining area are served from a central bar. Good value food is served 12–2 and 6–9 (Mon–Sat). Paella night is Thursday, courtesy of the Spanish chef. The restaurant has a children's certificate. Two guest beers are normally served in addition to the regular beers. A portable ramp is available on request for wheelchair users.
Q☜❀◐⌷♣P⅏

STOURPORT-ON-SEVERN

Holly Bush

54 Mitton Street, DY13 9AA
☼ 10-11; 12-10.30 Sun
☎ (01299) 879706

Banks's Original; Enville Ale; guest beers Ⓗ

The Holly Bush is the oldest pub in Stourport and the only family-owned free house. It comprises two drinking areas off the main bar with a restaurant upstairs. The guest beers are rotated from a list of 12, which include Black Sheep, Cannon Royall, Hobsons and Taylor Landlord. The pub opens for breakfast at 10am and food is served all day until 8.30pm. Located just off the High Street, it is close to the canal and a five-minute walk from the river.
♨☜❀◐▲♣☀⅏

Old Crown ✔

8 Bridge Street, DY13 8XB

☼ 10-11; 12-10.30 Sun
☎ (01299) 825693

Banks's Original; Hop Back Summer Lightning; Shepherd Neame Spitfire; Theakston Best Bitter; guest beers Ⓗ

The outside patio area at this Wetherspoon's pub overlooks one of James Brindley's historic river basins. The interior consists of one large room, with the bar down one side, plenty of seating, and a family area at the back where children are welcome until 9pm. One of the guest beers is from the Wood Brewery range.
Q❀◐க▲P⅏

UPHAMPTON

Fruiterer's Arms

Uphampton Lane, WR9 0JW (off A449 at Reindeer pub) OS839649
☼ 12.30 (12 Sat)-3, 7-11; 12-3, 7-10.30 Sun
☎ (01905) 620305

Cannon Royall Fruiterer's Mild, Arrowhead, Muzzle Loader, seasonal beers; John Smith's Bitter Ⓗ

This unspoilt country pub has a central dispense serving a cosy, homely lounge and a public bar. The Cannon Royall Brewery is situated behind the pub. The lounge has half-timbered walls and a wood-panelled bar. A mixture of old local pictures, antique sporting guns and horse brasses complete the decoration. Basic, home-cooked food, including excellent sandwiches and baguettes, is served at lunchtime. Down a short country lane, this is a little gem worth seeking out. Former local CAMRA Pub of the Year.
♨Q❀◐⌷♣P

UPTON SNODSBURY

French House Inn

Worcester Road, WR7 4NW
(near A422/B4082 jct) OS940544
☼ 12-3, 5.30-11; 12-10.30 Sun
☎ (01905) 381631

Beer range varies Ⓗ

Interesting and attractively decorated, this French-style pub comprises a bar and dining area, with a separate restaurant. An extensive collection of bottles lines the ceiling throughout. The licensees change the three imaginative guest beers weekly. An extensive menu is offered and the food is excellent quality and value. The New Year's Eve party is well worth attending.
♨Q❀☕◐P⅏

UPTON UPON SEVERN

White Lion Hotel

21 High Street, WR8 0HJ
☼ 11-11; 12-10.30 Sun
☎ (01684) 592551 website: www.whitelionhotel.biz

Greene King Abbot; guest beers Ⓗ

16th-century coaching inn with strong Civil War connections, located close to the River Severn. Two distinct drinking areas provide a bar with tables, comfortable chairs and upholstered bench seating and an adjoining lounge with plump sofas. Upmarket bar meals are served, except Saturday evening, alongside a full restaurant menu. Traditional Sunday lunches are popular. Three guest ales are chosen to offer a range of strengths with at least one from a local brewery. Spear dispense is used in the cellar to counter the threat from flooding. Q ❧ ❀ ⚓ ◖❙ ▲ P

WEATHEROAK

Coach & Horses
Weatheroak Hill, Alvechurch, B48 7EA
(Alvechurch-Wythall road)
❂ 11.30-2.30, 5.30-11; 11.30-11 Sat; 12-10.30 Sun
☎ (01564) 823386
Black Sheep Best Bitter; Weatheroak Light Oak, Ale, Redwood; Wood Shropshire Lad; Ⓗ **guest beers** Ⓗ/Ⓖ
This is an attractive rural pub with its own brewery. A quarry-tiled bar with a real fire and functional seating is complemented by a two-level lounge and modern restaurant (with wheelchair access) to the side. The surrounding gardens make it ideal for summer outings. As well as the Weatheroak ales, a good selection of guest beers is available and frequent beer festivals are held. It was awarded local CAMRA Pub of the Year in 1999, 2000, 2001 and 2002.
AQ ❧ ❀ ◖❙ ⚘ & ▲ ♣

WORCESTER

Bell
35 St Johns, WR2 5AG (W side of the Severn)
❂ 11-2, 5.30-11; 11-4, 7-11 Sat; 12-2.30, 7-10.30 Sun
☎ (01905) 424570
Fuller's London Pride; M&B Brew XI; guest beers Ⓗ
This is a pub for the connoisseur. The Bell consists of a frequently busy public bar, two side rooms (one of which can be used by families), a function room with access to a skittle alley, and an outside patio. Pub games and teams feature strongly with dominoes, darts and cribbage joining the skittles. The two guests frequently come from local micros and change every week or fortnight. ❧ ❀ ♣

Berkeley Arms
School Road, St Johns, WR2 4HF
❂ 11.30-3, 5-11; 11.30-11 Fri & Sat; 12-3, 7-10.30 Sun
☎ (01905) 421427
Banks's Hanson's Mild, Original, Bitter Ⓟ **guest beer** Ⓗ
A basic but friendly traditional local, it has a lounge at the front, and a public bar where most of the pub games are played, with a TV for sporting events. A third room at the rear provides a dartboard, and is available as a family room when not in use for darts matches. The guest beer is supplied by Wolverhampton & Dudley and comes from their stable or from an independent brewer.
❧ ❀ ⚘ ♣ P ☐

Bush ⊘
4 The Bull Ring, St Johns, WR2 5AD (W side of the Severn)
❂ 11-3, 5.30-11; 11-11 Sat; 12-3, 7-10.30 Sun
☎ (01905) 421086
Banks's Bitter; guest beers Ⓗ
Victorian pub comprising a public bar with etched and stained glass windows and a small lounge served from a hatch at the back of the bar. Four guest beers can be anything from the mundane to the obscure. It recently won a 'Worcester in Bloom' award for its impressive hanging baskets. Mulbury's restaurant upstairs opens Monday–Saturday evening and for Sunday

lunch, it offers a full vegetarian option. Bar snacks and lighter meals are available in the pub area during lunchtime and evenings except on Sunday. ◖❙ ⚘

Dragon Inn
51 The Tything, WR1 1JT
(300 yds from Foregate St Station, N of city centre)
❂ 12-3, 4.30-11; 12-11 Sat; 12.30-3, 7-10.30 Sun
☎ (01905) 25845 website: www.thedragoninn.com
Beer range varies Ⓗ
A beer drinker's paradise in a comfortable Grade II listed, Georgian town ale house, offering an ever-changing selection of seven ales including a stout or porter (Wednesday–Saturday only in summer). The beers are sourced almost exclusively from small independent breweries, many of which are brought direct to the pub in its own little red ale cart. Good value meals are available at lunchtime, 12–2.30, Monday–Saturday. Do not be put off by the life-size photograph of the landlord opposite the bar! Q ❀ ◖❙ ⇌ (Foregate St) ♣ ●

Plough
23 Fish Street, WR1 2HN (next to fire station)
❂ 12-2.30 (not Mon), 5-11; 8-10.30 (closed lunch) Sun (times may vary)
☎ (01905) 21381
Shepherd Neame Spitfire; guest beers Ⓗ
The landlord is an enthusiastic supporter of local micro-breweries, and fiercely proud of his Basque origins. He has earned himself the nickname Tony Neveropens because of eclectic opening hours. The Plough is a listed, two-roomed pub, with a patio for alfresco drinking (weather permitting). An interesting quirk is the 20p 'fine' for using a mobile phone – all proceeds are given to the local air ambulance. Q ❀ ⇌ (Foregate St)

Salmon's Leap
42 Severn Street, WR1 2ND
❂ 11-3, 5-11; 11-11 Fri, Sat & summer; 12-10.30 Sun
☎ (01905) 726260
website: www.thesalmonsleap.co.uk
Taylor Landlord; guest beers Ⓗ
This pub is ideally located near the cathedral, the River Severn and the Worcester Porcelain factory. A big screen inside the pub shows sports events or music videos. The selection of beers available is always changing, as the plethora of pump clips decorating the ceiling will testify. The garden has a fenced area for children to play in. Limited parking.
Q ❧ ❀ ◖❙ ⇌ (Foregate St) ♣ P ⅍

Burton beer makes me blythe,
French wine makes me sick.
I'm devoted to ale,
And to ale I will stick.
Henceforth let the grape
To the barleycorn bow;
Here's success to the farmer,
And God speed the plough.

Traditional

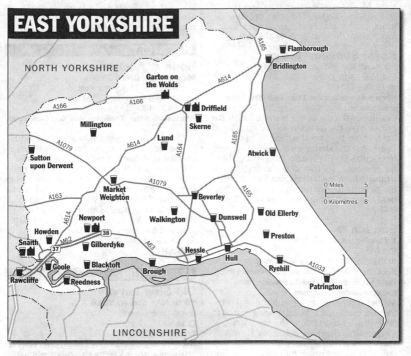

EAST YORKSHIRE

NORTH YORKSHIRE

Flamborough
Bridlington
Garton on the Wolds
A614
A165
Driffield
Skerne
Millington
Lund
Atwick
Sutton upon Derwent
A1079
A614
A164
A165
A166
A166
Market Weighton
A1079
Beverley
A165
Walkington
Dunswell
Old Ellerby
Newport
38
Howden
Preston
A163
A614
M62
Gilberdyke
A63
Hessle
Hull
Snaith
37
Goole
Blacktoft
Brough
Ryehill
A1033
Rawcliffe
Reedness
Patrington
0 Miles 5
0 Kilometres 8

LINCOLNSHIRE

Yorkshire (East)

ATWICK

Black Horse Inn
Church Street, YO25 8DQ
✪ 11.30-3, 6-11; 11.30-11 Sat; 12-10.30 Sun
☎ (01964) 532691
John Smith's Bitter; guest beer Ⓗ
Two miles north of Hornsea, overlooking the village green, this building dates from the mid-18th century and has a central hallway separating the extended bar and dining area. The cottage-style decor is enhanced by old pictures and low, beamed ceilings. A selection of home-cooked food is available; a specials board includes a vegetarian option. The pub fields darts, dominoes and cricket teams. It is only a short drive to the cliffs and beach. Watch out for the ducks crossing to the village pond. ✿Ⓞ▶♠♣P

BEVERLEY

Cornerhouse
2 Norwood, HU17 9ET (near bus station)
✪ 12-2.30, 5-11; 12-11 Fri; 11-11 Sat; 12-10.30 Sun
☎ (01482) 882652
Black Sheep Best Bitter; Greene King Abbot; Rooster's Yankee; Taylor Landlord; Tetley Bitter; guest beers Ⓗ
Former Tetley pub, known as the Valiant Soldier, this historic listed building was gutted by the previous owners before its re-birth as the Cornerhouse in 1999. This well-respected pub/café bar serves quality food in colourful surroundings. Guest beers, Westons Old Rosie cider, plus malt whiskies and cocktails add variety. Food is a speciality, mostly home-made and served until 8pm. Tuesday is curry night and the pub opens early on weekends for English breakfast (10–1). ✿Ⓞ▶♣P

Dog & Duck
33 Ladygate, HU17 8BH
✪ 11-4, 7-11; 11-11 Sat; 12-3, 7-10.30 Sun
☎ (01482) 862419 website: www.dog+duckinn.co.uk
Greene King Abbot; John Smith's Bitter; guest beer Ⓗ
Just off the main Saturday market, next to the historic picture playhouse. The Dog & Duck, built in the 1930s, has been in the same family for over 30 years. The interior comprises a former tap room with a period brick fireplace and bentwood seating, a lounge and a rear snug area, but dividing walls have been removed. The good value, home-made lunches are popular and include pensioners' specials. Accommodation is in the form of six purpose-built, self-contained rooms to the rear. 🏨🛏Ⓓ♣

Hodgson's
Flemingate, HU17 0NU
(opp. Army Transport Museum)
✪ 12-11; 12-10.30 Sun
☎ (01482) 880484 website: www.hodgsonspub.com
Tetley Bitter; guest beers Ⓗ
Surrounded by playing fields, this substantial former residence was converted last century into a social club. Following a major renovation it became a pub in 1996 and is now Beverley's only free house serving beers from independent micros. The tap room has a traditional feel in contrast to the large food/disco area to the rear, housing the town's only skittle

INDEPENDENT BREWERIES

Crown and Anchor Newport
Garton Garton on the Wolds
Old Mill Snaith
Wold Top Driffield

alley. Meals include pensioners' specials and Sunday carvery. The pub's upstairs function room is the venue for the annual folk festival, held in June. ⏸🍴🚃♣P

Royal Standard Inn ⊘
30 North Bar Within, HU17 8DL
⊕ 12-11; 12-10.30 Sun
☎ (01482) 882434
Jennings Cumberland Ale; Tetley Dark Mild, Bitter; guest beer Ⓗ
Classic town local by the historic North Bar and close to the racecourse. The small front bar features bentwood seating from the 1920s, but the Darley's window is a recent reproduction. The comfortable lounge to the rear hosts occasional live music. Award-winning hanging baskets and a bench on the pavement are a summer attraction. No food is served; bring your own sandwiches! Q🍴

Sun Inn ⊘
1 Flemingate, HU17 0NP
⊕ 12-11; 12-10.30 Sun
☎ (01482) 881547 website: www.suninnbeverley.co.uk
Black Sheep Best Bitter; Caledonian Deuchars IPA; Taylor Landlord; Theakston Old Peculier; York Yorkshire Terrier; guest beers Ⓗ
Medieval timber-framed building opposite the east front of the Minster and reputed to be Beverley's oldest pub. The Sun's spartan interior with flagstone floors, brick walls and wooden seating dates from a 1994 refurbishment. Known for its live music, it hosts trad jazz (Mon) and folk/rock (Sun) evenings, plus other sessions. Quiz night is Thursday. Lunches include Sunday roasts. A venue for the annual folk festival in June, this was CAMRA's East Yorkshire Pub of the Year 2002. 🌟⏸🚃♣⏸

White Horse Inn (Nellies) ☆
22 Hengate, HU17 8BL (next to bus station)
⊕ 11-11; 12-10.30 Sun
☎ (01482) 861973 website: www.nellies.co.uk
Samuel Smith OBB Ⓗ
One of Beverley's landmarks, this historic inn offers a multi-roomed interior with gas lighting and stone-flagged floors; all five rooms often have coal fires blazing. The building was owned by the Collinson family since the 1920s until the death of Miss Nellie in 1975, when the inn was acquired by Sam Smith's who, thankfully, only made minimal changes. Good value, home-made meals are served all day until 5pm, including Sunday roasts. Folk and jazz evenings are held weekly in the upstairs function room plus other live music nights. ♨Q🌟⏸🍴♣P⏸

Woolpack Inn
37 Westwood Road, HU17 8EN
(near Westwood Hospital)
⊕ 12-3 (not Mon), 5 (7 Mon)-11; 12-11 Sat; 12-3, 5-10.30 Sun
☎ (01482) 867095
Burtonwood Bitter, Top Hat; guest beer Ⓗ
Located in a Victorian residential street, west of the town centre, this inn started life as a pair of cottages built around 1830. The Woolpack was sensitively restored in late 2001, retaining its cosy snug plus a small extension into the garden. Enjoy tasty home-made meals (not served Sun eve) including specials, Monday curry nights,

Friday steak nights and a Sunday carvery. The guest beer changes monthly. Quiz night is Thursday. Q🌟⏸

Hope & Anchor
Main Street, DN14 7YW
(3½ miles S of Gilberdyke Station)
⊕ 4 (11 Wed-Sat)-11; 12-10.30 Sun
☎ (01430) 440441
John Smith's Bitter; Theakston Mild, Cool Cask; guest beer Ⓗ
Village local on the bank of the Ouse, with picnic tables looking out across the river to the Blacktoft Sands bird sanctuary. To the side there is a children's play area. The pub is on the Trans-Pennine trail link and is very popular with walkers and cyclists. It is also frequented by seamen who tie up at the nearby jetty. A mild is always available – usually Theakston's or Old Mill. The village is served by an occasional bus (Wed and Sat), South Cave–Goole, EYMS No. 160. 🌟⏸▲P

Old Ship Inn ⊘
90 St John Street, YO16 7JS
(1 mile NW of centre)
⊕ 11.30-11; 12-10.30 Sun
☎ (01262) 670466
Webster's Bitter; Worthington's Bitter; guest beers Ⓗ
Thriving former Vaux local, originally two dwellings with two rooms off the central corridor to the left, and three to the right. Alterations in the 1980s resulted in the present front lounge, front snug and a large rear bar. The lounge walls are adorned with prints of famous sailing ships. The front snug resembles a small Victorian parlour where photos show Yorkshire coastal scenes, towns and characters. The meals here are recommended. Q🌟⏸🍴♣⏸

Buccaneer
47 Station Road, HU15 1DZ
⊕ 12-2.30, 5-11; 12-11 Fri & Sat; 12-10.30 Sun
☎ (01482) 667435
Draught Bass; Black Sheep Best Bitter; Tetley Dark Mild, Bitter; guest beer Ⓗ
Friendly pub next to the station at the heart of the old village. It dates back to 1870 when it was the Railway Tavern. The pub was renovated in 2000 to provide a bar lounge (displaying old local photos) and a comfortable 45-seat dining room. The present name was introduced in 1968 after the aircraft built by the local Blackburn Aircraft Company (now BAE Systems). Delicious home-made food is served, including an excellent Friday lunchtime buffet. Overnight accommodation was added in summer 2003. 🌟🛏⏸🚃♣P

Bell Hotel
46 Market Place, YO25 6AN
⊕ 10-2.30, 6-11; 10-11 Thu; 12-3, 7-10.30 Sun
☎ (01377) 256661
Beer range varies Ⓗ
Historic coaching inn, situated in the town centre. The entrance hall opens on to a

long, wood-panelled bar to the right featuring red leather seating, substantial fireplaces, antiques and paintings which lend a quality feel. Two or three changing beers are available, usually from Daleside, Hambleton or Highwood breweries. Other micros are also represented, plus a choice of over 300 malt whiskies. A covered courtyard has bistro seating and old photographs of Driffield. The restaurant opens 7–9.30; Sunday lunch must be booked.
Q ⌂ ◑ ⊟ ♿ ⇌ P

Mariner's Arms
47 Eastgate South, YO25 6LR (near cattle market)
☼ 3 (12 Sat)-11; 12-4.30, 7-10.30 Sun
☎ (01377) 253708
Burtonwood Bitter; guest beer Ⓗ
Tenth consecutive year in this Guide for this traditional street-corner local, well worth seeking out as an alternative to the John Smith's outlets that dominate the 'capital of the Wolds'. Formerly part of the original Hull Brewery estate, with four small rooms, it now has two elongated rooms: a basic bar to the left of the central entrance and a more comfortable lounge. The long-standing licensees create a very friendly atmosphere. Driffield is well served by buses; the EYMS No. 121, Hull–Scarborough is the most regular. ⊛ ⊟ ⇌ ♣ P

Rose & Crown
North Street, YO25 6AS (400 yds N of centre)
☼ 11 (12 autumn & winter)-11; 12-10.30 Sun
☎ (01377) 253041
website: www.roseandcrowndriffield.co.uk
John Smith's Bitter; guest beers Ⓗ
Family-run pub, north of Driffield's central street, comprising a main bar/lounge and a pool room. Televised live sport is shown regularly and Thursday is quiz night. Numerous sports teams represent the pub throughout the week. The two guest beers are constantly changing, with one from an independent brewery. Benches are provided at the front and back for summer drinking. EYMS No. 121 Hull–Scarborough and other local bus services run regularly. ⊛ ♣ P

Ship Inn
Beverley Road, HU6 0AJ
☼ 11-11; 12-10.30 Sun
☎ (01482) 859160
John Smith's Bitter; Tetley Bitter, Burton Ale; guest beer (occasional) Ⓗ
This white-painted inn, fronting the old Hull–Beverley road, once served traffic on the nearby River Hull. Two log fires warm the welcoming interior which is partly divided to form a dining area with church pew seating. It is a rare local outlet for Tetley Burton Ale; beers from one of the local breweries are also occasionally available. Special events and barbecues are held in the adjoining paddock. The pub's name is reflected in the internal decor with nautical memorabilia. Evening meals are served until 7pm. ⋈ ⊛ ⌂ ◑ ♣ P

Seabirds
Tower Street, YO15 1PD
☼ 11.30-2-30, 7 (6.30 Sat)-11 (closed Mon eve, except summer); 12-3, 8-10.30 Sun
☎ (01262) 850242
John Smith's Bitter; guest beer Ⓗ
Just inside this pleasant seaside village pub stands a cabinet full of stuffed seabirds. The bar to the right bears a fishing theme, plus a collection of pump clips detailing the many guest beers previously offered. There is an emphasis on seafood and the special food board changes daily. All food is home cooked; meals are not served Sunday evening. The pub is popular with walkers and bird enthusiasts – spectacular cliffs and Bempton RSPB Sanctuary are close by.
⋈ ⊛ ◑ ⊟ ⚲ A P

Cross Keys Inn
Main Road, HU15 2SP
(on B1230, W edge of village)
☼ 12-11; 12-10.30 Sun
☎ (01430) 440310
Black Sheep Best Bitter; John Smith's Bitter; Tetley Bitter; guest beers Ⓗ
Village pub enjoying strong local support, situated on the old A63 (now bypassed by the M62). A listed building, dated 1750, it was originally known as Mook's Inn after its Dutch owners. There is a bar/lounge with a split-level snug displaying traditional brewery mirrors. A long-established beer house, it serves premium guest beers, draught Hoegaarden and one or two real ciders. ⋈ ⊛ ♣ ⚲ P

Macintosh Arms
13 Aire Street, DN14 5QW
☼ 11-11; 12-10.30 Sun
☎ (01405) 763850
John Smith's Bitter; Tetley Dark Mild, Bitter, Imperial; guest beer Ⓗ
Originally part of a courthouse, the pub retains a traditional feel from the heyday of Goole docks, whose builder, Sir Hugh Macintosh, gave the pub its name. It attracts a wide range of customers and can be busy on weekend evenings, but you can have a relaxing pint at lunchtime, maybe at the pavement tables if the weather is warm. Home to the Wobbly Goolies motorcycle club, whose exploits include charity fund-raising. Their many adventures can be followed in the photo gallery. A constantly-changing guest beer is stocked. ⊛ ⇌ ♣ P

Hase
5-7 Swinegate, HU13 9LG
☼ 11-3, 5-11; 11-11 Sat; 12-10.30 Sun
☎ (01482) 648559
Draught Bass; Black Sheep Best Bitter; Flowers IPA; Tetley Dark Mild; guest beer Ⓗ
Hessle lies in the shadow of the Humber Bridge. The pub, overlooking the church, is a former wine bar and offers a comfortable, welcoming atmosphere. Stone floors, a large open fireplace and photos and memorabilia of old Hessle feature; Hase is the Anglo-Saxon name for Hessle. A split-level dining area serves a full range of home-made dishes, including vegetarian and speciality fish dishes (no food Mon). Recently

introduced are monthly gourmet evenings (booking recommended). Live entertainment is staged on Friday evening. ✿ ◑ ≠ ♣

HOWDEN

Barnes Wallis
Station Road, North Howden, DN14 7LF
(on B1228, 1 mile N of town)
✪ 12-2 (not Mon), 5 (7 Mon)-11; 12-11 Sat; 12-10.30 Sun
☎ (01430) 430639
Black Sheep Best Bitter; Hambleton Bitter; guest beers Ⓗ

One-roomed pub, almost on the platform of Howden Station, named after one of Britain's greatest 20th-century inventors/engineers; the R100 airship, designed by Wallis was built nearby. The walls display pictures of British aviation history, especially WWII. A well-maintained garden and two roaring fires indoors add to its appeal. Three ever-changing guest beers tend to feature Yorkshire micros; more than 500 guest beers have been dispensed in the last three years. Sunday lunches must be booked. ♨ ✿ & ≠ ♣ P

HULL

Bay Horse
115-117 Wincolmlee, HU2 8AH
✪ 11-11; 12-10.30 Sun
☎ (01482) 329227
Bateman Mild, XB, XXXB, seasonal beers Ⓗ

Former two-roomed, street-corner local purchased by Bateman's in 1990. The present L-shaped bar was formed from the original layout and bears photographs of the city's two rugby league teams. The spectacular lofty stable lounge is the result of an extension into the adjoining building (formerly a garage and once a blacksmith's); it doubles as a dining area and displays brewery memorabilia. Home-cooked food is a speciality; try the home-made pies. No food is served Saturday. The pub fields a number of darts and rugby teams. ♨ ◑ ⊟ & ♣ P

Gardeners Arms
35 Cottingham Road, HU5 2PP
✪ 11-11; 12-10.30 Sun
☎ (01482) 342396
Tetley Bitter; guest beers Ⓗ

Local CAMRA Pub of the Year finalist for three consecutive years (2000–2002). The original front bar has seen many alterations over the years, but the matchwood ceiling has been retained and blends with the current ale house style. In contrast, the huge rear extension is comfortably furnished to form a bar with several pool tables. Good value food is served 12–2.30 and 5–7; 12–6 at weekends. It hosts a choice of quizzes: films (Mon), general knowledge (Wed), and music (Thu). Six guest ales are sold in the front bar. ✿ ◑ ⊟ ♣ ◔ P

Hole in the Wall
115 Spring Bank, HU3 1BH
✪ 12-11; 12-10.30 Sun
☎ (01482) 580354
Rooster's Yankee; guest beers Ⓗ

Former amusement arcade, converted into a two-room bar in 2001. It offers an excellent,

ever-changing range of five guest beers, mainly sourced from independents including local brews. One beer is always competitively priced. Featuring wood floors throughout, the spacious front bar has plenty of standing room and comfortable leather seating. Sport enthusiasts prefer the rear bar where a large-screen TV and pool table dominate. A rear patio was recently added. It is 15 minutes' walk from the recently built KC sports stadium. ✿ ⊠ & ♣

Minerva Hotel
Nelson Street, HU1 1XE
(near marina and Victoria Pier)
✪ 11-11; 12-10.30 Sun
☎ (01482) 326909
Tetley Bitter; guest beers Ⓗ

Overlooking the Humber estuary and Victoria Pier, this famous pub, built in 1835, is a great place to watch the ships go by. Superb photos and memorabilia are a reminder of the area's maritime past. The central bar serves various rooms, including a tiny, three-seater snug. Noted for its excellent home-made food (eve meals Mon–Thu); huge haddocks are a speciality. The pub is connected to the Deep visitor attraction by a footbridge at the mouth of the river. Local CAMRA Pub of the Year 2000–02. Guest beers often come from Scotland. ♨ ✿ ◑ ♣ ◔

Olde Black Boy ☆ ✅
150 High Street, HU1 1PS
✪ 12-11; 12-10.30 Sun
☎ (01482) 326516 website: www.yeoldeblackboy.com
Tetley Bitter; guest beers Ⓗ

Attractive, 14th-century Grade II listed building at the heart of the old town. The black front room snug (reputedly haunted) has items of special interest, including the front window and the carved head over the fireplace. The larger rear bar has rich chestnut varnished walls. The front upstairs bar opens on Friday and Saturday evenings; the rear upstairs room houses a pool table. Up to five guest ales are available at weekends, plus two ciders. The pub is on the city's Fish Trail walk around the old town and pier area. ♨ Q ⊟ ♣ ◔

Olde White Harte ☆
25 Silver Street, HU1 1JG
✪ 11-11; 12-10.30 Sun
☎ (01482) 326363
McEwan 80/-; Marston's Pedigree; Theakston Old Peculier; guest beer (occasional) Ⓗ

Historic, 16th-century courtyard pub, reputedly the residence of the Governor of Hull when he resolved to deny Charles I entry to the city. An impressive staircase leads up to the plotting room. Award-winning floral displays, superb dark woodwork, stained glass windows and sit-in fireplaces feature. In the old town, down an alleyway, it is at the heart of the commercial centre. Very busy at weekends with circuit drinkers, a covered, heated outdoor drinking area copes with the overspill. ✿ ◑

St John's Hotel
10 Queens Road, HU5 2PY
(off Beverley Road, A1079)
✪ 12-11; 12-10.30 Sun
☎ (01482) 343669

Banks's Riding Bitter, Banks's Bitter; Marston's Pedigree Ⓗ

Classic, street-corner local, boasting one of the least altered interiors in the city. Attracting a diverse cross-section of drinkers, it can get busy weekend evenings. The welcoming front corner public bar complements a quiet back room with original bench seating. A larger, basic third room, with juke box, doubles as a family area until 8pm, and leads to a secluded garden. Bring your own food or order a takeaway (menus provided). A major bus route (Beverley Road) passes nearby.
Q❀❀⚑⚸♣P

Three John Scott's
Lowgate, HU1 1XW
✪ 10-11; 12-10.30 Sun
☎ (01482) 381910
Bateman Mild; Black Sheep Special; Hop Back Summer Lightning; Shepherd Neame Spitfire; Theakston Best Bitter, Old Peculier (winter)**; guest beers** Ⓗ

Large, open-plan Wetherspoon's outlet with modern decor, in the old general post office building opposite Hull Crown Court. It is busy with mixed clientele at lunchtime and with circuit drinkers on Friday and Saturday evenings. Theakston Old Peculier is replaced by Westons Old Rosie cider, March–September. Wheelchair access by lift from the street is 10 yards to the left of the main entrance. Wetherspoon's curry club menu is offered on Tuesday and Thursday.
❀⚸⚑⚸

Whalebone
165 Wincolmlee, HU2 0PA
✪ 12-11; 12-10.30 Sun
☎ (01482) 327980
Highwood Tom Wood's Best Bitter; Taylor Landlord; guest beers Ⓗ

Built in 1805 on the site of the old Lockwood's Brewery, and changed somewhat since, it is basic and comfortable. The walls are adorned with old photos of Hull and several awards given to the licensee at his previous pub – the Eight Jolly Brewers in Gainsborough. The licensee is a champion of real ale and a new brewery, housed in the adjacent building, was due to be commissioned in 2003. Two quality ciders and three guest beers are normally available.
⚑♣⚭

White Hart
109 Alfred Gelder Street, HU1 1EP
(near Drypool Bridge)
✪ 12-11; 11-11 Sat; 12-10.30 Sun
☎ (01482) 228136
Marston's Pedigree; guest beers Ⓗ

Built in the grandiose 'gin palace' style for the Hull Brewery in 1904, the front bar has thankfully survived almost intact, with a wonderful semi-circular Doulton tiled bar and interesting bar back. Much of the original glass survives in the doors and windows. The long rear room, housing the pool table, is the result of an internal wall being demolished many years ago. It retains bench seating and provides a contrast to the front drinkers' bar.
❀♣

Wellington Inn
19 The Green, YO25 9TE
✪ 12-3 (not Mon), 6.30-11; 12-3, 6.30-10.30 Sun
☎ (01377) 217294
Black Sheep Best Bitter; John Smith's Bitter; Taylor Landlord; guest beer Ⓗ

The Wellington boasts a prime site on the green in this award-winning Wolds village. Most of the trade comes from the local farming community. It was totally renovated by the present licensee and features stone-flagged floors, beamed ceilings and three real fires. There is a no-smoking room, a games room and candlelit restaurant, serving evening meals, Tuesday–Saturday. Good quality food can be enjoyed at lunchtime from the bar menu and specials board. ⚑⚸⚑♣P✂

Carpenters Arms
56 Southgate, YO43 3BQ
✪ 12 (5 Mon & Tue)-11; 12-10.30 Sun
☎ (01430) 803321
John Smith's Bitter; guest beer Ⓗ

On the main road into the town as you enter from the east, this recently refurbished, family-run free house welcomes the local community and visitors alike. A split room, with pool table at one end, and a comfortable bar/lounge at the other, is served from a single bar. It fields darts and pool teams and has a very lively dominoes following. Alternating guest beers from a large portfolio are reasonably priced. Curry nights feature on alternate Tuesdays (5–7).
❀♣P

Gate Inn
Main Street, YO42 1TX
✪ 12-3.30 (not Mon-Fri), 7-11; 12-2.30, 7-10.30 Sun
☎ (01759) 302045
Black Sheep Best Bitter; John Smith's Bitter; Old Mill Bitter; Tetley Bitter Ⓗ

Millington is in a beautiful setting in the Yorkshire Wolds and has been inhabited since ancient times. The pub, which is at the centre of the village, has a single comfortable bar and adjoining pool room. Of special note is the old map of Yorkshire on the ceiling. It is popular with walkers as it is close to Millington Pastures and the two long-distance walks, the Wolds Way and the Minster Way. ⚑⚵❀⚑⚸♣P

Crown & Anchor
75 Main Street, HU15 2PR
✪ 3.30 (12 Fri & Sat)-11; 12-10.30 Sun
☎ (01430) 449757
website: www.crownandanchoryorks.co.uk
Crown & Anchor Newport Original, Newport Bridge IPA; Mansfield Dark Mild; guest beer Ⓗ

Comfortable village local on the old A63, by the Market Weighton Canal. This friendly, two-roomed pub offers good quality, home-cooked food (Fri–Sun lunchtimes and Tue–Sun eve until 8pm). Two open fires provide a warm welcome. The pub fields darts, cricket and football teams; fishing is possible in the canal and nearby ponds.

Guest beers are usually from Yorkshire's small independent breweries. The in-house brewery started production in November 2002 and the beers have proved popular in the pub. ⌂₼◑❶♿♣P⌷

OLD ELLERBY

Blue Bell Inn
Crabtree Lane, HU11 5AJ
☻ 12-4 (not Mon-Fri), 7-11; 12-5, 7-10.30 Sun
☎ (01964) 562364
Adnams Broadside; Black Sheep Best Bitter; Tetley Bitter; guest beers Ⓗ
This 16th-century, one-roomed inn has a games area to the rear and a snug area to the right of the bar. Tiled floors, beamed ceilings, and horse brasses are all features of this community-focused pub that holds many fundraising events. Morris dancers visit in summer and before Christmas. The patio area features attractive floral displays, while the large garden houses a bowling green, a children's play area and a large events field. The pub is on the EYMS 230/240 Hull–Hornsea bus route. ⌂Q❀▲P

PATRINGTON

Hildyard Arms
1 Market Place, HU12 0RA
☻ 12-11; 11-11 Sat; 12-10.30 Sun
☎ (01964) 630234
Draught Bass; Tetley Bitter; guest beer Ⓗ
Former coaching inn at the village centre, where a central bar serves a no-smoking restaurant, a pool and games room and a public bar, all of which boast a real fire. The interior is cottage style; the bar area is adorned with hops. All the food is freshly prepared; bar lunches are served Wednesday–Sunday, the restaurant opening times vary. It is conveniently situated for Patrington Haven holiday park and Spurn Point nature reserve. The pub is served by a regular bus service between Hull and Withernsea – EYMS Nos. 71, 75, 76 and 77. ⌂Q◑♿♣P

PRESTON

Cock & Bell
1 Main Street, HU12 8UB
☻ 6 (11 Fri & Sat)-11; 12-10.30 Sun
☎ (07989) 951276
Camerons Strongarm, Castle Eden Ale; Mansfield Dark Mild; guest beer Ⓗ
Cottage-style village pub that is over 200 years old. There is a main bar, a no-smoking games room, with pool table and a conservatory. The latter is used as a restaurant on Sunday and special occasions and as a function/meeting room for local organisations when required. There is a large outdoor patio area to the rear. The guest beer offered changes regularly. EYMS bus No. 277 (Hull–Hedon) serves Preston. ❀♣P⌇

RAWCLIFFE

Jemmy Hirst at the Rose & Crown
26 Riverside, DN14 8RN
☻ 6 (12 Sat)-11; 12-10.30 Sun
☎ (01405) 831038
Taylor Landlord; guest beer Ⓗ

White-painted, street-corner tavern opposite the river, reached, from the village green, by going down the lane next to the Neptune. As the licensees' first pub, it quickly gained a reputation for a warm welcome. There is a games room and the main lounge is spacious, yet homely, achieved by exposed beams, and many book shelves, in case you want to read by the log fire. In summer sit in the garden or on the river bank. Bar snacks are available. ⌂❀◑♣

REEDNESS

Half Moon Inn
Main Street, DN14 8ET (on A161, S of Goole)
☻ 12-2 (not Dec-Easter), 7-11; 12-11 Sat; 12-10.30 Sun
☎ (01405) 704484
Black Sheep Best Bitter; Cottage Norman's Conquest; guest beers Ⓗ
Two-roomed village local decorated in rural fashion with timber beams, plates and pot jugs, enhanced by red leather seating. A central bar serves a well-appointed bar and lounge/restaurant area. An extensive menu of home-cooked meals is available Wednesday–Saturday evenings and weekend lunchtimes. The Cottage beer has become something of a fixture after proving popular with customers. Camping and caravanning facilities are provided at the rear of the pub. The Blacktoft Sands RSPB bird reserve is nearby.
⌂Q❀◑♿♿▲♣P⌇⌷

RYEHILL

Crooked Billet
Pitt Lane, HU12 9NN
(400 yds off A1033, E of Thorngumbald)
☻ 11-11; 12-10.30 Sun
☎ (01964) 622303
Burtonwood Bitter, Top Hat; guest beer Ⓗ
Unspoilt, 17th-century coaching inn with a stone-flagged floor and comfortable upholstered seating areas, horse brasses and old pictures of the pub adorn the walls. This welcoming, two-roomed inn, with a real fire, is a peaceful retreat. The guest beer is from Burtonwood's monthly rotating list. Good quality, home-cooked food is served (no lunches Mon or Tue). At the centre of the local community, it fields cricket and dart teams and a Scrabble club. Regular buses run on the Hull–Withernsea route – EYMS Nos. 71, 75, 76 and 77. ⌂Q◑♣P

SKERNE

Eagle Inn ☆
Wansford Road, YO25 9HG
☻ 7-11; closed Mon; 12-3 Sun
☎ (01377) 252178
Camerons Bitter Ⓗ
This classic pub is a gem; a plain, white-painted village local surrounded by mature trees, it is much loved by regulars and visitors from near and far. The unspoilt, homely interior comprises a public bar with a matchboard ceiling, and a more comfortable parlour. Drinks are brought to your table from a cellar off the entrance corridor, dispensed from a Victorian cash register beer engine that serves a spectacular cone head. Outside WCs complete this time

warp pub, a Guide entry in every edition but one. ♨Q❀☕♣P☐

SNAITH

Brewers Arms
10 Pontefract Road, DN14 9JS
☼ 12-3, 5-11; 12-3, 6-10.30 Sun
☎ (01405) 862404
Old Mill Bitter, Old Curiosity, Bullion, seasonal beers ⌂
Old Mill's tap and showcase is just around the corner from the brewery. The well-appointed interior is split into several distinct areas, one of them smoke-free. An unusual feature is a deep floodlit glass-topped well, complete with a skeleton. The regular Old Mill beers are complemented by seasonal brews from the brewery's special reserve range. The beer quality is demonstrated by the array of awards displayed around the pub. Good food; no meals are served Monday lunchtime. ❀☞◑≠P✦

SUTTON UPON DERWENT

St Vincent Arms
Main Street, YO41 4BN (follow B1288 past Elvington)
☼ 11.30-3, 6-11; 12-3, 7-10.30 Sun
☎ (01904) 608349
Fuller's Chiswick, London Pride, ⌂ **ESB;** Ⓖ **John Smith's Bitter; Taylor Landlord; Wells Bombardier; guest beers** ⌂
Quintessential country inn, family-owned and run, which plays an integral part in village life. This striking, white building has several rooms. On the right is a cosy bar – little-changed over the years and often busy with groups of regulars. To the left is a smaller bar/dining room and two further dining areas – note the large Fuller, Smith & Turner mirror. The complete Fuller's range and their seasonal beers are kept at York CAMRA's Pub of the Year 2002. Q❀◑▲P

WALKINGTON

Barrel Inn
35 East End, HU17 8RX
☼ 4 (12 Sat)-11; 12-10.30 Sun
☎ (01482) 868494
Thwaites Mild, Bitter, Thoroughbred, Lancaster Bomber, seasonal beers ⌂
Welcoming local near the village pond. The front bar features a log fire, beamed ceiling and comfortable seating; a step up leads to the lounge, with dart area off. There is no food or music, but Sky TV is available for all major sporting events. Local football and cricket teams are based here. Acquired by Thwaites in 2002, it is their only pub in East Yorkshire. The village is served by an hourly bus service (EYMS 180/182) running between Beverley and Hessle. ♨❀⊟♣

Yorkshire (North)
(Including parts of Cleveland)

APPLETREEWICK

New Inn
Main Street, BD23 6DA
☼ 12-3 (not Mon or Tue), 7-11; 12-3, 7-10.30 Sun
☎ (01756) 720252
Daleside Bitter; John Smith's Bitter; guest beer (summer) ⌂

This rural pub has been in this Guide since 1988 with the same family in control since 1986. Renowned for its foreign beers, including three on draught and a menu of bottled beers, the guest beer is provided by Daleside. The home-cooked food is also much in demand. It is popular with walkers, being close to the Dales Way, and cyclists who can make use of the pub's cycle livery. The No. 74 Ilkley–Grassington bus passes outside. ♨Q❀☞◑▲P

AYSGARTH

Palmer Flatt Hotel
DL8 3SR
☼ 11.30-3, 6-11; 12-3, 6-10.30 Sun
☎ (01969) 663228
website: www.palmerflatthotel.co.uk
Black Sheep Best Bitter; John Smith's Bitter; Theakston Best Bitter; guest beers (occasional) ⌂
With the honeypot destination of Aysgarth Falls within 200 yards, this imposing Victorian hotel provides for both the weary traveller and local drinkers alike, as it has done since the railway arrived in the late 1800s, when it changed both its name and appearance to accommodate the tourists. The railway has long since gone but the visitors continue. A much-needed pint can be enjoyed after a walk back up the hill from the falls. ❀☞◑⊟▲♣P

BEDALE

Three Coopers
2 Emgate, DL8 1AH (just off main street)
☼ 11-11; 12-10.30 Sun
☎ (01677) 422153
Black Sheep Best Bitter; Jennings Bitter, Cumberland Ale, seasonal beers ⌂
Old pub, hidden down a side street near the ancient market cross of this town at the entrance to Wensleydale. Inside, the drinking area is partitioned into three sections, where a rustic look prevails, with bare brick, stone and woodwork abounding and two live fires. The landlord welcomes a varied clientele to this excellent watering-hole. ♨❀♣

BELLERBY

Cross Keys
DL8 5QS
(1 mile from Leyburn on A6108 to Richmond)
☼ 12-3, 6-11; 12-11 Fri & Sat; 12-10.30 Sun
☎ (01969) 622256
John Smith's Bitter; guest beers ⌂
Lively village pub, well supported by a good local and passing trade. The building dates back to 1740 and has an open, L-shaped bar lounge with exposed beams and a real fire. The adjoining field contains pot-bellied pigs, much photographed by overseas visitors. The guest beers are ever-changing; some are sourced from small, local breweries. Families are welcome and there are regular live music, quiz and food theme evenings (good food). ♨⚑❀◑ঌ♣P☐

BILBROUGH

Three Hares
Main Street, YO23 3PH
(off A64, York-Leeds road)
☼ 12-3, 7-11; closed Mon; 12-3 (closed eve) Sun

517

NORTH YORKSHIRE

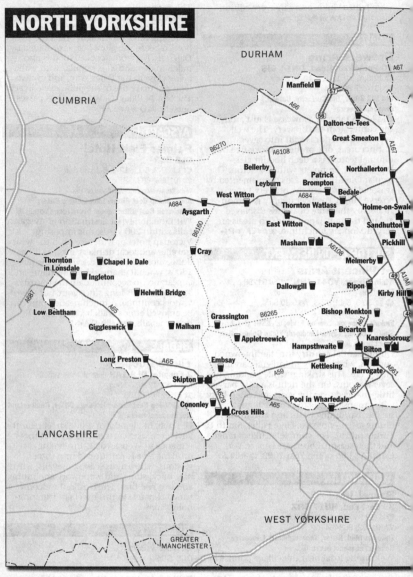

☎ (01937) 832128 website: www.thethreehares.co.uk
Black Sheep Best Bitter; Taylor Landlord; guest beers Ⓗ
Former blacksmith's shop with over 200 years' history. The pub provides excellent beers and food in a warm, friendly atmosphere. Roaring log fires in the winter and a summer garden terrace makes this an ideal all-year-round place to visit. Outstanding cellarmanship ensures that the beers are always on top form. Several food awards assure an excellent meal, served in the no-smoking restaurants or the bar.
⚆Q✿⊕♣P⚘⊟

BISHOP MONKTON

Lamb & Flag
Boroughbridge Road, HG3 3QN (off A61)
☼ 12-3, 5.30-11; 12-3, 7-10.30 Sun
☎ (01765) 677322

Daleside Bitter; Tetley Bitter; guest beer Ⓗ
Two-roomed, traditional village pub, full of knick-knacks and unusual brasses. It has a peaceful garden and tables in a suntrap at the front. It supports the village cricket team with fundraising throughout the year. An August bank holiday duck race is staged on the stream nearby. Ripon cathedral and racecourse, Studley Royal, and Fountains Abbey are all within striking distance.
⚆Q✥⊕Å♣P

Masons Arms
St John's Road, HG3 3QU (off A61)
☼ 12-3, 6.30-11; 12-3, 6.30-10.30 Sun
☎ (01765) 677427

Black Sheep Best Bitter; Tetley Bitter; guest beer Ⓗ
Set in a delightful village overlooking a stream which is home to some unusual crossbred ducks; look out for the duck race on August bank holiday. The pub, which

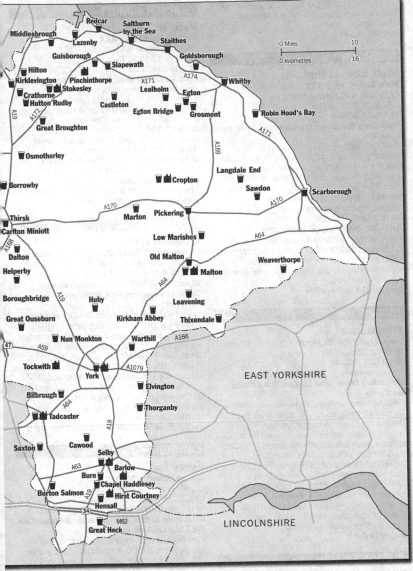

Map of Yorkshire (North) showing locations including: Middlesbrough, Redcar, Saltburn by the Sea, Lazenby, Staithes, Guisborough, Goldsborough, Slapewath, Hilton, Kirklevington, Pinchinthorpe, A171, A174, Whitby, Stokesley, Lealholm, Crathorne, Egton, Hutton Rudby, Castleton, Grosmont, Egton Bridge, Egton, Great Broughton, Robin Hood's Bay, A19, A172, Osmotherley, A169, A171, Borrowby, Cropton, Langdale End, Sawdon, Scarborough, Thirsk, A170, Marton, Pickering, A170, Carlton Miniott, A168, Low Marishes, A64, Dalton, Old Malton, Weaverthorpe, Helperby, Malton, A64, Boroughbridge, A19, Huby, Leavening, Great Ouseburn, Kirkham Abbey, Thixendale, A166, Nun Monkton, Warthill, 47, A59, EAST YORKSHIRE, Tockwith, York, A1079, Bilbrough, Elvington, A64, Thorganby, A19, Tadcaster, Saxton, Cawood, Selby, Barlow, Burn, Chapel Haddlesey, Burton Salmon, A19, Hirst Courtney, Hensall, 34, M62, LINCOLNSHIRE, Great Heck

0 Miles 10
0 Kilometres 16

---

made an appearance in TV's Touch of Frost, has a cosy interior with beamed ceilings and open fires. An extensive menu is served in the restaurant. Various Rudgate and Daleside beers are usually on tap.
🏛Q🏠🐕⊛◖▶♿♣P

BOROUGHBRIDGE

Black Bull
6 St James Square, YO51 9AR
🕐 11-11; 12-10.30 Sun
☎ (01423) 322413
Black Sheep Best Bitter; John Smith's Bitter; guest beer Ⓗ
Standing solidly in a corner of the square in the town centre, this venerable inn is white-painted with Georgian-style bay windows, the frontage is bedecked with hanging baskets in summer. The cosy main bar has a low, beamed ceiling, copper-topped tables

and a brick inglenook; the adjoining snug also has an open fire. A high quality popular restaurant is situated down a wood-panelled corridor (booking advised at weekends). Note the tiny servery in the main room. 🏛Q🏠◖▶

BORROWBY

Wheatsheaf
Main Street, YO7 4QP (1 mile from A19)
🕐 12-3 (not Mon-Fri), 5.30-11; 12-10.30 Sun
☎ (01845) 537274 website: www.borrowbypub.co.uk
John Smith's Bitter; Tetley Bitter; guest beer Ⓗ
Attractive, 17th-century pub in a village just off the A19. The low, beamed ceiling in the public bar is adorned with brass and copperware, while a real fire occupies the splendid stone fireplace, giving a very traditional feel. There is a room for dining and a newly-created third small drinking

area to the rear of the bar. Meals are served Tuesday–Sunday evening and Sunday lunchtime.
🏠Q🕙🍴🚬🅿♣♠

BREARTON

Malt Shovel Inn
Main Street, HG3 3BX (1 mile off B6165)
🕐 12-2.30, 6.45-11; closed Mon;
12-2.30, 6.45-10.30 Sun
☎ (01423) 862929

Black Sheep Best Bitter; Theakston Best Bitter; guest beers ⓗ

Unspoilt 16th-century village pub boasting a wealth of attractive features: an oak linen-fold bar, an ancient oak partition, beams, and a mix of tables. Excellent home-cooked food from a menu based on local produce includes vegetarian choices (arrive early if you want to eat, especially at weekends; no food Sun eve). A good wine list is reasonably priced, while a good range of whiskies, two guest beers and a summer cider mean a real choice for drinkers. Twenty years in this Guide, this real gem is always busy.
🏠Q🌳🕙🍴🚬🅲♣♠🍴🅿✗

BURN

Wheatsheaf
Main Road, YO8 8LJ (on A19, 3 miles S of Selby)
🕐 12-11; 12-10.30 Sun
☎ (01757) 270614
website: www.selbynet.co.uk/wheatsheaf.html

John Smith's Bitter; Taylor Landlord; Tetley Bitter; guest beers ⓗ

Roadside inn, built in 1896, which retains its narrow bar passage. A huge open fire dominates the main open lounge, which has an adjacent pool room. Agricultural memorabilia reflects the rural and WWII associations of the village – Burn aerodrome was a bomber base. The pub also boasts a large collection of Dinky toys. Home-cooked food is especially popular on Sunday lunchtime (evening meals served Thu–Sat). Mild is often a guest beer; regular beer festivals feature local and regional breweries.
🏠Q🚬🍴♣🅿

BURTON SALMON

Plough Inn
Main Street, LS25 5JS
(A162, 4 miles N of A1/M62 jct 33)
🕐 5 (12 Fri & Sat)-11; 12-10.30 Sun
☎ (01977) 672422
website: www.selbynet.co.uk/plough/inn.html

Banks's Original; Brown Cow Constellation; John Smith's Bitter; guest beers ⓗ

17th-century, privately-owned free house, in a quiet village close to the A1. It operates an ambitious guest beer policy and the house beer is from the local Brown Cow Brewery. Wood floors and open fires enhance the friendly welcome. The dining area serves a selection of home-cooked food. A base for the village cricket team, it also fields enthusiastic darts and dominoes teams. A quiz night is held Sunday and live folk music is performed monthly (second Tuesday).
🏠Q🚬🍴♣🅿

CARLTON MINIOTT

Vale of York
Carlton Road, YO7 4LX
(on A61, 1 mile W of Thirsk)
🕐 12-11; 12-10.30 Sun
☎ (01845) 523161

Black Sheep Best Bitter; John Smith's Bitter; Taylor Landlord; guest beers (summer) ⓗ

Enterprising and friendly free house, by Thirsk Station and separated from the town by Thirsk racecourse. The small public bar is dedicated to sports, displaying many trophies, with pool table and a separate snug. There is a large lounge and a restaurant that serves a Sunday carvery; no meals are served Wednesday. Quoits is played in the attractive garden. Accommodation in the 15 guest rooms is good value.
🚬🍴🛏🅲🚲🛏Å♣♠🅿✗

CASTLETON

Eskdale Inn
Station Road, YO21 2EU (just beyond bridge at Castleton Moor Station) OS685084
🕐 11 (7.30 Mon)-11; 12-10.30 Sun
☎ (01287) 660234 website: www.eskvalley.com

Camerons Strongarm; Tetley Bitter; guest beer (summer) ⓗ

Travel the half mile from Castleton village and enjoy the friendly welcome in this stone-built hotel with a patio, conservatory and a large garden leading down to the River Esk. Popular with walkers, anglers and cyclists, the bar on the right has tables and settles; the dining room is on the left. Pool and darts are played (children are admitted to the pool room). There are shops and a garage in Castleton village and bicycles can be hired nearby.
🏠Q🌳🚬🍴🅲🚂≠(Castleton Moor)♣🅿🍴

CAWOOD

Ferry Inn
2 King Street, YO8 3TL
(S side of river, near swing bridge)
🕐 12-11; 12-10.30 Sun
☎ (01757) 268515 website: www.ferryinn.f9.co.uk

Black Sheep Special; Camerons Bitter; Mansfield Cask Ale; Taylor Landlord; guest beers ⓗ

Low ceiling and inglenooks give a cosy atmosphere to this friendly, historic village inn, with a terrace and garden overlooking the river. The village has connections with Cardinal Wolsey who, as Archbishop of York, resided at Cawood Castle. Although the menu today is not as sumptuous as the great feast of 1464 – see details in the bar – it is exceptional value. The guest beer is often local. 🏠Q🚬🛏🍴Å♣🅿

CHAPEL HADDLESEY

Jug Inn
Main Street, YO8 8QQ (A19, 5 miles N of M62 jct 34)
🕐 12-3 (not Mon-Fri), 6-11; 12-3, 6-10.30 Sun
☎ (01757) 270307 website: www.thejuginn.co.uk

Brown Cow Bitter; Theakston Black Bull; guest beers ⓗ

Superb, 300-year-old, beamed village pub on the bank of the River Aire, well worth seeking out. Privately owned, it is popular for its ever-changing guest beers and fresh, home-made food, always based on local produce. A small central bar serves two rooms, both of which have real fires and there is a snug off the lounge, complete with chesterfield settees. The large garden backs on to the river. ⚲Q✿◖◗⊕P

CHAPEL LE DALE

Hill Inn
LA6 3AR (on B6255)
✪ 12-3, 6-11; 12-11 Sat & summer; 12-10.30 Sun
☎ (015242) 41256
Black Sheep Best Bitter, Special, Riggwelter; Dent Bitter, Aviator Ⓗ
Beloved of generations of hikers and potholers; well-worn paths run from here to both Whernside (Yorkshire's highest peak) and Ingleborough (its best-known). This pub has also become a destination for diners – booking is advisable for the restaurant. The bar has been carefully restored with wood and stonework. A folk evening is hosted on the last Friday of the month. The nearest public transport is Ribblehead Station (two miles).
⚲Q✿◖◗ ▲P⅄

CONONLEY

New Inn
Main Street, BD20 8NR
✪ 12-3, 5.30-11; 12-11 Sat; 12-10.30 Sun
☎ (01535) 636302
Taylor Golden Best, Best Bitter, Landlord, seasonal beers Ⓗ
Attractive, beamed Taylor's tied house at the centre of a quiet Dales village in South Craven. It is a pleasing example of vernacular architecture, where stone-mullioned windows complement the snug interior. There is a small garden at the rear. Although just two minutes' walk from the station, allow plenty of time to get over the level crossing if travelling south by train. It is also served by hourly buses (78A, 67 and 67A) from Keighley and Skipton.
⚲Q✿◖◗ ▲⇌♣

CRATHORNE

Crathorne Arms
TS15 0BA
✪ 11.30-2.30, 5-11; 11.30-11 Sat; 12-3, 7-10.30 Sun
☎ (01642) 701931
Black Sheep Best Bitter; Hambleton Bitter Ⓗ
Part of the Crathorne estate, and known locally as Free House Farm, the farm at the rear and the pub have been run hand-in-hand for over a century. Family-run, it caters for both village locals and visitors from much further afield as its reputation spreads. The photographs of turn-of-the-century village life come from Lord Crathorne's own collection. It comprises drinking areas, a large family/games room and a restaurant where a first-class menu is based on locally-sourced fresh meat and fish. ⚲Q⤢✿◖◗♿♣P⅄Ⓤ

CRAY

White Lion Inn
BD23 5JB
✪ 11-11; 12-10.30 Sun
☎ (01756) 760262 website: www.whitelioncray.com
Moorhouses Premier; Taylor Landlord; guest beers Ⓗ

Nestling beneath Buckden Pike in excellent walking country, this is the highest pub in Wharfedale. Formerly a drovers' inn dating from the early 17th century and once described by Wainwright as 'a tiny oasis', the main stone-flagged bar boasts original beams and an open log fire. There is also a small dining area serving good food, where children are welcome. Guest beers often come from local independent breweries.
⚲Q✿◖⇱◖◗♣P

CROPTON

New Inn
Woolcroft, YO18 8HH
(5 miles off A170, Pickering-Kirkby Moorside road)
✪ 11-11; 12-10.30 Sun
☎ (01751) 417330 website: www.croptonbrewery.co.uk
Cropton King Billy, Two Pints, Honey Gold, Scoresby Stout, Balmy Mild, Monkmans Slaughter Ⓗ
Situated at the edge of the North Yorkshire moors, the Heritage Coast and Pickering, the New Inn is a good stopping-off point and the accommodation makes it an ideal base for exploring the area. Locals and visitors mingle in the cosy bar, sampling beers from the outstanding brewery sited in the grounds. Downstairs, a large family room is also the venue for the annual beer festival held in November. Various local ciders are available throughout the year.
Q⤢✿◖⇱◖◗♿▲♣●P⒣

CROSS HILLS

Old White Bear
6 Keighley Road, BD20 7RN
✪ 11.30-11; 12-10.30 Sun
☎ (01535) 632115
Old Bear Original, seasonal beers; guest beer Ⓗ
Built in 1735 as a coaching inn, this popular pub has four rooms for drinkers with low, beamed ceilings; two of the beams came from the White Bear sailing ship. Ring the bull and darts are played. The dining room, serving good value food, has a window into the brewery, situated in the former stables. The beers are brewed using local well water (tours by arrangement). The upstairs rooms have been used as a court, council chamber and a brothel. ⚲✿◖◗♣P

INDEPENDENT BREWERIES

Abbey Bells Hirst Courtney
Black Sheep Masham
Brown Cow Barlow
Captain Cook Stokesley
Copper Dragon Skipton
Cropton Cropton
Daleside Harrogate
Franklin's Bilton
Hambleton Holme-on-Swale
Malton Malton
Marston Moor Tockwith (not currently brewing)
North Yorkshire Pinchinthorpe
Old Bear Cross Hills
Rooster's Knaresborough
Rudgate Tockwith
Selby Selby
Samuel Smith Tadcaster
York York

DALLOWGILL

Drovers' Inn

HG4 3RH (2 miles W of Laverton on Pateley Bridge road) OS210720

☼ 12-3 (summer only), 7 (6.30 Sat)-11; closed Mon; 12-3, 6.30-10.30 Sun

☎ (01765) 658510

Black Sheep Best Bitter; Hambleton Bitter; Old Mill Bitter Ⓗ

Small, stone inn situated high on the moors overlooking Nidderdale. As the name implies, the pub is adjacent to the old road where drovers took animals to the market in Pateley Bridge. Highly regarded for its good value, traditional, home-cooked meals, it is well used by walkers in summer and shooting parties from the moors. You are assured of a warm welcome at this cosy hostelry. ♨Q❀◑Å♣P

DALTON

Moor & Pheasant

YO7 3JD

☼ 12-11; 12-10.30 Sun

☎ (01845) 577268

John Smith's Bitter; guest beer Ⓗ

Formerly the Railway Inn (the London–Edinburgh line passes close by, but the station is now closed), this pub lies on the southern outskirts of the village, five miles south of Thirsk. A small front bar, with a pool table, shares a servery with the larger lounge that doubles as a dining area, serving good value meals (no food Sun eve). Outside is a large play area for children and a private static caravan site. ♨❀◑🛏&♣Pⓣ

DALTON-ON-TEES

Chequers Inn

DL2 2NS

☼ 12-3, 5.30-11; 12-11 Sat; 12-10.30 Sun

☎ (01325) 721213 website: www.thechequers.biz

John Smith's Bitter; guest beers Ⓗ

Traditional inn dating back to the 1840s, consisting of a bar, lounge and restaurant. Formerly known as the Crown & Anchor, this was once a Fryer's house, part of the now-defunct Fryer's Brewery. The landlord is passionate about real ale and at least two guest beers are available from micros countrywide. Regular gourmet evenings take place and a quiz is held every Wednesday. Q❀🛏◑&Å♣P⤬

EAST WITTON

Cover Bridge Inn

DL8 4SQ (on A6108, ¾ mile N of village)

☼ 11-11; 12-10.30 Sun

☎ (01969) 623250

website: www.thecoverbridgeinn.co.uk

Black Sheep Best Bitter; Taylor Landlord; Theakston Best Bitter, Old Peculier; guest beers Ⓗ

Dating from at least the 15th century and retaining many original features in several rooms, this inn enjoys a splendid location on the Cover near its confluence with the Ure. When you have puzzled out the escutcheon door latch you are met by a cosy atmosphere, log fires and bench seating. The sacked abbey of Jervaulx and ruins of Richard III's castle of Middleham are nearby, as well as good walks in all directions and fishing on the doorstep. It is

served weekdays by a Bedale–Leyburn bus and a Richmond–Ripon bus (Mon–Sat). ♨Q⏦❀🛏◑🛏Å♣P⤬ⓣ

EGTON

Wheatsheaf Inn

YO21 1TZ

☼ 11-3 (not Mon), 5.30-11; 11-11 Fri & Sat; 12-10.30 Sun

☎ (01947) 895271

Black Sheep Best Bitter; Theakston Best Bitter, Black Bull Ⓗ

In the middle of the village stands this Grade I listed pub. It has a small bar on the right, a central lounge and a no-smoking dining room with church pew-style seats, where children are welcome. Sit on the grass to enjoy your drink in the summer. The locals aid the Runswick inshore rescue boat. It is popular with visitors to the agricultural show and walkers and anglers on the River Esk nearby. Usually quiet – the TV is only turned on when there is rugby to watch. ♨Q❀🛏◑🛏&Å♣

EGTON BRIDGE

Horseshoe Hotel ⊘

YO21 1XE (from Egton Station, downhill, across river; bear right) OS801052

☼ 11-3, 6.30-11; 12-4, 7-10.30 Sun

☎ (01947) 895245

John Smith's Bitter; Theakston Best Bitter; guest beers Ⓗ

No visit to this part of the North Yorkshire Moors National Park is complete without a walk on the stepping stones and a pint in this justly popular old inn. A large garden, a recommended no-smoking restaurant, two intimate drinking areas and a good selection of ales are among its attractions. Go there by train or finish a walk on the moors in the bar to fully appreciate a peaceful pint. ♨Q⏦❀🛏◑🛏⇌♣P

ELVINGTON

Grey Horse

Main Street, YO41 4AG

(on B1228, 6 miles SE of York)

☼ 12-3, 5.30-11; 12-11 Sat; 12-10.30 Sun

☎ (01904) 608335

Black Sheep Best Bitter; John Smith's Bitter; Taylor Landlord; Theakston Black Bull; guest beers Ⓗ

Small pub where two rooms are served from a central bar. In summer there is outdoor seating at the front and in the yard; in winter two wood-burning stoves add to the comfortable atmosphere inside. The lounge displays photographs of the WWII bombers that used to fly from Elvington Aerodrome, next to the village (now the Yorkshire Air Museum). The guest beers change often. Recent renovations have provided accommodation and a restaurant (no meals are served Mon eve). ♨❀◑🛏Å♣P

EMBSAY

Elm Tree

5 Elm Tree Square, BD23 6RB

☼ 11.30-3, 5.30-11; 12-3, 7-10.30 Sun

☎ (01756) 790717

Goose Eye No-Eyed Deer; Tetley Bitter; guest beers Ⓗ

Former coaching inn, popular for both drink and food. Situated on the edge of the

Yorkshire Dales National Park, it is a handy base for walking on Barden Moor and Embsay Crag. The Embsay–Bolton Abbey steam railway runs nearby. The large main room has a smaller no-smoking side room used mainly by diners. The main menu is supplemented by a specials board. Look for the worn mounting steps at the front of the pub.

Q ✿ ⇔ ◖◗ P

GIGGLESWICK

Harts Head
Belle Hill, BD24 0BA (on B6480)
✿ 12-2.30, 5-11; 11-11 Sat; 12-10.30 Sun
☎ (01729) 822086
website: www.hotel52.freeserve.co.uk
Black Sheep Best Bitter; Taylor Landlord; Tetley Bitter; guest beers Ⓗ
Large, comfortably-furnished coaching inn, parts of which are 250 years old. Four drinking areas, a pool table and a full-sized snooker table are available. In the early 18th century the inn was the secret headquarters of the local Jacobite movement. A later owner was the local GP, Dr Buck. A talented amateur musician, the doctor formed a lasting friendship with Sir Edward Elgar, who was a regular visitor to the hotel. An imaginative menu and highly-rated en-suite accommodation complete the amenities here.

🏨 Q ✿ ⇔ ◖◗ ♣ P

GOLDSBOROUGH

Fox & Hounds
YO21 3RX (just out of village towards Whitby)
OS836145
✿ 12-3 (not winter Mon-Fri), 7-11; 12-3, 7-10.30 (may vary) Sun
☎ (01947) 893372
Black Sheep Best Bitter; guest beer (occasional) Ⓗ
Goldsborough is a farming hamlet in a quiet part of North Yorkshire. Jet and alum were once mined at nearby Kettleness and the Roman signalled from there. A good place to stop, just off the Cleveland Way, the pub is 400 years old, built of sandstone, with a small dining or children's room on the right and the bar on the left. At the back of the pub is the lounge/restaurant. It is decorated traditionally with beams and brasses. The garden has play equipment.

🏨 Q ☎ ✿ ◖◗ ⊟ ▲ ♣ P

GRASSINGTON

Foresters Arms ✪
20 Main Street, BD23 5AA
✿ 11-11; 12-10.30 Sun
☎ (01756) 752349
Black Sheep Best Bitter; Taylor Best Bitter; Tetley Mild, Bitter; guest beers Ⓗ
Originally a coaching inn, this village-centre local now has an opened-out feel. The bar and pool room/TV area are to the left; a second spacious seating area leads to the dining room where the menu includes a take-away option. Up to four guest beers are stocked. A quiz is held on Monday. Euros are accepted here. Traditional games include shove-ha'penny and devil among the tailors.

🏨 ☎ ✿ ⇔ ◖◗ ♣ P

GREAT BROUGHTON

Black Horse
2 Ingleby Road, TS9 7ER
✿ 6 (12 Sat)-11; 12-10.30 Sun
☎ (01642) 713962
Camerons Strongarm Ⓗ
Traditional, friendly local, popular with Coast-to-Coast and Cleveland Way walkers. Set in the middle of the picturesque village of Great Broughton, you can enjoy views of Crinkle Moor from the patio in the summer. The pub has a cosy lounge with a real fire and is decorated with hunting pictures and memorabilia. The bar/games room also has a real fire and hosts occasional live music. The pub has a warm, friendly atmosphere; children are welcome in the lounge until about 9pm. Meals are served in summer. 🏨 ✿ ⇔ ◖◗ ▲ ♣ P

GREAT HECK

Bay Horse
Main Street, DN14 0BQ
✿ 7-11; 12-2, 7-11 Fri & Sat; 12-2, 7-10.30 Sun
☎ (01977) 661125
Worthington's 1744; guest beer Ⓗ
On a bend in the road as you enter the village, from the A19, this quiet country pub is a compact, low-beamed former cottage dating from the 17th century. It has been knocked through, but retains three distinct areas; sympathetic renovations preserve a traditional, but light, look. The cosy feel is enhanced in winter by an open fire. Ideal for summer outings and lunchtime treats, this pub is also handy for users of the Aire and Calder Canal. Opening hours may vary in summer. 🏨 ✿ ◖◗ P

GREAT OUSEBURN

Crown Inn
YO26 9RF (on main street, B6265)
✿ 5 (12 Sat)-11; 12-10.30 Sun
☎ (01423) 330430
Black Sheep Best Bitter; John Smith's Bitter; Tetley Bitter Ⓗ
This is the only pub in this picturesque village. It offers Sunday lunches and an early bird menu in the bar – £9 for two courses, served 5–6.30, or you can dine in the restaurant. All the food is freshly prepared and cooked to order. Cosy and welcoming, the pub has open fires and is full of interesting wartime memorabilia. A little off the beaten track, but well worth a visit, it is situated between York and Boroughbridge. 🏨 Q ☎ ✿ ◖◗ P

GREAT SMEATON

Bay Horse
DL6 2EH (on A167)
✿ 12-2 (not Mon or Tue), 6-11; 11-11 Sat; 12-10.30 Sun
☎ (01609) 881466
John Smith's Bitter; guest beers Ⓗ
Small, 18th-century free house situated in the middle of a row of roadside cottages in an attractive village setting. It consists of a soft furnished lounge, with central fireplace and beams; a bustling little bar and a games room to the rear. Up to two guest beers are available from micro-breweries countrywide. This former CAMRA Rural Pub

of the Year has a charming, enclosed garden to the rear with small play area. No food is served Monday evening. ♨☙♿🌳🍴♣☗

GROSMONT

Crossing Club
Front Street, YO22 5QE (next to Co-op and Yorkshire Trading Post) OS828952
🕐 7 (11 Sat)-11; 12-10.30 Sun
☎ (01947) 895040
Banks's Original; Black Sheep Best Bitter; guest beers (summer) Ⓗ

Brilliant, comfortable conversion of the old Co-op delivery bay, undertaken by village volunteers, featuring splendid red walls and railway memorabilia, including its own indoor level crossing gate. Up to three real ales are sourced from independent breweries, usually including a mild. Members are proud of their club and very hospitable to visitors – ring the bell and ask to be signed in. Children are welcome until 9.30pm. Bar snacks are available. ♨☗

GUISBOROUGH

Anchor
16 Belmangate, TS14 7AB
🕐 11-11; 12-10.30 Sun
☎ (01287) 632715
Samuel Smith OBB Ⓗ

Small, quaint pub consisting of three rooms. On entering there is a corridor where a tap room runs off to the left and a lounge to the right (both burning real fires). A conservatory leads to the garden at the rear. Bar meals are served at lunchtime: a good selection of traditional food at reasonable prices. Children are welcome, but the pub does get smoky. Quoits is played here. ♨Q♿🌳🍴♣

Voyager
The Avenue, TS14 8DN (just off Stokesley road)
🕐 12-11.30; 12-10.30 Sun
☎ (01287) 634774
Banks's Bitter; Camerons Strongarm Ⓗ

Interesting, modern pub, rebuilt five years ago and reminiscent of a Swiss chalet. On entering there is a spacious lounge which includes the bar, leading to the family/no-smoking/dining area and a games area. It has low beams and brewing artefacts are displayed on ledges around the roof. Food is served all day from a varied menu, listed on chalkboards. A quiz is held every Tuesday.
🌳🍴♣P✖

HAMPSTHWAITE

Joiners Arms
High Street, HG3 2EU
🕐 11.30-2.30, 5.30-11; 11.30-11 Sat; 12-10.30 Sun
☎ (01423) 771673
John Smith's Bitter; Tetley Bitter; guest beer Ⓗ

This 200-year-old, comfortable village pub is close to the A59 and the Nidderdale Way. The two bars are connected by an unusual barrel-roofed snug. The dining area features an unusual collection of gravy boats; evening meals are served Wednesday–Saturday. Facilities in the main bar include, unusually, a Link cash dispenser.
🌳🍴☗P

HARROGATE

Coach & Horses
16 West Park, HG1 1BJ (facing the Stray)
🕐 11-11; 12-10.30 Sun
Black Sheep Best Bitter; Daleside Bitter, Blonde; Tetley Bitter; guest beers Ⓗ

The staff are rightly proud of the friendly atmosphere, quality beers and superb food here. This busy, popular pub consists of a central bar adorned by six handpumps where seating is arranged into snugs and alcoves. An agreement to showcase local brewery, Daleside in 2002 saw the introduction of the two regular beers, a third is featured as one of the two guests; Coniston Brewery and Rooster's Yankee complete the portfolio. Local CAMRA's Pub of the Season summer 2002.
🍴≢

Gardeners Arms ☆
Bilton Lane, HG1 4DH (1 mile off A59)
🕐 12-3, 6-11; 12-3, 7-10.30 Sun
☎ (01423) 506051
Samuel Smith OBB Ⓗ

Built in the 1500s, with thick stone walls and wood panelling, this totally unspoilt pub boasts a large stone fireplace and a tiny snug. A little gem, it is popular in summer for its excellent garden by a stream with much wildlife. It stands on the route of a bridle path used by Oliver Cromwell after destroying Knaresborough Castle. Fishing tickets are available for the River Nidd. No evening meals are served winter Sunday or Wednesday.
♨Q🌳🍴P

Old Bell Tavern
6 Royal Parade, HG1 2SZ
🕐 12-11; 12-10.30 Sun
☎ (01423) 507930
website: www.markettowntaverns.co.uk
Black Sheep Best Bitter; Taylor Landlord; guest beers Ⓗ

Long the site of an inn, the present building dates from 1846; see the documents relating to the original inn and memorabilia of Farrah's toffee shop into which the pub was extended to provide a no-smoking area. A range of eight real ales, usually including local products, is complemented by two foreign draught beers and an extensive range of continental bottled beers. Top quality food is available in the bar and upstairs no-smoking dining room.
Q🍴≢✖

Tap & Spile ⊘
Tower Street, HG1 1HS
(opp. multi-storey car park)
🕐 11-11; 12-10.30 Sun
☎ (01423) 526785
Big Lamp Bitter; Theakston Best Bitter, Old Peculier; guest beers Ⓗ

Well-established quality ale house, popular with all ages. The pub has three drinking areas, one of which is no-smoking, linked by a central bar. A mixture of wood panelling and exposed brick walls are used to display many old photographs of the town. Folk music on Tuesday evening and rock music (Thu eve) add to the atmosphere. No lunches are served on Sunday; the cider is Westons Old Rosie.
🌳🍴♣●✖

Winter Gardens ✓
4 Royal Baths, HG1 2RR
☼ 10-11; 12-10.30 Sun
☎ (01423) 877010
Greene King Abbot; Hop Back Summer Lightning; Shepherd Neame Spitfire; Theakston Best Bitter; guest beers Ⓗ

Formerly Harrogate's Lounge Hall, now an imposing Wetherspoon's conversion. You cannot fail to be impressed by the magnificent stairway leading down into the main part of the pub. The work put into the building reflects its former glory as a ballroom. In keeping with most Wetherspoon's pubs, food and drink offers excellent value for money. The pub is close to the town's Royal Hall and other conference facilities. Q ⑤ ❀ ◖◗ ᵹ ≠ ✂

HELPERBY

Half Moon
Main Street, YO61 2PS
☼ 5 (3 summer)-11; 12-11 Sat; 12-10.30 Sun
☎ (01423) 360270
Daleside Bitter; Greene King IPA Ⓗ

True village local that has served Helperby for at least 150 years. It concentrates on providing an interesting range of good beer, rather than on food, like so many other country pubs. The wood furniture and real fire in the main drinking area add to the traditional atmosphere and two smaller seating areas are located to the right of the bar. The house beer is Daleside Half Moon. ᐃ ♣ ♠ P

HELWITH BRIDGE

Helwith Bridge
BD24 0EH
☼ 11-11; 12-10.30 Sun
☎ (01729) 860220 website: www.helwithbridge.com
McEwan 80/-; Marston's Pedigree; Theakston Best Bitter; Webster's Bitter; Wells Bombardier; guest beers Ⓗ

Friendly, stone-flagged pub, full of character, backing on to the River Ribble, affording good views of the Settle–Carlisle Railway and Pen-y-Ghent. Recently partly divided to create a cosy alcove separate from the main bar, railway photos and paintings decorate the walls and a roaring fire is guaranteed in winter. Food is available all day, with a full menu Tuesday–Sunday 12–3 and 6–9. Guest beers are mainly from the Scottish Courage list. ᐃ ❀ ◖◗ ᐱ ♣ P

HENSALL

Anchor
Main Street, DN14 0QZ
☼ 5 (12 Sat)-11; 12-10.30 Sun
☎ (01977) 661634
Taylor Landlord; Tetley Bitter; guest beer (occasional) Ⓗ

Old village pub that has been thoroughly modernised, and is bigger than it looks from outside. It retains a traditional look and comfortable feel with beams, brassware, mirrors, bric-à-brac and real fire in winter. An open-plan layout is served by a central bar, but it retains discrete areas, including a restaurant, which offers an extensive, varied menu. This community pub serves Sunday lunches and evening meals Monday–Saturday (except Tue). ❀ ◖◗ P

HILTON

Falcon
Seamer Road, TS15 9LB
☼ 11.30-11; 12-10.30 Sun
☎ (01642) 592228
Beer range varies Ⓗ

Much extended village pub with a strong emphasis on food, but whose bar area is popular with village drinkers. The licensee has a long-standing reputation in the area for serving excellent real ale; guest beers are often from local micros, with North Yorkshire Brewing Company ales making frequent appearances. The restaurant draws customers from a wide area to enjoy the range of good value daily specials served all day. Occasional live music is performed. ᐃ ❀ ◖◗ ♣ P

HUBY

New Inn
Main Street, YO61 1HQ
(off B1363, 6 miles N of York) OS566656
☼ 5.30-11; 12-3, 6-11 Sat; 12-3, 6.30-10.30 Sun
☎ (01347) 810393
Black Sheep Best Bitter; John Smith's Bitter; Taylor Landlord; Tetley Bitter; guest beers Ⓗ

Three ancient cottages were converted to create this village local, north of York (not to be confused with the village of Huby near Harrogate). Many original features remain, notably ceiling beams and a fine Yorkshire range in the old kitchen area. Good value food is served each evening, with a dining room extension giving more formal surroundings. The decor commemorates its use by Canadian airmen during WWII. Today local customers are joined by visiting country sports enthusiasts. ᐃ Q ◖◗ ⊞ ♣ P ✂

HUTTON RUDBY

King's Head
36 North Side, TS15 0DA
☼ 12-11; 12-10.30 Sun
☎ (01642) 700342
Camerons Strongarm; Marston's Pedigree; guest beer Ⓗ

Set in an historic village, where scenic walks along the River Leven can be enjoyed, the pub stands on the north side of the broad main street. It is a traditional pub with beamed ceilings, a coal fire and brasses on the wainscotting. The bar is partially divided by a wooden partition to give a lounge and a no-smoking snug-cum-restaurant lies across the corridor where children are admitted. Meals are served 12–7. It hosts a quiz on Tuesday. Cleveland CAMRA Pub of the Year 2002. ᐃ Q ⑤ ❀ ♣ ✂ ⊟

INGLETON

Wheatsheaf ✓
22 High Street, LA6 3AD
☼ 12-11; 12-10.30 Sun
☎ (015242) 41275
Black Sheep Best Bitter, Special; Taylor Golden Best; Tetley Bitter Ⓗ

Towards the top end of the village, the Wheatsheaf is handy for the finish of the Waterfalls Walk. One long, narrow bar is divided into different areas, displaying a growing collection of stuffed animals. It is popular with tourists, who come especially for the accommodation or the restaurant. Birds of prey are kept in the garden. Ingleton is served by bus Nos. 80 and 80A to Lancaster and the infrequent No. 580 to Settle. ⌂❀⇌◑◐▲♣P

KETTLESING

Queen's Head

HG3 2LB (signed off A59 W of Harrogate) OS225574

11-11; 11-3, 6.30-11 Sat; 12-2.30, 6.30-10.30 Sun

☎ (01423) 770263

Black Sheep Best Bitter, Special; Theakston Old Peculier; guest beer Ⓗ

Located in a quiet village, this stone pub is noted for its food. An entrance lobby, dominated by a portrait of Queen Elizabeth I leads to two bars. One is a large L-shaped room while the smaller bar is decorated with cricketing memorabilia, presumably intended to baffle transatlantic real ale aficionados from the nearby American base. Outdoor facilities include benches at the front of the pub and a large patio area at the rear. ⌂Q❀⇌P

KIRBY HILL (BOROUGHBRIDGE)

Blue Bell

Leeming Lane, YO51 9DN

6-11; 12-5, 7-11 Sat; 12-4.30, 7-10.30 Sun

☎ (01423) 324180

Greene King Ruddles County; John Smith's Bitter; Tetley Bitter; Theakston Old Peculier Ⓗ

Alongside the old Great North Road, this imposing multi-roomed pub is spacious, yet homely. One area offers a pool table and piped music, while the lounge has wood panels, a piano and an open fire – a welcome retreat for travellers and locals alike from the nearby A1. Reasonably-priced accommodation is available in this pub, which is almost equidistant between London and Edinburgh. It hosts occasional beer festivals, one is held around Easter. No evening meals are served Sunday or Wednesday.

⌂Q❀⇌◑◐▲♣P⊁

KIRKHAM ABBEY

Stone Trough Inn

YO60 7JS (on A64, between York and Malton)

12-2.30, 6-11; closed Mon; 12-10.30 Sun

☎ (01653) 618713 website: www.stonetroughinn.co.uk

Black Sheep Best Bitter; Malton Golden Chance; Taylor Landlord; Tetley Bitter; guest beers Ⓗ

With a history dating back to 1120, the present pub was converted from a cottage in 1983. The terrace affords stunning views over Kirkham Priory, the River Derwent and the Vale of York. Inside, low, beamed ceilings, open fires and a flagged floor provide an inviting, cosy atmosphere. Renowned for its award-winning beers, the bar/restaurant is a gastronomic oasis, serving outstanding food (eve meals Tue–Sat). Malton Brewery provides the house beer.

⌂Q❀◑◐♣P

KIRKLEVINGTON

Crown

Thirsk Road, TS15 9LT (on A67 near A19 Crathorne interchange)

5 (12 Sat)-11; 12-10.30 Sun

☎ (01642) 780044

Castle Eden Ale; John Smith's Magnet Ⓗ

Old whitewashed pub overlooking a road junction in a quiet village, bypassed by the busy A19. The warm, welcoming interior is divided into two drinking areas: one area has a pool table and is popular with younger drinkers; the other is used for both drinking and dining and boasts a large ornate wooden fire surround. All meals – served Tuesday–Saturday evening and Sunday lunchtime – are prepared and cooked to order. A little off the beaten track, this pub is well worth searching out. Children are welcome. ⌂❀◐&♣P

KNARESBOROUGH

Blind Jack's

18a Market Place, HG5 8AL

4 (5.30 Mon; 12 Fri & Sat)-11; 12-10.30 Sun

☎ (01423) 869148

Black Sheep Best Bitter; Daleside Greengrass; Taylor Landlord; Village White Boar; guest beers Ⓗ

Wonderful bustling ale house in a characterful Georgian building. Bare brick walls, dark wood panelling and floorboards and breweriana on the walls help to create a warm, friendly drinking establishment. The pub is at the centre of this pretty market town and attracts many people who appreciate the traditional atmosphere where the only noise is lively conversation.

Q⇌⊁

LANGDALE END

Moorcock Inn

YO13 0BN OS938913

11-2, 6.30-11 (phone for winter hours); 12-3, 6.30-10.30 Sun

☎ (01723) 882268

Beer range varies Ⓗ

Classic example of a rural Yorkshire pub. Situated in a remote village, four miles from Scarborough, near Dalby Forest Drive, it is well off the beaten track but worth seeking out. The varied beer range is usually sourced from Yorkshire micros and small regional breweries. The beer is served through a hatch in both the rooms. Its beamed interior, with tiled floor and bench seating, is totally unspoilt. Excellent quality home-cooked food is served daily in summer.

⌂Q❀◑◐▲♣P

LAZENBY

Half Moon

High Street, TS6 8DX (off A174, close to the Wilton works)

11-11; 12-10.30 Sun

☎ (01642) 452752

Beer range varies Ⓗ

Located beneath the Eston Hills, the view from the patio at the rear of the pub is spectacular. The Half Moon is an Enterprise Inns free house, a traditional village inn enjoying an excellent reputation for home-cooked food, which is served daily (12–9). It stages occasional speciality food nights. You can eat in the no-smoking dining area where children are welcome. The pub keeps up to five cask ales that vary on a weekly basis. ⌖❀◗ ♿P

LEALHOLM

Board Inn
Village Green, YO21 2AJ OS762075
🕑 12-3 (not winter), 7-11; 11-11 Sat; 12-4, 7-10.30 Sun
☎ (01947) 897279
Camerons Strongarm; guest beer (summer) Ⓗ
Sandstone inn, dating from 1742, with a new restaurant, guest accommodation and toilets. A self-catering cottage is to let. This traditional country inn also has a games room and a large garden leading down to the River Esk. The pub sponsors the local football club. Ghosts have been seen – even by the sober. Quoits is played on the adjacent village green (but do not park there). Cross the stepping stones to the nursery or browse the secondhand bookshop. ♨Q⌖❀➠◗�̄➤⌔♣P✄

LEAVENING

Jolly Farmers
Main Street, YO17 9SA
🕑 12-3 (not Mon or Tue), 7-11; 12-4, 7-10.30 Sun
☎ (01653) 658276
John Smith's Bitter; Taylor Landlord; Tetley Bitter; guest beers Ⓗ
Between York and Malton on the edge of the Yorkshire Wolds, this former York CAMRA Pub of the Year dates from the 17th century. Although it has been extended, it retains the cosiness of its original multi-room layout. Guest beers often include strong ales from independent breweries and additional guest beers may be available directly from the cellar – ask. The restaurant specialises in locally-caught game. Accommodation is in a holiday cottage. ♨⌖❀➠◗♣P☗

LEYBURN

Black Swan Hotel
Market Place, DL8 5AS
🕑 11.30-11; 12-10.30 Sun
☎ (01969) 623131
Black Sheep Best Bitter; John Smith's Bitter; Taylor Landlord; guest beer (summer) Ⓗ
The ivy-clad exterior of this market town pub, dating from 1713, opens into a neatly divided interior with a decor of pictures and artefacts of local interest. One fascinating photograph shows the pub's exterior in 1870, when it was known as the Cornmarket. Friendly staff help create a cheerful atmosphere. The accommodation varies from basic single rooms to luxury double en-suites. From the wide range of home-cooked food the Sunday carvery is especially good value. The garden is safe for children.
♨Q⌖❀➠◗♿➤ (Wensleydale Rlwy) ♣P

LONG PRESTON

Maypole Inn
BD23 4PH
🕑 11-3, 6 (5 Sat)-11; (11-11 summer Sat); 12-10.30 Sun
☎ (01729) 840219 website: www.maypole.co.uk

Moorhouses Premier; Taylor Landlord; Tetley Bitter; guest beer Ⓗ
On the village green, opposite the maypole, this village local has won many CAMRA awards. The tap room boasts carved bench seating dating from 1875. The cosy lounge displays a list of the pub's licensees since 1695 and old photos of the village showing a quieter A65 road. Good value food (served all day Sun) can be eaten in the pub or in the no-smoking dining room. Dogs are welcome in the tap room.
♨Q❀➠◗➤♣●P

LOW BENTHAM

Sun Dial
LA2 7DS
🕑 11-3 (not Wed), 5-11, 11-11 Fri & Sat; 12-10.30 Sun
☎ (015242) 65132
Beer range varies Ⓗ
The Sun Dial remains what it has always been – a village local. It comprises a small, homely bar and an even smaller games room, which becomes a dining room in the summer. Note the old sundial that serves as an inn sign. Four draught beers often include a national brand, and brews from Everards, Jennings and Moorhouses. Bus Nos. 80 and 80A stop nearby. ❀◗♣P

LOW MARISHES

School House Inn
YO17 6RJ (800 yds from A169, Malton-Pickering road)
🕑 11.30-3, 6-11; 12-10.30 Sun
☎ (01653) 668247
Black Sheep Best Bitter; Hambleton Stallion, Nightmare; Tetley Bitter; guest beers Ⓗ
Cosy, multi-roomed pub offering excellent food. This wonderful, unspoilt inn is a little off the beaten track but worth finding. Eat in the dining room or conservatory and take drinks out on to the patio. Pool and darts are available in the games room, along with three on-line computers. Children (and dogs) are welcome here.
♨Q❀◗➤♣P

MALHAM

Lister Arms
BD23 4DB
🕑 12-3, 7-11; 12-11 Sat; 12-10.30 Sun
☎ (01729) 830330 website: www.listerarms.co.uk
Boddingtons Bitter; Marston's Pedigree; Taylor Landlord; guest beers Ⓗ
This 18th-century pub, dated 1702, is just off the village centre. A tiled entrance leads to the main bar area which faces the garden to the rear – a suntrap in summer. The front room looks towards the village. The accommodation and food are both of a high standard. It stocks up to three guest beers, plus a good range of foreign bottled beers and a draught cider in summer. Internet access is available and table football is played. ♨❀➠◗♠♣●P

MALTON

Crown Hotel (Suddaby's)
12 Wheelgate, YO15 0JJ
🕑 11-11; 12-4, 7-10.30 Sun
☎ (01653) 692038 website: www.suddabys.co.uk

Malton Double Chance, Golden Chance, seasonal beers; John Smith's Bitter; guest beers Ⓗ
This Grade II listed, town-centre building has been run by five generations of the Suddaby family since 1879. Many original features remain. Of its eight bedrooms, two en-suites are over the brewery annexe. Malton beers are regularly supplied to many outlets, near and far. The bar, with a horse-racing theme, is popular with the local stable lads. Lunches are served Saturday (sandwiches Mon–Fri). Live music, including jazz, folk, and piano recitals are performed in the conservatory; seasonal beer festivals are held. ▲Q⌂❀🖤◑≈♣P✠

MANFIELD

Crown Inn
Vicars Lane, DL2 2RF (500 yds from B6275)
✪ 5.30-11; 11-11 Sat; 12-10.30 Sun
☎ (01325) 374243
Village White Boar, Bull; guest beers Ⓗ
Attractive, 18th-century inn, situated in a quiet village. Consisting of the main lounge and a games room; the design of the bar allows both areas to be served. The mix of locals and visitors gives the pub a friendly atmosphere. Up to four guest beers come from micro-breweries countrywide, along with Dentergems wheat beer on draught. Local CAMRA Rural Pub of the Year 2003, it hosts two beer festivals a year. Snacks available. ▲Q❀◑♣P🍴

MARTON

Appletree
YO62 6RD (3 miles S of A170 between Pickering and Kirkbymoorside)
✪ 12-2.30, 6.30-11; closed Tue; 12-3, 7-10.30 Sun
☎ (01751) 431457
John Smith's Bitter; guest beers Ⓗ
Commodious, smart, village pub: two comfortable lounge bars with settees, beams and a huge fireplace, and two restaurants (both no-smoking). The absolutely immaculate dining room, has a further large room full of various sofas, where you can relax while waiting to dine, or browse through newspapers with a drink; this overlooks the patio and garden. Winner of Publican Magazine's Customer Service Pub of the Year award. ▲Q❀◑P

MASHAM

Black Sheep Brewery Visitors Centre
Wellgarth, HG4 4EN (follow tourist signs on A6108)
✪ 11-11; closed Mon & Tue in Jan/Feb; 12-5.30 Sun
☎ (01765) 680100 website: www.blacksheep.co.uk
Black Sheep Best Bitter, Special, Riggwelter, seasonal beers Ⓗ
Located in a former maltings this spacious, open-plan bistro is attached to the brewery, where regular tours are arranged. The bistro caters for passing tourists who just want a snack or coffee, or a more substantial meal, washed down with a pint of popular beers brewed here, followed by a browse around the 'sheepy shop'. Families are welcome during the day. What could be better in summer than to sit in the small garden surrounded by Lower Wensleydale's scenery?
❀◑占P

White Bear
12 Crosshills, HG4 4EN
✪ 11-11; 12-10.30 Sun
☎ (01765) 689319
Caledonian Deuchars IPA; Theakston Best Bitter, Black Bull, Old Peculier; guest beer Ⓗ
This attractive limestone inn is situated on the outskirts of Masham. It retains a traditional public bar which is popular with the locals and there is a spacious lounge that is often busy with diners. The whole place has a friendly community feel to it, but it is also highly regarded by visitors who enjoy the relaxed atmosphere. Occasional live music is staged. Admire the cooper at work in the stained glass panel behind the bar. ▲❀◑▣P

MELMERBY

George & Dragon
Main Street, HG4 5HA
✪ 5-11 (also opens 12-2 summer Thu & Fri); 12-11 Sat; 12-10.30 Sun
☎ (01765) 640970
Black Sheep Best Bitter; Hambleton Bitter; Tetley Bitter; guest beer Ⓗ
Cosy village pub in a listed building dating from the mid 1700s. Two beamed rooms, complete with coal fires, are situated either side of the island bar, both comfortably furnished. The new restaurant serves an imaginative home-cooked menu complemented by a good wine list (no food Mon). Crossword enthusiasts are welcome to join the communal puzzle solving around the bar each evening. ▲Q◑♣P

MIDDLESBROUGH

Doctor Brown's
135 Corporation Road, TS1 1NA
(opp. UGC Cinema, just off A66)
✪ 12-11; 12-10.30 Sun
☎ (01642) 213213
Courage Directors; Marston's Pedigree; guest beers Ⓗ
Large, friendly, end-of-terrace pub in a pedestrianised area of town. The pub is divided into three sections, and half can be partitioned off for group or party bookings. Live music is a major feature here, staging bands every Friday and Saturday evenings, plus some Thursdays and Sundays. Guest ales are from the SIBA range. The pub is handy for the new UGC Cinema, and the Riverside Stadium, so it can get very busy when Middlesbrough are playing at home. ❀◑占≈

Star & Garter
14 Southfield Road, TS1 3BZ
(opp. student union building)
✪ 11-11; 12-10.30 Sun
☎ (01642) 245307
Beer range varies Ⓗ
Former dockers' club, which won a CAMRA Pub Preservation Award for the conversion, although the bar has since been redecorated in a rather different style. Despite being close to the university, the pub attracts a wide-ranging clientele. It can be very busy at weekends and when Middlesbrough FC are on the large-screen TV. Four guest beers are available in the lounge, often from small independent brewers; the pub occasionally holds beer festivals. ❀◑▣占≈♣P

NORTHALLERTON

Station Hotel ✓
2 Boroughbridge Road, DL7 8AN
☼ 12-2.30, 5-11; 7-11 Sat; 12-3, 7-10.30 Sun
☎ (01609) 772053
website: www.stationhotel-northallerton.com
Tetley Bitter; guest beers Ⓗ
An imposing frontage reveals a pub of character close to the station and opposite North Yorkshire County Hall. The interior has been restored in recent years and etched windows proclaim its earlier name of the Railway Hotel. It offers good value accommodation and food, especially Sunday lunches (booking advised). Children are made welcome here.
🏤Q🐾❀⌂Ⓓ♿⇌♣P

Tithe Bar
2 Friarage Street, DL6 1DP (off High St)
☼ 12-11; 12-10.30 Sun
☎ (01609) 778482
website: www.markettowntaverns.co.uk
Black Sheep Best Bitter; Taylor Landlord; guest beers Ⓗ
Attractive, modern, yet traditional bar created in Belgian style with wood and panelling. Four constantly-changing guests and a wide variety of continental beers have helped the Tithe Bar win a number of awards. A brasserie upstairs serves excellent food based on local produce; snacks and meals are also available in the bar. This is an excellent example of how a new pub can thrive on fine beer and food. QⓊ♿⇌♣✂

NUN MONKTON

Alice Hawthorn
The Green, YO26 8EN
(off A59, York-Harrogate road)
☼ 12-2, 6-11; 12-10.30 Sun
☎ (01423) 330303 website: www.alicehawthorn.co.uk
Camerons Strongarm; John Smith's Bitter; Taylor Landlord; guest beers Ⓗ
At the end of a country lane, this cosy pub offers an excellent range of home-cooked food. Enjoy the view of the maypole and duckpond on the village green, or huddle around a log fire in winter. Named after a famous racehorse of the 1840s, it is a firm favourite with the fishing and boating fraternity from nearby rivers Ouse and Nidd. Walkers are welcome – local routes are available on request. Outside are patio tables and a children's playground.
🏤❀Ⓓ♿🅿️Ⓐ♣P

OLD MALTON

Wentworth Arms
Town Street, YO17 7HD
(200 yds off Malton bypass, A64)
☼ 11.30-2.30, 5-11; 11.30-11 Sat & summer; 12-10.30 Sun
☎ (01653) 692618
Tetley Bitter; guest beers Ⓗ
Originally an 18th-century coaching inn, the drinking area is in a low, beamed lounge. A no-smoking restaurant has been converted from an adjoining barn. The cask ales change often, with usually one from Durham Brewery; it hosts occasional mini beer festivals. Good value, home-cooked meals, including daily specials, make the most of local produce. Much frequented by locals, visitors are made welcome at this excellent stopping-off point, halfway between York and Scarborough.
🏤Q❀⌂Ⓓ♿♣P

OSMOTHERLEY

Golden Lion
6 West End, DL6 3AA
(1 mile E of A19 at A684 jct)
☼ 12-4, 6-11; 12-11 Sat; 12-10.30 Sun
☎ (01609) 883526
Hambleton Bitter; John Smith's Bitter; Taylor Landlord Ⓗ
This pub has simple decor and a warm, intimate atmosphere created by the use of low lighting and candles. The clever use of mirrors gives an illusion of size. Freshly cut flowers are usually found throughout, complementing the spectacular window boxes outside. On the edge of the National Park at the end of the Like Wake Walk, this is a popular watering-hole for walkers as well as locals. Although the emphasis here is on food, all prepared on the premises, drinkers are always welcome. 🏤❀ⓄⒶ

PATRICK BROMPTON

Green Tree
DL8 1JW
☼ 12-3 (not winter Mon-Wed), 6 (7 Sat)-11; 12-3, 7-10.30 Sun
☎ (01677) 450262
Black Sheep Best Bitter; Taylor Landlord; guest beer (summer) Ⓗ
Cosy, Grade II listed village pub overlooking the main A684 Wensleydale road, next to the parish church gates at the western edge of the village. The small, cosy bar has an open fire and brick-built bar; the rural ambience is continued in the restaurant. Beware of the narrow entrance to the car park. 🏤Q❀ⓄⓅ♣P

PICKERING

Bay Horse
Market Place, YO18 8AA
☼ 11-11; 12-10.30 Sun
☎ (01751) 472526
Greene King Old Speckled Hen; Tetley Bitter; guest beer Ⓗ
Friendly local, handy for the North Yorkshire Moors railway station. The quiet front bar boasts an open fire and window seats. The large multi-level bar at the rear has a pool table and juke box; it hosts a live disco on Friday evening and it can be noisy at the weekend. 🏤ⓄⓅ⇌♣P

PICKHILL

Nag's Head
YO7 4JG (between Bedale and Masham, turn off S on A1)
☼ 11-11; 12-10.30 Sun
☎ (01845) 567391
website: www.nagsheadpickhill.co.uk
Black Sheep Best Bitter; Hambleton Bitter; Tetley Bitter; guest beer Ⓗ
Comfortable country inn, winner of CAMRA and other awards and in the same hands for over 20 years. An imaginative menu has earned the restaurant a worthy reputation, and the lounge is popular with diners, but the public bar continues to

enjoy local custom – a welcome mix. Hambleton ales, brewed in the next village, were launched here; they usually supply the guest beer, too. Accommodation includes conference and riding facilities and the garden has a putting green.
🏨Q☆🛏🕪 ⊟&♣ ●P

POOL IN WHARFEDALE

Hunter's Inn
Harrogate Road, LS21 2PS
(on A658, 1/2 mile NE of village)
🕐 11-11; 12-10.30 Sun
☎ (0113) 284 1090
Tetley Bitter; Theakston Best Bitter; guest beers
This popular and well-patronised country inn is a detached single-storey building on a main bus route. The interior is open plan, with table and barside seating. There are nine real ales on offer at very reasonable prices, with local micro-breweries well represented. Saxon cider is available and the wine list is well-balanced: six red and six white. Food is available at lunchtime. Children are accepted until 9pm. There is a pool table at one end of the bar. 🏨☆🕪♣ ●P

REDCAR

Plimsoll Line ✿
138-142 High Street East, TS10 3DH
(2 minutes' walk from bus station)
🕐 10-11; 11-10.30 Sun
☎ (01642) 495250
Courage Directors; Greene King Abbot; Shepherd Neame Spitfire; Theakston Best Bitter, Old Peculier; guest beers Ⓗ
The pub follows the typical Wetherspoon's formula to an excellent standard. Based on the theme of the sea, it blends modern art with old black and white photographs. A regularly-changing guest beer choice complements the good food. In summer, a large sheltered patio area is perfect for a bite to eat and a drink in the sunshine.
Q☆🕪&≠(Central)

RIPON

One-Eyed Rat
51 Allhallowgate, HG4 1LQ (near bus station)
🕐 12-3.30 (not Mon-Wed), 6 (5.30 Fri)-11; 12-11 Sat; 12-3, 7-10.30 Sun
☎ (01765) 607704 website: www.oneeyedrat.co.uk
Black Sheep Best Bitter; Taylor Landlord; guest beers Ⓗ
Popular local situated in the oldest part of the city near the market square. Noted for its beer, with always four guests on tap, and its friendly atmosphere, it also stocks bottled beers from many countries, Biddenden cider and a large range of fruit wines. A garden, complete with pool table, is open in the summer. 🏨Q☆Å♣●

Wheatsheaf
Harrogate Road, HG4 2SB (by southern roundabout on city bypass)
🕐 12-3 (not Mon), 7-11; 12-3, 7-10.30 Sun
☎ (01765) 602410
Greene King IPA; Tetley Bitter Ⓗ
Small, cosy local in former quarrymen's cottages. The two-roomed interior is divided by an open fire. One side is quiet and the other houses the bar which features a lovely carved wood back – reputedly part of an

18th-century bed – and dummy drawers at the front. Looking at the outside, the pub is notable for its distinct lean towards what once was the quarry, and is now the sunken garden. 🏨☆♣P

ROBIN HOOD'S BAY

Dolphin Hotel
King Street, YO22 4SH
(down bottom of bank, turn left)
🕐 11 (12 winter)-11; 12-10.30 Sun
☎ (01947) 880337
Marston's Pedigree; John Smith's Bitter; Theakston Old Peculier; guest beer Ⓗ
The Dolphin is a friendly, old-fashioned village pub with a beamed bar downstairs and another room upstairs where children are welcome, and the folk club is held. Other musicians often play here, too. The food is fresh: 'only the scampi are frozen'. You can sit on benches outside and order beer through the window. No visit to this part of the coast is complete without seeing Robin Hood's Bay, a medieval fishing village at the bottom of a steep bank.
🏨Q⏱☆🕪⊟&♣

Victoria Hotel
Station Road, YO22 4RL
🕐 12-3, 6-11; 12-11 Fri, Sat & summer; 12-10.30 Sun
☎ (01947) 880205 website: www.thevictoriahotel.info
Camerons Bitter, Strongarm; guest beers Ⓗ
Impressive Victorian building on the cliff overlooking the bay and the village. Views from some of the 10 en-suite bedrooms are particularly spectacular. The comfortable bar bears a collection of guest pump clips. There is a no-smoking room and a dining room; the hotel has a well-deserved reputation for its home-cooked food. Walk along the old railway line to Whitby or Scarborough, or follow the Cleveland Way; this Cleveland CAMRA Pub of the Year 1999 and 2001 is excellent for families and walkers. 🏨Q⏱☆🛏🕪Å♣P

SALTBURN BY THE SEA

Saltburn Cricket, Bowls and Tennis Club
Marske Mill Lane, TS12 1HJ
(by Saltburn leisure centre)
🕐 8 (2 summer Sat)-11; 12-3, 8-10.30 Sun
☎ (01287) 622761
Tetley Bitter; guest beers Ⓗ
Friendly, private sports club, fielding cricket, tennis and bowls teams in local leagues. It has a spacious, well-furnished lounge and a games room; both areas afford a magnificent view of the cricket field. The club is open all day on match days. A large function area is available for special occasions. Casual visitors are welcome without joining. The club stocks a good range of cask ales, some local brews, and hosts occasional pub festivals. Frequent Cleveland CAMRA Pub of the Season winner. ☆Å≠P🍴

New Marine Hotel
Marine Parade, TS12 1DZ
🕐 11-11; 12-10.30 Sun
☎ (01287) 622695
Black Sheep Best Bitter; guest beer Ⓗ
Pub with a split personality: the bar caters for the young and livelier customers with

juke box, game machines (quiet), three pool tables and a couple of TV screens for sport or music. The lounge is quiet and undisturbed by the bar. Both bar and lounge are comfortably furnished to a high standard. At the front is a large patio with tables overlooking the North Sea, cliffs and the Tees estuary. The upstairs restaurant doubles as a function room.
Q ⊛ ◐ ⊟ ⊟ & 🅰 ⇌ ⊟

SANDHUTTON

King's Arms
Main Street, YO7 4RW (on A167, 4 miles W of Thirsk)
✪ 12-2.30, 5.30-11 Tue-Fri; 12-4, 6.30-11 Sat; closed Mon; 12-4, 6.30-10.30 Sun
☎ (01845) 587263
Black Sheep Best Bitter; John Smith's Bitter; Taylor Landlord; Tetley Bitter Ⓗ
This homely, friendly inn is all that can be expected of a village hostelry, offering a fine compromise between a local pub and an eating house. There is a comfortable lounge, workaday public bar and cosy dining room, each of quite different character. The home-cooked meals include a vast mixed grill served on an 18" stainless steel platter, for those with larger appetites. Q ⊛ ⇔ ◐ ♣ P ⅍

SAWDON

Anvil Inn
Main Street, YO13 3DY (follow signs to Sawdon off A170; 2 miles)
✪ 11-11; 12-10.30 Sun
☎ (01723) 859896
Wells Bombardier; guest beers Ⓗ
Restored in 1986, this former blacksmith's forge features the original anvil, old photos and memorabilia. The dining area provides excellent value, home-cooked food; barbecues are held in summer. With four en-suite rooms, it is conveniently located for outdoor pursuits in the Moors Forest and open country walking.
🏨 Q ⏃ ⊛ ⇔ ◐ ♣ P ⅍

SAXTON

Greyhound
Main Street, LS24 9PY (W of A162)
✪ 11.30-3, 5.30-11; 11-11 Sat; 12-10.30 Sun
☎ (01937) 557202
Samuel Smith OBB Ⓗ
This picturesque, 13th-century whitewashed village inn nestles by the church. It is said that many of the occupants of the graveyard still pop in for a quick one! This Grade II listed building was a teasle barn before becoming an inn. Enter through a low-ceilinged, stone-flagged corridor to a tiny cosy bar. Real fires blaze in two of the three rooms in winter. Note the extensive, colourful collection of wall plates.
🏨 Q ⊛ ⊟ ♣

SCARBOROUGH

Cellars
35-37 Valley Road, YO11 2LX
✪ 3 (12 Sat)-11 (11-11 summer); hours may vary; 12-10.30 Sun
☎ (01723) 367158
website: www.scarborough-brialene.co.uk
Black Sheep Special; Tetley Bitter; guest beers Ⓗ

Cosy, one-roomed, family-run pub situated beneath a restaurant and holiday apartments, within easy reach of South Bay centre and the spa complex. The bar has a wood floor while the adjoining lounge area provides more spacious, comfortable seating. One or two guest ales are available throughout the year; bar meals are served until early evening. Live music is performed on Sunday evening and occasionally at other times. ⊛ ⇔ ◐ ◐ & 🅰 ⇌ P

Cricketers ✅
119 North Marine Road, YO11 7HH
✪ 12 (3 winter Mon-Wed)-11; 12-10.30 Sun
☎ (01723) 365864
Caledonian Deuchars IPA; Taylor Landlord; Tetley Bitter; York Yorkshire Terrier; guest beers Ⓗ
Local CAMRA Town Pub of the Year 2002; opposite the cricket ground, it is Yorkshire Cricket Club's second home. Well patronised by cricket fans, it displays, naturally, cricket memorabilia in the bar. Excellent value, home-cooked food is served daily until late using locally-sourced ingredients; try the landlord's extra hot chilli. A large family room upstairs, affording picturesque views over North Bay, opens in summer. A large-screen TV is used for sports. ⏃ ⊛ ◐ ◐ 🅰 ⇌ ♣ ♠ P ⊟

Highlander
15-16 The Esplanade, YO11 2AF
✪ 11-11; 12-10.30 Sun
☎ (01723) 365627 website: www.highlandhotel.com
Flowers IPA; Hancock's HB; Tetley Bitter; Imperial; guest beers Ⓗ
This pub is an integral part of the Highlander Hotel and offers a Scottish-themed lounge, cellar bar and carvery. Enjoy superb views of South Bay from the patio. An extensive collection of malt whiskies is on show (800 bottles), 40–50 are regularly on sale, alongside three ever-changing guest beers. An excellent lunch menu and Sunday carvery draw a large local trade. No loud music or machines spoil the atmosphere. 🏨 Q ⏃ ⊛ ⇔ ◐ ⇌ ⅍

Indigo Alley
4 North Marine Road, YO12 7PD
✪ 4 (12 Sat)-11; 1-10.30 Sun
☎ (01723) 381900
Beer range varies Ⓗ
Lively, popular one-roomed pub offering six constantly-changing real ales, including a regular Rooster's brew. Belgian Leffe blonde and brown beers as well as Hoegaarden are also on draught. Live music is performed several times a week. It was voted local CAMRA Pub of the Year for three consecutive years; a real gem – not to be missed.

Old Scalby Mills
Scalby Mills Road, YO12 6RP
✪ 11-11; 12-10.30 Sun
☎ (01723) 500449
Tetley Burton Ale; guest beers Ⓗ
Popular with walkers and tourists in a seafront location, the building was originally a watermill but has seen many uses over the years; old photographs and prints chart its history. Admire the superb views of the North Bay and castle from the sheltered patio or from the lounge. The Cleveland Way reaches the seafront at this

point and there is a Sea Life Centre nearby. The pub holds a children's certificate for the lounge until 6pm, when smoking restrictions are lifted.
Q ⊃ ♿ ⊛ ⊟ ▲ ♣ ✂

Scholar's
Somerset Terrace, YO11 2PW
✪ 12-3, 5.30-11; 12-11 Fri & Sat; 12-10.30 Sun
☎ (01723) 360084
York Yorkshire Terrier; guest beers Ⓗ
Part of the Bedford Hotel, situated in an elegant Regency crescent, the entrance to the bar is on Somerset Terrace. This large, one-roomed pub was recently refurbished and has a warm, friendly atmosphere. Three constantly-changing guest ales often include one from Durham; Hoegaarden wheat beer is also on tap. The Scarborough Jazz Club give live performances (Tue eve), with other local musicians appearing at various times. Home-cooked food is available all day until early evening.
⋈ ◑ ♿ ≒

Tap & Spile ✿
94 Falsgrave Road, YO12 5AZ
✪ 11-11; 12-10.30 Sun
☎ (01723) 363837
Adnams Broadside; Big Lamp Bitter; Caledonian Deuchars IPA; Everards Tiger; Taylor Landlord; guest beers Ⓗ
Sympathetically restored coaching inn, not far from the centre, comprising three rooms, including a no-smoking snug, plus a large patio. Local memorabilia is displayed. Excellent value meals are served at lunchtime (not Wed), and Thursday–Saturday early evenings. Barbecues are held on the patio on summer Sunday afternoons. Live music, every Tuesday evening and Sunday afternoon and evening, is often blues-oriented. This thriving local has a friendly atmosphere; TV sport is shown in one bar.
Q ⊛ ◑ ≒ ♣ ⚰ P ✂

Valley
51 Valley Road, YO11 2LX
✪ 12-11; 12-10.30 Sun
☎ (01723) 372593
John Smith's Bitter; guest beer Ⓗ
Basement pub situated towards the top end of Valley Road. The pub has recently been renamed and given a new lease of life. The present owners have also introduced real ale, live music, plays, theme nights and excellent value, home-cooked food. There is a patio drinking area and no-smoking room. The interior is split level with an upstairs pool room. Pictures and drawings of scenes by local artists are for sale. ⊛ ⋈ ◑ ≒ ♣ ✂

SELBY

Albion Vaults
New Street, YO8 0PT
(A19, town side of River Ouse swing bridge)
✪ 11-11; 12-10.30 Sun
☎ (01757) 213817
Old Mill Bitter Ⓗ
Two-roomed pub, just off the town centre, on the street leading out of town towards York. Its pleasing Edwardian decor is characteristic of the style of this local independent brewery. The public bar has a pool table and TV for sporting events.

Although only serving the house bitter as a regular beer, occasionally specials from Old Mill are also on tap. ⋈ Q ⊛ ⊟ ≒ ♣

SKIPTON

Cock & Bottle
30 Swadford Street, BD23 1RD
✪ 11.30 (11 Sat)-11; 12-10.30 Sun
☎ (01756) 794734 website: www.cockandbottle.co.uk
Castle Eden Ale; Tetley Bitter; guest beers Ⓗ
Modernised, 18th-century coaching inn with a single long, split-level bar and original exposed beams. Taller customers should beware of the low beam above the step halfway along the bar. The three guest ales often include beers rarely found in Yorkshire. Note the unusual ground-floor 'cellar', visible through windows from the bar and from the street outside. Quiz night is Wednesday. This ex-Hogshead pub is thriving again under former managers who have returned as tenants. ⋈ ⊛ ◑ ≒ ♣

Commercial Inn
Water Street, BD23 1PB
✪ 11-11; 12-10.30 Sun
☎ (01756) 792847
website: www.paul@commercialpub.co.uk
Tetley Dark Mild, Bitter Ⓗ
It is worth walking out from the town centre to visit this lively, local community pub. Inside there are two rooms on the ground floor (one with a pool table and TV), plus a third room with a raised seating area. It is popular with dominoes players and sports enthusiasts. Mind the steps on the way out. ⋈ ≒ ♣

Narrow Boat
38 Victoria Street, BD23 1JE (alleyway off Coach St near canal bridge)
✪ 12-11; 12-10.30 Sun
☎ (01756) 797922
website: www.markettowntaverns.co.uk
Black Sheep Best Bitter; Taylor Landlord; guest beers Ⓗ
Excellent ale house, featuring old church pews, old brewery posters, mirrors and two eye-catching canal-themed murals. It brooks no piped music, juke boxes or gaming machines, but live jazz is staged (Tue eve) and folk on alternate Sundays. Smoking is only permitted on the upstairs balcony. Six rotating guest ales from Northern and Scottish independents are complemented by a selection of draught and bottled continental beers. Charity events are regularly organised by the community-minded licensees. Evening meals are served Sunday–Thursday. Q ⊛ ◑ ♿ ≒ ♣ ✂

SLAPEWATH

Fox & Hounds
TS14 6PX (on A171, Whitby road) OS643158
✪ 11-11; 12-10.30 Sun
☎ (01287) 632964 website: www.fox-and-hounds.com
Black Sheep Best Bitter; John Smith's Magnet; Tetley Bitter Ⓗ
Old coaching inn on the main moor road, between Guisborough and Whitby. The main bar/lounge with secluded areas is supplemented by a large dining area, nicely decorated with an olde-worlde feel to it. There is a choice of rooms available for weddings, including a conservatory; the

accommodation includes a four-poster bed. Children can let off steam in an open grassed area in front of the pub.
Q✿🚱🅾️P✓

SNAPE

Castle Arms ✪
DL8 2TB
☼ 12-3, 6-11; 12-3, 7-10.30 Sun
☎ (01677) 470270
Black Sheep Best Bitter; Hambleton Bitter; John Smith's Bitter; guest beer Ⓗ

This sleepy village, once home to Catherine Parr, the wife who outlived Henry VIII, nestles around a pretty beck; the queen's castle remains partly inhabited to this day. The 14th-century pub is full of character, with stone-flagged floors, low beams and an impressive fireplace. With its range of local beers, quality food in the bar or restaurant and comfortable accommodation in a converted barn, this is a deservedly popular inn, worth searching out. 🏨Q✿🚱🅾️Å♣P

STAITHES

Captain Cook Inn
60 Staithes Lane, TS13 5AD (200 yds from A174)
☼ 11-11; 12-10.30 Sun
☎ (01947) 840200
website: www.captaincookinn.co.uk
Daleside Bitter; John Smith's Magnet or Theakston Cool Cask; guest beers Ⓗ

Built in the late 19th century as the Station Hotel, it was renamed in the 1960s after closure of the railway line. The pub enjoys good views across Staithes Beck towards Boulby Cliffs, the highest in England at 660 feet. Guest beers come from micro-breweries in the Midlands. Staithes is a lovely olde-worlde fishing village, the home of Captain Cook and has a museum dedicated to him. A beer festival is held during lifeboat week (summer). Evening meals are served Friday–Sunday. 🏨Q🚲✿🚱🅾️🍴Å♣🚽

STOKESLEY

Spread Eagle
39 High Street, TS9 5AD
☼ 11-11; 12-10.30 Sun
☎ (01642) 710278
Camerons Strongarm; Marston's Pedigree; guest beer Ⓗ

Small, unspoilt, town-centre pub, originally a coaching inn dating from the 18th century. Excellent, genuinely home-cooked food is available all day from an interesting menu, with meat, game and poultry from the family butcher, real vegetables and imaginative salads; booking is advisable. An enclosed garden leads down to the River Leven. In the front room, only the real fire is permitted to smoke. Live music is performed on Tuesday evening, otherwise a fairly quiet pub. 🏨Q🅾️🚽✓🚽

White Swan
1 West End, TS9 5BL
☼ 11.30-3, 5.30-11; 12-3, 7-10.30 Sun
☎ (01642) 710263
website: www.thecaptaincookbrewery.co.uk/swan.htm
Captain Cook Navigation, Sunset, Slipway, Black Porter; Castle Eden Ale Ⓗ

Old-fashioned town pub with a J-shaped bar

(no-smoking at the back). An outlet for the adjacent prize-winning Captain Cook's Brewery, it also has an award for its cheese board. It lies just off West Green, maybe the prettiest part of this fine little market town. No juke box or fruit machine, but bar billiards is played. Children are welcome until 8pm. It is 200 yards from the bus station. 🏨Q♣✓

TADCASTER

Angel & White Horse
Bridge Street, LS24 9AW
☼ 11-3, 5-11; 11-5, 7-11 Sat; 12-3, 7-10.30 Sun
☎ (01937) 835470
Samuel Smith OBB Ⓗ

In the centre of town, this is Samuel Smith's brewery tap. An old coaching inn with a late-Georgian façade, the large, single bar has fine wood panelling and furnishings and affords good views of the brewery yard and stables at the rear. Tours of this independent Yorkshire brewery start from the pub and include a visit to the tack room with the chance to inspect the famous grey shire horses which haul Sam's dray around local streets. ✿🅾️♣

THIRSK

Golden Fleece Hotel
42 Market Place, YO7 1LL
☼ 11-2.30, 6-11; 12-3, 7-10.30 Sun
☎ (01845) 523108
website: www.goldenfleecehotel.com
Hambleton Bitter, Goldfield, Stud Ⓗ

Former coaching inn overlooking Thirsk's impressive market square. The current hotel dates from the 1790s but can trace its history back to Tudor times. Thirsk was the home of Alf Wight, better known as vet James Herriot, and the town boasts a museum in his former surgery. The split-level bar forms an exhibition for Hambleton beers and has a horse-racing theme in honour of the town's racecourse. There is also a smaller paddock bar and a dining room. 🏨Q🚱🅾️🍴P

THIXENDALE

Cross Keys
YO17 9TG
☼ 12-3, 6-11; 12-3, 7-10.30 Sun
☎ (01377) 288272
Jennings Bitter; Tetley Bitter; guest beers Ⓗ

Thixendale lies at the heart of the Yorkshire Wolds at the junction of several dry valleys. Inhabited since the Stone Age, many tracks established by Roman times are still used today by walkers on their way to the Cross Keys, which is an unspoilt, unpretentious village local. The single bar offers good value, home-cooked food and award-winning beer. Children are welcome in the garden. Accommodation is a new amenity, introduced in 2003. 🏨Q🚱🅾️Å♣

THORGANBY

Ferryboat Inn
YO19 6DD
(1 mile NE of village, SE of York) OS697426
☼ 12-3 (extended in summer), 7-11 (closed winter Mon; extended hours in summer); 12-3, 7-10.30 Sun
☎ (01904) 448224

Old Mill Bitter; guest beers Ⓗ

Just to the north of this village a signpost points down a country lane. At the end, situated by the River Derwent, you will come across this family-run inn. Popular with anglers and boaters, the large garden on the river bank is an ideal spot for quenching your thirst on sunny days. The welcoming bar and family room have lovely views of the garden. Two alternating guest beers often come from local brewers.

🏰Q☎🐾♿♣Å♣P🖫

THORNTON IN LONSDALE

Marton Arms ✓

LA6 3PB (¼ mile N of A65/A687 jct) OS685736

☻ 12-11; 12-10.30 Sun

☎ (015242) 41281 website: www.martonarms.co.uk

Black Sheep Best Bitter; Dent Bitter; Sharp's Doom Bar; Taylor Golden Best; guest beers Ⓗ

In a hamlet containing a parish church, old stocks and little else, the pub relies almost entirely on tourists, drawn by the 16 handpumps, although there are other interesting beverages, such as the stunning range of malt whiskies. Behind the 1679 datestone and old oak door, a flagged passage leads to a modern bar dominated by white wood and bus and rail memorabilia. Ten minutes' walk from the start of the Ingleton Waterfalls walk; buses 80 and 80A run along the main road.

☎🛏🕪Å♣P

THORNTON WATLASS

Buck Inn ✓

HG4 4AH

☻ 11-11; 12-10.30 Sun

☎ (01677) 422461

Black Sheep Best Bitter; John Smith's Bitter; Theakston Best Bitter; guest beers Ⓗ

This delightful Wensleydale inn overlooks the village green and its 100-year-old cricket pitch with unusual boundaries – outside the front door acts as position for deep third man. A small, comfortable bar has settles, old bottles and a gem of a bar servery. An excellent menu is served in the bar and informal no-smoking dining area. Sunday lunchtime trad jazz is performed fortnightly. The large garden has a children's play area and quoits pitches.

🏰☎🛏🕪🍴♣P

WARTHILL

Agar Arms

YO19 5XW (off A166, 5 miles NE of York)

☻ 11.30-2.30, 6.30-11; 12-3, 7-10.30 Sun

☎ (01904) 488142

Samuel Smith OBB Ⓗ

Converted from a blacksmith's shop in the 19th century, the Agar Arms provides a friendly atmosphere, with roaring fires, and in common with most of the pubs owned by this independent Yorkshire brewery, a traditional decor of horse brasses and oak beams. Tucked away from the road, with outdoor tables overlooking the duckpond, it is a popular stopping-place for cyclists and is renowned for its steaks. Look out for the indoor well.

🏰Q☎🐾🕪P🖫

534

WEAVERTHORPE

Star Inn

Main Street, YO17 8EY (off A64 at Sherburn traffic lights)

☻ 12-4 (not Mon & Tue), 7-11; 12-4, 7-10.30 Sun

☎ (01944) 738273 website: www.starinn.net

Camerons Bitter; John Smith's Bitter; Tetley Bitter; guest beers Ⓗ

One of CAMRA writer Susan Nowak's favourite rural pubs, listed in all editions of her Good Pub Food and Pub Super Chef publications. With good en-suite accommodation, it is ideally situated for visiting the Yorkshire coast, moors and national park. Bar/restaurant lunches are available every day and dinner is served Wednesday–Monday evenings, specialising in game, seafood and vegetarian dishes. It is advisable to book at weekends. A rural retreat for conversation and relaxation.

🏰Q☎🛏🕪🍴♣P✂

WEST WITTON

Fox & Hounds

Main Street, DL8 4LP

(A684, 3½ miles W of Leyburn)

☻ 12-4, 7-11 (may vary summer); 12-4, 7-10.30 Sun

☎ (01969) 623650

Black Sheep Best Bitter; John Smith's Bitter; Tetley Burton Ale; guest beers Ⓗ

In a village on a limestone terrace of Penhill Beacon, this 15th-century outpost of Jervaulx Abbey has been a pub for 300 years. Inside the Grade II listed building a stone fireplace divides the cosy drinking area. Good meals are served here, or in a dining room boasting an impressive chimney arch complete with bread oven. Each August, Witton feast includes the Burning of Bartle, when a straw effigy is paraded through the village before being set alight. Walkers are welcome. Daily bus service runs between Leyburn and Hawes.

🏰☎🛏🕪Å♣♣P🖫

WHITBY

Endeavour Hotel

66 Church Street, YO22 4AS (across swing bridge from centre, bear right)

☻ 11-11; 12-10.30 Sun

☎ (01947) 603557

Adnams Broadside; John Smith's Bitter Ⓗ

Bustling, friendly one-bar pub overlooking the inner harbour, backing on to a steep bank below the moor. The bar is divided into alcoves and has a beamed ceiling. Five music festivals are held a year (Irish and folk music) and the pub is popular in Folk and Regatta Weeks. Five minutes' walk from the beach and the historic town centre, at the other end of Church Street is the way up to the abbey; look at the glassblowing shop, or buy some jet jewellery nearby. 🏰⇌♣

Little Angel Hotel

18 Flowergate, YO21 3BA OS897110

☻ 11-11; 12-10.30 Sun

☎ (01947) 602514

Tetley Bitter; guest beer Ⓗ

On the corner of Brunswick Street and Flowergate, only three minutes' walk from the beach and harbour, two old buildings were put together to form this three-roomed pub. The beamed ceilings and leaded lights add to the atmosphere of this friendly local where charitable events are organised. It is a good place to relax after the Regatta, or during Folk Week. Lunches are available in summer. ◖⊞≉♣

YORK

Ackhorne
9 St Martins Lane, YO1 6LN (up cobbled lane by church at bottom of Micklegate)
✪ 12-11; 12-10.30 Sun
☎ (01904) 671421 website: www.ackhorne.com
Caledonian Deuchars IPA; Rooster's Yankee; guest beers Ⓗ
One of York's best-known pubs – despite (or because of) its slightly out-of-the-way location. A former York CAMRA Pub of the Year, it has a bare-boarded bar with comfortable bench seating and original stained glass windows. Beyond the bar is a carpeted snug which contains Civil War memorabilia featuring local hero Sir Thomas Fairfax. Do not miss the tiny garden – a real suntrap. No food Sunday. Q❁◖≉♣♠

Blue Bell ☆ ⊘
53 Fossgate, YO1 9TF
✪ 11-11; 12-10.30 Sun
☎ (01904) 654904 website: www.bluebellyork.co.uk
Caledonian Deuchars IPA; Camerons Strongarm; Greene King Abbot; John Smith's Bitter; Taylor Landlord; Wells Bombardier; guest beer Ⓗ
This tiny pub has a big heart – voted Morning Advertiser Fundraising Pub of the Year. It is also York CAMRA Pub of the Year, for the second time. The narrow, glazed brick-clad exterior leads to York's only perfectly intact Edwardian interior, dating from a 1903 refurbishment, that merits Grade II listed status. The dark wood panelling in the drinking corridor and two small rooms help create a cosy, welcoming atmosphere, enjoyed by all. Q⊞♣

Golden Ball ☆
2 Cromwell Road, YO1 6DU
✪ 4 (12 Sat)-11; 12-10.30 Sun
☎ (01904) 652211 website: www.goldenballyork.com
Greene King Ruddles Best; Marston's Pedigree; John Smith's Bitter, Magnet; Wells Bombardier; guest beers Ⓗ
Occupying a street-corner site in the residential Bishophill district, this is a fine community local. Victorian-built, it has an impressive glazed brick exterior. Extensively refurbished in 1929 by John Smith's, it merits an entry on CAMRA's National Inventory of pubs with interiors of outstanding historic interest. There are four different rooms, one with bar billiards and TV, and a hidden garden. Live music is staged Thursday and Sunday. Q❁⊞Å≉♣

Last Drop Inn
27 Colliergate, YO1 8BN
✪ 11-11; 12-10.30 Sun
☎ (01904) 621951 website: www.thelastdropinn.co.uk
York Stonewall, York Bitter, Yorkshire Terrier, Centurion's Ghost Ale, seasonal beers; guest beers Ⓗ
This former solicitor's office was converted by York Brewery into their first pub only three years ago, using mainly local materials. Its large plain glass windows afford drinkers a good view of King's Square where street performers entertain. Inside,

entertainment comes in the form of live music (Mon and Tue eves); there are no electronic amusements of any kind. Food, using mostly local ingredients, is available daily until 4pm. Q❁◖

Maltings
Tanners Moat, YO1 6HU (below Lendal Bridge)
✪ 11-11; 12-10.30 Sun
☎ (01904) 655387 website: www.maltings.co.uk
Black Sheep Best Bitter; guest beers Ⓗ
Now more than 10 years old, the Maltings is as solidly reliable as ever under the same guiding hands. During this time it has won more awards than could possibly be listed here, but there is no sign of complacency. The five guest beers are usually supplied by micro-brewers, whose products also feature at its nationally-renowned beer festivals. Recommended food is served in huge portions daily 12–2 (4 weekends). ◖≉♠

Minster Inn
24 Marygate, YO30 7BH (off Bootham, A19)
✪ 12 (11 Fri & Sat)-11; 12-10.30 Sun
☎ (01904) 624499 website: www.minsterinn.co.uk
John Smith's Bitter, Magnet; guest beers Ⓗ
Unspoilt, Edwardian local with a bar and three rooms off a central corridor. A pub for all types of visitor, especially those liking good beer and good conversation, it offers an adventurous range of guest ales. There is a no-smoking room and families are made welcome. Hidden outside the walls of the St Mary's Abbey and within easy reach of the city centre, it is a perfect place to while away an evening. ♨Q⊠❁⊞≉♣⌇

Royal Oak ⊘
18 Goodramgate, YO1 7LG
✪ 11-11; 12-10.30 Sun
☎ (01904) 653856
website: www.royal-oak-pub-york.co.uk
Greene King Abbot; Tetley Bitter; guest beers Ⓗ
There has been a pub on the site of the Royal Oak since 1783, but its 'Tudor' styling is due to a 1934 revamp by then-owners, John J Hunt, of nearby Aldwark. The long-standing incumbents run a cosy, intimate, little pub with three rooms off a staggered corridor. There is also a meeting room upstairs. Its food – of wide repute – is available from 11am (12 Sun) until 8pm daily. Q⊠◖♠⌇

Saddle Inn
Main Street, Fulford, YO10 4PJ
✪ 11.30-4, 5.45-11; 11.30-11 Sat; 12-10.30 Sun
☎ (01904) 633317
Banks's Bitter; Camerons Bitter Ⓗ
Comfortable, well-maintained suburban local. The spacious, L-shaped lounge bar has two cheery open fires. The dining area, where children are welcome, has a pool table at one end. Unusually for these parts, petanque has a strong following here and its devotees pursue their pastime on the attractively-sited terrains at the rear of the pub. No lunches are served Monday; evening meals available 6–8pm. ♨❁⌂◖♣P🖵

Sun Inn
The Green, Acomb, YO26 5LL (on B1224)
✪ 11-11; 12-10.30 Sun
☎ (01904) 798500
John Smith's Bitter; Wells Bombardier; guest beers Ⓗ

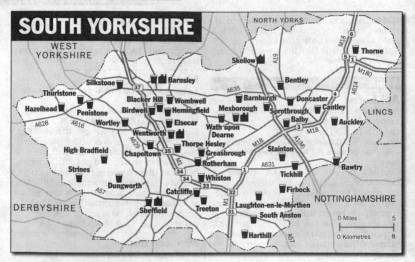

SOUTH YORKSHIRE

In a suburb on the western side of York, this traditional village pub stands next to Acomb Green and has been much improved in recent times following a sensitive refurbishment. The three drinking areas (one no-smoking) give an intimate and welcoming feeling. Picturesque views of the green make the Sun a pleasant stop for an outdoor drink and friendly management helps attract a good mixture of regulars and passing trade.
Q❀❍🌢♣P✶

Swan Inn ☆
16 Bishopgate Street, YO23 1JH
✪ 4 (12 Sat)-11; 12-10.30 Sun
☎ (01904) 634968
Greene King Abbot; Taylor Landlord; Tetley Bitter; guest beers Ⓗ
Classic street-corner local with a 'West Riding' layout, unusual for the city. The entrance corridor leads to a drinking lobby with a servery and two rooms also served from the main bar. A Tetley Heritage inn; it is one of three York pubs on CAMRA's National Inventory. Popular most evenings with the younger generation, it is usually quieter early evening and weekends. A paved, walled garden (large by York's standards) enjoys a pleasant, sunny aspect.
🏛❀🍴≠♣

Three-Legged Mare
15 High Petergate, YO1 7EN
✪ 11-11; 12-10.30 Sun
☎ (01904) 638246 website: www.thethreeleggedmare.co.uk
York Stonewall, York Bitter, Yorkshire Terrier, Centurion's Ghost Ale, seasonal beers; guest beers Ⓗ
York Brewery's second of their three pubs in the city (known locally as the Wonky Donkey) is rather ghoulishly named after a device for hanging three felons simultaneously – a replica can be seen in the garden. The bar and conservatory are modern in style and mercifully free of electronic gimmickry. There are always nine beers available and food is served until 3pm. Note that access to the toilets is via a tightly-twisting spiral staircase.
Q🍴♿

Wellington Inn
47 Alma Terrace, YO10 4DL
✪ 11-3 (not Mon), 6-11; 11-5, 7-11 Sat; 12-4, 7-10.30 Sun
☎ (01904) 645642
Samuel Smith OBB Ⓗ
Classic, back-street local, purpose-built in the mid-19th century. Previously Lawson's beer house and the Sir Colin Campbell, it was acquired by Samuel Smith's in 1887. The central, through corridor is flanked by a public bar and two small lounges, one with a pool table. Three modest refurbishments in the last 20 years or so have improved comfort without compromising the pub's utterly traditional character. 🏛Q🍴❀🍴♣

York Beer & Wine Shop
28 Sandringham Street, YO10 4BA
(off A19/Fishergate)
✪ 11 (6 Mon; 10 Sat)-10; 6-10 Sun
☎ (01904) 647136
Taylor Landlord; guest beers Ⓗ
Opened in 1985, this pioneering off-licence has been a Guide regular since then and was runner-up in Off-Licence News Independent Beer Retailer of the Year competition 2003. Along with the draught beers there are usually three ciders available – all of which may be taken away in any quantity. A fine array of bottled beers includes many English and continental classics. A well-stocked cheese counter – including weekly guests – provides some mouth-watering delights. ♣

Yorkshire (South)

AUCKLEY

Eagle & Child
24 Main Street, DN9 3HS
✪ 11.30-3, 5-11; 11.30-11 Sat; 7-10.30 Sun
☎ (01302) 770406
Barnsley Bitter; Boddingtons Bitter; John Smith's Bitter; Theakston Cool Cask; guest beers Ⓗ
Attractive, traditional country pub, well used by the village community. Locally-brewed Glentworth beers are now available here on a permanent basis, along with another ever-changing guest beer. The excellent meals are very popular, served in a

no-smoking area as well as throughout the pub. There is a quiz every Monday evening, and the pub won a special award in 2000 from the local CAMRA branch for services to real ale. Q❀◗P

BALBY

Winning Post
Warmsworth Road, DN4 0TR (on A630, by A1(M) jct 36)
✪ 12 (11 Sat)-11; 12-4, 7-10.30 Sun
☎ (01302) 853493
John Smith's Bitter; guest beer Ⓗ
Spacious, community local run by a capable licensee and his wife who were literally brought up in the trade. Opened in 1956 it retains a two-roomed layout, comprising a tap room, with pool and darts and a large, comfortable lounge, hosting regular quiz nights, with a quiet area to the rear. The landlord's Sunday lunches come highly recommended (no other food is served). Guest beers are sold at competitive prices.
❀�♣P

BARNBURGH

Coach & Horses ☆
High Street, DN5 7EP
✪ 12-5, 7.30-11; 12-11 Sat; 12-10.30 Sun
☎ (01709) 892306
John Smith's Bitter Ⓗ
When Whitworth, Son & Nephew, brewers of Wath upon Dearne, decided to build a pub in Barnburgh they specified a magnificent example. This four-roomed pub, opened in 1937, remains unaltered. Whitworth's Wheatsheaf motifs can still be seen in the leaded glass screens above the bars, while drawers on the bar back have polished brass handles. A visit to all rooms is essential. It is a recent addition to CAMRA's National Inventory of pub interiors of outstanding historic interest.
🏛❀⊞♣P

BARNSLEY

Courthouse Station ⦿
24 Regent Street, S70 2HG
✪ 10-11; 12-10.30 Sun
☎ (01226) 779056
Boddingtons Bitter; Theakston Best Bitter; guest beers Ⓗ
Popular, open-plan, split-level Wetherspoon's pub, once a courthouse and after that a railway station with the platform level on the first floor. The pub is divided into six drinking and dining areas. The walls display old pictures of Barnsley folk and its streets, alongside local history panels. The pub has lots of comfortable seating, however many people choose to stand. Children are welcome until 6pm.
Q⏱❀◗⅙⇌⌿

George & Dragon
41-43 Summer Lane, S70 2NW
(follow signs for hospital)
✪ 12-3, 7-11; 12-11 Fri & Sat; 12-4, 7-10.30 Sun
☎ (01226) 205609
John Smith's Bitter; guest beers Ⓗ
Popular edge-of-town boozer on a busy road. Brilliant white with hanging baskets, it is hard to miss. The pub picked up autumn Pub of the Season from the local

CAMRA branch in 2002. Its split-level interior divides a large open-plan drinkers' area (mostly standing) from the pool and darts room; plenty of seating is provided. Sports TV is popular (unlike the collection of teapots). Old photos of Barnsley cover the walls. Lunches are served Tuesday–Friday, booking is advised.
❀⊞⇌ (Interchange)♣P⌷

Keresforth Hall
Keresforth Hall Road, Kingstone, S70 6NH
✪ 11-3, 7-11; 12-10.30 Sun
☎ (01226) 287206 website: www.keresforthhall.co.uk
Clark's Classic Blonde; guest beers Ⓗ
Where town meets country: standing in its own grounds with spectacular views over open countryside, you find it hard to believe you are just a mile from the town centre. Keresforth Hall was a former country club; now a lot larger, it has three dining areas (seating from 50–350) used for conferences, weddings and parties. Between two of the restaurants, the Hall Bar serves an ever-changing choice of three cask ales. A welcoming lounge, large garden and varied menus complete the facilities.
Q❀◗⅙P

Moulders Arms
Summer Street, S70 2NU
(off Summer Lane, follow signs for hospital)
✪ 4.30 (2.30 Fri; 12 Sat)-11; 12-10.30 Sun
☎ (01226) 215767
John Smith's Bitter; guest beer Ⓗ
Wonderful back-street pub with a small, bustling bar. Drinking areas are split into three; two have TVs that usually show sport. Most of the drinkers are from the local area of town, however, the pub has been welcoming new faces since the addition of a guest beer. The local CAMRA branch presented the pub with the Pub of the Season for winter 2002/03. The guest beer for May is usually a mild in support of the mild campaign. ❀⇌ (Interchange)♣

BAWTRY

Turnpike
28-30 High Street, DN10 6JE
✪ 11-11; 12-10.30 Sun
☎ (01302) 711960
Greene King Ruddles Best; John Smith's Bitter; Marston's Pedigree; guest beers Ⓗ
The Turnpike is a homely pub; L-shaped, it is divided with wood-panelled partitions to form six seating areas of varying size in older style; the floors are part-flagstoned and part-carpeted. It has been in this Guide for the last 16 years, and has been three times winner of local CAMRA's Pub of the Season award. There is a good bus service to Bawtry from the surrounding towns with a bus stop nearby. Evening meals are available Wednesday and Thursday. ❀◗

INDEPENDENT BREWERIES

Abbeydale Sheffield
Concertina Mexborough
Crown Sheffield
Glentworth Skellow
Kelham Island Sheffield
Oakwell Barnsley
Wentworth Wentworth

BENTLEY

Three Horse Shoes
Town End, DN5 9AG
✪ 12-2, 6-11; 12-11 Sat; 12-3, 7-10.30 Sun
☎ (01302) 323571
Tetley Bitter Ⓗ
One of Doncaster's few remaining multi-roomed pubs. The central bar serves a public bar with pool and TV, a quieter lounge and a room adorned with old photographs of the pub. Although the present building dates from 1914, there has been a pub here since at least 1783. Formerly a Ward's house, it stands at the far end of the old North Bridge, which now carries only buses, cyclists and pedestrians. Live music is staged: folk (Mon eve) and monthly jazz (first Sat afternoon).
Q ⏚ ≊ P

BIRDWELL

Cock Inn
Pilley Hill, S70 5UD (off A61 towards Pilley)
✪ 12-3, 7-11; 12-3, 7-10.30 Sun
☎ (01226) 742155
Draught Bass; John Smith's Bitter; guest beer (occasional) Ⓗ
The Cock is a stone-built village local with an open coal fire. Traditional in style, with two main rooms; the larger one features a slate floor, beams, brassware and old photos of the village. The home-cooked bar meals and daily specials are popular; Sunday lunch must be booked (no food Sun eve). Quizzes are held on Monday and Thursday evenings, plus occasional gourmet nights (Wed). Garden barbecues are on offer in summer. The Triumph Spitfire Club meets here.
🚗 ❀ ◑ P

BLACKER HILL

Royal Albert
Wentworth Road, S74 0RL
(between Platts Common and Worsborough)
✪ 12 (6 Tue)-11; 12-10.30 Sun
☎ (01226) 742193
Wentworth WPA, Best Bitter, Oatmeal Stout Ⓗ
This cosy, ex-Ward's pub is the first owned by Wentworth Brewery and is the focal point of the village. The traditional wood-panelled snug has an unspoilt air; the classic lounge has been recently refurbished. The pub fields darts, pool, dominoes and cards teams and hosts regular games nights. It is the venue for clubs as diverse as metal detecting and ratting. There is a free quiz on Sunday evening. Q ❀ ◑ ⏚ ♣ P ⊟

CANTLEY

Paddock
Goodison Boulevard, DN4 6NL (on B1396 in Cantley estate by roundabout)
✪ 11-3, 5-11; 11-11 Fri & Sat; 12-4, 7-10.30 Sun
☎ (01302) 536433
Greene King Old Speckled Hen; John Smith's Bitter; guest beers Ⓗ
A local estate pub, the Paddock, as its name suggests, has a strong horse racing theme running throughout, with photos of famous horses. It has the usual pub games in the bar, but the lounge, which is entered through an unusual revolving door, is free

538

from music, and the fruit machine is silent. It is possible to enjoy the ancient art of conversation over a pint. Q ❀ ⏚ P

CATCLIFFE

Waverley
Brinsworth Road, S65 3RW
(B6067, 1 mile from M1 jct 33)
✪ 2 (12 Sat)-11; 12-4, 7-10.30 Sun
☎ (01709) 360906
Beer range varies Ⓗ
Modern, stone-built pub of three rooms: a small traditional tap, a spacious lounge and a large children's room. Set back from the road, it boasts a large patio and an outside play area. Up to four ever-changing ales are always available from breweries large and small. Beers from the Glentworth and Wentworth breweries can often be found at this local CAMRA Pub of the Year 2000. Excellent home-cooked meals are based on local produce. Family entertainment is staged on Friday and Saturday.
🚸 ❀ ◑ ⏚ ⅙ ♣ P

CHAPELTOWN

Commercial
107 Station Road, S35 2XF
✪ 12-3, 5.30-11; 12-11 Sat; 12-10.30 Sun
☎ (0114) 246 9066
Wentworth Needles Eye, WPA, Premium, Oatmeal Stout; guest beers Ⓗ
Built by the former Stroutts Brewery in 1890, it is now a regular outlet for Wentworth beers. A no-smoking snug, public/games room and a comfortable lounge are all served by a newly-restyled central bar, which serves up to four changing guest ales. Note the large pump clip collection on the walls of the snug. Popular and successful beer festivals are held in May and November. Meals are served all day Friday and Saturday (12–9); no evening meals Sunday.
🚗 ❀ ◑ ⏚ ⅙ ≊ ♣ ● P ⅙ ⊟

Wharncliffe Arms
365 Burncross Road, Burncross, S35 1SB
✪ 3 (2 Fri; 12 Sat)-11; 12-10.30 Sun
☎ (0114) 246 3807
Stones Bitter; guest beers Ⓗ
Unpretentious community local, which attracts sporting clientele and is home to several clubs. A small public bar on the right is served by the main bar, while a separate servery caters for the comfortable sunken lounge on the left, displaying a collection of photographs of old Chapeltown. An extensive enclosed garden houses a children's play area and an aviary; Bonfire Night is celebrated in November. Three changing guest beers are mostly sourced from regional brewers. Small car park.
❀ ⏚ ≊ ♣ P

DONCASTER

Corner Pin
145 St Sepulchre Gate West, DN1 3AH
✪ 11-11; 12-10.30 Sun
☎ (01302) 323159
John Smith's Bitter; guest beers Ⓗ
Local CAMRA Pub of the Year 2002 where a sympathetic recent refurbishment has retained its appeal as a traditional street-

corner boozer. It offers two weekly-changed guest beers from a wide range of breweries. The central bar serves the lounge and bar areas. Original etched glass windows are a pleasing feature of this pub. It supports a darts team and, unusually, an angling club. Its friendly atmosphere attracts a good mix of customers and enlivens an otherwise neglected part of town. ⌂≠♣

Leopard
1 West Street, DN1 3AA
✪ 11-11; 12-10.30 Sun
☎ (01302) 363054
Glentworth seasonal beers; John Smith's Bitter; guest beer Ⓗ

Street-corner pub, less than five minutes' walk from the station. An impressive tiled exterior recalls its former ownership by Warwick and Richardson's Brewery. A welcome regular outlet since 1999 for local Glentworth beers – one is always available. An eclectic range of music is played on the juke box in both the comfortable lounge (refurbished in 2003) and the lively bar/games room. The upstairs band room hosts regular music and comedy gigs. Meals are served 12–7 (1–4 Sunday). ❀◑⌂≠♣P

Masons' Arms
22 Market Place, DN1 1ND
✪ 11-11; 12-10.30 Sun
☎ (01302) 364391
Taylor Landlord; Tetley Bitter Ⓗ

Traditional market place pub, a Guide regular for many years. Where once only a superb pint of Tetley's was on offer, the additional beer has proved popular. Just over 200 years old, it has maintained its multi-roomed layout. The outstanding public bar has occasional background music and is complemented by two quieter, comfortable rooms (the back room is the headquarters of the local morris men). Worthington's White Shield is available. Q⌂≠

Plough
8 West Laith Gate, DN1 1SF
✪ 11-11; 12-3, 7-10.30 Sun
☎ (01302) 738310
Barnsley Bitter; Draught Bass; guest beers (occasional) Ⓗ

Old established drinkers' pub, on the edge of the town centre, which attracts more mature (and discerning) clients. Long-standing hosts promote a comfortable, friendly atmosphere, making it an ideal break from shopping. Choose between a light, informal bar or a relaxing, comfortable lounge. On nice days sit in the covered courtyard to admire the stained glass windows. One of the first pubs on the West End real ale trail, it is renowned for its Barnsley Bitter. Q⌂≠♣

Salutation
14 South Parade, DN1 2DR
✪ 12-11, 12-10.30 Sun
☎ (01302) 340705
Tetley Dark Mild, Bitter; guest beers Ⓗ

Coaching inn dating from 1745, the pub is now an ale house, consisting of a large open room divided into cosier drinking areas. There is a large function room upstairs, with its own bar, and a patio to the rear for outside drinking. A variety of guest beers is

always on offer, along with good value meals (evening meals Mon–Fri, 5–8pm). On Tuesday evening the quiz usually draws a good crowd. ❀◑♣P

Tut 'n' Shive ✓
6 West Laith Gate, DN1 1SF
✪ 11-11 (12-midnight Fri & Sat); 12-midnight Sun
☎ (01302) 360300
Black Sheep Best Bitter; Boddingtons Bitter; Marston's Pedigree; guest beers Ⓗ

Unusual decor in the style of a town-centre ale house. Well-kept ales and cider are complemented by a good pub food selection. It appeals to a cross-section of the public, but is frequented mainly by students and young people at night. An excellent juke box plays rock standards. Sunday and Wednesday are quiz nights; rock night on Sunday and Indie night on Tuesday (both with a disc jockey) can sometimes be noisy. This vibrant pub is well worth visiting. ◑≠♠

DUNGWORTH

Royal Hotel
Main Road, S6 6HF
✪ 5.30 (12 Sat)-11; 12-4, 7-10.30 Sun
☎ (0114) 285 1213
website: www.royalhotel-dungworth.co.uk
Tetley Bitter; guest beer Ⓗ

Cosy local in a small village north-west of Sheffield, affording panoramic views of the Loxley Valley. Built almost 200 years ago, it is compact with seating in and around the bar area, and another room to the left of the entrance. En-suite accommodation is available. An extensive pie menu is served daily (evening meals finish at 8pm). There are daily bus services from Hillsborough. 🏨Q❀🛏◑♣

ELSECAR

Fitzwilliam Arms
42 Hill Street, S74 8EL (down hill from station)
✪ 12-3 (not Mon), 7-11; 12-3.30, 7-11 Sat; 12-3.30, 7-10.30 Sun
☎ (01226) 742461
Camerons Strongarm; Tetley Bitter; guest beers Ⓗ

Former Ward's pub situated very close to Elsecar railway station, and conveniently placed for Elsecar's Heritage Centre. Comfortably-furnished rooms surround a central bar, creating a warm and friendly atmosphere. This popular local is happy to welcome all visitors. ❀≠♣P

FIRBECK

Black Lion
9 New Road, S81 8JY
✪ 11-3, 5-11; 11-11 Sat; 12-10.30 Sun
☎ (01709) 812575
Greene King Ruddles County; John Smith's Bitter; Stones Bitter; Tetley Bitter Ⓗ

17th-century pub in a quiet rural village. Pleasantly modernised with beamed ceilings, it comprises one large room with a little snug and a restaurant. All rooms are full of photos of local people, scenes and famous visitors. It lies close to the ancient monument of Roche Abbey and Langold Lake, where you can fish or walk. Good food includes a lunchtime carvery and six kinds of duck. Children are welcome until

9pm when dining. Note the two splendid sedan-type chairs. ♨️❀◑ 🐕P✂

GREASBROUGH

Prince of Wales
9 Potter Hill, S61 4NU
✪ 11-4, 7-11; 12-3, 7-10.30 Sun
☎ (01709) 551358
John Smith's Bitter; ℗ guest beer Ⓗ
Friendly, street-corner local with a warm atmosphere. It still manages to sell a low-priced, ever-changing guest beer and stocks up to 50 malt whiskies. There is a traditional tap room where a lively games culture prevails. The lounge is spacious and comfortable, decorated with china plates depicting the now-defunct local mining industry, and an extensive collection of water jugs. A regular Guide entry, it has thrice been local CAMRA Pub of the Season. Well served by public transport. **Q**❀🖢♣🍺

HARTHILL

Beehive
16 Union Street, S31 8YH (opp. church)
✪ 12-3 (not Mon), 6 (7 Sat)-11; 12-3, 7-10.30 Sun
☎ (01909) 770205
Taylor Landlord; Tetley Bitter; guest beer Ⓗ
Lively, friendly pub in an historic village. Two rooms are for drinking and dining; the back room houses a full-sized snooker table. Home to the famous Harthill morris dancers and a monthly folk club (first Fri), the function room hosts many other clubs and events. Good home-cooked food is made from local produce; a Braille menu is provided and children are welcome if dining, until 9pm. Rother Valley Country Park is close by, which offers camping and good walks. **Q**❀◑🐕♣P✂

HAZELHEAD

Dog & Partridge
Bord Hill, S36 4HH (on A628, 1¼ miles from A616)
✪ 12-11; 12-10.30 Sun
☎ (01226) 763173
website: www.dogandpatridgeinn.co.uk
Barnsley Bitter; Taylor Landlord; Tetley Bitter; guest beers Ⓗ
Set in high moorland country, just below the east side of Woodhead Pass, this 15th-century inn has recently been improved by adding 12 guest rooms and extending the food provision to both bar meals and a restaurant menu. The last pub before you leave the Barnsley area on the road to Manchester, you will want to linger to enjoy all four real ales, real fires, stone-flagged floors and the incredible atmosphere of such a bleak but beautiful setting. ♨️**Q**🚬❀🛏◑🐕▲♣P✂

HEMINGFIELD

Elephant & Castle
Tinglebridge Lane, S73 0NT
✪ 11-11; 12-10.30 Sun
☎ (01226) 755986
John Smith's Bitter; Tetley Bitter; guest beers Ⓗ
Attractive stone building, graced by a large fountain outside the front door. Inside is a well-lit seating area, as well as an open area for those who prefer to stand. The guest

beers change often, while an extensive menu offers daily specials and monthly theme nights; no evening meals Sunday. There is a disused canal outside and a drinking area; it is a short walk to Elsecar Heritage Centre. ❀◑🐕🚉♣P✂

Lundhill Tavern
Beech House Road, S73 0PF
✪ 12-11; 12-10.30 Sun
☎ (01226) 752283
Samuel Smith OBB; guest beers Ⓗ
This building served as pit offices in the 1850s. Steps up to a flagstoned area lead to the bar; to the right is a games room. Wood-panelled walls show the history of the pub and colliery pictures from 1857. It has two lounge areas; one admits children. Exposed beams and stonework feature throughout. This pub has won several CAMRA awards over the last 20-plus years. One entrance is in Wombwell and the other is in the village of Hemingfield. **Q**❀♣P

HIGH BRADFIELD

Old Horns
Towngate, S6 6LG
✪ 12-11; 12-4, 5.30-11 Mon, Tue & Thu; 12-10.30 Sun
☎ (0114) 285 1207
website: www.oldhorns@bradfield.co
Thwaites Bitter, Thoroughbred, Lancaster Bomber Ⓗ
Imposing building benefiting from panoramic views, in small scenic village north of Sheffield, served by daily bus service from Hillsborough. A single bar serves an L-shaped lounge. It now stocks the Thwaites range with possibly an occasional guest or seasonal beer. The landlord celebrated 10 years in the pub in October 2003. There is a newly-built restaurant adjacent and a function room upstairs, which has hosted occasional beer festivals. ❀◑🐕♣P✂

LAUGHTON-EN-LE-MORTHEN

St Leger Arms
4 High Street, S25 1YF
✪ 12-11; 12-10.30 Sun
☎ (01909) 562940
Barnsley Bitter; Boddingtons Bitter; Whitbread Trophy Bitter Ⓗ
Handy for walkers visiting Roche Abbey, this welcoming local is in a pleasant village. The small bar area for drinkers has a games section with a TV and pool table. Excellent home-cooked food is served in the busy restaurant (children welcome until 9pm if dining). The outside drinking area has a grassy play space for children. Reputedly haunted, beams and brasses abound in this old pub, which is popular with ramblers. ❀◑♣P

MEXBOROUGH

Concertina Band Club
9A Dolcliffe Road, S64 9AZ (off High St)
✪ 12-4, 7-11; 12-2, 7-10.30 Sun
☎ (01709) 580841
Concertina Club Bitter, Bengal Tiger, seasonal beers; John Smith's Bitter; guest beers Ⓗ
The Tina is just off the High Street, and as the name implies, it was the original home of the local concertina band. Old

photographs of the band can be seen in the club. There is a large concert room and a smaller games room with a TV and pool table. It was in 1992 that the owning family decided to install a brewing plant and over the years have brewed many award-winning beers. ⇌🖪

Falcon
12 Main Street, S64 9DW
🌣 11.30-11; 12-10.30 Sun
☎ (01709) 513084
Old Mill Bitter, seasonal beers Ⓗ

Town-centre, double-fronted pub, where the original leaded windows overlook a paved seating area at the front. Originally called the Old Mason's Arms, it closed for some time until bought by the Old Mill Brewery in 1990. After refurbishment, it reopened as the Falcon, and is now a lively pub. There is a large lounge with many corners and raised seating areas, plus a smaller tap room offering pub games. Guest beers are from the Old Mill range. ✿🍽️⇌♣

PENISTONE

Cubley Hall ✓
Mortimer Road, S36 9DF (2/3 mile due S of the centre of Penistone)
🌣 11-11; 12-10.30 Sun
☎ (01226) 766086
Tetley Bitter; guest beers Ⓗ

Originally a moorland farm on the Pennine packhorse routes of the 1700s, Cubley Hall evolved into a fine Victorian gentleman's residence, then a children's home, when resident ghost, Flora, was said to appear at the bedside of sick children. Sympathetically refurbished under the present owners, original mosaic floor tiles, oak panelling, stained glass and elaborate ceiling mouldings create a rich ambience. Good food is available throughout the day and ample grounds with a play area ensure its popularity with families. ⛲✿🛏️🍽️🅿️½

ROTHERHAM

Blue Coat ✓
The Crofts, S60 2DJ
🌣 10-11; 12-10.30 Sun
☎ (01709) 539500
Theakston Best Bitter; guest beers Ⓗ

Hidden behind the town hall, this has proved to be a very popular pub. Serving up to five regularly-changing guest beers, it is very CAMRA-friendly, with the local branch helping to choose the beers on occasions such as meetings and beer festivals. A modern conversion of an old school building, this pub goes from strength to strength and is well worth seeking out. Q✿🍽️&⇌(Central) 🅿️½

Rhinoceros ✓
35-37 Bridgegate, S60 1PL
🌣 10-11; 12-10.30 Sun
☎ (01709) 361422
Theakston Best Bitter; guest beers Ⓗ

Popular, town-centre pub where a mix of customers keeps it busy all day. Quality cask beers and food are provided at very reasonable prices; it is an ideal spot for a rest from shopping in the town. Old pictures provide an historical insight to the town; see the one of the rhinoceros vase which is

kept in the local museum and gave the pub its name.
Q✿🍽️&⇌(Central) ½

Banker's Draft ✓
1-3 Market Place, S1 2GH
🌣 10-11; 12-10.30 Sun
☎ (0114) 275 6609
Barnsley IPA; Courage Directors; Shepherd Neame Spitfire; Theakston Best Bitter; guest beers Ⓗ

Overlooking Sheffield's bustling Castle Square, this Wetherspoon's house features a range of habitats to suit all-comers. It ministers to a broad church of drinkers from shoppers in search of refreshment to friends meeting of an evening. The recent policy change by the chain to admit children has not spoilt the character of the pub. The usual range of national and regional beers at bargain prices are there, supplemented by guests from near and far.
Q🍽️&⇌(Midland) ⊖(Castle Sq) ●½

Devonshire Cat
49 Wellington Street, S1 4HG
🌣 11.30-11; 12-10.30 Sun
☎ (0114) 279 6700 website: www.devonshirecat.co.uk
Kelham Island Devonshire Cat Bitter; Ⓗ
guest beers Ⓗ/Ⓖ

Twelve handpumps are supplemented by casks on gravity in a novel, glass-sided cellar to provide a notable range of beers. These and the huge selection of continental beers, and a varied food menu are enjoyed by diverse clientele. The spacious and airy, purpose-built establishment finds itself home to those who are serious about their ale, those on a night out and even the occasional card school.
🍽️&⊖(West St) ●½

Fat Cat
23 Alma Street, S3 8SA
🌣 12-3, 5.30-11; 12-11 Sat; 12-10.30 Sun
☎ (0114) 249 4801 website: www.thefatcat.co.uk
Kelham Island Best Bitter, Pale Rider; Taylor Landlord; guest beers Ⓗ

Over the years, the area surrounding the Fat Cat has gone from grimy, post-industrial dereliction to being one of the most sought-after areas in the city, complete with warehouse conversions and executive apartments. How much of this is due to there being such a great pub in the vicinity is debatable, but the Cat's award-winning vegetarian food and long-established no-smoking room certainly have not driven anyone away. Very much a pub for all seasons.
🍺Q✿🍽️⊖(Shalesmoor) ●½

Kelham Island Tavern
62 Russell Street, S3 8RW
🌣 12 (3 Mon)-11; 12-3, 7-10.30 Sun
☎ (0114) 272 9463
Barnsley Bitter; Pictish Brewers Gold; guest beers Ⓗ

Located in a rapidly improving area near the river, this is the success story of taking a pub that had seen far better days and turning it into a real ale oasis. The L-shaped main room holds a bijou bar that nevertheless has room for eight handpumps, one of which mostly dispenses one or another of this country's great milds.
Q✿🍽️⊖(Shalesmoor) 🖪

Red Deer ✅
18 Pitt Street, S1 4DD
🕐 11.30-11; 12-3, 7-11 Sat; 7.30-10.30 Sun
☎ (0114) 272 2890
website: www.red-deer-sheffield.com
Black Sheep Best Bitter; Greene King Abbot, Old Speckled Hen; Marston's Pedigree; Taylor Landlord; guest beers Ⓗ
Traditional watering-hole, amid the university's engineering campus. A loyal local contingent and office types rub shoulders with the academic community over lunch or a pint. On several levels, with a central bar on the lower level, the interior swallows almost limitless punters, lending a relaxed atmosphere even on a busy evening. Where the decor deviates from the norm, it is simply following the theme inherent in the name. ❀◗⊖ (West St)

Red House
168 Solly Street, S1 4BB
🕐 12-2, 6 (7 Tue & Fri; 7.30 Thu & Sat)-11; 4-10.30 Sun
☎ (0114) 272 7926
Adnams Bitter; Greene King IPA; guest beers Ⓗ
Compact, comfortable pub divided into a pool/main room, a dark wood-panelled snug and a corner for the dominoes players. Deeply traditional, it is home to an amiable dog and regular live folk music. It has the distinct advantage that, despite being close to the city centre, it remains free of the circuit drinker and is one of Sheffield's better-kept pub secrets.
🏚◗⊖ (Netherthorpe)

Rutland Arms
86 Brown Street, S1 2BS
🕐 11.30-11; 12-10.30 Sun
☎ (0114) 272 9003
website: www.rutlandarms-sheffield.co.uk
Adnams Bitter; Black Sheep Bitter; Greene King Abbot; Marston's Pedigree; guest beers Ⓗ
Conveniently located for the station in Sheffield's cultural zone, this impressively-fronted corner establishment provides good, home-cooked food and of course beers for those visiting or working in this section of the city. Its award-winning garden provides one of the finest urban drinking environments available.
❀◛◗▶≒ (Midland) ⊖ (Castle Sq)

Ship Inn
312 Shalesmoor, S3 8UL
🕐 12-3, 7 (6 Fri; 7.30 Sat)-11; 12-3, 7.30-10.30 Sun
☎ (0114) 281 2204
Hardys & Hansons Best Bitter, seasonal beers Ⓗ
In permanent dry dock, within spitting distance of the ring road, this venerable man-o-war of the Sheffield pub fleet has heaved-to to sustain old beer dogs and those merely scanning the horizon for a Bristol-fashion pint of Kimberley. Spacious and comfortable, the decor incorporates both standard public house ephemera and maritime paraphernalia. ◗🖫

SHEFFIELD: *EAST*

Carlton
563 Attercliffe Road, S9 3RA
🕐 11-3, 7 (7.30 Sat)-11; 11.30-3.30, 7.30-11 Fri; 7.30-10.30 Sun
☎ (0114) 244 3287

John Smith's Bitter, Magnet; guest beer (occasional) Ⓗ
Former Gilmour's pub dating from 1862 with a deceptively small frontage. A free house for the last 14 years, a comfortable lounge around the main bar leads to a pool room at the rear. Weekend entertainment may include a singalong with the landlord at the organ, or karaoke. Once at the heart of a busy shopping centre, it remains a community pub redolent of a bygone era, with a swear box. Handy for the Don Valley Stadium and the Five Weirs Walk.
Q⊖ (Attercliffe/Woodbourne Rd) ♣🖫

Cocked Hat
75 Worksop Road, S9 3TG
🕐 11-11; 11-3, 7-11 Sat; 12-2, 7-10.30 Sun
☎ (0114) 244 8332
Marston's Bitter, Pedigree; guest beer Ⓗ
Street-corner pub built in the 1840s in the then-heart of the steel industry, now lying in the shadow of the Don Valley Stadium. Acquired by Marston's in the 1980s it was refurbished in traditional style, with stalled seating at the end of the bar (reserved for diners weekday lunchtimes). A raised area at the front houses one of Sheffield's few bar billiards tables. The pub is popular with players and fans from the sports stadium as well as walkers following the nearby Five Weirs walk. 🏚❀◗⊖ (Attercliffe) ♣

SHEFFIELD: *NORTH*

Cask & Cutler
1 Henry Street, Shalesmoor, S3 7EQ
🕐 12-2 (not Mon), 5.30-11; 12-11 Fri & Sat; 12-3, 7-10.30 Sun
☎ (0114) 249 2295
Beer range varies Ⓗ
Celebrating 10 years as a free house, this two-roomed, unspoilt pub has served more than 4,000 different guest beers from its nine handpumps, promoting small independent brewers, alongside traditional cider and a large selection of Belgian bottled beers. Three times winner of local CAMRA's Pub of the Year and twice regional runner-up, the house brewery (Port Mahon) is situated to the rear, next to the secluded garden. A popular beer festival is held in November. 🏚Q❀🖳⊖ (Shalesmoor) ●⊁🖫

Gardener's Rest
105 Neepsend Lane, S3 8AT
🕐 12-11; 12-10.30 Sun
☎ (0114) 272 4978
Taylor Golden Best, Porter, Best Bitter, Landlord; Wentworth Needles Eye, WPA; Ⓗ **guest beers** Ⓗ/Ⓖ
Now firmly established on the Upper Don Pathway, this pleasant three-roomed house offers four guest beers (two on gravity dispense) plus draught Belgian and German beers. Bar billiards and other games are available in the main room, which features live music and monthly art exhibitions. A smoke-free dram shop houses brewery memorabilia. The light and airy conservatory hosts local walking, running and history groups and leads to a secluded riverside garden.
Q❀&⊖ (Infirmary Rd) ♣●⊁🖫

Hillsborough Hotel
54-58 Langsett Road, S6 2UB
🕐 4.30-11; closed Mon-Wed; 4.30-10.30 Sun

☎ (0114) 232 2100
website: www.hillsboroughhotel.com
Crown HPA, Loxley Gold, Stannington Stout; guest beers Ⓗ/Ⓖ
Although primarily a hotel during the week, it opens up to the public at weekends to serve a large variety of guest beers. Usually 16 are available, through the handpumps or in jugs from the cellar, supplementing the house beers from its award-winning Crown Brewery. Local CAMRA's Pub of the Year 2002, the three main rooms – one no-smoking, one with TV – open on to a conservatory and a sun terrace to the rear which is popular in summer.
Q ❀ ✉ ⊖ (Langsett/Primrose View) ☛ P ✕

New Barrack Tavern
601 Penistone Road, Hillsborough, S6 2GA
✪ 12-11; 12-10.30 Sun
☎ (0114) 234 9148
Abbeydale Moonshine; Barnsley Bitter, IPA; John Smith's Magnet; guest beers Ⓗ
Three-roomed roadside pub recently sold to the Tynemill pub group and re-badged as a Castle Rock pub. The award-winning formula of the previous owner – a mix of local brews and five guest beers – has been retained. Popular with the discerning football fans on match days at Hillsborough, fanzines are available. A large selection of continental draught and bottled beers is available, alongside a rotating cider and a vast array of whiskies. Evening meals are served weekdays.
▲▲ Q ❀ ◑ ⊟ ⊖ (Bamford St) ♣ ✕

SHEFFIELD: SOUTH

Archer Road Beer Stop
57 Archer Road, S8 0JT
✪ 11-10; 12-2, 6-10 Sun
☎ (0114) 255 1356
Beer range varies Ⓗ
Small, corner shop-style real ale off-licence. Formerly known as Small Beer, it is now into its 22nd year of bringing real ale to the take-home market. Up to four, mainly local, beers are available on handpump. There are up to 200 bottled beers on show, including at least two dozen bottle-conditioned ales. Many world classics are stocked, with a good selection from Belgium and Germany.

Castle Inn
Twentywell Road, Bradway, S17 4PT
✪ 12 (11 Fri & Sat)-11; 12-10.30 Sun
☎ (0114) 236 2955
Boddingtons Bitter; Fuller's London Pride; Tetley Bitter; guest beers Ⓗ
Attractive, stone-fronted pub at the end of a row of cottages, dating from the 1860s. The original pub was recently extended into an adjoining cottage. Although very popular for meals, it is very much a pub which serves food rather than a restaurant serving beer. Despite being hidden way out in the suburbs, the friendly atmosphere and quality ale make this pub well worth seeking out. ❀ ◑ ⊟ ≈ ♣ P

Prince of Wales
150 Derbyshire Lane, S8 8SE
✪ 11-11; 12-10.30 Sun
☎ (0114) 255 0960
Flowers Original; Greene King Abbot; guest beers Ⓗ
Community local: a single L-shaped bar is split into small areas with a games area at one end. There is a strong commitment to family events, many held outside in the children's play area. Originally part of the Whitbread estate, now leased from Enterprise Inns, the present managers have experienced many changes but have maintained their enthusiasm for serving real ale in a relaxed, welcoming environment. Guest ales are usually chosen from small independent brewers. ❀ ◑ ⑤ ♣ P

Sheaf View
25 Gleadless Road, S2 3AA
✪ 12 (5 Mon)-11; 12-10.30 Sun
☎ (0114) 249 6455
Abbeydale Moonshine; Barnsley Bitter; Wentworth WPA; guest beers Ⓗ
Dating from 1871, the pub has experienced an interesting, but recently chequered, history. Reopened in 2000 after a period of dereliction, it was completely refurbished to include disabled facilities. A lounge, with pine floor and furniture, leads to a carpeted bar area, with mirrors and breweriana throughout. This free house always stocks four ever-changing guest beers, a traditional cider and an impressive range of bottled and draught continental beers. ❀ ⑤ ♣ ☛ P

White Lion
615 London Road, S2 4HT
✪ 12-11; 12-10.30 Sun
☎ (0114) 255 1500
Marston's Pedigree; Tetley Dark Mild, Bitter, Burton Ale; guest beers Ⓗ
Outstanding roadside pub, dating from the mid-19th century, featuring two delightful snugs, a superb no-smoking room with pictures and maps of old Heeley, a TV and games room and a large concert room. It retains many original features, including a tiled corridor. Part of the small Just Williams group, which has a strong commitment to real ale and good cellarmanship, it is popular with all ages. Guest beers are chosen from the Punch Group list. ❀ ♣ ☛ ✕

SHEFFIELD: WEST

Noah's Ark
94 Crookes, S10 1UG
✪ 12 (11 Sat)-11; 12-10.30 Sun
☎ (0114) 266 3300
Boddingtons Bitter; Castle Eden Ale; Flowers IPA; John Smith's Magnet; Tetley Bitter; guest beers Ⓗ
Busy community pub in a popular student area, with a variety of seating areas around a central bar. The decor features dark wood and warm red in the exposed brickwork and the ceiling. Of the many pictures, some show bygone Crookes. One of the first Whitbread pubs to re-introduce real ale in the 1980s, it now offers two guest beers, mainly from regional brewers. Despite having a pool table and TV, it is still a pub for quiet conversation. Evening meals are served 5–7pm. ❀ ◑ ♣

Old Heavygate
114 Matlock Road, S6 3RQ
✪ 1-4 (not Mon-Fri), 7-11; 12-4, 7-10.30 Sun
☎ (0114) 234 0003
Hardys & Hansons Best Bitter, seasonal beers Ⓗ
Occupying a former toll house and adjoining cottage, dating from 1696, the

pub is on the old pack horse route from Sheffield to Glossop. To the right is a comfortable lounge with pool table; the Oak Room on the left still has some of the original oak beams around the windows, where the thickness of the walls can be seen by the width of the window ledges. A photograph of the ox roast celebrating the 200 years of the pub hangs on the wall. Q✿♣P

Plough Inn
288 Sandygate Road, S10 5SE
✪ 11-11; 12-10.30 Sun
☎ (0114) 230 1802
Caledonian Deuchars IPA; Greene King Abbot; Marston's Pedigree; Taylor Landlord; guest beers Ⓗ
After the indignity of a spell as a Whitbread theme pub in the 1980s, the Plough has been restored to suit the upmarket suburb it serves. The long bar has raised seating areas at either end and a pool area. The wood-panelled walls are decorated with local pictures and bric-à-brac. Up to seven real beers are on tap, sometimes including guests from local micro-breweries. ✿◑&♣P✄

Ranmoor Inn
330 Fulwood Road, S10 3BG
✪ 12-11; 12-10.30 Sun
☎ (0114) 230 1325
Black Sheep Best Bitter; Taylor Landlord; Tetley Bitter; guest beer Ⓗ
Renovated Victorian local, close to Ranmoor Church in the leafy suburb of Fulwood. It is now open-plan, but has retained separate seating areas reflecting the old room layout. This friendly, old-fashioned pub serves proper pub food. Built on a corner site, it has a small garden at the front. Q✿◑

Star & Garter ❷
82-84 Winter Street, S3 7ND
✪ 11-11; 12-10.30 Sun
☎ (0114) 272 0694
Tetley Bitter; Greene King Abbot; guest beer Ⓗ
Open-plan pub in the shadow of the university arts tower. A pool table is at one end of the central bar and darts at the other. Busy lunchtime and early evening with staff and students from the university and adjacent St George's Hospital complex, later it reverts to a traditional community pub with thriving games teams and quiz nights (Thu and Sun). The windows are decorated with etched Star and Garter signs. The guest beer changes weekly; no meals are served Saturday. ✿◑♣

Walkley Cottage
46 Bole Hill Road, S6 5DD
✪ 11-11; 12-10.30 Sun
☎ (0114) 234 4968
Black Sheep Best Bitter; Taylor Landlord; Tetley Bitter; guest beers Ⓗ
Large roadhouse-style suburban local retaining two rooms: a good-sized tap room with snooker table and big-screen TV, and a comfortable L-shaped lounge that has a food servery and no-smoking area at meal times. Built for Gilmour's between the wars on a spacious site, its extensive garden affords good views over the Rivelin Valley. Usually three or four guest beers are from regional brewers and local micros. This

lively pub hosts a popular quiz on Thursday. No evening meals are served Sunday. ✿◑⊟♣P

SILKSTONE

Silkstone Lodge
Cone Lane, S75 4LY
(off A628 towards Silkstone Common)
✪ 5-12; 12-10.30 Sun
☎ (01226) 790456
John Smith's Bitter; Wentworth Best Bitter, Black Zac Ⓗ
Large, comfortable, chalet-style former working men's club, staging regular live music events, jazz and quiz nights. The stone interior has several bar areas and a large function room. The full-sized snooker table is regularly used for team matches, as is the crown green outside. Excellent home-cooked Sunday lunches are available. There is always the chance of running into Zac, the black labrador who has a real ale named after him! Q✿⊟& ⏃≠ (Silkstone Common) P

SOUTH ANSTON

Loyal Trooper Inn
34 Sheffield Road, S25 5DT (off A57, 3 miles from M1 jct 31)
✪ 12-3, 6-11; 12-11 Sat; 12-3, 7-10.30 Sun
☎ (01909) 562203
Adnams Bitter; Taylor Landlord; Tetley Bitter; guest beer Ⓗ
Village local in the old part of Anston, named after reputedly being used to house soldiers. Dating back to 1690, it comprises a public bar, snug and lounge (also known as the Dragoons Room). A function room upstairs caters for many local groups, including Anston Folk Club. Good value, home-cooked food is served Monday–Thursday evenings (6–8) and all lunchtimes except Sunday. Handy for Anston Stones Nature Reserve and Lindrick golf course, this has been local CAMRA Pub of the Year for the last two years. Q✿◑⊟♣P

STAINTON

Three Tuns
Stainton Lane, S66 7RB
✪ 11.30-2.30, 5-11; 12-10.30 Sun
☎ (01709) 812775
John Smith's Bitter; Marston's Pedigree; Wentworth Best Bitter Ⓗ
Traditional village pub, well used by locals and visitors alike. This split-level, open-plan pub has distinctive drinking areas, one no-smoking. It enjoys a good reputation for its excellent home-cooked food, ranging from bar meals to a full à la carte menu featuring many unusual dishes. It is one of the few Doncaster area outlets to regularly stock the locally-brewed Wentworth beers. ♨✿◑P✄

STRINES

Strines Inn
Bradfield Dale, Bradfield, S6 6JE (signed 2 miles from A57) OS222906
✪ 10.30-11; (10.30-3, 6-11 winter Mon-Fri); 10.30-10.30 Sun
☎ (0144) 285 1247
Kelham Island Pale Rider; Marston's Pedigree; guest beers Ⓗ

Originally a manor house, built in 1275, most of the current building dates from the 1550s. It has been an inn since 1771, yet never been owned by a brewery. An isolated pub, in walking country, its three drinking areas include a no-smoking room. En-suite accommodation is available. Meals are served all day in summer and at the weekend; it opens at 10.30 for coffee (it has its own blend). The inn is home to a collection of rescued animals.

🏠🅂🛏🍴🕩♣P⅍

THORNE

Canal Tavern
South Parade, DN8 5DZ (town side of flyover bridge on A614)
🕓 11.30-11; 12-10.30 Sun
☎ (01405) 813688
John Smith's Bitter; Tetley Bitter; Wells Bombardier; guest beers Ⓗ

Dating back to 1822, the hostelry stands on the banks of the Stainforth & Keadby Canal, making it popular with present-day boaters. Pictures of old Thorne and maps of its windmills line the walls, while the extensive menu may line your stomach walls. The array of pump clips signals the variety of guest beers served in this well-run free house.

🅂🕩P

THORPE HESLEY

Masons Arms
Thorpe Street, S61 2RP (1/2 mile from M1 jct 35)
🕓 12-3.30, 5.30-11; 12-3.30, 7-10.30 Sun
☎ (0114) 246 8079
John Smith's Bitter; Theakston Best Bitter, Cool Cask, Old Peculier; guest beer Ⓗ

Friendly, welcoming local where a pianist plays Wednesday and Thursday, and other live entertainment takes place on Tuesday. A collection of jugs above the bar, beamed ceilings and old local pictures characterise this pub. Children are welcome in the two snugs until 9pm. Once owned by Tennant Bros of Sheffield, and built in the 19th century, the pub is home to many local groups. Handy for the Coast-to-Coast walk, it serves good value, mainly home-cooked food on a varied menu.

🅂🕩♣&♣P

THURLSTONE

Huntsman
136 Manchester Road, S36 9QW (on A628)
🕓 12-3 (not Mon-Thu), 6-11; 12-11 Sat; 12-10.30 Sun
☎ (01226) 764892
Beer range varies Ⓗ

Stone pub at the heart of the village, retaining much of its original cottage architecture. Exposed beams and a log fire make the pub a home from home. The house beer (Huntsman) is brewed by Clark's. Two regular beer festivals, on April Fool's Day and Hallowe'en, see around 25 ales offered over the week. Guest ales change regularly, making the pub worth seeking out, while quality home-cooked food is an added draw (no evening meals served Sun). A guest cider is occasionally stocked.

🏠Q🕩🅰♣🍺⅍

TICKHILL

Carpenters Arms
Westgate, DN11 9NE (near A60/A631 jct)
🕓 11.45-3 (not Mon), 6 (6.30 Sat)-11; 12-5, 7-10.30 Sun
☎ (01302) 742839
John Smith's Bitter; guest beers Ⓗ

Situated close to the castle and impressive village church, this hostelry offers many drinking areas including a comfortable, multi-alcove lounge, a bar, an award-winning no-smoking family room, and a conservatory. The extensive garden has also won awards. Two guest beers are usually offered (rotated monthly). The wholesome food (served Tue–Sat) is reasonably priced. Tickhill boasts several real ale outlets, and a frequent bus service from Doncaster, Sheffield and Worksop. �🅂🕩♣P

Scarbrough Arms
Sunderland Street, DN11 9QJ
(near village Buttercross)
🕓 11-3, 6-11; 12-3, 7-10.30 Sun
☎ (01302) 742977
Greene King Abbot; John Smith's Bitter, Magnet; guest beers Ⓗ

A deserving Guide entry since 1990, this excellent three-roomed stone pub has won several local CAMRA awards, including Doncaster Pub of the Year 1997 and 2003. Originally a farm, the building dates back to the 16th century, although structural changes have inevitably taken place over the years. The pub's wonderfully cosy, timber-panelled no-smoking snug is a delight. Other attractions include its two rotating guest beers and interesting food (served Tue–Sat). 🏠Q🅂🕩♣P🍴

TREETON

The Station ⊘
1 Station Road, S60 5PN
🕓 12-11; 12-10.30 Sun
☎ (0114) 269 2631
website: www.stationhoteltreeton.co.uk
Beer range varies Ⓗ

Totally refurbished to a high standard, the pub has a traditional tap room and a large comfortable lounge, with a no-smoking area while food is being served. When real ale was re-introduced it proved to be a runaway success and two changing guests are now available at very reasonable prices. Their top quality has earned a rare Cask Marque accreditation in the area. Good home-cooked food is available in the bar and restaurant; try the excellent curries.

🅂🕩🕂♣P

WATH UPON DEARNE

Church House
Montgomery Square, S63 7RZ
🕓 10-11; 12-10.30 Sun
☎ (01709) 875918
Beer range varies Ⓗ

This impressive building was put up in 1870, originally for the local landowner, now a fully air-conditioned, modern single bar serves both floors (toilets upstairs) with the cheapest beer in Rotherham. Handy for the RSPB Wetlands Centre near Wombwell, the pub is at the centre of the pedestrianised precinct and now has an outside drinking

WEST YORKSHIRE

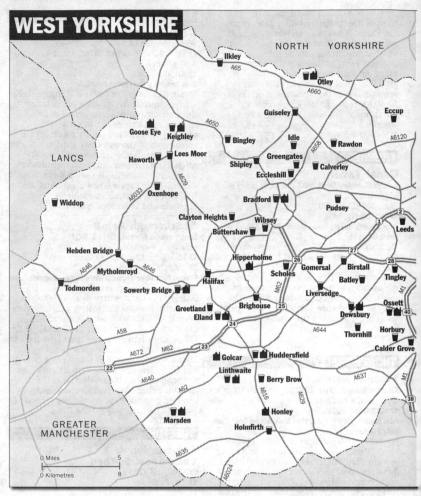

area. A varied menu is offered at excellent prices (two for £5.50 on certain choices); last orders for children is 5pm (they have to leave by 6pm). Q ❀ ◑ & P ⚞

WENTWORTH

George & Dragon
85 Main Street, S62 7TN
🕔 11-11; 12-10.30 Sun
☎ (01226) 742440
Taylor Landlord; Wentworth WPA; guest beers ⊞
Popular village pub partly dating back to the 16th century. Recently it has been the subject of discussion as the cellar appears to be haunted: strange goings-on have occurred, including casks being mysteriously moved. All this adds to the rich tapestry that this traditional local has to offer. Of six cask beers on tap, at least one is from the nearby Wentworth Brewery. One of Rotherham's gems, set in delightful countryside, it is well served by public transport. 🚶Q ❀ ◑ & P

Rockingham Arms
8 Main Street, S62 7TL
🕔 11-11; 12-10.30 Sun
☎ (01226) 742075

Wentworth Needles Eye, WPA; Theakston Old Peculier ⊞
Cosy pub in a charming village that retains a multi-roomed layout around a central bar. Mouth-watering food and entertainment are both provided. Attached to the pub is a large garden, and a bowling green adds to its appeal. Bed and breakfast accommodation is available, making it an ideal base for walking in the surrounding area and also the nearby Wentworth Park. 🚶Q 🛏 ❀ 🚄 ◑ P

WHISTON

Chequers Inn
Pleasley Road, S60 4AH (on A618, 2½ miles from Rotherham, 1½ miles from M1 jct 33)
🕔 11-11; 12-10.30 Sun
☎ (01709) 829168
Stones Bitter; Taylor Landlord; Tetley Bitter; guest beer ⊞
This brightly-painted local hosts a monthly jazz club (last Wed). Children are welcome until 7.30pm when eating (no eve meals Sun). A former Mr. Q theme pub, its fortunes were recently turned around by new licensees. Its range of real ales has been expanded; the guest beer is changed

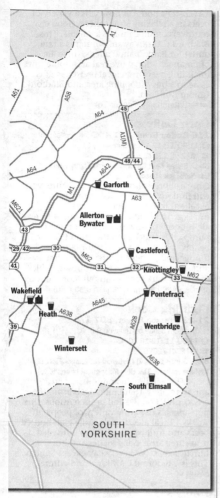

☎ (01226) 273820

Theakston Best Bitter; guest beers Ⓗ

This impressive town-centre pub was built at the start of the last century, replacing an earlier terraced pub (also called the Horseshoe), that was knocked down as a part of the redevelopment of the town-centre shopping area. The town's main disabled parking area is immediately outside the front doors. Rejuvenated by new owners, Wetherspoon's, it provides a welcome meeting-place for drinkers and shoppers, particularly since the relaxation of opening hours by local magistrates. Children are admitted until 6pm. Q ◑ & ⌽

WORTLEY

Wortley Arms
Halifax Road, S35 7DB (on A629)
✪ 12-11; 12-10.30 Sun
☎ (0114) 288 2245

Draught Bass; Oakwell Barnsley Bitter; Taylor Dark Mild, Landlord Ⓗ

Cosy, rambling, multi-roomed, old village hostelry, oozing with understated character and charm; gorgeous wood panelling, a huge inglenook and exposed stonework inlaid with a coat of arms. It offers two house beers from different breweries, plus a selection of bottled Belgian beers and a wide range of malt whiskies. Half a mile from the Trans-Pennine Trail, in excellent walking country, it is served by buses from Penistone and Sheffield.
🏯 Q ⬱ ✿ ⍝ ◑ ⊟ A P ⌽

Yorkshire (West)

ALLERTON BYWATER

Boat Inn
Boat Lane, WF10 2BX
✪ 11-11 (may close winter weekday afternoons);
12-10.30 Sun
☎ (01977) 552216 website: www.boatpub.co.uk

Boat Man in the Boat, seasonal beers; Tetley Bitter Ⓗ

A success story in an attractive setting next to the River Aire, the Boat was extended in 2003. This work has increased capacity for the famous pub food (booking advised), while also providing more room for those concentrating on the beers from the Boat Brewery (located in the car park). There is now full wheelchair access and a baby changing room. The Boat is run by Rugby League legend, Brian Lockwood and his family – note the mementos of his long career. ⬱ ✿ ◑ & A P ⌽

BATLEY

Wilton Arms
4 Commercial Street, WF17 5HH
(100 yds NW A652/B6124 jct)
✪ 11-11; 12-10.30 Sun
☎ (01924) 479996

Stones Bitter; Tetley Bitter Ⓗ

This 18th-century, Grade II listed, town-centre pub is run by one of the longest-serving licensees in the area. The function room once hosted a mayoral court and council room. Sporting traditions are reflected in the fine collection of Rugby League memorabilia and a strong ladies' hockey team. A vibrant tap room and quieter lounge welcome customers from

monthly with some rare brews for the area. Note the thatched medieval manorial barn close by in the older part of the village. Ulley Country Park is about two miles away. Q ✿ ◑ ♣ P

Sitwell Arms
Pleasley Road, S60 4AH (on A618, 2½ miles from Rotherham, 1½ miles from M1 jct 33)
✪ 12-11; 12-10.30 Sun
☎ (01709) 377003

Greene King Abbot; Tetley Bitter; guest beers Ⓗ

Welcoming local with beamed ceilings; originally a farm and ale house, it is centuries old in parts. Later a coaching inn, it is now a pub and restaurant serving good food (no meals Sun eve). Named after a local land-owning family, it lies close to an historic thatched manorial barn and the dyke, and boasts a garden; good local walks. it hosts regular quiz nights and other entertainments. A Link cash machine in the lounge is a useful amenity. ✿ ◑ & ♣ P

WOMBWELL

Horseshoe
High Street, S73 0AA (next to main post office)
✪ 10-11; 12-10.30 Sun

local shops and the innovative mill complex nearby, as well as stalwarts of Batley's 'Golden Mile'. No lunches served Sunday. ⊛◖⊡≢♣P

BERRY BROW

Berry Brow Liberal Club
6 Parkgate, HD4 7NF (on A616)
✪ 12-2 (not Tue or Thu), 8-11 (12-11 Sat in football season); 12-2, 8-10.30 Sun
☎ (01484) 662549
website: www.groups.msn.com/berrybrowliberalclub
Jennings Bitter, Cumberland Ale; guest beers Ⓗ
Small, stone-built CIU-affiliated club at the centre of Berry Brow. Good views can be enjoyed from the back of the club (known as the Vatican) down into the valley. Three open-plan areas are served from the central bar. Two snooker tables are hidden in the upstairs room. Limited parking is available on surrounding streets. Show this Guide or a CAMRA membership card to be signed in. ≢♣

BINGLEY

Brown Cow
Ireland Bridge, BD16 2QX
✪ 12-3, 5-11; 12-11 Sat; 12-10.30 Sun
☎ (01274) 564345
Taylor Golden Best, Dark Mild, Best Bitter, Landlord; guest beers Ⓗ
Extensively refurbished in 2001 following severe flooding, this riverside pub is extremely popular for excellent food and quality real ale. It often has all six Timothy Taylor draught beers, supplemented by guests from local micro-breweries, including Goose Eye, Brown Cow, Ossett and Daleside. Opening hours may be extended during summer. Booking is advisable for meals. Bradford CAMRA Pub of the Season winter 2002. ⋈⊛◖Ġ≢P

BIRSTALL

Black Bull
5 Kirkgate, WF17 9PB (off A652, near A643)
✪ 12-11; 12-3.30, 7-10.30 Sun
☎ (01274) 873039
Boddingtons Bitter; Whitbread Trophy Bitter; guest beer Ⓗ
Long, narrow inn, parts of which date from the 17th century. Once an important venue for auctions, elections and other functions, it has retained the magistrates' box and prisoner's dock last used in 1839 in the upstairs courtroom. Downstairs, the snug is good for a quiet drink and four other seating areas provide a cosy atmosphere. Local CAMRA Pub of the Year 2001 and 2002, it was voted Best Pub for food by the local newspapers (booking advised for weekend meals; eve meals Tue–Sat, 6–9). Q⊛◖♣P

BRADFORD

Castle Hotel
20 Grattan Road, BD1 2LU (off Westgate)
✪ 11.30-11; closed Sun
☎ (01274) 393166
website: www.thecastlehotel.britain-uk.com
Banks's Bitter; Barnsley Bitter; Fuller's ESB; guest beers Ⓗ
Imposing stone pub, built in 1898. Formerly a Webster's house, it now sells a variety of beers in a relaxing atmosphere. Good city-centre accommodation is available. This Bradford CAMRA award-winner is a rare outlet for Banks's and Fuller's; there are often an additional five real ales, sometimes including beers from local breweries. It is close to a busy shopping area and Bradford Colour Museum.
⇔≢ (Interchange/Forster Sq)

Corn Dolly ⊘
110 Bolton Road, BD1 4DE (off Forster Sq)
✪ 11.30-11; 12-10.30 Sun
☎ (01274) 720219
Black Sheep Best Bitter; Everards Tiger; Taylor Landlord; guest beers Ⓗ
Only a short walk from the city centre, you will find no smoothflow here at this excellent inn with mock country-style interior. The landlord's commitment to real ale is borne out by the large number of pump clips attached to the pub's fake roof beams. Divided into two distinct areas – lounge and games – it offers four guest ales and a house beer from Moorhouses. Tables in the car park serve as an outdoor drinking space. ⋈⊛◖≢ (Interchange/Forster Sq) ♣P

Fighting Cock
21-23 Preston Street, BD7 1JE
(1 mile from centre off Thornton Rd)
✪ 11.30-11; 12-10.30 Sun
☎ (01274) 726907
Black Sheep Special; Eastwood & Sanders First Light; Taylor Landlord; Thwaites Mild; guest beers Ⓗ
Drinkers' paradise in an industrial area, approximately 15 minutes' walk from the city centre. Popular and unpretentious, this pub appeals to a wide variety of people. It stocks 12 real ales, real cider, Belgian bottled beers and fruit wines. The pub is divided into three areas. Sandwiches and hot lunches are served every day except Sunday. This is a Bradford CAMRA award-winner. ⋈◖♣◗

Haigy's
31 Lumb Lane, BD8 7QU
✪ 5 (12 Fri & Sat)-1am; Sun opens 12
(closing time varies)
☎ (01274) 731644
Greene King Abbot; Tetley Bitter; guest beers Ⓗ
Unusual, but friendly, local situated in a difficult trading area for real ale. It is painted outside in the colours of the Bantams, Bradford City AFC. Haigy's has been a supporter of the Ossett Brewery for a number of years, and sells guest beers from that company's range. A cosy lounge, pool and music areas offer customers a choice of venue. A late licence applies every day except Sunday when closing time varies. ⊛≢ (Interchange/Forster Sq) ♣P

Melborn Hotel
104 White Abbey Road, BD8 8DP (on B6144, 1/2 mile from centre)
✪ 12 (4 Wed-Fri)-11; 12-10.30 Sun
☎ (01274) 726867
Moorhouses Premier; Tetley Bitter; guest beers Ⓗ
Ex-Tetley, ex-Melbourne pub, now a proper free house fully deserving its fine reputation as a venue for live music. This characterful house stands at a junction, inviting entry to the lively tap room and large music room, that hosts folk and blues nights almost

every evening. Many glass cabinets display curios and fascinating artefacts. Note, too, the musical instruments and biggest clock ever on the walls. ⏴⏵⬤&⇌ (Forster Sq) ♣P

New Beehive Inn ☆
171 Westgate, BD1 3AA (on B1644)
🕐 12-11; (2am Fri & Sat); 6-10.30 Sun
☎ (01274) 721784
Barnsley Bitter; Kelham Island Best Bitter; Ossett Silver King; Taylor Landlord; guest beers Ⓗ
Gaslit and multi-roomed, this fine building has been painstakingly brought back to its original standard. Noted for its original paintings by local artist, Jim Smith, the large mural depicting deceased rock stars is a stunner; is that really a picture of Gazza with a pint? Four rooms suit all tastes (including non-smokers) and the entrance hall is also used as a drinking area. It stocks a large range of single malts and boasts lots of handpumps. Often live music is staged.
⍨Q⊛⏴⬤⇌ (Forster Sq) ♣⬤P⌿

Prospect of Bradford
527 Bolton Road, BD3 0NW
🕐 2.30-5.30, 7-11; 2.30-11 Fri & Sat; 12-10.30 Sun
☎ (01274) 727018
Taylor Golden Best; Tetley Bitter Ⓗ
An imposing frontage, yet it is the rear that commands an outstanding view over the city. This Victorian house, built on the site of an earlier pub, has one bar, with a side hatch to serve two ground-floor rooms. The first-floor function room comfortably holds 60 people and is available for hire with excellent catering and a real ale bar. Singalong live music is a weekend speciality (guest singers welcome). Wednesday is games night. ⍨⇌ (Forster Sq) ♣P

Shoulder of Mutton
28 Kirkgate, BD1 1QI
🕐 11-11; 12-10.30 Sun
☎ (01274) 726038
Samuel Smith OBB Ⓗ
This small, multi-roomed, city-centre pub dates as a coach house from 1825. It is a popular lunchtime venue for business people, shoppers and locals who appreciate the good value food. Its appeal is enhanced in summer by a large, suntrap garden. The pub was refurbished without ruining its traditional atmosphere; pictures, photographs and drawings of the old city abound. It is the headquarters of Airedale quiz league.
⊛⬤⇌ (Forster Sq/Interchange)

Sir Titus Salt ⊘
Windsor Baths, Morley Street, BD7 1AQ (by Alhambra Theatre)
🕐 10-11; 12-10.30 Sun
☎ (01274) 732853
Boddingtons Bitter; Shepherd Neame Spitfire; Taylor Landlord; Theakston Best Bitter; guest beers Ⓗ
Spacious Wetherspoon's conversion of the original Windsor swimming baths. It is popular with a variety of customers, ranging from mature couples to students from the nearby university and colleges. An upstairs seating area overlooks the main pub. It is often very busy in the evenings at the end of the week as it is ideally situated for theatregoers, clubbers and many curry restaurants.
Q⌂⊛⬤& ⇌ (Interchange) ⌿

Steve Biko Bar
D floor, Richmond Building, University, Richmond Road, BD7 1DP (off Gt Horton Rd)
🕐 11 (4 Sat)-11; 4-10.30 Sun
☎ (01274) 233257
Greene King Old Speckled Hen; Stones Bitter; Worthington's 1744; guest beers Ⓗ
This large, open-plan bar offers snacks, coffee and soft drinks from 8am. Although run by the student union, it is open to the general public. Four or five ever-changing guest beers come from independent and local breweries, all sold at reasonable prices, with cheaper promotions on Monday evening. The bar can be noisy with special events such as comedy shows and other acts. Choice can be limited during student vacations. ⇌ (Interchange)

BRIGHOUSE

Crown
6 Lightcliffe Road, Waring Green, HD6 2DR
🕐 11-11; 12-10.30 Sun
☎ (01484) 715436
Courage Directors; Tetley Bitter; Theakston Dark Mild Ⓗ
You are assured of a warm welcome at this traditional family pub. With three comfortable seating areas and a large pool room, the Crown is the base for both the Brighouse old boys' football club and the famous Brighouse and Rastrick brass band. On Saturday evenings you can enjoy your favourite tunes, courtesy of the piano player. ♣P

Richard Oastler ⊘
9-11 Market Street, HD6 1JL
🕐 10-11; 12-10.30 Sun
☎ (01484) 401756
Boddingtons Bitter; Hop Back Summer Lightning; Shepherd Neame Spitfire; Taylor Landlord; Theakston Best Bitter; guest beers Ⓗ
Another successful Wetherspoon's conversion. The atmospheric former

INDEPENDENT BREWERIES

Anglo Dutch Dewsbury
Boat Allerton Bywater
Briscoe's Otley
Clark's Wakefield
Eastwood & Sanders Elland
John Eastwood Linthwaite
Egyptian Dewsbury
Fernandes Wakefield
Golcar Golcar
Goose Eye Keighley
Halifax Hipperholme
Linfit Linthwaite
Ossett Ossett
Rat & Ratchet Huddersfield
Red Lion Ossett
Riverhead Marsden
Ryburn Sowerby Bridge
Salamander Bradford
Taylor Keighley
Tigertops Wakefield
Turkey Goose Eye
Upper Agbrigg Honley
Whitley Bridge Wakefield

Wesleyan chapel in central Brighouse (built in 1878) has retained many original features, notably the organ and organ pipes. From the central seating area, view the magnificent circular upper floor (not used) with pews and an impressive mural on the ceiling. The beer range includes at least three guest beers. The pub holds two beer festivals a year, with 30 ales available over a four day period. Q✿◑❦❧≠✂

Round Hill Inn ✪
75 Clough Lane, Rastrick, HD6 3QL (on A6103)
✪ 5 (7 Sat)-11; 12-3, 7-10.30 Sun
☎ (01484) 713418 website: www.roundhillinn.com
Black Sheep Best Bitter; Taylor Golden Best, Landlord; guest beer Ⓗ
Cottage-style building set back from the main road. Two comfortably furnished lounges afford views over the cricket ground and the eponymous round hill. The low-ceilinged smaller lounge is non-smoking. It is a popular calling place on the way home in the early evening, when parking can be difficult. The guest beer comes from a regional or micro-brewery. ⚞P✂

BUTTERSHAW

Beehive Inn ✪
583 Halifax Road, BD6 2DU
✪ 11-11; 12-10.30 Sun
☎ (01274) 678550
Ansells Best Bitter; Tetley Bitter; guest beers Ⓗ
Lively, homely local where children are welcome until 7.30pm. A pool table dominates the side room and there is a large-screen TV for sporting events in the lounge. Guest beers change weekly; many are from local breweries such as Salamander, Daleside, Ossett and Taylors. Entertainment includes a disco every Friday and karaoke on Saturday; it hosts a games league evening on Tuesday. ✿❦♣

CALDER GROVE

Navigation
Broad Cut Road, Caldervale, WF4 3DS
✪ 12-11; 12-10.30 Sun
☎ (01924) 274361
Taylor Landlord; Tetley Bitter; guest beers (summer) Ⓗ
Aptly named pub, situated on an island between the River Calder and the Aire and Calder Navigation Canal. This historic two-roomed pub attracts both boaters and families with small children who enjoy the outdoor playground with bouncy castle, as well as indoor attractions in the no-smoking family room. Boats can be moored in front of the pub. ⚞Q⚑✿◑P✂

CALVERLEY

Thornhill Arms
18 Town Gate, LS28 5NF
✪ 11-11; 12-10.30 Sun
☎ (0113) 256 5492
Courage Directors; John Smith's Bitter; Theakston Cool Cask; guest beer Ⓗ
This traditional Yorkshire stone building is a former coaching inn. Situated near the church, the two are reputedly linked by an underground passage. A smart pub in a commuter village between Leeds and

Bradford, it is plushly decorated in beige and brown colours. Some of the comfy settles retain their bell pushes – no longer functional. Beware, the car park entrance is at an acute angle to a busy main road, making access tricky. Evening meals are served in an upstairs bistro. ✿◑❦♣P✂

CASTLEFORD

Early Bath
Wheldon Road, WF10 2SE (follow signs for Castleford Rugby League ground)
✪ 7-11 (all day match days); 12-3, 7-10.30 Sun
☎ (01977) 518389
Black Sheep Special; John Smith's Bitter; guest beer Ⓗ
An unprepossessing exterior opens to a friendly two-room boozer, close to the Jungle, home of Castleford Tigers, so Rugby League is in evidence everywhere. The pub's name is the traditional epithet for a sending-off in Rugby League. The pub's freehold belongs to the adjacent forklift truck firm, so that means no brewery ties or inflated beer prices. Ask to see the amazing Art Deco function suite. The accommodation is cheap, but no breakfast is available. ✿⚑♿P

Glass Blower ✪
15 Bank Street, WF10 1JD
✪ 11-11; 12-10.30 Sun
☎ (01977) 520390
Greene King Abbot; Shepherd Neame Spitfire; Taylor Landlord; Theakston Best Bitter; guest beers Ⓗ
The town's former post office, the Glass Blower is a large, bustling town pub, popular with all ages. The comfortable interior displays pictures of the town's history: coal, pottery and bottle making, while the route to the toilets celebrates sculptor, Henry Moore. A good range of guest beers is served by informed staff; beer festivals are held in spring and at Hallowe'en. It has a large garden at the rear and a children's licence applies until 5pm. It opens for breakfast at 10am. ✿◑♿≠✂

CLAYTON HEIGHTS

Old Dolphin
192 Highgate Road, BD13 1DR
(on A647, Bradford side of Queensbury)
✪ 12-3, 5.30-11; 12-11 Fri & Sat; 12-10.30 Sun
☎ (01274) 882202
Beer range varies Ⓗ
This 300-year-old coaching inn offers two guest beers, possibly from Durham, Eastwood & Sanders, Salamander, Goose Eye, Phoenix, Ossett or Boat. A good selection of home-cooked meals includes vegetarian and diabetic choices. The garden play area has barbecue facilities. Originally built around 1200 as a hospital in the War of the Roses, Cromwell's men were billeted here in 1650. John Foster performed here before creating the famous Black Dyke Mills band; 'cat's eyes' inventor, Percy Shaw, was a regular. ⚞✿◑P

DEWSBURY

Huntsman ✪
Chidswell Lane, Shaw Cross, WF12 7SW
(400 yds from A635/B6128 jct)
✪ 12-3 (not Mon), 5 (7 Sat)-11; 12-3, 7-10.30 Sun

☎ (01924) 275700

Black Sheep Special; Taylor Landlord; guest beer Ⓗ
This pub has a real local atmosphere. Formed from a couple of cottages, it boasts a traditional Yorkshire range in one room; old horse brasses and exposed beams give a warm feel to the bar. On the edge of the village, it benefits from spectacular views over open countryside, making it popular with walkers. Food is served Tuesday–Saturday (no eve meals Sat). The house beer, Chidswell Bitter, is brewed by Highwood and the guest beer is often from a small brewer. ♨❀ⓓ P

Leggers Inn
Robinsons Boatyard, Mill Street East, WF12 9BD (off B6409, S of centre)
🕐 11.30-11; 12-10.30 Sun
☎ (01924) 502846

Everards Tiger; guest beers Ⓗ
First-floor bar with a low, beamed ceiling, once a hayloft for stables housing horses that pulled barges along the canal. It overlooks a busy, residential canal basin with the Calder Lady trip boat. The Egyptian Sand & Gravel Brewery brews downstairs. Two of its beers are on the bar, alongside a Rooster's beer, several guests and a wheat beer. It also stocks a good range of Belgian bottled beers, wines and malt whiskies. Snacks are served all day. ♨❀♣P

West Riding Licensed Refreshment Rooms ❷
Railway Station, Wellington Road, WF13 1HF (on platform 2 of Dewsbury Station)
🕐 11-11; 12-10.30 Sun
☎ (01924) 459193 website: www.wrlrr.com

Black Sheep Best Bitter; Taylor Landlord; guest beers Ⓗ
A main stop on the Trans-Pennine rail ale trail, this popular pub is a 1993 conversion of the former waiting rooms in the Grade II listed station building. The main outlet for the local Anglo Dutch Brewery, it offers up to eight real ales, always including a local dark mild. Live music is a regular feature. The walls display much evocative railwayana. Excellent good value lunches are served weekdays; on Tuesday evening pie and peas are available, Wednesday is curry night. ♨❀ⓓ♣⇌P

Woodman Inn
6 Hartley Street, Batley Carr, WF13 2BJ (off A652, behind Vauxhall garage)
🕐 4-11; 11.30-11 Fri; 12-4, 7-11 Sat; 12-4, 7-10.30 Sun
☎ (01924) 463825

Tetley Mild, Bitter; guest beer Ⓗ
Back-street local, dating from 1680, probably the oldest pub in town. It has been extended by the current licensees who bought this ex-Bentley's house in 1984. It attracts working drinkers early in the evening and a very smart clientele at the weekend. Darts and dominoes are played in the large tap room that has Sky TV; a quiz is staged on Tuesday. ❀⊟♣P

Royal Oak
39 Stony Lane, BD2 2HN (¼ mile from A6176)
🕐 11-11; 12-10.30 Sun
☎ (01274) 639182

Taylor Landlord; Tetley Mild, Bitter Ⓗ
Friendly, village-style two-roomed local with separate entrances to the older lounge and more recent public bar where darts, dominoes and pool are played regularly. Quizzes are popular with the locals. The pub has been rewarded with Cellarman of the Year awards; customers are rewarded with regular money-off promotions. It is a rare outlet for mild. The heated patio at the rear of the pub is an asset on chillier summer evenings. ❀⊟♣P

New Inn
Eccup Lane, LS16 8AU
🕐 12-3, 6-11; 12-10.30 Sun
☎ (0113) 288 6335

Greene King Old Speckled Hen; Tetley Bitter; guest beer Ⓗ
Country pub on a minor road, but still close to the urban bustle of Lawnswood. Aimed mainly at diners, drinkers are still made welcome, especially in the public bar area. One end of the main bar is very much a restaurant. Just a few yards off the Dales Way, it is popular with walkers in summer, when the garden and children's play area also fill up. This fine pub is well worth a visit. No meals are served Sunday evening. ♨⭐❀ⓓ⊟A✕

Barge & Barrel
10-20 Park Road, 4X5 9AP (on A6025)
🕐 12-11; 12-10.30 Sun
☎ (01422) 373623

Black Sheep Best Bitter; Rooster's Yankee; Taylor Landlord; Tetley Bitter; guest beers Ⓗ
Large canalside/roadside pub with a central horseshoe-shaped bar. Many interior walls have been removed, some replaced by glazed screens. A raised seating area on the canal doubles as a stage for occasional live music on a Sunday evening. The original brewing plant is still in place, but most brewing now takes place at a larger plant across town. Up to seven guest beers come from micro-breweries, and Saxon perry or cider is stocked. ♨❀♣♣P

Gaping Goose
41 Selby Road, LS25 1LP
🕐 11-11; 12-10.30 Sun
☎ (0113) 286 2127

Tetley Mild, Bitter Ⓗ
Bustling local with three rooms and a lively atmosphere. You enter straight into the main bar; this and the Tudor Room are carpeted and comfortable, while the tap room is more basic. Interior doors bear octagonal windows with the room names on them. In the Tudor Room is a collection of plates and old photos, while the main bar displays horse brasses. This is a fine example of a nearly intact pub interior – increasingly rare in Leeds. ❀⊟P

Wheatsheaf
95 Gomersal Lane, Little Gomersal, BD19 4HY (off A643 between Gomersal and Cleckheaton)

❄ 12-3 (not Mon), 5.30-11; 12-11 Sat; 12-10.30 Sun
☎ (01274) 873661

Black Sheep Best Bitter; Tetley Bitter; guest beer Ⓗ
Modest pub, located in the hamlet of Little
Gomersal. Inside is a large collection of
brass and knick-knacks with many old
photos of landlords and regulars. There are
three lounge areas, one of which doubles as
restaurant and no-smoking room. A
tempting blackboard menu is available
Tuesday–Saturday and Sunday lunchtime.
The enclosed garden has swings. A friendly,
cosy village pub, it is popular with locals
and ideal for weary walkers, as it stands near
the end of the 26-mile Heritage Trail.
Q ❀ ◑ P ⊁

GREENGATES

Albion Inn ⊘
25 New Line, BD10 9AS
❄ 12-11; 12-10.30 Sun
☎ (01274) 613211

Barnsley Bitter; Tetley Dark Mild, Bitter, Imperial Ⓗ
Popular roadside inn on the main
Leeds–Keighley road (A657) near two
business centres. This compact local has a
warm and friendly atmosphere created by
staff and customers alike. An L-shaped
lounge leads to an old-fashioned games
room, which can be cramped on darts
nights. Bus No. 760 Leeds–Keighley passes
the pub. ⊟ ♣ P

GREETLAND

Druids Arms
2-4 Spring Lane, HX4 8JL (off Rochdale road,
B6113, opp. community centre)
❄ 5-11; 12-11 Sat; 12-10.30 Sun
☎ (01422) 372465

**Taylor Golden Best, Best Bitter, Landlord;
guest beers** Ⓗ
Popular, village free house, known to the
locals as the Rat. Local micro-breweries
feature strongly among the three guest beers
– future offerings are displayed on the board
opposite the bar. In winter the pub is
heated by two real fires, while for summer
drinking, doors open on to a decked area
affording impressive views across the valley.
Good quality, home-cooked food is served
evenings and Sunday lunchtime in the no-
smoking restaurant area. Regular live music
nights feature local bands. ᨔ ❀ ◑ P

Spring Rock ⊘
Rochdale Road, Upper Greetland, HX4 8PT
(on B6113, 2 miles from B6112 jct)
❄ 12-11; 12-10.30 Sun
☎ (01422) 377722

Black Sheep Best Bitter; Holt Bitter; guest beers Ⓗ
On Norland Moor, with open views, the
Spring Rock looks very like a traditional
Pennine farmhouse. The present owner
has quickly created a warm and
welcoming pub with a good reputation for
its food (no meals served Sun eve).
Essentially two rooms: the larger one
contains the bar, plus some comfy
armchairs; the smaller room is used for
families and functions. It stocks
continental bottled beers and a good
selection of wines. 'Knurr and spile', a
peculiar local game used to be played
here.
ᨔ Q ⌂ ❀ ◑ ▲ P ⊁

GUISELEY

Drop
29 Town Street, LS20 9DT
❄ 11.30-11; 12-10.30 Sun
☎ (01943) 874967
website: www.thedropinn@hotmail.com

Black Sheep Best Bitter; Tetley Bitter; guest beer Ⓗ
Prominent 1960s pub, with a steeply
pitched roof. The name relates to a former
nearby hostelry where hangings took place.
A central bar serves a comfortable lounge
area. The games room has satellite TV and is
popular with sports fans. The guest beer
comes from the Tapster's Choice list.
Evening meals (served in summer) finish at
7.30pm. ❀ ◑ ⊟ ઙ ⇌ ♣ P

Ings
45 Ings Lane, LS20 9HR
(off A65 at Guiseley Town FC)
❄ 11-11; 12-10.30 Sun
☎ (01943) 873315

Taylor Landlord; Tetley Bitter; guest beer Ⓗ
This attractive, well-patronised pub derives
its name from an adjoining area of
wetlands. The open-plan, well-appointed
lounge hosts a music quiz (Tue) and general
knowledge quiz (Thu). Airedale and
Wharfedale Motorcyle Club hold regular
meetings here. Its semi-rural setting and
proximity to Otley Chevin make it handy
for hikers. It has a heated outdoor patio and
secure garden, but no children are allowed
in the pub. ᨔ ❀ ⇌ ♣ P

HALIFAX

Big Six ⊘
10 Horsfall Street, Savile Park, HX1 3HG (off
Skircoat Moor road, A646, at King Cross)
❄ 5 (1 Fri)-11; 12-11.30 Sat; 12-5, 7-10.30 Sun
☎ (01422) 350169

Greene King IPA; Taylor Landlord; guest beers Ⓗ
Cosy, mid-terrace pub with a multi-room
layout, where original features include a
range from 1857. The history of the pub is
documented on the walls. Although tucked
away on a back street, this pub is hugely
popular with the local community and a
warm welcome is given to everyone
including cyclists, bikers and dog-walkers.
ᨔ ❀

Brown Cow Inn
569 Gibbet Street, Highroad Well, HX2 0AL
❄ 11.30-11; 12-10.30 Sun
☎ (01422) 361640

**Castle Eden Ale; Taylor Landlord; Tetley Bitter; guest
beer** Ⓗ
Community roadside inn that appeals to a
wide range of ages. Though open plan,
there are four distinct seating areas. Sport,
including Sky, features on the large-screen
TV in the games area, which is adorned
with Halifax Town Football Club
memorabilia. Local amateur football teams
meet here at weekends, and the pub has its
own golf society. Quiz night is Tuesday.
Weekday lunches include special offers for
pensioners. Chairs and benches on the
roadside cater for outdoor drinkers. ❀ ◑ ♣

Commercial Inn
23 Lower Skircoat Green, HX3 0TG
(1 mile S of centre)
❄ 12-2, 5-11; 12-3, 7-10.30 Sun

☎ (01422) 365078

Tetley Bitter; guest beer Ⓗ

Homely local that has been run by the Golthorpes for the past 33 years. The Commercial enjoys expansive views across the Calder Valley towards North Dean woods and the Norland hillside. Features include a rare 1950s Whitaker's fireplace complete with 'Cock of the North' embellishments. One or more interesting guest beers are always available from a wide variety of micro-breweries, both near and far. ❀♣

Shears Inn
Paris Gates, Boys Lane, HX3 9EZ (by river behind flats opp. football ground)
✪ 11.45-11; 12-10.30 Sun
☎ (01422) 362936

Taylor Golden Best, Best Bitter, Landlord, Ram Tam; Theakston Black Bull; guest beer Ⓗ

Tucked into the valley next to Hebble Brook and dwarfed by one of the few remaining working textile mills. It can take some finding initially, but is well worth the effort. A popular lunchtime venue for workers, locals come along in the evening. It is basically one room, but the central chimney piece and seating alcoves do create more intimate areas. It is home to soccer and cricket teams. Lunches are served Monday–Saturday. ⚐❀Ⓒ⇌♣P

Sportsman Inn
Bradford Old Road, Swalesmoor, HX3 6UG (off A647, 1 mile N of centre)
✪ 11.45-2.30, 6-11 (12 Fri); 11.45-12 Sat; 11.45-10.30 Sun
☎ (01422) 367000

Taylor Landlord; Tetley Bitter; Theakston Old Peculier; guest beer Ⓗ

In its hilltop position, benefiting from fine views, the Sportsman is a local pub/leisure centre. It offers not only an adventure playground, virtual golf and karting, but also a dry ski slope. The pub, which is separate from the various leisure facilities, has a bar, a large no-smoking family room and a dining room (no food Mon). It stages a folk club on Thursday and a quiz Friday evening. ⚐❦❀ⒸⒹP⅄

Three Pigeons Ale House
1 Sun Fold, South Parade, HX1 2LX
✪ 12-11; 12-10.30 Sun
☎ (01422) 347001
website: www.threepigeons.demon.co.uk

Black Sheep Best Bitter; Eastwood & Sanders Best Bitter; Jennings 1828; Taylor Best Bitter, Landlord; guest beers Ⓗ

Award-winning, family-owned free house; local CAMRA Pub of the Year 2002. Three rooms radiate off a central octagonal drinking area, or lobby, which boasts a ceiling painting depicting the birds which give the pub its name. Regular initiatives take place, such as showcasing guest beers from West Yorkshire over a month; brewers' tutored tastings and evenings devoted to rare pub games. The three guests, usually from micro-breweries, often include a mild. ⚐❀Ⓒ⇌♣

Windmill Tavern
1 Park Square, The Hough, Northowram, HX3 7BZ (off A6036)
✪ 12-11; 12-2, 4-11 Tue & Wed; 12-10.30 Sun

☎ (01422) 202464

Old Mill Bitter; Taylor Best Bitter, Landlord; guest beers Ⓗ

Built on the site of the old Windmill Brewery, this friendly, open-plan pub is a former local CAMRA Pub of the Season. The decor features a fish tank and fishing memorabilia. Pub games are encouraged and Thursday is quiz night. Small functions can be catered for, and the landlord can often be persuaded to order a curry to be brought in if pressed by enough of his customers.
❀♣P

Buffet Bar on K&WVLR
The Railway Station, BD22 8NJ (join at any station on Worth Valley Line)
✪ 11.15-6.30 weekends Mar-Oct; 11.25-5.20 midweek in summer
☎ (01535) 645214 website: www.kwvr.co.uk

Beer range varies Ⓗ

Scenic Pennine steam journey covering five miles from Oxenhope to Keighley. Always two guest beers are available in the buffet car that seats 44, specialising in local regional or micro-breweries, plus a wide range of local bottled beers. A beerfest is planned for October. Many other special events range from Thomas the Tank Engine and Santa specials, to enthusiasts' weekends and evening dining trains. The buffet bar was built in 1950s for use on the east coast mainline. Telephone Haworth Station for details of train times; park at Oxenhope or Ingrow. (⚐Q▲⇌Haworth/Oxenhope/Keighley/Ingrow/Oakworth) P⅄

Fleece Inn
67 Main Street, BD22 8DA
✪ 12 (11 summer)-11; 12-10.30 Sun
☎ (01535) 642172

Taylor Golden Best, Porter, Best Bitter, Landlord, Ram Tam Ⓗ

Former coaching inn at the village centre, popular with locals and tourists alike, recently sympathetically renovated, with the addition of seven en-suite bedrooms and a new no-smoking dining room. The bar area is stone-flagged and all rooms are comfortably appointed, featuring etched Taylors windows. The dining room is decorated with pictures from the Railway Children and has an oak floor. Excellent meals are served 12–9 daily in summer, lunch and evening in winter, except Monday (Sun 12–6). Children are welcome until 8pm.
⚐⇌ⒸⒹ♿▲⇌ (K&WVLR) ⅄

Haworth Old Hall ⊘
Sun Street, BD22 8BP (opp. park gates)
✪ 11-11; 12-10.30 Sun
☎ (01535) 642709

Jennings Bitter, Cumberland Ale, Cocker Hoop, Sneck Lifter, seasonal beers; Tetley Bitter Ⓗ

Old manor house, built in 1612, with mullioned windows and low ceilings. Warm and comfortable, children are welcome throughout. The bar area is wood panelled with a stone-flagged floor. Of its three rooms, the Tudor Room is no-smoking; the other two boast large inglenooks and are decorated with pictures of the village and surrounding area. Good quality, home-cooked food is served daily (12–8 Sun). Good access is provided for wheelchairs. ♨🍴⊛🚪◑ ☖▲≢(K&WVLR) P✂

HEATH

King's Arms
Heath Common, WF1 5SL
(off A655, Wakefield-Castleford road)
🕓 11.30-3, 5.30-11; 11.30-11 Sat; 12-10.30 Sun
☎ (01924) 377527
Clark's Classic Blonde; Taylor Landlord; Tetley Bitter ℍ

The King's Arms was acquired by Clark's Brewery for its chain of ale houses in 1989. Built in the early 1700s and converted into a public house in 1841, it consists of three oak-panelled rooms with gas lighting, plus a conservatory and gardens to the rear. In the summer months, you can sit outside and relax peacefully amid the acres of common grassland surrounding the area.
♨Q🍴⊛◑☖P

HEBDEN BRIDGE

Fox & Goose
9 Heptonstall Road, HX7 6AZ (at A646 jct)
🕓 11.30-3, 7 (6 Fri)-11; 12-3, 7-10.30 Sun
☎ (01422) 842649
Pictish Brewers Gold; guest beers ℍ

Traditional, cosy pub where sociable conversation comes second only to the appreciation of the ever-changing ales from independent breweries. If this on-going beer festival, uninterrupted by juke box or bandits, were not enough, there are also Czech and German bottled beers and 30 malt whiskies to choose from. This friendly pub is now celebrating 14 consecutive years in this Guide. Q⊛≢♣⊟

HOLMFIRTH

Farmers Arms
2-4 Liphill Bank Road, Burnlee, HD9 2LR
(off A635)
🕓 5 (12 Sat)-11; 12-10.30 Sun
☎ (01484) 683713
Adnams Bitter; Black Sheep Best Bitter; Fuller's London Pride; Taylor Landlord; Tetley Dark Mild, Bitter ℍ

Popular, friendly local, tucked away off the Manchester road, below Compo's Café. Discrete drinking areas have been tastefully linked and are served by one bar. There is a patio with tables at the front for use in summer. Regular beers include both local and national brands. The walls are hung with original watercolours of the surrounding area. ♨⊛♣P

Rose & Crown (Nook)
7 Victoria Square, HD9 1DA
(down alley off Hollowgate)
🕓 11.30-11; 12-10.30 Sun
☎ (01484) 683960
Black Sheep Best Bitter; Jennings Cumberland Ale; Moorhouses Black Cat; Taylor Best Bitter, Landlord; Tetley Bitter; guest beers ℍ

Friendly, no-frills village-centre pub that has changed little since its first appearance in this Guide in 1976. Family-run, now by the second generation, it retains a strong local identity while welcoming visitors. Choose between the garden or several rooms, ranging from a large drinking area at the

rear to a cosy front room, warmed by a roaring fire in winter. A folk club meets monthly on the first Thursday. ♨⊛♣

HORBURY

Boon's
6 Queen Street, WF4 6LP
(2 miles from M1 jct 40)
🕓 11-3, 5-11; 11-11 Fri & Sat; 12-10.30 Sun
☎ (01924) 280442
John Smith's Bitter; Taylor Landlord; Tetley Bitter; guest beers ℍ

Situated just off the High Street, this former keg-only pub was bought by Clark's Brewery who have turned it into a lively popular community pub. A large part of its success can be put down to the introduction of real ale; a Clark's beer is always on tap here. The pub is furnished in a traditional style with a large patio area around the back that hosts the annual beer festival.
♨⊛♣

HUDDERSFIELD

Dusty Miller Inn ✓
2 Gilhead Road, Longwood, HD3 4YH (take Longwood Edge Road off A640)
🕓 6 (12 Sat)-11; 12-10.30 Sun
☎ (01484) 651763
Black Sheep Best Bitter; Taylor Best Bitter, Landlord; Tetley Bitter; guest beer ℍ

This cosy pub was converted from four small cottages. The comfortable lounge contains the bar and has a no-smoking area. There are two pool rooms – one features a stone floor and exposed stone walls and beams. All the rooms have stone fireplaces; the lounge also boasts a kitchen range. A small, narrow area outside the front door with a couple of tables affords a view of the valley. An Ossett beer is usually stocked.
⊛♣✂

Fieldhead
219 Quarmby Road, HD3 4FB
🕓 4 (12 Fri & Sat)-11; 12-10.30 Sun
☎ (01484) 654581
Tetley Bitter; guest beers ℍ

Large inter-war pub in a prominent location, three miles from the town centre. The lounge, with generous seating, is served by a central horseshoe-shaped bar. A former tap room, now used for games, is supplemented by a light, spacious pool room. The garden overlooks the Colne Valley. Typically, three beers are on offer. Live music is performed most Tuesday and Friday evenings.
⊛♣P

Flyboat
6 Colne Street, Aspley, HD1 3BS
(opp. Aspley Marina)
🕓 5 (12 Fri & Sat)-11; 12-10.30 Sun
☎ (01484) 353494
Tetley Mild, Bitter ℍ

Formerly a bargees' watering-hole, this pub is in a quiet back street, minutes from the town centre, behind the university. The lounge, decorated with pictures of old Huddersfield, has a central bar. The games room houses a pool table, TV with Sky Sports and a dartboard. It hosts a quiz every Thursday; two pool teams and the Huddersfield Sub-Aqua Club meet here, and it is a favourite for rugby and football fans on match days. Occasional live music is staged. ≥ ♣

Head of Steam
St George's Square, HD1 1JB
(in the station buildings)
🕐 11-12.30am (2am Fri & Sat); 12-10.30 Sun
☎ (01484) 454533 website: www.theheadofsteam.com
Black Sheep Best Bitter; Highgate Dark; Holt Bitter; guest beers Ⓗ

This commodious pub adjoins the railway station. In all four rooms the walls are covered with railway memorabilia; one room is for non-smokers. Hot and cold food is served from opening time until late at night. Jazz and blues bands regularly play here, while beer festivals feature breweries from all over the country. Outside seating is provided on an area of the station.
🏮 ◑ ♿ ≥ ⊖ ✂

Marsh Liberal Club
31 New Hey Road, Marsh, HD3 4AL (on A640, 1½ miles from centre)
🕐 12-2; 7 (5 Fri)-11; 12-11 Sat; 12-10.30 Sun
☎ (01484) 420152 website: www.marshlib.co.uk
Taylor Best Bitter, Golden Best; Theakston Best Bitter; guest beers Ⓗ

This Grade II listed building, just outside the town centre, is the home of an impressive club – a national finalist in CAMRA's 2002 Club of the Year competition. Proud of the quality and range of its real ale, three guest beers are usually on the bar. A no-smoking room, and snooker room are available, plus Crown Green bowling. Wheelchair ramp access and a disabled WC are provided. Show this Guide or a CAMRA membership card to be signed in. Children are welcome until 9pm.
🛏 🏮 ♿ ♣ P ✂

Rat & Ratchet
40 Chapel Hill, HD1 3EB
(on A616, below ring road)
🕐 12 (3.30 Mon & Tue)-11; 12-10.30 Sun
☎ (01484) 516734 website: www.ratandratchet.co.uk
Greene King Abbot; Pictish Brewers Gold; Taylor Best Bitter, Landlord; guest beers Ⓗ

Popular brew-pub, boasting an enviable record for the quality and variety of its ales. With a choice of up to 14 beers, including a Rat beer brewed on the premises, it has arguably the widest selection locally, making it a regular entry in this Guide. There are several seating areas surrounded by brewery-related memorabilia. It is a popular meeting place for locals and students. Lunches are served Wednesday–Saturday; Wednesday is curry night. 🏮 ◑ ≥ ⊖ ♣ P

Star Inn
7 Albert Street, Follyhall, Lockwood, HD1 3PJ (off A616)
🕐 12-2 (not Tue-Thu), 5-11; 12-3, 6-11 Sat; closed Mon; 12-3, 7-10.30 Sun
☎ (01484) 545443
Eastwood & Sanders Best Bitter; Taylor Best Bitter, Landlord; guest beers Ⓗ

Recently transformed basic back-street boozer, this characterful pub offers a friendly atmosphere and good conversation, free from juke boxes or noisy gaming machines. An enviable reputation for good beer is due to an ever-changing range of

quality ales from varied micro-breweries. Three drinking areas are enhanced by a real fire and local pictures. Occasional beer festivals are held, the summer one being staged in the garden. 🏚 Q 🏮 ≥ (Lockwood) ●

Train Station Tavern
St George's Square, HD1 1JB
(in station buildings)
🕐 11.30-11; 12-10.30 Sun
☎ (01484) 511058
Black Sheep Best Bitter; Jennings Cumberland Ale; Taylor Best Bitter, Landlord; guest beers Ⓗ

Well-established, real ale pub in the Grade I listed Huddersfield railway station buildings. It comprises a large open-plan room with a stage, a games room with pool table and a snug next to the bar replete with military pictures. Home to the Savannah Jazz Band, it regularly stages blues and jazz on Wednesday and trad jazz on Thursday evenings. Regular mini-beer festivals feature local micro-breweries. ◑ ♿ ≥ ♣ P

White Cross Inn ⊘
2 Bradley Road, Bradley, HD2 1XD (on A62, Leeds road/Bradley road jct)
🕐 11.45-11; 12-10.30 Sun
☎ (01484) 425728
Caledonian Deuchars IPA; Tetley Bitter; guest beers Ⓗ

Huddersfield CAMRA's 2002 autumn Pub of the Season, is the town's oldest pub without a name change. Formerly a Bentley's Yorkshire Brewery inn, note the original tiles in the doorway. Extensive lounge sections radiate from a bare-boarded bar. The upstairs function room is a popular meeting place for various clubs, notably the Yorkshire Gundog Club and Kirklees Foster Carers. The pub fields both a pool team and Sunday league football team. A regular bus route serves the pub. 🏮 ◑ ♣ P

Idle Working Men's Club
23 High Street, BD10 8NB
🕐 12-4 (not Tue-Thu; 12-5 Sat); 7.30 (7 Fri & Sat)-11; 12-4, 7-10.30 Sun
☎ (01274) 613602
website: www.idleworkingmensclub.com
Tetley Mild, Bitter; guest beers Ⓗ

Popular club that attracts members because of its name; souvenir merchandise is available to buy. The club comprises a concert room, lounge and games room. The concert room hosts live entertainment weekend evenings; the lounge offers a quieter alternative. The downstairs games room houses two full-sized snooker tables plus big-screen TV and sometimes offers a different guest beer. Show this Guide or CAMRA membership to be signed in. Parking is difficult, but bus Nos. 610 and 612 pass close by. Q ♣

Symposium Ale & Wine Bar ⊘
7 Albion Road, BD10 9PY
🕐 12-2.30, 5.30-11; 12-11 Fri & Sat; 12-10.30 Sun
☎ (01274) 616587
Taylor Landlord; guest beers Ⓗ

Ever-changing ales from regional, independent breweries make this Market Town Tavern a CAMRA award-winner; it was Bradford's Pub of the Year in 2002 and 2003. It also stocks a good range of foreign bottled beers and a wide selection of wines.

The snug serves as a no-smoking room and can be hired for small meetings or functions. Seasonal meal and beer promotions are run on a regular basis. Q ◑ ▷ ½

ILKLEY

Bar T'at
7 Cunliffe Road, LS29 9DZ
✪ 12-11; 12-10.30 Sun
☎ (01943) 608888
Black Sheep Best Bitter; Caledonian Deuchars IPA; Taylor Landlord; guest beers Ⓗ
Popular side-street pub, renowned for its beer quality and choice. Guest ales tend to be from small Yorkshire breweries. A good choice of foreign beers is available, including three on draught. It is also a good pub for those who prefer wine or even fruit juice. Home-cooked food is served daily. Bar T'at is part of the Market Town Taverns chain, regular sponsors of Bradford CAMRA's beer festival. Q ✿ ◑ ▷ ≠ ½

Riverside Hotel
Riverside Gardens, Bridge Lane, LS29 9EU
✪ 11-11; 12-10.30 Sun
☎ (01943) 607338
Samuel Smith OBB; Taylor Best Bitter; Tetley Bitter Ⓗ
The hotel is 10 minutes' walk north-west from the rail and bus interchange. A large lounge, with open fire, forms the main drinking area. Happy hour happens daily (4–8pm). Selected live football games are shown on TV and quiz nights are held Wednesday and Sunday. Meals are served until early evening, and the fish and chip shop next to the hotel opens daily from 11.30am until mid-evening. The hotel patio overlooks the river, and the Riverside Park houses a children's play area. ⚌ ✿ ⇚ ◑ ▷ ≠ P

KEIGHLEY

Boltmakers Arms
117 East Parade, BD21 5HX
✪ 11-11; 12-10.30 Sun
☎ (01535) 661936
Taylor Golden Best, Best Bitter, Landlord; guest beers Ⓗ
Popular with locals and visitors alike, this pub's turnover is such that the three regular beers are sold in 36-gallon barrels. The split-level one-room pub displays pictures detailing the brewing and distilling processes. A coal fire is welcome in winter. Games are limited by lack of space, but the pub fields a football team in the local league. Good value hot snacks are available all day. ⚌ ≠ ♣

Brewery Arms ⊘
Longcroft, BD21 5AL (opp. Morrisons)
✪ 11.30 (4 Mon & Tue)-11; 12-10.30 Sun
☎ (07855) 826875/6
Clark's Classic Blonde; Goose Eye Barm Pot; guest beers Ⓗ
Run for real ale lovers, this former Worth Brewery pub is now a free house which normally has 10 draught beers from independent breweries on tap, plus a good selection of British bottled ales. The pub is quite spacious, with a central bar area, raised seating and separate pool and darts areas. The patio provides views of passing vintage trains on the Keighley & Worth

---

Valley Railway line. Regular brewery trips are organised. ✿ ◑ ▷ ≠ ♣ P

Cricketers
23 Coney Lane, BD21 5JE
✪ 11.30-11; 12-10.30 Sun
☎ (01535) 669912
Eastwood & Sanders First Light; Moorhouses Black Cat, Premier; guest beers Ⓗ
Originally three cottages, built in 1828, this compact, friendly, single-roomed free house was imaginatively refurbished by the former Worth Brewery in 1999. The original stone walls display some cricket memorabilia; note, too, the brass ship's portholes and Worth Brewery windows. The partly-carpeted interior features tram-style seating, complete with luggage racks. Len Hutton is depicted on the pub sign. Guest beers mainly come from north of England micros at this local CAMRA Pub of the Season winter 2002/03. Q ♿ ≠ ♣

Friendly
2 Aireworth Street, BD21 1NS
✪ 12-11; 12-5, 7.30-11 Sat; 12-10.30 Sun
☎ (01535) 672136
Taylor Golden Best, Best Bitter Ⓟ
Two-roomed local that really lives up to its name; what it lacks in size is compensated for in Yorkshire hospitality. A bright, relaxed place with 1960s background music, this Taylor's tied house serves the beer in oversized glasses. It hosts a quiz on Monday and 'play your cards right' Sunday afternoon and Monday evening. The view from the first-floor ladies' WC is awesome, due to the steep stairs. ♣ ⊟

KNOTTINGLEY

Steampacket Inn
2 Bendles, Racca Green, WF11 8AT (200 yds off A645, next to Aire & Calder Canal)
✪ 12-11; 12-10.30 Sun
☎ (01977) 677266
John Smith's Bitter; guest beer Ⓗ
Lively local, situated on the bank of the Aire & Calder Canal. The public bar is usually busy, while the large lounge hosts 'gameshow night' on Thursday. A pool room and large function room complete the facilities here. The pub fields darts, dominoes and pool teams. It was voted local CAMRA Pub of the Season winter 2001/02. Outside drinking takes place in summer on the grassy canal bank. ⚌ ✿ ⊟ ♿ ♣ P

LEEDS: *CITY*

Duck & Drake
43 Kirkgate, LS2 7DR
✪ 11-11; 12-10.30 Sun
☎ (0113) 246 5806
Old Mill Bitter; John Smith's Bitter; Taylor Landlord; Theakston Best Bitter, Old Peculier; guest beers Ⓗ
Archetypal CAMRA award-winning ale house. Offering up to seven guest beers, it has the city's widest choice of real ale and cider on draught. It is a basic bare-boarded, two-roomed pub with a central bar, where blazing fires warm both rooms and add to its character. Check the chalkboards and flyers for details of the regular music sessions on offer. Bar snacks are available weekday lunchtimes. ⚌ ≠ ♣ ♠

North Bar
24 New Briggate, LS1 6NU
🕐 12-2am (1am Mon & Tue); 12-10.30 Sun
☎ (0113) 242 4540 website: www.northbar.com
Beer range varies Ⓗ

Blink and you might miss this narrow café-bar near the North Bar – the city's old boundary stone. A long, narrow, single bar attracting predominantly, but by no means exclusively, younger customers, the decor is modern and unassuming, unlike the choice of beer. In addition to the changing British cask ale there is a veritable feast of foreign beers on draught or kept in the well-stocked fridges. Real art on the walls is for sale. Guest DJs appear on Friday and Saturday evenings. ◑▮

Palace
Kirkgate, LS2 7DJ
🕐 11-11; 12-10.30 Sun
☎ (0113) 244 5882
Draught Bass; Bateman Mild; Tetley Bitter, Burton Ale; guest beers Ⓗ

Formerly a four-roomed pub, now opened out; some Melbourne windows and some of the original tiles are still evident. Serving up to six guest ales, the pub is handy for the parish church and the bus station. The no-smoking area (restrictions lifted at 5pm) has the feel of a gentleman's club, with its burgundy-colour walls and dark leather banquettes, while the rest of the walls are resplendent in pistachio green. Meals are served 12–7. The garden has heaters.
❀◑▮&♣✂

Scarbrough Hotel
Bishopgate Street, LS1 5DY
🕐 11-11; 12-10.30 Sun
☎ (0113) 243 4590
Tetley Bitter; guest beers Ⓗ

Ex-Festival Ale House, now part of the Mitchells & Butlers estate, this pub has been in and out of this Guide like a yo-yo. Now under the new managership of an ex-Whitelocks licensee (where he won Leeds CAMRA Pub of the Season), it has regained its Guide status. Owned by the Bishop of Bristol until 1792, it became the King's Arms, an extensive hotel, until about 1863. In the late 1890s it was owned by Fred Wood, a noted theatre impresario. Four or five guest beers are usually available. ◑▮≈

Victoria Family & Commercial Hotel
28 Great George Street, LS1 3DL
🕐 11-11; 12-10.30 Sun
☎ (0113) 245 1386
Black Sheep Best Bitter; Tetley Bitter; guest beers Ⓗ

This fine Victorian pub, built in 1865, is situated behind the town hall which was opened in 1858 by Queen Victoria herself. Its three rooms can be crowded, especially on Fridays when the office workers lay seige. Jazz-lovers should visit on a Thursday evening. Those in pursuit of a quiet pint will find a corner in one of the cubicles where you can admire the excellent woodwork and glass screens. Evening meals finish early. ◑▮≈✂

Whitelock's First City Luncheon Bar ☆
6-8 Turks Head Yard, LS1 6HB (off Briggate)

🕐 11-11; 12-10.30 Sun
☎ (0113) 245 3950
Greene King Ruddles Best; John Smith's Bitter; Theakston Best Bitter, XB; guest beers Ⓗ

Down an alleyway, hidden from busy shoppers, this pub has been licensed since 1715. The main room is a palace of traditional wood and glass, and holds interest for the 'Titanic' historian. The yard serves as a garden and an overflow for the small main bar. Another room is used as a restaurant. The top bar is open at busy times and is available for hire. The range of guest ales was recognised by Leeds CAMRA, awarding it Pub of the Season (summer 2002). ♨Q❀◑▮≈

Wrens
59-61 New Briggate, LS2 8JD
🕐 11-11; 6-10.30 (may vary) Sun
☎ (0113) 245 8888
Black Sheep Best Bitter; Jennings Cumberland Ale; Taylor Landlord; Tetley Dark Mild, Bitter Ⓗ

Unspoilt, three-roomed house, popular with theatregoers, being the nearest pub to the Grand Theatre. The rooms set around a central bar include a tap room with wall seating and wood floor, a comfortably furnished lounge and a no-smoking theatre bar, decorated with associated memorabilia. Audience members may order drinks for the interval to avoid the inevitable crush. Sunday opening hours vary with performance times; the premises are also available for private hire on Sunday.
Q◑▮⊟♣✂

Eldon ✓
190 Woodhouse Lane, LS2 9DX
🕐 11.30 (12 Sat)-11; 12-10.30 Sun
☎ (0113) 245 3591
Tetley Dark Mild, Bitter; guest beers Ⓗ

An ever-changing range of up to seven real ales makes the Eldon popular with all. There are always plenty of students and staff from the university across the road, but there is still room for locals. The olde-worlde decor provides an ale house feel, with plenty of quiet alcoves. It gets very busy when there is football on, especially on Sunday when all beers are cheap all evening. The number of guest beers may be reduced outside university terms. ◑▮&

New Roscoe
Bristol Street, Sheepscar, LS7 1DH
🕐 11-11; 12-10.30 Sun
☎ (0113) 246 0778
Tetley Bitter; guest beers Ⓗ

Externally reminiscent of a Spanish hacienda, this ex-club and Indian restaurant was transformed internally as a reminder of the old Roscoe. The busy front bar has three pool tables and space for waiting players and spectators alike. The large bar/concert room plays host to bands from near and far; usually well attended, a small door charge is levied (ring for details). A small, quieter room is available for those who like to watch their TV sport in comfort. ❀▮♣P

Pack Horse
208 Woodhouse Lane, LS2 9DX
🕐 11-11; 12-10.30 Sun
☎ (0113) 245 3980

Taylor Landlord; Tetley Bitter; guest beers Ⓗ

Originally established to serve the packhorse route between Leeds and Otley, the multi-roomed layout boasts a mosaic in the entrance hall. Nowadays, the pub caters for students from the university across the road. It hosts regular live bands and at other times the upstairs room serves as a cinema. A refurbishment retained much of the layout, while making room for a big-screen TV. The guest beers are normally from the larger regional breweries. ✿◑⇦

LEEDS: SOUTH

Grove Inn
Back Row, Holbeck, LS11 5PL
✿ 12-11; 12-10.30 Sun
☎ (0113) 243 9254
Adnams Broadside; Bateman XB; Caledonian Deuchars IPA; Wells Bombardier; guest beers Ⓗ

Several rooms off a West Riding drinking corridor offer customers a choice of environment – whether you want a quiet drink in one of the side rooms, or to join the lively throng in the tap room. For those that enjoy live music there are performances in the music room most evenings and weekends (ring for details). With eight beers to choose from, one pump dedicated to mild and the recent introduction of Hoegaarden from Belgium, this is a pub not to miss. ᴀ✿◑⇦⇥♣

LEEDS: WEST

Highland
36 Cavendish Street, LS3 1LY (down steps next to Sentinel Towers on Burley Rd)
✿ 11.30-11; 12-10.30 Sun
☎ (0113) 242 8592
Taylor Landlord; Tetley Mild, Bitter Ⓗ

The Highland seems to defy the new buildings that now surround it. Once at the end of a Victorian terrace, the pub has an odd triangular shape. There are some leaded windows, throwing subtle light into the narrow main bar. Inside are two fine mirrors, one depicting the eponymous cow. Some benches provide a pleasant spot for outside drinking. This is a pub that almost seems caught in a time warp, and is none the worse for it. ✿♣

Jug & Barrel
56-58 Town Street, Stanningley, LS28 6EZ
✿ 12-11; 12-10.30 Sun
☎ (0113) 257 6877 website: www.thejug&barrel.com
Courage Directors; John Smith's Bitter, Magnet; Taylor Landlord; guest beer Ⓗ

Friendly local set in an industrial area. Originally two cottages, the property has been much extended and refurbished to provide comfortable surroundings. Note the numerous jugs hanging from the ceiling. An adjoining former printer's has been converted into a concert room, hosting band nights most weekends plus jam sessions Sunday afternoon and Monday evening. Meals are served 12-7. ᴀ✿◑♣P

Old Vic
17 Whitecote Hill, Bramley, LS13 3LB (400 yds from A657/B6157 jct)
✿ 4 (2 Fri; 11 Sat)-11; 12-3, 7-10.30 Sun
☎ (0113) 256 1207
Black Sheep Best Bitter, Special; Taylor Landlord;

Tetley Bitter; guest beers Ⓗ

Originally a vicarage, this deservedly popular watering-hole fosters a real community spirit. A central bar serves a lounge and two games rooms. A function room is well used by clubs and private parties. Pool and dominoes are popular, and a quiz is staged on Thursday evening. Two changing guest beers are usually available. ᴀQ✿♿♣P

West End House ⊘
26 Abbey Road, Kirkstall, LS5 3HS (next to sports centre)
✿ 11.30-11; 12-10.30 Sun
☎ (0113) 278 6332
Beer range varies Ⓗ

Sympathetically refurbished over the years, this open-plan pub retains well-defined spaces around an imposing central bar. To the front is a small TV area and a lounge with a light, airy feel thanks mainly to the bay window. To the rear of the bar are a number of quieter nooks and alcoves. Popular for its good food, it gets busy Sunday lunchtime and for its quizzes on Tuesday and Thursday evenings. The beer range varies, but is usually from the larger regional breweries. ✿◑⇥ (Headingley)

LEES MOOR

Quarry House Inn
Bingley Road, BD21 5QE (off A629/A6033 jct) OS054380
✿ 12-3, 7-midnight; 12-3, 7-10.30 Sun
☎ (01535) 642239
Taylor Golden Best, Best Bitter, Landlord; Tetley Bitter Ⓗ

Family-run, converted farmhouse set in open countryside, affording extensive views. The bar is a former pulpit set in a small, cosy area. Families are welcome at all times throughout this twice local CAMRA Pub of the Season. The restaurant provides an excellent 'global' menu, based on seasonal produce; try the soups or mixed grill (a speciality on Wed eve). It is advisable to book for Sunday lunch which is very popular. ✿◑♿ＡP

LINTHWAITE

Royal Oak
826 Manchester Road, HD7 5QS (on A62)
✿ 5 (4 Fri)-11 (may vary summer); 12-10.30 Sun
☎ (01484) 842469
Caledonian Deuchars IPA; Webster's Green Label; guest beers Ⓗ

Large roadside pub, set on the side of the Colne Valley. The central bar dominates the pub's three rooms, each of which bears interesting displays of jugs and plates. Home to darts, pool and dominoes teams, this friendly pub hosts regular Sunday barbecues during the summer. Popular with locals, this is an Enterprise Inns house. ✿♣P

Sair Inn ⊘
139 Lane Top, HD7 5SG (top of Hoyle Ing, off A62) OS100143
✿ 7 (5 Fri; 12 Sat)-11; 12-10.30 Sun
☎ (01484) 842370
Linfit Dark Mild, Bitter, Cascade, English Guineas Stout, seasonal beers Ⓗ

Set on a hillside overlooking the Colne

Valley, this brew-pub has won a plethora of awards, accolades and recommendations, including CAMRA's 1997 national Pub of the Year. A central bar overlooks four rooms, including one for non-smokers; the real fires are welcome in winter. Typically up to 10 beers are available. The pub has a 200-year history, with the current brewery on site for over 20 years. ⚶Q☎❀♣●⅄

LIVERSEDGE

Swan
380 Bradford Road, WF15 6JE
(at A62/A638 jct)
✪ 11-11; 12-10.30 Sun
☎ (01924) 401855
Boddingtons Bitter; Daleside Bitter; Greene King Old Speckled Hen; Taylor Landlord; guest beers Ⓗ
This modern, two-roomed pub was rebuilt in 1982 on the site of its smaller predecessor. It has a large lounge, serving good value meals in the afternoon, and a separate public bar. It stages a popular jazz night on Wednesday and lively karaoke on Thursday, Friday and Saturday. Home of the local Rugby League team, it has a friendly atmosphere throughout. ❀◖🍴♣P

MARSDEN

Riverhead Brewery Tap
2 Peel Street, HD7 6BR (off A62)
✪ 5 (4 Fri; 11 Sat)-11; 12-10.30 Sun
☎ (01484) 841270
Riverhead Sparth Mild, Butterley Bitter, Deer Hill Porter, Cupwith Light, March Haigh Special Ⓗ
Opened in 1995, this brew-pub, with riverside garden, has won deserved acclaim and several CAMRA awards. Located at the village centre, it is popular with ramblers and locals alike. It takes part in Marsden's jazz festival, and is close to the Pennine Way and Peak District. The beer range is varied, with the brews being named after local reservoirs; the gravity of the beer reflects the altitude of the reservoir. Related memorabilia adorns the pub walls.
Q❀♿⇌●

MYTHOLMROYD

Hinchliffe Arms
Cragg Vale, HX7 5TA (off B6138)
✪ 12-2.30, 6-11; closed Mon; 12-5 (closed eve) Sun
☎ (01422) 883256 website: www.hinchliffearms.com
Greene King Old Speckled Hen; Jennings Cumberland Ale; Taylor Landlord; Theakston Best Bitter; guest beers Ⓗ
Spacious, yet cosy, pub in a quiet rural hamlet. The lounge displays plates and pictures, while the replica Portuguese doubloons on the bar front reflect the area's former notoriety for coin clipping. The intimate restaurant, serving freshly-cooked meals admits children for Sunday lunch only. Set in a valley, the surrounding hills offer a network of footpaths benefiting from splendid views; the Calderdale Way passes the pub and the Pennine Way is nearby.
⚶❀🛏◖▲P

Shoulder of Mutton
New Road, HX7 5DZ
✪ 11.30-3, 7-11; 11-11 Sat; 12-10.30 Sun
☎ (01422) 883165
Black Sheep Best Bitter; Boddingtons Bitter; Castle

Eden Ale; Flowers IPA; Taylor Landlord Ⓗ
Roadside village inn, close to the station. The spacious bar area includes an attractive fireplace, and a display depicts the local 17th-century coin clipping 'industry', complete with tools of the trade. For rainy days, a very long run of coat hooks is provided. Two cottage-style rooms give a cosy dining area in which to enjoy the simple, freshly-made, wholesome meals; evening meals are served 7–8.30 (not Tue). A small, enclosed outside drinking area is at the rear. ❀◖▲⇌♣P⅄

OSSETT

Brewer's Pride
Low Mill Road, off Healey Road, WF5 8ND
(1½ miles from centre)
✪ 12-3, 5.30-11; 12-11 Fri & Sat; 12-10.30 Sun
☎ (01924) 273865
Ossett Excelsior; Taylor Landlord; guest beers Ⓗ
This popular free house has Ossett Brewery at the rear and always has eight beers on handpull. The pub is within five minutes' walk of the Calder & Hebble Canal, or can be reached from Wakefield using the No. 121 bus. Home-cooked food is available Monday–Saturday lunchtimes, plus Wednesday evenings. It holds a beer festival late in the year, offering over 30 beers. The local folk club meets each Thursday at this frequent local CAMRA Pub of the Season winner. ⚶Q◖▶●

Fleece
Spa Street, WF5 0HP
✪ 12-11; 12-10.30 Sun
☎ (01924) 273685
John Smith's Bitter; Tetley Bitter; guest beers Ⓗ
Quiet, three-roomed pub situated between Horbury and Ossett within easy reach of M1 junction 40. The landlord is a keen amateur musician himself and promotes live music evenings. The pub has a small garden for summer drinking. ⚶Q❀🍴♣P

Red Lion
273 Dewsbury Road, WF5 9NQ
(on old Flushdyke-Gawthorpe road, parallel to bypass)
✪ 12-11; 12-10.30 Sun
☎ (01924) 273487
Red Lion White Lion; John Smith's Bitter; guest beers Ⓗ
Although in a largely industrial area of town this stone building still has a farmhouse feel. The pub is cosy with plenty of nooks in which to settle. The Lonely Pub Company allows its tenants scope to make their pubs prosper, hence the choice of four cask ales from independent breweries. Generous portions of real food are served in a new extension for dining, keeping the bar for drinkers, but on Sunday the emphasis is on food. Outbuildings at the rear house the Red Lion Brewery. ◖▶P

OTLEY

Black Bull
Market Place, LS21 3AQ (near bus station)
✪ 11-11; 12-10.30 Sun
☎ (01943) 462288
Taylor Best Bitter, Landlord; Tetley Bitter Ⓗ
Bustling town-centre pub fronting on to the historic market place. Dating back in part to the 16th century, it retains an historic feel

with low ceiling, stone fireplace and sturdy timber front door. English Civil War paintings recall the pub's links with Cromwell's Ironsides. An L-shaped drinking area, divided into three distinct alcoves, is served from a single bar. ♿❀◖

Bowling Green
18 Bondgate, LS21 3AB (near bus station)
✪ 12-4, 7-11 (winter hours vary Mon & Tue); 2.30-10.30 Sun
☎ (01943) 461494
Beer range varies Ⓗ
Built in 1757, with many varied uses before becoming a pub in 1825, it now comprises an L-shaped main bar. Drinkers are surrounded by an array of curios from around the world. Up to four changing guest beers are available, including locally-brewed Briscoe's; an annual beer festival is held in September. A large outdoor area to the front is used for summer drinking. No children are permitted in the pub. ♿❀♣

Manor House
Walkergate, Cross Green, LS21 1HB
(off Boroughgate)
✪ 12 (3.30 Tue-Thu)-11; 12-10.30 Sun
☎ (01943) 463807
Thwaites Bitter Ⓗ
This traditional pub, within a terrace of houses, provides a friendly meeting place for locals. The large lounge benefits from partitions and alcoves to provide discrete drinking areas. A small tap room caters for those wishing to play darts and dominoes. A coal fire adds to the pub's ambience on a cold winter's evening. ♿Q❀◖♣

Red Lion
43-45 Kirkgate, LS21 3HN (near market square)
✪ 11-11; 12-10.30 Sun
☎ (01943) 461494
Courage Directors; Greene King Ruddles County; John Smith's Bitter; guest beer Ⓗ
Pleasant, late 18th-century, town-centre pub that gives some respite from the bustle of the nearby open market. An open-plan front lounge provides three comfortable drinking areas, served by a compact rear bar. A back room plays host to dominoes players and houses a TV. Local clubs regularly use the upstairs meeting room. A quiz is held on Sunday. The guest beer changes weekly. Q❀◖♣

Royalty
Yorkgate, LS21 3DG OS206440
✪ 11-11; 12-10.30 Sun
☎ (01943) 461156
Black Sheep Best Bitter; Taylor Landlord; Tetley Bitter; guest beer Ⓗ
Remote country pub on top of Otley Chevin. Extensive views of Airedale and Wharfedale attract walkers and drivers alike. A central bar serves a basic tap room, cosy lounge and family room (part of which is designated as the no-smoking area). Food is served Monday–Saturday evenings (5–8) and Sunday 12–6. Caravans are allowed on the adjoining camp site. ☞❀◖◗ ▣♣▲P✗

Whitakers
47 Kirkgate, LS21 3JY (near market square)
✪ 11.30 (11 Fri & Sat)-11; 12-10.30 Sun
☎ (01943) 462580
Black Sheep Best Bitter; Tetley Mild, Bitter; guest

beer Ⓗ
Dating from the late 18th-century, this busy town-centre pub has been refurbished to provide a long, narrow, split-level drinking area. Drawing a mixed clientele during the day, it is popular with younger drinkers on weekend evenings. The enclosed rear garden is recommended in summer. Meals are served until 5pm on Saturday and Sunday. The house beer is from Goose Eye. ♿❀◖♣

Woolpack
14 Bondgate, LS21 3AB (near bus station)
✪ 11.30-11; 12-10.30 Sun
☎ (01943) 462908
John Smith's Bitter; Stones Bitter; Tetley Bitter; Worthington's Bitter Ⓗ
Dating in part from the 17th century, this popular local regularly features in TV's Heartbeat. A central bar serves an L-shaped lounge and larger public bar, while a corridor provides an overspill drinking area. This is very much a community pub, with well-supported darts and dominoes teams. It stages live music Tuesday evening. An enclosed rear yard is used for outdoor drinking in summer. ❀⌂◖▣♣

OXENHOPE

Bay Horse
20 Uppertown, BD22 9LN (off A6033)
✪ 12-11; 12-10.30 Sun
☎ (01535) 642209
Taylor Landlord; Whitbread Trophy Bitter Ⓗ
Country pub, but close to the village centre, popular with locals. Of the four areas, one is next to the bar, one is for dining and the 'nannying hole' is aimed at younger customers, with a pool table. Upstairs is a no-smoking restaurant (no eve meals Mon or Tue). It is comfortably decorated with pictures of rural scenes and brasswork. Several magazines and newspapers are provided for customers. The games room displays pictures of the local football team over the decades. ❀◖◗ Å➤♣P

PONTEFRACT

Robin Hood
4 Wakefield Road, WF8 4HN (off A645)
✪ 11.30-3.30 (4.30 Fri & Sat), 7-11; 12.30-3.30, 7-10.30 Sun
☎ (01977) 702231
John Smith's Bitter; Tetley Bitter; guest beers Ⓗ
Friendly, welcoming pub at Town End near the traffic lights. The Robin has a very busy bar and three smaller drinking areas. It holds quizzes every Sunday and Tuesday evenings, and fields darts and dominoes teams. It stages a beer festival over August bank holiday weekend. Winner of local CAMRA Pub of the Year 1998, it has also won various Pub of the Season awards. ♿❀▣ & ➤(Tanshelf/Baghill) ♣

Tap & Barrel
13 Front Street, WF8 1AN (opp. court house)
✪ 11-11; 12-10.30 Sun
☎ (01977) 699918
Daleside Bitter; Greene King Old Speckled Hen; John Smith's Bitter; Tetley Bitter; Theakston Old Peculier Ⓗ
Pontefract's only genuine free house. Completely refurbished in early 2003, it

now comprises one large drinking area, fully carpeted throughout. Live music is performed on Saturday and Sunday evenings. Darts, dominoes and pool are all played here. ♨≠(Tanshelf) ♣

PUDSEY

Bankhouse
40-42 Bankhouse Lane, LS28 8EB
☼ 12-3, 5.30-11; 12-11 Sat; 12-10.30 Sun
☎ (0113) 256 4662
Black Sheep Best Bitter; Taylor Landlord; Tetley Bitter; guest beer Ⓗ
With its low, beamed ceilings, plates, brasses and dangling teapots, the Bankhouse is a cosy, rambling pub in the country style. There is much in the way of red upholstery and unusual knick-knacks. Situated at the end of a sloping lane through fields, the pub's terraced garden affords impressive views over Fulneck Valley. Once famous for terrier racing and lark singing competitions, it is now famed for its fine restaurant meals. The guest beer is supplied by Ossett. ⊛◑▶

World's End
2 Wesley Square, LS28 7AB
☼ 11-midnight; 11-10.30 Sun
☎ (0113) 255 1634
Daleside Bitter; Theakston Best Bitter, Old Peculier; guest beer Ⓗ
Multi-level pub, accessible from two alleyways, each leading to a different room. The upstairs room has a wood floor around the often crowded bar area; here there are both raised and sunken seating areas. The downstairs room has stone-flagged floors and two distinct seating areas, again on different levels. The pub is just over 20 years old, despite its olde-worlde feel – indeed the fabric of the building is 17th-century. See the chalkboards for music and food attractions. ⊛◑▶

RAWDON

Princess
Apperley Lane, LS19 6BJ (400 yds from A65 roundabout)
☼ 12-11; 12-10.30 Sun
☎ (0113) 250 2495
Tetley Bitter; guest beer Ⓗ
Originally two stone cottages, this well-appointed local caters for the more mature drinker. An L-shaped lounge and a TV room are served from a single bar where the handpumps date from 1942. Food is served Monday–Saturday evenings (5.30–8) and Sunday, 12–7. Quizzes are held Monday and Thursday evenings. The guest beer is either Greene King Abbot or Taylor Landlord. ⊛◑⁄

SCHOLES (CLECKHEATON)

Rising Sun
Scholes Lane, BD19 6NR
☼ 12-11; 12-10.30 Sun
☎ (01274) 874397
Boddingtons Bitter; Taylor Landlord; Whitbread Trophy Bitter; guest beer Ⓗ
Traditional-style local serving gourmet quality, good value food. Winner of the Kirklees Pubs in Bloom competition, it promises a relaxing visit in the summer

months as the garden leads on to popular cricket and football fields. The bar area is compact, with a pleasant lounge used for dining (booking is advised, especially for Sunday meals, served 12–6). A plain games room opens to the garden. ⊛◑♣P

SHIPLEY

Fanny's Ale & Cider House
63 Saltaire Road, BD18 3JN (on A657)
☼ 11.30 (5 Mon)-11; 12-10.30 Sun
☎ (01274) 591419
Taylor Golden Best, Landlord; Theakston Old Peculier; guest beers Ⓗ
This was a pet shop, then a beer shop before becoming a fully licensed free house. The cosy, nostalgic atmosphere downstairs is enhanced by gas lights, a log fire and old brewery memorabilia. An upstairs room increases the available space for drinking. It usually offers eight real ales, including some from local breweries, plus a range of foreign draught and bottled beers and Biddenden cider. The pub is close to the historic village of Saltaire. ♨Q♣♣♠

Shipley Pride
1 Saltaire Road, BD18 3HH
(250 yds from Fox Corner, A657/A6038 jct)
☼ 11.30 (11 Sat)-11; 12-10.30 Sun
☎ (01274) 585341
Taylor Landlord; Tetley Bitter; guest beers Ⓗ
Built in 1870 as the Beehive Hotel, the Shipley Pride is a genuine free house and friendly local. Its two traditional rooms are linked by a central bar. The rectangular lounge features wood panels, stained glass windows and a semi-circular bar. The games room has two pool tables that are well used by locals. Quiz nights are held every Thursday. Guest beers are usually local Red Lion ales. Home-made food is a speciality, served weekdays. ⊛◑≠♣P

Sun Hotel ⊘
3 Kirkgate, BD18 3QP (off Otley road, A6038)
☼ 10-11; 12-10.30 Sun
☎ (01274) 530757
Brains SA; Shepherd Neame Spitfire; Theakston Best Bitter; guest beers Ⓗ
Busy, town-centre Wetherspoon's, ideally situated for both train and bus services. The pub is on two floors, each with a bar and no-smoking area; the ground floor is available for family dining until 6pm. Good value food starts with breakfast from 10am. Three guest beers are usually on offer and it hosts occasional beer festivals. It is close to the Leeds–Liverpool Canal where summer cruises and towpath walks can be enjoyed. Q⊛◑≠⁄

SOUTH ELMSALL

Brookside Commercial Social Club
35 Barnsley Road, WF9 2RN
(near bus and train stations)
☼ 11.30-4, 6.30-11; 11-5, 6.30-11 Sat; 11-3, 6.30-10.30 Sun
☎ (01977) 643530
John Smith's Bitter; guest beers Ⓗ
An oasis for real ale in the town centre, this popular club is at the hub of the community and caters for all ages. It is proud to support independent breweries;

over 200 different beers have been sold. This local CAMRA Club of the Season winter 2001/02 is CIU affiliated, but CAMRA members can be signed in on production of a membership card. Parking is limited. ⅃≠♣P

SOWERBY BRIDGE

Moorcock Inn

Moor Bottom Lane, Norland, HX6 3RP (on Shaw Lane, by Norland Moor) OS055218

✪ 12-3, 8 (6.30 Wed; 5.30 Thu)-11; 12-11 Fri; 12-5, 7-11 Sat; 12-10.30 Sun

☎ (01422) 832103

Samuel Smith OBB; guest beer Ⓗ

Built around 1750, this traditional stone pub is on the edge of Norland Moor which offers fine views over Sowerby Bridge to Halifax. There are two cosy drinking areas and a restaurant serving good value, home-cooked food. Open land next to the pub is criss-crossed by footpaths – perfect for a stroll. Just off the Calderdale Way, walkers, cyclists and their dogs are assured a warm welcome. Please phone for restaurant times. ⋘Q❀◖P

Rams Head

26 Wakefield Road, HX6 2AZ (on A6026, 400 yds from A58)

✪ 12-2 (3 Sat), 5-11; 12-10.30 Sun

☎ (01422) 835876

Ryburn Best Bitter, Numpty Bitter, Luddite, Stabbers Ⓗ

Convivial local, with a relaxed atmosphere. The cosy bar, lounge and L-shaped dining area boast beamed ceilings, lots of woodwork and stone fireplaces. The Ryburn beers are brewed in the cellar – usually five or six are available, at competitive prices. The garden affords views across the Calder Valley. Good value, home-cooked food is served lunchtime and until 8.30pm in the evenings (12–7 Sun). The no-smoking area (until 9pm) is not exclusive to diners. Singalongs take place on Saturday evening. ⋘Q❀◖⅃♣P

White Horse

Burnley Road, Friendly, HX6 2UG (on A646, 3/4 mile from centre)

✪ 12-11; 12-10.30 Sun

☎ (01422) 831173

Eastwood & Sanders Nettlethrasher; Tetley Mild, Bitter Ⓗ

On the Halifax–Burnley road, the White Horse is unmissable most of the year because of its award-winning floral displays. This friendly, popular local has a large lounge (once two rooms), featuring pictures of old Sowerby Bridge, a 1944-45 excise licence and photos and certificates showing the generosity of its customers in aid of Muscular Dystrophy. Trophies are displayed in the tap room and there are seats outside at the front and back, overlooking the car park. ❀♣P

THORNHILL

Savile Arms (Church House)

Church Lane, WF12 0JZ (on B6117, 2½ miles S of Dewsbury)

✪ 5 (4 Fri)-11; 12-4, 7-11 Sat; 12-4, 7-10.30 Sun

☎ (01924) 463738

Black Sheep Best Bitter; Tetley Bitter; guest beers Ⓗ

This 600-year-old pub shares consecrated ground with the parish church of St Michael, famed for its medieval glass and the magnificent Savile family tombs. A friendly village inn, it has taken on a new lease of life under the present licensee. A thriving sporting tradition reigns among the friendly regulars – the games room is the oldest part of the pub. The multi-roomed layout makes it difficult for children, although they can use the large garden. The guest beers are often from smaller brewers. ❀♣P

TINGLEY

British Oak

407 Westerton Road, WF3 1AF (take A650 from M62 interchange; left at Hesketh Lane)

✪ 5 (1.30 Fri; 12 Sat)-11; 12-10.30 Sun

☎ (0113) 253 4792

Boddingtons Bitter; Castle Eden Bitter; John Smith's Bitter; guest beer Ⓗ

Popular local with a central island bar. Regular beers are supplemented by a changing guest, usually from a regional brewer. A quiz night three times a week gets a good turn-out; on Monday there is free supper. A pub that appeals to all ages: a big-screen TV is used for major sporting events but this does not intrude on those wishing for a quiet drink. The pub is easily reached by bus; Nos. 205 and 425 stop at the door, all through the day. ❀P

TODMORDEN

Masons Arms

1 Bacup Road, OL14 7PN (at A6033/A681 jct)

✪ 3 (12 Sat)-11; 12-10.30 Sun

☎ (01706) 812180

Barnsley Bitter; Tetley Bitter; guest beers Ⓗ

Traditional drinkers' pub attracting local sporting groups and impromptu folk music sessions. The unspoilt entrance corridor leads into a bar and lounge area notable for the laying-out tables. The walls bear framed articles and photographs featuring local events. Situated at the junction of two steep valleys, and dwarfed by a railway viaduct, the Masons has a small, enclosed, outside drinking area; the hills provide good walks. The guest beers are from small breweries. ❀Å≠ (Walsden) ♣

Staff of Life

550 Burnley Road, OL14 8JF (on A646, 1½ miles W of Todmorden)

✪ 7 (12 Sat)-11; 12-4, 7-10.30 Sun

☎ (01706) 812929 website: www.staffoflife.co.uk

Taylor Golden Best, Best Bitter, Landlord, Ram Tam Ⓗ

Set in a steep gorge, and part of a row of cottages, the Staff is popular with both diners and drinkers. Stone-flagged floors, beamed roofs, and walls crowded with pictures, brassware and bric-à-brac give a cosy feel. One room is an arched former ground-floor cellar. A car park next to the pub is accessed from Knotts Road. The en-suite guest bedrooms are light and modern. The menu offers Asian, Spanish, Mexican as well as British dishes (no meals Mon). ⋘❀⇔◖

Woodpecker ❂

222 Rochdale Road, OL14 7NU

✪ 12-11; 12-10.30 Sun

☎ (01706) 816088
Lees Bitter; Thwaites Bitter; guest beer ⓗ
Friendly, roadside free house local, at the end of a row of terraced houses. The comfortable drinking area is L-shaped and quite narrow by the bar. The Woodpecker fields two pool teams and a quiz team. The narrow valley bottom is built up, but a walk alongside the nearby canal is worthwhile, especially to or from Todmorden; the pub is by a public car park. The one or two guest beers are mainly from small breweries.
🏠Å⇌

WAKEFIELD

Alverthorpe WMC
111 Flanshaw Lane,
WF2 9JG
🕐 11.30-3.30, 6.30-11; 12-3, 7-10.30 Sun
☎ (01924) 374179
Adnams Broadside; Greene King Abbot; Tetley Mild, Bitter ⓗ
Multi-roomed club catering for all tastes with lounges, games rooms, a snooker room with a full-sized table and a concert/function room. Crown Green bowls fans have the use of a floodlit green. The regular beers are complemented by guest beers from regional and micro-breweries. CAMRA members are welcome on production of a current membership card.
🏠♣P

Fernandes Brewery Tap
5 Avisons Yard, Kirkgate,
WF1 1UA
🕐 5 (11 Fri & Sat)-11; 12-10.30 Sun
☎ (01924) 369547
Fernandes Malt Shovel Mild, Ale to the Tsar, To be Joyful; guest beers ⓗ
Winner of local CAMRA's Pub of the Year for the past four years and numerous other awards, the Brewery Tap crowned its achievements as Yorkshire CAMRA's Pub of the Year two years running (2001 and 2002). This convivial local is all that every real ale drinker has dreamed of. No strangers in this bar, just new friends we have not met. A constantly-changing draught cider is stocked. No meals are served, but soup and sandwiches are available Friday and Saturday lunchtimes.
Q⇌🍷

Harry's Bar
107B Westgate, WF2 9SW
🕐 4-11; 4-10.30 Sun
☎ (01924) 373773
Ossett Silver King; John Smith's Bitter; Taylor Landlord; guest beers ⓗ
Small, single-roomed pub hidden away just off Westgate, but certainly not aimed at the 'Westgate Run' crowd. It is named after the father-in-law, Harry Murphy, of the original owner. Harry played Rugby League for Wakefield Trinity and Great Britain in the 1940s and '50s as the photos around the pub bear witness. No bandits or juke box, but the pub hosts live music on Tuesday and Wednesday evenings. It is a must for anyone who enjoys a quiet drink.
🚂Q🏠♿⇌ (Westgate)

Henry Boon's
130 Westgate, WF2 9SR
🕐 11-11 (1am Fri & Sat); 12-10.30 Sun

☎ (01924) 378126
Clark's Classic Blonde, seasonal beers; Taylor Landlord; Tetley Bitter ⓗ
City-centre pub that is used by many people as the tap for Clark's Brewery. It does get very busy on Friday and Saturday evenings. Old hogshead barrels are used as tables and the canopy around the main bar is thatched. A pool table and juke box make this a popular place for both young and old. Two function rooms are for hire.
⇌(Westgate)♣

Labour Club
18 Vicarage Street,
WF1 1QX
(bottom of market car park)
🕐 12-5 (not Mon-Thu; 11-4 Sat), 7-11; 12-5 Sun
☎ (01924) 215626 website: www.theredshed.org.uk
Ossett Silver Shadow; guest beers ⓗ
This club has provided a base for Wakefield's Labour movement for many years, and unlike other Labour clubs has continued to have socialist leanings. As the backbone of organisational support for workers involved in a range of industrial struggles, it has played a vital part in the lives and history of the people of Wakefield. This small, friendly, award-winning club has become a favourite with ale drinkers, stocking a variety of beers from independent breweries.
🏠⇌(Westgate/Kirkgate) P🕐

O'Donoghues
60 George Street, WE1 1DL
🕐 5-11; 1-10.30 Sun
☎ (01924) 291326
Draught Bass; Greene King Old Speckled Hen; Ossett Silver Shadow, Excelsior; Wells Banana Bread Beer ⓗ
This traditional house lies 200 yards off Westgate. Live music evenings are a regular feature here and Ossett beers are usually on tap. The floor is all wood, giving it the feel of an old-style inn. This pub has won a number of CAMRA awards. A nice atmosphere is enhanced by friendly bar service. 🚂⇌(Westgate/Kirkgate)

Redoubt
28 Horbury Road,
WF2 8TS
(behind St Michael's Church)
🕐 12 (11 Sat)-11; 12-10.30 Sun
☎ (01924) 377085 website: www.theredoubt.co.uk
Taylor Landlord; Tetley Mild, Bitter ⓗ
This CAMRA award-winning is a rare outlet for Tetley Mild in Wakefield. The pub has strong sporting connections and is one of the oldest in Wakefield. A Tetley Heritage pub, comprising four cosy rooms, two are available midweek at no charge for private functions; a family room is available until 8pm. It has had the same name since 1882.
Q🛏🏠⇌(Westgate) P

WENTBRIDGE

Blue Bell
Great North Road, WF8 3JP (1 mile off A1)
🕐 11.30-3, 5-11; 12-10.30 Sun
☎ (01977) 620697
Taylor Landlord; Tetley Bitter; guest beer ⓗ
In the picturesque village of Wentbridge, on the old Great North Road, this former coaching inn was rebuilt in 1633. An

original inn sign hangs in the entrance. It stands at the head of Brock Dale, the smallest of the Yorkshire dales. It is known for its excellent range of food which includes several vegetarian options (booking is advisable at weekends). Comfortably furnished, it boasts Mousey Thompson tables and chairs. Q 🌣 🚪 ◖ ৬ P ⅍

WIBSEY

Gaping Goose
5-6 Slack Bottom Road, BD6 3RH
◷ 4 (2 Sat)-11; 2-10.30 Sun
☎ (01274) 601701
Black Sheep Best Bitter; Taylor Landlord; Tetley Bitter Ⓗ

Converted many years ago from two terraced houses, it has been altered internally but retains a homely feel. This popular village pub is a true, family-run free house. There is a comfortable lounge and a games-oriented tap room. Guest beers have appeared on occasions. There is very limited parking at the front of the pub. 🚪♣P

WIDDOP

Pack Horse Inn ✆
Widdop Road, HX7 7AT (midway between Hebden Bridge and Colne) OS952317
◷ 12-3 (not weekdays Oct-Easter), 7-11; closed Mon; 12-10.30 Sun
☎ (01422) 842803

Black Sheep Best Bitter, Special; Greene King Old Speckled Hen; Thwaites Bitter; guest beer (summer) Ⓗ

Converted old laithe farmhouse situated beside the old packhorse route between Colne and Heptonstall. Nicknamed the Ridge, this isolated inn is 300 yards from the Pennine Way and popular with walkers. Its traditional atmosphere and excellent food (no chips) attracts visitors from afar; an upstairs restaurant is open Saturday evening (booking recommended). The accommodation is not available winter weekdays. Over 100 single malt whiskies are stocked.
🛏Q🌣🚪◖ ♠P

WINTERSETT

Angler's Retreat
Ferrytop Lane, WF4 2EB
(between villages of Crofton and Ryhill) OS382157
◷ 12-3, 7-10.30; 12-11 Fri & Sat; 12-3, 7-10.30 Sun
☎ (01924) 862370
John Smith's Bitter; Samuel Smith OBB; Theakston XB; guest beer (summer) Ⓗ

Friendly local that features a stone-flagged floor in the public bar and an open fire. The lounge houses a collection of plates, old photographs and two stuffed birds in glass cases. Close by is Anglers Country Park. The guest beer is only available in summer months. Buses run from Wakefield bus station (Nos. 196 and 197 to Hemsworth or Newstead). 🛏Q🌣🚪P

The Praise of Yorkshire Ale

It warms in winter, in summer opes the pores,
'Twill make a Sovereign Salve 'gainst cuts and sores;
It ripens wit, exhillerates the mind,
Makes friends of foes, and foes of friends full kind;
It's physical for old men, warms their blood,
Its spirits makes the Coward's courage good:
The tatter'd Beggar being warmed with Ale,
Nor rain, hail, frost, nor snow can him assail,
He's a good man with him can then compare,
It makes a Prentise great as the Lord Mayor;
The Labouring man, that toiles all day full sore,
A pot of ale at night, doth him restore,
And makes him all his toil and paines forget,
And for another day's work, he's then fit.

G.M. Gent, York, 1697

Our Bud...Budvar

THE BELT AND BRACES OF CAMRA's work is promoting British cask-conditioned beer. But the Campaign, through its membership of the European Beer Consumers' Union, also supports such classic European beer styles as the Trappist ales and spontaneous lambic and gueuze beers of Belgium. CAMRA has also given its backing to the Czech Budweiser Budvar brewery in its campaign to remain independent.

Budvar is one of only a few European lager beers still brewed in the traditional manner. While many other lager breweries – including even Pilsner Urquell, the original golden lager from Pilsen – are having fermentation times drastically reduced, Budvar still enjoys a long, slow cold maturation (lagering) that lasts for three months in deep, icy cellars below the brewery.

For more than 100 years, Budvar has been locked in a trade mark dispute with the American brewer Anheuser-Busch, owner of the other Budweiser brand, a beer that lists rice before barley malt in its ingredients. A-B relentlessly pursues Budvar through the courts of the world in an attempt to register its rights to the full Budweiser trade mark. It has lost in many countries, including Britain.

Budweiser Budvar remains a state-owned brewery: successive Czech governments have said they will privatise the brewery only when a suitable partner comes along. But there were alarming developments in 2003.

While the Czech Ministry of Agriculture remains committed to the brewery, two members of the government – including the influential Minister of Finance – publicly declared that Budvar should be privatised and sold.

Most of the major breweries in the Czech Republic are now owned by global giants. Pilsner Urquell, Gambrinus and Velke Popovice are owned by SAB-Miller, while the Staropramen group is owned by Interbrew. If Budvar is privatised and sold, other global giants are waiting in the wings. If Anheuser-Busch were allowed to buy Budvar it would end the costly legal battles over trade mark rights. A-B record of acquiring other American breweries that produced beers labelled Budweiser does not inspire confidence: all were rapidly closed down. Even if Budvar fell into the hands of a different global brewer, the odds are that the beer would be cheapened and brewed more quickly.

CAMRA appeals to all beer lovers to join the campaign to keep Budweiser Budvar independent and to continue to brew this classic lager beer in the traditional manner. You can sign at petition by logging on to the CAMRA website: www/camra.org.uk/budvar. Or you can write direct to the Czech Ministry of Agriculture to express your support for the beer: Ministerstvo zemedelstvi, Tesnov 17, 117 05 Prague 1, Czech Republic. Website: www.mze.cz; email: posta@mze.cz.

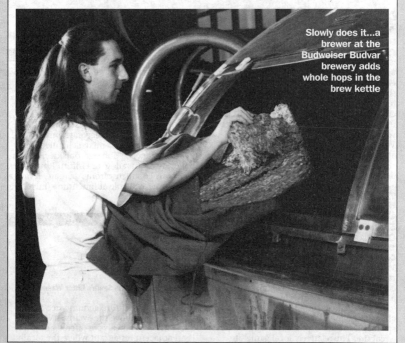

Slowly does it...a brewer at the Budweiser Budvar brewery adds whole hops in the brew kettle

GLAMORGAN

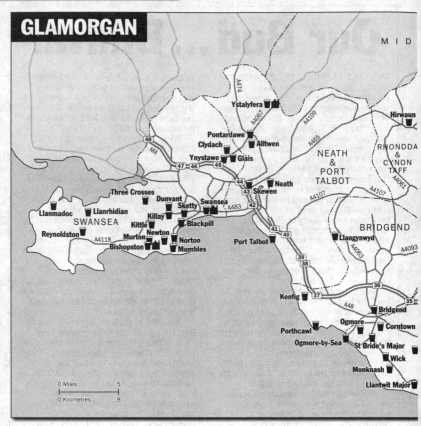

Authority areas covered: Bridgend UA, Caerphilly UA, Cardiff UA, Merthyr Tydfil UA, Neath & Port Talbot UA, Rhondda, Cynon, Taff UA, Swansea UA, Vale of Glamorgan UA

ABERAMAN

Aberaman Hotel ✓
Brynheulog Terrace, CF44 6EP
☻ 3 (2 Fri; 12 Sat)-11; 12-10.30 Sun
☎ (01685) 874695
Brains Rev James, seasonal beers; guest beer ⊞
Good example of a valleys' local, this single-bar pub offers a pleasant welcome to all. A lounge to one side allows the customer a chance of quiet drink. This is useful when the big-screen TV is tuned to sport. This is the first pub in the Cynon Valley to achieve Cask Marque accreditation. No evening meals are served on Tuesday or Thursday.
❀◑♣

ABERCARN

Old Swan
55 Commercial Road, NP11 5AJ
☻ 2.30 (11.30 Sat)-11; 11.30-11 Sun
☎ (01495) 243161
Courage Best Bitter; guest beer ⊞
Welcoming, roadside pub with a well-refurbished bar area, leading on to a comfortable lounge. Courage on gravity is a popular choice, known by the locals as 'cold tea'. A great supporter of a local charity, the pub has a strong community spirit and the atmosphere is enhanced by a real fire. The relatively local game of corks is played here, among the more usual pub games. A convenient bus stop is just outside. ☙♣

ABERDARE

Cambrian Inn
60 Seymour Street, CF44 7DL
☻ 11-5, 7-11; 11-11 Fri & Sat; 12-10.30 Sun
☎ (01685) 879120
Beer range varies ⊞
Fine, pleasant town pub, just a short stroll from the centre. Well decorated and furnished, it draws a mixed clientele from near and far. The pub sign outside portrays a picture of 'Caradog' or Griffith Rhys-Jones, a famous conductor from Aberdare. A range of meals is available at lunchtime (including Sun). ◑⇌♣

ALLTWEN

Butchers Arms
Alltwen Hill, SA8 3BP
(just off main road to Neath, A474)
☻ 12-11; 12-10.30 Sun
☎ (01792) 863100
Everards Original; John Smith's Bitter Wadworth 6X; guest beers ⊞
Welcoming, well-run, genuine free house situated high above the Swansea Valley. Substantial bar meals are offered and there is an adjacent restaurant where the locally-

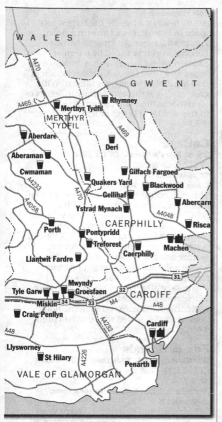

Boddingtons Bitter; Marston's Pedigree;
Wadworth 6X Ⓗ
Prominent pub/restaurant situated at the
side of the main Mumbles Road. Dating
from Victorian times, it has been extended
over the years to become a pleasantly-
appointed outlet. The restaurant area
includes a conservatory and offers
reasonably-priced meals with various special
deals. Meals are also served in the bar area,
which has a dartboard and large-screen TV
for sport. A quiz is held on Wednesday
evening. The pub is located at the entrance
to Clyne Gardens; well worth a visit.
✿ⓓ ዿP

BLACKWOOD

Rock & Fountain
**St David's Avenue, Woodfieldside,
NP12 0PN** (from High St turn into Bridge St, at end
turn right and follow round to pub)
✪ 3 (12 Fri & Sat)-11; 12-10.30 Sun
☎ (01495) 223907
Wadworth 6X; guest beer Ⓗ
This small, traditional pub is popular with
the locals. It is best described as a country
inn, based in a market town by a river. The
building, originally a counting house for
the mining industry, dates from the 1820s.
The bar is divided into three areas, one is for
non-smokers. Wooden floors and a real fire
enhance the congenial atmosphere.
Reasonably-priced food is served, including
'real chips' (no meals on Sun eve or Mon).
Diversions include a quiz night (Tue) and
live entertainment (occasional Sat). The
Sirhowy Valley walk passes the pub.
Benches are provided to the front for
summer drinking. ⚌Q ⓓ♣P✲

BRIDGEND

Wyndham Arms ❷
Dunraven Place, CF31 1JE
✪ 11-11; 12-10.30 Sun
☎ (01656) 663608
**Brains SA; Theakston Best Bitter; Worthington's
Bitter; guest beers** Ⓗ
A tempting outlet for real ale in a town that
has recently become something of a desert
for quality. Originally a coaching inn,
Wetherspoon's now offer accommodation
at this pub. Wood panelling and
photographs of old Bridgend adorn the
walls. Bridgend is an ideal place to stay
when exploring the nearby Vale of
Glamorgan. Q⇄ⓓዿ✲

CAERPHILLY

Masons Arms
Mill Road, CF83 3FE
✪ 12-11; 12-10.30 Sun
☎ (029) 2088 3353
Brains Bitter; guest beers Ⓗ
Busy, traditional pub with a contrasting bar

renowned meals are home made by the chef
who has served the pub for 14 years. The
hearth, with its real fire and gleaming
copper artefacts, complements the new
stone bar and substantial dark wood
furniture. Two guest ales usually accompany
the three regular beers. Unusually, half
pints are served in goblets. ⚌ⓓP

BISHOPSTON

Joiners Arms
50 Bishopston Road, SA3 3EJ
✪ 11.30-11; 12-10.30 Sun
☎ (01792) 232658
**Courage Best Bitter; Marston's Pedigree; Swansea
Bishopswood Bitter, Three Cliffs Gold, Original Wood;
guest beers** Ⓗ
Attractive, stone-built village pub with an
unusual spiral staircase in the bar. Licensed
since the 1860s, it is the home of the
popular Swansea Brewing Company. There
is a rear lounge and good value food is
served all day. It is a regular venue for
CAMRA visits, and was regional Pub of the
Year in 1999 and Branch Pub of the Year
2002 and 2003. Occasional beer festivals are
held and the local bus stops outside.
⚌Q✿ⓓ ⊟♣P

BLACKPILL

Woodman Inn
120 Mumbles Road, SA3 5AS
✪ 11-11; 12-10.30 Sun
☎ (01792) 402700

INDEPENDENT BREWERIES

Brains Cardiff
Bryncelyn Ystalyfera
Bullmastiff Cardiff
Carters Machen
Swansea Bishopston
Tomos Watkin Swansea

and lounge. The bar attracts a younger, lively crowd and has pool and dart teams. The relaxing atmosphere in the lounge means it is popular with all ages. A no-smoking section in part of the lounge is the focus for imaginative meals (not served Mon or Tue). The beer range is evolving as the pub finds new real ale converts. The Masons is well worth the short walk from the town centre and castle.
Q ✿ ❀ ⊕ ⇌ (Aber) ♣ P ⚲

CARDIFF

Black Pig/Mocyn Du
Sophia Close, CF11 9HW
(next to Wales Institute of Sport, off Cathedral Rd)
✪ 12-11; 12-10.30 Sun
☎ (029) 2037 1599
Brains Bitter, Rev James; Greene King Abbot Ⓗ
The transformation of this former, quiet Wolverhampton & Dudley back-street boozer has been quite remarkable. Close to the Welsh Institute of Sport, the National Cricket Centre and a leisurely riverside walk from the city centre, it is a firm favourite with Welsh students and residents alike. Bilingual signage throughout the bar, restaurant and garden areas helps Welsh speakers, learners and foreign visitors. Draught Hoegaarden and Leffe are an added bonus. This pub has a great atmosphere. ✿ ❀ ♠ P

Butchers Arms
29 Llandaff Road, Canton, CF5 1QD
(on B4267 off Cowbridge Road East)
✪ 11-11; 12-3, 7.30-10.30 Sun
☎ (029) 2022 7927
Brains Dark, Bitter, SA Ⓗ
In a world where the local city pub is often either a karaoke bar and/or a theme pub, this is a real local. It has a traditional street-corner location and comprises a separate bar and lounge. Various items of rugby memorabilia adorn the walls of the small bar which also boasts pews, darts and three TVs. The arched windows retain rare examples of the original Brains 'A1' logo. It is handy for the Chapter Arts Centre. Q ⊕ ♣

Cayo Arms
36 Cathedral Road, Pontcanna, CF11 9LL
(10 minutes' walk NW of city centre)
✪ 12-11; 12-10.30 Sun
☎ (029) 2039 1910
Tomos Watkin BB, OSB; Worthington's Bitter; guest beer Ⓗ
This popular pub was CAMRA Pub of the Year in 2001 and 2002 and has recently been acquired by the Celtic Inns pub chain. Although Tomos Watkin still forms the core of the beer range, the choice has been broadened to include a number of others. It is conveniently situated for the Millennium Stadium and Glamorgan County Cricket Club and attracts a mixed clientele including real ale enthusiasts. A fully-equipped conference room is available. Meals are served 12–3 and 5–8 daily.
✿ ❀ ♠ P ⚲

Chapter Arts Centre
Market Road, Canton, CF5 1QE
(off Cowbridge Road East)
✪ 6 (5 Thu)-11; 1-12.30am Fri; 1-11 Sat; 1-10.30 Sun
☎ (029) 2031 1050 website: www.chapter.org

Beer range varies Ⓗ
At the heart of allegedly the biggest arts space in Europe, lies a bar with a strong European flavour. An array of bottled European beers is joined by a regular rotation of real ales as well as draught 'real' lagers and weiss beers. A good selection of non-alcoholic beverages is offered. With great grub and the opportunity to see art or an arthouse film, you can imagine you are in the middle of Berlin or Barcelona.
✿ ♿ P ⚲

Cottage
25 St Mary's Street, CF10 1AA
✪ 11-11; 12-10.30 Sun
☎ (029) 2033 7194
Brains Dark, Bitter, SA Ⓗ
This pub occupies the ground floor of a tall, narrow building on one of Cardiff's principal streets. The large glazed window and mirrors along the side wall give the front area a light and airy aspect. A long bar is on one side of the pub, with further seating and a good serving area to the rear where a stained glass skylight provides further light. The pub attracts a mixed clientele of all ages and can get very busy when events are held at the nearby Millennium Stadium. Wholesome home-cooked food is served weekday lunchtimes.
⊕ ⇌ (Central)

Fox & Hounds
Old Church Road, Whitchurch, CF14 1AD
✪ 11-11; 12-10.30 Sun
☎ (029) 2069 3377
Brains Dark, Bitter, Ⓗ **SA,** Ⓟ **seasonal beers; guest beers** Ⓗ
Refurbished and enlarged in recent years, this pub still retains a cosy atmosphere as well as developing a popular restaurant. It has a garden drinking area at the rear and a more traditional bar area towards the front. Quiz night is Sunday. The bar area is often busy when sporting events are shown on the big screen. The enterprising landlord holds beer festivals in July and on other occasions. The guest beer is usually from independent family brewers. Part of the eating section is designated a no-smoking area. Q ✿ ❀ ♿ ⇌ P ⚲

Gatekeeper ✪
9-10 Westgate Street and Womanby Street, CF14 2SE
✪ 11-11; 12-10.30 Sun
☎ (029) 2064 6020
Brains SA; Greene King Abbot; Theakston Best Bitter; guest beers Ⓗ
This imaginative Wetherspoon's conversion of former auction rooms has three distinct floor areas served by a passenger lift. The pub's management are keen supporters of local micro-brewers Bullmastiff and Cwmbran whose products frequently feature as guests. Occasional Welsh beer festivals are held. The pub attracts visitors of all ages and can be very busy in the evening. The Gatekeeper won the CAMRA Best Conversion of Pub award.
Q ❀ ♿ ⇌ (Central) ⚲

Glamorgan Council & Staff Club
17 Westgate Street, CF10 1DD
(opp. Millennium Stadium)
✪ 11-11; 12-10.30 Sun

☎ (029) 2023 3216
Brains Dark, Bitter; guest beers Ⓗ
Victorian, red-brick building of historic interest, it has had many uses over the years. The club was established in 1963 as the Glamorgan County Council Staff Club. Currently midway through a refurbishment, it still gets busy on match days. Soon to have a skittle alley, it currently provides a pool table and a dartboard upstairs. A friendly welcome is assured for CAMRA members; please produce a membership card or this Guide if asked to do so. It is a regular outlet for beers from Bullmastiff Brewery. A family room is available on request. Q ⍽ ≠ (Central) ♣

Glass Works
4 Wharton Street, CF10 1AG
(at the side of Howells store, off St Mary's St)
✪ 11.30-11 (midnight Thu-Sat); 12-6 Sun
☎ (029) 2022 2114
Greene King IPA, Abbot, Old Speckled Hen; guest beers Ⓗ
An oasis of real ale in a city centre dominated by tied houses, the Glass Works was a real glass factory in a former life. This Greene King house offers four changing guest ales in addition to its own successful portfolio and Budweiser Budvar is served on draught. The single-room bar is divided into four sections on split levels, one is a no-smoking area until 7 pm. Visit during the real ale 'happy hour' (weekdays 5–7) when there is a substantial reduction. Meals are served 11.30–7 Monday–Saturday and 12–5 on Sunday.
◖◗ ≠ (Central) ⅄

Griffin ✓
Church Road, Lisvane, CF14 0SJ
✪ 11-11; 12-10.30 Sun
☎ (029) 2074 7399
Draught Bass; Brains SA; Flowers IPA; Fuller's London Pride; Marston's Pedigree; Wadworth 6X Ⓗ
A long central bar links the drinking area (with flagstones, a large fireplace and a TV) with two separate raised drinking sections. The relaxed atmosphere and local reputation for good food make this a popular pub. The beer range consists of well-known regional beers, national brands and an occasional guest. A small rear patio overlooks the car park, and additional seating is provided at the front of the building. This has been a pub for more than four centuries.
Q ❀ ◖◗ ⅋ P

Olde Butchers
22 Heol y Felin, Rhiwbina, CF14 6NB
✪ 12-11; 12-10.30 Sun
☎ (029) 2069 3526
Brains SA; Fuller's London Pride; Greene King Old Speckled Hen; Tetley Bitter Ⓗ
Lively, bustling pub with a central bar. Entertainment includes a regular quiz night, jazz (Thu) and a much-used skittle alley. The TV in one area contrasts with the quieter section on the other side of the pub. The licensee has a display of Cardiff City memorabilia on part of the bar. There is ample car parking and a pleasant garden at the rear. The kitchen remains busy providing the popular range of meals offered.
❀ ◖◗ ⅋ ♣ P

Owain Glyndŵr
St John's Square, CF10 2AU (by St John's Church, city centre)
✪ 12-11 (may extend Thu-Sat); 12-10.30 Sun
☎ (029) 2022 1980
Beer range varies Ⓗ
In the heart of the city, the Owain Glyndŵr is linked to the RSVP pub next door but has a totally different character. The fine guest beers, brown woodwork and slightly bohemian Welsh character are unusual in Cardiff. The juke box is one of the best in the area but is rarely so loud as to impede conversation. In the summer sit in the pedestrianised street and watch the world go by.
❀ ◖◗ ₺ ≠ ♣ ☗

Pendragon ✓
Excalibur Drive, Thornhill, CF14 9BB
✪ 11-11; 12-10.30 Sun
☎ (029) 2061 0550
Brains Dark, SA Ⓗ
Modern estate pub set on a rise with its own green belt and a fine mature monkey puzzle tree. The pub has a central bar area with three separate rooms, a quiet lounge with a no-smoking section, lively bar with pool and TV and a function room. A beer garden and children's play area have a fine view over Cardiff. The large car park is linked by its own driveway to the main estate road. The continuing dedication to quality makes this pub a splendid place to relax over food and a pint.
Q ❀ ◖◗ ⅋ P ⅄

Vulcan
10 Adam Street, CF24 2FH (opp. Cardiff prison)
✪ 11.30-11; 12-10.30 Sun
☎ (029) 2046 1580
Brains Bitter, SA Ⓗ
Unspoilt two-bar local situated a short distance from the city centre in an area that is currently the focus of residential redevelopment. The large front bar has a sawdust-covered floor and original Brains stained glass windows. Pictures and artefacts are displayed relating to Cardiff's past as a major port. The small rear lounge is served by a hatch. Lunchtime food is served Monday–Friday. The pub's name reflects the city's history of steel-making and has remained unchanged for over 150 years. The licensee is keen to preserve the traditional feel of the pub.
Q ◖◗ ⅋ ≠ (Central/Queen St)

Carpenters Arms
High Street, SA6 5LN
✪ 11-11; 12-10.30 Sun
☎ (01792) 843333
Brains Dark, seasonal beers; guest beers Ⓗ
Popular stone-fronted pub with a bustling public bar, and a split-level lounge/restaurant. Seasonal beer festivals are organised throughout the year with ales from regional brewers. Traditional pub games feature and it is also used as a meeting place for the local cyclists group. A pleasant patio garden is available with ample parking.
❀ ◖◗ ⅋ ♣ P

CORNTOWN

Golden Mile
Corntown Road, CF35 5BA (off A48, between Cowbridge and Bridgend) OS928774
☼ 11.30-3, 6-11; 12-4, 7-10.30 Sun
☎ (01656) 565 4884
Shepherd Neame Spitfire; Tomos Watkin Whoosh; Wells Bombardier Ⓗ
Set down below road level, this pub has a small, cosy bar with a TV, a lounge and a restaurant area. A real fire in the lounge and a warm welcome add to the relaxed atmosphere. Brassware adorns the fireplace and an outside drinking area has fine views over the adjacent fields. A similar view can be had from the large window in the bar. A pool table and dartboard provide the pub games. An award-winning chef adds to the appeal of this pub. Visit the café bar for a warm welcome from Dave the dog.
≜Q❀◑🖢♣P

CRAEG PENLLYN

Barley Mow
CF71 7RT OS978773
☼ 12-2.30 (not Mon or Tue; 3 Sat), 6-11; 12-3, 7-10.30 Sun
☎ (01446) 772558
Hancock's HB; guest beers Ⓗ
This old, established hostelry retains much of its original atmosphere. The pub continues to provide fine guest beers and prides itself in presenting them in good condition. The bar meals are reasonably priced and deservedly popular. Families are welcome and there is plenty of parking in the large car park opposite. In the winter a roaring log fire is a splendid sight, in summer the small beer garden at the rear is another useful facility. ≜Q❀◑🖢♣P

CWMAMAN

Falcon Inn
1 Incline Row, CF44 6LU OS008998
☼ 11-11; 12-10.30 Sun
☎ (01685) 873758 website: www.thefalconinn.net
Beer range varies Ⓗ
Nestled in the Aman Valley, the Falcon is close to the village, but feels quite isolated. The picturesque river setting ensures its popularity in the summer. Three beers are usually on offer. Built using wood and stone from a local chapel, it is a pub that once visited, remains in the memory.
❀🛏◑🖢♿P

DERI

Old Club
93 Bailey Street, CF81 9HX
☼ 7 (4.30 Fri; 12 Sat)-11; 12-10.30 Sun
☎ (01443) 830278
Beer range varies Ⓗ
Visitors are always welcome at this friendly, independent social club. Two guest beers are on offer, with a range and diversity which is unusual for the area. The cellar is managed by enthusiasts who take great pride in quality and presentation. The community spirit found here is infectious, and you will probably meet some of the locals, or be tempted to join in with one of the many events held. Local buses from Bargoed stop outside. ❀♿♣P

DUNVANT

Found Out Inn
Killan Road, SA21 7TD
(from Dunvant Square uphill towards Three Crosses)
☼ 12-3.30 (not Mon), 5.30-11; 12-3, 7-10.30 Sun
☎ (01792) 203596
Flowers Original; guest beers Ⓗ
This village local was rebuilt in the 1960s when the old pub was demolished. It was originally called the Dunvant Inn but was nicknamed the Found Out from the time when local colliers went straight from work to the pub on paydays, only to be found there by their wives and chased home! The pub is immaculately kept and the bar has darts, pool table, juke box and TV. Good value food is served and a quiz is held on Tuesday.
Q❀◑♣

GELLIHAF

Coal Hole
Bryn Road, NP12 2QE
(on A4049, S of Fleur de Lys) OS160958
☼ 12-3, 6.30-11; 11-11 Fri & Sat; 12-10.30 Sun
☎ (01443) 830280
Hancock's HB; guest beers Ⓗ
This comfortable, friendly one-bar pub, once a private house, has extensive views over the Rhymney Valley. Although rather food-based, this pub is well worth a visit, with two guest ales changing weekly. Drinkers are made to feel very welcome. A courtesy bus is available for use by customers in the local area. No meals are served on Sunday or Monday evenings.
≜◑P

GILFACH FARGOED

Capel
Park Place, CF81 8LW
☼ 12-4, 7-11; 12-11 Fri & Sat; 12-4, 8-10.30 Sun
☎ (01443) 830272
Brains SA; John Smith's Bitter; guest beers Ⓗ
Large, sociable, traditional Valleys' pub with many original features including a long bar and extensive wood panelling. Look out for the large decorated cast iron weighing scales in the lobby. Apart from being the focus of the local community, overnight accommodation is available. Guest beers are usually from craft brewers.
Q🛏◑♿≠ (Bargoed) ♣✂

GLAIS

Globe Inn
Birchgrove Road, SA7 9EN
☼ 12 (4 Mon)-11; 12-10.30 Sun
☎ (01792) 842655
Fuller's London Pride; Tomos Watkin OSB; guest beer Ⓗ
Attractively decorated, bright village pub with two bars in the heart of Glais. Food is served in both bars but oriented to the restaurant-style lounge. There is a large car park at the rear with an outdoor seating area for sunny days. Inexpensive food is served Tuesday–Saturday, 12–2.30 and 6–9 (plus Sun lunches from 12–2.30). For public transport users, service 145 runs from Swansea city centre to the stop outside.
❀◑♿♣P

GROESFAEN (PONTYCLUN)

Dynevor Arms ✪
Llantrisant Road, CF72 8NS (on A4119)
OS061810
☻ 11-11; 12-3, 7-10.30 Sun
☎ (029) 2089 1285
Adnams Broadside; Draught Bass; Hancock's HB; guest beer Ⓗ

The Dynevor Arms is a popular, roadside village pub. It is comfortable and well decorated on the inside while on the outside it is colourfully signposted and painted in traditional pub colours. Changing guest beers alternate between various brewers and brews. An area is set aside for darts, dominoes and cards and either live music or a quiz is held on Sunday evening. A dining area enhances the open-plan bar and a varied menu offers good value meals with special prices for senior citizens on Monday (no food Sun eve). A delightful pub with excellent parking facilities. ⊛◑♣P

HIRWAUN

Glancynon Inn
Swansea Road, CF44 9PH
☻ 11-11; 12-10.30 Sun
☎ (01685) 811043
Beer range varies Ⓗ

Large, welcoming, oak-beamed country pub on the outskirts of the village. It offers a well-appointed and pleasantly decorated lounge and a split-level public bar. A little way off the main roads, but easy to find, it is a haven for real ale in the area. Bookings are essential for Sunday lunch (no meals on Sun eve). ⊛◑⊟♣P

KENFIG

Prince of Wales Inn
CF33 4PR
☻ 11.30-4, 6-11; 11.30-11 Sat; 12-10.30 Sun
☎ (01656) 740356
Draught Bass; Worthington's Bitter; guest beer Ⓖ

Stone-built pub dating from 1440, this building has been the town hall, school and courtroom of the drowned town of Kenfig. It is allegedly haunted by one of the former inhabitants of the town. There is a visitor centre and nature reserve nearby. The Maid of Sker House first met her harpist lover here, later immortalised in a story by RD Blackmore. The pub may stay open longer in the afternoons when busy, as it tends to be in the summer, as customers enjoy their beer served straight from the barrel.
♨Q⊛◑P

KILLAY

Railway Inn
553 Gower Road, Upper Killay, SA2 7DS
☻ 12-2, 6-11; 12-11 Sat; 12-10.30 Sun
☎ (01792) 203946
Swansea Deep Slade Dark, Bishopswood Bitter, Original Wood; guest beers Ⓗ

Built in 1864 when the railway ran through the Clyne Valley, the railway closed in the 1960s but happily the pub soldiers on. It is a rare unspoilt gem with walls still adorned with railway memorabilia. A major outlet for Swansea Brewing Company, the pub guests at least four beers at any time, usually

including one from Wye Valley. Occasional beer festivals are held at local CAMRA's Pub of the Year, 2000. The old railway is now a popular cycle track and footpath.
♨⊛⊛⊟♣P

KITTLE (SWANSEA)

Beaufort Arms ✪
18 Pennard Road, SA3 3JS
☻ 11.30-11; 12-10.30 Sun
☎ (01792) 234521
Brains Buckley's Best Bitter, Rev James, seasonal beers Ⓗ

Reputedly the oldest pub in Gower, the original part of the building boasts a beamed ceiling and some early stonework. The pub has won a number of awards for its community focus and Gower in Bloom competitions. A Brains tenanted house with three bars and a function room, there is a large car park with outdoor seating and a children's play area. A quiz is held on Monday night and the pub hosts the local ladies' darts team. An extensive menu is served daily (11.30-3, 5-9.30 Mon-Thu, and 11.30-9.30 Fri-Sun). ⊱⊛◑⊟♣P

LLANGYNWYD

Old House/Yr Hen Dŷ ♪ ✪
CF34 95B (on top of hill) OS858889
☻ 11-11; 12-10.30 Sun
☎ (01656) 733310
Flowers Original; guest beer Ⓗ

Much-visited, atmospheric thatched pub, one of the oldest in Wales, dating back to1147. Large windows afford views across the Bryncynan Valley. The traditional 'Mari Lwyd' is depicted on the pub sign. The poet Wil Hopcyn (1701–41), visited the pub and courted Ann Thomas of Cefn Ydfa. Read about their story in the pub. The extensive garden incorporates an adventure playground. An unusual feature is a helicopter landing pad – please phone first if intending to use it!
♨Q⊱⊛◑ΔP

LLANMADOC (GOWER)

Britannia Inn
SA3 1DB
☻ 11-11; 12-10.30 Sun
☎ (01792) 386624
Marston's Pedigree; Wadworth 6X; guest beer Ⓗ

The last pub surviving in a village which was once a thriving little port. There are ship's timbers in the construction and two old bread ovens retained. 'The Mapsant', an ancient annual religious festival celebrating the patron saint of the parish, is still celebrated here every November. The pub has a good range of facilities for families including a menagerie in the grounds. Enjoy the extensive views over the estuary and pleasant walks nearby. Guest beers are available in the holiday periods and food is served all day in season.
♨Q⊛⊟◑⊟Δ♣P⅄

LLANRHIDIAN (GOWER)

Greyhound Inn
Oldwalls, SA3 1HA
☻ 11-11; 12-10.30 Sun
☎ (01792) 391027

Fuller's London Pride; Marston's Pedigree; Tomos Watkin BB, OSB; guest beers ⓗ

Attractive village pub situated on the North Gower Road, a favourite with diners who travel miles especially to try the local fish dishes. A free house with an excellent atmosphere, it can be very busy at peak holiday times. Families are welcome in the games room and food is served in all the bars and the restaurant. There is also a function room available. A large car park is provided. ♨Q⇆❀◑⊟♣P

LLANTWIT FARDRE

Bush Inn
Main Road, CF38 2EP
❂ 11-11; 12-10.30 Sun
☎ (01443) 203958
Hancock's HB; guest beers ⓗ

Small, single-bar village local, with a side room mainly used by the younger, but quiet, clientele. The pub features something on several nights, such as sixties' records, a quiz or darts. Regular trips to the races and other events are organised. Guest beers may include unusual choices for the area. ❀♣P

Ship
Efail Isaf, CF38 1BH (400 yds from A473)
❂ 11-11; 12-10.30 Sun
☎ (01443) 202341
Hancock's HB; guest beers ⓗ

Just about a country pub, but the houses are closing in. This welcoming, open-plan bar offers one or two guest beers, usually uncommon in the area. The long back bar has darts, pool and music at the weekends – this does not disturb the rest of the pub. An extensive menu attracts customers from a wide area, and booking is advisable for Sunday lunch. The patio is a summer suntrap, and a good spot to watch the world walk or ride slowly by. The adjacent nature trail is simple fun for visitors. ❀◑♣P

LLANTWIT MAJOR

King's Head
East Street, CF61 1XY
❂ 11-11; 12-10.30 Sun
☎ (01446) 792697
Brains Dark, Bitter, SA; Worthington's Bitter ⓗ

Excellent, two-bar, town-centre local. The basic public bar has a large-screen TV and is popular on race days due to the bookie's next door. Darts, pool and dominoes are played and live music and karaoke takes place (weekend eves). Good value home-cooked food is available in the comfortable lounge or no-smoking dining room. The pleasant garden is accessed via the lounge. Brains at its best. ♨Q⇆❀◑⊟♿A♣P

Old Swan Inn
Church Street, CF61 1XY (opp. old town hall)
❂ 12-11; 12-10.30 Sun
☎ (01446) 792230 website: www.oldswaninn.com
Beer range varies ⓗ

The oldest pub in the historic town of Llantwit Major, with a fine view of St Illtyd's Church (estd. 5th century), this ancient two-bar hostelry serves up to four real ales regularly, including beers from the Cottage Brewery. A large range of freshly-cooked and interesting good is available all day. The pub is home to the 'Swan 4 Sir

Tom' group that campaigned to make Tom Jones a knight. A pool table and a juke box are in the rear bar. The pub is supposed to be haunted by a large odorous, hirsute figure who stands at the bar, shrouded in a smoky haze. ♨❀◑⊟A♣P

LLYSWORNEY

Carne Arms
Llantwit Major Road, CF74 7NQ
(on B4268, off A48)
❂ 12-11 (12-3, 5-11 winter); 12-10.30 Sun
☎ (01446) 773553 website: www.thecarnearms.co.uk
Greene King Old Speckled Hen; Hancock's HB ⓗ

White-walled, friendly local situated at the southern end of the village on the B4268, 3¼ miles from Llantwit Major (according to the milestone outside). At the far end of the car park, children can be kept amused in the safe play area or animal garden. A covered mediterranean-style patio guards the main entrance to the two-roomed pub, both rooms boast inglenooks and were used during the war as soup kitchens. Main meals are served in the lounge, and special themed menus are regularly offered. A no-smoking area is in operation Friday–Sunday. ♨Q❀◑⊟♣P✧

MACHEN

White Hart
Nant y Ceisiad, CF83 8QQ
(100 yds N of A468 at W end of village) OS203892
❂ 12-3, 6.30-11; 12-11 Sat; 12-10.30 Sun
☎ (01633) 441005
Beer range varies ⓗ

Independent free house and brew-pub. Up to four guest beers from very diverse sources are offered. Carters beers are brewed on the premises, but not always on sale. This unusual building has rambling extensions and is fitted out with oak panels and features from the classic liner Empress of France. A wide range of meals is available at most times, but booking for Sunday lunch is advised. Occasional beer festivals are held. The pub is much easier to find from the recently opened cycle path, along the old railway embankment which hides the pub from the A468. ❀⇌◑♣P✧

MERTHYR TYDFIL

Dic Penderyn ⊘
102-103 High Street, CF47 8AQP
❂ 11-11; 12-10.30 Sun
☎ (01685) 385786
Brains Arms Park Ale, SA; Theakston Best Bitter; Worthington's Bitter; guest beer ⓗ

This busy Wetherspoon's pub is named after one of the leaders of the Merthyr riots. Dic was hanged in 1831 for stabbing a soldier in the leg. It is widely believed that he was innocent but hanged for his political activities. The premises have been converted from a very large 19th-century general store and display many historic photographs of Merthyr and its industrial heritage. Situated in the busy High Street, the railway and bus stations and a large car park are nearby. Q◑♿⇌✧

Rose & Crown ⊘
Morgan Street, CF47 8TP (off Brecon Rd, ½ mile S of Cyfarthfa Park)

✪ 12-11 (10 Mon); 12-10.30 Sun
☎ (01685) 723743
Brains Bitter; guest beers ⒣
Converted from cottages nearly 200 years ago, this pub hosted prayer meetings for local residents prior to the opening of the church in 1822. Black and white photographs of the local area in years gone by, along with a large selection of pump clips can be found on the walls. The visitors book is evidence that Welsh sporting celebrities regularly head for this pub in order to appreciate the fine selection of ever-changing guest ales. Well worth a visit. ⇌

MISKIN

Miskin Arms
Hensol Road, CF72 8JQ (180 yds off B4264)
✪ 11.30-11; 12-10.30 Sun
☎ (01443) 224346
Hancock's HB; guest beer ⒣
Dating from at least 1741, this is a listed building, and the sort of village pub you hope to see around the corner. The regular and guest beers complement the food, which includes daily curries (these can be very hot and spicy). Mayfields restaurant is known for good food, a bit different from traditional pub fare (no meals Sun lunchtime or Sun or Mon eves). Outside, you can sit on a raised decking area or choose the walled beer garden. Q ❀ ◑ ▲ P

MONKNASH

Plough & Harrow
CF71 7QQ
(off B4265, between Marcross and Broughton)
✪ 12-11; 12-10.30 Sun
☎ (01656) 890209
website: www.theploughandharrow.com
Shepherd Neame Spitfire; Worthington's Bitter; Wye Valley HPA; ⒣ **guest beers** ⒣/Ⓖ
Ancient former Welsh long house which has been runner-up in the CAMRA national Pub of the Year competition on several occasions, most recently in 2002. Five real ales are on handpump with up to six on gravity dispense. There are two rooms, the larger bar is dominated by an inglenook, and the smaller room acts as a restaurant for lunchtime and evening meals. A vast range of British bottled beers is available; the pub serves as the base for the licensee's internet-based beer sales business. ⚏ ❀ ◑ ▣ ♣ ♠ P

MUMBLES

Park Inn
23 Park Street, SA3 4DA
✪ 12-2.30 (not Mon), 4.30-11; 12-11 Sat; 12-10.30 Sun
☎ (01792) 366738
Worthington's Bitter; guest beers ⒣
Long-established, back-street pub sought out by all real ale lovers in Mumbles. A good selection of guest beers is always on tap, usually five; Wye Valley brews also feature. Good value home-cooked meals are available with daily specials and occasional theme nights. Regular 'open-mike' music nights are a favourite with locals and visitors alike. A light-hearted quiz is held on Thursday night. Note the interesting old pictures of the pub on the walls.

Addlestones cider is stocked. The Park Inn was local CAMRA Pub of the Year in 1999. Q ◑ ♣ ♠

Victoria Inn
21 Westbourne Place, SA3 4DB
✪ 12-11; 12-10.30 Sun
☎ (01792) 360111
Draught Bass; Greene King Old Speckled Hen; Worthington's Bitter; guest beers ⒣
Lovely, back-street, corner local dating from the mid-19th century, as the name implies. The pub retains some lovely stained glass windows and features an old pub well which was undoubtedly the water source when the pub brewed its own beer. A single-roomed pub but with two distinct sections – the bar area has darts and TV, while the other end is a little quieter. You can request 'flat' Bass to be served, if required. ❀ ♣

MURTON (GOWER)

Plough & Harrow
88 Oldway, SA3 3DJ
✪ 11-11; 12-10.30 Sun
☎ (01792) 234459
Courage Best Bitter, Directors; guest beers ⒣
One of the oldest pubs in Gower, which has been renovated and extended in recent times. It retains its character and manages to combine its popular food trade with its tradition as a village local. The bar has darts, TV and a pool table, and attracts younger customers, while the lounge is a quiet place to enjoy a chat or a bar meal. Quiz night is on Tuesday. Good value food is served daily. Q ❀ ◑ ♣ P

MWYNDY

Barn at Mwyndy
CF72 8PJ (down lane opp. Corner Park Garage on A4119) OS056816
✪ 11-3, 5-11; 11.30-11 Sat; 12-10.30 Sun
☎ (01443) 222333
Worthington's Bitter; guest beers ⒣
Converted, 16th-century long barn with an eclectic array of country memorabilia, including a coracle. The split-level bar has a log fire in winter. Amenities include a good, no-smoking restaurant (reservations advised), a garden with children's play area and a meeting room. Regular beer festivals, occasional music and a serious interest in petanque are other features. Up to six guests usually include Bullmastiff or Tomos Watkin or other Welsh beers. Local CAMRA Pub of the Year 2002.
⚏ ❀ ◑ ♿ P

NEATH

David Protheroe ✔
7 Windsor Road, SA11 1LS
✪ 11-11; 12-10.30 Sun
☎ (01639) 622130
Brains Dark, SA; Greene King Abbot; Theakston Best Bitter; guest beers ⒣
This popular Wetherspoon's outlet, situated directly opposite the railway station, was converted from the old police station. The name derives from the first policeman to be posted at the jail. Inside, the modern oversized seating makes customers resemble a Borrowers' convention. Friendly staff serve good value food and drink, two guest ales

are usually available. A children's eating area is located at the rear. Wheelchair WC and ramp. ♿🏠🍴◑♿⇌✗

RAFA Club
Astra House, 16 London Road, SA11 1LE
(150 yds from Victoria Gardens)
🕐 6 (12 Sat)-11; 12-3, 7-12.30 Sun
☎ (01639) 642444
Hancock's HB; guest beer H
Easily accessible on foot from the bus and train stations, this club has a comfortable lounge bar, function room and pool area downstairs and another function room upstairs. Entertainment includes a quiz on Sunday evening, bingo on Tuesday evening, old-time dancing on Thursday night, modern dancing on Saturday night and occasional concerts to raise funds for charities. CAMRA members are allowed access on production of their membership cards. ⇌♣P

Star Inn
83 Penydre, SA11 3HF (near Gnoll rugby ground)
🕐 12-11; 12-10.30 Sun
☎ (01639) 637745
Draught Bass; Hancock's HB; Taylor Landlord; guest beer H
Popular, well-run, back-street local where strangers are welcome. Beer is dispensed from 1940s beer engines. It is very busy when Neath RFC play at home and during televised rugby matches. The beer garden has a children's play area and boules piste. Neath Canal and a national cycle track are nearby. Charities are supported. This trouble-free, genuine free house is often described by visitors as a 'real pub'. ⊛⇌P✗

NEWTON (GOWER)

Newton Inn
New Well Lane, SA3 4SR
🕐 12-11; 12-10.30 Sun
☎ (01792) 365101
Draught Bass; H/G **Fuller's London Pride; Marston's Pedigree; Worthington's Bitter** H
Welcoming village local that retains a bar and lounge area in a semi open-plan layout. The pub offers very competitively-priced meals and is popular with diners both lunchtime and early evening. The bar has a big-screen TV and shows sporting events. Quizzes are held on Monday and Wednesday evenings. The draught Bass can be supplied straight from the cask on request. The small front patio draws many customers on summer evenings. ⊛◑🍴

NORTON

Beaufort Arms
1 Castle Road, SA3 5TF
(turn by Norton House Hotel, off Mumbles Rd)
🕐 11.30-11; 12-10.30 Sun
☎ (01792) 401319
Draught Bass; Worthington's Bitter; guest beer H
Village local dating from the 18th century, the Beaufort retains its friendly charm. A real fire features in both the bar and cosy, smaller lounge. A dartboard remains in the bar and a TV is turned on for sport. A quiz is held on Tuesday night. There are photographs on the walls of the annual Mumbles raft race which the pub strongly

supports, one year's entry was a raft in the form of a replica of the pub itself!
🍴Q⊛🍴♣

OGMORE

Pelican In Her Piety
Ewenny Road, CF32 0QP
🕐 11.30-11; 12-10.30 Sun
☎ (01656) 880049 website: www.pelicanpub.co.uk
Draught Bass; Greene King Abbot, Old Speckled Hen; Fuller's London Pride; Worthington's Bitter; guest beer H
Excellent roadside public house with a fine front patio, part of which affords splendid views of the ruins of Ogmore Castle opposite. It welcomes visitors and locals with a warming log fire in winter. Pride is taken in the quality of the real ales (ale served without sparklers). The food remains popular (not served Sun eve). A great deal of fundraising goes on in aid of an autistic children's charity. The pub has reverted to its original name (an heraldic symbol) under its current owners. 🍴♿⊛◑🍴P

OGMORE-BY-SEA

Sealawns Hotel
Slon Lane, CF32 0PN (on seaward side of B4524)
🕐 12-3, 6.30-11; 12-3; 7-10.30 Sun
☎ (01656) 880311
Felinfoel Double Dragon; Tomos Watkin OSB; Worthington's Bitter; guest beer (summer) H
Originally a 16th-century cottage, this building has been extended to form a clifftop hotel providing spectacular views across the channel to Devon and down the coast to Carmarthenshire. There is a cosy bar, a restaurant and a function room, used for parties and as an overflow for the restaurant at busy times. Enjoy a drink in the large, enclosed garden. Barbecues are held in summer on the patio.
🍴Q⊛🛏◑🍴🍴♣P

PENARTH

Windsor
Windsor Road, CF64 1JF
(downhill from town centre)
🕐 12-11; 12-10.30 Sun
☎ (02920) 702821
Hancock's HB; Taylor Landlord; Tomos Watkin OSB; guest beer H
Street-corner local just outside the centre of this Victorian seaside town. It comprises a large single room with bar servery and a raised area at one end which forms a stage for regular live music, including jazz. There is a restaurant area to the rear. The guest beers frequently feature ales from Welsh micro-breweries, including the local Bullmastiff. This pub stocks the best range of cask beers in Penarth.
⊛◑⇌(Dingle Rd)♣

PONTARDAWE

Pontardawe Inn
123 Herbert Street, SA8 4ED
🕐 12-11; 12-10.30 Sun
☎ (01792) 830791 website: www.come.to/gwachel
Brains Dark, Buckley's Best Bitter, Rev James, seasonal or guest beer H
This attractive two-bar village inn, with a riverside location, is known as the Gwachel.

Interesting notes on local history are displayed in the bar and live music is played (Fri and Sat eves). There is a large car park, family play area and boules court. Prize-winning hanging baskets grace the outdoor drinking areas. The pub was awarded CAMRA Neath and Bridgend Pub of the Year 2002. The riverside restaurant at the rear provides good home-cooked meals (no food Tue or Sun eves). Wheelchair WC. ✿◑🗗&♣P

PONTYPRIDD

Bunch of Grapes
Ynysangharad Road, CF37 4DA (under the A470 from the Llanover)
☼ 11-11; 12-10.30 Sun
☎ (01443) 402934
Draught Bass; guest beers Ⓗ

A short walk from the town centre, the frontage belies its size, with several drinking areas. The interior is fairly simple, but a warm welcome is guaranteed. Food is above-average quality in the bar and the separate non-smoking restaurant. It is one of those pubs where you feel that a quick pint will lead to a lasting relationship with the place. ⚅ゟ✿◑♣P

Llanover Arms
Bridge Street, CF37 4PE
☼ 12-11; 12-3, 7-10.30 Sun
☎ (01443) 403215
Brains Dark, Bitter, SA; Worthington's Bitter; guest beer Ⓗ

Opposite the renowned Ynysangharad Park, this 18th-century town pub has been kept by the same family for over a century. The current habitués are not the thirsty chainmakers and bargees of yore, but discerning drinkers from near and far, many of whom are attracted by the ever-changing guest ale. If using the car park, a ticket needs to be obtained from the bar – or your car may be clamped. ✿🗗≠♣P

PORTH

Rheola Hotel
Rheola Road, CF39 0LF (200 yds S of bus depot)
☼ 2 (1 Fri; 12 Sat)-11; 12-10.30 Sun
☎ (01443) 682633
Draught Bass; Wells Bombardier; guest beer Ⓗ

Comfortable, friendly, two-roomed pub, popular with locals and discerning drinkers from the Rhondda Valleys. The bar has a pool table and darts, the lounge offers background music. The pub is situated in Porth, the 'gateway' to the Rhondda Valleys, 400 yards from Porth railway station and 200 yards from the bus depot. Entertainment includes a quiz night on Monday and a singer in the bar on Thursday. A guest ale is on tap at weekends. ✿🗗≠♣P

PORTHCAWL

Lorelei Hotel
36-38 Esplanade Avenue, CF36 3YU
☼ 5 (12 Sat)-11; 12-10.30 Sun
☎ (01656) 788342 website: www.loreleihotel.co.uk
Draught Bass; Ⓖ **Shepherd Neame Spitfire; Wye Valley Butty Bach; guest beers** Ⓗ

This former local CAMRA Pub of the Year is well worth seeking out in a seaside town

devoted to keg beer. It is a regular and rare outlet for Bullmastiff Brewery. Several beer festivals are held throughout the year. Set back from the seafront, the hotel has a small front bar and a dining area to the rear. Evening meals and Sunday lunch are offered. ✿≠◑𝍫⛴

PORT TALBOT

Lord Caradoc ⊘
69-73 Station Road, SA16 1BN
☼ 10-11.30; 12-10.30 Sun
☎ (01639) 896007
Draught Bass; Brains SA; Theakston Best Bitter; guest beers Ⓗ

Spacious, open-plan pub with an L-shaped bar situated in the centre of Port Talbot, about two minutes' walk from the train station. There are usually four mainstream beers available all the time and two guest ales – these may include Greene King Abbot, Hop Back Summer Lightning or Worthington's 1744. This typical Wetherspoon's pub is quiet (with the 'no music' policy) and offers a separate dining area, beer garden and disabled facilities. Q✿◑&≠(Parkway)✂

QUAKERS YARD

Glan Taff
Cardiff Road, CF46 5AK
(on A4054 between Abercynon and Treharris)
☼ 12-4, 7-11; 12-4, 7-10.30 Sun
☎ (01443) 410822
Courage Best Bitter, Directors; guest beers Ⓗ

Comfortable inn displaying a large collection of water jugs, boxing memorabilia and photographs of local and historic interest. This well-appointed pub enjoys a warm and friendly atmosphere on the side of the River Taff and close to the Taff Trail. Walkers and cyclists break their journey here for refreshments, to sample the beer and the good food (no meals Sun eve). This is a long-standing Guide entry and well worth a visit. Q✿◑P

REYNOLDSTON (GOWER)

King Arthur Hotel
Higher Green, SA3 1AD
☼ 12-11; 12-10.30 Sun
☎ (01792) 390775
Draught Bass; Felinfoel Double Dragon; Worthington's Bitter Ⓗ

Imposing pub and hotel/restaurant in a semi-idyllic setting on a large village green. Locals and tourists flock here during the holiday period and it can be very busy on summer weekends. The pub is named after Arthur's Stone, an ancient monument on nearby Cefn Bryn hill. The hotel is in a pleasant spot in the middle of the Gower Peninsula and has a large outdoor drinking area. Meals are served in all bars, the family room and outside. It is reputedly haunted by two ghosts. ⚅Qゟ✿≠◑🗗𝍫♣P

RHYMNEY

Farmers Arms ⊘
Brewery Row, NP22 5EZ
☼ 12-11; 12-10.30 Sun
☎ (01685) 840257
Brains Bitter; Marston's Pedigree; guest beers Ⓗ

Comfortable and friendly pub with a separate dining area. Once a farmhouse, it was taken over by the former Rhymney Brewery to slake the thirst of the local iron workers and miners. The current furnishings and bric-à-brac reflect the pub's history – the photographs of the old brewery are particularly interesting.
⊛◑⇌♣P

RISCA

Commercial
Commercial Street, Pontyminster, NP11 6BA (on B4591)
☼ 11-11; 12-10.30 Sun
☎ (01633) 612608
Beer range varies Ⓗ
Large, bustling pub at the southern end of Risca. The single bar is divided into two distinct areas. The public bar offers darts, a pool table and fruit machines, while the more comfortable lounge is a quieter haven. Of the two ales usually available, one is often a stout. ⊛♣

Fox & Hounds
Park Road, NP11 6PW (adjacent to park)
☼ 11-11; 12-10.30 Sun
☎ (01633) 612937
Beer range varies Ⓗ
Busy village local just off the main road, with fine views over the local park. The single bar has a pool table at one end and a large TV screen at the other to keep sports fans happy. Beers tend to be from the smaller craft breweries and a menu displays forthcoming attractions. ⊛◑♣P

ST BRIDE'S MAJOR

Farmers Arms
Wick Road, CF32 0SE
☼ 12-3, 6-11; 12-10.30 Sun
☎ (01656) 880224
Courage Best Bitter; Usher's Best Bitter, Founders Ale, seasonal beers Ⓗ
Locally known as the Pub on the Pond which becomes obvious when you visit. A popular pub and restaurant where you can expect good beer and food with a friendly welcome, booking is advisable for the restaurant, especially at weekends. The pub is decorated in traditional style, with plenty of china, glass jugs and paintings. Tourists, passing trade and regulars ensure that this pub remains a lively local. If you visit the pond be careful, the swans can be quite vicious when they have cygnets. ⩜Q⊛◑P

ST HILARY

Bush Inn
CP7 7AD (off A48, E of Cowbridge)
☼ 11.30-11; 12-10.30 Sun
☎ (01446) 772745
Draught Bass; Greene King Old Speckled Hen; Ⓖ **Hancock's HB** Ⓗ
Splendid, 400-year-old thatched inn, a focal point in this attractive village. The small bar has larger rooms opening off to either side, the restaurant is to the right. In addition, there is a pleasant outside drinking area. A display of hops around the fireplace makes for a cosy winter atmosphere when the fire is lit. Please ask what beers are on, as the pump clips do not always show the current

beers on gravity. Well known for its good food – no meals are served on Sunday evening. Westons Old Rosie cider is stocked.
⩜Q⊛◑⊟♣P

SKETTY

Vivian ✅
6 Gower Road, SA2 9BZ
☼ 12-11; 12-10.30 Sun
☎ (01792) 516194
Brains Buckley's Best Bitter, SA, Rev James Ⓗ
Long-standing Guide entry situated on Sketty Cross. A Brains managed house, it has a one-bar layout but with a distinctive back area housing a large-screen TV for sport. The decor is dominated by wood and the walls are adorned with a mixture of modern art and pictures of old Swansea, it retains some stained glass windows. There is a relaxed atmosphere with piped music. Enjoy a pint in the pretty, walled garden on a sunny day. Lunches are served daily and evening meals Monday–Friday, 6–8. ⊛◑&

SKEWEN

Crown
216 New Road, SA10 6EW
☼ 12-11; 12-10.30 Sun
☎ (01792) 411270
Brains Dark, Bitter, SA Ⓗ
This cheery pub with traditional decor is in the centre of the village on the main road. It has a central bar separating two drinking areas. A big-screen TV shows major sporting events. There is seating outside and a snooker room upstairs. This pub offers the best range of Brains beer in the area and is well worth a visit. ⊛⊟&⇌♣⅄

SWANSEA

Brunswick Inn
3 Duke Street, SA1 4HS
☼ 12-11; 12-10.30 Sun
☎ (01792) 456676
Greenalls Bitter; Swansea Deep Slade Dark; Ⓗ **guest beers** Ⓖ
Long-established pub on the fringe of the city centre, it is now a Scottish Courage pub. Plenty of woodwork and many rural pictures provide a cosy atmosphere. Subdued piped music is played. A quiz is held on Monday and live music is staged twice a month. Guest beers are served straight from the barrel. Popular for food – especially lunches – evening meals are provided Monday–Saturday, 6–8.30. This is a regular outlet for the Swansea Brewing Company. ◑♣

Eli Jenkins Ale House
24 Oxford Street, SA1 3AQ
☼ 11-11; 12-10.30 Sun
☎ (01792) 630961
Badger Tanglefoot; Draught Bass; Worthington's Bitter; guest beer Ⓗ
Named after a character in Under Milkwood by Dylan Thomas, this is a large, modern, city-centre pub. Wooden alcoves and niches feature throughout and the walls are adorned with memorabilia and some references to Dylan Thomas. The guest beer is changed frequently. Popular with lunchtime diners, meals are served 11.30–7 Monday–Saturday and 12–3.30 on Sunday.

Quieter in the evenings, piped music is played, creating a relaxed atmosphere. ◑▷&

Westbourne Hotel
1 Bryn-y-mor Road, SA1 4JQ
✪ 12-2.30, 5.30-11; 12-11 Fri & Sat; 12-2.30, 7-10.30 Sun
☎ (01792) 476637
Draught Bass; Hancock's HB; guest beer Ⓗ
Comfortable Enterprise Inn house with an internal layout that manages to retain two separate areas (lounge and bar), and has a dartboard. The TV in the bar shows sport. The guest beer changes at least weekly and the pub boasts over 400 guests over the last eight years. Not surprisingly, it is a long-standing Guide entry, it lies 10 minutes' walk from the city centre and is handy for both rugby and football grounds. Meals are served every lunchtime and Monday–Friday evenings, 6–8. ❀◑▷&♣

THREE CROSSES

Poundffald Inn
SA4 3PB (in village centre)
✪ 12-11; 12-10.30 Sun
☎ (01792) 873428
Brains SA; Greene King Abbot, Old Speckled Hen; Marston's Pedigree; Worthington's Bitter; guest beer Ⓗ
Much-visited village local with a traditional public bar warmed by a homely fire in winter. It was awarded Real Fire Pub of the Year 2001. Note the interesting collection of horse bits and other rural implements. The name Poundffald refers to the old circular animal pound that was incorporated into the lounge. The 'ffald' half of the name is the Welsh word for pound and so we have the name in both languages together. The lounge is food-oriented and meals are offered all day. ⋓⪫❀◑▷⊟P

TREFOREST

Otley Arms
Forest Road, CF37 1SY
✪ 11-11; 12-10.30 Sun
☎ (01443) 402033 website: www.otleyltd.co.uk
Bullmastiff Gold; Cains Bitter; guest beers Ⓗ
Despite being close to the University of Glamorgan, the many distinct drinking areas in this large pub dilute the student influence and it retains its strong local following. Railway memorabilia and prints are on display but the main attractions are its lively atmosphere, keenly-priced beer and the multiple TVs which provide sports fans with a plethora of choice. ◑⇌♣P

TYLE GARW

Boar's Head Hotel
Coedcae Lane, CF72 9EZ (600 yds off A473)
✪ 12-11, 12-5, 7-10.30 Sun
☎ (01443) 225400
Brains Rev James; Ⓗ **guest beers** Ⓗ/Ⓖ
Built in 1875, to serve the local workers from the railway, iron ore mine, tin works and forge, now it has industrial units and new houses as neighbours, but retains an air of splendid isolation. Although a drinkers' pub, with a target of 200 beers a year, Sunday lunches and Wednesday night curries are popular. A place of character, with a welcome for all ages, it was local

CAMRA Pub of the Year 2003.
⋓❀◑▷⏃⇌ (Pontyclun) ♣☙P

WICK

Star
Ewenny Road, CF71 7QA
✪ 11-3 (not winter), 5-11; 12-10.30 Sun
☎ (01656) 890519
Hancock's HB; Shepherd Neame Spitfire; Young's Special Ⓗ
Alongside the main road through the village, this pub has a central bar with two separate rooms. The smaller one has a flagstone floor, TV and dartboard and is simply furnished. The larger lounge/dining area also has a stone floor. Special meals are based on seasonal events and main sporting occasions (no food on Sun eve). Barbecues feature in summer. The tasty home-cooked food has a growing reputation.
Q❀◑▷⊟&♣P

YNYSTAWE (SWANSEA)

Millers Arms
634 Clydach Road, SA6 5AX (next to school)
✪ 11.30-3, 6-11; 11.30-11 Sat; 12-3, 7-10.30 Sun
☎ (01792) 842614
Adnams Bitter; Taylor Landlord; Wells Bombardier Ⓗ
Welcoming roadside pub that is now a regular Guide entry. It is well known for its good food, served in the bar and adjoining restaurant. The beer list is unusual for the area and is proving popular with locals. Note the teapot collection on top of the bar. There is a car park at the rear of the pub, and for public transport users there is a frequent bus service from the city centre.
Q◑▷P⊁

YSTALYFERA

Wern Fawr Inn
47 Wern Road, SA9 2LX
✪ 7-11; 12.30-3, 7-11 Sun
☎ (01639) 843625
website: www.bryncelynbrewery.co.uk
Bryncelyn Buddy Marvellous, Cwrw Celyn, Oh Boy, Rave On, seasonal beers Ⓗ
From the outside this appears to be an ordinary valleys' pub, however, it is home to a multi-award winning brewery and collections of industrial and domestic curios. The pub name translates as Holly Hill and the landlord is a big Buddy Holly fan, hence the names of the home-brewed beers. There is a separate bar and lounge.
⋓❀⊟♣🏠

YSTRAD MYNACH

Royal Oak
Commercial Street, CF82 7DY
✪ 12-11; 12-10.30 Sun
☎ (01443) 862345
Draught Bass; guest beer Ⓗ
A warm welcome awaits visitors to this 'Brewers Tudor' style pub sited on a busy road junction. Famed for the quality of its Bass, the regularly-changing guest beer is of the same order. The public bar and lounge/dining areas are separate and both are invariably busy. An interesting selection of old photographs of the area is displayed. No food is served on Sunday evening.
◑▷⇌♣P

India Pale Ale

MANY MODERN BREWERS produce beers they call 'India Pale Ale' or IPA for short. Few have much in common with the great, revolutionary style of the early 19th century, though Marston's new Old Empire recalls a genuine Burton IPA.

The first English pale ales, which inspired even the lager pioneers of central Europe, were a product of the industrial revolution that enabled pale malt, cured over coke-fired ovens, to be made on a mass commercial scale.

Demand

The first pale beers coincided with a growing demand from India and other colonies for more refreshing beers than brown ales, porters and stouts. The first known brewer of pale ale was Hodgson in Bow, East London. Hodgson was based close to the East and West India Docks and sent his beer, at cheap rates, to India. When the great Burton brewers lost their lucrative trade in exported brown beers to the Baltic during the wars with France, they were encouraged by the powerful East India Company to emulate Hodgson and switch to pale ale production. Aided by the hard, salty waters of the Trent Valley, the likes of Allsopp and Bass quickly came to dominate an export trade with beers that were high in alcohol and massively hopped to help withstand three-month sea journeys in sailing ships.

In the early 1990s, Bass at Burton brewed a special IPA based on an 1850s recipe. It was 7.2% ABV and and had an astonishing bitterness level of 83 units. The recipe was made up of 90% pale malt and 10% brewing sugar. No dark malts were used and the finished beer was only fractionally darker than a Pilsner. The beer matured and improved for a year in cask. The 19th-century IPAs would have softened considerably and lost some of their bitterness during their sea journeys.

Export

IPA as an export style was driven out of the British colonies by the end of the 19th century by German brewers and their new golden lagers. The British brewers concentrated on the domestic market, but lowered both the strength and the hop rates to produce more acceptable pale ales. Pale ale was more expensive than mild ales and porters, and was promoted to the new, rising class of teachers and clerical workers who felt themselves a cut above the hoi-polloi and their brown beers.

The demand for pale ale was so enormous in the latter half of the 19th century that many London and provincial brewers opened second plants in Burton to avail themselves of the spring waters rich in gypsum and magnesium. But once scientists were able to evaluate water, it was possible to add salts to replicate Burton water without moving to the town. 'Burtonisation' of water led to IPA and pale ale being brewed throughout Britain: Edinburgh and Alloa became major brewers of the style.

Heavy taxation on beer in the 20th century and government imposition of lower levels of alcohol in World War One saw the rapid demise of true IPAs. Pale ale was also reduced in importance, becoming a bottled version of breweries' best bitters.

IPA lives on as a popular brand name and is also enthusiastically produced by many micro-brewers in the United States. But high levels of beer tax means we are unlikely to drink again true versions of a style that revolutionised brewing practice in the 19th century.

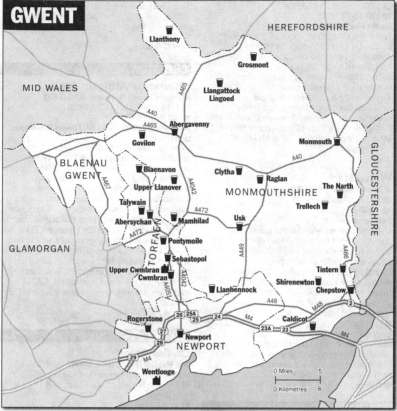

GWENT

HEREFORDSHIRE

MID WALES

Llanthony

Grosmont

Llangattock
Lingoed

Abergavenny

Govilon

Monmouth

BLAENAU
GWENT

Blaenavon

Clytha

Raglan

Upper Llanover

MONMOUTHSHIRE

The Narth

Talywain

A472

Trellech

Abersychan

Mamhilad

Usk

Pontymoile

GLAMORGAN

TORFAEN

Sebastopol

Upper Cwmbran
Cwmbran

Tintern

Shirenewton

Llanhennock

Chepstow

Rogerstone

26 25A
25

24

Caldicot

27

23A 23

28

Newport

NEWPORT

M4

29

Wentlooge

0 Miles   5

0 Kilometres   8

GLOUCESTERSHIRE

Authority areas covered: Blaenau Gwent UA, Monmouthshire UA, Newport UA, Torfaen UA

ABERGAVENNY

Coliseum ✓
Lion Street, NP7 5PE (off High St)
⌚ 11-11; 12-10.30 Sun
☎ (01873) 736960
Draught Bass; Brains Arms Park, SA; Greene King Abbot; Shepherd Neame Spitfire; Theakston Best Bitter; guest beers Ⓗ
Large pub converted from a former cinema.
A flight of stairs (chairlift assistance available for disabled) leads up to a light, open-plan bar with a high ceiling and skylights. There are several distinct areas, some no-smoking, with one set aside for families during the day. The walls feature locally commissioned work depicting local history, and copies of old film posters are a reminder of the pub's past. Interesting guest ales appear as well as those listed. Q ⓓ ♿ ✸

King's Head
60 Cross Street, NP7 5EU
⌚ 10.30 (10 Tue & Fri)-3, 7-11; 10.30-11 Sat;
12-3, 7-10.30 Sun
☎ (01873) 853575
Wells Bombardier; guest beer Ⓗ
Adjacent to the town hall and market, this popular bar attracts a good mix of customers, with early opening on Tuesday and Friday to cater for market folk. Behind the old etched windows lies a pleasantly decorated interior with wooden beams and a large fireplace. There is live music on Friday evening, and the background music

tends to be louder at weekends, making for a lively but friendly atmosphere. Lunches are served Monday–Saturday. Wells Bombardier arrived as a visitor and stayed!
🚪 ⓓ ♣

Somerset Arms
Victoria Street, NP7 5DT (at Merthyr Rd jct)
⌚ 12-11; 12-10.30 Sun
☎ (01873) 852158
Worthington's Bitter; guest beer Ⓗ
The perfect example of a traditional town pub, with separate public bar and lounge, each with its own individual feel. The bar, with sports TV and enthusiastic dart teams, is cosy, while the quieter lounge is the place for a chat, or some delicious home-cooked food. Colourful hanging baskets and a sheltered patio complete the picture. Many guests like to extend their visit by staying in the good value en-suite accommodation. Sunday night sees a popular quiz – the humour of the landlord adds to the fun. All in all a lively place that will not disappoint.
🛏 🚪 ⓓ ♣ ♠

ABERSYCHAN

Buck
8 Station Street, NP4 8PH

INDEPENDENT BREWERIES

Cwmbran Upper Cwmbran
Warcop Wentlooge

✪ 1 (12 Sat)-11; 12-10.30 Sun
☎ (01495) 772152
Greene King Abbot Ⓗ
From the main Pontypool to Blaenafon road, you enter an unspoilt village local. Although only one cask ale is sold, this is considered to be the best in the area. Behind the main bar is a games room with a skittle alley and pool table. No meals are served and no children are admitted. Regulars have contributed to a fine collection of keyrings displayed behind the bar. This is the kind of pub where you will be made very welcome by both landlord and customers.
✿♣

White Hart
2 Broad Street, NP4 7BQ
✪ 12-11; 12-10.30 Sun
☎ (01495) 772378
Beer range varies Ⓗ
Unspoilt village pub on the main road, the cosy front bar features an old serving hatch to the corridor which leads to a comfortable lounge with pool table. Home of the Torfaen Music Society, it features live bands each Friday, and an 'open mike' session on Sunday afternoon in the downstairs stable bar. Apparently the Chartists stored their gunpowder in this historic pub, en route to their fatal encounter in Newport in 1839. There is a skittle alley behind the lounge. The three handpumps serve a changing range of interesting guest ales. In summer a barrel of real cider will appear on the bar.
✿⊕♣♨

BLAENAVON

Pottery
Llanover Road, NP4 9HT
(off A4043 & Coed Road, turn right)
✪ 12-3 (not Mon or Tue), 6.30 (not Mon; 7 Tue)-11, 12-11 Fri & Sat; 12-10.30 Sun
☎ (01495) 790395
Brains Bitter; guest beer Ⓗ
Pleasant pub in a residential area, the front room is spacious and popular with diners who tuck in appreciatively to the food, which includes home-made fare. The split-level public bar is cosy; the higher level at the rear is occupied by a pool table and offers splendid mountain views. Once called the Oak, the pub takes its present name from the former Blaenavon blue pottery. Handy refreshment stop if visiting the local World Heritage sites.
✿⊕⊕♿♣P

CALDICOT

Cross
1 Newport Road, NP26 4BG
✪ 11-11; 12-10.30 Sun
☎ (01291) 420692
Courage Best Bitter; guest beer Ⓗ
Basic, but very popular, the Cross stands at the crossroads in the centre of the old part of the village. It has a strong local trade and can be very busy at weekends. The lounge has a central fireplace and on Thursday evening a raised area hosts live music acts. The smaller bar is oriented towards games – especially pool and darts.

The guest beer tends to be ABV 5%, or above, and will often prove an interesting choice for the area. Cider is served in summer.
♨✿⊕♣♨P

CHEPSTOW

Chepstow Athletic Club
Mathern Road, Bulwark, NP16 5JT
✪ 7 (12 Sat)-11; 12-2.30, 7-10.30 Sun
☎ (01291) 622126
Boddingtons Bitter; Brains SA; Flowers IPA, Original; guest beers Ⓗ
Whether the planned external refurbishment makes this 1960s block attractive, remains to be seen. Once inside, however, you will find a welcoming, friendly bar. To the rear is a patio overlooking the cricket field. Families are welcome in the bar and there is a function room upstairs. Apart from the regular beers, two guests are frequently changed. Look out for the unusual timepieces behind the bar. Two TV screens are usually showing live sport. A popular club, which, bearing in mind its friendly atmosphere and user-friendly prices, is not surprising. CAMRA members are welcome – show your card at the bar.
✿≷♣P

CLYTHA

Clytha Arms
Old Raglan Road, NP7 9BW
(on B4598, between Raglan and Abergavenny)
✪ 12-3 (not Mon), 6-11; 12-11 Sat; 12-4, 7-10.30 Sun
☎ (01873) 840206
website: www.lineone.net/~one.bev
Draught Bass; Hook Norton Best Bitter; guest beers Ⓗ
This superb pub is a legend in its own lifetime; several times Gwent CAMRA Pub of the Year and known over a wide area for food and accommodation as well as its beers, perry and cider. The individual styles of the bar and lounge, together with extensive grounds, cater for all tastes. Separate festivals for Welsh beers and ciders have become features. This free house really is a family business – the wife and husband have now been joined by their eldest daughter, all working hard to make this such a delightful place – enjoy it.
♨Q✿⊨⊕⊕♿♣P⊟

CWMBRAN

Commodore Hotel
Mill Lane, Llanyravon, NP44 8SH
(off Llanfrechfa Way, behind Crow's Nest pub))
✪ 12-3 (not Sat), 6.30-11 (Mary O'Brien's 3-11); 12-11 Fri & Sat); 7-10.30 (Mary O'Brien's 12-10.30) Sun
☎ (01633) 484091
Brains Arms Park; Cwmbran Double Hop, Crow Valley Bitter; guest beers Ⓗ
Comfortably furnished residential hotel set in wooded surroundings. Cask ales from independent breweries are sold in the soothing environment of Pillinger's lounge, with its dark wood and matching decor. This room leads on to a patio. Tasty bar meals can be had, or there is the popular Willows restaurant with a range of dishes to suit all tastes. Mary O'Brien's is a traditional

style of bar with more real ale and occasional entertainment. It is available for private functions. ✿🛏◑◗⊟♣P

Mount Pleasant
Wesley Street, NP44 3LX
✪ 4 (12 Sat)-11; 12-3, 7-10.30 Sun
☎ (01633) 484289
Brains SA; Greene King Abbot; guest beers Ⓗ
Cosy pub in the heart of the village that gave its name to the post-war new town. Haunt of local witches (look above the serving counter), it offers an alternative kind of spiritual comfort amid what could be called the ecclesiastical centre of Cwmbran, as it lies close to several churches and chapels. The interior is homely with pleasant decor. The split-level lounge attracts diners; the 'early bird' menu (4–7pm) is popular. ✿◑◗⊟♣P

GOVILON

Bridgend Inn ✓
Church Lane, NP7 9RP
✪ 12-4, 7-11; 12-4, 7-10.30 Sun
☎ (01873) 830177
Adnams Bitter; Draught Bass; Fuller's London Pride; guest beer Ⓗ
This village pub, with separate bar and lounge, gets better and better. Friday is folk night, the music led by the landlord, friends and guests. He and his wife are proud to display their cask marque sign. Some rare guest beers also feature regularly. A new development is a performance area to support live music, with arts funding. The Bridgend certainly shows that it is possible to create a thriving village-based pub. ◑◗⊟♣P

GROSMONT

Angel Inn
Main Street, NP7 8TP
(off A465 at Llanfihangel Crucorney or Llangua)
✪ 12-3 (1 Thu), 5-11; 12-10.30 Sun
☎ (01981) 240646
Wye Valley Butty Bach; guest beers Ⓗ
Situated in the heart of the ancient village, this inn is part of a row of old whitewashed cottages next to the tiny 'town hall'. In medieval times this was a flourishing borough, reflected in its castle ruins and church. A recent CAMRA Gwent Pub of the Year, there is one long room separated by a large central chimney. Guest beers are often from Tomos Watkin – not common locally. Meals are served daily (except Tue). It is a classic village pub, fully in keeping with its surroundings and providing a focus now sadly missing from many villages. Q✿🛏◑♣♣

LLANGATTOCK LINGOED

Hunter's Moon Inn
NP7 8RR (turn off the B4521 Abergavenny-Ross old road at Llanvetherine) OS363201
✪ 12-3 (not winter Mon or Wed), 6-11; 12-4, 7-10.30 Sun
☎ (01873) 821499
website: www.hunters-moon-inn.co.uk
Beer range varies Ⓖ
Tiny pub situated a stone's throw from Offa's Dyke in a secluded village. Its origins date back to the 13th century. Constantly

changing beers, usually from a local independent brewer, are served direct from a cask on the back of the bar. Inside, the bar is stone-flagged with bare stone walls and a woodburner for cold days. There is a cosy restaurant featuring local produce. Outside, a deck acts as a suntrap overlooking the ancient church, and a beautiful wild garden surrounds a small waterfall and stream. Many walkers and cyclists seek out this charming pub; with the good quality accommodation it provides an excellent base. 🛏Q✿🛏◑◗P

LLANHENNOCK

Wheatsheaf
NP18 1LT
(1 mile along Caerleon-Usk road, turn right) OS353927
✪ 11-11 (Wed closes 3-5); 12-3, 7-10.30 Sun
☎ (01633) 420468
Draught Bass; Worthington's Bitter; guest beer Ⓗ
Unspoilt, traditional village local within easy reach of town, it boasts fine views of the surrounding countryside. It is worth spending time looking at the interesting memorabilia in the bar, or relax in the comfortable lounge. The guest beer is usually from a micro, often local. Some sort of activity is always being organised. Boules (petanque) is played all year round, by those hardy enough. 🛏✿◑◗♣P

LLANTHONY

Half Moon
NP7 7NN (6 miles off A465, at Llanfihangel Crucorney) OS286279
✪ Summer 12-3 (not Tue), 7 (6 Sat)-11; Winter 12-3 (Sat & Sun only), 7-11 Fri & Sat; 12-3, 7-10.30 Sun
☎ (01873) 890611
Bullmastiff Gold, Son of a Bitch; guest beer (summer) Ⓗ
Situated amid stunning vistas, close to Llanthony Abbey ruins, with the valley floor below and towering ridges on both sides, this is a rare outlet for Bullmastiff beers. Addlestones Cloudy cider is stocked. The bar features a stone-flagged floor, with a lounge that looks like a sitting room – which it is! Winter opening is only at weekends, so phone to check hours before setting off. The pub is on a lane, four miles from a main road. Once you've been to Llanthony you won't forget it – it really is beer with a view, you'll love it. 🛏Q🛌✿🛏◑◗▲♣●P✕

MAMHILAD

Star Inn
Old Abergavenny Road, Folly Lane, NP4 0JF
(off A4042(T))
✪ 11.30-3, 6-11; 11-11 Sat & summer; 12-3, 7-10.30 Sun
☎ (01495) 785319
Draught Bass; Hancock's HB; guest beers Ⓗ
Welcoming country inn providing a social hub for the scattered community it serves. It is equally popular with regulars and casual visitors from further afield who savour the intimate atmosphere, excellent home-cooked food, and well-kept beer. Occasional beer festivals are held and the guest ales are usually from independent breweries. The pub is a short stroll from the Monmouthshire & Brecon Canal, providing

a welcoming pit stop for walkers in need of refreshment. A holiday cottage is available to let. ⚲❀⇌◑ⓓP

Green Dragon
St Thomas' Square, NP25 5ES
✪ 11-11; 12-10.30 Sun
☎ (01600) 712561
Draught Bass; Hancock's HB; Marston's Bitter, Pedigree; guest beer Ⓗ
An old Hancock's Toastmaster sign welcomes you to this two-bar pub, set on the western side of town, past the 13th-century fortified Monnow bridge. Decorative prints and plaster mouldings feature in the bar and lounge. A good selection of home-cooked food is available. Live music is played on Wednesday and Friday night. A visit to the gents' is sure to raise a laugh as a collection of cartoons livens up the walls. ❀◑ ⊟⚐P

Old Nag's Head
Granville Street, NP25 3DP
(off St James Square – follow signs to leisure centre)
✪ 12-3, 6 (5 Fri)-11; 12-11 Sat; 12-10.30 Sun
☎ (01600) 713782
website: www.theoldnagshead@aol.com
Brains Rev James; Fuller's London Pride Ⓗ
Situated on the eastern edge of town and incorporating a round tower from the town's medieval defences, this multi-roomed pub is well worth visiting. From street level, steps lead into this predominantly 18th-century pub, with its unspoilt, traditional layout. The bar is to the right, and straight ahead are the other areas; a games room (with pool, crib and darts) and separate family room. ⚐❀◑ ⊟♣

Trekkers
The Narth, near Monmouth, NP25 4QG
(2 miles down road, signed in Trellech) OS525064
✪ 11.30-3.30, 6-11; closed Mon-Wed; 11-11 Sat; 12-10.30 Sun
☎ (01600) 860367
Greene King IPA, Ruddles County; guest beer (occasional) Ⓗ
This unusual log cabin pub is open-plan, a central fire divides the drinking and dining areas. A skittle alley doubles as a family room. In one corner is a splendid collection of teddy bears. With excellent views from the large garden, the pub is a fine base for Wye Valley walks, and a large assortment of local guide books are available. Children's swings are an added bonus. An accommodation chalet opened in the summer of 2003. The food is fresh and locally produced (book in advance). ⚲Q⚐❀⇌◑▲♣P

Godfrey Morgan ✔
158 Chepstow Road, NP9 8EG (1 mile from town centre)
✪ 11-11; 12-10.30 Sun
☎ (01633) 221928
Brains Dark, SA; Greene King Abbot; Theakston Best Bitter; Worthington's Bitter Ⓗ
One of three Wetherspoon's outlets in the city. This one is noted for the best quality

and range of cask ales. Formerly a cinema and then a bingo hall, it has revitalised the pub scene in an area of high population. It appears deceptively small from the front, but stretches inwards along a compact area before expanding out into a spacious room where the single bar is located. Typical local scenes and history adorn the walls. Although quiet by the Guide definition, this pub can be very noisy in the evening and at the weekend when it is very busy. Check out both the mild and the unusual house beer (Wyre Piddle Piddle in Maindee) that are usually available; very competitive prices. Q⚐◑♿❀

Lyceum Tavern
110-112 Malpas Road, NP20 5PL
(just off M4 jct 26 towards town centre)
✪ 12-11; 12-10.30 Sun
☎ (01633) 858636
Courage Best Bitter; Greene King Old Speckled Hen; Theakston Old Peculier (winter)**; guest beers** Ⓗ
Celebrating its golden jubilee as a pub (formerly two private houses), this impressive-looking building has a single U-shaped bar where the original two bars have been combined. There are also small separate areas to the rear of both sides of the bar plus a large upstairs function room. Live music is performed every Saturday on the stage area of the bar, while every Thursday the upstairs room hosts the Newport folk club. The patio drinking area at the front gets busy in summer. This is a friendly pub, popular with the locals. ❀◑♿⇌

Olde Murenger House
53 High Street, NP20 1GA
✪ 11-3, 5.30-11; 11-11 Fri & Sat; 7-10.30 Sun
☎ (01633) 263977 website: www.murenger.com
Samuel Smith OBB Ⓗ
The haven in Newport's super-pub ghetto, the Murenger has recently undergone a sympathetic refurbishment under owners, Sam Smith's. This timber building dates back to Tudor times and was originally built as the town house of local landowners, the Herberts. It later became a pub (the Fleur-de-Lys) before acquiring its present name in Victorian times. The name of the pub is unique and comes from the tax or murage levied for the upkeep of the town walls. Popular with all ages for the last 500 years. ⇌

Red Lion
47 Stow Hill, NP20 1JH
✪ 11-11; 12-10.30 Sun
☎ (01633) 264398
Draught Bass; Usher's Best Bitter; guest beer Ⓗ
One of the few remaining traditional street-corner locals in the city centre, it is handy for the main shopping attractions. Very much a sporting pub, it hosts local teams and all major events are shown on a large-screen TV. Two huge casks suspended from the ceiling dominate the single bar. Comfortable furnishings are provided in different areas. A refreshing pint awaits you after the short steep climb from the main shopping street. A small paved area serves as a garden. ⚲❀⇌♣

St Julian Inn
Caerleon Road, NP18 1QA
✪ 11.30-11; 12-10.30 Sun

☎ (01633) 243548
Courage Best Bitter; John Smith's Bitter; guest beers Ⓗ

Highly regarded pub, in a superb location, served by frequent bus services. It dominates a bend of the River Usk giving panoramic views of the rural outskirts of Newport, historic Caerleon with its Roman ruins, and small craft at their moorings. Attractively furnished, the cosy lounge is fitted out with wood panelling and fixtures from the old liner, Doric. This area links with a spacious balcony, the bar and games areas, and downstairs the skittle alley/function room. ❀❶▷♣P

Tom Toya Lewis
108-112 Commercial Street, NP20 1LW
✪ 11-11; 12-10.30 Sun
☎ (01633) 245030
Brains SA; Greene King Abbot; Theakston Best Bitter; guest beers Ⓗ

The newest of three Wetherspoon's outlets in the city which has quickly established itself at the top end of the scale. Very popular in the day with shoppers and local office workers alike, when the meals are as much an attraction as the quality real ales. An excellent range of guest beers from all over the UK can be enjoyed. This huge split-level pub, with many distinct drinking areas, was converted from former retail outlets. Well worth the 15-minute walk from the railway station.
Q≿❀❶▷ঙ⅄

Horse & Jockey
Usk Road, NP4 0JB (off A4042(T))
✪ 12-11; 12-10.30 Sun
☎ (01495) 762721
Adnams Broadside; Greene King Abbot or Old Speckled Hen Ⓗ

Attractive 15th-century coaching inn with a long, low frontage and thatched roof. Once a favourite watering-hole for farmers en route to/from Pontypool market, it is now a hugely popular eating house although there is some space for drinkers near the bar. The menu is well-balanced and appetising; booking is advisable as it can get very busy, particularly at weekends. The beer garden at the rear is a peaceful spot to enjoy the tranquil countryside.
❀❶▷P⅄

Ship Inn
High Street, NP15 2DY
✪ 11 (12 Mon)-11; 12-10.30 Sun
☎ (01291) 690635
Adnams Bitter; guest beers Ⓗ

A former coach house, complete with preservation order, this old inn is approached via a small cobbled courtyard containing a disused water pump. To the right of the entrance is the main bar, to the left a smaller lounge. Running off the lounge is a separate dining room, a recent conversion from a lumber room. There is seating in the courtyard and a beer garden is planned. The guest beers are often from micro-breweries. The Newport–Monmouth and Monmouth–Abergavenny buses stop outside (no evening service). ▲❀❶▷◲♣

Tredegar Arms
57 Cefn Road, NP10 9AQ
✪ 12-3, 5.30-11; 11-11 Thu-Sat; 12-4, 7-10.30 Sun
☎ (01633) 664999
Draught Bass; Courage Best Bitter; guest beer Ⓗ

With a number of different rooms, this pub offers plenty of scope. A side entrance leads to a small, traditional pub bar, lounge and separate dining room. Down a couple of steps from here you will find the quiet snug, which in turn leads to a small, enclosed garden. The pub is popular with locals and is full of character with original flagstones and ceiling beams. It is close to many local attractions, so is handily placed to refresh visitors. A good, varied menu is available, with ample choice. Q≿❀❶▷◲P

Sebastopol Social Club
Wern Road, NP4 5DU (on jct with Austin Rd)
✪ 12-11; 12-3, 7-10.30 Sun
Tomos Watkin Whoosh; guest beers Ⓗ

South & Mid Wales CAMRA Club of the Year 2002, a cask ale mecca combining established club traditions with the attitude of a go-ahead free house. Most activity centres on the main bar where an impressive array of pump clips adorns the servery. Addlestones Cloudy cider is served. There is also a cosy smaller room, downstairs skittle alley (venue of occasional beer festivals) and upstairs function room – HQ of Torfaen Jazz Society, who give public performances on a Friday evening. CAMRA members and holders of this Guide are welcome. ❀❶♣♠P

Carpenters Arms
Usk Road, Mynydd Bach, NP16 6BU
(on B4235) OS485943
✪ 12-2.30; 6-11; 12-3, 7-10.30 Sun
☎ (01291) 641231
website: www.chepstow.co.uk/adverts/carps
Draught Bass; Flowers IPA; Fuller's London Pride; Wadworth 6X; guest beer Ⓗ

400-year-old hostelry which expanded over the years to take in the adjoining blacksmith's and carpenter's shop, creating the rambling seven-roomed building of today. Flagstone floors, low beams, log fires and many items that the landlord refers to as his 'clutter' create a homely atmosphere inside. The whitewashed exterior is even more attractive in summer when the hanging baskets are a blaze of colour. Good home-cooked food (not served Sun eve) and a choice of over 50 malt whiskies complete the picture for an excellent and popular pub. ▲Q≿❀❶▷♣P⅄

Tredegar Arms
The Square, NP16 6RQ
✪ 12-3, 6-11; 12-11 Sat; 12-4, 7-10.30 Sun
☎ (01291) 641274
Hancock's HB; Otter Bitter; guest beer Ⓗ

Popular, congenial pub in the heart of the village, next to the church. The public bar, which is decorated with old farming equipment and photographs, is the preferred choice of locals. The lounge, with its exposed stone walls, is favoured by diners – the pub enjoys a good reputation for its food. In summer, the whitewashed façade is enhanced by a spectacular floral display. ♨Q✿♿🚫🍴🐾P

TALYWAIN

Globe Inn
Commercial Road, NP4 7JH
(1½ miles along road from Abersychan)
☼ 7 (12 Sat)-11; 12-10.30 Sun
☎ (01495) 772053
Brains Bitter, Buckley's Best Bitter; guest beers Ⓗ
With its distinctive sign above the door, this is a traditional two-roomed local with strong community ties. The owners take great pride in their beers, and extend a warm welcome to all. Guest ales include those from micro-breweries when available. The pub is popular with walkers in the area, with good views across the neighbouring 'British' mountain. Live entertainment is staged on Saturday evening. Look out for the photographs in the lounge of the old railways that once served the area. The landlord will be pleased to give details! Real cider (Thatchers) is served in summer. Darts, crib and dominoes are played. ♨🍴🐾👆

TINTERN

Cherry Tree
Forge Road, NP16 6TH
(off A466 at Royal George Hotel) OS526001
☼ 12-11 (supper licence until midnight); 12-10.30 Sun
☎ (01291) 689292 website: www.thecherry.co.uk
Cottage Golden Arrow; Hancock's HB; Wye Valley Butty Bach; guest beer Ⓖ
This is the only Welsh pub to feature in every edition of this Guide. Now extended from the original single room, which has been retained for drinkers, there is now a new lounge and restaurant. Other recent innovations include four B&B rooms and a cooling system for the gravity dispensed ales. Thatchers and Bulmers cider are stocked. The food is organic and locally sourced. Note the old Hancock's Toastmaster pub sign. ♨Q✿🍴🚫🐾👆P

Wye Valley Hotel
NP16 6SQ (on A466)
☼ 11-3, 6-11; 12-3, 7-10.30 Sun
☎ (01291) 689441 website: www.wyevalleyhotel.co.uk
Wye Valley Bitter, Butty Bach Ⓗ
Smart hotel on the main road at the north end of this favoured tourist destination. It was originally built in 1835 as an ale house called the Carpenters Arms; it was extended and renamed in 1909. Non-residents are welcome in the bar, note the large bottle collection. Outdoor drinking is possible on the forecourt. The hotel offers a high standard of accommodation and excellent food, and is popular for short breaks – the surrounding countryside is perfect for walking holidays. ✿🚫🍴P

TRELLECH

Lion Inn
NP25 4PA (on B4293, Chepstow-Monmouth road)
☼ 12-3, 6 (7 Mon; 6.30 Sat)-11; 12-3 (closed eve) Sun
☎ (01600) 860322
Beer range varies Ⓗ
Situated in the ancient village of Trellech,

this is a thriving village pub. It is open-plan, with a raised dining area to the left and a public bar to the right. One Bath ale and two or three guests are stocked. In the last year, real cider, usually from small local producers, has been on offer. In 2003 a separate accommodation chalet was added, converted from a barn, this can be either self-catering or full board. The food can be highly exotic and Hungarian dishes are a speciality. ♨✿🚫🍴🐾P

UPPER LLANOVER

Goose & Cuckoo
NP7 9ER (2 miles off A4042, at Llanover)
OS292073
☼ 11.30-3, 7-11; 11-11 Fri & Sat; closed Mon;
12-10.30 Sun
☎ (01873) 880277
website: www.gooseandcuckoo.fsnet.co.uk
Bullmastiff Gold; guest beers Ⓗ
A remote pub at the end of a long, narrow lane – but what a joy to discover. The views open up for miles from the bar and, on warm days, the newly-developed garden, with its sheep, goats, ducks and other animals, offers a stunning sight. Not surprisingly, this is a popular pub with walkers – and if you feel in need of a chaser, to go with your pint, there is a choice of 64 single malts. The pub itself is basically a single room that pays scant regard to modernity. Next to the bar is a large woodburner for winter heat, while a brighter alcove on the other side provides a more modern feel. A real gem – make the effort to find it. ♨Q✿🚫🍴🐾P🚫

USK

King's Head Hotel
18 Old Market Street, NP15 1AL
☼ 11-11; 12-10.30 Sun
☎ (01291) 672963
Brains Rev James; Fuller's London Pride; Taylor Landlord Ⓗ
Popular residential hotel and free house in a quiet location. On entry a function room is to the right, but turn left into the main bar with a great fireplace as a focal point. The decor is dark and the room pleasantly cluttered with bric-à-brac gathered over the years, making for a relaxing environment. A collection of photos depicts the landlord's angling prowess and, needless to say, fish features on a well-balanced menu that attracts hungry diners.
♨🚫🍴🐾P

Nag's Head Inn ⊘
Twyn Square, NP15 1BH
☼ 11-3, 5.30-11; 12-3, 6.30-10.30 Sun
☎ (01291) 672820
Brains Buckley's Best Bitter, SA, Rev James Ⓗ
Charming 500-year-old hostelry with a beamed front room and snug, both having a cosy, intimate feel. The interior is adorned with pictures, lamps and a host of other interesting artefacts. The rear 'tack room' is used by families (when it is no-smoking) and displays a range of equine tack donated by the owners of Usk Castle. With the proud boast of its superb food and beer, mostly sourced locally, this old inn is a beacon of all-round quality.
Q🐾✿🍴🚫

MID WALES

NORTH-EAST WALES

NORTH-WEST WALES

Llanrhaeadr-ym-Mochnant
B4396
A458   A495
A470   Welshpool
Llanfair Caereinion   A490
Machynlleth   A470   Berriew
Montgomery
A489   Newtown
Llanidloes   A489
SHROPS
WEST WALES   A483
A470
Rhayader   A44
A483   Llandrindod Wells   Penybont   A44
A470
Llanafan Fawr   Howey
Hundred House
Aberedw   HEREFORDS
A470   A438
Pentre-bach
A40   Brecon
A4067   Llangorse
Talybont-on-Usk   GWENT
Penycae   Crickhowell   A40
Abercrave
0 Miles   10
GLAMORGAN   0 Kilometres   16

ABERCRAVE

Copper Beech Inn
133 Heol Tawe, SA9 1XS
(just off the main Swansea-Brecon road, A4067)
⊙ 11-11; 12-10.30 Sun
☎ (01639) 730269
Beer range varies Ⓗ
Large single-bar, village pub with partitions, separate dining area and a games room. Up to five real ales are available including many from micro-breweries. It holds occasional beer festivals, regular theme nights and a music club meets in the upstairs lounge every month. Budget lunchtime specials are served Monday–Friday and evening meals daily until 9pm. Families with children are welcome. Accommodation is two-star inn grade. Close to Brecon Beacons National Park. ⚏✿⌂◑P

ABEREDW

Seven Stars
LD2 3UW (on minor road off B4567, Builth Wells-Erwood)
⊙ 12-2.30 (may vary winter), 6.30-11; 12-3, 6-10.30 Sun
☎ (01982) 560494
Beer range varies Ⓗ
Much of the original character of the pub was retained during the conversion,

following years of neglect. The open stonework, flagstone floors and exposed beams combine with an open fire to give a comforting ambience. The Llywellyn bar (site of an old smithy) is named after the last native Prince of Wales. Legend has it that his horse was shod with reversed shoes by the smith to enable him to escape his pursuers. This ruse, if true, was unsuccessful because Llywellyn was killed at nearby Cilmeri. The pub has a good reputation for food and was 1997 regional CAMRA Pub of the Year. Post Office facilities are available on Thursday only, 2–8pm. The restaurant is open 6.30–9.30pm (not Mon in winter). ⚏Q⌂◑&♣

BERRIEW

Lion Hotel & Restaurant
SY21 8PQ (off A483)
⊙ 12-3, 5.45-11; 12-10.30 Sun
☎ (01686) 640452
Beer range varies Ⓗ
This village hotel has a small wooden beamed public bar with a friendly atmosphere. This compact area is dominated by a large stone inglenook and an unusual stove. The lounge bar is spacious and ideal for a relaxing drink. The entrances to the lounge and public bars are on different sides of the hotel. ⚏✿⌂◑

Talbot Hotel
SY21 8AH (off A483)
⊙ 4.30-11; 11-11 Sat & summer; 12-10.30 Sun
☎ (01686) 640881
Beer range varies Ⓗ
Delightful village local which draws a wide range of customers. A pool table and darts section are provided in the public bar. The bar area is beamed and offers a congenial atmosphere in which to enjoy your pint. Settees grace the small lounge area which leads to the restaurant. Fine, home-cooked meals are available Tuesday–Sunday and lunchtimes at the weekend. ⚏✿⌂◑♣

BRECON

Bull's Head
86 The Struet, LD3 7LS
(under the cathedral on the banks of River Honddu)
⊙ 12-2.30, 7-11; 12-3, 7-10.30 Sun
☎ (01874) 622044
Beer range varies Ⓗ
Well-respected and popular pub, the two bars actually provide three distinct drinking areas. The beer range varies from locally-produced Breconshire beers to occasional ales from Europe. A good selection of bottled beers is always available, including some that are vegetarian/vegan. Addlestones cider is served. Well worth visiting while in town, and take a look at the monthly magazine the pub publishes. ⌂◑⊟♠

Old Boar's Head
14 Ship Street, LD3 9AL (by bridge over River Usk)
⊙ 12-11 (will extend in summer); 12-10.30 Sun
☎ (01874) 622856

INDEPENDENT BREWERY
Breconshire Brecon

Breconshire WPA, Golden Valley, Ramblers Ruin; Fuller's London Pride; guest beers ⓗ

This is the tap for the Breconshire Brewery. New management and extensive redevelopment of the back bar look set to increase the popularity of this already much-used town-centre pub. The wood-panelled locals' bar to the front of the pub, has many photographs of floods in Brecon, while the beer garden at the rear overlooks the River Usk with views up into the Beacons. Opening hours may be extended in the summer, and food may also then be available. ♨❀☎⊞♣P

CRICKHOWELL

Bear Hotel
High Street, NP8 1BW
🕓 11-3, 6-11; 12-3, 7-10.30 Sun
☎ (01873) 810408 website: www.bearhotel.co.uk
Draught Bass; Brains Rev James; Greene King Old Speckled Hen; Hancock's HB ⓗ

Originally a 15th-century coaching inn, now a multi-award-winning hotel set in the Brecon Beacons National Park. A varied and inventive menu is available. The characterful, beamed bar area features a welcoming log fire in the winter months. Crickhowell is on the Brecon to Abergavenny bus route (no eve service) and is an ideal base for exploring the Black Mountains. ♨Q⌂☎❀⊲◑⊟P

HOWEY

Laughing Dog ⊘
LD1 5PT
🕓 12-2.30 (not Tue), 6.30-11; 12-3, 7-10.30 Sun
☎ (01597) 822406
website: www.thelaughingdog.ukpub.net
Brains Bitter; guest beers ⓗ

19th-century (1872) pub in an 18th-century (1750) building. The area occupied by the lounge/dining room/function room was the adjoining smithy. The no-nonsense, airy bar has sensible furniture and a collection of comic books for the younger visitor. There is a separate games room. A vigorous guest ale policy exists. The large stone outside the pub was used when visitors arrived on horseback, and was used for dismounting and remounting. ♨Q⌂☎❀◑⊟♣

HUNDRED HOUSE

Hundred House Inn
LD1 5RD
🕓 11-11 (Easter to late autumn); 12-10.30 Sun
☎ (01982) 570231
Wood Shropshire Lad; Worthington's Bitter; guest beers ⓗ

Former drovers' inn set in a prominent roadside position with fine views of the surrounding uplands. The Hundred was an ancient Anglo-Saxon administrative subdivision of a shire which continued sporadically to the 19th century; the inn was first listed as such in 1823. A more detailed explanation of a Hundred is on display in the cosy bar which has a tiled floor and a huge number of beer clips on display. The public bar and lounge retain original fireplaces. The games room and no-smoking restaurants (supper licence) are later additions. ♨Q❀⊲◑⊟&♣Å♣P

LLANAFAN FAWR

Red Lion
LD2 3PW
🕓 12-2 (closed Jan-Mar), 6-11; 12-2; 6-10.30 Sun
☎ (01597) 860204
Worthington's Bitter; guest beers ⓗ

Dating from 1189, the inn was used by Giraldus Cambrensis (the Welsh churchman, historian and patriot) and is the oldest in the Powys, and probably the oldest in Wales. The huge cruck beams, which are still visible, are thought to have been in place for over 500 years, and are secondhand! The shaped stones around the fireplace and the large floor slates may have come from the church opposite, which has a 2,000-year-old yew tree in its churchyard (certificate of authentication in the pub). The pub hosts the world amateur tippet championships and offers an excellent, varied menu. An informative booklet is available in the pub. ♨Q❀☎⊲◑⊟&Å♣P✂

LLANDRINDOD WELLS

Llanerch 16th-Century Inn
Llanerch Lane, LD1 6BG
(by police station, opp. railway station)
🕓 11.30-2.30, 6-11; 11.30-11 Fri & Sat; 12-10.30 Sun
☎ (01597) 822086
Marston's Bitter; guest beers ⓗ

Originally Llanerchderion – 'resting place by the glade for coaches' – the inn still retains many of its original features such as a Jacobean staircase and an inglenook in the bar, and is many-roomed with a split-level interior. The lounge is no-smoking until 8pm. It has easy access to the railway station and town centre. The inn has its own drive, car park and cycle storage, but limited wheelchair access.
Q⌂☎❀◑&⊨♣P✂

LLANFAIR CAEREINION

Goat Hotel
High Street, SY21 0QS (on A458)
🕓 11-11; 12-10.30 Sun
☎ (01938) 810428
Beer range varies ⓗ

Delightful, beamed inn with a welcoming atmosphere. Popular with locals and tourists, the Goat has a plush lounge with comfortable leather armchairs and settees. Three real ales are on offer and the lounge is dominated by a large inglenook and fire. There is a separate restaurant and a games area at the rear. The restaurant provides home-cooked food. ♨❀⊲◑♣P

LLANGORSE

Castle Inn
LD3 7UB (on B4500) OS136275
🕓 12-3, 6-11; 12-11 Sat; 12-10.30 Sun
☎ (01874) 658225
Breconshire Golden Valley; guest beers ⓗ

Warm and welcoming village local that always has three cask ales available, and occasionally, a cask cider on gravity. The outside drinking area provides views of Llangorse Lake and the surrounding Black Mountains. A stone-flagged public bar with solid fuel stove greets you on entry, with a lounge bar and eating area (all no-smoking) off to the left. A range of freshly-prepared food is available. ♨🏶🕓🕽 🍴 🍽 P 🚫

LLANIDLOES

Crown & Anchor Inn
41 Long Bridge Street, SY18 6EF
🕓 11-11; 12-10.30 Sun
☎ (01686) 412398
Brains Rev James; Hancock's HB Ⓗ
Traditional, no-frills town-centre local with wooden beams. This unspoilt pub still retains its public bar, lounge and snug. It offers a games room with pool and various games machines. Old posters decorate the walls of the main bar. The lounge and pool room are separated from the bar and snug by a central hallway. ♨ ♣

Royal Head
SY18 6EE (off A470)
🕓 12-11; 12-10.30 Sun
☎ (01686) 412583
Draught Bass; Courage Directors; M&B Mild; Theakston Old Peculier Ⓗ
Once two pubs, this appealing town-centre hostelry has two bars. Both are welcoming and have wooden beams. The main bar has subdued lighting and a large stone inglenook with seating inside. A number of TV sets are provided for sports fans. The second bar has a pool table and games area. Reasonably-priced accommodation is available. 🏶🛏🕽 🍴 P

LLANRHAEADR-YM-MOCHNANT

Hand Inn (Tafarn Llaw)
SY10 0JJ
🕓 12-11; 12-10.30 Sun
☎ (01691) 780413
Beer range varies Ⓗ
Multi-roomed village pub which has exposed beams and tiled floors. The bar is dominated by a large inglenook and real fire. Inglenooks are also found in the smaller, cosy lounge. A large function room is available. The inn offers accommodation at a fair price. It has recently changed its name to the Welsh language.
♨ 🛏 🏶🕽 🍴 A

MACHYNLLETH

Skinners Arms
Main Street, SY20 8EB (on A487)
🕓 11-11; 12-10.30 Sun
☎ (01654) 702354
Burtonwood Bitter; guest beer Ⓗ
Town-centre, timbered local, with a plush, stone-walled lounge bar and a no-smoking eating area. This is set around an impressive stone inglenook. The public bar has a friendly, cosy feel with a wooden floor, subdued lighting and a pool table. A good selection of food is provided in the lounge (not Sun eve) and bar snacks in the public bar. A patio garden is a bonus. 🏶🕽 🍴 ≈ ♣

MONTGOMERY

Dragon Hotel
Market Square, SY15 6PA
🕓 11-3, 6-11; 12-3, 7-10.30 Sun
☎ (01686) 668359 website: www.dragonhotel.com
Beer range varies Ⓗ
Delightful bar in a 17th-century coaching

inn. This hotel is a two-star establishment in the town centre. The bar walls are covered with bric-à-brac and the beams and masonry are reputedly from the local castle which was destroyed by Cromwell. The hotel has good facilities, including an indoor, heated swimming pool and a function room catering for 20–100 people. The beer range usually includes an ale from the Shropshire brewery, Wood.
Q 🏶🛏🕽 ♣ P

NEWTOWN

Railway Tavern
Old Kerry Road, SY16 1BH (off A483)
🕓 12-2.30, 6.30-11; 11-11 Tue, Fri & Sat; 12-10.30 Sun
☎ (01686) 626156
Draught Bass; Worthington's Bitter; guest beer Ⓗ
Unspoilt, compact, one-bar local close to the railway station. Much-visited, this cheery pub has beams and features one stone wall. The darts teams are successful as can be seen by the vast array of trophies displayed, there is a further collection in the cellar. On match nights the pub tends to be crowded. Beware of the cellar hatch which lies right in front of the dartboard! 🏶 ≈ ♣

Sportsman
17 Severn Street, SY16 2QA (off A483)
🕓 11-11; 12-10.30 Sun
☎ (01686) 625885
Adnams Broadside; Greene King Old Speckled Hen; Tetley Bitter; Theakston Best Bitter Ⓗ
This town-centre pub has once again become a popular watering-hole for after-work drinkers. It offers three distinct drinking areas: a comfortable lounge, a main bar area, equally comfortable, with wooden beams and a large fireplace, and a tiled drinking section that has a games machine and TV. 🏶🕽 ≈ ♣

PENTRE-BACH

Shoemakers Arms
Sennybridge, LD3 8UB
(follow signs 'country pub' from Sennybridge) OS908328
🕓 12-3 (not Mon & Tue), 6-11 (may open longer in summer); 12-3, 7-10.30 Sun
☎ (01874) 636508
Beer range varies Ⓗ
According to the road signs, 'The road to Pentre-bach is always open'. A little further along, the Eppynt firing range is encountered so the pub is a safe place to stop! Originally four cottages, this 18th-century pub was saved from closure by the local community who purchased and refurbished it. Now it is once again at the heart of this rural community. Two real ales are on sale, usually one is from Cottage Brewery. A varied menu is available. It received the CAMRA Best Pub in Powys award in 2003. Quoits is played.
♨ Q 🏶🕽 🍴 ♣ P

PENYBONT

Severn Arms
Llandrindod Wells, LD1 5UA
🕓 11-2.30, 6-11; 12-3, 7-10.30 Sun
☎ (01597) 851224
Draught Bass; Brains SA; Marston's Pedigree; guest beers Ⓗ

18th-century coaching inn named after John Cheesment Severn, the second squire of Penybont Hall and a stop-off point between Hereford and Aberystwyth. The large bar has access to the rear garden, while a games room, quiet lounge and a restaurant complete the picture. The restaurant is open evenings (7–9.30 all week) and on Sunday lunchtime, when booking is essential. The pub has six miles of fishing rights on the River Ithon (free to residents). Wales and border counties trotting racing takes place twice yearly on a nearby course. A good range of malt whiskies is provided. ⚌✿🍴◑ 🛏️⚁⚄ ⚄AP

PENYCAE

Ancient Briton
Brecon Road, SA9 1YY
(on main Swansea-Brecon road, A4067)
✪ 11-11; 12-10.30 Sun
☎ (01639) 730273
Beer range varies Ⓗ
Comfortable, open-plan country pub with a restaurant area and games facilities, close to Dan yr Ogof caves and Craig y Nos country park and castle. Up to six real ales are available, including Brains Buckley's Best Bitter, and real cider is sold in summer. Live entertainment can be enjoyed on occasional weekends. Families with children are welcome. There is a large play area with camping facilities at the rear of the pub. The landlord is a keen real ale enthusiast. Wheelchair WC.
✿🍴◑⚄Å♣P

RHAYADER

Crown Inn
North Street, LD6 5BT
✪ 11-11; 12-3, 7-10.30 Sun
☎ (01597) 811099
Brains Dark, Bitter; Rev James, seasonal beers Ⓗ
This 16th-century building has always been

a pub, and although horses were stabled, it was never a coaching inn; it was linked with the hiring of horses (livery) instead. Much of the internal timbering is still visible despite changes made in the 1970s. The linen-fold bar front was saved from a demolished house in Caersws. The bar is comfortable and lining the walls is a pictorial history of recent Rhayader, with text. Look out for the item referring to Major Stancombe, a former owner.
Q✿🍴◑⚄♣P⚄

TALYBONT-ON-USK

Star Inn
LD3 7YX
✪ 11-3, 6.30-11; 11-11 Sat; 12-3, 6.30-10.30 Sun
☎ (01874) 676635
Hancock's HB; Theakston Old Peculier; guest beers Ⓗ
Former CAMRA regional Pub of the Year, the Star has served many different beers through the years and their pump clips are displayed on the bar. A blues festival is held in the second week of August. Quiz night is Monday and live music is staged each Wednesday. There is a bus stop nearby for the Abergavenny–Brecon service, but as this is rural Wales there is no evening service.
⚌✿🍴◑⚄Å♣👜

WELSHPOOL

Royal Oak Hotel
The Cross, SY21 7DG (off A483)
✪ 11-3, 5.30-11; 11-midnight Fri & Sat; 12-10.30 Sun
☎ (01938) 552217
Worthington's Bitter; guest beer Ⓗ
Plush, town-centre, 300-year-old coaching inn, which was formerly the manor house of the Earls of Powis. There are two bars; a cosy, quiet Oak bar with a real fire and relaxing atmosphere and the Ostler bar with pool, music and TV. The Ostler bar has an extension on Friday and Saturday. The hotel has a separate restaurant. ⚌Q🍴◑≓

Pepys on the road

Thence (from Salisbury) about 6 o'clock, and with a guide went over the smooth plain indeed till night; and then by a happy mistake, and that looked like an adventure, we were carried out of our way to a town where we would lie, since we could not go as far as we would. And there with great difficulty came about 10 at night to a little inn, where we were fain to go into a room where a pedlar was in bed, and made him rise; and there wife and I lay, and in a truckle-bed, Betty Turner and Willet. But good beds, and the master of the house a sober, understanding man, and I had a pleasant discourse with him about country matters. Up, finding our beds good, but we lousy; which made us merry. We set out, the reckoning and servants coming to 9s. 6d.

Samuel Pepys (1633-1703), diary for Thursday and Friday, 11 and 12 June 1668

NORTH-EAST WALES

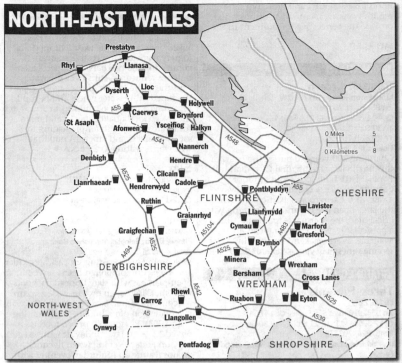

Authority areas covered: Denbighshire UA, Flintshire UA, Wrexham UA

Denbighshire

CARROG

Grouse Inn

LL21 9AT (on B5437, ½ mile from A5) OS113435
☼ 12-11; 12-10.30 Sun
☎ (01490) 430272

Lees Bitter, seasonal beers Ⓗ

A short walk from the western terminus of the Llangollen preserved railway via a narrow road bridge, the Grouse is in a superb location overlooking the River Dee from the bar and patio. There is a games room and small dining room where food is available 12–10 every day. Guesthouse accommodation is nearby, the pub will supply details. The last remaining pub in the village, it was originally a farm and brewhouse. Tends to be busy in summer.
❀◑Ⓓ▲♣P

CYNWYD

Blue Lion

Main Street, LL21 0LE
(on B4401, 2 miles SW of Corwen) OS056411
☼ 12-3, 6-11; 12-11 Fri & Sat; 12-10.30 Sun
☎ (01490) 412106 website: www.bluelionhotel.co.uk

Mansfield Dark Mild; Plassey Bitter; guest beers Ⓗ

Friendly, traditional local at the village crossroads near Cynwyd Forest and Waterfall. The building was part of the Rûg estate owned by Lord Newborough. The bar has a stone floor and a real fire. There is a smaller lounge where meals are served. The bar is often full with locals. A youth hostel is nearby, used by the many walkers in the forest. The River Dee is only 400 yards away and is spanned by a narrow road bridge. Dogs are not welcome.
▲▭❀◑Ⓓ⍟☖▲♣P

DENBIGH

Old Vaults

40-42 High Street, LL16 3RY
☼ 11-11; 12-10.30 Sun
☎ (01745) 815142

Greene King Abbot; Jennings Cumberland Ale Ⓗ

Town-centre pub, a single bar with an L-shaped room. Pictures on the walls include historical views of Denbigh town and the celebrated HM Stanley who was born in the town. Nearby attractions include the castle and the town walls are also worth the walk (a key can be obtained from the library). Denbigh is on the No. 51 bus service which runs from the resort town of Rhyl. The nearest railway station is also at Rhyl. ▲

DYSERTH

New Inn

Waterfall Road, LL18 6ET
(off A5151, 4 miles S of Rhyl) OS055796
☼ 12-11; 12-10.30 Sun
☎ (01745) 570482

Banks's Riding Bitter, Original, Bitter; Marston's Pedigree Ⓗ

Multi-roomed village inn, all areas are fed from a single bar. It is close to the waterfall that was featured in the film Holiday on the Buses. A short bus ride away are the local

resort towns of Rhyl and Prestatyn. The mouth-watering menu offers dishes which provide the perfect accompaniment to the real ale.
🏃Q🕷🍴◑P

GRAIANRHYD

Rose & Crown
Llanarmon Road, CH7 4QW
(on B5430, off A5104)
☼ 4-11 (1-11 summer Fri & Sat); 4 (1 summer)-10.30 Sun
☎ (01824) 780727
Flowers IPA Ⓗ
Charming 200-year-old pub at the heart of this small vilage in the rural Clwydian hills. Popular with both locals and outdoor pursuits fanatics, a warm welcome always awaits in the two rooms, particularly when the large open fire is burning. Teeming with bric-à-brac, the unusual teapot collection is a particular feature. Evening meals are available, as are weekend lunches, but serving times may vary. 🏃🏕🕷◑🍴♣P

GRAIGFECHAN

Three Pigeons
LL15 2EU
(on B5429, 3 miles S of Ruthin) OS147545
☼ 12-3, 5.30-11; 12-11 Sat; 12-10.30 Sun
☎ (01824) 703178
Draught Bass; Enville Ale; Hancock's HB; Plassey Fusilier Ⓗ
Spacious, rural pub with outstanding views of the Clwydian range and facilities to suit all tastes. There is a large outdoor area and separate rooms for dining (no food on Sun eve or Mon). The menu includes dishes cooked in Enville Ale, such as ham in honey. The four handpulled beers are often supplemented by other cask ales served straight from the jug. The Pant Ruth nature reserve, once one of four local limestone quarries, is situated nearby. Pub games are played including splat the rat.
🏃Q🕷◑🦽🅰♣P✠

HENDRERWYDD

White Horse
LL16 4LL (600 yds E of B5429, 1 mile S of Llandyrnog) OS121634
☼ 12-2.30, 6-11; 12-11 Sat; 12-10.30 Sun
☎ (01824) 790218 website: www.white-horse-wn.co.uk
Beer range varies Ⓗ
Traditional 17th-century inn in the foothills of the Clwydian range with an extensive restaurant offering an à la carte menu which changes every three weeks. Bar snacks are also available in the snug for customers with simpler tastes. This room features fly fishing and relics of other sporting pursuits. The games room is well equipped and can be used to help disoriented ramblers find their way back on track. Good value themed evenings are a regular event (ring for details).
🏃Q🕷◑🅰♣P

LLANGOLLEN

Corn Mill
Dee Lane, LL20 8PN (close to river bridge)
☼ 12-11; 12-10.30 Sun
☎ (01978) 869555

website: www.cornmillatbrunningandprice.co.uk
Boddingtons Bitter; Plassey Bitter; guest beers Ⓗ
Sympathetic conversion of a former mill building on the banks of the River Dee. Visitors will notice the excellent modern joinery work and impressive staircase connecting the two bars. The spectacular outdoor terrace, on stilts over the water, runs the entire length of the building, past the functioning water wheel and beyond, providing a perfect location to sit and watch the river. Good quality snacks and main meals are served with ample seating to satisfy drinkers and diners. A pub that is well worth visiting. Q🕷◑🦽🅰≈✠

Sun
49 Regent Street, LL20 8HN
(head E on A5, near town centre)
☼ 12-11 (may close weekday afternoons); 12-10.30 Sun
☎ (01978) 860233
website: www.suninnllangollen@btopenworld.com
Plassey Bitter; Salopian Shropshire Gold; guest beers Ⓗ
Welcoming pub boasting six cask ales, cider and a selection of foreign beers, served in an open-plan bar with slate floor (dirty boots welcome). Two open fires provide a warm welcome in winter. Seating around the walls is provided on old school benches (dating from 1903). Reasonably-priced food is served 12–9, Friday–Sunday. It tends to get busy on Friday evening when live rock groups feature and Saturday evening with rhythm and blues. A small snug provides a quieter refuge. Winner of local CAMRA Pub of the Year for the past two years, a covered courtyard serves as a garden.
🏃🕷◑🅰≈♣🚻

Wynnstay Arms
20 Bridge Street, LL20 8PF
☼ 12-3.30, 6-11; 12-11 Fri & Sat; 12-4, 7-10.30, (12-10.30 summer Sun)
☎ (01978) 860710
website: www.@wynnstay-arms.co.uk
Greene King IPA, Abbot; Tetley Burton Ale Ⓗ
Historic 16th-century, friendly, town-centre inn. The largely unaltered interior provides several small rooms including a games room with juke box. The main bar has a welcoming open fire in winter. The cosy dining room seats 30, and is also used as a family room and function area. Children's games and high chairs are available. There are five en-suite bedrooms plus a bunkhouse room that is often used by hikers, canoeists and cyclists. The pleasant enclosed beer garden is popular.
🏃Q🛏🕷◑🦽🅰≈♣P

LLANRHAEADR

King's Head
LL16 4NL
(off A525, 2 miles S of Denbigh) OS081635
☼ 12-3, 5-11; 12-11 Sat; 12-10.30 Sun
☎ (01745) 890278
Draught Bass; guest beer Ⓗ
16th-century pub just off the A525 on the way to Ruthin from the town of Denbigh. A single bar serves a small labyrinth of rooms. There is a collection of whisky containers in one corner. Opposite the pub is a church which has the locally-renowned 'Jesse Window' that was saved from the ravages of

Henry VIII during the Dissolution of Monasteries. ≥❀≠◖◗P

PRESTATYN

Royal Victoria
Sandy Lane, LL19 7SG
✪ 11.30-11; 12-10.30 Sun
☎ (01745) 854670
Burtonwood Bitter; guest beer Ⓗ
Close to the town centre and opposite the railway station, this popular local has a raised seating area in the main bar with a function room to the rear. Catering is possible for parties and meetings by arrangement. This pub is the first (or last) drinking establishment for walkers on Offa's Dyke. The guest beer changes weekly.
❀Å≠♣

RHEWL (LLANGOLLEN)

Sun Inn
LL20 7YT
(on B5103, follow signs from A542) OS178449
✪ 12-3, 6-11; 12-11 Sat; 12-10.30 Sun
☎ (01978) 861043
Beer range varies Ⓗ
Beautifully located high above the Dee Valley, four miles north of Llangollen, this classic 14th-century former drovers' inn is a perfect retreat. It is popular with locals and visitors enjoying the mountain walks and the nearby Horseshoe Falls. The central bar and hatch serve three rooms: a cosy and intimate public bar, a small rear snug, and the main lounge area with a warming, open fire. Good wholesome food is served.
ᄲQ≥❀◖◗⊟Å♣P

RHYL

Sussex ✿
20-26 Sussex Street, LL18 1SG
(between High St and Queen St)
✪ 10-11; 12-10.30 Sun
☎ (01745) 362910
Courage Directors; Greene King Abbot; Tetley Bitter; guest beers Ⓗ
The former Old Comrades' Club became the Sussex public house and was taken over by Wetherspoon's in 2001. The conversion has been undertaken in a manner which allows Rhyl's history as a resort to be portrayed through a series of pictorial wall plaques. Situated in a pedestrianised street, it has become popular and is often busy at weekends and during the evenings. Breakfast is served Monday–Saturday, 10-12. Children are welcome in the no-smoking area, last orders for children's meals is 5pm.
Q≥❀◖&≠⌿

Swan
13 Russell Road, LL18 3BS
(close to southern end of pedestrianised High St)
✪ 11-11; 12-10.30 Sun
☎ (01745) 336694
Thwaites Mild, Bitter, Lancaster Bomber Ⓗ
Reputed to be the oldest pub in town, the frontage displays the name of former brewery, Wilderspool Ales. The building was once a farmhouse and old photographs of Rhyl adorn the homely interior. Lunches are served 12–2.30, Monday–Saturday. The pub is popular with locals, who appreciate the level of service offered by the licensee

and his staff. Active darts and dominoes teams are supported, together with a popular quiz league. ❀◖◗≠♣

RUTHIN

Wine Vaults ✿
2 Castle Street, LL15 1DP (in town square)
✪ 12-11; 12-10.30 Sun
☎ (01824) 702067
Robinson's Best Bitter, seasonal beers Ⓗ
Town-centre pub with an Irish flavour – old Guinness posters are mounted on the walls of the main bar and sports bar. A front verandah serves as an outside drinking area and overlooks the historic courthouse (AD 1401), now converted into a bank. The local clientele are sports-oriented and regular promotional events take place. Live music features on Friday evening. ❀⊟ÅP

ST. ASAPH

Plough
The Roe, LL17 0LU
(on A525, off A55, 200 yds on entering town)
✪ 12-11; 12-10.30 Sun
☎ (01745) 585080
Plassey Bitter; guest beers Ⓗ
Large open-plan pub with a central bar. Tables have a range of heights and seating includes reclaimed church pews. The tables are named after well-known racehorses. This theme is continued in the Racecourse, one of the two first-floor restaurants. The other serves Italian meals. The pub is handy for the local cricket club ground.
ᄲ❀◖&P⌿

Flintshire

AFONWEN

Pwll-Gwyn
Denbigh Road, CH7 5UB
(on A541, Mold-Denbigh road) OS127717
✪ 12-2, 7-11 (not Mon); 12-3, 6-11 Sat; 12-3, 7-10.30 Sun
☎ (01352) 720227
Tetley Bitter; guest beers Ⓗ
Spacious roadside pub with one large bar and two dining areas, this 18th-century coaching inn was once owned by the Chester Northgate Brewery. Food features strongly with an extensive menu and interesting specials board. There are separate lunchtime and evening menus, both dining rooms are no-smoking. The pub is served by an hourly Mold–Denbigh bus service. Guest beers change twice weekly and are usually from micros. ᄲ❀◖&ÅP

BRYNFORD

Llyn-y-Mawn
Brynford Hill, CH8 8AD
(on B5121, 1 mile S of Holywell) OS181748
✪ 12-2.30, 5.30-11; 5.30-11 Fri; 12-11 Sat; 12-10.30 Sun
☎ (01352) 714367
John Smith's Bitter; guest beers Ⓗ
A former guesthouse for travellers, there has been a building on this site since the 14th century. The clientele are very competitive, with enthusiastic darts and dominoes teams. Ramblers and sportsmen from the nearby sports centre and golf club use the

facilities. There are two dining areas and a large no-smoking room. Entertainment is provided on Friday evening, and Wednesday is quiz night. Disabled access is via the dining room, to the rear of the pub. The pub can be seen from the A55 but is difficult to drive to; an OS map would be handy. ⋔❀◑⊟⅏P

CADOLE

Colomendy Arms
Village Road, CH7 5LL
(off A494, Mold-Ruthin road)
☼ 7 (6 Thu; 4 Fri; 12 Sat)-11; 12-10.30 Sun
☎ (01352) 810217
Shepherd Neame Master Brew Bitter; guest beers Ⓗ
A splendid example of how a pub can flourish when the licensees are committed to cask ale. Four interesting guest beers are always on offer to complement the Shepherd Neame, which is rare locally. Situated close to the Loggerheads Country Park (yes, that is where the saying comes from), this cosy and convivial two-roomed pub sets a benchmark for quality cask ale. The village name comes from the Cat's Hole, a mine – in fact potholers and cavers are often to be found in this pub. ⋔Q❀♣P

CILCAIN

White Horse
The Square, CH7 5NN (1 mile S of A541)
OS177652
☼ 12-3, 6.30-11; 12-11 Sat; 12-10.30 Sun
☎ (01352) 740142
Banks's Bitter; guest beers Ⓗ
Picturesque, whitewashed pub in an attractive village in the foothills of Moel Fammu in the Clwydian range. The public bar has a traditional quarry-tiled floor and welcomes walkers and dogs. Meals are served in a cosy split-level lounge (12–2 and 7–9) from an imaginative menu, and with changing specials. There are photographs of the old village and exterior signs from long-defunct breweries. Under 14s are not admitted. It is on the regular Mold to Denbigh bus route. ⋔Q❀◑⊟P

CYMAU

Talbot
Cymau Lane, LL11 5LB
☼ 7-11 Mon-Fri; 12-4, 7-11 Sat; 12-10.30 Sun
☎ (01978) 761410
Hydes Bitter; Ⓟ seasonal beers Ⓗ
Unchanging, whitewashed local on Hope mountainside, a long-standing Guide entry of defiant, no-frills character. From the front entrance porch, take your pick: to the left, a lively public bar with dominoes, darts and TV; to the right, a quieter, little two-room lounge of spartan but functional nature. The nearby country park offers spectacular panoramic views across the Cheshire plain. An uncomplicated, friendly drinkers' pub, where the only sign of food is a few baps at the weekend. Q⊟♣P

HALKYN

Britannia
Pentre Road, CH8 8BS (off A55, jct 32B)
☼ 11-11; 12-10.30 Sun
☎ (01352) 780272

Lees GB Mild, Bitter, seasonal beers Ⓗ
Only 400 yards from the main westbound A55 express way, this four-roomed pub has a relaxed, homely atmosphere and panoramic views over the Dee estuary. The conservatory restaurant is no-smoking and attracts visitors, while the locals congregate in the rear bar area. There is also a cosy front lounge and pool room. Warning signs in the car park alert customers to the crossing ducks. The Lees seasonal beers are subject to limited availability but are always worth a try. ⋔❀◑⅏Å♣P⅊

HENDRE

Royal Oak
Denbigh Road, CH7 5QE
(on A541, Mold-Denbigh road) OS191677
☼ 7 (12 Sat)-11; 12-10.30 Sun
☎ (01352) 741466
Black Sheep Best Bitter; Worthington's Bitter; guest beer Ⓗ
Roadside pub, close to several disused mines, limestone, lead and spa. The spa was used for road lines. The original hooter from the limestone mine is on display in the lounge, along with a fine array of mugs. The smaller bar features old village photographs and bottles from long-gone breweries. A pool table is in the games room. Walkers in the nearby Clwydian hills use the pub as a pit stop at the weekend. Special promotions are offered; on Wednesday an evening meal and a pint cost £3.99. ⋔Q❀⊟ÅP

HOLYWELL

Glan-yr-Afon
Dolphin, Milwr Road, CH8 8HE (off A5026, 1 mile S of Holywell, signed Dolphin) OS195739
☼ 12-3, 5.30-11; 12-10.30 Sun
☎ (01352) 710052
Tetley Bitter; guest beers Ⓗ
Traditional Welsh long house extended to provide accommodation. There are seven guest rooms, one with disabled facilities. The five drinking areas include a games room, a large dining area and a function room on the upper floor. Pepe, the Spanish landlord, hosts a Spanish language circle every last Thursday of the month. A quiz is held every Wednesday, and the pub fields a football team. Darts and shove ha'-penny are played. Regular beer festivals feature. The caves to the rear of the pub are not yet open. Ask about the Milwr dragon. ⋔⌂❀⇋◑⊟⅏Å♣P

Old Wine Vaults
3 Cross Street, CH8 7LP (just off High St)
☼ 11-11; 12-10.30 Sun
☎ (01352) 714801
Marston's Pedigree; John Smith's Bitter; guest beers Ⓗ
Busy town pub, the bar serves a large open-plan area on one side and two small rooms on the other. The tiny office in the main room is where local lead miners used to be paid 100 years ago, with the bonus of clay pipes and tobacco provided free for drinkers. The pub is close to the famous St Winefride's Holy Well, a shrine of unbroken pilgrimage since the 12th century and one of the ancient seven wonders of Wales. ⋔❀⊟

LLANASA

Red Lion

CH8 9NE (signed from A5151 at Trelawnyd)
OS105815
✪ 12-11; 12-10.30 Sun
☎ (01745) 854291
Courage Directors; Webster's Bitter; guest beer Ⓗ
Charming two-bar inn with open fires, and
a superb central location in this delightful
village that is a designated Conservation
Area. Close to the duckpond and parish
church, the pub has superb views to the
surrounding hills. There is a pool table off
the public bar, and a no-smoking dining
room with an extensive menu. Two regular
beers are served alongside a guest ale
(weekends). The Red Lion is about three
miles from Prestatyn. ♨Q❀⇄◑Å♣P

LLANFYNYDD

Cross Keys

LL11 5HH (on B5101)
✪ 7-11; closed Mon; 12-10.30 Sun
☎ (01978) 760333
Beer range varies Ⓗ
Traditional village pub with inviting fires
and well-regarded menu. This 300-year-old
former blacksmith's shop might only boast
one handpump but the beer it dispenses is
usually from a local micro-brewery. Lunch
is served on Sunday only. The enthusiastic
new licensee holds a monthly themed food
evening and occasional quiz night in the
cosy lounge which has attractive, intricately
carved settles. The quarry-tiled bar is more
basic but still welcoming. The opening
hours may extend in the summer – phone
to check. ♨❀◑♣P

LLOC

Rock Inn

St Asaph Road, CH8 8RD
(at A5026/A5151 jct, 1 mile from A55) OS144766
✪ 12-11; 12-10.30 Sun
☎ (01352) 710049
Burtonwood Bitter; guest beer Ⓗ
A slight diversion from the A55 western end
of the Holywell bypass, will bring you to
this appealing pub. There are three rooms: a
bar with a horse-racing theme; a lounge
with a collection of teapots (hanging from
the ceiling), a mural showing an
Elizabethan pub and a selection of cigarette
cards; the third room is the no-smoking
dining room. The local cricket team is
evident on Saturday. Darts and dominoes
are popular. Reasonably-priced meals are
served 12–2 and 6–9, Wednesday–Monday.
◑◱&♣P

NANNERCH

Cross Foxes

Village Road, CH7 5RD
(off A541, Mold-Denbigh road)) OS167695
✪ 6-11; 12-10.30 Sun
☎ (01352) 741293
Beer range varies Ⓗ
Traditional village pub with low, beamed
ceilings and a welcoming atmosphere. A
free house, with two beers which change
regularly, the public bar has an open fire
and tiled floor. The extended lounge (with
piano) is decorated with brassware. The

restaurant is only open at weekends with a
full menu plus a wide range of filled
baguettes. A curry and a pint for under a
fiver is a popular Tuesday night feature. Fly
fishing is available nearby, and the regular
Mold to Denbigh bus stops outside.
♨Q◑❀◱&P

PONTBLYDDYN

New Inn

Corwen Road, CH7 4HR (on A5104)
✪ 12-11; 12-10.30 Sun
☎ (01352) 771459
website: www.newinnpontblyddyn.fsnet.co.uk
Brains Rev James; guest beers Ⓗ
Much-improved 19th-century pub on a
winding and wooded road into the hills.
The bar offers pool and TV. The lounge on
the other hand is a tranquil sea of pink,
except when the folk club meets on
Tuesday or the Rally Club gets together on
Thursday. Food is extensive and varied with
cheap midweek deals. Meals are not served
on Monday unless it is a bank holiday.
There is an extra dining room upstairs.
Children are welcome until 9pm and there
is also an outdoor play area. The pub has a
car park on the opposite side of the road.
Two or three interesting cask ales are on
tap.
♨❀◑◱♣P🍴

YSCEIFIOG

Fox Inn ☆

The Village, CH8 8NJ
(signed from A541, also from B5121) OS152715
✪ 6 (12 Sat)-11; 12-10.30 Sun
☎ (01352) 720241
Beer range varies Ⓗ
This Grade II listed pub was built circa 1730
and was named after a local landowner
Ignatious Fox. It lay on the pilgrim's trail
from Shrewsbury to St Winefride's Holy
Well in Holywell. The Fox is on CAMRA's
National Inventory of Pub Interiors. Note
the seat under the bar. There are four
rooms: the bar, full of character; a lounge;
an intimate dining room and a room that
turns into a post office each Friday
morning. Best to reserve a table for the
popular weekend meals. The locals have
personalised glasses printed by the
landlord's wife. Worth finding – a rural
gem.
♨❀◑◱♣P🍴

Wrexham

BERSHAM

Black Lion Inn ⊘

Y-Ddol, LL14 4HN (off B5097)
✪ 12 (11.30 Sat)-11; 12-10.30 Sun
☎ (01978) 365588
Hydes Light, Bitter; guest beer Ⓗ
Travelling from Wrexham towards Y-Ddol
turn left just before the Bersham Heritage
Centre, the pub is on the bank of the River
Clywedog, and on the Clywedog heritage
trail. A cosy and welcoming pub, known
locally as the Hole in the Wall, it is popular
with locals and with hikers and visitors to
the heritage centre. It is a sympathetic
renovation of a parlour-style pub with a side
off-shoot and a separate pool room. Y-Ddol
means the meadow, and the pub garden

overlooks the wooded riverside, with the added bonus of a children's playground.
🏚Q🏠🕭🛗♣P

BRYMBO

George & Dragon
Ael y Bryn, LL11 5DA
🕛 12-11; 12-10.30 Sun
☎ (01978) 758515
Lees Bitter, seasonal beers Ⓗ

Charming, traditional local pub, that is very welcoming to strangers. Real fires warm the bar and the lounge; darts and dominoes are popular and there is a singalong to accompany an organ on a Friday evening. The landlord is a keen fisherman, note the picture of him with a 26½lb rainbow trout, which he caught and sold for charity. An attractive collection of toby jugs and a painting of the pub by a local artist grace the interior. At the entrance is a tiny bar named McGills bar, after a former regular. Children are allowed until 7pm.
🏚🏠🕭🛗♣P

CROSS LANES

Kagan's Brasserie
LL11 0TF (on A525, 1 mile from Marchwiel)
🕛 11-11; 12-10.30 Sun
☎ (01978) 780555 website: www.crosslanes.co.uk
Plassey Bitter Ⓗ

Large lounge, with central bar, in a mansion formerly known as Maes-y-Nant. A rare outlet for local Plassey, this upmarket hotel is set back from the road in six acres of gardens. From the front entrance, the bar is approached via a grand panelled hall with a 1618 staircase rescued from Emral Hall. Or, enter through the alternative side door. The bar has a dining area and is decorated with old prints and photographs. 🏚Q🛏🕦P

EYTON

Plassey Leisure Park
The Plassey, LL13 0SP
(off B5426, signed from A483)
🕛 11-11; 12-10.30 (will vary in winter) Sun
☎ (01978) 780019 website: www.theplassey.co.uk
Plassey Bitter Ⓗ

Atop a wooded hillock, this one-time Victorian dairy farm is now fully dedicated to the leisure industry. With a caravan park attached, there is plenty here for the family from craft shops, boutiques, salons and garden nurseries to nature trails, a blacksmith's and a swimming pool. Most importantly, it is the home of Plassey Brewery (shop on site). The bitter features in the Shippon restaurant/bar, Haybank Inn (the on-site golf course clubhouse) or the Treetops, the latter servicing the caravan site and open only in season. Children are welcome in the no-smoking conservatory at the Haybank Inn, or in a small family room at the Treetops. 🚼🏠🕦▲P½

GRESFORD

Griffin Inn
Church Green, LL12 8RG
🕛 3-11; 3-10.30 Sun
☎ (01978) 852231
Banks's Original; Greenalls Bitter; Wells Bombardier Ⓗ

This popular village pub is a true local, it stands opposite Gresford parish church. The bright interior features a large South African turtle shell, a poster with photographs of the 62 men who lost their lives in the Gresford pit disaster of 1934, and a lovely old piano. The landlady, who has been in the pub for 30 years, has been playing the piano since she was six, and will be delighted to play you a tune.
Q🏠♣P

Pant-yr-Ochain
Old Wrexham Road, LL12 8TY
(just off A534, follow sign to 'The Flash')
🕛 12-11; 12-10.30 Sun
☎ (01978) 853525
Boddingtons Bitter; Flowers Original; Plassey Bitter; Taylor Landlord; guest beer Ⓗ

Popular, upmarket, 16th-century hostelry set amid tranquil gardens and a lake, yet only three miles from Wrexham. The Pubco's policy of good cask ale and quality food is vindicated here. Local produce is used, and the imaginative menu changes regularly. A central bar serves a number of separate areas including a no-smoking back room, and a (normally) food-free bar. The pub is well-regarded for its food and is a staunch supporter of the local Plassey Bitter. Children are welcome until 6pm. Enjoy the beautiful outdoor drinking area or relax in the large conservatory.
🏚Q🏠🕦🛗P½

LAVISTER

Nag's Head
Old Chester Road, LL12 0DN
(on B5445, old Chester-Wrexham road)
🕛 5.30 (12 Fri & Sat)-11; 12-10.30 Sun
☎ (01244) 570486
Boddingtons Bitter; Taylor Landlord; Weetwood Best Bitter; guest beers Ⓗ

Large, extended roadside hostelry just inside the Welsh border. A plaque on the wall claims that the Nag's Head was the birthplace of CAMRA in 1971. A lively atmosphere usually prevails and the pub serves both the local community and visitors. There is a children's play area to the rear. The layout of the pub features a single large room with a central bar from which the ales are dispensed. An area is set aside for pool and darts.
🏚🏠🕦🛗♣P

MARFORD

Red Lion
Marford Hill, LL12 8SN (on B5445)
🕛 12-2 (not Mon & Tue), 5-11; 12-11 Sat;
12-10.30 Sun
☎ (01978) 853562
Burtonwood Bitter; guest beers Ⓗ

Friendly pub on the old Chester road that was a former coaching house. It comprises two distinct areas. The bar features a pool table and TV and has a splendid brick fireplace. The attractively decorated lounge is often busy with diners enjoying the Thai food which is a speciality of the pub. Bookings are recommended at weekends. Meals are served from Friday evening to Sunday lunchtime.
🏚🏠🕦♣P

MINERA

Tyn-y-Capel
Church Road, LL11 3DA (off B5426)
☼ 11.30-3 (not Tue), 5 (6.30 Tue)-11 (midnight Fri);
11.30-midnight Sat; 11.30-3, 5-10.30 Sun
☎ (01978) 757502
Tetley Bitter; guest beers Ⓗ

Former drovers' pub originally associated with the adjacent church. The attractive whitewashed exterior with sturdy stone-flanked windows and pretty little painted heraldic shields belies a semi-open modern interior. Step down, past a small area (with pool table) to the bar, marvel at the stunning views of Esclusham Mountain across the valley, the scenery can also be enjoyed from the beer garden. There is a separate restaurant, occasional live music and an unobtrusive tiny terrestrial TV. The pub is close to Minera lead mines and the start of the Clywedog Valley heritage trail.
❀◑♣P

PONTFADOG

Swan
LL20 7AR (on B4500, Glyn Ceiriog road)
☼ 12-3, 7-11; 12-3, 7-10.30 Sun
☎ (01691) 718273
Brains Bitter; guest beer Ⓗ

Popular roadside pub located in the beautiful Ceiriog Valley. The small intimate bar area has darts, table football and a juke box, while another room is reserved for diners. The friendly, welcoming landlord offers a rotating guest beer, usually from the nearby Plassey Brewery. Good simple bar food is available. An occasional quiz evening is held.
♨❀◑Å♣P

RUABON

Wynnstay Arms
High Street, LL14 6BL (on B5605)
☼ 11.30-3; 5.30-11; 12-11 Sat; 12-3, 7-10.30 Sun
☎ (01978) 822187
Robinson's Best Bitter, seasonal beers Ⓗ

This imposing red-brick hotel lies on a precarious bend in the High Street, immediately opposite St Mary's church. A large wrought iron sign overhanging the road may return. It is currently the victim of passing traffic as it has been hit several times, most famously by a Spitfire during WWII. Many varied areas are provided so the pub will suit most tastes. A strong local following frequents the back bar with its games area, while the wood-panelled lounge is more sedate. Families are particularly welcome in the front alcove.
♨❀⇔◑☒≠♣P

WREXHAM

Horse & Jockey
Hope Street, LL11 1BD
☼ 10-11; 12-10.30 Sun
☎ (01978) 351081
Tetley Bitter; guest beers Ⓗ

A welcome return to the Guide for this wonderful old thatched pub in the middle of Wrexham's shopping area. A central bar serves four small but characterful areas, including the rear lounge in which children are welcome during the day. Two regularly-changing guest beers ensure the pub is always busy, whether this is with escapees from the bustle of the shopping areas during the day, or aficionados of one of the few traditional pubs in Wrexham during the evening. ◑≠ (Central/General)

Tipper beer

I entered a little public-house near Newhaven harbour, and asked the man at the bar for bread and cheese and beer. 'Tipper, sir?' inquired the barman. Now I had long known of 'Newhaven Tipper' by repute, for who knows not 'Tipper' knows not Sussex. Old Tom Tipper invented the brew that has kept his name famous for a century and a half, and today the 'Tipper Brewery' carries on one of the principal industries of Newhaven town. The beer is brewed from the brackish water of a certain well; and is the colour of pale ale. So I ordered a glass of 'Tipper' to drink to the memory of the perpetuator. I found it good at that, the flavour full and pleasant and slightly brackish, though the barman told me that his customers generally drank it mixed with a milder ale, for 'Tipper' has virtues that are different from those of beers of more modern repute. The said virtues of 'Tipper' are these: a man may drink a glass and be merry, he may drink two glasses and be mighty; but if the little goddess that lurketh in the glass tempteth him to drink a third, and he drink again, then let him go out on the Downs, and may the Powers that are above preserve him.

Arthur Beckett, *The Spirit of the Downs,* 1909

NORTH-WEST WALES

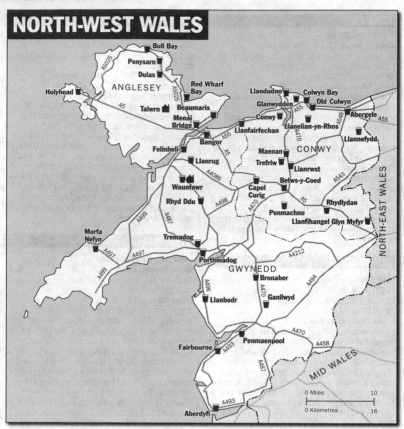

Authority areas covered: Anglesey UA, Conwy UA, Gwynedd UA

Anglesey/Ynys Môn

BEAUMARIS

George & Dragon
Church Street, LL58 8AA
☼ 11-11; 12-10.30 Sun
☎ (01248) 810491
Robinson's Best Bitter, seasonal beers Ⓗ
Welcoming local in the centre of the town and a short walk from the Menai Straits, castle and other historic buildings. According to tradition, this timber-framed inn was built in 1410 but architectural details suggest a date in the more settled prosperous days of Queen Elizabeth I. In the 1970s a remarkable series of wall paintings came to light during repair work. These have been restored and can be viewed on request. ⓦ◑♣⅍

Olde Bull's Head Inn
Castle Street, LL58 8AP
☼ 11-11; 12-10.30 Sun
☎ (01248) 810329
Draught Bass; Hancock's HB; Worthington's Bitter; guest beer Ⓗ
Grade II listed building that was the original posting house of the borough. In 1645 General Mytton, a Parliamentarian, commandeered the inn while his forces lay siege to the castle, which is a mere stone's throw away. The Royalists surrendered on 25th June, 1646. Dr Samuel Johnson and

Charles Dickens were famous guests and each individually-designed bedroom is named after a Dickens' character. The beamed bar has a large open fire and many antiques to create a genuine olde-worlde atmosphere. The inn has an excellent restaurant and brasserie (with wheelchair access). Very limited parking available. ♿◑

BULL BAY

Bull Bay Hotel
LL68 9SH
☼ 11-11; 12-10.30 Sun
☎ (01407) 830223 website: www.welshpubs.net
Lees GB Mild, Bitter, seasonal beers Ⓗ
Popular, residential hotel, the most northerly in Wales, in a commanding position on the coast of Anglesey. There are two comfortable lounges and a public bar/games room, all used by local interest groups for a wide range of activities, including indoor and outdoor musical events, quiz nights, pub games, rowing, fishing, golf and rambling. A wide ranging menu is available, the accent is on local produce, and includes seafood, and game in season. One of the guest rooms has a four-poster bed. An ideal base for exploring the island and its historic sites, with quick access to the mainland and Snowdonia, or Holyhead and the Irish ferries.
Q❀⇋◑♦⅃⚠♣P

DULAS

Pilot Boat Inn

LL70 9EX (on A5025)

☼ 11-11; 12-10.30 Sun

☎ (01248) 410205

Robinson's Best Bitter, seasonal beers Ⓗ

Friendly, rural, family pub with a play area and converted double-decker bus to keep the children amused. Originally a cottage-type building, now much extended, the lounge has an unusual bar created from half a boat. The pub is much used by walkers, the Anglesey coastal path passes through the car park. There are many worthwhile places to visit in the area, including Mynydd Bodafon for its spectacular views and Traeth Lligwy for the sands.

✿◖&Å♣P

HOLYHEAD

79

79 Market Street, LL65 1UW

☼ 11-11; 12-10.30 Sun

☎ (01407) 763939

Beer range varies Ⓗ

Comfortably furnished, popular town pub, overlooking the nearby ferry port, with several separate drinking areas, and a dining section that can be closed off for private functions. A local wholesaler supplies the rotating guest beers, mostly from regional breweries. A good year-round local trade is boosted by visitors, including rugby supporters on their way to Ireland. For those interested in local history, there is a small maritime museum just off the main promenade. ◖⇌♣

MENAI BRIDGE

Liverpool Arms

St George's Pier, LL59 5DD

(100 yds from square, towards pier)

☼ 11.30-3, 5.30-11; 12-3, 7-10.30 Sun

☎ (01248) 713335

Flowers IPA, Original, guest beer Ⓗ

Awarded local CAMRA Pub of the Year (Eryri a Môn) 2002/03, it offers first-rate B&B (12 rooms) with an excellent reputation for home-cooked food and Sunday lunches. This 150-year-old pub has a conservatory and several rooms served from three central bars. Old maps, antiquities and local photographs adorn the walls. This is a good base for touring Anglesey and Snowdonia. The narrow gauge Welsh Highland Railway is within easy reach. Sailing and fishing are popular locally. Locals, students and the sailing fraternity gather at this superb pub. A different guest bitter is offered every few days. Q⏚⌂◖

Tafarn y Bont

Telford Road, LL59 5DT

(on roundabout next to suspension bridge)

☼ 11-11; 12-10.30 Sun

☎ (01248) 716888

Greene King IPA; Wells Bombardier; guest beers Ⓗ

Recently refurbished, mid-19th-century shop and tea rooms, now a well-positioned pub with an excellent brasserie-style restaurant. Four cask bitters are on tap permanently. The beamed interior, and numerous small rooms with log fires create a welcoming ambience. The pub is situated on one of the main roads so is ideally placed to explore Anglesey. Snowdonia National Park is within easy reach and the Menai Straits a stone's throw away. The Welsh Highland Railway starts at nearby Caernarfon and runs to Rhyd Ddu at the foot of Snowdon, eventually running via Beddgelert to Porthmadog. ⚔✿◖⚥

Victoria Hotel

Telford Road, LL59 5DR

☼ 11-11; 12-10.30 Sun

☎ (01248) 712309

Draught Bass; Bragdy Ynys Môn Medra; guest beers Ⓗ

This 19-room residential hotel, with extensive gardens and patio, is situated 300 yards from the Menai suspension bridge, overlooking the Straits. Licensed for weddings, the spacious function room is also licensed to midnight. Regular live music is a feature. Wide-screen TV for sports is available. The local independent brewery Bragdy Ynys Môn supplies the hotel with excellent Welsh bitters. There is easy access to Snowdonia, the North Wales coast and the Welsh Highland Railway from Caernarfon. The resorts and beaches of Anglesey are all accessible en route to Holyhead and the Irish ferries sailing on the Menai Straits are close at hand. Fishing and sailing are popular pastimes.

⚔Q⏚✿⌂◖⊟&P

PENYSARN

Bedol

LL69 9YR (just off A5025)

☼ 12-11; 12-10.30 Sun

☎ (01407) 832590

Robinson's Hatters, Hartleys XB, seasonal beers Ⓗ

Built in 1984, the Bedol (Welsh for horseshoe) sold Greenalls, then Marston's, and is now a Robinson's tied house, selling most of their range on a rotating basis. Lunches are served in summer and at weekends. There is a comfortable lounge, with a smaller public bar/games room. It is a family-run, friendly community pub with live entertainment and quizzes, and a strong local following, supplemented by visitors in season, many of whom are exploring the island with its prehistoric sites, sandy beaches and industrial heritage trail. ⚔Q✿◖⊟Å♣P

RED WHARF BAY (TRAETH COCH)

Ship Inn

LL75 8RJ (1¹/₂ miles off A5025, near Benllech)

☼ 11-3, 6.30-11 (11-11 Sat & summer); 12-10.30 Sun

☎ (01248) 852568

Adnams Bitter; Greene King IPA; Tetley Dark Mild; guest beer Ⓗ

Renowned for its good food, Sunday lunches and upstairs restaurant, this mid-17th-century pub has superb views over the bay and homely log fires in winter. It was previously known as the Quay. Red Wharf Bay between 1700 and 1820 was a busy port in the days of sail, specialising in coal and

INDEPENDENT BREWERIES

Bragdy Ynys Môn Talwrn

Snowdonia Waunfawr

fertiliser. Today it is busy with locals and holidaymakers, bustling in summer. The beer garden affords panoramic views across the bay to south-east Anglesey. Comfortable walks can be made nearby. The summer resort of Benllech is about three miles away. Try the local Welsh bitter from Bragdy Ynys Môn in summer. ▲Q♿⚘☕◑▲P⚲

Conwy

ABERGELE

Bee Hotel
Market Street, LL22 7AA
✪ 11-11; 12-10.30 Sun
☎ (01745) 832300
Lees GB Mild, Bitter, seasonal beers Ⓗ

Locals' pub which is also a 10-room hotel. The bar serves a large lounge with a real coal fire, contributing to the warm welcome on offer. Evening social activity involves quizzes (Thu), karaoke (Fri) and live entertainment (Sat). There is a pool and TV room, and an upstairs function room. A pleasant rear garden with picnic tables overlooks St Michael's Church. Reasonably-priced lunchtime and evening meals are served all week, with Sunday lunches a speciality. The pub lies on coastal bus route 12. ▲⚘☕◑▶➤(Abergele & Pensarn) ♣P

BETWS-Y-COED

Glan Aber Hotel
Holyhead Road, LL24 0AB OS798562
✪ 11-11; 12-10.30 Sun
☎ (01690) 710325 website: www.betws-y-coed.co.uk
Greene King Old Speckled Hen; Tetley Dark Mild, Bitter; guest beer Ⓗ

Very popular, family-run, traditional Welsh stone-built hotel, located in the middle of a picturesque village. The back bar is open to visitors, as well as hotel residents. There are a number of lounge areas to cater for all tastes, each with interesting features and located on separate levels. The games room houses a display of plaques. The hotel aims to provide the guest beer from one of the Welsh breweries. Bunkhouse accommodation is available.
Q♿⚘☕◑▲➤♣P

Pont-y-Pair Hotel
Holyhead Road, LL24 0BN OS798562
✪ 11-11; 12-10.30 (11 summer) Sun
☎ (01690) 710407
Greene King Abbot; Marston's Pedigree; Tetley Bitter Ⓗ

Comfortable, family-run hotel opposite the famous Pont-y-Pair bridge (from which the hotel is named) over the Afon Llugwy. A warm welcome is offered to visitors, many of whom use the hotel as a base for their varied activities around Snowdonia. Relax in the lounge and bar areas, and enjoy a good selection of freshly-cooked meals, or opt for the separate no-smoking dining room. A small pool room lies to the rear, and the back courtyard has picnic tables. Very limited parking. Q⚘☕◑▲➤♣P

CAPEL CURIG

Cobden's Hotel
Holyhead Road, LL24 0EE OS732578
✪ 11-11; 12-10.30 Sun
☎ (01690) 720243

Brains Rev James; Greene King Old Speckled Hen; guest beer Ⓗ

This 200-year-old hotel is set in its own grounds in the middle of the village. The well-appointed front lounge, rear terraced climbers' bar with feature natural rock face, and separate restaurant cater for all visitors. The hotel (with 16 bedrooms) has built up a good reputation for its warm hospitality, comfortable informality and relaxed atmosphere, together with menus of freshly-prepared, hearty and healthy food. It is deservedly popular all year round.
▲Q⚘☕◑⊟▲♣P

COLWYN BAY

Pen-y-Bryn
Pen-y-Bryn Road, Upper Colwyn Bay, LL29 6DD (top of King's Rd, 1 mile from centre)
✪ 11.30-11; 12-10.30 Sun
☎ (01492) 533360
website: www.penybryn-colwynbay.co.uk
Fuller's London Pride; Taylor Landlord; Thwaites Bitter; guest beers Ⓗ

Built in old brick on the site of the old Colwyn Bay golf club, this large, modern, open-plan pub has lovely oak floors, open fires and old furniture. Outside is a stunning garden and terrace with panoramic views of the bay and the Great Orme. Imaginative bar food can be enjoyed in a relaxed atmosphere, the menu is updated daily on the website. Five handpumps offer guest beers from independent breweries. Occasionally beer festivals are hosted while jazz nights are a frequent Sunday feature.
▲⚘◑♿♣P⚲

CONWY

Bridge Inn/Bont
Rose Hill Street, LL32 8LD OS780778
✪ 11-11; 12-10.30 Sun
☎ (01492) 573482 website: www.bridge-conwy.co.uk
Banks's Bitter; guest beers Ⓗ

Traditional-style inn opposite Conwy Castle. An open-plan lounge with coal fire in the colder months surrounds a central bar. The pub displays a collection of beer badges and pump clips and there are framed caricatures of Victorian politicians, together with interesting artefacts highlighting the town's history. Two guest beers from independent breweries are regularly featured. Bar meals are available lunchtime and Friday and Saturday evening. Orders can be made by email – the address is on the website. Excellent value accommodation is offered. ▲☕◑➤⚲

Old White House
Bangor Road, LL32 8DP (on old A55)
OS770780
✪ 6 (11 Thu-Sat)-11; 11-10.30 Sun
☎ (01492) 573133
Thwaites Bitter Ⓗ

Located half a mile west of the town of Conwy, this 17th-century building was once a coach house stable for a now demolished neighbouring hotel. It features a large, welcoming log-burning stove and a high, beamed roof space – admire the ancient cobwebs! Pictures of local historical and nautical interest decorate the walls. A long central bar serves the open-plan front lounge, and rear, no-smoking eating area.

No meals are served on Monday or Tuesday. There is usually live entertainment on Saturday evening. The pub lies on the main bus routes 5 and 5X.

♨ ⅏ ❀ ◑ ▲ ≈ ♣ P

GLANWYDDEN

Queen's Head

LL31 9JP (follow Penrhyn Bay sign from A470, 1 mile, second right) OS810810
🕓 11-3, 6-11 (10.30 Mon); 12-10.30 Sun
☎ (01492) 546570
Tetley Bitter, Burton Ale; guest beer Ⓗ

Old village pub, beautifully maintained with a cosy ambience, well-patronised by locals and holidaymakers. It was formerly a wheelwright's cottage. The restaurant serves quality food using local Welsh produce in an olde-worlde pub atmosphere. Set menus are offered on special occasions to celebrate Valentine's Day and the arrival of Beaujolais Nouveau and there is a New Year's Day highland breakfast. The Queen's Head has had the same chef and landlord for 20 years, numerous food awards have been won. The central bar serves a comfortable lounge section, which doubles as a dining area on one side and a locals' bar on the other. A few tables are provided outside which are popular in summer. A one-bedroomed cottage is available to let.

♨ ❀ ≈ ◑ ⊞ ▲ P

LLANDUDNO

King's Arms

17 Mostyn Street, LL30 2NL
🕓 12-11; 12-10.30 Sun
☎ (01492) 875882
Draught Bass; Marston's Pedigree; Tetley Dark Mild, Bitter; guest beer Ⓗ

Traditional, town-centre pub, built in 1898, with mock Tudor-style frontage featuring attractive, frosted glass windows and a pavement drinking area for hardier customers. The central bar, with tiled floor surround, serves a timber-floored front lounge, which has a dartboard and TV. The rear raised dining area has a stone fireplace and displays interesting prints depicting historic scenes of the town. The pavement area to the front is used for summer drinking. The pub is served by the main bus routes 5, 5X and 12. ❀ ◑ ♣ ♠

Snowdon Hotel

11 Tudno Street, LL30 2HB
(Great Orme end of Mostyn St)
🕓 12-11; 12-10.30 Sun
☎ (01492) 872166 website: www.snowdonhotel.co.uk
Draught Bass; Taylor Landlord; Tetley Burton Ale; guest beers Ⓗ

Popular pub, just off the shopping area, that features a large, open-plan lounge with a central bar and coal fire. The engraved Snowdon mirror is impressive. Darts, dominoes and pool are played in the games area, which displays memorabilia from the days of tall ships. There are mini beer festivals held during May and August bank holiday weekends. Guest beers normally come from local independent breweries. The pub is handy for Gloddaeth Street which is served by all bus routes.

♨ ❀ ⊞ ≈ ♣

LLANELIAN-YN-RHOS

White Lion Inn

LL29 8YA (off B5383) OS860760
🕓 11.30-3, 6-11; 12-3, 6-10.30 Sun
☎ (01492) 515807 website: www.whitelioninn.co.uk
Marston's Bitter, Pedigree; guest beer Ⓗ

Next to the church, in the hills above the coast, this is an attractive, family-run, traditionally furnished inn. It has been extended to accommodate a no-smoking area for diners and boasts a slate-floored bar, a tiny snug and a lounge partly dating back to the 16th century. White lion statues are a feature, as is the collection of jugs hanging from the ceiling beams. The comfortable leather suite in front of a real log fire is especially welcome during the winter months. ♨ Q ⅏ ❀ ≈ ◑ ▲ P

LLANFAIRFECHAN

Virginia Inn

Mill Road, LL33 0TH
🕓 12-11; 12-3, 7-10.30 Sun
☎ (01248) 680584
Theakston Mild Ⓗ

Situated in the upper village, next to the fast-flowing River Ddu and the smithy, this 1880-built terraced pub, owned and run by the same family for over 30 years, is a pleasant and typical local. A quarry-tiled hallway leads to a small bar and three rooms furnished with basic period items. The old till and genuine Allsopp's Burton Ale mirror are worthy of note. The beer is served from a vertical stillage and is always a mild. Q ≈ ♣

LLANFIHANGEL GLYN MYFYR

Crown Inn

LL21 9UL (on B5105) OS992491
🕓 7 (12 Sat)-11; closed Mon; 12-5; 7-10.30 Sun
☎ (01490) 420209
Beer range varies Ⓗ

A warm welcome awaits in this lovely old inn situated beside the Afon Alwen. The front bar has an open fire and slate flooring. Across the corridor is the pool room, with darts and portable TV, and to the rear is a small room. Children are welcome in the pub, and in the terraced gardens beside the river, where in summer bar meals are served. Permits are available for trout fishing – the licensee owns the rights. There are camping facilities in the grounds of the pub. The beers are from small independent local breweries. Regional CAMRA Pub of the Year winner 2002; food is served by arrangement – best to phone. ♨ Q ❀ ▲ ♣ P

LLANNEFYDD

Hawk & Buckle Inn

LL16 5ED (signed from Henllan at jct of B5382/B5429) OS980712
🕓 12-3 (Wed & Sat only), 6-11; 12-3, 6-10.30 Sun
☎ (01745) 540249 website: www.welshinn.co.uk
Beer range varies Ⓗ

Welcoming, 17th-century coaching inn situated high in the hills on the old stagecoach route to Holyhead. Blackpool Tower is sometimes visible over 40 miles away. The long, knocked-through, black-beamed bar has comfy upholstered settles around the walls and by the open fire. The locals' side bar includes a pool table. Excellent meals using local produce are served in the front bar or restaurant at the rear. The guest beer is from an independent brewery normally from Wales, often Brains Arms Park or SA. ♨Q⇔◑❶⊟♿Å♣P⚲

LLANRWST

New Inn
Denbigh Street, LL26 0LL
🕐 11-11; 12-10.30 Sun
☎ (01492) 640476
Banks's Original; Marston's Bitter, seasonal beer or guest beer Ⓗ
Popular, traditional, terraced town pub. One bar centres on a U-shaped lounge and also serves a corner snug, which has an open coal fire and TV. There is a rear games room which has a pool table and juke box, from which, in the evenings, the volume can reach amazing levels. Outside, there is a small courtyard with a few picnic tables. This is a friendly pub appealing to young and old. ♨❀≈♣

Pen-y-Bryn
Ancaster Square, LL26 0LH
🕐 3 (11 Fri & Sat)-11; 12-10.30 Sun
☎ (01492) 640678
Greene King Abbot; Marston's Pedigree; guest beer Ⓗ
Traditional, stone-built pub, much favoured by the locals. The hospitable landlord and friendly regulars offer a warm welcome. A long bar serves a front lounge (which features an original inglenook) and a smaller rear lounge; the walls of both are decorated with interesting historic scenes. A rear garden is used as a picnic area and children's play space. Games activities include darts and dominoes and the pub is home to the local football team. Bar snacks are available during summer months.
❀◑≈♣

MAENAN

Maenan Abbey Hotel
LL26 0UL (on A470 just N of Llanrwst) OS788675
🕐 11-11; 12-10.30 Sun
☎ (01492) 660247 website: www.manab.co.uk
Beer range varies Ⓗ
Impressive, Victorian stone house built in 1850 on the site of the original Cistercian monastery. It has a large entrance hall with a magnificent staircase, comfortable public lounge bar and restaurant. The hotel is surrounded by picturesque gardens with a seating area. Accommodation comprises 14 bedrooms (Welsh Tourist Board four crowns and a caravan/camping site is adjacent. The guest beer is normally selected from an independent brewery. Pump clips of previous guests adorn the bar. The local Rotary Club holds regular meetings here.
♨Q❀⇔◑❶Å≈(North) P

OLD COLWYN

Red Lion
385 Abergele Road, LL29 9PL
🕐 5 (4 Fri; 12 Sat)-11; 12-10.30 Sun
☎ (01492) 515042
Banks's Riding Bitter, Original; guest beers Ⓗ
Serving up to seven ales from independent brewers, this ever-popular, genuine free house, boasts many CAMRA awards for its dedication to real ale. The L-shaped lounge, warmed by a real coal fire, features the history of the area in framed pictures around the walls, including a description of the origins of the pub. There is a separate bar with pool table, darts and TV as well as a rear stableyard for outdoor drinking. The pub stands on coastal bus route 12.
♨Q❀⊟♣

Sun Inn
383 Abergele Road, LL29 9PL
🕐 12-11; 12-10.30 Sun
☎ (01492) 517007
Mansfield Dark Mild; Marston's Bitter, Pedigree; guest beer Ⓗ
Genuine beer drinkers' local and the only original, unreconstructed pub building in Old Colwyn, dating from 1844. A central bar serves a cosy lounge area, with a welcoming real coal fire, paintings by a local artist and a piano for prominent display of CAMRA literature. There is also a side bar with TV and juke box as well as a large rear games/meeting room where occasional live music can be heard. The pub is served by coastal bus route 12.
♨♣

PENMACHNO

Eagles/Ty Uchaf
LL24 0UG OS787509
🕐 7 (1 Sat)-11; 1-10.30 Sun
☎ (01690) 760177
website: www.eaglespenmachno.co.uk
Greene King Ruddles Best; John Smith's Bitter; Theakston Mild; guest beer Ⓗ
Delightful, traditional village pub, recently attractively redecorated. A warm welcome awaits the visitor in the lounge, with its wood-burning stove. The piano is also a focal point, with the pub itself being the centre of many village activities in this isolated area. A no-smoking room is available, for drinking or dining, with its own bar, and there is cheap bunkhouse accommodation. The landlord uses lined glasses, and selects the guest beer from independent breweries.
♨Q❀⇔♣⚲⊟

RHYDLYDAN

Giler Arms Hotel
LL24 0LL OS895510
🕐 12 (11 summer)-2.30, 6.30 (6 summer)-11; 12-11 Sat; 12-2.30, 6.30-10.30 (12-10.30 summer) Sun
☎ (01690) 770612
Batham Mild, Best Bitter Ⓗ
Friendly, country hotel situated in the Hiraethog, in seven acres of grounds that offers a coarse fishing lake, small campsite, and pleasant gardens beside the Afon Merddwr. Welcoming bars are well stocked, the comfortable lounge has a large open stove; and the 60-seater restaurant overlooks the lake. Children are welcome. The public bar has a real fire, and there is a small pool room; both are popular with the locals. The pub is now owned by Batham Brewery – however, the annual summer beer festivals should continue.
♨Q❀⇔◑❶⊟Å♣P

TREFRIW

Old Ship/Yr Hen Llong
LL27 0JH (on B5106) OS788638
☼ 12-3, 6-11; 12-11 Sat; 12-10.30 Sun
☎ (01492) 640013 website: www.the-old-ship.co.uk
Banks's Bitter; Marston's Pedigree; guest beers H
Dating from the 16th century, this half-timbered former customs house (when the Conwy was navigable to here) is now a popular village local. A small central bar serves the cosy L-shaped lounge with open fire, unusual period furniture, brass ornaments and pictures of historical and nautical interest. There is a separate, attractive no-smoking dining room with inglenook. No gimmicks appear in this free house just real ale and good food. Take bus route 19 or 19A. ♨Q❀✿◑ ♠P

Gwynedd

ABERDYFI

Penhelig Arms Hotel
Terrace Road, Promenade, LL35 0LT
☼ 11-3.30, 6-11 (11-11 summer); 12-3.30, 6-10.30 Sun
☎ (01654) 767215 website: www.penheligarms.com
Tetley Bitter; guest beers H
Archetypal, small, friendly seaside hotel standing beside Penhelig harbour, with superb views across the Dyfi estuary. The building is of historical interest – today the 'Little Inn' has grown into a delightful hotel with a well-earned reputation. Located in a self-contained part of the building is the rather stylish, nautically-themed Fisherman's public bar, with a designated no-smoking area. Good food, including fish specialities and local meat dishes, is served in the excellent restaurant. The hotel has 14 comfortable bedrooms. ♨Q❀✿◑ ♠≈P¼

BANGOR

Belle Vue
Holyhead Road, LL57 2EU
☼ 11 (12 Sat)-11; 12.30-10.30 Sun
☎ (01248) 364439
Boddingtons Bitter; Flowers IPA; Marston's Pedigree; guest beer H
Traditional town pub situated near Bangor University, frequented by students, lecturers and locals. A good range of beers includes local Bragdy Ynys Môn brews. There is a wood-panelled lounge, and the bar boasts an old Welsh range and a piano. Regular quiz nights and outdoor summer music events are recent features at the pub. Generous helpings of home-made food are served at lunchtime when a no-smoking area is available. Sunday hours may vary outside term time. ❀◑♠≈

Black Bull/Tarw Du ✓
107 High Street, LL57 1NS
☼ 10-11; 12-10.30 Sun
☎ (01248) 387900
Courage Directors; Greene King Abbot; Shepherd Neame Spitfire; Tetley Bitter; Theakston Best Bitter; guest beers H
Wetherspoon's pub in a converted church and presbytery at the top of the High Street. It offers spacious drinking areas (large no-smoking section) with an outdoor patio overlooking Upper Bangor and the university. A good selection of real ales is

served. It is very busy during term time, especially at weekends. A lift is available for disabled access. A number of pictures show the history of the university and the Menai Bridge. Q❀◑&≈¼

Castell
Glanrafon, LL57 1LH (opp. Cathedral)
☼ 12-11; 12-10.30 Sun
☎ (01248) 355866
Boddingtons Bitter; guest beers H
Former Hogshead pub, this spacious one-roomed house is popular with locals and students. It is now a themed pub and tends to be noisy (with loud music) in the evenings. A large-screen TV is available for sporting fixtures. There are up to four guest ales available and food is served from 12–4. The pub stands in the more popular drinking area of Bangor, at the top of the High Street. ◑&≈

Tap & Spile
Garth Road, LL57 2SW
(off old A5, follow pier signs)
☼ 12-11.30; 12-10.30 Sun
☎ (01248) 370835
Draught Bass; Greene King IPA; Wells Bombardier; guest beers H
Very popular, multi-levelled pub overlooking the pier and the Menai Straits. It has a back-to-basics feel with no upholstered seats and several church pews. Be prepared for large-screen TV and fruit machines. Four guest beers a week, from small breweries, are from the Unique Cask Ale Club. ✿◑♣

BRONABER

Rhiw Goch
LL41 4UY
☼ 12-11; 12-10.30 Sun
☎ (01766) 540374 website: www.rhiwgoch.com
Tetley Bitter; guest beers H
The Rhiw Goch was originally built as a farmhouse in the 12th century, with later additions in 1610. The public bar has a feature fireplace and a big TV screen. Families are welcome in the separate lounge, and large restaurant. An extensive menu is available from 12–9 (8.30 Sun), throughout the year. There is a games room upstairs for the youngsters. Enjoy a beer in the small courtyard, just below the floodlit ski slope. Accommodation is available in the adjacent log cabin village, and mountain bikes can be hired. One guest beer is available in winter, and two in summer. ♨Q❀◑⊟♣P

FAIRBOURNE

Fairbourne Hotel
LL38 2HQ
☼ 11-3, 6-11; 12-3, 6-10.30 Sun
☎ (01341) 250203
Courage Directors; John Smith's Bitter; guest beer (summer) H
This large, 17th-century residential hotel is renowned for excellent food, a friendly atmosphere, and 20 comfortable bedrooms. The lounge bar is attractive, with subdued lighting and plenty of quiet corners, where bar meals are served. The terrace bar, which is no-smoking until 9pm, provides an ideal area for families. The restaurant, with its

comprehensive menu, has beautiful views over the gardens and estuary. Full disabled facilities are offered. The guest beer is normally from an independent brewery.
🏚Q🍴🕽🛇🚼🅿✂

FELINHELI

Gardd Fôn
Beach Road, LL56 4RQ
(off main road, by the Menai Straits)
🕒 11-11; 12-10.30 Sun
☎ (01248) 670359
Burtonwood Bitter; guest beer Ⓗ
Nautically-themed, 18th-century, friendly pub, which is very busy in summer and at weekends when locals are joined by numerous visitors. The new bistro (no-smoking) offers good food, booking is advisable at weekends. Splendid views of the Menai Straits can be enjoyed from the drinking area opposite the pub. The nearby marina is worth a visit. Q🕸🕽🛇♣

GANLLWYD

Tyn-y-Groes Hotel
LL40 2HN
🕒 12-11 (12-2.30, 6-11 winter); 12-3.30 (3 winter); 7-10.30 Sun
☎ (01341) 440275 website: www.tynygroes.co.uk
Flowers IPA; guest beer Ⓗ
Old coaching inn set in a hillside forest, on the A470, south of the village, with views across the valley. The cosy main bar has stone walls, oak beams, and a real fire. The restaurant, separate family room, and a roadside conservatory are all no-smoking. In the summer, the outdoor tables and seating in front of the hotel are popular. A true free house – the landlord normally selects the beer from an independent brewery. 🏚Q🛌🕸🍴🕽♣🅿✂

LLANBEDR

Tŷ Mawr Hotel
LL45 2NH (take Cwmbychan turn in centre of village)
🕒 11-11; 12-10.30 Sun
☎ (01341) 241440
Draught Bass; Worthington's Bitter; guest beers Ⓗ
Small country hotel set in its own grounds. The modern lounge bar has a slate-flagged floor and cosy wood-burning stove in winter. Unusual flying memorabilia points to connections with a local airfield. French windows lead on to a verandah and landscaped terrace with outdoor seating. The pub is popular with locals, walkers and real ale enthusiasts; dogs and children are welcome. Good value meals are offered. An interesting range of guest beers is stocked.
🏚🕸🍴🕽🅰🚾🅿

LLANRUG

Glyntwrog Inn
LL55 4AN (on A4086, towards Llanberis, approx ½ mile past Spar shop)
🕒 11-11; 12-10.30 Sun
☎ (01286) 671191
Greene King IPA; Young's Special Ⓗ
This spacious pub is situated just outside the village. It offers a games room, comfortable no-smoking area and children's playground. Popular with locals, it is open all year round with meals served every day, lunchtime and

evening. It is handy for Llanberis, Padarn Lake and Snowdonia National Park. The pub is served by bus services 83 and 88 from Caernarfon and service 86 from Bangor.
🕸🕽🅰♣🅿✂

MORFA NEFYN

Cliffs Inn
Beach Road, LL53 6BY OS283408
🕒 12-3, 6 (7 winter)-11; 12-3, 6-10.30 (not winter eve) Sun
☎ (01758) 720356
Draught Bass or Greene King Old Speckled Hen; guest beer Ⓗ
Spacious pub situated above the glorious beach with fine views of the unspoilt bay across to Porth Dinllaen (once planned as the ferry port for Ireland). Walk along the sands and watch the seals from the headland beyond the lifeboat station. Excellent value food is available with vegetarian options. There is dedicated disabled parking. The guest beer is normally from Brains. Self-catering accommodation is provided. Q🛌🕸🍴🕽🛇🅿

PENMAENPOOL

George III Hotel
LL40 1YD
🕒 11-11; 12-10.30 Sun
☎ (01341) 422525 website: www.george-3rd.co.uk
Greene King Ruddles Best; John Smith's Bitter; guest beer (summer) Ⓗ
This residential hotel (built circa 1650) is situated beside the Mawddach estuary, at a toll bridge crossing, and adjacent to the old railway line which is now a cycleway and footpath. The Cellar Bar, open in season, has a slate floor, oak-beamed ceiling, and panelled benches. It is ideal for families, as it has a children's licence and menu, and no-smoking policy. The separate, plush Dresser Bar lounge upstairs, and restaurant both offer fine views. 🏚Q🕸🍴🕽🚾🛇🅿

PORTHMADOG

Ship/Llong
14 Lombard Street, LL49 9AP
(near park and harbour)
🕒 11-11; 12-10.30 Sun
☎ (01766) 512990
Greene King Old Speckled Hen; Tetley Dark Mild, Bitter; guest beers Ⓗ
Two-roomed local with a no-smoking area at the rear. Both bars are attractively adorned with nautical memorabilia, early photographs and prints. Bar meals are available and there is a separate Italian restaurant upstairs. It is now under new management, maintaining the tradition of good beer at the Ship. 🏚🕽🅰🚾🔥✂

Spooner's Bar
Harbour Station, LL49 9NF
🕒 11-11; 12-10.30 Sun
☎ (01766) 516032 website: www.festrail.co.uk
Banks's Original; Marston's Bitter, Pedigree; guest beers Ⓗ
Forming part of the Porthmadog terminus of the world-famous Ffestiniog Railway, this popular bar hosts regular mini beer festivals. There is normally at least one guest ale available. Home-cooked food is provided daily at lunchtime and on winter

Thursday–Saturday evenings. There is a terrace for outdoor drinking off the platform, and the café area has a no-smoking section. Narrow gauge steam trains run from outside the door from Easter to the end of October, and most weekends in the winter – check the website for details. ⛲❀◑⟵⏦P⌇

RHYD DDU

Cwellyn Arms

LL54 6TL (on A4085 Caernarfon-Beddgelert road at foot of Snowdon)
◷ 11-11; 11-10.30 Sun
☎ (01766) 890321 website: www.snowdoninn.co.uk
Worthington's Bitter; guest beers Ⓗ

This beamed 200-year-old pub at the foot of Snowdon, with a roaring real fire, is open all year round. An excellent menu of tasty food is offered – try their home-made curried pizza! An ever-changing range of beers from smaller breweries on the eight pumps, makes this pub well worth a visit. B&B, bunkhouse and cottage accommodation is available, also camping is just 15 minutes' walk away. Situated in a beautiful national park location, this is ideal for walkers and ramblers. Railway enthusiasts will enjoy the Welsh Highland Railway, as it is virtually on the doorstep. The pub is served by Sherpa bus route 95. Local CAMRA Pub of the Year 2000. ⚏Q⛲❀⊠◑ Å⟵P

TREMADOG

Golden Fleece

The Square, LL49 9RB
(A487, 1 mile N of Porthmadog)

◷ 11.30-3, 6-11; 12-3, 6-10.30 Sun
☎ (01766) 512421
Draught Bass; guest beer Ⓗ

Situated in the old market square, this old coaching inn is now a friendly local. On the main bus routes, nearby attractions include rock climbing and narrow gauge railways. The lounge has a no-smoking area at the rear and there is a snug which may be reserved for local regulars occasionally. There is also an extensive covered area outside with decking and bench seating. An additional bistro is upstairs, booking is advised. Guest beers are from small independent breweries. Children are welcome.
⚏Q⛲❀⊠◑Å⌇

WAUNFAWR

Snowdonia Parc

LL55 4AQ (on A4085, Caernarfon-Beddgelert road, S of the village) OS527588
◷ 11-11; 12-10.30 Sun
☎ (01286) 650409
website: www.snowdonia-park.co.uk
Mansfield Dark Mild; Marston's Bitter; Snowdonia Welsh Highland Bitter Ⓗ

The home of the Snowdonia Brewery, this pub overlooks the station on the Welsh Highland Railway – see the famous Garratt articulated locomotives steam by. There are children's play areas both inside and outside the pub, and a large campsite which offers discounts for CAMRA members (bring your membership card). The Sherpa bus from Caernarfon to Beddgelert (route 95) stops close by. Try the filled rolls.
Q⛲❀◑⊟Å⟵♣P⌇

Fizz warning

Some national breweries produce both cask-conditioned and 'nitro-keg' versions of their beers. Boddingtons Bitter, John Smith's Bitter, Tetley's Bitter and Worthington fall into this category. Nitro-keg beers, often promoted as 'smooth' or 'cream-flow' products, are filtered and pasteurised in the brewery, and served in pubs by a mix of applied carbon dioxide and nitrogen gases. They are bland, served extremely cold, and any hop character is lost by the use of applied gas. To add insult to injury, the keg founts that serve such beers are often topped by small dummy handpumps. As a result of lobbying by CAMRA, some producers of cask and nitro versions of the same beer now include the word 'cask' on pump clips for the genuine article. For example, both John Smith's Bitter and Tetley's Bitter now carry the word 'cask' on pump clips for the real thing. For the sake of brevity, and as the Good Beer Guide lists only cask-conditioned beers, we refer simply to John Smith's Bitter and Tetley Bitter. The Interbrew brand, Worthington, is labelled Worthington Bitter in cask form, and – bizarrely – Worthington Best Bitter in the nitro-keg version. Always choose the living rather than the dead.

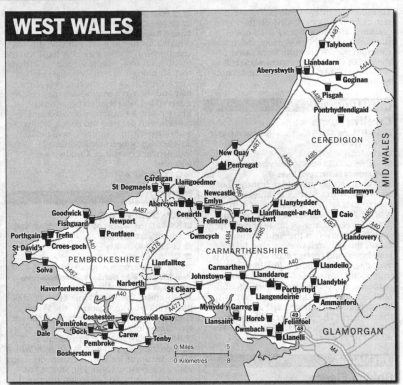

WEST WALES

Authority areas covered: Carmarthenshire UA, Ceredigion UA, Pembrokeshire UA

Carmarthenshire

AMMANFORD

Ammanford Hotel
**Wernolau House, 31 Pontamman Road,
SA18 2HX** (from Ammanford-Neath road,
50 yds past Murco garage)
☼ 5.30-11; 12-10.30 (7 winter) Sun
☎ (01269) 592598
Brains Buckley's Best Bitter; guest beers Ⓗ

The splendid choice of varying guest ales is
popular with locals. This was originally a
mine manager's house and was built in the
17th century. Five acres of landscaped
grounds and woodland surround this
residential hotel (open to non-residents).
There is a Victorian theme and open log
fires blaze in winter. A large function room
caters for weddings. Meals are available and
families welcome. Lions Club and Round
Table meetings are held here regularly.
♨Q❀⇔Å

CAIO

Brunant Arms
SA19 8RD
☼ 12 (6 Mon)-11; 12-10.30 Sun
☎ (01558) 650483
Beer range varies Ⓗ

The Brunant Arms is the only pub to
survive in Caio – a village that once had five
pubs. Situated at the end of a terrace, it is in
the centre of the village and close to the
Dolau Cothi goldmines. Regular pool and
quiz meetings are held. Good quality meals
are available. There is a pony-trekking

centre nearby and it is easy to call at the
pub en route and tether the horses to a rail
outside. A legendary Welsh wizard is buried
in the church opposite. ♨❀⇔◑ ÅP

CARMARTHEN

Queen's Hotel
Queen Street, SA31 1JR
☼ 12-11; 12-10.30 Sun
☎ (01267) 231800
Draught Bass; Worthington's Bitter; guest beers Ⓗ

Town-centre pub which is noted for the
quality of the Bass. Lunchtime meals are
served along with early evening offers. Darts
can be played in the public bar. Upstairs
meeting rooms and a dining section are
provided. An abundance of pump clips is
on display around the bar area. The pub is
leased from Punch Taverns. A patio can be
reached through the lounge, and is used for
summer drinking. ❀◑⇋

Stag & Pheasant
34 Spilman Street, SA31 1LQ
☼ 11-11; 12-10.30 Sun
☎ (01267) 236278
Worthington's Bitter; guest beers Ⓗ

Popular roadside pub which attracts many
local office workers. Once part of a stable
block belonging to the nearby Royal Hotel,
it is now a James Williams managed house.
A friendly atmosphere can be enjoyed at
this one-bar, open-plan inn where good
quality beer is the norm and tasty
lunchtime meals are served (including
Sunday). The TV is only used for sporting
events. Children are welcome. ◑⇋

CENARTH

Three Horseshoes

SA39 9JL (on A484, next to church)
☼ 11-11 (winter hours may vary);
12-10.30 (closed winter eve) Sun
☎ (01239) 710119
Ansells Mild; Brains Buckley's Best Bitter; Ⓗ
Greene King Abbot; Ⓖ **guest beer** (summer) Ⓗ
Homely pub in a village noted for its
waterfalls and gorge on the River Teifi. A
cosy bar leads to the two eating areas. A
guest beer is sold in summer and the mild,
which is always available, may vary. Meals
are served lunchtime and evening. An old
brewhouse is situated in the car park, which
is adjacent to Cenarth Coracle Centre. It is
popular with anglers as well as tourists.
ᛗQ❀◑Å♣P

CWMBACH

Farriers

Trimsaran Road, SA15 4PN
☼ 11-11; 12-10.30 Sun
☎ (01554) 774256
Draught Bass; Worthington's Bitter; guest beer Ⓗ
Small pub with an attractive garden, a
popular drinking area in summer as it
overlooks a stream. The main entrance to
the pub is down steps which lead to a
suspended walkway. A good reputation for
food is enjoyed with a varied and
interesting menu. The owner is a keen
golfer as can be seen by the memorabilia
adorning the pub. Parking is possible
opposite the pub. The Farriers is situated on
the Trimsaran to Furnace (Llanelli) road.
Q❀◑

CWMCYCH

Fox & Hounds

SA38 9RR OS276363
☼ 11-11 (not winter Mon); 12-10.30 Sun
☎ (01239) 698308
Draught Bass; Enville Ale; Worthington's Bitter Ⓗ
A few yards from the River Cych, in a rural
location, this inn is mainly used by the
hamlet's community and is heavily
involved with charity events and
fundraising. It has an open-plan bar/lounge
and games room, but retains the original
bar top (nice piece of wood). The old pub
game of bar skittles can be played, locals
often take up the challenge. The Fox &
Hounds attracts many tourists in summer.
Lunchtime and evening meals are offered
from April–September.
ᛗ❀◑Å♣P

FELINDRE

John y Gwâs

SA44 5XG (opp. school and church)
☼ 12-11; 12-10.30 Sun
☎ (01559) 370469
Beer range varies Ⓗ
The pub name translates from Welsh as
'John the Servant', and relates to a previous
owner (in the 1950s) whose portrait hangs
in the bar. A traditional, cosy, friendly,
village pub, it was formerly known as the
New Shop Inn. Built in the early 1800s,
there were once three shops on the site,
including a cobbler and a barber. Customers
can enjoy a drink in the bar, snug or pool

room; there are three rotating guest beers.
The pub is close to attractions such as the
National Woollen Museum of Wales.
ᛗQ◑ᵹÅ♣P

HOREB

Waunwyllt

Horeb Road, SA15 5AQ
(off B4309 at Five Roads, 3 miles from Llanelli)
☼ 12-3, 7 (6.30 Fri & Sat)-11 (12-11 summer);
12-3, 7-10.30 Sun
☎ (01269) 860209
Beer range varies Ⓗ
Superb country pub with a genuinely warm
welcome. The food is delicious and
reasonably priced; choose from a varied
menu and specials board. The landlord and
some of the locals are keen cyclists and have
taken part in several rides for charity. The
pub is close to the new cycle path from
Llanelli and now often attracts passing
cyclists. It was awarded Carmarthenshire
CAMRA Pub of the Year in 2000.
Accommodation is available. There are seats
outside at the front and a beer garden to the
rear. Q❀⇔◑ÅP

JOHNSTOWN

Friends Arms

St Clears Road, SA31 3HH
(jct of Johnstown-Picton Hill)
☼ 11-11; 12-3, 7-10.30 Sun
☎ (01267) 234073
Ansells Mild; Tetley Bitter, Burton Ale Ⓗ
There has been a pub on this site for 400
years, originally it was a blacksmith's with
attached stables and a nearby toll house
which is still standing. The smith was
owned by John Thomas in 1841 and he
took 60 years to become landlord. The pub
has low beams and a great deal of brassware
around the walls. Very much a community
local, it raises a substantial amount each
year for charity.
Q❀♣

LLANDEILO

Castle Hotel

113 Rhosmaen Street, SA19 6EN
☼ 11-11; 12-10.30 Sun
☎ (01558) 823446
Tomos Watkin Whoosh, BB, Merlin Stout, OSB,
seasonal beers; Worthington's Bitter Ⓗ
Originally the home of Tomos Watkin
Brewery, now relocated (to Swansea), this is
a multi-roomed pub with an increasing
reputation for good food. It is close to
several local tourist attractions including
the National Botanical Gardens at
Llanarthne. For more ideas, the local tourist
information office is based in the large
council car park behind the Castle Hotel.
Locals are friendly and will make all visitors
welcome. There is sometimes live music on
at weekends.
Q❀◑≅

INDEPENDENT BREWERIES

Bragdy Ceredigion Pentregat
Coles Llanddarog
Felinfoel Felinfoel
Nags Head Abercych

White Horse ✓
125 Rhosmaen Street, SA19 7AF
(off main street through arch)
🕐 11-11; 12-10.30 Sun
☎ (01558) 822424
Breconshire Brecon County Ale, Golden Valley; Wells Bombardier; guest beers Ⓗ

Charming, 16th-century, Grade II listed coaching inn which is a multi-roomed pub but does not serve food. It is popular with all ages and there are occasionally live bands. The beer garden at the rear leads into the main council car park. The courtyard to the front of the building houses seating which allows alfresco drinking. A good range of beers is normally available. Admire the Guinness memorabilia behind the bar. 🏠☸≥♣👍

LLANDOVERY

Castle Hotel
King's Road, SA20 0AP
🕐 11-11; 12-3, 7-10.30 Sun
☎ (01550) 720343
Worthington's Bitter; guest beer Ⓗ

Originally built in the 18th century, the pub has recently undergone extensive refurbishment. It is close to the castle (hence the name) and the livestock market. The nearby car park has ample space for visitors. There are 23 rooms which include two heritage rooms with four-poster beds. All the rooms have en-suite accommodation. There is an annual drovers' festival held in the town in September. Llandovery is situated on the River Towy. 🛏◑▷≥P

LLANDYBIE

Ivy Bush
18 Church Street, SA18 3HZ
🕐 12-11; 12-2.30, 7-10.30 Sun
☎ (01269) 850272
Greene King Old Speckled Hen; Tetley Burton Ale; guest beer Ⓗ

The oldest pub in the village, dating back nearly 300 years. Recently refurbished to an open-plan design, it has lost none of its local appeal. Darts are played on Tuesday and Thursday, and cards on Wednesday. Children and dogs are welcome. It is situated near the Heart of Wales railway line. B&B accommodation is available in the cottage adjacent which features an en-suite sauna. No food is served, just good honest ale. ◑≥

LLANELLI

Lemon Tree
2 Prospect Place, SA15 3PT
(off A476, at jct with A484)
🕐 12-11; 12-10.30 Sun
☎ (01554) 775121
Brains Buckley's Best Bitter; Tomos Watkin Whoosh; guest beer Ⓗ

End-of-terrace pub near the former site of Buckley's Brewery. It is a popular local with a strong sports following. The exterior artwork is interesting. The interior has been refurbished and is now open plan but retains the feel of a separate bar. The bowling green to the rear is now used for barbecue events when the weather permits.

606

A pool room is available at a lower level than the bar, and darts are played in the bar area. ♣

LLANFALLTEG

Plash Inn
SA34 0UN
(from A40 at Llanddew Velfrey, at the end of village)
🕐 12-3.30 (not Mon; closed all day Tue), 6-11; 12-10.30 Sun; 12-10.30 Sun
☎ (01437) 563472
website: www.plash@btinternet.com
Worthington's Bitter; guest beer Ⓗ

When the local mansion, Tegfynydd, burned down, English craftsmen were employed to repair it and, unable to pronounce the name (Plas y Pwdl – Puddle Palace), they referred to it as 'The Plash'. A traditional village free house the locals call it a 'talking pub'. A garden at the rear overlooks green fields and the River Taf. An attractive bar area, which came from a local outfitter's shop, serves ales (including a Wye Valley brew) while a small restaurant offers traditional home-made dishes (Wed–Sat lunchtime and eve meals). A brewery cottage in the grounds of the inn provides private accommodation. Darts, dominoes, crib and skittles are played. 🏠Q☸◑▷♣P

LLANFIHANGEL-AR-ARTH

Cross Inn
Cross Roads, SA39 9HX
🕐 5 (12 Sat)-11; 12-10.30 Sun
☎ (01559) 384838
Breconshire Golden Valley; Fuller's London Pride Ⓗ

Dating back to the 16th century, the Cross Inn was originally a drovers' stopping inn. A log fire greets you in the cosy bar which features some original beams. Under the bar the old railway tunnel remains, but since the line has closed the shaking has stopped. All the restaurant food is prepared and cooked on the premises, and well worth trying (lunches available on Sunday). 🏠☸◑▲♣P

LLANGENDEIRNE

Smiths Arms/y Gof
SA17 5EN (on main Carmarthen-Pontyberem road)
🕐 12-2.30 (not winter Mon-Fri), 6.30-11.30; 12-2.30, 6.30-10.30 Sun
☎ (01269) 871544
Brains Dark; guest beer Ⓗ

Situated in a pretty village, with splendid views of the river (the Gwendraeth Fawr), this friendly pub is on the main road. The bar area includes a games room where pool and darts can be played. The lounge has a large dining area with a no-smoking section. Tasty meals are offered and prove excellent value. Pump clips cover the walls, giving testament to the ever-changing range of guest ales available. The pub is the focal point of the village. ☸◑▷P

LLANSAINT

King's Arms
13 Maes yr Eglwys (behind church)
🕐 12-2.30, 6.30-11 (closed winter Tue); 12-2.30, 6.30-10.30 Sun
☎ (01267) 267487
Worthington's Bitter; guest beers Ⓗ

A log fire and fine welcome are the norm at this 200-year-old pub, situated close to the village's 11th-century church. An interesting collection of jugs adorns the low beams and local photographs hang on the walls. It is rumoured to be built from stone recovered from the lost village of St Ishmael's. Children are welcome and the food is good; handy for Carmarthen Bay Holiday Park.
🏠✿㈪⌾▲♣P

LLANYBYDDER

Albion Arms
Llansawel Road, SA40 9RN
(off A485, at Llanybydder to village of Glanduar)
✪ 5 (12 Sat)-11; 12-10.30 Sun
☎ (01570) 480781
Black Sheep Best Bitter; Boddingtons Bitter; guest beer Ⓗ
Unpretentious and cheerful, traditional Welsh market town pub. It is now being restored to include a restaurant on the second level. The name Albion is possibly from a ship-building connection. There has been a pub here for over 200 years serving the village of Glanduar, now encompassed by the town of Llanybydder. The extensive bar area provides a large-screen TV to show sports events. There is a separate pool room. Children and dogs are welcome.
🏠♣P

MYNYDD Y GARREG

Prince of Wales
SA17 4RP (1½ miles from Kidwelly bypass)
✪ 7 (5 Sat)-11; 12-3 Sun
☎ (01554) 890522
Beer range varies Ⓗ
Comfortable and welcoming, this small, isolated pub is definitely worth finding. The walls are covered with an extensive array of movie memorabilia. There is a small, no-smoking restaurant serving delicious food (Mon–Sat eves and Sun lunch). The pub does a good trade in take-home beers, bring your own container. Six ales are available at all times and present an ever-changing choice from small local breweries. This is the largest range of real ales in the area; it is a rare local outlet for Bullmastiff Brewery. Children under 14 are not allowed in the pub. Pembrey Country Park, Kidwelly Castle and Kidwelly Industrial Museum are close at hand. 🏠Q✿㈪

NEWCASTLE EMLYN

Bunch of Grapes
Bridge Street, SA38 9DU
(opp. provisions market)
✪ 12-11 (closed winter Mon); 12-3, 7-10.30 Sun
☎ (01239) 711185
Courage Directors; guest beers Ⓗ
Delightful, listed 17th-century town pub with many original features still retained: exposed beams, floors and stonework. A large grapevine covers the unusual indoor garden. A rear restaurant serves tasty home-made food. Book early for the Sunday roast as it proves popular. Entertainment includes live music on Thursday evening, and Celtic music on Monday, this appeals to customers of all age groups.
🏠✿㈪▲♣P✗

Plas Parke Inn
SA44 5AX
(on B4335 between Llandysul and Newcastle Emlyn)
✪ 2.30-11; 12-10.30 Sun
☎ (01559) 362684
Draught Bass; guest beer Ⓗ
Friendly village meeting place with a choice of three bars and cosy nooks and crannies. Gazebos in the garden provide sheltered outdoor seating in summer, whatever the weather. Evening meals and Sunday lunch are served in the 40-seater restaurant, which has a reputation for gargantuan helpings. Close to a local beauty spot, Alltcafan Bridge, it is much frequented by fly fishermen on the River Teifi and is handy for the canoeing centre at Llandysul. The Henllan Falls and the National Woollen Museum of Wales are both close by.
🏠✿㈪▲♣P

PORTHYRHYD

Mansel
Banc y Mansel, Drefach, SA32 8BS
(off A48, Drefach-Llanddarog road)
✪ 6 (2 Sat)-11; 12-4 Sun
☎ (01267) 275305
Beer range varies Ⓗ
Friendly, roadside pub with wood fires in each room. It is an 18th-century former coaching inn on the A48. A games room to the rear, where you can play pool and darts, used to be a killing room for pigs but the limestone slabs have been broken up and used in the fireplace. Low beams have been added to create a homely atmosphere. A fine collection of jugs hangs from the beams. Very much a locals' pub, you will receive a warm welcome here. 🏠Q㈪⊟♣P

RHANDIRMWYN

Royal Oak
SA20 0NY
✪ 11.30-3, 6-11 (times can vary); 12-2, 7-10.30 Sun
☎ (01550) 760201
Beer range varies Ⓗ
Built as a hunting lodge for the local landowner, this remote stone-flagged pub offers excellent views of the valley. It was awarded CAMRA South Wales Pub of the Year 2001–02. An excellent selection of whiskies and bottled beers can be sampled and the varying guest list (three to four in winter, and up to six in summer) is superb. Close to the Llyn Brianne Dam, the pub attracts a large number of ramblers and birdwatchers. 🏠Q✿⌾㈪▲♣P

RHOS

Lamb Inn
SA44 5EE
(on A484, Carmarthen-Newcastle Emlyn road)
✪ 12-2.30, 5.30-11; 12-11 Fri & Sat; 12-10.30 Sun
☎ (01559) 370055
Banks's Original; Greene King Old Speckled Hen; Taylor Landlord; guest beers Ⓗ
Spacious country inn, overlooking the Teifi Valley, with flagstoned floors and interesting interior and exterior brickwork. There has been a pub here for 300 years. It was extended in the 1970s, then known as 'the little Ritz in Wales', and has undergone

a recent, attractive refurbishment. Spend an hour browsing among the curios, including a collection of bottled beers. Children can play in what must be the smallest 'fun' village jail, HM Prison Rhos. Bottled beers include Wychwood Hobgoblin and Robinson's Old Tom. The restaurant seats 75. ♨☞❀✍◑ ♣ P ✂

ST CLEARS

Corvus
Station Road, SA33 4BG
🕐 11-11; 12-10.30 Sun
☎ (01994) 230965
Courage Best Bitter; Worthington's Bitter; guest beer Ⓗ

Busy, two-bar locals' pub in the centre of the village. There are cartoon caricatures of regulars in the bar. The lounge has many beer jugs and also a great deal of decorative brassware. It is the local haunt of many of the village's sportsmen and supports the local football team. Continuing the sporting theme, darts are played in the bar. Food is available in the evening with an interesting menu. Nearby is Heatherton Adventure Park which provides a great day out for the family. Q ◑ ⍫

Ceredigion

ABERYSTWYTH

Fountain Inn
Trefechan, SY23 1BE
(from Aberystwyth town centre, 1/4 mile S on A487)
🕐 12-11; 12-10.30 Sun
☎ (01970) 612430
Boddingtons Bitter; Brains Dark; guest beer Ⓗ

This small but cosy pub on the outskirts of Aberystwyth has a separate lounge and public bar. One guest beer is always available and changes regularly. Situated on the main A487, opposite the new marina development, this traditional pub has a cheery atmosphere and real local character. Until 1960 this was the brewery tap for the town's principal brewery – while little remains of this, photographs in the pub depict both the brewery itself and the history of this industrial quarter of Aberystwyth. For the energetic, the climb to nearby Pen Dinas iron age hill-fort should work up a thirst. ❀◑ ⍫ Å ♣ ♠

Hen Orsaf ◉
Alexandra Road, SY23 1LN
🕐 10-11; 12-10.30 Sun
☎ (01970) 636080
Banks's Bitter; Brains SA; Courage Directors; Shepherd Neame Spitfire; guest beers Ⓗ

The town's old station, a 1924 listed building, has been given a stylish Wetherspoon's make-over. Linked ground floor rooms and an attractive 'beer patio' (the old station concourse) provide light, airy drinking/eating areas with toilets upstairs. A fully specified disabled toilet is on the ground floor. The guest beer policy is less consistently adventurous than it was initially, and you may need to ask for a top-up (willingly given) as tight sparklers are used. Trains, buses, taxis and public car parks are all nearby. It can get very busy in the evening, especially at weekends.
Q ❀◑ ♿ Å ⇌ ✂

Ship & Castle
1 High Street, SY23 1JG
🕐 12-11; 12-10.30 Sun
☎ (01970) 612334
Beer range varies Ⓗ

The most consistently varied selection of real ales in town is to be found at this excellent free house. The beer range usually includes Six Bells Full Moon (4.5% ABV) and five other beers mostly from micros in Wales and the borders. Themed beer festivals are held in April and October. Sunday lunch is served (12–4) and children are welcome. Traditional Irish folk music is played on Wednesday night. Tara, the friendly pub Rottweiler somnolently maintains good order!
Å ⇌ ♣

CARDIGAN

Black Lion/Llew Du
High Street, SA43 1JW
🕐 10-11; 12-10.30 Sun
☎ (01239) 612532
Tomos Watkin Whoosh, OSB; Worthington's Bitter Ⓗ

Historic coaching inn in a busy, characterful town. It dates back to the 12th century, but the present building is 18th century. There is a main drinking area, a small panelled snug and a rear dining section. It is a welcome outpost for for Tomos Watkin beers. Good value food is available. A friendly meeting place for locals and visitors alike.
❀ ✍◑ Å ♣

Red Lion/Llew Coch
Pwllhai, SA43 1DB
(behind the Cardigan bus station)
🕐 11-11; 12-10.30 Sun
☎ (01239) 612482
Brains Buckley's Best Bitter, Rev James Ⓗ

Homely locals' pub where Welsh is the first language. Visitors are made to feel most welcome. The landlady is the longest-serving in Cardigan. The main bar area is complemented by a smaller, private lounge area and a separate games room. Welsh music is sold plus weekly live entertainment is staged. Tucked away behind the bus station, this pub is worth seeking out.
Q ❀ ❀ ♣

GOGINAN

Druid Inn
High Street, SY23 3NT
(on A44, 7 miles E of Aberystwyth)
🕐 11-11; 12-10.30 Sun
☎ (01970) 880650 website: www.goginan.co.uk
Banks's Bitter, Brains Bitter; guest beer Ⓗ

This enterprising free house, in a former lead-mining village, stands on the busy A44 trunk road. It overlooks the Melindwr Valley, with the Llywernog Mining Museum nearby. The L-shaped main bar includes a dining area, where food is available all day. The regular guest beer comes generally from a micro or regional brewery. Look out for the locally-made love spoons (main bar) and the fresh water wells at the back of the pub.
Q ❀ ❀ ✍◑ ♣ P

LLANBADARN

Black Lion
The Square, SY23 3RA
☼ 12-11; 12-10.30 Sun
☎ (01970) 623448
Banks's Original, Bitter; Marston's Pedigree; guest beer Ⓗ

Though heavily modernised, this village pub occupies an ancient site next to the village's historic parish church. The large main bar houses a pool table at one end, while the other end offers a traditional drinkers' environment with bench seating. It is a lively place, with darts, pool, or a quiz most nights, and an enthusiastic following for televised sport. A jazz band rehearses on Wednesday evening, and there are occasional live gigs in the rear function/family room, which is also much in demand by local societies. Custom is a good mix of locals and students. Aberystwyth town centre, a mile away, is easily accessible by bus. ⌂❀◑▲♣P

LLANGOEDMOR

Penllwyndu
SA43 2LY (on B4570, 4 miles E of Cardigan) OS241458
☼ 1-11; 12-10.30 Sun
☎ (01239) 682533
Brains Buckley's Best Bitter; guest beer Ⓗ

This old-fashioned ale house stands on the crossroads where Cardigan's wrong-doers were hanged! Do not be put off, the atmosphere is cheerful and welcoming today. The public bar has a slate floor and inglenook with wood-burning stove. Down the steps is a cosy restaurant. In summer, it is a treat to sit in the garden and admire superb views of the Preseli mountains. ⌂❀◑♣P

NEW QUAY

Cambrian Hotel
New Road, SA45 9SE
(on B4342 at E approach to town)
☼ 11-11; 12-10.30 Sun
☎ (01545) 560295
website: www.smoothhound.co.uk/hotels
Brains Buckley's Best Bitter; Felinfoel Double Dragon; Worthington's Bitter; guest beer Ⓗ

Named after a South Wales colliery, the Cambrian may well be the only pub in town not visited by Dylan Thomas (it was not a pub when he lived here). The comfortable bar in this former sea captain's house is tucked away behind the restaurant, and also has a separate side entrance. Or choose to sit in the lounge which has a TV. A guest beer is available in summer when trade flourishes from the holiday complex across the road and at certain busy times out of season. The pub's beer festival (first week in Aug) is now an established event. Aberystwyth to Cardigan buses stop outside (limited evening and Sunday service). Q❀≈◑▲P

PISGAH

Halfway Inn
Devil's Bridge Road, SY23 4NE
(7 miles E of Aberystwyth on A4120)

☼ 12-2 (not winter Mon-Fri), 6.30-11; 12-2, 6.30-10.30 Sun
☎ (01970) 880631
Badger Best; Felinfoel Double Dragon; Hancock's HB; guest beer (summer) Ⓗ

Commanding glorious upland views, this old wayside inn has long been known for its cask beers and has more recently developed a reputation for food and accommodation. Westons Old Rosie cider is sold in summer. Flanked by a smaller pool room, the main bar has a rustic feel with stone walls, flagstone floor and beams. While the pub has a loyal local following, its remoteness means it can be quiet in winter. For an unusual approach to the pub, take the steam-hauled Vale of Rheidol railway (Easter–October) and alight at Nantyronen Station for a stiff but rewarding uphill walk. ⌂⌂≈≈◑▲♣P

PONTRHYDFENDIGAID

Black Lion Hotel
Mill Street, SY25 6BE (off B4343) OS732666
☼ 12-11; 12-10.30 Sun
☎ (01974) 831624 website: www.blacklionatbont.co.uk
Beer range varies Ⓗ

Enthusiastic licensees are bringing back new life to this historic inn after years in which it has struggled to find a role. The recent refurbishment, its first since 1865, highlights historic features – oak panelling rescued from a manor house, floorboards from a church hall, inglenook, ancient furniture and original beams. The main bar is complemented by the old auction room at the rear, which serves as a function/family room. A separate dining room is planned, to preserve the main bar's identity as an area for drinkers. Two handpumped beers are sold in summer, and one or two in winter, mainly from micro-breweries. It makes a fine base for exploring a fascinating region. ⌂Q⌂❀≈◑♿▲♣P

TALYBONT

White Lion/Llew Gwyn
SY24 5ER
☼ 11-11; 12-10.30 Sun
☎ (01970) 832245
Banks's Original, Bitter Ⓗ

One of two Lions facing the village green, this welcoming pub functions well both as a local and as an ideal stop-off point for the traveller. Serious drinkers head for the traditional front bar, with a slate floor, bench seating and TV. The recently refurbished rear lounge is quiet and relaxing while some fascinating photographs of the area and a local history display lend interest. The family/pool room, dining room, and beer garden complete the picture. Curries are a speciality and can also be supplied to take away. Buses from Aberystwyth to Machynlleth stop outside (limited evening and Sunday service). Q❀≈◑⊟♿▲♣P✁

Pembrokeshire

ABERCYCH

Nags Head
SA37 0HJ
(on B4332, between Cenarth and Eglwyswrw)

✪ 11-3, 5.30-11; 11-11 Sat; 12-10.30 Sun
☎ (01239) 841200

Flowers Original; Nags Head Old Emrys; Worthington's Bitter; guest beers ⓗ

Well-restored old smithy, boasting a beamed bar, riverside beer garden and a micro-brewery. The Old Emrys Ale is not always available. The bar area is furnished with an interesting collection of old medical instruments, railway memorabilia and a range of timepieces giving the time in different parts of the world. Space is also found for an extensive collection of bottled beers. ⚲Q☕✿◑▶P

BOSHERTON

St Govan's Inn
SA71 5AN (signed from Pembroke)
✪ 11-3, 7-11 (11-11 summer); 12-3, 7-10.30 Sun
☎ (01646) 661311

Hancock's HB; Worthington's Bitter; guest beers ⓗ

A relatively modern pub, it takes its name from the saint who built a chapel on the cliffs close by. The pub is on the coast path and close to the internationally renowned Bosherston lily ponds. It is frequented by climbers who find the local cliffs irresistible. A short distance away is a safe sandy beach. The pub serves a variety of food to complement its range of real ales.
Q✿◑⊟♣P

CAREW

Carew Inn
SA70 8SL
(A477 to Carew, follow signs for Carew Cross)
✪ 12-3, 5-11 (11-11 summer); 12-10.30 Sun
☎ (01834) 651267

Brains Rev James; Worthington's Bitter; guest beers ⓗ

This pub lies in the centre of the village, close to the Celtic Carew Cross and Carew Castle, a short distance away is the restored tidal mill. In the middle of the Pembrokeshire Coast National Park, the pub makes an ideal stop-off when exploring the area; close by is the Oakwood Adventure and Leisure Park plus many other attractions. ⚲Q✿◑⊟♣P

COSHETON

Brewery Inn
SA72 4UD
(from A477, turn right to Cosheston, then right in village)
✪ 12-4, 6.30-11; 11-11 Sat; 12-3, 7-10.30 Sun
☎ (01646) 686678

Tomos Watkin OSB; Worthington's Bitter; guest beers ⓗ

As its name suggests this pub was originally the village brewery. It has now been extensively altered internally, to provide a comfortable bar with adjoining restaurant, specialising in Mexican cuisine as well as a good general menu. The old brewery has been converted to self-catering accommodation units. ⚲Q⇌◑&♣P

CRESSWELL QUAY

Cresselly Arms
SA68 0TE (follow signs for Lawrenny)
✪ 12-3, 5-11; 7-10.30 Sun
☎ (01646) 651210

Worthington's Bitter; guest beer ⓖ

Situated on a tributary of the western Cleddau, the Cresselly was originally a one-room pub. It has now been sympathetically extended without losing any of the character and charm of this friendly local. Beer is still dispensed from barrels on the back of the bar. The pub is the hub of the community and is the meeting place for most of the local sports teams. ⚲Q✿P⅊

CROES-GOCH

Artramont Arms
SA62 5JP (on A487 through road)
✪ 7-11 (12-3, 6-11 summer); 12-3, 6-10 Fri & Sat; 12-3, 7-10.30 Sun
☎ (01348) 831309

Brains SA; guest beer ⓗ

Appealing village local with a large public bar, separate lounge and dining section, plus a conservatory area. There is a no-smoking area for drinkers and a pleasant beer garden. Food is served lunchtime and evening from an imaginative menu. The pub acts as the central focus for village activities.
⚲✿◑⊟&P⅊

DALE

Griffin Inn
SA62 3RB (on seafront)
✪ 12-3, 6-11 (12-11 summer); 12-10.30 Sun
☎ (01646) 636227

Felinfoel Double Dragon; Worthington's Bitter; guest beer ⓗ

Harbourside establishment at the end of the bay, close to the slipway that is popular with locals and visitors alike. Table skittles are played. Relax over a drink outside, some of the seating is by the seawall.
⚲◑♣

FISHGUARD

Fishguard Arms
SA65 9HQ
✪ 12-3, 6.30-11; closed Mon; 12-10.30 Sun
☎ (01348) 872763

Worthington's Bitter; guest beer ⓖ

A small locals' pub with a distinctive dark blue-green painted exterior. There is no keg beer but a very interesting rotation of real ales. The only entertainment is conversation. A visit to this establishment is an experience not to be missed.
⚲Q⊟

Royal Oak
Market Square, SA65 9HA
(town centre roundabout, on A487)
✪ 11-11; 12-10.30 Sun
☎ (01348) 872514

Brains Dark, Bitter, SA, Rev James; guest beers ⓗ

Charming, friendly pub claiming historic connections (French forces surrendered here following the last invasion of mainlaind Britain in 1797). Some fascinating memorabilia from this time is worth a look. This pub is full of character and offers a separate public bar and attractive beer garden. Home-cooked meals are served at affordable prices from a varied menu. Camping facilities are available nearby. The local folk-singing fraternity meet here on Monday evening.
⚲◑⊟♣

GOODWICK

Rose & Crown
SA64 0BP
(on left uphill from ferry port entrance) OS947384
☼ 11-11; 12-10.30 Sun
☎ (01348) 874449
Brains Buckley's IPA; Worthington's Bitter; guest beer Ⓗ
Picturesque pub close to the ferry port and enjoying views of Goodwick harbour and the beach. It has a no-smoking dining section and offers meals at each session. The landlord is an active member of the Royal British Legion. Q✿⊛❁ ▲≈♣P

HAVERFORDWEST

Pembroke Yeoman
Hill Street, St Thomas's Green, SA61 1QF
☼ 11-11; 12-3, 7-10.30 Sun
☎ (01437) 762500
Flowers IPA; Worthington's Bitter; guest beers Ⓗ/Ⓖ
This well-supported, comfortable town local attracts a wide range of customers. It is very popular with all age groups and is a meeting place for a variety of local organisations. The guest ale can be served by jug or handpump and the sparkler will be removed on request. Enjoy the peaceful atmosphere, fine beers and traditional pub games. An imaginative menu is on offer.
♨❁♣

NARBERTH

Angel Inn
High Street, SA67 7AS
☼ 11-3, 5.30-11; 7-10.30 Sun
☎ (01834) 860215
Worthington's Bitter; guest beer Ⓗ
Cosy, modernised, town-centre pub that is very popular for food. It has a separate public bar.
Q❁⊟▲

Kirkland Arms
East Gate, St James Street, SA67 7BB
☼ 11-11; 11-10.30 Sun
☎ (01834) 860423
Felinfoel Best Bitter, Double Dragon; guest beer Ⓗ
Comfortable, two-roomed local on the edge of a one-way traffic system. No food is served other than barbecues for special occasions. Savour the exceptional beer quality. There are separate public and lounge bars and the pub has its own car park. If walking, it is the first stop-off point for a pint after a lengthy trek from the railway station. Camping facilities are available nearby.
⊟▲≈P

NEWPORT

Castle Hotel
Bridge Street, SA42 0TB (on A487 through road)
☼ 11-11; 12-10.30 Sun
☎ (01239) 820742
Wadworth 6X; Worthington's Bitter; guest beer Ⓗ
This friendly, popular local has an attractive bar with a real fire and a wealth of wood panelling. There is an extensive separate dining area serving food at all sessions. A large off-street car park is situated at the rear of the hotel.
♨➳✿⊟❁ ▲P

Golden Lion
East Street, SA40 2SY (on A487 through road)
☼ 11-11; 12-10.30 Sun
☎ (01239) 820321
Felinfoel Double Dragon; Tomos Watkin OSB; Worthington's Bitter Ⓗ
Another of Newport's social local pubs. This one reputedly has a resident ghost. A number of internal walls have been removed to form a spacious bar area with other distinct sections; the pub retains a cosy atmosphere.
Q❁▲P

Llwyngwair Arms
East Street, SA42 0SY (on A487 through road)
☼ Winter 5-11 (closed Mon); summer 11-11; 12-10.30 Sun
☎ (01239) 820267
Draught Bass; guest beers Ⓗ
This popular local has not been altered for some considerable time. It has a separate dining area serving inexpensive food, and there is a focus on bar meals. Both food and ales have a distinct Welsh emphasis. Parking is available through the archway on the opposite side of the road.
♨Q❁ ▲P

PEMBROKE

Old King's Arms Hotel
Main Street, SA71 4JS (next to town hall)
☼ 11-11; 12-10.30 Sun
☎ (01646) 683611
website: www.oldkingsarmshotel.co.uk
Worthington's Bitter; guest beer Ⓗ
Olde-worlde hotel located in the town centre about 100 yards from Pembroke Castle, the birthplace of Henry VII. The hotel consists of a large public bar, which can be busy at weekends, and a small lounge. The restaurant is recommended and specialises in steaks, and also serves a wide range of bar snacks. The car park is at the rear of the hotel. Q➳❁⊟❁P

Royal George Hotel
9 Northgate, SA71 4NR
☼ 11-3, 5-11; 11-11 Sat; 12-3, 7-10.30 Sun
☎ (01646) 682751
Worthington's Bitter; guest beers Ⓗ
Pleasant, cheery locals' pub on the old South Quay just outside the town centre. The pub building is part of the old town wall and is located directly below Pembroke Castle at what used to be the town's north gate. The interior consists of one large split-level, L-shaped room with a single bar. Current and future guest ales are listed on a blackboard by the bar. The sparkler will be removed on request. ➳≈♣

PEMBROKE DOCK

First & Last
London Road, SA72 6TX
(entrance to town on A477)
☼ 11-11; 12-10.30 Sun
☎ (01646) 682687
Worthington's Bitter; guest beers Ⓗ
Large, friendly, local pub on the outskirts of the town offering a good variety of guest ales and value-for-money bar food. Live music is staged on Saturday evening, plus a quiz night on Sunday. On the main route to

the Irish ferries, the pub is close to local castles and a short diversion from the Pembrokeshire coastal path. ♛❀◑⇌♣P

Station Inn

Apley Green, Dimond Street, SA72 6HN
(follow signs to railway station)
⏲ 11-3, 6.30-11; 12-3, 7-10.30 Sun
☎ (01646) 621255
Tomos Watkin BB; guest beers Ⓗ
Housed in a Victorian railway station with the trains still running on the adjoining lines, this town-centre pub is only a short distance from the Irish ferry terminal. The bar features a range of ales and its restaurant specialises in home-cooked meals using organic meats (served Wed–Sat 7–9). Bar meals are also on offer. Every Tuesday customers can sample the new beer on tap.
Q◑♿⇌P

PONTFAEN

Dyffryn Arms ☆

SA65 9SG (on B4313, Gwaun Valley road)
OS027341
⏲ hours vary
☎ (01348) 881305
Draught Bass or Tetley Burton Ale Ⓖ
This bar resembles a 1920s front room where time has stood still. The beer is still served by the jug through a sliding hatch. Conversation is the main form of entertainment. The landlady is in her eighties and there is a superb, relaxed atmosphere in this pub. It lies in the heart of the scenic Gwaun Valley between the Preseli Hills and Fishguard (Abergwaun).
♛Q❀⛺♣

PORTHGAIN

Sloop Inn

SA62 5BN
⏲ 11.30-3, 6-11 (11-11 summer); 12-4, 6-10.30 Sun
☎ (01348) 831449
Brains SA; Felinfoel Double Dragon; Worthington's Bitter Ⓗ
This sympathetically modernised old inn has served both the locally-based fishing industry and the now-defunct quarrying and stone exporting industries. The pub features quarrying and shipping ephemera as part of its decor. Holding hoppers for stone can be seen on the opposite side of the harbour. It is a popular pub with both locals and visitors, and offers a good variety of beers and reasonably-priced food, using local produce where possible. ♛❀◑♣P

ST DAVID'S

Farmers Arms

Goat Street, SA62 6RF (on road leading from Old Cross Square to St Justinians) OS751253
⏲ 11-11; 12-10.30 Sun
☎ (01437) 720328
Brains Bitter, Rev James; Worthington's Bitter Ⓗ
19th-century stone hostelry that retains many old features. It is popular with local farmers, fishermen and youngsters, with many tourists calling in during the summer season. The pub serves an interesting range of good, wholesome home-cooked food. Definitely worth a visit; there is often a singalong session on a Sunday evening.
♛Q❀◑⊞⛺

ST DOGMAELS

White Hart

Finch Street, SA43 3EA
(on B4546 through village)
⏲ 12-2.30 (not Tue), 7-11; 12-3, 7-10.30 Sun
☎ (01239) 612099
Wadworth IPA; guest beer Ⓗ
Cheery, welcoming, small village pub with a good local following. It is on the right-hand side of the road when entering St Dogmaels from Cardigan. The guest ale changes on a regular basis and frequently showcases a brewery not represented locally. Three guest ales are served in summer and two in winter. The landlord is a great rugby enthusiast. The opening hours are extended in the summer as the pub is a good stopping-off point if walking the coastal path.
♛◑⊞⛺♣

SOLVA

Harbour Inn

SA62 6RF
(on A487 through road adjoining harbour car park)
⏲ 11-11; 12-10.30 Sun
☎ (01437) 720013
Draught Bass; Greene King Old Speckled Hen; guest beer Ⓗ
This delightful seaside hostelry retains a traditional atmosphere, having remained unaltered for a considerable time. It is used as a base for many community activities and is popular with locals. Camping facilities are close by for both tents and caravans. Enjoy a quiet, relaxing pint in this attractive, unspoilt local. Entertainment is organised on an ad hoc basis.
♛Q❀🛏◑⛺

TENBY

Hope & Anchor

St Julian Street, SA70 7AX
(on main approach road to harbour)
⏲ 11 (12 winter)-11; 12-10.30 Sun
☎ (01834) 842131
Brains Rev James; Worthington's Bitter; guest beer Ⓗ
Small pub in the centre of the walled town, situated on the main approach road to the harbour, where you can take a boat trip to the monastery island of Caldey. Close to two sandy beaches and on the coastal path, the Hope & Anchor attracts both holidaymakers and locals. No lunches are served in winter.
♛❀◑⊞⛺⇌♣

TREFIN

Ship Inn

SA62 5AX (on unclassified coastal road) OS838325
⏲ 12-3, 6-11; 11-10.30 Sun
☎ (01348) 831445
Worthington's Bitter; guest beer Ⓗ
Congenial village local very close to the Pembrokeshire coastal path, it is a convenient refreshment point. The internal layout, with a distinct dining area and public bar, allows both drinkers and diners to be in a separate environment. The public bar has a warming fire to greet customers when the weather demands it.
♛Q❀◑⊞⛺P

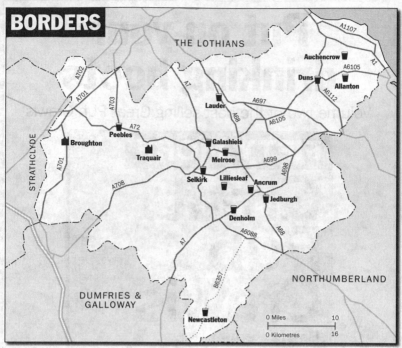

BORDERS

THE LOTHIANS

Auchencrow

Duns

Allanton

Lauder

STRATHCLYDE

Peebles

Broughton

Traquair

Galashiels

Melrose

Selkirk

Lilliesleaf

Ancrum

Jedburgh

Denholm

NORTHUMBERLAND

DUMFRIES &
GALLOWAY

Newcastleton

0 Miles		10
0 Kilometres		16

Authority area covered: The Borders UA

ALLANTON

Allanton Inn
TD11 3JZ (on B6437)
🌣 12-2.30, 6 (5 Fri)-11 (midnight Thu; 1am Fri);
12-1am Sat; 12-midnight Sun
☎ (01890) 818260
Beer range varies Ⓗ
Traditional, welcoming, Borders coaching
inn in a village surrounded by rolling
farmland. Hitching rings by the door are
useful if you arrive by horse. The front part
of the bar is quiet, cosy and functional with
flagstone flooring around the bar. The back
area has a juke box and a pool table. The
two real ales always prove an interesting,
varying selection, and the menu in the
restaurant features a wide range of dishes
using local ingredients. Families are
welcome.
🏚🏵🖛🕽 ♣ P

ANCRUM

Cross Keys Inn
The Green, TD8 6XH (on B6400, off A68)
🌣 6-11 (midnight Thu); 5-1am Fri; 12-midnight Sat;
12.30-11 Sun
☎ (01835) 830344
Beer range varies Ⓗ
Friendly village local with a bar that
remains nearly untouched from the
refurbishment by Jedburgh Brewery in
1908. It retains the pine panelling
through into the gantry, has compact but
comfortable seating and tables that have
been made from old sewing machines.
The spacious back lounge has been
sympathetically refurbished but retains
overhead tramlines from the former cellar.
A good, varied menu is supplemented by
daily specials. Lunches are served at

weekends only. The pub has a children's
certificate. 🏚Q🏵🖛🕽 ⊟♣P

AUCHENCROW

Craw Inn
TD14 5LS (on B6438, follow signs from A1)
🌣 12-2.30, 6-11 (midnight Fri); 12-midnight Sat;
12.30-11 Sun
☎ (018907) 61253
Beer range varies Ⓗ
Village inn, circa 1680. The beamed bar has
bench seating at one end and wooden
tables and chairs by the log-burning stove at
the other. The two beers are usually from
smaller breweries, and change regularly. The
no-smoking rear of the inn affords rural
views and is divided into a lounge-cum-
eating area and restaurant. Traditional
furniture gives a select feel. Local produce is
used in many dishes on the wide-ranging
menu. The pub has a children's certificate.
There are two areas for summer drinking,
the patio to the rear, and the green opposite
the pub which was voted CAMRA Borders
Pub of the Year 2003. 🏚Q🏵🖛🕽 ♣ P⚲

DENHOLM

Auld Cross Keys Inn
Main Street, TD9 8NU (on A698)
🌣 11-2.30 (not Mon), 5-11 (midnight Fri); 11-midnight
Sat; 12.30-11 Sun
☎ (01450) 870305
Beer range varies Ⓗ
This 18th-century inn stands by the village
green. The cosy main bar has a low ceiling,
real fire and a pool table. The scarlet macaw
and Robinson's Golly provide conversation
pieces. Through the back is an upmarket
lounge and dining area, which Tardis-style
opens through to a large function room.

Quizzes, folk music sessions and concerts are regular events. Those not wishing to dine must try the cheesy eggs. The pub was runner-up for the best bar food in the Borders award 2002. No meals are served on Monday. Children are allowed in the lounge. Pavement tables and chairs serve as a garden in summer. ♨☸⌂◑⎕♣P

Fox & Hounds Inn
Main Street, TD9 8NU (on A698)
🕐 11-3, 5-midnight (1am Fri); 11-1am Sat; 12.30-midnight Sun
☎ (01450) 870247
website: www.foxandhoundsinndenholm.co.uk
Beer range varies Ⓗ

This local, circa 1750, overlooks the village green. The main bar is light and retains the original beams, a real fire gives it a cosy feel in winter. Above the fire is the odd stuffed animal head and other hunting memorabilia. The rear lounge has a coffee house feel to it. A new dining room has been created upstairs. In summer the courtyard is used for sheltered outdoor drinking. Beers are usually from smaller breweries. Children are welcome in the dining room. ♨☸⌂◑⎕♣

DUNS

Whip & Saddle
Market Square, TD11 3BZ
🕐 11-11 (midnight Fri; 1am Sat); 12.30-11.30 Sun
☎ (01361) 883215
Caledonian Deuchars IPA; guest beer Ⓗ

This town-centre bar, dating from around 1790, has an airy interior due to the light wooden floor and leaded windows, which offer views across the square. The pub has modern decor, the bright vibrant colours contrasting with the 1950s photographs of local interest. Children are admitted. The upstairs dining room is pleasantly decorated. ◑▲♣✂

GALASHIELS

Ladhope Inn
33 High Buckholmside, TD1 2HR (on A7, ½ mile N of town centre)
🕐 11-3, 5-11; 11-11 Wed; 11-midnight Thu-Sat; 12.30-midnight Sun
☎ (01896) 752446
Caledonian Deuchars IPA; guest beer Ⓗ

Comfortable, friendly local with a vibrant Borders' atmosphere. Originating from around 1792, this inn has been altered considerably inside and comprises a single room with an alcove. The main area has a practical feel with TVs and slot machines and is decorated with whisky jugs. The alcove has an historical theme, displaying old photographs and a large inked map of the Borders area. The guest beer is often from Hadrian & Border but changes regularly. Toasties are available. Children are welcome. ☸▲♣

Salmon Inn
54 Bank Street, TD1 1EP
🕐 11-11 (midnight Thu; 1am Fri & Sat); 12.30-11 Sun
☎ (01896) 752577
Caledonian Deuchars IPA; Tetley Burton Ale; guest beer Ⓗ

Cosy, cheerful pub with a mixture of old and modern decoration. The bar displays historical photographs of the Galashiels area. The curvature of the room gives the impression of two rooms. Towards the back of the bar is more seating and a games machine. It is popular with the locals at lunchtime for meals; no food is served on Sunday. It stands opposite the fountain and gardens, close to the shopping area. The guest beer changes regularly. Children are admitted at lunchtime only. ☸◑▲♣

JEDBURGH

Cannon
8 Exchange Street, TD8 6BH
🕐 11-midnight (1am Fri); 12.30-11 Sun
☎ (01835) 863243
Hadrian & Border Gladiator; guest beer (summer) Ⓗ

Compact, town-centre pub with a traditional atmosphere. Inside is a welcoming real fire, an original stone wall and dark wooden beams. The long bar has a small, alcove-like area at the end. It is a local sporting man's watering-hole. The walls are adorned with rugby memorabilia interspersed with local historical material. Time can easily be spent reading the information on the walls or catching up with sporting events from the TV. Children are allowed until 8.30pm. ♨♣

LAUDER

Eagle Hotel
1 Market Place, TD2 6SR (on A68)
🕐 11-11 (midnight Thu-Sat); 12.30-11 Sun
☎ (01578) 722255
Caledonian Deuchars IPA; guest beer Ⓗ

Friendly hotel dating from 1665 in a small market town on the A68. The stone wall surrounding the fireplace and the ornate bar are features of the comfortable lounge where children are welcome. The more functional bar has an interesting mirror-backed gantry and a real fire. The bar can be cramped when big rugby games are played, as indicated by the Welsh rugby memorabilia hanging on the walls. ♨Q☸◑⎕▲♣

LILLIESLEAF

Plough Inn
15 Main Street, TD6 9JD
🕐 11 (12 Thu)-2 (closed Tue & Wed), 5-11 (midnight Fri); 11-midnight Sat; 12-11 Sun
☎ (01835) 870271
Beer range varies Ⓗ

Village local, with a very active social club, comprising a bar and dining room. The bar is housed in a square room, partly in the original building and partly a more recent extension. The modern, wood-panelled finish to the walls and counter gives it a plain feel but the recently re-upholstered bench seating, brass plates and horse brasses help brighten things up. The dining room is cheerfully decorated in pink and set out with wooden tables and chairs. It has a children's certificate. ☸⌂◑♣P

INDEPENDENT BREWERIES

Broughton Broughton
Traquair Traquair

MELROSE

Burt's Hotel
Market Square, TD6 9PL
⊙ 11-2, 5-11; 12-2, 6-11 Sun
☎ (01896) 822285
Caledonian Deuchars IPA, 80/-; guest beer Ⓗ
Elegant, family-run hotel in the main square. The decor of the plush lounge bar reflects the hunting and fishing interests of many of the clientele. The restaurant is expensive but serves award-winning food. The bar menu offers cheaper options. A comfortable seating area by the entrance is reserved for non-smokers. The pub has a children's certificate. Close by is the famous Melrose Abbey and the Teddy Bear Museum. Real ale may not be available during Melrose 7's rugby week.
᎙Q↠◑Ⅾ⅄AP⅃

King's Arms Hotel
High Street, TD6 9PB
⊙ 11-midnight; 12-11 Sun
☎ (01896) 822143
Tetley Bitter, Burton Ale; guest beer (summer) Ⓗ
Coaching inn, dating from 1793, with two separate rooms, near the rugby ground. The bar has a wooden floor and church pew seating, and is decorated with rugby memorabilia and old local photographs. There is a large-screen TV for sports events, and the room can get smoky. The contrasting lounge is comfortably furnished and has a lovely old carved door set into the ceiling. Children are welcome in the lounge until 8pm.
᎙Q↠◑Ⅾ⅄A♣

NEWCASTLETON

Liddesdale Hotel
Douglas Square, TD9 0QD
⊙ 11-11 (1am Fri & Sat); 12-11 Sun
☎ (01387) 375255
Greene King Old Speckled Hen Ⓗ
Small hotel with a split-level bar in the main square of a remote 18th-century planned weavers' village. The Waverley rail line from Edinburgh to Carlisle runs past, but was closed in 1969 so the only public transport now is the bus. The pub has a children's certificate. The upper level serves as a dining area while the lower area near the bar is more basic with Art Deco style wooden panelling. Prints of local hunting scenes and an old map decorate the walls.
᎙↠◑Ⅾ A♣

PEEBLES

Bridge Inn
Portbrae, EH45 8AW (W end of town centre)
⊙ 11-midnight; 12.30-midnight Sun
☎ (01721) 720589
Caledonian Deuchars IPA; Courage Directors; guest beer (summer) Ⓗ
Cheerful and welcoming, single-roomed, town-centre local, also known as the 'Trust', on the ground floor of a Tudor-style building. The mosaic floor in the entrance bears the pub's older name of the Tweedside Inn. The bright, comfortable, bar is decorated with memorabilia of outdoor pursuits and photographs of old Peebles. An interesting selection of jugs and bottles also catch the eye. The gents' is superb with

well-maintained original Twyford Adamant urinals. ⅄♣

Cross Keys Hotel
Northgate, EH45 8RS
⊙ 12-11 (midnight Sat); 11-midnight Sun
☎ (01721) 724000
Arran Blonde; guest beers Ⓗ
Just off the High Street, this old coaching inn has a large, L-shaped lounge bar. The ceiling is low but the light-coloured decor gives a spacious feel. The imposing bar and gantry were reclaimed from a demolished Edinburgh pub. Although generally relaxed, it can be boisterous during weekend evenings when the clientele is mainly younger. The guest beers are an eclectic mix from regional and micro-breweries throughout the UK. Children are welcome.
◑Ⅾ ⅄

Neidpath Inn
27–29 Old Town, EH45 8JF (on A72 to W of town centre)
⊙ 11-midnight (11 Mon); 12.30-midnight Sun
☎ (01721) 721721
Caledonian Deuchars IPA; guest beer Ⓗ
On the quieter, west side of Peebles, this airy, L-shaped bar provides a contrast for drinkers. The front bar area with a real fire provides a cosy area to enjoy a relaxing drink in traditional surroundings. The back bar area is popular with the younger clientele with a pool table and juke box close by. In contrast, the quieter lounge bar provides a safe haven away from distractions. The wood, glasswork and musical instruments throughout provide interesting touches. Peebles folk, chess and fishing clubs meet here. Darts, crib and dominoes are also played. Children are allowed in the lounge or garden until 7pm.
᎙✿⅄A♣

SELKIRK

Heatherlie House Hotel
Heatherlie Park, TD7 5AL (off A708, near town centre)
⊙ 11-11 (midnight Fri & Sat); 12.30-midnight Sun
☎ (01750) 721200
website: www.heatherlie.freeserve.co.uk
Caledonian Deuchars IPA; guest beer (summer) Ⓗ
This family-run hotel is set in tranquil surroundings. Once a Victorian villa, it retains a stately air of grandeur with a magnificent hand-carved fireplace depicting barn owls in the entrance and a beautiful cornice in the bar. Comfortable and airy, the bar is also a dining area. It has views through the large bay windows to the gardens. In winter, the single real ale is often from Caledonian. In the summer a choice is available. Children are welcome until 8pm. ᎙✿↠◑Ⅾ A♣P

Measures

1 butt = 108 gallons = 864 pints
1 hogshead = 54 gallons = 432 pints
1 barrel = 36 gallons = 288 pints
1 kilderkin = 18 gallons = 144 pints
1 firkin = 9 gallons = 72 pints
1 pin = 4½ gallons = 36 pints

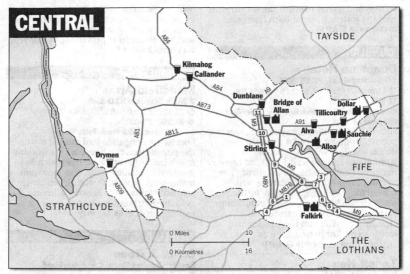

CENTRAL

Authority areas covered: Clackmannan UA, Falkirk UA, Stirling UA

ALVA

Cross Keys
12C Stirling Street, FK12 5EH (on main street)
🕓 11-11 (midnight Thu; 1am Fri & Sat); 11-11 Sun
☎ (01259) 760409
Beer range varies Ⓗ
Situated at the base of the Ochil Hills, this pub is well known for the quality and value of its food. It tends to get busy at weekends and it is worth booking for meals. It can be noisy Friday and Saturday nights. This is a popular area for hillwalkers and hang gliders. Occasional live music and theme nights are advertised locally. 🖾🌗🔌

BRIDGE OF ALLAN

Hyde's Bar
24 Henderson Street, FK9 4HP (on main street)
🕓 11-midnight (1am Fri & Sat); 11-midnight Sun
☎ (01786) 833268
Fuller's London Pride; Tetley Bitter Ⓗ
The bar is located down a narrow lane, behind the Queen's Hotel on the main street, and is of a modern bistro-style design with some unusual features. The town itself is the home of Stirling University, and is situated in an ideal location for exploring Central and the Highlands of Scotland. Good quality meals are available from the hotel and will be brought down to the bar. 🖾🌗🔌♿≠P

CALLANDER

Waverley Hotel
Main Street, FK17 8BD
🕓 11-midnight (1am Fri & Sat); 11-midnight Sun
☎ (01877) 330245
website: www.thewaverleycallander.com
Harviestoun Bitter & Twisted; guest beers Ⓗ
The Claymore Bar stocks a fine selection of ales from major and micro-brewers. This large bar also serves meals or, if preferred, try the restaurant. Situated at the gateway to the Highlands and Trossachs, it is well placed for golfing and fishing breaks. Week-long beer festivals

are held in September and December annually, featuring unusual ales. Westons Old Rosie cider is sold.
Q🖾🔌♣👣

DOLLAR

Castle Campbell
11 Bridge Street, FK14 7DE
🕓 11-11.30 (1am Fri & Sat); 12.30-11 Sun
☎ (01259) 742519
website: www.castle-campbell.co.uk
Harviestoun Bitter & Twisted; guest beer Ⓗ
Interesting hotel on the main street, it consists of a large lounge bar, well decorated with a gantry of whiskies. There are two comfortable lounges with fires and a bright, pleasant atmosphere. The restaurant sells tasty meals and is no-smoking. It is convenient for a walk up Dollar Glen and into the Ochil Hills, where you will pass the historic Castle Campbell.
🛏Q❀🖾🌗🔌♿P

DRYMEN

Winnock Hotel
The Square, G63 0BL
🕓 11 (12 Sun)-midnight
☎ (01360) 660245 website: www.winnockhotel.com
Caledonian Deuchars IPA, 80/-; Tetley Bitter; guest beer (summer) Ⓗ
Attractive, whitewashed hotel strung along the side of the village square, it dates back 300 years. There is a comfortable country hotel lounge and further rooms lead off to one side. The main bar is to the other side, characterful with wooden beams, and warmed by an open fire, it leads to a restaurant. Special packages are on offer for

INDEPENDENT BREWERIES

Bridge of Allan Bridge of Allan
Devon Sauchie
Eglesbrech Falkirk
Forth Alloa
Harviestoun Dollar

walkers and golfers to enjoy the countryside near the eastern shore of Loch Lomond.
🚶Q❀🐕◑🍺♿AP✉

DUNBLANE

Dunblane Hotel
16 Stirling Road, FK15 9EP
🟢 11-midnight (1am Fri & Sat); 11-midnight Sun
☎ (01786) 822178
Greene King Abbot, Old Speckled Hen; Tetley Burton Ale; guest beers Ⓗ
Situated next to the railway station, this is a popular stopping place for those on their way home from work. The bar is comfortable and decorated with old brewery mirrors. The lounge has an excellent view over the River Allan. Dunblane is well known for golfing and this may be the place to stay if you like small, cosy surroundings. Normally there are three frequently changing guest ales on tap, making this worth a visit just to find out what is on at any one time. 🛏❀🐕◑🍺≉P✉

Tappit Hen
Kirk Street, FK15 0AL
🟢 11-12.30am (1.15 am Fri & Sat); 12.30-12.15am Sun
☎ (01786) 825226
Belhaven Sandy Hunter's Ale; guest beers Ⓗ
Situated opposite Dunblane Cathedral, this pub has plenty of character. It offers the discerning drinker eight ales to sample – with a grand total of seven guests. This one-roomed pub, with its large number of beer clips decorating the walls, is popular with locals at any time of day or night. The name, Tappit Hen, is from the old Scots and refers to a Scottish quart. Well worth a visit if in the area or en route to the Highlands. ≉♣

FALKIRK

Wheatsheaf Inn
16 Baxter's Wynd, FK1 1PF (off High St)
🟢 11-11 (12.30am Fri & Sat); 12.30-4.30, 7.30-11 Sun
☎ (01324) 623716
Caledonian Deuchars IPA; guest beers Ⓗ
This building has always been a public house, starting off as a coaching inn in the 18th century, it has retained much of its character over the years. The bar is long and narrow with stools and small tables around the walls, which are decorated with caricatures of local worthies and old brewery mirrors. The pub stocks a good selection of whiskies. Well used by locals, the atmosphere is peaceful as there is no intrusive music or TV. Q

KILMAHOG

Lade Inn FK17 8HD
🟢 12-2.30, 5.30-11; 12-midnight Sat; 12.30-10.30 Sun
☎ (01877) 330152 website: www.theladeinn.com
Broughton Greenmantle; Cairngorm Wildcat Ⓗ
Situated in a superb position at the junction of the A84 and A821, the gateway to the Trossachs and the Highlands, this old coaching inn has a lovely, welcoming feel. There is ample space, including a large sun room and extensive grounds. Meals are available in all parts and are of excellent

quality and value. A ceilidh is held regularly in the public bar on Saturday evening. The walls of the large bar/lounge are adorned with photographs of film stars of yesteryear.
🚶Q🛏❀◑🍺♿AP

SAUCHIE

Mansfield Arms
7 Main Street, FK10 3JR
🟢 11-11 (12.30am Fri & Sat); 12.30-11 Sun
☎ (01259) 722020
Devon Original, Thick Black, Pride Ⓗ
Located in a one-time coal mining town, the pub projects this image with a working man's public bar and a lounge which has good value, quality meals. This brew-pub makes three types of Devon ale which are sold only in this pub. Brewery tours are available by arrangement with the management. 🛏◑🍺♿♣P

STIRLING

Birds & Bees
Easter Cornton Road, Causewayhead, FK9 5PB (Cornton area, W of town)
🟢 11-3, 5-midnight, 11-1am Fri & Sat; 12.30-midnight Sun
☎ (01786) 473663
Beer range varies Ⓗ
Busy and popular with local residents, this pub has a rural setting, although close to town (30 minutes) and the university (15 minutes). It is housed in a converted farm building as reflected in the interior design. Fleece-covered sheep seats and milk churn bar stools add character, while the walls are decorated with odd wrought iron birds and bees. A large restaurant and outside seating provide a good view of the Wallace Monument. The pub has regular happy hours and a Tuesday quiz. ❀◑P

Hogshead ⊘
2 Baker Street, FK8 1BJ
🟢 11-midnight (1am Fri & Sat); 11-midnight Sun
☎ (01786) 448722
Beer range varies Ⓗ
Bustling, noisy pub that is popular with local residents and students. A rustic atmosphere has been created with wooden floors and pine tables, the walls are adorned with old farm implements. Customers are actively encouraged by the staff to sample from the choice of eight ales before making a final decision. Unless, of course, you have decided to drink all on offer. Food is served all day, making this an obvious choice for visitors and locals, it is situated close to the town centre. A quiz is staged on Tuesday night, so expect things to be lively. ◑≉

Portcullis
Castle Wynd, FK8 1EG (next to castle)
🟢 11.30 (12.30 Sun)-midnight
☎ (01786) 472290 website: www.portcullishotel.com
Orkney Dark Island; guest beer Ⓗ
Built in 1787 as a grammar school, the Portcullis is a quiet but busy bar, situated next to Stirling Castle. Reasonably-priced food is served, and it is worth booking for the evening and weekend as during the tourist season it gets very busy. Weather permitting, a sheltered walled garden is available for food and drinks. Overall, a very peaceful pub that is popular with locals and

tourists, the gentle, relaxed atmosphere is enhanced in the evening with candelit tables. ♨♿◑ P

TILLICOULTRY

Woolpack Inn
Glassford Square
☼ 11-midnight (1am Fri & Sat); 12.30-11 Sun
☎ (01259) 750332
Beer range varies Ⓗ

Old Drovers' inn (dating back to 1784) with a basic bar area, a small lounge to the rear and a compact family room. This cheerful pub is very popular with hillwalkers and locals alike, and tends to be busy at weekends. Beers are sourced from both large and small breweries all over the UK. Ales from Scottish breweries such as Harviestoun or Caledonian feature. This hostelry is an ideal starting (or finishing) point for a walk up the glen to the Ochil Hills. Q ☺ ♿ ♣

The Globe Inn, Dumfries: where Burns caught a chill

They say – but I do not believe there is documentary evidence – that Burns after a carousal in the Globe collapsed on a step in the snow and caught a chill which hastened his end. I had the feeling that this public-house should be an annexe to the Burns National Museum. It has not changed by so much as the flicker of an eye since his day. The bar is very small. There is more room behind it where the bottles stand on shelves than there is on the side of custom. And the bar was full, that is to say, there were nine men present. It is not easy for a stranger to become admitted to such a gathering. I don't know how it happened, but quite soon I had accepted a drink from some one, and soon I was paying for a round of amazingly varied alcohol: Jock was drinking rum with a chaser of beer, the others were drinking beer or rum, and some one was drinking whisky escorted by a half of bitter. I was indeed in the heart of Burns country! I brought the conversation round to the poet, not quite sure how it would be received. (Had I mentioned Shakespeare in a public house in Stratford-upon-Avon there would have been no response). There was, however, an instant reaction. We were suddenly all talking about Burns.

H.V. Morton, *In Search of Scotland*, 1929

O Lord, since we have feasted thus,
Which we so little merit,
Let Meg now take away the flesh,
And Jock bring in the spirit!

Poem by Burns written for the landlord of the Globe, William Hislop

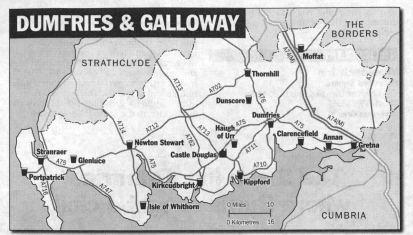

DUMFRIES & GALLOWAY

Authority area covered: Dumfries & Galloway UA

ANNAN

Blue Bell Inn
10 High Street, DG12 6AG
⊛ 11-11 (midnight Thu-Sat); 12.30-11 Sun
☎ (01461) 202385
Theakston Best Bitter; guest beers Ⓗ
Busy riverside pub on the edge of the town centre. A former coaching inn, it is built of sandstone and is easily identified by the large blue bell above the front door. This lively, friendly local serves a varied selection of real ales and usually has three guest beers available. It also offers a pool table, darts and a large-screen TV. A courtyard serves as a garden in summer. Look out for live music nights. Local CAMRA Pub of the Year 2002.
⊛Å≈♣

CLARENCEFIELD

Farmers Inn
Main Street, DG1 4NF (on B724)
⊛ 11-2.30, 6-11.30 (12.30am Fri); 12-12.30am Sat; 12.30-11.30 Sun
☎ (01387) 870675
Sulwarth Cuil Hill; guest beers Ⓗ
Late 16th-century coaching inn with a varied history. The current version opened in 1983 with the original bar area still in use. It was the post office and also housed the village's first telephone exchange. Robert Burns was a customer when he came on a visit to the Brow Well for health reasons. Nearby tourist attractions include the world's first savings bank at Ruthwell and the 8th-century Ruthwell Cross. Clarencefield is served by a regular bus service between Dumfries and Annan.
⋈Q⊛⋈◑⅊♣P

DUMFRIES

New Bazaar
39 Whitesands, DG1 2RS
⊛ 11-11 (midnight Thu-Sat); 11-11 Sun
☎ (01387) 268776
McEwan 80/-; Sulwath Knockendoch; guest beers Ⓗ
This traditional pub has a superb Victorian bar. The lounge is warmed by a welcoming fire during the winter months and has great views across the River Nith. A back room is available for meetings. It is convenient for the tourist attractions in this part of the town such as the Devorgilla Bridge, Old Bridge Museum, Robert Burns Centre and Camera Obscura. Buses depart from the Whitesands to all parts of the region.
⋈Q♣♠

Robert the Bruce ⊘
81-83 Buccleuch Street, DG1 1DJ
⊛ 11 (12.30 Sun)-midnight
☎ (01387) 270320
Caledonian Deuchars IPA; guest beers Ⓗ
Former episcopalian church originally consecrated in 1817 and sold 50 years later to local methodists. It remained empty and roofless for many years before a sympathetic conversion by Wetherspoon's. With its relaxed atmosphere the 'Bruce' has quickly established itself as a favourite meeting place, handy for the town cente. Beers from Sulwath and other Scottish breweres are among the guests. ◑▷≈

Ship Inn
97-99 St Michael Street, DG1 2PY
⊛ 11-2.30, 5-11; 12-2.30; 6.30-11 Sun
☎ (01387) 255189
Caledonian Deuchars IPA; Greene King Abbot, McEwan 80/-; guest beers Ⓗ
Very friendly and welcoming two-roomed free house. On display are a small collection of toby jugs and other artefacts, some with a nautical theme. For lovers of Robert Burns, his mausoleum is in St Michael's churchyard, opposite the pub; the house he lived in, now Burns House Museum, is only a short walk. Look out for the old-fashioned working till behind the bar. Q≈

Tam O'Shanter
113-117 Queensberry Street, DG1 1BH
⊛ 11-11 (midnight Fri & Sat); 12.30-11 Sun
☎ (01387) 254055
Caledonian Deuchars IPA; guest beers Ⓗ
The 'Tam' is a 17th-century former coaching inn named after one of Rabbie Burns' famous poems. The bar is small and decorated with prints of old Dumfries. A corridor leads to a small room that retains the original hearth, while the back room displays a number of brewery mirrors. Guest beers include Belhaven and Houston with a fine selection of ales from both sides of the

border. Occasionally traditional live music is staged at this local CAMRA Pub of the Year 2003. Q≹♣

DUNSCORE

George Hotel
DG2 0TB
⏲ 4.30 (12 Fri & Sat)-midnight; 12.30-midnight Sun
☎ (01387) 820250
Beer range varies Ⓗ
You will quickly find yourself engaged in conversation with the locals in this sociable pub that is a focal point for village life. The locals regularly provide informal evening entertainment ranging from music to storytelling. This is a popular watering-hole for cyclists of both the pedal and powered variety, and specialist events are held each year. One real ale is available during the winter months, with two in the summer. Meals are served Friday–Sunday. There is an infrequent bus service from Dumfries.
❀⇌◑◐♿♣P⅍

GLENLUCE

Kelvin House Hotel
53 Main Street, DG8 0PP (off A75)
⏲ 11-3, 6-11.30 (midnight Fri & Sat); 12.30-11.30 Sun
☎ (01581) 300303 website: www.kelvin-house.co.uk
Orkney Red MacGregor; guest beer Ⓗ
This small, friendly hotel was built in 1770 and is situated near Luce Bay in a village bypassed by the busy A75. The hotel's restaurant is renowned for its traditional Scottish fare, including local seafood and game dishes. The single guest beer changes regularly, as can be seen from the display of pump clips above the bar. The lounge is warmed by a real fire. ♨❀⇌◑◐⛺⅍

GRETNA

Solway Lodge Hotel
97-99 Annan Road, DG16 5DN
⏲ 11 (12 Sun)-11
☎ (01461) 338266
Tetley Bitter Ⓗ
Gretna is known as the gateway to Scotland and the Solway Lodge is less than 10 minutes' walk from the border. There is a comfortable homeliness about this hotel which is popular with locals and visitors. It is popular with wedding parties so expect to see vintage Rolls-Royces, or stretched limousines outside. Do not be surprised if someone asks you to witness their marriage at a few minutes' notice.
Q⚇❀⇌◑◐♿⛺≹(Gretna Green) P⅍

HAUGH OF URR

Laurie Arms Hotel
11-13 Main Street, DG7 3YA (on B794, 1 mile S of A75)
⏲ 11.45-2.30, 5.30-11 (midnight Thu-Sat); 11.45-3.30; 6-midnight Sun
☎ (01556) 660246
Beer range varies Ⓗ
This award-winning pub was CAMRA's Scottish Pub of the Year runner-up in 2002. It is situated on the main street of this quiet village in the Urr valley. A warm welcome is guaranteed in the bar, which features a large fireplace of local Dalbeattie granite. A wide selection of meals is available in both the bar and restaurant. There are up to four real ales on tap, with the local preference being for session beers. Look out for the collection of classic saucy postcards in the toilets. There is a regular bus service to Dumfries and Castle Douglas. ♨❀◑◐♣P

ISLE OF WHITHORN

Queen's Arms Hotel
22 Main Street, DG8 8LF
⏲ 11-11 (midnight Fri, Sat and summer); 11-11 Sun
☎ (01988) 500369
Houston Peter's Well; Sulwath Knockendoch Ⓗ
This sensitively restored hotel features comfortable seating, stone-clad walls, a separate pool room and a well-appointed restaurant. Real ales are only served in the bar and it is intended to keep the same regular beers rather than the previous owner's policy of having a guest. The restaurant bar has traditional tall founts but these dispense keg beer. ♨⇌◑◐

Steampacket Inn
Harbour Row, DG8 8LL (on A750)
⏲ 11-11 (11-2.30, 6-11 Mon-Thu winter); 11-1am Fri; 11-midnight Sat; 12-11 Sun
☎ (01988) 500334
Theakston XB; guest beer Ⓗ
This attractive harbourside inn has a small public bar with stone-clad walls, a large fireplace and flagstone floor. There is a larger lounge with a pool room off. Picture windows give good views of the harbour which attracts sailing craft from near and far. Both the Isle of Man and the Lake District can be seen from this picturesque, historic village. The menu features mainly local produce. ♨Q⚇❀⇌◑◐⊟♣

KIPPFORD

Anchor Hotel
DG5 4LN
⏲ 11-3, 6-11 (11-midnight summer); 11-3, 6-11 (11-midnight summer) Sun
☎ (01556) 620205
Beer range varies Ⓗ
Situated on the main street in the heart of the charming village of Kippford, a popular sailing centre, this friendly inn has fine views over the Urr estuary. The varied menu includes meals made with local produce and also has good vegetarian options. One real ale is available throughout the year, more during the tourist season, often from the Sulwath Brewery. A good path links the village with the more secluded bay at Rockcliffe. There is an infrequent bus service for those who wish to use public transport. ♨Q❀⇌◑◐⊟⛺♣

KIRKCUDBRIGHT

Masonic Arms
19 Castle Street, DG6 4JA
⏲ 11 (12.30 Sun)-midnight
☎ (01557) 330517
Beer range varies Ⓗ
A small, sociable bar that is welcoming to both locals and visitors. The tables, stools and bar-front are made from old barrels. In

INDEPENDENT BREWERY

Sulwath Castle Douglas

addition to the beers there are over 85 whiskies available. McLellan's Castle is nearby at the side of the Dee estuary. The historic town has a reputation for attracting artists to the area and the Tolbooth Art Centre is worth a visit. There are some wonderful walks locally. ♨ ♣

Selkirk Arms Hotel
High Street, DG6 4JG
✪ 11 (12 Sun)-midnight
☎ (01557) 330402
Sulwath Criffel; guest beers Ⓗ
This warm and welcoming hotel serves fine beer and good quality food. It has a comfortable lounge with an impressive plaque depicting the life of John Paul Jones, a local man who founded the US navy. Robert Burns is thought to have written his Selkirk Grace in this hotel. The historic fishing harbour is nearby. The real ales are served in the lounge bar but are brought through to the public bar on request.
♿ ❀ ⌂ ◑ ⊟ ♿

MOFFAT

Balmoral Hotel
High Street, DG10 9DL
✪ 11 (12.30 Sun)-11
☎ (01683) 220288
Caledonian 80/; guest beers Ⓗ
Fine, traditional hotel with a long lounge bar on two levels. A good range of reasonably priced food is available, and there are varied vegetarian options. Supervised children are welcome. Moffat is an excellent starting point for the scenic route to Edinburgh via the famous Devil's Beef Tub. There is good walking to be had in the area and the Southern Upland Way passes nearby. There are many tourist attractions in Moffat and the town is a regular stopping point for coach trips.
♨ ❀ ⌂ ◑ ♿ ▲ P

NEWTON STEWART

Creebridge House Hotel
Minigaff, DG8 6NP (on old main road, E of river)
✪ 12-2.30, 6-11.30 (midnight Sat); 12.30-11 Sun
☎ (01671) 402121 website: www.creebridge.co.uk
Beer range varies Ⓗ
This superb country house hotel sits in three acres of idyllic gardens and woodland. Built in 1760 as the home of the Earl of Galloway, it has been beautifully converted and is renowned for fine food and warm hospitality. The real ales (up to four in summer) are served in the Bridge Bar,

including some from the local Sulwath Brewery. Meals are available in the adjacent brasserie and in the more formal garden restaurant.
♿ ❀ ⌂ ◑ ⊟ ♣ P

PORTPATRICK

Harbour House Hotel
53 Main Street, DG9 8JW
✪ 11-11.15 (11.45 Fri & Sat); 11-11 Sun
☎ (01776) 810456
Houston Killellan; guest beer Ⓗ
Harbour-front hotel which has a popular lounge bar with superb views. It has been recently refurbished in a modern, but comfortable style and has seating outside. Opening hours are extended to 1am for live music most summer weekends.
❀ ⌂ ◑ ▲ ♣ P

STRANRAER

Ruddicot Hotel
London Road, DG4 8AJ (A75, 400 yds E of town centre)
✪ 11-2.30, 5-11 (midnight Thu-Sat); 12.30-2.30, 6.30-11 Sun
☎ (01776) 702684
Beer range varies Ⓗ
This small, family-run hotel is a detached sandstone building that used to be a girls' school. It is close to both the football ground and the Irish ferry terminal. The single real ale changes regularly and tends to be a national brand. The small bar features wooden screens that divide the bar seating from the eating area.
Q ❀ ◑ ▲ P

THORNHILL

Buccleugh & Queensberry Hotel
112 Drumlanrig Street, DG3 5LU
✪ 11-midnight (1am Thu-Sat); 12.30-midnight Sun
☎ (01848) 330215
Caledonian 80/-; guest beers Ⓗ
The paraphernalia of country pursuits decorate the ceilings and walls of the two main lounges, each warmed by a real fire. You may well find yourself swapping stories with friendly locals or visitors from all over Europe and beyond. The food is always hearty and watch the blackboard for (very) special dishes. The nearby Drumlanrig Castle is deserving of a visit in its own right and regularly hosts special events. There is a regular bus service between Thornhill and Dumfries. ♨ Q ⌂ ◑ ♿ P

Come back to the inn, love, and the lights and the fire,
And the fiddler's old tune and the shuffling of feet;
For there in a while shall be rest and desire,
And there shall the morrow's uprising be sweet.

William Morris (1834-96), from *The Message of the March Wind* in Poems by the Way, 1891

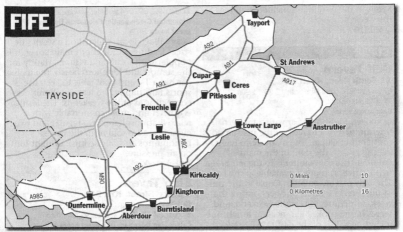

FIFE

Tayport
St Andrews
Cupar
Ceres
TAYSIDE
Pitlessie
A917
Freuchie
Lower Largo
Anstruther
Leslie
Kirkcaldy
0 Miles 10
0 Kilometres 16
Kinghorn
Dunfermline
Burntisland
Aberdour

Authority area covered: Fife UA

ABERDOUR

Aberdour Hotel
38 High Street, KY3 0SW
🕐 4-11; 3-11.45 Fri; 11-11.45 Sat; 12-11 Sun
☎ (01383) 860325 website: www.aberdourhotel.com
Broughton Greenmantle; Caledonian Deuchars IPA Ⓗ
Family-run, small hotel in a popular tourist
and commuter area. It has separate public
and lounge bars, the latter is used more as a
restaurant, open 6–9 each evening, and
offers a varied menu; weekend lunches are
also served. The hotel started life as a
coaching inn and many of the original
features remain. One handpump is in use
during winter, increasing to two in spring,
sometimes four during summer and the
proprietor runs a small beer festival in the
first week of August to coincide with the
village gala. Wheelchair access is via the rear
courtyard. ▲🍴🛏️🍴◑&🚭P

Cedar Inn
20 Shore Road, KY3 0TR
🕐 11-2.30, 5-midnight; 11-midnight Fri & Sat;
12.30-midnight Sun
☎ (01383) 860310
Caledonian Deuchars IPA; guest beers Ⓗ
A short stroll from the scenic harbour, this
small, family-run hotel is situated in a quiet
side street of Aberdour, on the north shore
of the Forth, a village renowned for its
'silver sands'. The public bar has a large-
screen TV and pool table; the smaller side
bar and no-smoking conservatory are
quieter. The hotel also offers a peaceful
lounge, a separate restaurant and a small
patio. One regular and three guest beers are
sold, changing on an almost daily basis.
Q🍴🛏️◑&🍴🚭≠P¥

ANSTRUTHER

Dreel Tavern
16 High Street, KY10 3DL
(on main road into town from the west)
🕐 11 (12.30 Sun)-midnight
☎ (01333) 310727
Orkney Dark Island; guest beers Ⓗ
An old stone building in the East Neuk of
Fife with crow step gables and a pantile
roof. It was previously called the Railway
Tavern; the railway, thanks to Dr Beeching,
is long gone. Starting life as a 16th-century
coaching inn, it was reputedly visited by
James V; the beamed ceiling looks old
enough. The public and lounge bars are
separated by an open fire, the conservatory
provides dining/family/no-smoking space; it
gets very busy at lunchtime and early
evening, serving good quality meals. One
regular and two guest beers are served from
three handpumps. ▲🍴🛏️♣◑♣¥

BURNTISLAND

Crown Tavern
17 Links Place, KY3 9DY
(on corner facing the links)
🕐 11 (12.30 Sun)-midnight
☎ (01592) 873697
Beer range varies Ⓗ
Two-roomed, traditional, small town pub
with a lively, spacious public bar and even
larger separate lounge. An attractive gantry,
wood panelling and splendid etched glass
windows create an old-fashioned and
relaxed atmosphere in the bar. The sports-
minded gravitate to the pool table in the
lounge. Three handpumps offer two guest
beers and, brewed exclusively for the
Crown, Inveralmond Bachanal. 🍴&≠♣

CERES

Ceres Inn
The Cross, KY15 5NE
🕐 12-3, 5-midnight (1am Fri); 12.30-midnight Sun
☎ (01334) 828305 website: www.ceresinn.uk
Beer range varies Ⓗ
Situated at a crossroads in rural Fife, it
probably started life as a coaching inn. This
pleasant, low-ceilinged bar was restored to
its original state in the 1990s, with beams
and exposed stone. One of two villages in
Scotland with a village green, Ceres hosts
the oldest highland games in the country
each June, when competitors try to throw
the Ceres stone, which is kept in the bar.
The range from two handpumps varies
continuously, featuring Houston,
Harviestoun and other small local breweries.

INDEPENDENT BREWERY

Fyfe Kirkcaldy

Meals in the restaurant, include high teas at the weekend.
Q ⊛ (⊟ ♣ P ⊬

CUPAR

Golf Tavern
11 South Road, KY15 5JF
✪ 11-midnight (1am Fri & Sat); 12.20-11 Sun
☎ (01334) 654233
Beer range varies Ⓗ
Compact, traditional bar with a modern interior, part of a terrace on the main road south out of Cupar. The main room has a seating area to the right of the main entrance, the bar counter is to the left and a small function room is available at the back. The only real ale outlet in Cupar at the time of the survey, it offers one beer during the week, sometimes two at the weekend, and serves home-cooked bar meals at lunchtime, including a dish of the day. Q ⌂ (♦ ⇌ ⊬

DUNFERMLINE

Commercial Inn
13 Douglas Street, KY12 7EB
(opp. the main post office)
✪ 11-11 (midnight Fri & Sat); 12.30-11 Sun
☎ (01383) 733876 website: www.commercialinn.co.uk
Caledonian Deuchars IPA; Courage Directors; McEwan 80/-; Theakston Old Peculier; guest beers Ⓗ
Cosy, town-centre pub with a long history as an ale house and coaching inn (it dates back to the 1820s). The recently refurbished bare floorboards and mellow paintwork create a warm, friendly atmosphere for the very mixed clientele, with the emphasis on conversation not music. Along with four regular Scottish Courage beers, four continually-changing guest ales from all over Britain are served, also augmented by a selection of continental bottled beers. It can get very busy on match day afternoons, and Friday and Saturday evenings. Lunches are served 11–2.30 daily, and evening meals 7–9, Monday–Thursday. (♦ ⇌

FREUCHIE

Albert Tavern
2 High Street, KY15 7EX
(just W of the A92 Kirkcaldy-Dundee road)
✪ 11-2, 5-11; 12-1am Fri & Sat; 12.30-11 Sun
☎ (01337) 857192
Beer range varies Ⓗ
Family-friendly village local that probably started life as a two-up, two-down house, the pub was reputedly a coaching inn when nearby Falkland Palace was a royal residence; an old photograph shows the property as a tavern, sometime in the 19th century. Both bar and lounge have beamed ceilings, the bar has wainscot panelling, the cosy upstairs restaurant seats about 20. Three handpumps offer guest beers. There is a small patio for summer drinking. Scottish CAMRA Pub of the Year 2002, it was runner-up for the UK award the same year.
⌂ Q ⊛ ( )

KINGHORN

Auld Hoose
6-8 Nethergate, KY3 9SY
(down a flight of steps from main street)
✪ 12 (11 Sat)-midnight; 12.30-midnight Sun
☎ (01592) 891074 website: www.theauldhoose.co.uk
Broughton Greenmantle; Caledonian Deuchars IPA; guest beers Ⓗ / Ⓐ
Busy village local, situated on a steep side street leading off Kinghorn main street, it is popular with locals and visitors. Handy for the station and Kinghorn beach, the main bar has a TV and pool table to keep the sports fans happy and features dominoes competitions at the weekends. The lounge is quieter and more comfortable with a relaxed atmosphere. Two regular and two guest beers are sold from the three handpumps and one Scottish upright font on air pressure.
⇌ ⊟ & ⇌ ♣

Ship Tavern
2 Bruce Street, KY3 9JT
✪ 12 (12.30 Sun)-midnight
☎ (01592) 890655 website: shiptavern.com
Caledonian Deuchars IPA; guest beers Ⓗ
One of the older buildings in Kinghorn, it was originally built as a house for Bible John, who printed the first bibles in Scotland. The rather unobtrusive entrance door, which faces the main road, opens into a fine timber-panelled interior, with a long bar counter and ornate gantry. The small jug bar is probably one of the finest surviving traditional interiors in Fife, a brass pressure gauge at one end of the gantry is evidence of an old water engine for the beer. A separate back room is ideal for meetings and private parties. Lunchtime and evening meals are served spring–autumn. ⌂ ( ) & ⇌

KIRKCALDY

Harbour Bar
471-475 High Street, KY1 1JL
✪ 11-3, 5-midnight; 11-midnight Thu-Sat; 12.30-midnight Sun
☎ (01592) 264270 website: www.e-fife.com/harbourbar
Beer range varies Ⓗ
On the ground floor of a tenement building, this lively, unspoilt local has a separate bar and lounge areas featuring timber panelling. Note the large murals depicting the town's whaling history. The bar has an ornate gantry stocked with a fine selection of malt whiskies and the beer range, served from six handpumps, continually changes. It features some ales from the Fyfe Brewing Company housed in premises to the rear. There are no meals but an interesting selection of bar snacks is available. CAMRA Scottish Pub of the Year 2000, it was Kingdom of Fife winner in 2003.

LESLIE

Burns Tavern
184 High Street, KY6 7DD
✪ 12 (11 Fri & Sat)-midnight; 12.30-midnight Sun
☎ (01592) 741345
Taylor Landlord; guest beer Ⓗ
Typical Scottish two-roomed main street local, the public bar is on two levels, the lower is lively and friendly, the upper has a large-screen TV and pool table. The lounge bar is more spacious and quieter, except on Thursday–Sunday evenings when karaoke and pub quizzes are held. One guest beer is generally from a small independent

brewery. Basic bar meals are available at lunchtime but there is no set menu.
🏨🍺◐🍴🚻

LOWER LARGO

Crusoe Hotel
The Harbour, KY8 6BT (on shore of River Forth)
☼ 11-midnight (11 Mon; 1am Sat); 12.30-11 Sun
☎ (01333) 320759
Caledonian Deuchars IPA Ⓗ
The name of this hotel should provide some clues as to its association. A small, friendly hotel that could not be any closer to the Firth of Forth, part of the building is an old mill, the public bar is on the ground floor. The hotel has an information and display area, resembling below decks on ship complete with creaky floorboards. It is dedicated to Alexander Selkirk, a native of the area whose real life adventures were the basis for Daniel Defoe's book, Robinson Crusoe. ◐🚻♿

Railway Tavern
1 Station Wynd, KY8 6BU
(near the harbour, below the old railway viaduct)
☼ 11-midnight; 12.30-11 Sun
☎ (01333) 320239
Fullers London Pride; guest beer Ⓗ
Small, two-roomed pub close to the harbour, the bar has a nautical theme, and is a focal point of this attractive coastal hamlet. Fuller's London Pride is the regular ale, with one guest usually on offer. There is a quiet room at the rear away from the main bar, suitable for meetings. Snacks are available lunchtime and evening. There is no longer a railway nearby – yet another Fife village to suffer under Dr Beeching.
◐🚻♿

PITLESSIE

Village Inn
Cupar Road, KY15 7SU
(on main road between Cupar and Glenrothes)
☼ 12-2, 5-midnight (1am Fri); 11-1am Sat; 12.30-midnight Sun
☎ (01337) 830595
Beer range varies Ⓗ
Typical Scottish village pub from the outside, the public bar is a nice surprise featuring bare stonework, an open fire and candles on the tables. Almost like a bothy, with bare wooden tables for dining, the menu combines traditional and exotic dishes, cooked to order. Several rooms, one with an old Raeburn cooker, provide space for families and pub games; the large function room at the rear is decked out in tartan. Three handpumps offer one regular and two guest beers. A quiz night is held every second Wednesday.
🏨Q🐶◐🍴🚻♿♣P🅿♿

ST ANDREWS

Aikman's Cellar Bar
32 Bell Street, KY16 9UK
☼ 6-midnight; 1-1am Sat; 6-midnight Sun
☎ (01334) 477425 website: www.cellarbar.co.uk
Beer range varies Ⓗ
Basement lounge bar, in this Guide since 1987, selling around 300 real ales each year, together with a variety of continental bottled beers. A week-long beer festival at Easter offers 20 ales. The rolled copper bar-top was salvaged from the White Star liner Oceanic (same shipping line as the Titanic). Opening hours outside term time can vary; the bar is closed most lunchtimes but cask ales are available on request in the Bistro upstairs where lunchtime meals are available. The pub can get very busy, particularly with students. ◐♣

Central Bar
77-79 Market Street, KY16 9NU
(overlooks market square)
☼ 11-11.45; 11-1am Fri & Sat; 12.30-11.45 Sun
☎ (01334) 478296
Caledonian Deuchars IPA; Greene King Old Speckled Hen; McEwan 80/-; Theakston Best Bitter, Old Peculier; guest beers Ⓗ
Student-oriented, town-centre pub that is also popular with the locals. It has a Victorian-style island bar, large windows and some ornate mirrors, creating a late-19th century feel. The only pub in town that serves food after 9pm, meals are available all day (until 10pm). The pavement tables are ideal for watching the world go by on a summer evening while enjoying a good range of regular and guest ales. 🍴◐♣

Whey Pat Tavern
2 Argyle Street, KY16 9EX
(just outside the old town from West Port)
☼ 11-11.30 (11.45 Fri & Sat); 12.30-11.30 Sun
☎ (01334) 477740
Beer range varies Ⓗ
Town-centre pub on a busy road junction just outside the old town walls. There has been a hostelry on this site for a few centuries, it was taken over by Belhaven in 2002 but with minimal changes. Unusually for St Andrews, this cheery, welcoming pub is popular with students, academics and townspeople alike, perhaps because of the superb sandwiches freshly made to order at lunchtime. Three handpumps offer an ever-changing range of beer. Wheelchair WC. Pub games include board games and darts.
◐♣

TAYPORT

Bell Rock Tavern
4-6 Dalgleish Street, DD6 9BB
☼ 11-midnight (1am Thu-Sat); 12.30-midnight Sun
☎ (01382) 552388
Caledonian Deuchars IPA; guest beer Ⓗ
Friendly, cosy, town local near the harbour. The bar is on three levels, each with a separate, mainly nautical theme of artefacts including old charts, photographs of ships and aircraft, old Dundee and the Tay ferries. One real ale is served throughout the year, increasing to two in the summer and during the festive season. This welcoming pub dispenses good cheer with good ales and excellent value home-cooked meals, such as mince and tatties at lunchtime, an ideal respite for people on the Fife coastal path.
Q🐶🍴◐♣

Beer site
Keep in touch with CAMRA:
www.camra.org.uk

Scottish Beer

JUST AS MONKS call their Lenten beers 'liquid bread', it's tempting to call traditional Scottish ales 'liquid porridge'. They are beers brewed for a cold climate, a country in which beer vies with whisky (uisge breatha – water of life) for nourishment and sustenance.

Brewers blend not only darker malts such as black and chocolate with paler grains, but also add oats, that staple of many foodstuffs in the country. In common with the farmer-brewers of the Low Countries and French Flanders in earlier centuries, domestic brewers in Scotland tended to use whatever grains, herbs and plants were available to make beer. The intriguing use of heather in the Fraoch range of ales recalls brewing practice in Scotland from bygone times.

Concentrate

The industrial revolution arrived later in Scotland than in England, and industry tended to concentrate in the Lowland belt around Alloa, Edinburgh and Glasgow. As a result, brewing remained a largely domestic affair for much longer and – as with early Irish ales – made little use of the hop, which could not grow in such inhospitable climes.

Brewing developed on a commercial scale in the Lowlands in the early 19th century at the same time as many French emigres, escaping the revolution, settled in the Scottish capital. They dubbed the rich, warming local ales 'Scottish Burgundy'. Real wine from France, always popular in Scotland as a result of the Auld Alliance, became scarce during the Napoleonic Wars, and commercial brewing grew rapidly to fill the gap and to fuel the needs of a growing class of thirsty industrial workers.

Different

Traditionally, Scottish ales were brewed in a different manner to English ones. Before refrigeration, beer was fermented at ambient temperatures far lower than in England. As a result, not all the sugars turned to alcohol, producing rich, full-bodied ales. As hops had to be imported from England at considerable cost, they were used sparingly. The result was a style of beer markedly different to English ones: vinous, fruity, malty and with only a gentle hop bitterness.

Many of the new breed of ales produced by micro-brewers in Scotland tend to be paler and more bitter than used to be the norm. For the true taste of traditional Scottish ales you will have to sample the products of the likes of Belhaven, Broughton, Caledonian and Traquair.

Complexities

The language of Scottish beers is different, too. The equivalent to English mild is called Light (even when it's dark

Caledonian's award-winning Deuchars IPA is served by a handpump. Traditional tall founts are now rare.

in colour), standard bitter is called Heavy, premium bitter Export, while strong old ales and barley wines (now rare) are called Wee Heavies.

To add to the complexities of the language differences, many traditional beers incorporate the word Shilling in their names. A Light may be dubbed 60 Shilling, a Heavy 70 Shilling, an Export 80 Shilling, and a Wee Heavy 90 Shilling. The designations stem from a pre-decimalisation method of invoicing beer in Victorian times. The stronger the beer, the higher the number of shillings.

Until recent times, cask-conditioned beer in Scotland was served by air pressure. In the pub cellar a water engine, which looks exactly the same as a lavatory cistern but works in reverse, used water to produce air pressure that drove the beer to the bar. Sadly, these wonderful Victorian devices are rarely seen, and the Sassenach handpump and beer engine dominate the pub scene.

GRAMPIAN

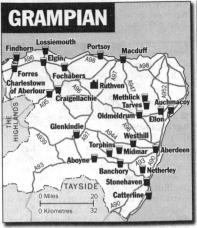

Authority areas covered: Aberdeenshire UA, City of Aberdeen UA, Moray UA

ABERDEEN

Carriages
Brentwood Hotel, 101 Crown Street, AB11 6HH
🕐 11-2.30, 4.30-midnight; 6-11 Sun
☎ (01224) 595440
website: www.brentwood-hotel.co.uk
Boddingtons Bitter; Caledonian Deuchars IPA; Castle Eden Ale; Courage Directors; Flowers Original; guest beers Ⓗ
Low-ceilinged basement bar below Brentwood Hotel. It offers a varied selection of ales in a relaxed atmosphere with comfortable sofas. The pub has a small function area and is very close to the railway station, ferries, Maritime Museum and main shopping areas. As the hotel attracts mainly midweek oil firm residential business, it can often be quieter to savour the choice of 10 ales at weekends. 🛏◑≠P

Globe Inn
13-15 North Silver Street, AB10 1RJ
🕐 12 (12.30 Sun)-midnight; closed 3-5 Mon-Wed and may close at 11, weeknights
☎ (01224) 624258
Houston Peter's Well; guest beer Ⓗ
Convivial, open-plan pub with a plethora of musical instruments decorating the walls. It offers a variety of musical events on a weekly basis. Admire the unusual stained glass light fitting. Allegedly the nicest gents' loos in the city once featured a prominent fireplace, it was moved during a recent refurbishment which, along with added accommodation, persuaded Belhaven to add the premises to its local portfolio. Convenient for both the theatre and music hall, the Globe also enjoys a substantial lunchtime food trade.
🛏◑&≠

Grill ☆
213 Union Street, AB11 6BA
🕐 10-midnight (1am Fri & Sat); 10-midnight Sun
Boddingtons Bitter; Caledonian 80/-; Courage Directors; Isle of Skye Red Cuillin Ⓗ
The only National Inventory pub north of Dundee, although it does seem to slowly be leaving the 19th century and does now have a ladies toilet! The pub is very central, directly opposite the music hall, so an ideal location. A large selection of malt whiskies could tempt you away from the beer. ≠

Moorings Bar
2 Trinity Quay, AB11 2AA
(facing the quayside at bottom of Market St)
🕐 12-midnight (1am Fri & Sat); 12.30-midnight Sun
☎ (01224) 587602
Beer range varies Ⓗ
Hard rock meets real ale in this laid-back dockside haven. Live and loud at weekends, the bar can also be quiet and relaxed midweek. Up to three handpumps dispense an ever-changing range of both familiar and unexpected ales from both Scotland and England. The staff can advise on an unusual range of spirits. Addlestones cider is available. Seating and decor are far from refined, but the bar is convenient for bus, rail and ferry, close to the Maritime Museum and multiplex cinema. The bar supports men's and ladies' darts teams and a pool team. ≠♣👝🖶

Old Blackfriars
52 Castle Street, AB11 5BB
🕐 11-midnight; 12.30-11 Sun
☎ (01224) 581922
Belhaven 80/-, St Andrew's Ale; Caledonian Deuchars IPA, 80/-; Inveralmond Ossian's Ale; guest beer Ⓗ
The first acquisition in Belhaven's burgeoning local empire, mimicking the ambience of a high quality continental café with its well-balanced mixture of bar and restaurant; the attractive furnishings and eclectic decor display religious overtones and contain some back-lit stained glass from Dunecht House. A multiple local CAMRA award-winner, it supplies food on its split levels until 9pm (8 Fri and Sat). It hosts occasional Czech and real ale festivals.
◑&≠

Prince of Wales
7 St Nicholas Lane, AB10 1HF
🕐 10-midnight; 12.30-11 Sun
☎ (01224) 640597
Caledonian 80/-; Courage Directors; Theakston Old Peculier; guest beers Ⓗ
Although recently transferred from private ownership to pub chain, life at the Prince continues much as before. A fine, traditional pub, most of the interior fittings are genuinely old (not all original to the Prince) and the effect is of organic growth. The guest beers currently come from Scottish micros, with regular price promotions, and the house ale is from Inveralmond. A folk session holds sway on Sunday evening. Q◑≠

Tilted Wig
55-56 Castle Street, AB11 5BA
🕐 12-midnight (1am Fri & Sat); 12.30-11 Sun
☎ (01224) 583248
Tetley Bitter, Burton Ale; guest beers Ⓗ
Former Festival ale house, now following a more idiosyncratic path. The guest beers tend to be supplied from the likes of Caledonian and Houston, and are competitively priced for the city-centre location. The layout, with a long narrow

INDEPENDENT BREWERY

Borve Ruthven (not currently brewing)

bar, means it can switch from feeling empty to busy in a very short time. The atmosphere can be boisterous when a live band performs. ◑ ≉

Under the Hammer
11 North Silver Street, AB10 1RJ
✪ 5 (4 Fri; 2 Sat)-midnight (1am Thu-Sat); 6.30-11 (if an event is on at music hall, otherwise closed) Sun
☎ (01224) 640253
Inveralmond Ossian's Ale; Taylor Landlord; guest beer Ⓗ
Compact and intimate basement bar, named for its location next to the city auction rooms. Midway between the music hall (Union Street) and HM Theatre (Rosemount viaduct), it often gets busy with patrons before and after shows, and has a brisk teatime trade from nearby offices. Ever-changing art displays decorate the walls and work may be purchased. The large notice board has posters advertising events in town. Beer prices are above average, even for Aberdeen. ≉

ABOYNE

Boat Inn
Charleston Road, AB34 5EL
(N bank of River Dee next to Aboyne bridge)
✪ 11-2.30, 5-11 (midnight Fri); 11-midnight Sat; 11-11 Sun
☎ (01339) 886137
Draught Bass; guest beers Ⓗ
Popular, riverside inn, especially for thirsty hillwalkers descending from nearby Glentanar. The lounge, which has an emphasis on food, features a spiral staircase leading to a mezzanine floor which caters for families. The local Rotary Club regularly meets here, and all customers are usually given the choice of two ales from Scottish micros. Accommodation is provided in a self-catering flat. Benches in the car park serve as an area for summer drinking.
🛏Q≿❀🚪◑⌂&♣P

AUCHMACOY

Poachers Rest
Denhead, AB41 8JL
(off A90 Ellon bypass, 2 miles E of Ellon)
✪ 11-2.30, 5-11 (midnight Thu-Sat); 12.30-11 Sun
☎ (01358) 722114
Inveralmond Thrappledouser Ⓗ
Converted from an old general merchant's store, an attractive restaurant in the front leads to the rear bar area. After a meal, parents can relax over a pleasant pint of ale while their children enjoy the bouncy castle outside in the play area. The single ale may vary. Q❀◑&♣P

BANCHORY

Ravenswood (British Legion)
Ramsay Road, AB31 5TS
✪ 11-2.30, 5-midnight (11 winter); 11-midnight Sat and Sun
☎ (01330) 822347
Beer range varies Ⓗ
Premier club for cask ale in the region, recently increased to two handpumps on all year round. The ales on offer are unpredictable, and tend to be interesting choices from Scottish micros. The front terrace offers a fine view of Banchory and

the surrounding Deeside Hills. Temporary members are accepted.
❀🚪◑⌐&♣P

CATTERLINE

Creel Inn
AB39 2UL (on coast, off A92, 5 miles S of Stonehaven) OS868781
✪ 12-3, 6-11 (midnight Fri & Sat) (closed Mon & Tue Nov-Mar); 12-3, 5.30-11 Sun
☎ (01569) 750254 website: www.thecreelinn.co.uk
Beer range varies Ⓗ
Busy village local perched on a cliff top, overlooking the harbour. The inn dates from 1838 and the low ceilings and wood fires create a traditional ambience. Well regarded locally for its cuisine – fish and shellfish feature prominently on the eclectic menu, including five tons of crab disposed of annually. Food is served in both the no-smoking restaurant and the (smoking) bar. B&B accommodation is available in two en-suite rooms converted from an old fishing cottage. Reservations are recommended.
🛏❀🚪◑ÅP

CHARLESTOWN OF ABERLOUR

Mash Tun
8 Broomfield Square, AB38 9QP
✪ 12-2.30, 5-11; 5-12.30am Fri; 12-12.30am Sat; 12-11 Sun
☎ (01340) 881771
Beer range varies Ⓗ
Built in 1896 as the Station Bar, this unusual round-ended pub has a light interior with extensive use of timber. The Speyside Way runs past the door and patrons may drink in the view and the ales, from the old station platform in summer. This former local CAMRA Country Pub of the Year offers up to three beers in the tourist season, it also stocks a wide variety of bottled beers. Good value food is available. ❀◑Å

CRAIGELLACHIE

Highlander Inn
2 Victoria Street, AB38 9SR
✪ 11-2.30, 5-11 (longer hours in tourist season); 11-12.30am Sat; 12-11 Sun
☎ (01340) 881446
Beer range varies Ⓗ
Cosy cellar bar that displays a fishing theme. The beer is overshadowed by the extensive selection of malt whiskies. Beers are usually from Aviemore or Isle of Skye. Pins are used in winter to maintain beer freshness. The excellent cuisine is a big attraction in the tourist season, as is the frequent live music. The inn lies on the Speyside Way and the Whisky Trail and runs an outdoor bar at the annual local Couthie Doo. 🚪◑P

ELGIN

Flanagan's
Shepherd's Close, 48a High Street, IV30 1BU (end of narrow alleyway opp. Farmfoods)
✪ 11-11 (11.45 Wed & Thu; 12.30am Fri & Sat); 12-11 Sun
☎ (01343) 549737
Beer range varies Ⓗ
This bar, with modern comfortable sofas

and tables has less emphasis on the Irish theme than previously. A large-screen TV dominates one end of the bar, usually showing Sky Sports. Up to three, generally Scottish, beers are available, and can also be obtained in the upstairs tapas restaurant. The ruins of Elgin Cathedral, destroyed by the 'Wolf of Badenoch' (Alexander Stewart, Earl of Moray) in 1390, are a short walk away.
◑⇌

Muckle Cross ⊘
34 High Street, IV30 1BU
❂ 11-11.45 (1.30am Fri & Sat); 12.30-11.45 Sun
☎ (01343) 559030
Caledonian 80/-; Courage Directors; Theakston Best Bitter; guest beers Ⓗ
Converted from a building which was previously a bicycle repair shop and latterly a branch of Halfords, this is a fairly typical small branch of Wetherspoon's. The long, wide bar offers a choice of fine ales, and has a bustling atmosphere at weekends.
◑ ⅙ ⇌ ✕

Sunninghill Hotel
Hay Street, IV30 1NH
❂ 11-11.15 (12.15 Fri & Sat); 11-11.15 Sun
☎ (01343) 547799 website: www.hotelselgin.co.uk
Beer range varies Ⓗ
Small, family-run hotel, just outside the city centre, near the railway station and Moray College. The five ales on tap complement the highly-rated menu, with families attracted by the children's certificate. The large selection of malts is another temptation.
❀⇦◑⇌P

ELLON

Tolbooth
23 Station Road, AB41 9AE
❂ 11-2.30, 5-11 (midnight Thu & Fri; 11.45 Sat); 6.30-11 Sun
☎ (01358) 721308
Draught Bass; guest beers Ⓗ
Comfortable lounge bar, split on two levels, with a spacious conservatory on the lower level leading to an enclosed patio. The generally mature clientele and the pub's refusal to admit children ensure a fairly relaxed and quiet atmosphere. A smaller attic bar is available for meetings. The Bass is complemented by three guests, generally from the larger English regional brewers.
Q❀⅙♣

FINDHORN

Kimberley Inn
94 Findhorn, IV36 3YG (on harbour front)
❂ 11-12.30 am (1.30am Fri & Sat); 12.30-12.30am Sun
☎ (01309) 690492
Beer range varies Ⓗ
Specialising in local, fresh seafood, this popular, friendly bar sells mainly English beers in winter and Scottish ones in summer. The patio offers glorious views of Findhorn Bay, famous for water sports. The nearby shop at the Findhorn Foundation is well worth a visit for its excellent selection of organic bottled beers.
⚏⭗❀◑⅙♣✕

FOCHABERS

Gordon Arms Hotel
80 High Street, IV32 7DH
(on A96, W end of village)
❂ 11 (12 Sun)-11
☎ (01343) 820508
website: www.gordonarmshotel.com
Caledonian Deuchars IPA; Marston's Pedigree Ⓗ
Rambling, low-ceilinged coaching inn on the main street of the village, offering an upmarket restaurant and accommodation. It is home to many local societies. Real ale pumps are in the public bar, but it can also be served in the lounge bar. The inn lies adjacent to Speyside Way and Baxters factory village. Meals are available between 12–2 and 5–7.
❀⇦◑⇱P

Red Lion Inn
67 High Street, IV32 7DU
❂ 11-11 (midnight Thu; 1.30am Fri & Sat); 12.30-11.30 Sun
☎ (01343) 820455
Caledonian Deuchars IPA Ⓗ
Traditional coaching inn which has been heavily modernised. The real ale is in the sport-dominated public bar, but is also available in the quieter lounge. Handy for the Speyside Way long-distance path and for fishing on the Spey, Baxter Soup visitor centre is one mile to the west.
⚏❀◑⇱A♣

FORRES

Carisbrooke Hotel
Drumduan Road, IV36 1BS
(¼ mile off A96, E end of town)
❂ 11-midnight (1.30am Fri & Sat); 12-midnight Sun
☎ (01309) 672585
Boddingtons Bitter; guest beers Ⓗ
Pleasant, family-run, two-bar hotel on the eastern outskirts of town. Families are welcome (children allowed until 9pm). Good food is available at competitive prices. Regular activities include quiz evenings and barbecues on the patio. The hotel specialises in golfing breaks and boasts very comfortable accommodation.
⚏❀⇦◑⇱♣P

GLENKINDIE

Glenkindie Arms Hotel
AB33 8SX (on A97, at E edge of village)
❂ 12-2 (not Tue), 5-11 (1am Fri) (closed winter Mon); 12-midnight Sat; 12-11 Sun
☎ (01975) 641288 website: www.glenkindiearms.co.uk
Beer range varies Ⓗ
This 400-year-old ancient drovers' inn is a tiny, listed building known locally as the Lodge, due to its former use as a Masonic lodge, evidence of which can still be seen. A vast selection of excellent food is served, with produce sourced locally (not available on Mon). Two ales are usually available in winter, and in summer beers tend to be from Greene King or Inveralmond. The inn stands on the castle trail and is convenient for the Lecht ski area. Phone to check the winter opening hours before travelling.
⚏❀⇦◑P

LOSSIEMOUTH

Clifton Bar
5 Clifton Road, IV31 6DJ
✪ 11-2.30, 5-midnight; 11-12.30am Fri & Sat; 12-midnight Sun
☎ (01343) 812100
Boddingtons Bitter; McEwan 80/-; guest beers Ⓗ
Two-roomed bar overlooking the River Lossie and harbour area, near the marina. The bar is favoured by personnel from the local RAF base, who provide enough trade for the licensee to concentrate on his ale and not have to offer meals. Accommodation is available in the adjoining guesthouse, which is under the same ownership.
🚾 ❀ 🛏 Ⓖ ♣ P

MACDUFF

Knowes Hotel
Market Street, AB44 1LL
✪ 12-12.30am; 12-midnight Sun
☎ (01261) 832229
Beer range varies Ⓗ
Spacious, detached, family-run hotel, dated 1879 but frequently extended, it stands on an elevated site affording tremendous panoramic views of the Moray Firth. The beer choice usually comprises one local micro-brew and one national brand. A price premium is levied on half pints. Nearby, Macduff Aquarium is of family interest, with its unusual open-air central tank.
Q ⛵ 🛏 Ⓓ P ⚥

METHLICK

Gight House Hotel
Sunnybrae, AB41 7BP
(over bridge and 1/2 mile up hill on New Deer Rd)
✪ 5-midnight (1am Fri); 12-12.30am Sat; 12-11 Sun
☎ (01651) 806389
website: www.gighthousehotel.co.uk
Beer range varies Ⓗ
This former free kirk manse, dates from 1850 and is reputedly home to the ghost of a minister. The welcoming ambience of the beamed lounge and reputation for good food at reasonable prices, make it popular with locals and visitors alike. Two attractive conservatories lead to a one-acre garden, complete with putting green and petanque court. Clay-pigeon shooting, loch and river fishing are abundant nearby, and accommodation is provided with three en-suite bedrooms.
🚾 Q ❀ 🛏 Ⓓ ♿ P

Ythanview Hotel
Main Street, AB41 7DT
✪ 11-2.30; 5-11 (1am Fri); 11-12.30am Sat; 11-11 Sun
☎ (01651) 806235 website: www.ythanview.com
Beer range varies Ⓗ
Comfortable, family-run hotel comprising a welcoming restaurant, enlivened by a real fire, and a smaller public bar. It has a real village local feel, even having its own cricket team and organising community fundraising events. Inexpensive meals tempt visitors and locals, with the landlord's hot chicken curry being something of a challenge.
🚾 Q ❀ 🛏 Ⓓ Ⓖ ♿ ♣ P ⚥

MIDMAR

Midmar Inn
AB51 7LX (on B9119, 2 miles W of Echt)
✪ 11-2.30, 5-11 (1am Fri; midnight Sat); 12.30-midnight Sun
☎ (01330) 860515
Beer range varies Ⓗ
Despite the scarcity of adjacent housing, this sociable pub is well frequented by locals, especially on Thursday's ceilidh night. It is popular for family meals at weekends (booking advised). The bar area has recently been renovated, but the building is a veritable warren of rooms, including a separate area housing a pool table. Q ❀ Ⓓ ♣ P

NETHERLEY

Lairhillock
AB39 3QS (signed off B979, 3 miles S of B9077)
✪ 11.30-2.30, 5-11 (midnight Fri); 11-midnight Sat; 12-11 Sun
☎ (01569) 730001 website: www.lairhillock.co.uk
Courage Directors; Taylor Landlord; guest beers Ⓗ
Set in the heart of beautiful countryside, the emphasis here is on quality, friendliness and families. The public bar, with its log fire, is ideal for a convivial drink, while both the lounge and conservatory tend to be used by diners. The conservatory, where the views are breathtaking whatever the season, is also a popular choice for customers with children. The lounge has a more intimate atmosphere. Look out for the 'inn' on the roof. 🚾 Q ⛵ ❀ Ⓓ Ⓖ ♿ ♣ P ⚥

OLDMELDRUM

Redgarth Hotel ✓
Kirk Brae, AB51 0DJ
(off A947, towards golf course)
✪ 11-2.30, 5-midnight; 12-2.30, 5-11 Sun
☎ (01651) 872353
Beer range varies Ⓗ/Ⓖ
Traditional, wood-panelled lounge bar, in an imposing position at the top of the village, enjoying panoramic views of the eastern Grampian mountains. It offers an imaginative selection of seasonal guest ales and a varied menu of home-cooked food. Occasional 'brewer-in-residence' evenings are an added attraction. A no-smoking room is available for diners or meetings. Families are welcome in the main lounge (children's certificate). Local CAMRA Pub of the Year 2003.
Q ⛵ ❀ 🛏 Ⓓ ♣ P ⚥

PORTSOY

Shore Inn
The Old Harbour, Church Street, AB45 2QR
✪ 10-11 (midnight Thu; 12.30am Fri & Sat); 10-11 Sun
☎ (01261) 842831
Beer range varies Ⓗ
This 18th-century coastal inn, situated at the oldest harbour on the Moray coast, exudes an old-time atmosphere with its low ceiling and dark wooden bar fittings. Up to three ales are stocked (only one in winter); the selection is unpredictable. The village hosts an annual boat festival, for which the pub runs an outdoor bar – the Shore Out.
🚾 Q ⛵ Ⓓ ♿ ♣

STONEHAVEN

Marine Hotel

9-10 Shorehead, AB39 2JY (harbour front)
☼ 11-midnight (1am Fri & Sat); 11-midnight Sun
☎ (01569) 762155
Inveralmond Ossian's Ale; Taylor Landlord; guest beers Ⓗ

Former Scottish CAMRA Pub of the Year whose picturesque harbour-front location makes it particularly appealing in summer. Downstairs consists of a simple wood-panelled bar. The adjacent lounge, furnished with armchairs and settees, together with a huge fire in winter, makes a comfortable contrast to the bustle of the small bar. Upstairs, the main eating area specialises in fresh, local produce, particularly fish dishes. Addlestones cider is sold. ㊙Q☙❀⊯◑◐⊟Å♣✂日

Ship Inn

5 Shorehead, AB39 2JY (harbour front)
☼ 11 (12.30 Sun)-midnight
☎ (01569) 762617
Caledonian Deuchars IPA; Orkney Dark Island; guest beers Ⓗ

Set on the picturesque harbour, this long, narrow pub was built in 1771. It is divided into three sections: bar, lounge and family room, all areas display a distinct nautical feel with brass fittings, wood panelling and old photographs of the harbour area. The tiny patio makes an ideal location for a summer pint. The large picture window enables you to enjoy the spectacular views when the weather is inclement. Good value meals are available, except on Sunday evening. Q☙❀◑◐⊟Å♣

TARVES

Aberdeen Arms Hotel

The Square, AB41 7GX
☼ 12-2.30 (not Mon), 5-11 (1am Fri); 12-11.45 Sat; 12.30-11 Sun
☎ (01651) 851214
website: www.aberdeenarmstarves.com

Beer range varies Ⓗ

Small, family-run hotel in the village conservation area. Note the fine mirrors in the public bar where a children's certificate operates until 8pm. Regular folk music evenings feature bagpipes and a zither! Food ranges from the cuisine of the north-east to the Far East. It is handy for Tolquhon Castle and Pitmedden Gardens, which were laid out in the 17th century by Sir Alexander Seddon, with elaborate flowerbeds, fountains and pavilions.
㊙Q☙❀◑◐⊟Å♣P✂

TORPHINS

Learney Arms Hotel

The Square, AB31 4GP
☼ 11-2.30, 5-11.30; 11-11.30 Sat; 12.30-11 Sun
☎ (01339) 882202
Beer range varies Ⓗ

Traditional, 19th-century hotel, originally a holiday resort on the defunct Deeside railway line. The decor displays a golfing theme. A range of over 100 malts is sure to tempt many customers. A price premium is levied on half pints.
Q❀❀◑◐⊟♣P

WESTHILL

Shepherd's Rest

Straik Road, Arnhall Business Park, AB32 6HF
☼ 11-11; 12.30-11 Sun
☎ (01224) 740208
Beer range varies Ⓗ

Part of Scottish Courage's Chef & Brewer chain, the kit-built interior is well done with differing serving areas surrounding the bar. The guest beer selection tends to be more adventurous than might be expected, as demonstrated by the pump clip display. Unsurprisingly, food dominates the proceedings, and the pub is popular with families at weekends. Accommodation is available in the adjoining commercial lodge. ㊙❀❀◑◐⅋P✂

HIGHLANDS & ISLANDS

SHETLAND

Baltasound

Whiteness
Scousburgh

Stornoway

THE WESTERN ISLANDS

Ullapool
Dundonell

Gairloch

Uig

Rosemarkie
Munlochy
Nairn
Inverness
GRAMPIAN

Waternish
SKYE
Plockton
Drumnadrochit

Sligachan
Carrbridge
Nethy Bridge
Aviemore

Inverie
Invergarry
Kingussie

Melvich
Thurso

Quoyloo
Kirkwall
Stromness

ORKNEY

Fort William
Onich
Kinlochleven
Ballachulish
Glencoe

0 Miles 20
0 Kilometres 32

Authority areas covered: Highland UA, Orkney Islands UA, Shetland Islands UA, Western Islands UA

AVIEMORE

Old Bridge Inn
Dalfaber Road, PA22 1PU
(100 yds from jct with Cairngorm ski road, B970)
✪ 11-midnight (1am Fri); 12.30-11 Sun
☎ (01479) 811137 website: www.bridgeinn.co.uk
Cairngorm Highland IPA; guest beer Ⓗ
Busy and popular pub with a developing catering trade, originally a cottage and now greatly enlarged. It lies to the south of the village, on the road leading to the Strathspey Steam Railway and attracts outdoor enthusiasts. It features two guest beers including one from the nearby Cairngorm Brewery. The pub has a children's certificate. There is a good choice of malt whiskies. A new self-catering bunkhouse adjoins the pub, it can accommodate 40 guests. ♨Q✿✍◑❺▲⇌P

BALLACHULISH

Laroch Bar & Bistro
Loanfern, East Laroch, PH49 4JB (off A82)
✪ 11-11.30 (1.30am Thu-Sat); 12.30-11.30 Sun
☎ (01855) 811900
Atlas Wayfarer Ⓗ
A new pub, built 11 years ago and extended more recently. Previously this attractive village by the bridge over Loch Leven had had no pub for over 50 years. The clean and uncluttered lounge bar is furnished in a modern style and decorated with prints. Space for eating is provided on a raised section. The public bar offers a large-screen and is popular with locals, some taking advantage of a designated driver scheme. ⏃◑❺P✕

BALTASOUND

Baltasound Hotel
ZE2 9DS
✪ 12-2.30, 5-midnight (1am Fri & Sat); 12.30-2.30, 5-11 Sun
☎ (01957) 711334
website: www.baltasound-hotel.shetland.co.uk
Valhalla White Wife, Simmer Dim, Auld Rock Ⓗ
Think remote, very remote – the island of Unst. The capital of Shetland, Lerwick, is 70 miles and two ferry rides away. At midsummer an almost perpetual daylight exists, known locally as 'simmer dim'. The Keen of Hamar nature reserve, home to some unique local species of flora, is within walking distance. The beers of the island's Valhalla Brewery are stocked in this, the most northerly hotel in Britain (25 guest rooms). ✍◑❺❺P

CARRBRIDGE

Cairn Hotel
PH23 AS (on B9153, formerly A9)
✪ 11.30-midnight (1am Fri & Sat);
12.30 (12 summer)-11 Sun
☎ (01479) 841212
website: www.cairncarrbridgelineone.net
Beer range varies Ⓗ
In the centre of a pleasant village, now bypassed by the busy A9 and convenient for the nearby landmark heritage park, this busy pub forms part of an hotel. It caters for locals and outdoor enthusiasts. The two beers are mainly Scottish, and include brews from Cairngorm, Isle of Skye, and Black Isle. In addition to bar meals, soup and toasties

are available all day; evening meals are served 6–8 (8.45 in summer).
🏨❀🏤🅍⊕≉P✁

DRUMNADROCHIT

Benleva Hotel
IV63 6UH (signed from A82)
🕐 12-midnight (1am Thu & Fri; 11.45 Sat); 12-11 Sun
☎ (01456) 450080 website: www.benleva.co.uk
Beer range varies Ⓗ

Popular village hotel catering for locals and visitors, an extended and refurbished 400-year-old former manse in extensive grounds, it is convenient for Urquart Castle, the Great Glen Way and looking for the Loch Ness Monster. Two Scottish beers are available; one from the Isle of Skye Brewery. The hotel offers a limited lunchtime menu and good evening meals. Regular quiz nights and occasional traditional music are staged. The sweet chestnut tree at the entrance was a former hanging tree. There is always a friendly welcome.
🏨Q❀🏤🅍⊕🌢A♣P✁

FORT WILLIAM

Grog & Gruel
66 High Street, PH33 6AE
🕐 11 (12 winter)-midnight (1am Thu-Sat);
5 (closed lunch)-midnight Sun
☎ (01397) 705078 website: www.grogandgruel.co.uk
Beer range varies Ⓗ

In the shadow of Britain's highest mountain, this bare-floored ale house with church pew seating, keeps up to six beers in summer, reducing to two in winter. Owned by the same family that owns the famous Clachaig Inn, it holds beer festivals at Easter, October and Christmas. Busy with tourists in summer, it also attracts locals. Home-cooked food is available in the upstairs dining room or from the more limited bar menu; no meals are prepared on Sunday lunchtime. ❀⊕A≉

Nevisport Bar
Tweedale, PH33 6EJ
(at N end of High St, under sports shop)
🕐 11.30-11.30 (11.30-1am Fri & Sat);
11.30-11.30 Sun
☎ (01397) 704921 website: www.nevisport.com
Beer range varies Ⓗ

A warming open fire welcomes winter visitors to this large but cosy bar, which attracts outdoor enthusiasts all year round. Situated at the north end of Fort William and convenient for Glen Nevis and Aonach Mor, this is a regular watering-hole for climbers, walkers and skiers. The walls of the informal lounge-style bar are adorned with large pictures of mountain scenery and mountain sports paraphernalia. Mainly Scottish beers are served, often from the Isle of Skye Brewery. 🏨🌢⊕🌢A≉

GAIRLOCH

Old Inn
IV21 2BD (opp. harbour)
🕐 11-1am (11.30 Sun); 12.30-11 Sun
☎ (01445) 712006 website: www/theoldinn.co.uk
Beer range varies Ⓗ

Up to eight real ales (three in winter) are served in this family-run hotel, which is in a delightful setting at the foot of Flowerdale Glen. Mainly Scottish ales are served, to accompany the enticing menu of home-cooked game and locally-caught seafood. Much of the seafood offered in the bistro and restaurant is landed at the nearby harbour. There is a pottery, a walker's lodge, and a natural climbing wall in the grounds. Spectacular murals adorn the bar.
🏨🌢❀🏤🅍⊕🌢A♣P🍴

GLENCOE

Clachaig Inn
PH49 4HX (1/2 mile off A82, on old road to Glencoe going west) OSNN128 567
🕐 11-11 (midnight Fri; 11.30 Sat); 11-11 Sun
☎ (01855) 811252 website: www.clachaig.com
Heather Fraoch Heather Ale; Tetley Bitter, Burton Ale; guest beers Ⓗ

Set amid the rugged mountainous beauty of Glencoe, this coaching inn dates back 300 years. The spacious bar has a stone floor, low stone dividers and rustic, wooden furniture. Here climbers and travellers can warm up by iron stoves and regain their strength. Away from the general melee are quieter corners, a no-smoking room and a comfy sofa lounge. At opposite ends, the long counter serves an impressive range of ales (nine guests) plus many bottled beers and food. 🏨Q🌢❀🏤🅍⊕🌢🌢AP✁

INVERGARRY

Invergarry Hotel
PH35 4HJ
🕐 12-2.30, 6-11 (midnight Fri); 12.30-2.30; 6-11 Sun
☎ (01809) 501206 website: www.invergarry.net
Beer range varies Ⓗ

Real ales are only served in the summer and at Christmas time at this fully modernised coaching inn, dating from the Victorian era. The bar at the side of the hotel has two handpumps; one from the Isle of Skye Brewery. It is handy for the Great Glen cycle route and new walkway, and on the road to Skye. These premises were once owned by John Anderson, the good friend of Rabbie Burns. Children are allowed until 8pm.
🏨🏤⊕🌢♣P

INVERIE

Old Forge
Knoydart by Mallaig, PH41 4PL
(accessible by ferry from Mallaig)
🕐 11-midnight (including Sun)
☎ (01678) 462267
Beer range varies Ⓗ

The most remote pub on mainland Britain is reached by ferry or by a 15-mile, hilly walk from Kinloch Hourn. In a spectacular

INDEPENDENT BREWERIES

An Teallach Dundonell
Atlas Kinlochleven
Black Isle Munlochy
Cairngorm Aviemore
Far North Melvich
Hebridean Stornoway
Isle of Skye Uig
Newtonmore & Kingussie Kingussie
Orkney Quoyloo
Valhalla Baltasound

setting on the shore of Loch Nevis, it provides an ideal base for walking the 'Rough Bounds' of Knoydart; moorings welcome waterborne visitors. An essential hub of the local community, it has two pumps serving mainly Isle of Skye beers. Specialities on the all-day menu include locally-caught seafood. An informal atmosphere prevails – dress code is wellies, waterproofs and midge cream. The landlord can arrange accommodation. ⚏Q⚛◑Å

INVERNESS

Blackfriars
93-95 Academy Street, IV1 1LU
✪ 11-midnight (12.30 Fri; 11.45 Sat); 12.30-11 Sun
☎ (01463) 233881
website: www.blackfriars.50megs.com
Courage Directors; Greene King Old Speckled Hen; McEwan 80/-; Marston's Pedigree; Theakston Old Peculier Ⓗ
Traditional, town-centre pub; one spacious room, with a large standing area at the bar and ample seating in comfortable alcoves around the room. Four guest ales usually include Scottish breweries, such as Isle of Skye. Inexpensive meals are home-cooked, using local produce; a vegetarian choice is always available. This music-oriented pub offers evenings of ethnic, traditional music, often featuring bagpipes, and poetry. Local bands appear regularly. ◑⑅≈

Clachnaharry Inn
17-19 High Street, IV3 6RH (on A862, Beauly Rd on outskirts of town)
✪ 11-11 (midnight Thu-Sat); 12.30-11.45 Sun
☎ (01463) 239806
Adnams Broadside; Courage Directors; Isle of Skye Red Cuillin; Ⓗ **Blaven;** Ⓗ/Ⓖ **McEwan 80/-; guest beers** Ⓗ
Locals and visitors enjoy the atmosphere at this cheerful, 17th-century coaching inn. Food is served all day and families are always welcome. The lounge and garden afford fine views across the Caledonian Canal sea lock and the Beauly Firth towards Ben Wyvis. Some beers are dispensed by gravity from wooden casks; a variety of house beers is brewed by the Isle of Skye Brewery. Regular local CAMRA town Pub of the Year winner, it was CAMRA Scottish Pub of the Year 2001.
⚏Q⚘⚛◑⑅Å♣P

Hootananny
67 Church Street, IV1 1ET
✪ 12-11 (if music staged 1am Wed-Sat); 7-11 (summer 12-11; 1am music) Sun
☎ (01463) 233651 website: www.hootananny.com
Black Isle Red Kite Ⓗ
This pub only opened a year ago, the building was originally a bank established in 1810. The large, sectioned bar has wood and newspaper wallpaper decoration. The one handpump supplies Red Kite, the only Black Isle beer in the city. Popular with all walks of life, customers are drawn by the friendly environment and lively traditional music that is played most nights. Tasty food is served, including daily specials. ◑⑆≈

Number 27
27 Castle Street, IV2 3DU (below castle)
✪ 11-11 (midnight Thu; 1am Fri; 11.45 Sat); 12.30-11 Sun

☎ (01463) 241999
Beer range varies Ⓗ
Bright, friendly, modern pub in the shadow of the castle. The bar has a comfortable seating area where beers on tap usually include a local ale, often from Black Isle or Isle of Skye. Only one beer is kept in winter. Meals, served in the attractive dining area and the main bar, are prepared using fresh local produce, including game and salmon in season. A large-screen TV shows sporting events. ◑≈

Palace Hotel
Palace Milton Hotel & Leisure Club, 8 Ness Walk, IV3 5NE
(100 yds from main bridge, opp. castle)
✪ 11.30-11 (including Sun)
☎ (01463) 223243 website: www.miltonhotels.com
Isle of Skye Red Cuillin Ⓗ
This 88-roomed, tourist-oriented, family-friendly hotel, enjoys a spectacular setting by the River Ness, opposite the castle. It is close to the centre of the city. It specialises in coach parties, but local trade includes families using the hotel's leisure centre and gymnasium. Just one spacious lounge with an island bar serves two, usually Scottish beers in summer. Food ranges from a sandwich to a steak meal, and is available in the bar, or large restaurant, both have splendid views of the river and castle.
⚿◑⚛Å≈P

Phoenix
108 Academy Street, IV1 1LP
✪ 11-1am (12.30am Sat); 11-midnight Sun
☎ (01463) 245990
Beer range varies Ⓗ
Established in 1894, the public bar has changed little, with wooden floor, wood-panelled walls and the original island bar with granite trough around the base. It is a gem. Beers are usually from Scottish breweries, two in the lounge and up to six in the public bar. Inexpensive food is available in the lounge bar, with a limited menu in the public bar all day. Children are welcome and a large-screen TV shows major football matches. ◑⑆Å≈

KINGUSSIE

Royal Hotel
29 High Street, PH21 1HX
✪ 11-midnight (1am Thu-Sat); 12.30-midnight Sun
☎ (01540) 661898
Beer range varies Ⓗ
Large, 51-roomed hotel, that is popular with coach parties. Located in a delightful holiday area, nearby attractions include the Cairngorms, Wildlife Park and Highland Folk Museum. It is the main outlet for the four beers brewed at the attached Newtonmore & Kingussie Brewery. Up to 10 handpumps are in use in summer (three in winter). A beer festival is held in November. Many locals use the large, extended bar area which hosts regular live music.
⚛⚿◑⚓Å≈P⚼

KINLOCHLEVEN

Tailrace Inn
Riverside Road, PA40 4QH (on B863)
✪ 11-11.30 (12.30am Thu-Sat); 12-11.30 Sun
☎ (01855) 831777 website: www.tailraceinn.co.uk

Beer range varies H

This friendly, modern pub has recently been refurbished. Fine food is served daily until 8pm winter and 9pm summer. Entertainment is staged on Thursday and Friday in summer. Two handpumps sell Atlas beers; the brewery is a short walk away. It has a marvellous setting, surrounded by the Mamore Mountains and midway between Glencoe and Ben Nevis on the West Highland Way. Guest rooms and self-catering accommodation are available. ⊛⇔◑⬥P

KIRKWALL

Bothy Bar
Albert Hotel, Mounthoolie Lane, KW15 1HW
(100 yds along Junction Rd from harbour)
✪ 11-11 (1am Thu-Sat); 12-1am Sun
☎ (01856) 876000

Orkney Red Macgregor, Dark Island H

The Bothy Bar is part of the Albert Hotel, and has the appearance, as the name suggests, of a bothy, complete with a very large open fire. It is handy for buses, North Isles ferries and Kirkwall's main shopping street. There is a regular early evening trade boosted at the weekend by the night club which is also part of the hotel. The car park is pay and display during the day. ⇔◑A

NAIRN

Invernairne Hotel
Thurlow Road, IV12 4EZ
✪ 11-midnight (12.30am Wed, Fri & Sat); 11-midnight Sun
☎ (01667) 452039

Isle of Skye Red Cuillin H

Family-owned hotel with reasonably-priced accommodation, tucked away in acres of secluded gardens overlooking the Moray Firth. The baronial-style lounge bar has cosy nooks, oak panelling and a roaring log fire (in winter). The real ale is usually supplied by the Isle of Skye Brewery. The excellent cuisine focuses on fresh local produce. A garden path leads to a beach. This is an ideal base for the 'Whisky Trail'. It is close to Nairn's two championship golf courses. Jazz music is staged every Wednesday night, and folk music once a month. The hotel has a children's certificate. ⇔⦁⊛◑⬥A⇌⬥P

NETHY BRIDGE

Heatherbrae Hotel
Dell Road, PH25 3DG (off B970)
✪ 5-11 (1am Fri); 12-1am Sat; 12-11 Sun
☎ (01479) 821345
website: www.nethybridge.com/heatherbraehotel.htm

Cairngorm Highland IPA H

Busy, welcoming pub forming part of a small hotel that is popular with locals, birdwatchers, walkers, fishermen, golfers and skiers. All meals are served in the dining room adjoining the bar. Bunkhouse and a variety of other accommodation is available nearby. Usually an additional Cairngorm beer is on offer alongside the Highland IPA. ⇔⦁⊛◑⬥P

ONICH

Four Seasons
PH33 6SE (signed from A82)

✪ 5.30-11.45 (12.45am Thu-Sat; closed Mon-Wed winter); 5.30-11.45 Sun
☎ (01855) 821287 website: www.inchreecentre.co.uk

Atlas Latitude; Isle of Skye Red Cuillin; guest beer H

Set in the Inchree holiday centre, halfway between Ben Nevis and Glencoe with plenty of chalets, camping and bunkhouse accommodation available, superb views of Loch Linnhe and the Ardgour Hills can be enjoyed. The business has been run by the same family for 30 years. It is not open at lunchtime, but serves meals in the evening. Two or three Scottish beers are stocked. The small bar opens out into a large area with tables. ⊛◑⬥A⬥P

Nether Lochaber Hotel
PH33 6SE
(by E terminal of Corran Ferry, 200 yds from A82)
✪ 11-2.30; 5-11 (midnight Fri & Sat); 12.30-2.30, 6-11 Sun
☎ (01855) 821235

Draught Bass H

A few yards only from the busy A82, it is well worth breaking your journey to visit this cosy and welcoming little bar, which is beside the slipway for the Corran Ferry. Once a Temperance hotel the bar was built on to the rear of the building, accessible from an outside door. This popular bar is close to Glencoe and convenient for the Ben Nevis area. Q⊛⇔◑A⬥P

PLOCKTON

Plockton Hotel
Harbour Street, IV52 8TN
✪ 11-midnight; 12.30-11 Sun
☎ (01599) 544274 website: www.plocktonhotel.co.uk

Caledonian Deuchars IPA H

This much-visited hotel is set among a row of traditional waterfront buildings in the picturesque village of Plockton, and boasts spectacular views over Loch Carron. Recently extended and refurbished, the hotel offers an award-winning menu of locally-landed seafood. Close to the Isle of Skye and to the mountains of Torridon, the village has much to offer and is a regular haunt for outdoor enthusiasts. Palm trees take advantage of the Gulf Stream warmed coastline. Q⇔⊛⇔◑⊟⬥⇌⬥⊁

ROSEMARKIE

Plough Inn
IV10 8UF
✪ 11-11.30 (12.30am Fri); 11-2.30, 6-11.30 (12.30am Fri) winter; 12.30-11.30 Sun
☎ (01381) 620164

Beer range varies H

Beautiful old country pub, in a pretty seaside village. Unmissable, with its distinctive leaning gable, it has a cosy wood-lined bar with an ancient marriage stone lintel (dated 1691) over the fireplace. Two attractive gardens lead to a sandy beach, also signposted is a walk through the local beauty spot, the Fairy Glen. The menu specialises in seafood and fresh local produce. ⇔⊛◑⊟A⬥P

SCOUSBURGH

Spiggie Hotel
ZE2 9JE
✪ 11-11 (midnight Wed-Sat); 12.30-11 Sun

☎ (01950) 460409 website: www.spiggie.co.uk
Valhalla Simmer Dim; guest beers Ⓗ
Recently restored, small hotel which was
originally built to service the Shetland ferry
in the 19th century. The compact bar has a
stone and wood floor. Up to three beers are
on offer in the tourist season and good
quality, locally-sourced food is served. A
virtual paradise for 'twitchers', local
amenities include the trout fishery in
Spiggie Lock and the archaeological sites of
Jarlshof and Scatness. ♨⌂◑♣☙P

SLIGACHAN

Sligachan Hotel
IV47 8SW (at A850/A863 jct)
◷ 9am-midnight; 11-11 Sun
☎ (01478) 650204
website: www.sligachan.demon.co.uk
Beer range varies Ⓗ
Situated next to the Cuillin Hills, this
superb, family-run, 19th-century hotel lies
in some of the most spectacular walking
and climbing country in Britain. There is a
fully-equipped campsite opposite and
children are welcome. Eight ales are
available during the summer, with a
reduced range in winter. Bar meals are
excellent value. The hotel hosts an autumn
real ale and music festival. Local CAMRA
Country Pub of the Year 2001.
♨⌺❀⌂◑⊟♧♣P

STROMNESS

Stromness Hotel
15 Victoria Street, KW16 3AA (set back from
harbour, 200 yds from ferry terminal)
◷ 11-11 (1am Fri & Sat); 12-11 Sun
☎ (01856) 850296 website: www.stromnesshotel.com
**Orkney Red MacGregor, Dark Island, seasonal beers;
guest beers** Ⓗ
The Stromness Hotel dominates the
pierhead, the first-floor location of the
lounge bar is great for people and boat
watching. Throughout the year there are
beer, blues and jazz festivals and a recent
innovation is themed food nights with
bottled beers to match. Prices are lower at
the weekend, outside the summer season.
♨Q❀⌂◑ÅP

THURSO

Central Hotel
Traill Street, KW14 8EJ
◷ 11-11.45 (1am Fri & Sat); 12.30-11.45 Sun
☎ (01847) 893129
Beer range varies Ⓗ
Town-centre hotel, two miles from Orkney
ferry terminal at Scrabster, on the
spectacular Pentland Firth coast. It attracts
many families with children who enjoy the
soft play area and bouncy castle, accessed

from the large upstairs bar/restaurant. No
children are admitted to the downstairs bar,
which, with a large-screen TV, is popular
with locals and frequented by Caithness
rugby club. The food is mainly home made
and served from 9am–8.30pm (takeaways
available). ♨◑⊟&Å⇌♣⅍

ULLAPOOL

Ferry Boat Inn
Shore Street, IV26 2UJ
◷ 11-11; 12.30-11 Sun
☎ (01854) 612366 website: www.ferryboat-inn.com
Beer range varies Ⓗ
This family-run, 18th-century inn is
situated in a wonderful setting on the shore
of Loch Broom, with stunning views across
the loch to the mountains of Wester Ross. A
mixture of locals and regularly returning
visitors enjoy the friendly and informal
atmosphere in this busy bar. Sunny summer
evenings spent sitting on the harbour wall
opposite are a real treat. Local fresh produce
is served in the bar (all year) and restaurant
(open spring–late autumn). ♨Q⛵⌂◑Å

WATERNISH

Stein Inn ⊘
Stein, IV55 8GA (N of Dunvegan on B886,
4½ miles from Fairy Bridge)
◷ 4-11 (midnight Fri); 12-midnight summer;
12-12.30am Sat; 12.30-11 Sun
☎ (01470) 592362 website: www.steininn.co.uk
Isle of Skye Red Cuillin; guest beers Ⓗ
This traditional Highland hostelry, set in a
row of cottages on the shores of Loch Bay, is
a well-rewarded, single-track detour from
the main Portree to Dunvegan road.
Locally-caught seafood, landed at the
nearby jetty, is served (Easter–Oct) in the
bar and restaurant. Both the bar and large
shoreside garden afford fine views across the
loch to Rubha Maol. Facilities for seafarers
include council moorings, showers, food
supplies (by arrangement), and message
relay services. ♨Q❀⌂Å♣P

WHITENESS

Inn on the Hill
Westings Hotel, Wormadale, ZE2 9LJ (on
A971, 10 miles NW of Lerwick) OS402464
◷ 12-2 (3 Sat), 5-11; 12-2.30, 5-11 Sun
☎ (01595) 840242
website: www.westings.shetland.co.uk
Beer range varies Ⓗ
Isolated, small hotel with tremendous sea
views of Weisdale Voe. One Valhalla beer
and two guests are dispensed in the Palm
Shack Bar, with the Green Room available
for families and non-smokers. Evening
meals are served from 7.15–8.15.
⛵⌂&Å♣P⅍

Drunk in the 1970s

Blathered, blotto, bollocksed, bullifants, drunk as a sack, foul fu'
(Scotland), full as a boot, fuzzled, mouldy, paralytic, pie-eyed, pissed
as arseholes (or as a fart, a handcart, a rat or a skunk), pixilated,
rotten, shickered, shonkered, sloshed, sozzled, stewed, taking both
sides of the road, tight as a drum, under the weather, zonked.

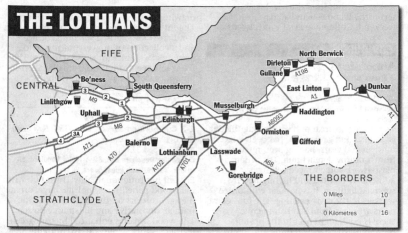

THE LOTHIANS

Authority areas covered: City of Edinburgh UA, East Lothian UA, Midlothian UA, West Lothian UA

BALERNO

Johnsburn House
64 Johnsburn Road, EH14 7BB (off A70)
☼ 12-3 (not Mon), 6-midnight (1am Fri); 12-1am Sat; 12.30-midnight Sun
☎ (0131) 449 3847
Caledonian Deuchars IPA; guest beers Ⓗ
Grade B listed baronial mansion dating from 1760, originally owned by Professor Adam Fergusson who reputedly brought together the two great men of Scottish literature, Robert Burns and Sir Walter Scott. The low-ceilinged, cosy bar has a convivial atmosphere with varied memorabilia and exposed beams. A passageway leads to a dark wood panelled dining room, beyond which a corridor leads to further rooms for diners. It enjoys a good reputation for award-winning meals. Children are welcome. Four guest beers are available.
ᴹᴬQ❀◑♣P

BO'NESS

Anchor Tavern
54 North Street, EH51 0AG (opp. town clock)
☼ 11-11 (11.45 Fri & Sat); 12.30-11 Sun
☎ (01506) 824717
website: www.bo-ness.org.uk/html/history/anchor
Caledonian Deuchars IPA; Orkney Dark Island Ⓗ
Built in 1891 and in its early days a popular haunt for sailors of all nationalities, it remains a popular watering-hole, offering a good selection of ales, lagers and whisky. It bustles with regular activity every time there is a quiz night, major football or rugby match. It is also a gathering point for local business people and visiting steam railway enthusiasts.

DIRLETON

Castle Inn
EH39 5EP (off A198)
☼ 11.30-midnight (1am Fri & Sat); 11.30-midnight Sun
☎ (01620) 850221
Caledonian Deuchars IPA; Orkney Dark Island Ⓗ
Attractive inn overlooking the village green and opposite the castle ruins. To the right of the front door is the public bar, with a games room to the rear. Of interest are historical mirrors from bygone breweries. Half a dozen people would make the bar feel snug. To the left is the comfortable lounge bar, dominated by a central stone fireplace. Alterations can be compared with a 1898 plan hanging in the lounge. No food is available on winter weekday evenings. Children are admitted until 7pm.
ᴹᴬ❀✍◑ 🍴⚘♣P

EAST LINTON

Bridgend Hotel
3 Bridge End, EH40 3AF (off A1)
☼ 12-2, 7-11 (1am Thu); 12-1am Fri & Sat; 12-midnight Sun
☎ (01620) 860202
website: www.bridgendhotel-restaurant.co.uk
Hadrian & Border Rampart; guest beer Ⓗ
Village pub with a public bar and a comfortable lounge. Hadrian & Border beers usually feature on the bar. The stained glass windows and rooftop statue hint that the pub was once the Red Lion. The bar has a light wood counter, musical instruments hanging on the wall and a pool table. The lounge-cum-dining room, offers evening meals on Friday and Saturday. Families are welcome.
✍◑🍴⚘♣🍴

Drovers Inn ✪
5 Bridge Street, EH40 3AG (off A1)
☼ 11.30-3, 5-11 (1am Thu & Fri); 11-1am Sat; 12.30-midnight Sun
☎ (01620) 860298
Adnams Broadside; Caledonian Deuchars IPA; guest beers Ⓗ
An oasis, with three or four serious ales, just off the A1 and the main East Coast rail line, which runs through the disused station at the foot of the main street. The inn is part of a row of stone-terraced, double-storey dwellings. The bar has a select feel with claret-coloured walls, dark wood decor, and is surveyed by a stuffed goat's head. A good

INDEPENDENT BREWERIES

Belhaven Dunbar
Caledonian Edinburgh

restaurant leads from the bar. Meals are served 12–2 and 6–9 and all day at the weekend. Children are welcome. 🚪🏠🜊♣

EDINBURGH

Abbotsford ☆
3 Rose Street, EH2 2PR
✪ 11-11; closed Sun
☎ (0131) 225 5276
Belhaven 80/-; Broughton Greenmantle; guest beers Ⓐ

Traditional Scottish pub with a magnificent island bar and gantry that has been a fixture for over 100 years, having been rescued from a nearby derelict pub. The ornate plasterwork and corniced ceiling is attractively painted and highlighted by subdued lighting. It is popular with office workers in the early evening. The four guest beers are often from Scottish micros. While there is no draught beer in the upstairs restaurant, the staff will bring you a pint from downstairs. Q◑➔(Waverley)

Bennets Bar ☆
1 Maxwell Street, Morningside, EH10 5HT
✪ 11-midnight; closed Sun
☎ (0131) 447 1903
Belhaven 70/-, 80/-; guest beers Ⓐ

Couthy back-street boozer in the douce suburb of Morningside, except that it is only yards from one of the city's busiest road junctions. The walls are adorned with photographs of old Edinburgh. It can be smoky when busy. Four guest beers are sold. Outdoor drinking is available in a paved area at the front of the pub. 🏠

Blue Blazer
2 Spittal Street, EH3 9DX (W side of centre)
✪ 11-1am; 12.30-1am Sun
☎ (0131) 229 5030
Caledonian Deuchars IPA, 80/-; Ⓐ **guest beers** Ⓗ

This two-roomed ale house was one of the first pubs in Edinburgh to have a sympathetic refurbishment by Ian White, a publican dedicated to the traditional style of the Scottish pub. Both rooms are cosy and convivial, but can be smoky when busy. Note the original Bernard's Brewery mirrors. The six guest beers are generally from Scottish micros. Q

Bow Bar
80 West Bow, EH1 2HH (off Grassmarket)
✪ 12-11.30; 12.30-11 Sun
☎ (0131) 226 7667
Belhaven 80/-; Caledonian Deuchars IPA; Taylor Landlord; guest beers Ⓐ

The original home of the 2002 Champion Beer of Britain, Deuchars IPA, for which it was originally brewed as a house beer. This one-roomed bar is situated in the heart of the historic Old Town, close to the temporary home of the Scottish Parliament. Five guests are stocked. Rare, old brewery mirrors and advertising ephemera adorn the walls. Q➔(Waverley)

Cask & Barrel
115 Broughton Street, EH1 3RZ (E edge of New Town)
✪ 11-12.30am (1am Thu-Sat); 12.30-12.30am
☎ (0131) 556 3132
Draught Bass; Boddingtons Bitter; Caledonian Deuchars IPA, 80/-; guest beers Ⓗ

Spacious and extremely busy ale house drawing a mainly local clientele of all ages. The interior features an imposing horseshoe bar, bare floorboards, a splendid cornice and a collection of brewery mirrors. Old barrels act as tables for those standing. The five guest beers, often from smaller Scottish breweries, feature a range of strengths. Sparklers are removed on request. 🏠◑&➔(Waverley)

Cumberland Bar ✪
1-3 Cumberland Street, EH3 6RT (New Town)
✪ 11 (12.30 Sun)-1am
☎ (0131) 558 3134
Caledonian Deuchars IPA, 80/-; Taylor Landlord; Ⓗ **Orkney Dark Island; guest beers** Ⓐ

Elegant but functional, New Town pub with half wood panelling. Exquisite, large, ornate brewery mirrors on the walls hang beside framed, decorative and illustrative posters. The wood finish is enhanced by dark green leather seating. There are two drinking areas linked by a wide corridor. Some of the beers are dispensed by traditional Scottish tall fount. Four guest ales are sold. Children are welcome in the back room during the day. 🚪Q🏠◑

Golden Rule ✪
30 Yeaman Place, Fountainbridge, EH11 1BU (1 mile W of centre)
✪ 11-11.30 (midnight Fri); 12.30-11 Sun
☎ (0131) 229 3413
Caledonian Deuchars IPA, 80/-; Harviestoun Bitter & Twisted; Taylor Landlord; Ⓗ

Split-level, local bar in a Victorian tenement tucked away just around the corner from the Fountain Park complex. A regular entry in this Guide for over 10 years, the two guest beers, usually from smaller breweries, generally include one at 4% ABV and one at 5%. The downstairs bar, Rule 2, caters for the trendier end of the market. Bar snacks are available all day. The Union Canal, being refurbished under the millennium project, runs close by. ➔(Haymarket) ♣

Guildford Arms ✪
1 West Register Street, EH2 2AA
(behind Burger King at E end of Princes St)
✪ 11-11 (midnight Fri & Sat); 12.30-11 Sun
☎ (0131) 556 4312
Belhaven 80/-; Ⓗ **Caledonian Deuchars IPA;** Ⓟ **Harviestoun Bitter & Twisted, Ptarmigan; Orkney Dark Island; guest beers** Ⓗ

Bustling, but orderly, city-centre pub notable for its ornate plasterwork. The high ceiling, cornices and friezes are spectacular, as are the window arches and screens. An unusual gallery above the main bar is noteworthy. The extensive range of four guests usually includes beers from smaller breweries. No food is served on Sunday. The piped music can be loud. ◑➔(Waverley) ♣

Leslie's Bar ☆ ✪
45 Ratcliffe Terrace, EH9 1SU
(Newington, 1½ miles S of centre)
✪ 11-11 (11.30 Thu; 12.30am Fri & Sat); 12.30-11.30 Sun
☎ (0131) 667 7205
Caledonian Deuchars IPA, 80/-; Taylor Landlord; guest beers Ⓗ

Oustanding Victorian pub, retaining its fine ceiling, cornice, leaded glasswork and half wood panelling. The island bar has a spectacular snob screen which divides the pub. Small 'ticket window' hatches allow customers to order drinks. A plaque near the fire gives further details of this busy, vibrant but orderly pub. The two guest beers are often from smaller breweries. Trad jazz is usually played on Monday evening at this local CAMRA Pub of the Year 2002. ⚠Q⊞♣

Malt & Hops
45 The Shore, Leith, EH6 6QU
☼ 12-11 (midnight Wed-Thu); 1am Fri-Sat); 12.30-11 Sun
☎ (0131) 555 0083
website: www.spidacom.co.uk/EDG/malthops/
Greene King Old Speckled Hen; Tetley Bitter, Burton Ale; guest beers Ⓗ
One-roomed public bar dating from 1749, in the heart of 'new' Leith's riverside restaurant district. The superb collection of pump clips, many from now defunct breweries, indicates the ever-changing range of six interesting guest beers served. The real fire is very welcoming in winter. Among the artefacts on view are an oil painting, showing Leith around 50 years ago. Children are admitted until 6pm. Lunches are served Monday–Friday. ⚠Q❀♣✦

Oxford Bar ☆
8 Young Street, EH2 4JB (off Charlotte Sq)
☼ 11-1am; 12.30-midnight Sun
☎ (0131) 539 7119 website: www.oxfordbar.co.uk
Belhaven 80/-; Caledonian Deuchars IPA Ⓗ
Tiny, yet vibrant New Town drinking shop, retaining signs of its 19th-century parlour arrangement. Decorated with Burns memorabilia, this is where the 'Professor' holds court in Ian Rankin's novels. Over the years, this has been the haunt of many a famous and infamous character. Some nights you may rub shoulders with Rankin or other fellow authors. Alternatively visit the website and contribute to a story. ♣

Spylaw Tavern ⊘
27 Spylaw Street, Colinton, EH13 0JT
(SW edge of city)
☼ 11-11.30 (midnight Thu-Sat); 12.30-11 Sun
☎ (0131) 441 2783
Caledonian Deuchars IPA, 80/-; guest beer Ⓗ
Attractive pub with bar, lounge, restaurant and secure beer garden set in historic Colinton village. The decor gives the bar a light, airy feel due to the use of light-coloured wood. The lounge is well appointed and the no-smoking restaurant has views over the Dell. All food is freshly-prepared on the premises, including a range of pies that is a speciality. Children are welcome if dining. The pub makes an ideal stop when walking the Water of Leith path, however, no dogs are allowed. Q❀◑♣♣

Stable Bar
Mortonhall Park, 30 Frogston Road East, EH16 6TJ (S edge of City, by campsite)
☼ 11-midnight; 12.30-11 Sun
☎ (0131) 664 0773 website: www.stablebar.co.uk
Caledonian Deuchars IPA, 80/-; Inveralmond Ossian's Ale Ⓗ
Friendly bar in an old stable block, approached through a cobbled courtyard. It is popular for food and is often busy in summer with visitors to the nearby campsite. Children are welcome. The comfortable main bar has stone walls on

two sides, and is dominated by a huge chimney and fireplace which contains a large log fire in winter. The counter, gantry and rear room are relatively modern in appearance. ⚠❀◑♣P✦

Starbank Inn
64 Laverockbank Road, EH5 3BZ (on foreshore, near Newhaven)
☼ 11-11 (midnight Thu-Sat); 12.30-11 Sun
☎ (0131) 552 4141
Belhaven Sandy Hunter's Ale, 80/-; Caledonian Deuchars IPA; Taylor Landlord; guest beers Ⓗ
Bright, airy, bare-boarded ale house, with an extended U-shaped layout and superb views across the Firth of Forth to Fife. Try a pint of prawns with your beer! Four guest ales are usually available and the uncluttered walls sport several rare brewery mirrors. The restaurant is no-smoking. Food is served until 9pm and children are welcome until 8.30pm. It hosts occasional jazz on Sunday. Q◑♣♣

Thomson's
182-184 Morrison Street, EH3 8EB (W edge of centre)
☼ 12-11.30; closed Sun
☎ (0131) 228 5700
Caledonian Deuchars IPA, 80/-; Taylor Landlord; guest beers Ⓐ
Award-winning refurbishment of a pub modelled on the style of Glasgow's forgotten architect, Alexander 'Greek' Thomson. The walls are liberally decorated with old adverts and rare mirrors from long-defunct Scottish breweries. Up to five guest beers are available, one of which is normally from either Atlas, Pictish or Oakham. No lunches are served on Saturday. Edinburgh CAMRA Pub of the Year 2003.
Q◑⇌ (Haymarket)

Winston's ⊘
20 Kirk Loan, Corstorphine, EH12 7HD
(3 miles W of centre, off St Johns Rd)
☼ 11-11.30 (midnight Thu-Sat); 12.30-11 Sun
☎ (0131) 539 7077
Caledonian Deuchars IPA; Tetley Burton Ale; guest beer Ⓗ
This comfortable lounge bar is situated in Corstorphine, a busy area of west Edinburgh about a mile from Murrayfield stadium and close to the zoo. The small, modern building houses a warm and welcoming, active community pub. The one room is used by old and young alike, with children welcome until 3pm. Wonderful home-made pies are sold, but no food is available on Sunday. ◑

Goblin Ha' Hotel
Main Street, EH41 4QH
☼ 11-2.30, 4.30-11; 11-midnight Fri & Sat; 11-11 Sun
☎ (01620) 810244 website: www.goblin-ha-hotel.co.uk
Caledonian Deuchars IPA; Hop Back Summer Lightning; guest beers Ⓗ
Large hotel in a picturesque village. The public bar has a mixture of church pew and leather-style covered banquettes. The ceiling is low and of painted wood planking, while the gantry is a mix of glass and wood. The pool room is to the side of the bar. At the front is a large comfortable lounge, mainly laid out for eating. A conservatory provides

additional space. The beer garden is popular with families in summer; children are admitted until 8pm. Lothian CAMRA Pub of the Year 2003. 🏚🏮🚲🌳🍴🚬

GOREBRIDGE

Stobbs Mill Inn
25 Powdermill Brae, EH23 4HX (S end of town)
🕐 11-3, 6-11 (11.30 Thu); 11-midnight Fri & Sat; 12.30-11.30 Sun
☎ (01875) 820202
Beer range varies Ⓗ
Built in 1866 as a public house, this two-storey detached building looks more like a private dwelling. The friendly, functional, locals' bar has three engraved wooden panels with sporting scenes, which separate it from an intriguingly tiny snug. Old photographs of the town adorn the walls. The lounge is only open when food is served on Friday and Saturday evening and Sunday lunchtime. Simple bar snacks are available at all times. Families may sit in the lounge or snug. ◑🍴🍀P

GULLANE

Old Clubhouse
East Links Road, EH31 2AF
🕐 11-11 (midnight Thu-Sat); 12-11 Sun
☎ (01620) 842008 website: www.oldclubhouse.com
Caledonian Deuchars IPA, 80/-; guest beer Ⓟ
Spacious, well-appointed, select bar decorated in warm colours and natural woods. The windows offer a wide view over the golf course to the Lammermuir Hills. There is an extensive bar meal menu and wine list. Children are allowed until 8pm. Numerous stuffed birds and animals and golfing memorabilia on the walls and many knick-knacks surround the bar gantry. 🏚🏮◑

HADDINGTON

Pheasant
73 Market Street, EH41 3JJ
🕐 11-11 (midnight Thu; 1am Fri & Sat); 12.30-midnight Sun
☎ (01620) 824428
website: www.spidacom.co.uk/EDG/pheasant/
Orkney Red MacGregor; Tetley Bitter, Burton Ale; guest beers Ⓗ
The Pheasant, housed in a 19th-century building, attracts a mixed clientele of town folk. The main bar has a serpentine counter winding through to the pool area, presided over by Basil the African Grey parrot. In addition to pool, crib, darts and dominoes are played. Vinyl banquettes line the walls, which are decorated with advertising tins and photographs of customers' revelries. Children are admitted until 5pm. 🍀

Tyneside Tavern
10 Poldrate, EH41 4DA (on A6137, S of centre)
🕐 11-11 (midnight Thu; 12.45am Fri & Sat); 12.30-midnight Sun
☎ (01620) 822221 website: www.tynesidetavern.co.uk
Caledonian Deuchars IPA; Courage Directors; guest beer Ⓗ
Cosy, convivial, town local; the bar is long and narrow, with a fine, stone fireplace beside the door. Rustic-style woodwork fronts the bar counter, which boasts a mahogany top and gantry behind. The

comfortable lounge has violet walls and off-pink cloth-covered banquettes. The building dates from 1819, although the interior looks more 1970s. It holds a children's certificate (children are welcome until 8pm when evening meals finish). 🏚🏮◑🍀

LASSWADE

Laird & Dog Hotel
5 High Street, EH18 1NA (on A768)
🕐 11-11.30 (11.45 Thu); 12.30am Fri & Sat; 12.30-11.30 Sun
☎ (0131) 663 9219
website: www.lairdanddog.btinternet.co.uk
Beer range varies Ⓗ
Comfortable village local catering for all tastes, from music-loving pool players to those who enjoy a quiet drink or meal. The food (served all day) is good and plentiful, with an extensive conservatory menu, daily specials and cheaper bar options satisfying most palates. Children are allowed until 8pm. An unusual bottle-shaped well, a real fire surrounded by armchairs and two real ales, usually from smaller breweries, complete the picture. 🏚🏮🚲◑🍴🍀P

LINLITHGOW

Four Marys
65-67 High Street, EH49 7ED
🕐 12-11 (11.45 Thu-Sat); 12.30-11 Sun
☎ (01506) 842171
Belhaven 80/-, St Andrew's Ale; Caledonian Deuchars IPA; guest beers Ⓗ
Named after the four ladies-in-waiting of Mary, Queen of Scots, who was born in the nearby Linlithgow Palace, it was built around 1500 as a private house. The pub has seen several uses through the years, such as a chemist's shop run by the Waldie family whose most famous member, David, established the anaesthetic properties of chloroform in 1847. It opened as a pub in 1975 and hosts beer festivals in May and October when the handpumps are increased from eight to 18. ◑🍽

Platform 3
1A High Street, EH49 7AB
🕐 11-midnight; 12.30-midnight Sun
☎ (01506) 847405
Caledonian Deuchars IPA; guest beers Ⓗ
Small, friendly pub on the railway station approach, originally the public bar of the hotel next door. It was purchased and renovated in 1998 as a pub in its own right and stages occasional live music. Note the interesting memorabilia displayed around the walls, a new feature is a train running above the bar. The two guest ales usually come from the Caledonian range. 🍽🍀

LOTHIANBURN

Steading
118-120 Biggar Road, EH10 7DU
(on A702, near Hillend ski centre)
🕐 10-midnight; 12.30-11 Sun
☎ (0131) 445 1128
Caledonian Deuchars IPA, 80/-; Orkney Dark Island; Taylor Landlord Ⓗ
Old stone cottages converted into an attractive bar and restaurant, with large conservatory extensions. The outside

drinking area affords good views to the Pentland Hills. Although it is a popular eating establishment, there is a sizeable bar area for drinkers where a condensed menu is available. This has a real fire and a large no-smoking section. It is a handy place for refreshment after a walk on the hills or a visit to the dry ski slope. Families are welcome.

MUSSELBURGH

Levenhall Arms
10 Ravensheugh Road, EH21 7PP
(on B1348, near racecourse roundabout)
12-11 (midnight Thu; 1am Fri & Sat); 12.30- midnight Sun
☎ (0131) 665 3220
Caledonian Deuchars IPA; Tetley Burton Ale; guest beer P

Busy pub, popular with locals, race-goers and visitors to the nearby golf course. This three-roomed former coaching inn dates from 1830. The public bar is half timber panelled and carpeted, and has a smaller section leading off, providing a dartboard. The lounge is used as a restaurant during the day. Food is served all day until 8.30pm when children are also expected to leave.
Q (Wallyford)

Volunteer Arms (Staggs)
81 North High Street, EH21 6JE
(behind Brunton Hall)
12-11 (11.30 Thu); 11-midnight Fri & Sat; closed Sun
☎ (0131) 665 9654
Caledonian Deuchars IPA, 80/-; guest beers H

This three-roomed pub has been run by the same family since 1858. The main bar is traditional with a tiled floor, dark wood panelling, wood and glass screens, along with mirrors from defunct local breweries. A superb gantry is topped with old casks. In the snug is a nascent history collection about local breweries. The rear lounge opens at the weekend. The single guest beer changes regularly, up to four times on a Saturday. Awarded national CAMRA Pub of the Year in 1998.

NORTH BERWICK

Auld Hoose
19 Forth Street, EH39 4HX
(on street parallel to Main St)
11-11 (1am Thu-Sat; midnight Sun)
☎ (01620) 892692
Beer range varies H

High-ceilinged, traditional Scottish drinking shop with bare floorboards around the mahogany bar. The three-bay gantry has carved pillars and supports six old whisky casks and various knick-knacks. A fine painting of the nearby Bass Rock overlooks the bar. Gas lighting remains as a back-up for power cuts. The lounge has a tiny dance floor and is decorated with prints of Islay distilleries. Children are admitted until 7.30pm.

Nether Abbey Hotel
20 Dirleton Avenue, EH39 4BQ
(on A198, just W of centre)
11-11 (midnight Thu; 1am Fri & Sat); 12-11 Sun
☎ (01620) 892802 website: www.netherabbbey.co.uk
Caledonian Deuchars IPA; Greene King Old Speckled Hen; guest beers P

Comfortable, family-run hotel in a Victorian villa. The drinking area is L-shaped with one arm being a carpeted lounge and the other a bar/dining section with bare floorboards. Dark wood and photographic prints with a maritime theme feature in the decor. In good weather the bar expands into an outdoor area with a retractable canvas roof. An annual real ale festival is held in February. Close to some legendary golf courses and good beaches, food is served all day in summer; the pub has a children's certificate.

ORMISTON

Hopetoun Arms Hotel
Main Street, EH35 5HX
11-11 (1am Fri & Sat); 12.30-11 Sun
☎ (01875) 610298
Taylor Landlord; guest beer H

Village local dating from 1737. The long, narrow public bar is warmed by a flame-effect fire. Many pictures of the village and local sports teams complement a collection of trophies. A raised area at the end of the bar has a dartboard. The small lounge bar does not have a separate counter. Evening meals are served on Friday and Saturday, 6–9. Children are allowed until 8pm.

SOUTH QUEENSFERRY

Ferry Tap
36 High Street, EH30 9HN
11.30-11.30 (midnight Thu, 12.30am Fri & Sat); 12.30-11.30 Sun
☎ (0131) 331 2000
Caledonian Deuchars IPA, 80/-; Orkney Dark Island; guest beers H

Ground-floor bar in a 328-year-old building in the historic part of the village, dominated by bridges. The comfortable, one-roomed, L-shaped bar boasts an unusual barrel-vaulted ceiling. Dark wood gives an intimate feel and numerous artefacts, many from bygone breweries, add interest. Enjoy the varied selection of meals served at lunchtime; evening meals are available on Wednesday and Saturday, plus winter Friday.
(Dalmeny)

UPHALL

Oatridge Hotel
2-4 East Main Street, EH52 5DA
(at A899/B8046 jct)
11 (12.30 Sun)-midnight
☎ (01506) 856465
Caledonian Deuchars IPA; guest beers H

Originally a 19th-century coach house, the hotel still serves the modern-day traveller as well as thirsty locals. Real ale is served in the public bar and up to four beers regularly feature Scottish micros. Note the large collection of ceramic vessels behind the bar. Pool can be played and TV sport is popular. Evening meals are served on Friday and Saturday.

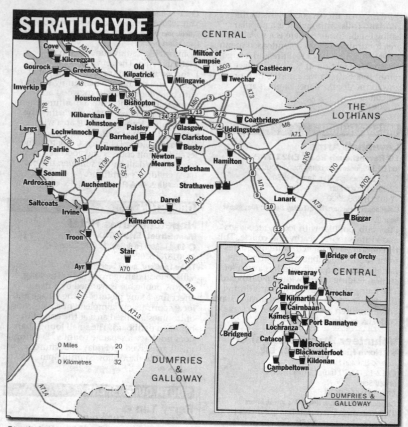

STRATHCLYDE

Strathclyde comprises Argyll and Bute, Ayrshire and Arran, Dunbartonshire, Glasgow, Lanarkshire and Renfrewshire

Argyll and Bute

ARROCHAR
Village Inn
G83 7AX (on A814, 3/4 mile S of A83 jct)
🕐 11-midnight (1am Fri & Sat); 12-midnight Sun
☎ (01301) 702279
Orkney Dark Island; guest beers Ⓗ
Idyllic inn, built in 1827 as the local manse, it is situated on the east shore of Loch Long, offering breathtaking views over the Arrochar Alps and the famous Cobbler. Recently expanded, it has retained its rustic feel, with bare floorboards, wood furniture and fireplaces constructed with stone from Greenock Esplanade. Beer from Fyne Brewery is occasionally available. It makes an ideal base for hillwalkers, and a stop-off point on the West Highland circuit.
🏚️❀🏚️◑&🅿️

BRIDGEND
Horseshoe Inn
PA31 82A (off A816) OS852927
🕐 12-11 (midnight Thu; 1am Fri & Sat); 11-11 Sun
☎ (01546) 606369
Beer range varies Ⓗ
Comfortable pub in which both lounge and bar have wood-burning fires and Art Nouveau stained glass door panels. The bar has bench seating, an upright piano for occasional music sessions and a TV. The lounge/diner has upholstered furniture, a stone fireplace and corner counter. There is also a pool room with a dartboard. Popular with locals, it is a welcome stop for tourists, too, offering a single draught beer and generous portions of tasty food.
🏚️❀🏚️◑🅿️

BRIDGE OF ORCHY
Bridge of Orchy Hotel ✓
PA36 4AD
🕐 11-11 (midnight Fri & Sat); 11-midnight Sun
☎ (01838) 400208
Caledonian Deuchars IPA, 80/-, guest beers Ⓗ
Possibly the most accessible, remote destination hotel in Scotland, it is a staging post on the road to Skye and the famous West Highland Way. The comfortably furnished Caley Bar offers panoramic views across the glen to the mountains on either side. Guest beers are mainly from Fyne and Harviestoun. With its modern bunkhouse, it provides a centre for outdoor activities, including salmon and trout fishing, kayaking, rafting, canoeing, walking and climbing (Munro and Corbett).
🏚️Q❀🏚️◑Å⇌🅿️✝

CAIRNBAAN

Cairnbaan Hotel
PA31 8SJ (off A816, on road to Crinan) OS839908
🕐 11-1am (including Sun)
☎ (01546) 603668
Fyne Piper's Gold, Highlander Ⓗ
This old coaching inn opened around 200 years ago, at the same time as the adjacent Crinan Canal. The bars are in a more recent annexe, nearest the main road. The bar itself is comfortable and carpeted and opens out on to an enclosed verandah furnished with comfortable sofas and low tables. A restaurant area leads off, but food is available throughout. Only one beer is usually on offer in winter.
Q🏠🛏️◖Ⓟ

CAMPBELTOWN

Commercial Inn
Cross Street, PA28 6HU
🕐 11-1am (including Sun)
☎ (01586) 553703
Caledonian Deuchars IPA; guest beer (summer) Ⓗ
Lively, friendly, traditional town pub of three rooms, that is family-run. The main bar is a jovial place where the locals discuss the issues of the day and keep abreast of sport on the corner TV. In the cosy, carpeted lounge, with subdued lighting and roof skylights, a more relaxed, meditative air prevails. Others may prefer to test their skill in the pool room. This locals' pub welcomes visitors. ◖♣

COVE

Knockderry House Hotel
204 Shore Road, G84 0NX (on B833)
🕐 11.30-midnight; 12.30-11 Sun
☎ (01436) 842283
website: www.knockderryhotel.co.uk
Beer range varies Ⓗ
Former Victorian Glasgow merchant's house, boasting one of the best local examples of works by William Leiper and Daniel Cottier. This stunning building features a recurring theme of the four seasons, in stained glass and wood. Situated on the rural Rosneath Peninsula, with safe anchorage and a large garden, it offers superb views over Loch Long towards Benmore and Strone. Kelburn Brewery beers are frequently on tap, with others from Belhaven's guest list. An hourly bus service runs to Helensburgh.
🏨🏠🛏️◖♣Ⓟ

INVERARAY

George Hotel
Main Street East, PA32 8TT
🕐 Lounge: 11 (12 Sun)-12.30am; Bar: 5 (11 Sat; 12 Sun)-11
☎ (01499) 302111 website: www.thegeorgehotel.co.uk
Beer range varies Ⓗ
This imposing building, built in 1775 and in the same family's hands for over 135 years, stands at the centre of this historic conservation town. The main bar retains its original flagstoned floors, which, with its interlinked side rooms and welcoming log and peat fires, cannot fail to impress. The lively, friendly public bar has restricted opening hours. Two guest beers are offered

in summer (one in winter), usually from Fyne Brewery. Excellent meals use the best of local produce. 🏨🏠🌳🛏️◖🍴🅐♣Ⓟ

KAMES

Kames Hotel
PA21 2AF OS671197
🕐 11.30-2am; 12-11 Sun
☎ (01700) 811489 website: www.kames-hotel.com
Fyne Piper's Gold; Marston's Pedigree Ⓗ
Originally a two-roomed bar, this 150-year-old, popular hotel is elegantly decorated throughout, with wood panels, stained glass and an interesting range of yachting photographs. Next to the defunct Kames pier, and not far from Tighnabruaich village, it offers magnificent views over the Kyles of Bute. Well worth visiting, the hotel also has free boat moorings, which cater for well over 1,000 boats a year. A water taxi service is available. Children are welcome in the no-smoking TV lounge.
🏨🌳🏠🛏️◖🅐🍴♣Ⓟ⌖

KILCREGGAN

Kilcreggan Hotel
Argyll Road, G84 0JP
🕐 12-midnight (1am Fri & Sat); 12.30-midnight Sun
☎ (01436) 842243
Theakston Best Bitter; guest beers Ⓗ
Stone Victorian village mansion, at the southern end of the rural Rosneath Peninsula, affording a stunning view over the Clyde Estuary to Arran. Built by a Glasgow stockbroker, it contains fine wood panelling, with stained glass windows, ornate bargeboards and balconies, and features a curious gabled and battlemented tower. Close to the pier, it is served by a regular passenger-only ferry to Gourock, an hourly bus service to Helensburgh and the paddle steamer Waverley (Fridays in summer).
🏨🏠🛏️◖🅐Ⓟ⌖

KILMARTIN

Kilmartin Hotel
PA31 8RQ
🕐 11-1am (5-midnight in mid-winter); 12-1am (5-midnight in mid-winter) Sun
☎ (01546) 510250 website: www.kilmartin-hotel.com
Caledonian 80/-; guest beer Ⓗ
This whitewashed, family-run hotel overlooks a linear set of burial cairns, the oldest of which date back more than 5,000 years. A stone circle and Neolithic monument lie beyond, and medieval grave slabs in the churchyard opposite add to the historic backdrop. The hotel has a small, cosy public bar leading to a games room at the rear and dining areas along a corridor. The bar is backed by an old gantry and brewery mirror.
🌳🛏️◖🅐Ⓟ

INDEPENDENT BREWERIES

Arran Brodick
Clockwork Glasgow
Fyne Cairndow
Heather Strathaven
Houston Houston
Kelburn Barrhead

PORT BANNATYNE

Port Royal Hotel
37 Marine Road, PA20 0LW
⊛ 12-1am (2am Sat); 12.30-1am Sun
☎ (01700) 505073 website: www.butehotel.com
Beer range varies Ⓖ

A little piece of Russia has been transported to a two-storey pierhead hotel in one of the most picturesque settings on the Firth of Clyde. This café-bar is run by a dedicated couple who serve beer from Scottish micro-breweries from bartop casks. An all-day menu comprises fresh, local ingredients cooked to Russian recipes. No keg lager or fizzy drinks – Warsteiner Premium Lager and Fentemans soft drinks are sold instead. One for the purists, it is very special indeed.
Q ⋈ ◑ ⬤

RHU

Ardencaple Hotel
Shore Road, G84 8LA (on A814)
⊛ 11-11 (midnight Fri & Sat); 11-11 Sun
☎ (01436) 820200
Caledonian Deuchars IPA, 80/- Ⓗ

Attractive, white-painted, 25-year-old former coaching inn, on the main road to Helensburgh. It benefits from fine views over the Gare Loch and River Clyde. The recently refurbished Caple Bar has retained its popular pool and darts area, also the TV projection screen, which is mainly used for sporting events. Handpumps are only available in this bar, but real ale can be brought to the comfortable lounge bar near the hotel's main entrance. Children are welcome in the tea room. ⌚ ⊛ ⋈ ◑ 🍴 ⅗ ♣ P

Ayrshire and Arran

ARDROSSAN

Lauriston Hotel
15 South Crescent Road, KA22 8EA
(on A738, seafront)
⊛ 11-11 (midnight summer Sat; 1am Fri); 11-11 Sun
☎ (01294) 463771 website: www.lauristonhotel.co.uk
Arran Ale, Dark, Blonde Ⓗ

Free-standing, red sandstone building with a large conservatory at the front, providing stunning sea views. The front door leads to an extensive restaurant area, with a lounge that accommodates drinkers. The public bar has its own side entrance and a different menu. There are always two Arran beers on tap, one in each bar, but the other will be brought through on request. The lounge beer prices are above average.
Q ⊛ ⋈ ◑ 🍴 ⅗ ≠ (S Beach) P

AUCHENTIBER

Blair Country Restaurant
KA13 7RR (at A736/B778 jct)
⊛ 11-3, 5-11; 11-11 Sat; 11-11 Sun
☎ (01294) 850237
Beer range varies Ⓗ

Traditional country inn on the Glasgow–Irvine road, six miles from both Irvine and Kilwinning. There are few houses nearby so it concentrates on food, with only limited space for drinkers during main mealtimes, but it does attract a loyal group of regular drinkers. Two rooms have traditional decor, one is no-smoking. Guest

beers come from anywhere in Britain, with the displayed pump clips showing an amazing variety. Well-cooked food makes it well worth the journey. Beer prices are above average. Q ⊛ ◑ ▸ P ⅏

AYR

Chestnuts Hotel
52 Racecourse Road, KA7 2UZ
(on A719, 1 mile S of centre)
⊛ 11-midnight (12.30am Fri & Sat); 12-midnight Sun
☎ (01292) 264393
Beer range varies Ⓗ

Reflecting its proximity to local courses, the wood-panelled lounge bar of this family-run hotel features a collection of golfing prints. The three real ales are usually a mix of beers from the larger regional brewers and local micros. High quality meals are served in the bar area or in the restaurant. The spacious garden boasts an excellent children's play area.
⌚ ⊛ ⋈ ◑

Geordie's Byre
103 Main Street, KA8 8BU
(over river, towards Prestwick)
⊛ 11-11 (midnight Thu-Sat); 12.30-11 Sun
☎ (01292) 264925
Caledonian Deuchars IPA; guest beers Ⓐ

This popular pub boasts a wealth of memorabilia, especially in the lounge (open Thu–Sat eve). Up to four guest ales are offered from a wide range of breweries. The landlord prides himself on his range of spirits, with over 100 malt whiskies and 28 rums on offer – ask for the menu. Although food is not served, the home-made pickled eggs are a speciality. Local CAMRA Pub of the Year 2002, previous Scottish Pub of the Year.
⬡ ≠ (Newton-on-Ayr)

Market Inn
2 Castlehill Road, KA7 2HT
⊛ 11-12.30am; 12.30-midnight Sun
☎ (01292) 280391
Draught Bass; guest beers Ⓗ

This prominent red sandstone building, opposite the rear exit from the railway station, was once an integral part of the cattle market (now a supermarket). Refurbishment has retained many original features including the listed horseshoe bar and gantry, tiled floor, fireplaces and stained glass windows. The guest beer (from the Houston Brewery) is not always available. Adequate car parking can be found nearby. ⬡ ⅗ ≠

BLACKWATERFOOT

Blackwaterfoot Lodge
KA27 8EU
⊛ 12-3 (not Oct-April), 6.30-11; 12-11.30 Sat;
12-3, 6-10 Sun
☎ (01770) 860202
website: www.blackwaterfoot-lodge.co.uk
Arran Ale Ⓗ

The Mariners is a small, cosy bar in what used to be a temperance hotel. Home-cooked food, using local produce, is served in the bar, the conservatory dining room or the garden. Local amenities include a golf course and an hotel swimming pool, open to the public. The village benefits from stunning views across to Campbeltown Loch, Kintyre and, on clear days, Northern Ireland. Q☆✍◑

BRODICK

Brodick Bar
Alma Road, KA27 8BU (off Shore Rd)
☼ 11-midnight; 12.30-midnight (summer only) Sun
☎ (01770) 302169
Arran Ale; guest beers P
Once described as the only pub in Arran, this long, white building next to the post office has two bars. The main bar is light with a contemporary feel; the other bar is more food-oriented, but extensive menus are available in both bars. The real ale founts are unmarked, so ask what is on.
🏚Q◑⬛

Mac's Bar
MacLaren Hotel, Shore Road, KA27 8AJ
(on seafront, 300 yds from ferry terminal)
☼ 11-midnight (including Sun)
☎ (01770) 302353
Arran Ale, Dark, Blonde; H /P
This is a large, comfortable bar attached to one of the main seafront hotels in Brodick. Popular with locals and visitors, it affords spectacular views across the bay towards Goat Fell. It offers a good basic menu, and regular music sessions are held, especially during the Arran Folk Festival. Formerly well known as Duncan's Bar in the Kingsley Hotel, this long-established real ale outlet now remains open all year under new ownership. 🏚☆✍◑⬛P

Ormidale Hotel
Knowe Road, KA27 8BY
(off A841, W end of village)
☼ 12-2.30 (not winter), 4.30-midnight; 12-midnight Sat & Sun
☎ (01770) 302293 website: www.ormidale-hotel.co.uk
Arran Ale, Blonde; guest beers A
Fine sandstone building – a small, friendly bar plus a large conservatory which is a real suntrap. The original tall founts on the boat-shaped bar serve two beers from the nearby Arran Brewery. Built in the 1850s as a summer house for the painter, Herring, it was converted to an hotel in 1935 by the present owner's grandparents. Discos and folk music are staged in the conservatory at weekends; quizzes are held twice weekly. The home-cooked bar meals are highly recommended. Accommodation is available in summer. 🏚Q☆✍◑⬛♣P

CATACOL

Catacol Bay Hotel
KA27 8HN
☼ 11-1am (midnight Sun)
☎ (01770) 830231 website: www.catacol.co.uk
Arran Blonde; Draught Bass H
This white building nestles in the hills opposite the shore, with grand views across the Kilbrannan Sound to Kintyre. It is adjacent to the Twelve Apostles, a listed terrace of former estate houses. Originally a manse, it has been run by the present owner for 25 years. Ideally situated for walking and climbing; for natural history lovers there is a richness of flora and fauna – glimpses of red deer and golden eagles are not unusual. 🏚⛵☆✍◑♣P

DARVEL

Loudounhill Inn
KA17 0LY (1 mile E of Darvel on A71)
☼ 12-2.30 (not Wed), 5-11 (not Tue); 12-midnight Sat; 12.30-2.30, 4.30-11 Sun
☎ (01560) 320275 website: www.loudoun-hill-inn.co.uk
Beer range varies H
Family-owned old coaching inn near Loudoun Hill, which is the site of an 11th-century battle and features a challenging rock-climbing face and interesting walks. The hotel has a cosy bar with an open fire and a larger lounge/restaurant, with a conservatory opening on to the garden.
🏚☆✍◑♣P

FAIRLIE

Mudhook ✓
46 Bay Street, KA29 0AL
☼ 11.30-11 (1am Fri & Sat); 11.30-11 Sun
☎ (01475) 568432
Draught Bass; guest beer H
This friendly village pub enjoys a lovely position, overlooking the Isles of Cumbrae and Arran. It has two bars, plus a restaurant with a conservatory. Bar meals are available and the restaurant offers an extensive menu. There is also a garden and a large car park. At least one guest beer is always on tap.
☆◑⬛⬛≢P⌿

IRVINE

Marina Inn
110 Harbour Street, KA12 8PZ
(400 yds W of station)
☼ 11.45-3, 5.45-midnight (11.45-midnight summer); 11.45-1am Fri & Sat; 12.30-midnight Sun
☎ (01294) 274079
Belhaven 80/- or St Andrew's Ale H
Busy harbourside lounge bar at the heart of Irvine's main tourist area, close to the Magnum leisure centre, the Scottish Maritime Museum, the Big Idea Inventor Centre and the Beach Park. It enjoys a good food trade at lunchtime, early evening and weekends. It hosts regular folk sessions on Tuesday evening, and occasional live music on Friday evening. The sheltered garden is a popular suntrap in summer.
☆◑≢

KILDONAN

Breadalbane Hotel
KA27 8SE (on loop road through village)
☼ 11-midnight (1am Thu-Sat); 11-midnight Sun; closed two weeks mid-Jan
☎ (01770) 820284
Arran Ale; guest beer H
Just behind the shore in a scattered village at the south end of the island, the hotel enjoys extensive views, especially from the front sun lounge, to Pladda and its lighthouse, Ailsa Craig and Loch Ryan. The main bar has a large stone fireplace and a pool table. Ales are from Scottish breweries, and food is served all day. En-suite rooms and self-catering flats are available. Named after a ship that sank in the North-West Passage, it is close to beaches renowned for seal spotting.
Q☆✍◑♣P

KILMARNOCK

Wheatsheaf ⊘
Unit 5, Portland Gate, KA1 5NQ
⊗ 11-midnight (opens 10am for breakfast);
12.30-midnight Sun
☎ (01563) 572483
**Courage Directors; Theakston Best Bitter;
guest beers** Ⓗ
Lying north of the main shopping areas and close to both rail and bus stations, this is mostly a new building, although the shell of the original inn can be seen at the rear. The interior is a vast, modern open-plan area, with wall displays related to Robert Burns and local history. The front patio affords views of the impressive railway viaduct. Children are allowed in the rear area until 6pm. The pub is very busy Thursday–Saturday evenings due to its proximity to night clubs. Q ☸ ◑ ᵬ ╪ ⅍

LARGS

Clachan
14 Bath Street, KA30 8BL (on B7025)
⊗ 11-midnight (1am Thu-Sat); 12.30-midnight Sun
☎ (01475) 672224
Beer range varies Ⓗ
This single-bar, town-centre pub normally features Belhaven ales, and stocks a good selection of whiskies. It hosts live music on Friday evening and a quiz on Monday. Its back door leads to the seafront, opposite the pier from where the Cumbrae car ferry leaves; the paddle steamer Waverley also calls in summer. Largs is one of the main 'Costa Clyde' resorts and boasts two good golf courses and the Vikingar Centre. ◑ ᵬ ╪

LOCHRANZA

Lochranza Hotel
Isle of Arran, KA27 8HL
⊗ 11 (5 winter)-1am; 11.30-1am Sun
☎ (01770) 830223 website: www.lochranza.co.uk
Arran Blonde; guest beer Ⓗ
In a tranquil village with spectacular views to Lochranza Castle and across the sea loch, the bar comprises two interconnecting rooms and stocks over 100 single malt whiskies. The front of the hotel has a large grassed area with tables, an ideal place to watch local wildlife, including red deer, seals and golden eagles. There are plenty of good walks in the area and the hotel is handy for the summer car ferry to Kintyre, Islay, Gigha and other islands.
≝ ⛺ ☸ ⋈ ◑ ▲ ╪ ⅍

SALTCOATS

Salt Cot ⊘
7 Hamilton Street, KA21 5DS
⊗ 11-midnight (1am Thu-Sat); 12.30-midnight Sun
☎ (01294) 465924
Beer range varies Ⓗ
This is a good conversion of a former cinema, decorated with photos of its heyday, and of old Saltcoats. Children are allowed in one area, and there is a family menu. Unusually for Wetherspoon's there are no regular beers, but Theakston Old Peculier and Greene King Old Speckled Hen are frequently on tap. The pub's name comes from the original cottages at the salt pans. Q ◑ ᵬ ╪ ⅍

SEAMILL

Waterside Inn
Ardrossan Road, KA23 9NG
(on A78 between Ardrossan and Seamill)
⊗ 11-11 (including Sun)
☎ (01294) 823238
Beer range varies Ⓗ
Former Brewer's Fayre that has continued the theme under private ownership, but has also restored real ale. It is located right on the beach, with wonderful sea views of the Firth of Clyde and Arran. Food is available all day and there are large indoor and outdoor children's play areas. ≝ ⛺ ◑ ᵬ P

STAIR

Stair Inn
Mauchline, KA5 5HN (on B730, 7 miles E of Ayr)
⊗ 12-3, 5-11; 12-1am Sat; 12-11 Sun
☎ (01292) 591650 website: www.stairinn.co.uk
Beer range varies Ⓗ
Family-run inn at the foot of a glen on the bank of the River Ayr. The bar has an open fire and a snug leading off. Built about 1700, this pub serves a district rather than a village, and it is close to Stair Bridge (single track on a tight corner – take care crossing). The area has many connections with Robert Burns and is well located for walks, golf and fishing. ≝ Q ⛺ ⋈ ◑ P

TROON

Ardneil Hotel
51 St Meddans Street, KA10 6NU
(next to station)
⊗ 11 (12 Sun)-midnight
☎ (01292) 311611
Draught Bass; Caledonian Deuchars IPA; guest beers Ⓗ
Smart and popular, privately-run hotel close to the town centre and other amenities, including the many golf courses in the area. Up to three guest ales are usually from Houston, Arran, Kelburn and Caledonian breweries. The hotel has two restaurants and a cocktail bar; the main bar has a lower level pool and darts area. There is a large garden. Quiz night is Wednesday. The hotel caters for locals and tourists alike.
⛺ ⋈ ◑ ╪ ♣ P

Dan McKay's Ale House
69 Portland Street, KA10 6QU (on A759)
⊗ 11-12.30am; 12.30-midnight Sun
☎ (01292) 311079
Caledonian Deuchars IPA; guest beers Ⓗ
Family-run, one-roomed lounge bar close to the centre of Troon. There is a regular rotation of up to three guest ales, plus a selection of foreign bottled beers and mini beer festivals are held occasionally. The bar attracts a mixed clientele, and can get noisy when the younger generation come in late at the weekends. There is a regular 5–7pm 'happy hour'. The beer garden is a suntrap. Note the rare Lorimer & Clark brewery sign on the wall. ⛺ ◑ ╪

Dunbartonshire

MILNGAVIE

Talbot Arms
62 Main Street, G62 6JG

11-11 (midnight Thu-Sat); 11-11 Sun
☎ (0141) 955 0981
Draught Bass; Caledonian Deuchars IPA, 80/-; guest beer Ⓗ

Renovated single room, decorated with Victoriana and separated into two drinking areas with a wooden partition. The bar is simply furnished with bare floorboards and a pool table. More seating is provided in the comfortable lounge, with easy chairs in the alcove. The name is taken from a breed of hunting dogs once raised on a nearby estate. This local is a useful starting point for a walk to the West Highlands.
🗢♿⇌P

MILTON OF CAMPSIE

Kincaid House Hotel
Birdston Road, G66 8BZ (on B757)
✪ 12-midnight (1am Fri); 12-midnight Sun
☎ (0141) 776 2226
Beer range varies Ⓗ

Impressive, pale stone building at the end of a long, wooded drive. Real ale is served in the bar area to the rear, but may be ordered from the conservatory. In summer, food and ale may be taken into the garden. The semi-divided carpeted lounge has upholstered furniture, beams bedecked with horse brasses, and a fine Alloa Brewery mirror. The bar area has a pool table. Popular with locals, and an ale oasis for visitors, three ales rotate on two handpumps, from Caledonian, Orkney and Timothy Taylor breweries.
🏨🏵🛏🗢♿♣P

OLD KILPATRICK

Ettrick
159 Dumbarton Road, G60 5JQ (on A814)
✪ 11-midnight (1am Fri & Sat); 12.30-midnight Sun
☎ (01389) 872821 website: www.theettrick.com
Caledonian Deuchars IPA; guest beers Ⓗ

Close to the Erskine Bridge, the pub takes its name from poet, James Hogg, the Ettrick Shepherd, a friend of Sir Walter Scott. It is situated on the site of the 19th-century Hogg building. Three handpumps serve ale in the small, lively, horseshoe-shaped public bar where darts and dominoes are played. The more comfortable lounge is no-smoking, when food is being served (all day, 12–8 Fri–Sun; lunch and evening Mon–Thu). Children are welcome.
🏵🗢🍴⇌♣P

TWECHAR

Lock, Stock & Barrel
Main Street, G65 9QE
✪ 11-11.30 (1am Fri); 11-11.30 Sun
☎ (01236) 821496
Theakston Best Bitter; guest beers Ⓗ

Traditional local that formed the heart of a one-time mining community where men were paid (and spent) their wages. Much remains, including the stoves and brewery mirror, though the name has changed. The busy public bar has a pool table and big-screen TV for sporting events to one side; the other side, separated by the entrance, is much quieter – good for meeting and talking. The lounge lies behind to one side.
Q🍴P

Glasgow

1901 Bar & Bistro
1534 Pollokshaws Road, G43 1RF
✪ 11.45-11 (midnight Fri & Sat); 12.30-11 Sun
☎ (0141) 632 0161
Caledonian Deuchars IPA; guest beers Ⓗ

When it opened in 1901, this pub was called the Old Swan Inn. On the ground floor of one of the first red sandstone tenements built in the area, it stands across from Pollok Park, where the world-famous Burrell Collection can be visited. There is ample seating and standing room in the bare-boarded bar area. The lounge bar was refurbished as a bistro restaurant two years ago. A good selection of German Weiss beers is stocked.
🗢♿⇌ (Shawlands/Pollokshaws W) ♣

Babbity Bowster
16-18 Blackfriars Street, G1 1PE
✪ 11 (12 Sun)-midnight
☎ (0141) 552 5055
Caledonian Deuchars IPA; Houston Peter's Well; guest beer Ⓟ

Hidden down a pedestrianised area off the High Street, Babbity's provides a quiet retreat from the city hubbub. The garden (rare in Glasgow), is pleasant in summer, offering barbecues and boules; a movable canopy copes with showers (common in Glasgow). Indoors the café-style decor is warmed in winter by a peat fire. The French chef prepares excellent food for the bar and upstairs restaurant. Used by locals, the press, business people, academics and visitors.
🏨Q🏵🍴⇌ (High St/Argyle St/Queen St) ⊖ (Buchanan St) ♣♦P

Blackfriars
36 Bell Street, G1 1LG
✪ 12 (12.30 Sun)-midnight
☎ (0141) 552 5924
Tetley Burton Ale; guest beers Ⓗ/Ⓟ

Low lighting and candles in this metropolitan bar provide a cosy atmosphere for live jazz at weekends. Large brass-framed mirrors are an unusual feature; seating is in the more common form of benches and tables. The raised corner café-bar area looks out on to the street. Food (until 11pm) includes dishes made with beer. Three local guest ales are complemented by foreign draught and bottled beers. The Blackfriars caters for students, local residents and city workers. 🗢⇌ (High St/Argyle St/Queen St) ⊖ (Buchanan St)

Bon Accord
153 North Street, G3 7DA (near Mitchell Library)
✪ 11-midnight; 12.30-11 Sun
☎ (0141) 248 4427
website: www.thebonaccord.freeserve.co.uk
Beer ranges varies Ⓗ

Glasgow CAMRA Pub of the Year 2003, the Bon Accord has risen from the ashes like a phoenix under the current forward-thinking management, assisted by the same cellarman who has been looking after the beers for the past 23 years. It celebrated 30 years of selling real ale in Feb 2003. Tuesday sees an open stage, with a quiz on Wednesday and live music every Saturday evening. Cheerful, well-

informed bar staff ensure everyone is made welcome. Meals are served 11–7 (children welcome).
◁▷ �&≈ (Charing Cross/Anderston) ♣

Clockwork Beer Co.
1153-1155 Cathcart Road, G42 9BH
☼ 11-11 (11.30 Tue; midnight Thu-Sat); 12.30-11 Sun
☎ (0141) 649 0184
Caledonian Deuchars IPA, 80/-; guest beers Ⓟ
Open-plan, modern bar, a short distance from Hampden Park, Scotland's national football stadium. It was completely rebuilt in 1997 to include a five-barrel brewery on the premises. A spiral staircase leads to an upper seated area where live music is performed. An extensive range of drinks includes German and Belgian bottled beers, draught Belgian and Czech beers, also their own ales which include fruit beers.
⏚◁▷�&≈ (Mt Florida) ♦P✗⊟

Crystal Palace ⊘
36 Jamaica Street, G1 1QB (near Central Station)
☼ 11 (12.30 Sun)-midnight
☎ (0141) 221 2624
Caledonian Deuchars IPA; Courage Directors; guest beers Ⓗ
Wetherspoon's have converted this ex-furniture store imaginatively into Glasgow's second largest pub. Massive windows, garden-style furniture and slab flooring create a near-outdoor effect. Spacious areas on two floors include three no-smoking areas. The original cage lift has been retained – handy for the infirm and wheelchairs. The friendly staff provide a warm welcome to a varied clientele including city workers, young clubbers, theatregoers, locals and regulars.
Q⏚◁▷�&≈ (Central) ⊖ (St Enoch) ✗

Samuel Dow's
69 Nithsdale Road, G41 2PZ
☼ 11-11 (midnight Fri & Sat); 12.30-11 Sun
☎ (0141) 423 0107
Caledonian Deuchars IPA; guest beer Ⓗ
Popular pub, on the south side of Glasgow. Bench seats border the bar which features two Ind Coope brewery mirrors behind the gantry. (Remember Skol lager and Double Diamond?) The guest ale rotates between Marston's Pedigree, Adnams Broadside and Charles Wells Bombardier. The function room at the rear of the pub frequently features live bands.
◁▷ ⊟≈ (Pollockshields W)

Sir John Moore ⊘
260 Argyle Street, G2 8QW
☼ 11-midnight (including Sun)
☎ (0141) 222 1780
Caledonian Deuchars IPA; Courage Directors; guest beers Ⓗ
The low ceiling of this Wetherspoon's pub, and the long, narrow room, create an effect closer to a 'local' than is usual for pub chains. Large patio doors give views of Argyle Street and can be opened up in summer. Wood is used extensively for partitions and contemporary furniture – a change from the metal and glass of many modern bars. Near Central Station, it is used by travellers, office staff, some students and young people going on to clubs. It opens at 7am for breakfast.
⚏Q◁▷�&≈ (Central) ⊖ (St Enoch) ✗

State Bar ⊘
148 Holland Street, G2 4NG
(near King's Theatre)
☼ 11 (12.30 Sun)-midnight
☎ (0141) 332 2159
Caledonian Deuchars IPA; Courage Directors; Houston Killellan; McEwan 80/-; guest beers Ⓗ
The proximity of this Victorian-style pub to the King's Theatre makes it popular with theatregoers, as well as city workers and locals. Pictures of theatrical personalities and old Glasgow adorn the wood-panelled walls, alongside a carved Glasgow coat of arms and two distillery mirrors. A fine oval island bar has hand and foot rails for those using the bar stools. Armchairs offer a comfortable alternative to wooden chairs and window seats. It hosts live blues (Tue) and comedy on Saturday.
◁≈ (Charing Cross) ⊖ (Cowcaddens)

Station Bar
55 Port Dundas Road, G4 0HF
☼ 11-midnight; 12.30-11.45 Sun
☎ (0141) 332 3117
Caledonian Deuchars IPA; guest beers Ⓗ
Away from the city centre, but worth finding, the bar features distinctive coloured glass panes in windows, plus backlit panels in the wooden bar back, illustrating a closed rail station and nearby fire and police offices. Workers from several office blocks make for a vibrant afternoon trade, later, regulars ensure the beer keeps flowing. The long room is semi-divided: the bar area has high circular tables and tall chairs, plus benches; the lounge has leather upholstered seating. ≈ (Queen St) ⊖ (Cowcaddens)

Tennents ⊘
191 Byres Road, G12 8TN
☼ 11-11 (midnight Fri & Sat); 12.30-11 Sun
☎ (0141) 341 1024
Broughton Old Jock; Caledonian 80/-; Cairngorm Wildcat; Orkney Dark Island; Taylor Landlord; guest beers Ⓗ
Spacious and popular bar for those who enjoy conversation, situated at the heart of the West End. Frequented by locals and staff from the nearby university, sporting enthusiasts are attracted by the large TV screens, switched on for major sporting events. The meals are good value, and extra seating is provided at lunchtime. Nine regular beers and three guests are on offer every week. ◁▷�&⊖ (Hillhead)

Three Judges ⊘
141 Dumbarton Road, G11 6PR
☼ 11-11 (midnight Fri; 11.45 Sat); 12.30-11 Sun
☎ (0141) 337 3055
Beer range varies Ⓗ
Typical corner-tenement Glasgow pub that has won many CAMRA awards over the years. The Judges recently celebrated 10 years of serving quality cask ales. Beers, too numerous to mention, mostly from independent and small craft breweries, grace this L-shaped bar every year. Pump clips are displayed above the bar, foreign banknotes adorn the gantry and local CAMRA awards line the walls. Real cider is often available on one of the nine pumps. Live jazz is performed every Sunday afternoon.
≈ (Partick) ⊖ (Kelvinhall) ♦

Toby Jug
97 Hope Street, G2 6LL
☼ 11-11 (midnight Thu & Fri); closed Sun
☎ (0141) 221 4159
Caledonian Deuchars IPA; Fuller's London Pride; Orkney Dark Island; guest beer Ⓗ
Town pub in a busy part of the city. The bar area has bench seats divided by wooden partitions, with framed prints of steam trains. Window seats offer views of Hope Street and Central Station. The bar sports brass pillars and coat-hooks for those on stools. To the rear, a step leads into the raised lounge area with long tables and historic pictures of Glasgow. Popular with city office workers, businessmen and rail travellers, weekday lunches are served.
◖&≠ (Central/Queen St) ⊖ (Buchanan St/St Enoch)

Lanarkshire

Crown Inn
109-111 High Street, ML12 6DL
☼ 11-1am (midnight Sat); 12.30-1am Sun
☎ (01899) 220116
Beer range varies Ⓗ
Friendly multi-roomed pub in the centre of an attractive border town that boasts the largest number of museums in the country in proportion to the population. The 300-year-old former coaching inn features many genuine old pictures of Biggar. The home-cooked meals are popular and children are fed for free. 1960s music is often featured on Sunday. The snug is the designated no-smoking area. ▨Q ੴ ❀◖▶ ⽆

Castlecary House Hotel
Main Street, G68 0HD (on B816 near A80 jct)
☼ 11-11.30 (11 Mon-Wed); 12.30-midnight Sun
☎ (01324) 840233 website: www.castlecaryhotel.com
Beer range varies Ⓗ
Private hotel in a village on the site of one of the major forts on the Antonine Wall. Three distinct drinking areas in the main building include a snug. Four real ales are kept in the Castle Lounge, but can be served in any of the bars, including the cocktail bar in the modern extension. The main bar, Poachers, is warmed by a real fire in winter. The bar food and high teas are highly recommended.
▨ੴ❀⊨◖▶ ◳P

St Andrews
37 Sunnyside Road, ML5 3DG
(between station and town centre)
☼ 11-midnight (1am Fri & Sat); 12.30-midnight Sun
☎ (01236) 423773
Beer range varies Ⓗ
Small pub, formerly called the Saloon Bar, the present owners took over in 1998. Recently renovated, the Art Deco features added in a 1930s restoration have been kept, but the less sympathetic revamp of the 1960s has largely been reversed and a Campbell, Hope and King mirror has been acquired. The pub has one of the best selections locally of Belgian bottled beers; it

was the Malt Whisky Pub of the Year and local CAMRA Pub of the Year in 2002.
≠ (Sunnyside)

George
18 Campbell Street, ML3 6AS
☼ 11 (12.30 Sun)-midnight
☎ (01698) 424225
Beer range varies Ⓗ
This family-run pub is local CAMRA's 2003 Pub of the Year and has won this title many times before. The present owners took over in 1991 and immediately restored its reputation as a first-class local, after a couple of years in the doldrums. A single public bar is supplemented by a smaller room to the rear. The pub holds its own beer festival twice a year. It sometimes stays open later on Friday.
ੴ❀&▲≠ (Central) ⽆

Clydesdale Inn ⊘
15 Bloomgate, ML11 9ET
☼ 10-midnight (1am Fri); 12.30-midnight Sun
☎ (01555) 678740
Beer range varies Ⓗ
Formerly the Clydesdale Hotel, it was taken over in 2000 by Wetherspoon's, who made a modest change to the name but huge alterations to the interior. It is now unrecognisable even to visitors from a few years ago, let alone Charles Dickens, who stayed here when it was a coaching inn. Many of the artefacts found in the pub have been moved to the museum along the street.
▨Q ੴ◖&≠⽆

Horse & Jockey
54 High Street, ML11 7ES
☼ 11-1am (midnight Sat); 12.30-1am Sun
☎ (01555) 664825
Beer range varies Ⓗ
Public bar, with a lounge/diner on the main street of this historic market town, where a pub has stood since 1740. The ambience of the pub was much improved by renovations in the 1990s. The pub name and some of the decor recall the town's long connection with the sport of kings, although the racecourse is now disused. An unusual feature is the list of previous owners on the wall. Evening meals are available on Saturdays.
◖≠

Weavers
3 Green Street, ML10 6LT
☼ 12 (4.30 Tue-Thu)-midnight (1am Fri & Sat); 7-1am Sun
☎ (01357) 522648 website: www.strathaven.com
Beer range varies Ⓗ
Listed building at the centre of an attractive small town, once known as the Crown Hotel, it reopened as the Weavers in 1980. The single bar is decorated with pictures of Hollywood icons such as Marlon Brando, Liz Taylor and a big chap in a gorilla suit. The local squash, climbing and motorcycle clubs all meet here. A range of bottled Belgian beers is stocked. Q

UDDINGSTON

Rowan Tree
60 Old Mill Road, G71 7PF
(next to Tunnocks Bakery)
☼ 11 (12.30 Sun)-11.45
☎ (01698) 812678
Beer range varies Ⓗ
Grade B listed building, boasting a superb wood-panelled interior, two fireplaces and some fine, rare mirrors, including one from Whitelaw's Brewery. Reputedly the oldest pub in Lanarkshire, this former staging inn has a genuine olde-worlde feel that no modern fake could ever emulate. Since the present owners bought it from Maclays in 1998, they have concentrated on selling beers from local micro-breweries. ﲀ≈P

Renfrewshire

BARRHEAD

Cross Stobs Inn
4 Grahamston Road, G78 1NS
☼ 11-11 (midnight Thu; 1am Fri; 11.45 Sat);
12.30-11 Sun
☎ (0141) 881 1581
Kelburn Goldihops, Carte Blanche Ⓗ
This inviting 18th-century coaching inn is the first building to greet you as you arrive by bus from Paisley. Retaining much of its charm, drinkers can choose from the public bar, with real coal fire, or the L-shaped lounge with easy chairs and a view of the garden. The unobtrusive pool room was once a second lounge, note the antique furniture and service bells. Good lunches and locally-brewed Kelburn beers complete the picture. Children are welcome at lunchtime. ﲀ☎❀⫱⨭≈

Waterside Inn
Glasgow Road, The Hurlet, G53 7TH
(on A736, near the Hurlet)
☼ 11-11 (midnight Fri & Sat); 12.30-11 Sun
☎ (0141) 881 2822
Beer range varies Ⓗ
Popular with couples and young families, this is more of a drinking area attached to a restaurant than a pub in its own right. Relax in easy chairs around a real fire in winter or enjoy a pleasant drink outside beside the Levern Water in summer. Still known locally as Jeanie Gebbie's, the bar boasts a stained glass gantry which pre-dates the most recent conversion. Guest beers are typically from Scottish micro-breweries. ﲀ❀⨭⨭P

BISHOPTON

Golf Inn
28-30 Greenock Road, PA7 5JN
(400 yds W of station)
☼ 12-2.30, 5-11 (midnight Fri & Sat);
12.30-2.30, 6.30-11 Sun
☎ (01505) 862303
Belhaven 80/-; guest beer Ⓟ
Unchanged for decades, this village local has rare character. The public bar is a plain room with an L-shaped bar and shelves for glasses on the walls opposite; seats are available in the TV/games room. A selection of foreign beers is kept in a fridge in the cellar. The lounge bar has its own entrance that is used when the bar is busy; it bears a similar simple decor to the public bar, furnished with wooden tables and chairs, and seating about 50. Q⫱⨭≈P

BUSBY

White Cart
61 East Kilbride Road, G76 8HX (on A726)
☼ 11 (12.30 Sun)-11
☎ (0141) 644 2711
Greene King Old Speckled Hen; guest beer Ⓗ
Built in 1996, this pub incorporates a much older building. Still surviving at the back are sections of the old stone walls, thought to have been part of the stables that once stood on the site. The exterior encapsulates a history that stretches back to the 18th century. The spacious interior is well divided, mainly by large oak beams, into cosy nooks. The decor is from an older era, incorporating old dressers and a grandfather clock. The guest beer is from Kelburn Brewery. ﲀQ❀⫱⨭≈P⨳

CLARKSTON

Busby Hotel
Field Road, G76 8RX (on road to Busby)
☼ 11-midnight (1am Thu-Sat); 12.30-midnight Sun
☎ (0141) 644 2661 website: www.busbyhotel.co.uk
Beer range varies Ⓗ
Large hotel, overlooking the White Cart River. Wood panelling and leather couches feature in a room that is dominated by a long bar on one side. Staff provide excellent service, whether you come for a meal or just a drink. The hotel's website is informative. ❀⨳⫱⨭≈ (Busby) P

EAGLESHAM

Crosskeys
1 Montgomery Street, G76 0AS
☼ 11-midnight (11 Mon); 12.30-11 Sun
☎ (01355) 302356
Beer range varies Ⓗ
Two real ales are kept in the lounge, but can be ordered in the public bar. The lounge serves meals at lunchtime and in the evening; children are welcome until 8pm. The bar boasts a large gantry holding an extensive range of whisky. Live music is performed monthly in the lounge (first Sat), a quiz and pool contest are also regular events. ⫱⨭

GOUROCK

Spinnaker Hotel
121 Albert Road, PH19 1BU
☼ 11-11.30 (midnight Thu; 1am Fri & Sat);
12.30-midnight Sun
☎ (01475) 633107 website: www.spinnakerhotel.co.uk
Beer range varies Ⓗ
Enjoy one of three real ales, or one of the 30-plus whiskies available in this friendly hotel bar which also serves meals; the menu includes vegetarian and children's choices, the latter are welcome until 8pm. Looking out on to the Firth of Clyde, the hotel offers fantastic scenery, beyond the Firth to the Cowal Hills. In a Victorian sandstone terrace, the hotel lies between the two Gourock Ferry Terminals and you may spot a submarine heading to or from the Holy Loch. Q❀⨳⫱⨭

GREENOCK

James Watt ⊘
80-92 Cathcart Street, PA15 1DD
⊘ 11-11 (midnight Thu; 1am Fri & Sat);
12.30-midnight Sun
☎ (01475) 722640
Courage Directors; Greene King Abbot; guest beers Ⓗ
Large Wetherspoon's in a former post office,
named after the famous inventor. All the
usual JDW trimmings are here, including
local history panels and patio heaters.
Handy for the station, it is a welcome beer
venue, in what is very much a keg town.
Two English ales are supplemented by local
guest beers. Once a thriving shipyard
community, the waterfront has now been
redeveloped; HM Customs and Excise
Museum, with its tales of smuggling and
bootlegging, is worth a visit.
Q ⊛ ◑ Ġ ⇌ (Central) P⅄

HOUSTON

Fox & Hounds
South Street, PA6 7EN
⊘ 11-midnight (1am Fri & Sat); 12.30-midnight Sun
☎ (01505) 612448
website: www.foxandhoundshouston.co.uk
**Houston Killellan, Barochan, Peter's Well, Texas;
guest beer** (occasional) Ⓗ
This 17th-century coaching inn is now the
home of the Houston Brewery. The lounge
bar, which is large and comfortable and
decorated with hunting memorabilia,
features a window to the brewery. The
stable bar has plainer light wood decor,
large alcoves with tables and benches, a
pool table, large-screen TV and a fruit
machine. Upstairs, the Huntsman's Bar and
Restaurant is really two restaurants offering
different menus; food is served all day
Saturday and Sunday. ⊟P⅄

INVERKIP

Inverkip Hotel
Main Street, PA16 0AS (off A78)
⊘ 11-11 (midnight Fri & Sat); 12.30-11 Sun
☎ (01475) 521478 website: www.inverkip.co.uk
Beer range varies Ⓗ
Well known for its marina, this small
coastal town lies between the ferry
terminals for the Isle of Bute and Dunoon.
The excellent restaurant, to the rear of the
hotel, uses fresh local produce (booking
recommended). Meals can also be taken in
the lounge which has several alcoves so that
you can usually find a quiet spot. The three
beers often include Orkney Dark Island and
Caledonian Deuchars IPA. Q⋈◑⊟⇌P

JOHNSTONE

Coanes ⊘
26-28 High Street, PA5 8AH
⊘ 11-11.30 (1am Fri; midnight Sat); 12.30-11.30 Sun
☎ (01505) 322925
**Boddingtons Bitter; Caledonian Deuchars IPA, 80/-;
Orkney Dark Island; guest beers** Ⓗ
This town house-style building has a cosy
local bar with fake beams and bric-à-brac.
The lounge doubles as a restaurant, with the
eating area on a higher level, affording a
degree of privacy, however, in the late
evening the dining and lounge areas merge,
when it tends to get busy, especially at the

weekend. Evening meals are served Friday
and Saturday, 6–9 (no food Sun). Usually
beers from the local Kelburn Brewery are
available. Local CAMRA Pub of the Year
2003. Q◑⊟Ġ⇌

KILBARCHAN

Glenleven Inn
25 New Street, PA10 2LN
⊘ 11-11 (midnight Thu; 1am Fri & Sat); 12.30-11 Sun
☎ (01505) 702481
Beer range varies Ⓗ
Friendly pub, in a conservation village, with
a restaurant and a games area as well as a
comfortable lounge. A well-stocked bar
supports the two local breweries, Houston
and Kelburn, always having one beer from
each. Regular entertainment includes local
groups and quizzes. ⊛◑Ġ♣P

Trust Inn
8 Low Barholm, PA10 2ET
⊘ 11.45-11.30; 11-1am Fri & Sat; 11.45-11.30 Sun
☎ (01505) 702401
**Caledonian Deuchars IPA; Tetley Burton Ale;
guest beers** Ⓗ
Olde-worlde pub set in a conservation
village, within easy walking distance of the
Glasgow–Irvine cycle track. The single
lounge bar bears old pictures of the village
and decorative brasses; low oak beams
feature throughout with intimate recesses. A
large-screen TV is used for major sporting
events, but when it is folded away the pub
retrieves its friendly village atmosphere.
Regular entertainment includes folk groups
and pub quizzes.
◑Ġ⇌ (Milliken Pk) ♣

LOCHWINNOCH

Brown Bull
33 Main Street, PA12 4AH
⊘ 12-11 (midnight Fri; 11.45 Sat); 12.30-11 Sun
☎ (01505) 843250
Beer range varies Ⓗ
Owned by Enterprise Inns, this friendly pub
on the main road is handy for the local
RSPB visitor centre and Castle Semple
Nature Reserve. Scenes from the BBC drama
Doctor Finlay's Casebook were filmed on
the premises. Meals are served 12.30–2.30
and 5.30–7.30, dogs are allowed so please
remember food is served if you take your
dog. The Glasgow–Irvine cycle track passes
nearby and the station is less than a mile
away. ♨◑Ġ

NEWTON MEARNS

Osprey
Stewarton Road, G77 6NP
⊘ 11 (12.30 Sun)-11
☎ (0141) 616 5071
Draught Bass; Caledonian Deuchars IPA Ⓗ
One of the Vintage Inn chain (Mitchells &
Butlers), where an olde-worlde feel has been
created by the judicious use of wood, brick
and stone, the oak bar, strewn with hops,
adds to the effect. Arched windows overlook
the large garden with adequate seating.
Quiet areas within the bar allow privacy,
while the main pub is oriented towards
family dining. Good food, a good
atmosphere and a warm welcome are
assured. ♨Q⊛◑Ġ⅄

PAISLEY

Gabriels
33 Gauze Street, PA1 1EX
☼ 11-midnight (1am Fri; 12.30am Sat);
12.30-midnight Sun
☎ (0141) 887 8204
Kelburn Carte Blanche; guest beers Ⓗ
Busy, town-centre lounge with an oval-shaped island bar, raised dining area and adjoining function suite. A combination of fresh daily meals and a children's certificate help create a family-friendly atmosphere during the day; no meals are served Sunday evening. Real ale handpumps located at the back corner can mean slow service when busy, although knowledgeable, friendly staff do an excellent job. ◑ ⑅ ≠ (Gilmour St)

Hamishes' Hoose
42 Old Sneddon Street, PA3 2AP
☼ 11-11 (midnight Wed & Thu; 1am Fri & Sat);
12.30-11 Sun
☎ (0141) 847 4613 website: www.hamisheshoose.com
Kelburn Red Smiddy Ⓗ
Two-roomed lounge bar under Gilmour St railway arch. During the day it has a strong family food focus, at night the emphasis changes, with live entertainment for grown-ups. The walls are adorned with pictures of old Paisley and a shawl made from the town's famous fabric. A play area and free food are provided for the under-12s. A large-screen TV dominates the bar area, while comfortable seating creates a more relaxed atmosphere in the lounge. No food is served Sunday evening. ◑ ≠ (Gilmour St)

Hogshead ⊘
45 High Street, PA1 2AH
☼ 12-midnight (1am Fri & Sat); 12-midnight Sun
☎ (0141) 840 4150
Boddingtons Bitter; Caledonian Deuchars IPA, 80/- Ⓗ
Centrally located, close to the university, a spacious split-level interior features wood flooring, comfortable sofas and a large-screen TV. It has a no-smoking area and a dining area. Music levels vary, but can be loud, especially at weekends. The atmosphere is generally lively and friendly, as the pub is a favourite with students. Although the ale variety is limited, the quality is good and prices reasonable.
◑ ⑅ ≠ (Gilmour St) ♣ ⑇

Last Post ⊘
2 County Square, PA1 1BP
☼ 11-midnight (1am Fri & Sat); 12.30-midnight Sun
☎ (0141) 849 6911
Caledonian Deuchars IPA; Shepherd Neame Spitfire; Greene King Abbot; guest beers Ⓗ
Typical Wetherspoon's conversion of this listed building, formerly a post office, into a split-level drinking area. The walls are decorated with pictures of Paisley's textiles and its world-famous Robertson's jam-making past. Guest ales change daily. Wheelchair access is from the station entrance of the building. With all Wetherspoon's usual attributes – all day food and a no-smoking area – children are admitted until 6pm. Q ◑ ⑅ ≠ (Gilmour St) ⑇

Wee Howf
53 High Street, PA1 2AH
☼ 11-11 (11.30 Wed & Thu; 1am Fri; midnight Sat);
closed Sun
☎ (0141) 889 2095
Caledonian Deuchars IPA; Tetley Burton Ale; guest beers Ⓗ
Small, town-centre pub near the university, showcasing guest beers from Houston and Kelburn breweries. The pub used to be called the Market Bar, and the present publican has been in all of the last 16 editions of this Guide. He was the first Burton Master Cellarman in Scotland.
≠ (Gilmour St)

UPLAWMOOR

Uplawmoor Hotel
66 Neilston Road, G78 4AF (off A736)
☼ 12-2.30, 5-11 (midnight Fri & Sat); 12-midnight Sun
☎ (01505) 850565 website: www.uplawmoor.co.uk
Beer range varies Ⓗ
Hotel bar and restaurant, situated in the highest village in Renfrewshire, catering mainly for local trade, but attracting many visitors, too. Opened in 1750 to serve travellers between Glasgow and the Clyde coast, this gem has been extended and improved; a former barn has been converted to form the restaurant. A copper canopied open fire forms the centrepiece of the cocktail bar, while the public bar has a charm of its own.
⇟ ⊛ ⊨ ◑ ⊟ ⑅ P

Nut Brown Ale

The nut-brown ale, the nut-brown ale,
Puts down all drink when it is stale*;
The toast, the nutmeg and the ginger
Will make a sighing man a singer.
Ale gives a buffet in the head,
But ginger under-props the brain:
When ale would strike a strong man dead,
The nutmeg tempers it again.
The nut-brown ale, the nut-brown ale,
Puts down all drink when it is stale.

John Marston (1576-1634), from his play, *Histrioamastix*,
written in 1599 and published 1610
*Stale is old or well-matured ale.

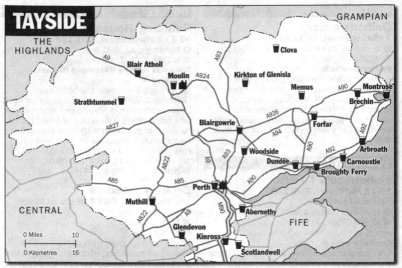

TAYSIDE

Authority areas covered: Angus UA, City of Dundee UA, Perth & Kinross UA

ABERNETHY

Cree's Inn
Main Street, PH2 9LA
🕒 11-2.30, 5-11; 11-11 Sat; 12.30-11 Sun
☎ (01738) 850714 website: www.creesinn.co.uk
Beer range varies Ⓗ

Warm, welcoming village local, within the shadow of a Pictish watch tower (one of only two in Scotland). Formerly a farmhouse, the building itself is now listed and has been sympathetically renovated to provide a long, L-shaped lounge bar and a small restaurant area. Using fresh local produce, the pub offers a varied menu at lunchtime and in the evening. Up to five ales are available, with a good mix of Scottish and English beers. ♨Q⇦◑ ▶P⍻

ARBROATH

Lochlands Bar
14 Lochlands Street, DD11 2AW
🕒 11-midnight (1am Fri & Sat); 12.30-midnight Sun
☎ (01241) 873286
Beer range varies Ⓗ

Busy, street-corner pub that displays strong sporting associations. In its public bar sports memorabilia adorn the walls while the two TV sets show sports programmes continuously. If you are not a fan, do not despair, as peace may be found in the small lounge where real ale is brought through from next door. Two ales are always on tap, from diverse breweries. ⏦⇌♣♣

BLAIR ATHOLL

Blair Atholl Hotel (Bothy Bar)
Old North Road, PH18 5SG (by station)
🕒 12-11 (including Sun)
☎ (01796) 481205 website: www.athollarmshotel.co.uk
Moulin Light, Braveheart, Ale of Atholl,
Old Remedial Ⓗ

Once owned by the Dukes of Atholl, this traditional highland hotel was built in 1832. The Bothy Bar was a relatively recent addition. The Bothy (meaning a place of refuge and comfort) is decorated using timbers and artefacts from the old stables. Excellent value meals are available all day. Blair Atholl is ideally situated, offering relaxation with a variety of outdoor activities. There are two caravan parks nearby. Why not visit Blair Castle – home of the Atholl Highlanders, Britain's only private army. ❄⇌◑▶Å⇌P

BLAIRGOWRIE

Ericht Alehouse
13 Wellmeadow, PH10 6NI
🕒 11-11 (11.45 Fri & Sat); 12.30-11 Sun
☎ (01250) 872469
Beer range varies Ⓗ

Friendly, traditional town-centre pub (established 1802). Its two seating areas are split by a small, well-stocked bar. Recently redecorated, the lounge area boasts a log-burning open fire. There are up to six ales on tap – with the range, from Scottish and English breweries, changing all the time. Addlestones cider is also stocked. Weekends can be busy, with live music performed occasionally. ♨Q♣🍺

Rosemount Golf Hotel
Golf Course Road, Rosemount, PH10 6LJ
🕒 11-11 (11.45 Fri & Sat); 12-11 Sun
☎ (01250) 872604 website: www.rosemountgolf.co.uk
Beer range varies Ⓗ

In a quiet area at the southern end of Blairgowrie, this traditional hotel is set back from the road, within its own mature gardens. It has a restaurant area and a comfortable lounge with open fire. Above the bar hangs an unusual array of golf tags. It stocks one or two beers, plus a large selection of malt whiskies. Popular with locals and visitors alike, it is an ideal base for walking and golf – some 80 golf courses can be reached within an hour's drive. ♨Q❄⇌◑♿P🍺

INDEPENDENT BREWERIES

Inveralmond Perth
Moulin Moulin

BRECHIN

Dalhousie Bar
1 Market Street, DD9 6BA
⚙ 11-midnight (1am Fri & Sat); 12.30-midnight Sun
☎ (01356) 622096
Beer range varies Ⓗ
A former city-centre hotel, this pub is a
useful refreshment stop for walkers from the
North Angus Hills. It has an unusual
horseshoe-shaped bar where one ale is
dispensed. The cathedral and round tower
are only 100 yards away, and worth a look.
✿♣

BROUGHTY FERRY

Fisherman's Tavern
10-12 Fort Street, DD5 2AD
(near lifeboat station)
⚙ 11-midnight (1am Fri & Sat); 12.30-midnight Sun
☎ (01382) 775941
website: www.fishermans-tavern-hotel.co.uk/
Beer range varies Ⓗ
This popular small hotel incorporates three
former fishermen's houses. The garden is
put to good use during the annual beer
festival (May/June), held in aid of the RNLI.
The original bar has changed little down the
years, with its low ceiling, corner dominoes
table, wooden partitions and swing doors.
The six beers on tap change often and
include local Scottish brews. A stronghold
of cask beer, it has appeared in 30 editions
of this Guide: there were no Scottish pubs
in the first edition.
🏨🛏✿🛋◐⇌ (limited service) ♣✁

CARNOUSTIE

Stag's Head
91 Dundee Street, DD7 7PG
(½ mile W of station)
⚙ 11-midnight (1am Fri & Sat); 12.30-midnight Sun
☎ (01241) 858777
Fuller's London Pride; guest beers Ⓗ
While totally changed from the days when
Billy Connolly drank here while on TA
camps at Barry, this is a popular local, very
busy at weekends. As well as locals, golfers
who appreciate a good pint will find
succour here, especially now Carnoustie is
back on the open circuit. It comprises a
large bar, a function suite, pool room and a
patio (by the car park).
🛏✿Å⇌♣P

CLOVA

Clova Hotel
Glen Clova, DD8 4QS (follow B955 from Kirriemuir)
⚙ 11-11 (1am Fri & Sat); 12.30-11 Sun
☎ (01575) 550350 website: www.clova.com
Caledonian Deuchars IPA, 80/- Ⓗ
This comfortable country hotel caters for
all visitors from the day-tripping family to
the serious climber. All country sports are
catered for, including falconry, and it is an
ideal centre for walking and birdwatching. A former drovers' inn, it stands
at the north end of the glen. Ales are kept
in the climbers' (public) bar, but may be
ordered from the lounge; the Deuchars
IPA may be replaced by a beer from
Houston Brewery. Meals are served all day
in high season.
🏨Q✿🛏◐⊟P

DUNDEE

Counting House ❷
67-71 Reform Street, DD1 1SP
⚙ 11-midnight; 12.30-11 Sun
☎ (01382) 322392
**Caledonian Deuchars IPA; Courage Directors;
guest beers** Ⓗ
Former bank opposite the McManus
Galleries in Albert Square, the elegance of its
former existence is maintained in the decor
and furnishings. The policy of lower priced
beers ensures a constantly busy atmosphere,
and attracts a complete cross-section of
customers. Good value meals are available
10–10 (12.30–10 Sun), on a typical
Wetherspoon's menu. ◐✁

Drouthy Neebors
142 Perth Road, DD1 4JW (opp. Art College)
⚙ 11-midnight; 12-midnight Sun
☎ (01382) 322392
Beer range varies Ⓗ
Small, friendly pub, with a split-level bar
plus a basement bar, which often stages live
music. Located at the heart of Dundee's
student area, both the university and art
college are nearby. Previously a car
showroom, it was turned into a Scottish
theme pub as a shrine to Dundee's anti-
poet, William McGonagall. It now
celebrates Scotland's true bard, Robert
Burns. Up to four ales include a mix of
Belhaven and guest beers. ◐⇌

Mickey Coyle's
21-23 Old Hawkhill, DD1 5DL
(by Hawkhill/West Port)
⚙ 11-3, 5-midnight; 11-midnight Fri & Sat;
7-midnight Sun
☎ (01382) 225871
Caledonian Deuchars IPA, 80/-; guest beer Ⓗ
Old, city-centre 'howff', closed for many
years, and named after a former owner.
Reopened as a students' club, it became a
pub again in the 1980s, called the Blue
Mountains after some local tenements. It
originally featured an amazingly high bar
(judge by the area near the east entrance). A
spirits mirror advertising house-bottled
products carries the name, MC, as such it
once appeared in the Guinness Book of
Records as the shortest pub name. Meals are
served weekdays (eves 5.30–7.30). ◐⇌

Phoenix
103 Nethergate, DD1 4JS (W of city centre)
⚙ 11-midnight; 12.30-midnight Sun
☎ (01382) 200014
**Caledonian Deuchars IPA; Orkney Dark Island; Taylor
Landlord; guest beer** Ⓗ
Long-standing real ale pioneer, now a
mellowed, but busy, city-centre bar. Its
traditional appearance, while a product of
refurbishment, is in keeping with a pub that
is at least 100 years old. The gantry and
some bar fittings reputedly come from a
now-demolished Cardiff hostelry. Handy for
the Repertory Theatre and Dundee
Contemporary Arts Centre, it serves meals
all day, until 7pm – try the chilli. The guest
beer usually comes from Houston Brewery.
◐⇌

Speedwell (Mennie's) ☆
165-167 Perth Road, DD2 1AS
(W of university)

✪ 11-midnight; 12.30-midnight Sun
☎ (01382) 667783
Beer range varies Ⓗ

This L-shaped Edwardian bar, better known as Mennie's after an earlier dynasty of owners, has truly been described as a gem. Opened in 1904, it is rich in mahogany – in the bar, gantry and dividing screens, the latter bearing glazed panels. Details like the ceiling, frieze and impressive gents', contribute to the stylish interior. The atmosphere is completed by a cross-section of clientele. Two rooms lead off the bar: one for TV, the other is a no-smoking area. Snacks are available.
Q ⬚ ♣ ✂

FORFAR

Baxter's Bar & Bistro
37-43 West High Street, DD8 1BE
✪ 11-midnight (1am Fri & Sat); 12.30-midnight Sun
☎ (01307) 464350
Beer range varies Ⓗ

Formerly O'Hara's, this pub retains its old character upstairs, where a traditional, cosy restaurant serves varied and exciting food. Downstairs, there is a spacious, modern bar, offering frequently-changed beers, mainly Scottish, and including brews from the Isle of Skye and Cairngorm. Regular live music is staged. On sunny days you can sit outside on the old town square.
Q ❀ ◑ ⬚ &

GLENDEVON

Tormaukin Hotel
FK14 7JY
✪ 11-11; 12-11 Sun
☎ (01259) 781252 website: www.tormaukin.com
Beer range varies Ⓗ

This 18th-century drovers' inn is situated in a peaceful rural setting, surrounded by the Ochil Hills. Tormaukin means 'hill of the mountain hare' in old Scots. The use of natural timbers and stone ensures a warm, welcoming atmosphere. Up to three ales are available in the rear lounge – usually two from Harviestoun (Bitter & Twisted, is a local favourite), plus one guest. An extensive bar menu is supplemented by the restaurant fare. The hotel is an ideal base for walking, golf and fishing. ♨ Q ⛵ ❀ 🚪 ◑ P

KINROSS

Kirklands Hotel
20 High Street, KY13 8AN
✪ 11-2.30, 5-11 (11.45 Sat); 12.30-11 Sun
☎ (01577) 863313
Beer range varies Ⓗ

Traditional, small town hotel, one of the original coaching inns. In the centre of Kinross, it has been fully refurbished to provide modern and comfortable accommodation. Two ales are usually on tap; Courage Directors is one of the local favourites. Why not visit the nearby Loch Leven Castle (where Mary, Queen of Scots was once imprisoned), or the Vane Farm Reserve – an RSPB property. ♨ 🚪 ◑ P

KIRKTON OF GLENISLA

Glenisla Hotel
PH11 8PH (on B591, 10 miles N of Alyth)

✪ 11-11 (12.30am Fri; 1am Sat); closed winter afternoons; 12.30-11 Sun
☎ (01575) 582223 website: www.glenisla-hotel.co.uk
Beer range varies Ⓗ

This 17th-century coaching inn has long been a focal point for travellers and today a wide variety of outdoor activities are catered for – golf, walking and fishing are just a few. Recently renovated and refurbished, it has retained its original character with a warm, welcoming oak beamed bar on two levels, and an open fire. A commitment to local beers means products from Inveralmond and other Scottish micro-breweries are often featured. The pub has a games room.
♨ ❀ 🚪 ◑ ♣ P

MEMUS

Drovers' Inn
DD8 3TY (5 miles N of Forfar, off B957)
✪ 12-2.30, 6-midnight; 12-midnight Sat; 12.30-midnight Sun
☎ (01307) 860322
Beer range varies Ⓗ

A pleasant bar bears pine-panelled walls, flagstones and an open fire, while a spacious restaurant, large garden, children's playground and car park complete the facilities here. The pub was formerly the local post office and it still serves as the local shop where groceries, newspapers and vegetables may be ordered; it also has an ATM. Opening hours may vary, so phone to check.
♨ ❀ ◑ ♣ P

MONTROSE

George Hotel
22 George Street, DD10 8EW
✪ 11-2, 5-11; 11-11 Sat; 12-11 Sun
☎ (01674) 675050
Beer range varies Ⓗ

Small hotel in the town centre, with a split-level bistro-style lounge/bar, warmed by an open gas fire. At least one ale is available all year round, and up to three in summer. Meals may be eaten in the lounge/bar or in the restaurant. High tea is served Sunday–Thursday, 5–9.30, and dinner on Friday and Saturday, 7–10pm.
❀ 🚪 ◑ ⇌ P

MOULIN

Moulin Inn
11-13 Kirkmichael Road, PH16 5EH
(¾ mile NE of Pitlochry)
✪ 12-11 (11.45 Fri & Sat); 12-11.45 Sun
☎ (01796) 472196 website: www.moulinhotel.co.uk
Moulin Light, Braveheart, Ale of Atholl, Old Remedial Ⓗ

On Moulin's village square, this country inn was established in 1695 and, although extended into an hotel, it retains character and charm. The oldest part is the original inn, a traditional pub with two log-burning fires. Moulin is an ancient crossroads, near Pitlochry, 'Gateway to the Highlands'. Good home-cooking is provided, along with beer from the brewery in the old coach house behind the inn. An excellent base for outdoor pursuits, a variety of marked walks pass nearby.
♨ Q ⛵ ❀ 🚪 ◑ ⬚ ♣ P

MUTHILL

Muthill Village Hotel
6 Willoughby Street, PH5 2AB
☼ 12-2.30, 5.30-11 (11.45 Sat); 12.30-2.30,
5.30-11 Sun; may vary; phone to check
☎ (01764) 681451
website: www.muthillvillagehotel.com
Orkney Dark Island; guest beers Ⓗ
18th-century coaching inn on the old
drovers' road from the Highlands, it is
located in the centre of the conservation
village of Muthill (boasting over 90 listed
buildings). The Bothy Bar is characterful,
with a large open fire and farming
implements; the restaurant area bears a
hunting theme. Up to four ales give
prominence to Scottish micro's products;
the house beer, Tapsman's Yill or Drovers'
Ale reflects historic links with the cattle
drovers (Tapsman being the name for a
head drover). ♨Q⏰⌖☕⇌◗P

PERTH

Cherrybank Inn
210 Glasgow Road, PH2 0NA
☼ 11-11 (11.45 Fri & Sat); 12.30-11 Sun
☎ (01738) 624349 website: www.cherrybankinn.co.uk
**Inveralmond Independence, Ossian's Ale; Tetley Bitter;
guest beer** Ⓗ
From its days as a drovers' inn over 200
years ago, the Cherrybank has been a
popular stop for passing travellers – situated
as it is on the Wester approach to Perth.
Thought to be one of the oldest public
houses in Perth, it has a well-appointed
lounge bar and a small public bar with three
adjacent rooms. Up to four real ales show a
strong commitment to the local
Inveralmond Brewery. Q⇌◗⏏⌖P

Greyfriars
15 South Street, PH2 8PG
☼ 11-11 (11.45 Fri & Sat); 12.30-11 Sun
☎ (01738) 633036
**Caledonian Deuchars IPA; Taylor Landlord;
guest beers** Ⓗ
One of the smallest lounge bars within the
city centre, it enjoys a vibrant, friendly
atmosphere. Good value lunches are served
in the bar and a small upstairs seating area.
Up to four ales are available, with the
popular house beer, Friar's Tipple, brewed
by Inveralmond. As a plaque says above the
bar, this is 'more of a club without
membership'. Ideally located, attractions
nearby include the Victorian Theatre, art
gallery, museum and the River Tay. ◗⇌

SCOTLANDWELL

Well Country Inn
Main Street, KY13 9JA
☼ 11-11 (11.45 Fri & Sat); 12-11 Sun
☎ (01592) 840444
website: www.thewellcountryinn.co.uk
Beer range varies Ⓗ
Family-run country inn, in a quiet village
that dates back to 84AD. Ideally situated for
country outdoor pursuits – shooting,
fishing, golfing and gliding – the inn has a
comfortable main lounge and a snug bar,
both warmed by open fires. Bar meals and
two restaurant areas (one no-smoking) offer
a choice ranging from traditional to
Mediterranean and Mexican dishes. Nearby
are the famous Tetley Tea Trail and one of
the last underground springwater wells still
working in Scotland. ♨Q⌖☕⇌◗⏏P

STRATHTUMMEL

Loch Tummel Inn
Strathtummel by Pitlochry, PH16 5RP
(on B8019, approx. 3 miles W of Queen's View)
☼ 11-11 (may close afternoons); 12.30-11 Sun;
inn closes Oct-mid March
☎ (01882) 634272
Moulin Braveheart Ⓗ
Former coaching inn, built by the Dukes of
Atholl, it is located on a remote stretch of
road overlooking Loch Tummel (part of the
romantic 'Road to the Isles') and boasts
some magnificent scenery. The bar area is in
what used to be the stables, with the
restaurant in a converted hayloft (where
you can try the inn's own smoked salmon).
Nearby is the panoramic viewpoint of
Queen's View. The inn may close
afternoons, so a phone call to check is
advised. ♨Q⌖☕⇌◗P

WOODSIDE

Woodside Inn
Main Street, PH13 9NP
(on A94, S of Coupar Angus)
☼ 11-2.30, 5-11; 11-11.45 Fri; 11-11 Sat;
12.30-11 Sun
☎ (01828) 670254
Beer range varies Ⓗ
Located at the north-east end of
Burrelton/Woodside, this small, but
welcoming, village local has a small public
bar serving up to four real ales which
regularly change. The restaurant area serves
an excellent choice of food, and children
are welcome to dine. Evening meals on
Sunday are served 4.30–6.30. ♨◗♣P

Honest ale-house

I'll now lead you to an honest
ale-house where we shall find
a cleanly room, lavender in
the windows, and twenty
ballads stuck about the wall;
there my hostess (which, I
may tell you, is both cleanly
and handsome, and civil)
hathe dressed many a one (a
chub) for me, and shall now
dress it after my fashion, and I
warrant it good meat.

Izaak Walton (1593-1683),
The Compleat Angler, 1653

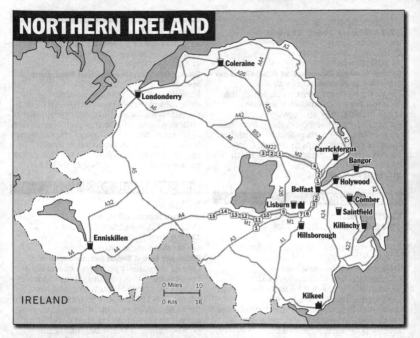

NORTHERN IRELAND

BANGOR

Esplanade
12 Ballyholme Esplanade, BT20 5LZ
☼ 11.30-11; 12.30-10 Sun
☎ (028) 9127 0954
website: www.gillespie-esplanade.com
Whitewater Glen Ale; guest beers Ⓗ
Comfortable, seaside pub which has
lounges and dining areas offering
commanding views over Ballyholme Bay.
There are handpumps in the public bar
only, but staff will serve real ale elsewhere.
Good food is served in the bar and lounge
as well as the upstairs dining room which
offers an à la carte menu. Wheelchair access
and WC are provided.
✿◑●🏠&≑

BELFAST

Crown ☆
46 Great Victoria Street, BT2 7BA
(opp. Europa Hotel and Gt Victoria St station)
☼ 11.30-12.30am; 12.30-11.30 Sun
☎ (028) 9027 9902
website: www.belfasttelegraph.co.uk/crown/
Whitewater Belfast Ale Ⓗ
The exterior façade, consisting of
polychromatic tiles, partially prepares
you for the riot of colours, textures and
materials of the interior. Highly
patterned and coloured mosaic tiles,
brocaded walls, ornate mirrors, vigorous
wood carving throughout and wood
columns with corinthian capitals
combine to complete an entirely
decorated interior. Dating to 1826 when
the first train ran from Belfast to Lisburn,
it is probably the most ornate pub in the
UK. Good pub grub is sold and there is a
separate upstairs restaurant. Live web-
cam conveys the goings-on to the rest of
the world!
◑●≑ (Gt Victoria St)

Kitchen Bar
16-18 Victoria Square, BT1 4QA
(off Cornmarket)
☼ 11.30-11; 12-7 Sun
☎ (028) 9032 4901
Beer range varies Ⓗ
This popular and historic pub in central
Belfast was voted CAMRA Northern Ireland
Pub of the Year 2003. Its days are numbered
due to redevelopment – despite CAMRA
protests for its preservation. One of the first
bars in the province to serve real ale, it is
famous locally for its traditional foods and
its olde-world charm, including a display of
photographs of the stars of the Empire
Music Hall, long since gone. Come and see
this rare treat before it too disappears.
Occasional music sessions are staged.
⛨◑●≑ (Central)

Rotterdam Bar
52-54 Pilot Street, BT1 5HZ (off Corporation
Street, at the far end of Pilot St))
☼ 11.30-11.30; 11.30-1am Fri & Sat; 4-midnight Sun
☎ (028) 9074 6021
Whitewater Belfast Ale Ⓗ
The rejuvenation of this famous docklands
tavern was a product of the bohemian
culture present in 1980s Belfast. The
clientele may have changed but the varied
present-day patrons still throng to the
regular music sessions. A low ceiling and
irregular floor add to the charm of this
country-style city pub and the real coal fire
offers a welcome on a cold winter's day.
Once difficult to find, the redevelopment of
the area now means a pleasant stroll
through the expanse of opened-up
docklands. ⛨◑●≑ (York St)

INDEPENDENT BREWERIES

Hilden Lisburn
Whitewater Kilkeel

Wetherspoon's
37-43 Bedford Street, BT2 4HF
(opp. BBC, Ormeau Ave)
🕓 10-1am; 12.30-midnight Sun
☎ (028) 9072 7890
Courage Directors; Theakston Best Bitter; Whitewater Belfast Ale; guest beers (occasional) Ⓗ

Large, bustling, city-centre pub which has recently been modernised to include a comfortable family area upstairs (until 6pm). There are two no-smoking areas and friendly staff. It boasts probably the highest number of handpumps in Belfast. Good food is served seven days a week – try the all day breakfast (Ulster fry).
🏚Q☎◑⇌(Gt Victoria St) ⑁

CARRICKFERGUS

Central Bar
13-15 High Street, BT38 7AN
(opp. Carrickfergus Castle)
🕓 10-11 (1am Thu-Sat); 12.30-midnight Sun
☎ (028) 9935 7840
Theakston Best Bitter; guest beers Ⓗ

Overlooking the 12th-century castle and Belfast Lough, this pub takes its name from the original bar on the site. It is conveniently situated near the town-centre shops and marinas. Typical, value-for-money pub fare is served all day, every day.
Q☎◑⑁

COLERAINE

Old Courthouse
Castlerock Road, BT51 3HP
(across the old bridge and 200 yds ahead)
🕓 10-11 (1am Thu-Sat); 12.30-midnight Sun
☎ (028) 7032 5820
Caledonian Deuchars IPA; Fuller's London Pride; guest beers Ⓗ

Wetherspoon's first building conversion in NI. An impressive, listed, former courthouse, circa 1852 with a spacious interior, disabled access and two no-smoking areas. A younger crowd gathers in the evening, replacing the mixed daytime clientele. Occasional beer festivals are held. The guest beers are of a more interesting nature due to the manager and real ale drinking locals have increased due to this. Good food is served all day, children are welcome until 9pm Monday–Wednesday, and 6pm Thursday–Sunday. A patio area surrounds the pub. Q✿◑⇌⑁

COMBER

North Down House
Belfast Road, BT23 5EN (Castle St roundabout)
🕓 12-midnight (1am Fri & Sat); 1-midnight Sun
☎ (028) 9187 2242
Beer range varies Ⓗ

The inside of this old pub (dating back over 100 years) reflects the history of the area. An extension to the main bar is the Comber Halt with its railway carriage-style seating. The quieter lounge is decorated with memorabilia of the old Comber whiskey distillery. Friendly staff look after customers of various ages. A DJ appears on Friday night and live entertainment features on Saturday. A pool table is provided; lunches are served 12–2.30, Monday–Friday, and 2–5, Saturday and Sunday. ◑♣

ENNISKILLEN

Linen Hall
11-13 Townhall Street, BT74 7BD
🕓 10-11 (1am Fri & Sat); 12.30-midnight Sun
☎ (028) 6634 0910
Courage Directors; Theakston Best Bitter; guest beers Ⓗ

Recently refurbished pub, now part of the expanding Wetherspoon's chain in NI. It is popular with locals and the large number of visitors who throng to this picturesque part of Ulster to take advantage of the excellent fishing in the area. Good value food is served at all times. There is a stair lift to the bar for disabled access. 🏚Q☎✿◑♿P⑁

HILLSBOROUGH

Hillside
21 Main Street, BT26 6AE
🕓 12-11.30 (1am Fri & Sat); 12-11 Sun
☎ (028) 9268 2765
website: www.carmichaelgroup.co.uk
Whitewater Belfast Belfast Ale; guest beers Ⓗ

One of the earliest purveyors of real ale in the province, this pub usually has four ales on tap, two from Whitewater, and two guests. Food is available in three areas of the pub: the Refectory, lunchtime and evening; a separate restaurant on Friday and Saturday (7.30–9.30); and in the bar during the afternoon. Jazz bands play on Sunday evening, and a beer festival is held in summer. This friendly, popular inn is a former CAMRA NI Pub of the Year.
🏚Q✿◑Ⓔ♿▲⑁

HOLYWOOD

Dirty Duck Ale House
2-4 Kinnegar Road, BT18 9JN
🕓 11.30-midnight (1am Fri & Sat); 12.30-midnight Sun
☎ (028) 9059 6666
Beer range varies Ⓗ

Cheerful pub on the County Down side of Belfast Lough. The picture windows of the bar and upstairs restaurant provide superb views across the Lough with its shipping, during the day, and the lights of the County Antrim coast at night. Four handpumps, good quality food and regular live music Thursday–Sunday, attract a wide range of customers. The pub hosts a summer beer festival when the seated area outside is served by a temporary covered bar. 🏚✿◑⇌

KILLINCHY

Daft Eddie's
Sketrick Island, BT23 6QH
(Whiterock Road, 2 miles N of Killinchy)
🕓 11.30-11.30 (1am Fri); 12-10.30 Sun
☎ (028) 9754 1615
Whitewater Belfast Belfast Ale Ⓗ

Appealing bar and restaurant adjacent to a small castle. Difficult to find – try following the signs to Sketrick Castle. The pub overlooks Whiterock Bay, a great spot for outdoor drinking in the summer. Inside, the decor reflects the sea-going nature of the surrounding area. As you might expect, the restaurant specialises in seafood, all the meals are highly recommended. Due to its popularity, booking is advised. A genuine hidden gem. Q✿◑Ⓔ♿P

LISBURN

Taproom
**Hilden Brewery, Hilden,
BT27 4TY**
(5-minute walk from Hilden railway halt)
☼ 12-2.30 (not Mon), 6-9 Fri & Sat; 12.30-3 Sun
☎ (028) 9266 3863
Hilden Ale, Molly Malone's Porter Ⓗ
Real ale has been brewed and sold here for
22 years. The licensed restaurant serves a
range of tasty food and Hilden's own ales
are crafted in the attached brewery. A visitor
centre tracks Hilden's brewing and linen
history, tours around the brewery can be
arranged. The function room is also
bookable and often hosts dining and wine-
tasting events, and a beer festival is held
annually. All of this occurs in the pleasing
surroundings of the Scullion family's
Georgian manor. The courtyard serves as a
garden for summer drinking.
🏚Q❀◑🖢≠ (Hilden) P

Tuesday Bell
**Units 1 & 2, Lisburn Square,
BT28 2TU**
(in new shopping centre)
☼ 11.30-11 (1am Tue-Sat); 12.30-midnight Sun
☎ (028) 9262 7390
**Courage Directors; Theakston Best Bitter; Whitewater
Belfast Ale** Ⓗ
Named after the bell that once sounded the
opening of the local market, the Tuesday
Bell has transformed the drinking landscape
in Lisburn. Unlike the other pubs, it is
bright and reasonably priced. It has greatly
increased the availability of real ale in the
town centre, with Theakston, Directors and
Whitewater ales. This new two-storey
building is the centrepiece of a complex
that features many trendy shops. It tends to
be busy on Friday and Saturday evenings.
Q◑≠⌿

LONDONDERRY

Diamond
**23-24 The Diamond,
BT48 6HP**
☼ 11-11 (1am Thu-Sat); 12-10 Sun
☎ (028) 7127 2880
**Courage Directors; Theakston Best Bitter; guest
beers** Ⓗ
Typical Wetherspoon's free house
converted from an old department store.
There are two floors with separate bars
and seating. The pub is situated at the
centre of NI's second city within the
perfectly complete city walls. The views
are wonderful as you walk around the
walls and the gates, on the streets leading
to the Diamond. Meals are served all day
until 10pm; there is a curry club on
Thursday evening.
Q◑🖢≠ (Waterside) ⌿

SAINTFIELD

White Horse
**Main Street,
BT24 7AB**
☼ 11.30-11.30; 12-10 Sun
☎ (028) 9751 1143
**Whitewater Mill Ale, Glen Ale, Belfast Ale, Knight
Porter; guest beers** Ⓗ
Cosy, cheerful inn dating to the 17th
century. Popular with locals and visitors, it
has been a frequent winner of CAMRA NI
Pub of the Year. It was recently acquired by
Whitewater Brewery, making it the first
micro-brewery tied house in the province.
As well as a good range of ales from
Whitewater, there are always at least two
guests from mainland UK. An excellent
restaurant is provided, but the previous off-
licence has been incorporated into the pub
as a coffee area.
🏚◑

Benefit of the hop

If your ale may endure for a fortnight, your beer through
the benefit of the hop shall endure a month, and what
grace it yieldeth to the taste, all men may judge that have
sense in their mouths. And if controversy be betwixt Beer
and Ale, which of them shall have the place of pre-
eminence, it sufficeth for the glory and commendation of
the Beer that, here in our own country, ale giveth place
unto it and that most part of our countrymen do abhor
and abandon ale as a loathsome drink.

Reynold Scot,
A Perfite Platforme for a Hoppe Garden,
1574

CHANNEL ISLANDS

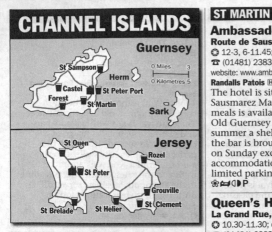

Guernsey

Jersey

Guernsey

CASTEL

Fleur du Jardin
Kings Mills, GY5 7JT
☼ 10.30-11.45; 12-3.15 Sun
☎ (01481) 257996
website: www.fleurdujardin.guernsey.net
Guernsey Sunbeam Ⓗ
Country pub with a good-sized sheltered garden, in an attractive setting. There is ample parking on site, but it can be busy during the summer. There are two bars: one small and cosy attached to the restaurant, the other large and airy; the same real ales are sold in both. The restaurant and bar menus feature fresh local produce, with daily changing specials to reflect availability. ▲Q◑◖P

Rockmount Hotel
Cobo, GY5 7HB
☼ 10.30-11.45; 12-3.30 Sun
☎ (01481) 256757
Randalls Patois Ⓗ
The hotel's large public bar is by the car park to the rear while the large lounge at the front is partitioned into two areas. Good quality food is served in the lounge. The pub is situated on the main coastal road, just across from one of the island's most popular beaches and provides an excellent watering-hole when you require a break from sunbathing!
◑ ◖P

FOREST

Venture Inn
New Road, GY8 0HG (2 minutes' drive from airport)
☼ 10.30-midnight; closed Sun
☎ (01481) 263211
Randalls Patois, seasonal beers Ⓗ
Popular, traditional, Guernsey hostelry, where the visitor is made to feel welcome in the lounge or busy public bar. The latter serves excellent food at lunchtime, with evening meals available Monday–Saturday during the summer; just Friday and Saturday in winter. Parking is available to the front and the rear; well worth a visit.
▲◑ ◖P

ST MARTIN

Ambassador Hotel
Route de Sausmarez, GY4 6SO
☼ 12-3, 6-11.45; 12-3.30 Sun
☎ (01481) 238336
website: www.ambassador.guernseynet
Randalls Patois Ⓗ
The hotel is situated just down from Sausmarez Manor. An excellent range of meals is available, either in the bar or the Old Guernsey conservatory. During the summer a sheltered patio area to the rear of the bar is brought into use. The bar is closed on Sunday except for hotel guests; the accommodation here is good value. There is limited parking to the front of the hotel.
❀⇌◑P

Queen's Hotel
La Grand Rue, GY4 6AA
☼ 10.30-11.30; closed Sun
☎ (01481) 238398
Randalls Patois, seasonal beers Ⓗ
The busy, locals' public bar is situated to the rear of the hotel, with access from the car park. The lounge bar, to the front, is adorned with posters of old film stars – Laurel and Hardy are the prime subjects. Note too, the old poster for Randalls beer in the lounge bar window. Good quality food is served, with a dining area provided for non-smokers.
❀⇌◑ ◖P

ST PETER PORT

Cock & Bull
Lower Hauteville, GY1 1LL
☼ 10-2.30, 4-11.45; 10-11.45 Fri & Sat; closed Sun
☎ (01481) 722660
Beer range varies Ⓗ
Popular pub, just up the hill from the town church. Five handpumps provide a changing range of beers which includes Ringwood brews. A large-screen TV shows sporting events in the main bar area, but the pub is on three levels, so there is plenty of choice in seating areas. The lower level houses a pool table. The pub stages regular beer festivals, some for charity, and live music Tuesday and Thursday. Snacks and good value meals are available at lunchtime. ◑

Cornerstone Café
2 La Tour Beauregard, GY1 1LQ
☼ 8am (9.30am Sat)-11.30pm; 9.30am-3.30pm Sun
☎ (01481) 713832
Flowers IPA; Randalls Patois; Tipsy Toad Jimmy's Bitter Ⓗ
This former restaurant has a small bar area to the front, but plenty of seating to the rear. The menu offers a wide selection of hot and cold food; note the collection of framed Giles cartoons and old advertising posters scattered around the bar. ◑◖

Dog House
Rohais, GY1 1YW
(main route out of town, 200 yds from Safeway)
☼ 10.30-11.45; 12-3.30, 6.30-11.45 Sun
☎ (01481) 721302 website: www.thedoghouse.gg
Badger Tanglefoot; Randalls Pale Ale Ⓗ
Free house on the edge of town, specialising in live music each evening and some lunchtimes. Comfortable seating is enhanced by interesting murals to look at.

There is a wood-panelled dining area, but this can be cramped when the pub is very busy. There is a small patio to the rear. Parking space is available at the front and rear, but beware of parking on others' property to avoid a ticket. ✿◖▶P

Randy Paddle
North Esplanade, GY1 2LQ
(opp. tourist board office)
✪ 10-11.45; closed Sun
☎ (01481) 725610
Badger Tanglefoot; Flowers IPA Ⓗ
Recently renovated, this bar is situated in an area that would originally have housed cargo from the old wooden sailing ships docked in the harbour across the road. It lies on the town crawl, but attracts a mixed crowd.

Ship & Crown
North Esplanade, GY1 2NB
(opp. Crown Pier car park)
✪ 10-11.45; 12-3.30, 6-10 Sun
☎ (01481) 721368
Draught Bass; Guernsey Sunbeam, seasonal beers Ⓗ
Providing picturesque views of the harbour, this pub is popular with locals and tourists alike. There is a convenient public car park opposite. It appeals to all ages at different times of the day, being popular in the evening with the younger crowd, on the town crawl. The walls display pictures of wartime occupation and local shipping disasters. A good range of bar meals come in generous portions. ◖

ST SAMPSON

La Fontaine Inn
Vale Road, GY2 4DS
✪ 10.30-11.30; closed Sun
☎ (01481) 247644
Randalls Mild Ⓗ
Popular with the local community, the inn has a small public bar. The large L-shaped lounge has its own bar, plus a small hatch further down the room for ordering beer from the public bar. A reasonably-sized car park stands to the rear, with a garden. The mild is sold as Cynfull, named after Cindy, the landlady. Shove-ha'penny can be played here. ✿🛋♣P

Jersey
GROUVILLE

Pembroke Inn
La Grande Route des Sablons, JE3 9FR
(by Royal Jersey Golf Club)
✪ 10-11; 11-11 Sun
☎ (01534) 855756
Draught Bass; Courage Directors; Wadworth 6X Ⓗ
The Pembroke is a large, friendly pub. Real ale is only available in the public bar, so ask if you do not see it. Food is popular here, and it is worth booking if your group is large. The public bar boasts a range of games, a pool table and a vast TV screen. The car park is small, but there is plentiful safe parking nearby. Outside drinking is on an enclosed patio. ⚲Q✿◖🛋&♣P

ROZEL

Rozel Bay Hotel
La Vallée de Rozel, JE3 6AJ

✪ 11-11; 11-11 Sun
☎ (01534) 863438
Draught Bass; Courage Directors; Wadworth 6X Ⓗ
The Rozel Bay is a favourite with customers, and deservedly so. It has an extremely cosy lounge bar where three real ales are served from a small corner bar. The public bar houses a pool table and a TV. A good pub menu is supplemented by a splendid restaurant upstairs. Evening meals are not served Sunday, except for summer barbecues. Outside is a delightful garden and an alfresco dining area (under cover). Car parking space is at a premium.
⚲Q✿◖🛋&♣P

ST BRELADE

Old Smugglers Inn ⊘
La Mont du Ouaisne, JE3 8AW
✪ 11-11; 11-11 Sun
☎ (01534) 741510
Draught Bass; guest beers Ⓗ
The Smugglers is a quaint, historic pub, nestling next to Ouaisne Bay, which is the home of the rare 'agile frog'. It is a busy, but cosy local. A stalwart of real ale, it was Jersey's only free house until 2001. The pub is recommended for the food and features a comprehensive menu, served in spacious dining areas. A fine beach is less than 100 yards away. Bar billiards is played here.
⚲Q✿♣

ST CLEMENT

Le Hocq Inn
La Grande Route de la Côte, JE2 6FP
✪ 11-11; 11-11 Sun
☎ (01534) 854924
Tipsy Toad Jimmy's Bitter; guest beer Ⓗ
This large, comfortable pub is situated on the south-east coast of the island, affording superb views over the bay from the front patio. Food is available, Monday–Saturday, in the lounge bar, and the excellent restaurant upstairs. The public bar houses a pool table, juke box and widescreen TV. There is a large public car park next to the pub and the beach is not far away. A good bus service runs into St Helier. ✿◖🛋♣

ST HELIER

Lamplighter
Mulcaster Street, JE2 3NJ
✪ 11-11; 11-11 Sun
☎ (01534) 723119
Draught Bass; Boddingtons Bitter; Courage Directors; Theakston Old Peculier; guest beers Ⓗ
The Lamplighter is an institution on Jersey's real ale scene. Unashamedly a drinkers' pub, this was Jersey CAMRA Pub of the Year 2000 and 2001, in recognition of consistently good quality. The Lamplighter is the only public house on the island to be gaslit, creating an intimate atmosphere in which to relax and socialise. Take time to look at the intricate detail on the exterior of the pub.
♣👜

INDEPENDENT BREWERIES

Randalls St Peter Port
Tipsy Toad St Peter

Original Wine Bar ✪
86 Bath Street, JE2 4SU
🕐 11-11; 4.30-11 Sun
☎ (01534) 871119
Draught Bass; Tipsy Toad Jimmy's Bitter; guest beers Ⓗ

This relaxed eating and drinking establishment has recently been refurbished. Popular with office workers from town, it offers a comprehensive wine list, but there is always a varied real ale choice too with up to five beers on tap. It has won various local CAMRA awards for the promotion of quality real ale in Jersey and has now been accredited with a Cask Marque. Meals are served Monday–Saturday. ◖◗

Prince of Wales Tavern
Hilgrove Street, JE2 4SL
🕐 10-11; 11-2 Sun
☎ (01534) 737378
Draught Bass; Wadworth 6X; guest beer Ⓗ

Busy, one-bar town pub next to the central market. An impressive bar, with stained glass inserts, dominates the room and frames a classic six-pump beer engine (but only three work). The back yard is a sun terrace, surrounding a little fountain, which offers sanctuary from bustling St Helier. The pub services town workers and is very busy at lunchtime, when meals are available. It is less hectic in the evening. Q☻◗

ST OUEN

Farmer's Inn
La Grande Route de St Ouen, JE3 2HY
🕐 10-11; 11-11 Sun
☎ (01534) 485311
Draught Bass; Guernsey Sunbeam; Tipsy Toad Jimmy's Bitter; guest beers Ⓗ

This is the quintessential local pub, set at the centre of the village, in the north-west of the island. The large public bar boasts four handpumps and an open fire. The smaller, yet cosy, lounge has a small hatch for ordering drinks from the public bar. An outside area is provided for drinking and eating in summer. There is a regular bus service into St Helier. Lunches are served Tuesday–Saturday, evening meals Friday and Saturday. ♨Q☻◖◗⊟♣♠P

Moulin de Lecq
Le Mont de la Greve de Lecq St Ouen, JE3 2DT
🕐 11-11; 11-11 Sun
☎ (01534) 482818
Guernsey Sunbeam; guest beers Ⓗ

This is one of Jersey's most picturesque public houses – a must for tourists. A converted 12th-century watermill, it features a working drive wheel behind the bar. The mill was used by the Germans to generate power during the occupation. The cosy lounge bar boasts a roaring fire in winter, while a large outdoor area hosts summer barbecues, and houses a play area for children. No meals are available Sunday evening. ♨☻◖◗♠P

ST PETER

Star & Tipsy Toad Brewery
La Route de Beaumont, JE2 7BQ
🕐 11-11; 11-11 Sun
☎ (01534) 485556
Tipsy Toad Jimmy's Bitter, seasonal beers Ⓗ

The Star is the home of the Tipsy Toad Brewery, Jersey's only remaining real ale producer. The Star is smart and bright, offering a variety of dining and drinking areas around a central bar. All the Tipsy Toad beers are served, but as the brewery is not large, sometimes only the award-winning Jimmy's Bitter may be on tap. The main bar features a stained glass roof. Live music is performed most Friday and Saturday evenings. Meals are served Monday–Saturday. ♨Q🛏☻◖◗♿♣♠P

Life, liberty – and beer

Beer, happy produce of our Isle
Can sinewy Strength impart,
And wearied with Fatigue and Toil
Can cheer each manly Heart.

Labour and Art upheld by Thee
Successfully advance,
We quaff thy balmy Juice with Glee
And Water leave to France.

Genius of Health, thy grateful Taste
Rivals the Cup of Jove,
And warms each English generous Breast
With Liberty and Love.

Verses by **James Townley** to accompany William Hogarth's engraving, *Beer Street*, 1751

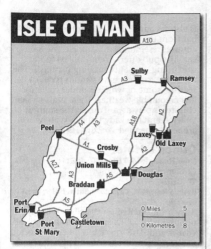

ISLE OF MAN

Crosby Hotel ✓
Peel Road, IM4 2PQ
🕑 12-2.30, 4.30-11; 12-midnight Fri & Sat;
12-3, 8-11 Sun
☎ (01624) 851293
Okells Mild, Bitter Ⓗ

This large free-standing building has a spacious lounge and smaller public bar. The lounge has traditional decor with comfy button-back seats. The far end of the lounge is a no-smoking area. A beautifully restored vintage MGP Norton stands in a glass case near the entrance. The Crosby is popular with bikers, young and old, and hosts a Boxing Day veteran bike rally. The Peel bus stops at the entrance to the car park making the Crosby an excellent venue to watch the TT races. The friendly locals and pleasant staff enhance the atmosphere at this worthy stop-off point between Douglas and Peel.
Q✿🕭🝔🅛🚶▲♣P⊬

Castle Arms (Gluepot)
The Quay, IM9 1LP (by Castle Rushen)
🕑 12-11 (midnight Fri & Sat); 12-3, 7-10.30 Sun
☎ (01624) 824673
John Smith's Bitter; Okells Bitter Ⓗ

Although not viable as a brewery pub, the Castle Arms, better known as the Gluepot, has thrived under new ownership. A nautical theme with models and pictures seems appropriate to its quayside location. Even though it has been extended, with comfortable seating in the small rooms, it is sometimes very busy in the evenings. Normal pub meals are complemented two evenings a week by Thai cuisine. 🝔▲≠(IMR)

Sidings
Victoria RoadIM9 1EF (by station)
🕑 12-11 (midnight Fri & Sat); 12-3, 7-10.30 Sun
☎ (01624) 823282
Bushy's Ruby Mild, Castletown Bitter, Old Bushy Tail; Marston's Pedigree; guest beers Ⓗ

After many years' benign neglect under brewery ownership, the refurbished Duck's Nest became the Sidings with an Isle of Man railway theme, appropriate to its situation adjacent to Castletown Station. An impressive and ornate wooden bar counter displays a large array of handpumps dispensing a wide range of ales, both Manx and imported. During fine weather the small, secluded garden area is ideal for those with children. It was awarded CAMRA Isle of Man Pub of the Year 2003. 🚲✿🝔≠(IMR)♣

Union Hotel
Arbory Street IM9 1LJ (near Castle Rushen)
🕑 11.30-11 (midnight Fri & Sat); 12-11 Sun
☎ (01624) 825286
Okells Mild, Bitter Ⓗ

Multi-roomed pub in the town centre – ideal for the serious drinker as there is no conflict with customers consuming meals. Well-supported by local residents, the Union is home to a branch of the Buffaloes as well as the charitable organisation, the Castletown Ale Drinkers' Society. Those who contemplate joining the latter may ponder on the fact that a dip in Castletown harbour on New Year's Day is one of the events held. 🚲♣

Albert Hotel
3 Chapel Row, IM1 2BJ (50 yds from quayside, next to bus depot)
🕑 10-11 (midnight Fri & Sat); 12-11 Sun
☎ (01624) 673632
Okells Mild, Bitter Ⓗ

Overlooking the main bus depot, this busy, unspoilt local is home to a thriving social club. A traditionally laid-out pub with a central bar serving the wood-lined lounge and vaults, karaoke at weekends adds to the lively atmosphere. The Albert Hotel is popular with TT visitors. The house brew, 'Jough' (Manx Gaelic for beer), is supplied by Okells. Q🝔≠(IMR)♣

Cat with no Tail
Hailwood Court, Hailwood Avenue, Governors Hill, IM2 7EA
🕑 12-11 (midnight Fri & Sat); 12-10.30 Sun
☎ (01624) 616364
Okells Bitter Ⓗ

Modern pub located in a housing estate shopping area. The lounge has alcove seating and a raised central area with distinctive stained glass. The seating is comfortable and the floor is carpeted. There is a no-smoking conservatory which admits children when food is being served. No evening meals are served on Sunday. At the back is a garden with seating and a children's play area. The public bar has a large-screen TV and a dartboard.
✿🝔🅛♣P⊬

Forester's Arms
St George's Street, IM1 1AJ (off Athol St)
🕑 11.30-11.30; 12-10.30 Sun
☎ (01624) 676509
Okells Mild, Bitter Ⓗ

Situated within the office district of the thriving financial sector, the regulars of this wonderfully unspoilt working man's pub fought and won a battle to convert the Forester's into a wine bar. A 1,000-plus

INDEPENDENT BREWERIES

Bushy's Braddan
Okells Douglas
Old Laxey Old Laxey

petition played no small part in the decision. A central bar serves the two rooms and an unusual tiny (no-smoking) snug. A larger side room hosts live music most weekends. Note the original Castletown Brewery windows, which are a reminder of its former heritage. ♨Q⊟≉(IMR) ♣⚓

Old Market Tavern
2 Chapel Row, IM1 2BJ
(between market hall and bus depot)
✪ 10-midnight; 11-midnight Sun
☎ (01624) 675202
Okells Bitter Ⓗ
Traditional back-street local with two small wood-panelled rooms served by a central bar. It is a friendly family-run pub with a strong community spirit. Dominoes, cribbage and darts are played. For many years (uniquely) it was jointly owned by Castletown and Okells breweries. It is very busy at weekends and visitors are made welcome. The pub specialises in loose packaged pipe tobaccos. ♨Q⊟≉(IMR) ♣

Rovers Return
11 Church Street, IM1 2AG (behind town hall)
✪ 12-11 (midnight Fri & Sat); 12-3, 7-10.30 Sun
☎ (01624) 676459
Bushy's Ruby Mild, Bitter, seasonal beers; guest beers Ⓗ
Previously the Albion Hotel, belonging to Castletown Brewery, now a back-street local, owned by Bushy's Brewery. An outside cobbled drinking area at the front has tables and chairs in the summer. The pub is named after the licensee's favourite Blackburn football team, and contains a room dedicated as a shrine to the players. The pub contains photos of many old Isle of Man pubs, and note the unusual handpumps – fire brigade brass branch pipes which came from the former fire station. ♨⊠≉(IMR)

Samuel Webbs
Marina House, 9-11 Marina Road, IM1 2HG
✪ 12-11 (midnight Fri & Sat); 12-11 Sun
☎ (01624) 675595
Courage Directors Ⓗ
Large free-standing building situated at the north end of the busy shopping street, known as The Strand. Locals can remember when it was a jewellers owned by the Webb family from which it gains its name. The one room is separated into three distinct areas. 'Sam's' is popular with members of the building trade and sports fans; different sports are shown in different bars simultaneously. The unusual patio door opens up the front of the building on warm days extending the views of the sea. Tourists and locals alike watch the passenger ferries come and go. Also for summer days, picnic benches are situated outside the front of the building. ✿

LAXEY

Mines Tavern
Captains Hill, IM4 7AA
✪ 11-11 (midnight Fri & Sat); 11-11 Sun
☎ (01624) 861484
Bushy's Bitter; Okells Mild, Bitter; guest beer Ⓗ
Adjacent to the delightful Laxey electric tram station and Snaefell mountain railway terminus, the Ramsey to Douglas bus stops

nearby. This popular, family-run tourist pub is also favoured by locals. Enter the public bar from the garden and you will find a counter resembling a Manx Electric Railway car. The pub offers home-cooked food (including speciality 'sizzling platters'). The attractive gardens have various types of seating, some of which is under cover for less favourable weather. There is also a safe children's play area. Trips to the summit of Snaefell and the Lady Isabella Waterwheel are recommended. ♨✿◑⊟⊖(MER)

Queen's Hotel
New Road, IM4 7BP (300 yds S of Laxey centre)
✪ 12-midnight; 12-11.30 Sun
☎ (01624) 861195
Bushy's Ruby Mild, Castletown Bitter, Bitter; guest beers Ⓗ
Busy local situated on the edge of Laxey, popular with locals and bike enthusiasts all year round. The interest in bikes is reflected in the numerous photos and pictures adorning the walls. Several depict the late Joey Dunlop, a famous TT rider. The Queen's has live music every Saturday and hosts barbecues on summer weekends on the large patio at the rear of the building. Toasties are available all year, as is B&B accommodation. However, you will need to book at least a year in advance for TT weeks. The enthusiasm for real ale is reflected in the large collection of beermats and pump labels mounted above the bar. When you have finished sampling the ale you can sit on the attractive iron benches and await the No. 3 bus to Douglas. ✿⌂⊖(MER) ♣P

OLD LAXEY

Shore Hotel
IM4 7DA
✪ 5 (12 summer)-11 (midnight Fri, Sat & summer); 12-11 Sun
☎ (01624) 861509
website: www.welcometo/shorehotel.com
Old Laxey Bosun Bitter Ⓗ
Situated on the banks of the River Laxey, this popular local has an ideal location for summer drinking. You can sit outside the Old Laxey Brewery on picnic benches next to the river, with nothing to disturb you apart from occasional harassment by the local ducks. Lunches are served during the summer. The building consists of one large room decorated with faded fishing boat pictures and fishing artefacts. There is a real fire in winter and comfortable traditional seating adding to the cosy atmosphere. The Shore Hotel has one of the largest selections of single malts on the island. The adjoining brewery producing Bosun Bitter is fully operational after recent flooding and tours will be available. ♨◑♣P

PEEL

Peveral Hotel
Quayside, IM5 1AY
✪ 12-midnight; 12-midnight Sun
☎ (01624) 842381
Okells Mild, Bitter Ⓗ
This well-known, family-run pub with open fires in two rooms, is situated on the picturesque quayside. Enjoy the views of Peel Hill and ancient castle, fishing boats and the easy walk to the safe, sandy shore.

A small museum is next door and it is a short walk to the world-famous House of Mananan Heritage Centre. You can also see Manx kipper curing by appointment. Fishermen frequent this pub which is close to the bus station and one mile from a campsite.
🏠Q❀⊕&▲♣

White House ⊘
2 Tynwald Road, IM5 1LA
(150 yds from bus station)
🕐 11-midnight (1am Fri & Sat); 11-midnight Sun
☎ (01624) 842252
Bushy's Bitter; Flowers Original; Okells Mild, Bitter; Taylor Landlord; guest beers Ⓗ
Multi-roomed town pub with a snug, public bar, pool room and music room, all around a central bar. Musicians meet most Saturday evenings to play Gaelic music at this popular local pub. A genuine free house, it hosts occasional 'Poets and Pints' nights. Serving one of the best pints on the island (awards adorn the walls), this family-run pub has remained unaltered since the 1930s. It boasts a large collection of old local photos. 🏠Q➤❀⊕▲♣P

PORT ERIN

Bay Hotel
Shore Road, IM9 6HC (on Port Erin lower promenade, beside beach)
🕐 12-midnight; 12-midnight Sun
☎ (01624) 832084 website: www.bushys.com
Bushy's Ruby Mild, Bitter, Old Bushy Tail, seasonal beers; guest beers Ⓗ
Large, established pub fronting on to the lower promenade and beach. It has a traditional feel with timber floors in an unspoilt interior, encompassing bar, lounge and separate vaults. A full range of Bushy's beers and guests are offered, together with a selection of imported bottled beers. A varied food menu is available; the atmosphere is friendly and welcoming. 🏠⊕&≠(IMR)✄

Falcon's Nest Hotel
Station Road, IM9 6AF (Spaldrick Promenade jct)
🕐 10.30-11 (midnight Fri & Sat); 10.30-11 Sun
☎ (01624) 834077
Bushy's Bitter; Okells Bitter; guest beers Ⓗ
Spacious, residential hotel situated at the junction of Station Road and Spaldrick Promenade, just a short walk from the steam railway station and bus station. There are two bars and cask ale is served in the front lounge bar which offers commanding views over the bay. Food is available in the bars and dining room. 🏠Q⊨⊕≠(IMR)

PORT ST MARY

Albert
Athol Street, IM9 5DS (next to harbour)
🕐 11-midnight (1am Fri & Sat); 12-midnight Sun
☎ (01624) 832118
Bushy's Bitter; Okells Bitter, seasonal beers; guest beers Ⓗ
Free house situated next to the harbour and bus terminus to Douglas. The bar offers modern pub games and satellite TV. The cosy lounge has an adjacent bistro-style eating area. Food is served in the bar and lounge during the day (up to 7.30pm). The Albert Hotel can get very busy at weekends. 🏠Q⊕⊕

RAMSEY

Trafalgar ⊘
West Quay, IM8 1DW
🕐 11-11 (midnight Fri & Sat); 12-3, 8-11 Sun
☎ (01624) 814601
Cains Mild, Bitter; guest beers Ⓗ
Small, cosy, quayside pub popular with young and old locals and visiting yachtsmen. A pleasant time can be had enjoying a good beer, watching a busy harbour operating. Note the interesting display of black and white photographs of bygone days around the harbour. The Trafalgar has been local CAMRA Pub of the Year twice. Choose varied lunchtime food from the inexpensive menu; no meals served Sunday or Monday. Also on West Quay the Ellan Vannin sells real ale. ➤⊕⊖(MER)♣

SULBY

Sulby Glen Hotel ⊘
Main Road, IM7 2HR (Sulby crossroads, A3)
🕐 12-midnight (1am Fri & Sat); 12-11 Sun
☎ (01624) 897240
Bushy's Bitter, seasonal beers; Okells Bitter; guest beers Ⓗ
Large roadside hotel on the famous Sulby Straight section of the TT course and in the centre of the village. The hotel was recently refurbished to give extra space in the bars which display many photographs of TT riders through the ages. The pub is closely linked to a German motorcycle club in Waltrop, with annual visits. Once the 'local' of a Manx giant who lived nearby 150 years ago, it is a former local CAMRA Pub of the Year.
🏠➤❀⊨⊕⊕&▲♣P

UNION MILLS

Railway Inn
Main Road, IM4 4NE (on Douglas-Peel road)
🕐 12-11 (midnight Fri & Sat); 12-10.30 Sun
☎ (01624) 853006 website: www.iomrailwayinn.com
Boddingtons Bitter; Okells Mild, Bitter; guest beers Ⓗ
Very pleasant village watering-hole, a true free house, this former Castletown Brewery tied house has been in the same family for over 100 years, and has never had a man's name over the door. Its former names include the Grapes and the Prince of Wales. It is an ideal spot to watch the TT races. A quiet pub without juke box, pool table or fruit machines, certainly a pub to quaff a good pint. Look out for original memorabilia in this Manx CAMRA Pub of the Year 2000.
🏠Q❀♣P

She drank good ale, good
 punch and wine,
And lived to the age of
 ninety-nine.

Epitaph to **Rebecca Freeland**
(died 1741) at Edwalton,
Nottinghamshire

Old Ale and Barley Wine

THEY ARE OFTEN LINKED in beer tastings, but Old Ale and Barley Wine are two separate styles. The modern linkage is the result of both styles being predominantly winter ones. Unlike barley wine, old ale does not necessarily have to be a beer of fearsome strength. Centuries ago, it acquired its maturity, flavour, ripe condition and smooth flavour as the result of ageing in great oak tuns. Today ageing is more likely to be in bottle or brewery conditioning tank. Historically, it was a beer brewed for blending with fresh pale and brown ales. Old or 'stale' was one of the key constituents of the early porter beers: see section on porter and stout.

Improve

The vatting of beer has long since disappeared, and the finest versions of old ale are now those that mature and improve on their yeasty sediment in bottle. Others are produced for the winter and Christmas period, cask-conditioned ales that gain in palate and flavour as the weeks go by. Among fine examples of the style are the prize-winning Old Tom brewed by Robinson's of Stockport. The 8.5% beer has been brewed since 1838 and is almost as old as the brewery. It's the result of a mash of Halcyon and Pipkin pale and crystal malts, flaked maize and torrefied wheat, with caramel for colour. It's boiled with Golding and Northdown hops and dry hopped in the cask with a further addition of Goldings. One of the best-known and certainly most widely available old ales in Theakston's Old Peculier (5.6%), while a classic of the style is the bottle-conditioned Prize Old Ale produced by George Gale of Horndean. It's matured in the brewery for a minimum of six months and is given a further addition of yeast when bottled. The 9% beer will improve in bottle for several years.

Counter

Barley wine came into use in the 18th century as brewers attempted to counter the impact of imported French wine. The new technologies of the industrial revolution made it possible to make strong but pale beers. The increasing use of lightly cured pale malt and the scientific culturing of pure strains of yeast gave brewers far greater control over the production of strong beers. These beers were variously described as October beers (brewed in the spring and stored until the autumn), malt liquors and malt wines. Eventually they were brought together under the generic title of barley wine.

The leading British barley wine for many years was Bass No 1, available only in small nip bottles. No 1 indicated that, at 10.5%, it was the strongest of all Bass's beers. It has been restored by the Museum Brewing Company in Burton-on-Trent, which specialises in recreating old Bass beers. The profile of barley wine was given a boost in 1995 when Norman's Conquest (7%) beat all-comers to pick up the Champion Beer of Britain award for the Cottage Brewery in Somerset. Other fine examples of the style are Fuller's Golden Pride (9.2%) – casks of the beer are rolled around the brewery yard to keep the yeast working – and J W Lees' 11.5% Harvest Ale, an annual bottled vintage. Visitors to the US are advised to seek out the 12% Big Foot barley wine brewed by the Sierra Nevada Brewery in California.

The Breweries

The Beer Seller
the home of good beer

BEER SELLER
CASK BEER SPECIALIST

The Beer Seller was formed over 20 years ago to supply cask beer to the local free trade market. We are still doing the same today, but despite the name, the Beer Seller now sells cask beer, wine and spirits (through its Folio division), lager and soft drinks to over 18,000 outlets across England. It is one of the leading wholesalers, but most people will know it for its excellent reputation for cask beer.

Cask beer & the future

The Beer Seller is certain of a future for cask beer, with choice and quality being the two key aspects that will both drive traffic in outlets and ensure that customers will come back for more. Consumers are being more selective about their drinks, but cask beer drinkers put it into the same group as red wine and Guinness as a choice, and are willing to pay more for a good pint. When choosing a beer, it is no longer for that funny or bizarre name. The trends for guest beers are moving towards quality regional brands and seasonal/special event beers from proven brewers with an ale heritage.

Quality & Cask Marque membership

Without paying attention to quality at each level of the chain the consumer will not get a perfect pint. That is why, at the Beer Seller,

we take quality to extra lengths. The company is currently the first company to work towards achievement of the Cask Marque Distributors Charter.

The Beer Seller has chilled storage at each cask-handling depot that no other distributor has installed at this time. It also issues quality guidance to staff and customers - such as Cask to Glass, an informative booklet detailing all angles on cask beer, including a recap quiz that could be used for training purposes. Additionally, the distribution system ensures that beer does not endure more than the recommended three movements.

Quality is also key for our customers. The Beer Seller offers a recommendation and subsidises the costs for Cask Marque accreditation, to enable our customers to reap the benefits and publicise their excellent quality standards.

Beer Festivals

We all know that beer festivals can be a great trade generator for pubs and a great social occasion for local communities, particularly when organised by CAMRA, and the Beer Seller is here to help. Working with a local representative, a pub or organisation can put together a large or small beer festival. Beer Seller will arrange the sourcing of beers, pump clips, help with equipment where necessary, and provide tasting notes and other point of sale. Themed off the shelf beer festivals, quality themes such as CAMRA Award Winners, SIBA beers and wacky themes like vicars & tarts, black and white, are ideal for pubs that are not used to beer festivals, or want an event to support other local activities or to drive sales at quiet times.

Guest beer programmes

The Beer Seller runs monthly guest programmes with at least 20 beers available on a national basis. There is a brewery of the month featuring two or three of their key beers, plus two price buster beers. The programme features all kinds of beers including seasonal, special event, award winners and favourites. The guest programme is available to all pubs that are open to buying a guest beer. Empty belly posters for guest ales are always available from your local depot on request.

Each local depot will also hold stock of our range of national and local favourites that are available all year round. This selection of beers will be able to support any pub at any time of the year.

Working with brewers to support regular stockists

There is more to selling cask beer than just the beer. Our excellent relationships with over 200 breweries means that we can provide you with the best deal, including point of sale, sales support and promotions, as well as being competitive on price.

> **"Thanks to the carefully chosen portfolio offered by the Beer Seller, it's possible to enjoy a wide range of beers from all parts of the country".**
> **Roger Protz**

With excellent service levels from local support teams and the brewers, the Beer Seller truly is first for cask – for regular stockists or for a community beer festival, the Beer Seller is there to help. For more information on any of the above please contact your local Beer Seller Depot:

The Beer Seller Depot Contacts

Birmingham	0121 505 6228	Leeds	0113 2319125
Bodmin	01208 77822	London	020 8838 4200
Bristol	01454 413712	Newbury	01635 40136
Chandlers Ford	02380 252299	Paignton	01803 559181
Chesterfield	01246 453333	Peterborough	01733 230167
Colchester	01206 577272	Sunderland	0191 521 3477
Cromer	01263 513545	Warrington	01925 212300
Hailsham	01323 847888	Wincanton	01963 34264

How to use The Breweries section

Breweries are listed in alphabetical order. The Independents (regional, smaller craft brewers and brew-pubs) are listed first, followed by the Nationals and finally the major non-brewing Pub Groups. Within each brewery entry, beers are listed in increasing order of strength. Beers that are available for less than three months of the year are described as 'occasional' or 'seasonal' brews. Bottle-conditioned beers are also listed: these are beers that have not been pasteurised and contain live yeast, allowing them to continue to ferment and mature in the bottle as a draught real ale does in its cask.

Symbols

⎕ A brew-pub: a pub that brews beer on the premises.

◆ CAMRA tasting notes, supplied by a trained CAMRA tasting panel. Beer descriptions that do not carry this symbol are based on more limited tastings or have been obtained from other sources.
Tasting notes are not provided for brew-pub beers that are available in fewer than five outlets, nor for other breweries' beers that are available for less than three months of the year.

⎕ A CAMRA Beer of the Year in the past three years.

▮ One of the 2003 CAMRA Beers of the Year, a finalist in the Champion Beer of Britain competition held during the Great British Beer Festival at Olympia in August 2003, or the Champion Winter Beer of Britain competition held earlier in the year.

☺ The brewery's beers can be acceptably served through a 'tight sparkler' attached to the nozzle of the beer pump, designed to give a thick collar of foam on the beer.

⊗ The brewery's beer should NOT be served through a tight sparkler. CAMRA is opposed to the growing tendency to serve southern-brewed beers with the aid of sparklers, which aerate the beer and tend to drive hop aroma and flavour into the head, altering the balance of the beer achieved in the brewery.

Abbreviations

OG stands for original gravity, the measure taken before fermentation of the level of 'fermentable material' (malt sugars and added sugars) in the brew. It is a rough indication of strength and is no longer used for duty purposes.

ABV stands for Alcohol by Volume, which is a more reliable measure of the percentage of alcohol in the finished beer. Many breweries now only disclose ABVs but the Guide lists OGs where available. Often the OG and the ABV of a beer are identical, ie 1035 and 3.5 per cent. If the ABV is higher than the OG, ie OG 1035, ABV 3.8, this indicates that the beer has been 'well attenuated' with most of the malt sugars turned into alcohol. If the ABV is lower than the OG, this means residual sugars have been left in the beer for fullness of body and flavour: this is rare but can apply to some milds or strong old ales, barley wines, and winter beers.

*The Breweries Section was correct at the time of going to press and every effort has been made to ensure that all cask-conditioned and bottle-conditioned beers are included.

The Independents

*Indicates new entry since last edition; SIBA indicates member of Society of Independent brewers; IFBB indicates member of Independent Family Brewers of Britain

ABBEY ALES SIBA

Abbey Ales Ltd, The Abbey Brewery, Camden Row, Bath, Somerset, BA1 5LB
Tel (01225) 444437
Fax (01225) 443569
E-mail am@abbeyales.co.uk
Website www.abbeyales.co.uk
Shop via website
Tours by arrangement

⊠ Abbey Ales is the first and only brewery in Bath for nearly 50 years and is the initiative of brewery sales and marketing manager Alan Morgan. He supplies more than 80 regular accounts within a 20-mile radius of Bath Abbey; selected wholesalers deliver the beers nationally. One tied house, the Star Inn, Bath, is listed on CAMRA's national inventory of heritage pubs; it was Bath and Borders CAMRA pub of the year for the second time in 2000-2001. The one regular cask beer, Bellringer, has won several CAMRA Beer of Festival awards and was a finalist in the 2001 Champion Beer of Britain competition. Seasonal beers: Bath Star (ABV 4.5%, spring), Chorister (ABV 4.5%, autumn), Resurrection (ABV 4.6%, April-June), Twelfth Night (ABV 5%, Christmas).

Bellringer
(OG 1042, ABV 4.2%) ◲◈
A notably hoppy ale, light to medium-bodied, clean-tasting, refreshingly dry, with a balancing sweetness. Citrus, pale malt aroma and dry, bitter finish. Consistent. Amber-gold in colour.

ABBEY BELLS*

Abbey Bells Brewery, 5 Main Road, Hirst Courtney, Selby, North Yorkshire, YO8 8QP
Tel (07940) 726658
E-mail abbeybells@aol.com
Website under construction
Tours by prior arrangement, in small numbers

⊠ The brewery was launched by Jules Dolan in July 2002 and was financed by the sale of his motorbike. The 2.5-barrel plant has cellar tanks from the defunct Brigg Brewery and other parts from a dairy maker in Congleton. The gantry that holds the mash tun came from a flour mill in Goole. The budget was so tight that even the pumpclips for the beer had to be made on a lathe that Jules inherited from his father. Some 25 outlets are supplied direct. Seasonal beers: Santa's Stocking Filler (ABV 4.5%), Black Satin (ABV 6.2%), winter.

Monday's Child
(OG 1035, ABV 3.7%)
An easy-drinking session beer, made with Maris Otter malt and Goldings hops. Pale and refreshing. The late addition of Goldings imparts a subtle banana flavour.

Hoppy Daze *(OG 1041, ABV 4.1%)*
Similar in colour to Monday's Child, the beer is hopped with Target, giving a wonderful hoppy tang.

Cordelia's Gift *(OG 1042, ABV 4.3%)*
The combination of Pearl and chocolate malts and Fuggles hops imparts a flavour reminiscent of dandelion and burdock.

Original Bitter *(OG 1044, ABV 5.1%)*
Made from Pearl malt with a dash of crystal and flavoured with Goldings hops.

ABBEYDALE SIBA

Abbeydale Brewery Ltd, Unit 8, Aizlewood Road, Sheffield, South Yorkshire, S8 0YX
Tel (0114) 281 2712
Fax (0114) 281 2713
E-mail admin@abbeydalebrewery.co.uk
Website www.abbeydalebrewery.co.uk

⊠ Founded in 1996 by Patrick Morton, originally from Kelham Island (qv), Abbeydale is based in an industrial unit in the south of the city in the Abbeydale area, which takes its name from Beauchief Abbey, a medieval monastery built by the murderers of Thomas Becket; hence the ecclesiastical theme of the beers. Early 2003 saw a major expansion, with the brew length increased from eight to more than 14 barrels, and a rise in the number of outlets supplied across the North and Midlands. Seasonal beers: Sanctuary (ABV 4.2%, Oct-Dec), Vespers (ABV 4.2%, April-June), Belfry (ABV 4.5%, Jan-March), Prophecy (ABV 4.5%, July-Sept), Resurrection (ABV 4.8%, April-June: awaiting Soil Association certificate as an organic beer), Redemption (ABV 5%, Jan-March), Mother's Ruin (ABV 5.1%, Oct-Dec), Ascension (ABV 5.3%, July-Sept), Hells Bells (ABV 5.8%, December).

Matins *(OG 1034.9, ABV 3.6%)*
Extremely pale and fully flavoured, but light in alcohol content, an excellent, hoppy session beer.

Best Bitter *(OG 1039, ABV 4%)*
A well-rounded bitter, reddish in colour, not too bitter, with lots of aromatic hops.

Moonshine *(OG 1041.2, ABV 4.3%)*
Pale premium beer balancing hints of sweetness and bitterness with full hop aromas. Pleasant grapefruit traces may be detected.

Absolution *(OG 1050, ABV 5.3%)*
Strong, pale, sweetish beer.

Black Mass *(OG 1065, ABV 6.6%)*
Strong black stout, quite bitter and dry but full-flavoured with a characteristic hop aroma.

Last Rites *(OG 1097, ABV 11%)*
A pale, strong barley wine bursting with flavour.

ADNAMS IFBB

Adnams plc, Sole Bay Brewery, Southwold, Suffolk, IP18 6JW
Tel (01502) 727200
Fax (01502) 727201
E-mail info@adnams.co.uk
Website www.adnams.co.uk
Shop 9-5

✖ The earliest recorded brewing on the site of Adnams was in 1345 by Johanna de Corby. The present brewery was taken over by George and Ernest Adnams in 1872 and turned into a public company in 1890. The Adnams family was joined by the Loftus family in 1902, and Adnams still has three members of the families working for the company: John Adnams, president, chairman Simon Loftus, and Jonathan Adnams, managing director. Adnams remains committed to brewing cask ale and unthemed pubs. Real ale is available in 84 of its 85 pubs, and it also supplies some 750 other outlets direct. New fermenting vessels were installed in 2001 to cope with increased demand. Seasonal beers: Regatta (ABV 4.3%, spring/summer), Tally Ho (ABV 7%, Christmas ✿), Oyster Stout (ABV 4.3%, autumn).

Bitter (OG 1036, ABV 3.7%) ✿✦
A definitive hoppy aroma with malty echoes introduces this copper-coloured bitter. This continues through to the initial taste where a hoppy bitterness competes for dominace with a noticeable malty sweetness. This satisfying balance of flavours continues through to a long, sustained finish that slowly turns to raspberry dryness.

Fisherman (OG 1047, ABV 4.5%)
Rich and complex, but clean and refreshing, deep copper-red ale. Roasted nuts and dark chocolate dominate the aroma, with lingering flavours of liquorice and dried fruits.

Broadside (OG 1049, ABV 4.7%) ✦✦
A mid-brown beer with a well-balanced flavour of fruit, malt and hops on a bitter-sweet base. The aroma is fruity, with some underlying malt and hops. Bitter fruit finish.

ALCAZAR SIBA

◻ **Alcazar Brewing Company,**
33 Church Street, Old Basford,
Nottingham, NG6 0GA
Tel/Fax (0115) 978 2282
E-mail dallen@alcazar.freeserve.co.uk
Website www.alcazarbrewingco.com
Tours by arrangement

✖ Alcazar Brewing Company was established in 1999 and is located behind its brewery tap, the Fox & Crown brew-pub. The name Alcazar is a Spanish word meaning palace, which relates to the crown in the brewery tap's name. The brewery is full mash with a 10-barrel brew length. Production is mainly for the Fox & Crown, with smaller quantities sold on demand to local free houses and beer festivals. Visitors are welcome at the brewery and regular tours are conducted on Saturdays, but prior arrangements are requested. Seasonal beer: Maple Magic (ABV 5.5%, winter); occasional beer: Alcazam (ABV 4.4%).

Black Fox (OG 1039, ABV 3.9%)
A dark ruby-coloured mild with distinctive fruit taste and aroma.

Alcazar Ale (OG 1040, ABV 4%)
A traditional session ale made with a blend of English and North American hops; pale, full-flavoured with a fruity aroma and finish.

Nottingham Nog (OG 1046, ABV 4.2%)
A dark session ale brewed with five kinds of malt and three varieties of hops; rich and smooth with fruit tones and a palate-pleasing finish.

New Dawn (OG 1045, ABV 4.5%)
Golden ale made with North American hops that give a unique fruit aroma and crisp, malty taste.

Brush Bitter (OG 1050, ABV 4.9%)
An amber bitter with a well-rounded flavour, maltiness on the palate and a distinctive hoppy finish.

Vixen's Vice (OG 1052, ABV 5.2%)
A pale, strong ale with a malt flavour balanced by a clean, crisp, hop taste.

ALES OF SCILLY SIBA

Ales of Scilly Brewery, Higher Trenoweth, St Mary's, Isles of Scilly, TR21 0NS
Tel (01720) 422419
E-mail mark@alesofscilly.co.uk
Tours by arrangement: not always available because of small number of employees.

The brewery was established in 2001 and has expanded to a five-barrel plant. There are plans to bottle Scuppered. Eight outlets are supplied.

Maiden Voyage (ABV 4%)

Three Sheets (ABV 4.1%)

Natural Beauty (ABV 4.2%)

Scuppered (ABV 4.7%)

ALEWIFE

Alewife Brewery, Starston, Harleston, Norfolk, IP20 9NN
Tel (01379) 855267
E-mail AlewifeBrewery@yahoo.co.uk
Website www.alewifebrewery.co.uk
Shop: mail order service

A small brewery set up in 2000 by Jane Taylor, who had been home-brewing for 20 years. Her friends so admired her Xmas brew that they encouraged her to brew commercially. She concentrates on bottle-conditioned beer as casks are too heavy for her to handle, though she brews cask beer occasionally when she has help. She supplies one pub, several off-licences and also sells by mail order. The beers listed are all available in bottle-conditioned form and are suitable for vegetarians.

Harvest Ale (ABV 4.5%)
A full-bodied, amber-coloured bitter brewed using lightly crushed malts, roast barley and Wye Challenger hops. Carageen, a type of seaweed, is used to ensure beer clarity during the brewing process.

Dark Skies Stout (ABV 4.6%)
A smooth stout made with generous

amounts of chocolate malt and roasted barley to give a subtle bitterness.

Festival Ale *(ABV 6.5%)*
A smooth, dark, fruity ale brewed using chocolate malt and a mixture of the finest English hops, including Goldings. It is matured for several months before bottling.

Hunters Moon *(ABV 7%)*
A reddish-coloured, mildly hopped ale.

ALL NATIONS
See Worfield

ALNWICK ALES
See Hadrian

ALTRINCHAM
Altrincham Brewing Company, Old Market Tavern, Old Market Place, Altrincham, Cheshire, WA14 4DN Tel 0771 2033886 (mobile) (0161) 9277062 (pub) E-mail dave_ward@connectfree.co.uk

Brewing suspended.

AN TEALLACH*
An Teallach Ale Company, Camusnagaul, Dundonell, By-Garve, near Ullapool, Ross-shire, IV23 2QT. Tel/Fax (01854) 633306. E-mail anteallachale@dundonnell. freeserve.co.uk

Wilma and David Orr started brewing at Easter 2003. They produce 20 barrels a week and supply 30 to 40 outlets in the Highlands and Islands.

Beinnderag *(ABV 3.8%)*

An Teallach *(ABV 4.2%)*

ANGLO DUTCH SIBA
The Anglo Dutch Brewery, Unit 12, Savile Bridge Mill, Mill Street East, Dewsbury, West Yorkshire, WF12 6QQ Tel (01924) 457772 Fax (01924) 507444 E-mail info@anglo-dutch-brewery.co.uk Website www.anglo-dutch-brewery.co.uk
Tours by arrangement

Paul Klos (Dutch) worked as a manager for Mike Field (Anglo), who runs the Refreshment Rooms at Dewsbury Station. When they found the right location, a brewery was born. The equipment came from the Rat & Ratchet in Huddersfield. The location used to be a dyehouse and the metal beams that used to hold block and tackle to lift lids of dye pans have been cut up and welded to make a platform for the fermenter. The pallet racking that makes the brewing platform came from the dye house as well. Most beers contain wheat except for Spike and Tabatha, which contain lager malt. It is intended to start bottling in 2004.

Best Bitter *(ABV 3.8%)*

Kletswater *(OG 1039, ABV 4%)*
Pale coloured beer with a hoppy nose and a good hop and citrus fruit flavour. An excellent session beer, full-bodied and smooth with a short dry finish. Kletswater is the Dutch for waffle water. Next question: what is waffle water?

Mild Rabarber *(ABV 4%)* ◆
Light-coloured brown mild with a malty, fruity flavour and moderate hop character. Refreshing and light bodied.

Mitch's Brew *(ABV 4.1%)* ◆
Amber bitter with malty, fruity and floral overtones but not citrussy. Slightly dry.

Spike's on 't' Way *(OG 1040.5, ABV 4.2%)* ◆
Pale bitter with citrus/orange flavour and dry, fruity finish.

Spikus *(OG 1040.5, ABV 4.2%)*

Grizzly Ghost *(OG 1041, ABV 4.3%)* ◆
Full-bodied pale bitter.

Jasperus *(OG 1042, ABV 4.4%)*

Ghost on the Rim *(OG 1043, ABV 4.5%)* ◆
Pale, dry and fruity.

Supreme Spicus *(OG 1043, ABV 4.5%)*

At 't' Ghoul and Ghost *(OG 1048, ABV 5.2%)* ◆
Pale golden bitter with strong citrus and hoppy aroma and flavour. The finish is long, dry, bitter and citrus.

Tabatha the Knackered *(OG 1054, ABV 6%)* ◆
Golden Belgian-style Tripel. With strong fruity, hoppy and bitter character. Powerful and warming, slightly thinnish with bitter, dry finish.

ANN STREET
See Jersey.

ARCHERS
Archers Brewing & Wholesale Ltd, Penzance Drive, Swindon, Wiltshire, SN5 7JL Tel (01793) 879929 Fax (01793) 879489
Shop 9-5 Mon-Fri; 9-12 Sat
Tours by arrangement

⊗ Under new ownership since autumn 2001, Archers is fast approaching its 25th anniversary, and has consolidated its position as one of the premier regional breweries in the south. Its position in a former weigh house adjoining the Great Western Railway makes it a Victorian landmark. The beers have gained many awards, including the gold medal at the 1996 Brewing Industry International Awards. Beers are supplied to the local free trade on a direct basis and on a national basis to pub groups, other breweries and wholesalers. The company supplies 200 free trade outlets direct and via wholesalers. Seasonal beers: Spring Ale (ABV 4.2%, March-May), Summer Ale (ABV 3.5%, June-Aug), Autumn Ale (ABV 4.5%, Sept-Oct), Winter Warmer (ABV 5.2%, Nov-Feb). Special beers: Marley's Ghost (ABV 7%, Nov-Dec), Black Jack Porter (ABV 4.6%, Nov-Jan), Dark Mild (ABV 3.6%) March-May. Bottle-conditioned beer: Archers Golden.

Village Bitter *(OG 1036, ABV 3.6%)* 🍷◈
A dry, well-balanced beer, with a full body for its gravity. Malty and fruity in the nose, then a fresh, hoppy flavour with balancing malt and a hoppy, fruity finish.

Best Bitter *(OG 1040, ABV 4%)* ◈
Slightly sweeter and rounder than Village, with a malty, fruity aroma and pronounced bitter finish.

Special Bitter *(OG 1044, ABV 4.3%)*
Tawny in colour, full-flavoured and well-balanced. Brewed with a blend of traditional English hops.

Golden Bitter *(OG 1046, ABV 4.7%)* ◈
A full-bodied, hoppy, straw-coloured brew with an underlying fruity sweetness. A gentle aroma, but a strong, distinctive bitter finish.

Swindon Strong Bitter (SSB)
(OG 1052, ABV 5%)

ARKELLS IFBB SIBA

Arkell's Brewery Ltd, Kingsdown, Swindon, Wiltshire, SN2 7RU
Tel (01793) 823026
Fax (01793) 828864
E-mail arkells@arkells.com
Website www.arkells.com
Tours by arrangement

⊗ Arkells was established in 1843 and is now one of the few remaining breweries whose shares are all held by one family: managing director James Arkell is a great-great-grandson of founder John Arkell. Gradually expanding its tied estate, mainly along the M4 corridor, the brewery is committed to a continual programme of upgrading and refurbishment for its pubs. All 96 tied pubs serve real ale, which is also supplied direct to around 200 free trade accounts. Some of the malt comes from James Arkell's own farm. Fuggles and Goldings hops are used, with pale ale malt and crystal malt. There is a higher proportion of crystal malt in 3B and Kingsdown, which are 'parti-gyled', i.e. made from the same mash but then reduced with 'liquor' [water] to the required strength. Occasional/seasonal beers: Summer Ale (ABV 4%), Peter's Porter (ABV 4.8%), Noel Ale (ABV 5.5%, Christmas), JRA (ABV 3.8%).

2B *(OG 1032, ABV 3.2%)* ◈
Light brown in colour, malty but with a smack of hops and an astringent aftertaste. An ideal lunchtime beer, it has good body for its strength.

3B *(OG 1040, ABV 4%)* ◈
A medium brown beer with a strong, sweetish malt/caramel flavour. The hops come through strongly in the aftertaste, which is lingering and dry.

Kingsdown Ale *(OG 1052, ABV 5%)* ◈
A rich deep russet-coloured beer, a stronger version of 3B. The malty/fruity aroma continues in the taste, which has a hint of pears. The hops come through in the aftertaste where they are complemented by caramel tones.

ARRAN SIBA

The Arran Brewery Co Ltd, Cladach, Brodick, Isle of Arran, KA27 8DE
Tel (01770) 302353
Fax (01770) 302653
E-mail info@arranbrewery.co.uk
Website www.arranbrewery.com
Shop 10am-7pm in summer, reduced hours in winter
Tours by prior arrangement

☺ The brewery started production in 2000. It steadily increased production, rising to 100 barrels a week. Production of bottled beer has increased and a seasonal beer is planned. Some 70-80 outlets are supplied direct.

Ale *(OG 1038, ABV 3.8%)* ◈
An amber summer ale, typical of new wave Scottish beers. The predominance of the hop produces a bitter beer with a subtle balancing sweetness of malt and an occasional hint of roast.

Dark *(OG 1042, ABV 4.3%)* ◈
A well-balanced malty beer with plenty of roast and hop in the taste and a dry, bitter finish.

Blonde *(OG 1048, ABV 5%)* 🍷◈
A hoppy beer with substantial fruit balance. The taste is balanced and the finish increasingly bitter. An aromatic strong bitter that drinks below its weight.

ARUNDEL SIBA

Arundel Brewery Ltd,
Unit C7, Ford Airfield Industrial Estate, Ford, Arundel, W Sussex, BN18 0HY
Tel (01903) 733111
Fax (01903) 733381
E-mail arundelbrewery@telinco.co.uk
Tours by prior arrangement

⊗ Set up in 1992, the town's first brewery in 60 years, Arundel supplies around 100 outlets. Under new ownership from September 1998, Arundel continues to serve and increase its range of occasional and seasonal beers. Occasional ales are on sale for one month each. Seasonal beers: Footslogger (ABV 4.4%), Summer Daze (ABV 4.7%), Black Beastie (ABV 4.9%), Bullseye (ABV 5%).

Gauntlet *(OG 1035, ABV 3.5%)*
A light, refreshing session beer. The carefully selected blend of malt and hops produce a low gravity bitter with excellent initial flavour and a pleasant bitter finish.

INDEND

Castle (OG 1038, ABV 3.8%) ◆
A pale tawny beer with fruit and malt
noticeable in the aroma. The flavour has a
good balance of malt, fruit and hops, with a
dry, hoppy finish.

Gold (OG 1042, ABV 4.2%) ◆
A light golden ale with a malty, fruity
flavour and a little hop in the finish.

Classic (OG 1045, ABV 4.5%)
A special bitter with a good hop and fruit
aroma. The use of roast malt gives way to a
fruity, hoppy, bitter-sweet finish.

Celebration Stout (OG 1046, ABV 4.6%)

Stronghold (OG 1047, ABV 4.7%)
A smooth, full-flavoured premium bitter. A
good balance of malt, fruit and hops come
through in this rich brew.

Old Knucker (OG 1055, ABV 5.5%)

ASTON MANOR

**Aston Manor Brewery Co Ltd,
173 Thimble Mill Lane, Aston,
Birmingham, W Midlands, B7 5HS
Tel (0121) 328 4336
Fax (0121) 328 0139**
Shop 10-6 Mon-Fri; 10-1 Sat

Aston Manor owns the Highgate Brewery in
Walsall (qv). Its own plant concentrates on
cider. Beer is bottled at Highgate but is not
bottle conditioned.

ATLAS SIBA

**Atlas Brewery Ltd, Lab Road,
Kinlochleven, Argyll, PH50 4SG
Tel (01855) 831111.
Fax (01855) 831122
E-mail info@atlasbrewery.com
Website www.atlasbrewery.com**
Shop Open office hours
Tours by prior arrangement

⊗ Founded in 2002, Atlas is a 20-barrel
brewery in a 100 year-old listed Victorian
industrial building on the banks of the River
Leven. The emphasis – as the name Atlas
suggests – is on brewing more modern,
more international beers. Scottish malts
(whole grain) and local Highland water are
complemented by whole hops from five
different countries. Seasonal beers:
Meridian (ABV 4%, spring), Tempest
(ABV 4.9%, autumn).

Latitude (OG 1037, ABV 3.6%) ◆
Dry, bitter summer ale with an intense
hoppiness throughout. Refreshing with a
taste of grapefruit and a slightly astringent
finish.

Three Sisters (OG 1043, ABV 4.2%)

Wayfarer (OG 1044, ABV 4.4%)
Refreshing, golden pale ale, hoppy with
some malt leading to a dry bitter finish.

B&T

**B&T Brewery Ltd, The Brewery,
Shefford, Beds, SG17 5DZ
Tel (01462) 815080
Fax (01462) 850841
E-mail brewery@banksandtaylor.com
Website www.banksandtaylor.com**
Tours by arrangement

⊗ Banks & Taylor, founded in 1981, was
restructured in 1994 under the name B&T
Brewery and has continued to produce an
extensive range of beers, including monthly
special brews together with contract
brewing for wholesalers and individual
public houses. 60 outlets are supplied direct
and two pubs are owned. There is an
extensive range of seasonal beers. Bottle-
conditioned beers: Black Dragon Mild,
Edwin Taylor's Extra Stout,
Shefford Old Strong, Black Old Bat, Old Bat.

Two Brewers Bitter (OG 1036, ABV 3.6%)
Hoppy, amber-brown session beer.

Shefford Bitter (OG 1038, ABV 3.8%)
A pleasant, predominantly hoppy session
beer with a bitter finish.

Shefford Dark Mild
(OG 1038, ABV 3.8%) ◆
A dark beer with a well-balanced taste.
Sweetish, roast malt aftertaste.

Black Dragon Mild (OG 1043, ABV 4.3%)
Dark, rich in flavour, with a strong roast
barley finish.

Dragonslayer (OG 1045, ABV 4.5%) ◆
A straw-coloured beer, dry, malty and
lightly hopped.

Edwin Taylor's Extra Stout
(OG 1045, ABV 4.5%) ☐◆
A pleasant, bitter beer with a strong roast
malt flavour. Champion Beer of East Anglia
2001.

Shefford Pale Ale (SPA)
(OG 1045, ABV 4.5%) ◆
A well-balanced beer with hop, fruit and
malt flavours. Dry, bitter aftertaste.

Fruit Bat (OG 1045, ABV 4.5%)
Raspberry flavoured, hoppy fruit beer.

Shefford Old Strong (SOS)
(OG 1050, ABV 5%) ☐■◆
A rich mixture of fruit, hops and malt is
present in the taste and aftertaste of this
beer. Predominantly hoppy aroma.

Shefford Old Dark (SOD)
(OG 1050, ABV 5%)
SOS with caramel added for colour, often
sold under house names.

Black Bat (OG 1060, ABV 6%) ◆
A powerful, sweet, fruity and malty beer for
winter. Fruity, nutty aroma; strong roast
malt aftertaste.

Old Bat (OG 1070, ABV 7%) ◆
A powerful-tasting, sweet winter beer, with
bitterness coming through in the aftertaste.
Fruit is present in both aroma and taste.

BADGER IFBB

**Hall & Woodhouse Ltd, The Brewery,
Blandford St Mary, Dorset, DT11 9LS
Tel (01258) 452141
Fax (01258) 459528
E-mail info@badgerbrewery.com
Website www.badgerbrewery.com**
Shop 9-6 Mon-Sat.
Tours by arrangement

⊗ The company was founded in 1777 as the
Ansty Brewery by Charles Hall. Charles's son
took George Woodhouse into partnership
and formed Hall & Woodhouse. They

moved to their present site at Blandford St Mary in 1899. Trading under the Badger name, it owns 263 pubs in the south of England including the Gribble Inn brew-pub at Oving, West Sussex (qv), and supplies 700 outlets direct. In 2000, Hall & Woodhouse bought King & Barnes of Horsham and closed the brewery. It matches some of K&B beers, which are available throughout the Badger estate as well as the former Horsham company's 57 pubs. Seasonal beers: King & Barnes Festive (ABV 5.4%, winter), Fursty Ferret (ABV 4.4%, summer).

King & Barnes Sussex Bitter
(OG 1033, ABV 3.5%) ◈
A rather thin, malty session beer, with a little hoppiness. The malty aroma leads through a balanced flavour to a predominantly bitter finish. A beer in the Badger style rather than that of the former K&B brewery.

IPA *(OG 1034, ABV 3.6%)*
A pale beer, light, refreshing and pleasantly hoppy. Served with a creamy head.

Badger Best *(OG 1039, ABV 4%)* ◈
A fine best bitter whose taste is strong in hop and bitterness, with underlying malt and fruit. Hoppy finish with a bitter edge.

Tanglefoot *(OG 1047, ABV 5.1%)*
A full-bodied beer, pale straw in colour with a characteristic fruitiness, medium bitterness and a slightly spicy finish.

For Interbrew
Flowers IPA *(OG 1035, ABV 3.6%)*

Flowers Original Bitter
(OG 1043, ABV 4.3%)

BALLARD'S SIBA

**Ballard's Brewery Ltd, The Old Sawmill,
Nyewood, Petersfield, GU31 5HA
Tel (01730) 821301/821362
Fax (01730) 821742
E-mail info@ballardsbrewery.org.uk
Website www.ballardsbrewery.org.uk**
Shop 8-4 Mon-Fri
Tours by arrangement

⊗ Founded in 1980 at Cumbers Farm, Trotton, Ballard's has been trading at Nyewood (in W Sussex, despite the postal address) since 1988 and now supplies around 60 free trade outlets. Seasonal beers: Golden Bine (ABV 4.2%, spring), Wheatsheaf (ABV 5%, summer), On the Hop (ABV 4.5%, autumn), Foxy (ABV 9.3%, winter). Bottle-conditioned beers: Best Bitter, Nyewood Gold, Wassail, Foxy.

Midhurst Mild *(OG 1035, ABV 3.5%)*
Traditional dark mild, well balanced, refreshing, with a biscuity flavour.

Trotton Bitter *(OG 1036, ABV 3.6%)* ◈
Amber, clean-tasting bitter. A roast malt aroma leads to a fruity, slightly sweet taste and a dry finish.

Best Bitter *(OG 1042, ABV 4.2%)* ◈
A copper-coloured beer with a malty aroma. A good balance of fruit and malt in the flavour gives way to a dry, hoppy aftertaste.

Wild *(ABV 4.7%)*
A blend of Mild and Wassail.

Nyewood Gold *(OG 1050, ABV 5%)* ⊡◈
Robust golden brown strong bitter, very hoppy and fruity throughout, with a tasty balanced finish.

Wassail *(OG 1060, ABV 6%)* ◈
A strong, full-bodied, fruity beer with a predominance of malt throughout, but also an underlying hoppiness. Tawny/red in colour.

BANK TOP SIBA

**Bank Top Brewery, The Pavilion, Ashworth Lane, Banktop, Bolton, Lancs, BL1 8RA
Tel/Fax (01204) 595800**

⊛ Bank Top was established in 1995 by John Feeney. The brewery has enjoyed gradual expansion and relocated in 2002. The beers are supplied to 60-80 outlets locally. Seasonal beer: Santa's Claws (ABV 5%, Christmas).

Brydge Bitter *(OG 1038, ABV 3.8%)*

Game Set & Match *(OG 1038, ABV 3.8%)*

Flat Cap *(OG 1040, ABV 4%)*

Gold Digger *(OG 1040, ABV 4%)* ◈
Golden coloured, with a citrus aroma, grapefruit and a touch of spiciness on the palate and a fresh, hoppy citrus finish.

Dark Mild *(OG 1040, ABV 4%)*

Samuel Crompton's Ale
(OG 1042, ABV 4.2%) ◈
Amber beer with a fresh citrus-peel aroma. Well-balanced with hops and a zesty grapefruit flavour, and a hoppy, citrus finish.

The Haka *(OG 1042, ABV 4.2%)*
Brewed with New Zealand hops.

Outback Bitter *(OG 1042, ABV 4.2%)*
Brewed with Australian hops.

Old Slapper *(OG 1042, ABV 4.2%)*

Volunteer Bitter *(OG 1042, ABV 4.2%)*
Brewed with American hops.

Cliff Hanger *(OG 1045, ABV 4.5%)*

Smoke Stack Lightning *(OG 1050, ABV 5%)*

BANKS'S

**Wolverhampton & Dudley Breweries plc, Park Brewery, Bath Road, Wolverhampton, W Midlands, WV1 4NY
Tel (01902) 711811
Fax (01902) 329136
Website www.fullpint.co.uk**

⊛ Wolverhampton & Dudley Breweries, Britain's biggest regional brewer, successfully defeated a hostile takeover bid by the Pubmaster group in August 2001. Pre-empting the bid, W&D's management appeased the City of London with its own

get-tough stance. It sold Camerons of
Hartlepool (qv) to the neighbouring Castle
Eden Brewery, while Mansfield Brewery
closed at the end of 2001, with Mansfield
brands switched to Wolverhampton.
Marston's of Burton-on-Trent (qv) remains
in production. W&D has sold most of its
managed pubs, and in total some 200 jobs
have disappeared. Banks's was formed in
1890 by the amalgamation of three local
companies. Hanson's was acquired in 1943,
but its Dudley brewery closed in 1991 and
its beers are now brewed at Wolverhampton,
though Hanson's pubs maintain their own
livery. In 1992, W&D bought Camerons
Brewery and 51 pubs from Brent Walker. In
1999 W&D turned itself into a 'super
regional' through the acquisition of
Marston's and Mansfield. The W&D estate
numbers 1,763, and almost all the pubs
serve traditional ales, though the group has
phased out the use of oversized lined
glasses. There is also extensive free trade
throughout the country, particularly in
pubs and clubs. W&D concentrates on such
key brands as Banks's Original and Bitter,
and Marston's Pedigree.

Hanson's Mild Ale
(OG 1035, ABV 3.2%) ◆
A mid-to dark brown mild with a malty
roast flavour and aftertaste.

Mansfield Dark Mild
(OG 1035, ABV 3.45%)

Banks's Original
(OG 1036, ABV 3.35%) ◆
An amber-coloured, well-balanced,
refreshing session beer.

Riding Bitter *(OG 1035, ABV 3.55%)*

Banks's Bitter *(OG 1038, ABV 3.7%)* ◆
A pale brown bitter with a pleasant balance
of hops and malt. Hops continue from the
taste through to a bitter-sweet aftertaste.

Mansfield Cask Ale *(OG 1038, ABV 3.9%)*

BARGE & BARREL
See Eastwood & Sanders

BARNGATES SIBA
**Barngates Brewery Ltd, Barngates,
Ambleside, Cumbria, LA22 0NG
Tel/Fax (015394) 36575
E-mail barngatesbrewery
@drunkenduckinn.co.uk
Website www.drunkenduckinn.co.uk**
Tours by prior arrangement

⊗ Barngates Brewery started brewing in
1997 as a one-barrel plant in the Drunken
Duck inn. Expansion in 1999 saw a brand
new five-barrel plant installed. Barngates
supplies 55 outlets in Cumbria, 25 in
Lancashire and 10 in North Yorkshire.
Bottle-conditioned beer: Tag Lag.

Cat Nap *(OG 1036, ABV 3.6%)*
A pale bitter with a strong hop aroma. Well-
balanced bittering leads to a long dry finish.
A fruity, zesty character throughout.

Cracker Ale *(OG 1038, ABV 3.9%)*
Subtle hoppy aroma, clean, smooth and
refreshing, developing into a long bitter
finish.

Tag Lag *(OG 1044, ABV 4.4%)* ◆
Light, golden bitter, citrus hints in the
flavour with a slight dry finish.

Chester's Strong & Ugly
(OG 1050, ABV 5.2%)
Slightly fruity, well-balanced roasted malt
and hop flavours.

BARNSLEY
**Barnsley Brewery Co, Powerhouse Square,
Heritage Centre, Wath Road, Elsecar,
Barnsley, South Yorkshire, S74 8HJ
Tel/Fax Brewery (01226) 741009
Office (01226) 731313**

Barnsley Brewery went into liquidation in
the spring of 2003. It may be relaunched
but all existing stock was transferred to a
new company, BBD, in Blackpool. See
Blackpool Brewery.

BARTRAMS SIBA
**Bartrams Brewery, Rougham Estate,
Rougham, Bury St Edmunds,
Suffolk, IP30 9LZ
Tel (01449) 737655
E-mail captainbill@lineone.net**
Tours by arrangement

⊗ Marc Bartram started his brewery in 1999
and has built up a good trade with locals.
Thirty-five outlets are supplied direct. He
uses a five-barrel plant purchased from
Buffy's Brewery. He currently produces 10
barrels a week but hopes to double the
amount. There was a Bartrams Brewery
between 1894 and 1902 run by Captain Bill
Bartram and his image graces the pump
clips. After three years in an industrial unit,
Marc is converting a barn into a brewery
and retail outlet. All the beers will shortly be
available in bottle-conditioned form. Marld
and Captain's Stout are suitable for
vegetarians. Marc is seeking Soil Association
accreditation for his organic beers.

Marld *(OG 1034, ABV 3.4%)*
A traditional mild.

Premier Bitter *(OG 1037, ABV 3.7%)*

Little Green Man *(ABV 3.8%)*
Made with organic ingredients.

Red Queen *(OG 1039, ABV 3.9%)*

Pierrot *(OG 1040, ABV 4%)*

Green Man *(ABV 4%)*
An organic beer, using West Country floor-
malted Maris Otter malt, New Zealand hops
and coriander.

Bees Knees *(OG 1042, ABV 4.2%)*

Jester Quick One *(OG 1044, ABV 4.4%)*
A darker than average best bitter that is
more malty than hoppy, with hints of fruit
in the aroma.

Captain's Stout *(OG 1048, ABV 4.8%)*
Overall champion at Cambridge Beer
Festival 2002, Best in Class at Regional SIBA
AGM. Best in class at national SIBA AGM.

Captain Bill Bartrams Best Bitter
(OG 1048, ABV 4.8%)

Damson/Cherry Stout
(OG 1048, ABV 4.8%)

BARUM SIBA

**Barum Brewery Ltd, c/o The Reform Inn,
Pilton, Barnstaple, Devon, EX31 1PD
Tel (01271) 329994
Fax (01271) 321590
E-mail info@barumbrewery.co.uk
Website www.barumbrewery.co.uk**
Tours by arrangement

⊠ Barum started brewing in 1996 and a new five-barrel plant was installed in 2001 at the Castle Inn, George Nympton, South Molton. Distribution is primarily within Devon. Seasonal beer: Gold (ABV 4%, summer). Bottle-conditioned beers: Original, Breakfast, Challenger, Barnstablasta.

XTC *(OG 1039, ABV 3.9%)*

Jester *(OG 1042, ABV 4.2%)*

Original *(OG 1044, ABV 4.4%)*

Breakfast *(OG 1050, ABV 5%)*

Barumberg *(OG 1051, ABV 5.1%)*

Challenger *(OG 1056, ABV 5.6%)*

Barnstablasta *(OG 1066, ABV 6.6%)*

For Thatch Inn, Croyde (seasonal):
Longboat *(OG 1038, ABV 3.8%)*

BATEMAN IFBB IBA

**George Bateman & Son Ltd,
Salem Bridge Brewery, Wainfleet All Saints,
Lincolnshire, PE24 4JE
Tel (01754) 880317
Fax (01754) 880939
E-mail jbateman@bateman.co.uk
Website www.bateman.co.uk**
Shop 11-4 daily
Tours By arrangement

⊠ A family-owned brewery established in 1874 by the present chairman's grandfather, Batemans is committed to brewing cask ale. To underscore this commitment, it opened a new brewhouse in 2002. The beers are sold throughout the country. Alongside the award-winning core brands, there is a large portfolio of seasonal and occasional beers. A visitor centre includes the fascinating Brewing Experience that allows visitors to follow the brewing system from malting to fermentation and cask filling. Batemans owns 68 pubs all serving cask ale. The seasonal beer range changes from year to year. Seasonal/Speciality ales: Loxley's Liquor (ABV 4.7%, Jan-Feb), Excalibur (ABV 4.4%, March-April), Hooker (ABV 4.5%, March-April), Victory Ale (ABV 5.2%, April), Godiva's Gold (ABV 4%, May-June), Summer Swallow (ABV 3.9%, May-Aug), Jewel in the Crown (ABV 4.5%, June), Yella Belly Organic Beer (ABV 4.2%, June), Marie Celeste (ABV 4.6%, July-Aug), Salem Porter (ABV 4.7%, Oct-May), Owd Nessie (ABV 5%, Nov), Rosey Nosey (ABV 4.9%, Dec). Bottle-conditioned beers: Yella Belly, Combined Harvest, XXXB, Victory Ale, Rosey Nosey.

Dark Mild *(OG 1032, ABV 3%)* ▥⬚◆
Characteristic orchard fruit and roasted nut nose with hops evident. One of the classic mild ales, although the lasting bitter finish may not be entirely true to type; nevertheless, a ruby-black gem.

Blackbeerd *(OG 1037, ABV 3.6%)*
A rich flavour is imparted from the roasted and chocolate malts, balanced with hops to give a lasting bitter-sweet finish.

XB Bitter *(OG 1037, ABV 3.7%)* ◆
A mid-brown balanced session bitter with malt most obvious in the finish. The taste is dominated by the house style apple hop, which also leads the aroma.

Lincolnshire Yella Belly Organic
(OG 1042, ABV 4.2%)
Organic malt and hops combine to produce a clean, refreshing, crisp pale ale with a rich spicy hop aroma and fruit character, with vanilla as a finishing taste.

Combined Harvest *(OG 1044, ABV 4.4%)*
A unique multi-grain blend of malted barley, oats, rye and wheat. Grainy tasting with a delightful floral start and finish.

Salem Porter *(OG 1047, ABV 4.7%)* ⬚◆
Ruby black with a brown tint to the head. The aroma is liquorice with a subtle hint of dandelion and burdock; the initial taste is hoppy and bitter, with a mellowing of all the elements in the finish.

XXXB *(OG 1048, ABV 4.8%)* ◆
A brilliant blend of malt, hops and fruit on the nose with a bitter bite over the top of a faintly banana maltiness that stays the course. A russet-tan brown classic.

BATH SIBA

**Bath Ales Ltd, (Admin) Hare on the Hill,
Dove St, Kingsdown, Bristol, BS2 5LK
Tel Office (0117) 9071797
Fax Office (0117) 9095140
E-mail Hare@bathales.co.uk
Website www.bathales.com/co.uk**
Tours by arrangement

⊠ Bath Ales started brewing in 1995, formed by two former Smiles brewers and a Hardington brewer. They began with rented equipment at the Henstridge Brewery near Wincanton, moved premises and upgraded to a full steam, 15-barrel plant in 1999. Situated between Bath and Bristol, all beer deliveries are direct to 100-plus outlets. Wholesalers are used in a limited way. Six pubs are owned, all serving cask ale. Bottle-conditioned beer: Gem (ABV 4.8%). Seasonal/occasional beers: Spa Extra (ABV 5%), Festivity, Rare Hare (ABV 5.2%).

Special Pale Ale (SPA)
(OG 1037, ABV 3.7%) ◆
Gold/yellow in colour, this is a light-bodied, dry, bitter beer. Pale and lager malts and citrus hop aroma. Long, pale, malty, bitter finish with some fruit and a slight sweetness. Refreshing, clean and complex.

Gem Bitter *(OG 1041, ABV 4.1%)* ◆
Well-balanced and complex, this medium-bodied bitter is malty (pale and crystal with a tiny hint of chocolate), fruity and hoppy throughout. Amber-coloured, it is drier and more bitter at the end.

Barnstormer *(OG 1045, ABV 4.5%)* ▥◆
Malt (roast and chocolate), hop and fruit aroma, with a similar taste. Mid-brown, well-balanced and smooth, with a complex malty and bitter, dry finish.

Festivity *(OG 1050, ABV 5%)* ⬚◆
Dark copper-brown, with crystal and roast

chocolate malt, hoppy and black cherry aroma and taste. Complex and full-bodied, there is some sweetness but it is bitter and quite dry with more chocolate and roast flavour in the finish.

BATHAM IFBB

Batham (Delph) Ltd, Delph Brewery, Delph Road, Brierley Hill, West Midlands, DY5 2TN
Tel (01384) 77229
Fax (01384) 482292
E-mail info@bathams.com
Website www.bathams.co.uk

⊛ A classic Black Country small brewery established in 1877 and now in its fifth generation of family ownership, run by Tim and Matthew Batham. Batham's sympathetic programme of upgrading and refurbishment in its tied estate has been rewarded by winning CAMRA's 1996 Joe Goodwin Award for pub refurbishment for the Vine, one of the Black Country's most famous pubs, and the site of the brewery. The brewery celebrated its 125th anniversary in 2002. Second place Best Bitter, West Midlands Beer of Year competition 2002. The company has 10 tied houses and supplies around 25 other outlets. Such is the demand for Batham's Bitter that the beer is stored in giant hogsheads. Seasonal beer: XXX (ABV 6.3%, Dec).

Mild Ale *(OG 1036.5, ABV 3.5%)* ◆
A fruity, dark brown mild with a malty sweetness and a roast malt finish.

Best Bitter *(OG 1043.5, ABV 4.3%)* 🍴🏠◆
A pale yellow, fruity, sweetish bitter, with a dry, hoppy finish. A good, light, refreshing beer.

BATTERSEA SIBA

The Battersea Brewery Co. Ltd.,
43 Glycena Road, London, SW11 5TP
Tel/Fax (020) 7978 7978
E-mail Stephen.nockolds@btclick.com
Tours by arrangement

Founded in 2001 by Stephen Nockolds to supply pubs in London and the South-east, the five-barrel plant is used to brew beer without adjuncts or chemicals. Stephen plans to introduce a range of seasonal and other speciality beers in the future.

Battersea Bitter *(OG 1042, ABV 4%)* ◆
A light drinking bitter with a clean finish.

BAZENS'* SIBA

Bazens' Brewing Co Ltd, Unit 6,
Knoll Street Industrial Estate,
Salford, M7 2BL
Tel (0161) 708 0247
Fax (0161) 708 0248
E-mail enquiries@bazensbrewery.co.uk
Website www.bazensbrewery.co.uk
Tours by arrangement

Richard Bazen, former head brewer at Bridgewater and then Phoenix breweries, set up Bazens' Brewery with his wife Jude in Swinton, near Manchester, in 2002. In March 2003 they moved to Salford, sharing plant and premises with the new Facers Brewery (qv) in an enterprise called the Salford Brewery Syndicate. No pubs are owned, but some 50 outlets are supplied direct. Seasonal beers are produced throughout the year.

Black Pig Mild *(OG 1037, ABV 3.6%)* 🍴◆
A dark brown beer with malt and fruit aromas. Dark roast and chocolate flavours, with an underlying bitterness, lead to a dry, malty aftertaste.

Pacific *(OG 1039, ABV 3.8%)*

Flatbac *(OG 1042, ABV 4.3%)*

Best Bitter *(OG 1045, ABV 4.5%)*

Knoll's Porter *(OG 1053, ABV 5.2%)*

TRADITIONAL BEERS
BAZENS' BREWERY
for modern tastes

BEARTOWN SIBA

AP Club, Beartown Brewery, Station Road, Holmes Chapel, Cheshire, CW4 8AA
Tel (01477) 537274
Fax (01477) 535439
E-mail steve@beartown42.freeserve.co.uk
Website www.beartownbrewery.co.uk

Congleton's links with brewing can be traced back to 1272, when the town received charter status. Two of its most senior officers at the time were Ale Taster and Bear Warden, hence the name of the brewery. During 1999/2000 the brewery acquired two pubs, the Beartown Tap in Congleton and the White Bull in Rossendale, and in 2001 the Navigation in Stockport. Seven pubs are now owned. The Navigation was previously an all-keg outlet and is now serving the full range of Beartown ales, plus a selection of Belgian, German and other bottled beers. The brewery also operates a private members' club at Holmes Chapel, Cheshire, where a range of the brewery's ales are served. The brewery will move to larger premises within Congleton in 2003 or 2004, while the office will remain in nearby Holmes Chapel at one of the tied outlets. The plan is to extend the tied estate by two to three outlets a year during the course of the next three years. Beartown supplies 50 outlets direct. Seasonal beers: Goldie Hops (ABV 3.5%), Santa's Claws (ABV 4.5%), IBA (ABV 4.8%), Blarney Bear (ABV 4.8%), Bruins Ruin (ABV 5%).

Ambeardextrous *(ABV 3.8%)*
Dark mild.

Ginger Bear *(ABV 4%)*
The flavours from the malt and hops blend with the added bite from the root ginger to produce a superbly quenching finish.

Bear Ass *(OG 1038, ABV 4%)* ◆
Dark ruby-red, malty bitter with good hop nose and fruity flavour with dry, bitter, astringent aftertaste.

Kodiak Gold *(ABV 4%)* ⬚◆
Well-balanced, straw-coloured and very drinkable with citrus fruit and hops aroma, and sharper bitter, clean, astringent aftertaste.

Bearskinful *(ABV 4.2%)* ◆
A tawny, malty beer, with a clean hop finish.

Polar Eclipse *(ABV 4.8%)* ◆
A smooth and roasty dark stout, with light hoppy notes and dry, bitter finish.

Wheat Beer *(OG 1050, ABV 5%)* ◆
A dry and bitter wheat beer. Initial fruitiness in aroma and taste with good wheat malt flavours. Long-lasting dry aftertaste.

Black Bear *(ABV 5%)* ⬚◆
Dark brown strong mild, some roast and malt flavours, with a mellow sweetish finish.

BECKSTONES*

Beckstones Brewery, Upper Beckstones Mill, The Green, Millom, Cumbria, LA18 5HL
Tel (01229) 775294
Tours by arrangement

⊗ Beckstones started brewing in December 2002 using equipment bought from the closed High Force Brewery. Owner David Taylor is supplying nearby free houses.

Bitter *(OG 1040, ABV 3.7%)*

Best Bitter *(OG 1045, ABV 4.2%)*

BEECHAM'S

Beecham's Bar & Brewery, St Helen's College, Water Street, St Helens, WA10 1PZ
Tel (01744) 623420
Fax (01744) 623400/412
Website www.sthelens.ac.uk/college/facilities /beechams.asp
Tours by arrangement

◉ Beecham's Brewery is a training establishment within St Helens College of Further Education. The brewing course has a recognised certificate validated by the National Open College Network. The bar and brewery are part of St Helen's College and courses are offered in Brewing and On-licensed Premises Management. Seasonal beers: Noir (ABV 4.5%, Oct-March), Epiphany (ABV 4.5%, Jan-Mar).

Crystal Wheat Beer *(OG 1048, ABV 5%)*
Light, fruity wheat beer with an aroma of citrus fruits, clean, hoppy palate, and a dry finish.

BEER ENGINE SIBA

⬚ **Beer Engine, Newton St Cyres, Exeter, Devon, EX5 5AX**
Tel (01392) 851282
Fax (01392) 851876
Website www.thebeerengine.co.uk
E-mail peterbrew@aol.com
Tours by arrangement

◉ Beer Engine, run by Peter and Jill Hawksley, started brewing in 1983 next to the Barnstaple branch railway line. The

brewery is visible behind glass downstairs. It uses the finest malts from Tuckers of Newton Abbot and quality English hops from Charles Faram of Newland. Two other outlets are supplied regularly and the beers are also distributed via agencies. Seasonal beers vary from year to year, but include Porter (ABV 4.8%), and Whistlemas (ABV 7.3%).

Rail Ale *(OG 1037, ABV 3.8%)* ◆
A straw-coloured beer with a fruity aroma and a sweet, fruity finish.

Piston Bitter *(OG 1043, ABV 4.3%)* ◆
A mid-brown, sweet-tasting beer with a pleasant, bitter-sweet aftertaste.

Sleeper Heavy *(OG 1052, ABV 5.4%)* ◆
A red-coloured beer with a fruity, sweet taste and a bitter finish.

Brewed for Agricultural Inn, Exeter
Speke Easy *(ABV 3.8%)*

BELHAVEN

Belhaven Brewing Co Limited, Dunbar, East Lothian, EH42 1RS
Tel (01368) 864488
Fax (01368) 865640
E-mail info@belhaven.co.uk
Website www.belhaven.co.uk
Shop open during tours.
Tours by arrangement

◉ Belhaven Brewery is located in Dunbar, some 30 miles east of Edinburgh on the beautiful East Lothian coast. The brewery lays claim to being the oldest independent brewery in Scotland and one of the oldest in Britain. Its history as a commercial brewery is well documented back to 1719, although it is probable that a brewery existed on site since at least the middle ages and is on the site of a former monastery where brewing took place. Belhaven owns 40 tied pubs and has about 2,500 direct accounts.

60/- Ale *(OG 1030, ABV 2.9%)* ⬚◆
A fine but virtually unavailable example of a Scottish light. This bitter-sweet, reddish-brown beer is dominated by fruit and malt with a hint of roast and caramel, and increasing bitterness in the aftertaste.

70/- Ale *(OG 1038, ABV 3.5%)* ◆
A fine Scottish ale. This pale brown beer has malt and fruit and some hop throughout, and is increasingly bitter-sweet in the aftertaste.

Sandy Hunter's Traditional Ale
(OG 1038, ABV 3.6%) ◆
A distinctive, medium-bodied beer named after a past chairman and head brewer. An aroma of malt and hops greets the nose. A hint of roast combines with the malt and hops to give a bitter-sweet taste and finish.

80/- Ale *(OG 1040, ABV 4.2%)* ◆
One of the remaining Scottish 80 Shillings, with malt the predominant flavour characteristic, though it is balanced by hop and fruit. Roast and caramel play a part in this complex beer. The soubriquet 'the claret of Scotland' hints at the depth and complexity of the flavours.

St Andrew's Ale *(OG 1046, ABV 4.9%)* ◆
A bitter-sweet beer with lots of body. The malt, fruit and roast mingle throughout with hints of hop and caramel.

For Maclay:
Maclay Signature (OG 1038, ABV 3.8%)
A pronounced malty note is followed by a digestive biscuit flavour. The beer has a late addition of Styrian and Goldings hops.

Kane's Amber Ale (ABV 4%)
A hoppy aroma gives way to a malty, yet slightly bitter flavour.

Wallace IPA (ABV 4.5%)
A classic IPA in both colour and style, with a long, dry finish.

Golden Scotch Ale (ABV 5%)
Brewed to an original Maclay's recipe, the emphasis is firmly on malt.

BELVOIR SIBA

Belvoir Brewery Ltd, Woodhill, Nottingham Lane, Old Dalby, Leicestershire, LE14 3LX
Tel/Fax (01664) 823455
E-mail sales@Belvoir-brewery.go-plus.net
Website www.belvoirbrewery.co.uk
Tours occasionally by arrangement

Belvoir (pronounced 'beaver') Brewery was set up in 1995 by Colin Brown, who previously brewed with Shipstone and Theakston. Long-term expansion has seen the introduction of a 20-barrel plant that can produce 50 barrels a week. Bottle-conditioned beers are now being produced using in-house bottling equipment. More than 100 outlets are supplied. Seasonal beers: Whippling Golden Bitter (ABV 3.6%, spring/summer), Peacock's Glory (ABV 4.7%, spring/summer), Old Dalby (ABV 5.1%, winter). Bottle-conditioned beers: Beaver Bitter, Peacock's Glory (ABV 4.7%), Old Dalby.

Mild Ale (OG 1034, ABV 3.4%)

Star Bitter (OG 1039, ABV 3.9%)
A beer designed to replicate the bitter flavour of the old Shipstone's Bitter.

Beaver Bitter (OG 1043, ABV 4.3%)
A light brown bitter that starts malty in both aroma and taste, but soon develops a hoppy bitterness. Appreciably fruity.

Gordon Bennett (OG 1041, ABV 4.1%)

BEOWULF SIBA

Beowulf Brewing Company, Chasewater Country Park, Craft Units 3 & 4, Pool Road, Brownhills, Staffs, NS8 7LN
Tel/Fax (01543) 454067
E-mail beowulfbrewing@yahoo.co.uk

After six successful years producing Birmingham's only real ale in a converted shop, the Beowulf Brewing Company continues to flourish and moved to new premises in 2003. Beowulf's beers appear as guest ales in the central region and all across the country. Seasonal beers: autumn and winter – Hurricane (ABV 4%, autumn and winter), Glutlusty (ABV 4.5%), Finn's Hall Porter (ABV 4.7%), Dragon Smoke Stout (ABV 4.7%), Blizzard (ABV 5%), Grendal's Winter Ale (ABV 5.8%); spring and summer – Wergild (ABV 4.3%), Fifty Winters (ABV 4.4%), Wuffa (ABV 4.5%), Mercian Blade (ABV 4.5%), Gold Work (ABV 5.1%).

Beorma (OG 1038, ABV 3.9%)
A pale session ale with a malty hint of fruit giving way to a lingering bitterness.

Noble Bitter (OG 1039, ABV 4%)
Gold colour, fruity aroma, hoppy taste with a dry finish.

Wiglaf (OG 1043, ABV 4.3%)
A golden bitter, with a malty flavour married to a pleasing bitterness, with three hop varieties used.

Swordsman (OG 1045, ABV 4.5%)
Pale gold, light fruity aroma, tangy hoppy flavour. Faintly hoppy finish.

Heroes Bitter (OG 1046, ABV 4.7%)
Gold colour, malt aroma, hoppy taste but sweetish finish.

Mercian Shine (OG 1048, ABV 5%)
Pale gold colour, citrus flavour with a full body and hoppy, dry finish.

BERROW SIBA

Berrow Brewery, Coast Road, Berrow, Burnham-on-Sea, Somerset, TA8 2QU
Tel (01278) 751345
Off licence 9-9
Tours by arrangement, limited numbers

The brewery started brewing in 1982. With the introduction of Topsy Turvy, its success was soon established and it remains very popular. Berrow Porter has also made its mark and is produced all year round. Berrow supplies 12 outlets direct. Seasonal beers: Christmas Ale (ABV 5%, winter), Carnivale (ABV 4.6%, Nov-Dec).

Best Bitter/4Bs (OG 1038, ABV 3.9-4%)
A pleasant, pale brown session beer, with a fruity aroma, a malty, fruity flavour and bitterness in the palate and finish.

Berrow Porter (OG 1047, ABV 4.6-4.7%)

Topsy Turvy (OG 1055, ABV 6%)
A gold-coloured beer with an aroma of malt and hops. Well-balanced malt and hops taste with a hoppy, bitter finish with some fruit notes.

BIG LAMP

Big Lamp Brewers, Grange Road, Newburn, Newcastle upon Tyne, NE15 8NL
Tel (0191) 2671689 Fax (0191) 2677387
E-mail brewers@biglampbrewers.freeserve.co.uk
Website www.biglampbrewers.com
Tours by arrangement

Big Lamp Brewers started in 1982 and relocated in 1997 to a 55-barrel former water pumping station. It is the oldest micro-brewery in the North-east of England. Twelve outlets are supplied and two pubs are owned. Seasonal/occasional beers: Sunny Daze (ABV 3.6%), Keelman Brown (ABV 5.7%), Old Genie (ABV 7.4%), Blackout (ABV 11%) g.

Bitter (OG 1039, ABV 3.9%)
A clean-tasting bitter, full of hops and malt, a hint of fruit, with a slightly dry aftertaste.

Double M (OG 1043, ABV 4.3%)

Summerhill Stout *(OG 1044, ABV 4.4%)* ◈
A tasty, rich, ruby stout with a lasting rich
roast feel and character. A malty mouthfeel
with a lingering finish.

Prince Bishop Ale
(OG 1048, ABV 4.8%) ▢◈
A golden-coloured, well-balanced fruity
beer. Plenty of hop flavours and strong
bitterness, with a spicy dry finish.

Premium *(OG 1052, ABV 5.2%)* ◈
A well-balanced, flavoursome bitter with a
big nose full of hops. The sweetness lasts
into a mellow, dry finish.

Embers *(OG 1055, ABV 5.5%)*

Blackout *(OG 1100, ABV 11%)* ◈
A strong bitter, fortified with roast malt
character and rich maltiness. Try it for its
mouthfeel and lasting bitterness.

BIRD IN HAND
See Wheal Ale Brewery

BITTER END
✇ **Bitter End brew-pub,**
15 Kirkgate, Cockermouth,
Cumbria, CA13 9PJ
Tel (01900) 828993
Email mike.askey@ talk21.com
Website www.visitcumbria.com/bitter

The brewery was founded, along with the
pub, in 1995. Brewer Mike Askey was
helped by Peter Yates, founder of Yates
Brewery, to put together the brewing kit;
Peter also supplied the brewing expertise. In
2001, Mike went into the long-distance
lorry-driving business, and barmaid Nicola
Farmer became Cumbria's first brewster
(woman brewer) and has expanded the
range. The brewery has a one-barrel capacity
but there are plans to increase this to two
barrels and to install a bigger gas-fired copper.

Old Neddy *(ABV 3.6%)*

Cocker Snoot *(ABV 3.8%)*

Farmers Ale *(ABV 3.8%)* ◈
A pale brown, slightly thin, malty, bitter,
fruity and sweet beer with a slight
astringency in the finish.

Wheat Beer *(ABV 4.1%)*

Call Out *(ABV 4.2%)*
Brewed to raise funds for Cockermouth
Rescue Team.

Czechumberland *(ABV 4.5%)*

Cuddy Lugs *(ABV 4.7%)* ◈
A malty aroma and sweet start quickly lead
to lingering bitter flavours.

Full English *(ABV 5%)*

Wordsworth 6X *(ABV 5%)*

Skinner's Old Strong *(ABV 5.5%)*

BLACK BULL
✇ **Black Bull (Haltwhistle Brewery),**
Market Square, Haltwhistle,
Northumberland, NE14 0BL
Tel (01434) 320463

Seasonal beers: Dark Mild (ABV 3.5%),
Fat Boys Bitter (ABV 3.7%), Captain O'Neill's

Intrepid Stout (ABV 3.8%), 1555 (ABV
4.4%), Special (ABV 4.6%), ESB (ABV 5.5%).

Bitter *(ABV 3.8%)*

Beastly Bitter *(ABV 4.5%)*

Bishop Ridley's Ale *(ABV 4.7%)*

BLACK DOG
Black Dog Brewery,
St Hilda's Business Centre, Whitby,
North Yorkshire, Y022 4EU
Tel (01947) 821464, 07785 541917(m)
Fax (01947) 603301
E-mail black_dog@lineone.net
Website www.synthesys.co.uk/black-dog

⊛ The Black Dog Brewery was established in
1997. Sales grew steadily and the beers
developed a loyal following but were never
able to achieve a sales volume that made
production viable. The brewery closed in
2001, but the Black Dog Brewery Company
continues and all beers are now produced
under licence by Hambleton Ales (qv).
Orders can be placed with Black Dog or
Hambleton. All beers are suitable for
vegetarians. Seasonal beers: Scallywag (ABV
3.6%, summer), First Out (ABV 4%,
summer), Synod (ABV 4.2%, spring),
Whitby Jet (ABV 5%, winter).

Scallywag *(OG 1036, ABV 3.6%)*
A light, hoppy summer session beer.

Whitby Abbey Ale *(OG 1036.7, ABV 3.8%)*
A light, hoppy bitter.

Schooner *(ABV 4.2%)*

Rhatas *(OG 1043.2, ABV 4.6%)*
A dark, malty bitter.

BLACK ISLE SIBA
Black Isle Brewery Ltd, Old Allangrange,
Munlochy, Ross-shire, IV8 8NZ
Tel (01463) 811871
Fax (01463) 811875
E-mail greatbeers@blackislebrewery.com
Website www.blackislebrewery.com
Shop 10-6 daily, closed Sundays in winter
Tours by prior arrangement

⊠ Black Isle Brewery was set up in 1998 in
the heart of the Scottish Highlands. The
five-barrel plant is based in converted farm
buildings on the Black Isle. The company
concentrates on organic production: the
beers have Soil Association certification,
while the bottle-conditioned beers are

certified by both the SA and the Vegetarian Society. Bottled beers are available by mail order to anywhere in mainland Britain. One pub is owned and 20 outlets are supplied. Bottle-conditioned beers: Wheat Beer (ABV 4.5%), Scotch Ale (ABV 4.5%), Porter (ABV 4.5%), Blonde (ABV 4.5%).

Yellowhammer *(OG 1042, ABV 4%)* ◆
A classic straw-coloured summer ale. Intense aroma of citrus fruits and hops, which is maintained through to the dry, bitter finish.

Red Kite *(OG 1041, ABV 4.2%)* ◆
A crisp, amber-coloured ale, steeped with Goldings hops to create a well-balanced citrus and malt-flavoursome ale. Bright, amber, with a light toasted orange aroma.

Wagtail Porter *(ABV 4.5%)*

Hibernator Wheat Beer *(ABV 4.5%)*

BLACK SHEEP

Black Sheep Brewery plc, Wellgarth, Masham, Ripon, North Yorkshire, HG4 4EN
Tel (01765) 689227 (brewery)
680100 (visitor centre)
Fax (01765) 689746
E-mail visitor.centre@blacksheep.co.uk
Website www.blacksheep.co.uk
Bistro & shop closed Mondays except July/Aug; closed Tuesdays in Jan & Feb. Tues 11am-5.30pm; Wed-Sat 11-11; Sundays 11am-5.30pm.
Tours by arrangement on shop opening days

☻ Set up in 1992 by Paul Theakston, a member of Masham's famous brewing family, in the former Wellgarth Maltings, Black Sheep has enjoyed continued growth and now supplies a free trade of around 600 outlets in the Yorkshire Dales and in an 80-mile radius of Masham, but owns no pubs. A limited number of wholesalers are also supplied. All the output is fermented in two-storey Yorkshire Square vessels; there are six slate ones and eight stainless steel Yorkshire 'round' squares. The Black Sheep complex includes video shows of the brewing process, a brewery shop, and a bistro.

Best Bitter *(OG 1039, ABV 3.8%)* ⌂◆
A hoppy and fruity beer with strong bitter overtones, leading to a long, dry, bitter finish.

Special Ale *(OG 1046, ABV 4.4%)* ◆
A well-rounded and warming bitter beer with a good helping of hops and fruit in the taste and aroma, leading to a moderately dry, bitter aftertaste.

Emmerdale Ale *(OG 1051, ABV 5%)*
New beer introduced in summer 2003. Brewed with pale malt, Goldings hops and demerara sugar, it has a blood-orange fruitiness, juicy malt and a hint of rum in the finish.

Riggwelter *(OG 1056, ABV 5.9%)* ◆
A fruity bitter, with complex underlying tastes and hints of liquorice and pear drops leading to a long, dry, bitter finish.

BLACKAWTON SIBA

Blackawton Brewery, Unit 7, Peninsula Park, Channon Road, Saltash, Cornwall, PL12 6LX
Tel (01752) 848777

Fax (01752) 848999
E-mail blackawtonbrewery@talk21.com
Tours by arrangement

⊗ What was once Devon's oldest operating brewery has relocated to Cornwall and moved to new premises in 2003. Run independently as a family business, the brewery is supplying ales to the free trade throughout Devon and Cornwall. A new range of bottle-conditioned beer was launched in 2001. Blackawton brews a house beer at ABV 4.8% for the Wetherspoon's outlet, the Isaac Merritt, in Paignton. Seasonal beers: Winter Fuel (ABV 5%, winter), Humbug (ABV 4.7%, Christmas), Golden Hind (ABV 4%), Dragon Heart (ABV 5%). Bottle-conditioned beers: Headstrong, Winter Fuel, Dragonheart (ABV 5%).

Original Bitter *(OG 1036, ABV 3.8%)*

Westcountry Gold *(OG 1038, 4.1%)*

44 Special *(OG 1044, ABV 4.5%)*

Exhibition Ale *(OG 1046, ABV 4.7%)*

Headstrong *(OG 1048, ABV 5.2%)*

BLACKDOWN

Blackdown Brewery Ltd, Units C5/C6, Dunkeswell Business Park, Dunkeswell, Honiton, Devon, EX14 0RA
Tel (01404) 891122 Fax (01404) 890097
E-mail swfabs@freeuk.com
Tours by arrangement

⊗ Blackdown is a purpose-built brewery, completed in 2002 by SW Fabrications, adjacent to its equipment production site at Dunkeswell. Seasonal beers will be developed. Approximately 60 outlets are supplied.

Bitter *(OG 1039, ABV 3.8%)*

Best *(OG 1041, ABV 4%)* ◆
A pale brown bitter with well-balanced malt and hops on the palate, and honey overtones, leading to a hoppy bitter finish.

Gold *(OG 1044, ABV 4.3%)*

Premium *(OG 1048, ABV 4.7%)*

BLACKPOOL

Blackpool Brewery Co Ltd, The Old Dairy, George Street, Blackpool, FY1 3RP
Tel (01253) 304999
Fax (01253) 304868
Tours by arrangement

☻ Blackpool is the first new brewery in the town for 30 years. The brewery produces up to 80 barrels a week and intends to produce a monthly beer in addition to its regular range. Seasonal beers: Lights Out (ABV 4.4%), Black Diamond (ABV 3.4%), Christmas Lights (ABV 4.3%), Crackle Porter (ABV 5%), Red Heart (ABV 4.1%). Blackpool also brews the beers for the closed Barnsley Brewery.

Golden Smile *(OG 1036.5, ABV 3.7%)*
Gold-coloured beer with a hoppy aroma; well-balanced with a fruity flavour.

Bitter *(OG 1039, ABV 4%)*
A golden beer with great depth of flavour.

BPA *(OG 1041, ABV 4.2%)*
A full-bodied, malty bitter with an agreeable flowery aroma.

For Barnsley Brewery:

Bitter *(OG 1038, ABV 3.8%)*

IPA *(OG 1041, ABV 4.2%)*

Black Heart Stout *(OG 1044, ABV 4.6%)*

Glory *(OG 1048, ABV 4.8%)*

BLANCHFIELDS

**Blanchfields, North Norfolk Brewery,
Orchard Workshops, Dereham Road,
Colkirk, Norfolk, NR21 7NU
Tel (01485) 578104
Fax (01485) 576039**
Tours by arrangement

⊠ After 20 years in the Bull, Fakenham, Graham Blanchfield moved his brewery to a small unit three miles out of town. He supplies half a dozen outlets plus beer festivals. Seasonal: White Bull Wheat Beer (ABV 4.4%, summer), Winter Warmer (ABV 6%, winter). Bottle-conditioned beers: Winter Warmer, Raging Bull Bitter.

Black Bull Mild *(OG 1040, ABV 3.6%)* ⬥
Light malty airs introduce this red-coloured, traditional mild. A dry fruity maltiness gives a hint of cocoa as the gentle malt base gives a counter-balance. Finish fades quickly although roasted malt remains.

Bull Best Bitter *(OG 1040, ABV 3.9%)* ⬥
A moderately bitter beer with a hoppy backbone that is not apparent in the delicate malty nose. Easy on the tongue, the finish contains a subtle blend of malt, hops and bitterness.

Raging Bull Bitter
(OG 1048, ABV 4.9%) ⬥
A heavy feeling beer redolent of fruits of the forest. Malt mixed with sweetness remains to the bitter end. The gentle malty aroma is at odds with the depth of flavour.

BLENCOWE SIBA

**Blencowe Brewing Company, c/o Exeter
Arms, Barrowden, Rutland, LE15 8EQ
Tel (01572) 747247
E-mail info@exeterarms.com
Website www.exeterarms.com**
Tours by arrangement

⊠ The brewery was set up in 1998 in a barn adjacent to the pub. The two-barrel plant was bought with the intention of supplying traditional beers for sale in the Exeter Arms bar and festivals only. An expansion programme in 2001 added one extra fermenting vessel but demand still outstrips production. Seasonal beers: Fun Boy Four (ABV 4.4%, summer), Bevin Boy (ABV 4.5%, winter), Spice Boys/Choir Boys/Naughty Boys (ABV 6%, Easter and Xmas), Fruity (ABV 3.6%, spring/summer).

Farmers Boy *(OG 1036, ABV 3.6%)*
A wheat beer.

Beach Boys *(OG 1040, ABV 3.8%)*
Fruit on the aroma; hoppy with a bitter finish.

Young Boy *(OG 1042, ABV 4.1%)*

Danny Boys *(OG 1046, ABV 4.5%)*
A rich, dark and creamy stout.

Golden Boy *(ABV 5%)*

BLEWITTS SIBA

**Blewitts Brewery Ltd, Loddiswell Road,
Kingsbridge, Devon, TQ7 4BP
Tel (01548) 855034,
Ship & Plough (01548) 852485
E-mail jeff@fredericks35.fsbusiness.co.uk**
Tours as part of Sorley Tunnel attraction

⊠ Steve Blewitt started his Kingsbridge brew-pub business in 1988 at the Ship and Plough. He has attracted national press coverage with amusing brews such as Hitler Blewitt for the VE day celebrations and Major Blewitt for the 1997 general election. Steve brews with local malted barley, Sorley Organic Farm's own pure spring water and cultures his own yeast. Seasonal beer: Blewitt's Top (ABV 5.5%, Christmas).

Premium *(ABV 3.8%)*

Wages *(ABV 4.5%)*

Head Off *(ABV 5%)*

BLINDMANS* SIBA

**Blindmans Brewery, Talbot Farm, Leighton,
nr Frome, Somerset, BA11 4PN
Tel/Fax (01749) 880094
E-mail blindmansbrewery@aol.com**
Tours by arrangement

Blindmans is located outside Shepton Mallet and started brewing in 2002, using the redundant five-barrel Tripple fff plant. Spring water is used to produce the unique flavours.

Golden Spring *(ABV 3.8%)*
A golden brew with light, flowery aroma.

Mine Beer *(ABV 4.2%)*
A copper-coloured ale with full body, leading to a long finish with fresh hoppy aroma.

BLUE ANCHOR SIBA

⇪ **Blue Anchor Inn, 50 Coinagehall Street,
Helston, Cornwall, TR13 8EL
Tel (01326) 562821
Fax (01326) 565765**
Tours by arrangement

⊠ Dating back to the 15th century, this is the oldest brewery in Cornwall and was originally a monk's hospice. After the dissolution of the monasteries it became a tavern brewing its own uniquely flavoured beer called Spingo at the rear of the premises. Brewing has continued to this day and people travel from all over the world to sample the delights of this wonderful inn untouched by time. The brewery has undergone complete refurbishment and the pub is also due for improvement, with careful attention to preserving its special character. Two outlets are supplied direct. Hosts Simon and Kim Stone have owned the Blue Anchor since 1993 and have done much to preserve its character. Seasonal: Spingo Bragget (ABV 6.1%, April-Oct), Spingo Easter Special (ABV 7.6%, two months), Spingo Christmas Special (ABV 7.6%, Dec-mid Jan). All draught beers are available in bottle-conditioned form. Bragget is a recreation of a medieval beer style.

Spingo Jubilee (IPA) *(OG 1045, ABV 4.6%)*

Spingo Middle *(OG 1050, ABV 5.1%)*
A deep copper-red beer with a big fruity

aroma of raisins and sultanas, a hint of vanilla and an earthy, peppery note from the hops. The palate is nutty, with a fruit cake note. The long bitter-sweet finish has a raspberry-like fruitiness balanced by the dryness of the hops.

Spingo Special *(OG 1066, ABV 6.7%)*
Darker than Middle with a pronounced earthy character on the nose balanced by rich fruit. Fruit and peppery hops dominate the mouth, followed by a big finish in which malt, fruit and hops vie for attention.

BLUE BELL

**Blue Bell Brewery Ltd,
Cranesgate South, Whaplode St Catherine,
Spalding, Lincs, PE12 6SN
Tel/Fax (01406) 540300**
Tours by arrangement

⊗ Ken Dixon, former head brewer at Bateman, and Mike Pilkington, landlord of the Blue Bell, started brewing in 2002. Ken has retired and Mike has carried on both the brewing and business since. He won the Peterborough Beer Festival New Brewer award with Olde Honesty in 2000. The brewery is behind the pub in a former potato store. One pub is owned and approximately 50 outlets are supplied direct.

Olde Session *(OG 1035, ABV 3.7%)*

Olde Honesty *(OG 1039, ABV 4.1%)*

Olde Fashioned *(OG 1045, ABV 4.8%)*

BLUE COW

▢ **Blue Cow Inn and Brewery, South Witham,
nr Grantham, Lincs, NG33 5QB
Tel/Fax (01572) 768432
E-mail Richard@thirlwell.fslife.co.uk
Website www.thebluecowinn.co.uk**
Tours by arrangement

☺ The Blue Cow opened in 1997 and is run by Dick Thirlwell, who brews only for the pub. The equipment came from Parish Brewery at Old Somerby in Leicestershire.

Thirlwell's Best *(OG 1040, ABV 3.8%)*

Thirlwell's Witham Wobler
(OG 1043, ABV 4.5%)

BLUE MOON

▢ **Blue Moon Brewery, Cock Inn, Watton
Road, Barford, Norfolk, NR9 4AS
Tel (01603) 757646**

⊗ Blue Moon stopped brewing for a while and its beer were contract-brewed by Buffy's. But Pete Turner moved his kit to the Cock Inn and has expanded his range. He supplies the Cock and some 60 free trade outlets. A new brewery, Spectrum (qv), run by Andy Mitchell, is now using the Blue Moon kit.

Easy Life *(OG 1040, ABV 3.8%)* ✦
A pale brown, easy-drinking session beer. Gentle toffee and malt aroma introduces a defined malty beginning. A soft fruity hoppiness supports the delicate balance of flavours to a swift but clean finish.

Sea of Tranquillity *(OG 1042, ABV 4.2%)* ✦
Solid malty taste matches the nose of this mid-brown, complex bitter. A bitter-sweet hoppiness develops to soften the malt that lasts to the long, rounded finish. Something for everyone.

Moon Dance *(ABV 4.7%)* ✦
A rich elderberry aroma is matched by a solid fruity taste in which the nutty malt flavours are slightly topped by well-defined hoppy overtones. Amber-coloured with a long, sustained finish.

Dark Side *(OG 1048)* ✦
Slightly scented, with fruit, hops and malt, this dark brown strong mild has plenty of body. A caramel sweetness gives balance to the dominant malty foundation. A long finish maintains the rich blend of flavours.

Hingham High *(OG 1050, ABV 5.2%)* ✦
A malt-based beer with a good balance of hops and bitterness. Roast notes provide background flavour as the finish lingers to a dry richness befitting the red-brown colouring. Dangerously smooth.

Milk of Amnesia *(OG 1055, ABV 5.2%)* ✦
A complex beer, mid-brown coloured, but the light malty nose gives little away. The taste has a port-like fluency, cinnamon and ginger jostle with pepper and citrus as the flavours continue to hold up well.

Liquor Mortis *(OG 1075, ABV 7.5%)* ✦
A heavy blackcurrant signature introduces this dark brown barley wine. A mature roast beginning counter-balances the fruity sweetness that carries through to a long, filling farewell with more than a hint of hops.

Total Eclipse *(ABV 9%)*

BLYTHE*

**Office: Blythe Brewery, 2 Rutherglen Close,
Rugeley, Staffs, WS15 2TA
Delivery: Blythe House Farm,
Hamstall Ridware, Rugeley,
Staffordshire, WS15 3QQ
Tel (01889) 586466 or 07773 747724
Fax (01889) 586466**

⊗ Robert Greenway started brewing in February 2003 in a converted barn on a farm in Hamstall Ridware. His beers are available in Northampton, as well as locally, as his best salesman is his brother, Phil, who also chairs the Northants branch of CAMRA. The equipment is a 2.5 barrel plant. Six outlets are supplied.

Chase Bitter *(OG 1041, ABV 4%)*

Blythe Bitter *(OG 1045, ABV 4.4%)*

BOAT SIBA

The Boat Brewery, Boat Lane, off Main Street, Allerton Bywater, Castleford, West Yorkshire, WF10 2BX
Tel (01977) 667788
Email ron@boatbrewery.co.uk
Website www.boatbrewery.co.uk
Tours by arrangement

☺ Founded in 1999 by Ron Ridout, Boat is in a building converted from a 19th-century stable block. The brewery supplies the Boat and the beers can be found in many parts of the country. Increased demand is ensuring continued expansion. Seasonal beer: Phesta (ABV 4.5%, winter).

Man in the Boat
(OG 1037, ABV 3.5%) 🍺🏷
A smooth, dark mild, full in flavour for its strength. Chocolate and dark fruit on the aroma and taste lead to a satisfying dry, fruity finish.

Black Pearl *(OG 1040, ABV 4%)*

Rattler *(OG 1041, ABV 4.3%)*

Yorkshire Belle *(OG 1045, ABV 4.5%)*

Eckythump *(OG 1045, ABV 4.5%)*

ELB *(OG 1047, ABV 4.7%)*

BODICOTE

⚲ **Bodicote Brewery, Plough Inn, Bodicote, Banbury, Oxon, OX15 4BZ**
Tel (01295) 262327
Fax (01295) 273010
Website www.banbury-cross.co.uk /bodicotebrewery
Tours by arrangement

⊗ Bodicote has been brewing since 1982 at the Plough, which has been in the Blencowe family since 1957. Jim and Doreen Blencowe retired in 2002 (Life Sentence was introduced to mark the occasion), leaving son Jim as head brewer and licensee with his wife, Denise. Seasonal beers: Bodicote Porter (ABV 4.7%, winter), Triple X (ABV 6.2%, winter).

Bitter *(OG 1035, ABV 3.3%)*

No 9 *(OG 1044, ABV 4.4%)*

Life Sentence *(ABV 5.1%)*

BOGGART HOLE CLOUGH

Boggart Hole Clough Brewing Co, Unit 13, Brookside Works, Clough Road, Moston, Manchester, M9 4SP
Tel/Fax (0161) 277 9666
E-mail mark@boggart-brewery.co.uk
Website www.boggart-brewery.co.uk
Tours by arrangement

☺ The brewery was set up in 2001 by Mark Dade, former brewer at Marble (qv), next to Boggart Hole Clough Park in North Manchester, which supplies timber from which the brewery's distinctive wooden pump clips are fashioned. Mark has increased the brew length to eight barrels. He has set up the Workshop Brewery that enables visitors to design and produce beers to their own specifications on a dedicated 2.5-barrel plant. Boggart Distribution was set up in 2003 and this allows Boggart beers

to be sold to more than 250 free houses throughout the country. Bottle-conditioned beer: Steaming Boggart (9%).

Boggart Bitter *(OG 1038, ABV 3.8%)*

Bog Standard *(OG 1040, ABV 4%)*

Log End *(OG 1040, ABV 4%)*

Angel Hill *(OG 1042, ABV 4.2%)*

Boggart Brew *(OG 1043, ABV 4.3%)*

Dark Side *(OG 1044, ABV 4.4%)*

Sun Dial *(OG 1047, ABV 4.7%)*

Steaming Boggart *(ABV 9%)*

BORVE

⚲ **Borve Brew House, Ruthven, Huntly, Aberdeenshire, AB54 4SG**
Tel (01466) 760343
E-mail grgrghughes@netscapeonline.co.uk
Tours by arrangement

Brewing suspended due to family illness.

BRAGDY CEREDIGION

Bragdy Ceredigion Brewery, Office: Bryn Hawk New Road, New Quay, Ceredigion, SA45 9SB
Brewery: Unit 2, Wervil Grange Farm, Pentregat, Ceredigion, SA44 6HW
Tel/Fax (01545) 561417
Tel (01239) 654888
E-mail brian@ceredigionbrewery.fs .business.co.uk
Website www.bestofruralwales.co.uk
Shop due to open summer 2003
Tours by arrangement

Bragdy Ceredigion Brewery is situated on the coastal belt of West Wales and housed in a converted barn on Wervil Grange Farm. The neighbouring unit has been taken over, which enabled a brewery shop to be opened. A family-run craft brewery established in 1997 by Brian and Julia Tilby, it produces bottle-conditioned and cask-conditioned ales. No chemical additives are used. The bottle-conditioned beers are suitable for vegans. The full-mash, five-barrel plant uses Maris Otter floor-malted barley, with Challenger, First Gold and Fuggles hops. An organic beer with certified pale malt and organic hops was added in 2001 and a range of organic fruit beers is planned. Bottle-conditioned beers: as for cask beers, save for the Spirit of the Forest. Occasional beer: Honey Beer (ABV 5%).

Ysbryd O'r Goeden/Spirit of the Forest
(OG 1036, ABV 3.8%)

Gwrach Ddu/Black Witch
(OG 1038, ABV 4%)

Draig Aur/Gold Dragon
(OG 1039, ABV 4.2%)

Barcud Coch/Red Kite
(OG 1040, ABV 4.3%)

Blodeuwedd/Flowerface organic beer
(OG 1043, ABV 4.5%)
Golden beer with a citrus hop and juicy malt aroma. Peppery hops dominate the palate, balanced by creamy malt, while the finish is hoppy and bitter with a continuing citrus fruit note.

Cwrw 2000/Ale 2000 *(OG 1049, ABV 5%)*

Yr Hen Darw Du/Old Black Bull
(OG 1058, ABV 6.2%)

BRAGDY YNYS MON SIBA

**Isle of Anglesey Brewery, Cae Cwta Mawr,
Talwrn, Anglesey, LI77 7SD**
Tel/Fax (01248) 723801
E-mail martyn@bragdyynysmonplus.com
Website angleseyale.co.uk
Shop available when brewery open. Please ring.
Tours by arrangement

☺ Martyn Lewis started brewing in summer
1999 in a converted outbuilding of a
farmhouse that faces the mountains of
Snowdonia. A bottling plant has been
added in a former stable. All the cask beers
are available in bottle-conditioned form and
are unfiltered. Organic Sosban Fach and all
bottled beers are made without finings and
are suitable for vegetarians and vegans.

Medra *(OG 1039, ABV 4%)* ✎
Attractive-looking, copper-coloured, soft,
malty bitter with hints of berries in the
short, dry finish.

Wennol *(OG 1040, ABV 4.1%)*
The name means Swallow. Golden toned
fruity beer with a lingering bitter finish.

Seuruik *(OG 1042, ABV 4.2%)*

Sosban Fach *(OG 1043, ABV 4.3%)*

Tarw Du *(OG 1045, ABV 4.5%)* ✎
The name means Black Bull. Inviting black
porter-style beer that has an earthy flavour
with some chocolate/coffee notes and a
long, dry aftertaste.

Amnesia *(OG 1048, ABV 4.9%)*
Full-bodied, rich hop and malt character
throughout with a delectable aftertaste.

BRAINS IFBB

**S A Brain & Company Ltd, The Cardiff
Brewery, Crawshay Street, Cardiff, CF10 5TR**
Tel (029) 2040 2060
Fax (029) 2041 4391
Email marketing@sabrain.com
Website www.sabrain.co.uk

☺ S A Brain began trading at the Old
Brewery in Cardiff in 1882 when Samuel
Arthur Brain and his uncle Joseph Benjamin
Brain purchased a site founded in 1713. The
company has remained in family ownership
ever since and in 1997 bought South Wales'
other leading independent, Crown Buckley,
formed from the merger of the Crown
Brewery of Pontyclun with Buckleys of
Llanelli. The full range of Brain's and
Buckley's ales are now produced at the
company's Cardiff Brewery (formerly
Hancock's), bought from Bass in 1999.
Brains owns 212 pubs, as well as having a
sizeable free trade, plus interests in hotel
and leisure projects in Wales and the West
Country. 390 outlets are supplied.

Buckley's IPA *(OG 1033.5, ABV 3.4%)*

Brains Dark *(OG 1035.5, ABV 3.5%)* ▣▥✎
A dark brown mild with a satisfying mix of
flavours, malt, caramel, roast and gentle
hop, bitter-sweet with a lasting finish. An
award-winning, traditional mild.

Brains Bitter *(OG 1036, ABV 3.7%)* ✎
A low aroma followed by a blend of malt,
hops and increasing bitterness, leading to a
clean, bitter finish.

Buckley's Best Bitter
(OG 1036.5, ABV 3.7%)

Arms Park *(OG 1040, ABV 4%)* ✎
Amber-coloured with a gentle malt and hop
aroma, leading to a mainly malty flavour
with some hop and fruit flavour. The finish
is malty with moderate bitterness.

SA *(OG 1042, ABV 4.2%)* ✎
Gentle, mainly malty aroma. Amber-colour
with a mellow blend of flavours, malt, hops
and fruit with a building moderate
bitterness.

Rev James *(OG 1045.5, ABV 4.5%)* ✎
Pale brown, faint fruit, hop and malt aroma.
Malt and fruit dominate the flavour with
hops in the background and moderate
bitterness.

BRAKSPEAR

See Burtonwood and Pub Companies.

BRANDY CASK

⛫ **Brandy Cask Pub & Brewery, Bridge
Street, Pershore, Worcs, WR10 1AJ**
Tel/Fax (01386) 552602
Tours by arrangement

☺ Brewing started in 1995 in a refurbished
bottle store in the garden of the pub. It was
run as a separate business until the
retirement of the brewer in 1998. Brewery
and pub now operate under one umbrella,
with brewing carried out by the
owner/landlord. Since the change, brewing
is restricted to the Brandy Cask but a return
to supplying other outlets in the future is
anticipated.

Whistling Joe *(ABV 3.6%)* ✎
Easy drinking, fruity and sweetish beer
balanced by a short, quenching dryness.
Some fruit remains in the shy finish.

Brandy Snapper *(ABV 4%)* ✎
A dry, lingering aftertaste to a smoothly
satisfying golden bitter. Subtle fruity hops
give the taste profile on the tongue and nose.

John Baker's Original *(ABV 4.8%)* ✎
A sweet tasting, fruity, deep brown beer
with contrasting bitter roast flavours. A thick
mouthfeel and a complex array of flavours.

Ale Mary *(ABV 4.8%)* ✎
Golden strong bitter with a sweet but subtle
blend of malt, fruit and hops and rapidly
fading bitter-sweet finish.

BRANSCOMBE VALE SIBA

**Branscombe Vale Brewery Ltd,
Great Seaside Farm, Branscombe,
Devon, EX12 3DP**
Tel/Fax (01297) 680511
E-mail branscombe.brew@btconnect.com
Tours by arrangement

⊠ The brewery was set up in 1992 by former
dairy workers Paul Dimond and Graham
Luxton in cowsheds owned by the National
Trust. Paul and Graham converted the
sheds and dug their own well. The NT has

built an extension for the brewery to ensure future growth. The first pub, the Old Inn at Kilmington, was purchased in 2002. Branscombe Vale currently supplies 60 regular outlets. Seasonal beers: Anniversary Ale (ABV 4.6%, Feb-March), Hells Belles (ABV 4.8%, winter), Summa That (ABV 5%, summer), Yo Ho Ho (ABV 6%, Christmas). Bottle-conditioned beer: Draymans (ABV 4.2%).

Branoc (OG 1035, ABV 3.8%) ◆
Light brown in colour, this is a good session bitter. Light fruity/malt taste and aroma with a well-rounded bitter finish.

Draymans (OG 1040, ABV 4.2%)
A mid-brown beer with hop and caramel notes, and a lingering finish.

BVB Own Label (OG 1046, ABV 4.6%) ◆
Reddy/brown-coloured beer with a fruity aroma and taste, and bitter/astringent finish.

BRECONSHIRE* SIBA

The Breconshire Brewery, Ffrwdgrech Industrial Estate, Brecon, Powys, LD3 8LA
Tel (01874) 623731 Fax (01874) 611434
E-mail info@breconshirebrewery.com
Website www.breconshirebrewery.com
Tours by prior arrangement

⊗ Breconshire was created by Howard Marlow in 2002 as part of CH Marlow, a wholesaler and distributor of ales in the South and West Wales areas for more than 30 years, and which owns eight pubs. The 10-barrel plant was commissioned in time to produce the first beers for Christmas 2002. To create 'Ales from the Heart of Wales', Optic malts are blended with a range of English whole hops by head brewer Justin 'Buster' Grant. Seasonal beers are planned.

Brecon County Ale (OG 1037.5, ABV 3.7%)

Golden Valley (OG 1042, ABV 4.2%)

Ramblers Ruin (OG 1050.5, ABV 5%)

BREWSTER'S SIBA

Brewster's Brewing Co Ltd, Penn Lane, Stathern, nr Melton Mowbray, Leicestershire, E14 4JA
Tel (01949) 861868
Fax (01949) 861901
E-mail sara@brewsters.co.uk
Website www.brewsters.co.uk
Tours by arrangement

⊗ Brewster is the old English term for a female brewer and Sara Barton is a modern example. A Master of Brewing trained at Heriot Watt Brewing School in Edinburgh, she worked with Courage before striking out alone. In 2000, she won the Small Business category of Country Living magazine's Enterprising Rural Women awards. Brewster's Brewery was set up in the heart of the Vale of Belvoir in 1998 with a five-barrel plant; this has since been upgraded to 10 barrels to cope with demand. Beer is supplied to some 250 pubs throughout central England and further afield via wholesalers. Seasonal beers: Claudia Wheat Beer (ABV 4.5%, summer), Wicked Women Range (ABV 4.8%), Frau Brau Lager (ABV 5%, summer), Brewster's Stocking (ABV 5.5%, Christmas), Vale T'Ales Range

(various ABVs). Bottle-conditioned beer: Vale Pale Ale.

Meek & Mild (OG 1034, ABV 3.5%)
A dark mild with a good balance of roast and fruit elements.

Hophead (OG 1036, ABV 3.6%)
A pale and hoppy brew, a very refreshing session beer with a fresh floral hop character.

Marquis (OG 1038, ABV 3.8%)
A pleasant quaffing beer with a light maltiness, balanced by a dry hoppy finish.

Monty's Mild (OG 1040, ABV 4%)
A full-bodied dark mild made with a blend of pale, chocolate and crystal malts as well as torrefied wheat. Lightly hopped with Progress.

Bitter (OG 1042, ABV 4.2%)
A well-balanced red ale with nutty malt character and aromatic hop flavour.

Vale Pale Ale (VPA) (OG 1045, ABV 4.5%)
A golden ale with a subtle biscuit malt flavour and citrus hop notes.

Wicked Woman (OG 1048, ABV 4.8%)
(Varies seasonally)

Belly Dancer (OG 1050, ABV 5.2%)
A rich tasting ruby beer with a blend of Bramling Cross and Fuggles hops.

BRIDGE OF ALLAN SIBA

Bridge of Allan Brewery Ltd, The Brewhouse, Queens Lane, Bridge of Allan, Stirlingshire, FK9 4NY
Tel (01786) 834555   Fax (01786) 833426
E-mail brewery@bridgeofallan.co.uk
Website www.bridgeofallan.co.uk
Shop 12-4 daily, Easter to October.
Tours by arrangement

⊛ Bridge of Allan Brewery was founded in 1997 and is located in the leafy Victorian spa town in the Forth Valley, with Stirling Castle, the Wallace Monument and the Trossochs close by. The five-barrel custom-built brewery, run by Douglas Ross, has recently been expanded. The owner also owns two village pubs and sells to more than 100 pubs in Scotland and also distributes to England and abroad via beer agencies. Seasonal beers: Sporran Warmer (ABV 4.8%, January), Summer Breeze (ABV 4.2%), Bramble Ale (ABV 4.2%, September), Aleoween (ABV 4.2%, October), Bronwyn Blonde Ale (ABV 5%, December). Bottle-conditioned beer: Brig o'Allan (ABV 4.2%) available only from brewery. Lomond Gold, Glencoe Stout and Ben Nevis are suitable for vegetarians and vegans.

Stirling Bitter (OG 1038, ABV 3.7%)
A full-flavoured beer with a nutty, fruity taste offering a relatively dry aftertaste. Bittered with Bramling Cross and Fuggles hops.

Ben Nevis (OG 1042, ABV 4%) ◆
A traditional Scottish 80 shilling, with a distinctive roast and caramel character. Bitter-sweet fruit throughout provides the sweetness typical of a Scottish Heavy.

Stirling Brig (OG 1042, ABV 4.1%)
Brewed to commemorate the 700th anniversary of the Battle of Stirling Brig in 1297. A full-bodied, rich, malty and slightly

sweet beer. A classic rich dark ruby red ale with a creamy head, typical of a traditional Scottish 80/-.

Bannockburn *(OG 1044, ABV 4.2%)*
A light-coloured ale brewed with Maris Otter and crystal malts. A hint of torrefied wheat is added, producing a satisfying and complex flavour. A fresh dry aftertaste is supported by a fairly hoppy character.

Glencoe Wild Oat Stout
(OG 1048, ABV 4.5%) ◆
A sweetish stout, not surprisingly dark in colour. Plenty of malt and roast balanced by fruit and finished with a hint of hop.

Lomond Gold *(OG 1054, ABV 5%)* ◆
A malty, bitter-sweet golden ale with plenty of fruity hop character.

BRIDGE STREET*

Bridge Street Brewery, 51 Bridge Street, Kington, Herefordshire, HR5 3DW.
Tel (015440 231993)

A new brewery using equipment from Moss Brew, based on the site vacated by Dunn Plowman (qv).

Four Seasons *(ABV 3.8%)*

Arrow *(ABV 4.5%)*

BRISCOE'S

Briscoe's Brewery, 16 Ash Grove, Otley, West Yorkshire, LS21 3EL
Tel/Fax (01943) 466515
E-mail briscoe.brewery@virgin.net

The brewery was launched in 1998 by microbiologist/chemist Dr Paul Briscoe in the cellar of his house with a one-barrel brew length. A new three-barrel brewery at the rear of the Bowling Green public house in Otley opened in 2000. The brew length increased to four barrels during 2002. The original one-barrel plant has been retained for special bottled beers. The beers are full mash, most being all malt. Eleven outlets are supplied direct. Most of the beer names are related to the brewer's other passion – long-distance running. Following a serious injury, Dr Briscoe is currently brewing on his original plant but hopes to return to full production. Seasonal beers: Rombalds Reviver (ABV 3.8%), Runner's Ruin (ABV 4.3%), Shane's Shamrock Stout (ABV 4.6%), Chevinbrau Pilsner-style lager (ABV 5.2%), Puddled and Barmy Ale (ABV 5.8%), Victorian Velvet (ABV 4.9%, winter).

Burnsall Classic Bitter *(OG 1040, ABV 4%)*
A full-flavoured, reddish coloured bitter with a good hop flavour.

Chevin Chaser *(OG 1043, ABV 4.3%)*
A refreshing, pale-coloured, all-malt bitter with a distinct hop finish.

Dalebottom Dark *(OG 1043, ABV 4.3%)*
A smooth and malty strong dark mild with a good hop character.

Otley Gold *(OG 1043, ABV 4.6%)*
A pale, fairly full-flavoured but soft beer brewed in the style of a lager.

Badger Stone Bitter *(OG 1044, ABV 4.4%)*
A classic English bitter, packed with the flavour of malt and hops.

Three Peaks Ale *(OG 1045, ABV 4.5%)*
A strong, pale premium bitter brewed with only pale malt and traditional hops.

Victorian Velvet *(OG 1048-49, ABV 4.9%)*
A malty, fruity and smooth copper-coloured special bitter. Small amounts are available in bottle-conditioned form from the brewery at Christmas.

BROADSTONE SIBA

Broadstone Brewing Company Ltd, Waterside Brewery, Rum Runner, Wharf Road, Retford, Notts, DN22 6EN
Tel/Fax (01777) 719797
E-mail broadstone@btconnect.com
Website www.broadstonebrewery.com
Tours by arrangement

⊠ Alan Gill, who founded Springhead Brewery, set up Broadstone in an industrial unit in Tuxford in 1999. The brewery was relocated to the back of his former business partner's pub, the Rum Runner in Retford, in 2002. From there, Alan supplies around 100 outlets directly. He also brews the Rum Runner's house beer, Two Water Grog (4%), which is served exclusively at the pub. Broadstone began bottling in 2002 and now supplies bottle-conditioned Gold, Black Abbot and Two Water Grog to two major supermarket chains, plus local off-licences. Seasonal beers: March Ale (ABV 5%, March), Mason's Field (ABV 3.6%, summer), Fletchers Ale (ABV 4.2%, spring).

Best Bitter *(OG 1039, ABV 3.8%)* ◆
An orange-brown session beer with a good hop backed by a malty nose that continues in the fairly bitter taste. The bitterness dries into a malty finish.

Stonebridge Mild *(OG 1041, ABV 4%)*

Priorswell Porter *(OG 1041, ABV 4%)*

Ladywell Ale *(OG 1042, ABV 4%)*

Two Water Grog *(OG 1042, ABV 4%)*

Charter Ale *(OG 1047, ABV 4.6%)* ◆
A light creamy head on a darkish brown beer. A beautiful coffee roast aroma and taste that lingers on through the hoppy, bitter finish. A fine use of amber malt.

Gold *(OG 1052, ABV 5%)*

Black Abbot *(OG 1052, ABV 5%)*

BROUGHTON SIBA

Broughton Ales Ltd, Broughton, Biggar, Peeblesshire, ML12 6HQ
Tel (01899) 830345
Fax (01899) 830474
E-mail beer@broughtonales.co.uk
Website www.broughtonales.co.uk
Shop 8-5 Mon – Fri
Tours by arrangement

⊚ Founded in 1979, the company went into receivership in 1995 and was taken over by Whim Brewery owner Giles Litchfield along with managing director Alastair Mouat. They have created the popular Clipper IPA and the new Greenmantle Original as well as 16 other cask ales. Expansion into new markets in England is going well. 55 per cent of production is bottled (not bottle-conditioned), 10 per cent of it is for export. A single tied house and 200 outlets in Scotland are supplied direct from the brewery. Seasonal/occasional beers: Scottish Oatmeal Stout (ABV 4.2%, winter), The Ghillie (ABV 4.5%, summer), Black Douglas (ABV 5.2%, spring/autumn), Winter Fire (ABV 4.2%, winter), Border Gold Organic Ale (ABV 4.2%). Border Gold and all bottled beers, stouts and lagers are suitable for vegetarians and vegans.

Greenmantle Original
(OG 1038, ABV 3.9%) ⬗
This tawny beer has strong malty characteristics with a bitter-sweet finish.

Broughton Special Bitter
(OG 1038, ABV 3.9%)

Clipper IPA *(OG 1042, ABV 4.2%)*
This light-coloured, crisp, hoppy beer bears all the hallmarks of an India Pale Ale, with a strong hop character and a clean taste.

Greenmantle IPA *(OG 1042, ABV 4.2%)*

Scottish Oatmeal Stout
(OG 1045, ABV 4.2%) ⬗
A rare pleasure, this wonderfully dry stout has a bitter aftertaste dominated by roast malt. A distinctive malt aroma is followed by a prominent roast note. Fruit is evident throughout.

Merlin's Ale *(OG 1042, ABV 4.2%)* ⬗
A well-hopped, fruity flavour is balanced by malt in the taste. The finish is bitter-sweet, light but dry.

Border Gold *(OG 1042, ABV 4.2%)*
Fruity hop aroma with citrus-lime hop flavour balanced by a malty sweetness. The finish is rich malt with grapefruit bitterness.

Bramling Cross *(OG 1042, ABV 4.2%)*

The Ghillie *(OG 1043, ABV 4.5%)* ⬗
A full-bodied ale. Hops, malt and fruit dominate the palate. The finish is dry and dominated by hops.

The Black Douglas
(OG 1053, ABV 5.2%)
Brewed using Maris Otter pale ale malt with the addition of roasted barley and maize, this ruby-coloured beer has a full malty flavour with a warm, strong finish.

Old Jock *(OG 1070, ABV 6.7%)*
Strong, sweetish and fruity in the finish. A classic Scottish strong ale.

BROWN COW

Brown Cow Brewery, Brown Cow Road, Barlow, Selby, North Yorkshire, YO8 8EH
Tel (01757) 618947
E-mail sue@browncowbrewery.f9.co.uk
Website www.browncowbrewery.f9.co.uk

Brown Cow was set up in 1997, with new plant added in 2002 that doubled capacity. Brewing takes place in a converted

outbuilding at the brewer's riverside home (the former Brown Cow inn). The brewery is run by Susan Simpson, who brews 10 barrels a week on the five-barrel plant. The beers can always be found at three local outlets and also as guest ales to free houses in the area. The beers are delivered from the brewery only and are not available via wholesalers. 100 outlets are supplied direct. Seasonal beers: Nimbus Wheat Beer (suitable for vegetarians and vegans, ABV 4.8%, spring/summer), Wassail Warmer (ABV 5%, Christmas).

Mistle Mild *(OG 1037, ABV 3.7%)* ⬗
Dark, malty and softly rounded.

Bitter *(OG 1038, ABV 3.8%)* ⬗
A well-hopped traditional session bitter.

Maiden Century *(OG 1040, ABV 4%)*

Simpsons No. 4
(OG 1043, ABV 4.4%) ⬗
Dark and bitter-sweet, full of roast barley character.

Wolfhound *(OG 1043, ABV 4.5%)* ⬗
Straw-coloured, full and rounded palate of malt and traditional English hops.

How Now *(OG 1044, ABV 4.5%)* ⬗
Pale, fruity and single hopped.

BRUNSWICK SIBA

◻ **The Brunswick Inn, 1 Railway Terrace, Derby, DE1 2RU**
Tel (01332) 290677
Fax (01332) 370226
E-mail grahamyates@work.gb.com
Tours by arrangement

⊗ The Brunswick is a purpose-built tower brewery attached to the Brunswick Inn, the first railwaymen's hostelry in the world, built in 1842 and just two minutes' walk from the main railway station. The triangular building is at the end of a terrace of cottages also built for railwayworkers. The inn was restored by the Derbyshire Historic Trust in 1987 and brewing started in 1991. The inn and brewery were bought by Everards in 2002 with a commitment to maintaining the unique ambience and real ales.

Mild *(OG 1035, ABV 3.6%)*

Triple Hop *(OG 1040, ABV 4%)*
A straw-coloured ale with a slightly sulphury aroma. An overtly bitter beer with pleasant mouth-puckering dryness.

Second/The Usual
(OG 1042, ABV 4.2%)
A dark copper colour, it drinks vinously with a lot of mouthfeel round the rich, clean malt. Dry aftertaste with a dash of orange.

Railway Porter *(OG 1043, ABV 4.3%)*
Chocolate aroma with spicy fruit notes. A complex, full-bodied brew with distinct coffee and fruity after character.

Triple Gold *(OG 1045, ABV 4.5%)*

Old Accidental *(OG 1050, ABV 5%)*
A light vinous floral hop aroma with underlying malt notes. Well-balanced, malty beer leading to a bitter finish with warming aftertaste.

Father Mike's Dark Rich Ruby
(OG 1056, ABV 5.8%)

BRYNCELYN

**Bryncelyn Brewery, 47 Wern Road,
Ystalyfera, Swansea, SA9 2LX
Tel (01639) 843625
E-mail bryncelynbrewery@aol.com
Website www.bryncelynbrewery.co.uk**
Tours by arrangement

☺ A one-quarter barrel brewery was opened in 1999 by William Hopton (owner) and Robert Scott (brewer). Capacity was increased to its present three-quarter capacity barrel in the same year. As the beer names imply, the owner is fond of Buddy Holly: February 1959 commemorates the singer's death. Seasonal beers: Feb 59 (ABV 3.7%), Peggy's Brew (ABV 4.2%, March), May B Baby (ABV 4.5%, May), That Will Be the Sleigh (ABV 7.2%, Dec-Jan).

Buddy Marvellous *(OG 1040, ABV 4%)* ◆
A robust and pleasing blend of malt and roast flavours with fruit throughout. Hop flavours emerge along with gentle bitterness to balance. A complex finish. Champion Beer of Wales 2002.

Buddy's Delight *(OG 1042, ABV 4.2%)*

Cwrw Celyn *(OG 1044, ABV 4.4%)*

Oh Boy *(OG 1045, ABV 4.5%)* ◆
This golden beer has an enticing aroma of hops and fruit. A moderate bitterness complements the burst of hop and fruit flavours with underlying malt. Refreshing and satisfying finish.

CHH *(OG 1045, ABV 4.5%)* ◆
An inviting aroma, a pale brown colour with hints of red malt and hop aroma, with fruit and bitterness adding to the flavour. The finish is clean and hoppily bitter.

Rave On *(OG 1050, ABV 5%)*

Buddy Confusing *(OG 1050, ABV 5%)*

BRYSON'S SIBA

**Bryson's Brews, 1 Summerside,
25 Oxcliffe Road, Heysham, Lancs, LA3 1PU
Tel (01524) 852150
E-mail brysonsbrews@supanet.com
Website www.brysonsbrews.co.uk**
Tours by prior arrangement

The brewery, opened in 2000, is owned and operated by Caroline and George Palmer. For the first year or so it was run as a part-time business while George worked at Heysham Power Station, but since early 2002 it has operated full time. The recipes are adapted from George's home-brews, developed over 20 years and the names all have local connections. The brewery now has a part time sales/delivery man, and sales are increasing towards the current plant's capacity. Some 50 outlets are supplied. Seasonal beer: Patrick's Porter (ABV 4.3%, winter), Castle (ABV 4.2%, spring), Memorial (ABV 4%, summer), Quayside (ABV 4.9%, autumn), Priory (ABV 5.7%, winter).

Tern's Tipple *(OG 1035, ABV 3.5%)*
Dark mild.

Shifting Sands *(OG 1038, ABV 3.8%)*
Hoppy session bitter.

Wammellers Wheat *(OG 1040, ABV 4%)*
Pale, lightly-hopped wheat beer.

Barrows Bitter *(OG 1042, ABV 4.2%)*
Traditional, well-hopped northern beer.

Acremoss Amber *(OG 1045, ABV 4.5%)*
Malty bitter.

Shrimpers Stout *(OG 1048, ABV 4.7%)*
Rich, full-bodied stout.

BUFFY'S

**Buffy's Brewery Ltd, Rectory Road,
Tivetshall St Mary, Norwich, NR15 2DD
Tel/Fax (01379) 676523
E-mail buffysbrewery@lineone.net
Website www.buffys.co.uk**
Tours by arrangement

⊠ Established in 1993, the brewing capacity stands at 45 barrels, but plans are in hand to move to bigger premises. The brewery has one pub, the Cherry Tree at Wickerwood, and plans to buy a second pub closer to home: the brewery will eventually move to these premises. Julie Savory (one half of the business) won a national award from Publican newspaper in 2002 to mark her efforts to save and restore the Cherry Tree. She also won the title of Businesswoman of the Year in competition with some of the biggest names in the business. Some 50 outlets are supplied. Seasonal beers: Sleigher (ABV 4.1%, Nov-Dec), Hollybeery (ABV 6% but changes each year), Festival 9X (ABV 9%, summer).

Norwich Terrier *(OG 1036, ABV 3.6%)* ◆
Light and crisp with a refreshing hoppy character. Grapefruit notes add a bouncy feel to this amber-coloured, easy-drinking bitter. An uncomplicated brew with a sustained finishing comprising hoppy bitterness softened by a rounded, malty counterpoint.

Bitter *(OG 1039, ABV 3.9%)* ◆
A comfortable, easy-drinking beer. A malt base with blackcurrant fruitiness matches the gentle fruity nose. As the taste develops, hops overtake malt as a partner to the refreshing fruitiness. Little flavour is lost as the finish develops a singular, hop-influenced bitterness that adds an edge to the mellow sweetness.

Mild *(OG 1042, ABV 4.2%)* ◆
Light roast malt airs introduce a solid old-style mild where sweetness vies with roast malt for dominance. A rich roast beefiness emerges from the long unwavering finish that complements the deep red hues of this ale.

Polly's Folly *(OG 1043, ABV 4.3%)* ◈
A full-flavoured bitter with malt the dominant flavour in both taste and nose. Hops, noticeable in the bouquet, provide a counter to the maltiness as the long finish develops a bitter-sweet fruitiness.

Hopleaf *(OG 1044.5, ABV 4.5%)* ◈
An amber brew with a smoothness often associated with larger breweries. Sweet hoppy notes with a hint of vanilla provide an easy-drinking feel. A gently fading finish with honey overtones.

India Ale *(OG 1046, ABV 4.6%)* ◈
Deceptively light on the tongue for its strength, this amber-coloured beer introduces itself with a vanilla ice-creamy aroma. This transforms to a rich blend of caramel, toffee and hops. Well-balanced with a malty thread throughout, the creamy texture fades slowly to leave a peppery, hop-influenced bitterness.

Norwegian Blue *(OG 1049, ABV 4.9%)* ◈
A gentle malt aroma with a hint of cherry introduces this predominantly malty brew. There is more than a hint of hops and bitterness in the background flavour but not enough to detract from the fruity malt character. A mid-brown beer with a quick finish in which coffee notes can be found.

Ale *(OG 1055, ABV 5.5%)* ◈
A tawny, old-fashioned Christmas pudding beer. Rich, plummy aroma emerges from a sweet fruity flavour laced with a malty platform. The finish continues through to a smooth malty flavour abetted by sweet bitterness.

Festival 9X *(OG 1090, ABV 9.0%)*
A fine, old-fashioned ale, dark amber in colour.

BULLMASTIFF SIBA

Bullmastiff Brewery, 14 Bessemer Close, Leckwith, Cardiff, CF11 8DL
Tel/Fax (029) 20665292

⊗ An award-winning small craft brewery run by the brothers Bob and Paul Jenkins since 1987. The name stems from their love of the bullmastiff breed. They have won many awards for the beers, including Champion Beer of Wales 1999 and 2000 and joint gold medal for Bitter at the 2000 Great British Beer Festival, but have no ambitions for expansion or owning any pubs, preferring to concentrate on quality control. 30 outlets are supplied. Seasonal beers: Summer Moult (ABV 4.3%), Mogadog (ABV 10%, winter).

Welsh Gold *(OG 1039, ABV 3.8%)* ◈◈◈
A hoppy aroma invites you to taste the blend of hop and fruit flavours with balancing bitterness. A refreshing, juicy hop finish.

Jack the Lad *(OG 1041, ABV 4.1%)*

Thoroughbred *(OG 1046, ABV 4.5%)* ◈
A tasty premium bitter with hops strong on the aroma and flavour balanced by fruit and malt with a bitter finish.

Welsh Red *(OG 1048, ABV 4.8%)*

Welsh Black *(OG 1050, ABV 4.8%)*

Brindle *(OG 1050, ABV 5.1%)* ◈

A full-bodied, flavoursome pale beer. Good hop aroma with a mix of malt, hops, fruit and bitterness in the taste. A lasting and satisfying finish.

Son Of A Bitch *(OG 1062, ABV 6%)* ◈
Amber-coloured, rich, warming, tasty and very drinkable. A complex blend of malt, hop and fruit with good bitterness. Lasting finish.

BUNTINGFORD SIBA

Buntingford Brewery Co Ltd, Unit 3A, Watermill Industrial Estate, Aspenden Road, Buntingford, Herts, SG9 9JS
Tel 07947 214058
E-mail steve@buntingford-brewery.co.uk
Website www.buntingford-brewery.co.uk
Tours by arrangement

⊗ The brewery was set up in 2001 as a part-time venture by Andrew Potter and Steve Banfield. Late in 2002 capacity was increased, and the brewery became a full-time commercial venture, focusing on producing beers using only whole hops, proper floor-malted barley and no chemical adjuncts or enhancers. No colouring additives are used beyond coloured malts. Various experiments are made with herbs, fruit or spirits as additional brewing materials. It is planned to move the brewery by 2004 to larger premises, allowing further developments, including a shop and visitor centre. Banfield Ales and Woodlands Brewery, which operated from the same address, have now been merged with Buntingford. Seasonal beers: Dark Times. Bottle-conditioned beers: Hertfordshire Honey (ABV 4.2%), Hurricane Force, Buntingford Gold, Watermill Stout, Bishop.

Highwayman Best Bitter *(OG 1036-38, ABV 3.7%)*
Pale-brown in colour, gentle smooth maltiness and a good hoppy character.

Tinker *(OG 1039-41, ABV 4%)*

Hurricane Force *(OG 1042-44, ABV 4.3%)*
Light brown in colour, this is a pleasantly hoppy beer with light malty undertones.

Buntingford Gold *(OG 1045-47, ABV 4.6%)*

Watermill Stout *(OG 1048-50, ABV 4.8%)*

Bishop *(OG 1048-52, ABV 5%)*

BUNTINGFORD
ESTD. 2001

BREWERY CO LTD

BURTON BRIDGE SIBA

Burton Bridge Brewery Ltd, 24 Bridge Street, Burton upon Trent, Staffs, DE14 1SY
Tel (01283) 510573
Fax (01283) 515594
E-mail bbb@burtonbridgebrewery.fsnet.co.uk
Website www.midlandspubs.co.uk /burtonbridge/brewery
Shop Bridge Inn sale in bar
Tours Wednesday evenings.

✪ A craft brewery established in 1982 by Bruce Wilkinson and Geoff Mumford, two refugees from Allied Breweries who finished up at Ind Coope of Romford. Burton Bridge now has four pubs in the town, including an enlarged brewery tap. It supplies 300 outlets. Seasonal beers: Old Expensive (ABV 6.5%) 🗂, Top Dog Stout (ABV 5%), Hearty Ale (ABV 5%), Battle Brew (ABV 5%), Knot Brown Ale (ABV 4.8%), Spring Ale (ABV 4.7%). Bottle-conditioned beers: Burton Porter 🍺, Bramble Stout (ABV 5% 🗂), Empire Pale Ale (ABV 7.5%), Tickle Brain (ABV 8%). Bottle-conditioned beers are brewed and bottled at the brewery and include commemorative beers.

Golden Delicious *(OG 1037, ABV 3.8%)* ✦
Gold-coloured and hoppy. Well-balanced with a dry, mouth-watering finish.

XL Bitter *(OG 1039, ABV 4%)* ✦
A golden, malty bitter, with a faint hoppy and fruity aroma. An excellent mix of flavours follows, with fruitiness dominating.

Bridge Bitter *(OG 1041, ABV 4.2%)* ✦
Pale brown coloured with hoppy aroma. Good bitter taste with hops lingering to give a long, bitter finish.

Porter *(OG 1044, ABV 4.5%)* 🗂✦
Dark red, with a faint roast aroma. The taste combines some liquorice flavour with hops and fruit; slightly sweet. A dry, astringent aftertaste.

Top Dog Stout *(OG 1049, ABV 5%)* 🍺✦
A winter-brew with a strong roast malt and fruit mix, developing into a potent malt and roast malt aftertaste.

Festival Ale *(OG 1054, ABV 5.5%)* ✦
A full-bodied, tawny-coloured, strong but sweet beer. The aroma is hoppy, malty and slightly fruity. Fruit and hops in the flavour give way to a fruity finish. Tremendous sparkling mouthfeel.

BURTONWOOD

**Thomas Hardy Burtonwood Ltd,
Bold Lane, Burtonwood, Warrington,
Cheshire, WA5 4PJ
Tel (01925) 225131
Fax (01925) 229033**
Tours by arrangement (charge)

✪ A family-run brewery that merged its brewing operation in 1998 with Thomas Hardy of Dorchester (qv) to form Thomas Hardy Burtonwood Ltd. The brewery is still 40% owned by Burtonwood Brewery plc, which is now a pub-owning group. The other 60% is owned by Thomas Hardy. Burtonwood is currently producing two Brakspear's brands for Refresh UK, following the closure of the Henley brewery. Occasional beers: Black Parrot (ABV 4%), Forshaws Bitter (ABV 4%), Hoppers (ABV 4.2%).

Bitter *(OG 1036.8, ABV 3.7%)* ✦
A well-balanced, refreshing, malty bitter, with good hoppiness. Fairly dry aftertaste.

Top Hat *(OG 1046, ABV 4.8%)* ✦
Soft, nutty, malty and a little sweet.

For Morrells of Oxford:

Oxford Blue *(OG 1036, ABV 3.7%)*

Varsity *(OG 1042, ABV 4.3%)*

Graduate *(OG 1048, ABV 4.8%)*

For Refresh UK:

Brakspear Bitter *(OG 1035.5, ABV 3.4%)*

Brakspear Special *(OG 1043.5, ABV 4.3%)*

BURY STREET

🍺 **Bury Street Brewery,
t/a The Stag Tavern, 44-46 Bury Street,
Stowmarket, Suffolk, IP14 1HF
Tel (01449) 613980**

Patrick Murphy built his small brewery in 2001. It has a nine-gallon brew length, and most of the beer is sold through the pub, with some going to CAMRA beer festivals.

Mr Murphy's Mild (Dark)
(OG 1036, ABV 3.6%)
A dark mild with distinct chocolate and slight roast notes. A soft medium/low bitterness.

Bridget's Best Bitter (BBB)
(OG 1037, ABV 3.7%)
Moderately but subtly bitter, slightly malty but dry with delicate late and dry hop.

Blonde Bombshell *(OG 1037, ABV 3.7%)*
Lager-coloured. Dry and bitter with a citrus late hop character. Very refreshing.

Tawny Owl *(OG 1037, ABV 3.7%)*
A darkish bitter with a touch of chocolate and a single hop bitterness. Slightly fruity.

Pat Murphy's Porter *(OG 1043, ABV 4%)*
Distinct roast and chocolate notes balanced by hop bitterness. Complex, fruity undertones.

Tawny Special *(OG 1040, ABV 4.2%)*
Big Brother of Tawny Owl. A totally separate brew with a bit more of the same in all respects, specially the fruity notes.

BUSHY'S SIBA

**The Mount Murray Brewing Co Ltd, Mount Murray, Braddan, Isle of Man, IM4 1JE
Tel Office (01624) 611101
Tel/Fax Brewery (01624) 611244
E-mail Bushys@enterprize.net
Website www.bushys.com**
Shop Available from our pubs
Tours by arrangement

☺ Set up in 1986 as a brew-pub, Bushy's moved to its present site in 1990 when demand outgrew capacity. It owns four tied houses and the beers – all brewed to the stipulations of the Manx Brewers' Act of 1874 that permits only malts, hops, brewing sugar, yeast and water – are also supplied to 25 other outlets. Bottle-conditioned beer: Bushys Premium Manx Ale (ABV 4.5%).

Ruby (1874) Mild *(OG 1035, ABV 3.5%)*

Castletown Bitter *(OG 1035, ABV 3.5%)*

Bushy's Export Bitter
(OG 1038, ABV 3.8%) ✦
An aroma full of pale malt and hops introduces you to a beautifully hoppy, bitter beer. Despite the predominant hop character, malt is also evident. Fresh and clean-tasting.

Manannan's Cloak *(OG 1039, ABV 4%)*

Oyster Stout *(OG 1042, ABV 4.2%)*

Classic *(OG 1042, ABV 4.3%)*

Piston Brew *(OG 1044, ABV 4.5%)*

Old Bushy Tail *(OG 1044, ABV 4.5%)*

BUTCOMBE SIBA

Butcombe Brewery Ltd, Butcombe, Bristol, BS40 7XQ
Tel (01275) 472240
Fax (01275) 474734
E-mail butcombebrewery@talk21.com
Tours by arrangement (trade only)

⊗ One of the most successful of the newer breweries, set up in 1978 by a former Courage Western director, Simon Whitmore, this West Country independent based in Somerset's Mendip hills has gained a considerable reputation with its quality beers and friendly service. During 1992-93, the brewery virtually doubled in size (for the third time) and, after 18 years of brewing just a single beer, a second ale went into production in 1996. Simon Whitmore retired in 2003; the company was bought by Guy Newell and Paul Horsley who set up The Beer Seller wholesale firm but left when it was bought by Bulmer. Butcombe has an estate of six houses (although none is tied) and it also supplies 350 other outlets. Butcombe's beers contain no added sugars, colourings or preservatives and are available directly from the brewery to outlets within a 50-mile radius and nationally via selected wholesalers and pub companies.

Bitter *(OG 1039, ABV 4%)* ◆
Amber coloured, malty and notably bitter beer, with subtle citrus fruit qualities. Hoppy, malty, citrus and a very slightly sulphur aroma, and a long, dry, bitter finish with light fruit notes. Consistent and refreshing.

Gold *(OG 1047, ABV 4.7%)* ⬧◆
Aroma of pale malt, citrus hops and fruit. Medium bodied, well-balanced, with good pale malt, hops and bitterness. Yellow-gold in colour, it is quite fruity, slightly sweet, with an abiding dryness.

BUTTS SIBA

Butts Brewery Ltd, Northfield Farm, Great Shefford, Hungerford, Berkshire, RG17 7BY
Tel (01488) 648133
Fax (0118) 375 9341
Tours by arrangement

⊗ The brewery was set up in a converted Dutch barn in 1994. Apart from pubs, Butts also supplies a handful of local supermarkets with bottle-conditioned beers, bottled by Butts on the premises. In 2002, the brewery took the decision to become dedicated to organic production: all the beers are brewed using organic malted barley and organic hops when suitable varieties are available. Barbus Barbus won the gold award for bottle-conditioned beer at the SIBA South-east competition in 2002. Seasonal beer: Golden Brown (ABV 5%, spring and autumn), Le Butts cask-conditioned lager (ABV 5%). Bottle-conditioned beers: Golden Brown (ABV 5%), Le Butts, Blackguard, Barbus Barbus.

Jester *(OG 1035, ABV 3.5%)* ⬧◆
This amber-coloured beer is fruity and slightly buttery, with an excellent hop aroma supported by pale malt. Aroma and bittering hops balance in the mouth, leading to a dry, hoppy finish.

Butts *(OG 1040, ABV 4%)* ◆
A traditional southern-style bitter, pale brown in colour with a good bitter hop character and some fruity tendencies.

Blackguard *(OG 1045, ABV 4.5%)* ◆
A rich, fruity red-brown porter with hints of crystal and chocolate malt in the mouth. A blackcurrant aroma and taste are well-balanced with bitterness and malt characters, followed by a dry, bitter and roast finish.

Barbus Barbus *(OG 1046, ABV 4.6%)* ⬧◆
The pale malt in this amber beer is tempered with a hint of crystal malt, well balanced by hops and fruit, leading to a long, complex and bitter-sweet finish. Very drinkable.

CAINS

Robert Cain Brewery Ltd, Stanhope Street, Liverpool, Merseyside, L8 5XJ
Tel (0151) 709 8734
Fax (0151) 708 8395
E-mail danuk@cainsbeers.com
Website www.cainsbeers.com
Shop Customer collections (10-3)
Tours by arrangement Mon-Thur evenings

◎ Robert Cain's brewery was established in 1850 and in 1922 was renamed Higson's. In 1985 Boddingtons acquired the brewery, which passed to Whitbread when it was taken over by the national group. Whitbread closed the site in 1991. It was reopened a year later and the Brewery Group Denmark purchased the site. In 2002, Denmark sold the brewery to new owners the Dusanj brothers, Ajmail and Sudarghara. Future plans include new seasonal ales. The new owners' commitment to cask beer can be seen by the installation of a new cask-washing line. Ten pubs are owned and around 300 outlets are served direct. Seasonal beers: Dragon Heart (ABV 5%), Sundowner (ABV 4.5%), Triple Hop (ABV 4.5%), Red (ABV 4.5%).

Dark Mild *(OG 1033.5, ABV 3.2%)* ⬧◆
A smooth, dry and roasty dark mild, with some chocolate and coffee notes.

Dr Duncans IPA *(OG 1036, ABV 3.5%)*

Traditional Bitter *(OG 1038.5, ABV 4%)* ◆
A darkish, full-bodied and fruity bitter, with a good hoppy nose and a dry aftertaste.

Formidable Ale *(OG 1048, ABV 5%)* ◆
A bitter and hoppy beer with a good dry aftertaste. Sharp, clean and dry.

CAIRNGORM SIBA

Cairngorm Brewery Co. Ltd., Unit 12, Dalfaber Industrial Estate, Aviemore, Inverness-shire, PH22 1PY
Tel (01479) 812222 Fax (01479) 811465
E-mail info@cairngormbrewery.com
Website www.cairngormbrewery.com
Shop 9-530, Mon-Fri
Tours by arrangement

☺ The Cairngorm Brewery Co was created in 2001 to produce beers from the former Aviemore and Tomintoul breweries. Seven regular cask-conditioned beers are produced and a series of seasonal ales are available throughout the year. Rebranding of all the beers under the Cairngorm name took place in the spring of 2003. 300 outlets are supplied direct. Seasonal beers: Ruthven (ABV 3.8%, summer), Black Gold (ABV 4.4%, spring and autumn), Strathspey Brew (ABV 4.2%, summer), Bard's Ale (ABV 4.4%, Jan-Feb), Santa's Sledgehammer (ABV 6.3%, winter).

Highland IPA *(OG 1036, ABV 3.6%)*
A light ale with a crisp freshness.

Ruthven Brew *(OG 1039, ABV 3.8%)* ◆
Copper-coloured ale with nice hop and roast balance, and a malty body. Good hoppy aftertaste.

Stag *(OG 1039.5, ABV 4.1%)* ◆
A powerful malty nose with less hop character on the palate than in early brews. This tawny brew has a lingering malty, gently bitter aftertaste.

Nessies Monster Mash
(OG 1044, ABV 4.4%) ◆
A mahogany-coloured, full malty brew with a creamy mouthfeel leading to a satisfying, fruity finish.

Black Gold *(OG 1048.5, ABV 4.4%)*
A Scottish stout with a rich dark colour, traditional smooth sweetness with underlying roast barley hints.

Gold *(OG 1046, ABV 4.5%)*
A golden beer with a good balance between continental hops and fine Scottish malt.

Sheepshagger *(ABV 4.5%)*
A delicious golden ale with a perfect balance between continental hops and the finest malt.

Witches Cauldron *(ABV 4.8%)*

Murdoch *(OG 1046, ABV 4.8%)*
A strong, robust, deep copper-coloured beer.

Bard's Ale *(ABV 4.4%)*

Wildcat *(OG 1049.5, ABV 5.1%)* ◆
A fruity aroma leads to a sweetish, fruity beer with much malt in evidence. Hops and caramel add complexity to this pale brown ale.

CALEDONIAN

**The Caledonian Brewing Company Ltd,
42 Slateford Road, Edinburgh, EH11 1PH
Tel (0131) 337 1286
Fax (0131) 313 2370
E-mail info@caledonian-brewery.co.uk
Website www.caledonian-brewery.co.uk**
Tours contact 0131 228 3688

☺ The brewery was established in 1869 as Lorimer & Clark and was taken over by Vaux of Sunderland in 1919. In 1985, when Vaux planned to close the site, it was bought by its management team. Under the Caledonian name, it now concentrates on cask beers, sold through the free trade. It also produces the Calders range from the closed Alloa Brewery. Caledonian's flagship brand, Deuchars IPA, won the champion Beer of Britain title in 2002. There are plans to increase distribution throughout Britain. Caledonian still brews in three direct-fired open coppers, the last of their type still in use. Beers are fermented in open squares and are all blessed by the Sabbath. The brewery supplies more than 650 outlets but does not own any pubs or bars of its own. Monthly seasonals: Burns Ale (ABV 4.7%, January), 6 Nations (ABV 4.2%, February), Lorimer & Clark (ABV 5.3%, March), Flying Scotsman (ABV 4.6%, April), Caledonian 1869 (ABV 4.5%, May), Nectar (ABV 4.3%, June), Scotch Mist (ABV 4%, July), Edinburgh Tattoo (ABV 4.2%, August), Mellow Yellow (ABV 4.7%, September), Double Amber (ABV 4.6%, October), Merman XXX (ABV 4.8%, November), Santas Little Helper (ABV 3.7%, December). Golden Promise Organic cask ale is suitable for vegetarians and vegans.

Deuchars IPA
(OG 1039, ABV 3.8%) ⌂🍺◆
An extremely tasty and refreshing session beer that is now much more consistent. Hops and fruit are very evident and are balanced by malt throughout. The lingering aftertaste is delightfully bitter and hoppy.

80/- *(OG 1042, ABV 4.1%)* ⌂◆
A predominantly malty, copper-coloured beer with hop and fruit. A Scottish heavy that now lacks the complex taste and hoppiness of old and is frequently dominated by caramel flavours.

Golden Promise Organic Ale
(OG 1043, ABV 4.4%)
The original organic beer, pale in colour, with pronounced hop character. Floral and fruity on the nose.

CAMBRINUS

**Cambrinus Craft Brewery, Home Farm,
Knowsley Park, Knowsley,
Merseyside, L31 4AQ
Tel (0151) 546 2226
E-mail cambrinus@talk21.com**
Tours by prior arrangement

☒ Cambrinus is based in part of farm buildings on a private estate. A five-barrel plant produces 250 hectolites a year. Some 45 outlets are supplied. Seasonal beers: Clogdance (ABV 3.6%, spring), Dark Harvest (ABV 4%, summer and autumn), Bootstrap (ABV 4.5%, spring and autumn), Lamp Oil (ABV 4.5%, winter), Celebrance (ABV 5.5%, Christmas).

Herald *(OG 1036, ABV 3.7%)*
Pale and bitter.

Yardstick *(OG 1040, ABV 4%)*
Dark, malty hints, refreshing.

Deliverance *(OG 1040, ABV 4.2%)*
Pale, bitter, dry.

Endurance *(OG 1045, ABV 4.3%)*
IPA-style, smooth and hoppy.

CAMERONS

**Camerons Brewery Limited, Lion Brewery,
Hartlepool, TS24 7QS
Tel (01429) 266666
Fax (01429) 890183
E-mail martindutoy@cameronsbrewery.com**
Tours by arrangement

⊚ Founded in 1865, Camerons expanded rapidly in the early 1900s and then again in the 1950s, reaching a peak in the early 70s. In 1975, Camerons became part of the Ellerman Shipping group and in 1985 was sold to the Barclay brothers. In 1989, Brent Walker became the new owner, and sold to to Wolverhampton & Dudley in 1992. In 2002, Castle Eden Brewery purchased Camerons and moved brewing from Castle Eden to Hartlepool. 25 pubs are owned, 15 selling cask-conditioned beer. Some 100 outlets are supplied. Seasonal beer: Camerons Cauldron (ABV 4%, Oct-Nov), Spring Knights Ale (ABV 4%, spring), Hollydaze (ABV 4%, December), Autumn Knights Ale (ABV 4.2%, autumn), Winter Knights Ale (ABV 5%, winter).

Camerons Bitter *(OG 1036, ABV 3.6%)* ◈
A light bitter, but well balanced, with hops and malt.

Strongarm *(OG 1041, ABV 4%)* ◈
A well-rounded, ruby-red ale with a distinctive, tight creamy head; initially fruity, but with a good balance of malt, hops and moderate bitterness.

Castle Eden Ale
(OG 1040, ABV 4.2%) ◈
A light, creamy, malty sweet ale with fruit notes and a mellow dry bitterness in the finish.

Nimmos XXXX *(OG 1043, ABV 4.4%)* ◈
Light golden beer with a well-balanced character derived from the best English malt and Goldings hops.

CANNON ROYALL SIBA

⌷ Cannon Royall Brewery,
Fruiterer's Arms, Uphampton Lane,
Ombersley, Droitwich,
Worcs, WR9 0JW
Tel (01905) 621161
Fax (01562) 743262
E-mail info@cannonroyall.co.uk
Tours by arrangement, but rarely

The first brew was in 1993 in a converted cider house behind the Fruiterer's Arms pub. It has increased capacity from five barrels to more than 16 a week. Cannon Royall supplies a number of outlets in the West Midlands and Worcestershire and plans to bottle. There are occasional seasonal and special beers.

Fruiterer's Mild
(OG 1037, ABV 3.7%) ◈
Fruity dark mild, full-bodied with plenty of roast malt coming through in the mouth. A classic mild, well-liked and respected.

King's Shilling *(OG 1038, ABV 3.8%)* ◈
A slightly dry aftertaste from this straw-coloured, aromatic session bitter. Bitter hops are the hallmark of this pungent and very popular drink.

Arrowhead *(OG 1039, ABV 3.9%)* ◈
Crisp drinking bitter with a powerful aroma of hops leading to a mixture of tastes dominated by a satisfying citrus hoppy bitterness.

Muzzle Loader *(OG 1042, ABV 4.2%)* ◈
A carefully balanced combination of fruity bitterness and light malt.

CAPTAIN COOK SIBA

⌷ Captain Cook Brewery Ltd,
The White Swan, 1 West End, Stokesley,
North Yorkshire, TS9 5BL
Tel (01642) 710263
Fax (01642) 714245
E-mail Joonanbri@aol.com
Website www.thecaptaincookbrewery.co.uk
Tours by arrangement

The 18th-century White Swan concentrated on promoting real ale for 10 years before taking on the challenge of becoming a brew-pub. The brewery, with a four-barrel plant, started operations in 1999 and was opened by White Swan regular James Cook on his 79th birthday. Plans to close the brewery were reversed in 2002 as a result of Chancellor Gordon Brown's reduction in duty for small brewers. The beer range is now supplied to other pubs and bottled beer production is under review. Seasonal beer: Black Porter (ABV 4.4%, spring, autumn and winter).

Navigation *(OG 1038, ABV 3.8%)*
A light session beer.

New Horizons *(OG 1039, ABV 3.9%)*

Sunset *(OG 1040, ABV 4%)*
An extremely smooth light ale with a good balance of malt and hops.

Slipway *(OG 1042, ABV 4%)*
A light-coloured hoppy ale with bitterness coming through from Challenger hops. A full-flavoured ale with a smooth malt aftertaste.

CAPTAIN GRUMPY

Captain Grumpy's Beer Company,
Grey House, Lynn Road, Stoke Ferry,
Norfolk, PE33 9SW
Tel (01366) 500767

The brewery was launched in 2002 at the Ship pub in Downham Market and moved to new premises in 2003. The brewery supplies the Ship and CAMRA festivals.

Best Bitter *(ABV 3.9%)*

Busted Flush *(ABV 4.5%)*

Golden Rivet *(ABV 5.1%)*

CARTERS

White Hart Inn,
White Hart Lane,
Machen, Caerphilly, CF83 8QQ
Tel (01633) 441005

⊗ Formerly trading as White Hart, Carters is a small plant currently supplying the White Hart plus occasional beer festivals only. Owner Alan Carter is currently looking for new plant and premises to expand production. Limited brew-lengths means that in-house beers are sometimes not available; phoning in advance will avoid disappointment.

Fawn *(ABV 3.8%)*

Rhymney Valley Bitter *(ABV 4%)*

Machen Bitter *(ABV 4.2%)*

T.U. *(ABV 5%)*

Gordon the Gofer *(ABV 5.2%)*

CASTLE ROCK SIBA

Castle Rock Brewery, Queensbridge Road, Nottingham, NG2 1NB
Tel (0115) 985 1615Fax (0115) 985 1611
Email castlerock@tynemill.co.uk
Website www.tynemill.co.uk
Tours by arrangement

☺ Close to Nottingham Midland Railway Station and situated next to the Vat & Fiddle public house, Castle Rock Brewery has been a trading division of pub group Tynemill since 2001. Capacity was increased in 2003 to a maximum of 100 barrels a week. The beers are distributed throughout the Tynemill estate, local free trade and by reciprocal swaps with micro and regional breweries nationwide. The brewery supplies 40 outlets. A different 'wildlife' beer is brewed each month to highlight an endangered species.

Black Gold *(ABV 3.5%)*
A dark mild with a slight bitterness and without undue sweetness.

Nottingham Gold *(ABV 3.5%)*
A golden beer with a distinct hop character derived from 100% Golding hops. Launched in 2001, it is the house beer in many Tynemill pubs with a house name, such as Meadows Gold for the Vat & Fiddle.

Hemlock *(ABV 4%)*
Mid strength, full bodied, fruity notes and a hop finish.

Snowhite *(ABV 4.2%)*
Well-balanced, golden brew.

Nottingham Dark Stout *(ABV 4.5%)*
Dark, heavy and well-hopped, with a full finish.

Elsie Mo *(ABV 4.7%)*
A blonde single malt beer, light in colour and refreshing on the palate.

CAYTHORPE

Caythorpe Brewery, Walnut Cottage, Boat Lane, Hoveringham, Nottingham, NG14 7JP.
Tel/Fax (0115) 966 4376

⊗ Caythorpe was set up in 1997 by an ex-Home Brewery employee, Geoff Slack, and his wife, Pam. The beers are brewed at the Black Horse, Caythorpe, and demand is high from local outlets. Occasional/seasonal beers: Christmas Light (ABV 3.7%), Too Grand (ABV 4.8%, winter), Santa's Stiffener (ABV 4.7%, winter), Saucy Susan (ABV 3.8%, summer).

Light Horse Bitter *(OG 1034.7, ABV 3.7%)*
Light in strength but richly coloured. A malty-flavoured session bitter with a dry finish. Dry hopped in cask for aroma.

Dover Beck Bitter *(OG 1037, ABV 4%)*
A light, dry, well-hopped beer, dry hopped in cask. The house beer at the Black Horse.

Old Nottingham Extra Pale Ale
(OG 1038.6, ABV 4.2%)
The recipe comes from a Home Brewery brewing book of 1914 and offers a taste of old Nottingham. Very light in colour, hoppy and crisp.

Birthday Brew *(OG 1040, ABV 4.5%)*
A golden-coloured bitter with a full malt feel. Late hopping in the copper using Styrian Goldings gives a pleasant aroma.

CHALK HILL

Chalk Hill Brewery, Rosary Road, Norwich, Norfolk, NR1 4DA
Tel/Fax (01603) 4770778
Tours by arrangement

⊗ Run by former Reindeer brew-pub owner Bill Thomas and his partners Tiny Little and Dave Blake, Chalk Hill began production with a 15-barrel plant in 1993. It is developing plans for expansion and new brews. Chalk Hill supplies its own two pubs and 20 local free trade outlets. The beers are also available nationwide via beer agencies. Occasional beer: IPA (ABV 5.3%).

Brewery Tap *(OG 1036, ABV 3.6%)* ◕
A copper-coloured session beer. The malty, hop-based aroma is matched by the first taste, which adds a gentle bitterness to the range. The lightness of flavour continues to the rather quick ending where an increasing bitterness gives a better balance to the overall feel.

CHB *(OG 1042, ABV 4.2%)* ◕
An even-tasting brew with equal amounts of malt and hops throughout the aroma and taste. The malt subsides as a growing bitter-sweet tang emerges in a lingering finish. Some honey notes can be found to dull the bitterness that emerges as the dominant flavour of this tawny-coloured best bitter.

Dreadnought *(OG 1050, ABV 4.9%)* ◕
A deep fruity beer with more than a hint of sweetness. Caramel, toffee and dates can be detected against a solid malty background. Although some bitter notes provide a counter to the heavy fruit bias, the finish holds up well to a palate-pleasing finale. Red-coloured with a solid and filling signature.

Flintknapper's Mild *(OG 1050, ABV 5%)* ◕
The light roast malt aroma disguises the solid roast backbone to this dark brown, rich-flavoured mild. Brooding chocolate overtones percolate through to give a greater depth to the taste. A certain sweetness adds complexity but quickly fades to a leave a filling, roast-dominated exit.

Old Tackle (*OG 1056, ABV 5.6%*) ✦
A sweet, fruity beer with a definite malty signature. A swirling interplay of malt, hops and a slowly increasing sweetness gives a heavy feel to this mid-brown old ale. A peppery tang develops towards the end to lighten the otherwise cloying heaviness.

CHERITON SIBA

◘ **Cheriton Brewhouse, Cheriton, Alresford, Hampshire, SO24 0QQ**
Tel /Fax (01962) 771166
E-mail bestbeer1@aol.com
Tours by arrangement

▩ The brewery was founded in 1993 by the owners of the adjacent Flower Pots pub, and two working partners, Ray Page and Martin Roberts. With an emphasis on quality rather than quantity the beers soon gained an appreciative audience in local pubs. Full capacity has been achieved. 45-50 outlets are supplied direct.

Pots Ale (*OG 1038.5, ABV 3.8%*) ✦
Pale brown, with a hoppy nose. A well-balanced bitter and hoppy taste leads through to the aftertaste.

Village Elder (*OG 1038.5, ABV 3.8%*) ▤

Cheriton Best Bitter
(*OG 1043, ABV 4.2%*) ✦
A malty and fruity taste continues into the aftertaste. A dark brown beer with a malty and fruity nose.

Diggers Gold (*OG 1044.5, ABV 4.6%*)
A golden beer with a citric, hoppy aroma; bitter and hoppy in all respects. A dry finish.

Turkey's Delight (*OG 1060, ABV 5.9%*)

CHILTERN SIBA

The Chiltern Brewery, Nash Lee Road, Terrick, Aylesbury, Bucks, HP17 0TQ
Tel (01296) 613647
Fax (01296) 612419
E-mail info@chilternbrewery.co.uk
Website www.chilternbrewery.co.uk
Shop 9-5 Mon-Sat.
Tours by arrangement

▩ Established by Richard and Lesley Jenkinson in 1980, the first brew, Chiltern Ale, was followed in 1982 by Beechwood Bitter. Three Hundred Old Ale joined the ranks in 1988 to celebrate the eighth anniversary, with Bodgers Barley Wine in 1990 for the 10th, and John Hampden's Ale in 1995 for the 15th anniversary. A brewery shop opened in 1989, followed by a small museum in 1994. Buckinghamshire County Celebration Ale has been replaced with Lord Lieutenant's Ale. Seasonal: Golden Sovereign Ale (ABV 3.7%, summer), Three Hundreds Old Ale (ABV 4.9%, winter), Stout & Gout (ABV 4.9%, winter). Bottle-conditioned beer: Bodgers Barley Wine (ABV 8.5%). The brewery now offers own label bottled beers for customers who choose a name or supply a design.

Chiltern Ale (*OG 1037, ABV 3.7%*) ✦
A refreshing session bitter, amber in colour, with a predominantly malty character. The aroma is of pale malt with a hint of grape, with some sweetness in the mouth and a short finish.

Beechwood Bitter (*OG 1043, ABV 4.3%*) ✦
A pale brown, refreshing beer with a rich butter-toffee aroma, lots of pale malt and fruit in the mouth and a finish that is more sweet and fruity than bitter.

Three Hundreds Old Ale
(*OG 1049/50, ABV 4.9%*) ✦
A strong old ale with some crystal malt and roast character plus hints of liquorice. Deceptively strong.

CHILTERN VALLEY SIBA

Chiltern Valley Winery and Brewery, Old Luxters Vineyard, Hambleden, Henley-on-Thames, Oxon, RG9 6JW
Tel (01491) 638330
Fax (01491) 638645
E-mail enquiries@chilternvalley.co.uk
Website www.chilternvalley.co.uk
Shop Mon-Fri 9-5, Sat/Sun 11-5
Tours by arrangement

▩ A traditional, full-mash, independent farm brewery – originally called Old Luxters –was established in 1990 in a 17th-century barn alongside a winery. Cask ales are supplied through the shop and private clients and some free trade customers. The brewery specialises in exclusive bottle-conditioned beers for specialist customers, such as Fortnum & Mason, and Royal Farm Shop. Bottle-conditioned beers: Barn Ale (ABV 5.4%), Dark Roast Ale (ABV 5%), Luxters Gold (ABV 5%), Damson Ale (ABV 7%), Old Windsor Gold, brewed for the Royal Household Farm Shop, Windsor (ABV 5%), Old Windsor Dark Ale (ABV 5%), 21-21 (ABV 4.5%), Fortnum & Mason Ale (ABV 5%). The brewery is in Buckinghamshire, despite the postal address.

Barn Ale Bitter (*OG 1038, ABV 4%*)
A fruity, aromatic, fairly hoppy, bitter beer.

Barn Ale Special (*OG 1042.5, ABV 4.5%*) ✦
The original Barn Ale: predominantly malty, fruity and hoppy in taste and nose, and tawny/amber in colour. Fairly strong in flavour: the initial, sharp, malty and fruity taste leaves a dry, bitter-sweet, fruity aftertaste. It can be slightly sulphurous.

Dark Roast Ale (*OG 1048, ABV 5%*)

Gold (*OG 1048, ABV 5%*)

CHURCH END SIBA

Church End Brewery Ltd, 109 Ridge Lane, Nuneaton, Warwickshire, CV10 0RD
Tel (01827) 713080
Fax (01827) 717328
Shop during tap opening hours
Tours by arrangement

▩ Church End opened in 1994 as a small brewery in a 350-year-old coffin shop adjacent to the Griffin Inn, Shustoke, with a four-barrel capacity. It moved to new premises in a former social club in Ridge Lane in 2001 with 10-barrel capacity that can be viewed from the tap room. The coffin shop heritage is reflected in a number of ecclesiastical names. Many unusual beers are produced during the year (eg damson, oregano, ginger and honey), mainly for beer festivals. There are a large number of occasional beers. 100-150 outlets are supplied.

Cuthberts *(OG 1038, ABV 3.8%)* ♦
A refreshing, hoppy beer, with hints of malt, fruit and caramel taste. Lingering bitter aftertaste.

Gravediggers *(OG 1038, ABV 3.8%)* ♦
A premium mild. Black and red in colour, with a complex mix of chocolate and roast flavours, it is almost a light porter.

Goat's Milk *(OG 1038, ABV 3.8%)*

Hop Gun *(OG 1041, ABV 4.1%)*

Without-a-Bix *(OG 1042, ABV 4.2%)* ♦
A wheat beer; clear, malty and pale, combining German hops and English wheat.

What the Fox's Hat *(OG 1043, ABV 4.2%)* ♦
A beer with a malty aroma, and a hoppy and malty taste with some caramel flavour.

Pooh Beer *(OG 1044, ABV 4.3%)* ♦
A bright golden beer brewed with honey. Sweet, yet hoppy.

Vicar's Ruin *(OG 1044, ABV 4.4%)* ♦
A straw-coloured best bitter with an initially hoppy, bitter flavour, softening to a delicate malt finish.

Stout Coffin *(OG 1046, ABV 4.6%)*

Fallen Angel *(OG 1050, ABV 5%)*

Rest in Peace *(OG 1070, ABV 7%)*

CITY OF CAMBRIDGE

**City of Cambridge Brewery Co Ltd,
Ely Rd, Chittering, Cambridge, CB5 9PH
Tel (01223) 864864
E-mail sales@cambridge-brewery.co.uk
Website www.cambridge-brewery.co.uk**

⊗ City of Cambridge opened in 1997 at Cheddars Lane with a five-barrel brew plant and moved in 2002 to a new site at Chittening. The company supplies 100 outlets.

Jet Black *(ABV 3.7%)*
A black beer, mild but full in flavour and body.

Boathouse Bitter *(ABV 3.8%)* ♦
Copper-brown and full-bodied session bitter, starting with impressive citrus and floral hop; grassy, fruity notes and cooked vegetables are present with finally a fading, gentle bitterness.

Rutherford IPA *(ABV 3.8%)* ♦
Satisfying session bitter with a soft hoppy, bitter-sweet balance and a light sulphury character after a fruity, malty start. This

amber brews ends dry and bitter with a light balance of malt and hops.

Hobson's Choice *(ABV 4.1%)* ⬠♦
A highly drinkable, golden brew with a pronounced hop aroma and taste, and a fruity, bitter balance in the mouth, finishing gently dry. Vegetable notes occur when young.

Atom Splitter *(ABV 4.7%)* ♦
Robust copper-coloured strong bitter with hop aroma and taste, and a distinct vegetable sulphury edge..

Darwin's Downfall *(ABV 5%)*
A blended, ruby-golden coloured beer. Hoppy with a fruity character and a refreshing citrus aftertaste.

Parkers Porter *(ABV 5.3%)* ♦
Impressive reddish brew with a defined roast character throughout, and short, fruity, bitter-sweet palate.

Bramling Traditional *(ABV 5.5%)*
Made with Bramling Cross hops, very fruity and delicious.

CLARK'S SIBA

**HB Clark & Co (Successors) Ltd,
Westgate Brewery, Wakefield,
W Yorkshire, WF2 9SW
Tel (01924) 373328
Fax (01924) 372306
E-mail phillip.owen@hbclark.co.uk
Website www.hbclark.co.uk**
Shop Mon-Fri 9-5pm
Tours by arrangement

☺ Founded in 1905, Clark's ceased brewing during the keg revolution of the 1960s and 1970s. It resumed cask ale production in 1982 and now supplies by direct delivery to more than 100 outlets, in addition to wholesalers and distributors throughout Britain. Clark's owns five pubs, four of which serve cask-conditioned beer. Specials are brewed every month. Seasonal beer: Loose Cannon (ABV 4.4%, February), Lauded Leprechaun (ABV 4.7%) and Code Red (ABV 4.2%, March-April), Nutcracker Barrel (ABV 4%) and Bursting Nectar (ABV 4.5%, May-June), Summer Ale (ABV 4.1%, August), Indian Summer (ABV 4%, October), Scrooges Brew (ABV 4.6%) and Christmas Moon (ABV 3.8%, December).

Classic Blonde *(OG 1039, ABV 3.9%)*
A light blond ale with a citrus and hoppy flavour, a distinctive grapefruit aroma and a dry finish.

Festival Ale *(OG 1042, ABV 4.2%)* ♦
A light, fruity, pleasantly hopped premium bitter with a good fruity, hoppy nose. Moderate bitterness follows, with a dry, fruity finish. Gold in colour.

Rams Revenge *(OG 1046, ABV 4.6%)* ♦
A rich, ruby-coloured premium ale, well-balanced with malt and hops, with a deep fruity taste and a dry hoppy aftertaste, with a pleasant hoppy aroma.

Golden Hornet *(OG 1050, ABV 5%)* ♦
A crisp golden premium beer with a full fruity taste, with full hop aroma and dry hop aftertaste.

Mulberry Tree *(OG 1050, ABV 5%)*

CLEARWATER SIBA

Clearwater Brewery, 2 Devon Units, Hatchmoor Industrial Estate, Great Torrington, Devon, EX38 7HP
Tel (01805) 625242
Tours by arrangement

⊗ Clearwater took on the closed St Giles in the Wood brewery in 1999 and has steadily grown since. The brewery has a 10-12 barrel capacity and the owners plan to bottle their beers. Around 80 outlets are supplied direct. Seasonal beer: Ebony & Ivory (ABV 4.2%, winter).

Cavalier *(OG 1041, ABV 4%)* ◆
Mid-brown, full-bodied best bitter with a burnt, rich malt aroma and taste, leading to a bitter, well-rounded finish.

Torridge Best *(OG 1044, ABV 4.4%)*

1646 *(OG 1047, ABV 4.8%)*

Oliver's Nectar *(OG 1051, ABV 5.2%)*

CLOCKWORK

⬭ **The Clockwork Beer Co,**
1153/55 Cathcart Road, Glasgow, G42 9HB
Tel/Fax (0141) 6490184
E-mail rhg@talk21.com
Tours by arrangement

Robin and Gay Graham, a husband-and-wife partnership, purchased a Glasgow pub in 1997, gutted it and rebuilt it to include a micro-brewery in the middle of the bar. Beers, which use primarily American hops, are: Amber IPA (ABV 3.8%), Red Alt Beer (ABV 4.4%), either Oregon IPA (ABV 5.5%) or Thunder and Lightning (ABV 6%) – the uncut versions of the Amber IPA and Red Alt Beer, Original Lager (ABV 4.8%), Hazy Daze fruit range (ABV 5%): Seriously Ginger is permanent, with others produced as the fruit is available (eg Kiwi, Raspberry and Banana). A German Weisse [wheat] Beer and a Raspberry Weisse Beer (both ABV 5%) are also produced. A Monthly Special (ABV 4.1/4.2%) is always available and uses European/British hops for customers who are not keen on the more flowery American hops. The Specials tend to be quite eclectic, ranging from Original Kelpie [seaweed] Ale, Scottish Oatmeal Stout to Organic Rowan Ale. They are on sale for approximately four weeks at a time. The ales are only available in the pub itself. All the beers are cold conditioned and, with the exception of the strong ales (ie 5.5% ABV plus) are sold from five-barrel conditioning tanks. The Original Lager, the Weisse beer and the Hazy Daze range are served under artificial CO2 pressure, while the Amber, Red Alt ale and the Special utilise a system in which they are covered with a blanket of the gasses naturally produced by their fermentation: no pressure

is involved. The strong ales (ie 5.5% plus) are cask conditioned and dispensed in the traditional Scottish spear extraction method.

COACH HOUSE SIBA

Coach House Brewing Company Ltd, Wharf Street, Howley, Warrington, WA1 2DQ
Tel (01925) 232800
Fax (01925) 232700
E-mail info@coach-house-brewing.co.uk
Tours by arrangement for CAMRA groups

☺ The brewery was founded in 1991 by four ex-Greenall Whitley employees. In 1995 Coach House increased its brewing capacity to cope with growing demand and it now delivers to some 250 outlets throughout England, Wales and Scotland, either direct or via wholesalers. The brewery also brews a large number of one-off and special beers. Seasonal beers: Ostlers Summer Pale Ale (ABV 4%, summer), Squires Gold (ABV 4.2%, spring), Summer Sizzler (ABV 4.2%, summer), Countdown (ABV 4.7%, 6 December onwards), Taverners Autumn Ale (ABV 5%, autumn), Blunderbus Old Porter (ABV 5.5% winter).

Coachman's Best Bitter
(OG 1037, ABV 3.7%) ◆
A well-hopped, malty bitter, moderately fruity with a hint of sweetness and a peppery nose.

Honeypot Bitter *(OG 1037, ABV 3.8%)*

Gunpowder Mild *(OG 1037, ABV 3.8%)* ◆
Dark brown, lightly hopped, malty mild with faint roast undertones. Easy drinking but not as characterful as it once was.

Turnpike *(OG 1037, ABV 3.8%)*

Dick Turpin *(OG 1042, ABV 4.2%)* ◆
Malty, hoppy pale brown beer with some initial sweetish flavours leading to a short, bitter aftertaste. Also sold under other names as a pub house beer.

Flintlock Pale Ale *(OG 1044, ABV 4.4%)*

Innkeeper's Special Reserve
(OG 1044, ABV 4.5%) ◆
A darkish, full-flavoured bitter. Quite fruity, with a strong, bitter aftertaste.

Postlethwaite *(OG 1045, ABV 4.6%)*

Gingernut Premium *(OG 1049, ABV 5%)*

Posthorn Premium *(OG 1049, ABV 5%)* ◆
Well-hopped and fruity, with bitterness and malt also prominent. Hoppy aroma and fruity aftertaste.

For John Joule of Stone

Old Knotty *(ABV 3.6%)*

Old Priory *(ABV 4.4%)*

Victory *(ABV 5.2%)*

COLES

⬭ **Coles Family Brewery,**
White Hart Thatched Inn & Brewery,
Llanddarog, Nr Carmarthen, SA32 8NT
Tel (01267) 275395
Tours by arrangement

⊗ Coles is based in an ancient inn built in 1371. Centuries ago it brewed its own beer, but only started brewing again in 1999. The site has its own water supply 320 feet below ground, free from pollution. Coles makes a large selection of cask ales due to a system that allows small-batch production. Two pubs are owned. Seasonal beers: Cwrw Nadolig (ABV 3%, Christmas), Summer Harvest (ABV 3.8%).

Nettle Ale *(OG 1039, ABV 3.8%)*

Oaten Barley Stout *(OG 1042, ABV 4%)*

Liquorice Stout *(OG 1042, ABV 4%)*

Black Stag *(OG 1042, ABV 4%)*

Amber Ale *(OG 1042, ABV 4%)*

Roasted Barley Stout *(OG 1042, ABV 4%)*

Cwrw Betys (Beetroot Ale) *(OG 1042, ABV 4%)*

Cwrw Llanddarog *(OG 1043, ABV 4.1%)*

Cwrw Blasus *(OG 1044, ABV 4.3%)*

Dewi Sant *(OG 1045, ABV 4.4%)*

CONCERTINA SIBA

◻ Concertina Brewery, 9A Dolcliffe Road, Mexborough, South Yorkshire, S64 9AZ
Tel (01709) 580841
Tours by arrangement

A club once famous for its concertina band, where brewing started in the cellar in 1992. The plant is continuously upgraded and produces eight barrels a week and supplies 25 outlets.

Club Bitter *(ABV 3.9%)* ◆
A fruity session bitter with a good bitter flavour.

Old Dark Attic *(OG 1038, ABV 3.9%)*
A dark brown beer with a fairly sweet, fruity taste.

Best Bitter *(OG 1038.5, ABV 3.9%)* ◆
This mid-brown bitter has lots of hops on the nose, a hoppy taste and a dry finish, plus gentle fruitiness throughout.

One-eyed Jack *(OG 1039, ABV 4%)*
Fairly pale in colour, with plenty of hop bitterness. Brewed with the same malt and hops combination as Bengal Tiger, but more of a session beer. Also known as Mexborough Bitter.

Bengal Tiger *(OG 1043, ABV 4.6%)* ◆
Light amber ale with an aromatic hoppy nose followed by a wonderful combination of fruit and bitterness. A very smooth finish.

Dictators *(OG 1044, ABV 4.7%)*

Ariel Square Four *(OG 1046, ABV 5.2%)*

CONISTON SIBA

◻ Coniston Brewing Co Ltd, Coppermines Road, Coniston, Cumbria, LA21 8HL
Tel (015394) 41133
Fax (015394) 41177
E-mail Coniston.brewery@kencomp.net
Website www.conistonbrewery.com
Shop 10-11.
Tours by arrangement.

☺ A 10-barrel brewery set up in 1995 behind the Black Bull inn, it achieved national fame when it won the Champion Beer of Britain competition in 1998 for

Bluebird Bitter. This was followed by SIBA North first prize in 2003. It is now brewing 30 barrels a week and supplies 30 local outlets direct. One pub is owned. Bottle-conditioned Bluebird is brewed at Hepworth in Horsham (qv). Seasonal beer: Blacksmith's Ale (ABV 5%, Dec-Mar).

Bluebird Bitter *(OG 1036, ABV 3.6%)* 🗋◆
A yellow-gold, predominantly hoppy and fruity beer, well-balanced with some sweetness and a rising bitter finish.

Opium *(OG 1039, ABV 4%)* ◆
Copper-coloured with distinctly fruity, hoppy aromas; a well-balanced flavour with malt, hops and fruit, and more bitter and astringent in the aftertaste.

Bluebird XB *(OG 1042, ABV 4.2%)* ◆
Well-balanced, hoppy and fruity golden bitter. Bitter-sweet in the mouth with dryness building.

Old Man Ale *(OG 1042, ABV 4.2%)* ◆
Delicious fruity, winey beer with complex, well-balanced richness.

COPPER DRAGON* SIBA

Copper Dragon Skipton Brewery Ltd, Snaygill Industrial Estate, Keighley Road, Skipton, North Yorkshire, BD23 2QR
Tel (01756) 702130
Fax (01756) 702136
E-mail sales@copperdragon.uk.com
Website www.copperdragon.uk.com

Copper Dragon is a new venture in a town that hasn't seen a brewery for a century. The first brew was delivered in March 2003. The directors are partners Steve Taylor (a craft brewer of 20 years) and Ruth Bennett. The head brewer is Gordon Wilkinson, formerly of Websters for 18 years and Oakwell (Barnsley) for six. The plant has a brew length of 10 barrels with the potential to be increased over the next two years. Early response to the beers in the local area has been very positive. Seasonal beers: Challenger (ABV 4.5%), Golden Pippin Ale.

Dark Ale *(ABV 3.5%)*
A recipe from days gone by, using coloured malts to give a rich roasted flavour.

Best Bitter *(ABV 3.8%)*
A refreshing amber best bitter, with a well-balanced malty and hoppy flavour.

Pale Ale *(ABV 4.4%)*
A traditional premium ale, full bodied and fruity with subtle hoppy undertones.

CORVEDALE SIBA

◻ Corvedale Brewery, The Sun Inn, Corfton, Craven Arms, Shropshire, SY7 9DF
Tel (01584) 861239
E-mail normanspride@aol.com
Website www.thesuninn.netfirms.com
Tours by arrangement

☺ Brewing started in 1999 in a building behind the pub. Landlord Norman Pearce is also the brewer and he uses only British malt and hops, with water from a local borehole. Corvedale swaps its beer with those of other small craft breweries, making them available in many parts of the country. One pub is owned and 10 outlets are supplied. Seasonal beer: Teresa Pride (ABV 4.3%, January). All beers are on sale in the pub in bottle-conditioned form and not fined, making them suitable for vegetarians and vegans.

Katie's Pride (OG 1040, ABV 4%)

Norman's Pride (OG 1043, ABV 4.3%)
A golden amber beer with a refreshing, slightly hoppy taste and a bitter finish.

Secret Hop (OG 1045, ABV 4.5%)
A clear, ruby bitter with a smooth malty taste. Customers are invited to guess the hop!

Dark and Delicious (OG 1045, ABV 4.6%)
A dark ruby beer with hops on the aroma and palate, and a sweet aftertaste.

COTLEIGH SIBA

Cotleigh Brewery, Ford Road, Wiveliscombe, Somerset, TA4 2RE
Tel (01984) 624086
Fax (01984) 624365
E-mail cotleigh@cloveruk.net
Website www.cotleighbrewery.co.uk
Tours Yes, but limited

⊗ Cotleigh Brewery is one of the oldest and most successful small breweries in the West Country. The brewery, which started trading in 1979, is housed in specially converted premises with a modern plant capable of producing 140 barrels a week. 150 pubs, mostly in Devon and Somerset, are supplied from the brewery; the beers are also widely available across the country via selected wholesalers. Seasonal beer: Old Buzzard (ABV 4.8%, Oct-March). In July 2003 the brewery was bought by Steve Heptinstall and Fred Domellof when founders John and Jenny Aries retired.

Tawny Bitter (OG 1038, ABV 3.8%) ◆
Well-balanced, tawny-coloured bitter with plenty of malt and fruitiness on the nose; malt to the fore followed by hop fruit, developing to a satisfying bitter finish.

Golden Eagle (OG 1042, ABV 4.2%) ◆
A gold, well-hopped premium bitter with a flowery hop aroma and fruity hop flavour, clean mouthfeel, leading to a dry, hoppy finish.

Barn Owl Bitter (OG 1045, ABV 4.5%) ◆
A pale to mid-brown beer with a good balance of malt and hops on the nose; a smooth, full-bodied taste with hops dominating, but balanced by malt, following through to the finish.

COTTAGE SIBA

The Cottage Brewing Co Ltd, The Old Cheese Dairy, Hornblotton Road, Lovington, Somerset, BA7 7PS
Tel (01963) 240551
Fax (01963) 240383
Website www.cottagebrewing.com
Tours by arrangement

⊗ The brewery, which celebrated its 10th anniversary in 2003, was founded in West Lydford in 1993 and upgraded to a 10-barrel plant in 1994. Owned by former airline pilot Chris Norman and his wife Helen, the company got off to a flying start when

Norman's Conquest won the Champion Beer of Britain title at the 1995 Great British Beer Festival. Other awards followed and, on the strength of this success, the brewery moved to larger premises in 1996, doubling the brewing capacity at the same time. In early summer 2001, Cottage installed a 30-barrel plant that enabled head brewer Daren Godfrey to brew four times a week, instead of six or seven times a week on the previous 20-barrel kit. 1,500 outlets are supplied. The malt used is Maris Otter and hops come mainly from Kent. In 1997 Golden Arrow won the silver medal for Best Bitter at the Great British Beer Festival. In 1999 Norman's Conquest won the Gold Medal for strong beers at the Great British Winter Beer Festival. No pubs are owned but the beers are supplied as far away as Liverpool and Yorkshire. The names of beers mostly follow a railway theme. Seasonal beers: Goldrush (ABV 5%), Santa's Steaming Ale (ABV 5.5%, Christmas). Norman's Conquest is also available in filtered bottled form.

Southern Bitter (OG 1039, ABV 3.7%) ◆
Gold-coloured beer with malt and fruity hops on the nose. Malt and hops in the mouth with a long fruity, bitter finish.

Champflower Ale (OG 1041, ABV 4.2%) ◆
Amber beer with fruity hop aroma, full hop taste and powerful bitter finish.

Somerset & Dorset Ale
(OG 1044, ABV 4.4%)
A well-hopped, malty brew, with a deep red colour.

Golden Arrow
(OG 1043, ABV 4.5%) ◆
A hoppy golden bitter with a powerful floral bouquet, a fruity, full-bodied taste and a lingering dry, bitter finish.

Norman's Conquest (OG 1066, ABV 7%) ◆
A dark strong ale, with plenty of fruit in the aroma and taste; rounded vinous, hoppy finish.

COUNTRY LIFE SIBA

Country Life Brewery, The Big Sheep Theme Park, Abbotsham, Bideford, Devon, EX39 5AP
Tel (01237) 420808/07971 267790
E-mail simon@countrylifebrewery .freeserve.co.uk
Website www.countrylifebrewery.co.uk
Shop open 7 days a week
Tours by arrangement

⊗ The original 2.5-barrel plant was bought from the Lundy Island brewery in the Bristol Channel and set up by Simon Lacey at the Pig on the Hill pub. Country Life then moved to the Big Sheep tourist attraction. The Lundy plant was replaced with a five-barrel one producing some 15 barrels a week. More than 30 outlets are supplied. Bottle-conditioned beers: occasional bottles are produced for sale in the brewery shop.

Old Appledore (OG 1038, ABV 3.7%)

Wallop (OG 1044, ABV 4.4%)

Golden Pig (OG 1046, ABV 4.7%)

Country Bumpkin (OG 1058, ABV 6%)

COX & HOLBROOK

Cox & Holbrook, Manor Farm, Brettenham Road, Buxhall, Suffolk, IP14 3DY
Tel/Fax (01449) 736323

Brewing suspended but hopes to re-start.

CROPTON SIBA

♥ **Cropton Brewery, Cropton, Nr Pickering, North Yorkshire, YO18 8HH**
Tel/Fax (01751) 417582
E-mail info@croptonbrewery.co.uk
Website www.croptonbrewery.co.uk
Shop merchandise available all year round at the New Inn
Tours by arrangement

☺ Brewing returned to Cropton in 1984 when the cellars of the pub were converted to accommodate a five-barrel plant. The plant was extended in 1988, but by 1994 it had outgrown the cellar and a purpose-built brewery was installed in the grounds of Woolcroft Farm behind the pub. Production fluctuates between 35 and 50 barrels a week according to the season. Cropton's nine additive-free beers are supplied to more than 100 independent outlets direct and nationwide through wholesalers. All the beers, with the exception of Balmy Mild and Yorkshire Moors Bitter, are available bottle-conditioned and can be purchased from the visitor centre attached to the pub. Bottled beers are suitable for vegetarians and vegans. Seasonal: Rudolph's Revenge (ABV 4.6%), Balmy Mild (ABV 4.4%).

King Billy *(OG 1038, ABV 3.6%)* ♦
A refreshing, straw-coloured bitter, quite hoppy, with a strong but pleasant bitter finish that leaves a clean, dry taste on the palate.

Endeavour Ale *(OG 1038, ABV 3.6%)*
A light session ale, made with the best quality hops, providing a refreshing drink with a delicately fruity aftertaste.

Two Pints *(OG 1040, ABV 4%)* ♦
A good, full-bodied bitter. Malt flavours initially dominate, with a touch of caramel, but the balancing hoppiness and residual sweetness come through.

Honey Gold Bitter *(OG 1042, ABV 4.2%)* ♦
A medium-bodied beer, ideal for summer drinking. Honey is apparent in both aroma and taste but does not overwhelm. Clean finish with a hint of hops.

Scoresby Stout *(OG 1042, ABV 4.2%)* ♥♦
A classic of the style. A jet-black stout whose roast malt and chocolate flavours contrast with a satisfying bitter finish.

Balmy Mild *(OG 1044, ABV 4.4%)* ♦
Dark and full-flavoured with a malty aroma and taste. Milk chocolate and slight coffee notes.

Uncle Sam's *(OG 1046, ABV 4.4%)* ♦
A clean-tasting and refreshing premium pale ale. The overriding characteristic is the fruity bouquet yielded by authentic American ingredients.

Yorkshire Moors Bitter
(OG 1046, ABV 4.6%)
A ruby beer brewed with Fuggles and Progress hops. A hoppy beer with a fruity aftertaste. Brewed to commemorate the North York Moors National Parks 50th Anniversary.

Monkmans Slaughter
(OG 1060, ABV 6%) ♦
Rich tasting and warming; fruit and malt in the aroma and taste, with dark chocolate, caramel and autumn fruit notes. Subtle bitterness continues into the aftertaste.

CROUCH VALE SIBA

Crouch Vale Brewery Limited,
12 Redhills Road, South Woodham Ferrers, Chelmsford, Essex, CM3 5UP
Tel (01245) 322744
Fax (01245) 329082
E-mail info@crouch-vale.co.uk
Website www.crouch-vale.co.uk
Tours by arrangement

⊗ Founded over 20 years ago by two CAMRA enthusiasts, Crouch Vale is now well established as a major craft brewer in Essex, still brewing in the original premises in the industrial area of South Woodham Ferrers. The company is also a major wholesaler of cask ale from other independent breweries, which they supply to more than 250 outlets as well as beer festivals throughout the region. Two tied houses are owned, both serving a range of Crouch Vale beers with additional guest ales. The beer range was substantially revamped in 2002. Seasonal beers: two beers are available each month, details on website.

Essex Boys Bitter *(OG 1035, ABV 3.5%)*
A pale brown beer with plenty of pleasing malt and hop flavour despite the low gravity.

Blackwater Mild
(OG 1037, ABV 3.7%) ♦
A fruity mild with a full body, in spite of its name.

Crouch Best *(OG 1040, ABV 4%)* ♦
Dry, copper-coloured beer with a gentle hoppiness throughout, and a bitter taste and astringent finish.

Brewers Gold *(OG 1040, ABV 4%)* ▣♦
Striking grapefruit nose leads to a beer of generally citrus hoppy character, underpinned by a perfumed sweetness and an aftertaste of orange wine gums.

Anchor Street Porter
(OG 1049, ABV 4.9%)
A strong and substantial dark ale, brewed using roasted malts and dry-hopped for a fuller flavour.

CROUCH VALE BREWERY

CROWN SIBA

⌂ Crown Brewery Sheffield,
Hillsborough Hotel, 54-58 Longsett Road,
Sheffield, S6 2UB
Tel/Fax (0114) 2322100
E-mail reception@hillsboroughhotel.com
Website www.crownbrewery.com
Tours by arrangement

Head brewer Brian Hendry has accumulated an impressive array of awards since brewing started in 2001. The five-barrel plant from Iceni Brewery uses steam power and is located in the cellar of the hotel. The brewery was extended in 2003 primarily to meet demand but also to allow the development of a porter and a wheat beer to complement the regular beer range. One pub is owned and 10 outlets are supplied.

Hillsborough Pale Ale (OG 1039, ABV 3.9%)
The combination of lager malt, wheat malt and American hops produce a pale, thirst-quenching, hoppy session beer.

Loxley Gold (OG 1045, ABV 4.5%)
Voted Beer of the Festival at the 2002 Great Welsh Beer Festival. This is a fine, crisp, well-balanced golden best bitter.

Stannington Stout (OG 1050, ABV 5%)
Chocolate and liquorice undertones complement the smooth rich texture. An award winner at the Great Yorkshire, Oakwood and Sheffield festivals.

CROWN AND ANCHOR*

⌂ Crown and Anchor Pub and Brewery,
75 Main Street, Newport, Brough,
East Yorkshire, HU15 2PR
Tel (01430) 449757
E-mail phil@crownandanchor.co.uk
Tours by prior arrangement

The brewery started in 2002 with a 2.5-barrel plant purchased from the Brown Cow brewery at Barlow and fitted in what was a large pool room. One pub is owned and various local pubs are supplied. Seasonal beers will be produced throughout the year.

Newport Original (OG 1036, ABV 3.6%)

Newport Bridge IPA (OG 1042, ABV 4.2%)

CUCKMERE HAVEN SIBA

Cuckmere Haven Brewery, Exceat Bridge,
Cuckmere Haven, East Sussex, BN25 4AB
Tel (01323) 892247
Fax (01323) 892555
E-mail info@goldengalleon.co.uk
Website goldengalleon.co.uk
Tours by arrangement

☺ Alan Edgar set up the brewery in 1994 adjacent to the Golden Galleon inn overlooking Cuckmere Haven. Hops from his own hop garden are used in production.

Downland Bitter (OG 1035, ABV 3.4%)
Light bitter brewed with Fuggles and Goldings hops. High proportion of old style amber malt for toffee notes in the aftertaste. Dry and hoppy on the palate.

Best Bitter (OG 1041, ABV 4.1%) ◆
Medium colour bitter. Dry hopping with full flower Goldings gives strong hop aroma and fruity aftertaste.

Saxon King Stout (OG 1042, ABV 4.2%)
Dark and rich. A nice balance between sharp and soft tastes.

Guvnor (OG 1045, ABV 4.7%)
Tawny strong ale. Dry hopped with Goldings for aroma.

Golden Peace (OG 1054, ABV 5.5%)
A light-coloured strong ale brewed originally in May 1995 as a celebration of the 50th anniversary of VE Day.

Saxon King Stout Extra (ABV 5.5%)

Saxon Berserker (ABV 7%)

CWMBRAN SIBA

Cwmbran Brewery, Gorse Cottage, Graig
Road, Upper Cwmbran, Torfaen, NP44 5AS
Tel (01633) 485233 or 482543

☺ Cwmbran Brewery is a craft brewery on the slopes of Mynydd Maen in Upper Cwmbran in Gwent's Eastern Valley. With an output of up to 24 barrels a week, the brewery is built alongside the brewer's cottage home. A mountain spring supplies the water used for brewing liquor. The brewery has produced a range of six cask beers that are all produced using traditional methods and ingredients. It is planned to install a larger mash tun to double output. 40-plus outlets are supplied. Seasonal beer: Santa's Tipple (ABV 4.8%, Christmas).

Double Hop (OG 1039, ABV 4%)

Crow Valley Bitter (OG 1042, ABV 4.2%) ◆
Gentle malt and hop aroma followed by a crisp, clean mix of malt, hop and fruit flavours. Moderate bitterness builds, leaving a lasting finish.

Crow Valley Stout/Deryn Du
(OG 1050, ABV 4-4.2%)

Four Seasons (OG 1047/49, ABV 4.8%)

Full Malty (OG 1047/49, ABV 4.8%)

Gorse Porter (OG 1048, ABV 4.8%)

DALESIDE

Daleside Brewery Ltd, Unit 1, Camwal Road,
Harrogate, North Yorkshire, HG1 4PT
Tel (01423) 880022 Fax (01423) 541717
E-mail dalesidebrewery@hotmail.com
Website www.dalesidebrewery.co.uk
Shop 9-5 Mon-Fri

☺ After years of gradual expansion, capacity at Daleside was greatly increased in 2000 when plant was bought from Vaux. Around 200 barrels a week are brewed, half of which is cask beer. Daleside has no tied pubs but the beers are available nationwide. 2002 saw the introduction of a range of seasonal styles brewed throughout the year. Some 400 outlets are supplied.

Bitter (OG 1038, ABV 3.7%) 🍷🍷◆
Pale brown in colour, this well-balanced, hoppy beer is pleasantly complemented with fruity bitterness and a hint of sweetness, leading to a moderately long, bitter finish.

Blonde (OG 1041, ABV 3.9%) ◆
A pale golden beer with a predominantly hoppy aroma and taste, leading to a refreshing hoppy, bitter but short finish.

Old Legover *(OG 1043, ABV 4.1%)* ◆
A well-balanced, mid-brown, refreshing beer that leads to an equally well-balanced, fruity and bitter aftertaste.

Greengrass Old Rogue Ale
(OG 1046, ABV 4.5%) ◆
Well-balanced, full-bodied amber bitter with strong hop and fruit overtones, the fruitiness carries through to the aftertaste, which has a long, dry, bitter finish.

Monkey Wrench *(OG 1053, ABV 5.3%)* ◆
A powerful strong ale, mid-brown to ruby in hue. Aromas of fruit, hops, malt and roast malt give way to well-balanced fruit, malt and hoppiness on the tongue, with some sweetness throughout. A very flavoursome beer.

Morocco Ale *(OG 1058, ABV 5.5%)* 🍴◆
A powerful, dark brew with malt and fruit in the taste. A spicy beer in which ginger predominates and can at times overpower. Brewed to an Elizabethan recipe found at Levens Hall in Cumbria and using a 'secret' spice, the beer is becoming increasingly more widely available.

For AVS Wholesalers of Gravesend:

Shrimpers *(OG 1043, ABV 4.1%)*
A mid-amber bitter with a malty nose and a hint of fruitiness. Hops and malt carry over to leave a clean, hoppy aftertaste.

DARK STAR SIBA

**Dark Star Brewing Co Ltd,
Moonhill Farm, Burgess Hill Road, Ansty, Haywards Heath,
W Sussex, RH17 5AH
Tel/Fax (01444) 412311
E-mail info@darkstarbrewing.co.uk
Website www.darkstarbrewing.co.uk**
Tours by arrangement

⊗ The brewery was originally set up in the cellar of the Evening Star pub in Brighton in 1995. Due to space restrictions and demand for the beers, a brand new 15-barrel brewhouse was built in a former dairy near Burgess Hill to supply 25 local outlets and selective wholesalers. One pub is owned (but with guest beers). During the past couple of years, the brewery has won a number of awards for its beers and sales continue to grow at a steady rate. Seasonal beers: Sunburst (ABV 4.8%), Meltdown (ABV 4.8%), City Porter (ABV 5.5%), Critical Mass (ABV 7%), Golden Gate (ABV 4.3%). Suitable for vegetarians/vegans: Natural Blonde Lager (unfiltered, ABV 4.5%).

Hophead *(OG 1036-1040, ABV 3.8%)* 🍴
A light, hoppy, refreshing bitter.

Over the Moon *(OG 1036-1040, ABV 3.8%)*

Landlords Wit *(OG 1039-1043, ABV 4.1%)*

Best *(OG 1039-1043, ABV 4.1%)*

Espresso Stout
(OG 1040-1044, ABV 4.2%)

Red Ale *(OG 1048-1052, ABV 5%)*
Malty, full-flavoured, dry-hopped red ale.

Dark Star *(OG 1048-1052, ABV 5%)* ◆
Dark full-bodied ale with a roast malt aroma and a dry, bitter stout-like finish.

Festival *(OG 1049-1053, ABV 5%)*

DARKTRIBE

**DarkTribe Brewery, 25 Doncaster Road, Gunness, Scunthorpe, Lincs, DN15 8TG
Tel (01724) 782324
Fax (01724) 782324
E-mail dixie@darktribe.co.uk
Website www.darktribe.co.uk**

⊗ The small brewery was built during the summer of 1996 in a workshop at the bottom of the garden by Dave 'Dixie' Dean. The beers generally follow a marine theme, recalling Dixie's days as a marine engineer in the Merchant Navy and his enthusiasm for sailing. DarkTribe merged with Duffield of Harmston, Lincs. The original brewhouse was been replaced by a bigger building but the original 2.5-barrel plant is still in use. Twelve outlets are supplied. Seasonal beers: Dixie's Midnight Runner (ABV 6.5%, Dec-Jan), Dark Destroyer (ABV 9.7%, August onwards).

Dixie's Mild *(ABV 3.6%)*

Honey Mild *(ABV 3.6%)*

Albacore *(ABV 3.8%)*

Full Ahead *(ABV 4%)* ◆
A malty smoothness backed by a slightly fruity hop give a good bitterness to this amber-brown bitter.

Red Duster *(ABV 4%)*

Bucket Hitch *(ABV 4.4%)*

Dr Griffin's Mermaid *(ABV 4.5%)*

Old Gaffer *(ABV 4.5%)*

Dixie's Bollards *(ABV 4.5%)*

Galleon *(ABV 4.7%)* 🍴◆
A tasty, golden, smooth, full-bodied ale with fruity hops and consistent malt. The thirst-quenching bitterness lingers into a well-balanced finish.

Twin Screw *(ABV 5.1%)* ◆
A fruity, rose-hip tasting beer, red in colour. Good malt presence with a dry, hoppy bitterness coming through in the finish.

DARWIN SIBA

**Darwin Brewery Ltd, 63 Back Tatham Street, Sunderland, SR1 2QE
Tel (0191) 514 4746
Fax (0191) 515 2531
E-mail info@darwinbrewery.com
Website www.darwinbrewery.com**
Tours by arrangement (including tasting at local venue)

☺ The Darwin Brewery first brewed in 1994 and expanded into larger scale production with the construction of its Wearside brewery in central Sunderland in 2002 after a move from the Hodges brewhouse in

Crook, Co Durham. The current brewery uses the brewplant from Butterknowle brewery and produces a range of high-quality beers with the strong individual character of the North-east region. Darwin Brewery specialises in historical recreations of past beers such as Flag Porter, a beer produced with yeast rescued from a shipwreck in the English Channel. The brewery also produces trial beers from the Brewlab training and research unit at the University of Sunderland, and experiments in the production of novel and overseas styles for occasional production. The brewery now produces the beers of the High Force Brewery in Teesdale. Bottle-conditioned beer: Cauldron Snout, Forest XB.

Ghost Ale *(OG 1037, ABV 4.1%)*

Sunderland Best *(OG 1041, ABV 3.9%)*

Evolution Ale *(OG 1042, ABV 4%)*
A dark amber, full-bodied bitter with a malty flavour and a clean, bitter aftertaste.

Durham Light Ale *(OG 1042, ABV 4%)*

Smugglers Mild *(OG 1044, ABV 4%)*

Richmond Ale *(OG 1048, ABV 4.5%)*

Saints Sinner *(OG 1052, ABV 5%)*
A rich, smooth-tasting, ruby-red ale with a fruity aroma and hop character in the taste.

Killer Bee *(OG 1054, ABV 6%)*

Imperial Stout *(OG 1072, ABV 7%)*

Extinction Ale *(OG 1086, ABV 8.3%)*

For High Force Hotel:

Teesdale Bitter
(OG 1040, ABV 3.8%)

Forest XB *(OG 1044, ABV 4.2%)*

Cauldron Snout *(OG 1056, ABV 5.6%)*

DENT SIBA

Dent Brewery, Hollins, Cowgill, Dent, Cumbria, LA10 5TQ
Tel (01539) 625326
Fax (01539) 625033
E-mail martin@dentbrew.u-net.com
Tours by arrangement (minimum six people)

☺ A brewery set up in a converted barn in the Yorkshire Dales National Park in 1990, originally to supply just three local pubs. It now has two tied houses and supplies 50 free trade outlets. Its own distribution company, Flying Firkin (01282 865923), delivers all over northern England and is making some inroads into the south. All Dent's beers are brewed using the brewery's own spring water.

Bitter *(OG 1036, ABV 3.7%)* ❧
Fruity throughout and lightly hopped. This beer has a pervading earthiness that is evident to a lesser extent in other Dent beers. A short, bitter finish.

Rambrau *(OG 1039, ABV 4.2%)*
A cask-conditioned lager.

Ramsbottom Strong Ale
(OG 1044, ABV 4.5%) ❧
This complex, mid-brown beer has a warming, dry, bitter finish to follow its unusual combination of roast, bitter, fruity and sweet flavours.

T'Owd Tup *(OG 1058, ABV 6%)* ⬚❧
A rich, fully-flavoured, strong stout with a coffee aroma. The dominant roast character is balanced by a warming sweetness and a raisiny, fruit-cake taste that linger on into the finish.

For Flying Firkin:
Aviator *(OG 1038, ABV 4%)* ⬚❧
This medium-bodied amber ale is characterised by strong citrus and hoppy flavours that develop into a long bitter finish.

Kamikaze *(OG 1048, ABV 5%)* ⬚❧
Hops and fruit dominate this full-bodied, golden, strong bitter, with a dry bitterness growing in the aftertaste.

DERWENT

Derwent Brewing Co,
Units 2a/2b Station Road Industrial Estate,
Silloth, Cumbria, CA5 4AG
Tel (016973) 31522
Fax (016973) 31523
Tours by arrangement

☺ Derwent was set up in 1996 in Cockermouth by Hans Kruger and Frank Smith, both former Jenning's employees, and moved to Silloth in 1998. It supplies beers throughout the north of England, with outlets in Cumbria, Lancashire, Yorkshire, Cheshire and the North-east. It organises the Silloth Beer Festival every September. It has supplied Carlisle State Bitter to the House of Commons, a beer that recreates one produced by the state-owned Carlisle Brewery. Seasonal beers: Derwent Summer Rose (ABV 4.2%), Derwent Spring Time (ABV 4.3%), Harvesters Ale (ABV 4.3%), Bill Monk (ABV 4.5%), Auld Kendal (ABV 5.7%, winter).

Carlisle State Bitter
(OG 1037, ABV 3.7%) ❧
A light hoppy beer with underlying malt and fruit and a dry, yeasty finish.

Parsons Pledge *(OG 1040, ABV 4%)*

W & M Kendal Pale Ale
(OG 1044, ABV 4.4%) ❧
A sweet, fruity, hoppy beer with a bitter finish.

DERWENT ROSE

⬚ **Derwent Rose Brewery, Grey Horse,**
115 Sherburn Terrace, Consett,
Co Durham, DH8 6NE
Tel (01207) 502585
E-mail paul@thegreyhorse.co.uk
Website www.thegreyhorse.co.uk

A micro-brewery based in Consett's oldest surviving pub, 154 years old in 2000, it produced its first brew in a former stable block behind the pub in 1997. Seasonal beer: St Patricks.

3 Giants *(ABV 3.2%)*

Mutton Clog *(ABV 3.8%)*

Steel Town *(ABV 3.8%)*

Target Ale *(ABV 4%)*

Conroy's Stout *(ABV 4.1%)*

Red Dust *(ABV 4.2%)*

Potts' Clock (*ABV 4.2%*)

Swordmaker (*ABV 4.5%*)

Angel Ale (*ABV 5%*)

Coast 2 Coast (*ABV 5%*)

Derwent Deep (*ABV 5%*)

DEVON

Devon Ales Ltd, Mansfield Arms,
7 Main Street, Sauchie, Alloa, FK10 3JR
Tel (01259) 722020
Fax (01259) 216636
E-mail john.gibson@btinternet.com
Tours by arrangement

This family-owned and run brewery was established to produce high quality ales in 1993 in outbuildings at the rear of the Mansfield Arms in Sauchie for the pub and The Inn at Muckhart.

Original (*OG 1037, ABV 3.7%*)

Thick Black (*OG 1042, ABV 4.2%*)

Pride (*OG 1046, ABV 4.8%*)

DOGHOUSE SIBA

Doghouse Brewery, Scorrier, Redruth,
Cornwall, TR16 5BN
Tel/Fax (01209) 822022
E-mail ian@startrax.fsbusiness.co.uk
Tours by arrangement

The brewery was launched in 2001 by two stalwart CAMRA members in a converted dog rescue kennel, hence the name of both brewery and beers. Boarding and breeding kennels still exist on the adjacent site making this, as described by a beer writer, 'One of the noisiest breweries I have ever visited, not from the banging of barrels, but from the dogs next door!' The five-barrel plant produces a full range of beers that expands as new recipes are tried out in the one pub owned by the brewery, free trade outlets in the county and beer festivals. Seasonal beers (both also bottle conditioned): Staffi Stout (ABV 4.7%, winter), Dingo Lager (ABV 5%, summer).

Wet Nose (*OG 1037, ABV 3.8%*)
A gold-coloured, quaffing bitter with plenty of hoppy bite in the aftertaste.

Retriever (*OG 1035, ABV 3.9%*)

Biter (*OG 1039, ABV 4%*)
Mid-brown, standard strength bitter.

Loyal Corgi (*OG 1043, ABV 4.5%*)
Gold-coloured beer first brewed for the Royal Jubilee but maintained.

Bow Wow (*OG 1048, ABV 5%*)
Dark ruby-coloured premium ale; well rounded maltiness gives way to a more bitter aftertaste.

DOLPHIN

The Dolphin Bar & Brewery, 48 St Michael's Street, Shrewsbury, SY1 2EZ
Tel (01743) 350419
E-mail brewers@thedolphinbrewery.co.uk
Website under construction

Dolphin was launched in 2000 by Peter Buy and Nigel Morton and was upgraded to 4.5 barrels in 2001. There are further plans to update the plant and install a small bottling line. One pub is owned. Porter is suitable for vegetarians and vegans.

Best Bitter (*OG 1043, ABV 4.2%*)

Gold (*OG 1044, ABV 4.5%*)

Porter (*OG 1045, ABV 4.6%*)

Brew (*OG 1046, ABV 4.8%*)

DONNINGTON IFBB

Donnington Brewery, Stow-on-the-Wold,
Cheltenham, Gloucestershire, GL54 1EP
Tel (01451) 830603

Thomas Arkell bought a 13th-century watermill in idyllic countryside in 1827, and he began brewing on the site in 1865. It is owned and run by a direct family descendant, Claude Arkell, and the millwheel is still used to drive small pumps and machinery. Donnington supplies its own 15 tied houses and a number of free trade outlets.

BB (*OG 1035, ABV 3.6%*) ◆
A pleasant amber bitter with a slight hop aroma, a good balance of malt and hops in the mouth and a bitter aftertaste.

SBA (*OG 1045, ABV 4.6%*) ◆
Malt dominates over bitterness in the subtle flavour of this premium bitter, which has a hint of fruit and a dry malty finish.

DONOGHUE

Donoghue Brewing Co, The Orchard,
Butt Gate, Grainthorpe, Louth,
Lincs, LN11 7HU
Tel (01472) 389543

Experimental brews were conducted in 1999 but brewing did not start on a regular basis until 2001. In 2002, the brewery left the Black Horse inn and is now operating from new premises, but it still supplies the pub.

Fiddlers Elbow (*ABV 3.5%*)

The Pipes (*ABV 3.7%*)

Danny Boy (*ABV 4%*)

DOW BRIDGE

Dow Bridge Brewery, 2-3 Rugby Road,
Catthorpe, Leics, LE17 6DA.
Tel/Fax (01788) 869121.
Tours by prior arrangement

Commercial brewing began in 2002, using equipment from two defunct micros. The current capacity is 2.5 barrels but expansion to five-barrel plant to meet demand is imminent. Beers are supplied mainly to outlets in Leicestershire, Northamptonshire and Warwickshire. 18 outlets are supplied.

Mild (*OG 1034, ABV 3.4%*)

Bitter (*OG 1037, ABV 3.8%*)

Ratae'd (*OG 1042, ABV 4.3%*)

DRIFTWOOD

Driftwood Spars Co Ltd,
Trevaunance Cove, Quay Rd, St Agnes,
Cornwall, TR5 0RT

Tel (01872) 552428/553323
Fax (01872) 553701
E-mail driftwoodspars@hotmail.com
Website www.driftwoodspars.com
Tours by arrangement

Gordon Treleaven started brewing in 2000 in this famous Cornish pub and hotel that dates back to 1660. The brewery is based in the former Flying Dutchman café across the road from the hotel. The Old Horsebridge one-barrel plant has been replaced by a state of the art, customised, five-barrel plant. Pale malt comes from Tuckers of Newton Abbott and the hops are Fuggles.

Cuckoo Ale *(OG 1045, ABV 4.5%)*

DUNN PLOWMAN SIBA

Dunn Plowman Brewery, Unit 1A, Arrow Court Industrial Estate, Hergest Road, Kington, Herefordshire, HR5 3ER
Tel (01544) 231993
E-mail dunnplowman.brewery@talk21.com
Tours by arrangement

⊗ The brewery was established in 1987 as a brew-pub, moved to Leominster in 1992, and to its present site in 2002, when Dunn Plowman bought SP Sporting Ales of Leominster. The brewery supplies the Old Tavern, its brewery tap, and 30 other outlets within a 50-mile radius. It is run by husband and wife team Steve and Gaye Dunn. Seasonal beers: Crooked Furrow (ABV 6.5%, Nov-Jan, all year in bottle), Parsons Nose (ABV 5.5%, Nov-Jan). Bottle-conditioned beers: Old Jake Stout (ABV 4.8%), Kyneton Ale (ABV 5%), Golden Haze Wheat Beer (ABV 5%), Crooked Furrow (ABV 6.5%). In 2002 Dunn Plowman bought SP Sporting Ales of Leominster and now uses that equipment as well.

Thomas Bewick Bitter *(OG 1036, ABV 3.7%)*

Brewhouse Bitter *(OG 1037, ABV 3.8%)*

Early Riser *(OG 1039, ABV 4%)*

Kingdom Bitter *(OG 1043, ABV 4.5%)*

Sting *(ABV 4.2%)*

Under the SP Sporting Ales name:

Winners *(ABV 3.5%)*

Olde Jake *(ABV 4.8%)*

DURHAM SIBA

Durham Brewery Ltd, Unit 5A, Bowburn North Industrial Estate, Bowburn, Co Durham, DH6 5PF
Tel (0191) 3771991 Fax (0191) 3770768
E-mail gibbs@durham-brewery.co.uk
Website www.durham-brewery.co.uk
Shop open during business hours.
Tours by arrangement

Established in 1994, Durham now has a portfolio of around 20 beers plus a bottle-conditioned range. Bottles can be purchased via the online shop and an own label/special message service is available. News from the brewery is delivered by e-mail newsletter by free subscription on the website. Bottle-conditioned beers (suitable for vegetarians): Evensong (ABV 5%), Sanctuary (ABV 6%), Benedictus (ABV

8.4%), Imperial Stout (ABV 10%).

Magus *(OG 1038.5, ABV 3.8%)* ✦
Golden, refreshing dry bitter. An excellent session and summer ale, with a medium fruity/dry aftertaste.

White Gold *(OG 1040, ABV 4%)*
Pale and aromatic, mouth-filling and thirst-quenching with citrus aromas and flavours.

White Velvet *(OG 1041.5, ABV 4.2%)* ✦
Smooth, golden bitter with a tangy hop and fruit taste. The aftertaste lingers with a pleasant fruitiness.

Prior's Gold *(OG 1044, ABV 4.5%)*
A very round, full hop aroma and flavour.

Evensong *(OG 1049.5, ABV 5%)*
A deep ruby bitter. Based on an original 1937 recipe with a traditional English character.

Sanctuary *(OG 1057, ABV 6%)*
A ruby-coloured traditional old ale. Named after the Sanctuary knocker at Durham Cathedral.

Benedictus *(OG 1072, ABV 8.4%)*
This barley wine is golden in colour with a luscious malty body. A complex blend of hops give an interesting depth and balancing bitterness. The finish lingers with a rich warmth.

Imperial Stout *(OG 1088, ABV 10%)*
Massive body and sense of alcohol. This classic beer is deep black with coffee and liquorice flavours.

EARL SOHAM SIBA

Earl Soham Brewery, The Street, Earl Soham, Woodbridge, Suffolk, IP13 7RL
Tel/Fax (01728) 684097
E-mail fram.station@btinternet.com
Website www.earlssohambrewery.co.uk
Shop Village store Tastelands next to brewery
Tours by previous arrangement

⊗ Earl Soham was set up by John Bjornson behind the Victoria pub in 1984 in an old chicken shed. In 2001 the brewery moved to a bigger shed, 200 metres down the road. The building also houses the village sub-post office. The Victoria and the Station Hotel in Framlingham keep the beers on a regular basis and, when there is spare stock, they are supplied to local free houses and beer festivals. The new plant has five times the capacity of the old site and enjoys healthy sales to the free trade. Seasonal beer: Jolabrugg (ABV 5%, December until finished).

Gannet Mild (OG 1034, ABV 3.3%)
An unusual, full-tasting mild with a bitter finish and roast flavours that compete with underlying maltiness.

Victoria Bitter (OG 1037, ABV 3.6%)
A characterful, well-hopped, malty beer with a tangy, hoppy aftertaste.

Sir Roger's Porter
(OG 1043, ABV 4.2%)
Full-flavoured dark brown malty beer with bitter overtones, and a fruity aftertaste.

Albert Ale (OG 1045, ABV 4.4%)
Hops dominate every aspect of this beer, but especially the finish. A fruity, astringent beer.

EASTWOOD & SANDERS SIBA

**Eastwood & Sanders (Fine Ales) Ltd,
The Brewery, Units 3-5 Heathfield
Industrial Estate, Heathfield Street,
Elland, West Yorkshire, HX5 9AE
Tel (01422) 377677
Fax (01422) 370922
E-mail admin@eastwood-sanders.fsnet.co.uk**
Tours by prior arrangement

Eastwood & Sanders was formed in 2002 as a result of the amalgamation of the Barge & Barrel Brewery Co and West Yorkshire Brewery. A 10-barrel plant has been installed in the site at Elland. The brewery has invested in new pump clips for its six core beers, and has bought a pub, the Oddfellows Arms in Elland Lane. More than 60 outlets are supplied. As well as the core brands, there is a rolling programme of special beers.

First Light (OG 1037, ABV 3.5%)
A pale, subtly-flavoured session beer with delicate hop flavours, balanced by underlying malt sweetness. A rare example of the Pennine light mild style.

Bargee (OG 1038, ABV 3.8%)
Pale bitter with a well-balanced malt, fruit and hoppy character, and slightly sweet citrus taste.

Beyond the Pale (OG 1040, ABV 4%)
Pale golden bitter with an intense citrus flavour that dominates the underlying biscuity malt and fruity character. The finish is long, dry and hoppy.

Best Bitter (OG 1041, ABV 4%)
Made with a single malt and English and American hops, this is a straw-coloured bitter with a strong hoppy aroma and taste. Fruity and malty in character, the dry citrus, bitter flavour lingers to the end.

Fireball (OG 1042, ABV 4.2%)
A copper-coloured bitter with crystal malt flavours and a long, hoppy finish.

Nettlethrasher (OG 1042, ABV 4.4%)
A premium bitter brewed with three different malts, and English and American hops.

JOHN EASTWOOD*

**The John Eastwood Brewery,
Unit 4, Linthwaite Business Centre,
Manchester Road,
Linthwaite, Huddersfield, West Yorkshire,
HD7 7QS
Tel (01484) 846429**
Tours by arrangement

A new brewery set up at the end of 2002 by John Eastwood following his departure from Eastwood & Sanders (above). John has produced a new range of beers based on his original recipes for the free trade and local free houses. This is John's sixth move since he started brewing in 1993. Ten outlets are served.

Olympian Bronze (ABV 3.8%)

Best Bitter (ABV 4%)

Eastwood's Gold (ABV 4.4%)

Eastwood's Silver (ABV 5%)

ECCLESHALL SIBA

**Eccleshall Brewing Co Ltd, 1-3 Castle Street, Eccleshall, Staffordshire, ST21 6DF
Tel (01785) 850300
Fax (01785) 851452**
Tours by arrangement

The brewery was started in 1994 by father and son, Andrew and Ged Slater. It has been extended twice and has won numerous competitions. One pub is owned and 250 outlets are supplied. Seasonal beer: Slaters Eccy Thumper (ABV 5%, winter).

Monkey Magic (OG 1034, ABV 3.4%)
Dark brown with a caramel and hop aroma. Zesty with satisfying aftertaste.

Slaters Bitter (OG 1036, ABV 3.6%)
'Murray Mint' caramel aroma; very hoppy with some fruit. Bitterness that lasts.

Slaters Original (OG 1040, ABV 4%)
Caramel aroma, complex taste with marmalade fruit hints. Well balanced with a bitter finish.

Slaters Top Totty (OG 1040, ABV 4%)
Hoppy aroma and taste with a bitter and astringent finish.

Slaters Premium (OG 1044, ABV 4.4%)
Hoppy aroma with malt beyond. Bitterness intensifies to astringency; malty to the end.

Slaters Shining Knight
(OG 1045, ABV 4.5%)
No flavours but hops and fruit combine to the bitter finish. A good session beer for its strength, so beware!

Slaters Supreme (OG 1047, ABV 4.7%)
Flowery hop taste developing into a bitter finish. Fruity and astringent.

EGLESBRECH

**Crispnew Ltd, 14 Melville Street,
Falkirk, FK 1HZ
Tel (01324) 633338
Fax (01324) 613258
Website www.behindthewall.co.uk**
Tours by prior arrangement

The brewery is part of an extension to the Ale House. Eglesbrech brews only for its own customers. Occasional special beers are made and a Falkirk Wheel Ale is planned to tie in with the area's newest tourist attraction, the Canal Boat Lift. Three pubs are owned, one of which serves cask beer.

Falkirk 400 (ABV 3.8%)

Golden Nectar (ABV 3.8%)

Antonine (ABV 3.9%)

Cascade (ABV 4.1%)

Stones Ginger Beer (ABV 4.2%)

Alt Bier (ABV 4.4%)

EGYPTIAN

**The Egyptian Sand & Gravel Co. Ltd.,
The Leggers Inn, Robinson's Boat Yard,
Mill Street East, Savile Town, Dewsbury,
West Yorkshire, WF12 9BD
Tel (01924) 502846**
Tours by arrangement

⊙ Previously called Sunset Cider & Wine, the brewery is based under the Leggers pub and brews twice a week. Beers are brewed for any beer festival or pub that provide a cask and collect it from the brewery.

Marriots Mild (OG 1040, ABV 4%)

Prospect Road (OG 1040, ABV 4%)

Golden Eye 700 (OG 1042, ABV 4.2%)
Pale golden bitter, lightly hopped, with well-balanced fruity and malty character, and smooth finish.

Pharaoh's Curse (OG 1046, ABV 4.6%)

Dark Old Ale (OG 1048, ABV 4.8%)

ELGOOD'S IFBB SIBA

**Elgood & Sons Ltd, North Brink Brewery,
Wisbech, Cambridgeshire, PE13 1LN
Tel (01945) 583160
Fax (01945) 587711
E-mail info@elgoods-brewery.co.uk
Website www.elgoods-brewery.co.uk**
Shop 1-5 Wed, Thur, Fri & Sun and Bank Holiday
Mondays; closed Sat (May-Sept). Tours by arrangement

⊗ The North Brink Brewery was established in 1795 and was one of the first classic Georgian breweries to be built outside London. In 1878 it came under the control of the Elgood family and is still run today as one of the few remaining independent family breweries, with the fifth generation of the Elgood family now helping to run the brewery. Belinda Sutton has become managing director, with her father, Nigel Elgood, as chairman. Elgood's stands on the north bank of the River Nene, in the heart of the Fens in Wisbech, Cambridgeshire. Over the years Elgood's has remained loyal to traditional brewing methods. The beers go to 43 Elgood's public houses within a 50-mile radius of the brewery and free-trade outlets throughout East Anglia, while wholesalers distribute nationally. Elgood's has a visitor centre, offering the opportunity to combine a tour of the brewery and the magnificent gardens. Seasonal beers: Old Black Shuck (ABV 4.5%, Nov-Dec.), Barleymead (ABV 4.8%, Sept-Oct), Reinbeer (ABV 5.9%, December), Wenceslas Winter Warmer (ABV 7.5%, December), Golden Newt (ABV 4.6%, March-April), Double Swan (ABV 4.5%, May-June), Mad Dog (ABV 4.4%, July-Aug), Thin Ice (ABV 4.7%, Jan-Feb).

Black Dog Mild (OG 1036, ABV 3.6%) 🍷◆
Muscular ruby/black, dry mild with a defined liquorice character. Raisin fruit, malt and hops are in balance, and the dry, bitter finish does not fade

Cambridge Bitter (OG 1038, ABV 3.8%) ◆
Impressive copper-coloured session bitter with a light fruity aroma, a malty palate and a long bitter, dry aftertaste.

Pageant Ale (OG 1043, ABV 4.3%)
A premium beer, with a good aroma of hops and malt, giving a well-balanced bitter-sweet flavour and a satisfying finish.

Golden Newt (OG 1046, ABV 4.6%) ◆
A well-balanced, but dry palate with very prominent bitterness; the unusual malted grain types used give a clean but slightly fruity depth to the finish of this dry, hopped beer.

Thin Ice (OG 1047, ABV 4.7%)
Fragrant hops and orange fruit aromas introduce this golden bitter. Citrus, resiny hop fills the mouth, and the finish is delightfully bitter, with hops and fruit persisting

North Brink Porter (ABV 5%)
Dark in colour resembling a dry stout, although less creamy and lighter in body with a coffeeish dryness.

Greyhound Strong Bitter
(OG 1052, ABV 5.2%) ◆
Full-bodied, tawny brew, with a mouth-filling blend of malty sweetness and fruit. Starts with berry fruits on the nose and ends surprisingly bitter.

ENVILLE SIBA

**Enville Ales, Enville Brewery,
Cox Green, Enville, Stourbridge,
W Midlands, DY7 5LG
Tel (01384) 873728
Fax (01384) 873770
E-mail info@envilleales.com
Website www.envilleales.com**

⊙ A brewery based on a picturesque Victorian farm complex. Using the same water source as the original village brewery (closed in 1919), the beers also incorporate more than three tons of honey annually, produced on the farm, using recipes passed down from the proprietor's great-great aunt. Enville's owner, H Constantine-Cort, had originally intended to go into full-time beekeeping with brewing as a sideline, but the position is now reversed. The brewery grows its own barley, too. Seasonal beer: Phoenix IPA (ABV 4.8%, April-Sept).

Chainmaker Mild (OG 1036-38, ABV 3.6%)

Bitter (OG 1036-38, ABV 3.8%) ◆
A straw-coloured, hoppy and bitter beer that leaves a malty, moreish aftertaste.

Simpkiss Bitter (OG 1036-38, ABV 3.8%) ◆
A medium-bodied, golden bitter. The refreshing, hoppy taste lingers.

Nailmaker Mild (OG 1040-42, ABV 4%)

Enville White (OG 1040-42, ABV 4.2%) ◆
A clean, well-balanced, golden, sweet bitter, light in flavour. An appealing beer.

Czechmate Saaz (OG 1041-43, ABV 4.2%)

Enville Ale (OG 1044-45, ABV 4.5%)
A pale gold, medium-bodied bitter. Light hops and sweet fruit in the taste; a hint of honey in the aroma and aftertaste.

Enville Porter (OG 1044-1045, ABV 4.5%)

Ginger Beer *(OG 1044-46, ABV 4.6%)*

Gothic *(OG 1050-52, ABV 5.2%)* ⬧
Malt, hops and caramel combine with a strong roast malt taste in this dark, stout-like beer. Well-balanced, with lurking hints of honey. Available Oct-March.

EVERARDS IFBB

Everards Brewery Ltd, Castle Acres, Narborough, Leicester, LE19 1BY
Tel (0116) 201 4100
Fax (0116) 281 4199
E-mail: mail@everards.co.uk
Website www.everards.co.uk/www
.tigermania.co.uk
Shop Mon-Fri 9-5.30, Sat 9-12.30.
Tours by arrangement – ring Marketing 0116 201 4184

⊗ An independent, family-owned brewery run by the great-great grandson of the founder. Based at Narborough on the outskirts of Leicester, Everards celebrated its 150th anniversary in 1999. A tenanted estate of 135 high-quality pubs is based largely in Leicestershire and surrounding counties. Nearly all the pubs serve a full range of cask-conditioned ales and many serve guest ales. The principal ales are all dry-hopped and conditioned for a week prior to dispatch from the brewery. Tiger Best Bitter is the most widely distributed ale and can be found all over Britain. Daytime weekday tours can be arranged for CAMRA branches. Some 500 outlets are supplied direct. Seasonal beers: Perfick (ABV 4.5%, spring), Terra Firma (organic: ABV 4.5%, spring and summer), Sleighbell (ABV 4.5%, winter), Equinox (ABV 4.8%, autumn), Tiger Triple Gold (ABV 5%, winter). Everards also brews Home Bitter (3.8% ABV) for S & N.

Beacon Bitter
(OG 1036, ABV 3.8%) ⬧
Light, refreshing, well-balanced pale amber bitter in the Burton style.

Tiger Best Bitter
(OG 1041, ABV 4.2%) ⬧ ⬧
A mid-brown, well-balanced best bitter crafted for broad appeal, benefiting from a long, bitter-sweet finish.

Original Bitter *(OG 1051, ABV 5.2%)* ⬧
Full-bodied, this mid-brown strong bitter is smooth and well-balanced. The malted bitterness continues into a long finish.

EVESHAM

⌂ **SM Murphy Associates Ltd,
t/a The Evesham Brewery,
r/o Green Dragon, 170 Oat Street,
Evesham, Worcestershire, WR11 4PJ**
Tel/Fax (01386) 443462
E-mail asumgold@aol.com
Tours by arrangement

☺ A brewery set up in 1992 in the old bottle store at the Green Dragon Inn in Evesham. The owner and licensee, Steve Murphy, currently supplies another four outlets. The brewery has become a tourist attraction, drawing thousands of visitors each year. 'Asum' in the beer names is the local pronunciation of Evesham. Seasonal beer: Santa's Nightmare (ABV 6%, Christmas).

Asum Ale *(OG 1038, ABV 3.8%)* ⬧
Dry, sharp tawny bitter with an inter-play of malt, hops and fruit in the aroma and taste. Fruit fades as a dry, almost harsh, finale develops.

Asum Gold *(OG 1052, ABV 5.2%)* ⬧
A well-balanced premium ale that has all the range of tastes from malt to a fruity hoppiness that make it a very satisfying drink.

EXE VALLEY SIBA

Exe Valley Brewery, Silverton, Exeter, Devon, EX5 4HF
Tel (01392) 860406
Fax (01392) 861001
E-mail guysheppard@supanet.com
Website www.sibasouthwest.co.uk/breweries
/exevalley
Brewery tours not available except to pre-arranged groups – charge made

⊗ Exe Valley was established as Barron's Brewery in 1984 by former publican Richard Barron, who retired from the business in 2003. Guy Sheppard, who came into the business in 1991, continues to run the brewery. The beers are all brewed traditionally using spring water, Devon malt and English hops. Direct deliveries are made to pubs within a 40-mile radius of the brewery; the beers are also available nationally via wholesalers. Some 60 outlets are supplied direct. Seasonal beers: Devon Summer (ABV 3.9%, June-Aug), Spring Beer (ABV 4.3%, March-May), Autumn Glory (ABV 4.5%, Sept-Nov), Devon Dawn (ABV 4.5%, Dec-New Year), Winter Glow (ABV 6%, Dec-Feb). Bottle-conditioned beer: Devon Glory.

Bitter *(OG 1036, ABV 3.7%)* ⬧
Mid-brown bitter, pleasantly fruity with underlying malt through the aroma, taste and finish.

Barron's Hopsit *(OG 1040, ABV 4.1%)* ⬧
Straw-coloured beer with strong hop aroma, hop and fruit flavour and a bitter hop finish.

Dob's Best Bitter *(OG 1040, ABV 4.1%)* ⬧
Light brown bitter. Malt and fruit predominate in the aroma and taste with a dry, bitter, fruity finish.

Devon Glory *(OG 1046, ABV 4.7%)*
Mid-brown, fruity-tasting pint with a sweet, fruity finish.

Mr Sheppard's Crook
(OG 1046, ABV 4.7%) ◈
Smooth, full-bodied, mid-brown beer with a
malty-fruit nose and a sweetish palate
leading to a bitter, dry finish.

Exeter Old Bitter *(OG 1046, ABV 4.8%)* ◈
Mid-brown old ale with a rich fruity taste
and slightly earthy aroma and bitter finish.

EXMOOR SIBA

**Exmoor Ales Limited,
Golden Hill Brewery, Wiveliscombe,
Somerset, TA4 2NY
Tel (01984) 623798
Fax (01984) 624572
E-mail info@exmoorales.co.uk
Website www.exmoorales.co.uk**
Tours by arrangement

⊠ Somerset's largest brewery was founded
in 1980 in the old Hancock's plant, which
had been closed since 1959. It quickly won
national acclaim, as its Exmoor Ale took the
Best Bitter award at CAMRA's Great British
Beer Festival that year, the first of many
prizes. The brewery has enjoyed many years
of continuous expansion and steadily
increasing demand. Around 250 pubs in the
South-west are supplied direct, and others
nationwide via wholesalers and pub chains.
Seasonal beers: Hound Dog (ABV 4%,
March-May), Wild Cat (ABV 4.4%, Sept-
Nov), Beast (ABV 6.6%, Oct-April), Exmas
(ABV 5%, Nov-Dec).

Ale *(OG 1039, ABV 3.8%)* ◈
A pale to mid-brown, medium-bodied
session bitter. A mixture of malt and hops
in the aroma and taste lead to a hoppy,
bitter aftertaste.

Fox *(OG 1043, ABV 4.2%)*
Crafted from a special blend of several malts
and hops to produce a mid-brown beer of
unusual subtlety and taste. The slight
maltiness on the tongue is followed by a
burst of hops with a lingering bitter-sweet
aftertaste.

Gold *(OG 1045, ABV 4.5%)* ◈
A yellow/golden best bitter, with a good
balance of malt and fruity hop on nose and
palate. The sweetness follows through to an
ultimately more bitter finish.

Hart *(OG 1049, ABV 4.8%)* ◈
A mid-to-dark brown beer with a mixture of
malt and hops in the aroma. A rich, full-
bodied malt and fruit flavour following
through to a clean, hoppy aftertaste.

Stag *(OG 1050, ABV 5.2%)* ◈
A pale brown beer, with a malty taste and
aroma, and a bitter finish.

FACERS*

**Facer's Brewery, Unit 6, Knoll Street
Industrial Estate, Knoll Street,
Salford, M7 2BL.
Tel (0161) 708 0247
Fax (0161) 708 0248**

David Facer is a former head brewer at
Boddingtons. He left to start his own small
brewery in 2003. He shares premises with
Bazens' Brewery (qv) and together they
form the Salford Brewery Syndicate, but use
different yeast strains and water treatment.
David's first beer was launched at the
Queen's Arms, Honey Street, Manchester.

First Draught *(ABV 4.1%)*

FAR NORTH SIBA

⌂ **Far North Brewery, Melvich Hotel,
Melvich, Thurso, KW14 7YJ
Tel (01641) 531206
Fax (01641) 531347
E-mail farnorthbrewery@aol.com
Website www.smoothhound.co.uk/hotels
/melvich**
Tours for hotel residents

⊠ The most northerly brew-pub in Britain,
it originally brewed just one cask a week for
hotel guests working at Dounray nuclear
power site. Far North now has a two-barrel
plant from Dark Star's original plant in
Brighton. Owner Peter Martin plans to add
a bottle-conditioned John o'Groats Ale for
summer tourist outlets.

Real Mackay *(OG 1038, ABV 3.8%)*

Split Stone Pale Ale *(OG 1042, ABV 4.2%)*

Special *(OG 1040, ABV 4.2%)*

Porter *(OG 1048, ABV 4.8%)*

Fast Reactor *(OG 1048, ABV 4.8%)*

Edge of Darkness *(OG 1065, ABV 7%)*

FEATHERSTONE

**Featherstone Brewery, Unit 3,
King Street Buildings, King Street,
Enderby, Leicestershire, LE9 5NT
Tel (0116) 275 0952
Mobile 0966 137762**

⊠ Small brewery that specialises in
supplying custom-brewed beers to pubs for
sale under house names. Personalised beers
are brewed to order, minimum volume four
barrels.

Howes Howler *(OG 1035, ABV 3.6%)*

Best Bitter *(OG 1041, ABV 4.2%)*

Vulcan Bitter *(OG 1048, ABV 5.1%)*

FEDERATION

**Northern Clubs Federation Brewery Ltd,
Lancaster Road, Dunston,
Tyne and Wear, NE11 9JR
Tel (0191) 460 9023
Fax (0191) 460 1297
Production (0191) 460 8853**

E-mail enquiries@federation-brewery.co.uk
Website www.federation-brewery.co.uk
Tours by arrangement to special interest groups

☺ A brewery owned by working-men's clubs that produces only bright beers. The Buchanans range of cask beers is produced under licence by Robinson's of Stockport. Seasonal ale: Tummy Tickler (ABV 5%).

Buchanan's Best Bitter
(OG 1035, ABV 3.5%)
A light balance of malt and hops in the mouth with a bitter-sweet finish. A delicate hop resin aroma.

Buchanan's Original *(OG 1041, ABV 4.2%)*
Rich and complex aromas of Goldings hops, malt and tart fruit. Superb mouth-feel of rich malt and hops, long dry finish with citrus fruit notes.

FELINFOEL IFBB

Felinfoel Brewery Co Ltd,
Farmers Row, Felinfoel, Llanelli,
Carmarthenshire, SA14 8LB
Tel (01554) 773357
Fax (01554) 752452
E-mail enquiries@felinfoel-brewery.com
Website www.felinfoel-brewery.com
Shop 9-5 Mon-Fri; 10-12 Sat

☺ Founded in 1830 by David John, the company is still family-owned and is now the oldest brewery in Wales. The present buildings are Grade II* listed and were built in the 1870s. Felinfoel was the first brewery in Europe to can beer in the 1930s. It supplies cask ale to half its 84 houses, though some use top pressure, and to approximately 350 free trade outlets.

Dragon Bitter Ale *(OG 1034, ABV 3.4%)*

Best Bitter *(OG 1038, ABV 3.8%)* ◕
A balanced beer, low aroma, bitter-sweet initially with an increasing moderate bitterness.

Double Dragon Ale
(OG 1042, ABV 4.2%) ◕
A fruity, malty aroma, a similar taste with moderate bitterness. Hops in background throughout, with a fruity finish.

FELSTAR

Felstar Brewery, Felsted Vineyard,
Crix Green, Felsted, Essex, CM6 3JT
Tel (01245) 361504, (07973) 315503
Fax (01245) 361504
Shop 10-dusk 7 days/week.
Ring to engage if on long journey.
Tours by arrangement

✖ The Felstar Brewery opened in 2001 and is based in the Felsted Vineyard, the oldest commercial vineyard in East Anglia. The brewery is in the old bonded stores and is a five-barrel plant. Seasonal beer: Haunted Hen (ABV 6%, Nov-Feb). Bottle-conditioned beers: Hop-Hop-Hurray, Hopsin, Felstar Glory (ABV 5%), Haunted Hen.

Rooster's Knight *(OG 1035, ABV 3.4%)*

Rooster's Ale *(OG 1037, ABV 3.8%)*

Hop-Hop-Hurray *(OG 1040, ABV 4%)*

Hopsin *(OG 1046, ABV 4.6%)*

Golden Egg *(OG 1052, ABV 5.4%)*

FENLAND

Fenland Brewery, Unit 4, Prospect Way,
Chatteris, Cambridgeshire, PE16 6TZ
Tel/Fax (01354) 696776 (brewery)
Tours by arrangement

✖ The brewery was set up in 1997 by Dr Rob Thomas and his wife, Liz. Rob was formerly a research chemist and lecturer in Switzerland, where he was born. He was a home brewer for 15 years before embarking on commercial brewing in Chatteris. Fenland became the first brewery in the town for 65 years, converting an industrial unit to a self-designed brewery. Demand and sales have expanded since a salesman was employed in 2000. Rob continues to experiment and has produced a number of experimental beers that may become part of the regular portfolio (eg Satisfaction 4%, Beerelzebub 4.1% and Sunset 4.2%). Beers are supplied throughout Bedfordshire, Cambridgeshire, Lincolnshire, Norfolk, and Northamptonshire, and have been steadily winning both awards and customer loyalty. 100-plus outlets are supplied. Seasonal beers: Tell Tale Pale Ale (ABV 3.6%, summer), Drayman's Draught (ABV 4%, autumn /winter), Paranoia (ABV 4.2%, autumn), Smokestack Lightning (ABV 4.2%, spring), Sparkling Wit (ABV 4.5%, May-Sept), Winter Warmer/Rudolph's Rocket Fuel (ABV 5.5%, Nov-Jan). This is the same beer; it's available as Winter Warmer but can be re-badged (publicans choice) as RRF in December.

Doctor's Orders *(ABV 5%)*
A russet best bitter with a ruby glint and a complex malty fruit aroma, with a blend of First Gold hops and three varieties of Norfolk malts.

FERNANDES SIBA

Fernandes Brewery, The Old Malt House,
5 Avison Yard, Kirkgate, Wakefield,
West Yorkshire, WF1 1UA
Tel (01924) 291709
Shop Mon,Wed, Thur 10.30-5, Fri 10.30-7,
Sat 10.30-5, Sun 12-2. Tours by arrangement

☺ The brewery opened in 1997 and is housed in a 19th-century malthouse. It incorporates a home-brew shop and a brewery tap that opened in 1999. It has won Wakefield CAMRA's Pub of the Year for 1999, 2000 and 2002, and has been awarded Yorkshire Regional Pub of the Year 2001 and 2002. One pub is owned and 10-15 outlets are supplied. Seasonal beer: 12 monthly special beers, named after the months, are brewed.

Boys Bitter *(OG 1035, ABV 3.2%)*
A light, hoppy session beer that belies its gravity, a long lasting hoppy finish. Some citrus notes.

Best Bitter (OG 1040, ABV 3.8%)
A light-coloured, spritzy, lightly hopped and refreshing session beer, with a long lasting hoppy finish.

Malt Shovel Mild (OG 1038, ABV 3.8%)
A dark, full-bodied, malty mild with an abundance of roast malt and chocolate flavours, leading to a lingering, dry, malty finish.

Partners in Crime (OG 1040, ABV 3.8%)
A pale coloured bitter beer with a clean, hoppy and smooth malty aftertaste, with some fruitiness.

Ale to the Tsar (OG 1042, ABV 4.1%)
A pale, smooth, well-balanced beer with some sweetness leading to a nutty, malty and satisfying aftertaste.

Lucasale (OG 1042, ABV 4.1%)
An extremely fruity, pale coloured beer with a refreshing, hoppy finish.

To be Joyfull (OG 1044, ABV 4.3%)
An extremely fruity and hoppy, bitter beer with a long lasting fruity aftertaste. Pale in colour.

Wakefield Pride (OG 1045, ABV 4.5%)
A light-coloured and full-bodied, clean-tasting malty beer with a good hop character leading to a dry, bitter finish.

Cascade (OG 1049, ABV 5%)
A light coloured, citrussy and spicy beer.

Empress of India (OG 1058, ABV 6%)
A strong, light-coloured, malty beer with a complex bitter palate. Fruit and malt dominate the aftertaste.

Double Six (OG 1062, ABV 6%)
A powerful, dark and rich strong beer with an array of malt, roast malt and chocolate flavours and a strong, lasting malty finish, with some hoppiness.

FILO SIBA

⚲ **First In Last Out Brewery, 14-15 High St., Old Town, Hastings, E Sussex, TN34 3EY**
Tel (01424) 425079 Fax (01424) 420802
E-mail mike@thefilo.co.uk
Website www.thefilo.co.uk
Tours by arrangement

⊗ The Filo Brewery has been brewing since 1985, using converted dairy equipment, with only a short break in 2000 when the brewery was refurbished, along with a new brewer, trained in-house. The pub has also added a covered brewery yard and a special window in the bar to observe the brewing. One pub is owned.

Crofters (OG 1040-1042, ABV 4-4.1%)

Cardinal (OG 1046, ABV 4.6%)

Gold (OG 1049-1050, ABV 4.7-4.9%)

FLAGSHIP

Flagship Brewery, Nelson Brewing Co, Unit 2 Building 64, The Historic Dockyard, Chatham, Kent, ME4 4TE
Tel (01634) 832828
Tours by arrangement

⊗ The brewery was established in 1995 by home-brewing enthusiast Andrew Purcell in partnership with his father-in-law. It became a limited company in 2000. It's located in Chatham's Historic Dockyard, a uniquely preserved Georgian dockyard and premier tourist attraction in the South-east. Production has steadily increased, with at least 75 regular outlets served direct and further outlets supplied by wholesalers and other breweries. The brewery now has its own tied house. Seasonal beers: Spring Pride (ABV 4.4%), Powder Monkey (ABV 4.4%), Moby Dick (ABV 4.4%), Pembroke Old Ale (ABV 4.4%), Pembroke Porter (ABV 4.4%), Shipwrecked (ABV 5%), Frigging Yuletide (ABV 5.5%), Old Sea Dog Stout (ABV 5.5%), Nelson's Blood (ABV 6%), Nelsons Blood Extra (ABV 7.1%).

Victory Mild (OG 1036, ABV 3.5%)

Admiral's Bitter (OG 1038, ABV 3.8%)

Trafalgar Bitter (OG 1040, ABV 4.1%)

Hardys Kiss (OG 1042, ABV 4.2%)

Spanker (OG 1042, ABV 4.2%)
A version of Ensign.

Friggin in the Riggin (OG 1045, ABV 4.7%)
A premium bitter with a smooth malt flavour and a bitter-sweet aftertaste.

Crow's Nest (OG 1048, ABV 4.8%)
A straw-coloured, sweet and fruity ale with a hoppy aroma.

Futtock (OG 1050, ABV 5.2%)
A fruity, ruby-coloured ale, with a roast malt aftertaste.

FORTH

Forth Brewery Co Ltd, Eglinton, Kelliebank, Alloa, FK10 1NU
Tel (01259) 725511 Fax (01259) 725522

☺ A brewing company set up by former partners when Maclay stopped brewing in 1999. Forth's beers are distributed by Belhaven, Caledonian, Beer Seller, Flying Firkin and Maclay. Forth will contract brew and bottle for micro-breweries that need to supplement their production.

Steamboat Ale (ABV 4%)

Puffer Ale (ABV 4.1%)

FOX

⚲ **Fox Brewery, Fox & Founds, 22 Station Road, Heacham, Norfolk, PE31 7EX**
Tel (01485) 570345

Brewery that opened in 2002 that brews for the pub and other outlets.

Heacham Gold (ABV 3.9%)

Grace & Favour (ABV 4.4%)

FOXFIELD

Foxfield Brewery, Prince of Wales Hotel, Foxfield, Broughton in Furness, Cumbria, LA20 6BX
Tel (01229) 716238
E-mail drink@princeofwalesfoxfield.co.uk
Website www.princeofwalesfoxfield.co.uk
Tours by arrangement

☺ Foxfield is a three-barrel plant run by Stuart and Lynda Johnson in old stables attached to the Prince of Wales inn. A few other outlets are supplied. The Johnsons also own Tigertops in Wakefield (qv). There are many occasional and seasonal beers. Dark Mild is suitable for vegetarians and vegans.

Sands *(OG 1038, ABV 3.4%)*
A pale, light, aromatic quaffing ale.

Fleur-de-Lys *(OG 1038, ABV 3.6%)*

Dark Mild *(OG 1040, ABV 3.7%)*

Brief Encounter *(OG 1040, ABV 3.8%)*
A fruity beer with a long, bitter finish.

Furness Flyer *(OG 1042, ABV 4.1%)*

Stuarts Stout *(OG 1042, ABV 4.2%)*

Muesli Mild *(OG 1044, ABV 4.4%)*

FRANKLIN'S

Franklin's Brewery, Bilton Lane, Bilton, Harrogate, North Yorkshire, HG1 4DH
Tel/Fax (01423) 322345
E-mail Tommy2Tom@yahoo.co.uk

A brewery set up in 1980 by Sean Franklin of Roosters (qv) and run by Leeds CAMRA founder-member Tommy Thomas and stepson Tim Osborne. 10-20 outlets are supplied. Seasonal beers: Summer Blotto (ABV 4.7%), Winter Blotto (ABV 4.7%).

Bitter *(OG 1038, ABV 3.8%)*
A tremendous hop aroma precedes a flowery hop flavour, combined with malt. Long, hoppy, bitter finish. A fine, unusual amber bitter.

DT's *(OG 1045, ABV 4.5%)*

My Better Half *(OG 1060, ABV 5%)*

FRANKTON BAGBY

The Old Stables Brewery, Green Lane, Church Lawford, Rugby, Warwickshire, CV23 9EF
Tel (02476) 540770
Tours by arrangement

Frankton Bagby was set up in 1999 by three local families. The five-barrel plant is housed in a small, 18th-century stable block that has been carefully renovated by Warwickshire craftsmen. A specialist micro-brewery engineer undertook the design and installation of the equipment for the brewhouse. More than 150 outlets are supplied direct. Seasonal beers: Dark Secret (ABV 4.8%, winter), Top Tipple (ABV 4.2%, summer), Christmas Pud (ABV 7%).

Peeping Tom *(OG 1038, ABV 3.8%)*
Light brown ale packed with a traditional hoppy, bitter flavour.

Old Chestnut *(OG 1040, ABV 4%)*
A chestnut-coloured bitter brewed using a combination of Green Bullet and Fuggles hops that give the beer a distinctive mellow flavour; the late addition of Styrian Goldings adds a fruity nose.

Chicken Tackle *(OG 1041, ABV 4.1%)*
A hoppy but mellow beer with a tantalising hint of ginger.

Squires Brew *(OG 1042, ABV 4.2%)*
A straw-coloured best bitter, smooth on the palate with a good, hoppy aftertaste. A mix of Challenger and Fuggles hops are used in the main brew and Styrian Goldings are added for late hopping.

Top Tipple *(OG 1042, ABV 4.2%)*
Brewed using American Liberty hops, which give this best bitter a unique flavour and a memorable aftertaste.

Rugby Special *(OG 1045, ABV 4.5%)*
A reddy-brown, full-bodied, well-balanced and pleasantly hoppy best bitter. First brewed in the borough of Rugby to celebrate Rugby Union's World Cup, the beer proved so popular it became a regular brew.

FREEDOM

Freedom Brewing Company Ltd, 11 Galena Road, Hammersmith, London, W6 0LT
Tel (0208) 748 0903
Fax (0208) 741 9637
E-mail info@freedombrewery.com
Website www.freedombrewery.com
Tours by arrangement

Freedom was established in Fulham in 1995 and was the first micro-brewery in England to specialise in brewing unpasteurised lager to the German Reinheitsgebot purity law. From small beginnings, delivering fresh draught lager to bars in South-west London, the company expanded its product range to include a 330ml bottle. Distribution of both bottles and draught grew to include Greater London and the South-east. In 1999 the brewery produced its first organic lager in its micro-brewery in Covent Garden. Initially this was only available in the bar itself, but demand soon grew and the company started producing organic lager in both kegs and bottles. Both products are certified by the Soil Association and are available nationally through third party wholesalers. Four pubs are owned and 12 outlets are supplied with organic lager. Bottle conditioned: Freedom Organic Beer (ABV 4.8%). The beers brewed at Freedom, 41 Earlham Street, Covent Garden, WC2 are: Soho Red (ABV 4.2%), Freedom Pale (ABV 4.3%). Freeedom Wheat (ABV 5%) and Freedom Pilsner (ABV 5%). Beers brewed at Zebranos, Granton Street, W1 are Freedom Pilsner and Freedom Wheat.

FREEMINER SIBA

Freeminer Brewery Ltd, Whimsey Road, Steam Mills, Cinderford, Gloucestershire, GL14 3JA
Tel (01594) 827989
Fax (01594) 829464
E-mail sales@freeminer.com
Website www.freeminer.com
Tours by arrangement

Freeminer Brewery celebrated 10 years of brewing in the Forest of Dean in 2002 and over this time has expanded from a five-barrel to a 40-barrel plant to cope with an increase in cask and bottle sales in Britain and abroad. A number of independent wholesalers are used to ensure a national distribution of the beers from its rural location. Some 40 outlets are supplied direct. New brews, such as Royal Union Steam Ale (ABV 4.5%), Resolution Pale Ale

(ABV 4.5%) and Tormentor (ABV 4.5%) have been added to the seasonal range such as Strip and At It (ABV 4%, summer), Iron Brew (ABV 4.2%, spring) and Celestial Steam Gale (ABV 5%, summer).

Bitter *(OG 1038, ABV 4%)* ◈
A light, hoppy session bitter with an intense hop aroma and a dry, hoppy finish.

Speculation *(OG 1047, ABV 4.8%)* ◈
An aromatic, chestnut-brown, full-bodied beer with a smooth, well-balanced mix of malt and hops, and a predominantly hoppy aftertaste.

Gold Standard *(OG 1049, ABV 5%)*

FROG ISLAND SIBA

Frog Island Brewery, The Maltings, Westbridge, St James' Road, Northampton, NN5 5HS
Tel (01604) 587772
Fax (01604) 750754
E-mail beer@frogislandbrewery.co.uk
Website www.frogislandbrewery.co.uk
Shop by arrangement
Tours by arrangement

⊗ Started in 1994 by home-brewer Bruce Littler and business partner Graham Cherry in a malt house built by the long-defunct brewery Thomas Manning & Co, Frog Island expanded by doubling its brew length to 10 barrels in 1998. It specialises in beers with personalised bottle labels, available by mail order. Up to 40 free trade outlets are directly supplied with the beer occasionally available through other micro-brewers. Seasonal beers: Fuggled Frog (ABV 3.5%, May), Head in the Clouds (ABV 4.5%, August). Bottle-conditioned beers: Natterjack, Fire Bellied Toad, Croak & Stagger. Bottled beers are available for sale in a shop on the brewery forecourt.

Best Bitter *(OG 1040, ABV 3.8%)* ◈
Blackcurrant and gooseberry enhance the full malty aroma with pineapple and papaya joining on the tongue. Bitterness develops in the fairly long Target/Fuggle finish.

Shoemaker *(OG 1043, ABV 4.2%)* ⬚◈
Cascade aroma hops create a cauldron of tastes and the full mouthfeel complements the strong orangy/malty aromas that precede the citrus and hoppy bitterness lasting into a long, dry finish. Amber.

That Old Chestnut *(OG 1044, ABV 4.4%)*
A malty, chestnut-brown ale brewed with Maris Otter pale malt, with a hint of crystal and malted wheat, and coloured with roast barley. Target is the bittering hop with Cascade as a late addition for aroma.

Natterjack *(OG 1048, ABV 4.8%)* ◈
Deceptively robust, golden and smooth. Fruit and hop aromas fight for dominance before the grainy astringency and floral palate give way to a long, dry aftertaste with a hint of lingering malt.

Fire Bellied Toad
(OG 1050, ABV 5%) ⬚◈
Amber-gold brew with an extraordinary long bitter/fruity finish. Huge malt and Phoenix hop flavours have a hint of apples after the pink grapefruit nose belies its punchy overall hit.

Croak & Stagger
(OG 1056, ABV 5.8%) ◈
The initial honey/fruit aroma is quickly overpowered by roast malt then bitter chocolate and pale malt sweetness on the tongue. Gentle, bitter-sweet finish. A dark winter brew.

FULLER'S IFBB

Fuller, Smith and Turner PLC,
The Griffin Brewery, Chiswick Lane South, Chiswick, London, W4 2QB
Tel (020) 8996 2000
Fax (020) 8995 0230
E-mail fullers@fullers.co.uk
Website www.fullers.co.uk
Shop 10-6 Mon-Fri, 10-5 Sat.
Tours Mon,Wed, Thur, Fri 11am, 12pm, 1pm, 2pm; must be booked on 020 8996 2063.

⊗ Fuller, Smith & Turner's Griffin Brewery in Chiswick has stood on the same site for more than 350 years. Messrs Fuller, Smith & Turner formed their partnership in 1845 and direct descendants of the founding families are still involved in the running of the company. In spite of technical advances, traditional brewing methods have been maintained. In the 24 years that CAMRA has held the Champion Beer of Britain competition, Fuller's has won the Beer of the Year award five times. The beers have been Best in Class no less than nine times and ESB has been voted Best Strong Ale an unprecedented seven times. All Fuller's 240 pubs, bars and hotels serve cask ales. Fuller's also supplies close to 600 free trade accounts. Fuller's Organic Honey Dew (cask and bottle), is the world's first honey-flavoured organic ale and its winter ale, Jack Frost, is made with the addition of blackberries. Fuller's has recently added new fermenters and maturation vessels. Beer sales continue to increase and more tanks will have to be added during 2004.
Seasonal beers: Summer Ale (ABV 3.9%, summer), Organic Honey Dew (ABV 4.3%, spring and autumn, suitable for vegetarians and vegans), Jack Frost (ABV 4.5%, winter). Bottle-conditioned beers: 1845 (ABV 6.3% ⬚▮), Vintage Ale (OG 1086.5, ABV 8.5%).

Chiswick *(OG 1034.5, ABV 3.5%)* ⬚◈
Hops and malt on the nose intensify on the palate leaving a clean, fruity hop finish and a bitterness that builds on drinking.

London Pride
(OG 1040.5, ABV 4.1%) ▮⬚◈
A tawny-coloured beer with malt notes balanced with hops. Fruity citrus orange is noticeable throughout, with a well-rounded, bitter finish.

ESB *(OG 1054.5, ABV 5.5%)* 🍺📖🌢
A rich, full-bodied, complex beer with malt, hops and fruit all in evidence. Marmalade bitter notes build, leaving a dry aftertaste.

FYFE SIBA

⊘ Fyfe Brewing Company, 469 High Street, Kirkcaldy, Fife, KY1 2SN
Tel/Fax (01592) 646211
E-mail fyfebrew@blueyonder.co.uk
Website www.e-fife.com/harbourbar
Tours by arrangement

☺ Established in 1995 behind the Harbour Bar, it was Fife's first brew-pub in the 20th century. Most of the output is taken by the pub, the remainder being sold direct to 10 local outlets and to the free trade via wholesalers. Seasonal beer: Cauld Turkey (ABV 6%, winter).

Rope of Sand *(OG 1037, ABV 3.7%)* 🌢
A quenching bitter. Malt and fruit throughout, with a hoppy, bitter aftertaste.

Auld Alliance *(OG 1040, ABV 4%)* 🌢
A very bitter beer with a lingering, dry, hoppy finish. Malt and hop, with fruit, are present throughout, fading in the finish.

Lion Slayer *(OG 1042, ABV 4.2%)*

First Lyte *(OG 1043, ABV 4.3%)*

Fyfe Fyre *(OG 1048, ABV 4.8%)*

FYNE SIBA

Fyne Ales, Achadunan, Cairndow, Argyll, PA26 8BJ
Tel/Fax (01499) 600238
E-mail jonny@fyneales.com
Website www.fyneales.com
Tours by arrangement

☺ Fyne Ales brewed for the first time on St Andrew's Day 2001. The 10-barrel plant was installed in a redundant milking parlour on a farm in Argyll. The brewery supplies outlets in the central belt and West Highlands as well as beer festivals south of the border.

Piper's Gold *(OG 1037.5, ABV 3.8%)* 🌢
An easy-drinking, golden session ale. Bitter-sweet taste with a hoppy finish.

Maverick *(OG 1040.5, ABV 4.2%)* 🌢
Smooth, nutty session beer with a sweet, fruity finish.

Highlander *(OG 1045.5, ABV 4.2%)*
A strong traditional ale with intense malt flavours and a citrus hop aroma.

GALE'S IFBB

George Gale & Co Ltd, The Hampshire Brewery, Horndean, Hampshire, PO8 0DA
Tel (02392) 571212
Fax (02392) 598641
E-mail gales@mcmail.com
Website www.gales.co.uk
Shop 9.30-5 Mon-Fri; 9.30-1.30 Sat.
Tours by arrangement

⊠ Richard Gale bought the Ship & Bell inn and its small brewery in 1847. His youngest son, George, expanded the business by buying local inns and the farm buildings next to the Ship & Bell, which he developed into a substantial brewery. In 1869 the brewery was destroyed by fire, but by the end of the year had been rebuilt; much of the present building results from that time. In 1896 George Gale sold his major share in the brewery to the Bowyer family, who still control the company today. All 110 tied houses serve cask ale. Gale's also supplies 600 free trade outlets direct. Seasonal beers: Frolic Bitter (ABV 4.4%), Hampshire Glory (ABV 4.3%), Summer Hog (ABV 3.8%), Christmas Ale (ABV 5%). Bottle-conditioned beers: Christmas Ale (ABV 8.5%), Trafalgar (ABV 9%), Prize Old Ale (ABV 9%), HSB (ABV 4.8%), Festival Mild (ABV 4.8%).

Butser Bitter
(OG 1034, ABV 3.4%) 🌢
A mid-brown chestnut beer. A slightly malty and fruity aroma preludes a sweet taste, with some fruit and malt. The aftertaste is sweet and fruity with a little bitterness.

GB *(OG 1040, ABV 4%)* 🌢
A medium-bodied, deep golden brown brew that is initially malty sweet, has a fruity middle period with a hint of burnt orange and a dry hop flower-tasting bitter finish. Brewed to be served through a tight sparkler, which can ruin the characteristics described.

Winter Brew *(OG 1044, ABV 4.2%)* 🌢
A rich winter ale, containing Prize Old Ale. Almost black in colour, it has a roast malt aroma with fruit and caramel, all of which are echoed in the taste and finish. Available Nov-March.

HSB *(OG 1050, ABV 4.8%)* 📖🌢
A mid-brown beer with a fruity aroma. The full-bodied, sweet and fruity taste, with some maltiness, follows through to the aftertaste. For those with a sweet tooth.

Festival Mild
(OG 1052, ABV 4.8%) 🍺📖🌢
Black in colour, with a red tinge. The aroma is fruity. A sweet, fruity and malty taste, with some caramel, carries through to the aftertaste, but with more bitterness.

GARDEN BARBER* SIBA

Garden Barber Brewery, PO Box 23, Hertford, SG14 3PZ
Tel (01992 504167

Small brewery operating from a residential site, supplying beer festivals and local trade The brew-length is 2.5 barrels. As the ABV indicates, the strength of the beer varies.

Readypops *(ABV 3.6-4.2%)*

GARTON

Garton Brewery, Station House, Station Road, Garton on the Wolds, Driffield, East Yorkshire, YO25 3EX
Tel (01377) 252340

A small brewery, set up in 2001 in former railway station buildings, by Richard Heptinstall, after a decade brewing for himself and friends using home-brew kits. The brewery has a five-barrel plant. Liquid Lobotomy is now available in five-litre cans and will be available at beer festivals where Lobotomy is featured.

Woldsman Bitter *(OG 1048, ABV 4.5%)* ◆
This refreshing bitter is gold in colour. This
full-bodied beer has a mix of hops and fruit
balancing sweetness. A dry, crisp finish.

Stunned Mullet Bitter *(OG 1053, ABV 5%)*
Strong bitter.

Goodnight Vienna *(OG 1077, ABV 8%)*
An India Pale Ale.

Liquid Lobotomy Stout *(OG 1081, ABV 8%)*
A heavy duty stout.

GLASTONBURY SIBA

**Glastonbury Ales, Grovers Brew House, Unit
10, Wessex Park, Somerton Business Park,
Somerton, Somerset, TA11 6SB
Tel (01458) 272244
E-mail glastonburyales@aol.com
Website www.glastonburyales.com/
www.glastonburyales.co.uk**
Tours by prior arrangement

⊗ Glastonbury Ales was established in 2002
by Greig Nicholls, after many years as a
home brewer. Having already won a few
awards for Mystery Tor (Champion of
Champions, St Albans) and Holy Thorn,
production has increased to 15 barrels a
week and is still rising. The five-barrel plant
produces quality ales using the best malt
from Tuckers of Newton Abbot and hops
from Charles Faram in Worcestershire.
Seasonal beers: Spring Loaded (ABV 4.4%,
Feb-June), Brue (ABV 4%, May-Oct). 50
outlets are supplied.

Mystery Tor *(OG 1040, ABV 3.8%)* ▨◆
A golden bitter with plenty of floral hop
and fruit on the nose and palate, the
sweetness giving way to a bitter hop finish.
Full-bodied for a session bitter.

Holy Thorn *(OG 1042, ABV 4.2%)*
An amber beer with a rich complex malt
flavour. Brewed with vanilla, chocolate and
French orange liqueur to give a subtle
festive flavour, which compliments a
powerful hop bitterness and aroma.

Lady of the Lake *(OG 1042, ABV 4.2%)* ◆
A full-bodied amber best bitter with plenty
of hops to the forefront balanced by a fruity
malt flavour and a subtle hint of vanilla,
leading to a clean, bitter hop aftertaste.

Ley Line *(OG 1042, ABV 4.2%)*
A dark bitter that combines the sweetness of
a mild with the richness of a porter.
Delicately hopped to give sweetness with a
light hoppy aftertaste.

Hedgemonkey *(OG 1048, ABV 4.6%)*
A ruby bitter with toffee/coffee undertones
that give way to a medium hopped, spicy
aftertaste supplied by Goldings hops.

Golden Chalice *(OG 1048, ABV 4.8%)*
Light and golden coloured best bitter with a
robust malt character. Strong bitterness
provided by Challenger hops gives way to a
light floral aftertaste, thanks to the late
addition of American Mount Hood hops.
Full of flavour and deceptively drinkable.

F.M.B. *(OG 1050, ABV 5%)*
Rich amber ale with the tangy complexities
of amber and crystal malts combining with
experimental hedgerow hops to give a tangy,
chewy malt flavour and a potent hop finish.

GLENTWORTH SIBA

**Glentworth Brewery, Glentworth House,
Crossfield Lane, Skellow, Doncaster,
South Yorkshire, DN6 8PL
Tel (01302) 725555
Fax (01302) 724133
E-mail glentworth.brewery
@btopenworld.com**

☺ The brewery was formed in 1996 and is
housed in dairy building. The five-barrel
plant supplies more than 80 pubs. Mainly
light-coloured, hoppy ale. Due to demand a
second cold room has been added, doubling
storage capacity. Seasonal beers (brewed to
order): Oasis (ABV 4.1%), Happy Hooker
(ABV 4.3%), North Star (ABV 4.3%), Perle
(ABV 4.4%), Dizzy Blonde (ABV 4.5%),
Whispers (ABV 4.5%).

Lightyear *(OG 1037, ABV 3.9%)*

GOACHER'S

**P&DJ Goacher, Unit 8, Tovil Green Business
Park, Maidstone, Kent, ME15 6TA
Tel (01622) 682112**
Tours by arrangement

⊗ A traditional brewery that uses all malt
and only Kentish hops for all its beers.
Established for 19 years, Phil and Debbie
Goacher have concentrated on brewing
good wholesome tasty beers without
gimmicks. The brewery has thrived, with its
high quality recognised with a silver award
for Gold Star in the strong ales category at
GBBF 2001. Two tied houses and around 25
free trade outlets in the mid-Kent area are
supplied. Special, a mix of Light and Dark
ales, is also available to pubs for sale under
house names. Seasonal beer: Old ☖.

Real Mild Ale *(OG 1033, ABV 3.4%)* ☖
A full-flavoured malty ale with a
background bitterness.

Fine Light Ale *(OG 1036, ABV 3.7%)* ☖◆
A pale, golden brown bitter with a strong,
floral, hoppy aroma and aftertaste. A hoppy
and moderately malty session beer.

Special (House Beer)
(OG 1037, ABV 3.8%)

Best Dark Ale *(OG 1040, ABV 4.1%)* ◆
An intensely bitter beer, balanced by a
moderate maltiness, with a complex
aftertaste.

Crown Imperial Stout *(OG 1044, ABV 4.5%)*
A classic Irish-style stout with a clean palate
and satisfying aftertaste from Kent Fuggles
hops.

Gold Star Ale *(OG 1050, ABV 5.1%)* ◆
A strong pale ale brewed from 100% Maris
Otter malt and all Kent hops.

Maidstone Porter *(OG 1050, ABV 5.1%)*
An occasional brew. A dark ruby winter beer
with a roast malt flavour.

GODDARDS SIBA

**Goddards Brewery Ltd, Barnsley Farm,
Bullen Road, Ryde, Isle of Wight, PO33 1QF
Tel (01983) 611011
Fax (01983) 611012
E-mail office@goddards-brewery.co.uk
Website www.goddards-brewery.co.uk**

⊗ Housed in a converted 18th-century barn on a farm near Ryde, the brewery went into production in 1993. Sales of its award-winning beers have been rising steadily and 2001 saw record sales. Around 40 outlets are supplied. Seasonal beers: Ale of Wight (ABV 4%, spring), Duck's Folly (ABV 5%, early autumn), Inspiration (ABV 5.2%), Winter Warmer (ABV 5.2%).

Special Bitter *(OG 1038.5, ABV 4%)* 🍺
A refreshing, straw-coloured, easy-drinking bitter with a wonderfully flowery hop aroma that carries right through to a satisfying aftertaste.

Fuggle-Dee-Dum *(OG 1048.5, ABV 4.8%)* 🍺
Tawny, full-flavoured, rich malty ale with a pleasing consistency of malty sweetness complemented by a hoppy bitterness that produces that essential bite that makes you want more.

Iron Horse *(OG 1049, ABV 4.8%)* 🍺
Superb roast old ale/porter style beer with complex roast malty-fruity bitterness consistent through the tasting experience – and what an experience. Available late autumn.

Inspiration Ale *(OG 1050, ABV 5.2%)* 🍺
Straw-coloured pale strong ale with a predominantly bitter fruity flavour balanced by a sweet undertone.

Winter Warmer *(OG 1052, ABV 5.2%)* 🍺
Good example of a winter ale with a refreshing bitterness that cleans the palate of the sweetness inherent in this style of beer.

GOFF'S SIBA

**Goff's Brewery Ltd, 9 Isbourne Way, Winchcombe, Cheltenham, Gloucestershire, GL54 5NS
Tel (01242) 603383 Fax (01242) 603959
E-mail goffsbrewery@yahoo.co.uk
Website www.goffs.biz**
Tours by arrangement

⊗ Goff's is a family concern that started brewing in 1994, using plant purchased from Nethergate Brewery. Now brewing to capacity, it supplies beer to 200 outlets and via wholesalers. Two pubs are owned in Cheltenham and Gretton. 'Ales of the Round Table' seasonal beers: Morored (ABV 4.2%, Jan-Feb), Launcelot (ABV 4.5%, March-April), Galahad (ABV 4.3%, May-June), Excalibur (ABV 3.8%, July), Lamorak (ABV 5%, August), Merlin (ABV 4.3%, Sept-Nov), Camelot (ABV 4.4%, Nov-Dec).

Jouster *(OG 1040, ABV 4%)* 🍺
A drinkable, tawny-coloured ale, with a light hoppiness in the aroma. It has a good balance of malt and bitterness in the mouth, underscored by fruitiness, with a clean, hoppy aftertaste.

Tournament *(OG 1038, ABV 4%)*
An amber-coloured, thirst-quenching session bitter with a delicate floral aroma and a bitter-sweet finish.

White Knight *(OG 1046, ABV 4.7%)* 🍺
A well-hopped bitter with a light colour and full-bodied taste. Bitterness predominates in the mouth and leads to a dry, hoppy aftertaste. Deceptively drinkable for its strength.

Black Knight *(OG 1053, ABV 5.3%)* 🍺
A dark, ruby-red tinted beer with a strong chocolate malt aroma. It has a smooth, dry, malty taste, with a subtle hoppiness, leading to a dry finish. A classic winter porter.

GOLCAR SIBA

**Golcar Brewery, Swallow Lane, Golcar, Huddersfield, West Yorkshire, HD7 4NB
Tel (01484) 644241/0797 0267555
E-mail jbltd111@aol.com**
Tours by arrangement

☺ Golcar started brewing in 2001. Production has increased to 2.4 barrels a week, mostly for the Rose and Crown brewery tap in Golcar. There were plans to further increase production during 2003.

Dark Mild *(OG 1033, ABV 3.2%)* 🍺
Dark mild with a light roasted malt and liquorice taste. Smooth and satisfying.

Pennine Gold *(OG 1038, ABV 3.8%)*

Best Bitter *(OG 1040, ABV 4%)* 🍺
Amber bitter with a hoppy, citrus taste, with fruity overtones and bitter finish.

Weavers Delight *(OG 1042, ABV 4.2%)*

Dark Angel *(OG 1044, ABV 4.4%)*

GOLDFINCH

**Goldfinch Brewery, 47 High East Street, Dorchester, DT1 1HU
Tel (01305) 264020**

⊗ A brewery established in 1987 at the rear of Tom Brown's public house in Dorchester. Originally a one-barrel plant, it has been increased to four barrels. The brewery supplies Tom Brown's pubs in Dorchester and Salisbury. Free trade outlets are supplied by wholesalers. Seasonal beer: Flashman's (ABV 4.5%, brewed alternately with Midnight Sun in summer).

Tom Brown's Best Bitter
(OG 1039, ABV 4%) 🍺
Clean, refreshing session beer. Moderate fruit and hops in the aroma and taste, balanced well with a little sweetness.

Midnight Sun *(OG 1045, ABV 4.5%)* 🍺
A well-balanced, golden bitter, light in body with hops, fruit and bitterness in moderation.

Flashman's Clout Strong Ale
(OG 1045, ABV 4.5%) 🍺
A tawny/mid-brown beer with an attractive, honeyed aroma, and a bitter-sweet taste with malt and some hops. Hoppiness continues through to give a bitter edge to the aftertaste.

Midnight Blinder *(OG 1050, ABV 5%)* 🍺
A reddish brown, full-bodied strong bitter. Dark malts dominate the bitter-sweet flavour, continuing into the hoppy aftertaste.

GOLDTHORN SIBA

**Goldthorn Brewery & Co, Imex Unit 60, Sunbeam Street, Wolverhampton, WV2 4NU
Tel/Fax (01902) 313018
E-mail paul@goldthornbrewery.co.uk
Website www.goldthornbrewery.co.uk**
Tours by arrangement

⊚ Goldthorn has a five-barrel plant based in the former Sunbeam car and motorcycle factory, home of the land speed record holders in the 1920s and 30s. Brewing started in 2001. There were plans to increase the five-barrel plant to 15 barrels in 2003, with the addition of bottling capacity. 80-plus outlets are supplied.

Ge It Sum Ommer (OG 1038, ABV 3.8%)

Sunbeam Bitter (OG 1040, ABV 4%)

Wulfrun Gold (OG 1043, ABV 4.3%)

Juniper Blonde (OG 1045, ABV 4.5%)

John Barleycorn (OG 1046, ABV 4.7%)

Goldthorn Premium (OG 1048, ABV 5%)

Deadly Nightshade (OG 1062, ABV 6%)

GOOSE EYE SIBA

**Goose Eye Brewery Ltd,
Ingrow Bridge, South Street, Keighley,
West Yorkshire, BD21 5AX
Tel/Fax (01535) 605807
Website www.goose-eye-brewery.co.uk**
Tours by arrangement

⊚ Goose Eye, run by Jack and David Atkinson since 1991, supplies 50-60 regular outlets, mainly in West and North Yorkshire, and Lancashire. The beers are also available through national wholesalers and pub chains. It produces an ever-expanding range of occasional beers, sometimes brewed to order, and is diversifying into wholesaling and bottled beers (filtered but not pasteurised). No-Eyed Deer is often re-badged under house names.

Barm Pot Bitter
(OG 1038, ABV 3.8%) ▉⬚◥
Hops and fruity flavours dominate the aroma and taste of this golden session beer, balanced by by a malty base throughout. The finish is hoppy and bitter.

No-Eye Deer (OG 1040, ABV 4%) ◥
A faint fruity and malty aroma. Hoppy fruit flavours, and a long, bitter finish characterise this refreshing, copper-coloured beer.

Bronte Bitter (OG 1040, ABV 4%) ◥
An amber bitter with a faint fruity, hoppy aroma. Bitterness dominates the taste with some background malt and hops. The lingering aftertaste is dry and bitter.

Wharfedale (OG 1045, ABV 4.5%) ◥
Malt and hops dominate the taste of this copper-coloured premium bitter. Bitterness comes through into the finish.

Golden Goose (OG 1045, ABV 4.5%)

Pommies Revenge (OG 1052, ABV 5.2%)
A light-coloured, full-bodied and fruity, strong bitter.

GRAINSTORE SIBA

**Davis'es Brewing Company Ltd,
The Grainstore Brewery, Station Approach,
Oakham, Rutland, LE15 6RE
Tel (01572) 770065
Fax (01572) 770068
E-mail grainstore@aol.com
Website www.rutnet.co.uk/grainstore**
Tours by arrangement

⊗ Grainstore, the smallest county's largest brewery, has been in production since 1995. The brewery's curious name comes from the fact that it was founded by Tony Davis and Mike Davies. After 30 years in the industry, latterly with Ruddles, Tony decided to set up his own business after finding a derelict Victorian railway grainstore building. The brewing is designed traditionally, relying on whole hops and Maris Otter barley malt. 60 outlets are supplied. Future plans include relocating and expanding the brewery, and incorporating a bottling line. Seasonal beers: Springtime (ABV 4.5%, March-May), Gold (ABV 4.5%, May-Oct), Harvest IPA (ABV 4.5%, Sept-Oct), Three Kings (ABV 4.5%, Nov-Dec), Winter Nip (ABV 7.3%, Nov-Dec).

Rutland Panther (OG 1034, ABV 3.4%) ◥
Black brew with the drinkability of a mild or light bitter, combined with the roast flavours associated with a stout.

Cooking Bitter (OG 1036, ABV 3.6%) ◥
A smooth, copper-coloured beer, full-bodied for its gravity. Malt and hops on the nose; malt and fruit to taste, with a malty aftertaste.

Triple B (OG 1042, ABV 4.2%) ◥
Initially, hops dominate over malt in both the aroma and taste, but fruit is there, too. All three linger in varying degrees in the sweetish aftertaste of this tawny brew.

Steamin' Billy Bitter
(OG 1043, ABV 4.3%)
Brewed for the Steaming Billy Brewing Co of Leicester (qv).

Ten Fifty (OG 1050, ABV 5%) ◥
This full-bodied, tawny beer is hoppy and fruity right into the aftertaste. A little malt on the nose and in the initial taste, with an underlying sweetness and an increasing bitterness.

GRAND UNION

**Grand Union Brewery Ltd,
Brewhouse Lock, 10 Abenglen,
Betam Road, Hayes, Middx, UB3 1SS
Tel (020) 8573 9888
Fax (020) 8573 8885
E-mail info@gubc.co.uk
Website www.gubc.co.uk**
Shop 10-4pm
Tours by prior arrangement

⊗ Grand Union started brewing in 2002. The 10-barrel plant came from the Mash & Air brew-restaurant in Manchester. Grand Union produces both ale and traditional, continental-style lagers. The lagers were intended for bottle only, but have been in demand as cask products. Some 45 outlets are supplied. Grand Union also brews some beers from the closed Old Kent brewery. They include Fine Edge (ABV 3.8%) and Opener (ABV 4.2%).

Bitter (OG 1036, ABV 3.7%)
Refreshing session ale.

Best (OG 1039, ABV 4.1%) ◥
An amber-brown, light drinking beer with some citrus notes. It is brewed with both English and east European hops, the latter giving the beer pleasant metallic notes.

Gold (*OG 1040, ABV 4.2%*) ◈
A yellow-coloured beer brewed with east European, German and American hops, giving fruity hop notes on the nose and in the flavour. The aftertaste is crisp and dry.

Special (*OG 1043, ABV 4.5%*)

Kolsch (*OG 1043, ABV 4.8%*)
A German-style ale from the Cologne region.

Pilsner (*OG 1047, ABV 5.2%*)
In the style of Pils from the Czech Republic, light tasting and thirst quenching, served from the cask.

Stout (*OG 1047, ABV 4.8%*) ◈
A sweetish black beer balanced with a dry, clean finish. There are chocolate and roasted coffee notes throughout.

GREAT GABLE

⛏ **Great Gable Brewing Co Ltd, Wasdale Head Inn, Gosforth, Cumbria, CA20 1EX**
Tel (019467) 26229 Inn 26333
Fax (019467) 26334
E-mail wasdaleheadinn@msn.com
Website www.greatgablebrewing.com
Tours by arrangement

☺ The Great Gable Brewery, the brainchild of Giles Holiday and Howard Christie, is based in Wasdale Head Inn, at the head of remote and unspoiled Wasdale at the foot of England's highest mountain and near its deepest lake. Brewing was due to start in 2001 but the foot and mouth epidemic delayed this until 2002. The brewery produces 4.5 barrels of Great Gable and three barrels of Wasd'ale a week. Seasonal: Wry'Nose (ABV 4%, Easter-Oct). There are plans to bottle the beers. All beers are fined with isinglass and Yewbarrow contains a little honey.

Great Gable (*OG 1035, ABV 3.7%*)
Made from Thomas Fawcett's pale malt with a little dark crystal malt. High alpha Challenger hops for bittering and another hop for aroma.

Burnmoor Pale Ale (*OG 1040, ABV 4.2%*)
Classic English pale bitter. The traditional, old-fashioned but distinctive hoppy bitterness is achieved through a combination of three different types of hop.

Wasd'ale (*OG 1042, ABV 4.4%*)
Ruby in colour with a fine aftertaste.

Scafell (*OG 1046, ABV 4.8%*)
Reminiscent of an old-fashioned ale, brewed with pale malt and a small amount of pale crystal. Hops are Bramling Cross.

Illgill IPA (*OG 1048, ABV 5%*)
A blend of pale malts, highly hopped with only aroma varieties.

Yewbarrow (*OG 1054, ABV 5.5%*)
A rich, dark, mellow stout with an unusual fruit flavour.

GREEN DRAGON

⛏ **Green Dragon, 29 Broad Street, Bungay, Suffolk, NR35 1EE**
Tel/Fax (01986) 892681
Tours by arrangement

⊗ The Green Dragon pub was purchased from Brent Walker in 1991 and the buildings at the rear converted to a brewery. In 1994 the plant was expanded and moved into a converted barn across the car park. The doubling of capacity allowed the production of a larger range of ales, including seasonal and occasional brews. The beers are available at the pub and three other outlets. A new cask beer is planned and the bottled range will be expanded. Seasonal beer: Wynter Warmer (ABV 6.5%). Bottle-conditioned beers: Dragon (ABV 5.5%), Wynter Warmer (ABV 7%).

Chaucer Ale (*OG 1037, ABV 3.7%*)

Bridge Street Bitter (*OG 1046, ABV 4.5%*)

GREENE KING

Greene King PLC, Westgate Brewery, Bury St Edmunds, Suffolk, IP33 1QT
Tel (01284) 763222
Fax (01284) 706502
Website www.greeneking.co.uk
Shop Mon-Sat 11-5
Tours Individual and party bookings welcome (01284 714297/714382)

⊗ Greene King has been brewing in the market town of Bury St Edmunds in the heart of rural Suffolk since 1799. It is now a 'super-regional' following the acquisition of Morland and Ruddles. Sales of its main cask beers continue to grow in line with a massive presence in East Anglia and the South-east. A 'Beer to Dine For' campaign launched in 2002 has attracted interest and support among food and drink enthusiasts. The brewery museum, shop and tours are open and available all year round. Greene King now owns 1,680 pubs in East Anglia, the Thames Valley and South-east England, 99 per cent of them serving cask beer. In 2002 it bought the bulk of the Morrells pub company outlets in the Thames Valley. 3,000 free trade outlets are supplied direct. Organic beer: Ruddles Organic Ale (ABV 5.1%). Bottle-conditioned beer: Hen's Tooth (ABV 6.5%).

XX Mild (*OG 1035, ABV 3%*) ◈
Smooth and sweet, with a bitter aftertaste. The beer is enjoying greater promotion and has increased sales.

GREENE KING
ESTD 1799

Beer to dine for ™

Greene King IPA *(OG 1036, ABV 3.6%)* ◆
A light, uncomplicated session bitter. Copper-coloured with a subtle malty nose and just a hint of hops. A light bitter introduction with sweetish malty undertones give a refreshing, lemonade-type feel. A long, tapering finish turns dryer and increases in bitterness.

Ruddles Best Bitter
(OG 1037, ABV 3.7%) ◆
An amber/brown beer, strong on bitterness but with some initial sweetness, fruit and subtle, distinctive Bramling Cross hop. Dryness lingers in the aftertaste.

Morland Original Bitter *(OG 1039, ABV 4%)*

Ruddles County *(OG 1048, ABV 4.3%)* ◆
Richer and slightly darker than Ruddles Best, this premium ale shares similar characteristics. Sweetness and fruit on the palate give way to bitterness and a distinctive hoppy, dry finish. Good body for its strength

Abbot Ale *(OG 1049, ABV 5%)* ◆
A full-bodied, very distinctive beer with a bitter-sweet aftertaste.

Old Speckled Hen *(OG 1050, ABV 5.2%)* ◆
Rich and cloying in both nose and taste. An intense malty nose with plummy overtones. The flavour spectrum matches this with a rich spicy maltiness overwhelming the latent bitterness. A solid mouthfeel helps retain the fruity sweetness as the heavy malt framework slowly turns to a light dryness.

GREENFIELD*

Greenfield Real Ale Brewery, Unit 8, Waterside Mills, Greenfield, Saddleworth, OL3 7NH
Tel (01457) 879789
E-mail percivalbrewer@hotmail.com
Tours by prior arrangement

The brewery started trading in 2002. Peter Percival, the former brewer at Saddleworth Brewery, with Mark Atherton and Richard Nankinson, set up the five/six-barrel plant supplied by Porter Brewing Co. The brewery is situated in a mill complex in a beautiful country location. 20-25 outlets are served.

Greenfield Ale *(OG 1040, ABV 4%)*

Bill's o' Jack's *(OG 1041, ABV 4.1%)*

Dobcross Bitter *(OG 1042, ABV 4.2%)*

GREEN TYE

Green Tye Brewery, Green Tye, Much Hadham, Hertfordshire, SG10 6JP
Tel/Fax (01279) 841041
E-mail enquiries@gtbrewery.co.uk
Website www.gtbrewery.co.uk
Tours by arrangement

⊗ Green Tye supplies direct to local outlets, nationally via a wholesaler, and by arrangement with other micros. Occasional beers include a mild, beers for special events and a spiced winter beer. Seasonal beers: Snowdrop (ABV 3.9%, spring), Mad Morris (ABV 4.2%, summer), Autumn Rose (ABV 4.2%, late autumn), Conkerer (ABV 4.7%, early autumn), Coal Porter (ABV 4.5%, winter). Bottle-conditioned beers (available direct from the brewery): Boy Stout, Union

Jack, Shot in the Dark, Mustang Mild, Uncle John's Ferret, Snowdrop, Smile for the Camera, Green Tiger, Mad Morris, Autumn Rose, Wheelbarrow, Coal Porter, Merry Maker, Citrus Sin.

Boy Stout *(OG 1040, ABV 3.1%)*
Deep, rich, coffee and chocolate flavours with a smooth and satisfying finish.

Shot in the Dark *(OG 1036, ABV 3.6%)*
A dark, hoppy bitter, with a pleasant, lingering aftertaste. Malt and toffee abound on the tongue, with a touch of fruit.

Union Jack *(OG 1036, ABV 3.6%)*
A copper-coloured bitter. Fruity, citrus taste and a hoppy, citrus aroma, with a balanced, bitter finish.

Mustang Mild *(OG 1038, ABV 3.7%)*
Named after the P-51 Mustangs that flew under British colours from a local airfield, this dark mild is brewed with only the best Maris Otter, crystal, brown and chocolate malts, and Fuggles hops.

Uncle John's Ferret *(OG 1040, ABV 3.8%)*
Easy drinking, ruby-brown mild, with light caramel on the nose, and malt fruit in the mouth.

Green Tiger *(OG 1042, ABV 4.2%)*
Light amber in colour, this all-Goldings brew has a lemony hop aroma and flavour, with a subtle addition of fresh root ginger.

Wheelbarrow *(OG 1044, ABV 4.3%)*
Amber-coloured beer with a soft, fruity nose and taste. Gentle malt, with underlying hop bitterness, with a fruity and slightly dry finish.

Coal Porter *(OG 1048, ABV 4.5%)*
Dark, easy drinking porter made with chocolate malt. Hints of liquorice and Bramling Cross hops add a spicy blackcurrant flavour and aroma, perfectly complementing the light bitter finish. Brewed for the winter.

Conkerer *(OG 1048, ABV 4.7%)*
A mid-brown best bitter hopped with a new hedgerow variety, Hilary. This hop is robust, full and rounded, with a refreshing, spicy aroma. Brewed early autumn.

GRIBBLE INN

⌂ **Gribble Brewery, Gribble Inn, Oving, nr Chichester, W Sussex, PO20 2BP**
Tel (01243) 786893
Fax (01243) 788841
E-mail brianelderfield@hotmail.com
Tours by arrangement

⊗ The Gribble Brewery has been on the site for 22 years. After a brief interlude, it has been in operation in its current form for 11 years. It is owned by Badger (Hall & Woodhouse, qv) but the brewer and manager are given a free hand in the production of their beers, which are distributed throughout the H&W estate, including the former King & Barnes houses. There are plans for a bottle-conditioned beer. Eight outlets are supplied, with a further 25-30 via Blandford. Seasonal beers: Wobbler (ABV 7.8%, winter), Porterhouse (ABV 5.2%, winter and spring), Plucking Pheasant (ABV 5.2%, spring and summer), Wobbler (7.8%, Nov-Feb).

Fursty Ferret
(OG 1041, ABV 4%)
For selected H & W houses, all year round. This fine golden beer with its light nutty and slightly hoppy flavour is very easy on the palate.

Gribble Ale *(OG 1041, ABV 4.1%)*
The original brewhouse bitter, second only to Fursty Ferret in popularity.

Reg's Tipple *(OG 1048, ABV 5%)*
Reg's Tipple was named after a customer from the early days of the brewery. It has a smooth nutty flavour with a very pleasant afterbite.

Pig's Ear *(OG 1060, ABV 5.8%)*
A full-bodied old ale with a rich ruby-brown colour.

For Hall & Woodhouse:

King & Barnes Mild Ale
(OG 1030, ABV 3.5%) ◄
A truly dark mild with a toffee, roast malt character that is present throughout. Short, sweet aftertaste. Nothing like the old K&B Mild, but pleasant nonetheless.

King & Barnes Sussex Bitter
(OG 1035, ABV 3.5%) ◄
Reasonably well-balanced, mid-brown bitter. Hints of pear fruit in the flavour.

GUERNSEY

See Tipsy Toad

HADRIAN & BORDER SIBA

**Alnwick Ales Ltd,
t/a Hadrian & Border Brewery,
Unit 10, Hawick Crescent
Industrial Estate,
Newcastle upon Tyne, NE6 1AS
Tel (0191) 276 5302
Fax (0191) 265 5312
E-mail border@rampart.freeserve.co.uk**
Tours by arrangement

☺ Hadrian & Border is the result of a merger between Border Brewery of Berwick-on-Tweed and Four Rivers of Newcastle. Shona and Andy Burrows of Border joined forces and the new company is based at the ex-Four Rivers 20-barrel site in Newcastle. There are plans to move to a new site. The new company's brands are available from Glasgow to Yorkshire, and nationally through wholesalers. They are hard to find on Tyneside, though the Sir John Fitzgerald group stocks them from time to time. Approximately 100 outlets are supplied.

Vallum Bitter *(OG 1034, ABV 3.6%)*
A well-hopped, amber-coloured bitter with a distinctive dry refreshing taste.

Gladiator *(OG 1036, ABV 3.8%)* ◄
Medium-bodied bitter with plenty of malt in the aroma and palate, leading to a strong bitter finish.

Farne Island Pale Ale
(OG 1038, ABV 4%) ◄
An amber/mid-brown bitter with a refreshing hop/malt balance.

Flotsam *(OG 1038, ABV 4%)*
Bronze coloured with a citrus bitterness and a distinctive floral aroma.

Legion Ale *(OG 1040, ABV 4.2%)* ◄
Well-balanced, amber-coloured beer, full bodied with good malt flavours. Well hopped with a long bitter finish.

Secret Kingdom *(OG 1042, ABV 4.3%)*
Dark, rich and full bodied, slightly roasted with a malty palate ending with a pleasant bitterness.

Reiver's IPA *(OG 1042, ABV 4.4%)*
Dark golden bitter with a clean citrus palate and aroma with subtle malt flavours breaking through at the end.

Northumbrian Gold *(OG 1043, ABV 4.5%)*
Dark golden coloured ale with a biscuity malt flavour countered with floral and citrus aromatic hops.

Centurion Best Bitter
(OG 1043, ABV 4.5%) ◄
Golden-coloured bitter with a distinct hop palate, some fruit, smooth, clean tasting and refreshing.

Rampart *(OG 1046, ABV 4.8%)* ◄
Golden bitter; complex hopping gives this beer a clean, refreshing taste with plenty of character.

Jetsam *(OG 1046, ABV 4.8%)*
Pale golden bitter, clean and fresh with a flowery, hoppy nose.

HAGGARDS SIBA

**Haggards Brewery Limited,
c/o 577 King's Road,
London, SW6 2EH
Tel (020) 7731 3845
Fax (020) 7731 3874
E-mail andrewhaggard@haggardsbrewery.
fsnet.co.uk**
Tours by arrangement

The brewery was set up in 1998 to supply beer to the Imperial pub on King's Road. It is owned and run by the Haggard brothers, who worked in the City of London but gave up their jobs to run the pub and establish the brewery. The brewery has a five-barrel capacity, and was designed by Rob Jones of Dark Star. One pub is owned and 10 outlets are supplied.

Horny Ale *(OG 1042, ABV 4.3%)* ◄
A lightly hopped, clean finishing, flavour packed session ale.

Imp Ale *(OG 1046, ABV 4.7%)*
This pale ale is well hopped with Cascade hops, providing punchy tropical fruit aromas and sweet-spicy flavours that last right to the bottom of the pint.

HALIFAX

**Halifax Steam Brewing Co Ltd,
Southedge Works, Hipperholme, Halifax,
West Yorkshire, HX3 8EF
Tel 07967 802488
Fax (01484) 715074 (Phone first)
E-mail davidearnshaw@blueyonder.co.uk**
Tours occasionally, by arrangement

⊛ David Earnshaw started brewing in 2001 in a converted garage, inspired by CAMRA's series of home-brewing books. He learnt his brewing skills at Barge & Barrel. He bought his five-barrel plant from the Fox & Firkin in Lewisham, south London, and has moved to new premises to meet demand. He supplies 12 pubs while Flying Firkin wholesales further afield. The beers are loosely based on old Whitaker's of Halifax brands, and one of Ramsden's beers.

Morning Glory *(ABV 3.8%)*

Pickel Hut Imposter *(ABV 4%)*
Cask lager.

Lilly Fogg *(ABV 4%)*
Straw-coloured beer.

Bantam *(OG 1043, ABV 4.1%)*

Cock o' t' North *(OG 1048, ABV 4.9%)*

Shirley Crabtree *(ABV 4.9%)*

HAMBLETON SIBA

**Nick Stafford Hambleton Ales, Holme-on-
Swale, Thirsk, North Yorkshire, YO7 4JE
Tel (01845) 567460
E-mail sales@hambletonales.co.uk
Website www.hambletonales.co.uk
Shop 9-4 Mon-Fri.
Tours by arrangement**

⊛ Hambleton was established in 1991 by Nick Stafford on the banks of the River Swale in the heart of the Vale of York. The bottling line caters for micro and large brewers, handling more than 20 brands. New brewing equipment was installed in 2000, doubling capacity to 100 barrels a week. A mail-order service for all bottle brands is available from the brewery or its website. 100 outlets are supplied. Hambleton brews beers under contract for the Village Brewer wholesale company (01325) 374887, and Black Dog of Whitby (qv).

Bitter *(OG 1036.5, ABV 3.6%)* 🍺◆
Rich, hoppy aroma rides through this light and drinkable beer. Taste is bitter with citrus and marmalade aroma and solid body. Ends dry with a spicy mouthfeel.

Goldfield *(OG 1040, ABV 4.2%)* ◆
A light amber bitter with good hop character and increasing dryness. A fine blend of malts gives a smooth overall impression.

Stallion *(OG 1040, ABV 4.2%)* ◆
A premium bitter, moderately hoppy throughout and richly balanced in malt and fruit, developing a sound and robust bitterness, with earthy hop drying the aftertaste.

Stud *(OG 1042, ABV 4.3%)* ◆
A strongly bitter beer, with rich hop and fruit. It ends dry and spicy.

Nightmare *(OG 1050, ABV 5%)* ◆
Fully deserving its acclaim, this impressively flavoured beer satisfies all parts of the palate. Strong roast malts dominate, but hoppiness rears out of this complex blend.

For Village Brewer:
White Boar *(OG 1037.5, ABV 3.7%)* ◆
A light, flowery and fruity ale; crisp, clean and refreshing, with a dry-hopped, powerful but not aggressive, bitter finish.

Bull *(OG 1039, ABV 4%)* ◆
A fairly thin, but well-hopped bitter, with a distinct dryness in the aftertaste.

Old Ruby *(OG 1048, ABV 4.8%)* ◆
A full-bodied, smooth, rich-tasting dark ale. A complex balance of malt, fruit character and creamy caramel sweetness offsets the bitterness. A classic old ale.

HAMPSHIRE SIBA

**Hampshire Brewery Ltd, 6-8 Romsey
Industrial Estate, Greatbridge Road, Romsey,
Hampshire, SO51 0HR
Tel (01794) 830529
Fax (01794) 830528
E-mail online@hampshirebrewery.com
Website www.hampshirebrewery.com**
Shop 9-5.30 Mon-Fri.
Tours by arrangement.

⊠ Hampshire was founded in 1992 and soon developed a strong reputation for the production of high-quality and consistent products. In 2002 Hampshire merged with the Millennium Bottling Co but it still operates as an independent brewery. The original brew, King Alfred, took its name from Alfred the Great whose parliament was based in Andover (the original home of the brewery). Later brews continued the theme of noble kings. The brewery moved in 1997 to a larger site in Romsey. Pride of Romsey was launched to celebrate the move and in 2000 won the Gold Medal in the Brewing Industry International Awards for Strong Ales. (The bottle-conditioned version has the distinction of winning a medal at three successive GBBFs). In 1999 the brewery relaunched Strong's Best Bitter, to the old Romsey Brewery's original recipe. Hampshire has now bought the title to the beer from Whitbread who last owned and closed Strong's Brewery. All the beers produced are available in bottle-conditioned form from a new, state-of-the-art bottling plant. The brewery produces some 22 seasonal beers: consult the website for full details.

King Alfred's *(OG 1037, ABV 3.8%)* ◆
A mid-brown beer, featuring a malty and hoppy aroma. A malty taste leads to a hoppy, malty and bitter finish.

Strong's Best Bitter *(OG 1037, ABV 3.8%)*
A deep copper-coloured bitter with rich

malt complexity brewed with classic English aroma hops.

Ironside *(OG 1041, ABV 4.2%)* ◆
A beer with little aroma, but some malt. The taste has solid fruit with lasting hops and malt. The aftertaste is more bitter and malty. Pale brown in colour.

Pride of Romsey *(OG 1048, ABV 5%)*
Abundant aroma of the fruit of the hop, citrus and fragrant with orange, grapefruit and lemon hints. Powerful hop aroma through to the aftertaste with distinctive bitterness complemented by good strength of malt character.

HANBY SIBA

Hanby Ales Ltd, New Brewery, Aston Park, Soulton Road, Wem, Shropshire, SY4 5SD
Tel/Fax (01939) 232432
E-mail hanby@dialpipex.com
Website www.hanbyales.co.uk
Tours by arrangement

⊗ Hanby was set up in 1988 by Jack Hanby following the closure of the Shrewbury & Wem Brewery. The aim was to continue the two-hundred-year tradition of brewing in the area. In 1990 the brewery was moved lock, stock and barrels to its present home, and has recently upgraded to 30-barrel production runs. Future plans include a re-launch with new pump clips and a brewery shop. Hanby supplies 204 outlets. Several seasonal beers are brewed: consult the website. Bottle-conditioned beers: Hanby Premium (ABV 4.6%), Rainbow Chaser (ABV 4.3%), Golden Honey (ABV 4.5%), Cherry Bomb (ABV 6%).

Drawwell Bitter *(OG 1039, ABV 3.9%)* ◆
A hoppy beer with excellent bitterness, both in taste and aftertaste. Beautiful amber colour.

Black Magic Plus Mild
(OG 1040, ABV 4%) ◆
A dark, reddish-brown mild, which is dry and bitter with a roast malt taste.

All Seasons Bitter *(OG 1042, ABV 4.2%)*
A light, hoppy bitter, well balanced and thirst quenching, brewed with a fine blend of Fuggles and Cascade hops.

Rainbow Chaser Bitter
(OG 1043, ABV 4.3%)
A pale beer brewed with Pioneer hops.

Golden Honey *(OG 1043, ABV 4.3%)*
A beer made with the addition of Australian honey.

Shropshire Stout *(OG 1044, ABV 4.4%)*
A full-bodied, rich ruby/black coloured stout. A blend of four malts produces a distinct chocolate malt dry flavour, with a mushroom-coloured head.

Wem Special Bitter *(OG 1044, ABV 4.4%)*
A pale, smooth, hoppy bitter.

Scorpio Porter *(OG 1045, ABV 4.5%)*
A dark porter with an interesting and complex palate introducing hints of coffee and chocolate contrasting and complementing the background hoppiness.

Cascade Bitter *(OG 1045, ABV 4.5%)*
A very pale beer, brewed with Cascade hops, producing a clean crisp flavour and a hoppy finish.

Hanby's Premium Bitter
(OG 1046, ABV 4.6%)
A pale brown beer that is sweeter and fruitier than most of the beers above. Slight malt and hop taste.

Old Wemian *(OG 1049, ABV 4.9%)*
Golden-brown colour with an aroma of malt and hops and a soft, malty palate.

Taverners Ale *(OG 1053, ABV 5.3%)*
A smooth and fruity beer full of body.

Cherry Bomb *(OG 1060, ABV 6%)*
Beer made with the addition of cherries.

Nutcracker *(OG 1060, ABV 6%)*
Very full tawny beer, a fine blend of malt and hops.

HANSON'S

See Banks's.

THOMAS HARDY

Thomas Hardy Brewery, Weymouth Avenue, Dorchester, Dorset, DT1 1QT
Tel (01305) 250255
Fax (01305) 258381
Website www.thomashardybrewery.co.uk

⊗ In March 1997, former Courage manager Peter Ward bought Dorchester Brewery from Eldridge Pope, which is now a pub company (qv). The next year Ward acquired the majority shares of Burtonwood Brewery (qv) and formed Thomas Hardy Burtonwood. The sale of the former Eldridge Pope site was conc̶l̶uded in March 2003 for £8.85 million. Ward has made it clear that he inte̶nds to brewing at Dorch̶ester ̶£3.5 million in the ̶Pope sold its minority ̶Hardy and 40% stake in ̶Packaging. Save for one solitary EP sh̶ Peter Ward is now the sole owner. In 2001, Eldridge Pope discontinued the contract with Ward to brew Royal Oak, Hardy Country Bitter and Popes Traditional: the first two beers are now brewed by O'Hanlon's (qv). Refresh UK's brands have left Dorchester and are now brewed at Burtonwood, Wychwood and Wadworth. The Morrells brands have also decamped to Burtonwood. Thomas Hardy declines to reveal any information about the beers it is currently brewing due to 'client confidentiality'.

CLOSED JULY 2003

HARDYS & HANSONS IFBB

Hardys & Hansons PLC, The Brewery, Kimberley, Nottingham, NG16 2NS
Tel (0115) 938 3611
Fax (0115) 945 9055
E-mail info@hardysandhansons.plc.uk
Website www.hardysandhansons.plc.uk
Tours by arrangement

☺ Established in 1832 and 1847 respectively, Hardys and Hansons were two competitive breweries until a merger in 1930 produced the present company, listed on the Stock Exchange in 1960. The brewery is still run by descendants of the original families. The majority of its 246 tied houses take its award-winning real ales, mostly drawn by metered dispense into oversized glasses, although Bitter is increasingly served by handpumps. 2003 saw the re-branding of beers and pubs, with the renaming of regular beers and the introduction of Olde Trip as a new premium beer: the name reflects the brewery's ownership of the Olde Trip to Jerusalem in Nottingham, the country's oldest tavern. As well as tied trade, around 75 other outlets are also supplied direct. A range of seasonal ales, with a rotation or new beer every month under the Cellarman's Cask banner, has extended. Occasional/seasonal beers: Old Kim (ABV 4.5%, January), Peak Perfection (ABV 4.1%, February), Peddlars Pride (ABV 4.3%, March), Spring Hop (ABV 4.4%, April), Original Gravity (ABV 4.1%, May), Vintage 1832 (ABV 4.6%, June), Guinea Gold (ABV 4.5%, July), Frolicking Farmer (ABV 4.2%, August), Swallows Return (ABV 4.1%, September), Guzzling Goose (ABV 4.4%, October), Classic (ABV 4.8%, November), Rocking Rudolph (ABV 5%, December).

Kimberley Mild *(OG 1035, ABV 3.1%)* ♦
A deep ruby mild dominated by chocolate malt. The fruitiness and caramel sweetness are well balanced in the taste, with a faintly hoppy finish.

Kimberley Bitter
(OG 1038, ABV 3.9%) ♦
A beer with a flowery, hoppy and fruity nose, although malt is never far away. Fruity hop is evident in the taste and there is a consistent bitterness.

Olde Trip *(OG 1043, ABV 4.3%)*

HART

⚲ Hart Brewery Co Ltd, Cartford Hotel, Cartford Lane, Little Eccleston, Preston, Lancs, PR3 0YP
Tel (01995) 671686
Fax (01772) 797069
Tours by arrangement Tue-Thur evenings

⊛ The brewery was founded in 1994 in a small private garage in Preston. It moved to its present site at the rear of the Cartford Hotel in 1995. With a 10-barrel plant, Hart now supplies around 100 outlets nationwide and does swaps with other breweries. It became a limited company in 2002. Seasonal beers: Indian Pale Ale (ABV 4.2%, summer), Bat out of Hell (ABV 4.5%, Halloween), No Balls (ABV 4.5%, winter).

Dishie Debbie *(OG 1040, ABV 4%)* ♦
An amber-coloured bitter. It has a smooth, creamy malt character with a subtle hoppiness.

Ice Maiden *(OG 1040, ABV 4%)*

Maysons Premier *(OG 1040, ABV 4%)*

Squirrels Hoard *(OG 1040, ABV 4%)*

Genesis *(OG 1042, ABV 4.2%)*

Mariners Mirage *(OG 1042, ABV 4.2%)*

Nemesis *(OG 1045, ABV 4.5%)*

Siren *(OG 1045, ABV 4.5%)*

HARVEYS IFBB

Harvey & Son (Lewes) Ltd, The Bridge Wharf Brewery, 6 Cliffe High Street, Lewes, East Sussex, BN7 2AH
Tel (01273) 480209
Fax (01273) 486074
E-mail maj@harveys.org.uk
Website www.harveys.org.uk
Shop 9.30-4.45 Mon-Sat
Tours by arrangement (two-year waiting list)

⊗ Established in 1790, this independent family brewery operates from the Bridge Wharf Brewery on the banks of the River Ouse in Lewes. The brewery was rebuilt in 1881. A major development in 1985 doubled the brewhouse capacity and subsequent additional fermenting capacity has seen production rise to in excess of 34,000 barrels a year. Harveys supplies real ale to all its 45 pubs and 400 free trade outlets in Sussex and Kent.
Seasonal beers: Knots of May Light Mild (ABV 3%, May), Sussex XXXX Old Ale (ABV 4.3%, Oct-May), Kiss (ABV 4.8%, February), Southdown Harvest Ale (ABV 5%, September), 1859 Porter (ABV 4.8%, March), Tom Paine (ABV 5.5%, July), Copperwheat Beer (ABV 4.8%, June), Bonfire Boy (ABV 5.8%, November), Christmas Ale ⬤ (ABV 8.1%, December). Bottle-conditioned beer: Imperial Extra Double Stout (ABV 9%), a brilliant recreation of a 19th-century strong stout exported to Russia.

Sussex XX Mild Ale
(OG 1030, ABV 3%) ⬤⬤♦
A dark copper-brown colour. Roast malt dominates the aroma and palate leading to a sweet, caramel finish.

Sussex Pale Ale
(OG 1033, ABV 3.5%) ⬤♦
An agreeable, light bitter with malt and hops dominating the aroma, while a hoppy bitterness develops throughout the taste, to dominate the finish.

Sussex Best Bitter
(OG 1040, ABV 4%) ⬤⬤♦
Full-bodied brown bitter. A hoppy aroma leads to a good malt and hop balance and a dry aftertaste.

Sussex XXXX Old Ale
(OG 1043, ABV 4.3%) ⬤⬤♦
A rich, dark beer with a good malty nose, with undertones of roast malt, hops and fruit. The flavour is a complex blend of roast malt, grain, fruit and hops with some caramel. Malty caramel finish with roast malt.

Armada Ale *(OG 1045, ABV 4.5%)* ⬤♦
Hoppy amber best bitter. Well-balanced fruit and hops dominate throughout with a fruity palate.

HARVIESTOUN SIBA

Harviestoun Brewery Ltd, Devon Road, Dollar, Clackmannanshire, FK14 7LX
Tel (01259) 742141
Fax (01259) 743141
E-mail harviestoun@talk21.com
Shop Mon-Fri 9-4.30

⊛ A new purpose-built brewery was being constructed in 2003, seven miles from Dollar in Hillfoots Industrial Estate, Alva, with a brew length of 50-60 barrels. The company was set up in 1985 by two home-brewing enthusiasts, and has grown to become one of Scotland's most successful craft breweries. Owner Ken Brooker's humour can be seen in the name of Bitter & Twisted and the choice of German hops in Schiehallion. Harviestoun now serves 70 outlets. Seasonal beers: Jack the Lad (ABV 4.1%, wheat beer, January), Ice Maiden (ABV 4.2%, February), Spring Fever (ABV 3.8%, March), IPA (ABV 4.1%, April), Belgian White (ABV 4.3%, wheat and malted oats, May), Navigator (ABV 4.3%, American Mount Hood hops, June), Natural Blonde (ABV 4%, July), Gold Rush (ABV 3.9%, Brewers Gold hops, August), Gremlin (ABV 4.3%, First Gold hops, September), American Red (ABV 4.1%, American Liberty and Willamette hops, October), Amarillo (ABV 4.2%, November) and Good King Legless (ABV 4.5%, December).

Brooker's Bitter & Twisted
(OG 1036, ABV 3.8%) ⬛🔲❖
Aggressively hoppy beer with fruit throughout. A bitter-sweet taste with a long bitter finish. A golden session beer, 2002 Champion Beer of Scotland.

Turnpike *(OG 1043, ABV 4.1%)*

Ptarmigan *(OG 1047, ABV 4.5%)* ❖
A well-balanced, bitter-sweet beer in which hops and malt dominate. The blend of malt, hops and fruit produces a clean, hoppy aftertaste.

Schiehallion
(OG 1045, ABV 4.8%) ⬛🔲❖
A Scottish cask lager, brewed using a lager yeast and Hersbrucker hops. A hoppy aroma, with fruit and malt, leads to a malty, bitter taste with floral hoppiness and a bitter finish.

Old Engine Oil *(OG 1066, ABV 6%)*

HAWKSHEAD SIBA
Hawkshead Brewery Co,
Town End, Hawkshead,
Cumbria, LA22 0JU
Tel/Fax (015394) 36111
E-mail alex.brodie@kencomp.net
Website www.hawksheadbrewery.co.uk
Tours By prior arrangement

☺ The brewery was launched in 2002 by BBC Radio presenter Alex Brodie, with a seven-eight barrel plant bought from Border Brewery, Berwick-on-Tweed, which in turn came originally from Hadrian. There are plans to extend the range of beers and to bottle. The brewery is housed in a restored, listed, disused dairy beside Esthwaite Water in the Lake District.

Hawkshead Bitter
(OG 1036.5-1037.5, ABV 3.7%)
A pale, hoppy and bitter session beer. It has a distinct fruity aroma with a dry and bitter finish. The hops are First Gold and Styrian Golding. Grains are Maris Otter pale ale malt with a little crystal.

Hawkshead Best Bitter
(OG 1041-1042.5, ABV 4.2%)
A reddish, malty, yet bitter, fuller-bodied English ale. It has a definite malty and spicy aroma and initial taste, but is not sweet as the maltiness suggests; rather it finishes dry and bitter. Grains are Maris Otter pale ale malt with crystal and dark crystal; hops are First Gold and Fuggles.

HAYWOOD*
Haywood Brewery, Callow Top Holiday Park,
Buxton Road, Sandybrook, Ashbourne,
Derbyshire, DE6 2AQ
Tel (01335) 344020
Fax (01335) 343726
E-mail enquiries@callowtop.freeserve.co.uk
Website www.callowtop.co.uk

Alan Palmer bought Haywood Farm in 1994 and turned a derelict barn into a brewery at the turn of the century. He began to brew at Easter 2003. He is conducting trial brews at present and hopes to get production up to one barrel a week. He is looking for outlets in the area.

Dr Samuel Johnson *(ABV 4.5%)*

Callowtop Imperial IPA *(ABV 5.25%)*

HEATHER SIBA
Heather Ale Ltd, Craigmill Brewery,
Strathaven, Lanarkshire, ML10 6PB
Tel (01357) 529529
Fax (01357) 522256
E-mail fraoch@heatherale.co.uk
Website heatherale.co.uk
Tours by arrangement

☺ The company operates under both the Heather Ale and Craigmill names. It's based in an 18th-century watermill on the banks of the River Avon, restored for use as a brewery in 1998. All cask beers are made on site while the bottled products are brewed and bottled by Forth Brewery (qv). Heather Ale is made with flowering heather, in addition to malt and hops. Craigmill Brewery focuses on a range of ales brewed with malt and hops with a bird theme. The brewery welcomes groups for tours. Some 35 outlets are supplied direct. Seasonal beers: Pidgin Pale Ale (ABV 3.9%, Oct-Nov), Barn Owl Bitter (ABV 4%, April-May), Pheasant Plucker 80/- (ABV 4.2%, Aug-Sept), Wheatear Spiced Wheat (ABV 4.2%, June-July), Black Grouse Stout (ABV 4.4%, Feb-March), Cock Sparra Red Ale (ABV 4.5%, Dec-Jan), Alba Pine Ale (ABV 6.1%, March-April). Kelpie Seaweed Ale (ABV 4.4%) is suitable for vegetarians and vegans.

Swallow IPA *(OG 1039, ABV 3.8%)*
A light fresh golden ale with a soft malt character and crisp hop finish.

Fraoch Heather Ale
(OG 1041, ABV 4.1%) ⬛🔲❖
The unique taste of heather flowers are very noticeable in this beer. A fine floral aroma and spicy taste give character to this very drinkable speciality beer.

HEBRIDEAN SIBA
Hebridean Brewing Company,
Bells Road, Stornoway,
Isle of Lewis, HS1 2RA
Tel (01851) 700123
Fax (01851) 700234
Website www.hebridean-brewery.co.uk

☺ The company was set up in 2001 by Andy Ribbens, whose family came from Lewis. The plant is steam powered with a 14-barrel brew length. An off-licence is attached to the brewery and the beers are now being bottled (not bottle conditioned).

Clansman Ale *(OG 1037, ABV 3.9%)*

Celtic Black Ale *(ABV 3.9%)*
A porter-style beer.

Islander Strong Premium Ale
(OG 1047, ABV 4.8%)
An Old Ale.

HEPWORTH

**Hepworth & Co (Brewers) Ltd/Welton's,
The Beer Station,
The Railway Yard, Horsham,
West Sussex, RH12 1DQ
Tel (01403) 269696
Fax (01403) 269690
E-mail mail@thebeerstation.co.uk
Website www.thebeerstation.co.uk**
Tours by arrangement

⊠ Andy Hepworth, former head brewer at King & Barnes, together with K&B's key personnel, set up his own brewery in Horsham in 2000 to continue a tradition and maintain quality of beer making. The company has expanded and employs former Brakspear staff. Sales are direct from the website to local pubs in South-east England. Welton's plans to move to separate premises in Horsham.

Pullman *(ABV 4.2%)*

For Welton's:

Pride & Joy *(ABV 2.8%)*

Kid 'n' Bard *(ABV 3.5%)* ◈
Mid-brown session beer, little aroma but a good balanced flavour of malt and hops that continues into a sharp, bitter finish.

Old Cocky *(ABV 4.3%)*

Horsham Old Ale
(ABV 4.5%)
Dark brown old ale with a full mix of flavours. A predominantly fruity, malty aroma leads into a good bitter flavour, with a noticeable hoppiness. The finish is sweet and malty with some balancing hops as the roastiness fades.

HESKET NEWMARKET SIBA

**Hesket Newmarket Brewery Ltd,
Old Crown Barn, Back Green,
Hesket Newmarket,
Cumbria, CA7 8JG
Tel/Fax (016974) 78066
E-mail breweryhesket@talk21.com
Website www.hesketbrewery.co.uk**
Tours Booking essential (016974) 78288

⊛ The brewery was established in 1988 by Jim and Liz Fearnley in the barn at the back of the Old Crown Inn. Sales were limited at first to the Old Crown, but gradually a small free trade developed. Jim and Liz sold the pub in 1996 but retained the brewery until 1999, when they retired and sold it to a co-operative of local villagers. It's now run by a brewery manager on their behalf. Plans are in hand to build a custom-designed beer store and expand the brewery to 50 barrels a week. Between 15 and 20 other outlets are supplied. In summer 2003, when the pub tenant announced his retirement, the villagers, including mountaineer Sir Chris Bonington, raised the funds to run the pub as a co-op, too.

Great Cockup Porter *(OG 1035, ABV 3%)*
A refreshing, dark and chocolatey porter with a dry finish.

Blencathra Bitter *(OG 1035, ABV 3.1%)* ◈
A malty, tawny ale, mild and mellow for a bitter, with a dominant caramel flavour.

Skiddaw Special Bitter
(OG 1035, ABV 3.7%)
An amber session beer, malty throughout, thin with a dryish finish.

Helvellyn Gold *(OG 1039, ABV 3.9%)* ◈
A fruity bitter with a full mouthfeel and a bitter finish.

Uld' Ale *(OG 1041, ABV 4.2%)*

Doris's 90th Birthday Ale
(OG 1045, ABV 4.3%) ◈
A full-bodied, nicely balanced malty beer with an increasing hop finish and butterscotch in the mouth.

Catbells Pale Ale *(OG 1050, ABV 5%)* ◈
A powerful golden ale with a well-balanced malty bitterness, ending with a bitter and decidedly dry aftertaste.

Old Carrock Strong Ale
(OG 1060, ABV 6%)
A dark red, powerful ale.

Ayala's Angel *(OG 1070, ABV 7%)*
A black, dark, strong beer, with a complex, nutty character.

HEXHAMSHIRE SIBA

**Hexhamshire Brewery, Leafields, Ordley,
Hexham, Northumberland, NE46 1YA
Tel (01434) 606577
E-mail hexhamshire@supanet.com**

⊠ Hexamshire was founded more than 10 years ago, but still owns just one pub. It has been under the present ownership for five years. Five beers are brewed regularly for the brewery tap and other free houses in a 50-mile radius. Some 20 outlets are supplied direct and sales reach a wider audience through SIBA and a small number of specialist independent wholesalers. Bottle-conditioned beers are planned.

Devil's Elbow *(OG 1036, ABV 3.6%)* ◈
Amber brew full of hops and fruit, leading to a bitter finish.

Shire Bitter *(OG 1037, ABV 3.8%)* ◈
Good balance of hops with fruity overtones, this amber beer makes an easy-drinking session bitter.

Devil's Water *(OG 1041, ABV 4.1%)* ◈
Copper-coloured best bitter, well-balanced with a slightly fruity, hoppy finish.

Whapweasel *(OG 1048, ABV 4.8%)* ⧉◈
An interesting smooth, hoppy beer with a fruity flavour. Amber in colour, the bitter finish brings out the fruit and hops.

Old Humbug *(OG 1055, ABV 5.5%)*

HIDDEN* SIBA

**The Hidden Brewery Ltd, Dinton Road,
Wylye, Salisbury, Wilts, SP3 5EU
Tel (01722) 716440
Fax (01202) 842885
E-mail sales@thehiddenbrewery.co.uk
Website www.thehiddenbrewery.co.uk**

Gary Lumber calls his brewery Hidden as it's in an obscure location and has no shop or presence. Gary used to brew at Oakhill and brings a wealth of experience to his craft. He is producing between five to 10 barrels a weeks and reports that demand is increasing dramatically. He supplies between 80 and 100 pubs, and plans to install a bottling line to produce bottle-conditioned beers.

Old Sarum
(OG 1042, ABV 4.1%)
A well-balanced bitter with a complex combination of malts and hops. The aroma is floral and spicy, full-flavoured with a dry bitterness. The colour is dark ruby-brown.

Quest *(OG 1043, ABV 4.2%)*
An amber-coloured bitter with a malt background, with a fruity aroma and a dry finish.

HIGH FORCE
See Darwin

HIGHGATE SIBA
**Highgate Brewery Ltd,
Sandymount Road, Walsall,
West Midlands, WS1 3AP
Tel (01922) 644453
Fax (01922) 644471**
Tours by arrangement

Built in 1898, Highgate was an independent brewery until 1938 when it was taken over by Mitchells & Butlers and subsequently became the smallest brewery in the Bass group. It was brought back into the independent sector in 1995 as the result of a management buy-out, and was subsequently bought by Aston Manor (qv) in 2000. Some of the original equipment in the traditional Victorian brewery is still in use, but a new racking line and laboratory have been added along with a visitor facility. Highgate has now acquired 10 tied houses towards a target of 50, including the City Tavern, a restored Victorian ale house off Broad Street in Birmingham. Five of the tied houses serve cask-conditioned beer. Around 200 outlets are supplied direct. The company also has a major contract to supply Mitchells & Butlers pubs. Seasonal beer: Old Ale (ABV 5.3%, winter).

Dark Mild
(OG 1036, ABV 3.4%)
A dark brown Black Country mild with a good balance of malt and hops, and traces of roast flavour following a malty aroma.

Special Bitter *(OG 1038, ABV 3.8%)*

Davenports Bitter *(OG 1040, ABV 4%)*

Saddlers Best Bitter
(OG 1044, ABV 4.3%)
A fruity, pale yellow bitter with a strong hop flavour and a light, refreshing bitter aftertaste.

Old Ale *(OG 1055, ABV 5.3%)*
A dark brown/ruby-coloured old ale, full-flavoured, fruity and malty, with a complex aftertaste with hints of malt, roast, hops and fruit.

For Coors:
M&B Mild *(OG 1034, ABV 3.2%)*

HIGHWOOD SIBA
**Highwood Brewery Ltd, Melton Highwood,
Barnetby, Lincs, DN38 6AA
Tel (01472) 691222
Fax (01472) 697935
E-mail tomwood@tom-wood.com
Website www.tom-wood.com**

Highwood – best known under the Tom Wood brand name – started brewing in a converted Victorian granary on the family farm in 1995. The brew-length was increased from 10 barrels to 30 in 2001, using plant from Ash Vine brewery. In 2002, Highwood bought Conway's Licensed Trade Wholesalers, intending to use this purchase to become the leading supplier of cask ale in Lincolnshire and Nottinghamshire. It now distributes Bateman's, Black Sheep, Everards, Greene King, Jennings, Shepherd Neame, Thwaites and most other regional and national cask beers. More than 200 outlets are supplied direct. Seasonal beers: Mill Race (ABV 4.2%, Jan-Feb), Wagoners Ale (ABV 4.8%, March-April), Barn Dance (4.2%, May-June), Summer Days (ABV 4.4%, July-Aug), Lincolnshire Longwool (4.4%, Sept-Oct), Jolly Ploughman (ABV 5%, Oct-Nov), Christmas Cheers (ABV 5%, December). Bottle-conditioned beers: Jolly Ploughman (ABV 5%), Father's Pride (ABV 4.5%); both are suitable for vegetarians and vegans.

Tom Wood's Dark Mild
(OG 1034, ABV 3.5%)

Tom Wood's Best Bitter
(OG 1034, ABV 3.5%)
A good citric passion fruit hop on the nose and taste, which dominates the background malt. A lingering hoppy and bitter finish makes this amber bitter very drinkable.

Tom Wood's Shepherd's Delight
(OG 1040, ABV 4%)
Malt is the dominant taste in this amber brew, although the fruity hop bitterness complements it all the way.

Tom Wood's Harvest Bitter
(OG 1042, ABV 4.3%)
A well-balanced amber beer where the hops and bitterness just about outdo the malt.

Tom Wood's Old Timber
(OG 1043, ABV 4.5%)
Hoppy on the nose, but featuring well-balanced malt and hops otherwise. A slight, lingering roast/coffee flavour develops, but this is generally a bitter, darkish brown beer.

Tom Wood's Bomber County
(OG 1046, ABV 4.8%)
An earthy malt aroma but with a complex underlying mix of coffee, hops, caramel and apple fruit. The beer starts bitter and intensifies but all its mahogany characteristics stay on until the end.

HILDEN
**Hilden Brewing Company,
Hilden House, Hilden, Lisburn,
Co Antrim, BT27 4TY
Tel (028 92) 663863
Fax (028 92) 603511
E-mail hilden.brewery@uk.gateway.net
Shop 10-5 Mon-Sat.**
Tours by arrangement

⊚ Hilden Brewery Company was established by Ann and Seamus Scullion in 1981 and is now the oldest independent brewery in Ireland. It is looking forward, in conjunction with the latest wave of small breweries on the island, to meet a growing demand for choice in a market dominated by a beer monopoly. Bottle-conditioned beer: Original (ABV 4.6%).

Hilden Ale *(OG 1038, ABV 4%)* ◆
An amber-coloured beer with an aroma of malt, hops and fruit. The balanced taste is slightly slanted towards hops, and hops are also prominent in the full, malty finish. Bitter and refreshing.

Molly Malone's Porter
(OG 1048, ABV 4.6%)
Dark ruby-red porter with complex flavours of hop bitterness and chocolate malt.

Scullion's Irish *(OG 1048, ABV 4.6%)*
Initially smooth on the palate, it finishes with a clean, hoppy aftertaste.

HILL ISLAND*

Hill Island Brewery, Unit 7, Fowlers Yard, Durham City, DH1 3RA
Tel (07740) 932584
E-mail mike@hillisland.freeserve.co.uk
Tours by arrangement

⊚ Hill Island started brewing in 2002. It's run by Michael Griffin, former brewer at Durham and more recently Cathedrals. The brewery moved a few yards in 2003 to bigger premises and is situated in the heart of Durham City. Regular one-off brews are produced as well as genuine, un-rebadged house beers. Michael plans to have visiting facilities on site. 14 outlets are supplied.

Miners Gala Bitter *(ABV 3.7%)*

Peninsula Pint *(ABV 3.7%)*

Dun Cow Bitter *(ABV 4%)*

Penny Ferry Porter *(ABV 4.5%)*

Castle Keep Strong Ale *(ABV 5.2%)*

HOBDEN'S SIBA

Hobden's Wessex Brewery, Rye Hill Farm, Longbridge Deverill, Warminster, Wilts, BA12 7HT
Tel/Fax (01985) 844532
E-mail wessexbrewery@tinyworld.co.uk
Tours by arrangement

⊠ Hobden's went into production in 2002 and 50 outlets are supplied. Seasonal beers are produced using the Wylye name, along

with beers named after members of the polecat family – ferrets, weasels, mink etc. The brewery is also producing beers for Nursery (qv), which has closed, possibly only temporarily

Naughty Ferret *(OG 1037, ABV 3.5%)*
A session bitter with full flavour. Tawny colour, spicy bitterness and citrus hop aroma.

Crockerton Classic *(OG 1041, ABV 4.1%)*
Full bodied, tawny, full flavoured; bitter, fruity and malty.

Warminster Warrior *(ABV 4.5%)*
Premium bitter brewed using malt from local barley. Subtle bitterness and balanced body makes the beer quaffable for its strength.

Wylye Warmer *(ABV 6%)*
Deep red in colour, and packed with bitter fruit flavours, this ale is deceptively easy to drink.

For Nursery Brewery:

Georgie Porgie *(OG 1038, ABV 3.7%)*

Three Blind Mice *(OG 1041, ABV 4.2%)*

Hey Diddle Diddle *(OG 1048, ABV 4.7%)*

Old Mother Hubbard *(OG 1050, ABV 5.2%)*

HOBSONS SIBA

Hobsons Brewery & Co Ltd, Newhouse Farm, Tenbury Road, Cleobury Mortimer, nr Kidderminster, Worcestershire, DY14 8RD
Tel (01299) 270837
Fax (01299) 270260
E-mail beer@hobsons-brewery.co.uk
Website www.hobsons-brewery.co.uk
Tours by arrangement

⊠ Established in 1993, Hobsons moved to its present site in 1996. Production was developed further in 2002, including the installation of bottling plant. 100 outlets are supplied. Bottle-conditioned beer: Old Henry.

Mild *(OG 1034.5, ABV 3.2%)*

Best Bitter *(OG 1038.5, ABV 3.8%)* ◆
A pale brown to amber, medium-bodied beer with strong hop character throughout. It is consequently bitter, but with malt discernible in the taste.

Town Crier *(OG 1044, ABV 4.5%)* ▤
An elegant straw-coloured bitter. The hint of sweetness is complemented by subtle hop flavours, leading to a dry finish.

Old Henry *(OG 1052, ABV 5.2%)*
Authentic winter ale. Complex malty flavours give a richness that is balanced by the clean, hoppy finish.

HOGGLEYS*

**Hoggleys Brewery, 30 Mill Lane, Kislingbury, Northampton, NN7 4BD.
Tel (01604) 831762
E-mail hoggleys@hotmail.com**

Roy Crutchley has been a keen home brewer for years, moving from kits to full mash. He moved into full-time commercial brewing in 2003, using both home-made and secondhand equipment. A winter beer is planned.

Mill Lane Mild *(ABV 4%)*
Brewed from pale, black and crystal malts and hopped with Fuggles and Goldings.

RGC Mild *(ABV 4%)*
A pale mild brewed for a local pub, the Royal George at Cottingham, but popular enough to become a regular brew. Brewed from pale and mild malts and hopped with Cascade and Fuggles.

Northamptonshire Bitter *(ABV 4%)*
A straw-coloured bitter brewed with pale malt only. The hops are Fuggles and Northdown and it's late hopped with Goldings for aroma.

HOGS BACK SIBA

**Hogs Back Brewery Ltd, Manor Farm, The Street, Tongham, Surrey, GU10 1DE
Tel (01252) 783000 Fax (01252) 782328
E-mail info@hogsback.co.uk
Website www.hogsback.co.uk**
Shop 10-6 Mon-Tue; 10-8.30 Wed-Fri; 9-6 Sat; 10-4.30 Sun.
Tours by arrangement 6.30 Wed-Fri; 11am and 2.30 Sat; 2.30 Sun

⊗ The traditional-style, purpose-built brewery has occupied a range of 18th-century farm building since 1992. The popularity of its ales – particularly the award-winning TEA – hastened the commissioning of new, larger brewing vessels, including a traditional copper and an automated bottling production line. Some 20 beers are brewed on a regular or occasional basis, all of which are available from the brewery off-licence in the newly refurbished 15th-century barn on site. The brewery shop and visitor centre will allow the range of bottled beers from around the world to be increased to more than 400. Exporting and e-commerce continue to grow and plans are afoot to build a brewery tap on site. Seasonal beers: Dark Mild (ABV 3.4%, May and Sept), Legend (ABV 4%, Sept-Oct), Spring Call (ABV 4%, spring), Easter Teaser (ABV 4.2%), Summer This (ABV 4.3%, summer), Blackwater Porter (ABV 4.4%, February ⬚), Advent Ale (ABV 4.4%, Christmas), Autumn Seer (ABV 4.8%), Rip Snorter (ABV 5%, winter), Santa Wobble (ABV 7.5%, Christmas). Bottle-conditioned beers: TEA, BSA (ABV 4.5%), Vintage Ale (ABV 6%), Brewster's Bundle (ABV 7.4%), Wobble in a Bottle (ABV 7.5%), A over T (ABV 9%), OTT (ABV 6%), Hop Garden Gold (ABV 4.6%).

Dark Mild *(OG 1036, ABV 3.4%)*
Dark mild, easy to drink, with a clean palate.

Hair of the Hog *(OG 1038, ABV 3.5%)* ◆
A smooth, light brown session bitter. Predominantly malty but balanced by some bitterness with a lemony hop character. A bitter-sweet finish.

Legend *(OG 1040, ABV 4%)* ◆
Complex and drinkable, this golden-coloured beer contains both wheat and lager malts, and has a dry, malty and bitter taste that lingers.

TEA or Traditional English Ale
(OG 1044, ABV 4.2%) ⬚◆
The brewery's flagship beer. Pale brown with an initial fruitiness, some hops and a noticeable maltiness in aroma and taste. A bitter-sweet finish.

Hop Garden Gold *(OG 1048, ABV 4.6%)* ⬚◆
Pale golden beer with a fruity, malty aroma. Delicate flowery-citrus hop flavours are balanced by malt and fruit. Hoppy bitterness grows in the aftertaste.

Autumn Seer *(OG 1050, ABV 4.8%)*
Autumnal colour, malty yet well balanced with hops.

Rip Snorter *(OG 1055, ABV 5%)* ◆
Strong, malty and fruity mid-brown premium bitter, rather sweet but with some balancing hops and bitterness.

HOLDEN'S IFBB

**Holden's Brewery Ltd, George Street, Woodsetton, Dudley, West Midlands, DY1 4LN
Tel (01902) 880051
Fax (01902) 665473
E-mail holdens.brewery@virgin.net
Website www.holdensbrewery.co.uk**
Tours by arrangement

☺ A family brewery going back four generations, Holden's began life as a brew-pub when Edwin and Lucy Holden took over the Park Inn (the brewery tap) in the 1920s; the inn has now been restored to its former Victorian heritage. Holden's also renovated a Grade II listed building in Codsall and has restored it to a traditional drinkers pub that will also interest railway fanatics. The newest addition to the Holden's estate is the Whitehouse in Hockley. Holden's reduced its beer prices in 2002 and were awarded a CAMRA 'Value for Money' award for their efforts. Holden's continues to grow with its 21 pubs tied estate and it supplies more than 50 other outlets with cask ales. Seasonal beer: Old Ale (ABV 7.2%, Nov-Jan).

Black Country Mild
(OG 1037, ABV 3.7%) ◆
A good, red/brown mild; a refreshing, light blend of roast malt, hops and fruit, dominated by malt throughout.

Black Country Bitter
(OG 1039, ABV 3.9%) ◨◆
A medium-bodied, golden ale; a light, well-balanced bitter with a subtle, dry, hoppy finish.

XB *(OG 1042, ABV 4.1%)* ◆
Named after founder Lucy Blanche Holden,

this is a sweeter, slightly fuller version of the Bitter. Sold in a number of outlets under different names.

Golden Glow *(OG 1045, ABV 4.4%)*
A pale golden beer, with a subtle hop aroma plus gentle sweetness and a light hoppiness.

Special Bitter *(OG 1052, ABV 5.1%)* ◆
A sweet, malty, full-bodied amber ale with hops to balance in the taste and in the good, bitter-sweet finish.

HOLLAND

Holland Brewery, 5 Browns Flatt, Brewery Street, Kimberley, Notts, NG16 2JU
Tel (0115) 938 2685
E-mail hollandbrew@btopenworld.com

⊗ Len Holland, a keen home-brewer for 30 years, went commercial in 2000, cheek-by-jowl with mighty Hardys & Hansons. He has a nine-gallon plant in his back yard. Seasonal beers: Holly Hop Gold (ABV 4.7%, Xmas), Dutch Courage (ABV 5%, winter), Glamour Puss (ABV 4.2%, spring), Blonde Belter (ABV 4.5%, summer).

Golden Blond *(OG 1040, ABV 4%)*

Lip Smacker *(OG 1040, ABV 4%)*

Cloghopper *(OG 1042, ABV 4.2%)*

Double Dutch *(OG 1045, ABV 4.5%)*

Mad Jack Stout *(ABV 4.5%)*

HOLT IFBB

Joseph Holt Group plc, Derby Brewery, Empire Street, Cheetham, Manchester, M3 1JD
Tel (0161) 834 3285
Fax (0161) 834 6458
Website www.joseph-holt.com
Tours 10-11.15am Sat, £10 per person donation to Holt Radium Institute at the Christie Hospital. Groups of 12-15 only.

☺ A family brewery established in 1849 by Joseph Holt, it celebrated 150 years in brewing in 1999. In recent years new equipment for the brewing process has been installed to cope with demand for the ever-expanding estate of pubs. Bitter is often delivered in 54-gallon hogsheads and the brewery hopes that one day there will be a demand for Mild in hogsheads, too. 127 pubs are owned, all serving cask-conditioned beer. Holts became a limited company in 1951 and was quoted on the Stock Exchange, but in 2000 the company applied to re-purchase all the shares and to become de-listed. This will make the company even more secure from takeovers, being family-run and truly independent once more. A new 30-barrel plant is being installed to produce small one-off brews to different recipes on an ad hoc basis.

Mild *(OG 1032, ABV 3.2%)* ◆
A dark brown beer with a fruity, malty nose and taste. Strong in bitterness for a mild, with a dry, hoppy finish.

Bitter *(OG 1040, ABV 4%)* ◆
Copper-coloured beer with malt and hops in the aroma and taste. The uncompromising bitterness can be a shock to the unwary.

HOME COUNTY

Home County Brewers, The Old Brewery, Wickwar Trading Estate, Station Road, Wickwar, Gloucestershire, GL12 8NB
Tel/Fax (01454) 294045
No shop Polypins to order
Tours by arrangement

⊗ The brewery opened in 1997. Production was stopped in its tracks when the Wickwar railway tunnel suffered a flood that breached the nearby brewery in 2000. There was a complication with insurers and the brewery did not re-open until 2001. Home County now brews five barrels a week. 24 outlets are supplied.

Golden Brown *(OG 1035, ABV 3.5%)* ◆
Gentle and clean-tasting ale. Golden brown in colour, this is a light malty ale with a very subtle aroma. Moderately bitter and slightly dry. Malty and dry finish.

Wichen *(OG 1042, ABV 4.2%)* ◆
Pale brown, this has a malty and fruity aroma with a little hop. Medium bodied, with a good, malty taste throughout, some hops and complex fruit, and a slightly dry, bitter finish.

Pit Orchard Pale *(OG 1045, ABV 4.5%)*

Old Tradition *(OG 1048, ABV 4.8%)* ◆
Malty throughout, but with balancing fruit and hops. Mid to full-bodied, brown in colour, and bitter-sweet. Predominantly malty aroma.

County Pride *(OG 1050, ABV 5%)* ◆
Pale and crystal malts and fruit aroma. Mid-brown and bitter-sweet tasting, with a slightly dry, malty aftertaste. Medium-bodied for its strength.

HOOK NORTON IFBB

Hook Norton Brewery Co Ltd, The Brewery, Hook Norton, Banbury, Oxon, OX15 5NY
Tel (01608) 737210/visitor centre
(01608) 730384
Fax (01608) 73029
Email info@hook-norton-brewery.co.uk
Website www.hook-norton-brewery.co.uk
Shop Mon-Fri 9-5 Tours by arrangement: visitor centre open 9am-5pm Mon-Fri.

⊗ The Hook Norton Brewery was founded in 1849 by John Harris, a farmer and maltster. The current premises were built in 1900, and Hook Norton is one of the finest examples of a Victorian tower brewery, with a 25hp steam engine for most of its motive power. The brewhouse is currently expanding, with new fermenters, copper, mash tun and racking plant. Hook Norton owns 42 pubs and supplies approximately 300 free trade accounts. All Hook Norton draught beers are cask conditioned and dry hopped. All the beers use water drawn from wells beneath the brewery, Maris Otter malt and English Challenger, Fuggles and Goldings hops. Seasonal beers: First Light (ABV 4.3%, May-June), Steaming On (ABV 4.4%, Sept-Oct), Copper Ale (ABV 4.8%, March-April), Double Stout (ABV 4.8%, Jan-Feb), Haymaker (ABV 5%, July-Aug), Twelve Days (ABV 5.5%, Nov-Dec).

Best Mild *(OG 1033, ABV 3%)* ◆
A dark, red/brown mild with a malty aroma

and a malty, sweetish taste, tinged with a faint hoppy balance. Malty in the aftertaste.

Best Bitter *(OG 1035, ABV 3.4%)* 🍷🌿
A fruity and hoppy aroma introduces this complex, well-crafted amber bitter. Moderate maltiness underpins the hops, leading to a long, bitter-sweet finish.

Generation *(OG 1041, ABV 4%)* 🌿
A pale brown best bitter, predominantly hoppy but balanced with moderate malt and banana fruit. The fruit and malt decline to a relatively short, hoppy finish.

Old Hooky *(OG 1048, ABV 4.6%)* 🌿
A well-balanced and full-bodied pale copper beer that is fruity with pale and crystal malt and hops on the aroma and taste. The hoppy character gives way to a sweet and fruity finish.

HOP BACK SIBA

**Hop Back Brewery plc,
Unit 22 Downton Business Centre,
Downton, Salisbury, Wilts, SP5 3HU
Tel (01725) 510986 Fax (01725) 513116
E-mail sales@hopback.co.uk
Website www.hopback.co.uk**
Tours by arrangement

⊠ Started by John Gilbert in 1987 at the Wyndham Arms in Salisbury, the brewery has expanded steadily ever since. It went public via a Business Expansion Scheme support plan in 1993, and has enjoyed rapid continued growth. Summer Lightning has won many awards. The brewery has eight tied houses and also sells to more than 200 other outlets. Seasonal beers are produced on a monthly basis. Bottle-conditioned beers: Thunderstorm (ABV 5%), Summer Lightning (ABV 5% 🍷🍶), Taiphoon (ABV 4.2%), Crop Circle (ABV 4.2%).

GFB/Gilbert's First Brew
(OG 1035, ABV 3.5%) 🌿
A golden beer, with the sort of light, clean quality that makes it an ideal session ale. A hoppy aroma and taste lead to a good, dry finish. Refreshing.

Best Bitter *(OG 1040, ABV 4%)*

Crop Circle *(OG 1041, ABV 4.2%)*

Entire Stout *(OG 1043, ABV 4.5%)* 🍷🍶🌿
A rich, dark stout with a strong roasted malt flavour and a long, sweet and malty aftertaste. A beer suitable for vegans. Also produced with ginger.

Thunderstorm *(OG 1048, ABV 5%)* 🍷🌿
A softly bitter, easy-drinking wheat beer.

Summer Lightning
(OG 1049, ABV 5%) 🍷🍶🌿
A pleasurable pale bitter with a good, fresh, hoppy aroma and a malty, hoppy flavour. Finely balanced, it has an intense bitterness leading to a long, dry finish. Though strong, it tastes like a session ale.

HOPDAEMON

**Hopdaemon Brewery Co, 18a-18b
Canterbury Hill, Tyler Hill, Canterbury, Kent,
CT2 9LS
Tel (01227) 784962
E-mail hopdaemon@supanet.com**
Tours by prior arrangement

Tonie Prins, former brewer at Swale Brewery, opened a 12-barrel plant in 2001 and within six months was supplying more than 30 pubs in the area, as well as exclusive bottled-conditioned, own-label beers for the British Museum and Southwark Cathedral, named Beer and Pilgrim's Pleasure respectively, and for the Science Museum, Deep Blue, all 5% ABV. Approximately 100 outlets are supplied direct. Bottle-conditioned beers: Skrimshander IPA (ABV 4.5%), Green Daemon Natural (ABV 5%), British Museum Beer (ABV 5%), Science Museum Beer Deep Blue (ABV 5%), Southwark Cathedral Beer Pilgrims Pleasure (ABV 5%) and Leviathan (ABV 6%).

Golden Braid *(OG 1039, ABV 3.7%)*

Incubus *(OG 1041, ABV 4%)*

Skrimshander IPA *(OG 1045, ABV 4.5%)*
Kentish Champion, Kent Beer Festival 2002.

Dominator *(OG 1050, ABV 5.1%)*

HOUSTON SIBA

**Houston Brewing Company, South Street,
Houston, Renfrewshire, PA6 7EN
Tel (01505) 614528
Fax (01505) 614133
E-mail ale@houston-brewing.co.uk
Website www.houston-brewing.co.uk**
Shop open pub hours, every day.
Tours by arrangement, includes dinner and tasting (£9.95)

⊠ Established in 1997 by Carl Wengel, who built the brewery on his family's pub/restaurant, the Fox and Hounds. The brewery has expanded rapidly and the beers are now available throughout Britain. Silver Medal winner Champion Beer of Scotland 2000 and 2001, and Bronze Medal winner, Best Bitter category, Champion Beer of Britain 2000, for Peter's Well. A mail order and personalisation service is available for bottles, polypins and cask ale. There is a special tour package that includes dinner and tastings. 300 outlets are supplied. Seasonal beers: Cheeky Wee Beastie (ABV 3.8%, January), Horny Wee Devil (ABV 4%, February), Black Beauty (ABV 5%, March), Hunny Bunny (ABV 4.1%, April), Big Lusty May (ABV 4.3%, May), Helga's Big Jugs (ABV 5%, June), Rambo the Mighty Midge (ABV 3.6% July), Big Tosser (ABV 3.9%, August).

Killellan *(OG 1037, ABV 3.7%)* ◆
A light session ale, with a floral hop and fruity taste. The finish of this amber beer is dry and quenching.

Blonde Bombshell *(OG 1040, ABV 4%)*
A gold-coloured ale with a fresh hop aroma and rounded maltiness.

Barochan *(OG 1041, ABV 4.1%)* ◆
A red, malty beer, in which fruit is balanced by roast and hop overtones; dry, bitter-sweet finish.

Peter's Well *(OG 1042, ABV 4.2%)* ⬚◆
Well-balanced fruity taste with sweet hop, leading to an increasingly bitter-sweet finish.

Texas *(OG 1045, ABV 4.5%)*
Amber coloured, made with American Cascade hops that merge with pale chocolate malt to produce a full-bodied ale.

SARAH HUGHES

⬚ **Sarah Hughes Brewery, 129 Bilston Street, Sedgley, West Midlands, DY3 1JE Tel (01902) 883380**
Tours by prior arrangement

☺ Opened originally in the 1860s behind the Beacon Hotel, Sarah Hughes bought the brewery in 1921 and started to brew the beer now called Dark Ruby. After lying idle for 30 years, the brewery was re-opened in 1987 by John Hughes, who continued the tradition and recipe of his grandmother. One pub is owned and more than 100 outlets are supplied direct. The beers are now exported to the United States. Seasonal beer: Snow Flake (ABV 8%). Bottle-conditioned beer: Dark Ruby.

Pale Amber *(OG 1038, ABV 4%)*
A well-balanced beer, initially slightly sweet but with hops close behind.

Sedgley Surprise *(OG 1048, ABV 5%)* ◆
A bitter-sweet, medium-bodied, hoppy ale with some malt.

Dark Ruby *(OG 1058, ABV 6%)* ▣⬚◆
A dark ruby strong ale with a good balance of fruit and hops, leading to a pleasant, lingering hops and malt finish.

HUMPTY DUMPTY

Humpty Dumpty Brewery, Church Road, Reedham, Norfolk, NR13 3TZ Tel (01493) 701818. Fax (01493) 700727 E-mail mick@humptydumptybrewery.com
Shop 9-6 daily
Tours by arrangement

✖ Humpty Dumpty Brewery was opened in 1998 by Mick Cottrell and it moved to its present site in 2001. Brewing capacity expanded from five to 11 barrels and the brewery is currently producing 25 to 35 barrels a week. The brewery shop sells a wide range of bottle-conditioned beers (their own and other breweries), and home-brew kits, plus a full off-licence. There are plans to develop other buildings on site for retail, and Mick is actively looking for a free house to buy. He sells to the Railway Tavern in Reedham and some 150 pubs nationwide. There is a full range of bottle-conditioned ales.

Nord Atlantic *(ABV 3.7%)* ◆
Tawny coloured with light fruity airs, giving little hint of the heavily-hopped bitterness that leaves little room for other flavours. A lingering finish with little appreciable diminishing of bitterness.

Little Sharpie *(ABV 3.8%)* ◆
A delicate hoppy aroma is a forerunner to a sweet hoppy, lagerish flavour. A clean golden yellow bitter with a finish in which bitterness grows.

Ferryman *(ABV 3.8%)*

Four Spot Chaser *(ABV 3.9%)*

Swallow Tail *(ABV 4%)*

Lemon and Ginger *(ABV 4%)*

Tender Behind *(ABV 4%)*

Swingbridge Ale *(ABV 4%)*

Humpty Dumpty *(ABV 4.1%)* ◆
A complex mix of delicate flavours. A malty fruitiness gives balance to the dry, hoppy bitterness. A light fruity nose and an amber colour generate a feeling of smooth bitterness with hoppy overtones.

'Ops on Train *(ABV 4.1%)*

Reed Cutter *(ABV 4.2%)*

Claud Hamilton *(ABV 4.3%)* ◆
With its dark brown colouration, this old-style oyster stout is a stirring mix of roast fruity sweetness. The bitter-sweet finish draws out a hint of caramelised toffee.

Brief Encounter *(ABV 4.3%)*

Iron Duke *(ABV 4.6%)*

Butt Jumper *(ABV 4.8%)* ◆
Toffee and malt dominate the aroma of this tawny-hued ale. Full-flavoured, with malt vying with a fruity bitterness for dominance. Long, lingering finish does not fade as a nutty bitterness becomes prevalent.

Spark Arrester *(ABV 4.8%)*

Railway Sleeper *(ABV 5%)* ◆
Hops with a citrus hint introduce this mid-brown strong bitter. This blend continues through the first taste, and although a bitter-sweet influence grows, later the strong hop character dominates a short ending.

Peto's Porter *(ABV 6%)*

Broadland Gold *(ABV 6%)* ◆
Easy-drinking and smooth, this old ale introduces itself with a well-rounded, fruity aroma. This is followed by a deep hoppy introduction with a bitter vine, fruity edge. A well-defined finish with lots of malt.

HYDES IFBB

Hydes' Brewery Ltd, 46 Moss Lane West, Manchester, M15 5PH Tel (0161) 226 1317 Fax (0161) 227 9593 E-mail pauljefferies@hydesbrewery.com Website www.hydesbrewery.com
Tours by arrangement

☺ Hydes has continued to increase its share of the market in both its tied houses and free trade operations. In particular, Hydes bi-monthly craft ale programme has been successful and, together with contract brewing for Interbrew, this has ensured a healthy increase in turnover and profits. 2002 year saw major investments in the brewery with a new copper whirlpool, and in the brewery's tied estate with the purchase of more pubs. Hydes owns 70 tied houses, supplying cask ale to all but two of these outlets. The brewery now has more than 200 free trade accounts. It's one of the few breweries to still brew three milds: XXXX is being brewed again due to popular demand. Seasonal beers: Malt & Mash (ABV 4.8%, Jan-Feb), Copper Hopper (ABV 4.2%, March-April), Hubble Bubble (ABV 4.4%, May-June), Rack'n'Ruin (ABV 4.1%, July-August), Firkin Fruity (ABV 4.5%, Sept-Oct), XXXX Dark Mild (ABV 3.5%, December), Rompers Rein (ABV 5%, Nov-Dec).

Light Mild *(OG 1033.5, ABV 3.5%)* ◈
A lightly-hopped, amber-coloured session beer with a fresh, fruity taste and a brief but dry finish.

Traditional Mild *(OG 1033.5, ABV 3.5%)* ◈
A mid-brown beer with malt and citrus fruit in the aroma and taste. Short dry aftertaste.

Dark Mild *(OG 1033.5, ABV 3.5%)* ☐◈
Dark brown/red in colour with a fruit and roast malt nose. Complex taste, including berry fruits, malt and hint of chocolate. Satisfying aftertaste.

Trophy Bitter *(OG 1036, ABV 3.8%)*
Now brewed for Interbrew, this is a beer with a mellow balance of hop, malt and grain flavours with a malty and light, floral hop aroma. Dry hop finish.

Traditional Bitter *(OG 1036.5, ABV 3.8%)* ◈
Amber beer with a fruity nose, citrus fruit and hops in the taste, and a good bitterness through to the finish.

Jekyll's Gold Premium Ale
(OG 1042, ABV 4.3%)
Pale gold in colour, with a fruity, hoppy nose. A well-balanced beer with hops, fruit and malt all in evidence, and a dry, hoppy finish.

ICENI SIBA

Iceni Brewery, 3 Foulden Road, Ickburgh, Mundford, Thetford, Norfolk, IP26 5BJ
Tel (01842) 878922 Fax (01842) 879216
E-mail icenibrewe@aol.com
Shop 830-230, Mon-Sat
Tours by arrangement

✖ Brendan Moore started the Iceni Brewery in 1995 after a dream in which Queen Boudicca stopped a lorry-load of duty-free French lager and then pointed to the pure waters of the Ickburgh spring. The brewery now has its own hop garden and barley plot aimed at amusing the many visitors that flock to the shop to buy the 28 different ales, stout and lagers bottled on-site. Beer as a gift is an increasingly important trend at Iceni. 35 outlets are supplied direct and Brendan also targets local farmers' markets and the tourist shop in nearby Thetford Forest. He has also set up a brewer's cooperative in East Anglia to sell craft brewers' beers more effectively. Special beers are brewed for festivals. All cask ales are bottle-conditioned. Deirdre of the Sorrows (ABV 4.4%) is suitable for vegetarians and vegans.

Thetford Forest Mild *(OG 1036, ABV 3.6%)*

Fine Soft Day *(OG 1038, ABV 4%)* ◈
Full-bodied and hoppy amber ale with a lingering aftertaste of hops and malt.

Celtic Queen *(OG 1038, ABV 4%)*
A light summer ale, packed with flavour.

Fen Tiger *(OG 1040, ABV 4.2%)*

It's a Grand Day *(OG 1040, ABV 4.5%)*

Gold *(OG 1045, ABV 5%)*
A strong ale, sun gold in colour. Crisp taste; smooth and deceptive for its strength.

Norfolk Lager *(OG 1046, ABV 5%)*

Raspberry Wheat *(OG 1046, ABV 5%)*

Men of Norfolk *(OG 1062, ABV 6.2%)*

INVERALMOND SIBA

Inveralmond Brewery Ltd,
1 Inveralmond Way, Perth, PH1 3UQ
Tel/Fax (01738) 449448
E-mail info@inveralmond-brewery.co.uk
Website www.inveralmond-brewery.co.uk
Shop 9-5

☺ Established in 1997, the Inveralmond Brewery was the first brewery in Perth for more than 30 years. The brewery has gone from strength to strength since opening with a string of awards, culminating in winning Champion Beer of Scotland in 2001 with Ossian's Ale. Around 150 outlets are supplied, with wholesalers taking beers nationwide. Ossian's Ale and Lia Fail are now also available in bottle (not bottle conditioned). Seasonal ales: Inkie Pinkie (ABV 3.7%), Amber Bead (ABV 4.1%), Pint Stowp (ABV 4.2%), Pundie (ABV 5%).

Independence *(OG 1040, ABV 3.8%)* ◈
A well-balanced Scottish ale with fruit and malt tones. Hop provides an increasing bitterness in the finish.

Ossian's Ale *(OG 1042, ABV 4.1%)* ☐◈
Well-balanced best bitter with a dry finish. This full-bodied amber ale is dominated by fruit and hop with a bitter-sweet character, although excessive caramel can distract from this. Champion Beer of Scotland 2001.

Thrappledouser *(OG 1043, ABV 4.3%)* ◈
A refreshing amber beer with reddish hues. The crisp, hoppy aroma is finely balanced with the tangy but quenching taste.

Lia Fail *(OG 1048, ABV 4.7%)* ◈
The name is the Gaelic title for the Stone of Destiny. A dark, robust, full-bodied beer with a deep malty taste. Smooth texture and balanced finish.

ISLE OF PURBECK*

⚲ **Isle of Purbeck Brewery, Bankes Arms, Watery Lane, Studland, Dorset, BH19 3AU**
Tel (01929) 450225

The 10-barrel brewing equipment from the former Poole Brewery has been installed at this famous Dorset pub that overlooks the sweep of Studland Bay. Only one beer is brewed at present but there are plans to add new brews and the size of the plant will enable the brands to be sold to other pubs.

Studland Bay Wreck *(ABV 4.5%)*

ISLE OF SKYE

Isle of Skye Brewing Company (Leann an Eilein), The Pier, Uig, Isle of Skye, IV51 9XP
Tel (01470) 542477
Fax (01470) 542488
E-mail info@skyebrewery.co.uk
Website www.skyebrewery.co.uk
Shop 10-6 Mon-Sat; 12.30-4.30 Sun Apr-Oct
Tours by arrangement

☺ Established in 1995 with a 10-barrel plant, the Isle of Skye Brewery has installed a new 20-barrel plant to enable it to meet rising demand. Once a real ale desert, the island now boasts 11 outlets serving cask ale (some seasonal). Beers are now available throughout Britain via wholesalers, while the brewery serves 80 outlets direct.

Young Pretender (OG 1039, ABV 4%) ◈
Golden amber ale with hop and fruit on the nose. The bitter taste is dominated by fruit and hop, the latter lingering into the dry, bitter finish.

Red Cuillin (OG 1041, ABV 4.2%) ◫◈
A burst of fruit with malt and hop notes introduce this tawny reddish beer. These characteristics continue into the wonderful bitter-sweet taste. A very dry and bitter finish.

Hebridean Gold
(OG 1041.5, ABV 4.3%) ◫◈
A superb golden-coloured beer that is brewed using oats. Hops and fruit dominate the bitter taste and increasingly dry, citrus finish.

Black Cuillin (OG 1044, ABV 4.5%) ◈
A complex beer with more of a stout taste to it than in the past. Predominately malty with roast malt and summer fruits in the taste. Plenty of bitterness in the long, dry finish.

Blaven (OG 1047, ABV 5%) ◈
A copper-brown beer with plenty of fruit throughout. Some bitterness in the dry finish.

Cuillin Beast (OG 1061.5, ABV 7%) ◈
A special brew to begin with, it proved so popular it became permanent. Sweet and fruity, and much more drinkable than the strength would suggest. Plenty of caramel throughout with a creamy, dry mouthfeel.

ITCHEN VALLEY SIBA

Itchen Valley Brewery Ltd, Unit 4, Shelf House, New Farm Road, Alresford, Hampshire, SO24 9QE
Tel (01962) 735111
Fax (01962) 735678
E-mail matthew@itchenvalley.com
Website www.itchenvalley.com
Shop 9-5 Mon-Fri.
Tours by arrangement

⊗ The brewery, founded in 1997, enjoyed immediate success by winning the bronze medal award for its Godfathers beer at the 1998 Great British Beer Festival, Olympia. This set a precedent for winning awards that continues today. Over the past few years, the brewery has expanded and its enlarged range of beers is now sold in more than 150 pubs across Hampshire, Surrey, Sussex and Berkshire. The brewery also offers bottle-conditioned ales, not only in supermarkets and independent off-licences but also direct to the public online and at farmers' markets and agricultural shows.

There is an extensive seasonal programme featuring at least 15 different cask ales each year, including Hambledon Bitter (ABV 4%), brewed with elderflower and honey extract.

Godfathers (OG 1039, ABV 3.8%) ◱
Brewed from a secret recipe using a unique combination of four hops. A crisp distinctive quaffing ale with a bitter-sweet edge. Full in flavour, golden in colour with a unique hoppiness.

Fagin's (OG 1042, ABV 4.1%)
Brewed from a traditional recipe using a combination of three hops. A light brown, well-balanced beer with fine malts, dry citrus flavours and well hopped.

Wykehams Glory (OG 1043, ABV 4.3%)
Nut brown in appearance, malty flavour, with a hoppy nose.

Treacle Stout (OG 1044, ABV 4.4%)
A wholesome stout, smooth on the palate, brewed with rolled oats, Maris Otter malt and roast barley, combined with a touch of treacle for a full-bodied and warming stout. Brewed with a blend of Fuggles and Progress hops.

Pure Gold (OG 1048, ABV 4.8%)
A light golden, refreshing beer, with a unique, deliciously hoppy nose.

JARROW* SIBA

Jarrow Brewery, Robin Hood Inn, Primrose Hill, Jarrow, Tyne and Wear, NE32 5UB
Tel (0191) 4285454
Fax (0191) 4836792
E-mail info@jarrowbrewery.co.uk
Website www.jarrowbrewery.co.uk
Tours by arrangement

☺ Brewing started in autumn 2002. Owners and brewers Jess and Alison McConnell also own two pubs, the Albion Inn, Bill Quay, and the Robin Hood, Jarrow; the 10-barrel plant is based at the latter. They supply some 50 outlets, mainly on Tyneside, with distribution handled by Flying Firkin.

Jarrow Bitter (OG 1037.5, ABV 3.8%)
A light session bitter with a delicate hop aroma.

Joblings Swinging Gibbet
(OG 1041, ABV 4.1%)
A copper-coloured, evenly balanced beer with a good hop aroma and a fruity finish.

Riley's Army (OG 1042, ABV 4.3%)
A copper-coloured, robust ale with a citrus hop aroma using American hops.

Old Cornelius (OG 1046, ABV 4.8%)
A rich ruby-red beer with a malty character.

JENNINGS IFBB

Jennings Bros PLC, Castle Brewery, Cockermouth, Cumbria, CA13 9NE
Tel (01900) 823214
Fax (01900) 827462
E-mail ggreen@jenningsbrewery.co.uk
Website www.jenningsbrewery.co.uk
Shop 9-5 Mon-Fri, 10-4 Sat, 10-5 Sun (July & Aug)
Tours by arrangement

☺ Founded in 1828, Jennings moved to its present idyllic site by the River Derwent and at the foot of Cockermouth Castle in 1874, where it still uses its own well water. Although there is no longer any family involvement, many of the company's shares are owned by local people. 120 pubs are owned and around 350 free trade outlets are supplied direct with many more via a network of wholesalers throughout the country. A £1 million investment programme, launched in 1999 to upgrade the brewery and increase output, was completed in the summer of 2002. Real ale is available in most of Jenning's tied estate, which has expanded outside Cumbria into the North-east and Lancashire. The company is committed to an integrated pub and brewery business, and has converted managed houses back to tenancies. Seasonal beers: J J No 1 (ABV 4.3%, spring), Crag Rat (ABV 4.3%, summer), Cross Buttock (ABV 4.5%, autumn), La'al Cockle Warmer (ABV 6.5%, winter).

Dark Mild (OG 1031, ABV 3.1%) ⬥
A well-balanced dark brown mild with a malty aroma, strong roast taste, not over-sweet, with some hops and a slightly bitter finish.

Bitter (OG 1035, ABV 3.5%) ⬥
A malty beer with good mouthfeel combined with roast flavours and a hoppy finish.

1828 (OG 1038, ABV 3.8%)

Cumberland Ale
(OG 1039, ABV 4%) ⬥
A light, creamy, hoppy beer with a dry aftertaste.

Cocker Hoop
(OG 1044, ABV 4.6%) 🗋⬥
A rich, creamy, copper-coloured beer with raisiny maltiness balanced with a resiny hoppiness, with a developing bitterness towards the end.

Sneck Lifter (OG 1051, ABV 5.1%) ⬥
A strong, dark brown ale with a complex balance of fruit, malt and full roast flavours right through to the finish.

ESTᴰ 1828
JENNINGS
BROTHERS PLC

JERSEY <small>SIBA</small>

Ann Street Brewery Co Ltd, t/a Jersey Brewery, 57 Ann Street, St Helier, Jersey, JE1 1BZ
Tel (01534) 731561
Fax (01534) 767033
Tours by arrangement

Jersey, better known as Ann Street, phased out cask ale after a brief flirtation in the 1980s and '90s. It has 50 tied houses, of which 12 take real ale. It has closed its subsidiary, Guernsey Brewery. Jersey Brewery also has an interest in the Tipsy Toad brew-pub (qv), which brews the former Guernsey beers.

JOHN O'GAUNT

John O'Gaunt Brewing Co Ltd, Unit 2 Rural Industries, John O'Gaunt, Melton Mowbray, Leicestershire, LE14 2RE
Tel (07812) 161439
Fax (01664) 820103
E-mail Brewery@John-o-gaunt-brewery.co.uk
Website www.john-o-gaunt-brewery.co.uk
Tours by prior arrangement

⊗ The brewery moved to new premises in 2002 in John O'Gaunt with a five-barrel plant. The company's pub, the Fox Inn, Thorpe Satchville, has been leased to Kevin and Denise Preston who stock John O'Gaunt and other guest ales. Seasonal beer: Glitter Bitter (ABV 5.2%). Bottled-conditioned beers: check the website.

Robin a Tiptoe (OG 1043, ABV 3.9%)

Duke of Lancaster (ABV 4.3%)
A light and refreshing drink, brewed to celebrate the opening of the new brewery.

Cropped Oak (OG 1047, ABV 4.4%)

Coat O' Red (OG 1052, ABV 5%)

JOLLYBOAT

Jollyboat Brewery (Bideford) Ltd, The Coach House, Buttgarden Street, Bideford, Devon, EX39 2AU
Tel (01237) 424343
Tours by arrangement

⊗ The brewery, named after sailors' leave boats, was established in 1995 by Hugh Parry and his son Simon. The brewery went into receivership in 2000 but brewing didn't stop, and the new company is now in the sole hands of Hugh. It is now expanding, with new beers added. It currently supplies some 204 outlets. Seasonal beer: Contraband (ABV 5.8%, Christmas). Bottle-conditioned beers: Privateer, Plunder.

Buccaneers (OG 1036, ABV 3.7%)
A pale brown summer bitter with a pleasant presence of hops and bitterness from the nose through to the aftertaste.

Grenville's Renown (ABV 3.8%)

Freebooter (OG 1040, ABV 4%)

Mainbrace (OG 1041, ABV 4.2%) ⬥
Pale brown brew with a rich fruity aroma and a bitter taste and aftertaste.

Privateer (OG 1046/48, ABV 4.8%)

Plunder
(OG 1046/48, ABV 4.8%) 🗋⬥
A good balance of malt, hops and fruit are present on the aroma and palate of this red/brown beer with a bitter finish. Winner of Best in Class at the 2001 Maltings Festival, Newton Abbot.

Contraband (OG 1054/56, ABV 5.8%)
A festive porter for Christmas. Complex meld of pale, crystal and black malt and definitely not sweet.

JUWARDS

Juwards Brewery, Unit 14G, Tonedale Business Park, Wellington, Somerset, TA21 0AW
Tel (01823) 667909

Brewing ceased following a serious accident to founder and brewer Ted Bishop. He has moved some of his brewing plant to Moor Beer Co of Bridgwater (qv) and there are plans for a possible merger with Moor, which will revive the Juwards' brands.

KELBURN SIBA

**Kelburn Brewing Company Ltd,
10 Muriel Lane, Barrhead,
East Renfrewshire, G78 1QB
Tel/Fax (0141) 881 2138 (Brewery),
(01505) 329720 (Office)
E-mail info@kelburnbrewery.com
Website www.kelburnbrewery.com**
Tours by arrangement

⊗ Kelburn Brewing is a family-run business formed in 2001. The 10-barrel plant is run by father and son, Derek and Ross Moore (both of whom formerly worked at Houston Brewery), Derek's partner Margaret and his daughter Karen. In the first six months of trade, Kelburn beers won six CAMRA-accredited awards. All beers are available for take-away in 17 or 34 pint polypins. There are plans to bottle some of the beers. More than 100 outlets are supplied.

Goldihops (OG 1038, ABV 3.8%)
Well-hopped session ale with a fruity taste and a bitter-sweet finish.

Red Smiddy (OG 1040, ABV 4.1%)
A smooth ale with a reddish hue and a citrus, fruity aftertaste. Winner of Best Beer Paisley Beer Festival 2002 and Watford Beer Festival 2002. Second in its category, South Devon Beer Festival 2002.

Dark Moor (OG 1044, ABV 4.5%)
A beautifully-balanced dark, fruity ale with undertones of liquorice and blackcurrant.

Carte Blanche (OG 1048, ABV 5%)
A golden, full-bodied ale with a wonderfully dry aftertaste. Winner of Best Beer Oxford Beer Festival 2002.

KELHAM ISLAND SIBA

**Kelham Island Brewery Ltd, 23 Alma Street,
Sheffield, South Yorkshire, S3 8SA
Tel (0114) 249 4804
Fax (0114) 249 4803
E-mail sales@kelhambrewery.co.uk
Website www.kelhambrewery.co.uk**
Tours by arrangement

☺ Kelham Island Brewery was purpose built in 1990 on land adjoining the Fat Cat pub in Alma Street. The area is known as Kelham Island as the land is on an island formed by a mill race, leaving then running back into the River Don. The brewing equipment was purchased from the Oxford Brewery and Bakehouse, and allowed for full-mash brewing of approximately 20 barrels a week. Kelham Island was the first new independent brewery in Sheffield in the last century. Due to its success in its early years, the brewery has now moved into new, purpose-built premises at Kelham Island, with five times the capacity of the original premises. More than 200 outlets are supplied and three pubs are owned.

Best Bitter (OG 1038.8, ABV 3.8%)
A clean, characterful, crisp, pale brown beer.

The nose and palate are dominated by refreshing hoppiness and fruitiness, which, with a good bitter dryness, lasts in the aftertaste.

Kelham Gold (OG 1038.8, ABV 3.8%)

Easy Rider (OG 1041.8, ABV 4.3%)
A pale, straw-coloured beer with a sweetish flavour and delicate hints of citrus fruits. A beer with hints of flavour rather than full-bodied.

Fat Cat Bitter (OG 1044, ABV 4.4%)

Pride of Sheffield (OG 1045, ABV 4.5%)
A full-flavoured, amber-coloured, premium strength bitter.

Pale Rider (OG 1050.8, ABV 5.2%)
A full-bodied, straw pale ale, with a good fruity aroma and a strong fruit and hop taste. Its well-balanced sweetness and bitterness continue in the finish.

Bete Noire (OG 1055, ABV 5.5%)

KELTEK SIBA

**Keltek Brewery, Unit 3A, Restormel
Industrial Estate, Liddicoat Road, Lostwithiel,
Cornwall, PL22 0HG
Tel/Fax (01208) 871199**
Tours by arrangement

⊗ Keltek Brewery moved to Lostwithiel in 1999 and started brewing again in March of that year. Monthly specials and house beers for pubs are brewed. 50 outlets in Cornwall and North Devon are supplied direct. Seasonal/occasional beers: Olde Smugglers Ale (ABV 4.2%, September), Olde Pirates Ale (ABV 4.8%, March). Bottle-conditioned beers: King (ABV 5.1%), Revenge (ABV 7%).

4K Mild (OG 1038, ABV 3.8%)
Dark and fruity.

Golden Lance (OG 1038, ABV 3.8%)
Light golden, refreshing brew.

Magik (OG 1042, ABV 4.2%)
Good balance of malt and hops. Tawny red in colour.

King (OG 1051, ABV 5.1%)
A light brown beer with a bitter taste, then a sweetness through the middle.

Revenge (OG 1066, ABV 7%)
Dark ruby in colour; sweetish with a bitter edge.

KEMPTOWN SIBA

**Kemptown Brewery Co Ltd,
33 Upper St James's Street, Kemptown,
Brighton, East Sussex, BN2 1JN
Tel (01932) 342663, (01273) 699595
Fax (01932) 344413
E-mail bev@kemptownbreweryltc.co.uk
Website www.kemptownbrewery.com**
Tours by arrangement

⊗ A brewery established in 1989 and built in the tower tradition behind the Hand in Hand, which is possibly the smallest pub in England with its own brewery. It takes its name and logo from the former Charrington's Kemptown Brewery 500 yards away, which closed in 1964. Six free trade outlets are supplied.

Black Moggy Mild (ABV 3.6%)

Brighton Bitter *(ABV 3.6%)* ◄
A refreshing, dry beer, with malt and hops in the flavour and a dry, hoppy finish.

Kemptown Bitter *(ABV 4%)*

Old Trout Ale *(OG 1045, ABV 4.5%)*

Dragons Blood *(ABV 5%)*

Old Grumpy *(ABV 6%)*

KHEAN*

**Khean Brewing Company,
Unit 4, Royle Park, Royle Street,
Congleton, Cheshire, CW12 1JJ
Tel/Fax (01260) 272144**
Tours by arrangement

Congleton's second micro-brewery was established in 2002 in an industrial unit in the centre of the town. Caught Behind was the runner-up in the Porter and Stout class at the Huddersfield Beer Festival. 30 outlets are supplied. Beers are named with a cricket theme.

All Rounder *(OG 1040, ABV 3.9%)*
Light golden, clean tasting, smooth session beer with a pleasant bitter finish.

Caught Behind *(OG 1044, ABV 4.2%)*
Smooth, traditional, easy-drinking stout with a dry roasted barley flavour.

Leg Spinner *(OG 1043, ABV 4.4%)*
Gold coloured beer with a sharp flavour and strong bitter finish.

Seamer *(OG 1045, ABV 4.5%)*
Conker-coloured smooth ale with a balanced malt and hops flavour, leaving a bitter aftertaste.

KING SIBA

**W J King & Co (Brewers),
Units 3-5 Jubilee Estate, Foundry Lane,
Horsham, West Sussex, RH13 5UE
Tel (01403) 272102
Fax (01403) 754455
E-mail office@kingfamilybrewers.co.uk
Website www.kingfamilybrewers.co.uk**

⊗ Brewing started in mid-2001 using former Firkin pub equipment. King, run by former King & Barnes managing director Bill King, has developed two main beers similar in style to the old K&B Sussex Bitter and Festive but deliberately different in flavour. After just six months, Bill was brewing to capacity of 20 barrels a week. Weekly capacity is now 40 barrels. A small bottle-conditioned beer line has been set up. One pub, the Lamb in Horsham, is owned and

Bill's long-term plan is to build an estate of five or six pubs by 2006. 150 outlets are supplied. Seasonal beers: Merry Ale (ABV 6.5%), Summer Ale (ABV 4%), Harvest Ale (ABV 4.1%), Valentine Ale (ABV 4.1%), Spring Ale (ABV 4.1%), Kings Old Ale (ABV 4.5%). Bottle-conditioned beers: Red River Ale, Kings Old Ale.

Horsham Best Bitter
(OG 1038, ABV 3.8%) ◄
Well-rounded session beer with nutty overtones. A good balance of malt and hops. Maltiness and bitterness build into a long aftertaste.

Red River Ale *(OG 1048, ABV 4.8%)* ◄
A rather sweet beer, full in flavour, predominantly malty with some fruit and a short finish.

KINGS HEAD

**Kings Head Brewing Co, Kings Head,
132 High Street, Bildeston, Ipswich,
Suffolk, IP7 7ED
Tel (01449) 741434
E-mail enquiries@bildestonkingshead.co.uk
Website www.bildestonkingshead.co.uk**
Shop Open pub hours
Tours By prior arrangement

⊗ Kings Head has been brewing since 1996 in the old stables at the back of the pub. The plant is approximately five barrels and brewing taking place twice a week. The brewery stages a beer festival in May (Late Spring Bank Holiday) every year where most of the 40 beers on offer are swapped with other micros around the country. Six other pubs and many beer festivals are supplied. Seasonal beer: Dark Vader (ABV 5.4%, winter). Bottle-conditioned beers: Blondie, Apache, Crowdie and Dark Vader.

Not Strong Beer (NSB)
(OG 1030, ABV 2.8%)

Best Bitter *(OG 1040, ABV 3.8%)*

Blondie *(OG 1040-1042, ABV 4%)*

First Gold *(OG 1044, ABV 4.3%)*

Apache *(OG 1046, ABV 4.5%)*

Crowdie *(OG 1050, ABV 5%)*

Dark Vader *(OG 1055, ABV 5.4%)*
Champion beer Ipswich Beer Festival 1999. Best in class Ipswich Beer Festival 2000.

LANGTON

⚲ **The Langton Brewery, Bell Inn,
Main Street, East Langton, Market
Harborough, Leicestershire, LE16 7TW
Tel (01858) 545278
Fax (01858) 545748
Website www.thebellinn.co.uk**
Tours by arrangement

☺ Langton is run by two partners, Alistair Chapman and Derek Hewitt, publican and customer respectively of the Bell Inn. Derek is a retired banker who brought his business experience to underscore Alistair's knowledge of the pub trade. They installed a 2.5-barrel brewing plant in outbuildings of the 17th century Bell. They now brew 90 gallons a time of Caudle Bitter (named after the range of local hills) and Bowler, which celebrates the Bell Inn's long association with Langton Cricket Club, whose ground is opposite the inn. Boxer Heavyweight is named after Jack Gardner, British Heavyweight champion, who was resident in the village. The brewery owns one pub and supplies eight outlets. The beers are available for take-away in nine-gallon casks or 10-litre polypins. Seasonal beers: Buzz Light Beer (brewed with honey, ABV 3.5%), Bankers Draught (ABV 4.2%), Langton Belle (ABV 4.5%) and Boxer Heavyweight porter (ABV 5.2%).

Caudle Bitter *(OG 1039, ABV 3.9%)*
A session bitter, close to a pale ale in style.

Bowler Strong Ale *(OG 1048, ABV 4.8%)*
A strong traditional ale with a deep red colour and a hoppy nose.

LARKINS SIBA

Larkins Brewery Ltd, Larkins Farm, Chiddingstone, Edenbridge, Kent, TN8 7BB
Tel (01892) 870328
Fax (01892) 871141
Tours by arrangement Nov-Feb

⊗ Larkins Brewery was founded in 1986 by the Dockerty family, farmers and hop growers, who bought the Royal Tunbridge Wells Brewery. The company moved to Larkins Farm in 1987. Since then production of three regular brews and a Porter in the winter months have steadily increased. Brews are made using only Kentish hops, yeast and malt; no sugars or brewing adjuncts are added to the beers. Larkins owns one pub, the Rock at Chiddingstone Hoath, and supplies around 70 free houses within a radius of 20 miles.

Traditional Ale *(OG 1035, ABV 3.4%)*
Tawny in colour, a full-tasting hoppy ale with plenty of character for its strength.

Chiddingstone *(OG 1040, ABV 4%)*
Named after the village where the brewery is based, Chiddingstone is a mid-strength, hoppy/fruity ale with a long, bitter-sweet aftertaste.

Best *(OG 1045, ABV 4.4%)* ◆
Full-bodied, slightly fruity and unusually bitter for its gravity.

Porter *(OG 1052, ABV 5.2%)* ◆
Each taste and smell of this potent black winter beer (Nov-April) reveals another facet of its character. An explosion of roasted malt, bitter and fruity flavours leaves a bitter-sweet aftertaste.

LEADMILL

The Leadmill Brewery, Park Hall, Park Hall Road, Denby, Derbyshire, DE5 8PX
Tel (01332) 883577 or 07971 189915 (m)
Email TLC@leadmill.fsnet.co.uk
Tours by arrangement; visitor centre pub hours 4pm-11pm Fri; 11-11 Sat, 12 noon-10.30pm Sun

⊗ The brewery has settled into a new home, and the beer range continues to expand on the two-barrel plant. A new visitor centre functions as a pub at weekends when at least 12 of Leadmill's beers can be sampled along with guest beers. Future plans include opening in the week and purchasing a local pub. Some 80 outlets are supplied. Seasonal

beers: Mistletoad (ABV 4.5%, Christmas), Mince Pie Eyed (ABV 4.8%, Christmas).

Maremay Mild *(OG 1036, ABV 3.6%)*

Wild Weasel *(OG 1038, ABV 3.8%)*

Wild Rover *(OG 1041, ABV 4.2%)*

Arc-Light *(OG 1041, ABV 4.2%)*

Rolling Thunder *(OG 1043, ABV 4.5%)*

Saigon *(OG 1043, ABV 4.5%)*

India Pale Ale *(OG 1044, ABV 4.5%)*

Linebacker *(OG 1045, ABV 4.6%)*

Curly Blonde *(OG 1045, ABV 4.6%)*

Red River *(OG 1046, ABV 4.6%)*

Derby Festival Stout *(OG 1046, ABV 4.7%)*

Call it a Day *(OG 1046, ABV 4.8%)*

Agent Orange *(OG 1047, ABV 4.9%)*

Sidewinder *(OG 1048, ABV 5%)*

Niagara *(OG 1048, ABV 5%)*

Firebird *(OG 1048, ABV 5%)*

Rampage *(OG 1049, ABV 5.1%)*

Apocalypse Now *(OG 1050, ABV 5.2%)*

B52 *(OG 1050, ABV 5.2%)*

Spit or Swallow *(OG 1053, ABV 5.5%)*

Park Hall Porter *(OG 1056, ABV 6%)*

LEATHERBRITCHES SIBA

⬭ **Leatherbritches Brewery,**
The Bentley Brook Inn, Fenny Bentley, Ashbourne, Derbyshire, DE6 1LF
Tel (01335) 350278
Fax (01335) 350422
E-mail all@bentleybrookinn.co.uk
Website www.bentleybrookinn.co.uk

☺ Leatherbritches Brewery is part of the Bentley Brook Inn, just north of Ashbourne. The inn and brewery are owned by David and Jeanne Allingham, with their son Edward as general manager, and David Corby as head brewer. Both cask-conditioned and bottle-conditioned beers are brewed. Production averages 10 barrels a week and supplies some 40 selected real ale specialist pubs in the Midlands and North West. Bottle-conditioned beer: Bespoke (ABV 5%), Ale Conners Porter (ABV 5.4%).

Goldings *(OG 1036, ABV 3.6%)*
A light hoppy session beer with a fruity finish.

Ashbourne Ale *(OG 1040, ABV 4%)*
Bitter with fruity hints from fresh Goldings hops with a crisp lasting taste.

Belter *(OG 1040, ABV 4.4%)*
Maris Otter malt produces a pale but interesting beer.

Hairy Helmet *(OG 1047, ABV 4.7%)*

Bespoke *(OG 1050, ABV 5%)*
Mid-brown in colour, with a well-balanced sweet finish. Full bodied.

LEEK*

The Leek Brewing Co. Ltd., 12 Bridge End, Leek, Staffs, ST13 8LG
Tel (01538) 388273
E-mail leekbrewery@hotmail.com

Leek was set up in 2002 in outbuildings behind the owner's house. The brew length is 4.5 barrels. The beer is available at the Bulls Head, Leek, and sold through the local free trade. Twenty outlets are supplied. Seasonal beer: Christmas Special (ABV 6.5%).

Staffordshire Gold *(ABV 4%)*

Staffordshire Bitter *(ABV 4.2%)*

St Edwards Ale *(ABV 4.6%)*

LEES IFBB

J W Lees & Co (Brewers) Ltd, Greengate Brewery, Middleton Junction, Manchester, M24 2AX
Tel (0161) 643 2487
Fax (0161) 655 3731
Website www.jwlees.co.uk
Tours by arrangement

Lees is a family-owned brewery founded in 1828 by John Lees and run by the sixth generation of the family. Brewing takes place in the 1876 brewhouse designed and built by John Willie Lees, the grandson of the founder. All 170 pubs (most in north Manchester) serve cask beer. Seasonal beers: Two-faced Janus (ABV 4.2%, Jan-Feb), Brooklyn Best (ABV 5%, March-April), 1828 Anniversary Ale (ABV 4.6%, May-June), Scorcher (July-Aug), Razzmatazz (ABV 4.4%, Sept-Oct), Plum Pudding (ABV 4.8%, Nov-Dec).

GB Mild *(OG 1032, ABV 3.5%)*
Malty and fruity in aroma. The same flavours are found in the taste, but do not dominate in a beer with a rounded and smooth character. Dry, malty aftertaste.

Bitter *(OG 1037, ABV 4%)*
An amber beer with a malty and citrus fruit aroma. Distinctive, malty, dry and slightly metallic taste. Clean, dry Lees finish.

Moonraker *(OG 1073, ABV 7.5%)*
A reddish-brown beer with a strong, malty, fruity aroma. The flavour is rich and sweet, with roast malt, and the finish is fruity yet dry. Available only in a handful of outlets.

LEITH HILL

Leith Hill Brewery, c/o The Plough Inn, Coldharbour Lane, Coldharbour, nr Dorking, Surrey, RH5 6HD
Tel (01306) 711793
Fax (01306) 710055
E-mail theploughinn@btinternet.com
Website www.ploughinn.com
Tours by arrangement

Leith Hill started in the summer of 1996 to supply the Plough Inn. Formerly using adapted, home-made vessels, a new 2.5-barrel, purpose made, ex-micro-brewery plant was installed in 2001 in another part of the pub to halve brewing time and improve consistency. There are plans to brew a third beer in the near future. One pub is owned.

Crooked Furrow *(OG 1040, ABV 4%)*
Sharp, tangy bitter with strong malt and some balancing hop flavours. A long, bitter aftertaste. The recipe continues to be tweaked.

Tallywhacker *(OG 1056, ABV 5.6%)*
Medium to full-bodied, dark brown old ale. Fruity aroma leads to a fruity sweet taste, balanced by some roast malt. Sweet malty finish with some sharpness.

LEYDEN SIBA

Leyden Brewery, Nangreaves, Bury, Lancs, BL9 6SP
Tel (0161) 764 6680
Fax (0161) 763 4371
Website leydenbrewery.com
Tours by arrangement

A brewery built by Brian Farnworth that started production in 1999. Additional fermenting vessels have been installed, allowing a maximum production of 12 barrels a week. One pub is owned. There are plans to bottle Raglan Sleeve.

Nanny Flyer *(OG 1040, ABV 3.8%)*
A drinkable session bitter with an initial dryness, a hint of citrus, followed by a strong, malty finish.

Black Pudding *(OG 1040, ABV 3.9%)*
A dark brown, creamy mild with a malty flavour, followed by a faint, balanced finish.

Light Brigade *(OG 1043, ABV 4.2%)*
Copper in colour with a citrus aroma. The flavour is a balance of malt, hops and fruit, with a bitter finish.

Forever Bury *(ABV 4.5%)*

Raglan Sleeve *(OG 1047, ABV 4.6%)*
Dark red/brown beer with a hoppy aroma and a dry, roasty, hoppy taste and finish.

Crowning Glory *(OG 1069, ABV 6.8%)*
A surprisingly smooth-tasting beer for its strength, ideal for cold winter nights.

LIDSTONES

Lidstones Brewery, Coltsfoot Green, Wickhambrook, Nr Newmarket, Suffolk, CB8 8UW
Tel (01440) 820232
E-mail Lidstones.brewery@btopenworld.com
Tours by arrangement

Lidstones was founded by Peter Fairhall in 1998. His sister, Jane, joined the business in 1999 to run sales and administration. In 2000 they took over the Kingston Arms in Cambridge, which was awarded Pub of the

Year status in 2001 by the Cambridge & District branch of CAMRA. While Jane runs the pub, Peter is concentrating on developing the brewery, bottling and wholesaling. One pub is owned. Seasonal beers: Old Ale (ABV 6%, winter).

Rowley Mild *(ABV 3.2%)* 🍺◆
Chocolate and toffee aromas lead into what, for its strength, is an impressively rich and flavoursome ale. The finish is pleasantly bitter-sweet.

Session Bitter *(ABV 3.7%)* ◆
Intensely aromatic, straw-coloured ale offering a superb balance of malt and hops on the tongue; an ideal session beer by any standards.

Lucky Punter *(ABV 4.1%)*
Golden ale with a hint of banana on the nose. The taste is clean, crisp and moreishly hoppy, with grapefruit flavours also present.

Suffolk Draught *(ABV 4.3%)*
A straw-coloured bitter with great depth of character with a strong fruit and hop aroma.

Kingston Bitter *(ABV 4.4%)*
Light copper in colour, an excellent example of a traditional bitter.

Oat Stout *(ABV 4.4%)*
Black beer brimming with a roasted chocolate aroma.

Rawalpindi IPA *(ABV 5%)*
Citrus flavours dominate both aroma and taste in this pale, smooth, refreshing beer; the aftertaste is quite dry.

LINFIT

🏠 Linfit Brewery, Sair Inn,
**139 Lane Top, Linthwaite, Huddersfield,
West Yorkshire, HD7 5SG
Tel (01484) 842370**

⊗ A 19th-century brew-pub that started brewing again in 1982, producing an impressive range of ales for sale at the pub. New plant installed in 1994 has almost doubled capacity. Linfit no longer supplies the free trade or beer festivals as a result of concerns over temperature and use of sparklers: beer can only be bought direct from the brewery. One pub is owned. Seasonal beers: Smoke House Ale (ABV 5%), Springbok Bier (ABV 5.7%), Xmas Ale (ABV 8%). Dark Mild and English Guineas Stout are suitable for vegetarians and vegans as isinglass finings are not used.

Dark Mild *(OG 1032, ABV 3%)* ◆
Roast grain dominates this straightforward dark mild, which has some hops in the aroma and a slightly dry flavour. Malty finish.

Bitter *(OG 1035, ABV 3.7%)* ◆
A refreshing session beer. A dry-hopped aroma leads to a clean-tasting, hoppy bitterness, then a long, bitter finish with a hint of malt.

Cascade *(OG 1038, ABV 4%)*
The use of Cascade hops from Washington State gives this a delightfully aromatic flavour, with citrus and fruity overtones. A very pale colour.

Gold Medal *(OG 1040, ABV 4.2%)*
Very pale and hoppy. Use of the new dwarf variety of English hops, First Gold, gives a unique flavour.

Special *(OG 1041, ABV 4.3%)* ◆
Dry-hopping provides the aroma for this rich and mellow bitter, which has a very soft profile and character: it fills the mouth with texture rather than taste. Clean, rounded finish.

Janet St Porter *(OG 1043, ABV 4.5%)*
This blend combines the bitterness of a bitter with the smoothness of a stout. Unlike many porters, this is dry and thirst-quenching.

Autumn Gold *(OG 1045, ABV 4.7%)* ◆
Straw-coloured best bitter with hop and fruit aromas, then the bitter-sweetness of autumn fruit in the taste and the finish.

English Guineas Stout
(OG 1050, ABV 5.3%) ◆
A fruity, roast aroma preludes a smooth, roasted barley, chocolatey flavour that is bitter but not too dry. Excellent appearance; good, bitter finish.

Old Eli *(OG 1050, ABV 5.3%)*
A well-balanced premium bitter with a dry-hopped aroma and a fruity, bitter finish.

Leadboiler *(OG 1060, ABV 6.6%)* ◆
Powerful malt, hop and fruit in good balance on the tongue, with a well-rounded bitter sweet finish.

Enoch's Hammer *(OG 1075, ABV 8%)* ◆
A straw-coloured beer with malt, hop and fruit aromas. Mouth-filling, smooth malt, hop and fruit flavours with a long, hoppy bitter finish. Dangerously drinkable.

LIVERPOOL

🏠 Liverpool Brewing Company Ltd.
**Subsidiary of Bispham Green Brewery Co
Ltd, 21-23 Berry Street, Liverpool, L1 9DF
Tel (0151) 709 5055
Fax (0151) 707 9926**
Shop Mon-Sat 12-2, Sun 12-1030. Ask bar staff.
Tours by arrangement

⊗ The Liverpool Brewing Company is based in the Brewery public house on Berry Street, 300 yards from Europe's largest Chinese arch. The brewhouse was installed at the front of the premises with views from the street, the bar and the entrance hall (via a porthole) in 1990, when the pub was called the Black Horse and Rainbow. In 1996 it was bought by the Bispham Green Brewing Company and continued to brew ales for sale on the premises. Seasonal beers are available and bottle-conditioned beers are planned. Six pubs are owned with three serving cask-conditioned beer. Six outlets area supplied direct. Seasonal beers: Berry Street Mild (ABV 3.4%, May), Lughnasadh (ABV 5%, cask-conditioned lager; pronounced 'lunacy').

Blondie *(OG 1040, ABV 4.1%)*
Creamy, light, best bitter.

First Gold *(OG 1041, ABV 4.2%)*
A light, single hop brew.

Scouse Mouse *(OG 1040, ABV 4.2%)*
A tawny, fruity best bitter.

Devil in Disguise *(OG 1047, ABV 4.8%)*
An amber ale with a spicy/peppery aftertaste.

Celebration *(OG 1048, ABV 4.8%)*
Premium bitter.

LOWES ARMS

⚲ Lowes Arms Brewery,
**The Lowes Arms, 301 Hyde Road,
Denton, Manchester, M31 3FF
Tel (0161) 336 3064
Fax (0161) 285 9015
E-mail brewer@thelab.biz
Web www.thelab.biz**
Shop during pub opening hours
Tours by arrangement

⊛ The brewery, known as 'the Lab', was set
up by Peter Wood, landlord of the Lowes,
who had brewed as a student, and Anthony
Firmin, a keen home-brewer. The brewery is
located in the cellars of the pub. It produces
a range of five beers named after local
landmarks and sites of interest. The brewery
is a 2.5 barrel system, but two new
fermenting vessels have been added to
enable Lab to brew four times a week, so
producing 10 barrels. A campaign to
wholesale the beer is planned.

Jet Amber *(OG 1040, ABV 3.5%)*
Brewed for the Stockport and Manchester
Mild challenge.

Frog Bog *(OG 1040, ABV 3.9%)*
A light, easy-drinking bitter with an orange
aroma and a light hoppy taste.

Wild Wood *(OG 1040-1046, ABV 4.1%)*
A spicy session bitter with a malty and
fruity aroma, and spicy hop tastes leading
to a tingling sensation on the tongue.

Broomstairs
(OG 1040-1046, ABV 4.3%)
A dark best bitter with distinct roast flavours
and a hoppy aftertaste.

Haughton Weave
(OG 1040-1046, ABV 4.5%)
Distinct tangerine aromas in this light-
coloured beer are followed by lots of
bitterness and hoppy tastes in the mouth.

McGUINNESS

**Thomas McGuinness Brewing Co,
Cask & Feather, 1 Oldham Road,
Rochdale, Lancs, OL16 1UA
Tel (01706) 711476
Fax (01706) 669654
E-mail tonycask@hotmail.com
Website www.mcguinnessbrewery.com**
Tours by arrangement

⊗ McGuinness opened in 1991 and now
averages 15-20 barrels a week. It supplies
real ale to its own pub and several other
outlets direct. There are various seasonal
beers at ABV 3.8-4.2%.

Feather Pluckers Mild *(ABV 3.4%)* ◈
A dark brown beer, with roast malt
dominant in the aroma and taste, with
hints of chocolate. Satisfying bitter and
roast finish.

Best Bitter *(ABV 3.8%)* ◈
Gold in colour with a hoppy aroma: a clean,
refreshing beer with hop and fruit tastes
and a hint of sweetness. Bitter aftertaste.

Utter Nutter *(ABV 3.8%)*

Special Reserve Bitter or SRB
(ABV 4%) ◈
A tawny beer, sweet and malty, with
underlying fruit and bitterness, and a bitter-
sweet aftertaste.

Junction Bitter *(ABV 4.2%)* ◈
Mid-brown in colour, with a malty aroma.
Maltiness is predominant throughout, with
some hops and fruit in the taste and
bitterness coming through in the finish.

Tommy Todd's Porter
(ABV 5%) ☐◈
A winter warmer, with a fruit and roast
aroma, leading to a balance of malt and
roast malt flavours, with some fruit. Not too
sweet for its gravity.

McMULLEN IFBB

**McMullen & Sons Ltd, 26 Old Cross,
Hertford, Hertfordshire, SG14 1RD
Tel (01992) 584911
Fax (01992) 553395**
Tours by arrangement

⊠ The future of Hertfordshire's oldest
independent brewery, in doubt for several
years, was assured in the summer of 2003.
The company is controlled by a series of
trusts, and in 2002 a majority of
shareholders decided to cash in their shares.
The sale of the company – brewery and tied
estate – was resisted passionately by David
and Fergus McMullen, who were determined
to maintain an integrated brewery and pub
business. As the dispute dragged on into
2003, McMullen reported record sales of its
cask beers and also continued to invest in its
tied estate. In June, McMullen announced
that the sale of non-brewing assets – mainly
commercial shops and offices – would
enable sufficient cash to be raised to meet
the 'liquidity demands' of the shareholders.
McMullen will remain an integrated
brewery-and-pubs operation. Contract
brewing will be phased out and the
company will concentrate solely on its own
cask beers. This will bring it below the
18,300 barrels-a-year ceiling and, as a result,
it will gain substantial cuts in beer duty
under the government's Progressive Beer
Duty. The company was founded in 1827 by
Peter McMullen, a cooper. He decided there
was a good future in beer itself, and he
started his own small brewery in Hertford.
Brewing 'liquor' (water) is still drawn from
three deep artesian wells. Cask ale is served
in all McMullen's 134 pubs in Hertfordshire,
Essex and London (although all managed
houses use cask breathers on all beers), and
also supplies direct to approximately 60 free
trade outlets. Seasonal beers are brewed for a
limited period under the banner of
McMullen Special Reserve. Gladstone,
formerly a regular brew, is now part of the
Special Reserve portfolio.

Original AK *(OG 1036, ABV 3.7%)* ◈
A pleasant mix of malt and hops leads to a
distinctive, dry aftertaste that isn't always as
pronounced as it used to be.

Country Best Bitter
(OG 1042, ABV 4.3%) ◈
A full-bodied beer with a well-balanced mix
of malt, hops and fruit throughout.

Strong Hart *(OG 1066-70, ABV 7%)*
Liquid Christmas Pudding, Champion of
CAMRA's Winter Beers of Britain awards
1997.

MALDON*

**The Maldon Brewing Co. Ltd,
also trading as Farmers Ales,
The Stable Brewery, Silver Street,
Maldon, Essex, CM9 4QE
Tel (01621) 840925
E-mail maldonbrewingco@aol.com**
Shop open for off sales on Saturdays and by appointment.
Tours by arrangement for small parties only

Situated in a refurbished Victorian stable
block behind the historic, 14th-century Blue
Boar coaching inn in Maldon, brewing
started in 2002 on a 2.5-barrel plant
supplied by Iceni Brewery. The brewery is
open part time, brewing on alternate
weekends. Beer is supplied to the Blue Boar
and other local free houses. It is also
available via Crouch Vale and Mighty Oak
breweries. There are plans for a summer
beer. Four outlets are supplied and the
number is growing. Bottle-conditioned
beers: Farmers First, Ploughboys.

Farmers First *(OG 1041, ABV 4%)*
Best bitter.

Ploughboys *(OG 1043, ABV 4.3%)*
Stout.

MALLARD SIBA

**Mallard Brewery, 15 Hartington Avenue,
Carlton, Nottingham, NG4 3NR
Tel/Fax (0115) 952 1289
E-mail Philip.mallard@ntlworld.com
Website www.mallard-brewery.co.uk**
Tours by arrangement (small groups)

⊗ Phil Mallard built and installed a two-
barrel plant in a shed at his home and
started brewing in 1995. The brewery is a
mere nine square metres and contains a hot
liquor tank, mash tun, copper, and three
fermenters. The brewery was launched at
the Nottingham Beer Festival in 1995. Since
then production has risen from one barrel a
week to between six or eight barrels, which
is the plant's maximum. Phil has no plans
at present to expand and now supplies
around 25 outlets, of which seven are on a
regular weekly basis. He has also launched a
small-scale bottling enterprise and plans to
produce bottled beers as limited editions
supplied direct from the brewery by mail
order. Seasonal beer: DA (ABV 5.8%,
winter), Quismas Quacker (ABV 6%,
Christmas). Bottle-conditioned beers: Owd

Duck (ABV 4.8%), Friar Duck (ABV 5%), DA
(ABV 5.8%), Quismas Quacker (ABV 6%),
Duckling (ABV 4.2%), Drake (ABV 4.5%),
Duckdown Stout (ABV 4.6%), Spittin'
Feathers (ABV 4.4%), Waddlers Mild (ABV
3.7%), Duck & Dive (ABV 3.7%), Feather
Light (ABV 4.1%)

Waddlers Mild *(OG 1039, ABV 3.7%)*
A dark ruby mild with a fruity chocolate
flavour in the mouth and a fruity finish.

Duck & Dive *(OG 1037, ABV 3.7%)*
A light single-hopped beer made from the
hedgerow hop, First Gold. A bitter beer with
a hoppy nose, good bitterness on the palate
and a dry finish.

Best Bitter *(OG 1038, ABV 4%)* ◗
Golden brown, fruity and hoppy to the
nose, with malt more apparent in the taste
than anywhere else. The fruity hop carries
through to a bitter, dry finish.

Feather Light *(OG 1039, ABV 4.1%)*
A very pale lager-style bitter, floral bouquet
and sweetish on the palate, a nice light
hoppy session beer.

Duckling *(OG 1039, ABV 4.2%)*
A crisp refreshing bitter with a hint of
honey and citrus flavour. Dry hopped.

Spittin' Feathers *(OG 1043, ABV 4.4%)*
A mellow, ruby bitter with a complex malt
flavour of chocolate, toffee and coffee,
complemented with a full and fruity/hoppy
aftertaste.

Drake *(OG 1044, ABV 4.5%)*
A full-bodied premium bitter, with malt and
hops on the palate, and a fruity finish.

Duck Down Stout *(OG 1045, ABV 4.6%)*
Black and fruity.

Owd Duck *(OG 1046, ABV 4.8%)*
A dark ruby bitter with a smooth mellow
smoky flavour and fruity finish.

Friar Duck *(OG 1048, ABV 5%)*
A pale full malt beer, hoppy with a hint of
blackcurrant flavour.

MALTON SIBA

**Malton Brewery Company Ltd, Rear of
Suddabys Crown Hotel, 12 Wheelgate,
Malton, North Yorkshire, YO17 7HP
Tel (01653) 697580
Fax (01653) 691812
E-mail suddaby@crownhotel.plus.com
Website www.maltonbrewery.com**
Tours by arrangement

⊗ The brewery was founded in the stable
block at the rear of Suddaby's Crown Hotel
in Wheelgate, Malton in 1984. The brewery
is now run by the Suddaby family with Alan
Brayshaw as brewer. The hotel itself and
upwards of 25 other outlets are supplied on
a regular basis as well as several beer
agencies. Seasonal beers: Auld Bob (ABV
6%), Pickwick's Porter (ABV 4.2%). Bottle-
conditioned beer: Auld Bob. Organic beer:
Golden Chance, suitable for vegetarians and
vegans.

Double Chance *(OG 1038, ABV 3.8%)* ◗
A clean-tasting, amber bitter in which hops
predominate. Little malt character, but hop
and fruit flavours lead to a smooth, bitter
finish.

Golden Chance *(OG 1039, ABV 4.2%)*
Golden-coloured bitter with a complex hoppy finish. Two distinct varieties of hops combine with English malts to make this mid-strength bitter distinctive and quaffable.

Ryedale Light *(OG 1044, ABV 4.5%)*

MALVERN HILLS SIBA

**Malvern Hills Brewery Ltd,
15 West Malvern Road,
Great Malvern,
Worcestershire, WR14 4ND
Tel (01684) 560165
Fax (01684) 577336
E-mail MHB.ales@tesco.net
Website www.malvernhillsbrewery.co.uk**

⊗ The brewery was established in 1997 using a converted dynamite store on the slopes of the Malvern Hills. It's now owned and operated by the sole proprietor, Julian Hawthornthwaite, who bought out his previous business partner. Production halted completely in September 2002 due to long-term illness, but a return to full production was expected during 2003. There is a strong past demand for products in the Black Country, a fact commemorated by the brewing of Black Country Wobble (ABV 4.5%) as a festival beer for the Worcester Beer Festival. Seasonal beer: Dr Gully's Winter Ale (ABV 5.2%).

Red Earl *(OG 1037, ABV 3.7%)* ◈
A very light beer that does not overpower the senses. A hint of apple fruit, it is ideal for slaking the thirst.

Worcestershire Whym
(OG 1042, ABV 4.2%)

Black Pear
(OG 1044, ABV 4.4%) ◈
Amber best bitter with a strong backbone of hops and fruit, and a short-lived malty sweetness that is overwhelmed by the growing and long-lasting bitter end.

Black Country Wobble
(OG 1045, ABV 4.5%) ◈
A sharp, clean-tasting golden beer with an aroma of hops challenged by fruit and malt, which hold up well in the mouth. A bitter dryness grows as the contrasting latent sweetness subsides.

MARBLE SIBA

**⛉ Marble Beers Ltd, (Marble Brewery),
73 Rochdale Road,
Manchester, M4 4HY
Tel/Fax (0161) 819 2694
E-mail vance@marblebeers.co.uk
Website www.marblebeers.co.uk**
Tours by arrangement

The Marble Brewery was designed by brewmaster Brendan Dobbin and opened in the Marble Arch Inn in 1997. As a result of the success of the brewery and a request to brew an organic beer for the Manchester Food Festival, the brewery has now gone totally organic and vegan, and is registered with the Soil Association and the Vegetarian Society. The five-barrel plant operates at full capacity, producing five regular beers plus seasonal brews. Five pubs are owned and

three outlets are supplied direct. Seasonal beer: Chocolate Heavy (ABV 5.5%, winter).

Chorlton-cum-Hazy *(OG 1038, ABV 3.8%)* ◈
Also sold as N/4. This golden-amber beer has a shy nose with some hops and fruit, a fresh hoppy palate, and a short, dry aftertaste.

Cloudy Marble *(OG 1040, ABV 4%)* ◈
Amber in colour, with as hoppy/fruity nose. Hops, fruit and bitterness in the mouth, with quite a strong bitter finish.

Manchester Bitter *(OG 1042, ABV 4.2%)*

Ginger Marble *(OG 1045, ABV 4.5%)*

Uncut Amber *(OG 1047, ABV 4.7%)* ◈
Red/brown beer with malt, coffee and fruit in the aroma. It has dark chocolate, malt and fruit on the palate, with a dry, roast finish.

Lagonda IPA *(ABV 5%)*
A classic pale ale, immense citrus and floral hop notes balanced against a dry bitter finish.

Chocolate Heavy *(OG 1055, ABV 5.5%)* ◈
Black in colour; chocolate, roast malt and fruit nose. A smooth chocolatey, roasty bitter taste with hops and fruit also in evidence. Dry, roast, hoppy finish.

MARCHES

**Marches Ales, Unit 6, Western Close,
Southern Avenue Industrial Estate,
Leominster, Herefordshire, HR6 0QD
Tel (01568) 610063**

⊗ Plans to expand the brewery in 2001 had to be put on hold as a result of foot-and-mouth disease in the locality, which meant that engineers could not get on to the site. By the summer of 2003, the owners were ready to brew again but were waiting for an entry road to be completed. Brewing will start again during the lifetime of this Guide.

MARSTON MOOR

**Marston Moor Brewery Ltd, Crown House,
Kirk Hammerton, York, YO26 8DD
Tel/Fax (01423) 330341
E-mail marston.moor.brewery@ic24.net**

☺ A small brewery established in 1983. The beers are currently brewed by Rudgate Brewery (qv) on a temporary basis, enabling Marston Moor to devote more time to the fabrication of small-scale brewing plant and associated activities. About 100 outlets are served. Bottle-conditioned beer: Brewers Droop.

Cromwell Bitter
(OG 1036, ABV 3.6%) ◈
A golden beer with hops and fruit in strong evidence on the nose. Bitterness as well as fruit and hops dominate the taste and long aftertaste.

Brewers Pride *(OG 1041, ABV 4.2%)* ◈
A light but somewhat thin, fruity beer, with a hoppy, bitter aftertaste.

Merriemaker *(OG 1044, ABV 4.5%)*

Musketeer *(OG 1044, ABV 4.5%)*

Brewers Droop *(OG 1048, ABV 5%)*
A pale, robust ale with hops and fruit notes in prominence. A long, bitter aftertaste.

Trooper *(OG 1048, ABV 5%)*

MARSTON'S

Marston, Thompson & Evershed, Shobnall Road, Burton upon Trent, Staffs, DE14 2BW
A subsidiary of Wolverhampton & Dudley Breweries
Tel (01902) 711811
Fax (01902) 429136
Website www.fullpint.co.uk
Shop 10-3 Mon-Fri; 10-12 Sat
Tours by arrangement, ring (01283) 504391

⊛ Marston's has been brewing in Burton on Trent since 1834 and it is still the home of Marston's Pedigree and 'The Cathedral of Brewing', the only working set of Burton Union oak fermenters. Marston's became part of Wolverhampton & Dudley Breweries in 1999 and the group underscored its commitment to the Burton brewery in 2003 with an investment of £1.7 million. Plant from the former Mansfield Brewery has been moved to Burton to help keep pace with demand, though the Unions will still be used to produce Pedigree and yeast for all other beers. In June 2003 Marston's launched a new premium pale ale, Old Empire, that recreates the colour and flavours of a true 19th-century India Pale Ale. If successful, it will become a regular member of the portfolio and will be brewed using the Unions. Cask beer is supplied to Marston's estate, which stretches from Hampshire to Yorkshire. There is also a substantial free trade.

Marstons Bitter (OG 1037, ABV 3.8%) ◆
A light, fruity beer with a touch of roast. Some bitterness later but little aroma.

Pedigree Bitter (OG 1043, ABV 4.5%) ◆
Sulphurous aroma gives way to hops. Tastes hoppy and fruity, and leaves a bitter aftertaste. The classic Burton pale ale rarely found in peak form.

Old Empire (ABV 5.7%)
An India Pale Ale launched in 2003, brewed with pale malt and Fuggles, Goldings and American Cascade hops.

MASH SIBA

⌷ **Mash Ltd, 19/21 Great Portland Street, London, W1W 8QB**
Tel (0207) 637 5555
Fax (0207) 637 7333
Tours by arrangement

The Mash micro-brewery is the centrepiece of the Mash bar and restaurant that opened in 1998. The New York-style brewery can be toured to inspect the process at close hand and the restaurant provides a tutored lunch or dinner where the beers are matched to food. The beers are not cask conditioned but are stored in cellar tanks using a CO2 system. Regular beer: Mash Wheat (ABV 5.2%). Other beers include a Blackcurrant Porter, Scotch, IPA, Peach, Extra Stout and Pils.

MAULDONS SIBA

Mauldons Brewery Ltd, 7 Addison Road, Chilton Industrial Estate, Sudbury, Suffolk, CO10 2YW
Tel/Fax (01787) 311055
E-mail sims@mauldons.co.uk
Website www.mauldons.co.uk
Tours by arrangement

⌧ The company was bought by Steve and Alison Sims in 2000 from founder Peter Mauldon. Steve is a former sales manager with Adnams. Using traditional methods and quality materials, Mauldons supplies ales throughout East Anglia. There are plans to purchase a brew-pub. Seasonal beers: May Bee (ABV 3.7%, May), Bah Humbug (ABV 4.9%, Christmas), Midsummer Gold (ABV 4%), Mid Autumn Gold (ABV 4.2%), Midwinter Gold (ABV 4.5%), Cuckoo (ABV 4.3%), Ploughmans (ABV 4.3%), Eatanswill Old (ABV 4%). There are also a large number of occasional and one-off brews. Bottle-conditioned beer: Black Adder.

Mauldons Bitter (OG 1036, ABV 3.6%)

Moletrap Bitter (OG 1037.8, ABV 3.8%) ◆
A well-balanced session beer with a crisp, hoppy bitterness balancing sweet malt.

Dickens (OG 1039.8, ABV 4%)
A light-coloured bitter with a fine distinctive hop nose, and a refreshingly dry, fruity finish.

Peggottys Porter (OG 1041, ABV 4.1%)

Pickwick (OG 1042, ABV 4.2%)
A best bitter with a rich rounded malt flavour with ripe aromas of hops and fruit. A bitter-sweet finish.

Suffolk Pride (OG 1048, ABV 4.8%) ◆
A full-bodied strong bitter. The malt and fruit in the aroma are reflected in the taste, and there is some hop character in the finish. Deep tawny/red in colour.

Black Adder (OG 1053.8, ABV 5.3%) ◆
A dark stout. Roast malt is strong in the aroma and taste, but malt, hop and bitterness provide an excellent balance and a lingering finish.

White Adder (OG 1053.8, ABV 5.3%) ◆
A pale brown, almost golden, strong ale. A warming, fruity flavour dominates and lingers into a dry, hoppy finish.

Suffolk Comfort (OG 1065.8, ABV 6.6%)
A clean, hoppy nose leads to a predominantly malty flavour in this full-bodied beer. Dry, hoppy aftertaste.

MAYFLOWER

Mayflower Brewery, Mayflower House, 15 Longendale Rd, Standish, Wigan, WN6 0UE
Tel (01235) 400605
E-mail info@mayflowerbrewery.co.uk
Website www.mayflowerbrewery.co.uk

⊛ Stewart Thompson, a northern brewer of 35 years' standing, started Mayflower Brewery in autumn 2001. It was housed in

the ex-canteen of a former bleach works, standing on concrete stilts over the River Douglas, but production ceased in June 2003 while new premises were sought: the brewery planned to move to the Royal Oak, Wigan, in autumn 2003. Some 30 outlets are supplied.

Black Diamond (OG 1035, ABV 3.4%)

Mayflower Bitter (OG 1037, ABV 3.8%)

Brewsters First (OG 1037, ABV 3.8%)

Wigan Bier (OG 1041, ABV 4.2%)

Hic-Bibi (OG 1049, ABV 5%)

MAYPOLE

Maypole Brewery, North Laithes Farm, Wellow Road, Eakring, Newark, Notts, NG22 0AN
Tel (01623) 871690
Tours by arrangement

⊗ The brewery was founded in 1995 in a converted 18th-century farm building. It was bought in 2001 by the Square & Compass Inn, Normanton-on-Trent, where at least two Maypole beers are usually on sale. It also supplies the Beehive, Maplebeck, which is reputedly the smallest pub in Nottinghamshire. Plans were in place to increase brewing capacity during 2003. Around 45 outlets are supplied on an occasional basis. Seasonal beers: Mayfair (ABV 3.8%, May-June), Flanagans Stout (ABV 4.4%, Feb-March), Donner and Blitzed (ABV 5.1%, Nov-Dec).

Normanton IPA
(OG 1037, ABV 3.6%)
A classic, golden coloured IPA.

Lion's Pride (OG 1038, ABV 3.8%)
A tawny brown beer with a malty aroma and taste. Fruity hop bitterness comes through in the finish.

Celebration
(OG 1040, ABV 4%) ◈
A ruddy-brown bitter in which malt dominates. Some fruity hop in the nose and taste, with an initial sweetness that dries into a bitter finish where the fruit and hops meet the malt.

Loxley Ale (OG 1041, ABV 4.2%)
A light golden ale made with local honey. Refreshing, but not too sweet, it has a subtle bitterness.

Brew Britannia (OG 1045, ABV 4.5%)
A tawny-coloured best bitter. Initial fruit and malt gives way to a bitter, hoppy finish.

Wellow Gold
(OG 1044, ABV 4.6%)
A blonde, Belgian-style beer where citrus flavours predominate in the nose and taste. A deceptively drinkable beer for its strength. Sells under the Mae West label in some existing outlets.

Ghost Train (OG 1047, ABV 4.7%)
A smooth, black porter, slight sweetness to begin with, giving way to a bitter finish.

Major Oak
(OG 1047, ABV 4.8%)
A well-balanced, full-bodied premium beer. Fruity nose and taste with a slightly burnt aftertaste.

MEANTIME SIBA

Meantime Brewing Co. Ltd., 2 Penhall Road, Greenwich, London, SE7 8RX
Tel (020) 8293 1111
Fax (020) 8293 4004
E-mail sales@meantime.co.uk
Website www.meantimebrewing.co.uk
Tours by arrangement

⊗ Meantime is dedicated to quality production of continental-style lagers and beers, supplying various style bars. It is the sole own-label supplier to Sainsbury's ground-breaking Taste the Difference range. One pub is owned in Greenwich with further additions to come. Meantime launched its first cask ale in 2003. Bottle-conditioned beer: Sainsbury's Taste the Difference Weiss Beer (ABV 5%).

Meantime Blonde (OG 1038-40, ABV 3.9%)

MIGHTY OAK SIBA

Mighty Oak Brewing Company Ltd, 14B, West Station Yard, Spital Road, Maldon, Essex, CM9 6TW
Tel (01621) 843713
Fax (01621) 840914
E-mail moakbrew@aol.com
Tours for evening group visits only

⊗ Founded in 1996 by former Ind Coope Romford brewer John Boyce and his partner Ruth O'Neill, a management accountant, Mighty Oak continues to grow, justifying its increased capacity of 70 barrels a week. The brewery moved to its current premises in 2001 where it has seen continuing success with four of its ales, Oscar Wilde, IPA, Burntwood Bitter and Spice, becoming CAMRA beers of the year for 2002. Mighty Oak Ales are supplied to around 200 customers in Essex as well as Beds, Gloucestershire, Herts, Kent, Wilts, Somerset, and Suffolk, plus North and East London. Additionally, Mighty Oak Ales are available from other breweries around the country through beer swaps and an increasing number of wholesalers. Each year, Mighty Oak produces a range of monthly ales that are based on a theme. For 2003 they were based on a Shakespeare theme celebrating the four-hundredth anniversary of the Bard's visit to Maldon with his band of players. Burntwood Bitter was Champion Beer of East Anglia in 1999, Champion Beer of Britain finalist 1999 and 2000.

IPA (OG 1036.1, ABV 3.5%) ▣⬚◈
Delicate honey and vanilla tones complement a moderate bitterness in this well-balanced, amber session beer.

Oscar Wilde
(OG 1039.5, ABV 3.7%) ⬚◈
Dark reddish mild with a biscuity aroma giving way to a smoky taste with suggestions of plain chocolate. Gentle hop character underpins a burnt-toast aftertaste. (In Cockney rhyming slang, Oscar Wilde equals Mild.)

Maldon Gold (OG 1039.5, ABV 3.8%)
Brewed using only Maris Otter pale malt for a light golden ale with biscuity malt flavours. Mount Hood and First Gold hops give a distinctive citrus character along with a long dry, bitter finish.

Burntwood Bitter *(OG 1040.9, ABV 4%)* 🍺◆
Tawny bitter with a grainy, roasty palate, dominated by a marked coffee character.

Simply The Best *(OG 1044.1, ABV 4.4%)* ◆
Complex and fruity best bitter with a solid, meaty taste.

English Oak *(OG 1047.9, ABV 4.8%)* ◆
Pale brown strong bitter. Initially a sweet beer, with a peach blossom aroma and a fruity taste. Increasingly, and surprisingly, bitter in the finish.

Spice *(OG 1069.4, ABV 7%)* 🔲◆
Beer brewed with fruits and spices, most obviously cinnamon and orange zest, which dominate over malt and hops.

MILK STREET SIBA

**The Milk Street Brewery, The Griffin, 25 Milk Street, Frome, Somerset, BA11 3DB
Tel (01373) 467766
E-mail the griffin@milkstreetbrewery .fsnet.co.uk**
Tours by arrangement

The brewery was commissioned in 1999 and has a capacity of 20 barrels a week. Four beers are brewed with seasonal brands every two months. Milk Street runs three outlets and plans to expand. 25 other outlets are supplied. Seasonal beers: Funky Monkey (ABV 4%), Mermaid (ABV 4.1%), Aldhelms (ABV 4.3%).

Gulp *(OG 1036, ABV 3.5%)*
An amber beer that is fresh and lively on the palate. The aroma is reminiscent of grapefruit peel and freshly-picked hawthorne leaves.

Natural Ale *(ABV 3.8%)*

B4 *(OG 1040, ABV 4%)*
Golden in colour, there is a softness on the palate due to the use of malted wheat. Smooth and well-rounded, the bitterness comes from American Liberty hops, with Goldings for aroma.

Nick's *(OG 1045, ABV 4.4%)*
A clean-drinking bitter, refreshing with an excellent balance of malt flavours. East Kent Goldings are used both for aroma and bitterness and create an excellent length of flavour.

MILLIS*

**The Millis Brewing Co Ltd,
St Margaret's Farm, South Darenth, Dartford, Kent, DA4 9LB
Tel/Fax (01474) 566903
E-mail john@millis-brewing.com
Website www.millis-brewing.co.uk**

⊗ Millis started with a half-barrel brew-length in a specially created brewery at home in a pilot plant. Demand outstripped the facility and Millis moved to a new site with a 10-barrel plant in March 2003. Seasonal beer: Santa's Sticky Bits (ABV 5.3%, Dec-Jan).

Chantry Bitter *(OG 1039, ABV 3.9%)*
A copper-coloured ale with a pale and crystal malt base, balanced by tart, tangy fruit flavours and Kentish-grown hops, ending with a distinctive, clean finish.

Capall Dubh *(OG 1043, ABV 4.3%)*
A full-bodied, straw-coloured premium beer. Clear, smooth and easy drinking, with a subtle balance of malt and finest Kentish aroma hops, leading to a tangy, clean, gentle bitter finish.

Burning Sun *(OG 1048, ABV 4.8%)*
A golden, smooth, full malt beer, with hops and fruit notes contributing towards a long, clean, bitter finish.

Bandraoi Bitter *(OG 1050, ABV 5%)*
A deep, dark, ruby-red beer with a full malt base. There are complex tangy fruit flavours balanced by generous hopping using Kent-grown medium alpha and aroma hops. Finally, like a dark cloak covering the beer, there is a background of chocolate roast flavours.

MILTON SIBA

**Milton Brewery, Cambridge, Ltd, 111 Cambridge Road, Milton, Cambs, CB4 6AT
Tel (01223) 226198
Fax (01223) 226199
E-mail enquiries@miltonbrewery.co.uk
Website www.miltonbrewery.co.uk**
Tours by arrangement

⊗ Founded in 1999, Milton Brewery now supplies more than 100 pubs within one hour of Cambridge. The brew length is 15 barrels and extra capacity was added in 2002 to cope with demand. The brewery has two tied houses, in Peterborough and London, and further expansion is anticipated. Seasonal beer: Mammon (ABV 7%, from December).

Minotaur *(OG 1035, ABV 3.3%)* ◆
Rich and very full-bodied for its strength, a malty chocolateyness predominates, but vanilla and liquorice flavours also surface.

Jupiter *(OG 1037, ABV 3.5%)* ◆
A light malty aroma and a delicate hoppy palate lead to a bitter finish. A light barley sugar aroma and taste underpin this amber session bitter

Neptune *(OG 1039, ABV 3.8%)* ◆
Delicious hop aromas introduce this well-balanced, nutty and refreshing copper-coloured ale. Good hoppy finish.

Pegasus *(OG 1043, ABV 4.1%)* 🍺◆
Clean-tasting amber best bitter with a malty, fruity and slightly sulphury start,

augmented by a gentle mix of hops and toffee in the mouth that persists in the sustained bitter ending.

Electra *(OG 1046, ABV 4.5%)* ♦
A restrained bitter and hoppy backbone with short, sweet, fruity undertones and a light malt flavour after a gentle, fruity aroma. This full-bodied amber premium bitter ends with a persistent hop bitterness.

Cyclops *(OG 1055, ABV 5.3%)*
Deep copper-coloured ale, with a rich hoppy aroma and full body; fruit and malt notes develop in the finish. Uses three different malts and four different hops.

MOLES SIBA

Moles Brewery (Cascade Drinks Ltd), 5 Merlin Way, Bowerhill, Melksham, Wilts, SN12 6TJ
Tel (01225) 704734/708842
Fax (01225) 790770
E-mail cascade@blueyonder.co.uk
Website molesbrewery.com
Shop 9-5.
Tours by arrangement

⊗ Moles Brewery was established in 1982 and produces beers for local pubs and also nationwide via other brewers and wholesalers. Over the past 20 years the range of beers has been expanded to meet consumer demand. Molennium (ABV 4.5%) was introduced at the appropriate time while Molecatcher (ABV 5%) was launched at the 2001 Bristol CAMRA Beer Festival. 14 pubs are now owned, 13 serving cask beer. 150 outlets are supplied. Seasonal beers: Barleymole (ABV 4.2%, summer), Molegrip (ABV 4.3%, autumn), Holy Moley (ABV 4.7%, spring), Moel Moel (ABV 6%, winter).

Tap Bitter *(OG 1035, ABV 3.5%)*
A session bitter with a smooth, malty flavour and clean bitter finish.

Best Bitter *(OG 1040, ABV 4%)*
A well-balanced amber-coloured bitter, clean, dry and malty with some bitterness and delicate floral hop flavour.

Landlords Choice *(OG 1045, ABV 4.5%)*
A dark, strong, smooth porter beer, with a rich fruity palate and malty finish.

Moles Molennium *(OG 1045, ABV 4.5%)*
Fruit, caramel and malty overtones in the aroma of this deep amber-coloured ale, balanced by a pleasant bitterness.

Molecatcher *(OG 1050, ABV 5%)*
This copper-coloured ale has a delightfully spicy hop aroma and taste with a long bitter finish.

MOONSTONE

▽ **Moonstone Brewery, Ministry of Ale, 9 Trafalgar Street, Burnley, Lancs, BB11 1TQ**
Tel (01282) 830909
Tours by arrangement

☺ The brewery was built in a pub that had been closed for three years, and the first brew appeared in 2001.

Black Star *(ABV 3.4%)*

MOOR SIBA

Moor Beer Company, Whitley Farm, Ashcott, Bridgwater, Somerset, TA7 9QW
Tel/Fax (01458) 210050
E-mail arthur@moorbeer.co.uk
Website www.moorbeer.co.uk
Tours by arrangement

⊗ Farmer Arthur Frampton and his wife Annette swapped beef for beer in 1996 when he set up a brewery in an old workshop on their former dairy farm. The 10-barrel operation has since thrived, selling beers to local pubs and further afield through their own wholesaling business. Bottle-conditioned beers are produced for sale at local farmers' markets while monthly specials with a rail tour theme are brewed. Some 50 outlets are supplied. Seasonal beer: Avalon (ABV 4%, spring/autumn), Santa Moors (ABV 4.8%, Christmas). Bottle-conditioned beers: Old Freddy Walker, Withy Cutter and Merlins Magic.

Withy Cutter *(OG 1037, ABV 3.8%)* ♦
A lightly malty, pale brown beer with a moderately bitter finish.

Merlin's Magic *(OG 1044, ABV 4.3%)* ♦
Dark amber-coloured, complex, full-bodied beer, with fruity notes.

Peat Porter *(OG 1045, ABV 4.5%)* ♦
Dark brown/black beer with an initially fruity taste leading to roast malt taste with a little bitterness. A slightly sweet malty finish.

Old Freddy Walker *(OG 1074, ABV 7.3%)* ♦
Rich, dark, strong ale with a fruity complex taste, leaving a fruitcake finish.

For Juwards (qv):

Juwards Bitter *(3.8%)*

Bishops Somerset Ale *(4%)*

MOORHOUSES SIBA

Moorhouses Brewery (Burnley) Ltd, 4 Moorhouse Street, Burnley, Lancs, BB11 5EN
Tel (01282) 422864/416004
Fax (01282) 838493
E-mail moorhouses@moorhouses
.fsbusiness.co.uk
Website www.moorhouses.co.uk
Tours by arrangement

☺ Established in 1865 as a drinks manufacturer, the brewery started brewing cask-conditioned ale in 1978 and has achieved recognition by winning more international and CAMRA awards than any other brewery of its size. The company owns seven pubs, all serving cask-conditioned beer, and supplies real ale to approximately 300 free trade outlets. Two new 30-barrel fermenters and a 7.5 ton dray were added in 2000 to keep up with demand. Seasonal beer: Owd Ale (ABV 6%, Nov-Feb). There is a selection of seasonal ales throughout the year, all of which are available for more than a month.

Black Cat *(OG 1035, ABV 3.4%)* ◻♦
An excellent dark, fruity ale. Smooth and well-balanced with fruity, chocolate and coffee flavours to complement the bitter roast character that lingers on in the aftertaste. Champion Beer of Britain 2000.

Premier Bitter *(OG 1036, ABV 3.7%)* ✦
A clean and satisfying bitter aftertaste
rounds off this consistent, well-balanced
hoppy, amber session bitter.

Pride of Pendle *(OG 1040, ABV 4.1%)*
A fine balance of malt and hops give this
beer a long, dry and extremely satisfying
finish.

Pendle Witches Brew
(OG 1049, ABV 5.1%) ✦
A faint malty nose leads into a rich,
sweetish nutty flavour with a subtle hoppy
bitterness. This develops into a delightful
lasting bitter finish.

MORDUE SIBA

**Mordue Brewery, Unit 21A, Oak Road,
West Chirton North Industrial Estate,
Shiremoor, Tyne & Wear, NE29 8SF
Tel/Fax (0191) 2961879
E-mail enquiries @morduebrewery.com
Website www.morduebrewery.com**
Shop see website
Tours by arrangement

⊛ Garry and Matthew Fawson were
enthusiastic home brewers when they
discovered the house they were living in
had been the former Mordue Brewery,
which closed in 1879. They decided to start
their own brewery using the old Mordue
name and purchased a five-barrel plant.
Their first commercial beers were Workie
Ticket and Five Bridge Bitter, which were
launched at the 1995 Newcastle Beer
Festival. Workie Ticket was voted Beer of
the Festival and subsequently went on to
win Champion Beer of Britain at the 1997
GBBF. In 1998 a move to larger premises
and a 20-barrel plant meant that production
could keep pace with demand. In the same
year Radgie Gadgie won the Strong Bitter
Award at GBBF. The full range of Mordue
Beers are distributed nationally and are
regular winners at beer festival throughout
the country. Seasonal ales: Summer Tyne
(ABV 3.6%), Millennium Bridge Ale (ABV
3.8%), Spring Tyne (ABV 4%), Autumn
Tyne (ABV 4%), A'l Wheat Pet (ABV 4.1%),
IPA (ABV 5%), Headmasters Xmas Sermon
(ABV 5.2%).

Five Bridge Bitter *(OG 1038, ABV 3.8%)* ✦
Crisp, golden beer with a good hint of hops.
The bitterness carries on in the aftertaste. A
good session bitter.

Geordie Pride *(OG 1042, ABV 4.2%)* ✦
Medium-bodied amber brew, well-balanced
and hoppy, with a long, bitter finish.

Workie Ticket
(OG 1045, ABV 4.5%) ⬡✦
Complex, tasty beer with plenty of malt and
hops. Long, satisfying, bitter finish.

Radgie Gadgie
(OG 1048, ABV 4.8%) ▮⬡✦
Strong, easy-drinking bitter. Plenty of fruit
and hops. The flavours extend into a long,
lingering finish.

MOULIN

⌂ **Moulin Hotel & Brewery, Kirkmichael
Road, Pitlochry, Perthshire, PH16 5EW
Tel (01796) 472196
Fax (01796) 474098
E-mail hotel@moulin.u-net.com
Website www.moulin.u-net.com**
Shop 12-3 daily. Tours by arrangement
Tours by prior arrangement

⊛ A small craft brewery, set up originally to
serve the 300-year-old inn, it now supplies
another hotel outlet and also sells bottle-
conditioned beers to visitors. Two pubs are
owned and six outlets are supplied. Bottle-
conditioned beer: Ale of Atholl.

Light *(OG 1036, ABV 3.7%)* ✦
Thirst-quenching, straw-coloured session
beer, with a light, hoppy, fruity balance
ending with a gentle, hoppy sweetness.

Braveheart *(OG 1039, ABV 4%)* ✦
An amber bitter, with a delicate balance of
malt and fruit and a Scottish-style sweetness.

Ale of Atholl *(OG 1043.5, ABV 4.5%)* ✦
A reddish, quaffable, malty ale, with a solid
body and a mellow finish.

Old Remedial *(OG 1050.5, ABV 5.2%)* ✦
A distinctive and satisfying dark brown old
ale, with roast malt to the fore and tannin
in a robust taste.

NAGS HEAD

⌂ **Nags Head Inn, Abercych, Boncath,
Pembrokeshire, SA37 0HJ
Tel (01239) 841200**

Pub-brewery producing just one brew for its
own consumption. Two outlets are supplied
direct.

Old Emrys *(OG 1038-40, ABV 3.8-4%)*

NATHAN'S

**Nathan's Fine Ales, the Queen's Arms,
Main Street, Taddington, nr Buxton,
Derbyshire, SK17 9UD
Tel (01298) 85245
E-mail nathanshome@hotmail.com**

Brewing was suspended when Nathan Gale
bought the Queen's Arms in 2003. He is
seeking planning permission to build at the
rear of the pub and will then start brewing
again.

NETHERGATE SIBA

**Nethergate Holdings Ltd, Nethergate
Brewery Ltd, 11-13 High Street, Clare,
Suffolk, CO10 8NY
Tel (01787) 277244
Fax (01787) 277123
E-mail orders@nethergate.co.uk
Website www.nethergate.co.uk**
Tours by arrangement (trade and CAMRA groups)

⊠ Nethergate Brewery was established in
1986 and has been in the forefront of
innovative brewing, while maintaining
strictly traditional methods. The 2002 move
to Progressive Beer Duty enabled Nethergate
to upgrade its brewing equipment, including
a new 'state of the art' cask washer, and
extended cold-store facilities. Old Growler,
introduced in 1989, heralded the new wave

of porters, while Umbel Ale reintroduced coriander as an English brewing ingredient for the first time in 150 years. Both these brews became Champion Beers of Great Britain in their respective categories. Nethergate supplies approximately 360 outlets on a direct basis, mainly in East Anglia, with seven regular ales, to which has been added a successful monthly beer programme produced by head brewer Tom Knox. Seasonal brews: Vixen (ABV 4.3%, January), Red Rooster (ABV 4.5%, February), Dr John's Panacea (ABV 4.3%, March), Wild Fox (ABV 4.3%, April), Painted Lady (ABV 4.2%, May), Hares Breadth (ABV 4.4%, June), Golden Gate (ABV 4.5%, July), Sheeps Eye (ABV 4.1%, August), Wild Goose (ABV 4.5%, September), Scutchers (ABV 4.3%, October), Monks Habit (ABV 4.2%, November), Dirty Dicks (ABV 5.2%, December). Bottle-conditioned beer: Augustinian Ale (ABV 5.2%: coriander is used and it is a different beer to the cask ale of the same name; brewed mainly for the American market.)

Priory Mild (OG 1036, ABV 3.5%) ◆
Distinctive, full-flavoured, very dark mild. Pronounced lingering roast and dry hop aftertaste.

IPA (OG 1036, ABV 3.5%) ◆
This amber-coloured session bitter is clean, crisp and very drinkable. Plenty of malt and hoppy bitterness together with some fruit are pleasing to the palate. Bitterness lingers in a long dry aftertaste.

Umbel Ale (OG 1039, ABV 3.8%) ⬛◆
Wort is percolated through coriander seeds to give a wonderful, warming, spicy fruit tang to both the taste and aroma. The hops are strong enough to make themselves known and a strong, bitter malt finish hits late.

Suffolk County Best Bitter
(OG 1041, ABV 4%) ◆
Formerly Nethergate Bitter, Suffolk County retains the classic Nethergate taste but not so intensely bitter as previously. Still a fine balanced beer with plenty of hops and malt.

Augustinian Ale (OG 1046, ABV 4.5%) ◆
A pale, refreshing, complex best bitter. Fruity aroma leads to a bitter-sweet flavour and aftertaste with predominance of citrus tones.

Old Growler (OG 1052, ABV 5%) ⬛⬛◆
A complex and satisfying porter, smooth and distinctive. Sweetness, roast malt and fruit feature in the palate, with bitter chocolate lingering. The finish is powerfully hoppy.

Umbel Magna (OG 1052, ABV 5%) ⬛
The addition of coriander to the Old Growler wort completes the original 1750s recipe for this distinctive dark beer. The powerful spiciness only adds to this porter's appeal.

NEWBY WYKE

Newby Wyke Brewery, Willoughby Arms Cottages, Station Road, Little Bytham, Lincolnshire, NG33 4RA
Tel/Fax (01780) 411119
Tours by arrangement

⊗ The brewery, named after a Hull trawler skippered by brewer Rob March's grandfather, was set up in a converted garage at his home in Grantham. Brewing started in 1998 with a 2.5-barrel plant. Rob moved in 2001 into purpose-built premises with a 10-barrel brewery and capacity for 30 barrels a week at the Willoughby Arms. 60 outlets are supplied. Stamford Gold (ABV 4.4%) is brewed regularly for the Green Man, Stamford; Lord Willoughby, named after another Hull trawler (ABV 4.8%), and Lord Ancaster (ABV 4.5%) are regular beers for the Willoughby Arms. Seasonal beers: Summer Session (ABV 3.8%, April-Sept), Winter Session (ABV 3.8%, Oct-March), Red Squall (ABV 4.4%, Oct-March), White Sea (ABV 5.2%, April-Sept), Kingston Amber (ABV 5.2%, June-Aug), Distant Grounds IPA (ABV 5.2%, Nov-March), Black Squall Bitter (ABV 4.6%, Oct-March), The Deep (ABV 5.4%, winter), Homeward Bound (ABV 6%, winter). A beer will be brewed for St George's Day.

Sidewinder (OG 1038, ABV 3.8%)

Decade (OG 1039, ABV 4%)

Lord Ancaster (OG 1039, ABV 4%)

Brutus (OG 1039, ABV 4%)

Bardia (OG 1039, ABV 4%)

Slingshot (OG 1041, ABV 4.2%)

Slipway (OG 1041, ABV 4.2%)

Bear Island (OG 1044, ABV 4.6%)

White Squall (OG 1045, ABV 4.8%)

NEWTONMORE & KINGUSSIE

⬚ **Newtonmore & Kingussie Brewery Ltd, Royal Hotel, 29 High Street, Kingussie, Inverness-shire, PH21 1HX**
Tel (01540) 661898
Fax (01540) 661061
E-mail info@kingussieroyal.fsnet.co.uk
Tours by prior arrangement

☺ NKB is a micro-brewery capable of producing five barrels a week. It has been in operation since 2001, having taken over and re-commissioned the Iris Rose Brewery. Two pubs are owned and 10 outlets are supplied.

Highland Mist (OG 1036, ABV 3.6%)

NKB 1 (OG 1038, ABV 4%)

Piper's Brew (OG 1040, ABV 4.2%)

Royale 12 (OG 1043, ABV 4.5%)

NORTH COTSWOLD

North Cotswold Brewery, Ditchford Farm, Moreton-in-Marsh, Glos, GL55 9RD
Tel (01608) 663947
E-mail northcotswold@breathe.com

☺ Brothers David and Roger Tilbrook started brewing in 1999 on a 2.5-barrel plant, bought from the closed Viking Brewery. A new 10-barrel plant was installed in 2000. The brewery is in Warwickshire, despite the Gloucestershire postal address, on the estate of Lord Willoughby De Broke. Two mainstream beers are produced with other seasonals planned and 12 outlets are supplied direct. Seasonal beer: Christmas Special (ABV 4.4%).

Solstice (OG 1037, ABV 3.7%)

Genesis (OG 1038, ABV 4%)

NORTH YORKSHIRE

North Yorkshire Brewing Co, Pinchinthorpe Hall, Pinchinthorpe, Guisborough, TS14 8HG
Tel/Fax (01287) 630200
E-mail nyb@pinchinthorpe.freeserve.co.uk
Website www.pinchinthorpehall.co.uk
Tours by arrangement

The brewery was founded in 1989 and moved in 1998 to Pinchinthorpe Hall, a moated, listed medieval monument near Guisborough that has its own spring water. The site also includes a hotel, restaurant and bistro. More than 100 free trade outlets are currently supplied. In 2002 the brewery converted to organic ingredients for all brews. A special monthly beer is produced together with three beers in the Cosmic range. Bottle-conditioned beers (all organic): Prior's Mild, Best Bitter, Ruby Ale, Boro Best, Golden Ale, Fools Gold, Lord Lees, Flying Herbert.

Prior's Ale *(OG 1036, ABV 3.6%)* ❧
Light, refreshing and surprisingly full-flavoured for a pale, low gravity beer, with a complex, bitter-sweet mixture of malt, hops and fruit carrying through into the aftertaste.

Best Bitter *(OG 1036, ABV 3.6%)*
Clean tasting, well hopped, pale-coloured traditional bitter.

Ruby Ale *(OG 1040, ABV 4%)*
A full-bodied beer with a malty aroma and a balanced malt and hops taste, with vanilla notes.

Boro Best *(OG 1040, ABV 4%)*
Northern-style, full-bodied beer.

Fools Gold *(OG 1046, ABV 4.6%)*
Hoppy, pale-coloured premium beer.

Golden Ale *(OG 1046, ABV 4.6%)* ❧
A well-hopped, lightly-malted, golden premium bitter, using Styrian and Goldings hops.

Flying Herbert *(OG 1047, ABV 4.7%)*
Full-flavoured premium bitter, smooth and well balanced.

Lord Lees *(OG 1047, ABV 4.7%)* ❧
A refreshing, red/brown beer with a hoppy aroma. The flavour is a pleasant balance of roast malt and sweetness that predominates over hops. The malty, bitter finish develops slowly.

NORTHUMBERLAND*

Northumberland Brewery Ltd, Earth Balance, West Sleekburn Farm, Bomarsund, Bedlington, Northumberland, NE22 7AD.
Tel/Fax (01670) 822112
Tours by arrangement

Based on the Earth Balance organic farm and visitor centre, Northumberland stopped brewing in 2002 but was revived in 2003 by new owner Dave Roberts. The brewery tap, the Lake Shore Inn, is an integral part of the project. The beers on sale are not fined with isinglass and are suitable for vegetarians and vegans. There's a folk club and community events at weekends. The brewery also sells to the free trade.

Castles *(ABV 3.8%)*

Reivers *(ABV 3.9%)*

County *(ABV 4%)*

Kitty Brewster *(ABV 4%)*

Bedlington Terrier *(ABV 4.2%)*

GNC *(ABV 4.3%)*

Original Northumberland Ale *(ABV 4.3%)*

Best Bitter *(ABV 4.5%)*

Sheep Dog *(ABV 4.7%)*

Bomar Bitter *(ABV 5%)*

Premium *(ABV 5%)*

NOTTINGHAM SIBA

The Nottingham Brewery, 17 St Peter's St, Radford, Nottingham, NG7 3EN
Tel (0115) 9422649 or 0781 5073447
Fax (0115) 9422649
Website www.nottinghambrewery.com
Shop All merchandise on sale through pub
Tours by arrangement

Formerly Bramcote Brewery, which went into partnership with Tynemill and became Castle Rock. The owners of Bramcote, Niven Balfour and Philip Darby, sold control to Tynemill, bought the name of Nottingham Brewery and built a purpose-built brewery behind their pub, the Plough Inn at Radford. The 10-barrel plant brews a range of beers based on recipes from the former Nottingham Brewery, which was closed by Whitbread in the 1950s. It supplies six outlets.

Rock Ale Mild Beer *(OG 1038, ABV 3.8%)*

Rock Ale Bitter Beer *(OG 1038, ABV 3.8%)*

Legend Best Bitter *(OG 1040, ABV 4%)*

Extra Pale Ale *(OG 1042, ABV 4.2%)*

Dreadnought *(OG 1045, ABV 4.5%)*

Bullion *(OG 1047, ABV 4.7%)*

Sooty Oatmeal Stout *(OG 1048, ABV 4.8%)*

Supreme Pale Amber *(OG 1052, ABV 5.2%)*

NURSERY SIBA

Nursery Brewing Co Ltd, Stockwood Vale, Keynsham, Bristol, BS31 2AL
Tel (0117) 986 1212

Closed, but may re-open. The beers are currently being brewed by Hobden (qv).

O'HANLON'S SIBA

O'Hanlon's Brewing Company Ltd, Great Barton Farm, Whimple, Devon, EX5 2LA
Tel (01404) 822412
Fax (01404) 833700
E-mail info@ohanlons.co.uk
Website www.ohanlons.co.uk
Tours by arrangement, summer weekdays only

Since moving to Whimple in Devon in 2000, O'Hanlon's has gone from strength to strength, winning the SIBA Champion Wheat Beer of Britain for the second time, and gaining a Silver Medal in the World Beer Cup with Port Stout. A recent export contract to America yielded a surprise dividend with the brewery being offered the rights to brew Thomas Hardy's Ale, Royal Oak and Country Bitter for both the bottle and cask market. The plant is being expanded in order to cope with these new products

without detriment to the existing range of fine ales. Some 150 outlets are supplied. Bottle-conditioned beers: Yellow Hammer (ABV 4.5%), Red Ale (ABV 4.5%), Port Stout ▇ (ABV 4.8%), Organic Rye (ABV 5%), Wheat Beer (ABV 4%). Organic Rye (ABV 5%) is suitable for vegetarians and vegans.

Fire Fly *(OG 1035, ABV 3.7%)* ◆
Malty and fruity light bitter. Hints of orange in the taste.

Double Champion Wheat
(OG 1037, ABV 4%) ◆
1999 & 2002 SIBA Champion Wheat Beer of Britain has a fine citrus taste.

Blakeley's Best *(OG 1040, ABV 4.2%)* ◆
Premium ale with complex flavours. Hoppy nose and finish are balanced by a fruity malt taste.

Dry Stout *(OG 1041, ABV 4.2%)* ◆
A dark malty, well-balanced stout with a dry, bitter finish and plenty of roast and fruit flavours up front.

Myrica Ale *(OG 1039, ABV 4.2%)* ◆
The use of honey and bog myrtle for flavour produce a sweet, malty yellow beer with no noticeable bitterness.

Hardy Country Bitter *(OG 1040, ABV 4.2%)*

Yellowhammer *(ABV 4.5%)*
Flavour-packed golden ale.

Port Stout *(OG 1041, ABV 4.8%)* ▇◆
A black beer with a roast malt aroma that remains in the taste but gives way to hoppy bitterness in the aftertaste. Silver Medal, World Beer Cup.

Red Ale *(OG 1044, ABV 4.5%)* ◆
A typical Irish red ale. Well-balanced but fruity with a good, dry, hoppy finish.

Royal Oak *(OG 1048, ABV 5%)*

Organic Rye Beer *(ABV 5%)*
Crisp, with a unique nutty flavour that goes wonderfully with bar food.

Contract brew and bottle for Phoenix Imports, Colorado, US:

Thomas Hardy's Ale *(OG 1125, ABV 12%)*
A world-classic bottle-conditioned Old Ale that will improve in bottle for many years.

OAKHAM SIBA
Oakham Ales, 80 Westgate, Peterborough, Cambs, PE1 2AA Tel (01733) 358300 Fax (01733) 892658

E-mail oakhamales@aol.com
Website www.oakhamales.co.uk
Tours by arrangement

⊠ 2002 was the fifth year in a row when Oakham won awards at the Great British Beer Festival. It also bought the Barton's Arms in Aston, Birmingham, which is on CAMRA's National Inventory. The future is still unclear for the brewery in Peterborough, with a threatened compulsory purchase to make way for re-development of the area. Oakham plans to find future pubs with character to slowly build a pub estate. Between 60 and 100 outlets are supplied. Seasonal beers: Five Leaves Left (ABV 4.5%, October), Harlequin (ABV 4.9%, April), Mompessons Gold (ABV 5%, May-June), Kaleidoscope (ABV 7%, February), Old Tosspot (ABV 5.2%, November), St Bibina (ABV 5.5%, September), Cold Turkey (ABV 6.3%, December).

Jeffrey Hudson Bitter or JHB
(OG 1038, ABV 3.8%) ▇◆
Impressive thirst-quenching yellow bitter with powerful aromatic grapefruity hop character. Mouthfilling grainy palate with a malty sweetness underpinning the hop bitterness. The citrus hop and malt persist as a deep enveloping dryness builds.

White Dwarf Wheat Beer
(OG 1043, ABV 4.3%) ▇◻
Full-bodied yellow-golden beer with a well-defined citrus hop, rounded off with a gentle underlying malty sweetness in the mouth but ending bone-dry with hops holding up well.

Bishops Farewell
(OG 1046, ABV 4.6%) ▇◆
A well-rounded, full-bodied strong bitter, yellow in colour with a strong hoppy aroma joined by floral fruity flavours in the mouth with a grainy background and a dry, fruity finish.

Helterskelter *(OG 1049, ABV 5%)*

OAKHILL
Oakhill Brewery, The Old Maltings, High Street, Oakhill, Radstock, Somerset, BA3 5BX
Tel (01749) 840340
Fax (01749) 840531
E-mail sales@oakhillbrewery.co.uk
Website www.oakhillbrewery.co.uk
Shop Informal, when brewery is open
Tours by arrangement Tue evening, £5.00 per person, max 25 people

⊠ Founded in 1767, Oakhill was a major brewery until 1924, when it closed following a catastrophic fire. The brewery was restarted in 1984 by a local businessman, with the business run for several years by a single brewer-cum-manager. The operation expanded in the early 1990s, taking on more full-time staff and acquiring a number of local pubs. In 1997 it moved from the old brewing site to the refurbished Oakhill Maltings, expanding its capacity to 300 barrels a week. In 2002 the owner received planning permission to develop the maltings site for housing. The future of the brewery is uncertain, as both the brewing business and the malting site are being offered for sale separately. Seasonal beers: Charioteer (ABV 4.2%, March-Sept), Merry Maltings (ABV 4.8%, December).

XXX Mature *(OG 1038, ABV 3.7%)*
A slightly darker beer that replaced Bitter.

Best Bitter *(OG 1040, ABV 4%)* ◆
A clean-tasting, tangy bitter, with a good hop content and citrus fruit and malt balance. Dry finish; light hop aroma. Very quenching.

Black Magic Stout *(OG 1045, ABV 4.5%)* ◆
A black/brown bitter stout with roast malt and a touch of fruit on the nose. Smooth roast malt and bitterness in the taste, with mellow coffee and chocolate.

Mendip Gold *(OG 1045, ABV 4.5%)*

Yeoman 1767 Strong Ale
(OG 1050, ABV 5%) ◆
A strong, pale brown, full-bodied bitter, with a floral hop palate and notable fruitiness. Dry, bitter, lasting finish.

Mendip Twister *(OG 1065, ABV 6.3%)*

OAKLEAF SIBA

Oakleaf Brewing Co Ltd, Unit 7,
Clarence Wharf Industrial Estate,
Mumby Road, Gosport,
Hants, PO12 1AJ
Tel (023) 9251 3222
Fax (023) 9251 0148
E-mail info@oakleafbrewing.co.uk
Website www.oakleafbrewing.co.uk
Tours by arrangement

Oakleaf Brewery

⊗ A family brewery founded in 2000 by Dave Pickersgill and his son-in-law Ed Anderson. Ed was a brewer at a Firkin brew-pub in Southsea before moving to brew for Winchester Ale Houses. Oakleaf Brewery has won awards from local beer festivals. Hole Hearted was voted CAMRA Champion Beer of Hampshire 2002 while Green Gold was Champion Beer of the Festival at Portsmouth in the same year. Oakleaf doesn't own any public houses but has contracts to sell to Innspired Inns. Some 100 outlets are supplied. Seasonal beers: Maypole Mild (ABV 3.8%, Feb-Sept), Stokers Stout (ABV 5%, Oct-Jan), IPA (ABV 5.5%), Blakes Heaven (ABV 7%, December), Green Gold Harvest Ale (ABV 4.3%), I Can't Believe It's Not Bitter (cask-conditioned lager ABV 4.9%). Bottle-conditioned beers: Hole Hearted, Blakes Gosport Bitter.

Farmhouse Ale *(ABV 3.5%)*

Oakleaf Bitter *(ABV 3.8%)*

Nuptu'ale *(ABV 4.2%)*

Squirrel's Delight *(ABV 4.4%)*

Hole Hearted *(ABV 4.7%)*

Blake's Gosport Bitter *(ABV 5.2%)*

OAKWELL

Oakwell Brewery, Pontefract Road,
Barnsley, South Yorkshire, ST1 1YX
Tel (01226) 296161 Fax (01226) 771457

☻ Brewing started in 1997, with plans for expansion. Oakwell supplies some 30 outlets.

Barnsley Bitter *(OG 1036, ABV 3.8%)*

ODCOMBE

⬭ Odcombe Ales, The Masons Arms,
41 Lower Odcombe, nr Yeovil,
Somerset, BA22 8TX
Tel (01935) 862591
E-mail charteris@odcombe41.freeserve.co.uk
Tours by arrangement

⊗ Oakham is a one-barrel plant installed in 2000 to produce beer for the pub. Originally it was anticipated that a brew a fortnight would be sufficient but the plant is now producing three beers with occasional specials. Brewing takes place three times a fortnight. The beers are occasionally found at local festivals. Seasonal beers: Buzz (ABV 4%, summer), Somerset (September), Donkey Path (ABV 5.4%, Christmas).

Lower Odcombe Ale *(OG 1040.5, ABV 4%)*
A golden ale, dry hopped and bitter.

Donne Lane *(OG 1042, ABV 4.2%)*

Higher Odcombe *(OG 1046, ABV 4.5%)*
Amber bitter with a fruit palate and a dry, hoppy finish.

OKELLS SIBA

Okell & Son Ltd, Kewaigue, Douglas,
Isle of Man, IM2 1QG
Tel (01624) 699400
Fax (01624) 624253
E-mail mac@okells.co.uk
Website www.okells.co.uk
Tours by arrangement

☻ Founded in 1874 by Dr Okell and formerly trading as Isle of Man Breweries, this is the main brewery on the island, having taken over and closed the rival Castletown Brewery in 1986. The brewery moved in 1994 to a new, purpose-built plant at Kewaigue. All the beers are produced under the Manx Brewers' Act 1874 (permitted ingredients: water, malt, sugar and hops only). All of the company's 55 pubs sell real ale and more than 70 free trade outlets are also supplied. Occasional beers: Castletown Bitter (ABV 4%), Manx Cat (ABV 4%), Wheel Ale (ABV 4.2%), Spring Ram (ABV 4.2%), Poleaxed (ABV 4.2%), Autumn Dawn (ABV 4.2%), Chequered Flag (ABV 4.2%), Summer Storm (ABV 4.2%), Hoptunaa (ABV 4.2%), Olde Skipper (ABV 4.5%), St Nick (ABV 4.5%), Falcon Strong Ale (ABV 5%).

Mild *(OG 1034, ABV 3.4%)* ◆
A genuine, well-brewed mild ale, with a fine aroma of hops and crystal malt. Reddish-brown in colour, this beer has a full malt flavour with surprising bitter hop notes and a hint of blackcurrants and oranges. Full, malty finish.

Bitter *(OG 1035, ABV 3.7%)*
A golden beer, malty and superbly hoppy in aroma, with a hint of honey. Rich and

malty on the tongue, it has a wonderful, dry, malt and hop finish. A complex but rewarding beer.

Heart-Throb *(OG 1042, ABV 4.5%)*

OLD BEAR

Old Bear Brewery, 6 Keighley Road, Cross Hills, Keighley, West Yorkshire, BD20 7RN
Tel/Fax (01535) 637451
E-mail sales@oldbearbrewery.com
Website www.oldbearbrewery.com
Tours by arrangement

☺ The brewery – originally Old White Bear – was founded in 1993 by former Goose Eye brewer Bryan Eastell, and was taken over by the Naylor family, who appointed Ian Cowling as brewer. The brewery is unusual as it is operated in property owned by Enterprise Inns, whose tie limits the beers on sale. The Naylors are seeking larger premises. Seven regular outlets are supplied.

Original *(OG 1038, ABV 3.9%)* ◆
A refreshing and easy-to-drink bitter. The balance of malt and hops gives way to a short, dry, bitter aftertaste.

Hibernator *(OG 1049, ABV 5%)*

OLD CANNON

Old Cannon Brewery Ltd, 86 Cannon Street, Bury St Edmunds, Suffolk, IP33 1JR
Tel (01284) 768769
Fax (01284) 701137
E-mail rej@btinternet.com
Website www.oldcannon.co.uk
Tours by arrangement

⊗ St Edmunds Head pub opened in 1845 with its own brewery. Brewing ceased in 1917, and Greene King closed the pub in 1995. It re-opened in 1999 complete with unique state-of-the-art brewery housed in the bar area. There are plans for bottling, further off-sales, more seasonal beers and the acquisition of a further pub. Seasonal beers: Black Pig (ABV 4.5%, winter), Old Chestnut (ABV 4.4%, autumn), Spring Ale (ABV 4.5%, spring), Summer Ale (ABV 4.2%, summer).

Best Bitter *(OG 1040, ABV 3.8%)* ◆
An excellent session bitter brewed using Styrian Goldings, giving a crisp grapefruit aroma and taste. Very refreshing and full of flavour.

Powder Monkey *(OG 1047, ABV 4.7%)*

Gunner's Daughter
(OG 1052, ABV 5.5%) ◆
A well-balanced strong ale with a complexity of hop, fruit, sweetness and bitterness in the flavour, and a lingering pleasant hoppy, bitter aftertaste.

OLD CHIMNEYS

Old Chimneys Brewery, The Street, Market Weston, Diss, Norfolk, IP22 2NZ (office). Brewery: Hopton End Farm, Church Road, Market Weston, Diss, Norfolk, IP22 2NX
Tel Office (01359) 221411 Brewery (01359) 221013
Fax (01359) 221843
Shop Open Fri 2-7pm, Sat 10am-1pm
Tours by arrangement

⊗ A craft brewery opened in 1995 by former Vaux/Greene King/Broughton brewer Alan Thomson. In 2001 the brewery moved to larger premises in a converted farm building in the same village. Despite the postal address, the brewery is in Suffolk. The beers produced are mostly named after endangered local species. Four bottle-conditioned beers are also brewed. Old Chimneys currently supplies 30 outlets. Seasonal beers: Polecat Porter (ABV 4.2%, winter), Black Rat Stout (ABV 4.4%, winter), Golden Pheasant (ABV 4.7%, summer), Natterjack Premium Ale (ABV 5%, winter), Winter Cloving (ABV 7.2%, winter), Corn Cleavers Ale (ABV 4.3%, spring/summer). Bottle-conditioned beers: Greenshank Organic (ABV 7%), Brimstone Lager (ABV 6.5%), Redshank Strong Ale (ABV 8.7%), Good King Henry Imperial Stout (ABV 9.6%), Great Raft Bitter (ABV 4.3%), Golden Pheasant (ABV 4.9%), Natterjack Premium Ale (ABV 5.4%). All bottle- conditioned beers are suitable for vegetarians and vegans.

Military Mild
(OG 1035, ABV 3.3%) ◆
A rich, dark mild with good body for its gravity. Sweetish toffee and light roast bitterness dominate, leading to a dry aftertaste.

Galingale *(OG 1041, ABV 3.9%)* ◆
This amber gold bitter has excellent body allied to a clean and refreshing character. Hops, malt and fruit combine to give a well-balanced, bitter-sweet flavour with hop in the early aftertaste, followed by a pleasing dry finish.

Great Raft Bitter
(OG 1043, ABV 4.2%)
Complex and satisfying for its gravity, this pale copper bitter is bursting with fruit throughout. Malt and hops add to the sweetish fruity flavour, which is nicely rounded off with hoppy bitterness in the aftertaste.

OLD COTTAGE

Burton Old Cottage Beer Co, Unit 9, Eccleshall Industrial Estate, Hawkins Lane, Burton-on-Trent, Staffs, DE14 1PT
Tel 07780 900006
Fax (01283) 511615
E-mail kevinjs@tesco.net
Tours by arrangement

⊗ Old Cottage was installed in the Heritage Brewery. When the site was taken over, Kevin Slater was evicted and set up in a modern industrial unit. Due to growth in sales, he has now moved to a larger unit in the same yard. He purchased his first pub in 2001. Six other outlets are supplied.

Oak *(OG 1040, ABV 4%)*

Stout *(OG 1047, ABV 4.7%)* ◆
Black but not heavy! Full roast aroma with hints of liquorice and chocolate malt; the roast flavours linger to a bitter finish.

Halcyon Daze
(OG 1050, ABV 5.3%) ◆
Strong, dark and full bodied, with hops, fruit and malt.

OLD KENT

Old Kent Brewery Ltd, 11-13 Western Road, Borough Green, Sevenoaks, Kent, TN15 8AL

Old Kent closed in summer 2003. Some of the beers are now produced by Grand Union (qv).

OLD LAXEY

Old Laxey Brewing Co, The Shore Hotel, Old Laxey, Isle of Man, IM4 7DA
Tel (01624) 861509
E-mail shore@advsys.co.uk
Website www.welcome.to/shorehotel
Tours by arrangement

The brewery was designed and constructed in 1997 by Peter Austin, the renowned 'father' of micro-brewing and founder of Ringwood Brewery. The five-barrel plant can be seen through the brewery bar. Various outlets on the island and in Britain are supplied.

Bosun Bitter *(OG 1038, ABV 3.8%)*
Crisp and fresh with a hoppy aftertaste.

OLD LUXTERS

See Chiltern Valley

OLD MILL

Old Mill Brewery, Mill Street, Snaith, East Yorkshire, DN14 9HU
Tel (01405) 861813 Fax (01405) 862789
Website www.oldmillbrewery.co.uk
Tours by arrangement to organisations only

Old Mill is a small craft brewery opened in 1983 in a 200-year-old former malt kiln and corn mill. A new brewhouse was installed in 1991 to increase the brew-length to 60 barrels. The brewery is building its tied estate (now 15 houses). The innovation of selling beer in plastic, non-returnable handicasks has meant that the beer can now be found nationwide. Around 80 free trade outlets are supplied direct from the brewery. A bottling plant installed in 1997 sees occasional use. Seasonal beers: Black Jack (ABV 5%, January), Cupid's Kiss (ABV 4.2%, February), Springs Eternal (ABV 4%, March), St George (ABV 4.2%, April), Willow Wood (ABV 4.2%, May), Old Man's Ale (ABV 4.1%, June), Summer Sunshine (ABV 4%, July), Nellie Dene (ABV 3.7%, August), Autumn Breezes (ABV 4.2%, September), Halloween Surprise (ABV 3.9%, October), Winter Warmer (ABV 4.5%, November), Midnight Moonshine (ABV 4.5%, December).

Mild *(OG 1034, ABV 3.4%)*
A satisfying roast malt flavour dominates this easy-drinking, quality dark mild.

Bitter *(OG 1038.5, ABV 3.9%)*
A malty nose is carried through to its initial flavour. Bitterness runs throughout.

Old Curiosity *(OG 1044.5, ABV 4.5%)*
Slightly sweet amber brew, malty to start with. Malt flavours all the way through.

Bullion *(OG 1047.5, ABV 4.7%)*
The malty and hoppy aroma is followed by a neat mix of hop and fruit tastes within an enveloping maltiness. Dark brown/amber in colour.

OLD STABLES*

The Old Stables Brewing Company, Sir William Peel, 39 High Street, Sandy, Beds, SG19 1AG.
Tel (Pub) (01767) 680607
(Office/Fax) (01767) 692151

A venture between pub landlord Dermot Hehir, who has since died, and regular customer Bob Trenholme. The pub will be run by Lindsey Hehir, wife of Dermot, and the brewery will be run by Bob. More beers will be added.

Stable Ale Best Bitter
(OG 1040, ABV 4.2%)

OLDE SWAN

Olde Swan Brewery, 87-89 Halesowen Road, Netherton, Dudley, West Midlands, DY2 9PY
Tel (01384) 253075
Shop Ask at bar
Tours by arrangement

The welcome return of a once-famous and much-loved brew-pub, best known in the old days as 'Ma Pardoe's', after the matriarch who ruled it for years. The pub has been licensed since 1835 and the present brewery and pub were built in 1863. Brewing continued until 1988, and restarted in 2001. The plant brews primarily for the on-site pub with some beer available to the trade. Some 15-20 outlets are supplied direct. Seasonal beer: Black Widow (ABV 6.7%, winter).

Original *(OG 1034, ABV 3.5%)*

Dark Swan *(OG 1041, ABV 4.2%)*
A rich dark mild full of flavour.

Entire *(OG 1043, ABV 4.4%)*
A premium bitter beer.

Bumblehole *(OG 1052, ABV 5.2%)*

OLD WHEELTON

Old Wheelton Brewery, Dressers Arms, Briers Brow, Wheelton, Chorley, Lancs, PR6 8HD
Tel (01254) 830041
Fax (01254) 832899
E-mail dressers.arms@virgin.net
Tours by arrangement

Brewing started at the Dresser's Arms in 2001. A purpose-built, two-barrel plant is situated in the brewery, built next to the pub with a glass-panelled viewing area behind the bar. The beers are currently only supplied to the Dresser's Arms and local beer festivals. Seasonal beer: Winterbrew (ABV 4.5%).

Big Frank's Bitter *(OG 1041, ABV 4.1%)*

Just a Flyer *(OG 1042, ABV 4.2%)*

Milk of Amnesia *(OG 1044, ABV 4.4%)*

OLDERSHAW SIBA

Oldershaw Brewery, 12 Harrowby Hall Estate, Grantham, Lincs, NG31 9HB
Tel (01476) 572135
Fax (01476) 572193
E-mail goldbrew@lineone.net
Website www.oldershawbrewery.co.uk
Tours by arrangement

⊗ Experienced home-brewer Gary Oldershaw and his wife Diane set up the brewery at their home in 1997. Grantham's first brewery for 30 years, Oldershaw now supplies 60 local free houses. It concentrates on supplying outlets direct and is enjoying steady growth. A third fermenting vessel was added in 1999 to increase capacity to 20 barrels a week. The Oldershaws plan to introduce some small-scale bottling, to include Old Boy, Yuletide, Royal Blonde and Grantham Stout. Seasonal beers: Sunnydaze (ABV 4%, summer wheat beer, May-Aug), Topers Tipple (ABV 4.5%, Nov-Feb), Yuletide (ABV 5.2%, Nov-Dec).

Mowbrays Mash (*OG 1037, ABV 3.7%*)

High Dyke (*OG 1039, ABV 3.9%*)
Golden and moderately bitter. A predominantly hoppy session beer.

Newton's Drop (*OG 1041, ABV 4.1%*) ◗
Balanced malt and hops but with a strong bitter, lingering taste in this mid-brown beer.

Ermine Ale (*OG 1042, ABV 4.2%*)
Golden brown with a fruity hop dominant feature on nose and taste giving a bitterness that lasts; malt plays a supporting role.

Caskade (*OG 1042, ABV 4.2%*)
Pale, golden beer brewed with American Cascade hops to give a distinctive floral, hoppy flavour and aroma, and a clean lasting finish.

Grantham Stout (*OG 1043, ABV 4.3%*) ▣
Dark brown and smooth with rich roast malt flavour, supported by some fruit and bitterness. A long, moderately dry finish.

Ahtanum Gold (*OG 1043, ABV 4.3%*)
A gold-coloured, fruity, hoppy beer balanced with some maltiness. Moderately bitter.

Regal Blonde (*OG 1043, ABV 4.4%*) ◗
Straw-coloured lager-style beer with a good malt/hop balance throughout; strong bitterness on the taste lingers.

Isaac's Gold (*OG 1044, ABV 4.5%*)

Old Boy (*OG 1047, ABV 4.8%*) ◗
A full-bodied amber ale, fruity and bitter with a hop/fruit aroma. The malt that backs the taste dies in the long finish.

ORGANIC SIBA

Organic Brewhouse, Unit 1, Higher Bochym Workshops, Cury Cross Lanes, Helston, Cornwall, TR12 7AZ
Tel (01326) 241555
Fax (01326) 241188
E-mail a.hamer@btclick.com
Tours by arrangement

⊗ Established by Andy Hamer in 2000, the brewery is dedicated to supplying exclusively organic beer, using its own source of natural mineral water. Laid out as a mini 'tower' system, production has increased to five regular beers. About 20 local outlets are supplied regularly, and the beers occasionally head north with wholesalers. Lizard Point won its class at St Ives Beer Festival 2000, as did Serpentine at Doncaster Beer Festival 2002. All the beers are also available bottle-conditioned and all are suitable for vegetarians.

Halzephron Gold (*OG 1033, ABV 3.6%*)

Lizard Point (*OG 1038, ABV 4%*)

Serpentine Dark Ale (*OG 1042, ABV 4.5%*)

Black Rock (*OG 1044, ABV 4.7%*)

Wolf Rock (*OG 1047, ABV 5%*)

ORKNEY SIBA

Orkney Brewery Ltd, Quoyloo, Sandwick, Orkney, KW16 3LT
Tel (01856) 841802
Fax (01856) 841754
E-mail beer@orkneybrewery.co.uk
Website www.orkneybrewery.co.uk

⊛ Set up in 1988 in an old school building by former licensee Roger White, the brewery was completely modernised in 1995 with new buildings replacing a single cramped room. The brewery is run along strict ecological lines with its own water supply and unique effluent control system. There are plans for a new fermenting room/visitor centre if funds will allow. 30 outlets are served and the beers are available nationwide via wholesalers. Occasional beer: White Christmas (ABV 5%, December).

Raven Ale (*OG 1038, ABV 3.8%*) ◗
Both citrus and hedgerow fruits are evident in this golden brown, quaffable bitter. Hops balance the sweetish taste and carry through to the satisfying dry, bitter finish.

Northern Light (*OG 1040, ABV 4%*) ◗
A lager-coloured beer, hoppy and refreshing. Fruity hop notes can develop a true lager nose. A late copper hop is intense without being cloying.

Dragonhead Stout (*OG 1040, ABV 4%*) ▣◗
A strong, dark malt aroma flows into the taste in this superb Scottish stout. The roast malt continues to dominate the aftertaste, and blends with chocolate to develop a strong, dry finish. Hard to find.

Red MacGregor (*OG 1040, ABV 4%*) ▣▣◗
A very well-balanced bitter with malt and hops predominating throughout. This tawny red ale also has a powerful smack of fruit and has a clean, fresh mouthfeel. Another thoroughbred from a successful stable.

Dark Island (*OG 1045, ABV 4.6%*) ▣◗
Well-balanced and full of malt, roast and fruit, with just a hint of caramel. A sweetish taste leads to a long-lasting roasted, slightly bitter finish. A full-bodied and deceptively drinkable old ale.

Skullsplitter *(OG 1080, ABV 8.5%)* 🍺🏠🔨
An intense velvet malt nose with hints of apple, nutmeg and spice. Hops to the fore balanced by satiny smooth malt with fruity spicy edges leading to a long dry finish with a hint of nut. Champion Winter Beer of Britain 2001.

OSSETT SIBA

**Ossett Brewing Company Ltd,
t/a Ossett Brewery, Low Mill Road,
Ossett, West Yorkshire, WF5 8ND
Tel (01924) 261333
Fax (01924) 261356
E-mail brewery@ossett.co.uk
Website Ossett-brewery.co.uk**
Tours by arrangement

⊗ Brewing started in 1998 at the rear of the Brewers Pride public house. The purpose-built brewery is wholly owned by Robert Lawson, an ex-Tetley brewer. When sales rose to 20 barrels a week, new fermenters were installed in mid-2000, increasing capacity to 35 barrels. Further expansion is due and bottled beers will be introduced. Direct delivery is made to more than 100 outlets and others through selected wholesalers. Excelsior was voted Supreme Champion of Great Britain at the SIBA Beer Competition in April 2003. Ossett is exporting beer to Japan and has opened its first pub, the Black Bull in Liversedge. Seasonal Beers: Silver Fox (ABV 4.1%, spring), Silver Link (ABV 4.6%, summer), Ace of Spades Porter (ABV 4.5%, winter), Ruby Mild (ABV 4.2%, autumn), Oregon Pale (ABV 4.7%, Sept-Oct), Hercules (ABV 6.5%, Jan-March), Winter Warmer (ABV 6%, Dec-March).

Pale Gold *(OG 1038, ABV 3.8%)*
A light, refreshing pale ale with a floral/spicy aroma derived from American hops.

Silver Shadow *(OG 1038, ABV 3.9%)*
A pale session beer of considerable character despite its low gravity. The first Ossett brew to use eco-friendly English hedgerow hops.

Silver King *(OG 1041, ABV 4.3%)*
A lager-style beer with a crisp, dry flavour and citrus fruity aroma.

Dazzler *(OG 1044, ABV 4.5%)*
A delicately-flavoured pale ale. The smooth, slightly spicy aroma is derived from use of classic English Goldings hops.

Fine Fettle *(OG 1048, ABV 4.8%)*
A strong yet refreshing pale ale with a crisp clean flavour and citrus fruity aroma.

Excelsior *(OG 1051, ABV 5.2%)*
A mellow yet full flavour that develops into fruity dryness on the palate. A fresh, hoppy aroma with citrus, toffee and floral characteristics.

OTTER

**Otter Brewery Ltd, Mathayes,
Luppitt, Honiton, Devon, EX14 4SA
Tel (01404) 891285 Fax (01404) 891124
E-mail info@otterbrewery.com
Website www.otterbrewery.com**
Tours by arrangement

⊗ The Otter Brewery was established in 1990 by David and Mary Ann McCaig. The brewery is located in the Blackdown Hills, between Taunton and Honiton, and makes the most of the local spring water that feeds the River Otter. David had previously brewed with Whitbread for 17 years and Mary Ann's family have been brewers for a number of generations. Steady growth over the years has resulted in a new brewery being commissioned in July 2003. Today, still maintaining its family roots, the brewery employs local friends and family and delivers Otter beers to more than 200 outlets within a 40-mile radius across the West Country.

Bitter *(OG 1036, ABV 3.6%)* 🏠🔨
Well-balanced amber session bitter with a fruity nose and bitter taste and aftertaste.

Bright *(OG 1039, ABV 4.3%)* 🔨
Fruit and hop aroma in a straw-coloured bitter with a strong bitter finish.

Ale *(OG 1043, ABV 4.5%)* 🏠🔨
Full-bodied best bitter. Malty aroma and taste predominate with a fruity taste and finish.

Head *(OG 1054, ABV 5.8%)*
Fruity aroma and taste with a pleasant bitter finish. Dark brown and full-bodied.

OULTON

**Oulton Ales Ltd, Lake Lothing Brewery,
Harbour Road, Oulton Broad, Lowestoft,
Suffolk, NR32 3LZ
Tel (01502) 587905
E-mail wayne@oultonales.co.uk**
Tours by arrangement

⊗ In December 2001, Green Jack changed to Oulton Ales and in 2002 director Tim Dunford left the brewery. The pumpclips were re-designed and several new names were chosen to reflect the nautical history of Oulton Broad and Lowestoft. Plans for the future are to enlarge the brewery plant and increase availability of bottles. 20 outlets are supplied as well as its own three pubs. Bottle-conditioned beers: Nautilus, Gone Fishing, Roaring Boy. Sunset and Bedazzled are suitable for vegetarians and vegans.

Oulton Bitter *(OG 1037, ABV 3.5%)*

Nutford Mild *(OG 1038, ABV 3.7%)*

Sunrise *(OG 1040, ABV 4%)*

Bedazzled *(OG 1040, ABV 4%)*

Nautilus *(OG 1042, ABV 4.2%)*

Sunset *(OG 1041, ABV 4.2%)*

Wet and Windy *(OG 1044, ABV 4.3%)*

Windswept *(OG 1044, ABV 4.5%)*

Excelsior *(OG 1045, ABV 4.6%)*

Gone Fishing *(OG 1049, ABV 5%)*

Keelhaul *(OG 1060, ABV 6.5%)*

Roaring Boy *(OG 1075, ABV 8.5%)*

OXFORD*

**Oxford Brewery Ltd, PO Box 256,
Kidlington, Oxon, OX5 2FR
Tel (01865) 841 839
E-mail info@oxfordbrewery.com
Website www.oxfordbrewery.com**

Oxford Brewery opened in 2002 with a two-barrel brew length. It is run by Will Eckhert from Toronto, Canada. He supplies pubs mainly in and around Oxford, though the beer has been seen farther afield via wholesalers. The two beers, Bitter and Draught, are meant to be examples of Thames Valley style ales, to help preserve this now endangered species. Some 20 outlets are served direct. The beers contain isinglass finings.

Bitter *(OG 1040, ABV 3.9%)*

Draught Ale *(OG 1044, ABV 4.4%)*

PACIFIC ORIENTAL SIBA

⌷ **Pacific Oriental, 1 Bishopsgate, London, EC2N 3AB**
Tel (020) 7621 9988

Pacific Oriental is a state-of-the-art boutique brewery based in the heart of the City of London. Brewing started in 1998 and the permanent brews are a Pilsner lager and a bitter with at least one other beer always on offer. These include a wheat beer, a golden ale and a red beer. The copper brewhouse is on full display at the front of the restaurant. The beers are filtered and served by mixed gas dispense. Beers: Bishops (ABV 4.5%), Pils (ABV 5%).

PACKHORSE

Packhorse Brewing Co Ltd, 5 Somers Road, Southsea, Portsmouth, Hampshire, PO5 4PR
Tel (02392) 750450
Fax (02392) 733350

Packhorse Brewery was resurrected in Portsmouth from the former Ashford Brewery. It started as a lager brewery and the present five-barrel equipment was acquired from the Flamingo & Firkin in Kingston, Surrey. The brewer retired in 2003 and a replacement had not been found when the guide went to press. As a result, the brewery is not currently operating.

Southern Star *(OG 1038, ABV 3.8%)*

Old Pompey *(OG 1046, ABV 4.8%)*

PALMER IFBB SIBA

JC & RH Palmer Ltd, The Old Brewery, Bridport, Dorset, DT6 4JA
Tel (01308) 422396 Fax (01308) 421149
E-mail enquiries@palmersbrewery.com
Website www.palmersbrewery.com
Shop Mon-Sat, 9-6 BST, Fri-Sat 9-8
Tours by arrangement (01308) 427500

⊠ Palmers Brewery has enjoyed sustained growth in real ale sales in the past two years and has continued to invest in the tenanted pubs, specially in ale dispense. The company has increased the pub estate when the opportunities have arisen. IPA is still the flagship beer, which has been supported by Copper Ale (launched Autumn 2001) and Dorset Gold (re-launched at a higher ABV in spring 2002). Some 56 pubs are owned and a further 200 outlets are supplied direct.

Bridport Bitter *(OG 1030, ABV 3.2%)* ❧
A light beer with a hoppy aroma, a bitter hoppy taste with some malt, and a bitter aftertaste.

Copper Ale *(OG 1036, ABV 3.7%)* ❧
Well-balanced session ale. Gentle fruit and caramel on the nose lead through a sweetish taste with hop bitterness developing.

IPA *(OG 1040, ABV 4.2%)* ❧
A deep copper beer that is hoppy and bitter throughout. Fruit and malt undertones give some balance in the aroma and taste, and there is a lingering bitter aftertaste.

Dorset Gold *(OG 1046, ABV 4.5%)*

200 *(OG 1052, ABV 5%)* ❧
Full-bodied, caramel sweetness and fruity aroma are balanced with a dry finish, not excessively bitter; a deep-copper ale, originally brewed to mark the brewery's 200th anniversary.

Tally Ho! *(OG 1057, ABV 5.5%)*

PARADISE SIBA

Paradise Brewery, 2 Creamery Industrial Estate, Wrenbury, Nantwich, Cheshire, CW5 8EX
Tel/Fax (01270) 780916

☺ Paradise was founded by partners John Wood and Nick Platt, who traded as Paradise Plastics and turned to brewing when there was a recession in the plastics industry. The brewery is based in a former creamery.

Marbury Mild *(ABV 3.6%)*

Shunter Best Bitter *(ABV 4%)*

Promised Land *(ABV 4.2%)*

Paradise Gold *(ABV 4.5%)*

Dabbers Gold *(ABV 5%)*

PARISH

⌷ **Parish Brewery, Courtyard of the Old Brewery Inn, Somerby, Leicestershire, LE14 2PZ**
Tel (01664) 454801
Shop Open noon-3pm & 7-11pm
Tours by arrangement

☺ Parish started life at Burrough on the Hill in 1982 and moved to its present location after expanding to a 20-barrel plant in 1992. The Parish Brewery was one of the first brew-pubs to start up in the Midlands and is famous for brewing the strongest beer in the world, with an ABV of 23%, as listed in the

Guinness Book of World Records. It has now been trading for 20 years and is not looking to expansion. Plans for the future are to help set up more brew-pubs. One pub is owned and Parish supplies 10 local outlets. Bottle-conditioned: Parish Special Bitter (ABV 4.3%), Baz's Bonce Blower (ABV 11%).

Mild *(OG 1039, ABV 3.9%)*

Parish Special Bitter or PSB
(OG 1039-42, ABV 4.2%)

Farm Gold *(OG 1043, ABV 4.3%)*

Somerby Premium *(OG 1043, ABV 4.3%)*

Poachers Ale *(OG 1060, ABV 6%)*

Baz's Bonce Blower *(OG 1100, ABV 11.5%)*

PHOENIX

Phoenix Brewery, Green Lane, Heywood, Greater Manchester, OL10 2EP
Tel (01706) 627009 Fax (01706) 623235
E-mail beer@phoenixbrewery.sagehost.co.uk

☺ A company established as Oak Brewery in 1982 at Ellesmere Port, it moved in 1991 to Heywood and changed its name in 1996 to Phoenix (after the original name of the brewery it occupies). It now supplies more than 450 free trade outlets mostly in the North-west and West Yorkshire. At the International Brewing Awards 2002, it achieved two out of three gold medals available in the Draught Beer Class (Navvy and Wobbly Bob). Seasonal beers: Black Shadow (ABV 4%, April-May), Flashflood (ABV 4.1%, Oct-Dec), Rip-Rap (ABV 4.1%, Oct-Nov), Jovian (ABV 4.2%, Jan-Feb), Snowbound (ABV 4.3%, Oct-Feb), Shamrock (ABV 4.3%, Feb-March), White Tornado (ABV 4.3%, Sept-Oct), March Hare (ABV 4.4%, Feb-March), May Fly (ABV 4.4%, April-May), Christmas Kiss (ABV 4.5%, Nov-Dec), Midsummer Madness (ABV 4.5%, May-Aug), Tennis Elbow (ABV 4.5%, May-Jun), Last Leaf (ABV 4.5%, Sept-Nov), Uncle Fester (ABV 4.5%, Oct-Nov), Sticky Wicket (ABV 4.7%, May-Aug), Struggling Monkey (ABV 4.7%, Sept-Oct), Fire Cracker (ABV 4.7%, Oct-Nov), Spooky Brew (ABV 4.7%, Oct-Nov), Porter (ABV 5%, Oct-Jan), Golden Glow (ABV 6.5%, Nov-Dec), Humbug (ABV 7%, Nov-Dec).

Bantam *(ABV 3.5%)* ◆
Light brown beer with a fruity aroma. Balance of malt, citrus fruit and hop in taste. Hoppy, bitter finish.

Navvy *(ABV 3.8%)*

Monkeytown Mild *(ABV 3.9%)*

Best Bitter *(ABV 3.9%)*

Arizona *(ABV 4.1%)* ▣◆
Yellow in colour with a fruity and hoppy aroma. A refreshing beer with citrus, hop and good bitterness, and a shortish dry aftertaste.

Pale Moonlight *(ABV 4.2%)*

Black Bee *(ABV 4.5%)*

White Monk *(ABV 4.5%)*

Old Oak Ale *(ABV 4.5%)* ◆
A well-balanced, brown beer with a multitude of mellow fruit flavours. Malt and hops balance the strong fruitiness in the aroma and taste, and the finish is malty, fruity and dry.

Thirsty Moon *(ABV 4.6%)*
Fruity, malty aroma to this amber beer. Malt, fruit and bitter taste and a dry, hoppy finish.

Double Dagger *(ABV 5%)* ◆
A pale brown, malty brew, more pleasantly dry and light than its gravity would suggest. Moderately fruity throughout; a hoppy bitterness in the mouth balances the strong graininess.

Double Gold *(ABV 5%)*

Wobbly Bob *(ABV 6%)* ◆
A red/brown beer with a malty, fruity aroma. Strongly malty and fruity in flavour and quite hoppy, with the sweetness yielding to a dryness in the aftertaste.

PICKS

Picks Brewery, Red Lion Hotel, Willows Lane, Green Haworth, Accrington, Lancashire, BB5 3SJ
Tel (01254) 233194
Tours by arrangement

☺ The brewery was originally based in 1998 in the cellar of the Red Lion pub in Green Haworth using home-made equipment, but in 2000 it moved into a nearby industrial unit, converting five-barrel beer tanks to make hot liquor tank, mash tun, copper, one fermenter and two conditioning tanks. Owner Steven Pickles has started supplying the free trade, with just some local outlets. Six regular beers are produced and he plans to produce a real lager for the summer.

Moorgate Mild *(OG 1035, ABV 3.5%)*
A smooth, grainy, chocolate and coffee cream mild. Red-brown in colour, it is not oversweet, with a long, gently hopped aftertaste.

Pale Ale *(OG 1036, ABV 3.7%)*
Soft lemon and honey notes at the beginning, with a lingering bitter-dry end. A straw-coloured refreshing pint.

Bedlam Bitter *(OG 1038, ABV 3.9%)*
Complex sour and barley sugar flavours. Astringent throughout, pepper-dry at the end. A red-gold bitter.

Lions Main *(OG 1041, ABV 4.2%)*

Porter *(OG 1042, ABV 4.5%)*
Impenetrably dark beer, it has an immediate strong black coffee flavour, leading to a dry finish. A pronounced, teeth-coating maltiness throughout.

Lions Pride *(OG 1049, ABV 5.4%)*
A pale premium bitter, strong but sweet and deceptively easy-drinking. Golden in colour, it builds to a malty finish.

PICTISH

Pictish Brewing Company, Unit 9, Canalside Industrial Estate, Woodbine Street East, Rochdale, Lancs, OL16 5LB
Tel/Fax (01706) 522227
Website www.pictish-brewing.co.uk
Tours by arrangement

☺ The brewery was established in 2000 by Richard Sutton, formerly senior brewer for the north with the Firkin Brewery until Punch Taverns took over the former Allied

Domecq estate and closed the Firkin chain in 1999. The brewery supplies free trade outlets in the North-west. Seasonal beers: Summer Solstice (ABV 4.7%, May-Aug), Porter (4.4%, Nov-March). There are regular monthly beers.

Brewers Gold *(OG 1038, ABV 3.8%)* ◆
Yellow in colour, with a hoppy, fruity nose. Soft maltiness and a strong hoppy/citrus flavour lead to a dry, bitter finish.

Celtic Warrior *(OG 1042, ABV 4.2%)* ◆
Tawny beer with malt and hops dominant in aroma and taste. Good bitter finish.

For Crown Inn, Bacup:

Bare Arts *(OG 1035, ABV 3.5%)*

IBA *(OG 1050, ABV 5%)*

PILGRIM SIBA

**Pilgrim Ales, The Old Brewery,
West Street, Reigate, Surrey, RH2 9BL
Tel (01737) 222651
Fax (01737) 225785
E-mail david@pilgrim.co.uk
Website www.pilgrim.co.uk**

Set up by Dave Roberts in 1982, and based in Reigate since 1985, Pilgrim has gradually increased its capacity and its beers have won both local and national awards, although sales are mostly concentrated in the Surrey area (around 60 outlets). Pilgrim owns one tied house, the Rising Sun, Epsom. Seasonal beers: Autumnal (ABV 4.5%, Sept-Oct), Excalibur (ABV 4.5%, March-May), Pudding (ABV 7.3%, Nov-Jan). Bottle-conditioned beers: Springbock (ABV 5.2%, brewed by Hepworth of Horsham), Pudding (ABV 6.8%). The draught version of Springbock, originally cask-conditioned, is now a pressurised keg beer.

Surrey Bitter *(OG 1037, ABV 3.7%)* ◆
Grapefruit and spicy aromas in a well-balanced session beer. Initial maltiness gives way to bitterness that becomes more pronounced in a refreshing finish.

Porter *(OG 1040, ABV 4%)* ◆
Black beer with a good balance of dark malts with hints of berry fruit. Roast character present throughout to give a bitter-sweet finish.

Progress *(OG 1040, ABV 4%)* ◆
A well-rounded, copper-coloured, malty best bitter that can be cloying. Medium-bodied with a subdued bitterness. The aftertaste dissipates quickly.

Crusader *(OG 1049, ABV 4.9%)*

Talisman *(OG 1049, ABV 5%)* ◆
A strong ale with a tawny red colour. Little aroma, but a sweet malty flavour, with a noticeable fruitiness and a faint hoppiness, which carries on to a short, bitter-sweet finish.

PITFIELD

**Pitfield Brewery, London Beer Co, 14
Pitfield Street, London, N1 6EY
Tel (020) 7739 3701
Website www.pitfieldbeershop.co.uk**
Shop 11-7 Tue-Fri; 10-4 Sat.
Tours by arrangement

Pitfield Brewery was established in 1982, two years after its sister business, the Beer Shop. In 1988, it won champion Beer of Britain with Dark Star (now renamed Black Eagle). To celebrate its 21st birthday, a range of non-organic beers have been brewed under the banner of the London Beer Co., to distinguish them from the organic Pitfield range. Pitfield's beers can be found on draught at the Wenlock Arms NI, where the beers are fined. Vegetarians are directed to the Duke of Cambridge NI, or to the bottled versions at the Beer Shop. Six outlets are supplied direct. Bottle-conditioned beers: Original, Shoreditch Stout, East Kent Goldings, Eco Warrior, Hoxton Best Bitter, Black Eagle, London Porter (ABV 5%), 21st Anniversary Ale (ABV 5.5%), Christmas Ale (ABV 6+% – recipe varies), Imperial Stout (ABV 10%). Except for London Porter, 21st Anniversary Ale and Imperial Stout, all are organic. All bottled beers are not fined. Draught Eco Warrior is brewed for Pitfield by Dark Star (qv).

Singhbolton *(ABV 3.7%)*
Brewed for the Singboulton organic pubs in London.

Shoreditch Stout *(OG 1040, ABV 4%)* ◆
Dark and malty, there are rich roast notes on the aroma and flavour, overlaid with some caramel notes. The aftertaste is dry and lingering.

East Kent Goldings *(ABV 4.2%)* ◆
The malt and sweetness are well balanced by the hoppy fruit character in this gold-coloured beer. The finish is slightly dry with bitter fruit notes.

Eco Warrior *(ABV 4.5%)*
A light-drinking, malty, yellow-coloured beer with bitterness building on the palate and aftertaste.

Hoxton Best Bitter *(ABV 4.8%)* ◆
Previously named Hoxton Heavy, a smooth, deceptively easy-drinking beer for the strength. Malt and fruit are well-balanced and pear notes persist in the dry aftertaste.

Black Eagle *(ABV 5%)* ◆
A light-drinking strong old ale, black with red hues, a lasting roast malt flavour and a malty, dryish aftertaste.

PLASSEY SIBA

**Plassey Brewery, The Plassey, Eyton,
Wrexham, LL13 0SP
Tel (01978) 781111
Fax (01978) 781219
Website www.plasseybrewery.co.uk**
Shop open on request
Tours by arrangement

The brewery founded in 1985 on the 250-acre Plassey Estate, which also incorporates a touring caravan park, craft centres, a golf course, three licensed outlets for Plassey's ales, and a brewery shop. 30 free trade outlets also take the beers. Seasonal beer: Ruddy Rudolph (ABV 4.5%, Christmas), Lager (ABV 4%). Bottle-conditioned beer: Royal Welch Fusilier (ABV 4.5%).

Bitter *(OG 1041, ABV 4%)* ◆
Full-bodied and distinctive best bitter. Good balance of hops and fruit flavours with a lasting dry bitter aftertaste.

Royal Welch Fusilier
(OG 1046, ABV 4.5%) 🍺

Cwrw Tudno *(OG 1048, ABV 5%)* 🍺
A mellow sweetish premium beer with classic Plassey flavours of fruit and hops.

Dragon's Breath *(OG 1060, ABV 6%)*
A fruity, strong bitter, smooth and quite sweet, though not cloying, with an intense, fruity aroma. A dangerously drinkable winter warmer.

PLOUGH INN

See Bodicote

POACHERS

Poachers Brewery, Unit 4, Swinderby Industrial Park, Swinderby, Lincs
Tel (01522) 510237
Website www.poachersbeer.co.uk

The brewery was established in 2001 by Ian Baker and George Batterbee on a former RAF station at Swinderby in Lincolnshire. Initially, a 2.5-barrel plant was used but this has now been replaced by a five-barrel one. Regular outlets are supplied direct throughout Lincolnshire and Norfolk with plans to gradually expand the area of operation. The brewery produces its own range of bottle-conditioned beers and also owns an off-licence on Lincoln High Street, which stocks bottled beers from micros as well as a selection of Belgian beers. Seasonal beer: Santas Come (ABV 6.5%, Christmas). All the draught beers are also available in bottle-conditioned form.

Trembling Rabbit *(OG 1034, ABV 3.4%)*
Rich dark mild with a smooth malty flavour and a slightly bitter finish.

Shy Talk *(OG 1037, ABV 3.7%)*
Clean-tasting session beer, pale gold in colour; slightly bitter finish, dry hopped.

Pride *(OG 1040, ABV 4%)*
Amber bitter brewed using American Cascade hops that produce a wonderful flavour and aroma that lingers.

Trail *(OG 1042, ABV 4.2%)* ❧
A flowery hop-nosed, mid-brown beer with a well-balanced but bitter taste that stays with the malt, becoming more apparent in the drying finish.

Den *(OG 1042, ABV 4.2%)* ❧
Pale amber with a musty fruit hop aroma that gives way to a citrus hoppiness in the taste, with a moderate bitterness that brings it to a nice malty aftertaste.

Dick *(OG 1045, ABV 4.5%)*
Ruby red bitter, smooth fruity flavour balanced by the bitterness of Goldings hops.

Black Crow *(OG 1045, ABV 4.5%)*
Dry stout with burnt toffee and caramel flavour.

Pytiak (Per-Tash) *(OG 1049, ABV 5%)*
Cask-conditioned lager brewed in the Czech style using Saaz hops and caramalt.

Jock's Trap *(OG 1050, ABV 5%)*

De Wilderer *(OG 1050, ABV 5.1%)*
Brewed using the famous smoked rauch malts from Bamberg. A smoked beer with

depth and character, dark ruby in colour with an intense lingering aftertaste.

For Bluebell, Tattershall Thorpe, Lincs

Pathfinders Ale *(ABV 4.4%)*

For the Sports & Social Club, North Hykeham, Lincs

Old Joe *(ABV 4.1%)*

POINTS WEST

Points West Brewery, Plymouth College of Further Education, Kings Road, Devonport, Plymouth, Devon, PL1 5QG
Tel (01752) 305700 Fax (01752) 305888
E-mail broome@scfe.ac.uk
Tours by prior arrangement

A college brewery created for catering students that produces five barrels once a fortnight. Occasional beers are sold to the free trade, but in general the beers are bottled and sold through the National Trust and Plymouth Argyle FC. The beers are also supplied to CAMRA beer festivals. Seasonal beers: Antibiotic (ABV 7.5%, winter), Wheat Beer (ABV 5.5%, summer).
Bottle-conditioned beers: Drakes Drum (ABV 4.8%), Antibiotic, Wheat Beer.

Pilgrim PA *(OG 1039, ABV 4%)*

Drakes Drum *(OG 1046, ABV 4.8%)*

PORT MAHON

⚑ **Port Mahon Brewery, Cask and Cutler, 1 Henry Street, Sheffield, South Yorkshire, S3 7EQ**
Tel (0114) 2492295

Brewing started in 2001 in a purpose-built brewery behind behind the Cask and Cutler, using a one-barrel plant. There are plans to install a four-barrel plant. The brewery produces one-off beers mainly for festivals and special occasions. It is planned to brew a permanent house bitter and a range of beer styles that will alternate with the other guest ales in the pub. The beer range is yet to be established.

PORTCHESTER SIBA

Portchester Brewery, 6 Audret Close, Portchester, Fareham, Hants, PO16 9ER
Tel/Fax (01329) 512918
E-mail gill.stone@portchesterbrewery.co.uk
Website www.portchesterbrewery.co.uk

A tiny brewery, able to produce just nine gallons a time, set up in the garage of Gill

Stone's home. After years of home-brewing, Gill was encouraged by her husband Graham (both are keen CAMRA members) to 'go commercial' in 2000, as they were fed up with over-priced beer in pubs. Dr Graham Stone used his knowledge from his biology and physics doctorate to help Gill make the perfect pint. She is now supplying a few pubs and clubs in the locality, and has upgraded to a 2.5-barrel plant. Five outlets are supplied. The beers are named in honour of Portchester Castle. Seasonal beers: Southsea Spice (ABV 4.4%, summer), Firepot (ABV 4%, autumn), XP (Xmas Pud) (ABV 6.2%, Christmas).

Bastion *(ABV 3.8%)*

Slingshot *(ABV 4.2%)*

Catapult *(ABV 4.8%)*

Battering Ram *(ABV 5%)*

PORTER

Porter Brewing Co Ltd, Rossendale Brewery, The Griffin Inn, 84-86 Hud Rake, Haslingden, Lancs, BB4 5AF
Tel/Fax (01706) 214021
Tours by arrangement

⊠ The Griffin Inn opened in 1994 and now has five tied houses. All four pubs sell a minimum of five house ales. All the pubs serve cask ale and a few other local outlets also take the beer. Occasional/seasonal beers: Timmy's Ginger Beer (ABV 4.2%, March and August), Stout (ABV 5.5%, Sept-Oct), Sleighed (ABV 6.5%, Dec-Jan), Celebration Ale (ABV 7.1%, July-Aug). All beers leave the brewery as vegan products.

Dark Mild *(OG 1033, ABV 3.3%)*
A true dark mild, with a slight maltiness and a good hint of roast in the finish.

Floral Dance *(OG 1035, ABV 3.6%)*
Pale and fruity.

Bitter *(OG 1037, ABV 3.8%)* ◆
Unusually dark for a standard bitter, this beer has a dry and assertively bitter character that develops in the finish.

Railway Sleeper *(OG 1040, ABV 4.2%)*
Intensely bitter and hoppy.

Rossendale Ale *(OG 1041, ABV 4.2%)* ◆
A malty aroma leads to a complex, malt-dominated flavour supported by a dry, increasingly bitter finish.

Porter *(OG 1050, ABV 5%)*
A rich beer with a slightly sweet, malty start, counter-balanced with sharp bitterness and a noticeable roast barley dominance.

Sunshine *(OG 1050, ABV 5.3%)*
An intensely hoppy and bitter golden ale, full-bodied with some malt, a robust mouthfeel and a lingering bitterness.

POTTON SIBA

Potton Brewery Company, 10 Shannon Place, Potton, Sandy, Beds, SG19 2PZ
Tel (01767) 261042
E-mail info@potton-brewery.co.uk
Website www.potton-brewery.co.uk
Shop via brewery, open 8-530
Tours by arrangement

⊠ Started in 1998 and run by Clive Towner and Robert Hearson, both ex-managers of Greene King at Biggleswade, they resurrected the Potton Brewery Company name after it disappeared as a result of a takeover in 1922. Some 100 outlets are supplied direct. Bottle-conditioned beers: Butlers Ale (ABV 4.3%), Shambles.

Shannon IPA *(OG 1035, ABV 3.6%)*

Shambles *(OG 1042, ABV 4.3%)*

Village Bike *(OG 1042, ABV 4.3%)*

Potton Gold *(OG 1047, ABV 4.8%)*

Pride of Potton
(OG 1057, ABV 6%) ◆
Impressive, robust amber ale with a malty aroma, malt and ripe fruit in the mouth, and a fading sweetness.

PRINCETOWN SIBA

Princetown Breweries Ltd, The Brewery, Tavistock Road, Princetown, Devon, PL20 6QF
Tel (01822) 890789
Fax (01822) 890719
Tours by arrangement

⊠ A brewery (claimed to be the highest in England at 1400 feet above sea level), established in 1994 by a former Gibbs Mew and Hop Back brewer, capacity is being increased to 45 barrels a week. It supplies two hotels owned by a sister company, the pub next door and 30 other local outlets. In 2003, it was planned to move the brewery a short distance to a new building and plant in Princetown. Bottle-conditioned beer: Jail Ale.

Dartmoor IPA *(OG 1039, ABV 4%)* ◆
Flowery hop aroma and taste with a bitter aftertaste to this full-bodied, amber-coloured beer.

Jail Ale *(OG 1047, ABV 4.8%)* ◆
Hops and fruit predominate in the flavour of this mid-brown beer, which has a slightly sweet aftertaste.

QUAY SIBA

Lapin Noir Ltd t/a The Quay Brewery, Hope Square, Weymouth, Dorset, DT4 8TR
Tel/Fax (01305) 777515
E-mail mail@quaybrewery.com
Website quaybrewery.com
Shop at Brewers Quay 10-5.30 daily
Tours by arrangement via Timewalk at Brewers Quay

⊠ Founded in 1996 by Giles Smeath, he brews on part of the site that was formerly the Devenish & Groves brewery. The rest of the site is open to visitors as a Timewalk attraction showing the history of Weymouth; much of the old brewing plant is still on view. Giles plans to add two new 10-barrel fermenters. Seasonal beers: Silent Knight (ABV 5.9%, winter), Summer Knight (ABV 3.8%). Bottle-conditioned beers: Quay Steam Beer, Old Rott, Silent Knight.

Weymouth Harbour Master
(OG 1036, ABV 3.6%) ◆
Well-balanced, nut-brown session beer, sweetish, but not cloying, thanks to the dry finish. May be badged by pubs as a house beer.

Weymouth Best Bitter
(OG 1038, ABV 3.9%) ◆
Light, sweetish session bitter, amber with a fruity aroma.

Weymouth JD 1742
(OG 1040, ABV 4.2%) ◆
Clean-tasting, easy-drinking bitter. Well-balanced with lingering bitterness after moderate sweetness.

Steam Beer *(OG 1043, ABV 4.5%)* ◆
Complex old ale with roast malt predominating from the nose to the long, bitter finish.

Jurassic *(OG 1045, ABV 4.7%)*

Old Rott *(OG 1048, ABV 5%)* ◆
Warming finish despite a rather light caramel and malt taste. Hint of sulphur and yeastiness throughout.

RAILWAY TAVERN

⌕ **Famous Railway Tavern Brewing Co, 58 Station Road, Brightlingsea, Essex, CO7 0DT**
Tel (01206) 302581
Website www.geocities.com/famousrailway
Tours by arrangement

⊠ The brewery started life as a kitchen-sink affair, with Crab & Winkle Mild the staple brew. Crouch Vale Brewery obtained two fermenters from Vaux for the Railway Tavern and today two barrels are brewed every fortnight. The future is likely to involve the development of a bitter being added to the existing range of dark ales. One pub is owned. Seasonal beer: Old Ale (ABV 4.7%, autumn), Fireside Porter (ABV 4.7%, winter/spring).

Crab & Winkle Mild *(OG 1040, ABV 3.7%)*

Bladderwrack Stout *(OG 1050, ABV 4.7%)*

RAINBOW

⌕ **Rainbow Inn & Brewery, 73 Birmingham Road, Allesley Village, Coventry, W Midlands, CV5 9GT**
Tel (024) 76402888
Fax (024) 76407415
E-mail rainbowinn@coventry.fsnet.co.uk
Tours by arrangement

⊛ Rainbow was set up in 1995 by Terry Rotherham. Since Unique Pub Co took over the lease in 1999, only one guest ale is allowed.

Piddlebrook *(OG 1038, ABV 3.8%)*

RAMSBOTTOM*

Ramsbottom Brewery,
10 Mount Pleasant, Nangreaves,
Bury, Lancs, BL9 6SP
Tel (07739) 507416
Fax (0161) 761 1776
Tours by arrangement

⊛ Ramsbottom has a five-barrel brew-length using equipment from the Ledbury Brewery. It was set up in premises that were the basement of the old Co-op. CAMRA member Paul Robinson currently brews once or twice a week, but hopes to brew full time in the future. 20 outlets are supplied.

Old Ground Mild *(OG 1040, ABV 3.8%)*

Rammy Mile *(OG 1040, ABV 3.8%)*

Tower Bitter *(OG 1042, ABV 4%)*

Provident *(OG 1048, ABV 4.5%)*

RAMSGATE

⌕ **Ramsgate Brewery, 98 Harbour Parade, Ramsgate, Kent, CT11 8LP**
Tel (07967) 660060
E-mail info@ramsgatebrewery.co.uk
Website ramsgatebrewery.co.uk
Tours by arrangement

⊠ Ramsgate Brewery is part of the Ramsgate Royal Harbour Brewhouse and Bakers, a café bar built by Andy Barrett and Eddie Gadd in an old restaurant building, unused for 30 years. It has a five-barrel capacity. Along with its own beer and bakery products, the site serves Belgian beers on draught and an ever-increasing number in bottle.

Gadds No. 7 Ramsgate Bitter
(OG 1038, ABV 3.8%)

Gadds No. 5 Ramsgate Best Bitter
(OG 1044, ABV 4.4%)

Gadds No. 3 Ramsgate Pale Ale
(OG 1048, ABV 5%)

RANDALLS SIBA

RW Randall Ltd, Vauxlaurens Brewery, St Julian's Avenue, St Peter Port, Guernsey, GY1 3JG
Tel (01481) 720134
Fax (01481) 713233
Shop 9-5
Tours by arrangement

⊠ Founded five generations ago, Randalls brewery in Guernsey has been brewing in the Channel Islands longer than anyone can remember. It is the last independent, family-owned brewery in the islands. Seventeen pubs are owned (10 serving cask-conditioned beer) and 18 outlets are supplied. Seasonal beer: Randalls Stout (ABV 5.5%, winter).

Mild *(OG 1034, ABV 3.4%)*

Pale Ale *(OG 1038, ABV 3.8%)*

Patois *(OG 1048, ABV 4.8%)* ◆
Amber in colour, with a hoppy aroma. Bitter and hoppy both in the palate and finish.

RAT & RATCHET

⌂ Rat & Ratchet, 40 Chapel Hill,
Huddersfield, West Yorkshire, HD1 3EB
Tel (01484) 516734
Fax (01484) 300196
E-mail mail@ratandratchet.co.uk
Website www.ratandratchet.co.uk
Tours by arrangement

☺ A brew-pub with an extensive range of beers, it has been brewing since 1994 to supply the pub and beer festivals. The 3.5-barrel brew plant is the ex-Firkin equipment from the Firecracker & Firkin in Crawley. The beers are generally named with a rodent theme and are rarely repeated.

White Mouse (ABV 3.8%)

Trap Tickler (ABV 4.1%) ◆
Straw-coloured pale bitter with an intense citrus flavour. Fruit and malt are evident throughout, leading to a dry, zesty and bitter finish.

RCH SIBA

RCH Brewery, West Hewish,
Weston-super-Mare,
Somerset, BS24 6RR
Tel (01934) 834447
Fax (01934) 834167
E-mail rchbrew@aol.com
Website www.rchbrewery.com
Shop. Mon-Fri 8.30-4

⊗ The brewery was originally installed by previous owners in the early 1980s behind the Royal Clarence Hotel at Burnham-on-Sea. But since 1993 brewing has taken place on a commercial basis in a former cider mill at West Hewish. A new 30-barrel plant was installed in 2000. RCH now supplies 75 outlets direct and the award-winning beers are available nationwide through its own wholesaling company, which also distributes beers from other small independent breweries. Seasonal beers: Steam Sale (ABV 4.5%, January), Steam Lovers (ABV 4.7%, February), Steam Spring (ABV 4.6%, March), Steam Showers (ABV 4.8%, April), Steam Pole (ABV 4.9%, May), Steam Flames (ABV 4.5%, June), Steam Special (ABV 5%, July), Steam Festival (ABV 4.5%, August), Steam Harvest (ABV 4.7%, September), Steam Fair (ABV 4.5%, October), Steam Carnival (ABV 4.7%, November), Steaming Santa (ABV 4.5%, December). Bottle-conditioned beers: Pitchfork ⬚, Old Slug Porter ⬚, Firebox, Ale Mary (ABV 6%).

Hewish IPA (ABV 3.6%) ⬚◆
Light, hoppy bitter with some malt and fruit, though slightly less fruit in the finish. Floral citrus hop aroma, pale/brown amber colour.

PG Steam (ABV 3.9%) ⬚◆
Amber-coloured, medium-bodied with a floral hop aroma with some fruit. Hoppy and bitter, with some malt, fruit and subtle sweetness. Finish is similar.

Pitchfork (ABV 4.3%) ⬚⬚◆
Floral citrus hop with pale malt. Yellow/gold in colour, hops predominate in a full-bodied taste, which is slightly sweet. Long finish – a class act.

Old Slug Porter (ABV 4.5%) ⬚⬚◆
Chocolate, coffee, roast malt and hops with lots of body and dark fruits. A complex, rich stout, dark brown in colour.

East Street Cream (ABV 5%) ⬚⬚◆
Superb premium ale, pale brown in colour, it is malty with chocolate hints, hoppy, fruity and bitter-sweet. All flavours vie for dominance in what is a notable and well-crafted ale.

Double Header (ABV 5.3%) ◆
Light brown, full-bodied strong bitter. Beautifully balanced flavours of malt, hops and tropical fruits, followed by a long, bitter-sweet finish. Very refreshing and easy drinking for its strength.

Firebox (ABV 6%) ◆
Aroma and taste of citric hops and pale crystal malt. A strong, complex, full-bodied, mid-brown beer with a well-balanced flavour of malt and hops.

Santa Fe (ABV 7.3%)

REBELLION SIBA

Rebellion Beer Company,
Marlow Brewery, Bencombe Farm,
Marlow Bottom, Bucks, SL7 3LT
Tel (01628) 476594
Fax (01628) 476617
E-mail info@rebellionbeer.co.uk
Website www.rebellionbeer.co.uk
Shop 8-530 Mon-Fri; 9-5 Sat
Tours by arrangement 1st Tue every month
at 7.15pm (£6)

⊗ Opened in 1993, Rebellion fills the gap left in Marlow by Whitbread, which shut down Wethereds in 1988. Rebellion moved to a new site in Marlow, and increased brewing capacity from 50 to 200 barrels a week, when it bought a pilot brewery from Courage at Reading. The new brewery will now allow Rebellion to grow and produce a much wider range of beer styles. Rebellion now has the lease of the Three Horseshoes pub, located a few hundred yards away. 160 outlets are supplied. Seasonal beers: Gold Digger (May), Blonde (ABV 4.3%, July-Aug), Rebellion Red (ABV 4.7%, Sept-Oct), Old Codger (ABV 5%, Nov-Dec), Roasted Nuts (ABV 4.6%, Christmas). Bottle-conditioned beer: White (ABV 4.5%).

IPA (OG 1039, ABV 3.7%) ⬚◆
Copper-coloured bitter, sweet and malty, with resinous and red apple flavours. Caramel and fruit decline to leave a dry, bitter and malty finish.

Smuggler (OG 1042, ABV 4.1%) ◆
A red-brown beer, well-bodied and bitter with an uncompromisingly dry, bitter finish.

Mutiny (OG 1046, ABV 4.5%) ◆
Tawny in colour, this full-bodied best bitter is predominantly fruity and moderately bitter with crystal malt continuing to a dry finish.

RECTORY SIBA

Rectory Ales Ltd, Streat Hill Farm, Streat Hill,
Streat, Hassocks, East Sussex, BN6 8RP
Tel/Fax (01273) 890570
E-mail sales@rectory-ales.co.uk
Tours by arrangement

⊗ Rectory was founded in 1995 by the Rector of Plumpton, the Rev Godfrey Broster, to generate funds for the maintenance of his three parish churches. 107 parishioners are shareholders. The brewing capacity is now 20 barrels a week. Some seasonal beers are produced. All outlets are supplied direct. Seasonal beer: Christmas Cheer (ABV 3.8%, December). Bottle-conditioned beer: Rector's Revenge (ABV 5.4%).

The Rector's Ale *(OG 1038, ABV 3.8%)*

Rector's Revenge *(OG 1054, ABV 5.4%)*
Copper-brown strong bitter with a complex aroma, becoming more hoppy in the mouth with a dry, bitter finish.

RED LION*

Red Lion Ales, The Red Lion, 73 Dewsbury Road, Ossett, West Yorkshire, WF5 9NQ
Tel (01924) 273487
Tours for small groups by arrangement

A five-barrel plant owned by Bob Hunter, who founded the Ossett Brewing Co before selling his share in 2001. The Red Lion is owned by the Lonely Pub Company, a Bradford-based firm that rents a former store for brewing at the rear of the pub. The brewery is only 17x11ft yet contains two fermenters and three conditioning tanks. In 2003 two additional rectangular five-barrel fermenters were added, doubling capacity to 10 barrels. Some 10 outlets are supplied.

White Lion *(OG 1043, ABV 4.3%)*
Very pale, flowery lager-style beer using Cascade hops.

Golden Lion *(OG 1045.5, ABV 4.5%)*
Robust, hoppy ale that uses a generous amount of East Kent Goldings.

Yakima Pale Ale *(OG 1045.5, ABV 4.5%)*
A hoppy and fairly bitter yellow premium beer that uses American hops.

Chardonnayle *(OG 1051.5, ABV 5.1%)*
Golden aromatic brew with American Willamette hops.

RED ROSE*

Red Rose Brewery, Royal Hotel, 2 Station Road, Gt Harwood, Lancashire, BB6 7BA
Tel (01254) 883541
Fax (01254) 877375
E-mail ente@streamline.uk.com

⊕ Started on a small scale in 2002 with an 18-gallon plant, Red Rose expanded to 2.75 barrels in 2003. The beers all have local names, except for Felix, named after the pub cat. One pub is owned and five outlets are supplied direct.

Bowley Best *(OG 1036, ABV 3.7%)*

Felix *(OG 1041, ABV 4.2%)*

Old Demdyke *(OG 1047, ABV 4.6%)*

Care Taker of History *(OG 1058, ABV 6%)*

REDRUTH

Redruth Brewery (1742) Ltd, The Brewery, Redruth, Cornwall, TR15 1RB
Tel (01209) 212244
Fax (01209) 210383
Website www.Redruth-brewery.fsnet.co.uk
Shop noon-6 Mon-Fri; 10-4 Sat

⊠ Redruth Brewery is owned by the Hong Kong based Sino-Cornwall Company. Cask-conditioned beer was re-established in 1998 after a break of nearly 10 years. It is a large brewery with the capacity to increase barrelage significantly when required. Redruth has no tied estate and most of the activity centres around bottling and canning. Cask beer is sold through Beer Seller on a seasonal basis. The brewery's sales force is now promoting cask-conditioned beer, starting with Cornish Rebellion.

Cornish Rebellion *(OG 1049, ABV 4.8%)*

Steam Brewed Bitter *(OG 1051, ABV 5%)*

RED SHOOT

⎗ **Red Shoot Inn Brewery, Toms Lane, Linwood, Ringwood, Hampshire, BH24 3QT**
Tel (01425) 475792
Website www.redshootinn.co.uk

The brewery, owned by Wadworth, was commissioned in 1998 with Forest Gold as the first brew. Tom's Tipple was introduced in 1998 as a winter brew and is now a permanent brand. Red Shoot would like to expand but the size of plant (2.5 barrels) makes this difficult, though some occasional beers are produced.

Forest Gold *(ABV 3.8%)*

Tom's Tipple *(ABV 4.8%)*

REEPHAM

Reepham Brewery, Unit 1, Collers Way, Reepham, Norwich, Norfolk, NR10 4SW
Tel (01603) 871091
Tours by arrangement

⊠ Norfolk's oldest working brewery is a family business established in 1983 by a chemical engineer and architect (father and son), who brought back the name and brewing to the small market town west of Norwich. The original Reepham Brewery was closed by Steward and Patteson. Some 20 outlets are supplied direct. Bottle-conditioned beers: Organic Honey Ale (brewed for Fat Cat pub, Norwich), Granary Bitter, Rapier Pale Ale.

Granary Bitter *(OG 1038, ABV 3.5%)* ⬠⬟
A gold-coloured beer with a light hoppy aroma followed by a malty sweetish flavour with some smoke notes. A well-balanced beer with a long, moderately hoppy aftertaste.

Rapier Pale Ale
(OG 1042, ABV 4.2%) 🏠🍺
Refreshingly clean tasting bitter with a delightful strawberry and hop nose. The first taste is overtly hoppy with smoky overtones and a soft, fruity background. Hops continue to dominate the taste as the fruit background fades to leave a dry, consistent finish.

Brewhouse *(OG 1052, ABV 5%)*

Velvet Sweet Stout
(OG 1045, ABV 4.5%) 🍺
A heavy roast influence in aroma and taste. A smoky malt feel to the taste produces an interesting combination that is both creamy and well-defined. Initial fruit and hop contributions indicate a subtle sweetness that soon fades to leave a growing dry bitterness.

St Agnes *(OG 1046, ABV 4.6%)* 🍺
A donation to a local church is made for every pint sold of this golden-hued, hoppy bitter. Bitterness combined with citrus notes provide a counter-balance to the inherent hoppiness. Complex, drawn-out, dry finish.

RIDLEYS IFBB SIBA

T D Ridley & Sons Ltd,
Hartford End Brewery, Chelmsford,
Essex, CM3 1JZ
Tel (01371) 820316
Fax (01371) 821216
E-mail philip.downes@ridleys.co.uk
Website www.ridleys.co.uk
Shop open via reception, 9-4
Tours by arrangement, min 10, max 25. Tours every Wednesday during the summer; booking not required. £6 per person with a free pint of beer.

⊗ Ridleys was established by Thomas Dixon Ridley in 1842 and has been passed down through succeeding generations and is still a family company. It has an estate of 75 pubs and also supplies some 700 other outlets. In 2002, Ridley's purchased the Tolly Cobbold brands, estate and distribution contacts. Seasonal beers: Cobbolds Conquest (ABV 4.2%, April-June), Cobbolds Cardinal (ABV 4.3%, Feb-March), Witchfinder Porter (ABV 4.3%, autumn-winter), Spectacular (ABV 4.6%, July-Sept), Tolly Old Strong (ABV 5.5%, December).

Tolly Mild *(OG 1035, ABV 3.5%)* 🍺
Sweet, dark mild, with malt and fruit balanced by a slight roastiness.

IPA *(OG 1035, ABV 3.5%)* 🍺
Well-balanced beer with an aroma redolent of grass and fennel. Initial complexity thins quickly to a lasting bitterness.

Tolly Original *(OG 1038, ABV 3.8%)*

Prospect *(OG 1042, ABV 4.1%)* 🍺
Bitter, hoppy, gold/amber beer with a deep citrus character throughout.

Rumpus *(OG 1049, ABV 4.5%)* 🍺
Initially sweet and vinous, with a drier, biscuity aftertaste. Now seems to be somewhat darker than in previous years.

Old Bob
(OG 1055, ABV 5.1%) 🏠🍺
Lightly hopped, full-bodied, grainy bitter with a very fruity taste, dominated by cherry fruits. Liquorice comes through towards the finish.

RING O' BELLS SIBA

Ring O' Bells Brewery Ltd, Pennygillam Way,
Pennygillam Industrial Estate,
Launceston, Cornwall, PL15 7ED
Tel (01566) 777787
Fax (01566) 777788
E-mail enquiries@ringobellsbrewery.co.uk
Website www.ringobellsbrewery.co.uk
Shop Mon-Fri 9-4.30
Tours by arrangement

⊗ The Ring O'Bells started trading in the 13th century as a cider farm-cum-alehouse for the stonemasons of St Torney Church, North Hill. It closed in 1918 and after 79 years of neglect new owners set about restoring the old ale house, and rebuilding the cider press and vat. Intensive research with the help of two micro-biologists re-cultured the old yeast strain that was trapped within the walls of the old vat, and is now used to ferment today's ales, some 600 years later. The success of the beers when launched in 1999 led to the brewery moving to new premises in Launceston, in 2001. Some 300 outlets are supplied direct.

Porkers Pride *(OG 1036, ABV 3.8%)*
A light, refreshing session ale that is well-balanced with a clean, hoppy finish.

Surf Boar *(OG 1038, ABV 4%)*

Bodmin Boar *(OG 1041.5, ABV 4.3%)*
Full-flavoured, darkish premium ale, with a fine aroma and malty finish.

Dreckly *(OG 1046, ABV 4.8%)*
A warm, ruby-coloured, strong premium ale fortified with gorse and heather, rich in malt with a spicy aroma and good malty after taste.

Tipsy Trotters *(OG 1048.3, ABV 5.1%)*
Amber-coloured, full-bodied, malty beer, slightly fruity.

Sozzled Swine *(OG 1051.8, ABV 5.5%)*

RINGWOOD IFBB SIBA

Ringwood Brewery Ltd,
138 Christchurch Road, Ringwood,
Hampshire, BH24 3AP
Tel (01425) 471177
Fax (01425) 480273
E-mail info@ringwoodbrewery.co.uk
Website www.ringwoodbrewery.co.uk
Shop 9.30-5 Mon-Fri; 9.30-12 Sat
Tours by arrangement

⊗ Ringwood, which celebated 25 years of brewing in 2003, was set up in 1978 by legendary micro-brewery builder Peter Austin. The brewery moved in 1986 to

attractive 18th-century buildings, formerly part of the old Tunks Brewery. A new brewhouse was commissioned at the end of 1994, and a new fermenting room completed in 1995. Additional fermenters were installed in 2002 along with cask-washing and cask-filling equipment. Six pubs are owned, all serving cask-conditioned beer and some 800 outlets are supplied. Ringwood's impressive success, under managing director David Welsh, has moved the brewery out of the ranks of micro-brewers and it's now a regional producing around 30,000 barrels a year. Seasonal beers: Boondoggle (ABV 4%, summer), Bold Forester (ABV 4.2%, spring), Huffkin (ABV 4.4%, autumn), 4X Porter (ABV 4.7%, winter ⬠). Bottle-conditioned beers: Fortyniner, XXXX Porter (ABV 4.7%).

Best Bitter *(OG 1037, ABV 3.8%)* ❧
A well-balanced, golden brown beer. A malty and hoppy aroma leads to a malty taste with some sweetness. Malty and bitter finish, with some fruit present.

Fortyniner *(OG 1048, ABV 4.9%)* ❧
Pale brown in colour. A malty and fruity aroma leads to a well-balanced taste of malt and hops. Fruity finish.

Old Thumper *(OG 1055, ABV 5.6%)* ❧
A mid-brown beer. A fruity aroma preludes a sweet, malty taste with some fruit. Surprisingly bitter aftertaste, with malt and fruit.

RIVERHEAD

⚲ Riverhead Brewery Ltd,
2 Peel Street, Marsden, Huddersfield, West Yorkshire, HD7 6BR
Tel (01484) 841270
Tours by arrangement

The Riverhead Brewery Tap is a brew-pub that opened in 1995 after its conversion from an old grocery store. The seven beers are named after local reservoirs with the height of the reservoir relating to the strength of the beer. Occasional specials such as Jazz Bitter (ABV 4%, for Marsden Jazz Festival), and Ruffled Feathers Bitter (ABV 4.2%, for Marsden Cuckoo Day) are brewed. The brewery also supplies six local outlets on an occasional basis.

Sparth Mild *(OG 1038, ABV 3.6%)* ⬠❧
A light-bodied, dry mild, with a dark ruby colour. Fruity aroma with roasted flavour and a dry finish.

Butterley Bitter *(OG 1038, ABV 3.8%)* ❧
A dry, amber-coloured, hoppy session beer.

Deer Hill Porter *(OG 1040, ABV 4%)*
A dark brown bitter with the characteristics of stout, but not as strong.

Cupwith Light Bitter *(OG 1042, ABV 4.2%)*
A very pale bitter with a distinctive bitter aftertaste.

Black Moss Stout *(OG 1043, ABV 4.3%)* ❧
Roast malt and fruit aromas from a lightly-hopped dry stout with a chocolatey finish.

March Haigh Special Bitter
(OG 1046, ABV 4.6%)
A smooth, rounded flavour appealing to the taste buds as a result of the interesting selection of hops used.

Redbrook Premium Bitter
(OG 1055, ABV 5.5%) ❧
A rich and malty strong beer, with malt and fruit, and a sweet, fruity aftertaste.

RIVERSIDE*

Riverside Brewery, Unit 1, Church Lane, Wainfleet All Saints, Lincolnshire.
Tel (01754) 881288

New brewery that opened in May 2003. Kenneth Dixon uses his 50 years' experience of brewing to help his son, John, the owner. Eight barrels a week are produced for local trade.

Major Bitter *(ABV 3.9%)*

JOHN ROBERTS SIBA

John Roberts Brewing Co Ltd,
16 Market Square, Bishops Castle, Shropshire, SY9 5BN
Tel (01588) 638392
Fax (01588) 638896
Shop Yes
Tours by prior arrangement

⊠ The brewery, formerly the Three Tuns, is a miniature Victorian tower, considered to be the oldest in Britain. The brewery has been saved from development into residential housing. Bottle-conditioned beers: Chocolate Stout (ABV 4.3%), Clerics Cure (ABV 5%).

Sexton *(OG 1036, ABV 3.7%)*

XXX *(OG 1041.5, ABV 4.3%)*

Offas *(OG 1048, ABV 4.9%)*

Old Scrooge *(OG 1062, ABV 6.5%)*

ROBINSON'S IFBB

Frederic Robinson Ltd, Unicorn Brewery, Stockport, Cheshire, SK1 1JJ
Tel (0161) 480 6571
Fax (0161) 476 6011
E-mail brewery@frederic-robinson.co.uk
Website www.frederic-robinson.com
Tours by arrangement

⊠ A major family brewery founded in 1838 in the Unicorn Inn and still run by the descendants of Frederic Robinson. The company moved to the present site in 1865. Robinson's bought Hartleys of Ulverston in 1982 and closed the brewery in 1991. The company supplies real ale to all its 398 tied houses in the North-west and North Wales, and to some 100 free trade outlets. Seasonal: Samuel Oldknow (ABV 3.5%, Jan-Feb), Stockport Arches (ABV 4%, March-April), Young Tom (ABV 4%, May-June), Whistling Will (ABV 4%, July-Aug), Coopers Bell (ABV 4%, Sept-Oct), Robin Bitter (ABV 4.5%, Nov-Dec).

Hatters *(OG 1032, ABV 3.3%)* ❧
A light mild with a fruity aroma, it has biscuity malt and a fresh fruitiness in the taste and finish. A darkened version is available in a handful of outlets and badged Dark Mild.

Old Stockport Bitter
(OG 1033.5, ABV 3.5%) ❧
A beer with a refreshing taste of malt, hops and citrus fruit, a fruity aroma, and a short, dry finish.

Hartleys XB *(OG 1039.5, ABV 4%)* ◆
An overly sweet and malty bitter with a bitter citrus peel fruitiness and a hint of liquorice in the finish.

Snowdon *(OG 1040.5, ABV 4%)*

Cumbria Way *(OG 1040.5, ABV 4.1%)*
A new pale, refreshing bitter marketed under the Hartley's name and first brewed for the Ulverston Ale Trail in 2001.

Best Bitter *(OG 1040, ABV 4.2%)* ◆
Amber beer with a fruity aroma. Hoppy, bitter and quite fruity to taste with a bitter finish.

Frederics *(OG 1048, ABV 5%)* ▭◆
A gold-coloured beer with an aroma of orange and a hint of spice. Citrus fruit and hops on the taste with a dry hoppy finish.

Old Tom *(OG 1079, ABV 8.5%)* ▯▭◆
A full-bodied, dark beer, it has malt, fruit and chocolate in the aroma. A delightfully complex range of flavours including dark chocolate, full maltiness, port and fruits lead to a long, bitter-sweet aftertaste.

ROCKINGHAM SIBA

Rockingham Ales, c/o 25 Wansford Road, Elton, Cambs, PE8 6RZ
Tel (01832) 280722
E-mail brian@rockinghamales.co.uk
Website www.rockinghamales.co.uk

✗ A part-time micro-brewery established in 1997, which operates from a converted farm building near Blatherwyke, Northamptonshire (business address as above). The two-barrel plant produces a prolific range of beers and supplies half a dozen local outlets. The regular beers are brewed on a rota basis, with special beers brewed to order. Seasonal beers: Fineshade (ABV 3.8%, autumn), Sanity Clause (ABV 4.3%, December), Old Herbaceous (ABV 4.5%, winter).

Forest Gold *(OG 1040, ABV 3.9%)*
A hoppy blonde ale with citrus flavours. Well-balanced and clean finishing.

Hop Devil *(OG 1040, ABV 3.9%)*
Six hop varieties give this light amber ale a bitter start and spicy finish.

A1 Amber Ale *(OG 1041, ABV 4%)*
A hoppy session beer with fruit and blackcurrant undertones.

Saxon Cross *(OG 1041, ABV 4.1%)*
A golden-red ale with nut and coffee aromas. Citrus hop flavours predominate.

Fruits of the Forest *(OG 1043, ABV 4.2%)*
A multi-layered beer in which summer fruits and several spices compete with a big hop presence.

Dark Forest *(OG 1050, ABV 5%)*
A dark and complex beer, similar to a Belgian Dubbel, with numerous malty/smoky flavours that give way to a fruity bitter finish.

ROOSTER'S SIBA

Rooster's Brewing Co Ltd, Unit 3, Grimbald Park, Wetherby Road, Knaresborough, North Yorkshire, HG5 8LJ
Tel/Fax (01423) 865959
E-mail sean@roosters.co.uk

Website www.roosters.co.uk

☺ Rooster's Brewery was opened in 1993 by Sean and Alison Franklin. Outlaw Brewery Co started in 1996 after the original Pioneer label was released. In 2001 the brewery was relocated to larger premises at Knaresborough. Production is close to 80 barrels a week. Under the Rooster's label, Sean and Alison make seven regular beers while Outlaw produces experimental beers. They change materials or process or both to make a new beer every two months. Sean Franklin is a devotee of hops and uses many varieties, including North American, in his brews. 500 outlets are supplied direct

Special *(OG 1038, ABV 3.9%)* ▭◆
Yellow in colour, a full-bodied, floral bitter with fruit and hop notes being carried over in to the long aftertaste. Hops and bitterness tend to increase in the finish.

Scorcher
(OG 1042, ABV 4.3%) ▭◆
Golden aromatic and fruity, with balancing bitterness. The fruitiness is carried through into the aftertaste, where the bitterness tends to increase. A well-balanced beer.

Yankee *(OG 1042, ABV 4.3%)* ◆
A straw-coloured beer with a delicate, fruity aroma leading to a well-balanced taste of malt and hops with a slight evidence of sweetness, followed by a refreshing, fruity/bitter finish.

Hooligan *(OG 1042, ABV 4.3%)* ▯◆
Pale and aromatic bitter, a citrus fruit aroma with hints of tangerine. The palate has pronounced fruit and hops with a hint of sweetness. Bitterness and hops linger in the aftertaste, accompanied with a background of fruit flavours.

Cream *(OG 1045, ABV 4.7%)* ◆
A pale-coloured beer with a complex, floral bouquet leading to a well-balanced refreshing taste. Fruit lasts throughout and into the aftertaste.

ROTHER VALLEY

Rother Valley Brewing Co, Gate Court Farm, Station Road, Northiam, East Sussex, TN31 6QT
Tel (01797) 252922
Fax (01797) 253550
Tours by arrangement
✗ Rother Valley was established in Northiam in 1993 on a hop farm overlooking the river that marks the boundary between Kent and Sussex. Special beers are brewed to order and 50 outlets are supplied. Occasional/seasonal beers: Wheat Beer (ABV 3.8%, summer), O.P.M. (ABV 4.2%, July-August), Blues (ABV 5%, winter), Holly Daze (ABV varies, Christmas).

Wealden Bitter
(OG 1038, ABV 3.7%)

Level Best *(OG 1040, ABV 4%)* ◆
Full-bodied tawny session bitter with a malt and fruit aroma, malty taste and a dry, hoppy finish.

Hoppers Ale *(OG 1044, ABV 4.4%)*

RUDDLES

See Greene King.

RUDGATE SIBA

**Rudgate Brewery Ltd,
2 Centre Park, Marston Business Park,
Tockwith, York, YO26 7QF
Tel/Fax (01423) 358382
E-mail sales@rudgate-beers.co.uk
Website www.rudgate-beers.co.uk**
Shop Mail-order available

☺ Rudgate was founded in 1992 and is located in an old armoury building on the edge of a disused World War Two airfield. It has a 15-barrel brew plant and three open square fermenters, currently producing around 30 barrels a week. It supplies more than 150 outlets. Seasonal beer: Rudolf's Ruin (ABV 4.6%, Christmas).

Viking Bitter *(OG 1038, ABV 3.8%)* 🍺◆
An initially warming and malty, full-bodied beer, with hops and fruit lingering into the aftertaste.

Battleaxe *(OG 1041, ABV 4.2%)* ◆
A well-hopped bitter with slightly sweet initial taste and light bitterness. Complex fruit character gives a memorable aftertaste.

Ruby Mild *(OG 1044, ABV 4.4%)* 🍺◻
Nutty rich ruby ale, stronger than usual for a mild.

Special *(OG 1043, ABV 4.5%)*

RYBURN SIBA

**◻ Ryburn Brewery, c/o Ram's Head,
Wakefield Road, Sowerby Bridge, Halifax,
West Yorkshire, HX6 2AZ
Tel (01422) 835413
Fax (01422) 836488
E-mail ryburnbrewery@talk21.com**

☺ The brewery was established during 1989 at Mill House, Sowerby Bridge, but has since been relocated beneath the company's sole tied house, the Rams Head. Some business is done with the local free trade but the chief market for the brewery's products is via wholesalers and the SIBA cooperative venture.

Best Mild *(OG 1033, ABV 3.3%)*

Best Bitter *(OG 1038, ABV 3.6%)*

Numpty Bitter *(OG 1044, ABV 4.2%)*

Rydale Bitter *(OG 1044, ABV 4.2%)*

Light Ale *(OG 1042, ABV 4.4%)*

Luddite *(OG 1048, ABV 5%)*

Stabbers Bitter *(OG 1052, ABV 5.2%)*

SADDLEWORTH

**◻ The Church Inn & Saddleworth Brewery,
Church Lane, Uppermill, Oldham, OL3 6LW
Tel (01457) 820902/872415**
Tours by arrangement

☺ Saddleworth started brewing in 1997 in a brewhouse closed for around 120 years. The first brew was Saddleworth More sold for £1 per pint; it now sells at £1.10. Brewery and inn are set in an historic location at the top of a valley overlooking the village of Saddleworth and next to St Chads Church, which dates back to 1215. Seasonal beers: Ayrton's Ale (ABV 4.1%, April-May), Robyn's Bitter (ABV 4.6%, Nov-Dec), Christmas Carol (ABV 7.5%), Harvest Moon (ABV 4.1%, Aug-Sept).

Saddleworth More *(ABV 3.8%)*

Bert Corner *(ABV 4%)*

Ayrton's Ale *(ABV 4.1%)*

Harvest Moon *(ABV 4.1%)*
A light golden beer, slightly sweet with bitter aftertaste.

Hop Smacker *(ABV 4.1%)*
A golden, refreshing bitter, brewed with five different varieties of hops.

Indian 2 Pale Ale *(ABV 4.1%)*

Robyns Bitter *(ABV 4.6%)*
A dark ruby bitter with a rich malty flavour.

Shaftbender *(ABV 5.4%)*
A black porter/stout bitter.

Christmas Carol *(ABV 7.5%)*

ST AUSTELL IFBB

**St Austell Brewery Co Ltd, 63 Trevarthian
Road, St Austell, Cornwall, PL25 4BY
Tel (01726) 74444
Fax (01726) 68965
E-mail info@staustellbrewery.co.uk
Website www.staustellbrewery.co.uk**
Shop 9-5 Mon-Fri
Visitor centre and tours (01726) 66022

St Austell Brewery celebrated 150 years of brewing in 2001. Founded by Walter Hicks in 1851, the company is still family-owned and run, with Walter Hicks' great-great-grandson, James Staughton, at the helm as managing director since 2000. He leads a young team, with head brewer Roger Ryman, and there is a powerful commitment to cask beer. The beer range has been overhauled, with new branding and pump clips in pubs. Cask beer is available in all 150 licensed houses, as well as an increasing presence in the free trade throughout Devon, Cornwall and Somerset. An attractive visitor centre offers guided tours and souvenirs from the brewery. The brewery hosts its own Celtic Beer Festival late in the year. Bottle-conditioned beer: Clouded Yellow (ABV 5%).

IPA *(OG 1034, ABV 3.4%)*
Copper/bronze in colour, the nose blossoms with fresh hops. The palate is clean and full-bodied with a hint of toffee caramel. The finish is short and crisp.

Black Prince
(OG 1041, ABV 4%) 🍺◆
Little aroma, but a strong, malty character. A caramel-sweetish flavour is followed by a good, lingering aftertaste that is sweet but with a fruity dryness.

Tinners Ale *(OG 1038, ABV 3.7%)* ◆
A deservedly popular, golden beer with an appetising malt aroma and a good balance of malt and hops in the flavour. Lasting finish.

Dartmoor Best Bitter
(OG 1039, ABV 3.9%)
A delicately hopped golden bitter. Originally brewed at the now-closed Ferguson Brewery in Plymouth, DBB was brewed by St Austell for Carlsberg-Tetley, but it is now owned by St Austell and is spearheading the Cornish company's increased presence in Devon.

Tribute *(OG 1043, ABV 4.2%)* ◆
Pale brown ale capable of a tight, persistent head. Aroma is of malt and fruity Oregon hops, with a balance of malt and hoppy bitterness in the mouth. The finish is moderately dry with malt. A refreshing best bitter aimed to expand beyond Cornwall.

Hicks Special Draught/HSD
(OG 1051, ABV 5%) ▣◆
An aromatic, fruity, hoppy bitter that is initially sweet and has an aftertaste of pronounced bitterness, but whose flavour is fully rounded. A good premium beer.

ST GEORGE'S

St George's Brewing Co Ltd, Bush Lane, Callow End, Worcester, WR2 4TF
Tel/Fax (01905) 831316;
07813 084171 (m)
E-mail stgeorges@btconnect.com
Website www.stgeorgesbrewery.com
Tours by arrangement

⊠ The brewery was established in 1998 by Martin Soden and his father. It then transferred ownership in to Brian McCluskie and David Butcher, who had long careers in the brewing industry. They have a strong commitment to traditional brewing and have revised the beer range, and plan to expand. When David Butcher retired, Brian McCluskie appointed Paul Hodgkinson as brewery manager, who also has had a career in the brewing and pub world. Seasonal beer: Paragon Steam (ABV 4%), Enigma (ABV 4.2%), A Winters Ale (ABV 4.6%). Some of the beer names pay homage to Sir Edward Elgar, who lived in the area and was inspired by the Malvern Hills.

Bitter *(OG 1037, ABV 3.7%)*
Light and refreshing, brewed using traditional English barley and hops.

Gold *(OG 1038, ABV 3.9%)*
A mellow bitter with pronounced taste and a richer colour.

War Drum *(OG 1042, ABV 4.1%)*
A pale ale with a multi-layered, ripe maltiness and long finish

Premium Bitter *(OG 1043, ABV 4.3%)* ◆
A strikingly bitter and hoppy golden ale. An underpinning fruity sweetness is cut short as the high alpha levels deliver a hoppy finish.

Special *(OG 1044, ABV 4.4%)*

Nimrod *(OG 1045, ABV 4.5%)*
A smoky taste and sharp hopping make for a pronounced character for this traditional ale.

Ruby XXX *(OG 1046, ABV 4.6%)*
Fruity in the mouth with great character and roundness in the finish.

Fire *(OG 1049, ABV 4.9%)*
Roasted and dark malts for full body.

ST PETER'S SIBA

St Peter's Brewery Co Ltd,
St Peter's Hall, St Peter South Elmham,
Bungay, Suffolk, NR35 1NQ
Tel (01986) 782322
Fax (01986) 782505
E-mail beers@stpetersbrewery.co.uk
Website www.stpetersbrewery.co.uk
Shop available 9-5
Tours by arrangement

⊠ St Peter's Brewery started brewing in 1996 using water from a deep-water bore hole on the site. A wide range of cask-conditioned beers are produced and the beer is also bottled on site. The medieval St Peter's Hall provides a dramatic back-drop to the brewery and is open as a bar and restaurant every Friday, Saturday and Sunday. Pubs in the Home Counties are supplied direct and elsewhere via distributors. Seasonal beers: Winter Ale (ABV 6.5%), Cinnamon & Apple Spiced Ale (ABV 6.5%), Summer Ale (ABV 6.5%).

Best Bitter *(OG 1038, ABV 3.7%)*
A traditional best bitter brewed with pale and crystal malts and Goldings aroma hops. The result is a full-bodied ale with distinctive fruity caramel notes.

Mild *(OG 1038, ABV 3.7%)*
A beer mild in hops but not in flavour. Sweetness is balanced by bitter chocolate malt.

Organic Best Bitter *(OG 1041, ABV 4.1)*
Soil Association accredited, organically-grown Chariot malted barley is used to make the mash for this beer, which is hopped with organic Hallertauer hops.

Extra *(OG 1044, ABV 4.3%)*
A premium beer with hop character is to the fore.

Organic Ale *(OG 1046, ABV 4.5%)*
Soil Association standard, light malted barley from Scotland, with organic Target hops create a refreshingly flavoured ale with a delicate character.

Golden Ale *(OG 1047, ABV 4.7%)*
English Halcyon malts are used together with pale malts, with Goldings hops providing the bitterness and aroma. The result is a highly distinctive light, golden ale.

Wheat Beer *(OG 1048, ABV 4.7%)*
A high proportion of premium wheat is used with modest amounts of Challenger and Goldings hop varieties to produce a light, smooth, clear and refreshing beer with a distinctive palate and a clean, crisp aftertaste.

Elderberry Fruit Beer
(OG 1048, ABV 4.7%)
This refreshing beer has a wheat beer base complemented by the addition of elderberry. This rare example of an English fruit beer has a delightfully floral fruit nose and refreshing dry finish.

Grapefruit Beer *(OG 1045, ABV 4.7%)*
Wheat Beer is the base for this refreshing beer. The zesty/pithy grapefruit is in complete harmony with the hops and malt. Excellent as an aperitif.

Lemon and Ginger Spiced Ale
(OG 1048, ABV 4.7%)
A traditional English ale with a light citrus aroma and a delicate ginger aftertaste.

Suffolk Gold *(OG 1050, ABV 4.9%)*
Suffolk-grown First Gold hops provide the inspiration for this premium beer, which is brewed with Suffolk malt to produce a full-bodied ale with a lasting hop aroma.

King Cnut Ale *(OG 1051, ABV 5%)*
This ale is based on a recipe from the first millennium and features roast barley, juniper berries, orange and lemon peel, spices and stinging nettles from a local hedgerow.

Old Style Porter
(OG 1051, ABV 5.1%)
This beer is a blend of a mature old ale with a younger light beer, just as a true Porter should be. The marriage produces an extremely characterful brew that is dark in colour and complex in taste.

Honey Porter *(OG 1051, ABV 5.1%)*
A traditional English porter finished with honey for a truly unique aroma and taste.

Strong Ale *(OG 1052, ABV 5.1%)*
A fine example of a traditional English strong ale. Challenger and Goldings hops act in perfect harmony with Suffolk malt.

Cream Stout *(OG 1065, ABV 6.5%)*
Challenger and Fuggles hops plus a blend of four local barley malts create an aromatic, strong, dark chocolate cream stout with a satisfying bitter-sweet aftertaste.

SALAMANDER

**Salamander Brewing Co Ltd,
22 Harry Street, Dudley Hill, Bradford,
West Yorkshire, BD4 9PH
Website www.salamanderbrewing.com
Tel (01274) 652323
Fax (01274) 680101**
Tours by arrangement

⊗ Chris Bee and Daniel Gent launched their brewery in 2001 in a former pie factory. Chris brewed at the Orange Brewery and the Yorkshire Grey brew-pubs in London, and Daniel honed his skills at Freedom, also in London. Their 10-barrel plant is made up of some vessels bought from Mitchells of Lancaster along with ex-dairy equipment. They have quickly established their business with 150 outlets in the North and Midlands. In 2001, more tanks were purchased and capacity doubled to meet growing demand. Most of the beer names have salamander connections. The brewery has recently extended its delivery area and is now supplying Nottingham and Liverpool.

Axolotl *(OG 1038, ABV 3.8%)*
A pale refreshing session ale with a pleasing Fuggles late hop character.

Young Buzzard *(OG 1038, ABV 3.8%)* ◆
A bitter, dry and slightly astringent finish rounds off this tawny, medium-bodied beer. Tart fruit and resinous hops dominate with a subtle malty sweetness. The nose is hoppy and fruity.

Mudpuppy *(OG 1042, ABV 4.2%)* ◆
A nicely balanced pale brown beer with a malty and slightly fruity nose giving way to

stronger hoppy, bitter flavours, leaving a long, dry finish.

Golden Salamander
(OG 1045, ABV 4.5%) ◆
A pleasant, hoppy aroma leads to a crisp, citrus-hoppy bitterness with malt undertones. The finish is long and bitter.

Stout *(OG 1045, ABV 4.5%)*

Porter *(OG 1048, ABV 4.8%)*

SALOPIAN SIBA

**Salopian Brewing Co Ltd, 67 Mytton Oak
Road, Shrewsbury, Shropshire, SY3 8UQ
Tel (01743) 248414**
Shop 9-5 weekdays
Tours by arrangement

☺ The brewery was opened in 1995 in an old dairy on the outskirts of Shrewsbury. Partners Wilf Nelson and brewer Martin Barry have developed cask sales locally and nationally through wholesalers. They have purchased two new fermenters, and capacity has been increased in size to 50 barrels. Bottle-conditioned beers are brewed at Hepworth of Horsham (qv). The brewery is actively seeking a brewery tap. Fifty-five outlets are supplied from the brewery.

Shropshire Gold *(OG 1037, ABV 3.8%)*

Proud Salopian *(OG 1044, ABV 4.5%)*

Heaven Sent *(OG 1044, ABV 4.5%)*

Puzzle *(OG 1047, ABV 4.8%)*

Golden Thread *(OG 1048, ABV 5%)*

Ironbridge Stout *(OG 1050, ABV 5%)*

SARAH'S HOP HOUSE SIBA

**Sarah's Hop House Brewery,
131 High Street, Golborne, Warrington,
Cheshire, WA3 3TG
Tel (01942) 606792
E-mail jim@tripp.fsnet.co.uk**
Tours by arrangement

☺ Sarah Porter worked in the pub trade for 20 years, bought her own free house eight years ago, and decided to go the next mile and brew her own beer. She learnt the brewing skills by working with John Feeney at Bank Top. Her five-barrel plant is situated in outbuildings behind the Railway Inn. She started brewing in 2000 with Hop House Bitter and supplies outlets (but steadily increasing) within the locality, plus some supplied by wholesalers.

CLOSED JULY 2003

Hop House Bitter *(OG 1038, ABV 3.9%)*
An amber beer with a fruity nose. A nice balance of orange fruit and hops with malt and bitterness in the mouth and a satisfyingly bitter, fruity finish.

Black Mamba Mild *(OG 1040, ABV 4%)*
A roast malt and chocolate aroma complements the dark red/brown colour. Hints of treacle toffee join the roast malt and chocolate in the taste, before a dry roast finish.

Hop To It *(OG 1042, ABV 4.2%)* ◆
Amber beer with a light citrus aroma. Bitter, malty palate with a bitter and very dry aftertaste.

Gordon's Amber Ale (OG 1042, ABV 4.2%)

Chocolate Stout (OG 1047, ABV 4.7%)
Dark red/brown beer with roast malt and chocolate on the aroma and flavour. Creamy, smooth palate and a fairly dry, roast aftertaste.

Wheels of Fire (OG 1047, ABV 4.7%)

Two Harleys (OG 1047, ABV 4.7%)

SAWBRIDGEWORTH

**Sawbridgeworth Brewery,
The Gate, 81 London Road,
Sawbridgeworth, Herts, CM21 9JJ
Tel (01279) 722313 Fax (01279) 726060**
Tours by arrangement

✖ A brew-pub run by former professional footballer Tommy Barnett (Crystal Palace, Orient and St Albans City) with equipment bought from Whitbread. Tommy started brewing in 2000 and he supplies beer festivals as well as the Gate.

Brown Bomber (ABV 3.7%)

Selhurst Park Flyer (ABV 3.7%)

Teflon (ABV 3.7%)

Is It Yourself (ABV 4.2%)

Brooklands Express (ABV 4.6%)

Lynne Pearce (ABV 5%)

Piledriver (ABV 5.3%)

SCARECROW

⌂ **Scarecrow Brewery Ltd, Arreton Craft Village, Arreton, Isle of Wight, PO30 3AA
Phone (01983) 856161**
Shop Open daily 10am-8pm

✖ Scarecrow Brewery, owned by Ventnor Brewery (qv), is located at Arreton Craft village alongside the Dairyman's Daughter Inn. Brewing takes place once a week and supplies four pubs and beer festivals. Brewing can be viewed from the Beer Emporium, which specialises in bottled beers from all over the country as well as breweriana. The beer shop has a full range of Ventnor Brewery products and merchandise and a wide range of beers from all over Britain. Bottle-conditioned beer: Scarecrow Best.

Scarecrow Best (OG 1042, ABV 4.2%)

SCATTOR ROCK

**Scattor Rock Brewery Ltd,
Unit 5 Gidley's Meadow, Christow,
Exeter, Devon, EX6 7QB
Tel (01647) 252120
E-mail keithscattorrock@aol.com
Website www.scattorrockbrewery.com**
Tours by arrangement

✖ The brewery was set up in 1998 and is based in the Dartmoor National Park, and named after a well-known local landmark. More than 60 outlets are supplied on a permanent or regular basis. Occasional beers: Quarryman Stout (ABV 4.9%), Scattor Brain (ABV 4.8%), Gidleys Bitter (ABV 4.4%), Completely and Utterly Brain Dead (ABV 9%). There is a seasonal beer available every month and branded as the 'Tor collection'.

Scatty Bitter (OG 1040, ABV 3.8%)

Teign Valley Tipple (OG 1042, ABV 4%)
A well-balanced, tawny-coloured beer with a hoppy aroma.

Skylark (OG 1043, ABV 4.2%)
A refreshing, light brown session ale.

Devonian (OG 1045, ABV 4.5%)
A strong, fruity, light-coloured ale.

Golden Valley
(OG 1046, ABV 4.6%)
A golden refreshing ale.

Valley Stomper (OG 1051, ABV 5%)
Light brown and deceptively drinkable.

SELBY

**Selby (Middlebrough) Brewery Ltd,
131 Millgate, Selby,
North Yorkshire, YO8 3LL
Tel (01757) 702826**
Shop 10-12 and 6-10 Mon-Sat

◉ And old family brewery that resumed brewing in 1972 after a gap of 18 years but which is now mostly involved in wholesaling. Its beers, which are brewed on an occasional basis, are available, while stocks last (only in bulk) at the shop and not at the company's single pub. They are also sold as guest beers in the local free trade.

No. 1 (OG 1040, ABV 4%)

No. 3 (OG 1040, ABV 4%)

Old Tom (OG 1065, ABV 6.5%)

SHARDLOW

**Shardlow Brewing Company Ltd,
The Old Brewery Stables,
British Waterways Yard, Cavendish Bridge,
Leicestershire, DE72 2HL
Tel/Fax (01332) 799188**
Tours by arrangement

✖ The brewery was established in 1993 and the present owner, Ron Morgan, bought the company in 1996. As a traditional ale fan, the company has expanded under his guidance to running two pubs and extending its customer base. More occasional and seasonal beers have been produced and the company still provides cask beers at large, outdoor events. 100 outlets are supplied direct.

Chancellors Revenge
(ABV 3.6%)
A light-coloured, refreshing, full-flavoured and well-hopped session bitter.

Cavendish Dark (ABV 3.7%)

Best Bitter (ABV 3.9%)
A well-balanced, amber-coloured, quaffable bitter.

Narrowboat (ABV 4.3%)
A pale amber bitter, with a short, crisp hoppy aftertaste.

Cavendish Gold (ABV 4.5%)
A premium pale bitter.

Reverend Eaton's Ale
(ABV 4.5%)
A smooth, medium-strong bitter, full of malt and hop flavours with a sweet aftertaste.

Mayfly (ABV 4.8%)

Whistle Stop *(OG 1050, ABV 5%)*
Maris Otter pale malt and two hops produce this smooth and surprisingly strong pale beer.

Five Bells *(ABV 5%)*

Platinum Blonde *(ABV 5%)*

Six Bells *(ABV 6%)*

SHARP'S SIBA

Sharp's Brewery, Rock, Wadebridge, Cornwall, PL27 6NU
Tel (01208) 862121 Fax (01208) 863727
E-mail enquiries@sharp'sbrewery.co.uk
Website www.sharpsbrewery.co.uk
Tours by arrangement

⊠ Founded in 1994 in one industrial unit, the brewery has enjoyed rapid expansion and now occupies nearly half the estate. It supplies the free trade in Devon and Cornwall, and the beers are also widely available via wholesalers. The brewery is upgrading its equipment to cope with continued demand for the beers. Some 350 outlets are supplied. Eden Ale is now being bottled with other beers from the range to follow.

Cornish Coaster
(OG 1032-38, ABV 3.6%) ◈
A smooth, easy-drinking beer, golden in colour, with a fresh hop aroma and dry malt and hops in the mouth. The finish starts malty but becomes dry and hoppy.

Doom Bar Bitter *(OG 1038-45, ABV 4%)* ◈
A rich, golden brown beer with a hint of barley. Dry malt and hops in the mouth. The malty finish becomes dry and hoppy. Fresh hop aroma.

Eden Ale *(OG 1042-48, ABV 4.4%)*
Brewed in celebration of Cornwall's Eden Project, it boasts a full and rounded flavour with a distinctively crisp and refreshing, dry hop finish.

Sharp's Own *(OG 1042-48, ABV 4.4%)* ◈
A deep golden brown beer with a delicate hops and malt aroma, and dry malt and hops in the mouth. Like the other beers, its finish starts malty but turns dry and hoppy.

Will's Resolve *(OG 1044-50, ABV 4.6%)*
A rich golden brown beer with fresh hop aroma and with dry malt and hops in the mouth.

Special *(OG 1050-54, ABV 5.2%)* ◈
Deep golden brown with a fresh hop aroma. Dry malt and hops in the mouth; the finish is malty but becomes dry and hoppy.

SHAWS

Shaws Brewery, The Old Stables, Park Road, Dukinfield, Cheshire, SK16 5LX
Tel (0161) 330 5471 Fax (0161) 343 1879

☻ The brewery is housed in the stables of William Shaws Brewery, closed by John Smiths in 1941. The five-barrel plant was designed and commissioned by the brewers Neil Hay and Phillip Windsor in consultation with Baz Parish of Parish Brewery. Brewing started in 2002. Beer is supplied to more than 30 local free trade and beer festivals.

Best Bitter *(OG 1038, ABV 4%)*

Tame Valley Ale *(OG 1040, ABV 4.3%)*

IPA *(OG 1044, ABV 4.8%)*

SHEPHERD NEAME IFBB

Shepherd Neame Ltd, 17 Court Street, Faversham, Kent, ME13 7AX
Tel (01795) 532206
Fax (01795) 538907
E-mail company@shepherd-neame.co.uk
Website www.shepherd-neame.co.uk
Shop 11-3 Mon-Fri.
Tours by arrangement

⊠ Kent's major independent brewery is believed to be the oldest continuous brewer in the country since 1698, but records show brewing began on the site as far back as the 12th century. The same water source is still used today, steam engines are still usable, and the mash is produced in two teak tuns that date from 1910. A visitors' reception hall is housed in a restored medieval hall (tours by arrangement). In 2000, Shepherd Neame invested £2.2 million in a new brewhouse that boosted production to 200,000 barrels a year. The company has 372 tied houses in the South-east, nearly all selling cask ale, but tenants are encouraged to keep beers under blanket pressure if the cask is likely to be on sale for more than three days. More than 2000 other outlets are also supplied. Seasonal beers: Early Bird (ABV 4.5%, spring), Late Red (ABV 4.5%, autumn), Goldings (ABV 4.7%, summer), Original Porter (ABV 4.8%, winter).

Master Brew Bitter
(OG 1032, ABV 3.7%) ◈
A distinctive bitter, mid-brown in colour, with a hoppy aroma. Well-balanced, with a nicely aggressive bitter taste from its hops, it leaves a hoppy/bitter finish, tinged with sweetness.

Master Brew Best Bitter
(OG 1036, ABV 4.1%) ◈
Mid-brown, with less marked characteristics than the bitter. However, the nose is very well-balanced and the taste enjoys a malty, bitter smokiness. Malty, well-rounded finish. It also appears under the name Canterbury Jack.

Spitfire *(OG 1039, ABV 4.5%)*
A commemorative Battle of Britain brew for the RAF Benevolent Fund's appeal, now a permanent feature.

Bishops Finger *(OG 1046, ABV 5%)*
A cask-conditioned version of a famous bottled beer, introduced in cask in 1989.

SHOES SIBA

Shoes Brewery, Three Horseshoes Inn, Norton Canon, Hereford, HR4 7BH
Tel/Fax (01544) 318375
Tours by arrangement

Landlord Frank Goodwin had long been a home brewer, but decided in 1994 to brew on a commercial basis for his pub. The beers are brewed from malt extract, stored in casks and dispensed under a blanket of mixed gas. Bottle-conditioned beer: Farriers Beer (ABV 15.1%).

Norton Ale *(OG 1038, ABV 3.6%)*

Canon Bitter *(OG 1040, ABV 4.1%)*

SHUGBOROUGH
See Titanic.

SIX BELLS
The Six Bells Brewery, Church Street, Bishop's Castle, Shropshire, SY9 5AA
Tel (01588) 638930 Fax (01588) 630132
Website bishops-castle.co.uk/SixBells /brewery
Tours by arrangement

⊗ Neville Richards – 'Big Nev' – started brewing in 1997 with a five-barrel brew length plant and two fermenters. Alterations in 1999 included two more fermenters, a new grain store and mashing equipment, and some automation. He currently supplies a number of customers both within the county and over the border in Wales. Seasonal beers: Old Recumbent (ABV 5.2%, Oct-spring), Spring Forward (ABV 4.6%, March-May), Seven Bells (ABV 5.5%, Christmas), Festival Pale (ABV 5.2%, June-July for town's annual beer festival).

Big Nev's *(OG 1037, ABV 3.8%)*
A pale, fairly hoppy bitter.

Roo Brew *(OG 1038, ABV 3.8%)*
Brewed exclusively for the Kangaroo Inn Aston on Clun, to the publican's recipe. Copper-coloured, hoppy and heavily late hopped with Goldings.

Marathon Ale *(OG 1040, ABV 4%)*
Dark ruby-coloured and malty.

Cloud Nine *(OG 1042, ABV 4.2%)*
Pale amber-colour with a slight citrus finish.

Duck & Dive *(OG 1044, ABV 4.6%)*
Pale and hoppy.

Brew 101 *(OG 1048, ABV 4.8%)*
A dark, fruity beer.

SKINNER'S SIBA
Skinner's Brewery, Riverside View, Newham, Truro, Cornwall, TR1 2SU
Tel (01872) 271885 Fax (01872) 271886
E-mail info@skinnersbrewery.com
Website www.skinnersbrewery.com
Tours by arrangement

⊗ A brewery founded in 1997 by Steve and Sarah Skinner, formerly of the Tipsy Toad Brewery in Jersey. The beer names are based on Cornish folklore characters. The brewery has won many awards in its short life, including Supreme Champion at the SIBA Maltings Festival, Newton Abbot, in 1998, with Cornish Knocker. This was followed in 1999 with a repeat performance with Betty Stogs. Also in 1999 Who Put the Lights Out? won a gold medal in the National Beauty of Hops competition. Ice Blonde won Beer of the Festival at the Cotswold Festival in 2000. Skinner's owns one pub, the Skinner's Ale House in Newquay. Occasional beer: Jingle Knockers (ABV 5.5%, Christmas), Mild Oatmeal Stout (ABV 4%, April-May). Bottle-conditioned beers: Who Put the Lights Out? (ABV 5%), Cornish Knocker Ale, Jingle Knockers (ABV 5.5%).

Coast Liner *(ABV 3.4%)*
A crisp, light brown, hoppy session bitter.

Spriggan Ale *(OG 1038, ABV 3.8%)* ◆
A light golden, hoppy bitter. Well-balanced with a smooth bitter finish.

Betty Stogs Bitter *(ABV 4%)* ⛃◆
A pale amber, mid-strength bitter with hoppy overtones.

Cornish Knocker Ale
(OG 1044.5, ABV 4.5%) ◆
A strong, clean-tasting golden ale. Distinctive flowery aroma with a lasting finish.

Figgy's Brew *(ABV 4.5%)* ◆
A classic, dark, premium-strength bitter. Full-flavoured with a smooth finish.

Who Put the Lights Out? *(ABV 5%)*
Strong single hop amber ale first brewed to mark the solar eclipse in 1999.

Cornish Blonde Wheat Beer
(OG 1050, ABV 5%)

Ice Blonde *(OG 1050, ABV 5%)*
Wheat beer served at 4 degrees C.

SMILES SIBA
Smiles Brewing Co Ltd, Colston Street, Colston St, Bristol, BS1 5BD
Tel (01275) 375 878
Fax (01275) 375 076
E-mail mort@smiles.co.uk/ chris@smiles.co.uk
Website www.smiles.co.uk
Tours by arrangement (01275) 375894

⊗ Built on the classic brewing principle, Smiles Brewery uses traditional methods and only the finest ingredients to brew fresh, natural, hand-crafted beers. Smiles started full-scale brewing in 1978 and has grown into a successful, independent brewery, having celebrated its silver jubilee in 2003. One pub is owned. There are some eight seasonal beers a year.

Original *(OG 1038, ABV 3.8%)* ◆
Aroma of pale/crystal malt, fruit and floral hop, with similar, bigger taste. Good dry bitterness, with a finish less sweet and more dry. Amber-coloured, it is light, hoppy, dry and refreshing.

Best *(OG 1041, ABV 4.1%)* ◆
Nicely balanced, mid-bodied and bitter-sweet ale, with malt, hops and fruit lasting throughout. Pale brown in colour.

Bristol IPA
(OG 1044, ABV 4.5%) ◆
Crisp, hoppy, dry bitter. Pale and crystal malts combine with peppery Styrian hops to create a pleasing tart acidity, balanced by malt. Long dry finish.

Heritage *(OG 1052, ABV 5.2%)* ◆
Aroma of malt, chocolate and hops, this is a medium to full-bodied, fruity ale, with a lasting, bitter-sweet finish. Red-brown in colour.

SAMUEL SMITH
Samuel Smith Old Brewery (Tadcaster), High Street, Tadcaster, North Yorkshire, LS24 9SB
Tel (01937) 832225 Fax (01937) 834673
Tours by arrangement

⊛ Although related to the nearby John Smith's, this fiercely independent, family-owned company is radically different. Tradition, quality and value are important here, resulting in traditional brewing without adjuncts and all real ale supplied in wooden casks. Unfortunately, nitro-keg has crept in, especially in London. Although processed, a fine range of bottled beers is produced. A filtered draught wheat beer is a recent addition. Some 200 pubs are owned.

Old Brewery Bitter (OBB)
(OG 1040, ABV 4%)
Malt dominates the aroma, with an initial burst of malt, hops and fruit in the taste, which is sustained in the aftertaste.

SNOWDONIA SIBA

Snowdonia Brewery, Snowdonia Parc Hotel, Waunfawr, Caernarfon, Gwynedd, LLS5 Tel/Fax (01286) 650409
Tours by arrangement

Snowdonia started brewing in spring 1998 in a two-barrel brew length brewhouse. The pub is the station master's house for the Welsh Highland Railway. Waunfawr station opened in summer 2000 and is now the railway terminus. The owners bought the Prince of Wales in Caernarfon, which is a second outlet for the brewery's beers.

Welsh Highland Bitter *(OG 1050, ABV 5%)*

SPECTRUM* SIBA

Spectrum Brewery, c/o 23 Briton Way, Wymondham, Norfolk, NR18 0TT
Tel (07949) 254383
E-mail andy@spectrumbrewery.co.uk
Website www.spectrumbrewery.co.uk

⊗ After escaping from the IT industry, proprietor and founder Andy Mitchell gained experience working for a number of East Anglian brewers, as well as gaining an MSc in brewing and distilling, before establishing Spectrum Brewery in 2002. It's the only East Anglian brewery to brew exclusively from organic malt and hops and attaining organic certification is planned. The brewery shares plant and premises with

Spectrum Brewery

Blue Moon Brewery and supplies more than 30 outlets. Seasonal beers: Light Fantastic (ABV 3.2%, summer), Reaper (ABV 4.4%, summer-autumn), Old Stoatwobbler (ABV6%, winter).

Light Fantastic *(OG 1032, ABV 3.2%)*
Thirst-quenching light bitter.

Bezants *(OG 1039.5, ABV 4%)* ◆
A well-hopped, clean-tasting bitter. Although some maltiness can be detected in both the aroma and taste, it is hops that dominate. A residual bitterness adds to a long aftertaste that ends in a lingering dryness.

42 *(OG 1042, ABV4.2%)*
Hoppy and easy-drinking best bitter.

Reaper *(OG 1044, ABV 4.4%)* ◆
A well-rounded brew with a soft fruity character that agrees with the red-brown colouring. A hint of lychees in the gentle, delicate aroma. Fruits of the vine are well to the fore in the taste throughout. Roast notes support the well-balanced fruitiness as the finish holds up well. Traces of hop provide a contrast to the overall mellowness of character.

Red Sickle *(OG 1044.5, ABV 4.5%)* ◆
Blackcurrant notes can be found throughout the aroma and taste of this easy-drinking ale. A gentle blend of flavours belies the strength of this red-hued brew. Malt, roast and hops provide a background to the fruity signature, although the finish quickly ends on a somewhat drier note.

Black Buffle *(OG 1046, ABV 4.5%)*
A stout, named after the brewer's cat.

Wizard *(OG 1048.5, ABV 4.9%)* ◆
A pungent sultana and malt aroma introduces this well-balanced but almost primitive mid-brown beer. Sweet dried fruit flavours dominate the taste through to the long, sustained finish. A dryish hop feel can be detected in the background, which helps to give a lighter character to this full-flavoured brew.

Old Stoatwobbler
(OG 1064.5, ABV 6%) ◆
Wonderfully complex brew with dark chocolate, morrello cherry, raisin and banana vying for dominance alongside hops and malt. A black-coloured brew with a solid fruity nose continuing to a well-balanced explosion of flavour ending in a sustained smooth but soft finish.

Trip Hazard *(OG 1064.5, ABV 6.5%)* ◆
Exceptionally malty but easy-drinking for its strength. Rich fruity flavours dominate throughout, date and sultana to the fore. A growing bitterness in the finish.

SPINNING DOG SIBA

⌕ **Spinning Dog Brewery, 88 St Owen's Street, Hereford, HR1 2QD**
Tel/Fax (01432) 342125
E-mail jfkenyon@aol.com
Tours by arrangement

⊛ The brewery was built in a room of the Victory in 2000 by Jim Kenyon, following the purchase of the pub. Initially the brewery served only the pub, but is now supplying some 500 other outlets. As a result of the closure of Flannery's of Aberystwyth, Jim has taken on some of its beers. One pub is owned. In 2002, the brewery expanded from its four-barrel plant to a 10-barrel one and extensive work was carried out on the brewhouse. There is a programme of monthly beers as well as the 10 regular ones.

Chase Your Tail (*OG 1036, ABV 3.6%*)
A good session beer with an abundance of hops and bitterness. Dry, with citrus aftertaste.

Mutleys Mongrel (*OG 1039, ABV 3.9%*)
Brewed with a blend of three different hops to create a very hoppy ale.

Mutleys Dark (*OG 1040, ABV 4%*)
A dark, malty mild with a hint of bitterness and a touch of roast caramel. A smooth drinkable ale.

Pit Stop (*OG 1040, ABV 4%*)
Pale in colour, light and refreshing with a fruity aftertaste.

Hereford Cathedral Bitter
(*OG 1040, ABV 4%*)
A crisp amber beer made with the finest Hereford hops, producing a well-rounded malt/hop bitterness throughout and a pleasing, lingering aftertaste.

Top Dog (*OG 1042, ABV 4.2%*)
A hoppy beer with both malt and fruit flavours, a hoppy aroma with a slight bitter, hoppy aftertaste.

Mutleys Oatmeal Stout
(*OG 1044, ABV 4.4%*)
Robust, full-bodied and satisfying.

Harvest Moon (*OG 1045, ABV 4.5%*)
A former seasonal brew that quickly became a best seller. Pale in colour with a malty, bitter, lingering aftertaste.

Celtic Gold (*OG 1045, ABV 4.5%*)
This beer was runner up in the People's Pint 2001 at St Albans beer festival and is proving to be a big seller.

Mutleys Revenge (*OG 1048, ABV 4.8%*)
A strong, smooth, premium, hoppy beer, amber in colour. Full-bodied with a dry, citrus aftertaste.

SPRINGHEAD SIBA

Springhead Brewery, Old Great North Road, Sutton-on-Trent, Newark, Notts, NG23 6QS
Tel (01636) 821000
Fax (01636) 821150
E-mail steve@springhead.co.uk
Website www.springhead.co.uk
Tours by arrangement

The brewery started life in 1990 as the country's smallest brewery. Rapid expansion has taken place in the past few years and, since the appointment of head brewer Shirley Reynolds in 2001, business has boomed with production up some 75% in the past year. The brewery plans to move to larger premises to realise its potential. Two pubs are owned. Cask ales are supplied to more than 400 outlets in the East and West Midlands, and Yorkshire.

Surrender 1646 (*OG 1038, ABV 3.6%*)
A burnished, copper-coloured bitter with a stunning combination of malt and hops. Long dry finish. Wonderfully refreshing.

Bitter (*OG 1041, ABV 4%*)
A clean-tasting, easy-drinking, hoppy beer.

Puritans Porter (*OG 1041, ABV 4%*)
A porter, dark but not heavy. Smooth with a lingering finish of roasted barley. Suitable for vegans.

Roundhead's Gold
(*OG 1042, ABV 4.2%*)
Golden light, made with wild flower honey. Refreshing but not too sweet with the glorious aroma of Saaz hops.

Rupert's Ruin (*OG 1042, ABV 4.2%*)
A coppery, complex beer with a fruity aroma and a long, malty aftertaste.

Goodrich Castle (*OG 1044, ABV 4.4%*)
Brewed following a 17th-century recipe using rosemary. Pale ale, light on the palate with a bitter finish and a delicate flavour.

Oliver's Army (*OG 1044, ABV 4.4%*)

Sweet Lips (*OG 1045, ABV 4.6%*)
A light, smooth and refreshing beer with some grapefruit notes from American Cascade hops.

Bare Bones (*OG 1046, ABV 4.7%*)

Newark Castle Brown (*OG 1049, 5%*)

Willys' Wheatbeer (*OG 1051, ABV 5.3%*)

Roaring Meg (*OG 1052, ABV 5.5%*)
Smooth and sweet with a dry finish and citrus honey aroma.

Cromwell's Hat (*OG 1056, ABV 6%*)

STANWAY

Stanway Brewery, Stanway, Cheltenham, Glos, GL54 5PQ
Tel (01386) 584320
Website www.stanwaybrewery.co.uk

Small brewery founded in 1993 with a five-barrel plant, which confines its sales to the Cotswolds area (around 25 outlets). Seasonal beers: Lords-a-Leaping (ABV 4.5%, Christmas), Cotteswold Gold (ABV 3.9%, summer).

Stanney Bitter (*OG 1042, ABV 4.5%*)
A light, refreshing, amber-coloured beer, dominated by hops in the aroma, with a bitter taste and a hoppy, bitter finish.

STEAMIN' BILLY

Steamin' Billy Brewing Co Ltd, 5 The Oval, Oadby, Leics, LE2 5JB
Tel (0116) 271 2616
E-mail enquiries@steaminbilly.co.uk
Website www.steaminbilly.co.uk

The Steamin' Billy Brewing Co, despite the name, doesn't brew any beer. It was set up to supply three pubs it owned in 1996. It now has just one outlet, but is planning to expand. The beers are brewed at Grainstore of Oakham. Seasonal beers: Lazy Summer (ABV 4.4%, summer), Robert Catesby (ABV 4.5%, autumn), Merry Christmas (ABV 4.4%, December), Knock Out (ABV 7.1%, winter).

Scrum Down Mild (*OG 1039, ABV 3.9%*)
A refreshing, dark, well-balanced mild whose chocolatey fruity flavours

complement its roasted bitter finish, with a hint of Golding hops coming through.

Country Bitter *(OG 1040, ABV 4%)*
A full-bodied, copper-coloured beer.

Billy the Porter *(OG 1042, ABV 4.2%)*
Smooth and dry with a bitter-sweet, roasted malt aftertaste.

Steamin' Billy Bitter *(OG 1043, ABV 4.3%)*
The floral flavour and aroma are derived from dry hopping with Golding hops. A well-rounded beer with a satisfying after-taste.

Skydiver *(OG 1050, ABV 5%)*
A strong, rich, mahogany-coloured beer with malty sweetness and pronounced hop bitterness.

STONEHENGE SIBA

Stonehenge Ales Ltd, The Old Mill, Netheravon, Salisbury, Wilts, SP4 9QB
Tel (01980) 670631
Fax (01980) 671187
E-mail stonehenge_ales@bigfoot.com
Website www.stonehengeales.co.uk
Shop off-licence Mon-Fri 8.30am-5.30pm
Tours by arrangement

⊗ A tower brewery, originally named Bunce's Brewery after late founder Tony Bunce, is housed in a listed building on the River Avon. It was established in 1984, and sold to Danish master brewer Stig Anker Andersen in 1993. Its cask-conditioned beers are delivered to around 60 free trade outlets within a radius of 50 miles, and a number of wholesalers are also supplied. Seasonal beers: Sign of Spring (ABV 4.6%), Second to None (ABV 4.6%), Old Smokey (ABV 5%), Rudolph (ABV 5%).

Benchmark *(OG 1035, ABV 3.5%)* ◆
A pleasant, bitter ale of remarkable character which maintains one's interest for a long time. The taste is malty, the aroma subtle and the very long finish is quite dry on the palate.

Pigswill *(OG 1040, ABV 4%)*
A full-bodied beer, rich in hop aroma, with warm amber colour.

Body Line *(OG 1042, ABV 4.3%)*

Heel Stone *(OG 1042, ABV 4.3%)*
A crisp, clean, refreshing bitter, deep amber in colour, well balanced with a fruity blackcurrant nose.

Danish Dynamite *(OG 1050, ABV 5%)*
A light golden, dry strong ale, slightly fruity with a well-balanced hop flavour and bitterness.

Old Smokey *(OG 1050, ABV 5%)* ◆
A delightful, warming, dark bitter ale, with a roasted malt taste and a hint of liquorice surrounding a developing bitter flavour.

STORM

Storm Brewing Co, 2 Waterside, Macclesfield, Cheshire, SK11 7HJ
Tel (01625) 432978
Tel/Fax (01625) 431234
Tours by arrangement

Storm started brewing in 1998 under the guidance of Brian Rides of Wickwar

Brewery. Two partners, Hugh Thompson and Dave Stebbings, have added two new fermenters and brew 15 barrels a week. They supply more than 60 outlets in Cheshire, Manchester and the Peak District.

Beauforts Ales *(ABV 3.8%)*

Desert Storm *(ABV 3.8%)*

Bitter Experience *(ABV 4%)*

Brainstorm *(ABV 4.1%)*

Bosley Cloud *(ABV 4.1%)*

Ale Force *(OG 1038, ABV 4.2%)* ◆
Amber, smooth-tasting, complex beer that balances malt, hop and fruit on the taste, leading to a roasty, slightly sweet aftertaste.

Windgather *(OG 1043, ABV 4.5%)*
Pale brown, refreshing, clean-tasting best bitter, complex and highly flavoured.

Storm Damage *(ABV 4.7%)*
A light-coloured, well-hopped beer with a distinct fruitiness from start to finish.

Silk of Amnesia *(ABV 4.7%)*

SULWATH SIBA

Sulwath Brewers Ltd, The Brewery, 209 King Street, Castle Douglas, Dumfries & Galloway, DG7 1DT
Tel/Fax (01556) 504525
E-mail allen@scottdavid98.freeserve.co.uk
Website www.sulwathbrewers.co.uk
Shop Mon-Sat 10-4. Tours Mon-Sat.

☺ Sulwath is a small, privately-owned company that started brewing in 1995. It sells cask ales direct to the licensed trade and currently has some 100 outlets and three wholesalers for draught. Seasonal/occasional beers: Sulwath Reinbeer (ABV 4.5%, Christmas), Tam o'Shanter (ABV 4.1%, Burns Night), Woozy Wabbit (ABV 4.6%, Easter), Saltire Cross (ABV 4.1%, St Andrews Day).

Cuil Hill *(OG 1036, ABV 3.6%)* ◆
Distinctively fruity session ale with malt and hop undertones. The taste is bitter-sweet with a long-lasting dry finish.

John Paul Jones *(OG 1035, ABV 4%)*

The Black Galloway *(OG 1043, ABV 4.4%)*
Named after the native cattle of Galloway, this dark porter derives its colour from the abundance of deeply roasted malts used.

Criffel *(OG 1044, ABV 4.4%)* ◆
Full-bodied beer with a distinctive bitterness. Fruit is to the fore of the taste, with hop becoming increasingly dominant in the taste and finish.

Knockendoch *(OG 1046, ABV 5%)* ◆
Dark, copper-coloured, reflecting a roast malt content, with bitterness from Challenger hops.

Galloway Gold (cask-conditioned lager) *(OG 1044, ABV 5%)* ◆
An unusual beer that will be too sweet for many despite being heavily hopped.

SUMMERSKILLS SIBA

Summerskills Brewery,
15 Pomphlett Farm Industrial Estate,
Broxton Drive, Billacombe,
Plymouth, Devon, PL9 7BG

Tel/Fax (01752) 481283
E-mail summerskills@aol.com

⊗ Originally established in a vineyard in 1983 at Bigbury-on-Sea, Summerskills moved to its present site two years later. National distribution via carefully vetted wholesalers ensures nationwide coverage for the company's prize-winning beers. Occasional/seasonal beers: Menacing Dennis (ABV 4.5%), Turkey's Delight (ABV 5.1%, Christmas).

Cellar Vee (OG 1037, ABV 3.7%)

Tamar (OG 1037, ABV 3.7%)
A tawny-coloured bitter with a fruity aroma, and a hop taste and finish.

Hopscotch (OG 1041, ABV 4.1%)

Best Bitter (OG 1042, ABV 4.3%) ◈
A mid-brown beer, with plenty of malt and hops through the aroma, taste and finish. A good session beer.

Whistle Belly Vengeance
(OG 1046, ABV 4.7%) ◈
A red/brown beer with a beautiful malt and fruit taste and a pleasant, malty aftertaste.

Indiana's Bones (OG 1055, ABV 5.6%)
A mid-brown beer with a good balance of fruit and malt in the aroma and taste, and a sweet, malty aftertaste.

SUSSEX

The Sussex Brewery, Pett Road, Pett, East Sussex, TN35 4HB
Tel (01424) 813927 Fax (01424) 813928
Tours by arrangement

⊗ Formerly Pett Brew Company, then Old Forge and now Sussex Brewery, run by Robbie Chapman. The brewery is sited in buildings in the grounds of the Two Sawyers public house in Pett. The equipment has a capacity to brew five barrels and normally brews on Mondays, Wednesdays and Fridays.

Forge Bitter (ABV 3.2%)

Brothers Best (ABV 3.9%)
A hoppy, amber-coloured, session beer.

Pett Progress (ABV 4.6%)
Hoppy aroma, full body and a slightly bitter aftertaste.

SUTTON

Sutton Brewing Co, 31 Commercial Road, Coxside, Plymouth, Devon, PL4 0LE
Tel/Fax (01752) 205010
E-mail nigel@suttonbrewing.fsnet.co.uk
Tours by arrangement

⊗ The brewery was built alongside the Thistle Park Tavern, near Plymouth's Sutton Harbour, in 1993. The brewery sells to more than 60 outlets in Plymouth and south Devon. The original plant was a five-barrel plant but was upgraded in 1998 to 10 barrels. Wholesalers are used to distribute products to other areas. One pub is owned. Occasional/seasonal beers: Wild Blonde (ABV 4.4%) and Hopnosis (ABV 4.5%, spring/summer), Madiba Stout (ABV 5%), Knickadroppa Glory (ABV 5.5%, autumn/winter). Bottle-conditioned beer: Madiba Stout.

Plymouth/Dartmoor Pride
(OG 1039, ABV 3.8%)

XSB (OG 1043, ABV 4.2%) ◈
Amber nectar with a fruity nose and a bitter finish.

Sutton Comfort (OG 1046, ABV 4.5%) ◈
Hoppy-tasting, mid-brown beer with a bitter hop finish underscored by malt and fruit.

Eddystone (OG 1050, ABV 4.8%)

SWAN

⌂ Swan on the Green, The Green, West Peckham, Kent, ME18 5JW
Tel (01622) 812271
Fax (0870) 0560556
E-mail goodbeer@swan-on-the-green.co.uk
Website www.swan-on-the-green.co.uk
Tours by arrangement

⊗ A pub brewery that opened in 2000 on a site that dates back to 1526, when an inn was first recorded. Over the centuries it has been variously known as the Millers Arms (when it included a bakery), the Myllers Arms on the Greene, and Honest Tom after landlord Thomas Oliver. It became the Swan in 1852. The current owner, Gordon Milligan, looked at micro-breweries in the US and Britain, and picked up brewing skills with Rob Jones at Dark Star in Brighton, honing the skills on courses with Brewlab at Sunderland University. Gordon built his two-barrel plant himself and supplies just the pub with beer. The pub stages a 'green beer' festival in September, offering four to six different beers made with hops harvested straight from the hop fields. There are plans for another brew of the popular special beer called Swan on the Port Side which has a bottle of port in each cask.

Whooper Pale (OG 1036, ABV 3.5%)
A light, fruity, refreshing pale ale.

Old Fashioned Mild (OG 1036, ABV 3.5%)

Ginger Swan (OG 1036, ABV 3.6%)

Organic Swan (ABV 4%)
A light, hoppy, session beer.

Trumpeter Best (OG 1040, ABV 4%)
Traditional hoppy bitter.

Stout (OG 1048, ABV 4.8%)

Parliament Ale (OG 1050, ABV 4.8%)
An excellent, strong bitter with just a hint of ginger and cinnamon.

Swan Porter (OG 1051, ABV 5.1%)

Bewick (OG 1054, ABV 5.3%)

SWANSEA SIBA

⌂ Swansea Brewing Company, Joiners Arms, 50 Bishopston Road, Bishopston, Swansea, SA3 3EJ
Office: 74 Hawthorne Avenue, Uplands, Swansea, SA2 0LY
Tel (01792) 232658 brewery, (01792) 290197 office
E-mail rorygowland@fsbdial.co.uk
Tours by arrangement

☺ Opened in 1996, it was the first commercial brewery in the Swansea area for almost 30 years and is Swansea's only brew-pub. It doubled its capacity within the first year and now produces four regular beers and occasional experimental ones. The founder, Rory Gowland, learned his trade working in the chemistry department of Swansea University. Four regular outlets are supplied direct plus free trade outlets in the South Wales area. Seasonal beers: St Teilo's Tipple (ABV 5.5%), Barland Strong (ABV 6%), Pwll Du XXXX (ABV 4.9%).

Deep Slade Dark *(OG 1034, ABV 4%)*

Bishopswood Bitter
(OG 1038, ABV 4.3%) 🍷♦
Pale brown, delicate aroma of hops and malt. A balanced mix of flavours and bitterness lead to a lasting dry, bitter finish.

Three Cliffs Gold *(OG 1042, ABV 4.7%)* ♦
A hop and fruity aroma leads to a tasty hop, fruit and malt mix. The pleasing finish has a good hop bitterness.

Original Wood *(OG 1046, ABV 5.2%)*

SWEET WILLIAM SIBA

☐ Sweet William Brewery, William IV, 816 High Road, Leyton, London, E10
Tel (020) 8556 2460
E-mail sweetwilliamivy@aol.com
Tours by arrangement

A brew-pub that came on stream in 2000. The beers are currently delivered to 20 regular outlets.

East London Mild *(OG 1039, ABV 3.6%)*

Just William *(OG 1039, ABV 3.8%)*

E10 Red Ale *(ABV 4.1%)*

William the Conqueror
(OG 1045, ABV 4.4%)

TALLY HO

☐ Tally Ho! Country Inn & Brewery,
14 Market Street, Hatherleigh,
Devon, EX20 3JN
Tel (01837) 810306
Fax (01837) 811079
E-mail tally.ho@virgin.net

Not currently brewing.

TAYLOR IFBB

Timothy Taylor & Co Ltd, Knowle
Spring Brewery, Belina Street, Keighley,
West Yorkshire, BD21 1AW
Tel (01535) 603139
Fax (01535) 691167
Website www.timothy-taylor.co.uk

One of the classic brewers of pale ale, Timothy Taylor is an independent family-owned company established in 1858. It moved to the site of the Knowle Spring in 1863. Its prize-winning ales, which use Pennine spring water, are served in all 23 of the brewery's pubs as well as 300-plus other outlets. In 2003 the brewery was given planning permission for a £1 million expansion programme that will include a new brewhouse. While organic beers are not yet produced, none of the ales contains animal products. Seasonal beer: Ram Tam (ABV 4.3%, winter).

Golden Best *(OG 1033, ABV 3.5%)* 🍷🍷♦
A clean-tasting and refreshing amber-

coloured mild with fruit on the nose, a light hoppy taste, a bitter finish and background malt throughout. A good session beer.

Dark Mild *(OG 1034, ABV 3.5%)* ♦
The hops of the underlying Golden Best combine with malt and a caramel sweetness and lead to a dry, bitter-sweet finish.

Porter *(OG 1041, ABV 3.8%)* ♦
Sweetness and caramel can dominate this beer if it is served too young. However, when mature, the sweetness is balanced by fruity flavours and bitterness in the finish.

Best Bitter *(OG 1038, ABV 4%)* 🍷♦
Hops and a citrus fruitiness combine well with a nutty maltiness in this drinkable bitter. Bitterness increases down the glass and lingers in the aftertaste.

Landlord *(OG 1042, ABV 4.3%)* 🍷🍷♦
An increasingly dry, bitter finish complements the spicy, citrus hop character and complex fruitiness of this full-flavoured and well-balanced beer.

TEIGNWORTHY SIBA

Teignworthy Brewery, The Maltings,
Teign Road, Newton Abbot,
Devon, TQ12 4AA
Tel (01626) 332066
Fax (01626) 330153
E-mail john@teignworthy.freeserve.co.uk
Shop 10-5 weekdays at Tuckers Maltings

Teignworthy Brewery was established in 1994 by John and Rachel Lawton and is located in part of the historic Tuckers Maltings. There are regular tours of the maltings from Easter to the end of October, which includes the brewery and a sample of beer (tel 01626 334734 or www.tuckersmaltings.com for details of tours). The brewery is a 15- barrel plant and produces an average of 30-35 barrels a week using malt from Tuckers: production has increased thanks to Progressive Beer Duty. It supplies about 75 outlets in Devon and Somerset, and some of the range of beers are bottled on site and are available from the Tuckers Maltings shop (also available by mail order). Seasonal beers: Maltster's Ale (ABV 5%, November), Christmas Cracker (ABV 6%, December). Bottle-conditioned beers (all suitable for vegans): Reel Ale (ABV 4%), Springtide (ABV 4.3%), Old Moggie (ABV 4.4%), Beachcomber (ABV 4.5%), Harvey's Ale (ABV 4.6%, April and October), Amy's Ale (ABV 4.8%, April and October), Maltster's Ale (ABV 5%, November), Martha's Mild (ABV 5.3%, April and October), Christmas Cracker (ABV 6%, December).

Reel Ale *(OG 1039.5, ABV 4%)* ♦
Clean, sharp-tasting bitter with lasting hoppiness; predominantly malty aroma.

Springtide *(OG 1043.5, ABV 4.3%)* ♦
An excellent, full and well-rounded, mid-brown beer with a dry, bitter taste and aftertaste.

Old Moggie *(OG 1044.5, ABV 4.4%)*
A golden, hoppy and fruity ale.

Beachcomber *(OG 1045.5, ABV 4.5%)* ♦
A pale brown beer with a light, refreshing fruit and hop nose, grapefruit taste and a dry, hoppy finish.

TEME VALLEY SIBA

◻ Teme Valley Brewery, Talbot Hotel,
Knightwick, Worcs, WR6 5PH
Tel (01886) 821235 ext 122
Fax (01886) 821060
E-mail info@the_talbot.co.uk
Website www.the_talbot.co.uk
Tours by arrangement

☺ The Teme Valley Brewery opened in 1997 behind the Talbot, with both brewery and inn owned by the farming and hop-growing Clift family. The brewery was the only privately-owned British brewery that grew and used its own hops, but in September 2000, after the hop harvest, Lulsley Court Estate was sold. The Clifts had grown hops at Lulsley Court since the late 19th century, had been heavily involved in the history of hop growing in the area, and were among the first to change to mechanical hop picking in 1947. The new owner at Lulsley Court continues to supply all the brewery's hops. With a 360-gallon weekly capacity, the brewery is on the smaller scale of micro plants, supplying some 40 outlets direct. Chris Gooch, the brewer, uses a full barley mash and ferments in traditional, open-topped fermenting vessels. Seasonal beers: 3 Pears (ABV 3.9%), Dark Stranger (ABV 4.2%), Hops Nouvelle (ABV 4.1%), Talbot Porter (ABV 4.4%), Wassail (ABV 6%), Spring Wot (ABV 4.7%), Fool's Gold (ABV 4.5%). Bottle-conditioned beers: This, That, Hops Nouvelle, Wassail, Wotever Next? (ABV 5%).

T'Other (OG 1035, ABV 3.5%) ◆
Easy-drinking tawny best bitter beginning with a powerful smack of hops and sustained balancing fruit and malt.

This (OG 1037, ABV 3.7%) ◆
Gold quaffing bitter with enjoyable hops and subtle malt balance in the mouth, ending with a strong bitter-sweet finale.

That (OG 1041, ABV 4.1%) ◆
Copper-coloured best bitter with a balance of malt and hops, and overlying fruitiness. Ending with a light, dry finish.

JOHN THOMPSON

◻ John Thompson Brewery, John Thompson Inn, Ingleby, Derbyshire, DE73 1HW
Tel (01332) 862469
Tours by arrangement

The departure of both Lichfield and Lloyds breweries has turned the site into a brew-pub, producing three beers for the inn.

JTS XXX (ABV 4.1%)

JTS Rich Porter (ABV 4.5%)

JTS Summer Gold (ABV 4.5%)

THREE B'S

Three B's Brewery, Unit 5,
Laneside Works, Stockclough Lane,
Feniscowles, Blackburn, Lancs, BB2 5JR
Tel (01254) 207686
Tours by arrangement

Robert Bell designed and began building his two-barrel brewery in 1997 and in 1998 he obtained premises in Hamilton Street, Blackburn, to set up the brewery and complete the project. It is now a 10-barrel

brewery. 20 outlets are supplied.

Stoker's Slake (ABV 3.6%)
A traditional dark mild with roast malt aromas and creamy chocolate notes.

Bobbin's Bitter (ABV 3.8%)
Warm aromas of malt, Goldings hops and nuts; a full, fruity flavour with a light dry finish.

Tackler's Tipple (ABV 4.3%)
A best bitter with full hop flavour, biscuit tones on the tongue and a deep, dry finish. A darker coloured ale with a fascinating blend of hops and dark malt.

Doff Cocker (ABV 4.5%)
Multi-layered delight of malt and hops in a flowery, refreshing taste. A yellow-coloured beer.

Pinch Noggin' (ABV 4.6%)
A luscious balance of malt, hops and fruit, with a lively, colourful spicy aroma of citrus fruit. A quenching golden beer.

Knocker Up (ABV 4.8%)
A porter with an exotic ebony texture and a deep, rich palate of roast barley and chocolate malt.

Shuttle Ale (ABV 5.2%)
A strong pale ale, light in colour with a balanced malt and hop flavour, and superb Goldings aroma, long dry finish and delicate fruit notes.

THREE TUNS

see John Roberts

THWAITES IFBB

Daniel Thwaites Brewery PLC, PO Box 50,
Star Brewery, Blackburn, Lancs, BB1 5BU
Tel (01254) 686868
Fax (01254) 681439
E-mail info@thwaites.co.uk
Website www.thwaites.co.uk
Tours by arrangement

☺ Founded by an excise officer, Thwaites Brewery has dominated the centre of Blackburn for more than 200 years. Its famous shire horses, which delivered beer to local pubs, are now only used for shows and publicity events. The number of local tied pubs has been reduced significantly through closures and sales, though new outlets have been developed further afield. The availability of cask beer, in particular the excellent Mild, has been hard hit by the promotion of nitro-keg 'smooth' beers, leading to questions being asked about Thwaites' commitment to cask. However, the quality and diversity of new and seasonal beers continues to increase. 450 pubs are owned, with 850 free trade accounts. Seasonal beers: Daniel's Hammer (ABV 5%, Sept-Oct), Good Elf (ABV 4.9%, Nov-Dec).

Mild (OG 1033, ABV 3.3%) ◆
Has become hard to find in cask form. A traditional dark mild presenting a thin, malty flavour and slight bitter finish.

Original Bitter (OG 1036, ABV 3.6%) ◆
A pale brown session bitter with a faint malt and hop aroma. The distinctive hop character has diminished and the taste is thin with a moderately bitter, dry finish.

Thoroughbred *(OG 1040, ABV 4%)*
A robust golden colour with a good hop aroma, with dry hops added to the cask.

Lancaster Bomber *(OG 1044, ABV 4.4%)*
A prominent hop aroma and bitterness throughout, finely balanced with a full malt flavour leading to a dry bitter finish.

TIGERTOPS SIBA

**Tigertops Brewery, 22 Oakes Street, Flanshaw Lane, Wakefield, West Yorkshire, WF2 9LN
Tel (01229) 716238 or (01924) 897728**
Tours by arrangement in August only

⊚ Tigertops was established in 1995 by Stuart Johnson, a former chairman of the Wakefield branch of CAMRA, and his wife, Lynda. The Johnsons also own the Foxfield Brewery in Cumbria. Barry 'Axeman' Smith, the brewer, produces continental beer styles, using imported malts and yeasts. The brewery supplies mainly beer festivals and three or four other outlets. Seasonal beer: Marzen (ABV 5%, March).

Dark Mild Wheat *(OG 1036, ABV 3.6%)*
An unusual mild made primarily with wheat malt.

Axeman's Light *(OG 1035, ABV 3.6%)*
A hoppy pale ale.

Axeman's Block *(OG 1036, ABV 3.6%)*
A malty beer with a good hop finish.

Blanche de Newland *(OG 1044, ABV 4.6%)*
A Belgian-style wheat beer.

Bock *(OG 1058, ABV 6.4%)*
A fruity, full-bodied complex beer.

TINDALL

**Tindall Ale Brewery, Toad Lane, Seething, Norfolk, NR35 2EQ
Tel/Fax (01508) 483844**
Tours by arrangement

⊗ Tindall Ales was established in 1998 and was situated on the edge of the medieval Tindall Wood. It moved to new premises at Seething in 2002. It is a family-run business with the main objective of producing good quality beer for local outlets. 12 outlets are supplied. All the beers are made from best local malt and the finest Kentish hops. Seasonal beers: Summer Loving (ABV 3.6%), Autumn Brew (ABV 4), Lovers' Ale (ABV 4%), Christmas Cheer (ABV 4%), IPA (ABV 3.6%), Suffolk 'n' See (ABV 4.6%). All the beers are available in bottle-conditioned form.

Mild *(ABV 3.7%)*
A good dark mild.

Best Bitter *(ABV 3.7%)* ✦
A hint of cocoa can be found in the light malty nose. This is borne out by the initial taste impression of malt backed by a bitter-sweet hoppiness and a hint of dark chocolate. The flavours drop off quickly to leave a dry bitterness tempered by a light shortbread sweetness. Copper-coloured and easy drinking.

Fuggled Up *(ABV 3.7%)*

Liberator *(ABV 3.8%)* ✦
This yellow bitter has a distinctly flowery bouquet. Citrus notes are well to the fore, acting as a counterpoint to the hoppy bitterness. Low malt notes in the background disappear to leave a long, bitter finish with hints of hop and resin.

Alltime *(ABV 4%)* ✦
A complex blend of flavours, none dominate but all contribute to give a light, grainy feel. Dark brown with a gentle nose comprising roast, malt and vine fruits lend a sweetness that provides depth and balance. The flavour wheel is completed by a distinct liquorice flurry that develops towards the end.

Mundham Mild *(ABV 4%)*

Ditchingham Dam *(OG 1042, ABV 4.2%)* ✦
Initial malt flavour with a treacle toffee edge adds to the rich malty aroma. Some hints of dried vine fruits develop before the quick finish gives a dryish roast farewell befitting a mid-brown coloured beer.

Ale Extra *(ABV 4.5%)* ✦
A sweet, fruity ale with a distinct malt beginning. This fades as bitterness comes through to give a quick, dry finish. Amber in colour, with low malt notes in a gentle hoppy aroma.

Norwich Dragon *(OG 1046, ABV 4.6%)* ✦
Hops dominate throughout this yellow, easy-drinking bitter. Citrus airs, combined with a malty backing, soften the aroma but are severely diminished by the powerful hoppy bitterness of the taste. A marmalade sweetness gives a better balance to the overall impression as the finish continues to a powerful hoppy ending.

Norfolk 'n' Good *(OG 1046, ABV 4.6%)*
Sold under that name in Norfolk, changed to Suffolk for sales over the border.

Honeydo *(ABV 5%)*

TIPSY TOAD

**▢ Tipsy Toad Brewery, St Peter's Village, Jersey, CI, JE3 7AA
Tel (01534) 485556
Fax (01534) 485559**
Tours by arrangement

⊗ A brew-pub launched in 1992 and taken over by Jersey Brewery in 1997. Jersey Brewery distributes the beers through its tied estate. Seasonal/rotating beers: Festive Toad (ABV 8%), Horny Toad (ABV 5%), Dixie's Wheat Beer (ABV 4%), Naomh Padraig's Porter (ABV 4.4%).

Tipsy Toad Ale *(OG 1038, ABV 3.8%)*

Jimmy's Bitter *(OG 1042, ABV 4.2%)*

For Guernsey Brewery:

Braye Mild *(OG 1037, ABV 3.8%)*

Pirates Ale *(OG 1042, ABV 4.2%)*

Sunbeam Bitter *(OG 1042, ABV 4.2%)*

TIRRIL SIBA

**Tirril Brewery Ltd, Brougham Hall, Brougham, Penrith, Cumbria, CA10 2DE
Tel (01768) 863219
Fax (01768) 863243
E-mail chris@tirrilbrewery.co.uk
Website www.tirrilbrewery.co.uk**
Tours by arrangement

⊛ Tirril started brewing 100 years after Siddle's Brewery closed in Tirril in 1899. It brewed to full capacity of 2.5 barrels a week at the Queens Head in Tirril, until in 2002 it moved to a 10-barrel plant in nearby Brougham Hall, which has a 19th-century brewhouse. The hall is the largest country house restoration in England. With the support of English Heritage, Tirril occupies the 1823 Brewing Rooms. One pub is owned.

John Bewsher's Best Bitter
(OG 1037.5, ABV 3.8%)
A lightly-hopped, golden brown session beer, named after the landlord and brewer at the Queen's Head Inn in the 1830s.

Brougham Ale *(OG 1038, ABV 3.9%)*
A gently hopped, amber bitter.

Charles Gough's Old Faithful
(OG 1039, ABV 4%)
Pale gold, aromatic and well-hopped, an ideal summer ale. Named after the dog of the hapless Gough who fell to his death in the area; the dog stayed by his body for several months.

1823 *(OG 1040, ABV 4.1%)*

Thomas Slee's Academy Ale
(OG 1040.5, ABV 4.2%)
A dark, full-bodied, traditional rich and malty ale. In the 1820s Mr. Slee's Academy was considered the equal of Oxford and Cambridge for the study of mathematics.

TITANIC SIBA

**Titanic Brewery, Unit 5,
Callender Place, Lingard Street,
Burslem, Stoke-on-Trent, Staffs, ST6 1JL
Tel (01782) 823447
Fax (01782) 823349
E-mail titanic@titanicbrewery.co.uk
Website www.titanicbrewery.co.uk**

⊛ Founded in 1985, the brewery is named in honour of Captain Smith who hailed from the Potteries, and had the misfortune to captain the Titanic. In 1996 Titanic Brewery resurrected the log-fired Victorian micro-brewery at Shugborough, home of Lord Lichfield, and brews for demonstration purposes there, producing one-off brews for festivals and special occasions. Titanic's increasing presence in the free trade led to another move to larger premises in 2002 and a visitor centre is planned. The company now supplies more than 250 free trade outlets as well as its own tied house, the Bulls Head in Burslem. For Shugborough Brewery: Coachman's Tipple (ABV 4.7%, Jan-Feb), Butler's Revenge (ABV 4.9%, March-April), Milady's Fancy (ABV 4.6%, May-June), Farmer's Half (ABV 4.8%, July-Aug), Gardener's Retreat (ABV 4.7%, Sept-Oct), Lordship's Own (ABV 5%, Nov-Dec). Shugborough brews are also available in bottle-conditioned form in the same periods. Titanic seasonal beers: A monthly seasonal beer is brewed, all named with Titanic connections.

Mild *(OG 1035, ABV 3.5%)* 🍺
A mild of classic style, full of roast malt flavours and balanced by delicate hops. True to type, it has rounded sweetness and a smooth, dry finish.

Best Bitter *(OG 1036, ABV 3.5%)* ◆
Fruit, notably grapes, are tasted in this well-balanced, smooth and light bitter that has developing bitterness after some nuttiness.

Lifeboat Ale *(OG 1040, ABV 4%)* ◆
A fruity and malty, dark red/brown beer, with a fruity finish.

Iceberg *(OG 1042, ABV 4.1%)* 🍺◆
Hoppy and fruity with a touch of malt. Strongly bitter, intensifying to a hoppy finish and supporting astringency.

Premium Bitter *(OG 1042, ABV 4.1%)* ◆
An impressive, well-balanced pale brown bitter with hops and fruit in the aroma, which develop into a full flavour and a dry, hoppy finish.

Stout *(OG 1046, ABV 4.5%)* ◆
Full roast with great liquorice taste. Hopped to give dryness and astringency, but roast is well balanced and lingers.

White Star *(OG 1050, ABV 4.8%)* ◆
Terrific straw colour, hoppy taste, astringent finish.

Captain Smith's *(OG 1054, ABV 5.2%)* ◆
A full-bodied, dark red/brown beer, hoppy and bitter with malt and roast malt flavours, and a long, bitter-sweet finish.

Wreckage *(ABV 7.2%)* ◆
This sweet malty winter ale has a port-like aroma and walnut aftertaste.

TOLLY COBBOLD
See Ridleys

TOWER SIBA

**Tower Brewery, The Old Water Tower,
Walsitch Maltings, Glensyl Way,
Burton-on-Trent, Staffs, DE14 1PZ
Tel/Fax (01283) 530695**
Tours by arrangement

⊠ The water tower that is the home of Tower Brewery was built in 1875 by Thomas Salt & Co and provided a water supply for Walsitch Maltings. The derelict building was converted into a working tower brewery and started trading in 2001. The conversion was awarded a Civic Society award for the restoration of a 'Historic Industrial Building'. Owner John Mills has 40 regular outlets for his beers. Seasonal beers: Sundowner (ABV 4%, May-Aug), Spring Equinox (ABV 4.6%, March-May), Autumn Equinox (ABV 4.6%, Sept-Nov), Winter Spirit (ABV 5%).

Thomas Salts Bitter *(OG 1038, ABV 3.8%)*

Tower Bitter *(OG 1042, ABV 4.2%)* ◆
Gold coloured with a malty aroma, with hops and caramel. A full hop and fruit taste with the fruit lingering; almost grassy fresh. A bitter and astringent finish that lingers.

Malty Towers
(OG 1044, ABV 4.4%) ◆
Yellow with a malty aroma as named, with a hint of tobacco. Strong hops give a long, dry, bitter finish with pleasant astringency.

Tower Pale Ale *(OG 1048, ABV 4.8%)*

Tower of Strength *(OG 1076, ABV 7.6%)*

TOWNES SIBA

◻ Townes Brewery, Speedwell Inn, Lowgates, Staveley, Chesterfield, Derbyshire, S43 3TT
Tel (01246) 472252
E-mail woodcurly@aol.com
Tours by arrangement

▩ Townes Brewery started in 1994 in an old bakery on the outskirts of Chesterfield using a five-barrel plant; it was the first brewery in the town for more than 40 years. After a period of steady progress, the Speedwell Inn at Staveley was bought and the plant was moved to the rear of the pub. Brewing at Staveley started in 1997 and, after a period of renovation, the pub opened a year later. It was the first brew-pub in north Derbyshire in the 20th century. Bottling is now established and there are plans to extend this part of the operation. More than 40 outlets are supplied on an occasional basis. Seasonal beers: Stargazer (ABV 5.5%, winter), Sunshine (ABV 3.7%, summer). A monthly special is available under the 'Real Gone' motif. Two seasonal milds are produced to increase interest in the style: Golden Bud (ABV 3.8%, summer) and Muffin Man (ABV 4.6%, winter). Staveley Cross, IPA, Pynot Porter, Oatmeal Stout, Staveleyan, and Essence are also available in bottle-conditioned form and are suitable for vegetarians and vegans.

Speedwell Bitter *(OG 1039, ABV 3.9%)*

Lowgate Light *(OG 1041, ABV 4.1%)*

Staveley Cross *(OG 1043, ABV 4.3%)*

IPA *(OG 1045, ABV 4.5%)*

Pynot Porter *(OG 1045, ABV 4.5%)*

Oatmeal Stout *(OG 1047, ABV 4.7%)*

Staveleyan *(OG 1049, ABV 4.9%)*

Essence *(OG 1051, ABV 5.1%)*

TOWNHOUSE

Townhouse Brewery, Studio 2, Town House Farm, Alsager Road, Audley, Staffs, ST7 8JQ
Tel (07976) 209437

☺ Established in spring 2002 in a converted stable block at Townhouse Farm, once a working farm, now converted to craft studios. With a new 2.5 barrel brewery, sales are steadily increasing and the beers are always available at three local outlets and as guest ales at various freehouses in the area. 10 outlets are supplied direct.

Audley Bitter *(OG 1038, ABV 3.8%)*
A pale, well-balanced session bitter.

Dark Horse *(OG 1042, ABV 4.3%)*
Dark ruby ale with dark malt character and late hoppy finish.

Audley Gold *(OG 1043, ABV 4.5%)*
Pale, golden bitter with malt and fruity character.

Parker's Pride *(OG 1044, ABV 4.6%)*
A copper coloured bitter, malty with a balanced hoppy taste.

Townhouse Special Bitter
(OG 1048, ABV 5%)
A balanced best bitter with floral hop palate and fruity, dry, bitter finish.

TRAQUAIR SIBA

Traquair House Brewery Ltd, Traquair Estate, Innerleithen, Peeblesshire, EH44 6PP
Tel (01896) 830323 & 831370
Fax (01896) 830639
E-mail enquiries@traquair.co.uk
Website www.traquair.co.uk
Shop and Brewery Museum 12.30-5.30 daily April-Oct, 10.30-5.30 daily June-Aug.
Tours by arrangement April-Sept

☺ The 18th-century brewhouse is based in one of the wings of the 1,000-year-old Traquair House, Scotland's oldest inhabited house, visited by Mary Queen of Scots and Prince Charles Edward Stuart. The brewhouse was rediscovered by the 20th Laird, the late Peter Maxwell Stuart, in 1965. He began brewing again using all the original equipment, which remained intact, despite having lain idle for more than 100 years. The brewery has been run by Peter's daughter, Catherine Maxwell Stuart, since his death in 1990. The Maxwell Stuarts are members of the Stuart clan, and the main Bear Gates will remain shut until a Stuart returns to the throne. All the beers are oak-fermented and 60 per cent of production is exported (mostly bottled Traquair House Ale and Jacobite Ale). Some five outlets take the cask beer. Seasonal beers: Stuart Ale (ABV 4.5%, summer), Bear Ale (ABV 5%, winter).

House Ale *(ABV 7.2%)*

Jacobite Ale *(ABV 8%)*

TRAVELLERS INN

◻ Travellers Inn, Tremerchion, Caerwys, Flintshire, CH7 5BL
Tel (01352) 720251

An intermittent brewer, Kevin Jones, who only brews when he feels like it. One pub is owned.

Roy Morgan's Original Ale *(ABV 4%)*

TRING SIBA

Tring Brewery Co Ltd, 81-82 Akeman Street, Tring, Herts, HP23 6AF
Tel (01442) 890721
Fax (01442) 890740
E-mail info@tringbrewery.com
Website www.tringbrewery.com
Tours by arrangement

⊠ Tring Brewery was founded in 1992 and, after a break of more than 50 years, restored brewing to the West Hertfordshire town. Richard Shardlow, who had brewed with Devenish, Greene King and Ruddles, started the company. Andrew Jackson from Whitbread joined Richard in 2000. A new range of beers has been developed for the 32-barrel plant, backed by contemporary marketing. The brewery supplies 60-100 outlets. As well as seasonal beers, there is a vast range of one-off specials and seasonal beers. Seasonal beers: Cuckoo's Coming (ABV 4.5%, Feb-April), Mother Haggy's Finest Summer Ale (ABV 4%, July-Sept), Reap the Rye (ABV 4.7%, Oct-Nov), Santa's Little Helper (ABV 4.8%, December). Ridgeway Bitter (ABV 4%), once a leading brand, is now only produced for a few pubs in the Tring area.

Side Pocket for a Toad
(OG 1036, ABV 3.6%)
Citrus notes from American Cascade hops balanced with a floral aroma and crisp, dry finish in a straw-coloured ale.

Jack O'Legs *(OG 1041, ABV 4.2%)*
A combination of four types of malt and two types of aroma hops provide a copper-coloured premium ale with full fruit and a distinctive hoppy bitterness.

Colley's Dog *(OG 1053, ABV 5.2%)*
Dark but not over-rich, strong yet drinkable, this premium ale has a long dry finish with overtones of malt and walnuts.

TRIPLE FFF SIBA

Triple fff Brewing Company, Unit 3, Old Magpie Works, Four Marks, Alton, Hampshire, GU34 5HN
Tel (01420) 561422
Fax (01420) 560159
E-mail triplefffbrewing@aol.com
Website www.triplefff.co.uk
Tours by arrangement

⊠ Opened in 1997 with a five-barrel plant, Triple fff is now in the sole ownership of Graham Trott, who also has the lease of the Railway Arms in Alton. There has been a steady expansion of output, which is now produced on a 18-barrel plant. One pub is owned and some 200 outlets are supplied direct. Seasonal beers: Little Red Rooster (ABV 5%), Snow Blind (ABV 4.2%), I Can't Remember (ABV 6.8%).

Alton's Pride *(ABV 3.8%)* ❚◱◈
Excellent, clean-tasting, golden brown session bitter, full-bodied for its strength. A strong hoppiness, with a pleasant citrus balance. Delicious hoppy aroma and a long, hoppy, bitter finish.

Pressed Rat & Warthog *(ABV 3.8%)* ❚◱◈
Rather hoppy for a mild. Dry, roasty and ruby in colour with a good body and hints of blackcurrant and caramel. Moderately bitter-sweet with a short but well-balanced aftertaste.

After Glow *(ABV 4%)* ◱◈
Straw/gold best bitter with malt and hop flavours throughout. Well-balanced with a superb hoppy aftertaste, which builds with bitterness into a long, dry finish.

Moondance *(ABV 4.2%)* ❚◱◈
An amber-coloured best bitter, wonderfully hopped, with a huge aromatic, citrus hop, balanced by an uncompromising bitterness and some malt. Bitterness increases in the finish as the fruit declines.

Apache Rose Peacock *(ABV 4.2%)*

Stairway to Heaven *(ABV 4.6%)* ◱◈
An aroma of pale and crystal malts introduces this pale brown beer with a flavour of summer fruits. Well-balanced, with a dry and fruity finish. Predominately bitter with a slightly sweet background.

Dazed and Confused *(ABV 4.6%)* ◈
A strongish bitter, pale yellow in colour, with pale and lager malts plus a suggestion of elderflower. Refreshing and only moderately bitter.

Comfortably Numb *(ABV 5%)*

TURKEY

◱ **Turkey Inn, Goose Eye, Oakworth, Keighley, West Yorkshire, BD22 0PD**
Tel (01535) 681339
Tours by arrangement

☺ A purpose-built brewhouse with walls four feet thick, built into the hillside at the back of the pub, it took three years to build. Some of the beers are named after local caves. Brewery trips are free, with a small donation to Upper Wharfdale Fell Rescue. Beer Festivals are staged every May Bank Holiday, finishes first Monday in May.

Turkey Bitter *(ABV 3.8%)*

Turkey Mild *(ABV 4.2%)*

Black Shiver *(ABV 4.2%)*

ULEY

Uley Brewery Ltd, The Old Brewery, 31 The Street, Uley, Glos, GL11 5TB
Tel (01453) 860120
Website www.uleybrewery.com

⊠ Brewing at Uley began in 1833 at Price's Brewery. After a long gap, the premises were restored and Uley Brewery opened in 1985. It has its own spring water, which is used to mash with Tuckers Maris Otter malt and boiled with Hereford hops. No sugar or additives are used. Uley serves 40-50 free trade outlets in the Cotswolds area and, says owner Chas Wright, contrary to 'decline in cask ales, we have never been busier!' Seasonal beer: Pigor Mortis (ABV 6%, Dec-Jan).

Hogshead PA
(OG 1036, ABV 3.5%) ◈
A pale-coloured, hoppy session bitter with a good hop aroma and a full flavour for its strength, ending in a bitter-sweet aftertaste.

Uley Bitter *(OG 1040, ABV 4%)* 🍺
A copper-coloured beer with hops and fruit in the aroma and a malty, fruity taste, underscored by a hoppy bitterness. The finish is dry, with a balance of hops and malt.

Laurie Lee's Bitter
(OG 1045, ABV 4.5%)

Old Ric *(OG 1045, ABV 4.5%)* 🍺
A full-flavoured, hoppy bitter with some fruitiness and a smooth, balanced finish. Distinctively copper-coloured. This is the house beer, solely for the Old Spot Inn, Dursley.

Old Spot Prize Ale
(OG 1050, ABV 5%) 🍺
A distinctive full-bodied, red/brown ale with a fruity aroma, a malty, fruity taste, with a hoppy bitterness, and a strong, balanced aftertaste.

Pig's Ear Strong Beer
(OG 1050, ABV 5%) 🍺
A pale-coloured beer, deceptively strong. Notably bitter in flavour, with a hoppy, fruity aroma and a bitter finish.

UNCLE STUARTS*

**Uncle Stuarts Brewery, Antoma, Pack Lane, Lingwood, Norwich, Norfolk, NR13 4DD
Tel (07732) 012112
E-mail stuartsbrewery@aol.com**
Tours by arrangement

⊗ The brewery started in 2002, selling bottle-conditioned beers and polypins direct to customers and mail orders. Since 2003, all the beers are available in nine-gallon casks. Seasonal beer: Xmas (ABV 7%).

Brew 1 *(OG 1037-39, ABV 4%)*

Brew 9 *(OG 1041-43, ABV 4.7%)*

Brew 3 *(OG 1049-51, ABV 5.6%)*

Brew 2 *(OG 1050-52, ABV 5.7%)*

UPPER AGBRIGG

**Upper Agbrigg Brewery,
Unit 12, Honley Business Centre,
New Mill Road, Honley, Holmfirth,
West Yorkshire, HD9 6QB
Tel (01484) 660008
Fax (01484) 663359
E-mail info@upperagbriggbrewery.co.uk**

⊛ Upper Agbrigg Brewery was founded in 2001 by Andrew Balmforth in the cellar of his house in the village of Holme. The popularity of his beer was such that Andrew has now teamed up with Clive Donald of Brupaks, a leading supplier of brewing equipment and ingredients, and installed a brand new brewery in Brupaks' warehouse in Honley. The beers listed are the result of the new partnership. Ten outlets are supplied direct.

Home Valley Bitter *(ABV 3.8-4%)*

Black Beauty Porter *(ABV 4.3-4.5%)*

Premium Ale *(ABV 4.5-4.8%)*

Keller Bier *(ABV 4.8-5%)*

Oat Meal Stout *(ABV 4.8-5%)*

Rauchbier *(ABV 4.8-5%)*

VALE SIBA

**Vale Brewery Company, Thame Road,
Haddenham, Bucks, HP17 8BY
Tel (01844) 290008 Fax (01844) 292505
E-mail valebrewery@ntlworld.com
Website www.valebrewery.co.uk**
Tours by arrangement

⊗ After many years working for large regional breweries and allied industries, brothers Mark and Phil Stevens opened a small, purpose-built brewery in Haddenham. This revived brewing in a village where the last brewery closed at the end of World War Two. The plant was expanded in 1996 and now has a capacity of 40 barrels. All the beer is traditionally brewed without adjuncts, chemicals, or preservatives. A bottling line has been added, now producing a range of 10 different ales plus own label beers in short runs and the cask beers are also available in bottle-conditioned form. Around 200 local outlets take the beers. Seasonal beers: Hadda's Spring Gold (ABV 4.6%), Hadda's Summer Glory (ABV 4%), Hadda's Autumn Ale (ABV 4.5%), Hadda's Winter Solstice (ABV 4.1%), Good King Senseless (ABV 5.2%). Bottle-conditioned beers: As for regular ales, except Notley Ale. All are suitable for vegetarians and vegans.

Black Swan Dark Mild
(OG 1033, ABV 3.3%)

Notley Ale *(OG 1033, ABV 3.3%)* 🍺
A refreshing, copper-coloured session bitter with some malt in the aroma and taste, and an uncompromisingly dry finish.

Best Bitter *(OG 1036, ABV 3.7%)*

Wychert Ale *(OG 1038, ABV 3.9%)*
A full-flavoured beer with nutty overtones.

Black Beauty Porter *(OG 1043, ABV 4.3%)*

Edgar's Golden Ale
(OG 1043, ABV 4.3%) 🍺
A golden, hoppy best bitter with some sweetness and a dry, bitter-sweet finish. An unpretentious and well-crafted beer.

Grumpling Premium Ale
(OG 1046, ABV 4.6%)

Hadda's Headbanger *(OG 1050, ABV 5%)*

VALHALLA

**Valhalla Brewery, Shetland Refreshments
Ltd, Baltasound, Unst, Shetland, ZE2 9DX
Tel/Fax (01957) 711658
Website www.valhallabrewery.co.uk**
Tours by arrangement

Valhalla Brewery opened in 1997 on the island of Unst in the Shetland Isles, making it the most northerly brewery in Great Britain. It is run by husband and wife team Sonny and Sylvia Priest plus some part-timers. The latest acquisition was a bottling plant in 1999, which has greatly increased sales.

White Wife *(ABV 3.8%)* 🍺
Predominantly malty aroma with hop and fruit, which remain on the palate. The aftertaste is increasingly bitter.

Simmer Dim *(ABV 4%)* 🍺
A light golden bitter, named after the long Shetland twilight. The sulphur features do

not mask the fruits and hops of this well-balanced beer.

Auld Rock (ABV 4.5%)
A full-bodied, dark Scottish-style best bitter, it has a rich malty nose but does not lack bitterness in the long dry finish.

Sjolmet Stout (ABV 5%)
Full of malt and roast barley, especially in the taste. Smooth, creamy, fruity finish, not as dry as some stouts.

VENTNOR SIBA

Ventnor Brewery Ltd, 119 High Street, Ventnor, Isle of Wight, PO38 1LY
Tel (01983) 856161
Website www.ventnorbrewery.co.uk
Shop 10-4 weekdays.
Tours groups by arrangement

Ventnor Brewery is situated on the south of the island. Beer has been made here since 1840. All the beers are brewed with St Boniface natural spring waters. Ventnor has introduced a new organic beer. Some 90 outlets are supplied direct. Bottle-conditioned ale: Old Ruby. Seasonal ales are also available, including Sandrock Smoked Ale (ABV 5.6%, winter).

Golden Bitter (OG 1039, ABV 4%)
Well-balanced, easy-drinking bitter with an interesting slight honey/yeasty aftertaste.

SunFire Bitter (OG 1043, ABV 4.3%)
A generously and distinctively bittered amber beer that could be toned down if pulled through a sparkler.

Oyster Stout (OG 1045, ABV 4.5%)
A thin stout/dark mild with real oysters in the brew.

Organic Hygeia Ale
(OG 1046, ABV 4.6%)

Old Ruby Ale (OG 1048, ABV 4.7%)
A deep ruby-coloured bitter, with a good body and well-balanced hop character.

Wight Spirit (OG 1050, ABV 5%)
Interesting pale, hoppy, strong bitter with a surprising reversal of flavours from taste to aftertaste.

VENTONWYN
See Wooden Hand

VERULAM SIBA

Verulam Brewery, 134 London Road, St Albans, Herts, AL1 1PQ
Tel (01727) 766702
Tours by arrangement

A brewery housed behind the Farmers Boy pub run by Viv and Tina Davies. There are monthly specials.

Best Bitter (OG 1035, ABV 3.5%)

Special (OG 1037, ABV 3.8%)
Well-balanced session beer with a dryish aftertaste.

IPA (OG 1039, ABV 4%)
Impressive straw-coloured, very hoppy beer.

Farmers Joy (OG 1043, ABV 4.5%)
A malty beer with overtones of sweetness.

WADWORTH IFBB

Wadworth & Co Ltd, Northgate Brewery, Devizes, Wilts, SN10 1JW
Tel (01380) 723361
Fax (01380) 724342
E-mail sales@wadworth.co.uk
Website www.wadworth.co.uk
Shop (reception) Mon-Fri. 9-5.30. Stables open weekday afternoons.
Tours Trade April-Oct. Public June-Sept (by arrangement).

A market town brewery set up in 1885 by Henry Wadworth, and one of the few remaining breweries to sell beer locally in oak casks; the brewery still employs a cooper. Though solidly traditional, with its own dray horses, it continues to invest in the future and to expand, producing up to 2,000 barrels a week to supply a wide-ranging free trade in the south of England, as well as its own 252 pubs. All the tied houses serve real ale. In spring 2003 Wadworth launched a £1 million promotion for 6X, with poster sites in the south-west and on London Underground. Up to 300 free trade outlets are supplied. Wadworth also owns a brew-pub, the Red Shoot (qv). Seasonal beers: Old Father Timer (ABV 5.8%, Nov-Dec), Malt n' Hops (ABV 4.5%, Sept-Oct), Summersault (ABV 4%, May-Sept).

Henry's IPA
(OG 1035, ABV 3.6%)
A golden brown-coloured beer with a gentle, malty and slightly hoppy aroma, a good balance of flavours, with maltiness gradually dominating, and then a long-lasting aftertaste to match, eventually becoming biscuity. A good session beer.

6X (OG 1041, ABV 4.3%)
Copper-coloured ale with a malty and fruity nose, and some balancing hop character. The flavour is similar, with some bitterness and a lingering malty, but bitter finish. Full-bodied and distinctive.

JCB (OG 1046 ABV 4.7%)
A deep amber, robust but perfectly balanced, traditional English ale with a rich, malty body, complex hop character and a hint of tropical fruit in the aroma and taste. A gentle 'boiled sweet'/barley sugar sweetness blends wonderfully with smooth nutty malt and rounded hop bitterness before a dry, biscuity, bitter finish.

For Refresh UK:

Ushers Best Bitter (ABV 3.8%)

WAPPING

Wapping Beers, The Baltic Fleet, 33A Wapping, Liverpool, L1 8DQ
Tel (0151) 709 3116
Fax (0151) 707 2242

Wapping uses a scaled-down plant from the former Passageway brewery. It was commissioned in 2002, installed in a cellar below the pub. An old smugglers' tunnel provides a cool conditioning area for racked beer. There is a room for another fermenter in the future to cope with increased demand.

Wapping Bitter (OG 1036, ABV 3.6%)
Light, easy-drinking session beer with a good, bitter finish.

Summer Ale (OG 1042, ABV 4.2%)
Golden/straw coloured, thirst-quenching with a bite in the finish.

Baltic Extra (OG 1045, ABV 4.5%)
Chestnut in colour with good body and intensely bitter finish.

Stout (OG 1050, ABV 5%)
Dark with hints of roasted coffee.

WARCOP

Warcop Country Ales, 9 Nellive Park, St Brides Wentlooge, S. Wales, NP10 8SE
Tel (01633) 680058 Fax (01633) 681089
E-mail williampicton@compuserve.com

A small brewery based in a converted milking parlour, with 30 outlets delivered direct and others supplied by two wholesalers. Seasonal beer brewed normally at Christmas: Red Hot Furnace (ABV 9%), Furnace Fire (ABV 7.2%), Oil Fire (ABV 6 or 6.7%). All the cask ales are also bottle-conditioned.

Pit Shaft (ABV 3.4%)
Dark mild.

Pitside (ABV 3.7%)
The delicate taste of malt beer.

Arc (ABV 3.8%)
Light session beer with a dry, hoppy taste.

Pit Prop (ABV 3.8%) ◈
Fruit and roast aroma, dark brown in colour. A mixture of roast, malt, caramel and fruit in taste and aftertaste. The bitterness builds, adding to the character.

Hackers (ABV 4%)
Pale yellow, lightly-hopped bitter.

Black and Amber (ABV 4%)
A traditional pale ruby bitter, lightly hopped and full of flavour.

Casnewydd (ABV 4%)
Light, easy-drinking beer.

Hilston Premier (ABV 4%)
Rustic coloured, medium dry, autumnal beer.

Drillers (ABV 4%)
A lightly hopped, golden-yellow ale.

Steelers (ABV 4.2%)
Light red, malty-tasting brew.

Raiders (ABV 4.3%)
A lightly hopped, strong yellow ale.

Zen (ABV 4.4%)
A light yellow ale with a dry finish.

Rollers (ABV 4.5%)
A light ruby-coloured, well-hopped bitter.

Riggers (ABV 4.5%)
A strongly hopped golden beer with body.

Refuge (ABV 4.5%)
A well hopped, golden-yellow strong ale using Fuggles hops.

Printers (ABV 4.6%)
Pale yellow strong ale.

Rockers (ABV 4.8%)
A pale yellow, refreshing strong ale.

Dockers (ABV 5%)
Golden, fruity, full-bodied beer with real taste.

Deep Pit (ABV 5%)
Ruby, full-bodied beer with distinctive taste.

Painters (ABV 5%)
Pale yellow, full-bodied strong ale.

QE2 (ABV 6%)
A pale yellow, full-bodied, strong ale.

WARWICKSHIRE

Warwickshire Beer Co Ltd, The Brewery, Queen Street, Cubbington, Leamington Spa, Warwickshire, CV32 7NA
Tel (01926) 450747
Fax (01926) 450763
E-mail warwickshirebeer@hotmail.com
Website www.warwickshirebeerco.co.uk
Shop 8-12 Sat (ring first)
Tours by arrangement

Warwickshire is a seven-barrel capacity brewery operating in a former village bakery since 1998. Brewing takes place four times a week and, in addition, some beer is produced under licence by Highgate Brewery. As well as the regular range of seven beers, monthly specials are also produced and King Maker is available as a bottle-conditioned beer. Warwick Market Ale was commissioned by Warwick District Council to commemorate the re-opening of the town's market place; 20p from the sale of each bottle is donated to the Guide Dogs for the Blind Association. The cask beers are available in approximately 80 directly supplied outlets as well as the brewery's only owned pub, the Market Tavern in Atherstone. Polypins and bottles are available from the brewery. Seasonal beer: Xmas Bare (ABV 4.9%). Bottle-conditioned beer: King Maker.

Best Bitter (OG 1039, ABV 3.9%)
A golden brown session bitter flavoured with First Gold hops.

Lady Godiva (OG 1042, ABV 4.2%)
Blond, gentle, and full-bodied.

St Patricks (OG 1044, ABV 4.4%)
A rich porter brewed in the Irish tradition.

Falstaff (OG 1044, ABV 4.4%)
A mahogany-coloured bitter flavoured with Cascade and First Gold hops.

Castle (OG 1046, ABV 4.6%)
A premium, full-bodied and malty bitter.

Golden Bear (OG 1049, ABV 4.9%)
Golden in colour with well-balanced bitterness and spicy/fruity notes.

King Maker (OG 1055, ABV 5.5%)
Its subtlety belies its strength with flavour dominated by Challenger hops.

TOMOS WATKIN SIBA

Hurns Brewing Co Ltd, Phoenix Brewery, Unit 3, Century Park, Valley Way, Swansea Enterprise Park, Swansea, SA6 8RP
Tel (01792) 797303
Fax (01792) 775779
E-mail enquiries@tomoswatkin.com
Website www.tomoswatkin.com
Tours by arrangement

☻ The brewery was established in Llandeilo in 1995, adopting the name of a Llandovery company that ceased production in 1928. In 2000, the brewery moved to Swansea and two years later was taken over by the Hurns drinks wholesaling group. Seasonal beers: Cwrw Ceridwen (ABV 4.2%, spring), Canon's Choice (ABV 4.5%, winter), Dewi Sant (ABV 4.3%, March-April), Cwrw Haf (ABV 4.2%), summer), Owain Glyndwr (ABV 4.2%), autumn), Cwrw Santa (ABV 4.6%, Dec-Jan).

Whoosh *(OG 1037.5, ABV 3.7%)*
Amber-coloured, gentle malt and hop aroma. A mix of hop, malt and fruit flavours with moderate bitterness leading to a finish that is similar but mellow.

Brewery Bitter
(OG 1040.5, ABV 4%)
Pale brown, a faint malt, hop and fruit aroma. A rounded mix of flavours is balanced by a pleasant bitterness that builds in the finish.

Merlin Stout
(OG 1043, ABV 4.2%)
Dark brown with an aroma of malt and roast. A satisfying mix of malt, roast and coffee flavours with hop and some caramel. A good malt and roast finish with moderate bitterness completes this creamy, mellow stout.

Old Style Bitter (OSB)
(OG 1045, ABV 4.5%)
Amber with an aroma of hops and malt that leads to a full-bodied mouthfeel with a satisfying blend of hop, fruit and malt flavours. The bitterness builds in the finish, which is long lasting.

WEATHEROAK

**Weatheroak Brewery,
Coach & Horses Inn, Weatheroak Hill, Alvechurch, Birmingham, B48 7NX
Tel (07798) 773894 (day),
(0121) 445 4411 (eves)
E-mail dave@weatheroakales.co.uk
Website www.weatheroakales.co.uk**
Shop Real Ale Off-Licence, Alvechurch.
Tue-Fri 5.30-830. Fri-Sat 5-9.
Tours by arrangement

The brewery was set up in 1997, in an outhouse of the Coach & Horses, by Dave and Pat Smith by arrangement with pub owners Phil and Sheila Meads. The first brew was produced in 1998. A real ale off-licence has been opened in nearby Alvechurch. Weatheroak supplies 40 outlets direct.

Light Oak *(ABV 3.6%)*
A golden, well-hopped quaffing bitter with a hoppy aroma, a sharp, hoppy, fruity palate, giving way to a dry, lingering, hop-induced bitter aftertaste.

Weatheroak Ale *(ABV 4.1%)*
A well-hopped gold best bitter with plenty of fruity undertones and building hop bitterness, ending with a dry memory.

Redwood *(ABV 4.7%)*
The rich red colour heralds a wealth of flavours from the fruity bitter hops to the roast malt. A full bitter-sweet palate fades quickly.

Triple Tee *(ABV 5.1%)*
Potent amber strong bitter. A light fruity hop aroma explodes into a swirling mix of malt and hops in the mouth and a developing bitterness that fades rapidly.

WEETWOOD

**Weetwood Ales, Weetwood Grange, Weetwood, Tarporley, Cheshire, CW6 0NQ
Tel (01829) 752805
or Tel/Fax (01829) 752377
E-mail sales@weetwoodales.co.uk
Website www.weetwoodales.co.uk**

The brewery was set up at an equestrian centre in 1993. In 1998, the five-barrel plant was replaced by a 10-barrel kit. Around 100 regular customers are now supplied.

Best Bitter *(OG 1038.5, ABV 3.8%)*
A clean, dry and malty bitter with little aroma. Bitterness dominates the finish.

Eastgate Ale *(OG 1043.5, ABV 4.2%)*
Well-balanced, pale, refreshing beer with malty, fruity taste and short, dry finish.

Old Dog Bitter
(OG 1045, ABV 4.5%)
A fuller-bodied version of the bitter: fruitier, with a hint of sweetness.

Ambush Ale *(OG 1047.5, ABV 4.8%)*
Smooth, dark, amber-coloured beer with the fruity flavour balanced by the addition of Styrian Goldings hops.

Oasthouse Gold *(OG 1050, ABV 5%)*
Sweet, golden beer with some light malt and hop flavours. Typical Weetwood sharp aftertaste. It is deceptively drinkable for a beer of this strength.

WELLS IFBB

**Charles Wells Ltd, The Eagle Brewery, Havelock Street, Bedford, MK40 4LU
Tel (01234) 272766
Fax (01234) 279000
E-mail postmaster@charleswells.co.uk
Website www.charleswells.co.uk**
Tours by prior arrangement

The largest independent, family-owned brewery in the country established in 1876 and still run by descendants of the founder. The brewery has been on this site since 1976 and owns 257 pubs, of which 218 serve cask beer. Wells also supplies around 150 other outlets, while wholesalers distribute the beers nationally. Bombardier is now one of Britain's biggest-selling premium cask beers. In 2001 it launched cask-conditioned Bombardier in vented cans for supermarket sales. Seasonal beers: Summer Solstice (ABV 4.1, June), Lock Stock and Barrel (ABV 4.3%, September), Naked Gold (ABV 4.5%, December), Banana Bread Beer (ABV 4.5%, February).

Eagle IPA *(OG 1034, ABV 3.6%)*
A refreshing, amber session bitter with pronounced citrus hop aroma and palate, faint malt in the mouth, and a lasting dry, bitter finish.

Bombardier Premium Bitter
(OG 1042, ABV 4.3%)
Gentle citrus hop is balanced by traces of malt in the mouth, and this pale brown best bitter ends with a lasting dryness. Sulphur often dominates the aroma, particularly with younger casks.

WELTONS

See Hepworth.

WENTWORTH SIBA

Wentworth Brewery Ltd, The Powerhouse, Gun Park, Wentworth, Rotherham, South Yorkshire, S62 7TF
Tel (01226) 747070
Fax (01226) 747050
E-mail info@wentworth-brewery.com
Website www.wentworth-brewery.com
Tours by arrangement

⊗ Wentworth was built during the summer of 1999, using equipment from two defunct Sheffield breweries, Stones and Wards. Brewing started in 1999 and the first brew, WPA, won Best Beer of the Festival at CAMRA's Sheffield festival. Wentworth has installed three 15-barrel fermenters, boosting production to 70 barrels. One pub is owned and the owners plan to create a small tied estate. Approximately 300 outlets are supplied direct. A bottling plant is now being built. Bottle-conditioned beers: WPA (ABV 4.8%), Oatmeal Stout, Moores Magic (ABV 5.5%), Rampant Gryphon.

Needles Eye (OG 1035, ABV 3.6%)
A session bitter with a rather bitter taste that dominates the aftertaste.

WPA (OG 1039.5, ABV 4%) ◆
An extremely well-hopped IPA-style beer that leads to some astringency. A very bitter beer.

Best Bitter (OG 1040, ABV 4.1%) ◆
A hoppy, bitter beer with hints of citrus fruits. A bitter taste dominates the aftertaste.

Premium Bitter (OG 1044, ABV 4.4%)

Rock Spalt (OG 1045, ABV 4.5%)
Straw-coloured, aromatic, dry and drinkable. Spalt is the German variety of hop used.

Black Zac (OG 1046, ABV 4.6%)
A mellow, dark ruby-red ale with chocolate and pale malts leading to a bitter taste, with a coffee finish.

Oatmeal Stout (OG 1050, ABV 4.8%) ▥◆
Black, smooth, with roast and chocolate malt and coffee overtones.

Gold (OG 1049, ABV 5%)

Rampant Gryphon (OG 1062, ABV 6.2%) ◆
A strong, well-balanced golden ale with hints of fruit and sweetness but which retains a hoppy character.

WEST BERKSHIRE SIBA

West Berkshire Brewery Co Ltd, The Old Bakery, Yattendon, Thatcham, Berks, RG18 OUE
Tel/Fax (01635) 202968
E-mail dave@wbbrew.co.uk
Website www.wbbrew.co.uk
Tours strictly by arrangement only

⊗ A brewery established in 1995 by Dave and Helen Maggs at the rear of the Pot Kiln. The pub soon outgrew the plant and the Maggs added a 25-barrel plant in Yattendon, a mile away, although they retained the five-barrel plant at the Pot Kiln. They are now trying to buy pubs and will probably seek a new site to house a larger brewery in the near future. The brewery is committed to cask-conditioned beers but also produces some bottle-conditioned beer. There is a small craft shop at Yattendon that sells brewery pint tankards, mugs, sweat-shirts and T-shirts. Some 120 outlets are supplied direct. Seasonal specials are brewed on a changing, monthly basis, all in the range 4.1-4.6% ABV and a spiced porter is available each Christmas.

Old Father Thames (OG 1036, ABV 3.4%)

Mr Chubb's Lunchtime Bitter
(OG 1039, ABV 3.7%)
A traditional beer with all English hops and a good bitterness balanced by Maris Otter malts from Wiltshire and Suffolk. This beer is named in memory of the brewer's father who was the lock-keeper at Whitchurch-on-Thames and sometimes nick-named Mr. Chubb.

Maggs Magnificent Mild
(OG 1040, ABV 3.8%) ◆
An easy-to-drink southern mild with a good balance of malt and hops for the style. This dark red-brown beer has a short, dry finish.

Good Old Boy (OG 1042, ABV 4%) ◆
A well-balanced, fruity and hoppy beer with some sweetness in the finish.

Dr Hexter's Wedding Ale
(OG 1043, ABV 4.1%)
There are hints of grapefruit in this pale-coloured beer, with strong hop aromas and a long, bitter finish.

Full Circle (OG 1047, ABV 4.5%) ▤

Dr Hexter's Healer (OG 1052, ABV 5%) ◆
A full-bodied, vinous and sweet, end-of-the-evening beer that tastes stronger than it is. Tawny in colour, fruity and warming, with masses of malt and roast character.

WHEAL ALE

Wheal Ale Brewery, Paradise Park, Trelissick Road, Hayle, Cornwall, TR27 4HY.

Founded in 1980 as Parkside Brewery, the small brewhouse is behind a large pub, the Bird in Hand at the entrance to the Paradise Park bird sanctuary.

Millers's Ale (OG 1045, ABV 4.3%)

Old Speckled Parrot (OG 1052, ABV 5.5%)

WHIM SIBA

Whim Ales, Whim Farm, Hartington, Nr Buxton, Derbyshire, SK17 OAX
Tel (01298) 84991 Fax (01298) 84702

⊗ A brewery opened in 1993 in outbuildings at Whim Farm by Giles Litchfield who bought Broughton Brewery (qv) in 1995. Whim's beers are available in 50-70 outlets and the brewery's tied house, the Wilkes Head in Leek, Staffs. Some one-off brews are produced. Occasional/seasonal beers: Snow White (ABV 4.5%, a wheat beer), Special Ale (ABV 4.7%), Old Izaak (ABV 5%, winter), Black Christmas (ABV 6.5%, winter).

Arbor Light (OG 1035, ABV 3.6%)
Light-coloured bitter, sharp and clean with lots of hop character and a delicate light aroma.

Magic Mushroom Mild
(OG 1037, ABV 3.8%)
Ruby-black in colour, well-balanced with a complex mix of flavours and a sweet finish.

Hartington Bitter (OG 1038, ABV 4%)
A light, golden-coloured, well-hopped session beer. A dry finish with a spicy, floral aroma.

Hartington IPA (OG 1045, ABV 4.5%)
Pale and light-coloured, smooth on the palate allowing malt to predominate. Slightly sweet finish combined with distinctive light hop bitterness. Well rounded.

WHITE

White Brewing Company, The 1066 Country Brewery, Pebsham Farm Industrial Estate, Pebsham Lane, Bexhill, E Sussex, TN40 2RZ
Tel (01424) 731066
Fax (01424) 732995
E-mail whitebrewing@fsbdial.co.uk
Tours by arrangement

Brewery founded in 1995 by husband-and-wife team David and Lesley White to serve local free trade outlets and some wholesalers, brewing five to 10 barrels a week. A small, experimental bottling plant has been installed and the Whites hope to produce bottle-conditioned beer and to bottle for other craft brewers in this area. Some 20 or so outlets are supplied. Seasonal beer: White Gold (ABV 4.9%, summer); it appears under various labels, all with 'millennium' in the name.

1066 Country Bitter (OG 1040, ABV 4%)
Amber-gold in colour, a light, sweetish beer with good malt and hop balance, and a bitter, refreshing finish.

White Dark (OG 1040, ABV 4%)

WHITEWATER

Whitewater Brewing Co, 40 Tullyframe Road, Kilkeel, Co Down, N Ireland, BT34 4RZ
Tel/Fax (02841) 769449
E-mail kerrysloan@hotmail.co.uk
Website www.whitewaterbrewing.co.uk
Tours by arrangement
⊗ Set up in 1996 and nestling in the idyllic setting of the heart of the Mourne Mountains, Whitewater is now the largest micro-brewery in Northern Ireland. It produces 11 different cask-conditioned ales. The plant was designed and built by Kerry and Bernard Sloan and, with an expansion in 2000, it now boasts a 15-barrel brew length. With its stainless-steel construction, the plant has fermenting capacity of 2,000 gallons a week. The brewery is currently supplying 18 outlets in Northern Ireland and owns one pub. Seasonal beers: Summer Solstice (ABV 4%), Glen Ale (ABV 4.2%), All that Jazz (ABV 4.2%), Nut Brown Ale (ABV 4.2%), Dappled Mare (ABV 4.3%), Snake Drive Bitter (ABV 4.3%), Sanity Claus (ABV 4.5%), Bee's Endeavour (ABV 4.8%), Knight Porter (ABV 5%).

Mill Ale (OG 1038, ABV 3.7%)

Natural Blonde Lager
(OG 1037, ABV 3.7%)

Belfast Ale (OG 1046, ABV 4.5%)

WHITLEY BRIDGE*

**Whitley Bridge Brewing Co,
c/o 3 George Street, Outwood, Wakefield, West Yorkshire, WF1 2LR.**
Tel (01924) 825836
E-mail big.neil@virgin.net

The brewery was launched in April 2003. It produces some four barrels a week and supplies three beer agencies and six pubs.

Nelly's Ale (OG 1043, ABV 4.2%)

Gunslingers (OG 1043, ABV 4.2%)

Three Kings Royal Ale
(OG 1043, ABV 3.9-4%)

Kneesknocker (OG 1043, ABV 3.9-4%)

WHITSTABLE*

Whitstable Brewery, Little Telpits Farm, Woodcock Lane, Grafty Green, Kent, ME17 2AT

⊗ Whitstable Brewery took over the Swale Brewery plant and started brewing in the summer of 2003 at the old site until plans are finalised to move the brewery to Whitstable at one of the restaurants owned by Whitstable Oyster & Fisheries. The beers are for the company's own outlets. Bottle-conditioned beers are planned.

Bitter (ABV 3.8%)

WHITTINGTON'S*

Whittington's Brewery, Three Choirs Vineyards Ltd, Newent, Gloucestershire, GL18 1LS.
Tel (01531) 890555
E-mail info@whittingtonbrewery.co.uk
Website www.whittingtonbrewery.co.uk
Tours available; shop, restaurant and eight guest rooms.

Dick Whittington came from Newent, hence the name of the brewery. Five barrels a week are produced and are supplied mainly to Cellar Supplies in Cheltenham for the Gloucester area.

Cats Whiskers (ABV 4.1%)

WICKED HATHERN

Wicked Hathern Brewery Ltd, The Willows, 46 Derby Road, Hathern, Loughborough, Leics, LE12 5LD
Tel (01509) 842585
E-mail Beer@Hathern.com
Website www.wicked-hathern.co.uk
Tours by arrangement, £3 charge (includes one pint each of two beers)

⊗ Opened in the first month of the new millennium, the 2.5-barrel brewery is owned and operated by four men, John and Marc Bagley, John Worsfold and Sean O'Neill, in their spare time. They supply beers on a guest basis to many local pubs and beer festivals, and brew commissioned beers for special occasions, such as beer festivals. Since 2002 they have bottled their beers to supply mainly their local shop, as the guest beer policies of the owners of pubs in Hathern preclude the brewery having a regular village outlet. In 2003, the brewery created and supplied Albion Special, a light copper coloured bitter, exclusively for the Albion in Loughborough. Seasonal beers: Doble's Dog (ABV 3.5%, autumn-winter), Hawthorn Gold (ABV 3.5%, spring-summer), Gladstone Tidings (ABV 5.1%, Christmas). Bottled beers: with the exception of Albion Special, all beers are available in bottles from selected off-licences (see website) and from Hathern Village Shop; ABVs are higher.

Doble's Dog (OG 1036, ABV 3.5%)
A full-bodied, stout-like dark mild, good head retention, with fruit and nut flavours on the palate.

Hawthorn Gold (OG 1035, ABV 3.5%)
A light golden, easy-drinking beer with a good balance of hops and malt.

WHB (Wicked Hathern Bitter) (OG 1038, ABV 3.8%)
A light-tasting session bitter with a dry palate and good hop aroma.

Albion Special (OG 1041, ABV 4%)
A light, copper-coloured bitter with a nutty aroma with a smoky malty taste, hops leading through.

Cockfighter (OG 1043, ABV 4.2%)
A pale bitter with a pronounced maltiness offset by a delicate hop flavour.

Soar Head (OG 1048, ABV 4.8%)
A dark ruby bitter with a complex rich fruit taste and a mellow aroma.

Gladstone Tidings (OG 1051, ABV 5.1%)
A dark bitter having a deep rounded finish with a strong hop presence and a rich full taste.

WICKWAR SIBA

Wickwar Brewing Co Ltd, The Old Brewery, Station Road, Wickwar, Glos, GL12 8NB
Tel/Fax (01454) 294168
E-mail bob@wickwarbrewing.co.uk
Website www.wickwarbrewing.co.uk
Shop 9.30-4.30 Mon-Fri, 10-12 Sat.
Tours by arrangement

⊗ Having set up Wickwar Brewing Co in 1990, in the cooper's shed of the old Arnold Perrett & Co Brewery, it was always Ray Penny's dream to move into the main brewery building across the road, built around 1840, but which spent most of the 20th century as a cider factory and more recently as a bonded warehouse. This dream will be realised in 2003/4 when the business expands into the old brewery with a new 60-barrel brew-length plant. Three pubs are owned in Bristol and some 250 outlets are supplied. Seasonal beers: Spring Ale (ABV 3.8%, April-May), Sunny Daze (ABV 4.2%, June-Aug), Autumnale (ABV 4.5%, Sept-Nov). Bottle-conditioned beers: Cotswold Way, Old Arnold, Station Porter, Brand Oak Bitter (BOB), Mr Perretts Traditional Stout.

Coopers WPA (OG 1036.5, ABV 3.5%) ▢◥
Golden-coloured, this well-balanced beer is light, refreshing, with hops, citrus fruit, apple/pear flavour and notable pale malt character. Bitter, dry finish. A crisp and quenching ale.

Brand Oak Bitter (BOB) (OG 1039, ABV 4%) ◥
Amber-coloured, this has a distinctive blend of hop, malt and apple/pear citrus fruits. The slightly sweet taste turns into a fine, dry bitterness, with a similar malty-lasting finish.

Cotswold Way (OG 1043, ABV 4.2%) ◥
Amber-coloured, it has a pleasant aroma of pale malt, hop and fruit. Good dry bitterness in the taste with some sweetness. Similar though less sweet in the finish, with good hop content.

Old Arnold (OG 1045.5, ABV 4.6%)
Named after the founder of the original brewery, around 1800, this is a ruby-red ale, sweetish with malt and bitter overtones, and Challenger hops providing rich fruitiness. It is brewed to a similar recipe used by Arnold in his Strong Old Beer.

Olde Merryford Ale (OG 1049, ABV 4.8%) ◥
Full-flavoured and well-balanced ale, with malt, hops and cherry fruit throughout. Amber/pale brown, it is slightly sweet, with a long-lasting, malty, dry, fruity and increasingly bitter finish.

Mr Perretts Traditional Stout (OG 1059, ABV 5.9%) ◥
Aroma and taste of smoky chocolate malts and peppery hops. Dark fruits of black cherry and blackcurrant give hints of sweetness to the dry, quite bitter, slightly spicy, well-balanced taste.

Station Porter (OG 1062, ABV 6.1%) ◥
Available Oct-Feb, this is a rich, smooth, dark ruby-brown ale. Starts with roast malt; coffee, chocolate and dark fruit then develop a complex, spicy, bitter-sweet taste and a long roast finish.

WILLY'S SIBA

Willy's Brewery Ltd, 17 High Cliff Road, Cleethorpes, Lincs, DN35 8RQ
Tel (01472) 602145
Fax (01472) 603578
Tours by arrangement

☺ The brewery opened in 1989 to provide beer for two outlets in Grimsby and Cleethorpes. It has a five-barrel plant with maximum capacity of 15 barrels a week. The brewery can be viewed at any time from pub or street.

Original Bitter (OG 1038, ABV 3.8%) ◥
A light brown 'sea air' beer with a fruity, tangy hop on the nose and taste, giving a strong bitterness tempered by the underlying malt.

Burcom Bitter *(OG 1044, ABV 4.2%)* ◆
A dark ruby colour, sometimes known as
Mariner's Gold, although the beer is dark
ruby in colour. It is a smooth and creamy
brew with a sweet chocolate-bar maltiness,
giving way to an increasingly bitter finish.

Last Resort *(OG 1044, ABV 4.3%)*

Weiss Buoy *(OG 1045, ABV 4.5%)*
A cloudy wheat beer.

Coxswains Special *(OG 1050, ABV 4.9%)*

Old Groyne *(OG 1060, ABV 6.2%)* ◆
An initial sweet banana fruitiness blends
with malt to give a vanilla quality to the
taste and slightly bitter aftertaste. A copper-
coloured beer reminiscent of a Belgian ale.

WINTER'S SIBA

**Winter's Brewery, 8 Keelan Close,
Norwich, NR6 6QZ
Tel/Fax (01603) 787820
E-mail sales@wintersbrewery.com
Website www.wintersbrewery.com**

⊗ Daved Winter, who has had previous
award-winning success as brewer for both
Woodforde's and Chalk Hill breweries,
decided to set up his own brewery in 2001.
He purchased the brewing plant from the
now defunct Scott's Brewery in Lowestoft.
He produces five ales at present, and sells
direct to the local free trade.

Mild *(OG 1036.5, ABV 3.6%)*
Mild in strength but strong in flavour; roast
tones come through.

Bitter *(OG 1039.5, ABV 3.8%)* ◆
A session beer with a pronounced hoppy
character. Although some malt can be
detected in the aroma, this is masked
throughout by the dominating hoppiness.
This leads to a bitter feel that overcomes a
latent malty sweetness that fades quickly.
The finish of this mid-brown brew
continues the hoppy theme through a
lingering dryness.

Golden *(ABV 4.1%)* ▧◆
Golden in name and colour, this
refreshingly fruity beer has a light but
satisfying character. An aroma redolent of
citrus fruits leads into an array of differing
but well-balanced flavours. Mandarin jostles
with apricot and peach as the citrus notes
more than match the slightly bitter
maltiness. The gently tapering fruitiness
continues as the flavours meld into a
complex yet satisfying finale.

Revenge *(OG 1047, ABV 4.7%)* ◆
Well-balanced and fruity with a smoky,
mellow character. A plummy malt body
underpins a wide-ranging taste spectrum. A
hoppy bitterness provides a low backing
that tempers the inherent sweetness that is
prevalent throughout the range of this beer.
The sweet malty signature continues with
little fading as the feel of this mid-brown
brew remains light despite the fullness of
flavour.

Storm Force *(OG 1053, ABV 5.3%)* ◆
A rich malty brew with a pronounced
sweetness throughout. Tawny-coloured
with a heavy malt nose that continues into
the strawberry sweet introduction. Light on
the tongue but with a distinctively malty

character, the flavour subsides quickly to a
gentle fruity glow.

Tempest *(OG 1062, ABV 6.2%)*

WIZARD*

**Wizard Ales, The Norman Knight, Whichford,
Shipston on Stour, Warwickshire, CV36 5PE
Tel/Fax (01608) 684621
E-mail wizardales@thenormanknight.co.uk
Website www.thenormanknight.co.uk**
Tours by prior arrangement

⊗ A new 1.25-barrel brewery housed in a
barn behind the pub, brewing solely for the
pub but it may sell locally to other free
houses in the future.

Apprentice *(OG 1038, ABV 3.5%)*
Amber-coloured session beer with a dry finish.

Whichford Bitter *(OG 1038, ABV 3.6%)*
Pale-coloured session beer.

One For The Toad *(OG 1041, ABV 3.8%)*
A light-coloured beer with a good hop
flavour.

Mother in Law *(OG 1043, ABV 4%)*
A rich, darkish beer with a strong hop
flavour.

WOLD TOP* SIBA

**Wold Top Brewery, Hunmanby Grange, Wold
Newton, Driffield, East Yorkshire, YO25 3HS
Tel (01723) 891636
Fax (01723) 892229
E-mail enquiries@woldtopbrewery.co.uk
Website www.woldtopbrewery.co.uk**

Wold Top started production in May 2003
and is run by two farming families, the
Mellors and the Grays. Both farms produce
high-quality malting barley and the farm at
which the brewery is based has a supply of
pure chalk-filtered water. The brewing
equipment was built in Yorkshire. Bottled as
well as draught beers will be produced and
customised beers for such special occasions
as weddings, anniversaries and birthdays
can be ordered.

Bitter *(OG 1037.2, ABV 3.7%)*
Maris Otter pale and a small amount of
crystal malt form the basis of the beer, with
Northdown hops for aroma and bitterness.

Falling Stone *(ABV 4.2%)*
A full-bodied and well-rounded beer, the
rich colour produced by adding a small
amount of chocolate malt to the mash,
which is based around Maris Otter pale
malt. Progress are used for aroma.

WOLF SIBA

**Wolf Brewery Ltd, 10 Maurice Gaymer Road,
Attleborough, Norfolk, NR17 2QZ
Tel (01953) 457775 Fax (01953) 457776
E-mail info@wolf-ales.co.uk
Website www.wolf-brewery.ltd.uk**
Tours by arrangement

⊗ The brewery was founded by Wolf
Witham, the former owner of the Reindeer
Brewery in 1996, using a 20-barrel plant
housed on the site of the old Gaymer's cider
orchard. 200 outlets are supplied direct. All
the beers are also sold in bottle-conditioned
form.

Golden Jackal (*OG 1039, ABV 3.7%*) ◆
With a colour fitting the name, this well-balanced session bitter starts with a light honeyish aroma and a bitter-sweet hoppiness. A light finish as the bitterness fades behind a smooth, hop-influenced sweetness.

Wolf In Sheeps Clothing
(*OG 1039, ABV 3.7%*) ◆
A malty aroma with fruity undertones introduces this reddish-hued mild. Malt, with a bitter Bisto-like background that remains throughout, is the dominant flavour of this clean-tasting beer.

Bitter (*OG 1041, ABV 3.9%*) ◆
Malt and hops mix well throughout this copper-coloured brew. A consistent mix in both aroma and taste is overshadowed by a growing bitterness in the aftertaste. Some dryness develops at the end.

Coyote Bitter (*OG 1044, ABV 4.3%*) ⌂◆
A pale brown bitter with light, fruit-enhanced hoppy vapours. A complex but well-balanced mix of hops and malt with more than a hint of citrus leads on to a crisp, well-hopped finale.

Newshound 2001 (*ABV 4.5%*) ◆
Copper coloured with a light hop and malt nose. Malt takes the edge off the bitter backbone of this solid tasting beer. Vanilla and citrus hints can be detected as the long finish grows into a dry hoppiness.

Woild Moild (*OG 1048, ABV 4.8%*) ◆
A big roast coffee bean aroma leads into a distinctively roasted barley base. A good balance of malt with a liquorice bitterness aids this dark-red mild towards a smoky, dark and long-lasting rich finish.

Granny Wouldn't Like It
(*OG 1049, ABV 4.8%*) ⌂◆
Dark red, rich and filling, the swirling mix of flavours produces a complex but satisfying experience. Both the nose and taste have a fruity blend of malt and bitter-sweet hoppiness with smoky overtones.

Lupus Lupus (*ABV 5%*) ◆
A soft blackcurrant nose introduces this red-coloured brew. Hops vie with bitterness in the initial taste. Fruity malt notes soon fade to leave a long bitter finish with just a hint of blackcurrant fruitiness.

Timber Wolf (*OG 1060, ABV 5.8%*) ◆
A rich and warming winter ale. A solid currant bun aroma combines with a rich fruit and nut beginning to give this red-hued beer a sweet, spicy feel. A long, drawn-out bitter-sweet finale completes the experience.

WOLVERHAMPTON & DUDLEY
See Banks's and Marston's.

WOOD SIBA
Wood Brewery Ltd, Wistanstow, Craven Arms, Shropshire, SY7 8DG
Tel (01588) 672523
Fax (01588) 673939
E-mail mail@woodbrewery.co.uk
Website www.woodbrewery.co.uk
Shop. Goods available at brewery, working hours and by mail
Tours by arrangement

⊠ The brewery opened in 1980 in buildings next to the Plough Inn, still the brewery's only tied house. Steady growth over the years included the acquisition of the Sam Powell Brewery and its beers in 1991. Building work started in 2002 to enlarge fermentation, storage and office space. Production averages 60 barrels a week. 200 outlets are supplied direct. Seasonal beers: Summer That! (ABV 3.9%, summer), Woodcutter (ABV 4.2%, autumn), Saturnalia (ABV 4.2%, Jan-Feb), Get Knotted (ABV 4.7%, February), Hopping Mad (ABV 4.7%, March), Anniversary Ale (ABV 5%, April), Christmas Cracker (ABV 6%, Nov-Dec), plus a series under the Shropshire Heroes label. Bottle-conditioned beers: Hopping Mad, Shropshire Lad.

Wallop (*OG 1035, ABV 3.4%*)

Sam Powell Original Bitter
(*OG 1038, ABV 3.7%*)

Parish Bitter (*OG 1040, ABV 4%*) ◆
A blend of malt and hops with a bitter aftertaste. Pale brown in colour.

Special Bitter (*OG 1042, ABV 4.2%*) ◆
A tawny brown bitter with malt, hops and some fruitiness.

Shropshire Lad (*OG 1045, ABV 4.5%*)
Full-bodied, with roasted malts evident in palate, moderate hop bitterness and a dryish finish.

Sam Powell Old Sam (*OG 1047, ABV 4.6%*)

Wonderful (*OG 1048, ABV 4.8%*) ◆
A mid-brown, fruity beer, with a roast and malt taste.

WOODEN HAND*
Wooden Hand Brewery, Unit 2b, Grampound Road Industrial Estate, Grampound Road, Truro, Cornwall, TR2 4TB
Tel (01726) 881318

Wooden Hand has taken over the plant from the former Ventonwyn Brewery. The company is run by Anglo-Swedish businessman Rolf Munding, who owns the Zatec Brewery in the Czech Republic. Brewing is on an irregular basis for a limited local market.

Bitter (*ABV 4.1%*)

WOODFORDE'S SIBA
Woodforde's Norfolk Ales
(t/a Woodforde's Ltd),
Broadland Brewery, Woodbastwick,
Norwich, Norfolk, NR13 6SW
Tel (01603) 720353
Fax (01603) 721806
E-mail info@woodfordes.co.uk
Website www.woodfordes.co.uk
Shop 10.30-4.30 Mon-Fri; open most weekends & Bank Holidays, telephone 01603 722218 to confirm.
Tours Tuesday and Thursday evenings

⊠ Founded in 1981 in Drayton near Norwich, Woodforde's moved to Erpingham, near Aylsham, in 1982, and then moved again to a converted farm complex, with greatly increased production capacity, in the picturesque Broadland village of Woodbastwick in 1989. A major expansion of Broadland Brewery took place

Woodforde's
Norfolk Ales

in 2001/2002 to more than double production capacity and included a new brewery shop and visitor centre. Woodforde's brews an extensive range of beers and runs three tied houses with some 300 other outlets supplied on a regular basis. Bottle-conditioned beers: Wherry Best Bitter, Great Eastern, Nelson's Revenge, Admiral's Reserve, Norfolk Nog, Headcracker ⬡, Norfolk Nip. Admiral's Reserve was added to the range in 2002 to celebrate Woodforde's 21st Anniversary.

Mardler's *(OG 1035, ABV 3.5%)* ✦
A traditional dark brown Norfolk mild with a definite roast and caramel aroma. This is continued in the initial taste where the roast and caramel are softened by a light hoppiness and gentle sweetness. The flavours soon subside to a pleasant blend of flavours in which an increased malt presence can be detected.

Kett's Rebellion *(OG 1034.4, ABV 3.6%)* ✦
Brewed to celebrate the 450th anniversary of Kett's land workers' rebellion, this moderately bitter session beer retains a hoppiness to the finish. Sweet caramel notes fade in the finish.

Fur & Feather *(OG 1035.4, ABV 3.6%)* ✦
House beer for the brewery tap. Copper coloured with a soft fruity aroma that leads to a well-balanced sweet, malty flavour with bitter echoes. The quick finish sustains the maltiness but loses bitterness.

Wherry Best Bitter
(OG 1037.4, ABV 3.8%) 🍴🗂✦
Pale brown in colour with a sustained fruity character in both nose and taste. A hint of caramel and roast in the aroma are overtaken by a first taste that has rather more hop and malt background. The fruity character fades towards the finish as a more defined hoppiness becomes apparent. Easy drinking with a consistent character.

Great Eastern *(OG 1039.8, ABV 4.3%)* ✦
Citrus notes are to the fore in this golden-hued brew. A consistent hop flavour gives this beer a clean, easy-drinking feel. Although the citrus notes fade, enough remain to soften the hoppiness and help the beer retain a refreshing lightness.

Nelson's Revenge
(OG 1042.7, ABV 4.5%) 🗂✦
A rich fruity beer with a good balance of flavours. The sultana sweetness is challenged by a dry bitterness that gives a rich, filling mouthfeel. The malty bitterness is retained to the end as the fruitiness recedes.

Norfolk Nog *(OG 1046.8, ABV 4.6%)* 🍴🗂✦
A dark brown beer with a heavy roast framework. A deep fruity bitterness hangs on to the roast notes to give depth to the taste. The nose is full of roast and dried fruits well in keeping with the flavour profile. The bitterness takes over towards the end to lighten the somewhat heavy, filling mouthfeel.

Admiral's Reserve *(OG 1050, ABV 4.6%)* ✦
A crisp malty aroma introduces this well-balanced and flavoursome, copper-coloured ale. A stirring mix of malt, hops and bitterness is heightened by a sweet fruitiness. Little noticeable loss of flavour as the beer develops a vinous character that cleans the palate.

Headcracker *(OG 1065.7, ABV 7%)* 🍴🗂✦
Surprisingly clean-tasting for a barley wine. A booming, plummy aroma buttressed with malt continues through to become the dominant taste throughout. A pleasant winey bitterness provides a counterpoint and lightens the mouthfeel as the beer develops a slowly-fading maturity. A warming, dry sultana plumminess provides a fitting finale.

WORFIELD

Worfield Brewing Co, All Nations Brewhouse, Coalport Road, Madeley, Shropshire, TF7 5DP
Tel (01952) 585747

☺ Set up in 1994 at the Davenport Arms, Worfield, by licensee Mike Handley, it moved to Bridgnorth in 1998. Following the reopening of the All Nations in Madeley, the brewery relocated there in the autumn of 2003. Worfield brews for the All Nations as well as free trade outlets. Dabley Ale is only available at the All Nations. Some 100 outlets are supplied. Seasonal beers: Winter Classic (January), Spring Classic (ABV 4.5%, March), Summer Classic (June), Autumn Classic (September), Ploughman's (ABV 4.4%), Waggoner's (ABV 4.6%), Harvest Ale (ABV 4.6%).

Hopstone Bitter *(OG 1040, ABV 4%)*

OBJ *(OG 1043, ABV 4.2%)*

Shropshire Pride *(OG 1045, ABV 4.5%)*

Burcote Premium Pale
(OG 1049, ABV 4.9%)

For All Nations:
Dabley Ale *(OG 1040, ABV 3.8%)*

WYCHWOOD SIBA

The Wychwood Brewery Ltd, Eagle Maltings, The Crofts, Witney, Oxon, OX28 4DP
Tel (01993) 890800
Fax (01993) 772553
E-mail imray@wychwood.co.uk
Website www.wychwood.co.uk
Shop 9-5
Tours only for CAMRA branch visits

⊗ Wychwood was started in 1983 by Chris Moss and Paddy Glenny. A chain of Hobgoblinn pubs was created in the 1990s. As a result of the death of Chris Moss in 2000, the pubs and brewery were sold. The brewery is now owned by Refresh UK, which also owns the Brakspear brands. 100 outlets are supplied and nine seasonal beers are produced. Wychwood also brews Brakspear's seasonal beers.

Shires Best Bitter *(OG 1034, ABV 3.7%)* ✦
A copper-coloured session beer with a fruity and malty aroma and admirable hop character. Good body for its strength. Fruit declines to a dry finish.

Fiddler's Elbow Bitter
(OG 1039, ABV 4.1%) ◆
A spicy amber beer, complex, with a spicy hop aroma and a suggestion of cinnamon. Easy to drink, with a crisp and refreshing finish.

Hobgoblin Best Bitter
(OG 1043, ABV 4.5%) ◆
Powerful, full-bodied, copper-red, well-balanced brew. Strong in roasted malt, with a moderate, hoppy bitterness and a slight fruity character.

For Usher's pubs owned by InnSpired (qv)

Winter Storm *(OG 1038, ABV 4%)*

Spring Fever *(OG 1038, ABV 4%)*

Summer Madness *(OG 1038, ABV 4%)*

Autumn Frenzy *(OG 1038, ABV 4%)*

WYE VALLEY SIBA

Wye Valley Brewery Ltd, Stoke Lacy, Herefordshire, HR7 4HG
Tel (01885) 490505
Fax (01885) 490595
E-mail wvb@freeuk.com
Website www.wyevalleybrewery.co.uk
Tours by arrangement

⊠ Wye Valley Brewery was founded in 1985 by Peter Amor at the Nags Head in Canon Pyon. In 1986, the brewery moved to the outbuildings at the Barrels pub in Hereford. 2002 saw another move 10 miles north to Stoke Lacy where it was completely re-equipped and now has a daily output of 80

NEW BREWERIES

The following new breweries have been notified to the Guide and should come on stream in 2003/2004:

Acorn, Wombwell, Barnsley

Anchor Brewery, King's Lynn, Norfolk

Bedrock, Toppesfield, Essex

Belfast Brewery, Belfast

Borough Arms, Crewe

Bragdy Ty Crwr Glan yr Afon, Holywell, Flintshire

Briarsway, Edinburgh

Brimstage Brewing Co, Thornton Heath, Merseyside

Carpenters Arms, Slapton, Bucks

Cross Hands, near Ammanford, Dyfed

Edale Brewery, Edale, Derbyshire

Gretna Green, Cumbria

Joule's, Stone, Staffs

Kingston Arms, Kingston Street, Cambridge

Matfen, Newcastle upon Tyne

Nantwich, Cheshire

Pheasant Inn, Broseley, Telford, Shropshire

Queen's Head, Earsham, Norfolk

Slaughterhouse Brewery, Warwick

Stanton, Northumberland

Star Inn, Crowlas, Penzance, Cornwall

Tickenham, Somerset

barrels. Beers are distributed locally every week and monthly to many parts of the country. Two pubs are owned and 300 outlets are supplied. Seasonal beers: Golden Ale (ABV 4.2%, March-Oct), Winter Tipple (ABV 4.4%, Nov-Feb), Christmas Ale (ABV 6%, Nov-Dec). Bottle-conditioned beers: DG Golden Ale, DG Wholesome Stout.

Bitter *(OG 1037, ABV 3.7%)* ◆
A beer whose aroma gives little hint of the bitter hoppiness that follows right through to the aftertaste.

Hereford Pale Ale *(OG 1040, ABV 4%)* ◆
A pale, hoppy, malty brew with a hint of sweetness before a dry finish.

Dorothy Goodbody's Golden Ale
(OG 1042, ABV 4.2%)
A light, gold-coloured, refreshing ale with a hint of malty sweetness from the pale crystal malt, balancing well with the aroma and flavour of the classic English hop varieties used.

Butty Bach *(OG 1046, ABV 4.5%)*
A burnished gold, full-bodied premium ale.

Dorothy Goodbody's Wholesome Stout
(OG 1046, ABV 4.6%) ⬚◆
A smooth and satisfying stout with a bitter edge to its roast flavours. The finish combines roast grain and malt.

WYLAM SIBA

Wylam Brewery Ltd, South Houghton, Heddon on the Wall, Northumberland, NE15 0EZ
Tel (01661) 853377
E-mail john@wylambrew.co.uk
Website www.wylambrew.co.uk
Tours by arrangement

⊠ Wylam was set up by John Boyle and Robin Leighton in a disused farm dairy in 2000. Originally a five-barrel plant, the brew-length is now eight barrels, and a 10-barrel plant is being sought. The brewery delivers to more than 150 local outlets. Seasonal beers: Spring Thing (ABV 3.4%, spring), Wylam Autumn (ABV 4.9%, autumn).

Bitter *(OG 1039, ABV 3.8%)*
A refreshing lighter version of the 4.4 Rocket using similar ingredients but producing a beer with its own distinctive character.

Gold Tankard *(OG 1041.5, ABV 4%)* ◆
Fresh, clean flavour, full of hops, this golden ale has a hint of citrus in the finish.

Turbinia *(OG 1041.5, ABV 4%)* ⬚
Rich, ruby-coloured beer full of hops, with a long, bitter finish.

80/- *(OG 1045, ABV 4.5%)*
A traditional brown beer in the style favoured in Scotland and the North-east by the 'old school' of beer connoisseurs. Smooth with complex malts and subtle hops.

Bohemia Pilsner
(OG 1046.5, ABV 4.6%) ⬚◆
Deep gold in colour with a heady bouquet of malt and hops, and a deep finish of fruit.

Haugh *(OG 1046.5, ABV 4.6%)* ◆
A smooth velvet porter packed with flavour. Roast malt and a slight fruitiness provide a satisfying pint with a smooth finish.

WYRE PIDDLE

Wyre Piddle Brewery, Highgrove Farm, Peopleton, Nr Pershaw, Worcs, WR10 2LF
Tel/Fax (01905) 841853

A brewery established in a converted stable by a former publican and master builder in 1992. Some 200 pubs in the Midlands take the beer. The brewery relocated and upgraded its equipment in 1997 and has now moved again to Highgrove Farm. It also brews for Green Dragon, Malvern: Dragon's Downfall (ABV 3.9%), Dragon's Revenge (ABV 4%). For Severn Valley Railway: Royal Piddle (ABV 4.2%). Seasonal beers: Piddle in the Sun (ABV 5.2%, summer), Yule Piddle (ABV 4.5%, Christmas). Bottle-conditioned beer: Piddle in the Hole (ABV 4.6%).

Piddle in the Hole *(OG 1039, ABV 3.9%)*
Copper-coloured and quite dry, with lots of hops and fruitiness throughout.

Piddle in the Wind *(ABV 4.5%)*
This drink has a superb mix of flavours. A nice hoppy nose through to a lasting aftertaste makes it a good, all-round beer.

Piddle in the Dark *(ABV 4.5%)*
A rich ruby red bitter with a smooth flavour.

Piddle in the Snow *(ABV 5.2%)*
A dry, strong taste all the way through draws your attention to the balance between malt and hops in the brew. A glorious way to end an evening's drinking.

YATES

Yates Brewery Ltd, Ghyll Farm, Westnewton, Wigton, Cumbria, CA5 3NX
Tel (016973) 21081
E-mail enquiry@yatesbrewery.co.uk
Website yatesbrewery.co.uk
Tours by arrangement

Established in 1986 in a range of outbuildings at Ghyll Farm, Westnewton, the brewery was bought in 1998 by Graeme and Caroline Baxter, who had previously owned High Force Brewery in Teesdale. More beers have been added to the range and direct distribution now includes Tyneside and Wearside, in addition to the traditional stronghold of the Lake District. 40 outlets are supplied direct. Feverpitch has been added to the portfolio of permanent beers this year and is proving to be very successful – a lager style cask beer using lager malt and hops, but still using the Yates yeast. Seasonal beers: Summer Fever (ABV 3.9%), Autumn Fever (ABV 4%), Winter Fever (ABV 4%), No. 3 (ABV 4.2%), Spring Fever (ABV 4.7%), Best Cellar (ABV 5.8%, winter).

Bitter *(OG 1035, ABV 3.7%)*
A balanced beer with a sweet start that leads to hops and a long bitter finish.

Fever Pitch *(OG 1041, ABV 3.9%)*

XB *(OG 1043, ABV 4.5%)*

Premium *(OG 1048, ABV 5.2%)*
A golden beer with hops and lingering fruity sweetness. Rising bitterness with some malt and good mouthfeel.

YATES SIBA

Yates Brewery, The Inn at St Lawrence, Undercliff Drive, St Lawrence, Ventnor, Isle of Wight, PO38 1XG
Tel (01983) 854689
E-mail info@yates-brewery.fsnet.co.uk
Website www.yates-brewery.co.uk
Tours by arrangement

David Yates previously worked for the original Burts Brewery in Ventnor, which went into receivership in 1992. He started brewing for Hartridge at the Island Brewery. Hartridge sold its pubs and brewery to Usher's of Trowbridge and Dave was made redundant four months later. He has now installed his own five-barrel brewery at The Inn at St Lawrence. Brewing started in 2000 and he now has regular outlets on the Isle of Wight. Seasonal beer: Xmas Pud (ABV 5%).

Undercliff Experience *(OG 1042, ABV 4.1%)*

Holy Joe *(OG 1050, ABV 4.9%)*

Wight Winter Ale *(OG 1052, ABV 5%)*

YORK SIBA

York Brewery Company Ltd, 12 Toft Green, Micklegate, York, YO1 6JT
Tel (01904) 621162 Fax (01904) 621216
E-mail andrew@yorkbrew.co.uk
Website www.yorkbrew.co.uk
Shop Mon-Sat 11.30-7 daily.
Tours Mon-Sat 12.30, 2.00, 3.30, 5.00 daily

York started production in 1996, the first brewery in the city for 40 years. A visitor centre, gift shop and bar were added in 1997. It is designed as a show brewery, with a gallery above the 20-barrel brew plant giving visitors a view of the fermenting and conditioning rooms. In 2000, York, in partnership with Tynemill, set up 'The Mildly Mad Pub Co' and opened The Last Drop Inn in Colliergate; a second pub opened in 2001, the Three-Legged Mare in High Petergate, and in 2002 a third pub opened, the Rook & Gaskill, Lawrence Street. More than 400 pubs take the beers. Seasonal beers: Swing Low (ABV 4.8%, Feb-March), Final Whistle (ABV 3.9%, April-June), Busy Lizzie (ABV 4.1%, May-June), York IPA (ABV 5%, July-Sept), Golden Reign (ABV 4.1%, July-Aug), Black Bess Stout (ABV 4.2%, Oct-Nov), Wonkey Donkey (ABV 4.5%, Sept- Feb), Stocking Filler (ABV 4.8%, December), Guzzler (ABV 3.6%, Jan-Feb).

Stonewall *(OG 1037, ABV 3.7%)*
A light amber bitter with little maltiness but strong hop and fruit aromas and flavours.

Clean-tasting, its hoppiness leads to a dry, bitter finish.

York Bitter (OG 1039, ABV 4%) ◥
A fine, easy-drinking session beer with a fresh floral aroma, well-balanced malt and hops in the mouth, and a hint of marmalade in the aftertaste.

Yorkshire Terrier
(OG 1041, ABV 4.2%) ⬚◥
Refreshing and distinctive, well-balanced fruit and hops in the aroma and taste, with a background of malt. Hoppy bitterness remains assertive in the aftertaste of this amber-gold brew.

Centurion's Ghost Ale
(OG 1045, ABV 5.4%) ◥
Dark ruby in colour, full-tasting with mellow roast malt character balanced by bitterness that lingers into the aftertaste.

YOUNG'S IFBB

**Young & Co's Brewery PLC,
The Ram Brewery, High Street,
Wandsworth, London, SW18 4JD
Tel (020) 8875 7000
Fax (020) 8875 7100
E-mail sales@youngs.co.uk
Website www.youngs.co.uk**
Shop 11-6, Mon-Fri.
Tours by prior arrangement

⊗ Beer has been brewed continuously alongside the River Wandle since 1581, making it the oldest site in Britain for beer production. The present brewery was founded in 1675 and bought by Charles Young & Anthony Bainbridge in 1831; the business was continued by the Young family and, although it is a public company, it remains very much a family affair. The company brews award-winning beers in the traditional manner and also produces up to four seasonal beers. 450 free-trade outlets are supplied throughout Britain, concentrated in London and the South-east. Young's growing tied estate stands at 203 pubs. The brewery has outlawed pouring back spilt or unsold beer in its tied houses, and recommends the use of cask breathers only if its smallest casks cannot be consumed within three days. Bottle-conditioned beer: Special London Ale (OG 1068.8, ABV 6.4% ⬚⬚).

Bitter (OG 1036.8, ABV 3.7%) ⬚◥
With some hops and malt throughout, this refreshing beer has hints of citrus on the palate and a lingering, dry, bitter finish.

Special (OG 1042.8, ABV 4.5%)
A clean-drinking, smooth best bitter. Malt on the nose and palate giving way to citrus hops and a dry, lingering, bitter finish. (The beer was reformulated in 2003.)

Waggle Dance (OG 1049.8, ABV 5%) ⬚ ◥
With honey on the nose and palate, this amber beer is sweet but is tempered by malt and fruit notes, leaving a rich finish.

Winter Warmer
(OG 1055.8, ABV 5%) ⬚◥
A full-flavoured, ruby black beer with caramelised fruit on the nose and in the flavour, but the malt and bitterness build on the palate to leave a pleasant dry finish.

ZERODEGREES SIBA

**⌂ Zerodegrees Micro-brewery,
29-31 Montpelier Vale, Blackheath,
London, SE3 0TJ
Tel (020) 8852 5619
Fax (020) 8852 4463
E-mail info@zerodegrees-microbrewery.co.uk
Website www.zerodegrees-
microbrewery.co.uk**

⊗ Brewing started in 2000. The brewery incorporates a state-of-the-art, computer-controlled German plant, producing unfiltered and unfined ales and lagers, served from tanks using air pressure (not CO_2). The brewery has won several awards, including Best Lager, Best Ale and Best Beer at the SIBA Championship 2001 and at Reading CAMRA Beer Festival 2002. The company plans to open a new micro-brewery in Bristol. Five pubs are owned and a further five outlets are supplied. All beers are suitable for vegetarians and vegans.

Wheat Ale
(OG 1042-45, ABV 4.2-4.4%)

Pale Ale (OG 1045, ABV 4.6%) ◥
A dry, hoppy beer with malt notes initially and then a bitterness that lingers. Becomes sweeter on warming.

Pilsner (OG 1048, ABV 4.8%)

Black Lager (OG 1052, ABV 4.8%)

R.I.P.

The following breweries have closed, gone out of business, suspended operations, or merged with another company since the 2003 Guide was published:

**Ales of Kent
Aviemore
Bragdy Ty Bach
Cape Hill (Bass, Mitchells & Butlers)
Castle Eden
Cox's Yard
Crewkerne
Dark Horse
Frome Valley
Grimsdale
Henry's Butcher's Yard
Heritage
Hoskins & Oldfield
Hull
Lakeland
Lichfield
Lloyds
Millers Thumb
Northumberland
Orchard (Lincs)
Passageway
Payn
Pembroke
Reading Lion
Shraley Brook
Spinnaker
SP Sporting Ales
Strawberry Bank
Swaled Ale
Tolly Cobbold
Trimdon
Woodbury
Woodhampton**

Global giants

Eight out of ten pints of beer brewed in Britain today come from the groups listed below...

ANHEUSER-BUSCH UK

**Anheuser-Busch UK, Thames Link House,
1 Church Road, Richmond,
Surrey, TW9 2QW.
Tel (020) 8332 2302**

The company brews 'American' Budweiser at the Stag Brewery, Lower Richmond Road, Mortlake, London SW14 7ET, the former Watneys plant. Budweiser, bottle, can and keg, is brewed from rice (listed first on the label), malt and hops, with planks of wood – the famous beechwood chips – used to clarify the beer. Not to be confused with the classic Czech lager, Budweiser Budvar.

CARLSBERG-TETLEY

**Carlsberg-Tetley Brewing Ltd, PO Box 142,
The Brewery, Leeds, W Yorkshire, LS1 1QG
Tel (0113) 259 4594
Fax (0113) 259 4000
E-mail comms.website@carlsbergtetley.co.uk
Website www.carlsbergtetley.co.uk**

A wholly-owned subsidiary of Carlsberg Breweries A/S of Copenhagen, Denmark. Carlsberg is an international giant best known for its pale lagers, though in Denmark it brews a large range of beers, including brown lagers and a porter-stout, all made by cold fermentation. In Britain its lagers are brewed at a dedicated plant in Northampton, while Carlsberg-Tetley in Leeds produces ales and some Carlsberg products. Some 250,000 barrels are produced annually.

Tetley's Dark Mild
(OG 1031, ABV 3.2%) ◆
A reddish, mid-brown beer with a light malt and caramel aroma. A well-balanced taste of malt and caramel follows, with good bitterness and a satisfying finish.

Tetley's Mild *(OG 1034, ABV 3.3%)* ◆
A mid-brown beer with a light malt and caramel aroma. A well-balanced taste of malt and caramel follows, with good bitterness and a satisfying finish.

Ansells Mild *(OG 1035, ABV 3.4%)*

Ansells Best Bitter *(OG 1035, ABV 3.7%)*

Tetley's Cask Bitter
(OG 1035, ABV 3.7%) ◆
A variable, amber-coloured light, dry bitter with a slight malt and hop aroma, leading to a moderate bitterness with a hint of fruit, ending with a dry and bitter finish.

Tetley's Imperial *(ABV 4.3%)*

Burton Ale *(OG 1047, ABV 4.8%)* ◆
A beer with hops, fruit and malt present throughout, and a lingering complex afteraste, but lacking some hoppiness compared to its Burton original.

Carlsberg-Tetley also brews Greenalls Mild (ABV 3.3%), and Greenalls Bitter (ABV 3.8%) for former Greenalls pubs supplied by Scottish & Newcastle Retail and other wholesalers.

COORS

**Coors Brewers Ltd,
137 High Street, Burton-on-Trent,
Staffs, DE14 1JZ.
Tel (01283) 511000
Fax (01283) 513873
Website www.coorsbrewers.com**

Coors of Colorado is a giant brewer in the United States but has a much lower profile outside the US than Anheuser-Busch (Budweiser) or Miller, the latter now owned by South African Breweries. In 2002 Coors established itself in Europe by buying part of the former Bass brewing empire, when Interbrew was instructed by the British government to divest itself of some of its interests in Bass. Coors now owns several cask ale brands. It brews 110,000 barrels of cask beer a year and also provides a further 50,000 barrels of cask beer from other breweries. Coors closed the Mitchells & Butlers brewery in Birmingham in 2002.

M&B Mild *(OG 1034, ABV 3.2%)*
Brewed under licence by Highgate Brewery, Walsall

Stones Bitter *(OG 1037, ABV 3.7%)*
Brewed for Coors by Everards

Hancock's HB *(OG 1037, ABV 3.6%)* ◆
A pale brown, slightly malty beer whose initial sweetness is balanced by bitterness but lack a noticeable finish. A consistent if inoffensive Welsh beer brewed for Coors by Brains.

Worthington's Bitter *(OG 1038, ABV 3.6%)*
A pale brown bitter of thin and unremarkable character.

M&B Brew XI *(OG 1039.5, ABV 3.8%)*
A sweet, malty beer with a hoppy, bitter aftertaste, brewed under licence by Brains of Cardiff.

Worthington's 1744 *(OG 1044, ABV 4.4%)*
A premium bitter launched in 2002, as a head-to-head competitor with Draught Bass, owned by Interbrew.

Worthington's White Shield *(ABV 5.6%)* 🍺🔑
Brewed virtually unchanged since 1829. A bottle-conditioned IPA with a clean fruit aroma and a fruity/nutty taste.

St Modwen... a new seasonal beer launched July 2003

MUSEUM BREWING CO
White Shield Brewery, Horninglow Street, Burton-on-Trent, Staffs, DE14 1YQ
Tel (0845) 6000598
Fax (01283) 513509
E-mail brewery@museum.brewers.bass.com
Website www.bass-museum.com
Shop (in Bass Museum) 9.30-4.30
Tours by arrangement

The Museum Brewing Co, based in the Museum of Brewing, is part of Coors but has a large degree of independence. It began brewing in 1994 and recreates some of the older Bass beers that have been discontinued. The brewery dates from 1920 with some equipment going back to 1840. It has a maximum capacity of 60 barrels a week. Production is divided 50:50 between cask and bottled beers. As well as historic beers, the brewery produces seasonal brands and creates ales for CAMRA festivals.

Victoria Ale *(ABV 3.5%)* 🔑
Aroma of malt and fruit leads to a well-balanced beer with a bitter-sweet, almost dry aftertaste.

Offilers Bitter *(ABV 4%)* 🔑
An amber beer with a hint of malt leading to a fruity start developing into hoppiness.. The hops linger without astringency.

Joules Bitter *(ABV 4.1%)* 🔑
Malty with a bitter finish.

Massey's Bitter *(ABV 4.1%)*
Easy-drinking golden bitter with a hoppy bite.

Centennial *(ABV 4.3%)*
A light golden bitter, refreshing and aromatic. It is named after the American hop variety used for bittering.

Five Hides *(ABV 4%)* 🔑
Little aroma but a flowery taste initially leading to a sharp hoppiness that lingers.

Bullion *(ABV 6.6%)*
Bottle-conditioned beer, winner of the Tesco Challenge 2002

P2 Imperial Stout *(ABV 8%)*
A black, sweetish, complex stout. Available in bottle and draught.

No 1 Barley Wine *(ABV 10.5%)* 🍺
A dark ruby winter beer brewed in summer and fermented in casks for 12 months. Available in bottle and on draught.

GUINNESS
Guinness Brewing GB,
Park Royal Brewery,
London, NW10 7RR
Tel (020) 8965 7700
Fax (020) 8963 5120

An Anglo-Irish giant with world-wide brewing operations and distribution. In London it brews draught keg and pasteurised bottled stouts only.

INTERBREW
Interbrew UK Ltd, Porter Tun House,
500 Capability Green, Luton, Beds, LU1 3LS
A wholly-owned subsidiary of Interbrew
of Leuven/Louvain, Belgium.
Tel (01582) 391166
Fax (01582) 397397
E-mail name.surname@interbrew.co.uk
Website www.interbrew.com

Interbrew of Belgium is a major player in the European market with such lager brands as Stella Artois and Jupiler, and internationally with Labatt and Molson of Canada. It has some interest in ale brewing with the cask- and bottle-conditioned wheat beer, Hoegaarden, and the Abbey beer Leffe. It has a ruthless track record of closing plants and disposing of brands. In the summer of 2000 it bought both Bass's and Whitbread's brewing operations, giving it a 32 per cent market share. The British government told Interbrew to dispose of parts of the Bass brewing group, which were bought by Coors (qv). In 2003 Interbrew said it would spend £17 million on a promotion for Draught Bass and Boddingtons. Draught Bass has declined to 150,000 barrels a year: it once sold several million barrels a year, but was sidelined by the Bass empire. Only 30 per cent of draught Boddingtons is now in cask form. Anything that revives the fortunes of these revered cask beers has to be applauded, though a hefty proportion of the £17 million will go on promoting the nitro-keg version of Boddingtons. Interbrew also announced that when the contract with Coors to brew Draught Bass expired it would look for another brewer 'in the Burton area' to produce it, opening up the intriguing possibility of Marston's brewing its main competitor. Marston's, however, denied that any talks had taken place with Interbrew.

Draught Bass (*OG 1043.3, ABV 4.4%*)
Amber-coloured, with some sweet fruit
aroma. A touch of caramel and malt with
the hoppy bitterness developing later.

BODDINGTONS
**Boddingtons Brewery, PO Box 23,
Strangeways, Manchester, M60 3WB
Tel (0161) 828 2000
Fax (0161) 828 2213
Website www.boddingtons.com
Tours by arrangement**

Founded in 1778, acquired by the
Boddington family in 1835, sold to
Whitbread in 1989, the brewery became
part of Interbrew in 2000. Following the
closure of the Cheltenham Brewery, Flowers
brands have been transferred to
Manchester.

Boddingtons Bitter
(*OG 1035, ABV 3.8%*) ✎
A golden straw-coloured beer in which the
grainy malt, hop and bitter character can be
spoiled by a cloying sweetness.

Flowers IPA (*OG 1035, ABV 3.6%*)
Brewed under licence by Hall &
Woodhouse/Badger (qv).

Flowers Original Bitter
(*OG 1043, ABV 4.3%*)
Brewed under licence by Hall &
Woodhouse/Badger (qv).

FELLOWS, MORTON & CLAYTON
**Fellows, Morton & Clayton Brewhouse
Company, 54 Canal Street,
Nottingham, NG1 7EH
Tel (0115) 950 6795
Fax (0115) 953 9838
E-mail fellowsgalley@aol.co.uk
Website www.galleyrestaurant.co.uk**

Ownership transferred to Enterprise Inns.

Fellows (*OG 1039, ABV 3.8%*)

Post Haste (*OG 1048, ABV 4.5%*)

FROG & PARROT
**Frog & Parrot Brewhouse, Division Street,
Sheffield, South Yorkshire, S1 4GF
Tel (0114) 272 1280**

Brew-pub launched in 1982; ownership
transferred to Laurel Pub Company. The
beers are brewed from malt extract. Brewing
is suspended during long students'
vacations. Occasional/one-off brews. Beer:
Roger & Out (ABV 12.5%).

LASS O'GOWRIE
**Lass O'Gowrie Brewhouse,
36 Charles Street, Manchester, M1 7DB
Tel (0161) 273 6932**
Tours by arrangement

Victorian pub that was revamped and
reopened as a malt extract brew-pub in
1983; ownership transferred to Laurel Pub
Company. The brewery in the cellar is
visible from the bar and the beer is now
stored in casks. Occasional/one-off brews.
Beers: Lass Ale (ABV 4.1%), Mukka
(ABV 4.4%).

SCOTTISH COURAGE
**Fountain House, 160 Dundee Street,
Edinburgh, EH11 1DQ
Tel (0131) 656 5000
Fax (0131) 656 5217**

Scottish Courage is Britain's biggest brewing
group with close to 30 per cent of the
market. It joined the ranks of the global
brewers in 2000 when it negotiated to buy
Brasseries Kronenbourg and Alken Maes
from the French group Danone;
Kronenbourg is the biggest French beer
brand and is exported internationally.
Alken Maes is a major Belgian group that
produces lagers and the Grimbergen abbey
beer range. The group also has extensive
brewing interests in Russia and the Baltic
States through a consortium, BBH, formed
with Carlsberg. BBH owns the biggest
brewery in Russia, Baltika. Scottish &
Newcastle was formed in 1960, a merger
between Scottish Brewers (Younger and
McEwan) and Newcastle Breweries. In 1995
it bought Courage from its Australian
owners, Foster's. Since the merger that
formed Scottish Courage, the group has
rationalised by closing its breweries in
Nottingham, Halifax and the historic
Courage [George's] Brewery in Bristol. The
remaining beers were transferred to John
Smith's in Tadcaster. In 2003 Scottish
Courage announced it planned to sell its
entire retail estate of 1,400 outlets in order
to concentrate on brewing. It also bought
the financially stricken Bulmer's Cider
group, which includes the Beer Seller
wholesale group.

FOUNTAIN

Fountain Brewery, 159 Fountainbridge, Edinburgh, EH3 9YY
Tel (0131) 229 9377
Fax (0131) 228 9522

The once-legendary home of McEwan's and Younger's cask ales has now axed all its real ales save for one.

McEwan's 80/- *(OG 1042, ABV 4.2%)*
A balanced malty beer lacking in character. Bitter-sweet with caramel notes. Occasionally labelled Younger's IPA.

JOHN SMITH'S

Scottish Courage Brewing Ltd, John Smith's Brewery, Tadcaster, North Yorkshire, LS24 9SA
Tel (01937) 832091
Fax (01937) 833766
Tours by arrangement.

The brewery was built in 1879 by a relative of Samuel Smith (qv). John Smith's became part of the Courage group in 1970. Major expansion has taken place since the formation of Scottish Courage, with 11 new fermenting vessels installed. Traditional Yorkshire 'square' fermenters have been replaced by conical vessels.

Webster's Green Label Best *(OG 1031.8, ABV 3.2%)*

Webster's Bitter *(OG 1034.8, ABV 3.5%)*

John Smith's Bitter *(OG 1035.8, ABV 3.8%)*
A copper-coloured beer, well-balanced but with no dominating features. It has a short hoppy finish.

Courage Best Bitter *(OG 1038.3, ABV 4%)*
Pale brown beer with hops throughout and a bitter aftertaste.

John Smith's Magnet *(OG 1039,8, ABV 4%)*
An almost ruby-coloured beer with a complex aroma of hops, malt and citrus fruit. Malt dominates the taste and aftertaste.

Courage Directors Bitter *(OG 1045.5, ABV 4.8%)*
Fruity, medium-bodied, pale brown beer with hoppy and yeasty notes throughout.

THEAKSTON

T&R Theakston Ltd, Wellgarth, Masham, Ripon, North Yorkshire, HG4 4YD
Tel (01765) 680000
Fax (01765) 689414
Website www.theakstons.co.uk
Shop April-Oct, open every day; Nov-Dec limited opening.
Brewery tours (01765) 684333

Founded in 1827 and based on the present site since 1875, Theakston became part of S&N in 1987. More than £1 million has been invested in the brewery and in developing a museum of brewing, but most of Theakston's production now takes place in Newcastle (see below). Best Bitter and Cool Cask are brewed exclusively at Tyne; all packaged Old Peculier is also brewed at Tyne. The same pump clips are used for both Masham and Newcastle beers so the consumer is not told where the beers are sourced. The brewery still employs a cooper. Masham has started a seasonal ale programme in which each of these beers among others (ABV 4.5%) is available for a month: Youngers No 3, Masham Ale (ABV 6.6%), Hogshead (ABV 4.1%) and Lightfoot (ABV 5.4%).

Mild Ale *(OG 1035, ABV 3.6%)*
A rich and smooth mild ale with a creamy body and a rounded liquorice taste. Dark ruby/amber in colour, with a mix of malt and fruit on the nose, and a dry, hoppy aftertaste. (This is a seasonal not a regular beer.)

Black Bull Bitter *(OG 1037, ABV 3.9%)*
A distinctively hoppy aroma leads to a bitter, hoppy taste with some fruitiness and a short bitter finish. Rather thin.

XB *(OG 1044, ABV 4.6%)*
A sweet-tasting bitter with background fruit and spicy hop. Some caramel character gives this ale a malty dominance.

Old Peculier *(OG 1057, ABV 5.7%)*
A rich, full-bodied, dark brown, strong ale. Slightly malty but with hints of roast coffee and liquorice. A smooth caramel overlay and a complex fruitiness lead to a bitter chocolate finish.

TYNE

Tyne Brewery, Gallowgate, Newcastle upon Tyne, Tyne & Wear, NE99 1RA
Tel (0191) 232 5091
Fax (0191) 261 2301

Home of Newcastle Breweries formed in 1890 from the amalgamation of five local companies. Cask ale production started in the 1970s.

Theakston Mild Ale *(OG 1035, ABV 3.6%)*

Theakston Best Bitter *(OG 1036, ABV 3.6%)*
A dry and metallic bitter with light hop character when fresh. Older samples lose character and end watery and pale.

Theakston Cool Cask *(OG 1042, ABV 4.2%)*
A beer served through special cooling equipment at 10 degrees C.

Theakston XB *(OG 1044, ABV 4.6%)*

Theakston Old Peculier *(OG 1057, ABV 5.7%)*

Pub Groups

Pubs groups or 'Pubcos' [pub companies] now dominate beer retailing in Britain. The national brewers have largely disengaged from running pubs, preferring to sell beer to the pub groups. As a result of the deep discounts demanded by the pubcos, most sell beers mainly from the nationals, thus restricting drinkers' choice, and forming a barrier to regional and micro-breweries. The biggest pub companies are Enterprise, Mitchells & Butlers, Punch and Pubmaster, owning more than 13,000 pubs.

AVEBURY

Avebury Taverns Ltd, Sterling House, 20 Station Road, Gerrards Cross, Bucks, SL9 8EL
Tel (01753) 482600

Avebury operates 800 tenanted and leased pubs throughout England and Wales. All pubs trade as independent free houses with tenants able to choose 'market-leading brands' supplied by national, regional and local brewers. Its main suppliers are Coors, Carlsberg-Tetley, Interbrew, and Scottish Courage. Cask beers include Marston's Pedigree.

BARRACUDA

Barracuda Group Ltd, Henley Road, Medmenham, Marlow, Bucks, SL7 2ER
Tel (0845) 345 2528
Fax (0845) 345 2527

Barracuda was formed in 2000. It runs 131 managed outlets. The main pub brands in Barracuda are the 20-strong Smith & Jones chain and Varsity student bars. It takes its main cask beers from Adnams, Coors, Interbrew, Greene King, and Scottish Courage.

BARTER

Barter Inns, 132 Gypsy Hill, London, SE19 1PW
Tel (020) 8670 7001.
Email barterinns@aol.com

Barter has 27 managed pubs in the South-east. It takes ales from Interbrew and Scottish Courage, but its best-selling beer is Fuller's London Pride.

BRAKSPEAR

W H Brakspear & Sons plc, The Bull Courtyard, Bell Street, Henley-on-Thames, Oxon, RG9 2BA.
Tel (01491) 570200
Fax (01491) 470201
E-mail frontoffice@brakspear.co.uk
Website www.brakspear.co.uk

A pub company is all that remains of one of Britain's greatest independent brewers. The directors exited from brewing for the proverbial mess of potage, selling the prime site in Henley for £10 million to make way

for luxury apartments overlooking the Thames. The brewery closed in the summer of 2002. It sold the brands to Refresh UK: Brakspear Bitter and Special are currently brewed at Burtonwood, with seasonals brewed at Wychwood (qv). The company runs some 103 pubs. The only cask beers sold are the reconstituted Brakspear brands.

BURTONWOOD

Burtonwood Brewery plc, Bold Lane, Burtonwood, Warrington, WA5 4PJ
Tel (01925) 225131
Brewing at the Burtonwood, Cheshire site is operated by Thomas Hardy Burtonwood, a joint venture formed in 1998 between Burtonwood Brewery and Thomas Hardy Brewery of Dorchester. Burtonwood operates 480 pubs, the majority of which are traditional tenancies. Burtonwood's cask ales and a monthly changing cask beer from an independent brewer are made available to all Burtonwood tenancies. Fewer than half the Burtonwood estate stocks cask ale.

CALEDONIAN HERITABLE

4 Hope Street, Edinburgh, EH2 4DB.
Tel (0131) 220 5511.
Fax (0131) 225 6546

A group with 16 tenanted pubs, 42 managed and 66 leased, all in Scotland. Beers come mainly from Scottish Courage, but the best-selling ale is Caledonian Deuchars IPA.

CATMERE

Catmere Group, Station Road, Scunthorpe, Lincs, DN15 6PY
Tel (01724) 861703
Fax (01724) 861708

Catmere owns eight pubs in Leicestershire and Lincolnshire. Five serve cask beer from both national and regional brewers.

CCT

CCT Group, 76 Mitcham Road, Tooting, London, SW17 9NG.
Tel (020) 8767 8967.
Fax (020) 8767 3675
A South-east based company with 38 managed pubs. Beer is supplied by Scottish Courage and Greene King.

TOM COBLEIGH

**Tom Cobleigh, Spencer House,
Cliftonville Road,
Northampton, NN1 5BU
Tel (01604) 745000**

Established in 1992 with just two pubs, the estate has grown to 116 across England. The company was taken over by the Rank Group in 1996 but was bought by its management. Licensees choose beers from a head office range of national and regional ales, with Scottish Courage as the main supplier. A list of rotating guest beers is also offered.

COMMER INNS

**Commer Group Ltd, Commer House, Station Road, Tadcaster, North Yorkshire, LS24 9JF
Tel (01937) 833311
Fax (01937) 834236
E-mail commer@commer.co.uk
Website www.commer.co.uk**

Commer has scaled down its pub operation from 75 to just five outlets but plans to buy a further 20.

CONQUEST INNS

**14 Theobald Steet, Borehamwood,
Herts, WD6 4SE
Tel (020) 8207 5656.
Fax (020) 8207 1211
Email info@conquest-inns.co.uk
Website www.conquest-inns.co.uk
Tel (01992) 717718 Fax (01992) 717788**

A company with 66 pubs in London, the South-east and East Anglia. Beers are supplied by Interbrew, Scottish Courage and Greene King.

JT DAVIES

**JT Davies & Sons Ltd, 7 Aberdeen Road,
Croydon, Surrey, CR0 1EQ
Tel (020) 8681 3222
Fax (020) 8760 0390**

Wine merchants now controlling 51 tenancies and leased houses in the South-east. Its main suppliers are Interbrew and Scottish Courage, with some beers from Fuller's and Harveys. In June 2002, the company bought a 28% share of Henley brewer W H Brakspeare now a pub retailer (qv).

DAVY'S

**Davy's, 59-63 Bermondsey Street,
London, SE1 3XF
Tel (020) 7407 9670
Fax (020) 7407 5844**

Wine merchants and shippers since 1870, Davy's has been opening wine bars and restaurants in the London area since 1965, taking previously unlicensed properties and creating a Dickensian, sawdust, nooks-and-crannies type of establishment. Its Davy's Old Wallop (ABV 4.8%) is a re-badged brew of undeclared origin (though Courage Directors fits the bill). This is usually served in pewter tankards or copper jugs. The company currently runs around 50 outlets, including a few pubs.

ELDRIDGE POPE

**Eldridge Pope & Co plc, Weymouth Avenue,
Dorchester, ST1 1QT**

Founded as the Green Dragon Brewery in 1837, Eldridge Pope divorced itself from brewing in 1996 when it split into two wings, the brewing side becoming known as Thomas Hardy Brewery (see Independents). The company now runs 188 pubs, 124 managed, the rest tenanted. It has axed Eldridge Pope beers from Thomas Hardy and has supply agreements with Coors, Interbrew and Scottish Courage. It is now attempting to sell off its pubs and exit from retailing as well as brewing. Greene King are thought to be interested in buying the pubs. See also Burtonwood.

ENTERPRISE INNS

**Enterprise Inns plc, Cranmore Avenue,
Shirley, Solihull,
W Midlands, B90 4LE
Tel (0121) 733 7700
Fax (0121) 733 6447**

Formed in 1991 with an initial acquisition of 372 pubs from Bass, the company has grown rapidly and is now Britain's biggest pub group. In 2002 it bought the former Whitbread tenanted pub estate known as Laurel Inns, and has a 20% stake in New Company, which has acquired the Unique and Voyager pub estates from Nomura. Enterprise has an option to buy both estates. Enterprise previously purchased pubs from John Labatt Retail, Discovery Inns, Gibbs Mew, Mayfair Taverns, Century Inns (Tap & Spile), and Swallow Inns. Enterprise added to this number by buying 439 former Whitbread pubs, and then in June 2001 bought 432 managed houses from Scottish & Newcastle, taking its estate to 3,400. Chief Executive Ted Tuppen says he plans to build an estate of 6,500. A range of cask beers from all the major brewers, as well as many of the regionals, is available through the Enterprise central distribution network.

FITZGERALD

**Sir John Fitzgerald Ltd,
Cafe Royal Buildings, 8 Nelson Street,
Newcastle upon Tyne, NE1 5AW
Tel (0191) 232 0664
Fax (0194) 261 4509**

Long-established, family-owned property and pubs company. Its pubs convey a free house image, most offering a good choice of cask beers, including guest ales from smaller craft breweries. The 31 pubs are mainly in the North-east but there are also outlets in Edinburgh, Harrogate and London.

GRAY

**Gray & Sons (Chelmsford) Ltd,
Rignals Lane, Galleywood, Chelmsford,
Essex, CM2 8RE
Tel (01245) 475181
Fax (01245) 475182**

Former Chelmsford brewery that ceased production in 1974 and which now supplies its 49 tied houses in Essex with a choice of cask beers from Adnams, Greene King and Mighty Oak. The tenants are also free to choose from a monthly guest list that features at least 10 different ales.

HEAD OF STEAM

The Head of Steam,
GRS Inns Ltd,
31 Haverscroft Industrial Estate,
New Road, Attleborough,
Norfolk, NR17 1YE.
Tel (01953) 450000
Fax (01953) 450100
Website www.theheadofsteam.com

Founded by CAMRA activist Tony Brookes, Head of Steam has pubs based on railway station concourses at London Euston, Huddersfield, Newcastle-on-Tyne, Scarborough and Liverpool. All the outlets serve a wide range of cask beers and they stage regular beer festivals.

HEAVITREE

Heavitree Brewery plc, Trood Lane,
Matford, Exeter, EX2 8YP
Tel (01392) 217733
Fax (01392) 229939

A West Country brewery, established in 1790, which gave up production in 1970 to concentrate on running pubs. The current estate, which is mainly confined to Devon, stands at 112: 12 managed, and the rest tenanted or leased. The pubs are tied to beers from Interbrew.

HERITAGE

Heritage Pub Co, Donnington House,
Riverside Road, Pride Park,
Derby, DE24 8HY
Tel (01332) 384808
Fax (01332) 384818
Email heritage@heritagepubs.com

Heritage runs 65 tenanted pubs in the East Midlands. Its main suppliers are Hardy's & Hansons and Interbrew. Its best-selling cask beer is Marston's Pedigree.

HOBGOBLINNS

Hobgoblinns, Eagle Maltings,
The Crofts, Corn Street, Witney,
Oxon, OX8 7AZ
Tel (01993) 702574
Fax (01993) 772553
Email intray@hobgoblinns.co.uk
Website www.hobgoblinns.co.uk

Formerly the pub-owning subsidiary of Wychwood Brewery. But Wychwood was bought by Refresh UK in June 2002 and the pub group now stands alone. It has 31 managed houses aimed primarily at young people. The main beer supplier is Wychwood.

HONEYCOMBE

Honeycombe Leisure, Muldoons, 50 Water
Lane, Ashton, Preston, Lancs, PR2 2NL
Tel (01772) 723764

This 25 year-old company bought the Devonshire Pub Co in 2000 and now has 89 managed houses. Beers are supplied by the nationals plus Burton Bridge, Eccleshall, Moorhouses, Phoenix and Timothy Taylor, and most micro-brewers in the North-west. It is one of the biggest sellers of Black Sheep, Moorhouses and Timothy Taylor in the north of England. Honeycombe also has its own micro-brewery based in Salford.

INN BUSINESS

See Punch

INN PARTNERSHIP

See Pubmaster

INNSPIRED

InnSpired Pubs & Taverns,
Wiltshire Drive, Trowbridge,
Wilts, BA14 0TT
Tel (01225) 763171
Website www.innspired.co.uk

InnSpired represents the remains of Ushers of Trowbridge, a famous West Country brewery founded in 1824. Ushers became part of Grand Metropolitan in 1960. The brewery passed into Courage's control, but a management buy-out restored its independence in 1991. In 1999 Ushers merged with the Alehouse Company of Southampton. With the involvement of the Alchemy group, it was always likely that the new owners would opt to concentrate on real estate and retailing. Brewing ceased early in 2000. InnSpired has an estate of more than 1,000 pubs. It bought 50 outlets in the North of England and plans to grow the estate to 2,000. Usher's cask beers are brewed for InnSpired by Wadworth; other brands, such as Manns Brown Ale and the Lowenbrau range of lagers, are brewed by Burtonwood. A separate company, Refresh UK, retails the Usher's brands, and bought the Wychwood Brewery in June 2002. Under new tenancy agreements, InnSpired's landlords can offer a wide range of beers that often includes ales from specialist and local breweries.

INNTREPRENEUR

Once a mighty pub company created by Courage and Grand Metropolitan, it was bought by Nomura, which sold its entire pub estate in 2002. See Enterprise.

LAUREL

Porter Tun House,
500 Capability Green, Luton,
Beds, LU1 3LS
Tel (01582) 391166

Laurel was created in 2001 by Morgan Grenfell/Deutsche Bank, who bought the Whitbread pub estate. Laurel sold the tenanted pubs to Enterprise Inns (qv) a year later, but kept the managed houses, including the Hogshead chain. They are being re-branded as Hogs Head and no longer specialise in cask beer. Laurel now operates from the Interbrew head office in Luton.

MACLAY

Maclay Group plc, Thistle Brewery, Alloa, FK10 1ED
Tel (01259) 723387
Fax (01259) 216511

Maclay, founded in 1830, stopped brewing in September 1999. It owns 35 pubs and its full range of cask ales is brewed under licence by Belhaven (qv).

McMANUS

McManus Taverns, Kingsthorpe Road, Northampton, NN2 6HT
Tel (01604) 713601

Company with 19 pubs in the East Midlands, Essex and Kent. Half serve cask beer mainly from ScotCo and Wadworth.

MERCURY

Mercury Management (UK) Ltd, Mercury House, Amber Business Village, Amington, Tamworth, Staffs, B77 4RP
Tel (01827) 62345
Fax (01827) 64166
E-mail headoffice@mercurymanagement .co.uk
Website www.mercurymanagement.co.uk

Mercury Management is the result of a 1999 buy-out of Mercury Taverns. It has slimmed down its estate from 45 pubs to 16.

MILL HOUSE

Mill House Inns, Century House, Westcott Venture Park, Westcott, Bucks, HP18 0XB
Tel (01296) 652600
Fax (01296) 652626

Mill House has 54 managed pubs nationwide, ranging from town bars to country pubs and family pub-diners. Its main supply agreement is with Interbrew.

MITCHELLS & BUTLERS

Mitchells & Butlers, Cape Hill, PO Box 27, Birmingham, B16 0PQ.
Tel (0121) 558 1481
Fax (0121) 558 2515

In the curious world of modern beer retailing, M&B is the new name for Six Continents. When the Bass empire was sold off, Coors closed the giant M&B Brewery in Birmingham but a year later the name resurfaced as...a pub company.M&B owns more than 2,000 pubs, bars and restaurants. Its brands include Vintage Inns, Ember Inns, and Goose. All these pubs serve cask beer and Ember also holds mini-beer festivals. Most pubs stock Draught Bass and also offer a choice of cask beers from Coors and some regionals. M&B is thought to be keen to buy the Scottish Courage pub estate, but City analysts suggest that if M&B becomes too big it could become a target for even bigger retailers in North America.

MORRELLS

Morrells of Oxford Ltd, Ferry Hinksey Road, Oxford, OX2 0ES
Tel (01865) 727722
Fax (01865) 794262

Morrells of Oxford was bought by Greene King in June 2002 for £60 million, from Michael Cannon, who bought the 132 pubs from Morrells. The pubs are all that remain of the once much-loved Oxford brewery that closed in 1998 following a boardroom split and the eviction of two members of the Morrell family. Morrells beers are brewed by Thomas Hardy Burtonwood.

NOBLE HOUSE

Noble House Pub Company, 4 Thameside Centre, Kew Bridge, Brentford, Mddx TW8 0HF
Tel (020) 8847 9100

A subsidiary of Noble House Leisure, which owns hotels and restaurants. The group is run by Robert Breare, who masterminded the exit from brewing by Ushers of Trowbridge to become the pub company InnSpired (qv). Mr Breare was interested in making a bid for Wolverhampton & Dudley in 2000, but withdrew to allow Pubmaster to make its own unsuccessful bid. Noble House owns 240 managed pubs.

OLD ENGLISH

Old English was bought by Greene King for £59 million in 2001.

PUB ESTATE

Pub Estate Company Ltd, 3-5 Ashfield Road, Chorley, Lancs, PR7 1LH
Tel (01257) 238800
Fax (01257) 233918

A company established with the purchase of 230 pubs from Scottish & Newcastle, it currently has 335 pubs (28 managed, the rest tenanted or leased) based in the north of England and Scotland. The pubs offer beers from Coors, Interbrew, Carlsberg-Tetley and Scottish Courage but some licensees have guest beer rights. The company's aim is to convert all pubs to three-year leases that would offer no guest beer entitlement and would mean all pubs being served by a favoured supplier, probably Scottish Courage.

PUBMASTER

Pubmaster Ltd, Greenbank, Hartlepool, TS24 7QS
Tel (01429) 266699
Fax (01429) 278457
Website www.pubmaster.co.uk

Pubmaster was formed in 1991 to take over the pub estate of Brent Walker, the property group that also owned Cameron's and Tolly Cobbold breweries in the 1980s. Following a management buy-out in 1996, Pubmaster continued to grow, with acquisitions from Mercury Taverns, Devonshire Pub Company and Swallow. Swallow, the remnant of the Vaux brewing group, sold 662 pubs to Pubmaster. In 2000, the initial investors in the group sold their stake to West LB (a German financial company), First Principal Finance Group/Nomura of Japan, Rotch Property Group, and St Modwen Properties. Nomura sold all its pub interests in 2002, with the exception of Wizards Inns (qv).

Pubmaster acquired 1,200 Inn Partnership outlets from Nomura as a result, followed by 38 pubs from Pub.com in Scotland. In the summer of 2002, it bought the 45-strong pub estate of White Rose of Leeds. It is currently operating more than 3,200 pubs and stocks beers from Coors, Interbrew, Carlsberg-Tetley, and some independents.

PUNCH GROUP

Punch was formed in 1998 by a team led by Hugh Osmond, founder of Pizza Express, with the purchase of the Bass leased pub estate. In 1999, Punch, with the backing of Bass, bought Allied Domecq's pub estate. It sold 550 former managed houses to Bass and now owns some 5,000 pubs itself. Punch claims its lessees are free to take guest beers, but brewers who supply the group are closely monitored and have to offer substantial discounts to be accepted. In 2001, Punch launched a specialist cask ale initiative to supply some of its pubs with a wider portfolio of beers but the problem of discounts restricts the number of participating brewers. The main cask ales sold by Punch are Tetley and Worthington, with guest ales from a number of regionals.

SPIRIT GROUP

107 Station Road, Burton-on-Trent, Staffs, DE14 1BZ
Tel (01283) 545320
Website www.spiritgroup.co.uk

The new name (previously Punch Retail) for the managed side of the business, based in the former offices of Allied Domecq. It operates 1,046 pubs.

PUNCH PUB COMPANY

Lincoln House, Wellington Crescent, Fradley Park, Lichfield, Staffs, WS13 8RZ
Tel (01543) 443500
Fax (01543) 443502
Website www.punchpubs.co.uk

Punch Pub Co, which includes the Inn Business estate, is the tenanted and leased division of the Punch Pub Company. It owns some 4,000 pubs.

PYRAMID

Pyramid Pub Co Ltd, Suite H3, Steam Mill Business Centre, Steam Mill Street, Chester, CH3 5AN
Tel (01244) 321171.
Fax (01244) 317665
Email amandab@pyramidpub.co.uk

Manages 475 pubs, formerly known as Paramount and bought from Royal Bank of Scotland. The pub estate is widely spread, mainly in towns and cities. Beers are supplied by Burtonwood, Interbrew, Scottish Courage and Wolverhampton & Dudley. Banks's is the leading cask ale.

RANDALL VAUTIER

Randall Vautier Ltd, PO Box 43, Clare Street, St Helier, Jersey, JE4 8NZ
Tel (01534) 887788
Fax (01534) 888350

A brewery that ceased production in 1992. It now runs 30 pubs on Jersey selling beers from Interbrew, Scottish Courage, and Marston's. Not to be confused with Randalls of Guernsey (see Independents).

REGENT INNS

Regent Inns plc, 77 Muswell Hill, London, N10 3PJ
Tel (020) 8375 3000
Fax (020) 8375 3001
Website www.regentinns.co.uk

Founded in 1980, Regent owns 123 managed pubs in London and the Home Counties, and is growing by 20 pubs a year. Expansion into the Midlands and the north is taking place. Most of the pubs are unbranded, are allowed to retain their own identities, and are not tied to any supplier. Most pubs feature a wide range of national, local and seasonal cask ales chosen by managers. The company has contracts with Coors, Interbrew and Scottish Courage plus half a dozen regional breweries, but licensees can also take beer from the Beer Seller wholesaler. Branded pubs include Walkabout Inns and Jongleurs.

RYAN

Ryan Elizabeth Holdings plc, Ryan Precinct, 33 Fore Street, Ipswich, IP4 1JL
Tel (01473) 217458
Fax (01473) 258237

The company's 63 pubs in East Anglia, many bought from national brewers, are mostly leased to individual operators on 35-year contracts, although eight are managed. The pubs are generally free of the tie but some have a tie to Interbrew. A subsidiary company, Elizabeth Hotels, operates independent bars/pubs in its hotels with a local community focus, offering four to five real ales and live entertainment. The main beer supplier is Interbrew but Adnams, Greene King, and Nethergate also supply beers.

SCORPIO INNS

Scorpio Inns Ltd, Commerce House, Abbey Road, Torquay, TQ2 5PJ
Tel (01803) 296111
Fax (01803) 296202

Formed in 1991, it now runs 111 pubs (nearly all tenanted). These stock beers from Interbrew and are located in South Wales, the Bristol and Hereford areas, and along the M4 corridor to Swindon.

SFI

SFI Group plc, SFI House, 165 Church Street East, Woking, Surrey, GU21 1HJ
Tel (01483) 227900
Fax (01483) 227903

Established in 1986, the SFI Group, formerly Surrey Free Inns, runs around 180 pubs and café bars in England, Scotland and Wales. The number is set to increase, with further acquisitions planned. Beers come from national brewers and a range of smaller regional brewers. Cask ale is a feature of the Litten Trees outlets. Not all the pubs are branded: around 20, such as the Ostrich Inn, at Colnbrook, near Heathrow, have kept their own identity. SFI bought the Slug & Lettuce group in 2000.

TYNEMILL

Tynemill Ltd, 2nd Floor, Victoria Hotel, Dovecote Lane, Beeston, Nottingham, NG9 1JG
Tel (0115) 925 3333
Fax (0115) 922 6741

Founded by former CAMRA chairman Chris Holmes, Tynemill has been established in the East Midlands for more than 20 years, and now owns 17 pubs. It has a 'pubs for everyone' philosophy, avoiding trends and gimmicks, and concentrating on quality cask ales and food in good surroundings, including public bars where space permits. It sold more than 1,500 different cask ales during 2000, thought to be more than anyone else in the industry. Managers have complete autonomy on guest beers they sell. During 2000, Tynemill entered into two joint ventures: the Mildly Mad Pub Co with York Brewery, to develop an estate in the York region, and with Breakthroughpoint in Nottingham. Tynemill is now the sole owner of the Castle Rock Brewery in Nottingham (qv). Regional and micro-brewers make up the bulk of Tynemill's products.

UNIQUE

See Enterprise

WETHERSPOON

JD Wetherspoon plc, PO Box 616, Watford, WD1 1YN
Tel (01923) 477777
Fax (01923) 219810
Website www.jdwetherspoon.co.uk

Wetherspoon is a vigorous and independent pub retailer that currently owns more than 580 managed pubs, with rapid plans for expansion. No music is played in any of the pubs, all offer no-smoking areas, and food is served all day. Two standard beers from Scottish Courage are available to managers: Theakston Best Bitter and Courage Directors. Each pub also stocks regional ales from the likes of Cains, Fuller's, Greene King, Shepherd Neame and Wolverhampton & Dudley, plus at least two guest beers. There are usually two beer festivals a year, one in the spring, the other in the autumn, at which up to 30 micro-

brewery beers are stocked over a four-day period. Wetherspoon joined the Cask Marque scheme in 2000 and now enjoys CM accreditation in more than 435 pubs.

WHARFEDALE

Wharfedale Taverns Ltd, Highcliffe Court, Greenfold Lane, Wetherby, West Yorkshire, LS22 6RG
Tel (01937) 580805
Fax (01937) 580806
E-mail wharfedale_taverns @compuserve.com

A company set up in 1993 by former Tetley employees to lease 90 pubs from that company, it currently owns 60 pubs, mainly in the north. The main beers come from Carlsberg-Tetley; guest beers are from C-T's Tapster's Choice.

WHITE ROSE

See Pubmaster

WILLIAMS

James Williams (Narberth), 7 Spring Gardens, Narberth, Pembrokeshire, SA67 7BP
Tel (01834) 862200
Fax (01834) 862202

A privately-owned concern that operates 55 pubs in West and mid-Wales. Tenants are mainly supplied by Coors, Interbrew, Brains, and Carlsberg-Tetley. A house ale, James Williams IPA, brewed by Brains, is also available. Regional brands are also supplied, including beers from Adnams, Banks, Bateman, Everards, Jennings and Shepherd Neame. The company has a regular, extensive guest cask beer policy.

WIZARD INNS

City Gate, 17 Victoria Street, St Albans, Herts, AL1 3JJ
Tel (01727) 792200
Fax (01727) 792210

Former CAMRA national chairman Chris Hutt, also the ex-boss of Midsummer Inns and Unicorn Inns, purchased 30-40 former Phoenix Inns pubs to set up this new company. Nomura, the Japanese bank that owned Unique Pub company, has a £9.5 million stake. Wizard Inns operates traditional, unbranded pubs. All the pubs, now numbering 46, are managed and serve a selection of real ales.

YATES'S

Yates's Wine Lodges Ltd, Peter Yates House, Manchester Road, Bolton, BL3 2PY
Tel (01204) 373737
Fax (01204) 388383

Company founded in Oldham in 1884 by wine merchant Peter Yates, it now runs 150 managed pubs in locations from Scotland to London. Beers are mainly from Coors, Interbrew and Scottish Courage, with some regional ales also featured. Boddingtons Bitter is sold at one price nationwide but many branches do not serve real ale.

J·D·WETHERSPOON

The Beers Index

Over 2,000 beers are listed. They refer to beers in bold type in the Breweries section

Bespoke Leatherbritches *741*
Bete Noire Kelham Island *738*
Betty Stogs Bitter Skinner's *775*
Bewick Swan *779*
Beyond the Pale Eastwood & Sanders *709*
Bezants Spectrum *776*
Big Frank's Bitter Old Wheelton *756*
Big Nev's Six Bells *775*
Bill's o' Jack's Greenfield *722*
Billy the Porter Steamin' Billy
(Grainstore) *778*
Birthday Brew Caythorpe *697*
Bishop Buntingford *692*
Bishop Ridley's Ale Black Bull *682*
Bishops Farewell Oakham *753*
Bishops Finger Shepherd Neame *774*
Bishops Somerset Ale Juwards (Moor) *749*
Bishopswood Bitter Swansea *780*
Biter Doghouse *707*
Bitter Experience Storm *778*
Black Abbot Broadstone *689*
Black Adder Mauldons *746*
Black and Amber Warcop *788*
Black Bat B&T *675*
Black Bear Beartown *680*
Black Beauty Porter Upper Agbrigg *786*
Vale *786*
Black Bee Phoenix *760*
Black Buffle Spectrum *776*
Black Bull Bitter Theakston
(Scottish Courage) *802*
Black Bull Mild Blanchfields *684*
Black Cat Moorhouses *749*
Black Country Bitter Holden's *731*
Black Country Mild Holden's *731*
Black Country Wobble Malvern Hills *745*
Black Crow Poachers *762*
Black Cuillin Isle of Skye *736*
Black Diamond Mayflower *747*
Black Dog Mild Elgood's *710*
The Black Douglas Broughton *690*
Black Dragon Mild B&T *675*
Black Eagle Pitfield *761*
Black Fox Alcazar *672*
The Black Galloway Sulwath *778*
Black Gold Cairngorm *695*
Castle Rock *697*
Black Heart Stout Barnsley (Blackpool) *684*
Black Knight Goff's *719*
Black Lager Zerodegrees *798*
Black Magic Mild Hanby *725*
Black Magic Stout Oakhill *754*
Black Mamba Mild Sarah's Hop House *772*
Black Mass Abbeydale *671*
Black Moggy Mild Kemptown *738*
Black Moss Stout Riverhead *768*
Black Pear Malvern Hills *745*
Black Pearl Boat *686*
Black Pig Mild Bazens' *679*
Black Prince St Austell *770*
Black Pudding Leyden *741*
Black Rock Organic *757*
Black Shiver Turkey *785*
Black Stag Coles *701*
Black Star Moonstone *749*
Black Swan Dark Mild Vale *786*
Black Witch Bragdy Ceredigion *686*
Black Zac Wentworth *790*
Blackbeerd Bateman *678*
Blackguard Butts *694*
Blackout Big Lamp *682*
Blackwater Mild Crouch Vale *703*
Bladderwrack Stout Railway Tavern *764*
Blake's Gosport Bitter Oakleaf *754*
Blakeley's Best O'Hanlon's *753*
Blanche de Newland Tigertops *782*
Blaven Isle of Skye *736*

Blencathra Bitter Hesket Newmarket *728*
Blodeuwedd Bragdy Ceredigion *686*
Blonde Arran *674*
Daleside *704*
Meantime *747*
Blonde Bombshell Bury Street *693*
Houston *734*
Blondie Kings Head *739*
Liverpool *742*
Bluebird Bitter Coniston *701*
Bluebird XB Coniston *701*
Boathouse Bitter City of Cambridge *699*
BOB Wickwar *792*
Bobbin's Bitter Three B's *781*
Bock Tigertops *782*
Boddingtons Bitter Interbrew *801*
Bodmin Boar Ring O' Bells *767*
Body Line Stonehenge *778*
Bog Standard Boggart Hole Clough *686*
Boggart Bitter Boggart Hole Clough *686*
Boggart Brew Boggart Hole Clough *686*
Bohemia Pilsner Wylam *796*
Bomar Bitter Northumberland *752*
Bombardier Premium Bitter Wells *789*
Border Gold Broughton *690*
Boro Best North Yorkshire *752*
Bosley Cloud Storm *778*
Bosun Bitter Old Laxey *756*
Bow Wow Doghouse *707*
Bowler Strong Ale Langton *740*
Bowley Best Red Rose *766*
Boy Stout Green Tye *722*
Boys Bitter Fernandes *713*
BPA Blackpool *683*
Brainstorm Storm *778*
Brakspear Bitter Refresh UK
(Burtonwood) *693*
Brakspear Special Refresh UK
(Burtonwood) *693*
Bramling Cross Broughton *690*
Bramling Traditional City of Cambridge *699*
Brand Oak Bitter Wickwar *792*
Brandy Snapper Brandy Cask *687*
Branoc Branscombe Vale *688*
Braveheart Moulin *750*
Braye Mild Tipsy Toad *782*
Breakfast Barum *678*
Brecon County Ale Breconshire *688*
Brew Dolphin *707*
Brew 1 Uncle Stuarts *786*
Brew 2 Uncle Stuarts *786*
Brew 3 Uncle Stuarts *786*
Brew 9 Uncle Stuarts *786*
Brew 101 Six Bells *775*
Brew Britannia Maypole *747*
Brewers Droop Marston Moor *745*
Brewers Gold Crouch Vale *703*
Pictish *761*
Brewers Pride Marston Moor *745*
Brewery Bitter Tomos Watkin *789*
Brewery Tap Chalk Hill *697*
Brewhouse Reepham *767*
Brewhouse Bitter Dunn Plowman *708*
Brewsters First Mayflower *747*
Bridge Bitter Burton Bridge *693*
Bridge Street Bitter Green Dragon *721*
Bridget's Best Bitter Bury Street *693*
Bridport Bitter Palmer *759*
Brief Encounter Foxfield *715*
Humpty Dumpty *734*
Bright Otter *758*
Brighton Bitter Kemptown *739*
Brindle Bullmastiff *692*
Bristol IPA Smiles *775*
Broadland Gold Humpty Dumpty *734*
Broadside Adnams *672*
Bronte Bitter Goose Eye *720*

County Pride Home County *732*
Courage Best Bitter Scottish Courage *802*
Courage Directors Bitter
Scottish Courage *802*
Coxswains Special Willy's *793*
Coyote Bitter Wolf *794*
Crab & Winkle Mild Railway Tavern *764*
Cracker Ale Barngates *677*
Cream Rooster's *769*
Cream Stout St Peter's *772*
Criffel Sulwath *778*
Croak & Stagger Frog Island *716*
Crockerton Classic Hobden's *730*
Crofters Filo *714*
Cromwell Bitter Marston Moor *745*
Cromwell's Hat Springhead *777*
Crooked Furrow Leith Hill *741*
Crop Circle Hop Back *733*
Cropped Oak John O'Gaunt *737*
Crouch Best Crouch Vale *703*
Crow Valley Bitter Cwmbran *704*
Crow Valley Stout Cwmbran *704*
Crow's Nest Flagship *714*
Crowdie Kings Head *739*
Crown Imperial Stout Goacher's *718*
Crowning Glory Leyden *741*
Crusader Pilgrim *761*
Crystal Wheat Beer Beecham's *680*
Cuckoo Ale Driftwood *708*
Cuddy Lugs Bitter End *682*
Cuil Hill Sulwath *778*
Cuillin Beast Isle of Skye *736*
Cumberland Ale Jennings *737*
Cumbria Way Robinson's *769*
Cupwith Light Bitter Riverhead *768*
Curly Blonde Leadmill *740*
Cuthberts Church End *699*
Cwrw Betys Coles *701*
Cwrw Blasus Coles *701*
Cwrw Celyn Bryncelyn *691*
Cwrw Llanddarog Coles *701*
Cwrw Tudno Plassey *762*
Cwrw 2000 Bragdy Ceredigion *687*
Cyclops Milton *749*
Czechmate Saaz Enville *710*
Czechumberland Bitter End *682*

D

Dabbers Gold Paradise *759*
Dabley Ale All Nations (Worfield) *795*
Dalebottom Dark Briscoe's *689*
Damson Stout Bartrams *677*
Danish Dynamite Stonehenge *778*
Danny Boy Donoghue *707*
Danny Boys Blencowe *684*
Dark and Delicious Corvedale *702*
Dark Angel Golcar *719*
Dark Forest Rockingham *769*
Dark Horse Townhouse *784*
Dark Island Orkney *757*
Dark Mild Wheat Tigertops *782*
Dark Moor Kelburn *738*
Dark Roast Ale Chiltern Valley *698*
Dark Ruby Sarah Hughes *734*
Dark Side Blue Moon *685*
    Boggart Hole Clough *686*
Dark Skies Stout Alewife *672*
Dark Star Dark Star *705*
Dark Swan Olde Swan *756*
Dark Vader Kings Head *739*
Dartmoor Best Bitter St Austell *770*
Dartmoor IPA Princetown *763*
Dartmoor Pride Sutton *779*
Darwin's Downfall City of Cambridge *699*
Davenports Bitter Highgate *729*

Davy's Old Wallop Davy's *804*
Dazed and Confused Triple fff *785*
Dazzler Ossett *758*
De Wilderer Poachers *762*
Deadly Nightshade Goldthorn *720*
Decade Newby Wyke *751*
Deep Pit Warcop *788*
Deep Slade Dark Swansea *780*
Deer Hill Porter Riverhead *768*
Deliverance Cambrinus *695*
Den Poachers *762*
Derby Festival Stout Leadmill *740*
Derwent Deep Derwent Rose *707*
Deryn Du Cwmbran *704*
Desert Storm Storm *777*
Deuchars IPA Caledonian *695*
Devil in Disguise Liverpool *743*
Devil's Elbow Hexhamshire *728*
Devil's Water Hexhamshire *728*
Devon Glory Exe Valley *711*
Devonian Scattor Rock *773*
Dewi Sant Coles *701*
Dick Poachers *762*
Dick Turpin Coach House *700*
Dickens Mauldons *746*
Dictators Concertina *701*
Diggers Gold Cheriton *698*
Dishie Debbie Hart *726*
Ditchingham Dam Tindall *782*
Dixie's Bollards DarkTribe *705*
Dixie's Mild DarkTribe *705*
Dob's Best Bitter Exe Valley *711*
Dobcross Bitter Greenfield *722*
Doble's Dog Wicked Hathern *792*
Dockers Warcop *788*
Dr Duncans IPA Cains *694*
Dr Griffin's Mermaid DarkTribe *705*
Dr Hexter's Healer West Berkshire *790*
Dr Hexter's Wedding Ale
West Berkshire *790*
Dr Samuel Johnson Haywood *727*
Doctor's Orders Fenland *713*
Doff Cocker Three B's *781*
Dominator Hopdaemon *733*
Donne Lane Odcombe *754*
Doom Bar Bitter Sharp's *774*
Doris's 90th Birthday Ale
Hesket Newmarket *728*
Dorothy Goodbody's Golden Ale
Wye Valley *796*
Dorothy Goodbody's Wholesome Stout
Wye Valley *796*
Dorset Gold Palmer *759*
Double Champion Wheat
O'Hanlon's *753*
Double Chance Malton *744*
Double Dagger Phoenix *760*
Double Dragon Ale Felinfoel *713*
Double Dutch Holland *732*
Double Gold Phoenix *760*
Double Header RCH *765*
Double Hop Cwmbran *704*
Double M Big Lamp *681*
Double Six Fernandes *714*
Dover Beck Bitter Caythorpe *697*
Downland Bitter Cuckmere Haven *704*
Dragon Bitter Ale Felinfoel *713*
Dragon's Breath Plassey *762*
Dragonhead Stout Orkney *757*
Dragons Blood Kemptown *739*
Dragonslayer B&T *675*
Draig Aur Bragdy Ceredigion *686*
Drake Mallard *744*
Drakes Drum Points West *762*
Draught Bass Interbrew (Coors) *801*
Drawwell Bitter Hanby *725*
Draymans Branscombe Vale *688*

Frederics Robinson's 769
Freebooter Jollyboat 737
Friar Duck Mallard 744
Friggin in the Riggin Flagship 714
Frog Bog Lowes Arms 743
Fruit Bat B&T 675
Fruiterer's Mild Cannon Royall 696
Fruits of the Forest Rockingham 769
Fuggle-Dee-Dum Goddards 719
Fuggled Up Tindall 782
Full Ahead DarkTribe 705
Full Circle West Berkshire 790
Full English Bitter End 682
Full Malty Cwmbran 704
Fur & Feather Woodforde's 795
Furness Flyer Foxfield 715
Fursty Ferret Gribble Inn 723
Futtock Flagship 714
Fyre Fyfe 717

G

Gadds No. 3 Ramsgate 764
Gadds No. 5 Ramsgate 764
Gadds No. 7 Ramsgate 764
Galingale Old Chimneys 755
Galleon DarkTribe 705
Galloway Gold Sulwath 778
Game Set & Match Bank Top 676
Gannet Mild Earl Soham 709
Gauntlet Arundel 674
GB Gale's 717
GB Mild Lees 741
Ge It Sum Ommer Goldthorn 720
Gem Bitter Bath 678
Generation Hook Norton 733
Genesis Hart 726
   North Cotswold 751
Geordie Pride Mordue 750
Georgie Porgie Nursery (Hobden's) 730
GFB Hop Back 733
The Ghillie Broughton 690
Ghost Ale Darwin 706
Ghost on the Rim Anglo Dutch 673
Ghost Train Maypole 747
Gilbert's First Brew Hop Back 733
Ginger Bear Beartown 679
Ginger Beer Enville 711
Ginger Marble Marble 745
Ginger Swan 779
Gingernut Premium Coach House 700
Gladiator Hadrian & Border 723
Gladstone Tidings Wicked Hathern 792
Glencoe Wild Oat Stout Bridge of Allan 689
Glory Barnsley (Blackpool) 684
GNC Northumberland 752
Goat's Milk Church End 699
Godfathers Itchen Valley 736
Gold Arundel 675
   Blackdown 683
   Broadstone 689
   Buntingford 692
   Butcombe 694
   Cairngorm 695
   Chiltern Valley 698
   Digger Bank Top 676
   Dolphin 707
   Exmoor 712
   Filo 714
   Grand Union 721
   Iceni 735
   Paradise 759
   Potton 763
   St George's 771
   Wentworth 790
Gold Dragon Bragdy Ceredigion 686

Gold Medal Linfit 742
Gold Standard Freeminer 716
Gold Star Ale Goacher's 718
Gold Tankard Wylam 796
Golden Winter's 793
Golden Ale North Yorkshire 752
   St Peter's 771
Golden Arrow Cottage 702
Golden Bear Warwickshire 788
Golden Best Taylor 780
Golden Bitter Archers 674
   Ventnor 787
Golden Blond Holland 732
Golden Boy Blencowe 684
Golden Braid Hopdaemon 733
Golden Brown Home County 732
Golden Chalice Glastonbury 718
Golden Chance Malton 745
Golden Delicious Burton Bridge 693
Golden Eagle Cotleigh 702
Golden Egg Felstar 713
Golden Eye 700 Egyptian 710
Golden Glow Holden's 732
Golden Goose Goose Eye 720
Golden Honey Hanby 725
Golden Hornet Clark's 699
Golden Jackal Wolf 794
Golden Lance Keltek 738
Golden Lion Red Lion 766
Golden Nectar Eglesbrech 709
Golden Newt Elgood's 710
Golden Peace Cuckmere Haven 704
Golden Pig Country Life 702
Golden Promise Organic Ale
Caledonian 695
Golden Rivet Captain Grumpy 696
Golden Salamander Salamander 772
Golden Scotch Ale Maclay (Belhaven) 681
Golden Smile Blackpool 683
Golden Spring Blindmans 684
Golden Thread Salopian 772
Golden Valley Breconshire 688
   Scattor Rock 773
Goldfield Hambleton 724
Goldihops Kelburn 738
Goldings Leatherbritches 741
Gone Fishing Oulton 758
Good Old Boy West Berkshire 790
Goodnight Vienna Garton 718
Goodrich Castle Springhead 777
Gordon Bennett Belvoir 681
Gordon the Gofer Carters 696
Gordon's Amber Ale
Sarah's Hop House 773
Gorse Porter Cwmbran 704
Gothic Enville 711
Grace & Favour Fox 714
Graduate Morrells (Burtonwood) 693
Granary Bitter Reepham 766
Granny Wouldn't Like It Wolf 794
Grantham Stout Oldershaw 757
Grapefruit Beer St Peter's 771
Gravediggers Church End 699
Great Cockup Porter
Hesket Newmarket 728
Great Eastern Woodforde's 795
Great Gable Great Gable 721
Great Raft Bitter Old Chimneys 755
Green Man Bartrams 677
Green Tiger Green Tye 722
Greengrass Old Rogue Ale Daleside 705
Greenmantle IPA Broughton 690
Greenmantle Original Broughton 690
Grenville's Renown Jollyboat 737
Greyhound Strong Bitter Elgood's 710
Gribble Ale Gribble Inn 723
Grizzly Ghost Anglo Dutch 673

Jet Black City of Cambridge 699
Jetsam Hadrian & Border 723
JHB Oakham 753
Jimmy's Bitter Tipsy Toad 782
Joblings Swinging Gibbet Jarrow 736
Jock's Trap Poachers 762
John Baker's Original Brandy Cask 687
John Barleycorn Goldthorn 720
John Bewsher's Best Bitter Tirril 783
John Paul Jones Sulwath 778
John Smith's Bitter Scottish Courage 802
John Smith's Magnet Scottish Courage 802
Joules Bitter Museum (Coors) 800
Jouster Goff's 719
JTS Rich Porter John Thompson 781
JTS Summer Gold John Thompson 781
JTS XXX John Thompson 781
Junction Bitter McGuinness 743
Juniper Blonde Goldthorn 720
Jupiter Milton 748
Jurassic Quay 764
Just a Flyer Old Wheelton 756
Just William Sweet William 780

K

Kamikaze Flying Firkin (Dent) 706
Kane's Amber Ale Maclay (Belhaven) 681
Katie's Pride Corvedale 702
Keelhaul Oulton 758
Kelham Gold Kelham Island 738
Keller Bier Upper Agbrigg 786
Kett's Rebellion Woodforde's 795
Kid 'n' Bard Welton's (Hepworth) 728
Killellan Houston 734
Killer Bee Darwin 706
Kimberley Bitter Hardys & Hansons 726
Kimberley Mild Hardys & Hansons 726
King Keltek 738
King & Barnes Mild Ale Badger
(Gribble Inn) 723
King & Barnes Sussex Bitter Badger 676
King & Barnes Sussex Bitter Badger
(Gribble Inn) 723
King Alfred's Hampshire 724
King Billy Cropton 703
King Cnut Ale St Peter's 772
King Maker Warwickshire 788
King's Shilling Cannon Royall 696
Kingdom Bitter Dunn Plowman 708
Kingsdown Ale Arkell's 674
Kingston Bitter Lidstones 742
Kitty Brewster Northumberland 752
Kletswater Anglo Dutch 673
Kneesknocker Whitley Bridge 791
Knockendoch Sulwath 778
Knocker Up Three B's 781
Knoll's Porter Bazens' 679
Kodiak Gold Beartown 680
Kolsch Grand Union 721

L

LAD Lager Iceni 735
Lady Godiva Warwickshire 788
Lady of the Lake Glastonbury 718
Ladywell Ale Broadstone 689
Lagonda IPA Marble 745
Lancaster Bomber Thwaites 782
Landlord Taylor 780
Landlords Choice Moles 749
Landlords Wit Dark Star 705
Last Resort Willy's 793
Last Rites Abbeydale 671
Latitude Atlas 675
Laurie Lee's Bitter Uley 786

Leadboiler Linfit 742
Leg Spinner Khean 739
Legend Hogs Back 731
Legend Best Bitter Nottingham 752
Legion Ale Hadrian & Border 723
Lemon and Ginger Humpty Dumpty 734
Lemon and Ginger Spiced Ale
St Peter's 772
Level Best Rother Valley 769
Ley Line Glastonbury 718
Lia Fail Inveralmond 735
Liberator Tindall 782
Life Sentence Bodicote 686
Lifeboat Ale Titanic 783
Light Brigade Leyden 741
Light Fantastic Spectrum 776
Light Horse Bitter Caythorpe 697
Light Oak Weatheroak 789
Lightyear Glentworth 718
Lilly Fogg Halifax 724
Lincolnshire Yella Belly Organic
Bateman 678
Linebacker Leadmill 740
Lion Slayer Fyfe 717
Lion's Pride Maypole 747
Lions Main Picks 760
Lions Pride Picks 760
Lip Smacker Holland 732
Liquid Lobotomy Stout Garton 718
Liquor Mortis Blue Moon 685
Liquorice Stout Coles 701
Little Green Man Bartrams 677
Little Sharpie Humpty Dumpty 734
Lizard Point Organic 757
Log End Boggart Hole Clough 686
Lomond Gold Bridge of Allan 689
London Pride Fuller's 716
Longboat Barum 678
Lord Ancaster Newby Wyke 751
Lord Lees North Yorkshire 752
Lower Odcombe Ale Odcombe 754
Lowgate Light Townes 784
Loxley Ale Maypole 747
Loxley Gold Crown 704
Loyal Corgi Doghouse 707
Lucasale Fernandes 714
Lucky Punter Lidstones 742
Luddite Ryburn 770
Lupus Lupus Wolf 794
Lynne Pearce Sawbridgeworth 773

M

M&B Brew XI Coors (Brains) 799
M&B Mild Coors (Highgate) 729
Machen Bitter Carters 696
Mad Jack Stout Holland 732
Maggs Magnificent Mild
West Berkshire 790
Magic Mushroom Mild Whim 791
Magik Keltek 738
Magus Durham 708
Maiden Century Brown Cow 690
Maiden Voyage Ales of Scilly 672
Maidstone Porter Goacher's 718
Mainbrace Jollyboat 736
Major Bitter Riverside 768
Major Oak Maypole 747
Maldon Gold Mighty Oak 747
Malt Shovel Mild Fernandes 714
Malty Towers Tower 784
Man in the Boat Boat 686
Manannan's Cloak Bushy's 693
Manchester Bitter Marble 745
Mansfield Cask Ale Banks's 677
Mansfield Dark Mild Banks's 677

O

Oak Old Cottage 755
Oasthouse Gold Weetwood 789
Oat Meal Stout Upper Agbrigg 786
Oat Stout Lidstones 742
Oaten Barley Stout Coles 701
Oatmeal Stout Townes 784
Wentworth 790
OBB Samuel Smith 776
OBJ Worfield 795
Offas John Roberts 768
Offilers Bitter Museum (Coors) 800
Oh Boy Bryncelyn 691
Old Accidental Brunswick 690
Old Appledore Country Life 702
Old Arnold Wickwar 792
Old Bat B&T 675
Old Black Bull Bragdy Ceredigion 687
Old Bob Ridleys 767
Old Boy Oldershaw 757
Old Brewery Bitter Samuel Smith 776
Old Bushy Tail Bushy's 694
Old Carrock Strong Ale
Hesket Newmarket 728
Old Chestnut Frankton Bagby 715
Old Cocky Welton's (Hepworth) 728
Old Cornelius Jarrow 736
Old Curiosity Old Mill 756
Old Dark Attic Concertina 701
Old Demdyke Red Rose 766
Old Dog Bitter Weetwood 789
Old Eli Linfit 742
Old Empire Marston's 746
Old Emrys Nags Head 750
Old Engine Oil Harviestoun 727
Old Fashioned Mild Swan 779
Old Father Thames West Berkshire 790
Old Freddy Walker Moor 749
Old Gaffer DarkTribe 705
Old Ground Mild Ramsbottom 764
Old Growler Nethergate 751
Old Groyne Willy's 793
Old Grumpy Kemptown 739
Old Henry Hobsons 731
Old Hooky Hook Norton 733
Old Humbug Hexhamshire 728
Old Jock Broughton 690
Old Joe Poachers 762
Old Knotty John Joule (Coach House) 700
Old Knucker Arundel 675
Old Legover Daleside 705
Old Man Ale Coniston 701
Old Moggie Teignworthy 780
Old Mother Hubbard Nursery
(Hobden's) 730
Old Neddy Bitter End 682
Old Nottingham Extra Pale Ale
Caythorpe 697
Old Oak Ale Phoenix 760
Old Peculier Theakston
(Scottish Courage) 802
Old Pompey Packhorse 759
Old Priory John Joule (Coach House) 700
Old Remedial Moulin 750
Old Ric Uley 786
Old Rott Quay 764
Old Ruby Village (Hambleton) 724
Old Ruby Ale Ventnor 787
Old Sarum Hidden 729
Old Scrooge John Roberts 768
Old Slapper Bank Top 676
Old Slug Porter RCH 765
Old Smokey Stonehenge 778
Old Speckled Hen Greene King 722
Old Speckled Parrot Wheal Ale 790
Old Spot Prize Ale Uley 786

Old Stoatwobbler Spectrum 776
Old Stockport Bitter Robinson's 768
Old Style Bitter Tomos Watkin 789
Old Style Porter St Peter's 772
Old Tackle Chalk Hill 698
Old Thumper Ringwood 768
Old Tom Robinson's 769
Selby 773
Old Tradition Home County 732
Old Trout Ale Kemptown 739
Old Wemian Hanby 725
Olde Fashioned Blue Bell 685
Olde Honesty Blue Bell 685
Olde Jake SP Sporting Ales
(Dunn Plowman) 707
Olde Merryford Ale Wickwar 792
Olde Session Blue Bell 685
Olde Trip Hardys & Hansons 726
Oliver's Army Springhead 777
Oliver's Nectar Clearwater 700
Olympian Bronze John Eastwood 709
One For The Toad Wizard 793
One-eyed Jack Concertina 701
Opium Coniston 701
'Ops on Train Humpty Dumpty 734
Organic Ale St Peter's 771
Organic Best Bitter St Peter's 771
Organic Hygeia Ale Ventnor 787
Organic Rye Beer O'Hanlon's 753
Organic Swan Swan 779
Original AK McMullen 743
Original Northumberland Ale
Northumberland 752
Original Wood Swansea 780
OSB Tomos Watkin 789
Oscar Wilde Mighty Oak 747
Ossian's Ale Inveralmond 735
Otley Gold Briscoe's 689
Outback Bitter Bank Top 676
Over the Moon Dark Star 705
Owd Duck Mallard 744
Own Sharp's 774
Oxford Blue Morrells (Burtonwood) 693
Oyster Stout Bushy's 693
Ventnor 787

P

P2 Imperial Stout Museum (Coors) 800
Pacific Bazens' 679
Pageant Ale Elgood's 710
Painters Warcop 788
Pale Amber Sarah Hughes 734
Pale Gold Ossett 758
Pale Moonlight Phoenix 760
Pale Rider Kelham Island 738
Parish Bitter Wood 794
Park Hall Porter Leadmill 740
Parker's Pride Townhouse 784
Parkers Porter City of Cambridge 699
Parliament Ale Swan 779
Parsons Pledge Derwent 706
Partners in Crime Fernandes 714
Pat Murphy's Porter Bury Street 693
Pathfinders Ale Poachers 762
Patois Randalls 764
Peat Porter Moor 749
Pedigree Bitter Marston's 746
Peeping Tom Frankton Bagby 715
Pegasus Milton 748
Peggottys Porter Mauldons 746
Pendle Witches Brew Moorhouses 750
Peninsula Pint Hill Island 730
Pennine Gold Golcar 719
Penny Ferry Porter Hill Island 730
Per-Tash Poachers 762

Reivers Northumberland 752
Rest in Peace Church End 699
Retriever Doghouse 707
Rev James Brains 687
Revenge Keltek 738
  Winter's 793
Reverend Eaton's Ale Shardlow 773
RGC Mild Hoggleys 731
Rhatas Black Dog 682
Rhymney Valley Bitter Carters 696
Richmond Ale Darwin 706
Riding Bitter Banks's 677
Riggers Warcop 788
Riggwelter Black Sheep 683
Riley's Army Jarrow 736
Rip Snorter Hogs Back 731
Roaring Boy Oulton 758
Roaring Meg Springhead 777
Roasted Barley Stout Coles 701
Robin a Tiptoe John O'Gaunt 737
Robyns Bitter Saddleworth 770
Rock Ale Bitter Beer Nottingham 752
Rock Ale Mild Beer Nottingham 752
Rock Spalt Wentworth 790
Rockers Warcop 788
Rollers Warcop 788
Rolling Thunder Leadmill 740
Roo Brew Six Bells 775
Rooster's Ale Felstar 713
Rooster's Knight Felstar 713
Rope of Sand Fyfe 717
Rossendale Ale Porter 763
Roundhead's Gold Springhead 777
Rowley Mild Lidstones 742
Roy Morgan's Original Ale
Travellers Inn 784
Royal Oak O'Hanlon's 753
Royal Welch Fusilier Plassey 762
Royale 12 Newtonmore & Kingussie 751
Ruby (1874) Mild Bushy's 693
Ruby Ale North Yorkshire 752
Ruby Mild Rudgate 770
Ruby XXX St George's 771
Ruddles Best Bitter Greene King 722
Ruddles County Greene King 722
Rugby Special Frankton Bagby 715
Rumpus Ridleys 767
Rupert's Ruin Springhead 777
Rutherford IPA City of Cambridge 699
Ruthven Brew Cairngorm 695
Rutland Panther Grainstore 720
Rydale Bitter Ryburn 770
Ryedale Light Malton 745

S

SA Brains 687
Saddlers Best Bitter Highgate 729
Saddleworth More Saddleworth 770
Saigon Leadmill 740
St Andrew's Ale Belhaven 680
St Agnes Reepham 767
St Edwards Ale Leek 741
St Patricks Warwickshire 788
Saints Sinner Darwin 706
Salem Porter Bateman 678
Sam Powell Old Sam Wood 794
Sam Powell Original Bitter Wood 794
Samuel Crompton's Ale Bank Top 676
Sanctuary Durham 708
Sands Foxfield 715
Sandy Hunter's Traditional Ale
Belhaven 680
Santa Fe RCH 765
Saxon Berserker Cuckmere Haven 704
Saxon Cross Rockingham 769

Saxon King Stout Cuckmere Haven 704
Saxon King Stout Extra
Cuckmere Haven 704
SBA Donnington 707
Scallywag Black Dog 682
Scatty Bitter Scattor Rock 773
Scafell Great Gable 721
Schiehallion Harviestoun 727
Schooner Black Dog 682
Scorcher Rooster's 769
Scoresby Stout Cropton 703
Scorpio Porter Hanby 725
Scottish Oatmeal Stout Broughton 690
Scouse Mouse Liverpool 742
Scrum Down Mild Steamin' Billy
(Grainstore) 777
Scullion's Irish Hilden 730
Scuppered Ales of Scilly 672
Sea of Tranquillity Blue Moon 685
Seamer Khean 739
Second Brunswick 690
Secret Hop Corvedale 702
Secret Kingdom Hadrian & Border 723
Sedgley Surprise Sarah Hughes 734
Selhurst Park Flyer Sawbridgeworth 773
Serpentine Dark Ale Organic 757
Session Bitter Lidstones 742
Seuruik Bragdy Ynys Môn 687
Sexton John Roberts 768
Shaftbender Saddleworth 770
Shambles Potton 763
Shannon IPA Potton 763
Sheep Dog Northumberland 752
Sheepshagger Cairngorm 695
Shefford Bitter B&T 675
Shefford Dark Mild B&T 675
Shefford Old Dark B&T 675
Shefford Old Strong B&T 675
Shefford Pale Ale B&T 675
Shifting Sands Bryson's 691
Shire Bitter Hexhamshire 728
Shires Best Bitter Wychwood 795
Shirley Crabtree Halifax 724
Shoemaker Frog Island 716
Shoreditch Stout Pitfield 761
Shot in the Dark Green Tye 722
Shrimpers AVS (Daleside) 705
Shrimpers Stout Bryson's 691
Shropshire Gold Salopian 772
Shropshire Lad Wood 794
Shropshire Pride Worfield 795
Shropshire Stout Hanby 725
Shunter Best Bitter Paradise 759
Shuttle Ale Three B's 781
Shy Talk Poachers 762
Side Pocket for a Toad Tring 785
Sidewinder Leadmill 740
  Newby Wyke 751
Signature Maclay (Belhaven) 681
Silk of Amnesia Storm 778
Silver King Ossett 758
Silver Shadow Ossett 758
Simmer Dim Valhalla 786
Simpkiss Bitter Enville 710
Simply The Best Mighty Oak 748
Simpsons No. 4 Brown Cow 690
Singhbolton Pitfield 761
Sir Roger's Porter Earl Soham 709
Siren Hart 726
Six Bells Shardlow 774
6X Wadworth 787
1646 Clearwater 700
Sjolmet Stout Valhalla 787
Skiddaw Special Bitter
Hesket Newmarket 728
Skinner's Old Strong Bitter End 682
Skrimshander IPA Hopdaemon 733

Tap Bitter Moles 749
Target Ale Derwent Rose 706
Tarw Du Bragdy Ynys Môn 687
Taverners Ale Hanby 725
Tawny Bitter Cotleigh 702
Tawny Owl Bury Street 693
Tawny Special Bury Street 693
TEA Hogs Back 731
Teesdale Bitter High Force Hotel (Darwin) 706
Teflon Sawbridgeworth 773
Teign Valley Tipple Scattor Rock 773
Tempest Winter's 793
Ten Fifty Grainstore 720
1066 Country Bitter White 791
Tender Behind Humpty Dumpty 734
Tern's Tipple Bryson's 691
Tetley's Cask Bitter Carlsberg-Tetley 799
Tetley's Dark Mild Carlsberg-Tetley 799
Tetley's Imperial Carlsberg-Tetley 799
Tetley's Mild Carlsberg-Tetley 799
Texas Houston 734
That Teme Valley 781
That Old Chestnut Frog Island 716
Theakston Best Bitter
Scottish Courage 802
Theakston Cool Cask
Scottish Courage 802
Theakston Mild Ale Scottish Courage 802
Theakston Old Peculier
Scottish Courage 802
Theakston XB Scottish Courage 802
Thetford Forest Mild Iceni 735
Thick Black Devon 707
Thin Ice Elgood's 710
Thirlwell's Best Blue Cow 685
Thirlwell's Witham Wobler Blue Cow 685
Thirsty Moon Phoenix 760
This Teme Valley 781
Thomas Bewick Bitter Dunn Plowman 708
Thomas Hardy's Ale Phoenix Imports (O'Hanlon's) 753
Thomas Salts Bitter Tower 784
Thomas Slee's Academy Ale Tirril 783
Thoroughbred Bullmastiff 692
   Thwaites 782
Thrappledouser Inveralmond 735
3B Arkell's 674
Three Blind Mice Nursery (Hobden's) 730
Three Cliffs Gold Swansea 780
3 Giants Derwent Rose 706
Three Hundreds Old Ale Chiltern 698
Three Kings Royal Ale Whitley Bridge 791
Three Peaks Ale Briscoe's 689
Three Sheets Ales of Scilly 672
Three Sisters Atlas 675
Thunderstorm Hop Back 733
Tiger Best Bitter Everards 711
Timber Wolf Wolf 794
Tinker Buntingford 692
Tinners Ale St Austell 770
Tipsy Trotters Ring O' Bells 767
To be Joyfull Fernandes 714
Tolly Mild Ridleys 767
Tolly Original Ridleys 767
Tom Brown's Best Bitter Goldfinch 719
Tom Wood's Best Bitter Highwood 729
Tom Wood's Bomber County
Highwood 729
Tom Wood's Dark Mild Highwood 729
Tom Wood's Harvest Bitter
Highwood 729
Tom Wood's Old Timber Highwood 729
Tom Wood's Shepherd's Delight
Highwood 729
Tom's Tipple Red Shoot 766
Tommy Todd's Porter McGuinness 743

Top Dog Spinning Dog 777
Top Dog Stout Burton Bridge 693
Top Hat Burtonwood 693
Top Tipple Frankton Bagby 715
Topsy Turvy Berrow 681
Torridge Best Clearwater 700
Total Eclipse Blue Moon 685
Tournament Goff's 719
Tower Bitter Ramsbottom 764
Tower of Strength Tower 784
Town Crier Hobsons 730
Traditional English Ale Hogs Back 731
Trafalgar Bitter Flagship 714
Trail Poachers 762
Trap Tickler Rat & Ratchet 765
Treacle Stout Itchen Valley 736
Trembling Rabbit Poachers 762
Tribute St Austell 771
Trip Hazard Spectrum 776
Triple B Grainstore 720
Triple Gold Brunswick 690
Triple Hop Brunswick 690
Triple Tee Weatheroak 789
Trooper Marston Moor 745
Trophy Bitter Interbrew (Hydes) 735
Trotton Bitter Ballard's 676
Trumpeter Best Swan 779
Turbinia Wylam 796
Turkey's Delight Cheriton 698
Turnpike Coach House 700
   Harviestoun 727
Twin Screw DarkTribe 705
2B Arkell's 674
Two Brewers Bitter B&T 675
Two Harleys Sarah's Hop House 773
200 Palmer 759
Two Pints Cropton 703
Two Water Grog Broadstone 689

Readers' recommendations
Suggestions for pubs to be included or excluded

All pubs are surveyed by local branches of the Campaign for Real Ale. If you would like to comment on a pub already featured, or any you think should be featured, please fill in the form below (or copy it), and send it to the address indicated. Your views will be passed on to the branch concerned. Please mark your envelope with the county where the pub is, which will help us to sort the suggestion efficiently.

Pub name:

Address:

Reason for recommendation/criticism:

Pub name:

Address:

Reason for recommendation/criticism:

Pub name:

Address:

Reason for recommendation/criticism:

Your name and address:

Pub name:

....

Address:

....

Reason for recommendation/criticism:

....

....

....

....

....

Pub name:

....

Address:

....

Reason for recommendation/criticism:

....

....

....

....

....

Pub name:

....

Address:

....

Reason for recommendation/criticism:

....

....

....

....

Pub name:

....

Address:

....

Reason for recommendation/criticism:

....

....

....

....

Your name and address:

....

....

Please send to: [Name of county] Section, Good Beer Guide,
230 Hatfield Road, St Albans, Hertfordshire AL1 4LW

CAMRA Books and Gifts

CAMRA Books (non-members' prices)	Price	Quantity	Total
Good Beer Guide 2003	£3.00		
Good Beer Guide 2002	£3.00		
Good Beer Guide 2001	£3.00		
Good Beer Guide 2000	£3.00		
Good Beer Guide 1999	£3.00		
50 Pub Crawls	£9.99		
Heritage Pubs (Hardback)	£15.00		
Pubs for Families (4th edition)	£9.99		
London Pub Guide (3rd edition)	£8.99		
Guide to Northern France	£7.99		
Guide to Home Brewing (3rd edition)	£7.99		
Brew British Real Ales at Home	£7.99		
Brew Classic European Beers at Home	£7.99		
Homebrew Classics – India Pale Ale	£8.99		
Homebrew Classics – Stout & Porter	£8.99		
CAMRA Guide to Good Pub Food (5th edition)	£8.99		
Good Bottled Beer Guide (Hardback – 4th edition)	£8.99		
Room at the Inn (3rd edition)	£9.99		
Landlord's Tale	£6.99		
Guide to Belgium & Holland (4th edition)	£11.99		
Real Ale Almanac (5th edition)	£4.99		
Pub Superchefs	£7.99		
Good Cider Guide (4th edition)	£9.99		
Dictionary of Beer	£9.99		
Kegbuster Remembers by Bill Tidy	£1.00		
Cidermaking on a Small Scale	£5.95		
Ciders Story Rough and Smooth	£9.99		
All the World's a Pub	£6.99		
Bamberg & Franconia	£9.99		
Heavenly Beer	£8.99		
Organic Beer Guide	£8.99		
Strangest Pubs in Britain	£6.99		
West Country Ales	£18.99		
	TOTAL		

- Add £1 per book in United Kingdom
- Add £2 per book in European Union (£4 for the Good Beer Guide)
- Add £4 per book elsewhere (£7 for the Good Beer Guide)

Credit Card Orders can be placed by calling **01727 867201**
or via our website **www.camra.org.uk**
■ Please visit the website for new items

- **Please allow up to 21 days for delivery, up to 35 days for delivery overseas**

Please send your order for books, CAMRA products and clothing to:
CAMRA, 230 Hatfield Road,
St Albans,
Hertfordshire AL1 4LW

(cheques made payable to CAMRA must accompany all orders). To place a credit card order, phone (01727) 867201 and ask for the Products Secretary.

NAME

ADDRESS

Postcode

CAMRA Products	Price	Quantity	Total
Spinning Key Fob	£2.95		
CAMRA Lapel Badge (New hand pump style)	£2.50		
Cider Lapel Badge	£2.50		
LADS Lapel badge	£2.50		
GBBF 10 Year @ Olympia Badge Set (Limited Edition)	£19.95		
CAMRA Bar Towel *Black* (10 for £12.50)	£2.00		
CAMRA Tea Towel (How a Brewery Works)	£3.00		
Hop Lady Beach Towel	£9.95		
CAMRA Hanging Neck Pen	£1.50		
CAMRA Ballpoint Pen	£0.50		
Embroidered Material Badge *Red and Black*	£2.00		
CAMRA Handpump Bookmark	£1.00		
Bottle Opener/Fridge Magnet (2 in 1)	£2.00		
Fridge Magnet – Hop Lady	£1.50		
Fridge Magnet _ Pulling Power	£1.50		
CAMRA Wallet (Embroidered Logo) *Red*	£3.75		
PVC Glass Cooler *Red*	£3.00		
PVC Good Beer Guide Cover *Burgundy*	£2.95		
CAMRA Squezzy Stress Bottle	£2.95		
CAMRA Notelets with Holder	£4.95		
CAMRA Darts Flights (pack of 3)	£1.00		
Beanie Bear	£3.00		
Desk Clock	£6.50		
Wall Clock	£17.50		
CAMRA Mouse Mat	£3.00		
CAMRA Coaster (6 for £8.50)	£1.75		
CAMRA Model Van *Red*	£9.50		
Ask if it's Cask Model Van *White*	£9.50		
Metal Waiters Tray	£14.95		
Golf Umbrella	£16.75		
Messenger Bag *Black with Grey and Red*	£14.95		
Mini Football	£3.95		
Jewellery – Drop Earrings (boxed)	£5.75		
Jewellery – Stud Earrings (boxed)	£4.95		
Jewellery – Cuff Links (boxed)	£7.50		
6 in 1 Travel Games Compendium	£9.99		
Postcards GBBF or Hop Lady	£0.50		
Cuddly Toys (Cat, Dog, Rabbit, Bear)	£9.00		

CAMRA Clothing			
CAMRA Tie (Help Save Real Ale) *Navy Blue*	£8.50		
CAMRA T-Shirt Embroidered Logo *Red/Back/Green* (M to XXL)	£9.50		
Pub is for Life (not just Christmas) *White* (S to XXL)	£8.50		
Life's Simple T-Shirt *Sky Black* (S to XXL)	£8.50		
Beer Warriors Rugby Shirt *Blue* (L to XXL)	£29.95		
CAMRA Sweatshirt *Navy Blue* (M to XXL)	£12.50		
CAMRA Polo Shirt *Crimson* (S to XXL)	£16.50		
Life Member Polo Shirt *Crimson* (M to XXL)	£16.50		
Lads Polo Shirt (Light and Dark Supporters) *Green* (S to XXL)	£17.50		
EBCU Polo Shirt *Blue* (M to XXL)	£14.50		
CAMRA Fleece *Red or Green* (M to XXL)	£24.95		
Rain Poncho	£3.95		
Scarf *Red or Blue*	£6.50		
Pomona T-Shirt *White* S-XXL	£8.50		
Dark Ages T-Shirt *Stone* S-XXL	£8.50		
Female Campaigner T-Shirt *Black* S-XXL	£8.50		
Female Campaigner Skinny Fit *Black or Pink S-L*	£10.50		
Invaders T-Shirt *Sand* S-XXL	£8.50		
George & Dragon T-Shirt S-XXL	£8.50		
Apron (Champion Beers of Britain) *White*	£9.50		
Children's 'Half Pint Kids' T-Shirt *Red*	£5.00		
(3 – 13 years old; Please state age required)			
		TOTAL	

- Prices include postage and packing to the UK
- Please add £2.00 per item In European Union ● Please add £4.00 per item elsewhere

● **Please allow up to 21 days for delivery** ● **Please allow up to 35 days for delivery overseas**

An offer for CAMRA members

GOOD BEER GUIDE
Annual Subscription

Being a CAMRA member brings many benefits, not least the big discount on the Good Beer Guide. Now you can take advantage of an even bigger discount on the Guide by taking out an annual subscription.

Simply fill in the form below and the Direct Debit form opposite (photocopies will do if you don't want to spoil your book), and send them to CAMRA at the usual St Albans address.

You will then receive the *Good Beer Guide* automatically every year. It will be posted to you before the official publication date and before any other postal sales are processed.

You won't have to bother with filling in cheques every year and you will receive the book at a lower price than other CAMRA members (the 2002 edition, for instance, was sold to annual subscribers at only £7.50).

So sign up now and be sure of receiving your copy early every year.

Note: This offer is open only to CAMRA members and is only available through using a Direct Debit instruction to a UK bank (use the form opposite, or copy it if you do not want to spoil your book). This offer applies to the 2004 *Guide* onwards.

Name
....

CAMRA Membership No.
....

Address and Post code
....

....

....

....

I wish to purchase the *Good Beer Guide* annually by Direct Debit and I have completed the Direct Debit instructions to my bank which are enclosed.

Signature   Date
....

Instruction to your bank or building society to pay by Direct Debit

Please fill in and send to the Campaign for Real Ale Limited, 230 Hatfield Road, St Albans, Herts AL1 4LW

Name and full postal address of your bank or building society

To the manager   Bank or building society

Address

Postcode

Name(s) of Account Holder(s)

Bank or building society account number

☐☐☐☐☐☐☐☐

Branch sort code

☐☐ ☐☐ ☐☐

Reference number

☐☐☐☐☐☐☐☐☐☐☐☐☐☐☐☐☐☐

Banks and building societies may not accept Direct Debit instructions for some types of account

---

Originator's identification number

9 2 6 1 2 9

For CAMRA official use only

This is not part of the instruction to your bank or building society

Membership number

Name

Postcode

Instruction to your bank or building society

Please pay CAMRA Direct Debits from the account detailed on this instruction subject to the safeguards assured by the Direct Debit Guarantee. I understand this instruction may remain with CAMRA and, if so, will be passed electronically to my bank/building society.

Signature(s)

Date

Postcode

Direct Debit

This Guarantee should be detached and retained by the payer.

The Direct Debit Guarantee

● This Guarantee is offered by all banks and building societies that take part in the Direct Debit Scheme. The efficiency and security of the scheme is monitored and protected by your own bank or building society.

● If the amounts to be paid or the payment dates change, CAMRA will notify you within ten working days in advance of your account being debited or as otherwise agreed.

● If an error is made by CAMRA or your bank or building society, you are guaranteed a full and immediate refund from our branch of the amount paid.You can cancel a Direct Debit at any time by writing to your bank or building society. Please also send a copy of your letter to CAMRA.

829

Join CAMRA
Free for three months!

- Has a pub near you been closed or ruined?
- Has your local brewery been taken over or its beers lost their flavour?
- Are you concerned about the price of a pint?

If you can answer 'yes' to any or all of these questions you are sure to benefit from becoming a member of CAMRA.

The Campaign for Real Ale is a voluntary organisation consisting of over 67,000 drinkers, run by an unpaid, elected National Executive and backed by a small core of professional executives. It speaks for drinkers everywhere in fighting to save pubs and breweries from closure, and in attempting to improve quality and to ensure pub standards are raised.

- As a member you can have your say about issues which effect you. You can stand for election to office, attend the annual conference to speak and vote, and help organise local campaigns.
- You can help select pubs for the Good Beer Guide, help out at beer festivals and enjoy some excellent social activities.
- You can receive big discounts on the Good Beer Guide and other CAMRA books and products, free or reduced price admission to CAMRA beer festivals, plus the What's Brewing newspaper, delivered to your door each month. All new members receive the Members' Handbook as soon as they are registered.

All this is available at the bargain price of just £16 per year (£19 per year for two people living at the same address).

- What's more if you join by Direct Debit you will receive three month's membership free, so you can see for yourself how worthwhile being a member can be.
- Fill in the application form below (or a photocopy of it) and the Direct Debit form on the previous page. If after three months of membership you decide not to continue just write to CAMRA, cancel your membership and you will owe nothing. Note: If you do not wish to take up the trial offer, but wish to join CAMRA anyway, fill in the application form and return it to us with a cheque for your first years subscription. To pay by credit card, contact the Membership Secretary on (01727) 867201 (or Join online on our National Web-site at www.camra.org.uk)
- Full annual membership £16
- Joint annual membership (two people at the same address) £19
- Life membership £192 (single)/£288 (joint)
- Under-26 membership £9 single/£12 joint.

Concessionary rates available on request.

Please delete as appropriate:
- ❏ I/We wish to take advantage of the trial membership, and have completed the instructions overleaf.
- ❏ I/We wish to become members of CAMRA
- ❏ I/We agree to abide by the memorandum and articles of association of the company.
- ❏ I/We enclose a cheque/PO for £   (payable to CAMRA)

NAME(S)

Address and Post Code

Date of birth   E-mail address

Signature(s)

- ❏ Tick here if you would like to receive occasional e-mails from CAMRA. (At no point will your details be released to a third party)   Opt-in

Signature(s)

To: CAMRA, 230 Hatfield Road, St Albans, Hertfordshire AL1 4LW